PHILIP'S

EASYREAD London

Contents

II Our Top 10 tips to avoid parking penalties
V Mobile speed camera sites
VI **Key to map pages**
VIII Administrative and Postcode boundaries
X **Route planning**

XXVIII **Key to map symbols**
1 **Street maps**

228 **Keys to enlarged map pages and symbols**
229 **Enlarged street maps**

271 **Index**
429 **List of numbered locations**

445 Hospitals
446 Shopping, theatres, cinemas
448 Central London buses
450 Local rail and London Underground
452 Places of interest

Digital Data

The exceptionally high-quality mapping found in this atlas is available as digital data in TIFF format, which is easily convertible to other bitmapped (raster) image formats.

The index is also available in digital form as a standard database table. It contains all the details found in the printed index together with the National Grid reference for the map square in which each entry is named.

For further information and to discuss your requirements, please contact victoria.dawbarn@philips-maps.co.uk

First published 2000 by

Philip's, a division of
Octopus Publishing Group Ltd
2–4 Heron Quays
London E14 4JP

Third edition 2007
Third impression 2008
LONCC

To the best of the Publishers' knowledge, the information in this atlas was correct at the time of going to press. No responsibility can be accepted for any errors or their consequences.

The representation in this atlas of a road, track or path is no evidence of the existence of a right of way.

The information for the speed camera locations is used with permission of the London Safety Camera Partnership and is correct at the time of publishing. New sites will be installed by the LSCP, for the latest list visit www.lscp.org.uk

Printed in China.

Our Top 10 Tips to avoid parking penalties

David Willis / Alamy

When it comes to parking, London's streets are mean and its traffic regulators keen. Lucky motorists might find a marked bay, or at night a patch of single line, but that could just be the start of the problem. It's all too easy to pick the wrong space or the wrong time of day.

Getting a ticket for over-staying, or using a suspended bay or a resident's only space, is invariably expensive and sometimes the pain doesn't end there. What's the worst that can happen? Well, the car could be clamped or towed away. But in either case it's excruciatingly costly and time-consuming to retrieve the vehicle, especially after 10pm, when London black cab prices go through the roof.

Why has parking become so hazardous? The whole process used to be much less complex, and far easier to understand. The hours of parking control were fairly standard right across the capital, and enforcement was also uniform, with traffic wardens attached to the police service. Then came the Road Traffic Act 1991, which took responsibility away from the police and into the hands of local authorities.

The post-code lottery

Since 1994 parking in London has been run by the borough councils. Most choose to employ private contractors to operate the parking penalty service. In common with all other companies, these outfits are in pursuit of profit – and they haven't been disappointed. Parking fines are big business in London these days.

Latest figures show that more than five million parking penalties were levied on motorists in 2005/6 (see table). In bald terms, that's nearly one for every person living in Greater London. These penalties produced an income for the boroughs of some £279 million in a year. Once the operators have taken their slice, the money goes into the coffers of London's 33 boroughs as well as Transport for London, which has recently stepped up its enforcement activities, especially on red routes.

There is huge variation among the 32 boroughs, with central London by far the riskiest place to park. Westminster held the 2005 record for issuing the greatest number of fines, even though its total of 715,085 was about 100,000 less than the previous year. The fewest parking fines were given in the City of London.

There is one piece of good news. A third fewer cars were clamped than in 2004/5 – nearly 50,000 fewer. But there was a sharp 18% increase in cars removed to pounds. To acknowledge this grim statistic, Philip's London street atlases are now the first to locate Car Pounds on the maps using this symbol: [car pound symbol]

The figures also reveal the trend-setters among the boroughs:

Camden for the most cars clamped.

Parking fines 2005/6

	Borough	fines
1	**Westminster**	715085
2	**Camden**	448085
3	**Kensington and Chelsea**	294932
4	**Lambeth**	255066
5	**Wandsworth**	245475
6	**Ealing**	212656
7	**Islington**	210685
8	**Newham**	188465
9	**Barnet**	168681
10	**Hammersmith and Fulham**	165196
11	**Hackney**	140966
12	**Waltham Forest**	140216
13	**Southwark**	135045
14	**Haringey**	134551
15	**Brent**	133561
16	**Enfield**	100087
17	**Redbridge**	95966
18	**Hounslow**	92764
19	**Croydon**	86534
20	**Harrow**	83303
21	**Tower Hamlets**	72858
22	**Richmond upon Thames**	72526
23	**Bromley**	69538
24	**Bexley**	65739
25	**Kingston upon Thames**	63980
26	**Lewisham**	63250
27	**Hillingdon**	61211
28	**Merton**	56860
29	**Sutton**	48965
30	**Greenwich**	48892
31	**Barking and Dagenham**	42416
32	**Havering**	40141
33	**City of London**	37478
34	**Transport for London**	304305
		5,095,478

Westminster for the most cars removed to pounds.

The boroughs where the number of tickets issued grew the fastest were: Ealing (+55%), Enfield (+47%) and Hackney (+46%).

The boroughs who saw the biggest falls were: Greenwich (-21%), Richmond (-25%) and Islington (-26%).

The sheer number of different authorities shelling out penalties can make the London street parking issue seem baffling. Arrangements in Richmond

Top 10 Tips

1 Check borough boundaries. One common pitfall for London's drivers is to pump cash into a meter belonging to one borough while being parked in another. This is especially problematic around the London museums. Numerous visitors perfectly willing to pay the charge have fed money into a meter belonging to the Royal Borough of Kensington and Chelsea when they have inadvertently parked in a bay operated by Westminster council. The signage, campaigners claim, is inadequate – so beware.

2 Keep plenty of loose change if you intend to use parking meters. If a parking attendant happens along while you have toddled off to find the correct coinage you have no defence against a ticket.

3 If you've been caught fair and square, pay the ticket within 14 days to take advantage of the cash discount scheme. Prompt settlement usually means coughing up just half the full amount.

4 Assume nothing. Just because you are often permitted to park on single yellow lines after 6.30 doesn't mean it is always so. There are an increasing number of parking places reserved for 'residents only' and these are frequently governed by a 10pm rule. Moreover some zones are 24 hour no parking areas. Look for signs to indicate what rules apply to the parking space before moving into it. Don't forget that some parking areas are watched by cameras that can capture your licence plate, so don't imagine you are safe to contravene regulations on the basis that parking attendants will have ended their shift. If you have received a penalty charge notice in an area where the signs outlining the regulations on parking are obscured by trees or even missing then you may have grounds for appeal. Take photographs as evidence before embarking on the appeals process.

5 If you return to your vehicle while a parking attendant is in the process of writing the ticket don't hesitate to drive off if you can do so without endangering anyone. Parking offences are not criminal offences, so you are not leaving the scene of a crime. The relevant legislation makes it clear that the completed ticket must be either given to the driver or attached to the vehicle. If not, the ticket is invalid.

6 There are loopholes in parking regulations to capitalise upon. A ticket is invalid if the parking attendant is not wearing full uniform, including a hat, or if his identification number is not clearly visible. There might be discrepancies in the ticket regarding the timings or your vehicle. Sometimes the markings on the road are awry or the position of the meter is misleading. If the parking attendant is present request that he makes a note of your objections as this may assist in any pending appeals process.

7 Don't be afraid to appeal against a penalty that in your view has been wrongly issued. The number of appeals is surprisingly small (fewer than 1%) and yet more than 60% are successful. It generally costs nothing to appeal so what have you got to lose? At first glance the process is daunting but stick with it if you feel you have been unfairly targeted with a ticket. Whatever you do, don't ignore it! See 'How to appeal' on the following page.

8 When cars are clamped or towed retrieve the vehicle fast – within 24 hours if possible. This is an expensive business because drivers must pay the penalty charge notice as well as a fee to release the vehicle. If it's not recovered promptly expect a daily charge for 'storage' on top. Afterwards, study the timings on the ticket. Most councils permit a 15 or 20 minute grace period after a parking ticket has run out before clamping or towing. Anything less than that is grounds for appeal. Remember, if you return to your vehicle before the clamp is locked or before the wheels are raised from the ground if it is being towed then the penalty charge notice is invalid.

9 Look out for cashless parking zones. Some are already on trial in central London. Drivers can ring a database to establish an arrival time. Then the clock starts running until the driver calls again to signal departure. The amount due is automatically debited from the driver's account. There's no doubt that new technology will play its part on the parking scene in the over-crowded capital. And it's sensible recognition at last that drivers may have many talents but are not as yet blessed with the foresight to know the precise moment that they will return to their vehicles.

10 Don't forget the other offences. London drivers not only have to be careful about parking. There's the congestion charge to consider as well as fines for using bus lanes illegally and other moving traffic fines orchestrated by local authorities. Congestion charge boundaries, bus lanes, red lights and yellow box junctions are generally monitored by enforcement cameras and evidence is extremely difficult to dispute.

Dominic Burke / Alamy

Parking on a suspended bay will almost certainly result in your car being towed to the borough pound.

may be substantially different to those in Redbridge. Charges and hours of operation for meters and ticket machines vary hugely, sometimes even on opposite sides of the same street. So there's 'stranger danger' not only for those from outside London, or suburbanites driving into central London, but even for Inner Londoners crossing borough borders.

But that isn't what most alarms the average motorist. There's a widely held belief that wardens have quotas to fill, and can get bonuses for over-achieving. Examples of predatory behaviour are

legendary. Favourite times for ticketing are the first and last 10 minutes of the controlled period, when wardens are often seen out in large numbers. There have been reports of tickets being issued to removal vans during house moves, to security company vans when rogue burglar alarms are clanging, and to numerous traders unloading goods for their shops – sometimes in the middle of the night.

In short, it is not only motorists who have broken parking regulations that are being fined, but also the unwary and the downright unlucky - in the right place, at the right time but with a wrong-minded attendant in the vicinity.

Some of the villains have been weeded out. Certain boroughs are ensuring those patrolling the streets have undergone a re-education process that will cast them as a friend to the motorist rather than a foe. It's not in your best interest to assume the whole system is unfair and take out your frustrations upon the parking attendant who just might have ticketed you legitimately.

However, the activities of a few parking regulators deserve close scrutiny. Clampers in particular have earned themselves a cowboy image that is finally arousing the interest of the legislators. A House of Commons Transport Committee Report has urged that operators should 'consider restricting clamping to persistent offenders and unregistered vehicles'. There's even talk in the document that towing a car may be incompatible with our human rights. That's perhaps why the number of cars being clamped in the capital has gone down by some 50,000.

Of course, there are always reasons to justify a harsh parking regime. It keeps London traffic on the move, making journey times more predictable and curtailing traffic mayhem. That's the official line – which never mentions just how valuable the income generated by parking penalties is to the enforcers. Further, authorities don't talk about targets in relation to parking fines, rather 'baseline performance indicators'.

So if you are going to park in London, especially in the centre, beware, be aware – and know your rights. If you do get fined and you think you have a case, be prepared to appeal. Fewer than 1% of motorists did appeal in 2004/5 (do we detect money-raising by inertia?), but over 60% of those appeals were allowed. Remember, if you do not get a response to your appeal within 56 days, your appeal is automatically allowed.

How to appeal

Begin with a letter sent by recorded delivery within 14 days. That generally means the clock will stop on the prompt payment discount scheme and it will still be available if the initial appeal is unsuccessful – although some councils claim the reduced amount isn't open to those who embark on this route. Keep copies of the correspondence and any supporting evidence you send with it. Always quote the Penalty Charge Notice number. If you hear nothing for more than 56 days then the council is deemed out of time and the ticket should be cancelled.

Do not pay any part of the fine if you are intending to appeal. Once payment is received by the authority the case is closed.

If your appeal is turned down don't accept a letter couched in general terms. Write back to ask about the specifics of your case. The council will either stand by the notice and issue a Notice of Rejection or allow the appeal.

If the authority endorses the ticket its next step is to issue a Notice to Owner and that should happen within six months. According to the Road Traffic Act of 1991 the owner is liable for violations linked to his vehicle. Disturbingly, it is only at this stage that many motorists discover they are being pursued for a parking offence. If you are the sole driver of a vehicle that hasn't been stolen the ticket has clearly not been either attached to the vehicle or handed to you, the driver, as the law demands. Respond within 28 days filing the relevant information. This is known as Formal Representation. (If you do not answer in the specified time the council may well up the fine and send in the bailiffs to recover the amount.)

If this petition is rejected by the local authority then it's time to take the case to the Parking and Traffic Appeals Service. You can select a postal or personal adjudication. Internet advice favours face time with the adjudicator as local councils are known to frequently cave in at the prospect of putting evidence before an official tribunal on the grounds of cost, although there's no guarantee of this happening. The adjudicator's decision is final as there is no recourse to law.

Clamping rates are falling but you are still at risk – especially in Camden and Westminster.

Dominic Burke / Alamy

Helpful information

The Knowledge A telephone advisory service run by off-duty London taxi drivers. They will help with problems including parking and directions. The number is 0906 265 6565 (premium rate) or try *www.theknowledge.com*

Transport for London (TfL) Responsible for 360 miles of roads, 4,600 traffic lights and London's red routes. It is also a fine-issuing authority. Contact Tfl on 0207 222 1234 or *www.tfl.gov.uk.*

www.ticketbusters.co.uk is a website devoted to assisting London motorists, offering tailored advice on parking ticket appeals.

www.parkingticket.co.uk also offers support for London drivers.

Mobile speed camera sites

This table lists the sites where the local safety camera partnership may enforce speed limits through the use of mobile cameras or detectors. These are usually set up on the roadside or a bridge spanning the road and operated by a police or civilian enforcement officer.

Barking & Dagenham
A13
Alfreds Way IG11
Alfreds Way IG12
Ripple Rd IG11
Ripple Rd RM9
A406
Barking Relief Rd IG11
A1153
Porters Avenue RM8
B178
Ballards Rd RM10

Barnet
A5
Hendon Broadway NW9
A406
North Circular Rd N3
Unclassified
Oakleigh Rd South N11

Bexley
A20
Sidcup Rd SE9
Unclassified
Abbey Rd DA17
Bellegrove Rd DA16
Erith Rd DA17
Farady Avenue DA14
King Harolds Way DA17
Lower Rd DA17
Penhill Rd DA5
Pickford Lane DA7
Well Hall Rd SE9
Woolwich Rd DA17

Brent
A5
Edgware Rd NW2
A406
North Circular Rd NW2
North Circular Rd NW10
A4006
Kenton Rd HA3
Unclassified
Crest Rd NW2
Fryent Way, Kingsbury NW9
Hillside NW10
Kingsbury Rd NW9
Watford Rd, Wembley HA0
Watford Rd, Sudbury HA0
Woodcock Hill HA3

Bromley
A20
Sidcup By-Pass DA14
A213
Croydon Rd SE20
A222
Bromley Rd BR2
Bromley Rd BR3
Unclassified
Beckenham Rd BR3
Burnt Ash Lane BR1
Crystal Palace Park Rd SE26
Elmers End Rd BR3
Main Rd TN16
Sevenoaks Way BR5
Wickham Way BR3

Camden
A501
Euston Rd NW1

Chadwell
M11
Chadwell IG8

City of Westminster
A40
Westway W2
Unclassified
Great Western Rd W11
Millbank SW1
Vauxhall Bridge Rd SW1

Croydon
A22
Godstone Rd CR8
A215
Beulah Hill SE19
A217
Garratt Lane SW18
Unclassified
Brigstock Rd CR7
Coulsdon Rd, Coulsdon CR5
Long Lane, Addiscombe CR0
Portnalls Rd, Coulsdon CR5
Thornton Rd CR0

Ealing
A40
Perivale UB6
Western Avenue UB5
Western Avenue UB6
Unclassified
Greenford Rd, Greenford UB6
Greenford Rd, Southall UB1
Horn Lane W3
Lady Margaret Rd UB1
Ruislip Rd UB5
Uxbridge Rd UB2

Egham
M25
Egham TW20

Elmbridge
M25
Byfleet KT14

Enfield
A10
Great Cambridge Rd N18
A110
Enfield Rd EN2
Unclassified
Fore Street N9

Forest Hill
Unclassified
Stanstead Rd SE23

Greenwich
A20
Sidcup Rd SE9
Unclassified
Beresford Street SE18
Court Rd SE9
Creek Rd SE10
Glenesk Rd SE9
Rochester Way SE3
Rochester Way SE9
Woolwich Church Street SE18

Hackney
A10
Stamford Hill N16
Unclassified
Clapton Common E5
Seven Sisters Rd N4
Upper Clapton Rd E5

Hammersmith & Fulham
A40
Westway W2
Westway W12
A219
Scrubs Lane W12
Unclassified
Fulham Palace Rd SW6
Uxbridge Rd W12

Haringey
A503
Seven Sisters Rd N15
Unclassified
Belmont Rd N15
Bounds Green Rd N11
Seven Sisters Rd N4
White Hart Lane N22

Harrow
Unclassified
Alexandra Avenue HA2
Harrow View HA3
Honeypot Lane NW9
Porlock Avenue HA2
Uxbridge Rd, Harrow Weald HA3
Watford Rd HA1

Havering
Unclassified
Brentwood Rd, Romford RM1
Chase Cross Rd RM5
Eastern Avenue RM14
Eastern Avenue East RM14
Hall Lane RM14
Ingrebourne Gardens, Upminster RM14
Ockenden Rd RM14
Parkstone Avenue, Hornchurch RM11
Wingletye Lane RM11

Hillingdon
M25
Colnbrook SL3
West Drayton UB7
A40
Western Avenue, Ruislip UB10
A312
Hayes UB3
Unclassified
Church Hill, Harefield UB9
Cowley Rd, Uxbridge UB8
Cowley High Rd UB8
Joel Street, Northwood Hills HA6
Kingshill Avenue, Hayes UB4
Park Rd UB8
Stockley Rd UB7
Uxbridge Rd, Hayes UB4

Hounslow
A4
Great West Rd, Brentford TW8
Great West Rd, Hounslow TW7
Great West Rd, Hounslow W4
A315
High Street TW8
Unclassified
Castle Way, Hanworth TW13
Great West Rd TW5
Harlington Rd West TW14
Hatton Rd, Bedfont TW14

Islington
Unclassified
Holloway Rd N19
Seven Sisters Rd N4
Upper Street N1

Kensington & Chelsea
Unclassified
Barlby Rd W10
Chelsea Embankment SW3
Chesterton Rd W10
Holland Park Avenue W11
Holland Villas Rd W14
Kensington Park Rd W11
Kensington Rd SW7
Ladbroke Grove W11
Latimer Rd W10
Royal Hospital Rd SW3
Sloane Street SW1
St Helens Gardens W10

Kingston upon Thames
A3
Kingston By-Pass SW20
A240
Kingston Rd KT4
Unclassified
Manor Drive North KT3
Richmond Rd KT2

Lambeth
Unclassified
Atkins Rd SW12
Brixton Hill SW2
Brixton Rd SW9
Clapham Rd SW9
Herne Hill Rd SE24
Kennington Park Rd SE11
Kings Avenue SW4
Streatham High Rd SW16

Lewisham
A21
Bromley Rd BR1
Unclassified
Brockley Rd SE4
Brockley Rd SE23
Bromley Rd SE6
Brownhill Rd SE6
Burnt Ash Hill SE12
Lee High Rd SE12
Lewisham Way SE4
Westwood Hill SE26

Merton
A298
Bushey Rd SW20
Unclassified
Central Rd SM4
High Street, Colliers Wood SW19
Hillcross Avenue SM4
London Rd CR4
Martin Way SM4
Martin Way SW20
Ridgway Place SW19
West Barnes Lane SW20

Newham
A13
Alfreds Way IG11
A124
Barking Rd E6
A1020
Royal Albert Dock Way E6
Royal Docks Rd E6
Unclassified
Barking Rd E13
Romford Rd E7

Redbridge
A406
Southend Rd IG8
Unclassified
Manford Way, Hainault IG7
Woodford Avenue IG8
Woodford Rd E18

Richmond upon Thames
A205
Upper Richmond Rd West SW14
Unclassified
Kew Rd TW9
Sixth Cross Rd TW2
Uxbridge Rd TW12

Ruislip
Unclassified
Field End Rd HA4

Runnymeade
M25
Runnymede TW20

Southwark
Unclassified
Albany Rd SE5
Alleyn Park SE21
Brenchley Gardens SE15
Camberwell New Rd SE5
Denmark Hill SE5
Kennington Park Rd SE11
Linden Grove SE15
Old Kent Rd SE1
Old Kent Rd SE14
Old Kent Rd SE17
Peckham Rye SE15
Salter Rd SE16
Southwark Pk Rd SE16
Sunray Avenue SE24

Spelthorne
M25
Staines TW18

Sutton
A232
Cheam Rd SM1
B272
Foresters Drive SM6
B278
Green Lane SM4
B279
Tudor Drive SM4
Unclassified
Malden Rd SM3
Middleton Rd SM5
Beddington Lane CR0
Cheam Common Rd KT4

Tower Hamlets
A102
Homerton High Street E9
Unclassified
Bow Rd E3
Cambridge Heath Rd E2
Manchester Rd E14
Mile End Rd E1
Upper Clapton Rd E5
Westferry Rd E14

Waltham Forest
Unclassified
Chingford Rd E4
Chingford Rd E17
Hoe Street E17
Larkshall Rd E4

Wandsworth
A3
Kingston Rd SW15
A214
Trinity Rd SW18
A3220
Latchmere Rd SW11
Unclassified
Battersea Park Rd SW11
Garratt Lane SW18
Upper Richmond Rd SW15

Windsor & Maidenhead
M25
Wraysbury TW19

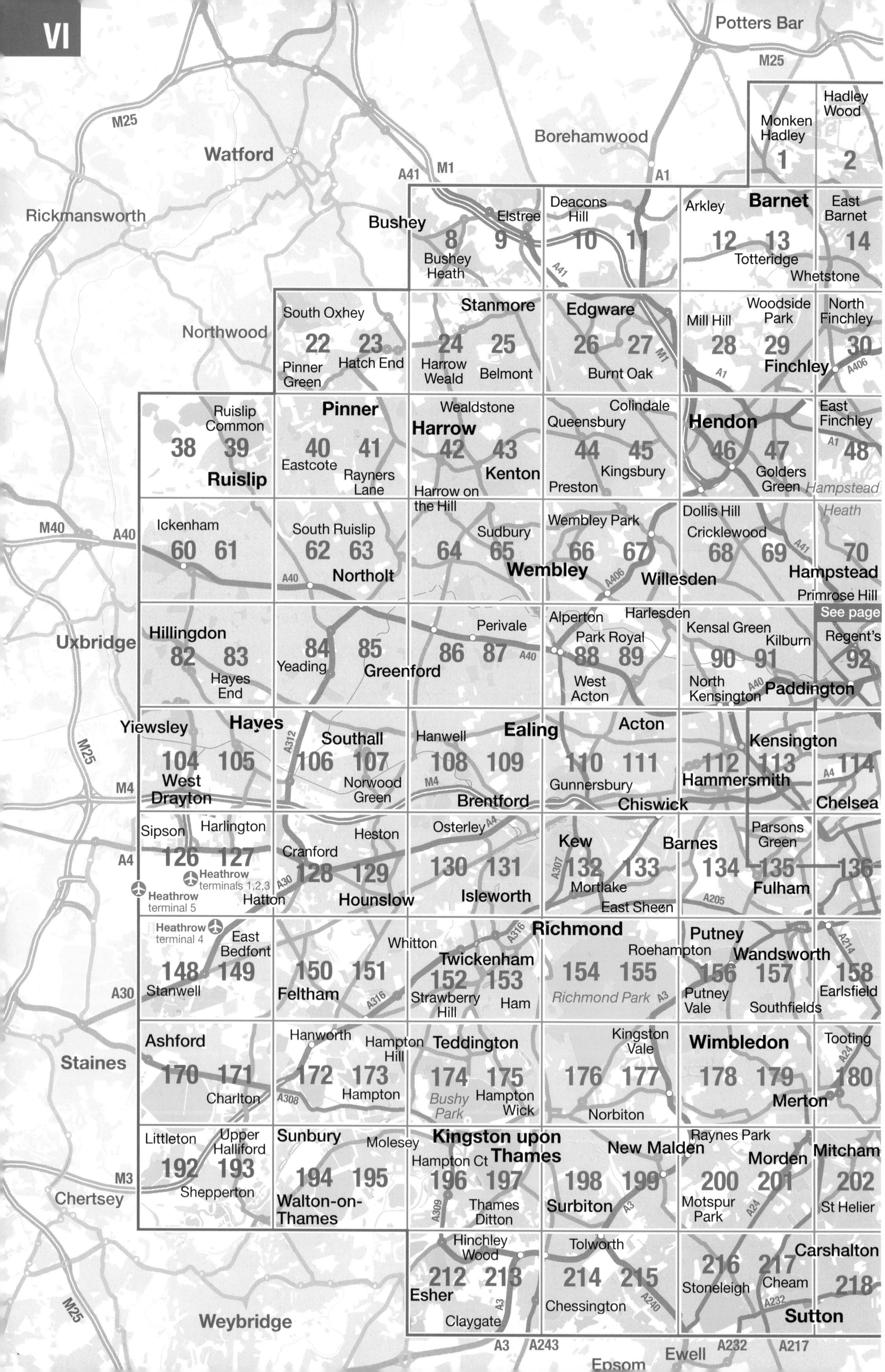
Potters Bar
M25
Hadley Wood
Monken Hadley
1
2
Borehamwood
Watford
A41
M1
A1
Rickmansworth
Bushey
Elstree
8
9
Bushey Heath
Deacons Hill
10
11
A41
Arkley
Barnet
12
13
Totteridge
East Barnet
14
Whetstone
South Oxhey
22
23
Pinner Green
Hatch End
Northwood
Stanmore
24
25
Harrow Weald
Belmont
Edgware
26
27
Burnt Oak
M1
Mill Hill
Woodside Park
28
29
A1
Finchley
North Finchley
30
A406
Ruislip Common
38
39
Ruislip
Pinner
40
41
Eastcote
Rayners Lane
Wealdstone
Harrow
42
43
Kenton
Harrow on the Hill
Colindale
Queensbury
44
45
Kingsbury
Preston
Hendon
46
47
Golders Green
East Finchley
A1
48
Hampstead Heath
M40
A40
Ickenham
60
61
South Ruislip
62
63
A40
Northolt
64
Sudbury
65
Wembley
Wembley Park
66
67
A406
Willesden
Dollis Hill
Cricklewood
68
69
A41
70
Hampstead
Primrose Hill
See page
Uxbridge
Hillingdon
82
83
Hayes End
84
Yeading
85
Greenford
Perivale
86
87
A40
Alperton
Harlesden
Park Royal
88
89
West Acton
Kensal Green
Kilburn
90
91
North Kensington
A40
Paddington
Regent's
92
Yiewsley
Hayes
A312
Southall
106
107
Norwood Green
M25
M4
104
105
West Drayton
Hanwell
Ealing
108
109
M4
Brentford
Acton
110
111
Gunnersbury
Chiswick
112
Kensington
113
Hammersmith
A4
114
Chelsea
Sipson
Harlington
126
127
A4
Heathrow terminals 1,2,3
Heathrow terminal 5
Hatton
Cranford
Heston
128
129
A30
Hounslow
Osterley
A4
130
131
Isleworth
Kew
A307
132
133
Mortlake
East Sheen
Barnes
134
A205
Parsons Green
135
Fulham
136
Heathrow terminal 4
East Bedfont
148
149
Stanwell
A30
150
151
Feltham
A316
Whitton
Twickenham
152
153
Strawberry Hill
Ham
A316
Richmond
154
155
Richmond Park
A3
Roehampton
Putney
Wandsworth
156
157
Putney Vale
Southfields
A214
158
Earlsfield
Staines
Ashford
170
171
Charlton
Hanworth
Hampton Hill
172
173
A308
Hampton
Teddington
174
175
Bushy Park
Hampton Wick
Kingston Vale
176
177
Norbiton
Wimbledon
178
179
Merton
Tooting
A24
180
Littleton
Upper Halliford
192
193
Shepperton
M3
Chertsey
Sunbury
Molesey
194
195
Walton-on-Thames
Kingston upon Thames
Hampton Ct
196
197
A309
Thames Ditton
New Malden
198
199
Surbiton
A3
Raynes Park
Morden
200
201
Motspur Park
A24
Mitcham
202
St Helier
Hinchley Wood
212
213
Esher
A3
Claygate
Tolworth
214
215
Chessington
A240
216
217
Stoneleigh
Cheam
A232
Carshalton
218
Sutton
M25
Weybridge
A3
A243
Epsom
Ewell
A232
A217

Key to map pages

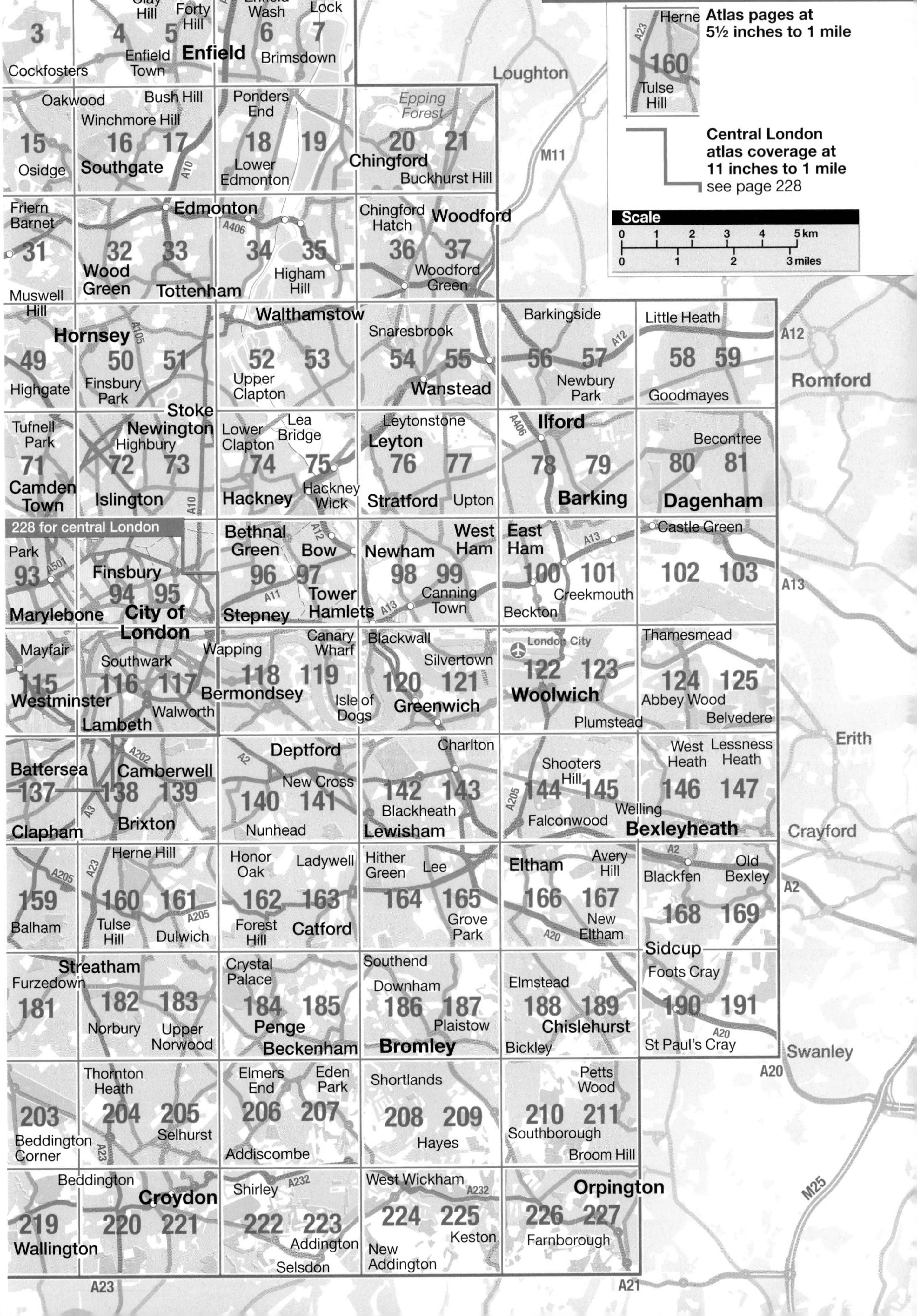
Herne Hill
160
Tulse Hill
A23
Atlas pages at 5½ inches to 1 mile
Central London atlas coverage at 11 inches to 1 mile
see page 228
Scale
0 1 2 3 4 5 km
0 1 2 3 miles
M25
A10
3 Cockfosters
4 Clay Hill
5 Forty Hill Enfield Town Enfield
6 Enfield Wash
7 Enfield Lock Brimsdown
Loughton
15 Oakwood Osidge
16 17 Bush Hill Winchmore Hill Southgate
18 19 Ponders End Lower Edmonton
20 21 Epping Forest Chingford Buckhurst Hill
M11
31 Friern Barnet Muswell Hill
32 33 Edmonton Wood Green Tottenham
34 35 A406 Higham Hill
36 37 Chingford Hatch Woodford Woodford Green
49 Highgate Hornsey
50 51 A105 Finsbury Park
52 53 Walthamstow Upper Clapton
54 55 Snaresbrook Wanstead
56 57 Barkingside Newbury Park A12
58 59 Little Heath Goodmayes
A12 Romford
71 Tufnell Park Camden Town
72 73 Stoke Newington Highbury Islington
74 75 Lower Clapton Lea Bridge Hackney Hackney Wick
76 77 Leytonstone Leyton Stratford Upton
78 79 A406 Ilford Barking
80 81 Becontree Dagenham
228 for central London
93 Park A501 Marylebone
94 95 Finsbury City of London
96 97 Bethnal Green Bow A12 A11 Stepney Tower Hamlets
98 99 Newham West Ham Canning Town A13
100 101 East Ham A13 Creekmouth Beckton
102 103 Castle Green
A13
115 Mayfair Westminster
116 117 Southwark Walworth Lambeth
118 119 Wapping Canary Wharf Bermondsey Isle of Dogs
120 121 Blackwall Silvertown Greenwich
122 123 London City Woolwich Plumstead
124 125 Thamesmead Abbey Wood Belvedere
Erith
137 Battersea Clapham
138 139 A202 Camberwell A3 Brixton
140 141 A2 Deptford New Cross Nunhead
142 143 Charlton Blackheath Lewisham
144 145 A205 Shooters Hill Falconwood Welling
146 147 West Heath Lessness Heath Bexleyheath
Crayford
159 A205 Balham
160 161 Herne Hill A23 A205 Tulse Hill Dulwich
162 163 Honor Oak Ladywell Forest Hill Catford
164 165 Hither Green Lee Grove Park
166 167 Eltham Avery Hill A20 New Eltham
168 169 A2 Blackfen Old Bexley Sidcup
A2
181 Streatham Furzedown
182 183 Norbury Upper Norwood
184 185 Crystal Palace Penge Beckenham
186 187 Southend Downham Plaistow Bromley
188 189 Elmstead Chislehurst Bickley
190 191 Foots Cray A20 St Paul's Cray
Swanley
A20
203 Beddington Corner
204 205 Thornton Heath A23 Selhurst
206 207 Elmers End Eden Park Addiscombe
208 209 Shortlands Hayes
210 211 Petts Wood Southborough Broom Hill
219 Beddington Wallington
220 221 Croydon
222 223 Shirley A232 Addington Selsdon
224 225 West Wickham A232 Keston New Addington
226 227 Orpington Farnborough
M25
A23
A21

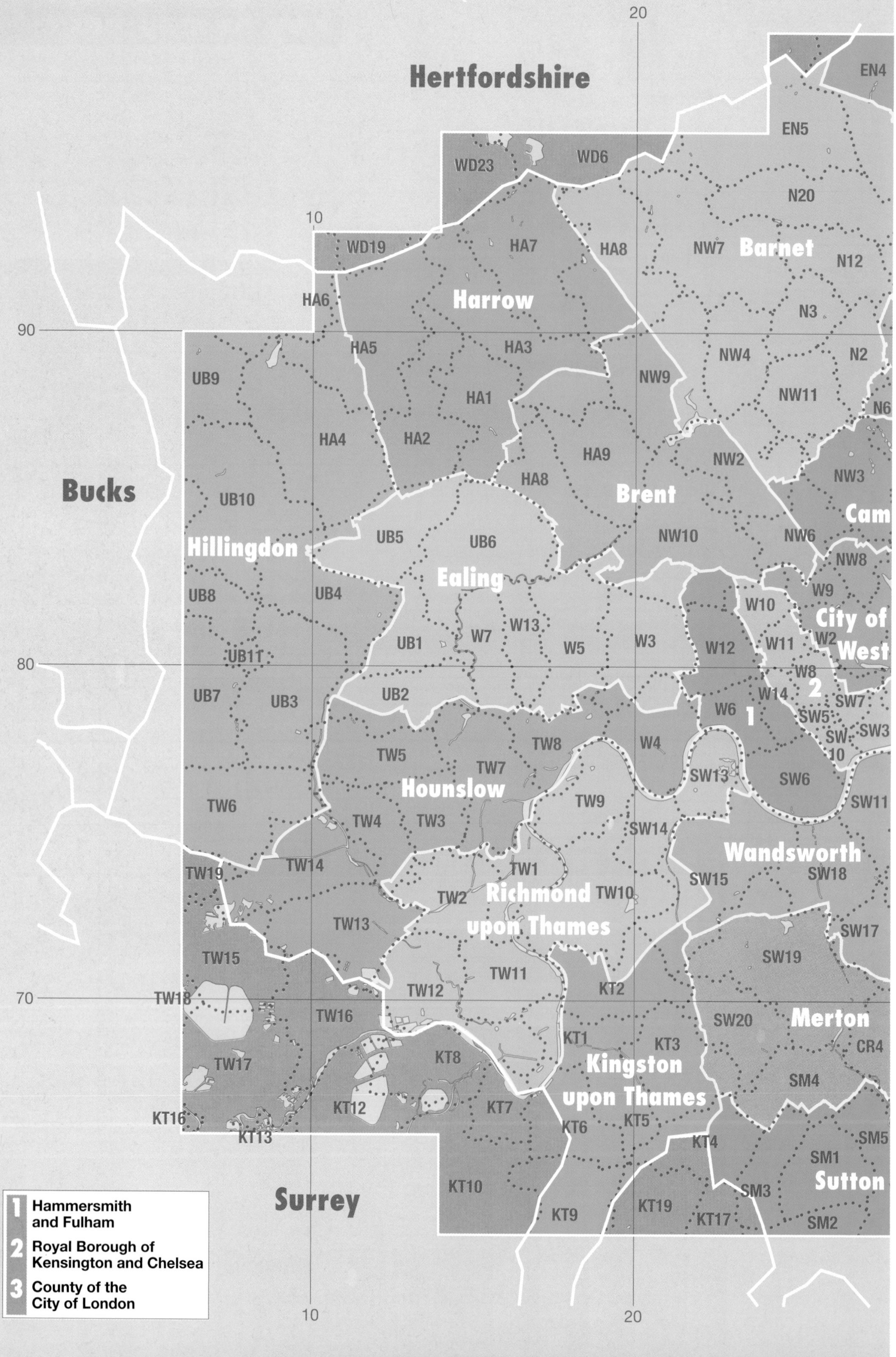
Hertfordshire
Bucks
Surrey
Hillingdon
Harrow
Barnet
Brent
Ealing
Hounslow
Richmond upon Thames
Kingston upon Thames
Wandsworth
Merton
Sutton
City of West
Cam
EN4
EN5
WD23
WD6
WD19
N20
N12
N3
N2
N6
NW7
NW4
NW11
NW9
NW2
NW3
NW10
NW6
NW8
HA6
HA7
HA8
HA5
HA3
HA1
HA4
HA2
HA9
UB9
UB10
UB5
UB6
UB8
UB4
UB11
UB1
UB7
UB3
UB2
W7
W13
W5
W3
W12
W10
W9
W11
W2
W8
W14
W6
W4
SW7
SW5
SW10
SW3
SW13
SW6
SW11
SW14
SW15
SW18
SW17
SW19
SW20
TW5
TW7
TW8
TW6
TW4
TW3
TW9
TW19
TW14
TW1
TW2
TW10
TW13
TW15
TW11
TW18
TW12
TW16
TW17
KT2
KT1
KT3
KT8
KT7
KT12
KT16
KT13
KT6
KT5
KT4
KT10
KT9
KT19
KT17
CR4
SM4
SM5
SM1
SM3
SM2
1
2
10
20
70
80
90
Hammersmith and Fulham
Royal Borough of Kensington and Chelsea
County of the City of London

Major administrative and Postcode boundaries

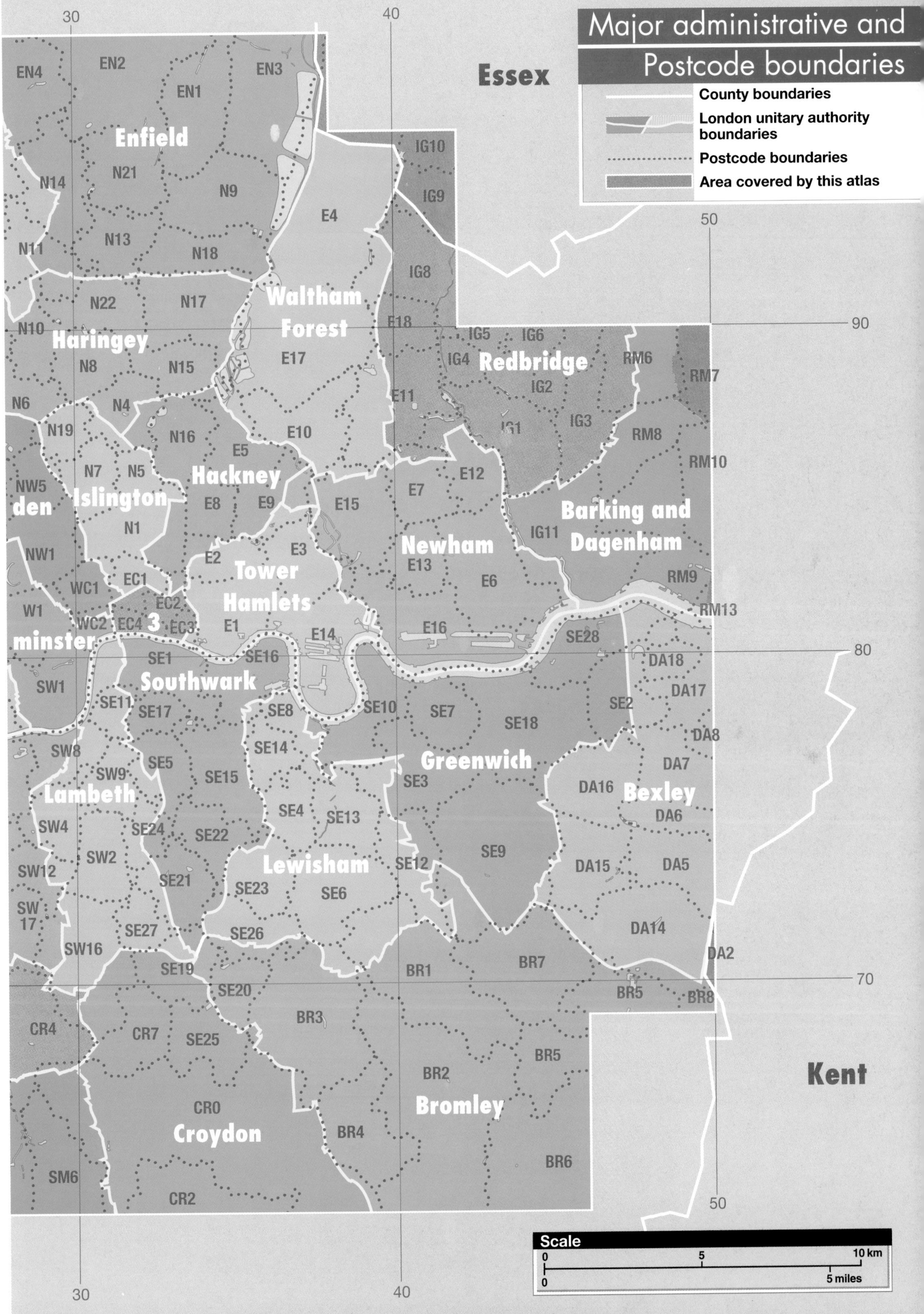
County boundaries
London unitary authority boundaries
Postcode boundaries
Area covered by this atlas
Essex
Kent
Enfield
Haringey
Waltham Forest
Redbridge
Hackney
Islington
den
Tower Hamlets
Newham
Barking and Dagenham
minster
3
Southwark
Greenwich
Bexley
Lambeth
Lewisham
Bromley
Croydon
EN4
EN2
EN1
EN3
N14
N21
N9
N11
N13
N18
N22
N17
N10
N8
N15
N6
N4
N19
N16
N7
N5
NW5
N1
NW1
WC1
EC1
EC2
W1
WC2
EC4
EC3
E1
E2
E3
E4
E5
E8
E9
E10
E11
E12
E13
E14
E15
E16
E17
E18
E6
E7
IG10
IG9
IG8
IG5
IG6
IG4
IG2
IG1
IG3
IG11
RM6
RM7
RM8
RM10
RM9
RM13
SE1
SE16
SE11
SE17
SE8
SE10
SE7
SE18
SE28
SE2
SE14
SE5
SE15
SE3
SE4
SE13
SE24
SE22
SE12
SE9
SE21
SE23
SE6
SE27
SE26
SE19
SE20
SE25
SW1
SW8
SW9
SW4
SW2
SW12
SW 17
SW16
DA18
DA17
DA8
DA7
DA16
DA6
DA15
DA5
DA14
DA2
BR1
BR7
BR5
BR8
BR3
BR2
BR4
BR6
CR4
CR7
CR0
CR2
SM6
30
40
50
90
80
70
Scale
0
5
10 km
5 miles

Route planning

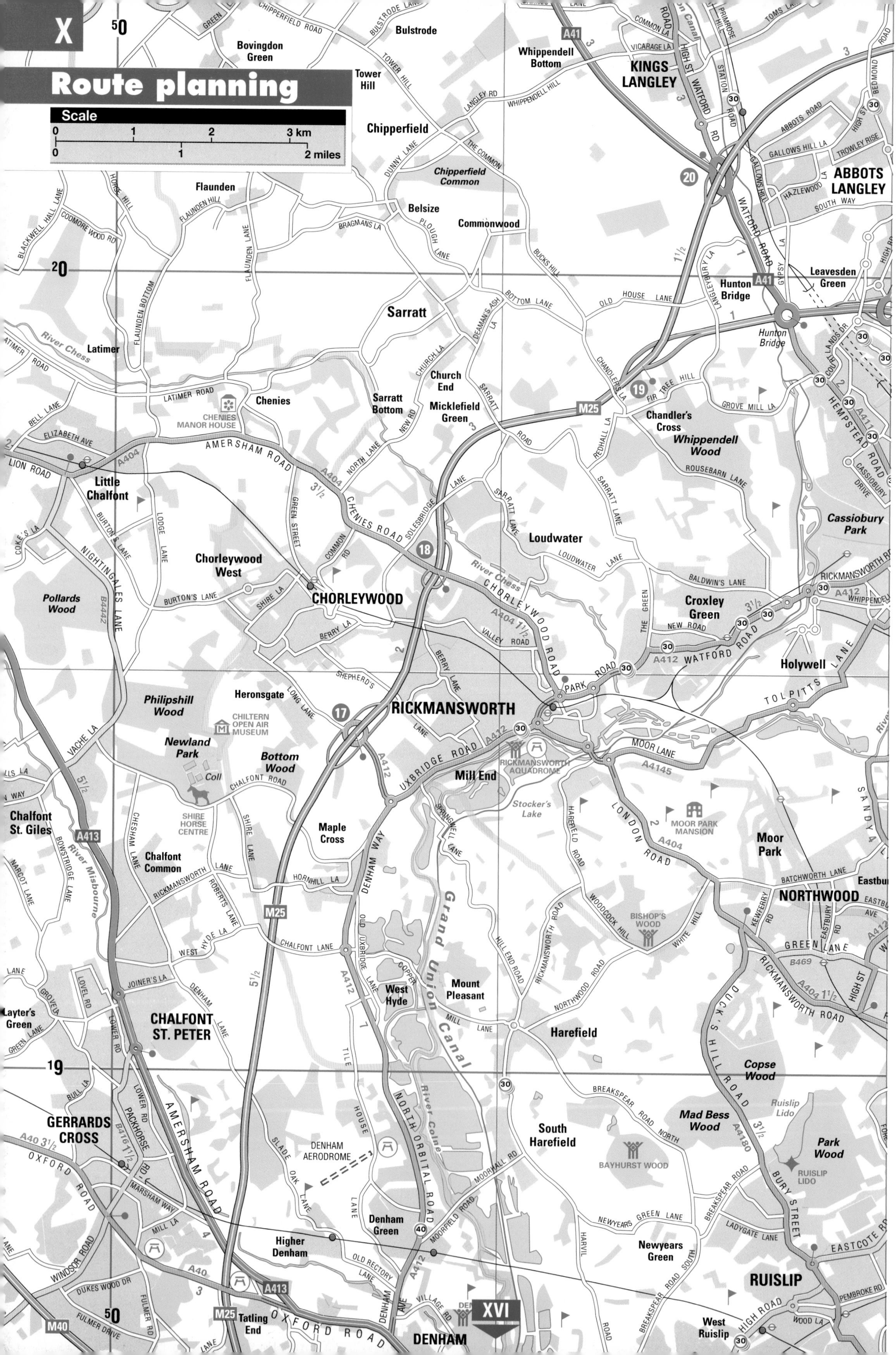
Scale
0 1 2 3 km
0 1 2 miles
Bovingdon Green
Bulstrode
Tower Hill
Chipperfield
Chipperfield Common
Whippendell Bottom
KINGS LANGLEY
ABBOTS LANGLEY
Flaunden
Belsize
Commonwood
Leavesden Green
Hunton Bridge
Sarratt
Latimer
River Chess
Chenies
CHENIES MANOR HOUSE
Church End
Sarratt Bottom
Micklefield Green
Chandler's Cross
Whippendell Wood
Little Chalfont
Loudwater
Cassiobury Park
Chorleywood West
CHORLEYWOOD
Pollards Wood
Croxley Green
Holywell
Heronsgate
Philipshill Wood
CHILTERN OPEN AIR MUSEUM
RICKMANSWORTH
Newland Park
Bottom Wood
Mill End
RICKMANSWORTH AQUADROME
Stocker's Lake
Chalfont St. Giles
SHIRE HORSE CENTRE
Maple Cross
MOOR PARK MANSION
Moor Park
Chalfont Common
NORTHWOOD
BISHOP'S WOOD
Grand Union Canal
West Hyde
Mount Pleasant
CHALFONT ST. PETER
Harefield
Layter's Green
Copse Wood
Ruislip Lido
GERRARDS CROSS
South Harefield
Mad Bess Wood
Park Wood
DENHAM AERODROME
BAYHURST WOOD
RUISLIP LIDO
Denham Green
Higher Denham
Newyears Green
RUISLIP
Tatling End
DENHAM
West Ruislip
River Colne
River Misbourne
M25
A41
A404
A412
A413
A4145
A4180
A40
M40
B4442
B469
B416
AMERSHAM ROAD
CHENIES ROAD
CHORLEYWOOD ROAD
WATFORD ROAD
UXBRIDGE ROAD
LONDON ROAD
MOOR LANE
DENHAM WAY
NORTH ORBITAL ROAD
OXFORD ROAD
HEMPSTEAD ROAD
RICKMANSWORTH ROAD
DUCK'S HILL ROAD
BURY STREET
HIGH ROAD
XVI
20
19

XI
52
M25
How Wood
Frogmore
Broad Colney
THE DE HAVILLAND AIRCRAFT HERITAGE CENTRE & MOSQUITO MUSEUM
Waterdale
BRICKET WOOD
Colney Street
Shenleybury
Woodside
Shenley
Garston
Radlett
20
WATFORD
North Watford
Dome Rdbt
Meriden
Berrygrove Interchange
Aldenham
River Colne
Catherine Bourne
Well End
Letchmore Heath
Patchetts Green
Watford Junction
BOREHAMWOOD
Film Studios
ELSTREE AERODROME
Hilfield Park Reservoir
ALDENHAM
BUSHEY
OXHEY
Bushey Heath
Elstree
Deacons Hill
Stirling Corner
Scratchwood
XII
Brockley Hill
Edgeware Bury
LONDON GATEWAY SERVICES
Stanmore Common
Carpenders Park
South Oxhey
Oxhey Woods
Apex Corner
EDGWARE
Mill Hill Circus
Canons Park
STANMORE
Hatch End
Harrow Weald
Little Stanmore
Burnt Oak
Graham Park
Headstone Lane
Headstone
Belmont
19
HARROW MUSEUM
Queensbury
Colindale
PINNER
Civic Centre
Wealdstone
HARROW
KENTON
Eastcote Village
North Harrow
Greenhill
Kingsbury
West Harrow
Eastcote
Northwick Park
Preston Road
Barn Hill
FRYENT
Ruislip Manor
Rayners Lane
Harrow on the Hill
Roxeth
XVII
North Wembley
Brent Reservoir (Welsh Harp)
FORTY LANE
52

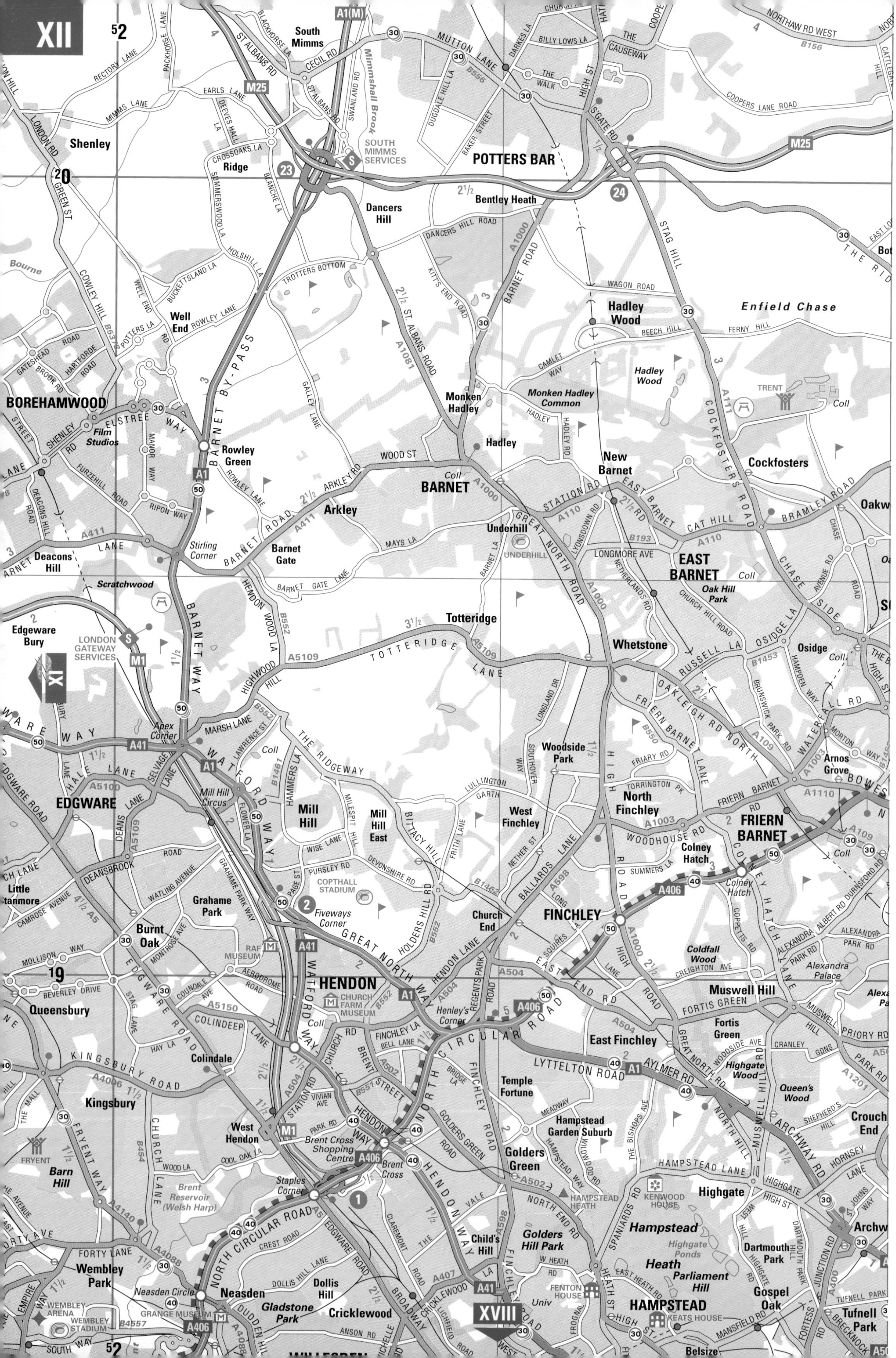
South Mimms
Shenley
Ridge
SOUTH MIMMS SERVICES
POTTERS BAR
Bentley Heath
Dancers Hill
Enfield Chase
Hadley Wood
Monken Hadley Common
Monken Hadley
Hadley
BOREHAMWOOD
Elstree Film Studios
Well End
Rowley Green
BARNET
Arkley
Cockfosters
New Barnet
Underhill
Barnet Gate
EAST BARNET
Oak Hill Park
Deacons Hill
Scratchwood
Stirling Corner
Edgware Bury
LONDON GATEWAY SERVICES
Totteridge
Whetstone
Osidge
Apex Corner
Woodside Park
Arnos Grove
EDGWARE
Mill Hill Circus
Mill Hill
Mill Hill East
West Finchley
North Finchley
FRIERN BARNET
Colney Hatch
Little Stanmore
Grahame Park
COPTHALL STADIUM
Fiveways Corner
Church End
FINCHLEY
Burnt Oak
RAF MUSEUM
HENDON
CHURCH FARM MUSEUM
Coldfall Wood
Alexandra Palace
Queensbury
Henley's Corner
Muswell Hill
Fortis Green
Colindale
East Finchley
Kingsbury
Temple Fortune
Highgate Wood
Queen's Wood
West Hendon
Hampstead Garden Suburb
Crouch End
Brent Cross Shopping Centre
Brent Cross
Golders Green
FRYENT
Barn Hill
Brent Reservoir (Welsh Harp)
Staples Corner
HAMPSTEAD HEATH
KENWOOD HOUSE
Highgate
Hampstead
Highgate Ponds
Child's Hill
Golders Hill Park
Heath
Parliament Hill
Dartmouth Park
Wembley Park
Neasden Circle
Neasden
Dollis Hill
Gospel Oak
WEMBLEY ARENA
WEMBLEY STADIUM
GRANGE MUSEUM
Gladstone Park
Cricklewood
FENTON HOUSE
HAMPSTEAD
KEATS HOUSE
Tufnell Park
Belsize
XVIII

Bury Green
CHESHUNT
LEE VALLEY
River Lea
Cattlegate
WALTHAM ABBEY
Waltham Cross
Holdbrook
Wood Green
HONEY LANE
M25
Crews Hill
Whitewebbs Park
CAPEL MANOR
Freezy Water
FORTY HALL
Clay Hill
Forty Hill
Enfield Wash
Enfield Lock
Sewardstone
High Beach
Gordon Hill
QUEEN ELIZABETH STADIUM
Enfield Highway
Brimsdown
King George's Reservoir
ENFIELD
World's End
Ponders End
Sewardstonebury
Grange Park
Bush Hill Park
Chingford Green
SOUTHGATE
Grovelands Park
Winchmore Hill
William Girling Reservoir
CHINGFORD
Friday Hill
PICKETT'S LOCK
Lower Edmonton
Palmers Green
Great Cambridge Junction
Pymmes Park
Cooks Ferry
Woodford Wells
Broomfield Park
Angel Edmonton
Hall Lane
Chingford Hatch
EDMONTON
Higham's Park
WOODFORD
Bowes Park
Clockhouse Junction
NEW RIVER STADIUM
Banbury Reservoir
Hale End
WALTHAMSTOW STADIUM
WOOD GREEN
BRUCE CASTLE MUSEUM
WHITE HART LANE
Crooked Billet
Woodford Green
Higham Hill
Waterworks Corner
Noel Park
TOTTENHAM
Bruce Grove
Reservoirs
West Green
Tottenham Hale
The Bell
WALTHAMSTOW
Snaresbrook
Seven Sisters
VESTRY HOUSE MUSEUM
HORNSEY
Harringay
South Tottenham
Stroud Green
Stamford Hill
Upper Clapton
WANSTEAD
Green Man Interchange
Finsbury Park
Leytonstone
Clapton
STOKE NEWINGTON
Lea Bridge
Hackney Marsh
LEYTON
Wanstead Flats
EMIRATES STADIUM
Shacklewell
Highbury
Nags Head
Clapton Park
Lea Interchange
Homerton
XIV
XIX
19
20

Claverhambury
Almes Green
Cobbins Brook
EPPING
Coopersale
Coopersale Street
Gaynes Park
Bell Common
Ivy Chimneys
Copthall Green
Upshire
WALTHAM ABBEY
Wood Green
Fiddlers Hamlet
Mount End
M25
M11
Wakearms Rdbt
Theydon Garnon
Hobbs Cross
Theydon Mount
Theydon Bois
Debden Green
Epping Forest
High Beach
STAPLEFORD AERODROME
Abridge
Debden
LOUGHTON
Sewardstonebury
River Roding
Nature Reserve
Lambourne End
CHINGFORD
Friday Hill
Buckhurst Hill
Chigwell Row
HAINULT FOREST
CHIGWELL
Woodford Wells
Chingford Hatch
Grange Hill
WOODFORD
Hale End
Woodford Bridge
Hainault
Woodford Green
Fairlop
Waterworks Corner
Charlie Browns Rdbt
Clayhall
Fulwell Cross
FAIRLOP WATERS
Marks Gate
Collier Row
Snaresbrook
Little Heath
Barkingside
Moby Dick
Redbridge
Gants Hill
Newbury Park
Seven Kings Park
Chadwell Heath
Redbridge Rdbt
WANSTEAD
Valentines Park
Seven Kings
Green Man Interchange
Wanstead Park
Cranbrook
Goodmayes
Leytonstone
XIII
XX

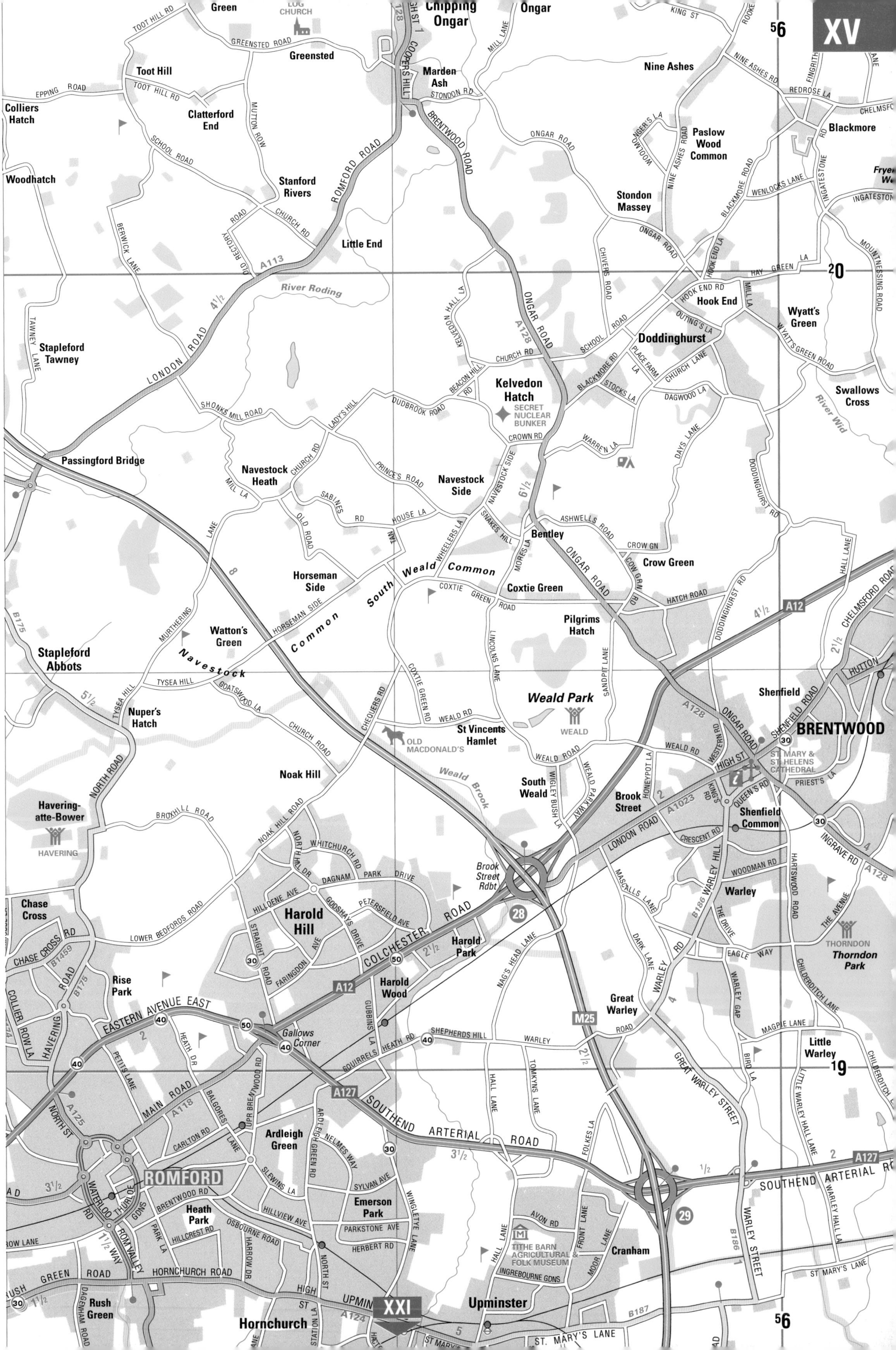

Chipping Ongar
Ongar
Green
LOG CHURCH
Greensted
GREENSTED ROAD
TOOT HILL RD
Toot Hill
Marden Ash
STONDON RD
Nine Ashes
NINE ASHES RD
REDROSE LA
Blackmore
CHELMSFORD
Colliers Hatch
EPPING ROAD
Clatterford End
MUTTON ROW
SCHOOL ROAD
COOPERS HILL
BRENTWOOD ROAD
ROMFORD ROAD
ONGAR ROAD
Paslow Wood Common
NINE ASHES ROAD
BLACKMORE ROAD
WENLOCKS LANE
INGATESTONE RD
INGATESTONE
Woodhatch
Stanford Rivers
CHURCH RD
OLD RECTORY ROAD
BERWICK LANE
Little End
Stondon Massey
CHIVERS ROAD
HOOK END LA
MOUNTNESSING ROAD
A113
River Roding
HAY GREEN LA
HOOK END RD
Hook End
MILL LA
Wyatt's Green
WYATT'S GREEN ROAD
OUTING'S LA
Doddinghurst
KELVEDON HALL LA
A128
CHURCH RD
SCHOOL ROAD
TAWNEY LANE
Stapleford Tawney
LONDON ROAD
BLACKMORE RD
PLACE FARM LA
CHURCH LANE
STOCKS LA
DAGWOOD LA
Swallows Cross
River Wid
BEACON HILL RD
Kelvedon Hatch
SECRET NUCLEAR BUNKER
CROWN RD
SHONKS MILL ROAD
DUDBROOK ROAD
LADY'S HILL
WARREN LA
DAYS LANE
Passingford Bridge
Navestock Heath
CHURCH RD
MILL LA
PRINCE'S ROAD
Navestock Side
NAVESTOCK SIDE
DODDINGHURST RD
SABINES RD
HOUSE LA
OLD ROAD
SNAKES HILL
ASHWELLS ROAD
Bentley
CROW GN
WHEELERS LA
MORES LA
COW GRN RD
Crow Green
HALL LANE
Horseman Side
South Weald Common
Coxtie Green
COXTIE GREEN ROAD
HATCH ROAD
A12
CHELMSFORD ROAD
Pilgrims Hatch
DODDINGHURST RD
HORSEMAN SIDE
Watton's Green
MURTHERING LANE
B175
Stapleford Abbots
Navestock
COXTIE GREEN RD
LINCOLNS LANE
SANDPIT LANE
HUTTON
TYSEA HILL
GOATSWOOD LA
Shenfield
Weald Park
WEALD
Nuper's Hatch
CHURCH ROAD
CHEQUERS RD
WEALD RD
St Vincents Hamlet
OLD MACDONALD'S
WEALD ROAD
WEALD RD
ONGAR ROAD
SHENFIELD ROAD
BRENTWOOD
ST MARY & ST HELENS CATHEDRAL
HIGH ST
WESTERN RD
NORTH ROAD
Weald Brook
Noak Hill
South Weald
WIGLEY BUSH LA
WEALD PARK WAY
HONEYPOT LA
Brook Street
A1023
KING'S RD
QUEEN'S RD
PRIEST'S LA
Havering-atte-Bower
HAVERING
BROXHILL ROAD
NOAK HILL ROAD
NORTH HILL DR
WHITCHURCH RD
LONDON ROAD
CRESCENT RD
Shenfield Common
INGRAVE RD
A128
DAGNAM PARK DRIVE
Brook Street Rdbt
WARLEY HILL
WOODMAN RD
HARTSWOOD ROAD
Chase Cross
HILLDENE AVE
GODSHAYS DRIVE
PETERSFIELD AVE
Harold Hill
COLCHESTER ROAD
Harold Park
MASCALLS LANE
Warley
THE DRIVE
THE AVENUE
THORNDON
Thorndon Park
LOWER BEDFORDS ROAD
CHASE CROSS RD
B1459
STRAIGHT ROAD
FARINGDON AVE
NAG'S HEAD LANE
DARK LANE
WARLEY RD
EAGLE WAY
CHILDERDITCH LANE
Rise Park
HAVERING ROAD
B175
COLLIER ROW LA
A12
Harold Wood
M25
Great Warley
WARLEY GAP
EASTERN AVENUE EAST
GUBBINS LA
Gallows Corner
HEATH DR
HEATH RD
SHEPHERDS HILL
WARLEY ROAD
MAGPIE LANE
Little Warley
PETITS LANE
SQUIRRELS HEATH LA
BIRD LA
A125
MAIN ROAD
A118
BALGORES LANE
UPR BRENTWOOD RD
A127
SOUTHEND ARTERIAL ROAD
HALL LANE
TOMKYNS LANE
GREAT WARLEY STREET
LITTLE WARLEY HALL LANE
CHILDERDITCH
NORTH ST
CARLTON RD
Ardleigh Green
ARDLEIGH GREEN RD
NELMES WAY
FOLKES LA
SOUTHEND ARTERIAL RD
SLEWINS LA
SYLVAN AVE
ROMFORD
WATERLOO RD
THURLOE GDNS
BRENTWOOD RD
Emerson Park
WINGLETYE LANE
AVON RD
FRONT LANE
WARLEY HALL LA
WARLEY STREET
Heath Park
HILLVIEW AVE
PARKSTONE AVE
ROW LANE
ROM VALLEY WAY
PARK LA
HILLCREST RD
OSBOURNE ROAD
HARROW DR
HERBERT RD
HALL LANE
TITHE BARN AGRICULTURAL & FOLK MUSEUM
MOOR LANE
Cranham
B186
ST MARY'S LANE
RUSH GREEN ROAD
HORNCHURCH ROAD
NORTH ST
INGREBOURNE GDNS
HIGH ST
UPMINSTER
Upminster
B187
Rush Green
DAGENHAM ROAD
STATION LA
Hornchurch
A124
ST MARY'S LANE
XXI

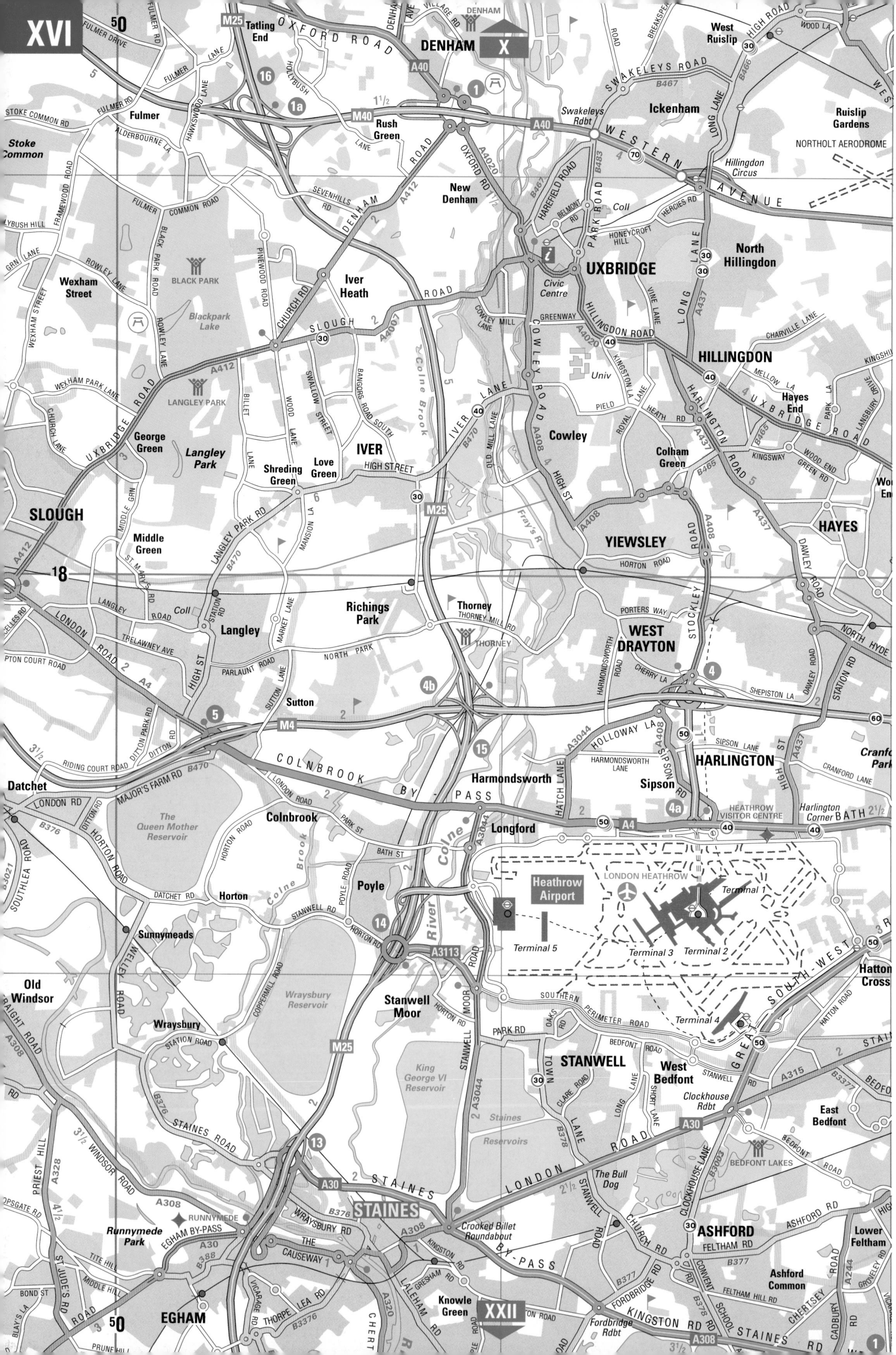

Tatling End
OXFORD ROAD
DENHAM
X
Fulmer
Stoke Common
Rush Green
West Ruislip
Ickenham
Ruislip Gardens
NORTHOLT AERODROME
SWAKELEYS ROAD
Swakeleys Rdbt
WESTERN AVENUE
Hillingdon Circus
New Denham
UXBRIDGE
North Hillingdon
Coll
Civic Centre
Wexham Street
BLACK PARK
Blackpark Lake
Iver Heath
SLOUGH ROAD
HILLINGDON ROAD
HILLINGDON
Univ
LANGLEY PARK
George Green
Langley Park
UXBRIDGE ROAD
Shreding Green
Love Green
IVER
HIGH STREET
Cowley
Colham Green
Hayes End
SLOUGH
Middle Green
YIEWSLEY
HAYES
Richings Park
Thorney
THORNEY
Langley
WEST DRAYTON
LONDON ROAD
Sutton
HARLINGTON
Harmondsworth
Sipson
COLNBROOK BY-PASS
The Queen Mother Reservoir
Colnbrook
Longford
HEATHROW VISITOR CENTRE
Harlington Corner
BATH
Datchet
LONDON HEATHROW
Heathrow Airport
Terminal 1
Terminal 2
Terminal 3
Terminal 5
Terminal 4
Horton
Poyle
River Colne
Sunnymeads
Wraysbury Reservoir
Stanwell Moor
Old Windsor
Wraysbury
King George VI Reservoir
STANWELL
West Bedfont
Clockhouse Rdbt
East Bedfont
Hatton Cross
GREAT SOUTH-WEST
Staines Reservoirs
BEDFONT LAKES
The Bull Dog
STAINES
RUNNYMEDE
Runnymede Park
EGHAM BY-PASS
Crooked Billet Roundabout
ASHFORD
Lower Feltham
Ashford Common
Knowle Green
XXII
EGHAM
Fordbridge Rdbt
KINGSTON RD
STAINES RD
M25
M40
M4
A40
A4
A30
A308
A3113
A3044
A412

XVII
52
XI
XVIII
XXIII
18
Roxeth
South Harrow
North Wembley
Wembley Park
Neasden Circle
Sudbury
WEMBLEY
WEMBLEY ARENA
WEMBLEY STADIUM
GRANGE MUSEUM
South Ruislip
Polish War Memorial
NORTHOLT
Target Rdbt
Stonebridge Park
Stonebridge
Alperton
Perivale
Greenford Rdbt
White Hart Rdbt
GREENFORD
LONDON MOTORCYCLE MUSEUM
Hangar Lane
Park Royal
Yeading
West Acton
Gipsy Corner
East Acton
EALING
Ossie Garvin Rdbt
Drayton Green
Hayes Town
Dormer's Wells
ACTON
SOUTHALL
West Ealing
HANWELL
South Acton
Grand Union Canal
Norwood Green
Northfields
Gunnersbury Park
Chiswick Rdbt
Osterley Park
HESTON SERVICES
OSTERLEY PARK (N.T.)
BRENTFORD
GRIFFIN PARK
STEAM MUS.
Kew Bridge
CHISWICK
HESTON
Gillette Corner
MUSIC MUS.
Kew
Public Record Office
North Hyde
Osterley
Grove Park
Syon Park
SYON HOUSE
ROYAL BOTANIC GARDENS (KEW)
Waggoners Rdbt
Cranford
Henlys Rdbt
Civic Centre
North Sheen
Chiswick Br
Hounslow West
Woodlands
Chalkers Corner
Mortlake
HOUNSLOW
Richmond Circus
Old Deer Park
Manor Circus
ISLEWORTH
East Sheen
Twickenham Br
RICHMOND
RUGBY MUS.
TWICKENHAM
Hounslow Heath
Richmond Br
St Margarets
Richmond Hill
Whitton
THE STOOP
MARBLE HILL HOUSE
TWICKENHAM
Roads in Richmond Park open in daylight hours only
Richmond Park
FELTHAM
Petersham
HAM HOUSE (N.T.)
River Thames
Hanworth Park
Ham
Apex Corner
Robin Hood
Kingston Vale
HANWORTH
TEDDINGTON

XVIII
XII
XXIV
WILLESDEN
Cricklewood
West Hampstead
Swiss Cottage
Belsize Park
Kentish Town
CAMDEN TOWN
Brondesbury
Kilburn
Harlesden
Stonebridge
Stonebridge Park
Kensal Rise
Primrose Hill
Regents Park
LONDON ZOO
St. John's Wood
Maida Vale
Park Royal
Old Oak Common
Wormwood Scrubs Park
LINFORD CHRISTIE STADIUM
Grand Union Canal
Marylebone
MARYLEBONE
MADAME TUSSAUD'S
West Acton
Gipsy Corner
East Acton
Westbourne Park
PADDINGTON
Paddington
ACTON
White City
LOFTUS ROAD
Notting Hill
Bayswater
MUSEUM OF BRANDS
Hyde Park
Kensington Gardens
KENSINGTON PALACE
Mayfair
Green Park
BUCKINGHAM PALACE
St James's Park
Westfield London
Shepherd's Bush
South Acton
Bedford Park
Holland Park
Knightsbridge
ROYAL ALBERT HALL
NATURAL HISTORY
HAMMERSMITH
Olympia
CHELSEA
Victoria
Pimlico
Chiswick Rdbt
CHISWICK
Hogarth Rdbt
Hammersmith Br
Hammersmith Broadway
Earl's Court
THE QUEEN'S CLUB
CHISWICK HOUSE
Public Record Office
Kew Bridge
Grove Park
FULHAM
Parsons Green
STAMFORD BRIDGE
NATIONAL ARMY MUSEUM
Chelsea Br
Albert Br
CHILDREN'S ZOO
Battersea Park
Battersea Br
BATTERSEA
WETLANDS CENTRE
River Thames
BARNES
CRAVEN COTTAGE
Barnes Br
Chiswick Br
North Sheen
Mortlake
Chalkers Corner
Manor Circus
Putney Br
Hurlingham Park
WESTLAND HELIPORT
Wandsworth Br
Clapham Junction
CLAPHAM
Clapham Common
RICHMOND
East Sheen
Red Rover
PUTNEY
Wandsworth Gyratory
WANDSWORTH
Roehampton
Putney Heath
West Hill
Wandsworth Common
Richmond Hill
Tibbet's Corner
Balham
Grange Mills
Roads in Richmond Park open in daylight hours only
Richmond Park
Southfields
Earlsfield
River Wandle
Upper Tooting
Tooting Bec Common
Tooting Bec
Putney Vale
Robin Hood
WIMBLEDON L.T.A.
Wimbledon Park
TENNIS MUSEUM
WIMBLEDON STADIUM
Kingston Vale
Wimbledon Common
WIMBLEDON
Tooting
Furzedown
Crooked Billet
Collier's Wood
KINGSTON UPON THAMES
Coombe
Coombe Lane
Norbiton
NEW MALDEN
MITCHAM

XIX
54
XIII
XX
XXV
17
18
Highbury
Canonbury
Clapton Park
Lea Interchange
Temple Mills
STRATFORD
Forest Gate
HACKNEY
Hackney Wick
Dalston
Upton
West Ham Park
Victoria Park
WEST HAM
ISLINGTON
SHOREDITCH
Old Ford
BOW
Kings Cross
BETHNAL GREEN
FINSBURY
Plaistow
Bromley
Spitalfields
Holborn
Liverpool St
Stepney
POPLAR
Canning Town
Prince Regent
Law Courts
City Thameslink
Aldgate
Limehouse
Blackwall
Blackwall Tunnel
EXCEL CENTRE
Royal Victoria Dock
Charing Cross
Blackfriars Br
Millennium Br
Southwark Br
London Br
Cannon St
Fenchurch St
Waterloo Br
TOWER OF LONDON
Wapping
Rotherhithe Tunnel
Canary Wharf
West India Docks
MILLENNIUM DOME
North Greenwich
TATE MODERN
GLOBE THEATRE & EXHIBITION
HAY'S GALLERIA
Tower Br
LONDON EYE
Govt Offices
Westminster Br
Waterloo
London Bridge
DESIGN MUS
BRUNEL ENGINE HOUSE MUSEUM
Rotherhithe
ISLE OF DOGS
Millwall
Houses of Parliament
BERMONDSEY
Surrey Quays
River Thames
THAMES BARRIER VISITOR CENTRE
IMPERIAL WAR MUSEUM
Lambeth Br
LAMBETH
Elephant & Castle
Walworth
THE NEW DEN
CUTTY SARK
RN Coll
Vauxhall Cross
THE OVAL
DEPTFORD
GREENWICH
NATIONAL MARITIME MUSEUM
Greenwich Park
GREENWICH OBSERVATORY
Kennington
LIVESEY MUSEUM
Peckham
New Cross
Sun in the Sands Rdbt
Camberwell Green
CAMBERWELL
BLACKHEATH
BRIXTON
East Dulwich
Nunhead
Brockley
Blackheath Park
LEWISHAM
Peckham Rye Park
Honor Oak
Ladywell
Hither Green
Brockwell Park
Lee
Catford Gyratory
Dulwich Park
PICTURE GALLERY
CATFORD
HORNIMAN MUSEUM
Forest Hill
Tulse Hill
West Dulwich
Dulwich
Mottingham
STREATHAM
Bellingham
Bell Green
Grove Park
Downham
CRYSTAL PALACE NATIONAL SPORTS CENTRE
PENGE
Norwood
Streatham Common
Beckenham Place Park
Plaistow
Norbury
Anerley
BECKENHAM
BROMLEY

ILFORD
Redbridge Museum
Ilford Interchange
Loxford
Wanstead Flats
Manor Park
Forest Gate
Little Ilford
Fair Cross
Becontree
Mayesbrook Park
Plashet
Upton
Upton Park
West Ham Park
BARKING
Barking Flyover
Castle Green
Eastbury Manor House
Ripple Road
Heathway
Movers Lane
WEST HAM
Boleyn Gd (Upton Park)
Wallend
EAST HAM
Plaistow
Gas Museum
Creekmouth
Barking Creek
Beckton Alps
Beckton
Prince Regent
Canning Town
Custom House
River Thames
Crossness Pumping Station
Blackwall
Blackwall Tunnel
ExCeL Centre
Royal Victoria Dock
Royal Albert Dock
City Airport
King George V Dock
Thamesmead
Millennium Dome
North Greenwich
Silvertown
Thames Barrier
North Woolwich
Old Station Railway Museum
Woolwich Ferry
Thames Barrier Visitor Centre
WOOLWICH
Abbey Wood
Plumstead
Belvedere
The Valley
GREENWICH
National Maritime Museum
Greenwich Park
Greenwich Observatory
Charlton
Woolwich Common
Bostall Woods
West Heath
Lessness Heath
East Wickham
Sun in the Sands Rdbt
Shooters Hill
Kidbrooke
Eltham Common
Welling
BLACKHEATH
Kidbrooke Intc
Oxleas Wood
Blackheath Park
Falconwood
Bexleyheath
LEWISHAM
Hither Green
Danson Park
The Red House
Danson Interchange
ELTHAM
BEXLEY
Yorkshire Grey
Lee
Cliftons Rdbt
Avery Hill
Blackfen
Eltham Palace
Old Bexley
New Eltham
Mottingham
Grove Park
Longlands
SIDCUP
North Cray
Downham
Elmstead Wood
Elmstead
Plaistow
Sundridge
Chislehurst
Frognal Corner
Scadbury Park Nature Reserve
Foots Cray
Upper
XIV
XIX
XXVI
54

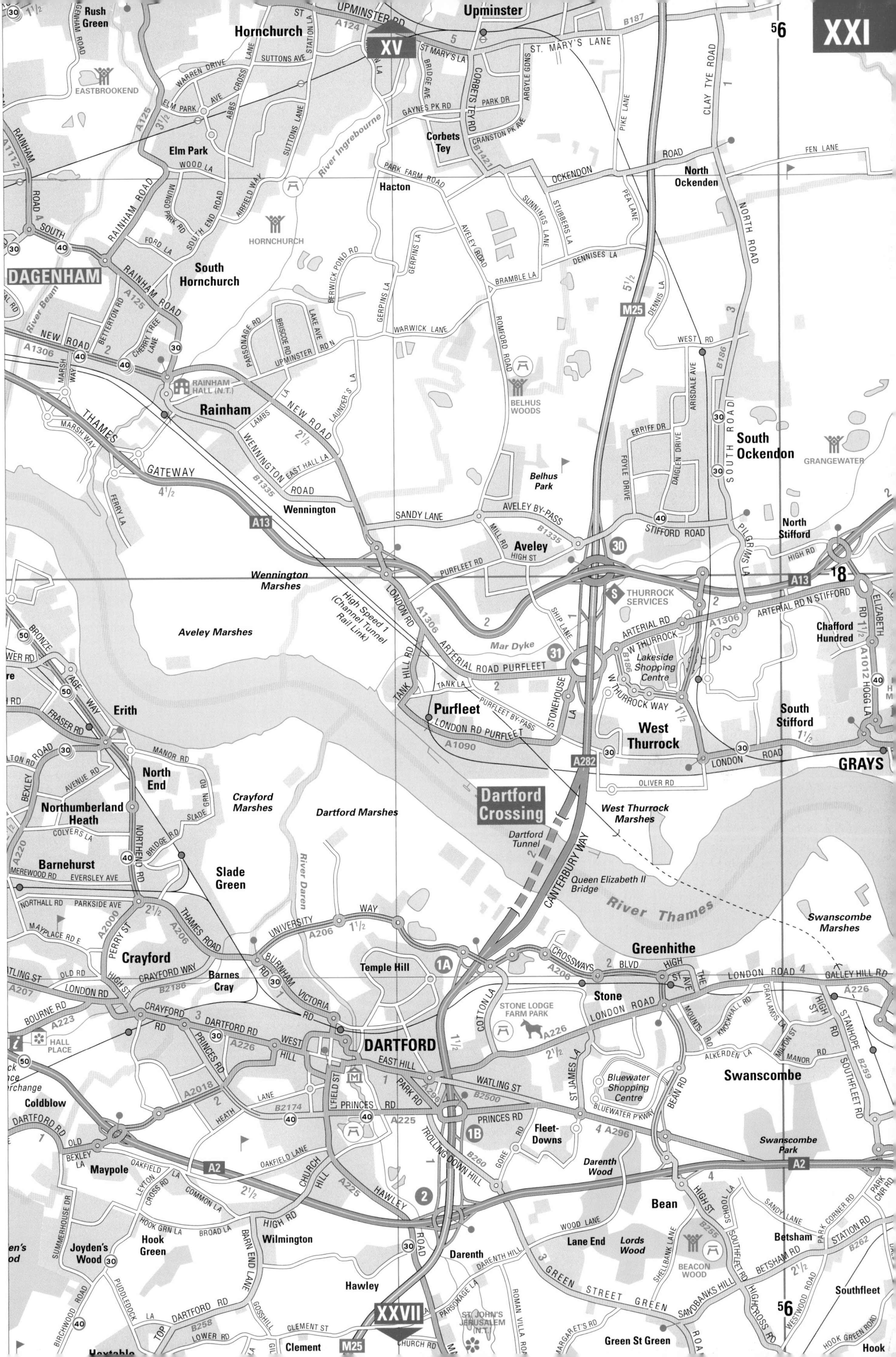

Rush Green
Upminster
Hornchurch
EASTBROOKEND
Elm Park
Corbets Tey
Hacton
North Ockenden
HORNCHURCH
DAGENHAM
South Hornchurch
River Ingrebourne
River Beam
Rainham
RAINHAM HALL (N.T.)
BELHUS WOODS
South Ockendon
GRANGEWATER
Belhus Park
Wennington
North Stifford
Aveley
Wennington Marshes
THURROCK SERVICES
Chafford Hundred
High Speed 1 (Channel Tunnel Rail Link)
Aveley Marshes
Mar Dyke
Lakeside Shopping Centre
Erith
Purfleet
South Stifford
West Thurrock
GRAYS
North End
Crayford Marshes
Dartford Marshes
Dartford Crossing
Dartford Tunnel
West Thurrock Marshes
Northumberland Heath
Barnehurst
Slade Green
River Darent
Queen Elizabeth II Bridge
River Thames
Swanscombe Marshes
Crayford
Temple Hill
Greenhithe
Barnes Cray
Stone
STONE LODGE FARM PARK
HALL PLACE
DARTFORD
Swanscombe
Bluewater Shopping Centre
Coldblow
Fleet-Downs
Swanscombe Park
Darenth Wood
Maypole
Bean
Hook Green
Joyden's Wood
Wilmington
Darenth
Lane End
Lords Wood
BEACON WOOD
Betsham
Hawley
Southfleet
ST JOHN'S JERUSALEM (N.T.)
Clement
Green St Green
Hook
Hextable
XV
XXVII
M25
A13
A2
A282
56

XVI
EGHAM
Milton Park
Knowle Green
Fordbridge Rdbt
Queen Mary Reservoir
Charlton
Stroude
Callow Hill
Longside Lake
Thorpe
Thorpe Park
Marina
River Thames
Laleham
Littleton
Shepperton Green
Upper Halliford
Virginia Water
Shepperton
Lower Halliford
Marina
Chertsey Museum
CHERTSEY
Chertsey Br
Walton Br
Lyne
Chertsey Common
Addlestonemoor
Woburn Park
Coll
Broad Water
WEYBRIDGE
Oatlands Park
Elmbridge Museum
ADDLESTONE
Ottershaw
Row Town
River Wey
R Navigation
Coll
Brooklands Museum
New Haw
St George's Hill
Fairoaks Aerodrome
Woodham
Brooklands
Whiteley Village
Anningsley Park
Dartnell Park
Horsell Common
Sheerwater
River Navigation
West Byfleet
Cobham Bus Museum
Silver Mere
Byfleet
Cheapside
Pain's Hill
Painshill Park
Horsell
Pyrford
Foxwarren Park
Wisley
Maybury
Pyrford Green
Wisley Common
Telegraph Hill
Bolder Mere
R.H.S. Garden Wisley
WOKING
Elm Corner
Hook Heath
Ripley Green
Bridge End
Martyr's Green
Old Woking
Ripley
Westfield
River Wey
Ockham Park
Church End
Ockham
Mayford
Cartbridge
Send
Send Marsh
Hungry Hill
Sutton Green
East
M25
M3
A3
A308
A320
A317
A319
A245
A3046
A3050
A318
A244
A247
B3376
B388
B377
B376
B389
B3366
B375
B387
B386
B3121
B385
B373
B372
B374
B365
B382
B367
B380
B2215
B368
B2039
London Rd
Prune Hill
Christchurch Road
Sandhills La
Kingston Rd
Staines Rd West
Shepperton Rd
Laleham Rd
Chertsey Rd
Russell Rd
Guildford Road
Chobham Road
Woodham Lane
Portsmouth Road
Ripley By-Pass
Ockham Road North
Send Road
Egley Road
Kingfield Rd
High St
Victoria Way

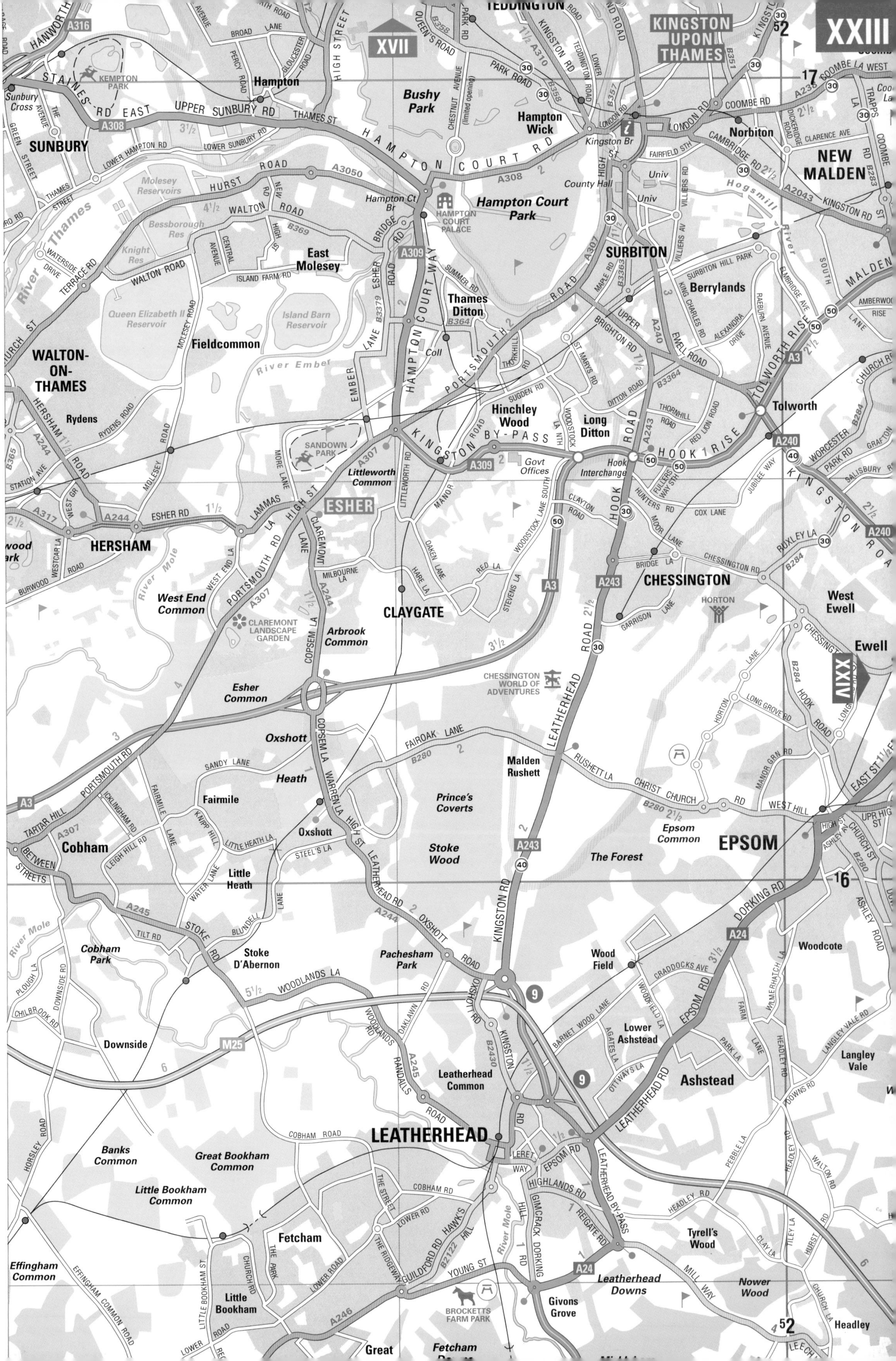
XXIII
XVII
XXIV
KINGSTON UPON THAMES
TEDDINGTON
Hampton
Bushy Park
Hampton Wick
SUNBURY
Sunbury Cross
KEMPTON PARK
Norbiton
NEW MALDEN
Kingston Br
County Hall
Hampton Court Park
HAMPTON COURT PALACE
Hampton Ct Br
Molesey Reservoirs
Bessborough Res
Knight Res
East Molesey
SURBITON
Berrylands
River Thames
Queen Elizabeth II Reservoir
Island Barn Reservoir
Thames Ditton
Fieldcommon
River Ember
WALTON-ON-THAMES
Rydens
Hinchley Wood
Long Ditton
Tolworth
SANDOWN PARK
Littleworth Common
Govt Offices
Hook Interchange
ESHER
HERSHAM
CHESSINGTON
West End Common
CLAREMONT LANDSCAPE GARDEN
Arbrook Common
CLAYGATE
HORTON
West Ewell
Ewell
River Mole
Esher Common
CHESSINGTON WORLD OF ADVENTURES
Oxshott
Heath
Malden Rushett
Fairmile
Prince's Coverts
Stoke Wood
Epsom Common
EPSOM
The Forest
Cobham
Little Heath
Cobham Park
Stoke D'Abernon
Pachesham Park
Wood Field
Woodcote
Downside
Lower Ashstead
Langley Vale
Leatherhead Common
Ashstead
LEATHERHEAD
Banks Common
Great Bookham Common
Little Bookham Common
Fetcham
Tyrell's Wood
Effingham Common
Little Bookham
Leatherhead Downs
Nower Wood
BROCKETTS FARM PARK
Givons Grove
Headley
Great
Fetcham Downs
HAMPTON COURT RD
KINGSTON BY-PASS
HOOK RISE
LEATHERHEAD ROAD
PORTSMOUTH RD
M25
A3
A243
A24
A309
A307
A308
A244
A245
A246
A240
A3050
17
16
52

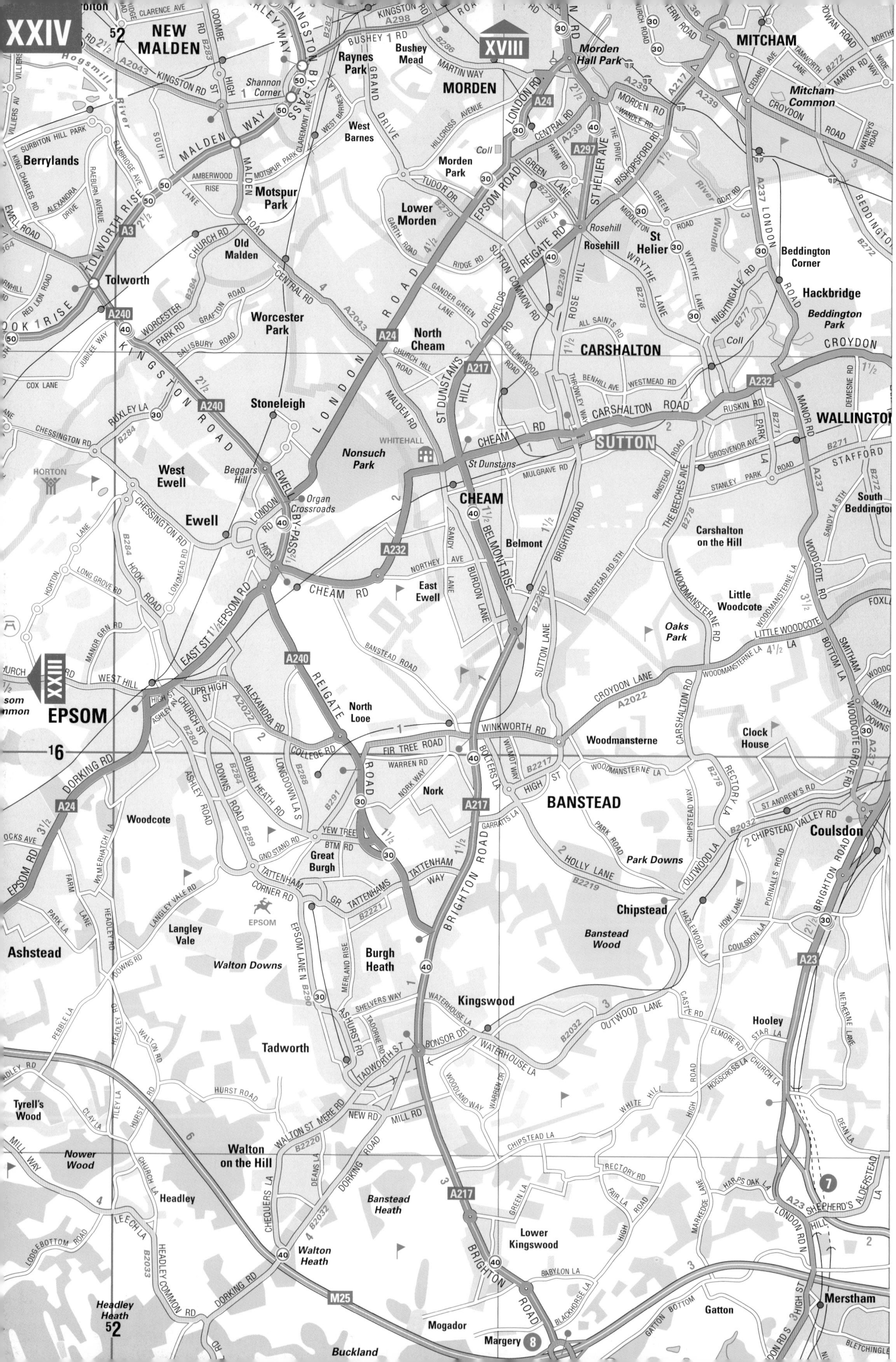
NEW MALDEN
Raynes Park
Bushey Mead
MORDEN
Morden Hall Park
MITCHAM
Mitcham Common
West Barnes
Berrylands
Morden Park
Motspur Park
Lower Morden
Old Malden
Rosehill
St Helier
Beddington Corner
Hackbridge
Beddington Park
Tolworth
Worcester Park
North Cheam
CARSHALTON
Stoneleigh
WALLINGTON
SUTTON
Nonsuch Park
West Ewell
Beggars Hill
Organ Crossroads
CHEAM
South Beddington
Ewell
Belmont
Carshalton on the Hill
East Ewell
Little Woodcote
Oaks Park
EPSOM
North Looe
Woodmansterne
Clock House
Nork
BANSTEAD
Woodcote
Coulsdon
Great Burgh
Park Downs
Chipstead
Langley Vale
Ashstead
Walton Downs
Burgh Heath
Banstead Wood
Kingswood
Hooley
Tadworth
Tyrell's Wood
Nower Wood
Walton on the Hill
Headley
Banstead Heath
Lower Kingswood
Walton Heath
Headley Heath
Mogador
Margery
Gatton
Merstham
Buckland
XVIII
XXIII
52
16

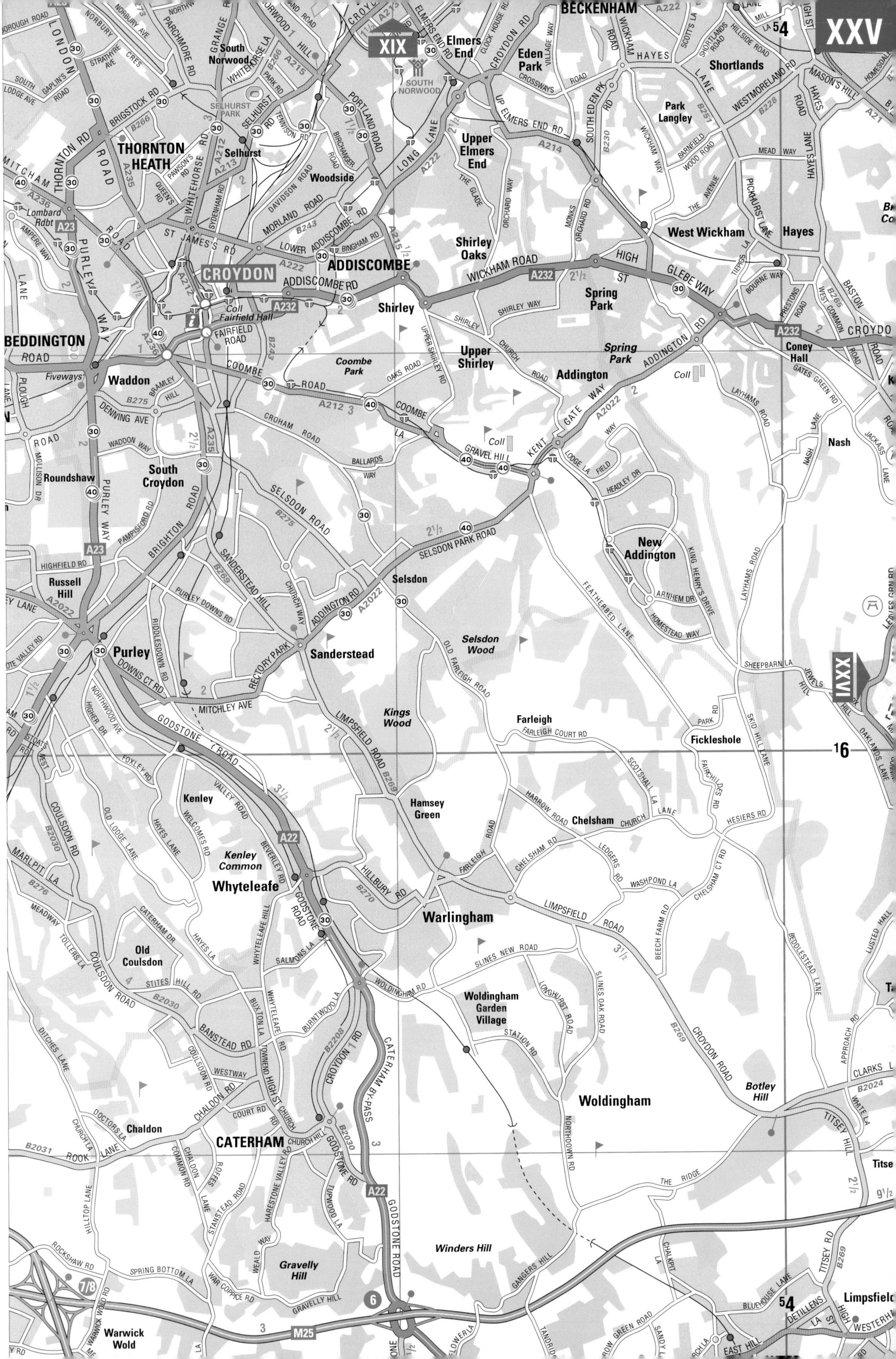
XXV
XIX
XXVI
54
16
BECKENHAM
Elmers End
Eden Park
Shortlands
Park Langley
South Norwood
THORNTON HEATH
Selhurst
Woodside
Upper Elmers End
West Wickham
Hayes
Shirley Oaks
CROYDON
ADDISCOMBE
Shirley
Spring Park
Coney Hall
BEDDINGTON
Coombe Park
Upper Shirley
Spring Park
Addington
Waddon
Fiveways
Nash
South Croydon
Roundshaw
New Addington
Selsdon
Russell Hill
Purley
Sanderstead
Selsdon Wood
Kings Wood
Farleigh
Fickleshole
Kenley
Hamsey Green
Chelsham
Kenley Common
Whyteleafe
Warlingham
Old Coulsdon
Woldingham Garden Village
Botley Hill
Woldingham
Chaldon
CATERHAM
Titsey
Winders Hill
Gravelly Hill
Warwick Wold
Limpsfield
A23
A22
A232
A2022
A212
A235
M25
B269
B2030
Coll
Fairfield Hall
Lombard Rdbt

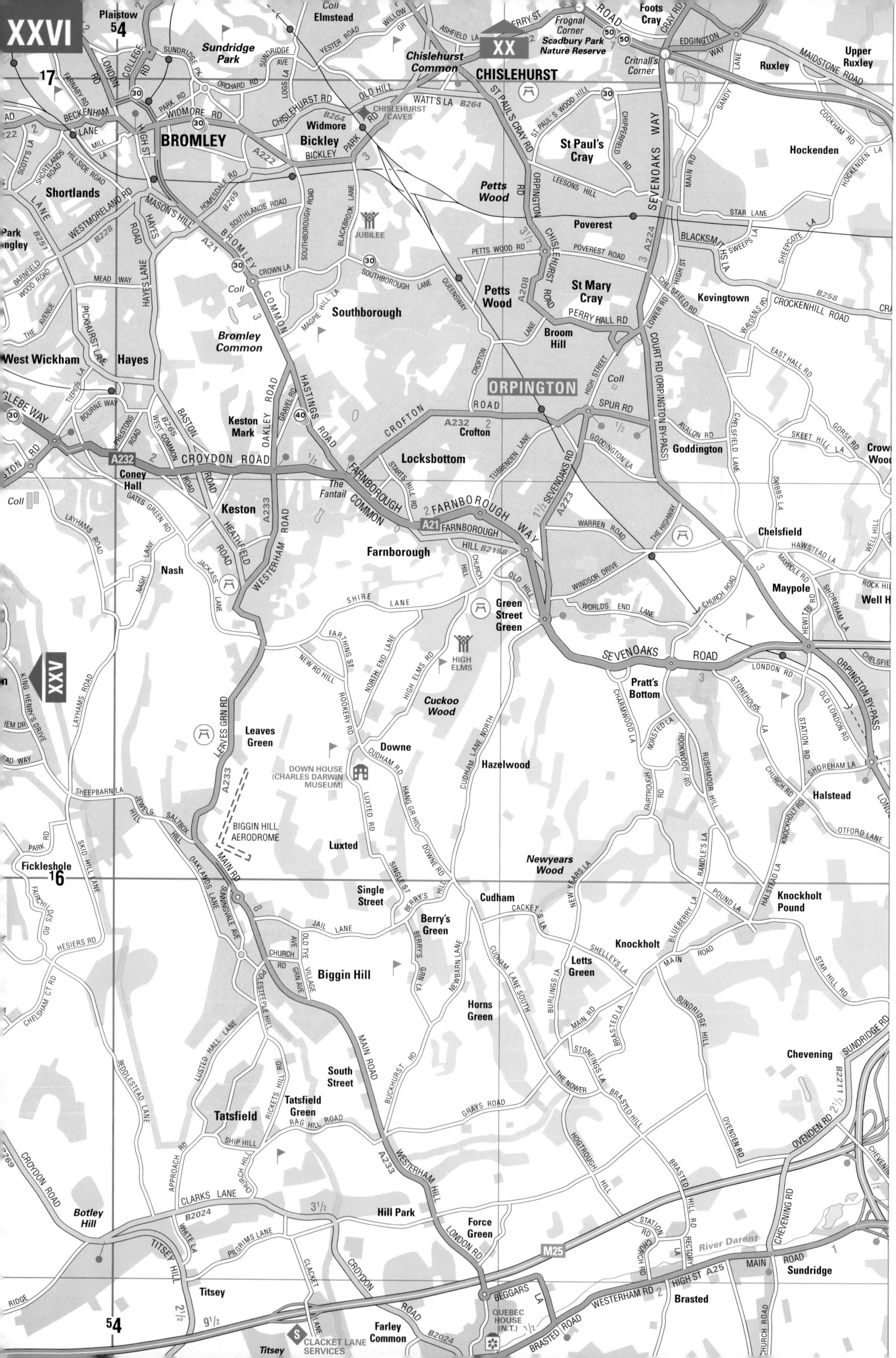
Plaistow
54
Coll
Elmstead
Frognal Corner
Scadbury Park Nature Reserve
Foots Cray
XX
Sundridge Park
Chislehurst Common
CHISLEHURST
Critnall's Corner
Upper Ruxley
Ruxley
MAIDSTONE ROAD
17
BECKENHAM LANE
WIDMORE RD
Widmore
Bickley
BROMLEY
CHISLEHURST CAVES
OLD HILL
WATT'S LA
B264
ST PAUL'S CRAY RD
St Paul's Cray
SEVENOAKS WAY
Hockenden
Shortlands
WESTMORELAND RD
MASON'S HILL
HOMESDALE RD
SOUTHLANDS ROAD
SOUTHBOROUGH ROAD
BLACKBROOK LANE
JUBILEE
Petts Wood
ORPINGTON RD
LEESONS HILL
STAR LANE
Poverest
A224
BLACKSMITHS LA
Park Langley
B251
B228
MEAD WAY
HAYES LANE
BROMLEY COMMON
CROWN LA
SOUTHBOROUGH LANE
QUEENSWAY
PETTS WOOD RD
POVEREST ROAD
CHISLEHURST ROAD
A208
St Mary Cray
PERRY HALL RD
Kevingtown
B258
CROCKENHILL ROAD
Coll
Southborough
Bromley Common
Broom Hill
West Wickham
Hayes
PICKHURST LANE
EAST HALL RD
ORPINGTON
HIGH STREET
COURT RD (ORPINGTON BY-PASS)
GLEBE WAY
Keston Mark
OAKLEY ROAD
HASTINGS ROAD
CROFTON ROAD
A232
Crofton
SPUR RD
Goddington
AVALON RD
GODDINGTON LA
CHELSFIELD LANE
SKEET HILL LA
GORSE RD
Crown Wood
A232
CROYDON ROAD
Coney Hall
Locksbottom
TUBBENDEN LANE
SEVENOAKS RD
A223
Keston
The Fantail
FARNBOROUGH COMMON
A21
FARNBOROUGH WAY
FARNBOROUGH HILL
B2158
WARREN ROAD
THE HIGHWAY
Chelsfield
HAWSTEAD LA
Coll
LAYHAMS ROAD
Nash
WESTERHAM ROAD
HEATHFIELD ROAD
JACKASS LANE
Farnborough
SHIRE LANE
CHURCH HILL
OLD HILL
WINDSOR DRIVE
Green Street Green
WORLDS END LANE
CHURCH ROAD
Maypole
SHOREHAM LA
Well Hill
FARTHING ST
NEW RD HILL
NORTH END LANE
HIGH ELMS RD
HIGH ELMS
SEVENOAKS ROAD
LONDON RD
ORPINGTON BY-PASS
XXV
KING HENRY'S DRIVE
Pratt's Bottom
CHARMWOOD LA
STONEHOUSE LA
OLD LONDON RD
STATION RD
Cuckoo Wood
ROOKERY RD
Leaves Green
LEAVES GRN RD
Downe
CUDHAM RD
DOWN HOUSE (CHARLES DARWIN MUSEUM)
Hazelwood
CUDHAM LANE NORTH
MORSTED LA
HOOKWOOD RD
RUSHMORE HILL
SHOREHAM LA
Halstead
SHEEPBARN LA
JEWELS HILL
SALTBOX HILL
A233
BIGGIN HILL AERODROME
LUXTED RD
HANG GR HILL
FAIRTROUGH RD
KNOCKHOLT RD
OTFORD LANE
Luxted
DOWNE RD
Newyears Wood
NEW YEARS LA
RANDLE'S LA
HALSTEAD LA
Fickleshole
16
SKID HILL LANE
OAKLANDS LANE
MAIN RD
Single Street
SINGLE ST
Cudham
Knockholt Pound
POUND LA
BLUEBERRY LA
CACKET'S LA
Berry's Green
JAIL LANE
HESIERS RD
CHURCH RD
OLD TYE AVE
Biggin Hill
BERRY'S GRN LA
NEWBARN LANE
CUDHAM LANE SOUTH
Knockholt
SHELLEYS LA
Letts Green
MAIN ROAD
STAR HILL RD
CHELSHAM CT RD
POLESTEEPLE HILL
Horns Green
BURLINGS LA
MAIN RD
BRASTED LA
SUNDRIDGE HILL
SUNDRIDGE RD
LUSTED HALL LANE
BEDDLESTEAD LANE
RICKETS HILL RD
South Street
MAIN ROAD
BUCKHURST RD
STONEINGS LA
THE NOWER
BRASTED HILL
Chevening
B2211
Tatsfield
Tatsfield Green
RAG HILL ROAD
GRAYS ROAD
OVENDEN RD
SHIP HILL
A233
WESTERHAM HILL
HOGTROUGH HILL
CROYDON ROAD
APPROACH RD
CHURCH HILL
CLARKS LANE
B2024
Botley Hill
Hill Park
Force Green
LONDON RD
STATION RD
CHURCH RD
BRASTED HILL RD
RECTORY LA
River Darent
CHEVENING RD
M25
PILGRIMS LANE
TITSEY HILL
WHITE LA
CLACKET LANE
CROYDON ROAD
BEGGARS LA
A25
MAIN ROAD
Sundridge
HIGH ST
WESTERHAM RD
Brasted
RIDGE
Titsey
54
QUEBEC HOUSE (N.T.)
BRASTED ROAD
Farley Common
B2024
CLACKET LANE SERVICES
Titsey
CHURCH ROAD

XXVII
XXI
56
17
16
Hextable
Clement Street
Sutton-at-Hone
ST. JOHN'S JERUSALEM (N.T.)
Green St Green
Hook Green
South Darenth
Pinden
Longfield
Swanley Village
Swanley
Farningham Wood
Horton Kirby
Hartley
Hartley Green
Farningham
Crockenhill
Horton Wood
EYNSFORD CASTLE
Eynsford
BIRD OF PREY CENTRE
LULLINGSTONE ROMAN VILLA
LULLINGSTONE CASTLE
Fawkham Green
New Ash Green
Beechen Wood
Maplescombe
BRANDS HATCH
Ash
High Castle Wood
West Kingsdown
Timberden Bottom
River Darent
Knatts Valley
Stansted
Shoreham
Romney Street
Magpie Bottom
Woodlands
Twitton
Otford
Crowdleham
Heaverham
Wrotham
KEMSING
Kemsing
Dunton Green
Longford
Greatness
Seal
Styants Bottom
Oldbury
Ightham
Borough Green
Chipstead
Riverhead
Wildernesse
Basted
Seal Chart
Godden Green
Stone Street
Ightham Common
Kippington
SEVENOAKS
Ivy Hatch
Lower Bitchet
Bitchet
Yopps
KNOLE (N.T.)
M25
M20
M26
A20
A225
A224
A25
A227
B258
B260
B2173
B2019
DARTFORD RD
CLEMENT ST
LOWER RD
MAIN ROAD
ST MARGARET'S RD
GILL'S ROAD
SHIP LANE
DEVON RD
STATION RD
RABBITS ROAD
MAIN ROAD
LONDON ROAD
LONDON ROAD
EYNSFORD ROAD
CROCKENHILL LANE
MAIN ROAD GORSE HILL
LONDON ROAD
FAWKHAM ROAD
CASTLE FARM RD
SHACKLANDS RD
REDMANS LANE
BOWER LANE
KNATTS VALLEY ROAD
PILGRIMS WAY
SHOREHAM RD
OTFORD RD
SEVENOAKS RD
HEAVERHAM RD
HONEYPOT LA
SEAL RD
BRADBOURNE VALE RD
MAIDSTONE RD
SEVENOAKS ROAD
IGHTHAM BY-PASS
TONBRIDGE ROAD
LONDON RD
TUBS HILL
DARTFORD RD
ST JOHN'S HILL
SEAL HOLLOW RD
BLACKHALL LANE
LONDON RD
MAIDSTONE

Key to map symbols

Roads

- **Motorway with junction number** (22a)
- **Primary route** – single, dual carriageway
- **A road** – single, dual carriageway
- **B road** – single, dual carriageway
- **Through-route** – single, dual carriageway
- **Minor road** – single, dual carriageway
- **Road under construction**
- **Rural track, private road or narrow road in urban area**
- **Path, bridleway, byway open to all traffic, restricted byway**
- **Tunnel, covered road**
- **Speed camera** – single, multiple (30)
- **Congestion Charge Zone boundary** Roads within the zone are outlined in green
- **Gate or obstruction, car pound**
- **Parking, park and ride** (P, P&R)
- **Road junction name** (Crooked Billet)
- **Pedestrianised, restricted access area**

Public transport

- **Railway station, private rail station**
- **London Underground station, Docklands Light Railway station**
- **Tramway or miniature railway**
- **Bus or coach station, tram stop**

Scale

5½ inches to 1 mile 1:11520

0 220yds 440yds 660yds ½ mile

0 250m 500m 750m 1km

Emergency services

- **Ambulance, police, fire station**
- **Hospital, accident and emergency entrance** (H)

General features

- **Market, public amenity site**
- **Sports stadium, shopping centre**
- **Information centre, post office** (i, PO)
- **Roman, non-Roman antiquity** (VILLA, House)
- **House number, spot height** – metres (100, .304)
- **Christian place of worship**
- **Mosque, synagogue**
- **Other place of worship**
- **Houses, important buildings**
- **Woods, parkland/common**
- **Adjoining page number** (123)

Leisure facilities

- **Camp site, caravan site**
- **Golf course, picnic site, view point**

Boundaries

- **Postcode boundaries** (NW6)
- **County and unitary authority boundaries** (Westminster)

Water features

- **Water name** (Barking Creek)
- **Tidal water**
- **River or canal** – minor, major
- **Stream**
- **Water**

Abbreviations

Acad	**Academy**
Allot Gdns	**Allotments**
Bndstd	**Bandstand**
Btcl	**Botanical**
Bwg Gn	**Bowling**
Cemy	**Cemetery**
Ctr	**Centre**
C Ctr	**Civic Centre**
CH	**Club House**
Ctry Pk	**Country Park**
Coll	**College**
Ct	**Court**
Crem	**Crematorium**
Crkt	**Cricket**
Ent	**Enterprise**
Ex H	**Exhibition Hall**
Fball	**Football**
Gdns	**Gardens**
Glf C	**Golf Course**
Glf Crs	**Golf Course**
Drv Rng	**Golf Driving Range**
Gn	**Green**
Gd	**Ground**
Hort	**Horticultural**
Ind Est	**Industrial Estate**
Inst	**Institute**
Int	**Interchange**
Ct	**Law Court**
L Ctr	**Leisure Centre**
LC	**Level Crossing**
Liby	**Library**
Mkt	**Market**
Meml	**Memorial**
Mon	**Monument**
Mus	**Museum**
Nat Res	**Nature Reserve**
Obsy	**Observatory**
Pav	**Pavilion**
Pk	**Park**
Pl Fld	**Playing Field**
Pal	**Royal Palace**
PH	**Public House**
Recn Gd	**Recreation Ground**
Resr	**Reservoir**
Ret Pk	**Retail Park**
Sch	**School**
Sh Ctr	**Shopping Centre**
Sp	**Sports**
Stad	**Stadium**
Sw Pool	**Swimming Pool**
Tenn Cts	**Tennis**
TH	**Town Hall**
Trad Est	**Trading Estate**
Univ	**University**
YH	**Youth Hostel**

A1000 Potters Bar
A
B
C
D
1
99
6
5
98
4
2
3
97
2
1
96
Wrotham Park
Home Farm
Cockshot Hill
Ganwick Farm
WAGON RD
Lower Kitt's End Farm
KITT'S END RD
Kitt's End
Kitt's End Farm
BARNET RD
A1000
Bartram's Quash
Hertfordshire Enfield
Pl Fld
Hadley Wood
BARTRAMS LA
CRESCENT W
Great Broad Hill
GREENACRE CL
BEAUMONT PL
EN4
Barnet Enfield
Hertfordshire Barnet
LANGLEY ROW
HADLEY HIGHSTONE
Old Fold Manor
TAYLOR'S LA
OLD FOLD CL
FOLD LA
MILL CNR
Tenn Cts
BOUNDARY CL
Monken Hadley CE Prim Sch
St Martha's Senior Sch
CAMLET WAY
HATHERLEIGH CL
PAGITTS GR
BROADGATES AVE
BURWOOD
PARKGATE AVE
PARKGATE CRES
EN5
Hadley Green
Convent
DURY RD
Allot Gdns
A1081 Hatfield (A1(M)), M25
ST ALBANS RD
Monken Hadley
HADLEY GN W
SYDNEY CHAPMAN WAY
HADLEY GREEN RD
HADLEY GN
Bournwell Hill
Monken Hadley Common
Priddeon's Hill
HADLEY WOOD RD
BAKERS HILL
SUNSET VIEW
Cemy
WROTHAM RD
FALKLAND RD
PULLER RD
HADLEY GR
GLADSMUIR RD
CHRIST CHURCH LA
LIVINGSTONE CT
FIRE STATION AL
London Loop
THE CRESCENT
THE SPINNEY
HADLEY HTS
The Tudor
LATIMER RD
LOWNDES CT
HADLEYVALE CT
SEBRIGHT RD
TA Ctr
LUCAN RD
A1081
Barnet Mkt
GROVE CT
HADLEY RIDGE
WYBURN AVE
EAST VIEW
Hadley
King George's Field
SHAKESPEARE CT
VINCENT CL
Allot Gdns
CLIFFORD RD
Tudor Sp Gd
CH
Tenn Cts
ALSTON RD
STRAFFORD RD
Liby
CHIPPING CL
BRUCE RD
BELGRAVIA CL
BATH PL
TUDOR RD
SLADE CT
GALDANA AVE
CARNARVON RD
PENRAY
SALISBURY RD
The Spires
HYDE CL
High Barnet
HURST RISE
JULIAN CL
NORFOLK RD
SANDFORD CT
RONALD CT
HADLEY RD
ORCHARD CT
Allot Gdns
BOLEYN WAY
MORREL CL
Cromer Road Sch
WENTWORTH CT
THE DRIVE
STAPYLTON RD
HART LO
GREAT NORTH RD
MOON LA
SOUTH CL
MOXON ST
Pl Fld
BOSWORTH RD
CATHERINE CT
DENBY CT
THE AVENUE
THORNTON RD
UNION ST
Sch
TAPSTER ST
VICTORS WAY
Barnet Trad Est
Tenn Cts
MEADWAY CL
BURNSIDE CL
ST MARK'S CL
PEARSON CL
WOODVILLE RD
CROMER RD
SHAFTESBURY AVE
LEE CL
GILLINGS CT
PARK RD
QUEEN ELIZABETH CT
MEADWAY
MARTINS MOUNT
POTTER'S RD
SHERIDAN LO
Pl Flds
EN5
BARNARD LO
A1 Borehamwood, A411
WOOD ST
A411
HIGH ST
Mus
MANOR CL
Barnet Coll
GORDON WAY
Queen Elizabeth's Sch
CRABTREE CT
HEXHAM RD
HADRIAN CT
HUGHENDON
BARON CT
SHELDON CT
BULWER RD
BULWER GDNS
MASEFIELD CT
HASTINGS
CATTLEY CL
SUTHERLAND CL
Bwg Gns
ORCHARD RD
ELM DR
VICTORIA LA
LAWN MANS
KINGSMEAD
HILLARY RISE
High Barnet
KING EDWARD RD
SCHOLARS CL
PINECROFT CR
MANORSIDE
Chipping Barnet
AVENUE MANS
HILLSIDE MANS
A1000
BARNET HILL
POTTER'S LA
PROSPECT RD
LEAF HO
WARWICK RD
VALE CT
LEICESTER RD
PLANTAGENET RD
DUNCAN CL
FALCON CT
LEECROFT RD
RODINGS ROW
HILLSIDE GDNS
WILLOW DR
MANOR RD
Tenn Cts
FITZJOHN AVE
NEWLYN RD
NORMANDY AVE
BEDFORD AVE
Sch
BRACKENWOOD LO
RAVENSCROFT COTTS
ESMOND CT
ABBOTS RD
THE HIGHLANDS
WINDERMERE HO
MERTON CT
BARNES CT
A110
MOWBRAY RD
ASHLEY CT
COLGATE CT
ELLESMERE GR
HILTON AVE
WOODFALL AVE
ELTON AVE
VALE DR
MARSTON
TELFORD CT
HIGHWOOD CT
HIGHLANDS RD
Highlands Gdns
COLLINGWOOD
STATION RD
SOMERSET RD
NORTH LO
THE THOMAS WATSON COTTAGE HOMES
CEDAR
BARNET
25
13
UNDERHILL CT
POTTERIES
HOMESTEAD CT
A1000
A110
26
New Barnet
Lyonsdown
RICHMOND

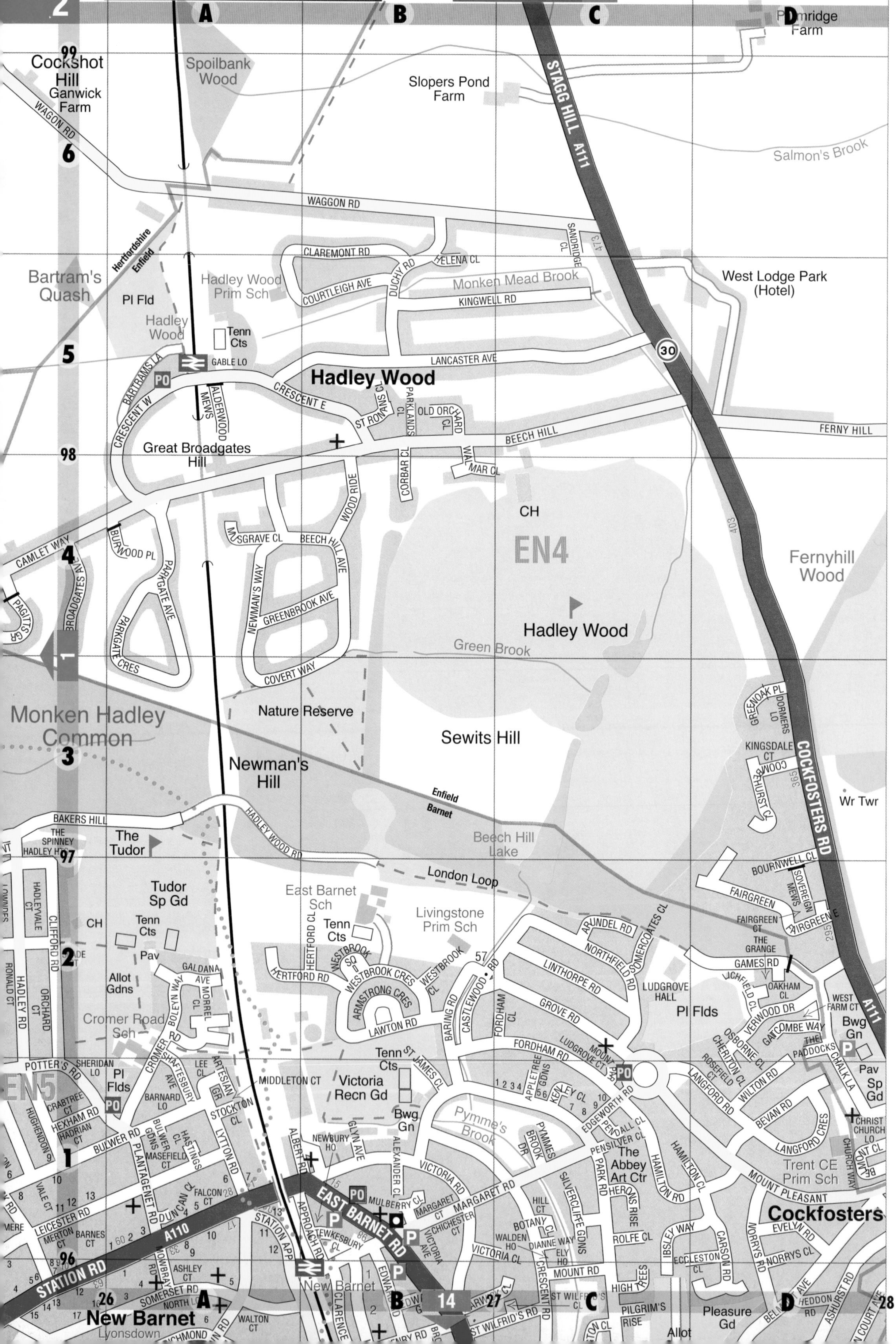
A
B
C
D
Plumridge Farm
99
Cockshot Hill
Ganwick Farm
WAGON RD
Spoilbank Wood
Slopers Pond Farm
STAGG HILL
A111
Salmon's Brook
6
WAGGON RD
SANDRIDGE CL
473
CLAREMONT RD
DUCHY RD
HELENA CL
Hertfordshire
Enfield
Bartram's Quash
Pl Fld
Hadley Wood Prim Sch
Monken Mead Brook
West Lodge Park (Hotel)
COURTLEIGH AVE
KINGWELL RD
Hadley Wood
Tenn Cts
5
GABLE LO
LANCASTER AVE
30
BARTRAMS LA
PO
Hadley Wood
CRESCENT E
CRESCENT W
ALDERWOOD MEWS
ST RONANS CL
PARKLANDS CL
OLD ORCHARD CL
FERNY HILL
BEECH HILL
Great Broadgates Hill
98
CORBAR CL
WALMAR CL
WOOD RIDE
CH
403
MUSGRAVE CL
BEECH HILL AVE
BURWOOD PL
EN4
CAMLET WAY
4
BROADGATES AVE
PARKGATE AVE
Fernyhill Wood
PAGITTS GR
NEWMAN'S WAY
GREENBROOK AVE
Hadley Wood
PARKGATE CRES
1
Green Brook
COVERT WAY
GREENOAK PL
DORMERS LO
Monken Hadley Common
Nature Reserve
3
Sewits Hill
KINGSDALE CT
COCKFOSTERS RD
Newman's Hill
COWDRAY
HURST CL
365
Enfield
Barnet
Wr Twr
BAKERS HILL
HADLEY WOOD RD
THE SPINNEY
HADLEY HTS
The Tudor
97
Beech Hill Lake
London Loop
BOURNWELL CL
HADLEYVALE CT
CLIFFORD RD
Tudor Sp Gd
East Barnet Sch
HERTFORD CL
Livingstone Prim Sch
FAIRGREEN
SOVEREIGN MEWS
CH
Tenn Cts
Tenn Cts
ARUNDEL RD
SOMERCOATES CL
FAIRGREEN CT
FAIRGREEN E
295
2
RONALD CL
HADLEY RD
ORCHARD CT
Pav
WESTBROOK SQ
WESTBROOK CRES
WESTBROOK CL
NORTHFIELD RD
THE GRANGE
GAMES RD
Allot Gdns
GALDANA AVE
MORREL CL
HERTFORD RD
57
CASTLEWOOD RD
LINTHORPE RD
LUDGROVE HALL
LICHFIELD CL
OAKHAM CL
ARMSTRONG CRES
BARING RD
FORDHAM CL
GROVE RD
Pl Flds
VERWOOD DR
WEST FARM CT
A111
Cromer Road Sch
BOLEYN WAY
LAWTON RD
GATCOMBE WAY
Bwg Gn
CROMER RD
FORDHAM RD
LUDGROVE CT
MOUNT PARK
OSBORNE CL
CHERITON CL
THE PADDOCKS
POTTER'S RD
SHERIDAN LO
Pl Flds
SHAFTESBURY AVE
LEE CL
ARTESIAN GR
MIDDLETON CT
Tenn Cts
ST JAMES CL
Victoria Recn Gd
PO
ROSEFIELD CL
WILTON RD
CHALK LA
Pav Sp Gd
EN5
CRABTREE CT
HEXHAM RD
HADRIAN CT
BARNARD LO
STOCKTON CL
APPLETREE GDNS
KENLEY CL
EDGEWORTH RD
PENDALL CL
LANGFORD RD
BEVAN RD
HUGHENDON
PO
Bwg Gn
Pymme's Brook
PYMMES BROOK DR
PENSILVER CL
HAMILTON CL
LANGFORD CRES
CHRIST CHURCH LO
BULWER RD
BULWER GDNS
HASTINGS CL
MASEFIELD CT
LYTTON RD
ALBERT RD
NEWBURY HO
GLYN AVE
ALEXANDER CL
The Abbey Art Ctr
CHURCH WAY
1
PLANTAGENET RD
VICTORIA RD
PARK RD
HAMILTON RD
Trent CE Prim Sch
VALE CT
FALCON CT
DUNCAN CL
EAST BARNET RD
PO
MULBERRY CL
MARGARET CT
MARGARET RD
SILVERCLIFFE GDNS
HERONS RISE
MOUNT PLEASANT
LEICESTER RD
MERTON CT
BARNES CT
A110
STATION APP
APPROACH RD
TEWKESBURY CL
CHICHESTER CT
VICTORIA AVE
HILL CT
BOTANY CL
WALDEN HO
DIANNE WAY
ELY HO
ROLFE CL
IBSLEY WAY
CARSON RD
Cockfosters
EVELYN RD
NORRYS RD
NORRYS CL
96
STATION RD
MOWBRAY RD
ASHLEY CT
SOMERSET RD
NORTH LO
EDWARD
New Barnet
VICTORIA CL
CRESCENT RD
MOUNT RD
HIGH TREES
ECCLESTON CL
BELMONT AVE
ASHURST RD
WEDDON RD
New Barnet
Lyonsdown
WALTON CT
CLARENCE
ST WILFRID'S CL
ST WILFRID'S RD
PILGRIM'S RISE
Pleasure Gd
Allot

Hertfordshire STREET ATLAS
A1005 Potters Bar, M25
3
A
B
C
D
Vault Hill Wood
Wood
Botany Bay Farm
Botany Bay
A1005
THE RIDGEWAY
99
Roundhedge Hill
Salmon's Brook
EN2
6
Duncan's Wood
Ash Wood
Cuc
Park Farm
5
FERNY HILL
Ferny Hill Farm
Obelisk
Moat Wood
Parkside Farm
HADLEY RD
98
Ride Wood
Leeging Beech G
Rough Lot
EN4
Enfield Chase
4
London Loop
Seedfield Spinney
Icehouse Wood
Williams Wood
Trent Country Park
Middlesex Univ Trent Park
3
Oak Wood
SHAWS WOOD COTTS
Shaws Wood
ROOKERY COTTS
97
Pav
Sp Gd
Church Wood
2
Merryhills Brook
South Lodge Farm
Triangular Wood
Cemy
Trent Park Equestrian Ctr
EASTPOLE COTTS
A110
SNAKES LA
Trent Park
Cockfosters
PO
COCKFOSTERS RD
COCKFOSTERS PAR
NORFOLK CL
WEST CL
EAST CL
GALVA CL
CHADDLEWOOD
MOUNT CL
BRAEMORE CT
STATION PAR
GLOUCESTER GDNS
KENT DR
WESTPOLE AVE
EASTPOLE COTTS
N14
CH
LONSDALE DR
SOUTH LODGE CRES
LAKESIDE
GREYSTOKE GDNS
NETHERBY GDNS
LOWTHER
CULGAITH GDNS
1
MERRYHILLS DR
BRAYTON GDNS
CURTHWAITE GDNS
BRANTWOOD GDNS
CLIFTON GDNS
WOODEND GDNS
96
BELGRAVE GDNS
GROSVENOR GDNS
BELGRAVE CT
BRAMLEY RD
RIDGEVIEW CT
Oakwood
GERRARDS CL
BETJEMAN CT
TAVERNERS LO
HEDDON CT
ESTON GDNS
A111
Southgate Sch
Pl Fld
SUSSEX WAY
28
29
15
30
D
LONSDALE
BEVERIDGE CT
JENNER CT

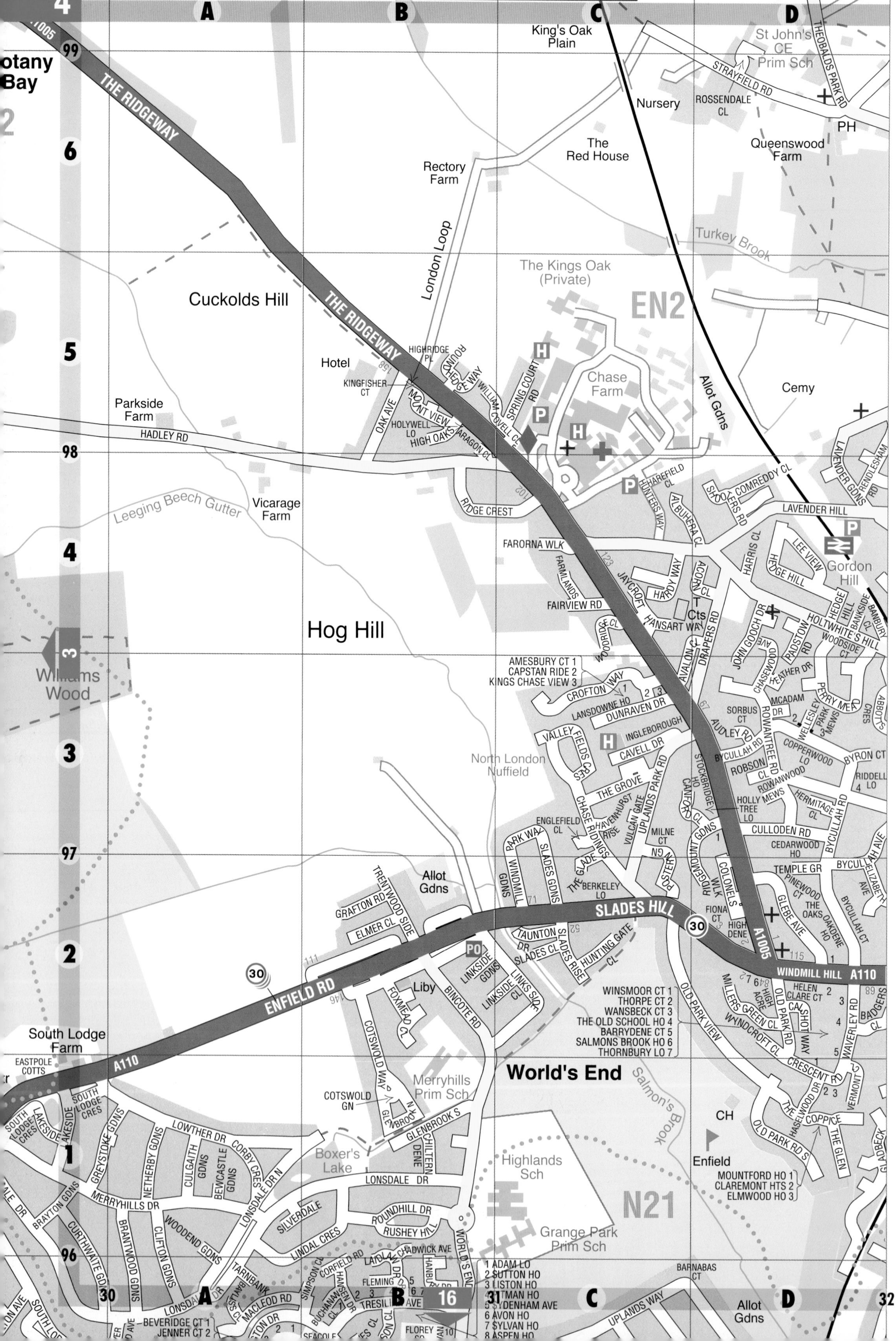
A
B
C
D
King's Oak Plain
St John's CE Prim Sch
THEOBALDS PARK RD
STRAYFIELD RD
ROSSENDALE CL
Nursery
PH
Botany Bay
THE RIDGEWAY
A1005
99
6
The Red House
Queenswood Farm
Rectory Farm
Turkey Brook
London Loop
The Kings Oak (Private)
EN2
Cuckolds Hill
5
Hotel
HIGHRIDGE PL
ROUNDHEDGE WAY
WILLIAM COVELL CL
SPRING COURT RD
Chase Farm
Allot Gdns
Cemy
KINGFISHER CT
OAK AVE
MOUNT VIEW
HOLYWELL LO
HIGH OAKS
ARAGON CL
Parkside Farm
HADLEY RD
98
HAREFIELD CL
HUNTERS WAY
SHOOTERS RD
COMREDDY CL
LAVENDER GDNS
RENDLESHAM RD
RIDGE CREST
ALBUHERA CL
LAVENDER HILL
Leeging Beech Gutter
Vicarage Farm
FARORNA WLK
HARRIS CL
LEE VIEW
Gordon Hill
4
FARMLANDS
JAYCROFT
HARDY WAY
ACORN CL
HEDGE HILL
Hog Hill
FAIRVIEW RD
HANSART WAY
Cts
DRAPERS RD
JOHN GOOCH DR
PADSTOW RD
HOLTWHITE'S HILL
BANKSIDE CL
BAMBURY CL
WOODSIDE CT
Williams Wood
3
WOODRIDGE CL
AVALON CL
AMESBURY CT 1
CAPSTAN RIDE 2
KINGS CHASE VIEW 3
CROFTON WAY
LANSDOWNE HO
DUNRAVEN DR
CHASEWOOD AVE
HEATHER DR
PERRY MEAD
ABBOTS CRES
MCADAM DR
SORBUS CT
WELLESLEY PARK MEWS
VALLEY FIELDS CRES
INGLEBOROUGH
CAVELL DR
AUDLEY RD
BYCULLAH RD
COPPERWOOD LO
BYRON CT
North London Nuffield
THE GROVE
UPLANDS PARK RD
STOCKBRIDGE HO
CANFORD CL
ROBSON CL
ROWANTREE RD
ROWANWOOD MEWS
RIDDELL LO
ENGLEFIELD CL
CHASE RIDINGS
HAVENHURST RISE
VULCAN GATE
HOLLY TREE LO
HERMITAGE CL
BYCULLAH RD
PARK WAY
SLADES GDNS
MILNE CT
RIDGEMOUNT GDNS
CULLODEN RD
CEDARWOOD HO
97
TRENTWOOD SIDE
Allot Gdns
WINDMILL GDNS
THE GLADE
BERKELEY LO
POSTERN GN
COLONELS WLK
TEMPLE GR
PINEWOOD CT
GLEBE AVE
THE OAKS
OAKDENE HO
BYCULLAH AVE
ELIZABETH AVE
BYCULLAH CT
GRAFTON RD
ELMER CL
SLADES HILL
FIONA CT
HIGH DENE
TAUNTON DR
SLADES CL
SLADES RISE
HUNTING GATE CL
2
PO
LINKSIDE GDNS
LINKSIDE CL
LINKS SIDE
WINDMILL HILL
A110
ENFIELD RD
Liby
FOXMEAD CL
BINCOTE RD
WINSMOOR CT 1
THORPE CT 2
WANSBECK CT 3
THE OLD SCHOOL HO 4
BARRYDENE CT 5
SALMONS BROOK HO 6
THORNBURY LO 7
OLD PARK VIEW
MILLERS GREEN CL
HIGH ACRE
OLD PARK RD
CALSHOT WAY
HELEN CLARE CT
WAVERLEY RD
BADGERS CL
WYNDCROFT CL
CRESCENT RD
VERMONT CL
South Lodge Farm
EASTPOLE COTTS
A110
COTSWOLD WAY
Merryhills Prim Sch
World's End
Salmon's Brook
THE HASELWOOD DR
COPPICE
THE GLEN
OLD PARK RD S
SOUTH LODGE CRES
LAKESIDE
GREYSTOKE GDNS
LOWTHER DR
CORBY CRES
COTSWOLD GN
GLENBROOK N
GLENBROOK S
CHILTERN DENE
CH
Enfield
1
NETHERBY GDNS
CULGAITH GDNS
BEWCASTLE GDNS
LONSDALE DR N
Boxer's Lake
Highlands Sch
GLADBECK
MOUNTFORD HO 1
CLAREMONT HTS 2
ELMWOOD HO 3
MERRYHILLS DR
BRAYTON GDNS
CURTHWAITE GDNS
BRANTWOOD GDNS
CLIFTON GDNS
WOODEND GDNS
LONSDALE DR
SILVERDALE
ROUNDHILL DR
RUSHEY HILL
LINDAL CRES
N21
Grange Park Prim Sch
96
CHADWICK AVE
WORLD'S END
TARNBANK
SIMPSON CL
CORFIELD RD
HANSEN DR
BUCHANAN CL
FLEMING
TRESILIAN AVE
MACLEOD RD
LONSDALE DR
BEVERIDGE CT 1
JENNER CT 2
1 ADAM LO
2 SUTTON HO
3 LISTON HO
5 SYDENHAM AVE
6 AVON HO
7 SYLVAN HO
8 ASPEN HO
FLOREY
BARNABAS CT
UPLANDS WAY
Allot Gdns
30
31
16

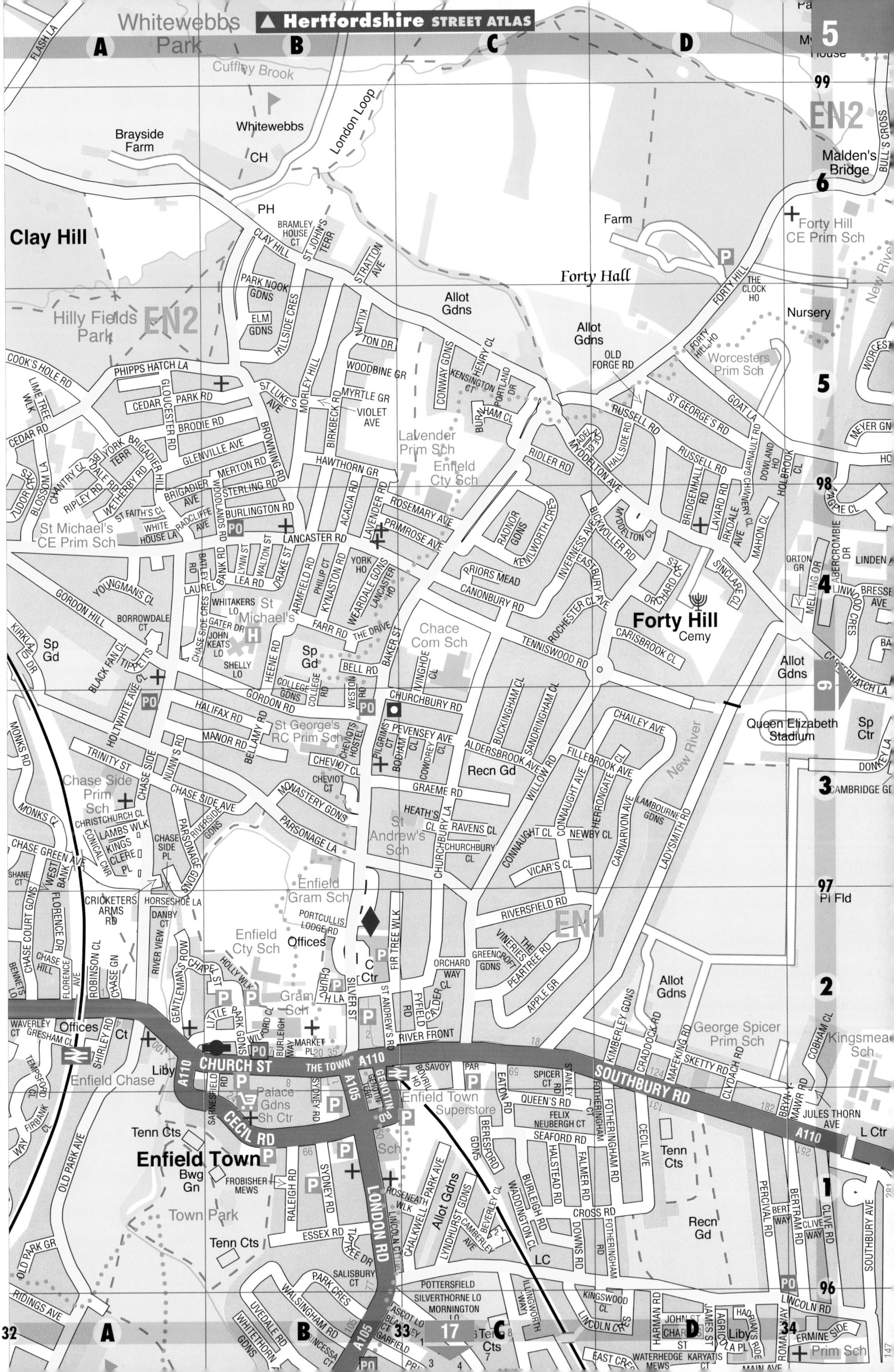
A
B
C
D
Whitewebbs Park
FLASH LA
Cuffley Brook
Whitewebbs
Brayside Farm
CH
London Loop
PH
Clay Hill
BRAMLEY HOUSE CT
ST JOHN'S TERR
CLAY HILL
STRATTON AVE
PARK NOOK GDNS
ELM GDNS
HILLSIDE CRES
Hilly Fields Park
EN2
KILVINTON DR
WOODBINE GR
MYRTLE GR
VIOLET AVE
Allot Gdns
Forty Hall
Farm
FORTY HILL
THE CLOCK HO
Forty Hill CE Prim Sch
Nursery
OLD FORGE RD
FORTY HILL HO
Worcesters Prim Sch
GOAT LA
ST GEORGE'S RD
RUSSELL RD
Malden's Bridge
BULL'S CROSS
99
6
5
98
4
3
97
2
1
96
COOK'S HOLE RD
LIME TREE WLK
PHIPPS HATCH LA
CEDAR
PARK RD
GLOUCESTER RD
BRODIE RD
GLENVILLE AVE
ST LUKE'S AVE
MORLEY HILL
BIRKBECK RD
CONWAY GDNS
HENRY CL
KENSINGTON CT
PORTLAND DR
BURNHAM CL
Lavender Prim Sch
Enfield Cty Sch
RIDLER RD
MYDDELTON AVE
HALLSIDE RD
BRIDGENHALL RD
LAYARD RD
GARNAULT RD
CHIMNEY CL
DOWLAND HO
HOLBROOK CL
MAGPIE CL
CEDAR RD
TUDOR CL
BLOSSOM LA
CHANTRY CL
YORK TERR
DALE RD
RIPLEY RD
WETHERBY RD
BRIGADIER HILL
BRIGADIER AVE
MERTON RD
STERLING RD
WOODLANDS RD
BROWNING RD
HAWTHORN GR
ACACIA RD
LAVENDER RD
ROSEMARY AVE
PRIMROSE AVE
RADNOR GDNS
KENILWORTH CRES
INVERNESS AVE
BICKWOLLER RD
MYDDELTON CL
IRKDALE AVE
MAHON CL
ABERCROMBIE DR
LINDEN
ORTON GR
MELLING DR
LINWOOD CRES
BRESSEY AVE
St Michael's CE Prim Sch
ST FAITH'S CL
WHITE HOUSE LA
RADCLIFFE AVE
BURLINGTON RD
LANCASTER RD
PO
BATLEY RD
BANK RD
LYNN ST
WALTON ST
DRAKE ST
ARMFIELD RD
PHILIP CT
KYNASTON RD
YORK HO
WEARDALE GDNS
LANCASTER HO
PRIORS MEAD
CANONBURY RD
EASTBURY AVE
ROCHESTER CL
ORCHARD CL
SINCLARE CL
Forty Hill Cemy
YOUNGMANS CL
GORDON HILL
LAUREL
WHITAKERS LO
St Michael's
CHASE SIDE CRES
GATER DR
JOHN KEATS LO
SHELLY LO
BORROWDALE CT
FARR RD
THE DRIVE
BAKER ST
Chace Com Sch
TENNISWOOD RD
CARISBROOK CL
Allot Gdns
CARTERHATCH LA
KIRKLAND DR
Sp Gd
BLACK FAN CL
TIPPETTS
HEENE RD
BELL RD
IVINGHOE CL
COLLEGE GDNS
COLLEGE RD
WESTON RD
CHURCHBURY RD
BUCKINGHAM CL
SANDRINGHAM CL
CHAILEY AVE
Queen Elizabeth Stadium
Sp Ctr
DONKEY LA
HOLTWHITE AVE
GORDON RD
HALIFAX RD
BELLAMY RD
St George's RC Prim Sch
CHEVIOTS HOSTEL
PILGRIMS CT
BODIAM CL
PEVENSEY AVE
COWDREY CL
ALDERSBROOK AVE
WILLOW RD
FILLEBROOK AVE
HERRONGATE CL
New River
CAMBRIDGE GDNS
TRINITY ST
CHASE SIDE
NUNN'S RD
MANOR RD
CHEVIOT CL
CHEVIOT CT
GRAEME RD
Recn Gd
CONNAUGHT AVE
LAMBOURNE GDNS
LADYSMITH RD
Chase Side Prim Sch
CHASE SIDE AVE
MONASTERY GDNS
HEATH'S CL
CHURCHBURY LA
RAVENS CL
CONNAUGHT CL
NEWBY CL
CARNARVON AVE
MONKS RD
MONKS CL
CHRISTCHURCH CL
LAMBS WLK
KINGS CLERE PL
CONICAL CNR
RIVERSIDE GDNS
PARSONAGE LA
St Andrew's Sch
CHURCHBURY CL
VICAR'S CL
CHASE GREEN AVE
SHANE CT
WEST BANK
CHASE SIDE PL
PARSONAGE GDNS
Enfield Gram Sch
RIVERSFIELD RD
Pl Fld
CHASE COURT GDNS
FLORENCE DR
CRICKETERS ARMS RD
HORSESHOE LA
DANBY CT
PORTCULLIS LODGE RD
EN1
THE VINERIES
PEARTREE RD
BENNETTS
CHASE HILL
FLORENCE AVE
ROBINSON CL
CHASE GN
RIVER VIEW
GENTLEMAN'S ROW
CHAPEL ST
HOLLY WLK
Enfield Cty Sch
Offices
C Ctr
FIR TREE WLK
ORCHARD WAY
GREENCROFT GDNS
APPLE GR
Allot Gdns
KIMBERLEY GDNS
CRADDOCK RD
MAFEKING RD
George Spicer Prim Sch
CLYDACH RD
COBHAM CL
Kingsmead Sch
WAVERLEY CT
GRESHAM CL
Offices
SHIRLEY RD
Ct
LITTLE PARK GDNS
CHURCH LA
Gram Sch
SILVER ST
ST ANDREW'S RD
FYFIELD RD
CALDER CL
RIVER FRONT
SKETTY RD
BURLEIGH WAY
MARKET PL
A110
CHURCH ST
THE TOWN
SAVOY
PAR
SPICER CT
STANLEY RD
SOUTHBURY RD
Enfield Chase
Liby
TEMPSFORD CL
FIRBANK CL
SARNESFIELD RD
Palace Gdns Sh Ctr
SYDNEY RD
A105
GENOTIN TERR
GENOTIN RD
BOVRIL HO
Enfield Town Superstore
EATON RD
QUEEN'S RD
FELIX NEUBERGH CT
FOTHERINGHAM RD
CECIL AVE
BRYN-Y-MAWR RD
JULES THORN AVE
L Ctr
CECIL RD
Tenn Cts
Enfield Town
Bwg Gn
FROBISHER MEWS
RALEIGH RD
SYDNEY RD
Sch
LONDON RD
ROSENEATH WLK
CHALKWELL PARK AVE
Allot Gdns
LYNDHURST GDNS
CAMBERLEY AVE
BEVERLEY CL
BERESFORD GDNS
SEAFORD RD
HALSTEAD RD
WADDINGTON CL
BURLEIGH RD
FALMER RD
CROSS RD
DOWNS RD
Tenn Cts
Recn Gd
PERCIVAL RD
BERTRAM RD
BERT WAY
CLIVE WAY
CLIVE RD
SOUTHBURY AVE
WAY
OLD PARK AVE
Town Park
ESSEX RD
TREE DR
LINCOLN CT
LC
OLD PARK GR
SALISBURY CT
PARK CRES
POTTERSFIELD
SILVERTHORNE LO
MORNINGTON LO
ILLINGWORTH WAY
KINGSWOOD CL
LINCOLN CRES
LINCOLN RD
RIDINGS AVE
WALSINGHAM RD
ASCOT LO
UVEDALE RD
WHITEHORN GDNS
PRINCESSA CT
GARFIELD
HARMAN RD
JOHNS T CHARLES ST
JAMES ST
AGRICOLA PL
HADRIAN'S RIDE
Liby
ROMANY WAY
ERMINE SIDE
Prim Sch
EAST CRES
WATERHEDGE MEWS
KARYATIS CT
MAIN AVE
Cts

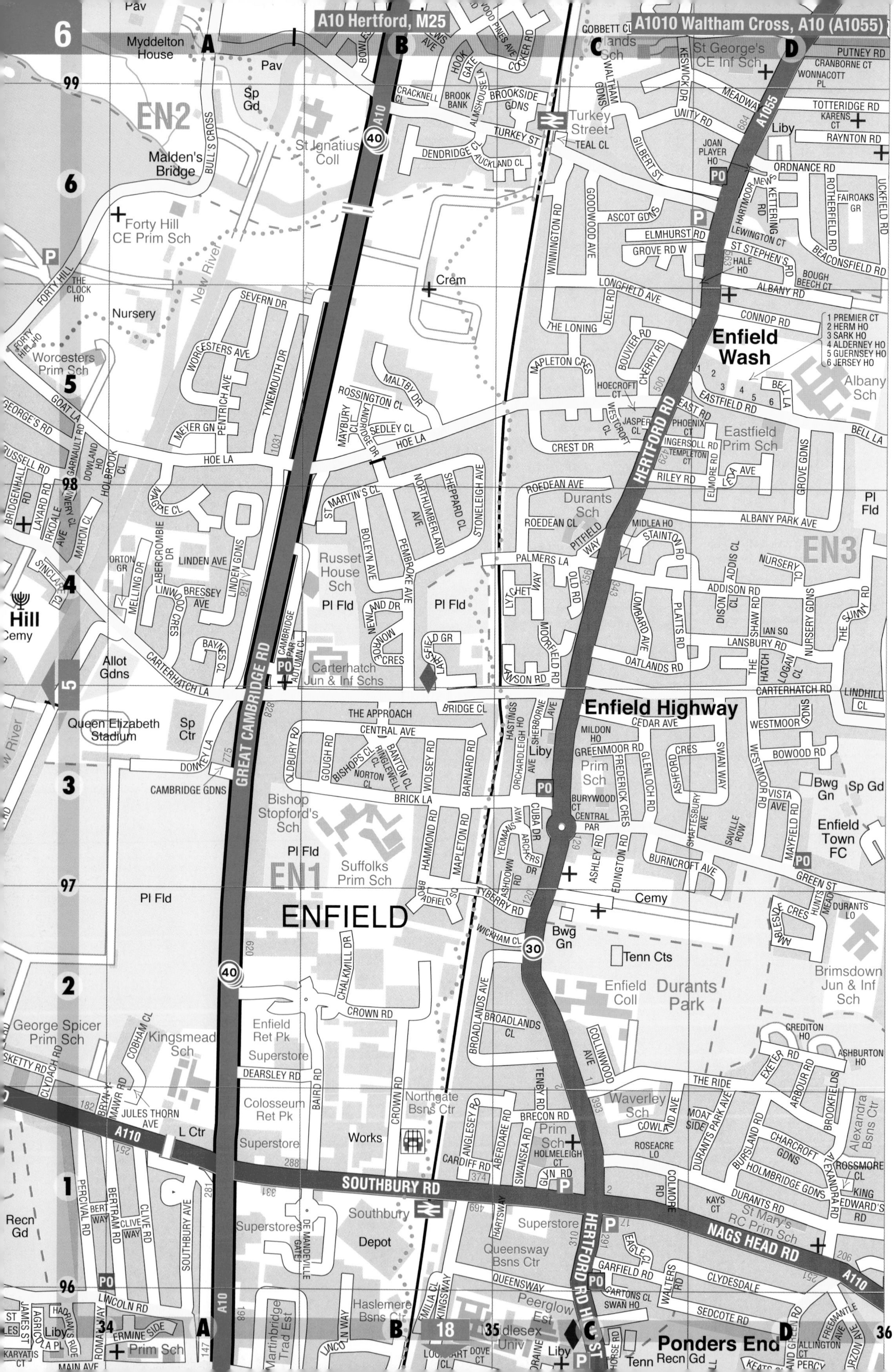

6
A10 Hertford, M25
A1010 Waltham Cross, A10 (A1055)
Myddelton House
Pav
Sp Gd
EN2
St Ignatius Coll
Malden's Bridge
BULL'S CROSS
Forty Hill CE Prim Sch
FORTY HILL
THE CLOCK HO
FORTY HILL HO
Nursery
New River
Worcesters Prim Sch
GOAT LA
GEORGE'S RD
RUSSELL RD
BRIDGENHALL RD
LAYARD RD
IRKDALE AVE
MAHON CL
GARNAULT RD
DOWLAND HO
HOLBROOK CL
SEVERN DR
WORCESTERS AVE
TYNEMOUTH DR
PENTRICH AVE
MEYER GN
HOE LA
MAGPIE CL
ABERCROMBIE DR
LINDEN AVE
LINDEN GDNS
MELLING DR
LINWOOD CRES
BRESSEY AVE
BAYNES CL
SINCLAIR CL
Hill Cemy
Allot Gdns
CARTERHATCH LA
Queen Elizabeth Stadium
Sp Ctr
DONKEY LA
CAMBRIDGE GDNS
GREAT CAMBRIDGE RD
Pl Fld
EN1
ENFIELD
George Spicer Prim Sch
Kingsmead Sch
COBHAM CL
CLYDACH RD
BRYN-Y-MAWR RD
JULES THORN AVE
A110
L Ctr
PERCIVAL RD
BERTRAM RD
CLIVE RD
CLIVE WAY
SOUTHBURY AVE
Recn Gd
LINCOLN RD
HADRIAN'S RIDE
ERMINE SIDE
ROMAN WAY
JAMES ST
AGRICOLA PL
Liby
Prim Sch
MAIN AVE
KARYATIS CT
CRACKNELL CL
BROOK BANK
ALMSHOUSE LA
BROOKSIDE GDNS
HOOK GATE
WOOD PINES AVE
COCKER RD
BOWLES
DENDRIDGE CL
AUCKLAND CL
TURKEY ST
Turkey Street
TEAL CL
Crem
MALTBY DR
ROSSINGTON CL
MAYBURY CL
LANDRIDGE DR
SEDLEY CL
ST MARTIN'S CL
NORTHUMBERLAND AVE
SHEPPARD CL
STONELEIGH AVE
BOLEYN AVE
PEMBROKE AVE
Russet House Sch
MONROE CRES
LARKSFIELD GR
CAMBRIDGE PAR
AUTUMN CL
Carterhatch Jun & Inf Schs
THE APPROACH
BRIDGE CL
CENTRAL AVE
OLDBURY RD
GOUGH RD
BISHOPS CL
BANTON CL
RINGLEWELL CL
NORTON CL
WOLSEY RD
BARNARD RD
BRICK LA
Bishop Stopford's Sch
HAMMOND RD
MAPLETON RD
Suffolks Prim Sch
BROADFIELD SQ
LYBERRY RD
WICKHAM CL
CHALKMILL DR
CROWN RD
Enfield Ret Pk
Superstore
DEARSLEY RD
BAIRD RD
Colosseum Ret Pk
Northgate Bsns Ctr
Works
ANGLESEY RD
ABERDARE RD
SWANSEA RD
CARDIFF RD
SOUTHBURY RD
Southbury
Depot
DE MANDEVILLE GATE
Martinbridge Trad Est
Haslemere Bsns Ctr
KINGSWAY
LOCKHART CL
DOVE CT
Middlesex Univ
18
COBBETT CL
St George's CE Inf Sch
WALTHAM GDNS
KESWICK DR
MEADWAY
UNITY RD
GILBERT ST
A1055
JOAN PLAYER HO
PUTNEY RD
CRANBORNE CT
WONNACOTT PL
TOTTERIDGE RD
KARENS CT
RAYNTON RD
ORDNANCE RD
MEWS
KETTERING RD
HARTMOOR
ROTHERFIELD RD
FAIROAKS GR
UCKFIELD RD
LEWINGTON CT
ST STEPHEN'S RD
HALE HO
BEACONSFIELD RD
BOUGH BEECH CT
ALBANY RD
WINNINGTON RD
GOODWOOD AVE
ASCOT GDNS
ELMHURST RD
GROVE RD W
LONGFIELD AVE
DELL RD
THE LONING
CONNOP RD
1 PREMIER CT
2 HERM HO
3 SARK HO
4 ALDERNEY HO
5 GUERNSEY HO
6 JERSEY HO
Enfield Wash
MAPLETON CRES
BOUVIER RD
CHERRY RD
HOECROFT CT
WESTCROFT CL
JASPER CL
PHOENIX CT
EAST RD
EASTFIELD RD
BELLA
Albany Sch
BELL LA
HERTFORD RD
INGERSOLL RD
TEMPLETON CT
CREST DR
Eastfield Prim Sch
RILEY RD
ELMORE RD
LEDA AVE
GROVE GDNS
ROEDEAN AVE
Durants Sch
ROEDEAN CL
PITFIELD WAY
MIDLEA HO
STAINTON RD
ALBANY PARK AVE
Pl Fld
EN3
PALMERS LA
LYTCHET WAY
OLD RD
ADDIS CL
NURSERY CL
ADDISON RD
DISON CL
LOMBARD AVE
PLATTS RD
SHAW RD
IAN SQ
NURSERY GDNS
THE SUNNY RD
MOORFIELD RD
LANSBURY RD
OATLANDS RD
LAWSON RD
THE HATCH
LOGAN CL
CARTERHATCH RD
LINDHILL CL
Enfield Highway
CEDAR AVE
WESTMOOR GDNS
MILDON HO
GREENMOOR RD
HASTINGS
ORCHARDLEIGH AVE
SHERBORNE AVE
FREDERICK CRES
GLENLOCH RD
ASHFORD CRES
SWAN WAY
WESTMOOR RD
BOWOOD RD
Prim Sch
BURYWOOD CT
CENTRAL PAR
SHAFTESBURY AVE
SAVILLE ROW
VISTA AVE
MAYFIELD RD
Bwg Gn
Sp Gd
Enfield Town FC
YEOMANS WAY
CUBA DR
ARCHERS DR
ASHDOWN RD
ASHLEY RD
EDINGTON RD
BURNCROFT AVE
GREEN ST
HUNTS MEAD
DURANTS LO
AMBLESIDE CRES
Cemy
Bwg Gn
Tenn Cts
Enfield Coll
Durants Park
Brimsdown Jun & Inf Sch
BROADLANDS AVE
BROADLANDS CL
COLLINWOOD AVE
CREDITON HO
ASHBURTON HO
EXETER RD
ARBOUR RD
BROOKFIELDS
Alexandra Bsns Ctr
THE RIDE
Waverley Sch
COWLAND AVE
MOAT SIDE
DURANTS PARK AVE
BURSLAND RD
CHARCROFT GDNS
ALEXANDRA RD
ROSSMORE CL
KING EDWARD'S RD
HOLMBRIDGE GDNS
DURANTS RD
TENBY RD
BRECON RD
HOLMELEIGH CT
GLYN RD
ROSEACRE LO
COLMORE RD
KAYS CT
St Mary's RC Prim Sch
NAGS HEAD RD
HARTSWAY
Superstore
Queensway Bsns Ctr
EAGLE CL
GARFIELD RD
WALTERS RD
CLYDESDALE
QUEENSWAY
Peerglow Est
CARTONS CL
SWAN HO
SEDCOTE RD
HERTFORD RD
HIGH ST
FREEMANTLE
Ponders End
Recn Gd
Tenn
ALLINGTON CT
PERCY
KEATS
A
B
C
D
99
98
97
96
1
2
3
4
5
6
34
35
36

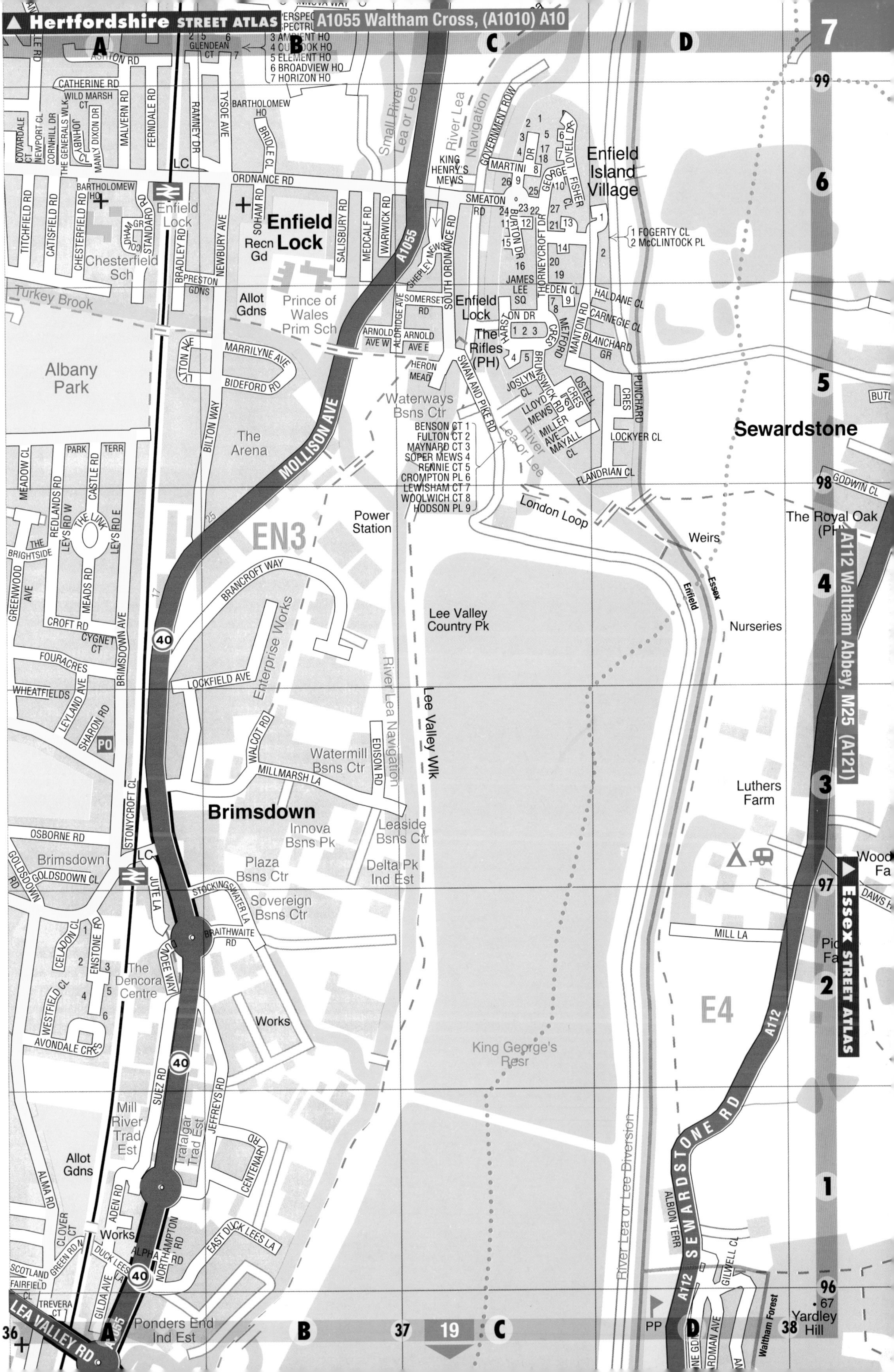
A
B
C
D
99
6
5
98
4
3
97
2
1
96
ASHTON RD
CATHERINE RD
WILD MARSH CT
GLENDEAN CT
2 AMBIENT HO
4 CUBROOK HO
5 ELEMENT HO
6 BROADVIEW HO
7 HORIZON HO
BARTHOLOMEW HO
MALVERN RD
FERNDALE RD
RAMNEY DR
TYSOE AVE
BRIDLE CL
COVARDALE CT
NEWPORT CL
CORNHILL DR
THE GENERALS WLK
JOHNBY CL
MANLY DIXON DR
LC
ORDNANCE RD
Enfield Lock
Enfield Lock
Recn Gd
TITCHFIELD RD
CATISFIELD RD
CHESTERFIELD RD
STANDARD RD
BRADLEY RD
NEWBURY AVE
SOHAM RD
SALISBURY RD
MEDCALF RD
WARWICK RD
Chesterfield Sch
PRESTON GDNS
Turkey Brook
Allot Gdns
Prince of Wales Prim Sch
A1055
Small River Lea or Lee
River Lea Navigation
GOVERNMENT ROW
KING HENRY'S MEWS
SMEATON RD
SHEPLEY MEWS
SOUTH ORDNANCE RD
MARTINI DR
GEORGE LOVELL DR
FISHER CL
BURTON DR
THORNEYCROFT DR
JAMES LEE SQ
Enfield Island Village
1 FOGERTY CL
2 McCLINTOCK PL
THEEDEN CL
HALDANE CL
CARNEGIE CL
BLANCHARD GR
MANTON RD
METFORD CRES
Enfield Lock
The Rifles (PH)
SOMERSET RD
ALDRIDGE AVE
ARNOLD AVE W
ARNOLD AVE E
HERON MEAD
SWAN AND PIKE RD
JOSLYN CL
LLOYD MEWS
BRUNSWICK RD
MILLER AVE
MAYALL CL
OSTELL CRES
PUNCHARD CRES
LOCKYER CL
FLANDRIAN CL
Albany Park
MARRILYNE AVE
BIDEFORD RD
LYTTON AVE
BILTON WAY
The Arena
Waterways Bsns Ctr
BENSON CT 1
FULTON CT 2
MAYNARD CT 3
SOPER MEWS 4
RENNIE CT 5
CROMPTON PL 6
LEWISHAM CT 7
WOOLWICH CT 8
HODSON PL 9
River Lea or Lee
London Loop
Sewardstone
GODWIN CL
The Royal Oak (PH)
Weirs
MOLLISON AVE
Power Station
EN3
MEADOW CL
PARK TERR
CASTLE RD
REDLANDS RD
LEYS RD W
LEYS RD E
THE LINK
MEADS RD
THE BRIGHTSIDE
GREENWOOD AVE
CROFT RD
CYGNET CT
BRIMSDOWN AVE
FOURACRES
WHEATFIELDS
LEYLAND AVE
SHARON RD
PO
BRANCROFT WAY
Enterprise Works
LOCKFIELD AVE
Lee Valley Country Pk
Enfield
Essex
Nurseries
A112 Waltham Abbey, M25 (A121)
River Lea Navigation
Lee Valley Wlk
WALCOT RD
Watermill Bsns Ctr
EDISON RD
MILLMARSH LA
STONYCROFT CL
OSBORNE RD
Brimsdown
Brimsdown
GOLDSDOWN RD
GOLDSDOWN CL
JUTE LA
Innova Bsns Pk
Leaside Bsns Ctr
Plaza Bsns Ctr
Delta Pk Ind Est
Luthers Farm
STOCKINGSWATER LA
Sovereign Bsns Ctr
BRAITHWAITE RD
MILL LA
▲ Essex STREET ATLAS
CELADON CL
ENSTONE RD
The Dencora Centre
WESTFIELD CL
AVONDALE CRES
Works
E4
King George's Resr
A112
40
SUEZ RD
Trafalgar Trad Est
JEFFREYS RD
Mill River Trad Est
CENTENARY RD
Allot Gdns
ALMA RD
ADEN RD
Works
CLOVER CT
GREEN RD
SCOTLAND GREEN RD N
DUCK LEES LA
NORTHAMPTON RD
ALPHA RD
EAST DUCK LEES LA
FAIRFIELD CL
TREVERA CT
GILDA AVE
LEA VALLEY RD
Ponders End Ind Est
River Lea or Lee Diversion
SEWARDSTONE RD
ALBION TERR
GILWELL CL
A112
PP
Waltham Forest
67
Yardley Hill

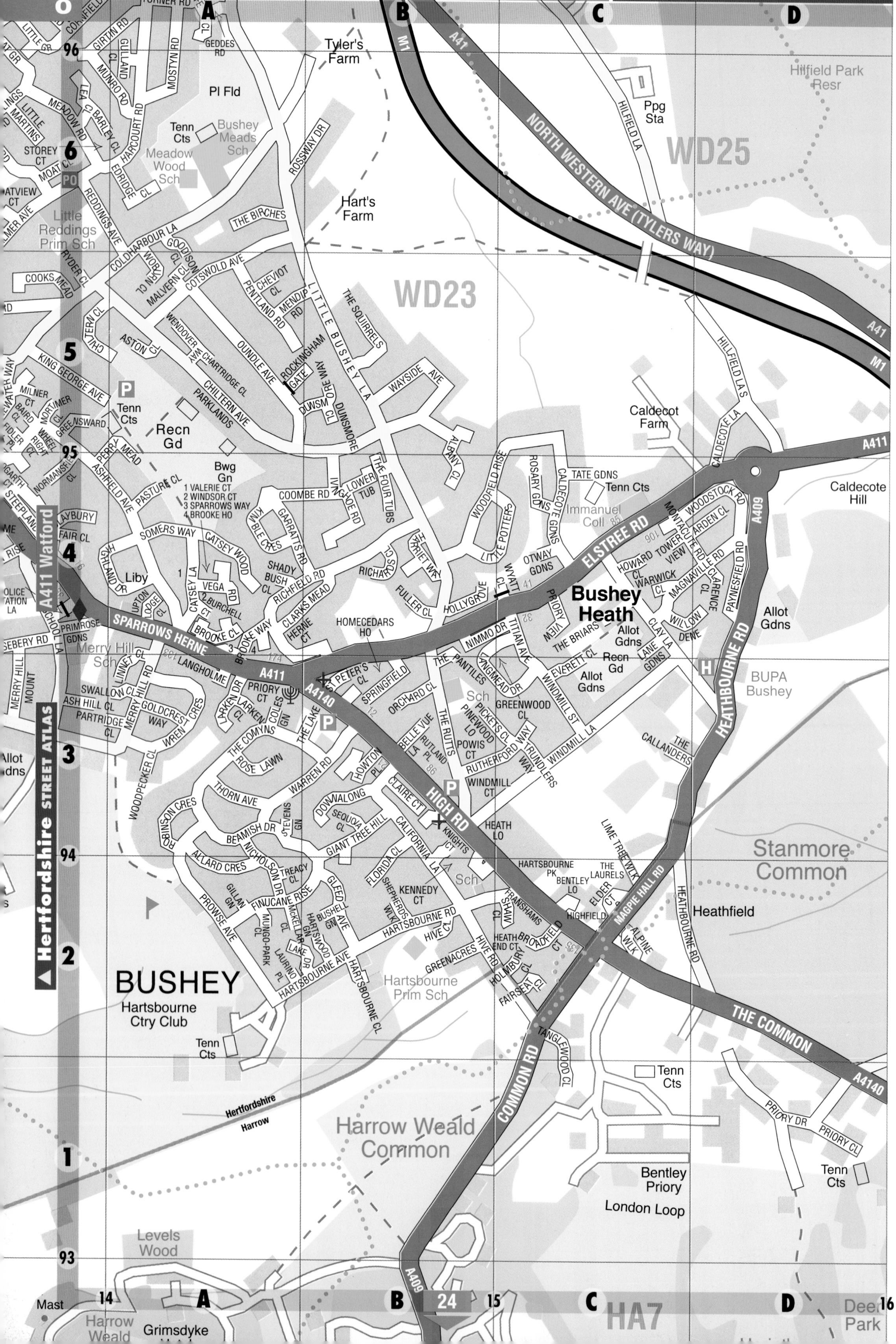
A
B
C
D
96
6
5
95
4
3
94
2
1
93
14
15
16
Tyler's Farm
Hilfield Park Resr
Ppg Sta
WD25
NORTH WESTERN AVE (TYLERS WAY)
A41
M1
HILFIELD LA
Pl Fld
Tenn Cts
Bushey Meads Sch
Meadow Wood Sch
Hart's Farm
Little Reddings Prim Sch
WD23
LITTLE BUSHEY LA
THE SQUIRRELS
ROSSWAY DR
THE BIRCHES
COLDHARBOUR LA
GOODISON CL
COTSWOLD AVE
CHEVIOT CL
PENTLAND RD
MENDIP RD
MALVERN CL
WORCESTER CL
ASTON CL
WENDOVER WAY
CHARTRIDGE CL
OUNDLE AVE
ROCKINGHAM GATE
CHILTERN AVE
PARKLANDS
KING GEORGE AVE
Recn Gd
Bwg Gn
1 VALERIE CT
2 WINDSOR CT
3 SPARROWS WAY
4 BROOKE HO
PASTURE CL
ASHFIELD AVE
PERRY MEAD
GREENSWARD
WAYSIDE AVE
ALBANY CL
DUNSMORE
THE FOUR TUBS
LOWER TUB
IVINGHOE RD
COOMBE RD
GARRATTS RD
KIMBLE CRES
SOMERS WAY
CATSEY WOOD
CATSEY LA
VEGA RD
BURCHELL CT
BROOKE CL
Liby
UPTON LODGE CL
HIGHLAND DR
SHADY BUSH CL
RICHFIELD RD
CLARKS MEAD
HERNE CT
RICHARDS CL
HARRIET WAY
FULLER CL
HOLLYGROVE
WYATT CL
WOODFIELD RISE
LITTLE POTTERS
ROSARY GDNS
CALDECOTE GDNS
TATE GDNS
Immanuel Coll
OTWAY GDNS
ELSTREE RD
PRIORY VIEW
Bushey Heath
HOWARD CL
WARWICK CL
TOWER VIEW
MONTAGUE RD
WOODSTOCK RD
ARDEN CL
MAGNAVILLE RD
CLARENCE CL
PAYNESFIELD RD
WILLOW DENE
CLAY LA
THE BRIARS
Allot Gdns
Caldecot Farm
CALDECOTE LA
HILLFIELD LA S
A411
Caldecote Hill
A409
HEATHBOURNE RD
BUPA Bushey
A411 Watford
SPARROWS HERNE
LAYBURY
FAIR CL
PRIMROSE GDNS
Merry Hill Sch
LANGHOLME
LINNET CL
MERRY HILL RD
SWALLOW CL
ASH HILL CL
PARTRIDGE CL
GOLDCREST WAY
WREN CRES
PRIORY CT
COLES GN
LARKEN DR
LARKEN CL
HOMECEDARS HO
ST PETER'S CL
SPRINGFIELD
ORCHARD CL
THE LAKE
A4140
THE COMYNS
ROSE LAWN
WARREN RD
HOWTON PL
THORN AVE
WOODPECKER CL
ROBINSON CRES
BEAMISH DR
DOWNALONG
SEQUOIA CL
GIANT TREE HILL
CLAIRE CT
CALIFORNIA LA
HIGH RD
KNIGHTS CT
BELLE VUE LA
RUTLAND PL
THE RUTTS
THE PANTILES
NIMMO DR
TITIAN AVE
LANGMEAD DR
PINEWOOD LO
POWIS CT
PICKETS CL
GREENWOOD CL
RUTHERFORD WAY
WINDMILL CT
TRUNDLERS WAY
WINDMILL LA
WINDMILL ST
EVERETT CL
Recn Gd
Sch
LANE GDNS
THE CALLANDERS
HEATH LO
Stanmore Common
HARTSBOURNE PK
BENTLEY LO
THE LAURELS
LIME TREE WLK
MAGPIE HALL RD
ELDER CT
HIGHFIELD
Heathfield
ALPINE WLK
ALLARD CRES
NICHOLSON DR
TREACY CL
FINUCANE RISE
GILLAN GN
PROWSE AVE
MUNGO-PARK CL
MCKELLAR CL
HARTSWOOD GN
BUSHELL GN
GLEED AVE
FLORIDA CL
SHEPHERDS WLK
KENNEDY CT
HARTSBOURNE RD
HIVE CL
HIVE RD
SHAW CL
FRANSHAMS
BROADFIELD CT
HEATH END CT
GREENACRES
HOLMBURY CT
FAIRSEAT CL
LAKE DR
LAURINO PL
HARTSBOURNE AVE
HARTSBOURNE CL
Hartsbourne Prim Sch
BUSHEY
Hartsbourne Ctry Club
Tenn Cts
THE COMMON
TANGLEWOOD CL
COMMON RD
A4140
PRIORY DR
PRIORY CL
Hertfordshire
Harrow
Harrow Weald Common
Bentley Priory
London Loop
Levels Wood
Mast
Harrow Weald
Grimsdyke
HA7
Deer Park
24

A
B
C
D
Home Farm
Allot Gdns
96
Aldenham Ctry Pk
LISTER COTTS
P
Laboratory
A5183
B5378
ALLUM LA
6
Cemy
DAGGER LA
ALDENHAM RD
Aldenham Resr
Sailing Club
Pav
ELSTREE HILL N
ROMELAND CT
THE BARTONS
St Nicholas CE Prim Sch
ROMELAND
4
Sp Gd
Tenn Cts
ST NICHOLAS CL
WD6
LANDS' END
1
NEW RD
Elstree
OAK TREE CT
GEORGES MEAD
YEW TREE CT
5
WATFORD RD
HIGH ST
SCHUBERT RD
2
PO
FOX CL
BRITTEN CL
3
A411
PH
RODGERS CL
SUMMER GR
ELSTREE RD
SULLIVAN WAY
DELIUS CL
WEBBER CL
BEEHIVE
WEST VIEW GDNS
VALENTINE CT
Lismirrane Ind Pk
MAY GDNS
FORTUNE LA
BEETHOVEN RD
ELSTREE HILL S
Tenn Cts
95
The Le
DYLAN CL
COATES RD
ELGAR CL
Edgwarebury House Farm
NORTH WESTERN AVE (WATFORD BY-PASS)
CENTENNIAL AVE
Centennial Pk
4
Ter Ct
WD23
Hertfordshire
Harrow
A5183
Centennial Ct
10
Hertfordshire
Barnet
M1
A5
4
Brockleyhill Farm
3
Sp Gd
Brockley Grange
London Loop
Tenn Cts
BROCKLEY HILL HO
94
HA8
Works
HA7
SIR HENRY FLOYD CT
Royal National Orthopaedic
H
Annandale
NUTT GR
A41 EDGWARE WAY (WATFORD BY-PASS)
Grove Farm
Pear Wood Cottages
2
BROCKLEY HILL
THE LIMES
Limes House
Wood Farm
WARREN LA
WOOD LA
Pear Wood
Crkt Gd
CH
LANCASTER HO
Pav
Tenn Cts
Brockley Hill
NEWLANDS CL
GRANTHAM CL
HAMLYN CL
Barnet
Harrow
Tenn Cts
Cloisters Wood
Springbok House
PIPERS GREEN LA
1
SPRINGFIELD CL
PARK LA
HILLTOP WAY
LITTLE COMMON
BROOMFIELD HO 1
FALLOWFIELD CT 2
HILL HO 3
WELLINGTON HO 4
STANMORE HILL
DENNIS LA
JULIUS CAESAR WAY
CLAUDIUS CL
AUGUSTUS CL
BROCKLEY AVE
FALLOWFIELD
AYLMER CL
Stanmore Hall
30
A4140
FAUNA CL
CHEVALIER CL
93
A5
PARTRIDGE CL
AYLWARDS RISE
AYLMER DR
HERIOTS CL
PINE CL
HALL F CL
BERRY HILL
REES DR
16
17
25
18

A
B
C
D
96
6
5
95
4
3
94
2
1
93
Elstree
Allot Gdns
WOODSIDE
BLATTNER CL
B5378
ALLUM LA
A5183
ELSTREE HILL
HILL CREST LO
FIR TREE CT
KNOWL PK
KNOWL WAY
TAUBER CL
LODGE AVE
GRANGE RD
BISHOPS AVE
Cemy
Furzehill Sch
CEDARS CL
OAKWOOD
ELMWOOD AVE
Allot Gdns
Sch
CAVENDISH CRES
LAKESIDE
AUDEN DR
HARTFIELD AVE
DEACON'S HILL RD
BERKELEY CL
WORDSWORTH GDNS
ASCOT CL
HARTFIELD AVE
HARTFIELD CL
BYRON AVE
MELROSE AVE
TENNISON AVE
MILTON DR
VALE AVE
MASEFIELD AVE
LULLINGTON GARTH
CARRINGTON AVE
THE RISE
WENTWORTH AVE
SHIREMEADE
SHERATON CL
LOWTHER CL
NICHOLAS RD
HADLEY CL
ALLWYN CL
CLARE CL
BELMOR
SUMMER HILL
London Loop
ROMELAND CT
ROMELAND
THE BARTONS
St Nicholas CE Prim Sch
ST NICHOLAS CL
Elstree
NEW RD
HIGH ST
OAK TREE CT
GEORGES MEAD
PO
SUMMER GR
VALENTINE CT
FORTUNE LA
MAY GDNS
WEST VIEW GDNS
Tenn Cts
A411
BARNET LA
DEACONS HTS
Deacons Hill
Abbotsbury
WD6
Elstree Tunnel
Woodcock Hill
Tenn Cts
Edgwarebury House Farm
The Leys
Penniwells Farm
Tenn Cts
Tenn Cts
Edgwarebury Ctry Club
Hertfordshire
Barnet
NW7
9
M1
Hertfordshire
Barnet
M1
Edgwarebury Farm
Bury Farm
Edgware Bury
DUNBLANE CL 1
KINROSS CL 2
MOIDART CT 3
MALLAIG CT 4
OBAN CT 5
ARRAN CT 6
TORRIDON CT 7
ROSS CT 8
EDGWAREBURY LA
Clay La
WARRENS SHAWE LA
MEADFIELD
MEADFIELD GN
BUSHFIELD CL
BUSHFIELD CRES
BURRELL CL
Cemy
Pav
Pl Fld
HARTLAND CL
HARTLAND DR
Broadfields Prim Sch
PENTLAND AVE
HAMONDE CL
CROMARTY RD
RANNOCH CL
KINGSLEY CT
TAYSIDE DR
MORAY CL
ALDRIDGE AVE
A41 EDGWARE WAY (WATFORD BY-PASS)
HA8
GLENDEVON CL
Sch
PO
Edgwarebury Park
PARSONS CRES
PARSONS GR
WOLMER GDNS
FRANCKLYN GDNS
HARROWES MEADE
FAIRCROFT RD
BROADFIELD CT
GLENGALL RD
MIDSUMMER CT
BULLESCROFT RD
BEULAH CL
CRANMER RD
ASHFORD CT
MARLBOROUGH AVE
WYRE GR
ROSENS WLK
LYNFORD GDNS
CROSSGATE
BROADFIELDS AVE
WINDSOR AVE
Tenn Cts
Pav
CH
GRANTHAM CL
NEWLANDS CL
HAMLYN CL
PIPERS GREEN LA
Barnet
Harrow
CH
Edgwarebury
JULIUS CAESAR WAY
CLAUDIUS CL
AUGUSTUS CL
BROCKLEY AVE
HA7
FAUNA CL
CHEVALIER CL
A5
PARTRIDGE CL
BERRY HILL
PARKLANDS PL 6
COMPASS CL 7
A41
A410
SPUR RD
GOLDSMITH CT
COLLINSON CT
SPALDING CT
EATON CT
PARKSIDE DR
BLACKWELL GDNS
MOWBRAY RD
HURSTMEAD CT
GRENVILLE CT
BROADHURST AVE
Sch
Sch
18
CANONS CNR
1 WARE CT
2 WAKEMAN HO
3 ABINGDON CT
4 CHICHELE HO
GARRICK CT
MARTYN CT
Pl Fld
26
1950
EDGWARE WAY (WATFORD BY-PASS)
RANELAGH CL
20

A
B
C
D
96
95
94
93
6
5
4
3
2
1
20
21
22
27
12
Arkley
Rowley Bank Nurseries
EN5
Memorial Sp Ctr
Rowley Lodge
Wr Twr
Pav
Windmill (dis)
Tenn Cts
Sp Gd
Barnet Gate
MOUNTVIEW COTTS
BARNET RD
BARNET LA
BOREHAMWOOD
WD6
Furze Hill
Saffron Green Prim Sch
Stirling Ind Ctr
Stirling Ret Pk
Stirling Cnr
Hertfordshire
Barnet
ELSTREE PK
GREENLANDS
ARKLEY PK
PH
Scratch Wood
Scratchwood Open Space
Nature Trail
Thistle Wood
London Loop
Hyver Hall
Hyver Farm
Barnet Gate Wood
Moat Mount Open Space
NW7
Mote End Farm
Mill Hill
London Gateway Service Area
Motel
Dean's Brook
Hemmings Wood
Nut Wood
Tenn Cts
Mill Hill Cty High Sch
Stoney Wood Lake
Fairway Prim Sch
Northway Sch
CH
Sch
Pl Fld
EDGWARE
Highwood House
Highwood Hill
Allot Gdns
Lawrence Green
St Joseph's Coll
Stoneyfields Park
OAKTREES HOSTEL
BARNET BY-PASS
BARNET WAY (BARNET BY-PASS)
A1
M1
A411
A5109
B552
A41
EDGWAREWAY (WATFORD BY-PASS)
NORTHWAY CIR
Apex Cnr
MARSH LA
HIGHWOOD HILL
B552 HIGHWOOD HILL
NAN CLARK'S LA
ON WOOD LA
1 WILLOW GN
2 HUNTER WLK
3 CLYDESDALE PATH
4 DALES PATH
5 SADDLERS PATH
ARUNDEL DR
PARSONAGE CT
GRANTHAM GN
ASHLEY DR
RIPON WAY
CLYDESDALE CL
SUFFOLK CL
HALTER CL
FARRIERS WAY
DALES RD
SADDLERS CL
PINTO CL
PERCHERON RD
SHETLAND CL
COBB CL
HUNTER CL
CONNEMARA CL
FROGHALL COTTS
STIRLING WAY
CARLTON CL
BALMORAL DR
ELY GDNS
NICOLL WAY
LINCOLN CT
RICHMOND CL
STANGATE CRES
MONKSWOOD GDNS
TINWELL MEWS
DACRE GDNS
BURGHLEY AVE
ST PAUL'S CL
CRANES WAY
CLEVELAND CRES
GRAVELEY
HAMPTON CL
OAK FARM
FURZEHILL RD
LINSTER GR
CARRINGTON CL
HACKNEY CL
ROWLEY LA
ROWLEY GREEN RD
MEADOWBANKS
KATES CL
LYNFORD CL
WINDMILL CL
DINGLE CL
ROCKWAYS
WYLO DR
HAWTHORN GR
BRICKFIELD LA
WINIFRED CL
CHANTRY CL
BARNET GATE LA
ALTHORP CL
HYVER HILL
CROWN CL
HENDON PK COTTS
SPRINGWOOD CRES
MORLEY CRES
MAYTREE CL
BELLAMY CL
LUTHER CL
KENILWORTH RD
HARCOURT AVE
FAIRMEAD CRES
CEDAR CT
WARWICK AVE
RIVERDENE
LANGLEY CRES
MOUNT GR
PARNELL CL
THE FAIRWAY
FAIRWAY CT
LALEHAM AVE
WESTMERE DR
LAUREL GDNS
ELLESMERE AVE
FERNSIDE AVE
NORTH DENE
MOUNT VIEW
MIDDLE DENE
SOUTH DENE
PIKE RD
COURTLAND AVE
ROBIN CL
HANKINS LA
STOCKTON GDNS
WESTFIELD RD
CROFT CL
BEDFORD RD
RAMILLIES RD
WORCESTER CRES
NORBURY GR
GLENWOOD RD
BRABOURNE HTS
AUSTELL HTS
AUSTELL GDNS
TRETAWN GDNS
TRETAWN PK
GREENDALE
MARSH CL
HORNBEAM CL
ABBEY VIEW
THE LINCOLNS
LAWRENCE GDNS
THE REDDINGS
REDDINGS CL
HOLCOMBE HILL
ABBOTSVIEW CT
LAWRENCE ST
NORTHWAY CT
UPHILL

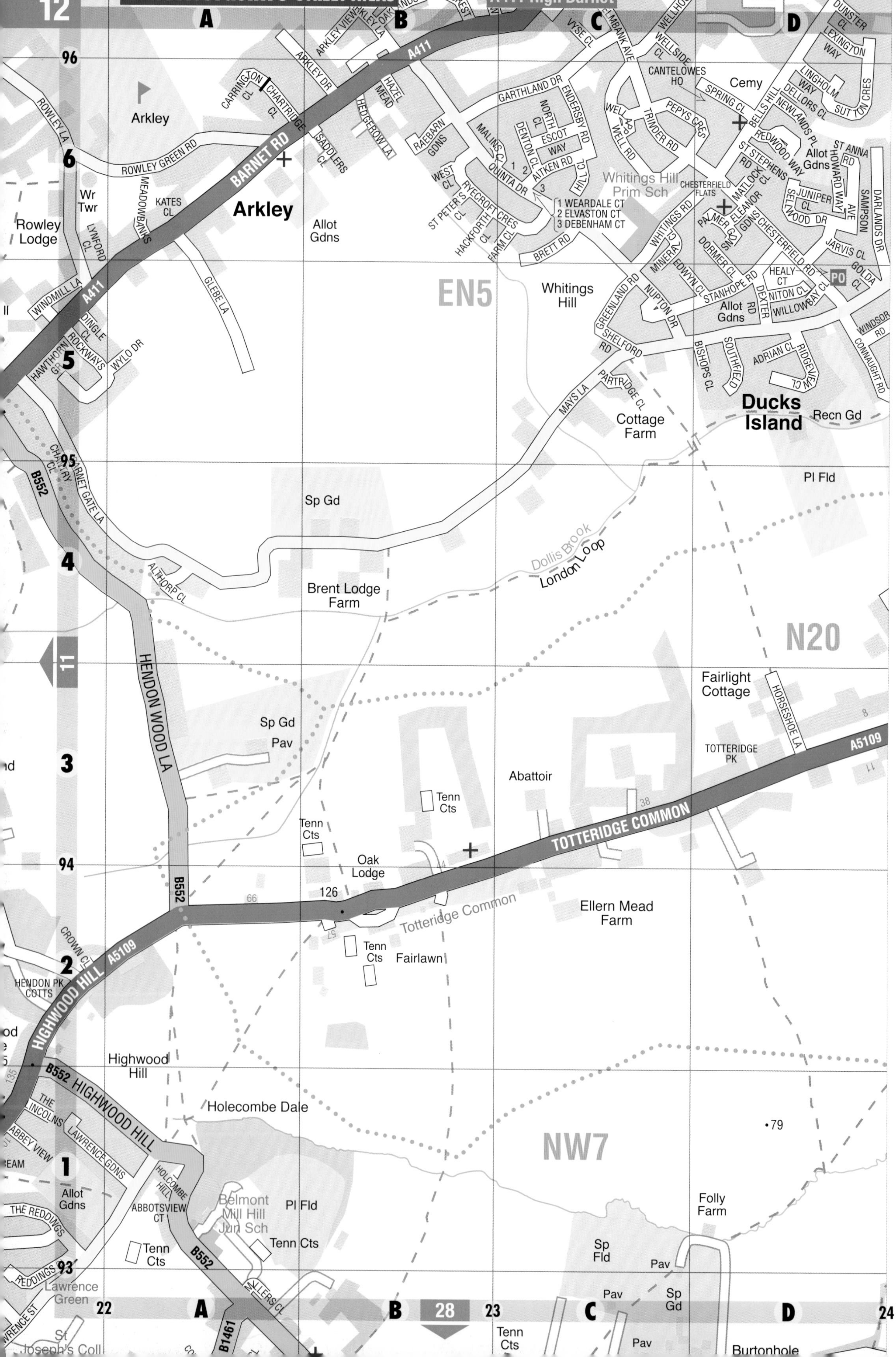
A411 High Barnet
A
B
C
D
96
Arkley
ROWLEY LA
ROWLEY GREEN RD
CARRINGTON CL
CHARTRIDGE CL
BARNET RD
A411
ARKLEY DR
ARKLEY VIEW
OAKLANDS LA
HILLCREST
HAZEL MEAD
HEDGEROW LA
SADDLERS CL
RAEBARN GDNS
GARTHLAND DR
ENDERSBY RD
NORTH CL
ESCOT WAY
DENTON CL
AITKEN RD
HILL CL
MALINS CL
QUINTA DR
WEST CL
RYECROFT CRES
ST PETER'S CL
HACKFORTH CL
FARM CL
BRETT RD
1 WEARDALE CT
2 ELVASTON CT
3 DEBENHAM CT
Whitings Hill Prim Sch
VYSE CL
ELMBANK AVE
WELLHOUSE LA
WELLSIDE CL
CANTELOWES HO
Cemy
SPRING CL
PEPYS CRES
TRINDER RD
WELL RD
BELLS HILL
DUNSTER CL
LEXINGTON WAY
LINGHOLM WAY
DELLORS CL
NEWLANDS PL
SUTTON CRES
REDWOOD WAY
ST STEPHENS RD
ST ANNA RD
Allot Gdns
HOWARD WAY
JUNIPER CL
SELLWOOD DR
SAMPSON AVE
DARLANDS DR
CHESTERFIELD FLATS
MATLOCK CL
ELEANOR GDNS
PALMER GDNS
WHITINGS RD
MINERAL CL
DORMER CL
CHESTERFIELD RD
JARVIS CL
GOLDA CL
HEALY CT
PO
EDWYN CL
STANHOPE RD
NITON CL
WILLOWBAY CL
DEXTER RD
6
Wr Twr
Rowley Lodge
MEADOWBANKS
KATES CL
Arkley
Allot Gdns
LYNFORD CL
WINDMILL LA
A411
DINGLE CL
ROCKWAYS
WYLD DR
HAWTHORN GR
GLEBE LA
5
EN5
Whitings Hill
GREENLAND RD
NUPTON DR
Allot Gdns
WINDSOR RD
CONNAUGHT RD
SHELFORD RD
BISHOPS CL
SOUTHFIELD
ADRIAN CL
RIDGEVIEW CL
PARTRIDGE CL
MAYS LA
Cottage Farm
Ducks Island
Recn Gd
95
B552
CHANTRY CL
BARNET GATE LA
Pl Fld
Sp Gd
Dollis Brook
London Loop
4
ALTHORP CL
Brent Lodge Farm
N20
11
HENDON WOOD LA
Fairlight Cottage
HORSESHOE LA
Sp Gd
Pav
3
TOTTERIDGE PK
A5109
Abattoir
Tenn Cts
Tenn Cts
TOTTERIDGE COMMON
Oak Lodge
94
B552
126
Ellern Mead Farm
Totteridge Common
Tenn Cts
Fairlawn
2
CROWN CL
A5109
HENDON PK COTTS
HIGHWOOD HILL
Highwood Hill
B552 HIGHWOOD HILL
Holecombe Dale
THE LINCOLNS
ABBEY VIEW
LAWRENCE GDNS
•79
NW7
1
Allot Gdns
HOLCOMBE HILL
ABBOTSVIEW CT
Belmont Mill Hill Jun Sch
Pl Fld
Folly Farm
THE REDDINGS
Tenn Cts
Tenn Cts
B552
Sp Fld
Pav
93
REDDINGS
Lawrence Green
MILLERS CL
Pav
Sp Gd
22
A
B
28
23
C
D
24
B1461
St Joseph's Coll
Tenn Cts
Pav
Burtonhole

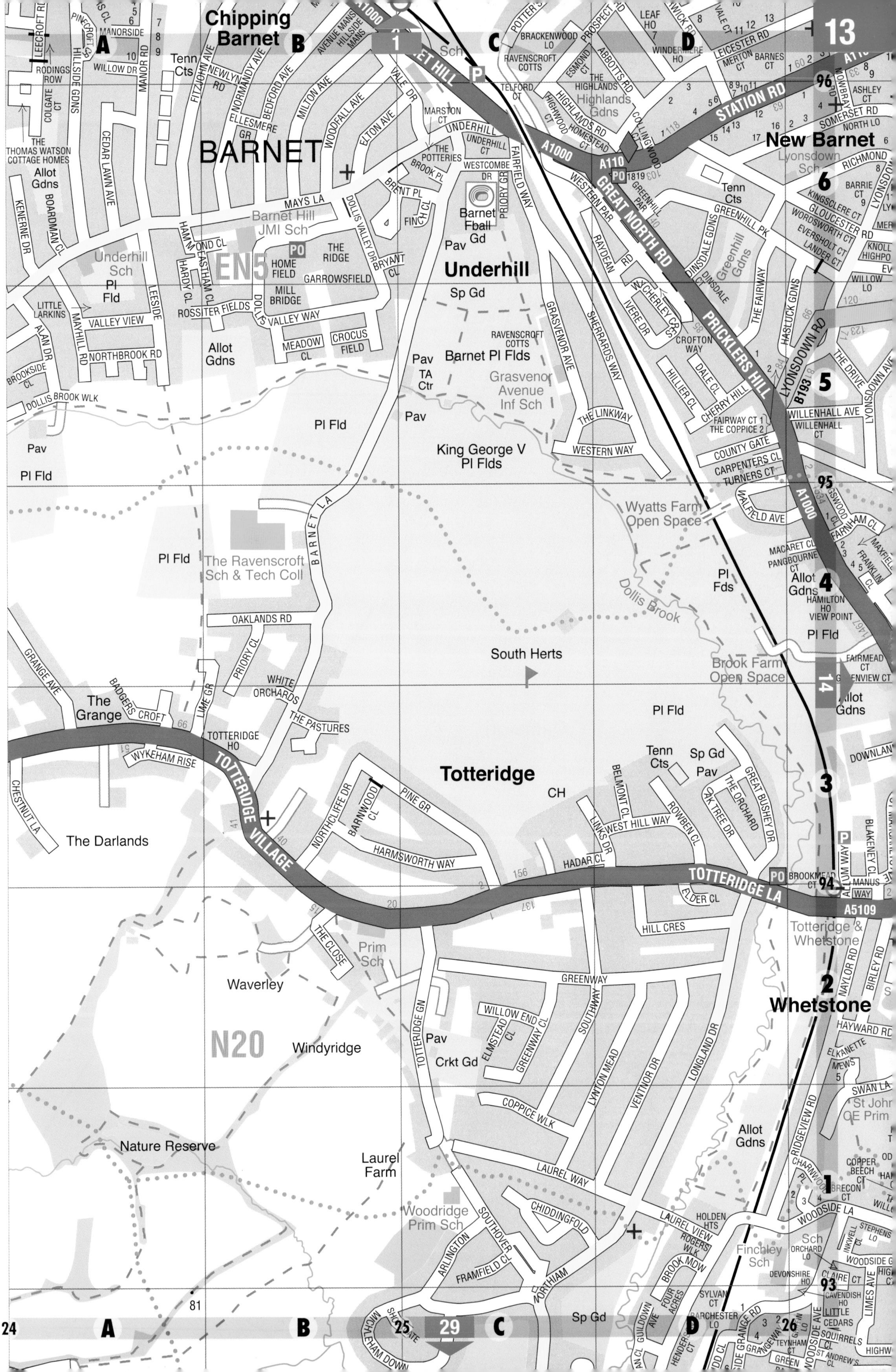
A
B
C
D
1
Chipping Barnet
BARNET
New Barnet
Underhill
Totteridge
Whetstone
EN5
N20
A1000
A110
A5109
B193
STATION RD
GREAT NORTH RD
PRICKLERS HILL
TOTTERIDGE VILLAGE
TOTTERIDGE LA
LYONSDOWN RD
MAYS LA
BARNET LA
UNDERHILL
FAIRFIELD WAY
LEECROFT RD
PINCROFT CT
MANORSIDE
MANOR RD
RODINGS ROW
WILLOW DR
HILLSIDE GDNS
COLGATE CT
THE THOMAS WATSON COTTAGE HOMES
CEDAR LAWN AVE
FITZJOHN AVE
NEWLYN RD
NORMANDY AVE
BEDFORD AVE
ELLESMERE GR
MILTON AVE
WOODFALL AVE
AVENUE MANS
HILLSIDE MANS
VALE DR
ELTON AVE
MARSTON CT
THE POTTERIES
BROOK PL
WESTCOMBE DR
PRIORY GR
BRENT PL
FINCH CL
DOLLIS VALLEY DR
BRYANT CL
KENERNE DR
BOARDMAN CL
Allot Gdns
Tenn Cts
Barnet Hill JMI Sch
Underhill Sch
Pl Fld
HAMMOND CL
HARDY CL
EASTHAM CL
LEESIDE
HOME FIELD
MILL BRIDGE
THE RIDGE
GARROWSFIELD
Barnet Fball Gd
Pav
Sp Gd
LITTLE LARKINS
ALAN DR
MAYHILL RD
VALLEY VIEW
ROSSITER FIELDS
DOLLIS VALLEY WAY
MEADOW CL
CROCUS FIELD
NORTHBROOK RD
BROOKSIDE CL
DOLLIS BROOK WLK
RAVENSCROFT COTTS
Barnet Pl Flds
TA Ctr
Grasvenor Avenue Inf Sch
GRASVENOR AVE
SHERRARDS WAY
THE LINKWAY
WESTERN WAY
King George V Pl Flds
POTTERS
BRACKENWOOD LO
RAVENSCROFT COTTS
TELFORD CT
HIGHWOOD CT
ESMOND CT
THE HIGHLANDS
Highlands Gdns
ABBOTTS RD
HOMESTEAD CT
COLLINGWOOD CT
LEAF HO
WINDERMERE HO
LEICESTER RD
MERTON CT
BARNES CT
ASHLEY CT
SOMERSET RD
NORTH LO
MOWBRAY RD
Lyonsdown Sch
RICHMOND
BARRIE CT
KINGSCLERE CT
GLOUCESTER RD
WORDSWORTH CT
EVERSHOLT CT
LANDER CT
KNOLL
HIGHPO
WILLOW LO
WESTERN PAR
GREENHILL PAR
RAYDEAN RD
GREENHILL PK
DINSDALE GDNS
Greenhill Gdns
DINSDALE CT
THE FAIRWAY
HASLUCK GDNS
WYCHERLEY CRES
IVERE DR
CROFTON WAY
HILLIER CL
DALE CL
CHERRY HILL
FAIRWAY CT
THE COPPICE
COUNTY GATE
CARPENTERS CL
TURNERS CT
WILLENHALL AVE
WILLENHALL CT
THE DRIVE
LYONSDOWN AVE
WALFIELD AVE
Wyatts Farm Open Space
MACARET CL
PANGBOURNE CT
FARNHAM CL
FRANKLIN CL
MAXFIELD
HAMILTON HO
VIEW POINT
Dollis Brook
Pl Fds
Pl Fld
Brook Farm Open Space
FAIRMEAD CT
GREENVIEW CT
14
South Herts
The Ravenscroft Sch & Tech Coll
OAKLANDS RD
PRIORY CL
WHITE ORCHARDS
THE PASTURES
GRANGE AVE
The Grange
BADGERS CROFT
LIME GR
TOTTERIDGE HO
WYKEHAM RISE
CHESTNUT LA
The Darlands
NORTHCLIFFE DR
BARNWOOD CL
PINE GR
HARMSWORTH WAY
CH
BELMONT CL
LINKS DR
WEST HILL WAY
ROWBEN CL
OAK TREE DR
THE ORCHARD
GREAT BUSHEY DR
HADAR CL
ELDER CL
HILL CRES
BROOKMEAD CT
ALLUM WAY
MANUS WAY
BLAKENEY CL
DOWNLAN
Totteridge & Whetstone
NAYLOR RD
BIRLEY RD
HAYWARD RD
ELKANETTE MEWS
SWAN LA
St John CE Prim
THE CLOSE
Prim Sch
Waverley
Windyridge
Nature Reserve
GREENWAY
SOUTHWAY
WILLOW END
ELMSTEAD CL
GREENWAY CL
TOTTERIDGE GN
Crkt Gd
COPPICE WLK
LYNTON MEAD
VENTNOR DR
LONGLAND DR
LAUREL WAY
Laurel Farm
Woodridge Prim Sch
SOUTHOVER
CHIDDINGFOLD
ARLINGTON
FRAMFIELD CL
NORTHIAM
LAUREL VIEW
HOLDEN HTS
ROGERS WLK
BROOK MDW
FOUR ACRES
GUILDOWN AVE
SYLVAN CT
DARCHESTER LO
Sp Gd
Finchley Sch
RIDGEVIEW RD
CHARNWOOD PL
COPPER BEECH CT
BRECON CT
WOODSIDE LA
ORCHARD LO
INKWELL CL
STEPHENS LO
WOODSIDE G
DEVONSHIRE HO
CLAIRE CT
CAVENDISH HO
LITTLE CEDARS
LIMES AVE
SQUIRRELS
TEYNHAM CT
ST ANDREW'S CL
WOODSIDE AVE
GREEN
HIGHW
MICHLEHAM DOWN
25
29
26
81

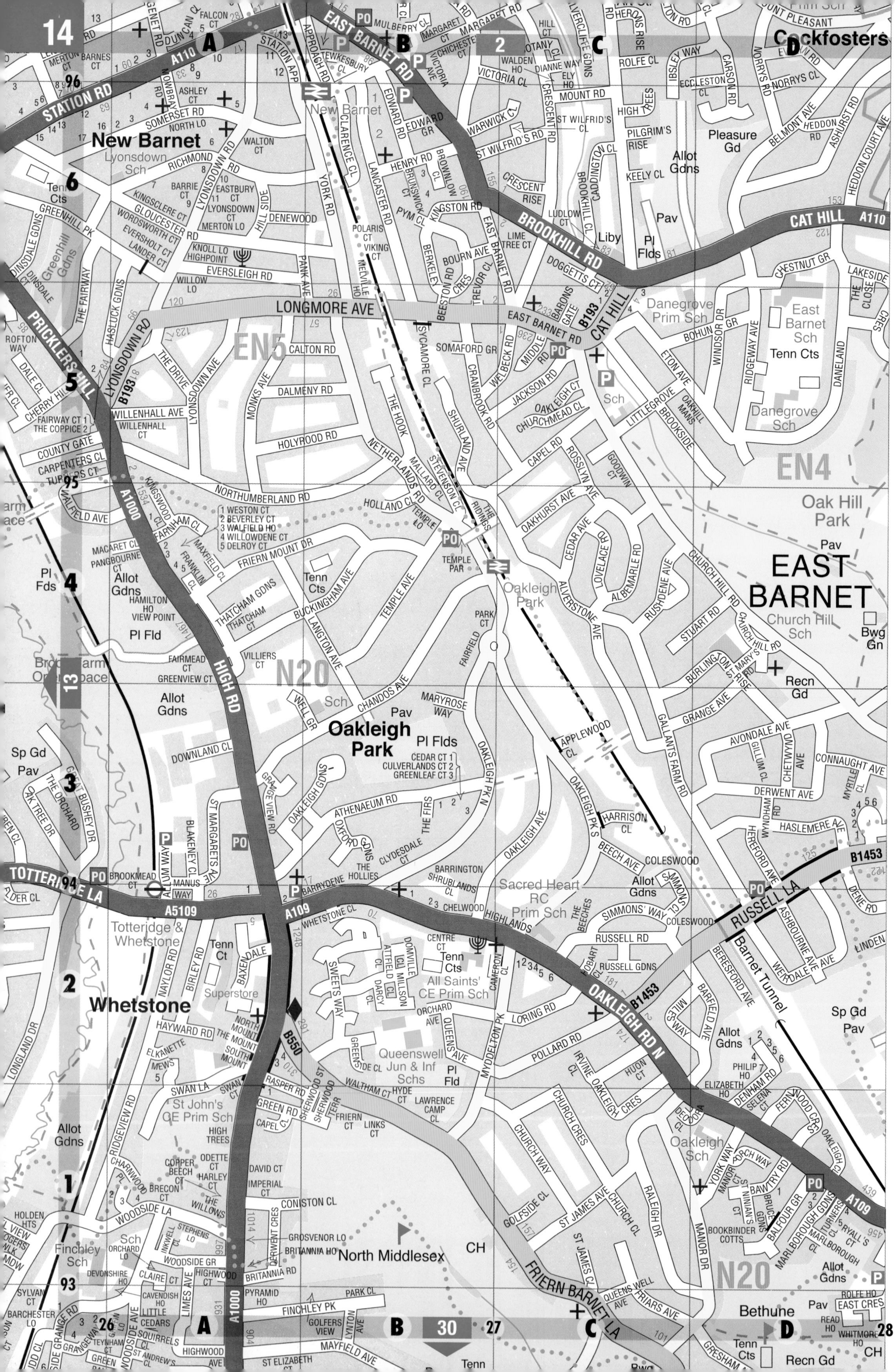
New Barnet
Cockfosters
EAST BARNET
Oakleigh Park
Whetstone
North Middlesex
EN5
EN4
N20
Oak Hill Park
STATION RD
EAST BARNET RD
BROOKHILL RD
CAT HILL
A110
LONGMORE AVE
PRICKLERS HILL
LYONSDOWN RD
HIGH RD
A1000
TOTTERIDGE LA
A5109
A109
OAKLEIGH RD N
B1453
RUSSELL LA
FRIERN BARNET LA
B550
B193
NORTHUMBERLAND RD
FRIERN MOUNT DR
CHURCH HILL RD
WOODSIDE LA
FINCHLEY PK
MAYFIELD AVE
Danegrove Prim Sch
East Barnet Sch
Church Hill Sch
Sacred Heart RC Prim Sch
All Saints' CE Prim Sch
Queenswell Jun & Inf Schs
St John's CE Prim Sch
Oakleigh Sch
Totteridge & Whetstone
Barnet Tunnel
Bethune
Finchley Sch
Lyonsdown Sch
Pleasure Gd
Allot Gdns
Recn Gd
Sp Gd
2
13
30
26
27
28
93
94
95
96

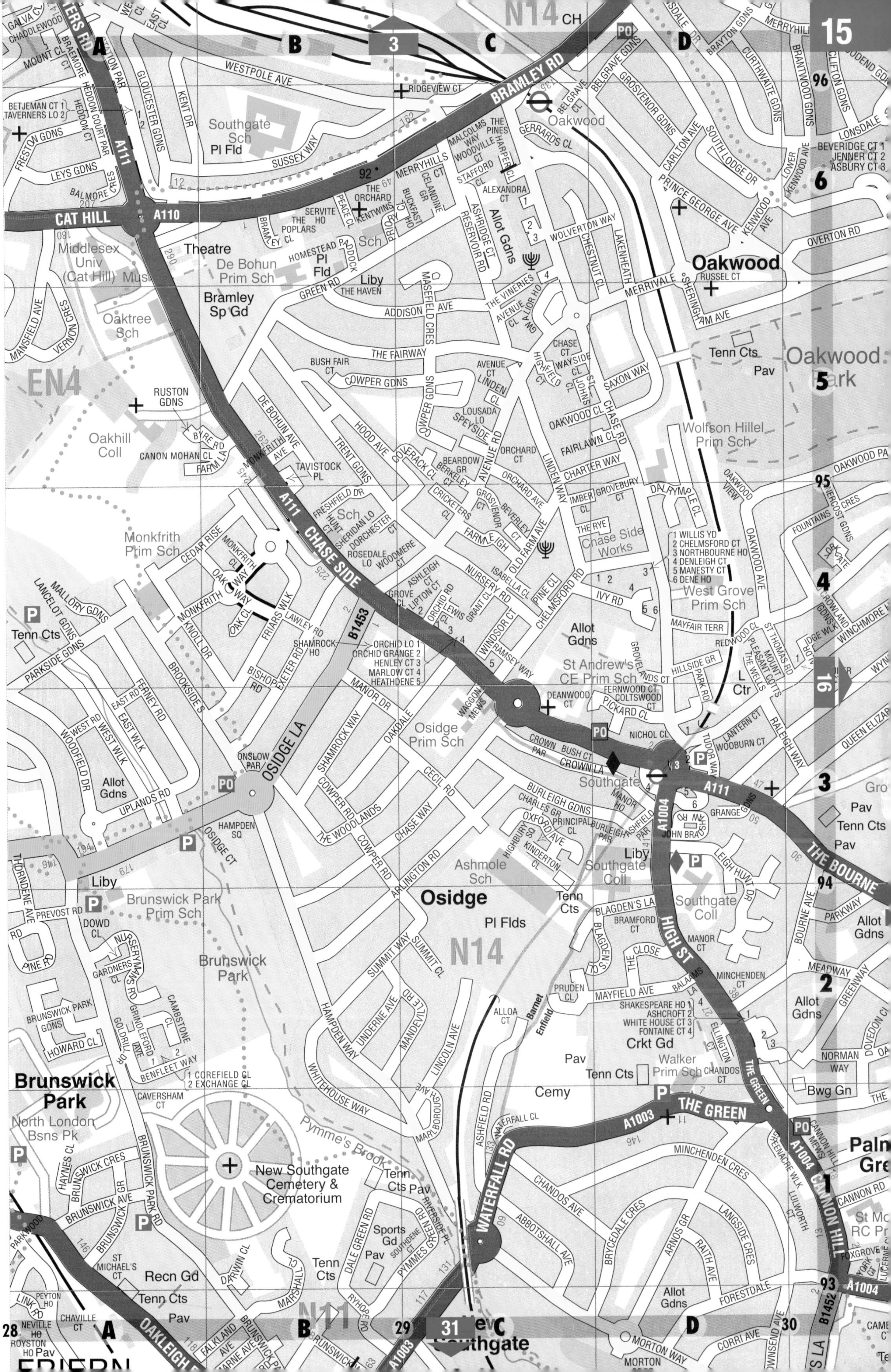

A
B
C
D
3
N14
EN4
N11
BRAMLEY RD
WESTPOLE AVE
RIDGEVIEW CT
Southgate Sch
Pl Fld
SUSSEX WAY
GLOUCESTER GDNS
KENT DR
CAT HILL
A110
A111
FRESTON GDNS
LEYS GDNS
BALMORE CRES
BETJEMAN CT 1
TAVERNERS LO 2
HEDDON COURT PAR
HEDDON CT
BRAEMORE
MOUNT CL
CHADDLEWOOD
GALVA CL
Middlesex Univ (Cat Hill)
Mus
Theatre
De Bohun Prim Sch
Bramley Sp Gd
Oaktree Sch
MANSFIELD AVE
VERNON CRES
RUSTON GDNS
Oakhill Coll
CANON MOHAN CL
BYRE RD
FARM LA
MERRYHILLS CT
THE ORCHARD
CELANDINE GR
BUCKFAST CT
KENTWINS
SERVITE HO
THE POPLARS
PEACE CL
BRAMLEY CL
HOMESTEAD PADDOCK
Sch
Pl Fld
Liby
THE HAVEN
GREEN RD
ADDISON AVE
MASEFIELD CRES
THE FAIRWAY
BUSH FAIR CT
COWPER GDNS
AVENUE CT
LINDEN CL
LOUSADA LO
SPEYSIDE
AVENUE RD
ORCHARD CT
ORCHARD AVE
MALCOLMS WAY
WOODVILLE CT
THE PINES
HARPER CL
STAFFORD CL
ALEXANDRA CT
ASHRIDGE CT
RESERVOIR RD
Allot Gdns
THE VINERIES
AVENUE CL
GERRARDS CL
Oakwood
BELGRAVE CL
BELGRAVE GDNS
GROSVENOR GDNS
CARLTON AVE
SOUTH LODGE DR
PRINCE GEORGE AVE
KENWOOD AVE
WOLVERTON WAY
CHESTNUT CL
LAKENHEATH
MERRIVALE
SHERINGHAM AVE
RUSSEL CT
Oakwood
OVERTON RD
LONSDALE
BEVERIDGE CT 1
JENNER CT 2
ASBURY CT 3
BRAYTON GDNS
CURTHWAITE GDNS
BRANTWOOD GDNS
CLIFTON GDNS
MERRYHILLS
96
6
Tenn Cts
Pav
Oakwood Park
5
Wolfson Hillel Prim Sch
CHASE CT
WAYSIDE
HIGHFIELD CT
ST JOHNS CL
SAXON WAY
OAKWOOD CL
CHASE RD
FAIRLAWN CL
CHARTER WAY
IMBER CL
GROVEBURY CT
DALRYMPLE CL
THE RYE
Chase Side Works
1 WILLIS YD
2 CHELMSFORD CT
3 NORTHBOURNE HO
4 DENLEIGH CT
5 MANESTY CT
6 DENE HO
West Grove Prim Sch
IVY RD
MAYFAIR TERR
CHELMSFORD RD
LINDEN WAY
OAKWOOD VIEW
OAKWOOD AVE
95
FOUNTAINS CRES
MERCOST GDNS
OAKWOOD PA
4
CROWLAND GDNS
WINCHMORE
IDGE WLK
ST THOMAS RD
MOUNT PLEASANT COTTS
THE WELLS
REDWOOD CL
HILLSIDE GR
PARK RD
GROVELANDS CT
L Ctr
16
WYN
QUEEN ELIZAB
RALEIGH WAY
LANTERN CT
WOOBURN CT
TUDOR WAY
NICHOL CL
FERNWOOD CT
COLTSWOOD CT
PICKARD CL
St Andrew's CE Prim Sch
Allot Gdns
DEANWOOD CT
Monkfrith Prim Sch
CEDAR RISE
MONKFRITH CL
MONKFRITH WAY
OAK WAY
OAK CL
FRIARS WLK
LAWLEY RD
DE BOHUN AVE
MONKFRITH AVE
TAVISTOCK PL
TRENT GDNS
HOOD AVE
COVERACK CL
BEARDOW GR
BERKELEY
CRICKETERS CL
GROSVENOR CT
BEVERLEY CT
FARMLEIGH
OLD FARM AVE
NURSERY RD
ISABELLA CL
PINE CL
CHASE SIDE
FRESHFIELD DR
HUNT CT
SHERIDAN LO
DORCHESTER CT
ROSEDALE LO
WOODMERE CT
ASHLEIGH CT
LIPTON CT
GROVE CL
ORCHID RD
LEWIS GR
GRANT CL
WINDSOR CT
RAMSEY WAY
SHAMROCK HO
ORCHID LO 1
ORCHID GRANGE 2
HENLEY CT 3
MARLOW CT 4
HEATHDENE 5
B1453
EXETER RD
BISHOP RD
MALLORY GDNS
LANCELOT GDNS
Tenn Cts
PARKSIDE GDNS
KNOLL DR
BROOKSIDES
FERNEY RD
EAST RD
EAST WLK
WEST RD
WEST WLK
WOODFIELD DR
Allot Gdns
UPLANDS RD
ONSLOW PAR
OSIDGE LA
MANOR DR
SHAMROCK WAY
OAKDALE
WAGGON MEWS
Osidge Prim Sch
CROWN PAR
BUSH CT
CROWN LA
Southgate
MANOR HO
BURLEIGH GDNS
CHARLES GR
PRINCIPAL CL
BURLEIGH PAR
ASHFIELD PAR
OXFORD AVE
HIGHBURY SQ
KINDERTON CL
A1004
JOHN BRAY
GRANGE GDNS
A111
Pav
Tenn Cts
Pav
THE BOURNE
3
Gro
LEIGH HUNT DR
Liby
Southgate Coll
HAMPDEN SQ
OSIDGE CT
COWPER RD
THE WOODLANDS
CECIL RD
CHASE WAY
ARLINGTON RD
Ashmole Sch
Osidge
Pl Flds
Tenn Cts
BLAGDEN'S LA
BLAGDEN'S CL
BRAMFORD CT
HIGH ST
Southgate Coll
MANOR CT
THE CLOSE
94
BOURNE AVE
PARKWAY
Allot Gdns
THORNDENE AVE
PREVOST RD
Liby
Brunswick Park Prim Sch
DOWD CL
NURSERYMANS RD
PINE RD
GARDNERS CL
GRINDLEFORD AVE
CAMBSTONE CL
GOLDRILL DR
BRUNSWICK PARK GDNS
HOWARD CL
BENFLEET WAY
1 COREFIELD CL
2 EXCHANGE CL
Brunswick Park
N14
SUMMIT WAY
SUMMIT CL
HAMPDEN WAY
UNDERNE AVE
MANDEVILLE RD
LINCOLN AVE
WHITEHOUSE WAY
MARLBOROUGH AVE
ALLOA CT
Barnet
Enfield
PRUDEN CL
MAYFIELD AVE
BALAAMS LA
MINCHENDEN CT
SHAKESPEARE HO 1
ASHCROFT 2
WHITE HOUSE CT 3
FONTAINE CT 4
Crkt Gd
ELLINGTON CT
Walker Prim Sch
CHANDOS CT
Pav
Tenn Cts
Cemy
THE GREEN
A1003
MEADWAY
GREENWAY
2
Allot Gdns
NORMAN WAY
DOVEDON CL
Bwg Gn
Brunswick Park
North London Bsns Pk
CAVERSHAM CT
New Southgate Cemetery & Crematorium
Pymme's Brook
HAYNES CL
BRUNSWICK CRES
BRUNSWICK GR
BRUNSWICK AVE
BRUNSWICK PARK RD
PARKWOOD
ST MICHAEL'S CT
Recn Gd
Tenn Cts
Pav
DARWIN CL
MARSHALL CL
Tenn Cts
Tenn Cts
Pav
Sports Gd
Pav
DALE GREEN RD
SOUTHDENE CT
PYMMES GREEN RD
RIVERSIDE PL
WATERFALL RD
WATERFALL CL
ASHFIELD RD
CHANDOS AVE
ABBOTSHALL AVE
BRYCEDALE CRES
ARNOS GR
RAITH AVE
LANGSIDE CRES
MINCHENDEN CRES
GREENACRE WLK
LULWORTH CT
CANNON HILL
CANNON MEWS
A1004
Paln Gre
1
CANNON RD
St Mo RC Pr
FOXGROVE
YORK CT
93
B1452
Allot Gdns
FORESTDALE
TOWNSEND AVE
CORRI AVE
MORTON WAY
MORTON
CAME
PEYTON HO
LINK RD
CHAVILLE CT
NEVILLE HO
ROYSTON HO
Pav
OAKLEIGH
FALKLAND AVE
BRUNSWICK
RYHOPE RD
A1003
New Southgate
28
29
31
30

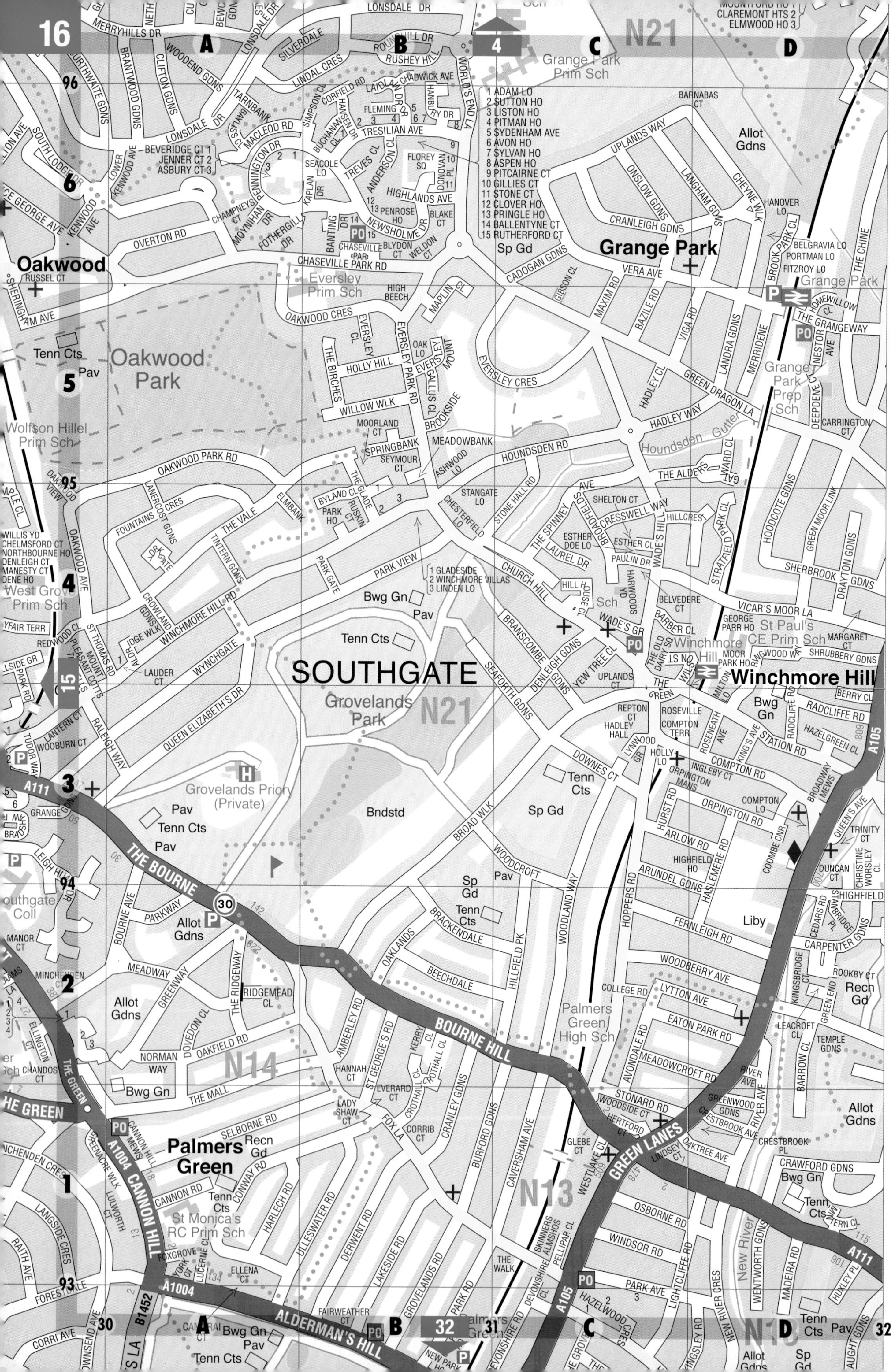
N21
Grange Park Prim Sch
1 ADAM LO
2 SUTTON HO
3 LISTON HO
4 PITMAN HO
5 SYDENHAM AVE
6 AVON HO
7 SYLVAN HO
8 ASPEN HO
9 PITCAIRNE CT
10 GILLIES CT
11 STONE CT
12 CLOVER HO
13 PRINGLE HO
14 BALLENTYNE CT
15 RUTHERFORD CT
Sp Gd
Grange Park
Oakwood
Eversley Prim Sch
Oakwood Park
Tenn Cts
Pav
Wolfson Hillel Prim Sch
West Grove Prim Sch
Grange Park Prep Sch
Houndsden Gutter
Allot Gdns
SOUTHGATE
Grovelands Park
Grovelands Priory (Private)
Bndstd
Bwg Gn
Winchmore Hill
St Paul's CE Prim Sch
Palmers Green High Sch
Palmers Green
St Monica's RC Prim Sch
N14
N13
1 GLADESIDE
2 WINCHMORE VILLAS
3 LINDEN LO
THE BOURNE
BOURNE HILL
GREEN LANES
ALDERMAN'S HILL
CANNON HILL
CHASEVILLE PARK RD
OAKWOOD PARK RD
WINCHMORE HILL RD
HOUNDSDEN RD
GREEN DRAGON LA
VICAR'S MOOR LA
STATION RD
COMPTON RD
WORLD'S END LA
A111
A105
A1004
Liby
Southgate Coll
New River
A B C D
1 2 3 4 5 6
4 15 32

A
B
C
D
5
Town Park
Tenn Cts
ESSEX RD
OLD PARK GR
RIDINGS AVE
OLD PARK RIDINGS
BushHill Park
CH
SALISBURY CT
PARK CRES
WALSINGHAM RD
UVEDALE RD
WHITETHORN GDNS
PRINCESSA CT
ANWELL CL
RIVERDALE CT
BROOKLANDS CT
CASTLELEIGH CT
A105
PO
POTTERSFIELD
SILVERTHORNE LO
MORNINGTON LO
ASCOT LO
BLAKENEY
GARFIELD
PRIVATE RD
Riverside Park
Tenn Cts
ROWLEY CT
VILLAGE RD
ESKDALE
LAURA CL
FORSYTH PL
REGENCY CT
PARK AVE
WALNUT GR
RINGMER PL
CARRS LA
BUSH HILL
QUAKERS WLK
THE ORCHARD
ORCHARDMEDE
MEWS
New River
MYLNE HO 1
FREAME HO 2
AISLABIE HO 3
TRITTON HO 4
BRAIKENRIDGE HO 5
METHERELL HO 6
HALLIWICK HO 7
Bush Hill
ELMSCOTT GDNS
HARTLAND CL
CLARENDON WAY
PARK DR
GRANGE PARK AVE
MYDDELTON GDNS
CUNARD CRES
BUSH HILL RD
BERKELEY GDNS
CRANWICH AVE
FAVERSHAM AVE
TEYNHAM AVE
SITTINGBOURNE AVE
BORDEN AVE
VILLAGE RD
WESTWOOD CT
CONIFER GDNS
QUEEN ANNE'S GR
SUMMERHILL GR
GARDENIA RD
CONSTANCE RD
EDENBRIDGE RD
Bush Hill Park
MANORWAY
EN1
THE BRACKENS
CROSSWAY
BRENDON WAY
BIDEFORD GDNS
WELLINGTON RD
ASH GR
RAGLAN RD
Raglan Jun & Inf Schs
SENNEN RD
AMBERLEY RD
BAGSHOT RD
COUNTISBURY AVE
DELHI RD
LYNMOUTH AVE
WINCHESTER CL
WENTWORTH HO
PEACOCK CT
LINGFIELD CL
ROYAL CT
QUEEN ANNE'S GDNS
WOODLEA LO
APSLEY HO
FOXWOOD GREEN CL
FRAMFIELD CT
ST STEPHENS CT
ANSTEY LO
CANNOCK LO
DRYDEN RD
KENWOOD HO
NUTCHFORD
PARK AVE
SAMBROOKE CT
JOANNE CT
QUEEN ANNE'S PL
LONGLEAT RD
SADLERS HO
ATHOLE GDNS
Bwg Gn
Tenn Cts
ABBEY RD
ILLINGWORTH WAY
DOWNS RD
CROSS RD
FOTHERINGHAM RD
LC
Recn Gd
KINGSWOOD CL
LINCOLN CRES
EAST CRES
HARMAN RD
JOHN ST
CHARLES ST
JAMES ST
AGRICOLA PL
HADRIAN'S RIDE
Liby
WATERHEDGE MEWS
KARYATIS CT
MAIN AVE
ROMAN WAY
LINCOLN RD
ERMINE SIDE
Prim Sch
SECOND AVE
FIRST AVE
THIRD AVE
ST MARK'S RD
MILLAIS RD
POYNTER RD
LANDSEER RD
AYLEY CROFT
LEIGHTON RD
TWEEDY
Bush Hill Park
PASTERS CT
LADBROKE RD
ALBERTA RD
HAZELWOOD RD
TRINITY AVE
HAILEYBURY AVE
INGRAM CT
WENDY CL
MELBOURNE WAY
HARROW AVE
WOODGRANGE TERR
A10
DIMSDALE DR
HAZEL GR
CHATSWORTH
ST EDMUNDS RD
HAMILTON AVE
HAMILTON RD
LATHKILL CL
Edmonton Cty Upper Sch
EDWARD CL
LAWN CL
WARREN CRES
HICKORY CL
BURY ST
18
TRANMERE RD
DARLEY RD
HARROW DR
RUGBY AVE
FALMAN CL
BURY ST
JUBILEE CL
Recn Gd
Churchfield Prim Sch
LANCING GDNS
LATYMER RD
MALVERN TERR
STOWE GDNS
MARLBOROUGH RD
GLASTONBURY
CHICHESTER RD
WINCHESTER RD
SALMONS RD
CROYLAND
Allot Gdns
Salmon's Brook
GREAT CAMBRIDGE RD
BURY HALL VILLAS
SHEPPARD TERR
CAMBRIDGE TERR
PORLOCK RD
CRAWLEY RD
LYNTON GDNS
AMBERLEY GDNS
BURY ST W
CLOVELLY GDNS
WESTVIEW CRES
BLAKESWARE GDNS
LITTLE BURY ST
RAMSCROFT CL
Recn Gd
Pav
ALDER LODGE
LYNFORD TERR
Bwg Gn
Edmonton Cty Lower Sch
ALDBURY MEWS
CHURCHILL CT
AINSLEY CL
Allot Gdns
B154
BUSH HILL PAR
AVENUE PAR
CAMBRIDGE GDNS
OXFORD GDNS
DEVONSHIRE GDNS
BRIDGE PAR
Tenn Cts
RIDGE AVE
Liby
YORK RD
PEGASUS CT
Tenn Cts
PEGASUS LO
RIDGE TERR
BRIDGE GATE
ELSIEDENE RD
PERCY RD
SOLNA RD
KENT RD
COLNE RD
GRIFFINS CL
RIVER BANK
MURLEY CT
ELM PARK RD
BEAULIEU GDNS
FIRS LA
BLENHEIM CL
CARLTON HO
Pav
Tenn Cts
The Paulin Gd
N21
RIDGE RD
ROWANTREE RD
ROWANTREE CL
HALSTEAD RD
HALSTEAD GDNS
FORD'S GR
FIRS PARK AVE
FIRS PARK GDNS
HYDEFIELD CL
BEVERLEY CL
FARM RD
Pl Fld
Highfield Prim Sch
BRENDON VILLAS
WELBECK VILLAS
LABURNUM GR
LABURNUM GDNS
HYDE PARK GDNS
HYDE PARK AVE
Edmonton Cemy
Tenn Cts
Tenn Cts
Bwg Gn
Pav
Sp Gds
Allot Gdns
CHURCH ST
HYDEFIELD CT
CEDARS CT
TILLOTSON RD
ARTHUR RD
STANLEY RD
STREAMSIDE CL
ST ANN'S RD
ST JOAN'S RD
CYPRUS RD
WYLDFIELD GDNS
Winchmore Sch
Recn Gd
Pav
N9
GATWARD GN
LABURNUM AVE
HAWTHORNE WAY
HYDESIDE GDNS
HYDE WAY
HYDETHORPE AVE
Latymer All Saints CE Prim Sch
ALL SAINTS CL
ALMSHOUSES
CHURCH ST
GRANHAM GDNS
GARTH DR
CHURCH LA
WIMBORNE RD
DURHAM RD
RUSKIN WLK
MILESTONE CL
LICHFIELD RD
LAMB'S CL
LION RD
COSGROVE CL
FIRTREE LODGE
Sp Gd
Pav
BARROWELL GN
FIRS LA
Firs Farm Pl Flds
KIPLING TERR
LAMB'S TERR
WHEATLEY GDNS
LATYMER WAY
The Latymer Sch
NORTHERN AVE
DEANSWAY
CENTRAL AVE
DUNHOLME GN
NEWSTEAD HO
NORTHUMBERLAND GDNS
WEST CL
MALDON RD
BEDEVERE RD
GALAHAD RD
SALISBURY MANS
CHAUNCEY CL
GAWAIN CL
TRISTRAM DR
BARBOT CL
Allot Gdns
FARNDALE AVE
ENSIGN DR
Allot Gdns
ASH GR
Firs Farm Prim Sch
RAYLEIGH RD
RAYLEIGH CL
HARLOW RD
THE FAIRWAY
FIRSCROFT
THE LARCHES
Pl Fld
THE ROWANS
BIRCH AVE
MYRTLE RD
BRIAR CL
HAZEL CL
CONISCLIFFE RD
PEMBROKE RD
RYLSTON RD
NEW PARK AVE
West Lea Sch
PERRY GDNS
BANSTEAD GDNS
PURLEY RD
SELHURST RD
BEXLEY GDNS
BECKENHAM GDNS
Hazelbury Jun & Inf Schs
VICTOR VILLAS
CHALFONT GN
SWEET BRIAR GR
CHALFONT RD
DUNHOLME RD
SOUTH EASTERN AVE
PYMMES GDNS N
PYMMES GDNS S
HAZELBURY LA
HAZELBURY GN
BRIARY LA
SWEET BRIAR GN
DUNHOLME LA
WESTERHAM AVE
ORPINGTON GDNS
KESTON CL
BROMLEY RD
SHORTLANDS CL
CHEDDINGTON RD
HUXLEY RD
HASELBURY RD
PARK LA
SWEET BRIAR WLK
VICTORIA RD
SUNNYSIDE RD N
SUNNYSIDE RD E
SUNNYSIDE RD S
LEONARD RD
PYCROFT WAY
SHRUBBERY RD
Liby
A1010
HEDGE LA
Tatem Park
PARKSIDE TERR
HARINGTON TERR
A10
Hollywood
Aylward
Lopen
Pl Flds
Pymmes Park
32
33
34
96
95
94
93
6
4
3
2
1
40
N21

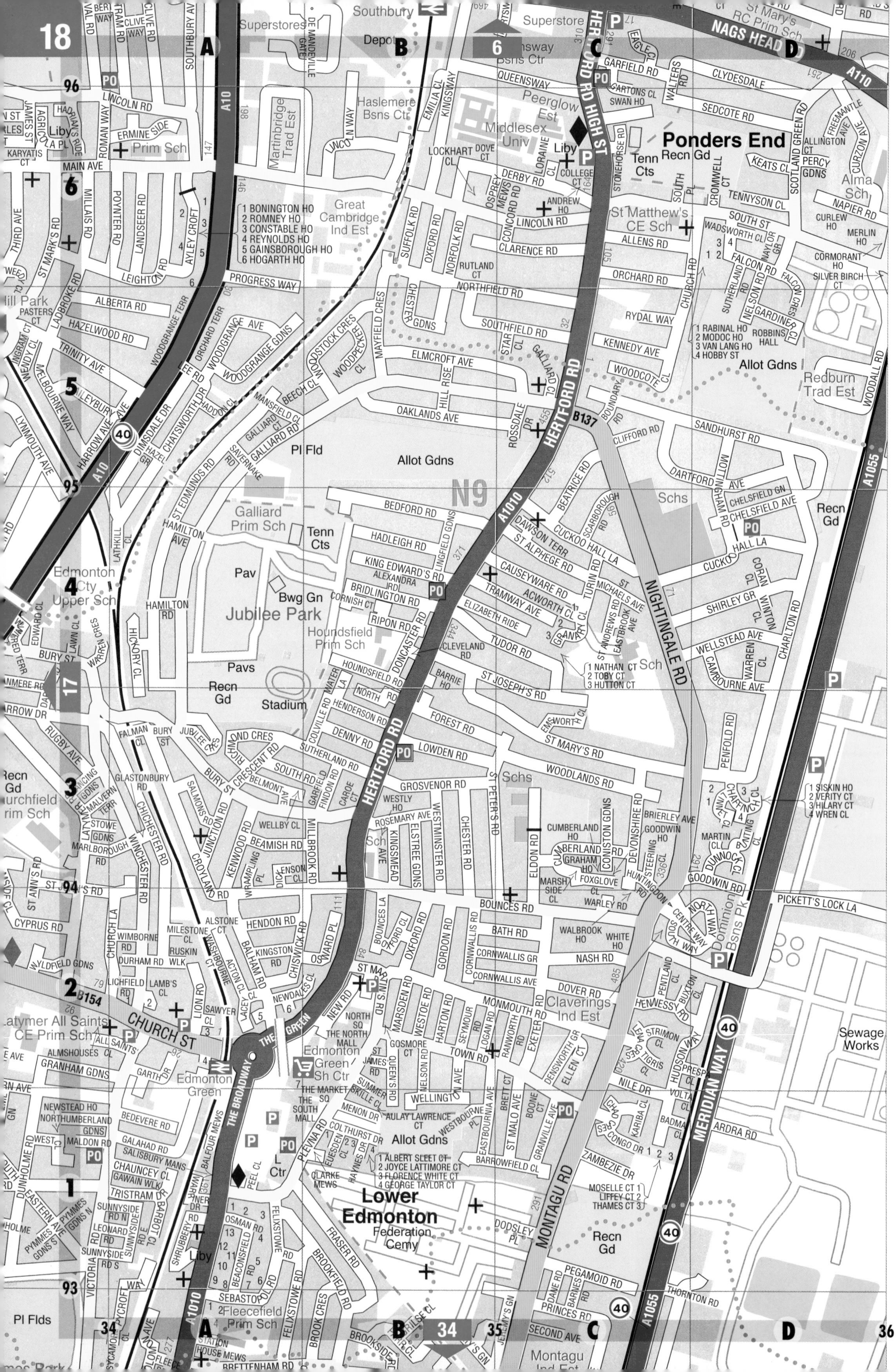
Southbury
Superstores
Depot
6
Superstore
Queensway Bsns Ctr
NAGS HEAD RD
A110
GARFIELD RD
CLYDESDALE
SEDCOTE RD
QUEENSWAY
Peerglow Est
Middlesex Univ
Haslemere Bsns Ctr
Martinbridge Trad Est
Ponders End
Tenn Cts
Recn Gd
LINCOLN RD
ERMINE SIDE
Prim Sch
MAIN AVE
Liby
Great Cambridge Ind Est
1 BONINGTON HO
2 ROMNEY HO
3 CONSTABLE HO
4 REYNOLDS HO
5 GAINSBOROUGH HO
6 HOGARTH HO
AYLEY CROFT
LEIGHTON RD
PROGRESS WAY
St Matthew's CE Sch
TENNYSON CL
SOUTH ST
ALLENS RD
ORCHARD RD
NORTHFIELD RD
SOUTHFIELD RD
RYDAL WAY
KENNEDY AVE
WOODCOTE CL
ELMCROFT AVE
OAKLANDS AVE
1 RABINAL HO
2 MODOC HO
3 VAN LANG HO
4 HOBBY ST
Allot Gdns
Redburn Trad Est
Alma Sch
ALBERTA RD
HAZELWOOD RD
TRINITY AVE
Hill Park
A10
A1010
HERTFORD RD
B137
SANDHURST RD
CLIFFORD RD
Pl Fld
Allot Gdns
N9
Galliard Prim Sch
Tenn Cts
BEDFORD RD
HADLEIGH RD
KING EDWARD'S RD
Schs
CHELSFIELD AVE
CUCKOO HALL LA
Recn Gd
Edmonton Cty Upper Sch
Pav
Bwg Gn
Jubilee Park
Houndsfield Prim Sch
NIGHTINGALE RD
SHIRLEY GR
WELLSTEAD AVE
CAMBOURNE AVE
TUDOR RD
ST JOSEPH'S RD
1 NATHAN CT
2 TOBY CT
3 HUTTON CT
Sch
Pavs
Recn Gd
Stadium
FOREST RD
ST MARY'S RD
LOWDEN RD
WOODLANDS RD
GROSVENOR RD
Schs
1 SISKIN HO
2 VERITY CT
3 HILARY CT
4 WREN CL
Recn Gd
Churchfield Prim Sch
BOUNCES RD
PICKETT'S LOCK LA
Dominion Bsns Pk
NASH RD
DOVER RD
Claverings Ind Est
Sewage Works
MERIDIAN WAY
A1055
CHURCH ST
B154
Latymer All Saints CE Prim Sch
Edmonton Green
THE GREEN
THE BROADWAY
Edmonton Green Sh Ctr
THE NORTH MALL
THE SOUTH MALL
Allot Gdns
1 ALBERT SLEET CT
2 JOYCE LATTIMORE CT
3 FLORENCE WHITE CT
4 GEORGE TAYLOR CT
Lower Edmonton
Federation Cemy
L Ctr
MONTAGU RD
MOSELLE CT 1
LIFFEY CT 2
THAMES CT 3
Recn Gd
PEGAMOID RD
THORNTON RD
Fleecefield Prim Sch
SECOND AVE
Montagu
Pl Flds
34
35
36
A
B
C
D
96
95
94
93
1
2
3
4
5
6
17

A
B
C
D
7
Works
CLOVER CT
GREEN RD N
SCOTLAND GREEN RD N
FAIRFIELD CL
TREVERA CT
GILDA AVE
LEES
ALPHA RD
NORTHAMPTON RD
EAST DUCK LEES LA
40
LEA VALLEY RD
A1055
A110
Ponders End Ind Est
River Lea or Lee
KESTREL HO
Ponders End
WHARF RD
Valleylink Est
Riverside Est
Works
MORSON RD
P
EN3
River Lea or Lee
ION TERR
GILWELL CL
A112
PP
Waltham Forest
96
67
Yardley Hill
SEWARDSTONE GDNS
BOARDMAN AVE
ANTLERS HILL
SEWARDSTONE RD
6
DEERLEAP GR
YARDLEY CL
YARDLEY LA
HAWKWOOD CRES
Yardley Prim Sch
Allot Gdns
HAWKDENE
EPPING GLADE
5
172
EPPING WAY
ALBANY CT 1
RIVERSIDE CT 2
CHELWOOD CL
AMESBURY DR
DRYSDALE AVE
MARK AVE
MARGARET AVE
REDWOOD GDNS
DELLS CL
SOUTH AVE
95
Horse Ride
MARKFIELD GDNS
HARFORD CL
HARFORD RD
Chingford Green
Pole Hill
BAYTREE HO 3
STONEHILL CT 4
WINGROVE HO
PO
LAUREL GDNS
MERRYHILL CL
HOMEBUSH HO
HOLLY DR
4
Enfield
Waltham Forest
MAIDA WAY
MAIDA AVE
KINGS HEAD HILL
HAWKSMOUTH
BLANDFORD CRES
Enterprise
SOLE HILL RD
SUNNY
LOW HALL CL
COLLEGE GDNS
20
A110
Pl Fld
A1037
MANSFIELD HILL
SEYMOUR RD
SUNSET AVE
COLLEGE GDNS
HUNGERDOWN
ST EGBERTS WAY
E4
MOUNT ECHO DR
3
P
TH
VALLEY SIDE
Mansfield Pk
ECHO HTS
MEADOW CL
MOUNT ECHO AVE
Chingford Foundation Sch
NEVIN DR
THE RIDGEWAY
94
BOSGROVE
WARREN RD
Lee Valley Wlk
Lee Valley L Ctr
Lee Valley Leisure
N9
River Lee Navigation
William Girling Resr
VALLEY SIDE PAR
BELLE STAINES PLEASAUNCE
SILVERTHORN GDNS
MULBERRY CL
B169
GREENBANK CL
2
EATONS MEAD
LAWRENCE HILL
LAMBOURNE GDNS
DENNER RD
Ridgeway Park
PEEL CL
ENDLE
Pickett's Lock
DOVE HOUSE GDNS
LANSDOWNE RD
ST CATHERINES RD
GOLDSBOROUGH CRES
HERIOT AVE
WALMER CL
RETINGHAM WAY
MARESBY HO
WALTHAM WAY
WELLINGTON AVE
Wellington Prim Sch
HEATHCOTE GR
LEADALE AVE
CHINGFORD AVE
BRINDWOOD RD
MISTRAL CT 1
MAGNOLIA LODGE 2
PHOENIX CT 3
ALDBOROUGH CT 4
CELANDINE CT 5
INGREBOURNE CT 6
MORELAND WAY
HALE CL
HEATHFIELD
PRIORY CL
MAYHEW CL
RAMPTON CL
RECTORY CL
OLD CHURCH RD
Cemy
GUNNERS GR
PRIORY AVE
1
OAKLEY CL 1
NAVESTOCK CL 2
BOOTHBY CT 3
CHERRYDOWN CL
MIDDLETON CL
MIDDLETON AVE
CHERRYDOWN AVE
HURST CL
HURST AVE
CHURCHILL TERR
WINTER'S CT
MORRIS CT
ALPHA RD
FLAXEN RD
SALISBURY RD
Allot Gdns
FLAXEN CL
GROVE RD
HAROLD RD
STAPLEFORD
TIPTREE C
MOUNT AVE
SUFFIELD RD
93
WOODVIEW
LEE PARK WAY
River Lea or Lee Diversion
TEMPLETON AVE
THE RIDGES
Larkswood Prim Sch
CHIVERS RD
ST JOHN'S RD
36
A
A1037
B
MARMION CL
37
35
MARMION AVE
C
PO
A112
BROOK CRES
WINDSOR RD
D
38
NEW RD
A1009
MAYA ANGELOU

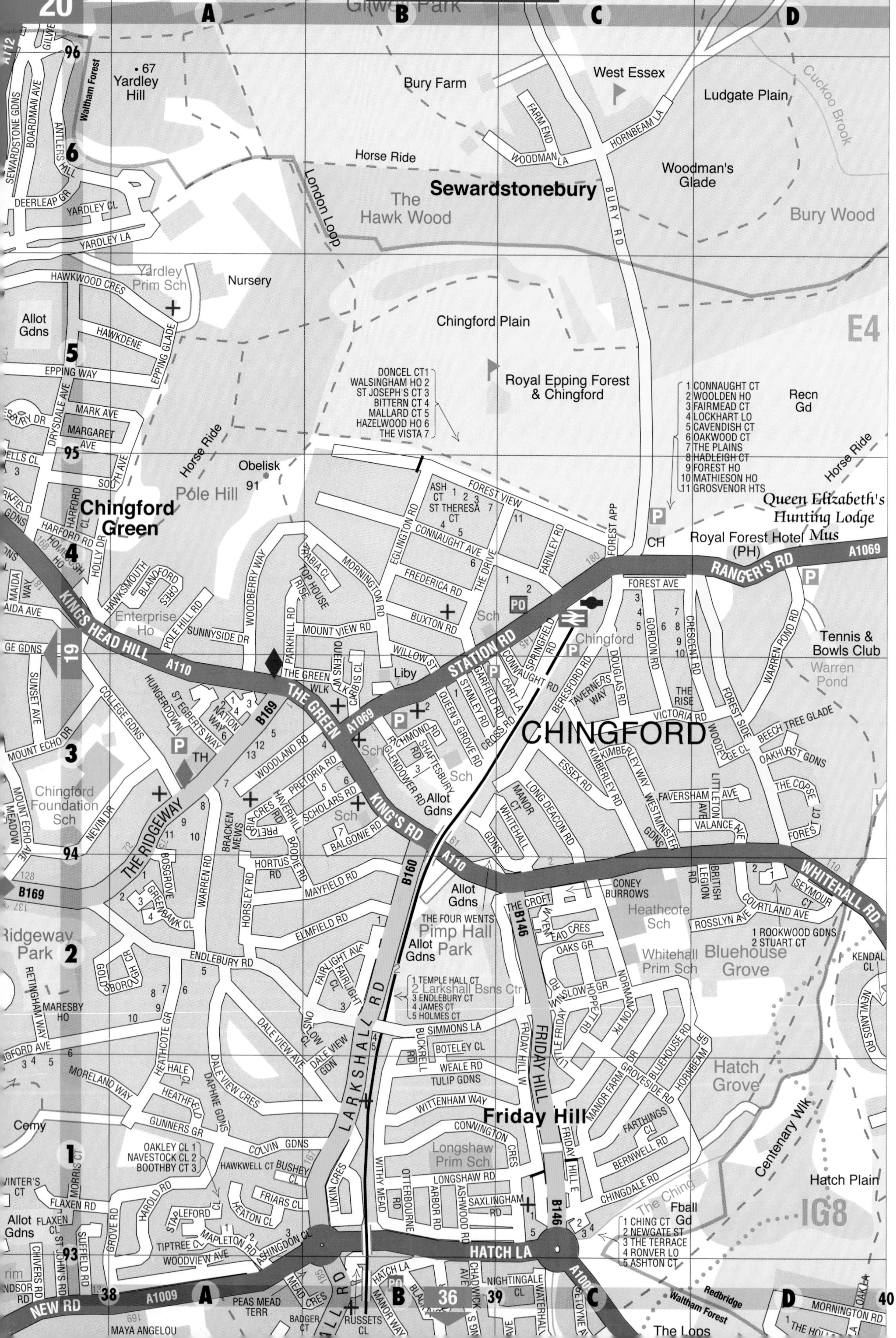
A
B
C
D
Gilwell Park
96
6
5
4
3
2
1
95
94
93
Waltham Forest
Yardley Hill
Bury Farm
West Essex
Ludgate Plain
Cuckoo Brook
FARM END
HORNBEAM LA
WOODMAN LA
Horse Ride
London Loop
Sewardstonebury
Woodman's Glade
The Hawk Wood
Bury Wood
BURY RD
SEWARDSTONE GDNS
BOARDMAN AVE
ANTLERS HILL
DEERLEAP GR
YARDLEY CL
YARDLEY LA
Yardley Prim Sch
Nursery
HAWKWOOD CRES
Allot Gdns
HAWKDENE
EPPING GLADE
Chingford Plain
E4
EPPING WAY
DONCEL CT 1
WALSINGHAM HO 2
ST JOSEPH'S CT 3
BITTERN CT 4
MALLARD CT 5
HAZELWOOD HO 6
THE VISTA 7
Royal Epping Forest & Chingford
1 CONNAUGHT CT
2 WOOLDEN HO
3 FAIRMEAD CT
4 LOCKHART LO
5 CAVENDISH CT
6 OAKWOOD CT
7 THE PLAINS
8 HADLEIGH CT
9 FOREST HO
10 MATHIESON HO
11 GROSVENOR HTS
Recn Gd
DRYSDALE AVE
MARK AVE
MARGARET AVE
Horse Ride
Obelisk
Pole Hill
SOUTH AVE
Chingford Green
HARFORD RD
HOLLY DR
ASH CT
ST THERESA CT
FOREST VIEW
EGLINGTON RD
CONNAUGHT AVE
FARNLEY RD
FOREST APP
Queen Elizabeth's Hunting Lodge Mus
CH
Royal Forest Hotel (PH)
RANGER'S RD
A1069
HAWKSMOUTH
BLANDFORD CRES
WOODBERRY WAY
ARABIA CL
TOP HOUSE RISE
MORNINGTON RD
FREDERICA RD
THE DRIVE
FOREST AVE
GORDON RD
CRESCENT RD
WARREN POND RD
Tennis & Bowls Club
Warren Pond
KINGS HEAD HILL
Enterprise Ho
POLE HILL RD
SUNNYSIDE DR
PARKHILL RD
MOUNT VIEW RD
BUXTON RD
PO
Sch
STATION RD
Chingford
SPRINGFIELD RD
DOUGLAS RD
19
A110
SUNSET AVE
COLLEGE GDNS
HUNGERDOWN
ST EGBERTS WAY
NATION WAY
THE GREEN
QUEENS WALK
CARBIS CL
WILLOW ST
Liby
GARFIELD RD
CART LA
CONNAUGHT RD
BERESFORD RD
TAVERNERS WAY
THE RISE
FOREST SIDE
VICTORIA RD
BEECH TREE GLADE
MOUNT ECHO DR
B169
TH
WOODLAND RD
A1069
RICHMOND RD
STANLEY RD
QUEEN'S GROVE RD
CROSS RD
CHINGFORD
ESSEX RD
KIMBERLEY RD
KIMBERLEY WAY
WOODBERRY CL
OAKHURST GDNS
THE COPSE
Chingford Foundation Sch
MOUNT ECHO AVE
MEADOW
NEVIN DR
THE RIDGEWAY
PRETORIA RD
HAVERHILL
SCHOLARS RD
SHAFTESBURY
GLENDOWER RD
KING'S RD
Allot Gdns
MANOR CT
WHITEHALL GDNS
LONG DEACON RD
WESTMINSTER GDNS
FAVERSHAM AVE
LITTLETON AVE
VALANCE AVE
FOREST CT
BRACKEN MEWS
BALGONIE RD
HORTUS RD
BRODIE RD
WARREN RD
BOSGROVE
B160
A110
CONEY BURROWS
BRITISH LEGION RD
WHITEHALL RD
SEYMOUR CT
COURTLAND AVE
Heathcote Sch
ROSSLYN AVE
1 ROOKWOOD GDNS
2 STUART CT
GREENBANK CL
MAYFIELD RD
HORSLEY RD
THE CROFT
YEW TREE CL
OAKS GR
Ridgeway Park
ELMFIELD RD
THE FOUR WENTS
Pimp Hall Park
B146
Whitehall Prim Sch
Bluehouse Grove
KENDAL CL
ENDLEBURY RD
Allot Gdns
GOLDSBOROUGH CR
RETINGHAM WAY
MARESBY HO
FAIRLIGHT AVE
FAIRLIGHT CL
1 TEMPLE HALL CT
2 Larkshall Bsns Ctr
3 ENDLEBURY CT
4 JAMES CT
5 HOLMES CT
WINSLOW GR
HOPPETT RD
NORMANTON PK
NEWLANDS RD
KINGFORD AVE
HEATHCOTE GR
DALE VIEW AVE
ONSLOW CL
DALE VIEW GDN
LARKSHALL RD
SIMMONS LA
BUCKRELL RD
BOTELEY CL
WEALE RD
TULIP GDNS
FRIDAY HILL W
FRIDAY HILL
LITTLE FRIDAY RD
MANOR FARM DR
GROVESIDE RD
BLUEHOUSE RD
HORNBEAM GR
Hatch Grove
MORELAND WAY
HALE CL
HEATHFIELD
DAPHNE GDNS
DALE VIEW CRES
WITTENHAM WAY
Friday Hill
FARTHINGS CL
Centenary Wlk
Cemy
GUNNERS GR
CONNINGTON CRES
BERNWELL RD
OAKLEY CL 1
NAVESTOCK CL 2
BOOTHBY CT 3
COLVIN GDNS
HAWKWELL CT
BUSHEY CL
Longshaw Prim Sch
FRIDAY HILL E
Hatch Plain
MORRIS CT
WINTER'S CT
HAROLD RD
FRIARS CL
LUKIN CRES
WITHY MEAD
OTTERBOURNE RD
LONGSHAW RD
ARBOR RD
ASHWOOD RD
CHINGDALE RD
The Ching
IG8
FLAXEN RD
STAPLEFORD CL
HEATON CL
SAXLINGHAM RD
Fball Gd
Allot Gdns
FLAXEN CL
ST JOHN'S RD
SUFFIELD RD
GROVE RD
MAPLETON RD
TIPTREE C
ASHINGDON CL
1 CHING CT
2 NEWGATE ST
3 THE TERRACE
4 RONVER LO
5 ASHTON CT
CHIVERS RD
WOODVIEW AVE
HATCH LA
B146
NEW RD
A1009
38
A
PEAS MEAD TERR
MEAD CRES
HATCH LA
B
36
39
NIGHTINGALE CL
WATERHALL
C
A1009
Redbridge
Waltham Forest
D
40
MORNINGTON RD
OAK LA
BADGER CT
RUSSETS CL
MANOR WAY
MAYA ANGELOU
The Loos

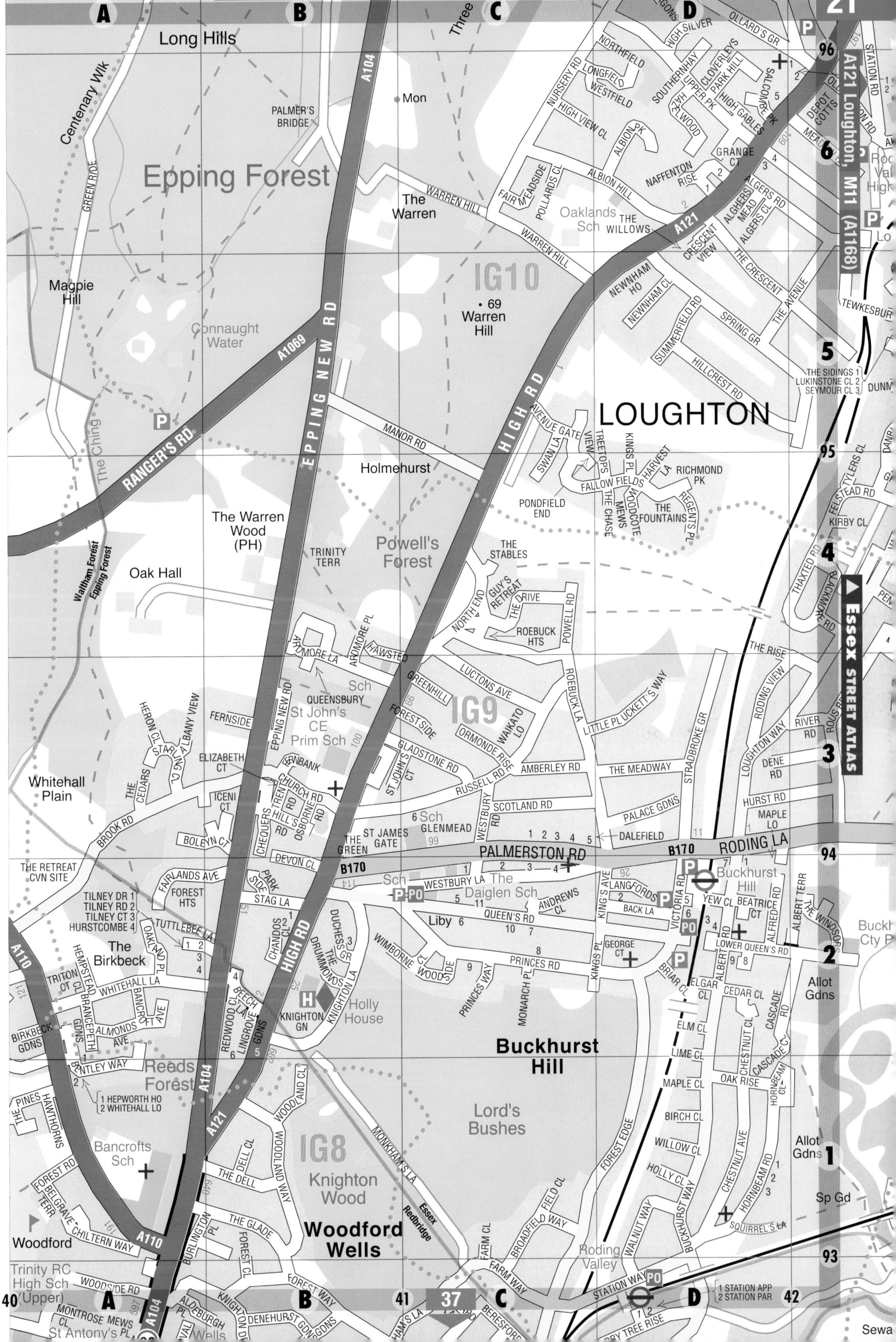
A
B
C
D
Long Hills
Centenary Wlk
GREEN RIDE
Mon
PALMER'S BRIDGE
Epping Forest
The Warren
WARREN HILL
Magpie Hill
Connaught Water
IG10
69 Warren Hill
EPPING NEW RD
A1069
RANGER'S RD
A104
HIGH RD
A121
MANOR RD
Holmehurst
The Ching
The Warren Wood (PH)
Oak Hall
TRINITY TERR
Powell's Forest
Waltham Forest
Epping Forest
LOUGHTON
NORTHFIELD
LONGFIELD
WESTFIELD
NURSERY RD
HIGH VIEW CL
HIGH SILVER
SOUTHERNHAY
UPPER PK
HAZELWOOD
CLOVERLEYS
PARK HILL
HIGH GABLES
SALCOMBE PK
ALBION PK
ALBION HILL
FAIR MEADSIDE
POLLARDS CL
NAFFENTON RISE
GRANGE CT
Oaklands Sch
THE WILLOWS
CRESCENT VIEW
ALGERS RD
ALGERS MEAD
ALGERS CL
THE CRESCENT
THE AVENUE
NEWNHAM HO
NEWNHAM CL
SUMMERFIELD RD
SPRING GR
HILLCREST RD
OLLARD'S GR
CONNAUGHT AVE
DEPOT COTTS
STATION RD
A121 Loughton, M11 (A1168)
TEWKESBURY
THE SIDINGS 1
LUKINSTONE CL 2
SEYMOUR CL 3
AVENUE GATE
SWAN LA
VIEW
TREETOPS
KINGS PL
HARVEST LA
RICHMOND PK
FALLOW FIELDS
THE CHASE
MEWS
WOODCOTE
THE FOUNTAINS
REGENT'S PL
PONDFIELD END
TYLERS CL
FELSTEAD RD
KIRBY CL
THAXTED RD
BLACKMORE RD
THE STABLES
NORTH END
GUY'S RETREAT
THE DRIVE
POWELL RD
ROEBUCK HTS
ROEBUCK LA
ARDMORE LA
ARDMORE PL
HAWSTED
GREENHILL
LUCTONS AVE
Sch
QUEENSBURY
St John's CE Prim Sch
IG9
FOREST SIDE
ORMONDE RISE
WAIKATO LO
LITTLE PLUCKETT'S WAY
STRADBROKE GR
THE RISE
RODING VIEW
LOUGHTON WAY
RIVER RD
DENE RD
HURST RD
MAPLE LO
Essex STREET ATLAS
HERON CL
ALBANY VIEW
STARLING CL
FERNSIDE
EPPING NEW RD
ELIZABETH CT
FERNBANK
CHURCH RD
GLADSTONE RD
ST JOHN'S CT
RUSSELL RD
AMBERLEY RD
THE MEADWAY
Whitehall Plain
THE CEDARS
ICENI CT
TRENT RD
HILLS RD
OSBORNE RD
CHEQUERS
Sch
GLENMEAD
WESTBURY RD
SCOTLAND RD
PALACE GDNS
DALEFIELD
BROOK RD
BOLEYN CT
ST JAMES GATE
THE GREEN
DEVON CL
B170
PALMERSTON RD
RODING LA
Buckhurst Hill
THE RETREAT CVN SITE
FAIRLANDS AVE
PARK SIDE
WESTBURY LA
The Daiglen Sch
LANGFORDS
VICTORIA RD
YEW CL
BEATRICE CT
ALFRED RD
ALBERT TERR
THE WINDSORS
TILNEY DR 1
TILNEY RD 2
TILNEY CT 3
HURSTCOMBE 4
FOREST HTS
STAG LA
Liby
QUEEN'S RD
ANDREWS CL
KING'S AVE
BACK LA
Buckh Cty P
TUTTLEBEE LA
OAKLAND PL
CHANDOS CL
DUCHESS GR
THE DRUMMONDS
WIMBORNE CL
WOODSIDE
GEORGE CT
ALBERT RD
LOWER QUEEN'S RD
The Birkbeck
HEMPSTEAD CL
TRITON CT
WHITEHALL LA
BRANCEPETH GDNS
BANCROFT AVE
PRINCES RD
PRINCES WAY
MONARCH PL
KINGS PL
BRIAR CL
ELGAR CL
CEDAR CL
CASCADE RD
Allot Gdns
A110
REDWOOD CL
BEECH LA
LINGROVE GDNS
KNIGHTON GN
KNIGHTON LA
Holly House
ALMONDS AVE
BIRKBECK GDNS
BENTLEY WAY
Reeds Forest
ELM CL
LIME CL
CHESTNUT CL
CASCADE CL
Buckhurst Hill
MAPLE CL
OAK RISE
HORNBEAM CL
1 HEPWORTH HO
2 WHITEHALL LO
THE PINES
HAWTHORNS
WOODLAND CL
MONKHAMS LA
Lord's Bushes
IG8
WOODLAND WAY
DELL CL
THE DELL
Knighton Wood
FOREST EDGE
BIRCH CL
WILLOW CL
HOLLY CL
BUCKHURST WAY
CHESTNUT AVE
HORNBEAM RD
Allot Gdns
Sp Gd
Bancrofts Sch
FOREST RD
BELGRAVE TERR
CHILTERN WAY
Woodford
BURLINGTON PL
THE GLADE
FOREST CL
Woodford Wells
Essex
Redbridge
FARM CL
FARM WAY
BROADFIELD WAY
FIELD CL
WALNUT WAY
Roding Valley
SQUIRREL'S LA
STATION WAY
1 STATION APP
2 STATION PAR
Trinity RC High Sch (Upper)
WOODSIDE RD
MONTROSE CL
MEWS
St Antony's PL
ALDEBURGH PL
KNIGHTON DR
DENEHURST GDNS
FOREST WAY
MONKHAMS LA
BERESFORD
CHERRY TREE RISE
Sewa

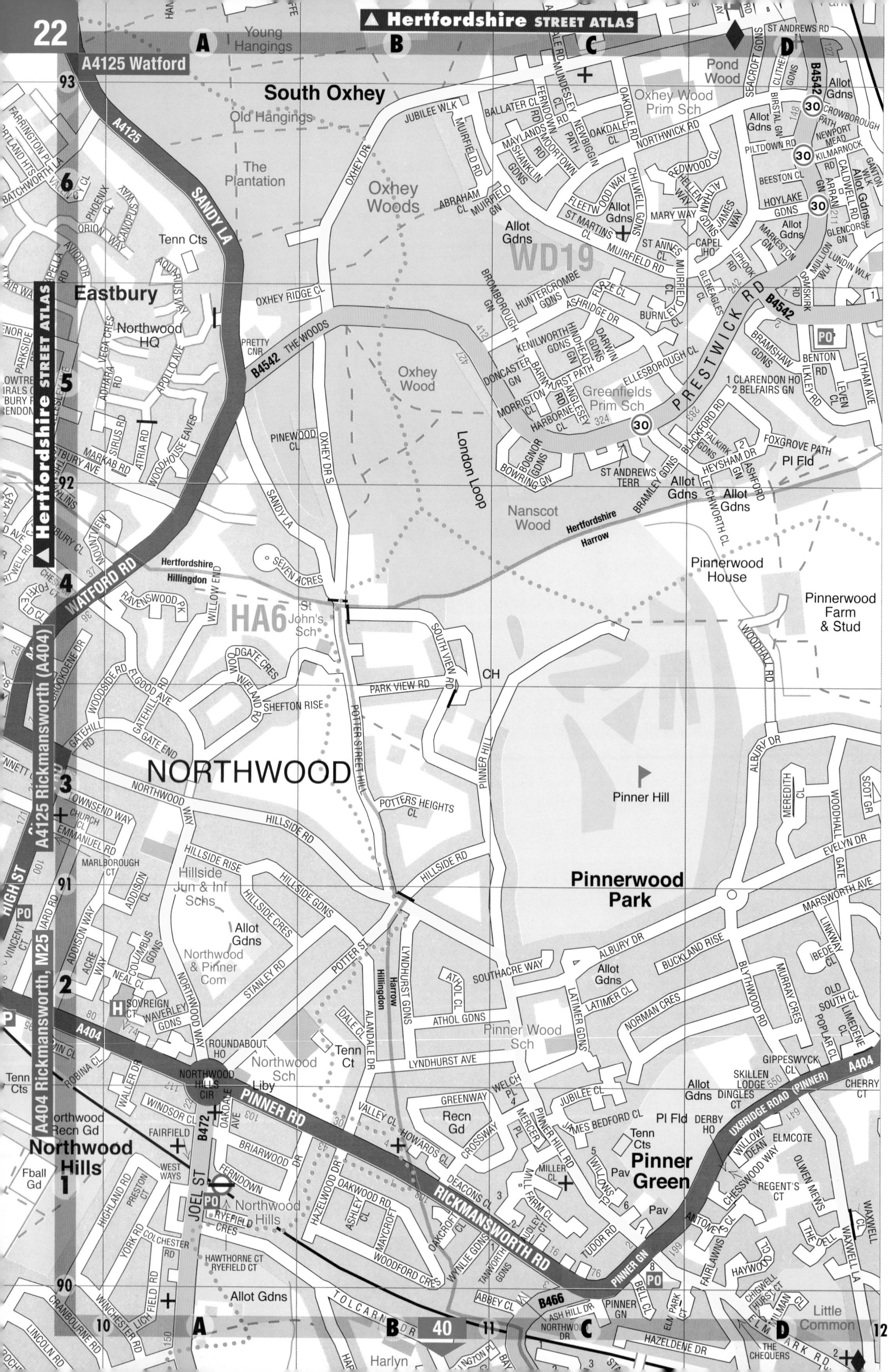
A4125 Watford
Young Hangings
South Oxhey
Old Hangings
The Plantation
Oxhey Woods
Oxhey Wood
Pond Wood
Oxhey Wood Prim Sch
WD19
Eastbury
Northwood HQ
Tenn Cts
SANDY LA
B4542 THE WOODS
PRETTY CNR
OXHEY RIDGE CL
OXHEY DR
JUBILEE WLK
MUIRFIELD RD
BALLATER CL
FERNDOWN RD
MUNDESLEY CL
NEWBIGGIN PATH
OAKDALE RD
OAKDALE CL
NORTHWICK RD
SEACROFT GDNS
CLITHEROE GDNS
ST ANDREWS RD
B4542
CROWBOROUGH PATH
NEWPORT MEAD
KILMARNOCK
PILTDOWN RD
BIRSTAL GN
BEESTON CL
HOYLAKE GDNS
ARRAN GN
CALDWELL RD
GANTON WLK
GLENCORSE GN
MULLION WLK
LUNDIN WLK
ORMSKIRK
PRESTWICK RD
REDWOOD CL
HELLEN WAY
ALTHAM GDNS
JAMES WAY
MARY WAY
CHILWELL GDNS
FLEETWOOD WAY
ST MARTINS CL
ST ANNES CL
CAPEL HO
LIPHOOK
GLENEAGLES
MUIRFIELD RD
MAYLANDS RD
SHANKLIN GDNS
MOORTOWN RD
ABRAHAM CL
MUIRFIELD GN
BROMBOROUGH GN
HUNTERCROMBE GDNS
ASHRIDGE DR
FURZE CL
BURNLEY CL
KENILWORTH GDNS
HINDHEAD GN
DARWIN GDNS
ELLESBOROUGH CL
DONCASTER GN
BARNHURST PATH
MORRISTON CL
HARBORNE CL
ANGLESEY RD
Greenfields Prim Sch
BOGNOR GDNS
BOWRING GN
ST ANDREWS TERR
BRAMLEY GDNS
BLACKFORD RD
FALKIRK GDNS
HEYSHAM DR
ASHFORD GN
FOXGROVE PATH
1 CLARENDON HO
2 BELFAIRS GN
BRAMSHAW GDNS
BENTON RD
ILKLEY RD
LEVEN CL
LYTHAM AVE
Pl Fld
Allot Gdns
LETCHWORTH CL
London Loop
Nanscot Wood
Hertfordshire
Harrow
Hillingdon
Pinnerwood House
Pinnerwood Farm & Stud
WOODHALL RD
PINEWOOD CL
OXHEY DR S
SEVEN ACRES
WILLOW END
RAVENSWOOD PK
HA6
St John's Sch
SOUTH VIEW RD
PARK VIEW RD
CH
PINNER HILL
Pinner Hill
WOODGATE CRES
WIELAND RD
SHEFTON RISE
POTTER STREET HILL
POTTERS HEIGHTS CL
WOODSIDE RD
ELGOOD AVE
GATEHILL RD
GATE END
NORTHWOOD
PHOENIX CL
CANOPUS WAY
ORION WAY
AVIOR DR
AQUARIUS WAY
VEGA CRES
ADHARA RD
APOLLO AVE
SIRIUS RD
ATRIA RD
WOODHOUSE EAVES
MARKAB RD
MOUNTVIEW
WATFORD RD
BROOKDENE DR
A4125 Rickmansworth (A404)
NORTHWOOD WAY
TOWNSEND WAY
CHURCH CL
EMMANUEL RD
MARLBOROUGH CT
HILLSIDE RD
HILLSIDE RISE
Hillside Jun & Inf Schs
HILLSIDE GDNS
HILLSIDE CRES
ADDISON CL
ADDISON WAY
ACRE WAY
COLUMBUS GDNS
NEAL CL
Allot Gdns
Northwood & Pinner Com
STANLEY RD
POTTER ST
SOVREIGN CT
WAVERLEY GDNS
A404
ROUNDABOUT HO
Northwood Sch
DALE CL
ALANDALE DR
Tenn Ct
LYNDHURST GDNS
ATHOL CL
ATHOL GDNS
LYNDHURST AVE
SOUTHACRE WAY
Pinnerwood Park
ALBURY DR
BUCKLAND RISE
LATIMER CL
LATIMER GDNS
NORMAN CRES
BLYTHWOOD RD
MURRAY CRES
MEREDITH CL
WOODHALL GATE
SCOT GR
EVELYN DR
MARSWORTH AVE
LINKWAY
IBEDEY CL
OLD SOUTH CL
LIMEDENE CL
POPLAR CL
Pinner Wood Sch
GIPPESWYCK CL
SKILLEN LODGE
CHERRY CT
A404 UXBRIDGE ROAD (PINNER)
HIGH ST
PO
A404 Rickmansworth, M25
Tenn Cts
ROBINA CL
WALLER DR
NORTHWOOD HILLS CIR
Liby
PINNER RD
WINDSOR CL
OAKDALE AVE
FAIRFIELD
Northwood Recn Gd
Northwood Hills
Fball Gd
WEST WAYS
JOEL ST
B472
BRIARWOOD DR
FERNDOWN
RYEFIELD CRES
Northwood Hills
HIGHLAND RD
PRESTON CT
YORK RD
COLCHESTER RD
HAWTHORNE CT
RYEFIELD CT
Allot Gdns
LICHFIELD RD
WINCHESTER RD
CRANBOURNE RD
LINCOLN RD
HAZELWOOD DR
OAKWOOD RD
ASHLEY CL
MAYCROFT
WOODFORD CRES
VALLEY CL
HOWARDS CL
OAKCROFT CL
WYNLIE GDNS
TAMWORTH GDNS
RICKMANSWORTH RD
GREENWAY
WELCH PL
Recn Gd
CROSSWAY
DEACONS CL
MERCER PL
MILL FARM CL
AUDLEY CT
PINNER HILL RD
MILLER CL
JUBILEE CL
JAMES BEDFORD CL
Pl Fld
Tenn Cts
Pav
WILLOWS CL
Pinner Green
TUDOR RD
PINNER GN
Allot Gdns
DINGLES CT
DERBY HO
WILLOW DEAN
ELMCOTE
CHESSWOOD WAY
REGENT'S CT
OLWEN MEWS
ANTONEY'S CL
FAIRLAWNS CL
HAYWOOD CL
THE DELL
WAXWELL CL
WAXWELL LA
CHIGWELL HURST CT
MILMAN CL
Little Common
ABBEY CL
B466
ASH HILL DR
PINNER GN
BELL CL
ELM PARK CT
ELM PARK RD
NORTHWOOD DR
HAZELDENE DR
THE CHEQUERS
TOLCARNE DR
Harlyn
40
A B C D
10 11 12
93 92 91 90

Mutton Wood
Levels Wood
Carpenders Park Cemy
BELLINGDON
COMPTON PL
ST GEORGE'S DR
HARROW WAY
ROMILLY DR
OULTON WAY
WOODHALL LA
Woodhall Prim Sch
LITTLE OXHEY LA
B4542
A4008
London Loop
Valley View Farm
Burnt Oak Farm
CH
Grims Dyke
Oxheylane Farm
Hertfordshire
Harrow
WD19
HA3
HA5
HA2
Mast
Harrow Weald Common
Grimsdyke Hotel
ASS HOUSE LA
OLD REDDING
Weald Wood
Stony Wood
CHERRY HILLS
Pl Fld
Sir James Altham Pool
OXHEY LA
WHITE CRAIG CL
ROYSTON PARK RD
SADDLERS CL
Saddlers Mead
Pav
HIGHBANKS RD
MEADWAY CL
WEALDWOOD GDNS
SEQUOIA PK
PINEWOOD CL
PINEWOOD AVE
OXHEY LA
NEWLAND CL
SYLVIA AVE
DERWENT AVE
LYNDON AVE
Grimsdyke Fst & Mid Sch
COLBURN AVE
HILLVIEW RD
HILLVIEW CL
THORNDYKE CT
MARDON
WITNEY CL
KENNEDY CL
ARGENT HO
OAKLEIGH RD
THE AVENUE
ROYSTON GR
LANGWORTHY
CLONARD WAY
THORNTON GR
ASHCROFT
Tenn Cts
OAKMEADE
HAZELCROFT
ROWLANDS AVE
WALPOLE CL
CEDAR DR
LIMETREE CT
FURHAM FIELD
THE LAWNS
SHERINGTON AVE
RANDOLPH CT
BRAESIDE CL
RIDGEWAY CT
MILNE FIELD
Pl Fld
Hatch End
STAPLEFIELD CL
FERNDOWN CL
GRIMSDYKE RD
WESSEX DR
BROADMEAD CL
LANGLAND DR
ALBURY DR
HALLAM GDNS
WOODRIDINGS CL
LEEWAY CL
FELDEN CL
LONSDALE CL
WESTFIELD PK
ELM HATCH
OAKDENE CL
UXBRIDGE ROAD (HATCH END)
A410
DOVE PK
BEETON CL
GABLE CL
GILDEA CL
Hatch End
Superstore
BONIFACE WLK
UFFORD RD
UFFORD CL
BONIFACE GDNS
TILLOTSON RD
CHICHELEY GDNS
LANGTON
WHITTLESEA CL
Hatch End High Sch
Pl Flds
Pav
WINSTON CT
MULLION CL
WEST CHANTRY
CHANTRY RD
HEADSTONE LA
Shaftesbury Sch
St Teresa's Sch
COURTENAY AVE
ST BARNABAS
Athletics Tk
Bar
LYTTON RD
ALTHAM RD
TOOKE CL
TOWERS RD
WOODHALL DR
THE BROADWAY
CORNWALL RD
HELSTON CL
ANSELM RD
PARK VIEW
DEVONSHIRE RD
WELLINGTON RD
WELLINGTON AVE
1 DEVONSHIRE CT
2 AVON MEWS
3 BENEDICT CT
4 TRURO HO
LITTLECOTE PL
SEYMOUR CL
CAVAN PL
BAYFORD LODGE
WOODRIDINGS AVE
NUGENTS CT
NUGENT'S PK
ST THOMAS' CT
UXBRIDGE ROAD (PINNER) A404
OLD HALL DR
OLD HALL CL
ST THOMAS' DR
HOLLY GR
BRIANTS CL
River Pinn
Pl Fld
Rugby Gd
Sp Gd
Pav
JUXON CL
THEOBALD CRES
BANCROFT GDNS
AUGUSTINE RD
SECKER CRES
Headstone Lane
PARKFIELD HO
LITTLE ORCHARD CL
WOODHALL AVE
BARROW POINT LA
BURHILL GR
OAKHILL AVE
BARROWDENE CL
LAWN VALE
LITTLE MOSS LA
GEORGE V AVE
MOSS CL
MOSS LA
PAINE'S LA
BARROW POINT AVE
EAST END WAY
Pinner Park Farm
RANDON CL
BROADFIELDS
FERNLEIGH CT
BARMOR CL
Pav
LAURA CL
TENSFORD RD
PARKFIELD AVE
PARKFIELD CRES
Model Rly
Tenn Cts
Bwg Gn
Sp Gd
Pav
Allot Gdns
Pl Fld
Pinner Park Schs
VERWOOD RD
FULBECK WAY
ALMOND WAY
WILLOW CT
PINNER PK
HOLMWOOD CL
MELBOURNE AVE
PARKFIELD GDNS
GREYSTOKE AVE
MANOR PARK DR
Open Air Theatre
LOVE LA
AVENUE RD
Cemy
LEIGHTON AVE
BLOOMSBURY CT
CHISWICK CT
A404
41
24
A B C D
93 92 91 90
6 5 4 3 2 1
12 13 14

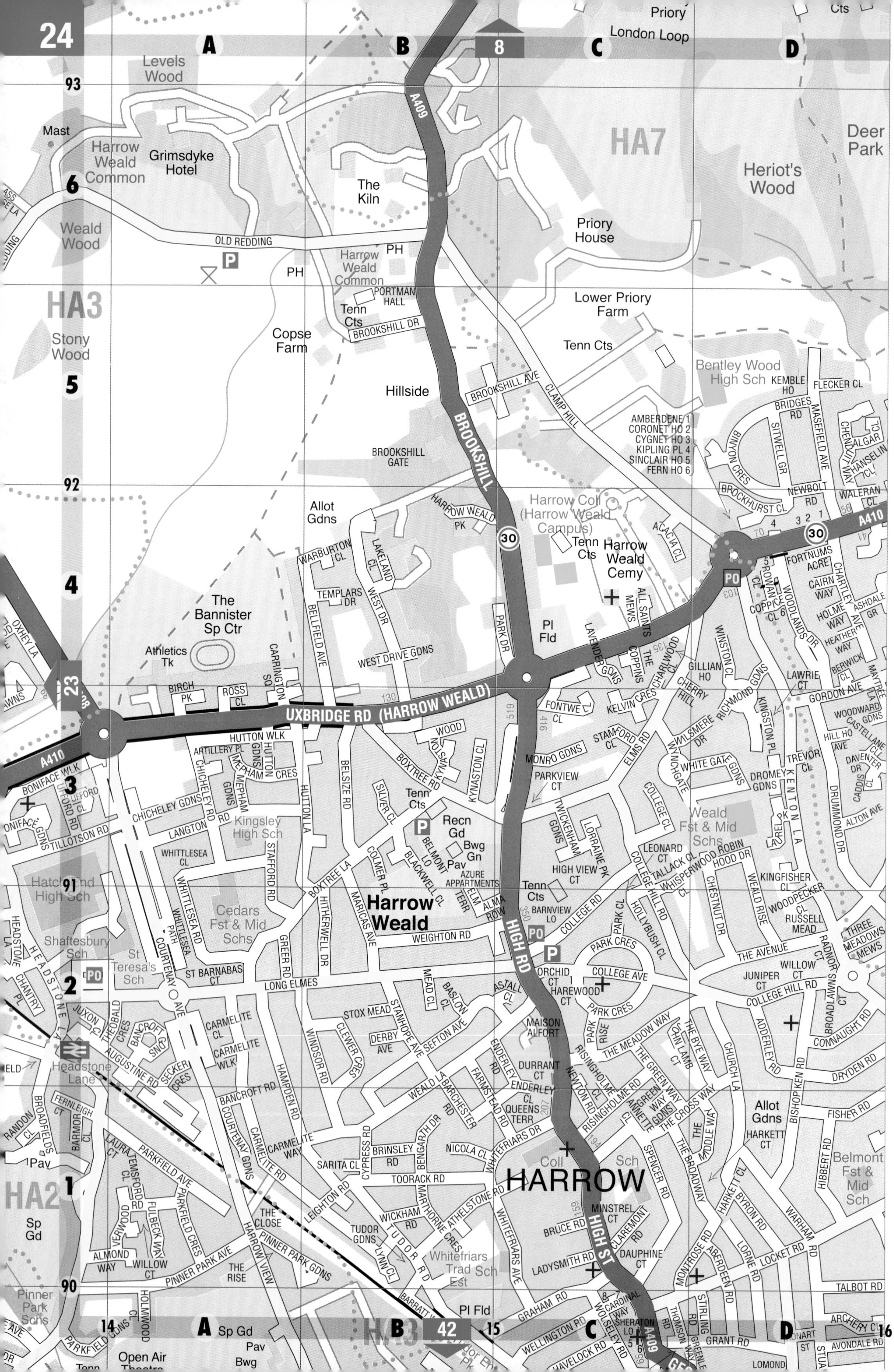
A
B
8
C
D
Priory
London Loop
Cts
Levels Wood
93
Mast
Harrow Weald Common
Grimsdyke Hotel
The Kiln
A409
HA7
Deer Park
Heriot's Wood
6
Weald Wood
OLD REDDING
Priory House
PH
Harrow Weald Common
HA3
PORTMAN HALL
Tenn Cts
BROOKSHILL DR
Copse Farm
Lower Priory Farm
Stony Wood
Tenn Cts
5
Hillside
BROOKSHILL AVE
CLAMP HILL
Bentley Wood High Sch
KEMBLE HO
FLECKER CL
BRIDGES RD
AMBERDENE 1
CORONET HO 2
CYGNET HO 3
KIPLING PL 4
SINCLAIR HO 5
FERN HO 6
BROOKSHILL
BROOKSHILL GATE
SITWELL GR
MASEFIELD AVE
BINYON CRES
CHENDUIT WAY
ALGAR CL
HANSELIN CL
92
BROCKHURST CL
NEWBOLT RD
WALERAN CL
Allot Gdns
HARROW WEALD PK
Harrow Coll (Harrow Weald Campus)
30
A410
Tenn Cts
Harrow Weald Cemy
ACACIA CL
WARBURTON CL
LAKELAND CL
FORTNUMS ACRE
CAIRN WAY
CHARTLEY AVE
ASHDALE GR
4
TEMPLARS DR
WEST DR
PO
ROWAN CL
COPPICE CL
WOODLANDS DR
HOLME WAY
The Bannister Sp Ctr
BELLFIELD AVE
PARK DR
Pl Fld
ALL SAINTS MEWS
LAVENDER GDNS
THE COPPINS
HEATHER WAY
Athletics Tk
CARRINGTON SQ
WEST DRIVE GDNS
WINSTON CL
BERWICK CL
OXHEY LA
GILLIAN HO
CHARLWOOD CL
LAWRIE CT
GORDON AVE
23
BIRCH PK
ROSS CL
UXBRIDGE RD (HARROW WEALD)
FONTWELL CL
KELVIN CRES
CHERRY HILL
RICHMOND GDNS
KINGSTON PL
WOODWARD GDNS
HUTTON WALK
WOOD CT
STAMFORD CL
ELMS RD
WILSMERE DR
HILL HO AVE
CASTELLANE CL
A410
ARTILLERY PL
HUTTON GDNS
KYNASTON CT
KYNASTON CL
MONRO GDNS
WHITE GATE GDNS
TREVOR CL
DAVENTER DR
BONIFACE WLK
MEPHAM CRES
BOXTREE RD
PARKVIEW CT
WYNCHGATE
DROMEY GDNS
CADDIS CL
3
UFFORD CL
CHICHELEY RD
HUTTON LA
BELSIZE RD
SILVER CL
Tenn Cts
COLLEGE CL
KENTON LA
DRUMMOND DR
ALTON AVE
CHICHELEY GDNS
MEPHAM GDNS
TWICKENHAM GDNS
LORRAINE PK
Weald Fst & Mid Schs
BONIFACE GDNS
TILLOTSON RD
LANGTON RD
Kingsley High Sch
Recn Gd
LAUREL PK
WHITTLESEA CL
STAFFORD RD
BELMONT LO
Bwg Gn
LEONARD CT
TALLACK CL
ROBIN HOOD DR
COLLEGE HILL RD
WHISPERWOOD CL
BLACKWELL CL
Pav
AZURE APPARTMENTS
HIGH VIEW CT
KINGFISHER CL
Hatch End High Sch
91
BOXTREE LA
COLMER PL
ELM TERR
CHESTNUT DR
WEALD RISE
WOODPECKER CL
Tenn Cts
RUSSELL MEAD
WHITTLESEA PATH
Cedars Fst & Mid Schs
MARICAS AVE
Harrow Weald
ALMA ROW
BARNVIEW LO
COLLEGE RD
HOLLYBUSH CL
THREE MEADOWS MEWS
HEADSTONE LA
Shaftesbury Sch
GREER RD
HITHERWELL DR
WEIGHTON RD
HIGH RD
PO
PARK CL
PARK CRES
THE AVENUE
RADNOR CT
St Teresa's Sch
P
WILLOW CT
PO
COURTENAY AVE
ST BARNABAS CT
ORCHID CT
COLLEGE AVE
JUNIPER CT
2
LONG ELMES
MEAD CL
BASLOW CL
ASTALL CL
HAREWOOD CT
COLLEGE HILL RD
SWANNS CT
CHANTRY PL
THEOBALD CRES
JUXON CL
CARMELITE CL
STOX MEAD
STANHOPE AVE
PARK CRES
BROADLAWNS CT
BANCROFT CL
WINDSOR RD
CLEWER CRES
DERBY AVE
MAISON ALFORT
PARK RISE
THE MEADOW WAY
ADDERLEY RD
CONNAUGHT RD
AUGUSTINE RD
SECKER CRES
CARMELITE WLK
SEFTON AVE
ENDERLEY RD
DURRANT CT
RISINGHOLME CL
JOHN LAMB CT
THE BYE WAY
CHURCH LA
DRYDEN RD
Headstone Lane
BANCROFT RD
HAMPDEN RD
WEALD LA
BARCHESTER RD
FARMSTEAD RD
ENDERLEY CL
NEWTON RD
RISINGHOLME RD
THE GREEN WAY
GREEN WAY GDNS
BISHOP KEN RD
FISHER RD
FERNLEIGH CT
BROADFIELDS
BARMOR CL
COURTENAY GDNS
CARMELITE WAY
QUEENS TERR
ANNETTE CL
THE CROSS WAY
Allot Gdns
LAURA CT
TEMSFORD CL
PARKFIELD AVE
CARMELITE RD
BRINSLEY RD
BENGARTH DR
NICOLA CL
WHITEFRIARS DR
SPENCER RD
THE MIDDLE WAY
THE BROADWAY
HARKETT CT
Pav
SARITA CL
CYPRESS RD
TOORACK RD
Coll
Sch
HARROW
HIBBERT RD
Belmont Fst & Mid Sch
1
HA2
VERWOOD RD
FULBECK WAY
PARKFIELD CRES
LEIGHTON RD
MARTHORNE CRES
WICKHAM RD
ATHELSTONE RD
WHITEFRIARS AVE
HIGH ST
MINSTREL CT
CLAREMONT RD
HARKETT CL
BYRON RD
WARHAM RD
Sp Gd
ALMOND WAY
WILLOW CT
THE CLOSE
TUDOR GDNS
LYNN CL
TUDOR RD
BRUCE RD
DAUPHINE CT
LOCKET RD
MONTROSE RD
ABERDEEN RD
LORNE RD
PINNER PARK AVE
THE RISE
HARROW VIEW
PINNER PARK GDNS
Whitefriars Trad Est
LADYSMITH RD
90
Pinner Park Schs
HOLMWOOD CL
BARRATT WAY
Pl Fld
GRAHAM RD
CARDINAL WAY
WOLSELEY RD
THOMSON RD
STIRLING RD
TALBOT RD
14
A
Sp Gd
B
42
15
C
D
ARCHERY CL
16
PARKFIELD GDNS
Pav
WELLINGTON RD
SHERATON LO
GRANT RD
AVONDALE RD
Open Air Theatre
Bwg
HAVELOCK RD
LOMOND
MONART ST

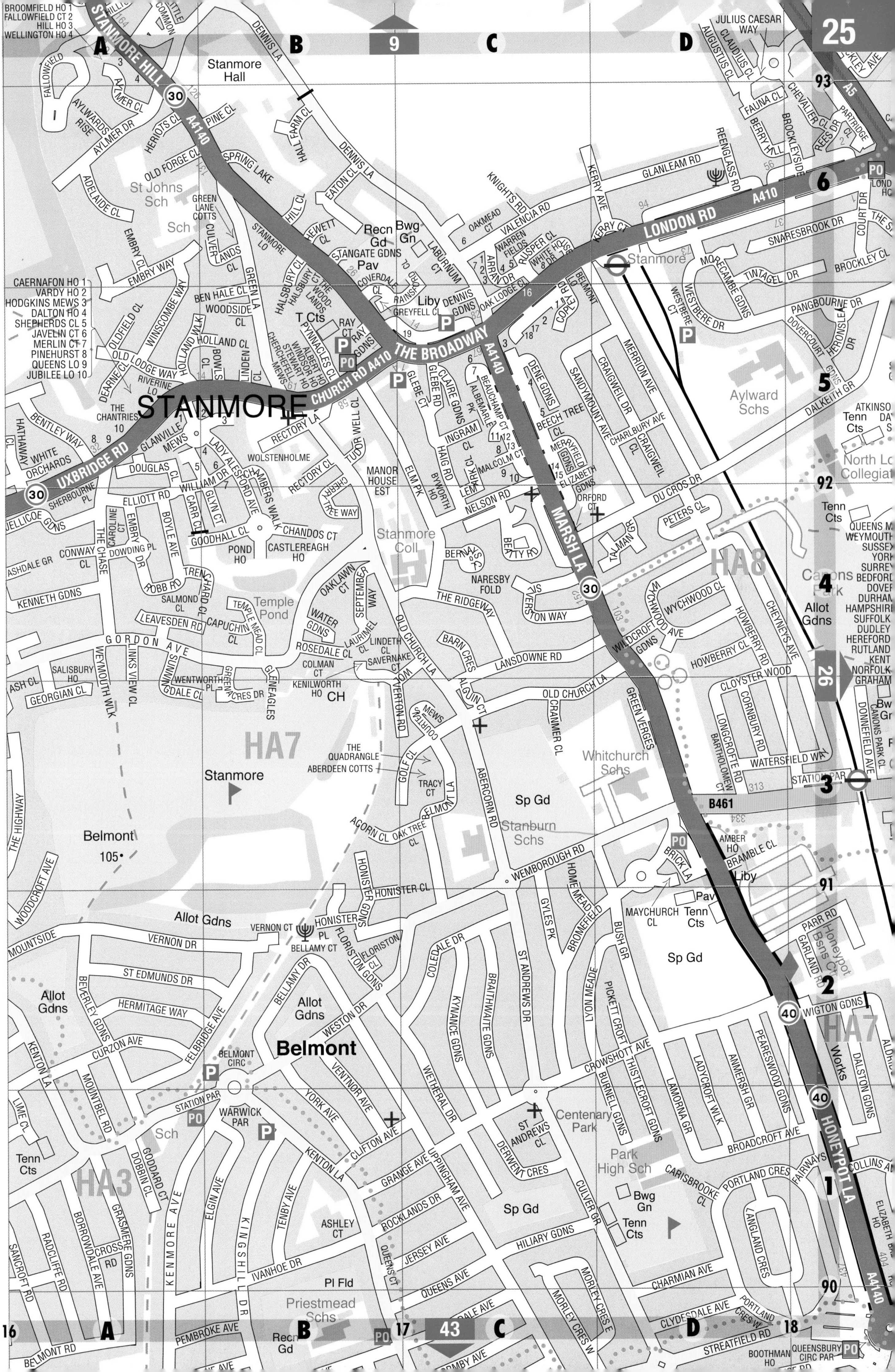

9
43
26
A
B
C
D
1
2
3
4
5
6
16
17
18
90
91
92
93
STANMORE
Belmont
HA7
HA8
HA3
Stanmore Hall
St Johns Sch
Sch
STANMORE HILL
A4140
UXBRIDGE RD
CHURCH RD A410
THE BROADWAY
LONDON RD
A410
MARSH LA
HONEYPOT LA
A5
B461
BROOMFIELD HO 1
FALLOWFIELD CT 2
HILL HO 3
WELLINGTON HO 4
CAERNAFON HO 1
VARDY HO 2
HODGKINS MEWS 3
DALTON HO 4
SHEPHERDS CL 5
JAVELIN CT 6
MERLIN CT 7
PINEHURST 8
QUEENS LO 9
JUBILEE LO 10
DENNIS LA
HALL FARM CL
EATON CL
HILL CL
HEWETT CL
Recn Gd
Bwg Gn
STANGATE GDNS
Pav
LABURNUM CT
Liby
DENNIS GDNS
GREYFELL CL
RAINSFORD
COVERDALE CL
T Cts
RAY CT
RAY GDNS
PO
P
FALLOWFIELD
AYLWARDS RISE
AYLMER DR
AYLMER CL
HERIOTS CL
PINE CL
OLD FORGE CL
SPRING LAKE
ADELAIDE CL
EMBRY CL
EMBRY WAY
GREEN LANE COTTS
CULVERLANDS CL
STANMORE LO
GREEN LA
WINSCOMBE WAY
BEN HALE CL
WOODSIDE CL
HOLLAND CL
HOLLAND WLK
OLDFIELD CL
OLD LODGE WAY
DEARNE CT
RIVERINE LO
BOWLS CL
LINDEN CL
HALSBURY CL
HALSBURY CT
THE WOODLANDS
PYNNACLES CL
ALBERT HO
WINDSOR HO
STEWART HO
CHERCEFELL MEWS
THE CHANTRIES
BENTLEY WAY
HATHAWAY CL
WHITE ORCHARDS
GLANVILLE MEWS
RECTORY LA
LADY ALESFORD AVE
WOLSTENHOLME
TUDOR WELL CL
RECTORY CL
CHERRY TREE WAY
DOUGLAS CL
WILLIAM DR
SHERBOURNE PL
JELLICOE GDNS
ELLIOTT RD
CAROLINE CT
EMBRY DR
BOYLE AVE
CARR CL
GLYN CT
CHAMBERS WALK
GOODHALL CL
CHANDOS CT
POND HO
CASTLEREAGH HO
THE CHASE
CONWAY CL
DOWDING PL
ASHDALE GR
ROBB RD
TRENCHARD CL
KENNETH GDNS
SALMOND CL
LEAVESDEN RD
TEMPLE MEAD CL
CAPUCHIN CL
Temple Pond
OAKLAWN CT
SEPTEMBER WAY
WATER GDNS
LAURIMEL CL
LINDETH CL
ROSEDALE CL
COLMAN CT
SAVERNAKE CT
KENILWORTH HO
CH
GORDON AVE
LINKS VIEW CL
WEYMOUTH WLK
SALISBURY HO
ASH CL
GEORGIAN CL
WENTWORTH PL
SUNNINGDALE CL
GREENACRES DR
GLENEAGLES
MANOR HOUSE EST
Stanmore Coll
ELM PK
GLEBE CT
GLEBE RD
CLAIRE GDNS
ALBEMARLE PK
BEAUCHAMP CT
INGRAM CL
HAIG RD
BYWORTH HO
YORK CL
LEMON
MALCOLM CT
NELSON RD
BEATTY RD
BERNAYS CL
NARESBY FOLD
THE RIDGEWAY
BARN CRES
LANSDOWNE RD
OLD CHURCH LA
TOM OVERTON RD
COURTENS MEWS
ALGUIN CT
THE QUADRANGLE
ABERDEEN COTTS
GOLF CL
TRACY CT
BELMONT LA
OAK TREE CL
ACORN CL
Stanmore
Belmont 105
THE HIGHWAY
WOODCROFT AVE
Allot Gdns
HONISTER GDNS
HONISTER CL
HONISTER PL
VERNON CT
BELLAMY CT
FLORISTON CL
FLORISTON GDNS
MOUNTSIDE
VERNON DR
ST EDMUNDS DR
HERMITAGE WAY
BEVERLEY GDNS
FELBRIDGE AVE
CURZON AVE
KENTON LA
MOUNTBEL RD
LIME CL
BELMONT CIRC
STATION PAR
WARWICK PAR
Tenn Cts
GODDARD CT
DOBBIN CL
BELLAMY DR
WESTON DR
VENTNOR AVE
YORK AVE
CLIFTON AVE
KENMORE AVE
ELGIN AVE
KINGSHILL DR
TENBY AVE
ASHLEY CT
GRASMERE GDNS
BORROWDALE AVE
CROSS RD
RADCLIFFE RD
SANCROFT RD
IVANHOE DR
Pl Fld
Priestmead Schs
PEMBROKE AVE
Recn Gd
BELMONT RD
GRANGE AVE
UPPINGHAM AVE
ROCKLANDS DR
JERSEY AVE
QUEENS CT
QUEENS AVE
WETHERAL DR
KYNANCE GDNS
COLEDALE DR
BRAITHWAITE GDNS
ST ANDREWS DR
GYLES PK
HOMEMEAD
BROMEFIELD
WEMBOROUGH RD
ABERCORN RD
Stanburn Schs
Sp Gd
CRANMER CL
Whitchurch Schs
GREEN VERGES
ST ANDREWS CL
DERWENT CRES
Centenary Park
CULVER GR
HILIARY GDNS
MORLEY CRES
MORLEY CRES W
LYON MEADE
PICKETT CROFT
BUSH GR
CROWSHOTT AVE
BURNELL GDNS
THISTLECROFT GDNS
LAMORNA GR
LADYCROFT WLK
ANMERSH GR
PEARESWOOD GDNS
BROADCROFT AVE
Park High Sch
Bwg Gn
CARISBROOKE CL
PORTLAND CRES
LANGLAND CRES
FAIRWAYS
CHARMIAN AVE
CLYDESDALE AVE
PORTLAND CRES W
STREATFIELD RD
BOOTHMAN HO
QUEENSBURY CIRC PAR
MAYCHURCH CL
BRICK LA
AMBER HO
BRAMBLE CL
PARR RD
GARLAND RD
Honeypot Bsns Cte
WIGTON GDNS
Works
DALSTON GDNS
COLLINS AVE
ELIZABETH HO
JULIUS CAESAR WAY
AUGUSTUS CL
CLAUDIUS CL
FAUNA CL
CHEVALIER CL
BERRY HILL
BROCKLEYSIDE
REES DR
PARTRIDGE CL
REENGLASS RD
GLANLEAM RD
KERRY AVE
KERRY CT
KNIGHTS RD
OAKMEAD CT
VALENCIA RD
WARREN FIELDS
RUSPER CL
WHITE HOUSE DR
ARRAN DR
OAK LODGE CL
BELMONT LO
COPLEY RD
Stanmore
WESTBERE CT
WESTBERE DR
MORECAMBE GDNS
TINTAGEL DR
SNARESBROOK DR
COURT DR
BROCKLEY CL
PANGBOURNE DR
DOVERCOURT GDNS
HERONSLEA DR
DALKEITH GR
Aylward Schs
DENE GDNS
BEECH TREE CL
MERRYFIELD GDNS
ELIZABETH GDNS
ORFORD CT
SANDYMOUNT AVE
CRAIGWEIL DR
MERRION AVE
CHARLBURY AVE
CRAIGWEIL CL
DU CROS DR
PETERS CL
TALMAN GR
ATKINSON Tenn Cts
North London Collegiate
QUEENS M
WEYMOUTH
SUSSEX
YORK
SURREY
BEDFORD
DOVER
DURHAM
HAMPSHIRE
SUFFOLK
DUDLEY
HEREFORD
RUTLAND
KENT
NORFOLK
GRAHAM
Canons Park
Allot Gdns
WYCHWOOD CL
WYCHWOOD AVE
WILDCROFT GDNS
HOWBERRY CL
HOWBERRY RD
CHEYNEYS AVE
CLOYSTER WOOD
CORNBURY RD
LONGCROFTE RD
BARTHOLOMEW CT
WATERSFIELD WAY
STATION PAR
DONNEFIELD AVE
CANONS PARK CL
IVERSON WAY

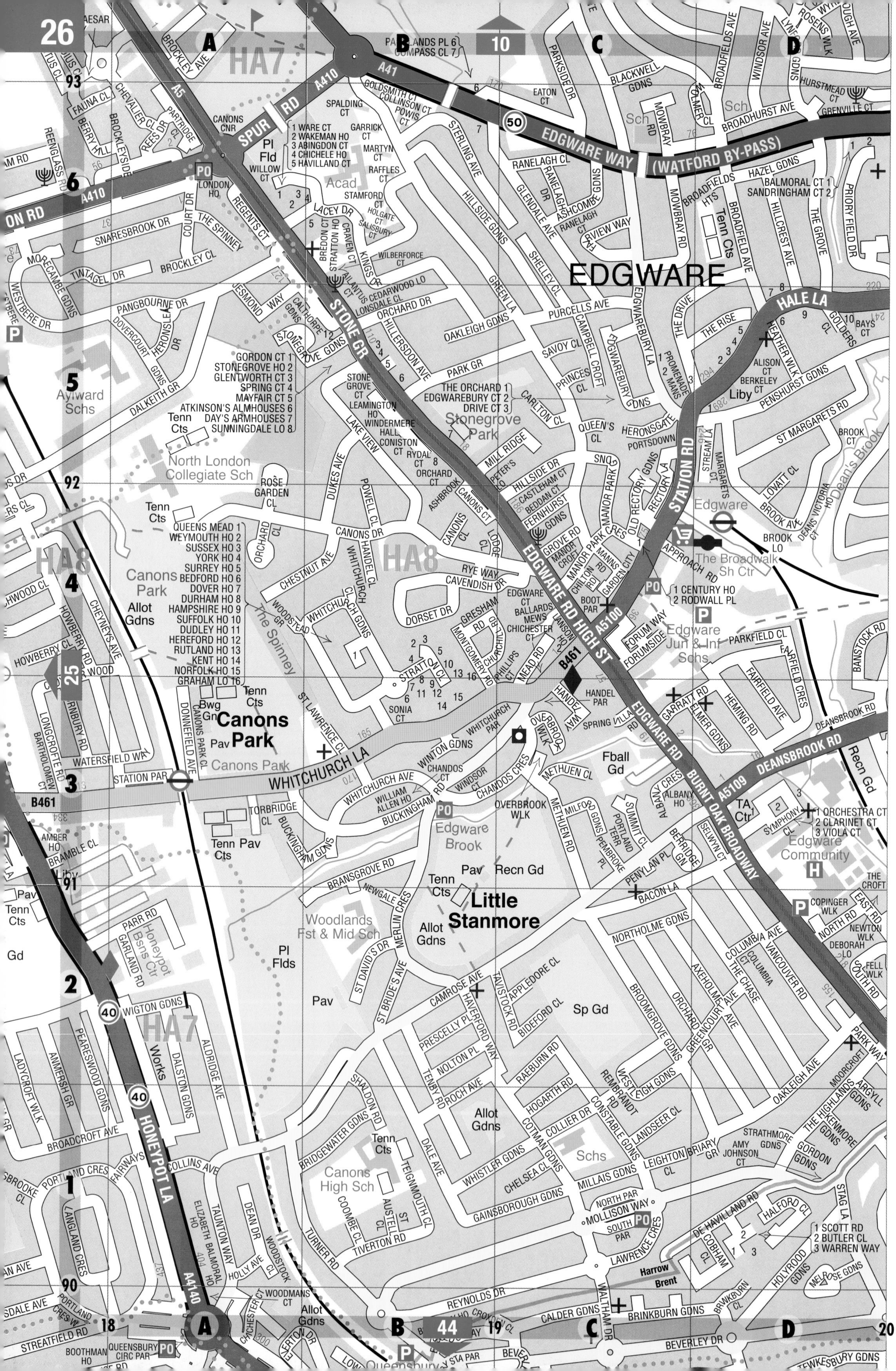

A
B
C
D
10
HA7
HA8
EDGWARE
EDGWARE WAY
(WATFORD BY-PASS)
A41
A410
A5
SPUR RD
STONE GR
EDGWARE RD HIGH ST
EDGWARE RD BURNT OAK BROADWAY
A5100
A5109
B461
STATION RD
HALE LA
DEANSBROOK RD
WHITCHURCH LA
HONEYPOT LA
A4140
CANONS CNR
LONDON HO
THE SPINNEY
REGENTS CT
BROCKLEY AVE
BROCKLEY CL
BROCKLEYSIDE
BROCKLEY HILL
FAUNA CL
CHEVALIER CL
REES DR
PARTRIDGE CL
SNARESBROOK DR
COURT DR
MORECAMBE GDNS
TINTAGEL DR
WESTBERE DR
PANGBOURNE DR
DOVERCOURT GDNS
HERONSLEA DR
JESMOND WAY
DALKEITH GR
Aylward Schs
Tenn Cts
North London Collegiate Sch
ROSE GARDEN CL
QUEENS MEAD 1
WEYMOUTH HO 2
SUSSEX HO 3
YORK HO 4
SURREY HO 5
BEDFORD HO 6
DOVER HO 7
DURHAM HO 8
HAMPSHIRE HO 9
SUFFOLK HO 10
DUDLEY HO 11
HEREFORD HO 12
RUTLAND HO 13
KENT HO 14
NORFOLK HO 15
GRAHAM LO 16
Canons Park
Allot Gdns
The Spinney
Bwg Gn
Pav
Canons Park
STATION PAR
WATERSFIELD WAY
DONNEFIELD AVE
CANONS PARK CL
HOWBERRY RD
HOWBERRY CL
CHEYNEYS AVE
LONGCROFTE RD
BARTHOLOMEW CT
AMBER HO
BRAMBLE CL
Liby
Tenn Cts
Gd
PARR RD
GARLAND RD
Honeypot Bsns Ctr
WIGTON GDNS
PEARESWOOD GDNS
ANMERSH GR
LADYCROFT WLK
DALSTON GDNS
ALDRIDGE AVE
Works
BROADCROFT AVE
FAIRWAYS
COLLINS AVE
PORTLAND CRES
LANGLAND CRES
TAUNTON WAY
ELIZABETH HO
BALMORAL HO
DEAN DR
HOLLY AVE
WOODSTOCK
WOODMANS CT
CHICHESTER CT
STREATFIELD RD
QUEENSBURY CIRC PAR
BOOTHMAN HO
Allot Gdns
Queensbury
44
19
18
20
1 WARE CT
2 WAKEMAN HO
3 ABINGDON CT
4 CHICHELE HO
5 HAVILLAND CT
SPALDING CT
GARRICK CT
MARTYN CT
RAFFLES CT
STAMFORD CT
HOLGATE CT
SALISBURY CT
WILBERFORCE CT
GOLDSMITH CT
COLLINSON CT
POWIS CT
Acad
Pl Fld
WILLOW CT
LACEY DR
BREDON CT
STRATTON HO
CRAVEN CT
KINGS DR
ATLANTUS CL
CEDARWOOD LO
LONSDALE CL
ORCHARD DR
CALTHORPE GDNS
STONEGROVE GDNS
HILLERSDON AVE
GORDON CT 1
STONEGROVE HO 2
GLENTWORTH CT 3
SPRING CT 4
MAYFAIR CT 5
ATKINSON'S ALMHOUSES 6
DAY'S ARMHOUSES 7
SUNNINGDALE LO 8
STONE GROVE CT
LEAMINGTON HO
WINDERMERE HALL
CONISTON CT
RYDAL CT
ORCHARD CT
LAKE VIEW
DUKES AVE
POWELL CL
CANONS DR
HANDEL CL
WHITCHURCH CL
CHESTNUT AVE
ORCHARD CL
WOODSTEAD GR
WHITCHURCH GDNS
HA8
RYE WAY
CAVENDISH DR
DORSET DR
GRESHAM RD
MONTGOMERY RD
CHURCHILL RD
PHILLIPS CT
MEAD RD
STRATTON CL
SONIA CT
ST LAWRENCE CL
WHITCHURCH PAR
WINTON GDNS
CHANDOS CT
WHITCHURCH AVE
WILLIAM ALLEN HO
BUCKINGHAM RD
WINDSOR CT
CHANDOS CRES
OVERBROOK WLK
TORBRIDGE CL
BUCKINGHAM GDNS
Tenn Pav Cts
Edgware Brook
BRANSGROVE RD
NEWGALE GDNS
MERLIN CRES
Woodlands Fst & Mid Sch
Pl Flds
Pav
ST DAVID'S DR
ST BRIDE'S AVE
Tenn Cts
Pav
Recn Gd
Little Stanmore
Allot Gdns
CAMROSE AVE
HAVERFORD WAY
TAVISTOCK RD
APPLEDORE CL
BIDEFORD CL
Sp Gd
PRESCELLY PL
NOLTON PL
TENBY RD
BROCH AVE
RAEBURN RD
HOGARTH RD
REMBRANDT RD
CONSTABLE GDNS
COLLIER DR
COTMAN GDNS
LANDSEER CL
SHALDON RD
BRIDGEWATER GDNS
Tenn Cts
Canons High Sch
DALE AVE
TEIGNMOUTH CL
AUSTELL GDNS
ST AUSTELL CL
COOMBE CL
TIVERTON RD
TURNER RD
WHISTLER GDNS
CHELSEA CL
GAINSBOROUGH GDNS
MILLAIS GDNS
Schs
Allot Gdns
NORTH PAR
MOLLISON WAY
SOUTH PAR
LAWRENCE CRES
Harrow
Brent
REYNOLDS DR
CROYDON CL
CALDER GDNS
WALTHAM DR
BRINKBURN GDNS
BRINKBURN CL
BEVERLEY DR
TEWKESBURY GDNS
STA PAR
LEIGHTON CL
BRIARY GR
AMY JOHNSON CT
STRATHMORE GDNS
GORDON GDNS
KENMORE GDNS
THE HIGHLANDS
ARGYLL GDNS
MOORCROFT
OAKLEIGH AVE
PARK WAY
DE HAVILLAND RD
HALFORD CL
COBHAM CL
HOLYROOD GDNS
MELROSE GDNS
STAG LA
1 SCOTT RD
2 BUTLER CL
3 WARREN WAY
EATON CT
PARKSIDE DR
STERLING AVE
HILLSIDE GDNS
GLENDALE AVE
RANELAGH CL
RANELAGH DR
ASHCOMBE GDNS
RIVERVIEW WAY
SHELLEY CL
GREEN LA
OAKLEIGH GDNS
PURCELLS AVE
CAMPBELL CROFT
EDGWAREBURY LA
EDGWAREBURY GDNS
SAVOY CL
PRINCES CL
PARK GR
THE ORCHARD 1
EDGWAREBURY CT 2
DRIVE CT 3
Stonegrove Park
CARLTON CL
MILL RIDGE
PETER'S CL
HILLSIDE DR
CASTLEHAM CT
BEDDAN CT
FERNHURST GDNS
QUEEN'S CL
HERONSGATE
PORTSDOWN
MANOR PARK GDNS
MANOR PARK CRES
OLD RECTORY GDNS
RECTORY LA
GROVE RD
MANOR CROFT
MANNS RD
CHILTON RD
GARDEN CITY
BOOT PAR
EDGWARE CT
BALLARDS MEWS
CHICHESTER CT
LANSON HO
ASHBROOK
CANONS CT
CANONS CL
LODGE CL
HANDEL PAR
HANDEL WAY
SPRING VILLA RD
FORUM WAY
FORUMSIDE
Edgware Jun & Inf Schs
PARKFIELD CL
FAIRFIELD CRES
FAIRFIELD AVE
HEMING RD
GARRATT RD
ELMER GDNS
Fball Gd
METHUEN CL
METHUEN RD
MILFORD GDNS
PEMBROKE PL
PORTLAND TERR
SUMMIT CL
ALBANY CRES
ALBANY HO
BERRIDGE GN
SELWYN CT
PENYLAN PL
BACON LA
NORTHOLME GDNS
BROOMGROVE GDNS
ORCHARD GR
AXHOLME AVE
GREENCOURT AVE
THE CHASE
COLUMBIA AVE
COLUMBIA CT
VANCOUVER RD
WESTLEIGH GDNS
TA Ctr
SYMPHONY CL
1 ORCHESTRA CT
2 CLARINET CT
3 VIOLA CT
Edgware Community
H
THE CROFT
COPINGER WLK
NORTH RD
EAST RD
NEWTON WLK
DEBORAH LO
FELL WLK
SOUTH RD
Recn Gd
BANSTOCK RD
APPROACH RD
1 CENTURY HO
2 RODWALL PL
The Broadwalk Sh Ctr
Edgware
BROOK AVE
BROOK LO
DEANS CL
VICTORIA CT
Deans Brook
LOVATT CL
BROOK CT
ST MARGARETS RD
MARGARETS
STREAM LA
PENSHURST GDNS
ALISON CT
BERKELEY CT
Liby
HEATHER WLK
BAYS CT
GOLDERS CL
THE RISE
THE DRIVE
PROMENADE MANS
BROADFIELD AVE
BROADFIELDS HTS
Tenn Cts
HILLCREST AVE
THE GROVE
PRIORY FIELD DR
BALMORAL CT 1
SANDRINGHAM CT 2
HAZEL GDNS
MOWBRAY RD
BLACKWELL GDNS
FULMER CL
BROADHURST AVE
HURSTMEAD CT
GRENVILLE CT
WINDSOR AVE
LYNFORD GDNS
ROSENS WLK
BROADFIELDS AVE
Sch
PARKLANDS PL 6
COMPASS CL 7
REENGLASS RD
25
93
92
91
90
6
5
4
3
2
1

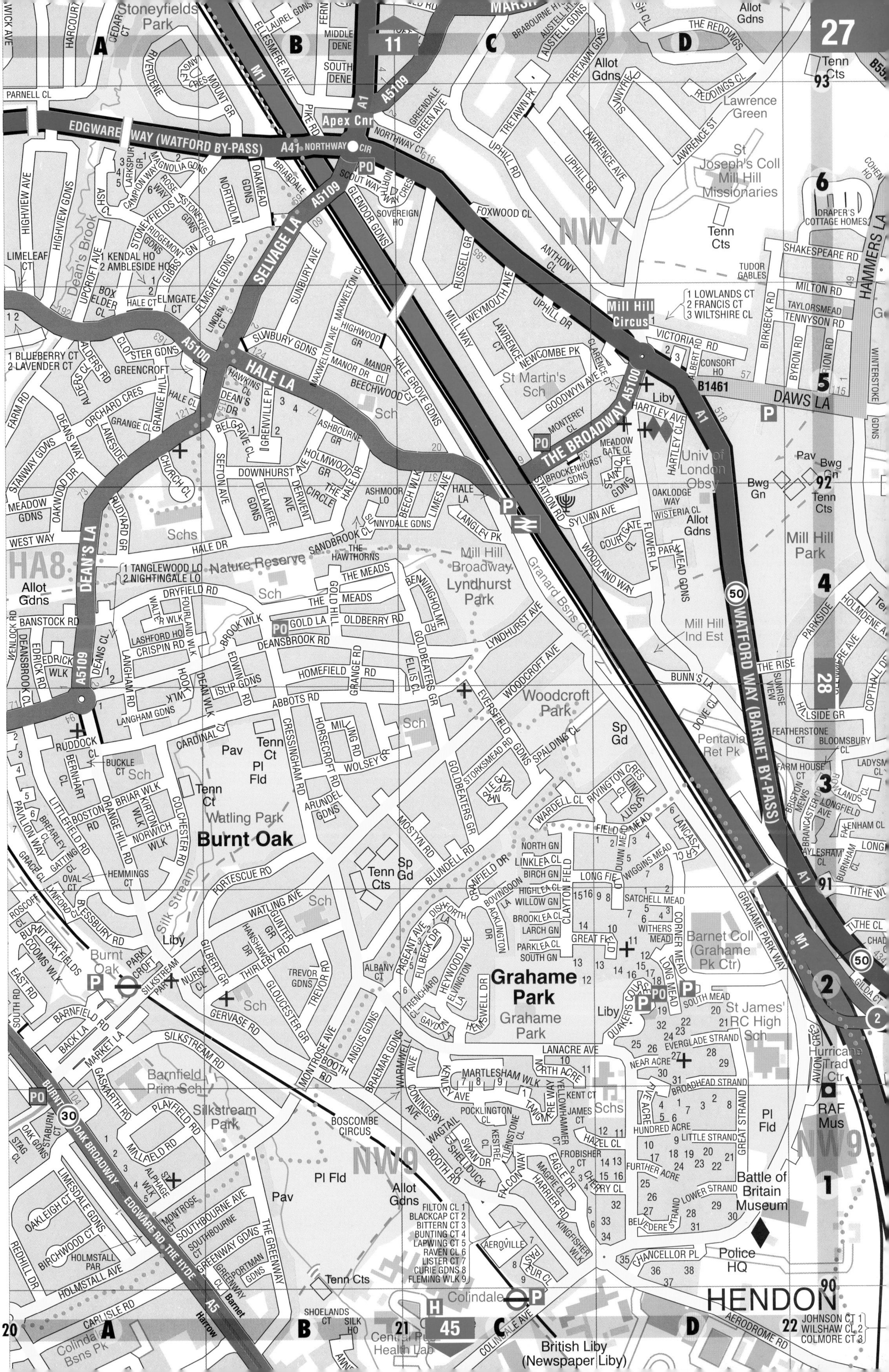
A
B
C
D
11
M1
A1
A5109
A41
Apex Cnr
NORTHWAY CIR
EDGWARE WAY (WATFORD BY-PASS)
Stoneyfields Park
PARNELL CL
HIGHVIEW AVE
HIGHVIEW GDNS
LIMELEAF CT
Dean's Brook
UPCROFT AVE
1 KENDAL HO
2 AMBLESIDE HO
ELMGATE CT
ELMGATE GDNS
SELVAGE LA
SUNBURY AVE
SUNBURY GDNS
MAXWELTON AVE
HIGHWOOD GR
MANOR DR
BEECHWOOD CL
HALE GROVE GDNS
HALE LA
A5100
1 BLUEBERRY CT
2 LAVENDER CT
GREENCROFT
CLOISTER GDNS
ORCHARD CRES
GRANGE CL
GRANGE HILL
HALE CL
DEAN'S DR
BELGRAVE CL
GRENVILLE PL
ASHBOURNE GR
HOLMWOOD GR
DOWNHURST AVE
DELAMERE GDNS
DERWENT AVE
THE CIRCLE
THE HALE DR
ASHMOOR LO
BEECH WLK
LIMES AVE
LANGLEY PK
SUNNYDALE GDNS
FARM RD
STANWAY GDNS
DEANS WAY
MEADOW GDNS
OAKWOOD DR
WEST WAY
Schs
HALE DR
CHURCH CL
RUDYARD GR
SEFTON AVE
SANDBROOK CL
THE HAWTHORNS
1 TANGLEWOOD LO
2 NIGHTINGALE LO
Nature Reserve
HA8
Allot Gdns
DEAN'S LA
DRYFIELD RD
THE MEADS
GOLD HILL
BENNINGHOLME RD
Mill Hill Broadway
Lyndhurst Park
Granard Bsns Ctr
LYNDHURST AVE
WALTER WLK
FOURLAND WLK
LASHFORD HO
CRISPIN RD
BROOK WLK
GOLD LA
OLDBERRY RD
DEANSBROOK RD
BANSTOCK RD
WENLOCK RD
DEANSBROOK CL
EDRICK RD
EDRICK WLK
DEANS CL
LANGHAM RD
HOOK WLK
DEAN WLK
ISLIP GDNS
EDWIN RD
HOMEFIELD RD
GRANGE RD
ELLIS CL
GOLDBEATERS GR
WOODCROFT AVE
Woodcroft Park
EVERSFIELD GDNS
LANGHAM GDNS
ABBOTS RD
CARDINAL
RUDDOCK CL
BUCKLE CT
BERNHART CL
Pav
Tenn Ct
Pl Fld
CRESSINGHAM RD
HORSECROFT RD
MILLING RD
WOLSEY GR
Sch
STORKSMEAD RD
SPALDING CL
Sp Gd
RIVINGTON CRES
UNIVERSITY CL
WARDELL CL
MAPLE GDNS
PAVILION WAY
LITTLEFIELD RD
BOSTON RD
ORANGE HILL RD
BRIAR WLK
KIRTON WLK
NORWICH WLK
COLCHESTER RD
Watling Park
Burnt Oak
ARUNDEL GDNS
MOSTYN RD
GOLDBEATERS GR
BLUNDELL RD
FIELD MEAD
DUNN MEAD
LANCASTER CL
WIGGINS MEAD
NORTH GN
LINKLEA CL
BIRCH GN
HIGHLEA CL
WILLOW GN
BROOKLEA CL
LARCH GN
PARKLEA CL
SOUTH GN
CLAYTON FIELD
LONG FIELD
SATCHELL MEAD
WITHERS MEAD
CORNER MEAD
GREAT FIELD
Barnet Coll (Grahame Pk Ctr)
GRAHAME PARK WAY
LONG MEAD
SOUTH MEAD
St James' RC High Sch
GRACE CL
OVAL CT
HEMMINGS CT
FORTESCUE RD
Tenn Cts
Sp Gd
CRANFIELD DR
BOVINGDON LA
ACKLINGTON DR
ROSCOFF CL
LYNFORD CL
BLESSBURY RD
BURNT OAK FIELDS
COOMS WLK
Silk Stream
Liby
WATLING AVE
GUNTER GR
HANSHAW DR
THIRLEBY RD
TREVOR GDNS
TREVOR RD
ALBANY CT
PAGEANT AVE
FULBECK DR
DISHFORTH LA
HEYWOOD AVE
ELVINGTON LA
HENSWELL DR
TRENCHARD CL
GAYDON LA
Grahame Park
QUAKERS COURSE
EAST RD
SOUTH RD
BARNFIELD RD
BACK LA
MARKET LA
PARK CROFT
SILKSTREAM PAR
NURSE CL
GILBERT GR
GERVASE RD
GLOUCESTER GR
SILKSTREAM RD
MONTROSE AVE
BOOTH RD
ANGUS GDNS
BRAEMAR GDNS
WARMWELL AVE
LANACRE AVE
MARTLESHAM WLK
NORTH ACRE
KENLEY AVE
NEAR ACRE
EVERGLADE STRAND
BROADHEAD STRAND
Hurricane Trad Ctr
RAF Mus
BURNT OAK BROADWAY
Barnfield Prim Sch
GASKARTH RD
PLAYFIELD RD
MILLFIELD RD
Silkstream Park
ALPHAGE WLK
STAG CL
OAK GDNS
STABURN CT
CONINGSBY AVE
BOSCOMBE CIRCUS
POCKLINGTON CL
KESTREL CL
TURNSTONE CL
YELLOWHAMMER CT
KENT CT
JAMES CT
FIVE ACRE
HUNDRED ACRE
LITTLE STRAND
GREAT STRAND
Pl Fld
NW9
LIMESDALE GDNS
OAKLEIGH CT
BIRCHWOOD CT
HOLMSTALL PAR
HOLMSTALL AVE
REDHILL DR
EDGWARE RD THE HYDE
A5
SOUTHBOURNE AVE
MONTROSE CT
SOUTHBOURNE CRES
GREENWAY GDNS
PORTMAN GDNS
THE GREENWAY
Pl Fld
Pav
Allot Gdns
WAGTAIL CL
SHELDUCK CL
SWAN DR
FALCON WAY
MAGPIE CL
HARRIER RD
EAGLE DR
FROBISHER CT
CHERRY CL
HAZEL CL
FURTHER ACRE
LOWER STRAND
Battle of Britain Museum
KINGFISHER WLK
FILTON CL 1
BLACKCAP CT 2
BITTERN CT 3
BUNTING CT 4
LAPWING CT 5
RAVEN CL 6
LISTER CT 7
CURIE GDNS 8
FLEMING WLK 9
AEROVILLE
CHANCELLOR PL
BELVEDERE STRAND
Police HQ
HENDON
Tenn Cts
Colindale
CARLISLE RD
Colindale Bsns Pk
SHOELANDS CT
SILK HO
Central Public Health Lab
COLINDALE AVE
British Liby (Newspaper Liby)
AERODROME RD
JOHNSON CT 1
WILSHAW CL 2
COLMORE CT 3
20
21
22
45
HAMMERS LA
Allot Gdns
THE REDDINGS
REDDINGS CL
Lawrence Green
LAWRENCE ST
St Joseph's Coll Mill Hill Missionaries
Tenn Cts
DRAPER'S COTTAGE HOMES
SHAKESPEARE RD
TUDOR GABLES
MILTON RD
TAYLORSMEAD
TENNYSON RD
1 LOWLANDS CT
2 FRANCIS CT
3 WILTSHIRE CL
Mill Hill Circus
VICTORIA RD
ALBERT RD
CONSORT HO
BIRKBECK RD
BYRON RD
B1461
DAWS LA
NW7
TRETAWN GDNS
TRETAWN PK
UPHILL RD
UPHILL GR
LAWRENCE AVE
SUNNYFIELD
FOXWOOD CL
RUSSELL GR
ANTHONY CL
WEYMOUTH AVE
LAWRENCE CT
NEWCOMBE PK
UPHILL DR
MILL WAY
St Martin's Sch
GOODWYN AVE
CLARENCE CT
MONTEREY CL
THE BROADWAY
HARTLEY AVE
HARTLEY CL
Univ of London Obsy
MEADOW GATE CL
BROCKENHURST GDNS
STATION RD
SYLVAN AVE
OAKLODGE WAY
WISTERIA CL
COURTGATE CL
FLOWER LA
PARK MEAD GDNS
WOODLAND WAY
Allot Gdns
Bwg Gn
Tenn Cts
Mill Hill Park
WATFORD WAY (BARNET BY-PASS)
Mill Hill Ind Est
BUNN'S LA
DOVE CL
Pentavia Ret Pk
THE RISE
SUNRISE VIEW
HILLSIDE GR
FEATHERSTONE CT
BLOOMSBURY CL
FARM HOUSE CT
BRISTOW MEWS
BRANCASTER DR
ROWLANDS CL
LONGFIELD AVE
AYLESHAM CL
BURNHAM CL
PARKSIDE
HOLMDENE AVE
COPTHALL DR
SOUTHERN CROSS
MIDDLE DENE
SOUTH DENE
ELLESMERE AVE
LAUREL GDNS
PIKE RD
GREENDALE
GREEN AVE
NORTHWAY CT
SCOUT WAY
NORTHWAY CRES
SOVEREIGN HO
GLENDOR GDNS
BRIARDALE
OAKMEAD GDNS
NORTHOLM GDNS
MAGNOLIA GDNS
CAMPION WAY
LARKSPUR
ROSE WAY
STONEYFIELDS LA
STONEYFIELDS GDNS
RIDGEMONT GDNS
GIBBS GN
RIVERDENE
MOUNT GR
LANGLEY CRES
BRABOURNE HTS
AUSTELL HTS
AUSTELL GDNS
28
50
30
NW9
HA8
93
92
91
90
1
2
3
4
5
6

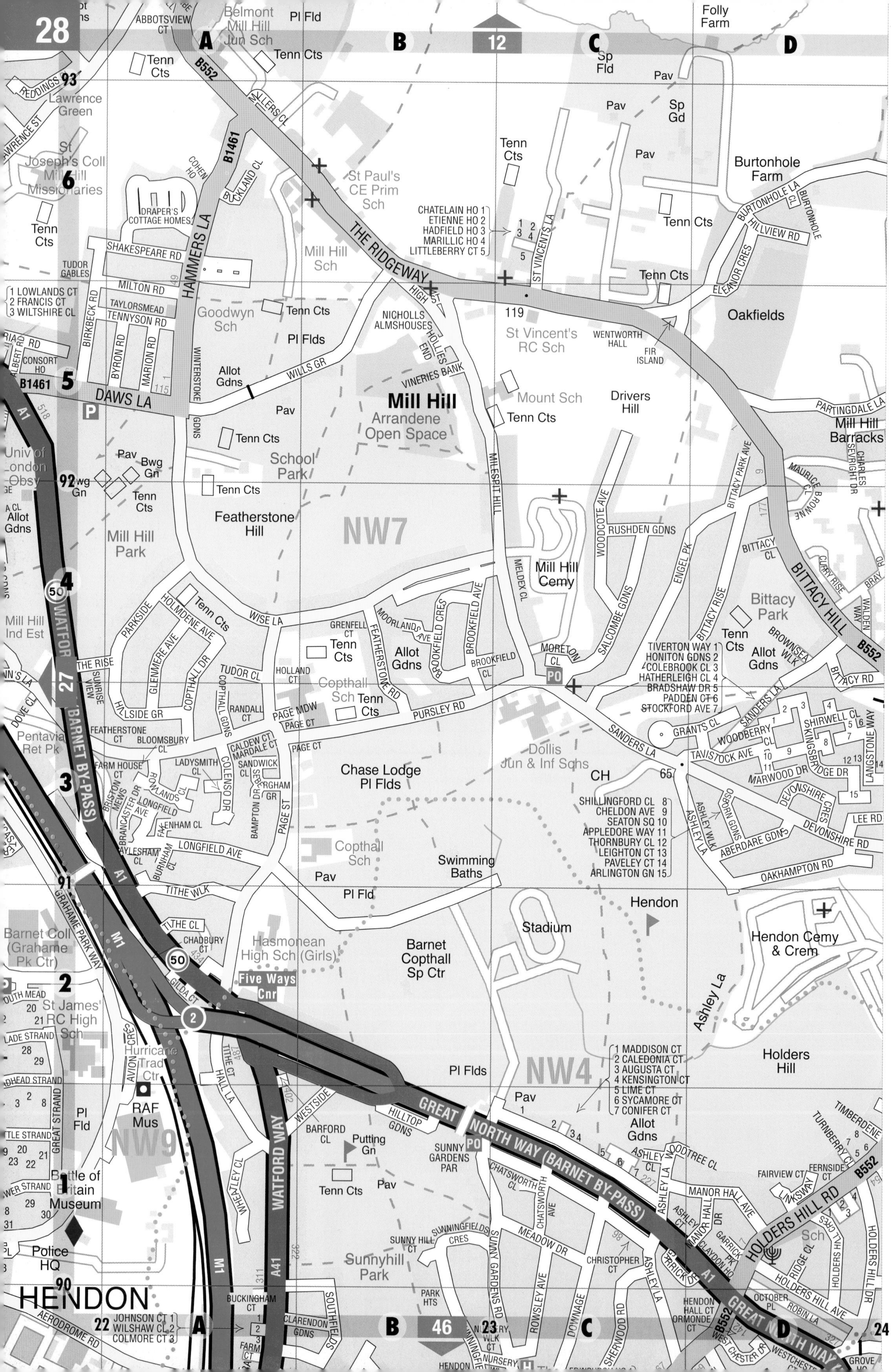
A
B
12
C
D
Belmont
Mill Hill
Jun Sch
Pl Fld
Folly
Farm
ABBOTSVIEW CT
Tenn Cts
Tenn Cts
93
REDDINGS
Lawrence
Green
LAWRENCE ST
St Joseph's Coll
Mill Hill
Missionaries
6
Tenn
Cts
B552
B1461
COHEN HO
BUCKLAND CL
DRAPER'S COTTAGE HOMES
HAMMERS LA
SHAKESPEARE RD
TUDOR GABLES
MILTON RD
1 LOWLANDS CT
2 FRANCIS CT
3 WILTSHIRE CL
TAYLORSMEAD
TENNYSON RD
BIRKBECK RD
BYRON RD
MARION RD
WINTERSTOKE GDNS
CONSORT HO
B1461
5
DAWS LA
St Paul's
CE Prim
Sch
Mill Hill
Sch
THE RIDGEWAY
Goodwyn
Sch
Tenn Cts
Pl Flds
Allot
Gdns
WILLS GR
Pav
Tenn Cts
Tenn Cts
School
Park
Featherstone
Hill
Pav
Bwg
Gn
Tenn
Cts
92
Univ of
London
Obsy
Allot
Gdns
Mill Hill
Park
4
50
Mill Hill
Ind Est
WATFORD
27
(BARNET BY-PASS)
A1
Sp
Fld
Pav
Sp
Gd
Pav
Pav
Tenn
Cts
CHATELAIN HO 1
ETIENNE HO 2
HADFIELD HO 3
MARILLIC HO 4
LITTLEBERRY CT 5
ST VINCENTS LA
Burtonhole
Farm
BURTONHOLE LA
BURTONHOLE CL
HILLVIEW RD
Tenn Cts
ELEANOR CRES
Tenn Cts
Oakfields
HIGH ST
NICHOLLS
ALMSHOUSES
HOLLIES END
VINERIES BANK
119
St Vincent's
RC Sch
WENTWORTH
HALL
FIR
ISLAND
Mill Hill
Arrandene
Open Space
Mount Sch
Tenn Cts
Drivers
Hill
PARTINGDALE LA
Mill Hill
Barracks
CHARLES SEVRIGHT DR
MAURICE BROWNE CL
MILESPIT HILL
NW7
Mill Hill
Cemy
MELDEX CL
WOODCOTE AVE
RUSHDEN GDNS
SALCOMBE GDNS
ENGEL PK
BITTACY PARK AVE
BITTACY CL
BITTACY HILL
CURRY RISE
BRAY RD
WALDEN WAY
Bittacy
Park
BITTACY RISE
Tenn
Cts
Allot
Gdns
BROWNSEA WLK
B552
BITTACY RD
PARKSIDE
HOLMDENE AVE
Tenn Cts
WISE LA
GLENMERE AVE
THE RISE
SUNRISE VIEW
COPTHALL DR
TUDOR CL
HOLLAND CT
GRENFELL CT
Tenn
Cts
MOORLANDS AVE
FEATHERSTONE RD
Allot
Gdns
BROOKFIELD CRES
BROOKFIELD AVE
BROOKFIELD CL
MORETON CL
PO
TIVERTON WAY 1
HONITON GDNS 2
COLEBROOK CL 3
HATHERLEIGH CL 4
BRADSHAW DR 5
PADDEN CT 6
STOCKFORD AVE 7
Copthall
Sch
Tenn
Cts
HILLSIDE GR
COPTHALL GDNS
RANDALL CT
PAGE MDW
PAGE CT
PURSLEY RD
SANDERS LA
GRANTS CL
WOODBERRY CL
SHIRWELL CL
LANGSTONE WAY
TAVISTOCK AVE
KINGSBRIDGE DR
MARWOOD DR
DOVE CL
Pentavia
Ret Pk
FEATHERSTONE CT
BLOOMSBURY CL
CALDEW CT
MARDALE CT
PAGE CT
Dollis
Jun & Inf Schs
CH
65
FARM HOUSE CT
LADYSMITH CL
SANDWICK CL
COLENSO DR
SEDGE CL
BERGHAM GR
Chase Lodge
Pl Flds
3
BRISTON MEWS
ROWLANDS CL
BRANCASTER DR
LONGFIELD AVE
FAKENHAM CL
BAMPTON DR
PAGE ST
SHILLINGFORD CL 8
CHELDON AVE 9
SEATON SQ 10
APPLEDORE WAY 11
THORNBURY CL 12
LEIGHTON CT 13
PAVELEY CT 14
ARLINGTON GN 15
ASHLEY WLK
ASHLEY LA
OSBORN GDNS
ABERDARE GDNS
DEVONSHIRE CRES
DEVONSHIRE RD
LEE RD
OAKHAMPTON RD
AYLESHAM CL
BURNHAM CL
LONGFIELD AVE
Copthall
Sch
Swimming
Baths
91
GRAHAME PARK WAY
A1
TITHE WLK
Pav
Pl Fld
Hendon
Stadium
Hendon Cemy
& Crem
Barnet Coll
(Grahame
Pk Ctr)
M1
THE CL
CHADBURY CT
50
Hasmonean
High Sch (Girls)
Five Ways
Cnr
Barnet
Copthall
Sp Ctr
Ashley La
2
SOUTH MEAD
St James'
RC High
Sch
GILDA CT
2
Hurricane
Trad
Ctr
AVION CRES
TITHE CT
HALL LA
GLADE STRAND
MEADHEAD STRAND
RAF
Mus
NW9
Pl
Fld
GREAT STRAND
WESTSIDE
WATFORD WAY
A41
HILLTOP GDNS
Pl Flds
NW4
1 MADDISON CT
2 CALEDONIA CT
3 AUGUSTA CT
4 KENSINGTON CT
5 LIME CT
6 SYCAMORE CT
7 CONIFER CT
Holders
Hill
Pav
GREAT NORTH WAY (BARNET BY-PASS)
BARFORD CL
Putting
Gn
SUNNY GARDENS PAR
PO
Allot
Gdns
ASHLEY CL
WOODTREE CL
TIMBERDENE
TURNBERRY CL
FERNSIDE CT
FAIRVIEW CT
B552
1
Battle of
Britain
Museum
TOWER STRAND
Tenn Cts
Pav
CHATSWORTH CL
CHATSWORTH AVE
WHEATLEY CL
MANOR HALL AVE
LINKSWAY
HOLDERS HILL RD
MANOR HALL DR
ASHLEY CT
CLAYDON HO
GARRICK PK
Sch
HOLDERS HILL CRES
RIDGE CL
HOLDERS HILL DR
Police
HQ
SUNNY HILL CT
SUNNINGFIELDS CRES
MEADOW DR
SUNNY GARDENS RD
Sunnyhill
Park
CHRISTOPHER CT
ASHLEY LA
GARRICK DR
A1
HOLDERS HILL AVE
OCTOBER PL
ROBIN LA
90
HENDON
BUCKINGHAM CT
PARK HTS
ROWSLEY AVE
DOWNAGE
SHERWOOD RD
HENDON HALL CT
ORMONDE CT
B552
GREAT NORTH WAY
AERODROME RD
22
JOHNSON CT 1
WILSHAW CL 2
COLMORE CT 3
A
CLARENDON GDNS
SOUTHFIELDS
B
46
23
NURSERY WLK CT
C
D
24
FARM CT
HENDON
NURSERY
WEST CHESTER DR
WESTCHESTER
GROVE

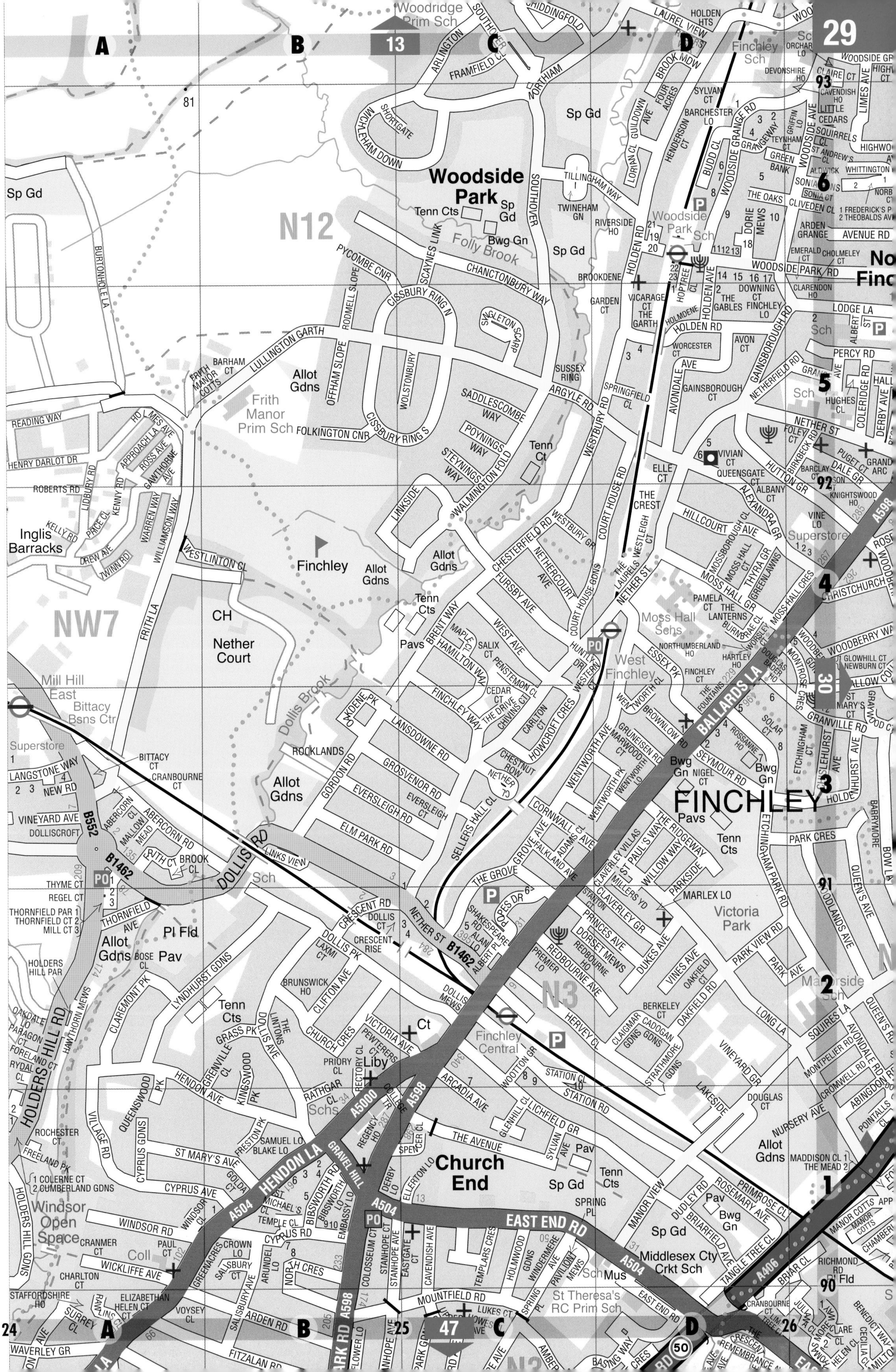
A
B
13
C
D
Woodridge Prim Sch
Woodside Park
N12
NW7
N3
FINCHLEY
Church End
Finchley
Inglis Barracks
Mill Hill East
Bittacy Bsns Ctr
Superstore
Frith Manor Prim Sch
Allot Gdns
Sp Gd
Tenn Cts
Bwg Gn
Folly Brook
Dollis Brook
CH
Nether Court
Pavs
West Finchley
Moss Hall Schs
Finchley Central
Victoria Park
Woodside Park Sch
Finchley Sch
Windsor Open Space
Coll
St Theresa's RC Prim Sch
Middlesex Cty Crkt Sch
Mus
Liby
Schs
Pl Fld
Pav
Ct
Manorside Sch
ARLINGTON
FRAMFIELD CL
NORTHIAM
SOUTHOVER
MICHLEHAM DOWN
SHORTGATE
TILLINGHAM WAY
TWINEHAM GN
RIVERSIDE HO
HOLDEN RD
HOLDEN AVE
BROOKDENE
VICARAGE CT
THE GARTH
GARDEN CT
CHANCTONBURY WAY
SCAYNES LINK
PYCOMBE CNR
CISSBURY RING N
CISSBURY RING S
RODMELL SLOPE
OFFHAM SLOPE
WOLSTONBURY
SINGLETON SCARP
SUSSEX RING
ARGYLE RD
SADDLESCOMBE WAY
POYNINGS WAY
STEYNINGS WAY
WALMINGTON FOLD
LINKSIDE
FOLKINGTON CNR
LULLINGTON GARTH
BARHAM CT
FRITH MANOR COTTS
BURTONHOLE LA
READING WAY
HENRY DARLOT DR
ROBERTS RD
KELLY RD
DREW AVE
TWINN RD
WILLIAMSON WAY
WARREN WAY
WESTLINTON CL
FRITH LA
BITTACY CT
CRANBOURNE CT
LANGSTONE WAY
NEW RD
VINEYARD AVE
DOLLISCROFT
B552
B1462
ABERCORN RD
DOLLIS RD
LINKS VIEW
THYME CT
REGEL CT
THORNFIELD AVE
HOLDERS HILL RD
HOLDERS HILL PAR
HAWTHORN MEWS
CLAREMONT PK
LYNDHURST GDNS
GRASS PK
DOLLIS AVE
VICTORIA AVE
CHURCH CRES
CLIFTON AVE
BRUNSWICK HO
DOLLIS PK
CRESCENT RD
CRESCENT RISE
NETHER ST
GORDON RD
ROCKLANDS
LANSDOWNE RD
GROSVENOR RD
EVERSLEIGH RD
ELM PARK RD
FINCHLEY WAY
HAMILTON WAY
BRENT WAY
WEST AVE
FURSBY AVE
CHESTERFIELD RD
NETHERCOURT AVE
WESTBURY RD
COURT HOUSE RD
COURT HOUSE GDNS
SPRINGFIELD CL
THE CREST
THE LAURELS
WESTLEIGH CT
HOWCROFT CRES
CARLTON CT
SELLERS HALL CL
THE GROVE
GROVE AVE
CORNWALL AVE
FALKLAND AVE
WENTWORTH AVE
WENTWORTH PK
BALLARDS LA
A598
A5000
A504
A406
HENDON LA
HENDON AVE
GRAVEL HILL
REGENCY HO
ST MARY'S AVE
CYPRUS AVE
CYPRUS GDNS
WINDSOR RD
WICKLIFFE AVE
VILLAGE RD
QUEENSWOOD PK
EAST END RD
THE AVENUE
ARCADIA AVE
LICHFIELD GR
STATION RD
WOOTTON GR
HERVEY CL
REDBOURNE AVE
DORSET MEWS
PRINCES AVE
CLAVERLEY GR
CLAVERLEY VILLAS
ST PAUL'S WAY
WILLOW WAY
THE RIDGEWAY
PARKSIDE
MARLEX LO
DUKES AVE
VINES AVE
OAKFIELD RD
BERKELEY CT
PARK VIEW RD
PARK AVE
ETCHINGHAM PARK RD
LONG LA
SQUIRES LA
VINEYARD GR
LAKESIDE
DOUGLAS CT
NURSERY AVE
PRIMROSE CL
ROSEMARY AVE
DUDLEY RD
BRIARFIELD AVE
MANOR VIEW
TANGLE TREE CL
SPRING PL
MOUNTFIELD RD
HOLMWOOD GDNS
WINDERMERE AVE
PAVILION MEWS
TEMPLARS CRES
CAVENDISH AVE
EASTGATE CT
STANHOPE AVE
COLOSSEUM CT
ARDEN RD
FITZALAN RD
WAVERLEY GR
STAFFORDSHIRE HO
SURREY CL
VOYSEY CL
NORTH CRES
SALISBURY AVE
ARUNDEL CL
BIBSWORTH RD
EMBASSY LO
HILLCOURT AVE
MOSSBOROUGH CL
MOSS HALL GR
MOSS HALL CRES
THYRA GR
GREENLAWNS
ALEXANDRA GR
HUTTON GR
QUEENSGATE
NETHER ST
ESSEX PK
BROWNLOW RD
SEYMOUR RD
ROSSANNE HO
CHRISTCHURCH
WOODBERRY WAY
GRANVILLE RD
ETCHINGHAM CT
GAINSBOROUGH RD
GAINSBOROUGH CT
AVONDALE AVE
NETHERFIELD RD
PERCY RD
WOODSIDE PARK RD
WOODSIDE GRANGE RD
WOODSIDE AVE
DOWNING CT
THE GABLES
FINCHLEY LO
AVENUE RD
CLIVEDEN CL
ARDEN GRANGE
HIGHWOOD
BUDD CL
HENDERSON CT
LORIAN CL
GUILDOWN AVE
FOUR ACRES
BROOK MDW
LAUREL VIEW
HOLDEN HTS
CHIDDINGFOLD
SOUTHOVER
24
25
26
30
47
50
81
90
91
92
93

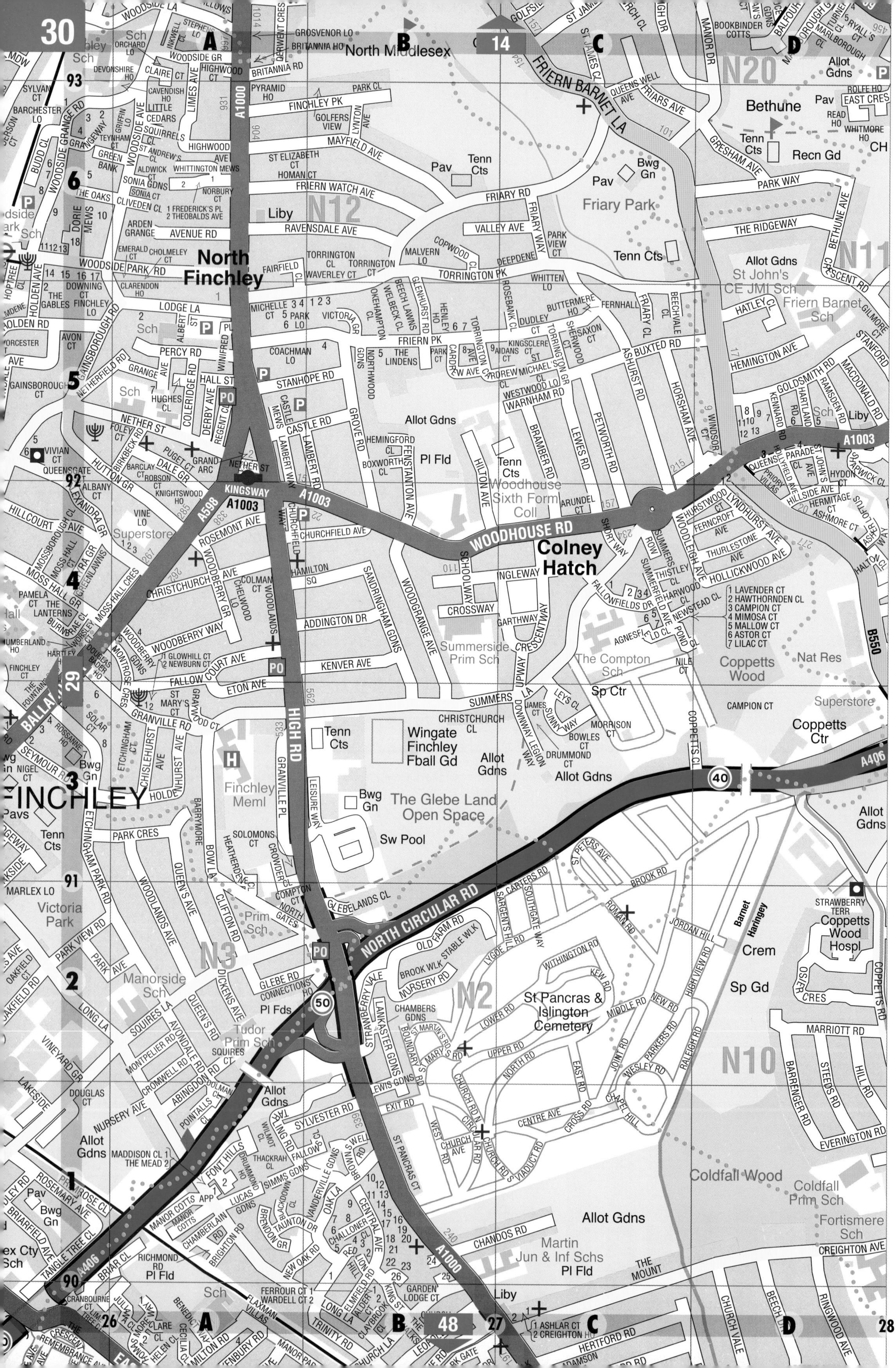
North Middlesex
14
FRIERN BARNET LA
N20
Bethune
Recn Gd
Friary Park
N12
North Finchley
A1000
Liby
FRIARY RD
TORRINGTON PK
WOODSIDE PARK RD
LODGE LA
FRIERN PK
WOODHOUSE RD
A1003
Colney Hatch
Woodhouse Sixth Form Coll
Summerside Prim Sch
The Compton Sch
Coppetts Wood
Nat Res
Superstore
Coppetts Ctr
A406
40
N11
St John's CE JMI Sch
Friern Barnet Sch
KINGSWAY
A598
HIGH RD
Wingate Finchley Fball Gd
The Glebe Land Open Space
Sw Pool
Finchley Meml
FINCHLEY
Victoria Park
Manorside Sch
N3
NORTH CIRCULAR RD
50
N2
St Pancras & Islington Cemetery
Crem
Sp Gd
N10
Coppetts Wood Hospl
Coldfall Wood
Coldfall Prim Sch
Fortismere Sch
Martin Jun & Inf Schs
Tudor Prim Sch
Allot Gdns
Pl Fld
Barnet
Haringey
B550
29
48
A
B
C
D
28

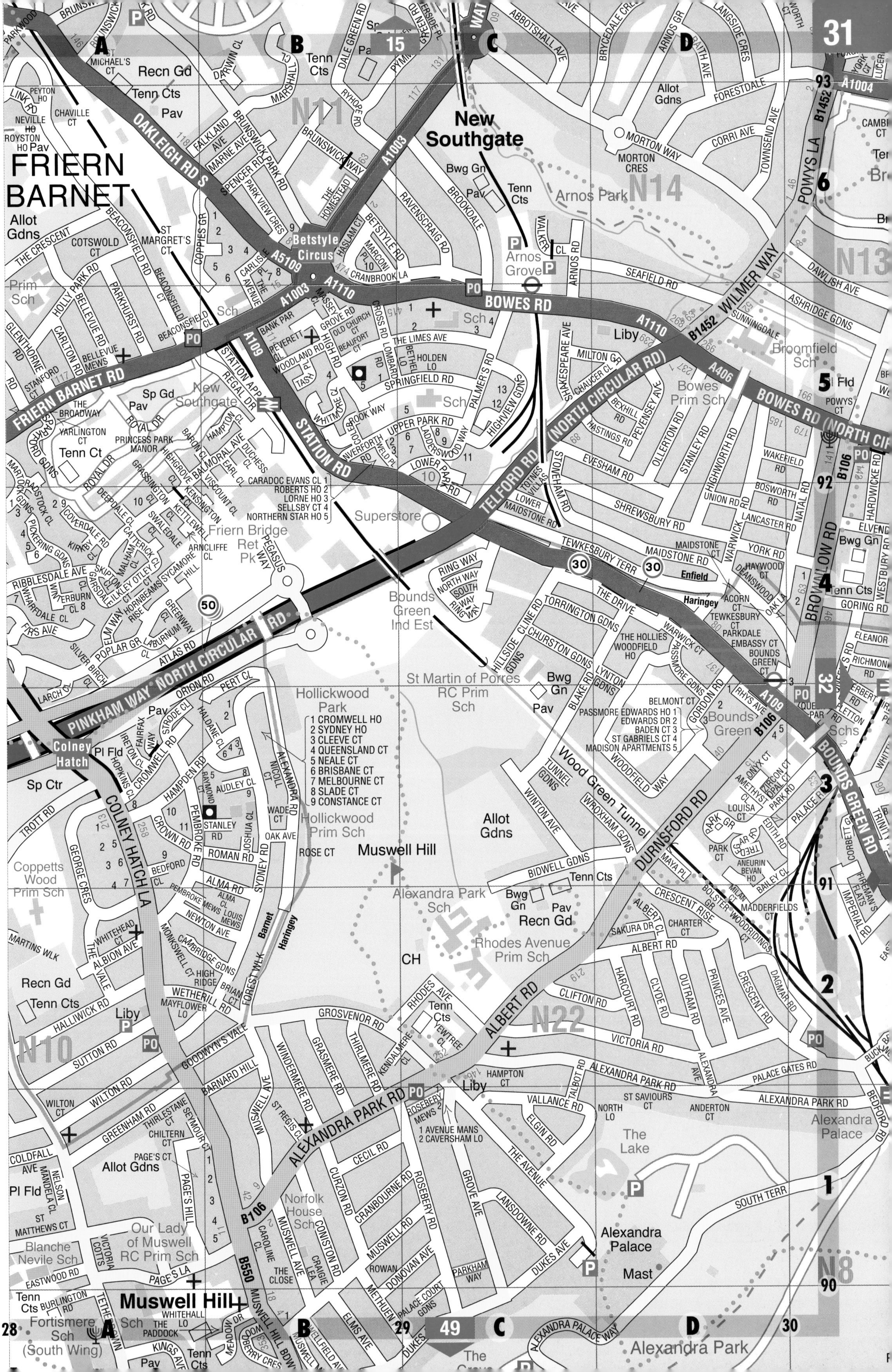
15
49
32
A
B
C
D
FRIERN
BARNET
New
Southgate
N11
N14
N13
N22
N10
N8
Muswell Hill
OAKLEIGH RD S
FRIERN BARNET RD
BOWES RD
STATION RD
TELFORD RD (NORTH CIRCULAR RD)
PINKHAM WAY NORTH CIRCULAR RD
COLNEY HATCH LA
ALEXANDRA PARK RD
ALBERT RD
DURNSFORD RD
BOUNDS GREEN RD
BROWNLOW RD
WILMER WAY
POWYS LA
MUSWELL HILL BDWY
Betstyle Circus
Colney Hatch
Arnos Park
Arnos Grove
Friern Bridge Ret Pk
Bounds Green Ind Est
Superstore
Hollickwood Park
Hollickwood Prim Sch
St Martin of Porres RC Prim Sch
Wood Green Tunnel
Alexandra Park Sch
Rhodes Avenue Prim Sch
Coppetts Wood Prim Sch
Our Lady of Muswell RC Prim Sch
Blanche Nevile Sch
Norfolk House Sch
Fortismere Sch (South Wing)
Bowes Prim Sch
Broomfield Sch
Alexandra Palace
The Lake
Mast
Alexandra Park
Bounds Green
1 CROMWELL HO
2 SYDNEY HO
3 CLEEVE CT
4 QUEENSLAND CT
5 NEALE CT
6 BRISBANE CT
7 MELBOURNE CT
8 SLADE CT
9 CONSTANCE CT
CARADOC EVANS CL 1
ROBERTS HO 2
LORNE HO 3
SELLSBY CT 4
NORTHERN STAR HO 5
BELMONT CT 1
PASSMORE EDWARDS HO 1
EDWARDS DR 2
BADEN CT 3
ST GABRIELS CT 4
MADISON APARTMENTS 5
1 AVENUE MANS
2 CAVERSHAM LO
Enfield
Haringey
Barnet
28
29
30
90
91
92
93

16
A
B
C
D
St Monica's RC Prim Sch
ALDERMAN'S HILL
A1004
Palmers Green
Broomfield Park
Bndstd
Sp Gd
N13
WILMER WAY
B1452
POWYS LA
Broomfield Sch
BOWES RD (NORTH CIRCULAR RD)
A406
NORTH CIRCULAR RD
Bowes Park
Clockhouse Junction
Tottenhall Inf Sch
St Michael-at-Bowes CE Jun Sch
Hazelwood Jun & Inf Schs
St Annes Catholic High Sch for Girls (Upper)
Pymme's Brook
Allot Gdns
HIGH RD
BOUNDS GREEN RD
A109
B106
Bounds Green
N22
New River Sp & Recn Ctr
St Georges Ind Est
Woodside Park
St Thomas More Sch
Earlham Prim Sch
White Hart Lane Sec Sch
WOOD GREEN
LORDSHIP LA
Noel Park
Noel Park Prim Sch
Alexandra Palace
Wood Green Common
Alexandra Prim Sch
STATION RD
B138
MAYES RD
A105
WESTBURY AVE
A1080
Olympia Ind Est
N8
1 KOBLENZ HO
2 WAT TYLER HO
3 NEWLAND HO
4 GOODWIN CT
5 GILLETT HO
6 MYDDELTON HO
7 CAMPSFIELD HO
50
31
30
32
90
91
92
93

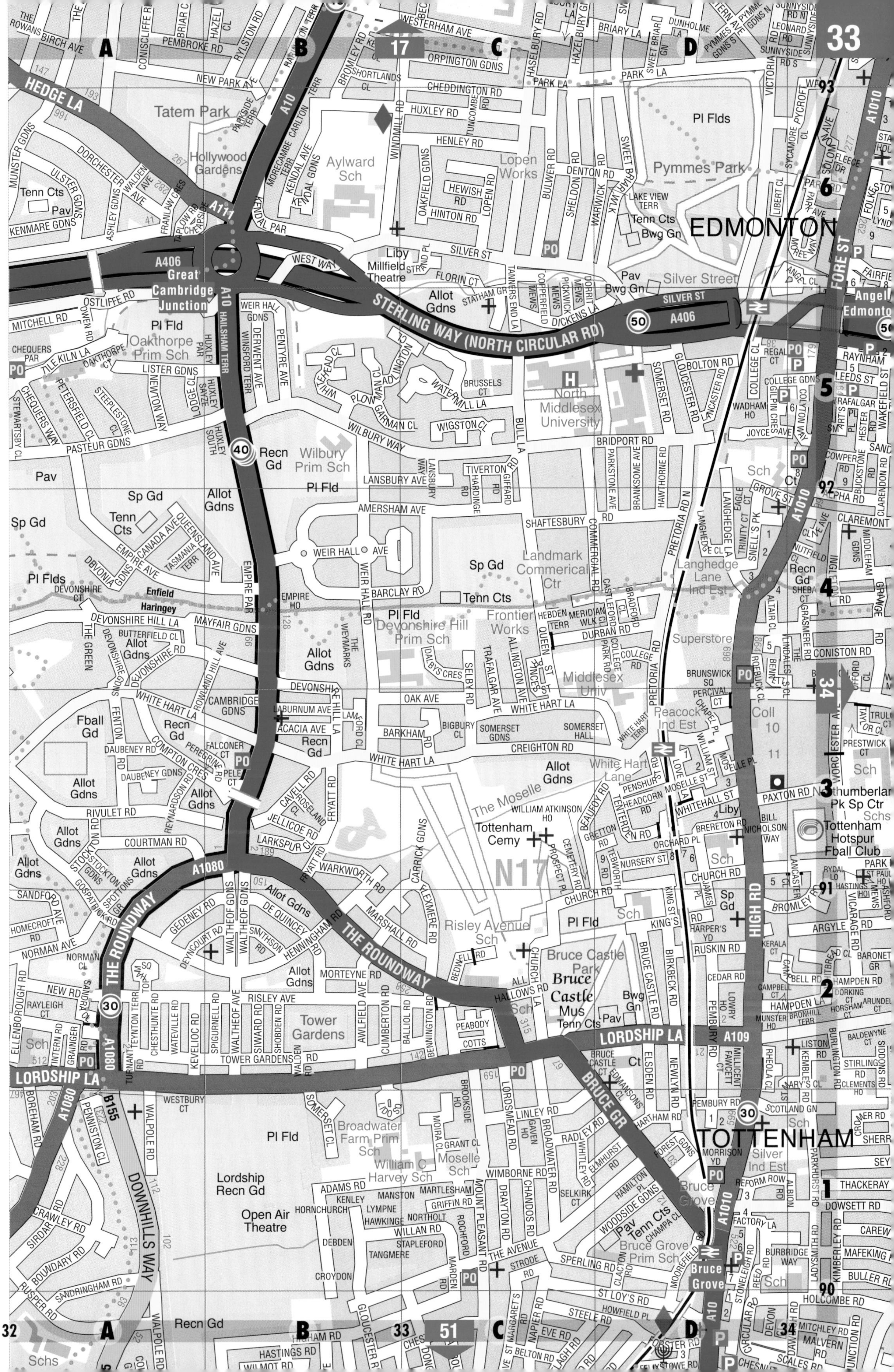
17
51
32
34
EDMONTON
TOTTENHAM
N17
Great Cambridge Junction
Tatem Park
Hollywood Gardens
Tenn Cts
Pav
Aylward Sch
Lopen Works
Pl Flds
Pymmes Park
Lake View Terr
Bwg Gn
Silver Street
Liby
Millfield Theatre
Allot Gdns
Pl Fld
Oakthorpe Prim Sch
North Middlesex University
Recn Gd
Wilbury Prim Sch
Sp Gd
Landmark Commerical Ctr
Langhedge Lane Ind Est
Enfield
Haringey
Frontier Works
Devonshire Hill Prim Sch
Superstore
Middlesex Univ
Peacock Ind Est
Coll
Fball Gd
White Hart Lane
The Moselle
Tottenham Cemy
Risley Avenue Sch
Bruce Castle Park
Bruce Castle Mus
Tottenham Hotspur Fball Club
Northumberland Pk Sp Ctr
Tower Gardens
Broadwater Farm Prim Sch
William C Harvey Sch
Moselle Sch
Lordship Recn Gd
Open Air Theatre
Bruce Grove Prim Sch
Bruce Grove
Silver Ind Est
Schs
A10
A406
A111
A1010
A1080
A109
B155
HEDGE LA
STERLING WAY (NORTH CIRCULAR RD)
SILVER ST
FORE ST
HIGH RD
THE ROUNDWAY
LORDSHIP LA
BRUCE GR
DOWNHILLS WAY
WESTERHAM AVE
ORPINGTON GDNS
PEMBROKE RD
BIRCH AVE
NEW PARK AVE
CHEDDINGTON RD
HUXLEY RD
HENLEY RD
HEWISH RD
HINTON RD
SILVER ST
PARK LA
BRIARY LA
DUNHOLME
DORCHESTER AVE
ULSTER GDNS
MUNSTER GDNS
KENMARE GDNS
WEST WAY
FLORIN CT
OSTLIFFE RD
MITCHELL RD
TILE KILN LA
LISTER GDNS
PASTEUR GDNS
BOLTON RD
BRIDPORT RD
WILBURY WAY
LANSBURY AVE
AMERSHAM AVE
WEIR HALL AVE
SHAFTESBURY
BARCLAY RD
EMPIRE AVE
DEVONSHIRE HILL LA
MAYFAIR GDNS
WHITE HART LA
OAK AVE
CREIGHTON RD
RIVULET RD
COURTMAN RD
WARKWORTH RD
CHURCH RD
RISLEY AVE
TOWER GARDENS RD
ADAMS RD
LORDSHIP LA
WIMBORNE RD
THE AVENUE
SPERLING RD
ST LOY'S RD
STEELE RD
HOLCOMBE RD
ARGYLE RD
THACKERAY
DOWSETT RD
RAYNHAM
CLAREMONT
CONISTON RD
PAXTON RD
SCOTLAND GN
PRETORIA RD N
PRETORIA RD
BULL LA
COMMERCIAL RD
HIGHAM RD
HASTINGS RD
RECN GD

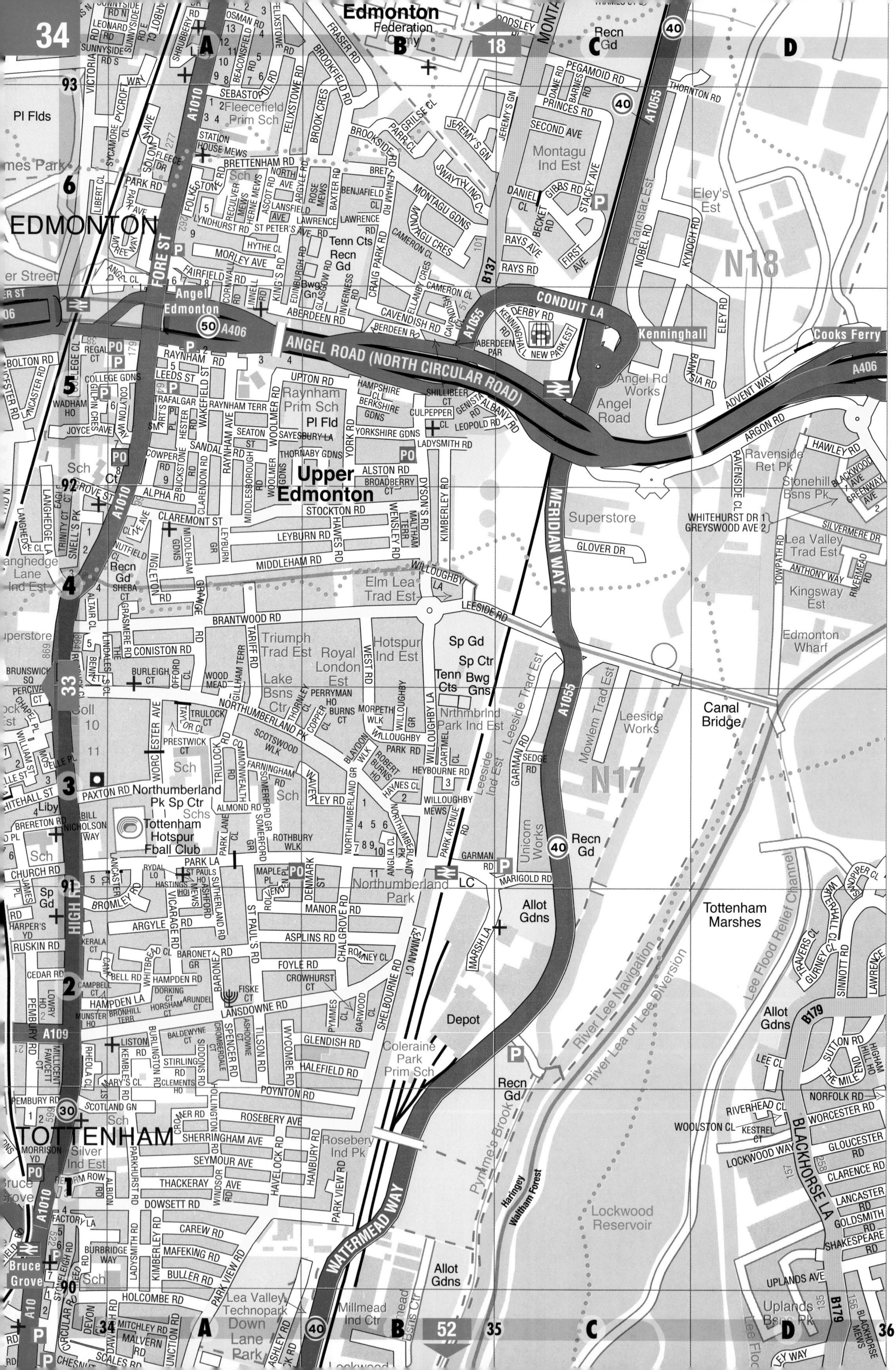

Edmonton
Federation
A
B
18
C
D
Recn Gd
PEGAMOID RD
THORNTON RD
PRINCES RD
SECOND AVE
Montagu Ind Est
Eley's Est
N18
SEBASTOPOL RD
Fleecefield Prim Sch
BRETTENHAM RD
STATION HOUSE MEWS
PYCROFT WAY
Pl Flds
EDMONTON
FORE ST
A1010
A1055
B137
JEREMY'S GN
SWAYTHLING CL
MONTAGU GDNS
MONTAGU CRES
CAMERON CL
RAYS AVE
RAYS RD
DANIEL CL
GIBBS RD
STACEY AVE
FIRST AVE
Rainstar Est
NOBEL RD
KYNOCH RD
ELEY RD
Tenn Cts
Recn Gd
Bwg Gn
CRAIG PARK RD
FAIRFIELD RD
MORLEY AVE
HYTHE CL
LYNDHURST RD
ST PETER'S AVE
LANSFIELD AVE
LAWRENCE RD
KING'S RD
ABERDEEN RD
CAVENDISH RD
BERDEEN RD
CONDUIT LA
DERBY RD
KENNINGHALL RD
NEW PARK EST
Kenninghall
Cooks Ferry
A406
ANGEL ROAD (NORTH CIRCULAR ROAD)
Angel Edmonton
50
Angel Rd Works
Angel Road
ADVENT WAY
ARGON RD
HAWLEY RD
Ravenside Ret Pk
Stonehill Bsns Pk
BLACKWOOD AVE
GREENWAY AVE
BOLTON RD
COLLEGE GDNS
RAYNHAM RD
LEEDS ST
UPTON RD
Raynham Prim Sch
HAMPSHIRE CL
BERKSHIRE GDNS
SHILLIBEER CT
CULPEPPER CL
LEOPOLD RD
ALBANY RD
Pl Fld
YORKSHIRE GDNS
LADYSMITH RD
TRAFALGAR PL
RAYNHAM TERR
SEATON ST
SAYESBURY LA
THORNABY GDNS
JOYCE AVE
WADHAM HO
COWPER RD
SANDAL RD
ALSTON RD
BROADBERRY CT
Upper Edmonton
ALPHA RD
GROVE ST
CLAREMONT ST
STOCKTON RD
MIDDLESBOROUGH RD
WOOLMER RD
YORK RD
DYSON'S RD
KIMBERLEY RD
MALTHAM TERR
WENSLEY RD
HAWES RD
LEYBURN RD
MIDDLEHAM RD
MIDDLEHAM GDNS
MERIDIAN WAY
Superstore
GLOVER DR
WHITEHURST DR
GREYSWOOD AVE
SILVERMERE DR
Lea Valley Trad Est
ANTHONY WAY
RIVERMEAD RD
TOWPATH RD
Kingsway Est
Edmonton Wharf
Recn Gd
SHEBA CT
INGLETON RD
GRANGE RD
WILLOUGHBY LA
Elm Lea Trad Est
LEESIDE RD
BRANTWOOD RD
TARIFF RD
Triumph Trad Est
Royal London Est
Hotspur Ind Est
WEST RD
Sp Gd
Sp Ctr
Tenn Cts
Bwg Gns
CONISTON RD
BURLEIGH CT
WOOD MEAD
GILLHAM TERR
Lake Bsns Ctr
PERRYMAN HO
BURNS CT
NORTHUMBERLAND PK
TRULOCK CT
TAYOR CL
PRESTWICK CT
WORCESTER AVE
SCOTSWOOD WLK
MORPETH WLK
WILLOUGHBY GR
WILLOUGHBY PARK RD
Nrthmbrlnd Park Ind Est
Leeside Ind Est
Leeside Trad Est
GARMAN RD
SEDGE RD
Mowlem Trad Est
Leeside Works
Canal Bridge
N17
Soll
33
PAXTON RD
Northumberland Pk Sp Ctr
Schs
Tottenham Hotspur Fball Club
FARNINGHAM RD
SOMERFORD GR
WAVERLEY RD
BLAYDON WLK
ROBERT BURNS HO
HEYBOURNE RD
HAWES CL
WILLOUGHBY MEWS
PARK AVENUE RD
ALMOND RD
ROTHBURY WLK
PARK LA
GARMAN RD
MARIGOLD RD
Unicorn Works
40
Recn Gd
LC
Northumberland Park
ANGLIA CL
MAPLE PL
DENMARK ST
MANOR RD
CHALGROVE RD
ASPLINS RD
ROMNEY CL
FOYLE RD
CROWHURST CT
ST PAUL'S RD
SUTHERLAND RD
VICARAGE RD
BROMLEY RD
ARGYLE RD
BARONET RD
HAMPDEN RD
FISKE CT
LANSDOWNE RD
HAMPDEN LA
BRONHILL TERR
Allot Gdns
MARSH LA
Tottenham Marshes
Depot
Lee Flood Relief Channel
River Lee Navigation
River Lea or Lee Diversion
HIGH RD
91
CHURCH RD
RUSKIN RD
CEDAR RD
A109
LISTON RD
BURLINGTON RD
STIRLING RD
CLEMENTS RD
SIDDONS RD
SPENCER RD
TILSON RD
WYCOMBE RD
GLENDISH RD
HALEFIELD RD
POYNTON RD
Coleraine Park Prim Sch
Recn Gd
Pymme's Brook
Allot Gdns
B179
SUTTON RD
THE MILE END
LEE CL
NORFOLK RD
RIVERHEAD CL
WORCESTER RD
WOOLSTON CL
KESTREL CT
LOCKWOOD WAY
GLOUCESTER RD
CLARENCE RD
BLACKHORSE LA
LANCASTER RD
GOLDSMITH RD
SHAKESPEARE RD
UPLANDS AVE
Uplands Bsns Pk
BLACKHORSE MEWS
SCOTLAND GN
ROSEBERY AVE
SHERRINGHAM AVE
SEYMOUR AVE
THACKERAY AVE
DOWSETT RD
CAREW RD
MAFEKING RD
BULLER RD
HOLCOMBE RD
Rosebery Ind Pk
HAVELOCK RD
HANBURY RD
PARK VIEW RD
WATERMEAD WAY
Haringey
Waltham Forest
Lockwood Reservoir
TOTTENHAM
Silver Ind Est
Bruce Grove
A10
Lea Valley Technopark
Down Lane Park
Millmead Ind Ctr
Allot Gdns
52
35
36
MITCHLEY RD
MALVERN RD
SCALES RD

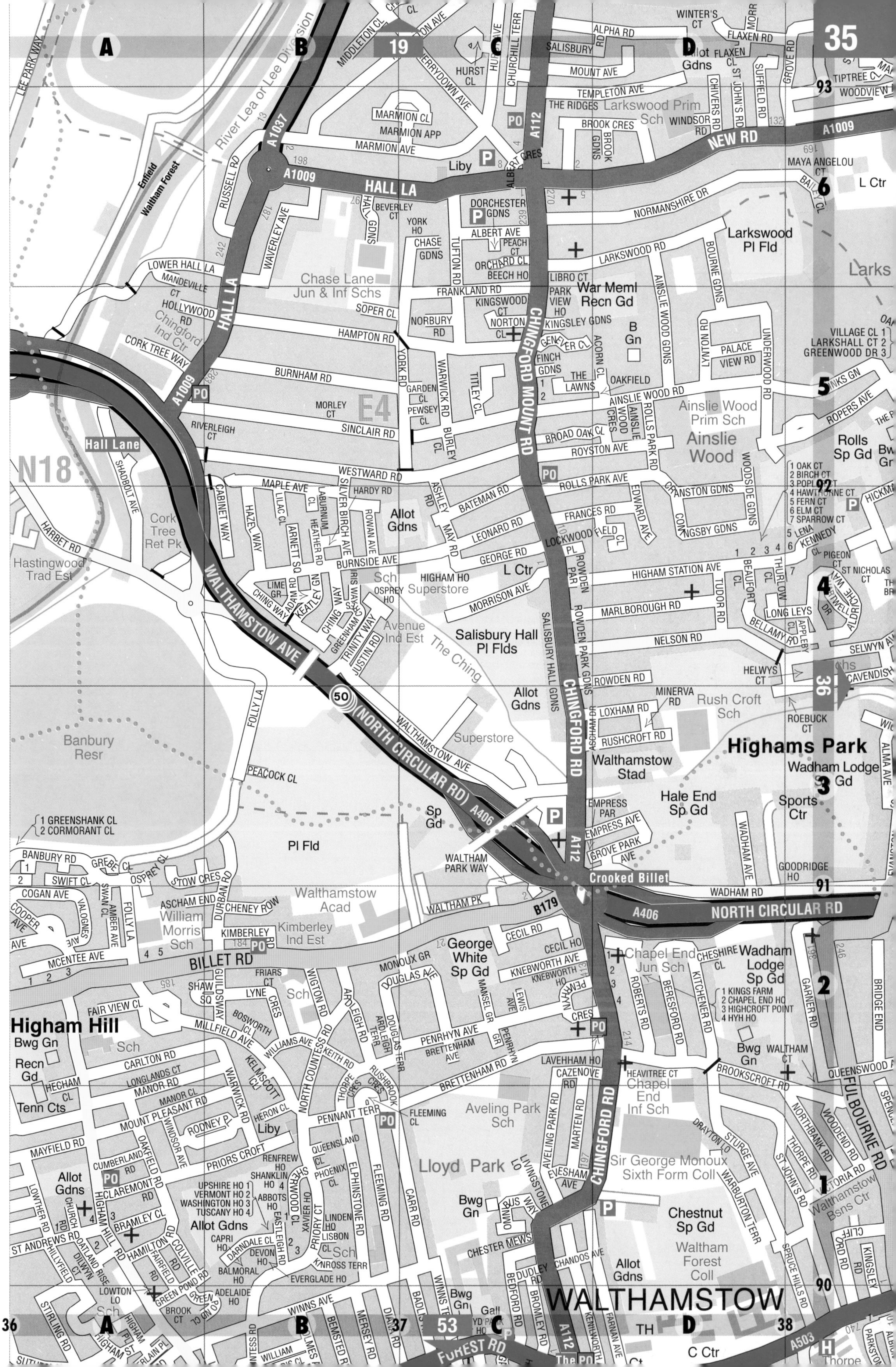
A
B
C
D
19
53
36
37
38
90
91
92
93
1
2
3
4
5
6
E4
N18
Enfield
Waltham Forest
River Lea or Lee Diversion
LEE PARK WAY
A1037
A1009
HALL LA
HALL LA
A112
NEW RD
MIDDLETON CL
MARMION CL
MARMION APP
MARMION AVE
HURST CL
CHURCHILL TERR
ALPHA RD
SALISBURY RD
MOUNT AVE
TEMPLETON AVE
THE RIDGES
Larkswood Prim Sch
BROOK CRES
BROOK GDNS
WINDSOR RD
WINTER'S CT
FLAXEN RD
FLAXEN CL
Allot Gdns
CHIVERS RD
ST JOHN'S RD
SUFFIELD RD
GROVE RD
TIPTREE CL
WOODVIEW
MAYA ANGELOU CT
BAILEY CL
L Ctr
RUSSELL RD
WAVERLEY AVE
HALL GDNS
BEVERLEY CT
YORK HO
CHASE GDNS
TUFTON RD
DORCHESTER GDNS
ALBERT AVE
ALBERT CRES
PEACH CT
ORCHARD CL
BEECH HO
Liby
NORMANSHIRE DR
Larkswood Pl Fld
LARKSWOOD RD
Larks
LOWER HALL LA
MANDEVILLE CT
HOLLYWOOD RD
Chingford Ind Ctr
CORK TREE WAY
Chase Lane Jun & Inf Schs
SOPER CL
HAMPTON RD
BURNHAM RD
YORK RD
NORBURY RD
FRANKLAND RD
KINGSWOOD CT
NORTON CL
LIBRO CT
PARK VIEW HO
War Meml Recn Gd
KINGSLEY GDNS
GENEVER CL
FINCH GDNS
THE LAWNS
ACORN CL
OAKFIELD
B Gn
AINSLIE WOOD GDNS
BOURNE GDNS
LYNTON RD
PALACE VIEW RD
UNDERWOOD RD
VILLAGE CL 1
LARKSHALL CT 2
GREENWOOD DR 3
LINKS GN
ROPERS AVE
CHINGFORD MOUNT RD
MORLEY CT
GARDEN CL
PEWSEY CL
WARWICK RD
TITLEY CL
BURLEY CL
SINCLAIR RD
RIVERLEIGH CT
Hall Lane
AINSLIE WOOD RD
AINSLIE WOOD CRES
ROLLS PARK RD
Ainslie Wood Prim Sch
Ainslie Wood
BROAD OAK CL
ROYSTON AVE
Rolls Sp Gd
WESTWARD RD
MAPLE AVE
HARDY RD
LILAC CL
LABURNUM CL
SILVER BIRCH AVE
CABINET WAY
HAZEL WAY
ARNETT SQ
HEATHER RD
ROWAN AVE
Allot Gdns
ASHLEY RD
MAY RD
BATEMAN RD
LEONARD RD
ROLLS PARK AVE
FRANCES RD
LOCKWOOD PL
FIELD CL
EDWARD AVE
CRANSTON GDNS
CONINGSBY GDNS
WOODSIDE GDNS
1 OAK CT
2 BIRCH CT
3 POPLAR CT
4 HAWTHORNE CT
5 FERN CT
6 ELM CT
7 SPARROW CT
LENA KENNEDY CL
HICKMAN
PIGEON CT
ST NICHOLAS CT
SHADBOLT AVE
Cork Tree Ret Pk
HARBET RD
Hastingwood Trad Est
BURNSIDE AVE
GEORGE RD
ROWDEN PAR
L Ctr
HIGHAM STATION AVE
TUDOR RD
BEAUFORT CL
THURLOW CL
LIME GR
CHING WAY
ADAM RD
KEATLEY GN
IRIS WAY
Sch
HIGHAM HO
Superstore
OSPREY HO
MORRISON AVE
MARLBOROUGH RD
LONG LEYS
BELLAMY RD
APPLEBY CL
NELSON RD
SELWYN AVE
WALTHAMSTOW AVE
GREENHAM CL
TRINITY WAY
JUSTIN RD
Avenue Ind Est
The Ching
Salisbury Hall Pl Flds
SALISBURY HALL GDNS
ROWDEN PARK GDNS
ROWDEN RD
HELWYS CT
CAVENDISH
Allot Gdns
MINERVA RD
Rush Croft Sch
ROEBUCK CT
50
(NORTH CIRCULAR RD)
A406
FOLLY LA
Banbury Resr
WALTHAMSTOW AVE
Superstore
LOXHAM RD
RUSHCROFT RD
ASCHAM DR
Highams Park
Wadham Lodge Sp Gd
Walthamstow Stad
CHINGFORD RD
PEACOCK CL
Sp Gd
Hale End Sp Gd
Sports Ctr
1 GREENSHANK CL
2 CORMORANT CL
Pl Fld
EMPRESS PAR
EMPRESS AVE
GROVE PARK AVE
WADHAM AVE
BANBURY RD
SWIFT CL
GREBE CL
OSPREY CL
STOW CRES
WALTHAM PARK WAY
Crooked Billet
GOODRIDGE HO
WADHAM RD
COGAN AVE
VALOGNES AVE
SWAN CL
COOPER AVE
AMBER AVE
FOLLY LA
ASCHAM END
DURBAN RD
CHENEY ROW
William Morris Sch
Walthamstow Acad
WALTHAM PK
B179
NORTH CIRCULAR RD
KIMBERLEY RD
Kimberley Ind Est
George White Sp Gd
CECIL RD
CECIL HO
MCENTEE AVE
BILLET RD
FRIARS CT
MONOUX GR
DOUGLAS AVE
KNEBWORTH AVE
KNEBWORTH HO
Chapel End Jun Sch
CHESHIRE CL
Wadham Lodge Sp Gd
SHAW SQ
GUILDSWAY
LYNE CRES
WIGTON RD
ARDLEIGH RD
MANSEL GR
LEWIS AVE
ROBERTS RD
BERESFORD RD
KITCHENER RD
1 KINGS FARM
2 CHAPEL END HO
3 HIGHCROFT POINT
4 HYH HO
GARNER RD
BRIDGE END
FAIR VIEW CL
MILLFIELD AVE
BOSWORTH CL
WILLIAMS AVE
Higham Hill
Bwg Gn
Sch
Recn Gd
HECHAM CL
Tenn Cts
CARLTON RD
LONGLANDS CT
MANOR RD
MANOR CL
MOUNT PLEASANT RD
KELMSCOTT CL
NORTH COUNTESS RD
KEITH RD
ARDLEIGH TERR
DOUGLAS TERR
PENRHYN AVE
BRETTENHAM AVE
PENRHYN GR
CRES
LAVEHHAM HO
CAZENOVE RD
HEAVITREE CT
Bwg Gn
WALTHAM CT
BROOKSCROFT RD
QUEENSWOOD
FULBOURNE RD
THORPE CRES
RUSHBROOK CRES
BRETTENHAM RD
Chapel End Inf Sch
DRAYTON LO
STURGE AVE
NORTHBANK RD
WOODEND RD
WARWICK RD
RODNEY PL
HERON CL
Liby
PENNANT TERR
FLEEMING CL
Aveling Park Sch
AVELING PARK RD
MARTEN RD
MAYFIELD RD
CUMBERLAND RD
WINDSOR AVE
PRIORS CROFT
OAKFIELD RD
RENFREW HO
SHANKLIN HO
QUEENSLAND AVE
PHOENIX CL
ELPHINSTONE RD
FLEEMING RD
Lloyd Park
LIVINGSTONE LO
EVESHAM AVE
Sir George Monoux Sixth Form Coll
WARBURTON TERR
THORPE RD
ST JOHN'S RD
VICTORIA RD
Walthamstow Bsns Ctr
Allot Gdns
CLAREMONT RD
UPSHIRE HO 1
VERMONT HO 2
WASHINGTON HO 3
TUSCANY HO 4
ABBOTS HO
HERWOOD CL
XAVIER HO
PRIORY CT
LINDEN HO
LISBON CL
CARR RD
Bwg Gn
OMNIBUS WAY
Chestnut Sp Gd
LOWTHER RD
CHURCH HILL RD
BRAMLEY CL
HAMILTON RD
COLVILLE RD
FAIRFIELD RD
ST ANDREWS RD
HILLYFIELD
OATLAND RISE
DILWYN CL
CAPRI HO
DARNDALE CL
DEVON HO
EASTLEIGH RD
Sch
KINROSS TERR
CHESTER MEWS
CHANDOS AVE
Waltham Forest Coll
SPRUCE HILLS RD
CLIFF
KINGSLEY
BALMORAL HO
EVERGLADE HO
LOWTON LO
GREEN POND RD
ADELAIDE HO
BROOK CT
Sch
Allot Gdns
DUDLEY RD
BEDFORD RD
BROMLEY RD
Bwg Gn
WALTHAMSTOW
STIRLING RD
HIGHAM ST
WINNS AVE
BEMSTED RD
MERSEY RD
DIANA RD
BADLIS RD
WINNS TERR
FOREST RD
Gall
KENILWORTH
FARNAN AVE
TH
C Ctr
A503
PARKSTONE
Thorpe
WILLIAM

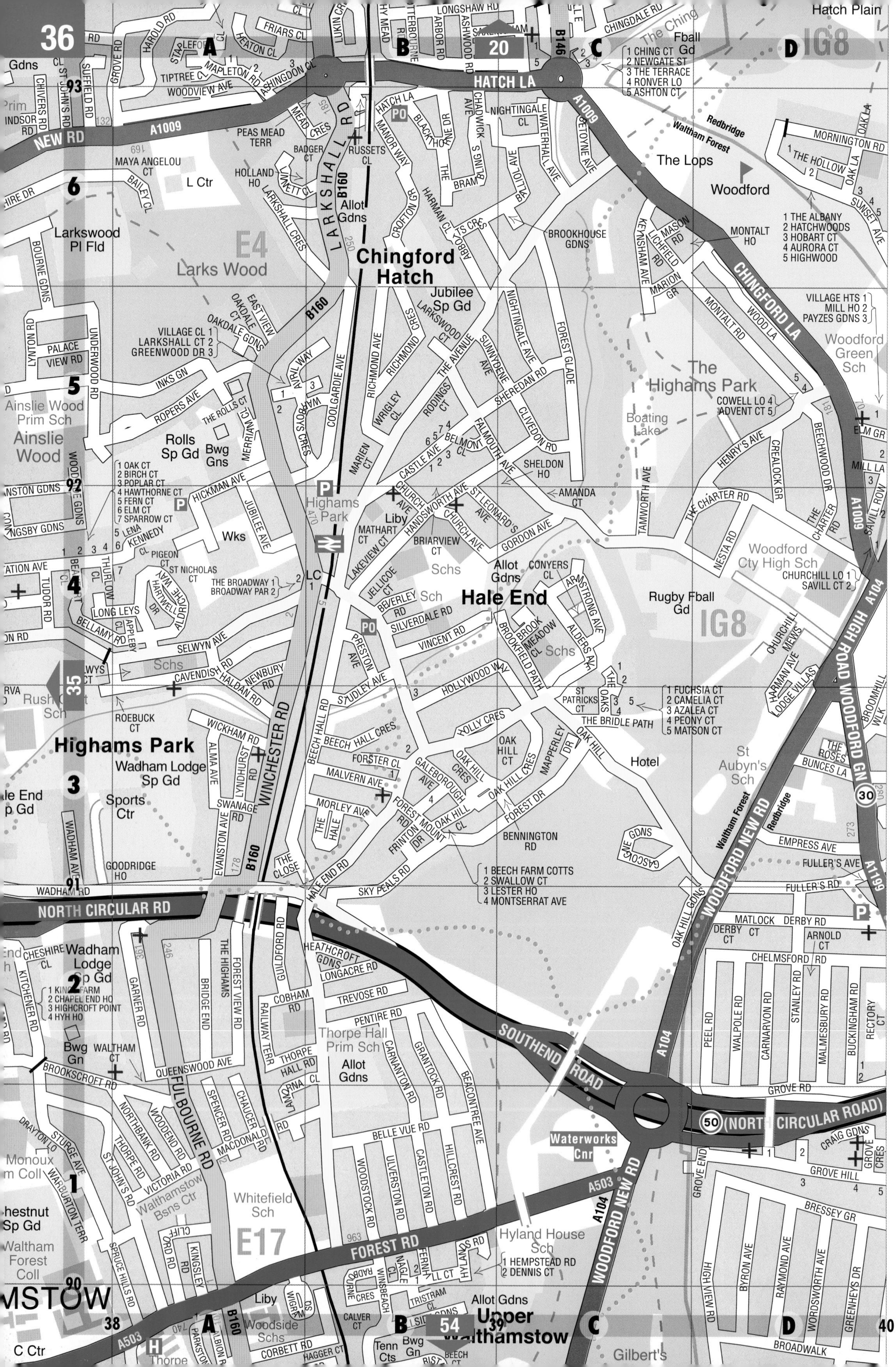
Hatch Plain
IG8
LONGSHAW RD
CHINGDALE RD
The Ching
Fball Gd
1 CHING CT
2 NEWGATE ST
3 THE TERRACE
4 RONVER LO
5 ASHTON CT
HAROLD RD
FRIARS CL
HEATON CL
GROVE RD
MAPLETON RD
ASHINGDON CL
TIPTREE C
WOODVIEW AVE
SUFFIELD RD
ST JOHN'S RD
CHIVERS RD
Gdns
Prim
NEW RD
A1009
HATCH LA
B146
20
LUKIN CR
HY MEAD
ARBOR RD
ASHWOOD RD
PEAS MEAD TERR
MEAD CRES
BADGER CT
RUSSETS CL
HATCH LA
PO
MANOR WAY
BLACKTHORNE DR
CHADWICK AVE
NIGHTINGALE CL
WATERHALL AVE
BETOYNE AVE
Redbridge
Waltham Forest
The Lops
Woodford
MORNINGTON RD
THE HOLLOW
OAK LA
SUNSET AVE
1 THE ALBANY
2 HATCHWOODS
3 HOBART CT
4 AURORA CT
5 HIGHWOOD
MAYA ANGELOU CT
BAILEY CL
L Ctr
HOLLAND HO
LINNETT CL
LARKSHALL CRES
LARKSHALL RD
B160
Allot Gdns
CROFTON GR
HARMAN CL
THE BRAMBLINGS
BALLIOL AVE
ABBOTTS CRES
BROOKHOUSE GDNS
KEYNSHAM AVE
LICHFIELD RD
MASON RD
MONTALT HO
CHINGFORD LA
Larkswood Pl Fld
E4
Larks Wood
Chingford Hatch
Jubilee Sp Gd
MARION GR
MONTALT RD
WOOD LA
VILLAGE HTS 1
MILL HO 2
PAYZES GDNS 3
Woodford Green Sch
BOURNE GDNS
LYNTON RD
PALACE VIEW RD
UNDERWOOD RD
OAKDALE CT
EAST VIEW
OAKDALE GDNS
VILLAGE CL 1
LARKSHALL CT 2
GREENWOOD DR 3
AVRIL WAY
WARBOYS CRES
COOLGARDIE AVE
RICHMOND AVE
RICHMOND CRES
LARKSWOOD CT
THE AVENUE
SUNNYDENE AVE
NIGHTINGALE AVE
FOREST GLADE
The Highams Park
COWELL LO 4
ADVENT CT 5
INKS GN
ROPERS AVE
THE ROLLS CT
MERRIAM CL
Ainslie Wood Prim Sch
Ainslie Wood
Rolls Sp Gd
Bwg Gns
WRIGLEY CL
RODINGS CT
SHEREDAN RD
CLIVEDON RD
Boating Lake
HENRY'S AVE
CREALOCK GR
BEECHWOOD DR
ELM GR
MILL LA
SAVILL ROW
1 OAK CT
2 BIRCH CT
3 POPLAR CT
4 HAWTHORNE CT
5 FERN CT
6 ELM CT
7 SPARROW CT
HICKMAN AVE
JUBILEE AVE
P
Higham's Park
MARIEN CT
CASTLE AVE
BELMONT CL
FALMOUTH AVE
SHELDON HO
AMANDA CT
TAMWORTH AVE
THE CHARTER RD
THE CHARTER RD
A1009
WOODLE GDNS
NGSBY GDNS
LENA KENNEDY CL
Wks
CHURCH AVE
HANDSWORTH AVE
ST LEONARD'S AVE
CHURCH AVE
GORDON AVE
NESTA RD
Woodford Cty High Sch
CHURCHILL LO 1
SAVILL CT 2
A104
PIGEON CT
ST NICHOLAS CT
ALDRICH WAY
HARTWELL DR
THURLOW
TUDOR RD
BEAUFORT CL
LONG LEYS
APPLEBY CL
BELLAMY RD
THE BROADWAY 1
BROADWAY PAR 2
LC
MATHART CT
LAKEVIEW CT
BRIARVIEW CT
Schs
Allot Gdns
CONYERS CL
ARMSTRONG AVE
Hale End
Rugby Fball Gd
IG8
JELLICOE CT
BEVERLEY RD
Sch
SILVERDALE RD
VINCENT RD
PRESTON AVE
BROOK MEADOW CL
BROOKFIELD PATH
ALDERS AVE
Schs
CHURCHILL MEWS
HARMAN AVE
LODGE VILLAS
HIGH ROAD WOODFORD GN
BROOMHILL WLK
SELWYN AVE
Schs
CAVENDISH RD
HALDAN RD
NEWBURY RD
35
Rush Croft Sch
ROEBUCK CT
STUDLEY AVE
HOLLYWOOD WAY
ST PATRICKS CT
THE OAKS
1 FUCHSIA CT
2 CAMELIA CT
3 AZALEA CT
4 PEONY CT
5 MATSON CT
THE BRIDLE PATH
OAK HILL
Highams Park
WICKHAM RD
ALMA AVE
LYNDHURST RD
WINCHESTER RD
BEECH HALL RD
BEECH HALL CRES
HOLLY CRES
OAK HILL CT
MAPPERLEY DR
Hotel
St Aubyn's Sch
THE ROSES
BUNCES LA
30
Wadham Lodge Sp Gd
Sports Ctr
SWANAGE RD
FORSTER CL
MALVERN AVE
GALEBOROUGH AVE
OAK HILL CRES
FOREST DR
WOODFORD NEW RD
Redbridge
Waltham Forest
EVANSTON AVE
MORLEY AVE
THE HALE
FOREST MOUNT RD
OAK HILL CL
FRINTON DR
BENNINGTON RD
GASCOYNE GDNS
EMPRESS AVE
FULLER'S AVE
A1199
WADHAM AVE
GOODRIDGE HO
B160
THE CLOSE
HALE END RD
SKY PEALS RD
1 BEECH FARM COTTS
2 SWALLOW CT
3 LESTER HO
4 MONTSERRAT AVE
OAK HILL GDNS
FULLER'S RD
WADHAM RD
NORTH CIRCULAR RD
MATLOCK CT
DERBY RD
DERBY CT
ARNOLD CT
P
CHESHIRE CL
Wadham Lodge Sp Gd
KITCHENER RD
1 KING FARM
2 CHAPEL END HO
3 HIGHCROFT POINT
4 HYH HO
GARNER RD
BRIDGE END
THE HIGHAMS
FOREST VIEW RD
GUILDFORD RD
HEATHCROFT GDNS
LONGACRE RD
TREVOSE RD
COBHAM RD
PENTIRE RD
RAILWAY TERR
Thorpe Hall Prim Sch
SOUTHEND ROAD
CHELMSFORD RD
PEEL RD
WALPOLE RD
CARNARVON RD
STANLEY RD
MALMESBURY RD
BUCKINGHAM RD
RECTORY CT
Bwg Gn
WALTHAM CT
BROOKSCROFT RD
QUEENSWOOD AVE
FULBOURNE RD
THORPE HALL RD
Allot Gdns
CARNANTON RD
GRANTOCK RD
BEACONTREE AVE
LANCASTER CL
A104
GROVE RD
50
(NORTH CIRCULAR ROAD)
NORTHBANK RD
WOODEND RD
SPENCER RD
CHAUCER RD
MACDONALD RD
DRAYTON RD
STURGE AVE
Monoux Coll
BELLE VUE RD
Waterworks Cnr
CRAIG GDNS
GROVE CRES
GROVE END
GROVE HILL
THORPE RD
ST JOHN'S RD
VICTORIA RD
Walthamstow Bsns Ctr
WARBURTON TERR
Whitefield Sch
WOODSTOCK RD
ULVERSTON RD
CASTLETON RD
HILLCREST RD
A503
WOODFORD NEW RD
A104
BRESSEY GR
Chestnut Sp Gd
Waltham Forest Coll
SPRUCE HILLS RD
CLIFFORD RD
KINGSLEY RD
E17
FOREST RD
HYLANDS RD
Hyland House Sch
1 HEMPSTEAD RD
2 DENNIS CT
BYRON AVE
RAYMOND AVE
WORDSWORTH AVE
GREENHEYS DR
HIGH VIEW RD
MSTOW
Liby
WIGRAM
TRISTRAM CL
Allot Gdns
Upper Walthamstow
38
A
B
C
D
54
39
40
A503
B160
Woodside Schs
CALVER CT
CORBETT RD
HAGGER CT
Tenn Cts
Bwg Gn
BROADWALK
Gilbert's
C Ctr
H
Thorpe

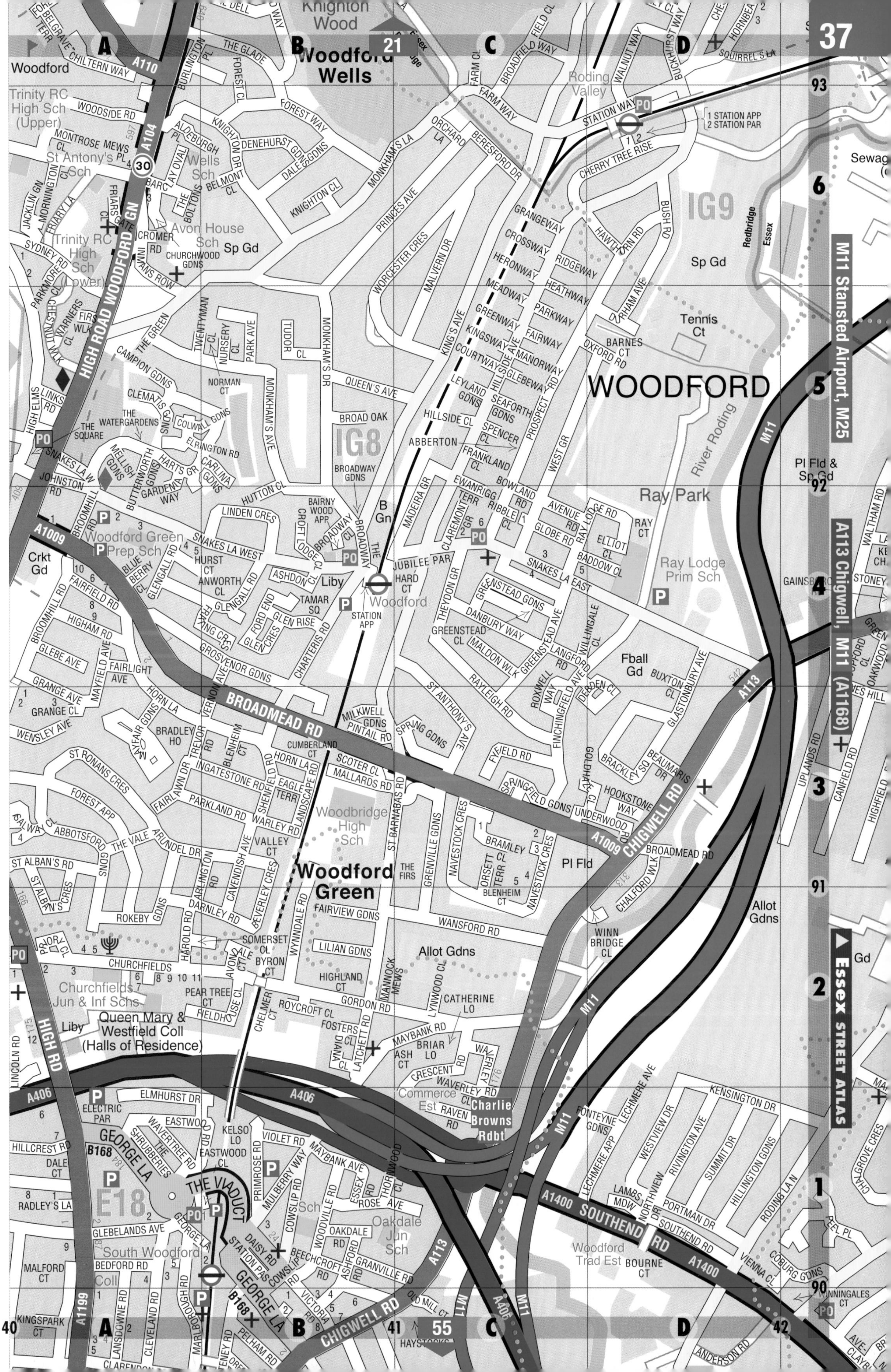

Woodford Wells
Knighton Wood
21
WOODFORD
Woodford Green
Woodford
Roding Valley
Ray Park
River Roding
IG8
IG9
E18
South Woodford
Trinity RC High Sch (Upper)
Trinity RC High Sch (Lower)
St Antony's Sch
Wells Sch
Avon House Sch
Woodford Green Prep Sch
Woodbridge High Sch
Ray Lodge Prim Sch
Churchfields Jun & Inf Schs
Queen Mary & Westfield Coll (Halls of Residence)
Oakdale Jun Sch
Woodford Trad Est
Commerce Est
Charlie Browns Rdbt
Allot Gdns
Pl Fld
Pl Fld & Sp Gd
Fball Gd
Tennis Ct
Sp Gd
Crkt Gd
Liby
Sewag
HIGH ROAD WOODFORD GN
HIGH RD
BROADMEAD RD
CHIGWELL RD
SOUTHEND RD
GEORGE LA
THE VIADUCT
SNAKES LA EAST
SNAKES LA WEST
SNAKES LA W
PRINCES AVE
MONKHAM'S LA
MONKHAM'S DR
MONKHAM'S AVE
KING'S AVE
MALVERN DR
WORCESTER CRES
BROADWAY
THE BROADWAY
GRANGEWAY
CROSSWAY
HERONWAY
MEADWAY
GREENWAY
KINGSWAY
COURTWAY
RIDGEWAY
HEATHWAY
PARKWAY
FAIRWAY
MANORWAY
GLEBEWAY
HILLSIDE AVE
PROSPECT RD
WEST GR
OXFORD RD
BUSH RD
HAWTHORN RD
CHERRY TREE RISE
STATION WAY
BERESFORD DR
FARM WAY
BROADFIELD WAY
FOREST WAY
KNIGHTON DR
KNIGHTON CL
DENEHURST GDNS
DALE GDNS
BELMONT CL
THE BOLTONS
CHILTERN WAY
WOODSIDE RD
MONTROSE MEWS
ALDEBURGH PL
FRIARS CL
CHURCHWOOD GDNS
CROMER RD
THE GREEN
CAMPION GDNS
CLEMATIS GDNS
COLWALL GDNS
ELRINGTON RD
CARLINA GDNS
HARTS GR
BUTTERWORTH GDNS
MELLISH GDNS
THE WATERGARDENS
THE SQUARE
JOHNSTON RD
BROOMHILL RD
HUTTON CL
LINDEN CRES
TWENTYMAN CL
NURSERY CL
PARK AVE
TUDOR CL
NORMAN CT
QUEEN'S AVE
BROAD OAK
BROADWAY GDNS
BAIRNY WOOD APP
CROFT LODGE CL
JUBILEE PAR
HARD CT
STATION APP
ASHDON CL
TAMAR SQ
GLEN RISE
GLEN CRES
FORD END
GLENGALL RD
ANWORTH CL
HURST CT
FAIRFIELD RD
HIGHAM RD
GLEBE AVE
FAIRLIGHT AVE
GRANGE AVE
GRANGE CL
WENSLEY AVE
GROSVENOR GDNS
CHARTERIS RD
HORN LA
MAYFAIR GDNS
BRADLEY HO
VERNON AVE
TREVOR RD
BLENHEIM CT
MILKWELL GDNS
PINTAIL RD
CUMBERLAND CT
SCOTER CL
MALLARDS RD
EAGLE TERR
LANDSCAPE RD
SHENFIELD RD
INGATESTONE RD
PARKLAND RD
WARLEY RD
VALLEY CT
ST RONANS CRES
FOREST APP
ABBOTSFORD GDNS
THE VALE
ARUNDEL DR
ST ALBAN'S RD
ST ALBAN'S CRES
CAVENDISH AVE
BEVERLEY CRES
ARLINGTON RD
DARNLEY RD
ROKEBY GDNS
PRIORY CL
CHURCHFIELDS
HAROLD RD
SOMERSET CL
BYRON CT
PEAR TREE CT
FIELDHOUSE CL
AVONDALE CT
CHELMER CT
WYNNDALE RD
FAIRVIEW GDNS
LILIAN GDNS
HIGHLAND CT
ROYCROFT CL
GORDON RD
FOSTERS CL
DIANA CL
LATCHETT RD
MANNOCK MEWS
LYNWOOD CL
CATHERINE LO
MAYBANK RD
BRIAR LO
ASH CT
CRESCENT RD
WAVERLEY RD
RAVEN RD
ST BARNABAS RD
THE FIRS
GRENVILLE GDNS
NAVESTOCK CRES
BRAMLEY CL
ORSETT TERR
BLENHEIM CT
WANSFORD RD
SPRING GDNS
ST ANTHONY'S AVE
RAYLEIGH RD
FYFIELD RD
SPRINGFIELD GDNS
UNDERWOOD RD
HOOKSTONE WAY
BRACKLEY SQ
BEAUMARIS DR
GLASTONBURY AVE
BUXTON CL
DEBDEN CL
FINCHINGFIELD AVE
ROXWELL WAY
LANGFORD RD
WILLINGALE CL
GREENSTEAD AVE
GREENSTEAD GDNS
GREENSTEAD CL
MALDON WLK
DANBURY WAY
THEYDON GR
CLAREMONT GR
EWANRIGG TERR
RIBBLE CL
BOWLAND RD
FRANKLAND CL
ABBERTON
SPENCER CL
SEAFORTH GDNS
LEYLAND GDNS
HILLSIDE CL
MADEIRA GR
AVENUE RD
GLOBE RD
RAY LODGE RD
ELLIOT CL
BADDOW CL
RAY CT
BARNES CT
CHALFORD WLK
WINN BRIDGE CL
ELMHURST DR
ELECTRIC PAR
EASTWOOD RD
EASTWOOD CL
KELSO LO
VIOLET RD
PRIMROSE RD
MULBERRY WAY
MAYBANK AVE
ESSEX RD
ROSE AVE
THORNWOOD CL
WOODVILLE RD
OAKDALE RD
ASHFORD RD
GRANVILLE RD
BEECHCROFT RD
COWSLIP RD
DAISY RD
STATION PAS
VICTORIA RD
SHRUBBERIES
WAVERTREE RD
HILLCREST RD
DALE CT
RADLEY'S LA
GLEBELANDS AVE
BEDFORD RD
MALFORD CT
KINGSPARK CT
LANSDOWNE RD
CLEVELAND RD
MARLBOROUGH RD
PELHAM RD
LINCOLN RD
FONTEYNE GDNS
LECHMERE AVE
LECHMERE APP
WESTVIEW DR
RIVINGTON AVE
SUMMIT DR
HILLINGTON GDNS
KENSINGTON DR
RODING LA N
LAMBS MDW
NORTHVIEW DR
PORTMAN DR
SOUTHEND RD
BOURNE CT
VIENNA CL
COBURG GDNS
UPLANDS RD
CANFIELD RD
HIGHFIELD RD
WALTHAM RD
GAINSBOROUGH
STONEY
OAKWOOD
OLD MILL CT
HAYSTOCKS
55
41
40
42
93
92
91
90
A
B
C
D
1
2
3
4
5
6
A110
A104
A1009
A113
A406
A1400
A1199
B168
M11
M11 Stansted Airport, M25
A113 Chigwell, M11 (A1168)
Essex STREET ATLAS
Redbridge
Essex
1 STATION APP
2 STATION PAR

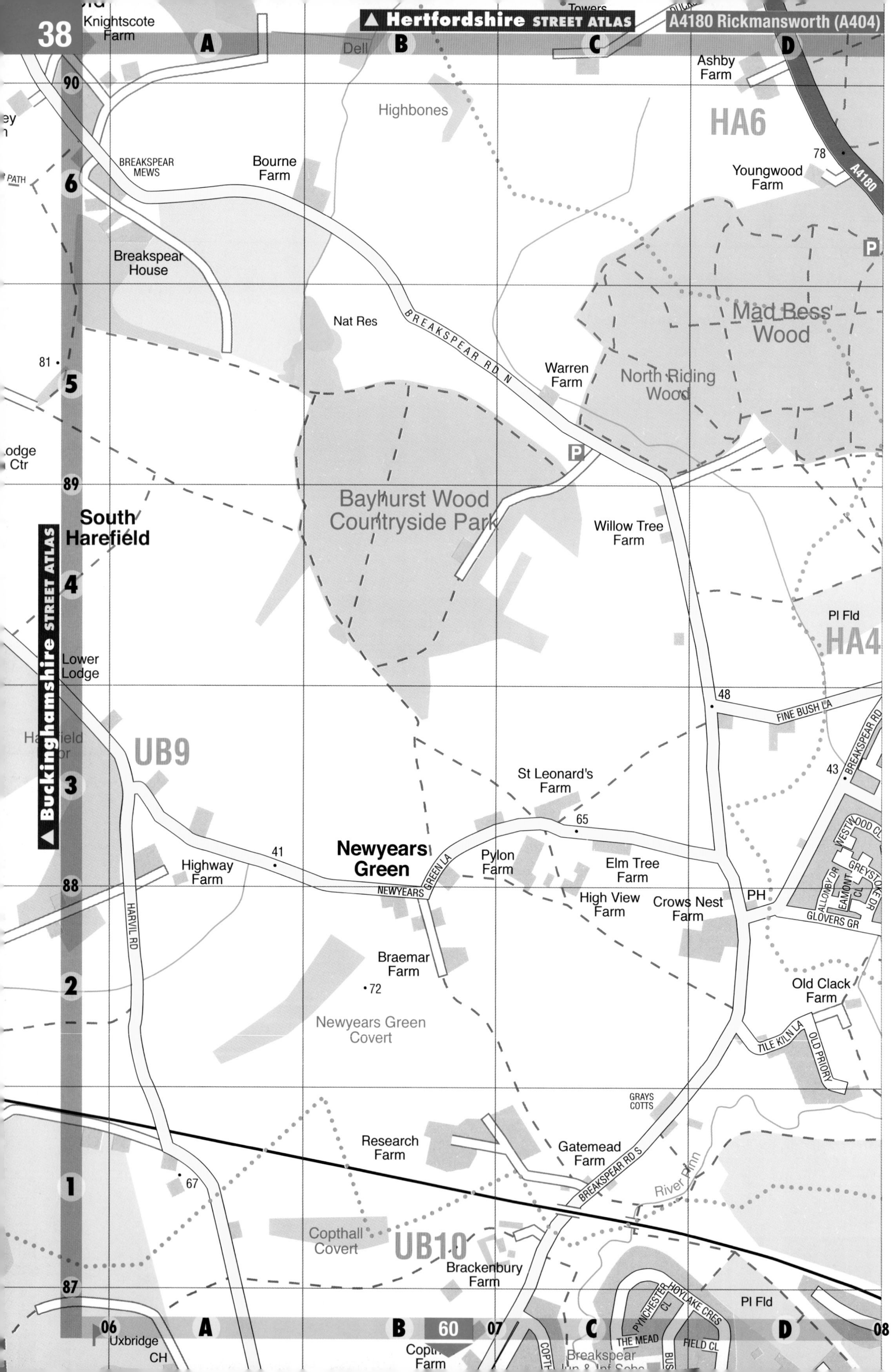
A
B
C
D
Knightscote Farm
Dell
Towers
Ashby Farm
90
Highbones
HA6
78
A4180
Youngwood Farm
BREAKSPEAR MEWS
PATH
Bourne Farm
6
Breakspear House
P
Nat Res
Mad Bess Wood
BREAKSPEAR RD N
81
5
Warren Farm
North Riding Wood
Lodge Ctr
P
89
Bayhurst Wood Countryside Park
South Harefield
Willow Tree Farm
4
Pl Fld
HA4
Lower Lodge
48
FINE BUSH LA
UB9
BREAKSPEAR RD
43
3
St Leonard's Farm
65
WESTWOOD CL
41
Newyears Green
GREEN LA
Pylon Farm
Elm Tree Farm
GREYSTOKE DR
Highway Farm
88
NEWYEARS
High View Farm
Crows Nest Farm
PH
ALLONBY DR
EAMONT CL
GLOVERS GR
HARVIL RD
Braemar Farm
2
72
Old Clack Farm
Newyears Green Covert
TILE KILN LA
OLD PRIORY
GRAYS COTTS
Research Farm
Gatemead Farm
BREAKSPEAR RD S
1
67
River Pinn
Copthall Covert
UB10
Brackenbury Farm
87
PYNCHESTER CL
HOYLAKE CRES
Pl Fld
06
A
B
60
07
C
D
08
THE MEAD
FIELD CL
Uxbridge CH
Copthall Farm
Breakspear
Buckinghamshire STREET ATLAS

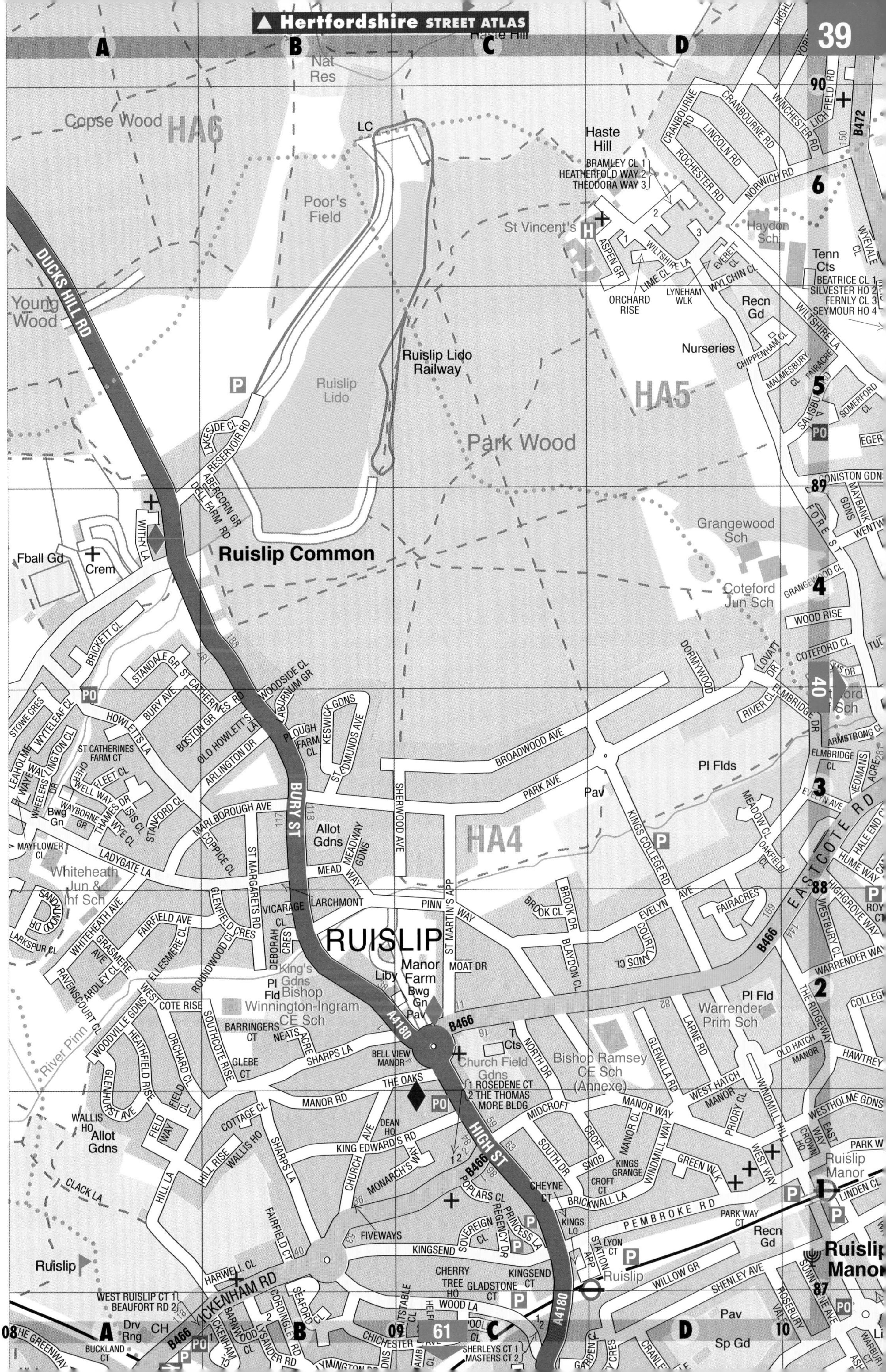
A
B
C
D
Haste Hill
Nat Res
Copse Wood
HA6
LC
Poor's Field
Haste Hill
BRAMLEY CL 1
HEATHERFOLD WAY 2
THEODORA WAY 3
CRANBOURNE RD
LINCOLN RD
ROCHESTER RD
WINCHESTER RD
LICHFIELD RD
NORWICH RD
B472
90
6
St Vincent's
ASPEN GR
WILTSHIRE LA
LIME CL
EVERETT CL
WYLCHIN CL
ORCHARD RISE
LYNEHAM WLK
Haydon Sch
Tenn Cts
BEATRICE CL 1
SILVESTER HO 2
FERNLY CL 3
SEYMOUR HO 4
Recn Gd
DUCKS HILL RD
Young Wood
Ruislip Lido
Ruislip Lido Railway
Nurseries
CHIPPENHAM CL
MALMESBURY CL
FAIRACRE
SALISBURY RD
SOMERFORD CL
HA5
5
PO
EGERTON
Park Wood
LAKESIDE CL
RESERVOIR RD
ABERCORN GR
DELL FARM RD
WITHY LA
CONISTON GDNS
89
MAYBANK GDNS
FORE ST
WENTWORTH
Grangewood Sch
Fball Gd
Crem
Ruislip Common
Coteford Jun Sch
GRANGEWOOD CL
4
WOOD RISE
COTEFORD CL
BRICKETT CL
STANDALE GR
ST CATHERINES RD
WOODSIDE CL
LABURNUM GR
DORMYWOOD
LOVATT DR
RIVER CL
ELMBRIDGE DR
40
PO
HOWLETTS LA
BURY AVE
BOSTON GR
OLD HOWLETTS LA
ARLINGTON DR
PLOUGH FARM CL
KESWICK GDNS
ST EDMUNDS AVE
BROADWOOD AVE
ARMSTRONG CL
ELMBRIDGE CL
YEOMANS ACRE
STOWE CRES
WYTELEAF CL
LEAHOLME WAYE
WHEELERS DR
ST CATHERINES FARM CT
FLEET CL
CHELWELL WAY
THAMES DR
ISIS CL
WYE CL
WAYBORNE GR
Bwg Gn
STANFORD CL
MARLBOROUGH AVE
BURY ST
SHERWOOD AVE
PARK AVE
Pav
KINGS COLLEGE RD
Pl Flds
MEADOW CL
3
EVELYN AVE
EASTCOTE RD
HALE END CL
HUME WAY
MAYFLOWER CL
LADYGATE LA
COPPICE CL
ST MARGARETS RD
Allot Gdns
MEADWAY GDNS
MEAD WAY
HA4
OAKFIELD CL
Whiteheath Jun & Inf Sch
SANDALWOOD DR
LARKSPUR CL
WHITEHEATH AVE
FAIRFIELD AVE
GRASMERE AVE
ELLESMERE CL
GLENFIELD CRES
VICARAGE CL
LARCHMONT
PINN WAY
ST MARTIN'S APP
BROOK CL
BROOK DR
EVELYN AVE
FAIRACRES
COURTLANDS CL
88
HIGHGROVE WAY
WESTBURY CL
B466
RAVENSCOURT CL
ARDLEY CL
ROUNDWOOD CL
DEBORAH CRES
RUISLIP
King's Gdns
Manor Farm
Liby
Bwg Gn
Pav
MOAT DR
BLAYDON CL
WARRENDER WAY
2
THE RIDGEWAY
COLLEGE
WOODVILLE GDNS
WEST END RD
COTE RISE
HEATHFIELD RISE
ORCHARD CL
SOUTHCOTE RISE
Pl Fld
Bishop Winnington-Ingram CE Sch
BARRINGERS CT
NEATS ACRE
SHARPS LA
A4180
B466
T Cts
Church Field Gdns
NORTH DR
Bishop Ramsey CE Sch (Annexe)
Pl Fld
Warrender Prim Sch
LARNE RD
GLENALLA RD
OLD HATCH MANOR
HAWTREY
River Pinn
GLENHURST AVE
FIELD CL
GLEBE CT
BELL VIEW MANOR
THE OAKS
1 ROSEDENE CT
2 THE THOMAS MORE BLDG
MIDCROFT
MANOR WAY
WEST HATCH MANOR
PRIORY CL
WINDMILL HILL
WESTHOLME GDNS
WALLIS HO
Allot Gdns
FIELD WAY
COTTAGE CL
MANOR RD
PO
DEAN HO
HIGH ST
SOUTH DR
CROFT GDNS
MANOR CL
KINGS GRANGE
WINDMILL WAY
GREEN WLK
WEST WAY
EAST WAY
CROWN HO
PARK W
Ruislip Manor
HILL RISE
WALLIS HO
SHARPS LA
CHURCH AVE
KING EDWARD'S RD
MONARCH'S WAY
CHEYNE CT
CROFT CT
BRICKWALL LA
CLACK LA
HILL LA
FAIRFIELD CT
POPLARS CL
SOVEREIGN CL
REGENCY DR
PRINCESS LA
FIVEWAYS
KINGS LO
STATION APP
PEMBROKE RD
PARK WAY CT
Recn Gd
LINDEN CL
1
Ruislip
KINGSEND
LYON CT
Ruislip
WILLOW GR
SHENLEY AVE
ROSEBURY VALE
SUNNINGDALE AVE
Ruislip Manor
87
CHERRY TREE HO
GLADSTONE CT
KINGSEND CT
HARWELL CL
WEST RUISLIP CT 1
BEAUFORT RD 2
ICKENHAM RD
CORDINGLEY RD
SEAFORD CL
WOOD LA
Pav
Sp Gd
08
Drv Rng
CH
THE GREENWAY
BUCKLAND CT
BARNWOOD CL
LYSANDER RD
CHICHESTER AVE
09
61
SHERLEYS CT 1
MASTERS CT 2
D
10

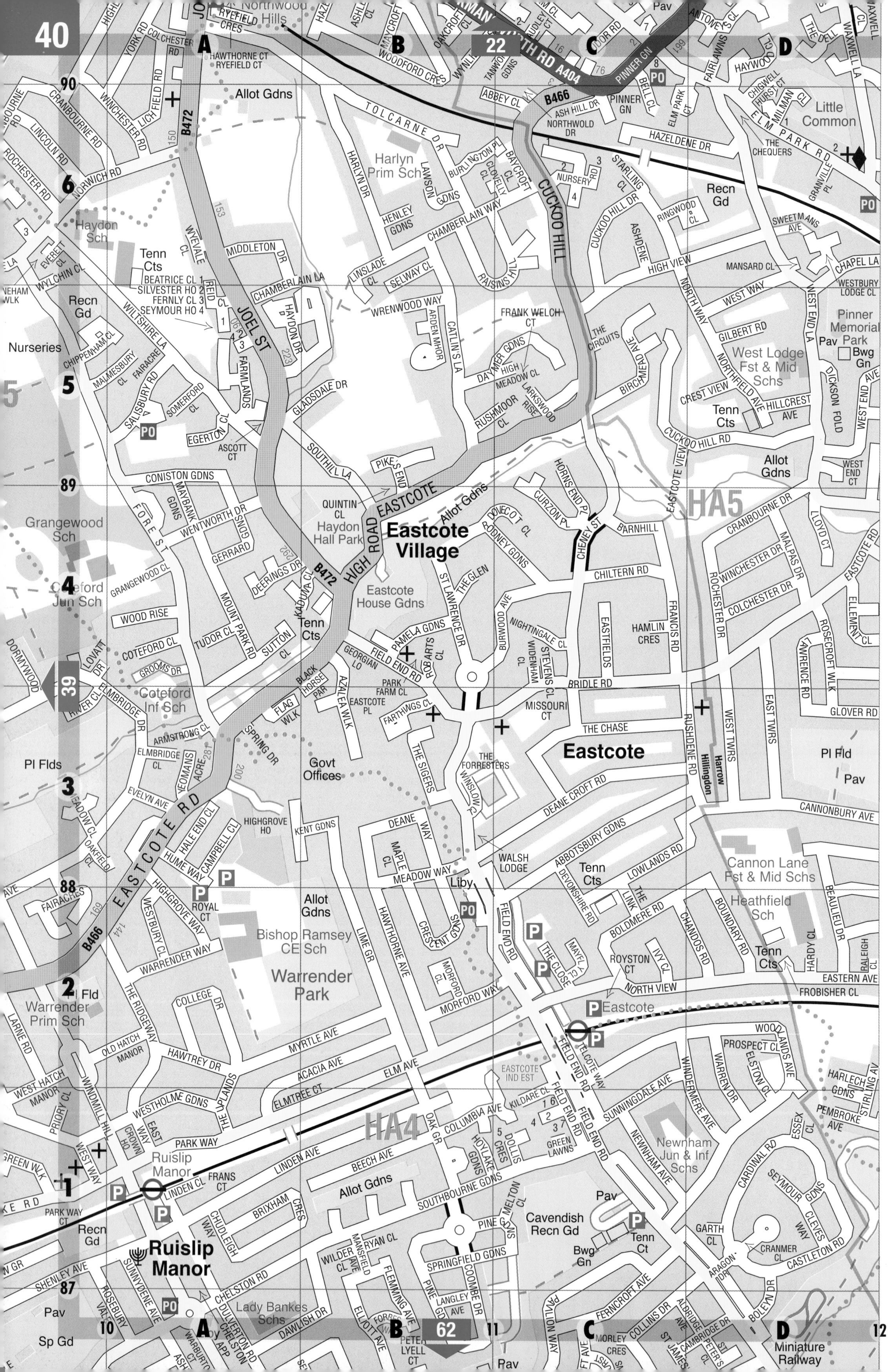
A
B
C
D
22
62
39
10
11
12
90
89
88
87
6
5
4
3
2
1
HA5
HA4
Eastcote Village
Eastcote
Ruislip Manor
Little Common
Northwood Hills
PINNER RD A404
PINNER GN
B466
B472
JOEL ST
CUCKOO HILL
HIGH ROAD EASTCOTE
EASTCOTE RD
FIELD END RD
TOLCARNE DR
HAZELDENE DR
ELM PARK RD
Harlyn Prim Sch
Haydon Sch
Recn Gd
Nurseries
Tenn Cts
Allot Gdns
Grangewood Sch
Coteford Jun Sch
Coteford Inf Sch
Pl Flds
Haydon Hall Park
Eastcote House Gdns
Govt Offices
Bishop Ramsey CE Sch
Warrender Park
Warrender Prim Sch
Pinner Memorial Park
West Lodge Fst & Mid Schs
Cannon Lane Fst & Mid Schs
Heathfield Sch
Newnham Jun & Inf Schs
Cavendish Recn Gd
Lady Bankes Schs
Miniature Railway
Liby
PO
Pav
Bwg Gn
Sp Gd
EASTCOTE IND EST
Harrow
Hillingdon
BRIDLE RD
THE CHASE
CHILTERN RD
DEANE CROFT RD
CANNONBURY AVE
SUNNINGDALE AVE
WINDERMERE AVE
NEWNHAM AVE
PARK WAY
LINDEN AVE
BEECH AVE
ELM AVE
ACACIA AVE
MYRTLE AVE
SOUTHBOURNE GDNS
SPRINGFIELD GDNS
CASTLETON RD
CARDINAL RD
SEYMOUR GDNS
CRANMER CL
BOLEYN DR
ARAGON DR
HIGHGROVE WAY
WARRENDER WAY
THE RIDGEWAY
HAWTREY DR
COLLEGE DR
WILTSHIRE LA
NORWICH RD
CRANBOURNE RD
LINCOLN RD
ROCHESTER RD
WINCHESTER RD
COLCHESTER RD
YORK RD
CONISTON GDNS
WENTWORTH DR
MOUNT PARK RD
WOOD RISE
COTEFORD CL
GRANGEWOOD CL
ELMBRIDGE DR
WEST END LA
CUCKOO HILL RD
NORTHFIELD AVE
HIGH VIEW
WEST WAY
NORTH WAY
CHAMBERLAIN WAY
WRENWOOD WAY
GLADSDALE DR
SOUTHILL LA
ST LAWRENCE DR
CATLIN'S LA
RUSHMOOR CL
LARKSWOOD RISE
DAYMER GDNS
FRANCIS RD
EASTFIELDS
HAMLIN CRES
RUSHDENE RD
WEST TWRS
EAST TWRS
ROCHESTER DR
WINCHESTER DR
COLCHESTER DR
MALPAS DR
ROSECROFT WLK
GLOVER RD
BEAULIEU DR
HARDY CL
EASTERN AVE
FROBISHER CL
NORTH VIEW
ROYSTON CT
BOLDMERE RD
CHANDOS RD
BOUNDARY RD
LOWLANDS RD
ABBOTSBURY GDNS
DEVONSHIRE RD
MEADOW WAY
DEANE WAY
HAWTHORNE AVE
LIME GR
MORFORD WAY
CRESCENT GDNS
KENT GDNS
WINSLOW CL
THE SIGERS
FIELD END RD
PAMELA GDNS
ROBARTS CL
AZALEA WLK
SPRING DR
FLAG WLK
EVELYN AVE
HUME WAY
HALE END CL
CAMPBELL CL
WESTBURY CL
WESTHOLME GDNS
THE UPLANDS
WINDMILL HILL
PRIORY CL
ELMTREE CT
COLUMBIA AVE
OAK GR
HOYLAKE GDNS
DOLLIS CRES
GREEN LAWNS
BRIXHAM CRES
CHUDLEIGH WAY
CHELSTON RD
DULVERTON RD
SUNNYDENE AVE
ROSEBURY VALE
SHENLEY AVE
DAWLISH DR
ELLIOTT AVE
FLEMMING AVE
PINE GR
COOMBE DR
LANGLEY AVE
PINE GDNS
RYAN CL
MANSFIELD AVE
WILDER CL
PAVILION WAY
FERNCROFT AVE
COLLINS DR
ALDRIDGE AVE
CAMBRIDGE DR
MORLEY CRES
GARTH CL
ESSEX CL
PEMBROKE AVE
HARLECH GDNS
PROSPECT CL
WOODLANDS AVE
ELSTON CL
WARREN DR
TELCOTE WAY

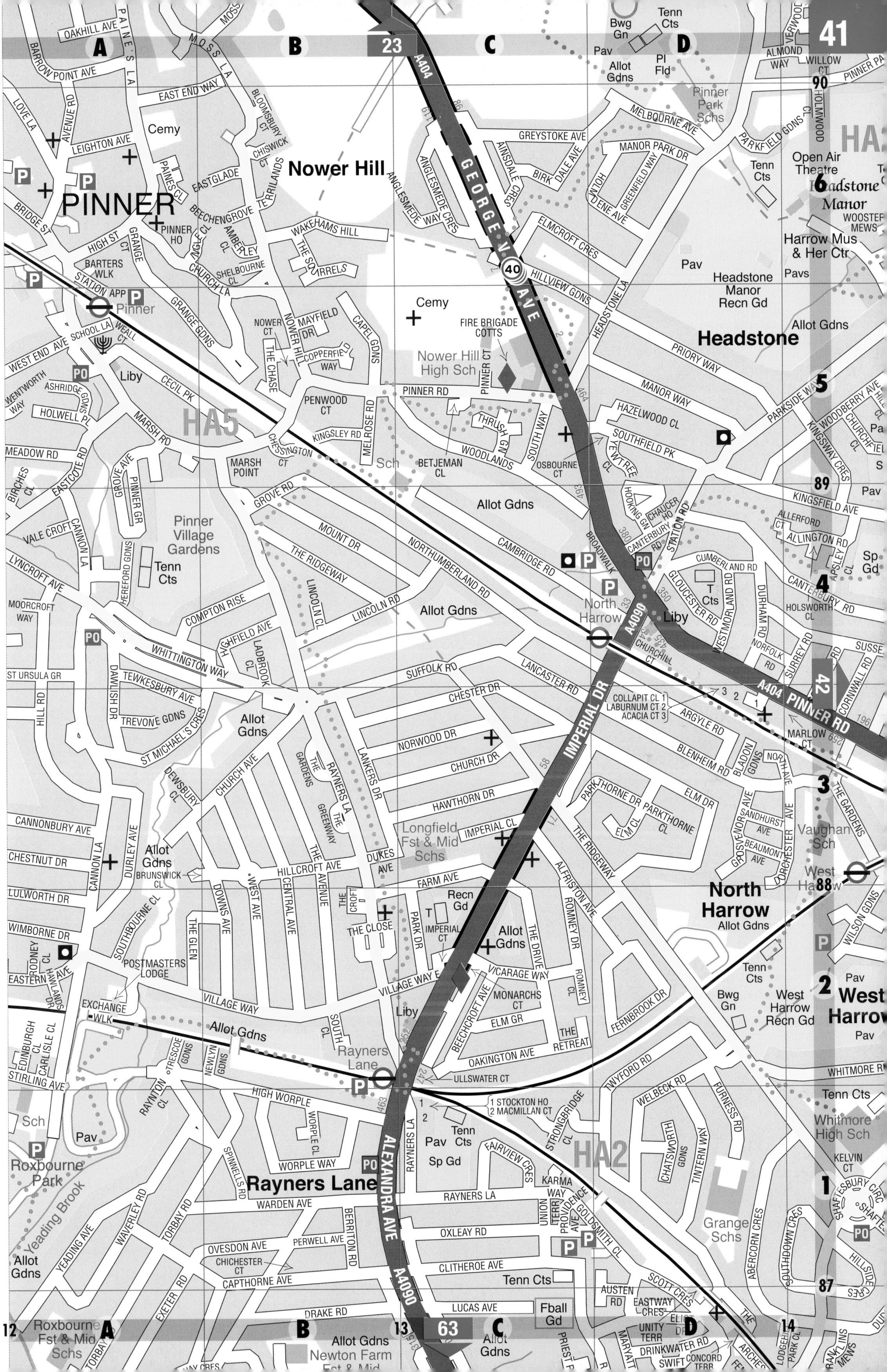
A
B
C
D
23
63
42
PINNER
Nower Hill
Headstone
North Harrow
West Harrow
Rayners Lane
HA5
HA2
Headstone Manor
A404
A4090
GEORGE V AVE
IMPERIAL DR
ALEXANDRA AVE
PINNER RD
OAKHILL AVE
PAINE'S LA
MOSS LA
BARROW POINT AVE
EAST END WAY
LOVE LA
AVENUE RD
LEIGHTON AVE
Cemy
BLOOMSBURY CT
CHISWICK CT
TERRILANDS
EASTGLADE
BEECHENGROVE
BRIDGE ST
HIGH ST
BARTERS WLK
GRANGE CT
PINNER HO
AMBERLEY CL
CHURCH LA
SHELBOURNE CL
STATION APP
Pinner
WAKEHAMS HILL
THE SQUIRRELS
ANGLESMEDE CRES
ANGLESMEDE WAY
AINSDALE CRES
GREYSTOKE AVE
BIRKDALE AVE
MELBOURNE AVE
MANOR PARK DR
HOLLY DENE AVE
GREENFIELD WAY
ELMCROFT CRES
HILLVIEW GDNS
HEADSTONE LA
PARKFIELD GDNS
HOLMWOOD CL
Bwg Gn
Tenn Cts
Pav
Allot Gdns
Pl Fld
Pinner Park Schs
ALMOND WAY
WILLOW CT
PINNER PARK
VERNWOOD
Open Air Theatre
WOOSTER MEWS
Harrow Mus & Her Ctr
Pavs
Headstone Manor Recn Gd
PRIORY WAY
MANOR WAY
PARKSIDE WAY
HAZELWOOD CL
SOUTHFIELD PK
YEWTREE CL
OSBOURNE CT
SOUTH WAY
THRUSH GN
WOODLANDS
BETJEMAN CL
PINNER RD
PINNER CT
FIRE BRIGADE COTTS
Nower Hill High Sch
CAPEL GDNS
MAYFIELD DR
COPPERFIELD WAY
NOWER CT
NOWER HILL
THE CHASE
PENWOOD CT
KINGSLEY RD
MELROSE RD
GRANGE GDNS
SCHOOL LA
WEALL CT
WEST END AVE
WENTWORTH WAY
ASHRIDGE GDNS
HOLWELL PL
Liby
CECIL PK
MARSH RD
CHESSINGTON CT
MARSH POINT
MEADOW RD
BIRCHES CL
EASTCOTE RD
GROVE AVE
PINNER GR
Pinner Village Gardens
VALE CROFT
CANNON LA
HEREFORD GDNS
LYNCROFT AVE
MOORCROFT WAY
GROVE RD
MOUNT DR
THE RIDGEWAY
NORTHUMBERLAND RD
CAMBRIDGE RD
BROADWALK
HOOKING GN
CHAUCER HO
CANTERBURY RD
STATION RD
KINGSFIELD AVE
WOODBERRY AVE
KINGSWAY CRES
CHURCHFIELD
ALLERFORD CT
ALLINGTON RD
APSLEY CL
CUMBERLAND RD
GLOUCESTER RD
WESTMORLAND RD
DURHAM RD
CANTERBURY RD
HOLSWORTH CL
NORFOLK RD
SURREY RD
SUSSEX RD
CORNWALL RD
T Cts
COMPTON RISE
LINCOLN CL
LINCOLN RD
HIGHFIELD AVE
LADBROOK CL
WHITTINGTON WAY
ST URSULA GR
TEWKESBURY AVE
TREVONE GDNS
ST MICHAEL'S CRES
DAWLISH DR
HILL RD
SUFFOLK RD
LANCASTER RD
CHURCHILL CT
CHESTER DR
COLLAPIT CL 1
LABURNUM CT 2
ACACIA CT 3
ARGYLE RD
BLENHEIM RD
BLADON GDNS
NORTH AVE
MARLOW CT
PINNER RD
NORWOOD DR
CHURCH DR
HAWTHORN DR
PARKTHORNE DR
PARKTHORNE CL
ELM DR
ELM CL
SANDHURST AVE
BEAUMONT AVE
GROSVENOR AVE
DORCHESTER AVE
THE GARDENS
Vaughan Sch
DEWSBURY CL
CHURCH AVE
THE GARDENS
RAYNERS LA
THE GREENWAY
LANKERS DR
Longfield Fst & Mid Schs
IMPERIAL CL
THE RIDGEWAY
ALFRISTON AVE
ROMNEY DR
CANNONBURY AVE
CHESTNUT DR
LULWORTH DR
WIMBORNE DR
DURLEY AVE
BRUNSWICK CL
SOUTHBOURNE CL
HILLCROFT AVE
DOWNS AVE
WEST AVE
CENTRAL AVE
THE AVENUE
DUKES AVE
FARM AVE
THE CROFT
THE CLOSE
PARK DR
Recn Gd
IMPERIAL CT
THE DRIVE
ROMNEY CL
Allot Gdns
RODNEY CL
EASTERN AVE
HAWLANDS DR
POSTMASTERS LODGE
THE GLEN
VILLAGE WAY
VILLAGE WAY E
VICARAGE WAY
MONARCHS CT
BEECHCROFT AVE
ELM GR
THE RETREAT
OAKINGTON AVE
ULLSWATER CT
FERNBROOK DR
Tenn Cts
Bwg Gn
West Harrow Recn Gd
WILSON GDNS
EXCHANGE WLK
EDINBURGH CL
CARLISLE CL
STIRLING AVE
TRESCOE GDNS
NEWLYN GDNS
SOUTH CL
Rayners Lane
RAYNTON CL
HIGH WORPLE
WORPLE CL
WORPLE WAY
SPINNELLS RD
Sch
Pav
Roxbourne Park
Yeading Brook
YEADING AVE
WAVERLEY RD
TORBAY RD
WARDEN AVE
BERRITON RD
OVESDON AVE
PERWELL AVE
CHICHESTER CT
CAPTHORNE AVE
EXETER RD
DRAKE RD
RAYNERS LA
1 STOCKTON HO
2 MACMILLAN CT
Sp Gd
FAIRVIEW CRES
STRONGBRIDGE CL
TINYFORD RD
WELBECK RD
FURNESS RD
CHATSWORTH GDNS
TINTERN WAY
KARMA WAY
UNION TERR
PROVIDENCE AVE
GOLDSMITH CL
RAYNERS LA
OXLEAY RD
CLITHEROE AVE
Tenn Cts
AUSTEN RD
EASTWAY CRES
SCOTT CRES
ELIOT DR
LUCAS AVE
Fball Gd
UNITY TERR
DRINKWATER RD
SWIFT CONCORD TERR
PRIEST PK
MARYATT
Grange Schs
ABERCORN CRES
SOUTHDOWN CRES
HILLSIDE CRES
SHAFTESBURY CIRC
WHITMORE RD
Whitmore High Sch
KELVIN CT
LODGE PARK CL
Roxbourne Fst & Mid Schs
Newton Farm Fst & Mid
12
13
14
87
88
89
90

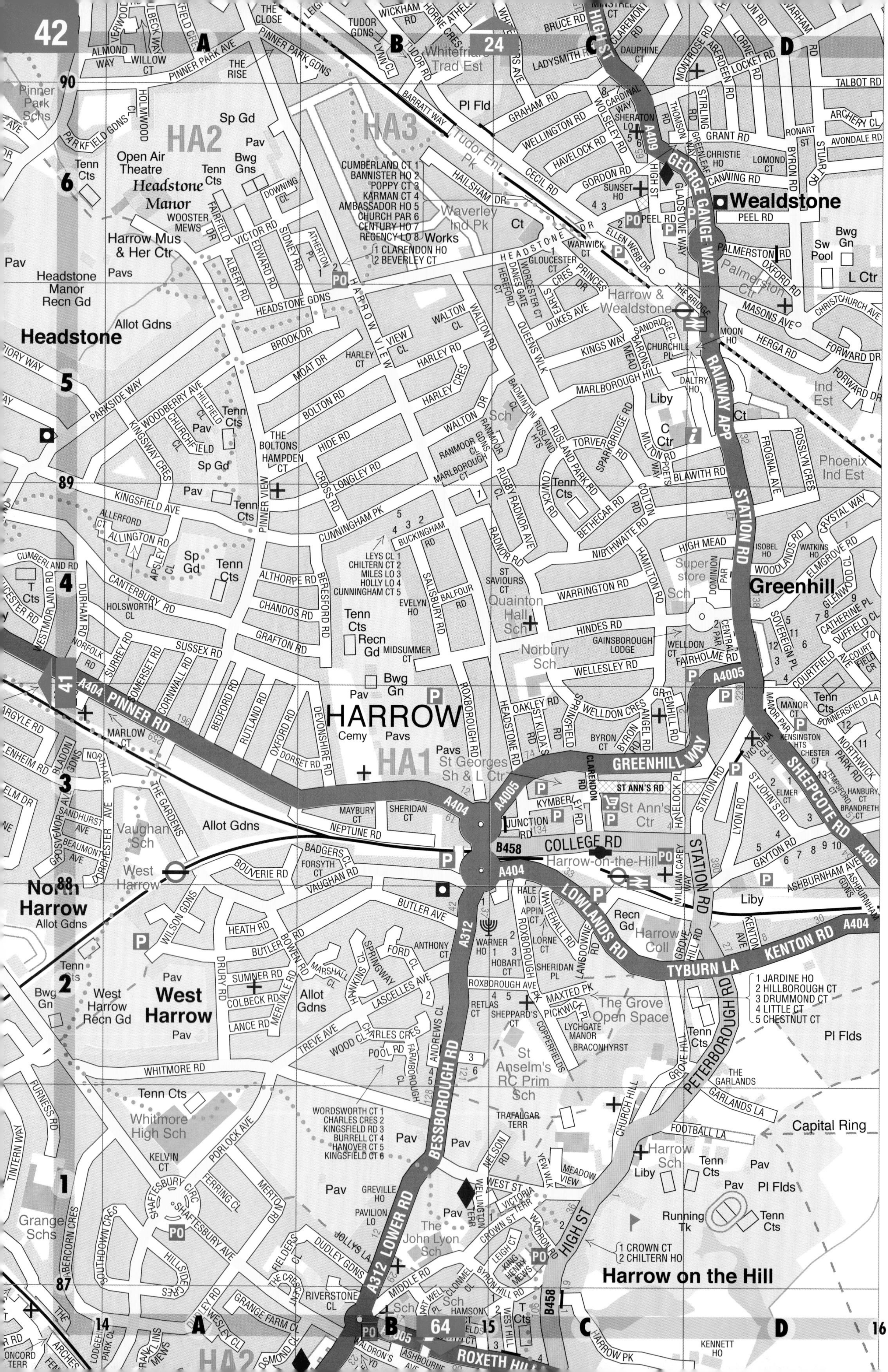

24
41
64
A
B
C
D
90
89
88
87
6
5
4
3
2
1
14
15
16
HA1
HA2
HA3
HARROW
Headstone
Wealdstone
Greenhill
North Harrow
West Harrow
Harrow on the Hill
Headstone Manor
Headstone Manor Recn Gd
Harrow Mus & Her Ctr
Open Air Theatre
Pinner Park Schs
Whitefriars Trad Est
Tudor Ent Pk
Waverley Ind Pk
Harrow & Wealdstone
Phoenix Ind Est
Palmerston Ctr
Quainton Hall Sch
Norbury Sch
St Georges Sh & L Ctr
St Ann's Ctr
Harrow-on-the-Hill
Vaughan Sch
West Harrow
Whitmore High Sch
Grange Schs
St Anselm's RC Prim Sch
The John Lyon Sch
Harrow Coll
Harrow Sch
The Grove Open Space
Running Tk
Capital Ring
West Harrow Recn Gd
PINNER RD
PINNER PARK AVE
PINNER PARK GDNS
PINNER VIEW
HEADSTONE GDNS
HEADSTONE DR
HEADSTONE RD
HARROW VIEW
KINGSFIELD AVE
CUNNINGHAM PK
HIGH ST
GEORGE GANGE WAY
RAILWAY APP
STATION RD
SHEEPCOTE RD
GREENHILL WAY
COLLEGE RD
ST ANN'S RD
LOWLANDS RD
KENTON RD
TYBURN LA
PETERBOROUGH RD
BESSBOROUGH RD
LOWER RD
WHITMORE RD
BUTLER AVE
SHAFTESBURY CIRC
ROXETH HILL
GROVE HILL RD
CHURCH HILL
FOOTBALL LA
GARLANDS LA
MARLBOROUGH HILL
HEADSTONE GDNS
PARKSIDE WAY
WALTON RD
BYRON HILL RD
WEST ST
HARROW PK
1 CUMBERLAND CT 2 BANNISTER HO 3 POPPY CT 4 KARMAN CT 5 AMBASSADOR HO 6 CHURCH PAR 7 CENTURY HO 8 REGENCY LO
1 CLARENDON HO 2 BEVERLEY CT
1 LEYS CL 2 CHILTERN CT 3 MILES LO 4 HOLLY LO 5 CUNNINGHAM CT
1 JARDINE HO 2 HILLBOROUGH CT 3 DRUMMOND CT 4 LITTLE CT 5 CHESTNUT CT
1 WORDSWORTH CT 2 CHARLES CRES 3 KINGSFIELD RD 4 BURRELL CT 5 HANOVER CT 6 KINGSFIELD CT
1 CROWN CT 2 CHILTERN HO

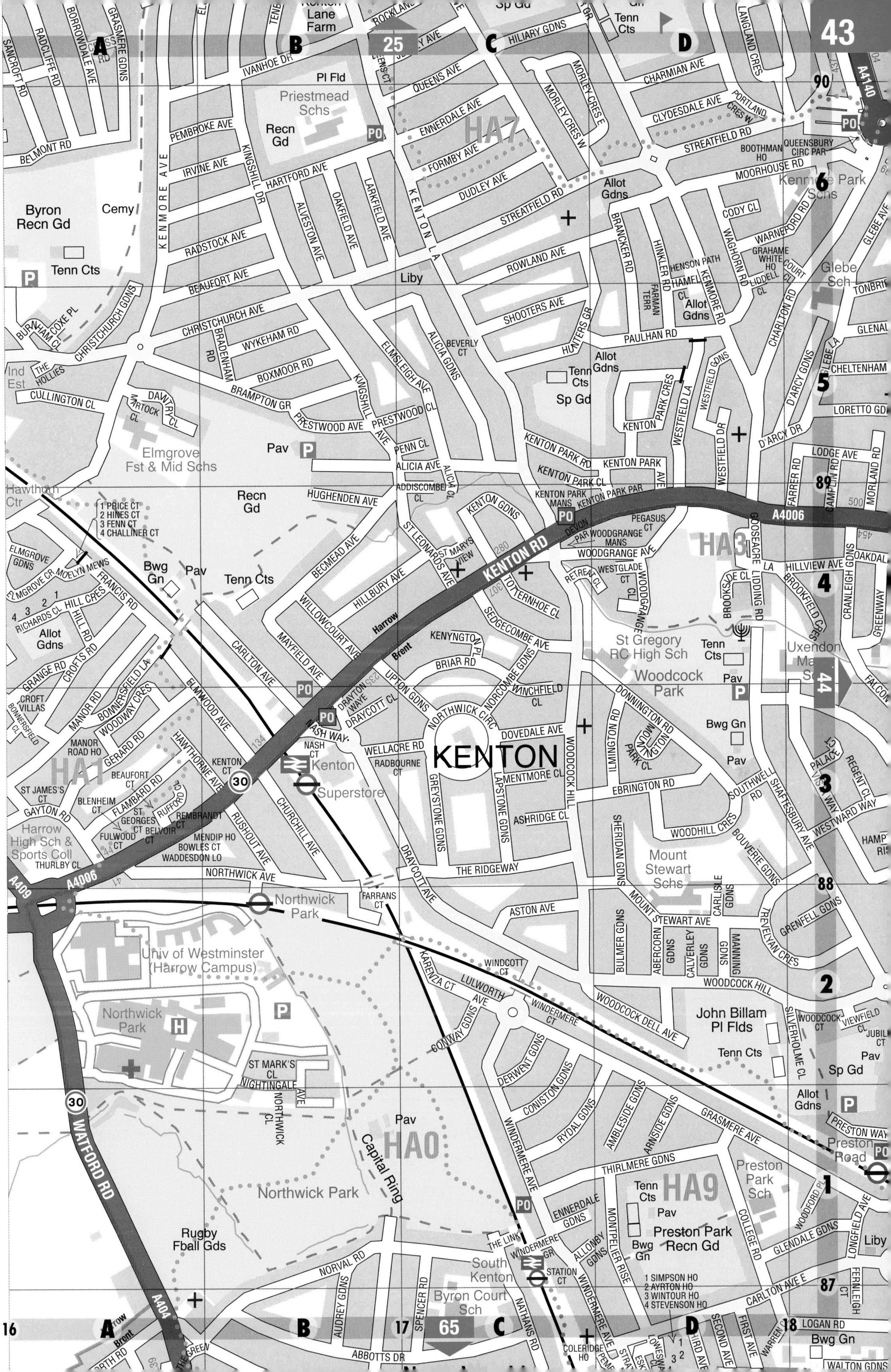

A
B
C
D
25
65
44
16
17
18
90
89
88
87
1
2
3
4
5
6
HA7
HA3
HA1
HA0
HA9
KENTON
Kenton Lane Farm
Tenn Cts
SANCROFT RD
RADCLIFFE RD
BORROWDALE AVE
GRASMERE GDNS
IVANHOE DR
ROCKLANDS
HILIARY GDNS
LANGLAND CRES
A4140
Pl Fld
Priestmead Schs
Recn Gd
PO
QUEENS AVE
CHARMIAN AVE
MORLEY CRES E
MORLEY CRES W
CLYDESDALE AVE
PORTLAND CRES
STREATFIELD RD
BOOTHMAN HO
QUEENSBURY CIRC PAR
MOORHOUSE RD
Kenmore Park Schs
BELMONT RD
PEMBROKE AVE
IRVINE AVE
KENMORE AVE
KINGSHILL DR
HARTFORD AVE
ENNERDALE AVE
FORMBY AVE
DUDLEY AVE
Allot Gdns
Byron Recn Gd
Cemy
Tenn Cts
P
RADSTOCK AVE
ALVESTON AVE
OAKFIELD AVE
LARKFIELD AVE
KENTON LA
STREATFIELD RD
BRANCKER RD
HINKLER RD
WAGHORN RD
CODY CL
WARNEFORD RD
GRAHAME WHITE HO
COURT
LIDDELL CL
HENSON PATH
HAMEL CL
KENMORE RD
FARMAN TERR
ROWLAND AVE
Liby
Glebe Sch
TONBRIDGE
GLEBE AVE
BEAUFORT AVE
SHOOTERS AVE
CHRISTCHURCH GDNS
CHRISTCHURCH AVE
WYKEHAM RD
BRADENHAM RD
BOXMOOR RD
BRAMPTON GR
ELMSLEIGH AVE
ALICIA GDNS
BEVERLY CT
HUNTERS GR
PAULHAN RD
CHARLTON RD
GLENALLA
GLEBE LA
D'ARCY GDNS
CHELTENHAM
BURNHAM CL
COXE PL
THE HOLLIES
Ind Est
CULLINGTON CL
DAWTRY CL
MARTOCK CL
Sp Gd
PARK CRES
WESTFIELD LA
WESTFIELD GDNS
WESTFIELD DR
KENTON
D'ARCY DR
LORETTO GDNS
Elmgrove Fst & Mid Schs
Pav
PRESTWOOD AVE
KINGSHILL AVE
PRESTWOOD CL
PENN CL
ALICIA AVE
ALICIA CL
ADDISCOMBE CL
KENTON PARK RD
KENTON PARK CL
KENTON PARK AVE
KENTON PARK MANS
KENTON PARK PAR
LODGE AVE
FARRER RD
CAMPLIN RD
MORLAND RD
A4006
Hawthorn Ctr
1 PRICE CT
2 HINES CT
3 FENN CT
4 CHALLINER CT
HUGHENDEN AVE
KENTON GDNS
DEVON PAR
PEGASUS CT
WOODGRANGE MANS
WOODGRANGE AVE
GOOSEACRE LA
HILLVIEW AVE
CRANLEIGH GDNS
OAKDALE
ELMGROVE GDNS
ELMGROVE CR
MOELYN MEWS
FRANCIS RD
Bwg Gn
BECMEAD AVE
ST LEONARDS AVE
ST MARYS VIEW
KENTON RD
RETREAT CL
WESTGLADE CT
WOODGRANGE CL
BROOKSIDE CL
LIDDING RD
BROOKFIELD CRES
GREENWAY
HILL CRES
RICHARDS CL
HILL RD
WILLOWCOURT AVE
HILLBURY AVE
TOTTERNHOE CL
SEDGECOMBE AVE
St Gregory RC High Sch
Uxendon Manor Sch
Allot Gdns
GRANGE RD
CROFTS RD
CARLTON AVE
MAYFIELD AVE
Harrow
Brent
KENYNGTON PL
BRIAR RD
Woodcock Park
FALCON
CROFT VILLAS
BONNERSFIELD CL
MANOR RD
BONNERSFIELD LA
WOODWAY CRES
ELMWOOD AVE
DRAYTON WAYE
DRAYCOTT CL
UPTON GDNS
NORTHWICK CIRC
NORCOMBE GDNS
WINCHFIELD CL
ILMINGTON RD
DONNINGTON RD
MOUNTINGTON PARK CL
MANOR ROAD HO
GERARD RD
HAWTHORNE AVE
NASH WAY
NASH CT
Kenton
WELLACRE RD
DOVEDALE AVE
WOODCOCK HILL
PALACE CT
REGENT CL
BEAUFORT CT
KENTON CT
RADBOURNE CT
Superstore
GREYSTONE GDNS
MENTMORE CL
EBRINGTON RD
SOUTHWELL RD
SHAFTESBURY AVE
VISTA WAY
ST JAMES'S CT
FLAMBARD RD
RUFFORD CL
BLENHEIM CT
ST GEORGES CT
BELVOIR CT
REMBRANDT CT
GAYTON RD
LAPSTONE GDNS
ASHRIDGE CL
WESTWARD WAY
Harrow High Sch & Sports Coll
THURLBY CL
FULWOOD CT
MENDIP HO
BOWLES CT
WADDESDON LO
RUSHOUT AVE
CHURCHILL AVE
SHERIDAN GDNS
WOODHILL CRES
BOUVERIE GDNS
HAMPTON RISE
A409
NORTHWICK AVE
DRAYCOTT AVE
THE RIDGEWAY
Mount Stewart Schs
CARLISLE GDNS
Northwick Park
FARRANS CT
ASTON AVE
MOUNT STEWART AVE
GRENFELL GDNS
Univ of Westminster (Harrow Campus)
BULMER GDNS
ABERCORN GDNS
CALVERLEY GDNS
MANNING GDNS
TREVELYAN CRES
KARENZA CT
WINDCOTT CT
LULWORTH AVE
WOODCOCK HILL
Northwick Park
H
WINDERMERE CT
WOODCOCK DELL AVE
John Billam Pl Flds
SILVERHOLME CL
WOODCOCK CT
VIEWFIELD CL
JUBILEE CT
CONWAY GDNS
DERWENT GDNS
Tenn Cts
Sp Gd
ST MARK'S CL
NIGHTINGALE AVE
NORTHWICK CL
CONISTON GDNS
RYDAL GDNS
AMBLESIDE GDNS
ARNSIDE GDNS
GRASMERE AVE
PRESTON WAY
Preston Road
30
WATFORD RD
Capital Ring
Northwick Park
WINDERMERE AVE
THIRLMERE GDNS
Preston Park Sch
Pav
Preston Park Recn Gd
ENNERDALE GDNS
MONTPELIER RISE
COLLEGE RD
WOODFORD PL
LONGFIELD AVE
Rugby Fball Gds
THE LINK
WINDERMERE GR
ALLONBY GDNS
GLENDALE GDNS
Liby
NORVAL RD
South Kenton
STATION CT
1 SIMPSON HO
2 AYRTON HO
3 WINTOUR HO
4 STEVENSON HO
CARLTON AVE E
FERNLEIGH CT
A404
AUDREY GDNS
SPENCER RD
Byron Court Sch
NATHANS RD
SECOND AVE
FIRST AVE
WARREN CL
LOGAN RD
THE GREEN
ABBOTTS DR
COLERIDGE HO
WALTON GDNS

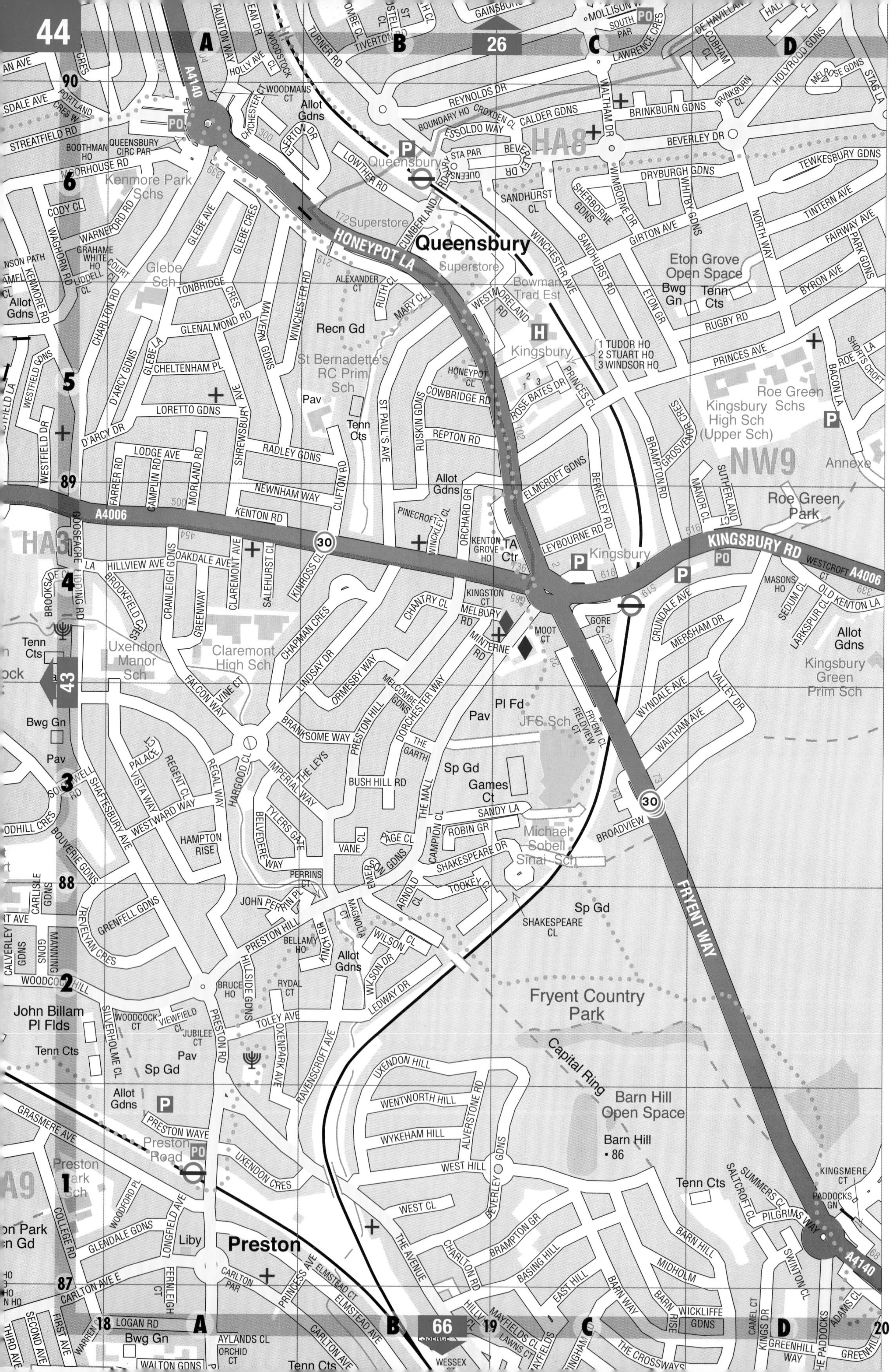

A
B
C
D
26
43
66
A4140
A4006
Queensbury
HONEYPOT LA
Kenmore Park Schs
Glebe Sch
Recn Gd
St Bernadette's RC Prim Sch
Pav
Tenn Cts
Allot Gdns
Superstore
Bowman Trad Est
Kingsbury
1 TUDOR HO
2 STUART HO
3 WINDSOR HO
HA8
HA3
NW9
Eton Grove Open Space
Bwg Gn
Roe Green Park
Kingsbury High Sch (Upper Sch)
Roe Green Schs
Annexe
KINGSBURY RD
Kingsbury Green Prim Sch
Uxendon Manor Sch
Claremont High Sch
TA Ctr
JFS Sch
Michael Sobell Sinai Sch
Pl Fd
Sp Gd
Games Ct
Fryent Country Park
Capital Ring
Barn Hill Open Space
Barn Hill
• 86
FRYENT WAY
John Billam Pl Flds
Preston Road
Preston
Liby
REYNOLDS DR
BOUNDARY HO
CROXDEN CL
ESSOLDO WAY
CALDER GDNS
BRINKBURN GDNS
BEVERLEY DR
TEWKESBURY GDNS
DRYBURGH GDNS
TINTERN AVE
FAIRWAY AVE
BYRON AVE
RUGBY RD
PRINCES AVE
GIRTON AVE
ETON GR
SANDHURST RD
WINCHESTER AVE
LOWTHER RD
CUMBERLAND RD
SANDHURST CL
WESTMORELAND RD
ROSE BATES DR
PRINCES CL
ELMCROFT GDNS
BERKELEY RD
LEYBOURNE RD
BRAMPTON RD
GROSVENOR CRES
MANOR CL
SUTHERLAND CT
CRUNDALE AVE
MERSHAM DR
WYNDALE AVE
WALTHAM AVE
VALLEY DR
BROADVIEW
FRYENT CL
FIELDVIEW CT
MOOT CT
GORE CT
MASONS HO
SEDUM CL
LARKSPUR CL
OLD KENTON LA
WESTCROFT CT
STREATFIELD RD
MOORHOUSE RD
CODY CL
WARNEFORD RD
GRAHAME WHITE HO
LIDDELL CL
KENMORE RD
CHARLTON RD
TONBRIDGE CRES
GLENALMOND RD
GLEBE AVE
GLEBE CRES
GLEBE LA
D'ARCY GDNS
D'ARCY DR
CHELTENHAM PL
LORETTO GDNS
SHREWSBURY AVE
MALVERN GDNS
WINCHESTER RD
ALEXANDER CT
RUTH CL
MARY CL
ST PAUL'S AVE
RUSKIN GDNS
HONEYPOT CL
COWBRIDGE RD
REPTON RD
RADLEY GDNS
NEWNHAM WAY
CLIFTON RD
KENTON RD
LODGE AVE
FARRER RD
CAMPLIN RD
MORLAND RD
PINECROFT
WINCKLEY CL
ORCHARD GR
KENTON GROVE HO
KINGSTON CT
MELBURY RD
MINTERNE RD
HILLVIEW AVE
OAKDALE AVE
CLAREMONT AVE
SALEHURST CL
KINROSS CL
BROOKFIELD CRES
CRANLEIGH GDNS
GREENWAY
CHAPMAN CRES
CHANTRY CL
LINDSAY DR
ORMESBY WAY
MELCOMBE GDNS
DORCHESTER WAY
BRANKSOME WAY
PRESTON HILL
THE GARTH
THE MALL
BUSH HILL RD
THE LEYS
IMPERIAL WAY
HARGOOD CL
FALCON WAY
VINE CT
REGAL WAY
PALACE CT
VISTA WAY
REGENT CL
WESTWARD WAY
SHAFTESBURY AVE
HAMPTON RISE
TYLERS GATE
BELVEDERE WAY
VANE CL
PAGE CL
CAMPION CL
ROBIN GR
SANDY LA
SHAKESPEARE DR
EMERSON GDNS
TOOKEY CL
ARNOLD CL
SHAKESPEARE CL
PERRINS CT
JOHN PERRIN PL
MAGNOLIA CT
BELLAMY HO
KINCH GR
WILSON CL
WILSON DR
LEDWAY DR
GRENFELL GDNS
TREVELYAN CRES
BOUVERIE GDNS
WOODCOCK HILL
BRUCE HO
RYDAL CT
HILLSIDE GDNS
PRESTON RD
TOLEY AVE
OXENPARK AVE
RAVENSCROFT AVE
SILVERHOLME CL
WOODCOCK CT
VIEWFIELD CL
JUBILEE CT
GRASMERE AVE
PRESTON WAYE
UXENDON CRES
UXENDON HILL
WENTWORTH HILL
WYKEHAM HILL
ALVERSTONE RD
WEST HILL
BEVERLEY GDNS
WEST CL
THE AVENUE
CHARLTON RD
BRAMPTON GR
BASING HILL
EAST HILL
BARN WAY
MIDHOLM
BARN HILL
BARN RISE
WICKLIFFE GDNS
SUMMERS CL
SALTCROFT CL
PILGRIMS WAY
SWINTON CL
KINGSMERE CT
PADDOCKS GN
ADAMS CL
THE PADDOCKS
GREENHILL WAY
KINGS DR
CAMEL CT
THE CROSSWAYS
MAYFIELDS CL
LAWNS CT
HILLVIEW CL
ELMSTEAD CT
ELMSTEAD AVE
CARLTON AVE
PRINCESS AVE
CARLTON PAR
FERNLEIGH CT
LONGFIELD AVE
GLENDALE GDNS
WOODFORD PL
COLLEGE RD
CARLTON AVE E
FIRST AVE
SECOND AVE
THIRD AVE
WARREN
LOGAN RD
AYLANDS CL
ORCHID CT
WALTON GDNS
WESSEX
18
19
20
90
89
88
87
6
5
4
3
2
1

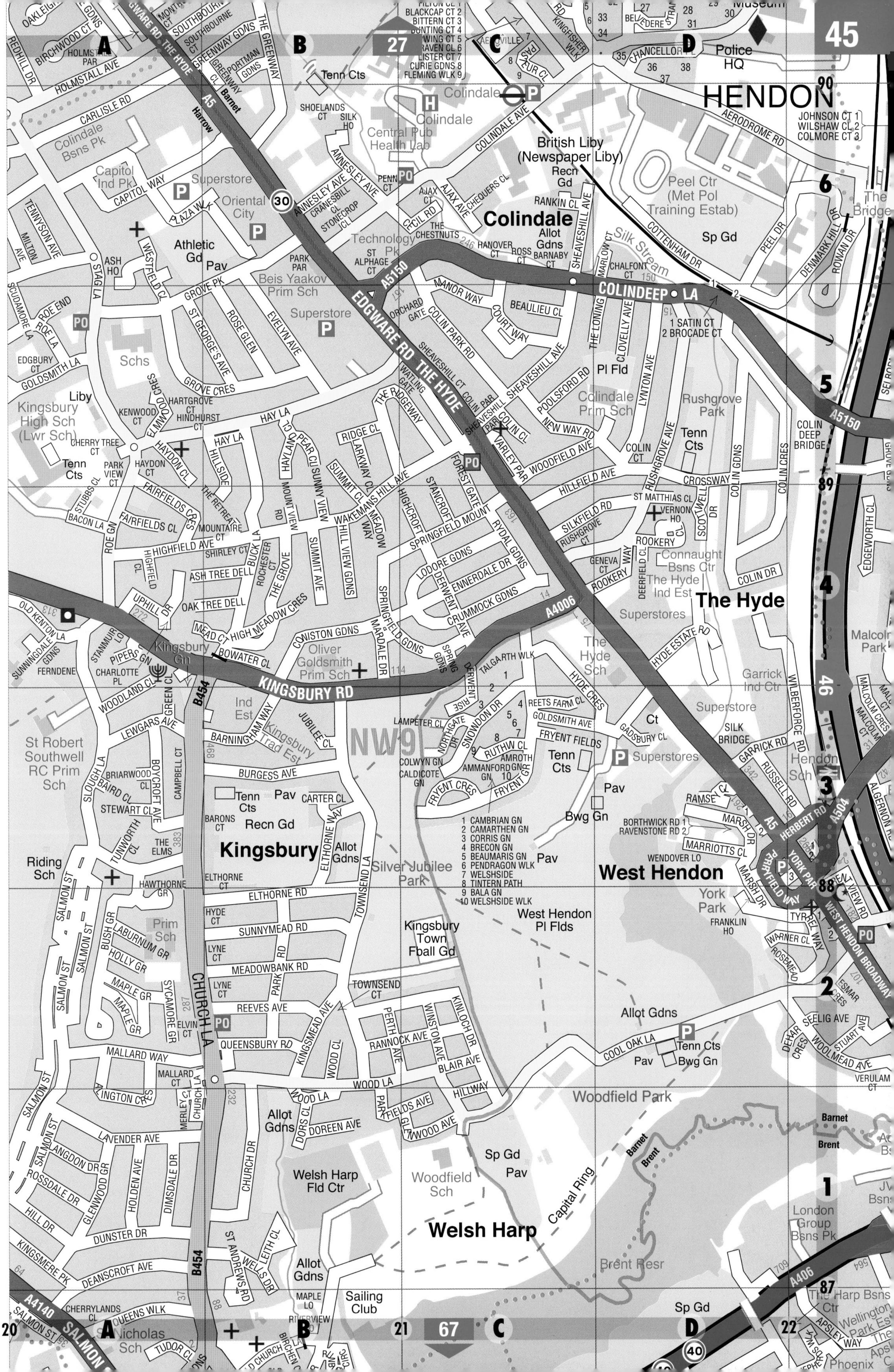
A
B
27
C
D
HENDON
Police HQ
Colindale
Colindale Bsns Pk
Capitol Ind Pk
Superstore
Oriental City
Athletic Gd
Pav
Beis Yaakov Prim Sch
Central Pub Health Lab
Technology Pk
British Liby (Newspaper Liby)
Peel Ctr (Met Pol Training Estab)
Sp Gd
Silk Stream
COLINDEEP LA
EDGWARE RD THE HYDE
AERODROME RD
COLINDALE AVE
CAPITOL WAY
CARLISLE RD
HOLMSTALL AVE
GROVE PK
ST GEORGE'S AVE
ROSE GLEN
EVELYN AVE
ANNESLEY AVE
SHEAVESHILL AVE
COTTENHAM DR
MANOR WAY
COLIN PARK RD
Schs
Liby
Kingsbury High Sch (Lwr Sch)
Tenn Cts
HAY LA
Colindale Prim Sch
Rushgrove Park
Pl Fld
LYNTON AVE
CLOVELLY AVE
THE LONING
POOLSFORD RD
WOODFIELD AVE
HILLFIELD AVE
CROSSWAY
COLIN GDNS
COLIN CRES
COLIN DEEP BRIDGE
A5150
The Hyde
Connaught Bsns Ctr
The Hyde Ind Est
Superstores
HIGHFIELD AVE
ASH TREE DELL
OAK TREE DELL
SPRINGFIELD MOUNT
A4006
KINGSBURY RD
Oliver Goldsmith Prim Sch
Kingsbury Gn
Ind Est
Kingsbury Trad Est
NW9
The Hyde Sch
HYDE ESTATE RD
Garrick Ind Ctr
Superstore
SILK BRIDGE
Hendon Sch
St Robert Southwell RC Prim Sch
BURGESS AVE
Kingsbury
Recn Gd
Allot Gdns
Silver Jubilee Park
West Hendon
West Hendon Pl Flds
York Park
Riding Sch
Prim Sch
ELTHORNE RD
SUNNYMEAD RD
MEADOWBANK RD
REEVES AVE
QUEENSBURY RD
MALLARD WAY
WOOD LA
Kingsbury Town Fball Gd
Allot Gdns
COOL OAK LA
Woodfield Park
CHURCH LA
B454
Welsh Harp Fld Ctr
Woodfield Sch
Welsh Harp
Capital Ring
Brent Resr
Sailing Club
London Group Bsns Pk
A406
The Harp Bsns Ctr
1 CAMBRIAN GN
2 CAMARTHEN GN
3 CORRIS GN
4 BRECON GN
5 BEAUMARIS GN
6 PENDRAGON WLK
7 WELSHSIDE
8 TINTERN PATH
9 BALA GN
10 WELSHSIDE WLK
20
21
67
22
40
St Nicholas Sch

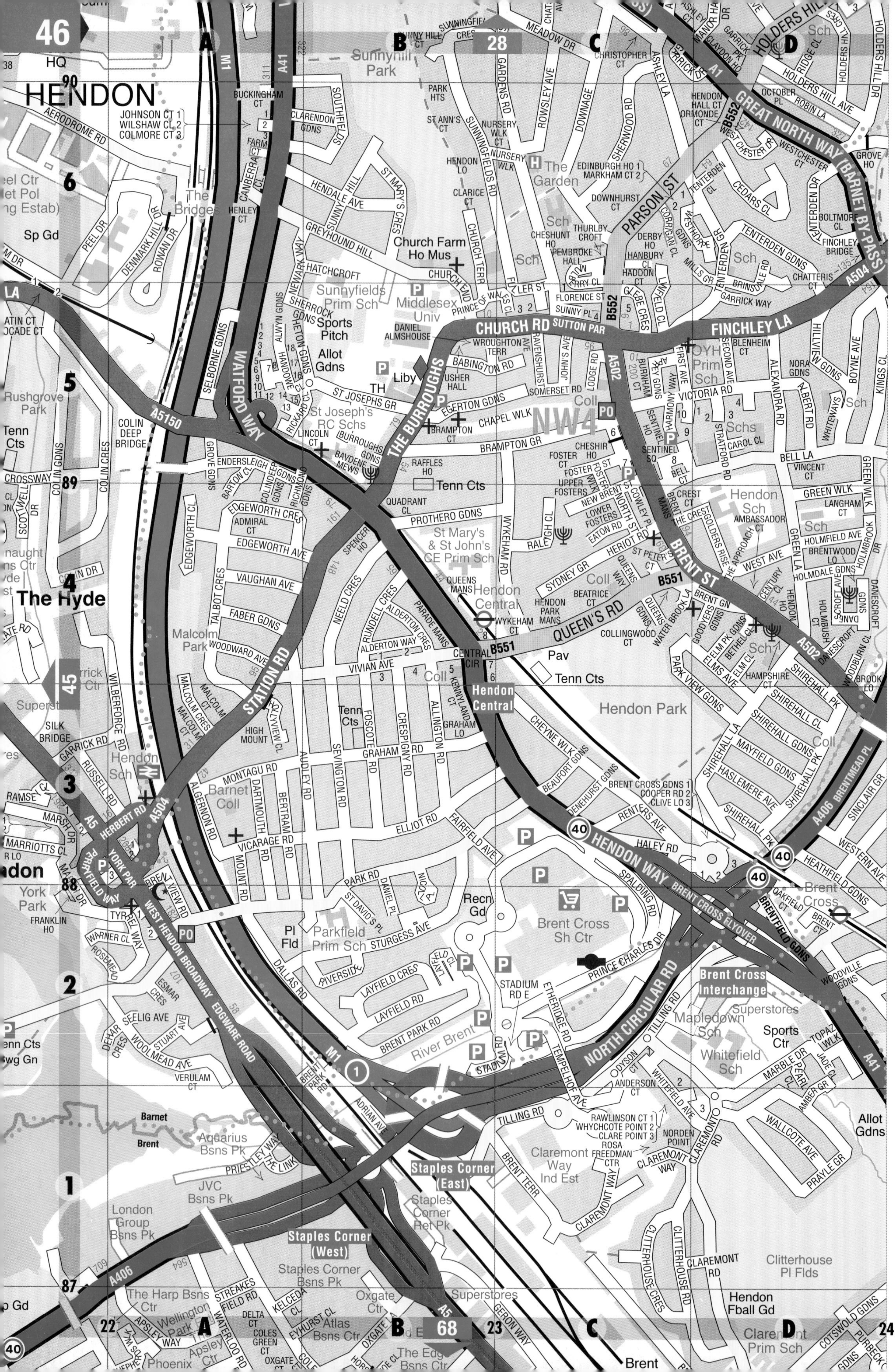
HENDON
The Hyde
NW4
28
68
45
A
B
C
D
6
5
4
3
2
1
90
89
88
87
22
23
24
HQ
Aerodrome Rd
Sunnyhill Park
Buckingham Ct
Johnson Ct 1
Wilshaw Cl 2
Colmore Ct 3
Clarendon Gdns
Southfields
Farm Ct
Canberra Cl
The Bridges
Henley Ct
Sp Gd
Peel Dr
Denmark Hill Dr
Rowan Dr
Sunny Hill Ct
Sunningfields Cres
Meadow Dr
Christopher Ct
Ashley La
Holders Hill
Holders Hill Ave
Holders Hill Cres
Ridge Cl
October Pl
Robin La
Great North Way (Barnet By-Pass)
Westchester Dr
Grove Ho
Park Hts
St Ann's Ct
Sunningfields Rd
Nursery Wlk Ct
Nursery Wlk
Rowsley Ave
Downage
Sherwood Rd
Hendon Hall Ct
Ormonde Ct
B552
Parson St
Edinburgh Ho 1
Markham Ct 2
Downhurst Ct
Tenterden Cl
Cedars Cl
Tenterden Dr
Boltmore Cl
Finchley Bridge
Tenterden Gdns
Tenterden Gr
Chatteris Ct
A504
Hendale Ave
Sunny Hill
St Mary's Cres
Greyhound Hill
Church Farm Ho Mus
Hatchcroft
Newark Way
Sherrock Gdns
Sunnyfields Prim Sch
Middlesex Univ
Daniel Almshouse
Hendon Lo
Clarice Ct
Church Terr
Church End
The Garden
Sch
Cheshunt Ho
Thurlby Croft
Pembroke Hall
Derby Ho
Hanbury Cl
Haddon Ct
Westhorpe Gdns
Corrigan Cl
Mills Gr
Brinsmead
Garrick Way
Florence St
Sunny Pl
Fuller St
Prince of Wales Cl
Church Rd
Sutton Par
Finchley La
Blenheim Ct
Hillview Gdns
Boyne Ave
Kings Cl
Nora Gdns
Alexandra Rd
Selborne Gdns
Watford Way
Alwyn Gdns
Handowe Cl
Sheaton Gdns
Sports Pitch
Allot Gdns
TH
Liby
The Burroughs
Wroughton Terr
Babington Rd
Usher Hall
Ravenshurst Ave
John's Ave
Lodge Rd
A502
Burnham Ct
Harmony Way
First Ave
Second Ave
OYH Prim Sch
Victoria Rd
Albert Rd
Whiteways
Rushgrove Park
Tenn Cts
Colin Deep Bridge
A5150
St Josephs Gr
St Joseph's RC Schs
Lincoln Ct
Rickard Cl
Egerton Gdns
Chapel Wlk
Somerset Rd
Coll
PO
Brampton Ct
Brampton Gr
Cheshir Ho
Sentinel Ho
Sentinel Sq
Schs
Stratford Rd
Carol Cl
Bell La
Vincent Ct
Green Wlk
Crossway
Colin Gdns
Colin Cres
Scotwell Dr
Grove Gdns
Endersleigh Gdns
Barton Cl
Colindeep Gdns
Richmond Gdns
Burroughs Gdns
Bavdene Mews
Raffles Ho
Tenn Cts
Foster Ct
Fosters Upper
Fosters Cl
New Brent St
North St
Cowley Pl
Bell Ct
Crest Ct
Brent Mans
The Crest
Golders Rise
Hendon Sch
Ambassador Ct
Langham Ct
Edgeworth Cl
Edgeworth Cres
Admiral Ct
Edgeworth Ave
Quadrant Cl
Prothero Gdns
St Mary's & St John's CE Prim Sch
Raleigh Cl
Lower Fosters
Eaton Rd
Heriot Rd
St Peter's Ct
Brent St
The Approach
West Ave
Century Cl
Green La
Holmfield Ave
Brentwood Lo
Holmdale Gdns
Holmbrook Dr
Spencer Ho
Talbot Cres
Vaughan Ave
Faber Gdns
Malcolm Park
Woodward Ave
Neeld Cres
Rundell Cres
Alderton Cres
Parade Mans
Queens Mans
Hendon Central
Sydney Gr
Queens Way
Beatrice Ct
Hendon Park Mans
Wykeham Ct
B551
Queen's Rd
Collingwood Ct
Queens Gdns
Water Brook La
Brent Gn
Goodyers Gdns
Elm Pk Gdns
Bethel Cl
Elm Cl
Elms Ave
Holmbush Ct
Dane Ct
Danescroft
Danescroft Ave
Danescroft Gdns
Woodburn Cl
Brook Lo
Alderton Way
Vivian Ave
Central Cir
Kennyland Ct
Pav
Tenn Cts
Hampshire Ct
Shirehall Pk
Shirehall Cl
Shirehall Gdns
Station Rd
Malcolm Ct
Malcolm Cres
Hollyview Cl
High Mount
Foscote Rd
Crespigny Rd
Allington Rd
Graham Lo
Cheyne Wlk
Hendon Park
Park View Gdns
Shirehall La
Mayfield Gdns
Haslemere Ave
Shirehall Pk
A406
Brentmead Pl
Sinclair Gr
Silk Bridge
Garrick Rd
Wilberforce Rd
Russell Rd
Hendon Sch
Superstore
Graham Rd
Audley Rd
Sevington Rd
Beaufort Gdns
Denehurst Gdns
Brent Cross Gdns 1
Cooper Rd 2
Clive Lo 3
Renters Ave
Western Ave
Heathfield Gdns
Ramsey Cl
Marsh Dr
Marriotts Cl
Herbert Rd
A5
A504
Montagu Rd
Dartmouth Rd
Bertram Rd
Barnet Coll
Algernon Rd
Elliot Rd
Fairfield Ave
Hendon Way
Haley Rd
Spalding Rd
Brent Cross Flyover
Brentfield Gdns
Oakfield Ct
Brent Ct
Brent Cross
York Par
Perryfield Way
York Park
Franklin Ho
Tyrrel Way
Brent View Rd
West Hendon Broadway
Mount Rd
Vicarage Rd
Park Rd
Daniel Pl
Nicoll Pl
St David's Pl
Recn Gd
Brent Cross Sh Ctr
Pl Fld
Parkfield Prim Sch
Sturgess Ave
Prince Charles Dr
Warner Cl
Rosemead
Esmar Cres
Dallas Rd
Riverside
Layfield Cres
Layfield Cl
Layfield Rd
Stadium Rd E
Etheridge Rd
Brent Cross Interchange
Woodville Gdns
Superstores
Mapledown Sch
Whitefield Sch
Sports Ctr
Topaz Wlk
Marble Dr
Jade Cl
Pearl Cl
Amber Gr
A41
Seelig Ave
Stuart Ave
Dehar Cres
Woolmead Ave
Verulam Ct
Edgware Road
Brent Park Rd
M1
Brent Park Rd
River Brent
Stadium Rd
Tempelhof Ave
North Circular Rd
Tilling Rd
Dyson Ct
Anderson Ct
Whitefield Ave
Claremont Rd
Wallcote Ave
Prayle Gr
Allot Gdns
Barnet
Brent
Aquarius Bsns Pk
Priestley Way
The Link
Adrian Ave
Rawlinson Ct 1
Whychcote Point 2
Clare Point 3
Rosa Freedman Ctr
Norden Point
Claremont Way
Claremont Way Ind Est
Brent Terr
JVC Bsns Pk
London Group Bsns Pk
Staples Corner (East)
Staples Corner Ret Pk
Staples Corner (West)
Staples Corner Bsns Pk
Clitterhouse Cres
Clitterhouse Rd
Claremont Rd
Clitterhouse Pl Flds
Hendon Fball Gd
Claremont Prim Sch
Cotswold Gdns
A406
The Harp Bsns Ctr
Wellington Park
Apsley Way
Streakes Field Rd
Waterloo Rd
Delta Ct
Coles Green Ct
Oxgate Ct
Kelceda Cl
Eyhurst Cl
Atlas Bsns Ctr
Oxgate Ctr
Oxgate La
Superstores
Geron Way
The Edge Bsns Ctr
Phoenix
Apsley Ctr
Brent

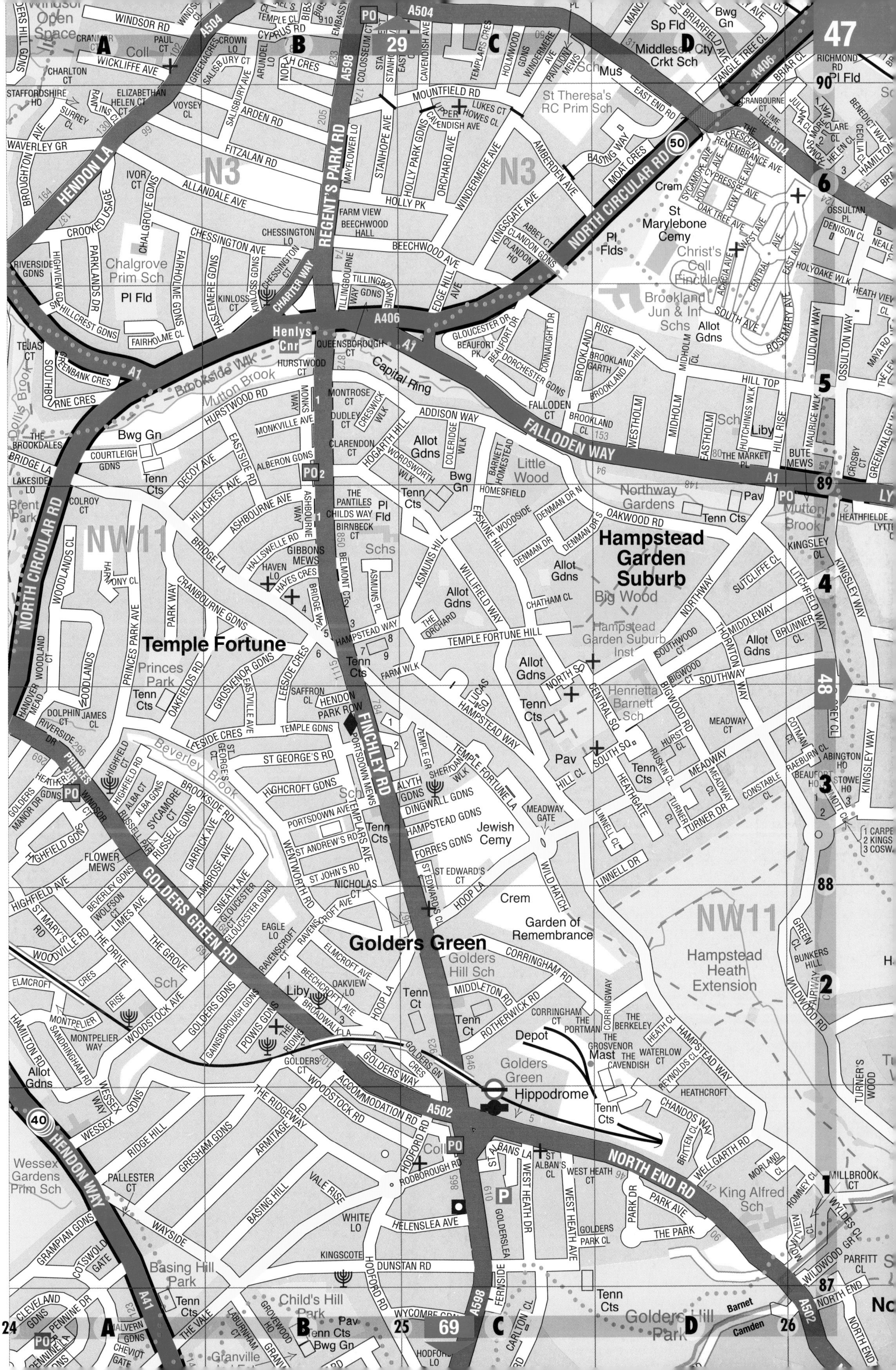
A
B
C
D
29
A504
A598
A406
A1
A502
A41
A5
N3
NW11
Windsor Open Space
WINDSOR RD
WICKLIFFE AVE
CHARLTON CT
STAFFORDSHIRE HO
ELIZABETH CT
HELEN CT
VOYSEY CL
SURREY CL
WAVERLEY GR
HENDON LA
BROUGHTON AVE
IVOR CT
CROOKED USAGE
CHALGROVE GDNS
Chalgrove Prim Sch
Pl Fld
RIVERSIDE GDNS
HIGHVIEW GDNS
PARKLANDS DR
FAIRHOLME GDNS
HASLEMERE GDNS
KINLOSS CT
KINLOSS GDNS
CHESSINGTON AVE
CHESSINGTON LO
CHESSINGTON CT
CHARTER WAY
HILLCREST GDNS
FAIRHOLME CL
ALLANDALE AVE
FITZALAN RD
ARDEN RD
SALISBURY AVE
ARUNDEL GDNS
NORTH CRES
REGENT'S PARK RD
MAYFLOWER LO
FARM VIEW
BEECHWOOD HALL
TILLINGBOURNE WAY
TILLINGBOURNE GDNS
BEECHWOOD AVE
STANHOPE AVE
HOLLY PARK GDNS
HOLLY PK
ORCHARD AVE
MOUNTFIELD RD
LUKES CT
HOWES CL
CAVENDISH AVE
CAVENDISH DR
WINDERMERE AVE
KINGSGATE AVE
ABBEY CT
CLANDON GDNS
CLANDON HO
AMBERDEN AVE
EDGE HILL AVE
St Theresa's RC Prim Sch
Middlesex Cty Crkt Sch
Mus
Sp Fld
Bwg Gn
EAST END RD
BASING WAY
MOAT CRES
NORTH CIRCULAR RD
50
Crem
St Marylebone Cemy
Christ's Coll Finchley
Brookland Jun & Inf Schs
Allot Gdns
Pl Flds
TANGLE TREE CL
BRIARFIELD AVE
RICHMOND RD
Pl Fld
CRANBOURNE CT
REMEMBRANCE AVE
SYCAMORE AVE
HOLLY AVE
CYPRESS AVE
YEW TREE AVE
OAK TREE AVE
WEST AVE
ACACIA AVE
CENTRAL AVE
EAST AVE
SOUTH AVE
ROSEMARY AVE
LUDLOW WAY
OSSULTON WAY
OSSULTAN PL
DENISON CL
HOLYOAKE WLK
HEATH VIEW
HAMILTON RD
Henlys Cnr
QUEENSBOROUGH CT
HURSTWOOD CT
GLOUCESTER DR
BEAUFORT DR
BEAUFORT PK
DORCHESTER GDNS
CONNAUGHT DR
BROOKLAND RISE
BROOKLAND GARTH
BROOKLAND HILL
BROOKLAND CL
MIDHOLM CL
MIDHOLM
WESTHOLM
EASTHOLM
HILL TOP
HUTCHINGS WLK
HILL RISE
THE MARKET PL
BUTE MEWS
MAURICE WLK
Liby
Sch
FALLODEN WAY
FALLODEN CT
Capital Ring
Mutton Brook
Brookside Wlk
TEJAS CT
GREENBANK CRES
SOUTHBOURNE CRES
Dollis Brook
HURSTWOOD RD
MONKS WAY
MONTROSE CT
DUDLEY CT
CRESWICK WLK
MONKVILLE AVE
ADDISON WAY
CLARENDON CT
HOGARTH HILL
WORDSWORTH WLK
COLERIDGE WLK
BARNETT HOMESTEAD
Little Wood
Northway Gardens
OAKWOOD RD
Tenn Cts
Pav
PO
Mutton Brook
HEATHFIELDE
KINGSLEY CL
Bwg Gn
THE BROOKDALES
COURTLEIGH GDNS
BRIDGE LA
LAKESIDE LO
Brent Park
COLROY CT
DECOY AVE
HILLCREST AVE
EASTSIDE RD
ALBERON GDNS
ASHBOURNE AVE
ASHBOURNE WAY
THE PANTILES
CHILDS WAY
BIRNBECK CT
Pl Fld
Schs
HOMESFIELD
ERSKINE HILL
WOODSIDE
DENMAN DR N
DENMAN DR S
DENMAN DR
Hampstead Garden Suburb
Big Wood
Allot Gdns
CHATHAM CL
NORTHWAY
SUTCLIFFE CL
LITCHFIELD WAY
KINGSLEY WAY
HALLSWELLE RD
GIBBONS MEWS
HAVEN LO
HAYES CRES
BRIDGE WAY
BELMONT CT
ASMUNS PL
ASMUNS HILL
WILLIFIELD WAY
THE ORCHARD
TEMPLE FORTUNE HILL
Hampstead Garden Suburb Inst
SOUTHWOOD CT
MIDDLEWAY
THORNTON WAY
BRUNNER CL
HARMONY CL
WOODLANDS CL
PARK WAY
CRANBOURNE GDNS
BRIDGE LA
Temple Fortune
PRINCES PARK AVE
Princes Park
OAKFIELDS RD
GROSVENOR GDNS
LEESIDE CRES
EASTVILLE AVE
HAMPSTEAD WAY
FARM WLK
LUCAS SQ
NORTH SQ
CENTRAL SQ
Henrietta Barnett Sch
BIGWOOD CT
BIGWOOD RD
SOUTHWAY
MEADWAY CT
COTMAN CL
48
HANOVER MEAD
WOODLAND CT
WOODLANDS
DOLPHIN CT
JAMES CL
RIVERSIDE DR
SAFFRON CL
HENDON PARK ROW
TEMPLE GDNS
LEESIDE CRES
ST GEORGE'S RD
FINCHLEY RD
PORTSDOWN MEWS
TEMPLE GR
SHERIDAN WLK
TEMPLE FORTUNE LA
SOUTH SQ
HILL CL
RUSKIN CL
HURST CL
MEADWAY
HEATHGATE
CONSTABLE CL
RAEBURN CL
ABINGTON HO
BEAUFORT HO
STOWE HO
KINGSLEY WAY
PRINCES PDE
WINDSOR RD
HIGHFIELD RD
HIGHFIELD CT
ALBA CT
ALBA GDNS
SYCAMORE CT
RUSSELL GDNS
RUSSELL PDE
BROOKSIDE RD
Beverley Brook
GARRICK AVE
AMBROSE AVE
HIGHCROFT GDNS
ALYTH GDNS
DINGWALL GDNS
HAMPSTEAD GDNS
Jewish Cemy
MEADWAY GATE
PORTSDOWN AVE
TEMPLARS AVE
ST ANDREW'S RD
FORRES GDNS
LINNELL CL
LINNELL DR
TURNER CL
TURNER DR
1 CARPE
2 KINGS
3 COSW
88
GOLDERS MANOR DR
HEATHFIELD GDNS
HIGHFIELD GDNS
FLOWER MEWS
GOLDERS GREEN RD
HIGHFIELD AVE
ST MARY'S RD
BEVERLEY GDNS
WOLFSON CL
LIMES AVE
SNEATH AVE
GLOUCESTER CT
GLOUCESTER GDNS
WENTWORTH RD
ST JOHN'S RD
NICHOLAS CT
ST EDWARD'S CT
ST EDWARDS CL
HOOP LA
WILD HATCH
Crem
Garden of Remembrance
NW11
Hampstead Heath Extension
GREEN CL
BUNKERS HILL
WILDWOOD RD
FAIRWAY
WOODVILLE RD
THE DRIVE
THE GROVE
EAGLE LO
RAVENSCROFT AVE
RAVENSCROFT CT
ELMCROFT AVE
Golders Green
Golders Hill Sch
CORRINGHAM RD
ELMCROFT
CRES
RISE
Sch
GOLDERS GDNS
BEECHCROFT AVE
OAKVIEW LO
Liby
HOOP LA
Tenn Ct
MIDDLETON RD
ROTHERWICK RD
CORRINGHAM CT
THE PORTMAN
CORRINGWAY
THE BERKELEY
HEATH CL
HAMPSTEAD WAY
HAMILTON RD
MONTPELIER RISE
SANDRINGHAM RD
MONTPELIER WAY
WOODSTOCK AVE
GAINSBOROUGH GDNS
POWIS GDNS
THE RIDING
BROADWALK LA
GOLDERS GN CRES
GOLDERS WAY
Depot
THE GROSVENOR
Mast
THE CAVENDISH
WATERLOW CT
REYNOLDS CL
HEATHCROFT
Golders Green Hippodrome
Allot Gdns
WESSEX GDNS
WESSEX WAY
40
HENDON WAY
THE RIDGEWAY
WOODSTOCK RD
ACCOMMODATION RD
GOLDERS CT
A502
Tenn Cts
CHANDOS WAY
BRITTEN CL
WELLGARTH RD
NORTH END RD
MORLAND CL
ROMNEY CL
MILLBROOK CT
WYLDES CL
RIDGE HILL
GRESHAM GDNS
ARMITAGE RD
HODFORD RD
Coll
RODBOROUGH RD
ST ALBANS LA
ST ALBAN'S CL
WEST HEATH CT
WEST HEATH DR
WEST HEATH AVE
King Alfred Sch
PARK DR
PARK AVE
THE PARK
Wessex Gardens Prim Sch
PALLESTER CT
BASING HILL
VALE RISE
WHITE LO
HELENSLEA AVE
GOLDERSLEA
GOLDERS PARK CL
WILDWOOD GR
PARFITT CL
GRAMPIAN GDNS
WAYSIDE
COTSWOLD GATE
Basing Hill Park
KINGSCOTE
DUNSTAN RD
87
NORTH END
Tenn Cts
Child's Hill Park
Pav
Golders Hill Park
Barnet
Camden
CLEVELAND GDNS
PENNINE DR
MALVERN GDNS
CHEVIOT GATE
PENNINE LA
THE VALE
LABURNHAM CT
GROVEWOOD HO
Bwg Gn
Granville
WYCOMBE GDNS
FERNSIDE
CARLTON CL
HODFORD LO
NORTH END RD
24
25
69
26

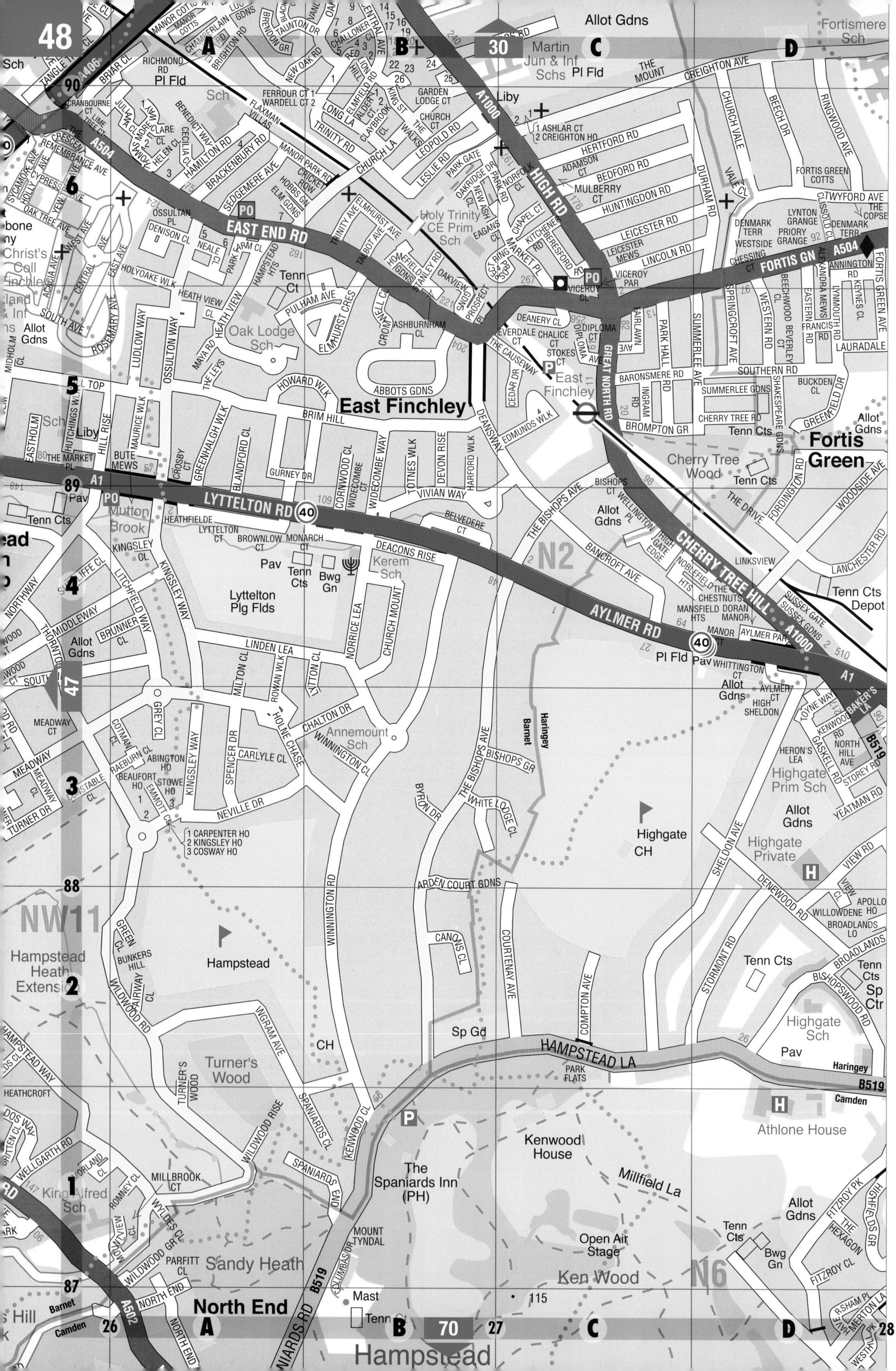
30
Allot Gdns
Martin Jun & Inf Schs
Fortismere Sch
Pl Fld
THE MOUNT
CREIGHTON AVE
A B C D
A406
A504
A1000
HIGH RD
EAST END RD
RICHMOND RD
Pl Fld
Sch
FERROUR CT
WARDELL CT
LONG LA
GARDEN LODGE CT
CHURCH CT
LEOPOLD RD
TRINITY RD
CHURCH LA
Liby
1 ASHLAR CT
2 CREIGHTON HO
HERTFORD RD
ADAMSON CT
BEDFORD RD
MULBERRY CT
HUNTINGDON RD
LEICESTER RD
LEICESTER MEWS
LINCOLN RD
CHURCH VALE
BEECH DR
RINGWOOD AVE
DURHAM RD
FORTIS GREEN COTTS
TWYFORD AVE
THE COPSE
FORTIS GN
DENMARK TERR
WESTSIDE
LYNTON GRANGE
PRIORY GRANGE
CHESSING CT
ANNINGTON RD
KEYNES CL
FORTIS GREEN AVE
Holy Trinity CE Prim Sch
SEDGEMERE AVE
HAMILTON RD
BRACKENBURY RD
MANOR PARK RD
CRICKET ROW
HOBBS GN
ELM GDNS
OSSULTAN PL
DENISON CL
NEALE CL
PARK FARM CL
HAMPSTEAD HTS
TRINITY AVE
ELMHURST AVE
TALBOT AVE
STANLEY RD
OAKVIEW GDNS
PROSPECT PL
MARKET PL
KITCHENER RD
BERESFORD RD
VICEROY CL
VICEROY PAR
CHAPEL CT
PARK GATE
OAKRIDGE DR
NORFOLK CL
EAGANS CL
Christ's Coll Finchley
CENTRAL AVE
EAST AVE
HOLYOAKE WLK
SOUTH AVE
ROSEMARY AVE
Allot Gdns
HEATH VIEW
LUDLOW WAY
OSSULTON WAY
MAYA RD
THE LEYS
Oak Lodge Sch
Tenn Ct
PULHAM AVE
ELMHURST CRES
CROMWELL CL
ASHBURNHAM CL
ABBOTS GDNS
DEANERY CL
CHALICE CT
DIPLOMA CT
DIPLOMA AVE
EVERDALE CT
THE CAUSEWAY
STOKES CT
CEDAR DR
East Finchley
GREAT NORTH RD
FAIRLAWN AVE
PARK HALL RD
SUMMERLEE AVE
SPRINGCROFT AVE
WESTERN RD
BEECHWOOD AVE
BEVERLEY CL
EASTERN RD
FRANCIS RD
LAURADALE
SOUTHERN RD
BUCKDEN CL
BARONSMERE RD
INGRAM RD
SUMMERLEE GDNS
SHAKESPEARE GDNS
CHERRY TREE RD
GREENFIELD DR
BROMPTON GR
Tenn Cts
Allot Gdns
Fortis Green
East Finchley
HOWARD WLK
BRIM HILL
EDMUNDS WLK
HILL TOP
HUTCHINGS WLK
HILL RISE
MAURICE WLK
GREENHALGH WLK
BLANDFORD CL
Liby
EASTHOLM
THE MARKET PL
BUTE MEWS
CROSBY CT
GURNEY DR
CORNWOOD CL
WIDECOMBE CT
WIDECOMBE WAY
TOTNES WLK
DEVON RISE
HARFORD WLK
DEANS WAY
VIVIAN WAY
Cherry Tree Wood
Tenn Cts
THE DRIVE
FORDINGTON RD
WOODSIDE AVE
A1
LYTTELTON RD
40
Pav
Mutton Brook
Tenn Cts
HEATHFIELDE
LYTTELTON CT
BROWNLOW CT
MONARCH CT
BELVEDERE CT
DEACONS RISE
THE BISHOPS AVE
BISHOPS CT
WELLINGTON PL
Allot Gdns
N2
BANCROFT AVE
HIGHGATE EDGE
NOBLEFIELD HTS
THE CHESTNUTS
CHERRY TREE HILL
LINKSVIEW
LANCHESTER RD
Tenn Cts Depot
SUSSEX GATE
SUSSEX GDNS
KINGSLEY CL
KINGSLEY WAY
Pav
Tenn Cts
Bwg Gn
Kerem Sch
Lyttelton Plg Flds
NORRICE LEA
CHURCH MOUNT
AYLMER RD
MANSFIELD HTS
DORAN MANOR
MANOR CT
AYLMER PAR
Pl Fld
Pav
WHITTINGTON CT
Allot Gdns
AYLMER CT
HIGH SHELDON
NORTHWAY
MIDDLEWAY
LITCHFIELD WAY
BRUNNER CL
Allot Gdns
LINDEN LEA
MILTON CL
ROWAN WLK
HOLNE CHASE
CHALTON DR
WINNINGTON CL
Annemount Sch
MEADWAY CT
GREY CL
COTMAN CL
RAEBURN CL
ABINGTON HO
BEAUFORT HO
STOWE HO
EMMOTT CL
KINGSLEY WAY
SPENCER DR
CARLYLE CL
NEVILLE DR
Haringey
Barnet
BISHOPS GR
BYRON DR
WHITE LODGE CL
TOYNE WAY
KENWOOD RD
BAKER'S LA
NORTH HILL AVE
B519
HERON'S LEA
GASKELL RD
Highgate Prim Sch
STOREY RD
YEATMAN RD
Allot Gdns
Highgate CH
MEADWAY
CONSTABLE CL
TURNER DR
1 CARPENTER HO
2 KINGSLEY HO
3 COSWAY HO
SHELDON AVE
Highgate Private
VIEW RD
DENEWOOD RD
APOLLO HO
WILLOWDENE
BROADLANDS LO
NW11
Hampstead Heath Extension
GREEN CL
BUNKERS HILL
FAIRWAY CL
WILDWOOD RD
Hampstead
WINNINGTON RD
ARDEN COURT GDNS
CANONS CL
COURTENAY AVE
COMPTON AVE
STORMONT RD
Tenn Cts
BROADLANDS RD
Tenn Cts
Sp Ctr
BISHOPSWOOD RD
Highgate Sch
WIGRAM AVE
CH
Sp Gd
HAMPSTEAD LA
PARK FLATS
Pav
Haringey
Camden
B519
HAMPSTEAD WAY
HEATHCROFT
Turner's Wood
TURNER'S WOOD
SPANIARDS CL
KENWOOD CL
Athlone House
WELLGARTH RD
MORLAND CL
King Alfred Sch
ROMNEY CL
MILLBROOK CT
WILDWOOD RISE
SPANIARDS END
The Spaniards Inn (PH)
Kenwood House
Millfield La
MOUNT TYNDAL
WYLDES CL
WILDWOOD GR
PARFITT CL
Sandy Heath
Open Air Stage
Ken Wood
N6
Allot Gdns
Tenn Cts
Bwg Gn
FITZROY PK
THE HEXAGON
FITZROY CL
A502
NORTH END
North End
Mast
115
Tenn Cts
Barnet
Camden
26
27
28
70
Hampstead
SPANIARDS RD

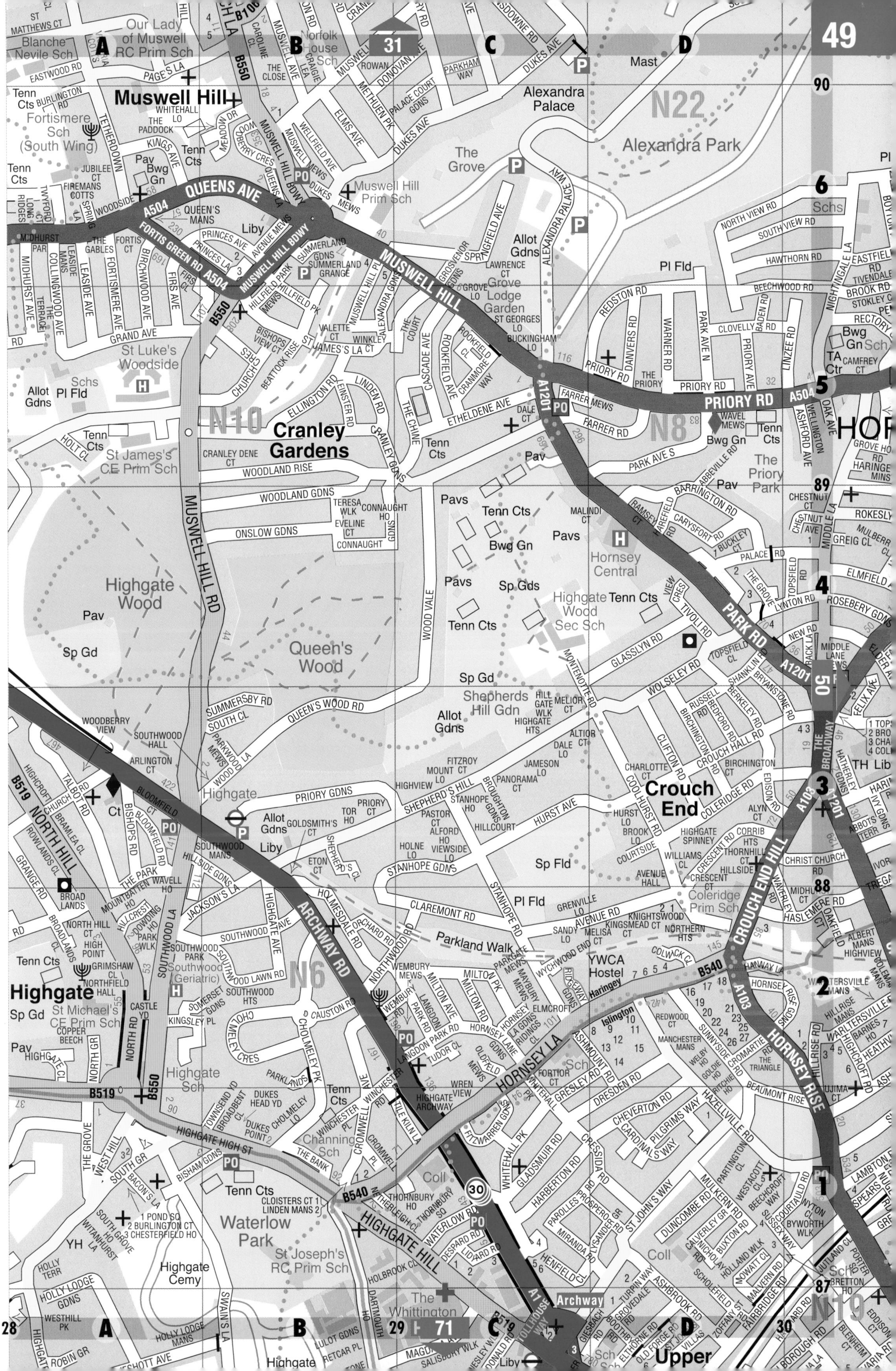

Muswell Hill
Alexandra Palace
Alexandra Park
N22
The Grove
Queens Ave
Muswell Hill Bdwy
Muswell Hill
Muswell Hill Rd
Priory Rd
Park Rd
N10
Cranley Gardens
N8
Highgate Wood
Queen's Wood
Hornsey Central
Highgate Wood Sec Sch
Shepherds Hill Gdn
Crouch End
Crouch End Hill
Hornsey Rise
Hornsey La
Archway Rd
N6
Highgate
North Hill
Highgate High St
Highgate Hill
Waterlow Park
Highgate Cemy
Parkland Walk
YWCA Hostel
Channing Sch
St Michael's CE Prim Sch
St Joseph's RC Prim Sch
The Whittington
Archway
Upper
N19
Fortismere Sch (South Wing)
St Luke's Woodside
St James's CE Prim Sch
Muswell Hill Prim Sch
Coleridge Prim Sch
Highgate Sch
Mast

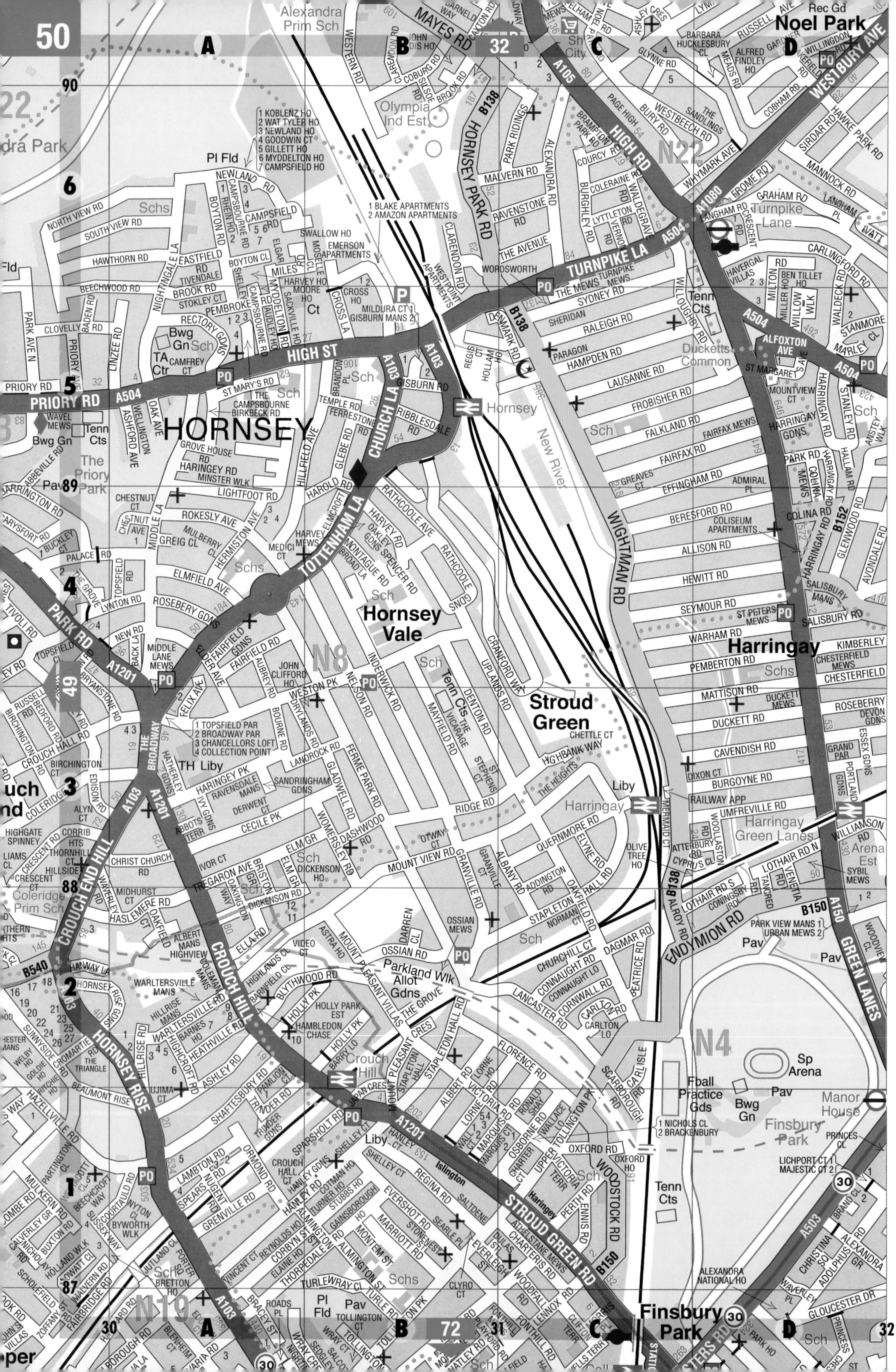

A
B
C
D
32
72
49
30
31
90
89
88
87
6
5
4
3
2
1
HORNSEY
Hornsey Vale
Stroud Green
Harringay
Noel Park
N22
N8
N4
N19
Alexandra Prim Sch
Olympia Ind Est
Hornsey
Harringay
Harringay Green Lanes
Crouch Hill
Finsbury Park
Manor House
Turnpike Lane
Ducketts Common
New River
The Priory Park
Parkland Wlk
Sp Arena
Fball Practice Gds
TURNPIKE LA
HIGH ST
PRIORY RD
HIGH RD
WESTBURY AVE
GREEN LANES
TOTTENHAM LA
CHURCH LA
PARK RD
THE BROADWAY
CROUCH END HILL
CROUCH HILL
HORNSEY RISE
STROUD GREEN RD
WIGHTMAN RD
HORNSEY PARK RD
MAYES RD
ENDYMION RD
HARRINGAY RD
MOUNT VIEW RD
FERME PARK RD
A504
A103
A1201
A105
A1080
B138
B150
B152
A503
B540
Islington
Haringey

TOTTENHAM
Recn Gd
West Green
Downhills Recn Gd
Downhills Park
Chestnuts Recn Gd
St Ann's General
South Tottenham
Seven Sisters
Bruce Grove
Stamford Hill
Arena Bsns Ctr
Crusader Ind Est
East Resr
West Resr
Capital Ring
Abney Park Cemy
STOKE
Stoke Newington
Open Air Theatre
The Moselle
N17
N15
N4
N16
WEST GREEN RD
BROAD LA
HIGH RD
STAMFORD HILL
SEVEN SISTERS RD
AMHURST PK
ST ANN'S RD
PHILIP LA
MONUMENT WAY
FOUNTAYNE RD
MANOR RD
LORDSHIP PK
DOWNHILLS PARK RD
DOWNHILLS WAY
BELMONT RD
A1080
A504
A503
A10
A1055
A107
A105
B155
B153
B152
B105
Haringey
Hackney
33
52
73
32
34

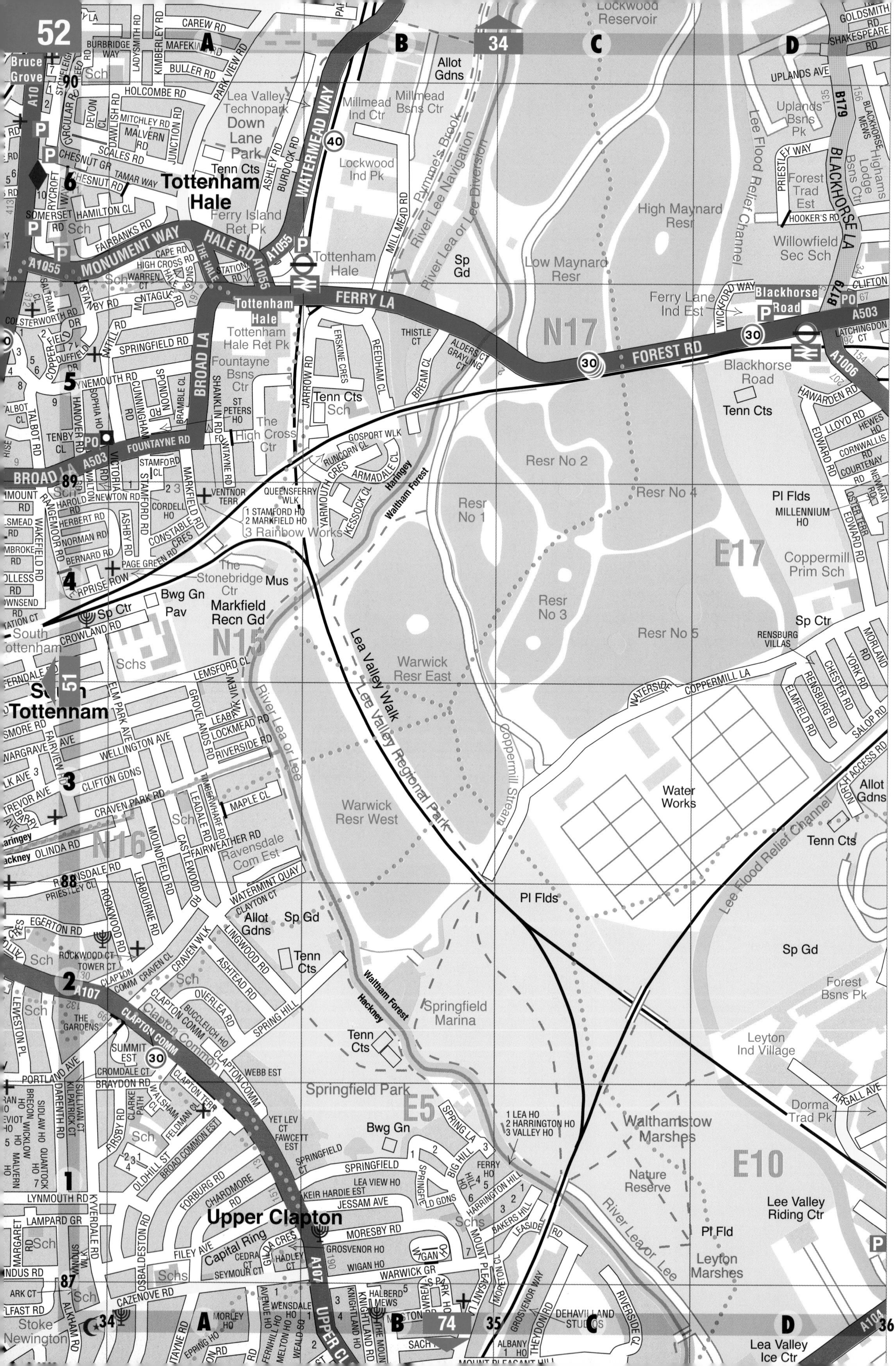
A
B
C
D
34
Lockwood Reservoir
Allot Gdns
Millmead Ind Ctr
Millmead Bsns Ctr
Lea Valley Technopark
Down Lane Park
Lockwood Ind Pk
WATERMEAD WAY
Pymme's Brook
River Lee Navigation
River Lea or Lee Diversion
MILL MEAD RD
High Maynard Resr
Low Maynard Resr
Sp Gd
Tottenham Hale
Tenn Cts
Ferry Island Ret Pk
MONUMENT WAY
HALE RD
THE HALE
A1055
FERRY LA
FOREST RD
A503
N17
Lee Flood Relief Channel
Uplands Bsns Pk
UPLANDS AVE
Forest Trad Est
Higham Lodge Bsns Ctr
BLACKHORSE LA
B179
Willowfield Sec Sch
Ferry Lane Ind Est
Blackhorse Road
WICKFORD WAY
Tottenham Hale Ret Pk
Fountayne Bsns Ctr
BROAD LA
FOUNTAYNE RD
The High Cross Ctr
St Peters Ho
Tenn Cts
Sch
Resr No 1
Resr No 2
Resr No 3
Resr No 4
Resr No 5
Pl Flds
Millennium Ho
E17
Coppermill Prim Sch
Sp Ctr
Rensburg Villas
COPPERMILL LA
WATERSIDE
Water Works
Coppermill Stream
The Stonebridge Ctr
Mus
Bwg Gn
Pav
Markfield Recn Gd
South Tottenham
N15
Haringey
Waltham Forest
Warwick Resr East
Warwick Resr West
Lea Valley Walk
Lee Valley Regional Park
River Lea or Lee
Ravensdale Com Est
N16
Hackney
WATERMINT QUAY
Allot Gdns
Sp Gd
Tenn Cts
Pl Flds
Sp Gd
Forest Bsns Pk
Leyton Ind Village
Springfield Marina
Springfield Park
E5
Bwg Gn
Walthamstow Marshes
Nature Reserve
E10
Lee Valley Riding Ctr
Dorma Trad Pk
ARGALL AVE
Pl Fld
Leyton Marshes
Upper Clapton
Capital Ring
CLAPTON COMM
Clapton Common
A107
UPPER CLAPTON RD
Stoke Newington
Summit Est
Webb Est
35
36
74
51
Lea Valley Ice Ctr
A104
DEHAVILLAND STUDIOS

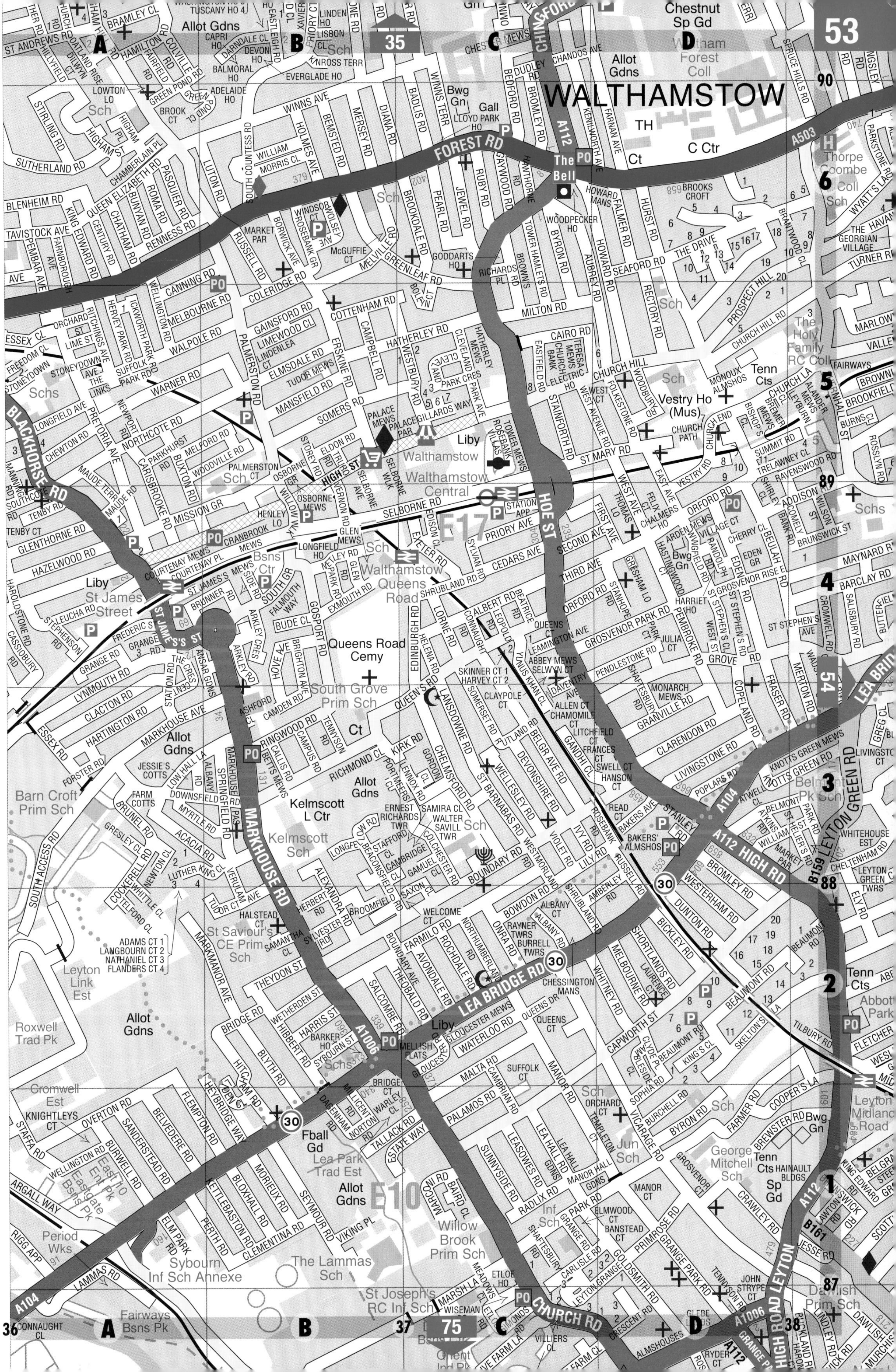
53
35
75
54
36
37
38
A
B
C
D
1
2
3
4
5
6
87
88
89
90
WALTHAMSTOW
E17
E10
Chestnut Sp Gd
Waltham Forest Coll
Allot Gdns
FOREST RD
A503
A112
The Bell
HOE ST
HIGH ST
Walthamstow Central
Walthamstow Queens Road
St James Street
BLACKHORSE RD
ST JAMES'S ST
Queens Road Cemy
South Grove Prim Sch
Kelmscott L Ctr
Kelmscott Sch
MARKHOUSE RD
A1006
LEA BRIDGE RD
A104
A112 HIGH RD
LEYTON GREEN RD
B159
HIGH ROAD LEYTON
CHURCH RD
B161
Leyton Midland Road
Barn Croft Prim Sch
Leyton Link Est
Roxwell Trad Pk
Cromwell Est
St Saviour's CE Prim Sch
Lea Park Trad Est
Willow Brook Prim Sch
The Lammas Sch
Sybourn Inf Sch Annexe
Period Wks
Fairways Bsns Pk
St Joseph's RC Inf Sch
George Mitchell Sch
Vestry Ho (Mus)
The Holy Family RC Coll
Thorpe Coombe Coll
Dawlish Prim Sch
Walthamstow Palace Mews
Liby
Fball Gd

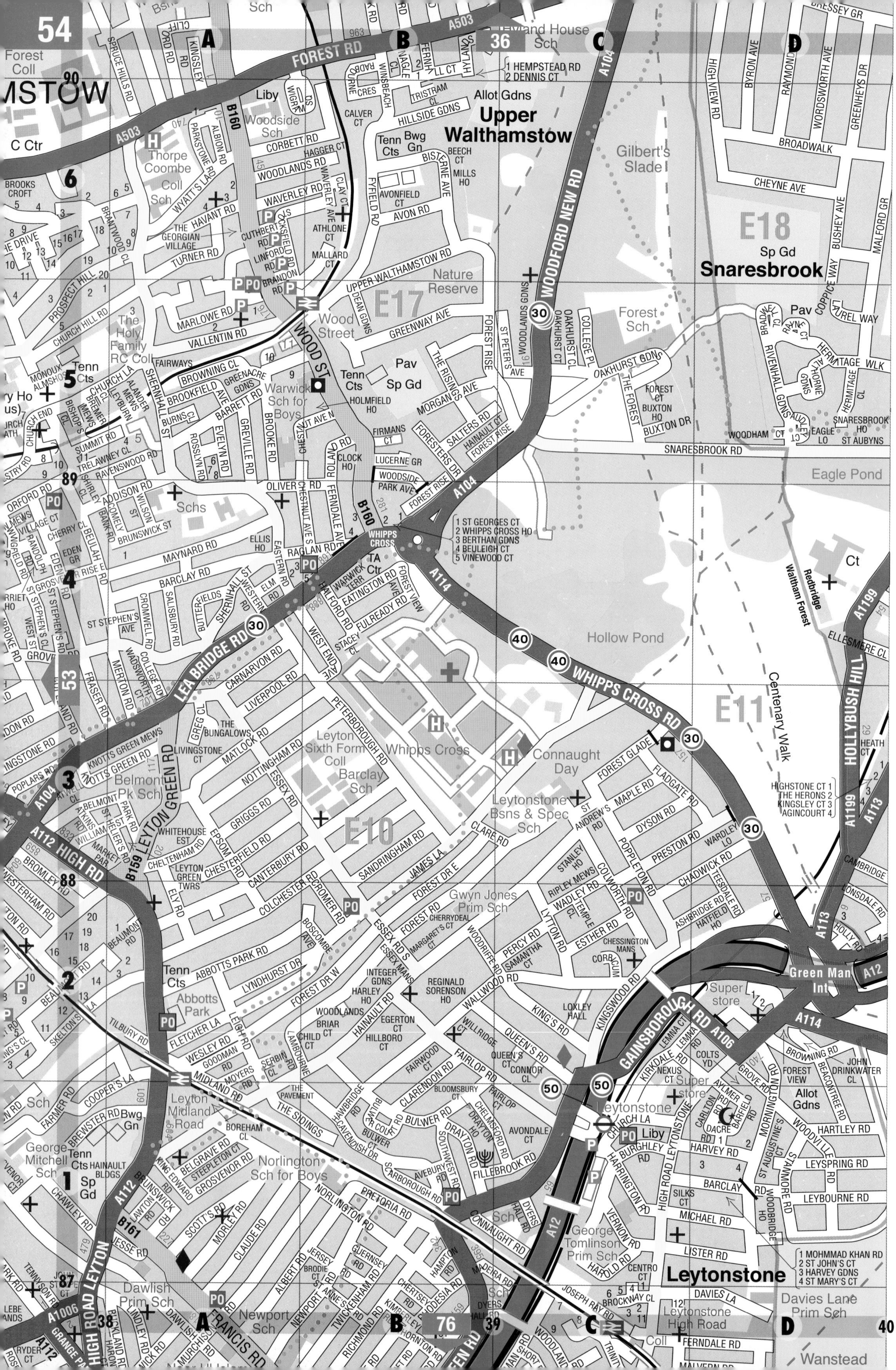
Upper Walthamstow
Snaresbrook
Leytonstone
E17
E18
E11
E10
FOREST RD
A503
WOODFORD NEW RD
A104
WHIPPS CROSS RD
A114
LEA BRIDGE RD
HIGH RD
A112
LEYTON GREEN RD
B159
WOOD ST
B160
SNARESBROOK RD
GAINSBOROUGH RD
A106
HOLLYBUSH HILL
A1199
A113
A12
HIGH ROAD LEYTON
HIGH ROAD LEYTONSTONE
Gilbert's Slade
Nature Reserve
Eagle Pond
Hollow Pond
Centenary Walk
Whipps Cross
Green Man Int
Leyton Midland Road
Leytonstone High Road
Forest Sch
Woodside Sch
Thorpe Coombe
The Holy Family RC Coll
Warwick Sch for Boys
Leyton Sixth Form Coll
Barclay Sch
Belmont Pk Sch
Leytonstone Bsns & Spec Sch
Connaught Day
Gwyn Jones Prim Sch
Abbotts Park
Norlington Sch for Boys
George Mitchell Sch
Dawlish Prim Sch
Newport Sch
George Tomlinson Prim Sch
Davies Lane Prim Sch
Wanstead
Redbridge
Waltham Forest
Allot Gdns
Sp Gd
Tenn Cts
Pav
Liby
1 HEMPSTEAD RD
2 DENNIS CT
1 ST GEORGES CT
2 WHIPPS CROSS HO
3 BERTHAN GDNS
4 BEULEIGH CT
5 VINEWOOD CT
HIGHSTONE CT 1
THE HERONS 2
KINGSLEY CT 3
AGINCOURT 4
1 MOHMMAD KHAN RD
2 ST JOHN'S CT
3 HARVEY GDNS
4 ST MARY'S CT
A
B
C
D
1
2
3
4
5
6
36
53
76
38
39
40
87
88
89
90

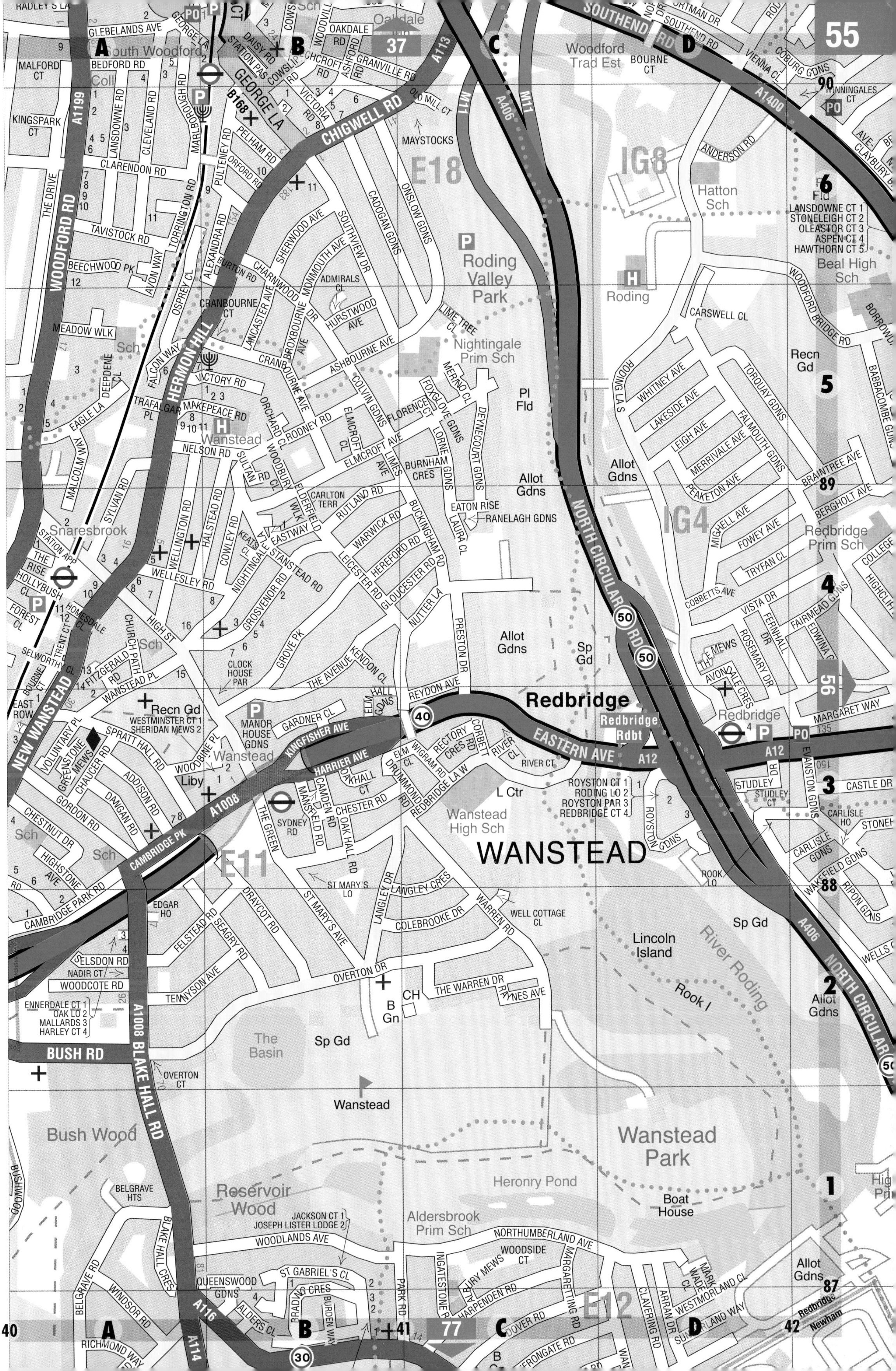
A
B
C
D
South Woodford
Woodford Trad Est
E18
IG8
IG4
E11
E12
Roding Valley Park
Nightingale Prim Sch
Redbridge
Redbridge Rdbt
WANSTEAD
Wanstead
Snaresbrook
Wanstead Park
Wanstead High Sch
Lincoln Island
River Roding
Rook I
Heronry Pond
Boat House
Bush Wood
Reservoir Wood
The Basin
Aldersbrook Prim Sch
Hatton Sch
Beal High Sch
Redbridge Prim Sch
Roding
Allot Gdns
Sp Gd
Recn Gd
L Ctr
Liby
Pl Fld
MAYSTOCKS
GLEBELANDS AVE
GEORGE LA
BEDFORD RD
MALFORD CT
KINGSPARK CT
WOODFORD RD
NEW WANSTEAD
HERMON HILL
CHIGWELL RD
NORTH CIRCULAR RD
EASTERN AVE
SOUTHEND RD
BUSH RD
BLAKE HALL RD
CAMBRIDGE PK
CAMBRIDGE PARK RD
KINGFISHER AVE
HARRIER AVE
WOODLANDS AVE
NORTHUMBERLAND AVE
WOODFORD BRIDGE RD
OVERTON DR
THE WARREN DR
WARREN RD
HIGH ST
WANSTEAD PL
NIGHTINGALE LA
ONSLOW GDNS
CADOGAN GDNS
SOUTHVIEW DR
CHARNWOOD DR
ASHBOURNE AVE
CRANBOURNE AVE
ELMCROFT AVE
FLORENCE CT
DEYNECOURT GDNS
BUCKINGHAM RD
PRESTON DR
REYDON AVE
RECTORY CRES
EVANSTON GDNS
MARGARET WAY
CASTLE DR
NORTHUMBERLAND AVE
PARK RD
INGATESTONE RD
HARPENDEN RD
CLAVERING RD
ARRAN DR
WESTMORLAND CL
SUNDERLAND WAY
DOVER RD
BELGRAVE RD
WINDSOR RD
RICHMOND WAY
QUEENSWOOD GDNS
ST GABRIEL'S CL
BRADING CRES
ALDERS CL
A406
A12
A113
A1008
A1199
A116
A114
A1400
M11
B168
37
77
56
40
41
42
90
89
88
87
1
2
3
4
5
6

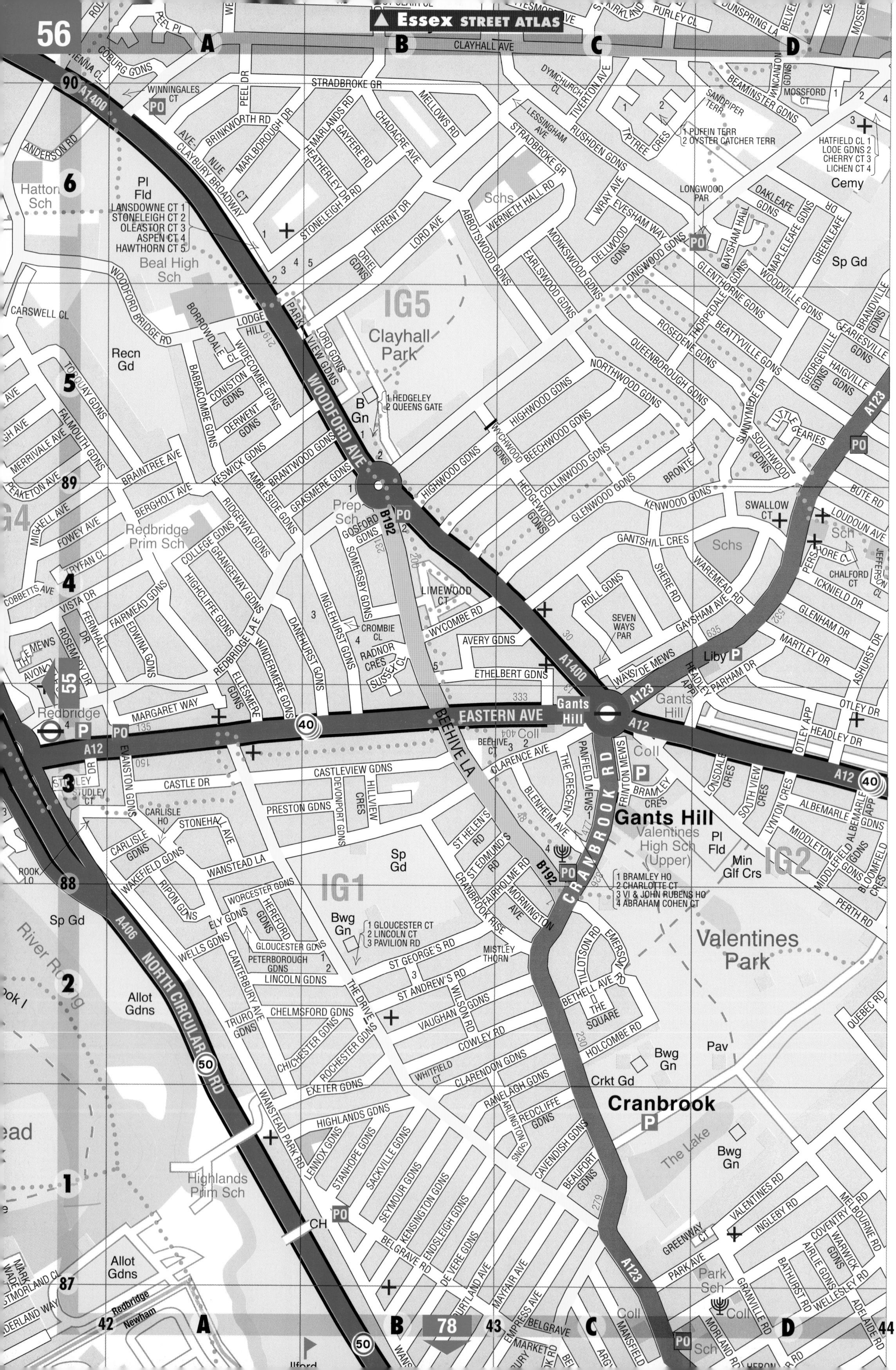
A
B
C
D
CLAYHALL AVE
STRADBROKE GR
WINNINGALES CT
PO
PEEL DR
PEEL PL
COBURG GDNS
ANDERSON RD
Hatton Sch
A1400
90
6
5
4
3
2
1
89
88
87
BRINKWORTH RD
MARLBOROUGH DR
CLAYBURY BROADWAY
MARLANDS RD
GAYFERE RD
CHADACRE AVE
MELLOWS RD
HEATHERLEY DR
STONELEIGH RD
HERENT DR
LORD AVE
ORIEL GDNS
ABBOTSWOOD GDNS
WERNETH HALL RD
STRADBROKE GR
LESSINGHAM AVE
DYMCHURCH CL
TIVERTON AVE
RUSHDEN GDNS
TIPTREE CRES
SANDPIPER TERR
1 PUFFIN TERR
2 OYSTER CATCHER TERR
BEAMINSTER GDNS
WINCANTON GDNS
MOSSFORD CT
HATFIELD CL 1
LOOE GDNS 2
CHERRY CT 3
LICHEN CT 4
Cemy
PURLEY CL
KIRKLAND
SUNSPRING LA
Pl Fld
LANSDOWNE CT 1
STONELEIGH CT 2
OLEASTOR CT 3
ASPEN CT 4
HAWTHORN CT 5
Beal High Sch
WOODFORD BRIDGE RD
CARSWELL CL
Recn Gd
BORROWDALE CL
LODGE HILL
WIDECOMBE GDNS
CONISTON GDNS
DERWENT GDNS
BABBACOMBE GDNS
PARK VIEW GDNS
LORD GDNS
IG5
Clayhall Park
Schs
EARLSWOOD GDNS
MONKSWOOD GDNS
DELLWOOD GDNS
WRAY AVE
EVESHAM WAY
LONGWOOD GDNS
LONGWOOD PAR
GAYSHAM HALL
OAKLEAFE GDNS
MAPLELEAFE GDNS
GREENLEAFE DR
Sp Gd
GLENTHORNE GDNS
WOODVILLE GDNS
BRANDVILLE GDNS
GEARIESVILLE GDNS
GEORGEVILLE GDNS
HAIGVILLE GDNS
ROSEDENE GDNS
THORPEDALE GDNS
BEATTYVILLE GDNS
QUEENBOROUGH GDNS
NORTHWOOD GDNS
SUNNYMEDE DR
LITTLE GEARIES
SOUTHWOOD GDNS
A123
TORQUAY GDNS
FALMOUTH GDNS
MERRIVALE AVE
PEAKETON AVE
MICHELL AVE
FOWEY AVE
BRAINTREE AVE
BERGHOLT AVE
KESWICK GDNS
AMBLESIDE GDNS
BRANTWOOD GDNS
GRASMERE GDNS
WOODFORD AVE
B Gn
1 HEDGELEY
2 QUEENS GATE
HIGHWOOD GDNS
WYCHWOOD GDNS
BEECHWOOD GDNS
COLLINWOOD GDNS
HEDGEWOOD GDNS
GLENWOOD GDNS
BRONTE CL
KENWOOD GDNS
SWALLOW CT
BUTE RD
LOUDOUN AVE
Sch
PERSHORE CL
JEFFERSON CL
CHALFORD CT
Schs
GANTSHILL CRES
ICKNIELD DR
GLENHAM DR
MARTLEY DR
ASHURST DR
Redbridge Prim Sch
COLLEGE GDNS
GRANGEWAY GDNS
RIDGEWAY GDNS
HIGHCLIFFE GDNS
Prep Sch
GOSFORD GDNS
SOMERSBY GDNS
B192
LIMEWOOD CT
WYCOMBE RD
BRYFAN CL
VISTA DR
COBBETTS AVE
FERNHALL DR
FAIRMEAD GDNS
EDWINA GDNS
REDBRIDGE LA E
WINDERMERE GDNS
DANEHURST GDNS
INGLEHURST GDNS
CROMBIE CL
RADNOR CRES
SUSSEX CL
AVERY GDNS
ETHELBERT GDNS
ROLL GDNS
SHERE RD
SEVEN WAYS PAR
WAREMEAD RD
GAYSHAM AVE
Liby
PARHAM DR
HEADLEY APP
WAYSIDE MEWS
THE MEWS
AVONDALE
ROSEMARY DR
55
Redbridge
MARGARET WAY
ELLESMERE GDNS
EASTERN AVE
A12
40
BEEHIVE LA
Gants Hill
Gants Hill
Coll
OTLEY DR
HEADLEY DR
OTLEY APP
BEEHIVE CT
CLARENCE AVE
EVANSTON GDNS
CASTLE DR
CASTLEVIEW GDNS
DEVONPORT GDNS
HILLVIEW CRES
PRESTON GDNS
STUDLEY CT
CARLISLE HO
STONEHALL AVE
CARLISLE GDNS
WAKEFIELD GDNS
RIPON GDNS
WANSTEAD LA
ROOKWOOD
Sp Gd
IG1
THE CRESCENT
PANFIELD MEWS
CRANBROOK RD
FRINTON MEWS
BRAMLEY CRES
LONSDALE CRES
SOUTH VIEW CRES
LYNTON CRES
ALBEMARLE GDNS
ALBEMARLE APP
MIDDLEFIELD GDNS
MIDDLETON GDNS
BLOOMFIELD CRES
Valentines High Sch (Upper)
Pl Fld
Min Glf Crs
IG2
1 BRAMLEY HO
2 CHARLOTTE CT
3 VI & JOHN RUBENS HO
4 ABRAHAM COHEN CT
PERTH RD
ST HELEN'S RD
ST EDMUND'S RD
BLENHEIM AVE
FAIRHOLME RD
MORNINGTON AVE
CRANBROOK RISE
WORCESTER GDNS
HEREFORD GDNS
ELY GDNS
WELLS GDNS
Bwg Gn
1 GLOUCESTER CT
2 LINCOLN CT
3 PAVILION RD
GLOUCESTER GDNS
PETERBOROUGH GDNS
LINCOLN GDNS
ST GEORGE'S RD
MISTLEY THORN
ST ANDREW'S RD
WILSON RD
TILLOTSON RD
EMERSON RD
BETHELL AVE
THE SQUARE
Valentines Park
River Roding
Allot Gdns
A406
NORTH CIRCULAR RD
50
CANTERBURY AVE
TRURO GDNS
CHELMSFORD GDNS
THE DRIVE
VAUGHAN GDNS
COWLEY RD
CHICHESTER GDNS
ROCHESTER GDNS
HOLCOMBE RD
Bwg Gn
Pav
QUEBEC RD
WHITFIELD CT
CLARENDON GDNS
EXETER GDNS
RANELAGH GDNS
ARLINGTON GDNS
REDCLIFFE GDNS
Crkt Gd
Cranbrook
The Lake
Bwg Gn
HIGHLANDS GDNS
WANSTEAD PARK RD
LENNOX GDNS
STANHOPE GDNS
SACKVILLE GDNS
SEYMOUR GDNS
KENSINGTON GDNS
ENDSLEIGH GDNS
CAVENDISH GDNS
BEAUFORT GDNS
Highlands Prim Sch
CH
BELGRAVE RD
DE VERE GDNS
PORTLAND AVE
MAYFAIR AVE
EMPRESS AVE
GREENWAY CT
VALENTINES RD
INGLEBY RD
MELBOURNE RD
COVENTRY RD
WARWICK GDNS
AIRLIE GDNS
BATHURST RD
WELLESLEY RD
ADELAIDE RD
GRANVILLE RD
PARK AVE
Park Sch
Coll
MORLAND RD
MANSFIELD
BELGRAVE
MARKET
A123
Allot Gdns
WESTMORLAND CL
Redbridge
Newham
42
43
44
78
Ilford
Sch
PO

Fairlop Waters Ctry Pk
Fairlop Plain
Ilford Jewish Prim Sch
Sch of Riding
Barkingside
IG6
Recn Gd
Fullwood Prim Sch
Superstore
Fball Gd
Aldborough Hatch
Aldborough Hall Farm
Aldborough House Farm
Allot Gdns
Pl Fld
William Torbitt Prim Sch
IG2
Bwg Gn
Sports Gd
Oaks Park High Sch
Newbury Park
Seven Kings Park
Farnham Green Prim Sch
Sp Gd
Seven Kings High Sch
Downshall Prim Sch
Westwood Rec Gd
Seven Kings
IG1
IG3
Christchurch Prim Sch
St Aidan's RC Sch
Canon Palmer RC Sch
HIGH ST
HIGH RD
EASTERN AVE
A12
A118
A123
A1083
STATION RD
ALDBOROUGH RD
ALDBOROUGH RD N
ALDBOROUGH RD S
HORNS RD
WESTMINSTER GDNS
WAVERLEY GDNS
FREMANTLE RD
CRAVEN GDNS
HEYBRIDGE DR
TANNERS LA
CARLTON DR
RAILWAY COTTS
CARLTON CT
PRINCES RD
DUKE RD
CROWN RD
OAKS LA
CHEVIOT WAY
SEVEN KINGS RD
GOODMAYES RD

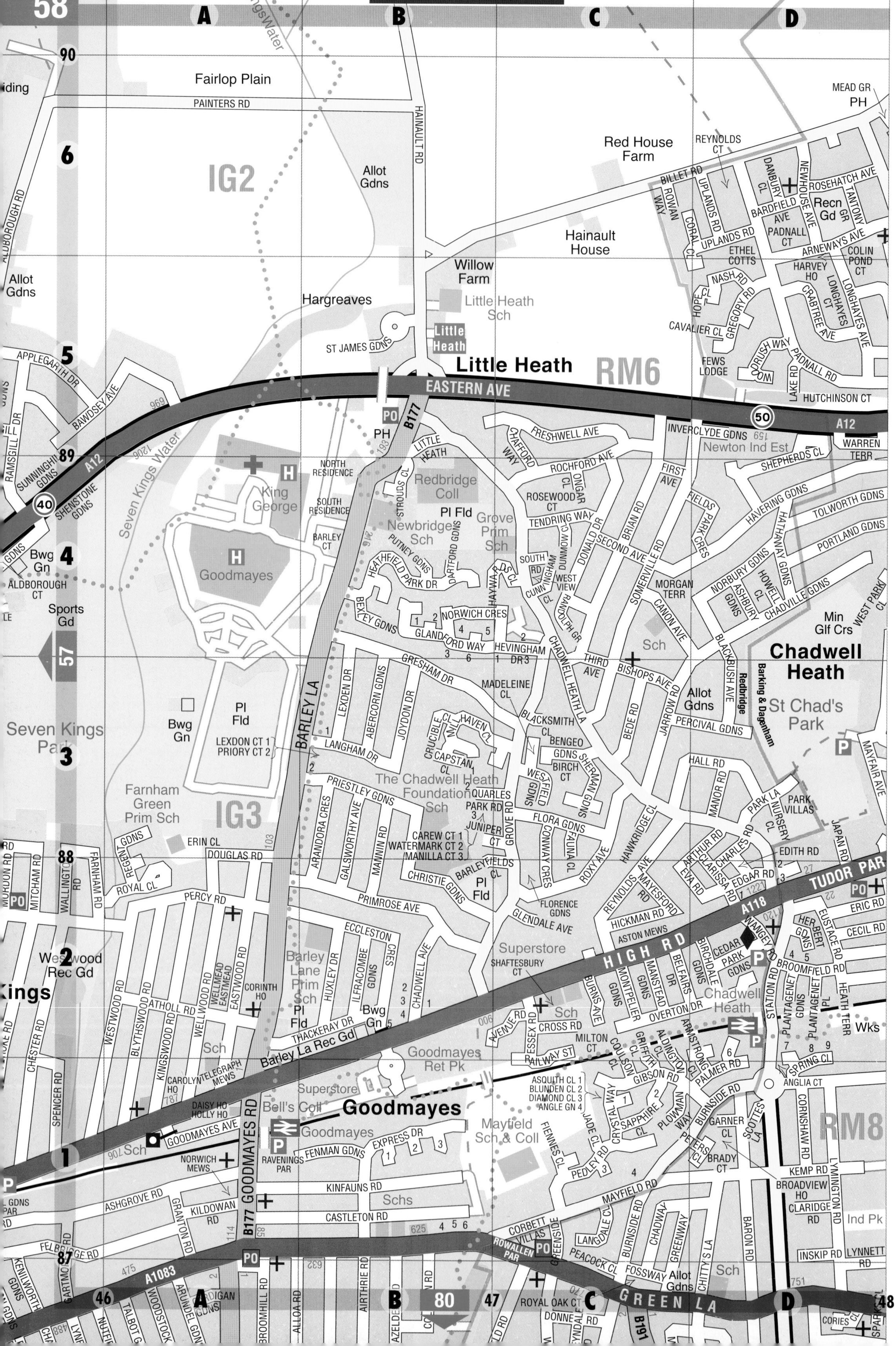
A
B
C
D
90
89
88
87
6
5
4
3
2
1
57
80
46
47
48
Fairlop Plain
PAINTERS RD
HAINAULT RD
IG2
Allot Gdns
Red House Farm
REYNOLDS CT
MEAD GR
PH
BILLET RD
ROWAN WAY
CORAL CL
UPLANDS RD
DANBURY CL
BARDFIELD AVE
NEWHOUSE AVE
ROSEHATCH AVE
TANTONY GR
Recn Gd
PADNALL CT
ARNEWAYS AVE
ETHEL COTTS
COLIN POND CT
HARVEY HO
Hainault House
Willow Farm
Little Heath Sch
Little Heath
Hargreaves
NASH RD
HOPE CL
GREGORY RD
CRABTREE AVE
LONGHAYES CT
LONGHAYES AVE
CAVALIER CL
ST JAMES GDNS
Little Heath
RM6
FEWS LODGE
RUSH WAY
PADNALL RD
LAKE RD
HUTCHINSON CT
APPLEGARTH DR
BAWDSEY AVE
EASTERN AVE
A12
50
INVERCLYDE GDNS
Newton Ind Est
WARREN TERR
SHEPHERDS CL
ALDBOROUGH RD
Allot Gdns
RAMSGILL DR
SUNNINGHILL GDNS
SHENSTONE GDNS
40
Seven Kings Water
King George
H
Goodmayes
NORTH RESIDENCE
SOUTH RESIDENCE
BARLEY CT
PO
PH
B177
LITTLE HEATH
STROUDS CL
Redbridge Coll
Pl Fld
Newbridge Sch
Grove Prim Sch
CHAFFORD WAY
FRESHWELL AVE
ROCHFORD AVE
ONGAR CL
ROSEWOOD CT
TENDRING WAY
FIRST AVE
FIELDS PARK CRES
HAVERING GDNS
TOLWORTH GDNS
HATHAWAY GDNS
PORTLAND GDNS
SECOND AVE
BRIAN RD
DONALD DR
DUNMOW CL
SOUTH RD
CUNNINGHAM CL
WEST VIEW
RANDOLPH GR
SOMERVILLE RD
MORGAN TERR
NORBURY GDNS
ASHBURY GDNS
HOWELL CL
CHADVILLE GDNS
WEST PARK CL
Min Glf Crs
Chadwell Heath
PUTNEY GDNS
DARTFORD GDNS
HEATHFIELD PARK DR
HAYWARDS CL
NORWICH CRES
BEXLEY GDNS
GLANDFORD WAY
HEVINGHAM DR
CANON AVE
Sch
THIRD AVE
BISHOPS AVE
BLACKBUSH AVE
Redbridge
Barking & Dagenham
Bwg Gn
ALDBOROUGH CT
Sports Gd
GRESHAM DR
MADELEINE CL
CHADWELL HEATH LA
Allot Gdns
St Chad's Park
Seven Kings Park
Bwg Gn
Pl Fld
LEXDON CT 1
PRIORY CT 2
BARLEY LA
LEXDEN DR
ABERCORN GDNS
JOYDON DR
CRUCIBLE CL
MILL HAVEN CL
CAPSTAN CL
BLACKSMITH CL
BENGEO GDNS
BIRCH CT
SHERMAN GDNS
BEDE RD
JARROW RD
PERCIVAL GDNS
HALL RD
MAYFAIR AVE
LANGHAM DR
The Chadwell Heath Foundation Sch
QUARLES PARK RD
WESTFIELD GDNS
Farnham Green Prim Sch
IG3
PRIESTLEY GDNS
ARANDORA CRES
GALSWORTHY AVE
MANNIN RD
JUNIPER CT
GROVE RD
FLORA GDNS
CONWAY CRES
FAUNA CL
ROXY AVE
HAWKRIDGE CL
MANOR RD
PARK LA
NURSERY CL
PARK VILLAS
JAPAN RD
ERIN CL
DOUGLAS RD
REGENT GDNS
CAREW CT 1
WATERMARK CT 2
MANILLA CT 3
BARLEY FIELDS CL
ARTHUR RD
CHARLES RD
CLARISSA RD
EVA RD
EDGAR RD
EDITH RD
TUDOR PAR
FARNHAM RD
WALLINGTON RD
MITCHAM RD
ROYAL CL
CHRISTIE GDNS
Pl Fld
REYNOLDS AVE
MAYESFORD RD
A118
ERIC RD
PERCY RD
PRIMROSE AVE
FLORENCE GDNS
GLENDALE AVE
HICKMAN RD
ASTON MEWS
WANGEY RD
HERBERT GDNS
EUSTACE RD
CECIL RD
Westwood Rec Gd
Kings
ECCLESTON CRES
Barley Lane Prim Sch
Pl Fld
HUXLEY DR
ILFRACOMBE GDNS
CHADWELL AVE
Superstore
SHAFTESBURY CT
HIGH RD
BURNS AVE
MONTPELIER GDNS
MANSTEAD GDNS
BELFAIRS DR
BIRCHDALE GDNS
CEDAR PARK GDNS
STATION RD
BROOMFIELD RD
PLANTAGENET GDNS
PLANTAGENET PL
HEATH TERR
WESTWOOD RD
BLYTHSWOOD RD
ATHOLL RD
WELLWOOD RD
WELLMEAD
EASTMEAD
EASTWOOD RD
CORINTHIAN HO
Bwg Gn
THACKERAY DR
Barley La Rec Gd
Sch
ESSEX RD
AVENUE RD
CROSS RD
OVERTON DR
Chadwell Heath
Wks
CHESTER RD
KINGSWOOD RD
TELEGRAPH MEWS
CAROLYN HO
Goodmayes Ret Pk
MILTON CT
RAILWAY ST
COULSON CL
GRIFFITH CL
ALDINGTON CL
ARMSTRONG CL
PALMER RD
SPRING CL
ANGLIA CT
SPENCER RD
Superstore
ASQUITH CL 1
BLUNDEN CL 2
DIAMOND CL 3
ANGLE GN 4
GIBSON RD
SAPPHIRE CL
PLOWMAN WAY
BURNSIDE RD
DAISY HO
HOLLY HO
Bell's Coll
Goodmayes
Goodmayes
GOODMAYES AVE
EXPRESS DR
Mayfield Sch & Coll
CRYSTAL WAY
JADE CL
FIENNES CL
PETERS CL
GARNER CL
SCOTTES LA
CORNSHAW RD
RM8
Sch
NORWICH MEWS
RAVENINGS PAR
FENMAN GDNS
PEDLEY RD
BRADY CT
KEMP RD
BROADVIEW HO
CLARIDGE RD
LYMINGTON RD
Ind Pk
ASHGROVE RD
KILDOWAN RD
GRANTON RD
GOODMAYES RD
KINFAUNS RD
Schs
CASTLETON RD
MAYFIELD RD
LANGDALE CL
BURNSIDE RD
CHADWAY
GREENWAY
CHITTY'S LA
BARON RD
CORBETT VILLAS
ROWALLEN PAR
GREENSIDE
PEACOCK CL
FOSSWAY
Allot Gdns
Sch
INSKIP RD
LYNNETT RD
FELBRIGGE RD
A1083
GARTMORE RD
KENILWORTH GDNS
TALBOT GDNS
WOODSTOCK
ARUNDEL GDNS
CARDIGAN GDNS
BROOMHILL RD
ALLOA RD
AIRTHRIE RD
AZELEIGH
ROYAL OAK CT
DONNE
GREEN LA
B191
CORIES CL
SPARKS CL

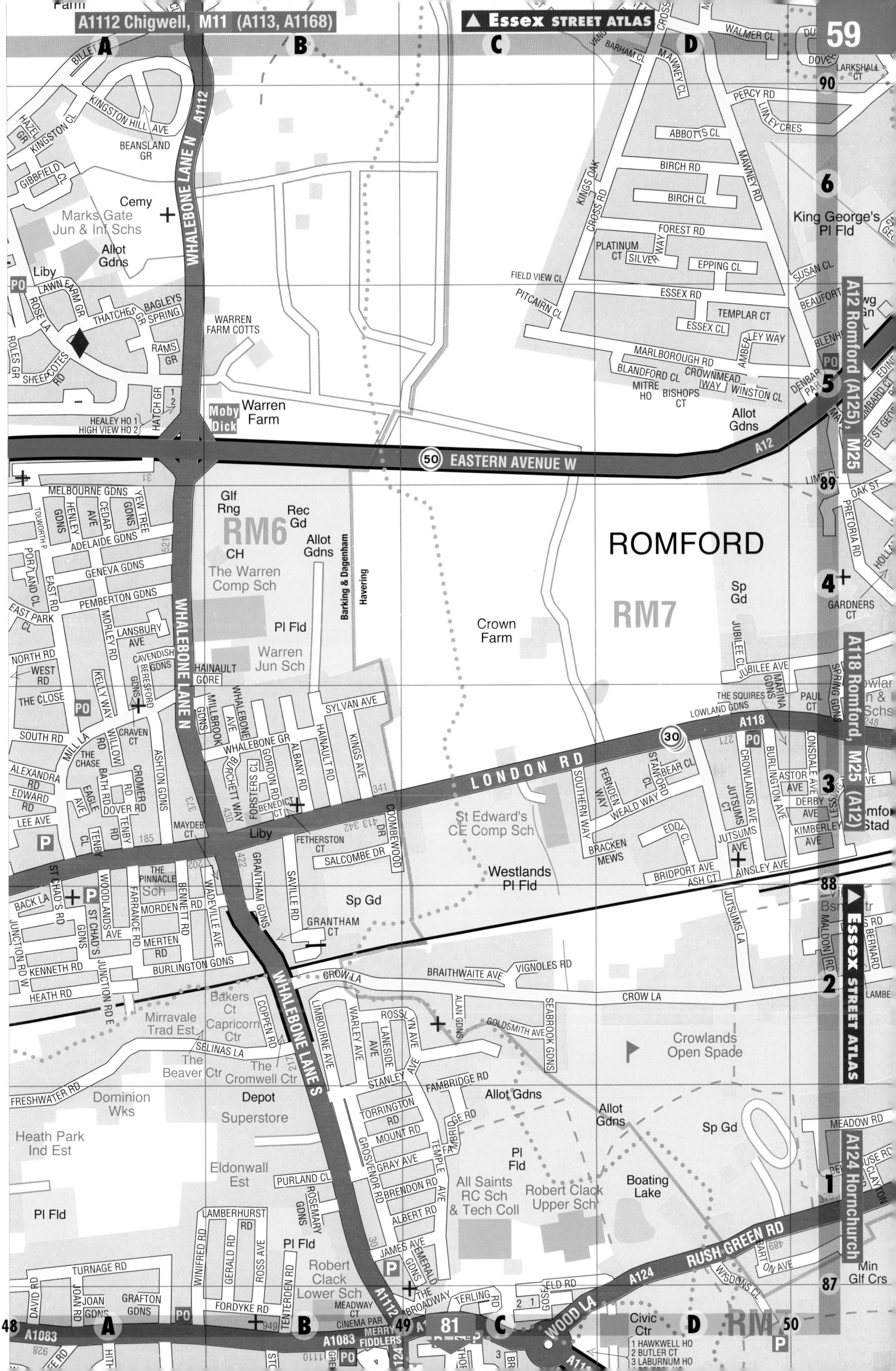
A1112 Chigwell, M11 (A113, A1168)
A
B
C
D
WALMER CL
BARHAM CL
MAWNEY CL
CROSS
LARKSHALL CT
90
PERCY RD
LINLEY CRES
ABBOTTS CL
BIRCH RD
BIRCH CL
MAWNEY RD
KINGS OAK
CROSS RD
6
King George's Pl Fld
FOREST RD
PLATINUM CT
SILVER WAY
EPPING CL
FIELD VIEW CL
PITCAIRN CL
ESSEX RD
SUSAN CL
BEAUFORT
TEMPLAR CT
ESSEX CL
AMBERLEY WAY
MARLBOROUGH RD
BLANDFORD CL
CROWNMEAD WAY
WINSTON CL
MITRE HO
BISHOPS CT
DENBAR PDE
5
Allot Gdns
A12 Romford (A125), M25
BILLET
HAZEL GR
KINGSTON CL
KINGSTON HILL AVE
BEANSLAND GR
GIBBFIELD CL
Cemy
Marks Gate Jun & Inf Schs
Allot Gdns
Liby
PO
LAWN FARM GR
ROSE LA
THATCHES GR
BAGLEYS SPRING
RAMS GR
ROLES GR
SHEEPCOTES RD
HATCH GR
HEALEY HO 1
HIGH VIEW HO 2
WHALEBONE LANE N
A1112
WARREN FARM COTTS
Moby Dick
Warren Farm
50
EASTERN AVENUE W
A12
89
OAK ST
PRETORIA RD
MELBOURNE GDNS
HENLEY GDNS
CEDAR AVE
YEW TREE GDNS
TOLWORTH P
Glf Rng
Rec Gd
RM6
CH
Allot Gdns
ADELAIDE GDNS
GENEVA GDNS
PORTLAND CL
EAST RD
The Warren Comp Sch
Barking & Dagenham
Havering
ROMFORD
Sp Gd
4
GARDNERS CT
RM7
EAST PARK CL
PEMBERTON GDNS
MORLEY RD
LANSBURY AVE
Pl Fld
Crown Farm
NORTH RD
CAVENDISH GDNS
BERESFORD GDNS
WEST RD
KELLY WAY
Warren Jun Sch
HAINAULT GORE
JUBILEE CL
JUBILEE AVE
A118 Romford, M25 (A12)
THE CLOSE
PO
MILLBROOK GDNS
WHALEBONE AVE
SYLVAN AVE
THE SQUIRES
MARINA GDNS
PAUL CT
SPRING GDNS
LOWLAND GDNS
A118
30
SOUTH RD
MILL LA
WILLOW RD
CRAVEN CT
THE CHASE
WHALEBONE GR
HAINAULT RD
KINGS AVE
PO
ALEXANDRA RD
BATH RD
CROMER RD
ASHTON GDNS
BURCHETT WAY
FORSTERS CL
GORDON RD
ALBANY RD
LONDON RD
SOUTHERN WAY
FERNDEN WAY
STANFORD CL
BEAR CL
CROWLANDS AVE
BURLINGTON AVE
ASTOR AVE
3
EDWARD RD
EAGLE AVE
DOVER RD
BENEDICT CT
341
DERBY AVE
LONSDALE AVE
LEE AVE
MAYDEB CT
373
WEALD WAY
JUTSUMS CT
KIMBERLEY AVE
P
TENBY CL
TENBY RD
185
430
Liby
FETHERSTON CT
COOMBEWOOD DR
St Edward's CE Comp Sch
EDDY CL
JUTSUMS AVE
SALCOMBE DR
BRACKEN MEWS
BRIDPORT AVE
ASH CT
AINSLEY AVE
ST CHAD'S RD
THE PINNACLE Sch
202
422
Westlands Pl Fld
88
BACK LA
P
WOODLANDS AVE
FARRANCE RD
BENNETT RD
WADEVILLE AVE
GRANTHAM GDNS
SAVILLE RD
Sp Gd
JUTSUMS LA
MALDON RD
BERNARD RD
ST CHAD'S GDNS
MORDEN RD
GRANTHAM CT
▲ Essex STREET ATLAS
JUNCTION RD W
MERTEN RD
BURLINGTON GDNS
KENNETH RD
JUNCTION RD E
BRAITHWAITE AVE
VIGNOLES RD
2
HEATH RD
WHALEBONE LANE S
CROW LA
CROW LA
LAMBE
Bakers Ct
Mirravale Trad Est
Capricorn Ctr
COPPEN RD
LIMBOURNE AVE
WARLEY AVE
ROSSLYN AVE
LANESIDE
ALAN GDNS
GOLDSMITH AVE
SEABROOK GDNS
Crowlands Open Space
SELINAS LA
The Beaver Ctr
The Cromwell Ctr
STANLEY AVE
FRESHWATER RD
Dominion Wks
Depot
FAMBRIDGE RD
Allot Gdns
Allot Gdns
Superstore
TORRINGTON RD
MOUNT RD
Sp Gd
MEADOW RD
Heath Park Ind Est
GROSVENOR RD
TEMPLE AVE
Pl Fld
GRAY AVE
Eldonwall Est
PURLAND CL
BRENDON RD
All Saints RC Sch & Tech Coll
Robert Clack Upper Sch
Boating Lake
1
CLAYTON
A124 Hornchurch
Pl Fld
ROSEMARY GDNS
ALBERT RD
LAMBERHURST RD
RUSH GREEN RD
WINIFRED RD
GERALD RD
ROSS AVE
Pl Fld
JAMES AVE
EMERALD GDNS
A124
BARTON AVE
Robert Clack Lower Sch
P
TURNAGE RD
DAVID RD
JOAN RD
JOAN GDNS
GRAFTON GDNS
TENTERDEN RD
WISDONS CL
87
Min Glf Crs
THE BROADWAY
TERLING RD
MEADWAY CT
A1112
FORDYKE RD
CINEMA PAR
PO
48
A1083
A
949
B
49
A1083
MERRY FIDDLERS
81
C
WOOD LA
Civic Ctr
D
RM7
50
1 HAWKWELL HO
2 BUTLER CT
3 LABURNUM HO
PO
P

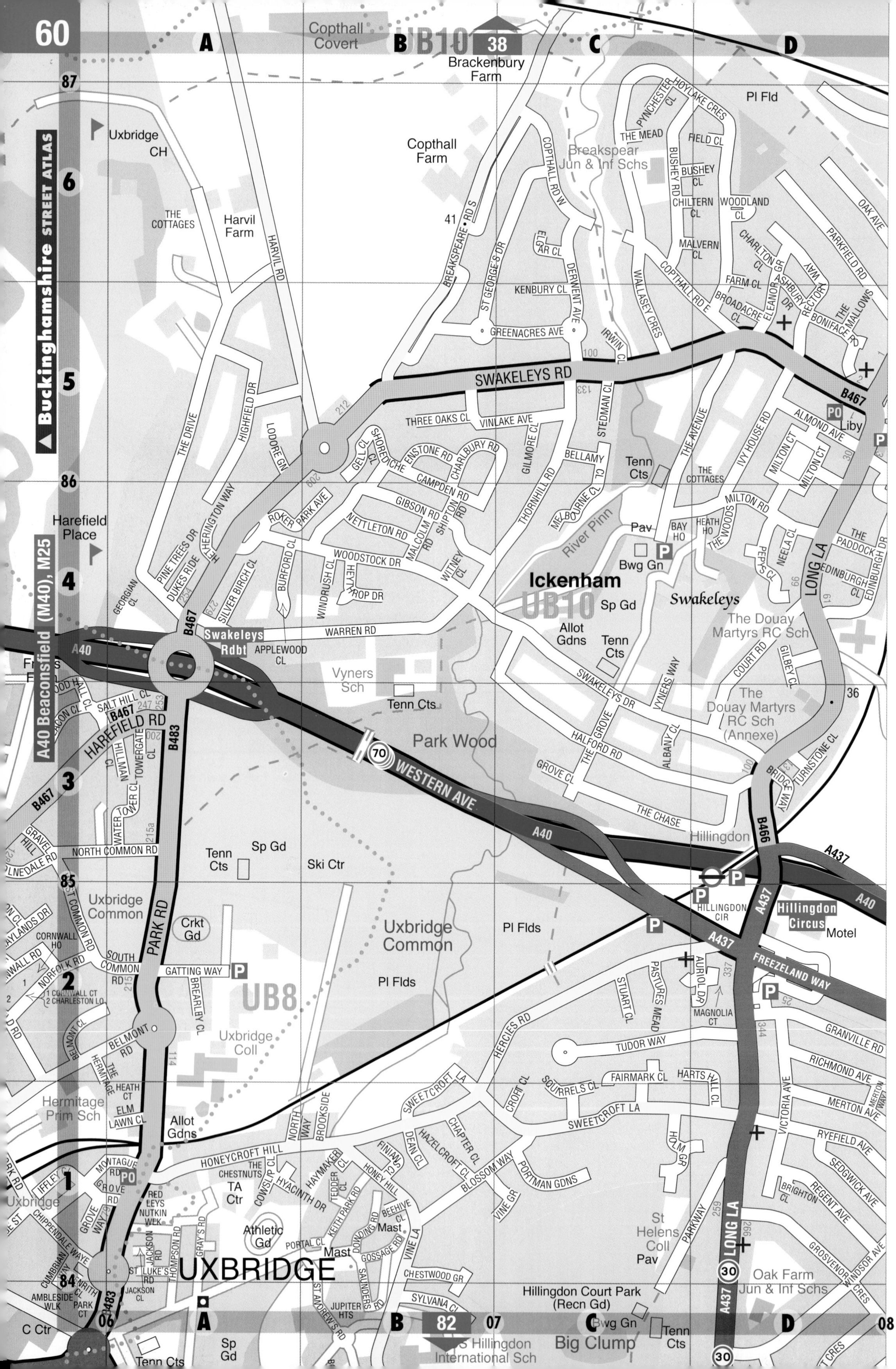
Buckinghamshire STREET ATLAS
A40 Beaconsfield (M40), M25
UB10
38
82
Copthall Covert
Brackenbury Farm
Copthall Farm
Uxbridge CH
THE COTTAGES
Harvil Farm
HARVIL RD
Breakspear Jun & Inf Schs
COPTHALL RD W
BREAKSPEARE RD S
ST GEORGE'S DR
ELGAR CL
KENBURY CL
DERWENT AVE
GREENACRES AVE
IRWIN CL
WALLASEY CRES
PYNCHESTER CL
HOYLAKE CRES
THE MEAD
FIELD CL
BUSHEY RD
BUSHEY CL
CHILTERN CL
WOODLAND CL
MALVERN CL
COPTHALL RD E
CHARLTON CL
FARM CL
BROADACRE CL
ELEANOR GR
ASHBURY DR
RECTORY WAY
BONIFACE RD
THE MALLOWS
PARKFIELD RD
OAK AVE
Pl Fld
SWAKELEYS RD
B467
PO
Liby
ALMOND AVE
MILTON CT
MILTON RD
IVY HOUSE RD
THE AVENUE
THE COTTAGES
STEDMAN CL
THREE OAKS CL
VINLAKE AVE
GILMORE CL
BELLAMY CL
MELBOURNE CL
THORNHILL RD
CHARLBURY RD
ENSTONE RD
CAMPDEN RD
SHOREDITCH RD
GELL CL
GIBSON RD
SHIPTON RD
NETTLETON RD
MALCOLM RD
ROKER PARK AVE
WOODSTOCK DR
WITNEY CL
HEYTHROP DR
HIGHFIELD DR
THE DRIVE
LODORE GN
HERINGTON WAY
PINE TREES DR
DUKES RIDE
Harefield Place
GEORGIAN CL
SILVER BIRCH CL
BURFORD CL
WINDRUSH CL
WARREN RD
Swakeleys Rdbt
APPLEWOOD CL
Tenn Cts
Pav
River Pinn
BAY HO
HEATH HO
THE WOODS
Bwg Gn
Ickenham
Sp Gd
Allot Gdns
Swakeleys
The Douay Martyrs RC Sch
The Douay Martyrs RC Sch (Annexe)
PEPYS CL
NEELA CL
THE PADDOCK
EDINBURGH DR
EDINBURGH CL
LONG LA
COURT RD
GILBEY CL
VYNERS WAY
SWAKELEYS DR
THE GROVE
HALFORD RD
ALBANY CL
GROVE CL
THE CHASE
TURNSTONE CL
BRIDGE WAY
B466
Hillingdon
Vyners Sch
Park Wood
70
WESTERN AVE
A40
A437
HILLINGDON CIR
Hillingdon Circus
Motel
FREEZELAND WAY
B467
HAREFIELD RD
SALT HILL CL
HILLMAN CL
TOWERGATE CL
B483
WATER TOWER CL
GRAVEL HILL
NORTH COMMON RD
Ski Ctr
Uxbridge Common
Crkt Gd
PARK RD
SOUTH COMMON RD
CORNWALL HO
NORFOLK RD
1 CORNWALL CT
2 CHARLESTON LO
GATTING WAY
BREARLEY CL
UB8
Uxbridge Coll
Pl Flds
BELMONT RD
BELMONT CL
HERMITAGE CL
THE HERMITAGE
HEATH CT
ELM LAWN CL
Hermitage Prim Sch
Allot Gdns
HERCIES RD
STUART CL
PASTURES MEAD
AURIOL DR
MAGNOLIA CT
GRANVILLE RD
TUDOR WAY
RICHMOND AVE
FAIRMARK CL
HARTS HILL CL
SQUIRRELS CL
CROFT CL
SWEETCROFT LA
MERTON AVE
MERTON WAY
VICTORIA AVE
RYEFIELD AVE
HOLM GR
SEDGWICK AVE
BRIGHTON CL
REGENT AVE
GROSVENOR CRES
WINDSOR AVE
HONEYCROFT HILL
NORTH WAY
BROOKSIDE
FINIAN CL
DEAN CL
HAZELCROFT CL
CHAPTER CL
BLOSSOM WAY
PORTMAN GDNS
VINE GR
PARKWAY
St Helens Coll
Pav
MONTAGUE RD
GROVE RD
THE CHESTNUTS
TA Ctr
COWSLIP CL
HYACINTH DR
HAYMAKER CL
TEDDER CL
HONEY HILL
BEEHIVE CL
KEITH PARK RD
DOWDING RD
Mast
GOSSAGE RD
VINE LA
Athletic Gd
PORTAL CL
RED LEYS
NUTKIN WLK
JACKSON RD
THOMPSON RD
GRAY'S RD
ST LUKE'S RD
JACKSON CL
UXBRIDGE
ST ANDREW'S RD
SAUNDERS RD
JUPITER HTS
CHESTWOOD GR
SYLVANA CL
Hillingdon Court Park (Recn Gd)
Oak Farm Jun & Inf Schs
Bwg Gn
Tenn Cts
Big Clump
Hillingdon International Sch
Sp Gd
Tenn Cts
C Ctr
IFFLEY CL
Uxbridge
CHIPPENDALE WAYE
GROVE WAY
CUMBRIAN WAY
PENRITH CL
AMBLESIDE WLK
PARK CT
06
07
08
A
B
C
D
87
86
85
84
6
5
4
3
2
1

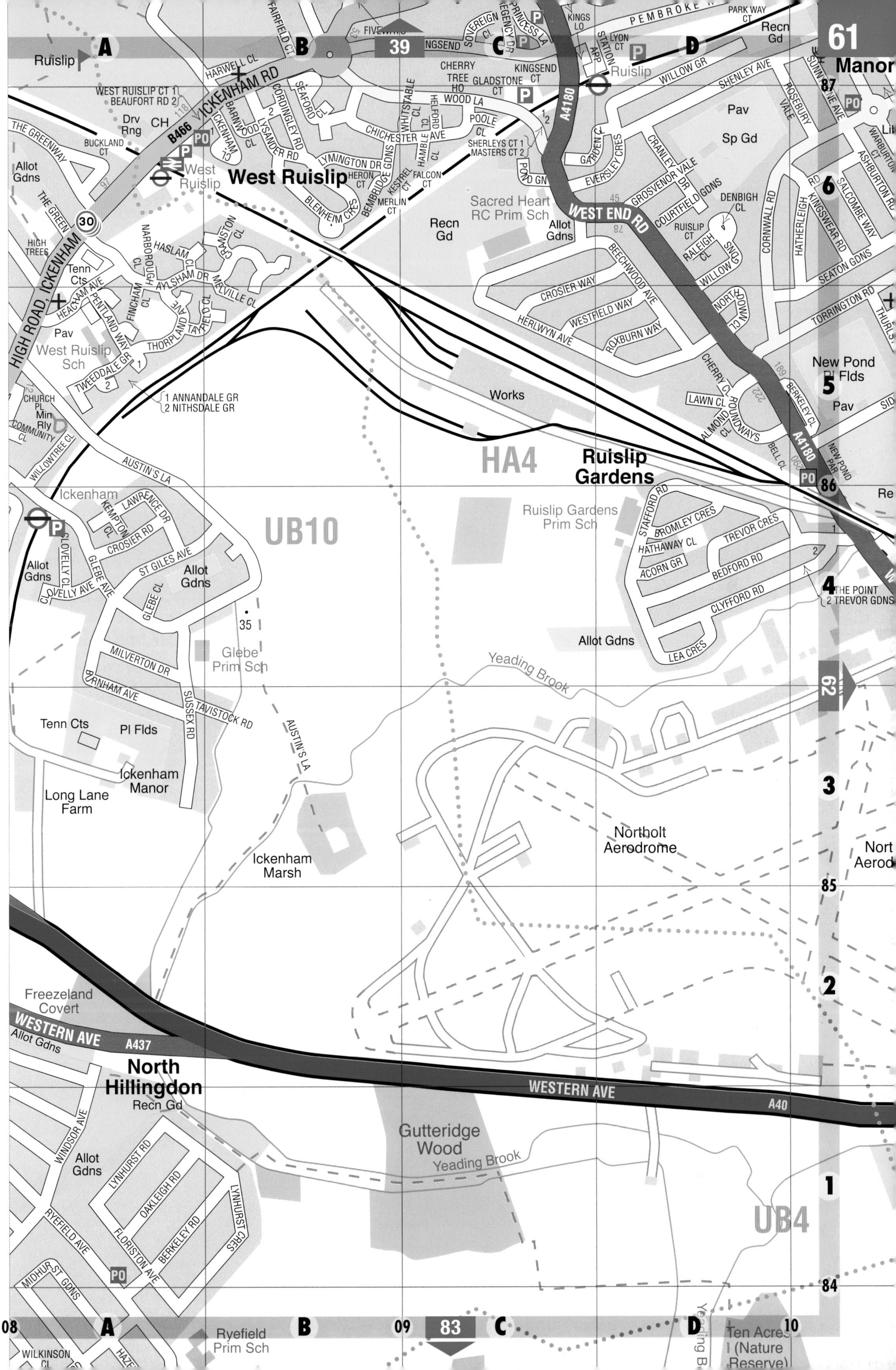
39
83
62
A
B
C
D
08
09
10
87
86
85
84
6
5
4
3
2
1
Ruislip
Manor
West Ruislip
Ruislip Gardens
North Hillingdon
Ickenham
HA4
UB10
UB4
ICKENHAM RD
B466
HIGH ROAD, ICKENHAM
WEST END RD
A4180
WESTERN AVE
A437
A40
PEMBROKE
PARK WAY CT
KINGS LO
LYON CT
STATION APP
PRINCESS LA
REGENCY DR
SOVEREIGN CL
KINGSEND
FIVEWAYS
FAIRFIELD CT
HARWELL CL
WEST RUISLIP CT 1
BEAUFORT RD 2
Drv Rng
CH
BUCKLAND CT
THE GREENWAY
Allot Gdns
THE GREEN
HIGH TREES
CORDINGLEY RD
SEAFORD CL
BARNWOOD CL
LYSANDER RD
ICKENHAM CL
CHERRY TREE HO
GLADSTONE CT
KINGSEND CT
WOOD LA
WHITSTABLE CL
HELFORD CL
CHICHESTER AVE
HAMBLE CL
POOLE CL
SHERLEYS CT 1
MASTERS CT 2
LYMINGTON DR
HERON CT
BEMBRIDGE GDNS
KESTREL CT
FALCON CT
MERLIN CT
BLENHEIM CRES
POND GN
WILLOW GR
SHENLEY AVE
SUNNINGDALE AVE
ROSEBURY VALE
Pav
Sp Gd
Recn Gd
GARDEN CL
EVERSLEY CRES
CRANLEY DR
GROSVENOR VALE
COURTFIELD GDNS
DENBIGH CL
RUISLIP CT
RALEIGH CL
WILLOW GDNS
CORNWALL RD
HATHERLEIGH RD
KINGSWEAR RD
SALCOMBE WAY
ASHBURTON RD
WARBURTON CL
SEATON GDNS
TORRINGTON RD
THURLSTONE
Sacred Heart RC Prim Sch
Tenn Cts
NARBOROUGH CL
HASLAM CL
CRANSTON CL
AYLSHAM DR
MELVILLE CL
HEACHAM AVE
PENTLAND WAY
FINCHAM CL
TAYFIELD CL
THORPLAND AVE
TWEEDDALE GR
1 ANNANDALE GR
2 NITHSDALE GR
West Ruislip Sch
CROSIER WAY
BEECHWOOD AVE
WESTFIELD WAY
HERLWYN AVE
ROXBURN WAY
NORTH DOWN CL
CHERRY CL
LAWN CL
ALMOND CL
ROUNDWAYS
BELL CL
BERKELEY CL
NEW POND PAR
New Pond Pl Flds
Works
CHURCH PL
Min Rly
COMMUNITY CL
WILLOWTREE CL
AUSTIN'S LA
LAWRENCE DR
KEMPTON CL
CROSIER RD
ST GILES AVE
CLOVELLY CL
CLOVELLY AVE
GLEBE AVE
GLEBE CL
STAFFORD RD
BROMLEY CRES
HATHAWAY CL
TREVOR CRES
ACORN GR
BEDFORD RD
CLYFFORD RD
LEA CRES
Ruislip Gardens Prim Sch
THE POINT
2 TREVOR GDNS
35
Glebe Prim Sch
MILVERTON DR
BURNHAM AVE
TAVISTOCK RD
SUSSEX RD
Yeading Brook
Tenn Cts
Pl Flds
Ickenham Manor
Long Lane Farm
Ickenham Marsh
Northolt Aerodrome
Freezeland Covert
Recn Gd
WINDSOR AVE
LYNHURST RD
OAKLEIGH RD
RYEFIELD AVE
FLORISTON AVE
BERKELEY RD
LYNHURST CRES
MIDHURST GDNS
Gutteridge Wood
WILKINSON CL
Ryefield Prim Sch
Ten Acres (Nature Reserve)
PO
P
30

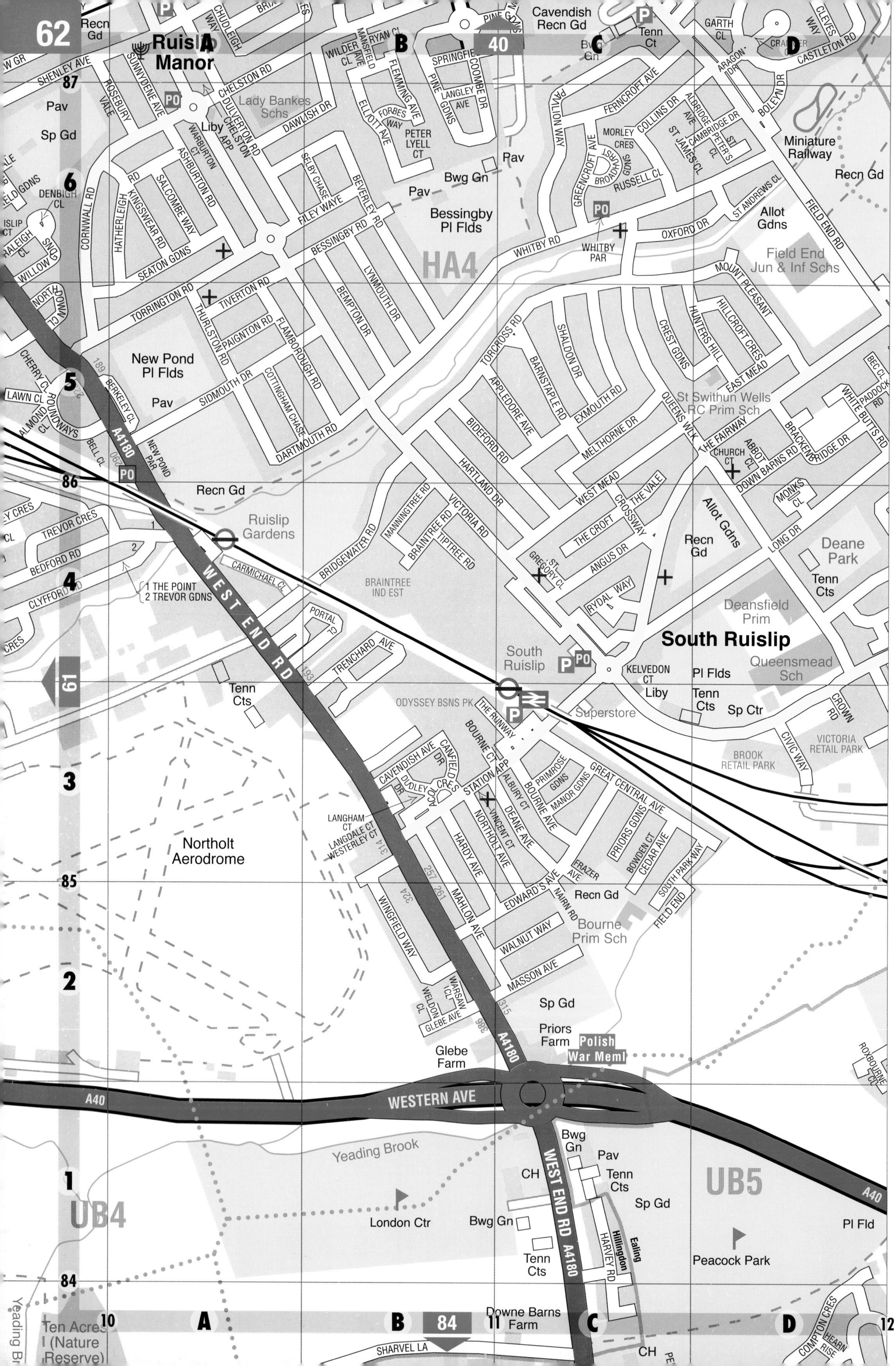

Ruislip Manor
South Ruislip
HA4
UB4
UB5
Ruislip Gardens
South Ruislip
Northolt Aerodrome
New Pond Pl Flds
Bessingby Pl Flds
Lady Bankes Schs
Field End Jun & Inf Schs
St Swithun Wells RC Prim Sch
Deansfield Prim
Queensmead Sch
Bourne Prim Sch
Miniature Railway
Deane Park
Peacock Park
London Ctr
Priors Farm
Glebe Farm
Downe Barns Farm
Polish War Meml
Yeading Brook
Ten Acres (Nature Reserve)
BRAINTREE IND EST
ODYSSEY BSNS PK
BROOK RETAIL PARK
VICTORIA RETAIL PARK
Superstore
WEST END RD
WESTERN AVE
A4180
A40
Cavendish Recn Gd
SHENLEY AVE
SUNNYDENE AVE
ROSEBURY VALE
CHELSTON RD
DULVERTON RD
CHELSTON APP
DAWLISH DR
WARBURTON CT
ASHBURTON RD
SALCOMBE WAY
KINGSWEAR RD
HATHERLEIGH RD
CORNWALL RD
SEATON GDNS
TORRINGTON RD
THURLSTON RD
TIVERTON RD
PAIGNTON RD
SIDMOUTH DR
COTTINGHAM CHASE
FLAMBOROUGH RD
DARTMOUTH RD
BESSINGBY RD
BEMPTON DR
LYNMOUTH DR
BEVERLEY RD
FILEY WAYE
SELBY CHASE
WHITBY RD
WHITBY PAR
OXFORD DR
ST ANDREWS CL
MOUNT PLEASANT
HILLCROFT CRES
HUNTERS HILL
CREST GDNS
EAST MEAD
SHALDON DR
TORCROSS RD
BARNSTAPLE RD
APPLEDORE AVE
EXMOUTH RD
BIDEFORD RD
HARTLAND DR
MELTHORNE DR
QUEENS WLK
THE FAIRWAY
WEST MEAD
THE VALE
CROSSWAY
THE CROFT
ANGUS DR
RYDAL WAY
ST GREGORY CL
VICTORIA RD
MANNINGTREE RD
BRAINTREE RD
TIPTREE RD
BRIDGEWATER RD
CARMICHAEL CL
PORTAL CL
TRENCHARD AVE
BERKELEY CL
ROUNDWAYS
BELL CL
NEW POND PAR
TREVOR CRES
BEDFORD RD
CLYFFORD RD
1 THE POINT
2 TREVOR GDNS
CHERRY CL
LAWN CL
ALMOND CL
NORTHDOWN CL
WILLOW GDNS
RALEIGH CL
DENBIGH CL
FERNCROFT AVE
PAVILION WAY
GREENCROFT AVE
BROADHURST GDNS
MORLEY CRES
RUSSELL CL
COLLINS DR
ALBRIDGE AVE
CAMBRIDGE DR
ST JAMES CL
ST PETERS CL
BOLEYN DR
FIELD END RD
CASTLETON RD
ARAGON DR
GARTH CL
SPRINGFIELD
COOMBE DR
LANGLEY AVE
PINE GDNS
FORBES WAY
ELLIOTT AVE
PETER LYELL CT
FLEMMING AVE
MANSFIELD AVE
WILDER CL
RYAN CL
CHUDLEIGH WAY
ABBOT CL
DOWN BARNS RD
BRACKENBRIDGE DR
CHURCH CT
MONKS CL
LONG DR
WHITE BUTTS RD
PADDOCK RD
KELVEDON CT
CROWN RD
CIVIC WAY
THE RUNWAY
BOURNE CT
STATION APP
CAVENDISH AVE
CANFIELD DR
DUDLEY DR
ACOL CRES
ALBURY CT
PRIMROSE GDNS
MANOR GDNS
BOURNE AVE
GREAT CENTRAL AVE
PRIORS GDNS
BOWDEN CT
CEDAR AVE
SOUTH PARK WAY
FIELD END
FRAZER AVE
VINCENT CT
NORTHOLT AVE
DEANE AVE
HARDY AVE
MAHLON AVE
EDWARD'S AVE
NAIRN RD
WALNUT WAY
MASSON AVE
LANGHAM CT
LANGDALE CT
WESTERLEY CT
WINGFIELD WAY
WELDON CL
WARSAW CL
GLEBE AVE
HARVEY RD
SHARVEL LA
COMPTON CRES
HEARN RISE
ROXBOURNE CL
Hillingdon
Ealing
40
61
84

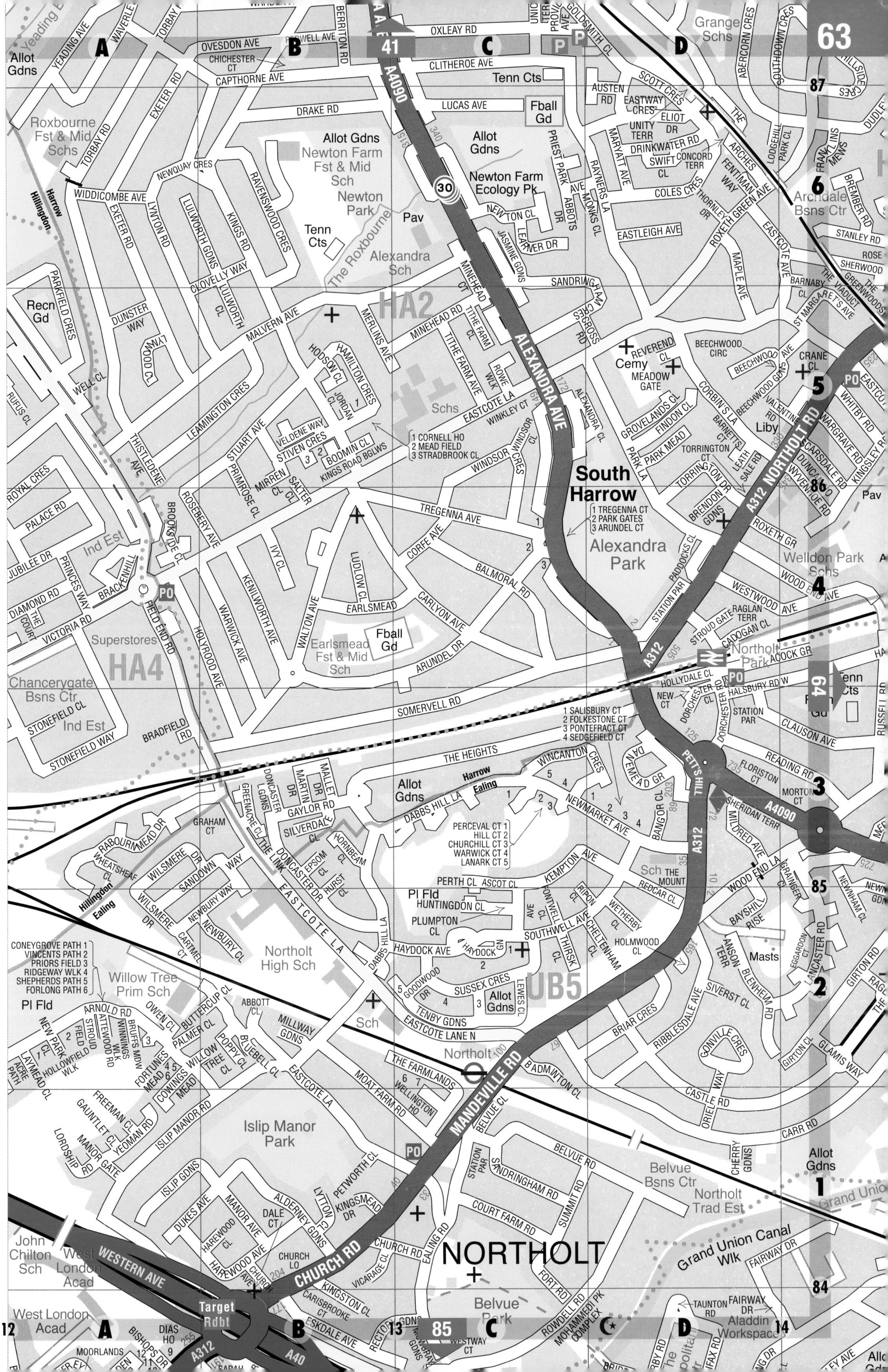

A
B
C
D
41
85
64
12
13
14
87
86
85
84
6
5
4
3
2
1
South Harrow
NORTHOLT
HA2
HA4
UB5
A4090
A312
A40
ALEXANDRA AVE
NORTHOLT RD
MANDEVILLE RD
CHURCH RD
WESTERN AVE
Target Rdbt
PETTS HILL
Allot Gdns
Roxbourne Fst & Mid Schs
Newton Farm Fst & Mid Sch
Newton Park
Newton Farm Ecology Pk
Alexandra Sch
Recn Gd
Cemy
Liby
Alexandra Park
Earlsmead Fst & Mid Sch
Superstores
Chancerygate Bsns Ctr
Ind Est
Northolt High Sch
Willow Tree Prim Sch
Islip Manor Park
John Chilton Sch
West London Acad
Belvue Bsns Ctr
Northolt Trad Est
Belvue Park
Grand Union Canal
Grand Union Canal Wlk
Aladdin Workspace
Welldon Park Schs
Archdale Bsns Ctr
Grange Schs
Northolt Park
Northolt
Harrow
Hillingdon
Ealing

Harrow on the Hill
Roxeth
HA2
HA1
UB5
UB6
42
86
63
16
14
15
A
B
C
D
87
86
85
84
6
5
4
3
2
1
1 CROWN CT
2 CHILTERN HO
The John Lyon Sch
Running Tk
Tenn Cts
Pavilion Lo
Pav
High St
B458
A312
A4005
A4090
A4127
A4005
Roxeth Hill
London Rd
Sudbury Hill
Greenford Rd
Northolt Rd
Whitton Ave W
Wood End Rd
South Hill Ave
Harrow Pk
Kennett Ho
Bowden House (Private)
The Woodlands
Julian Hill
Rama Ct
The Clementine Churchill
St George's RC Prim Sch
St Dominic's Coll(RC)
Orley Farm Sch
Pl Fld
Capital Ring
Sp Gds
Tenn Cts
Archdale Bsns Ctr
Superstore
South Harrow
Allot Gdns
Toll Gates
Oakmead
Roxeth Recn Gd
Welldon Park Schs
Harrow
Ealing
Sudbury Hill Harrow
Sudbury Hill
Sudbury Hill Pl Flds
Northolt Park
Recn Gd
Ealing Northern Sp Ctr
Bwg Gn
Liby
Schs
ATHENA CL 1
BRICKFIELDS 2
WEST HILL HALL 3
THE MOAT LODGE 4
EDWARD CT 5
CHYNGTON CT 6
BLAKE HO 7
KEATS HO 8
LANGTON HO 9
SYCAMORE LODGE 10
1 HUTTON CL
2 BRASHER CL
3 HEMERY RD
4 TESSA SANDERSON WAY
5 HAMMOND CL
THOMAS HEWLETT HO 1
JEM PATERSON CT 2
GREENBANKS 3
LYDIA LODGE 4
WALTON CROFT 5
Horsenden Prim Sch
The Ballot Box (PH)
Masts
Grand Union Canal Paddington Branch
Grand Union Canal Walk
Grand Union Canal Wlk
Northolt Trad Est
Greenford
Rockware Bsns Ctr
Sears Ret Pk
Aladdin Workspace
Berkeley Ave
Oldfield Lane N
Horsenden Lane N
Station App
Allington Cl
Carr Rd

43
87
66
A
B
C
D
1
2
3
4
5
6
16
17
18
84
85
86
87
North Wembley
Sudbury
WEMBLEY
HA0
UB6
South Kenton
Preston Park Recn Gd
Rugby Fball Gds
Byron Court Sch
Wembley Commercial Ctr
Gec Est
East Lane Bsns Pk
Wembley High Tech Coll
Tenn Cts
Vale Farm Sp Gd
Sp Arena
Vale Farm Sp Ctr
Fball Gd
Sudbury Prim Sch
Butler's Gn
Maybank Open Space
Sudbury & Harrow Road
Barham Park
Old Court (Mus & Liby)
Sudbury Town
Barham Prim Sch
Horsenden Hill
Horsenden Farm
Grand Union Canal Paddington Branch
Grand Union Canal Walk
Alperton Cemy
Alperton Lower Sch
Alperton
Rec Gd
Allot Gdns
King Edward VII Park
WATFORD RD
HARROW RD
EAST LA
SUDBURY COURT DR
WHITTON AVE E
BRIDGEWATER RD
EALING RD
A404
A4088
A4127
A4005
A4089
A4090
BRIDGEWATER CT 1
SUNNYDENE GDNS 2
ATHERTON HTS 3
1 SIMPSON HO
2 AYRTON HO
3 WINTOUR HO
4 STEVENSON HO
1 CRESSWELL
2 LOXLEY
3 KIRK HO
4 BELL HO

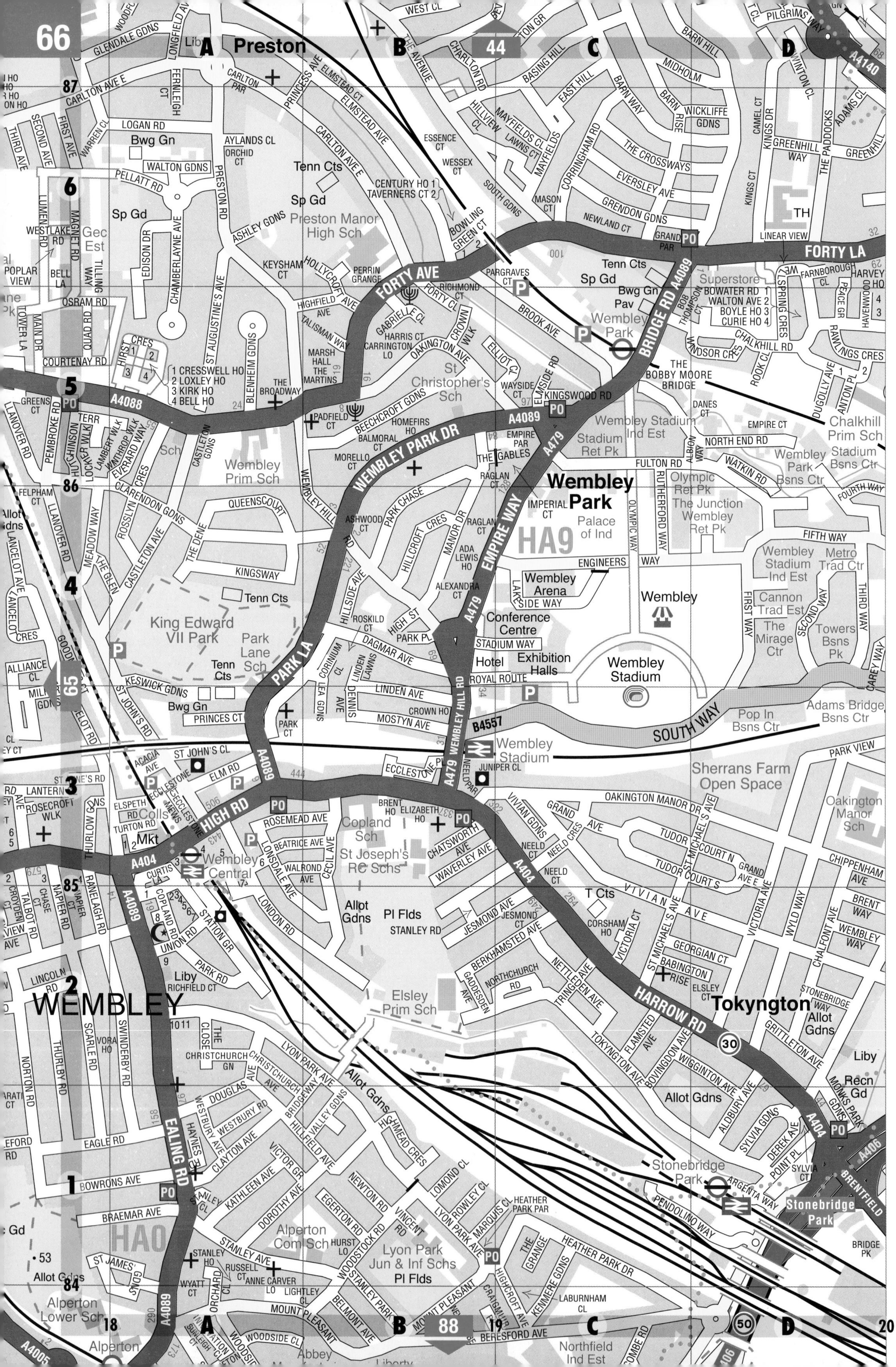
A
B
C
D
Preston
44
88
65
87
86
85
84
6
5
4
3
2
1
18
19
20
Wembley Park
Wembley
WEMBLEY
Tokyngton
Alperton
HA9
HA0
Preston Manor High Sch
Wembley Prim Sch
King Edward VII Park
Park Lane Sch
St Christopher's Sch
Wembley Stadium
Wembley Arena
Conference Centre
Exhibition Halls
Hotel
Palace of Ind
Wembley Stadium Ind Est
Stadium Ret Pk
Olympic Ret Pk
The Junction Wembley Ret Pk
Wembley Park Bsns Ctr
Stadium Bsns Ctr
Chalkhill Prim Sch
Wembley Stadium Ind Est
Metro Trad Ctr
Cannon Trad Est
The Mirage Ctr
Towers Bsns Pk
Pop In Bsns Ctr
Adams Bridge Bsns Ctr
Sherrans Farm Open Space
Oakington Manor Sch
Copland Sch
St Joseph's RC Schs
Elsley Prim Sch
Alperton Com Sch
Lyon Park Jun & Inf Schs
Alperton Lower Sch
Wembley Central
Wembley Stadium
Stonebridge Park
Northfield Ind Est
Superstore
Allot Gdns
Pl Flds
Tenn Cts
Sp Gd
Bwg Gn
Liby
Recn Gd
Mkt
Colls
FORTY AVE
FORTY LA
A4088
A4089
A479
A404
A4140
A406
A4005
B4557
EMPIRE WAY
BRIDGE RD
WEMBLEY PARK DR
WEMBLEY HILL RD
PARK LA
HIGH RD
EALING RD
HARROW RD
SOUTH WAY
OLYMPIC WAY
ENGINEERS WAY
FULTON RD
NORTH END RD
FIFTH WAY
FOURTH WAY
FIRST WAY
SECOND WAY
THIRD WAY
CARLTON AVE E
PRESTON RD
THE AVENUE
CHARLTON RD
BASING HILL
BARN HILL
MIDHOLM
PILGRIMS WAY
THE CROSSWAYS
EVERSLEY AVE
GRENDON GDNS
NEWLAND CT
CORRINGHAM RD
CHALKHILL RD
BOBBY MOORE BRIDGE
RAWLINGS CRES
DUGOLLY AVE
KINGSWAY
QUEENSCOURT
CLARENDON GDNS
CASTLETON AVE
ROSSLYN CRES
THE DENE
MEADOW WAY
KESWICK GDNS
ST JOHN'S RD
PRINCES CT
DAGMAR AVE
LINDEN AVE
MOSTYN AVE
HILLSIDE AVE
MANOR DR
OAKINGTON AVE
OAKINGTON MANOR DR
TUDOR COURT N
TUDOR COURT S
VIVIAN AVE
ST MICHAEL'S AVE
VICTORIA AVE
GEORGIAN CT
BABINGTON RISE
LONSDALE AVE
ROSEMEAD AVE
CECIL AVE
LONDON RD
STANLEY RD
PARK RD
UNION RD
STATION GR
LYON PARK AVE
DOUGLAS AVE
EAGLE RD
BOWRONS AVE
BRAEMAR AVE
STANLEY AVE
MOUNT PLEASANT
BERESFORD AVE
HEATHER PARK DR
PENDOLINO WAY
ARGENTA WAY
WIGGINTON AVE
ALDBURY AVE
TOKYNGTON AVE
BRENTFIELD

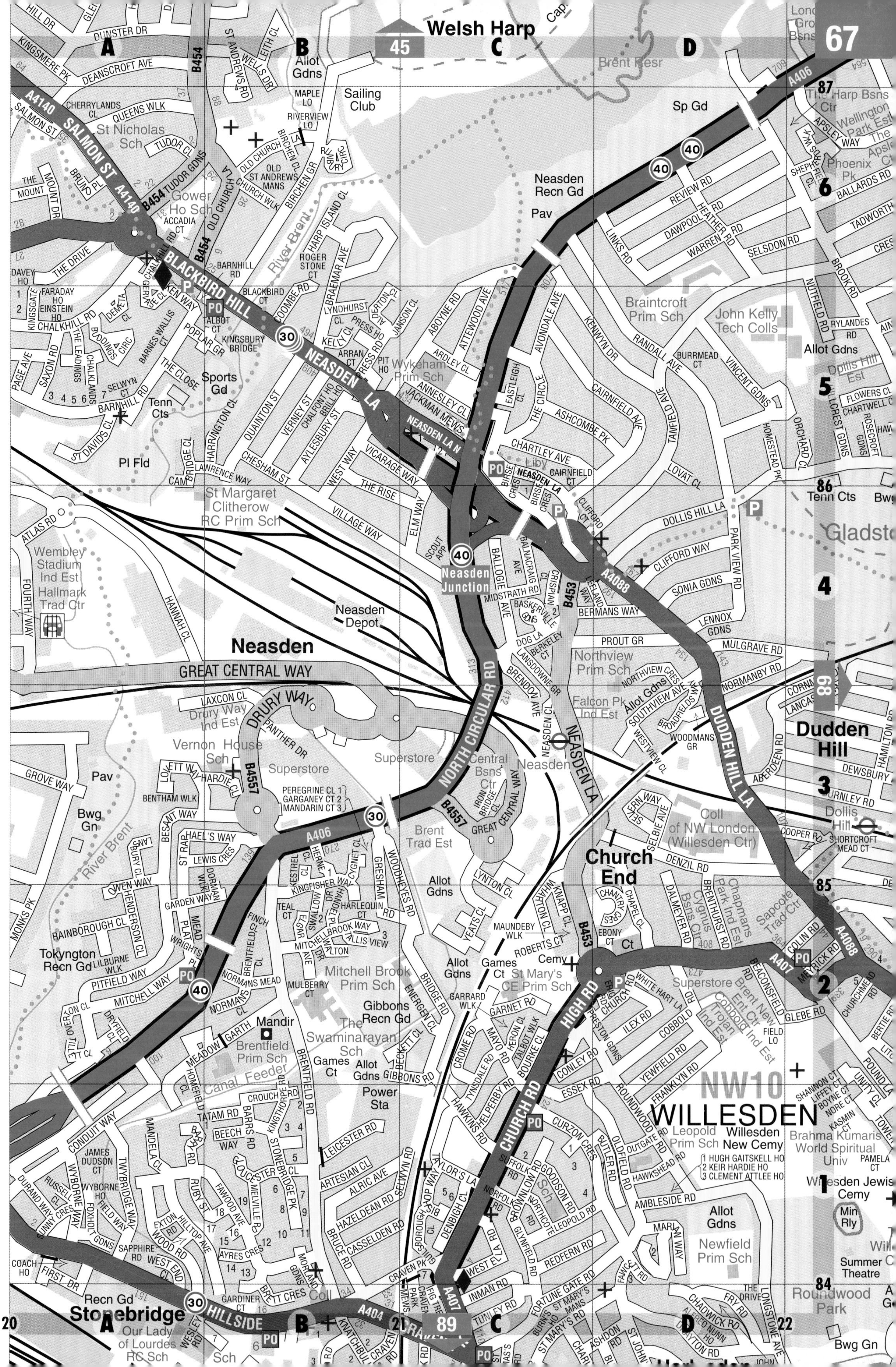
Welsh Harp
45
A
B
C
D
Brent Resr
Sailing Club
Sp Gd
Neasden Recn Gd
Pav
St Nicholas Sch
Gower Ho Sch
SALMON ST
A4140
B454
BLACKBIRD HILL
NEASDEN LA
NORTH CIRCULAR RD
A406
Wykeham Prim Sch
Braintcroft Prim Sch
John Kelly Tech Colls
Sports Gd
Tenn Cts
Pl Fld
St Margaret Clitherow RC Prim Sch
Wembley Stadium Ind Est
Hallmark Trad Ctr
Neasden Depot
Neasden
Neasden Junction
GREAT CENTRAL WAY
DRURY WAY
Drury Way Ind Est
Vernon House Sch
Superstore
Central Bsns Ctr
Northview Prim Sch
Falcon Pk Ind Est
DUDDEN HILL LA
A4088
Dudden Hill
Dollis Hill
Gladstone
Coll of NW London (Willesden Ctr)
Church End
Brent Trad Est
Tokyngton Recn Gd
Mitchell Brook Prim Sch
Gibbons Recn Gd
The Swaminarayan Sch
Mandir
Brentfield Prim Sch
Power Sta
Canal Feeder
St Mary's CE Prim Sch
HIGH RD
CHURCH RD
A407
Cygnus Bsns Ctr
Chapmans Park Ind Est
Sapcote Trad Ctr
Brent New Ent Ctr
Cobbold Ind Est
NW10
WILLESDEN
Leopold Prim Sch
Willesden New Cemy
Brahma Kumaris World Spiritual Univ
Willesden Jewish Cemy
Newfield Prim Sch
Roundwood Park
Summer Theatre
Stonebridge
Our Lady of Lourdes RC Sch
HILLSIDE
A404
89
20
21
22
87
86
85
84
68

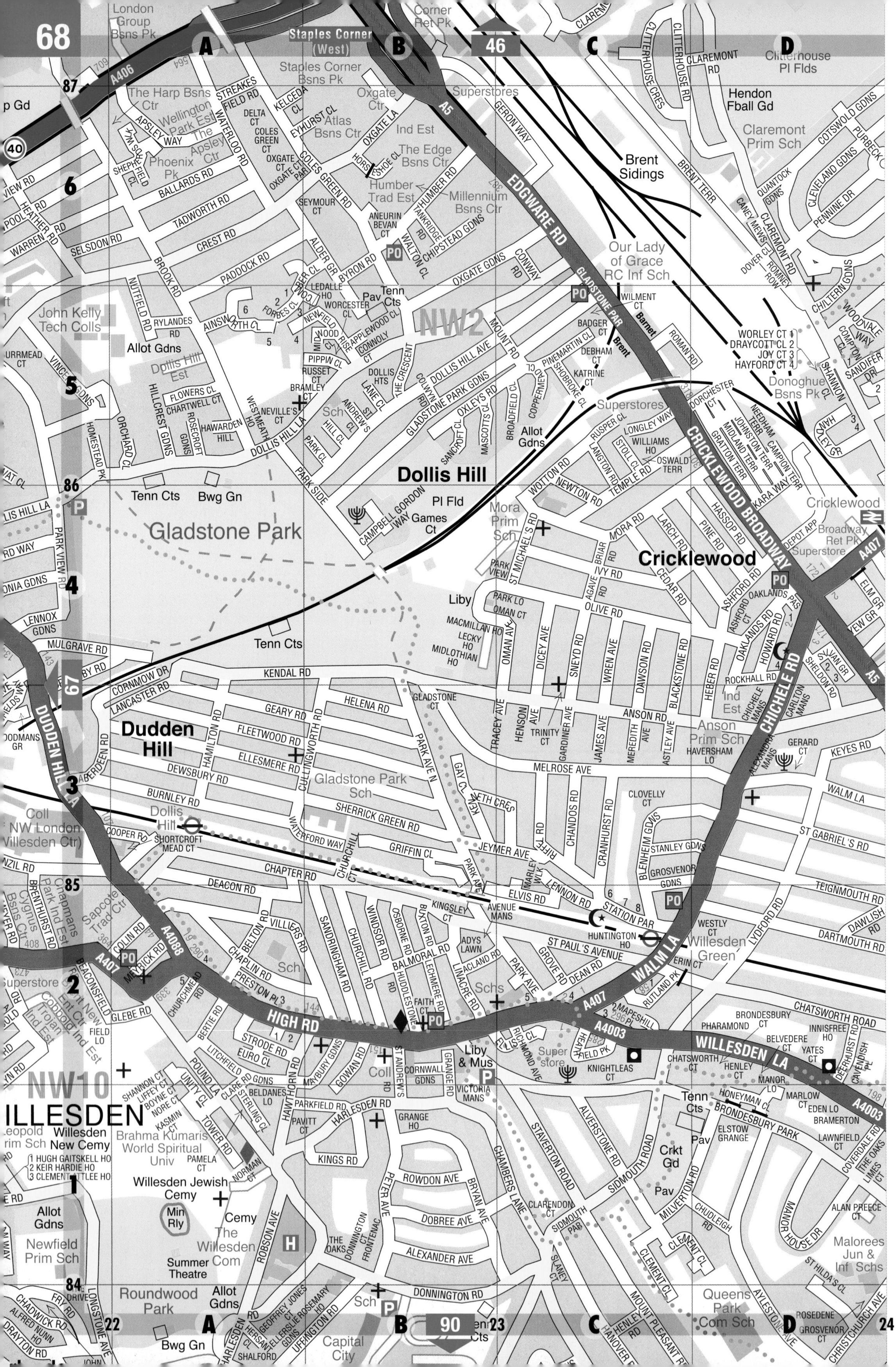

Staples Corner (West)
46
A B C D
London Group Bsns Pk
Corner Ret Pk
Staples Corner Bsns Pk
Superstores
Clitterhouse Pl Flds
Hendon Fball Gd
Claremont Prim Sch
The Harp Bsns Ctr
Wellington Park Est
The Apsley Ctr
Phoenix Pk
Oxgate Ctr
Atlas Bsns Ctr
Ind Est
The Edge Bsns Ctr
Humber Trad Est
Millennium Bsns Ctr
Brent Sidings
A406
A5
EDGWARE RD
STREAKES FIELD RD
WATERLOO RD
KELCEDA CL
EYHURST CL
DELTA CT
COLES GREEN CT
OXGATE CT
OXGATE CT PDE
COLES GREEN RD
OXGATE LA
HORSESHOE CL
HUMBER RD
GERON WAY
CLAREMONT RD
CLITTERHOUSE CRES
CLITTERHOUSE RD
BRENT TERR
COTSWOLD GDNS
PURBECK
CLEVELAND GDNS
PENNINE DR
QUANTOCK GDNS
CANEY MEWS
DOVER CL
ROMNEY ROW
APSLEY WAY
SHEPHERD CL
BALLARDS RD
TADWORTH RD
CREST RD
SELSDON RD
WARREN RD
HEATHER RD
POOL RD
VIEW RD
PADDOCK RD
BROOK RD
NUTFIELD RD
RYLANDES RD
AINSWORTH CL
SEYMOUR CT
ANEURIN BEVAN CT
TANKRIDGE RD
WALTON CL
CHIPSTEAD GDNS
ALDER GR
BYRON RD
OXGATE GDNS
CONWAY RD
GLADSTONE PAR
WILMENT CT
BADGER CT
DEBHAM CT
KATRINE CT
PINEMARTIN CL
SHOBROKE CL
COPPERMEAD CL
ROMAN RD
Our Lady of Grace RC Inf Sch
Barnet
Brent
CHILTERN GDNS
WOODVALE WAY
COMPTON CL
SANDIFER DR
SHANNON CL
HADLEY GR
WORLEY CT 1
DRAYCOTT CL 2
JOY CT 3
HAYFORD CT 4
Donoghue Bsns Pk
DORCHESTER CT
NEEDHAM TERR
JOHNSTON TERR
MIDLAND TERR
GRATTON TERR
CAMPION TERR
KARA WAY
Cricklewood
Broadway Ret Pk
Superstore
A407
ELM GR
YEW GR
John Kelly Tech Colls
Allot Gdns
Dollis Hill Est
URRMEAD CT
VINCENT GDNS
FLOWERS CL
CHARTWELL CT
ROSECROFT GDNS
HAWARDEN HILL
HILLCREST GDNS
ORCHARD CL
HOMESTEAD PK
FORBES CL
LEDALLE HO
WORCESTER CT
NEWFIELD RISE
WOOD CL
MIDCROFT
APPLEWOOD CL
CONNOLLY CT
PIPPIN CL
RUSSET CT
BRAMLEY CT
DOLLIS HTS
THE CRESCENT
DOLLIS HILL AVE
COLWYN RD
GLADSTONE PARK GDNS
MOUNT RD
OXLEYS RD
BROADFIELD CL
SANCROFT CL
MASCOTTS CL
Pav
Tenn Cts
NW2
Sch
ANDREW'S CL
LANE CL
ST HILL CL
PARK CL
NEVILLE'S CT
WESTMEATH HO
DOLLIS HILL LA
PARK SIDE
Allot Gdns
Superstores
RUSPER CL
LONGLEY WAY
WILLIAMS HO
OSWALD TERR
STOLL CL
LANGTON RD
TEMPLE RD
WOTTON RD
NEWTON RD
CRICKLEWOOD BROADWAY
HASSOP RD
PINE RD
LARCH RD
CEDAR RD
MORA RD
Dollis Hill
Pl Fld
Games Ct
CAMPBELL GORDON WAY
Mora Prim Sch
ST MICHAEL'S RD
PARK VIEW
BRIAR RD
AGAVE RD
IVY RD
OLIVE RD
Cricklewood
ASHFORD RD
ASHFORD CT
OAKLANDS RD
OAKLANDS PAS
HOWARD RD
DEPOT APP
86
Tenn Cts
Bwg Gn
Gladstone Park
PARK VIEW RD
LIS HILL LA
RD WAY
ONIA GDNS
LENNOX GDNS
MULGRAVE RD
BY RD
4
Liby
PARK LO
OMAN CT
MACMILLAN HO
LECKY HO
MIDLOTHIAN HO
OMAN AVE
DICEY AVE
SNEYD RD
WREN AVE
DAWSON RD
BLACKSTONE RD
HEBER RD
Tenn Cts
CHICHELE RD
ROCKHALL RD
SYLVAN GR
SHELDON RD
A5
67
CORNMOW DR
LANCASTER RD
KENDAL RD
HELENA RD
GEARY RD
GLADSTONE CT
Dudden Hill
FLEETWOOD RD
ELLESMERE RD
DEWSBURY RD
HAMILTON RD
CULLINGWORTH RD
PARK AVE N
TRACEY AVE
HENSON AVE
TRINITY CT
GARDINER AVE
JAMES AVE
MEREDITH AVE
ASTLEY AVE
ANSON RD
Ind Est
CHICHELE MANS
CARLTON MANS
Anson Prim Sch
HAVERSHAM LO
ALEXANDRA MANS
GERARD CT
KEYES RD
DUDDEN HILL LA
ODMANS GR
ABERDEEN RD
3
BURNLEY RD
Gladstone Park Sch
GAY CL
KEN
NETH CRES
MELROSE AVE
CLOVELLY CT
WALM LA
Coll of NW London (Willesden Ctr)
Dollis Hill
COOPER RD
SHORTCROFT MEAD CT
SHERRICK GREEN RD
WATERFORD WAY
GRIFFIN CL
CHURCHILL CT
JEYMER AVE
PARK AVE
MARLEY WLK
RIFFEL RD
CHANDOS RD
CRANHURST RD
BLENHEIM GDNS
STANLEY GDNS
GROSVENOR GDNS
ST GABRIEL'S RD
NZIL RD
85
CHAPTER RD
DEACON RD
ELVIS RD
LENNON RD
STATION PAR
TEIGNMOUTH RD
Cygnus Bsns Ctr
Chapmans Park Ind Est
BRENTHURST RD
Sapcote Trad Ctr
COLIN RD
A4088
BELTON RD
VILLIERS RD
SANDRINGHAM RD
CHURCHILL RD
WINDSOR RD
OSBORNE RD
BUXTON RD
KINGSLEY CT
AVENUE MANS
HUNTINGTON HO
Willesden Green
LYDFORD RD
DAWLISH RD
DARTMOUTH RD
A407
MELROSE RD
CHAPLIN RD
PRESTON PL
BALMORAL RD
ADYS LAWN
ACLAND RD
GROVE RD
ST PAUL'S AVENUE
DEAN RD
ERIN CT
Sch
LECHMERE RD
HUDDLESTONE RD
LINACRE RD
Schs
PARK AVE
RUTLAND PK
Superstore
BEACONSFIELD RD
2
CHURCHMEAD RD
GLEBE RD
Cobbold Ind Est
Trojan Ind Est
Ent Ctr
New Ind Est
FIELD LO
HIGH RD
FAITH CT
BERTIE RD
STRODE RD
EURO CL
LITCHFIELD GDNS
POUND LA
UNITY CL
MAYBURY GDNS
GOWAN RD
ST ANDREW'S RD
Coll
CORNWALL GDNS
GRANGE RD
Liby & Mus
VICTORIA MANS
RICHMOND AVE
ELLIS CL
HEATHFIELD PK
Super store
KNIGHTLEAS CT
MAPESHILL PL
A4003
BRONDESBURY CT
PHARAMOND
CHATSWORTH ROAD
CHATSWORTH CT
HENLEY CT
BELVEDERE CT
WILLESDEN LA
YATES CT
INNISFREE HO
DEERHURST RD
CAVENDISH RD
MANOR LO
HONEYMAN CL
MARLOW CT
EDEN LO
BRAMERTON
BRONDESBURY PARK
A4003
NW10
WILLESDEN
SHANNON CT
LIFFEY CT
BOYNE CT
NORE CT
KASMIN CT
CLARE RD
STERLING CL
BELDANES LO
HAWTHORN RD
PARKFIELD RD
HARLESDEN RD
PAVITT CT
GRANGE HO
ALVERSTONE RD
STAVERTON ROAD
CHAMBERS LANE
SIDMOUTH ROAD
Tenn Cts
Pav
Crkt Gd
ELSTOW GRANGE
LAWNFIELD CT
COVERDALE RD
THE OAKS
LIMES CT
Leopold Prim Sch
Willesden New Cemy
1 HUGH GAITSKELL HO
2 KEIR HARDIE HO
3 CLEMENT ATTLEE HO
Brahma Kumaris World Spiritual Univ
PAMELA CT
TOWER RD
NORMAN CT
KINGS RD
ROWDON AVE
BRYAN AVE
DOBREE AVE
Willesden Jewish Cemy
Min Rly
Cemy
1
Allot Gdns
Newfield Prim Sch
The Willesden Com
Summer Theatre
ROBSON AVE
H
THE OAKS
DONNINGTON CT
FRONTENAC
PETER AVE
ALEXANDER AVE
CLARENDON CT
SIDMOUTH PAR
SLANEY CT
CLEMENT CL
MILVERTON RD
CHUDLEIGH RD
Pav
MANOR HOUSE DR
ALAN PREECE CT
Malorees Jun & Inf Schs
84
Roundwood Park
Allot Gdns
DONNINGTON RD
Sch
ST HILDA'S CL
CHADWICK RD
FRY RD
ALFRED NUNN HO
DRAYTON RD
LONGSTONE AVE
22
A
HARLESDEN RD
GEOFFREY JONES CT
ELLERSLIE GDNS
ROSEMARY HO
UFFINGTON RD
B
90
23
C
HENLEY RD
MOUNT PLEASANT RD
Queens Park Com Sch
AYLESTONE AVE
D
ROSEDENE
GROSVENOR CT
CHRISTCHURCH AVE
24
Bwg Gn
Capital City
SHALFORD
HANOVER RD

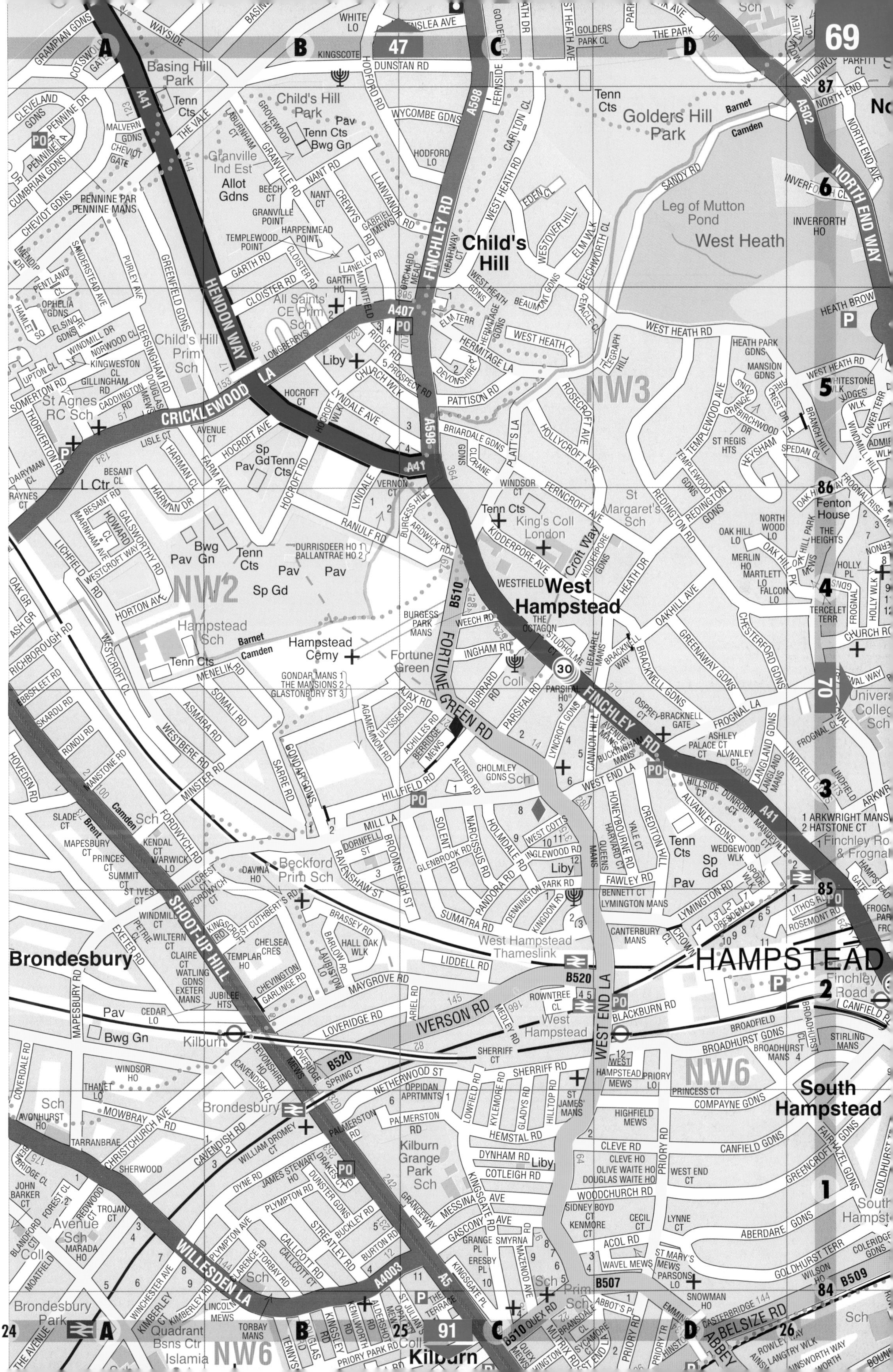
47
WHITE LO
ENSLEA AVE
KINGSCOTE
DUNSTAN RD
GOLDERS PARK CL
THE PARK
WAYSIDE
GRAMPIAN GDNS
COTSWOLD GATE
Basing Hill Park
Tenn Cts
THE VALE
A41
HENDON WAY
Child's Hill Park
Pav
Tenn Cts
Bwg Gn
HODFORD RD
WYCOMBE GDNS
HODFORD LO
FINCHLEY RD
A598
FERNSIDE
CARLTON CL
Tenn Cts
Golders Hill Park
Barnet
Camden
SANDY RD
Leg of Mutton Pond
West Heath
A502
NORTH END WAY
NORTH END AVE
NORTH END
WILDWOOD
PARFITT CL
INVERFORTH CL
INVERFORTH HO
CLEVELAND GDNS
PENNINE DR
CUMBRIAN GDNS
CHEVIOT GDNS
MALVERN GDNS
CHEVIOT GATE
PENNINE PAR
PENNINE MANS
Granville Ind Est
Allot Gdns
LABURNHAM CT
GROVEWOOD HO
GRANVILLE RD
BEECH CT
NANT RD
NANT CT
CREWYS RD
LLANVANOR RD
GABRIEL MEWS
GRANVILLE POINT
HARPENMEAD POINT
TEMPLEWOOD POINT
GARTH RD
CLOISTER RD
LLANELLY RD
GARTH HO
MOUNTFIELD RD
ORCHARD MEAD
All Saints' CE Prim Sch
A407
WEST HEATH RD
EDEN CL
WESTOVER HILL
ELM WLK
BEECHWORTH CL
Child's Hill
HEATHWAY CT
WEST HEATH GDNS
HERMITAGE GDNS
BEAUMONT GDNS
CENTRE CL
ELM TERR
HERMITAGE LA
WEST HEATH CL
DEVONSHIRE PL
HEATH BROW
HEATH PARK GDNS
MANSION GDNS
WHITESTONE WLK
JUDGES' WLK
LOWER TERR
PENTLAND CL
SAUNDERSTEAD AVE
PURLEY AVE
GREENFIELD GDNS
OPHELIA GDNS
ELSINORE GDNS
HAMLET SQ
WINDMILL DR
NORWOOD CL
Child's Hill Prim Sch
KINGWESTON CL
UPTON CL
GILLINGHAM RD
SOMERTON RD
CADDINGTON RD
DERSINGHAM RD
St Agnes RC Sch
CRICKLEWOOD LA
LONGBERRYS
RIDGE RD
Liby
CHURCH WLK
PROSPECT RD
HOCROFT CT
LYNDALE AVE
PATTISON RD
ROSECROFT AVE
TELEGRAPH HILL
NW3
TEMPLEWOOD AVE
GRANGE GDNS
BIRCHWOOD DR
ST REGIS HTS
HEYSHAM LA
SPEDAN CL
BRANCH HILL
WINDMILL HILL
THORVERTON RD
DAIRYMAN CL
RAYNES CT
LISLE CT
AVENUE CT
HOCROFT AVE
HOCROFT RD
Sp Gd
Tenn Cts
Pav
BRIARDALE GDNS
CRANE GDNS
PLATT'S LA
HOLLYCROFT AVE
BESANT CL
L Ctr
HARMAN CL
HARMAN DR
FARM AVE
VERNON CT
LYNDALE
BURGESS HILL
RANULF RD
WINDSOR CT
FERNCROFT AVE
Tenn Cts
King's Coll London
St Margaret's Sch
REDINGTON RD
REDINGTON GDNS
TEMPLEWOOD GDNS
OAK HILL LO
NORTH WOOD LO
OAK HILL WAY
OAK HILL PARK
Fenton House
THE HEIGHTS
FROGNAL RISE
MARNHAM AVE
HOWARD CL
GALSWORTHY RD
WESTCROFT WAY
LICHFIELD RD
Bwg Gn
Pav
Tenn Cts
DURRISDEER HO
BALLANTRAE HO
Pav
Sp Gd
NW2
ARDWICK RD
KIDDERPORE AVE
Croft Way
KIDDERPORE GDNS
HEATH DR
MERLIN HO
MARTLETT LO
FALCON LO
HOLLY PL
HOLLY WLK
OAK GR
ASH GR
HORTON AVE
WESTFIELD
West Hampstead
OAKHILL AVE
CHESTERFORD GDNS
TERCELET TERR
FROGNAL
CHURCH ROW
RICHBOROUGH RD
WESTCROFT CL
Hampstead Sch
Barnet
Camden
Tenn Cts
Hampstead Cemy
BURGESS PARK MANS
WEECH RD
B510
FORTUNE GREEN RD
INGHAM RD
THE OCTAGON
STUDHOLME CT
ALBEMARLE MANS
BRACKNELL WAY
GREENAWAY GDNS
Fortune Green
Coll
30
FINCHLEY RD
MENELIK RD
GONDAR MANS
THE MANSIONS
GLASTONBURY ST
BURRARD RD
PARSIFAL RD
PARSIFAL HO
BRACKNELL GDNS
OSPREY CT
BRACKNELL GATE
FROGNAL LA
70
University Coll Sch
EBBSFLEET RD
SKARDU RD
RONDU RD
SOMALI RD
ASMARA RD
WESTBERE RD
AJAX RD
ULYSSES RD
ACHILLES RD
AGAMEMNON RD
BERRIDGE MEWS
LYNCROFT GDNS
CANNON HILL
AVENUE MANS
BUCKINGHAM MANS
ASHLEY PALACE CT
ALVANLEY CT
LANGLAND GDNS
LANGLAND MANS
LINDFIELD GDNS
FROGNAL CL
HOVEDEN RD
MANSTONE RD
MINSTER RD
SARRE RD
GONDAR GDNS
ALDRED RD
CHOLMLEY GDNS
Sch
WEST END LA
HILLFIELD RD
HILLSIDE CT
DUNROBIN CT
A41
MANDEVILLE CT
ARKWRIGHT RD
1 ARKWRIGHT MANS
2 HATSTONE CT
Camden
Brent
Sch
SLADE CT
MAPESBURY CT
PRINCES CT
SUMMIT CT
ST IVES CT
KENDAL CT
WARWICK LO
FORDWYCH RD
HILLCREST CT
FORDWYCH CT
DAVINA HO
Beckford Prim Sch
MILL LA
DORNFELL ST
RAVENSHAW ST
BROOMSLEIGH ST
SOLENT RD
GLENBROOK RD
NARCISSUS RD
HOLMDALE RD
WEST COTTS
INGLEWOOD RD
Liby
HONEYBOURNE RD
HARVARD CT
QUEENS MANS
YALE CT
CREDITON HILL
ALVANLEY GDNS
Tenn Cts
Sp Gd
Pav
WEDGEWOOD WLK
SPODE WLK
Finchley Rd & Frognal
HAMPSTEAD GATE
FAWLEY RD
BENNETT CT
LYMINGTON MANS
LYMINGTON RD
DRESDEN CL
PANDORA RD
DENNINGTON PARK RD
KINGDON RD
ST CUTHBERT'S RD
BRASSEY RD
WINDMILL CT
PETRIE CL
WILTERN CT
CLAIRE CT
WATLING GDNS
EXETER MANS
JUBILEE HTS
KINGSCROFT RD
CHELSEA CRES
HALL OAK WLK
BARLOW RD
LAURISTON LO
SUMATRA RD
CANTERBURY MANS
CROWN CL
LITHOS RD
ROSEMONT RD
FROGNAL PARADE
SHOOT-UP HILL
EXETER RD
TEMPLAR HO
CHEVINGTON
GARLINGE RD
LIDDELL RD
West Hampstead Thameslink
B520
HAMPSTEAD
Finchley Road
Brondesbury
MAYGROVE RD
ROWNTREE CL
West Hampstead
BLACKBURN RD
CANFIELD GDNS
MAPESBURY RD
Pav
CEDAR LO
Bwg Gn
Kilburn
LOVERIDGE RD
ARIEL RD
IVERSON RD
MEDLEY RD
BROADFIELD
BROADHURST GDNS
BROADHURST MANS
BROADHURST CL
STIRLING MANS
WINDSOR HO
THANET LO
DEVONSHIRE HO
CAVENDISH CL
LOVERIDGE MEWS
B520
SPRING CT
SHERRIFF CT
SHERRIFF RD
WEST HAMPSTEAD MEWS
PRIORY LO
NW6
South Hampstead
COVERDALE RD
Sch
AVONHURST HO
MOWBRAY RD
Brondesbury
NETHERWOOD ST
OPPIDAN APRTMNTS
LOWFIELD RD
KYLEMORE RD
GLADYS RD
HILLTOP RD
ST JAMES' MANS
PRINCESS CT
COMPAYNE GDNS
TARRANBRAE
CHRISTCHURCH AVE
CAVENDISH RD
WILLIAM DROMEY CT
PALMERSTON RD
PALMERSTON RD
HEMSTAL RD
HIGHFIELD MEWS
CLEVE RD
CANFIELD GDNS
SHERWOOD
BRIDGE CL
JOHN BARKER CT
FOREST CL
REDWOOD CT
TROJAN CT
DYNE RD
JAMES STEWART HO
DUNSTER GDNS
DRAKES CTYD
Kilburn Grange Park
Sch
DYNHAM RD
Liby
COTLEIGH RD
CLEVE HO
OLIVE WAITE HO
DOUGLAS WAITE HO
WEST END CT
PRIORY RD
GREENCROFT GDNS
FAIRHAZEL GDNS
GOLDHURST TERR
Avenue Sch
MARADA HO
Coll
BLANDFORD CT
MOATFIELD
PLYMPTON RD
BUCKLEY RD
GRANGEWAY
MESSINA AVE
KINGSGATE RD
WOODCHURCH RD
SIDNEY BOYD CT
KENMORE CT
CECIL CT
LYNNE CT
ABERDARE GDNS
South Hampstead
WILLESDEN LA
WINCHESTER AVE
KIMBERLEY RD
PLYMPTON AVE
CLARENCE RD
TORBAY RD
CALLCOTT RD
CALLCOTT CT
STREATLEY RD
BURTON RD
GASCONY AVE
GRANGE PL
SMYRNA RD
ERESBY PL
MAZENOD AVE
ACOL RD
WAVEL MEWS
ST MARY'S MEWS
PARSONS LO
COLERIDGE GDNS
A4003
A5
Sch
KINGSGATE PL
Prim Sch
B507
ABBOT'S PL
SNOWMAN HO
WILSON HO
B509
Brondesbury Park
THE AVENUE
Quadrant Bsns Ctr
Islamia
LINCOLN MEWS
TORBAY MANS
KINGSLEY RD
KENILWORTH RD
ALDERSHOT RD
ST JULIAN'S RD
THE TERRACE
25
91
Coll
Kilburn
PRIORY PARK RD
B510
QUEX RD
QUEX MEWS
MUTRIX RD
BRANSDALE CL
SYCAMORE CT
WEST END LA
PRIORY TERR
ABBEY
CASTERBRIDGE
BELSIZE RD
26
ROWLEY WAY
LANGTRY WLK
AINSWORTH WAY
Sch
NW6
A
B
C
D
1
2
3
4
5
6
84
85
86
87

Sandy Heath
North End
Mast
Tenn Ct
Open Air Stage
Ken Wood
N6
Hampstead Heath
Parliament Hill
Highgate Ponds
West Heath
Leg of Mutton Pond
Inverforth HO
North End Way
Spaniards Rd
Heath Brow
East Heath
Vale of Health
Queen Mary's
The Pryors
Hampstead Ponds
NW3
South Hill Pk
2 Willow Road
Keates House Mus
Hampstead Heath
Nassington Rd
Allot Gdns
Fenton House
Heath St
Hampstead High St
Hampstead
Rosslyn Hill
Hampstead Com Mkt
University College Sch
Royal Free
Fleet Rd
Mansfield
Pond St
Belsize New Tunnel
Belsize Tunnel
Belsize Park
Haverstock Hill
Maitland Park
Fitzjohn's Ave
The Freud Mus
Finchley Road & Frognal
HAMPSTEAD
Finchley Road
NW6
South Hampstead
Finchley Rd
Swiss Cottage
Adelaide Rd
Primrose Hill
Primrose Hill Tunnels
St Paul's CE Prim Sch
The Central Sch of Speech & Drama
Belsize Park Gardens
Eton Ave
Belsize Rd
Abbey
Boundary Rd
A502
A41
B519
B511
B518
B517
B509
B525
A
B
C
D
1
2
3
4
5
6
84
85
86
87
26
27
28
48
69
229
92
230

Waterlow Park
St Joseph's RC Prim Sch
Highgate Cemy
Highgate Cemy
The Whittington
Archway
Upper Holloway
Archway
Upper Holloway
Holloway Rd
Whittington Park
Yerbury Prim Sch
Dartmouth Park
Brookfield Prim Sch
Holly Village
Saint Union RC Sec Sch
William Ellis Sch
Parliament Hill Sch
Tenn Cts
Bwg Gn
Athletics Gd
Sw Pool
Gospel Oak
Gospel Oak
N6
N19
N7
NW5
NW1
N1
Tufnell Park
Tufnell Park Hall
Tufnell Park
Tufnell Park Prim Sch
Holloway Sch
Acland Burghley Sch
Junction Rd
Fortess Rd
Brecknock Rd
Camden Rd
Kentish Town Rd
Highgate Rd
Dartmouth Park Hill
Chalk Farm Rd
York Way
Hillway
Swain's La
Highgate West Hill
Highgate Rd
Oakeshott Ave
Makepeace Ave
Langbourne Ave
Bromwich Ave
Gordon House Rd
Lady Somerset Rd
Leighton Rd
Torriano Ave
Hilldrop Cres
Dalmeny Ave
Camden Park Rd
Agar Gr
City Farm
Carlton Prim Sch
The Interchange
Kentish Town
Kentish Town
Kentish Town West
The Camden Sch for Girls
Roundhouse Theatre
Camden Town
Camden Mkt
Superstore
Utopia Village
Juniper Cres
Randolph St
Royal College St
St Pancras Way
Chalk Farm
A1
A400
A5200
A5202
A503
A502
B519
B518
B517
B509
28
29
30
A
B
C
D
49
231
93
231
72
84
85
86
87
1
2
3
4
5
6

50
A
B
C
D
N19
N4
N7
N5
N1
Finsbury Park
Highbury
Emirates (Arsenal FC)
Arsenal
Gillespie Park
Drayton Park
Holloway Road
Nags Head
Lower Holloway
HM Prison
Caledonian Road
Caledonian Park
Hall of Residence
Paradise Park
ISLINGTON
Highbury Fields
Highbury Pool
Highbury & Islington
Highbury Corner
Barnsbury
Caledonian Road & Barnsbury
Copenhagen Junction
Acorn Production Ctr
Fball Gd
Tenn Cts
Rech Gd
HOLLOWAY RD
HOLLOWAY RD
SEVEN SISTERS RD
BLACKSTOCK RD
HORNSEY RD
TOLLINGTON RD
CAMDEN RD
CALEDONIAN RD
LIVERPOOL RD
UPPER STREET
YORK WAY
HIGHBURY PK
HIGHBURY GR
CANONBURY RD
STROUD GREEN RD
ISLEDON RD
PARKHURST RD
HILLMARTON RD
TUFNELL PARK RD
MERCERS RD
HIGHBURY CNR
HIGHBURY STATION RD
BARNSBURY PK
BRIDGEMAN RD
MARKET RD
BREWERY RD
A1
A103
A503
A5203
A5200
A1201
A1200
B515
B150
B105
A104
87
86
85
84
6
5
4
3
2
1
71
30
31
32
233
94
234

73
A
B
C
D
51
STOKE NEWINGTON
Abney Park Cemy
Stoke Newington
LORDSHIP PK
MANOR RD
BROWNSWOOD RD
GREEN LANES
STOKE NEWINGTON CHURCH ST
Clissold Park
N16
N4
N5
N1
E8
STOKE NEWINGTON HIGH ST
RECTORY RD
EVERING RD
MANSE RD
Shacklewell
Rectory Road
ALBION RD
NEWINGTON GREEN RD
MILDMAY GR N
MILDMAY GR S
Canonbury
ST PAUL'S RD
BALLS POND RD
Kingsland
Dalston Kingsland
Dalston Jct
Dalston
KINGSLAND HIGH ST
KINGSLAND RD
QUEENSBRIDGE RD
SOUTHGATE RD
ESSEX RD
De Beauvoir Town
Essex Road
DALSTON LA
74
6
5
4
3
2
1
32
235
33
95
34

Upper Clapton
Capital Ring
A
B
C
D
52
River Lea or Lee
Pl Fld
Lee Valley Riding Ctr
Leyton Marshes
Stoke Newington
UPPER CLAPTON RD
A107
NORTHWOLD RD
B111
N16
RECTORY RD
Rectory Road
Clapton
LEA BRIDGE RD
A104
30
Recn Gd
Lea Valley Ice Ctr
Nature Reserve
Lea Valley Wlk
E5
Lea Bridge
Mandeville Prim Sch
Shacklewell
Hackney Downs
Mossbourne Com Acad
The Petchey Acad
CRICKETFIELD RD
PEMBURY RD
LOWER CLAPTON RD
Lower Clapton
Clapton Park
Clapton Girls Tec Coll
Homerton University
HOMERTON HIGH ST
A106
Sutton House
Hackney Central
DALSTON LA
AMHURST RD
GRAHAM RD
A1207
MORNING LA
WICK RD
Dalston
E8
HACKNEY
Homerton
QUEENSBRIDGE RD
B108
London Fields
MARE ST
WELL ST
E9
Well Street Common
VICTORIA PARK RD
CASSLAND RD
A102
96
34
35
36

53
Period Wks
Sybourn Inf Sch Annexe
The Lammas Sch
Willow Brook Prim Sch
Fairways Bsns Pk
St Joseph's RC Inf Sch
Leyton Bsns Ctr
Orient Ind Pk
Pl Flds
E10
Running Track
CHURCH RD
GRANGE PARK RD
HIGH ROAD LEYTON
A1006
A112
A104
LAMMAS RD
CONNAUGHT CL
ORIENT WAY
Waltham Forest
Hackney
Allot Gdns
Leyton Orient Fball Gd
Dawlish Prim Sch
Noor Ul Prim
Bndstd
Liby
Leyton Town Ctr
Bwg Gn
MARKET PAVILION
New Spitalfields Market
RUCKHOLT RD
Superstore
Leyton Mills
THE SQUARE
COW BRIDGE
E5
1 ASHBOURNE CT
2 MELBORNE CT
3 KEDELSTON CT
4 MONSAL CT
Hackney Marsh
Recn Gds
Lea Valley Wlk
River Lee Navigation Hackney Cut
River Lea or Lee
1 IRONSIDE HO
2 EDRED HO
3 ETHELBERT HO
4 TEMPLEMEAD HO
5 RUNNYMEDE HO
6 FAIRMEAD HO
7 KINGSMEAD HO
8 EDWY HO
9 ATHELSTAN HO
10 WATERMEAD HO
11 MALMSMEAD HO
12 ASHMEAD HO
13 RIVERMEAD HO
Kingsmead Prim Sch
Recn Gd
EASTWAY
Lee Valley Sp Ctr
Tenn Cts
A12
A106
B112
HOMERTON RD
Lea Int
TEMPLE MILLS RD
QUARTERMILE LA
Temple Mills
CLAYS LA
CRABTREE CT 1
BAMFORD CT 2
TEMPLARS HO 3
Cycle Circuit
1 TWEEDALE
2 TAYLOR C
3 SMITHIES
4 HOWARTH
5 HOLT CT
6 COOPER C
7 DALY CT
8 BROOK C
9 CLAYS LA
CVN SIT
MARSHGATE BRIDGE
TOWPATH WLK
E9
Fball Gds
1 ADELAIDE CT
2 CASTLE CL
3 BRENTON CT
4 TYNTE CT
5 SALISBURY CT
6 HILLYFIELD CL
7 BERESFORD CT
Hackney Marsh
EAST CROSS ROUTE
WATERDEN RD
Channelsea River
Allot Gdns
Depot
MARSH HILL
STUDLEY CL 2
NEWBURY CT 3
Hackney
Hackney Wick
KENWORTHY RD
1 SOUTHMOOR WAY
2 WINDSOR WHARF
Recn Gd
Gainsborough Prim Sch
Hackney Stadium
E15
Hackney Wick
East Cross Ctr
WICK RD
A102
B113
A106
CHAPMAN RD
A115
COWDRY RD
WHITE POST LA
QUEENS YD
KINGS YD
Hackney
Tower Hamlets
CARPENTER'S RD
Carpenters Bsns Pk
Hamlet Ind Est
Omega Works
Bow Ind Pk
River Lea or Lee
Waterworks River
City Mill River
Victoria Park Ind Ctr
RISEHOLME CT
CADOGAN CL
TYSSON HO
QUEENS GATE VILLAS
Tenn Cts
Bwg Gn
Sp Gd
WINFORD HO
Victoria Park
Swan Wharf
Crown Wharf
Stratford Marsh
Victoria Fntn
Gunmakers
ARTILLERY HO 1
PINE HO 2
ARMOURY HO 3
CONNAUGHT WORKS 4
36
37
97
38
A
B
C
D
1
2
3
4
5
6
76
84
85
86
87

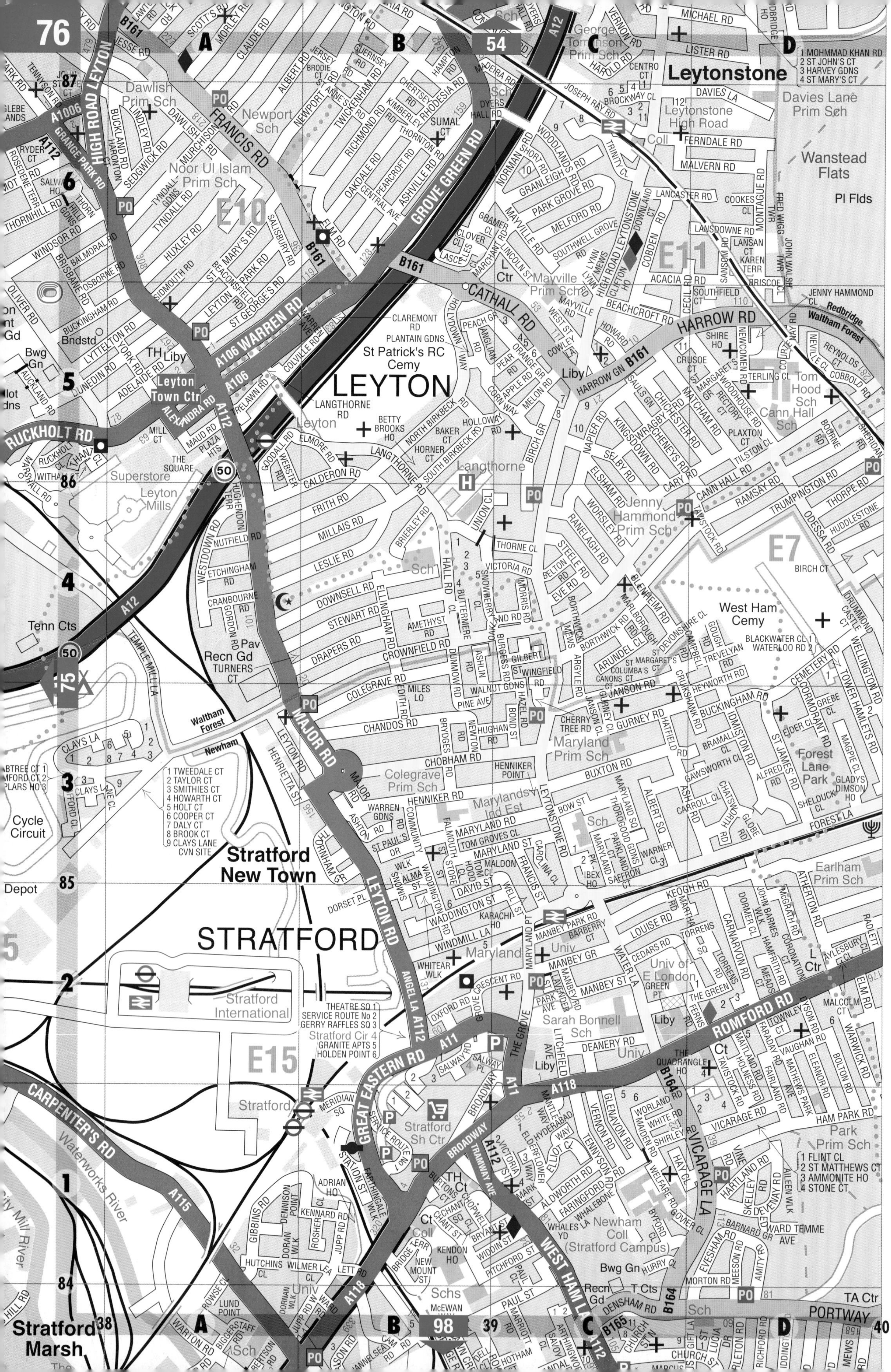
54
Leytonstone
LEYTON
STRATFORD
Stratford New Town
E10
E11
E7
E15
HIGH ROAD LEYTON
GROVE GREEN RD
FRANCIS RD
A106 WARREN RD
RUCKHOLT RD
LEYTON RD
MAJOR RD
CATHALL RD
HARROW RD
HARROW GN
CANN HALL RD
ROMFORD RD
GREAT EASTERN RD
ANGEL LA
BROADWAY
WEST HAM LA
VICARAGE LA
CARPENTER'S RD
PORTWAY
Waterworks River
City Mill River
Dawlish Prim Sch
Newport Sch
Noor Ul Islam Prim Sch
St Patrick's RC Cemy
Leyton Town Ctr
Superstore
Leyton Mills
Tenn Cts
Recn Gd
Cycle Circuit
Langthorne
Jenny Hammond Prim Sch
West Ham Cemy
Maryland Prim Sch
Colegrave Prim Sch
Forest Lane Park
Earlham Prim Sch
Davies Lane Prim Sch
Leytonstone High Road
Wanstead Flats
Pl Flds
Tom Hood Sch
Cann Hall Sch
Mayville Prim Sch
Stratford International
Stratford
Stratford Sh Ctr
Sarah Bonnell Sch
Univ of E London
Newham Coll (Stratford Campus)
Park Prim Sch
Stratford Marsh
Depot
Waltham Forest
Newham
Redbridge
1 TWEEDALE CT
2 TAYLOR CT
3 SMITHIES CT
4 HOWARTH CT
5 HOLT CT
6 COOPER CT
7 DALY CT
8 BROOK CT
9 CLAYS LANE CVN SITE
THEATRE SQ 1
SERVICE ROUTE No 2
GERRY RAFFLES SQ 3
Stratford Cir 4
GRANITE APTS 5
HOLDEN POINT 6
1 MOHMMAD KHAN RD
2 ST JOHN'S CT
3 HARVEY GDNS
4 ST MARY'S CT
1 FLINT CL
2 ST MATTHEWS CT
3 AMMONITE HO
4 STONE CT
98
75
38
39
40

Aldersbrook
Aldersbrook Prim Sch
Wanstead Flats
Centenary Walk
E12
E7
Manor Park
The Manor Park Cemy & Crem
City of London Cemy
Crem
Forest Gate
Plashet
Plashet Jewish Cemy
Plashet Park
East Ham Meml
Upton
West Ham Park
Woodgrange Park
Woodgrange Park Cemy
Wanstead Park
Godwin Sch
Woodgrange Sch
Kubrick Bsns Est
William Davies Sch
Monega Sch
Stratford Sch
St Angela's Sch
Elmhurst Sch
St Bonaventure's Sch
Azhar Acad
ALDERSBROOK RD
CENTRE RD
WOODFORD RD
WOODGRANGE RD
ROMFORD RD
FOREST DR
STATION RD
HIGH ST N
GREEN ST
KATHERINE RD
UPTON LA
PLASHET RD
PLASHET GR
DAMES RD
LAKE HOUSE RD
BLAKE HALL CRES
NORTHUMBERLAND AVE
WOODLANDS AVE
PARK RD
DOVER RD
CAPEL RD
Redbridge
Newham
Horse Ride
A114
A116
A117
A118
B161
B109
B165
B167
55
99
A
B
C
D
1
2
3
4
5
6
40
41
42
84
85
86
87
78

56
ILFORD
IG1
Ilford
Manor Park
City of London Cemy
Crem
Allot Gdns
Redbridge
Newham
Alders Brook
Ilford Interchange
Maytime Sch
ILFORD HILL
The Exchange
NORTH CIRCULAR RD
ROMFORD RD
LITTLE ILFORD LA
ILFORD LA
FOREST DR
STATION RD
HIGH ST N
E12
Little Ilford
Little Ilford Park
Rec Gd
Uphall Prim Sch
Plashet
Plashet Jewish Cemy
Plashet Park
East Ham Meml
Woodgrange Park Cemy
Essex Prim Sch
Kensington Prim Sch
EAST AVE
East Ham
E6
IG11
Riverside Works
Pacific Wharf
River Roding
Superstore
Sports Gd
Barking Flyover
Recn Gd
WANSTEAD PARK RD
COURTLAND AVE
MAYFAIR AVE
BELGRAVE RD
SELBORNE RD
ARGYLE RD
MANSFIELD RD
GRANVILLE RD
BROWNING RD
SHAKESPEARE CRES
STEVENAGE RD
LONDON RD
ABBEY RD
A406
A118
A123
A124
A117
A116
B165
B109
100
42
43
44

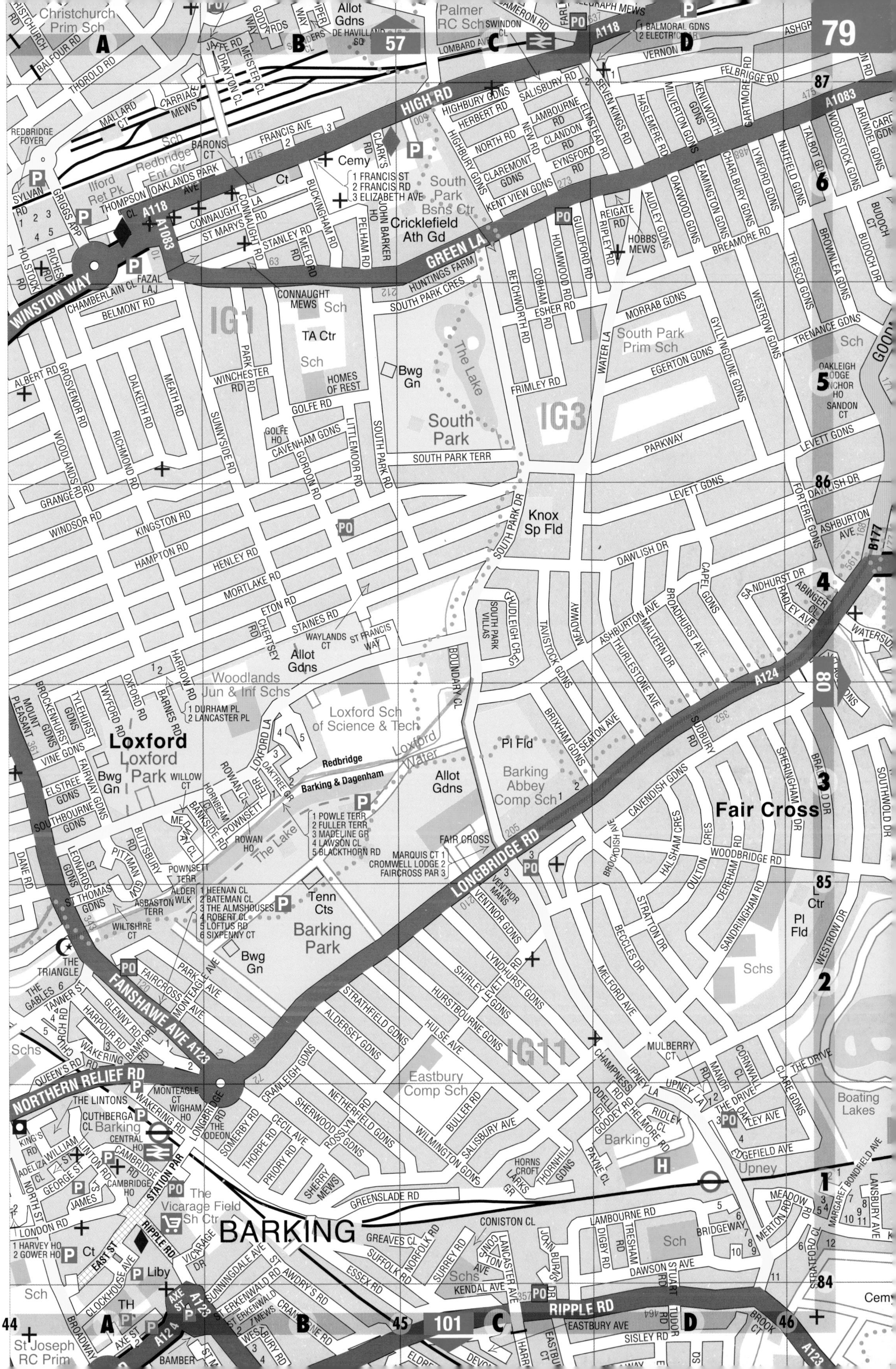
Christchurch Prim Sch
Allot Gdns
Palmer RC Sch
57
BALFOUR RD
THOROLD RD
DE HAVILLAND SQ
LOMBARD AVE
CAMERON RD
SWINDON CL
A118
1 BALMORAL GDNS
2 ELECTRIC
VERNON
FELBRIGGE RD
87
A1083
JAFFE RD
DRAYTON CL
MEISTER CL
MALLARD CT
CARRIAGE MEWS
HIGH RD
HIGHBURY GDNS
HERBERT RD
SALISBURY RD
LAMBOURNE RD
SEVEN KINGS RD
HASLEMERE RD
MILVERTON GDNS
KENILWORTH GDNS
GARTMORE RD
TALBOT GDNS
WOODSTOCK GDNS
ARUNDEL GDNS
REDBRIDGE FOYER
FRANCIS AVE
BARONS CT
Redbridge Ent Ctr
Ilford Ret Pk
OAKLANDS PARK AVE
Cemy
CLARK'S
NORTH RD
CLANDON RD
EYNSFORD RD
ELMSTEAD RD
LEAMINGTON GDNS
CHARLBURY GDNS
LYNFORD GDNS
NUTFIELD GDNS
6
SYLVAN RD
GRIGGS APP
THOMPSON CL
CONNAUGHT LA
CONNAUGHT RD
ST MARYS RD
1 FRANCIS ST
2 FRANCIS RD
3 ELIZABETH AVE
South Park Bsns Ctr
CLAREMONT GDNS
KENT VIEW GDNS
REIGATE RD
HOBBS MEWS
AUDLEY GDNS
OAKWOOD GDNS
BREAMORE RD
BUDOCH CT
BUDOCH DR
HOLSTOCK RD
RICHES RD
STANLEY RD
MELFORD RD
BUCKINGHAM RD
JOHN BARKER HO
PELHAM RD
Cricklefield Ath Gd
GREEN LA
GUILDFORD RD
HOLMWOOD RD
RIPLEY RD
WESTROW GDNS
TRESCO GDNS
BROWNLEA GDNS
WINSTON WAY
FAZAL LAJ
CHAMBERLAIN CL
BELMONT RD
CONNAUGHT MEWS
Sch
HUNTINGS FARM
SOUTH PARK CRES
BETCHWORTH RD
COBHAM RD
ESHER RD
MORRAB GDNS
TRENANCE GDNS
IG1
TA Ctr
Bwg Gn
The Lake
South Park Prim Sch
WATER LA
GYLLYNGDUNE GDNS
EGERTON GDNS
ALBERT RD
GROSVENOR RD
DALKEITH RD
MEATH RD
WINCHESTER RD
PARK RD
HOMES OF REST
FRIMLEY RD
IG3
OAKLEIGH LODGE
ANCHOR HO
SANDON CT
5
GOLFE RD
SUNNYSIDE RD
South Park
WOODLANDS RD
RICHMOND RD
GOLFE HO
CAVENHAM GDNS
LITTLEMOOR RD
SOUTH PARK RD
PARKWAY
LEVETT GDNS
SOUTH PARK TERR
GORDON RD
GRANGE RD
86
DAWLISH DR
FORTERIE GDNS
WINDSOR RD
KINGSTON RD
Knox Sp Fld
ASHBURTON AVE
HAMPTON RD
HENLEY RD
SOUTH PARK DR
B177
MORTLAKE RD
ETON RD
STAINES RD
CHERTSEY RD
WAYLANDS CT
ST FRANCIS WAY
CAPEL GDNS
SANDHURST DR
ABINGER CL
RADLEY AVE
4
WATERSIDE
CHUDLEIGH CRES
SOUTH PARK VILLAS
TAVISTOCK GDNS
MEADWAY
BROADHURST AVE
MALVERN DR
THURLESTONE AVE
HARROW RD
Allot Gdns
BOUNDARY CL
Woodlands Jun & Inf Schs
80
A124
BROCKENHURST GDNS
MOUNT PLEASANT
TYLEHURST GDNS
TWYFORD RD
OXFORD RD
BARNES RD
1 DURHAM PL
2 LANCASTER PL
Loxford Sch of Science & Tech
BRIXHAM GDNS
SEATON AVE
SUDBURY RD
Loxford
Loxford Park
VINE GDNS
ELSTREE GDNS
FAIRWAY GDNS
Bwg Gn
WILLOW CT
ROWAN CL
LOXFORD LA
OAKTREE GR
Redbridge
Barking & Dagenham
Loxford Water
Allot Gdns
Pl Fld
Barking Abbey Comp Sch
CAVENDISH GDNS
SHERINGHAM DR
3
Fair Cross
SOUTHWOLD DR
SOUTHBOURNE GDNS
HORNBEAM CL
BANKSIDE RD
POWNSETT TERR
1 POWLE TERR
2 FULLER TERR
3 MADELINE GR
4 LAWSON CL
5 BLACKTHORN RD
ROWAN HO
The Lake
FAIR CROSS
MARQUIS CT 1
CROMWELL LODGE 2
FAIRCROSS PAR 3
LONGBRIDGE RD
BROCKDISH AVE
HALSHAM CRES
OULTON CRES
WOODBRIDGE RD
DEREHAM RD
DANE RD
ST LEONARDS GDNS
PITTMAN GDNS
BUTTSBURY RD
ALDER WLK
1 HEENAN CL
2 BATEMAN CL
3 THE ALMSHOUSES
4 ROBERT CL
5 LOFTUS RD
6 SIXPENNY CT
Tenn Cts
VENTNOR MANS
VENTNOR GDNS
STRATTON DR
SANDRINGHAM RD
85
L Ctr
Pl Fld
WESTROW DR
ST THOMAS GDNS
ASBASTON TERR
WILTSHIRE CT
Barking Park
LYNDHURST GDNS
BECCLES DR
THE TRIANGLE
FAIRCROSS AVE
PARK AVE
MONTEAGLE AVE
Bwg Gn
STRATHFIELD GDNS
SHIRLEY GDNS
LEVETT GDNS
HURSTBOURNE GDNS
MELFORD AVE
Schs
2
THE GABLES
TANNER ST
CHURCH RD
HARPOUR RD
GLENNY RD
FANSHAWE AVE A123
ALDERSEY GDNS
HULSE AVE
IG11
Schs
WAKERING RD
BAMFORD RD
QUEEN'S RD
NORTHERN RELIEF RD
Eastbury Comp Sch
CHAMPNESS RD
UPNEY LA
MULBERRY CT
MANOR RD
CORNWALL CL
THE DRIVE
CLARE GDNS
Boating Lakes
THE LINTONS
MONTEAGLE CT
WIGHAM HO
CRANLEIGH GDNS
NETHERFIELD RD
BULLER RD
SALISBURY AVE
ODELL CL
GODEY RD
HELMORE RD
RIDLEY CL
THE OAK
LEY AVE
CUTHBERGA CL
Barking
CENTRAL HO
KING'S RD
LONGBRIDGE RD
THE ODEON
SOMERBY RD
SHERWOOD GDNS
ROSSLYN RD
NETHERFIELD GDNS
WILMINGTON GDNS
Barking
EDGEFIELD AVE
Upney
ADELIZA CL
WILLIAM ST
LINTON RD
CAMBRIDGE RD
CAMBRIDGE HO
STATION PAR
THORPE RD
CECIL AVE
PRIORY RD
SHERRY MEWS
HORNS CROFT
THORNHILL GDNS
PAYNE CL
LARKS GR
MARGARET BONDFIELD AVE
LANSBURY AVE
1
NORTH ST
GEORGE ST
ST JAMES
The Vicarage Field Sh Ctr
GREENSLADE RD
MEADOW RD
MERTON RD
LONDON RD
RIPPLE RD
BARKING
CONISTON CL
LAMBOURNE RD
DIGBY RD
TRESHAM RD
BRIDGEWAY
1 HARVEY HO
2 GOWER HO
Ct
EAST ST
VICARAGE DR
SUNNINGDALE AVE
GREAVES CL
SUFFOLK RD
NORFOLK RD
SURREY RD
CONISTON AVE
LANCASTER AVE
JOHN BURNS DR
Sch
DAWSON AVE
STUART RD
STRATFORD CL
Liby
CLOCKHOUSE AVE
ST ERKENWALD RD
AWDRY'S RD
ESSEX RD
Schs
KENDAL AVE
84
Cem
Sch
AXE ST
A123
ST ERKENWALD MEWS
CRANBROOK RD
RIPPLE RD
TUDOR RD
TH
44
St Joseph RC Prim
BROADWAY
A124
WESTBURY RD
45
101
EASTBURY AVE
SISLEY RD
BROOK CT
46
A123
BAMBER

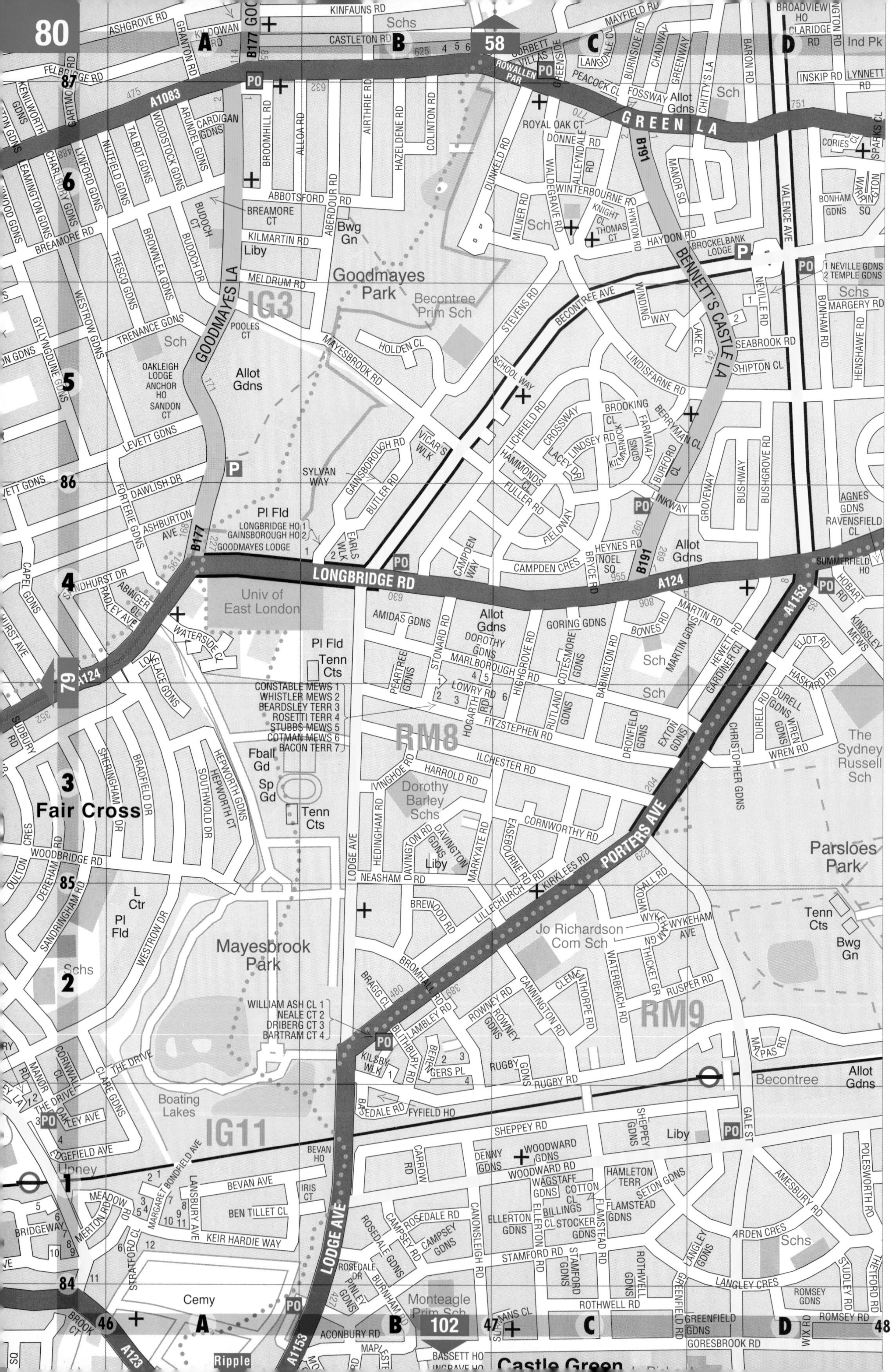
58
A
B
C
D
KINFAUNS RD
ASHGROVE RD
KILDOWAN RD
GRANTON RD
CASTLETON RD
Schs
MAYFIELD RD
BROADVIEW HO
CLARIDGE RD
Ind Pk
CORBETT VILLAS
ROWALLEN PAR
LANGDALE CL
BURNSIDE RD
CHADWAY
GREENWAY
BARON RD
FELBRIDGE RD
87
A1083
KENILWORTH GDNS
GARTMORE RD
PO
INSKIP RD
LYNNETT RD
PEACOCK CL
FOSSWAY
Allot Gdns
CHITTY'S LA
Sch
GREEN LA
ROYAL OAK CT
DONNE PL
ALLEYNDALE RD
B191
MANOR SQ
CORIES CL
SPARKS CL
CARDIGAN GDNS
ARUNDEL GDNS
WOODSTOCK GDNS
TALBOT GDNS
NUTFIELD GDNS
LYNFORD GDNS
CHARLBURY GDNS
LEAMINGTON GDNS
BROOMHILL RD
ALLOA RD
AIRTHRIE RD
HAZELDENE RD
COLINTON RD
DUNKELD RD
WALDEGRAVE RD
WINTERBOURNE RD
KNIGHT CL
THOMAS CT
HYNTON RD
VALENCE AVE
BONHAM GDNS
WARRINGTON SQ
6
ABBOTSFORD RD
ABERDOUR RD
BREAMORE CT
BUDOCH CT
KILMARTIN RD
Liby
Bwg Gn
MILNER RD
HAYDON RD
BROCKELBANK LODGE
P
NEVILLE GDNS 1
TEMPLE GDNS 2
BREAMORE RD
TRESCO GDNS
BROWNLEA GDNS
BUDOCH DR
MELDRUM RD
Goodmayes Park
Becontree Prim Sch
STEVENS RD
BECONTREE AVE
WINDING WAY
BENNETT'S CASTLE LA
NEVILLE RD
Schs
MARGERY RD
IG3
GOODMAYES LA
WESTROW GDNS
GYLLYNGDUNE GDNS
TRENANCE GDNS
Sch
POOLES CT
MAYESBROOK RD
HOLDEN CL
SCHOOL WAY
LAKE CL
SEABROOK RD
BONHAM RD
HENSHAWE RD
5
OAKLEIGH LODGE
ANCHOR HO
SANDON CT
Allot Gdns
LINDISFARNE RD
SHIPTON CL
LEVETT GDNS
LICHFIELD RD
CROSSWAY
BROOKING CL
FARMWAY
BERRYMAN CL
GAINSBOROUGH RD
VICAR'S WLK
LACEY DR
LINDSEY RD
KILMARNOCK GDNS
BURFORD CL
BUSHGROVE RD
BUSHWAY
GROVEWAY
HAMMONDS CL
86
DAWLISH DR
SYLVAN WAY
BUTLER RD
FULLER RD
LINKWAY
AGNES GDNS
FORTERIE GDNS
ASHBURTON AVE
Pl Fld
LONGBRIDGE HO 1
GAINSBOROUGH HO 2
GOODMAYES LODGE
EARLS WLK
FIELDWAY
RAVENSFIELD CL
B177
CAMPDEN WAY
HEYNES RD
NOEL SQ
Allot Gdns
SUMMERFIELD HO
HOBART RD
CAMPDEN CRES
BRYCE RD
955
4
SANDHURST DR
RADLEY AVE
ABINGER CL
LONGBRIDGE RD
A124
A1153
Univ of East London
AMIDAS GDNS
STONARD RD
Allot Gdns
DOROTHY GDNS
GORING GDNS
BOWES RD
MARTIN RD
MARTIN GDNS
HEWETT RD
GARDINER CL
KINGSLEY MEWS
ELIOT RD
HASKARD RD
CAPEL GDNS
WATERSIDE CL
LOVELACE GDNS
Pl Fld
Tenn Cts
PEARTREE GDNS
MARLBOROUGH RD
HIGHGROVE RD
COTESMORE GDNS
BABINGTON RD
Sch
DURELL RD
DURELL GDNS
WREN GDNS
WREN RD
79
CONSTABLE MEWS 1
WHISTLER MEWS 2
BEARDSLEY TERR 3
ROSETTI TERR 4
STUBBS MEWS 5
COTMAN MEWS 6
BACON TERR 7
LOWRY RD
HOGARTH RD
RUTLAND GDNS
FITZSTEPHEN RD
DRONFIELD GDNS
EXTON GDNS
CHRISTOPHER GDNS
The Sydney Russell Sch
RM8
SUDBURY RD
SHERINGHAM DR
BRADFIELD DR
HEPWORTH GDNS
HEPWORTH CT
SOUTHWOLD DR
Fball Gd
Sp Gd
Tenn Cts
IVINGHOE RD
HARROLD RD
ILCHESTER RD
Dorothy Barley Schs
3
Fair Cross
HEDINGHAM RD
DAVINGTON RD
DAVINGTON GDNS
MARKYATE RD
EASEBOURNE RD
CORNWORTHY RD
PORTERS AVE
Parsloes Park
WOODBRIDGE RD
DEREHAM RD
LODGE AVE
Liby
KIRKLEES RD
NEASHAM RD
85
SANDRINGHAM RD
L Ctr
Pl Fld
WESTROW DR
BREWOOD RD
LILLECHURCH RD
ROXWELL RD
WYKEHAM AVE
Tenn Cts
Bwg Gn
Mayesbrook Park
Jo Richardson Com Sch
THICKET GR
Schs
2
BROMHALL RD
BRAGG CL
CANNINGTON RD
CLEMENTHORPE RD
WATERBEACH RD
RUSPER RD
RM9
WILLIAM ASH CL 1
NEALE CT 2
DRIBERG CT 3
BARTRAM CT 4
LAMBLEY RD
ROWNEY RD
ROWNEY GDNS
MAPLESTEAD RD
MANOR RD
CORNWALL CL
CLARE GDNS
THE DRIVE
KILSBY WLK
BLITHBURY RD
BERENGERS PL
RUGBY GDNS
RUGBY RD
Becontree
Allot Gdns
Boating Lakes
OAKLEY AVE
IG11
BASEDALE RD
FYFIELD HO
SHEPPEY RD
SHEPPEY GDNS
Liby
GALE ST
FAGEFIELD AVE
MARGARET BONDFIELD AVE
BEVAN HO
CARROW RD
DENNY GDNS
WOODWARD GDNS
WOODWARD RD
POLESWORTH RD
Upney
1
BEVAN AVE
IRIS CT
WAGSTAFF GDNS
COTTON CL
HAMLETON TERR
SETON GDNS
AMESBURY RD
MEADOW RD
MERTON RD
LANSBURY AVE
BEN TILLET CL
ROSEDALE RD
CAMPSEY RD
CANONSLEIGH RD
ELLERTON GDNS
ELLERTON RD
BILLINGS CL
STOCKER GDNS
FLAMSTEAD RD
FLAMSTEAD GDNS
BRIDGEWAY
KEIR HARDIE WAY
CAMPSEY GDNS
ARDEN CRES
Schs
STRATFORD CL
LODGE AVE
ROSEDALE GDNS
STAMFORD RD
STAMFORD GDNS
ROTHWELL GDNS
LANGLEY GDNS
84
ROSEDALE DR
PINLEY GDNS
BURNHAM RD
Monteagle Prim Sch
GREENFIELD RD
LANGLEY CRES
ROMSEY GDNS
STUDLEY RD
THETFORD RD
Cemy
ROTHWELL RD
BROOK CT
46
A123
A
PO
ACONBURY RD
B
102
47
SUTHERLANDS CL
C
GREENFIELD GDNS
D
WIX RD
ROMSEY RD
48
Ripple
A1153
MAPLESTEAD
BASSETT HO
GORESBROOK RD
Castle Green

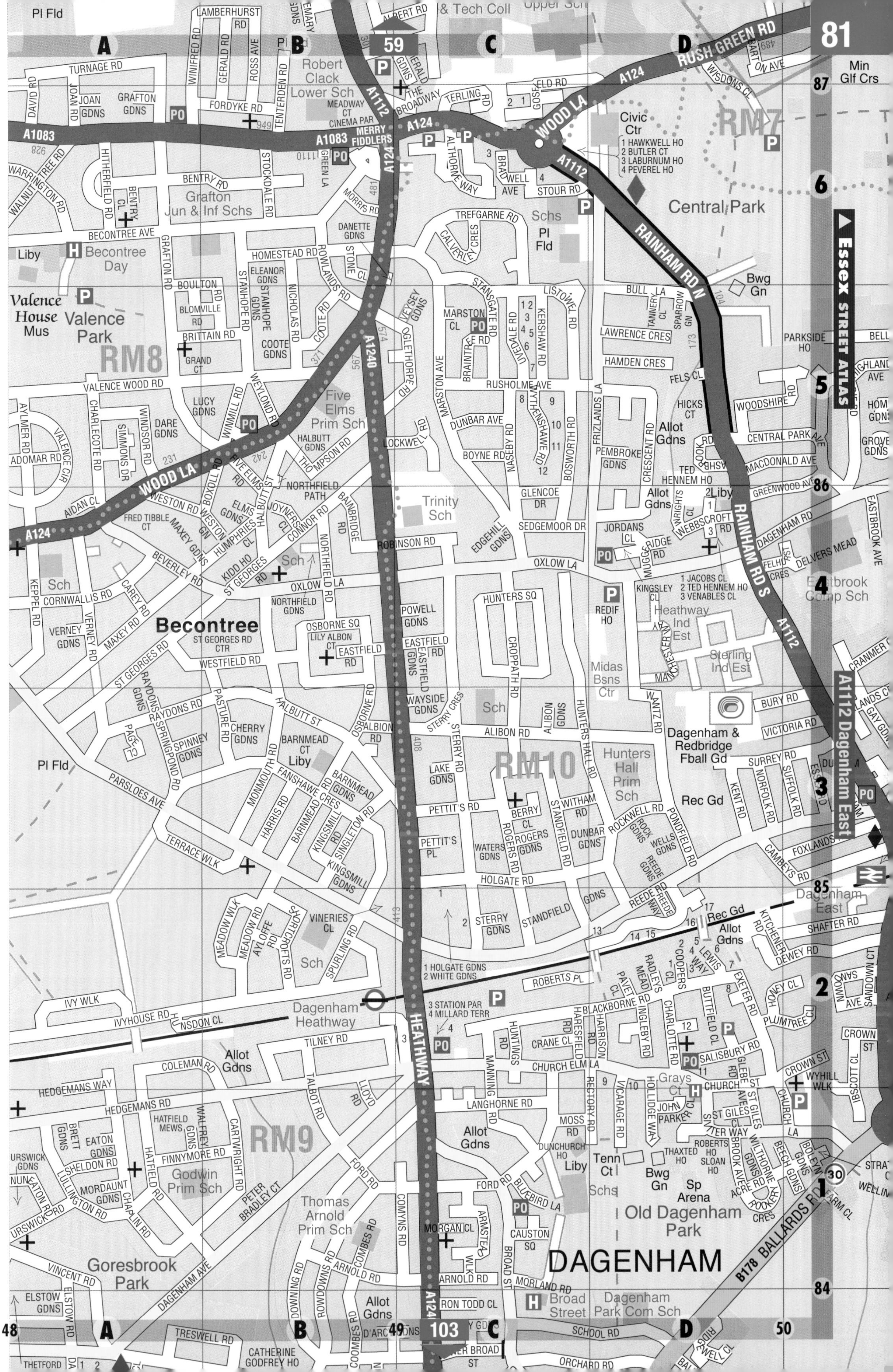
A
B
C
D
59
103
87
86
85
84
6
5
4
3
2
1
48
49
50
Essex STREET ATLAS
RM8
RM7
RM10
RM9
Becontree
DAGENHAM
A1083
A124
A1112
A1240
B178
WOOD LA
RUSH GREEN RD
RAINHAM RD N
RAINHAM RD S
HEATHWAY
BALLARDS RD
A1112 Dagenham East
Dagenham Heathway
Dagenham East
Valence House Mus
Valence Park
Becontree Day
Grafton Jun & Inf Schs
Robert Clack Lower Sch
Five Elms Prim Sch
Trinity Sch
Central Park
Civic Ctr
1 HAWKWELL HO
2 BUTLER CT
3 LABURNUM HO
4 PEVEREL HO
Heathway Ind Est
Sterling Ind Est
Midas Bsns Ctr
Dagenham & Redbridge Fball Gd
Hunters Hall Prim Sch
Eastbrook Comp Sch
Rec Gd
Allot Gdns
Godwin Prim Sch
Thomas Arnold Prim Sch
Goresbrook Park
Old Dagenham Park
Sp Arena
Tenn Ct
Broad Street
Dagenham Park Com Sch
Grays Ct
1 JACOBS CL
2 TED HENNEM HO
3 VENABLES CL
1 HOLGATE GDNS
2 WHITE GDNS
3 STATION PAR
4 MILLARD TERR
Min Glf Crs
Bwg Gn
Liby
Pl Fld
Sch
Schs
TURNAGE RD
BECONTREE AVE
VALENCE WOOD RD
OXLOW LA
WESTFIELD RD
HALBUTT ST
PARSLOES AVE
TERRACE WLK
IVYHOUSE RD
TILNEY RD
HEDGEMANS RD
HEDGEMANS WAY
FINNYMORE RD
CHURCH ELM LA
ALIBON RD
HOLGATE RD
PETTIT'S RD
RUSHOLME AVE
SEDGEMOOR DR
VICTORIA RD
BURY RD
SURREY RD
CENTRAL PARK AVE
MACDONALD AVE
DAGENHAM RD
DELVERS MEAD
EASTBROOK AVE
CRAMMER CT
SALISBURY RD
CROWN ST
CHURCH ST
CHURCH LA
MORLAND RD
ARNOLD RD
FORD RD
BLUEBIRD LA
SCHOOL RD
ORCHARD RD
TRESWELL RD
VINCENT RD
DAGENHAM AVE
CHAPLIN RD
HATFIELD RD
CARTWRIGHT RD
COMYNS RD
TALBOT RD
LANGHORNE RD
RECTORY RD
VICARAGE RD
ROBERTS PL
ST GEORGES RD
CORNWALLIS RD
MAXEY RD
BEVERLEY RD
RAYDONS RD
MONMOUTH RD
OSBORNE RD
STERRY RD
CROPPATH RD
BOSWORTH RD
FRIZLANDS LA
HUNTERS HALL RD
WANTZ RD
POND FIELD RD
REEDE RD
KENT RD
NORFOLK RD
SUFFOLK RD
FOXLANDS
SHAFTER RD
DEWEY RD
EXETER RD
BUTTFIELD CL
CHARLOTTE RD
HARRISON RD
INGLEBY RD
HARESFIELD RD
MANNING RD
BROAD ST
RON TODD CL
MORGAN CL
ARMSTEAD WLK
CAUSTON SQ
DUNCHURCH HO
MOSS RD
JOHN PARKER CL
SISTER WAY
ST GILES CL
BROOK AVE
WILTHORNE GDNS
BEECH GDNS
BOLEYN GDNS
ACRE RD
ROOKERY CRES
FARM CL
WELLINGTON DR
SANDOWN CT
SCOTT CL
WYHILL WLK
PLUMTREE CL
HONEY CL
BECONTREE
GRAFTON RD
STOCKDALE RD
BENTRY RD
FORDYKE RD
LAMBERHURST RD
GERALD RD
ROSS AVE
TENTERDEN RD
WINIFRED RD
STOUR RD
TREFGARNE RD
STANSGATE RD
LISTOWEL RD
KERSHAW RD
MARSTON AVE
DUNBAR AVE
BOYNE RD
GLENCOE DR
LAWRENCE CRES
HAMDEN CRES
WOODSHIRE RD
BULL LA
FELS CL
HICKS CT
PEMBROKE GDNS
CRESCENT RD
JORDANS CL
MUGGERIDGE RD
WEBBSCROFT RD
KINGSLEY CL
REDIF HO
HUNTERS SQ
POWELL GDNS
EASTFIELD RD
EASTFIELD GDNS
WAYSIDE GDNS
LILY ALBON CT
OSBORNE SQ
NORTHFIELD RD
NORTHFIELD GDNS
NORTHFIELD PATH
ROBINSON RD
BAINBRIDGE RD
CONNOR RD
THOMPSON RD
HALBUTT GDNS
WEYLOND RD
WINMILL RD
DARE GDNS
LUCY GDNS
WINDSOR RD
SIMMONS DR
CHARLECOTE RD
AYLMER RD
ADOMAR RD
VALENCE CIR
AIDAN CL
WESTON RD
FRED TIBBLE CT
KEPPEL RD
VERNEY GDNS
VERNEY RD
CAREY RD
KIDD HO
HUMPHRIES CL
BARNMEAD CT
BARNMEAD GDNS
BARNMEAD RD
FANSHAWE CRES
HARRIS RD
KINGSMILL RD
KINGSMILL GDNS
SINGLETON RD
VINERIES CL
SHORTCROFTS RD
AYLOFFE RD
MEADOW WLK
SPURLING RD
IVY WLK
COLEMAN RD
LLOYD RD
HATFIELD MEWS
WALFREY GDNS
EATON GDNS
BRETT GDNS
SHELDON RD
MORDAUNT GDNS
LULLINGTON RD
NUNEATON RD
URSWICK RD
URSWICK GDNS
PETER BRADLEY CT
ELSTOW GDNS
ELSTOW RD
THETFORD RD
CATHERINE GODFREY HO
COMBES RD
COMBES RD
ROWDOWNS RD
DOWNING RD
SPINNEY GDNS
SPRINGPOND RD
PAGE CL
CHERRY GDNS
PASTURE RD
LAKE GDNS
WATERS GDNS
ROGERS RD
ROGERS GDNS
BERRY CL
STANDFIELD RD
STANDFIELD
WITHAM RD
DUNBAR GDNS
ROCKWELL RD
ROCK GDNS
WELLS GDNS
REEDE GDNS
STERRY GDNS
STERRY CRES
ALIBON GDNS
EDGEHILL GDNS
CRANE CL
HUNTINGS RD
BLACKBORNE RD
RADLEYS MEAD
PAYET CL
COOPERS CL
LEWIS WAY
KITCHENER RD
CAMBEYS RD
THAXTED HO
ROBERTS HO
SLOAN HO
HOLLIDGE WAY
TERLING RD
THE BROADWAY
MEADWAY CT
CINEMA PAR
MERRY FIDDLERS
ALTHORNE WAY
BRADWELL AVE
DANETTE GDNS
HOMESTEAD RD
ROWLANDS RD
STONE CL
COOTE RD
COOTE GDNS
NICHOLAS RD
STANHOPE GDNS
STANHOPE RD
ELEANOR GDNS
BOULTON RD
BLOMVILLE RD
BRITTAIN RD
GRAND CT
JOAN GDNS
GRAFTON GDNS
DAVID RD
HITHERFIELD RD
WARRINGTON RD
WALNUT TREE RD
VESEY GDNS
OGLETHORPE RD
LOCKWELL RD
MARSTON CL
BRAINTREE RD
UVEDALE RD
WYTHENSHAWE RD
NASEBY RD
WISDONS CL
BARTON AVE
PARKSIDE HO
GREENWOOD AVE
FELHURST CRES
ST GEORGES RD CTR
PI Fld

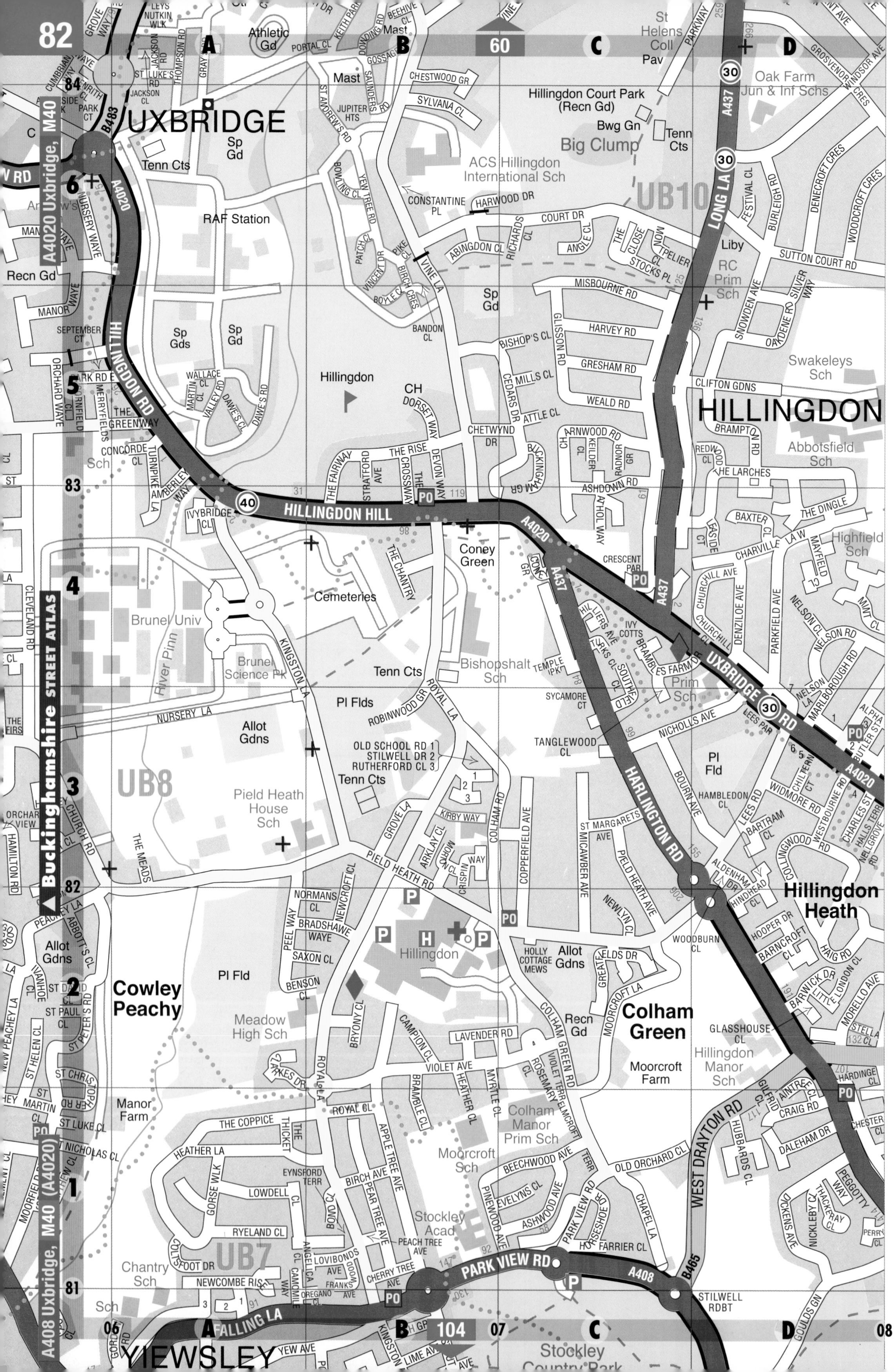

A
B
60
C
D
UXBRIDGE
HILLINGDON
UB10
UB8
UB7
Athletic Gd
Mast
St Helens Coll Pav
Oak Farm Jun & Inf Schs
Hillingdon Court Park (Recn Gd)
Bwg Gn
Tenn Cts
Big Clump
ACS Hillingdon International Sch
Sp Gd
Tenn Cts
RAF Station
Recn Gd
Sp Gds
Hillingdon
CH
Liby
RC Prim Sch
Swakeleys Sch
Abbotsfield Sch
Highfield Sch
HILLINGDON HILL
Coney Green
Cemeteries
Brunel Univ
River Pinn
Brunel Science Pk
Tenn Cts
Bishopshalt Sch
Prim Sch
Pl Flds
Allot Gdns
Pl Fld
Pield Heath House Sch
Hillingdon Heath
Hillingdon
Allot Gdns
Cowley Peachy
Pl Fld
Meadow High Sch
Recn Gd
Colham Green
Moorcroft Farm
Hillingdon Manor Sch
Manor Farm
Colham Manor Prim Sch
Moorcroft Sch
Stockley Acad
Chantry Sch
Sch
PARK VIEW RD
FALLING LA
STILWELL RDBT
YIEWSLEY
Stockley Country Park
104
06
07
08
UXBRIDGE RD
HARLINGTON RD
LONG LA
WEST DRAYTON RD
HILLINGDON RD
A4020
A437
A408
B465
B483
OLD SCHOOL RD 1
STILWELL DR 2
RUTHERFORD CL 3
A4020 Uxbridge, M40
A408 Uxbridge, M40 (A4020)
Buckinghamshire STREET ATLAS

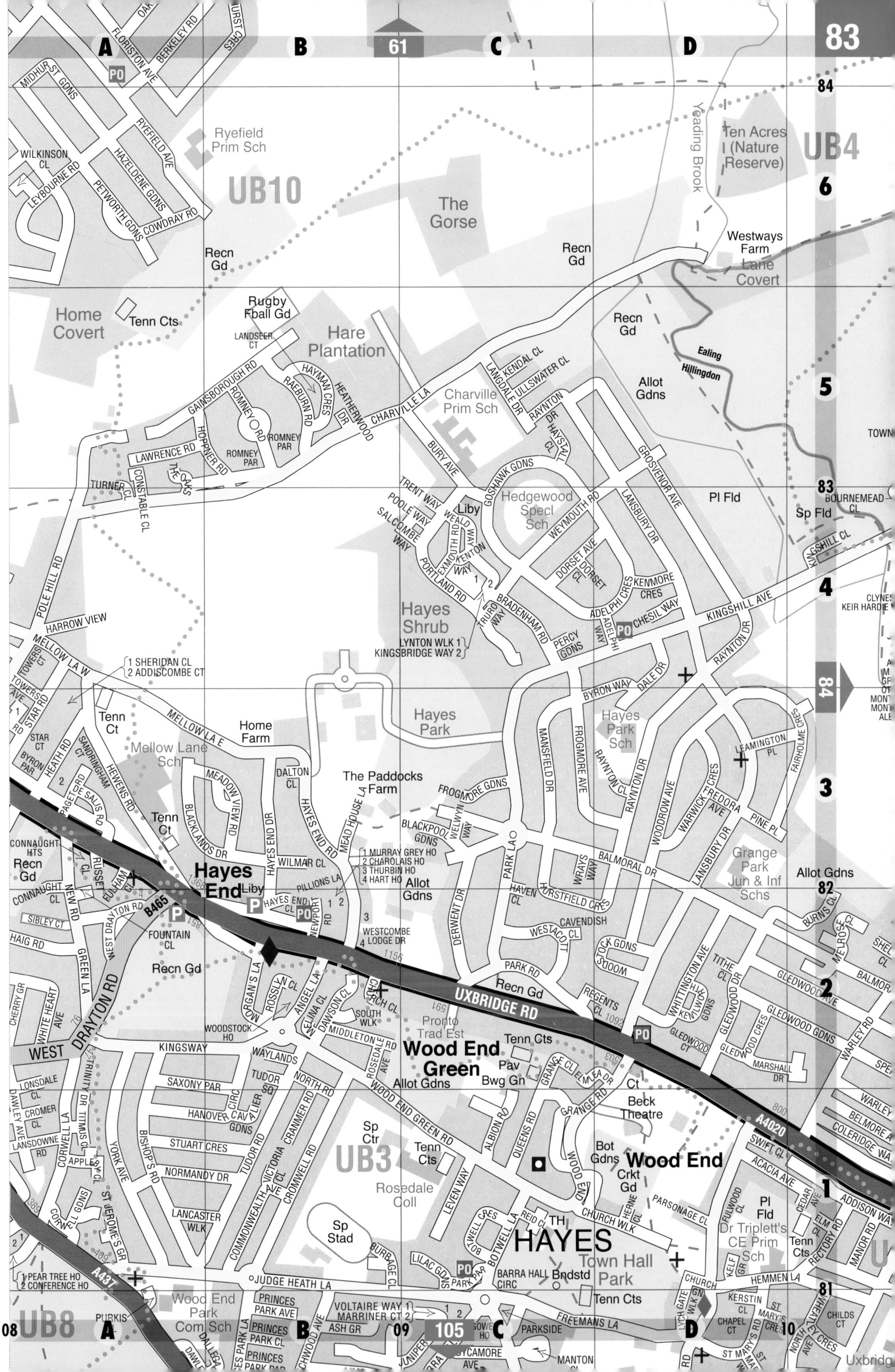
A
B
61
C
D
84
UB10
UB4
UB3
UB8
Ryefield Prim Sch
The Gorse
Ten Acres (Nature Reserve)
Yeading Brook
Westways Farm
Lane Covert
Recn Gd
Home Covert
Tenn Cts
Rugby Fball Gd
Hare Plantation
Charville Prim Sch
Allot Gdns
Ealing
Hillingdon
Hedgewood Specl Sch
Liby
Pl Fld
Sp Fld
Hayes Shrub
Hayes Park
Hayes Park Sch
Home Farm
Mellow Lane Sch
The Paddocks Farm
Grange Park Jun & Inf Schs
Hayes End
Wood End Green
Pronto Trad Est
Pav
Bwg Gn
Beck Theatre
Bot Gdns
Wood End
Crkt Gd
Sp Ctr
Rosedale Coll
Sp Stad
HAYES
TH
Town Hall Park
Bndstd
Dr Triplett's CE Prim Sch
Wood End Park Com Sch
UXBRIDGE RD
B465
A4020
A437
WEST DRAYTON RD
CHARVILLE LA
KINGSHILL AVE
MELLOW LA W
MELLOW LA E
BALMORAL DR
JUDGE HEATH LA
WOOD END GREEN RD
CHURCH WLK
KINGSWAY
1 SHERIDAN CL
2 ADDISCOMBE CT
LYNTON WLK 1
KINGSBRIDGE WAY 2
1 MURRAY GREY HO
2 CHAROLAIS HO
3 THURBIN HO
4 HART HO
1 PEAR TREE HO
2 CONFERENCE HO
VOLTAIRE WAY 1
MARRINER CT 2
105
08
09
10
6
5
4
3
2
1
83
82
81
Uxbridg

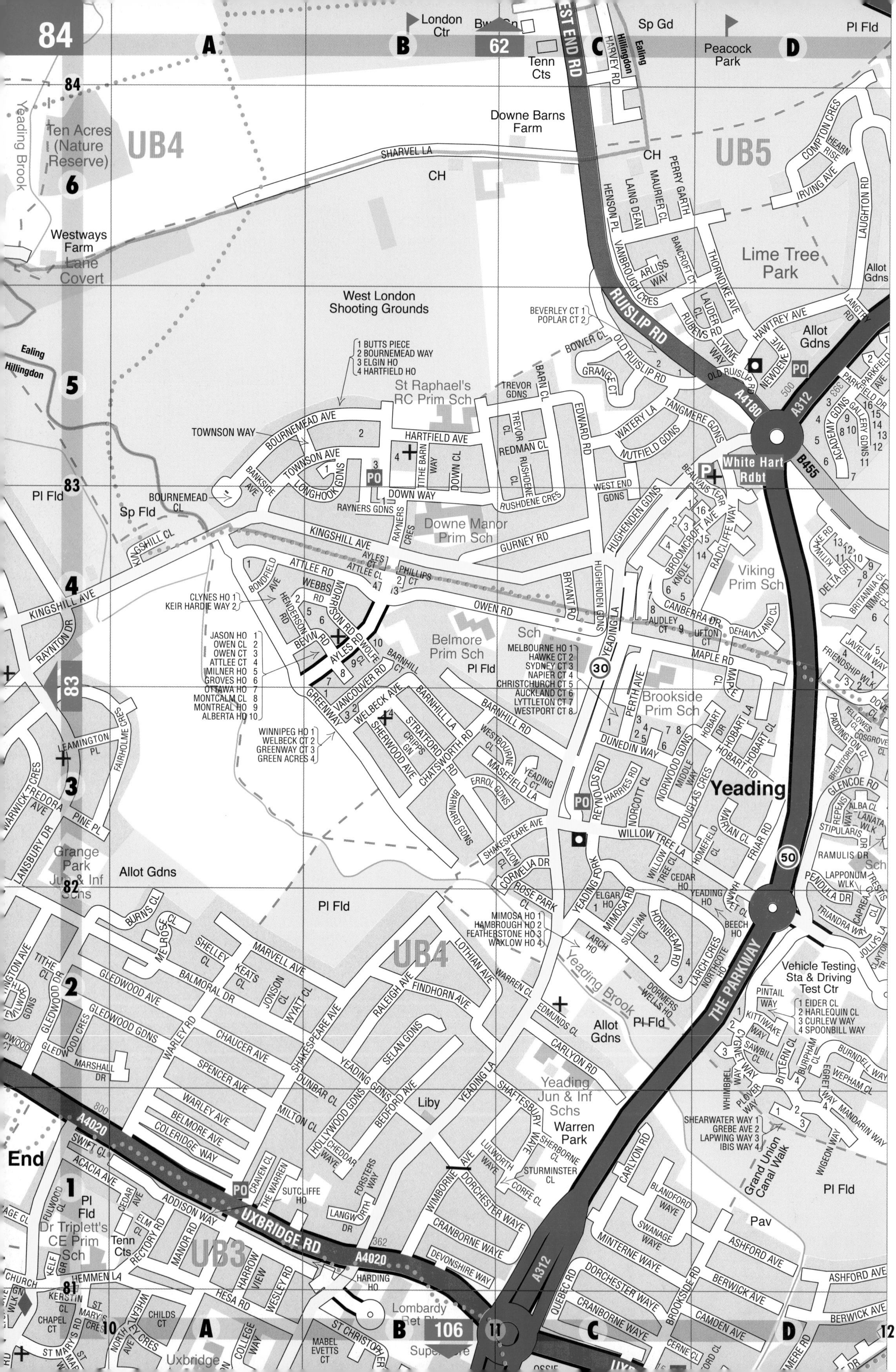
A
B
C
D
62
106
London Ctr
Tenn Cts
Sp Gd
Pl Fld
Peacock Park
WEST END RD
Hillingdon
Ealing
HARVEY RD
Downe Barns Farm
Yeading Brook
Ten Acres (Nature Reserve)
UB4
UB5
UB3
SHARVEL LA
CH
Westways Farm
Lane Covert
HENSON PL
LAING DEAN
MAURIER CL
PERRY GARTH
COMPTON CRES
HEARN RISE
IRVING AVE
LAUGHTON RD
Lime Tree Park
Allot Gdns
West London Shooting Grounds
ARLISS WAY
BANCROFT CT
THORNDIKE AVE
VANBROUGH CRES
LAUDER CL
RUBENS RD
LYNNE WAY
HAWTREY AVE
NEWDENE AVE
LANGTRY RD
RUISLIP RD
OLD RUISLIP RD
BEVERLEY CT 1
POPLAR CT 2
BOWER CL
GRANGE CT
1 BUTTS PIECE
2 BOURNEMEAD WAY
3 ELGIN HO
4 HARTFIELD HO
St Raphael's RC Prim Sch
TREVOR GDNS
BARN CL
EDWARD RD
WATERY LA
TANGMERE GDNS
MUTFIELD GDNS
A4180
A312
B455
PO
White Hart Rdbt
ACADEMY GDNS
GALLERY GDNS
PARKFIELD DR
PARKFIELD AVE
TOWNSON WAY
BOURNEMEAD AVE
HARTFIELD AVE
TITHE BARN WAY
DOWN CL
TREVOR CL
REDMAN CL
RUSHDENE CL
RUSHDENE CRES
TOWNSON AVE
LONGHOOK GDNS
BANKSIDE AVE
BOURNEMEAD CL
DOWN WAY
RAYNERS GDNS
RAYNERS CRES
Downe Manor Prim Sch
GURNEY RD
WEST END GDNS
HUGHENDEN GDNS
BEAUVAIS TERR
BROOMCROFT AVE
RADCLIFFE WAY
KNOLE CT
Viking Prim Sch
Pl Fld
Sp Fld
KINGSHILL CL
KINGSHILL AVE
AYLES CT
ATTLEE CL
ATTLEE RD
PHILLIPS CT
BONDFIELD AVE
WEBBS RD
MORRISON RD
HENDERSON RD
BEVIN RD
AYLES RD
WOLFE CL
CLYNES HO 1
KEIR HARDIE WAY 2
OWEN RD
BRYANT RD
YEADING LA
CANBERRA DR
AUDLEY CT
UFTON CT
DEHAVILLAND CL
DELTA GR
KITTIWAKE RD
BRITANNIA CL
NIMROD CL
JAVELIN WAY
FRIENDSHIP WLK
RAYNTON DR
JASON HO 1
OWEN CL 2
OWEN CT 3
ATTLEE CT 4
MILNER HO 5
GROVES HO 6
OTTAWA HO 7
MONTCALM CL 8
MONTREAL HO 9
ALBERTA HO 10
Belmore Prim Sch
Sch
MELBOURNE HO 1
HAWKE CT 2
SYDNEY CT 3
NAPIER CT 4
CHRISTCHURCH CT 5
AUCKLAND CT 6
LYTTLETON CT 7
WESTPORT CT 8
MAPLE RD
MAPLE CL
PERTH AVE
Brookside Prim Sch
BARNHILL CT
BARNHILL RD
BARNHILL LA
GREENWAY
VANCOUVER RD
WELBECK AVE
SHERWOOD AVE
STRATFORD RD
CRIPPS GN
CHATSWORTH RD
WESTBOURNE CL
MASEFIELD LA
YEADING CT
ERROL GDNS
BARNARD GDNS
WINNIPEG HO 1
WELBECK CT 2
GREENWAY CT 3
GREEN ACRES 4
LEAMINGTON PL
FAIRHOLME CRES
FREDORA AVE
WARWICK CRES
PINE PL
LANSBURY DR
DUNEDIN WAY
HOBART DR
HOBART LA
HOBART CL
HOBART RD
REYNOLDS RD
HARRIES RD
NORCOTT CL
NORWOOD GDNS
MIDDLE WAY
DOUGLAS CRES
Yeading
MARIAN CL
FRIAR RD
WILLOW TREE LA
WILLOW TREE CL
HOMEFIELD CL
CEDAR HO
YEADING HO
BEECH HO
SHAKESPEARE AVE
AVON CL
CORNELIA DR
ROSE PARK CL
YEADING FORK
ELGAR HO
MIMOSA RD
SULLIVAN CL
HORNBEAM RD
LARCH HO
LARCH CRES
NORTHCOTE HO
GLENCOE RD
ALBA CL
LANATA WLK
STIPULARIS DR
RAMULIS DR
PENDULA DR
LAPPONUM WLK
TRIANDRA WAY
CAPREA CL
JOLLYS LA
FELLOWES CL
COSGROVE CL
PADDINGTON CL
BRENTFORD CL
Grange Park Jun & Inf Schs
Allot Gdns
MIMOSA HO 1
HAMBROUGH HO 2
FEATHERSTONE HO 3
WAXLOW HO 4
THE PARKWAY
Vehicle Testing Sta & Driving Test Ctr
BURNS CL
MELROSE CL
SHELLEY CL
KEATS CL
MARVELL AVE
LOTHIAN AVE
TITHE CL
GLEDWOOD DR
GLEDWOOD AVE
GLEDWOOD CRES
GLEDWOOD GDNS
BALMORAL DR
JONSON CL
WYATT CL
RALEIGH AVE
FINDHORN AVE
WARREN CL
Yeading Brook
DORMERS WELLS HO
Allot Gdns
Pl Fld
PINTAIL WAY
KITTIWAKE WAY
1 EIDER CL
2 HARLEQUIN CL
3 CURLEW WAY
4 SPOONBILL WAY
EDMUNDS CL
CARLYON RD
CYGNET WAY
SAWBILL CL
BITTERN CL
BURPHAM CL
BURNDELL WAY
WEPHAM CL
EGRET WAY
MANDARIN WAY
WHIMBREL WAY
PLOVER WAY
WARLEY RD
CHAUCER AVE
SHAKESPEARE AVE
SELAN GDNS
SPENCER AVE
WARLEY AVE
BELMORE AVE
COLERIDGE WAY
MARSHALL DR
YEADING GDNS
DUNBAR CL
MILTON CL
BEDFORD AVE
Liby
YEADING LA
SHAFTESBURY WAYE
Yeading Jun & Inf Schs
Warren Park
SHEARWATER WAY 1
GREBE AVE 2
LAPWING WAY 3
IBIS WAY 4
WIGEON WAY
Grand Union Canal Walk
A4020
SWIFT CL
ACACIA AVE
End
Pl Fld
FULWOOD CL
CEDAR AVE
ELM CL
HOLLYWOOD GDNS
CHEDDAR WAYE
FORSTERS WAY
WIMBORNE AVE
DORCHESTER WAYE
LULWORTH WAYE
SHERBORNE CL
STURMINSTER CL
CORFE CL
CARLYON RD
BLANDFORD WAYE
SWANAGE WAYE
Pav
Pl Fld
CRAVEN CL
THE WARREN
SUTCLIFFE HO
ADDISON WAY
LANGWORTH DR
CRANBORNE WAYE
MINTERNE WAYE
ASHFORD AVE
Dr Triplett's CE Prim Sch
Tenn Cts
RECTORY RD
MANOR RD
UXBRIDGE RD
HARROW VIEW
WESLEY RD
DEVONSHIRE WAY
A312
QUEBEC RD
DORCHESTER WAYE
BROOKSIDE RD
BERWICK AVE
ASHFORD AVE
CHURCH
KELF GR
HEMMEN LA
HARDING HO
KERSTIN CL
ST MARY'S CRES
CHAPEL CT
CHILDS CT
HESA RD
WHEATLEY CRES
NORTH AVE
COLLEGE WAY
Lombardy Ret Pk
MABEL EVETTS CT
ST CHRISTOPHER
Superstore
CRANBORNE WAYE
CAMDEN AVE
CERNE CL
BERWICK AVE
ST MARY'S RD
Uxbridge
30
50
84
83
82
81
6
5
4
3
2
1
10
11
12

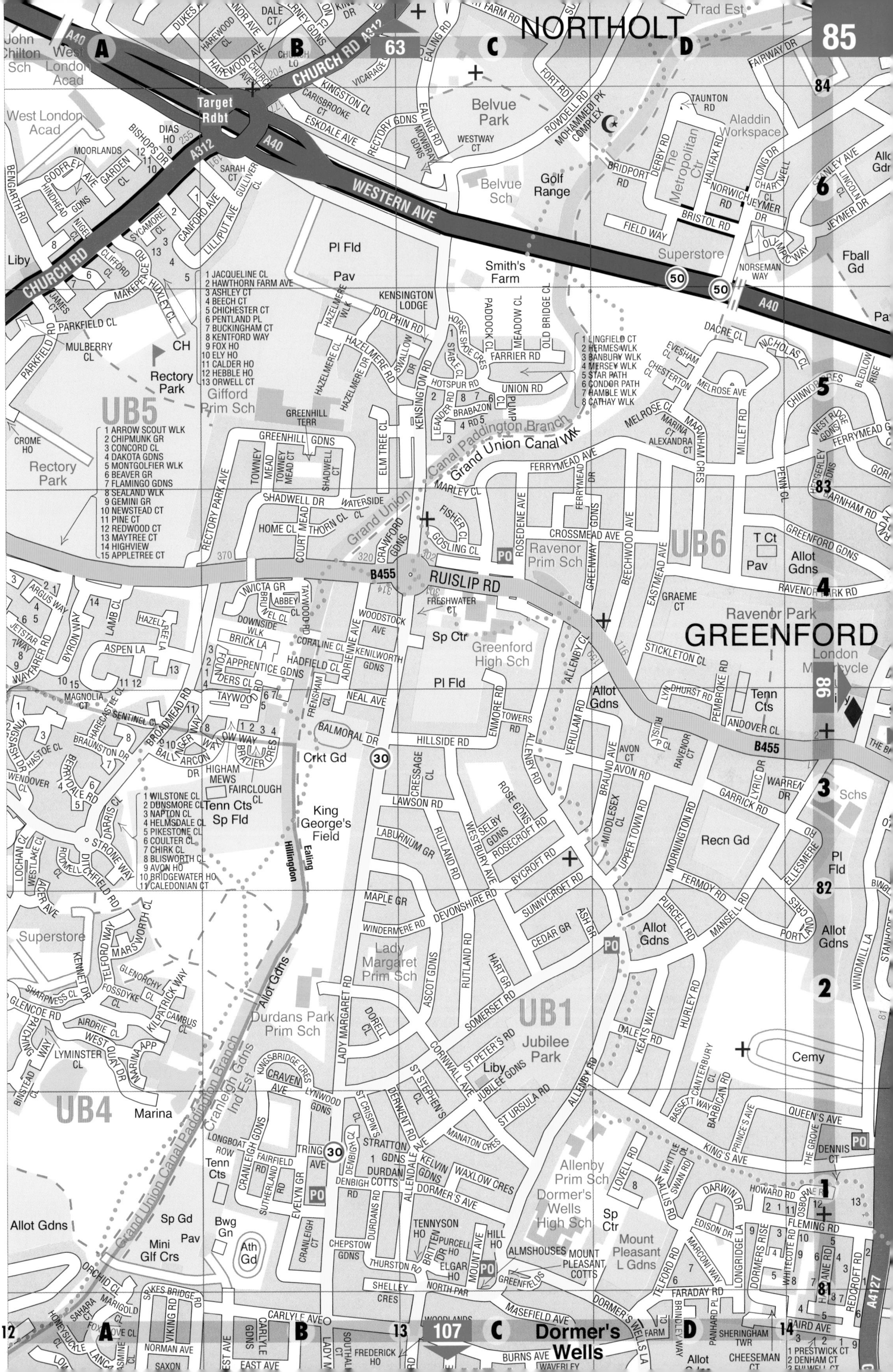
NORTHOLT
GREENFORD
Dormer's Wells
63
107
84
98
A
B
C
D
6
5
4
3
2
1
83
82
81
12
13
14
UB5
UB6
UB1
UB4
John Chilton Sch
West London Acad
Target Rdbt
CHURCH RD
WESTERN AVE
A40
A312
B455
A4127
RUISLIP RD
Belvue Park
Belvue Sch
Golf Range
Smith's Farm
Kensington Lodge
Pl Fld
Pav
Rectory Park
Gifford Prim Sch
Superstore
Aladdin Workspace
The Metropolitan Ctr
Fball Gd
Grand Union Canal Wlk
Grand Union Canal Paddington Branch
Ravenor Prim Sch
Ravenor Park
Greenford High Sch
Sp Ctr
Allot Gdns
Tenn Cts
Crkt Gd
King George's Field
Lady Margaret Prim Sch
Durdans Park Prim Sch
Jubilee Park
Recn Gd
Cemy
Allenby Prim Sch
Dormer's Wells High Sch
Mount Pleasant L Gdns
Cranleigh Gdns Ind Est
Marina
Mini Glf Crs
Sp Gd
Bwg Gn
Ath Gd
Hillingdon
Ealing
Liby
CH
Schs
London Motorcycle
1 JACQUELINE CL
2 HAWTHORN FARM AVE
3 ASHLEY CT
4 BEECH CT
5 CHICHESTER CT
6 PENTLAND PL
7 BUCKINGHAM CT
8 KENTFORD WAY
9 FOX HO
10 ELY HO
11 CALDER HO
12 HEBBLE HO
13 ORWELL CT
1 ARROW SCOUT WLK
2 CHIPMUNK GR
3 CONCORD CL
4 DAKOTA GDNS
5 MONTGOLFIER WLK
6 BEAVER GR
7 FLAMINGO GDNS
8 SEALAND WLK
9 GEMINI GR
10 NEWSTEAD CT
11 PINE CT
12 REDWOOD CT
13 MAYTREE CT
14 HIGHVIEW
15 APPLETREE CT
1 LINGFIELD CT
2 HERMES WLK
3 BANBURY WLK
4 MERSEY WLK
5 STAR PATH
6 CONDOR PATH
7 HAMBLE WLK
8 CATHAY WLK
1 WILSTONE CL
2 DUNSMORE CL
3 NAPTON CL
4 HELMSDALE CL
5 PIKESTONE CL
6 COULTER CL
7 CHIRK CL
8 BLISWORTH CL
9 AVON HO
10 BRIDGEWATER HO
11 CALEDONIAN CT
1 PRESTWICK CT
2 DENHAM CT
FERRYMEAD AVE
CROSSMEAD AVE
BEECHWOOD AVE
EASTMEAD AVE
ALLENBY RD
HILLSIDE RD
DEVONSHIRE RD
SOMERSET RD
CORNWALL AVE
KING'S AVE
QUEEN'S AVE
WINDMILL LA
CARLYLE AVE
BURNS AVE
MASEFIELD AVE
DORMER'S WELLS LA
FARADAY RD
FLEMING RD
KENSINGTON RD
EALING RD
BRISTOL RD
FIELD WAY
NORWICH RD
DACRE CL
NICHOLAS CL
MELROSE AVE
MILLET RD
RAVENOR PARK RD
GREENFORD GDNS
STICKLETON CL
PEMBROKE RD
ANDOVER CL
GARRICK RD
MORNINGTON RD
FERMOY RD
MANSELL RD
PURCELL RD
HURLEY RD
KEATS WAY
UPPER TOWN RD
MIDDLESEX CL
AVON RD
BRAUND AVE
VERULAM RD
ENMORE RD
WESTBURY AVE
ROSECROFT RD
BYCROFT RD
SUNNYCROFT RD
CEDAR GR
RUTLAND RD
LAWSON RD
LABURNUM GR
MAPLE GR
WINDERMERE RD
ASCOT GDNS
HART GR
LADY MARGARET RD
DORELL CL
KINGSBRIDGE CRES
CRAVEN AVE
LYNWOOD GDNS
DERWENT RD
ST STEPHEN'S CL
ST PETER'S RD
JUBILEE GDNS
ST URSULA RD
MANATON CRES
KELVIN GDNS
WAXLOW CRES
DORMER'S AVE
TENNYSON HO
CHEPSTOW GDNS
THURSTON RD
SHELLEY CRES
NORTH PAR
GREENFIELDS
ALMSHOUSES
MOUNT PLEASANT COTTS
LONGBOAT ROW
FAIRFIELD RD
CRANLEIGH GDNS
SUTHERLAND RD
EVELYN GR
TRING AVE
STRATTON GDNS
DURDAN COTTS
DENBIGH RD
HIGHAM MEWS
FAIRCLOUGH CL
BALMORAL DR
NEAL AVE
KENILWORTH GDNS
WOODSTOCK AVE
FRESHWATER CT
INVICTA GR
ABBEY CL
DOWNSIDE WLK
BRICK LA
CORALINE CL
HADFIELD CL
APPRENTICE GDNS
TAYWOOD RD
BROADMEAD RD
SENTINEL CL
MAGNOLIA CT
BRAUNSTON DR
BERRYDALE RD
WENDOVER CL
STRONE WAY
DITCHFIELD RD
ROWDELL RD
WESTLAKE CL
LOCHAN CL
AUGER AVE
TELFORD WAY
KENNET DR
MARSWORTH CL
GLENORCHY CL
FOSSDYKE CL
KILPATRICK WAY
CAMBUS CL
AIRDRIE CL
SHARPNESS CL
GLENCOE RD
PATCHING WAY
LYMINSTER CL
WEST QUAY DR
MARINA APP
BINSTEAD CL
ORCHID CL
SPIKES BRIDGE RD
VIKING RD
NORMAN AVE
SAXON
HONEYSUCKLE CL
SAHARA CT
MARIGOLD CL
LANCASTER
SOUTHALL
FREDERICK HO
WOODLANDS
EAST AVE
LADY MARGARET
ASPEN LA
LAMB CL
BYRON WAY
HAZEL TREE LA
WAYFARER RD
JETSTAR WAY
ARGUS WAY
SHADWELL DR
WATERSIDE
HOME CL
THORN CL
COURT MEAD
RECTORY PARK AVE
TOWNEY MEAD
GREENHILL GDNS
GREENHILL TERR
ELM TREE CL
DOLPHIN RD
HAZELMERE RD
HAZELMERE WLK
SWALLOW DR
HORSE SHOE CRES
STABLE CL
HOTSPUR RD
FARRIER RD
UNION RD
PADDOCK CL
MEADOW CL
OLD BRIDGE CL
BRABAZON RD
LEANDER RD
MARLEY CL
FISHER CL
GOSLING CL
ROSEDENE AVE
GREENWAY GDNS
PARKFIELD RD
PARKFIELD CL
MULBERRY CL
CROME HO
MAKEPEACE RD
HUXLEY CL
CLIFFORD RD
SYCAMORE CL
CANFORD AVE
LILLIPUT AVE
GULLIVER CL
SARAH CT
DIAS HO
BISHOPS DR
MOORLANDS
GODFREY AVE
GARDEN CL
HINDHEAD GDNS
BENGARTH RD
NIGEL CL
JAMES CT
KINGSTON CL
CARISBROOKE CT
ESKDALE AVE
VICARAGE
RECTORY GDNS
MOWBRAY GDNS
WESTWAY CT
ROWDELL RD
FORT RD
MOHAMMEDI PK COMPLEX
TAUNTON RD
DERBY RD
HALIFAX RD
BRIDPORT RD
LONG DR
CHARTWELL CL
JEYMER DR
OLYMPIC WAY
NORSEMAN WAY
STANLEY AVE
LINCOLN
FAIRWAY DR
EVESHAM CL
CHESTERTON CL
MARINA CT
ALEXANDRA CT
MARNHAM CRES
CHINNOR CRES
BLEDLOW RISE
WEST RIDGE GDNS
FERRYMEAD GDNS
HENGERLEY GDNS
PENN CL
BARNHAM RD
GRAEME CT
LYNDHURST RD
RUISLIP CL
RAVENOR CT
AVON CT
LYRIC DR
WARREN DR
ELLESMERE RD
PORTLAND CRES
STANHOPE
DARWIN DR
HOWARD RD
EDISON DR
MARCONI WAY
LONGRIDGE LA
DORMERS RISE
WHITECOTE RD
REDCROFT RD
BASSETT WAY
CANTERBURY CL
BARBICAN RD
PRINCE'S AVE
THE GROVE
DENNIS CT
LOVELL RD
WHITTLE
SWAN RD
WALLIS RD
TELFORD RD
SHERINGHAM TWR
CHEESEMAN CT
BAIRD AVE
PANHARD PL
BRINDLEY WAY
FARM
PO
Pl Fld
T Ct
Allot Gdns
Sp Ctr

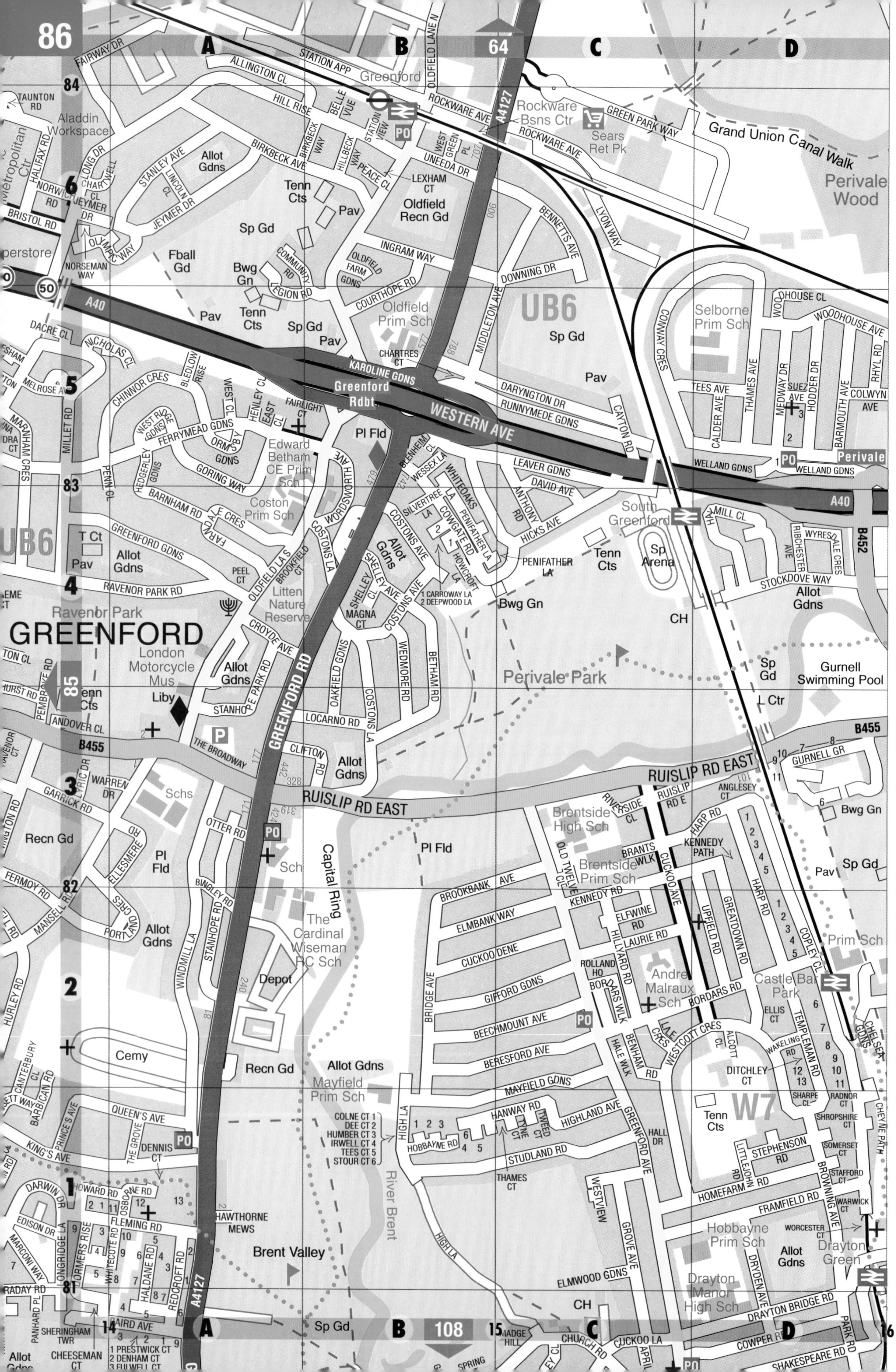
A
B
C
D
64
108
84
83
82
81
6
5
4
3
2
1
14
15
16
85
FAIRWAY DR
ALLINGTON CL
STATION APP
Greenford
OLDFIELD LANE N
HILL RISE
BELLE VUE
STATION VIEW
ROCKWARE AVE
A4127
Rockware Bsns Ctr
GREEN PARK WAY
Sears Ret Pk
Grand Union Canal Walk
Perivale Wood
TAUNTON RD
Aladdin Workspace
Metropolitan Ctr
HALIFAX RD
LONG DR
CHARTWELL CL
STANLEY AVE
LINCOLN CL
JEYMER DR
JEYMER AVE
NORWICH RD
BRISTOL RD
OLYMPIC WAY
NORSEMAN WAY
perstore
Allot Gdns
BIRKBECK AVE
BIRKBECK WAY
HILLBECK WAY
PEACE CL
LEXHAM CT
WEST GREEN PL
UNEEDA DR
Tenn Cts
Pav
Oldfield Recn Gd
LYON WAY
BENNETTS AVE
Sp Gd
Fball Gd
Bwg Gn
COMMUNITY RD
LEGION RD
INGRAM WAY
OLDFIELD FARM GDNS
COURTHOPE RD
DOWNING DR
MIDDLETON AVE
UB6
A40
DACRE CL
NICHOLAS CL
Oldfield Prim Sch
CHARTRES CT
KAROLINE GDNS
Greenford Rdbt
WESTERN AVE
DARYNGTON DR
RUNNYMEDE GDNS
CAYTON RD
CONWAY CRES
Selborne Prim Sch
WOODHOUSE CL
WOODHOUSE AVE
RHYL RD
COLWYN AVE
TEES AVE
THAMES AVE
MEDWAY DR
HODDER DR
SUEZ AVE
CALDER AVE
BARMOUTH AVE
WELLAND GDNS
Perivale
MELROSE AVE
MILLET RD
MARNHAM CRES
CHINNOR CRES
BLEDLOW RISE
WEST CL
HENLEY CL
EAST CL
FAIRLIGHT CT
WEST RIDGE GDNS
FERRYMEAD GDNS
ORMESBY GDNS
GORING WAY
Edward Betham CE Prim Sch
Pl Fld
WORDSWORTH AVE
BLENHEIM CL
WESSEX CL
WHITEOAKS LA
LEAVER GDNS
DAVID AVE
ANTHONY RD
HICKS AVE
South Greenford
MILL CL
RIBCHESTER AVE
WYRESDALE CRES
B452
PENN CL
HEDGERLEY GDNS
BARNHAM RD
FARMDALE CRES
Coston Prim Sch
COSTONS LA
SILVERTREE LA
COWGATE RD
PENIFATHER LA
HOWCROFT LA
COSTONS AVE
PENIFATHER LA
Tenn Cts
Sp Arena
STOCKDOVE WAY
T Ct
GREENFORD GDNS
PEEL CT
OLDFIELD LA S
BROOKFIELD CT
Litten Nature Reserve
SHELLEY AVE
SHELLEY CL
MAGNA CT
1 CARROWAY LA
2 DEEPWOOD LA
Bwg Gn
CH
RAVENOR PARK RD
Ravenor Park
GREENFORD
CROYDE AVE
London Motorcycle Mus
Liby
Perivale Park
Sp Gd
Gurnell Swimming Pool
L Ctr
PEMBROKE RD
ANDOVER CL
B455
THE BROADWAY
P
STANHOPE PARK RD
GREENFORD RD
OAKFIELD GDNS
WEDMORE RD
BETHAM RD
COSTONS LA
LOCARNO RD
CLIFTON RD
GURNELL GR
RUISLIP RD EAST
ANGLESEY CT
Bwg Gn
LYRIC DR
WARREN DR
GARRICK RD
Schs
Recn Gd
ELLESMERE RD
OTTER RD
PO
Sch
Capital Ring
Pl Fld
Brentside High Sch
RIVERSIDE CL
RUISLIP RD E
HARP RD
KENNEDY PATH
BRANTS WLK
Brentside Prim Sch
OLD TWELVE CL
BROOKBANK AVE
ELMBANK WAY
CUCKOO DENE
GIFFORD GDNS
BEECHMOUNT AVE
BERESFORD AVE
MAYFIELD GDNS
KENNEDY RD
ELFWINE RD
LAURIE RD
HILLYARD RD
CUCKOO AVE
UPFIELD RD
GREATDOWN RD
COPLEY CL
Prim Sch
Pav
Sp Gd
Castle Bar Park
ROLLAND HO
BORDARS WLK
Andre Malraux Sch
BORDARS RD
ELLIS CT
TEMPLEMAN RD
FERMOY RD
MANSELL RD
PORTLAND CRES
Allot Gdns
WINDMILL LA
STANHOPE RD
BINGLEY RD
The Cardinal Wiseman RC Sch
Depot
BRIDGE AVE
HALE WLK
BENHAM RD
LALE CRES
WESTCOTT CRES
ALCOTT CL
WAKELING RD
DITCHLEY CT
CHELSEA GDNS
HURLEY RD
Cemy
Recn Gd
Allot Gdns
Mayfield Prim Sch
HIGH LA
CANTERBURY CL
BARBICAN RD
QUEEN'S AVE
PRINCE'S AVE
THE GROVE
DENNIS CT
KING'S AVE
COLNE CT 1
DEE CT 2
HUMBER CT 3
IRWELL CT 4
TEES CT 5
STOUR CT 6
HOBBAYNE RD
HANWAY RD
LYNNE CT
TWEED CT
HIGHLAND AVE
GREENFORD AVE
HALL DR
STUDLAND RD
THAMES CT
W7
Tenn Cts
SHARPE CL
RADNOR CT
SHROPSHIRE CT
CHEYNE PATH
STEPHENSON RD
LITTLEJOHN RD
SOMERSET CT
STAFFORD CT
HOMEFARM RD
BROWNING AVE
WARWICK CT
FRAMFIELD RD
DARWIN DR
HOWARD RD
OSBORNE RD
FLEMING RD
EDISON DR
MARCONI WAY
LONGRIDGE LA
FORMERS RISE
WHITECOTE RD
HALDANE RD
REDCROFT RD
HAWTHORNE MEWS
River Brent
Brent Valley
WESTVIEW
GROVE AVE
Hobbayne Prim Sch
WORCESTER CT
Allot Gdns
Drayton Green
ELMWOOD GDNS
DRYDEN AVE
Drayton Manor High Sch
DRAYTON BRIDGE RD
FARADAY RD
PANHARD PL
SHERINGHAM TWR
BAIRD AVE
1 PRESTWICK CT
2 DENHAM CT
CHEESEMAN CT
Allot Gdns
Sp Gd
MADGE HILL
CH
CHURCH RD
CUCKOO LA
COWPER RD
PARK RD
SHAKESPEARE RD
SPRING

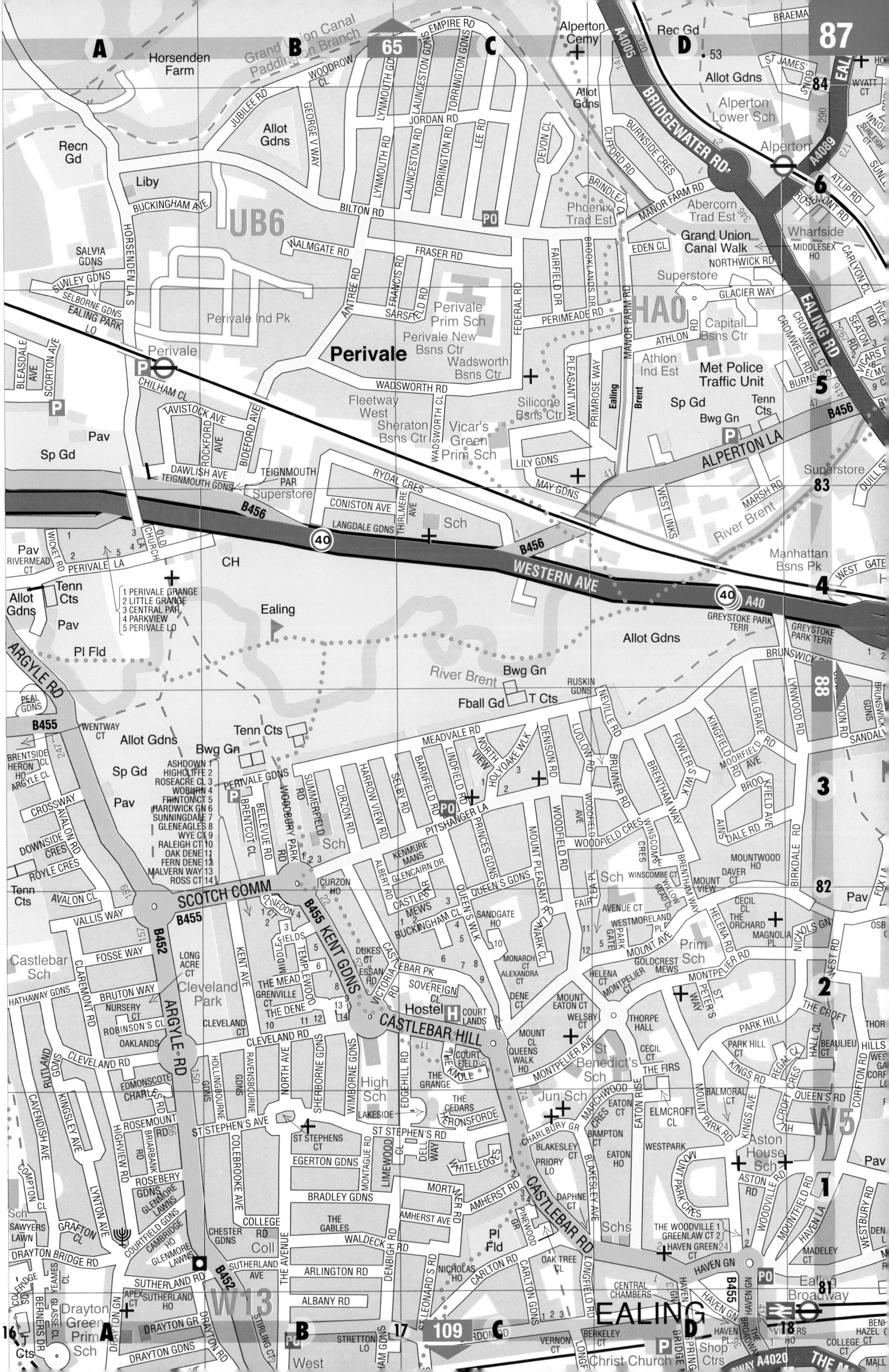
A
B
C
D
65
109
Horsenden Farm
Grand Union Canal Paddington Branch
Recn Gd
Allot Gdns
Liby
UB6
HA0
W5
W13
Perivale
Perivale Ind Pk
Perivale Prim Sch
Perivale New Bsns Ctr
Wadsworth Bsns Ctr
Fleetway West
Sheraton Bsns Ctr
Vicar's Green Prim Sch
Silicone Bsns Ctr
Phoenix Trad Est
Abercorn Trad Est
Grand Union Canal Walk
Alperton Cemy
Alperton Lower Sch
Alperton
Rec Gd
Wharfside
Superstore
Capital Bsns Ctr
Athlon Ind Est
Met Police Traffic Unit
Sp Gd
Tenn Cts
Bwg Gn
Manhattan Bsns Pk
River Brent
Ealing
Allot Gdns
Pl Fld
Fball Gd
T Cts
CH
Pav
Castlebar Sch
Cleveland Park
High Sch
Hostel
Jun Sch
St Benedict's Sch
Aston House Sch
Prim Sch
Coll
Schs
Drayton Green Prim Sch
Ealing Broadway
EALING
Christ Church
Shop Ctrs
West
HORSENDEN LA S
BUCKINGHAM AVE
JUBILEE RD
WOODROW CL
GEORGE V WAY
LYNMOUTH GD
LAUNCESTON GDNS
TORRINGTON GDNS
EMPIRE RD
JORDAN RD
LAUNCESTON RD
TORRINGTON RD
LEE RD
DEVON CL
BILTON RD
WALMGATE RD
FRASER RD
ANTREE RD
FRANCIS RD
SARSFIELD RD
FEDERAL RD
FAIRFIELD DR
BROOKLANDS DR
PERIMEADE RD
MANOR FARM RD
WADSWORTH RD
WADSWORTH CL
PLEASANT WAY
PRIMROSE WAY
LILY GDNS
MAY GDNS
CLIFFORD RD
BURNSIDE CRES
BRINDLEY CL
BRIDGEWATER RD
EDEN CL
ATHLON RD
GLACIER WAY
NORTHWICK RD
MIDDLESEX HO
CARLYON CL
EALING RD
ALPERTON LA
WEST LINKS
MARSH RD
ATLIP RD
ROSEMONT RD
ST JAMES' GDNS
WYATT CT
SALVIA GDNS
SUNLEY GDNS
SELBORNE GDNS
EALING PARK LO
BLEASDALE AVE
SCORTON AVE
CHILHAM CL
TAVISTOCK AVE
ROCKFORD AVE
BIDEFORD AVE
DAWLISH AVE
TEIGNMOUTH GDNS
TEIGNMOUTH PAR
RYDAL CRES
CONISTON AVE
THIRLMERE AVE
LANGDALE GDNS
WESTERN AVE
A40
B456
A4005
A4089
B455
B452
A4020
WICKET RD
RIVERMEAD CT
PERIVALE LA
OLD CHURCH LA
1 PERIVALE GRANGE
2 LITTLE GRANGE
3 CENTRAL PAR
4 PARKVIEW
5 PERIVALE LO
GREYSTOKE PARK TERR
BRUNSWICK
ARGYLE RD
PEAL GDNS
WENTWAY CT
BRENTSIDE
HERON HO
ARGYLE CL
CROSSWAY
AVALON RD
DOWNSIDE CRES
ROYLE CRES
AVALON CL
VALLIS WAY
ASHDOWN 1
HIGHCLIFFE 2
ROSEACRE CL 3
WOBURN 4
FRINTON CT 5
HARDWICK GN 6
SUNNINGDALE 7
GLENEAGLES 8
WYE CT 9
RALEIGH CT 10
OAK DENE 11
FERN DENE 12
MALVERN HO 13
ROSS CT 14
PERIVALE GDNS
BRENTCOT CL
BELLEVUE RD
WOODBURY PARK RD
SUMMERFIELD RD
CURZON RD
HARROW VIEW RD
SELBY RD
BARNFIELD RD
LINDFIELD RD
MEADVALE RD
NORTH VIEW
HOLYOAKE WLK
DENISON RD
LUDLOW RD
NEVILLE RD
RUSKIN GDNS
BRUNNER RD
BRENTHAM WAY
FOWLER'S WLK
KINGSFIELD RD
MOORFIELD RD
MULGRAVE RD
LYNWOOD RD
BROOKFIELD AVE
AINSDALE RD
BIRKDALE RD
MOUNTWOOD HO
DAVER CT
PITSHANGER LA
PRINCES GDNS
MOUNT PLEASANT RD
WOODFIELD RD
WOODFIELD AVE
WOODFIELD CRES
WINSCOMBE CRES
SCOTCH COMM
CURZON HO
KENT GDNS
KENT AVE
KENMURE MANS
GLENCAIRN DR
ALBERT RD
CASTLEBAR MEWS
QUEEN'S GDNS
QUEEN'S WLK
SANDGATE HO
BUCKINGHAM CL
CASTLEBAR PK
SOVEREIGN CL
COURT LANDS
CASTLEBAR HILL
CASTLEBAR RD
MONARCH CT
ALEXANDRA CT
DENE CT
MOUNT EATON CT
WELSBY CT
PARK CL
FAIRLEA PL
AVENUE CT
WESTMORELAND PL
PARK GATE
MOUNT AVE
GOLDCREST MEWS
HELENA CT
MONTPELIER CT
MONTPELIER RD
MONTPELIER AVE
ST PETER'S WAY
THORPE HALL
HELENA RD
CECIL CL
THE ORCHARD
MAGNOLIA PL
NICHOLS GN
MOUNT VIEW
PARK HILL
THE CROFT
PARK HILL CT
KINGS RD
REGAL CT
BALMORAL CT
QUEEN'S RD
BEAULIEU
HILLCREST RD
CORFTON RD
ASTON RD
WOODVILLE RD
MOUNTFIELD RD
HAVEN LA
MADELEY CT
WESTBURY RD
FOSSE WAY
LONG ACRE CT
CLAREMONT RD
HATHAWAY GDNS
BRUTON WAY
NURSERY CT
ROBINSON'S CL
OAKLANDS
CLEVELAND RD
CLEVELAND CT
EDMONSCOTE
CHARLES RD
ROSEMOUNT RD
BRIARBANK RD
HIGHVIEW RD
ROSEBERY GDNS
GLENMORE LAWNS
LYNTON AVE
KINGSLEY AVE
CAVENDISH AVE
RUTLAND GDNS
COMPTON CL
SAWYERS LAWN
GRAFTON CL
DRAYTON BRIDGE RD
COURTFIELD GDNS
CAMBRIDGE GDNS
SUTHERLAND RD
SUTHERLAND HO
SUTHERLAND AVE
APEX CT
DRAYTON GR
DRAYTON GDNS
DRAYTON GN
DRAYTON RD
HOLLINGBOURNE GDNS
RAVENSBOURNE GDNS
NORTH AVE
SHERBORNE GDNS
WIMBORNE GDNS
COLEBROOKE AVE
ST STEPHEN'S AVE
ST STEPHENS CT
ST STEPHEN'S RD
EGERTON GDNS
BRADLEY GDNS
THE GABLES
WALDECK RD
ARLINGTON RD
ALBANY RD
COLLEGE RD
CHESTER GDNS
THE AVENUE
STIRLING CT
STRETTON LO
LIMEWOOD CL
MONTAGUE RD
DENBIGH RD
EDGEHILL RD
LAKESIDE
DELL WAY
THE CEDARS
HERONSFORDE
WHITELEDGES
MORTIMER RD
AMHERST AVE
AMHERST RD
NICHOLAS HO
ST LEONARD'S RD
CARLTON RD
CARLTON GDNS
VERNON CT
THE GRANGE
THE KNOLL
COURTFIELD
THE MEAD
GRENVILLE CT
THE DENE
TEMPLEWOOD
MIDDLEFIELDS
CLEVELAND RD
DUKES CT
ESSAN HO
VICTORIA RD
MOUNT CL
QUEENS WALK HO
MARCHWOOD CRES
EATON CT
EATON RISE
BAMPTON CT
EATON HO
BLAKESLEY CT
BLAKESLEY AVE
CHARLBURY GR
PRIORY LO
DAPHNE CT
PINEWOOD GR
OAK TREE CL
LONGFIELD RD
THE FIRS
CECIL CT
ELMCROFT CL
WESTPARK
MOUNT PARK RD
MOUNT PARK CRES
KINGS AVE
THE WOODVILLE 1
GREENLAW CT 2
HAVEN GREEN CT
HAVEN GN
HAVEN PL
THE BROADWAY
CENTRAL CHAMBERS
BERKELEY CT
SPRING BRIDGE
COLLEGE CT
HAZEL CT
VILLIERS HO
BENHAM
THE MALL
ST LEONARD'S

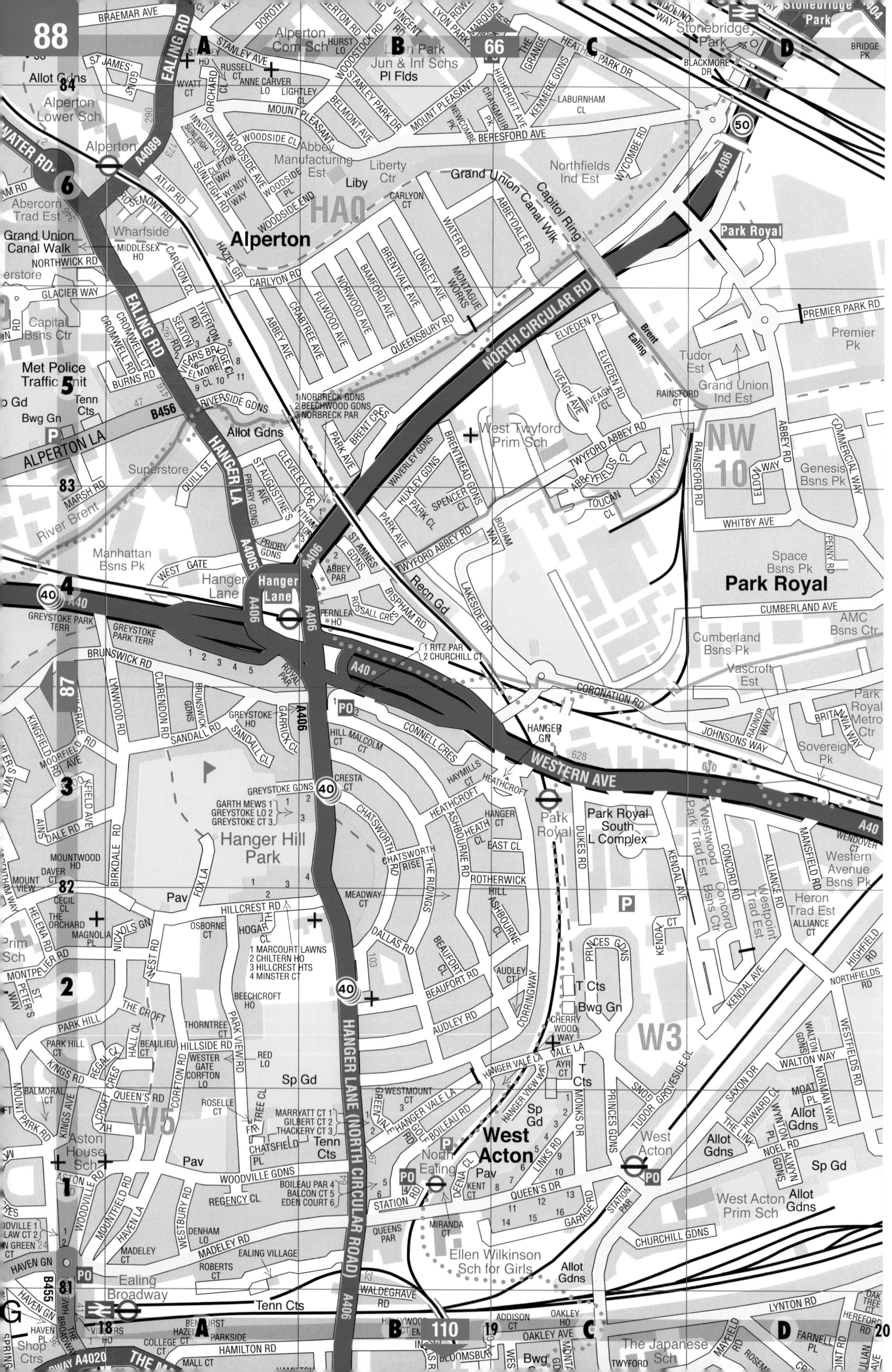
Alperton
Alperton Lower Sch
Alperton Com Sch
Lyon Park Jun & Inf Schs
Pl Flds
66
Stonebridge Park
Stonebridge Park
BRIDGE PK
BLACKMORE DR
HEATHER PARK DR
BRAEMAR AVE
EALING RD
STANLEY AVE
ST JAMES' GDNS
Allot Gdns
WYATT CT
RUSSELL CT
ANNE CARVER LO
LIGHTLEY CL
MOUNT PLEASANT
WOODSTOCK RD
STANLEY PARK DR
BELMONT AVE
HIGHCROFT AVE
KENMERE GDNS
LABURNHAM CL
BERESFORD AVE
WYCOMBE RD
Northfields Ind Est
Grand Union Canal Wlk
Capitol Ring
Abbey Manufacturing Est
Liberty Ctr
Liby
HA0
Alperton
Abercorn Trad Est
Grand Union Canal Walk
Wharfside
MIDDLESEX HO
NORTHWICK RD
GLACIER WAY
Capital Bsns Ctr
Met Police Traffic Unit
Tenn Cts
Bwg Gn
ALPERTON LA
B456
RIVERSIDE GDNS
Allot Gdns
Superstore
HANGER LA
A4005
A406
NORTH CIRCULAR RD
CARLYON RD
CARLYON CT
ABBEY AVE
CRABTREE AVE
FULWOOD AVE
NORWOOD AVE
BAMFORD AVE
BRENTVALE AVE
LONGLEY AVE
WATER RD
MONTAGUE WORKS
ABBEYDALE RD
QUEENSBURY RD
1 NORBRECK GDNS
2 BEECHWOOD GDNS
3 NORBRECK PAR
PARK AVE
BRENT CRES
ELVEDEN PL
ELVEDEN RD
IVEAGH AVE
IVEAGH CL
West Twyford Prim Sch
TWYFORD ABBEY RD
ABBEYFIELDS CL
MOYNE PL
TOUCAN CL
RAINSFORD CT
RAINSFORD RD
Grand Union Ind Est
Tudor Est
Park Royal
PREMIER PARK RD
Premier Pk
NW10
ABBEY RD
ELDON WAY
Genesis Bsns Pk
COMMERCIAL WAY
WHITBY AVE
Space Bsns Pk
PENNY RD
Park Royal
CUMBERLAND AVE
AMC Bsns Ctr
Cumberland Bsns Pk
Vascroft Est
Park Royal Metro Ctr
BRITANNIA WAY
RADNOR WAY
JOHNSONS WAY
Sovereign Pk
CORONATION RD
River Brent
Manhattan Bsns Pk
WEST GATE
Hanger Lane
Hanger Lane
A40
GREYSTOKE PARK TERR
BRUNSWICK RD
FERNLEA HO
ROSSALL CRES
BISPHAM RD
Recn Gd
LAKESIDE DR
BODIAM WAY
1 RITZ PAR
2 CHURCHILL CT
PO
CONNELL CRES
HANGER GN
WESTERN AVE
628
610
87
KINGSFIELD RD
MOORFIELD AVE
LYNWOOD RD
CLARENDON RD
BRUNSWICK GDNS
GREYSTOKE HO
SANDALL RD
SANDALL CL
GARRICK CL
HILL CT
MALCOLM CT
CRESTA CT
GREYSTOKE GDNS
GARTH MEWS 1
GREYSTOKE LO 2
GREYSTOKE CT 3
Hanger Hill Park
CHATSWORTH RD
CHATSWORTH RISE
THE RIDINGS
HEATHCROFT
ASHBOURNE RD
HEATH CL
EAST CL
HANGER CT
ROTHERWICK HILL
Park Royal
Park Royal South L Complex
DUKES RD
KENDAL AVE
CONCORD RD
Concord Bsns Ctr
Westwood Park Trad Est
Westpoint Trad Est
ALLIANCE RD
MANSFIELD RD
Western Avenue Bsns Pk
Heron Trad Est
ALLIANCE CT
BIRKDALE RD
MOUNTWOOD HO
DAVER CT
MOUNT VIEW
CECIL CL
THE ORCHARD
MAGNOLIA PL
HELENA RD
Pav
FOX LA
HILLCREST RD
OSBORNE CT
HOGARTH CL
1 MARCOURT LAWNS
2 CHILTERN HO
3 HILLCREST HTS
4 MINSTER CT
MEADWAY CT
DALLAS RD
BEAUFORT CL
BEAUFORT RD
AUDLEY CT
CORRINGWAY
PRINCES GDNS
T Cts
Bwg Gn
CHERRY WOOD WAY
KENDAL CT
W3
HIGHFIELD RD
NORTHFIELDS RD
WESTFIELDS RD
WALTON GDNS
WALTON WAY
NORMAN WAY
2
MONTPELIER RD
WEST RD
BEECHCROFT HO
THE CROFT
PARK HILL
PARK HILL CT
THORNTREE CT
HILLSIDE RD
PARK VIEW RD
BEAULIEU CT
AUDLEY RD
HANGER VALE LA
VALE LA
AYR CT
T Cts
KINGS RD
WESTER GATE
CORFTON LO
RED LO
Sp Gd
REGAL CRES
QUEEN'S RD
BALMORAL CT
MOUNT PARK RD
KINGS AVE
CORFTON RD
ROSELLE CT
TREE CL
W5
MARRYATT CT 1
GILBERT CT 2
THACKERY CT 3
WESTMOUNT CT
GREEN VALE
BOILEAU RD
HANGER VIEW WAY
Sp Gd
West Acton
MONKS DR
LINKS RD
TUDOR GDNS
GROVESIDE CL
SAXON DR
HOWARD CL
MOAT PL
Allot Gdns
THE LINK
Allot Gdns
NOEL RD
Aston House Sch
Pav
CHATSFIELD PL
Tenn Cts
HANGER LANE (NORTH CIRCULAR ROAD)
North Ealing
DEENA CL
KENT CT
West Acton
PO
Sp Gd
1
WOODVILLE RD
MOUNTFIELD RD
HAVEN LA
WESTBURY RD
WOODVILLE GDNS
REGENCY CL
BOILEAU PAR 4
BALCON CT 5
EDEN COURT 6
STATION RD
QUEEN'S DR
GARAGE RD
STATION PAR
West Acton Prim Sch
Allot Gdns
DENHAM LO
MADELEY RD
MADELEY CT
QUEENS PAR
MIRANDA CT
CHURCHILL GDNS
HAVEN GN
EALING VILLAGE
ROBERTS CT
Ellen Wilkinson Sch for Girls
Allot Gdns
B455
PO
Ealing Broadway
WALDEGRAVE RD
Tenn Cts
ADDISON CT
OAKLEY HO
LYNTON RD
OAK TREE CT
HEREFORD RD
18
HAVEN PL
PARKSIDE
110
19
OAKLEY AVE
MAYFIELD RD
FARNELL PL
20
Shop Ctrs
COLLEGE CT
HAMILTON RD
A4020
MALL CT
BLOOMSBURY
The Japanese Sch
TWYFORD
Bwg
A
B
C
D
6
5
4
3
2
1
84
83
82
81
40
50

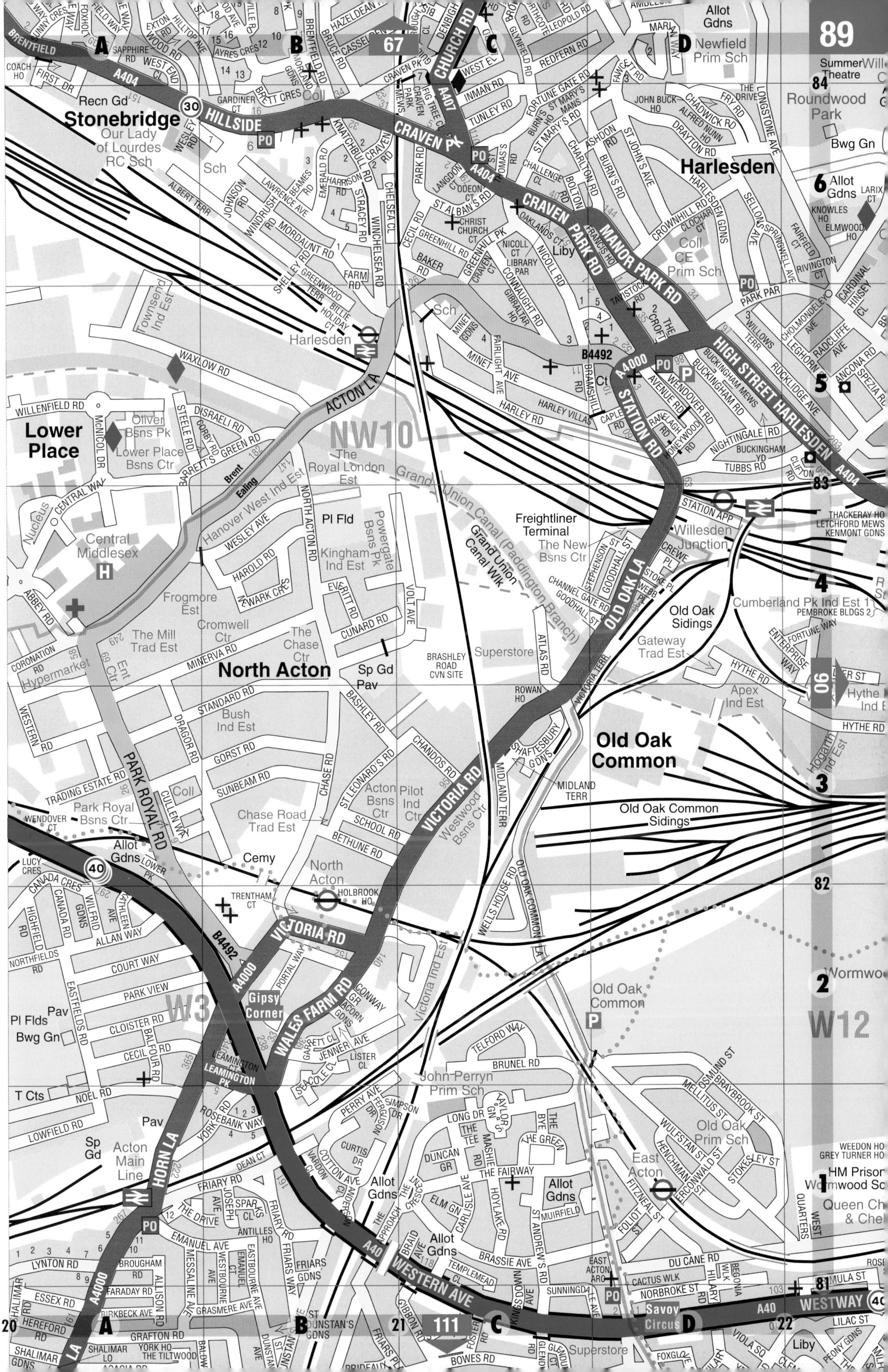
Stonebridge
Harlesden
Lower Place
North Acton
Old Oak Common
NW10
W3
W12
HILLSIDE
CRAVEN PK
CHURCH RD
CRAVEN PARK RD
MANOR PARK RD
HIGH STREET HARLESDEN
STATION RD
ACTON LA
OLD OAK LA
VICTORIA RD
PARK ROYAL RD
WALES FARM RD
WESTERN AVE
WESTWAY
HORN LA
A404
A4000
A40
A407
B4492
Grand Union Canal (Paddington Branch)
Grand Union Canal Wlk
Freightliner Terminal
Old Oak Sidings
Old Oak Common Sidings
Willesden Junction
Central Middlesex
Gipsy Corner
Savoy Circus
East Acton
Acton Main Line
North Acton
Harlesden
Roundwood Park
John Perryn Prim Sch
Old Oak Prim Sch
Newfield Prim Sch
The Royal London Est
Hanover West Ind Est
Park Royal Bsns Ctr
Cumberland Pk Ind Est
Apex Ind Est
Gateway Trad Est
Chase Road Trad Est
Acton Bsns Ctr
Westwood Bsns Ctr
Brashley Road Cvn Site
HM Prison Wormwood Scrubs
Superstore
Hypermarket

68
112
69
24
22
23
A
B
C
D
84
83
82
81
6
5
4
3
2
1
Harlesden
Willesden Green
Brondesbury Park
Kensal Rise
Kensal Green
College Park
North Kensington
White City
NW6
W10
W12
Roundwood Park
Capital City Acad
Willesden Sp Ctr
Recn Gd
Cardinal Hinsley RC High Sch (Boys)
The Willesden Com
Allot Gdns
Summer Theatre
Bwg Gn
Tenn Cts
Queens Park Com Sch
Malorees Jun & Inf Schs
HIGH STREET HARLESDEN
HARROW RD
MORTIMER RD
HARVIST RD
KILBURN LA
CHAMBERLAYNE RD
COLLEGE RD
DONNINGTON RD
ALEXANDER AVE
DOBREE AVE
DOYLE GDNS
HAYCROFT GDNS
ALL SOULS' AVE
HARDINGE RD
LEIGHTON GDNS
LIDDELL GDNS
WHITMORE GDNS
LEIGH GDNS
CLIFFORD GDNS
HERBERT GDNS
BUCHANAN GDNS
BATHURST GDNS
PALERMO RD
PURVES RD
ASHBURNHAM RD
BURROWS RD
Rutland Studios
Cumberland Pk Ind Est
Star Works
Hythe Road Ind Est
HYTHE RD
Hogarth Ind Est
Cemy
Crem
Kensal Green Cemy (All Souls)
Grand Union Canal Wlk
Grand Union Canal (Paddington Branch)
MITRE BRIDGE
Gas Works
Superstore
Westgate Bsns Ctr
CANAL WAY
HUMBER DR
LADBROKE GR
SCRUBS LA
Mitre Bridge Ind Pk
MITRE WAY
Little Wormwood Scrubs (Recn Gd)
Wormwood Scrubs Park
The Lindford Christie Stadium
Fball Gd
Burlington Danes Sch
Pl Fld
Wood Lane High Sch
HM Prison Wormwood Scrubs
Hammersmith
Queen Charlottes & Chelsea
DU CANE RD
WOOD LA
ST QUINTIN AVE
Kensington Meml Pk
Princess Louise
St Charles'
Old Oak Prim Sch
WESTWAY
WESTWAY (ELEVATED ROAD)
A40
A404
A219
A3220
B412
B450
B451
B413
Latimer Road
Canberra Prim Sch
Heart Raido
Liby
Sch
Prim Sch
PO
Brent
Hammersmith & Fulham
Kensington & Chelsea
City of Westminster
30
40

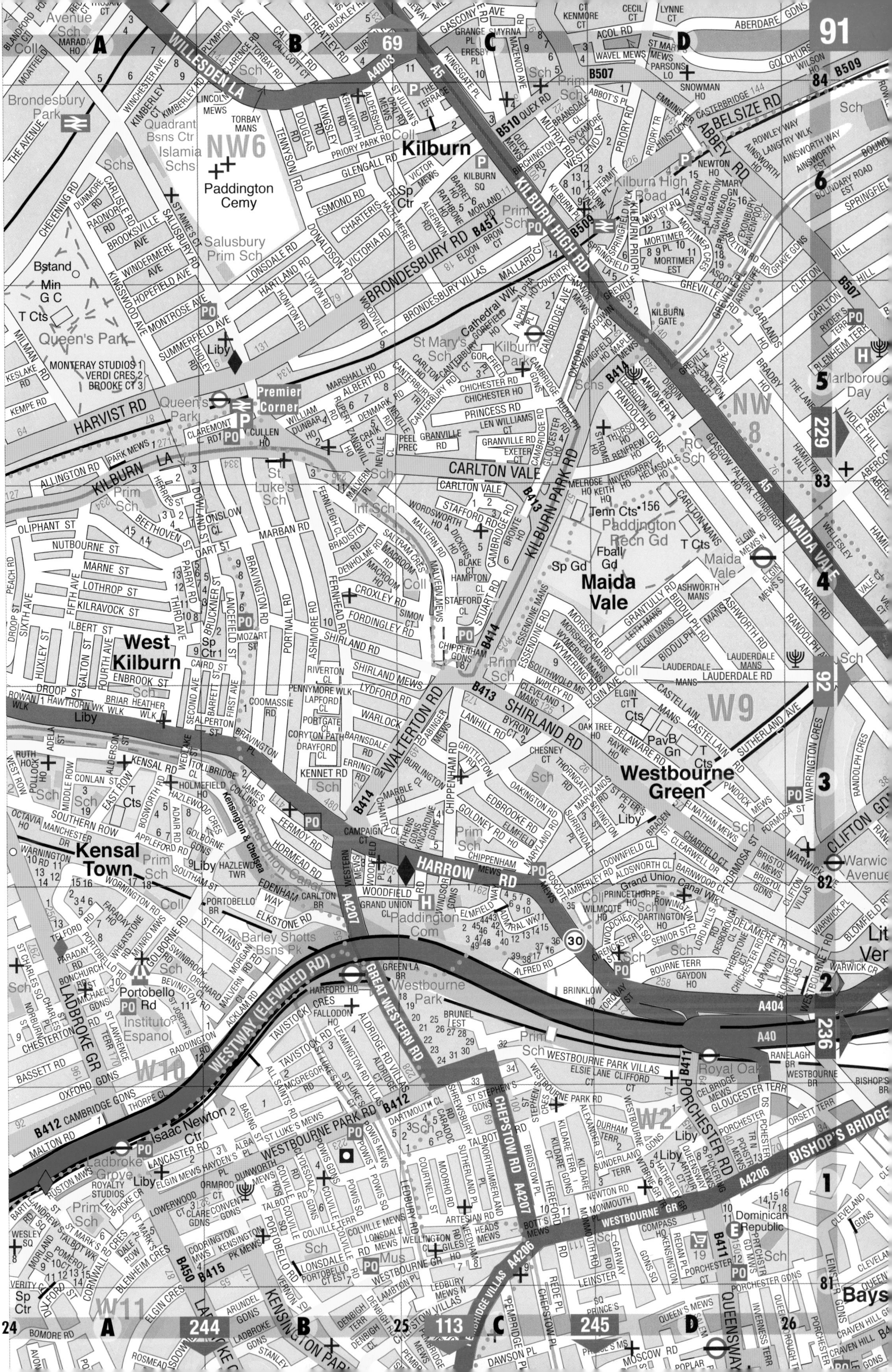

91
A
B
C
D
69
1
2
3
4
5
6
229
92
236
83
82
81
84
24
25
26
244
113
245
NW6
NW8
W9
W10
W11
W2
Kilburn
Maida Vale
West Kilburn
Kensal Town
Westbourne Green
Paddington Cemy
Queen's Park
Brondesbury Park
Westbourne Park
Royal Oak
Ladbroke Grove
Portobello Rd
Kilburn High Road
Kilburn Park
Warwick Avenue
Dominican Republic
Premier Corner
Quadrant Bsns Ctr
Islamia Schs
Salusbury Prim Sch
Paddington Recn Gd
Paddington Com
Barley Shotts Bsns Pk
Instituto Espanol
Isaac Newton Ctr
Grand Union Canal
Kensington & Chelsea
WILLESDEN LA
KILBURN HIGH RD
BRONDESBURY RD
BRONDESBURY VILLAS
HARVIST RD
KILBURN LA
CARLTON VALE
KILBURN PARK RD
SHIRLAND RD
WALTERTON RD
HARROW RD
MAIDA VALE
BELSIZE RD
ABBEY RD
WESTWAY (ELEVATED RD)
GREAT WESTERN RD
WESTBOURNE PARK RD
WESTBOURNE PARK VILLAS
WESTBOURNE GR
CHEPSTOW RD
PORCHESTER RD
BISHOP'S BRIDGE RD
LADBROKE GR
CLIFTON GDNS
SUTHERLAND AVE
ELGIN AVE
A5
A40
A404
A4003
A4206
A4207
B412
B413
B414
B415
B450
B451
B507
B509
B510
B411

Hampstead
A
B
C
D
70
230
NW6
NW3
NW8
NW1
W9
W2
Primrose Hill
Primrose Hill Tunnels
St Paul's
Barrow Hill
BELSIZE RD
BOUNDARY RD
SPRINGFIELD RD
LOUDOUN ROAD
MARLBOROUGH HILL
AVENUE RD
PRINCE ALBERT RD
FINCHLEY RD
WELLINGTON RD
ABBEY RD
MAIDA VALE
GROVE END RD
ST JOHN'S WOOD ROAD
St John's Barracks
St John's Wood
St John & Elizabeth
The Wellington
Marlborough Day
Lord's (MCC & Middlesex Cty Crkt Gd)
Crkt Mus
Grand Union Canal
(Regent's Canal)
OUTER CIRCLE
Winfield House
London Central Mosque
Boating Lake
The Holme
London Business Sch
PARK RD
LISSON GR
Lisson Grove
Antq Mkt
Marylebone
Govt Offices
Charter Nightingale
Western Eye
MARYLEBONE RD
Baker Street
BAKER ST
GLOUCESTER PL
Warwick Avenue
Little Venice
CLIFTON GDNS
HARROW RD
WESTWAY (ELEVATED) HARROW RD (UNDER)
A40 MARYLEBONE FLYOVER
Marylebone Flyover
PADDINGTON
Paddington Basin
St Mary's
Paddington
Royal Oak
BISHOP'S BRIDGE RD
EASTBOURNE TERR
PRAED ST
EDGWARE RD
SUSSEX GDNS
Edgware Road
Dominican Republic
Bayswater
QUEENSWAY
Art Gall
SEYMOUR ST
Marble Arch
Speakers' Corner
NORTH CARRIAGE DR
114
237
26
27
28
229
91
236

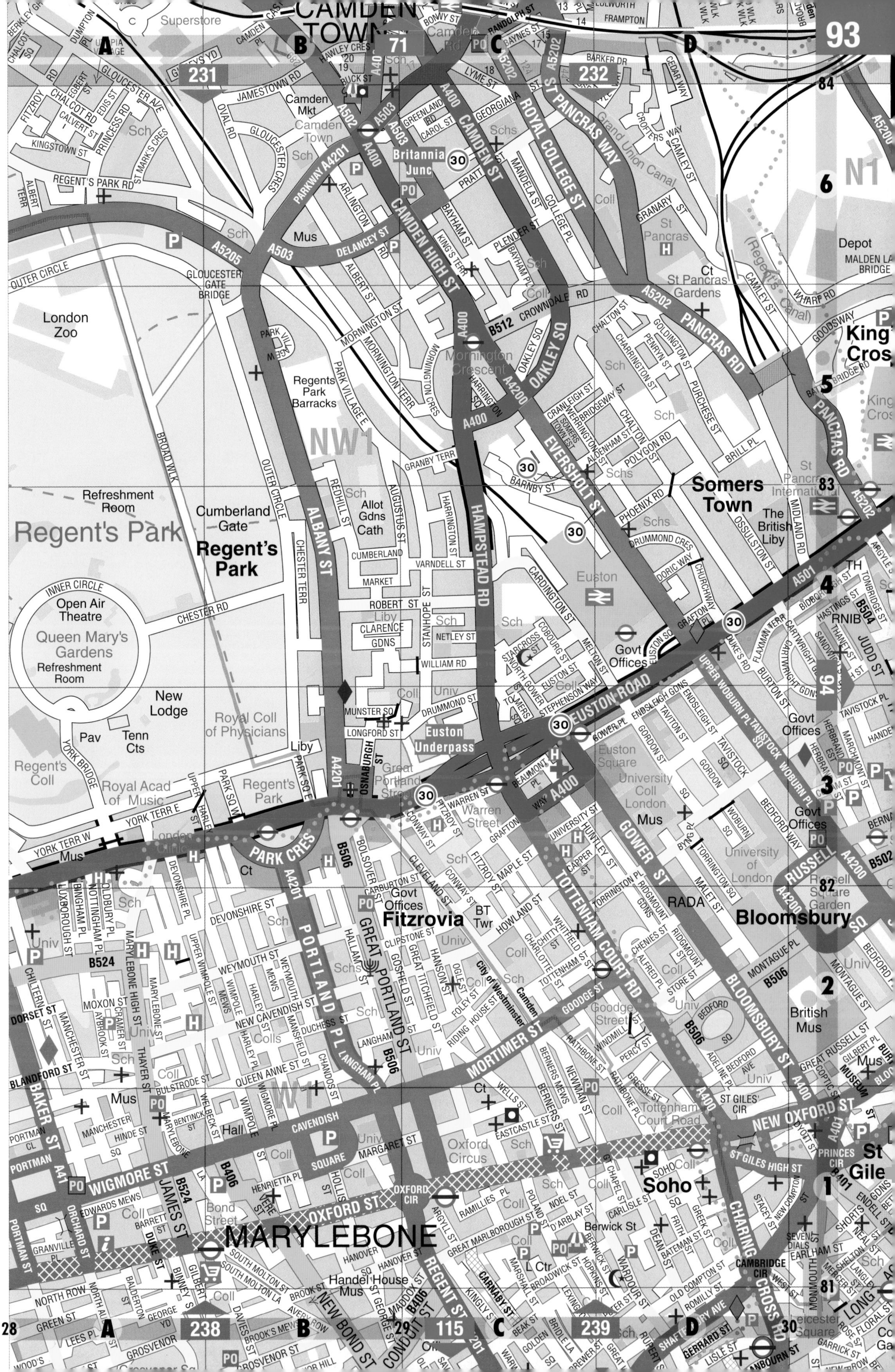
CAMDEN TOWN
Superstore
A
B
C
D
71
231
232
Camden Rd
Camden Mkt
Camden Town
JAMESTOWN RD
GLOUCESTER AVE
GLOUCESTER CRES
OVAL RD
PARKWAY A4201
ARLINGTON
CAMDEN HIGH ST
CAMDEN ST
ROYAL COLLEGE ST
ST PANCRAS WAY
Grand Union Canal
Britannia Junc
PRATT
REGENT'S PARK RD
KINGSTOWN ST
PRINCESS RD
FITZROY
CHALCOT RD
ALBERT TERR
OUTER CIRCLE
GLOUCESTER GATE BRIDGE
A5205
A503
DELANCEY ST
Mus
BAYHAM ST
PLENDER ST
MANDELA ST
COLLEGE PL
GRANARY ST
St Pancras
Ct
St Pancras Gardens
Depot
MALDEN LA BRIDGE
WHARF RD
CAMLEY ST
Regent's Canal
GOODSWAY
King's Cross
PANCRAS RD
A5202
CROWNDALE RD
B512
OAKLEY SQ
MORNINGTON ST
MORNINGTON TERR
Mornington Crescent
London Zoo
Regents Park Barracks
PARK VILLAGE E
NW1
N1
EVERSHOLT ST
CHALTON ST
GOLDINGTON ST
PURCHESE ST
POLYGON RD
PHOENIX RD
BRILL PL
Somers Town
The British Liby
St Pancras International
OSSULSTON ST
MIDLAND RD
HAMPSTEAD RD
GRANBY TERR
BARNBY ST
DRUMMOND CRES
CHURCHWAY
DORIC WAY
Euston
CARDINGTON ST
Refreshment Room
Cumberland Gate
Regent's Park
BROAD WLK
ALBANY ST
CHESTER TERR
REDHILL ST
AUGUSTUS ST
Allot Gdns
Cath
HARRINGTON ST
CUMBERLAND
MARKET
VARNDELL ST
ROBERT ST
CLARENCE GDNS
STANHOPE ST
NETLEY ST
WILLIAM RD
INNER CIRCLE
Open Air Theatre
Queen Mary's Gardens
CHESTER RD
New Lodge
Royal Coll of Physicians
Pav
Tenn Cts
YORK BRIDGE
Regent's Coll
Royal Acad of Music
Regent's Park
PARK SQ E
Liby
MUNSTER SQ
LONGFORD ST
Great Portland Street
Euston Underpass
DRUMMOND ST
Govt Offices
EUSTON ROAD
GOWER ST
Euston Square
University Coll London
Mus
UPPER WOBURN PL
ENDSLEIGH GDNS
TAVISTOCK SQ
GORDON SQ
BEDFORD WAY
WOBURN PL
TAVISTOCK PL
JUDD ST
RNIB
HASTINGS ST
Govt Offices
94
University of London
RUSSELL SQ
A4200
82
83
84
6
5
4
3
2
1
81
YORK TERR E
YORK TERR W
PARK CRES
WARREN ST
Warren Street
CONWAY ST
FITZROY ST
GRAFTON WAY
A400
TOTTENHAM COURT RD
MAPLE ST
HOWLAND ST
CLEVELAND ST
BOLSOVER ST
B506
Govt Offices
Fitzrovia
BT Twr
GREAT PORTLAND ST
PORTLAND PL
A4201
DEVONSHIRE ST
WEYMOUTH ST
NEW CAVENDISH ST
DUCHESS ST
LANGHAM
RADA
Bloomsbury
MONTAGUE PL
British Mus
BLOOMSBURY ST
BEDFORD SQ
Goodge Street
GOODGE ST
MORTIMER ST
RATHBONE PL
CHARLOTTE ST
City of Westminster
Camden
MARYLEBONE HIGH ST
B524
CHILTERN ST
DORSET ST
MANCHESTER ST
BLANDFORD ST
BAKER ST
THAYER ST
WELBECK ST
WIMPOLE ST
QUEEN ANNE ST
HARLEY ST
W1
CAVENDISH SQUARE
MARGARET ST
Oxford Circus
OXFORD CIR
OXFORD ST
WIGMORE ST
JAMES ST
Bond Street
MARYLEBONE
PORTMAN ST
ORCHARD ST
DUKE ST
Handel House Mus
NEW BOND ST
REGENT ST
CONDUIT ST
CARNABY ST
GREAT MARLBOROUGH ST
POLAND ST
NOEL ST
Berwick St
WARDOUR ST
Soho
SOHO SQ
FRITH ST
GREEK ST
DEAN ST
CHARING CROSS RD
NEW OXFORD ST
ST GILES' CIR
Tottenham Court Road
ST GILES HIGH ST
St Giles
SEVEN DIALS
CAMBRIDGE CIR
SHAFTESBURY AVE
GERRARD ST
Leicester Square
238
115
239
28
29
30

ISLINGTON
Pentonville
FINSBURY
King's Cross
St Pancras
Somers Town
Bloomsbury
Clerkenwell
Gray's Inn
Holborn
St Giles
Camden Pas
Angel
N1
WC1
WC2
EC1
YORK WAY
CALEDONIAN RD
PENTONVILLE RD
KING'S CROSS RD
GRAY'S INN RD
ROSEBERY AVE
FARRINGDON RD
CLERKENWELL RD
GOSWELL RD
ST JOHN ST
UPPER ST
LIVERPOOL RD
ESSEX RD
COPENHAGEN ST
BARNSBURY RD
CHAPEL MKT
WHITE LION ST
GUILFORD ST
THEOBALD'S RD
HIGH HOLBORN
HOLBORN
HOLBORN VIADUCT
NEW OXFORD ST
KINGSWAY
CHANCERY LA
SOUTHAMPTON ROW
RUSSELL SQ
BLOOMSBURY ST
BLOOMSBURY WAY
CHARING CROSS RD
LONG ACRE
ALDWYCH
FLEET ST
NEW BRIDGE ST
FARRINGDON ST
SHOE LA
NEW FETTER LA
CHARTERHOUSE ST
NEWGATE
LUDGATE HILL
ARGYLE ST
JUDD ST
HUNTER ST
EUSTON RD
PANCRAS RD
MIDLAND RD
OSSULSTON ST
Depot
MALDEN LANE BRIDGE
Regent's Canal
Basin
Mus
Barnard Park
Chapel Mkt
King's Cross St Pancras International
The British Liby
Russell Square
Russell Square Garden
British Mus
Coram's Fields
Eastman Dental
Family Records Ctr
City Univ
Leather Lane
Chancery Lane
Smithfield Mkt
St Barts
Lincoln's Inn Fields
Lincoln's Inn
Royal Courts of Justice
Covent Garden
Inner Temple Garden
Farringdon
City Thameslink
Bsns Design Ctr
Govt Offices
Somerset
233
234
72
240
116
241

SHOREDITCH
Hoxton
Haggerston
St Luke's
Barbican
Broadgate
Spitalfields
Whitechapel
Brick Lane
Shoreditch Park
Haggerston Park
Grand Union Canal
(Regent's Canal)
City Road Basin
Old Street
Liverpool Street
Moorgate
Aldgate
Aldgate East
Tower Hill
Tower Gateway
Fenchurch Street
Cannon Street
Bank
Monument
Mansion House
St Paul's
St Paul's Cath
Guildhall
Barbican Arts & Con Ctr
Tower 42
Swiss Re Bldg
Lloyds Bldg
Petticoat Lane
Old Spitalfields
Columbia Rd
Essex Road
NEW NORTH RD
KINGSLAND RD
QUEENSBRIDGE RD
HACKNEY RD
CITY RD
EAST RD
OLD ST
PITFIELD ST
SHOREDITCH HIGH ST
GREAT EASTERN ST
BETHNAL GREEN RD
COMMERCIAL ST
BISHOPSGATE
LONDON WALL
ALDERSGATE ST
WHITECHAPEL HIGH ST
MINORIES
LEMAN ST
UPPER THAMES ST
BUNHILL ROW
CHISWELL ST
COLUMBIA RD
HOUNDSDITCH
GRACECHURCH ST
EC2
EC3
EC4
E1
E2
E8
A
B
C
D
1
2
3
4
5
6
32
33
34
73
84
117
235
242
243

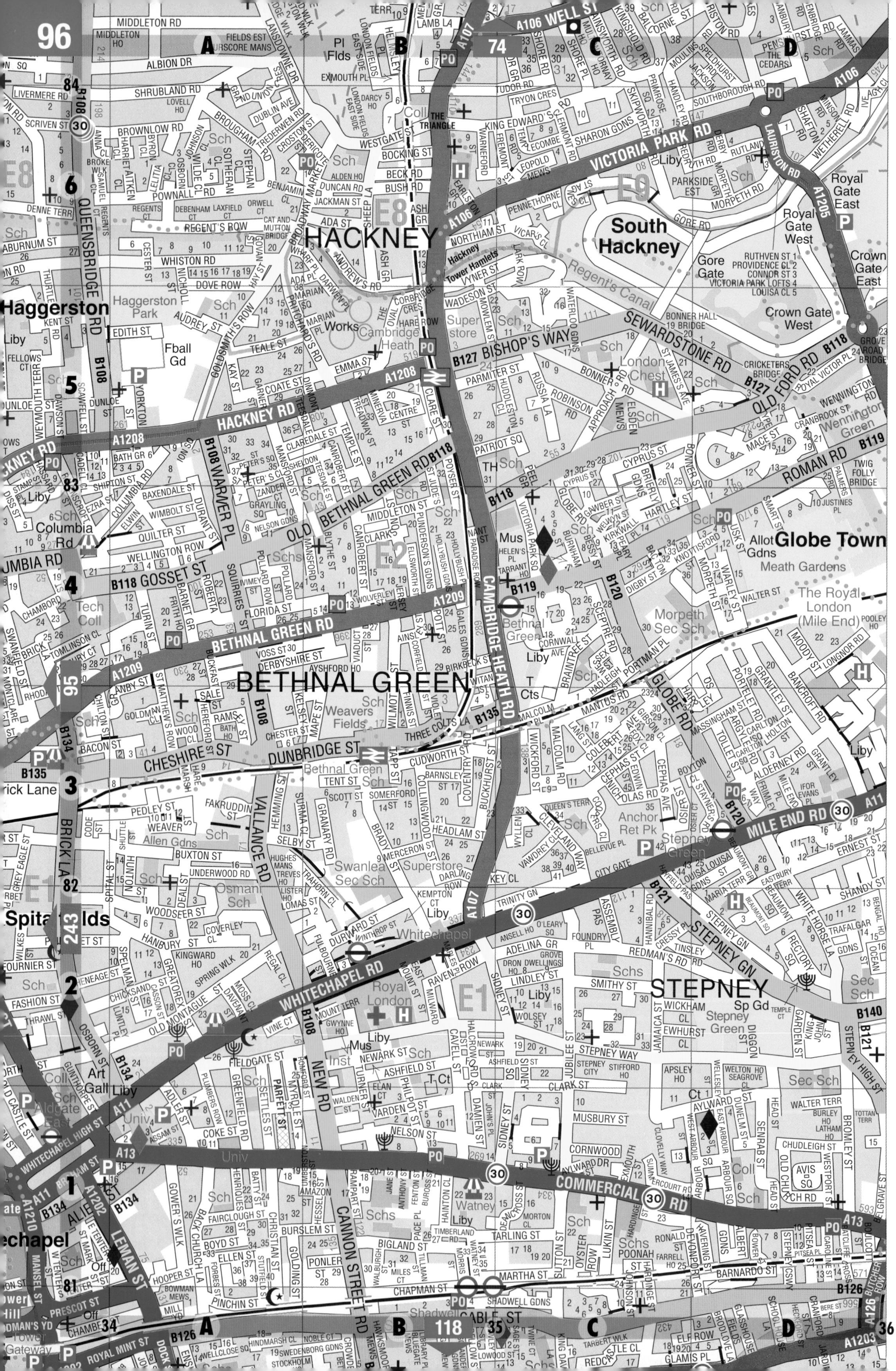
HACKNEY
South Hackney
Haggerston
BETHNAL GREEN
Globe Town
STEPNEY
Spitalfields
E8
E9
E2
E1
HACKNEY RD
VICTORIA PARK RD
BETHNAL GREEN RD
OLD BETHNAL GREEN RD
CAMBRIDGE HEATH RD
MILE END RD
WHITECHAPEL RD
COMMERCIAL RD
ROMAN RD
OLD FORD RD
SEWARDSTONE RD
BISHOP'S WAY
GOSSET ST
CHESHIRE ST
DUNBRIDGE ST
VALLANCE RD
QUEENSBRIDGE RD
BRICK LA
CANNON STREET RD
NEW RD
GLOBE RD
LEMAN ST
CABLE ST
WARNER PL
Regent's Canal
Haggerston Park
Weavers Fields
Meath Gardens
Allen Gdns
Royal Gate East
Royal Gate West
Gore Gate
Crown Gate East
Crown Gate West
Royal London
The Royal London (Mile End)
Stepney Green
Bethnal Green
Cambridge Heath
Whitechapel
Shadwell
Aldgate East
Columbia Rd
A
B
C
D
1
2
3
4
5
6
74
118
95
243
84
83
82
81
34
35
36

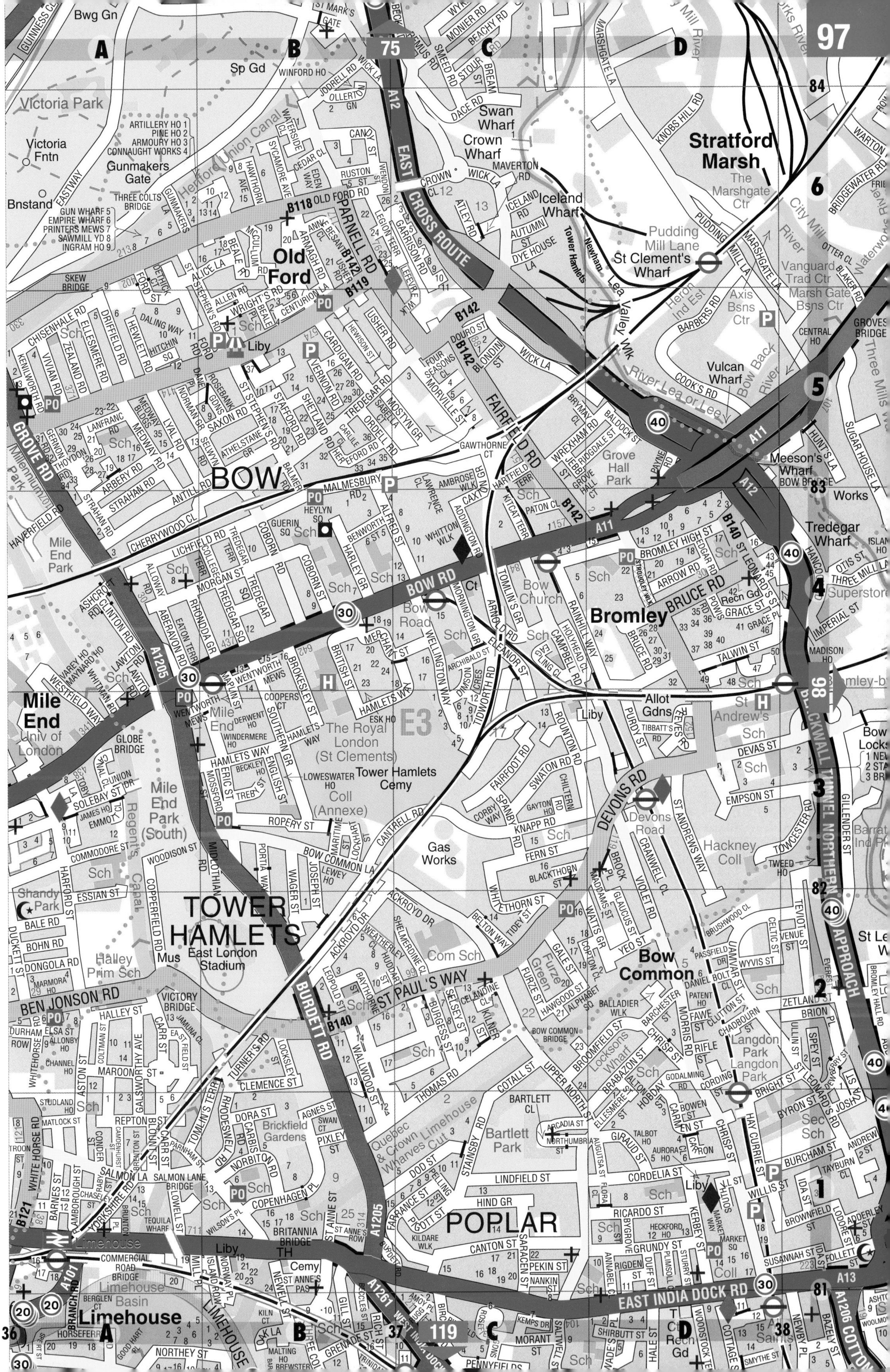

A
B
C
D
75
Victoria Park
Victoria Fntn
Gunmakers Gate
Bnstand
Hertford Union Canal
Old Ford
Swan Wharf
Crown Wharf
Iceland Wharf
Stratford Marsh
The Marshgate Ctr
Pudding Mill Lane
St Clement's Wharf
Heron Ind Est
Axis Bsns Ctr
Vanguard Trad Ctr
Marsh Gate Bsns Ctr
Vulcan Wharf
River Lea or Lee
Bow Back River
City Mill River
EAST CROSS ROUTE
A12
B118
B119
B142
B140
A11
A1205
BOW
BOW RD
Grove Hall Park
Meeson's Wharf
Tredegar Wharf
Superstore
Works
Bromley
Bow Church
Bow Road
Mile End
Mile End Park
Mile End Park (South)
Univ of London
GROVE RD
Millennium Park
E3
The Royal London (St Clements)
Tower Hamlets Cemy
Coll (Annexe)
Gas Works
Devons Road
Hackney Coll
St Andrew's
Allot Gdns
Bow Locks
BLACKWALL TUNNEL NORTHERN APPROACH
TOWER HAMLETS
East London Stadium
Mus
Halley Prim Sch
Shandy Park
Regent's Canal
BEN JONSON RD
ST PAUL'S WAY
BURDETT RD
Com Sch
Furze Green
Bow Common
Langdon Park
Brickfield Gardens
Limehouse Cut
Quebec & Crown Wharves
Bartlett Park
POPLAR
Limehouse
Limehouse Basin
COMMERCIAL ROAD
EAST INDIA DOCK RD
A13
A101
A1261
A1206
WEST INDIA DOCK
All Saints
Rech Gd
36
37
119
38
84
83
82
81
98
6
5
4
3
2
1

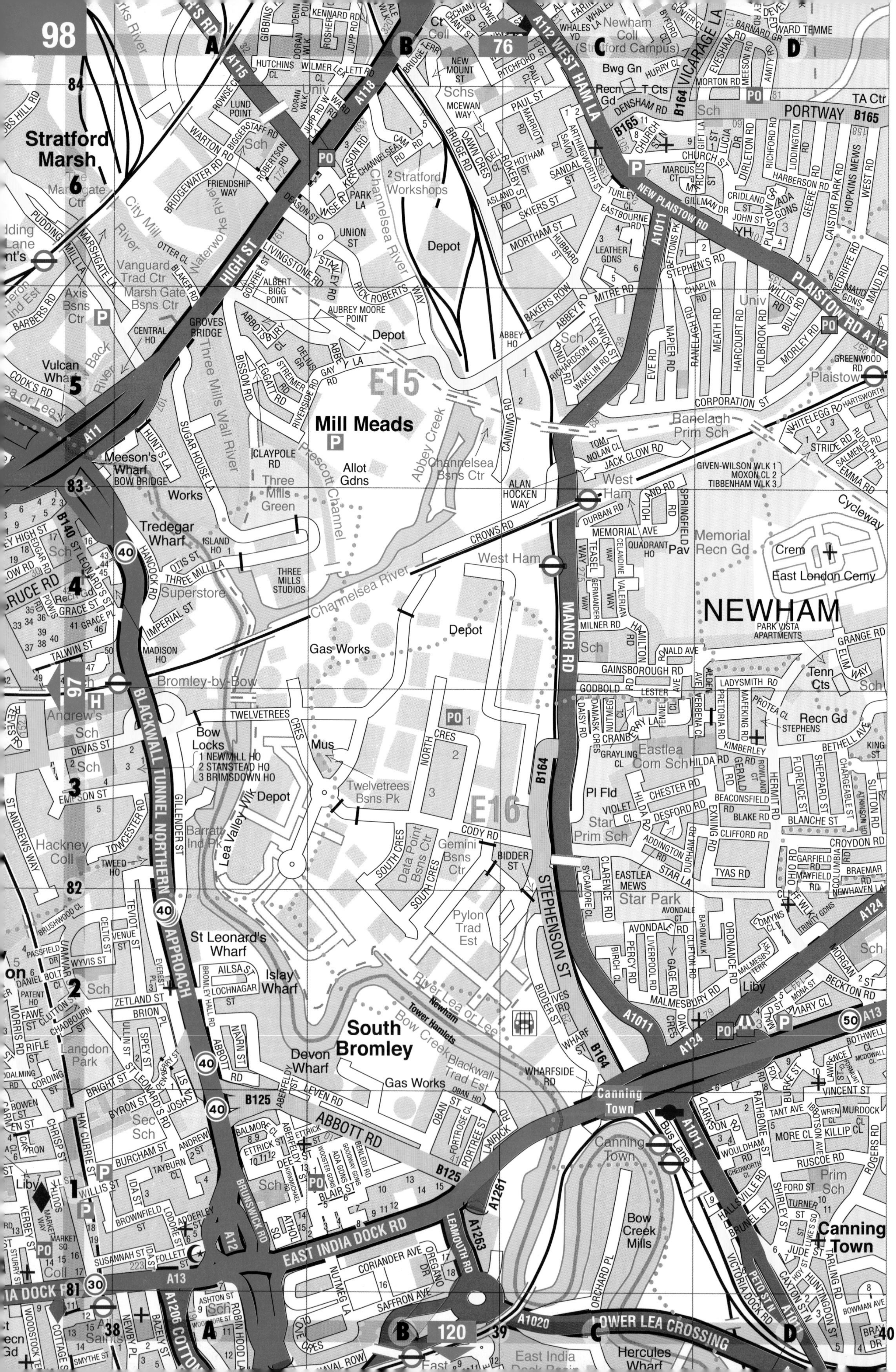
A
B
C
D
76
Stratford Marsh
Marshgate Ctr
City Mill
Vanguard Trad Ctr
Marsh Gate Bsns Ctr
Axis Bsns Ctr
Vulcan Wharf
HIGH ST
A11
A12
A13
A112
A118
A115
WEST HAM LA
Newham Coll (Stratford Campus)
Stratford Workshops
Channelsea River
Depot
Union St
Rick Roberts Way
Abbey Creek
Mill Meads
E15
E16
Prescott Channel
Three Mills Green
Three Mills Studios
Three Mills Wall River
Allot Gdns
Channelsea Bsns Ctr
Tredegar Wharf
Meeson's Wharf
Bow Bridge
Superstore
Gas Works
Bromley-by-Bow
Bow Locks
Twelvetrees Bsns Pk
Lea Valley Wlk
Barratt Ind Pk
Data Point Bsns Ctr
Gemini Bsns Ctr
Pylon Trad Est
St Leonard's Wharf
Islay Wharf
Devon Wharf
South Bromley
Blackwall Trad Est
River Lea or Lee
Bow Creek
Tower Hamlets
Newham
BLACKWALL TUNNEL NORTHERN APPROACH
EAST INDIA DOCK RD
ABBOTT RD
Langdon Park
Hackney Coll
West Ham
MANOR RD
STEPHENSON ST
B164
Memorial Recn Gd
Crem
East London Cemy
NEWHAM
Plaistow
PLAISTOW RD
NEW PLAISTOW RD
PORTWAY
VICARAGE LA
Corporation St
Eastlea Com Sch
Star Prim Sch
Star Park
Recn Gd
Tenn Cts
Canning Town
Bow Creek Mills
LOWER LEA CROSSING
A1011
A124
A1020
A1261
A1263
120
East India
Hercules Wharf
Cycleway
97
38
39
40

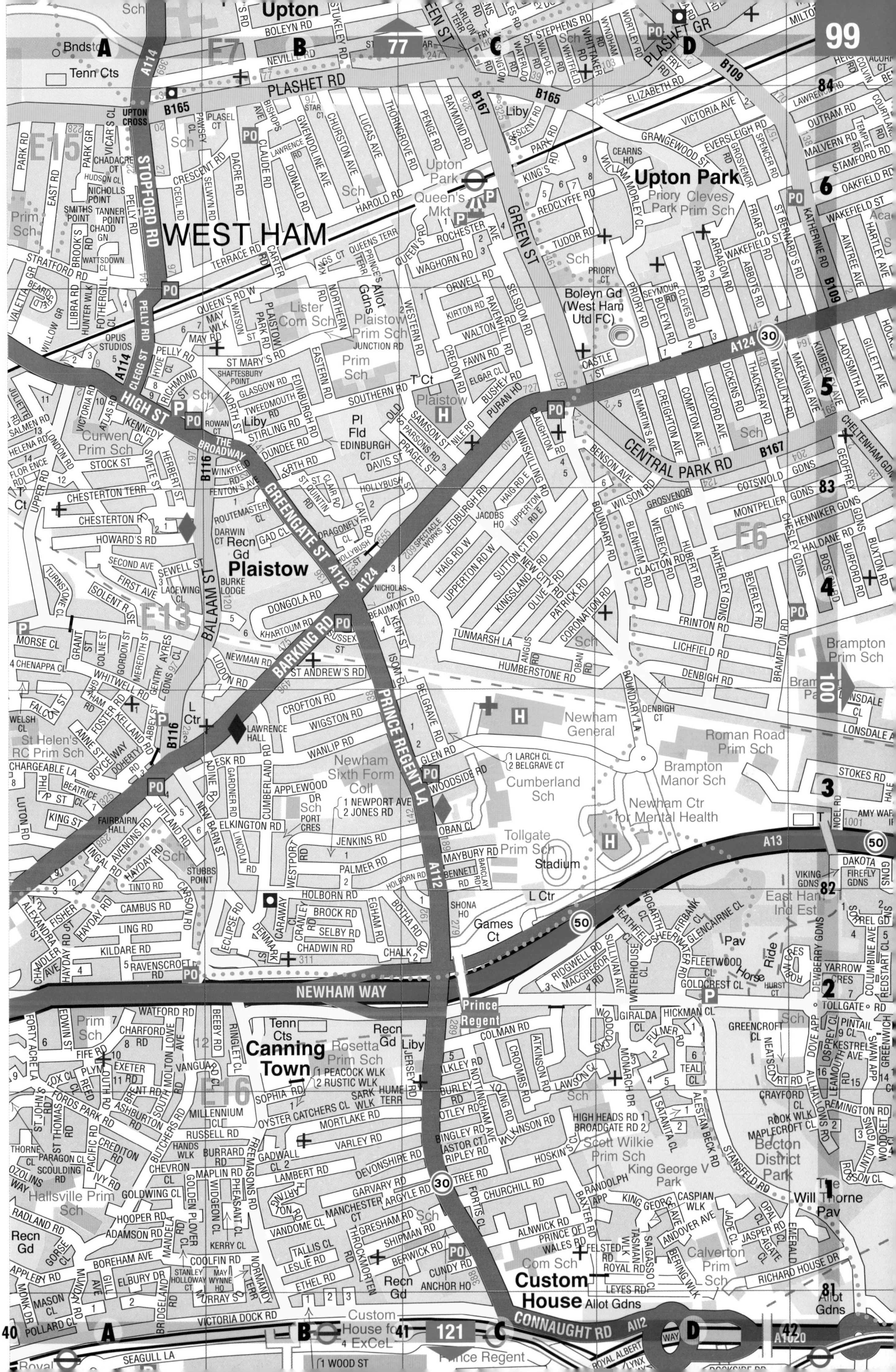
Upton
WEST HAM
Upton Park
Plaistow
Canning Town
Custom House
E15
E13
E6
E16
E7
STOPFORD RD
HIGH ST
THE BROADWAY
GREENGATE ST
BARKING RD
PRINCE REGENT LA
GREEN ST
PLASHET RD
CENTRAL PARK RD
NEWHAM WAY
CONNAUGHT RD
BALAAM ST
Newham General
Cumberland Sch
Boleyn Gd (West Ham Utd FC)
Queen's Mkt
Newham Sixth Form Coll
Tollgate Prim Sch
Stadium
Newham Ctr for Mental Health
Beckton District Park
King George V Park
Custom House for ExCeL
Prince Regent
77
100
121
40
41
42

A
B
C
D
78
E6
MILTON AV
THE FIRS
HEIGHAM RD
ACORN CT
BENDISH RD
COLVIN RD
CLEMENTS RD
CAULFIELD RD
THE WILLOWS
HART CT
LONDON RD
A12
Superstore
PI Fld
River Roding
ABBEY RD
A124
IG11
B109
84
VICTORIA AVE
LAWRENCE RD
OUTRAM RD
COURTLAND RD
HOLME RD
RON LEIGHTON WAY
A117
EVERSLEIGH RD
GROSVENOR RD
SPENCER RD
MALVERN RD
TEMPLE RD
STAMFORD RD
OAKFIELD RD
KEPPEL RD
SKEFFINGTON RD
CALEDON RD
HOLLAND RD
ALTMORE AVE
KEMPTON RD
HALL RD
NORFOLK RD
BEDFORD RD
CALVERTON RD
ST OLAVE'S RD
Barking Flyover
Recn Gd
NORTH CIRCULAR RD
A406
HIGHBRIDGE RD
WEST BANK
TOWN QUAY
Town Quay Wharf
HIGHBRIDGE RD
Fresh Wharf Est
FRESH WHARF RD
Barking & Dagenham
Newham
Park
Cleves Prim Sch
6
FRIAR'S RD
ST BERNARD'S RD
KATHERINE RD
WAKEFIELD ST
CAMPBELL RD
HARTLEY AVE
Acad
HIGH ST N
MYRTLE RD
THORPE RD
STREATFEILD AVE
LATIMER AVE
CANBERRA RD
DUKES RD
DUKES CT
1 MALDON CT
2 WALL END CT
3 TRAFALGAR CT
4 ANGLIA WLK
ARRAGON RD
PARR RD
ABBOTS RD
WAKEFIELD ST
AINTREE AVE
WINTER AVE
ST JOHN'S RD
LLOYD RD
BARKING RD
DIDSBURY CL
DRAKES WLK
Wallend
LANGDON RD
NELSON ST
SUSSEX RD
Langdon Sch
TH
L Ctr
Liby
NELSON ST
WELLINGTON RD
MELBOURNE RD
NAPIER RD
RANELAGH RD
PARK AVE
LANGDON CRES
B109
NAVARRE RD
ST BARTHOLOMEW'S RD
Coll
POULETT RD
TALBOT RD
MARKET ST
A124
30
THACKERAY RD
DICKENS RD
MACAULAY RD
MAFEKING AVE
KIMBERLEY AVE
LADYSMITH AVE
GILLETT AVE
HOCKLEY AVE
ERNALD AVE
BARTLE AVE
HENRY RD
CENTRAL PARK RD
DORAN CT
TIPPETT CT
MARKET ST
HOWARD RD
ARTHUR RD
TILBURY RD
HASTINGWOOD CT
Flanders PI Fld
SIDNEY ELSON WAY 1
MATHEWS AVE 2
PI Fld
HANDTROUGH WAY
5
COMPTON AVE
LOXFORD AVE
Sch
CHELTENHAM GDNS
Central Park
EAST HAM
SOUTHCHURCH RD
SOUTH CHURCH CT
FLANDERS RD
DARWELL CL
WELLSTEAD RD
PICKERING AVE
3 ATHELSTAN CT
4 WADHURST CT
PARK RD
B167
GOSWOLD GDNS
GEOFFREY GDNS
Bwg Gn
Tenn Cts
RANCLIFFE RD
B167
83
MONTPELIER GDNS
HENNIKER GDNS
BASIL AVE
PULLEYNS AVE
ASCOT RD
HIGH ST S
WHITE HORSE RD
GRESHAM RD
TYRONE RD
MOUNTFIELD RD
TELHAM RD
BREDE CL
EDWIN AVE
FOLKESTONE RD
HATHERLEY GDNS
CHESLEY GDNS
HALDANE RD
BURFORD RD
EUSTACE RD
MITCHAM RD
BUTTERFLY CT 1
CRICKET CT 2
VICARAGE LA
BRIGHTON RD
PAUL ROBESON CL
Allot Gdns
HUBERT RD
4
BOSTON RD
BUXTON RD
MASTERMAN RD
SUNNINGDALE CL
MARLOW RD
ELDERBERRY WAY
ALEXANDRA RD
ST ALBAN'S AVE
BECKET AVE
LANGTON AVE
EASTBOURNE RD
GOOSELEY LA
BLANEY CRES
BRINTON RD
HOLLINGTON RD
HERTFORD CT
MANOR FARM CT
MANBROUGH AVE
CHARLEMONT RD
WOLSEY AVE
A13
BRAMPTON RD
East Ham Jewish Cemy
Brampton Prim Sch
MORTIMER RD
HOLLOWAY RD
JOHNSTONE RD
SKIPSEY AVE
BURNELS AVE
BREAM GDNS
Gooseley's PI Flds
A1020
DENBIGH RD
99
Brampton Park
LONSDALE CL
SANDFORD CL 1
ST GEORGES CT 2
ST MARYS CT 3
MONMOUTH RD
SANDFORD RD
CHARLTON CT
MELFORD RD
E6
Bwg Gn
Beckton Triangle Ret Pk
Roman Road Prim Sch
LONSDALE AVE
NORMAN RD
HAMEWAY
BROOKS AVE
GREATFIELD AVE
Nat Res
Superstore
CLAPS GATE LA
3
STOKES RD
HALE RD
FABIAN ST
SAXON RD
SILVER BIRCH GDNS
50
1 MAGDALENE GDNS
2 MASEFIELD GDNS
3 HARTSHORN GDNS
Gateway Ret Pk
Ctr Health
NOEL RD
AMY WARNE CL 1
ROMAN RD
IRIS CL 2
THE LABURNUMS
A13
50
NEWHAM WAY
Beckton Alps
Ski Ctr
Greenway
ROYAL DOCKS RD
VIKING GDNS
DAKOTA GDNS
FIREFLY GDNS
EVELYN DENINGTON RD
BEGONIA CL
ALBATROSS CL
EASTBURY RD
82
East Ham Ind Est
SORREL GDNS
NIGHTINGALE WAY
North Beckton Prim Sch
WHITINGS WAY
Alpine Bsns Ctr
HILLCROFT RD
GLENCAIRNE CL
EISENHOWER DR
KINGFISHER ST
BERYL AVE
PEMBROKE RD
Pav
FLEETWOOD CL
DEWBERRY GDNS
YARROW CRES
COLUMBINE AVE
REDSTART CL
PERIDOT ST
VALIANT WAY
HARRIER WAY
HALLYWELL CRES
ALPINE WAY
Beckton Ret Pk
RODING RD
GOLDCREST CL
HURST CT
Ride
Horse
2
SWALLOW ST
BRACKEN CL
SADOR DR
VISCOUNT DR
CONCORDE DR
SOUTH ST
DERIFALL CL
BOWYER CL
PEPPER CL
AARON HILL RD
HAREBELL DR
COUNTY RD
TOLLGATE RD
AMBASSADOR GDNS
ANGELICA DR
HENRY ADDLINGTON CL
GREENCROFT CL
PINTAIL CL
GREENWICH CRES
WAVERLEY GDNS
LINDAL RD
LONGAGE APP
WINSOR TERR
EDMUND HURST DR
SEARLES DR
MAPLE CT
DOVE APP
OSPREY CL
KESTREL AVE
SWAN APP
OLIVER GDNS
BRADLEY STONE RD
IRELAND PL
KINGSFORD WAY
LION RD
East Beckton Dist Ctr
STONEWALL
Beckton
Beckton
NEATSCOURT RD
LEAMOUTH RD
COWAN CL
LATHAM CL
MITCHELL WLK
Liby
MARY ROSE MALL
CRAYFORD CL
ALLHALLOWS RD
REMINGTON RD
KIRKHAM RD
FROBISHER RD
NEWARK KNOK
SUDBURY
BEAUFORT
WARWALL
TUNNAN LEYS
Gallions Prim Sch
ROOK WLK
MAPLECROFT CL
Becton District Park
LINTON GDNS
WOODGET CL
BARRY RD
SALTLEY CL
DUNNOCK RD
HADLEIGH WLK
NORTHUMBERLAND RD
CHARDWELL CL
Kingsford Com Sch
TRIUMPH RD
THOMAS CRIBB MEWS
ASHEN
DOWNINGS
COW LEAZE
HORSE LEAZE
BRADYMEAD
TYNEMOUTH CL
OXLEAS
PEVEREL
HIDE
COVELEES WALL
WHEATFIELDS
ALESTAN BECK RD
STANSFELD RD
The Will Thorne Pav
ROBSON CL
ANDREWES GDNS
CHESTER CL
CHELMSFORD CL
GUILDFORD RD
EXETER RD
Horse Ride
ARMSTRONG CL
NEWLING CL
BRANDRETH RD
PEARL CL
WOOLWICH MANOR WAY
40
1
CASPIAN WLK
JADE CL
OPAL CL
JASPER RD
AGATE CL
EMERALD
BOULTWOOD RD
HARPER RD
BAYNE CL
TRUSEDALE RD
BATTEN CL
PORTER RD
OAKES CL
SAVAGE GDNS
Tenn Cts
EAST HAM MANOR WAY
BESSIE LANSBURY CL
VULCAN CL
Allot Gdns
Calverton Prim Sch
RICHARD HOUSE DR
YORK CL
PARRY AVE
New Becton Park
Bwg Gn
Winsor Prim Sch
PENNYROYAL AVE
ALISON CL
TANSY CL
HEATHER CL
FERNDALE ST
TRADER RD
40
81
Allot Gdns
PI Fld
STRAIT RD
PION CL
REW CL
LEAROYD GDNS
AGNES CL
BASING CL
DEVALLS CL
CYPRUS PL
YEOMAN
Gallions Reach
A1020
A117
42
A
B
122
43
C
D
44
A1020
ROYAL ALBERT WAY
ROYAL ALBERT WAY
Cyprus
DOCKSIDE RD
Beckton Park

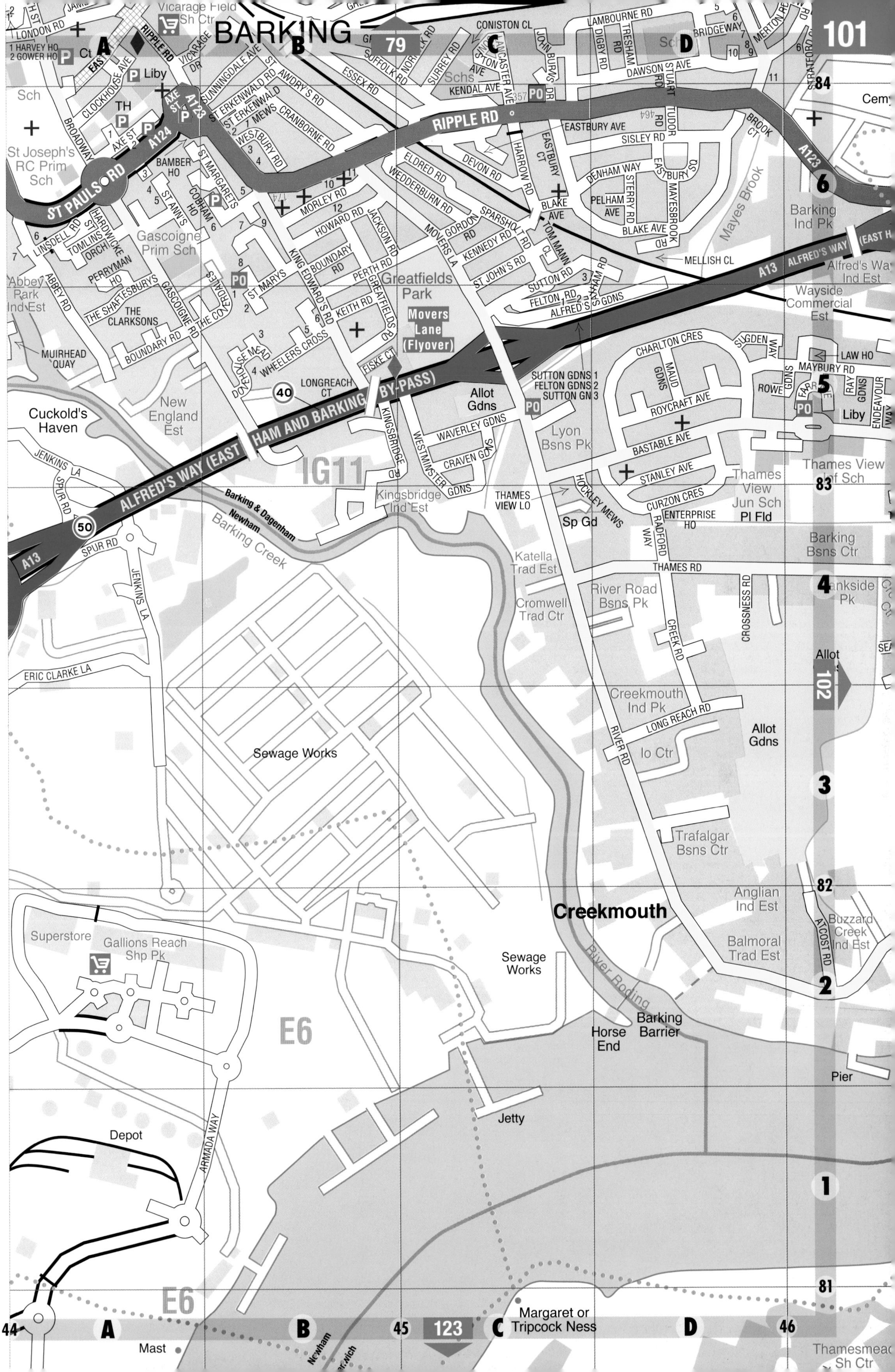
BARKING
79
A
B
C
D
LONDON RD
1 HARVEY HO
2 GOWER HO
Vicarage Field Sh Ctr
RIPPLE RD
VICARAGE DR
EAST ST
Liby
Ct
Sch
TH
CLOCKHOUSE AVE
BROADWAY
AXE ST
A124
A123
St Joseph's RC Prim Sch
ST PAULS RD
BAMBER HO
ST MARGARETS
COBHAM HO
ST ANN'S
Gascoigne Prim Sch
LINSDELL RD
TOMLINS ORCH
HARDWICKE ST
PERRYMAN HO
Abbey Park Ind Est
ABBEY RD
THE SHAFTESBURYS
THE CLARKSONS
GASCOIGNE RD
BOUNDARY RD
THE COVERDALES
MUIRHEAD QUAY
SUNNINGDALE AVE
ST AWDRY'S RD
ST ERKENWALD RD
ST ERKENWALD MEWS
CRANBORNE RD
WESTBURY RD
MORLEY RD
HOWARD RD
JACKSON RD
KING EDWARD'S RD
BOUNDARY RD
PERTH RD
ST MARYS
KEITH RD
GREATFIELDS RD
Greatfields Park
Movers Lane (Flyover)
WHEELERS CROSS
DOVEHOUSE MEAD
FISKE CT
LONGREACH CT
40
ESSEX RD
SUFFOLK RD
NORFOLK RD
SURREY RD
ELDRED RD
WEDDERBURN RD
MOVERS LA
GORDON RD
KENNEDY RD
SPARSHOLT RD
ST JOHN'S RD
CONISTON CL
LANCASTER AVE
KENDAL AVE
Schs
357
PO
JOHN BURNS DR
LAMBOURNE RD
DIGBY RD
TRESHAM RD
DAWSON AVE
STUART RD
BRIDGEWAY
MERTON RD
STRATFORD RD
84
Cem
EASTBURY AVE
SISLEY RD
TUDOR RD
464
BROOK CT
A123
DEVON RD
HARROW RD
EASTBURY CT
DENHAM WAY
EASTBURY SQ
PELHAM AVE
STERRY RD
MAYESBROOK RD
BLAKE AVE
TOM MANN CL
Mayes Brook
Barking Ind Pk
6
MELLISH CL
A13
ALFRED'S WAY
Alfred's Way Ind Est
Wayside Commercial Est
SUTTON RD
AXHAM RD
FELTON RD
ALFRED'S GDNS
SUTTON GDNS 1
FELTON GDNS 2
SUTTON GN 3
CHARLTON CRES
SUGDEN WAY
LAW HO
MAYBURY RD
MAUD GDNS
ROWE GDNS
FARR AVE
RAY GDNS
ENDEAVOUR WAY
5
Liby
ROYCRAFT AVE
Allot Gdns
PO
Lyon Bsns Pk
WAVERLEY GDNS
CRAVEN GDNS
WESTMINSTER GDNS
KINGSBRIDGE RD
BASTABLE AVE
STANLEY AVE
Thames View Jun Sch
Thames View Inf Sch
83
CURZON CRES
ENTERPRISE HO
Pl Fld
Cuckold's Haven
JENKINS LA
SPUR RD
ALFRED'S WAY (EAST HAM AND BARKING BY-PASS)
IG11
Kingsbridge Ind Est
THAMES VIEW LO
HOCKLEY MEWS
Sp Gd
RADFORD WAY
Barking & Dagenham
Newham
Barking Creek
50
A13
SPUR RD
Katella Trad Est
THAMES RD
Barking Bsns Ctr
4
Bankside Pk
Cromwell Trad Ctr
River Road Bsns Pk
CROSSNESS RD
CREEK RD
Allot
102
ERIC CLARKE LA
Creekmouth Ind Pk
LONG REACH RD
Allot Gdns
RIVER RD
Io Ctr
Sewage Works
3
Trafalgar Bsns Ctr
82
Anglian Ind Est
Creekmouth
Buzzard Creek Ind Est
ATCOST RD
Balmoral Trad Est
Superstore
Gallions Reach Shp Pk
Sewage Works
River Roding
2
Barking Barrier
Horse End
E6
Pier
Jetty
Depot
ARMADA WAY
1
81
E6
Margaret or Tripcock Ness
44
45
123
46
Mast
Newham
Thamesmead Sh Ctr

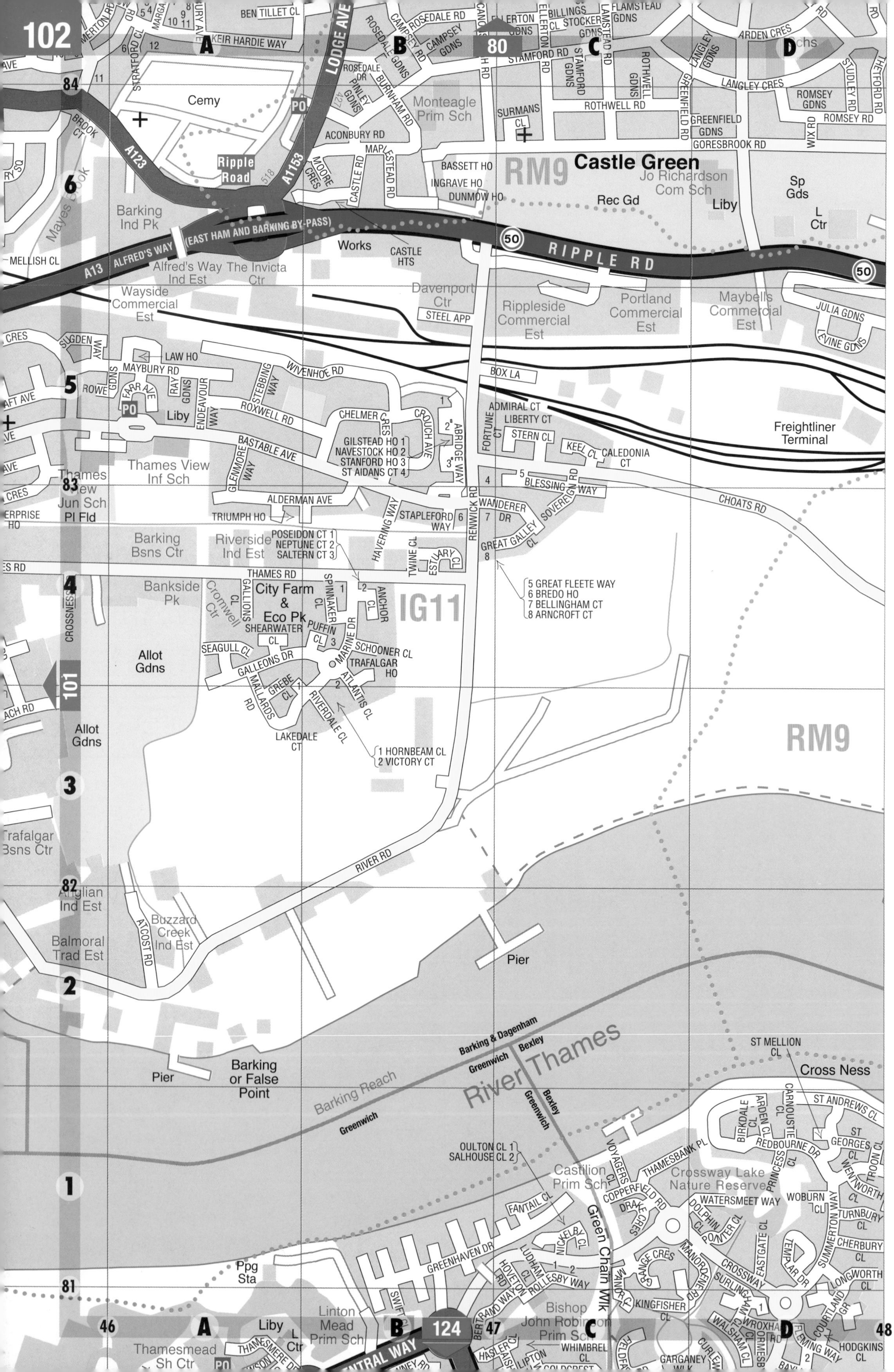
A
B
C
D
80
KEIR HARDIE WAY
BEN TILLET CL
LODGE AVE
ROSEDALE RD
CAMPSEY GDNS
STAMFORD RD
ELLERTON RD
BILLINGS CL
STOCKER GDNS
FLAMSTEAD GDNS
LAMSTEAD RD
ARDEN CRES
LANGLEY GDNS
LANGLEY CRES
ROMSEY GDNS
ROMSEY RD
STUDLEY RD
THETFORD RD
Cemy
Monteagle Prim Sch
ROSEDALE DR
PINLEY GDNS
BURNHAM RD
SURMANS CL
ROTHWELL RD
ROTHWELL GDNS
STAMFORD GDNS
GREENFIELD GDNS
GREENFIELD RD
WIX RD
GORESBROOK RD
ACONBURY RD
MAPLESTEAD RD
MOORE CRES
CASTLE RD
BASSETT HO
INGRAVE HO
DUNMOW HO
RM9
Castle Green
Jo Richardson Com Sch
Rec Gd
Liby
Sp Gds
L Ctr
BROOK CT
A123
A1153
Ripple Road
Mayes Brook
Barking Ind Pk
MELLISH CL
A13
ALFRED'S WAY
(EAST HAM AND BARKING BY-PASS)
Works
CASTLE HTS
50
RIPPLE RD
Alfred's Way Ind Est
The Invicta Ctr
Wayside Commercial Est
Davenport Ctr
STEEL APP
Rippleside Commercial Est
Portland Commercial Est
Maybells Commercial Est
JULIA GDNS
LEVINE GDNS
CRES
SUGDEN WAY
LAW HO
MAYBURY RD
ROWE GDNS
FARR AVE
RAY GDNS
ENDEAVOUR WAY
STEBBING WAY
WIVENHOE RD
ROXWELL RD
PO
Liby
BOX LA
ADMIRAL CT
LIBERTY CT
FORTUNE CT
STERN CL
KEEL CL
CALEDONIA CT
Freightliner Terminal
CHELMER CRES
CROUCH AVE
ABRIDGE WAY
GILSTEAD HO 1
NAVESTOCK HO 2
STANFORD HO 3
ST AIDANS CT 4
BASTABLE AVE
GLENMORE WAY
Thames View Inf Sch
Thames View Jun Sch
Pl Fld
ALDERMAN AVE
TRIUMPH HO
HAVERING WAY
STAPLEFORD WAY
RENWICK RD
BLESSING WAY
SOVEREIGN RD
WANDERER DR
GREAT GALLEY CL
CHOATS RD
ERPRISE HO
Barking Bsns Ctr
Riverside Ind Est
POSEIDON CT 1
NEPTUNE CT 2
SALTERN CT 3
TWINE CL
ESTUARY CL
THAMES RD
5 GREAT FLEETE WAY
6 BREDO HO
7 BELLINGHAM CT
8 ARNCROFT CT
Bankside Pk
Cromwell Ctr
GALLIONS CL
City Farm & Eco Pk
SPINNAKER CL
ANCHOR CL
IG11
CROSSNESS
SHEARWATER CL
PUFFIN CL
MARINE DR
SCHOONER CL
TRAFALGAR HO
SEAGULL CL
GALLEONS DR
Allot Gdns
101
MALLARDS RD
GREBE CL
ATLANTIS CL
RIVERDALE CL
LAKEDALE CT
1 HORNBEAM CL
2 VICTORY CT
RM9
Trafalgar Bsns Ctr
RIVER RD
82
Anglian Ind Est
Buzzard Creek Ind Est
ATCOST RD
Balmoral Trad Est
Pier
Barking or False Point
Barking Reach
River Thames
Barking & Dagenham
Greenwich
Bexley
ST MELLION CL
Cross Ness
CARNOUSTIE CL
ST ANDREWS CL
BIRKDALE CL
ARDEN CL
REDBOURNE DR
ST GEORGES CL
TROON CL
WENTWORTH CL
OULTON CL 1
SALHOUSE CL 2
VOYAGERS CL
THAMESBANK PL
Castilion Prim Sch
Crossway Lake Nature Reserve
PRINCESS CL
COPPERFIELD RD
DRAKE CRES
WATERSMEET WAY
WOBURN CL
SUMMERTON WAY
TURNBURY CL
FANTAIL CL
NICKELBY CL
Green Chain Wlk
DOLPHIN CL
POINTER CL
EASTGATE CL
TEMPLAR DR
CHERBURY CL
GREENHAVEN DR
LUDHAM CL
HOVETON RD
ROLLESBY WAY
GRANGE CRES
MANORSIDE RD
CROSSWAY
LONGWORTH CL
Ppg Sta
81
SURLINGHAM CL
SWIFT CL
BERTRAND WAY
KINGFISHER CL
COURTLAND GR
Linton Mead Prim Sch
Bishop John Robinson Prim Sch
WROXHAM RD
WALSHAM CL
FLEMING WAY
46
47
48
124
Liby
L Ctr
Thamesmead Sh Ctr
THAMESMERE DR
PO
CENTRAL WAY
WHIMBREL CL
HASLER CL
GARGANEY WLK
CURLEW
ORMESBY
HODGKINS CL

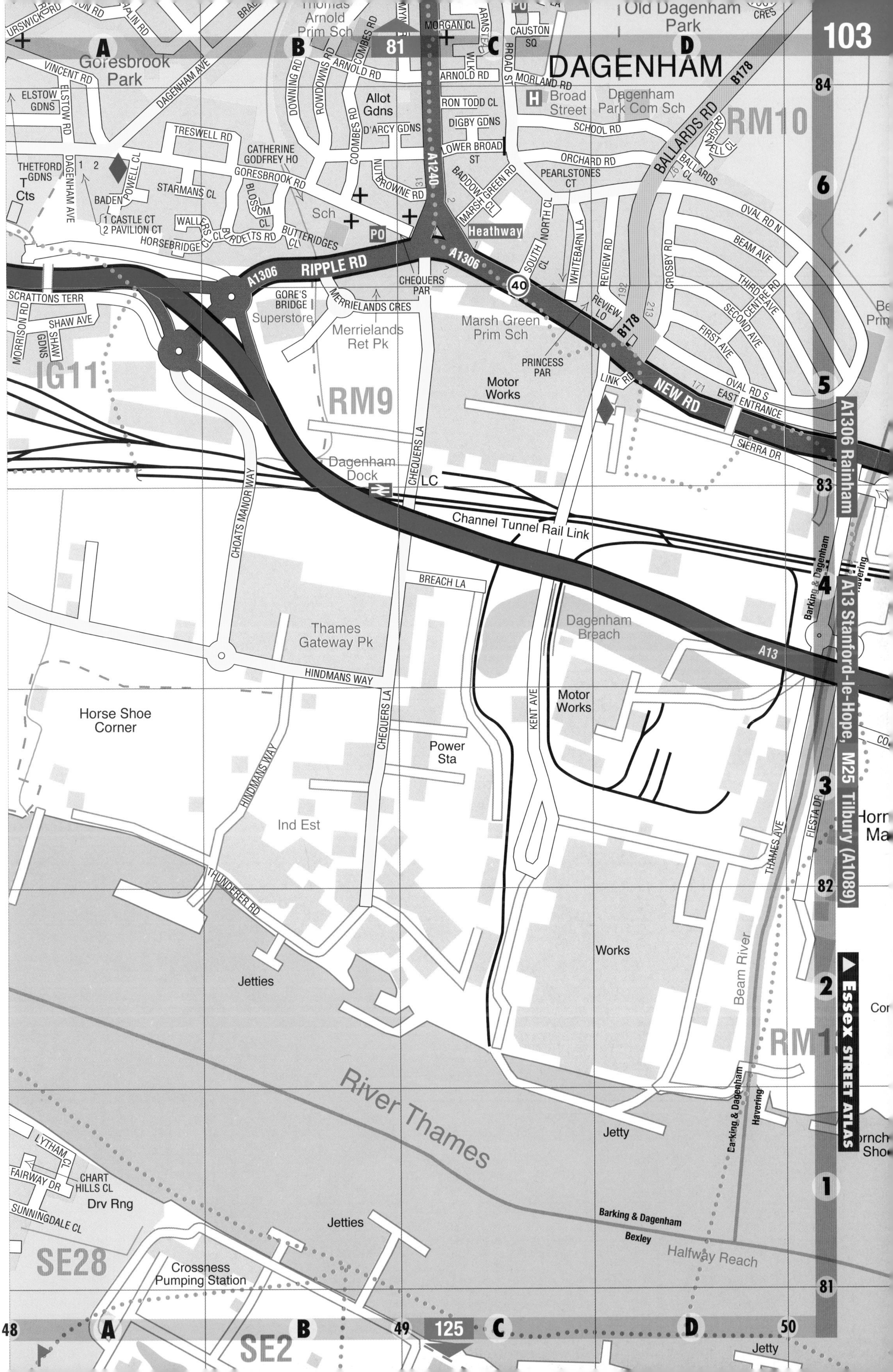

A
B
C
D
81
Goresbrook Park
Thomas Arnold Prim Sch
Old Dagenham Park
DAGENHAM
VINCENT RD
ELSTOW GDNS
ELSTOW RD
DAGENHAM AVE
TRESWELL RD
CATHERINE GODFREY HO
THETFORD GDNS
T Cts
BADEN
POWELL CL
STARMANS CL
1 CASTLE CT
2 PAVILION CT
WALLERS CL
HORSEBRIDGE CL
BURDETTS RD
BLOSSOM CL
BUTTERIDGES CL
GORESBROOK RD
DOWNING RD
ROWDOWNS RD
ARNOLD RD
COMBES RD
COOMBES RD
Allot Gdns
D'ARCY GDNS
NUTBROWNE RD
Sch
PO
MORGAN CL
ARMSTEAD WLK
CAUSTON SQ
BROAD ST
MORLAND RD
RON TODD CL
DIGBY GDNS
LOWER BROAD ST
Broad Street
Dagenham Park Com Sch
SCHOOL RD
ORCHARD RD
PEARLSTONES CT
BALLARDS RD
BALLARDS CL
B178
RM10
A1240
BADDOW CL
MARSH GREEN RD
Heathway
NORTH CL
SOUTH CL
WHITEBARN LA
REVIEW RD
REVIEW LO
CROSBY RD
OVAL RD N
BEAM AVE
THIRD AVE
CENTRE RD
SECOND AVE
FIRST AVE
OVAL RD S
EAST ENTRANCE
SIERRA DR
A1306
RIPPLE RD
CHEQUERS PAR
40
SCRATTONS TERR
MORRISON RD
SHAW AVE
SHAW GDNS
GORE'S BRIDGE
Superstore
MERRIELANDS CRES
Merrielands Ret Pk
Marsh Green Prim Sch
PRINCESS PAR
LINK RD
NEW RD
Motor Works
IG11
RM9
Dagenham Dock
LC
CHEQUERS LA
CHOATS MANOR WAY
Channel Tunnel Rail Link
BREACH LA
Thames Gateway Pk
Dagenham Breach
A13
HINDMANS WAY
Horse Shoe Corner
KENT AVE
Motor Works
Power Sta
Ind Est
THUNDERER RD
THAMES AVE
FIESTA DR
Jetties
Works
Beam River
RM13
River Thames
Jetty
LYTHAM CL
FAIRWAY DR
CHART HILLS CL
Drv Rng
SUNNINGDALE CL
Jetties
Barking & Dagenham
Bexley
Halfway Reach
Havering
SE28
Crossness Pumping Station
SE2
Jetty
A1306 Rainham
A13 Stanford-le-Hope, M25 Tilbury (A1089)
Essex STREET ATLAS
84
6
5
83
4
3
82
2
1
81
48
49
50
125

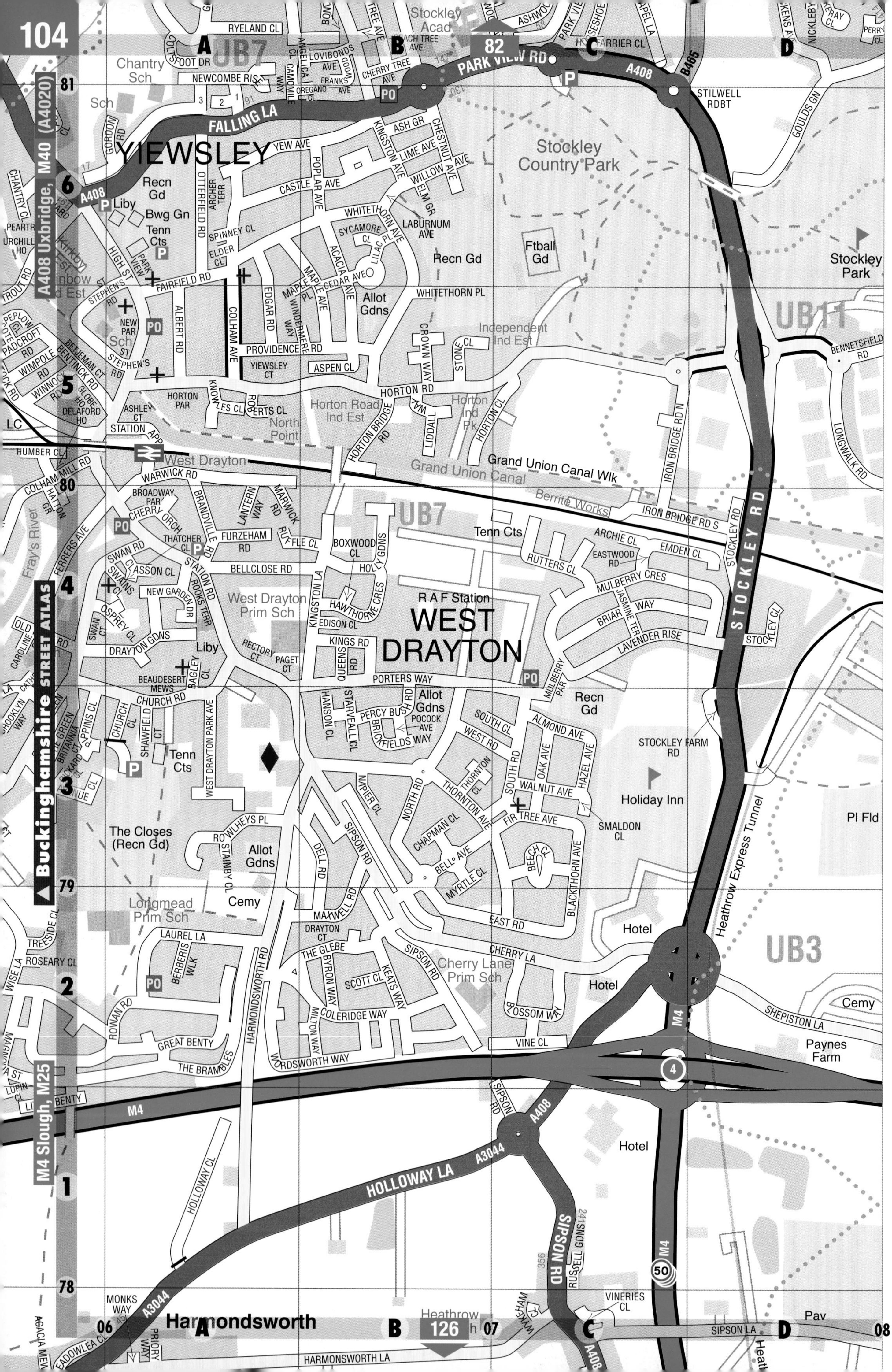
A408 Uxbridge, M40 (A4020)
82
126
Buckinghamshire STREET ATLAS
M4 Slough, M25
YIEWSLEY
WEST DRAYTON
Harmondsworth
UB7
UB11
UB3
RYELAND CL
CHANTRY Sch
COLTSFOOT DR
NEWCOMBE RISE
LOVIBONDS AVE
FRANKS AVE
ANGELICA CL
CAMOMILE WAY
OREGANO CL
CHERRY TREE AVE
BEACH TREE AVE
Stockley Acad
PARK VIEW RD
FARRIER CL
A408
B465
STILWELL RDBT
GOULDS GN
NICKLEBY CL
PERRY CL
FALLING LA
GORDON RD
YEW AVE
KINGSTON AVE
ASH GR
LIME AVE
CHESTNUT AVE
WILLOW AVE
ELM GR
CASTLE AVE
POPLAR AVE
OTTERFIELD RD
ARCHER TERR
Recn Gd
Liby
Bwg Gn
Tenn Cts
SPINNEY CL
ELDER CL
WHITETHORN AVE
SYCAMORE CL
LILAC PL
LABURNUM AVE
ACACIA AVE
CEDAR AVE
MAPLE AVE
MAPLE PL
WINDERMERE WAY
EDGAR RD
Stockley Country Park
Ftball Gd
Stockley Park
FAIRFIELD RD
HIGH ST
ST STEPHEN'S RD
NEW PAR
ALBERT RD
COLHAM AVE
PROVIDENCE RD
YIEWSLEY CT
ASPEN CL
Allot Gdns
WHITETHORN PL
CROWN WAY
STONE CL
Independent Ind Est
BENNETSFIELD RD
LONGWALK RD
PEPLOW CL
PADCROFT RD
WIMPOLE RD
WINNOCK RD
BETJEMAN CT
BENTINCK RD
GLOBE HO
DELAFORD HO
HORTON PAR
KNOWLES CL
ROBERTS CL
HORTON RD
Horton Road Ind Est
North Point
HORTON BRIDGE RD
LIDDALL WAY
Horton Ind Pk
HORTON CL
IRON BRIDGE RD N
ASHLEY CT
STATION APP
HUMBER CL
West Drayton
Grand Union Canal
Grand Union Canal Wlk
Berrite Works
IRON BRIDGE RD S
COLHAM MILL RD
HATTON GR
WARWICK RD
BROADWAY PAR
CHERRY ORCH
BRANDVILLE RD
LANTERN WAY
MARWICK RD
RUFFLE CL
BOXWOOD CL
HOLLY GDNS
Tenn Cts
ARCHIE CL
EMDEN CL
EASTWOOD RD
RUTTERS CL
STOCKLEY RD
Fray's River
FERRERS AVE
SWAN RD
THATCHER CL
FURZEHAM RD
STATION RD
ROOKS TERR
BELLCLOSE RD
ASSON CL
SWANS CL
NEW GARDEN DR
OSPREY CL
SWAN CT
West Drayton Prim Sch
KINGSTON LA
HAWTHORNE CRES
EDISON CL
RAF Station
MULBERRY CRES
JASMINE TER
BRIAR WAY
LAVENDER RISE
STOCKLEY CL
OLD
CAROLINE
DRAYTON GDNS
RECTORY CT
PAGET CT
KINGS RD
QUEENS RD
PORTERS WAY
MULBERRY PAR
Recn Gd
BEAUDESERT MEWS
BAGLEY CL
CHURCH RD
CHURCH CL
SHAWFIELD CT
WEST DRAYTON PARK AVE
HANSON CL
STARVEALL CL
PERCY BUSH RD
POCOCK AVE
BRICKFIELDS WAY
SOUTH CL
WEST RD
ALMOND AVE
OAK AVE
HAZEL AVE
STOCKLEY FARM RD
Holiday Inn
THE GREEN
BRITANNIA
Tenn Cts
NAPIER CL
NORTH RD
THORNTON CL
THORNTON AVE
SOUTH RD
WALNUT AVE
FIR TREE AVE
SMALDON CL
Heathrow Express Tunnel
Pl Fld
The Closes (Recn Gd)
ROWLHEYS PL
STAINBY CL
Allot Gdns
DELL RD
SIPSON RD
CHAPMAN CL
BELL AVE
MYRTLE CL
BEECH CL
BLACKTHORN AVE
Cemy
Longmead Prim Sch
MAXWELL RD
EAST RD
Hotel
TREESIDE CL
ROSEARY CL
LAUREL LA
BERBERIS WLK
DRAYTON CT
THE GLEBE
BYRON WAY
SCOTT CL
KEATS WAY
SIPSON RD
CHERRY LA
Cherry Lane Prim Sch
Hotel
WISE LA
ROWAN RD
HARMONDSWORTH RD
COLERIDGE WAY
MILTON WAY
BOSSOM WAY
VINE CL
SHEPISTON LA
Cemy
Paynes Farm
GREAT BENTY
THE BRAMBLES
WORDSWORTH WAY
M4
4
LUPIN CL
BENTY
SIPSON RD
A3044
HOLLOWAY LA
HOLLOWAY CL
Hotel
RUSSELL GDNS
50
MONKS WAY
PRIORY WAY
MEADOWLEA CL
ACACIA MEWS
WYKHAM CL
VINERIES CL
SIPSON LA
Pav
HARMONDSWORTH LA
Heathrow
81
80
79
78
6
5
4
3
2
1
A
B
C
D
06
07
08

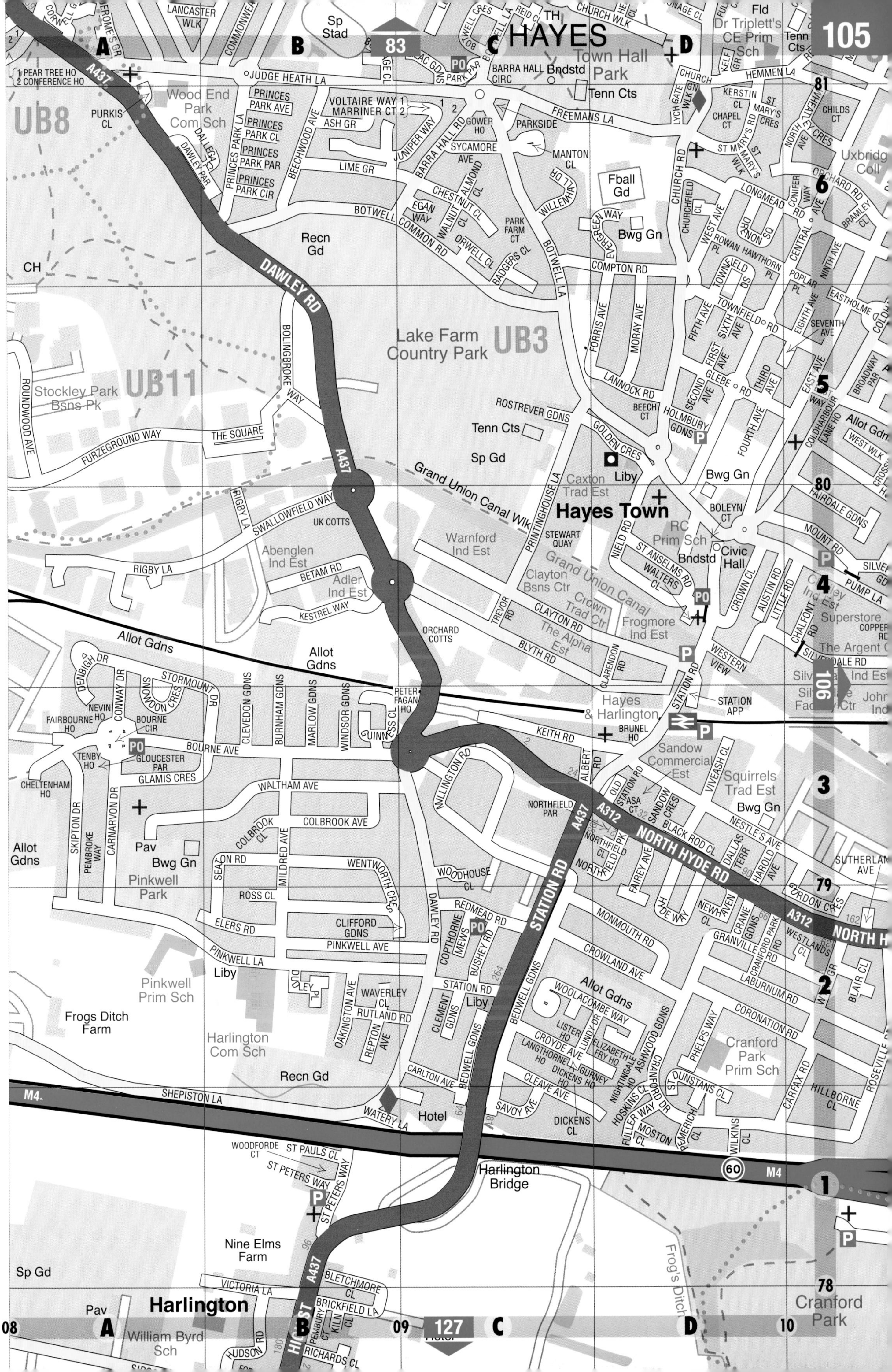
HAYES
Hayes Town
Harlington
UB8
UB3
UB11
A437
A312
M4
DAWLEY RD
STATION RD
NORTH HYDE RD
HIGH ST
Lake Farm Country Park
Stockley Park Bsns Pk
Grand Union Canal
Grand Union Canal Wlk
Hayes & Harlington
Harlington Bridge
Town Hall Park
Wood End Park Com Sch
Dr Triplett's CE Prim Sch
Uxbridge Coll
Pinkwell Park
Pinkwell Prim Sch
Harlington Com Sch
William Byrd Sch
Frogs Ditch Farm
Nine Elms Farm
Cranford Park
Cranford Park Prim Sch
Warnford Ind Est
Abenglen Ind Est
Adler Ind Est
Clayton Bsns Ctr
Crown Trad Ctr
The Alpha Est
Frogmore Ind Est
Caxton Trad Est
Sandow Commercial Est
Squirrels Trad Est
RC Prim Sch
Civic Hall
Bndstd
Liby
Recn Gd
Sp Gd
Tenn Cts
Fball Gd
Bwg Gn
Allot Gdns
Pav
Hotel
CH
Sp Stad
JUDGE HEATH LA
BOTWELL COMMON RD
BOTWELL LA
BARRA HALL RD
FREEMANS LA
CHURCH RD
COMPTON RD
TOWNFIELD RD
LANNOCK RD
ROSTREVER GDNS
GOLDEN CRES
PRINTINGHOUSE LA
NIELD RD
CLAYTON RD
BLYTH RD
KEITH RD
BOURNE AVE
WALTHAM AVE
COLBROOK AVE
PINKWELL AVE
PINKWELL LA
SHEPISTON LA
WATERY LA
FURZEGROUND WAY
SWALLOWFIELD WAY
RIGBY LA
BOLINGBROKE WAY
THE SQUARE
ROUNDWOOD AVE
STORMOUNT DR
CONWAY DR
CARNARVON DR
SKIPTON DR
CLEVEDON GDNS
BURNHAM GDNS
MARLOW GDNS
WINDSOR GDNS
WENTWORTH CRES
MILDRED AVE
STATION RD
BEDWELL GDNS
WOOLACOMBE WAY
CROWLAND AVE
MONMOUTH RD
CORONATION RD
LABURNUM RD
WESTLANDS CL
CLEAVE AVE
SAVOY AVE
DICKENS CL
VICTORIA LA
BLETCHMORE CL
BRICKFIELD LA
ST PETERS WAY
ST PAULS CL
83
127
106
A B C D
08 09 10
81 80 79 78
1 2 3 4 5 6

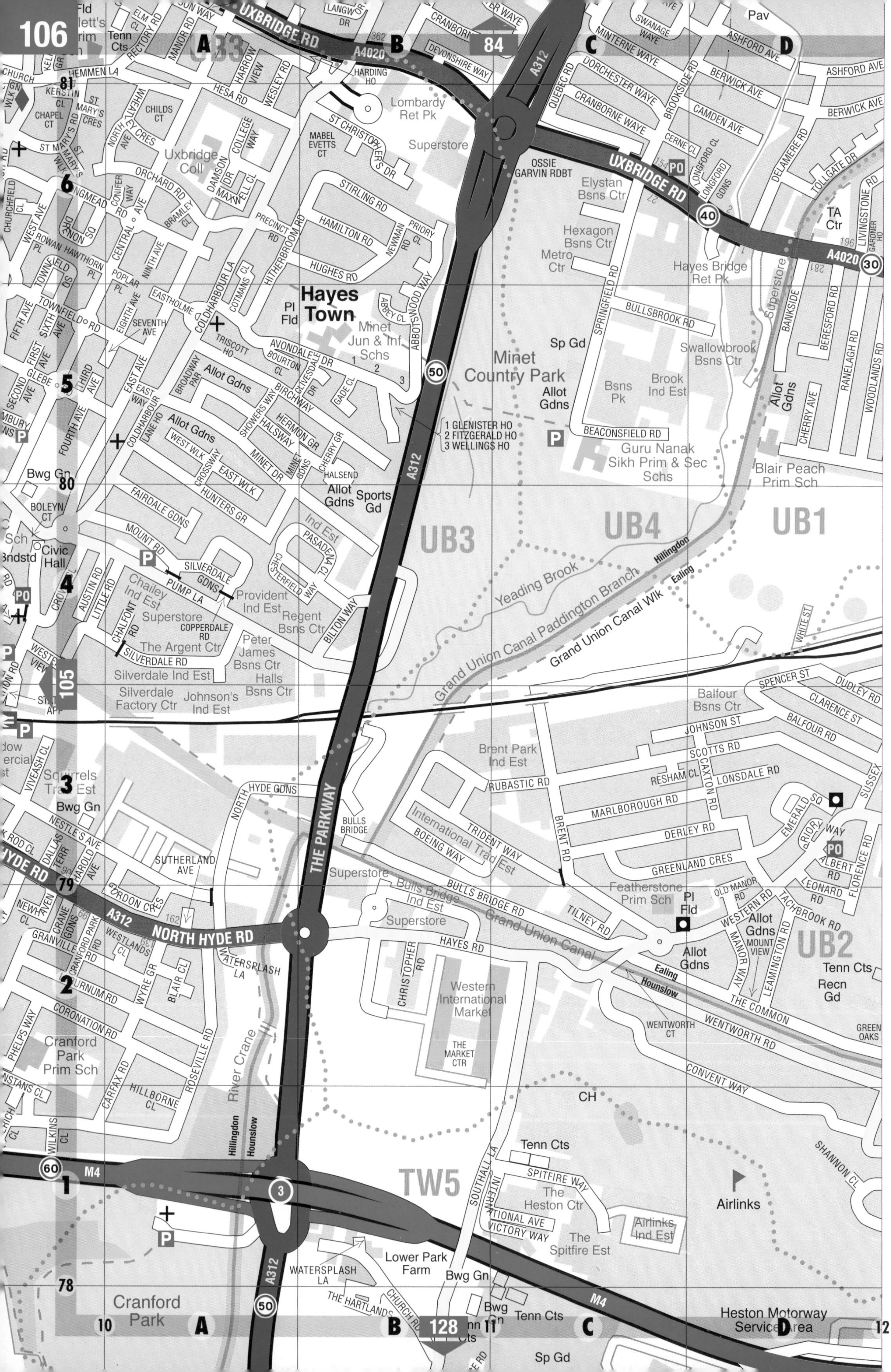

UXBRIDGE RD
A4020
84
A312
Lombardy Ret Pk
Superstore
OSSIE GARVIN RDBT
Elystan Bsns Ctr
Hexagon Bsns Ctr
Metro Ctr
Hayes Bridge Ret Pk
TA Ctr
Uxbridge Coll
Hayes Town
Pl Fld
Minet Jun & Inf Schs
Minet Country Park
Sp Gd
Allot Gdns
Bsns Pk
Brook Ind Est
Swallowbrook Bsns Ctr
Guru Nanak Sikh Prim & Sec Schs
Blair Peach Prim Sch
1 GLENISTER HO
2 FITZGERALD HO
3 WELLINGS HO
UB3
UB4
UB1
UB2
TW5
Yeading Brook
Grand Union Canal Paddington Branch
Grand Union Canal Wlk
Hillingdon
Ealing
Hounslow
Chailey Ind Est
Superstore
The Argent Ctr
Silverdale Ind Est
Silverdale Factory Ctr
Johnson's Ind Est
Provident Ind Est
Regent Bsns Ctr
Peter James Bsns Ctr
Halls Bsns Ctr
Civic Hall
Balfour Bsns Ctr
Brent Park Ind Est
International Trad Est
Bulls Bridge Ind Est
Western International Market
THE MARKET CTR
Featherstone Prim Sch
Squirrels Trad Est
THE PARKWAY
NORTH HYDE RD
Grand Union Canal
River Crane
Cranford Park Prim Sch
M4
The Heston Ctr
The Spitfire Est
Airlinks Ind Est
Airlinks
Lower Park Farm
Cranford Park
Heston Motorway Service Area
Tenn Cts
Recn Gd
Bwg Gn
Sp Gd
CH
105
128
A
B
C
D
1
2
3
4
5
6
78
79
80
81
10
11
12

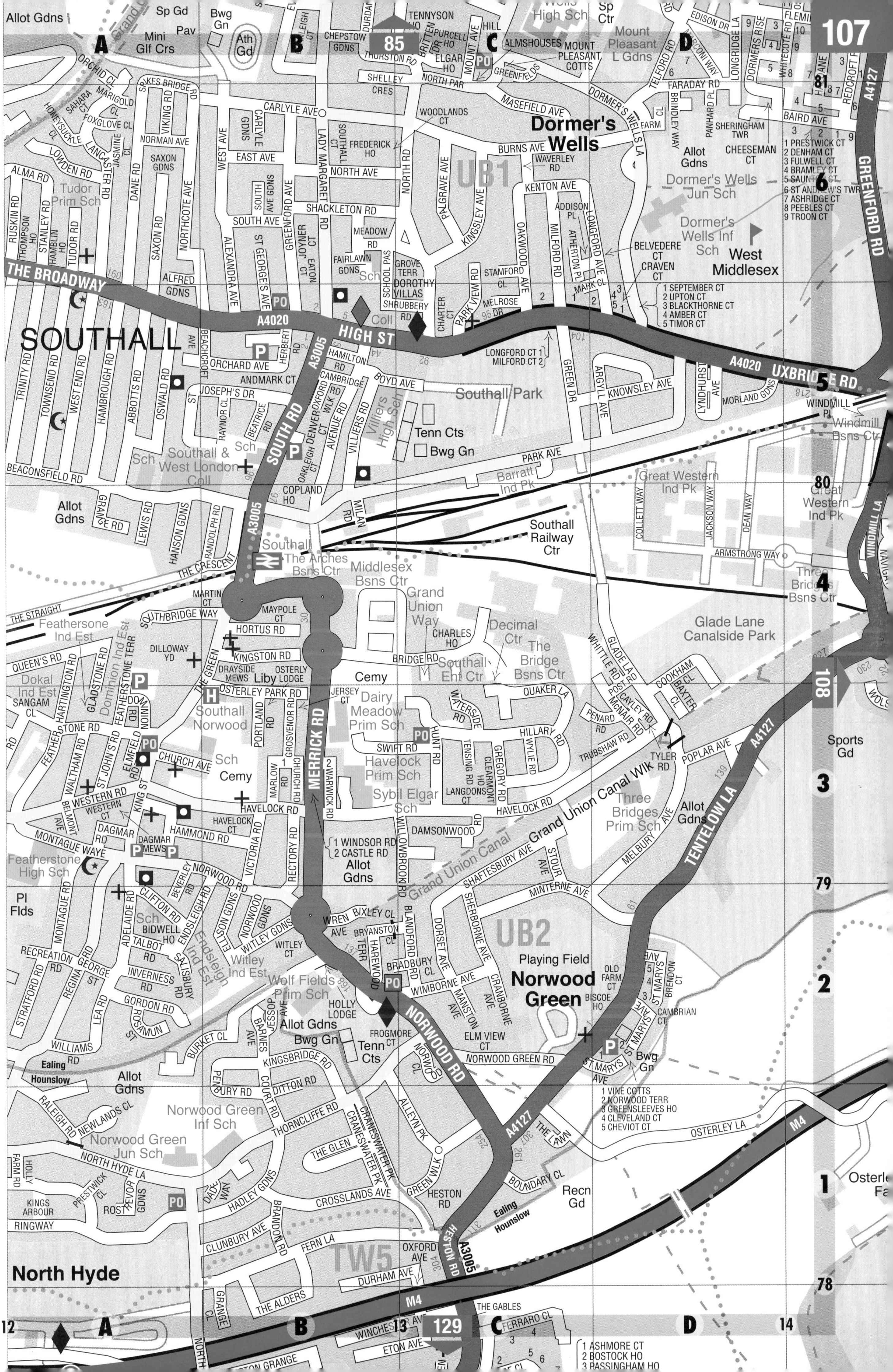
SOUTHALL
Dormer's Wells
West Middlesex
Norwood Green
North Hyde
UB1
UB2
TW5
THE BROADWAY
A4020
HIGH ST
A4020 UXBRIDGE RD
GREENFORD RD
A4127
A3005
SOUTH RD
MERRICK RD
NORWOOD RD
HESTON RD
TENTELOW LA
M4
Grand Union Canal
Grand Union Canal Wlk
Southall Park
Southall
Southall Railway Ctr
Great Western Ind Pk
Glade Lane Canalside Park
Three Bridges Bsns Ctr
Windmill Bsns Ctr
The Arches Bsns Ctr
Middlesex Bsns Ctr
Grand Union Way
Decimal Ctr
The Bridge Bsns Ctr
Southall Ent Ctr
Featherstone Ind Est
Dominion Ind Est
Dokal Ind Est
Endsleigh Ind Est
Witley Ind Est
Barratt Ind Pk
Tudor Prim Sch
Dormer's Wells Jun Sch
Dormer's Wells Inf Sch
Villiers High Sch
Southall & West London Coll
Featherstone High Sch
Dairy Meadow Prim Sch
Havelock Prim Sch
Sybil Elgar Sch
Three Bridges Prim Sch
Wolf Fields Prim Sch
Norwood Green Inf Sch
Norwood Green Jun Sch
Southall Norwood
Playing Field
Recn Gd
Sports Gd
Allot Gdns
Cemy
Tenn Cts
Bwg Gn
Mount Pleasant L Gdns
Mini Glf Crs
Ath Gd
Pl Flds
Ealing
Hounslow
85
108
129
A
B
C
D
1
2
3
4
5
6
12
13
14
78
79
80
81
1 PRESTWICK CT
2 DENHAM CT
3 FULWELL CT
4 BRAMLEY CT
5 SAUNTON CT
6 ST ANDREW'S TWR
7 ASHRIDGE CT
8 PEEBLES CT
9 TROON CT
1 SEPTEMBER CT
2 UPTON CT
3 BLACKTHORNE CT
4 AMBER CT
5 TIMOR CT
1 WINDSOR RD
2 CASTLE RD
1 VINE COTTS
2 NORWOOD TERR
3 GREENSLEEVES HO
4 CLEVELAND CT
5 CHEVIOT CT
1 ASHMORE CT
2 BOSTOCK HO
3 PASSINGHAM HO

A
B
C
D
86
130
14
15
16
81
80
79
78
6
5
4
3
2
1
107
Brent Valley
Hobbayne Prim Sch
Drayton Green
Drayton Manor High Sch
Allot Gdns
FLEMING RD
HAWTHORNE MEWS
DORMERS RISE
WHITECOTE RD
HALDANE RD
REDCROFT RD
FARADAY RD
PANHARD PL
BAIRD AVE
SHERINGHAM TWR
CHEESEMAN CT
1 PRESTWICK CT
2 DENHAM CT
3 FULWELL CT
4 BRAMLEY CT
5 SAUNTON CT
6 ST ANDREW'S TWR
7 ASHRIDGE CT
8 PEEBLES CT
9 TROON CT
Dormer's Wells Jun Sch
Dormer's Wells Inf Sch
West Middlesex
A4127
GREENFORD RD
CH
Sp Gd
HIGH LA
GROVE AVE
ELMWOOD GDNS
WORCESTER CT
DRYDEN AVE
DRAYTON BRIDGE RD
COWPER RD
SHAKESPEARE RD
PARK RD
MILTON RD
ALLINGHAM CL
TENNYSON RD
1 SHERIDAN CT
2 KIPLING CT
MADGE HILL
CHURCH RD
CUCKOO LA
APRIL CL
PO
GLEBE CT
SPRING CT
BRENT CT
BRIERLEY CT
HIGHTREES CT
OAKLEY CL
LIME TERR
HOLBROOK CT
GOLDEN CT
TESTWOOD CT
COURT RD
MANOR CT
BRENTMEAD CL
ALWYNE RD
GOLDEN MANOR
BLAGDON CT
CAMPBELL CT
CAMPBELL RD
Churchfields Recn Gd
T Cts
Bwg Gn
Hanwell
UB1
1 ALDERSON PL
2 IRON BRIDGE CL
3 ALEXANDER CL
A4020 UXBRIDGE RD
LYNDHURST AVE
MORLAND GDNS
WINDMILL PL
Windmill Bsns Ctr
Triangle Ctr
WHARNCLIFFE DR
BRENTVALE AVE
BLACKMORE AVE
Allot Gdns
River Brent
YORK AVE
Schs
SPRINGFIELD RD
STATION RD
CONOLLY RD
LAWN GDNS
MYRTLE GDNS
LAUREL GDNS
HALF ACRE RD
CLAIRVILLE GDNS
BALFOUR AVE
YORK CL
CHERINGTON RD
CHURCH RD
HOLLY PARK RD
NETHERAVON RD
BAKER HO
NIGHTINGALE RD
AZALEA CT
AZALEA CL
SHIRLEY GDNS
Liby
Cemy
BROADWAY
Hanwell
UXBRIDGE RD
MICHAEL GAYNOR CL
BARCHESTER CL
HAYDON HO
FILANCO CT
ST GEORGE'S RD
City of Westminster Cemy
30
HALLIDAY SQ
ELLIS RD
WEST PARK RD
Western Pk
JACKSON WAY
DEAN WAY
Great Western Ind Pk
CUBITT SQ
WINDMILL AVE
WILLIAM CL
GRAND DR
LOCK CL
CHEVY RD
OSTERLEY GDNS
OSTERLEY VIEWS
Ealing
H
WINDMILL LA
NAVIGATOR DR
RIVER CL
ARMSTRONG WAY
Three Bridges Bsns Ctr
Grand Union Canal Wlk
1 WATER LILY CL
2 COMER CRES
3 TULIP CL
WINDMILL BRIDGE
Glade Lane Canalside Park
WALKER CL
FACTORY YD
MAUDESVILLE COTTS
WESTMINSTER RD
GEORGE ST
A4001 BOSTON RD
JESSAMINE RD
WILMOT PL
MONTAGUE AVE
LOWER BOSTON RD
ADELAIDE CT
A3002
MONTAGUE RD
DEAN'S RD
Sch
CAMBRIDGE RD
DENE CT
EDINBURGH RD
SOUTHFIELD COTTS
OAKLANDS RD
CUMBERLAND RD
Capital Ring
MOUNT OLIVE CT
GREEN LA
ST ANDREW'S RD
BISHOP'S RD
ST MARK'S RD
BOSTON RD
ST DUNSTAN'S RD
THORPE RD
ROSEBANK RD
OSTERLEY PARK VIEW RD
STUDLEY GRANGE RD
CARLTON CT
HUMES AVE
LAMBOURN CL
OAK COTTS
ST MARGARET'S RD
BILLETS HART CL
ROSEDALE CL
THE BEECHES
TOMLIN CL
BELVEDERE RD
TRUMPERS WAY
MURRAY CT
1 THORNWELL CT
2 ST MARK"S CT
3 DU BURSTOW TERR
4 CHURCHFIELD RD
5 MALLARD CL
6 QUEENS TERR COTTS
Bnstand
W7
Elthorne Park
Elthorne Park High Sch
UB2
B454
WOLSEY CL
A4127
POPLAR AVE
TENTELOW LA
Allot Gdns
Sports Gd
Sp Ctr
Pl Fld
Waterside Trad Ctr
Boston Bsns Pk
River Brent Bsns Pk
Pl Fld
The Aviary
River Brent
Grand Union Canal
WINDMILL LA
Osterley Lock
M4
40
Trumper's Wood
OSTERLEY LA
Hare & Hounds (PH)
Osterley Park Farm
TW7
Osterley Park
Osterley Park House
Tenn Cts
Bwg Gn
Sp Gd
Wyke Green
CH
B454 SYON LA
T Cts
Pav
P

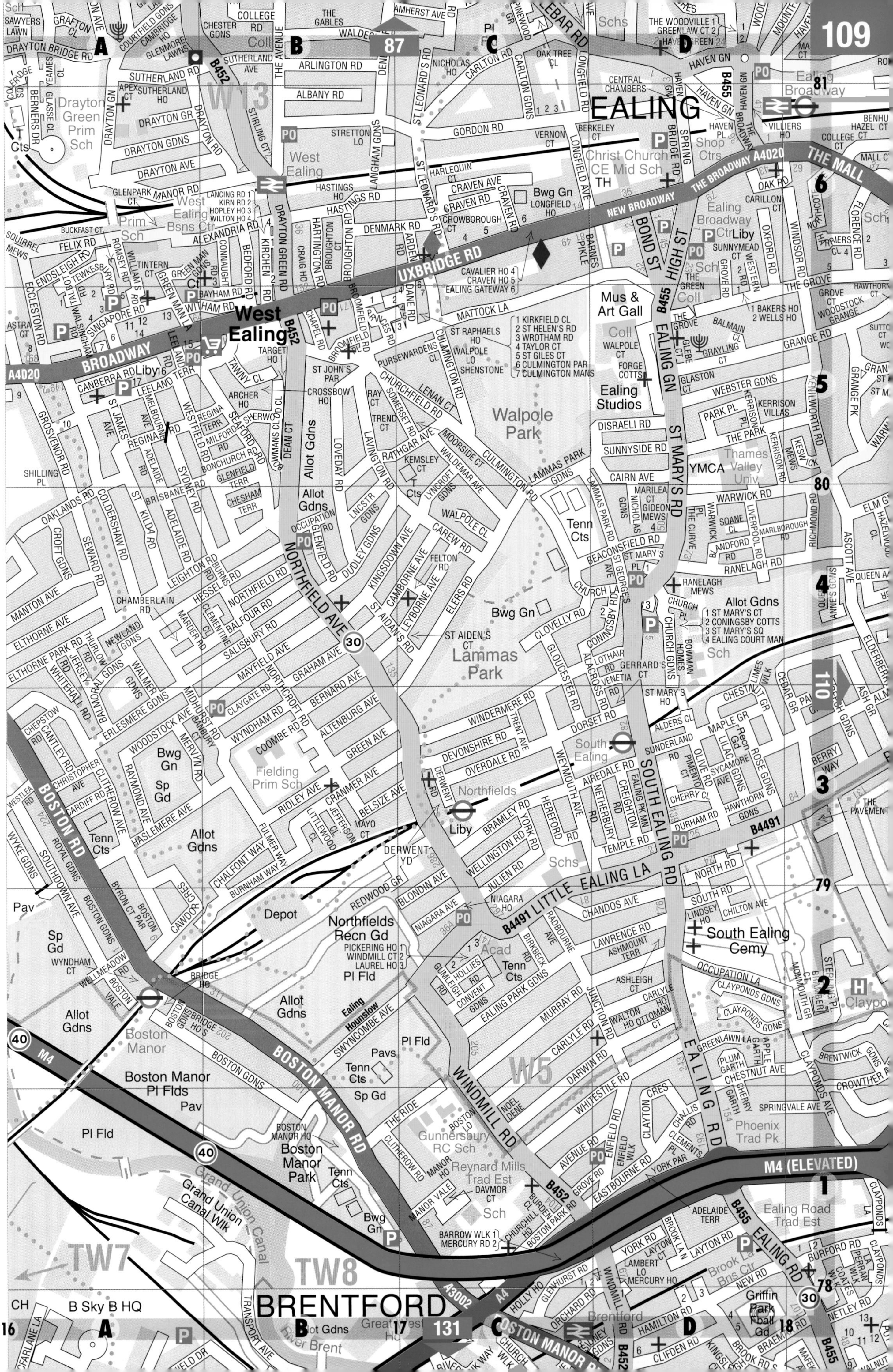
EALING
West Ealing
BRENTFORD
W13
W5
TW7
TW8
UXBRIDGE RD
BROADWAY
NEW BROADWAY
THE BROADWAY A4020
THE MALL
A4020
NORTHFIELD AVE
SOUTH EALING RD
ST MARY'S RD
EALING GN
HIGH ST
BOND ST
BOSTON RD
BOSTON MANOR RD
WINDMILL RD
LITTLE EALING LA
B4491
B452
B455
M4
M4 (ELEVATED)
A4
A3002
DRAYTON GREEN RD
DRAYTON GDNS
DRAYTON AVE
DRAYTON RD
CULMINGTON RD
CHURCHFIELD RD
SOMERSET RD
LAVINGTON RD
LOVEDAY RD
DUDLEY GDNS
KINGSDOWN AVE
CAMBORNE AVE
LEYBORNE AVE
ELERS RD
MAYFIELD AVE
GRAHAM AVE
BERNARD AVE
ALTENBURG AVE
GREEN AVE
CRANMER AVE
BELSIZE AVE
RIDLEY AVE
JEFFERSON CL
WINDERMERE RD
DEVONSHIRE RD
OVERDALE RD
WEYMOUTH AVE
BRAMLEY RD
YORK RD
HEREFORD RD
WELLINGTON RD
JULIEN RD
BLONDIN AVE
NIAGARA AVE
RADBOURNE AVE
EALING PARK GDNS
MURRAY RD
CARLYLE RD
DARWIN RD
WHITESTILE RD
AVENUE RD
ENFIELD RD
CLAYTON CRES
CLEMENTS PL
YORK PAR
Walpole Park
Lammas Park
LAMMAS PARK GDNS
Northfields Recn Gd
South Ealing Cemy
Boston Manor Park
Boston Manor Pl Flds
Gunnersbury RC Sch
Reynard Mills Trad Est
Phoenix Trad Pk
Ealing Road Trad Est
Thames Valley Univ
Ealing Studios
Mus & Art Gall
Ealing Broadway
Fielding Prim Sch
Drayton Green Prim Sch
Christ Church CE Mid Sch
South Ealing
Northfields
Boston Manor
Grand Union Canal
Grand Union Canal Wlk
Brentford
B Sky B HQ
Great West Rd
River Brent
Depot
Walpole Park
1 KIRKFIELD CL
2 ST HELEN'S RD
3 WROTHAM RD
4 TAYLOR CT
5 ST GILES CT
6 CULMINGTON PAR
7 CULMINGTON MANS
1 ST MARY'S CT
2 CONINGSBY COTTS
3 ST MARY'S SQ
4 EALING COURT MAN
87
131
110
A
B
C
D
16
17
18

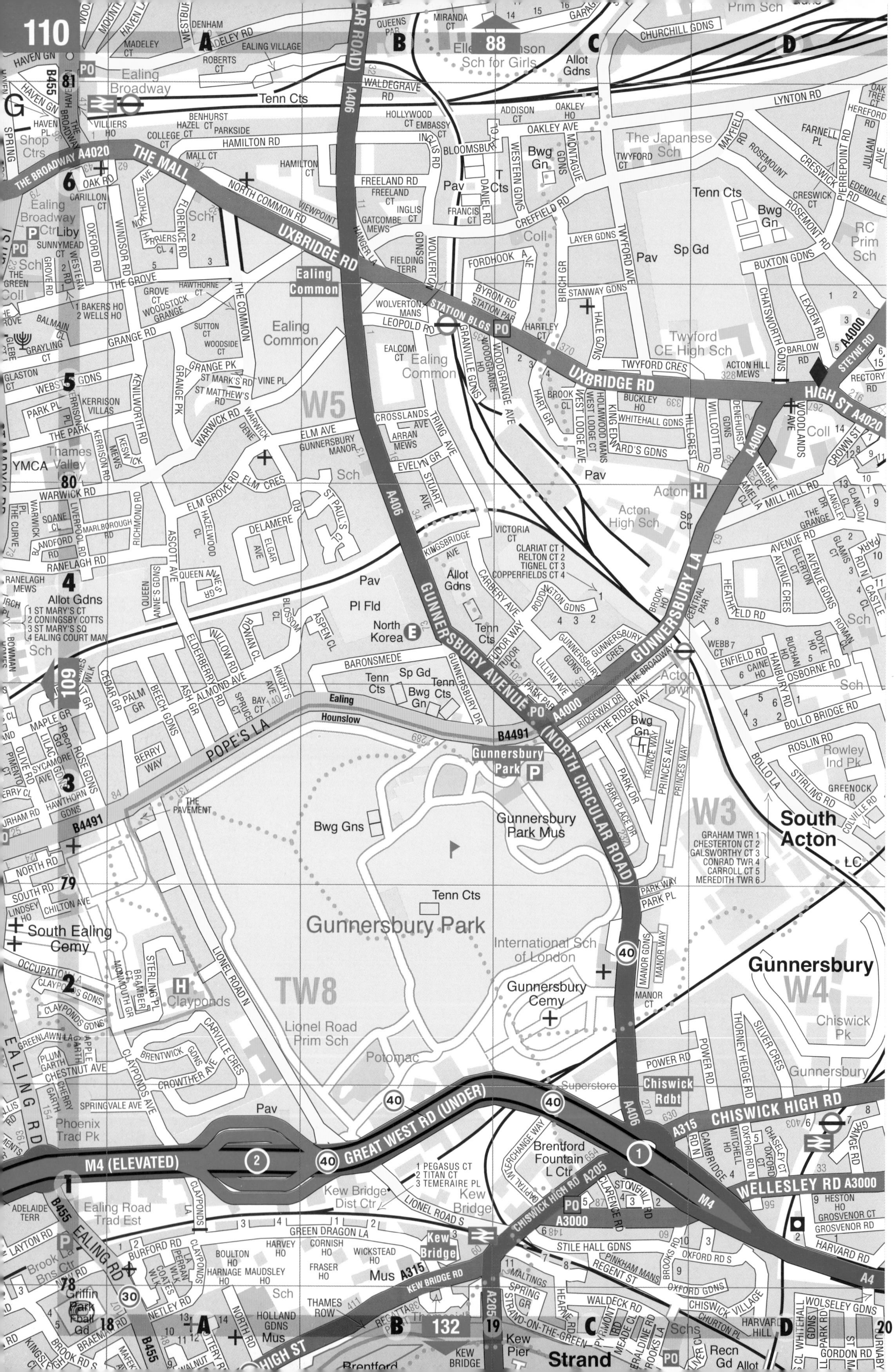
88
132
109
A
B
C
D
1
2
3
4
5
6
Ealing Broadway
Ealing Common
W5
W3
W4
TW8
South Acton
Gunnersbury
Gunnersbury Park
Gunnersbury Park Mus
Gunnersbury Cemy
International Sch of London
South Ealing Cemy
Claypond
Lionel Road Prim Sch
Potomac
Phoenix Trad Pk
Ealing Road Trad Est
Brentford Fountain L Ctr
Kew Bridge Dist Ctr
Kew Bridge
Chiswick Rdbt
Chiswick Pk
Acton Town
Acton High Sch
Twyford CE High Sch
The Japanese Sch
Rowley Ind Pk
North Korea
Ealing Village
Ellen Wilkinson Sch for Girls
Thames Valley
YMCA
Griffin Park Fball Gd
Strand
Kew Pier
Brentford
THE MALL
THE BROADWAY
UXBRIDGE RD
A4020
A406
A4000
GUNNERSBURY AVENUE (NORTH CIRCULAR ROAD)
GUNNERSBURY LA
POPE'S LA
B4491
M4 (ELEVATED)
GREAT WEST RD (UNDER)
CHISWICK HIGH RD
WELLESLEY RD A3000
A315
A205
A3000
A4
EALING RD
B455
KEW BRIDGE RD
HIGH ST
STEYNE RD
HIGH ST A4020
WARWICK RD
RANELAGH RD
GRANGE RD
ELM AVE
CROSSLANDS AVE
BARONSMEDE
LIONEL ROAD N
LIONEL ROAD S
GREEN DRAGON LA
STILE HALL GDNS
POWER RD
BOLLO BRIDGE RD
BOLLO LA
AVENUE RD
TWYFORD AVE
TWYFORD CRES
HAMILTON RD
OAKLEY AVE
LYNTON RD
CHURCHILL GDNS
ROSEMONT RD
MILL HILL RD
GRAHAM TWR 1
CHESTERTON CT 2
GALSWORTHY CT 3
CONRAD TWR 4
CARROLL CT 5
MEREDITH TWR 6
1 PEGASUS CT
2 TITAN CT
3 TEMERAIRE PL
1 ST MARY'S CT
2 CONINGSBY COTTS
3 ST MARY'S SQ
4 EALING COURT MAN
CLARIAT CT 1
RELTON CT 2
TIGNEL CT 3
COPPERFIELDS CT 4
40
30

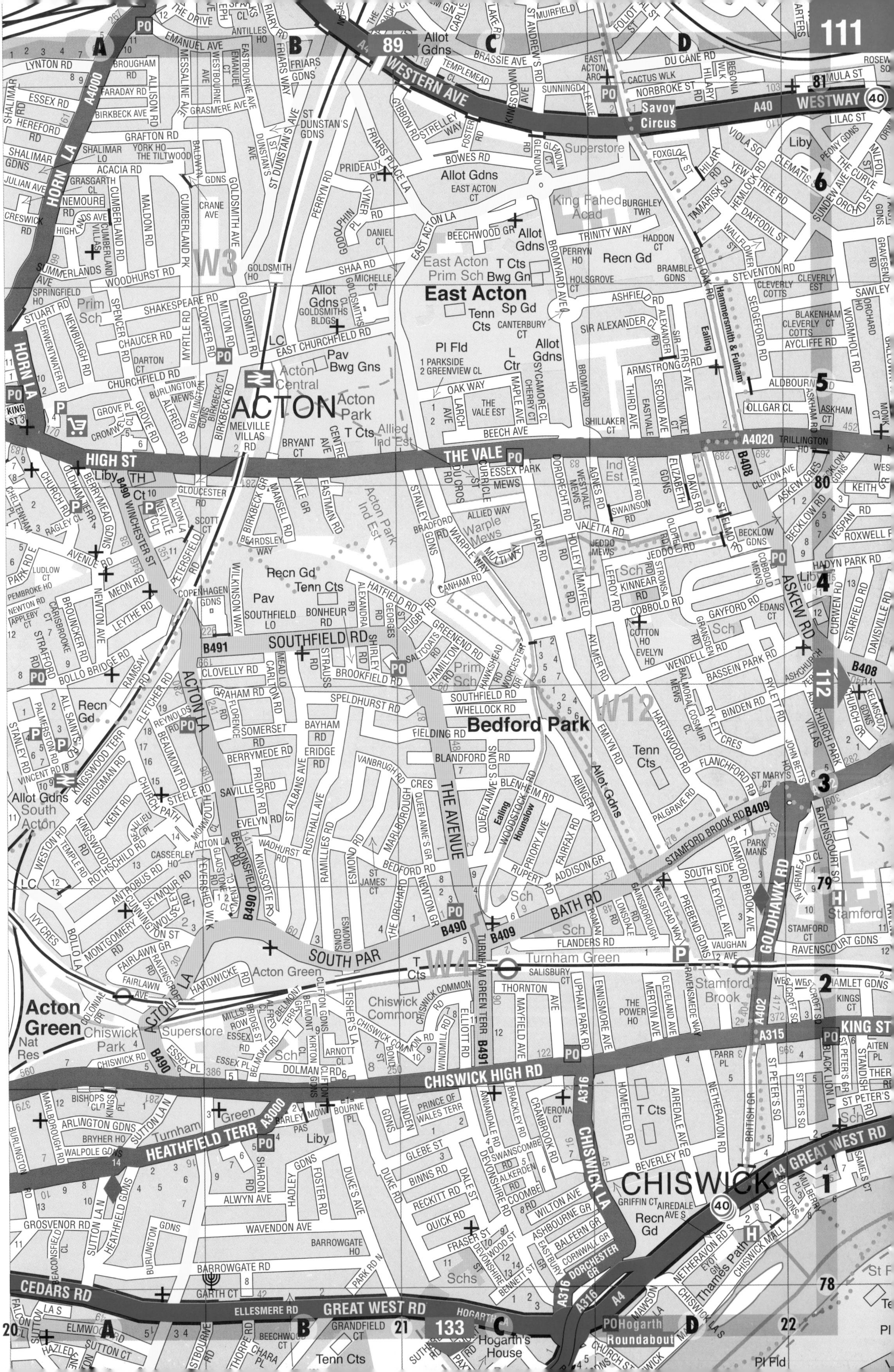
89
WESTERN AVE
A40
WESTWAY
Savoy Circus
ACTON
Acton Central
East Acton
Bedford Park
W3
W12
W4
HIGH ST
THE VALE
A4020
HORN LA
A4000
SOUTHFIELD RD
B491
ACTON LA
THE AVENUE
BATH RD
B409
SOUTH PAR
B490
Turnham Green
Stamford Brook
GOLDHAWK RD
A402
KING ST
A315
CHISWICK HIGH RD
CHISWICK LA
A316
HEATHFIELD TERR
A3000
GREAT WEST RD
A4
CEDARS RD
CHISWICK
Acton Green
Chiswick Common
Chiswick Park
Acton Park
Acton Park Ind Est
Allied Ind Est
King Fahed Acad
East Acton Prim Sch
Recn Gd
Allot Gdns
Superstore
Hammersmith & Fulham
Ealing
Hounslow
112
133
Hogarth Roundabout
Hogarth's House
Thames Path
South Acton
Liby
Sch
Tenn Cts
Pl Fld
78
79
80
81
20
21
22

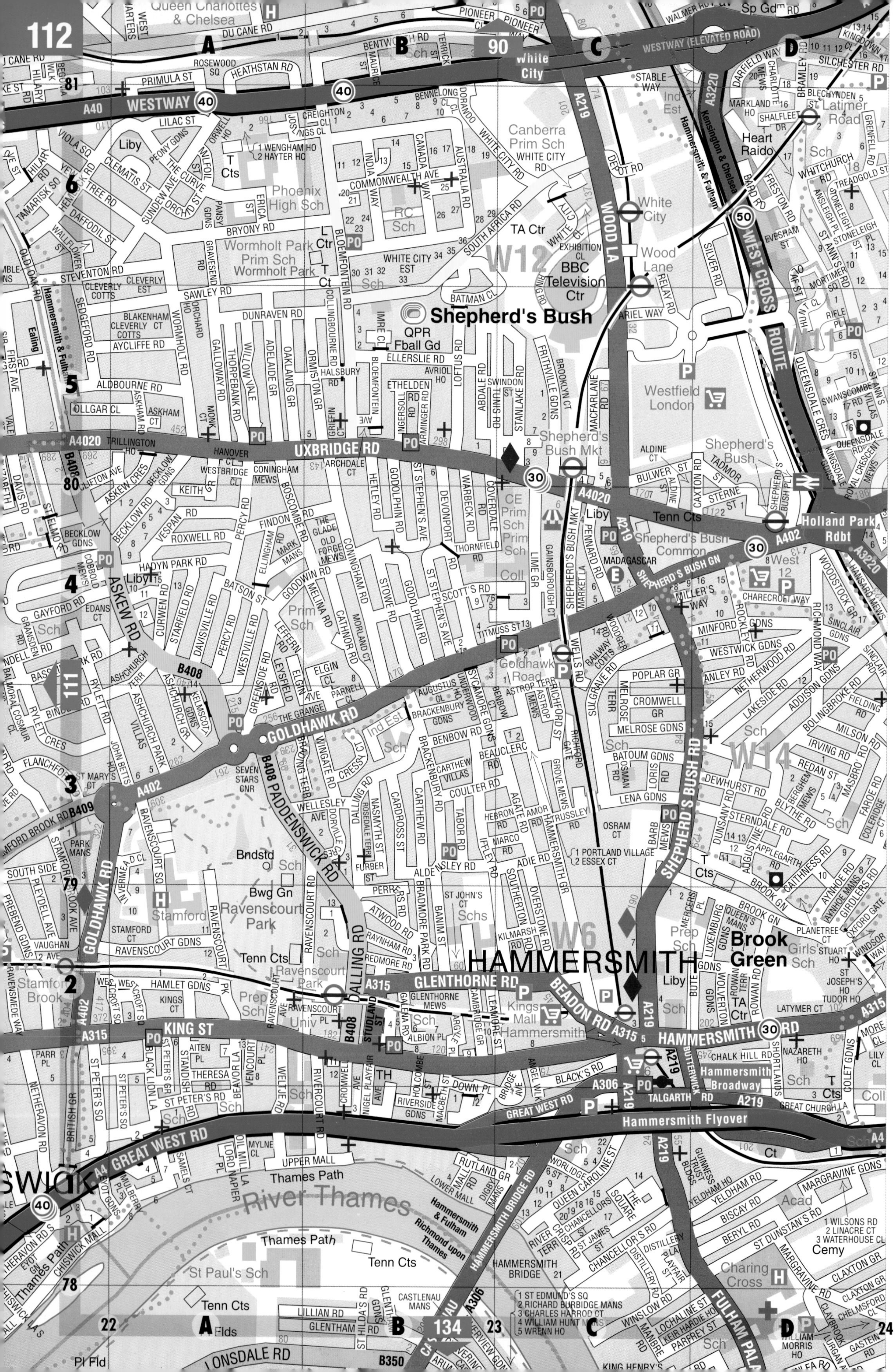
Shepherd's Bush
HAMMERSMITH
Brook Green
W12
W6
W14
White City
Westway
Westway (Elevated Road)
Wood La
Uxbridge Rd
Goldhawk Rd
King St
Glenthorne Rd
Great West Rd
Hammersmith Flyover
Shepherd's Bush Rd
Shepherd's Bush Gn
Shepherd's Bush Common
Hammersmith Rd
Hammersmith Bridge Rd
Fulham Palace Rd
West Cross Route
Holland Park Rdbt
Paddenswick Rd
Askew Rd
Du Cane Rd
Westfield London
BBC Television Ctr
QPR Fball Gd
Ravenscourt Park
Stamford Brook
Goldhawk Road
Shepherd's Bush Mkt
Wood Lane
Latimer Road
Hammersmith Broadway
Charing Cross
Thames Path
River Thames
Kings Mall
Wormholt Park
Phoenix High Sch
St Paul's Sch
Queen Charlotte's & Chelsea
90
111
134
22
23
24
78
79
80
81

Notting Hill
W11
Ladbroke Square Gardens
Avondale Park
Holland Park
Holland Park Sch
Holland Park Tenn Gd
The Orangery Gall
KENSINGTON
W8
Kensington Palace
Kensington Palace Green
Round Pond
Diana Princess of Wales Memorial Walk
Bayswater
Queensway
Notting Hill Gate
Orme Square Gate
Black Lion Gate
Inverness Terrace Gate
Palace Gate
High Street Kensington
Kensington Olympia
Olympia Ex Ctr
W14
West Kensington
Barons Court
Cemy
The Queen's Club
Earl's Court
Earl's Court Ex Ctr
SW5
SW10
West Brompton
Gloucester Road
South Ke
NOTTING HILL GATE
HOLLAND PARK AVE
KENSINGTON HIGH ST
KENSINGTON CHURCH ST
HAMMERSMITH RD
WARWICK GDNS
PEMBROKE RD
CROMWELL RD
WEST CROMWELL RD
TALGARTH RD
NORTH END RD
EARL'S COURT RD
OLD BROMPTON RD
HOLLAND RD
ADDISON RD
LADBROKE GR
PEMBRIDGE VILLAS
QUEENSWAY
KENSINGTON PARK RD
CAMPDEN HILL RD
GLOUCESTER RD
FINBOROUGH RD
REDCLIFFE GDNS
HYDE PARK GA
A402
A315
A3220
A4
A4204
A4206
A3218
B450
B415
B411
B405
B316
B317
B325
B410
91
245
244
114
254
135
255
A
B
C
D
1
2
3
4
5
6
24
25
26
78
79
80
81

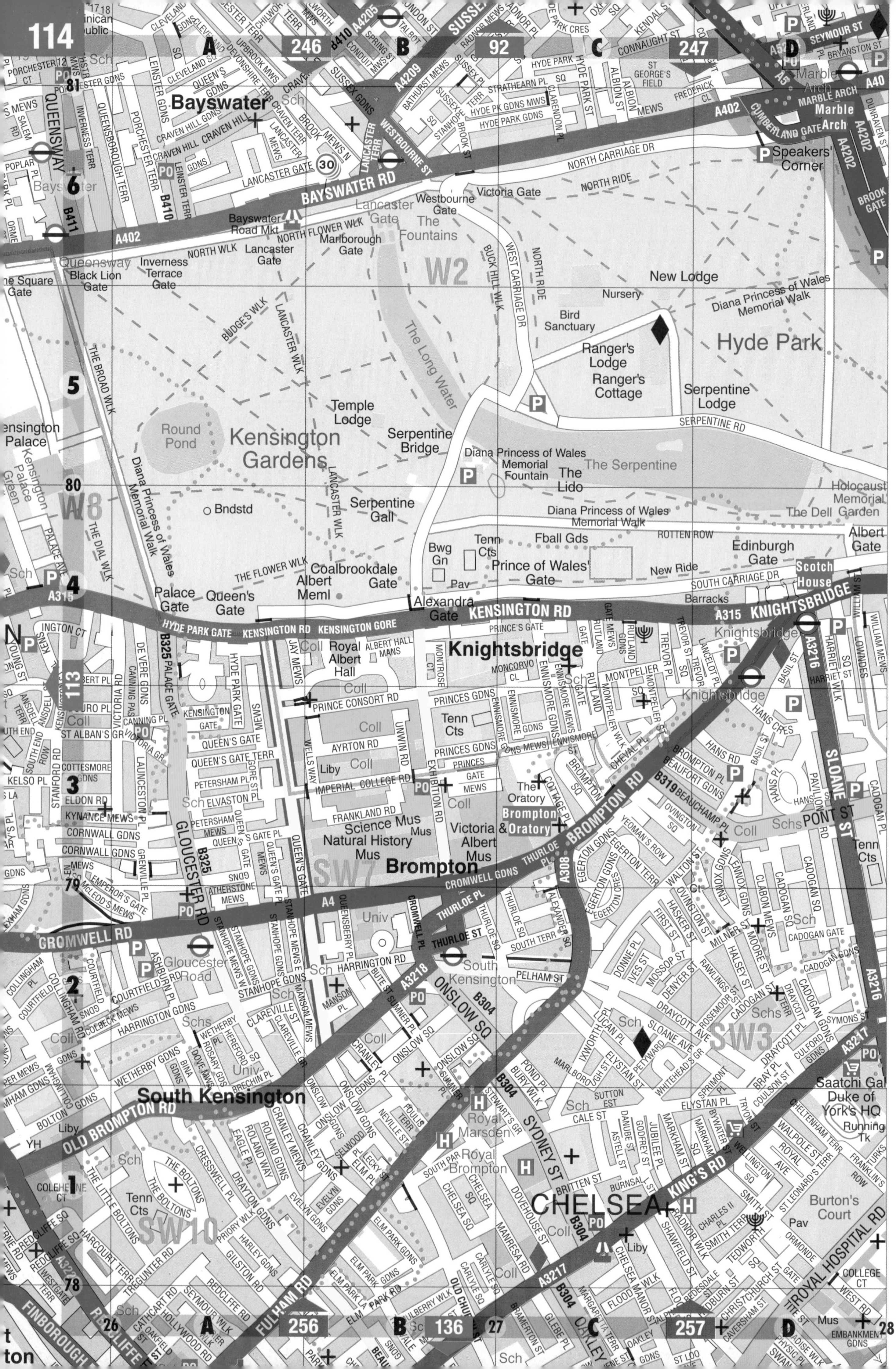
A
B
C
D
246
92
247
6
5
4
3
2
1
Bayswater
QUEENSWAY
BAYSWATER RD
A402
Lancaster Gate
Marble Arch
MARBLE ARCH
Speakers' Corner
NORTH CARRIAGE DR
NORTH RIDE
Victoria Gate
Westbourne Gate
The Fountains
W2
Hyde Park
New Lodge
Nursery
Bird Sanctuary
Ranger's Lodge
Ranger's Cottage
Serpentine Lodge
SERPENTINE RD
The Long Water
Kensington Gardens
Round Pond
Kensington Palace
Temple Lodge
Serpentine Bridge
Diana Princess of Wales Memorial Fountain
The Serpentine
The Lido
Serpentine Gall
Holocaust Memorial Garden
The Dell
Diana Princess of Wales Memorial Walk
ROTTEN ROW
Albert Gate
Edinburgh Gate
Prince of Wales' Gate
Alexandra Gate
Albert Meml
Coalbrookdale Gate
Palace Gate
Queen's Gate
KENSINGTON RD
KNIGHTSBRIDGE
Knightsbridge
KENSINGTON GORE
HYDE PARK GATE
Royal Albert Hall
PRINCE CONSORT RD
IMPERIAL COLLEGE RD
Science Mus
Natural History Mus
Victoria Albert Mus
Brompton Oratory
Brompton
BROMPTON RD
SW7
CROMWELL RD
CROMWELL GDNS
GLOUCESTER RD
Gloucester Road
South Kensington
ONSLOW SQ
OLD BROMPTON RD
SLOANE ST
PONT ST
SW3
SYDNEY ST
KING'S RD
CHELSEA
Royal Marsden
Royal Brompton
FULHAM RD
SW10
THE BOLTONS
Saatchi Gal
Duke of York's HQ
Burton's Court
ROYAL HOSPITAL RD
FINBOROUGH
A
B
C
D
256
136
257
26
27
28

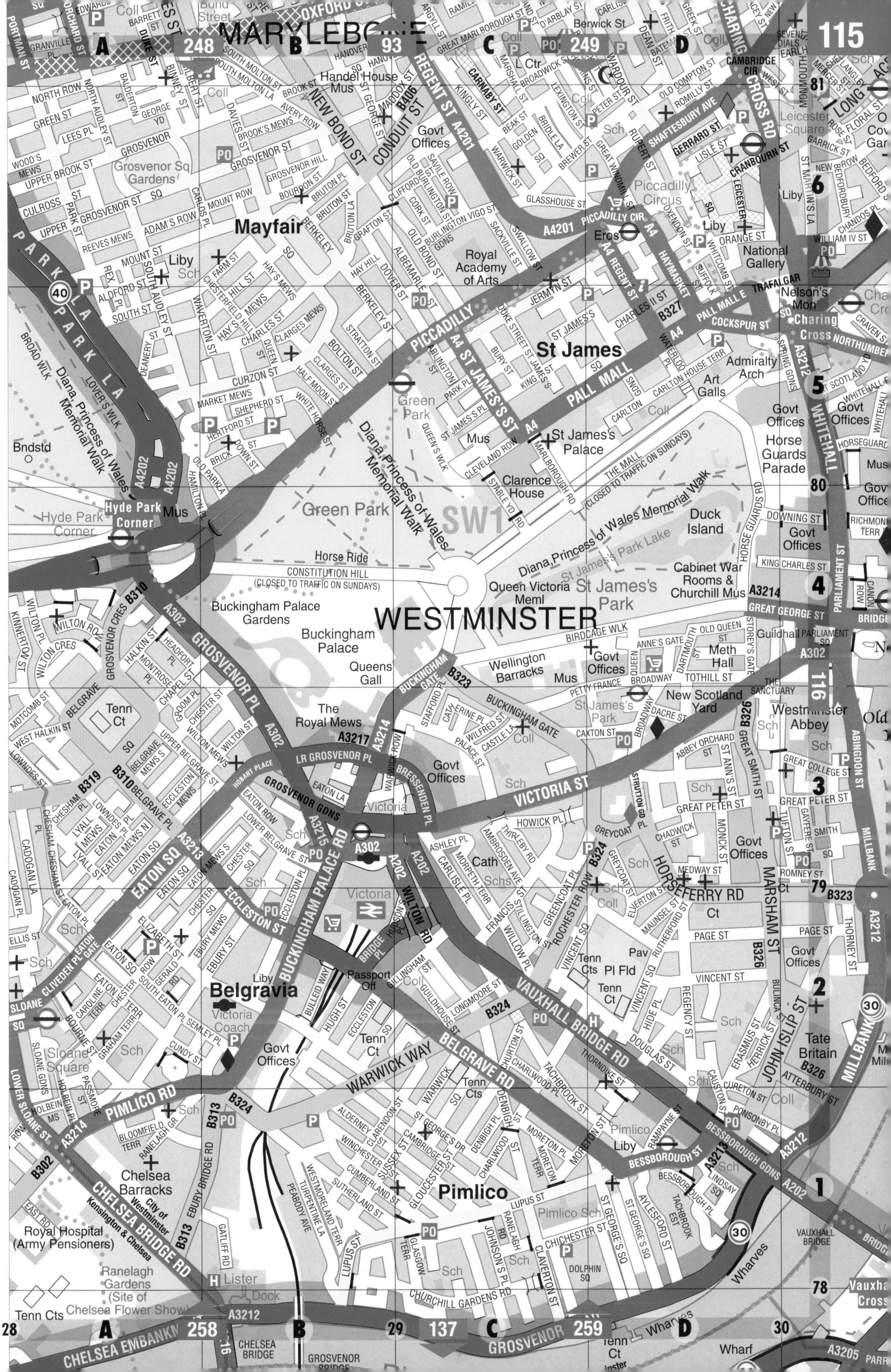
MARYLEBONE
248
93
249
A
B
C
D
Mayfair
St James
WESTMINSTER
Belgravia
Pimlico
SW1
OXFORD ST
REGENT ST A4201
NEW BOND ST
CONDUIT ST
CARNABY ST
Berwick St
SHAFTESBURY AVE
CHARING CROSS RD
CAMBRIDGE CIR
Leicester Square
GERRARD ST
CRANBOURN ST
LONG ACRE
Handel House Mus
Govt Offices
Grosvenor Sq Gardens
GROSVENOR ST
UPPER BROOK ST
NORTH ROW
GREEN ST
MOUNT ST
CURZON ST
PICCADILLY
Piccadilly Circus
PICCADILLY CIR
Eros
Royal Academy of Arts
National Gallery
Nelson's Mon
TRAFALGAR
Charing Cross
PALL MALL E
COCKSPUR ST
HAYMARKET
PALL MALL
JERMYN ST
ST JAMES'S ST
Green Park
Admiralty Arch
Art Galls
WHITEHALL
Horse Guards Parade
St James's Palace
Clarence House
THE MALL (CLOSED TO TRAFFIC ON SUNDAYS)
Diana, Princess of Wales Memorial Walk
Duck Island
St James's Park Lake
Cabinet War Rooms & Churchill Mus
St James's Park
Queen Victoria Meml
Hyde Park Corner
PARK LA
Bndstd
Horse Ride
CONSTITUTION HILL (CLOSED TO TRAFFIC ON SUNDAYS)
Buckingham Palace Gardens
Buckingham Palace
Queens Gall
The Royal Mews
Wellington Barracks
BIRDCAGE WLK
New Scotland Yard
Westminster Abbey
PARLIAMENT ST
GREAT GEORGE ST
BRIDGE ST
Guildhall
GROSVENOR PL
VICTORIA ST
BUCKINGHAM PALACE RD
Victoria
WILTON RD
VAUXHALL BRIDGE RD
HORSEFERRY RD
MARSHAM ST
Cath
EATON SQ
ECCLESTON ST
Sloane Square
SLOANE SQ
LOWER SLOANE ST
PIMLICO RD
WARWICK WAY
BELGRAVE RD
Victoria Coach
Passport Off
Tate Britain
MILLBANK
JOHN ISLIP ST
Chelsea Barracks
Royal Hospital (Army Pensioners)
Ranelagh Gardens (Site of Chelsea Flower Show)
CHELSEA BRIDGE RD
Lister
Dock
CHELSEA EMBANKMENT
GROSVENOR RD
Wharves
Wharf
VAUXHALL BRIDGE
CHURCHILL GARDENS RD
LUPUS ST
Pimlico Sch
BESSBOROUGH ST
City of Westminster
Kensington & Chelsea
Tenn Cts
28
A
258
B
29
137
C
259
D
30
116
81
80
79
78
6
5
4
3
2
1

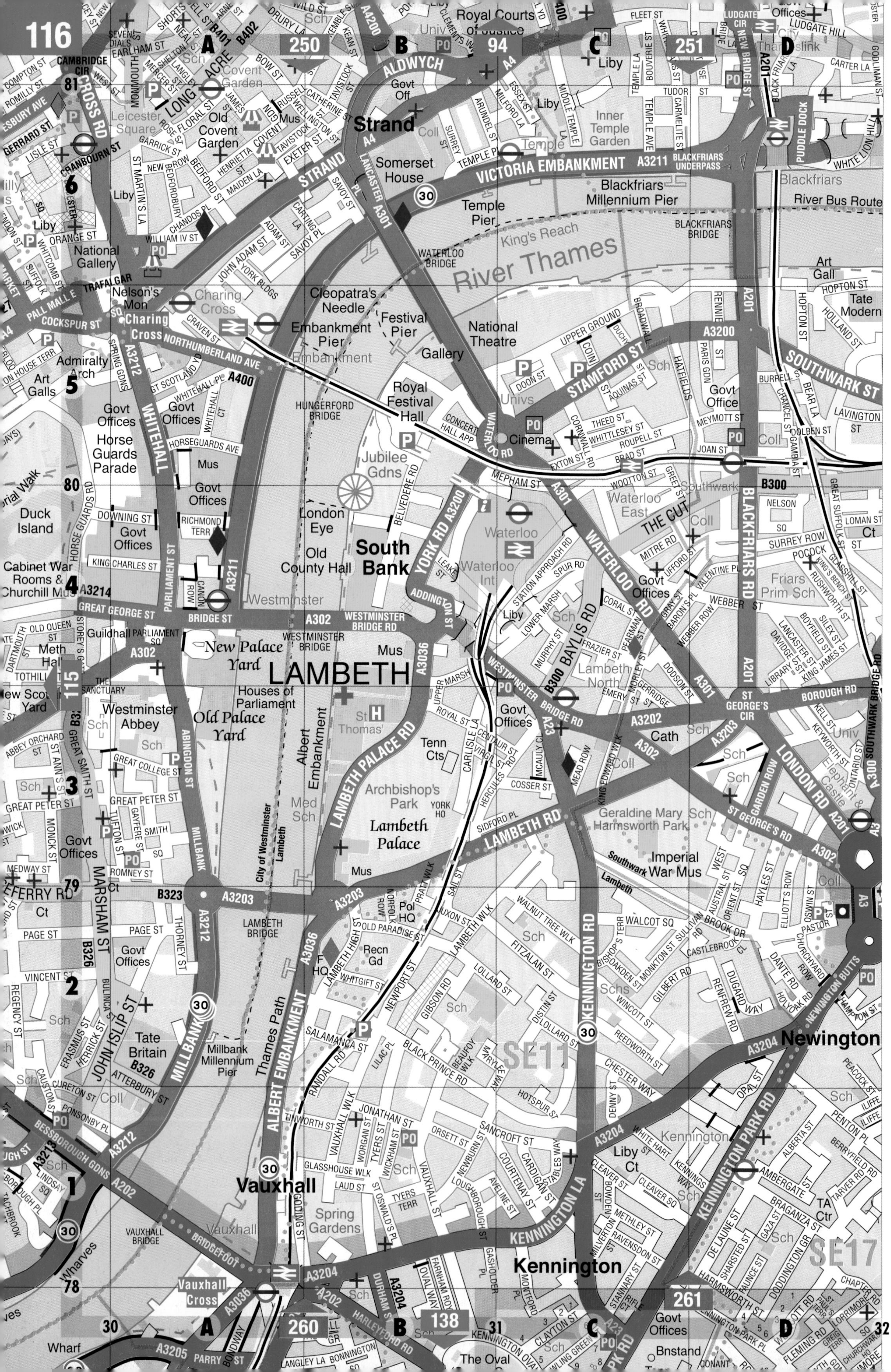
A
B
C
D
250
94
251
Royal Courts of Justice
Aldwych
Strand
Long Acre
Covent Garden
Old Covent Garden
Leicester Square
Cambridge Circ
Charing Cross Rd
Cranbourn St
Somerset House
Victoria Embankment
Blackfriars Underpass
Blackfriars
Blackfriars Millennium Pier
River Bus Route
Blackfriars Bridge
Temple Pier
Inner Temple Garden
King's Reach
River Thames
Waterloo Bridge
National Gallery
Trafalgar Sq
Nelson's Mon
Charing Cross
Pall Mall E
Cockspur St
Northumberland Ave
Cleopatra's Needle
Embankment Pier
Embankment
Festival Pier
National Theatre
Gallery
Stamford St
Upper Ground
Art Gall
Tate Modern
Southwark St
Admiralty Arch
Art Galls
Whitehall
Govt Offices
Horse Guards Parade
Hungerford Bridge
Royal Festival Hall
Jubilee Gdns
London Eye
South Bank
Old County Hall
York Rd
Waterloo
Waterloo East
The Cut
Blackfriars Rd
Southwark
Duck Island
Horse Guards Rd
Cabinet War Rooms & Churchill Mus
Downing St
King Charles St
Great George St
Bridge St
Westminster
Westminster Bridge Rd
Westminster Bridge
New Palace Yard
Lambeth
Houses of Parliament
Old Palace Yard
Westminster Abbey
Guildhall
Parliament Sq
New Scotland Yard
Abingdon St
Albert Embankment
St Thomas'
Lambeth Palace Rd
Archbishop's Park
Lambeth Palace
Baylis Rd
Waterloo Rd
Lambeth North
St George's Cir
Borough Rd
London Rd
Elephant & Castle
Geraldine Mary Harmsworth Park
Imperial War Mus
Lambeth Rd
Kennington Rd
Millbank
Marsham St
Horseferry Rd
Lambeth Bridge
Tate Britain
Millbank Millennium Pier
Thames Path
John Islip St
Vauxhall
Vauxhall Bridge
Vauxhall Cross
Bessborough Gdns
Spring Gardens
Kennington Ln
Kennington
Kennington Park Rd
Newington
Newington Butts
SE11
SE17
Wharves
Harleyford Rd
The Oval
115
260
138
261
30
31
32
1
2
3
4
5
6
78
79
80
81

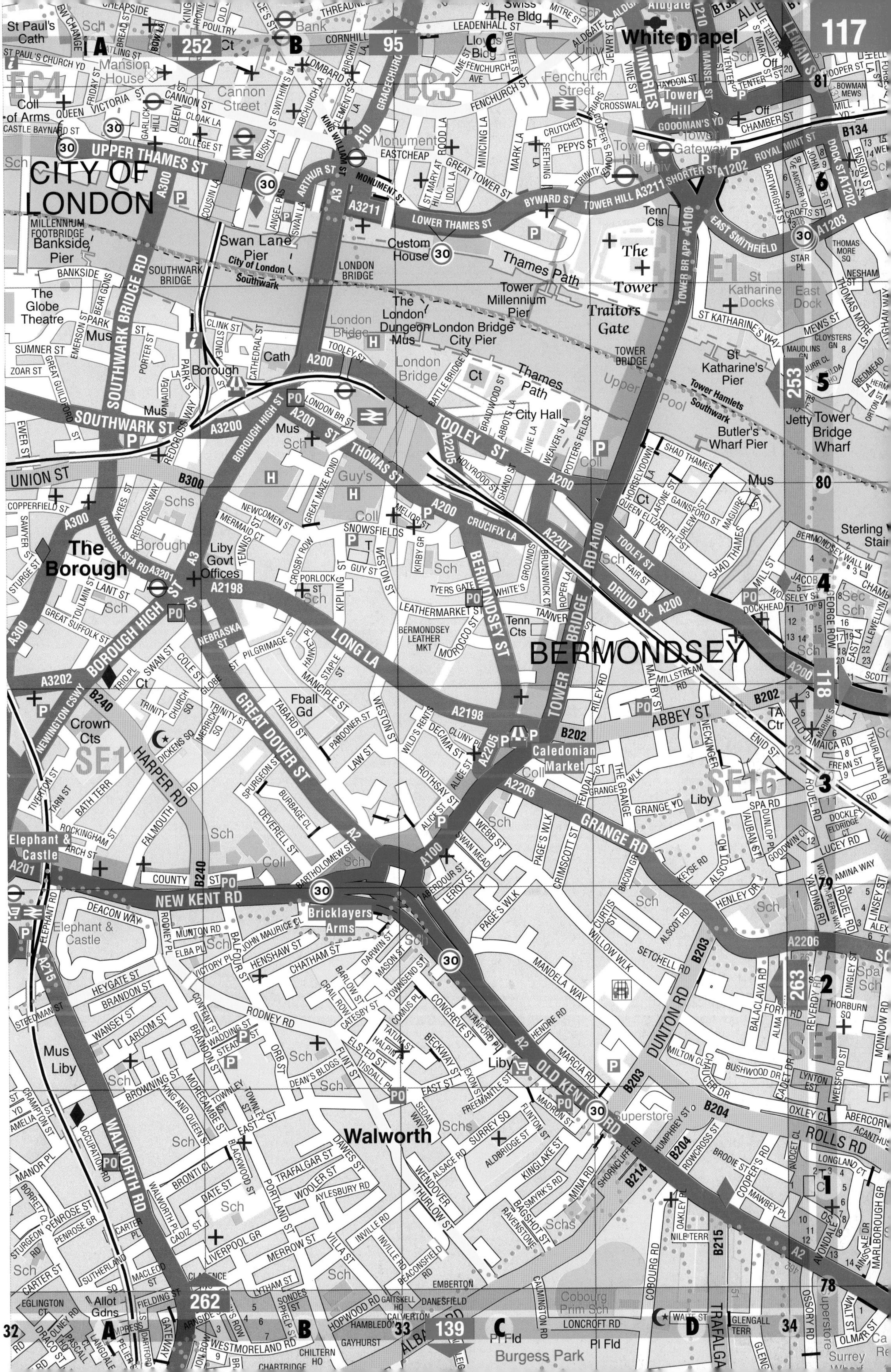
A
B
C
D
252
95
St Paul's Cath
Mansion House
Cannon Street
EC4
EC3
Whitechapel
Fenchurch Street
Tower Hill
Tower Gateway
CITY OF LONDON
UPPER THAMES ST
LOWER THAMES ST
MILLENNIUM FOOTBRIDGE
Bankside Pier
Swan Lane Pier
City of London
Southwark
LONDON BRIDGE
SOUTHWARK BRIDGE
Custom House
Monument
EASTCHEAP
GREAT TOWER ST
BYWARD ST
TOWER HILL
Thames Path
The Tower
Traitors Gate
Tower Millennium Pier
The London Dungeon Mus
London Bridge City Pier
TOWER BRIDGE
The Globe Theatre
SUMNER ST
ZOAR ST
Borough
Cath
London Bridge
City Hall
Upper Pool
Tower Hamlets
Southwark
St Katharine's Pier
Jetty
Tower Bridge Wharf
Butler's Wharf Pier
St Katharine Docks
East Dock
E1
253
SOUTHWARK ST
UNION ST
TOOLEY ST
BOROUGH HIGH ST
THOMAS ST
Guy's
CRUCIFIX LA
BERMONDSEY ST
The Borough
Liby Govt Offices
LONG LA
BERMONDSEY LEATHER MKT
BERMONDSEY
DRUID ST
ABBEY ST
GREAT DOVER ST
Fball Gd
Crown Cts
SE1
HARPER RD
Caledonian Market
GRANGE RD
SE16
118
Elephant & Castle
NEW KENT RD
Bricklayers Arms
COUNTY ST
DEACON WAY
MANDELA WAY
DUNTON RD
263
OLD KENT RD
WALWORTH RD
Walworth
Superstore
ROLLS RD
262
139
Cobourg Prim Sch
Burgess Park
Pl Fld
LONCROFT RD
GLENGALL TERR
TRAFALGAR
32
33
34
78
79
80
81
1
2
3
4
5
6

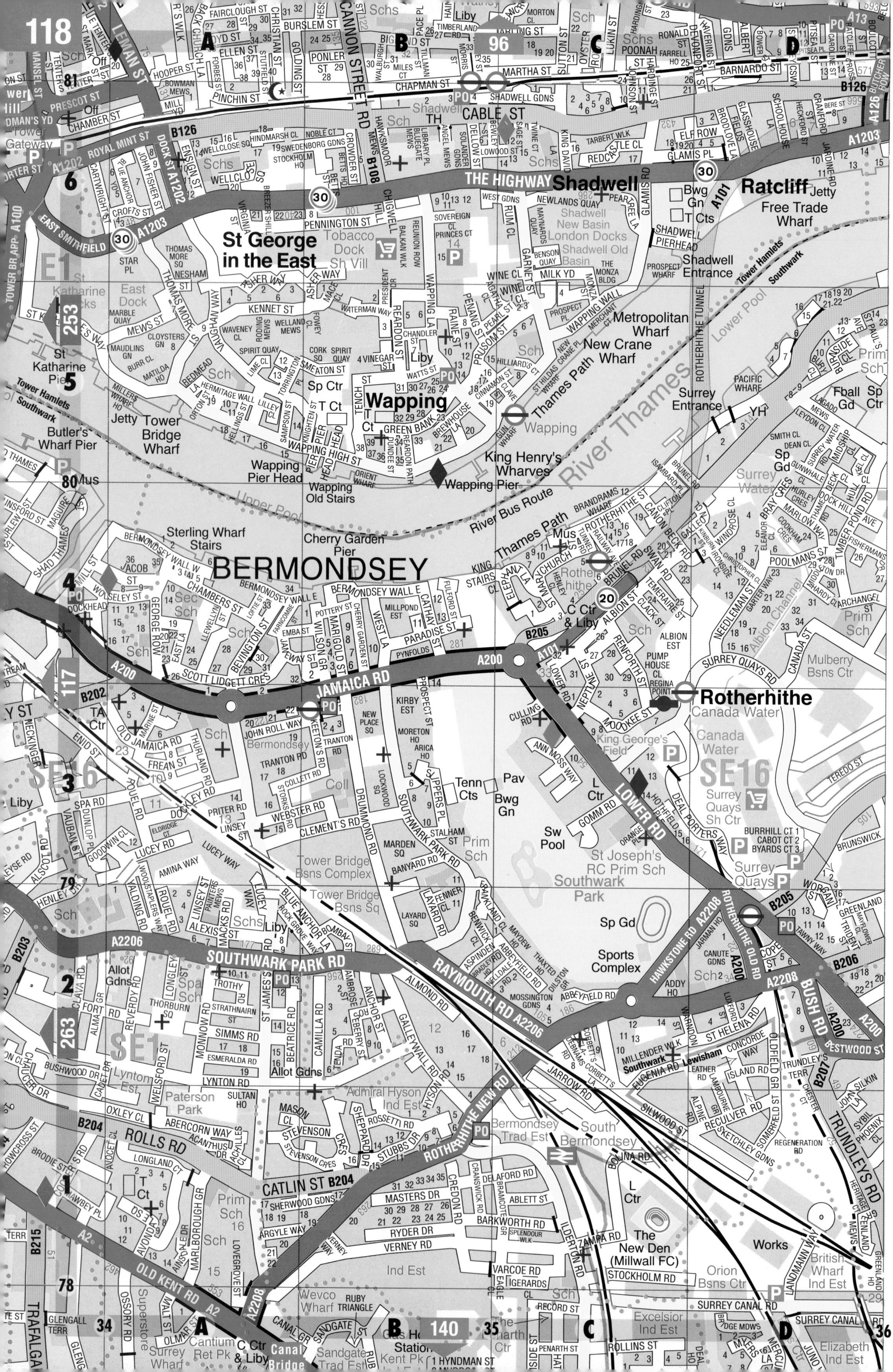
96
St George in the East
Shadwell
Ratcliff
Free Trade Wharf
THE HIGHWAY
CABLE ST
CANNON STREET RD
ROYAL MINT ST
EAST SMITHFIELD
Tobacco Dock
Shadwell Basin
London Docks
Wapping
WAPPING HIGH ST
WAPPING LA
Metropolitan Wharf
New Crane Wharf
Thames Path
River Thames
Lower Pool
Upper Pool
River Bus Route
Wapping Pier
King Henry's Wharves
Tower Bridge Wharf
Butler's Wharf Pier
St Katharine Pier
Sterling Whart Stairs
Cherry Garden Pier
BERMONDSEY
JAMAICA RD
LOWER RD
Rotherhithe
Canada Water
Surrey Quays Sh Ctr
Southwark Park
Sports Complex
SOUTHWARK PARK RD
RAYMOUTH RD
ROTHERHITHE NEW RD
Tower Bridge Bsns Complex
South Bermondsey
The New Den (Millwall FC)
OLD KENT RD
ROLLS RD
CATLIN ST
SE16
SE1
E1
Tower Hamlets
Southwark
Lewisham
A
B
C
D
1
2
3
4
5
6
34
35
36
117
140
253
263

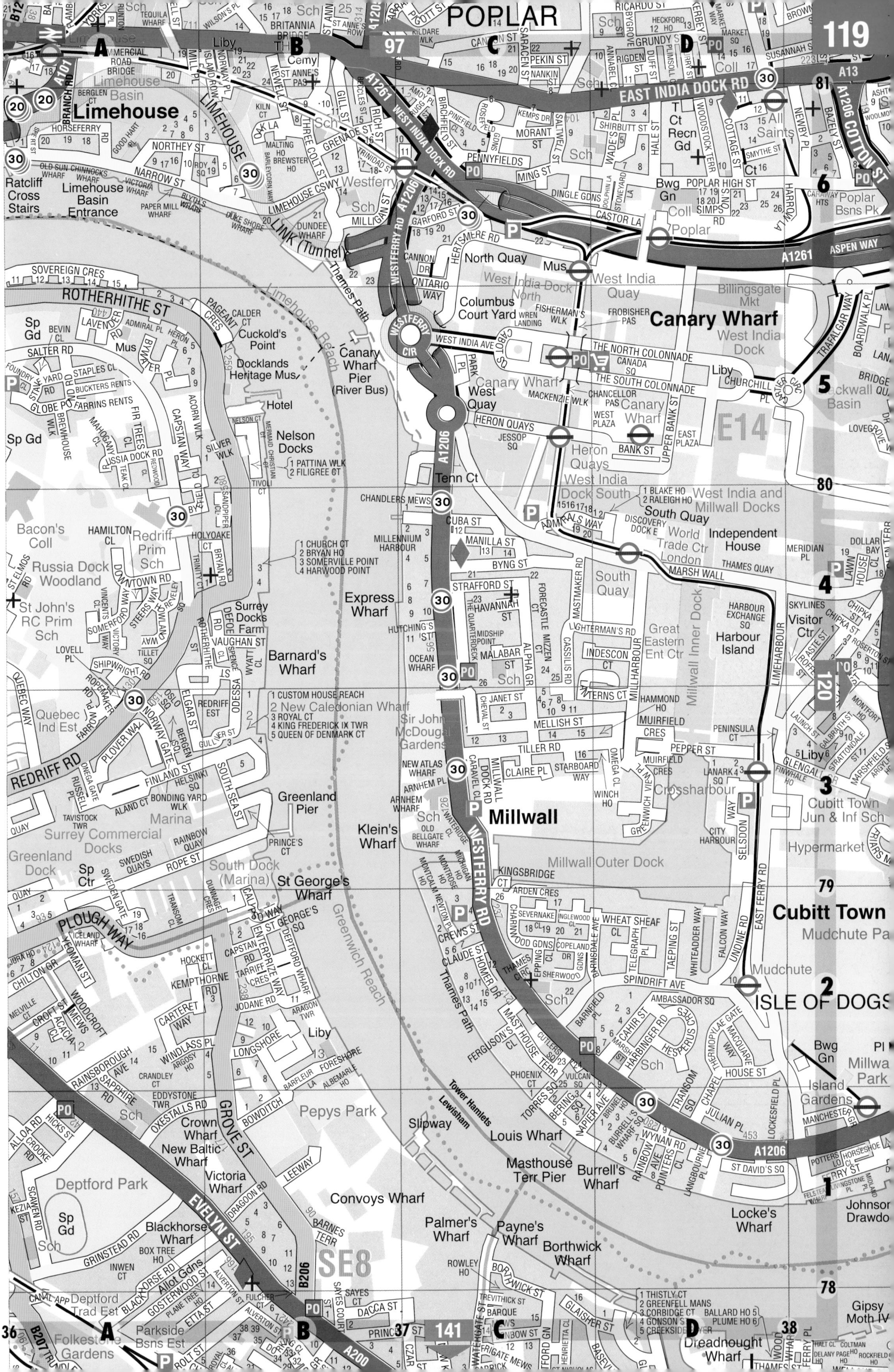
POPLAR
Limehouse
Limehouse Basin
Ratcliff Cross Stairs
Limehouse Basin Entrance
LIMEHOUSE LINK (Tunnel)
EAST INDIA DOCK RD
WEST INDIA DOCK RD
WESTFERRY RD
WESTFERRY CIR
POPLAR HIGH ST
ASPEN WAY
North Quay
West India Quay
Canary Wharf
Billingsgate Mkt
West India Dock
Columbus Court Yard
Canary Wharf Pier (River Bus)
Docklands Heritage Mus
Cuckold's Point
Limehouse Reach
ROTHERHITHE ST
SALTER RD
Nelson Docks
Heron Quays
West India Dock South
South Quay
Independent House
World Trade Ctr London
MARSH WALL
Harbour Island
Great Eastern Ent Ctr
Millwall Inner Dock
Express Wharf
Barnard's Wharf
Surrey Docks Farm
Russia Dock Woodland
Bacon's Coll
Redriff Prim Sch
St John's RC Prim Sch
Quebec Ind Est
REDRIFF RD
Surrey Commercial Docks
Greenland Dock
Greenland Pier
South Dock (Marina)
St George's Wharf
Klein's Wharf
Sir John McDougal Gardens
Millwall
Millwall Outer Dock
Crossharbour
Cubitt Town
Cubitt Town Jun & Inf Sch
Mudchute
ISLE OF DOGS
Island Gardens
Greenwich Reach
Thames Path
Louis Wharf
Masthouse Terr Pier
Burrell's Wharf
Locke's Wharf
Slipway
Pepys Park
Convoys Wharf
Palmer's Wharf
Payne's Wharf
Borthwick Wharf
Dreadnought Wharf
Crown Wharf
New Baltic Wharf
Victoria Wharf
Blackhorse Wharf
Deptford Park
EVELYN ST
GROVE ST
PLOUGH WAY
SE8
E14
Deptford Trad Est
Parkside Bsns Est
Folkestone Gardens
Tower Hamlets
Lewisham
A1261
A1206
A13
A200
B206
97
141
120

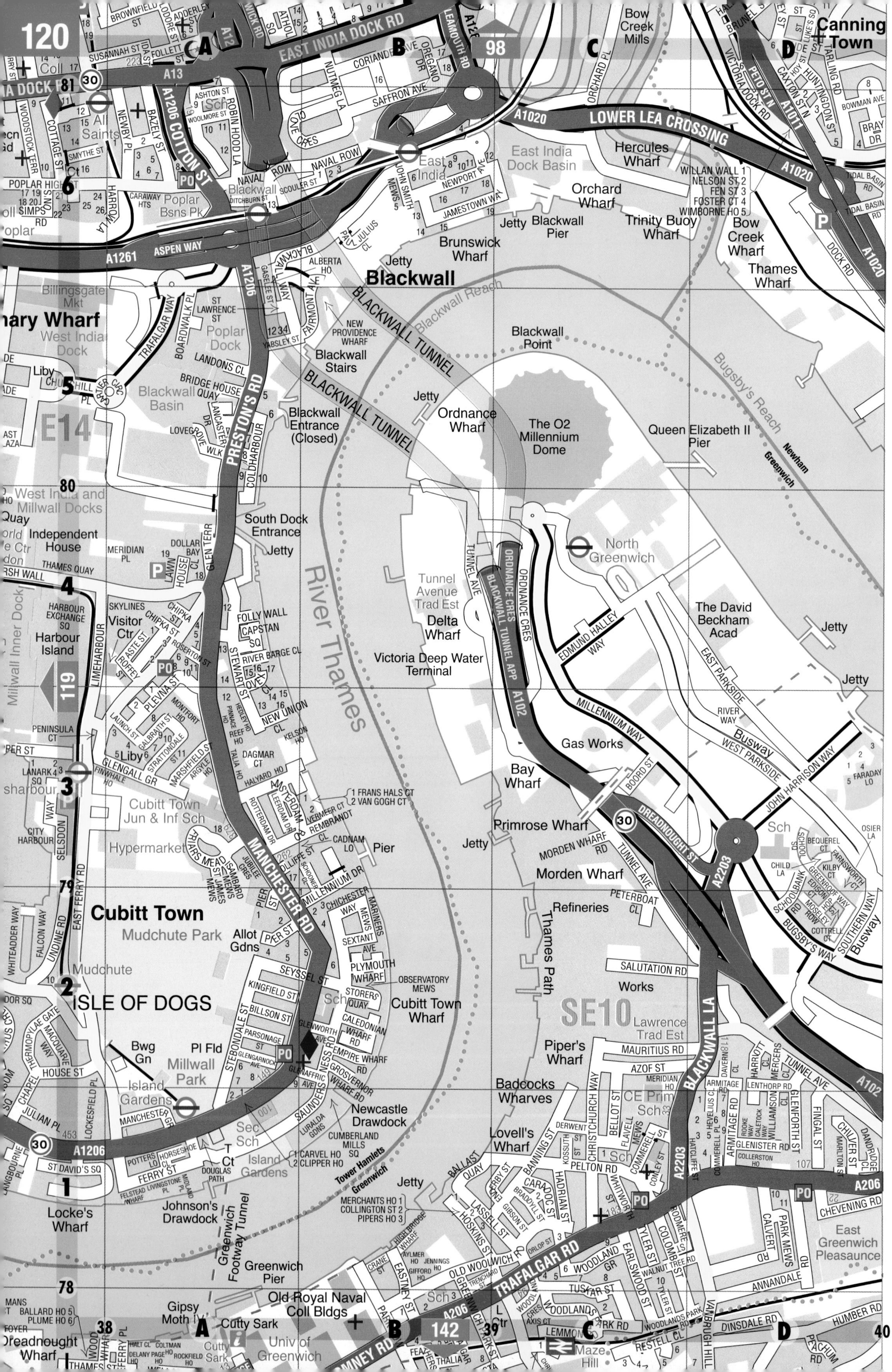
EAST INDIA DOCK RD
98
Bow Creek Mills
Canning Town
A B C D
LOWER LEA CROSSING
A1020
Hercules Wharf
East India Dock Basin
Orchard Wharf
Trinity Buoy Wharf
Bow Creek Wharf
Thames Wharf
Blackwall Pier
Brunswick Wharf
Jetty
Blackwall
East India
Poplar Bsns Pk
All Saints
Poplar
ASPEN WAY
A1261
A1206
COTTON ST
LEAMOUTH RD
SAFFRON AVE
NAVAL ROW
NEWPORT AVE
JAMESTOWN WAY
Blackwall Reach
BLACKWALL TUNNEL
Billingsgate Mkt
Canary Wharf
West India Dock
Poplar Dock
Blackwall Basin
Blackwall Stairs
Blackwall Entrance (Closed)
Blackwall Point
Bugsby's Reach
Ordnance Wharf
The O2 Millennium Dome
Queen Elizabeth II Pier
Newham
Greenwich
E14
PRESTON'S RD
TRAFALGAR WAY
West India and Millwall Docks
Independent House
South Dock Entrance
River Thames
North Greenwich
Tunnel Avenue Trad Est
Delta Wharf
The David Beckham Acad
Victoria Deep Water Terminal
BLACKWALL TUNNEL APP
A102
EDMUND HALLEY WAY
MILLENNIUM WAY
EAST PARKSIDE
WEST PARKSIDE
JOHN HARRISON WAY
Busway
Gas Works
Bay Wharf
Primrose Wharf
Harbour Island
Visitor Ctr
119
LIMEHARBOUR
Cubitt Town Jun & Inf Sch
Hypermarket
MANCHESTER RD
Cubitt Town
Mudchute Park
Mudchute
ISLE OF DOGS
Allot Gdns
Morden Wharf
Refineries
Thames Path
DREADNOUGHT ST
A2203
Works
SE10
Lawrence Trad Est
Piper's Wharf
Badcocks Wharves
Lovell's Wharf
BLACKWALL LA
Cubitt Town Wharf
Newcastle Drawdock
Millwall Park
Island Gardens
Bwg Gn
Pl Fld
Johnson's Drawdock
Locke's Wharf
Greenwich Footway Tunnel
Greenwich Pier
Tower Hamlets
Old Royal Naval Coll Bldgs
Gipsy Moth IV
Cutty Sark
Univ of Greenwich
TRAFALGAR RD
A206
East Greenwich Pleasaunce
CHEVENING RD
WOODLAND GR
Maze Hill
142
38
39
40
78
79
80
81

A
B
C
D
99
Custom House
Custom House for ExCeL
Prince Regent
Royal Victoria
Connaught Rd
A112
A1020
Royal Albert
6
Dockside Rd
Victoria Dock Rd
Seagull La
Western Gateway
Hotel
Warehouse W
Royal Victoria Sq
1 Wood St
2 Betts Rd
3 Chauntler Cl
4 Sandstone La
ExCel Ex Ctr
Royal Victoria Dock
E16
Connaught Bridge
Festoon Way
Royal Albert Way
Lynx Way
Airport Rdbt
Royal Connaught Apts
London City Airport
Hartmann Rd
Camel Rd
5
Silvertown Way
North Woolwich Rd
Western Beach Apts
Hanover Ave
Fitzwilliam Mews
Southey Mews
Keats Ave
Fairfax Mews
Constable Ave
Southampton Mews
Portsmouth Mews
Wesley Ave
Evelyn Rd
Hanameel St
Boxley St
Fort St
Mill Rd
Prim Sch
Mill
Bell La
Burt Rd
Charles St
Oriental Rd
Ind Est
North Woolwich Rdbt
Thames Rd
Wards Wharf App
West Silvertown
Knights Rd
Bradfield Rd
Tenn Cts
Greenshields Ind Est
Silvertown
Barrier Point Rd
Pontoon Dock
Thames Barrier Park
Thames Road Ind Est
Thameside Ind Est
80
Kierbeck Bsns Complex
Lyle Park
Wharves
4
The Thames Barrier
Bugsby's Reach
Woolwich Reach
Newham
Greenwich
122
River Thames
Barrier Gdns Pier
Thames Barrier Visitor Ctr
Mirfield St
Eastmoor Pl
Faraday Way
Unity Way
Mast
Mellish Ind Est
Harrington Way
Bywater Ho
Reddings Ho
Warspite Rd
Bowater Rd
3
Howick Mans
Westminster Ind Est
Thames Path
Wharf
Riverside
GREENWICH
Anchorage Point Ind Est
Herringham Rd
New Lydenburg St
New Lydenburg Comm Est
Ashleigh Comm Est
Holgate St
Westmoor St
Eastmoor St
Penhall Rd
Aldington Ferranti
Siemens Rd
Swan Rd
Westfield St
Yateley St
A206
Kency Cl
Tamar
79
West Parkside
SE10
Peartree Way
Horn Link Way
Lombard Wall
SE7
Derrick Gdns
Atlas Gdns
Anchor & Hope La
VIP Trad Est
Meridian Trad Est
Lombard Trad Est
Stone Lake Ind Pk
Ropery Bsns Pk
Stone Lake Ret Pk
Brocklebank Road Ind Est
Brocklebank Rd
Willoughby Way
Bugsby's Way
Tenn Cts
2
Green Chain Wlk
Maryon Park
Trinity Ct
New Charlton
Charlton Gate Bsns Pk
Greenwich Sh Pk
Peninsular Park Rd
Gallions Rd
Hickin Cl
Prentiss Ct
Pound Park Rd
Woodland Terr
Horn La
Aldeburgh Pl
Angerstein Bsns Pk
Superstore
Maritime Ind Est
Woolwich Rd
Gallon Cl
Harvey Gdns
Thorntree Inf Sch
Hasted Rd
Coxmount Rd
Ramac Ind Est
Ramac Way
Felltram Way
Alderburgh St
Fearon St
Barney Cl
Charlton
Troughton Rd
Reynolah Gdns
The Valley (Charlton Athletic FC)
Wolfe Cres
Thorntree Rd
Heathwood Gdns
Kinveachy Gdns
Denham St
Liby
Floyd Rd
Valley Gr
Sam Bartram Cl
Charlton La
Maryon Wilson Park
1
Farmdale Rd
Fairthorn Rd
Rainton Rd
Hardman Rd
Dupree Rd
Gurdon Rd
Rathmore Rd
Delafield Rd
Sundorne Rd
Lansdowne Mews
Kemsing Rd
Combedale Rd
Halstow Rd
Sch
Swallowfield Rd
Priolo Rd
Wellington Gdns
Charlton Church La
Lansdowne Workshops
1 Plane Tree Ho
2 Valleyside
3 St Paul's Cl
McCall Cres
Flamsteed Rd
Ormiston Rd
Westcombe Park
Station Cres
SE3
Bernard Ashley Dr
Fossdene Rd
Inverine Rd
Calydon Rd
Prim Sch
Nadine St
The Heights
Lansdowne La
Beacham Cl
78
A102
The Birches
Victoria Way
Elliscombe Rd
Warren Ct
Fred Styles Ho
Joyce Page Cl
Fletching Rd
Fairfield Gr
St Alfege Rd
Guild Rd
B210
40
41
42
143
Mycenae Rd
Westcombe Hill
Eastcombe Ave
Sandtoft Rd
Eversley Rd
Tallis Gr
Allot Gdns
The Village
Mulberry Cl
Charlton Park Rd
Pav
Adamson Rd
Hooper Rd
Boreham Ave
Elbury Dr
Coolfin Rd
Murray Sq
Victoria Dock Rd
Mason Cl
Pollard Cl
Monk Dr
Appleby Rd
Munday Rd
Recn Gd
Bridgeland Rd
Vandome Cl
Leslie Rd
Ethel Rd
Throckmorten Rd
Gresham Rd
Cundy Rd
Anchor Ho
Alnwick Rd
Prince of Wales Rd
Felsted Rd
Royal Rd
Leyes Rd
Com Sch
Allot Gdns
Andover Ave
Jasper Rd
Richard House Dr
Calverton Prim Sch
81

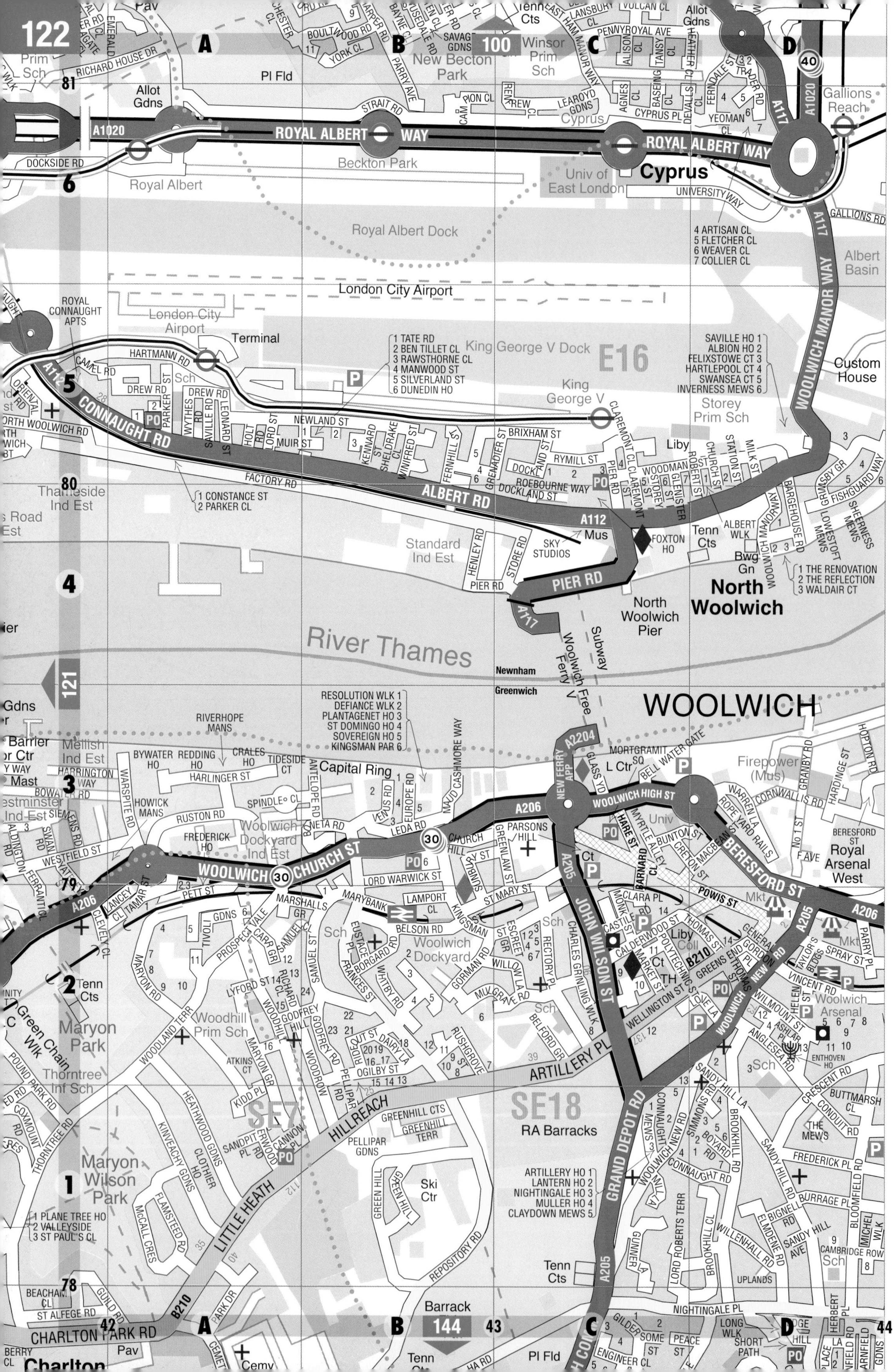

A
B
C
D
100
40
81
80
79
78
6
5
4
3
2
1
121
144
42
43
44
Pl Fld
Allot Gdns
Prim Sch
RICHARD HOUSE DR
EMERALD
BOULTWOOD RD
YORK CL
PARRY AVE
SAVAGE GDNS
New Becton Park
Tenn Cts
Winsor Prim Sch
EAST HAM MANOR WAY
LANSBURY
VULCAN CL
PENNYROYAL AVE
ALISON CL
TANSY CL
HEATHER CL
BASEING CL
AGNES CL
DEVALLS CL
CYPRUS PL
LEAROYD GDNS
Cypress
REW
CAM
PION CL
STRAIT RD
FERNDALE ST
TRADER RD
YEOMAN CL
Gallions Reach
A1020
A117
ROYAL ALBERT WAY
DOCKSIDE RD
Royal Albert
Beckton Park
Univ of East London
Cyprus
UNIVERSITY WAY
GALLIONS RD
4 ARTISAN CL
5 FLETCHER CL
6 WEAVER CL
7 COLLIER CL
Royal Albert Dock
Albert Basin
London City Airport
ROYAL CONNAUGHT APTS
London City Airport
Terminal
HARTMANN RD
CAMEL RD
DREW RD
PARKER ST
Sch
1 TATE RD
2 BEN TILLETT CL
3 RAWSTHORNE CL
4 MANWOOD ST
5 SILVERLAND ST
6 DUNEDIN HO
King George V Dock
E16
King George V
SAVILLE HO 1
ALBION HO 2
FELIXSTOWE CT 3
HARTLEPOOL CT 4
SWANSEA CT 5
INVERNESS MEWS 6
Custom House
WOOLWICH MANOR WAY
Storey Prim Sch
CONNAUGHT RD
A112
ORIENTAL RD
NORTH WOOLWICH RD
WYTHES RD
SAVILLE RD
LEONARD ST
HOLT RD
LORD ST
NEWLAND ST
MUIR ST
KENNARD ST
SHELDRAKE CL
WINIFRED ST
FERNHILL ST
GRENADIER ST
BRIXHAM ST
DOCKLAND ST
RYMILL ST
ROEBOURNE WAY
DOCKLAND ST
PIER RD
CLAREMONT CL
CLAREMONT ST
WOODMAN ST
STOREY ST
GLENISTER ST
ROBERTS ST
CHURCH ST
STATION ST
MILK ST
Liby
BARGEHOUSE RD
GRIMSBY GR
FISHGUARD WAY
LOWESTOFT MEWS
SHEERNESS MEWS
WOOLWICH MANORWAY
FACTORY RD
ALBERT RD
Thameside Ind Est
1 CONSTANCE ST
2 PARKER CL
Standard Ind Est
HENLEY RD
STORE RD
SKY STUDIOS
Mus
FOXTON HO
Tenn Cts
ALBERT WLK
Bwg Gn
1 THE RENOVATION
2 THE REFLECTION
3 WALDAIR CT
PIER RD
North Woolwich Pier
North Woolwich
Subway
Woolwich Free Ferry
River Thames
Newnham
Greenwich
WOOLWICH
RESOLUTION WLK 1
DEFIANCE WLK 2
PLANTAGENET HO 3
ST DOMINGO HO 4
SOVEREIGN HO 5
KINGSMAN PAR 6
RIVERHOPE MANS
Gdns
Barrier
Mellish Ind Est
BYWATER HO
REDDING HO
CRALES HO
TIDESIDE CT
HARRINGTON WAY
HARLINGER ST
Capital Ring
Mast
BOWATER RD
WARSPITE RD
HOWICK MANS
SPINDLE CL
ANTELOPE RD
VENUS RD
EUROPE RD
MAUD CASHMORE WAY
RUSTON RD
FREDERICK HO
Woolwich Dockyard Ind Est
BONETA RD
LEDA RD
A2204
NEW FERRY APP
GLASS YD
MORTGRAMIT SQ
L Ctr
BELL WATER GATE
Firepower (Mus)
GRANBY RD
HARDINGE ST
HOPTON RD
WOOLWICH HIGH ST
WARREN LA
ROPE YARD RAILS
CORNWALL IS RD
No 1 ST
F AVE
BERESFORD ST
Royal Arsenal West
A206
WESTFIELD ST
WOOLWICH CHURCH ST
CHURCH HILL
PARSONS HILL
GREENLAW ST
SUNBURY ST
HARE ST
BARNARD CL
MYRTLE ALLEY
Univ
BUNTON ST
CRETON ST
MACBEAN ST
POWIS ST
Mkt
SIEMENS RD
SWAN RD
ALDINGTON RD
FERRANTI CL
LANCEY CL
TAMAR ST
PETT ST
MARSHALLS GR
LORD WARWICK ST
MARYBANK
LAMPORT CL
KINGSMAN ST
ST MARY ST
BELSON RD
ESCREET GR
RECTORY PL
JOHN WILSON ST
CLARA PL
MONK ST
CASTILE RD
CALDERWOOD ST
THOMAS ST
POLYTECHNIC ST
Liby
Coll
B210
Ct
TH
GREENS END
GENERAL GORDON PL
NEW RD
TAYLOR'S BLDGS
SPRAY ST
PARRY PL
VINCENT RD
HELEN ST
WILMOUNT ST
Woolwich Arsenal
ENTHOVEN HO
ASHLAR PL
ANGLESEA RD
CLEVELY CL
TIVOLI GDNS
PROSPECT VALE
CARR GR
SAMUEL CL
SAMUEL ST
EUSTACE PL
BORGARD RD
FRANCES ST
Woolwich Dockyard
GORMAN RD
WILLOW LA
MULGRAVE RD
CHARLES GRINLING WLK
WELLINGTON ST
LOVE LA
WOOLWICH NEW RD
MARYON RD
Tenn Cts
LYFORD ST
RICHARD CL
WOODHILL
GODFREY HILL
GODFREY RD
WHITBY RD
DAIRY LA
RIDOUT ST
OGILBY ST
RUSHGROVE ST
BELFORD GR
ARTILLERY PL
Maryon Park
Green Chain Wlk
POUND PARK RD
COXMOUNT RD
Thorntree Inf Sch
WOODLAND TERR
Woodhill Prim Sch
MARYON GR
ATKINS CT
KIDD PL
WOODROW
PELLIPAR RD
HILLREACH
SE7
SE18
RA Barracks
GRAND DEPOT RD
A205
CONNAUGHT MEWS
SIMMONS RD
SANDY HILL LA
BROOKHILL RD
BOYARD RD
CRESCENT RD
BUTTMARSH CL
CONDUIT RD
THE MEWS
FREDERICK PL
BLOOMFIELD RD
SANDY HILL RD
THORNTREE RD
HEATHWOOD GDNS
KINVEACHY GDNS
CLOTHIER HO
SANDPIT PL
ERWOOD RD
CANNON RD
GREENHILL CTS
GREENHILL TERR
PELLIPAR GDNS
Maryon Wilson Park
FLAMSTEED RD
McCALL CRES
LITTLE HEATH
GREEN HILL
Ski Ctr
REPOSITORY RD
ARTILLERY HO 1
LANTERN HO 2
NIGHTINGALE HO 3
MULLER HO 4
CLAYDOWN MEWS 5
CONNAUGHT RD
MILL LA
GUNNER LA
LORD ROBERTS TERR
BROOKHILL CL
WILLENHALL RD
ELMDENE RD
BIGNELL RD
BURRAGE PL
SANDY HILL AVE
CAMBRIDGE ROW
MICHEL WLK
Sch
UPLANDS
1 PLANE TREE HO
2 VALLEYSIDE
3 ST PAUL'S CL
BEACHAM CL
ST ALFEGE RD
GUILD RD
CHARLTON PARK RD
PARK DR
Barrack
Tenn Cts
NIGHTINGALE PL
GILDERSOME ST
PEACE ST
ENGINEER CL
LONG WLK
SHORT PATH
HERBERT PL
Pl Fld
Cemy
Pav
Charlton
BERRY CL

A
B
101
C
D
81
E6
Margaret or
Tripcock Ness
Mast
Newham
Greenwich
Gallions Reach
Thamesmead
Sh Ctr
6
NAVIGATION CT
EBB CT
SE28
River Thames
E16
BRIDGE HO
DEFENCE CL
HILL HO
MURRAY CL
WARRIOR CL
TUMP HO
BAILEY CL
TOR GR
1 MARTINS WLK
2 MARTINS PL
3 SHEPHERDS LA
4 CROWFOOT CL
5 LONGMARSH LA
HIGH TOR VIEW
BARNHAM DR
WATERSIDE CL
BARNHAM DR
GRASSHAVEN WAY
NEWMARSH RD
FLOTHAVEN CL
BIRCHDENE DR
SILVER BIRCH CL
LAKESIDE AVE
5
TRICORN HO 1
TIDEHAM HO 2
TRIDENT HO 3
STRAND HO 4
TIDESLEA PATH
MILES CL
MILES DR
MARTIN ST
HILL VIEW DR
TEASEL CRES
FOXGROVE PATH
1 HULL PL
2 SUNDERLAND POINT
3 INVERNESS MEWS
NARROW BOAT CL
MERBURY CL
BLUEBIRD WAY
DELISLE RD
MERBURY RD
NEW ACRES RD
BATTERY RD
MARATHON WAY
BELLERMINE CL
A2041
80
A2016
PRINCESS ALICE WAY
WARE POINT DR
RIDGE CL
BATTERY RD
KENTLEA RD
ANSON PL
FISHERMANS WLK
TUGBOAT ST
THAMES REACH
WESTERN WAY
Cobalt
4
HARNESS RD
NATHAN WAY
TIDESLEA TWR 1
SARK TWR 2
GRANARY MANS 3
BENDISH POINT 4
TIDELOCK HO
CUMBERLAND HO
GALLIONS VIEW RD
GADWALL WAY
NUTHATCH GDNS
WREN PATH
Ct
MARLBOROUGH RD
EREBUS DR
CAMELOT CL
LIVESEY CL
TEMPLE CL
PIER WAY
HARRIER MEWS
REDWING PATH
WIDGEON PATH
AVOCET MEWS
WHINCHAT RD
GOLDFINCH RD
CHARLESMERE GDNS
HM Prison
Belmarsh
PURLAND RD
124
MERGANSER GDNS
Mast
ARGYLL RD
TUPPY ST
HARDINGE CRES
ARMSTRONG RD
CARRONADE PL
GOOSANDER WAY
GRIFFIN WAY
NATHAN WAY
KELLNER RD
WHITE HART AVE
3
CADOGAN RD
HASTINGS ST
ARSENAL WAY
ALLENBY RD
PETTACRE CL
BROADWATER RD
GARRICK DR
Heronsgate
Prim
Sch
Royal
Arsenal
East
BOUGHTON RD
West
Thamesmead
Bsns Pk
Sienna
St Thomas
a Beckett
RC Prim Sch
Allot
Gdns
Io
Ctr
Royal Arsenal
West
DUKE OF WELLINGTON AVE
CHAMBERLAIN CL
GARSIDE CL
A206 PETTMAN CRES
A2016
GRIFFIN MANOR WAY
HADDEN RD
Works
GUNNERY TERR
CORNWALLIS RD
SKEFFINGTON ST
SEYMOUR ST
TOM CRIBB RD
Gateway
Bsns Ctr
1 PASSFIELD HO
2 LENTON ST
3 FORELAND ST
Sports
Gd
Bwg
Gn
Tenn
Cts
79
NORTH RD
Plumstead
PLUMSTEAD RD
Coll
POLTHORNE GR
DAVE RAMSEY HO
GILL CT
BURRAGE GR
JESSUP CL
WALKER CL
MAXEY RD
SAMSON HO
INVERMORE PL
VILLAS RD
CLENDON WAY
WALMER TERR
Plumstead
HEVERHAM RD
REIDHAVEN RD
GUNNING ST
WHITE HART RD
BARTH MEWS
MARMADON RD
SE18
CHURCH MANOR WAY
BIRKDALE RD
2
ARTHUR GR
RICHMOND PL
OLIVER CT
ROBERT ST
SOUTHPORT RD
ELMLEY ST
ANN ST
MOUNT PLEASANT PL
ABERY ST
GARIBALDI ST
HARTVILLE RD
KENTMERE RD
BARTH RD
BANNOCKBURN RD
BALGOWAN ST
HYLTON ST
BROOKDENE RD
DAWSON CL
ABEL HO 1
MAYNARD HO 2
CROWN HO 3
GLYNDON RD
EARL RISE
RISE WAY
Sch
MINERAL ST
HECTOR ST
BEBBINGTON RD
GALLOSSON RD
OLD TRAMYARD
PO
PLUMSTEAD HIGH ST
Bannockburn
Prim Sch
BENARES RD
AMAR CT
CERES RD
AMARDEEP CT
ST NICHOLAS RD
CAMROSE ST
MANTON RD
MYRA ST
RUDDSTREET CL
BURRAGE RD
SANDBACH PL
SWETENHAM WLK
PATTISON WLK
VICARAGE RD
Sch
SOUTH RD
CONWAY RD
Liby &
Mus
STRANDFIELD CL
STRAND CL
SPERANZA ST
QUILTER ST
RAGLAN RD
GRIFFIN RD
COXWELL RD
INGLEDEW RD
LIFFLER RD
MIRIAM RD
ORISSA RD
WILLOW FIELDS CL
TEWSON RD
DRAWELL CL
KASHGAR RD
RIPPOLSON RD
A206
MYRTLEDENE RD
ST JAMES'S CL
HUDSON PL
COUPLAND PL
VICARAGE RD
MANTHORPE RD
DURHAM RISE
WAVERLEY RD
MAJENDIE RD
ANCONA RD
BREWERY RD
Sports
Ctr
GRANITE ST
BARGATE CL
SPINEL CL
A209
GATLING RD
1
DENEHOLE HO
THE DELL
CONGLETON GR
BRAMBLEBURY RD
BURWASH RD
EMMANUEL HO
CONGO RD
LEGHORN RD
LAKEDALE RD
HAWKSMOOR CL
TYNEMOUTH RD
RIVERDALE RD
SAUNDERS RD
PURRETT RD
FELSPAR CL
GROSMONT RD
ROCKMOUNT RD
BASTION RD
GLENDOWN RD
ST MARGARET'S TERR
VICARAGE PK
GOSSAGE RD
TUSCAN RD
PIEDMONT RD
CHESTNUT RISE
PARKDALE RD
SLADEDALE RD
PHILIMORE CL
LAND RD
VIEW CL
Gallions
Mount
Prim Sch
MARBLE HO 1
CRYSTAL HO 2
BERYL HO 3
GALENA HO 4
HEATH VILLAS
St Margaret's
CE Prim Sch
Tenn
Cts
HEAVITREE CL
HEAVITREE RD
WAVERLEY CRES
Sch
ROYDENE RD
78
THE OAKS
ST MARGARET'S GR
Bwg Gn
ST JOHN'S TERR
Tenn
Cts
INVERARY PL
WINN COMMON RD
Plumstead Common
44
GLOBE TERR
BLENDON TERR
PO
WERNBROOK ST
MILL RD
WARWICK TERR
45
145
46
PLUMSTEAD COMMON RD
Plumstead
Manor/Negus
CHURCH HYDE
BLEAK HILL LA
Pav
SANDYCROFT
RUTHERGLEN RD

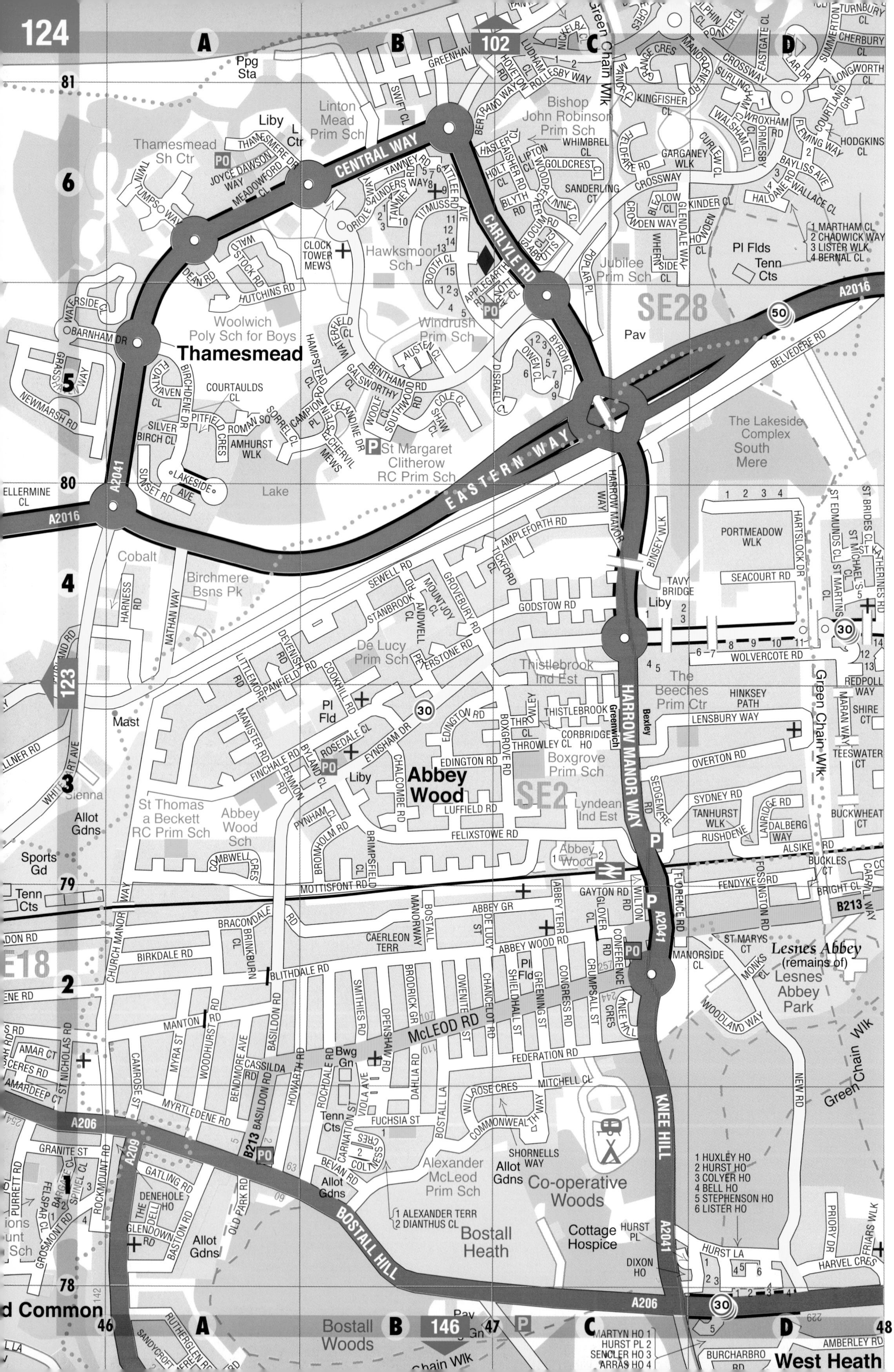
A
B
C
D
102
123
146
81
80
79
78
46
47
48
6
5
4
3
2
1
Ppg Sta
Thamesmead Sh Ctr
PO
Liby
L Ctr
Linton Mead Prim Sch
SWIFT CL
GREENHAVEN
HOVETON RD
LUDHAM CL
NICKELBY CL
ROLLESBY WAY
BERTRAND WAY
Green Chain Wlk
GRANGE CRES
MANORDENE RD
CROSSWAY
EASTGATE CL
POYNTER CL
TURNBURY CL
CHERBURY CL
LONGWORTH CL
SUMMERTON WAY
LAR DR
SURLINGHAM CL
KINGFISHER CL
Bishop John Robinson Prim Sch
WHIMBREL CL
GOLDCREST CL
SANDERLING CT
GARGANEY WLK
FIELDFARE RD
CURLEW CL
WROXHAM RD
ORMESBY
WALSHAM CL
COURTLAND GR
FLEMING WAY
HODGKINS CL
BAYLISS AVE
WALLACE CL
HALDANE RD
1 MARTHAM CL
2 CHADWICK WAY
3 LISTER WLK
4 BERNAL CL
Pl Flds
Tenn Cts
KINDER CL
GLENDALE WAY
HOWDEN CL
WHERNSIDE CL
BLEADLOW CL
CROWDEN WAY
POPLAR PL
Jubilee Prim Sch
SE28
A2016
50
Pav
BELVEDERE RD
THAMESMERE DR
JOYCE DAWSON WAY
MEADOWFORD CL
TWIN TUMPS WAY
CENTRAL WAY
TAWNEY RD
SAUNDERS WAY
ORIOLE WAY
TITMUSS AVE
ATTLEE RD
HASLER CL
HOLT CL
BLYTH RD
FAIRHOLME? RD
LIPTON
WOODPECKER RD
LINNET CL
SLOCUM CL
GABBOTTS CL
CARLYLE RD
CLOCK TOWER MEWS
Hawksmoor Sch
BOOTH CL
APPLEGARTH RD
NOTT CL
WALDSTOCK RD
DEAN RD
HUTCHINS RD
WATERSIDE CL
BARNHAM DR
Woolwich Poly Sch for Boys
Thamesmead
WATERFIELD CL
Windrush Prim Sch
AUSTEN CL
BENTHAM RD
BYRON CL
OWEN CL
DISRAELI CL
GRASSHAVEN WAY
NEWMARSH RD
FLOATHAVEN CL
BIRCHDENE DR
COURTAULDS CL
PITFIELD CRES
ROMAN SQ
SORREL CL
HAMPSTEAD RD
CAMPION PL
GALSWORTHY RD
CELANDINE DR
WOOLF CL
SOUTHWOOD RD
SHAW CL
COLE CL
SILVER BIRCH CL
AMHURST WLK
CHERVIL MEWS
St Margaret Clitherow RC Prim Sch
The Lakeside Complex South Mere
EASTERN WAY
SUNSET RD
LAKESIDE AVE
Lake
ELLERMINE CL
A2041
HARROW MANOR WAY
BINSEY WLK
1 2 3 4
PORTMEADOW WLK
HARTSLOCK DR
ST EDMUNDS CL
ST BRIDES CL
ST MICHAELS CL
ST KATHERINES RD
ST MARTINS CL
AMPLEFORTH RD
TICKFORD CL
Cobalt
Birchmere Bsns Pk
HARNESS RD
NATHAN WAY
SEWELL RD
STANBROOK RD
MOUNTJOY CL
ANDWELL CL
GROVEBURY RD
GODSTOW RD
TAVY BRIDGE
Liby
SEACOURT RD
30
WOLVERCOTE RD
DEVENISH RD
LITTLEMORE RD
PANFIELD RD
COOKHILL RD
De Lucy Prim Sch
PERSTONE RD
Thistlebrook Ind Est
The Beeches Prim Ctr
HINKSEY PATH
Green Chain Wlk
REDPOLL WAY
MARAN WAY
SHIRE CT
Mast
Pl Fld
MANISTER RD
EYNSHAM DR
EDINGTON RD
THROWLEY CL
BOXGROVE RD
THISTLEBROOK
CORBRIDGE HO
Greenwich
Bexley
LENSBURY WAY
TEESWATER CT
FINCHALE RD
BYLAND CL
ROSEDALE CL
PENMON RD
CHALCOMBE RD
EDINGTON RD
Abbey Wood
Boxgrove Prim Sch
OVERTON RD
SE2
SEDGEMERE
SYDNEY RD
TANHURST WLK
LANRIDGE RD
DALBERG WAY
BUCKWHEAT CT
RUSHDENE
ALSIKE RD
WHITEHART AVE
Sienna
Allot Gdns
St Thomas a Beckett RC Prim Sch
Abbey Wood Sch
PYNHAM CL
BROMHOLM RD
LUFFIELD RD
Lyndean Ind Est
FELIXSTOWE RD
BRIMPSFIELD CL
Sports Gd
COMBWELL CRES
Tenn Cts
MOTTISFONT RD
ABBEY TERR
GAYTON RD
WILTON RD
FLORENCE RD
FENDYKE RD
BUCKLES CT
CARRILL WAY
BRIGHT CL
B213
CHURCH MANOR WAY
BRACONDALE RD
MANORWAY
BOSTALL MANORWAY
ABBEY GR
DE LUCY ST
GLOVER CL
CONFERENCE RD
A2041
FOSSINGTON RD
ST MARYS CT
MONKS CL
Lesnes Abbey (remains of)
Lesnes Abbey Park
E18
BIRKDALE RD
BRINKBURN CL
CAERLEON TERR
ABBEY WOOD RD
Pl Fld
MANORSIDE CL
BLITHDALE RD
BASILDON RD
SMITHIES RD
BRODRICK GR
OPENSHAW RD
OWENITE ST
CHANCELOT RD
SHIELDHALL ST
GREENING ST
CONGRESS RD
CRUMPSALL ST
CRES
KNEE HILL
WOODLAND WAY
MANTON RD
MYRA ST
WOODHURST RD
BENDMORE AVE
McLEOD RD
CAMROSE ST
CASSILDA RD
HOWARTH RD
ROCHDALE RD
Bwg Gn
VIOLA AVE
DAHLIA RD
FEDERATION RD
MITCHELL CL
NEW RD
Green Chain Wlk
AMAR CT
SCERES RD
AMARDEEP CT
ST NICHOLAS RD
MYRTLEDENE RD
WILLROSE CRES
COMMONWEALTH WAY
Tenn Cts
FUCHSIA ST
BOSTALL LA
A206
A209
GRANITE ST
BARGATE CL
SPINEL CL
FELSPAR CL
PURRETT RD
GROSMONT RD
ROCKMOUNT RD
GATLING RD
DENEHOLE HO
THE DELL
GLENDOWN RD
BASTION RD
OLD PARK RD
B213 BASILDON RD
PO
CARNATION ST
COLTNESS CRES
BEVAN RD
Allot Gdns
Alexander McLeod Prim Sch
SHORNELLS WAY
Allot Gdns
Co-operative Woods
1 HUXLEY HO
2 HURST HO
3 COLYER HO
4 BELL HO
5 STEPHENSON HO
6 LISTER HO
1 ALEXANDER TERR
2 DIANTHUS CL
Bostall Heath
Cottage Hospice
HURST PL
DIXON HO
BOSTALL HILL
Allot Gdns
HURST LA
PRIORY DR
FRIARS WLK
HARVEL CRES
d Common
Pav
Bostall Woods
Chain Wlk
MARTYN HO 1
HURST PL 2
SENCLER HO 3
ARRAS HO 4
BURCHARBRO RD
AMBERLEY RD
West Heath
SANDYCROFT
RUTHERGLEN RD

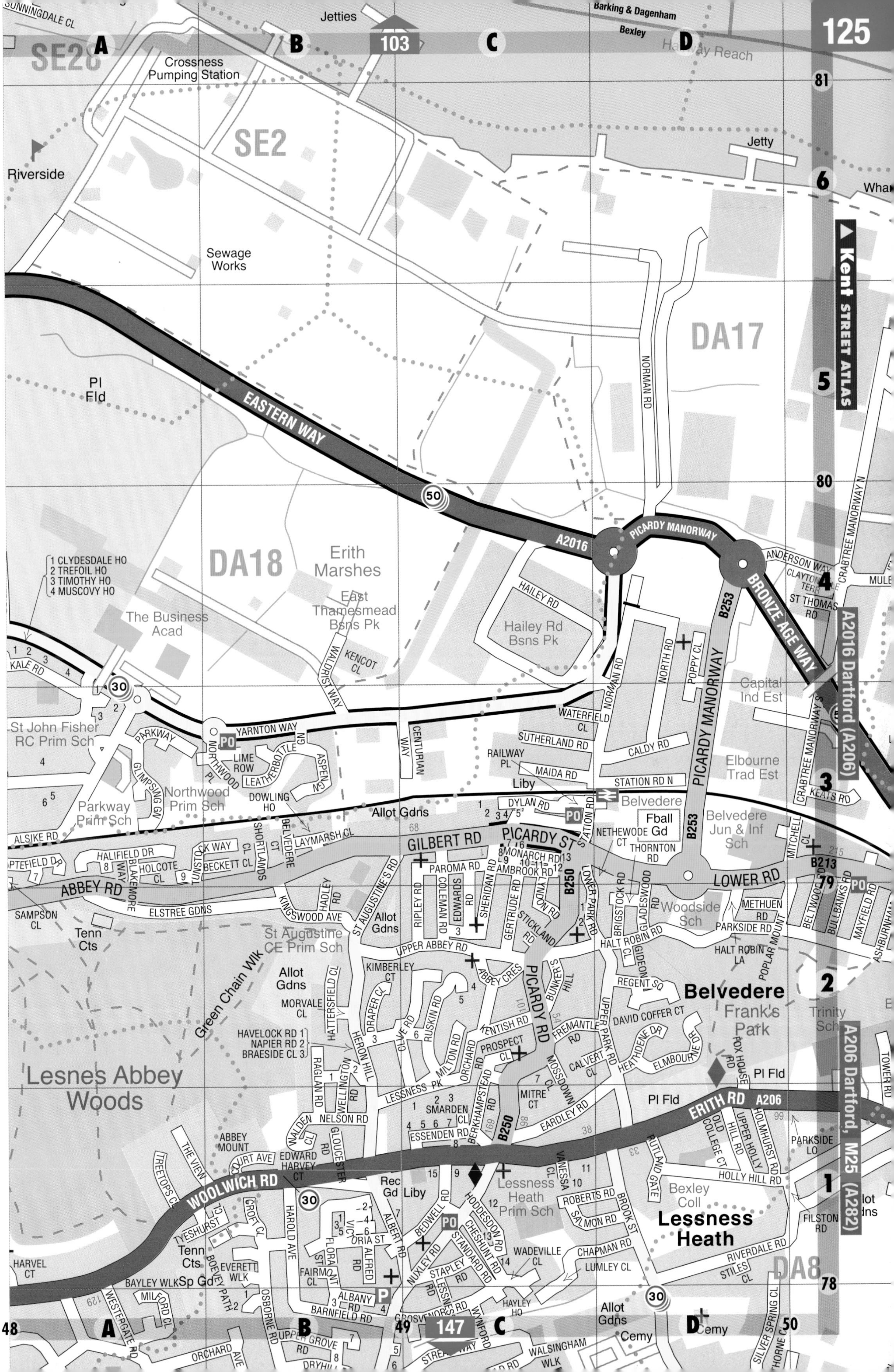
SUNNINGDALE CL
Jetties
Barking & Dagenham
Bexley
103
Halfway Reach
SE28
Crossness
Pumping Station
SE2
Jetty
Riverside
Sewage
Works
Wha
Kent STREET ATLAS
DA17
NORMAN RD
Pl
Fld
EASTERN WAY
50
A2016
PICARDY MANORWAY
ANDERSON WAY
CLAYTON TERR
ST THOMAS RD
CRABTREE MANORWAY N
MULE
DA18
Erith
Marshes
East
Thamesmead
Bsns Pk
1 CLYDESDALE HO
2 TREFOIL HO
3 TIMOTHY HO
4 MUSCOVY HO
The Business
Acad
HAILEY RD
Hailey Rd
Bsns Pk
B253
BRONZE AGE WAY
A2016 Dartford (A206)
KALE RD
KENCOT CL
WALDRIST WAY
NORMAN RD
NORTH RD
POPPY CL
Capital
Ind Est
30
St John Fisher
RC Prim Sch
PARKWAY
YARNTON WAY
NORTHWOOD PL
LIME ROW
LEATHERBOTTLE GN
ASPEN GN
CENTURIAN WAY
WATERFIELD CL
SUTHERLAND RD
RAILWAY PL
MAIDA RD
CALDY RD
STATION RD N
Elbourne
Trad Est
CRABTREE MANORWAY S
KEATS RD
GLIMPSING GN
Northwood
Prim Sch
Parkway
Prim Sch
DOWLING HO
Liby
Belvedere
DYLAN RD
STATION RD
Allot Gdns
Fball
Gd
Belvedere
Jun & Inf
Sch
ALSIKE RD
SHORTLANDS CL
BELVEDERE CT
LAYMARSH CL
GILBERT RD
PICARDY ST
NETHEWODE CT
THORNTON RD
MITCHELL CL
B213
HALIFIELD DR
TUNSTOCK WAY
BECKETT CL
MONARCH RD
AMBROOK RD
PAROMA RD
LOWER RD
PTEFIELD DR
HOLCOTE CL
BLAKEMORE WAY
ABBEY RD
B250
LOWER PARK RD
BRIGSTOCK RD
GLADESWOOD RD
Woodside
Sch
METHUEN RD
PARKSIDE RD
BELTWOOD RD
BULLBANKS RD
MAYFIELD RD
ASHBURNHAM
SAMPSON CL
ELSTREE GDNS
KINGSWOOD AVE
HADLEY RD
ST AUGUSTINE'S RD
RIPLEY RD
COLEMAN RD
EDWARDS RD
SHERIDAN RD
GERTRUDE RD
LYNDON RD
STICKLAND RD
Allot Gdns
Tenn
Cts
St Augustine
CE Prim Sch
UPPER ABBEY RD
HALT ROBIN RD
GIDEON CL
HALT ROBIN LA
POPLAR MOUNT
Green Chain Wlk
Allot
Gdns
KIMBERLEY CT
ABBEY CRES
PICARDY RD
BUNKERS HILL
REGENT SQ
Belvedere
Frank's
Park
Trinity
Sch
MORVALE CL
HATTERSFIELD CL
DRAPER CL
CLIVE RD
RUSKIN RD
KENTISH RD
FREMANTLE RD
UPPER PARK RD
DAVID COFFER CT
HEATHDENE DR
ELMBOURNE DR
FOX HOUSE RD
Pl Fld
A206 Dartford, M25 (A282)
TOWER RD
HAVELOCK RD 1
NAPIER RD 2
BRAESIDE CL 3
HERON HILL
MILTON RD
ORCHARD RD
PROSPECT CL
MOSSDOWN CL
CALVERT CL
Lesnes Abbey
Woods
RAGLAN RD
WELLINGTON RD
LESSNESS PK
MITRE CT
SMARDEN CL
BERKHAMPSTEAD RD
EARDLEY RD
Pl Fld
ERITH RD
A206
OLD COLLEGE CT
HILL RD
UPPER HOLLY HILL RD
HOLMHURST RD
PARKSIDE LO
NELSON RD
WALDEN CL
GLOUCESTER RD
ESSENDEN RD
ABBEY MOUNT
COURT AVE
EDWARD HARVEY CT
THE VIEW
TREETOPS CL
RUTLAND GATE
VANESSA CL
HOLLY HILL RD
WOOLWICH RD
Rec Gd
Liby
Lessness
Heath
Prim Sch
ROBERTS RD
SALMON RD
BROOK ST
Bexley
Coll
Lessness
Heath
FILSTON RD
TYESHURST CL
CROFT CL
HAROLD AVE
VICTORIA ST
FLORA ST
ALFRED RD
ALBERT RD
BEDWELL RD
HODDESDON RD
CHESHUNT RD
STANDARD RD
WADEVILLE CL
CHAPMAN RD
LUMLEY CL
RIVERDALE RD
STILES CL
HARVEL CT
Tenn
Cts
BOEVEY PATH
EVERETT WLK
FAIRMONT CL
NUXLEY RD
STAPLEY RD
DA8
BAYLEY WLK
Sp Gd
MILFORD CL
ALBANY RD
BARNFIELD RD
LESSNESS RD
HAYLEY HO
WYNFORD
Allot
Gdns
Cemy
SILVER SPRING CL
WESTERGATE RD
OSBORNE RD
UPPER GROVE RD
GROSVENOR RD
147
STREAM WAY
WALSINGHAM WLK
ORCHARD AVE
DRYHILL
HORNE
A
B
C
D
48
49
50
78
79
80
81
1
2
3
4
5
6

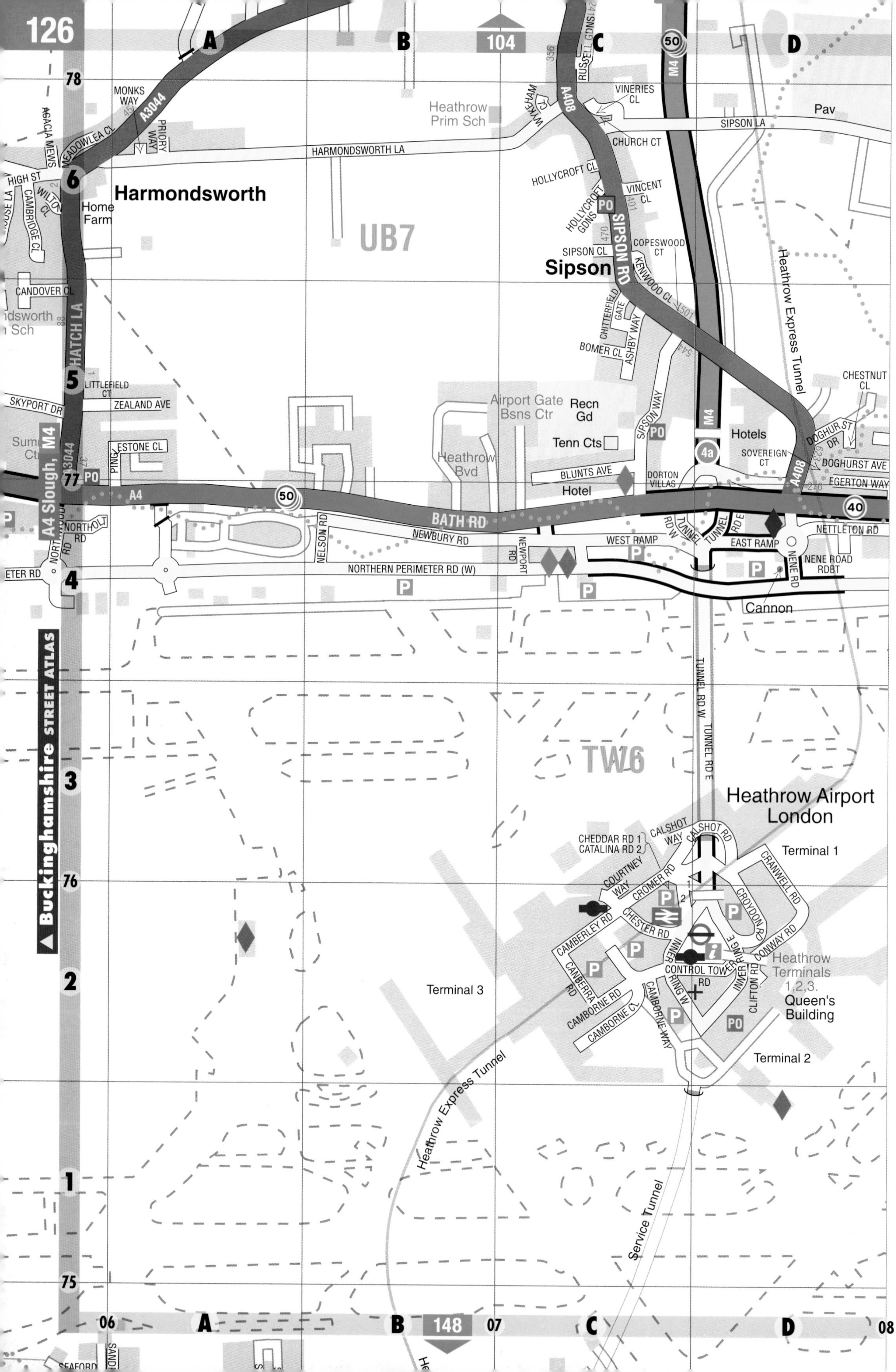
104
148
A
B
C
D
78
77
76
75
06
07
08
6
5
4
3
2
1
Harmondsworth
Sipson
UB7
TW6
Heathrow Airport
London
MONKS WAY
A3044
PRIORY WAY
MEADOWLEA CL
ACACIA MEWS
HIGH ST
WILTON CL
CAMBRIDGE CL
Home Farm
HARMONDSWORTH LA
Heathrow Prim Sch
CANDOVER CL
HATCH LA
LITTLEFIELD CT
SKYPORT DR
ZEALAND AVE
ESTONE CL
A4 Slough, M4
A4
BATH RD
NEWBURY RD
NELSON RD
NORTHOLT RD
NORTHERN PERIMETER RD (W)
NEWPORT RD
Airport Gate Bsns Ctr
Heathrow Bvd
Recn Gd
Tenn Cts
BLUNTS AVE
Hotel
WEST RAMP
EAST RAMP
TUNNEL RD W
TUNNEL RD E
NENE RD
NENE ROAD RDBT
NETTLETON RD
Cannon
RUSSELL GDNS
WYKEHAM CL
A408
VINERIES CL
CHURCH CT
SIPSON LA
Pav
HOLLYCROFT CL
HOLLYCROFT GDNS
VINCENT CL
SIPSON RD
SIPSON CL
COPESWOOD CT
KENWOOD CL
CHITTERFIELD GATE
ASHBY WAY
BOMER CL
SIPSON WAY
M4
Hotels
SOVEREIGN CT
DORTON VILLAS
DOGHURST DR
DOGHURST AVE
EGERTON WAY
CHESTNUT CL
Heathrow Express Tunnel
Terminal 1
Terminal 2
Terminal 3
CHEDDAR RD 1
CATALINA RD 2
CALSHOT WAY
CALSHOT RD
COURTNEY WAY
CROMER RD
CHESTER RD
CAMBERLEY RD
CANBERRA RD
CAMBORNE RD
CAMBORNE CL
CAMBORNE WAY
INNER RING W
INNER RING E
CONTROL TOWER RD
CROYDON RD
CRANWELL RD
CONWAY RD
CLIFTON RD
Heathrow Terminals 1,2,3.
Queen's Building
Service Tunnel

Buckinghamshire STREET ATLAS

A
B
C
D
105
Nine Elms Farm
Sports Gd
Pav
William Byrd Sch
VICTORIA LA
BLETCHMORE CL
BRICKFIELD LA
PEMBURY CT
KILN CL
Hotel
HUDSON RD
HIGH ST
A437
RICHARDS CL
SIPSON LA
FORGE CL
GOTHIC CT
FELLOWES CT
SHORTLANDS
Harlington
PO
FELBRIDGE CT
MANOR LA
PONDSIDE CL
MANSE CL
Frog's Ditch
78
6
Cranford Park
UB3
Gravel Pits
CRANFORD LA
PROVIDENCE CT
PROVIDENCE LA
OAKLEY CT
THE CRESCENT
GILPIN WAY
WEST END LA
HIGH STREET HARLINGTON
Poultry Farm
The White House
ACORN GR
Tenn
RAYWOOD CL
TASKER CL
CROFT CL
HARLINGTON CL
GRAMPIAN CL
QUANTOCK CL
LITTLE ELMS
SAUNTON AVE
5
Sp Gd
PENNINE WAY
WARNER CL
BROWNING RD
GRAVES RD
PENDELL AVE
STRATHEARN AVE
LANGLEY CRES
VANTAGE CT
MARLBOROUGH CRES
DAVID CL
CAROLINE PL
BOLTON'S LA
NEW RD
BRENDON CL
HALL LA
OXFORD AVE
ETON RD
MENDIP CL
CHEVIOT CL
HEATH CL
WINCHESTER RD
PARK RD
MONDIAL WAY
Hotel
Hotels
NOBEL DR
WINDSOR PARK RD
MALVERN RD
CRANESWATER
PARK LA
TRIUMPH CL
Harlington Cnr
Hotels
Hotel
Hotel
A4
The White Hart (PH)
BATH RD
40
Visitor Ctr
World Bsns Ctr
Hotel
P
NEWALL RD
NEPTUNE RD
HATTON RD N
NORTHROP RD
NORTHERN PERIMETER RD
CRANFORD LA
DUDSET LA
4
Hounslow
Hillingdon
128
London Loop
ENFIELD ROAD RDBT
ENFIELD RD
EPSOM SQ
ELY RD
ESHER CRES
EASTERN PERIMETER RD
ELGIN CRES
Eastern Bsns Pk
TW6
3
EASTCHURCH ROAD RDBT
EXETER WAY
VANGUARD WAY
EXETER RD
EXETER RD
EASTCHURCH RD
76
TW6
EASTERN PERIMETER RD
ELECTRA AVE
EAGLE RD
ELMDON RD
2
CRANFORD LA
Hotel
HATTON CROSS RDBT
EASTERN PERIMETER RD
A30
VISCOUNT WAY
Hatton Cross
LITHGOW'S RD
DICK TURPIN WAY
GREAT SOUTH-WEST RD
STEAM FARM LA
SOUTHERN PERIMETER RD
DOCKWELL CL
1
GREEN MAN LA
FAGG'S RD
Radius Pk
ST THERESA'S RD
HATTON RD
Hatton
ST ANTHONY'S WAY
HATTON GN
MYRTLE AVE
A30
75
08
09
10
149
WELLINGTON RD
PERIMETER RD
Tenn

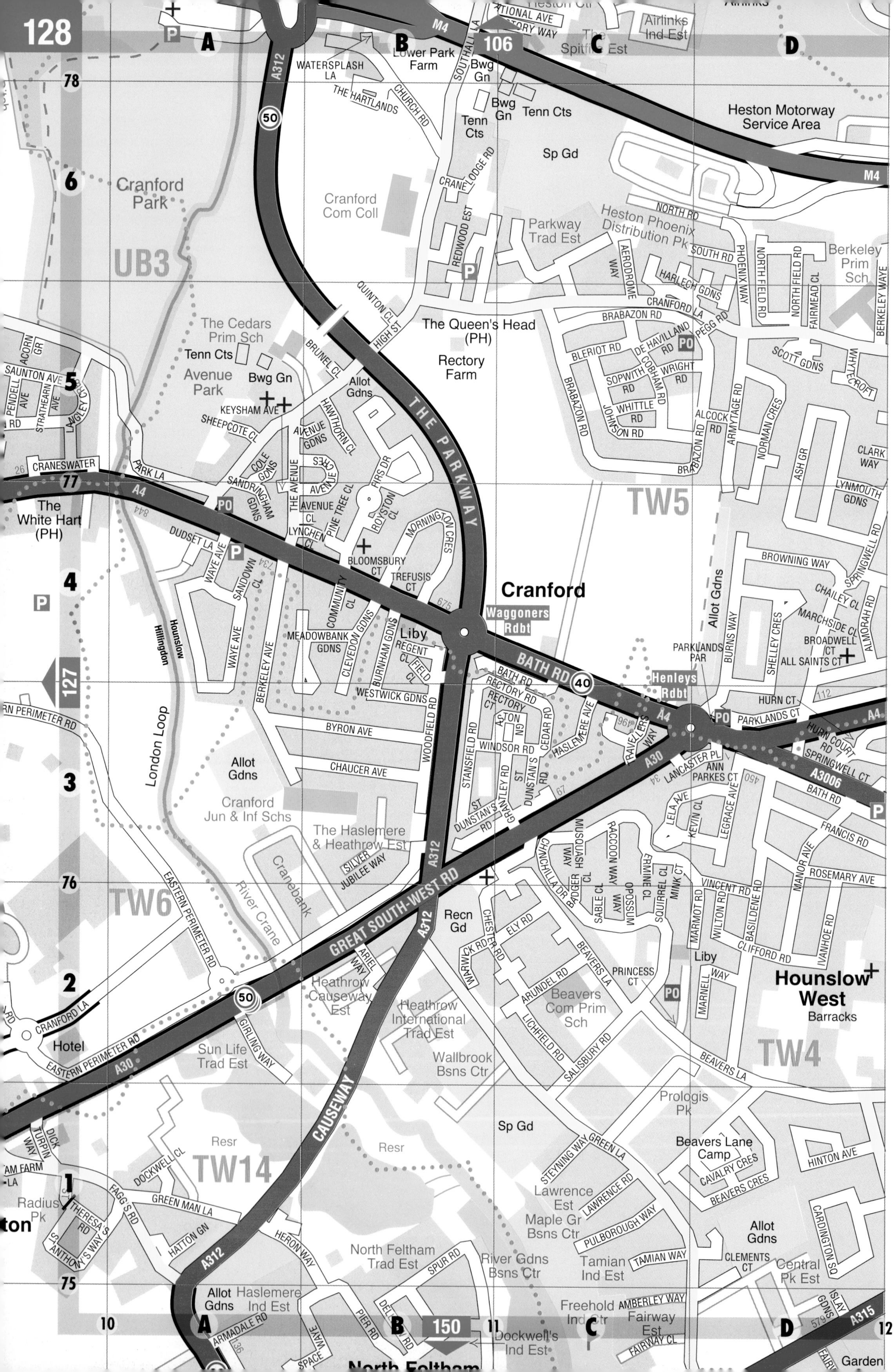
A
B
C
D
106
M4
78
6
5
77
4
3
76
2
1
75
10
11
12
127
150
UB3
TW5
TW6
TW4
TW14
Lower Park Farm
Airlinks Ind Est
The Spitfire Est
Heston Motorway Service Area
WATERSPLASH LA
THE HARTLANDS
CHURCH RD
SOUTHALL LA
Bwg Gn
Tenn Cts
Sp Gd
CRANE LODGE RD
Cranford Park
Cranford Com Coll
REDWOOD EST
Parkway Trad Est
Heston Phoenix Distribution Pk
NORTH RD
SOUTH RD
AERODROME WAY
PHOENIX WAY
NORTH FIELD RD
NORTHFIELD RD
FAIRMEAD CL
BERKELEY WAYE
Berkeley Prim Sch
HARLECH GDNS
CRANFORD LA
BRABAZON RD
PEGG RD
QUINTON CL
HIGH ST
The Queen's Head (PH)
Rectory Farm
The Cedars Prim Sch
Avenue Park
BRUNEL CL
Allot Gdns
THE PARKWAY
BLERIOT RD
DE HAVILLAND RD
COBHAM RD
WRIGHT RD
SOPWITH RD
WHITTLE RD
JOHNSON RD
ALCOCK RD
ARMYTAGE RD
NORMAN CRES
SCOTT GDNS
WHYTECROFT
ACORN GR
SAUNTON AVE
PENDELL AVE
STRATHEARN AVE
LANGLEY CRES
KEYSHAM AVE
SHEEPCOTE CL
HAWTHORN CL
AVENUE GDNS
AVENUE CRES
COLE GDNS
SANDRINGHAM GDNS
THE AVENUE
FIRS DR
ROYSTON CL
PINE TREE CL
LYNCHEN CL
CRANESWATER
PARK LA
A4
The White Hart (PH)
DUDSET LA
WAYE AVE
SANDOWN CL
BLOOMSBURY CT
TREFUSIS CT
MORNINGTON CRES
ASH GR
CLARK WAY
LYNMOUTH GDNS
BROWNING WAY
SPRINGWELL RD
CHAILEY CL
MARCHSIDE CL
ALMORAH RD
BROADWELL CT
ALL SAINTS CT
Cranford
Waggoners Rdbt
COMMUNITY CL
MEADOWBANK GDNS
CLEVEDON GDNS
BURNHAM GDNS
Liby
REGENT CL
FIELD CL
BATH RD
Henleys Rdbt
PARKLANDS PAR
BURNS WAY
SHELLEY CRES
HURN CT
PARKLANDS CT
HURN COURT RD
SPRINGWELL CT
A3006
London Loop
Hillingdon
Hounslow
BERKELEY AVE
WESTWICK GDNS
RECTORY RD
RECTORY CT
ACTON GN
CEDAR RD
HASLEMERE AVE
TRAVELLERS WAY
WOODFIELD RD
BYRON AVE
CHAUCER AVE
WINDSOR RD
STANSFIELD RD
GRANTLEY RD
ST DUNSTAN'S RD
A30
LANCASTER PL
ANN PARKES CT
LELA AVE
KEVIN CL
LEGRACE AVE
FRANCIS RD
RN PERIMETER RD
Cranford Jun & Inf Schs
The Haslemere & Heathrow Est
SILVER JUBILEE WAY
A312
CHINCHILLA DR
MUSQUASH WAY
RACCOON WAY
BADGER CL
SABLE CL
OPOSSUM WAY
ERMINE CL
SQUIRREL CL
MINK CT
MANOR AVE
ROSEMARY AVE
EASTERN PERIMETER RD
Cranebank
River Crane
GREAT SOUTH-WEST RD
Recn Gd
CHESTER RD
ELY RD
WARWICK RD
BEAVERS LA
VINCENT RD
MARMOT RD
WILTON RD
BASILDENE RD
IVANHOE RD
CLIFFORD RD
ARIEL WAY
ARUNDEL RD
PRINCESS CT
MARNELL WAY
Hounslow West
Barracks
CRANFORD LA
Hotel
Heathrow Causeway Est
Heathrow International Trad Est
Beavers Com Prim Sch
LICHFIELD RD
SALISBURY RD
GIRLING WAY
Sun Life Trad Est
Wallbrook Bsns Ctr
Prologis Pk
CAUSEWAY
Resr
DICK TURPIN WAY
STEYNING WAY
GREEN LA
Beavers Lane Camp
CAVALRY CRES
BEAVERS CRES
HINTON AVE
DOCKWELL CL
FAGG'S RD
GREEN MAN LA
Radius Pk
THERESA'S RD
ST ANTHONY'S WAY
Lawrence Est
LAWRENCE RD
Maple Gr Bsns Ctr
PULBOROUGH WAY
Allot Gdns
CARDINGTON SQ
HATTON GN
HERON WAY
North Feltham Trad Est
SPUR RD
River Gdns Bsns Ctr
Tamian Ind Est
TAMIAN WAY
CLEMENTS CT
Central Pk Est
Haslemere Ind Est
ARMADALE RD
PIER RD
SPACE WAYE
Freehold Ind Ctr
AMBERLEY WAY
Fairway Est
FAIRWAY CL
Dockwell's Ind Est
ISLAY GDNS
A315
Garden
North Feltham

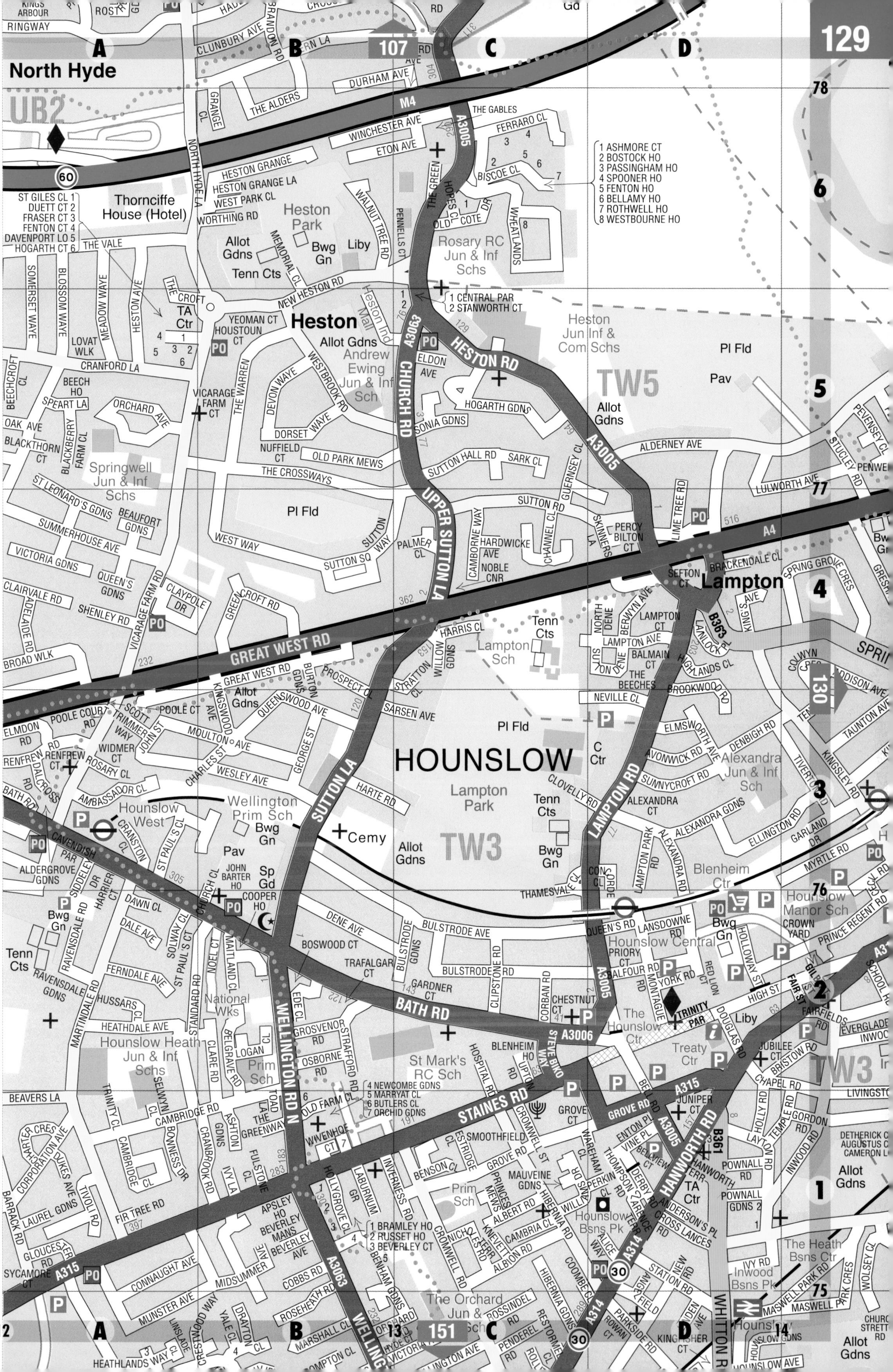
North Hyde
Heston
Lampton
HOUNSLOW
TW5
TW3
UB2
1 ASHMORE CT
2 BOSTOCK HO
3 PASSINGHAM HO
4 SPOONER HO
5 FENTON HO
6 BELLAMY HO
7 ROTHWELL HO
8 WESTBOURNE HO
ST GILES CL 1
DUETT CT 2
FRASER CT 3
FENTON CT 4
DAVENPORT LO 5
HOGARTH CT 6
1 CENTRAL PAR
2 STANWORTH CT
4 NEWCOMBE GDNS
5 MARRYAT CL
6 BUTLERS CL
7 ORCHID GDNS
1 BRAMLEY HO
2 RUSSET HO
3 BEVERLEY CT
Thorncliffe House (Hotel)
Heston Park
Hounslow West
Hounslow Central
Hounslow Heath Jun & Inf Schs
GREAT WEST RD
STAINES RD
BATH RD
HESTON RD
LAMPTON RD
WELLINGTON RD N
UPPER SUTTON LA
CHURCH RD
M4
A4
A3005
A3063
A315
A3006
107
130
151

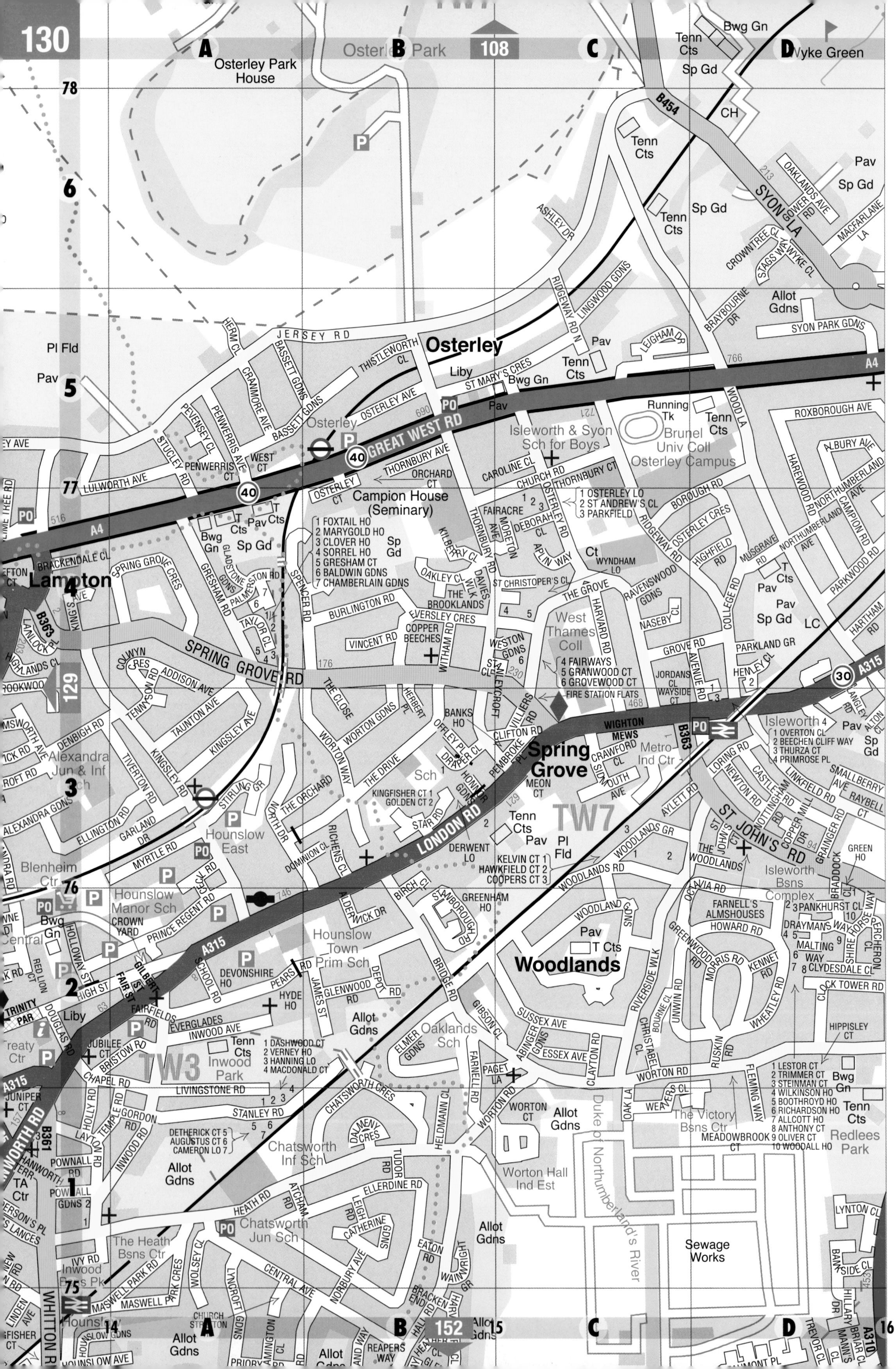
A
B
C
D
108
152
78
77
76
75
6
5
4
3
2
1
14
15
16
129
Osterley Park House
Osterley Park
Bwg Gn
Tenn Cts
Sp Gd
Wyke Green
B454
CH
SYON LA
OAKLANDS AVE
GOWER RD
MACFARLANE LA
CROWNTREE CL
STAGS WAY
WYKE CL
Pav
ASHLEY DR
RIDGEWAY RD N
LINGWOOD GDNS
BRAYBOURNE DR
Allot Gdns
SYON PARK GDNS
LEIGHAM DR
JERSEY RD
HERM CL
BASSETT GDNS
CRANMORE AVE
THISTLEWORTH CL
Osterley
ST MARY'S CRES
Liby
A4
Pl Fld
PEVENSEY CL
PENWERRIS AVE
STUCLEY RD
OSTERLEY AVE
PO
GREAT WEST RD
40
WEST CT
PENWERRIS CT
LULWORTH AVE
THORNBURY AVE
ORCHARD CT
OSTERLEY CT
Campion House (Seminary)
Isleworth & Syon Sch for Boys
Running Tk
Brunel Univ Coll Osterley Campus
WOOD LA
ROXBOROUGH AVE
ALBURY AVE
HAREWOOD RD
NORTHUMBERLAND AVE
CAROLINE CL
CHURCH RD
THORNBURY CT
1 OSTERLEY LO
2 ST ANDREW'S CL
3 PARKFIELD
BOROUGH RD
RIDGEWAY RD
OSTERLEY CRES
CAMPION RD
1 FOXTAIL HO
2 MARYGOLD HO
3 CLOVER HO
4 SORREL HO
5 GRESHAM CT
6 BALDWIN GDNS
7 CHAMBERLAIN GDNS
FAIRACRE
MORETON AVE
DEBORAH CL
OSTERLEY RD
APLIN WAY
Ct
WYNDHAM LO
HIGHFIELD RD
MUSGRAVE RD
PARKWOOD RD
Bwg Gn
Pav
BRACKENDALE CL
Lampton
SPRING GROVE CRES
GRESHAM RD
GLADSTONE GDNS
PALMERSTON RD
SPENCER RD
KILBERRY CL
OAKLEY CL
DAVIES WLK
THE BROOKLANDS
ST CHRISTOPHER'S CL
THE GROVE
RAVENSWOOD GDNS
COLLEGE RD
Sp Gd
LC
HARTHAM RD
B363
KING'S AVE
LANLOCK PL
HIGHLANDS CL
BURLINGTON RD
EVERSLEY CRES
COPPER BEECHES
VINCENT RD
WITHAM RD
TAYLOR CL
West Thames Coll
HARVARD RD
NASEBY CL
GROVE RD
AVENUE RD
PARKLAND GR
HEMLEY CL
A315
30
COLWYN CRES
ADDISON AVE
SPRING GROVE RD
TENNYSON RD
WESTON GDNS
STANLEY CL
4 FAIRWAYS
5 GRANWOOD CT
6 GROVEWOOD CT
FIRE STATION FLATS
JORDANS CL
WAYSIDE CT
LANGLEY CL
TAUNTON AVE
KINGSLEY AVE
THE CLOSE
WORTON GDNS
HERBERT PL
BANKS HO
LINDLEYCROFT
VILLIERS RD
WIGHTON MEWS
Isleworth
1 OVERTON CL
2 BEECHEN CLIFF WAY
3 THURZA CT
4 PRIMROSE PL
ALTON CL
DENBIGH RD
Alexandra Jun & Inf Sch
TIVERTON RD
KINGSLEY RD
STIRLING GR
WORTON WAY
THE DRIVE
OFFLEY PL
DRAPER CL
CLIFTON RD
PEMBROKE PL
Spring Grove
CRAWFORD CL
SIDMOUTH AVE
Metro Ind Ctr
LORING RD
NEWTON RD
CASTLE WAY
LINKFIELD RD
SMALLBERRY AVE
RAYBELL CT
ALEXANDRA GDNS
ELLINGTON RD
GARLAND DR
Hounslow East
NORTH DR
THE ORCHARD
Sch
KINGFISHER CT 1
GOLDEN CT 2
STAR RD
HONOR GDNS
LONDON RD
MEON CT
Tenn Cts
TW7
AYLETT RD
ST JOHN'S CT
NOTTINGHAM CT
COPPER MILL DR
GRAINGER RD
ST JOHN'S RD
GREEN HO
MYRTLE RD
Blenheim Ctr
DOMINION CL
RICHENS CL
DERWENT LO
Pl Fld
KELVIN CT 1
HAWKFIELD CT 2
COOPERS CT 3
WOODLANDS GR
THE WOODLANDS
Isleworth Bsns Complex
BRADDOCK CL
Hounslow Manor Sch
CROWN YARD
PRINCE REGENT RD
CECIL RD
ALDERWICK DR
BIRCH CL
STANBOROUGH RD
GREENHAM HO
WOODLANDS RD
OCTAVIA RD
FARNELL'S ALMSHOUSES
HOWARD RD
2 3 PANKHURST CL
DRAYMANS WAY
SHIRE HORSE WAY
PERCHERON CL
MALTING WAY
CLYDESDALE CL
HOLLOWAY ST
Central
RED LION CT
A315
SCHOOL RD
DEVONSHIRE HO
Hounslow Town Prim Sch
PEARS RD
JAMES ST
DEPOT RD
GLENWOOD RD
BRIDGE RD
WOODLAND GDNS
T Cts
Woodlands
GREENWOOD RD
MORRIS RD
KENNET RD
WHEATLEY RD
CLOCK TOWER RD
HIGH ST
GILBERT ST
FAIR ST
TRINITY PAR
DOUGLAS RD
FAIRFIELDS RD
HYDE HO
EVERGLADES
INWOOD AVE
Oaklands Sch
GIBSON CL
SUSSEX AVE
RIVERSIDE WLK
UNWIN RD
BOURNE CL
HIPPISLEY CT
Treaty Ctr
JUBILEE CT
BRISTOW RD
TW3
Inwood Park
1 DASHWOOD CT
2 VERNEY HO
3 HANNING LO
4 MACDONALD CT
ELMER GDNS
FARNELL RD
ABINGER GDNS
ESSEX AVE
CLAYTON RD
CHRISTABEL CL
RUSKIN RD
FLEMING WAY
1 LESTOR CT
2 TRIMMER CT
3 STEINMAN CT
4 WILKINSON HO
5 BOOTHROYD HO
6 RICHARDSON HO
7 ALLCOTT HO
8 ANTHONY CT
9 OLIVER CT
10 WOODALL HO
JUNIPER CT
CHAPEL RD
LIVINGSTONE RD
CHATSWORTH CRES
PAGET LA
WORTON RD
WEAVERS CL
The Victory Bsns Ctr
MEADOWBROOK CT
Redlees Park
HANWORTH RD
B361
HOLLY RD
TEMPLE RD
GORDON RD
STANLEY RD
DALMENY CRES
HELDMANN CL
WORTON CT
Allot Gdns
OAK LA
Duke of Northumberland's River
LAYTON RD
INWOOD RD
DETHERICK CT 5
AUGUSTUS CT 6
CAMERON LO 7
Chatsworth Inf Sch
TUDOR RD
Worton Hall Ind Est
POWNALL RD
POWNALL GDNS 2
TA Ctr
HEATH RD
ATCHAM RD
ELLERDINE RD
LEIGH GDNS
CATHERINE GDNS
Sewage Works
LYNTON CL
The Heath Bsns Ctr
Chatsworth Jun Sch
WOLSEY CL
LYNGROFT GDNS
CENTRAL AVE
NORBURY AVE
EATON RD
WAINWRIGHT GR
BANKSIDE CL
IVY RD
Inwood Bsns Pk
MASWELL PARK RD
MASWELL PARK CRES
BRACKEN END
HALL RD
HILLARY DR
LINDEN AVE
WHITTON RD
Hounslow
CHURCH STREATON
SLOW GDNS
AMINGTON CL
AND WAY
REAPERS WAY
TREVOR CL
BRIAR CL
MANNS CL
A310
FISHER CT
HOUNSLOW AVE
PRIORY

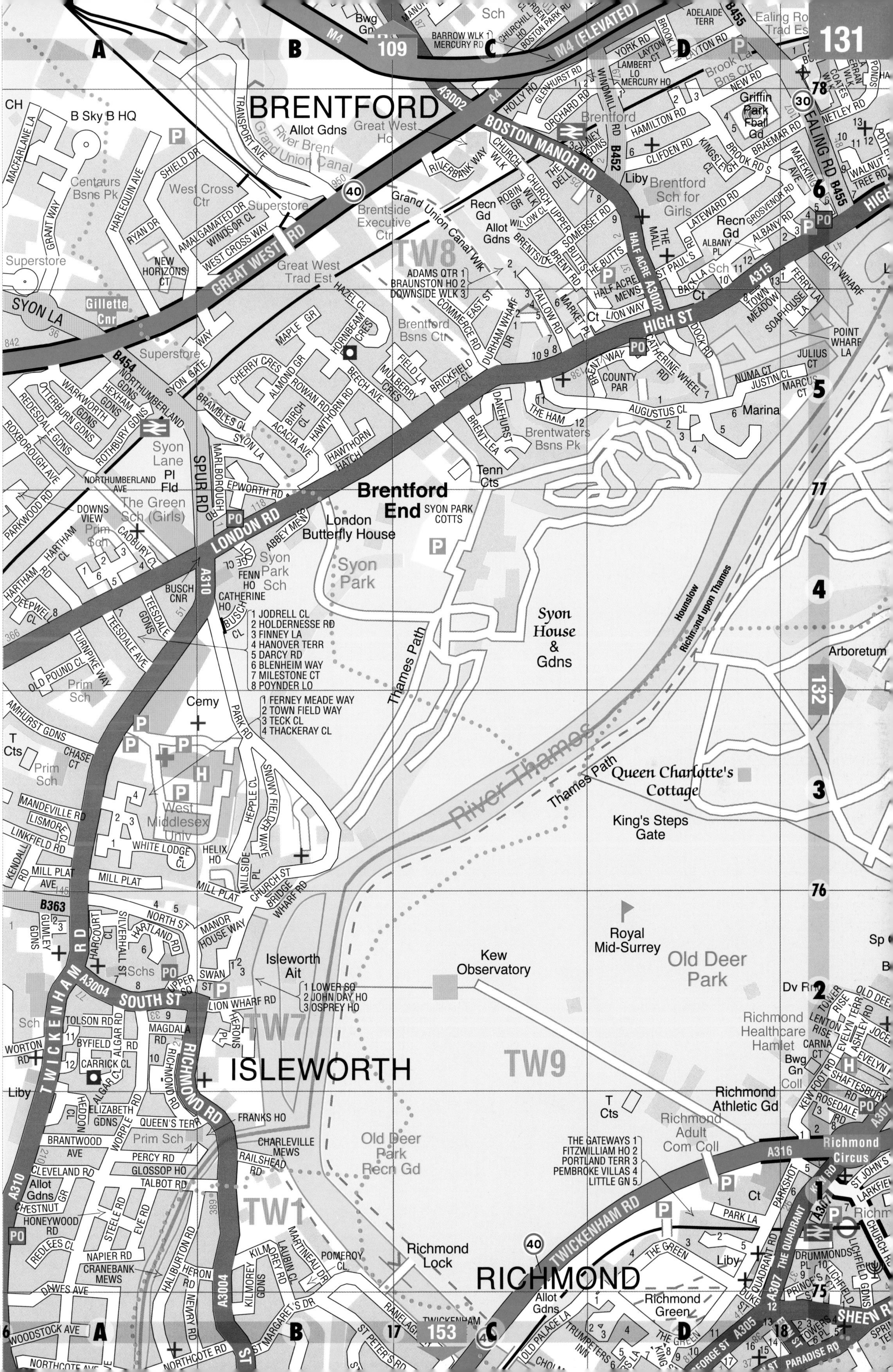
BRENTFORD
ISLEWORTH
RICHMOND
Brentford End
TW8
TW7
TW9
TW1
M4 (ELEVATED)
GREAT WEST RD
BOSTON MANOR RD
HIGH ST
LONDON RD
SPUR RD
TWICKENHAM RD
SOUTH ST
RICHMOND RD
HALF ACRE A3002
EALING RD B455
SYON LA
Syon Lane
Syon House & Gdns
Syon Park
London Butterfly House
River Thames
Thames Path
Queen Charlotte's Cottage
King's Steps Gate
Kew Observatory
Royal Mid-Surrey
Old Deer Park
Old Deer Park Recn Gd
Richmond Lock
Richmond Athletic Gd
Richmond Green
Richmond Circus
Arboretum
Grand Union Canal
River Brent
West Middlesex Univ
Isleworth Ait
Brentwaters Bsns Pk
Brentford Bsns Ctr
Great West Trad Est
Centaurs Bsns Pk
B Sky B HQ
Gillette Cnr
Marina
Hounslow
Richmond upon Thames
1 JODRELL CL
2 HOLDERNESSE RD
3 FINNEY LA
4 HANOVER TERR
5 DARCY RD
6 BLENHEIM WAY
7 MILESTONE CT
8 POYNDER LO
1 FERNEY MEADE WAY
2 TOWN FIELD WAY
3 TECK CL
4 THACKERAY CL
1 LOWER SQ
2 JOHN DAY HO
3 OSPREY HO
ADAMS QTR 1
BRAUNSTON HO 2
DOWNSIDE WLK 3
THE GATEWAYS 1
FITZWILLIAM HO 2
PORTLAND TERR 3
PEMBROKE VILLAS 4
LITTLE GN 5
A
B
C
D
109
132
153
16
17
18

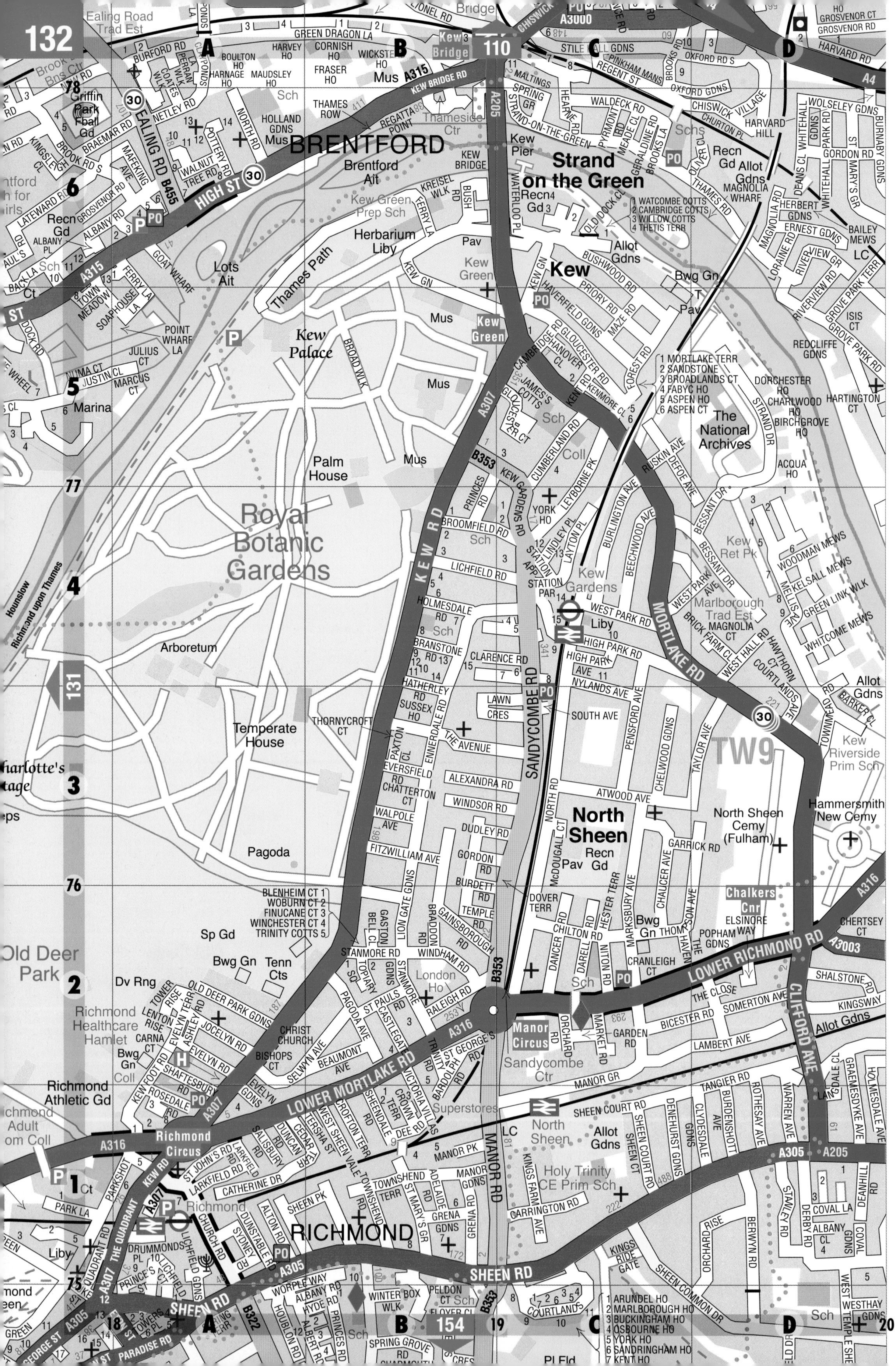
BRENTFORD
Strand on the Green
Kew
Brentford Ait
Lots Ait
Kew Palace
Royal Botanic Gardens
Palm House
Temperate House
Arboretum
Pagoda
Herbarium Liby
Thames Path
Kew Bridge
Kew Green
The National Archives
Kew Gardens
Marlborough Trad Est
North Sheen
North Sheen Cemy (Fulham)
Hammersmith New Cemy
Chalkers Cnr
Manor Circus
Sandycombe Ctr
Old Deer Park
Richmond Healthcare Hamlet
Richmond Athletic Gd
Richmond Circus
RICHMOND
Holy Trinity CE Prim Sch
Kew Riverside Prim Sch
TW9
KEW BRIDGE RD
HIGH ST
EALING RD
KEW RD
SANDYCOMBE RD
MORTLAKE RD
LOWER RICHMOND RD
LOWER MORTLAKE RD
CLIFFORD AVE
MANOR RD
SHEEN RD
KEW GARDENS RD
STATION PAR
NORTH RD
A315
A205
A307
A316
A305
A3003
A3000
A4
B353
B455
B322
110
131
154
Hounslow
Richmond upon Thames

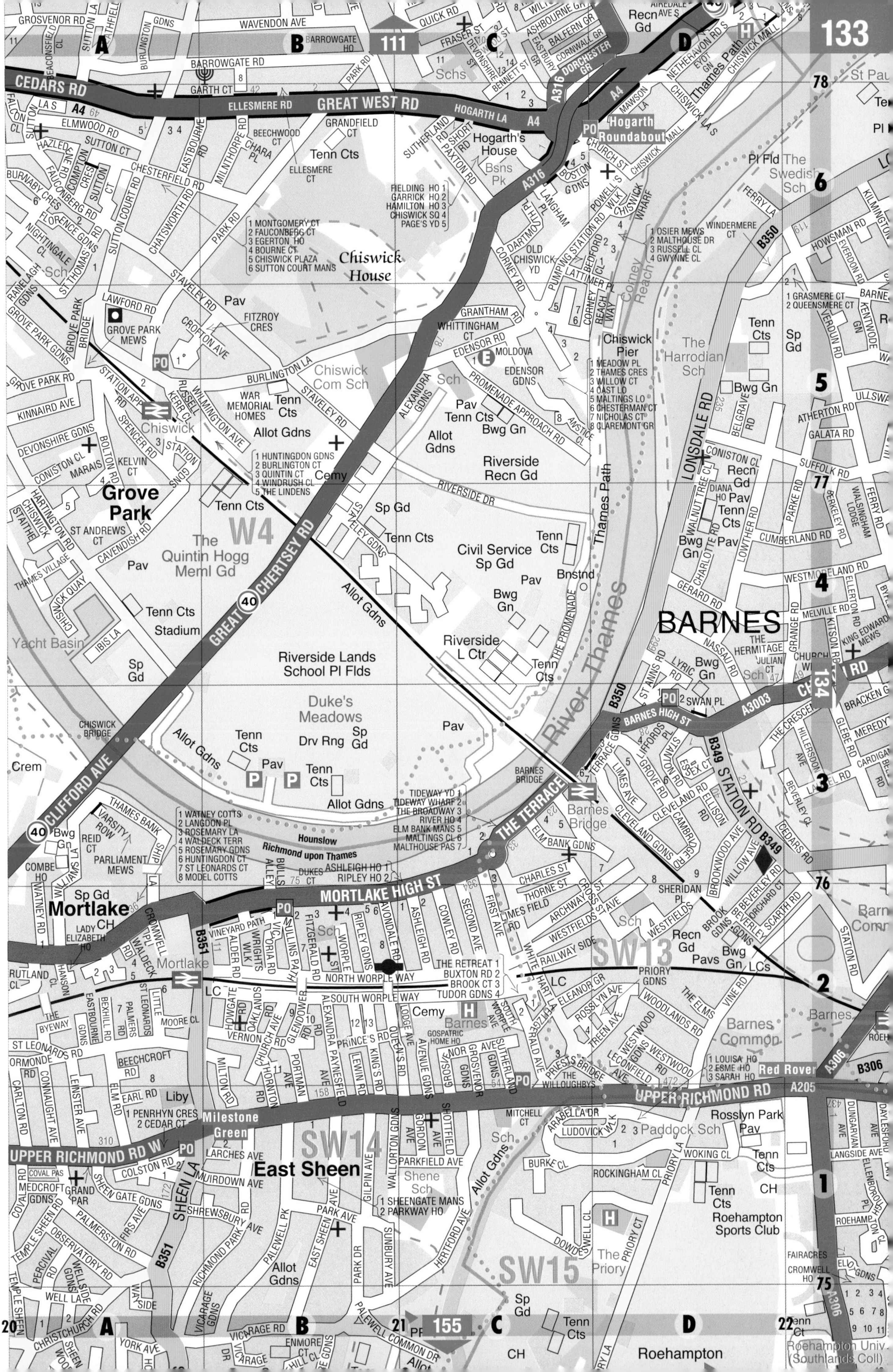
Chiswick House
Grove Park
Chiswick
W4
The Quintin Hogg Meml Gd
Riverside Lands School Pl Flds
Duke's Meadows
Civil Service Sp Gd
Riverside Recn Gd
River Thames
Thames Path
BARNES
Barnes Bridge
Mortlake
East Sheen
SW13
SW14
SW15
Barnes Common
Roehampton
Roehampton Sports Club
The Harrodian Sch
The Swedish Sch
Hogarth Roundabout
Hogarth's House
CEDARS RD
GREAT WEST RD
GREAT CHERTSEY RD
CLIFFORD AVE
MORTLAKE HIGH ST
UPPER RICHMOND RD
UPPER RICHMOND RD W
LONSDALE RD
BARNES HIGH ST
STATION RD
THE TERRACE
SHEEN LA
NORTH WORPLE WAY
SOUTH WORPLE WAY
BURLINGTON LA
STAVELEY RD
Milestone Green
Chiswick Pier
Chiswick Bridge
Barnes Bridge
Hounslow
Richmond upon Thames
Red Rover
The Priory
Paddock Sch
Yacht Basin
Crem
A B C D
20 21 22
111
155
134
78 77 76 75
6 5 4 3 2 1

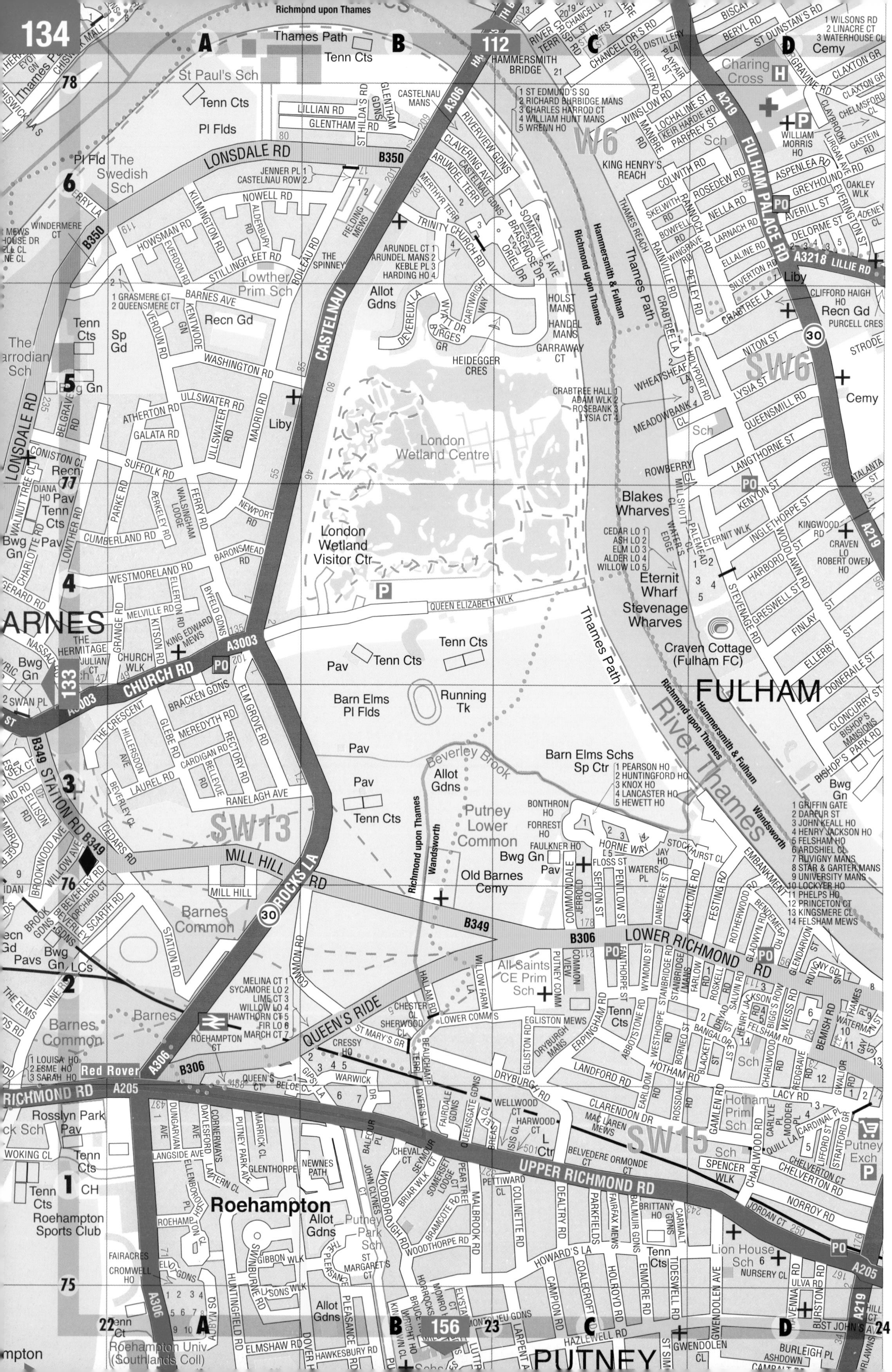

Richmond upon Thames
Thames Path
Tenn Cts
St Paul's Sch
Pl Flds
112
HAMMERSMITH BRIDGE
A B C D
Cemy
Charing Cross
LILLIAN RD
GLENTHAM RD
CASTELNAU MANS
LONSDALE RD
B350
The Swedish Sch
JENNER PL
CASTELNAU ROW
NOWELL RD
KILMINGTON RD
HOWSMAN RD
EVERDON RD
ALDERBURY RD
BOILEAU RD
STILLINGFLEET RD
Lowther Prim Sch
BARNES AVE
Recn Gd
WASHINGTON RD
ULLSWATER RD
ATHERTON RD
GALATA RD
MADRID RD
SUFFOLK RD
Liby
CASTELNAU
A306
THE SPINNEY
FIELDING MEWS
TRINITY CHURCH RD
ARUNDEL TERR
RIVERVIEW GDNS
CLAVERING AVE
SOMERVILLE AVE
Allot Gdns
DEVEREUX LA
WYATT DR
BURGES GR
CARTWRIGHT WAY
HEIDEGGER CRES
HOLST MANS
HANDEL MANS
GARRAWAY CT
London Wetland Centre
London Wetland Visitor Ctr
QUEEN ELIZABETH WLK
Hammersmith & Fulham
Richmond upon Thames
Thames Path
W6
KING HENRY'S REACH
WINSLOW RD
LOCHALINE ST
KEIR HARDIE HO
PARFREY ST
COLWITH RD
ROSEDEW RD
NELLA RD
LARNACH RD
ELLALINE RD
SILVERTON RD
CRABTREE LA
RAINVILLE RD
FULHAM PALACE RD
A219
A3218 LILLIE RD
ASPENLEA RD
GREYHOUND RD
AVERILL ST
DELORME ST
CLIFFORD HAIGH HO
Recn Gd
PURCELL CRES
NITON ST
SW6
LYSIA ST
QUEENSMILL RD
LANGTHORNE ST
WHEATSHEAF LA
MEADOWBANK
ROWBERRY CL
KENYON ST
INGLETHORPE ST
Blakes Wharves
Eternit Wharf
Stevenage Wharves
STEVENAGE RD
HARBORD ST
GRESWELL ST
FINLAY ST
ELLERBY ST
DONERAILE ST
Craven Cottage (Fulham FC)
FULHAM
River Thames
Wandsworth
BISHOP'S PARK RD
ARNES
CHURCH RD
A3003
WESTMORELAND RD
MELVILLE RD
KITSON RD
GRANGE RD
THE HERMITAGE
CHURCH WLK
BRACKEN GDNS
ELM GROVE RD
MEREDITH RD
THE CRESCENT
GLEBE RD
CARDIGAN RD
RECTORY RD
LAUREL RD
RANELAGH AVE
B349 STATION RD
SW13
MILL HILL RD
ROCKS LA
Barnes Common
Pav
Tenn Cts
Barn Elms Pl Flds
Running Tk
Beverley Brook
Allot Gdns
Putney Lower Common
Old Barnes Cemy
Barn Elms Schs Sp Ctr
B306
LOWER RICHMOND RD
EMBANKMENT
QUEEN'S RIDE
COMMON RD
HALLAM RD
WILLOW FARM LA
All Saints CE Prim Sch
Barnes
ROEHAMPTON CT
Red Rover
A205
RICHMOND RD
UPPER RICHMOND RD
SW15
Rosslyn Park Pav
Roehampton
Roehampton Sports Club
Putney Park Sch
DRYBURGH RD
CLARENDON DR
HOTHAM RD
LANDFORD RD
Hotham Prim Sch
LACY RD
Putney Exch
Lion House Sch
NORROY RD
CHELVERTON RD
HOWARD'S LA
Allot Gdns
156
22 23 24
PUTNEY
Roehampton Univ (Southlands Coll)

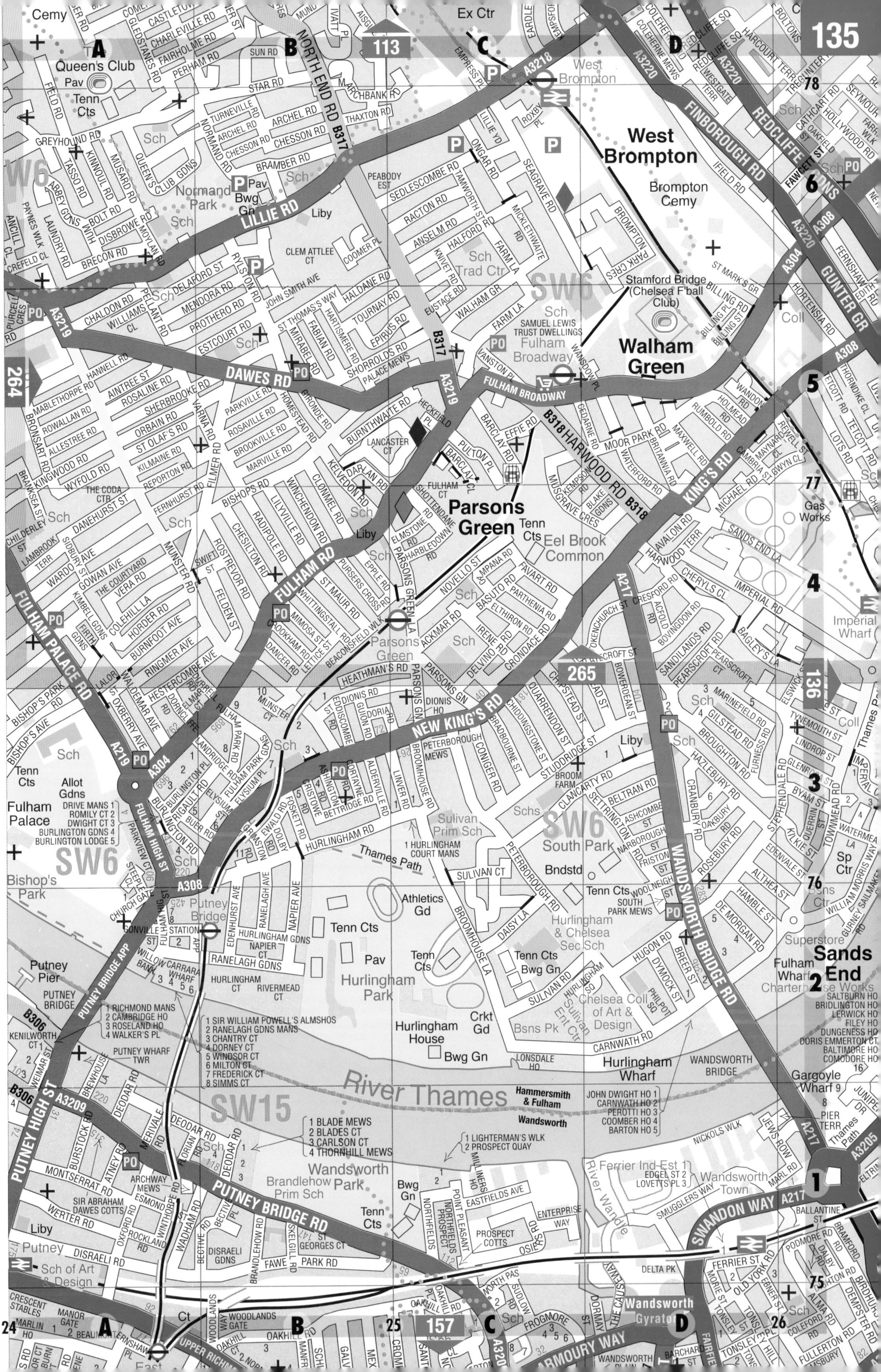
Queen's Club
West Brompton
Brompton Cemy
Walham Green
Stamford Bridge (Chelsea F'ball Club)
Parsons Green
Eel Brook Common
Normand Park
Fulham Palace
Bishop's Park
Putney Bridge
Putney Pier
SW6
SW15
River Thames
Hurlingham Park
Hurlingham House
South Park
Wandsworth Park
Sands End
Fulham Wharf
Imperial Wharf
Gas Works
Hurlingham Wharf
Wandsworth Bridge
Wandsworth Town
Wandsworth Gyratory
Gargoyle Wharf
Putney
Hammersmith & Fulham
Wandsworth
LILLIE RD
DAWES RD
FULHAM RD
FULHAM BROADWAY
NORTH END RD
KING'S RD
NEW KING'S RD
FULHAM PALACE RD
FULHAM HIGH ST
PUTNEY BRIDGE APP
PUTNEY BRIDGE RD
PUTNEY HIGH ST
WANDSWORTH BRIDGE RD
HARWOOD RD
SWANDON WAY
REDCLIFFE GDNS
FINBOROUGH RD
GUNTER GR
A3218
A3219
A3220
A308
A304
A217
A219
A3209
A3205
B317
B318
B306
113
264
265
136
157
A
B
C
D
1
2
3
4
5
6
24
25
26
75
76
77
78

SW10
A
B
C
D
114
CHELSEA
6
5
4
3
2
1
78
77
76
75
26
27
28
158
266
267
135
FULHAM RD
FINBOROUGH RD
REDCLIFFE GDNS
KING'S RD
GUNTER GR
EDITH GR
CHEYNE WLK
CREMORNE RD
OLD CHURCH ST
BEAUFORT ST
OAKLEY ST
ROYAL HOSPITAL RD
CHELSEA EMB
Thames Path
Cadogan Pier
Chelsea Reach
ALBERT BRIDGE (SUSPENSION)
Terrace Wlk
THE PARADE
Fountain Lake
CARRIAGE DRIVE N
CENTRAL AVE
Festival Pleasure Gardens
Recn Gd
SW11
BATTERSEA
Sp Gd
PRINCE OF WALES DR
Kensington & Chelsea
Wandsworth
BATTERSEA BRIDGE
Bridge Wharf
Ransome's Dock
Old Ferry Wharf
Chelsea Wharf
Cremorne Wharf
River Thames
Chelsea Creek
Gas Works
Imperial Wharf
(under construction, opening 2010)
Hammersmith & Fulham
Wandsworth
BATTERSEA BRIDGE RD
ALBERT BRIDGE RD
WESTBRIDGE RD
VICARAGE CRES
SURREY LA
Chelsea Harbour Pier
Chelsea & Westminster
BATTERSEA HIGH ST
BATTERSEA PARK RD
Regent Wharf
LOMBARD RD
York Road Bsns Ctr
Heliport
YORK RD
Battersea Reach
Sands End
Fulham Wharf
Charterhouse Works
Sherwood Wharf
Gargoyle Wharf
WANDSWORTH BRIDGE
WANDSWORTH BRIDGE RD
1 GREENSWARD HO
2 CHAPLOW CL
3 ARCADIAN HO
4 POTTERS RD
1 SALTBURN HO
2 BRIDLINGTON HO
3 LERWICK HO
4 FILEY HO
5 DUNGENESS HO
6 DORIS EMMERTON CT
7 BALTIMORE HO
8 COMODORE HO
9 Wandsworth Town
SWANDON WAY
EAST HILL
NORTH SIDE WANDSWORTH COMMON
ST JOHN'S HILL
Clapham Junction
FALCON RD
LATCHMERE RD
Falcon Park
Christ Church CE Prim Sch
THE VILLAGE 1
BATTERSEA HTS 2
BATTERSEA RISE
ELSPETH RD
LAVENDER HILL
CLAPHAM COMMON
BARNARD MEWS 1
CARRINGTON CT 2
ABYSSINIA CL 3
CLAPHAM JUNCTION EST
GILMORE HO 1
GROVE MANS 2
Belleville Prim Sch

Royal Hospital (Army Pensioners)
Ranelagh Gardens (Site of Chelsea Flower Show)
Lister
Dock
Tenn Cts
Pimlico Sch
CHICHESTER ST
CHURCHILL GARDENS RD
GROSVENOR ROAD
A3212
Wharves
Wharf
Thames Path
River Thames
City of Westminster
Wandsworth
CHELSEA BRIDGE
GROSVENOR BRIDGE
Battersea Wharf
Jetty
New Covent Garden Flower Mkt
NINE ELMS LA
Tideway Ind Est
South Bank Bsns Ctr
Battersea Power Station (disused)
Nine Elms
John Milton Prim Sch
SW8
QUEENSTOWN RD
CARRIAGE DRIVE N
Athletic Gd
Children's Zoo
Recn Gd
CENTRAL AVE
Battersea Dogs Home
Boating Lake
Battersea Park
Queen's Cir
A3216
New Covent Garden Fruit & Vegetable Market
WANDSWORTH RD
A3036
Larkhall Park
PRINCE OF WALES DR
BATTERSEA PARK RD
A3205
Queenstown Road
Sir James Barrie Prim Sch
268
269
138
115
159
Wandsworth Road
Parkfield Ind Est
Heathbrook Park
SILVERTHORNE RD
B224
SW4
LAVENDER HILL
CLAPHAM
OLD TOWN
CEDARS RD
NORTH ST
Clapham High Street
CLAPHAM HIGH ST
CLAPHAM PARK RD
CLAPHAM COMMON NORTH SIDE
LONG RD
A3
Clapham Common
BEDFORD RD
A2217
Ellerslie Ind Est
Windmill on the Common (PH)
Lambeth Coll
Bndstd
Recn
1 ST SAVIOURS
2 LYNCOTT CRES
3 SALCOMBE GDNS
4 BARKER MEWS
5 WOODLANDS
6 OKEOVER MANOR
A B C D
1 2 3 4 5 6

A
B
C
D
116
261
270
137
160
Kennington
SE17
SE11
SW8
SW4
SW9
Vauxhall
Vauxhall Bridge
Vauxhall Cross
Spring Gardens
Wharves
Wharf
New Covent Garden Flower Mkt
South Bank Bsns Ctr
Vauxhall Park
Tenn Cts
Bwg Gn
The Oval
Kennington Oval
Kennington Park
Fball Gd
Govt Offices
Bnstnd
Liby
Sch
PO
Coll
Univ
Larkhall Park
South Lambeth
Stockwell
Stockwell Park Sch
Allot Gdns
Mostyn Gdns
Myatt's Fields Pk
Prim Sch
YMCA
BRIXTON
Brixton
Loughborough Junc
Clapham High Street
Clapham North
Lambeth
Ellerslie Ind Est
Works
Bsns Ctr
Ret Pk
TA Ctr
KENNINGTON LA
KENNINGTON PK RD
KENNINGTON OVAL
HARLEYFORD RD
WANDSWORTH RD
SOUTH LAMBETH RD
CLAPHAM RD
BRIXTON RD
STOCKWELL RD
CAMBERWELL NEW RD
COLDHARBOUR LA
ACRE LA
EFFRA RD
ATLANTIC RD
BEDFORD RD
MILKWOOD RD
LOUGHBOROUGH RD
LANSDOWNE WAY
STOCKWELL PARK RD
BRIXTON STATION RD
HIGH ST
PARRY ST
A3
A23
A202
A203
A204
A2217
A3036
A3204
A3205
B221
B223

262
117
263
A
B
C
D
CAMBERWELL
Camberwell Green
Burgess Park
SE15
SE5
CAMBERWELL RD
CAMBERWELL CHURCH ST
PECKHAM RD
SOUTHAMPTON WAY
ALBANY RD
TRAFALGAR AVE
PECKHAM HILL ST
OLD KENT RD
COLDHARBOUR LA
DENMARK HILL
CHAMPION PK
GROVE LA
DOG KENNEL HILL
GROVE VALE
HERNE HILL
East Dulwich
Peckham Rye
Ruskin Park
The Maudsley
Denmark Hill
King's College
Lucas Gdns
Cobourg Prim Sch
Gloucester Prim Sch
Print Village Ind Est
Bellenden Rd Bsns Ctr
Coldharbour Ind Est
The Weston Ed Ctr
William Booth Meml Trng Coll
Bessemer Grange Prim Sch
The Charter Sch
Herne Hill
140
161
A202
A215
A2216
A2214
A2217
B214
B215
B216
B217
32
33
34

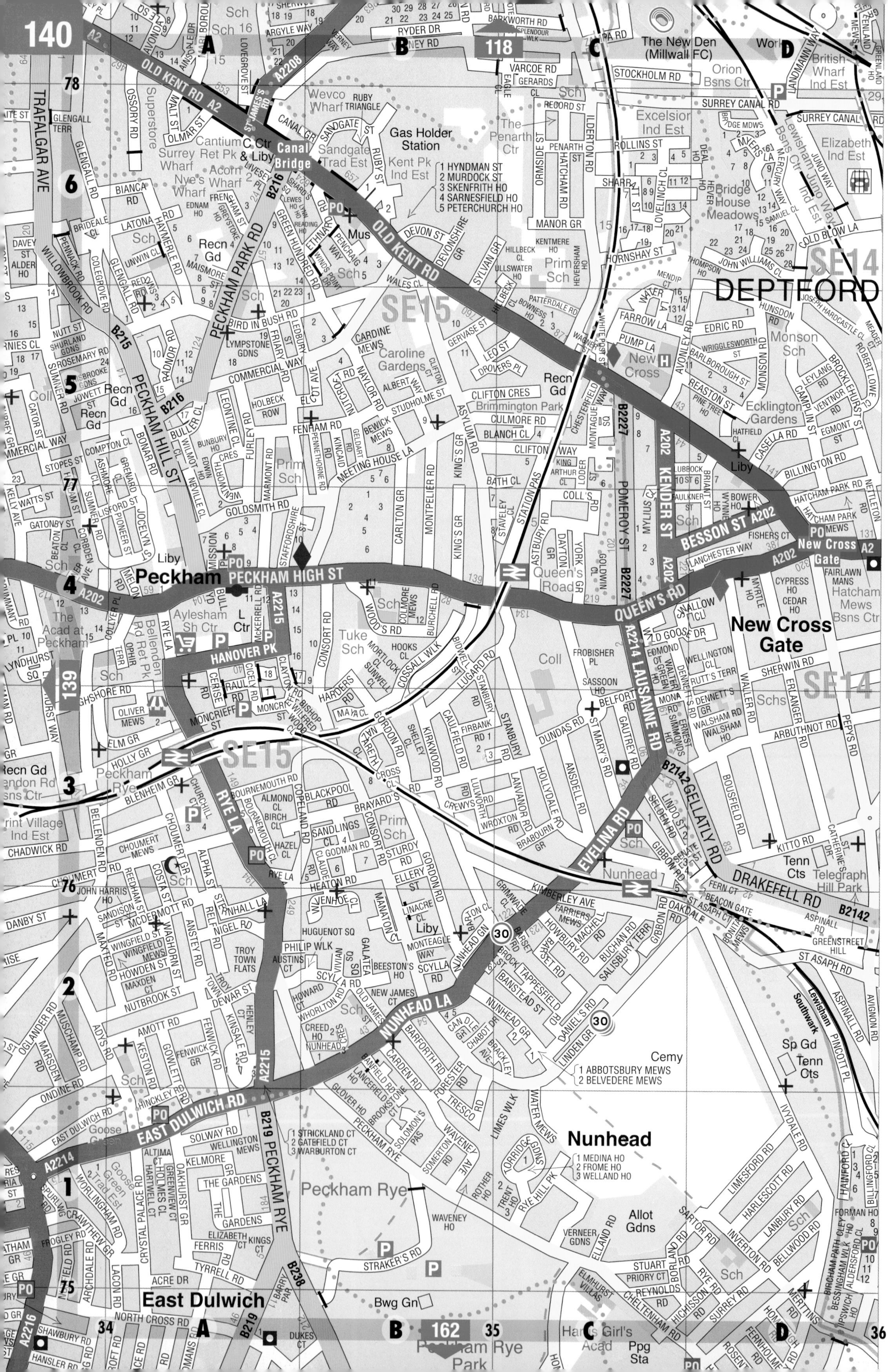

The New Den
(Millwall FC)
118
OLD KENT RD
A2
Canal Bridge
Gas Holder Station
Kent Pk Ind Est
1 HYNDMAN ST
2 MURDOCK ST
3 SKENFRITH HO
4 SARNESFIELD HO
5 PETERCHURCH HO
SE15
SE14
DEPTFORD
Caroline Gardens
Brimmington Park
Ecklington Gardens
New Cross
Peckham
PECKHAM HIGH ST
A202
PECKHAM PARK RD
PECKHAM HILL ST
TRAFALGAR AVE
Aylesham Sh Ctr
HANOVER PK
Queen's Road
QUEEN'S RD
KENDER ST
A202
BESSON ST
New Cross Gate
A2214 LAUSANNE RD
B2142 GELLATLY RD
EVELINA RD
Nunhead
DRAKEFELL RD
Telegraph Hill Park
Peckham Rye
RYE LA
139
NUNHEAD LA
EAST DULWICH RD
A2214
A2215
B219 PECKHAM RYE
Goose Green
Peckham Rye
1 STRICKLAND CT
2 GATEFIELD CT
3 WARBURTON CT
1 ABBOTSBURY MEWS
2 BELVEDERE MEWS
1 MEDINA HO
2 FROME HO
3 WELLAND HO
Nunhead
Cemy
Allot Gdns
East Dulwich
Lewisham
Southwark
162
Peckham Rye Park
34
35
36
A
B
C
D

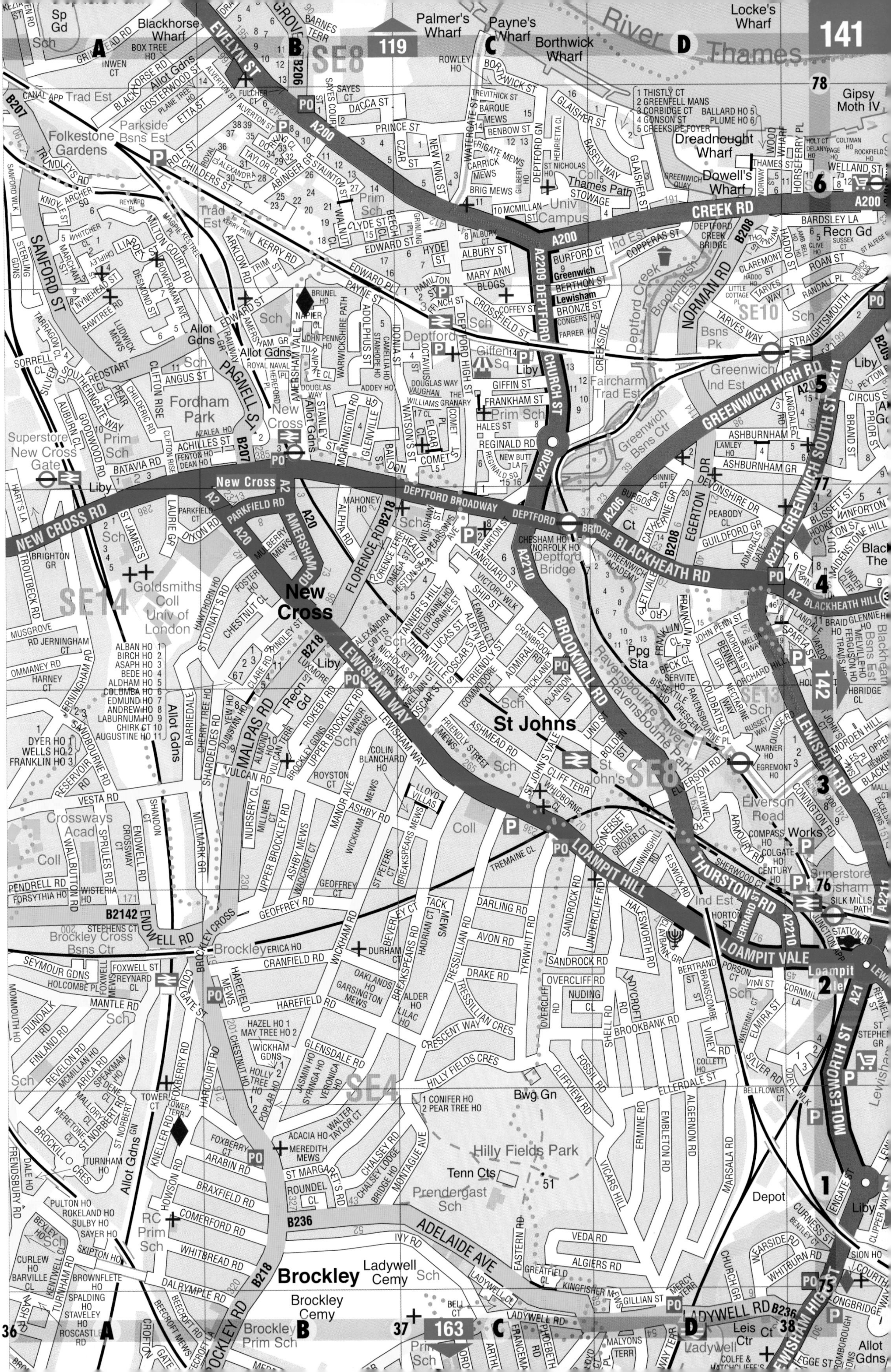
River Thames
Palmer's Wharf
Payne's Wharf
Borthwick Wharf
Locke's Wharf
Blackhorse Wharf
Dreadnought Wharf
Dowell's Wharf
Gipsy Moth IV
119
78
SE8
SE10
SE13
SE14
SE4
A
B
C
D
6
5
4
3
2
1
EVELYN ST
GROVE ST
CREEK RD
DEPTFORD CHURCH ST
DEPTFORD HIGH ST
DEPTFORD BROADWAY
DEPTFORD BRIDGE
NEW CROSS RD
New Cross
New Cross Gate
GREENWICH HIGH RD
GREENWICH SOUTH ST
BLACKHEATH RD
BLACKHEATH HILL
LEWISHAM WAY
LEWISHAM RD
LOAMPIT HILL
LOAMPIT VALE
THURSTON RD
BROOKMILL RD
MALPAS RD
BROCKLEY RD
BROCKLEY CROSS
ENDWELL RD
ADELAIDE AVE
LADYWELL RD
MOLESWORTH ST
LEWISHAM HIGH ST
AMERSHAM RD
PAGNELL ST
SANFORD ST
NORMAN RD
EGERTON DR
WICKHAM RD
TRESSILLIAN RD
HILLY FIELDS CRES
Folkestone Gardens
Fordham Park
Goldsmiths Coll Univ of London
Deptford Bridge
St Johns
Ravensbourne River
Ravensbourne Park
Elverson Road
Hilly Fields Park
Brockley
Brockley Cemy
Ladywell Cemy
Prendergast Sch
Crossways Acad
Brockley Cross Bsns Ctr
Greenwich Bsns Ctr
Faircharm Trad Est
Parkside Bsns Est
Thames Path
Deptford Creek
Depot
Superstore
Lewisham
36
37
163
38
75
76
77
142

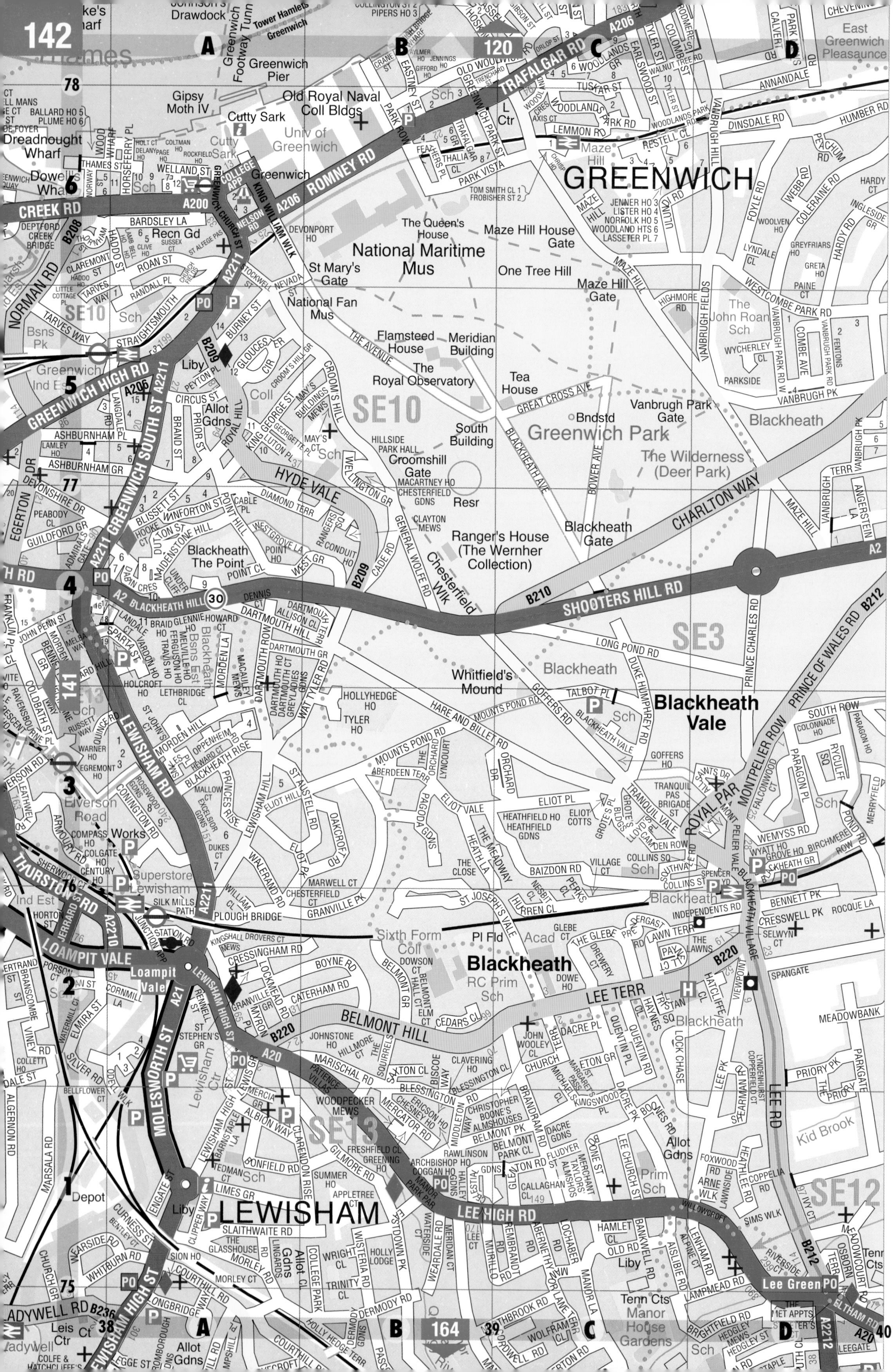
A
B
C
D
120
Greenwich Pier
Old Royal Naval Coll Bldgs
Gipsy Moth IV
Cutty Sark
Univ of Greenwich
Dreadnought Wharf
Dowells Wharf
CREEK RD
ROMNEY RD
TRAFALGAR RD
KING WILLIAM WLK
GREENWICH CHURCH ST
PARK ROW
GREENWICH
East Greenwich Pleasaunce
The Queen's House
National Maritime Mus
Maze Hill House Gate
One Tree Hill
Maze Hill Gate
St Mary's Gate
National Fan Mus
Flamsteed House
Meridian Building
The Royal Observatory
Tea House
SE10
Bndstd
Greenwich Park
Vanbrugh Park Gate
Blackheath
The Wilderness (Deer Park)
South Building
Croomshill Gate
Resr
Ranger's House (The Wernher Collection)
Blackheath Gate
CHARLTON WAY
SHOOTERS HILL RD
GREAT CROSS AVE
BLACKHEATH AVE
THE AVENUE
CROOM'S HILL
HYDE VALE
GREENWICH HIGH RD
GREENWICH SOUTH ST
BLACKHEATH HILL
SE3
Whitfield's Mound
Blackheath Vale
LONG POND RD
PRINCE CHARLES RD
PRINCE OF WALES RD
MONTPELIER ROW
ROYAL PAR
LEWISHAM RD
HARE AND BILLET RD
MOUNTS POND RD
ELIOT VALE
BLACKHEATH RISE
LEWISHAM HILL
Superstore Lewisham
LOAMPIT VALE
Loampit Vale
THURSTON RD
LEWISHAM HIGH ST
MOLESWORTH ST
BELMONT HILL
LEE TERR
Blackheath RC Prim Sch
Sixth Form Coll
Blackheath
Kid Brook
SE12
SE13
LEWISHAM
LEE HIGH RD
LEE RD
Lee Green
Manor House Gardens
LADYWELL RD
141
164
4
3
2
1
5
6

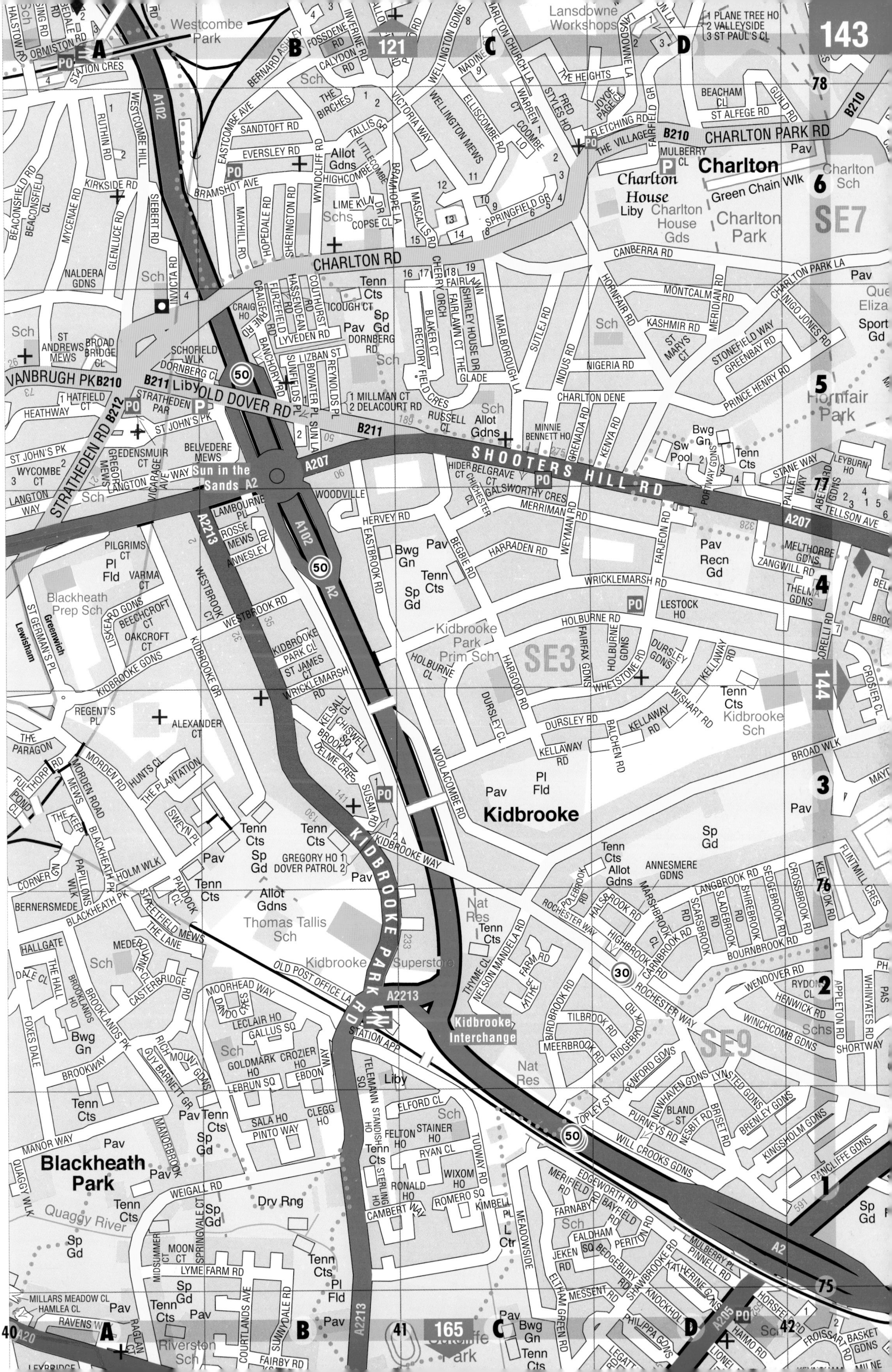
Westcombe Park
121
Lansdowne Workshops
1 PLANE TREE HO
2 VALLEYSIDE
3 ST PAUL'S CL
A
B
C
D
Charlton
Charlton House
Charlton House Gds
Charlton Park
Charlton Sch
Green Chain Wlk
SE7
CHARLTON PARK RD
CHARLTON RD
CHARLTON CHURCH LA
THE VILLAGE
B210
A102
B211
A207
A2
A2213
B212
OLD DOVER RD
VANBRUGH PK
STRATHEDEN RD
SHOOTERS HILL RD
Sun in the Sands
Hornfair Park
SE3
Kidbrooke
Kidbrooke Park Prim Sch
Kidbrooke Sch
Blackheath Prep Sch
Greenwich
Lewisham
KIDBROOKE PARK RD
KIDBROOKE WAY
ROCHESTER WAY
Thomas Tallis Sch
Kidbrooke Superstore
Kidbrooke Interchange
SE9
Blackheath Park
Quaggy River
Riverston Sch
144
165
40
41
42
1
2
3
4
5
6
75
76
77
78

A
B
C
D
122
166
143
42
43
44
78
77
76
75
6
5
4
3
2
1
Charlton
Charlton Park
Charlton Sch
SE7
SE18
SE9
CHARLTON PARK RD
B210
BEACHAM CL
ST ALFEGE RD
GUILD RD
LITTLE HEATH
PARK DR
CEMETERY LA
Cemy
Green Chain Wlk
CHARLTON PARK LA
Pav
REPOSITORY RD
Barrack Fld Pav
Tenn Cts
HA-HA RD
CIRCULAR WAY
Pl Fld
WOOLWICH COMM
A205
CLAYDOWN MEWS 5
GUNNER LA
LORD ROBERTS TER
BROOK HILL CL
WILLENHALL RD
ELMDENE RD
BIGNELL RD
SANDY HILL AVE
CAMBRIDGE ROW
MICHEL WLK
UPLANDS
Sch
NIGHTINGALE PL
GILDERSOME ST
PEACE ST
ENGINEER CL
NIGHTINGALE VALE
JACKSON ST
KEMPT ST
RITTER ST
FENNELL ST
LONG WLK
SHORT PATH
EDGE HILL
HERBERT PL
MAYPLACE LA
BARNFIELD RD
BARNFIELD GDNS
EGLINTON RD
WESTDALE RD
ETHEL BROOKS HO
COOPER CT
BARN FIELD
RIXON HO
KEEBLE CL
REEVES RD
RIPON RD
PAGET TERR
HERBERT RD
CANTWELL HO
DALLIN RD
HIGHVIEW
Woolwich Common
Woolwich Stad
STADIUM RD
Queen Elizabeth
Sports Gd
SHRAPNEL CL
MERIDIAN RD
INIGO JONES RD
STONEFIELD WAY
GREENBAY RD
PRINCE HENRY RD
Hornfair Park
MANSERGH CL
ACADEMY RD
ORDNANCE RD
LLANOVER RD
WHITWORTH RD
PAGET RISE
CANTWELL RD
SANTANA
BRENT RD
EGLINTON HILL
MAYPLACE LA
BRINKLOW CRES
DELVAN CL 1
KEEMOR CL 2
MATCHLESS DR
GARRISON CL
GRAHAM HO
CONDOVER CRES
DOWNEND
BUSHMOOR CRES
THE OLD FIRE STATION
Green Chain Wlk
Bwg Gn
Tenn Cts
PORTWAY GDNS
STANE WAY
PALLET WAY
ABERFORD GDNS
LEYBURN HO
BAKER RD
GREENWICH HTS
TELLSON AVE
GALTON HO 1
FLORENCE HO 2
SIDNEY HO 3
ROBERTSON HO 4
MENNIE HO 5
GODWIN HO 6
PANBRO HO 7
SUTHERLAND HO 8
IMPERIAL RD
RED LION LA
SPRINGWATER CL
DONALDSON RD
ANKERDINE CRES
MOORDOWN
OCCUPATION LA
RIVERVIEW HTS
EAGLESFIELD RD
A207
Pav
Recn Gd
MELTHORPE GDNS
ZANGWILL RD
THELMA GDNS
SHOOTERS HILL RD
EDITH CAVELL WAY
BELL
CAIRNS MEWS
ELIZABETH FRY PL
KENDALL RD
BROOK SQ
BARLOW DR
HOWERD WAY
CORELLI RD
CROSIER CL
GILBERT CL
ACADEMY PL
BARRINGTON VILLAS
CONSTITUTION RISE
CAMPBELL CL
RED LION PL
VYVYAN HO
HILL END
RAYLEAS CL
SHREWSBURY LA
FOXCROFT RD
CLEANTHUS RD
Recn Gd
THE CHESTNUTS
CLEANTHUS CL
LINKS VIEW
THE LEAS
SHOOTERS HILL
Castlewood Day Sch
KELLAWAY RD
Kidbrooke Sch
Recn Gd
Eltham Common
CRAIGHOLM
Mast
Memorial
KENILWORTH GDNS
CROWN WOOD LA
BROAD WLK
MAYDAY GDNS
Severndroog Castle
STONEY ALLEY
Green Chain Wlk
Jackwood
Pav
Sp Gd
Cemy
WELL HALL RD
PO
DUNBLANE RD
ALLENSWOOD RD
HEATHERBANK
CASTLEWOOD DR
FLINTMILL CRES
LANGBROOK RD
SLADEBROOK RD
SCARSBROOK RD
FIREBROOK RD
SEDGEBROOK RD
CROSSBROOK RD
KELBROOK RD
BOURNBROOK RD
ARBROATH RD
MAUDSLAY RD
MARTIN BOWES RD
ARSENAL RD
GRANBY RD
CORNWALLIS WLK
LITTLECROFT
CROOKSTON RD
ROSS WAY
PHINEAS PETT RD
FRANKLIN PAS
WHINYATES RD
APPLETON RD
DOWNMAN RD
LOVELACE GN
SHRAPNEL RD
BROME RD
GRANGEHILL PL
GARNETT CL
DAIRSIE RD
GLENHEAD CL
GLENBAR CL
GLENDAL CL
Tenn Cts
ENDOVER RD
RYDONS CL
HENWICK RD
WINCHCOMB GDNS
Schs
DICKSON RD
SHORTWAY
COBBETT RD
Deansfield Prim Sch
ROCHESTER WAY
DUMBRECK RD
BERRYHILL
CONGREVE RD
PRINCE RUPERT RD
ADMIRAL SEYMOUR RD
MORA RD
GRANGEHILL RD
WESTMOUNT RD
ELIBANK RD
BERRYHILL GDNS
Eltham Park North
LYNSTED GDNS
BRENLEY GDNS
BRISET RD
KINGSHOLM GDNS
RANCLIFFE GDNS
A208
TOM COOMBS CL
ODEON PAR
TUDOR PAR
ELMBROOK GDNS
BRICKYARD PATH
CRAIGTON RD
EARLSHALL RD
Sch
PLEASAUNCE CT
KIDBROOKE LA
Sp Gd
Pav
Tenn Cts
Well Hall Pleasaunce
GREENVALE RD
ELTHAM PARK GDNS
GLENESK RD
A2
PO
DUNVEGAN RD
WELL HALL PAR
MULBERRY PL
PINNELL RD
Bwg Gns
GLENLEA RD
GLENLYON RD
Eltham Park South
HORSFELD RD
A205
HAIMO RD
FROISSART RD
BASKET GDNS
Eltham
GLENSHIEL RD
Recn Gd
Tenn Cts
Green Chain Wlk
PULLMAN PL
St Mary's
CONNIFFE

A
B
C
D
123
167
44
45
46
78
77
76
75
6
5
4
3
2
1
146
St Margaret's CE Prim Sch
ST MARGARET'S TERR
ST MARGARET'S GR
VICARAGE PK
Tenn Cts
Bwg Gn
ST JOHN'S TERR
GLOBE CT
PO
BLENDON TERR
WERNBROOK ST
PLUMSTEAD COMMON RD
HEAVITREE RD
HEAVITREE CL
WAVERLEY CRES
GOSSAGE RD
TUSCAN RD
INVERARY PL
OLD MILL RD
WARWICK TERR
Plumstead Manor/Negus Sch
TORMOUNT RD
MERVYN CT
CHURCH HYDE
ROYDENE RD
SLADEDALE RD
PARKDALE RD
PHILIMORE CL
MARBLE HO
CRYSTAL HO
BERYL HO
GALENA HO
HEATH VILLAS
Gallions Mount Prim Sch
GROSMONT RD
WINN COMMON RD
Plumstead Common
BLEAK HILL LA
A209
WICKHAM LA
THE SLADE
RAVINE GR
SUTCLIFFE RD
MALTON MEWS
MALTON ST
MELLING ST
HEATHFIELD TERR
BASSANT RD
KING'S HIGHWAY
REVELL RISE
GILBOURNE RD
KINGSDALE RD
Rockliffe Manor Prim Sch
BRICKFIELD COTTS
Superstore
Acad
SANDYCROFT
OAKMERE RD
RUTHERGLEN RD
VERDUN RD
ALLIANCE RD
RADNOR CRES
WROTTESLEY RD
VERNHAM RD
VAMBERY RD
ISLA RD
KIRK LA
PALMERSTON RD
JAGO CL
ADMASTON RD
CRES
ENNIS RD
MACOMA RD
MACOMA TERR
ERINDALE TERR
ERINDALE
Sch
Liby
MANDELA HO
TUAM RD
PENDRELL ST
NYANZA ST
MOUNTBATTEN CL
KIRKHAM ST
TIMBERCROFT LA
ALBATROSS ST
PEGWELL ST
LUCKNOW ST
CARDIFF ST
ALABAMA ST
FLAXTON RD
ANCASTER ST
GENESTA RD
UPTON RD
OLVEN RD
HINSTOCK RD
WREKIN RD
NITHDALE RD
ROWTON RD
PLUM LA
Allot Gdns
CHELSWORTH DR
CHERITON DR
ST MERRYN CL
GARLAND RD
CLOTHWORKERS RD
WOOD RETREAT
RAYMERE GDNS
LANDSTEAD RD
DORAN GR
ACLAND CL
HATTON CL
DOTHILL RD
SE18
Green Chain Wlk
Shrewsbury Park
ASHRIDGE CRES
MEREWORTH DR
KINLET RD
IRWIN AVE
THORNHILL AVE
BARDEN ST
EASTVIEW AVE
SWINGATE LA
Cemy
SOUTHLAND RD
CAMDALE RD
Pl Fld
Tenn Cts
The William Barefoot Garden
HIGHMEAD
EDISON GR
COMBESIDE
DUNCROFT
WELTON RD
WARLAND RD
VOCE RD
HIGH GR
Pav
East Wickham Open Space
DRYDEN RD
MILTON RD
GLENMORE RD
Willow Dene Sch
TENNYSON CL
KEATS RD
EDISON RD
WYCLIFFE
BLENHEIM DR
CHAUCER RD
BURNS CL
WORDSWORTH RD
SHELLEY DR
BROWNING CL
BLAKE CL
PEREGRINE CT
ROSEMARY RD
East Wickham Schs
RIPPERSLEY RD
Tenn Cts
CH
EAGLESFIELD RD
Shooters Hill
Recn Gd
239
DOVER RD
Woodlands Farm
DA16
Greenwich
Bexley
PETERS CL
WICKHAM CT
MARINA DR
SANDRINGHAM DR
WICKHAM ST
HONITON RD
EXETER RD
TIDFORD RD
MONKTON RD
AWLISCOMBE RD
CENTRAL AVE
CRAMONDE CT
NORFOLK PL
DOVEDALE CL
CAMBORNE RD
NEWLYN RD
BALTIMORE PL
MARYVILLE
LULWORTH RD
MULBERRY CT
CLEVELAND RD
VAUGHAN RD
BENNETT CL
STATION APP
RUSKIN GR
RUSKIN AVE
RUSKIN DR
318
415
204
265
ROKESBY CL
HILL VIEW DR
SHERWOOD RD
BELLEGROVE CL
BELLEGROVE RD
BELLEGROVE PAR
MONTROSE CL
A207
OXLEAS CL
EASTCOTE RD
SUNDRIDGE AVE
BELMONT AVE
SHERWOOD RD
FALCONWOOD AVE
ASHMORE GR
Oxleas Wood Nature Reserve
Eastcote Prim Sch
SOUTHCROFT AVE
KELVIN RD
FARADAY RD
DARWIN RD
ST QUENTIN RD
TYNDALL RD
CAVENDISH AVE
MARNE AVE
NEWTON RD
WELLING WAY
CONISTON AVE
MONTROSE AVE
NORTHUMBERLAND AVE
CORNWALL AVE
HUXLEY RD
MAXWELL RD
Falconwood Field
SE9
Falconwood
SHEPHERDS LEAS
MABEL CROUT CT
LINGFIELD CRES
MILLBROOK AVE
BRAYWOOD RD
WINCROFTS DR
Bishop Ridley CE Prim Sch
Coll
WESTMORELAND AVE
CUMBERLAND AVE
CAMBRIDGE AVE
BUCKINGHAM AVE
DORSET AVE
THE GREEN
FALCONWOOD PAR
Tenn Ct
WESTWOOD LA
YORKLAND AVE
GLOUCESTER AVE
SOMERSET AVE
KENT AVE
HOOK LA
MERLIN RD
CLINTON AVE
BRENDENHAM AVE
FAIRWATER AVE
SUTHERLAND AVE
Cemy
978
870
596
50
EAST ROCHESTER WAY
A2
724
RIEFIELD RD
COLEPITS WOOD RD
Crown Woods
RIDGEWAY W

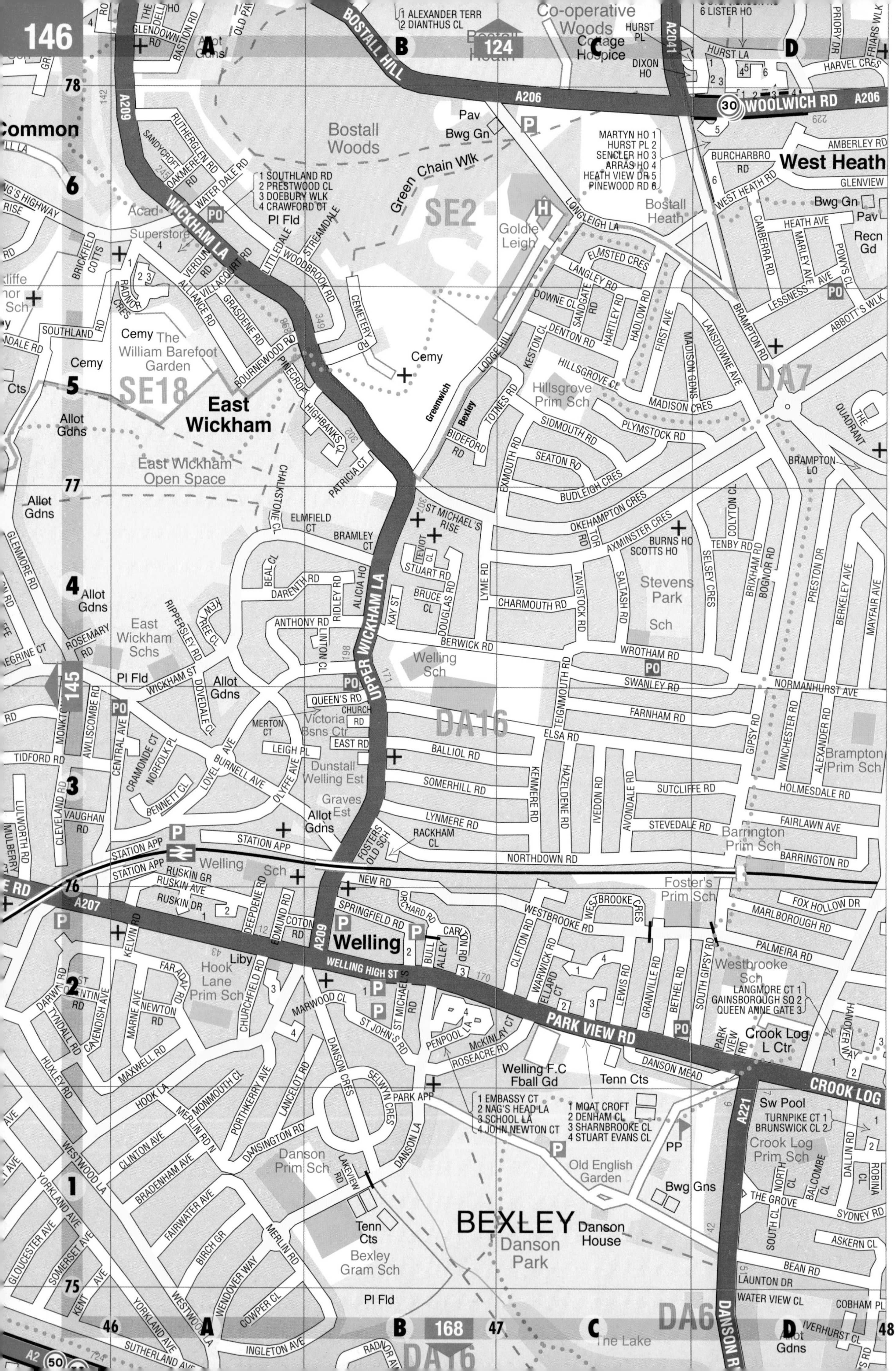
A
B
C
D
124
168
145
1
2
3
4
5
6
75
76
77
78
46
47
48
Common
West Heath
East Wickham
Welling
BEXLEY
SE2
SE18
DA7
DA16
DA6
1 ALEXANDER TERR
2 DIANTHUS CL
Co-operative Woods
Cottage Hospice
Bostall Heath
BOSTALL HILL
A206
A2041
A209
A207
A221
A2
HURST PL
DIXON HO
6 LISTER HO
HURST LA
PRIORY DR
FRIARS WLK
HARVEL CRES
WOOLWICH RD
MARTYN HO 1
HURST PL 2
SENCLER HO 3
ARRAS HO 4
HEATH VIEW DR 5
PINEWOOD RD 6
AMBERLEY RD
BURCHARBRO RD
GLENVIEW
WEST HEATH RD
Bwg Gn
Pav
HEATH AVE
Recn Gd
CANBERRA RD
MARLEY AVE
PONYS CL
LESSNESS AVE
ABBOTT'S WLK
BRAMPTON RD
LANSDOWNE AVE
Bostall Woods
Green Chain Wlk
Goldie Leigh
LONGLEIGH LA
ELMSTED CRES
LANGLEY RD
DOWNE CL
SANDGATE RD
HARTLEY RD
HADLOW RD
FIRST AVE
MADISON GDNS
DENTON RD
KESTON CL
HILLSGROVE CL
Hillsgrove Prim Sch
MADISON CRES
THE QUADRANT
BRAMPTON LO
GLENDOWN RD
BASTION RD
OLD PARK
Allot Gdns
RUTHERGLEN RD
SANDYCROFT
OAKMERE RD
WATER DALE RD
1 SOUTHLAND RD
2 PRESTWOOD CL
3 DOEBURY WLK
4 CRAWFORD CT
Pl Fld
WICKHAM LA
STREAMDALE
LITTLEDALE
WOODBROOK RD
VILLACOURT RD
VERDUN RD
ALLIANCE RD
GRASDENE RD
Acad
Superstore
BRICKFIELD COTTS
RADNOR CRES
KING'S HIGHWAY
SOUTHLAND RD
Cemy
The William Barefoot Garden
BOURNEWOOD RD
PINECROFT
HIGHBANKS CL
CEMETERY RD
Greenwich
Bexley
LODGE HILL
TOTNES RD
BIDEFORD RD
EXMOUTH RD
SIDMOUTH RD
SEATON RD
PLYMSTOCK RD
BUDLEIGH CRES
OKEHAMPTON CRES
TOR RD
AXMINSTER CRES
BURNS HO
SCOTTS HO
TENBY RD
COLYTON CL
BRIXHAM RD
BOGNOR RD
SELSEY CRES
PRESTON DR
BERKELEY AVE
MAYFAIR AVE
Stevens Park
Sch
East Wickham Open Space
CHALKSTONE CL
PATRICIA CT
ELMFIELD CT
BRAMLEY CT
ST MICHAEL'S RISE
TEVIOT CL
STUART RD
BRUCE CL
DOUGLAS RD
KAY ST
LYME RD
CHARMOUTH RD
TAVISTOCK RD
SALTASH RD
BEAL CL
DARENTH RD
RIDLEY RD
ALICIA HO
ANTHONY RD
LINTON CL
UPPER WICKHAM LA
BERWICK RD
WROTHAM RD
SWANLEY RD
NORMANHURST AVE
GLENMORE RD
East Wickham Schs
RIPPERSLEY RD
YEW TREE CL
ROSEMARY RD
PEREGRINE CT
WICKHAM ST
DOVEDALE CL
Welling Sch
TEIGNMOUTH RD
FARNHAM RD
ELSA RD
QUEEN'S RD
CHURCH RD
MERTON CT
Victoria Bsns Ctr
EAST RD
LEIGH PL
Dunstall Welling Est
Graves Est
BALLIOL RD
SOMERHILL RD
LYNMERE RD
KENMERE RD
HAZELDENE RD
IVEDON RD
AVONDALE RD
SUTCLIFFE RD
STEVEDALE RD
GIPSY RD
WINCHESTER RD
ALEXANDER RD
Brampton Prim Sch
HOLMESDALE RD
FAIRLAWN AVE
Barrington Prim Sch
BARRINGTON RD
MONKTON RD
AWLISCOMBE RD
CENTRAL AVE
CRAMONDE CT
NORFOLK PL
LOVEL AVE
BURNELL AVE
OLYFFE AVE
BENNETT CL
TIDFORD RD
LULWORTH RD
MULBERRY
CLEVELAND RD
VAUGHAN RD
STATION APP
FOSTERS OLD SCH
RACKHAM CL
NORTHDOWN RD
RUSKIN GR
RUSKIN AVE
RUSKIN DR
DEEPDENE RD
EDMUND RD
COTON RD
NEW RD
ORCHARD RD
SPRINGFIELD RD
Foster's Prim Sch
WESTBROOKE CRES
WESTBROOKE RD
FOX HOLLOW DR
MARLBOROUGH RD
PALMEIRA RD
KELVIN RD
Liby
FARADAY RD
Hook Lane Prim Sch
CHURCHFIELD RD
BULL ALLEY
CARLTON RD
WELLING HIGH ST
CLIFTON RD
WARWICK RD
ELLARD CT
LEWIS RD
GRANVILLE RD
BETHEL RD
SOUTH GIPSY RD
Westbrooke Sch
LANGMORE CT 1
GAINSBOROUGH SQ 2
QUEEN ANNE GATE 3
DARWIN RD
CONSTANTINE RD
CAVENDISH AVE
MARNE AVE
NEWTON RD
TYNDALL RD
MARWOOD CL
ST JOHN'S RD
ST MICHAEL'S RD
PENPOOL LA
McKINLAY CT
PARK VIEW RD
PARK VIEW RD
Crook Log L Ctr
HANOVER WAY
HUXLEY RD
MAXWELL RD
ROSEACRE RD
Welling F.C Fball Gd
Tenn Cts
DANSON MEAD
CROOK LOG
Sw Pool
TURNPIKE CT 1
BRUNSWICK CL 2
HOOK LA
MONMOUTH CL
MERLIN RD N
PORTHKERRY AVE
LANCELOT RD
DANSON CRES
SELWYN CRES
PARK APP
1 EMBASSY CT
2 NAG'S HEAD LA
3 SCHOOL LA
4 JOHN NEWTON CT
1 MOAT CROFT
2 DENHAM CT
3 SHARNBROOKE CL
4 STUART EVANS CL
PP
Crook Log Prim Sch
NORTH CL
BALCOMBE CL
DALLIN RD
ROBINA CL
WESTWOOD LA
CLINTON AVE
BRADENHAM AVE
DANSINGTON RD
Danson Prim Sch
LAKEVIEW RD
DANSON LA
Old English Garden
Bwg Gns
THE GROVE
SOUTH CL
SYDNEY RD
YORKLAND AVE
FAIRWATER AVE
Tenn Cts
Danson House
Danson Park
ASKERN CL
GLOUCESTER AVE
SOMERSET AVE
BIRCH GR
MERLIN RD
Bexley Gram Sch
BEAN RD
LAUNTON DR
WATER VIEW CL
WENDOVER WAY
COWPER CL
KENT AVE
Pl Fld
COBHAM PL
IVERHURST CL
DANSON RD
The Lake
SUTHERLAND AVE
INGLETON AVE
RADNOR AVE

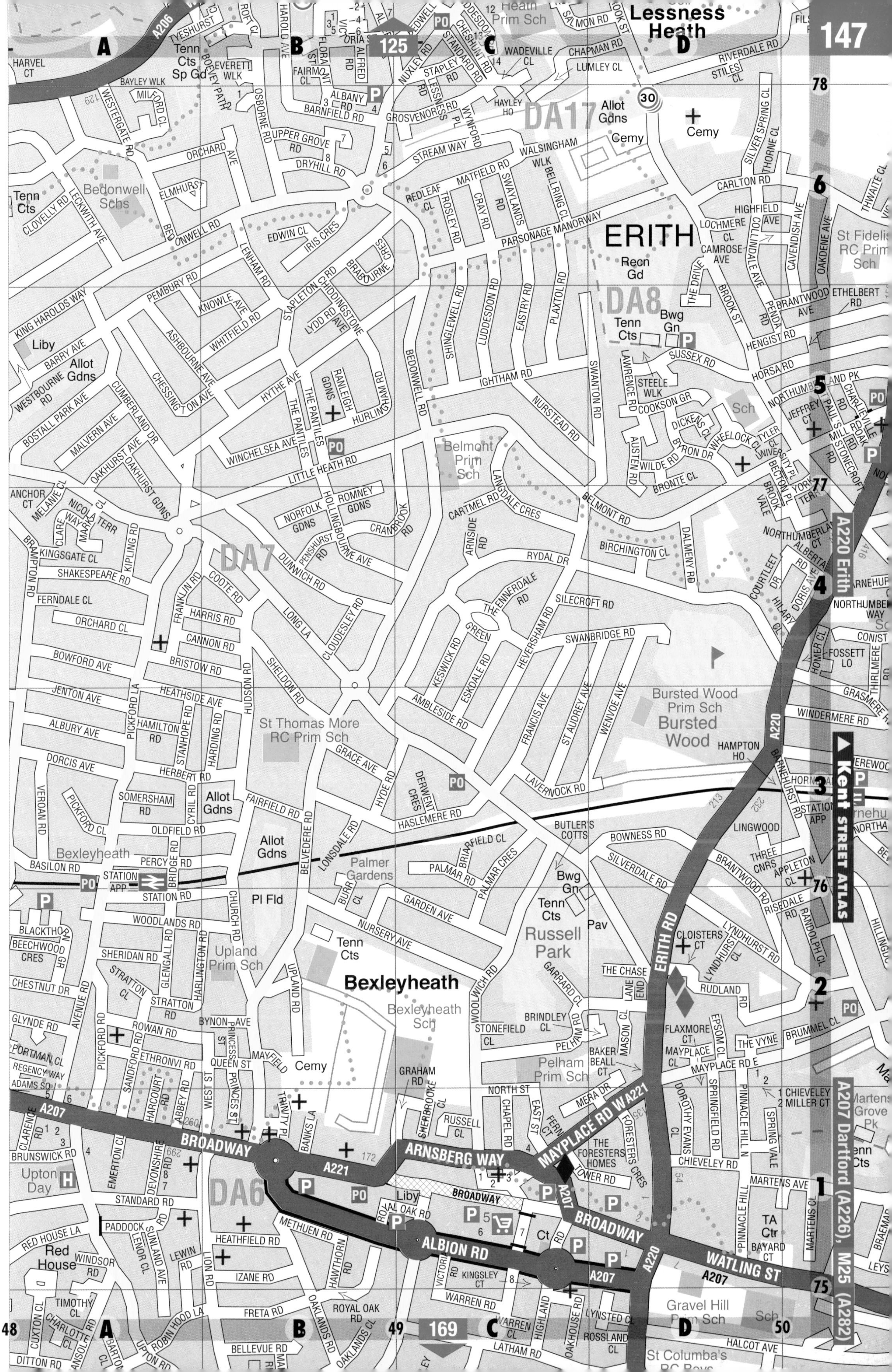
Lessness Heath
ERITH
Bexleyheath
DA17
DA8
DA7
DA6
A206
A207
A220
A221
A220 Erith
A207 Dartford (A226), M25 (A282)
Kent STREET ATLAS
125
169
A
B
C
D
78
77
76
75
48
49
50
6
5
4
3
2
1
Tenn Cts Sp Gd
Bedonwell Schs
Liby
Allot Gdns
Cemy
Recn Gd
Bwg Gn
Tenn Cts
Sch
St Fidelis RC Prim Sch
Belmont Prim Sch
St Thomas More RC Prim Sch
Bursted Wood Prim Sch
Bursted Wood
Bexleyheath
Palmer Gardens
Pl Fld
Upland Prim Sch
Bexleyheath Sch
Russell Park
Pav
Pelham Prim Sch
Upton Day
Red House
Gravel Hill Prim Sch
St Columba's
Martens Grove Pk
TA Ctr
HARVEL CT
TYESHURST
EVERETT WLK
BAYLEY WLK
MILFORD CL
WESTERGATE RD
BOEVEY PATH
HAROLD AVE
FAIRMONT CL
ALBANY RD
BARNFIELD RD
OSBORNE RD
UPPER GROVE RD
DRYHILL RD
ORCHARD AVE
ELMHURST
BEDONWELL RD
CLOVELLY RD
LECKWITH AVE
NUXLEY RD
STAPLEY RD
LESSNESS RD
GROSVENOR RD
WYNFORD PL
STREAM WAY
WADEVILLE CL
CHAPMAN RD
LUMLEY CL
HAYLEY HO
RIVERDALE RD
STILES CL
WALSINGHAM WLK
MATFIELD RD
SWAYLANDS RD
BELLRING CL
REDLEAF CL
TROSLEY RD
CRAY RD
PARSONAGE MANORWAY
SILVER SPRING CL
THORNE CL
CARLTON RD
THWAITE CL
LOCHMERE CL
HIGHFIELD AVE
COLLINDALE AVE
CAVENDISH AVE
OAKDENE AVE
CAMROSE AVE
THE DRIVE
BROOK ST
PENDA RD
BRANTWOOD AVE
ETHELBERT RD
HENGIST RD
HORSA RD
EDWIN CL
IRIS CRES
LENHAM RD
BRADBOURNE CRES
PEMBURY RD
KNOWLE AVE
WHITFIELD RD
STAPLETON RD
CHIDDINGSTONE AVE
LYDD RD
SHINGLEWELL RD
LUDDESDON RD
EASTRY RD
PLAXTOL RD
SWANTON RD
LAWRENCE RD
SUSSEX RD
STEELE WLK
COOKSON GR
DICKENS CL
BYRON DR
WHEELOCK CL
AUSTEN RD
WILDE RD
BRONTE CL
TYLER CL
UNIVERSITY PL
BECTON PL
NORTHUMBERLAND PK
JEFFREY CT
PAULS CT
MILL RD
CHARLIEVILLE RD
KING HAROLDS WAY
BARRY AVE
WESTBOURNE RD
BOSTALL PARK AVE
CUMBERLAND DR
ASHBOURNE AVE
CHESSINGTON AVE
HYTHE AVE
THE PANTILES
RANLEIGH GDNS
HURLINGHAM RD
BEDONWELL RD
IGHTHAM RD
NURSTEAD RD
MALVERN AVE
OAKHURST AVE
OAKHURST GDNS
WINCHELSEA AVE
LITTLE HEATH RD
ANCHOR CT
MELANIE CL
NICOLA TERR
CLARE WAY
MARK CL
KINGSGATE CL
KIPLING RD
SHAKESPEARE RD
BRAMPTON RD
FERNDALE CL
ORCHARD CL
BOWFORD AVE
JENTON AVE
ALBURY AVE
DORCIS AVE
VERDAN RD
PICKFORD CL
PICKFORD LA
HOLLINGBOURNE AVE
ROMNEY GDNS
NORFOLK GDNS
CRANBROOK RD
PENSHURST RD
DUNWICH RD
CARTMEL RD
LANGDALE CRES
ARNSIDE RD
BELMONT RD
BIRCHINGTON CL
DALMENY RD
YORK TERR
BROOK VALE
NORTHUMBERLAND CT
ALBERTA RD
COURTLEET DR
DORIS AVE
HILARY CL
RYDAL DR
THE GREEN
ENNERDALE RD
SILECROFT RD
HEVERSHAM RD
SWANBRIDGE RD
FRANKLIN RD
COOTE RD
HARRIS RD
CANNON RD
BRISTOW RD
HEATHSIDE AVE
HAMILTON RD
STANHOPE RD
HARDING RD
HUDSON RD
LONG LA
CLOUDESLEY RD
SHELDON RD
KESWICK RD
ESKDALE RD
AMBLESIDE RD
FRANCIS AVE
ST AUDREY AVE
WENVOE AVE
HOMER CL
FOSSETT LO
WINDERMERE RD
GRASMERE RD
HAMPTON HO
GRACE AVE
HERBERT RD
SOMERSHAM RD
CYRIL RD
FAIRFIELD RD
HYDE RD
DERWENT CRES
HASLEMERE RD
LAVERNOCK RD
BARNEHURST RD
LINGWOOD
OLDFIELD RD
PERCY RD
BASILON RD
STATION APP
STATION RD
BELVEDERE RD
LONSDALE RD
BUTLER'S COTTS
BRIARFIELD CL
PALMAR RD
PALMAR CRES
BOWNESS RD
SILVERDALE RD
BRANTWOOD RD
THREE CNRS
APPLETON CL
RISEDALE RD
RANDOLPH CL
BLACKTHORN GR
BEECHWOOD CRES
WOODLANDS RD
CHURCH RD
BURR CL
GARDEN AVE
NURSERY AVE
SHERIDAN RD
GLENGALL RD
HARLINGTON RD
CHESTNUT DR
STRATTON CL
STRATTON RD
UPLAND RD
WOOLWICH RD
GARRARD CL
THE CHASE
LANE END
ERITH RD
CLOISTERS CT
LYNDHURST CL
LYNDHURST RD
RUDLAND RD
GLYNDE RD
AVENUE RD
ROWAN RD
BYNON AVE
PRINCESS ST
PORTMAN CL
REGENCY WAY
ADAMS SQ
ETHRONVI RD
SANDFORD RD
QUEEN ST
MAYFIELD
STONEFIELD CL
BRINDLEY CL
PELHAM RD
MASON CL
FLAXMORE CT
MAYPLACE CL
EPSOM CL
THE VYNE
BRUMMEL CL
BAKER BEALL CT
MAYPLACE RD E
MAYPLACE RD W
CHIEVELEY CT
MILLER CT
CLARENCE RD
HARCOURT RD
ABBEY RD
WEST ST
PRINCES ST
TRINITY PL
BANKS LA
GRAHAM RD
SHERBROOKE CL
RUSSELL CL
NORTH ST
CHAPEL RD
EAST ST
FERN CT
MERA DR
THE FORESTERS HOMES
FORESTERS CRES
DOROTHY EVANS CL
SPRINGFIELD RD
PINNACLE HILL N
SPRING VALE
CHIEVELEY RD
MARTENS AVE
BRUNSWICK RD
BROADWAY
ARNSBERG WAY
EMERTON CL
DEVONSHIRE RD
STANDARD RD
TOWER RD
PADDOCK CL
LENOR CL
SUNLAND AVE
RED HOUSE LA
WINDSOR RD
LEWIN RD
LION RD
HEATHFIELD RD
METHUEN RD
ROYAL OAK RD
ALBION RD
IZANE RD
HAWTHORN RD
VICTORIA RD
KINGSLEY CT
WARREN RD
HIGHLAND RD
OAKHOUSE RD
LYNSTED CL
ROSSLAND CL
WATLING ST
BAYARD CT
PINNACLE HILL
MARTENS CL
TIMOTHY CL
CHARLOTTE CL
CUXTON CL
ANSOLL RD
UPTON RD
ROBIN HOOD LA
FRETA RD
OAKLANDS RD
OAKLANDS CL
ROYAL OAK RD
BELLEVUE RD
WARREN CL
LATHAM RD
HALCOT AVE
DITTON RD

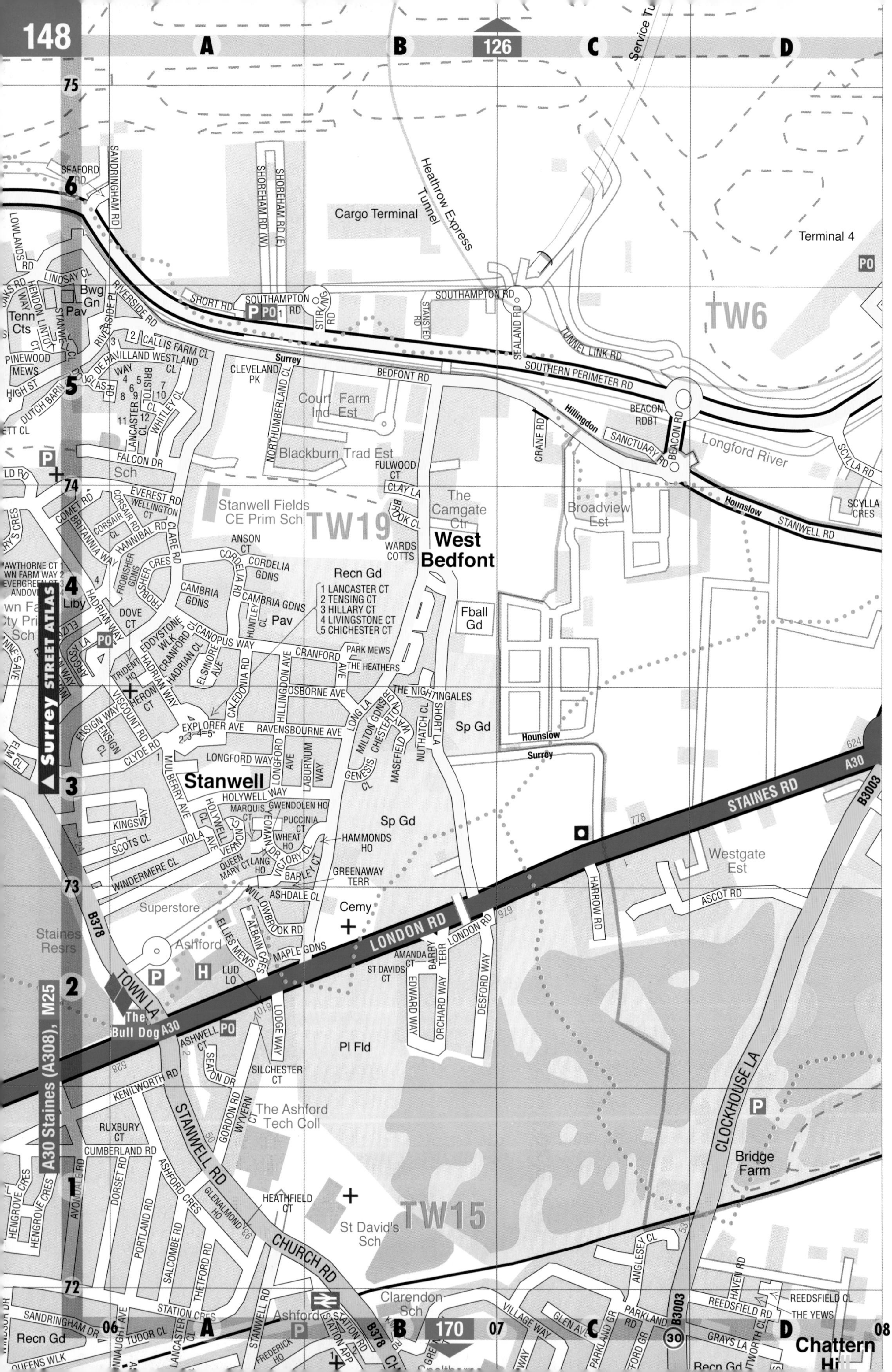
A
B
126
C
D
Service Tunnel
75
6
5
74
4
3
73
2
72
Heathrow Express Tunnel
Cargo Terminal
Terminal 4
PO
TW6
SEAFORD RD
SANDRINGHAM RD
SHOREHAM RD (W)
SHOREHAM RD (E)
LOWLANDS RD
LINDSAY CL
HENDON WAY
LINTOTT CT
Bwg Gn
Pav
Tenn Cts
STANWELL CL
RIVERSIDE PL
RIVERSIDE RD
SHORT RD
SOUTHAMPTON RD
STIRLING RD
STANSTED RD
SEALAND RD
TUNNEL LINK RD
SOUTHERN PERIMETER RD
PINEWOOD MEWS
HIGH ST
DUTCH BARN CL
CALLIS FARM CL
DE HAVILLAND WAY
WESTLAND CL
BRISTOL CL
LANCASTER CL
WHITLEY CL
CLEVELAND PK
NORTHUMBERLAND CL
Surrey
BEDFONT RD
Court Farm Ind Est
Blackburn Trad Est
BEACON RDBT
BEACON RD
Hillingdon
CRANE RD
SANCTUARY RD
Longford River
SCYLLA RD
SCYLLA CRES
Hounslow
STANWELL RD
FALCON DR
Sch
EVEREST RD
WELLINGTON CT
COMET RD
CORSAIR CL
CORSAIR RD
BRITANNIA WAY
HANNIBAL RD
CLARE RD
Stanwell Fields CE Prim Sch
TW19
FULWOOD CT
CLAY LA
BROOK CL
The Camgate Ctr
Broadview Est
WARDS COTTS
West Bedfont
ANSON CT
CORDELIA RD
CORDELIA GDNS
FROBISHER GDNS
FROBISHER CRES
CAMBRIA GDNS
CAMBRIA CT
Recn Gd
1 LANCASTER CT
2 TENSING CT
3 HILLARY CT
4 LIVINGSTONE CT
5 CHICHESTER CT
Fball Gd
Liby
DOVE CT
HADRIAN WAY
ELIZABETH WAY
ARGOSY LA
PO
HUNTLEY CL
Pav
EDDYSTONE WLK
CRANFORD CL
CANOPUS WAY
HADRIAN CL
ELSINORE AVE
CALEDONIA RD
HILLINGDON AVE
CRANFORD AVE
PARK MEWS
THE HEATHERS
OSBORNE AVE
TRIDENT HO
HERON CT
VISCOUNT RD
ENSIGN WAY
ENSIGN CL
EXPLORER AVE
RAVENSBOURNE AVE
LONG LA
MILTON GDNS
CHESTERTON DR
WALDON DR
MASEFIELD RD
THE NIGHTINGALES
NUTHATCH CL
SHORT LA
Sp Gd
Hounslow
Surrey
CLYDE RD
LONGFORD WAY
LONGFORD AVE
LABURNUM WAY
GENESIS CL
A30
STAINES RD
B3003
778
Stanwell
MULBERRY AVE
HOLYWELL WAY
GWENDOLEN HO
MARQUIS CT
PUCCINIA CT
WHEAT HO
HAMMONDS HO
KINGSWAY
SCOTS CL
VIOLA AVE
HOLYWELL CL
VERNON CL
YEOMAN DR
VICTORY CL
BARLEY CT
WINDERMERE CL
QUEEN MARY CT
LANG HO
GREENAWAY TERR
Westgate Est
HARROW RD
ASCOT RD
B378
Superstore
ASHDALE CL
WILLOWBROOK RD
Cemy
Staines Resrs
Ashford
ELLIES MEWS
ALBAIN CRES
MAPLE GDNS
LONDON RD
AMANDA CT
BARRY TERR
ST DAVIDS CT
EDWARD WAY
ORCHARD WAY
DESFORD WAY
TOWN LA
LUD LO
The Bull Dog
ASHWELL CT
PO
LODGE WAY
Pl Fld
SEATON DR
SILCHESTER CT
KENILWORTH RD
STANWELL RD
GORDON RD
WYVERN CT
The Ashford Tech Coll
CLOCKHOUSE LA
Bridge Farm
RUXBURY CT
CUMBERLAND RD
AVONDALE RD
DORSET RD
ASHFORD CRES
PORTLAND RD
SALCOMBE RD
GLENALMOND HO
HEATHFIELD CT
St David's Sch
TW15
HENGROVE CRES
CHURCH RD
THETFORD RD
ANGLESEY CL
HAVEN RD
REEDSFIELD CL
REEDSFIELD RD
THE YEWS
Clarendon Sch
STATION CRES
SANDRINGHAM DR
STANWELL RD
Ashford
STATION APP
STATION RD
VILLAGE WAY
GLEN AVE
PARKLAND GR
PARKLAND RD
GRAYS LA
Recn Gd
TUDOR CL
LANCASTER CL
FREDERICK RD
06
170
07
08
Chattern Hill
Recn Gd
QUEENS WLK
Surrey STREET ATLAS
A30 Staines (A308), M25

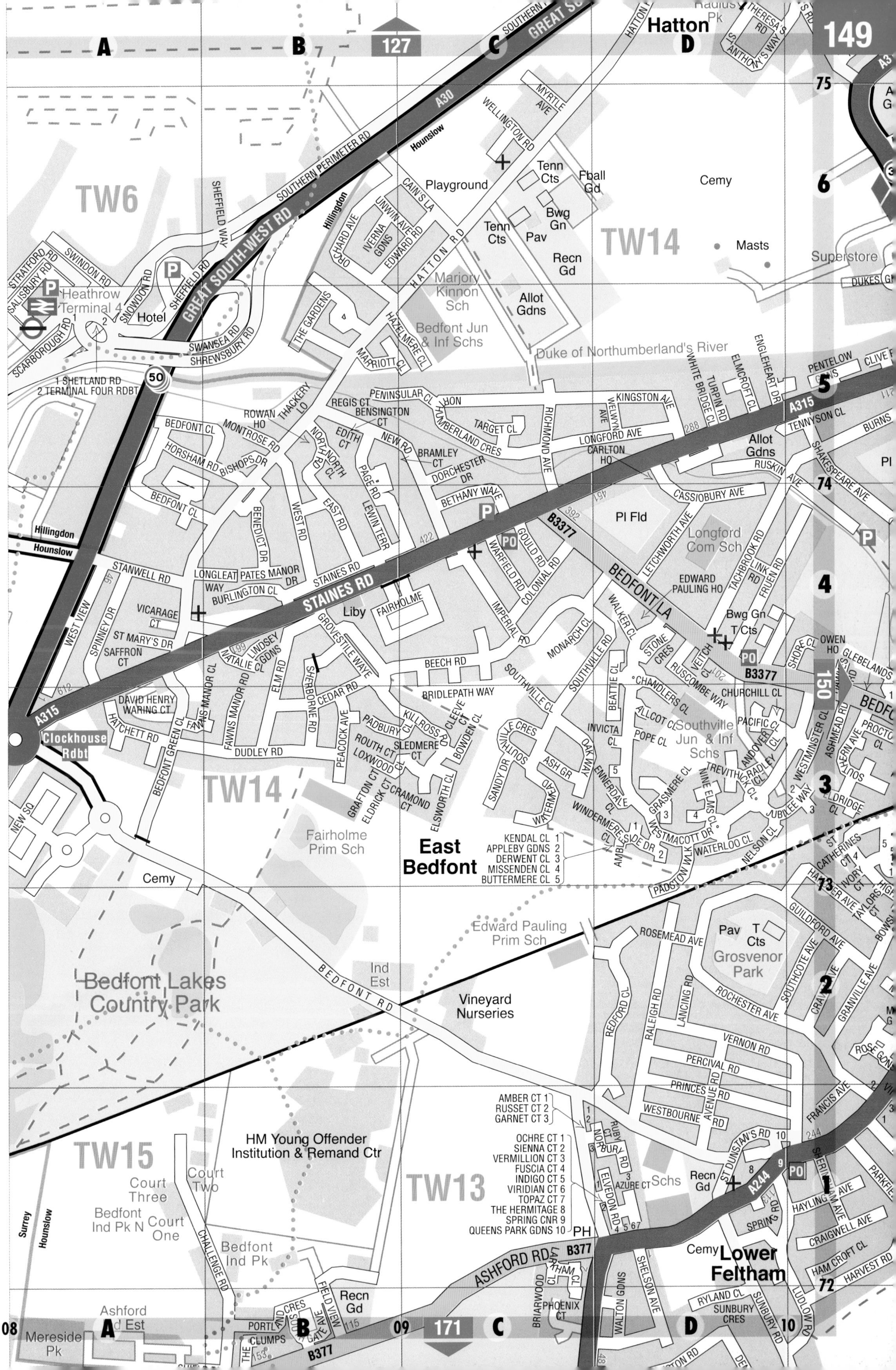

A
B
127
C
D
Hatton
TW6
TW14
Heathrow Terminal 4
Hotel
GREAT SOUTH-WEST RD
A30
SOUTHERN PERIMETER RD
SHEFFIELD WAY
SHEFFIELD RD
SWINDON RD
STRATFORD RD
SALISBURY RD
SCARBOROUGH RD
SNOWDON RD
SWANSEA RD
SHREWSBURY RD
1 SHETLAND RD
2 TERMINAL FOUR RDBT
Hillingdon
Hounslow
Playground
Tenn Cts
Fball Gd
Bwg Gn
Pav
Recn Gd
Allot Gdns
Cemy
Masts
Superstore
Marjory Kinnon Sch
Bedfont Jun & Inf Schs
Duke of Northumberland's River
HATTON RD
WELLINGTON RD
MYRTLE AVE
CAIN'S LA
UNWIN AVE
IVERNA GDNS
EDWARD RD
ORCHARD AVE
THE GARDENS
HAZELMERE CL
MARRIOTT CL
THACKERY LO
ROWAN HO
REGIS CT
BENSINGTON CT
PENINSULAR CL
NORTHUMBERLAND CRES
TARGET CL
RICHMOND AVE
KINGSTON AVE
WELWYN AVE
LONGFORD AVE
CARLTON HO
WHITE BRIDGE CL
TURPIN RD
ELMCROFT CL
ENGLEHEART DR
PENTELOW GDNS
CLIVE RD
A315
TENNYSON CL
BURNS
Allot Gdns
RUSKIN AVE
SHAKESPEARE AVE
Pl
CASSIOBURY AVE
Pl Fld
Longford Com Sch
LETCHWORTH AVE
TACHBROOK RD
LINK RD
FRUEN RD
EDWARD PAULING HO
BEDFONT LA
B3377
Bwg Gn
T Cts
VEITCH CL
STONE CRES
RUSCOMBE WAY
CHANDLERS CL
CHURCHILL CL
ALLCOT CL
POPE CL
Southville Jun & Inf Schs
PACIFIC CL
ANDOVER CL
RADLEY CL
TREVITHICK CL
NINE ELMS CL
GRASMERE CL
WESTMACOTT DR
JUBILEE WAY
WATERLOO CL
NELSON CL
PADSTOW WLK
WESTMINSTER CL
ASHMEAD RD
SOUTHERN AVE
PROCTOR CL
ELDRIDGE CL
SHORE CL
OWEN HO
GLEBELANDS
150
BEDFONT
BEDFONT CL
MONTROSE RD
HORSHAM RD
BISHOPS DR
NORTH RD
NORTH CL
EDITH CT
NEW RD
BRAMLEY CT
DORCHESTER DR
BETHANY WAYE
PAGE RD
LEWIN TERR
EAST RD
WEST RD
BENEDICT DR
STANWELL RD
LONGLEAT WAY
PATES MANOR DR
STAINES RD
BURLINGTON CL
STAINES RD
PO
GOULD RD
WARFIELD RD
COLONIAL RD
IMPERIAL RD
MONARCH CL
WALKER CL
SOUTHVILLE RD
SOUTHVILLE CL
SOUTHVILLE CRES
BEATTIE CL
INVICTA CL
OAK WAY
ASH GR
SANDY DR
WATERMILL WAY
ENNERDALE CL
WINDERMERE CL
AMBLESIDE DR
Liby
FAIRHOLME
GROVESTILE WAYE
BEECH RD
BRIDLEPATH WAY
WEST VIEW
SPINNEY DR
VICARAGE CT
ST MARY'S DR
SAFFRON CT
LINDSEY GDNS
NATALIE CL
ELM RD
SHERBORNE RD
CEDAR RD
PADBURY CL
KILLROSS RD
CLEEVE CT
BOWDEN CL
ROUTH CT
SLEDMERE CT
LOXWOOD CL
PEACOCK AVE
GRAFTON CT
ELDRICK CT
CRAMOND CT
ELSWORTH CL
DAVID HENRY WARING CT
HATCHETT RD
BEDFONT GREEN CL
FAWNS MANOR CL
FAWNS MANOR RD
DUDLEY RD
Clockhouse Rdbt
NEW SQ
Cemy
Fairholme Prim Sch
East Bedfont
KENDAL CL 1
APPLEBY GDNS 2
DERWENT CL 3
MISSENDEN CL 4
BUTTERMERE CL 5
Edward Pauling Prim Sch
Ind Est
Vineyard Nurseries
BEDFONT RD
Bedfont Lakes Country Park
ROSEMEAD AVE
Pav
T Cts
Grosvenor Park
REDFORD CL
RALEIGH RD
LANCING RD
ROCHESTER AVE
SOUTHCOTE AVE
CRAVEN AVE
GRANVILLE AVE
GUILDFORD AVE
ST CATHERINES CT
IVORY CT
HAMPSHER AVE
TAYLORS CT
VERNON RD
PERCIVAL RD
PRINCES RD
AVENUE RD
WESTBOURNE RD
FRANCIS AVE
ST DUNSTAN'S RD
AMBER CT 1
RUSSET CT 2
GARNET CT 3
OCHRE CT 1
SIENNA CT 2
VERMILLION CT 3
FUSCIA CT 4
INDIGO CT 5
VIRIDIAN CT 6
TOPAZ CT 7
THE HERMITAGE 8
SPRING CNR 9
QUEENS PARK GDNS 10
RUBY CT
NORBURY RD
ELVEDON RD
AZURE CT
Schs
Recn Gd
PO
A244
SPRING RD
SHERINGHAM AVE
HAYLING AVE
CRAIGWELL AVE
HAM CROFT CL
HARVEST RD
PARKFIELD
HM Young Offender Institution & Remand Ctr
TW15
TW13
Court Three
Court Two
Court One
Bedfont Ind Pk N
Bedfont Ind Pk
CHALLENGE RD
Surrey
Hounslow
ASHFORD RD
B377
LARKHAM CL
BRIARWOOD CL
PHOENIX CT
PH
WALTON GDNS
SHELSON AVE
Cemy
Lower Feltham
RYLAND CL
SUNBURY CRES
SUNBURY RD
LUDLOW RD
Recn Gd
FIELD VIEW
GATE AVE
CRES
PORTLAND CRES
THE CLUMPS
Ashford Ind Est
Mereside Pk
08
09
171
10
75
74
73
72
6
5
4
3
2
1

North Feltham
FELTHAM
Lower Feltham
Hanworth
TW14
TW13
North Feltham Trad Est
River Gdns Bsns Ctr
Tamian Ind Est
Central Pk Est
Haslemere Ind Est
Freehold Ind Ctr
Fairway Est
Dockwell's Ind Est
Mercury Ctr
Willow Ho
Duke of Northumberland's River
Griffin Ctr
Hounslow Heath
London Loop
Sparrow Farm Schs
Longford Com Sch
Feltham Arena
Southville Jun & Inf Schs
Victoria Jun Sch
The Centre
Grosvenor Park
Feltham Com Sch
Feltham Bsns Complex
Feltham Corporate Ctr
Felthambrook Ind Est
Hanworth Park House
Hanworth Park
STAINES RD
A315
A312
A244
A314
B3377
FAGG'S RD
HARLINGTON RD W
HARLINGTON RD E
HOUNSLOW RD
BEDFONT LA
HANWORTH RD
UXBRIDGE RD
HIGH ST
NEW RD
1 FRANK TOWELL CT
2 BRASSEY CL
3 EASTLEIGH WAY
4 ORCHARD RD
5 PEACH RD
6 ALMOND CL
7 HAZEL GR
8 HUNTER HO
9 HAWTHORN RD
10 TILLEY RD
11 PLUM CL
12 ARCHER CT
13 MAGNOLIA CT
14 LEMON GR
15 BELVEDERE HO
16 QUINCE HO
17 CAMELLIA HO
1 BERGENIA HO
2 AZALEA HO
3 HAMLYN HO
1 BROOKLYN CT
2 DEVONSHIRE CT
1 PARKFIELD PAR
2 ROCHESTER PAR
3 THE VINEYARDS
4 CHERVIL CL
1 BLAKEWOOD CL
2 SHAKESPEARE WAY
128
149
172

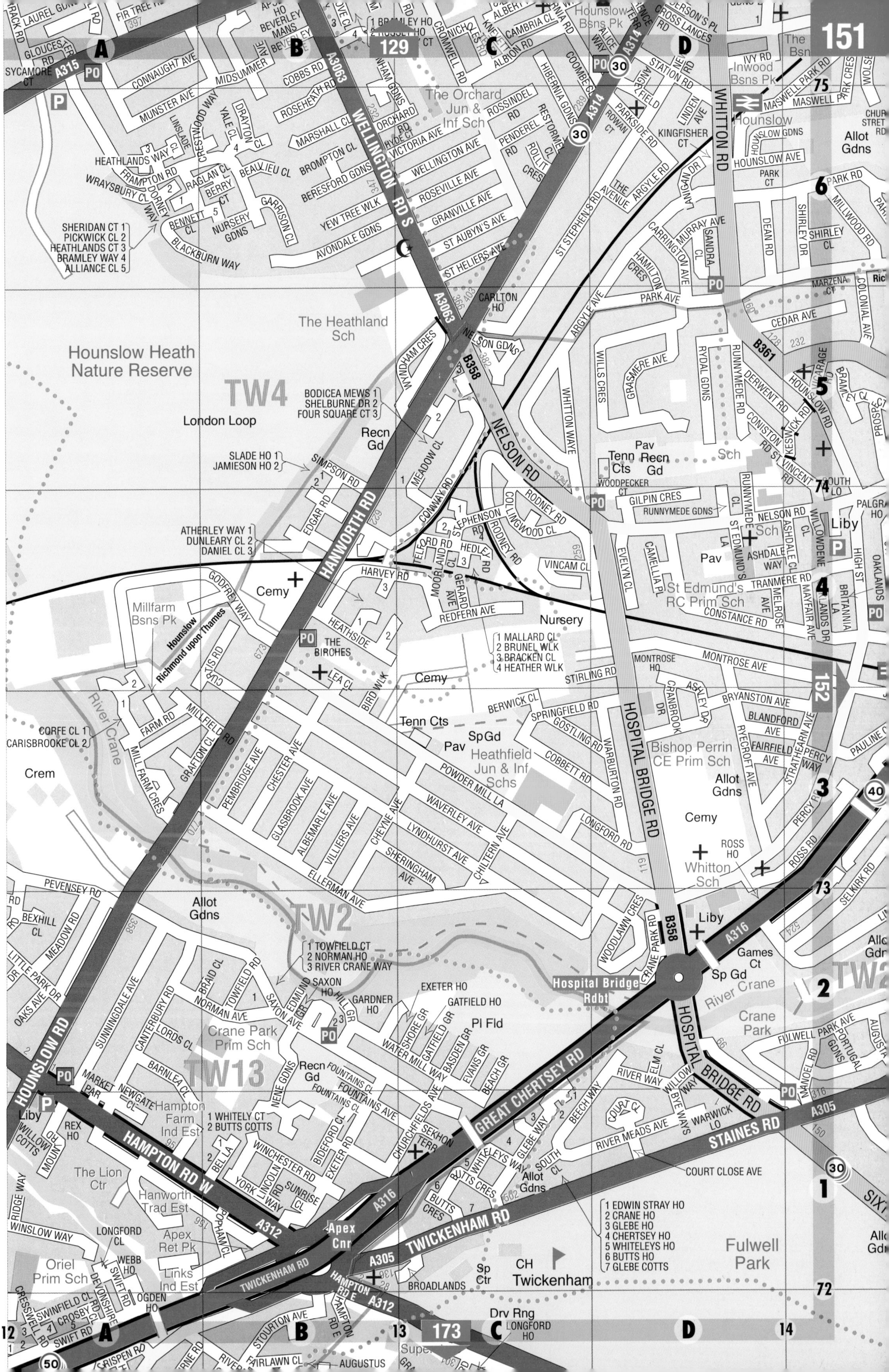

Hounslow Heath Nature Reserve
TW4
London Loop
The Heathland Sch
Hounslow Bsns Pk
The Orchard Jun & Inf Sch
Inwood Bsns Pk
Hounslow
Allot Gdns
WELLINGTON RD S
A3063
A314
A315
WHITTON RD
HANWORTH RD
NELSON RD
B358
B361
HOSPITAL BRIDGE RD
GREAT CHERTSEY RD
A316
STAINES RD
A305
TWICKENHAM RD
HAMPTON RD W
A312
HOUNSLOW RD
Hospital Bridge Rdbt
Apex Cnr
TW2
TW13
Recn Gd
Cemy
Millfarm Bsns Pk
Hounslow
Richmond upon Thames
River Crane
Crem
Heathfield Jun & Inf Schs
Bishop Perrin CE Prim Sch
St Edmund's RC Prim Sch
Whitton Sch
Crane Park Prim Sch
Crane Park
Hampton Farm Ind Est
The Lion Ctr
Hanworth Trad Est
Apex Ret Pk
Links Ind Est
Oriel Prim Sch
CH Twickenham
Fulwell Park
Drv Rng
Sp Ctr
Nursery
Tenn Cts
Pav
Pl Fld
Games Ct
Sp Gd
Liby
SHERIDAN CT 1
PICKWICK CL 2
HEATHLANDS CT 3
BRAMLEY WAY 4
ALLIANCE CL 5
BODICEA MEWS 1
SHELBURNE DR 2
FOUR SQUARE CT 3
SLADE HO 1
JAMIESON HO 2
ATHERLEY WAY 1
DUNLEARY CL 2
DANIEL CL 3
1 MALLARD CL
2 BRUNEL WLK
3 BRACKEN CL
4 HEATHER WLK
CORFE CL 1
CARISBROOKE CL 2
1 TOWFIELD CT
2 NORMAN HO
3 RIVER CRANE WAY
1 WHITELY CT
2 BUTTS COTTS
1 EDWIN STRAY HO
2 CRANE HO
3 GLEBE HO
4 CHERTSEY HO
5 WHITELEYS HO
6 BUTTS HO
7 GLEBE COTTS
129
173
152
A
B
C
D
75
74
73
72
12
13
14
6
5
4
3
2
1

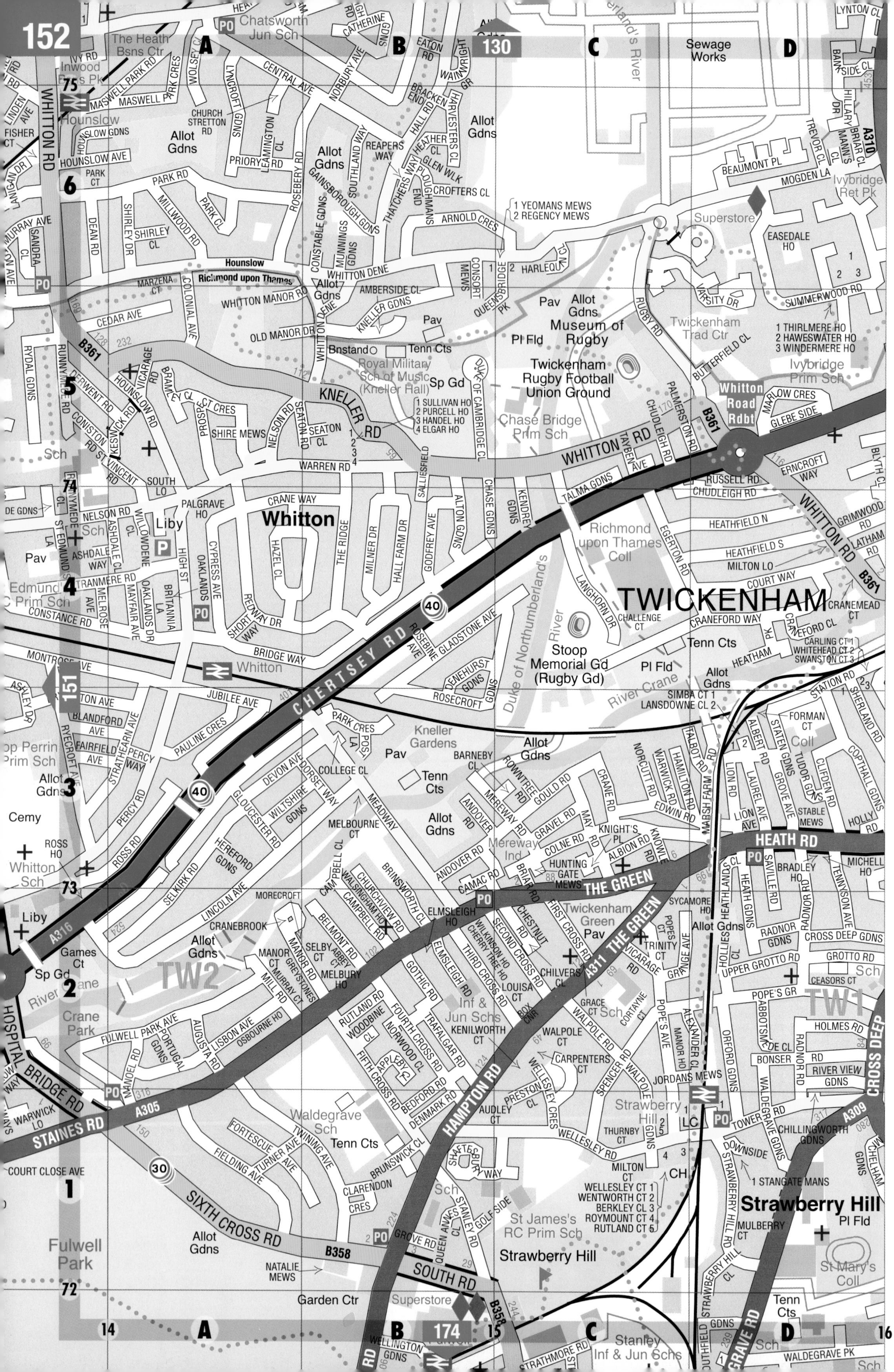
A
B
C
D
130
174
151
14
15
16
Whitton
TWICKENHAM
Strawberry Hill
TW2
TW1
Chatsworth Jun Sch
The Heath Bsns Ctr
Inwood Bsns Pk
Hounslow
Sewage Works
Ivybridge Ret Pk
Superstore
Easedale Ho
Twickenham Trad Ctr
Ivybridge Prim Sch
Whitton Road Rdbt
Museum of Rugby
Twickenham Rugby Football Union Ground
Royal Military Sch of Music (Kneller Hall)
Chase Bridge Prim Sch
Richmond upon Thames Coll
Stoop Memorial Gd (Rugby Gd)
River Crane
Kneller Gardens
Mereway Ind
Twickenham Green
Waldegrave Sch
Crane Park
Fulwell Park
St James's RC Prim Sch
St Mary's Coll
Stanley Inf & Jun Schs
Garden Ctr
Duke of Northumberland's River
WHITTON RD
KNELLER RD
CHERTSEY RD
HEATH RD
THE GREEN
STAINES RD
HAMPTON RD
SIXTH CROSS RD
SOUTH RD
CROSS DEEP
HOSPITAL BRIDGE RD
WALDEGRAVE RD
A316
A305
A311
A309
A310
B361
B358

131
175
154
A
B
C
D
RICHMOND
Richmond Lock
Richmond Green
St Margarets
Twickenham
Cambridge Park
Marble Hill Park
Marble Hill House
Ham House
Ham
Sudbrook
TW1
TW7
TW10
River Thames
River Crane
Eel Pie Island
Thames Path
Ferry P
St Helena Pier
Richmond Landing Stage
Orleans Park Sch
Orleans House Gallery
York House
St Mary's CE Prim Sch
The German Sch
The Russell Sch
Strathmore Sch
Grey Court Sch
St Catherine's Sch
St James Ind Sch for Boys
Meadlands Prim Sch
Moor Mead Gd
St Margarets Rdbt
London Road Rdbt
TWICKENHAM BRIDGE
RICHMOND BRIDGE
THE AVENUE
ST MARGARET'S RD
CHERTSEY RD
RICHMOND RD
CROWN RD
LONDON RD
YORK ST
KING ST
CROSS DEEP
STRAWBERRY VALE
TWICKENHAM RD
PETERSHAM RD
HILL RISE
HILL ST
GEORGE ST
RED LION ST
PARADISE RD
THE QUADRANT
SHEEN RD
HAM COMM
SANDY LA
RIVERSIDE
RIVERSIDE DR
A3004
A316
A310
A305
A307
B321
B352
Allot Gdns
Tenn Cts
Bwg Gn
Sp Gd
Pl Fld
Liby
Mus
Sch
Cemy
1 WINCHESTER HO
2 PARKVIEW CT
3 BIRNHAM HO
1 CAMBRIDGE PARK CT
2 MEADOWSIDE
1 SUTHERLAND HO
2 SCOTT HO
3 WIGGINS LA
ALBANY CT 1
ST RICHARDS CT 2
1 HAWKESLEY CL
2 CLAVERING CL
3 CHATSWORTH PL
4 WOODVILLE CL
5 MARLOW HO
6 FAIRWATER HO
7 REGATTA HO
16
17
18
72
73
74
75
1
2
3
4
5
6

RICHMOND
132
SHEEN RD
A305
A307
B322
B353
B321
B352
SHEEN RD
GEORGE ST
RED LION ST
PARADISE RD
HILL ST
BRIDGE ST
QUADRANT RD
THE QUADRANT
ETON ST
DRUMMONDS PL
PRINCE'S ST
LICHFIELD GDNS
DUNSTABLE RD
ALTON RD
SYDNEY RD
WORPLE WAY
ALBANY RD
HYDE RD
ALBERT RD
PRINCES RD
HOUBLON RD
SPRING TERR
WINTER BOX WLK
PELDON CT
FLOYER CL
QUEENS CRES
SPRING GROVE RD
CHARMOUTH CT
King's House Sch
DENBIGH GDNS
KINGS RD
AUDLEY RD
MARCHMONT RD
PRESTON PL
CHURCH RD
DYNEVOR RD
MOUNT ARARAT RD
GROSVENOR RD
GROSVENOR AVE
HALFORD RD
THE VINEYARD
ONSLOW AVE
ROYSTON RD
ONSLOW RD
CHISLEHURST RD
LANCASTER PK
ELLERKER GDNS
HILL RISE
HERMITAGE
ORMOND RD
Richmond Hill
RICHMOND HILL
FRIARS STILE RD
MONTAGUE RD
CARDIGAN RD
MARLBOROUGH RD
ROSEMONT RD
CHESTER AVE
QUEEN'S RISE
QUEEN'S RD
PARK RD
GREVILLE RD
LOWER GROVE RD
PYRLAND RD
PARK HILL
MANNING PL
KING GEORGE SQ
GROVE RD
KINGSMEAD
CAMBRIAN RD
HOBART PL
SAYER'S WLK
STAFFORD PL
Richmond Coll
The Vineyard Sch
TERRACE LA
PARK HO
HOWSON TERR
ROBINS CT
BLADE HO
HAVERSHAM CL
Richmond Landing Stage
PETERSHAM RD
COMPASS HILL
NIGHTINGALE LA
Star & Garter Home
STAR AND GARTER HILL
RICHMOND GATE
SAWYER'S HILL
Horse Ride
Capital Ring
CAMBRIDGE PARK CT
MEADOWSIDE
Bwg Gn
T Cts
153
RIVER LA
RUTLAND DR
PETERSHAM RD
The German Sch
Petersham
FORGE LA
MEADOW CL
CEDAR HTS
ASHFIELD CL
BUTE AVE
SUDBROOK LA
The Russell Sch
SANDPITS RD
PETERSHAM CL
HENLOW PL
CLIFFE RD
DICKENS CL
Pembroke Lodge
Petersham Park
Sudbrook Park
CH
Richmond
LAUDERDALE DR
BISHOPS CL
SUDBROOK GDNS
HAM GATE AVE
Cemy
CARRINGTON RD
KINGS RIDE GATE
COURTLANDS
1 ARUNDEL HO
2 MARLBOROUGH HO
3 BUCKINGHAM HO
4 OSBOURNE HO
5 YORK HO
6 SANDRINGHAM HO
7 KENT HO
8 NORFOLK HO
9 RUNNYMEDE HO
10 CARISBROOKE HO
11 GLOUCESTER HO
Pl Fld
Allot Gdns
Christ's Sch
Cemy
SHEEN COMMON DR
ORCHARD RISE
BERWYN RD
DERBY RD
COVAL LA
ALBANY CL
COVAL GDNS
WEST TEMPLE SHEEN
WESTHAY GDNS
LONGFIELD DR
MONROE DR
UPLANDS CL
East Sheen Common
Fball Gd
Pl Fld
Tenn Cts
Bwg Gn
The Bog
Bog Lodge
Saw Pit Plantation
TW10
Sidmouth Wood
Pen Ponds
Pond Plantation
Pond Slade
Hamcross Plantation
Isabella Plantation
176
18
19
20

A
B
C
D
133
SW15
The Priory
Roehampton Sports Club
SHREWSBURY AVE
PARK AVE
2 PARKWAY HO
PALMERSTON RD
OBSERVATORY RD
TEMPLE SHEEN RD
FIRS AVE
RICHMOND PARK RD
PALEWELL PK
EAST SHEEN
HERTFORD AVE
PRIORY CT
DOWDESWELL CL
PERCIVAL RD
WELLSIDE GDNS
TEMPLE SHEEN
WELL LA
WAYSIDE
VICARAGE GDNS
Allot Gdns
PARK DR
PALEWELL COMMON DR
PP
Sp Gd
Tenn Cts
CH
Roehampton
CHRISTCHURCH RD
SHEEN WOOD
THE MALL
YORK AVE
HOOD AVE
SHEEN LA
B351
VICARAGE RD
ENMORE CT
ENMORE GDNS
STONEHILL CL
STONEHILL RD
PARKGATE GDNS
CLARE LAWN AVE
PARKLANDS CL
1 MARTINDALE
2 SPENCER GDNS
FIFE RD
Palewell Fields
Palewell Common
PRIORY LA
BANK LA
ROEDEAN CRES
ROEHAMPTON GATE
Richmond upon Thames
Wandsworth
ALLENFORD HO 1
SWAYTHLING HO 2
TATCHBURY HO 3
PENWOOD HO 4
BRAMLEY HO 5
SHALDEN HO 6
DUNBRIDGE HO 7
DENMEAD HO 8
CHARCOT HO 9
PORTSWOOD PL 10
BROCKBRIDGE HO 11
HURSTBOURNE HO 12
Roehampton Univ (Froebel Coll)
Roehampton Univ (Southlands Coll)
Roehampton Univ (Digby Stuart Coll)
ROEHAMPTON LA
A306
CROMWELL HO
Pl Fld
East Sheen Gate
Adam's Pond
Horse Ride
Ibstock Place Sch
CLARENCE LA
HIGHCLIFFE DR
SHERFIELD GDNS
WINCHFIELD HO
BINLEY HO
CEDARS CT
South Thames Coll
Roehampton Gate
WARNFORD HO
TUNWORTH CRES
DANEBURY AVE
EGBURY HO
TANGLEY GR
ELLISFIELD DR
KINGSCLERE CL
HARBRIDGE AVE
LAVERSTOKE GDNS
CLEEVE WAY
CHADWICK CL
CLARE PL
SWANWICK CL
MINSTEAD GDNS
Old House
Roehampton
SW14
Polo Field
FINCHDEAN HO 1
HOLMSLEY HO 2
OVERTON HO 3
REDENHAM HO 4
MOUNT ANGELUS RD 5
Liby
Univ
The Huntercombe Roehampton
156
KIMPTON HO
CRONDALL HO
RUNNYMEDE CT
ARNEWOOD CL
IBSLEY GDNS
ALTON
SW15
Beverley Brook
Richmond Park
The Royal Ballet Sch (White Lodge)
REDWOOD
POCKLINGTON
Richmond Park
Deer Park
Pen Ponds
TW10
Chohole Gate
NORSTEAD PL
A3
Spankers Hill Wood
ROEHAMPTON VALE
Superstore
STAG LA
FRIARS AVE
FRENSHAM DR
STROUD CRES
PALLISTER TERR
FLORENCE TERR 1
EBOR COTTS 2
Horse Ride
Kingston Univ Roehampton Vale Campus
Robin Hood Gate
BEVERLEY COTTS
FUSION CT
A308
Robin Hood
War Meml
Allot Gdns
KINGSTON VALE
PO
VALE CRES
KT2
ROBIN HOOD
MARYDALE CL
DERWENT
177
Kingston
Pl Fld
20
21
22
75
74
73
72
6
5
4
3
2
1

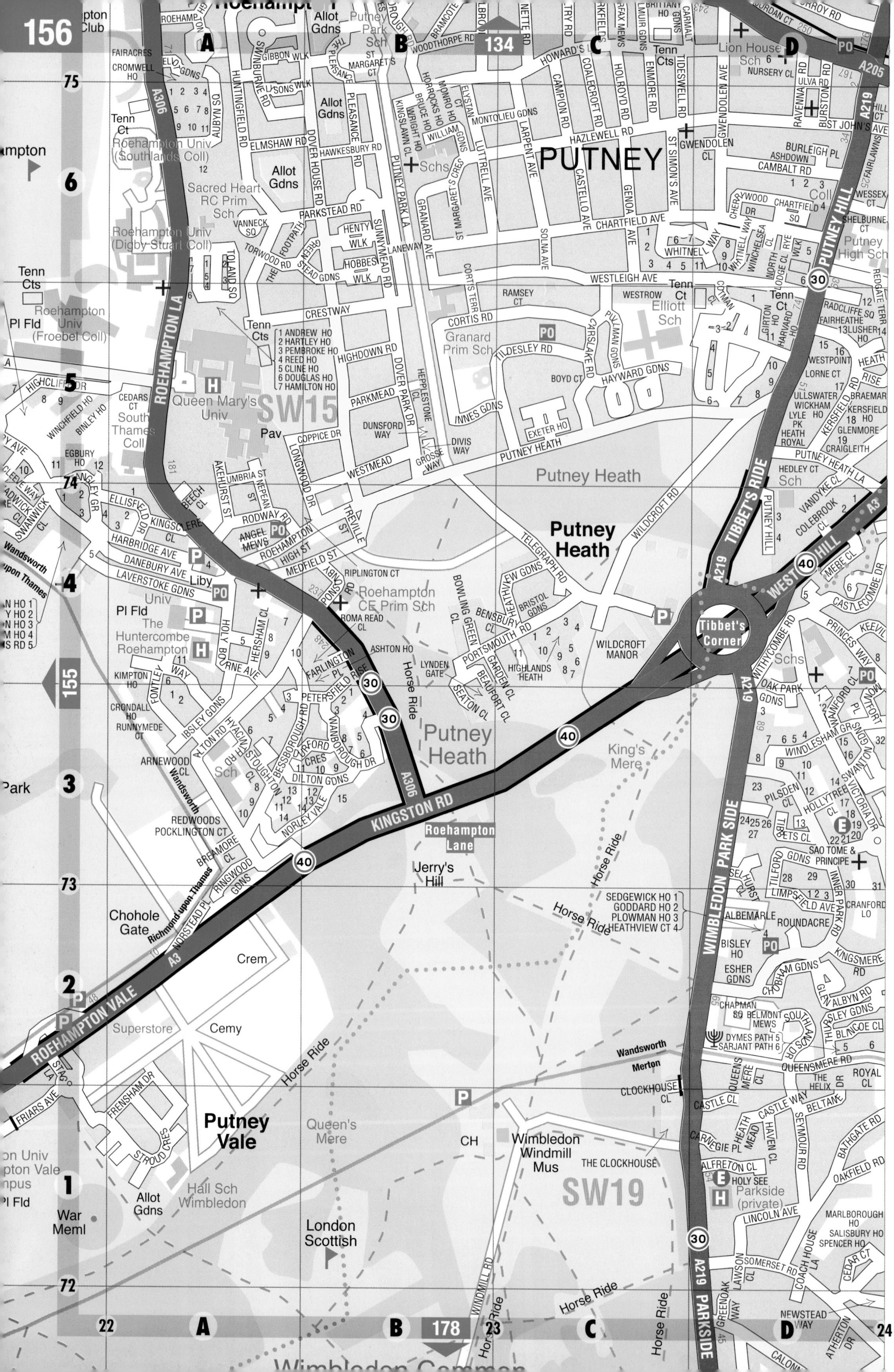
PUTNEY
Putney Heath
SW15
SW19
Putney Vale
Roehampton Lane
Jerry's Hill
Tibbet's Corner
Queen Mary's Univ
Roehampton Univ (Southlands Coll)
Roehampton Univ (Digby Stuart Coll)
Roehampton Univ (Froebel Coll)
Sacred Heart RC Prim Sch
Roehampton CE Prim Sch
Granard Prim Sch
Elliott Sch
Putney High Sch
Lion House Sch
Hedley Ct Sch
The Huntercombe Roehampton
Wimbledon Windmill Mus
London Scottish
Queen's Mere
King's Mere
Hall Sch Wimbledon
Parkside (private)
Chohole Gate
Crem
Cemy
Superstore
War Meml
Allot Gdns
Tenn Cts
Wildcroft Manor
The Clockhouse
Horse Ride
ROEHAMPTON LA
ROEHAMPTON VALE
KINGSTON RD
PUTNEY HILL
TIBBET'S RIDE
WIMBLEDON PARK SIDE
PARKSIDE
WEST HILL
PUTNEY HEATH
PUTNEY PARK LA
DOVER HOUSE RD
DOVER PARK DR
HIGHDOWN RD
CRESTWAY
PARKSTEAD RD
WESTLEIGH AVE
CHARTFIELD AVE
HAZLEWELL RD
HOWARD'S LA
WOODTHORPE RD
WILDCROFT RD
TELEGRAPH RD
PORTSMOUTH RD
HIGH ST
QUEENSMERE RD
CASTLE WAY
WINDMILL RD
A3
A306
A219
A205
134
155
178
A B C D
22 23 24
72 73 74 75
1 2 3 4 5 6
Wandsworth
Merton
Richmond upon Thames

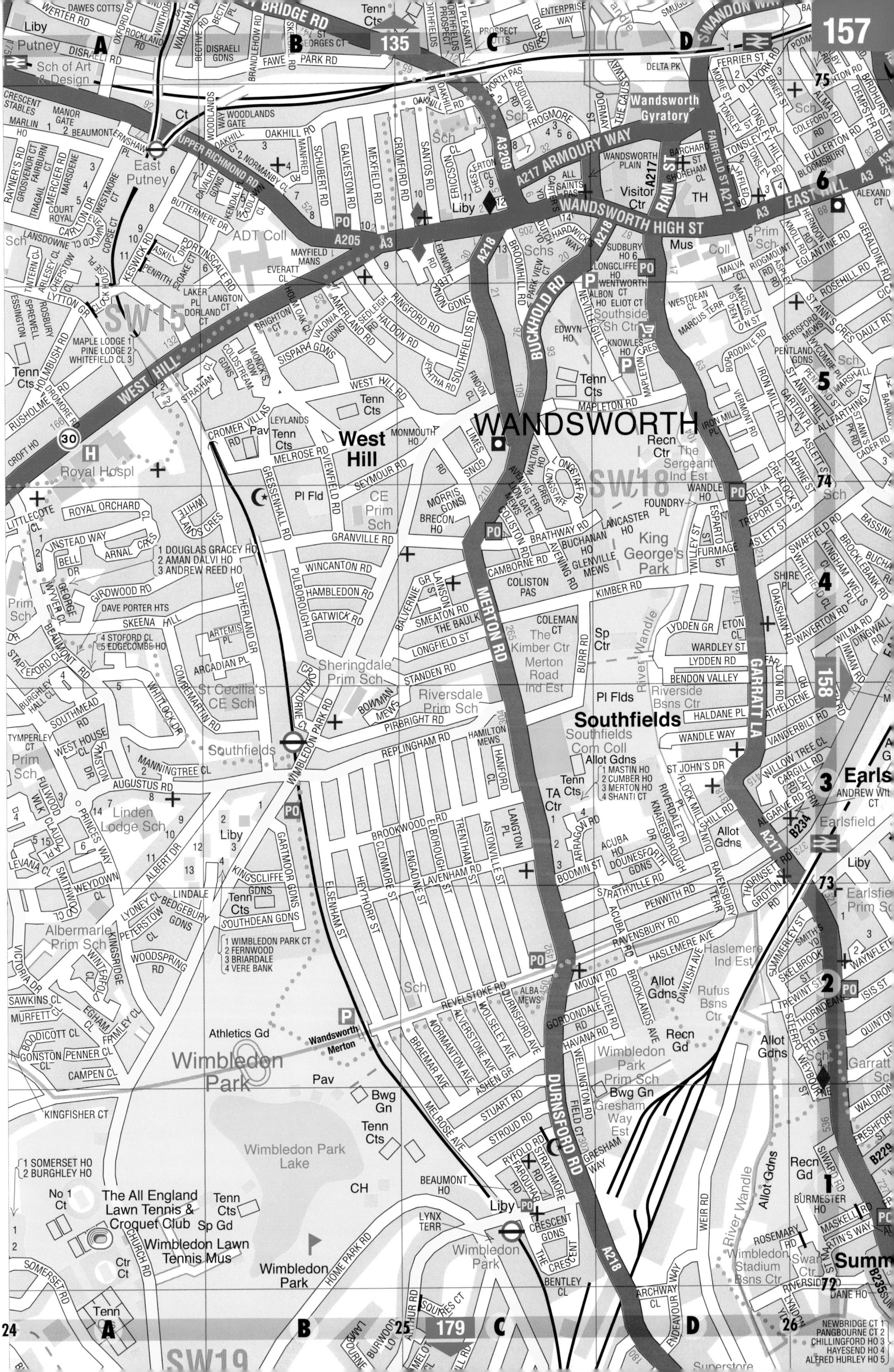
WANDSWORTH
West Hill
Southfields
Putney
East Putney
SW15
SW18
SW19
Wimbledon Park
Wimbledon Park Lake
The All England Lawn Tennis & Croquet Club
Wimbledon Lawn Tennis Mus
King George's Park
Wandsworth Gyratory
WANDSWORTH HIGH ST
WEST HILL
UPPER RICHMOND RD
A217 ARMOURY WAY
EAST HILL
MERTON RD
DURNSFORD RD
GARRATT LA
BUCKHOLD RD
WIMBLEDON PARK RD
RAM ST
FAIRFIELD ST A217
SWANDON WAY
Royal Hospl
Sheringdale Prim Sch
Riversdale Prim Sch
St Cecilia's CE Sch
Southfields Com Coll
Albermarle Prim Sch
Linden Lodge Sch
Wimbledon Park Prim Sch
Earlsfield
Earlsfield Prim Sch
Haslemere Ind Est
Rufus Bsns Ctr
Gresham Way Est
Wimbledon Stadium Bsns Ctr
Southside Sh Ctr
The Kimber Ctr
Merton Road Ind Est
Riverside Bsns Ctr
The Sergeant Ind Est
River Wandle
Athletics Gd
Wandsworth Merton
CE Prim Sch
ADT Coll
Visitor Ctr
135
158
179
24
25
26
A
B
C
D
1
2
3
4
5
6
72
73
74
75
NEWBRIDGE CT 1
PANGBOURNE CT 2
CHILLINGFORD HO 3
HAYESEND HO 4
ALFRED HURLEY HO 5

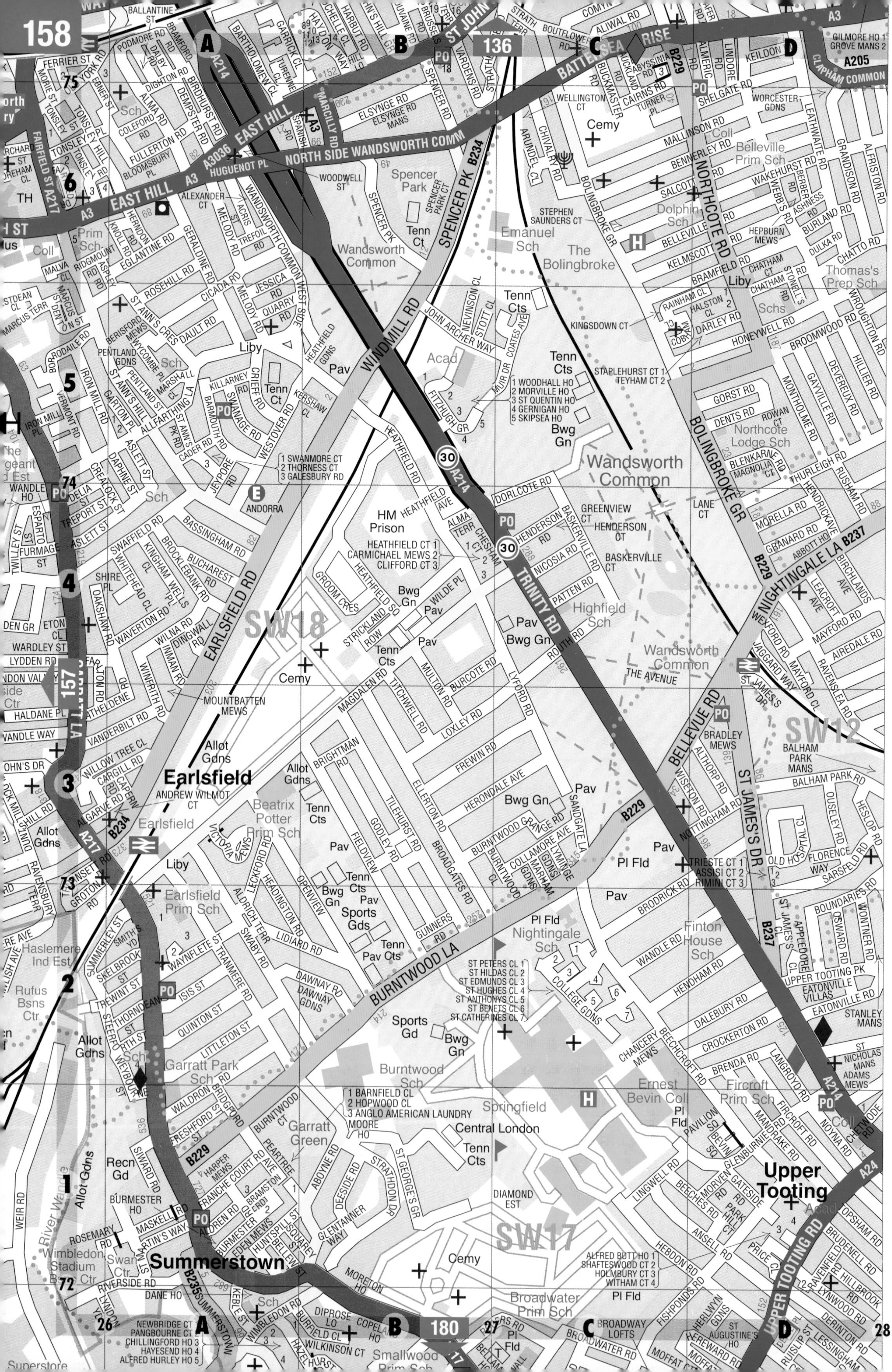
A
B
C
D
136
180
157
26
27
28
75
74
73
72
6
5
4
3
2
1
SW18
SW12
SW17
ST JOHN'S HILL
BATTERSEA RISE
A3
A205
CLAPHAM COMMON
GILMORE HO 1
GROVE MANS 2
EAST HILL
A3036
NORTH SIDE WANDSWORTH COMM
HUGUENOT PL
SPENCER PK
B234
Spencer Park
Wandsworth Common
WANDSWORTH COMMON WEST SIDE
WINDMILL RD
A214
TRINITY RD
Emanuel Sch
The Bolingbroke
Wandsworth Common
Cemy
NORTHCOTE RD
Belleville Prim Sch
Dolphin Sch
BOLINGBROKE GR
B229
Northcote Lodge Sch
Thomas's Prep Sch
NIGHTINGALE LA
B237
HM Prison
EARLSFIELD RD
Earlsfield
Highfield Sch
THE AVENUE
BELLEVUE RD
ST JAMES'S DR
BALHAM PARK RD
Beatrix Potter Prim Sch
Earlsfield Prim Sch
Haslemere Ind Est
Rufus Bsns Ctr
BURNTWOOD LA
Nightingale Sch
Finton House Sch
Burntwood Sch
Garratt Park Sch
Garratt Green
Springfield
Central London
Ernest Bevin Coll
Fircroft Prim Sch
Upper Tooting
UPPER TOOTING RD
A24
A217
Summerstown
B235
SUMMERSTOWN
Wimbledon Stadium Bsns Ctr
River Wandle
DIAMOND EST
Broadwater Prim Sch
Smallwood Prim Sch
ALFRED BUTT HO 1
SHAFTESWOOD CT 2
HOLMBURY CT 3
WITHAM CT 4
NEWBRIDGE CT 1
PANGBOURNE CT 2
CHILLINGFORD HO 3
HAYESEND HO 4
ALFRED HURLEY HO 5
ST PETERS CL 1
ST HILDAS CL 2
ST EDMUNDS CL 3
ST HUGHES CL 4
ST ANTHONYS CL 5
ST BENETS CL 6
ST CATHERINES CL 7
1 BARNFIELD CL
2 HOPWOOD CL
3 ANGLO AMERICAN LAUNDRY
1 WOODHALL HO
2 MORVILLE HO
3 ST QUENTIN HO
4 GERNIGAN HO
5 SKIPSEA HO
1 SWANMORE CT
2 THORNESS CT
3 GALESBURY RD
HEATHFIELD CT 1
CARMICHAEL MEWS 2
CLIFFORD CT 3
TRIESTE CT 1
ASSISI CT 2
RIMINI CT 3

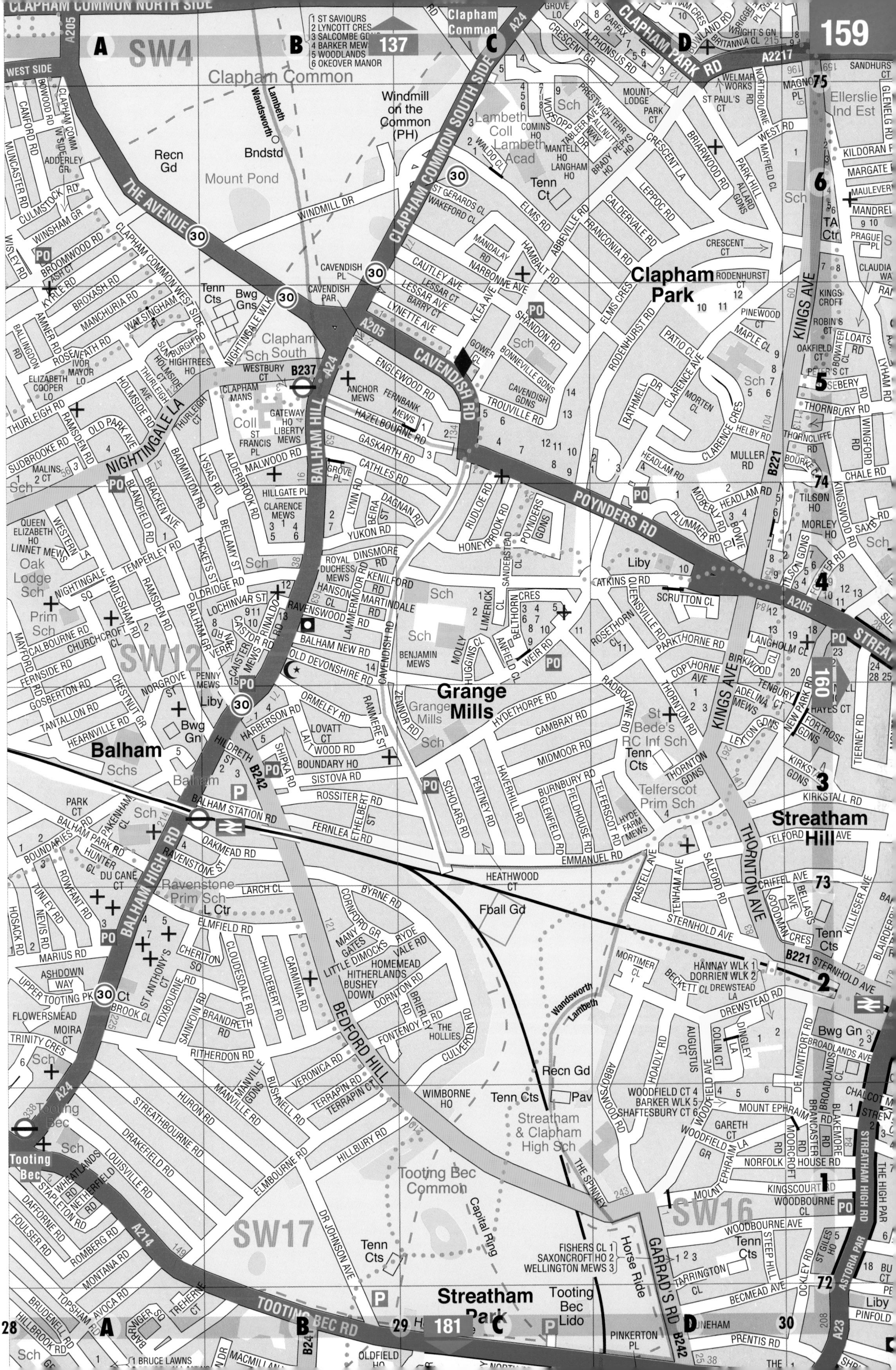

CLAPHAM COMMON NORTH SIDE
SW4
137
1 ST SAVIOURS
2 LYNCOTT CRES
3 SALCOMBE GDNS
4 BARKER MEWS
5 WOODLANDS
6 OKEOVER MANOR
Clapham Common
WEST SIDE
Windmill on the Common (PH)
Recn Gd
Bndstd
Mount Pond
Lambeth
Wandsworth
THE AVENUE
CLAPHAM COMMON SOUTH SIDE
CLAPHAM COMMON WEST SIDE
CLAPHAM PARK RD
A2217
A205
A24
WINDMILL DR
CAVENDISH PL
CAVENDISH PAR
Clapham South
WESTBURY CT
B237
Clapham Park
CAVENDISH RD
POYNDERS RD
KINGS AVE
B221
NIGHTINGALE LA
BALHAM HILL
BALHAM HIGH RD
BALHAM NEW RD
BALHAM STATION RD
Balham
SW12
Grange Mills
HILDRETH ST
B242
BEDFORD HILL
Streatham Hill
THORNTON AVE
STERNHOLD AVE
STREATHAM HIGH RD
160
SW16
SW17
Tooting Bec Common
Tooting Bec
Capital Ring
Streatham & Clapham High Sch
Recn Gd
Tenn Cts
Pav
Horse Ride
GARRAD'S RD
Streatham Park
Tooting Bec Lido
TOOTING BEC RD
A214
A23
181
Ellerslie Ind Est
Telferscot Prim Sch
St Bede's RC Inf Sch
Ravenstone Prim Sch
Oak Lodge Sch
Prim Sch
Fball Gd
Liby
Bwg Gn
1 BRUCE LAWNS

ACRE LA
A2217
ST MATTHEW'S RD
EFFRA RD
A204
Works
Ellerslie Ind Est
Lambeth Coll
BRIXTON WATER LA
A2214
DULWICH RD
RAILTON RD
Brockwell Lido
Brockwell Park
SE24
Tulse Hill
TULSE HILL
BRIXTON HILL
HM Prison
Allot Gdns
Sp Gd
KINGS AVE
STREATHAM PL
A205
CHRISTCHURCH RD
SW2
Streatham Hill
STREATHAM HILL
A23
NORWOOD RD
A215
STREATHAM HIGH RD
SW16
SE27
THORNTON AVE
B221
STERNHOLD AVE
LEIGHAM VALE
LEIGHAM COURT RD
KNOLLY'S RD
LANSDOWNE HILL
YORK HILL
The Adare Ctr
Dunraven Sch
Herne Hill
Tulse Hill
A
B
C
D
1
2
3
4
5
6
138
182
159
30
31
32

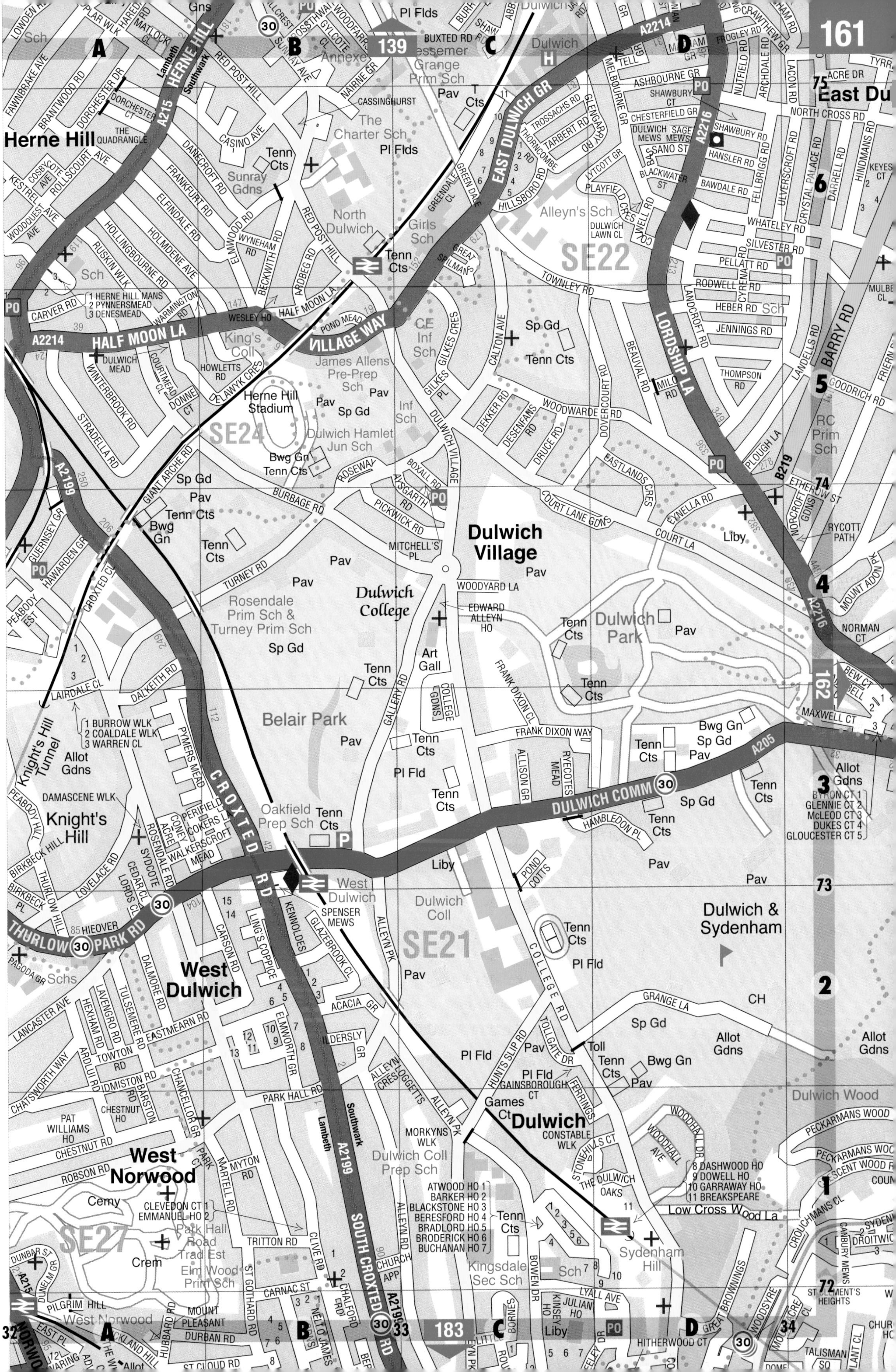
Herne Hill
A215
HERNE HILL
Lambeth
Southwark
A2214
HALF MOON LA
RED POST HILL
North Dulwich
VILLAGE WAY
EAST DULWICH GR
A2216
LORDSHIP LA
East Du
SE22
SE24
SE21
SE27
Herne Hill Stadium
King's Coll
James Allens Pre-Prep Sch
Dulwich Hamlet Jun Sch
The Charter Sch
Alleyn's Sch
Dulwich Village
Dulwich College
Dulwich Park
Belair Park
Rosendale Prim Sch & Turney Prim Sch
Art Gall
Oakfield Prep Sch
West Dulwich
Dulwich Coll
DULWICH COMM
A205
CROXTED RD
A2199
SOUTH CROXTED RD
THURLOW PARK RD
Knight's Hill
Knight's Hill Tunnel
West Norwood
Cemy
Crem
Kingsdale Sec Sch
Dulwich Coll Prep Sch
Dulwich & Sydenham
Dulwich Wood
Sydenham Hill
Low Cross Wood La
COLLEGE RD
GRANGE LA
BARRY RD
139
183
162
32
33
34
A
B
C
D
1
2
3
4
5
6
72
73
74
75

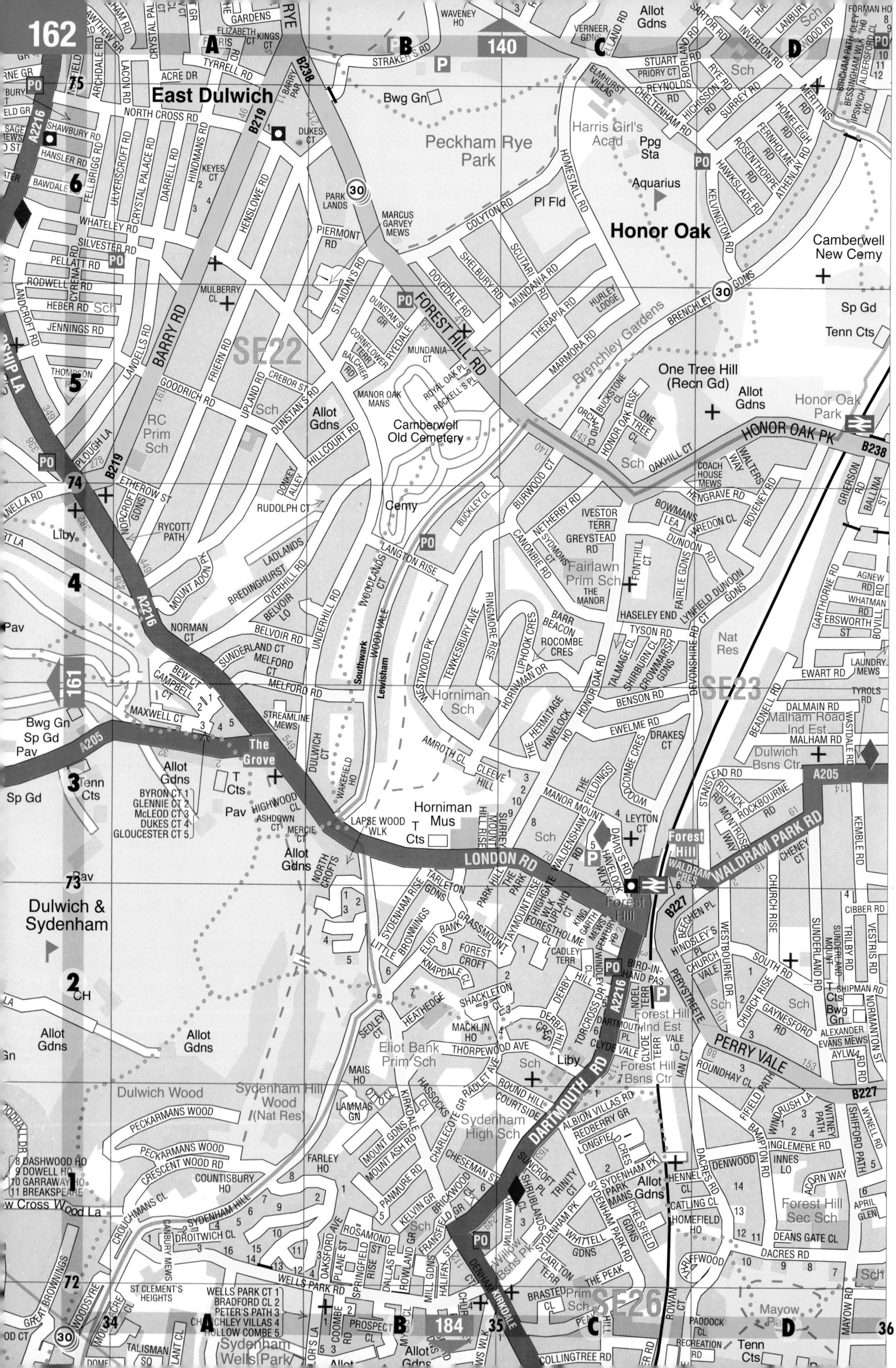
East Dulwich
Peckham Rye Park
Honor Oak
SE22
SE23
SE26
Camberwell Old Cemetery
One Tree Hill (Recn Gd)
Honor Oak Park
Camberwell New Cemy
Horniman Mus
Forest Hill
Dulwich & Sydenham
Sydenham Hill Wood (Nat Res)
Dulwich Wood
Sydenham Wells Park
LONDON RD
DARTMOUTH RD
PERRY VALE
FOREST HILL RD
HONOR OAK PK
WALDRAM PARK RD
140
161
184
34
35
36

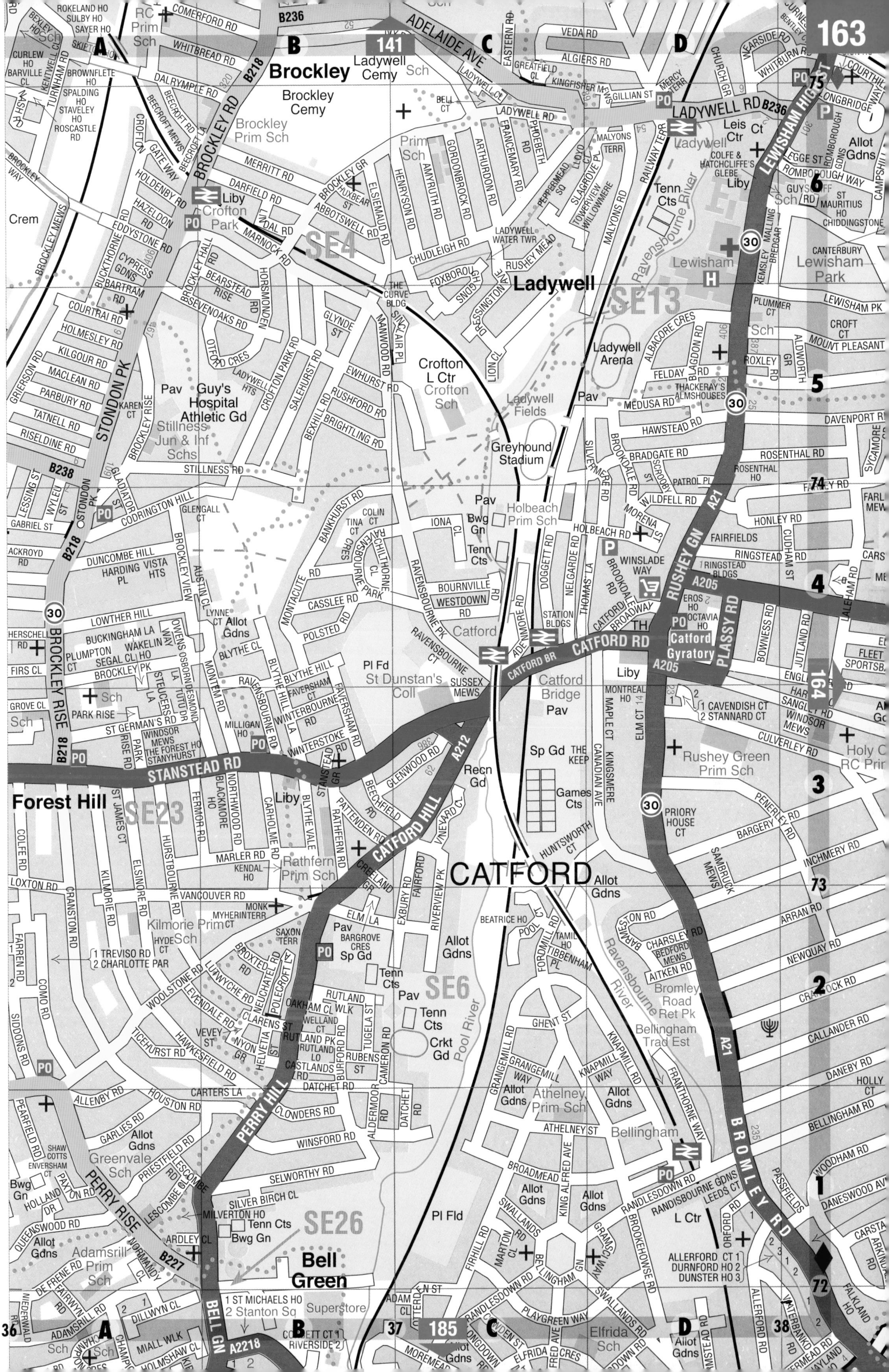

Brockley
Brockley Cemy
Ladywell Cemy
Brockley Prim Sch
Crofton Park
Crem
SE4
Ladywell
SE13
Lewisham
Lewisham Park
Ladywell Arena
Ladywell Fields
Greyhound Stadium
Crofton L Ctr
Crofton Sch
Guy's Hospital Athletic Gd
Stillness Jun & Inf Schs
Holbeach Prim Sch
Catford
Catford Gyratory
Catford Bridge
St Dunstan's Coll
Forest Hill
SE23
Rathfern Prim Sch
Kilmorie Prim Sch
CATFORD
SE6
Pool River
Ravensbourne River
Rushey Green Prim Sch
Bromley Road Ret Pk
Bellingham Trad Est
Athelney Prim Sch
Bellingham
Greenvale Sch
Adamsrill Prim Sch
SE26
Bell Green
Superstore
Elfrida Sch
BROCKLEY RD
STONDON PK
BROCKLEY RISE
STANSTEAD RD
CATFORD HILL
PERRY HILL
PERRY RISE
BELL GN
LADYWELL RD
ADELAIDE AVE
LEWISHAM HIGH ST
RUSHEY GN
CATFORD RD
BROMLEY RD
B236
B218
B238
B227
A21
A205
A212
A2218
141
164
185
36
37
38

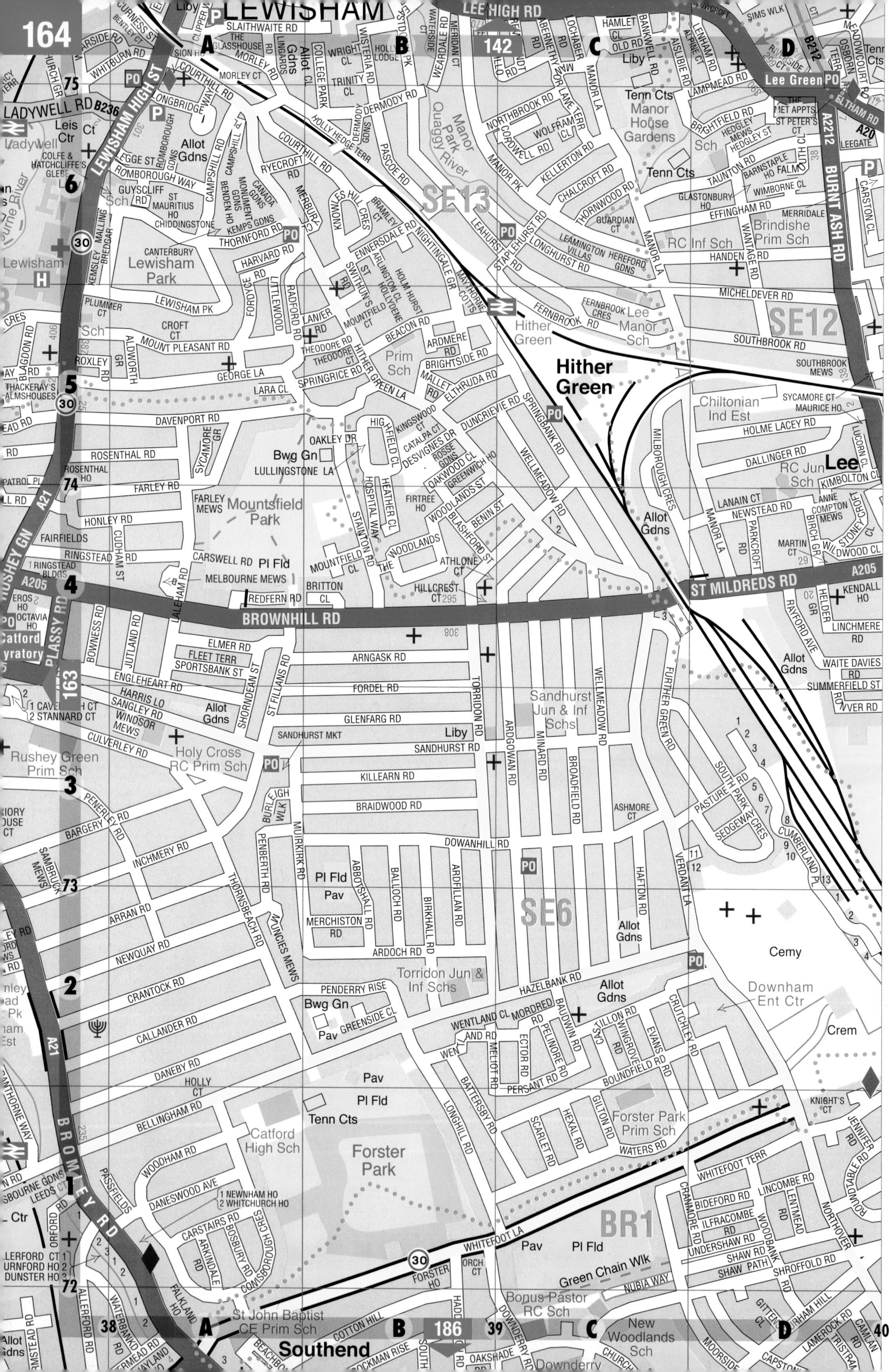
LEWISHAM
LEE HIGH RD
142
A
B
C
D
SLAITHWAITE RD
THE GLASSHOUSE
MORLEY RD
MORLEY CT
COURTHILL RD
LINGARDS RD
Allot Gdns
COLLEGE PARK
WRIGHT CL
HOLLY LODGE
TRINITY CL
WISTERIA RD
WEARDALE RD
MERIDIAN CT
WATERSIDE CT
ABERNETHY RD
LOCHABER RD
HAMLET CL
OLD RD
Liby
BANKWELL RD
AISLIBIE RD
ALPINE CT
LENHAM RD
SIMS WLK
B212
MEADOWCOURT RD
OSBORN TERR
Tenn Cts
Lee Green
PO
ELTHAM RD
A20
A2212
THE MET APPTS
ST PETER'S CT
LEEGATE
LAMPMEAD RD
75
LADYWELL RD
B236
LEWISHAM HIGH ST
Leis Ctr
Ladywell
LONGBRIDGE WAY
P
ROMBOROUGH GDNS
EGGE ST
COLFE & HATCHCLIFFE'S GLEBE
Allot Gdns
ROMBOROUGH WAY
GUYSCLIFF RD
ST MAURITIUS HO
CHIDDINGSTONE
CAMPSHILL RD
BENDEN HO
MONUMENT GDNS
CANADA GDNS
KEMPS GDNS
THORNFORD RD
6
Sch
30
Lewisham
H
KEMSLEY
MALLING
BREDGAR
CANTERBURY
Lewisham Park
LEWISHAM PK
PLUMMER CT
CRES
BLAGDON RD
Sch
CROFT CT
MOUNT PLEASANT RD
ALDWORTH GR
ROXLEY RD
GEORGE LA
LARA CL
THACKERAY'S ALMSHOUSES
5
DAVENPORT RD
SYCAMORE GR
ROSENTHAL RD
ROSENTHAL HO
PATROL PL
74
FARLEY RD
FARLEY MEWS
Mountsfield Park
HONLEY RD
FAIRFIELDS
CUDHAM ST
RINGSTEAD RD
RINGSTEAD BLDGS
A21
RUSHEY GN
A205
4
EROS HO
OCTAVIA HO
Catford Gyratory
PLASSY RD
LALEHAM RD
MELBOURNE MEWS
CARSWELL RD
Pl Fld
REDFERN RD
BRITTON CL
BROWNHILL RD
BOWNESS RD
JUTLAND RD
ELMER RD
FLEET TERR
SPORTSBANK ST
ENGLEHEART RD
HARRIS LO
SANGLEY RD
1 CAVELL CT
2 STANNARD CT
WINDSOR MEWS
SHORNDEAN ST
Allot Gdns
CULVERLEY RD
Holy Cross RC Prim Sch
Rushey Green Prim Sch
163
3
PENERLEY RD
BARGERY RD
INCHMERY RD
SAMBRUCK MEWS
73
ARRAN RD
NEWQUAY RD
2
CRANTOCK RD
CALLANDER RD
DANEBY RD
HOLLY CT
BELLINGHAM RD
WOODHAM RD
DANESWOOD AVE
1 NEWNHAM HO
2 WHITCHURCH HO
CARSTAIRS RD
ARKINDALE RD
BOSBURY RD
COMSBOROUGH CRES
PASSFIELDS
BROMLEY RD
1
72
LEERFORD CT
URNFORD HO
DUNSTER HO
ORFORD RD
ALLERFORD RD
WATERBANK RD
FALKLAND HO
38
A
St John Baptist CE Prim Sch
Southend
COTTON HILL
B
186
39
C
New Woodlands Sch
D
40
RYECROFT RD
MERBURY CL
HOLLY HEDGE TERR
DERMODY RD
DERMODY GDNS
PASCOE RD
Manor Park
Quaggy River
KNOWLES HILL CRES
BRAMLEY CT
ENNERSDALE RD
NIGHTINGALE GR
ARLINGTON CL
HOLLYDENE
SWITHUN'S CT
HOLM HURST
MOUNTFIELD CT
MAYTHORNE COTTS
HARVARD RD
FORDYCE RD
LITTLEWOOD
RADFORD RD
LANIER RD
THEODORE RD
THEODORE CT
BEACON RD
ARDMERE RD
BRIGHTSIDE RD
Prim Sch
SPRINGRICE RD
HITHER GREEN LA
MALLET RD
ELTHRUDA RD
SE13
NORTHBROOK RD
CORDWELL RD
WOLFRAM CL
MANOR LA TERR
MANOR LA
Tenn Cts
Manor House Gardens
KELLERTON RD
CHALCROFT RD
THORNWOOD RD
MANOR PK
LEAHURST RD
STAPLEHURST RD
GUARDIAN CT
LEAMINGTON VILLAS
HEREFORD GDNS
LONGHURST RD
PO
FERNBROOK RD
FERNBROOK CRES
Lee Manor Sch
Hither Green
Hither Green
BRIGHTFIELD RD
HEDGLEY MEWS
HEDGLEY ST
Sch
Tenn Cts
TAUNTON RD
BARNSTAPLE HO
FALMOUTH CL
WIMBORNE CL
GLASTONBURY HO
EFFINGHAM RD
MERRIDALE
Brindishe Prim Sch
RC Inf Sch
HANDEN RD
WANTAGE RD
BURNT ASH RD
CARSTON CL
MICHELDEVER RD
SE12
SOUTHBROOK RD
SOUTHBROOK MEWS
SYCAMORE CT
MAURICE HO
Chiltonian Ind Est
HOLME LACEY RD
DALLINGER RD
RC Jun Sch
Lee
LUCORN CL
KIMBOLTON CL
ANNE COMPTON MEWS
LANAIN CT
NEWSTEAD RD
MILBOROUGH CRES
Allot Gdns
MANOR LA
PARKCROFT RD
BIRCH GR
STONEY CROFT
MARTIN CT
WILDWOOD CL
A205
ST MILDREDS RD
KENDALL HO
RAYFORD AVE
HELDER GR
LINCHMERE RD
Allot Gdns
WAITE DAVIES RD
SUMMERFIELD ST
IVVER RD
OAKLEY DR
HIGHFIELD CL
KINGSWOOD CT
CATALPA CT
DESVIGNES DR
ROSSE GDNS
DUNCRIEVIE RD
SPRINGBANK RD
PO
Bwg Gn
LULLINGSTONE LA
OAKWOOD CL
GREENWICH HO
GREENLANDS ST
WELLMEADOW RD
FIRTREE HO
HOSPITAL WAY
HEATHER CL
STAINTON RD
WOODLANDS
BLASHFORD ST
BENIN ST
MOUNTFIELD CL
THE
ATHLONE CT
HILLCREST CT
ARNGASK RD
FORDEL RD
GLENFARG RD
SANDHURST MKT
Liby
SANDHURST RD
ST FILLANS RD
TORRIDON RD
PO
KILLEARN RD
BRAIDWOOD RD
BURLEIGH WLK
MURKIRK RD
PENBERTH RD
THORNSBEACH RD
MUNCIES MEWS
DOWANHILL RD
Pl Fld
Pav
ABBOTSHALL RD
BALLOCH RD
BIRKHALL RD
ARDFILLAN RD
MERCHISTON RD
ARDOCH RD
Torridon Jun & Inf Schs
PENDERRY RISE
Bwg Gn
Pav
GREENSIDE CL
Pav
Pl Fld
Tenn Cts
Catford High Sch
Forster Park
Sandhurst Jun & Inf Schs
ARDGOWAN RD
MINARD RD
BROADFIELD RD
WELLMEADOW RD
ASHMORE CT
SE6
PO
HAFTON RD
Allot Gdns
FURTHER GREEN RD
VERDANT LA
SOUTH PARK CRES
PASTURE RD
SEDGEWAY
CUMBERLAND PL
Cemy
Downham Ent Ctr
Crem
HAZELBANK RD
Allot Gdns
WENTLAND CL
MORDRED RD
BAUDWIN RD
PELLINORE RD
CASTILLON RD
WINGROVE RD
EVANS RD
CRUTCHLEY RD
ECTOR RD
MELIOT RD
BATTERSBY RD
PERSANT RD
BOUNDFIELD RD
LONGHILL RD
SCARLETT RD
HEXAL RD
GILTON RD
Forster Park Prim Sch
WATERS RD
KNIGHT'S CT
JENNIFER RD
WHITEFOOT TERR
LINCOMBE RD
BIDEFORD RD
ILFRACOMBE RD
LENTMEAD RD
UNDERSHAW RD
SHAW RD
SHAW PATH
WOODBANK RD
NORTHOVER
ROUNDTABLE RD
SHROFFOLD RD
BR1
Pav
Pl Fld
WHITEFOOT LA
Green Chain Wlk
NUBIA WAY
FORSTER HO
ORCHARD CT
Bonus Pastor RC Sch
CRANMORE RD
DOWNDERRY RD
OAKSHADE RD
Downderry
BEACHBOROUGH
BROCKMAN RISE
LAMEROCK RD
CAMLAN RD
TRISTRAM RD
MOORSIDE RD
CAPSTONE
GITTENS CL
DURHAM HILL

143
187
166
A
B
C
D
75
6
5
74
4
3
73
2
1
72
40
41
42
ELTHAM RD
A20
A210
A2213
A2212
A205
WESTHORNE AVE
ELTHAM HILL
SIDCUP RD
BARING RD
CHINBROOK RD
B226
GROVE PARK RD
Sutcliffe Park
Running Tk
Riverston Sch
Colfe's Sch
Lee
Cliftons Roundabout
Yorkshire Grey
Eltham Green Specialist Sports Coll
Moatbridge Sch
Eltham Green
Eltham Hill Te Coll for Gir
Horn Park
Northbrook Park
Mottingham Farm
Hadlow Coll
Hadlow Coll Nature Reserve
Eltham Coll Jun Sch
Eltham Coll
Quaggy River
SE12
SE9
BR1
Mottingham
Grove Park
Green Chain Wk
Lewisham
Greenwich
Bromley
ELTHAM PALACE RD
MIDDLE PARK AVE
KINGSGROUND
MOTTINGHAM LA
WINN RD
SIBTHORPE RD
HORN PARK LA
UPWOOD RD
CROWN CT
ALWOLD CRES
CEDARHURST DR
MARVELS LA
COURT FARM RD
ELMHURST RD
HALL VIEW
CEDAR MOUNT
WOODYATES RD
BURNT ASH HILL
KINGSAND RD
SOMERTREES AVE
LUFFMAN RD
ROBINS CT
DUNKERY RD
DOWNHAM WAY
Haberdashers' Aske's Knights

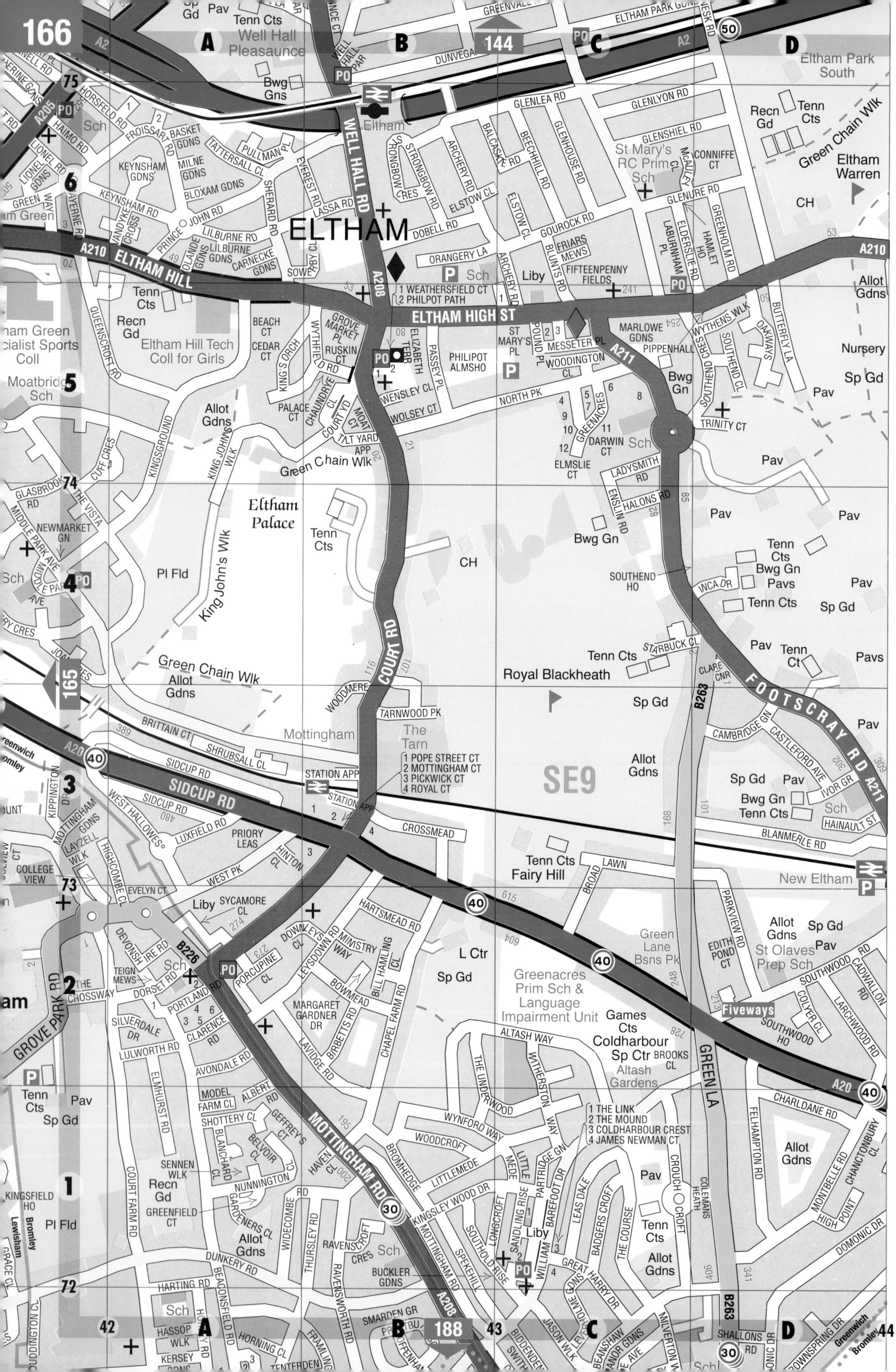
A
B
C
D
144
50
Well Hall Pleasaunce
Eltham Park South
Eltham
ELTHAM
WELL HALL RD
GLENLEA RD
GLENLYON RD
GLENSHIEL RD
St Mary's RC Prim Sch
Recn Gd
Tenn Cts
Green Chain Wlk
Eltham Warren
CH
KEYNSHAM GDNS
MILNE GDNS
BLOXAM GDNS
KEYNSHAM RD
PULLMAN PL
TATTERSALL CL
STRONGBOW RD
ARCHERY RD
ELSTOW CL
DOBELL RD
LASSA RD
SHERARD RD
EVEREST RD
BALCASKIE RD
BEECHHILL RD
GLENHOUSE RD
GOUROCK RD
GLENURE RD
LABURNHAM PL
ELDERSLIE RD
GREENHOLM RD
A210
ELTHAM HILL
ELTHAM HIGH ST
ORANGERY LA
1 WEATHERSFIELD CT
2 PHILPOT PATH
FRIARS MEWS
FIFTEENPENNY FIELDS
Liby
Sch
Allot Gdns
Recn Gd
Eltham Hill Tech Coll for Girls
Eltham Green Specialist Sports Coll
QUEENSCROFT RD
BEACH CT
CEDAR CT
KING'S ORCH
WYTHFIELD RD
GROVE MARKET PL
RUSKIN CT
ELIZABETH TERR
PASSEY PL
PHILIPOT ALMSHO
ST MARY'S PL
POUND PL
MESSETER PL
WOODINGTON CL
MARLOWE GDNS
PIPPENHALL
WYTHENS WLK
SOUTHEND CRES
SOUTHEND CL
OAKWAYS
BUTTERFLY LA
A211
Bwg Gn
Nursery
Sp Gd
Pav
Moatbridge Sch
Allot Gdns
KINGSGROUND
KING JOHN'S WLK
PALACE CT
CHAUNDRYE CL
COURT YD
MOAT CT
TILT YARD APP
WENSLEY CL
WOLSEY CT
NORTH PK
GREENACRES
DARWIN CT
ELMSLIE CT
LADYSMITH RD
HALONS RD
ENSLIN RD
TRINITY CT
Green Chain Wlk
Eltham Palace
Tenn Cts
CH
Bwg Gn
SOUTHEND HO
INCA DR
King John's Wlk
Pl Fld
GLASBROOK RD
CUFF CRES
THE VISTA
NEWMARKET GN
MIDDLE PARK AVE
COURT RD
Green Chain Wlk
Allot Gdns
Royal Blackheath
STARBUCK CL
CLARE CNR
FOOTSCRAY RD
B263
WOODMERE
TARNWOOD PK
Mottingham
The Tarn
BRITTAIN CT
SHRUBSALL CL
SIDCUP RD
A20
40
165
STATION APP
1 POPE STREET CT
2 MOTTINGHAM CT
3 PICKWICK CT
4 ROYAL CT
SE9
CAMBRIDGE GN
CASTLEFORD AVE
IVOR GR
HAINAULT ST
BLANMERLE RD
KIPPINGTON DR
MOTTINGHAM GDNS
LAYZELL WLK
WEST HALLOWES
LUXFIELD RD
PRIORY LEAS
HINTON CL
CROSSMEAD
Tenn Cts
Fairy Hill
BROAD LAWN
New Eltham
COLLEGE VIEW
HIGHCOMBE CL
EVELYN CT
WEST PK
Liby
SYCAMORE CL
HARTSMEAD RD
LEYSDOWN RD
MIMSTRY WAY
DOWNLEYS CL
BILL HAMLING CL
L Ctr
Sp Gd
Green Lane Bsns Pk
PARKVIEW RD
EDITH POND CT
Allot Gdns
St Olaves Prep Sch
SOUTHWOOD RD
CADWALLON RD
COLYER CL
LARCHWOOD RD
SOUTHWOOD HO
Fiveways
DEVONSHIRE RD
TEIGN MEWS
DORSET RD
THE CROSSWAY
B226
PORCUPINE CL
BOWMEAD
MARGARET GARDNER DR
BIRBETTS RD
CHAPEL FARM RD
Greenacres Prim Sch & Language Impairment Unit
Games Cts
Coldharbour Sp Ctr
Altash Gardens
BROOKS CL
ALTASH WAY
GREEN LA
GROVE PARK RD
SILVERDALE DR
PORTLAND RD
CLARENCE RD
LULWORTH RD
AVONDALE RD
ELMHURST RD
MODEL FARM CL
ALBERT RD
SHOTTERY CL
GEFFREY'S CT
BLANCHARD CL
BELVOIR CL
LAVIDGE RD
MOTTINGHAM RD
THE UNDERWOOD
WITHERSTON WAY
1 THE LINK
2 THE MOUND
3 COLDHARBOUR CREST
4 JAMES NEWMAN CT
WYNFORD WAY
WOODCROFT
BROMHEDGE
LITTLEMEDE
LITTLE MEDE
PARTRIDGE GN
CHARLDANE RD
FELHAMPTON RD
Allot Gdns
MONTBELLE RD
CHANCTONBURY CL
HIGH POINT
DOMONIC DR
Tenn Cts
Pav
Sp Gd
Recn Gd
SENNEN WLK
NUNNINGTON CL
GREENFIELD CT
GARDENERS CL
KINGSFIELD HO
Pl Fld
Allot Gdns
COURT FARM RD
WIDECOMBE RD
THURSLEY RD
HAVEN CL
RAVENSCROFT CRES
Sch
KINGSLEY WOOD DR
SPEKEHILL
SOUTHOLD RISE
LONGCROFT
SANDLING RISE
WILLIAM BAREFOOT DR
LEAS DALE
BADGERS CROFT
THE COURSE
CROUCH CROFT
COLEMANS HEATH
Liby
GREAT HARRY DR
Tenn Cts
Allot Gdns
30
BUCKLER GDNS
RAVENSWORTH RD
DUNKERY RD
HARTING RD
BEACONSFIELD RD
72
42
43
44
188
A208
SMARDEN GR
HASSOP WLK
KERSEY GDNS
HORNING CL
TENTERDEN
FRAMLINGHAM
BIDDENDEN
JASON WLK
BEANSHAW
MANOR GDNS
MILVERTON WAY
SHALLONS RD
DOWNSPRING DR
Greenwich
Bromley
Lewisham
73
74
75
1
2
3
4
5
6

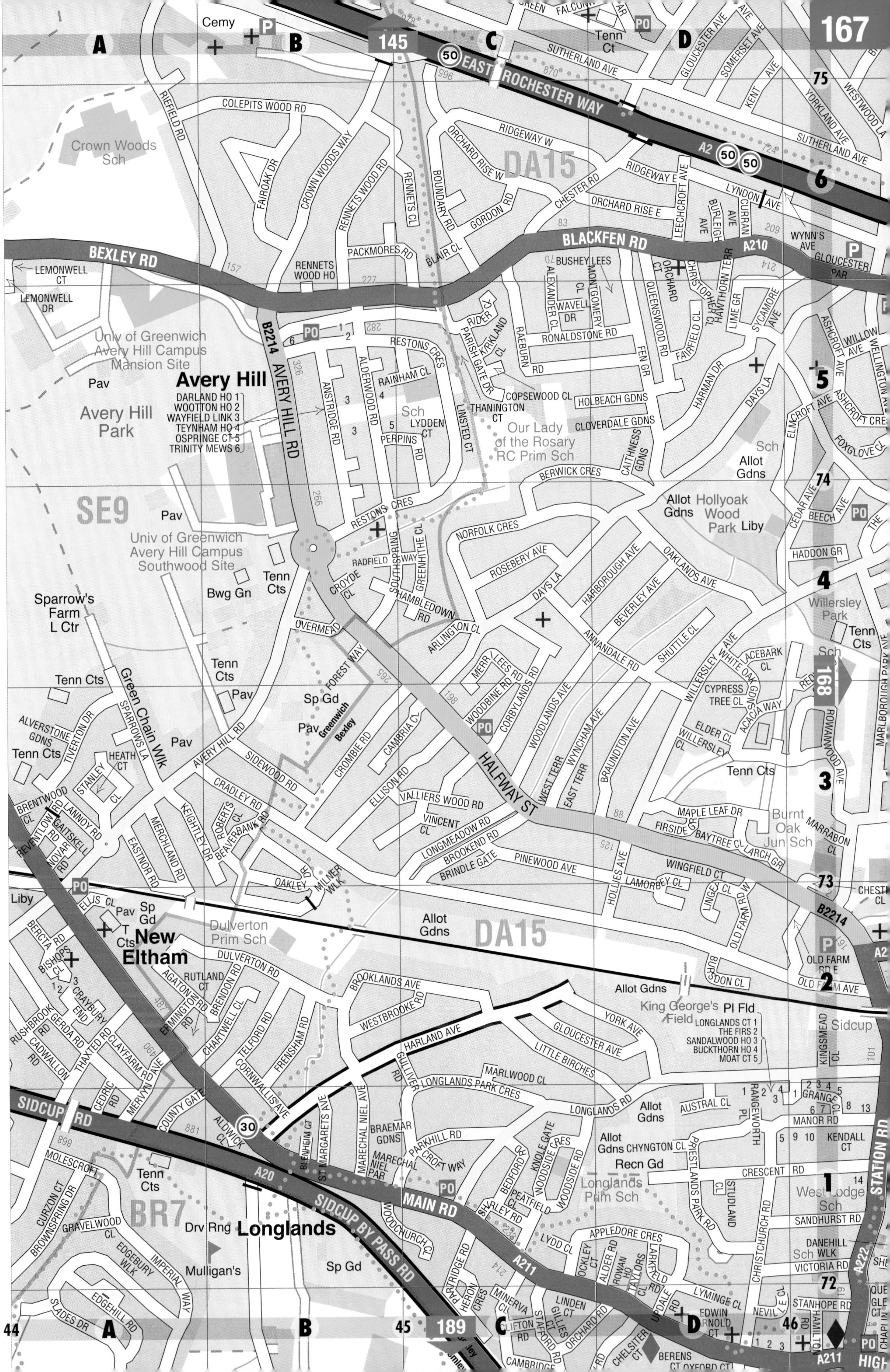

145
EAST ROCHESTER WAY
A2
DA15
Crown Woods Sch
Cemy
RIEFIELD RD
COLEPITS WOOD RD
FAIROAK DR
CROWN WOODS WAY
RENNETS WOOD RD
RENNETS CL
BOUNDARY RD
ORCHARD RISE W
GORDON RD
RIDGEWAY W
CHESTER RD
RIDGEWAY E
ORCHARD RISE E
LEECHCROFT AVE
BURLEIGH AVE
CURRAN AVE
LYNDON AVE
SUTHERLAND AVE
GLOUCESTER AVE
SOMERSET AVE
KENT AVE
YORKLAND AVE
WESTWOOD LA
WYNN'S AVE
GLOUCESTER PAR
BEXLEY RD
BLACKFEN RD
A210
LEMONWELL CT
LEMONWELL DR
RENNETS WOOD HO
PACKMORES RD
BLAIR CL
BUSHEY LEES
ALEXANDER CL
MONTGOMERY CL
WAVELL DR
RONALDSTONE RD
RAEBURN RD
QUEENSWOOD RD
ORCHARD CT
CHRISTOPHER CL
HAWTHORN TERR
LIME GR
SYCAMORE AVE
FAIRFIELD CL
FEN GR
HARMAN DR
DAYS LA
ASHCROFT AVE
WILLOW AVE
WELLINGTON AVE
ELMCROFT AVE
FOXGLOVE CL
Univ of Greenwich Avery Hill Campus Mansion Site
Avery Hill
DARLAND HO 1
WOOTTON HO 2
WAYFIELD LINK 3
TEYNHAM HO 4
OSPRINGE CT 5
TRINITY MEWS 6
Avery Hill Park
B2214
AVERY HILL RD
ANSTRIDGE RD
ALDERWOOD RD
RAINHAM CL
RESTONS CRES
LYDDEN CT
PERPINS RD
LINSTED CT
PARISH GATE DR
KIRKLAND CL
RIDER CL
THANINGTON CT
COPSEWOOD CL
HOLBEACH GDNS
CLOVERDALE GDNS
CAITHNESS GDNS
Our Lady of the Rosary RC Prim Sch
Allot Gdns
Hollyoak Wood Park
Liby
CEDAR AVE
BEECH AVE
HADDON GR
SE9
Univ of Greenwich Avery Hill Campus Southwood Site
Tenn Cts
Bwg Gn
Sparrow's Farm L Ctr
BERWICK CRES
NORFOLK CRES
ROSEBERY AVE
RADFIELD WAY
SOUTHSPRING
GREENHITHE CL
CROYDE CL
HAMBLEDOWN RD
OVERMEAD
ARLINGTON CL
DAYS LA
HARBOROUGH AVE
OAKLANDS AVE
BEVERLEY AVE
ANNANDALE RD
SHUTTLE CL
WILLERSLEY AVE
WHITE OAK GDNS
ACEBARK CL
Willersley Park
CYPRESS TREE CL
ACACIA WAY
ELDER CL
WILLERSLEY CL
ROWANWOOD AVE
MARLBOROUGH PARK AVE
168
FOREST WAY
Sp Gd
Greenwich
Bexley
MERRILEES RD
WOODBINE RD
CORBYLANDS RD
WOODLANDS AVE
WYNCHAM AVE
BRAUNDTON AVE
WEST TERR
EAST TERR
HALFWAY ST
Green Chain Wlk
SPARROWS LA
ALVERSTONE GDNS
TIVERTON DR
HEATH CT
STANLEY CL
BRENTWOOD CL
REVENTLOW RD
LANNOY RD
GAITSKELL RD
NOVAR RD
SIDEWOOD RD
CRADLEY RD
CROMBIE RD
CAMBRIA CL
ELLISON RD
VALLIERS WOOD RD
VINCENT CL
LONGMEADOW RD
BROOKEND RD
BRINDLE GATE
PINEWOOD AVE
HOLLIES AVE
LAMORBEY CL
WINGFIELD CT
LINGEY CL
OLD FARM RD W
MAPLE LEAF DR
FIRSIDE GR
BAYTREE CL
LARCH GR
Burnt Oak Jun Sch
MARRABON CL
CHESTER CL
EASTNOR RD
MERCHLAND RD
KEIGHTLEY DR
ROBERTS CL
BEAVERBANK RD
OAKLEY DR
MILNER WLK
ELLIS CL
New Eltham
Dulverton Prim Sch
BERCTA RD
BISHOPS CL
CRAYBURY END
RUTLAND CT
AGATON RD
DULVERTON RD
BRENDON RD
ERMINGTON RD
CHARTWELL CL
TELFORD RD
FRENSHAM RD
CORNWALLIS AVE
BROOKLANDS AVE
WESTBROOKE RD
HARLAND AVE
GULLIVER RD
LONGLANDS PARK CRES
MARLWOOD CL
LONGLANDS RD
LITTLE BIRCHES
GLOUCESTER AVE
YORK AVE
King George's Field
Pl Fld
LONGLANDS CT 1
THE FIRS 2
SANDALWOOD HO 3
BUCKTHORN HO 4
MOAT CT 5
KINGSMEAD CL
Sidcup
OLD FARM RD E
OLD FARM AVE
BURSDON CL
RUSHBROOK RD
GERDA RD
CADWALLON RD
THAXTED RD
CLAYFARM RD
MERVYN AVE
CEDRIC RD
COUNTY GATE
ALDWICK CL
SIDCUP RD
A20
SIDCUP BY PASS RD
MOLESCROFT
CURZON CT
BROWNSPRING DR
GRAVELWOOD CL
EDGEBURY WLK
IMPERIAL WAY
SLADES DR
EDGEHILL RD
BR7
Drv Rng
Longlands
Mulligan's
BLENHEIM CT
ST MARGARETS AVE
MARECHAL NIEL AVE
MARECHAL NIEL PAR
BRAEMAR GDNS
PARKHILL RD
CROFT WAY
MAIN RD
A211
WOODCHURCH CL
PARTRIDGE RD
HERON CRES
MINERVA CL
BEDFORD RD
SHIRLEY RD
PEATFIELD CL
KNOLE GATE
WOODSIDE CRES
WOODSIDE RD
LYDD CL
Longlands Prim Sch
Recn Gd
CHYNGTON CL
PRIESTLANDS PARK RD
STUDLAND CL
AUSTRAL CL
RANGEWORTH PL
GRANGE CL
MANOR RD
KENDALL CT
CRESCENT RD
CHRISTCHURCH RD
West Lodge Sch
SANDHURST RD
DANEHILL WLK
VICTORIA RD
STANHOPE RD
NEVILLE CL
HAMILTON RD
APPLEDORE CRES
OCKLEY CT
ALDER RD
ROWAN HO
TAYLORS CL
LARKFIELD
UPDALE RD
LYMINGE CL
EDWIN ARNOLD CT
LINDEN CT
GILLIES CT
STAFFORD RD
ORCHARD RD
CHELSITER CT
BERENS CT
OXFORD CT
CAMBRIDGE
STATION RD
A222
189

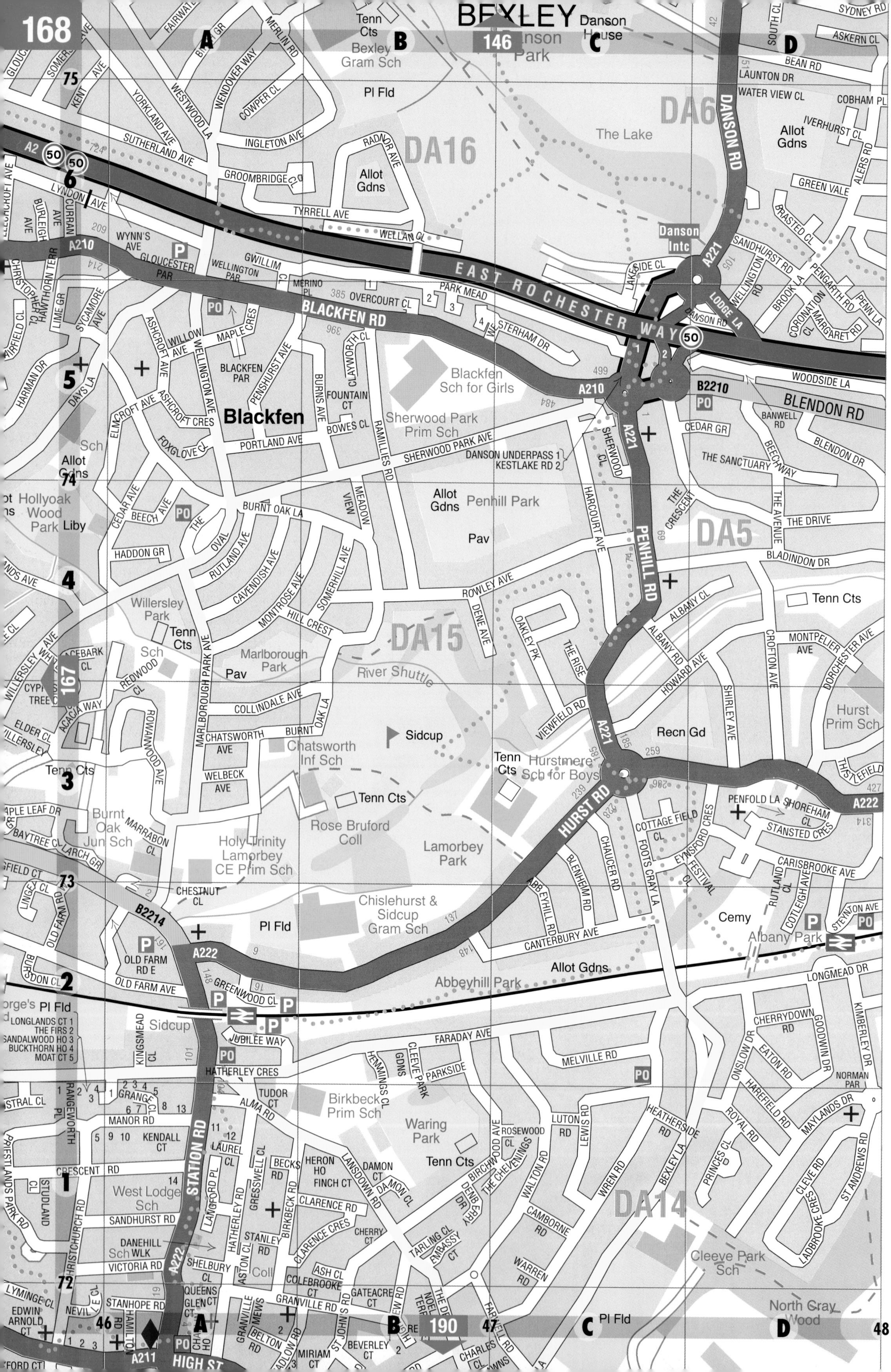
BEXLEY
146
Danson House
Danson Park
Tenn Cts
Bexley Gram Sch
Pl Fld
DA6
DA16
The Lake
DANSON RD
Allot Gdns
A2
50
6
5
4
3
2
1
75
74
73
72
A
B
C
D
SYDNEY RD
ASKERN CL
SOUTH CL
BEAN RD
LAUNTON DR
WATER VIEW CL
COBHAM PL
IVERHURST CL
ALERS RD
GREEN VALE
BRASTED CL
SANDHURST RD
PENGARTH RD
PENN LA
MARGARET RD
CORONATION CL
BROOK LA
WELLINGTON RD
LODGE LA
DANSON RD
Danson Intc
A221
EAST ROCHESTER WAY
BLACKFEN RD
A210
B2210
BLENDON RD
BLENDON DR
WOODSIDE LA
BANWELL RD
CEDAR GR
BEECHWAY
THE SANCTUARY
THE AVENUE
THE DRIVE
THE CRESCENT
DA5
BLADINDON DR
FAIRWATER
MERLIN RD
WENDOVER WAY
COWPER CL
WESTWOOD LA
YORKLAND AVE
SUTHERLAND AVE
INGLETON AVE
RADNOR AVE
GROOMBRIDGE CL
TYRRELL AVE
WELLAN CL
LYNDON AVE
CURRAN AVE
BURLEIGH AVE
WYNN'S AVE
GLOUCESTER PAR
WELLINGTON PAR
GWILLIM CL
MERINO PL
OVERCOURT CL
PARK MEAD
WESTERHAM DR
HAWTHORN TERR
CHRISTOPHER CL
LIME GR
SYCAMORE AVE
HARMAN DR
DAYS LA
ASHCROFT AVE
WILLOW AVE
MAPLE CRES
WELLINGTON AVE
BLACKFEN PAR
PENSHURST AVE
BURNS AVE
CLAYWORTH CL
FOUNTAIN CT
BOWES CL
RAMILLIES RD
Blackfen Sch for Girls
Sherwood Park Prim Sch
SHERWOOD PARK AVE
DANSON UNDERPASS 1
KESTLAKE RD 2
SHERWOOD CL
HARCOURT AVE
PENHILL RD
Blackfen
ELMCROFT AVE
ASHCROFT CRES
FOXGLOVE CL
PORTLAND AVE
Sch
Allot Gdns
Hollyoak Wood Park
Liby
CEDAR AVE
BEECH AVE
PO
THE OVAL
BURNT OAK LA
MEADOW VIEW
Allot Gdns
Penhill Park
Pav
HADDON GR
RUTLAND AVE
CAVENDISH AVE
MONTROSE AVE
SOMERHILL AVE
HILL CREST
ROWLEY AVE
DENE AVE
OAKLEY PK
THE RISE
ALBANY CL
ALBANY RD
HOWARD AVE
SHIRLEY AVE
CROFTON AVE
MONTPELIER AVE
DORCHESTER AVE
Tenn Cts
Willersley Park
Tenn Cts
DA15
Marlborough Park
MARLBOROUGH PARK AVE
River Shuttle
Pav
Sch
ACEBARK CL
REDWOOD CL
ROWANWOOD AVE
ACACIA WAY
167
WILLERSLEY AVE
CYPRESS TREE CL
ELDER CL
COLLINDALE AVE
BURNT OAK LA
CHATSWORTH AVE
WELBECK AVE
Chatsworth Inf Sch
Sidcup
VIEWFIELD RD
Recn Gd
Hurst Prim Sch
THISTLEFIELD
Tenn Cts
Hurstmere Sch for Boys
Tenn Cts
Rose Bruford Coll
HURST RD
A222
PENFOLD LA
SHOREHAM CL
STANSTED CRES
COTTAGE FIELD CL
EYNSFORD CRES
FESTIVAL CL
MAPLE LEAF DR
BAYTREE CL
LARCH GR
Burnt Oak Jun Sch
MARRABON CL
Holy Trinity Lamorbey CE Prim Sch
Lamorbey Park
ABBEYHILL RD
BLENHEIM RD
CHAUCER RD
FOOTS CRAY LA
RUTLAND CL
COTLEIGH AVE
CARISBROOKE AVE
STEYNTON AVE
Cemy
Albany Park
LINGEY CL
OLD FARM RD
CHESTNUT CL
B2214
Chislehurst & Sidcup Gram Sch
Pl Fld
CANTERBURY AVE
Allot Gdns
OLD FARM RD E
OLD FARM AVE
BURSDON CL
GREENWOOD CL
Abbeyhill Park
LONGMEAD DR
Pl Fld
LONGLANDS CT 1
THE FIRS 2
SANDALWOOD HO 3
BUCKTHORN HO 4
MOAT CT 5
Sidcup
KINGSMEAD CL
JUBILEE WAY
FARADAY AVE
HEMMINGS CL
CLEEVE PARK GDNS
PARKSIDE
MELVILLE RD
CHERRYDOWN RD
ONSLOW DR
EATON RD
GOODWIN DR
KIMBERLEY DR
NORMAN PAR
HATHERLEY CRES
RANGEWORTH PL
GRANGE CL
MANOR RD
KENDALL CT
TUDOR CT
ALMA RD
Birkbeck Prim Sch
Waring Park
ROSEWOOD CL
LUTON RD
LEWIS RD
HEATHERSIDE RD
HAREFIELD RD
ROYAL RD
MAYLANDS DR
LAUREL CL
STATION RD
CRESCENT RD
STUDLAND CL
West Lodge Sch
SANDHURST RD
PRIESTLANDS PARK RD
CHRISTCHURCH RD
DANEHILL WLK
VICTORIA RD
LANGFORD PL
HATHERLEY RD
GRESSWELL CL
BECKS RD
HERON HO
FINCH CT
LANSDOWN RD
DAMON CT
DAMON CL
BIRKBECK RD
CLARENCE RD
CLARENCE CRES
STANLEY RD
CHERRY CT
Tenn Cts
BIRCHWOOD AVE
THE CHEVENINGS
DENBERRY DR
WALTON RD
WREN RD
BEXLEY LA
DA14
PRINCES CL
CLEVE RD
ST ANDREWS RD
LADBROOKE CRES
CAMBORNE RD
WARREN RD
TARLING CL
EMBASSY CT
Cleeve Park Sch
SHELBURY CL
ASTON CL
Coll
ASH CL
COLEBROOKE CT
GATEACRE CT
A222
LYMINGE CL
NEVILLE CL
STANHOPE RD
EDWIN ARNOLD CT
QUEENS CT
GLEN CT
HAMILTON RD
GRANVILLE MEWS
GRANVILLE RD
ST JOHN'S RD
BELTON RD
MIRIAM CT
BEVERLEY CT
CHARLES CT
North Cray Wood
Pl Fld
190
46
47
48
A211
HIGH ST

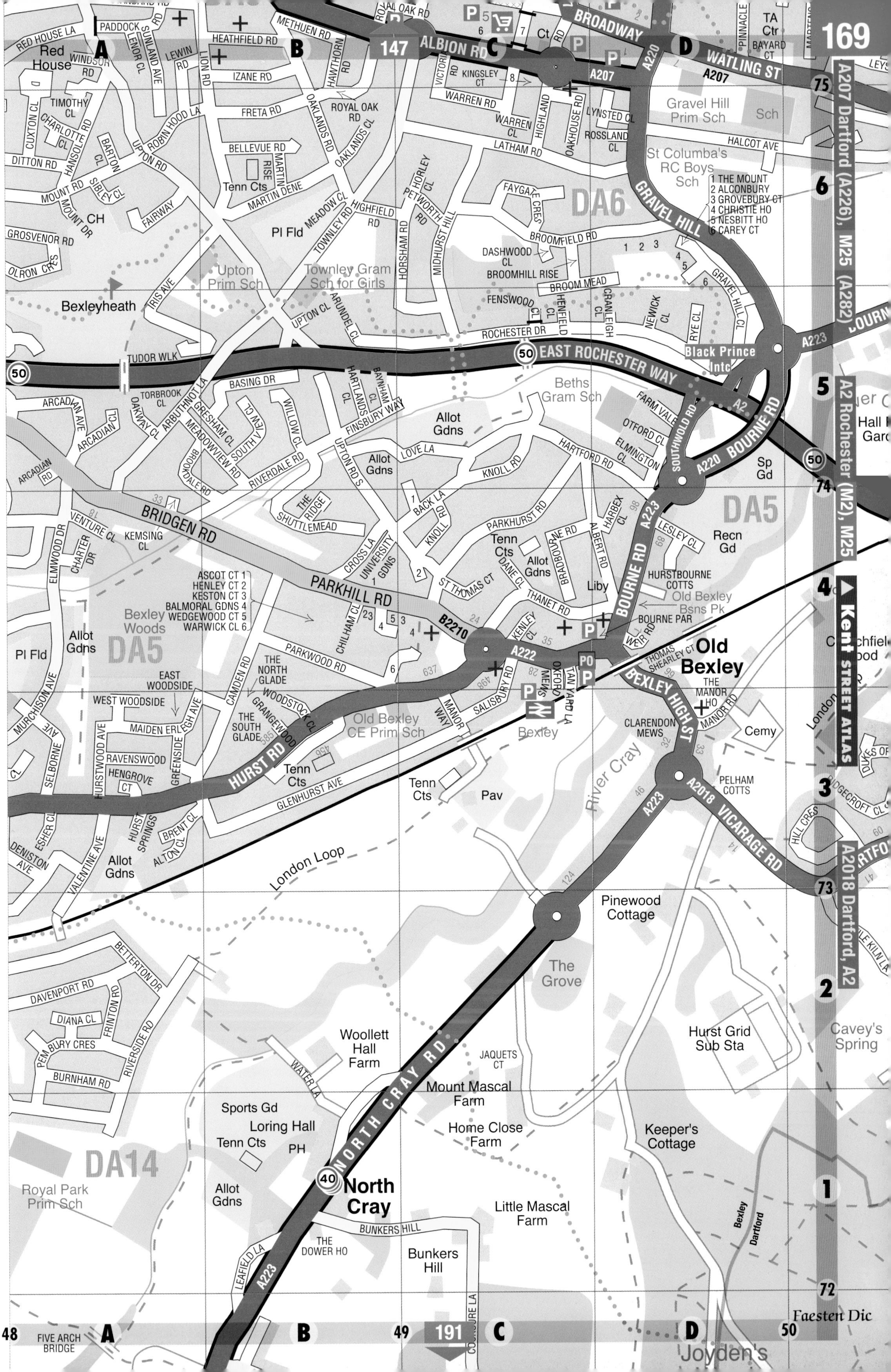
A
B
C
D
147
191
48
49
50
75
6
5
74
4
3
73
2
1
72
A207 Dartford (A226), M25 (A282)
A2 Rochester (M2), M25
Kent STREET ATLAS
A2018 Dartford, A2
Red House
RED HOUSE LA
PADDOCK CL
SUNLAND AVE
LENOR CL
WINDSOR RD
LEWIN RD
LION RD
HEATHFIELD RD
METHUEN RD
HAWTHORN RD
IZANE RD
FRETA RD
ROYAL OAK RD
OAKLANDS RD
OAKLANDS CL
BELLEVUE RD
MARTIN RISE
MARTIN DENE
Tenn Cts
TIMOTHY CL
CHARLOTTE CL
HANSOL RD
CUXTON CL
DITTON RD
BARTON CL
SIBLEY CL
ROBIN HOOD LA
UPTON RD
MOUNT RD
MOUNT DR
CH
FAIRWAY
GROSVENOR RD
OLRON CRES
Bexleyheath
Upton Prim Sch
Townley Gram Sch for Girls
IRIS AVE
UPTON CL
ARUNDEL CL
MEADOW CL
TOWNLEY RD
HIGHFIELD RD
Pl Fld
HORSHAM RD
PETWORTH RD
HORLEY CL
MIDHURST HILL
ALBION RD
BROADWAY
WATLING ST
A207
A220
VICTORIA RD
KINGSLEY CT
WARREN RD
WARREN CL
HIGHLAND RD
OAKHOUSE RD
LYNSTED CL
ROSSLAND CL
LATHAM RD
TA Ctr
BAYARD CT
PINNACLE
Gravel Hill Prim Sch
Sch
HALCOT AVE
St Columba's RC Boys Sch
1 THE MOUNT
2 ALCONBURY
3 GROVEBURY CT
4 CHRISTIE HO
5 NESBITT HO
6 CAREY CT
DA6
GRAVEL HILL
GRAVEL HILL CL
FAYGATE CRES
BROOMFIELD RD
DASHWOOD CL
BROOMHILL RISE
BROOM MEAD
FENSWOOD CL
HENFIELD CL
CRANLEIGH CL
NEWICK CL
RYE CL
ROCHESTER DR
EAST ROCHESTER WAY
Black Prince Intc
A223
A2
50
TUDOR WLK
BASING DR
TORBROOK CL
HARTLANDS CL
BAYNHAM CL
FINSBURY WAY
Beths Gram Sch
FARM VALE
OTFORD CL
ELMINGTON CL
SOUTHWOLD RD
BOURNE RD
Sp Gd
ARCADIAN AVE
ARCADIAN CL
ARCADIAN RD
OAKWAY CL
ARBUTHNOT LA
GRESHAM CL
SOUTH VIEW CL
MEADOWVIEW RD
BROOKDALE RD
WILLOW CL
RIVERDALE RD
UPTON RD S
Allot Gdns
LOVE LA
HARTFORD RD
KNOLL RD
BACK LA
THE RIDGE
SHUTTLEMEAD
BRIDGEN RD
VENTURE CL
KEMSING CL
ELMWOOD DR
CHARTER DR
PARKHURST RD
HARBEX CL
DA5
LESLEY CL
Recn Gd
CROSS LA
UNIVERSITY GDNS
ASCOT CT 1
HENLEY CT 2
KESTON CT 3
BALMORAL GDNS 4
WEDGEWOOD CT 5
WARWICK CL 6
PARKHILL RD
Bexley Woods
B2210
ST THOMAS CT
DANE CL
BRADBOURNE RD
ALBERT RD
Liby
HURSTBOURNE COTTS
Old Bexley Bsns Pk
THANET RD
KENLEY CL
BOURNE PAR
WEIR RD
CHILHAM CL
A222
Pl Fld
PARKWOOD RD
THE NORTH GLADE
EAST WOODSIDE
WEST WOODSIDE
CAMDEN RD
WOODSTOCK CL
GRANGEWOOD
THE SOUTH GLADE
MURCHISON AVE
SELBORNE AVE
MAIDEN ERLEGH AVE
RAVENSWOOD
HENGROVE CT
HURSTWOOD AVE
GREENSIDE
HURST RD
Old Bexley CE Prim Sch
MANOR WAY
SALISBURY RD
OXFORD MEWS
TAN YARD LA
PO
Bexley
THOMAS SHEARLEY CT
Old Bexley
BEXLEY HIGH ST
THE MANOR HO
MANOR RD
CLARENDON MEWS
Cemy
GLENHURST AVE
Tenn Cts
Pav
River Cray
PELHAM COTTS
A2018
VICARAGE RD
HILL CRES
RIDGECROFT CL
DENISTON AVE
ESHER CL
VALENTINE AVE
HURST SPRINGS
BRENT CL
ALTON CL
London Loop
Pinewood Cottage
The Grove
BETTERTON DR
DAVENPORT RD
FRINTON RD
DIANA CL
PEMBURY CRES
RIVERSIDE RD
BURNHAM RD
WATER LA
Woollett Hall Farm
NORTH CRAY RD
JAQUETS CT
Mount Mascal Farm
Hurst Grid Sub Sta
Cavey's Spring
Sports Gd
Loring Hall
PH
Home Close Farm
Keeper's Cottage
DA14
Royal Park Prim Sch
Allot Gdns
40
North Cray
Little Mascal Farm
Bexley
Dartford
BUNKERS HILL
THE DOWER HO
Bunkers Hill
LEAFIELD LA
FIVE ARCH BRIDGE
Faesten Dic
Joyden's

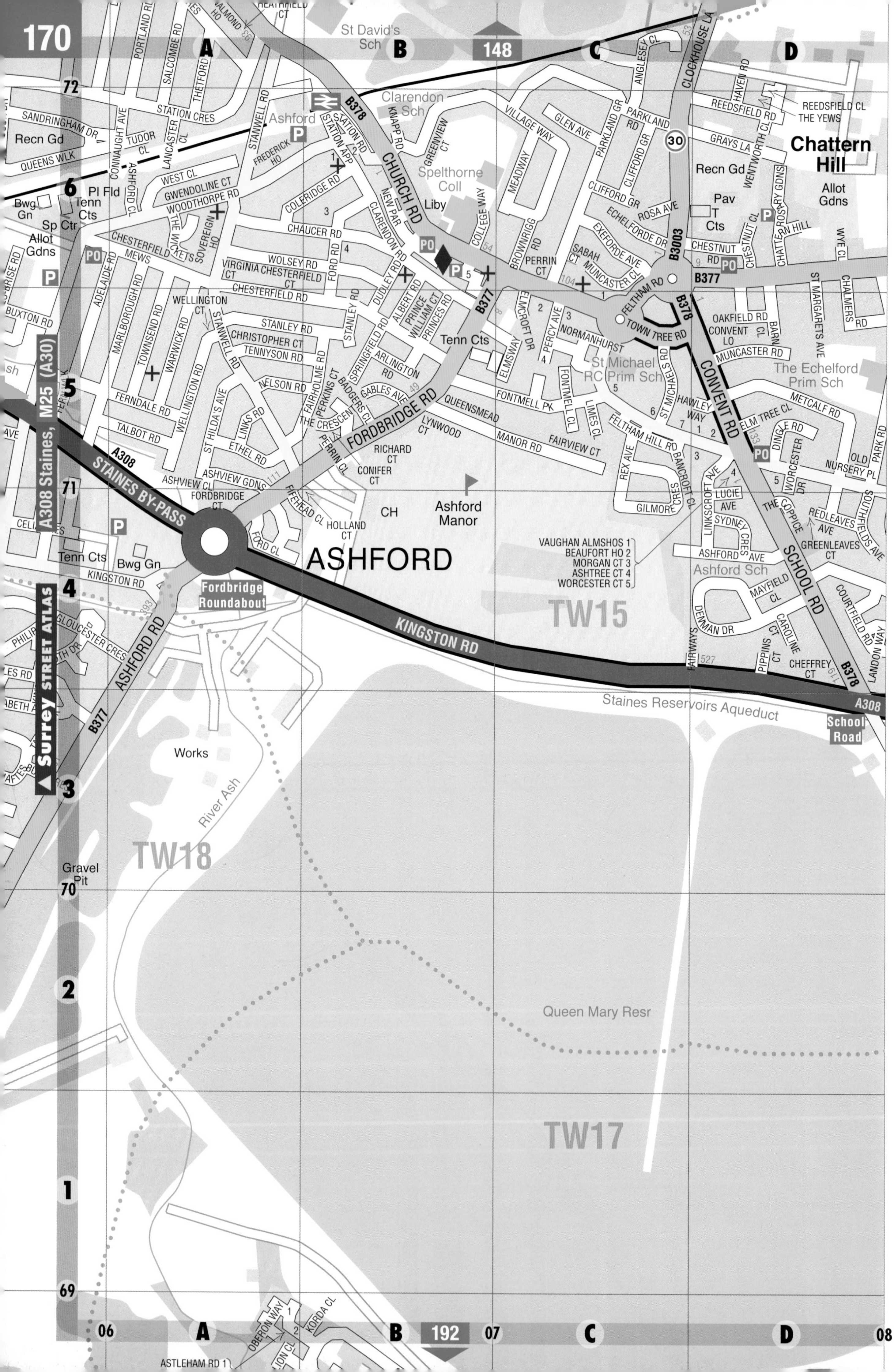

148
192
A
B
C
D
72
71
70
69
06
07
08
6
5
4
3
2
1
St David's Sch
Clarendon Sch
Spelthorne Coll
Liby
Ashford
Chattern Hill
Recn Gd
Allot Gdns
Pav
T Cts
Pl Fld
Tenn Cts
Bwg Gn
Sp Ctr
PO
P
ASHFORD
Ashford Manor
CH
St Michael RC Prim Sch
The Echelford Prim Sch
Ashford Sch
TW15
TW18
TW17
Fordbridge Roundabout
School Road
Works
River Ash
Gravel Pit
Queen Mary Resr
Staines Reservoirs Aqueduct
KINGSTON RD
STAINES BY-PASS
FORDBRIDGE RD
CHURCH RD
CONVENT RD
SCHOOL RD
CLOCKHOUSE LA
ASHFORD RD
A308
B377
B378
B3003
30
A308 Staines, M25 (A30)
Surrey STREET ATLAS
SANDRINGHAM DR
QUEENS WLK
CONNAUGHT AVE
TUDOR CL
LANCASTER CL
ASHFORD CL
STATION CRES
PORTLAND RD
SALCOMBE RD
THETFORD RD
STANWELL RD
FREDERICK HO
WEST CL
GWENDOLINE CT
WOODTHORPE RD
THE WICKETS
SOVEREIGN HO
CHESTERFIELD MEWS
ADELAIDE RD
MARLBOROUGH RD
TOWNSEND RD
WARWICK RD
WELLINGTON CT
WELLINGTON RD
FERNDALE RD
TALBOT RD
ASHVIEW CL
ASHVIEW GDNS
FORDBRIDGE CT
STATION RD
STATION APP
COLERIDGE RD
CHAUCER RD
WOLSEY RD
VIRGINIA CT
CHESTERFIELD CT
CHESTERFIELD RD
STANLEY RD
CHRISTOPHER CT
TENNYSON RD
NELSON RD
ST HILDA'S AVE
LINKS RD
ETHEL RD
FAIRHOLME RD
PERKINS CT
BADGERS CL
THE CRESCENT
PERRIN CL
FIFEHEAD CL
HOLLAND CT
FORD CL
FORD RD
STANLEY RD
DUDLEY RD
ALBERT RD
PRINCE WILLIAM CT
PRINCES RD
SPRINGFIELD RD
ARLINGTON RD
GABLES AVE
RICHARD CT
CONIFER CT
LYNWOOD CT
QUEENSMEAD
MANOR RD
FAIRVIEW CT
FONTMELL PK
FONTMELL CL
LIMES CL
ELMSWAY
ELMCROFT DR
PERCY AVE
NORMANHURST
PERRIN CT
BROWNRIGG RD
MEADWAY
VILLAGE WAY
COLLEGE WAY
KNAPP RD
GREENVIEW CT
CLARENDON RD
NEW PAR
GLEN AVE
PARKLAND GR
PARKLAND RD
CLIFFORD GR
ANGLESEY CL
ROSA AVE
ECHELFORDE DR
EXEFORDE AVE
SABAH CT
MUNCASTER CL
FELTHAM RD
TOWN TREE RD
ST MICHAELS RD
HAWLEY WAY
FELTHAM HILL RD
REX AVE
BANCROFT CL
GILMORE CRES
LINKSCROFT AVE
LUCIE AVE
SYDNEY CRES
ASHFORD AVE
MAYFIELD CL
DENMAN DR
FAIRWAYS
PIPPINS CT
CAROLINE CT
CHEFFREY CT
COURTFIELD RD
LANDON WAY
THE COPPICE
REDLEAVES AVE
GREENLEAVES CT
SOUTHFIELDS AVE
WORCESTER DR
DINGLE RD
ELM TREE CL
METCALF RD
OLD NURSERY PL
PARK RD
OAKFIELD RD
CONVENT LO
BARN CL
MUNCASTER RD
ST MARGARETS AVE
CHALMERS RD
WYE CL
CHESTNUT RD
CHESTNUT CL
CHATTERN HILL
ROSARY GDNS
GRAYS LA
WENTWORTH CL
REEDSFIELD RD
REEDSFIELD CL
THE YEWS
HAVEN RD
VAUGHAN ALMSHOS 1
BEAUFORT HO 2
MORGAN CT 3
ASHTREE CT 4
WORCESTER CT 5
KINGSTON RD
GLOUCESTER CRES
BUXTON RD
ASTLEHAM RD 1
OBERON WAY
KORDA CL

A
B
C
D
149
193
Bedfont Ind Pk N
Court One
Bedfont Ind Pk
Ashford Ind Est
Mereside Pk
Recn Gd
ASHFORD RD
FELTHAM RD
Allot Gdns
TW13
TW15
TW16
Lower Feltham
Cemy
Felthamhill
Sp Gd
Hounslow
Surrey
Meadhurst Sports Club
Tenn Cts
Ashford Common
Spelthorne Inf & Jun Schs
Kenyngton Manor Prim Sch
Sunbury Common
Spelthorne Sports Club
Littleton Common
STAINES RD W
CHERTSEY RD
CADBURY RD
WINDMILL RD
Superstore
Windmill Bsns Village
Sunbury Int Bsns Ctr
West Surrey Est
Action Ct
Water Works
The Dolphin Est
Springfield Prim Sch
Upper Halliford
Charlton
The Bishop Wand CE Sch
Hawkedale Inf Sch
Sunbury Cross
Sunbury
St Ignatius Prim
A244
A308
B377
M3
08
09
10

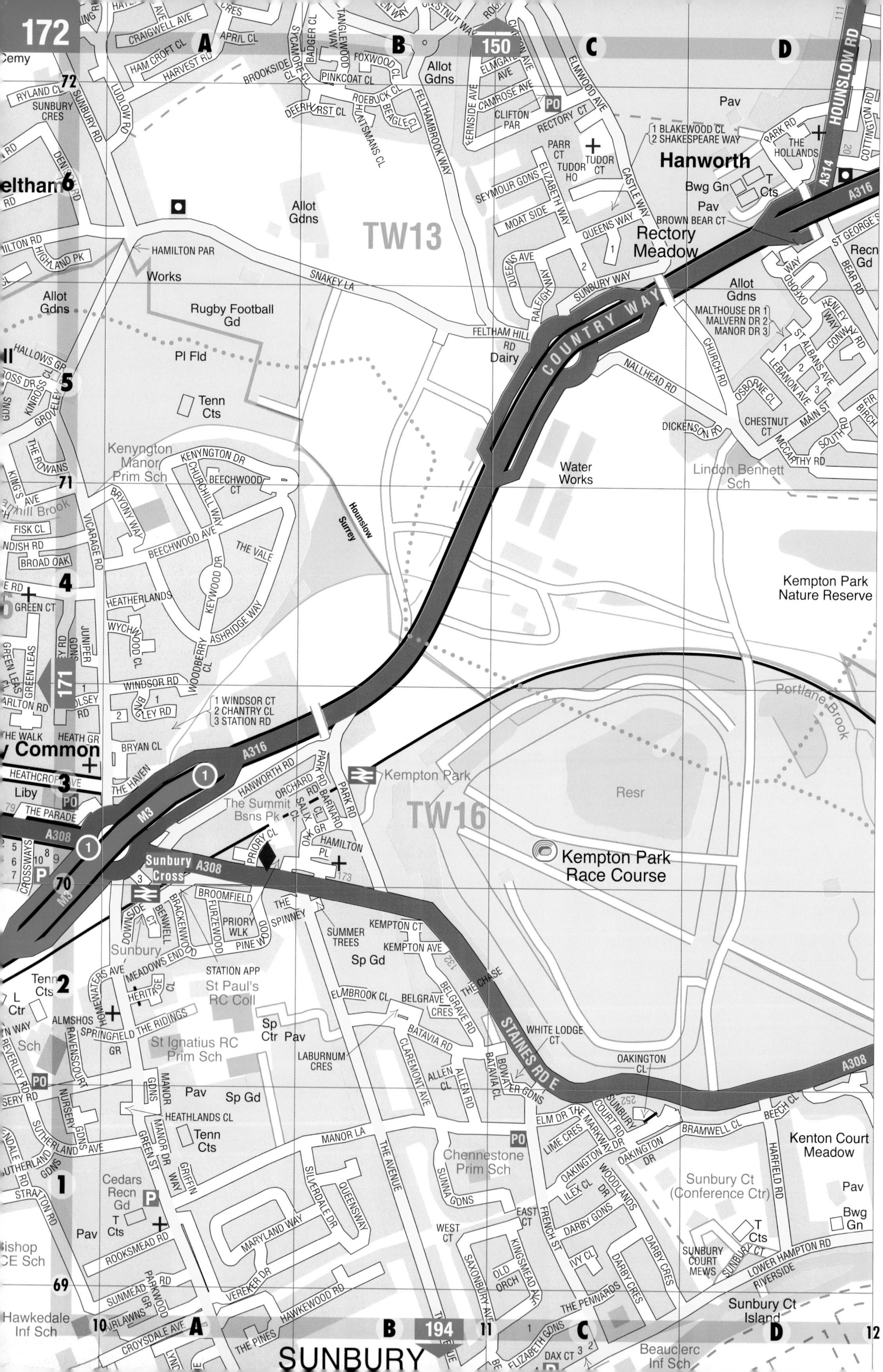
A
B
C
D
150
Cemy
CRAIGWELL AVE
APRIL CL
HAM CROFT CL
HARVEST RD
BROOKSIDE
SYCAMORE CL
BADGER CL
TANGLEWOOD WAY
FOXWOOD CL
PINKCOAT CL
Allot Gdns
ELMGATE AVE
CAMROSE AVE
FERNSIDE AVE
CLIFTON PAR
PO
RECTORY CT
ELMWOOD AVE
RYLAND CL
SUNBURY CRES
SUNBURY RD
LUDLOW RD
DEERHURST CL
ROEBUCK CL
BEAGLE CL
HUNTSMANS CL
FELTHAMBROOK WAY
1 BLAKEWOOD CL
2 SHAKESPEARE WAY
Pav
PARK RD
THE HOLLANDS
HOUNSLOW RD
COTTINGTON RD
A314
A316
Hanworth
PARR CT
TUDOR HO
TUDOR CT
Bwg Gn
T Cts
Pav
DENISON RD
Feltham
6
72
Allot Gdns
TW13
SEYMOUR GDNS
ELIZABETH WAY
MOAT SIDE
CASTLE WAY
QUEENS WAY
BROWN BEAR CT
Rectory Meadow
ST GEORGE'S
Recn Gd
BEAR RD
HILTON RD
HIGHLAND PK
HAMILTON PAR
Works
SNAKEY LA
QUEENS AVE
RALEIGH WAY
SUNBURY WAY
COUNTRY WAY
OXFORD WAY
Allot Gdns
MALTHOUSE DR 1
MALVERN DR 2
MANOR DR 3
HENLEY WAY
CONWAY RD
Allot Gdns
Rugby Football Gd
FELTHAM HILL RD
Dairy
CHURCH RD
ST ALBANS AVE
LEBANON AVE
HALLOWS GR
ROSS DR
KINROSS CL
GROVELEY
5
Pl Fld
NALLHEAD RD
OSBORNE CL
FIR
BIRCH
Tenn Cts
DICKENSON RD
CHESTNUT CT
MAIN ST
SOUTH RD
McCARTHY RD
THE ROWANS
Kenyngton Manor Prim Sch
KENYNGTON DR
CHURCHILL WAY
BEECHWOOD CT
Water Works
Lindon Bennett Sch
KING'S AVE
71
Hounslow
Surrey
FISK CL
BRYONY WAY
BEECHWOOD AVE
THE VALE
VICARAGE RD
BROAD OAK
4
Kempton Park Nature Reserve
GREEN CT
HEATHERLANDS
KEYWOOD DR
WYCHWOOD CL
ASHRIDGE WAY
JUNIPER
GREEN LEAS
171
WOODBERRY CL
WINDSOR RD
BINGLEY RD
Portlane Brook
HEATH GR
1 WINDSOR CT
2 CHANTRY CL
3 STATION RD
THE WALK
Common
BRYAN CL
A316
HEATHCROFT AVE
3
Liby
PO
THE PARADE
THE HAVEN
HANWORTH RD
ORCHARD RD
PARK RD
BARNARD CL
SALIX CL
Kempton Park
Resr
The Summit Bsns Pk
TW16
M3
A308
PRIORY CL
OAK GR
HAMILTON PL
CROSSWAYS
P
70
Sunbury Cross
A308
Kempton Park Race Course
BROOMFIELD
THE SPINNEY
DOWNSIDE
BENWELL CT
BRACKENWOOD
FURZEWOOD
PRIORY WLK
PINE WOOD
SUMMER TREES
KEMPTON CT
KEMPTON AVE
Sp Gd
Sunbury
MEADOWS END
STATION APP
2
Tenn Cts
L Ctr
HOMEWATERS AVE
HERITAGE CL
St Paul's RC Coll
ELMBROOK CL
BELGRAVE CRES
BELGRAVE RD
THE CHASE
STAINES RD E
WHITE LODGE CT
ALMSHOS
SPRINGFIELD GR
THE RIDINGS
Sch
Sp Ctr
Pav
BATAVIA RD
St Ignatius RC Prim Sch
LABURNUM CRES
CLAREMONT AVE
ALLEN CL
ALLEN RD
BATAVIA CL
BOWATER GDNS
OAKINGTON CL
A308
RAVENSCOURT
PO
MANOR GDNS
Pav
Sp Gd
HEATHLANDS CL
NURSERY GDNS
SUTHERLAND AVE
MANOR DR
GREEN ST
Tenn Cts
MANOR LA
THE AVENUE
PO
Chennestone Prim Sch
ELM DR
THE MARKWAY
LIME CRES
SUNBURY COURT RD
OAKINGTON DR
BRAMWELL CL
BEECH CL
HARFIELD RD
Kenton Court Meadow
1
GRIFFIN WAY
SILVERDALE DR
QUEENSWAY
SUNNA GDNS
ILEX CL
WOODLANDS DR
Sunbury Ct (Conference Ctr)
Pav
Bwg Gn
Cedars Recn Gd
P
T Cts
MARYLAND WAY
EAST CT
FRENCH ST
DARBY GDNS
T Cts
Pav
WEST CT
KINGSMEAD AVE
OLD ORCH
SAXONBURY AVE
IVY CL
DARBY CRES
SUNBURY COURT MEWS
SUNBURY CT
LOWER HAMPTON RD
RIVERSIDE
Bishop CE Sch
ROOKSMEAD RD
PARKWOOD GR
69
SUNMEAD RD
VEREKER DR
HAWKEWOOD RD
THE PENNARDS
Sunbury Ct Island
Hawkedale Inf Sch
10
CROYSDALE AVE
THE PINES
194
11
ELIZABETH GDNS
DAX CT
Beauclerc Inf Sch
12
SUNBURY

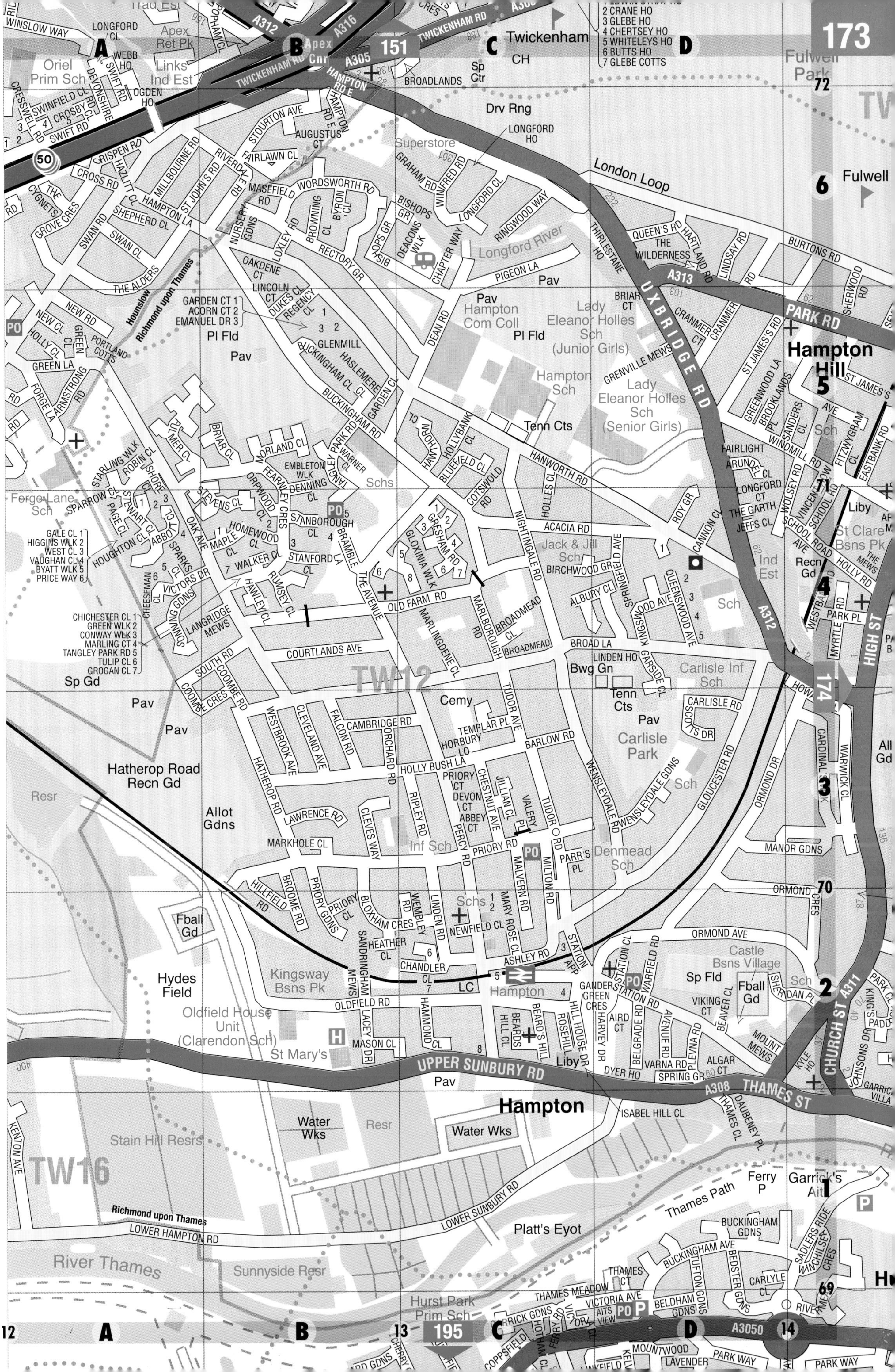

Twickenham
Apex Cnr
Apex Ret Pk
Links Ind Est
Oriel Prim Sch
TWICKENHAM RD
HAMPTON RD E
Sp Ctr
CH
Drv Rng
Superstore
LONGFORD HO
London Loop
Fulwell Park
Fulwell
TW
Longford River
PIGEON LA
Pav
Hampton Com Coll
Lady Eleanor Holles Sch (Junior Girls)
Lady Eleanor Holles Sch (Senior Girls)
Hampton Sch
UXBRIDGE RD
PARK RD
Hampton Hill
Tenn Cts
HANWORTH RD
Forge Lane Sch
Schs
Jack & Jill Sch
ACACIA RD
OLD FARM RD
COURTLANDS AVE
TW12
Cemy
Bwg Gn
Carlisle Inf Sch
Carlisle Park
Ind Est
St Clare Bsns Pk
Liby
HIGH ST
Sp Gd
Hatherop Road Recn Gd
Resr
Allot Gdns
Inf Sch
Denmead Sch
Fball Gd
Hydes Field
Kingsway Bsns Pk
Oldfield House Unit (Clarendon Sch)
St Mary's
Hampton
Castle Bsns Village
Sp Fld
UPPER SUNBURY RD
THAMES ST
CHURCH ST
Water Wks
Stain Hill Resrs
TW16
LOWER SUNBURY RD
LOWER HAMPTON RD
Richmond upon Thames
River Thames
Sunnyside Resr
Platt's Eyot
Thames Path
Ferry P
Garrick's Ait
Hurst Park Prim Sch
A312
A313
A316
A305
A308
A311
A3050

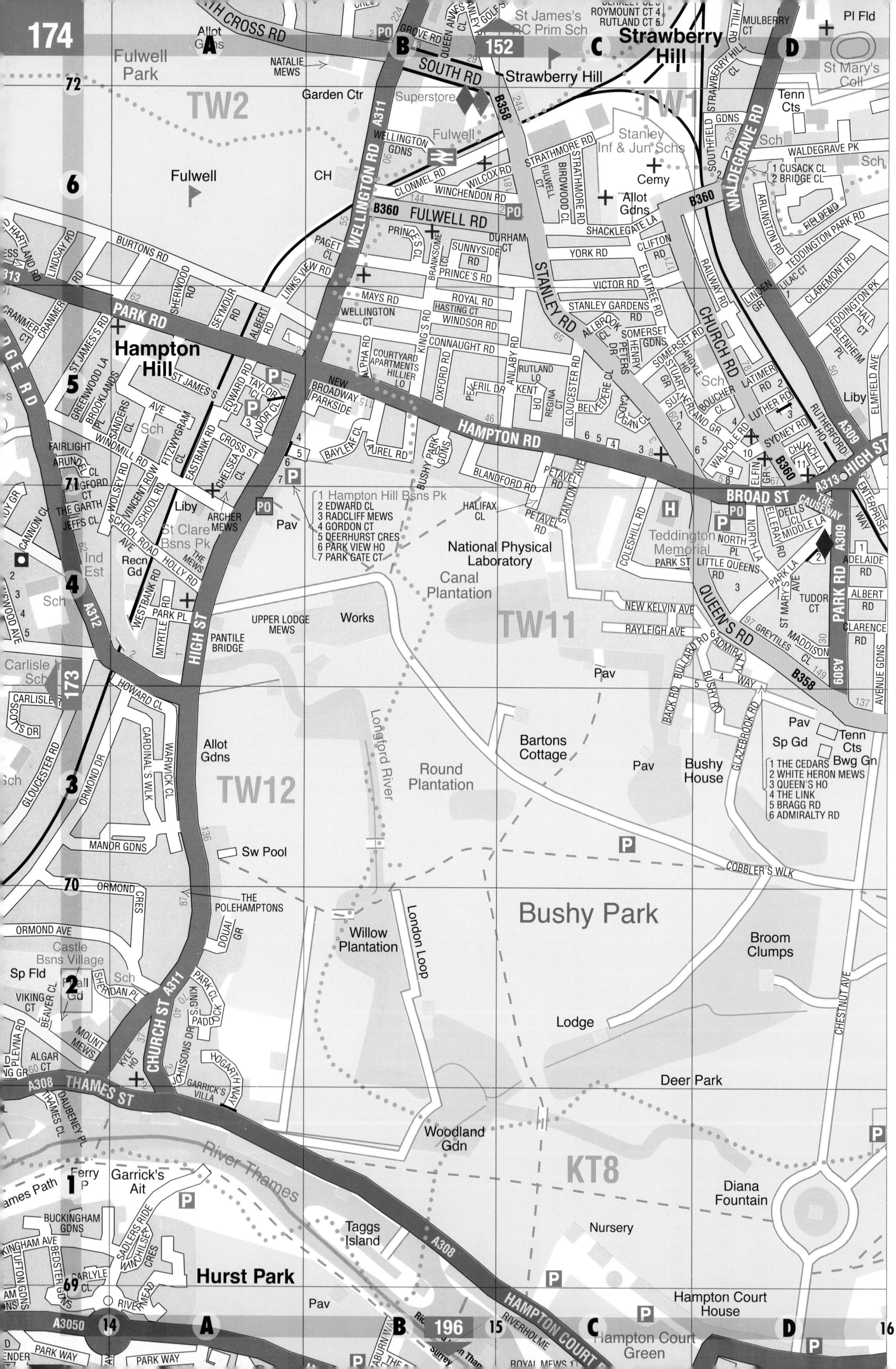
A
B
C
D
152
Strawberry Hill
St James's RC Prim Sch
ROYMOUNT CT 4
RUTLAND CT 5
MULBERRY CT
Pl Fld
St Mary's Coll
Allot Gdns
Fulwell Park
72
NATALIE MEWS
SOUTH RD
GROVE RD
QUEEN ANNES CL
Garden Ctr
Superstore
B358
TW2
TW1
Tenn Cts
Stanley Inf & Jun Schs
STRAWBERRY HILL CL
SOUTHFIELD GDNS
WALDEGRAVE RD
WALDEGRAVE PK
Sch
1 CUSACK CL
2 BRIDGE CL
A311
WELLINGTON GDNS
Fulwell
6
Fulwell
CH
CLONMEL RD
WILCOX RD
WINCHENDON RD
STRATHMORE RD
FULWELL CT
BIRDWOOD CL
Cemy
Allot Gdns
B360
FULWELL RD
WELLINGTON RD
PAGET CL
PRINCE'S CL
BRANKSOME CL
SUNNYSIDE RD
DURHAM CT
SHACKLEGATE LA
ARLINGTON RD
FIELDEND
TEDDINGTON PARK RD
BURTONS RD
LINDSAY RD
HARTLAND RD
CLIFTON RD
YORK RD
STANLEY RD
PRINCE'S RD
LINKS VIEW RD
LINDEN GR
LILAC CT
CLAREMONT RD
B313
SHERWOOD RD
SEYMOUR RD
MAYS RD
ROYAL RD
VICTOR RD
RAILWAY RD
ELMTREE RD
PARK RD
CRANMER CT
CRANMER RD
ALBERT RD
WELLINGTON CT
HASTING CT
WINDSOR RD
STANLEY GARDENS RD
TEDDINGTON PK
HALL CT
BLENHEIM PL
Hampton Hill
ST JAMES'S RD
CONNAUGHT RD
ALLBROOK CL
PETERS DR
HENRY
SOMERSET GDNS
SOMERSET RD
CHURCH RD
GREENWOOD LA
BROOKLANDS
ST JAMES'S
EDWARD RD
TAYLOR CL
NEW BROADWAY
PARKSIDE
ALPHA RD
COURTYARD APARTMENTS
HILLIER LO
KING'S RD
OXFORD RD
RUTLAND LO
ANLABY RD
KENT DR
REGINA CT
GLOUCESTER RD
BELVEDERE CL
CADOGAN CL
STUART GR
ARGYLE HO
SUTHERLAND GR
BOUCHER CL
LATIMER RD
LUTHER RD
ELMFIELD AVE
Liby
5
SANDERS CL
AVE
Sch
FITZWYGRAM CL
TUDOR CL
PERYL DR
RUTHERFORD
A309
5
FAIRLIGHT
ARUNDEL CL
WINDMILL RD
EASTBANK RD
CROSS ST
BAYLEAF CL
LAUREL RD
BUSHY PARK GDNS
HAMPTON RD
WALPOLE RD
SYDNEY RD
CHURCH LA
HIGH ST
71
LONGFORD CT
THE GARTH
JEFFS CL
WOLSEY RD
VINCENT ROW
SCHOOL RD
CHELSEA CL
BLANDFORD RD
PETAVEL RD
STANTON AVE
ELFIN
B360
A313
BROAD ST
THE CAUSEWAY
ENTERPRISE WAY
CANNON CL
Liby
ARCHER MEWS
1 Hampton Hill Bsns Pk
2 EDWARD CL
3 RADCLIFF MEWS
4 GORDON CT
5 DEERHURST CRES
6 PARK VIEW HO
7 PARK GATE CT
HALIFAX CL
Pav
COLESHILL RD
Teddington Memorial
NORTH LA
NORTH PL
DELLS CL
MIDDLE LA
ELLERAY RD
St Clare Bsns Pk
SCHOOL ROAD AVE
THE MEWS
HOLLY RD
Ind Est
Recn Gd
National Physical Laboratory
PARK ST
LITTLE QUEENS RD
ADELAIDE RD
4
WESTBANK RD
Sch
Canal Plantation
PARK LA
ST MARY'S AVE
TUDOR CT
ALBERT RD
PARK RD
A312
MYRTLE RD
PARK PL
HIGH ST
UPPER LODGE MEWS
Works
TW11
NEW KELVIN AVE
RAYLEIGH AVE
QUEEN'S RD
GREYTILES
MADDISON CL
CLARENCE RD
PANTILE BRIDGE
BULLARD RD
ADMIRALTY WAY
Carlisle Inf Sch
173
HOWARD CL
CARLISLE RD
SCOTTS DR
Pav
BUSHY RD
BACK RD
B358
AVENUE GDNS
CARDINAL'S WLK
WARWICK CL
Allot Gdns
Bartons Cottage
GLAZEBROOK RD
Pav
Sp Gd
Tenn Cts
Bwg Gn
Longford River
GLOUCESTER RD
ORMOND DR
3
TW12
Round Plantation
Pav
Bushy House
1 THE CEDARS
2 WHITE HERON MEWS
3 QUEEN'S HO
4 THE LINK
5 BRAGG RD
6 ADMIRALTY RD
MANOR GDNS
Sw Pool
COBBLER'S WLK
70
ORMOND CRES
THE POLEHAMPTONS
ORMOND AVE
Castle Bsns Village
DOUAI GR
Bushy Park
Willow Plantation
London Loop
Broom Clumps
Sp Fld
2
Sch
SHERIDAN PL
VIKING CT
BEAVER CL
MOUNT MEWS
CHURCH ST
PARK CL
KING'S PADDOCK
JOHNSONS DR
Lodge
CHESTNUT AVE
PLEVNA RD
ALGAR CT
KYLE HO
HOGARTH WAY
GARRICK'S VILLA
Deer Park
A308
THAMES ST
THAMES CL
DAUBENEY PL
River Thames
Woodland Gdn
KT8
1
Ferry
Garrick's Ait
Diana Fountain
BUCKINGHAM GDNS
SADLERS RIDE
WINCHILSEA CRES
Taggs Island
Nursery
BEDSTER GDNS
CARLYLE CL
69
Hurst Park
RIVERMEAD
A308
HAMPTON COURT RD
Hampton Court House
Pav
A3050
14
196
15
Hampton Court Green
16
PARK WAY
RIVERHOLME
ROYAL MEWS

TEDDINGTON
KINGSTON UPON THAMES
Hampton Wick
Teddington Lock
Teddington Weir
Thames Path
River Thames
TROWLOCK ISLAND
TW11
KT1
153
176
197
STRAWBERRY VALE
TWICKENHAM RD
MANOR RD
HIGH ST
KINGSTON RD
UPPER TEDDINGTON RD
UPPER HAM RD
HAM COMM
FERRY RD
BROOM RD
BROOM WATER W
STANLEY RD
PARK RD
B358 PARK RD
SANDY LA
BUSHY PARK RD
HAMPTON COURT RD
HORSE FAIR
WOOD ST
KINGSTON HALL RD
LOWER TEDDINGTON RD
LOWER HAM RD
RICHMOND RD
Meadlands Prim Sch
Cassel
St George's Ind Est
Tiffin Girls' Sch
Fern Hill Prim Sch
Collis Prim Sch
Sacred Heart RC Prim Sch
Teddington Sch
Hampton Wick Inf Sch
Athletic Gd
Sw Pool
Recn Gd
Marina
Warren Plantation
Oval Plantation
Heron Pond
Boating Lake
Cobbler's Wlk
The Royal Paddocks
Bushy Lodge
Hampton Wick Pond
Old Icehouse
KINGSTON BRIDGE
OLD BRIDGE ST
Superstore
Bsns Ctr
The Griffin Ctr
Richmond upon Thames
Kingston upon Thames
Teddington
Cemy
Allot Gdns

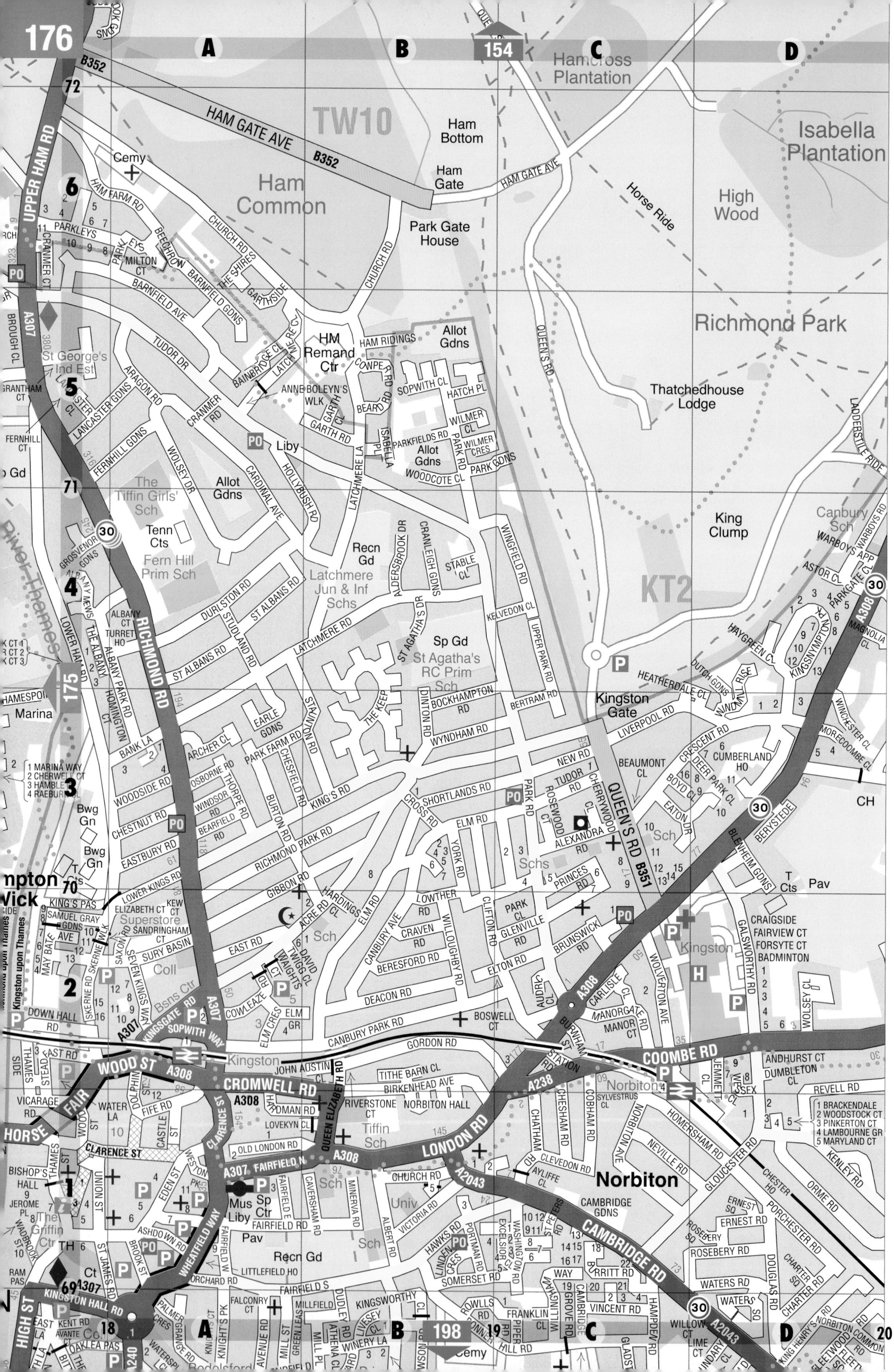
A
B
C
D
154
198
175
Hamcross Plantation
Isabella Plantation
TW10
KT2
HAM GATE AVE
B352
Ham Bottom
Ham Gate
Ham Common
Park Gate House
High Wood
Horse Ride
Richmond Park
Thatchedhouse Lodge
King Clump
Canbury Sch
HM Remand Ctr
Allot Gdns
UPPER HAM RD
RICHMOND RD
A307
QUEEN'S RD
B351
Kingston Gate
St George's Ind Est
The Tiffin Girls' Sch
Tenn Cts
Fern Hill Prim Sch
Latchmere Jun & Inf Schs
Recn Gd
Sp Gd
St Agatha's RC Prim Sch
River Thames
Marina
Superstore
Coll
Bsns Ctr
Kingston
WOOD ST
CROMWELL RD
A308
CLARENCE ST
QUEEN ELIZABETH RD
LONDON RD
A238
A2043
COOMBE RD
CAMBRIDGE RD
Norbiton
Tiffin Sch
Mus
Liby
Sp Ctr
Pav
Univ
HIGH ST
KINGSTON HALL RD
The Griffin Ctr
Cemy
LATCHMERE RD
KING'S RD
RICHMOND PARK RD
CANBURY PARK RD
GORDON RD
PARK RD
ELM RD
SHORTLANDS RD
TUDOR DR
CHURCH RD
HAM FARM RD
CHURCH RD
LIVERPOOL RD
GLOUCESTER RD
KINGSTON HILL
BLENHEIM GDNS
HOMERSHAM RD
FAIRFIELD RD
WHEATFIELD WAY
COOMBE RD
CRAIGSIDE
FAIRVIEW CT
FORSYTE CT
BADMINTON
1 BRACKENDALE
2 WOODSTOCK CT
3 PINKERTON CT
4 LAMBOURNE GR
5 MARYLAND CT
1 MARINA WAY
2 CHERWELL CT
3 HAMBLE ST
4 RAEBURN CL

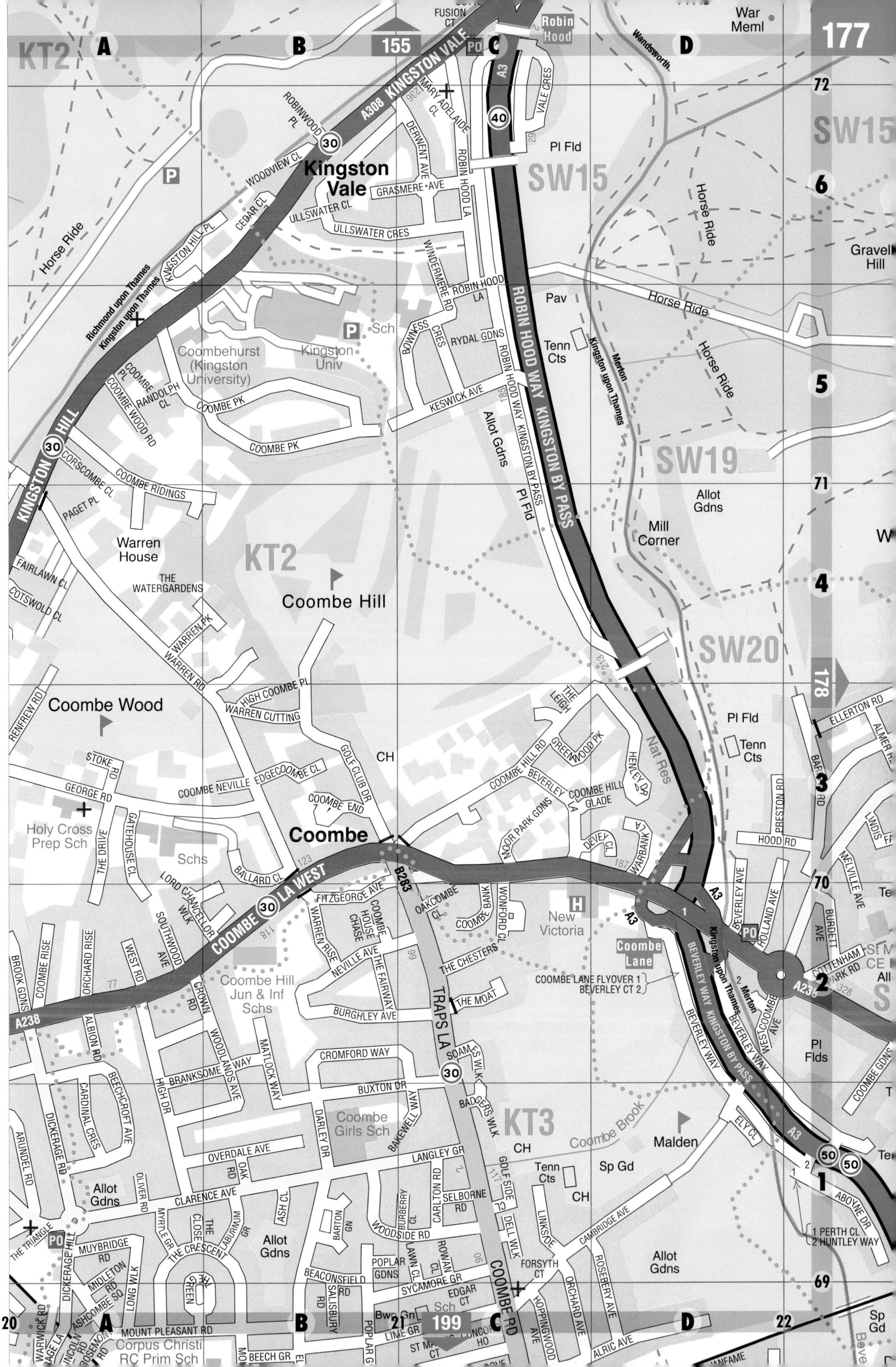
KT2
A
B
155
C
D
Robin Hood
War Meml
Wandsworth
72
SW15
FUSION CT
A308 KINGSTON VALE
MARY CL
ADELAIDE
ROBINWOOD PL
DERWENT AVE
VALE CRES
Pl Fld
Kingston Vale
WOODVIEW CL
GRASMERE AVE
ROBIN HOOD LA
SW15
6
Horse Ride
CEDAR CL
ULLSWATER CL
ULLSWATER CRES
KINGSTON HILL PL
WINDERMERE RD
ROBIN HOOD LA
Gravel Hill
Horse Ride
Richmond upon Thames
Kingston upon Thames
Pav
Horse Ride
Sch
Kingston Univ
Coombehurst (Kingston University)
BOWNESS CRES
RYDAL GDNS
Tenn Cts
Kingston upon Thames
Merton
Horse Ride
COOMBE PL
RANDOLPH CL
COOMBE WOOD RD
COOMBE PK
KESWICK AVE
ROBIN HOOD WAY KINGSTON BY PASS
5
KINGSTON HILL
CORSCOMBE CL
COOMBE PK
Allot Gdns
SW19
COOMBE RIDINGS
PAGET PL
Pl Fld
71
Allot Gdns
Mill Corner
Warren House
KT2
FAIRLAWN CL
THE WATERGARDENS
Coombe Hill
4
COTSWOLD CL
WARREN PK
WARREN RD
SW20
178
Coombe Wood
RENFREW RD
HIGH COOMBE PL
WARREN CUTTING
THE LEIGH
GREENWOOD PK
HENLEY DR
Nat Res
Pl Fld
ELLERTON RD
Tenn Cts
CH
GOLF CLUB DR
STOKE RD
EDGECOOMBE CL
GEORGE RD
COOMBE NEVILLE
COOMBE END
COOMBE HILL RD
BEVERLEY LA
COOMBE HILL GLADE
3
BARNES RD
PRESTON RD
Holy Cross Prep Sch
GATEHOUSE CL
THE DRIVE
Schs
Coombe
MOOR PARK GDNS
DEVEY CL
WARBANK LA
HOOD RD
BALLARD CL
LORD CHANCELLOR WLK
COOMBE LA WEST
B283
FITZGEORGE AVE
OAKCOMBE CL
COOMBE BANK
WONFORD CL
H
New Victoria
A3
A3
BEVERLEY AVE
HOLLAND AVE
70
MELVILLE AVE
BURDETT AVE
SOUTHWOOD AVE
WARREN RISE
COOMBE HOUSE CHASE
Coombe Lane
PO
BROOK GDNS
COOMBE RISE
ORCHARD RISE
WEST RD
NEVILLE AVE
THE FAIRWAY
THE CHESTERS
COOMBE LANE FLYOVER 1
BEVERLEY CT 2
BEVERLEY WAY
Kingston upon Thames
Merton
COTTENHAM PARK RD
A238
2
A238
CROWN RD
Coombe Hill Jun & Inf Schs
TRAPS LA
THE MOAT
BURGHLEY AVE
BEVERLEY WAY KINGSTON BY PASS
WEST COOMBE AVE
Pl Flds
ALBION RD
WOODLANDS AVE
MATLOCK WAY
CROMFORD WAY
SOAMES WLK
BRANKSOME WAY
COOMBE GDNS
BEECHCROFT AVE
CARDINAL CRES
HIGH DR
BUXTON DR
BAKEWELL WAY
BADGERS WLK
ARUNDEL RD
DICKERAGE RD
Coombe Girls Sch
DARLEY DR
KT3
Coombe Brook
Malden
ELY CL
A3
OVERDALE AVE
OAK RD
LANGLEY GR
CH
Tenn Cts
Sp Gd
50
50
1
ABOYNE DR
OLIVER RD
Allot Gdns
CLARENCE AVE
ASH CL
CARLTON RD
SELBORNE RD
GOLF SIDE CL
CH
MYRTLE GR
THE CLOSE
LABURNUM GR
BURBERRY CL
CAMBRIDGE AVE
THE TRIANGLE
PO
DICKERAGE HILL
MUYBRIDGE RD
THE CRESCENT
Allot Gdns
BARTON GN
WOODSIDE RD
DELL WLK
LINKSIDE
1 PERTH CL
2 HUNTLEY WAY
MIDLETON RD
LONG WLK
THE GREEN
POPLAR GDNS
LAWN CL
ROWAN CL
ROSEBERY AVE
Allot Gdns
ASHCOMBE SQ
BEACONSFIELD RD
SALISBURY RD
SYCAMORE GR
EDGAR CT
Sch
FORSYTH CT
ORCHARD AVE
69
COOMBE RD
HOPPINGWOOD AVE
20
WARWICK RD
A
MOUNT PLEASANT RD
B
21
199
C
D
22
Sp Gd
Corpus Christi RC Prim Sch
BEECH GR
POPLAR GR
LIME GR
ALRIC AVE
Beve

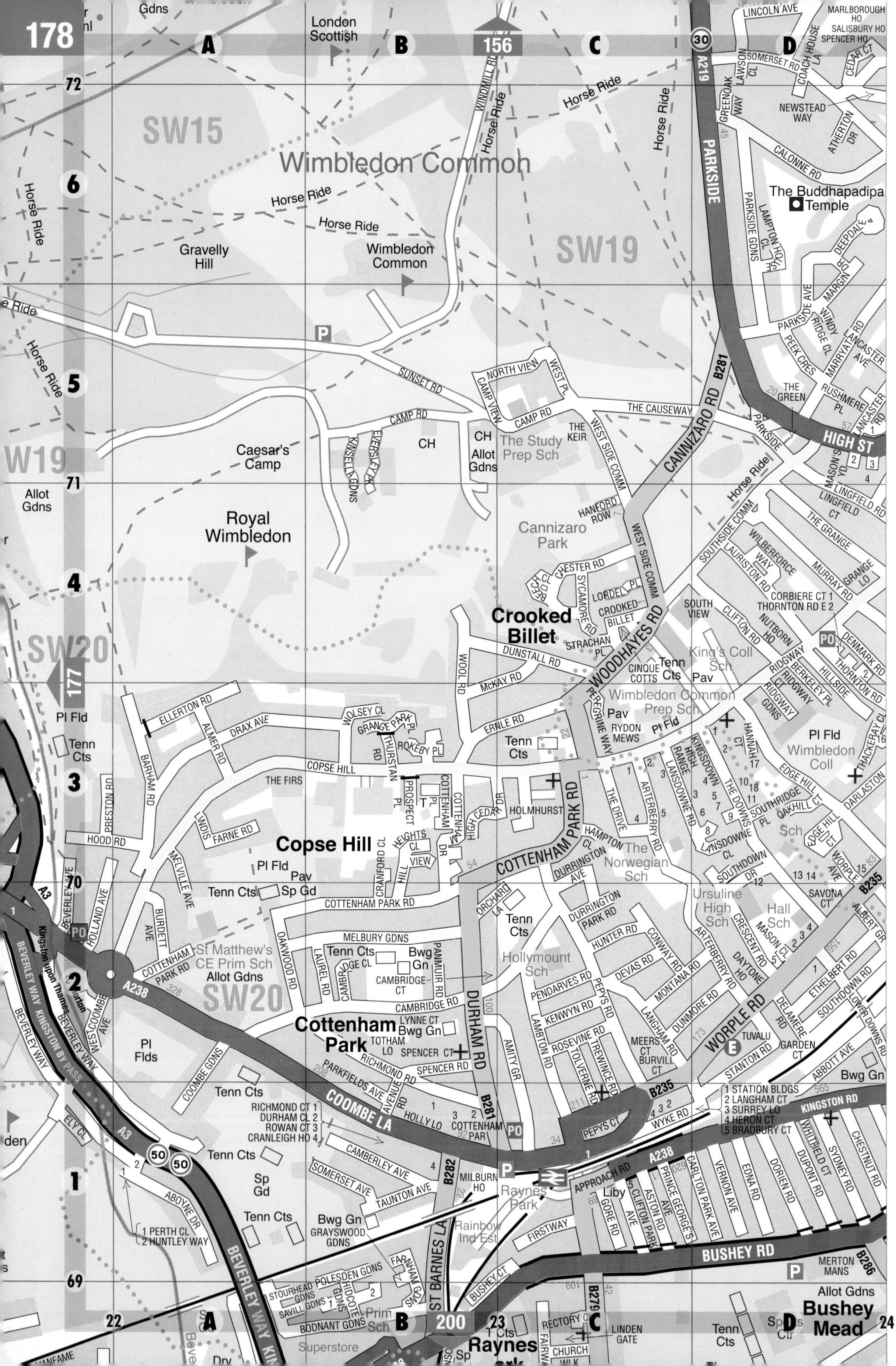
A
B
C
D
156
72
6
5
71
4
3
70
2
1
69
22
23
24
200
177
SW15
SW19
SW20
W19
Wimbledon Common
London Scottish
Horse Ride
Gravelly Hill
Wimbledon Common
Caesar's Camp
Royal Wimbledon
Allot Gdns
Pl Fld
Tenn Cts
WINDMILL RD
SUNSET RD
CAMP RD
CAMP VIEW
NORTH VIEW
WEST PL
THE CAUSEWAY
THE KEIR
The Study Prep Sch
WEST SIDE COMM
CANNIZARO RD
B281
A219
PARKSIDE
LINCOLN AVE
MARLBOROUGH HO
SALISBURY HO
SPENCER HO
SOMERSET RD
COACH HOUSE LA
CEDAR CT
LAWSON CL
GREENOAK WAY
NEWSTEAD WAY
ATHERTON DR
CALONNE RD
The Buddhapadipa Temple
PARKSIDE GDNS
LAMPTON HOUSE CL
DEEPDALE
MARGIN DR
WINDY RIDGE CL
PARKSIDE AVE
PEEK CRES
MARRYAT RD
LANCASTER AVE
THE GREEN
RUSHMERE PL
LANCASTER RD
HIGH ST
MASON'S YD
LINGFIELD RD
LINGFIELD CT
THE GRANGE
KINSELLA GDNS
EVERSLEY PK
CH
Allot Gdns
HANFORD ROW
Cannizaro Park
SOUTHSIDE COMM
WILBERFORCE WAY
LAURISTON RD
MURRAY RD
GRANGE LO
CORBIERE CT 1
THORNTON RD E 2
BEECH CL
CHESTER RD
SYCAMORE RD
LORDELL PL
CROOKED BILLET
STRACHAN PL
Crooked Billet
WOODHAYES RD
SOUTH VIEW
CLIFTON RD
NUTBORN HO
DENMARK RD
RIDGWAY
BERKELEY PL
HILLSIDE
THORNTON RD
King's Coll Sch
Pav
CINQUE COTTS
Wimbledon Common Prep Sch
RIDGWAY GDNS
Pl Fld
Wimbledon Coll
THACKERAY CL
DUNSTALL RD
WOOL RD
McKAY RD
ERNLE RD
ELLERTON RD
DRAX AVE
WOLSEY CL
GRANGE PARK PL
THURSTAN RD
ROKEBY PL
ALMER RD
BARHAM RD
COPSE HILL
THE FIRS
PRESTON RD
PROSPECT PL
COTTENHAM PL
RYDON MEWS
PEREGRINE WAY
KINGSDOWN HIGH RANGE
LANSDOWNE RD
HANNAH CT
THE DOWNS
EDGE HILL
SOUTHRIDGE PL
OAKHILL CT
DARLASTON RD
COTTENHAM PARK RD
HOLMHURST
HIGH CEDAR DR
THE DRIVE
ARTERBERRY RD
LANSDOWNE CL
EDGE HILL CT
WORPLE AVE
Sch
HOOD RD
LINDIS
FARNE RD
MELVILLE AVE
Copse Hill
CRANFORD CL
HEIGHTS CL
HILL VIEW
COTTENHAM DR
HAMPTON CL
The Norwegian Sch
DURRINGTON AVE
SOUTHDOWN DR
SAVONA CT
B235
Ursuline High Sch
Hall Sch
Sp Gd
BEVERLEY AVE
HOLLAND AVE
PO
A3
Kingston upon Thames
Merton
BURDETT AVE
ORCHARD LA
DURRINGTON PARK RD
HUNTER RD
CONWAY RD
CRESCENT RD
MASON CL
DAYTONE HO
ALBERT GR
St Matthew's CE Prim Sch
MELBURY GDNS
OAKWOOD RD
LAUREL RD
CAMBRIDGE CL
Bwg Gn
PANMUIR RD
CAMBRIDGE CT
Hollymount Sch
DEVAS RD
MONTANA RD
ETHELBERT RD
SOUTHDOWN RD
A238
BEVERLEY WAY
WEST COOMBE AVE
CAMBRIDGE RD
DURHAM RD
PENDARVES RD
KENWYN RD
PEPYS RD
DUNMORE RD
WORPLE RD
DELAMERE RD
LOWER DOWNS RD
Cottenham Park
LYNNE CT
TOTHAM LO
SPENCER CT
SPENCER RD
AMITY GR
LAMBTON RD
ROSEVINE RD
TOLVERNE RD
TREWINCE RD
MEERS CT
BURVILL CT
LANGHAM RD
TUVALU
STANTON RD
GARDEN CT
ABBOTT AVE
Pl Flds
COOMBE GDNS
RICHMOND RD
PARKFIELDS AVE
AVENUE RD
COOMBE LA
HOLLY LO
COTTENHAM PAR
RICHMOND CT 1
DURHAM CL 2
ROWAN CT 3
CRANLEIGH HO 4
ELY CL
KINGSTON BY PASS
PEPYS CT
WYKE RD
1 STATION BLDGS
2 LANGHAM CT
3 SURREY LO
4 HERON CT
5 BRADBURY CT
KINGSTON RD
WHITFIELD CT
SYDNEY RD
CHESTNUT RD
50
CAMBERLEY AVE
SOMERSET AVE
TAUNTON AVE
B282
MILBURN HO
Raynes Park
APPROACH RD
Liby
GORE RD
CLIFTON PARK AVE
ASTON RD
PRINCE GEORGE'S AVE
CARLTON PARK AVE
VERNON AVE
EDNA RD
DORIEN RD
DUPONT RD
Sp Gd
ABOYNE DR
1 PERTH CL
2 HUNTLEY WAY
Bwg Gn
GRAYSWOOD GDNS
ST BARNES LA
Rainbow Ind Est
FIRSTWAY
BUSHEY RD
MERTON MANS
B286
FARNHAM GDNS
POLESDEN GDNS
STOURHEAD GDNS
HIDCOTE GDNS
SAVILL GDNS
BODNANT GDNS
Prim Sch
BUSHEY CT
B279
RECTORY CL
LINDEN GATE
Allot Gdns
Bushey Mead
Sports Ctr
Superstore
Raynes Park
CHURCH WLK
BEVERLEY WAY

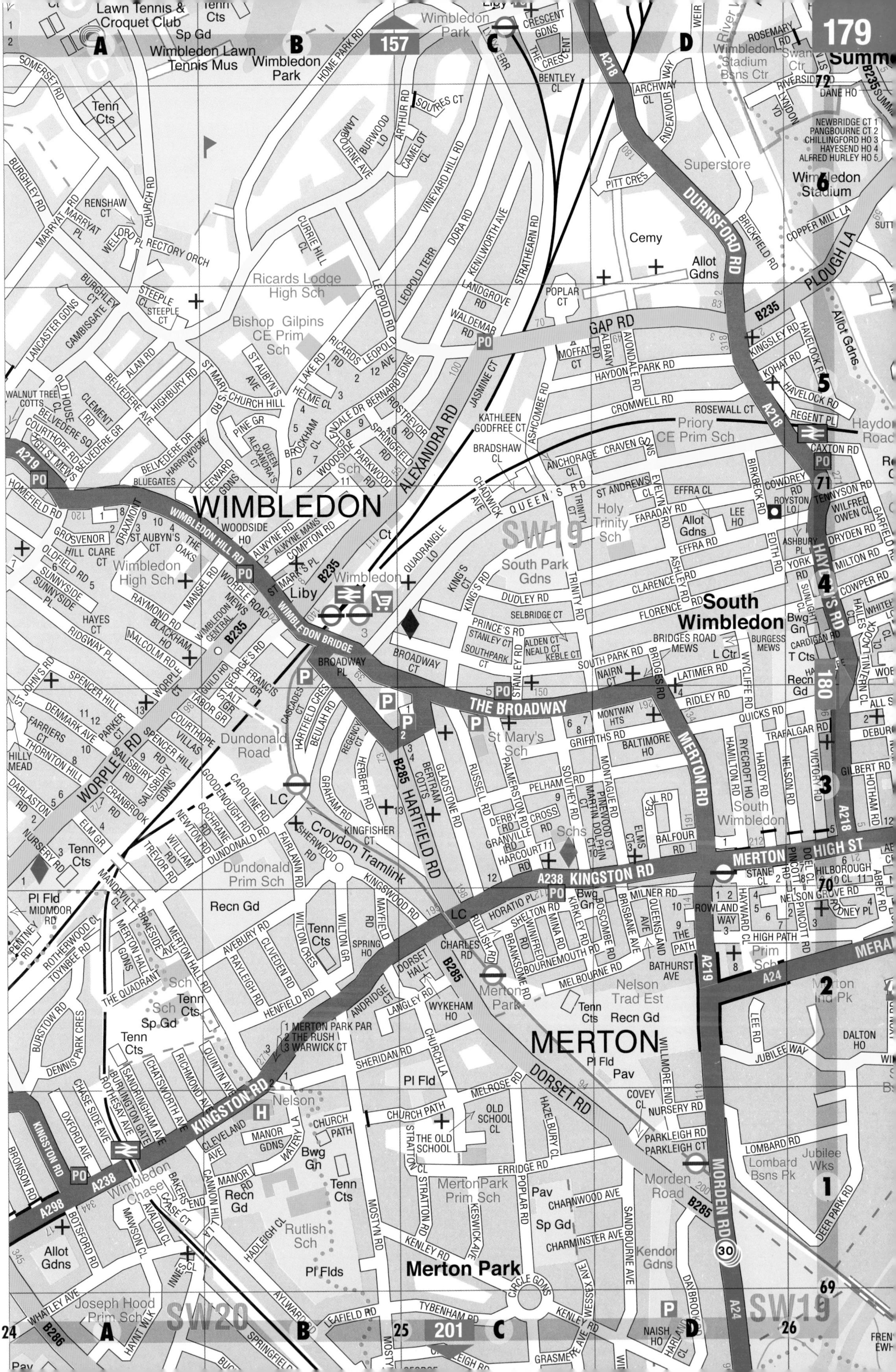
157
Lawn Tennis & Croquet Club
Sp Gd
Wimbledon Lawn Tennis Mus
Wimbledon Park
Wimbledon Park
CRESCENT GDNS
THE CRESCENT
BENTLEY CL
ARCHWAY CL
ENDEAVOUR WAY
WEIR
River Wandle
ROSEMARY RD
Wimbledon Stadium Bsns Ctr
Swan Ctr
RIVERSIDE RD
DANE HO
NEWBRIDGE CT 1
PANGBOURNE CT 2
CHILLINGFORD HO 3
HAYESEND HO 4
ALFRED HURLEY HO 5
Superstore
Wimbledon Stadium
SOMERSET RD
HOME PARK RD
SQUIRES CT
ARTHUR RD
BURWOOD LO
LAMBOURNE AVE
CAMELOT CL
Tenn Cts
BURGHLEY RD
RENSHAW CT
MARRYAT RD
MARRYAT PL
WELFORD PL
CHURCH RD
RECTORY ORCH
CURRIE HILL CL
VINEYARD HILL RD
DORA RD
KENILWORTH AVE
STRATHEARN RD
PITT CRES
Cemy
Allot Gdns
DURNSFORD RD
BRICKFIELD RD
COPPER MILL LA
PLOUGH LA
Ricards Lodge High Sch
LEOPOLD RD
LEOPOLD TERR
LANDGROVE RD
WALDEMAR RD
POPLAR CT
GAP RD
B235
BURGHLEY CT
CAMBISGATE
STEEPLE CL
STEEPLE CT
Bishop Gilpins CE Prim Sch
LANCASTER GDNS
ALAN RD
BELVEDERE GR
HIGHBURY RD
ST MARY'S RD
ST AUBYN'S AVE
LAKE RD
RICARDS RD
LEOPOLD AVE
BERNARD GDNS
JASMINE CT
MOFFAT CT
ALBANY
AVONDALE RD
HAYDON PARK RD
KINGSLEY RD
HAVELOCK RD
KOHAT RD
Allot Gdns
WALNUT TREE COTTS
OLD HOUSE CL
CLEMENT RD
BELVEDERE SQ
BELVEDERE AVE
CHURCH HILL
HELME CL
KATHLEEN GODFREE CT
ASHCOMBE RD
CROMWELL RD
ROSEWALL CT
REGENT PL
Priory CE Prim Sch
Haydons Road
COURTHOPE RD
HIGH ST MEWS
BELVEDERE DR
HARROWDENE CT
PINE GR
QUEEN ALEXANDRA'S CT
BROCKHAM CL
GLENDALE DR
SPRINGFIELD RD
ROSTREVOR RD
ALEXANDRA RD
BRADSHAW CL
ANCHORAGE CL
CRAVEN GDNS
CAXTON RD
A219
BLUEGATES
LEEWARD GDNS
WOODSIDE
PARKWOOD RD
Sch
QUEEN'S RD
ST ANDREWS CL
EVELYN RD
EFFRA CL
BIRKBECK RD
COWDREY RD
ROYSTON LO
TENNYSON RD
WILFRED OWEN CL
HOMEFIELD RD
WIMBLEDON HILL RD
WIMBLEDON
DRAMONT
WOODSIDE HO
ALWYNE RD
ALWYNE MANS
COMPTON RD
CHADWICK AVE
QUADRANGLE LO
TRINITY CT
Holy Trinity Sch
FARADAY RD
Allot Gdns
LEE HO
EFFRA RD
EDITH RD
ASHBURY PL
GARFIELD RD
DRYDEN RD
SW19
GROSVENOR HILL
CLARE CT
ST AUBYN'S CT
THE OAKS
OLDFIELD RD
SUNNYSIDE
SUNNYSIDE PL
Wimbledon High Sch
ST MARK'S PL
Wimbledon
Liby
KING'S CT
KING'S RD
South Park Gdns
DUDLEY RD
TRINITY RD
CLARENCE RD
ASHLEY RD
YORK RD
HAYDONS RD
MILTON RD
COWPER RD
HAYES CT
RIDGWAY PL
RAYMOND RD
MANSEL RD
WORPLE ROAD MEWS
WIMBLEDON BRIDGE
SELBRIDGE CT
FLORENCE RD
South Wimbledon
Bwg Gn
SUNLIGHT CL
HAILES CL
BLACKHAM HO
WIMBLEDON CENTRAL
MALCOLM RD
PRINCE'S RD
STANLEY CT
SOUTHPARK CT
ALDEN CT
NEALD CT
KEBLE CT
BROADWAY CT
BRIDGES ROAD MEWS
BURGESS MEWS
L Ctr
CARDIGAN RD
T Cts
ST JOHN'S RD
SPENCER HILL
GUILD HO
ST GEORGE'S RD
FRANCIS GR
BROADWAY PL
SOUTH PARK RD
NAIRN CT
BRIDGES RD
LATIMER RD
WYCLIFFE RD
Recn Gd
180
DENMARK AVE
PARKER CT
WORPLE RD
SALT CT
TABOR GR
COURTHOPE VILLAS
CASCADES CT
HARTFIELD CRES
BEULAH RD
THE BROADWAY
MONTWAY HTS
RIDLEY RD
QUICKS RD
FARRIERS CT
THORNTON HILL
HILLY MEAD
DARLASTON RD
SPENCER HILL RD
SALISBURY RD
SALISBURY GDNS
Dundonald Road
REGENCY CT
St Mary's Sch
GRIFFITHS RD
BALTIMORE HO
MERTON RD
TRAFALGAR RD
HAMILTON RD
RYECROFT HO
HARDY RD
NELSON RD
VICTORY RD
GILBERT RD
HOTHAM RD
CRANBROOK RD
GOODENOUGH RD
CAROLINE RD
HERBERT RD
B285 HARTFIELD RD
BERTRAM COTTS
GLADSTONE RD
RUSSELL RD
PALMERSTON RD
SOUTHEY RD
MONTAGUE RD
PELHAM RD
DERBY RD
CROSS RD
PINEWOOD CT
MARTIN DOLPHIN CT
CECIL RD
South Wimbledon
NURSERY RD
ELM GR
NEWTON RD
COCHRANE RD
WILLIAM RD
TREVOR RD
LC
GRAHAM RD
DUNDONALD RD
Croydon Tramlink
KINGFISHER CT
GRANVILLE RD
HARCOURT RD
Schs
ELMS CT
BALFOUR RD
MERTON HIGH ST
STANE CL
PINCOTT RD
DOEL CL
HILBOROUGH CL
ABBEY RD
Tenn Cts
MANDEVILLE CL
SHERWOOD CT
FAIRLAWN RD
Dundonald Prim Sch
KINGSWOOD RD
A238 KINGSTON RD
Bwg Gn
MILNER RD
NELSON GROVE RD
ROWLAND WAY
HAYWARD CL
DEBURGH RD
Pl Fld
MIDMOOR RD
PENTNEY RD
ROTHERWOOD CL
TOYNBEE RD
MERTON HALL GDNS
BRAESIDE AVE
MERTON HALL RD
Recn Gd
AVEBURY RD
RAYLEIGH RD
CLIVEDEN RD
WILTON CRES
Tenn Cts
WILTON GR
SPRING HO
MAYFIELD RD
HORATIO PL
SHELTON RD
WINIFRED RD
MINA RD
KIRKLEY RD
BOSCOMBE RD
BRISBANE AVE
QUEENSLAND AVE
THE PATH
HIGH PATH
Prim Sch
MERANTUN WAY
THE QUADRANT
Sch
Tenn Cts
Sp Gd
HENFIELD RD
DORSET HALL
CHARLES RD
RUTLISH RD
BRANKSOME RD
BOURNEMOUTH RD
MELBOURNE RD
BATHURST AVE
A24
Merton Ind Pk
BURSTOW RD
DENNIS PARK CRES
Tenn Cts
QUINTIN AVE
ANDRIDGE CT
LANGLEY RD
WYKEHAM HO
Merton Park
Tenn Cts
Nelson Trad Est
Recn Gd
LEE RD
DALTON HO
1 MERTON PARK PAR
2 THE RUSH
3 WARWICK CT
SHERIDAN RD
CHURCH LA
MERTON
Pl Fld
Pav
WILLMORE END
JUBILEE WAY
CHASE SIDE AVE
SANDRINGHAM AVE
CHATSWORTH AVE
RICHMOND AVE
BURLINGTON GATE
ROTHESAY AVE
Pl Fld
MELROSE RD
DORSET RD
HAZELBURY CL
KINGSTON RD
Nelson
CHURCH PATH
OLD SCHOOL CL
COVEY CL
NURSERY RD
KINGSTON RD
OXFORD AVE
CLEVELAND RD
MANOR GDNS
WATERY LA
Bwg Gn
THE OLD SCHOOL
STRATTON CL
PARKLEIGH RD
PARKLEIGH CT
LOMBARD RD
Jubilee Wks
Lombard Bsns Pk
BRONSON RD
A238
Wimbledon Chase
BAKERS END
MANOR RD
Recn Gd
Tenn Cts
ERRIDGE RD
MertonPark Prim Sch
Pav
CHARNWOOD AVE
Morden Road
MORDEN RD
DEER PARK RD
A298
CASE CT
MAWSON CL
AVALON CL
CANNON HILL LA
HADLEIGH CL
Rutlish Sch
STRATTON RD
KESWICK AVE
POPLAR RD
Sp Gd
CHARMINSTER AVE
SANDBOURNE AVE
B285
Allot Gdns
BOTSFORD RD
INNES CL
MOSTYN RD
KENLEY RD
Merton Park
Pl Flds
CIRCLE GDNS
WESSEX AVE
Kendor Gdns
DAYBROOK RD
WHATLEY AVE
Joseph Hood Prim Sch
SW20
AYLWARD RD
LEAFIELD RD
TYBENHAM RD
KENLEY RD
SW19
B286
HAYNT WLK
SPRINGFIELD
201
NAISH HO
HARLAND CL
GRASMERE AVE
FRENCH
Pav
A B C D
24 25 26
69 70 71 72
1 2 3 4 5 6

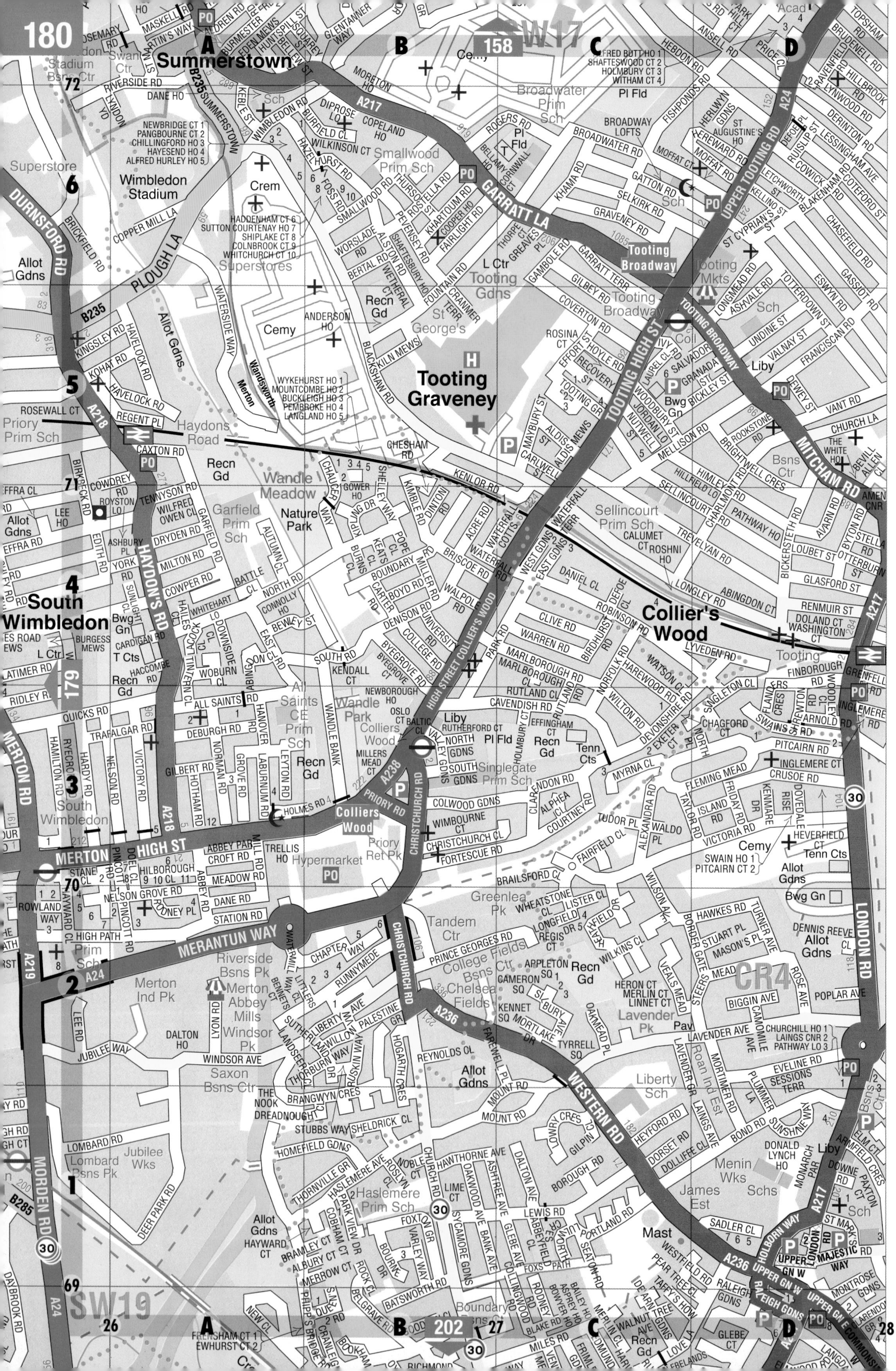
Summerstown
SW17
158
Wimbledon Stadium
Crem
Cemy
Superstores
Tooting Graveney
Tooting Broadway
Upper Tooting Rd
Garratt La
Durnsford Rd
Plough La
Haydon's Rd
Haydons Road
Wandle Meadow Nature Park
South Wimbledon
179
Merton High St
Merton Rd
Colliers Wood
High Street Collier's Wood
Collier's Wood
Tooting
Mitcham Rd
London Rd
Christchurch Rd
Merantun Way
Merton Ind Pk
Western Rd
CR4
Morden Rd
SW19
202
Wandsworth
Merton
A
B
C
D
1
2
3
4
5
6
26
27
28
69
70
71
72

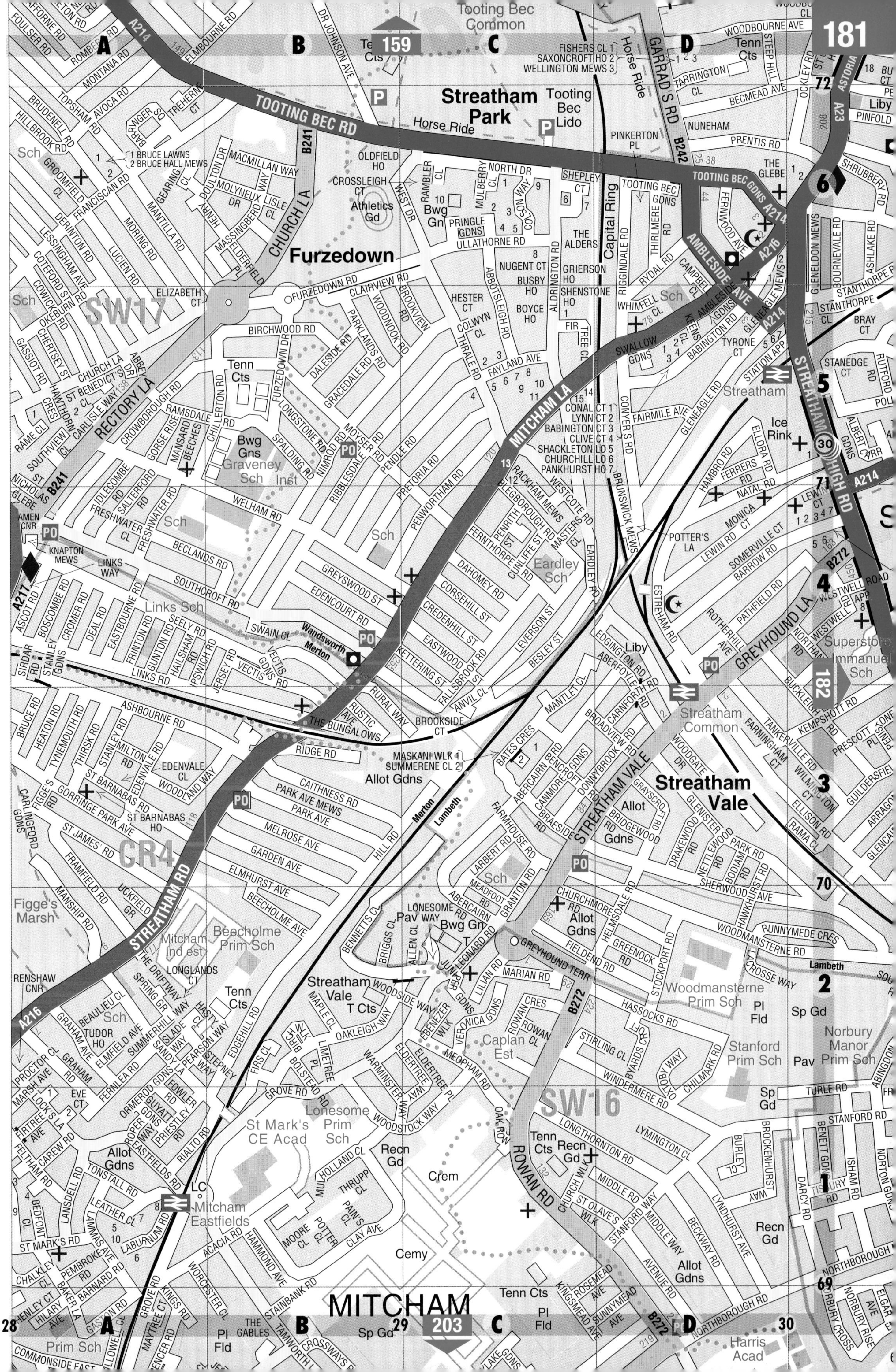

Tooting Bec Common
159
A B C D
Streatham Park
Tooting Bec Lido
Horse Ride
TOOTING BEC RD
A214
A23
A216
B241
B242
B272
A217
FISHERS CL 1
SAXONCROFT HO 2
WELLINGTON MEWS 3
GARRAD'S RD
WOODBOURNE AVE
Tenn Cts
TARRINGTON CL
BECMEAD AVE
NUNEHAM
PRENTIS RD
PINKERTON PL
Liby
PINFOLD
ASTORIA
OCKLEY RD
STEEP HILL
SHRUBBERY RD
THE GLEBE
TOOTING BEC GDNS
1 BRUCE LAWNS
2 BRUCE HALL MEWS
FOULSER RD
MONTANA RD
ROMBERG RD
ELMBOURNE RD
TOPSHAM RD
AVOCA RD
TREHERNE CT
BARRINGER SQ
BRUDENELL RD
HILLBROOK RD
GROOMFIELD CL
FRANCISCAN RD
GEARING CL
MANTILLA RD
MORING RD
LUCIEN RD
DOULTON DR
MACMILLAN WAY
MOLYNEUX DR
MASSINGBERD WAY
LISLE CL
DERINTON RD
LESSINGHAM AVE
COTEFORD ST
COWICK RD
OKEBURN RD
CHURCH LA
OLDFIELD HO
CROSSLEIGH CT
Athletics Gd
WEST DR
RAMBLER CL
Bwg Gn
PRINGLE GDNS
ULLATHORNE RD
MULBERRY CL
NORTH DR
COLSON WAY
SHEPLEY CT
TOOTING BEC GDNS
THIRLMERE RD
FERNWOOD AVE
AMBLESIDE AVE
Capital Ring
THE ALDERS
GRIERSON HO
SHENSTONE HO
NUGENT CT
BUSBY HO
BOYCE HO
ALDRINGTON RD
RIGGINDALE RD
RYDAL RD
CAMPBELL
GLENEAGLE MEWS
Furzedown
SW17
ELIZABETH CT
FURZEDOWN RD
CLAIRVIEW RD
WOODNOOK RD
BROOKVIEW RD
HESTER CT
COLWYN CL
ABBOTSLEIGH RD
FIR TREE CL
WHIMFELL CL
Sch
BIRCHWOOD RD
PARKLANDS RD
DALESIDE RD
GRACEDALE RD
THRALE RD
FAYLAND AVE
SWALLOW GDNS
BABINGTON RD
TYRONE CT
STATION APP
Streatham
STANEDGE CT
RUTFORD RD
GLENELDON MEWS
BOURNEVALE RD
ASHLAKE RD
STANTHORPE RD
BRAY CT
GASSIOT RD
CHERTSEY ST
HAWTHORN CRES
ST BENEDICT'S CL
CARLISLE WAY
ABBEY DR
RECTORY LA
Tenn Cts
CHILLERTON RD
FURZEDOWN DR
LONGSTONE RD
MOYSER RD
MITCHAM LA
CONAL CT 1
LYNN CT 2
BABINGTON CT 3
CLIVE CT 4
SHACKLETON LO 5
CHURCHILL LO 6
PANKHURST HO 7
CONYER'S RD
FAIRMILE AVE
GLENEAGLE RD
Ice Rink
ELLORA RD
HAMBRO RD
FERRERS RD
NATAL RD
LEWIN RD
MONICA CT
STREATHAM HIGH RD
ALBERT CARR GDNS
RAME CL
SOUTHVIEW CL
CROWBOROUGH RD
RAMSDALE RD
GORSE RISE
MANSARD BEECHES
Bwg Gns
Graveney Sch
Inst
SPALDING RD
NIMROD RD
RIBBLESDALE RD
PENDLE RD
PRETORIA RD
PENWORTHAM RD
RACKHAM MEWS
BLEGBOROUGH RD
WESTCOTE RD
BRUNSWICK MEWS
POTTER'S LA
SOMERVILLE CT
BARROW RD
ST NICHOLAS GLEBE
AMEN CNR
KNAPTON MEWS
LINKS WAY
IDLECOMBE RD
SALTERFORD RD
FRESHWATER CL
FRESHWATER RD
WELHAM RD
BECLANDS RD
SOUTHCROFT RD
GREYSWOOD ST
EDENCOURT RD
FERNTHORPE RD
PENRITH ST
CUNLIFFE ST
MASTERS CL
EARDLEY RD
Eardley Sch
DAHOMEY RD
CORSEHILL ST
CREDENHILL ST
EASTWOOD ST
LEVERSON ST
BESLEY ST
ESTREHAM RD
ROTHERHILL AVE
PATHFIELD RD
GREYHOUND LA
WESTWELL RD
NORTHANGER RD
Superstore
Immanuel Sch
182
ASCOT RD
BOSCOMBE RD
CROMER RD
DEAL RD
EASTBOURNE RD
Links Sch
FRINTON RD
GUNTON RD
SEELY RD
HAILSHAM RD
IPSWICH RD
JERSEY RD
VECTIS GDNS
VECTIS RD
SWAIN CL
Wandsworth
Merton
KETTERING ST
FALLSBROOK RD
ANVIL CL
EDGINGTON RD
ABERFOYLE RD
CARNFORTH RD
Liby
SIRDAR RD
STANLEY GDNS
LINKS RD
BRUCE RD
HEATON RD
TYNEMOUTH RD
THIRSK RD
STANLEY RD
ASHBOURNE RD
MILTON RD
EDENVALE RD
EDENVALE CL
WOODLAND WAY
RURAL WAY
RUSTIC AVE
THE BUNGALOWS
BROOKSIDE CT
MANTLET CL
BROADVIEW RD
Streatham Common
KEMPSHOTT RD
TANKERVILLE RD
FARNINGHAM CT
PRESCOTT CL
RIDGE RD
MASKANI WLK 1
SUMMERENE CL 2
Allot Gdns
BATES CRES
BENCROFT RD
ABERCAIRN RD
CANMORE GDNS
DONNYBROOK RD
STREATHAM VALE
WOODGATE DR
Streatham Vale
GUILDERSFIELD RD
WILMINGTON CT
ELLISON RD
RAMA CL
ARRAGON
GLENCAIRN
CARLINGFORD GDNS
FIGGE'S RD
GORRINGE PARK AVE
ST BARNABAS RD
ST BARNABAS HO
CAITHNESS RD
PARK AVE MEWS
PARK AVE
MELROSE AVE
GARDEN AVE
ELMHURST AVE
BEECHOLME AVE
HILL RD
Merton
Lambeth
FARMHOUSE RD
BRAESIDE RD
Allot
GRAYSCROFT RD
GLENISTER PARK RD
DRAKEWOOD RD
NETTLEWOOD RD
BODIAM RD
BRIDGEWOOD RD
SHERWOOD AVE
HAWKHURST RD
CR4
ST JAMES' RD
FRAMFIELD RD
MANSHIP RD
UCKFIELD GR
STREATHAM RD
Figge's Marsh
Beecholme Prim Sch
Mitcham Ind est
LARBERT RD
MEADFOOT RD
ABERCAIRN RD
GRANTON RD
CHURCHMORE RD
HELMSDALE RD
GREENOCK RD
STOCKPORT RD
RUNNYMEDE CRES
WOODMANSTERNE RD
Lambeth
ACROSSE WAY
LONESOME WAY
Pav
Bwg Gn
BENNETTS CL
BRIGGS CL
ALLEN CL
LEONARD RD
GREYHOUND TERR
FIELDEND RD
MARIAN RD
Woodmansterne Prim Sch
Pl Fld
Sp Gd
Norbury Manor Prim Sch
RENSHAW CNR
THE DRIFTWAY
SPRING GR
LONGLANDS CT
Tenn Cts
Streatham Vale T Cts
WOODSIDE WAY
MAPLE CL
LILIAN RD
JUNIPER GDNS
HASSOCKS RD
BEAULIEU CL
TUDOR HO
GRAHAM AVE
ELMFIELD AVE
SUMMERHILL WAY
SLADE WAY
HASTY CL
PEARSON WAY
EDGEHILL RD
OAKLEIGH WAY
LIMETREE PL
EBENEZER WLK
VERONICA GDNS
ROWAN CRES
ROWAN CL
Caplan Est
STIRLING CL
BYARDS CROFT
POLBY WAY
CHILMARK RD
Stanford Prim Sch
PROCTOR CL
MARSH AVE
GRAHAM RD
FERNLEA RD
SANDY LA
STEPNEY WAY
FIRS CL
WARMINSTER WAY
ELDERTREE WAY
ELDERTREE PL
MEOPHAM RD
WINDERMERE RD
TURLE RD
SW16
EVE CT
LOCKS LA
FIRTREE AVE
ORMEROD GDNS
ROPER WAY
GUYATT GDNS
FOWLER CL
PRIESTLEY RD
GROVE RD
BOLSTEAD RD
Lonesome Prim Sch
WOODSTOCK WAY
OAK ROW
LONGTHORNTON RD
LYMINGTON CL
BURLEY CL
BROCKENHURST WAY
STANFORD RD
BENETT GDNS
ISHAM RD
NORTON GDNS
CAREW RD
FELTHAM RD
Allot Gdns
EASTFIELDS RD
RIALTO RD
St Mark's CE Acad
Recn Gd
MULHOLLAND CL
THRUPP CL
Crem
Tenn Cts
Recn Gd
CHURCH WLK
MIDDLE RD
ROWAN RD
TISBURY RD
DARCY RD
BEDFONT CL
TONSTALL RD
LANSDELL RD
LEATHER CL
LABURNUM RD
LC
Mitcham Eastfields
MOORE CL
POTTER CL
PAIN'S CL
CLAY AVE
ST OLAVE'S WLK
STANFORD WAY
MIDDLE WAY
BECKWAY RD
LYNDHURST AVE
Recn Gd
ST MARK'S RD
PEMBROKE AVE
LAMMAS AVE
ACACIA RD
HAMMOND AVE
Cemy
AVENUE RD
Allot Gdns
NORTHBOROUGH RD
CHALKLEY CL
HENLEY CT
HILARY AVE
BAKER LA
BARNARD RD
GROVE RD
KINGS RD
WORCESTER CL
STAINBANK RD
MITCHAM
Tenn Cts
ROSEMEAD AVE
SUNNYMEAD AVE
KINGSMEAD AVE
NORBURY CROSS
NORBURY RISE
ELGAR AVE
28 A B 29 C D 30
Prim Sch
COMMONSIDE EAST
GASTON RD
MAYTREE CT
Pl Fld
THE GABLES
TAMWORTH
CROSSWAYS RD
Sp Gd
203
Pl Fld
Harris Acad

STREATHAM
Norbury
Streatham Vale
SE27
SW16
STREATHAM HIGH RD
STREATHAM COMMON N
STREATHAM COMMON S
CROWN LA
LONDON RD
GREEN LA
KNIGHT'S HILL
GREYHOUND LA
Streatham Common
Norwood Grove
Norbury Park
Capital Ring
Horse Ride
Bishop Thomas Grant RC Sec Sch
Sunnyhill Prim Sch
Julian's Prim Sch
St Andrews RC Prim Sch
Crown Lane Prim Sch
St Joseph's RC Coll
Immanuel Sch
Superstore
Norbury Manor Bsns & Enterprise Coll for Girls
Norbury Manor Prim Sch
Stanford Prim Sch
Woodmansterne Prim Sch
Kensington Avenue Prim Sch
St James The Great RC Prim Sch
Norbury Trad Est
Harris Acad
Dunraven Sch
Ice Rink
Liby
Allot Gdns
Tenn Cts
Bwg Gn
Pl Fld
Sp Gd
Recn Gd
Com Ctr
Pav
1 ELPHINSTONE CT
2 RIDLEY CT
3 BLADON CT
4 COMMONSIDE CT
5 SANDERS HO
6 BYRON CL
7 HAMBLY MANS
8 ST JOHNS HO
A23
A214
A215
A216
B242
B272
B273
160
181
204

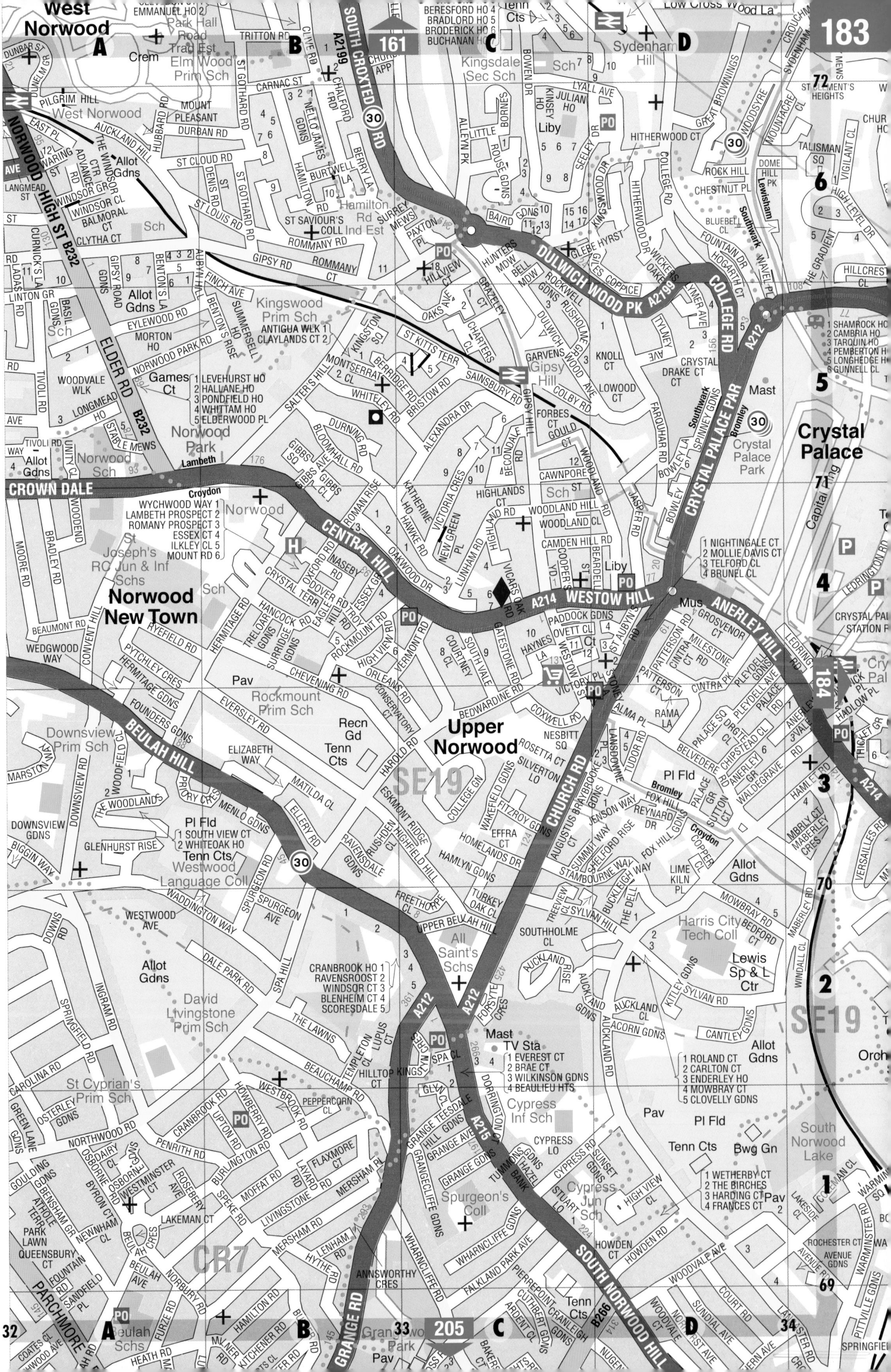
West Norwood
A
B
C
D
161
Crem
Park Hall Road Trad Est
Elm Wood Prim Sch
TRITTON RD
SOUTH CROXTED RD
A2199
BERESFORD HO 4
BRADLORD HO 5
BRODERICK HO 6
BUCHANAN HO
Tenn Cts
Sydenham Hill
Low Cross Wood La
Kingsdale Sec Sch
Sch
LYALL AVE
JULIAN HO
KINSEY HO
Liby
PO
HITHERWOOD CT
GREAT BROWNINGS
WOODSYRE
MOUNTACRE CL
ST CLEMENT'S HEIGHTS
72
TALISMAN SQ
DOME HILL PK
ROCK HILL
CHESTNUT PL
Lewisham
Southwark
BLUEBELL CL
FOUNTAIN DR
HOGARTH CT
WAVEL PL
THE GRADIENT
HIGH LEVEL DR
VIGILANT CL
HILLCREST
6
PILGRIM HILL
West Norwood
DUNBAR ST
DUNELM GR
EAST PL
WARING ST
AUCKLAND HILL
THE WINDSOR CTR
Allot Gdns
MOUNT PLEASANT
DURBAN RD
HUBBARD RD
CARNAC ST
NELLO JAMES GDNS
CHALFORD RD
CLIVE RD
ST GOTHARD RD
ST CLOUD RD
DENIS RD
BURTWELL LA
BERRY LA
HAMILTON RD
Hamilton Rd Ind Est
SURREY MEWS
PAXTON PL
ST SAVIOUR'S COLL
ROMMANY RD
ROMMANY CT
GIPSY RD
ST LOUIS RD
LITTLE BORNES
ALLEYN PK
ROUSE GDNS
SEELEY DR
KINGSWOOD DR
BAIRD GDNS
HITHERWOOD DR
COLLEGE RD
WICKERS OAKE
GLEBE HYRST
GILES COPPICE
DULWICH WOOD PK
A2199
HUNTERS MDW
BELL MDW
ROCKWELL GDNS
LANGMEAD ST
NORWOOD HIGH ST B232
WINDSOR GR
WINDSOR CL
BALMORAL CT
CLYTHA CT
Sch
CURNICK'S LA
LADAS RD
LINTON GR
GIPSY ROAD GDNS
BENTON'S LA
AUBYN HILL
FINCH AVE
BENTON'S RISE
SUMMERSELL HO
Kingswood Prim Sch
ANTIGUA WLK 1
CLAYLANDS CT 2
HILLVIEW CT
OAKS AVE
GRAZELEY CT
CHARTERS CL
ST KITTS TERR
KINGSTON SQ
MONTSERRAT CL
BERRIDGE RD
BRISTOW RD
WHITELEY RD
SAINSBURY RD
Gipsy Hill
GIPSY HILL
GARVENS
DULWICH WOOD AVE
RUSHOLME GR
KNOLL CT
LOWOOD CT
COLBY RD
FORBES CT
GOULD CT
TYLNEY AVE
LYMER AVE
CRYSTAL DRAKE CT
COLLEGE RD
A212
CRYSTAL PALACE PAR
Mast
Crystal Palace Park
Crystal Palace
Bromley
1 SHAMROCK HO
2 CAMBRIA HO
3 TARQUIN HO
4 PEMBERTON H
5 LONGHEDGE H
6 GUNNELL CL
5
BASIL GDNS
Sch
EYLEWOOD RD
MORTON HO
NORWOOD PARK RD
ELDER RD
B232
TIVOLI RD
WOODVALE WLK
LONGMEAD HO
Games Ct
1 LEVEHURST HO
2 HALLANE HO
3 PONDFIELD HO
4 WHITTAM HO
5 ELDERWOOD PL
STABLE MEWS
Norwood Park
Lambeth
TIVOLI RD
UNITY CL
Allot Gdns
Norwood Sch
CROWN DALE
SALTER'S HILL
DURNING RD
BLOOMHALL RD
GIBBS SQ
GIBBS AVE
GIBBS CL
ALEXANDRA DR
BECONDALE RD
WOODLAND RD
CAWNPORE ST
Sch
FARQUHAR RD
BOWLEY LA
SPINNEY GDNS
71
Capital Ring
Croydon
WYCHWOOD WAY 1
LAMBETH PROSPECT 2
ROMANY PROSPECT 3
ESSEX CT 4
ILKLEY CL 5
MOUNT RD 6
Norwood
ROMAN RISE
CENTRAL HILL
KATHERINE HO
HAWKE RD
VICTORIA CRES
NEW GREEN PL
HIGHLANDS CT
HIGHLAND RD
WOODLAND HILL
WOODLAND CL
CAMDEN HILL RD
JASPER RD
BOWLEY
1 NIGHTINGALE CT
2 MOLLIE DAVIS CT
3 TELFORD CL
4 BRUNEL CL
P
LEDRINGTON RD
MOORE RD
BRADLEY RD
WOODEND
St Joseph's RC Jun & Inf Schs
H
OXFORD RD
NASEBY RD
CRYSTAL TERR
DOVER RD
ESSEX GR
OAKWOOD DR
LUNHAM RD
VICARS OAK RD
COOPER'S YD
BEARDELL ST
Liby
A214
WESTOW HILL
Mus
ANERLEY HILL
GROSVENOR CT
4
CRYSTAL PALACE STATION RD
Norwood New Town
Sch
BEAUMONT RD
CONVENT HILL
HERMITAGE RD
TRELOAR GDNS
HANCOCK RD
EAGLE HILL
TROY RD
SURRIDGE GDNS
ROCKMOUNT RD
HIGH VIEW RD
VERMONT RD
COURTNEY CL
SOUTH VALE
GATESTONE RD
PADDOCK GDNS
OVETT CL
HAYNES LA
WESTOW ST
ST AUBYN'S RD
PATTERSON RD
CINTRA CT
MILESTONE RD
PLEYDELL GDNS
LEDRINGTON RD
WEDGWOOD WAY
RYEFIELD RD
PYTCHLEY CRES
HERMITAGE GDNS
Pav
Rockmount Prim Sch
CHEVENING RD
ORLEANS RD
CONSERVATORY CT
BEDWARDINE RD
COXWELL RD
VICTORY PL
STONEY
ALMA PL
PATTERSON CT
CINTRA PK
RAMA LA
PALACE SQ
PLEYDELL AVE
PALACE RD
184
HADLOW PL
THICKET GR
PO
A214
FOUNDERS GDNS
EVERSLEY RD
Recn Gd
Tenn Cts
Upper Norwood
NESBITT SQ
ROSETTA CT
SILVERTON LO
LANSDOWNE PL
TUDOR RD
BELVEDERE RD
CHIPSTEAD CL
ANERLEY GR
WALDEGRAVE RD
Downsview Prim Sch
BEULAH HILL
MARSTON WAY
DOWNSVIEW RD
WOODFIELD CL
ELIZABETH WAY
MATILDA CL
HAROLD RD
SE19
COLLEGE GN
CHURCH RD
BRAYBROOKE GDNS
Pl Fld
Bromley
FOX HILL
REYNARD DR
SUTTON GR
PALACE GR
HAMLET RD
3
THE WOODLANDS
PRIORY CRES
MENLO GDNS
ELLERY RD
ESKMONT RIDGE
WAKEFIELD GDNS
FITZROY GDNS
AUGUSTUS CT
JENSON WAY
SHELFORD RISE
FOX HILL GDNS
Croydon
COPPER CL
MBRLY CT
MABERLEY CRES
VERSAILLES RD
DOWNSVIEW GDNS
GLENHURST RISE
Pl Fld
1 SOUTH VIEW CT
2 WHITEOAK HO
Tenn Cts
Westwood Language Coll
30
RAVENSDALE GDNS
RUSHDEN CL
HIGHFIELD HILL
EFFRA CT
HOMELANDS DR
HAMLYN GDNS
SUMMIT WAY
STAMBOURNE WAY
BUCKLEIGH WAY
LIME KILN PL
Allot Gdns
70
BIGGIN WAY
WADDINGTON WAY
SPURGEON RD
SPURGEON AVE
FREETHORPE CL
TURKEY OAK CL
TREEVIEW CL
SYLVAN HILL
THE DELL
MOWBRAY RD
BEDFORD CT
MABERLEY RD
WESTWOOD AVE
UPPER BEULAH HILL
All Saint's Schs
SOUTHHOLME CL
AUCKLAND RISE
Harris City Tech Coll
Lewis Sp & L Ctr
DOWNS RD
Allot Gdns
DALE PARK RD
SPA HILL
CRANBROOK HO 1
RAVENSROOST 2
WINDSOR CT 3
BLENHEIM CT 4
SCORESDALE 5
A212
FORSYTE CRES
AUCKLAND GDNS
AUCKLAND RD
AUCKLAND CL
ACORN GDNS
KITLEY GDNS
SYLVAN RD
CANTLEY GDNS
WINDALL CL
2
SE19
David Livingstone Prim Sch
INGRAM RD
SPRINGFIELD RD
THE LAWNS
TEMPLETON CL
LUPUS CT
PO
SPA CL
Mast
TV Sta
1 EVEREST CT
2 BRAE CT
3 WILKINSON GDNS
4 BEAULIEU HTS
1 ROLAND CT
2 CARLTON CT
3 ENDERLEY HO
4 MOWBRAY CT
5 CLOVELLY GDNS
Allot Gdns
Orch
CAROLINA RD
St Cyprian's Prim Sch
BEAUCHAMP RD
HILLTOP CT
KINGS
DORRINGTON CT
Cypress Inf Sch
WESTBROOK RD
PEPPERCORN CL
GLYN CL
GRANGE TEESDALE
HILL GDNS
GRANGE AVE
A215
Pav
Pl Fld
South Norwood Lake
GREEN LANE GDNS
OSTERLEY GDNS
NORTHWOOD RD
CRANBROOK RD
HOWBERRY RD
PO
UPTON RD
PENRITH RD
BURLINGTON RD
FLAXMORE CT
GRANGE GDNS
GRANGECLIFFE GDNS
TUMMONS GDNS
HAZEL BANK
CYPRESS LO
CYPRESS RD
SUNSET GDNS
Cypress Jun Sch
HIGH VIEW CL
Tenn Cts
Bwg Gn
GOULDING GDNS
BENSHAM GR
DAIRY CL
OSBORNE GDNS
WESTMINSTER CT
ROSEBERY AVE
MOFFAT RD
LAYARD RD
MERSHAM PL
Spurgeon's Coll
STUART LO
1 WETHERBY CT
2 THE BIRCHES
3 HARDING CT
4 FRANCES CT
Pav
LAKESIDE CL
COLEMAN CL
1
ATHOLE TERR
BYRON CT
PARK LAWN
QUEENSBURY CT
NEWNHAM CL
LAKEMAN CT
SPEKE RD
LIVINGSTONE RD
MERSHAM RD
WHARNCLIFFE GDNS
HOWDEN CT
HOWDEN RD
ROCHESTER CT
AVENUE GDNS
WARMINSTER RD
FOUNTAIN RD
BEULAH CRES
CR7
LENHAM RD
HYTHE RD
ANNSWORTHY CRES
FALKLAND PARK AVE
PIERREPOINT RD
CRANLEIGH GDNS
CUTHBERT GDNS
SOUTH NORWOOD HILL
B266
WOODVALE AVE
WOODVALE CT
COURT RD
69
PITTVILLE GDNS
PARCHMORE
SANDFIELD PL
BEULAH AVE
NORBURY RD
FURZE RD
PO
Beulah Schs
HAMILTON RD
KITCHENER RD
GRANGE RD
Grangewood Park
Pav
205
33
ARDENT CL
Tenn Cts
SUNDIAL AVE
34
32
HEATH RD
COATES CL
SPRINGFIELD

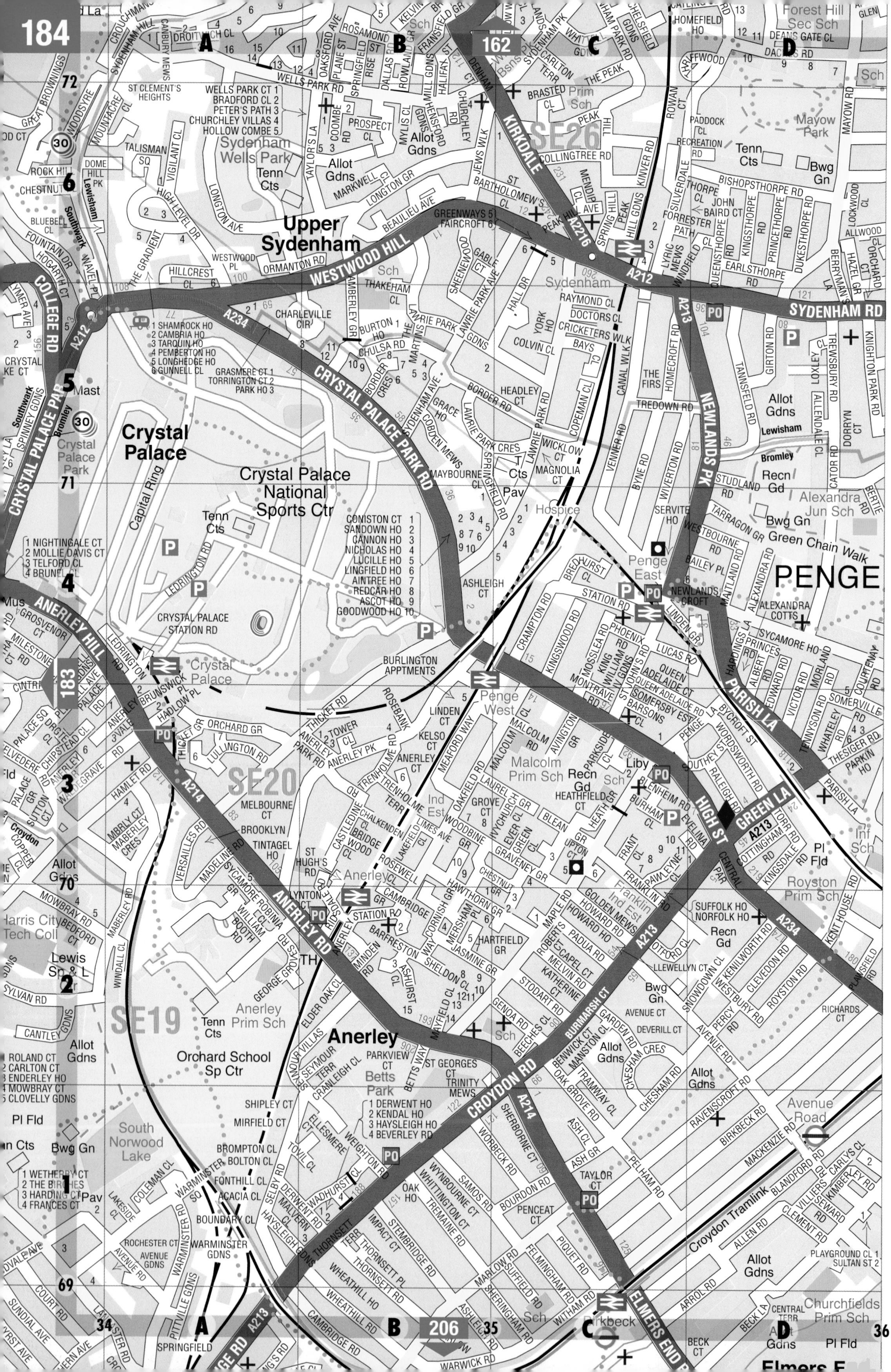
162
Upper Sydenham
Sydenham Wells Park
SE26
Kirkdale
Sydenham Pk
Westwood Hill
Sydenham
Sydenham Rd
Crystal Palace
Crystal Palace Park
Crystal Palace National Sports Ctr
Crystal Palace Park Rd
Crystal Palace Station Rd
College Rd
Crystal Palace Par
Anerley Hill
183
SE20
Penge East
Penge West
PENGE
Newlands Pk
Parish La
High St
Green La
Malcolm Prim Sch
Alexandra Jun Sch
Green Chain Walk
Anerley
Anerley Rd
Anerley Prim Sch
SE19
South Norwood Lake
Orchard School Sp Ctr
Betts Park
Croydon Rd
Croydon Tramlink
Avenue Road
Birkbeck
Elmers End
Royston Prim Sch
Churchfields Prim Sch
Harris City Tech Coll
Capital Ring
206
A B C D
34 35 36

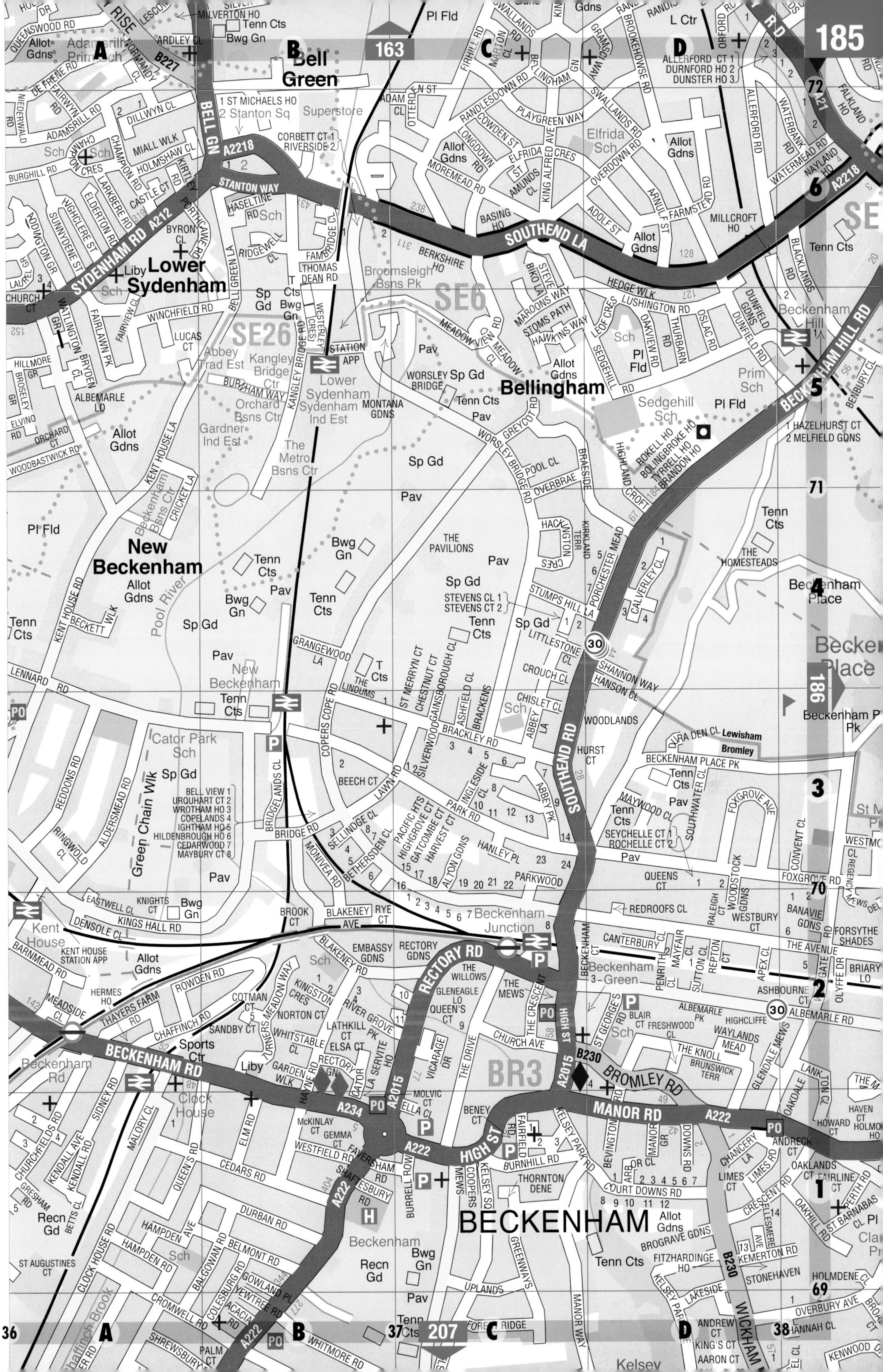
163
Bell Green
Lower Sydenham
SE26
SE6
Bellingham
New Beckenham
Beckenham Junction
BR3
BECKENHAM
Beckenham Hill
Beckenham Place
Beckenham Place Pk
Kent House
Clock House
Beckenham Rd
Lower Sydenham
Cator Park Sch
Sedgehill Sch
Elfrida Sch
Broomsleigh Bsns Pk
Kangley Bridge Ctr
Abbey Trad Est
Orchard Bsns Ctr
Gardner Ind Est
Sydenham Ind Est
The Metro Bsns Ctr
Beckenham Bsns Ctr
Superstore
SOUTHEND LA
SOUTHEND RD
SYDENHAM RD
BECKENHAM RD
BECKENHAM HILL RD
MANOR RD
BROMLEY RD
HIGH ST
RECTORY RD
STANTON WAY
BELL GN
KENT HOUSE RD
BRIDGE RD
LENNARD RD
WORSLEY BRIDGE RD
KANGLEY BRIDGE RD
BRACKLEY RD
PARK RD
CROOKED BILLET
Green Chain Wlk
Pool River
Chaffinch Brook
A2218
A212
A21
A2015
A222
A234
B227
B230
Lewisham
Bromley
186
207
36
37
38
69
70
71
72

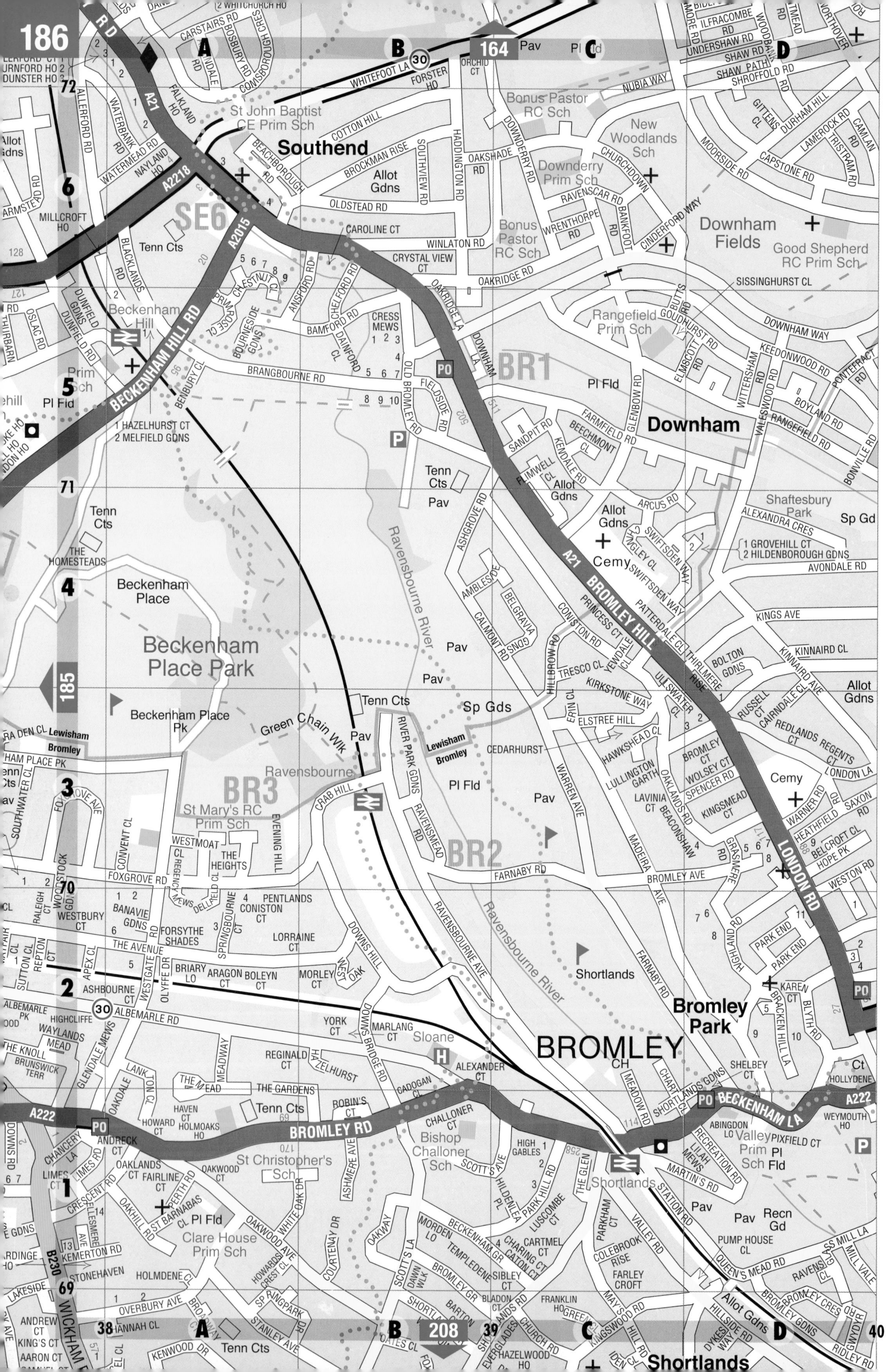
A
B
C
D
164
Pav
Pl Fld
30
6
5
4
3
2
1
72
71
70
69
185
208
38
39
40
Southend
SE6
BR1
BR3
BR2
Downham
Downham Fields
Bromley Park
BROMLEY
Shortlands
Beckenham Place Park
Beckenham Place
Beckenham Place Pk
Beckenham Hill
Ravensbourne
Ravensbourne River
Green Chain Wlk
Lewisham
Bromley
Sloane
St John Baptist CE Prim Sch
Bonus Pastor RC Sch
New Woodlands Sch
Downderry Prim Sch
Good Shepherd RC Prim Sch
Rangefield Prim Sch
St Mary's RC Prim Sch
St Christopher's Sch
Bishop Challoner Sch
Clare House Prim Sch
Valley Prim Sch
Shaftesbury Park
Allot Gdns
Tenn Cts
Sp Gds
Sp Gd
Cemy
Recn Gd
BECKENHAM HILL RD
BROMLEY HILL
LONDON RD
BROMLEY RD
BECKENHAM LA
WICKHAM
A21
A2218
A2015
A222
B230
WHITEFOOT LA
CARSTAIRS RD
BOSBURY RD
CONSBOROUGH CRES
FALKLAND HO
WATERBANK RD
ALLERFORD RD
WATERMEAD RD
NAYLAND HO
COTTON HILL
BEACHBOROUGH RD
BROCKMAN RISE
SOUTHVIEW RD
HADDINGTON RD
OAKSHADE RD
DOWNDERRY RD
CHURCHDOWN
RAVENSCAR RD
WRENTHORPE RD
BANKFOOT RD
CINDERFORD WAY
OLDSTEAD RD
CAROLINE CT
WINLATON RD
CRYSTAL VIEW CT
OAKRIDGE RD
OAKRIDGE LA
NUBIA WAY
ILFRACOMBE RD
UNDERSHAW RD
SHAW RD
SHAW PATH
SHROFFOLD RD
WOODBANK RD
GITTENS CL
DURHAM HILL
LAMEROCK RD
TRISTRAM RD
CAMLAN RD
MOORSIDE RD
CAPSTONE RD
FORSTER HO
ORCHID CT
MILLCROFT HO
ARMSTEAD RD
BLACKLANDS RD
DUNFIELD GDNS
DUNFIELD RD
OSLAC RD
THURBARN RD
CHESTNUT CL
PRIMROSE CL
AINSFORD RD
CHELFORD RD
BOURNESIDE GDNS
BAMFORD RD
DAINFORD CL
CRESS MEWS
BRANGBOURNE RD
BENBURY CL
OLD BROMLEY RD
FIELDSIDE RD
DOWNHAM LA
1 HAZELHURST CT
2 MELFIELD GDNS
SISSINGHURST CL
GOUDHURST RD
BUTTS RD
DOWNHAM WAY
KEEDONWOOD RD
ELMSCOTT RD
WITTERSHAM RD
VALESWOOD RD
BOYLAND RD
PONTEFRACT RD
RANGEFIELD RD
BONVILLE RD
GLENBOW RD
FARMFIELD RD
BEECHMONT CL
SANDPIT RD
KEMDALE RD
FLIMWELL CL
ASHGROVE RD
ARCUS RD
ALEXANDRA CRES
1 GROVEHILL CT
2 HILDENBOROUGH GDNS
AVONDALE RD
SWIFTSDEN WAY
CHINGLEY CL
PATTERDALE CL
KINGS AVE
KINNAIRD CL
KINNAIRD AVE
AMBLESIDE
BELGRAVIA GDNS
CALMONT RD
CONISTON RD
PRINCESS CT
YEWDALE CL
HILLBROW RD
TRESCO CL
KIRKSTONE WAY
ERIN CL
ULLSWATER CL
THIRLMERE RISE
BOLTON GDNS
RUSSELL CT
CAIRNDALE CL
REDLANDS CT
REGENTS CT
LONDON LA
ELSTREE HILL
HAWKSHEAD CL
CEDARHURST
LULLINGTON GARTH
BROMLEY CT
WOLSEY CT
SPENCER RD
OAKLANDS RD
LAVINIA CT
BEACONSHAW
KINGSMEAD CT
WARREN AVE
MADEIRA AVE
GRASMERE RD
WARNER RD
HEATHFIELD RD
SAXON RD
BELCROFT CL
HOPE PK
WESTON RD
BROMLEY AVE
HIGHLAND RD
PARK END
KAREN CT
BRACKEN HILL LA
BLYTH RD
FARNABY RD
RIVER PARK GDNS
RAVENSMEAD RD
RAVENSBOURNE AVE
CRAB HILL
EVENING HILL
WESTMOAT CL
THE HEIGHTS
REGENCY MEWS
DELLFIELD CL
FOXGROVE AVE
FOXGROVE RD
CONVENT CL
SOUTHWATER CL
WOODSTOCK GDNS
RALEIGH CT
WESTBURY CT
BANAVIE GDNS
FORSYTHE SHADES
SPRINGBOURNE CT
PENTLANDS
CONISTON CT
LORRAINE CT
THE AVENUE
SUTTON CL
REPTON CT
APEX CL
WESTGATE RD
OLYFFE DR
BRIARY LO
ARAGON CT
BOLEYN CT
MORLEY CT
WEST OAK
DOWNS HILL
ASHBOURNE CT
ALBEMARLE RD
ALBEMARLE PK
HIGHCLIFFE
WAYLANDS MEAD
THE KNOLL
BRUNSWICK TERR
GLENDALE MEWS
MEADWAY
YORK CT
MARLANG CT
DOWNS BRIDGE RD
REGINALD CT
HAZELHURST
LANKTON CL
OAKDALE
THE MEAD
THE GARDENS
HAVEN CT
HOLMOAKS HO
HOWARD CT
ROBIN'S CT
CADOGAN CL
ALEXANDER CT
CHALLONER CT
MEADOW RD
CHARTS CL
SHORTLANDS GDNS
SHELBEY CT
HOLLYDENE
WEYMOUTH HO
PIXFIELD CT
ABINGDON LO
RECREATION RD
LILAH MEWS
MARTIN'S RD
STATION RD
PUMP HOUSE CL
GLASS MILL LA
MILL VALE
QUEEN'S MEAD RD
RAVENS CL
BROMLEY CRES
BROMLEY GDNS
WYDR RD
RIDLEY RD
HILLSIDE RD
DYKES WAY
ANDRECK CT
CHANCERY LA
LIMES RD
LIMES CT
OAKLANDS CT
FAIRLINE CT
OAKWOOD CT
PERTH RD
ST BARNABAS CL
OAKHILL RD
CRESCENT RD
ELLESMERE AVE
KEMERTON RD
STONEHAVEN
HOLMDENE CT
OVERBURY AVE
LAKESIDE
ANDREW CT
KING'S CT
AARON CT
HANNAH CL
KENWOOD DR
STANLEY AVE
SPRINGPARK DR
HOWARDS CREST CL
OAKWOOD AVE
WHITE OAK DR
ASHMERE AVE
COURTENAY DR
OAKWAY
SCOTT'S LA
SCOTT'S AVE
DAWN WLK
SHORTLANDS
OATES CL
MORDEN LO
TEMPLEDENE
BECKENHAM GR
BROMLEY GR
BLADON CT
BARTON
HIGH GABLES
HILDENLEA PL
PARK HILL RD
LUSCOMBE CT
CARTMEL CT
CHARING CT
CATON CT
SIBLEY CT
EVERGLADES
CHURCH RD
HAZELWOOD HO
FRANKLIN HO
GREENCL
KINGSWOOD RD
THE GLEN
PARKHAM CT
COLEBROOK RISE
FARLEY CROFT
VALLEY RD
MAYS HILL RD
SHORTLANDS RD
DOWNS RD
CH
H
PO
P

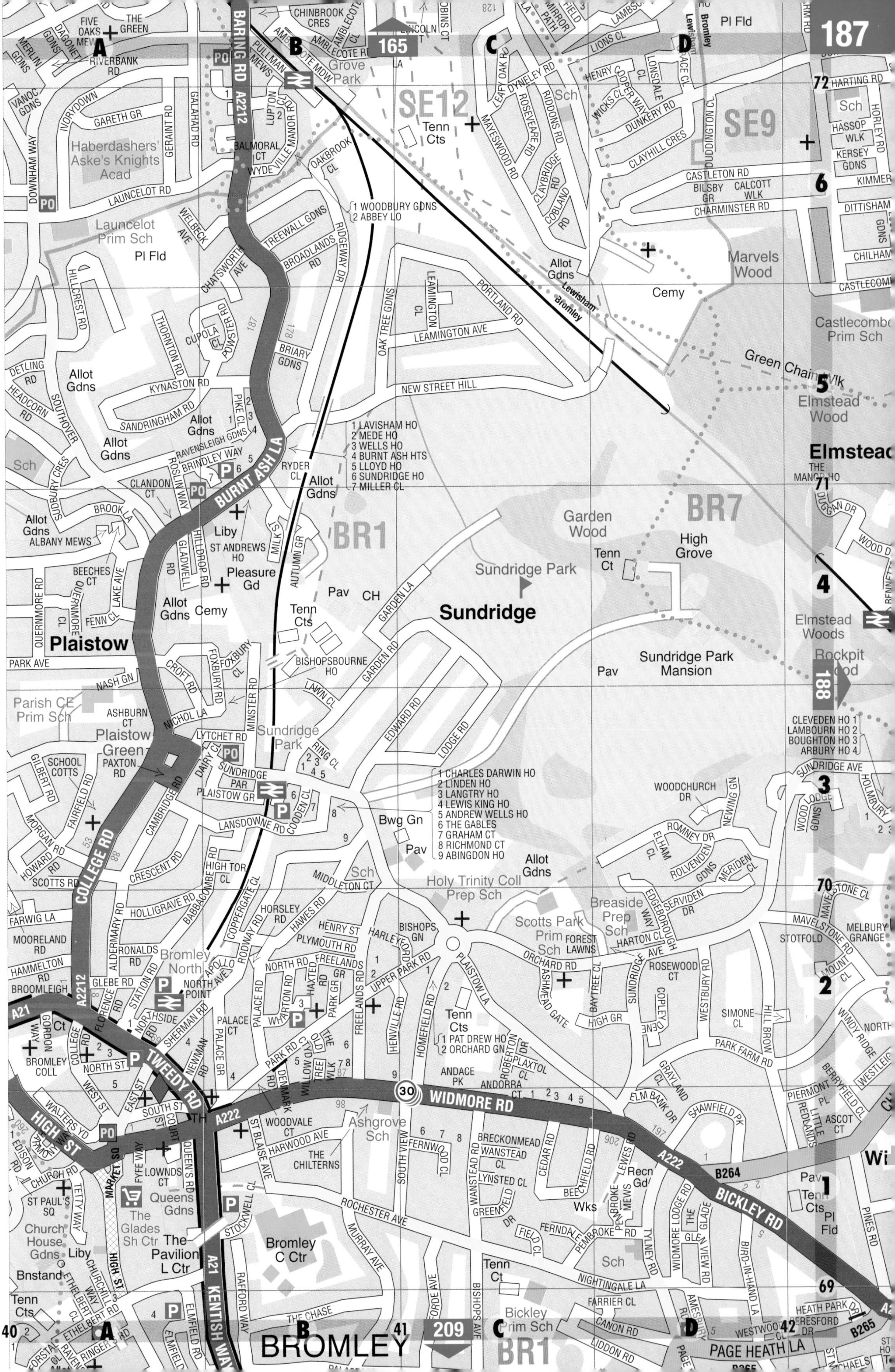
SE12
SE9
BR1
BR7
Plaistow
Sundridge
Elmstead
Sundridge Park
Sundridge Park Mansion
Garden Wood
High Grove
Elmstead Wood
Elmstead Woods
Marvels Wood
Plaistow Green
Grove Park
BROMLEY
Haberdashers' Aske's Knights Acad
Launcelot Prim Sch
Parish CE Prim Sch
Holy Trinity Coll Prep Sch
Scotts Park Prim Sch
Breaside Prep Sch
Castlecombe Prim Sch
Bromley Coll
Bromley C Ctr
The Glades Sh Ctr
The Pavilion L Ctr
Bickley Prim Sch
Ashgrove Sch
Bromley North
Green Chain Wlk
BARING RD
A2212
BURNT ASH LA
COLLEGE RD
TWEEDY RD
HIGH ST
A21
KENTISH WAY
WIDMORE RD
A222
BICKLEY RD
B264
B265
PAGE HEATH LA
LAUNCELOT RD
GARETH GR
IVORYDOWN
DOWNHAM WAY
RIVERBANK RD
WYDEVILLE MANOR RD
BALMORAL CT
OAKBROOK CL
RIDGEWAY DR
BROADLANDS RD
TREEWALL GDNS
CHATSWORTH AVE
WELBECK AVE
HILLCREST RD
THORNTON RD
CUPOLA CL
POWSTER RD
KYNASTON RD
SANDRINGHAM RD
BRIARY GDNS
LEAMINGTON AVE
LEAMINGTON CL
PORTLAND RD
OAK TREE GDNS
NEW STREET HILL
RAVENSLEIGH GDNS
BRINDLEY WAY
CLANDON CT
ROSLIN WAY
BROOK LA
ALBANY MEWS
BEECHES CT
QUERNMORE RD
QUERNMORE CL
FENN CL
LAKE AVE
PARK AVE
NASH GN
CROFT RD
FOXBURY RD
FOXBURY CL
MINSTER RD
NICHOL LA
ASHBURN CT
PAXTON RD
SCHOOL COTTS
GILBERT RD
FAIRFIELD RD
MORGAN RD
HOWARD RD
SCOTTS RD
FARWIG LA
MOORELAND RD
HAMMELTON RD
BROOMLEIGH
CAMBRIDGE RD
CRESCENT RD
HOLLIGRAVE RD
ALDERMARY RD
RONALDS RD
GLEBE RD
FLORENCE RD
STATION RD
NORTHSIDE RD
SHERMAN RD
NORTH POINT
GARDEN LA
GARDEN RD
EDWARD RD
LODGE RD
LAWN CL
RING CL
BISHOPSBOURNE HO
LYTCHET RD
DAIRY CL
SUNDRIDGE PAR
PLAISTOW GR
CODDEN CL
LANSDOWNE RD
HIGH TOR CL
BABBACOMBE RD
COPPERGATE CL
RODWAY RD
HORSLEY RD
HAWES RD
MIDDLETON CT
HENRY ST
HARLEYFORD
BISHOPS GN
PLYMOUTH RD
NORTH RD
FREELANDS RD
UPPER PARK RD
PLAISTOW LA
HOMEFIELD RD
HENVILLE RD
PALACE RD
PALACE GR
PALACE CT
PARK RD
DENMARK RD
ORCHARD RD
FOREST LAWNS
ASHMEAD GATE
BAYTREE CL
SUNDRIDGE AVE
ROSEWOOD CT
COPLEY DENE
WESTBURY RD
HIGH GR
HARTON CL
EDGEBOROUGH WAY
SERVIDEN DR
WOODCHURCH DR
NEWING GN
ROMNEY DR
ELTHAM CL
ROLVENDEN GDNS
MERIDEN CL
PARK FARM RD
HILL BROW
SIMONE CL
GRAYLAND CL
ELM BANK DR
SHAWFIELD PK
ANDORRA CT
ANDACE PK
PLAXTOL CL
ROBERTON DR
WOODVALE CT
HARWOOD AVE
THE CHILTERNS
ST BLAISE AVE
STOCKWELL CL
SOUTH VIEW
FERNWOOD CL
BRECKONMEAD
WANSTEAD RD
WANSTEAD CL
LYNSTED CL
CEDAR RD
BEECHFIELD RD
LEWES RD
PEMBROKE RD
FERNDALE
FIELD CL
TYLNEY RD
WIDMORE LODGE RD
THE GLADE
GLEN VIEW RD
BIRD-IN-HAND LA
ROCHESTER AVE
MURRAY AVE
NIGHTINGALE LA
FARRIER CL
CANON RD
LIDDON RD
AMESBURY RD
WESTWOOD CL
BERESFORD DR
HEATH PARK DR
PINES RD
THE CHASE
RAFFORD WAY
ELMFIELD RD
RINGERS RD
ETHELBERT RD
CHURCHILL WAY
ST PAUL'S SQ
CHURCH RD
MARKET SQ
FYFE WAY
LOWNDS CT
QUEEN'S RD
EAST ST
WEST ST
NORTH ST
SOUTH ST
WALTERS YD
EDISON RD
GORDON WAY
DYNELEY RD
LEAFY OAK RD
MAYESWOOD RD
ROSEVEARE RD
RIDDONS RD
CLAYBRIDGE RD
COBLAND RD
DUNKERY RD
CLAYHILL CRES
DUDDINGTON CL
CASTLETON RD
BILSBY GR
CALCOTT WLK
CHARMINSTER RD
HARTING RD
HASSOP WLK
KERSEY GDNS
KIMMERIDGE
DITTISHAM
CHILHAM
CASTLECOMBE
SUNDRIDGE AVE
HOLMBURY
WOOD LODGE GDNS
MAVELSTONE CL
MAVELSTONE RD
MELBURY GRANGE
STOTFOLD
MOUNT CL
WINDY RIDGE
PIERMONT PL
BERRYFIELD CL
LITTLE REDLANDS
ASCOT CT
DUGGAN DR
THE MANOR HO
CHINBROOK CRES
AMBLECOTE RD
AMBLECOTE CL
PULLMAN MEWS
LUPTON CL
FIVE OAKS MEWS
THE GREEN
DAGONET GDNS
MERLIN GDNS
VANOC GDNS
1 WOODBURY GDNS
2 ABBEY LO
1 LAVISHAM HO
2 MEDE HO
3 WELLS HO
4 BURNT ASH HTS
5 LLOYD HO
6 SUNDRIDGE HO
7 MILLER CL
1 CHARLES DARWIN HO
2 LINDEN HO
3 LANGTRY HO
4 LEWIS KING HO
5 ANDREW WELLS HO
6 THE GABLES
7 GRAHAM CT
8 RICHMOND CT
9 ABINGDON HO
CLEVEDEN HO 1
LAMBOURN HO 2
BOUGHTON HO 3
ARBURY HO 4
1 PAT DREW HO
2 ORCHARD GN
165
188
209

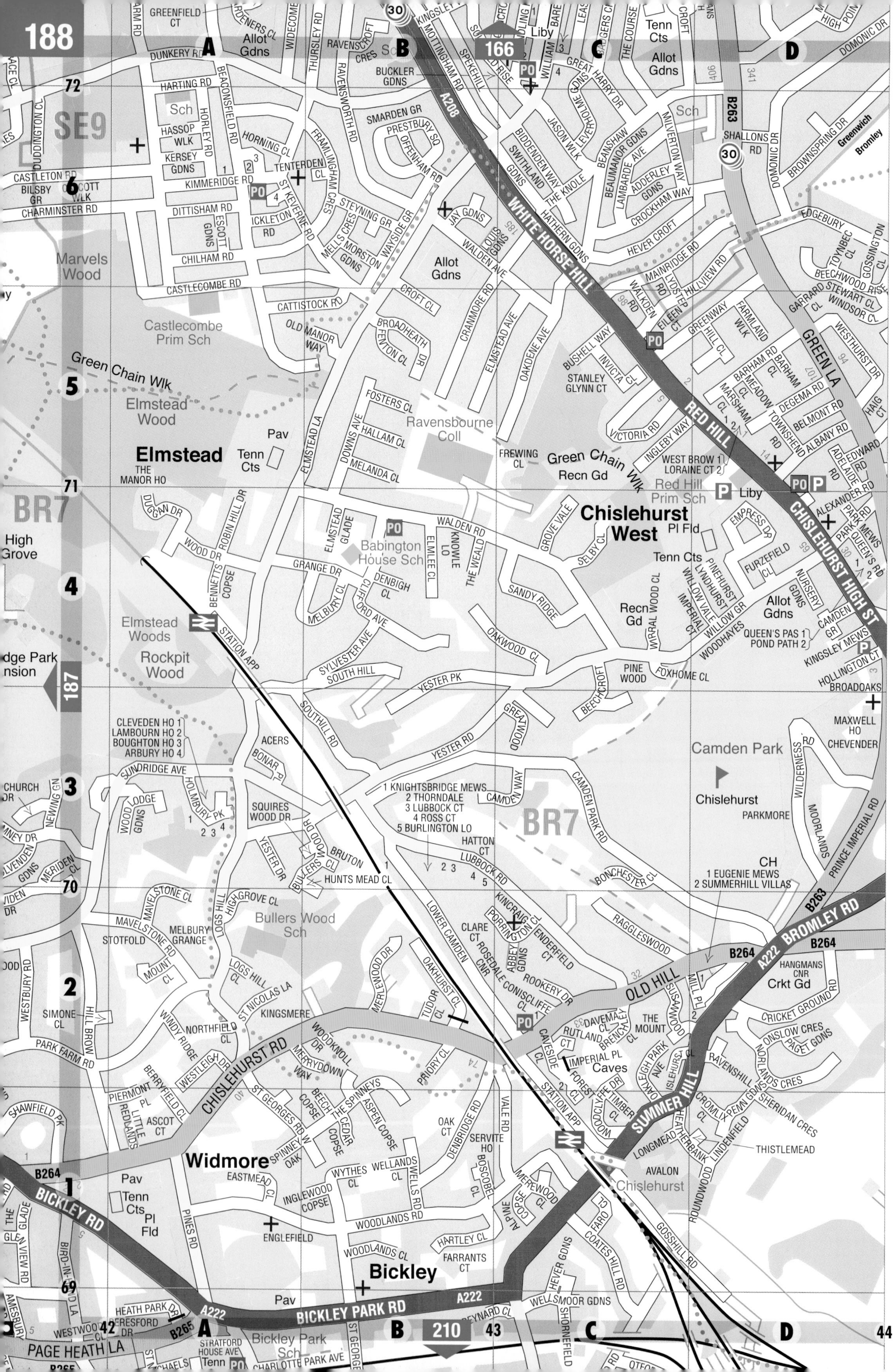

A
B
C
D
166
210
187
72
71
70
69
6
5
4
3
2
1
42
43
44
SE9
BR7
Elmstead
Chislehurst West
Widmore
Bickley
Marvels Wood
Elmstead Wood
Elmstead Woods
Rockpit Wood
Castlecombe Prim Sch
Green Chain Wlk
Ravensbourne Coll
Babington House Sch
Bullers Wood Sch
Red Hill Prim Sch
Camden Park
Chislehurst
Caves
Bickley Park Sch
Allot Gdns
Tenn Cts
Recn Gd
Pl Fld
Crkt Gd
Pav
Sch
Liby
PO
CH
THE MANOR HO
WHITE HORSE HILL
RED HILL
CHISLEHURST HIGH ST
GREEN LA
BICKLEY RD
BICKLEY PARK RD
CHISLEHURST RD
OLD HILL
SUMMER HILL
BROMLEY RD
PRINCE IMPERIAL RD
A208
A222
B263
B264
B265
DUNKERY RD
HARTING RD
BEACONSFIELD RD
HORLEY RD
HASSOP WLK
KERSEY GDNS
CASTLETON RD
KIMMERIDGE RD
CHARMINSTER RD
DITTISHAM RD
CHILHAM RD
CASTLECOMBE RD
CATTISTOCK RD
OLD MANOR WAY
HORNING CL
TENTERDEN CL
ST KEVERNE RD
ICKLETON RD
ESCOTT GDNS
FRAMLINGHAM CRES
STEYNING GR
MELLS CRES
MORSTON GDNS
WAYSIDE GR
RAVENSWORTH RD
SMARDEN GR
PRESTBURY SQ
OFFENHAM RD
BUCKLER GDNS
RAVENSCROFT CRES
THURSLEY RD
WIDECOMBE
MOTTINGHAM RD
SPEKEHILL
JAY GDNS
LOUIS GDNS
WALDEN AVE
CROFT CL
BROADHEATH DR
FENTON CL
CRANMORE RD
ELMSTEAD AVE
OAKDENE AVE
ELMSTEAD LA
FOSTERS CL
DOWNS AVE
HALLAM CL
MELANDA CL
BIDDENDEN WAY
SWITHLAND GDNS
JASON WLK
LEVERHOLME GDNS
THE KNOLE
HATHERN GDNS
BEANSHAW
BEAUMANOR GDNS
LAMBARDE AVE
ADDERLEY GDNS
CROCKHAM WAY
MILVERTON WAY
HEVER CROFT
GREAT HARRY DR
THE COURSE
SHALLONS RD
DOMONIC DR
BROWNSPRING DR
EDGEBURY
TOYNBEC CL
GOSSINGTON CL
BEECHWOOD RISE
STEWART CL
WINDSOR CL
GARRARD CL
WESTHURST DR
HAIG CT
MAINRIDGE RD
LYDSTEP RD
HILLVIEW RD
WALKDEN RD
EILEEN CT
GREENWAY
HILL CL
FARMLAND WLK
BUSHELL WAY
INVICTA CL
STANLEY GLYNN CT
VICTORIA RD
INGLEBY WAY
BARHAM RD
BARHAM CL
MEADOW CL
MARSHAM CL
TOWNSHEND RD
DEGEMA RD
BELMONT RD
ALBANY RD
ADELAIDE RD
EDWARD RD
ALEXANDER RD
PARK MEWS
QUEEN'S RD
WEST BROW 1
LORAINE CT 2
FREWING CL
DUGGAN DR
WOOD DR
ROBIN HILL DR
BENNETTS COPSE
ELMSTEAD GLADE
GRANGE DR
ELMLEE CL
KNOWLE LO
THE WEALD
WALDEN RD
DENBIGH CL
MELBURY CL
CLIFFORD AVE
GROVE VALE
SELBY CL
SANDY RIDGE
EMPRESS DR
FURZEFIELD CL
PINEHURST
LYNDHURST
WILLOW VALE
IMPERIAL CL
WILLOW GR
WIRRAL WOOD CL
WOODHAYES
NURSERY GDNS
CAMDEN GR
QUEEN'S PAS 1
POND PATH 2
KINGSLEY MEWS
HOLLINGTON CT
BROADOAKS
STATION APP
SYLVESTER AVE
SOUTH HILL
YESTER PK
OAKWOOD CL
PINE WOOD
FOXHOME CL
BEECHCROFT
SOUTHILL RD
GREAT WOOD
YESTER RD
MAXWELL HO
CHEVENDER
WILDERNESS RD
MOORLANDS
PARKMORE
CLEVEDEN HO 1
LAMBOURN HO 2
BOUGHTON HO 3
ARBURY HO 4
ACERS
BONAR PL
SUNDRIDGE AVE
HOLMBURY PK
WOOD LODGE GDNS
SQUIRES WOOD DR
YESTER DR
WOOD DR
BRUTON CL
BULLERS CL
HUNTS MEAD CL
1 KNIGHTSBRIDGE MEWS
2 THORNDALE
3 LUBBOCK CT
4 ROSS CT
5 BURLINGTON LO
CAMDEN WAY
CAMDEN PARK RD
HATTON CT
LUBBOCK RD
BONCHESTER CL
1 EUGENIE MEWS
2 SUMMERHILL VILLAS
RAGGLESWOOD
LOWER CAMDEN
KINCRAIG DR
PORRINGTON CL
ENDERFIELD CT
CLARE CT
ROSEDALE CNR
ABBEY GDNS
CONISCLIFFE CL
ROOKERY DR
HANGMANS CNR
CRICKET GROUND RD
ONSLOW CRES
PAGET GDNS
NORLANDS CRES
RAVENSHILL
SHERIDAN CRES
CROMLIX CL
PENN GDNS
LINDENFIELD
THISTLEMEAD
HEATHERBANK
LONGMEAD
AVALON
ROUNDWOOD
MILL PL
SUSAN WOOD
THE MOUNT
DAVEMA CL
BRENCHLEY CL
RUTLAND CT
CAVESIDE CL
IMPERIAL PL
FOREST CL
WOODCLYFFE DR
TIMBER CL
OAKLEIGH PARK AVE
ISLEHURST CL
HIGHGROVE CL
MAVELSTONE CL
MAVELSTONE RD
MELBURY GRANGE
STOTFOLD
LOGS HILL
LOGS HILL CL
MOUNT CL
ST NICOLAS LA
KINGSMERE
NORTHFIELD CL
WINDY RIDGE
WESTLEIGH DR
BERRYFIELD CL
PIERMONT PL
LITTLE REDLANDS
ASCOT CT
WESTBURY RD
SIMONE CL
HILL BROW
PARK FARM RD
SHAWFIELD PK
MERLEWOOD DR
WOODKNOLL DR
MERRYDOWN WAY
ST GEORGES RD W
BEECH COPSE
CEDAR COPSE
THE SPINNEYS
ASPEN COPSE
SPINNEY OAK
PRIORY CL
TUDOR CL
OAKHURST CL
OAK CT
DENBRIDGE RD
SERVITE HO
VALE RD
BOSCOBEL CL
MEREWOOD CL
ALPINE COPSE
FARO CL
COATES HILL RD
GOSSHILL RD
EASTMEAD CL
INGLEWOOD COPSE
WYTHES CL
WELLANDS CL
WELLS RD
WOODLANDS RD
WOODLANDS CL
HARTLEY CL
FARRANTS CT
ENGLEFIELD
PINES RD
HEVER GDNS
WELLSMOOR GDNS
SHORNEFIELD
HEATH PARK DR
BERESFORD DR
WESTWOOD
PAGE HEATH LA
STRATFORD HOUSE AVE
CHARLOTTE PARK AVE
ST GEORGE
REYNARD CL
THE GLADE
GLENVIEW RD
BIRD-IN-HAND LA
AMESBURY
DUDDINGTON CL
BILSBY GR
ESCOTT WLK
CHURCH DR
NEWING GN
MERIDEN CL
High Grove
Greenwich
Bromley

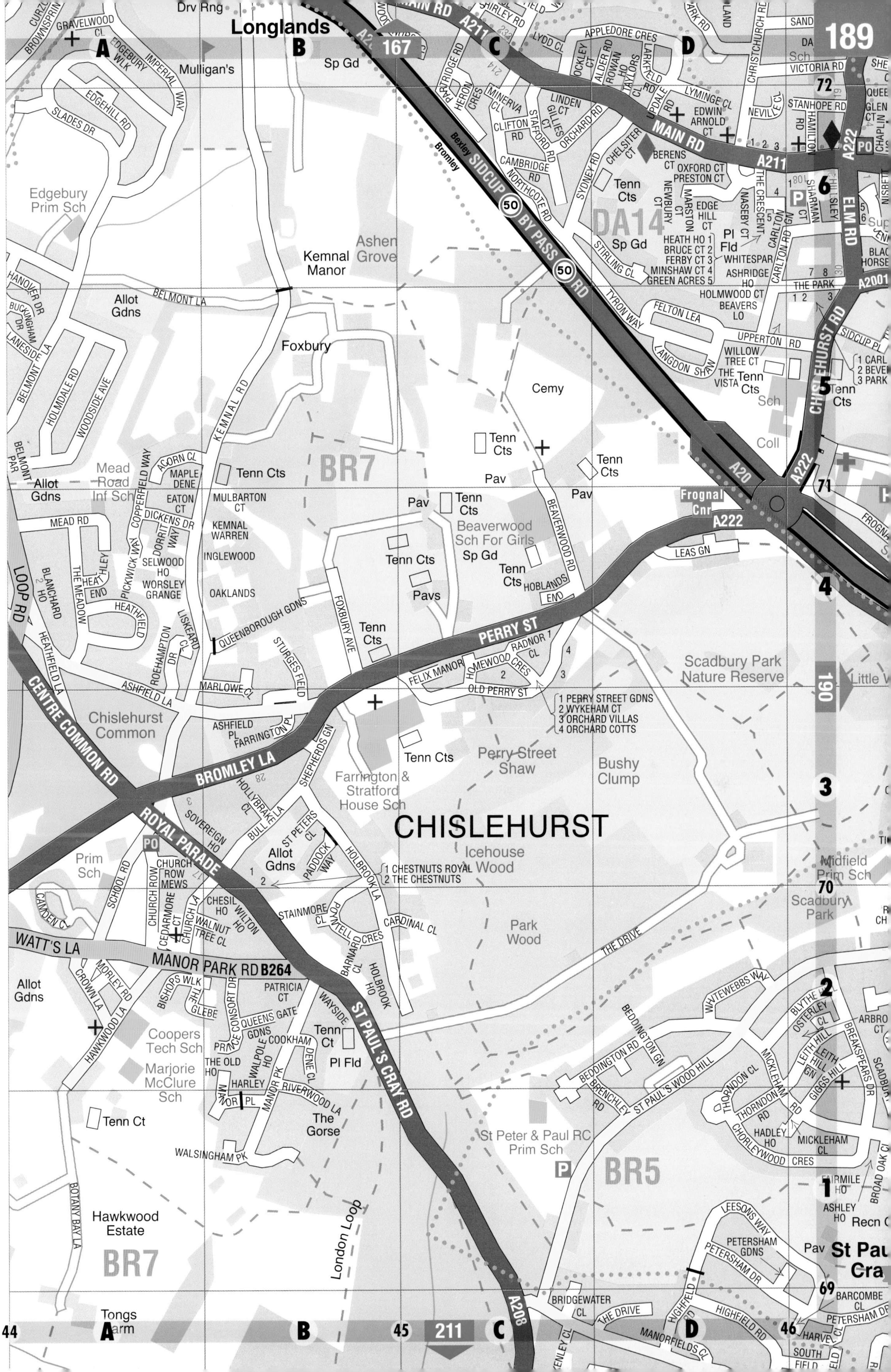
Longlands
Drv Rng
Mulligan's
Sp Gd
167
A20
A211
MAIN RD
SIDCUP BY PASS RD
Bexley
Bromley
50
GRAVELWOOD CL
EDGEBURY WLK
IMPERIAL WAY
EDGEHILL RD
SLADES DR
Edgebury Prim Sch
Kemnal Manor
Ashen Grove
BELMONT LA
Allot Gdns
Foxbury
HANOVER DR
BUCKINGHAM DR
LANESIDE
BELMONT LA
HOLMDALE RD
WOODSIDE AVE
KEMNAL RD
BELMONT PAR
Mead Road Inf Sch
ACORN CL
MAPLE DENE
EATON CT
COPPERFIELD WAY
DICKENS DR
DORRIT WAY
SELWOOD HO
WORSLEY GRANGE
MULBARTON CT
KEMNAL WARREN
INGLEWOOD
OAKLANDS
Tenn Cts
BR7
MEAD RD
LOOP RD
BLANCHARD HO
THE MEADOW
HEATHLEY END
PICKWICK WAY
HEATHFIELD
LISKEARD CL
ROEHAMPTON DR
QUEENBOROUGH GDNS
STURGES FIELD
FOXBURY AVE
HEATHFIELD LA
ASHFIELD LA
MARLOWE CL
CENTRE COMMON RD
Chislehurst Common
ASHFIELD PL
FARRINGTON PL
BROMLEY LA
HOLLYBRAKE CL
SHEPHERDS GN
SOVEREIGN HO
BULL LA
ROYAL PARADE
PO
Prim Sch
SCHOOL RD
CHURCH ROW
CHURCH ROW MEWS
CAMDEN CL
CEDARMORE CT
CHURCH LA
CHESIL HO
WILTON HO
WALNUT TREE CL
ST PETERS CL
PADDOCK WAY
Allot Gdns
HOLBROOK LA
STAINMORE CL
POWDRELL CRES
CARDINAL CL
BARNARD CL
HOLBROOK HO
1 CHESTNUTS ROYAL
2 THE CHESTNUTS
WATT'S LA
MANOR PARK RD B264
Allot Gdns
CROWN LA
MORLEY RD
HAWKWOOD LA
BISHOPS WLK
THE GLEBE
CONSORT DR
PATRICIA CT
QUEENS GATE
PRINCE GDNS
COOKHAM DENE CL
WAYSIDE
ST PAUL'S CRAY RD
Tenn Ct
Pl Fld
Coopers Tech Sch
Marjorie McClure Sch
THE OLD HO
WALPOLE HO
HARLEY HO
MANOR PK
MANOR PL
RIVERWOOD LA
The Gorse
WALSINGHAM PK
Tenn Ct
BOTANY BAY LA
Hawkwood Estate
BR7
London Loop
Tongs Farm
A208
211
SHIRLEY RD
PARTRIDGE RD
HERON CRES
MINERVA CL
CLIFTON RD
STAFFORD RD
CAMBRIDGE RD
NORTHCOTE RD
LYDD CL
APPLEDORE CRES
OCKLEY CT
ALDER RD
ROWAN HO
TAYLORS CL
LARKFIELD RD
UPDALE RD
LINDEN CT
GILLIES CT
ORCHARD RD
SYDNEY RD
CHELSITER CT
LYMINGE CL
EDWIN ARNOLD CT
NEVILLE CL
CHRISTCHURCH RD
VICTORIA RD
STANHOPE RD
HAMILTON RD
BERENS CT
OXFORD CT
PRESTON CT
Tenn Cts
DA14
Sp Gd
NEWBURY CT
MARSTON CT
EDGE HILL CT
NASEBY CT
THE CRESCENT
CARLTON GN
CARLTON RD
SHARMAN CT
HILLSLEY
ELM RD
A222
A211
PO
Pl Fld
WHITESPAR
ASHRIDGE HO
HEATH HO 1
BRUCE CT 2
FERBY CT 3
MINSHAW CT 4
GREEN ACRES 5
STIRLING CL
TYRON WAY
HOLMWOOD CT
BEAVERS LO
THE PARK
FELTON LEA
LANGDON SHAW
UPPERTON RD
WILLOW TREE CT
THE VISTA
Tenn Cts
Sch
Coll
CHISLEHURST RD
SIDCUP PL
1 CARL
2 BEVE
3 PARK
Tenn Cts
A2001
Cemy
Tenn Cts
Pav
Pav
Tenn Cts
Pav
Tenn Cts
Beaverwood Sch For Girls
Sp Gd
BEAVERWOOD RD
Tenn Cts
HOBLANDS END
Pavs
Tenn Cts
A20
Frognal Cnr
A222
LEAS GN
PERRY ST
RADNOR CL
HOMEWOOD CRES
FELIX MANOR
OLD PERRY ST
1 PERRY STREET GDNS
2 WYKEHAM CT
3 ORCHARD VILLAS
4 ORCHARD COTTS
Scadbury Park Nature Reserve
190
Little
Tenn Cts
Farrington & Stratford House Sch
Perry Street Shaw
Bushy Clump
CHISLEHURST
Icehouse Wood
Park Wood
THE DRIVE
Midfield Prim Sch
Scadbury Park
WHITEWEBBS WAY
BEDDINGTON GN
BEDDINGTON RD
BRENCHLEY RD
ST PAUL'S WOOD HILL
BLYTHE
OSTERLEY CL
LEITH HILL
LEITH HILL GN
BREAKSPEARS DR
ARBRO CT
MICKLEHAM RD
THORNDON CL
THORNDON RD
GIGGS HILL
HADLEY HO
MICKLEHAM CL
CHORLEYWOOD CRES
St Peter & Paul RC Prim Sch
BR5
FAIRMILE HO
ASHLEY HO
BROAD OAK CL
Recn
LEESONS WAY
PETERSHAM GDNS
PETERSHAM DR
Pav
St Pau
Cra
BARCOMBE CL
PETERSHAM DR
BRIDGEWATER CL
THE DRIVE
HIGHFIELD RD
HIGHFIELD RD
MANORFIELDS CL
SOUTH FIELD
A
B
C
D
1
2
3
4
5
6
45
46
69
70
71
72

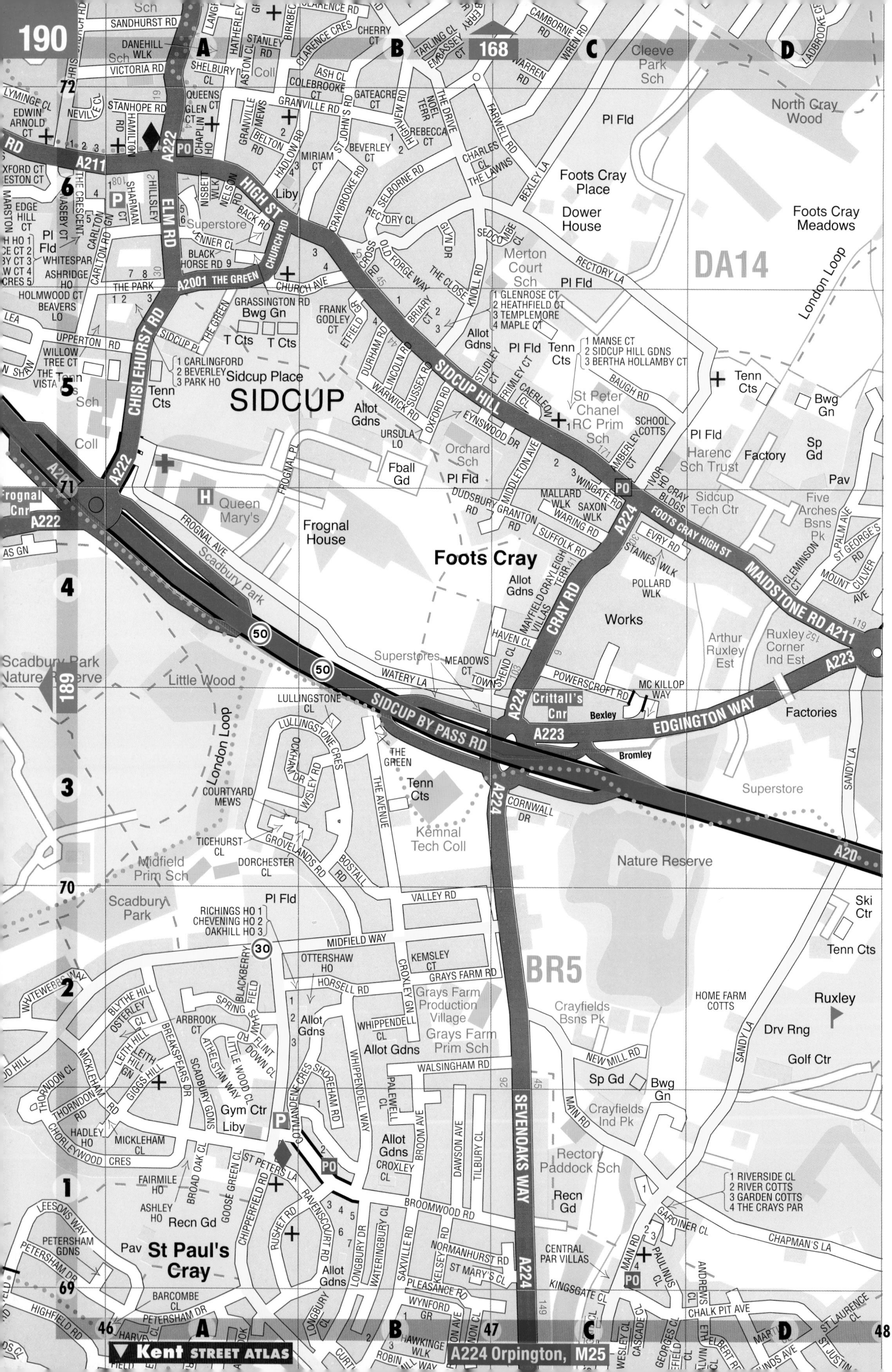

168
A
B
C
D
SIDCUP
Foots Cray
St Paul's Cray
DA14
BR5
Sidcup Place
Foots Cray Place
Dower House
Foots Cray Meadows
North Cray Wood
Cleeve Park Sch
Merton Court Sch
Frognal House
Queen Mary's
Scadbury Park
Scadbury Park Nature Reserve
Little Wood
London Loop
Nature Reserve
Kemnal Tech Coll
Midfield Prim Sch
Grays Farm Production Village
Grays Farm Prim Sch
Crayfields Bsns Pk
Crayfields Ind Pk
Rectory Paddock Sch
Ruxley
Ruxley Corner Ind Est
Arthur Ruxley Est
Five Arches Bsns Pk
Harenc Sch Trust
Sidcup Tech Ctr
St Peter Chanel RC Prim Sch
Orchard Sch
Crittall's Cnr
Frognal Cnr
Superstore
Superstores
Factories
Factory
Works
Drv Rng
Golf Ctr
Ski Ctr
Tenn Cts
Bwg Gn
Sp Gd
Pl Fld
Allot Gdns
Fball Gd
Recn Gd
Gym Ctr
Liby
Coll
Sch
Pav
HIGH ST
ELM RD
CHISLEHURST RD
SIDCUP HILL
FOOTS CRAY HIGH ST
MAIDSTONE RD A211
SIDCUP BY PASS RD
EDGINGTON WAY
CRAY RD
SEVENOAKS WAY
A20
A211
A222
A223
A224
A2001 THE GREEN
CHURCH RD
CHURCH AVE
RECTORY LA
BEXLEY LA
FROGNAL AVE
FROGNAL PL
WATERY LA
POWERSCROFT RD
MIDFIELD WAY
VALLEY RD
HORSELL RD
GRAYS FARM RD
WALSINGHAM RD
BROOMWOOD RD
CHAPMAN'S LA
SANDY LA
CHALK PIT AVE
KINGSGATE CL
MAIN RD
NEW MILL RD
CORNWALL DR
THE AVENUE
GROVELANDS RD
BOSTALL RD
LULLINGSTONE CRES
WISLEY RD
COTMANDENE CRES
WHIPPENDELL WAY
ST PETERS LA
RAVENSCOURT RD
CHIPPERFIELD RD
BROOM AVE
DAWSON AVE
TILBURY CL
SAXVILLE RD
LONGBURY DR
WATERINGBURY CL
PLEASANCE RD
NORMANHURST RD
ST MARY'S CL
WYNFORD GR
HAWKINGE WLK
PETERSHAM DR
HIGHFIELD RD
LEESONS WAY
CHORLEYWOOD CRES
MICKLEHAM RD
BREAKSPEARS DR
SCADBURY GDNS
FAIRMILE HO
ASHLEY HO
1 RIVERSIDE CL
2 RIVER COTTS
3 GARDEN COTTS
4 THE CRAYS PAR
1 MANSE CT
2 SIDCUP HILL GDNS
3 BERTHA HOLLAMBY CT
1 GLENROSE CT
2 HEATHFIELD CT
3 TEMPLEMORE
4 MAPLE CT
1 CARLINGFORD
2 BEVERLEY
3 PARK HO
RICHINGS HO 1
CHEVENING HO 2
OAKHILL HO 3
189
46
47
48
72
71
70
69
6
5
4
3
2
1

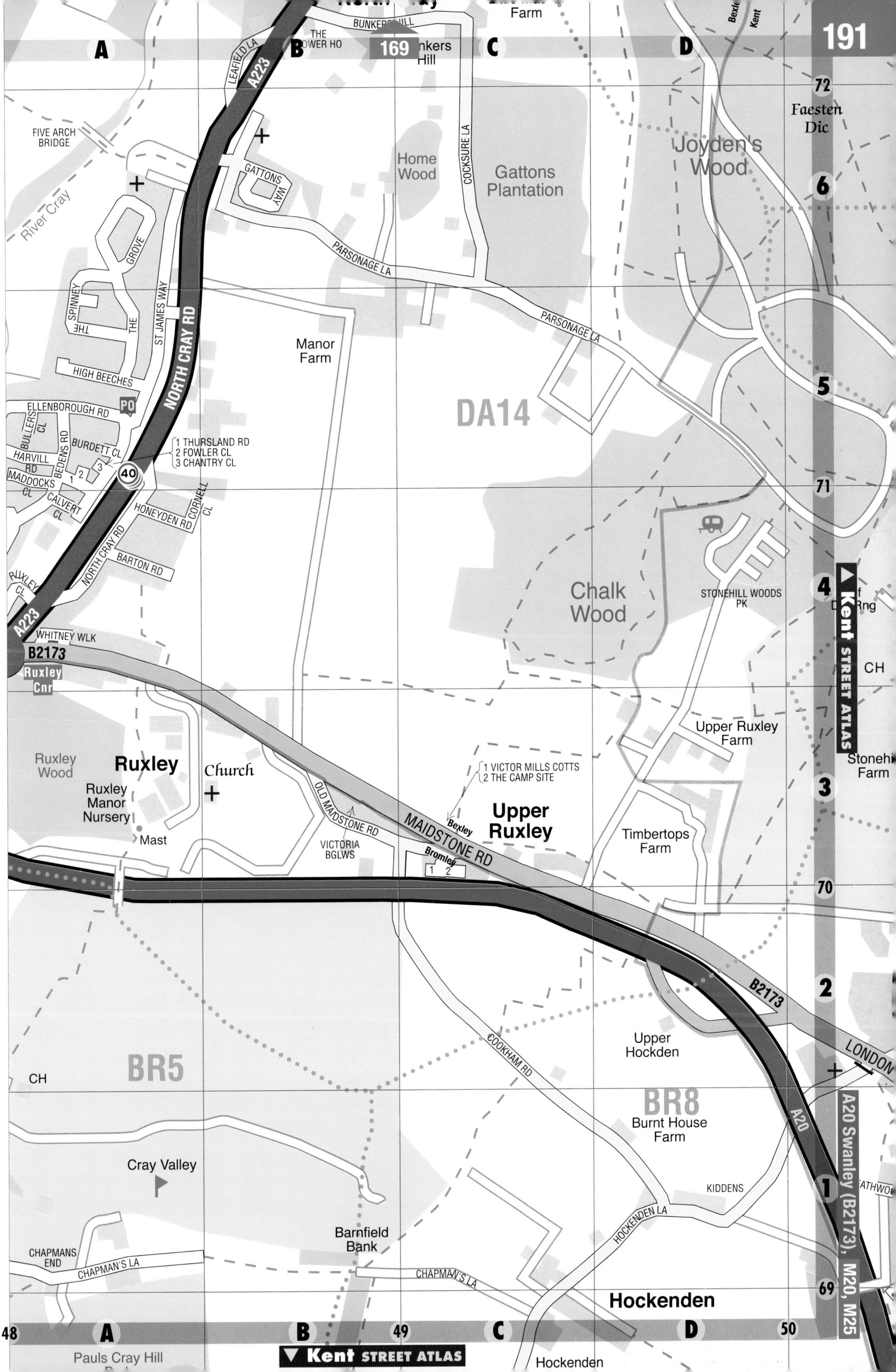
A
B
C
D
169
THE TOWER HO
BUNKERS HILL
Bunkers Hill
Farm
LEAFIELD LA
A223
FIVE ARCH BRIDGE
River Cray
GATTONS WAY
Home Wood
COCKSURE LA
Gattons Plantation
Joyden's Wood
Faesten Dic
72
6
GROVE
THE SPINNEY
THE
ST JAMES WAY
NORTH CRAY RD
PARSONAGE LA
Manor Farm
HIGH BEECHES
ELLENBOROUGH RD
PO
BULLERS CL
BEDENS RD
BURDETT CL
HARVILL RD
MADDOCKS CL
CALVERT CL
1 THURSLAND RD
2 FOWLER CL
3 CHANTRY CL
40
HONEYDEN RD
CORNELL CL
BARTON RD
RUXLEY CL
DA14
5
71
Chalk Wood
STONEHILL WOODS PK
4
Kent STREET ATLAS
CH
WHITNEY WLK
B2173
Ruxley Cnr
Ruxley Wood
Ruxley
Church
Ruxley Manor Nursery
Mast
OLD MAIDSTONE RD
VICTORIA BGLWS
1 VICTOR MILLS COTTS
2 THE CAMP SITE
Bexley
Bromley
MAIDSTONE RD
Upper Ruxley
Upper Ruxley Farm
Stonehill Farm
3
Timbertops Farm
70
2
B2173
LONDON
BR5
CH
COOKHAM RD
Upper Hockden
BR8
Burnt House Farm
A20
A20 Swanley (B2173), M20, M25
Cray Valley
KIDDENS
1
HOCKENDEN LA
Barnfield Bank
CHAPMANS END
CHAPMAN'S LA
69
Hockenden
48
49
50
Kent STREET ATLAS
Pauls Cray Hill

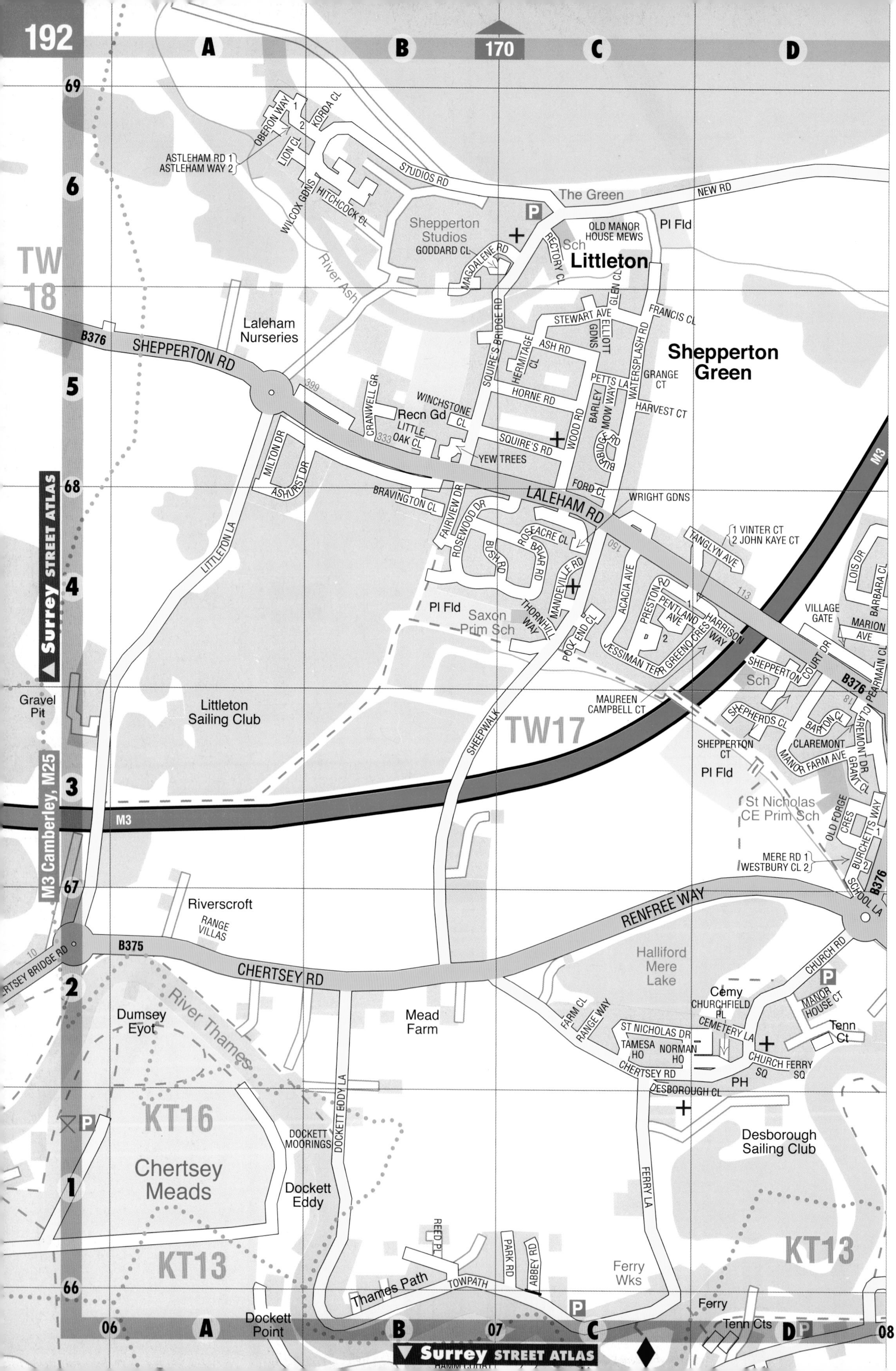
A
B
170
C
D
69
6
5
68
4
3
67
2
1
66
06
07
08
TW
18
Surrey STREET ATLAS
M3 Camberley, M25
ASTLEHAM RD 1
ASTLEHAM WAY 2
OBERON WAY
KORDA CL
LION CL
WILCOX GDNS
HITCHCOCK CL
STUDIOS RD
The Green
NEW RD
Shepperton
Studios
GODDARD CL
MAGDALENE RD
RECTORY CL
Sch
OLD MANOR
HOUSE MEWS
Pl Fld
Littleton
River Ash
GLEN CL
FRANCIS CL
STEWART AVE
ELLIOTT
GDNS
SQUIRE'S BRIDGE RD
HERMITAGE
CL
ASH RD
WATERSPLASH RD
Shepperton
Green
Laleham
Nurseries
B376
SHEPPERTON RD
399
CRANWELL GR
WINCHSTONE
CL
Recn Gd
LITTLE
OAK CL
333
HORNE RD
PETTS LA
GRANGE
CT
BARLEY
MOW WAY
HARVEST CT
WOOD RD
SQUIRE'S RD
YEW TREES
BURBIDGE RD
MILTON DR
ASHURST DR
BRAVINGTON CL
FAIRVIEW DR
ROSEWOOD DR
LALEHAM RD
FORD CL
WRIGHT GDNS
1 VINTER CT
2 JOHN KAYE CT
ROSEACRE CL
BUSH RD
BRIAR RD
150
TANGLYN AVE
LITTLETON LA
MANDEVILLE RD
ACACIA AVE
PRESTON RD
PENTLAND
AVE
HARRISON
WAY
113
M3
LOIS DR
BARBARA CL
VILLAGE
GATE
MARION
AVE
Pl Fld
Saxon
Prim Sch
THORNHILL
WAY
POUND END CL
JESSIMAN TERR
GREENO CRES
SHEPPERTON COURT DR
PEARMAIN CL
Sch
B376
Gravel
Pit
Littleton
Sailing Club
MAUREEN
CAMPBELL CT
SHEEPWALK
TW17
SHEPHERDS CL
BARTON CL
CLAREMONT DR
CLAREMONT
SHEPPERTON
CT
MANOR FARM AVE
GRANT CL
Pl Fld
St Nicholas
CE Prim Sch
OLD FORGE
CRES
BURCHETTS WAY
MERE RD 1
WESTBURY CL 2
SCHOOL LA
B376
M3
Riverscroft
RANGE
VILLAS
RENFREE WAY
B375
CHERTSEY RD
CHERTSEY BRIDGE RD
10
Halliford
Mere
Lake
CHURCH RD
Dumsey
Eyot
River Thames
Mead
Farm
FARM CL
RANGE WAY
Cemy
CHURCHFIELD
PL
CEMETERY LA
MANOR
HOUSE CT
Tenn
Ct
ST NICHOLAS DR
TAMESA
HO
NORMAN
HO
CHERTSEY RD
CHURCH
SQ
FERRY
SQ
PH
DESBOROUGH CL
KT16
DOCKETT
MOORINGS
DOCKETT EDDY LA
Chertsey
Meads
Dockett
Eddy
Desborough
Sailing Club
FERRY LA
REED PL
PARK RD
ABBEY RD
KT13
KT13
Ferry
Wks
Thames Path
TOWPATH
Ferry
Dockett
Point
Tenn Cts
Surrey STREET ATLAS

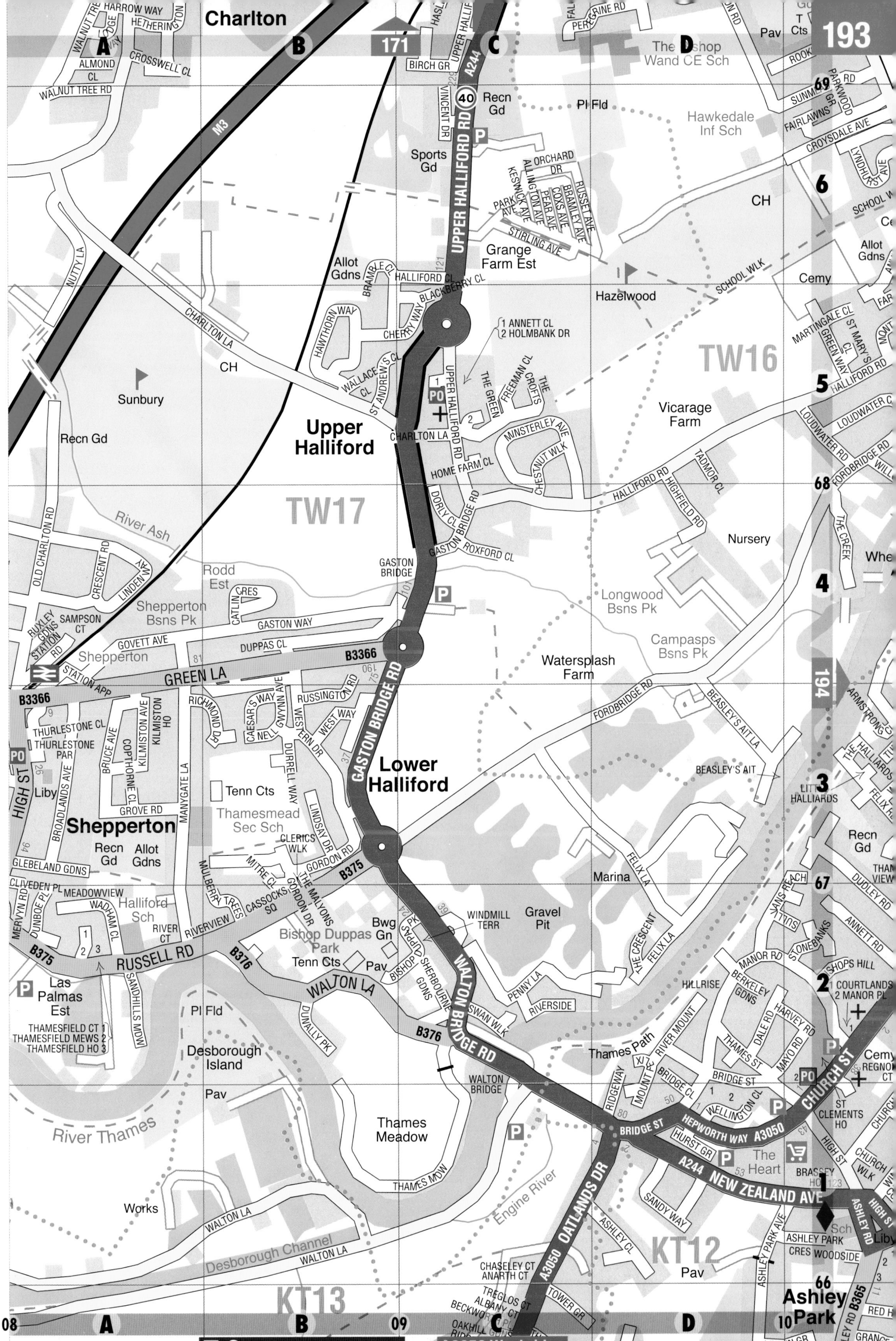

Charlton
171
A
B
C
D
M3
A244
40
HARROW WAY
HETHERINGTON
WALNUT TREE
ALMOND CL
CROSSWELL CL
WALNUT TREE RD
BIRCH GR
UPPER HALLIFORD
VINCENT DR
Recn Gd
PERGRINE RD
The Bishop Wand CE Sch
Pl Fld
Hawkedale Inf Sch
Pav
T Cts
ROOK
69
PARKWOOD
SUNMEAD
FAIRLAWNS
CROYSDALE AVE
LYNDHURST AVE
SCHOOL WLK
6
CH
Allot Gdns
Cemy
Sports Gd
UPPER HALLIFORD RD
ORCHARD DR
ALLINGTON AVE
KESWICK AVE
PARK AVE
COXS AVE
PEAR AVE
BRAMLEY AVE
RUSSET AVE
STIRLING AVE
Grange Farm Est
Allot Gdns
BRAMBLE CL
HALLIFORD CL
BLACKBERRY CL
Hazelwood
SCHOOL WLK
HAWTHORN WAY
CHERRY WAY
WALLACE'S CL
ST ANDREW'S CL
1 ANNETT CL
2 HOLMBANK DR
CHARLTON LA
CH
Sunbury
TW16
MARTINGALE CL
GREEN WAY
ST MARY'S CL
HALLIFORD RD
5
THE GREEN
FREEMAN CL
THE CROFTS
PO
Upper Halliford
Recn Gd
CHARLTON LA
MINSTERLEY AVE
Vicarage Farm
LOUDWATER RD
LOUDWATER CL
FORDBRIDGE RD
HOME FARM CL
CHESTNUT WLK
HALLIFORD RD
HIGHFIELD RD
TADMOR CL
68
TW17
DORLY CL
GASTON BRIDGE RD
River Ash
OLD CHARLTON RD
CRESCENT RD
LINDEN WAY
Nursery
THE CREEK
ROXFORD CL
GASTON BRIDGE
Rodd Est
CATLIN CRES
4
Longwood Bsns Pk
RUXLEY GDNS
SAMPSON CT
STATION RD
Shepperton Bsns Pk
GASTON WAY
GOVETT AVE
DUPPAS CL
B3366
Campasps Bsns Pk
Shepperton
STATION APP
GREEN LA
Watersplash Farm
194
B3366
RICHMOND DR
CAESAR'S WAY
GWYNN AVE
RUSSINGTON RD
FORDBRIDGE RD
BEASLEY'S AIT LA
ARMSTRONG CL
THURLESTONE CL
THURLESTONE PAR
BRUCE AVE
KILMISTON AVE
KILMISTON HO
COPTHORNE CL
NELL GWYNN AVE
WESTERN DR
WEST WAY
GASTON BRIDGE RD
PO
HIGH ST
Liby
BROADLANDS AVE
GROVE RD
MANYGATE LA
Tenn Cts
DURRELL WAY
Lower Halliford
BEASLEY'S AIT
THE HALLIARDS
3
LITTLE HALLIARDS
Shepperton
Thamesmead Sec Sch
LINDSAY DR
Recn Gd
Allot Gdns
CLERICS WLK
GORDON RD
Recn Gd
GLEBELAND GDNS
B375
MITRE CL
Marina
FELIX LA
CLIVEDEN PL
MEADOWVIEW
MULBERRY TREES
THE MALYONS
GORDON DR
CASSOCKS SQ
67
DUDLEY RD
MERVYN RD
DUNBOE PL
WADHAM CL
Halliford Sch
RIVER CT
RIVERVIEW
Bishop Duppas Park
Bwg Gn
WINDMILL TERR
Gravel Pit
THE CRESCENT
FELIX LA
SULLIANS REACH
STONEBANKS
ANNETT RD
B375
RUSSELL RD
B376
Tenn Cts
Pav
BISHOP DUPPAS PK
SHERBOURNE GDNS
WALTON BRIDGE RD
MANOR RD
BERKELEY GDNS
HILLRISE
SHOPS HILL
1 COURTLANDS
2 MANOR PL
2
Las Palmas Est
SANDHILLS MDW
WALTON LA
DUNALLY PK
PENNY LA
RIVERSIDE
SWAN WLK
HARVEY RD
DALE RD
THAMESFIELD CT
THAMESFIELD MEWS
THAMESFIELD HO
Pl Fld
Desborough Island
B376
Thames Path
RIVER MOUNT
THAMES ST
MAYO RD
Cemy
Pav
WALTON BRIDGE
RIDGEWAY
MOUNT PL
BRIDGE CL
BRIDGE ST
WELLINGTON CL
PO
CHURCH ST
ST CLEMENTS HO
River Thames
Thames Meadow
BRIDGE ST
HEPWORTH WAY
A3050
HURST GR
The Heart
BRASSEY HO
HIGH ST
CHURCH WLK
A244
NEW ZEALAND AVE
1
Works
THAMES MDW
Engine River
OATLANDS DR
SANDY WAY
ASHLEY PARK AVE
ASHLEY RD
HIGH ST
WALTON LA
Desborough Channel
WALTON LA
ASHLEY CL
KT12
ASHLEY PARK CRES
WOODSIDE
Sch
Liby
CHASELEY CT
ANARTH CT
A3050
Pav
66
Ashley Park
B365
TREGLOS CT
ALBANY CT
BECKWORTH
OAKHILL
TOWER GR
KT13
RED H
LINDEN GR
GRANGE
08
09
10

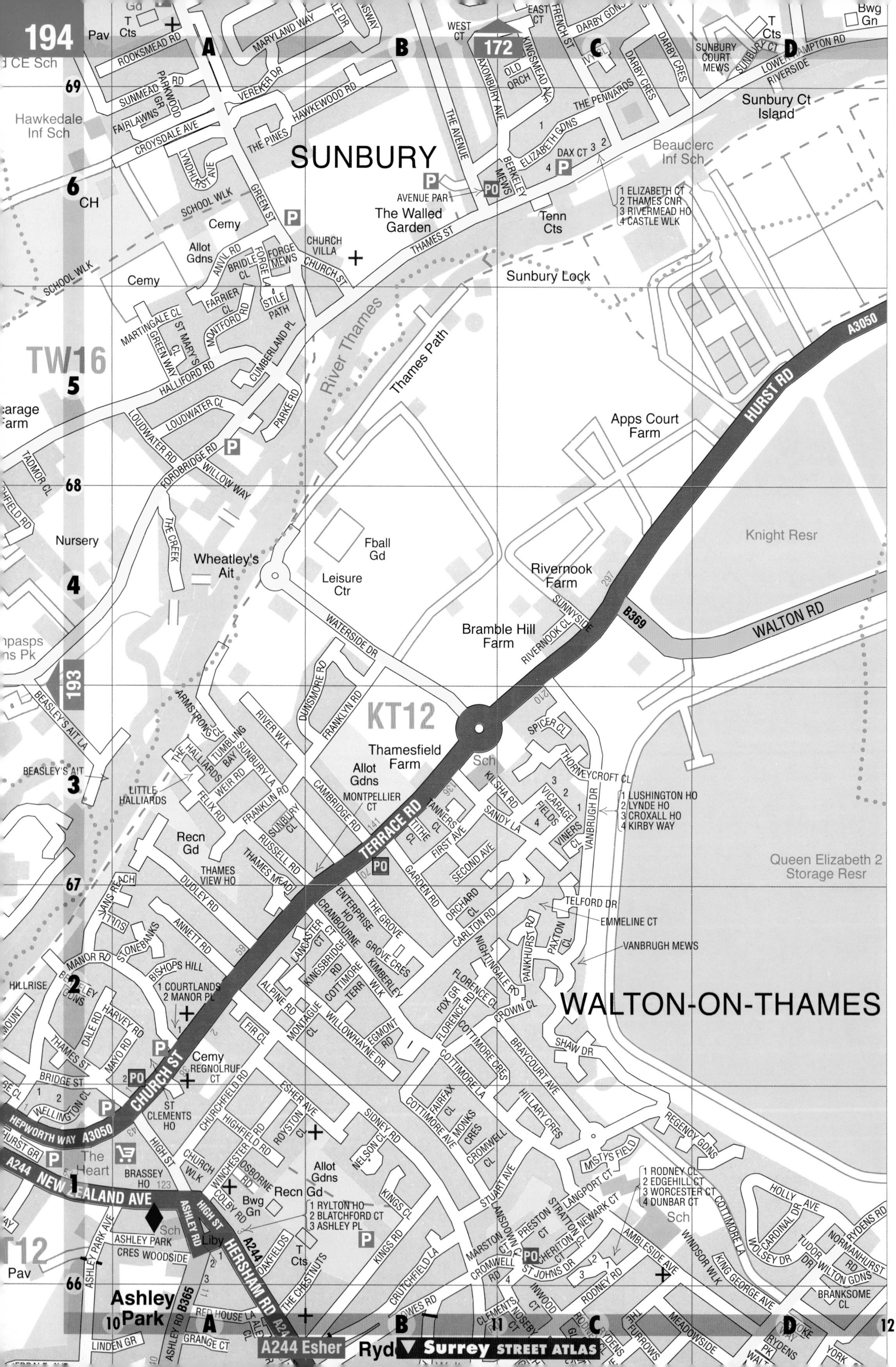
SUNBURY
WALTON-ON-THAMES
TW16
KT12
172
193
A
B
C
D
69
6
5
68
4
3
67
2
1
66
10
11
12
Pav
T Cts
CE Sch
ROOKSMEAD RD
MARYLAND WAY
WEST CT
EAST CT
FRENCH ST
DARBY GDNS
Bwg Gn
SUNBURY COURT MEWS
SUNBURY CT
LOWER HAMPTON RD
RIVERSIDE
Sunbury Ct Island
KINGSMEAD AVE
OLD ORCH
DARBY CRES
THE PENNARDS
VEREKER DR
HAWKEWOOD RD
SUNMEAD RD
PARKWOOD GR
FAIRLAWNS
Hawkedale Inf Sch
CROYSDALE AVE
THE PINES
LYNDHURST AVE
THE AVENUE
ACKONBURY AVE
BERKELEY MEWS
ELIZABETH GDNS
DAX CT
Beauclerc Inf Sch
AVENUE PAR
PO
1 ELIZABETH CT
2 THAMES CNR
3 RIVERMEAD HO
4 CASTLE WLK
CH
SCHOOL WLK
GREEN ST
Cemy
The Walled Garden
Tenn Cts
THAMES ST
Allot Gdns
ANVIL RD
BRIDLE CL
FORGE LA
FORGE MEWS
CHURCH VILLA
CHURCH ST
Sunbury Lock
FARRIER CL
STILE PATH
MARTINGALE CL
GREEN WAY
ST MARY'S CL
MONTFORD RD
CUMBERLAND PL
River Thames
Thames Path
A3050
HALLIFORD RD
Vicarage Farm
LOUDWATER CL
PARKE RD
HURST RD
Apps Court Farm
TADMOR CL
LOUDWATER RD
FORDBRIDGE RD
WILLOW WAY
ASHFIELD RD
THE CREEK
Nursery
Wheatley's Ait
Fball Gd
Leisure Ctr
Knight Resr
Rivernook Farm
SUNNYSIDE
297
B369
WALTON RD
Bramble Hill Farm
RIVERNOOK CL
Lindsay's Pk
WATERSIDE DR
DUNSMORE RD
FRANKLYN RD
BEASLEY'S AIT LA
ARMSTRONG CL
TUMBLING BAY
RIVER WLK
210
SPICER CL
THE HALLIARDS
Thamesfield Farm
Sch
BEASLEY'S AIT
SUNBURY LA
WEIR RD
Allot Gdns
KILSHA RD
THORNEYCROFT CL
LITTLE HALLIARDS
FELIX RD
FRANKLIN RD
CAMBRIDGE RD
MONTPELLIER CT
TANNERS CL
VICARAGE FIELDS
VANBRUGH DR
1 LUSHINGTON HO
2 LYNDE HO
3 CROXALL HO
4 KIRBY WAY
SUNBURY CL
TERRACE RD
TITHE CL
FIRST AVE
SANDY LA
VINERS CL
Recn Gd
RUSSELL RD
SECOND AVE
Queen Elizabeth 2 Storage Resr
THAMES VIEW HO
THAMES MEAD
GARDEN RD
VANS REACH
DUDLEY RD
ENTERPRISE HO
THE GROVE
ORCHARD CL
TELFORD DR
EMMELINE CT
SULL
CRANBOURNE CT
CARLTON RD
PANKHURST RD
PAXTON CL
ANNETT RD
STONEBANKS
LANCASTER CT
KINGSBRIDGE RD
GROVE CRES
NIGHTINGALE RD
VANBRUGH MEWS
MANOR RD
BISHOPS HILL
KIMBERLEY WLK
FLORENCE CL
HILLRISE
BERKELEY GDNS
1 COURTLANDS
2 MANOR PL
ALPINE RD
COTTIMORE TERR
FOX GR
FLORENCE RD
CROWN CL
DALE RD
HARVEY RD
FIR CL
MONTAGUE CL
WILLOWHAYNE DR
EGMONT RD
COTTIMORE CRES
BRAYCOURT AVE
SHAW DR
MOUNT
THAMES ST
MAYO RD
REGNOLRUF CT
COTTIMORE LA
BRIDGE ST
CHURCHFIELD RD
ESHER AVE
SIDNEY RD
HILLARY CRES
WELLINGTON CL
CHURCH ST
ST CLEMENTS HO
HIGHFIELD RD
ROYSTON CL
FAIRFAX CL
MONKS CRES
CROMWELL CL
REGENCY GDNS
HEPWORTH WAY
HURST GR
The Heart
HIGH ST
CHURCH WLK
WINCHESTER RD
OSBORNE RD
NELSON CL RD
COTTIMORE AVE
MISTYS FIELD
1 RODNEY CL
2 EDGEHILL CT
3 WORCESTER CT
4 DUNBAR CT
HOLLY AVE
BRASSEY HO
A244
NEW ZEALAND AVE
Allot Gdns
Recn Gd
KINGS CL
STUART AVE
LANGPORT CT
COLBY RD
Bwg Gn
1 RYLTON HO
2 BLATCHFORD CT
3 ASHLEY PL
LANSDOWN CL
STRATTON CL
NEWARK CT
COTTIMORE LA
CARDINAL DR
RYDENS RD
ASHLEY PARK AVE
Sch
ASHLEY RD
HIGH ST
Liby
ASHLEY PARK CRES
WOODSIDE
HERSHAM RD
OAKFIELDS
KINGS RD
PRESTON CT
CHERITON CT
AMBLESIDE AVE
WINDSOR WLK
WOLSEY DR
TUDOR DR
NORMANHURST RD
Pav
T Cts
THE CHESTNUTS
CRUTCHFIELD LA
MARSTON CT
CROMWELL RD
ST JOHNS DR
RODNEY RD
KING GEORGE AVE
WILTON GDNS
Ashley Park
B365
RED HOUSE LA
INWOOD CT
BRANKSOME CL
LINDEN GR
GRANGE CT
NOSEBY CT
CLEMENTS CT
HURST GR
RYDENS
MEADOWSIDE
THE FURROWS
YORK

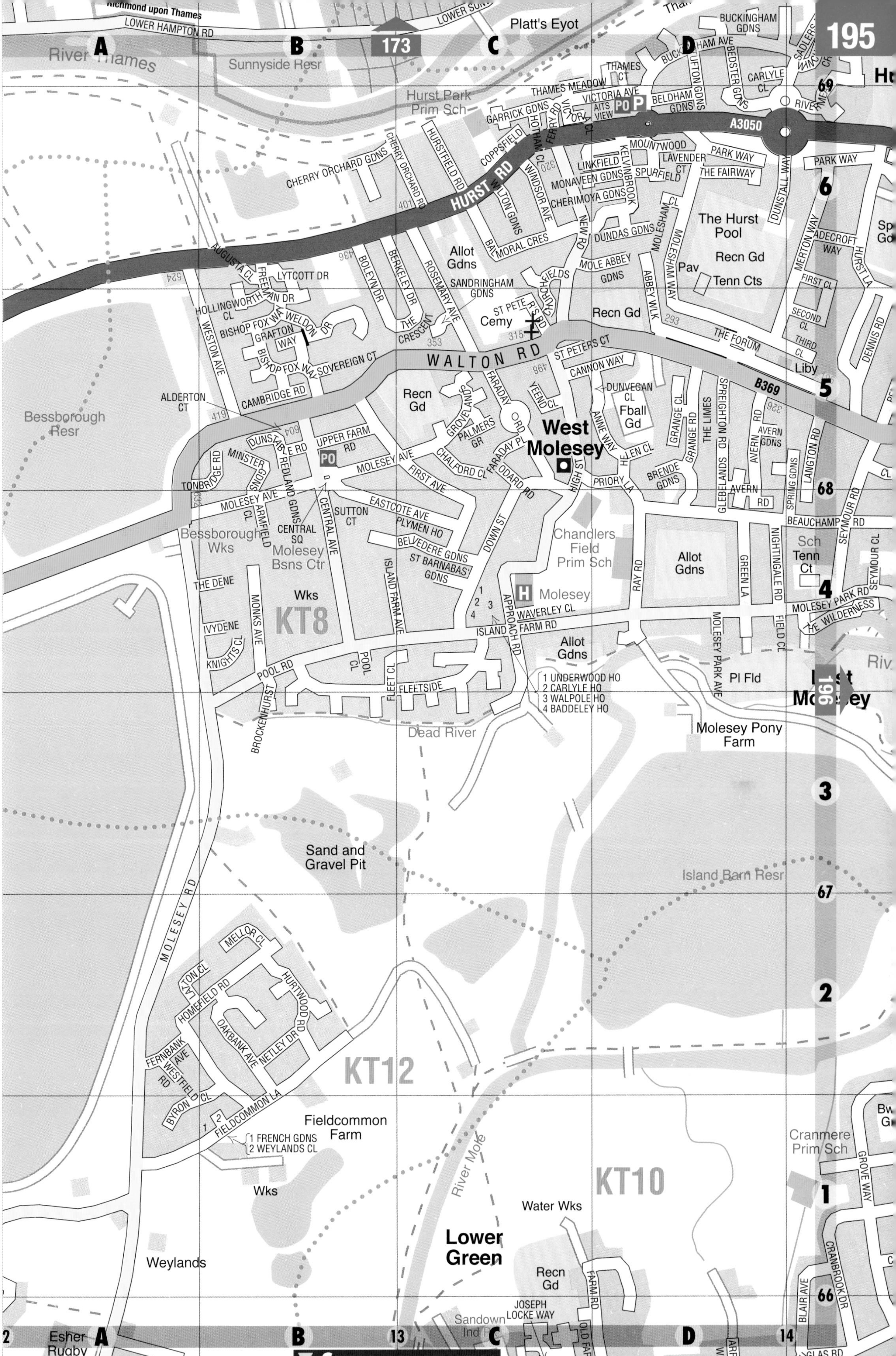

Richmond upon Thames
LOWER HAMPTON RD
173
Platt's Eyot
River Thames
Sunnyside Resr
BUCKINGHAM GDNS
THAMES CT
THAMES MEADOW
VICTORIA AVE
Hurst Park Prim Sch
GARRICK GDNS
BELDHAM GDNS
CARLYLE CL
A3050
COPPSFIELD
HURST RD
CHERRY ORCHARD GDNS
CHERRY ORCHARD RD
HURSTFIELD RD
WINDSOR AVE
LINKFIELD
MOUNTWOOD
LAVENDER CT
PARK WAY
THE FAIRWAY
SPURFIELD
MONAVEEN GDNS
CHERIMOYA GDNS
KELVINBROOK
MOLESHAM CL
The Hurst Pool
Recn Gd
Pav
Tenn Cts
DUNSTALL WAY
MERTON WAY
ADECROFT WAY
HURST LA
FIRST CL
SECOND CL
THIRD CL
DENNIS RD
WALTON GDNS
BALMORAL CRES
DUNDAS GDNS
NEW RD
MOLE ABBEY GDNS
ABBEY WLK
MOLESHAM WAY
Allot Gdns
SANDRINGHAM GDNS
BOLEYN DR
BERKELEY DR
ROSEMARY AVE
AUGUSTA CL
LYTCOTT DR
FREEMAN DR
HOLLINGWORTH CL
BISHOP FOX WAY
WELDON DR
GRAFTON WAY
WESTON AVE
THE CRESCENT
Cemy
Recn Gd
THE FORUM
Liby
B369
WALTON RD
ST PETERS CT
CANNON WAY
DUNVEGAN CL
Fball Gd
VEEND CL
FARADAY RD
SOVEREIGN CT
CAMBRIDGE RD
ALDERTON CT
Bessborough Resr
Recn Gd
GROVELANDS
PALMERS GR
West Molesey
ANNIE WAY
HELEN CL
GRANGE CL
GRANGE RD
THE LIMES
SPREIGHTON RD
AVERN RD
AVERN GDNS
LANGTON RD
UPPER FARM RD
PO
MOLESEY AVE
FIRST AVE
CHALFORD CL
FARADAY PL
ODARD RD
HIGH ST
PRIORY LA
BRENDE GDNS
GLEBELANDS RD
SPRING GDNS
68
MINSTER GDNS
TONBRIDGE RD
REDLAND GDNS
ARMFIELD CL
CENTRAL SQ
CENTRAL AVE
SUTTON CT
EASTCOTE AVE
PLYMEN HO
BELVEDERE GDNS
ST BARNABAS GDNS
DOWN ST
Chandlers Field Prim Sch
RAY RD
Allot Gdns
GREEN LA
NIGHTINGALE RD
BEAUCHAMP RD
SEYMOUR RD
Sch
Tenn Ct
SEYMOUR CL
Bessborough Wks
Molesey Bsns Ctr
THE DENE
MONKS AVE
Wks
ISLAND FARM AVE
KT8
Molesey
WAVERLEY CL
ISLAND FARM RD
APPROACH RD
MOLESEY PARK RD
THE WILDERNESS
FIELD CL
IVYDENE
KNIGHTS CL
POOL RD
POOL CL
FLEET CL
FLEETSIDE
Allot Gdns
1 UNDERWOOD HO
2 CARLYLE HO
3 WALPOLE HO
4 BADDELEY HO
MOLESEY PARK AVE
Pl Fld
196
BROCKENHURST
Dead River
Molesey Pony Farm
Sand and Gravel Pit
Island Barn Resr
67
MOLESEY RD
MELLOR CL
HURTWOOD RD
LAYTON CL
HOMEFIELD RD
OAKBANK AVE
NETLEY DR
FERNBANK AVE
WESTFIELD RD
BYRON CL
FIELDCOMMON LA
KT12
1 FRENCH GDNS
2 WEYLANDS CL
Fieldcommon Farm
River Mole
KT10
Cranmere Prim Sch
GROVE WAY
Wks
Water Wks
Lower Green
Weylands
Recn Gd
FARM RD
JOSEPH LOCKE WAY
Sandown Ind Est
OLD FARM CL
ARRAN WAY
CRANBROOK DR
BLAIR AVE
66
DOUGLAS RD
WOODEND
Esher Rugby Fball Gd
North Weylands
A
B
C
D
12
13
14
6
5
4
3
2
1

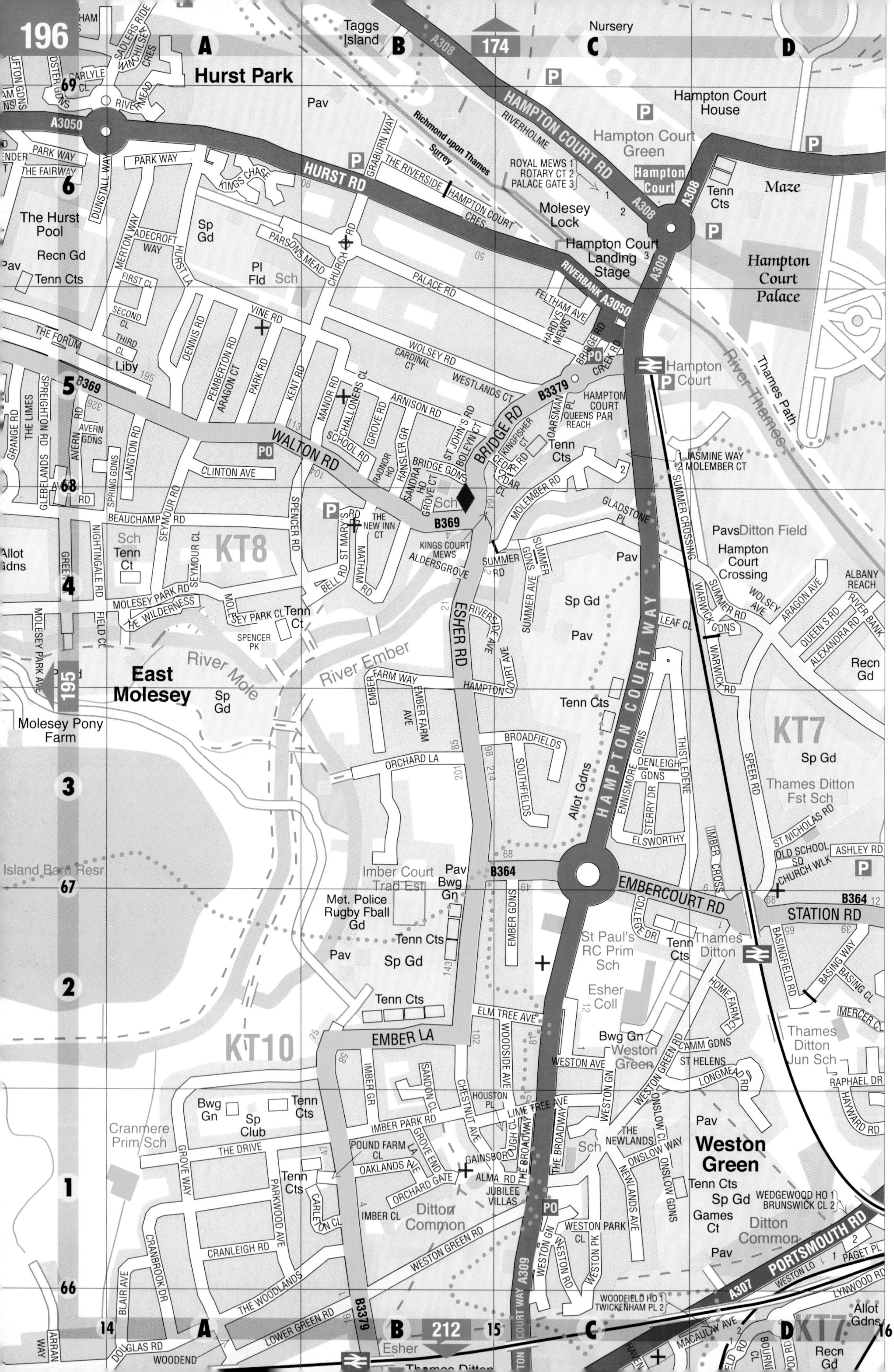
Hurst Park
Taggs Island
Nursery
174
Hampton Court House
Hampton Court Green
Hampton Court
Maze
Tenn Cts
Molesey Lock
Hampton Court Landing Stage
Hampton Court Palace
River Thames
Thames Path
HAMPTON COURT RD
HURST RD
RIVERBANK A3050
A3050
A308
A309
B369
B3379
B364
WALTON RD
BRIDGE RD
ESHER RD
HAMPTON COURT WAY
EMBERCOURT RD
STATION RD
PORTSMOUTH RD
A307
The Hurst Pool
Recn Gd
Tenn Cts
Sp Gd
Pl Fld
Sch
Liby
KT8
KT7
KT10
East Molesey
River Mole
River Ember
Molesey Pony Farm
Island Barn Resr
195
Imber Court Trad Est
Met. Police Rugby Fball Gd
Ditton Field
Hampton Court Crossing
Allot Gdns
Thames Ditton Fst Sch
St Paul's RC Prim Sch
Esher Coll
Thames Ditton
Thames Ditton Jun Sch
Weston Green
Ditton Common
Cranmere Prim Sch
Sp Club
Games Ct
Esher
212
Recn Gd
A B C D
1 2 3 4 5 6
14 15 16
66 67 68 69

175
213
198
A
B
C
D
KINGSTON UPON THAMES
SURBITON
Hampton Court Park
Thames Ditton
Long Ditton
Seething Wells
Southborough
Giggs Hill Green
KT1
KT6
KT7
KT8
The Royal Paddocks
Bushy Lodge
Hampton Wick Pond
Old Icehouse
Stud House
The Wilderness
Parkfield
Home Park
The Pavilion
Pavilion Terrace
Thames Ditton Island
Boyle Farm Island
Thames Path
River Thames
Barge Walk
Raven's Ait
Ferry P
CH
Richmond upon Thames
Kingston upon Thames
HAMPTON COURT RD
A308
A307
A243
A240
B3365
B3370
B364
PORTSMOUTH RD
BRIGHTON RD
VICTORIA RD
HIGH ST
PENRHYN RD
KINGSTON HALL RD
SURBITON RD
UPPER BRIGHTON RD
CLAREMONT RD
WATTS RD
THE HERMITAGE 1
TYNAMARA 2
MILESTONE HO 3
BROOKLANDS CT 4
PENRHYN GDNS 5
HOLYHEAD CT 6
ARUNDALE 7
MARLOWE HO 8
GROVELANDS 9
RAVENSIDE 1
THAMES HAVEN 2
EMBASSY CT 3
RAVENSVIEW CT 4
ST LEONARD'S SQ 5
SPRING COTTS 6
CHATSWORTH HO 7
1 THAMES SIDE
2 CITY WHARF HO
3 CLAREMONT TERR
4 SOUTHBANK
5 CRITERION BLDGS
SYCAMORE CT 3
CHESTNUT CT 4
BEECH CT 5
CROWN ARC 4
APPLE MKT 5
BATH PAS 6
TAGGS HO 7
RAVENS HO 8
STEVENS HO 9
GARRICKS HO 10
County Hall
Kingston Univ
Kingston House Est
Seething Wells Halls of Residence
St Mary's CE Prim Sch
Long Ditton Inf Sch
Recn Gd
Tenn Cts
Sports Gd
Allot Gdns
Cemy
Manor House
Hinchley Wood
RIVERSIDE CL
ANGLESEA RD
PALACE RD
BELGRAVIA MEWS
UXBRIDGE RD
WESTFIELD CT
CATHERINE RD
ANGLERS REACH
GROVE RD
CADOGAN RD
ST LEONARD'S RD
CLEAVELAND RD
WESTFIELD RD
THE MALL
ST ANDREW'S SQ
ST JAMES RD
MAPLE RD
THE CRESCENT
ADELAIDE RD
ST MARK'S
COTTAGE GR
ELECTRIC PAR
VICTORIA AVE
LOCKESLEY SQ
LOVELACE GDNS
LOVELACE RD
ALBANY CT
TERRAPINS
MARLBOROUGH GDNS
LOWER SAND HILLS
BEECHWOOD CL
ST CHADS CL
FLEECE RD
POUND CL
WINDMILL LA
EFFINGHAM RD
CHADWICK PL
SAVERY DR
JENNINGS CL
BALACLAVA RD
ENDSLEIGH GDNS
PROSPECT RD
SIMPSON WAY
WATER PL
ALSTON CL
HOWARD ST
HOUSTON RD
VAUGHAN RD
WINTERS RD
CHOLMLEY RD
FERRY RD
KING'S DR
QUEEN'S DR
LYNTON RD
RIVER AVE
BURTENSHAW RD
FITZGERALD RD
BOYLE FARM RD
ST LEONARD'S RD
PORTSMOUTH AVE
DITTON CL
RYTHE CT
STAGS CT
ASHDOWN PL
HIGH ST
SUMMER RD
BURTON CT
CHURCH LA
RIVERSDALE RD
THORKHILL RD
THORKHILL GDNS
WESTVILLE RD
SOUTHVILLE RD
RUSHETT RD
RUSHETT CL
EWELL RD
ORCHARD CL
GIGGS HILL GDNS
QUINTON AVE
OAKDENE AVE
ANGEL RD
DITTON LAWN
GLOUCESTER CL
SAVILLE CL
ATWELL PL
HOLLY COTTS
CLAYGATE LA
BROOKLANDS RD
GREENWOOD CL
GREENWOOD RD
MANORDENE CL
MANOR RD N
DENE CL
ORCHARD AVE
MAYFIELD CL
BANKSIDE DR
ST ANDREWS CL
SCOTT FARM CL
SUGDEN RD
CLAYTON RD
BETTS WAY
RECTORY LA
RECTORY CL
KING'S RD
DITTON HILL RD
CHALCOTT GDNS
CHURCH RD
HIGHFIELD CL
SAXONBURY GDNS
ST MARY'S RD
DEMPSTER CL
SHARON CL
LISSANT CL
GENESIS HO
DITTON GRANGE DR
DITTON GRANGE CL
DITTON HILL
SAFFRON WAY
MANDEVILLE DR
DEVONSHIRE DR
OAKS WAY
LANGLEY AVE
REDWOOD WLK
DITTON RD
ASHCOMBE AVE
SOUTHBOROUGH CL
SOUTHBOROUGH RD
COPSE GLADE
SYLVAN GDNS
WOODLANDS RD
WOODVILLE GDNS
HAILSHAM CL
CORKRAN RD
CROYLANDS DR
THE DRIVE
ARLINGTON RD
GLENBUCK RD
SAXON CL
WALPOLE RD
OAK HILL GR
THE CLOSE
KIRKLEAS RD
DUNTON CL
MALCOLM DR
THE LANE
SHREWSBURY CL
WARWICK CL
SHERWOOD
WENTWORTH CL
Surbiton

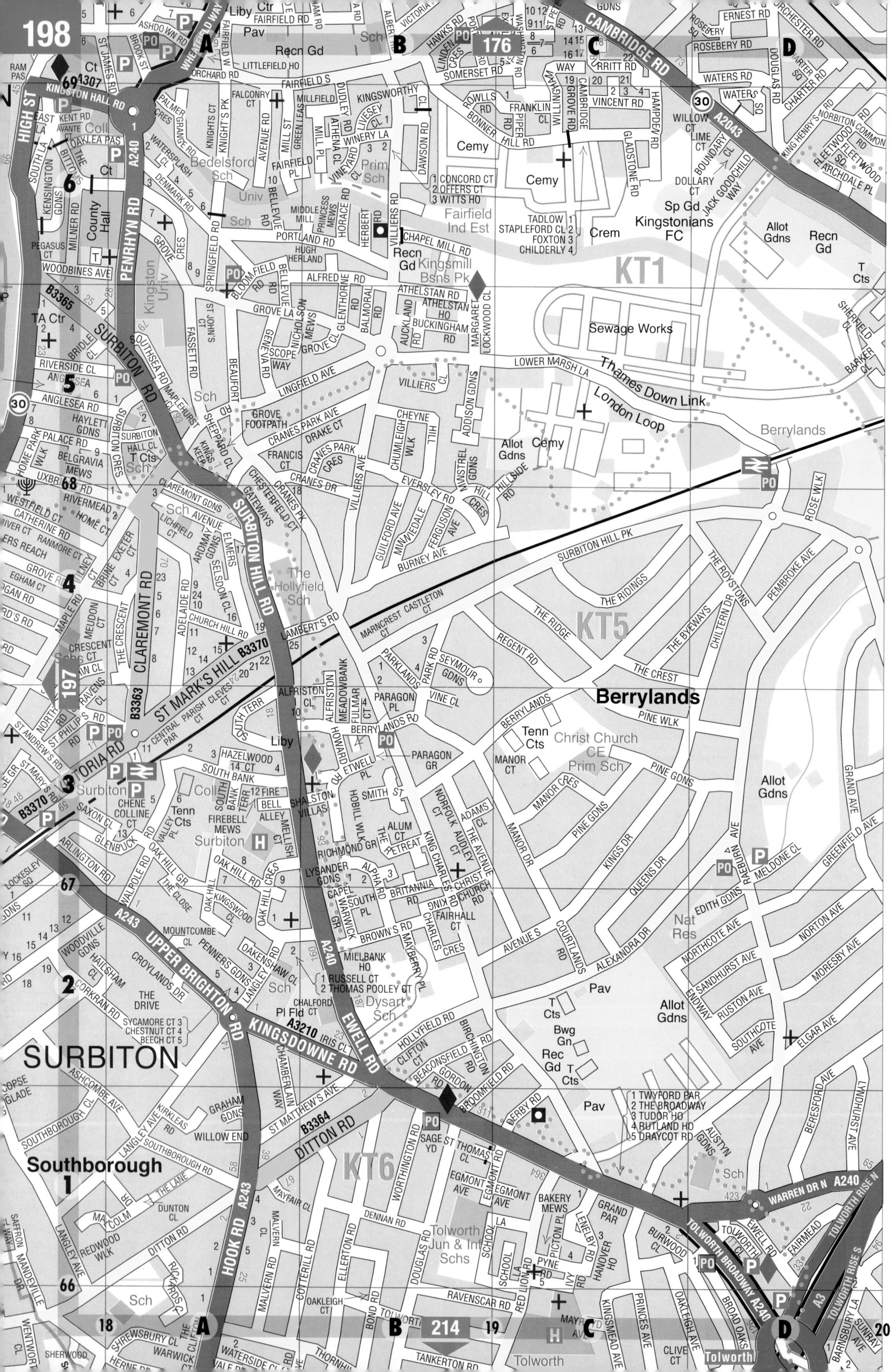

A
B
C
D
176
214
197
18
19
20
1
2
3
4
5
6
66
67
68
69
KT1
KT5
KT6
SURBITON
Southborough
Berrylands
Surbiton
Tolworth
CAMBRIDGE RD
A2043
KINGSTON HALL RD
HIGH ST
A240
PENRHYN RD
SURBITON RD
B3365
SURBITON HILL RD
ST MARK'S HILL
B3370
B3363
CLAREMONT RD
VICTORIA RD
UPPER BRIGHTON RD
A243
KINGSDOWNE RD
A3210
EWELL RD
HOOK RD
DITTON RD
B3364
TOLWORTH BROADWAY
WARREN DR N
TOLWORTH RISE N
TOLWORTH RISE S
A3
LOWER MARSH LA
Thames Down Link
London Loop
SURBITON HILL PK
Sewage Works
Sp Gd
Kingstonians FC
Crem
Cemy
Fairfield Ind Est
Kingsmill Bsns Pk
Recn Gd
Allot Gdns
Bedelsford Sch
Univ
Kingston Univ
County Hall
Coll
TA Ctr
The Hollyfield Sch
Christ Church CE Prim Sch
Tenn Cts
Nat Res
Pav
Surbiton
Dysart Sch
Tolworth Jun & Inf Schs
Liby
Sch
Pl Fld
Bwg Gn
Rec Gd
1 CONCORD CT
2 OFFERS CT
3 WITTS HO
TADLOW 1
STAPLEFORD CL 2
FOXTON 3
CHILDERLY 4
1 RUSSELL CT
2 THOMAS POOLEY CT
SYCAMORE CT 3
CHESTNUT CT 4
BEECH CT 5
1 TWYFORD PAR
2 THE BROADWAY
3 TUDOR HO
4 RUTLAND HO
5 DRAYCOT RD
FAIRFIELD RD
FAIRFIELD S
FAIRFIELD PL
PORTLAND RD
CHAPEL MILL RD
ALFRED RD
ATHELSTAN RD
GROVE LA
LINGFIELD AVE
CRANES PARK AVE
CRANES DR
VILLIERS AVE
EVERSLEY RD
BURNEY AVE
GUILFORD AVE
THE RIDGE
THE RIDINGS
REGENT RD
THE CREST
THE ROYSTONS
PEMBROKE AVE
CHILTERN DR
THE BYEWAYS
PINE WALK
PINE GDNS
MANOR DR
KINGS DR
QUEENS DR
ALEXANDRA DR
COURTLANDS RD
AVENUE S
RAEBURN AVE
GREENFIELD AVE
NORTHCOTE AVE
SANDHURST AVE
RUSTON AVE
SOUTHCOTE AVE
ELGAR AVE
MORESBY AVE
NORTON AVE
EDITH GDNS
BERESFORD AVE
LYNDHURST AVE
AUSTYN GDNS
DERBY RD
BROOMFIELD RD
HOLLYFIELD RD
BIRCHINGTON RD
ST MATTHEW'S AVE
WORTHINGTON RD
DOUGLAS RD
ELLERTON RD
COTTERILL RD
MALVERN RD
RAVENSCAR RD
TOLWORTH RD
KINGSMEAD AVE
PRINCES AVE
OAKLEIGH AVE
BROAD OAKS
SOUTHBOROUGH RD
ASHCOMBE AVE
LANGLEY AVE
CROYLANDS DR
HAILSHAM CL
OAK HILL RD
SOUTH BANK
BERRYLANDS RD
SURBITON CRES
ANGLESEA RD
UXBRIDGE RD
PALACE RD
RIVERSIDE CL
MAPLE RD
CRESCENT
THE CRESCENT
ADELAIDE RD
CHURCH HILL RD
LAMBERT'S RD
ROSE WLK
GRAND AVE

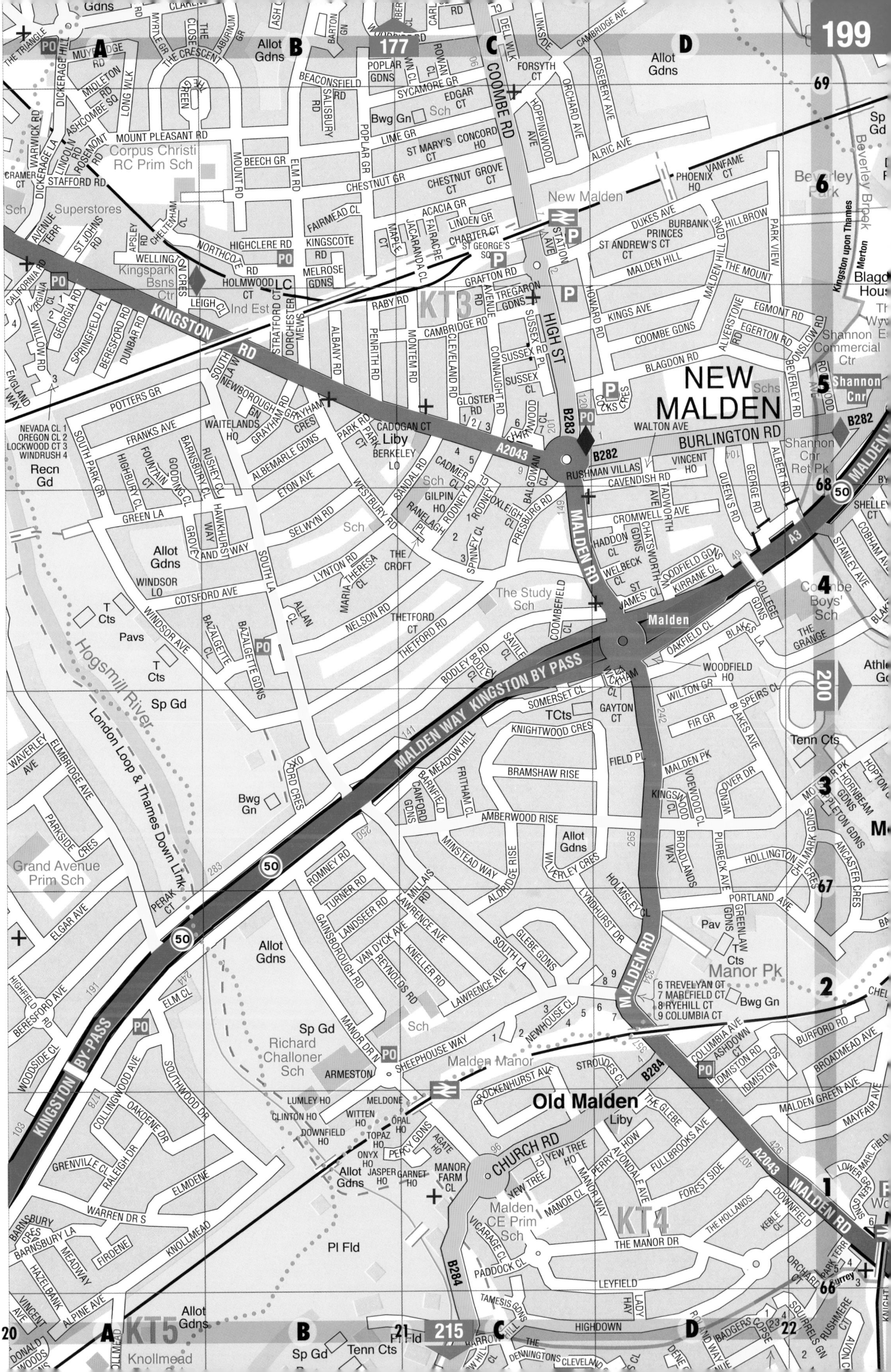

177
215
200
A
B
C
D
NEW MALDEN
Old Malden
Malden Manor
New Malden
KT3
KT4
KT5
KINGSTON RD
A2043
KINGSTON BY PASS
MALDEN WAY
KINGSTON BY-PASS
COOMBE RD
HIGH ST
B283
B282
BURLINGTON RD
MALDEN RD
B284
CHURCH RD
A3
Malden
Hogsmill River
London Loop & Thames Down Link
Corpus Christi RC Prim Sch
Grand Avenue Prim Sch
Richard Challoner Sch
Malden CE Prim Sch
The Study Sch
Coombe Boys' Sch
Kingspark Bsns Ctr
Shannon Commercial Ctr
Shannon Cnr Ret Pk
Beverley Park
Manor Pk
Recn Gd
Allot Gdns
Sp Gd
Pl Fld
Liby
Knollmead
Kingston upon Thames
Merton
NEVADA CL 1
OREGON CL 2
LOCKWOOD CT 3
WINDRUSH 4
6 TREVELYAN CT
7 MARLFIELD CT
8 RYEHILL CT
9 COLUMBIA CT

178
BUSHEY RD
B286
MERTON MANS
Allot Gdns
Bushey Mead
Tenn Cts
Sports Ctr
Pl Fld
SW20
Fball Gd
Cannon Hill Common
Allot Gdns
Cannon Hill
1 PERTH CL
2 HUNTLEY WAY
Tenn Cts
Bwg Gn
GRAYSWOOD GDNS
FIRSTWAY
BEVERLEY WAY KINGSTON BY-PASS
WEST BARNES LA
STOURHEAD GDNS
POLESDEN GDNS
SAVILL GDNS
HIDCOTE GDNS
BODNANT GDNS
Prim Sch
Superstore
Sp Gd
Drv Rng
Beverley Park
Beverley Brook
VANFAME CT
PHOENIX HO
HILLBROW
PARK VIEW
THE MOUNT
MALDEN HILL GDNS
Kingston upon Thames
Merton
Blagdon House
The Wyvern Est
Shannon Commercial Ctr
EGMONT RD
EGERTON RD
ALVERSTONE RD
ONSLOW RD
BEVERLEY RD
ROOKWOOD AVE
NEW MALDEN
Schs
Shannon Cnr
BURLINGTON RD
B282
Shannon Cnr Ret Pk
MALDEN WAY
A3
A298
B282
Sch
Superstore
BUSHEY CT
T Cts
Raynes Park
Sp Gd
1 PETWORTH GDNS
2 NYMANS GDNS
3 TRAFALGAR CT
4 MALDEN CT
FAIRWAY
RECTORY CL
LINDEN GATE
CHURCH WLK
MICHAELMAS CL
COPPICE CL
B279
RAYNESFIELD
BLENHEIM RD
BLENHEIM CL
CANNON CL
BERRYLANDS
PADDOCK CT
HEATH DR
LINKWAY
BROOK CL
BARNSCROFT
WESTWAY CL
Sp Gd
Tenn Cts
ORCHARD CL
ELM CL
GRAND DR
GREENWAY
MEADWAY
MEADOW CL
WOODLANDS
ELM WLK
PARKWAY
CROSSWAY
OAKWAY
SOUTHWAY
WESTWAY
LC
PO
GRESHAM HO
ESTELLA AVE
DOUGLAS AVE
ADELA AVE
SEAFORTH AVE
KT3
CLAREMONT AVE
CAVENDISH AVE
BELMONT AVE
BARNARD GDNS
ERROL GDNS
BYFIELD CT
SHELLEY CT
CONSFIELD AVE
BYRON AVE
COBHAM AVE
STANLEY AVE
BLAKES TERR
BARNES END
WEST BARNES LA
ALBERT RD
GEORGE RD
QUEEN'S RD
KINGSWAY
MEADOWSWEET CL
PHYLLIS AVE
TENNYSON AVE
Motspur Park
Liby
STATION RD
ARTHUR RD
MARINA AVE
PO
West Barnes
Pav
Tenn Cts
Pl Fld
Pav
THORNTON CT
CANNON HILL LA
QUEEN MARY AVE
GLENTHORPE RD
CAMBORNE RD
EDINBURGH CT
Allot Gdns
Coombe Boys' Sch
THE GRANGE
COLLEGE GDNS
BLAKES LA
Athletic Gd
LC
Sp Gd
St John Fisher RC Prim Sch
Allot Gdns
DERWENT RD
CONISTON CL
BUTTERMERE CL
Pav
Bwg Gn
Tenn Cts
Pl Fld
Crem
Morden Cemy
SM4
TUDOR DR
B279
CRANMER CL
ARAGON RD
Tenn Cts
Tenn Cts
Pav
Sp Gd
MOTSPUR PK
HORNBEAM GDNS
APPLETON GDNS
HOPTON GDNS
CHILMARK GDNS
ANCASTER CRES
HOLLINGTON CRES
Motspur Park
PURBECK AVE
PORTLAND AVE
BARGATE CL
FIR GR
WENSLEYDALE DR
Allot Gdns
Kingston upon Thames
LOWER MORDEN LA
WYDELL CL
ALLGOOD CL
CARLINGFORD RD
ROSEBERY CL
ESSEX CL
GARTH CL
Aragon Prim Sch
KINGSHILL AVE
HUGHENDEN RD
RISBOROUGH DR
Green Lane Prim Sch
Allot Gdns
GREEN LA
Merton & Sutton Joint Cemy
BEAVER CL
Pyl Brook
LYNMOUTH AVE
KINGSBRIDGE RD
SEYMOUR AVE
Pav
GREENLAW GDNS
T Cts
Manor Pk
Bwg Gn
CHELSEA CL
PRIMROSE CT
LANCASTER CL
LEWISTON CL
CANTERBURY HALL
AMENITY WAY
Beverley Trad Est
CLEVELAND
Midas Metro Ctr
The Garth Road Ind Ctr
GARTH RD
COLUMBIA AVE
ASHDOWN CT
IDMISTON RD
IDMISTON SQ
BURFORD RD
BROADMEAD AVE
MALDEN GREEN AVE
MAYFAIR AVE
PEMBURY AVE
CAVERLEIGH WAY
PORTLAND CL
SHERBROOKE WAY
BEAUMONT DR
SUTHERLAND GDNS
LINCOLN RD
Merton
Sutton
CONRAD DR
1 HANDSIDE CL
2 STANTON CL
SALCOMBE DR
DUNSTER AVE
A2043
MALDEN RD
DOWNFIELD
KEBLE CL
THE HOLLANDS
LOWER GREEN GDNS
MARLFIELD CL
T Cts
Bwg Gn
P
Worcester Park
Sp Gd
PO
GREEN LA
HAZELMERE GDNS
LONGFELLOW RD
CALDBECK AVE
WASHINGTON RD
BROWNING AVE
KT4
Recn Gd
Allot Gdns
BUCKLAND WAY
MERRILANDS RD
DELCOMBE AVE
AMESBURY CL
BISLEY CL
BOSCOMBE RD
CHARMINSTER RD
INVERNESS RD
ROSE END
SOUTHWOOD CL
CARTERS CL
CRESTON WAY
TRAFALGAR AVE
St Anthony's
H
DORCHESTER RD
Sch
WIMBORNE CL
ORCHARD CT
PARK TERR
Surrey
ROLAND WAY
BADGERS COPSE
SQUIRRELS GN
RUSHMERE CT
AVON CL
CENTRAL RD
A2043
Liby
BRINKLEY RD
DALEWOOD
ST PHILIP'S
216
BRECON CL
COTSWOLD WAY
MENDIP CL
CHILTERN CL
HAMBLETON CL
ANDREWS CL
CANTERBURY CL
CLARKS
WINCHESTER MEWS
St Cecilia's RC Prim Sch
A B C D
22 23 24
66 67 68 69
1 2 3 4 5 6
199
50

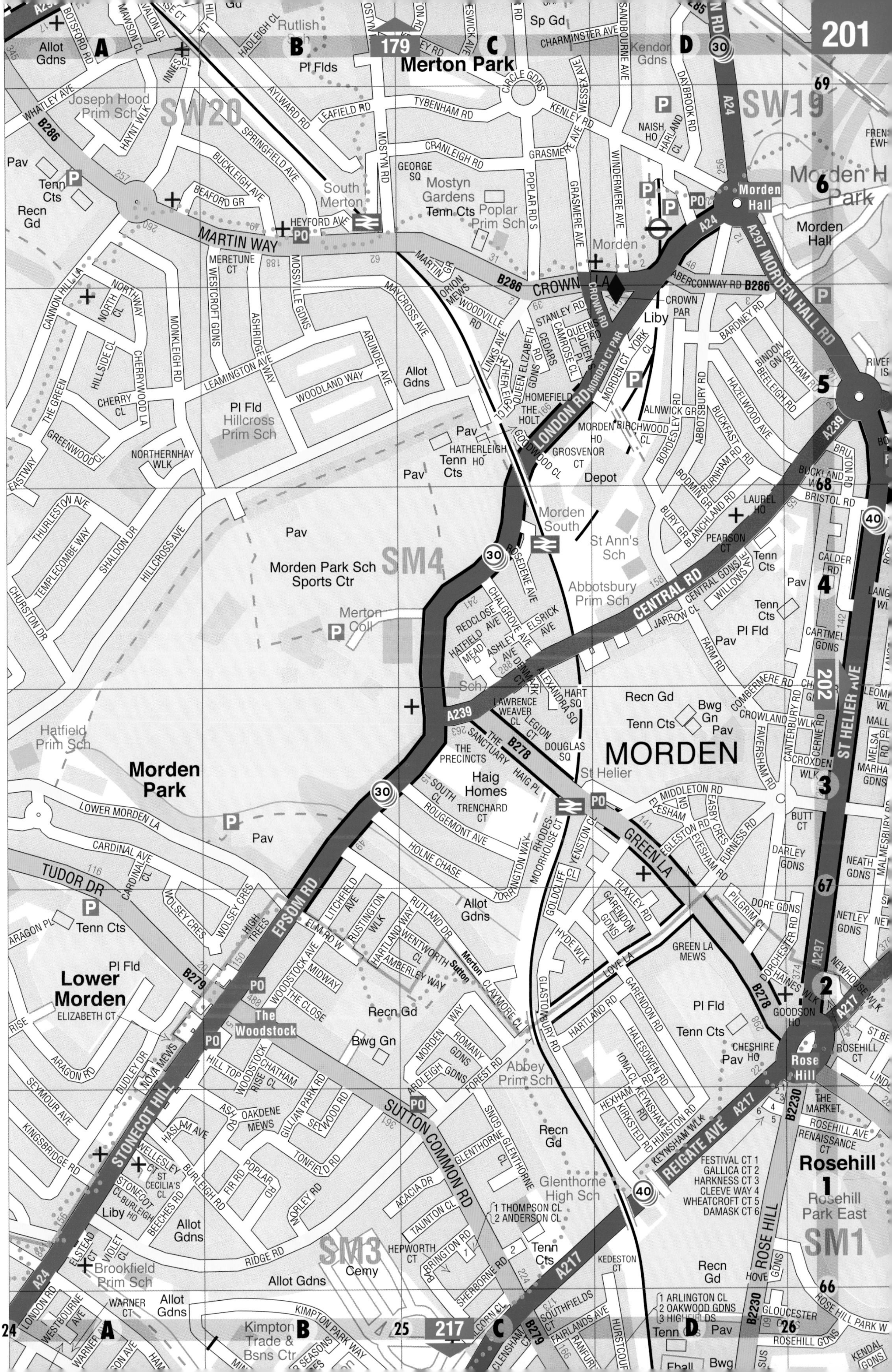
A
B
C
D
179
Merton Park
SW20
SW19
SM4
SM3
SM1
Joseph Hood Prim Sch
Rutlish Sch
Pl Flds
Kendor Gdns
Allot Gdns
BOTSFORD RD
WHATLEY AVE
B286
MARTIN WAY
South Merton
HEYFORD AVE
AYLWARD RD
LEAFIELD RD
MOSTYN RD
TYBENHAM RD
CRANLEIGH RD
GEORGE SQ
Mostyn Gardens
Tenn Cts
Poplar Prim Sch
POPLAR RD S
GRASMERE AVE
WINDERMERE AVE
CIRCLE GDNS
KENLEY RD
WESSEX AVE
SANDBOURNE AVE
CHARMINSTER AVE
DAYBROOK RD
NAISH HO
HARLAND CL
Morden Hall
Morden Hall Park
MORDEN HALL RD
A297
A24
Morden
CROWN LA
CROWN RD
ABERCONWAY RD
CROWN PAR
Liby
BARDNEY RD
BINDON GN
BAYHAM RD
BEELEIGH RD
HAZELWOOD AVE
BUCKFAST RD
ABBOTSBURY RD
ALNWICK GR
BIRCHWOOD CL
MORDEN HO
BORDESLEY RD
BODMIN GR
BURNHAM RD
BLANCHLAND RD
BURY GR
LAUREL HO
PEARSON CT
BUCKLAND WLK
BRISTOL RD
CALDER RD
LONDON RD
MORDEN CT PAR
YORK CL
QUEEN ELIZABETH GDNS
STANLEY RD
CAMROSE CL
QUEENS PL
CEDARS RD
HOMEFIELD
THE HOLT
GOODWOOD CL
GROSVENOR CT
Depot
Morden South
St Ann's Sch
Abbotsbury Prim Sch
CENTRAL RD
CENTRAL GDNS
WILLOWS AVE
JARROW CL
FARM RD
Pl Fld
Pav
CARTMEL GDNS
202
ST HELIER AVE
COMBERMERE RD
CROWLAND RD
FAVERSHAM RD
CANTERBURY RD
CERNE RD
CROXDEN WLK
MIDDLETON RD
EVESHAM GN
EASBY CRES
EGLESTON RD
EVESHAM RD
FURNESS RD
BUTT CT
DARLEY GDNS
DORE GDNS
PILGRIM CL
DORCHESTER RD
HAINES WLK
GOODSON HO
NEWHOUSE WLK
A217
Rose Hill
ROSEHILL CT
THE MARKET
ROSEHILL AVE
RENAISSANCE CT
Rosehill
Rosehill Park East
FESTIVAL CT 1
GALLICA CT 2
HARKNESS CT 3
CLEEVE WAY 4
WHEATCROFT CT 5
DAMASK CT 6
ROSE HILL
B2230
REIGATE AVE
KEYNSHAM WLK
HUNSTON RD
KIRKSTED RD
HEXHAM RD
IONA CL
HALESOWEN RD
GARENDON RD
HARTLAND RD
GLASTONBURY RD
CHESHIRE HO
Pl Fld
Tenn Cts
MORDEN
St Helier
GREEN LA
GREEN LA MEWS
LOVE LA
FLAXLEY RD
GARENDON GDNS
HYDE WLK
GOLDCLIFF CL
YENSTON CL
MOORHOUSE CT
RHODES
TORRINGTON WAY
Recn Gd
Bwg Gn
HART SQ
DOUGLAS SQ
LEGION CT
LAWRENCE WEAVER CL
ALEXANDRA SQ
B278
HAIG PL
THE SANCTUARY
THE PRECINCTS
Haig Homes
TRENCHARD CT
SOUTH CL
ROUGEMONT AVE
HOLNE CHASE
A239
DENMARK CT
ASHLEY AVE
HATFIELD MEAD
REDCLOSE AVE
CHALGROVE AVE
ELSRICK AVE
ROSEDENE AVE
Sch
Merton Coll
Morden Park Sch Sports Ctr
Hillcross Prim Sch
HATHERLEIGH HO
WOODLAND WAY
ARUNDEL AVE
LEAMINGTON AVE
MAYCROSS AVE
ORION MEWS
WOODVILLE RD
LINKS AVE
MOSSVILLE GDNS
ASHRIDGE WAY
WESTCROFT GDNS
MERETUNE CT
NORTHWAY
NORTH CL
CANNON HILL LA
HILLSIDE CL
CHERRY CL
CHERRYWOOD LA
MONKLEIGH RD
THE GREEN
GREENWOOD CL
NORTHERNHAY WLK
EASTWAY
THURLESTON AVE
TEMPLECOMBE WAY
SHALDON DR
HILLCROSS AVE
CHURSTON DR
Hatfield Prim Sch
Morden Park
LOWER MORDEN LA
CARDINAL AVE
CARDINAL CL
TUDOR DR
WOLSEY CRES
HIGH TREES
EPSOM RD
ARAGON PL
Lower Morden
ELIZABETH CT
B279
ARAGON RD
DUDLEY DR
NOVA MEWS
STONECOT HILL
SEYMOUR AVE
KINGSBRIDGE RD
WELLESLEY CT
ST CECILIA'S CL
STONECOT CL
BURLEIGH HO
Liby
HASLAM AVE
BURLEIGH RD
BEECHES RD
Brookfield Prim Sch
ELSTEAD CT
VIOLET CL
LONDON RD
WESTBOURNE AVE
WARNER CT
The Woodstock
WOODSTOCK AVE
MIDWAY
THE CLOSE
ELM RD W
LITCHFIELD AVE
RUSTINGTON WLK
RUTLAND DR
HARTLAND WAY
WENTWORTH CL
AMBERLEY WAY
Merton
Sutton
CLAYMORE CL
MORDEN WAY
ROMANY GDNS
ARDLEIGH GDNS
FOREST RD
Abbey Prim Sch
HILL TOP
WOODSTOCK RISE
CHATHAM CL
OAKDENE MEWS
ASH RD
GILLIAN PARK RD
SELWOOD RD
TONFIELD RD
POPLAR RD
FIR RD
MORLEY RD
SUTTON COMMON RD
GLENTHORNE CL
GLENTHORNE GDNS
Glenthorne High Sch
1 THOMPSON CL
2 ANDERSON CL
ACACIA DR
TAUNTON CL
HEPWORTH CT
BRINGTON RD
SHERBORNE RD
RIDGE RD
Cemy
Allot Gdns
KEDESTON CT
1 ARLINGTON CL
2 OAKWOOD GDNS
3 HIGHFIELDS
HOVE GDNS
GLOUCESTER RD
ROSE HILL PARK W
ROSEHILL GDNS
SOUTHFIELDS CT
FAIRLANDS AVE
HURSTCOURT
Kimpton Trade & Bsns Ctr
KIMPTON PARK WAY
217
24
25
26
66
67
68
69
1
2
3
4
5
6

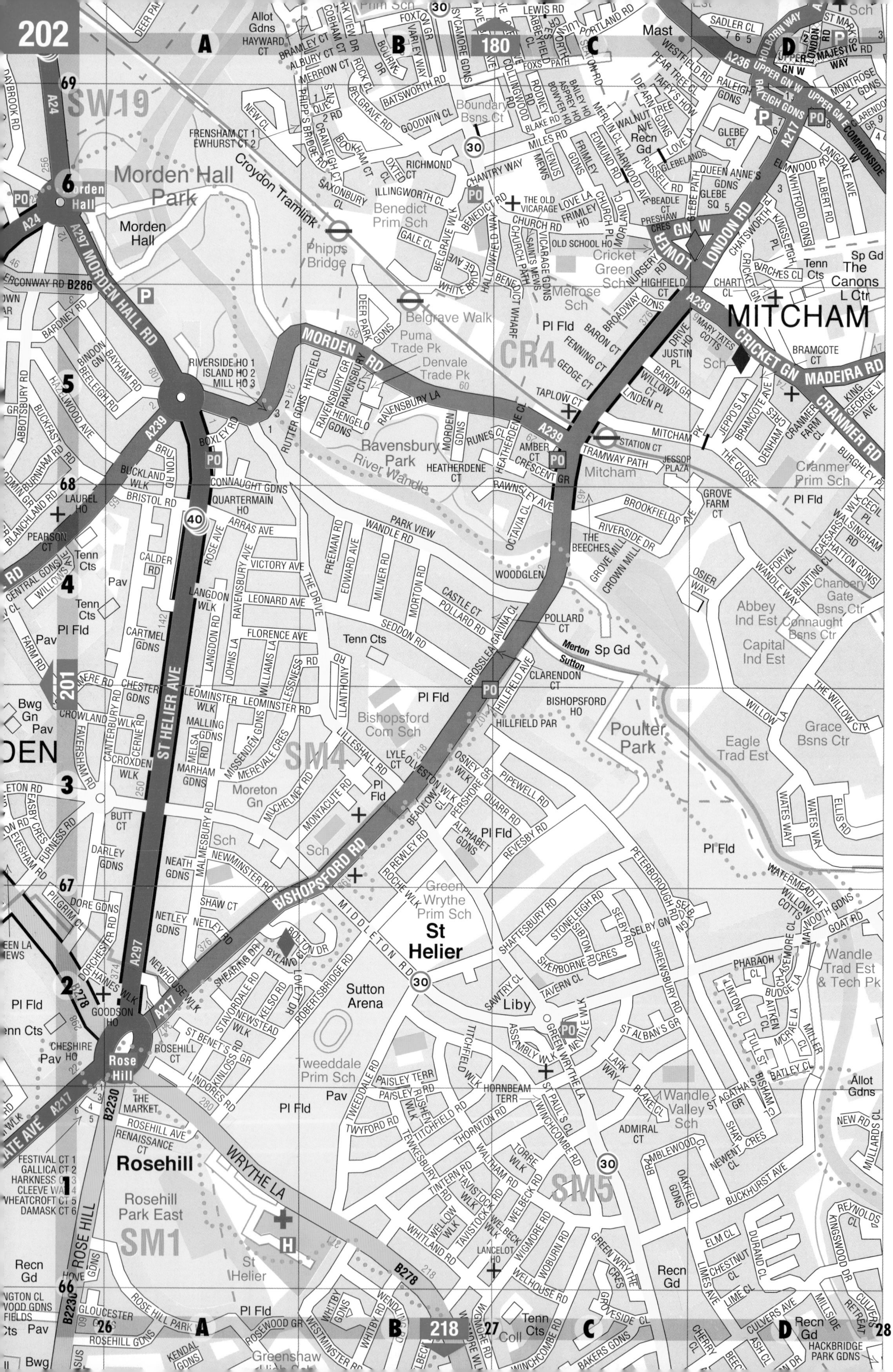
SW19
Morden Hall Park
Morden Hall
Croydon Tramlink
Phipps Bridge
Belgrave Walk
Benedict Prim Sch
Boundary Bsns Ct
Puma Trade Pk
Denvale Trade Pk
Cricket Green Sch
Melrose Sch
MITCHAM
The Canons L Ctr
CR4
Ravensbury Park
River Wandle
Mitcham
Cranmer Prim Sch
MORDEN RD
MORDEN HALL RD
LONDON RD
MADEIRA RD
CRANMER RD
CRICKET GN
ST HELIER AVE
BISHOPSFORD RD
Abbey Ind Est
Connaught Bsns Ctr
Chancery Gate Bsns Ctr
Capital Ind Est
Poulter Park
Eagle Trad Est
Grace Bsns Ctr
Merton
Sutton
Bishopsford Com Sch
SM4
Moreton Gn
Green Wrythe Prim Sch
St Helier
Sutton Arena
Tweeddale Prim Sch
Wandle Valley Sch
Wandle Trad Est & Tech Pk
Rose Hill
Rosehill
Rosehill Park East
SM1
SM5
WRYTHE LA
Greenshaw
A
B
C
D
180
218
201
26
27
28

MITCHAM
Mitcham Eastfields
181
A
B
C
D
Recn Gd
Allot Gdns
Tenn Cts
Pl Fld
Sp Gd
THE GABLES
Prim Sch
COMMONSIDE EAST
Pav
Tenn Cts
Harris Acad
William Morris Prim Sch
Garden Prim Sch
THE WOODLANDS 1
HEATHLANDS CT 2
Sp Gd
Pav
MANOR RD
MANOR WAY
NORTHBOROUGH RD
B272
PO
Liby
CR4
A239
A236
COMMONSIDE W
The Sherwood Sch
Pav
Recn Gd
Tenn Cts
Windmill Trad Est
WINDMILL RD
Allot Gdns
SHERWOOD PARK RD
CR4
A237
CARSHALTON RD
A239 CRANMER RD
MITCHAM GARDEN VILLAGE
WILLOW LA
Pl Flds
Mill House
Pl Flds
Mitcham
Mitcham Common
CROYDON RD
CH
Mitcham Junction
Allot Gdns
WATNEYS RD
1 POWEL
2 PERAL
3 BUCKI
4 BUCKI
5 LINCO
6 SUSSE
7 LINCO
204
Pl Flds
Croydon Tramlink
Works
DRAKE RD
RED HOUSE RD
Merton
Sutton
Beddington Lane
Brookmead Ind Est
LC
BROOKMEAD RD
JESSOPS WAY
ELBERON AVE
HOMEMEAD RD
OAKMEAD RD
ROCHFORD WAY
GOAT RD
Mill Green Bsns Pk
MILL GREEN RD
COOMBER WAY
The Tramsheds Ind Est
CR0
Allot Gdns
Beddington Corner
PORTLAND COTTS
THERAPIA LA
GREENLAND WAY
Prologis Pk
BEDDINGTON LA
BEDDINGTON CROSS
Valley Point Ind Est
1 SANDMARTIN WAY
2 OAK WLK
3 DUNSTER WAY
OAKLEY CT
LONDON RD
Beddington Farm
Beddington Sewage Treatment Works
MILE RD
SM6
Sch
Pioneers Ind Pk
B277
Soho Mills
Sch
THE GREEN
HACKBRIDGE RD
Hackbridge
WANDLE LODGE
Felnex Trad Est
Hackbridge
28
29
219
30

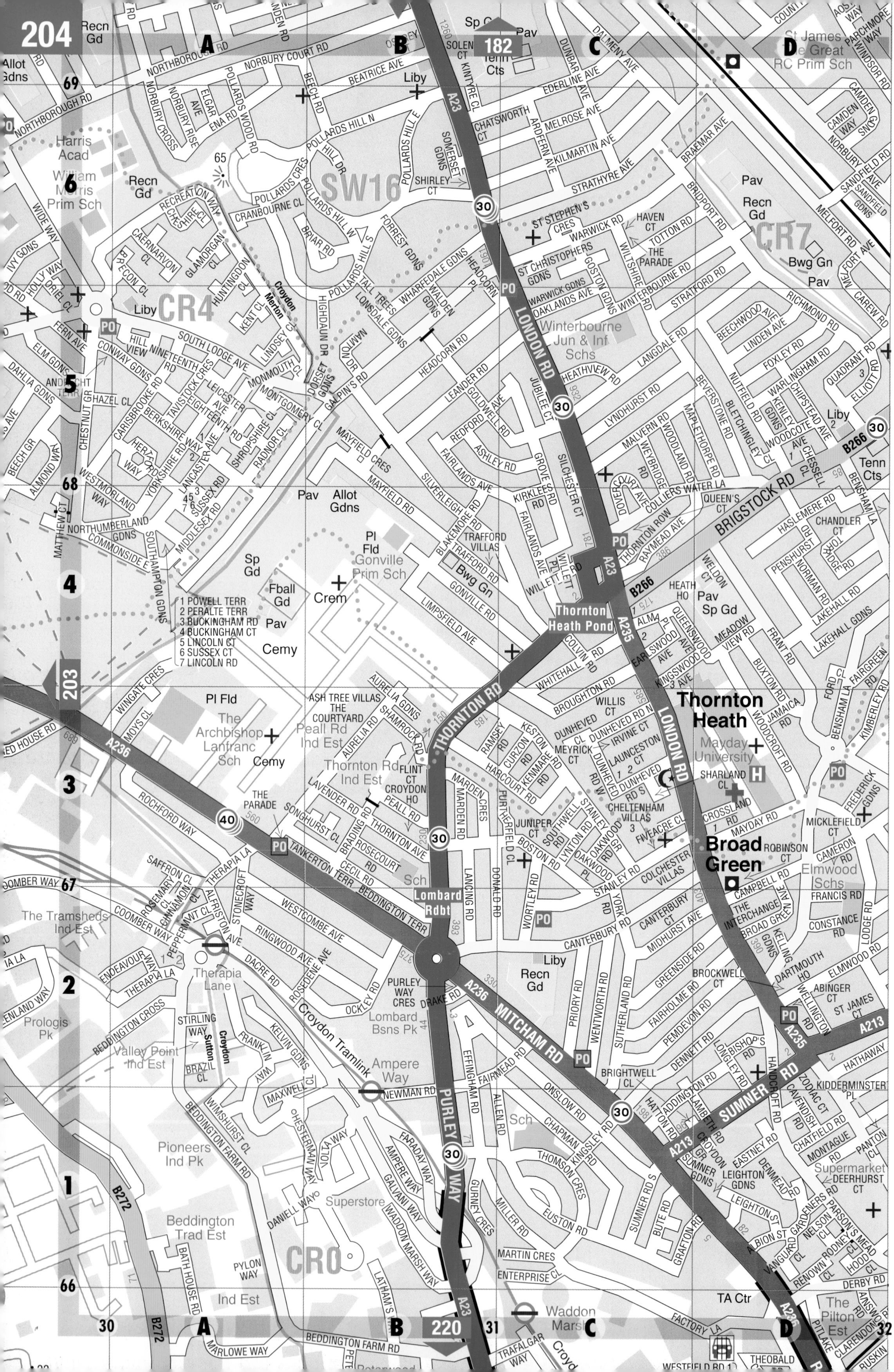
182
A
B
C
D
Recn Gd
Allot Gdns
69
NORTHBOROUGH RD
NORBURY COURT RD
BEATRICE AVE
Liby
SOLEN CT
KINTYRE CL
Tenn Cts
DALMENY AVE
DUNBAR AVE
EDERLINE AVE
St James the Great RC Prim Sch
A23
CHATSWORTH
MELROSE AVE
KILMARTIN AVE
POLLARDS HILL N
POLLARDS WOOD RD
NORBURY CROSS
NORBURY RISE
ELGAR AVE
ENA RD
BEECH RD
Harris Acad
William Morris Prim Sch
6
65
Recn Gd
SW16
POLLARDS CRES
SHIRLEY CT
SOMERSET GDNS
STRATHYRE AVE
BRAEMAR AVE
BRIDPORT RD
Pav
Recn Gd
CR7
Bwg Gn
Pav
RECREATION WAY
CHESHIRE CL
CAERNARVON CL
GLAMORGAN CL
BRECON CL
CRANBOURNE CL
BRIAR RD
FORREST GDNS
ST STEPHEN'S CRES
WARWICK RD
HAVEN CT
TOTTON RD
THE PARADE
WILTSHIRE RD
ST CHRISTOPHERS GDNS
WINTERBOURNE RD
STRATFORD RD
RICHMOND RD
MELFORT RD
MELFORT AVE
CAREW RD
HUNTINGDON CL
KENT CL
Croydon
Merton
CR4
Liby
PO
HILL VIEW
NINETEENTH RD
SOUTH LODGE AVE
FERN AVE
ELM GDNS
DAHLIA GDNS
5
CONWAY GDNS
HAZEL CL
CHESTNUT GR
CARISBROOKE RD
BERKSHIRE WAY
TAVISTOCK CRES
LEICESTER AVE
EIGHTEENTH RD
MONKMOUTH CL
MONTGOMERY CL
DORSET GDNS
GALPIN'S RD
LONSDALE GDNS
WHARFEDALE GDNS
WALDEN GDNS
HEADCORN RD
LONDON RD
WARWICK GDNS
OAKLANDS AVE
Winterbourne Jun & Inf Schs
HEATHVIEW RD
LANGDALE RD
BEECHWOOD AVE
LINDEN AVE
FOXLEY RD
WARLINGHAM RD
QUADRANT RD
ELLIOTT RD
30
Liby
Tenn Cts
B266
BRIGSTOCK RD
HERTFORD WAY
YORKSHIRE RD
SHROPSHIRE CL
RADNOR CL
LANCASTER AVE
SUSSEX RD
MIDDLESEX RD
WESTMORLAND WAY
68
NORTHUMBERLAND GDNS
COMMONSIDE E
MATTHEW CT
MAYFIELD CRES
MAYFIELD RD
LEANDER RD
REDFORD AVE
GOLDWELL RD
ASHLEY RD
FAIRLANDS AVE
SILVERLEIGH RD
JUBILEE CT
SILCHESTER CT
LYNDHURST RD
MALVERN RD
WEYBRIDGE RD
WOODLAND RD
MAPLETHORPE RD
BEVERSTONE RD
NUTFIELD RD
BLETCHINGLEY CL
WOODCOTE AVE
CHESSELL CL
BENSHAM LA
Pav
Allot Gdns
Pl Fld
Gonville Prim Sch
Sp Gd
Fball Gd
Crem
Pav
Cemy
4
BLAKEMORE RD
TRAFFORD VILLAS
TRAFFORD RD
Bwg Gn
GONVILLE RD
LIMPSFIELD AVE
KIRKLEES RD
GROVE RD
FAIRLANDS AVE
WILLETT PL
WILLETT RD
DOVERCOURT AVE
COLLIERS WATER LA
QUEEN'S CT
THORNTON ROW
RAYMEAD AVE
HASLEMERE RD
CHANDLER CT
PENSHURST RD
NORMAN RD
HEATH HO
WELDON CT
Pav
Sp Gd
LAKEHALL RD
LAKEHALL GDNS
SOUTHAMPTON GDNS
1 POWELL TERR
2 PERALTE TERR
3 BUCKINGHAM RD
4 BUCKINGHAM CT
5 LINCOLN CT
6 SUSSEX CT
7 LINCOLN RD
Thornton Heath Pond
A235
COLVIN RD
WHITEHALL RD
ALMA PL
EARLSWOOD AVE
QUEENSWOOD AVE
MEADOW VIEW RD
FRANT RD
BUXTON RD
FORD CL
BENSHAM LA
FAIRGREEN RD
KIMBERLEY RD
203
WINGATE CRES
Pl Fld
The Archbishop Lanfranc Sch
Cemy
ASH TREE VILLAS
THE COURTYARD
Peall Rd Ind Est
AURELIA GDNS
AURELIA RD
SHAMROCK RD
THORNTON RD
BROUGHTON RD
WILLIS CT
KINGSWOOD AVE
Thornton Heath
Mayday University
JAMAICA RD
WOODCROFT RD
PO
MOYS CL
A236
3
ROCHFORD WAY
Thornton Rd Ind Est
FLINT CT
CROYDON HO
PEALL RD
LAVENDER RD
SONGHURST CL
THE PARADE
40
PO
RAMSEY RD
CURZON RD
KESTON RD
KENMARE RD
HARCOURT RD
MARDEN CRES
MARDEN RD
DUNHEVED CL
DUNHEVED RD N
IRVINE CT
LAUNCESTON CT
DUNHEVED RD S
DUNHEVED RD W
MEYRICK CT
SHARLAND CL
H
CROSSLAND RD
MAYDAY RD
MICKLEFIELD CT
FREDERICK GDNS
CHELTENHAM VILLAS
FIVEACRE CL
JUNIPER CT
SOUTHWELL RD
STANLEY GR
OAKWOOD RD
OAKWOOD PL
LYNTON RD
Broad Green
ROBINSON CT
CAMERON RD
Elmwood Schs
FRANCIS RD
BRADING RD
ROSECOURT RD
THORNTON AVE
CECIL RD
TANKERTON TERR
BEDDINGTON TERR
Sch
Lombard Rdbt
LANCING RD
DONALD RD
FURTHERFIELD CL
BOSTON RD
WORTLEY RD
PO
STANLEY RD
COLCHESTER VILLAS
YORK RD
CANTERBURY CT
MIDHURST AVE
CANTERBURY RD
CAMPBELL RD
THE INTERCHANGE
BROAD GREEN AVE
KELLING GDNS
CONSTANCE RD
LODGE RD
SAFFRON CL
ROSEMARY CL
CINNAMON CL
THERAPIA LA
STONECROFT WAY
ALFRISTON AVE
PEPPERMINT CL
WESTCOMBE AVE
RINGWOOD AVE
COOMBER WAY
67
The Tramsheds Ind Est
ENDEAVOUR WAY
THERAPIA LA
Therapia Lane
DACRE RD
ROSEDENE AVE
OCKLEY RD
PURLEY WAY CRES
DRAKE RD
Liby
Recn Gd
PRIORY RD
WENTWORTH RD
SUTHERLAND RD
GREENSIDE RD
BROCKWELL CT
FAIRHOLME RD
PEMDEVON RD
DARTMOUTH HO
ELMWOOD RD
ABINGER CT
WELLINGTON RD
ST JAMES CT
A213
HATHAWAY
2
Prologis Pk
BEDDINGTON CROSS
STIRLING WAY
Sutton
Croydon
Valley Point Ind Est
BRAZIL CL
FRANKLIN WAY
KELVIN GDNS
Croydon Tramlink
Lombard Bsns Pk
Ampere Way
A236
MITCHAM RD
PO
FAIRMEAD RD
EFFINGHAM RD
ALLEN RD
ONSLOW RD
BRIGHTWELL CL
DENNETT RD
LONGLEY RD
BISHOP'S RD
HANDCROFT RD
SUMNER RD
ZODIAC CT
CAVENDISH RD
KIDDERMINSTER PL
MAXWELL CL
NEWMAN RD
PURLEY WAY
30
Sch
CHAPMAN RD
THOMSON CRES
KINGSLEY RD
HATTON RD
ADDINGTON RD
LAMBETH RD
CROYDON GR
SUMNER GDNS
EASTNEY RD
DENMEAD RD
LEIGHTON GDNS
CHATFIELD RD
MONTAGUE RD
PANTON CL
Supermarket
DEERHURST CT
1
Pioneers Ind Pk
WIMSHURST CL
BEDDINGTON FARM RD
VOLTA WAY
FARADAY WAY
AMPERE WAY
GALVANI WAY
Superstore
DANIELL WAY
WADDON MARSH WAY
GURNEY CRES
MILLER RD
EUSTON RD
SUMNER RD S
BUTE RD
GRAFTON RD
LEIGHTON ST
ALBION ST
VANGUARD CL
GARDENERS RD
NELSON CL
PARSON'S MEAD
RODNEY CL
HOOD CL
RENOWN CL
B272
Beddington Trad Est
CR0
PYLON WAY
MARTIN CRES
ENTERPRISE CL
DERBY RD
66
BATH HOUSE RD
Ind Est
LATHAM'S WAY
A23
Waddon Marsh
TA Ctr
The Pilton Est
AINSWORTH RD
PITLAKE
CLARENDON RD
30
220
31
32
MARLOWE WAY
BEDDINGTON FARM RD
TRAFALGAR WAY
FACTORY LA
WESTFIELD RD
THEOBALD RD
RUSKIN

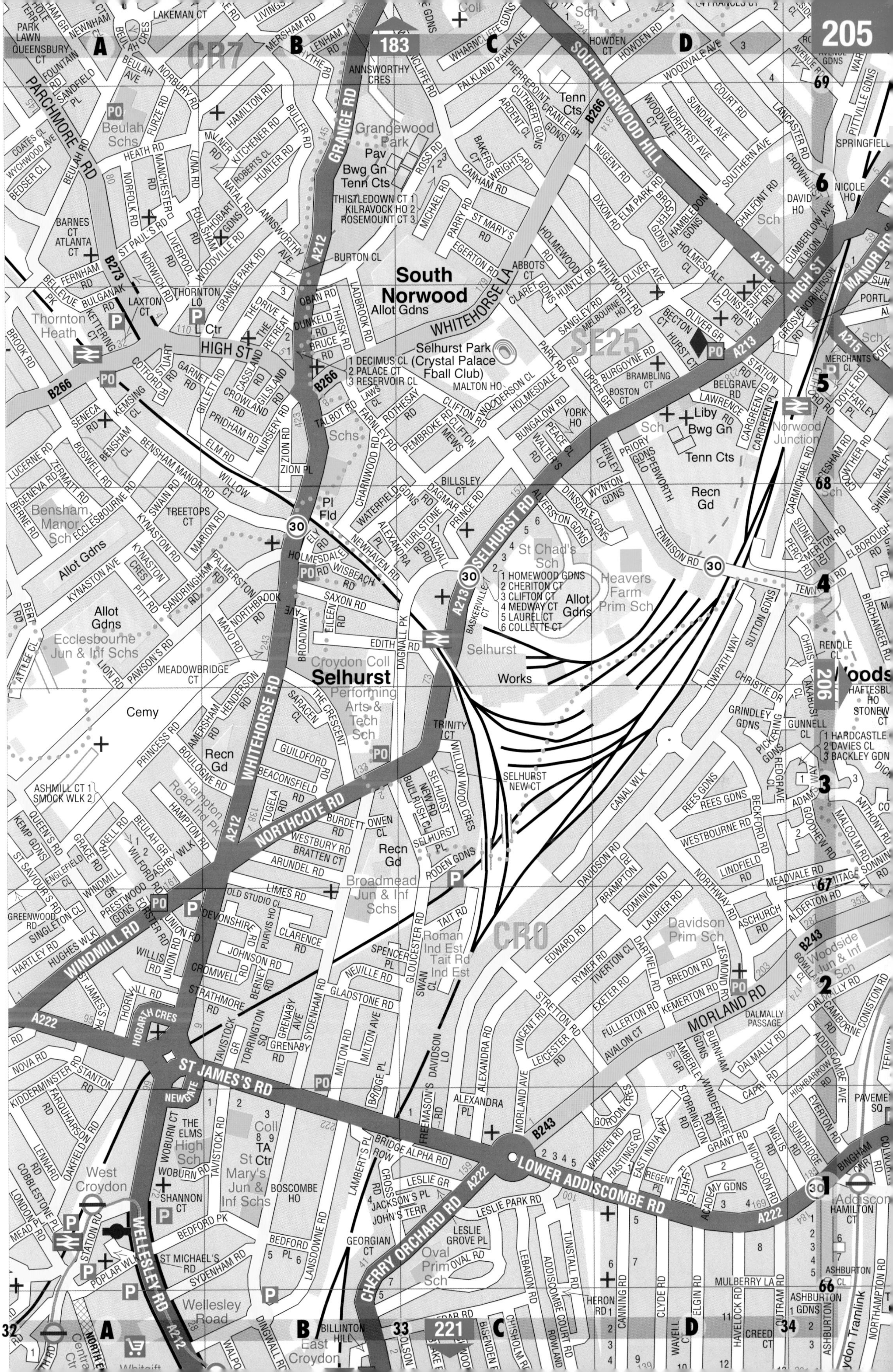

A
B
C
D
183
CR7
SE25
CR0
206
221
32
33
34
1
2
3
4
5
6
66
67
68
69
South Norwood
Selhurst
Thornton Heath
Norwood Junction
West Croydon
East Croydon
Woods
GRANGE RD
WHITEHORSE RD
SELHURST RD
SOUTH NORWOOD HILL
WHITEHORSE LA
NORTHCOTE RD
WINDMILL RD
ST JAMES'S RD
LOWER ADDISCOMBE RD
CHERRY ORCHARD RD
WELLESLEY RD
MORLAND RD
HIGH ST
PARCHMORE RD
BEULAH RD
BENSHAM MANOR RD
CANAL WLK
TOWPATH WAY
A212
A213
A215
A222
B243
B266
B273
Selhurst Park (Crystal Palace Fball Club)
Grangewood Park
Croydon Coll
Performing Arts & Tech Sch
Ecclesbourne Jun & Inf Schs
Bensham Manor Sch
Beulah Schs
St Chad's Sch
Heavers Farm Prim Sch
Broadmead Jun & Inf Schs
Davidson Prim Sch
Woodside Jun & Inf Sch
Oval Prim Sch
Elms High Sch
St Mary's Jun & Inf Schs
Hampton Road Ind Pk
Roman Ind Est
Tait Rd Ind Est
Wellesley Road
Selhurst Works
Cemy
Allot Gdns
Recn Gd
Tenn Cts
Bwg Gn
Liby
Pav
L Ctr
Whitgift Centre
Croydon Tramlink
Addiscombe

184
222
205
A
B
C
D
Elmers End
Birkbeck
Crem
Cemy
Harrington Road
BR3
South Norwood Country Park
SE25
Norwood Junction
Woodside
Long Lane Wood
Nat Res
Croydon Road Ind Est
Superstore
Chaffinch Bsns Pk
Monks Orchard Sch
Sports Arena
Ryelands Prim Sch
Golf Ctr
Arena
CR0
Ashburton Park
Ashburton Learning Village
Shirley Oaks
Addiscombe
Shirley
Blackhorse Lane
Churchfields Prim Sch
PENGE RD
HIGH ST
MANOR RD
PORTLAND RD
SPRING LA
LONG LA
SHIRLEY RD
LOWER ADDISCOMBE RD
WOODSIDE GN
ELMERS END RD
Croydon Tramlink

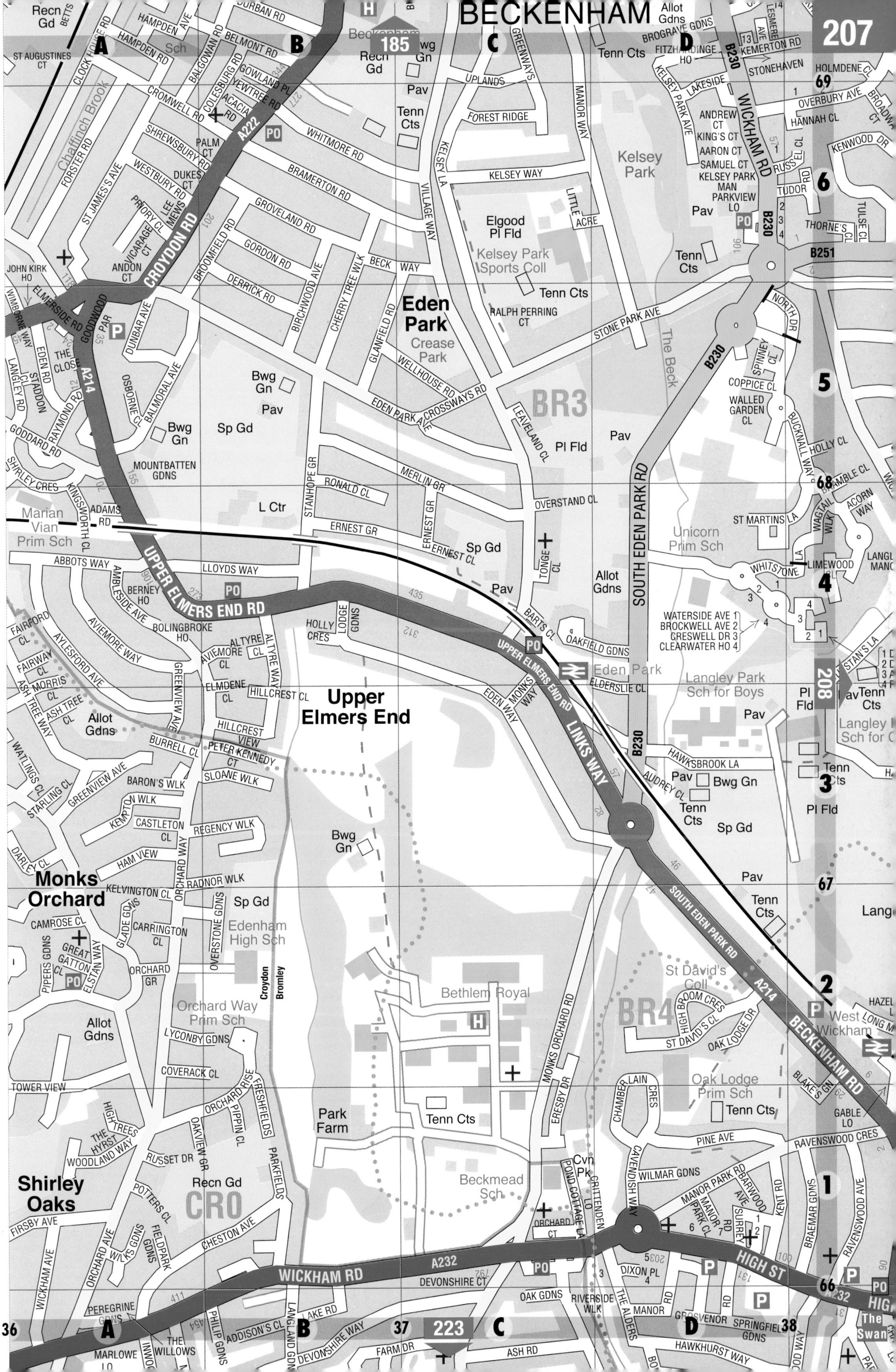

BECKENHAM
185
208
223
A
B
C
D
1
2
3
4
5
6
66
67
68
69
36
37
38
Eden Park
Upper Elmers End
Monks Orchard
Shirley Oaks
BR3
BR4
CR0
Kelsey Park
Crease Park
Elgood Pl Fld
Kelsey Park Sports Coll
Unicorn Prim Sch
Langley Park Sch for Boys
Edenham High Sch
Orchard Way Prim Sch
Bethlem Royal
Park Farm
Beckmead Sch
St David's Coll
Oak Lodge Prim Sch
Marian Vian Prim Sch
West Wickham
The Swan
Croydon
Bromley
CROYDON RD
A222
A214
A232
B230
B251
UPPER ELMERS END RD
LINKS WAY
SOUTH EDEN PARK RD
WICKHAM RD
BECKENHAM RD
HIGH ST
STONE PARK AVE
EDEN PARK AVE
WHITMORE RD
BRAMERTON RD
GROVELAND RD
GORDON RD
DERRICK RD
BEAUMONT WAY
KELSEY WAY
KELSEY LA
VILLAGE WAY
UPLANDS
FOREST RIDGE
MANOR WAY
GREENWAYS
CROMWELL RD
SHREWSBURY RD
WESTBURY RD
ST JAMES'S AVE
FORSTER RD
CLOCK HOUSE RD
HAMPDEN AVE
HAMPDEN RD
BELMONT RD
BALGOWAN RD
COLESBURG RD
GOODWOOD PAR
ELMERSIDE RD
DUNBAR AVE
OSBORNE CL
BALMORAL AVE
MOUNTBATTEN GDNS
ABBOTS WAY
LLOYDS WAY
AMBLESIDE AVE
AVIEMORE WAY
AYLESFORD AVE
GREENVIEW AVE
BURRELL CL
HILLCREST VIEW
SLOANE WLK
BARON'S WLK
ORCHARD WAY
MONKS ORCHARD RD
CHESTON AVE
FIRSBY AVE
WICKHAM AVE
PARKFIELDS
RAVENSWOOD CRES
PINE AVE
WILMAR GDNS
MANOR PARK RD
HAWKSBROOK LA
AUDREY CL
OAKFIELD GDNS
ELDERSLIE CL
HOLLY CRES
STANHOPE GR
ERNEST GR
MERLIN GR
RONALD CL
OVERSTAND CL
LEAVELAND CL
WELLHOUSE RD
CROSSWAYS RD
GLANFIELD RD
CHERRY TREE WLK
BIRCHWOOD AVE
BROOMFIELD RD
ST MARTINS LA
WATERSIDE AVE
BROCKWELL AVE
CRESWELL DR
CLEARWATER HO
DEVONSHIRE WAY
ASH RD
HAWKHURST WAY

186
224
207
A
B
C
D
1
2
3
4
5
6
38
39
40
66
67
68
69
Shortlands
Park Langley
BR2
BR3
BR4
Clare House Prim Sch
Pl Fld
Pav
Recn Gd
PUMP HOUSE CL
QUEEN'S MEAD RD
GLASS MILL LA
MILL VALE
RAVENS CL
BROMLEY CRES
BROMLEY GDNS
GWYDYR RD
RIDLEY RD
Allot Gdns
HILLSIDE RD
DYKES WAY
KERRY CL
VALLEY RD
PARKHALL CT
LUSCOMBE CT
CARTMEL CT
COLEBROOK RISE
FARLEY CROFT
SIBLEY CT
BLADON CT
FRANKLIN HO
GREEN CL
KINGSWOOD RD
MAY'S HILL RD
IDEN CL
FIRTREE CT
OCTOBER CT
WINCHESTER PK
WINCHESTER CL
WINCHESTER RD
ST MARY'S AVE
QUEEN ANNE AVE
DURHAM RD
MADISON GDNS
BAYDON CT
FRESHAM HO
Tenn Cts
Sch
SHORTLANDS RD
SHORTLANDS GR
CHURCH RD
EVERGLADES
HAZELWOOD HO
DEEPDENE CT
CASTLE CL
DARRELL CT
PELLINGS CL
CELTIC AVE
VALAN LEAS
CUMBERLAND RD
MERLIN CT
HIGHFIELD DR
PINE TREE LO
CHILTERN GDNS
SPRUCE PK
CAYGILL CL
B228
RUTLAND GATE
OAKHAM DR
STAMFORD DR
Highfield Jun & Inf Schs
BLENHEIM CT
DURHAM AVE
LANCASTER CL
MORLEY CT
FLORIDA CT
BROOKWOOD CL
SUFFOLK HO
NORFOLK HO
BODIAM CT
WESTMORELAND RD
DEEPDALE AVE
LANGHAM PK PL
KINGSLEIGH WLK
STONE RD
TALL ELMS CL
SOUTH HILL RD
ROMANHURST AVE
ROMANHURST GDNS
TOOTSWOOD RD
Bwg Gn
Recn Gd
BRANSCOMBE CT
BROADOAKS WAY
ELVINGTON GN
MEREWORTH CL
HAYESFORD PARK DR
PENSHURST GN
BARNHILL AVE
PO
WOODLEA DR
PICKHURST PK
BRAMBLEDOWN CL
CULVERSTONE CL
STANSTEAD CL
BRENCHLEY CL
Cupola Wood
Pickhurst Jun Sch
Pickhurst Inf Sch
EASTRY AVE
DRAVEN CL
SEDGEWOOD CL
MALLING WAY
BOUGHTON AVE
PEMBURY CL
MOUNTHURST RD
PICKHURST GN
PICKHURST MEAD
CONSTANCE CRES
Pickhurst Green
PICKHURST LA
CREST RD
Allot Gdns
HILLDOWN RD
COURTLANDS AVE
HAYES HILL RD
BRIAR GDNS
HURSTDENE AVE
HURST CL
B251
Hayes
SAVILLE ROW
KEMSING CL
HILLSIDE LA
HOLLAND CL
BOURNE WAY
PRICKLEY WOOD
TIEPIGS LA
NORTH CL
DEER PARK WAY
CHATSWORTH
MARWELL
HEPBURN GDNS
HAYES HILL
HAYES MEAD RD
PONDFIELD RD
Sp Gd
Hawes Down Schs
KESWICK RD
RYDAL DR
WINDERMERE RD
MOUNT CT
HAWES LA
MARTINS CL
LINDEN LEAS
THE MEAD
LINKS RD
HAWES LA
PICKHURST RISE
THE DRIVE
LANGLEY WAY
WICKHAM CHASE
THE AVENUE
RED LODGE RD
HAZELWOOD LO
LONG MEADOW CL
RAYS RD
RED LO
Sw Pool
STATION RD
A214
GABLE LO
BLAKE'S GN
RAVENSWOOD CRES
PINE AVE
West Wickham
Oak Lodge Prim Sch
BECKENHAM RD
OAK LODGE DR
A214
David's Coll
SOUTH EDEN PARK RD
Langley Park
HAYES CHASE
GOODHART WAY
THE CRESCENT
WEST WAY
BARNFIELD WOOD CL
BARNFIELD WOOD RD
CH
FAIRWAY GDNS
BUSHEY WAY
OVERHILL WAY
WOODMERE WAY
TOP PK
HAYES LA
DEN RD
DEN CL
FYFIELD CL
DRUIDS WAY
KINGSWOOD AVE
HENGIST WAY
HAYES WAY
WHITECROFT CL
WHITECROFT WAY
ELWILL WAY
MALMAINS WAY
MALMAINS CL
BRABOURNE RISE
STYLES WAY
WICKHAM WAY
HAWKSBROOK LA
Langley Park Sch for Girls
ST DUNSTAN'S LA
1 DEVERAUX CL
2 DORRINGTON WAY
3 ADAMSON WAY
4 RAWLINGS CL
LANGLEY MANOR
LIMEWOOD CL
WHITSTONE LA
ACORN WAY
WAGTAIL WLK
BRAMBLE CL
HOLLY CL
BUCKNALL WAY
ST MARTINS LA
Unicorn Prim Sch
WALLED GARDEN CL
SPINNEY CL
NORTH DR
B230
B251
WICKHAM RD
Liby
WALDRON GDNS
FOXES DALE
OATES CL
WESTPOINT
BARTON CT
BROMLEY GR
TEMPLEDENE
MORDEN LO
OAKWAY
SCOTT'S LA
DAWN WLK
SHORTLANDS GR
SPRINGPARK DR
STANLEY AVE
HOWARDS CREST CL
COURTENAY DR
OAKWOOD AVE
FERGUSON CL
QUINTON CL
TULSE CL
THORNE'S CL
KENWOOD DR
BROADWAY CT
HANNAH CL
OVERBURY AVE
HOLMDENE CL
STONEHAVEN
LAKESIDE
ANDREW CT
KING'S CT
AARON CT
SAMUEL CT
KELSEY PARK MAN
PARKVIEW LO
TUDOR
RUSSELL CL
KEMERTON RD
LESMERE RD
Sp Gd
Bwg Gn
HAWKSBROOK LA
MANOR PARK RD
MANOR PARK CL
SURREY AVE
BRAEMAR GDNS
RAVENSWOOD AVE
KENT RD
HIGH ST
A232
Liby
The Swan
CROFT AVE
OAK GR
ASH GR
GLEBE WAY
WICKHAM CRES
SPRINGFIELD GDNS
GROSVENOR RD
HAWKHURST WAY
Allot

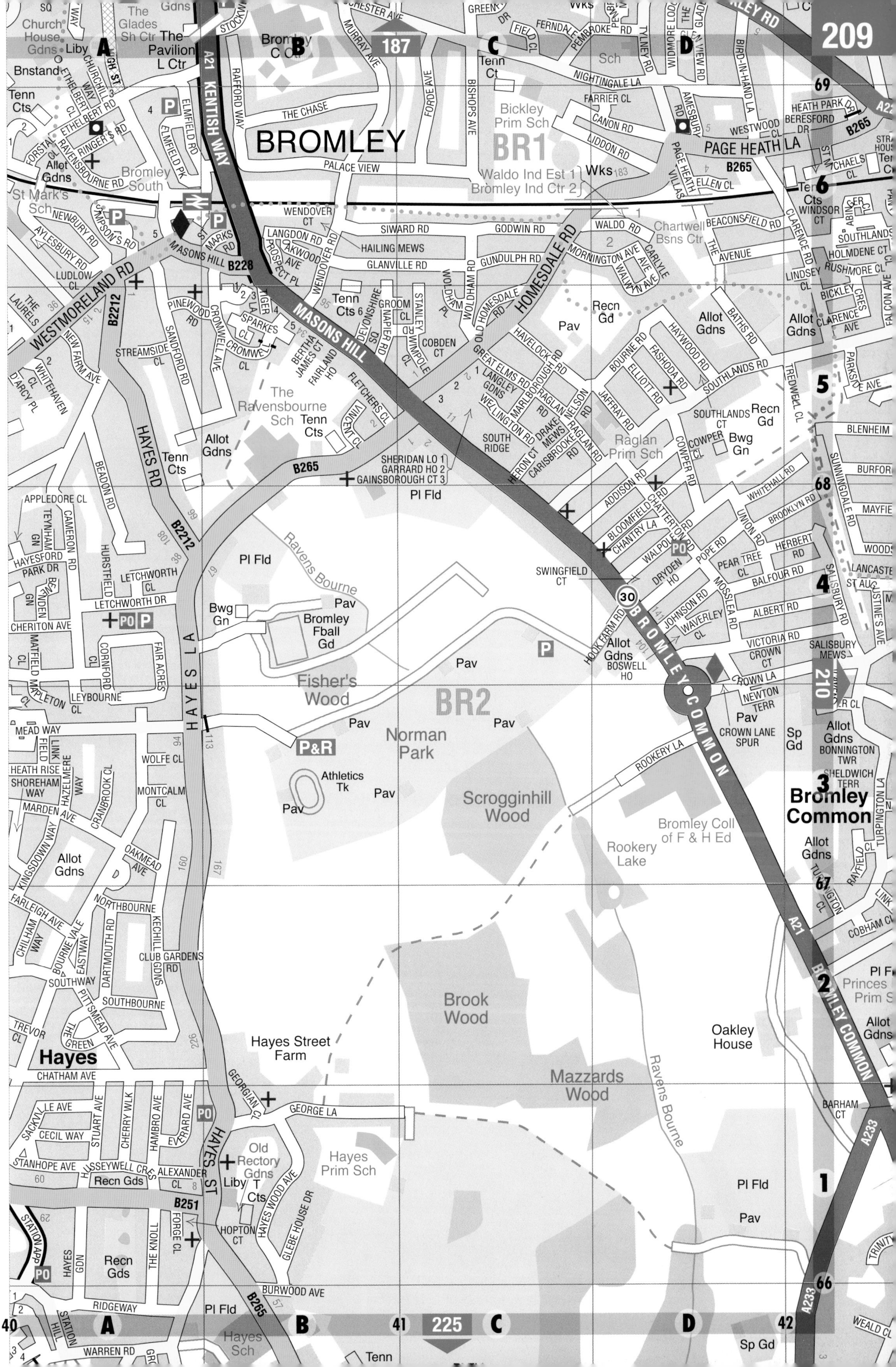
187
225
210
A
B
C
D
40
41
42
1
2
3
4
5
6
66
67
68
69
BROMLEY
BR1
BR2
Hayes
Bromley Common
Church House Gdns
Liby
The Glades Sh Ctr
The Pavilion L Ctr
Bromley C Of
Bnstand
Tenn Cts
Allot Gdns
Bromley South
St Mark's Sch
KENTISH WAY
A21
RAFFORD WAY
MURRAY AVE
FORDE AVE
BISHOPS AVE
THE CHASE
PALACE VIEW
Bickley Prim Sch
Tenn Ct
Sch
NIGHTINGALE LA
FARRIER CL
CANON RD
LIDDON RD
Waldo Ind Est 1
Bromley Ind Ctr 2
Wks
AMESBURY RD
PAGE HEATH VILLAS
PAGE HEATH LA
B265
WESTWOOD
HEATH PARK DR
BERESFORD DR
ELLEN CL
WINDSOR CT
SOUTHLANDS
HOLMDENE CT
RUSHMORE CL
LINDSEY CL
BICKLEY CRES
CLARENCE AVE
CLARENCE RD
WENDOVER CT
SIWARD RD
GODWIN RD
WALDO RD
Chartwell Bsns Ctr
BEACONSFIELD RD
THE AVENUE
LANGDON RD
HAILING MEWS
GLANVILLE RD
GUNDULPH RD
MORNINGTON AVE
CARLYLE AVE
WALWYN AVE
HOMESDALE RD
OLD HOMESDALE RD
WOLDHAM RD
WOLDHAM PL
MASONS HILL
B228
WESTMORELAND RD
NEWBURY RD
AYLESBURY RD
SIMPSON'S RD
LUDLOW CL
THE LAURELS
B2212
PINEWOOD RD
CROMWELL AVE
SPARKES CL
TIGER LA
DEVONSHIRE SQ
GROOM CL
NAPIER RD
STANLEY RD
WIMPOLE CL
COBDEN CT
Tenn Cts
Recn Gd
Pav
HAVELOCK RD
GREAT ELMS RD
LANGLEY GDNS
MARLBOROUGH RD
RAGLAN RD
NELSON RD
BOURNE RD
FASHODA RD
HAYWOOD RD
BATHS RD
SOUTHLANDS RD
TREDWELL CL
PARKSIDE AVE
ELLIOTT RD
JAFFRAY RD
STREAMSIDE CL
SANDFORD RD
NEW FARM AVE
WHITEHAVEN CL
D'ARCY PL
BERTHA JAMES CT
FAIRLAND HO
FLETCHERS CL
VINCENT CL
The Ravensbourne Sch
SOUTH RIDGE
WELLINGTON RD
DRAKE MEWS
CARISBROOKE RD
HERON CT
Raglan Prim Sch
COWPER RD
COWPER CL
SOUTHLANDS CT
Recn Gd
Bwg Gn
BLENHEIM
BURFORD
MAYFIELD
WOODS
LANCASTER
SUNNINGDALE RD
HAYES RD
BEADON RD
SHERIDAN LO 1
GARRARD HO 2
GAINSBOROUGH CT 3
Pl Fld
ADDISON RD
CHATTERTON RD
BLOOMFIELD RD
CHANTRY LA
WALPOLE RD
WHITEHALL RD
UNION RD
BROOKLYN RD
HERBERT RD
PEAR TREE CL
BALFOUR RD
POPE RD
DRYDEN HO
SWINGFIELD CT
30
BROMLEY COMMON
JOHNSON RD
MOSSLEA RD
WAVERLEY CL
ALBERT RD
VICTORIA RD
CROWN CT
CROWN LA
NEWTON TERR
SALISBURY RD
SALISBURY MEWS
ST AUGUSTINE'S AVE
APPLEDORE CL
TEYNHAM GN
CAMERON RD
HURSTFIELD
LETCHWORTH CL
LETCHWORTH DR
HAYESFORD PARK DR
BENENDEN GN
CHERITON AVE
MATFIELD CL
CORNFORD CL
FAIR ACRES
LEYBOURNE CL
APPLETON CL
Ravens Bourne
Pav
Bwg Gn
Bromley Fball Gd
Fisher's Wood
HOOK FARM RD
Allot Gdns
BOSWELL HO
Norman Park
P&R
Athletics Tk
HAYES LA
MEAD WAY
LINK FIELD
HEATH RISE
SHOREHAM WAY
HAZELMERE WAY
CRANBROOK CL
WOLFE CL
MONTCALM CL
MARDEN AVE
KINGSDOWN WAY
OAKMEAD AVE
Scrogginhill Wood
ROOKERY LA
CROWN LANE SPUR
Sp Gd
Bromley Coll of F & H Ed
Rookery Lake
BONNINGTON TWR
SHELDWICH TERR
TURPINGTON LA
RAYFIELD CL
TURPINGTON CL
COBHAM CL
LINK
NORTHBOURNE
KECHILL GDNS
FARLEIGH AVE
CHILHAM WAY
BOURNE VALE
EASTWAY
DARTMOUTH RD
CLUB GARDENS RD
SOUTHWAY
PITTSMEAD AVE
SOUTHBOURNE
TREVOR CL
THE GREEN
Brook Wood
Hayes Street Farm
Mazzards Wood
Princes Prim Sch
Oakley House
CHATHAM AVE
SACKVILLE AVE
STUART AVE
CHERRY WLK
HAMBRO AVE
EVERARD AVE
CECIL WAY
GEORGIAN CL
GEORGE LA
HAYES ST
Old Rectory Gdns
Hayes Prim Sch
BARHAM CT
A233
STANHOPE AVE
HUSSEYWELL CRES
ALEXANDER CL
Recn Gds
B251
Liby
T Cts
HAYES WOOD AVE
GLEBE HOUSE DR
STATION APP
HAYES GDN
THE KNOLL
FORGE CL
HOPTON CT
BURWOOD AVE
RIDGEWAY
STATION HILL
WARREN RD
Hayes Sch
Tenn
Sp Gd
WEALD CL

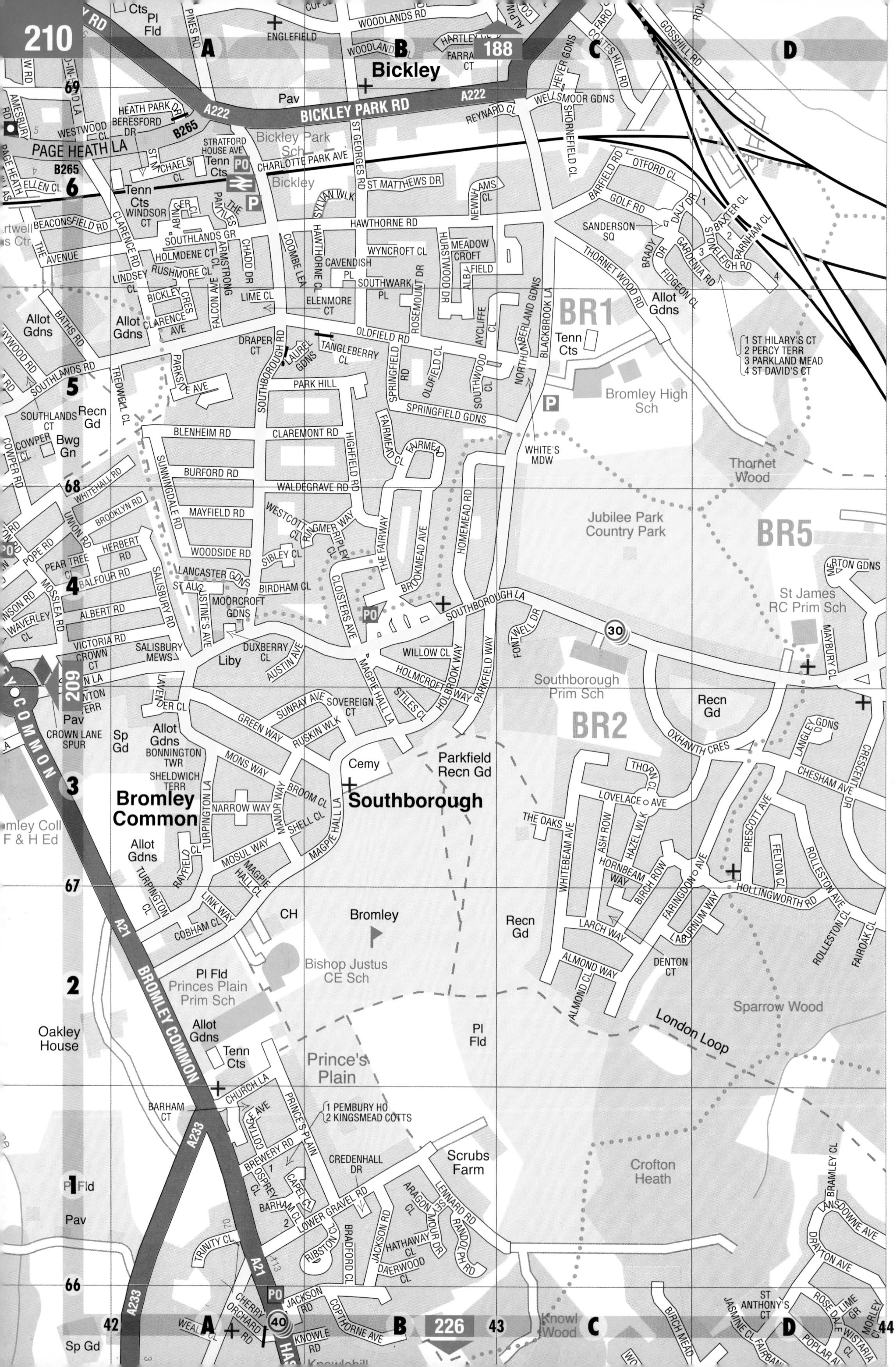

188
226
209
A
B
C
D
42
43
44
69
6
5
68
4
3
67
2
1
66
Bickley
Southborough
Bromley Common
BR1
BR2
BR5
BICKLEY PARK RD
A222
B265
PAGE HEATH LA
WOODLANDS RD
ENGLEFIELD
PINES RD
HARTLEY
FARRA CT
HEYER GDNS
COATES HILL RD
GOSSHILL RD
WELLSMOOR GDNS
REYNARD CL
SHORNEFIELD CL
HEATH PARK DR
BERESFORD DR
WESTWOOD CL
AMESBURY RD
STRATFORD HOUSE AVE
CHARLOTTE PARK AVE
Bickley Park Sch
Bickley
Pav
Tenn Cts
ST GEORGES RD
ST MATTHEWS DR
ST MICHAELS CL
ELLEN CL
NEWMANS CL
SYLVAN WLK
BARFIELD RD
OTFORD CL
GOLF RD
DALY DR
BAXTER CL
FARNHAM CL
STONELEIGH RD
GARDENIA RD
BRADY DR
FIDGEON CL
SANDERSON SQ
THORNET WOOD RD
WINDSOR CT
ABINGER CL
THE PANTILES
BEACONSFIELD RD
THE AVENUE
SOUTHLANDS GR
HOLMDENE CT
RUSHMORE CL
ARMSTRONG CL
CHADD DR
COOMBE LEA
HAWTHORNE RD
HAWTHORNE CL
WYNCROFT CL
CAVENDISH PL
SOUTHWARK PL
ROSEMOUNT DR
HURSTWOOD DR
MEADOW CROFT
ALBYFIELD
LINDSEY CL
BICKLEY CRES
CLARENCE RD
CLARENCE AVE
FALCON AVE
LIME CL
ELENMORE CT
AYCLIFFE CL
NORTHUMBERLAND GDNS
BLACKBROOK LA
Allot Gdns
BATHS RD
DRAPER CT
OLDFIELD RD
TANGLEBERRY CL
LAUREL GDNS
SOUTHBOROUGH RD
SPRINGFIELD RD
OLDFIELD CL
SOUTHWOOD CL
1 ST HILARY'S CT
2 PERCY TERR
3 PARKLAND MEAD
4 ST DAVID'S CT
Bromley High Sch
SOUTHLANDS RD
TREDWELL CL
PARKSIDE AVE
PARK HILL
SPRINGFIELD GDNS
SOUTHLANDS CT
Recn Gd
COWPER CL
Bwg Gn
BLENHEIM RD
CLAREMONT RD
HIGHFIELD RD
FAIRMEAD CL
FAIRMEAD RD
WHITE'S MDW
Thornet Wood
Jubilee Park Country Park
WHITEHALL RD
BURFORD RD
WALDEGRAVE RD
HOMEMEAD RD
SUNNINGDALE RD
BROOKLYN RD
UNION RD
MAYFIELD RD
WESTCOTT CL
RINGMER WAY
RIPLEY CL
THE FAIRWAY
BROOKMEAD AVE
HERBERT RD
POPE RD
PEAR TREE CL
WOODSIDE RD
SIBLEY CL
BALFOUR RD
LANCASTER GDNS
BIRDHAM CL
CLOISTERS AVE
SALISBURY RD
MOSSLEA RD
ST AUGUSTINE'S AVE
MOORCROFT GDNS
SOUTHBOROUGH LA
FONTWELL DR
ALBERT RD
WAVERLEY CL
VICTORIA RD
SALISBURY MEWS
DUXBERRY CL
AUSTIN AVE
Liby
WILLOW CL
HOLMCROFT WAY
HOLBROOK WAY
PARKFIELD WAY
Southborough Prim Sch
MERTON GDNS
St James RC Prim Sch
MAYBURY CL
CROWN CT
CROWN LA
CROWN LANE SPUR
LAVENDER CL
SUNRAY AVE
SOVEREIGN CT
STILES CL
MAGPIE HALL LA
GREEN WAY
RUSKIN WLK
Sp Gd
BONNINGTON TWR
SHELDWICH TERR
MONS WAY
Cemy
Parkfield Recn Gd
OXHAWTH CRES
LANGLEY GDNS
CHESHAM AVE
CRESCENT DR
THORN CL
LOVELACE AVE
THE OAKS
NARROW WAY
MANOR WAY
BROOM CL
SHELL CL
TURPINGTON LA
ASH ROW
HAZEL WLK
WHITEBEAM AVE
HORNBEAM WAY
BIRCH ROW
FARINGDON AVE
PRESCOTT AVE
FELTON CL
ROLLESTON AVE
HOLLINGWORTH RD
RAYFIELD CL
MOSUL WAY
MAGPIE HALL CL
TURPINGTON CL
LINK WAY
COBHAM CL
CH
Bromley
LABURNUM WAY
LARCH WAY
DENTON CT
ROLLESTON CL
FAIROAK CL
ALMOND WAY
ALMOND CL
A21
BROMLEY COMMON
Bishop Justus CE Sch
Pl Fld
Princes Plain Prim Sch
Oakley House
Sparrow Wood
London Loop
Prince's Plain
CHURCH LA
BARHAM CT
A233
COTTAGE AVE
PRINCE'S PLAIN
1 PEMBURY HO
2 KINGSMEAD COTTS
BREWERY RD
OSPREY CL
CAPEL CL
BARHAM CL
CREDENHALL DR
Scrubs Farm
Crofton Heath
LOWER GRAVEL RD
ARAGON CL
SEYMOUR DR
LENNARD RD
RANDOLPH RD
JACKSON RD
BRADFORD CL
RIBSTON CL
HATHAWAY CL
DAERWOOD CL
TRINITY CL
BRAMLEY CL
LANSDOWNE AVE
DRAYTON AVE
ST ANTHONY'S CT
JASMINE CL
ROSEDALE
LIME GR
WISTARIA CL
MORLEY CL
POPLAR AV
FAIRBANK
BIRCH MEAD
Knowl Wood
CHERRY ORCHARD RD
COPTHORNE AVE
KNOWLE RD
WEALD CL
PO
P
CROFTON LA

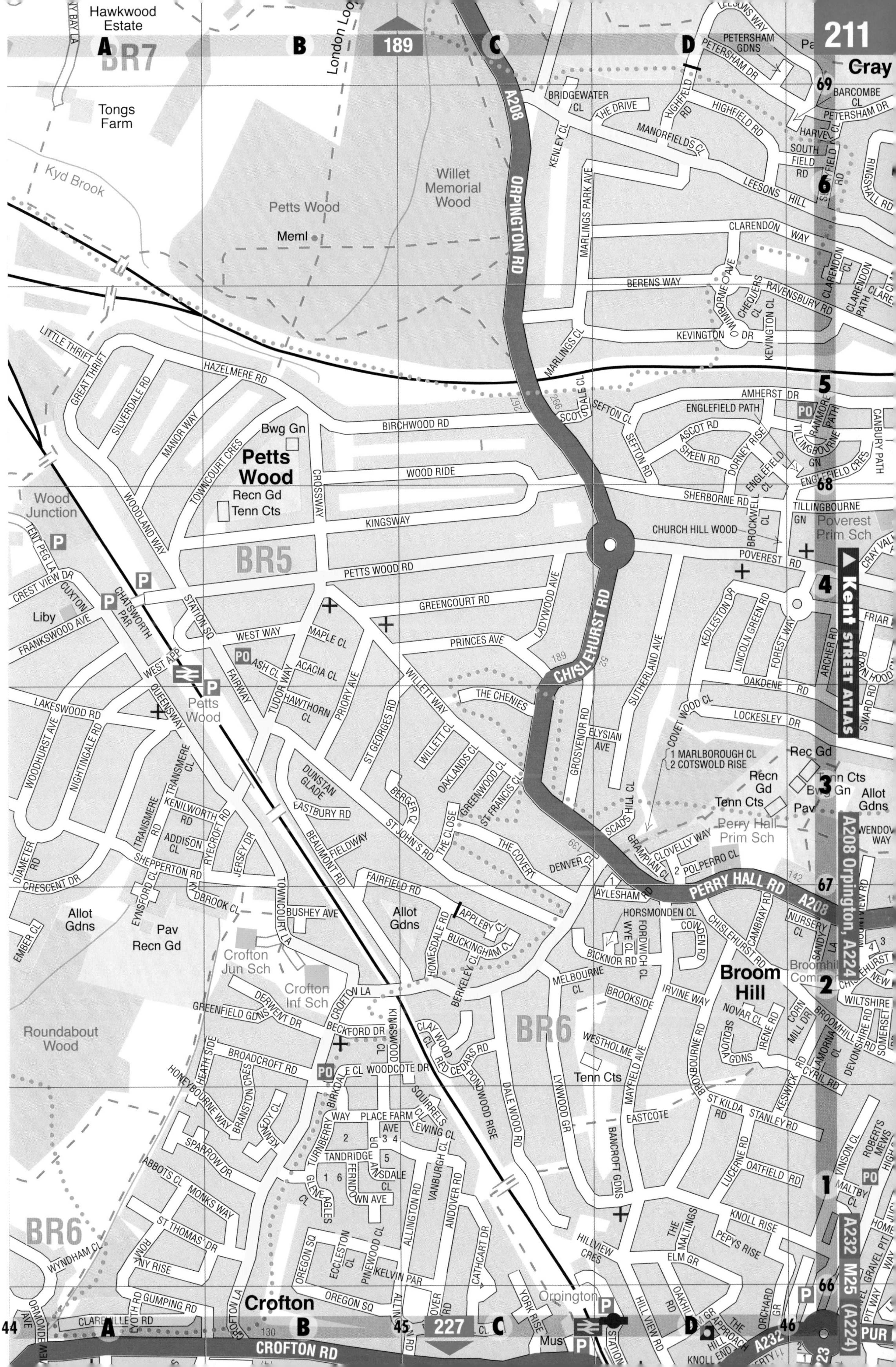
Hawkwood Estate
A
B
189
C
D
BR7
Cray
Tongs Farm
Kyd Brook
Petts Wood
Meml
Willet Memorial Wood
A208
ORPINGTON RD
BRIDGEWATER CL
THE DRIVE
HIGHFIELD RD
MANORFIELDS CL
KENLEY CL
MARLINGS PARK AVE
LEESONS HILL
PETERSHAM GDNS
PETERSHAM DR
LEESONS WAY
BARCOMBE CL
HARVEL CL
SOUTHFIELD RD
RINGSHALL RD
69
6
CLARENDON WAY
BERENS WAY
WIMBORNE AVE
CHEQUERS CL
RAVENSBURY RD
KEVINGTON CL
KEVINGTON DR
CLARENDON CL
CLARENDON PATH
MARLINGS CL
5
AMHERST DR
ENGLEFIELD PATH
SEFTON CL
SEFTON RD
SCOTSDALE CL
ASCOT RD
SHEEN RD
DORNEY RISE
ENGLEFIELD CL
ENGLEFIELD CRES
TILLINGBOURNE GN
RANMORE PATH
CANBURY PATH
68
LITTLE THRIFT
GREAT THRIFT
HAZELMERE RD
SILVERDALE RD
MANOR WAY
TOWNCOURT CRES
WOODLAND WAY
Bwg Gn
Petts Wood
Recn Gd
Tenn Cts
BIRCHWOOD RD
WOOD RIDE
CROSSWAY
KINGSWAY
SHERBORNE RD
BROCKWELL CL
TILLINGBOURNE GN
Poverest Prim Sch
CHURCH HILL WOOD
Wood Junction
TENT PEG LA
BR5
PETTS WOOD RD
POVEREST RD
CRAY VALLEY
4
Kent STREET ATLAS
CREST VIEW DR
CUXTON
CHATSWORTH PAR
Liby
FRANKSWOOD AVE
STATION SQ
GREENCOURT RD
LADYWOOD AVE
KEDLESTON DR
LINCOLN GREEN RD
FOREST WAY
FRIAR RD
WEST WAY
MAPLE CL
PRINCES AVE
CHISLEHURST RD
SUTHERLAND AVE
ARCHER RD
ROBIN HOOD
ASH CL
ACACIA CL
WEST APP
PO
OAKDENE RD
LAKESWOOD RD
QUEENSWAY
Petts Wood
FAIRWAY
TUDOR WAY
HAWTHORN CL
PRIORY AVE
WILLETT WAY
THE CHENIES
LOCKESLEY DR
SWARD RD
COVET WOOD CL
WOODHURST AVE
NIGHTINGALE RD
TRANSMERE CL
ST GEORGES RD
WILLETT CL
OAKLANDS CL
GREENWOOD CL
ST FRANCIS CL
GROSVENOR RD
ELYSIAN AVE
1 MARLBOROUGH CL
2 COTSWOLD RISE
Rec Gd
Recn Gd
Tenn Cts
Bwg Gn
Allot Gdns
Pav
3
DUNSTAN GLADE
BERGER CL
KENILWORTH RD
TRANSMERE RD
ADDISON CL
RYECROFT RD
JERSEY DR
EASTBURY RD
THE CLOSE
SCADS HILL CL
Perry Hall Prim Sch
WENDOVER WAY
DIAMETER RD
SHEPPERTON RD
BEAUMONT RD
FIELDWAY
ST JOHN'S RD
THE COVERT
DENVER CL
GRAMPIAN CL
CLOVELLY WAY
2 POLPERRO CL
CRESCENT DR
KYDBROOK CL
FAIRFIELD RD
AYLESHAM RD
PERRY HALL RD
A208
67
A208 Orpington, A224
EYNSFORD CL
Allot Gdns
Pav
Recn Gd
BUSHEY AVE
TOWNCOURT LA
Allot Gdns
APPLEBY CL
HORSMONDEN CL
WYE CL
FORDWICH CL
COWDEN RD
CAMBRAY RD
NURSERY CL
SANDY LA
EMBER CL
Crofton Jun Sch
HOMESDALE RD
BUCKINGHAM CL
BERKELEY CL
BICKNOR RD
CHISLEHURST RD
Broom Hill
Broomhill Comm
Crofton Inf Sch
CROFTON LA
MELBOURNE CL
BROOKSIDE
IRVINE WAY
NOVAR CL
IRENE RD
CORN MILL DR
2
WILTSHIRE
Roundabout Wood
GREENFIELD GDNS
DERWENT DR
BECKFORD DR
KINGSWOOD CL
CLAYWOOD CL
BR6
WESTHOLME
SEQUOIA GDNS
BROOMHILL RD
LAMORNA CL
SOMERSET
DEVONSHIRE RD
HEATH SIDE
BROADCROFT RD
WOODCOTE DR
CEDARS RD
POND WOOD RISE
DALE WOOD RD
LYNWOOD GR
MAYFIELD AVE
Tenn Cts
BROXBOURNE RD
KESWICK RD
CYRIL RD
HONEYBOURNE WAY
BRANSTON CRES
KENNEDY CL
BIRKDALE
SQUIRRELS CL
EASTCOTE
ST KILDA RD
STANLEY RD
PLACE FARM AVE
EWING CL
TURNBERRY WAY
SPARROW DR
TANDRIDGE DR
ANSDALE CL
FERNDOWN AVE
VANBURGH CL
BANCROFT GDNS
LUCERNE RD
OATFIELD RD
VINSON CL
ROBERTS MEWS
ABBOTS CL
MONKS WAY
GLENEAGLES CL
ALLINGTON RD
ANDOVER RD
CATHCART DR
1
MALTBY CL
BR6
ST THOMAS' DR
ROMANY RISE
WYNDHAM CL
OREGON SQ
ECCLESTON CL
PINEWOOD CL
KELVIN PAR
HILLVIEW CRES
THE MALTINGS
ELM GR
KNOLL RISE
PEPYS RISE
A232 M25 (A224)
GRAVEL PIT WAY
Crofton
GUMPING RD
CROFTON LA
OREGON SQ
YORK RISE
Orpington
HILL VIEW RD
OAKHILL RD
THE APPROACH
ORCHARD GR
66
ORMONDE AVE
CLAREVILLE RD
LYCOTH RD
44
A
B
45
227
C
D
46
CROFTON RD
Mus
STATION RD
KNOLL END
A232
PUR

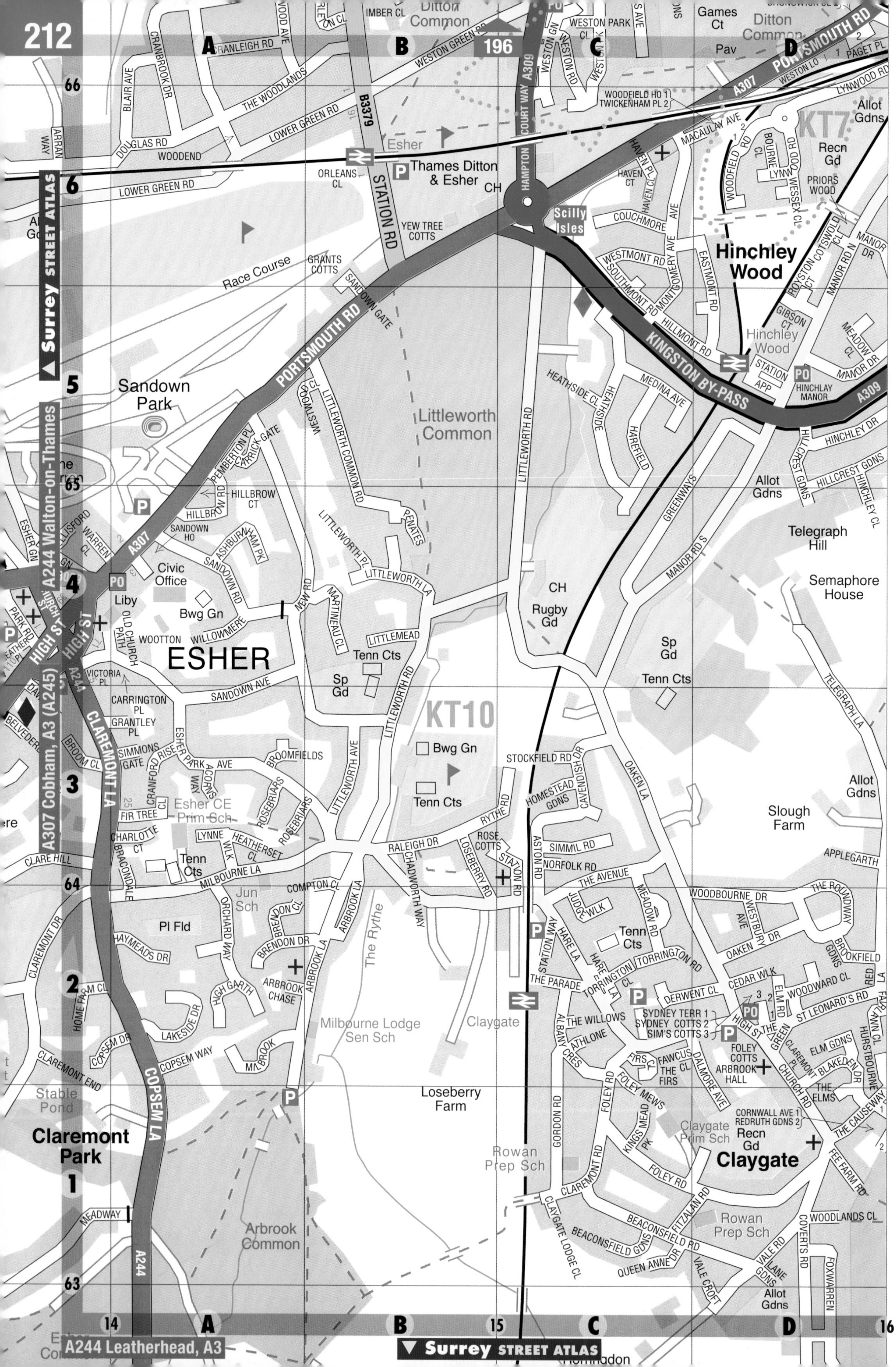

A
B
C
D
196
66
6
5
65
4
3
64
2
1
63
14
15
16
Surrey STREET ATLAS
A244 Walton-on-Thames
A307 Cobham, A3 (A245)
A244 Leatherhead, A3
Ditton Common
Games Ct
Pav
PORTSMOUTH RD
IMBER CL
CRANLEIGH RD
CRANBROOK DR
WESTON GREEN RD
WESTON PARK CL
WESTON GN
WESTON RD
PAGET PL
WESTON LO
LYNWOOD RD
BLAIR AVE
THE WOODLANDS
LOWER GREEN RD
DOUGLAS RD
WOODEND
ARRAN WAY
B3379
Esher
COURT WAY A309
HAMPTON
WOODFIELD HO 1
TWICKENHAM PL 2
A307
MACAULAY AVE
HAVEN PL
HAVEN CT
WOODFIELD RD
BOURNE CL
LYNN
WOOD RD
WESSEX CL
KT7
Allot Gdns
Recn Gd
PRIORS WOOD
ORLEANS CL
Thames Ditton & Esher
CH
STATION RD
YEW TREE COTTS
Scilly Isles
COUCHMORE AVE
MONTGOMERY AVE
WESTMONT RD
SOUTHMONT RD
EASTMONT RD
Hinchley Wood
COTSWOLD CL
ROYSTON CT
MANOR RD N
MANOR DR
Race Course
GRANTS COTTS
SANDOWN GATE
HILLMONT RD
KINGSTON BY-PASS
GIBSON CT
STATION APP
MEADOW CL
HINCHLAY MANOR
A309
Sandown Park
PORTSMOUTH RD
WESTWOOD CL
LITTLEWORTH COMMON RD
Littleworth Common
LITTLEWORTH RD
HEATHSIDE CL
HEATHSIDE
MEDINA AVE
HAREFIELD
GREENWAYS
HINCHLEY DR
HILLCREST GDNS
HINCHLEY CL
Allot Gdns
PEMBERTON PL
CARRICK GATE
HILLBROW RD
HILLBROW CT
SANDOWN HO
ASHBURNHAM PK
SANDOWN RD
PENATES
LITTLEWORTH PL
LITTLEWORTH LA
MANOR RD S
Telegraph Hill
Semaphore House
ESHER GN
WARREN CL
Civic Office
Liby
Bwg Gn
NEW RD
MARTINEAU CL
LITTLEMEAD
CH
Rugby Gd
PARK RD
HIGH ST
OLD CHURCH PATH
WOOTTON
WILLOWMERE
ESHER
Tenn Cts
Sp Gd
Sp Gd
Tenn Cts
VICTORIA PL
CARRINGTON PL
GRANTLEY PL
SANDOWN AVE
KT10
TELEGRAPH LA
CLAREMONT LA
BELVEDERE
BROOM CL
SIMMONS GATE
CRANFORD RISE
ESHER PARK AVE
ACORNS WAY
BROOMFIELDS
LITTLEWORTH AVE
Bwg Gn
STOCKFIELD RD
CAVENDISH DR
OAKEN LA
Allot Gdns
FIR TREE CL
Esher CE Prim Sch
ROSEBRIARS
HOMESTEAD GDNS
Tenn Cts
RYTHE RD
Slough Farm
CHARLOTTE CT
LYNNE WLK
HEATHERSET CL
RALEIGH DR
CHADWORTH WAY
ROSE COTTS
SIMMIL RD
CLARE HILL
BRACONDALE
Tenn Cts
MILBOURNE LA
ASTON RD
NORFOLK RD
APPLEGARTH
LOSEBERRY RD
STATION RD
THE AVENUE
Jun Sch
COMPTON CL
ARBROOK LA
JUDGE WLK
MEADOW RD
WOODBOURNE DR
WESTBURY AVE
THE ROUNDWAY
Pl Fld
ORCHARD WAY
BRENDON CL
BRENDON DR
The Rythe
STATION WAY
HARE LA
Tenn Cts
OAKEN DR
BROOKFIELD GDNS
CLAREMONT DR
HAYMEADS DR
TORRINGTON RD
TORRINGTON CL
HOME FARM CL
HIGH GARTH
ARBROOK CHASE
THE PARADE
DERWENT CL
CEDAR WLK
ELM RD
WOODWARD CL
RED LA
ST LEONARD'S RD
FAIRLAWN CL
LAKESIDE DR
Milbourne Lodge Sen Sch
Claygate
ALBANY CRES
THE WILLOWS
SYDNEY TERR 1
SYDNEY COTTS 2
SIM'S COTTS 3
HIGH ST
THE GREEN
CLAREMONT PL
ELM GDNS
HURSTBOURNE
COPSEM DR
COPSEM WAY
MILBROOK
ATHLONE
FIRS CL
FAWCUS CL
THE FIRS
DALMORE AVE
FOLEY COTTS
ARBROOK HALL
BLAKEDEN DR
CHURCH RD
THE ELMS
CLAREMONT END
FOLEY RD
FOLEY MEWS
Loseberry Farm
Stable Pond
Claremont Park
COPSEM LA
GORDON RD
KINGSMEAD PK
Claygate Prim Sch
CORNWALL AVE 1
REDRUTH GDNS 2
Recn Gd
Claygate
THE CAUSEWAY
Rowan Prep Sch
CLAREMONT RD
FOLEY RD
FITZALAN RD
FEE FARM RD
MEADWAY
Arbrook Common
CLAYGATE LODGE CL
BEACONSFIELD GDNS
BEACONSFIELD RD
Rowan Prep Sch
WOODLANDS CL
COVERTS RD
VALE RD
QUEEN ANNE DR
VALE CROFT
GDNS LANE
Allot Gdns
FOXWARREN
A244

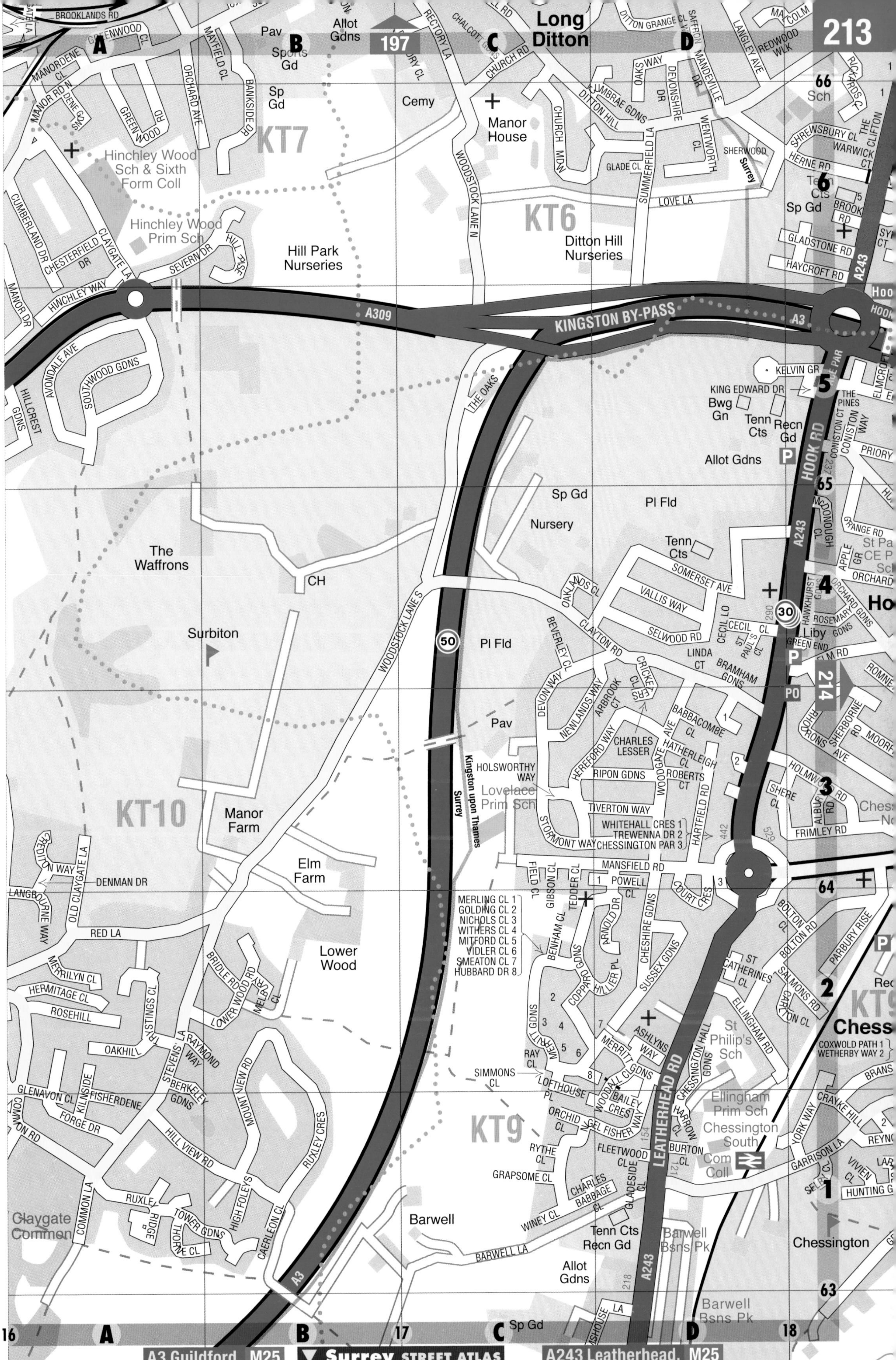

197
Long Ditton
A
B
C
D
BROOKLANDS RD
GREENWOOD CL
MANORDENE CL
MANOR RD N
DENE GDNS
MAYFIELD CL
ORCHARD AVE
GREENWOOD RD
BANKSIDE DR
Pav
Allot Gdns
Sports Gd
Sp Gd
KT7
Hinchley Wood Sch & Sixth Form Coll
Hinchley Wood Prim Sch
CUMBERLAND DR
CHESTERFIELD DR
CLAYGATE LA
SEVERN DR
HILL RISE
HINCHLEY WAY
MANOR DR
RECTORY LA
CHALCOTT GDNS
CHURCH RD
Cemy
Manor House
WOODSTOCK LANE N
Hill Park Nurseries
DITTON GRANGE CL
SAFFRON WAY
MANDEVILLE DR
OAKS WAY
DEVONSHIRE DR
CUMBRAE GDNS
DITTON HILL
CHURCH MDW
SUMMERFIELD LA
GLADE CL
WENTWORTH CL
SHERWOOD
Surrey
LOVE LA
KT6
Ditton Hill Nurseries
LANGLEY AVE
REDWOOD WLK
MALCOLM
RICHARDS CL
66
Sch
SHREWSBURY CL
THE CLIFTON
WARWICK CT
HERNE RD
Tenn Cts
6
Sp Gd
BROOK RD
GLADSTONE RD
HAYCROFT RD
A243
A309
KINGSTON BY-PASS
A3
AVONDALE AVE
SOUTHWOOD GDNS
HILLCREST GDNS
THE OAKS
KELVIN GR
KING EDWARD DR
5
Bwg Gn
Tenn Cts
Recn Gd
THE PINES
CONISTON CT
CONISTON WAY
PRIORY
Allot Gdns
HOOK RD
65
McDONOUGH CL
GRANGE RD
Sp Gd
Pl Fld
Nursery
The Waffrons
CH
Tenn Cts
SOMERSET AVE
OAKLANDS CL
VALLIS WAY
St Paul CE Prim Sch
APPLE GR
ORCHARD
4
HAWKHURST GDNS
ORCHARD GDNS
ROSEMARY GDNS
30
Surbiton
WOODSTOCK LANE S
50
Pl Fld
BEVERLEY CL
CLAYTON RD
SELWOOD RD
CECIL CL
CECIL LO
ST PAUL'S CL
LINDA CT
Liby
GREEN END
ELM RD
BRAMHAM GDNS
214
PO
DEVON WAY
NEWLANDS WAY
ARBROOK CT
CRICKETERS CL
BABBACOMBE CL
Pav
CHARLES LESSER
HEREFORD WAY
WOODGATE AVE
HATHERLEIGH CL
SHERBORNE RD
RHODRONS AVE
HOLSWORTHY WAY
Kingston upon Thames
Surrey
RIPON GDNS
ROBERTS CT
HARTFIELD RD
HOLMWOOD RD
SHERE CL
ALBURY RD
3
KT10
Manor Farm
Lovelace Prim Sch
TIVERTON WAY
WHITEHALL CRES 1
TREWENNA DR 2
CHESSINGTON PAR 3
STORMONT WAY
FRIMLEY RD
Elm Farm
MANSFIELD RD
FIELD CL
GIBSON CL
TEDDER CL
POWELL CL
COURT CRES
64
CREDITON WAY
LANGBOURNE WAY
DENMAN DR
OLD CLAYGATE LA
RED LA
MERLING CL 1
GOLDING CL 2
NICHOLS CL 3
WITHERS CL 4
MITFORD CL 5
VIDLER CL 6
SMEATON CL 7
HUBBARD DR 8
BENHAM CL
ARNOLD DR
CHESHIRE GDNS
BOLTON CL
BOLTON RD
PARBURY RISE
Lower Wood
BRIDLE RD
LOWER WOOD RD
MELBURY CL
COPPARD GDNS
HILLIER PL
SUSSEX GDNS
ST CATHERINES CL
SALMONS RD
CARLTON CL
2
Chess
MERRILYN CL
HERMITAGE CL
ROSEHILL
TRYSTINGS CL
ELLINGHAM RD
MERRITT GDNS
ASHLYNS WAY
St Philip's Sch
COXWOLD PATH 1
WETHERBY WAY 2
OAKHILL
STEVENS LA
RAYMOND WAY
RAY CL
SIMMONS CL
LOFTHOUSE PL
WOODHALL CL
BAILEY CRES
NIGEL FISHER WAY
CHESSINGTON HALL GDNS
HARROW CL
Ellingham Prim Sch
BRANS
CRAYKE HILL
YORK WAY
GLENAVON CL
KILNSIDE
FISHERDENE
BERKELEY GDNS
FORGE DR
COMMON RD
MOUNT VIEW RD
HILL VIEW RD
ORCHID CL
KT9
RYTHE CL
FLEETWOOD CL
LEATHERHEAD RD
BURTON CL
Chessington South
Com Coll
GARRISON LA
REYNOLDS
VIVIEN CL
HUNTING G
1
RUXLEY CRES
HIGH FOLEYS
GRAPSOME CL
CHARLES BABBAGE CL
GLADESIDE CL
SELBY CL
RUXLEY RIDGE
TOWER GDNS
THORNE CL
CAERLEON CL
Barwell
WINEY CL
Tenn Cts
Recn Gd
Barwell Bsns Pk
Claygate Common
COMMON LA
BARWELL LA
Allot Gdns
Chessington
63
Barwell Bsns Pk
LA
Sp Gd
16
17
18

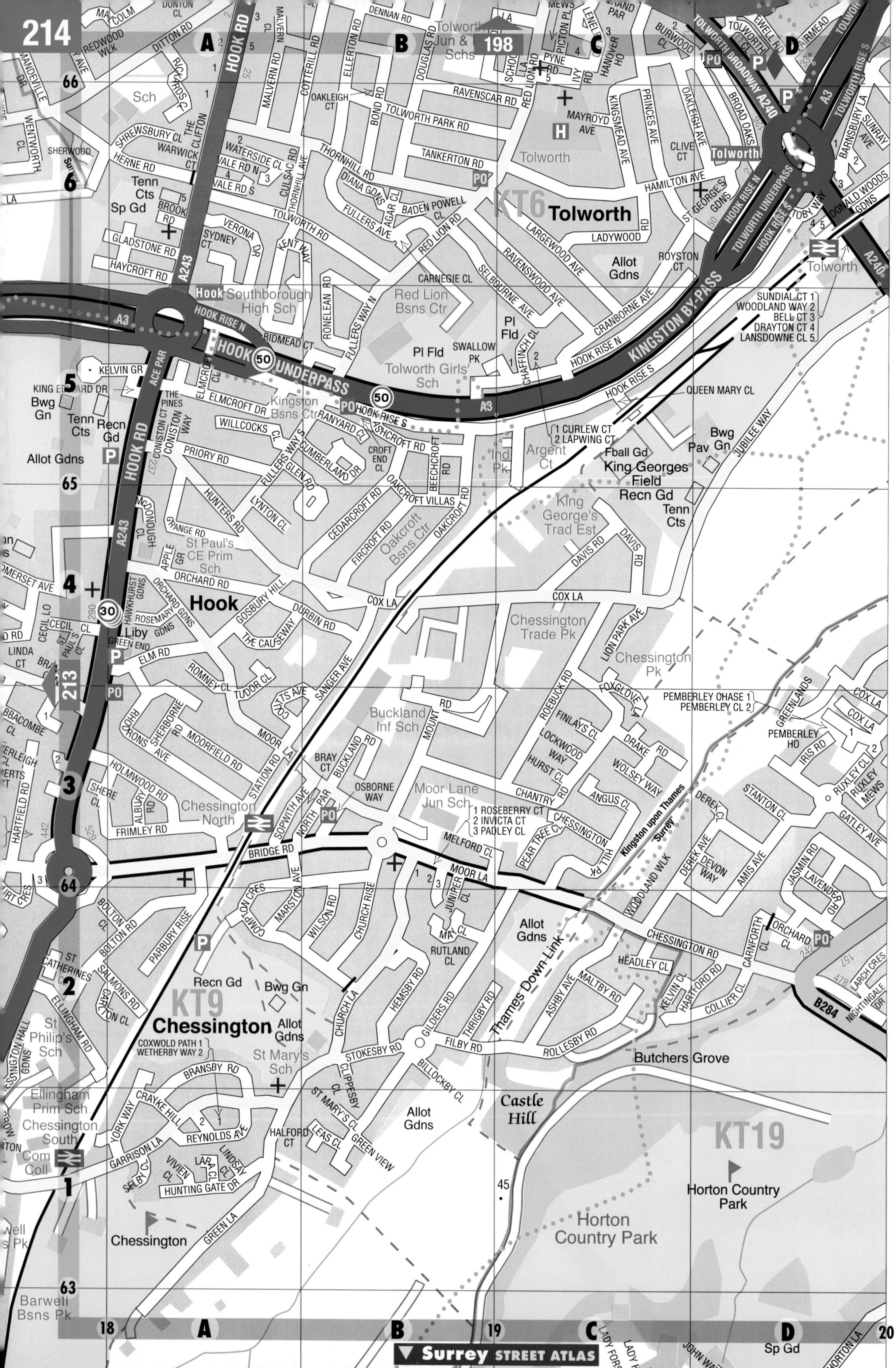
A
B
C
D
198
213
66
6
5
65
4
3
64
2
1
63
18
19
20
HOOK RD
A243
DITTON RD
REDWOOD WLK
MANDEVILLE DR
WENTWORTH CL
SHERWOOD
Sch
RICHARDS CL
THE CLIFTON
SHREWSBURY CL
WARWICK CT
HERNE RD
Tenn Cts
Sp Gd
BROOK RD
GLADSTONE RD
HAYCROFT RD
MALVERN RD
MALVERN CL
COTTERILL RD
ELLERTON RD
DENNAN RD
DOUGLAS RD
Tolworth Jun & Inf Schs
OAKLEIGH CT
BOND RD
TOLWORTH PARK RD
RAVENSCAR RD
WATERSIDE CL
VALE RD N
VALE RD S
CULSAC RD
THORNHILL AVE
THORNHILL RD
DIANA GDNS
FULLERS AVE
AGAR CL
BADEN POWELL CL
TANKERTON RD
TOLWORTH RD
KENT WAY
SYDNEY CT
VERONA DR
RED LION RD
PYNE RD
PICTON PL
IVY RD
HANOVER HO
MAYROYD AVE
KINGSMEAD AVE
PRINCES AVE
OAKLEIGH AVE
BROAD OAKS
TOLWORTH BROADWAY A240
BURWOOD CL
TOLWORTH CL
EWELL RD
FAIRMEAD
TOLWORTH RISE S
A3
BARNSBURY LA
SUNRAY AVE
CLIVE CT
Tolworth
KT6
Tolworth
HAMILTON AVE
LADYWOOD RD
ST GEORGE'S GDNS
HOOK RISE N
TOLWORTH UNDERPASS
HOOK RISE S
TOBY WAY
DONALD WOODS GDNS
A240
LARGEWOOD AVE
RAVENSWOOD AVE
SELBOURNE AVE
Allot Gdns
ROYSTON CT
KINGSTON BY-PASS
CARNEGIE CL
RONELEAN RD
FULLERS WAY N
Red Lion Bsns Ctr
Pl Fld
CRANBORNE AVE
SUNDIAL CT 1
WOODLAND WAY 2
BELL CT 3
DRAYTON CT 4
LANSDOWNE CL 5
Hook
Southborough High Sch
HOOK RISE N
BIDMEAD CT
HOOK UNDERPASS
SWALLOW PK
CHAFFINCH CL
Tolworth Girls' Sch
QUEEN MARY CL
KELVIN GR
KING EDWARD DR
Bwg Gn
Tenn Cts
Recn Gd
Allot Gdns
ACE PAR
THE PINES
ELMCROFT CL
ELMCROFT DR
Kingston Bsns Ctr
RANYARD CL
ASHCROFT RD
CONISTON CT
CONISTON WAY
WILLCOCKS CL
PRIORY RD
FULLERS WAY S
CUMBERLAND DR
GLEN RD
CROFT END CL
BEECHCROFT RD
1 CURLEW CT
2 LAPWING CT
Ind Pk
Argent Ct
Fball Gd
King Georges Field
Recn Gd
Pav
Bwg Gn
Tenn Cts
JUBILEE WAY
HUNTERS RD
LYNTON CL
CEDARCROFT RD
OAKCROFT VILLAS
OAKCROFT RD
FIRCROFT RD
Oakcroft Bsns Ctr
King George's Trad Est
DAVIS RD
MCDONOUGH CL
GRANGE RD
St Paul's CE Prim Sch
APPLE GR
ORCHARD RD
SOMERSET AVE
HAWKHURST GDNS
ROSEMARY GDNS
ORCHARD GDNS
Hook
GOSBURY HILL
DURBIN RD
COX LA
Chessington Trade Pk
LION PARK AVE
Chessington Pk
CECIL CL
CECIL RD
ST PAUL'S CL
LINDA CT
Liby
GREEN END
ELM RD
THE CAUSEWAY
ROMNEY CL
TUDOR CL
COUTTS AVE
SANGER AVE
Buckland Inf Sch
MOUNT RD
ROEBUCK RD
FOXGLOVE LA
FINLAYS CL
LOCKWOOD WAY
DRAKE RD
HURST CL
WOLSEY WAY
PEMBERLEY CHASE 1
PEMBERLEY CL 2
GREENLANDS
PEMBERLEY HO
IRIS RD
COX LA
RUXLEY CL
RUXLEY MEWS
STANTON CL
GATLEY AVE
BABBACOMBE CL
HARTFIELD RD
RHODRONS AVE
SHERBORNE RD
MOORFIELD RD
MOOR LA
STATION RD
BRAY CT
BUCKLAND RD
OSBORNE WAY
Moor Lane Jun Sch
1 ROSEBERRY CT
2 INVICTA CT
3 PADLEY CL
CHANTRY RD
ANGUS CL
CHESSINGTON HILL PK
PEAR TREE CL
Kingston upon Thames
Surrey
DEREK CL
DEREK AVE
DEVON WAY
AMIS AVE
JASMIN RD
LAVENDER RD
HOLMWOOD RD
SHERE CL
ALBURY RD
Chessington North
FRIMLEY RD
SOPWITH AVE
NORTH PAR
BRIDGE RD
MELFORD CL
JUNIPER CL
MAY CL
RUTLAND CL
WOODLAND WLK
Allot Gdns
Thames Down Link
CHESSINGTON RD
CARNFORTH CL
ORCHARD CL
BOLTON CL
BOLTON RD
PARBURY RISE
COMPTON CRES
MARSTON AVE
WILSON RD
CHURCH RISE
ST CATHERINES CT
SALMONS RD
CARLTON CL
ELLINGHAM RD
Recn Gd
Bwg Gn
KT9
Chessington
Allot Gdns
CHURCH LA
HEMSBY RD
GILDERS RD
THRIGBY RD
ASHBY AVE
MALTBY RD
HEADLEY CL
KELVIN CL
HARTFORD RD
COLLIER CL
B284
LARCH CRES
NIGHTINGALE DR
St Philip's Sch
COXWOLD PATH 1
WETHERBY WAY 2
St Mary's Sch
STOKESBY RD
FILBY RD
ROLLESBY RD
Butchers Grove
BRANSBY RD
BILLOCKBY CL
CLIPPESBY CL
Ellingham Prim Sch
Chessington South
Com Coll
CRAYKE HILL
YORK WAY
REYNOLDS AVE
ST MARY'S CL
Allot Gdns
Castle Hill
KT19
HALFORD CT
LEAS CL
GREEN VIEW
GARRISON LA
VIVIEN CL
LARA CL
LINDSAY DR
SELBY CL
HUNTING GATE DR
Horton Country Park
Horton Country Park
Chessington
GREEN LA
Barwell Bsns Pk
LADY FORSDYKE WAY
JOHN WATKIN
Sp Gd
HORTON LA

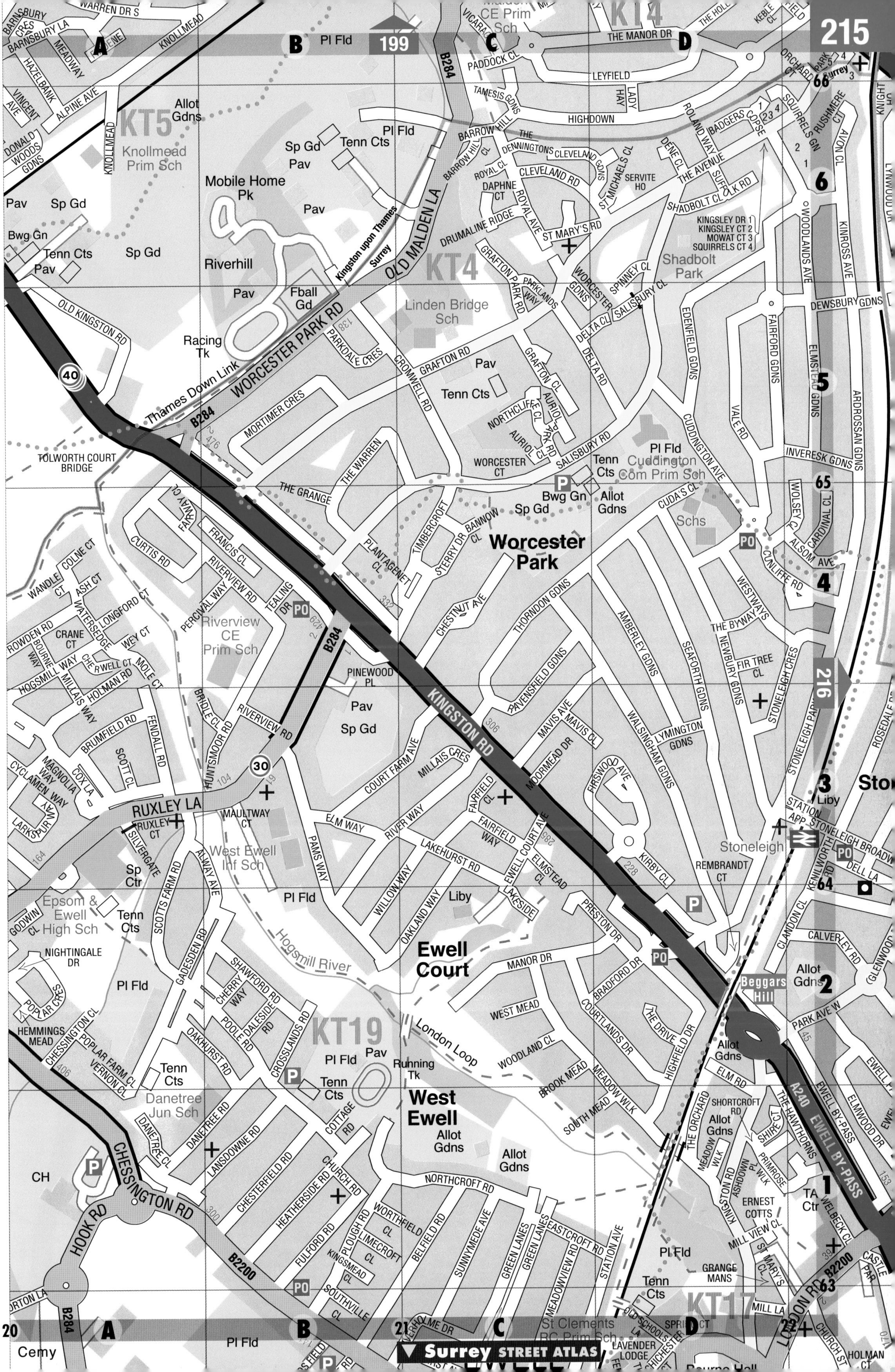
199
216
KT5
KT4
KT19
KT17
KT14
A
B
C
D
1
2
3
4
5
6
63
64
65
66
20
21
22
Worcester Park
Ewell Court
West Ewell
Stoneleigh
Beggars Hill
Knollmead Prim Sch
Linden Bridge Sch
Cuddington Com Prim Sch
Riverview CE Prim Sch
West Ewell Inf Sch
Epsom & Ewell High Sch
Danetree Jun Sch
St Clements RC Prim Sch
Shadbolt Park
Mobile Home Pk
Riverhill
Racing Tk
Running Tk
Hogsmill River
London Loop
Thames Down Link
Kingston upon Thames
Surrey
TOLWORTH COURT BRIDGE
OLD MALDEN LA
WORCESTER PARK RD
KINGSTON RD
OLD KINGSTON RD
RUXLEY LA
CHESSINGTON RD
HOOK RD
EWELL BY-PASS
A240
B284
B2200
THE MANOR DR
LEYFIELD
HIGHDOWN
BARROW HILL
CLEVELAND RD
DRUMALINE RIDGE
ST MARY'S RD
GRAFTON RD
CROMWELL RD
SALISBURY RD
DELTA RD
EDENFIELD GDNS
CUDDINGTON AVE
FAIRFORD GDNS
ELMSTEAD GDNS
ARDROSSAN GDNS
INVERESK GDNS
DEWSBURY GDNS
WOODLANDS AVE
KINROSS AVE
THE AVENUE
THE GRANGE
THE WARREN
MORTIMER CRES
PARKDALE CRES
TIMBERCROFT
PLANTAGENET CL
STERRY DR
CHESTNUT AVE
THORNDON GDNS
AMBERLEY GDNS
SEAFORTH GDNS
NEWBURY GDNS
WESTWAYS
THE BYWAY
FIR TREE CL
STONELEIGH CRES
STONELEIGH PARK
STONELEIGH BROADWAY
STATION APP
PAVENSFIELD GDNS
MAVIS AVE
MOORMEAD DR
FIRSWOOD AVE
WALSINGHAM GDNS
LYMINGTON GDNS
KIRBY CL
REMBRANDT CT
COURT FARM AVE
MILLAIS CRES
FAIRFIELD CL
FAIRFIELD WAY
ELM WAY
RIVER WAY
LAKEHURST RD
EWELL COURT AVE
ELMSTEAD CL
LAKESIDE
WILLOW WAY
OAKLAND WAY
PAMS WAY
PRESTON DR
MANOR DR
BRADFORD DR
COURTLANDS DR
THE DRIVE
HIGHFIELD DR
WEST MEAD
WOODLAND CL
BROOK MEAD
MEADOW WLK
SOUTH MEAD
RIVERVIEW RD
PERCIVAL WAY
FRANCIS CL
CURTIS RD
HOGSMILL WAY
MILLAIS WAY
HOLMAN RD
BRUMFIELD RD
FENDALL RD
SCOTT CL
HUNTSMOOR RD
BRIDLE CL
MAGNOLIA WAY
CYCLAMEN WAY
LARKSPUR WAY
SILVERGATE
SCOTTS FARM RD
ALWAY AVE
GADESDEN RD
SHAWFORD RD
CHERRY WAY
DALESIDE RD
POOLE RD
CROSSLANDS RD
OAKHURST RD
NIGHTINGALE DR
POPLAR CRES
HEMMINGS MEAD
CHESSINGTON CL
POPLAR FARM CL
VERNON CL
DANETREE RD
DANETREE CL
LANSDOWNE RD
CHESTERFIELD RD
HEATHERSIDE RD
CHURCH RD
COTTAGE RD
FULFORD RD
PLOUGH RD
KINGSMEAD CL
LIMECROFT CL
WORTHFIELD CL
BELFIELD RD
NORTHCROFT RD
SUNNYMEDE AVE
GREEN LANES
MEADOWVIEW RD
EASTCROFT RD
STATION AVE
SOUTHVILLE CL
THE ORCHARD
ELM RD
SHORTCROFT RD
THE HAWTHORNS
SHIREFCT
PRIMROSE WLK
ERNEST COTTS
MILL VIEW CL
GRANGE MANS
ST MARY'S CL
WELBECK CL
LONDON RD
CASTLE PAR
CHURCH ST
MILL LA
HOLMAN CT
CALVERLEY RD
CLANDON CL
KENILWORTH RD
DELL LA
PARK AVE W
GLENWOOD
ELMWOOD DR
EWELL PARK
ROSEDALE
LAVENDER LODGE
CHICHESTER
Bourne Hall
Cemy
CH
Allot Gdns
Pl Fld
Sp Gd
Pav
Tenn Cts
Bwg Gn
Fball Gd
Sp Ctr
TA Ctr
Liby
Schs
Pt

North Cheam
Stoneleigh
Nonsuch Park
Cheam Park
KT4
KT17
SM3
SM2
CENTRAL RD
CHEAM COMMON RD
LONDON RD
MALDEN RD
EWELL BY-PASS
EWELL RD
CHEAM RD
STONELEIGH PARK RD
STONELEIGH AVE
STONELEIGH BROADWAY
SPARROW FARM RD
THE AVENUE
Nonsuch Prim Sch
Nonsuch High Sch for Girls
Harefield Bridge
Organ Crossroads
Superstore
Recn Gd
Allot Gdns
A24 Epsom
A232 Epsom (A24)
Surrey STREET ATLAS
200
215

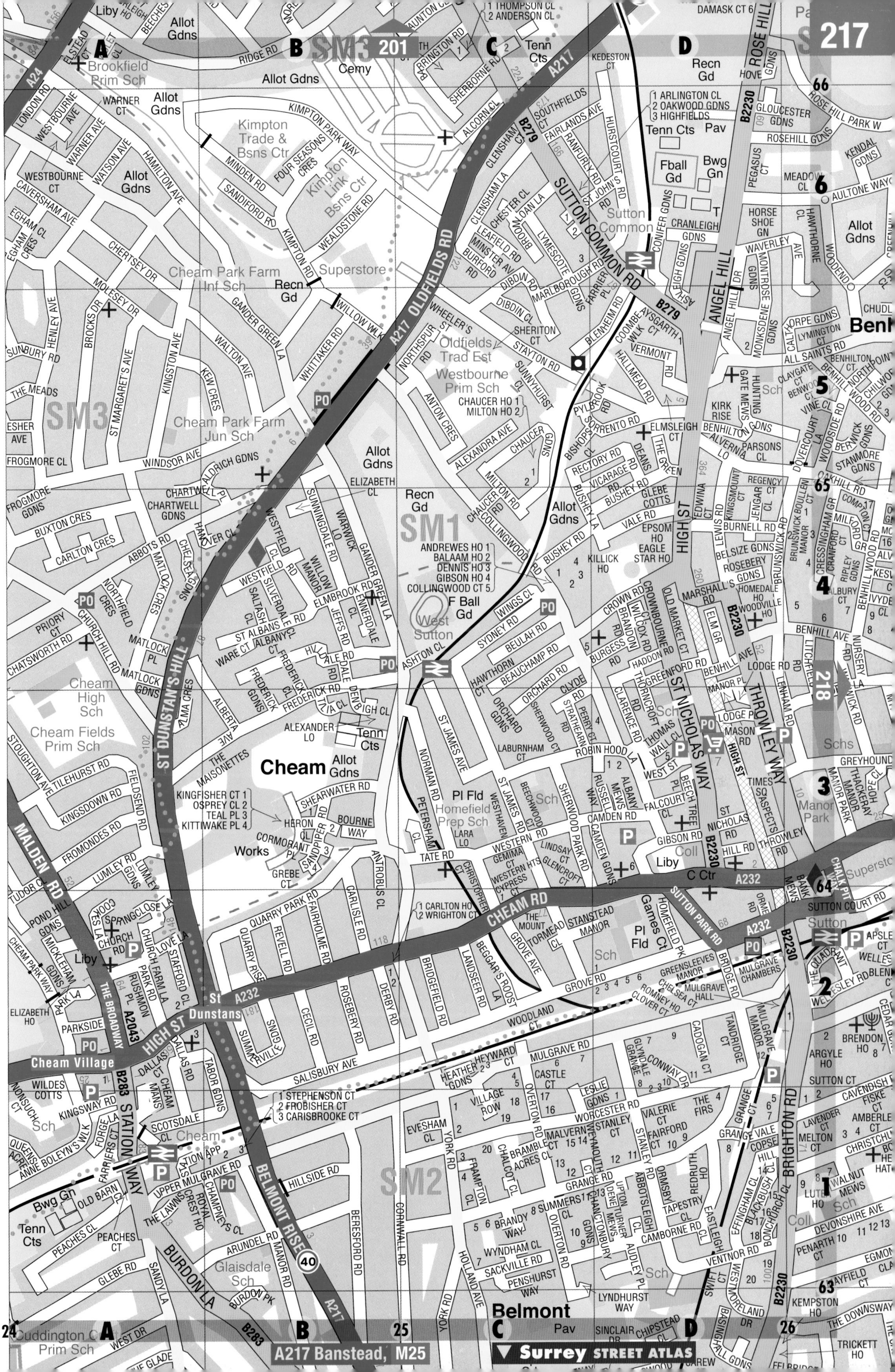
SM3
201
Liby
Allot Gdns
Brookfield Prim Sch
Ridge Rd
Cemy
Tenn Cts
Damask Ct
Recn Gd
Rose Hill
A217
A24
London Rd
Westbourne Ave
Warner Ct
Warner Ave
Watson Ave
Hamilton Ave
Kimpton Trade & Bsns Ctr
Kimpton Link Bsns Ctr
Kimpton Park Way
Four Seasons Cres
Minden Rd
Sandiford Rd
Kimpton Rd
Wealdstone Rd
Alcorn Cl
Sherborne Rd
Barrington Rd
Southfields
Fairlands Ave
Ranfurly Rd
Hurstcourt Rd
Kedeston Ct
1 Arlington Cl
2 Oakwood Gdns
3 Highfields
Tenn Cts
Pav
Fball Gd
Bwg Gn
B2230
Gloucester Gdns
Rosehill Gdns
Rose Hill Park W
Kendal Gdns
Pegasus Ct
Meadow Cl
Aultone Way
Westbourne Ct
Caversham Ave
Egham Cl
Egham Cres
Chertsey Dr
Cheam Park Farm Inf Sch
Superstore
Recn Gd
Molesey Dr
Clensham La
Clensham Ct
Chester Cl
Leafield Rd
Minster Av
Burford Rd
Brook Rd
Loan La
Lymescote Gdns
Sutton Common Rd
Sutton Common
St John's Rd
Conifer Gdns
Cranleigh Gdns
Horse Shoe Gn
Hawthorne Cl
Allot Gdns
Waverley Ave
Montrose Gdns
Ashleigh Gdns
Angel Hill
Angel Hill Dr
Marlborough Rd
Farrier Pl
Dibdin Rd
Dibdin Cl
Gander Green La
Willow Wlk
Oldfields Rd
Wheeler's La
Northspur Rd
Oldfields Trad Est
Westbourne Prim Sch
Sheriton Ct
Stayton Rd
Blenheim Rd
Coombe Wlk
Aysgarth Ct
Vermont Rd
Hallmead Rd
Monksdene Gdns
Calthorpe Gdns
Lymington Ct
All Saints Rd
Benhilton Ct
Northpoint
Benh
Sunbury Rd
Henley Ave
Brocks Dr
St Margaret's Ave
Kingston Ave
Walton Ave
Kew Cres
Whittaker Rd
The Meads
SM3
PO
Cheam Park Farm Jun Sch
Esher Ave
Frogmore Cl
Windsor Ave
Aldrich Gdns
Anton Cres
Chaucer Ho
Milton Ho
Alexandra Ave
Chaucer Gdns
Sunnyhurst Cl
Pylbrook Rd
Sorrento Rd
Bishopsford
Elmsleigh Ct
The Green
Kirk Rise
Gate Mews
Hunting Gdns
Claygate Ct
Benwood Ct
Benhilton Gdns
Parsons Cl
Alverna Lo
Vine Cl
Dovercourt La
Woodside Rd
Berwick Gdns
Stanmore Gdns
Frogmore Gdns
Chartwell Pl
Chartwell Gdns
Westfield Cl
Sunningdale Rd
Warwick Lo
Elizabeth Cl
Recn Gd
SM1
Milton Rd
Collingwood Rd
Rectory Rd
Vicarage Rd
Bushey Rd
Glebe Cotts
Vale Rd
Epsom Ho
Eagle Star Ho
High St
Edwina Ct
Lewis Rd
Kingsmount Ct
Regency Ct
Jengar Cl
Burnell Rd
Belsize Gdns
Rosebery Gdns
Homedale Ho
Woodville Ho
Brunswick Rd
Cressingham Gr
Milford Gdns
Buxton Cres
Carlton Cres
Abbots Rd
Chelsea Gdns
Matlock Cres
Northfield Cres
Willow Manor
Gander Green La
Andrewes Ho
Balaam Ho
Dennis Ho
Gibson Ho
Collingwood Ct
F Ball Gd
Killick Ho
Crown Rd
Crownbourne Ct
Old Market Ct
Marshall's Rd
Elm Gr
Benhill Ave
Priory Ct
Church Hill Rd
Chatsworth Rd
Matlock Pl
Matlock Gdns
Cheam High Sch
Cheam Fields Prim Sch
Westfield Rd
Saltash Cl
Silverdale Rd
St Albans Rd
Elmbrook Rd
Jeffs Rd
Ennerdale Cl
West Sutton
Ashton Cl
Wings Cl
Sydney Rd
Beulah Rd
Wilcox Rd
Brandon Rd
Burgess Rd
Haddon Rd
Greenford Rd
St Nicholas Way
Lodge Rd
Litchfield Rd
Nursery Rd
218
Hillsdale Rd
Frederick Gdns
Frederick Rd
Frederick Cl
Denbigh Cl
Alexander Lo
Tenn Cts
Hawthorn Ct
Beauchamp Rd
Orchard Rd
Clyde Rd
Sherwood Ct
Strathearn Rd
Perry Ct
Clarence Rd
Thorncroft Rd
Thomas Wall Cl
Manor Pl
Lodge Pl
Mason Rd
Throwley Way
Schs
Greyhound
Stoughton Ave
Tilehurst Rd
Kingsdown Rd
Fromondes Rd
Fieldsend Rd
St Dunstan's Hill
Alma Cres
Alberta Ave
The Maisonettes
Cheam
Allot Gdns
Kingfisher Ct
Osprey Cl
Teal Pl
Kittiwake Pl
Shearwater Rd
Heron Cl
Bourne Way
Cormorant Pl
Sandpiper Rd
Works
Grebe Ct
Norman Rd
Petersham Cl
St James Ave
Orchard Gdns
Laburnham Ct
Pl Fld
Homefield Prep Sch
Lara Lo
Westhaven
Beechwood Ct
Sherwood Park Rd
Russell Way
Robin Hood La
Albany Mews
Camden Rd
West St
Falcourt Cl
Beech Tree Pl
St Nicholas Rd
Gibson Rd
Coll
Liby
Hill Rd
Throwley Rd
Times Sq
Aspects
Manor Park
Thackeray Manor
Malden Rd
Lumley Rd
Lumley Gdns
Tudor Cl
Pond Hill Gdns
Mickleham Gdns
Cheam Park Way
Spring Close La
Church Rd
Church Farm La
Love La
Stafford Cl
Quarry Park Rd
Quarry Rise
Revell Rd
Fairholme Rd
Carlisle Rd
Antrobus Cl
Tate Rd
Christopher
1 Carlton Ho
2 Wrighton Ct
Western Rd
Gemima Ct
Western Hts
Cypress Ct
Lindsay Ct
Glencroft
Camden Gdns
Cheam Rd
The Mount
Tormead Cl
Stanstead Manor
Grove Ave
Games Ct
Pl Fld
Homefield Pk
Sutton Park Rd
A232
C Ctr
Bank Mews
Chalk Pit Way
Superstore
Orme Rd
Sutton Court Rd
Sutton
Apsley Ct
Welle
The Quadrant
Wellesley Rd
Blen
Rushmon Pl
The Broadway
Liby
Park La
Elizabeth Ho
Parkside
Cheam Village
High St
St Dunstans
A2043
B283
Dallas Rd
Tabor Gdns
Summerville Gdns
Cecil Rd
Rosebery Rd
Derby Rd
Bridgefield Rd
Landseer Rd
Beggar's Roost La
Grove Rd
Greensleeves Manor
Chelsea Ct
Romney Ho
Clover Ct
Mulgrave Hall
Bridge Rd
Mulgrave Chambers
Woodland Ct
Heyward Ct
Heather Gdns
Mulgrave Rd
Castle Ct
Leslie Gdns
Glyndale Grange
Conway Dr
Cadogan Ct
Tandridge Ct
Mulgrave Manor
Brendon Ho
Argyle Ho
Sutton Ct
Cavendish
Fiske Ct
Amberley Ct
Wildes Cotts
Nonsuch Ct
Kingsway Rd
Forge La
Cheam Mans
Scotsdale Cl
Salisbury Ave
1 Stephenson Ct
2 Frobisher Ct
3 Carisbrooke Ct
Village Row
Overton Rd
Worcester Rd
Valerie Ct
Fairford Ct
The Firs
Grange Ct
Grange Vale
Copse Hill
Lavender Ct
Melton Ct
Christchurch
Sch
Queens Acre
Anne Boleyn's Wlk
Farriers Ct
Station Way
Cheam
Station App
Upper Mulgrave Rd
Evesham Cl
York Rd
Bramble Acres Cl
Chalcot Cl
Malvern Ct
Stanley Ct
Weymouth Ct
Stanley Rd
SM2
Frampton Cl
Grange Rd
Ormsby
Redruth Ho
Tapestry Cl
Effingham Cl
Blackbush Cl
Bonchurch Cl
Brighton Rd
Walnut Mews
Luten Ho
Devonshire Ave
Bwg Gn
Old Barn Cl
Tenn Cts
Peaches Cl
Peaches Ct
The Lawns
Crest Ho
Royal Ct
Champneys Cl
Hillside Rd
Belmont Rise
Beresford Rd
Cornwall Rd
Brandy Way
Summers Cl
Upton Ct
Dene Mews
Turner Cl
Chanctonbury Gdns
Abbotsleigh Cl
Camborne Rd
Eastleigh Cl
Wyndham Cl
Sackville Rd
Penshurst Way
Audley Pl
Sch
Ventnor Rd
Swift Ct
Westmoreland Dr
Penarth Ct
Egmont
Mayfield Ct
Kempston Ho
B2230
Glebe Rd
Sandy La
Burdon La
Arundel Rd
Manor Rd
Glaisdale Sch
Burdon Pk
40
Holland Ave
Lyndhurst Way
Belmont
Pav
Sinclair Ct
Chipstead Cl
Basinghall Gdns
The Downsway
Trickett Ho
Cuddington C
Prim Sch
West Dr
A217 Banstead, M25
Felbridge
Carew
Surrey STREET ATLAS
A
B
C
D
24
25
26
6
5
4
3
2
1
66
65
64
63

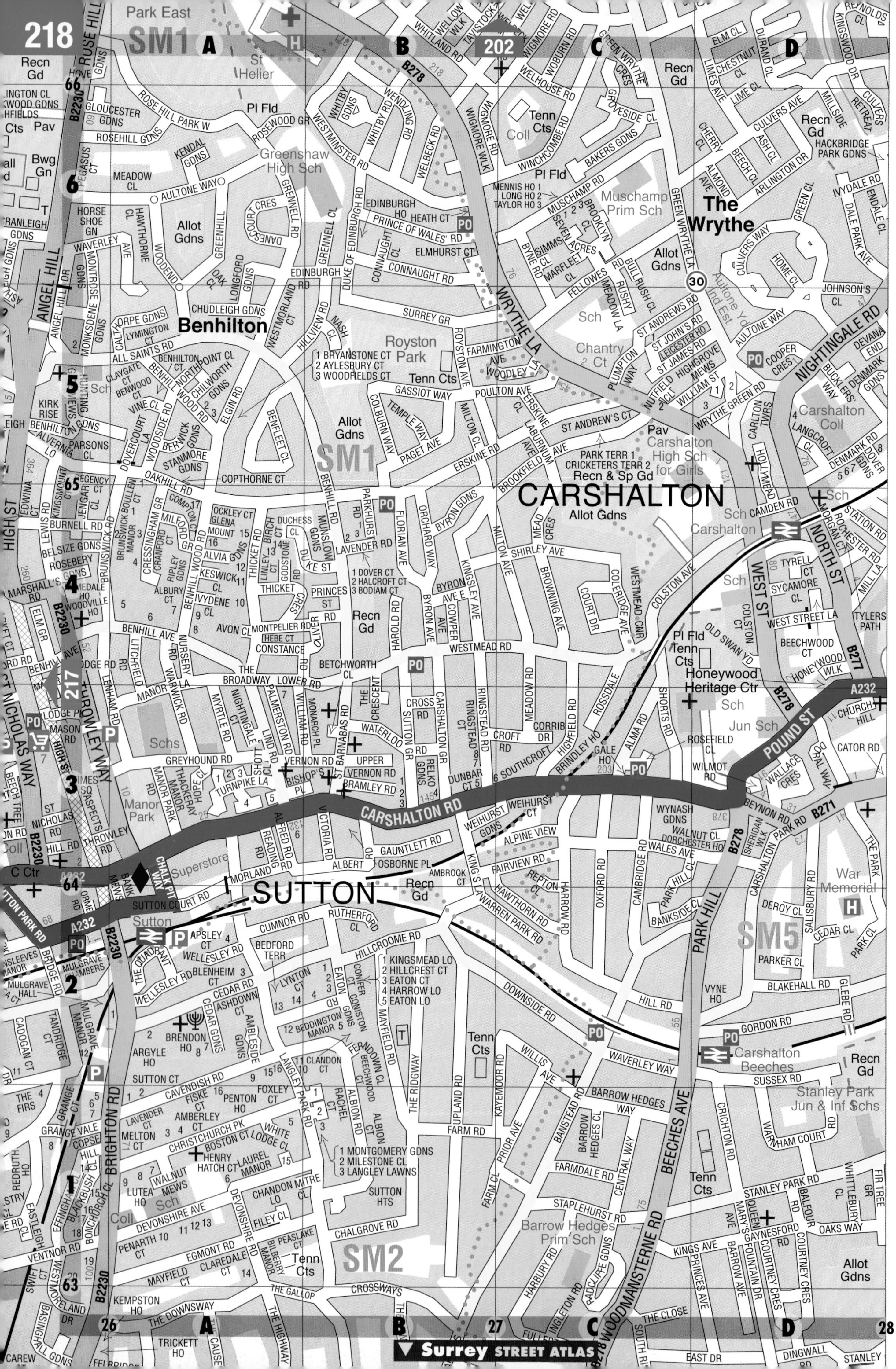
SM1
A
B
C
D
202
Park East
St Helier
Recn Gd
ROSE HILL
GLOUCESTER GDNS
ROSE HILL PARK W
ROSEHILL GDNS
Pl Fld
ROSEWOOD GR
Greenshaw High Sch
KENDAL GDNS
MEADOW CL
AULTONE WAY
HORSE SHOE GN
HAWTHORNE
Allot Gdns
DANESBURY CRES
GRENNELL RD
GREENHILL
WOODEND
WAVERLEY AVE
MONTROSE GDNS
ANGEL HILL
ANGEL HILL DR
MONKSDENE GDNS
CHUDLEIGH GDNS
Benhilton
LYMINGTON CT
ALL SAINTS RD
WESTMORLAND CT
HILLVIEW RD
WHITBY GDNS
WHITBY RD
WENDLING RD
WESTMINSTER RD
WELBECK RD
WIGMORE WLK
WIGMORE RD
WHITLAND RD
TAVISTOCK
B278
EDINBURGH HO
HEATH CT
PRINCE OF WALES' RD
PO
ELMHURST CT
CONNAUGHT RD
DUKE OF EDINBURGH RD
EDINBURGH RD
SURREY GR
ROYSTON AVE
Royston Park
1 BRYANSTONE CT
2 AYLESBURY CT
3 WOODFIELDS CT
Tenn Cts
FARMINGTON AVE
WOODLEY LA
WRYTHE LA
GASSIOT WAY
POULTON AVE
TEMPLE WAY
COLBURN WAY
PAGET AVE
MILTON CL
ERSKINE RD
LABURNUM
BROOKFIELD AVE
ST ANDREW'S CT
Coll
Tenn Cts
WINCHCOMBE RD
BAKERS GDNS
GROVESIDE CL
GREEN WRYTHE CRES
WELHOUSE RD
WOBURN RD
MENNIS HO 1
LONG HO 2
TAYLOR HO 3
MUSCHAMP RD
Muschamp Prim Sch
SEVEN ACRES
BROOKLYN
SIMMS CL
MARFLEET CL
FELLOWES RD
MEADOW LA
RUSHY
BULLRUSH CL
Allot Gdns
Sch
Chantry Ct
PLUMPTON WAY
ST ANDREWS RD
ST JOHN'S RD
LEICESTER HO
ST JAMES RD
HIGHGROVE MEWS
NUTFIELD CL
WILLIAM ST
WRYTHE GREEN RD
GREEN WRYTHE LA
The Wrythe
30
Aultone Yd Ind Est
AULTONE WAY
Recn Gd
ELM CL
CHESTNUT CL
LIMES AVE
LIME CL
DURAND CL
CHERRY
ALMOND AVE
BEECH CL
ASH CL
CULVERS AVE
ARLINGTON DR
Recn Gd
HACKBRIDGE PARK GDNS
MILLSIDE
CULVERS RETREAT
KINGSWOOD DR
REYNOLDS CL
IVYDALE RD
ENDALE CL
DALE PARK AVE
CULVERS WAY
HOME CL
GREEN CL
JOHNSON'S CL
NIGHTINGALE RD
DEVANA END
DENMARK GDNS
COOPER CRES
BUCKLERS' WAY
Carshalton Coll
LANGCROFT CL
DENMARK RD
DOVER RD
CARLTON TWRS
HOLLYMEAD
CAMDEN RD
MORGAN CT
STATION RD
ROCHESTER RD
Pav
Carshalton High Sch for Girls
PARK TERR 1
CRICKETERS TERR 2
Recn & Sp Gd
CARSHALTON
Allot Gdns
Sch
Carshalton
NORTH ST
WEST ST
Sch
TYRELL CT
SYCAMORE CL
WEST STREET LA
MILL LA
TYLERS PATH
BEECHWOOD CT
HONEYWOOD WLK
B277
A232
CHURCH HILL
CATOR RD
POUND ST
B278
Honeywood Heritage Ctr
Sch
Jun Sch
Pl Fld
Tenn Cts
OLD SWAN YD
COLSTON CT
COLSTON AVE
WESTMEAD CNR
COLERIDGE AVE
COURT DR
BROWNING AVE
MEAD CRES
SHIRLEY AVE
MILTON AVE
KINGSLEY AVE
BYRON AVE
BYRON GDNS
ORCHARD WAY
FLORIAN AVE
PARKHURST RD
LAVENDER RD
MUNSLOW GDNS
DUKE ST
BENHILL RD
SM1
1 DOVER CT
2 HALCROFT CT
3 BODIAM CT
PRINCES ST
OLIVER RD
Recn Gd
HAROLD RD
COWPER AVE
WESTMEAD RD
BETCHWORTH CL
PO
THE CRESCENT
CROSS RD
SUTTON GR
CARSHALTON GR
RINGSTEAD RD
RINGSTEAD CT
MEADOW RD
HIGHFIELD RD
ROSSDALE
ALMA RD
SHORTS RD
ROSEFIELD CL
WILMOT RD
WALLACE CRES
DORAL WAY
CORRIB DR
CROFT RD
BRINDLEY HO
GALE HO
DUNBAR CT
RELKO GDNS
SOUTHCROFT
WATERLOO
UPPER VERNON RD
BRAMLEY RD
ST BARNABAS RD
MONARCH PL
WILLIAM RD
PALMERSTON RD
LIND RD
NIGHTINGALE CT
MYRTLE RD
BISHOP'S PL
VERNON RD
TURNPIKE LA
GREYHOUND RD
Schs
THACKERAY MANOR
MANOR PARK
Manor Park
CARSHALTON RD
THE BROADWAY
LOWER RD
NURSERY RD
WARWICK RD
MANOR LA
LENHAM RD
LITCHFIELD RD
THROWLEY WAY
THROWLEY RD
BENHILL AVE
AVON CL
MONTPELIER RD
HEBE CT
CONSTANCE
IVYDENE CL
ALBURY CT
RIPLEY GDNS
CRESSINGHAM GR
BRUNSWICK MANOR
BOULLEN
COMPTON CT
MILFORD GR
OCKLEY CT
GLENA MOUNT
ALVIA GDNS
KESWICK
THICKET RD
LINLEY CT
BIRCH CT
GODSTONE RD
DUCHESS CT
THICKET CRES
OAKHILL RD
COPTHORNE CT
STANMORE GDNS
BERWICK GDNS
WOODSIDE RD
DOVERCOURT LA
VINE CL
BENHILL WOOD RD
CHILWORTH GDNS
NORTHPOINT CL
BENHILTON CT
CLAYGATE CT
BENWOOD CT
ELGIN RD
BENFLEET CL
KIRK RISE
BENHILTON GDNS
ALVERNIA LO
PARSONS CL
REGENCY CT
JENGAR CL
KINGSMOUNT CT
EDWINA CT
LEWIS RD
BURNELL RD
BELSIZE GDNS
ROSEBERY GDNS
MARSHALL'S RD
ELM GR
MEDALE HO
WOODVILLE HO
B2230
HIGH ST
ST NICHOLAS WAY
LODGE PL
MASON RD
TIMES SQ
ASPECTS
ST NICHOLAS RD
HILL RD
C Ctr
A232
ORME RD
BANK MEWS
CHALK PIT WAY
Superstore
MORLAND RD
READING RD
ALFRED RD
VICTORIA RD
GAUNTLETT RD
ALBERT RD
OSBORNE PL
AMBROOK CT
Recn Gd
SUTTON
SUTTON COURT RD
Sutton
APSLEY CT
WELLESLEY RD
THE QUADRANT
B2230
BRIDGE RD
MULGRAVE CHAMBERS
MULGRAVE HALL
MULGRAVE MANOR
TANDRIDGE CT
CADOGAN CT
CUMNOR RD
BEDFORD TERR
RUTHERFORD CL
HILLCROOME RD
1 KINGSMEAD LO
2 HILLCREST CT
3 EATON CT
4 HARROW LO
5 EATON LO
LYNTON CT
BLENHEIM CT
CEDAR RD
ASHDOWN CT
CEDAR GDNS
AMBLESIDE GDNS
EATON RD
CONIFER GDNS
CONISTON
BEDDINGTON MANOR
MAYFIELD RD
FERNDOWN CL
BRENDON HO
ARGYLE HO
SUTTON CT
CAVENDISH RD
FISKE CT
PENTON HO
FOXLEY CT
CLANDON CT
RACHEL CT
ALBION RD
BEECHWOOD CT
ALBION CT
THE RIDGWAY
LANGLEY PARK RD
AMBERLEY CT
LAVENDER CT
MELTON CT
CHRISTCHURCH PK
WHITE LODGE CL
BOSTON CT
HENRY HATCH CT
LAUREL MANOR
1 MONTGOMERY GDNS
2 MILESTONE CL
3 LANGLEY LAWNS
GRANGE CT
THE FIRS
GRANGE VALE
COPSE HILL
BLACKBUSH CL
BONCHURCH CL
BRIGHTON RD
WALNUT MEWS
LUTEA HO
Sch
Coll
DEVONSHIRE AVE
DEVONSHIRE RD
CHANDON LO
MITRE CL
FILEY CL
SUTTON HTS
CHALGROVE RD
PENARTH CT
EGMONT RD
CLAREDALE CT
MAYFIELD CT
BILBERRY MANOR
PEASLAKE CT
Tenn Cts
SM2
VENTNOR RD
WESTMORELAND DR
EFFINGHAM CT
EASTLEIGH CL
KEMPSTON HO
THE DOWNSWAY
THE GALLOP
CROSSWAYS
TRICKETT HO
CAUSE
THE HIGHWAY
BASINGHALL GDNS
CAREW
FELBRIDGE
26
27
28
A
B
C
D
WEIHURST GDNS
WEIHURST CT
ALPINE VIEW
FAIRVIEW RD
KING'S LA
REPTON CL
HAWTHORN RD
WARREN PARK RD
HARROW RD
OXFORD RD
CAMBRIDGE RD
WYNASH GDNS
WALNUT CL
DORCHESTER HO
WALES AVE
PARK HILL CL
BANKSIDE CL
PARK HILL
B278
SHERIDAN WLK
CARSHALTON PARK RD
B271
BEYNON RD
THE PARK
SALISBURY RD
War Memorial
DEROY CL
CEDAR CL
PARK CL
SM5
PARKER CL
VYNE HO
BLAKEHALL RD
GLEBE RD
HILL RD
DOWNSIDE RD
GORDON RD
PO
Carshalton Beeches
Recn Gd
WAVERLEY WAY
SUSSEX RD
Stanley Park Jun & Inf Schs
Tenn Cts
WILLIS AVE
UPLAND RD
KAYEMOOR RD
BARROW HEDGES WAY
BANSTEAD RD
BARROW HEDGES CL
CENTRAL WAY
BEECHES AVE
CRICHTON RD
WARNHAM COURT RD
FARM RD
PRIOR AVE
FARMDALE RD
Tenn Cts
FARM CL
STAPLEHURST RD
Barrow Hedges Prim Sch
WOODMANSTERNE RD
STANLEY PARK RD
WHITTLEBURY CL
FIR TREE GR
BALFOUR RD
OAKS WAY
QUEEN MARY'S AVE
GAYNESFORD RD
COURTNEY CRES
KINGS AVE
PRINCES AVE
BARROW AVE
FOUNTAIN DR
RADCLIFFE GDNS
HARBURY RD
INGLETON RD
THE CLOSE
SOUTH RD
Allot Gdns
DINGWALL RD
EAST DR
STANLEY

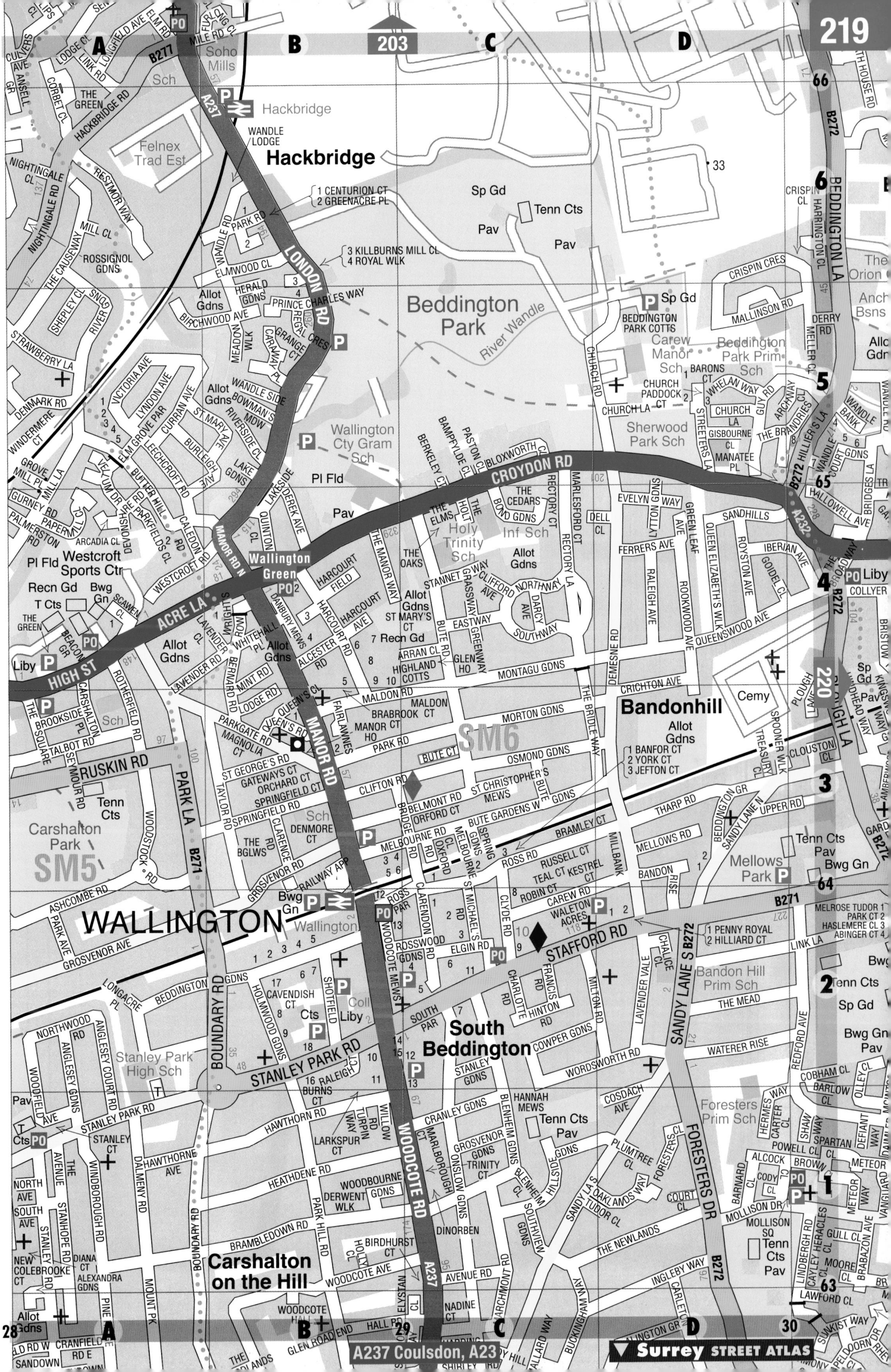
203
A
B
C
D
Hackbridge
Soho Mills
Felnex Trad Est
WANDLE LODGE
1 CENTURION CT
2 GREENACRE PL
3 KILLBURNS MILL CL
4 ROYAL WLK
Sp Gd
Tenn Cts
Pav
Beddington Park
River Wandle
BEDDINGTON PARK COTTS
Carew Manor Sch
Beddington Park Prim Sch
Sherwood Park Sch
CHURCH PADDOCK CT
CHURCH LA
CROYDON RD
Wallington Cty Gram Sch
Pl Fld
Holy Trinity Sch
Inf Sch
Allot Gdns
Wallington Green
LONDON RD
MANOR RD N
MANOR RD
ACRE LA
HIGH ST
Westcroft Sports Ctr
Recn Gd
Bwg Gn
T Cts
Liby
Bandonhill
Cemy
SM6
SM5
Carshalton Park
PARK LA
RUSKIN RD
WALLINGTON
Wallington
STAFFORD RD
South Beddington
SANDY LANE S
FORESTERS DR
Bandon Hill Prim Sch
Mellows Park
Foresters Prim Sch
STANLEY PARK RD
Stanley Park High Sch
BOUNDARY RD
WOODCOTE RD
Carshalton on the Hill
BEDDINGTON LA
The Orion
B272
B271
A237
A232
220
1
2
3
4
5
6
63
64
65
66
28
29
30
A237 Coulsdon, A23

Beddington
Waddon
Roundshaw
Wandle Park
Waddon Marsh
Croydon Tramlink
PURLEY WAY
CROYDON RD
DUPPAS HILL RD
STAFFORD RD
BEDDINGTON LA
PLOUGH LA
ROMAN WAY
OLD TOWN
DENNING AVE
Fiveways
Croydon Airport Ind Est
Roundshaw Park
Purley Way Pl Fld
Haling Manor High Sch
1 WINDSOR GDNS
2 KINGSTON GDNS
3 PETERSHAM TERR
4 OLD FORD HO
5 WANDLE LO
6 WANDLE CT
7 BEACON PL
8 CAMDEN HO
9 MARLOW HO
10 CAVERSHAM HO
WESTFIELD RD 1
LOWER CHURCH ST 2
BOURNE ST 3
RAMSEY CT 4
LATIMER RD 1
CROMWELL HO 2
1 CENTRAL PAR
2 STAFFORD CT
DOWNES HO 1
ARNOLD HO 2
HILLSIDE HO 3
ELIS DAVID ALMSHOUSES 4
MORRIS CT 5
KEELING CT 6
MESSER CT 7
MELROSE TUDOR 1
PARK CT 2
HASLEMERE CL 3
ABINGER CT 4
1 PENNY ROYAL
2 HILLIARD CT
FAYGATE CT 1
PENSHURST CT 2
HARTFIELD CT 3
CR0
SM6
CR2
204
219
A23 Redhill, M23, M25

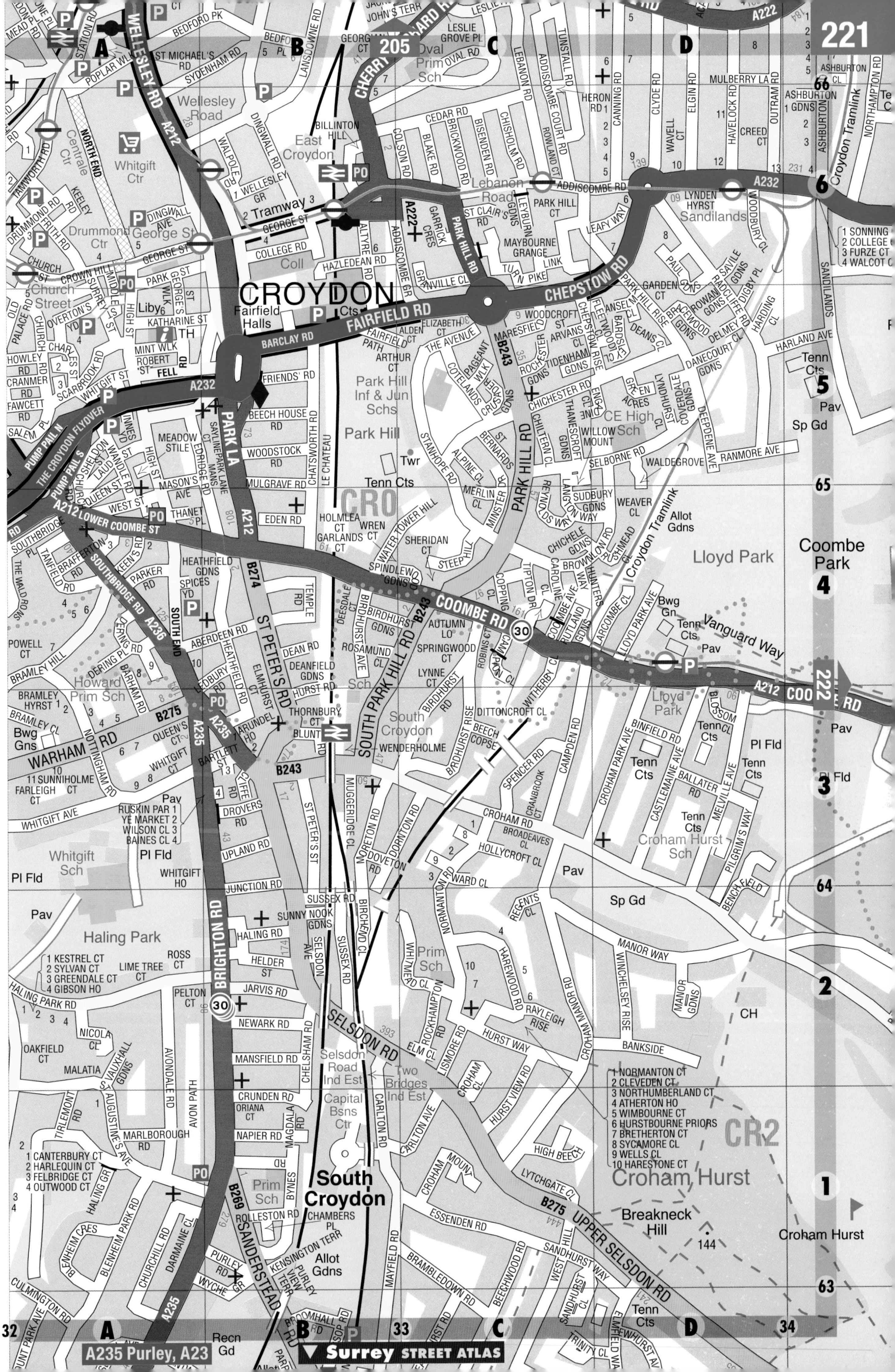
CROYDON
CR0
CR2
South Croydon
East Croydon
West Croydon
Wellesley Road
Centrale Ctr
Whitgift Ctr
Drummond Ctr
George St
Church Street
Fairfield Halls
Lebanon Road
Sandilands
Lloyd Park
Coombe Park
Croham Hurst
Breakneck Hill
Haling Park
Park Hill
Park Hill Inf & Jun Schs
Whitgift Sch
Howard Prim Sch
Croham Hurst Sch
CE High Sch
Oval Prim Sch
Selsdon Road Ind Est
Two Bridges Ind Est
Capital Bsns Ctr
Croydon Tramlink
Vanguard Way
Tramway
WELLESLEY RD
FAIRFIELD RD
CHEPSTOW RD
ADDISCOMBE RD
COOMBE RD
PARK LA
PARK HILL RD
SOUTH PARK HILL RD
ST PETER'S RD
BRIGHTON RD
SOUTH END
SOUTHBRIDGE RD
LOWER COOMBE ST
BARCLAY RD
GEORGE ST
WARHAM RD
SELSDON RD
UPPER SELSDON RD
SANDERSTEAD RD
CROHAM RD
MANOR WAY
BEDFORD PK
LESLIE GROVE PL
MULBERRY LA
HARLAND AVE
RANMORE AVE
WALDEGROVE
SELBORNE RD
HIGH ST
PUMP PAIL N
PUMP PAIL S
THE CROYDON FLYOVER
A212
A232
A222
A235
A236
B243
B274
B275
B269
A235 Purley, A23
205
222
32
33
34
63
64
65
66
1
2
3
4
5
6
A
B
C
D

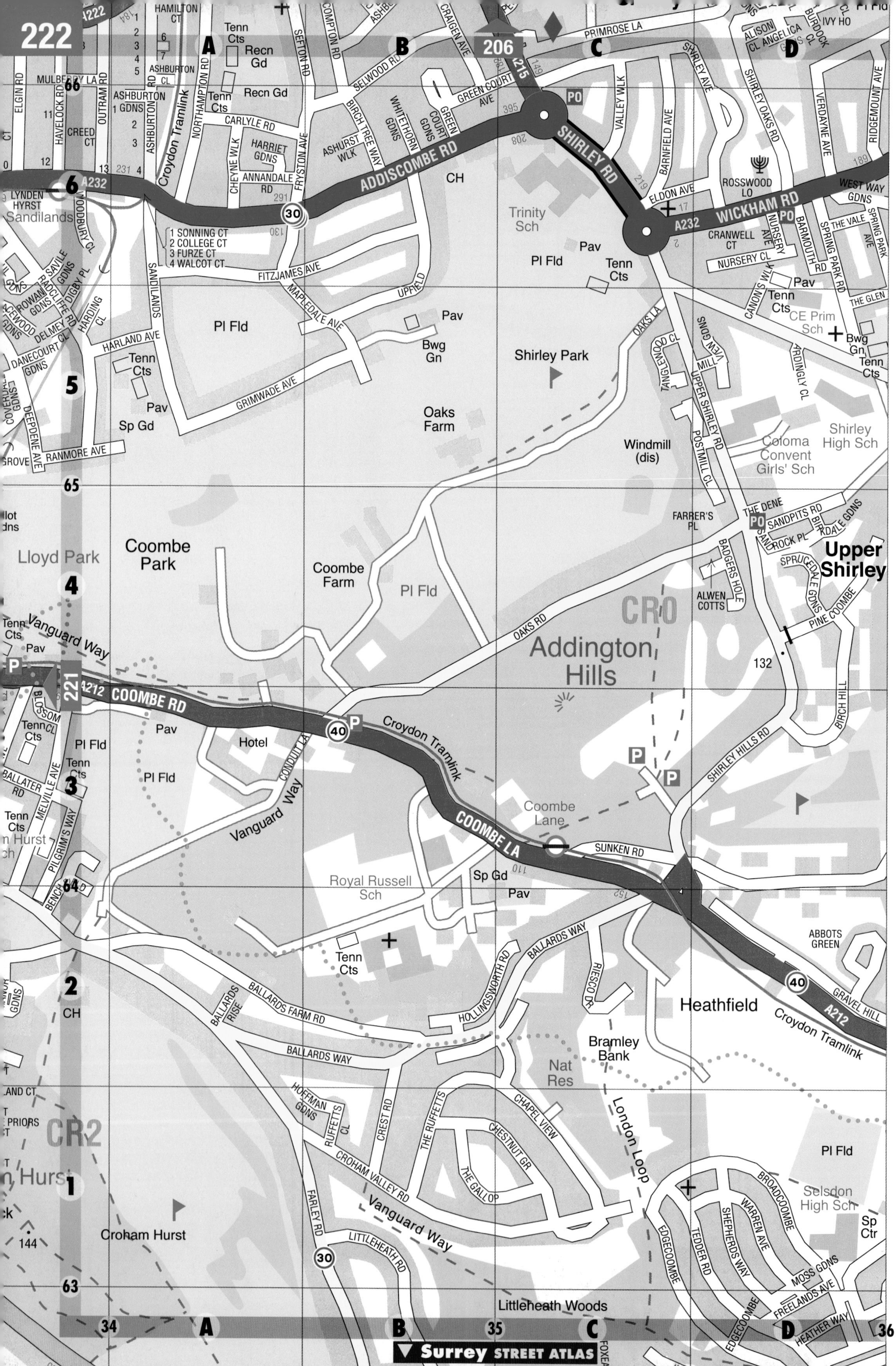
206
A
B
C
D
HAMILTON CT
Tenn Cts
Recn Gd
ASHBURTON CL
MULBERRY LA
ELGIN RD
HAVELOCK RD
OUTRAM RD
CREED CT
ASHBURTON GDNS
ASHBURTON RD
Croydon Tramlink
NORTHAMPTON RD
CARLYLE RD
CHEYNE WLK
HARRIET GDNS
ANNANDALE RD
FRYSTON AVE
SEFTON RD
COMPTON RD
SELWOOD RD
BIRCH TREE WAY
ASHURST WLK
WHITETHORN GDNS
COURT GDNS
GREEN COURT AVE
CRAIGEN AVE
PRIMROSE LA
ADDISCOMBE RD
A232
SHIRLEY RD
A215
PO
VALLEY WLK
SHIRLEY AVE
BARNFIELD AVE
SHIRLEY OAKS RD
ALISON CL
ANGELICA GDNS
BURDOCK CL
IVY HO
VERDAYNE AVE
RIDGEMOUNT AVE
ROSSWOOD LO
ELDON AVE
WICKHAM RD
WEST WAY GDNS
CRANWELL CT
NURSERY AVE
BARMOUTH RD
SPRING PARK RD
THE VALE
SPRING PARK AVE
NURSERY CL
CANON'S WLK
THE GLEN
CE Prim Sch
Bwg Gn
Tenn Cts
Pav
CH
Trinity Sch
Pl Fld
LYNDEN HYRST
Sandilands
WOODBURY CL
1 SONNING CT
2 COLLEGE CT
3 FURZE CT
4 WALCOT CT
FITZJAMES AVE
SANDILANDS
MAPLEDALE AVE
UPFIELD
SAVILE GDNS
ROWAN GDNS
RADCLIFFE RD
DIGBY PL
DELMEY CL
HARDING CL
DANECOURT GDNS
HARLAND AVE
GRIMWADE AVE
Shirley Park
OAKS LA
TANGLEWOOD CL
MILL VIEW GDNS
UPPER SHIRLEY RD
POSTMILL CL
ARDINGLY CL
Oaks Farm
Windmill (dis)
Sp Gd
RANMORE AVE
DEEPDENE AVE
COVERDALE GDNS
Coloma Convent Girls' Sch
Shirley High Sch
THE DENE
SANDPITS RD
BIRKDALE GDNS
ROCK PL
FARRER'S PL
Upper Shirley
SPRUCEDALE GDNS
PINE COOMBE
BADGERS HOLE
ALWEN COTTS
CR0
Lloyd Park
Coombe Park
Coombe Farm
OAKS RD
Addington Hills
132
BIRCH HILL
SHIRLEY HILLS RD
Vanguard Way
221
A212
COOMBE RD
P
BLOSSOM CL
Hotel
CONDUIT LA
Croydon Tramlink
BALLATER RD
MELVILLE AVE
PILGRIM'S WAY
BENCHAM CL
Coombe Lane
COOMBE LA
SUNKEN RD
Royal Russell Sch
BALLARDS WAY
HOLLINGSWORTH RD
RIESCO DR
ABBOTS GREEN
GRAVEL HILL
Heathfield
BALLARDS RISE
BALLARDS FARM RD
Bramley Bank
Nat Res
London Loop
HOFFMAN GDNS
RUFFETTS CL
CREST RD
THE RUFFETTS
CHAPEL VIEW
CHESTNUT GR
THE GALLOP
CROHAM VALLEY RD
FARLEY RD
LITTLEHEATH RD
Littleheath Woods
Croham Hurst
144
CR2
EDGECOOMBE
TEDDER RD
SHEPHERDS WAY
WARREN AVE
BROADCOOMBE
Selsdon High Sch
Sp Ctr
MOSS GDNS
FREELANDS AVE
HEATHER WAY
34
35
36
65
64
63
1
2
3
4
5
6

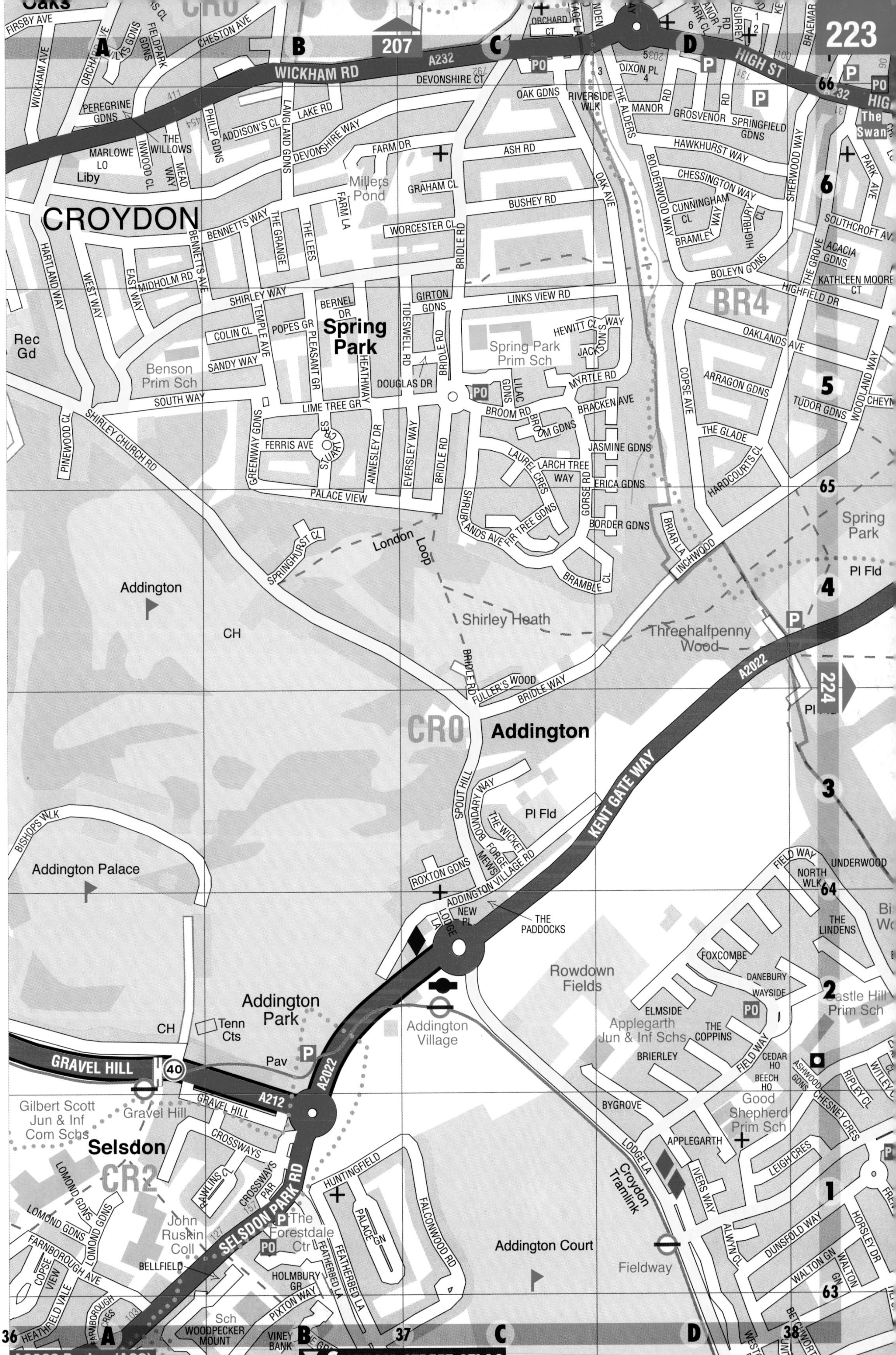
207
224
36
37
38
A
B
C
D
1
2
3
4
5
6
63
64
65
66
CROYDON
Spring Park
Addington
Selsdon
BR4
CR0
CR2
WICKHAM RD
A232
HIGH ST
FIRSBY AVE
CHESTON AVE
WICKHAM AVE
ORCHARD AVE
FIELDPARK GDNS
PEREGRINE GDNS
MARLOWE LO
Liby
THE WILLOWS
INWOOD CL
MEAD WAY
PHILIP GDNS
ADDISON'S CL
LANGLAND GDNS
LAKE RD
DEVONSHIRE WAY
DEVONSHIRE CT
FARM DR
Millers Pond
GRAHAM CL
OAK GDNS
RIVERSIDE WLK
ASH RD
BUSHEY RD
WORCESTER CL
BRIDLE RD
OAK AVE
THE ALDERS
DIXON PL
MANOR RD
GROSVENOR RD
SPRINGFIELD GDNS
HAWKHURST WAY
CHESSINGTON WAY
BOLDERWOOD WAY
CUNNINGHAM CL
BRAMLEY WAY
HIGHBURY CL
SHERWOOD WAY
SOUTHCROFT AV
ACACIA GDNS
KATHLEEN MOORE CT
HIGHFIELD DR
BOLEYN GDNS
THE GROVE
PARK AVE
The Swan
HARTLAND WAY
BENNETTS WAY
BENNETTS AVE
THE GRANGE
THE LEES
FARM LA
MIDHOLM RD
WEST WAY
EAST WAY
SHIRLEY WAY
BERNEL DR
GIRTON GDNS
LINKS VIEW RD
HEWITT CL
JACKSON'S WAY
OAKLANDS AVE
ARRAGON GDNS
COPSE AVE
Rec Gd
COLIN CL
POPES GR
TEMPLE AVE
SANDY WAY
PLEASANT GR
HEATHWAY
TIDESWELL RD
DOUGLAS DR
Spring Park Prim Sch
MYRTLE RD
LILAC GDNS
BRACKEN AVE
TUDOR GDNS
WOODLAND WAY
Benson Prim Sch
SOUTH WAY
LIME TREE GR
BROOM RD
BROOM GDNS
THE GLADE
HARDCOURTS CL
PINEWOOD CL
SHIRLEY CHURCH RD
GREENWAY GDNS
FERRIS AVE
STUART CRES
ANNESLEY DR
EVERSLEY WAY
LAUREL CRES
LARCH TREE WAY
JASMINE GDNS
GORSE RD
ERICA GDNS
PALACE VIEW
SHRUBLANDS AVE
FIR TREE GDNS
BORDER GDNS
BRIAR LA
INCHWOOD
Spring Park
Pl Fld
SPRINGHURST CL
London Loop
BRAMBLE CL
Addington
CH
Shirley Heath
Threehalfpenny Wood
FULLER'S WOOD
BRIDLE WAY
A2022
Addington
SPOUT HILL
BOUNDARY WAY
THE WICKET
FORGE MEWS
ADDINGTON VILLAGE RD
KENT GATE WAY
ROXTON GDNS
BISHOPS WLK
Addington Palace
NEW PL
LODGE LA
THE PADDOCKS
FIELD WAY
NORTH WLK
UNDERWOOD
THE LINDENS
FOXCOMBE
DANEBURY
WAYSIDE
Castle Hill Prim Sch
Rowdown Fields
Addington Park
Addington Village
ELMSIDE
Applegarth Jun & Inf Schs
THE COPPINS
BRIERLEY
CEDAR HO
BEECH HO
ASHWOOD GDNS
CHESNEY CRES
RIPLEY CL
Good Shepherd Prim Sch
BYGROVE
APPLEGARTH
LEIGH CRES
Tenn Cts
Pav
GRAVEL HILL
A212
40
Gilbert Scott Jun & Inf Com Schs
Gravel Hill
CROSSWAYS
CROSSWAYS PAR
RAWLINS CL
LOMOND GDNS
SELSDON PARK RD
HUNTINGFIELD
PALACE GN
FALCONWOOD RD
Croydon Tramlink
IVERS WAY
ALWYN CL
DUNSFOLD WAY
HORSLEY DR
WALTON GN
John Ruskin Coll
The Forestdale Ctr
FARNBOROUGH AVE
COPSE VIEW
BELLFIELD
HOLMBURY GR
FEATHERBED LA
Addington Court
Fieldway
HEATHFIELD VALE
FARNBOROUGH CRES
PIXTON WAY
Sch
WOODPECKER MOUNT
VINEY BANK
WESTCOTT
BETCHWORTH WAY

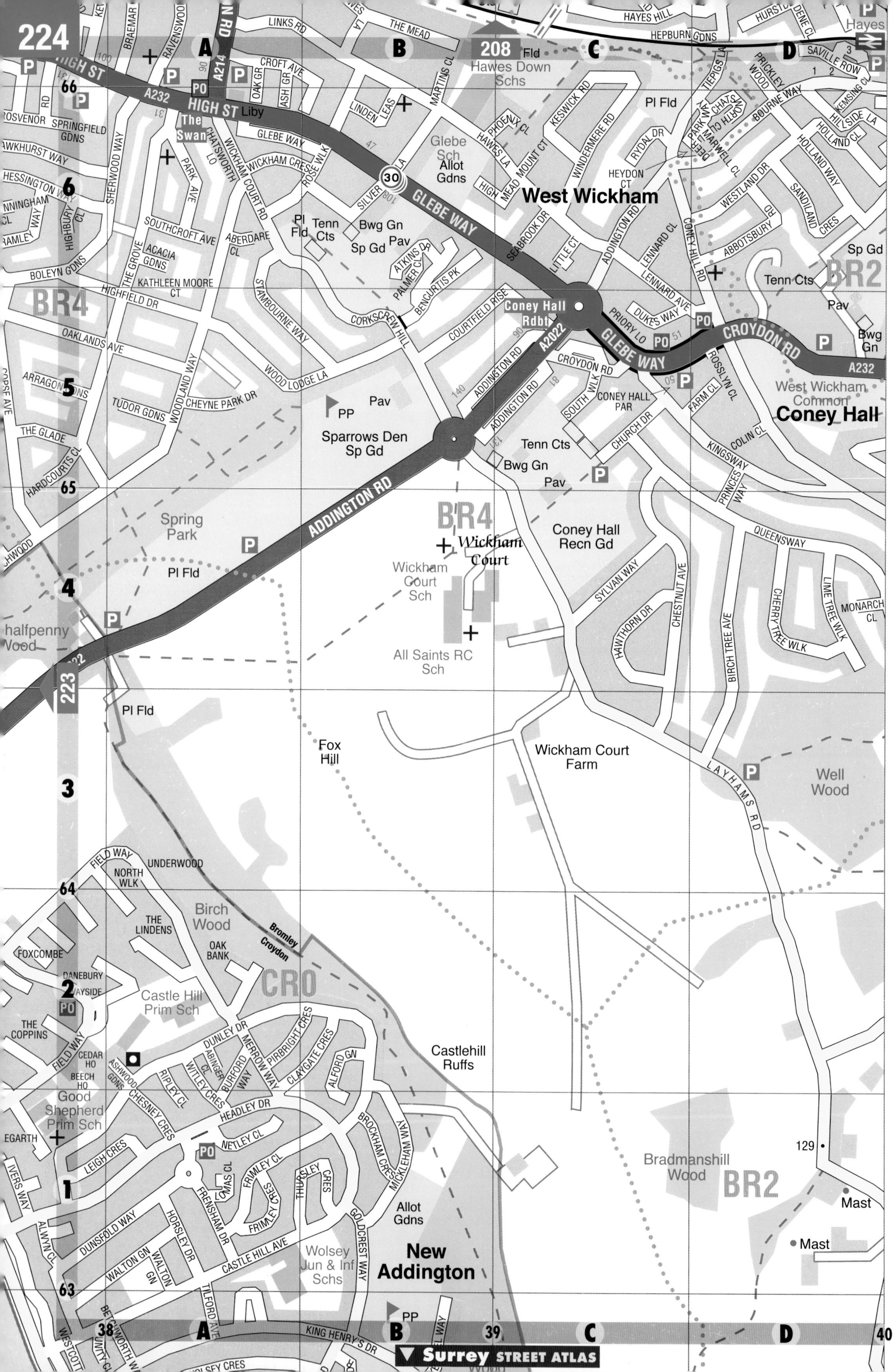
208
Hawes Down Schs
Hayes
HAYES HILL
HEPBURN GDNS
LINKS RD
THE MEAD
HIGH ST
A232
A214
The Swan
Liby
CROFT AVE
OAK GR
ASH GR
LINDEN LEAS
MARTINS CL
GLEBE WAY
WICKHAM CRES
ROSE WLK
SILVER LA
Glebe Sch
Allot Gdns
PHOENIX CL
HAWES LA
KESWICK RD
WINDERMERE RD
MEAD MOUNT CT
HIGH
Pl Fld
RYDAL DR
HEYDON CT
West Wickham
SEABROOK DR
LITTLE CT
ADDINGTON RD
LENNARD CL
LENNARD AVE
CONEY HILL RD
DUKES WAY
PRIORY LO
PO
CROYDON RD
ROSSLYN CL
FARM CL
COLIN CL
KINGSWAY
PRINCES WAY
QUEENSWAY
TIEPIGS LA
PRICKLEY WOOD
BOURNE WAY
SAVILLE ROW
KEMSING CL
HILLSIDE LA
HOLLAND CL
HOLLAND WAY
WESTLAND DR
SANDILAND CRES
ABBOTSBURY RD
MARWELL CL
DEER PARK WAY
Sp Gd
Tenn Cts
Pav
Bwg Gn
BR2
West Wickham Common
Coney Hall
Coney Hall Rdbt
A2022
CONEY HALL PAR
SOUTH WLK
CHURCH DR
Tenn Cts
Bwg Gn
Pav
Coney Hall Recn Gd
SYLVAN WAY
CHESTNUT AVE
HAWTHORN DR
BIRCH TREE AVE
CHERRY TREE WLK
LIME TREE WLK
MONARCH CL
ROSVENOR
SPRINGFIELD GDNS
HAWKHURST WAY
HESSINGTON WAY
SHERWOOD WAY
HIGHBURY CL
BRAEMAR
RAVENSWOOD
PARK AVE
CHATSWORTH LO
WICKHAM COURT RD
SOUTHCROFT AVE
ABERDARE CL
ACACIA GDNS
THE GROVE
KATHLEEN MOORE CT
BOLEYN GDNS
HIGHFIELD DR
BR4
OAKLANDS AVE
ARRAGON GDNS
TUDOR GDNS
WOODLAND WAY
CHEYNE PARK DR
STAMBOURNE WAY
WOOD LODGE LA
CORKSCREW HILL
BENCURTIS PK
ATKINS DR
PALMER CL
COURTFIELD RISE
Pl Fld
Tenn Cts
Bwg Gn
Sp Gd
Pav
30
THE GLADE
HARDCOURTS CL
PP
Pav
Sparrows Den Sp Gd
ADDINGTON RD
Spring Park
Pl Fld
halfpenny Wood
223
Wickham Court
Wickham Court Sch
All Saints RC Sch
Pl Fld
Fox Hill
Wickham Court Farm
LAYHAMS RD
Well Wood
FIELD WAY
UNDERWOOD
NORTH WLK
THE LINDENS
Birch Wood
OAK BANK
Bromley
Croydon
CR0
FOXCOMBE
DANEBURY
WAYSIDE
Castle Hill Prim Sch
THE COPPINS
CEDAR HO
BEECH HO
ASHWOOD GDNS
DUNLEY DR
ABINGER CL
WITLEY CRES
BURFORD WAY
MERROW WAY
PIRBRIGHT CRES
CLAYGATE CRES
ALFORD GN
RIPLEY CL
CHESNEY CRES
HEADLEY DR
Castlehill Ruffs
Good Shepherd Prim Sch
EGARTH
IVERS WAY
LEIGH CRES
NETLEY CL
LOMAS CL
FRIMLEY CL
FRIMLEY CRES
THURSLEY CRES
BROCKHAM CRES
MICKLEHAM WAY
FRENSHAM DR
GOLDCREST WAY
Allot Gdns
Bradmanshill Wood
BR2
129
Mast
Mast
ALWYN CL
DUNSFOLD WAY
HORSLEY DR
WALTON GN
CASTLE HILL AVE
Wolsey Jun & Inf Schs
New Addington
TILFORD AVE
PP
KING HENRY'S DR
WESTCOTT
BETCHWORTH
A
B
C
D
6
5
4
3
2
1
66
65
64
63
38
39
40

209
A
B
C
D
Recn Gds
PO
Pav
STATION APP
HAYES GDN
THE KNOLL
FORGE CL
HOPTON CT
GLEBE HOUSE
BURWOOD AVE
RIDGEWAY
STATION HILL
WARREN RD
B265
Pl Fld
Hayes Sch
Tenn Cts
Pl Fld
Pav
Sp Gd
Bwg Gn
Pav
Baston Sch
Tenn Cts
1 LARKFIELD CL
2 WENTWORTH CL
3 HAWTHORNDENE CL
4 HAWTHORNDENE RD
5 WARREN WOOD CL
The Priory
GROVE CL
HAYES CL
Pav
Sp Gd
Tenn Cts
REDGATE DR
Barnet Wood
Keston Mark
BARNET WOOD RD
PRESTONS RD
Pav
Pl Fld
Ravens Wood Sch
Ravens Bourne
BASTON RD
FIVE ELMS RD
Hayes Court
WEST COMMON RD
Hayes Common
Simpson's Cott
Colyers Wood
Allot Gdns
THE DRIFT
THE AVENUE
HARVEST BANK RD
CROYDON RD
A232
OAKLEY RD
A233
WEALD CL
CROSS RD
DOVES CL
GRAVEL RD
THE LIMES
Recn Gd
Allot Gdns
CEDAR CL
OAKLEY DR
KEMBLE DR
CHEYNE CL
CEDAR CL
Keston Park
ROBINS GR
HARTFIELD CRES
HARVEST BANK RD
HARTFIELD RD
RODNEY GDNS
LAWRENCE RD
BASTON MANOR RD
QUIET NOOK
PHOENIX DR
THANET DR
THE DALE
RUSHLEY CL
MARK CL
GATES GREEN RD
Wickham Common Prim Sch
Pl Fld
Hast Hill House
Baston Manor
P
COMMONSIDE
OAKFIELD LA
BEECHWOOD DR
LONGDON WOOD
BROCKDENE DR
HASSOCK WOOD
Ravensbourne Bsns Ctr
BR4
STOUR CL
KESTON GDNS
WINDMILL DR
LAKES RD
Keston
SWIRES SHAW
COLLIERS SHAW
POULTERS WOOD
HOLMSDEN WAY
226
Rouse Farm
PH
PO
HEATHFIELD CL
KESTON AVE
Keston CE Prim Sch
FOX LA
HERITAGE HILL
LEAFY GR
GREYS PARK CL
REGENTS DR
HEATHFIELD RD
FISHPONDS RD
London Loop
WESTERHAM RD
BR2
Windmill
Keston Common
64
Caesa Cam
Nash
NORTH POLE LA
NASH LA
JACKASS LA
Fuller's Wood
James's Wood
THE COURTYARD
Holw
Tenn Cts
ROMAN MAUSOLEUM
Keston Court
RECTORY RD
LAYHAMS RD
Milchden
CHURCH RD
BLACKNESS LA
ORCHARD PL
63
40
41
42
DOWNE RD
A233 Biggin Hill
66
65
6
5
4
3
2
1

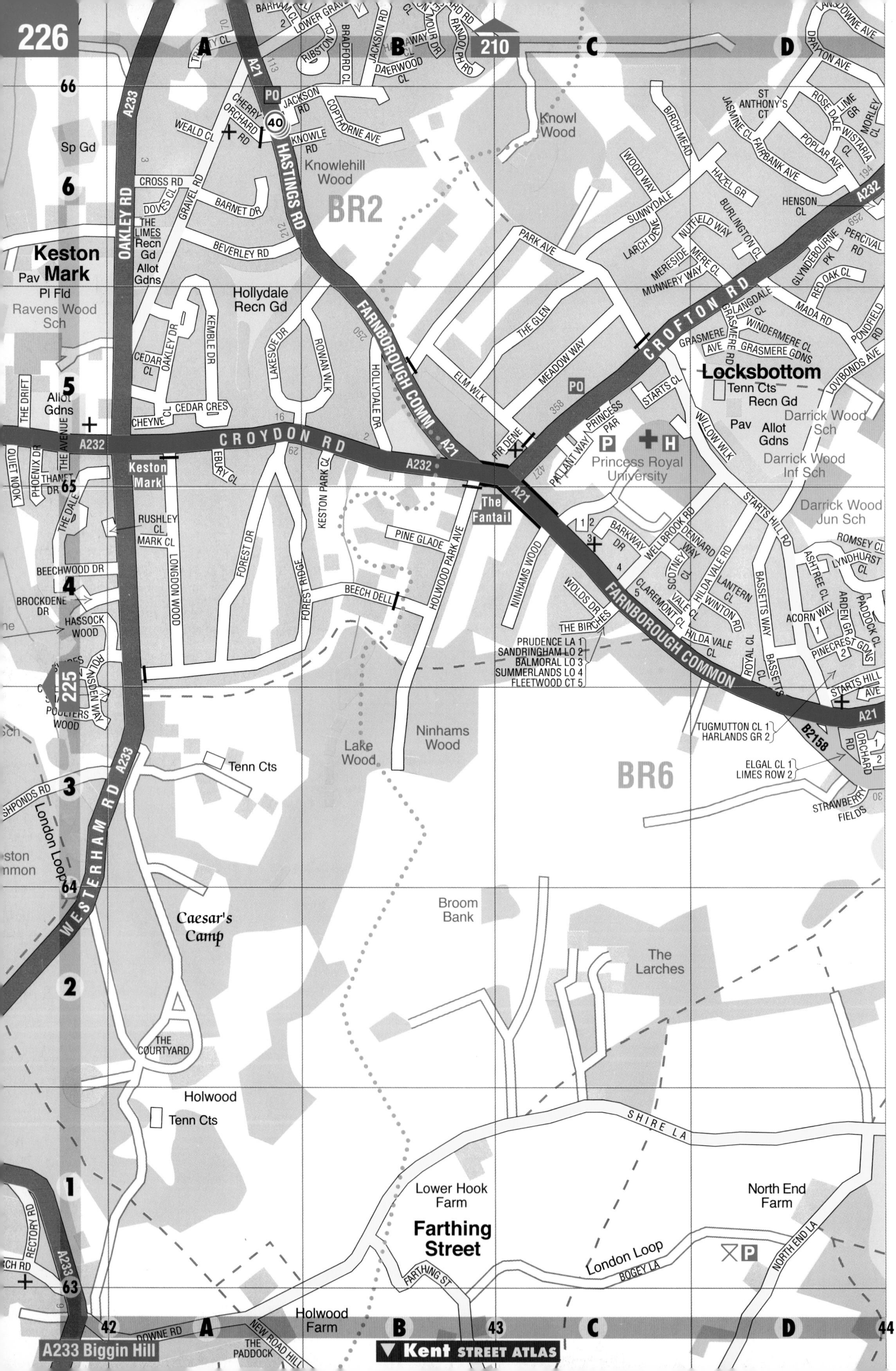
210
225
A
B
C
D
66
6
5
65
4
3
64
2
1
63
42
43
44
Keston Mark
Sp Gd
Pav
Pl Fld
Ravens Wood Sch
Allot Gdns
The Limes Recn Gd
Allot Gdns
Hollydale Recn Gd
Knowlehill Wood
Knowl Wood
BR2
BR6
PO
Locksbottom
Tenn Cts
Recn Gd
Darrick Wood Sch
Pav
Allot Gdns
Darrick Wood Inf Sch
Darrick Wood Jun Sch
Princess Royal University
The Fantail
Keston Mark
Ninhams Wood
Lake Wood
Tenn Cts
Caesar's Camp
The Courtyard
Holwood
Tenn Cts
Broom Bank
The Larches
Lower Hook Farm
Farthing Street
North End Farm
London Loop
Holwood Farm
The Paddock
A233 Biggin Hill
OAKLEY RD
A233
A21
HASTINGS RD
FARNBOROUGH COMM
CROYDON RD
A232
CROFTON RD
FARNBOROUGH COMMON
WESTERHAM RD
B2158
SHIRE LA
BOGEY LA
FARTHING ST
NORTH END LA
DOWNE RD
NEW ROAD HILL
RECTORY RD
TRINITY CL
LOWER GRAVEL
RIBSTON CL
BRADFORD CL
JACKSON RD
DAERWOOD CL
RANDOLPH RD
JACKSON RD
COPTHORNE AVE
KNOWLE RD
CHERRY ORCHARD RD
WEALD CL
CROSS RD
DOVES CL
GRAVEL RD
BARNET DR
BEVERLEY RD
OAKLEY DR
KEMBLE DR
CEDAR CL
CEDAR CRES
CHEYNE CL
LAKESIDE DR
ROWAN WLK
HOLLYDALE DR
KESTON PARK CL
EBURY CL
THE DRIFT
THE AVENUE
QUIET NOOK
PHOENIX DR
THANET DR
THE DALE
RUSHLEY CL
MARK CL
LONGDON WOOD
FOREST DR
FOREST RIDGE
PINE GLADE
HOLWOOD PARK AVE
BEECH DELL
BEECHWOOD DR
BROCKDENE DR
HASSOCK WOOD
ROLINSDEN WAY
POULTERS WOOD
SHIPONDS RD
PARK AVE
THE GLEN
ELM WLK
MEADOW WAY
FIR DENE
PALLANT WAY
PRINCESS PAR
STARTS CL
SUNNYDALE
LARCH DENE
WOOD WAY
BIRCH MEAD
HAZEL GR
BURLINGTON CL
NUTFIELD WAY
MERESIDE
MERE CL
MUNNERY WAY
HENSON CL
DRAYTON AVE
LANSDOWNE AVE
ST ANTHONY'S CT
JASMINE CL
FAIRBANK AVE
ROSE DALE
LIME GR
MORLEY CL
WISTARIA CL
POPLAR AVE
GLYNDEBOURNE PK
PERCIVAL RD
RED OAK CL
MADA RD
PONDFIELD RD
LOVIBONDS AVE
LANGDALE CL
WINDERMERE CL
GRASMERE GDNS
GRASMERE AVE
GRASMERE RD
WILLOW WLK
STARTS HILL RD
WELLBROOK RD
DENNARD WAY
SCOTNEY CL
VALE CL
HILDA VALE RD
HILDA VALE CL
LANTERN CL
WINTON RD
BARKWAY DR
CLAREMONT CL
WOLDS DR
THE BIRCHES
NINHAMS WOOD
BASSETTS WAY
BASSETTS CL
ROYAL CL
ROMSEY CL
LYNDHURST CL
ASHTREE CL
ACORN WAY
ARDEN GR
PADDOCK CL
PINECREST GDNS
STARTS HILL AVE
ORCHARD RD
STRAWBERRY FIELDS
PRUDENCE LA 1
SANDRINGHAM LO 2
BALMORAL LO 3
SUMMERLANDS LO 4
FLEETWOOD CT 5
TUGMUTTON CL 1
HARLANDS GR 2
ELGAL CL 1
LIMES ROW 2

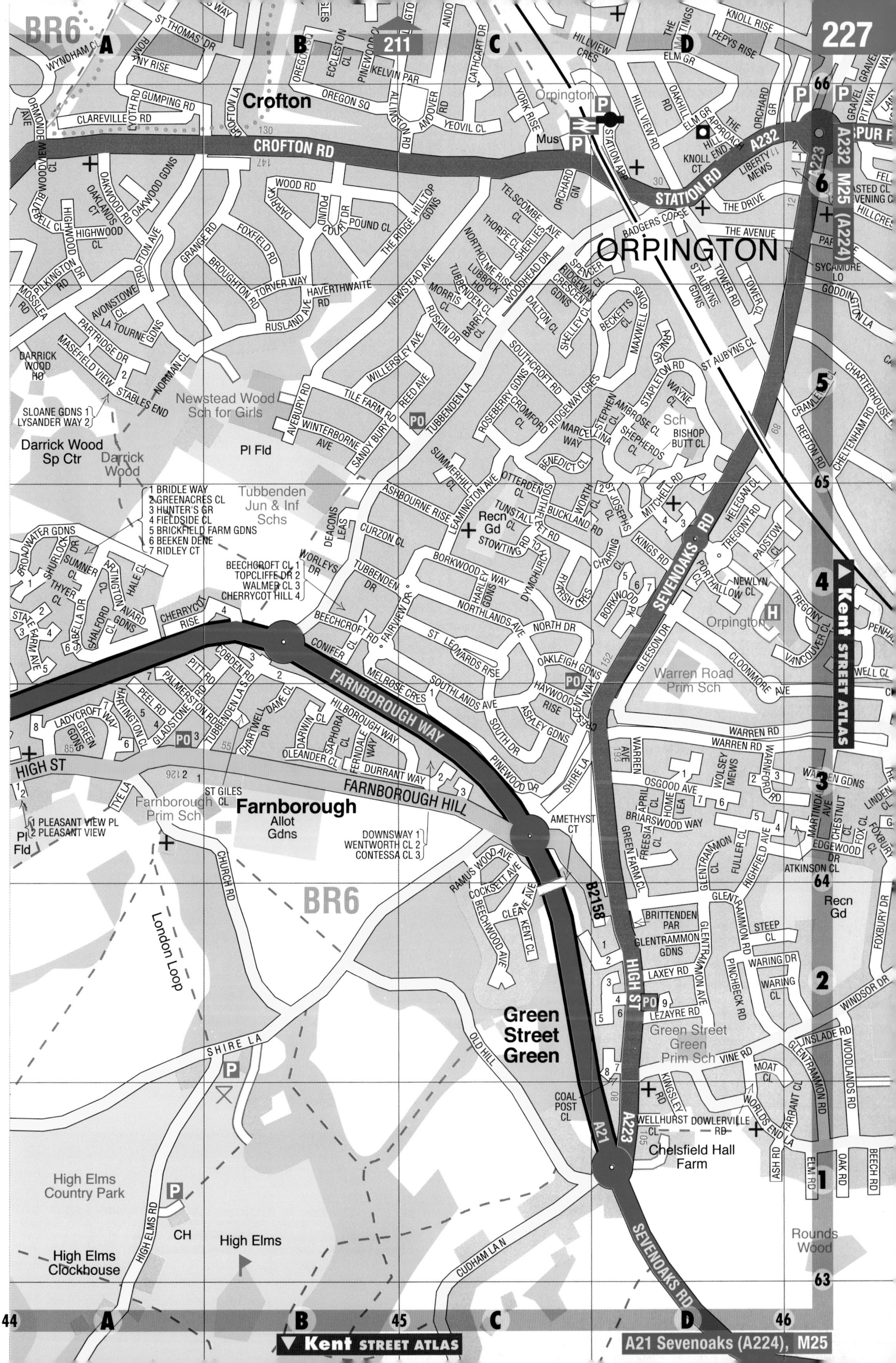
BR6
A
B
C
D
211
Crofton
CROFTON RD
WYNDHAM CL
ST THOMAS' DR
GUMPING RD
CLAREVILLE RD
OREGON SQ
ECCLESTON CL
PINEWOOD CL
KELVIN PAR
ALLINGTON RD
ANDOVER RD
YEOVIL CL
CATHCART DR
HILLVIEW CRES
KNOLL RISE
PEPYS RISE
THE MALTINGS
ELM GR
Orpington
Mus
STATION APP
HILL VIEW RD
OAKHILL RD
HILL END
KNOLL CT
THE APPROACH
ORCHARD GR
A232
STATION RD
LIBERTY MEWS
THE DRIVE
BADGERS COPSE
THE AVENUE
ORPINGTON
ST AUBYNS GDNS
TOWER RD
TOWER CL
ST AUBYNS CL
SYCAMORE LO
GODDINGTON LA
A232 M25 (A224)
A223
SPUR RD
GRAVEL PIT WAY
HILLCREST
OAKLANDS CT
OAKWOOD RD
OAKWOOD GDNS
HIGHWOOD CL
HIGHWOOD DR
BELL CL
WOODVIEW CL
ORMONDE AVE
PILKINGTON RD
MOSSLEA RD
CROFTON AVE
GRANGE RD
BROUGHTON RD
FOXFIELD RD
WOOD RD
DARRICK CL
POUND CT DR
POUND CL
THE RIDGE
HILLTOP GDNS
TORVER WAY
HAVERTHWAITE RD
RUSLAND AVE
NEWSTEAD AVE
AVONSTOWE CL
LA TOURNE GDNS
PARTRIDGE DR
MASEFIELD VIEW
STABLES END
NORMAN CL
DARRICK WOOD HO
SLOANE GDNS 1
LYSANDER WAY 2
Darrick Wood Sp Ctr
Darrick Wood
Newstead Wood Sch for Girls
Pl Fld
AVEBURY RD
TILE FARM RD
WILLERSLEY AVE
REED AVE
WINTERBORNE AVE
SANDY BURY
PO
TUBBENDEN LA
RUSKIN DR
MORRIS CL
TUBBENDEN CL
BARRY CL
LUBBOCK HO
NORTHOLME RISE
THORPE CL
TELSCOMBE AVE
SHERLIES AVE
WOODHEAD DR
ORCHARD GN
SPENCER CL
RIDGEWAY CRESCENT GDNS
DALTON CL
SHELLEY CL
BECKETTS CL
MAXWELL GDNS
ARNE GR
STAPLETON RD
WAYNE CL
SOUTHCROFT RD
ROSEBERRY GDNS
CROMFORD CL
RIDGEWAY CRES
MARCELLINA WAY
STEPHEN CL
AMBROSE CL
SHEPHERDS CL
Sch
BISHOP BUTT CL
SUMMERHILL CL
ASHBOURNE RISE
LEAMINGTON AVE
OTTERDEN CL
BENEDICT CL
WORTH CL
ST JOSEPHS CL
MITCHELL RD
BUCKLAND RD
SOUTHFLEET RD
Recn Gd
TUNSTALL CL
STOWTING RD
CHARING CL
KINGS RD
SEVENOAKS RD
HELEGAN CL
TREGONY RD
PADSTOW CL
CRANLEIGH
CHARTERHOUSE RD
CHELTENHAM RD
REPTON RD
1 BRIDLE WAY
2 GREENACRES CL
3 HUNTER'S GR
4 FIELDSIDE CL
5 BRICKFIELD FARM GDNS
6 BEEKEN DENE
7 RIDLEY CT
Tubbenden Jun & Inf Schs
DEACONS LEAS
CURZON CL
WORLEYS DR
TUBBENDEN DR
BORKWOOD WAY
HARLEY GDNS
DYMCHURCH CL
RYARSH CRES
BORKWOOD PK
NORTHLANDS AVE
NORTH DR
PORTHALLOW CL
NEWLYN CL
TREGONY
Orpington
H
PENHALL
BROADWATER GDNS
SHURLOCK DR
SUMNER CL
THYER CL
ARTINGTON CL
HALE CL
AVARD GDNS
SHALFORD CL
ISABELLA DR
STATE FARM AVE
BEECHCROFT CL 1
TOPCLIFFE DR 2
WALMER CL 3
CHERRYCOT HILL 4
CHERRYCOT RISE
BEECHCROFT RD
CONIFER CL
FAIRVIEW DR
ST LEONARDS RISE
OAKLEIGH GDNS
GLEESON DR
Warren Road Prim Sch
CLOONMORE AVE
VANCOUVER CL
WELL CL
FARNBOROUGH WAY
MELROSE CRES
SOUTHLANDS AVE
HAYWOOD RISE
CRESCENT WAY
ASHLEY GDNS
SOUTH DR
WARREN RD
PITT RD
COBDEN RD
PALMERSTON RD
PEEL RD
HARTINGTON CL
GLADSTONE RD
TUBBENDEN LA S
CHARTWELL DR
DAME CL
DARWIN CL
SAPHORA CL
HILBOROUGH WAY
FERNDALE WAY
OLEANDER CL
DURRANT WAY
LADYCROFT WAY
GREEN GDNS
HIGH ST
FARNBOROUGH HILL
PINEWOOD DR
SHIRE LA
WARREN AVE
OSGOOD AVE
WOLSEY MEWS
WARNFORD RD
WARREN GDNS
APRIL CL
HOME LEA
BRIARSWOOD WAY
GREEN FARM CL
FREESIA CL
GLENTRAMMON CL
FULLER CL
HIGHFIELD AVE
MARTINDALE AVE
CHESTNUT CL
FOX CL
FOXBURY
LINDEN
EDGEWOOD DR
ATKINSON CL
TYE LA
1 PLEASANT VIEW PL
2 PLEASANT VIEW
Pl Fld
Farnborough Prim Sch
ST GILES CL
Farnborough
Allot Gdns
DOWNSWAY 1
WENTWORTH CL 2
CONTESSA CL 3
AMETHYST CT
RAMUS WOOD AVE
COCKSETT AVE
CLEAVE AVE
BEECHWOOD AVE
KENT CL
B2158
BR6
CHURCH RD
London Loop
BRITTENDEN PAR
GLENTRAMMON GDNS
GLENTRAMMON RD
GLENTRAMMON AVE
PINCHBECK RD
STEEP CL
WARING DR
WARING CL
Recn Gd
FOXBURY DR
WINDSOR DR
LAXEY RD
LEZAYRE RD
Green Street Green Prim Sch
Green Street Green
VINE RD
INSLADE RD
WOODLANDS RD
MOAT CL
FARRANT CL
WORLDS END LA
KINGSLEY RD
SHIRE LA
OLD HILL
COAL POST CL
A21
WELLHURST CL
DOWLERVILLE RD
Chelsfield Hall Farm
ASH RD
ELM RD
OAK RD
BEECH RD
High Elms Country Park
HIGH ELMS RD
CH
High Elms
High Elms Clockhouse
CUDHAM LA N
SEVENOAKS RD
Rounds Wood
66
6
5
65
4
3
64
2
1
63
44
45
46
Kent STREET ATLAS
A21 Sevenoaks (A224), M25

Key to enlarged map pages

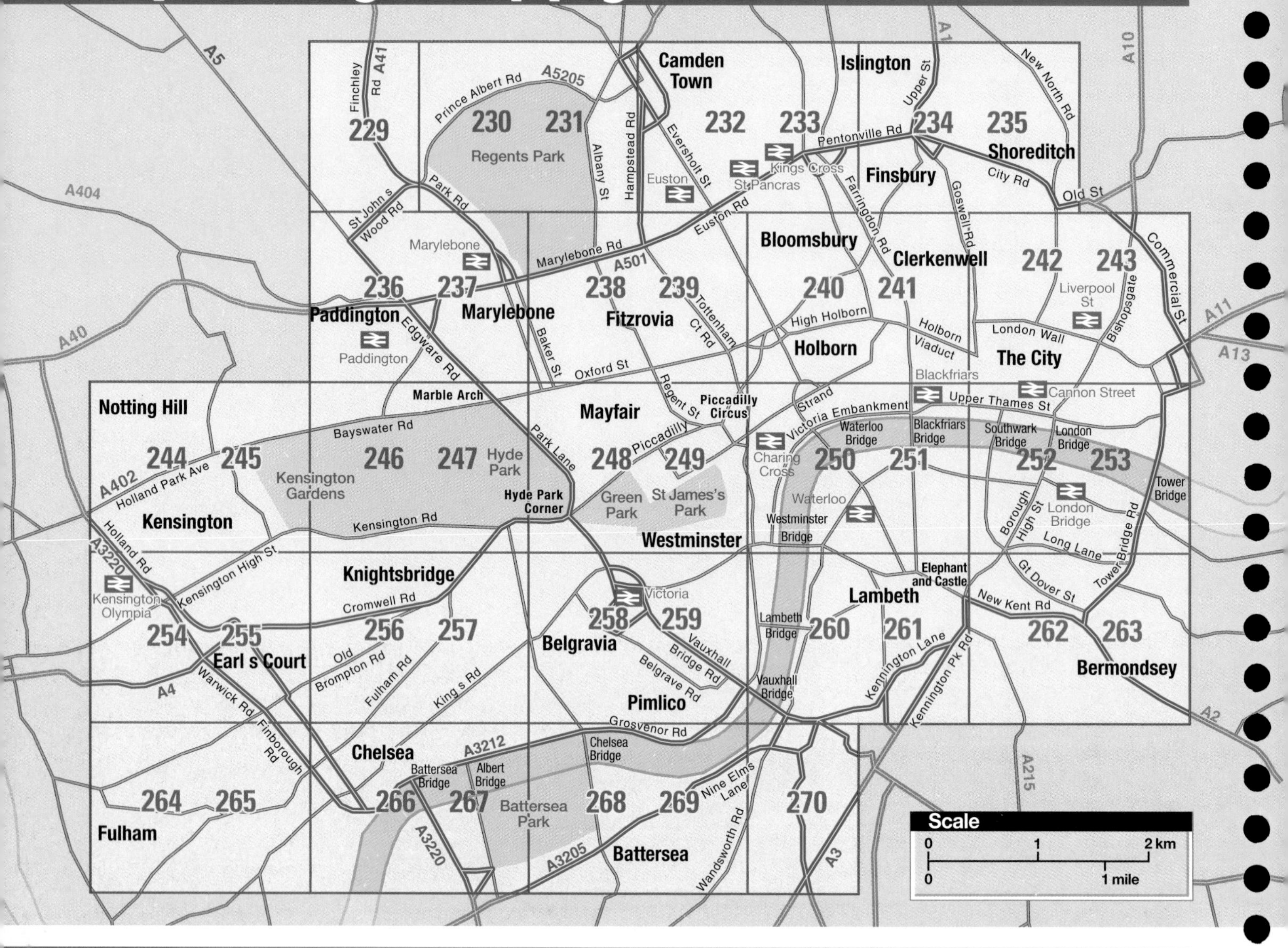
A5
A41
Finchley Rd
229
Prince Albert Rd
A5205
230
231
Regents Park
Albany St
Hampstead Rd
Camden Town
Eversholt St
232
233
Islington
Upper St
A1
234
235
New North Rd
A10
A404
Euston
St Pancras
Kings Cross
Pentonville Rd
Finsbury
Shoreditch
City Rd
Old St
Goswell Rd
Farringdon Rd
St John s Wood Rd
Park Rd
Marylebone
Euston Rd
Bloomsbury
Clerkenwell
242
243
Commercial St
Marylebone Rd
A501
236
237
238
239
240
241
Liverpool St
Bishopsgate
A11
A40
Paddington
Marylebone
Fitzrovia
Tottenham Ct Rd
High Holborn
Holborn Viaduct
London Wall
The City
A13
Edgware Rd
Baker St
Oxford St
Holborn
Blackfriars
Cannon Street
Marble Arch
Regent St
Piccadilly Circus
Strand
Upper Thames St
Notting Hill
Mayfair
Victoria Embankment
Waterloo Bridge
Blackfriars Bridge
Southwark Bridge
London Bridge
Bayswater Rd
Park Lane
Piccadilly
244
245
246
247
Hyde Park
248
249
Charing Cross
250
251
252
253
Tower Bridge
A402
Holland Park Ave
Kensington Gardens
Hyde Park Corner
Green Park
St James's Park
Waterloo
London Bridge
Kensington
Kensington Rd
Westminster Bridge
Westminster
Borough High St
Long Lane
Tower Bridge Rd
Holland Rd
A3220
Kensington High St
Knightsbridge
Elephant and Castle
Gt Dover St
Kensington Olympia
Cromwell Rd
Victoria
Lambeth
New Kent Rd
254
255
256
257
258
259
Lambeth Bridge
260
261
262
263
Earl s Court
Old Brompton Rd
Fulham Rd
Belgravia
Vauxhall Bridge Rd
Kennington Lane
Bermondsey
A4
Warwick Rd
King s Rd
Belgrave Rd
Pimlico
Vauxhall Bridge
Kennington Pk Rd
A2
Finborough Rd
Grosvenor Rd
Chelsea
A3212
Chelsea Bridge
Battersea Bridge
Albert Bridge
Nine Elms Lane
A215
264
265
266
267
Battersea Park
268
269
270
Fulham
A3220
A3205
Battersea
Wandsworth Rd
A3
Scale
0
1
2 km
1 mile

Additional symbols on enlarged maps

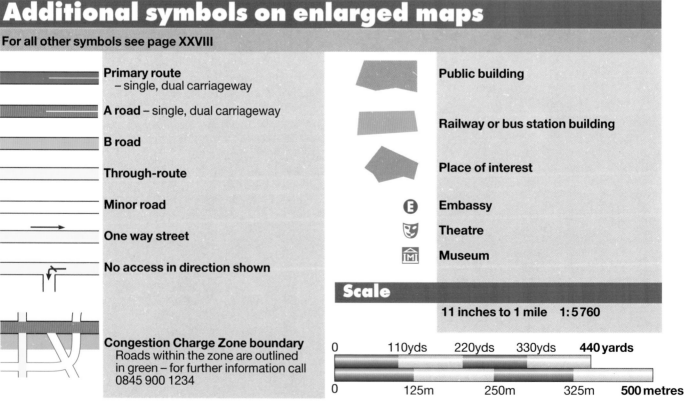

For all other symbols see page XXVIII

Primary route – single, dual carriageway

A road – single, dual carriageway

B road

Through-route

Minor road

One way street

No access in direction shown

Congestion Charge Zone boundary
Roads within the zone are outlined in green – for further information call 0845 900 1234

Public building

Railway or bus station building

Place of interest

Embassy

Theatre

Museum

Scale

11 inches to 1 mile 1:5760

0 | 110yds | 220yds | 330yds | **440 yards**

0 | 125m | 250m | 325m | **500 metres**

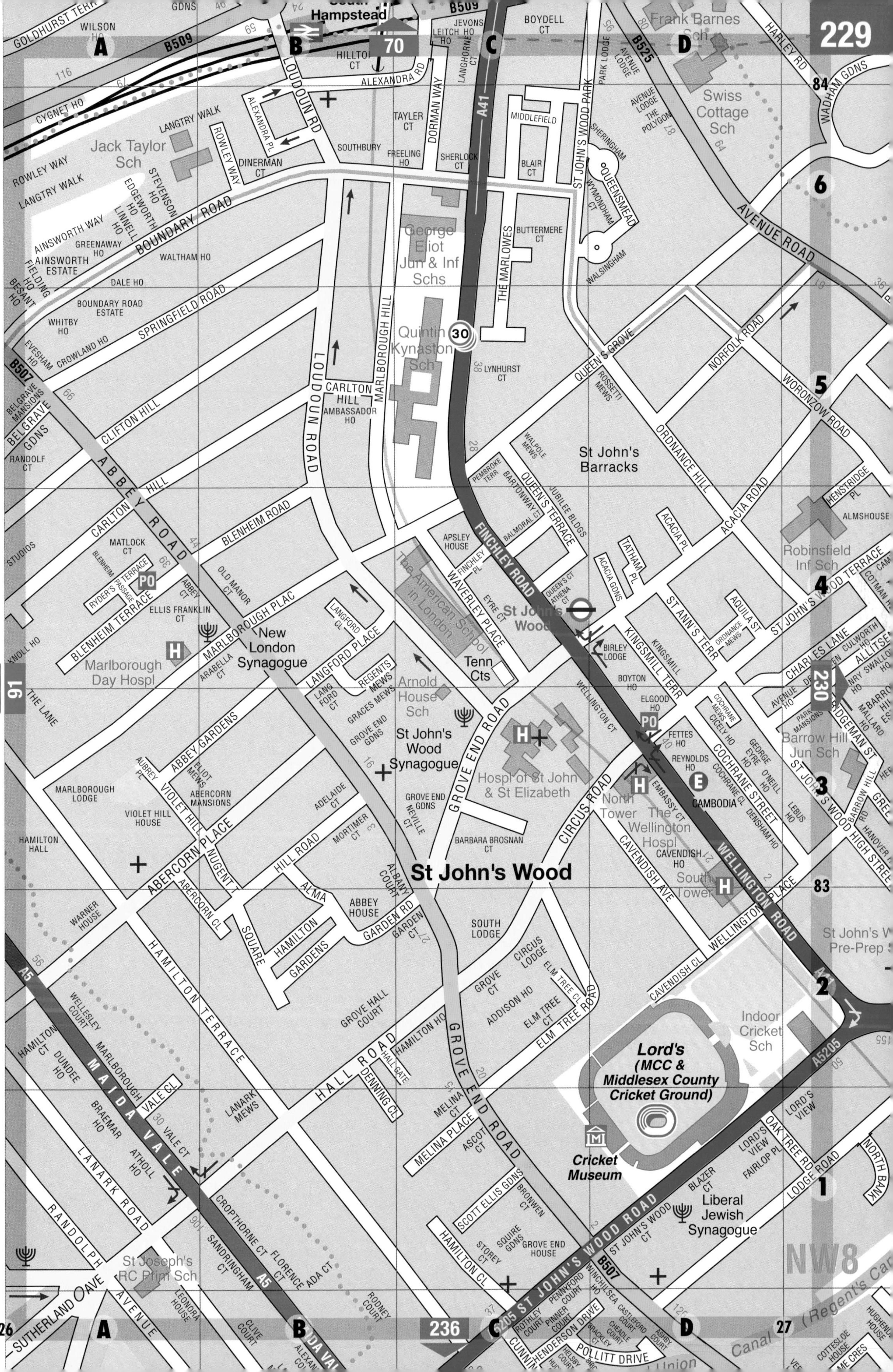

South Hampstead
70
A
B
C
D
B509
B525
A41
B507
A5
A5205
Goldhurst Terr
Wilson Ho
Cygnet Ho
Loudoun Rd
Alexandra Rd
Alexandra Pl
Hilltop Ct
Jevons Ho
Leitch Ho
Langhorne Ct
Boydell Ct
Park Lodge
Avenue Lodge
Frank Barnes Sch
Harley Rd
Wadham Gdns
Swiss Cottage Sch
Avenue Lodge
The Polygon
Langtry Walk
Jack Taylor Sch
Rowley Way
Dinerman Ct
Southbury
Tayler Ct
Dorman Way
Freeling Ho
Sherlock Ct
Middlefield
Blair Ct
St John's Wood Park
Sheringham
Queensmead
Wymondham Ct
Stevenson Ho
Edgeworth Ho
Linnell Ho
Ainsworth Way
Greenaway Ho
Ainsworth Estate
Boundary Road
Waltham Ho
Fielding Ho
Besant Ho
Dale Ho
Boundary Road Estate
Whitby Ho
Springfield Road
Evesham Ho
Crowland Ho
George Eliot Jun & Inf Schs
The Marlowes
Buttermere Ct
Walsingham
Avenue Road
6
Quintin Kynaston Sch
Lynhurst Ct
Queen's Grove
Norfolk Road
Rossetti Mews
5
Woronzow Road
Belgrave Mansions
Belgrave Gdns
Randolf Ct
Clifton Hill
Loudoun Road
Marlborough Hill
Carlton Hill
Ambassador Ho
Walpole Mews
St John's Barracks
Ordnance Hill
Abbey Road
Carlton Hill
Pembroke Terr
Bartonway Ct
Queen's Terrace
Jubilee Bldgs
Acacia Road
Henstridge Pl
Almshouse
Robinsfield Inf Sch
Studios
Matlock Ct
Blenheim Road
Apsley House
Finchley Road
Balmoral Ct
Acacia Pl
Tatham Pl
St John's Wood Terrace
4
Blenheim Terrace
Ryder's Terrace
Passage
PO
Abbey Ct
Old Manor Ct
Ellis Franklin Ct
Marlborough Place
Langford Cl
Langford Place
The American School in London
Finchley Pl
Waverley Place
Eyre Ct
Queen's Ct
Athena Ct
St John's Wood
Acacia Gdns
Aquila St
Ordnance Mews
St Ann's Terr
Kingsmill
Kingsmill Terr
Charles Lane
Knoll Ho
Marlborough Day Hospl
Arabella Ct
New London Synagogue
Regents Mews
Arnold House Sch
Tenn Cts
Birley Lodge
Boyton Ho
Elgood Ho
Wellington Ct
Allitsen
91
230
The Lane
Lang Ford Ct
Graces Mews
Grove End Gdns
St John's Wood Synagogue
Grove End Road
Hospl of St John & St Elizabeth
Fettes Ho
Reynolds Ho
Cochrane Mews
Cicely Ho
Cochrane Street
George Eyre Ho
O'Neill Ho
Barrow Hill Jun Sch
St John's Wood High Street
3
Abbey Gardens
Aubrey Pl
Eliot Mews
Abercorn Mansions
Marlborough Lodge
Violet Hill House
Violet Hill
Adelaide Ct
Mortimer Ct
Grove End Gdns
Neville Ct
Circus Road
North Tower
The Wellington Hospl
Embassy Ct
Cambodia
Cochrane Cl
Densham Ho
Lebus Ho
Barrow Hill Rd
Hanover
Hamilton Hall
Abercorn Place
Nugent
Hill Road
Alma
Albany Court
Barbara Brosnan Ct
St John's Wood
Cavendish Ho
Cavendish Ave
South Tower
Wellington Road
Wellington Place
83
Warner House
Abercorn Cl
Abbey House
Garden Rd
Garden Ct
South Lodge
Circus Lodge
Square
Hamilton Gardens
Hamilton Terrace
Cavendish Cl
St John's Wood Pre-Prep
Grove Ct
Elm Tree Cl
Grove Hall Court
Addison Ho
Elm Tree Ct
Elm Tree Road
2
Indoor Cricket Sch
Wellesley Court
Hamilton Ct
Dundee Ho
Marlborough Ct
Maida Vale
Vale Cl
Braemar Ho
Hall Road
Hamilton Ho
Hall Gate
Denning Cl
Grove End Road
Lanark Mews
Melina Ct
Melina Place
Ascot Ct
Lord's (MCC & Middlesex County Cricket Ground)
Cricket Museum
Lord's View
Oak Tree Rd
Lodge Road
North Bank
1
Vale Ct
Atholl Ho
Lanark Road
Randolph
Cropthorne Ct
Florence Ct
Ada Ct
Scott Ellis Gdns
Bronwen Ct
Hamilton Cl
Storey Ct
Squire Gdns
Grove End House
St John's Wood Road
St John's Wood Ct
Blazer Ct
Fairlop Pl
Liberal Jewish Synagogue
NW8
St Joseph's RC Prim Sch
Sandringham Ct
Sutherland Ave
Avenue
Leonora House
Rodney Court
Clive Court
236
Rothley Court
Pinner Court
Pennyford Court
Henderson Drive
Winchilsea Ho
Castleford Court
Cheadle Court
Brackley Ct
Ashby Court
Pollitt Drive
Canal (Regent's Canal)
Cotteslowe House
Hughes House
26
27

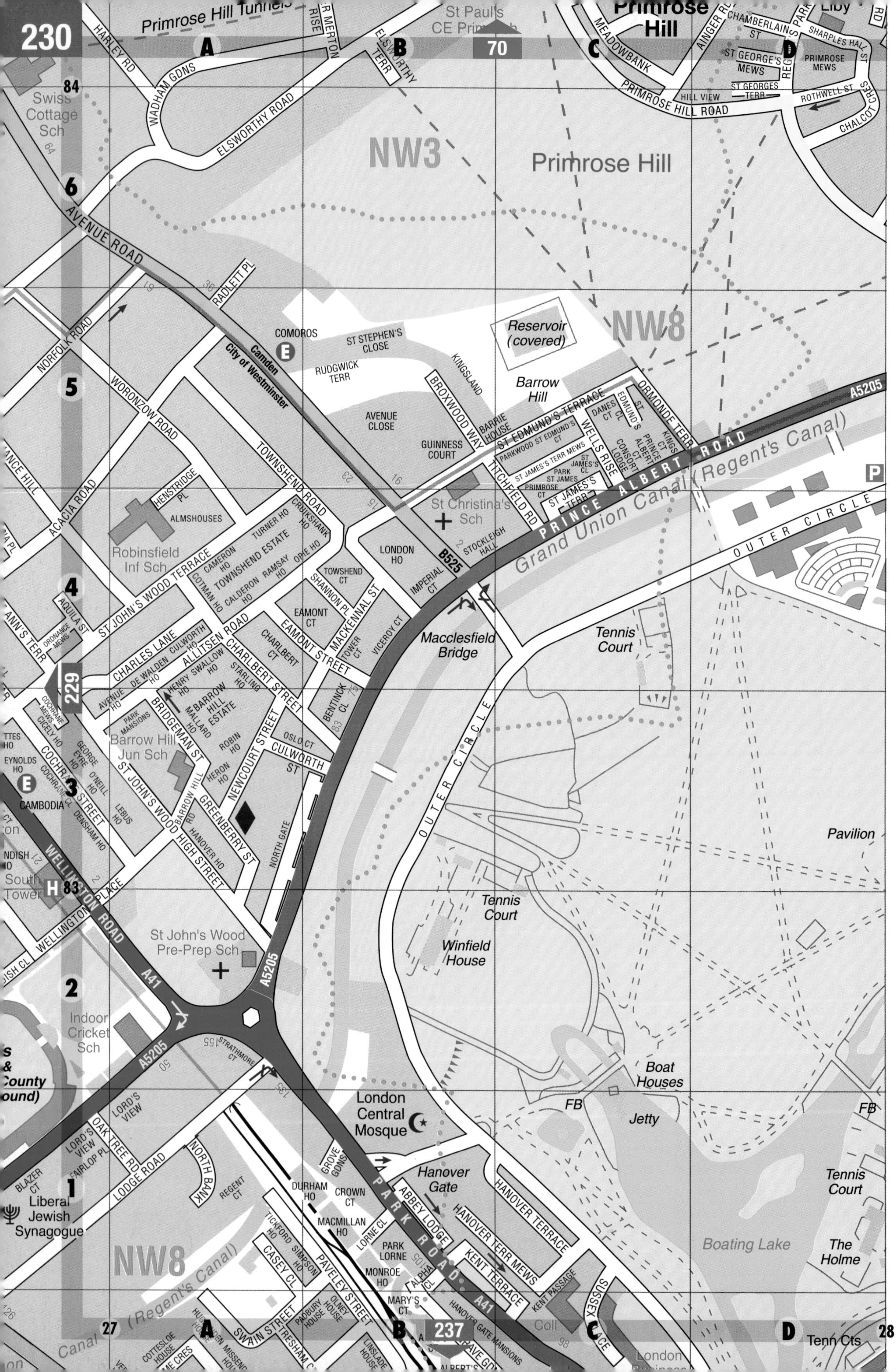
Primrose Hill Tunnels
St Paul's CE Prim Sch
70
Primrose Hill
Liby
Harley Rd
Wadham Gdns
Elsworthy Road
Elsworthy Terr
Merton Rise
Meadowbank
Ainger Rd
Chamberlain St
St George's Mews
Regent's Park Rd
Primrose Mews
Sharples Hall St
Hill View
St Georges Terr
Primrose Hill Road
Rothwell St
Chalcot Cres
Swiss Cottage Sch
NW3
Primrose Hill
Avenue Road
Radlett Pl
Norfolk Road
Comoros
St Stephen's Close
Rudgwick Terr
Kingsland
Reservoir (covered)
NW8
Barrow Hill
Camden
City of Westminster
Woronzow Road
Avenue Close
Broxwood Way
Barrie House
Guinness Court
St Edmund's Terrace
Danes Ct
Edmund's Cl
St Edmund's Ct
Prince Albert Ct
Ormonde Terr
Kings Ct
Wells Rise
Consort Lodge
Parkwood
St James's Terr Mews
Park St James
Primrose Ct
St James's Terr
Prince Albert Road
A5205
Grand Union Canal (Regent's Canal)
P
Outer Circle
Townshend Road
Acacia Road
Henstridge Pl
Almshouses
Robinsfield Inf Sch
St Christina's Sch
Titchfield Rd
Stockleigh Hall
London Ho
Imperial Ct
B525
Cruikshank Ho
Turner Ho
Townshend Estate
Cameron Ho
Calderon Ho
Ramsay Ho
Opie Ho
Cotman Ho
Townshend Ct
Shannon Pl
St John's Wood Terrace
Aquila St
Ordnance Mews
Eamont Ct
Eamont Street
Mackennal St
Tower Ct
Viceroy Ct
Macclesfield Bridge
Tennis Court
Charles Lane
Culworth Ho
Allitsen Road
De Walden Ho
Henry Swallow Ho
Starling Ho
Charlbert Ct
Charlbert Street
Bentinck Cl
229
Avenue Ho
Park Mansions
Barrow Hill Estate
Mallard Ho
Bridgeman St
Robin Ho
Heron Ho
Barrow Hill Jun Sch
Oslo Ct
Culworth St
Newcourt Street
Cochrane Mews
Cicely Ho
George Eyre Ho
O'Neill Ho
Cochrane Street
Reynolds Ho
Cambodia
St John's Wood Road
Barrow Hill Rd
Greenberry St
Lebus Ho
Densham Ho
Hanover Ho
North Gate
St John's Wood High Street
Wellington Road
South Tower
H
Wellington Place
Pavilion
Tennis Court
Winfield House
St John's Wood Pre-Prep Sch
A5205
A41
Indoor Cricket Sch
Strathmore Ct
Boat Houses
FB
Jetty
FB
London Central Mosque
Lord's View
Oak Tree Rd
Fairlop Pl
Blazer Ct
Lodge Road
North Bank
Regent Ct
Grove Gdns
Durham Ho
Crown Ct
Hanover Gate
Abbey Lodge
Park Road
Hanover Terrace
Hanover Terr Mews
Tennis Court
Liberal Jewish Synagogue
Macmillan Ho
Lorne Cl
Park Lorne
Tickford Ho
Simpson Ho
Casey Cl
Paveley Street
Monroe Ho
Alpha Cl
Kent Terrace
Kent Passage
Sussex Place
Boating Lake
The Holme
NW8
Canal (Regent's Canal)
27
Mary's Ct
Padbury House
Olney House
Swain Street
Tresham Cres
Linslade House
Hanover Gate Mansions
Cottesloe House
237
A
B
C
D
1
2
3
4
5
6
28
Tenn Cts
London Business
Coll

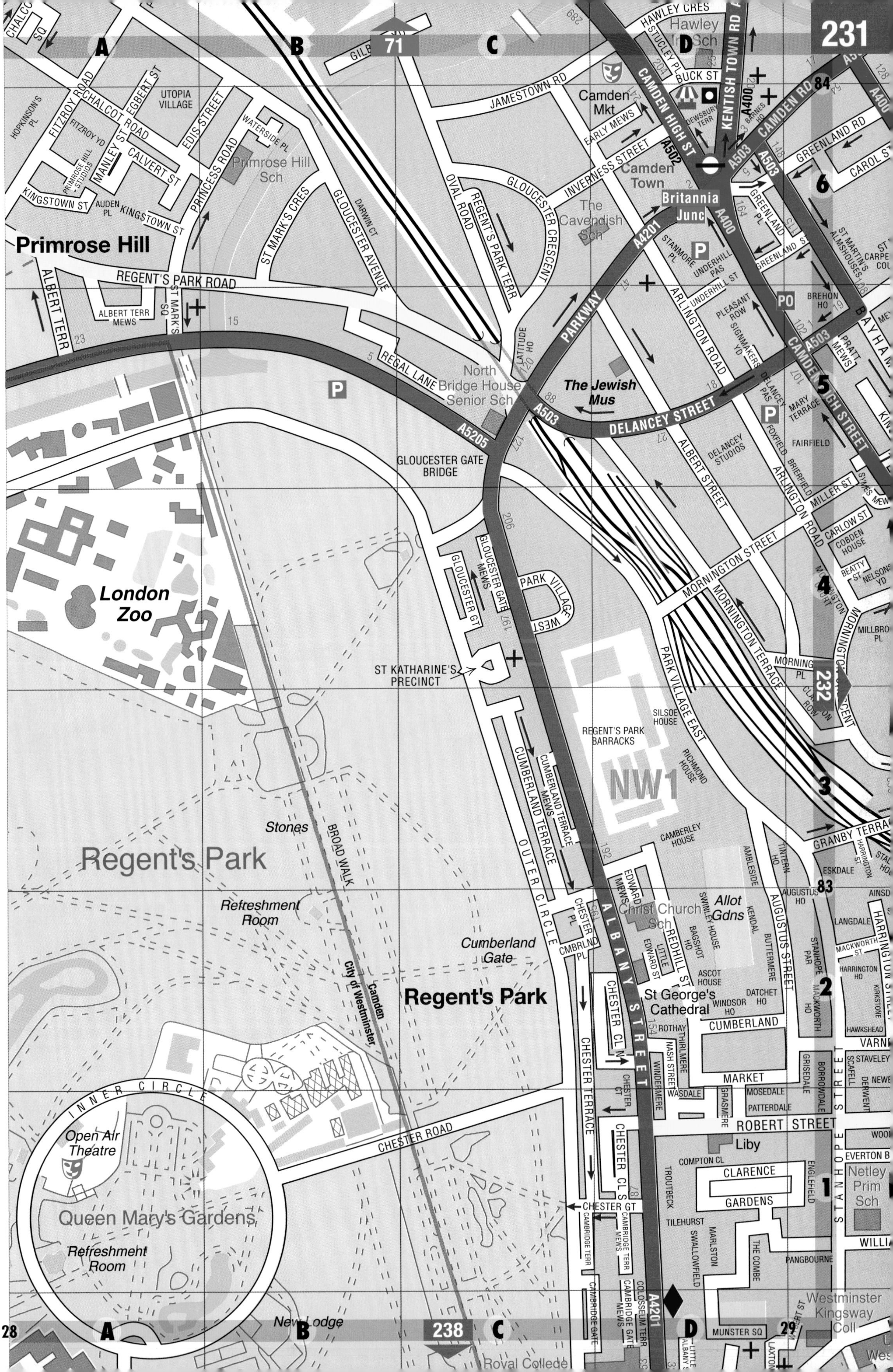
A
B
C
D
71
238
232
Primrose Hill
FITZROY ROAD
CHALCOT ROAD
EGBERT ST
UTOPIA VILLAGE
EDIS STREET
MANLEY ST
CALVERT ST
KINGSTOWN ST
PRINCESS ROAD
Primrose Hill Sch
WATERSIDE PL
ST MARK'S CRES
GLOUCESTER AVENUE
REGENT'S PARK ROAD
ALBERT TERR
ALBERT TERR MEWS
REGAL LANE
OVAL ROAD
REGENT'S PARK TERR
GLOUCESTER CRESCENT
JAMESTOWN RD
INVERNESS STREET
Camden Mkt
Camden Town
CAMDEN HIGH ST
KENTISH TOWN RD
CAMDEN RD
HAWLEY CRES
BUCK ST
Britannia Junc
The Cavendish Sch
PARKWAY
ARLINGTON ROAD
North Bridge House Senior Sch
The Jewish Mus
DELANCEY STREET
ALBERT STREET
GLOUCESTER GATE BRIDGE
London Zoo
MORNINGTON STREET
MORNINGTON TERRACE
PARK VILLAGE EAST
PARK VILLAGE WEST
ST KATHARINE'S PRECINCT
REGENT'S PARK BARRACKS
NW1
CUMBERLAND TERRACE
OUTER CIRCLE
Regent's Park
Stones
BROAD WALK
Refreshment Room
Cumberland Gate
City of Westminster
Camden
ALBANY STREET
St George's Cathedral
Christ Church Sch
Allot Gdns
AUGUSTUS STREET
GRANBY TERRACE
CHESTER TERRACE
CHESTER ROAD
INNER CIRCLE
Open Air Theatre
Queen Mary's Gardens
New Lodge
Royal College
ROBERT STREET
Liby
CLARENCE GARDENS
STANHOPE STREET
Netley Prim Sch
Westminster Kingsway Coll
MUNSTER SQ
28
29

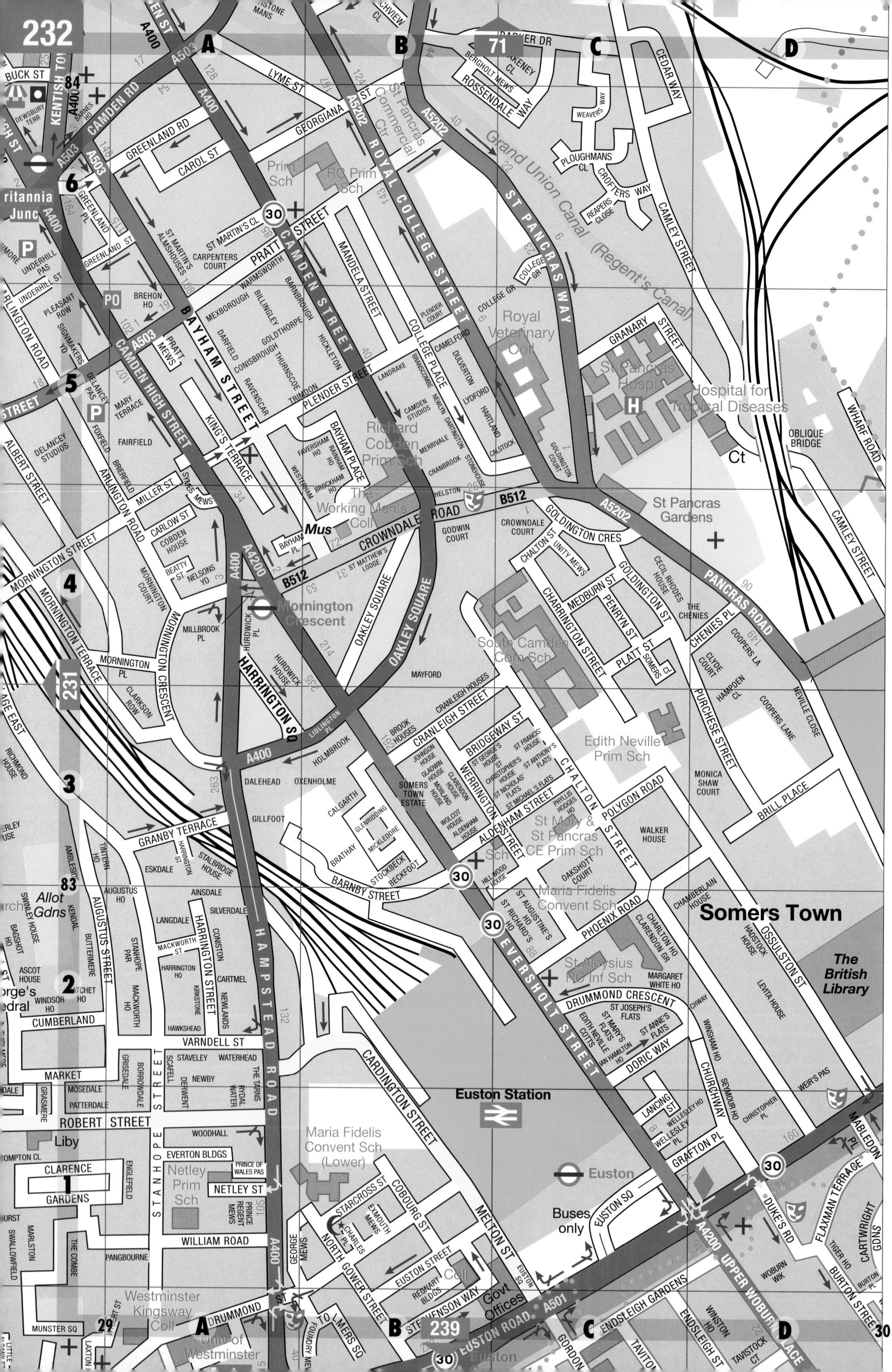

71
231
239
A
B
C
D
1
2
3
4
5
6
CAMDEN RD
KENTISH TOWN
BUCK ST
DEWSBURY TERR
GREENLAND RD
CAROL ST
LYME ST
GEORGIANA ST
St Pancras Commercial Ctr
ROYAL COLLEGE STREET
ST PANCRAS WAY
Grand Union Canal (Regent's Canal)
BARKER DR
BERGHOLT MEWS
ROSSENDALE WAY
WEAVERS WAY
PLOUGHMANS CL
CROFTERS WAY
REAPERS CLOSE
CEDAR WAY
CAMLEY STREET
Britannia Junc
UNDERHILL PAS
GREENLAND PL
GREENLAND ST
ST MARTIN'S ALMSHOUSES
ST MARTIN'S CL
CARPENTERS COURT
PRATT STREET
CAMDEN STREET
MANDELA STREET
Prim Sch
RC Prim Sch
PLEASANT ROW
SIGNMAKERS YD
BREHON HO
BAYHAM STREET
MEXBOROUGH
WARMSWORTH
BILLINGLEY
BARNBOROUGH
DARFIELD
GOLDTHORPE
CONISBROUGH
THURNSCOE
HICKLETON
RAVENSCAR
TRIMDON
PLENDER STREET
PLENDER COURT
COLLEGE PLACE
COLLEGE GR
COLLEGE GROVE
Royal Veterinary Coll
GRANARY STREET
St Pancras Hospl
Hospital for Tropical Diseases
OBLIQUE BRIDGE
WHARF ROAD
Ct
ARLINGTON ROAD
CAMDEN HIGH STREET
PRATT MEWS
DELANCEY PAS
DELANCEY STUDIOS
MARY TERRACE
FAIRFIELD
KING'S TERRACE
LANDRAKE
BRANSCOMBE
CAMELFORD
DULVERTON
LYDFORD
HARTLAND
CAMDEN STUDIOS
NEWLYN
DARTINGTON
MERRIVALE
CRANBROOK
STONEHOUSE
CALSTOCK
GOLDINGTON COURT
Richard Cobden Prim Sch
FAVERSHAM HO
RAINHAM HO
BAYHAM PLACE
WESTERHAM
BROCKHAM HO
ALBERT STREET
BRIERFIELD
FOXFIELD
MILLER ST
SYMES MEWS
CARLOW ST
COBDEN HOUSE
The Working Men's Coll
Mus
BAYHAM PL
CROWNDALE ROAD
B512
HELSTON
GODWIN COURT
CROWNDALE COURT
GOLDINGTON CRES
A5202
St Pancras Gardens
MORNINGTON STREET
MORNINGTON TERRACE
BEATTY ST
NELSONS YD
MORNINGTON COURT
ST MATTHEW'S LODGE
OAKLEY SQUARE
Mornington Crescent
MILLBROOK PL
HURDWICK PL
HURDWICK HOUSE
HARRINGTON SQ
MORNINGTON PL
MORNINGTON CRESCENT
CLARKSON ROW
MAYFORD
CHALTON ST
UNITY MEWS
CHARRINGTON STREET
MEDBURN ST
PENRYN ST
GOLDINGTON ST
CECIL RHODES HOUSE
THE CHENIES
CHENIES PL
PANCRAS ROAD
South Camden Com Sch
PLATT ST
SOMERS CL
COOPERS LA
CLYDE COURT
HAMPDEN CL
COOPERS LANE
NEVILLE CLOSE
PURCHESE STREET
RICHMOND HOUSE
LIDLINGTON PL
HOLMBROOK
BROOK HOUSES
CRANLEIGH HOUSES
CRANLEIGH STREET
BRIDGEWAY ST
Edith Neville Prim Sch
MONICA SHAW COURT
BRILL PLACE
DALEHEAD
OXENHOLME
SOMERS TOWN ESTATE
JOHNSON HOUSE
GLADWIN HOUSE
MIDLAND HOUSE
CLARENDON HOUSE
WERRINGTON STREET
CHALTON STREET
POLYGON ROAD
CALGARTH
GLENRIDDING
MICKLEDORE
WOLCOT HOUSE
ALDENHAM HOUSE
ALDENHAM STREET
PHYLLIS HODGES HO
St Mary & St Pancras CE Prim Sch
WALKER HOUSE
GRANBY TERRACE
GILLFOOT
BRATHAY
STOCKBECK
BECKFOOT
HARRINGTON ST
STALBRIDGE HOUSE
ESKDALE
TINTERN HO
AMBLESIDE
BARNBY STREET
Sch
HILLWOOD HOUSE
OAKSHOTT COURT
Maria Fidelis Convent Sch
Allot Gdns
KENDAL
AUGUSTUS HO
AUGUSTUS STREET
AINSDALE
SILVERDALE
LANGDALE
HARRINGTON STREET
CONISTON
ST AUGUSTINE'S HO
ST RICHARD'S HO
EVERSHOLT STREET
PHOENIX ROAD
CHARLTON HO
CLARENDON GR
CHAMBERLAIN HOUSE
Somers Town
HADSTOCK HOUSE
OSSULSTON ST
The British Library
SWINLEY HOUSE
BAGSHOT HO
BUTTERMERE
STANHOPE PAR
MACKWORTH ST
HARRINGTON HO
CARTMEL
KIRKSTONE
NEWLANDS
ASCOT HOUSE
WINDSOR HO
HATCHET HO
MACKWORTH HO
HAWKSHEAD
St Aloysius RC Inf Sch
MARGARET WHITE HO
DRUMMOND CRESCENT
ST JOSEPH'S FLATS
ST MARY'S FLATS
EDITH NEVILLE COTTS
ST ANNE'S FLATS
IAN HAMILTON HO
DORIC WAY
CHWAY
WINSHAM HO
SEYMOUR HO
LEVITA HOUSE
CUMBERLAND
VARNDELL ST
STAVELEY
WATERHEAD
SCAFELL
MARKET
MOSEDALE
GRISEDALE
BORROWDALE
DERWENT
NEWBY
RYDAL WATER
THE TARNS
HAMPSTEAD ROAD
CARDINGTON STREET
PATTERDALE
GRASMERE
ROBERT STREET
Euston Station
LANCING ST
WELLESLEY HO
WELLESLEY PL
CHURCHWAY
CHRISTOPHER PL
WEIR'S PAS
WOODHALL
Liby
COMPTON CL
CLARENCE GARDENS
ENGLEFIELD
STANHOPE STREET
EVERTON BLDGS
PRINCE OF WALES PAS
Netley Prim Sch
NETLEY ST
PRINCE REGENT MEWS
Maria Fidelis Convent Sch (Lower)
STARCROSS ST
EXMOUTH MEWS
COBOURG ST
CHARLES PL
Euston
EUSTON SQ
Buses only
GRAFTON PL
MABLEDON PL
FLAXMAN TERRACE
DUKE'S RD
CARTWRIGHT GDNS
MARLSTON
SWALLOWFIELD
THE COMBE
PANGBOURNE
WILLIAM ROAD
GEORGE MEWS
NORTH GOWER STREET
EUSTON STREET
MELTON ST
Coll
REGNART BLDGS
STEPHENSON WAY
Govt Offices
A501
UPPER WOBURN PLACE
A4200
WOBURN WLK
TIGER HO
BURTON PL
BURTON STREET
Westminster Kingsway Coll
MUNSTER SQ
DRUMMOND ST
ENDSLEIGH GARDENS
WINSTON HO
ENDSLEIGH ST
TAVISTOCK CT
Univ of Westminster
EUSTON ROAD
GORDON
TAVITON
LAXTON
FOUNDRY MEWS
TOLMERS SQ
A400
A503
A5202
A4200
B512
30

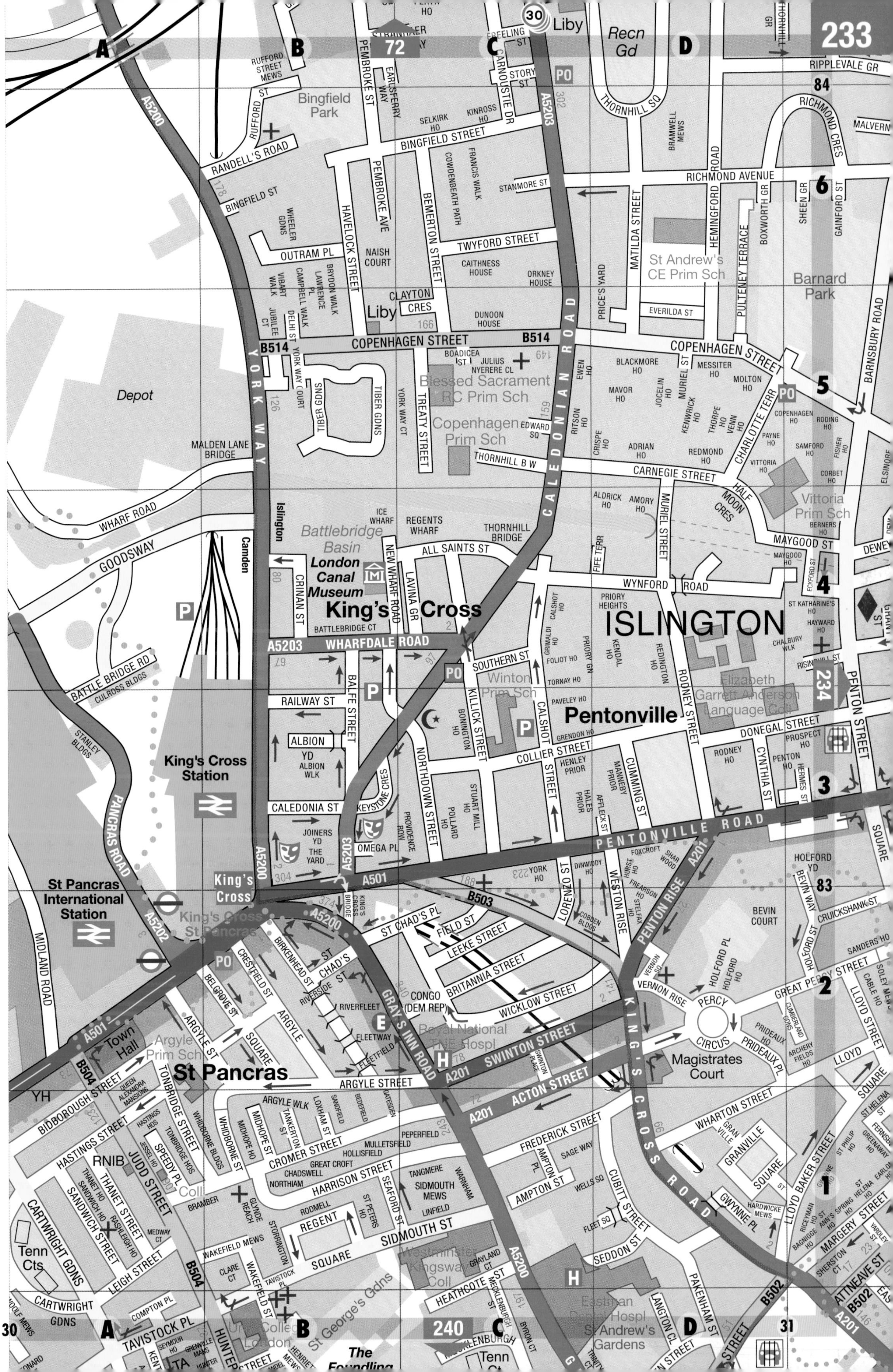
A
B
C
D
72
Liby
Recn Gd
RUFFORD STREET MEWS
PEMBROKE ST
EARLSFERRY WAY
FREELING ST
CARNOUSTIE DR
STORY ST
PO
THORNHILL GR
RIPPLEVALE GR
84
RICHMOND CRES
MALVERN
THORNHILL SQ
BRAMWELL MEWS
A5200
A5203
Bingfield Park
RUFFORD ST
RANDELL'S ROAD
SELKIRK HO
KINROSS HO
BINGFIELD STREET
COWDENBEATH PATH
FRANCIS WALK
STANMORE ST
HEMINGFORD ROAD
RICHMOND AVENUE
MATILDA STREET
6
BOXWORTH GR
SHEEN GR
GAINFORD ST
BINGFIELD ST
WHEELER GDNS
HAVELOCK STREET
PEMBROKE AVE
BEMERTON STREET
TWYFORD STREET
PULTENEY TERRACE
OUTRAM PL
NAISH COURT
CAITHNESS HOUSE
ORKNEY HOUSE
St Andrew's CE Prim Sch
Barnard Park
VIBART WALK
JUBILEE CT
CAMPBELL WALK
DELHI ST
BRYDON WALK
LAWRENCE PL
CLAYTON CRES
PRICE'S YARD
EVERILDA ST
DUNOON HOUSE
BARNSBURY ROAD
B514
COPENHAGEN STREET
COPENHAGEN STREET
BOADICEA ST
JULIUS NYERERE CL
Blessed Sacrament RC Prim Sch
EWEN HO
BLACKMORE HO
MURIEL ST
MESSITER HO
MOLTON HO
5
Depot
YORK WAY
YORK WAY COURT
TIBER GDNS
TIBER GDNS
YORK WAY CT
TREATY STREET
Copenhagen Prim Sch
EDWARD SQ
CALEDONIAN ROAD
RITSON HO
MAVOR HO
JOCELIN HO
KENWRICK HO
THORPE HO
VENN HO
CHARLOTTE TERR
COPENHAGEN HO
RODING HO
PAYNE HO
SAMFORD HO
FISHER HO
MALDEN LANE BRIDGE
THORNHILL B W
CRISPE HO
ADRIAN HO
REDMOND HO
CARNEGIE STREET
VITTORIA HO
CORBET HO
ELSINORE
ALDRICK HO
AMORY HO
MURIEL STREET
HALF MOON CRES
Vittoria Prim Sch
BERNERS HO
WHARF ROAD
Islington
Camden
ICE WHARF
REGENTS WHARF
THORNHILL BRIDGE
Battlebridge Basin
GOODSWAY
ALL SAINTS ST
FIFE TERR
MAYGOOD ST
MAYGOOD HO
DEWEY
CRINAN ST
London Canal Museum
NEW WHARF ROAD
LAVINA GR
WYNFORD ROAD
ECKFORD ST
4
King's Cross
PRIORY HEIGHTS
ISLINGTON
ST KATHARINE'S HO
HAYWARD HO
BATTLEBRIDGE CT
A5203
WHARFDALE ROAD
CALSHOT HO
GRIMALDI HO
PRIORY GN
KENDAL HO
REDINGTON HO
CHALBURY WLK
BATTLE BRIDGE RD
CULROSS BLDGS
SOUTHERN ST
FOLIOT HO
RISINGHILL ST
234
PENTON STREET
BALFE STREET
Winton Prim Sch
TORNAY HO
RODNEY STREET
Elizabeth Garrett Anderson Language Coll
RAILWAY ST
KILLICK STREET
PAVELEY HO
Pentonville
BONINGTON HO
CALSHOT STREET
GRENDON HO
DONEGAL STREET
ALBION YD
ALBION WLK
PROSPECT HO
STANLEY BLDGS
COLLIER STREET
RODNEY HO
PENTON HO
King's Cross Station
KEYSTONE CRES
NORTHDOWN STREET
HENLEY PRIOR
MAINEBY PRIOR
CUMMING ST
CYNTHIA ST
HERMES ST
3
STUART MILL HO
POLLARD HO
HALES PRIOR
AFFLECK ST
PANCRAS ROAD
CALEDONIA ST
JOINERS YD
THE YARD
PROVIDENCE ROW
OMEGA PL
PENTONVILLE ROAD
FOXCROFT
SHARWOOD
SQUARE
St Pancras International Station
King's Cross
A501
YORK HO
DINWIDDY HO
HURST HO
FREARSON HO
STELFAX HO
A201
HOLFORD YD
BEVIN WAY
83
King's Cross St Pancras
A5202
A5200
KING'S CROSS BRIDGE
B503
ST CHAD'S PL
FIELD ST
LORENZO ST
COBDEN BLDGS
WESTON RISE
PENTON RISE
BEVIN COURT
CRUICKSHANK ST
MIDLAND ROAD
PO
CRESTFIELD ST
BIRKENHEAD ST
ST CHAD'S ST
LEEKE STREET
BRITANNIA STREET
VERNON SQ
HOLFORD PL
HOLFORD HO
HOLFORD ST
SANDERS HO
GREAT PERCY STREET
2
CABLE HO
LLOYD STREET
BELGROVE ST
ARGYLE SQUARE
RIVERSIDE
RIVERFLEET
GRAY'S INN ROAD
CONGO (DEM REP)
WICKLOW STREET
VERNON RISE
PERCY CIRCUS
CUMBERLAND GDNS
PRIDEAUX PL
PRIDEAUX HO
ARCHERY FIELDS HO
A501
Town Hall
Argyle Prim Sch
ARGYLE ST
FLEETWAY
FLEETFIELD
Royal National TNE Hospl
SWINTON STREET
SWINTON PLACE
KING'S CROSS ROAD
Magistrates Court
LLOYD SQUARE
B504
St Pancras
ARGYLE STREET
A201
ACTON STREET
YH
BIDBOROUGH STREET
QUEEN ALEXANDRA MANSIONS
TONBRIDGE STREET
ARGYLE WLK
LOXHAM ST
SANDFIELD
BEDEFIELD
GATESDEN
WHARTON STREET
ST HELENA ST
HASTINGS STREET
HASTINGS HOS
WHIDBORNE BLDGS
WHIDBORNE ST
MIDHOPE HO
MIDHOPE ST
TANKERTON ST
CROMER STREET
HOLLISFIELD
MULLETSFIELD
PEPERFIELD
FREDERICK STREET
GRANVILLE SQUARE
GRAN VILLE
FERNSBY
RNIB
JUDD STREET
JESSEL HO
SPEEDY PL
TONBRIDGE HOS
GREAT CROFT
CHADSWELL
NORTHAM
HARRISON STREET
SEAFORD ST
TANGMERE
SIDMOUTH MEWS
WARNHAM
AMPTON PL
SAGE WAY
AMPTON ST
WELLS SQ
CUBITT STREET
LLOYD BAKER STREET
ST PHILIP HO
GREENAWAY HO
1
Coll
THANET HO
THANET STREET
SANDWICH HO
SANDWICH STREET
RASHLEIGH HO
CARTWRIGHT GDNS
MEDWAY CT
BRAMBER
GLYNDE REACH
RODMELL
REGENT SQUARE
ST PETERS HO
LINFIELD
SIDMOUTH ST
FLEET SQ
GWYNNE PL
HARDWICKE MEWS
RICEYMAN HO
BAGNIGGE HO
ANN'S SPRING HO
ST HELENA HO
CARLOW HO
MARGERY STREET
YARDLEY ST
Tenn Cts
LEIGH STREET
WAKEFIELD MEWS
CLARE CT
STORRINGTON
Westminster Kingsway Coll
GRAYLAND CT
SEDDON ST
PAKENHAM ST
SHERSTON CT
ATTNEAVE ST
B502
CARTWRIGHT GDNS
COMPTON PL
TAVISTOCK CT
WAKEFIELD ST
HEATHCOTE ST
MECKLENBURGH PL
H
Eastman Dental Hospl
LANGTON CL
B502
A201
30
A
TAVISTOCK PL
SEYMOUR HO
GRENVILLE MEWS
HUNTER
Univ Coll London
B
St George's Gdns
240
C
BYRON CT
St Andrew's Gardens
D
31
The Foundling
MECKLENBURGH
Tenn

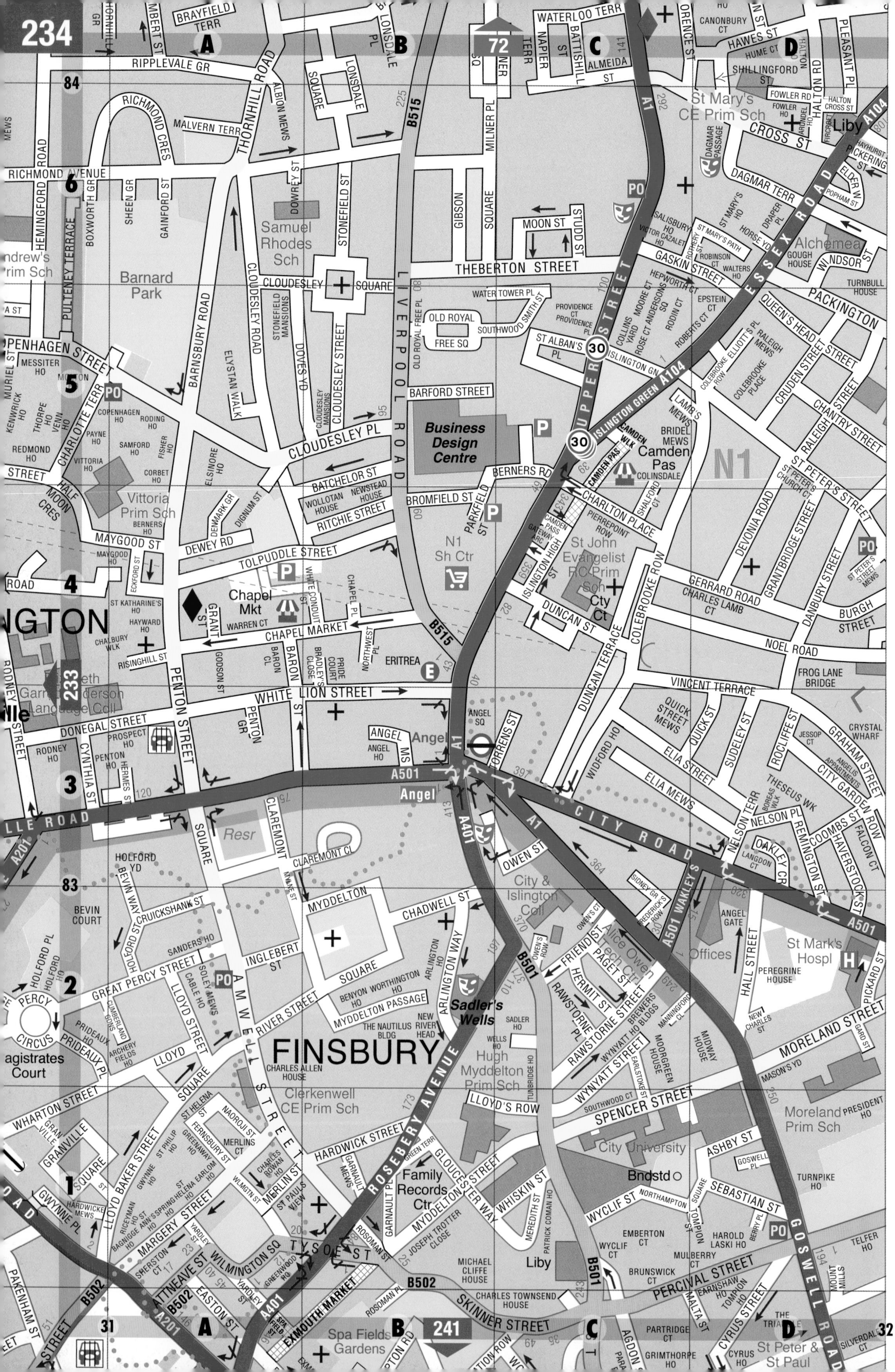
A
B
C
D
72
84
6
5
4
3
2
1
83
233
241
31
32
BRAYFIELD TERR
RIPPLEVALE GR
RICHMOND CRES
MALVERN TERR
RICHMOND AVENUE
THORNHILL ROAD
ALBION MEWS
LONSDALE SQUARE
LONSDALE PL
HEMINGFORD ROAD
PULTENEY TERRACE
BOXWORTH GR
SHEEN GR
GAINFORD ST
DOWREY ST
STONEFIELD ST
Samuel Rhodes Sch
Barnard Park
CLOUDESLEY SQUARE
CLOUDESLEY ROAD
CLOUDESLEY STREET
CLOUDESLEY PL
BARNSBURY ROAD
ELYSTAN WALK
STONEFIELD MANSIONS
DOVES YD
LIVERPOOL ROAD
B515
GIBSON SQUARE
MILNER PL
MILNER SQ
WATERLOO TERR
BATTISHILL ST
NAPIER TERR
ALMEIDA ST
CANONBURY CT
HAWES ST
HUME CT
SHILLINGFORD ST
HALTON RD
PLEASANT PL
St Mary's CE Prim Sch
FOWLER RD
FOWLER HO
HALTON CROSS ST
CROSS ST
Liby
DAGMAR PASSAGE
DAGMAR TERR
PICKERING
ELDER W
POPHAM ST
A104
ESSEX ROAD
MOON ST
STUDD ST
THEBERTON STREET
PO
SALISBURY HO
VICTOR CAZALET HO
ST MARY'S PATH
ST MARY'S HO
HORSE YD
DRAPER PL
Alchemea
GOUGH HOUSE
WINDSOR
TURNBULL HOUSE
GASKIN STREET
ROBINSON CT
WALTERS HO
HEPWORTH CT
EPSTEIN CT
PACKINGTON
A1
UPPER STREET
WATER TOWER PL
OLD ROYAL FREE SQ
OLD ROYAL FREE PL
SOUTHWOOD SMITH ST
PROVIDENCE CT
PROVIDENCE PL
ST ALBAN'S PL
ISLINGTON GN
ISLINGTON GREEN
COLLINS YARD
MOORE CT
ROSE CT
ANDERSONS SQ
RODIN CT
ROBERTS CT
COLEBROOKE ROW
ELLIOTT'S PL
RALEIGH MEWS
QUEEN'S HEAD STREET
COLEBROOKE PLACE
CRUDEN STREET
RALEIGH STREET
CHANTRY STREET
BARFORD STREET
Business Design Centre
30
CAMDEN WLK
LAMB'S MEWS
BRIDEL MEWS
Camden Pas
CAMDEN PAS
COLINSDALE
N1
BERNERS RD
BATCHELOR ST
WOLLOTAN HOUSE
NEWSTEAD HOUSE
RITCHIE STREET
BROMFIELD ST
PARKFIELD ST
CHARLTON PLACE
SHALFORD CT
PIERREPOINT ROW
ST PETER'S STREET
ST PETER'S CHURCH CT
DEVONIA ROAD
GRANTBRIDGE STREET
DANBURY STREET
ST PETER'S STREET MEWS
N1 Sh Ctr
CAMDEN PASS
GATEWAY ARC
ISLINGTON HIGH ST
St John Evangelist RC Prim Sch
Cty Ct
GERRARD ROAD
CHARLES LAMB CT
BURGH STREET
OPENHAGEN STREET
MESSITER HO
MORTON HO
MURIEL ST
KENWRICK HO
THORPE HO
VENN HO
CHARLOTTE TERR
COPENHAGEN HO
RODING HO
PAYNE HO
SAMFORD HO
FISHER HO
REDMOND HO
VITTORIA HO
CORBET HO
ELSINORE HO
DENMARK GR
DIGNUM ST
HALF MOON CRES
Vittoria Prim Sch
BERNERS HO
MAYGOOD ST
MAYGOOD HO
DEWEY RD
TOLPUDDLE STREET
ECKFORD ST
ST KATHARINE'S HO
HAYWARD HO
CHALBURY WLK
RISINGHILL ST
Chapel Mkt
GRANT ST
WARREN CT
WHITE CONDUIT ST
CHAPEL PL
CHAPEL MARKET
NORTHWEST PL
BARON CL
BARON ST
BRADLEY'S CLOSE
PRIDE COURT
GODSON ST
ERITREA
DUNCAN ST
DUNCAN TERRACE
NOEL ROAD
FROG LANE BRIDGE
VINCENT TERRACE
QUICK STREET MEWS
QUICK ST
SUDELEY ST
ROCLIFFE ST
JESSOP CT
CRYSTAL WHARF
GRAHAM STREET
GTON
Garrett Anderson Language Coll
PENTON STREET
WHITE LION STREET
PENTON GR
DONEGAL STREET
PROSPECT HO
RODNEY HO
CYNTHIA ST
PENTON HO
HERMES ST
RODNEY ST
ANGEL MS
ANGEL HO
Angel
ANGEL SQ
TORRENS ST
WIDFORD HO
ELIA STREET
ELIA MEWS
ANGELIS APARTMENTS
CITY GARDEN ROW
THESEUS WK
BOREAS WLK
NELSON TERR
NELSON PL
REMINGTON ST
COOMBS ST
HAVERSTOCK ST
FALCON CT
OAKLEY CR
LANGDON CT
A501
PENTONVILLE ROAD
A201
CLAREMONT SQUARE
Resr
CLAREMONT CL
MYLNE ST
A401
OWEN ST
CITY ROAD
HOLFORD YD
BEVIN WAY
CRUICKSHANK ST
BEVIN COURT
HOLFORD ST
SANDERS HO
MYDDELTON SQUARE
CHADWELL ST
City & Islington Coll
OWEN'S CT
OWEN'S HO
SIDNEY GR
FREDERICK'S ROW
WAKLEY ST
ANGEL GATE
Offices
HALL STREET
St Mark's Hospl
H
PICKARD ST
HOLFORD PL
HOLFORD HO
GREAT PERCY STREET
CABLE HO
SOLEY MEWS
AMWELL STREET
INGLEBERT ST
ARLINGTON HO
ARLINGTON WAY
FRIEND ST
Alice Owen Tech Ctr
PAGET ST
HERMIT ST
RAWSTORNE PL
RAWSTORNE STREET
BREWERS HO
MANNINGFORD CL
MIDWAY HOUSE
PEREGRINE HOUSE
NEW CHARLES ST
MORELAND STREET
GARD ST
PERCY CIRCUS
CUMBERLAND GDNS
PRIDEAUX PL
ARCHERY FIELDS HO
LLOYD STREET
RIVER STREET
BENYON HO
WORTHINGTON HO
MYDDELTON PASSAGE
Sadler's Wells
B501
SADLER HO
THE NAUTILUS BLDG
NEW RIVER HEAD
WELLS HO
WYNYATT HO BLDGS
WYNYATT STREET
EARLSTOKE ST
MOORGREEN HOUSE
MASON'S YD
Magistrates Court
LLOYD SQUARE
FINSBURY
CHARLES ALLEN HOUSE
Hugh Myddelton Prim Sch
TUNBRIDGE HO
Clerkenwell CE Prim Sch
ROSEBERY AVENUE
LLOYD'S ROW
SOUTHWOOD CT
SPENCER STREET
Moreland Prim Sch
PRESIDENT HO
WHARTON STREET
GRANVILLE SQUARE
LLOYD BAKER STREET
ST HELENA
NAOROJI ST
FERNSBURY ST
MERLINS CT
GREENAWAY HO
ST PHILIP HO
HARDWICK STREET
GREEN TERR
GARNAULT MEWS
GLOUCESTER WAY
WHISKIN ST
City University
ASHBY ST
GOSWELL PL
GWYNNE PL
HARDWICKE MEWS
RICEYMAN HO
BAGNIGGE HO
GWYNNE HO
ANN'S HO
SPRING HO
HELENA HO
EARLOM HO
CHARLES ROWAN HO
MERLIN ST
WILMGTN ST
ST PAUL'S VIEW
Family Records Ctr
GARNAULT PL
MYDDELTON STREET
MEREDITH ST
PATRICK COMAN HO
Bndstd
TURNPIKE HO
NORTHAMPTON SQUARE
SEBASTIAN ST
WYCLIF ST
TOMPION ST
BERRY PL
MARGERY STREET
YARDLEY ST
SHERSTON CT
ATTNEAVE ST
WILMINGTON SQ
GREENWOOD HO
TYSOE ST
ROSOMAN ST
JOSEPH TROTTER CLOSE
MICHAEL CLIFFE HOUSE
Liby
WYCLIF CT
EMBERTON CT
HAROLD LASKI HO
MULBERRY CT
BRUNSWICK CT
TELFER HO
GOSWELL ROAD
PAKENHAM ST
B502
EASTON ST
A401
EXMOUTH MARKET
SPA FIELD ST
ROSOMAN PL
Spa Fields Gardens
SKINNER STREET
CHARLES TOWNSEND HOUSE
PERCIVAL STREET
EARNSHAW HO
TOMPION HO
MALTA ST
CYRUS STREET
THE TRIANGLE
PARTRIDGE CT
GRIMTHORPE HO
CYRUS HO
St Peter & St Paul
SILVERDALE CT
AGDON ST

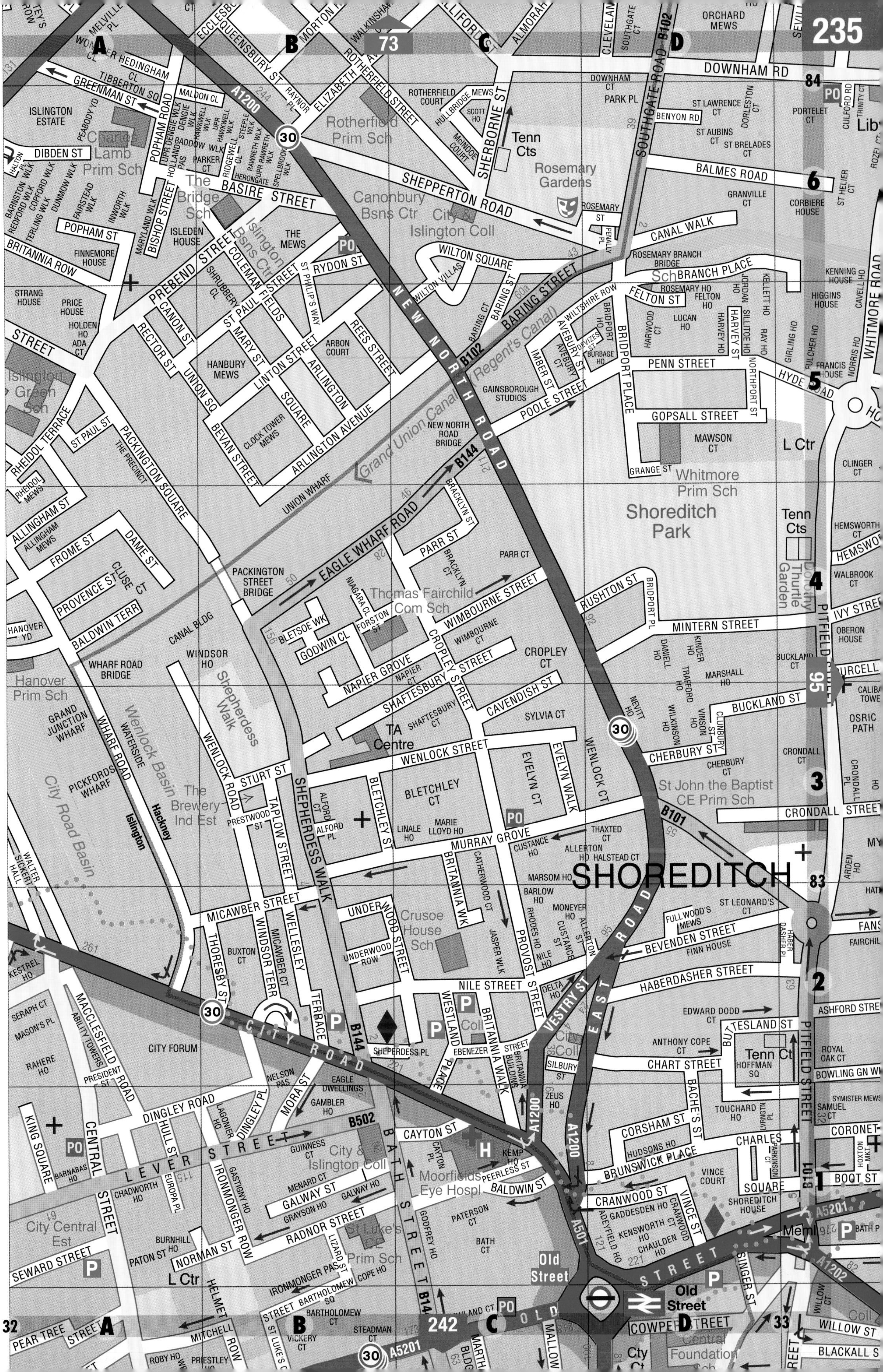

A
B
C
D
73
ISLINGTON ESTATE
DIBDEN ST
Charles Lamb Prim Sch
GREENMAN ST
TIBBERTON SQ
HEDINGHAM CL
POPHAM ROAD
POPHAM ST
BASIRE STREET
The Bridge Sch
ISLEDEN HOUSE
BRITANNIA ROW
FINNEMORE HOUSE
PREBEND STREET
Islington Bsns Ctr
A1200
ELIZABETH AV
ROTHERFIELD STREET
Rotherfield Prim Sch
ROTHERFIELD COURT
SHERBORNE ST
Tenn Cts
Rosemary Gardens
SHEPPERTON ROAD
Canonbury Bsns Ctr
City & Islington Coll
SOUTHGATE ROAD
B102
DOWNHAM RD
DOWNHAM CT
PARK PL
ST LAWRENCE CT
BENYON RD
ST AUBINS CT
ST BRELADES CT
BALMES ROAD
GRANVILLE CT
CORBIERE HOUSE
PORTELET CT
CANAL WALK
ROSEMARY BRANCH BRIDGE
BRANCH PLACE
WILTON SQUARE
BARING STREET
NEW NORTH ROAD
Grand Union Canal (Regent's Canal)
NEW NORTH ROAD BRIDGE
GAINSBOROUGH STUDIOS
POOLE STREET
FELTON ST
BRIDPORT PLACE
PENN STREET
GOPSALL STREET
MAWSON CT
HYDE ROAD
L Ctr
Whitmore Prim Sch
Shoreditch Park
WHITMORE ROAD
Tenn Cts
Dorothy Thurtle Garden
HANBURY MEWS
LINTON STREET
ARLINGTON AVENUE
ARBON COURT
REES STREET
CLOCK TOWER MEWS
BEVAN STREET
UNION WHARF
CANON ST
RECTOR ST
UNION SQ
Islington Green Sch
RHEIDOL TERRACE
ST PAUL ST
PACKINGTON SQUARE
ALLINGHAM ST
FROME ST
DAME ST
CLUSE CT
PROVENCE ST
BALDWIN TERR
HANOVER YD
Hanover Prim Sch
PACKINGTON STREET BRIDGE
EAGLE WHARF ROAD
B144
PARR ST
PARR CT
BRACKLYN ST
Thomas Fairchild Com Sch
WIMBOURNE STREET
RUSHTON ST
MINTERN STREET
PITFIELD STREET
CANAL BLDG
WINDSOR HO
WHARF ROAD BRIDGE
GRAND JUNCTION WHARF
WHARF ROAD
Wenlock Basin
City Road Basin
PICKFORDS WHARF
Shepherdess Walk
GODWIN CL
NAPIER GROVE
SHAFTESBURY STREET
CROPLEY STREET
CROPLEY CT
CAVENDISH ST
SYLVIA CT
TA Centre
WENLOCK STREET
WENLOCK ROAD
STURT ST
The Brewery Ind Est
SHEPHERDESS WALK
TAPLOW STREET
BLETCHLEY CT
BLETCHLEY ST
EVELYN CT
EVELYN WALK
WENLOCK CT
MURRAY GROVE
BUCKLAND ST
CHERBURY ST
St John the Baptist CE Prim Sch
CRONDALL STREET
B101
SHOREDITCH
EAST ROAD
MICAWBER STREET
WINDSOR TERR
BUXTON CT
UNDERWOOD STREET
Crusoe House Sch
BRITANNIA WK
JASPER WALK
PROVOST STREET
BEVENDEN STREET
HABERDASHER STREET
NILE STREET
VESTRY ST
CITY ROAD
CITY FORUM
MACCLESFIELD ROAD
SHEPHERDESS PL
EBENEZER ST
BRITANNIA WALK
City Coll
CHART STREET
BACHE'S ST
Tenn Ct
CORSHAM ST
BRUNSWICK PLACE
CHARLES SQUARE
DINGLEY ROAD
LEVER STREET
B502
CAYTON ST
City & Islington Coll
Moorfields Eye Hospl
BALDWIN ST
BATH STREET
GALWAY ST
RADNOR STREET
St Luke's CE Prim Sch
IRONMONGER ROW
KING SQUARE
CENTRAL STREET
City Central Est
SEWARD STREET
L Ctr
CRANWOOD ST
SHOREDITCH HOUSE
Old Street
OLD STREET
A5201
A1202
242
32
33
PEAR TREE STREET

229
A
B
C
D
6
5
4
3
2
1
W9
W2
PADDINGTON
Little Venice
Bayswater
Lauderdale Road
Sutherland Ave
Randolph Avenue
Warrington Crescent
Randolph Crescent
Maida Vale
A5
A5205 St John's Wood Road
B507
Clifton Road
B413
Clifton Gardens
Warwick Avenue
Warwick Avenue
Formosa Street
Clifton Villas
Bristol Gdns
Bristol Mews
Warwick Place
Blomfield Road
Maida Avenue
Grand Union Canal Wlk
Grand Union
Canal
Delamere Terrace
Westbourne Terrace Rd
Warwick Crescent
Harrow Rd
Harrow Road
A404
A40
Westway (Elevated) Harrow Rd (Under)
A4206
A4205
Bishop's Bridge Road
Ranelagh Bridge
Westbourne Bridge
Bishop's Road Bridge
Sheldon Sq
(Paddington Branch)
Paddington Basin
North Wharf Road
South Wharf Road
Harbet Road
Hermitage St
Dudley St
Dudley House
Paddington Acad
Alexander Fleming Laboratory Mus
St Mary's Hosp
Medical Sch
Praed Street
Paddington (Hammersmith & City)
Heathrow Express Terminal Paddington Station
Eastbourne Terrace
Eastbourne Mews
Westbourne Terrace
Gloucester Terrace
Orsett Terrace
Porchester Square
Porchester Terrace N
Gloucester Gdns
Cleveland Gdns
Cleveland Square
Leinster Gardens
Leinster Pl
Hallfield Jun & Inf Schs
Chilworth Street
Chilworth Mews
Craven Road
Craven Hill
London St
Spring St
Conduit Mews
Sussex Gardens
Sussex Place
Norfolk Square
Norfolk Place
Bathurst Mews
Hilton London Paddington Hotel
Paddington
B410
A4209
Hyde Park
St Mary's Gardens
City of Westminster Coll
Paddington Green Prim Sch
St Mary's Terr
Park Place Villas
Howley Place
Church Street
Edgware Road
Crompton Street
Hall Place
Aberdeen Place
Lyons Place
Northwick Terr
Cunningham Pl
Henderson Drive
Pollitt Drive
Fisherton Street
Capland Street
Frampton Street
Luton Street
Penfold Street
Boscobel St
Venables St
Hatton St
Adpar Street
Newcastle Pl
Gateway Prim Sch
St Joseph's RC Prim Sch
Jewish Synagogue
Grove End House
Hamilton Cl
Orchardson Street
Lilestone Estate
Fisherton Street Estate
Bedlow Cl
Paddington Green
26
27
246

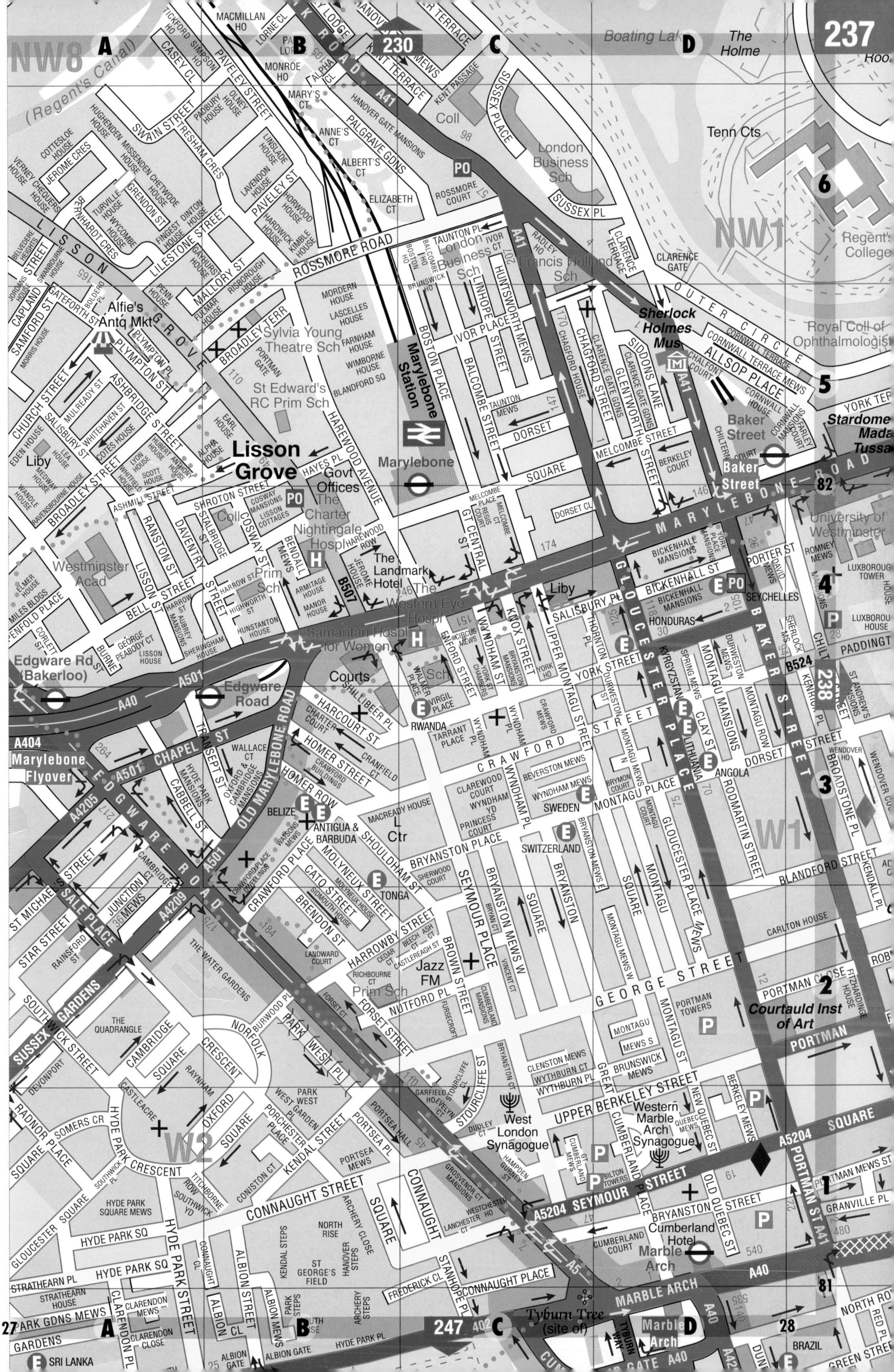
NW8
A
B
230
C
D
Boating Lake
The Holme
(Regent's Canal)
MACMILLAN HO
LORNE CL
MONROE HO
PAVELEY STREET
SWAIN STREET
TRESHAM CRES
JEROME CRES
LISSON GROVE
LILESTONE STREET
ROSSMORE ROAD
ROSSMORE COURT
PALGRAVE GDNS
HANOVER GATE MANSIONS
KENT TERRACE
KENT PASSAGE
SUSSEX PLACE
SUSSEX PL
Coll
London Business Sch
Tenn Cts
6
NW1
Regent's College
CLARENCE GATE
OUTER CIRCLE
Royal Coll of Ophthalmologists
Sherlock Holmes Mus
ALLSOP PLACE
CORNWALL TERRACE MEWS
5
YORK TERRACE
Stardome Madame Tussauds
Baker Street
MARYLEBONE ROAD
82
University of Westminster
Francis Holland Sch
CHAGFORD STREET
GLENTWORTH STREET
SIDDONS LANE
MELCOMBE STREET
DORSET SQUARE
IVOR PLACE
BALCOMBE STREET
BOSTON PLACE
Marylebone Station
Marylebone
Alfie's Antq Mkt
Sylvia Young Theatre Sch
St Edward's RC Prim Sch
HAREWOOD AVENUE
BROADLEY TERR
BROADLEY STREET
CHURCH STREET
SALISBURY ST
ASHBRIDGE STREET
Lisson Grove
Govt Offices
The Charter Nightingale Hospl
The Landmark Hotel
The Western Eye Hospl
Samaritan Hospl for Women
Westminster Acad
BELL STREET
LISSON ST
Edgware Rd (Bakerloo)
Edgware Road
A501
A40
A404
Marylebone Flyover
CHAPEL ST
EDGWARE ROAD
OLD MARYLEBONE ROAD
Courts
HARCOURT ST
HOMER STREET
HOMER ROW
CRAWFORD STREET
WYNDHAM PL
UPPER MONTAGU STREET
YORK STREET
GLOUCESTER PLACE
BAKER STREET
BICKENHALL ST
PORTER ST
LUXBOROUGH TOWER
4
PADDINGTON
238
B524
DORSET STREET
3
W1
BLANDFORD STREET
MONTAGU PLACE
MONTAGU SQUARE
BRYANSTON SQUARE
BRYANSTON PLACE
SEYMOUR PLACE
MOLYNEUX STREET
SHOULDHAM ST
CRAWFORD PLACE
HARROWBY STREET
Jazz FM
GEORGE STREET
PORTMAN CLOSE
2
Courtauld Inst of Art
PORTMAN SQUARE
SALE PLACE
SUSSEX GARDENS
THE WATER GARDENS
THE QUADRANGLE
CAMBRIDGE SQUARE
NORFOLK CRESCENT
OXFORD SQUARE
HYDE PARK CRESCENT
W2
UPPER BERKELEY STREET
West London Synagogue
Western Marble Arch Synagogue
SEYMOUR STREET
A5204
BRYANSTON STREET
1
CONNAUGHT STREET
CONNAUGHT SQUARE
HYDE PARK SQ
HYDE PARK STREET
Cumberland Hotel
Marble Arch
A40
81
CONNAUGHT PLACE
Tyburn Tree (site of)
MARBLE ARCH
A5
27
A
B
247
C
D
28
SRI LANKA
BRAZIL

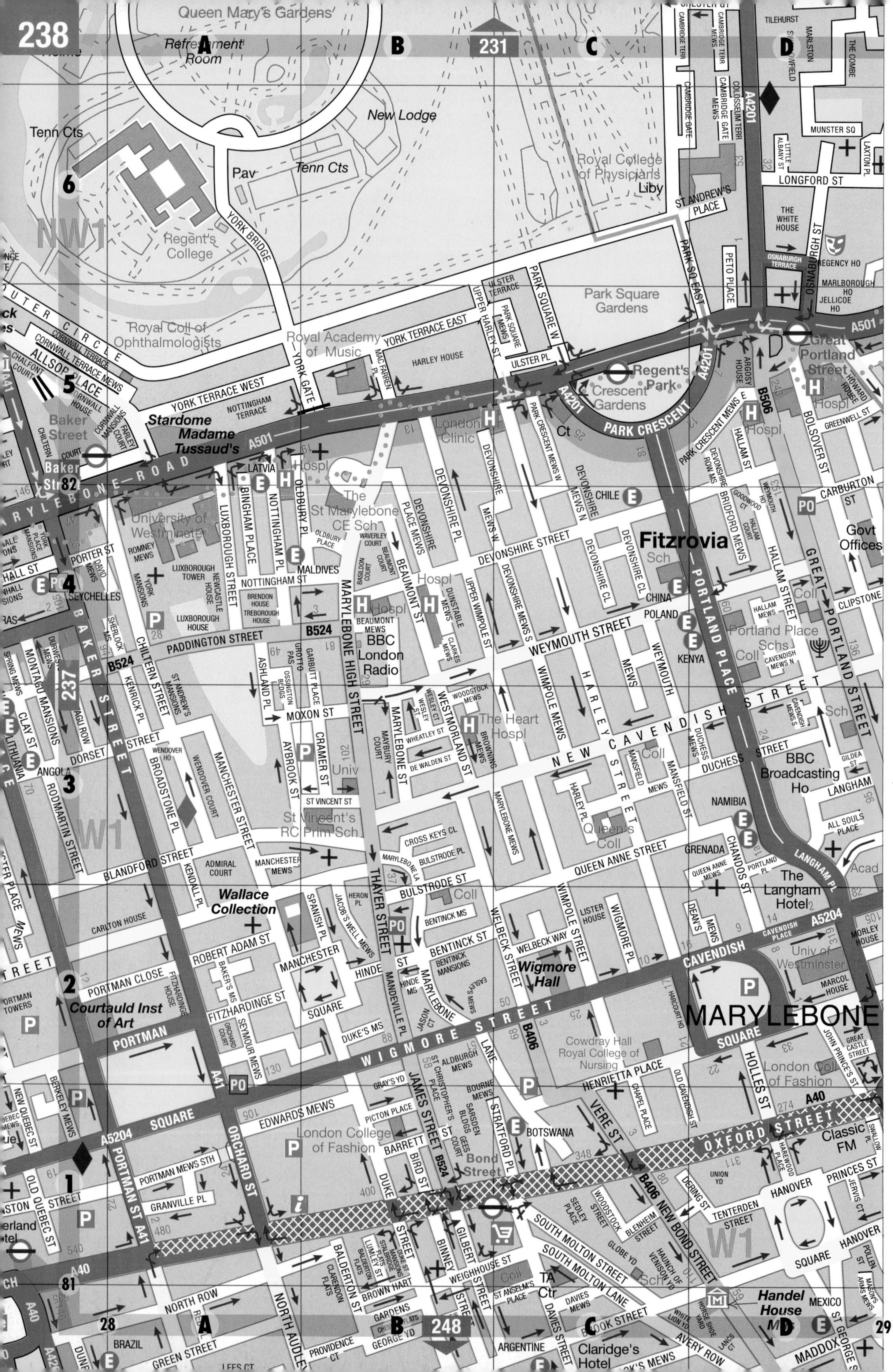
A
B
C
D
231
Queen Mary's Gardens
Refreshment Room
New Lodge
Tenn Cts
Pav
Tenn Cts
NW1
Regent's College
YORK BRIDGE
Royal College of Physicians
Liby
ST ANDREW'S PLACE
CAMBRIDGE TERR
CAMBRIDGE TERR MEWS
CAMBRIDGE GATE MEWS
COLOSSEUM TERR
CAMBRIDGE GATE
A4201
TILEHURST
MARLSTON
THE COMBE
MUNSTER SQ
LITTLE ALBANY ST
LAXTON PL
LONGFORD ST
THE WHITE HOUSE
OSNABURGH ST
OSNABURGH TERRACE
REGENCY HO
MARLBOROUGH HO
JELLICOE HO
PETO PLACE
PARK SQ EAST
Park Square Gardens
PARK SQUARE W
OUTER CIRCLE
CORNWALL TERRACE
CORNWALL TERRACE MEWS
ALLSOP PLACE
CHALFONT COURT
CORNWALL HOUSE
CORNWALL MANSIONS
FARLEY COURT
Royal Coll of Ophthalmologists
Royal Academy of Music
YORK GATE
YORK TERRACE EAST
YORK TERRACE WEST
NOTTINGHAM TERRACE
HARLEY HOUSE
MACFARREN PL
ULSTER TERRACE
UPPER HARLEY ST
PARK SQUARE MEWS
ULSTER PL
Regent's Park
Crescent Gardens
PARK CRESCENT
A501
Great Portland Street
ARGOSY HOUSE
HOWARD HOUSE
Hospl
GREENWELL ST
BOLSOVER ST
Baker Street
CHILTERN COURT
Stardome
Madame Tussaud's
MARYLEBONE ROAD
LATVIA
BINGHAM PLACE
NOTTINGHAM PL
OLDBURY PL
OLDBURY PLACE
London Clinic
DEVONSHIRE MEWS W
PARK CRESCENT MEWS W
PARK CRESCENT MEWS E
DEVONSHIRE MEWS N
CHILE
DEVONSHIRE ROW MS
DEVONSHIRE PL
DEVONSHIRE PLACE MEWS
The St Marylebone CE Sch
WAVERLEY COURT
BASILDON COURT
BEAUMONT COURT
University of Westminster
ROMNEY MEWS
LUXBOROUGH STREET
LUXBOROUGH TOWER
NEWCASTLE HOUSE
YORK MANSIONS
LUXBOROUGH HOUSE
NOTTINGHAM ST
BRENDON HOUSE
TREBOROUGH HOUSE
MALDIVES
PORTER ST
DAVID MEWS
SEYCHELLES
YORK PLACE MANSIONS
BAKER STREET
SHERLOCK MS
CHILTERN STREET
PADDINGTON STREET
B524
MARYLEBONE HIGH STREET
BEAUMONT MEWS
BEAUMONT ST
BBC London Radio
DUNSTABLE MEWS
CLARKES MEWS
UPPER WIMPOLE ST
DEVONSHIRE STREET
DEVONSHIRE MEWS S
Fitzrovia
Sch
DEVONSHIRE CL
CHINA
POLAND
KENYA
PORTLAND PLACE
HALLAM ST
BRIDFORD MEWS
GOODWOOD CT
HALLAM CT
WEYMOUTH MEWS
WEYMOUTH STREET
HALLAM STREET
HALLAM MEWS
Coll
Portland Place Schs
CAVENDISH MEWS N
GREAT PORTLAND STREET
CARBURTON ST
Govt Offices
CLIPSTONE
B506
Hospl
ASHLAND PL
OSSINGTON BLDGS
GROTTO PAS
GARBUTT PLACE
MOXON ST
AYBROOK ST
CRAMER ST
Univ
ST VINCENT ST
St Vincent's RC Prim Sch
MANCHESTER STREET
WENDOVER COURT
WENDOVER HO
BROADSTONE PL
KENRICK PL
ST ANDREW'S MANSIONS
DORSET STREET
ANGOLA
MONTAGU MANSIONS
MONTAGU ROW
DURWESTON MEWS
SPRING MEWS
CLAY ST
LITHUANIA
RODMARTIN STREET
237
W1
MARYLEBONE ST
MAYBURY COURT
WESLEY ST
WESTMORLAND ST
WOODSTOCK MEWS
WHEATLEY ST
DE WALDEN ST
The Heart Hospl
BROWNING MEWS
WIMPOLE MEWS
HARLEY STREET
NEW CAVENDISH STREET
MARYLEBONE MEWS
HARLEY PL
MANSFIELD MEWS
MANSFIELD ST
Queen's Coll
DUCHESS MEWS
DUCHESS STREET
CAVENDISH MEWS S
BBC Broadcasting Ho
GILDEA ST
LANGHAM
NAMIBIA
ALL SOULS PLACE
CROSS KEYS CL
MARYLEBONE LA
BULSTRODE PL
BULSTRODE ST
THAYER STREET
BLANDFORD STREET
KENDALL PL
ADMIRAL COURT
MANCHESTER MEWS
QUEEN ANNE STREET
GRENADA
QUEEN ANNE MEWS
CHANDOS ST
PORTLAND PL
The Langham Hotel
LANGHAM PL
Acad
Wallace Collection
HERON PL
SPANISH PL
JACOB'S WELL MEWS
BENTINCK MS
CARLTON HOUSE
ROBERT ADAM ST
BAKER'S MS
MANCHESTER SQUARE
HINDE ST
MANDEVILLE PL
BENTINCK ST
BENTINCK MANSIONS
WELBECK STREET
WELBECK WAY
WIMPOLE STREET
LISTER HOUSE
WIGMORE PL
DEAN'S MEWS
CAVENDISH PLACE
A5204
Univ of Westminster
MORLEY HOUSE
PORTMAN CLOSE
FITZHARDINGE HOUSE
FITZHARDINGE ST
ORCHARD COURT
SEYMOUR MEWS
Courtauld Inst of Art
PORTMAN SQUARE
HINDE MS
JASON CT
MARYLEBONE LANE
EASLEY'S MEWS
Wigmore Hall
WIGMORE STREET
B406
DUKE'S MS
HARCOURT HO
CAVENDISH SQUARE
MARYLEBONE
MARCOL HOUSE
JOHN PRINCE'S ST
GREAT CASTLE STREET
Cowdray Hall Royal College of Nursing
HENRIETTA PLACE
CHAPEL PLACE
OLD CAVENDISH ST
HOLLES ST
London Coll of Fashion
A40
NEW QUEBEC ST
BERKELEY MEWS
A41
EDWARDS MEWS
ALDBURGH MEWS
ST CHRISTOPHER'S PLACE
GRAY'S YD
JAMES STREET
BOURNE MEWS
SARSDEN BLDGS
GEES COURT
STRATFORD PL
BOTSWANA
VERE ST
OXFORD STREET
Classic FM
SWALLOW PL
HAREWOOD PLACE
PICTON PLACE
London College of Fashion
BARRETT ST
BIRD ST
Bond Street
PORTMAN MEWS STH
GRANVILLE PL
PORTMAN ST
ORCHARD ST
OLD QUEBEC ST
BRYANSTON STREET
DUKE STREET
UNION YD
DERING ST
TENTERDEN STREET
HANOVER SQUARE
PRINCES ST
JERVIS CT
SEDLEY PLACE
WOODSTOCK STREET
BLENHEIM STREET
NEW BOND STREET
GLOBE YD
HAUNCH OF VENISON YD
SOUTH MOLTON STREET
SOUTH MOLTON LANE
NORTH ROW
NORTH AUDLEY ST
BALDERTON STREET
CLARENDON FLATS
BALDERTON FLATS
LUMLEY ST
BROWN HART GARDENS
BINNEY STREET
GILBERT STREET
WEIGHHOUSE ST
TA Ctr
ST ANSELM'S PLACE
DAVIES MEWS
DAVIES STREET
BROOK STREET
HORSE SHOE YARD
LANCASHIRE CT
Handel House Mus
MEXICO
ST GEORGE
POLLEN ST
MASON'S ARMS MEWS
MADDOX
AVERY ROW
Claridge's Hotel
ARGENTINE
BRAZIL
GREEN STREET
PROVIDENCE CT
GEORGE YD
248
28
29
1
2
3
4
5
6
81
82

A
B
C
D
232
249
240
29
30
6
5
4
3
2
1
Buses only
WILLIAM ROAD
PANGBOURNE
DRUMMOND ST
Westminster Kingsway Coll
Univ of Westminster
Euston Underpass
EUSTON TWR
REGENT'S PL
TRITON SQ
EUSTON ROAD A501
Euston Square
GOWER PLACE
GOWER STREET
STEPHENSON WAY
Govt Offices
Univ Coll Hosp
BEAUMONT PLACE
University College London
Petrie Mus of Egyptian Archaeology
Grant Mus of Zoology
Warren Street
GRAFTON WAY
A400
WARREN STREET
FITZROY SQ
St Luke's Hospl
CROATIA
MOZAMBIQUE
LIBERIA
Bell Language Sch
CLEVELAND STREET
CONWAY ST
MAPLE ST
FITZROY STREET
BT Tower
HOWLAND ST
TOTTENHAM COURT ROAD
Elizabeth Garrett Anderson Hospl
UNIVERSITY ST
CAPPER ST
HUNTLEY STREET
CHENIES MEWS
TORRINGTON PLACE
RIDGMOUNT GDNS
GOWER STREET
ENDSLEIGH GARDENS
TAVITON STREET
ENDSLEIGH ST
ENDSLEIGH PLACE
GORDON SQUARE
Gordon Square Gdn
Tavistock Square Gdn
TAVISTOCK SQUARE
UPPER WOBURN PLACE A4200
BEDFORD WAY
WOBURN SQUARE
TORRINGTON SQUARE
University of London
MALET PL
BYNG PL
Royal Academy of Dramatic Art
MALET STREET
Bloomsbury
Russell Sq Garden
RUSSELL SQ
WOBURN PL
CORAM ST
Govt Offices
HERBRAND STREET
KEPPEL ST
MONTAGUE PLACE
British Museum
GREAT RUSSELL ST
BLOOMSBURY STREET
BEDFORD SQUARE
BEDFORD AVENUE
Aga Khan Univ
STORE STREET
Cavendish Coll
RADA
ALFRED PLACE
CHENIES STREET
RIDGMOUNT ST
Goodge Street
GOODGE ST A5204
CHARLOTTE ST
WHITFIELD ST
University College London
Univ of Westminster
Blake Coll
All Souls Sch
OGLE STREET
FOLEY STREET
RIDING HOUSE STREET
HANSON STREET
GREAT TITCHFIELD ST
GOSFIELD ST
MORTIMER ST
NEW ACAD GALL
WINDMILL ST
PERCY STREET
RATHBONE ST
BAYLEY ST
MORWELL STREET
Time Out Magazine
ADELINE PL
Birkbeck Coll
Nickelodeon
RATHBONE PL
HANWAY ST
Tottenham Court Road
BARBADOS
ST GILES' CIRCUS
BAINBRIDGE ST
NEW OXFORD ST
A40
Centre Point
ST GILES HIGH ST
DENMARK ST
BUCKNALL
Law Ct
ST ANDREWS CHAMBERS
WELLS STREET
BERNERS ST
NEWMAN STREET
BERNERS MEWS
LITTLE PORTLAND ST
ELSALVADOR
TURKMENISTAN
MARYLEBONE PASSAGE
MARGARET STREET
EASTCASTLE STREET
MARKET PLACE
Magic Kiss FM
Plaza Sh Ctr
OXFORD STREET
OXFORD CIRCUS
Oxford Circus
Radcliffe Coll
RAMILLIES PLACE
The Callan Sch
HOLLEN ST
SOHO ST
SOHO SQUARE
Soho
SUTTON ROW
GREEK ST
CHARING CROSS ROAD
FLITCROFT ST
STACEY ST
NEW COMPTON ST
SHAFTESBURY AVE
CAMBRIDGE CIRCUS
SEVEN DIALS
MONMOUTH STREET B404
GREAT MARLBOROUGH STREET
London Coll of Beauty Therapy
POLAND STREET
NOEL ST
D'ARBLAY ST
BERWICK STREET
Berwick Street
WARDOUR STREET
CARLISLE ST
DEAN STREET
FRITH ST
Coll of Art & Design
OLD COMPTON STREET
ROMILLY STREET
MOOR ST
Carnaby Street
MARSHALL STREET
BROADWICK ST
KINGLY STREET
REGENT STREET A4201
ARGYLL ST
Westminster Coll
SHAFTESBURY AVENUE

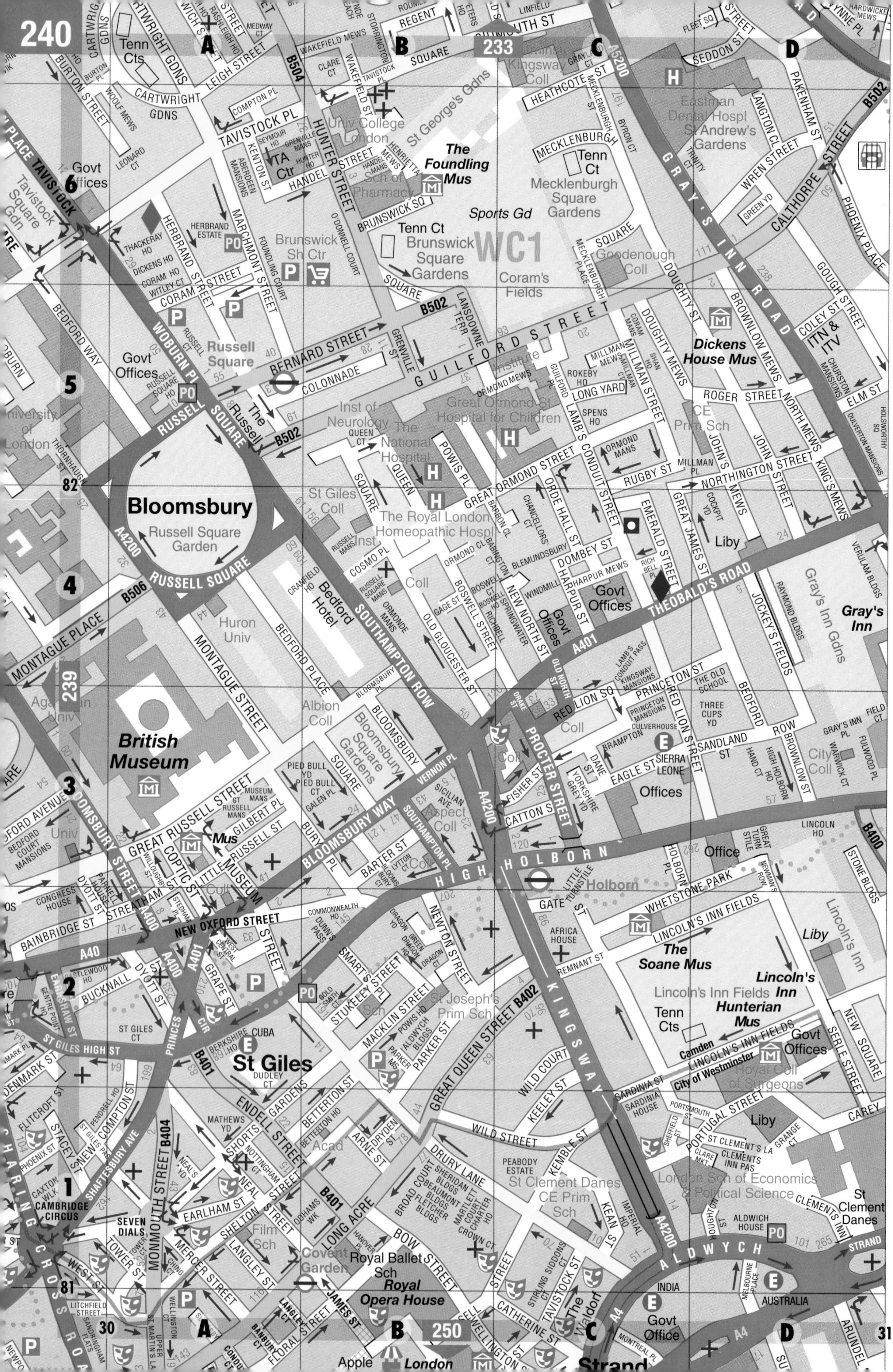

233
WC1
Bloomsbury
Russell Square Garden
British Museum
The Foundling Mus
Brunswick Square Gardens
Mecklenburgh Square Gardens
Coram's Fields
Sports Gd
Great Ormond St Hospital for Children
The National Hospital
The Royal London Homeopathic Hospl
Dickens House Mus
Gray's Inn
Gray's Inn Gdns
Lincoln's Inn
Lincoln's Inn Fields
The Soane Mus
Hunterian Mus
Royal Coll of Surgeons
London Sch of Economics & Political Science
St Clement Danes
St Giles
Seven Dials
Cambridge Circus
Covent Garden
Royal Ballet Sch
Royal Opera House
Holborn
Russell Square
High Holborn
New Oxford Street
Kingsway
Aldwych
Strand
Theobald's Road
Southampton Row
Gray's Inn Road
Guilford Street
Shaftesbury Ave
Charing Cross Road
Drury Lane
Long Acre
Great Queen Street
Bloomsbury Way
Tavistock Place
Woburn Pl
250
239

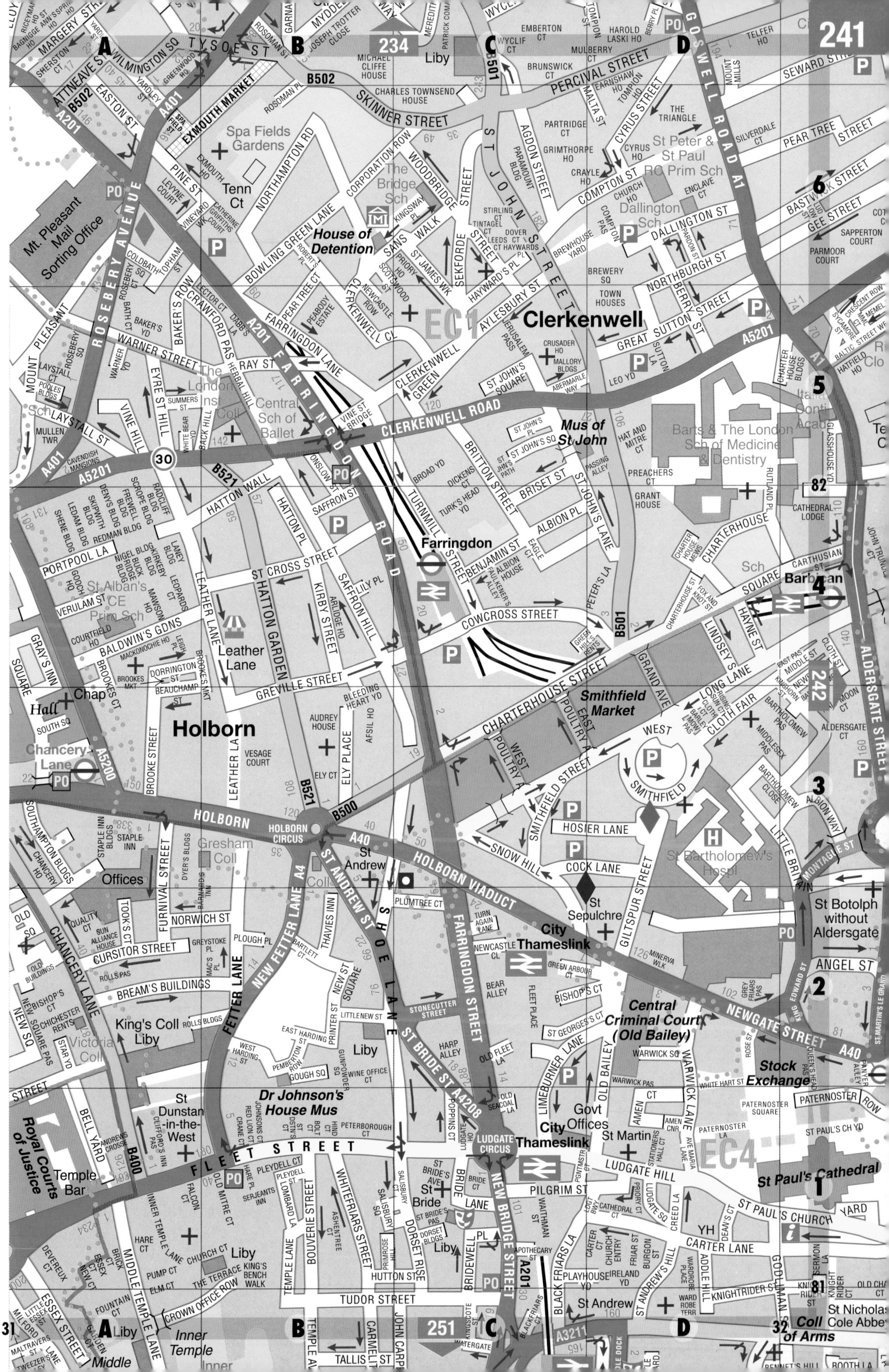

A
B
C
D
234
Liby
EMBERTON CT
HAROLD LASKI HO
TELFER HO
TYSOE ST
WILMINGTON SQ
MARGERY ST
ROSOMAN ST
JOSEPH TROTTER CLOSE
WYCLIF CT
MICHAEL CLIFFE HOUSE
B502
MULBERRY CT
BRUNSWICK CT
PERCIVAL STREET
GOSWELL ROAD A1
SEWARD STREET
ATTNEAVE ST
EASTON ST
A201
A401
EXMOUTH MARKET
CHARLES TOWNSEND HOUSE
SKINNER STREET
B501
MALTA ST
CYRUS STREET
THE TRIANGLE
Spa Fields Gardens
NORTHAMPTON RD
CORPORATION ROW
WOODBRIDGE STREET
ST JOHN STREET
AGDON STREET
PARTRIDGE CT
GRIMTHORPE HO
CYRUS HO
St Peter & St Paul RC Prim Sch
SILVERDALE CT
PEAR TREE STREET
PO
PINE ST
Tenn Ct
The Bridge Sch
COMPTON ST
CRAYLE HO
ENCLAVE CT
6
BASTWICK STREET
GEE STREET
Mt. Pleasant Mail Sorting Office
ROSEBERY AVENUE
P
BOWLING GREEN LANE
House of Detention
KINGSWAY PL
SANS WALK
SEKFORDE STREET
Dallington Sch
DALLINGTON ST
SAPPERTON COURT
PARMOOR COURT
COLDBATH SQ
TOPHAM ST
ST JAMES WK
BREWHOUSE YARD
NORTHBURGH ST
BERRY ST
BREWERY SQ
TOWN HOUSES
PEAR TREE CT
CLERKENWELL CL
EC1
Clerkenwell
AYLESBURY ST
JERUSALEM PASS
GREAT SUTTON ST
SUTTON LA
A5201
MOUNT PLEASANT
WARNER STREET
BAKER'S ROW
CRAWFORD PAS
FARRINGDON LANE
RAY ST
FARRINGDON ROAD
CLERKENWELL GREEN
ST JOHN'S SQUARE
CRUSADER HO
MALLORY BLDGS
ABERMARLE WAY
LEO YD
5
LAYSTALL ST
EYRE ST HILL
VINE HILL
The London Inst Coll
Central Sch of Ballet
VINE ST BRIDGE
CLERKENWELL ROAD
Mus of St John
HAT AND MITRE CT
Barts & The London Sch of Medicine & Dentistry
GLASSHOUSE YD
MULLEN TWR
CAVENDISH MANSIONS
A5201
30
B521
HATTON WALL
SAFFRON ST
TURNMILL STREET
BRITTON STREET
DICKENS CT
TURK'S HEAD YD
BRISET ST
ST JOHN'S LANE
PREACHERS CT
GRANT HOUSE
RUTLAND PL
82
CATHEDRAL LODGE
PORTPOOL LA
LEATHER LANE
HATTON PL
Farringdon
BENJAMIN ST
ALBION PL
CHARTERHOUSE
CARTHUSIAN STREET
JOHN TRUNDLE CT
ST CROSS STREET
HATTON GARDEN
KIRBY STREET
SAFFRON HILL
LILY PL
PETER'S LA
Sch
Barbican
4
St Alban's CE Prim Sch
VERULAM ST
GRAY'S INN SQUARE
BALDWIN'S GDNS
Leather Lane
COWCROSS STREET
B501
HAYNE ST
LINDSEY ST
BROOKES CT
DORRINGTON ST
GREVILLE STREET
BLEEDING HEART YD
CHARTERHOUSE STREET
Smithfield Market
GRAND AVE
LONG LANE
CLOTH FAIR
242
ALDERSGATE STREET
Hall
Chap
Holborn
AUDREY HOUSE
ELY PLACE
WEST POULTRY AVE
EAST POULTRY AVE
WEST
SOUTH SQ
VESAGE COURT
ELY CT
SMITHFIELD
BARTHOLOMEW CLOSE
ALDERSGATE CT
Chancery Lane
A5200
BROOKE STREET
B521
B500
SMITHFIELD STREET
3
ALBION WAY
HOLBORN
HOLBORN CIRCUS
A40
HOSIER LANE
H
STAPLE INN
Gresham Coll
St Andrew
HOLBORN VIADUCT
SNOW HILL
COCK LANE
St Bartholomew's Hospl
MONTAGUE ST
LITTLE BRITAIN
Offices
FURNIVAL STREET
NEW FETTER LANE
ST ANDREW ST
SHOE LANE
PLUMTREE CT
FARRINGDON STREET
St Sepulchre
GILTSPUR STREET
St Botolph without Aldersgate
NORWICH ST
CURSITOR STREET
PLOUGH PL
City Thameslink
MINERVA WLK
CHANCERY LANE
FETTER LANE
BREAM'S BUILDINGS
NEW ST SQUARE
BEAR ALLEY
FLEET PLACE
BISHOP'S CT
ANGEL ST
2
Central Criminal Court (Old Bailey)
NEWGATE STREET
King's Coll Liby
Victoria Coll
STONECUTTER STREET
ST BRIDE ST A4208
HARP ALLEY
ST GEORGE'S CT
LIMEBURNER LANE
OLD BAILEY
WARWICK SQ
WARWICK LANE
A40
Liby
GOUGH SQ
WINE OFFICE CT
Stock Exchange
PATERNOSTER ROW
PATERNOSTER SQUARE
Royal Courts of Justice
BELL YARD
St Dunstan -in-the- West
Dr Johnson's House Mus
PETERBOROUGH CT
Govt Offices
City Thameslink
St Martin
AMEN CT
ST PAUL'S CH YD
EC4
B400
FLEET STREET
LUDGATE CIRCUS
LUDGATE HILL
St Paul's Cathedral
1
Temple Bar
PO
St Bride
BRIDE LANE
NEW BRIDGE STREET
PILGRIM ST
CREED LA
ST PAUL'S CHURCH YARD
WHITEFRIARS STREET
BOUVERIE STREET
DORSET RISE
BRIDEWELL PL
CARTER LANE
INNER TEMPLE LANE
Liby
HUTTON ST
A201
BLACK FRIARS LA
PLAYHOUSE YD
ADDLE HILL
GODLIMAN ST
KNIGHTRIDER ST
81
MIDDLE TEMPLE LANE
CROWN OFFICE ROW
TEMPLE LANE
TUDOR STREET
JOHN CARPENTER ST
St Andrew
St Nicholas Cole Abbey
ESSEX STREET
Liby
Inner Temple
251
A3211
Coll of Arms
Middle
TALLIS ST

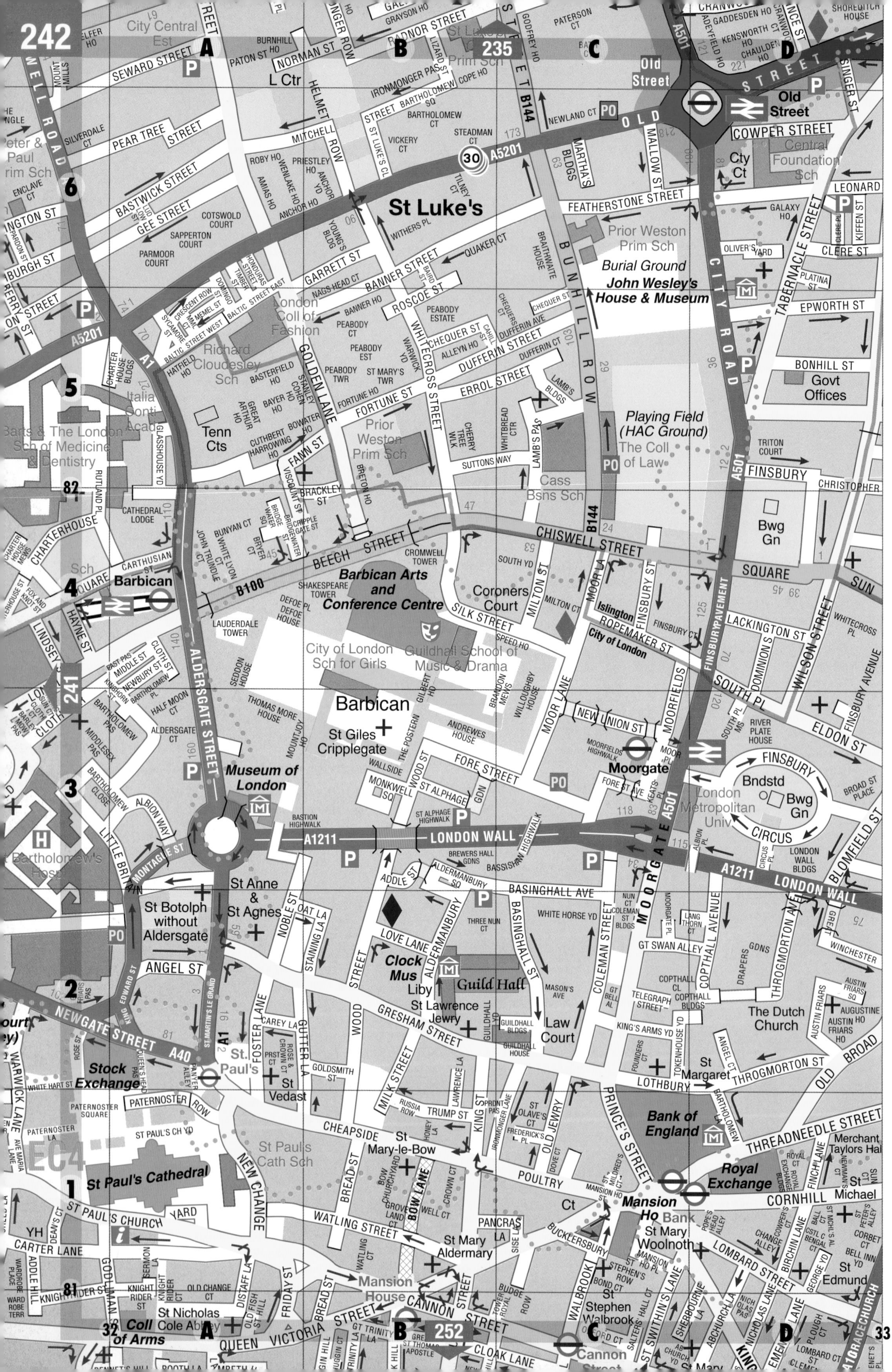

235
Old Street
St Luke's
Featherstone Street
Prior Weston Prim Sch
Burial Ground
John Wesley's House & Museum
Bunhill Row
City Road
Old Street
Central Foundation Sch
Cowper Street
Tabernacle Street
Epworth St
Bonhill St
Govt Offices
Playing Field (HAC Ground)
The Coll of Law
Cass Bsns Sch
Finsbury Square
Chiswell Street
Beech Street
Barbican Arts and Conference Centre
Barbican
Silk Street
Cromwell Tower
Shakespeare Tower
Lauderdale Tower
Guildhall School of Music & Drama
City of London Sch for Girls
Barbican
St Giles Cripplegate
Golden Lane
Whitecross Street
Goswell Road
Aldersgate Street
Charterhouse Square
Barts & The London Sch of Medicine & Dentistry
Richard Cloudesley Sch
London Coll of Fashion
Peabody Estate
Fortune St
Errol Street
Dufferin Street
Seward Street
Pear Tree Street
Bastwick Street
Gee Street
Banner Street
Roscoe St
Garrett St
Radnor Street
Mitchell Row
Museum of London
London Wall
A1211
Moorgate
Moor Lane
Moorfields
Fore Street
Wood St
Finsbury Circus
London Metropolitan Univ
Bndstd
Bwg Gn
South Pl
Eldon St
Wilson Street
Finsbury Avenue
Blomfield St
Throgmorton Ave
Old Broad St
Throgmorton St
Copthall Avenue
Coleman Street
Basinghall St
Basinghall Ave
Aldermanbury
Clock Mus
Guild Hall
Liby
St Lawrence Jewry
Law Court
Gresham Street
Lothbury
Bank of England
Threadneedle Street
Royal Exchange
Cornhill
Mansion Ho
Bank
St Mary Woolnoth
Lombard Street
Poultry
Cheapside
St Mary-le-Bow
Bow Lane
Bread St
Watling Street
St Mary Aldermary
Queen Victoria Street
Cannon Street
Mansion House
Walbrook
St Stephen Walbrook
St Swithin's Lane
Cannon
Gracechurch
King St
Milk Street
Old Jewry
Prince's Street
Ironmonger Lane
Stock Exchange
St Paul's
St Vedast
Newgate Street
A40
Angel St
St Botolph without Aldersgate
St Anne & St Agnes
St Martin's le Grand
Little Britain
Montague St
St Bartholomew's Hosp
St Paul's Cathedral
EC4
St Paul's Church Yard
St Pauls Cath Sch
New Change
Paternoster Row
Warwick Lane
Carter Lane
Godliman St
Knightrider St
St Nicholas Cole Abbey
Coll of Arms
Friday St
Distaff La
The Dutch Church
St Margaret
Austin Friars
St Edmund
St Michael
Merchant Taylors Hal
252
241
A
B
C
D
1
2
3
4
5
6
33

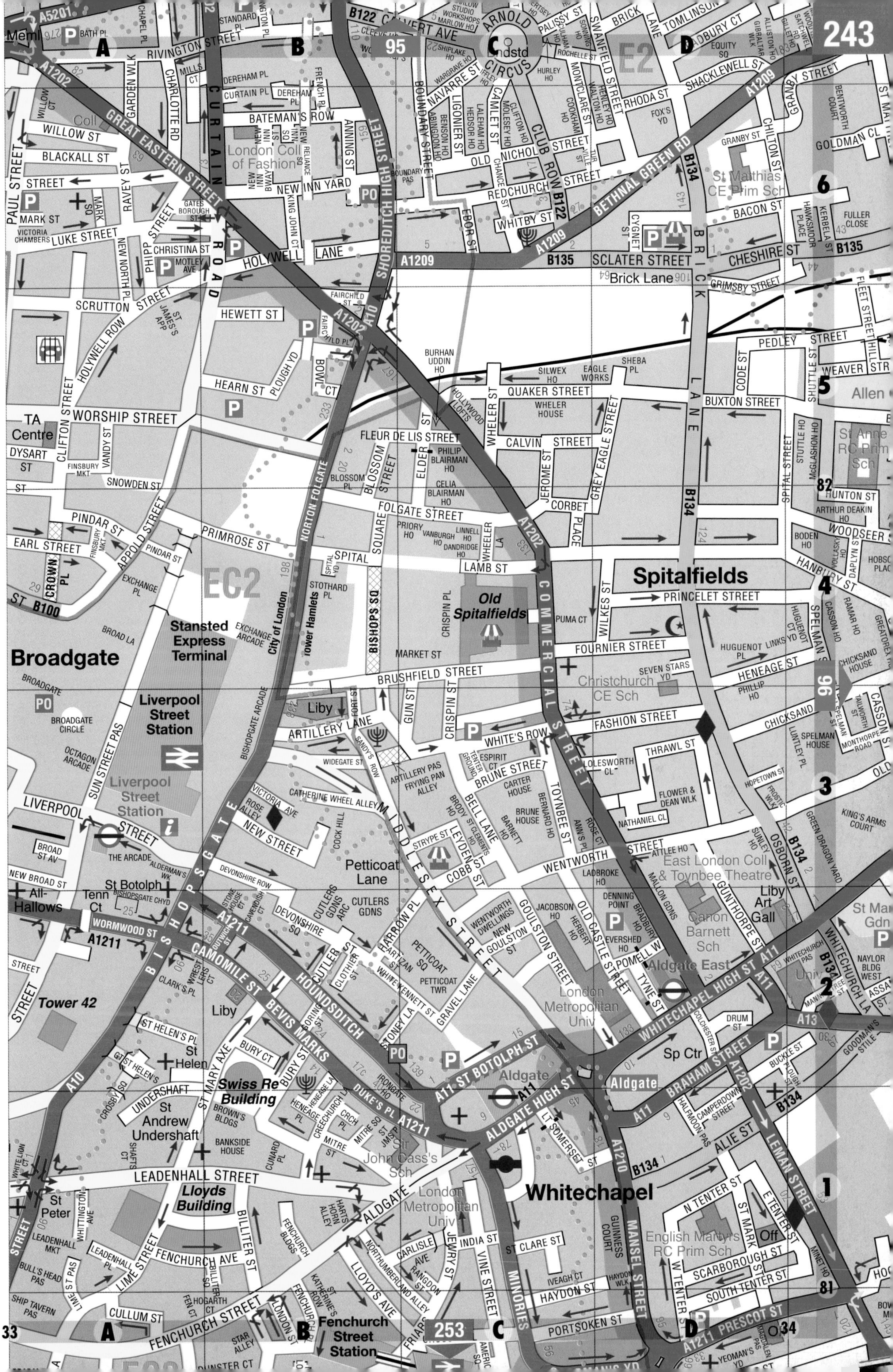

95
253
96
33
34
A
B
C
D
1
2
3
4
5
6
E2
EC2
Broadgate
Spitalfields
Whitechapel
Petticoat Lane
Old Spitalfields
Stansted Express Terminal
Liverpool Street Station
Liverpool Street Station
Fenchurch Street Station
Tower 42
Swiss Re Building
Lloyds Building
London Coll of Fashion
St Matthias CE Prim Sch
St Anne RC Prim Sch
Christchurch CE Sch
East London Coll & Toynbee Theatre
Canon Barnett Sch
London Metropolitan Univ
English Martyrs RC Prim Sch
Sir John Cass's Sch
Aldgate East
Aldgate
Shoreditch
Brick Lane
TA Centre
Liby
Sp Ctr
St Botolph
All-Hallows
St Helen
St Andrew Undershaft
St Peter
Allen
Arnold Circus
Bndstd
GREAT EASTERN STREET
CURTAIN ROAD
SHOREDITCH HIGH STREET
NORTON FOLGATE
BISHOPSGATE
COMMERCIAL STREET
BRICK LANE
BETHNAL GREEN RD
SCLATER STREET
CHESHIRE ST
HOLYWELL LANE
WORSHIP STREET
SCRUTTON STREET
HEWETT ST
HEARN ST
PRIMROSE ST
APPOLD STREET
EARL STREET
CROWN PL
LIVERPOOL STREET
WORMWOOD ST
CAMOMILE ST
HOUNDSDITCH
BEVIS MARKS
DUKE'S PL
ALDGATE HIGH ST
ST BOTOLPH ST
WHITECHAPEL HIGH ST
LEADENHALL STREET
FENCHURCH AVE
FENCHURCH STREET
LIME STREET
BILLITER ST
ST MARY AXE
MIDDLESEX STREET
GOULSTON STREET
WENTWORTH STREET
TOYNBEE ST
BRUSHFIELD STREET
FOURNIER STREET
PRINCELET STREET
FASHION STREET
FOLGATE STREET
QUAKER STREET
HANBURY ST
HERITAGE ST
MINORIES
MANSEL STREET
LEMAN STREET
PRESCOT ST
ALIE ST
BRAHAM STREET
PORTSOKEN ST
RIVINGTON STREET
CHARLOTTE RD
OLD NICHOL STREET
REDCHURCH STREET
CALVERT AVE
BOUNDARY STREET
CLUB ROW
CHILTON ST
GRANBY STREET
BUXTON STREET
PEDLEY STREET
WEAVER STR
WHEELER ST
CALVIN STREET
FLEUR DE LIS STREET
LAMB ST
ARTILLERY LANE
WHITE'S ROW
BRUNE STREET
BELL LANE
NEW STREET
DEVONSHIRE SQ
CUTLER ST
STONEY LA
GRAVEL LANE
JEWRY ST
VINE STREET
INDIA ST
ST CLARE ST
HAYDON ST
A1202
A10
A1209
A1211
A11
A13
A5201
B122
B134
B135
B100
A1210

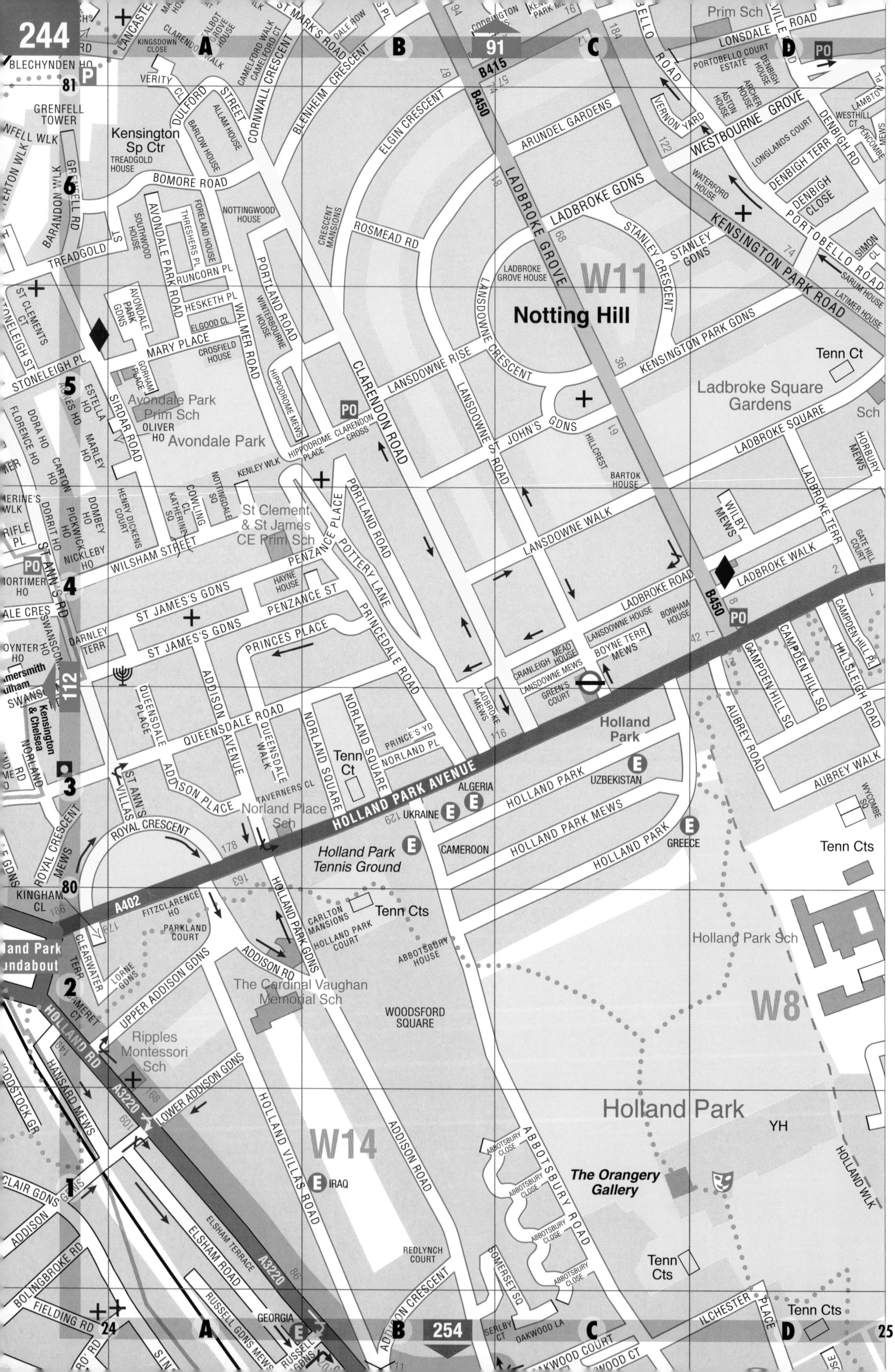
Notting Hill
W11
W14
W8
Holland Park
Kensington Sp Ctr
Ladbroke Square Gardens
Avondale Park
Avondale Park Prim Sch
St Clement & St James CE Prim Sch
Norland Place Sch
Holland Park Tennis Ground
The Cardinal Vaughan Memorial Sch
Ripples Montessori Sch
Holland Park Sch
The Orangery Gallery
Prim Sch
GRENFELL TOWER
HOLLAND PARK AVENUE
LADBROKE GROVE
CLARENDON ROAD
PORTLAND ROAD
WALMER ROAD
LANSDOWNE CRESCENT
LANSDOWNE ROAD
KENSINGTON PARK ROAD
KENSINGTON PARK GDNS
LADBROKE SQUARE
LADBROKE GDNS
LADBROKE ROAD
LADBROKE WALK
LADBROKE TERR
WESTBOURNE GROVE
PORTOBELLO ROAD
ELGIN CRESCENT
BLENHEIM CRESCENT
ARUNDEL GARDENS
ROSMEAD RD
STANLEY CRESCENT
STANLEY GDNS
ST JOHN'S GDNS
LANSDOWNE RISE
LANSDOWNE WALK
POTTERY LANE
PRINCEDALE ROAD
PENZANCE PLACE
PENZANCE ST
ST JAMES'S GDNS
QUEENSDALE ROAD
ADDISON AVENUE
NORLAND SQUARE
ROYAL CRESCENT
HOLLAND PARK
HOLLAND PARK MEWS
ADDISON ROAD
HOLLAND VILLAS ROAD
HOLLAND PARK GDNS
ABBOTSBURY ROAD
CAMPDEN HILL SQ
AUBREY ROAD
AUBREY WALK
HOLLAND WLK
UPPER ADDISON GDNS
LOWER ADDISON GDNS
HOLLAND RD
RUSSELL GDNS MEWS
ELSHAM ROAD
ILCHESTER PLACE
OAKWOOD COURT
ST ANN'S RD
BOMORE ROAD
TREADGOLD ST
WILSHAM STREET
MARY PLACE
Holland Park Roundabout
A402
A3220
B450
B415
UKRAINE
ALGERIA
UZBEKISTAN
CAMEROON
GREECE
IRAQ
GEORGIA
91
254
112
A B C D

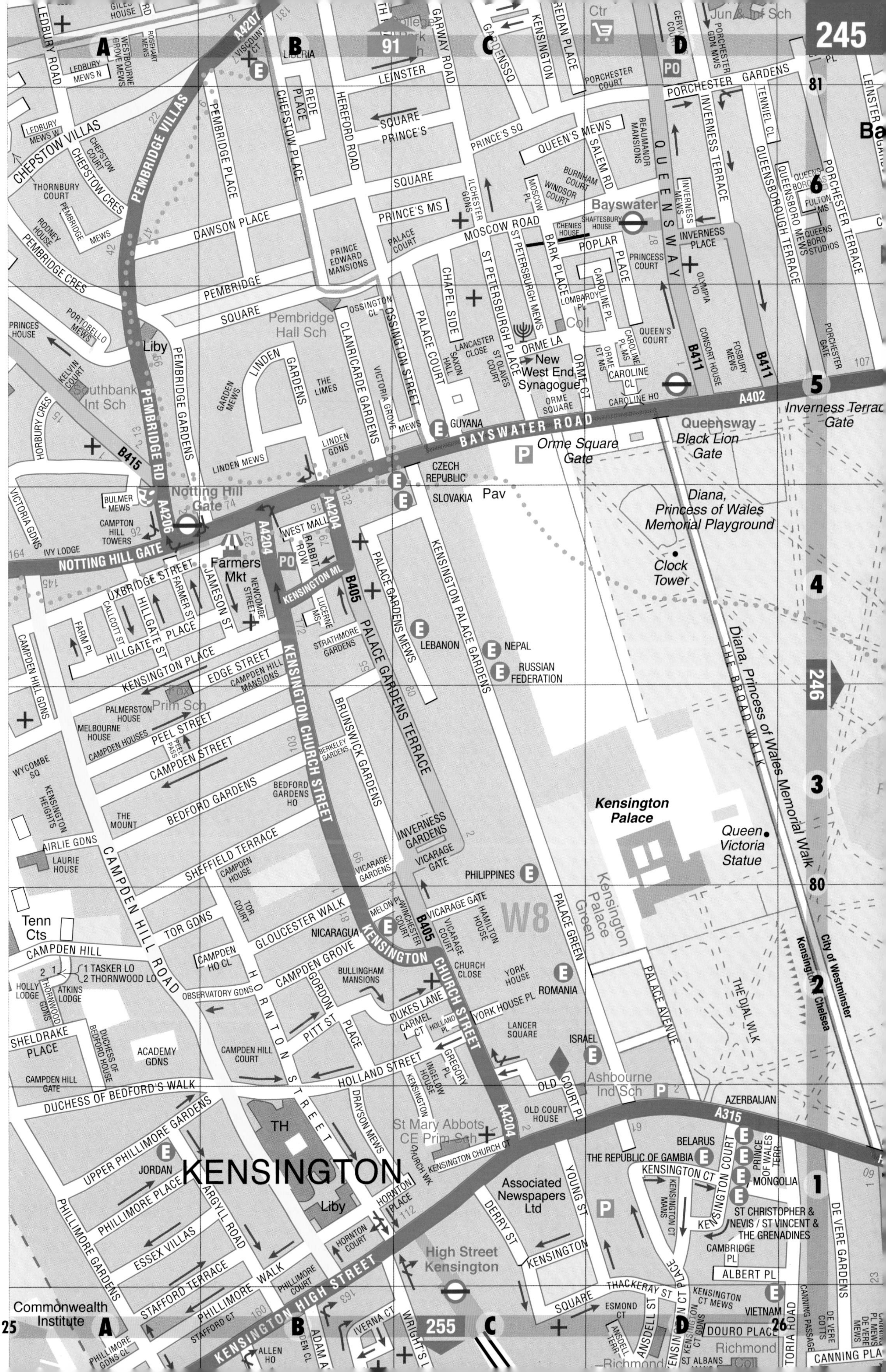
A
B
C
D
91
255
81
6
5
4
3
2
1
80
107
246
25
26
KENSINGTON
W8
Kensington Palace
Kensington Palace Green
Queen Victoria Statue
Diana, Princess of Wales Memorial Playground
Diana, Princess of Wales Memorial Walk
Clock Tower
Inverness Terrace Gate
Queensway Black Lion Gate
Orme Square Gate
Bayswater
Notting Hill Gate
High Street Kensington
City of Westminster
Kensington & Chelsea
THE BROAD WALK
THE DIAL WALK
BAYSWATER ROAD
A402
NOTTING HILL GATE
KENSINGTON HIGH STREET
A315
KENSINGTON CHURCH STREET
A4204
B405
PEMBRIDGE VILLAS
PEMBRIDGE RD
A4206
A4207
B415
B411
QUEENSWAY
LEDBURY ROAD
LEDBURY MEWS N
LEDBURY MEWS W
WESTBOURNE GROVE MEWS
ROSEHART MEWS
GILES HOUSE
VISCOUNT CT
LIBERIA
CHEPSTOW VILLAS
CHEPSTOW COURT
CHEPSTOW CRES
CHEPSTOW PLACE
THORNBURY COURT
RODNEY HOUSE
PEMBRIDGE MEWS
PEMBRIDGE CRES
PEMBRIDGE PLACE
PEMBRIDGE SQUARE
PEMBRIDGE GARDENS
DAWSON PLACE
REDE PLACE
HEREFORD ROAD
LEINSTER SQUARE
PRINCE'S SQUARE
PRINCE'S MS
PRINCE'S SQ
GARWAY ROAD
KENSINGTON GARDENS SQ
REDAN PLACE
PORCHESTER COURT
PORCHESTER GARDENS
PORCHESTER GDN MWS
PORCHESTER TERRACE
PORCHESTER GATE
CERVANTES COURT
INVERNESS TERRACE
INVERNESS MEWS
INVERNESS PLACE
TENNIEL CL
QUEENSBOROUGH TERRACE
QUEENSBORO MEWS
QUEENS BORO STUDIOS
FULTON MS
LEINSTER GARDENS
QUEEN'S MEWS
SALEM RD
BEAUMANOR MANSIONS
BURNHAM COURT
WINDSOR COURT
MOSCOW PL
MOSCOW ROAD
ILCHESTER GDNS
PALACE COURT
PRINCE EDWARD MANSIONS
CHENIES HOUSE
SHAFTESBURY HOUSE
POPLAR PLACE
PRINCESS COURT
OLYMPIA YD
ST PETERSBURGH PLACE
ST PETERSBURGH MEWS
BARK PLACE
LOMBARDY PL
CAROLINE PL
CAROLINE PL MS
CAROLINE CL
CAROLINE HO
QUEEN'S COURT
CONSORT HOUSE
FOSBURY MEWS
CHAPEL SIDE
LANCASTER CLOSE
SAXON HALL
ST OLAVES COURT
ORME LA
ORME CT
ORME CT MS
ORME SQUARE
New West End Synagogue
OSSINGTON CL
OSSINGTON STREET
CLANRICARDE GARDENS
VICTORIA GROVE MEWS
Pembridge Hall Sch
LINDEN GARDENS
LINDEN MEWS
LINDEN GDNS
GARDEN MEWS
THE LIMES
GUYANA
CZECH REPUBLIC
SLOVAKIA
Pav
PRINCES HOUSE
PORTOBELLO MEWS
KELVIN COURT
Southbank Int Sch
HORBURY CRES
Liby
Ctr
Jun & Inf Sch
College Park Sch
Col
PO
P
BULMER MEWS
CAMPTON HILL TOWERS
VICTORIA GDNS
IVY LODGE
Farmers Mkt
WEST MALL
RABBIT ROW
KENSINGTON ML
UXBRIDGE STREET
FARMER ST
HILLGATE ST
HILLGATE PLACE
JAMESON ST
NEWCOMBE STREET
CALLCOTT ST
FARM PL
CAMPDEN HILL GDNS
KENSINGTON PLACE
EDGE STREET
CAMPDEN HILL MANSIONS
LUCERNE MS
STRATHMORE GARDENS
PALACE GARDENS MEWS
PALACE GARDENS TERRACE
KENSINGTON PALACE GARDENS
LEBANON
NEPAL
RUSSIAN FEDERATION
Fox Prim Sch
PALMERSTON HOUSE
MELBOURNE HOUSE
CAMPDEN HOUSES
PEEL STREET
PEEL PASS
CAMPDEN STREET
WYCOMBE SQ
KENSINGTON HEIGHTS
BEDFORD GARDENS
BEDFORD GARDENS HO
BERKELEY GARDENS
BRUNSWICK GARDENS
THE MOUNT
AIRLIE GDNS
LAURIE HOUSE
SHEFFIELD TERRACE
CAMPDEN HOUSE
INVERNESS GARDENS
VICARAGE GATE
VICARAGE GARDENS
PHILIPPINES
Tenn Cts
TOR COURT
TOR GDNS
GLOUCESTER WALK
NICARAGUA
MELON PL
WINCHESTER COURT
VICARAGE COURT
HAMILTON HOUSE
CAMPDEN HILL
CAMPDEN HILL ROAD
1 TASKER LO
2 THORNWOOD LO
HOLLY LODGE
THORNWOOD GDNS
ATKINS LODGE
CAMPDEN HO CL
CAMPDEN GROVE
OBSERVATORY GDNS
BULLINGHAM MANSIONS
CHURCH CLOSE
YORK HOUSE
ROMANIA
PALACE GREEN
PALACE AVENUE
HORNTON STREET
GORDON PLACE
PITT ST
DUKES LANE
CARMEL CT
HOLLAND PL
YORK HOUSE PL
LANCER SQUARE
ISRAEL
SHELDRAKE PLACE
DUCHESS OF BEDFORD HOUSE
ACADEMY GDNS
CAMPDEN HILL COURT
HOLLAND STREET
INGELOW HOUSE
GREGORY PL
KENSINGTON CHURCH WK
OLD COURT PL
OLD COURT HOUSE
Ashbourne Ind Sch
AZERBAIJAN
CAMPDEN HILL GATE
DUCHESS OF BEDFORD'S WALK
UPPER PHILLIMORE GARDENS
JORDAN
TH
DRAYSON MEWS
St Mary Abbots CE Prim Sch
KENSINGTON CHURCH CT
BELARUS
THE REPUBLIC OF GAMBIA
KENSINGTON COURT
KENSINGTON CT
KENSINGTON CT MANS
PRINCE OF WALES TERR
MONGOLIA
ST CHRISTOPHER & NEVIS / ST VINCENT & THE GRENADINES
CAMBRIDGE PL
ALBERT PL
Associated Newspapers Ltd
PHILLIMORE PLACE
PHILLIMORE GARDENS
ARGYLL ROAD
ESSEX VILLAS
HORNTON PLACE
HORNTON COURT
DERRY ST
YOUNG ST
KENSINGTON SQUARE
THACKERAY ST
KENSINGTON CT PLACE
KENSINGTON CT MEWS
VIETNAM
DE VERE GARDENS
DE VERE COTTS
DE VERE MEWS
CANNING PLACE
CANNING PASSAGE
VICTORIA ROAD
DOURO PLACE
Richmond Col
ST ALBANS
ESMOND CT
ANSDELL ST
ANSDELL TERR
STAFFORD TERRACE
STAFFORD CT
PHILLIMORE WALK
PHILLIMORE COURT
PHILLIMORE GDNS CL
Commonwealth Institute
IVERNA CT
ALLEN HO
WRIGHT'S L
ADAM & EVE

A
B
C
D
236
Bayswater
St James's & St Michael's CE Prim Sch
CLEVELAND SQUARE
LEINSTER PL
TAUNTON HOUSE
PORCHESTER GARDENS
INVERNESS TERRACE
QUEENSBOROUGH TERRACE
TENNIEL CL
LEINSTER GARDENS
QUEEN'S GARDENS
DEVONSHIRE TERR
UPBROOK MEWS
CRAVEN ROAD
CRAVEN HILL MS
CRAVEN HILL GDNS
CRAVEN HILL
CRAVEN LODGE
BROOK MEWS NTH
CRAVEN TERRACE
LANCASTER MEWS
SMALLBROOK MEWS
WESTBOURNE CRES
WESTBOURNE CRESCENT MEWS
SUSSEX GDNS
A4209
CERNEY MEWS
MAITLAND COURT
GARSON HO
GILRAY HO
CARROLL HOUSE
ELMS MEWS
LANCASTER TERR
WESTBOURNE STREET
Royal Lancaster Hotel
BATHURST MEWS
BATHURST ST
SUSSEX SQUARE
SUSSEX MEWS W
SUSSEX PLACE
CLIFTON PL
SUSSEX LODGE
STANHOPE TERRACE
HYDE PARK GDNS
BROOK ST
HYDE PARK
GLOUCESTER
RADNOR LODGE
INVERNESS MEWS
INVERNESS PLACE
QUEENS BORO PAS
QUEENSBORO MEWS
FULTON MS
QUEENS BORO STUDIOS
PORCHESTER TERRACE
LEINSTER TERR
B410
LEINSTER MEWS
PO
SPIRE HOUSE
LANCASTER GATE
COSTA RICA
LANCASTER COURT
BARRIE HOUSE
OLYMPIA YD
CONSORT HOUSE
FOSBURY MEWS
B411
HYDE PARK TOWERS
PORCHESTER GATE
BAYSWATER ROAD
A402
Victoria Gate
Westbourne Gate
Lancaster Gate
Marlborough Gate
NORTH FLOWER WALK
St Agnes' Well
The Fountains
Lancaster Gate
Bayswater Road Mkt
Bayard's Watering Place (site of)
W2
Inverness Terrace Gate
NORTH WALK
Queensway
Black Lion Gate
Diana, Princess of Wales Memorial Playground
BUCK HILL WALK
Speke's Monument
Peter Pan Statue
BUDGE'S WALK
LANCASTER WALK
The Long Water
Diana, Princess of Wales Memorial Walk
245
Physical Engery Statue
Temple Lodge
Serpentine Bridge
Round Pond
Kensington Gardens
Queen Victoria Statue
P
Diana, Princess of Wales Memorial Fountain
Serpentine Gallery
Bandstand
Kensington & Chelsea
City of Westminster
DIAL WLK
Tenn Cts
Bwg Gn
Pav
THE FLOWER WALK
Albert Memorial
Coalbrookdale Gate
AZERBAIJAN
A315
Palace Gate
Queen's Gate
Alexandra Gate
BELARUS
KENSINGTON COURT
PRINCE OF WALES TERR
HYDE PARK GATE
KENSINGTON ROAD
KENSINGTON GORE
TUNISIA
PRINCES GATE
IRAN
AFGHANISTAN
ETHIOPIA
UNITED ARAB EMIRATES
MONGOLIA
FIJI
B325
THORNEY COURT
BROADWALK HOUSE
NETHERLANDS
Royal Coll of Art
Royal Albert Hall
ALBERT HALL MANSIONS
Royal Geographical Society
Polish Inst & Sikorski Museum
ST CHRISTOPHER & NEVIS / ST VINCENT & THE GRENADINES
ZAMBIA
DE VERE GARDENS
JAY MEWS
PRINCES GATE COURT
MONTROSE CT
CAMBRIDGE PL
RESTON PLACE
Royal Coll of Organists
ALBERT PL
ESTONIA
HYDE PARK GATE
HYDE PARK GATE MEWS
CHANCELLOR HOUSE
QUEEN'S GATE MEWS
ALBERT COURT
JAMAICA
KENSINGTON CT MEWS
VIETNAM
CANNING PASSAGE
DE VERE COTTS
PALACE GATE
BREMNER RD
Royal College of Science
PRINCE CONSORT ROAD
PRINCES GARDENS
DOURO PLACE
Richmond
ST ALBANS
CANNING PLACE
KENSINGTON GATE
256
Royal College of Music
Tenn Cts
SW7
26
27

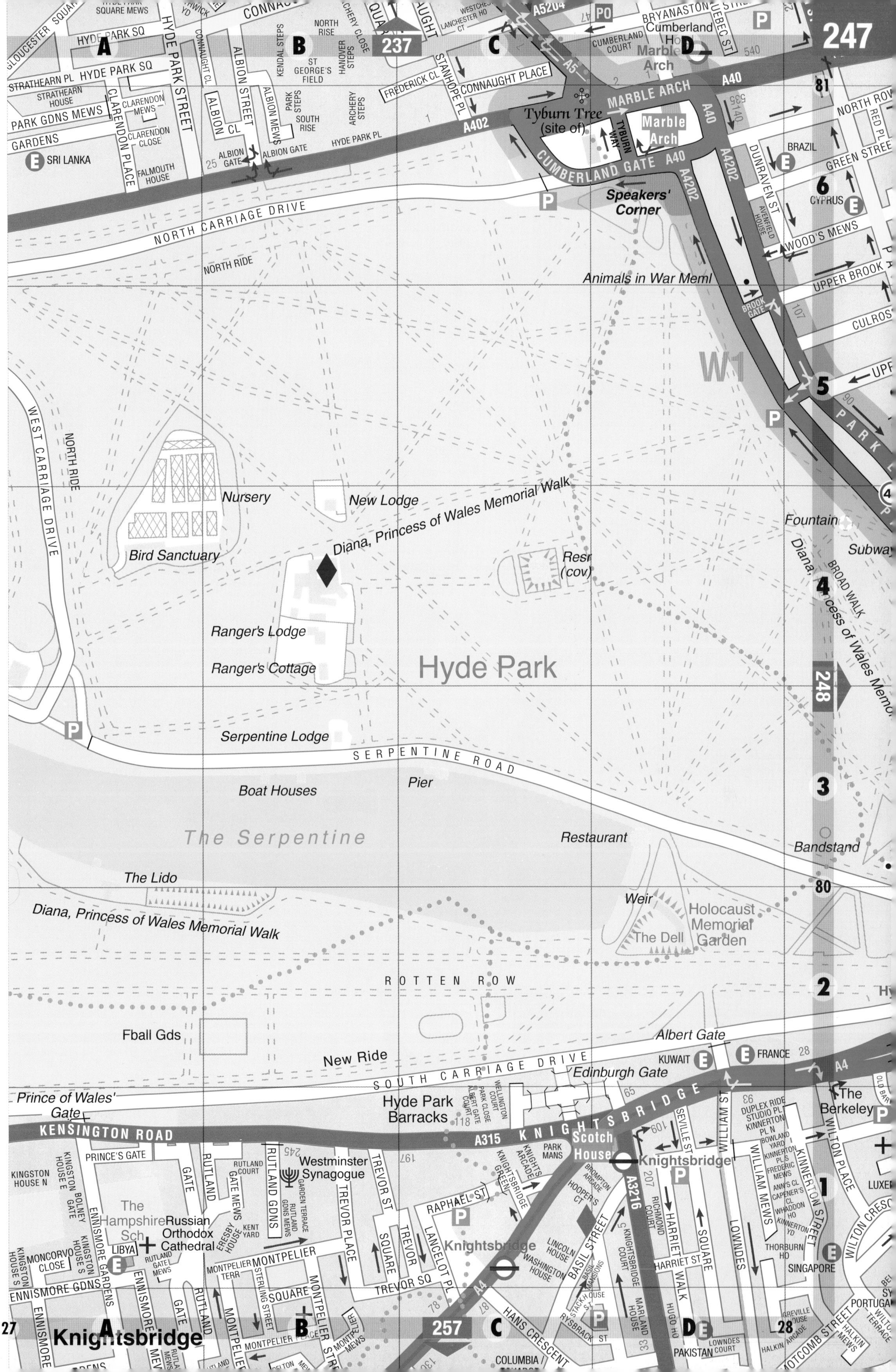
Hyde Park
The Serpentine
W1
North Carriage Drive
North Ride
West Carriage Drive
Nursery
Bird Sanctuary
New Lodge
Diana, Princess of Wales Memorial Walk
Ranger's Lodge
Ranger's Cottage
Resr (cov)
Serpentine Lodge
Serpentine Road
Boat Houses
Pier
Restaurant
The Lido
Weir
Holocaust Memorial Garden
The Dell
Rotten Row
Fball Gds
New Ride
South Carriage Drive
Albert Gate
Edinburgh Gate
Prince of Wales' Gate
Hyde Park Barracks
Kensington Road
Knightsbridge
Animals in War Meml
Speakers' Corner
Marble Arch
Tyburn Tree (site of)
Cumberland Gate
Park Lane
Fountain
Subway
Broad Walk
Bandstand
Hyde Park Sq
Hyde Park Street
Connaught Place
Albion Street
Albion Gate
Hyde Park Pl
Stanhope Pl
Frederick Cl
Bryanston St
Cumberland Ho
Great Cumberland Pl
North Row
Green Street
Upper Brook St
Wood's Mews
Dunraven St
Sri Lanka
Brazil
Cyprus
Kuwait
France
Libya
Singapore
Westminster Synagogue
Russian Orthodox Cathedral
The Hampshire Sch
Scotch House
Knightsbridge Green
Brompton Arcade
Basil Street
Hans Crescent
Sloane Street
Trevor Place
Trevor Square
Montpelier Square
Rutland Gate
Ennismore Gardens
Raphael St
Lancelot Pl
William St
Lowndes Square
Kinnerton Street
Wilton Place
The Berkeley
Knightsbridge
237
248
257
27
28
A
B
C
D
1
2
3
4
5
6

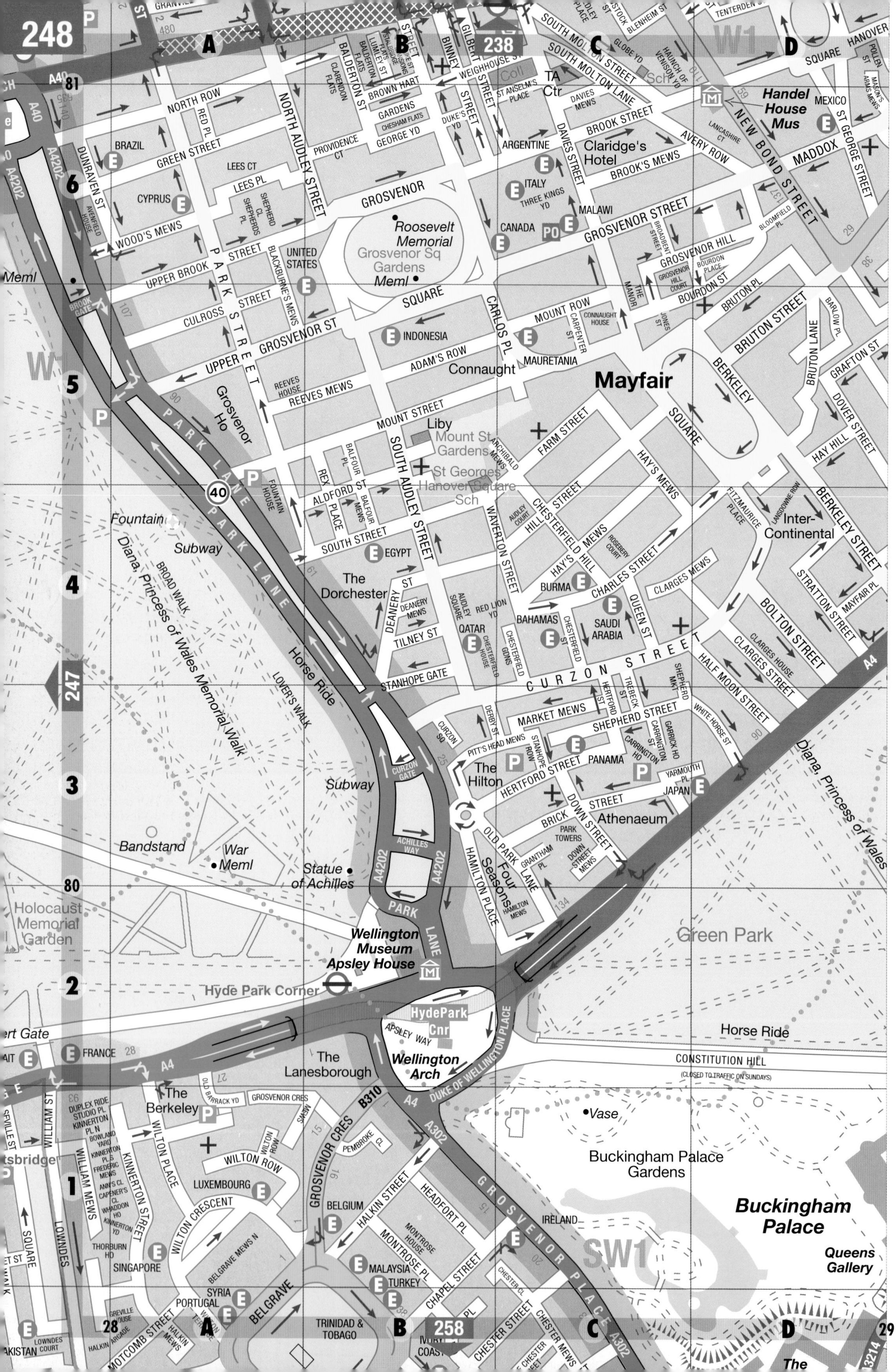
A
B
C
D
238
W1
Mayfair
Grosvenor Square
Roosevelt Memorial
Grosvenor Sq Gardens Meml
North Audley Street
South Audley Street
North Row
Green Street
Lees Pl
Wood's Mews
Upper Brook Street
Culross Street
Upper Grosvenor St
Park Street
Reeves Mews
Mount Street
Adam's Row
Connaught
Liby
Mount St Gardens
St Georges Hanover Square Sch
Brook Street
Claridge's Hotel
Brook's Mews
Avery Row
New Bond Street
Handel House Mus
Maddox
St George Street
Grosvenor Street
Grosvenor Hill
Bourdon St
Bruton Pl
Bruton Street
Bruton Lane
Berkeley Square
Grafton St
Dover Street
Hay Hill
Farm Street
Hill Street
Hay's Mews
Chesterfield Hill
Charles Street
Queen St
Curzon Street
Bolton Street
Clarges Street
Half Moon Street
Berkeley Street
Stratton Street
Inter-Continental
Waverton Street
Carlos Pl
Davies Street
South Molton Street
South Molton Lane
Binney Street
Gilbert Street
Weighhouse St
Balderton St
Brown Hart Gardens
Duke's Yd
Argentine
Italy
Canada
Malawi
Indonesia
Mauretania
United States
Brazil
Cyprus
Egypt
Burma
Bahamas
Saudi Arabia
Qatar
Panama
Japan
The Dorchester
Deanery St
Tilney St
Stanhope Gate
Aldford St
South Street
Rex Place
Balfour Pl
Market Mews
Shepherd Street
Hertford Street
Brick Street
Down Street
Old Park Lane
Hamilton Place
Four Seasons
The Hilton
Athenaeum
Park Lane
Grosvenor Ho
Fountain
Subway
Diana, Princess of Wales Memorial Walk
Broad Walk
Lover's Walk
Horse Ride
Bandstand
War Meml
Statue of Achilles
Holocaust Memorial Garden
Curzon Gate
Achilles Way
A4202
A4
A40
Wellington Museum Apsley House
Hyde Park Corner
HydePark Cnr
Apsley Way
Wellington Arch
Duke of Wellington Place
Green Park
Horse Ride
Constitution Hill
(CLOSED TO TRAFFIC ON SUNDAYS)
Diana, Princess of Wales
Vase
Buckingham Palace Gardens
Buckingham Palace
Queens Gallery
SW1
The Lanesborough
The Berkeley
Wilton Place
Wilton Row
Wilton Crescent
Luxembourg
Singapore
Grosvenor Cres
Halkin Street
Headfort Pl
Belgium
Montrose Pl
Malaysia
Turkey
Chapel Street
Chester Street
Chester Mews
Grosvenor Place
A302
B310
Ireland
Belgrave
Syria
Portugal
Kinnerton Street
William Mews
William St
Lowndes
France
Motcomb Street
Trinidad & Tobago
247
258
28
29
80
81
1
2
3
4
5
6

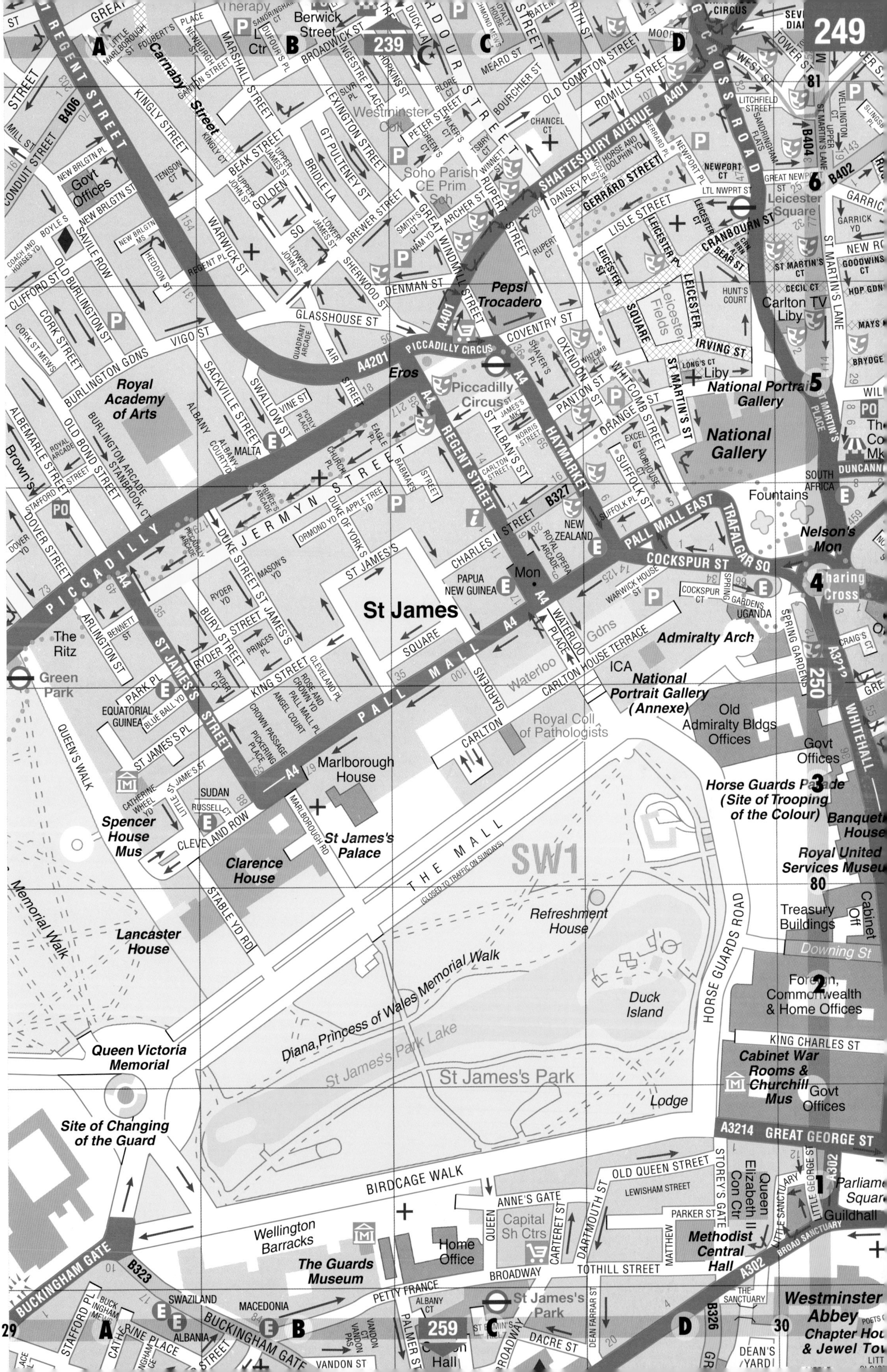
239
A
B
C
D
Berwick Street
Carnaby Street
REGENT STREET
BROADWICK ST
MARSHALL STREET
WARDOUR STREET
OLD COMPTON STREET
SHAFTESBURY AVENUE
CHARING CROSS ROAD
Westminster Coll
Soho Parish CE Prim Sch
Govt Offices
SAVILE ROW
GOLDEN SQ
BREWER STREET
GREAT WINDMILL STREET
GERRARD STREET
LISLE STREET
Leicester Square
LEICESTER SQUARE
Leicester Fields
CRANBOURN ST
ST MARTIN'S LANE
Carlton TV
Liby
Pepsi Trocadero
COVENTRY ST
DENMAN ST
GLASSHOUSE ST
VIGO ST
BURLINGTON GDNS
PICCADILLY CIRCUS
Piccadilly Circus
Eros
A4201
A401
Royal Academy of Arts
SACKVILLE STREET
ALBANY
OLD BOND STREET
ALBEMARLE STREET
DOVER STREET
PICCADILLY
JERMYN STREET
DUKE STREET ST JAMES'S
HAYMARKET
OXENDON ST
WHITCOMB STREET
ORANGE ST
IRVING ST
National Portrait Gallery
National Gallery
SOUTH AFRICA
Fountains
Nelson's Mon
TRAFALGAR SQ
COCKSPUR ST
PALL MALL EAST
Charing Cross
NEW ZEALAND
PAPUA NEW GUINEA
UGANDA
Mon
St James
ST JAMES'S SQUARE
PALL MALL
A4
B327
The Ritz
Green Park
ST JAMES'S STREET
KING STREET
ARLINGTON ST
EQUATORIAL GUINEA
ST JAMES'S PL
Admiralty Arch
ICA
National Portrait Gallery (Annexe)
Old Admiralty Bldgs Offices
CARLTON HOUSE TERRACE
WATERLOO PLACE
Waterloo Gdns
Royal Coll of Pathologists
CARLTON GARDENS
Marlborough House
MARLBOROUGH RD
St James's Palace
Clarence House
SUDAN
Spencer House Mus
CLEVELAND ROW
QUEEN'S WALK
Lancaster House
STABLE YD RD
THE MALL
(CLOSED TO TRAFFIC ON SUNDAYS)
SW1
Memorial Walk
250
WHITEHALL
A3212
Govt Offices
Horse Guards Parade (Site of Trooping of the Colour)
Banqueting House
Royal United Services Museum
Treasury Buildings
Cabinet Off
Downing St
HORSE GUARDS ROAD
Refreshment House
Duck Island
Diana, Princess of Wales Memorial Walk
Foreign, Commonwealth & Home Offices
KING CHARLES ST
Cabinet War Rooms & Churchill Mus
St James's Park Lake
St James's Park
Lodge
Queen Victoria Memorial
Site of Changing of the Guard
A3214
GREAT GEORGE ST
BIRDCAGE WALK
OLD QUEEN STREET
LEWISHAM STREET
QUEEN ANNE'S GATE
Capital Sh Ctrs
DARTMOUTH ST
STOREY'S GATE
Queen Elizabeth II Con Ctr
Parliament Square
Guildhall
Wellington Barracks
The Guards Museum
Home Office
BROADWAY
TOTHILL STREET
Methodist Central Hall
A302
BROAD SANCTUARY
THE SANCTUARY
Westminster Abbey
Chapter House & Jewel Tower
BUCKINGHAM GATE
B323
SWAZILAND
MACEDONIA
PETTY FRANCE
St James's Park
ALBANIA
CATHERINE PLACE
STAFFORD PL
VANDON ST
PALMER ST
DACRE ST
DEAN FARRAR ST
DEAN'S YARD
259
29
30

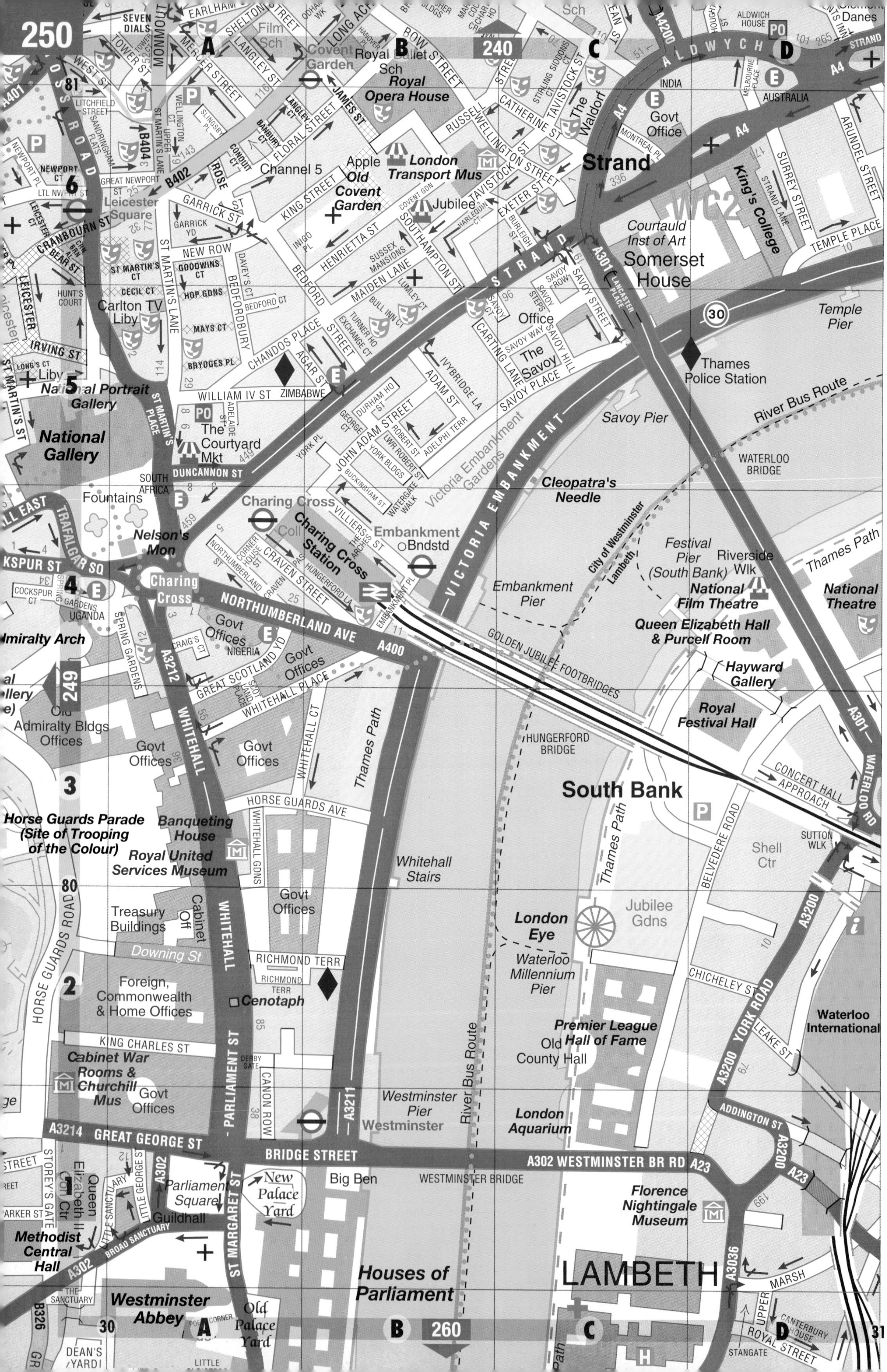

SEVEN DIALS
EARLHAM ST
SHELTON STREET
LONG ACRE
BOW STREET
240
ALDWICH HOUSE
PO
ALDWYCH
STRAND
MONMOUTH ST
MERCER STREET
LANGLEY ST
Film Sch
Covent Garden
Royal Ballet Sch
Royal Opera House
JAMES ST
FLORAL STREET
RUSSELL ST
CATHERINE ST
WELLINGTON STREET
TAVISTOCK ST
The Waldorf
INDIA
Govt Office
AUSTRALIA
MONTREAL PL
ARUNDEL STREET
SURREY STREET
STRAND LANE
A4
TOWER ST
WEST ST
81
LITCHFIELD STREET
CHARING CROSS ROAD
NEWPORT PL
NEWPORT CT
GREAT NEWPORT ST
LTL NWPRT ST
CRANBOURN ST
Leicester Square
SLINGSBY PL
UPPER ST MARTIN'S LN
B404
B402
ROSE ST
CONDUIT CT
BANBURY CT
LANGLEY CT
Channel 5
Apple
Old Covent Garden
London Transport Mus
Strand
King's College
WC2
GARRICK ST
GARRICK YD
KING STREET
INIGO PL
HENRIETTA ST
SOUTHAMPTON ST
Jubilee
TAVISTOCK ST
EXETER ST
BURLEIGH ST
Courtauld Inst of Art
Somerset House
TEMPLE PLACE
NEW ROW
ST MARTIN'S CT
GOODWINS CT
DAVEY'S CT
BEDFORD ST
SUSSEX MANSIONS
MAIDEN LANE
LUMLEY CT
BULL INN CT
STRAND
SAVOY ROW
SAVOY STEPS
SAVOY STREET
A301
LANCASTER PLACE
30
Temple Pier
LEICESTER ST
BEAR ST
HUNT'S COURT
CECIL CT
HOP GDNS
BEDFORD CT
Carlton TV Liby
MAYS CT
BEDFORDBURY
CHANDOS PLACE
TURNER HO
EXCHANGE CT
SAVOY CT
CARTING LANE
SAVOY WAY
Office
The Savoy
SAVOY HILL
SAVOY PLACE
IRVING ST
LONG'S CT
Liby
BRYDGES PL
AGAR ST
IVYBRIDGE LA
ADAM ST
Thames Police Station
National Portrait Gallery
ST MARTIN'S PLACE
WILLIAM IV ST
ZIMBABWE
DURHAM HO ST
ADELPHI TERR
Savoy Pier
River Bus Route
ST MARTIN'S ST
National Gallery
ADELAIDE ST
PO
The Courtyard Mkt
GEORGE CT
JOHN ADAM STREET
ROBERT ST
LWR ROBERT ST
YORK BLDGS
YORK PL
Victoria Embankment Gardens
VICTORIA EMBANKMENT
WATERLOO BRIDGE
SOUTH AFRICA
DUNCANNON ST
BUCKINGHAM ST
WATERGATE WALK
Cleopatra's Needle
Fountains
MALL EAST
TRAFALGAR SQ
Charing Cross
VILLIERS ST
Embankment
Bndstd
City of Westminster
Lambeth
Festival Pier (South Bank)
Riverside Wlk
Thames Path
Nelson's Mon
Coll
Charing Cross Station
THE ARCHES
COCKSPUR ST
COCKSPUR CT
SPRING GARDENS
UGANDA
NORTHUMBERLAND ST
CORNER HOUSE ST
CRAVEN PAS
CRAVEN STREET
HUNGERFORD LA
EMBANKMENT PL
Embankment Pier
National Film Theatre
National Theatre
Queen Elizabeth Hall & Purcell Room
NORTHUMBERLAND AVE
A400
GOLDEN JUBILEE FOOTBRIDGES
Admiralty Arch
Govt Offices
NIGERIA
CRAIG'S CT
GREAT SCOTLAND YD
SCOTLAND PLACE
WHITEHALL PLACE
Hayward Gallery
Royal Festival Hall
249
A3212
WHITEHALL
Old Admiralty Bldgs Offices
WHITEHALL CT
Thames Path
HUNGERFORD BRIDGE
CONCERT HALL APPROACH
WATERLOO RD
South Bank
3
HORSE GUARDS AVE
Horse Guards Parade (Site of Trooping of the Colour)
Banqueting House
Royal United Services Museum
WHITEHALL GDNS
Whitehall Stairs
BELVEDERE ROAD
Shell Ctr
SUTTON WLK
80
HORSE GUARDS ROAD
Treasury Buildings
Cabinet Off
London Eye
Jubilee Gdns
A3200
Downing St
RICHMOND TERR
Waterloo Millennium Pier
CHICHELEY ST
YORK ROAD
2
Foreign, Commonwealth & Home Offices
Cenotaph
Premier League Hall of Fame
Old County Hall
LEAKE ST
Waterloo International
KING CHARLES ST
PARLIAMENT ST
DERBY GATE
CANON ROW
Cabinet War Rooms & Churchill Mus
Westminster Pier
Westminster
A3211
River Bus Route
London Aquarium
ADDINGTON ST
A3214
GREAT GEORGE ST
BRIDGE STREET
A302 WESTMINSTER BR RD
A23
STOREY'S GATE
Queen Elizabeth II Con Ctr
LITTLE GEORGE ST
A302
Parliament Square
Guildhall
New Palace Yard
Big Ben
WESTMINSTER BRIDGE
Florence Nightingale Museum
PARKER ST
Methodist Central Hall
BROAD SANCTUARY
LITTLE SANCTUARY
ST MARGARET ST
Houses of Parliament
LAMBETH
A3036
MARSH
UPPER MARSH
THE SANCTUARY
Westminster Abbey
POETS' CORNER
Old Palace Yard
260
CANTERBURY HOUSE
ROYAL STREET
STANGATE
B326
30
DEAN'S YARD

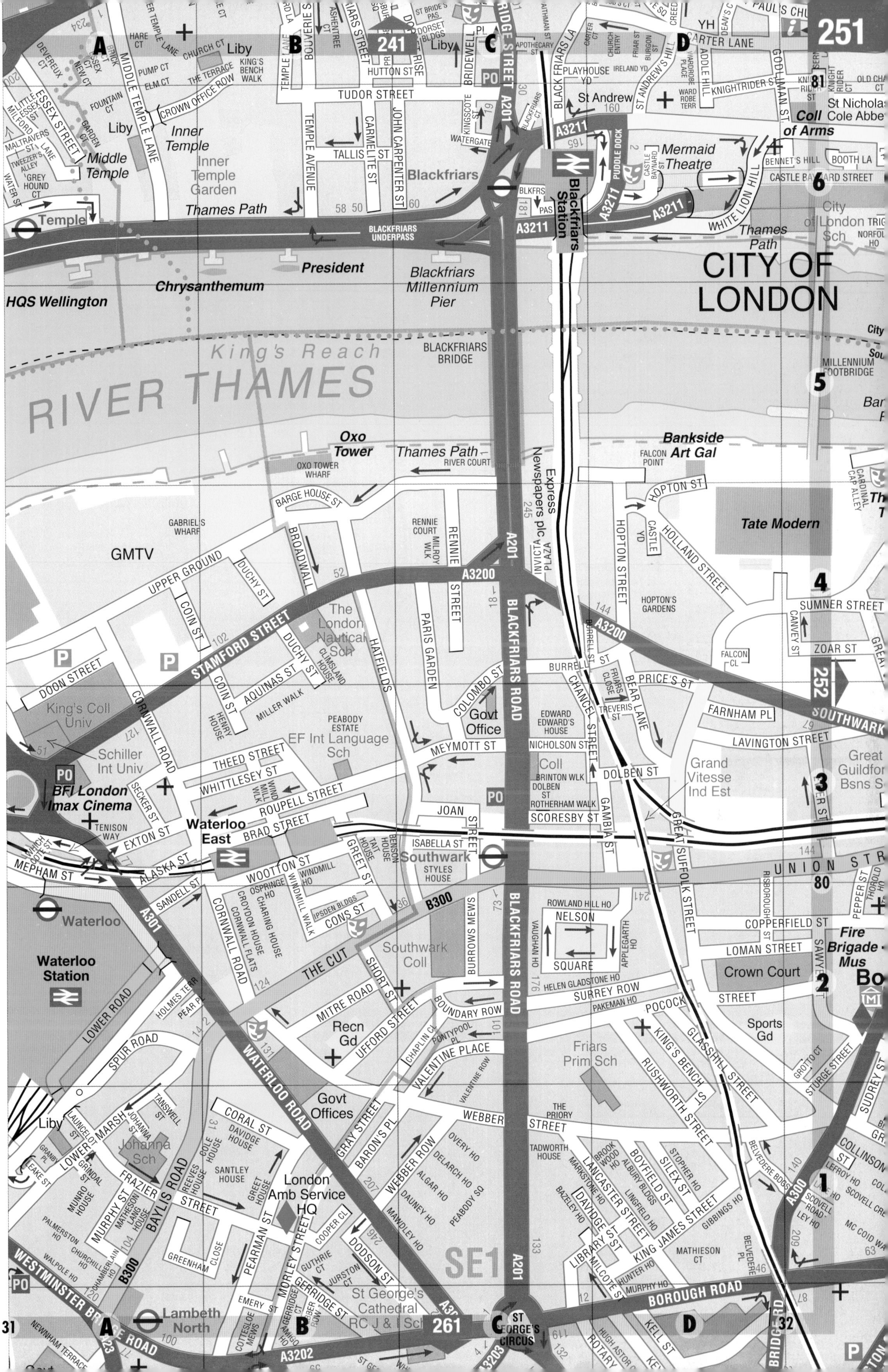
A
B
C
D
241
Liby
Inner Temple
Middle Temple
Inner Temple Garden
Thames Path
Temple
Essex Street
Middle Temple Lane
Crown Office Row
King's Bench Walk
Church Ct
The Terrace
Devereux Ct
Fountain Ct
Garden Ct
Maltravers St
Milford Lane
Tweezer's Alley
Grey Hound Ct
Water St
Brick Ct
Hare Ct
Pump Ct
Elm Ct
Temple Lane
Bouverie St
Whitefriars Street
Temple Avenue
Tudor Street
Hutton St
Tallis St
Carmelite St
John Carpenter St
Dorset Rise
Bridewell Pl
New Bridge Street
A201
PO
Blackfriars
Blackfriars Underpass
Kingscote St
Watergate
Apothecary St
Black Friars La
Playhouse Yd
Church Entry
Carter Lane
St Andrew
Ireland Yd
St Andrew's Hill
Friar St
Burgon St
Wardrobe Place
Ward Robe Terr
Addle Hill
Knightrider St
Godliman St
YH
Puddle Dock
A3211
Blackfriars Station
Blkfrs Pas
Mermaid Theatre
Castle Baynard St
White Lion Hill
Bennet's Hill
Booth La
Castle Baynard Street
Coll of Arms
St Nicholas Cole Abbey
City of London Sch
Thames Path
CITY OF LONDON
President
Chrysanthemum
HQS Wellington
Blackfriars Millennium Pier
Blackfriars Bridge
King's Reach
RIVER THAMES
Millennium Footbridge
Oxo Tower
Oxo Tower Wharf
Thames Path
River Court
Bankside Art Gal
Falcon Point
Express Newspapers plc
Hopton St
Tate Modern
Gabriel's Wharf
GMTV
Barge House St
Broadwall
Rennie Court
Milroy Walk
Rennie Street
A3200
Invicta Plaza
Upper Ground
Duchy St
Coin St
Stamford Street
The London Nautical Sch
Hatfields
Paris Garden
Blackfriars Road
Hopton Street
Castle Yd
Holland Street
Hopton's Gardens
Sumner Street
Canvey St
Zoar St
Falcon Cl
252
Southwark
Doon Street
King's Coll Univ
Cornwall Road
Aquinas St
Miller Walk
Henry House
Clims Land House
Peabody Estate
EF Int Language Sch
Colombo St
Govt Office
Burrell St
Chancel Street
Friars Close
Bear Lane
Price's St
Treveris St
Farnham Pl
Edward Edward's House
Lavington Street
Schiller Int Univ
BFI London Imax Cinema
Theed Street
Whittlesey St
Windmill Walk
Roupell Street
Meymott St
Nicholson St
Coll
Brinton Wlk
Dolben St
Rotherham Walk
Dolben St
Grand Vitesse Ind Est
Great Guildford Bsns Sq
Secker St
Tenison Way
Exton St
Waterloo East
Brad Street
Joan Street
Scoresby St
Gambia St
Isabella St
Southwark
Great Suffolk Street
Union Street
Mepham St
Alaska St
Sandell St
Wootton St
Ospringe Ho
Windmill Ho
Greet Street
Tait House
Benson House
Styles House
Charing House
Croydon House
Cornwall Flats
Waterloo
Waterloo Station
A301
Cons St
Ipsden Bldgs
B300
Burrows Mews
Rowland Hill Ho
Nelson Square
Vaughan Ho
Applegarth Ho
Risborough St
Copperfield St
Loman Street
Sawyer St
Crown Court
Street
Fire Brigade Mus
Pepper St
Thorold
The Cut
Southwark Coll
Short St
Helen Gladstone Ho
Surrey Row
Pakeman Ho
Pocock
Lower Road
Holmes Terr
Pear Pl
Mitre Road
Ufford Street
Boundary Row
Recn Gd
Chaplin Cl
Pontypool Pl
Valentine Place
King's Bench St
Glasshill Street
Sports Gd
Friars Prim Sch
Rushworth Street
Grotto Ct
Sturge Street
Spur Road
Waterloo Road
Valentine Row
Govt Offices
Webber Street
The Priory
Tadworth House
Brook Wood Ho
Boyfield St
Silex St
Stopher Ho
Belvedere Bldgs
Collinson St
Liby
Launcelot St
Lower Marsh
Tanswell St
Johanna St
Johanna Sch
Coral St
Davidge House
Cole House
Santley House
Greet House
Gray Street
Baron's Pl
Webber Row
Overy Ho
Delarch Ho
Algar Ho
Dauney Ho
Peabody Sq
Markstone Ho
Lancaster Street
Albury Bldgs
Lingfield Ho
King James Street
Gibbings Ho
Lefroy Ho
Scovell Road
Scovell Cres
Ley Ho
Mc Coid Way
Grindal St
Frazier Street
Baylis Road
Reeves House
Murphy St
Matheson Lang House
Munro House
London Amb Service HQ
Pearman St
Morley Street
Cooper Cl
Dodson St
Mandley Ho
Davidge St
Library St
Milcote St
Bazeley Ho
Mathieson Ct
Belvedere Pl
A300
Palmerston Ho
Churchill Ho
Chamberlain Ho
Walpole Ho
Greenham Close
Guthrie Ct
Jurston Ct
Hunter Ho
Murphy Ho
Borough Road
SE1
Westminster Bridge Road
Lambeth North
Emery St
Gerridge St
St George's Cathedral RC J & I Sch
Cottesloe Mews
261
St George's Circus
Hugh Astor Ct
Rotary
Kell St
Bridge Rd
Newnham Terrace
A3202
A3203
A23
31
32
1
2
3
4
5
6
80
81
P

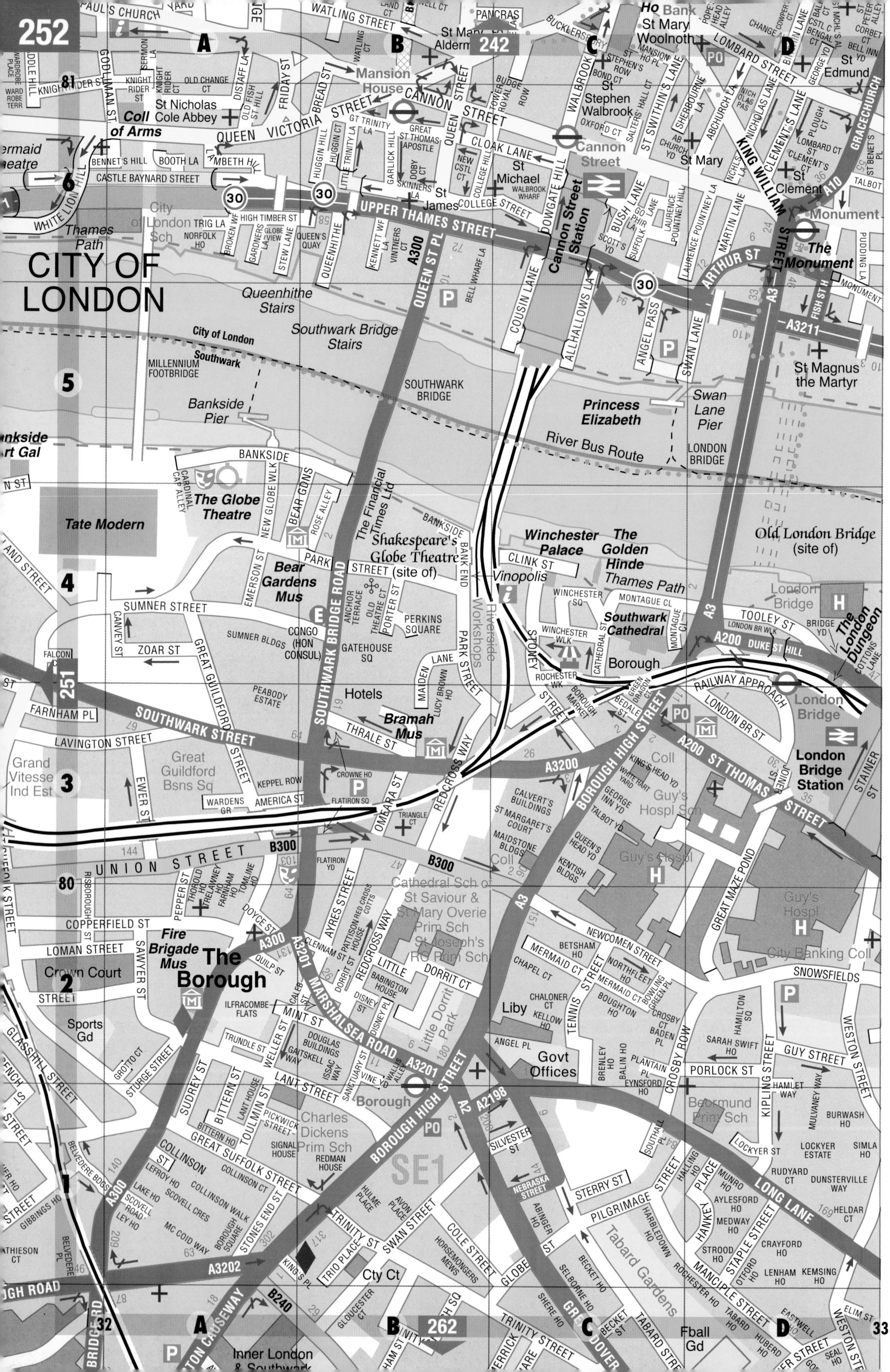

A
B
C
D
242
262
81
80
32
33
6
5
4
3
2
1
CITY OF LONDON
City of London
Southwark
SE1
Watling Street
Queen Victoria Street
Cannon Street
Upper Thames Street
Lombard Street
King William Street
Gracechurch
Arthur St
Queen St Pl
Knightrider St
Godliman St
Old Change Ct
Friday St
Bread St
Distaff La
Old Fish St Hill
St Nicholas Cole Abbey
Coll of Arms
Mansion House
St Mary Aldermary
Bucklersbury
Walbrook
St Stephen Walbrook
Bank
St Mary Woolnoth
St Edmund
Mermaid Theatre
Bennet's Hill
Booth La
Lambeth Hill
Castle Baynard Street
White Lion Hill
Huggin Hill
Little Trinity La
Garlick Hill
Great St Thomas Apostle
Cloak Lane
College Hill
St Michael
St James
Skinners La
College Street
Dowgate Hill
Cannon Street
Cannon Street Station
Oxford Ct
Salters' Hall Ct
St Swithin's Lane
Sherbourne La
Abchurch La
Nicholas Lane
Clement's Lane
Lombard Ct
St Clement
St Mary Abchurch
Bush Lane
Laurence Pountney Hill
Laurence Pountney La
Martin Lane
Monument
The Monument
Pudding La
Fish St H
A10
A3
A3211
A300
Thames Path
City of London Sch
High Timber St
Trig La
Norfolk Ho
Broken Wf
Gardners La
Globe View
Stew Lane
Queen's Quay
Queenhithe
Kennett Wf La
Vintners Ct
Bell Wharf La
Cousin Lane
Allhallows La
Angel Pass
Swan Lane
Queenhithe Stairs
Southwark Bridge Stairs
Millennium Footbridge
Southwark Bridge
Bankside Pier
Princess Elizabeth
Swan Lane Pier
River Bus Route
London Bridge
St Magnus the Martyr
Bankside Art Gal
Bankside
Cardinal Cap Alley
The Globe Theatre
New Globe Wlk
Bear Gdns
Rose Alley
Tate Modern
The Financial Times Ltd
Shakespeare's Globe Theatre (site of)
Park Street
Bank End
Clink St
Winchester Palace
The Golden Hinde
Thames Path
Vinopolis
Riverside Workshops
Old London Bridge (site of)
Bear Gardens Mus
Emerson St
Sumner Street
Canvey St
Zoar St
Congo (Hon Consul)
Sumner Bldgs
Southwark Bridge Road
Anchor Terrace
Old Theatre Ct
Porter St
Perkins Square
Gatehouse Sq
Winchester Sq
Montague Cl
Southwark Cathedral
Stoney St
Winchester Wlk
Cathedral St
Borough
Rochester Wk
Borough Market
Green Dragon Ct
Bedale St
Tooley St
London Br Wlk
Bridge Yd
The London Dungeon
Duke St Hill
A200
Railway Approach
London Br St
London Bridge
London Bridge Station
Joiner St
St Thomas Street
Stainer St
Great Guildford Street
Falcon Cl
Southwark Street
Farnham Pl
Peabody Estate
Hotels
Maiden Lane
Lucy Brown Ho
Bramah Mus
Thrale St
Redcross Way
A3200
Lavington Street
Grand Vitesse Ind Est
Great Guildford Bsns Sq
Ewer St
Keppel Row
Wardens Gr
America St
Crowne Ho
Flatiron Sq
O'Meara St
Triangle Ct
King's Head Yd
White Hart Yard
George Inn Yd
Talbot Yd
Queen's Head Yd
Calvert's Buildings
St Margaret's Court
Maidstone Bldgs
Kentish Bldgs
Coll
Guy's Hospl Sch
Guy's Hospl
Union Street
B300
Risborough St
Pepper St
Thorold Ho
Trelawney Ho
Farnham Ho
Tomline Ho
Copperfield St
Doyce St
Flatiron Yd
Ayres Street
Pattison House
Red Cross Cotts
Cathedral Sch of St Saviour & St Mary Overie Prim Sch
St Joseph's RC Prim Sch
Great Maze Pond
City Banking Coll
Snowsfields
Newcomen Street
Betsham Ho
Mermaid Ct
Northfleet Ho
Chapel Ct
Bowling Green Pl
Loman Street
Sawyer St
Fire Brigade Mus
The Borough
Crown Court
Quilp St
Glennam St
Dorrit St
Redcross Way
Little Dorrit Ct
Babington House
Disney St
Disney Pl
Little Dorrit Park
Marshalsea Road
A3201
Chaloner Ct
Kellow Ho
Liby
Tennis Street
Boughton Ho
Crosby Ct
Baden Pl
Crosby Row
Hamilton Sq
Weston Street
Kipling Street
Sarah Swift Ho
Guy Street
Porlock St
Hamlet Way
Mulvaney Way
Burwash Ho
Sports Gd
Glasshill Street
Grotto Ct
Sturge Street
Ilfracombe Flats
Mint St
Caleb St
Trundle St
Weller St
Douglas Buildings
Gaitskell Way
Issac Way
Sanctuary St
Vine Yd
Wallis Alley
Angel Pl
Govt Offices
Brenley Ho
Balin Ho
Plantain Pl
Eynsford Ho
Bermondsey
Prim Sch
Lant Street
Sudrey St
Bittern St
Lant House
Toulmin St
Pickwick Street
Charles Dickens Prim Sch
Signal House
Redman House
Borough
Borough High Street
A2
A2198
Silvester St
Southall Pl
Lockyer St
Lockyer Estate
Simla Ho
Rudyard Ct
Dunsterville Way
Long Lane
Heldar Ct
Bittern Ho
Collinson
Great Suffolk Street
Collinson Ct
Collinson Walk
Lefroy Ho
Lake Ho
Scovell Cres
Scovell Road
Ley Ho
Mc Coid Way
Borough Square
Stones End St
Belvedere Bldgs
Gibbings Ho
Mathieson Ct
Belvedere Pl
Hulme Place
Avon Place
Swan Street
Trinity St
Trio Place
Cole Street
Horsemongers Mews
Nebraska Street
Sterry St
Abinger Ho
Pilgrimage Street
Harbledown Ho
Hankey Place
Halling Ho
Munro Ho
Aylesford Ho
Medway Ho
Strood Ho
Staple Street
Crayford Ho
Lenham Ho
Kemsing Ho
Otford Ho
Rochester Ho
Mancipie Street
Tabard Gardens
Becket Ho
Selborne Ho
Globe St
A3202
King's Pl
Cty Ct
Gloucester Ct
B240
Trinity Street
Shere Ho
Great Dover
Becket St
Tabard Street
Fball Gd
Tabard Ho
Huber Ho
Eastwell Ho
Elim St
Weston St
Seal Ho
Borough Road
Bridge
Newington Causeway
Inner London & Southwark
Swan St

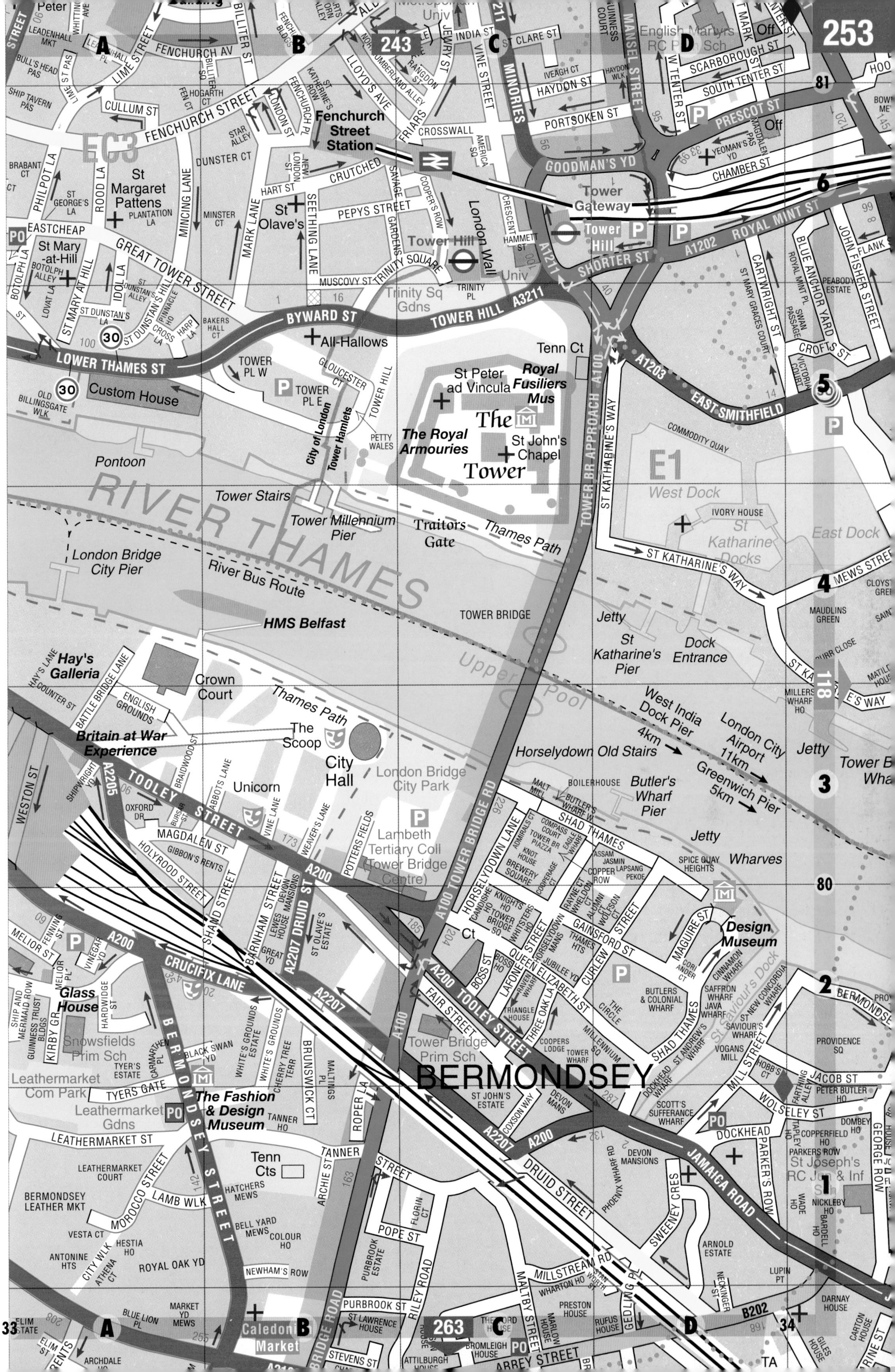

243
A
B
C
D
FENCHURCH AV
BILLITER ST
LEADENHALL MKT
LIME STREET
INDIA ST
ST CLARE ST
MINORIES
MANSEL STREET
English Martyrs RC Prim Sch
SCARBOROUGH ST
SOUTH TENTER ST
HAYDON ST
IVEAGH CT
PORTSOKEN ST
PRESCOT ST
CHAMBER ST
YEOMAN'S YD
BULL'S HEAD PAS
SHIP TAVERN PAS
CULLUM ST
FENCHURCH STREET
LLOYD'S AVE
JEWRY ST
VINE STREET
Fenchurch Street Station
CROSSWALL
AMERICA SQ
EC3
BRABANT CT
PHILPOT LA
ROOD LA
St Margaret Pattens
PLANTATION LA
MINCING LANE
DUNSTER CT
STAR ALLEY
HART ST
CRUTCHED
MARK LANE
MINSTER CT
St Olave's
SEETHING LANE
PEPYS STREET
SAVAGE GARDENS
COOPER'S ROW
London Wall
CRESCENT
GOODMAN'S YD
Tower Gateway
Tower Hill
HAMMETT ST
SHORTER ST
A1202
ROYAL MINT ST
CARTWRIGHT ST
ST MARY GRACES COURT
BLUE ANCHOR YARD
JOHN FISHER STREET
PEABODY ESTATE
EASTCHEAP
St Mary-at-Hill
BOTOLPH LA
GREAT TOWER STREET
IDOL LA
ST MARY AT HILL
LOVAT LA
ST DUNSTAN'S HILL
HARP LA
BAKERS HALL CT
MUSCOVY ST
TRINITY SQUARE
Trinity Sq Gdns
TRINITY PL
Univ
BYWARD ST
TOWER HILL
A3211
All-Hallows
LOWER THAMES ST
Custom House
OLD BILLINGSGATE WLK
TOWER PL W
TOWER PL E
GLOUCESTER CT
TOWER HILL
PETTY WALES
City of London
Tower Hamlets
Tenn Ct
St Peter ad Vincula
Royal Fusiliers Mus
The Tower
The Royal Armouries
St John's Chapel
TOWER BR APPROACH
A100
ST KATHARINE'S WAY
A1203
EAST SMITHFIELD
COMMODITY QUAY
E1
West Dock
IVORY HOUSE
St Katharine Docks
East Dock
CROFTS ST
Pontoon
RIVER THAMES
Tower Stairs
Tower Millennium Pier
Traitors Gate
Thames Path
London Bridge City Pier
River Bus Route
HMS Belfast
TOWER BRIDGE
Jetty
St Katharine's Pier
Dock Entrance
MAUDLINS GREEN
MEWS STREET
Upper Pool
West India Dock Pier 4km
London City Airport 11km
Greenwich Pier 5km
Horselydown Old Stairs
Butler's Wharf Pier
Hay's Galleria
HAY'S LANE
BATTLE BRIDGE LANE
ENGLISH GROUNDS
Crown Court
Britain at War Experience
The Scoop
City Hall
London Bridge City Park
Unicorn
TOOLEY STREET
A2205
WESTON ST
SHIPWRIGHT YD
OXFORD DR
MAGDALEN ST
GIBBON'S RENTS
HOLYROOD STREET
ABBOTS LANE
VINE LANE
WEAVER'S LANE
POTTERS FIELDS
Lambeth Tertiary Coll (Tower Bridge Centre)
A200
TOWER BRIDGE RD
HORSELYDOWN LANE
SHAD THAMES
BOILERHOUSE
SPICE QUAY HEIGHTS
Wharves
Design Museum
MAGUIRE ST
GAINSFORD ST
SHAND STREET
BARNHAM STREET
A2207 DRUID ST
ST OLAVE'S ESTATE
MELIOR ST
VINEGAR YD
CRUCIFIX LANE
Glass House
HARDWIDGE ST
KIRBY GR
Snowsfields Prim Sch
BERMONDSEY STREET
BLACK SWAN YD
WHITE'S GROUNDS
CHERRY TREE TERR
BRUNSWICK CT
MALTINGS PL
QUEEN ELIZABETH ST
THREE OAK LA
FAIR STREET
Tower Bridge Prim Sch
BERMONDSEY
CURLEW STREET
BUTLERS & COLONIAL WHARF
SAFFRON WHARF
JAVA WHARF
ST SAVIOUR'S WHARF
VOGANS MILL
MILL STREET
PROVIDENCE SQ
JACOB ST
PETER BUTLER HO
WOLSELEY ST
DOCKHEAD
PARKER'S ROW
St Joseph's RC Jun & Inf Sch
JAMAICA ROAD
Leathermarket Com Park
TYERS GATE
TYER'S ESTATE
Leathermarket Gdns
The Fashion & Design Museum
TANNER HO
ROPER LA
LEATHERMARKET ST
LEATHERMARKET COURT
BERMONDSEY LEATHER MKT
MOROCCO STREET
LAMB WLK
Tenn Cts
TANNER STREET
ARCHIE ST
HATCHERS MEWS
BELL YARD MEWS
COLOUR HO
POPE ST
FLORIN CT
PURBROOK ESTATE
RILEY ROAD
DRUID STREET
DEVON MANSIONS
PHOENIX WHARF RD
SWEENEY CRES
ARNOLD ESTATE
MILLSTREAM RD
VESTA CT
HESTIA HO
ANTONINE HTS
CITY WLK
ROYAL OAK YD
NEWHAM'S ROW
BLUE LION PL
MARKET YD MEWS
Caledonian Market
PURBROOK ST
ST LAWRENCE HOUSE
STEVENS ST
263
MALTBY STREET
GEDLING PL
B202
ABBEY STREET
ARCHDALE
33
34
118
1
2
3
4
5
6
80
81

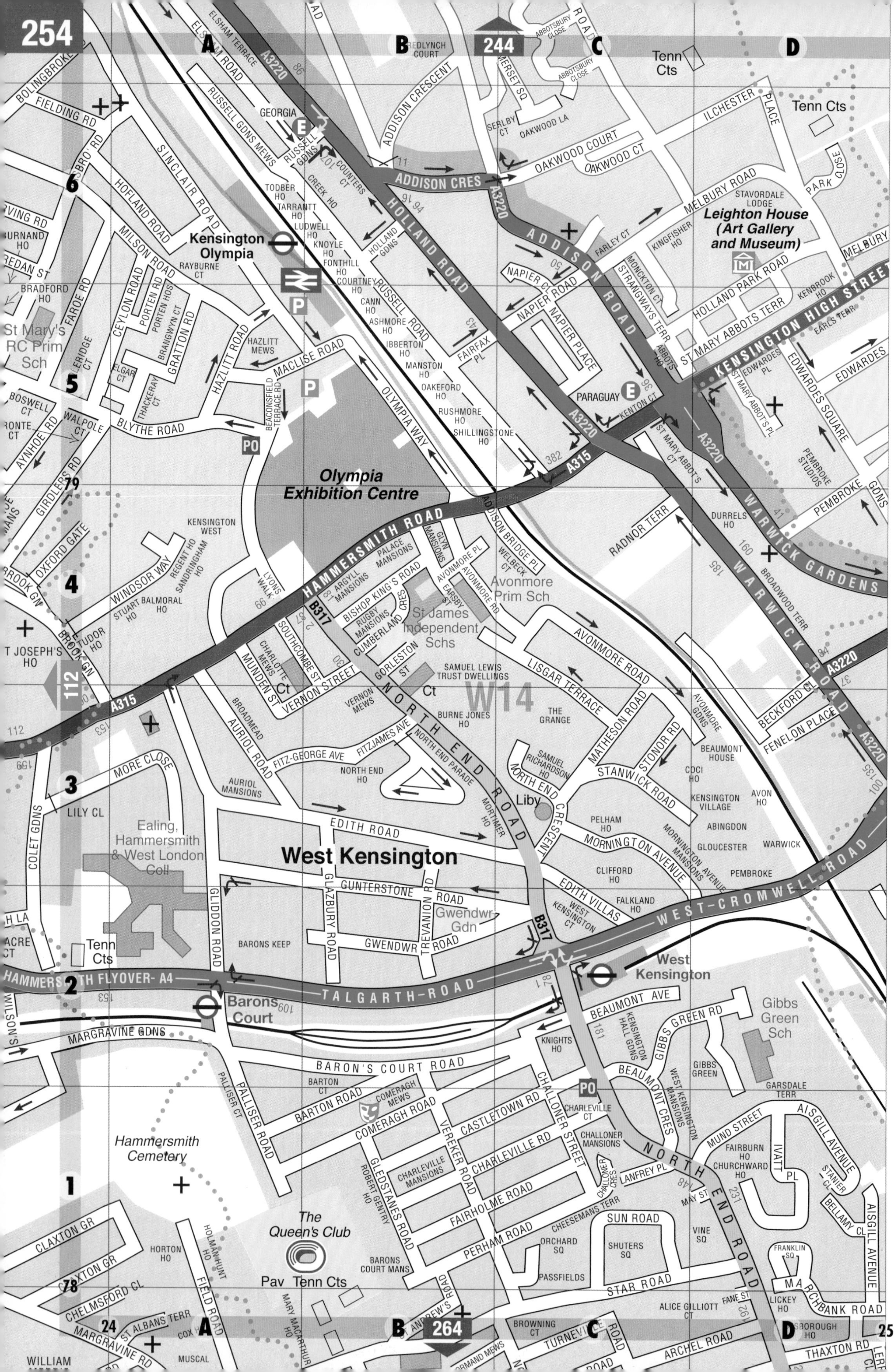
A
B
C
D
244
264
112
24
25
1
2
3
4
5
6
78
79
West Kensington
W14
Olympia Exhibition Centre
Kensington Olympia
Leighton House (Art Gallery and Museum)
The Queen's Club
Hammersmith Cemetery
Ealing, Hammersmith & West London Coll
St James Independent Schs
Avonmore Prim Sch
St Mary's RC Prim Sch
Gibbs Green Sch
Barons Court
West Kensington
Tenn Cts
Pav
Liby
PO
P
HAMMERSMITH ROAD
A315
A3220
B317
HAMMERSMITH FLYOVER- A4
TALGARTH-ROAD
WEST-CROMWELL ROAD
NORTH END ROAD
HOLLAND ROAD
ADDISON ROAD
ADDISON CRES
ADDISON CRESCENT
KENSINGTON HIGH STREET
WARWICK GARDENS
WARWICK ROAD
RUSSELL ROAD
OLYMPIA WAY
ELSHAM ROAD
ELSHAM TERRACE
RUSSELL GDNS MEWS
SINCLAIR ROAD
HOFLAND ROAD
MILSON ROAD
BLYTHE ROAD
MACLISE ROAD
HAZLITT ROAD
HAZLITT MEWS
BEACONSFIELD TERRACE RD
GRATTON RD
CEYLON ROAD
FIELDING RD
BOLINGBROKE
FAROE RD
GIRDLERS RD
AYNHOE RD
WALPOLE CT
OXFORD GATE
WINDSOR WAY
BROOK GN
MELBURY ROAD
ILCHESTER PLACE
OAKWOOD COURT
OAKWOOD CT
OAKWOOD LA
ABBOTSBURY ROAD
HOLLAND PARK ROAD
ST MARY ABBOTS TERR
EDWARDES SQUARE
PEMBROKE GDNS
NAPIER ROAD
NAPIER PLACE
STRANGWAYS TERR
RADNOR TERR
AVONMORE ROAD
AVONMORE PL
LISGAR TERRACE
MATHESON ROAD
STONOR RD
STANWICK ROAD
NORTH END CRESCENT
MORNINGTON AVENUE
EDITH VILLAS
EDITH ROAD
GUNTERSTONE ROAD
GWENDWR ROAD
GLAZBURY ROAD
TREVANION RD
GLIDDON ROAD
AURIOL ROAD
FITZ-GEORGE AVE
FITZJAMES AVE
NORTH END PARADE
VERNON STREET
MUNDEN ST
SOUTHCOMBE ST
BISHOP KING'S ROAD
GORLESTON ST
BECKFORD CL
FENELON PLACE
MORE CLOSE
LILY CL
COLET GDNS
MARGRAVINE GDNS
BARON'S COURT ROAD
BARTON ROAD
COMERAGH ROAD
PALLISER ROAD
CASTLETOWN RD
CHARLEVILLE RD
FAIRHOLME ROAD
PERHAM ROAD
CHALLONER STREET
GLEDSTANES ROAD
VEREKER ROAD
BEAUMONT AVE
BEAUMONT CRES
GIBBS GREEN RD
MUND STREET
AISGILL AVENUE
IVATT PL
SUN ROAD
STAR ROAD
MARCHBANK ROAD
ARCHEL ROAD
TURNEVILLE ROAD
THAXTON RD
CLAXTON GR
CHELMSFORD CL
ST ALBANS TERR
MARGRAVINE RD
FIELD ROAD
BARONS KEEP
Gwendwr Gdn

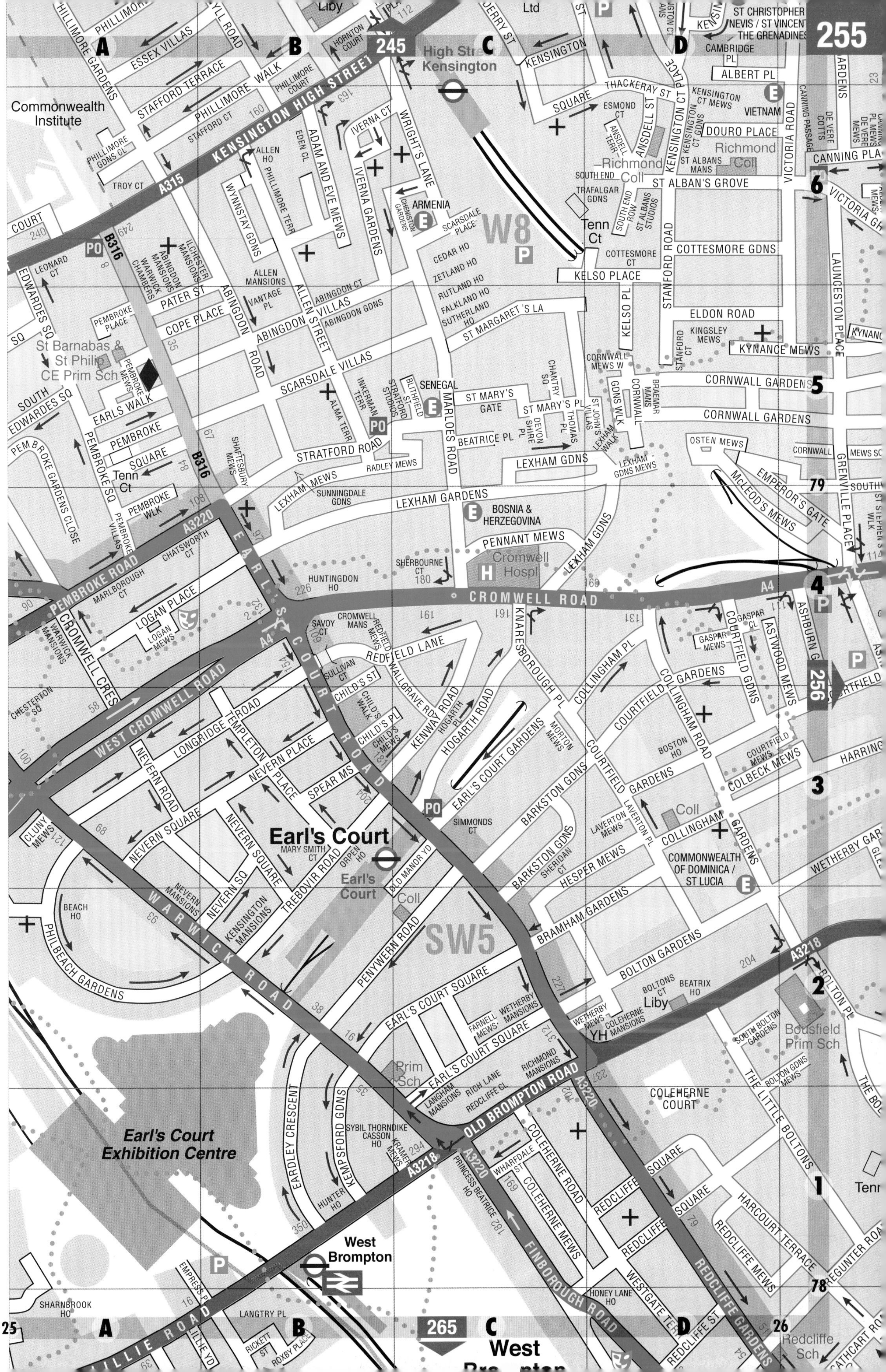

High Street Kensington
Commonwealth Institute
KENSINGTON HIGH STREET
A315
B316
W8
SW5
PHILLIMORE GARDENS
ESSEX VILLAS
STAFFORD TERRACE
PHILLIMORE WALK
PHILLIMORE COURT
HORNTON COURT
STAFFORD CT
PHILLIMORE GDNS CL
TROY CT
ALLEN HO
EDEN CL
ADAM AND EVE MEWS
IVERNA CT
IVERNA GARDENS
WRIGHT'S LANE
PHILLIMORE TERR
WYNNSTAY GDNS
ARMENIA
CHENISTON GARDENS
SCARSDALE PLACE
CEDAR HO
ZETLAND HO
RUTLAND HO
FALKLAND HO
SUTHERLAND HO
ST MARGARET'S LA
KENSINGTON SQUARE
THACKERAY ST
ESMOND CT
ANSDELL TERR
ANSDELL ST
KENSINGTON CT PLACE
KENSINGTON CT GDNS
KENSINGTON CT MEWS
VIETNAM
ALBERT PL
CAMBRIDGE PL
ST CHRISTOPHER NEVIS / ST VINCENT THE GRENADINES
DOURO PLACE
Richmond Coll
ST ALBANS MANS
SOUTH END
SOUTH END ROW
ST ALBANS STUDIOS
TRAFALGAR GDNS
ST ALBAN'S GROVE
VICTORIA ROAD
CANNING PASSAGE
DE VERE COTTS
CANNING PLACE
VICTORIA GROVE
Tenn Ct
COTTESMORE CT
COTTESMORE GDNS
KELSO PLACE
KELSO PL
STANFORD ROAD
ELDON ROAD
KINGSLEY MEWS
STANFORD CT
KYNANCE MEWS
LAUNCESTON PLACE
CORNWALL MEWS W
CORNWALL GDNS WLK
BRAEMAR MANS
CORNWALL GARDENS
CHANTRY SQ
ST MARY'S GATE
ST MARY'S PL
DEVONSHIRE PL
ST THOMAS WLK
ST JOHN'S VILLAS
LEXHAM WALK
LEXHAM GDNS MEWS
LEXHAM GDNS
BEATRICE PL
OSTEN MEWS
EMPEROR'S GATE
McLEOD'S MEWS
GRENVILLE PLACE
COURT
LEONARD CT
EDWARDES SQ
SOUTH EDWARDES SQ
ILCHESTER MANSIONS
ABINGDON MANSIONS
WARWICK CHAMBERS
PATER ST
ALLEN MANSIONS
VANTAGE PL
ABINGDON CT
ABINGDON VILLAS
ABINGDON GDNS
ABINGDON ROAD
ALLEN STREET
PEMBROKE PLACE
COPE PLACE
St Barnabas & St Philip CE Prim Sch
PEMBROKE MEWS
EARLS WALK
SCARSDALE VILLAS
INKERMAN TERR
ALMA TERR
STRATFORD STUDIOS
BLITHFIELD ST
SENEGAL
MARLOES ROAD
STRATFORD ROAD
RADLEY MEWS
SHAFTESBURY MEWS
PEMBROKE SQUARE
PEMBROKE GARDENS CLOSE
PEMBROKE SQ
PEMBROKE WLK
PEMBROKE VILLAS
LEXHAM MEWS
SUNNINGDALE GDNS
LEXHAM GARDENS
BOSNIA & HERZEGOVINA
PENNANT MEWS
LEXHAM GDNS
A3220
PEMBROKE ROAD
CHATSWORTH CT
MARLBOROUGH CT
LOGAN PLACE
LOGAN MEWS
HUNTINGDON HO
SHERBOURNE CT
Cromwell Hospl
CROMWELL ROAD
A4
WARWICK MANSIONS
CROMWELL CRES
SAVOY CT
CROMWELL MANS
REDFIELD MEWS
REDFIELD LANE
SULLIVAN CT
CHILD'S ST
CHILD'S WALK
CHILD'S PL
CHILD'S MEWS
WALLGRAVE RD
KENWAY ROAD
HOGARTH PL
HOGARTH ROAD
KNARESBOROUGH PL
COLLINGHAM PL
GASPAR CL
GASPAR MEWS
COURTFIELD GDNS
ASTWOOD MEWS
ASHBURN G
COURTFIELD GARDENS
COLLINGHAM GARDENS
COLLINGHAM ROAD
BOSTON HO
COURTFIELD MEWS
COLBECK MEWS
HARRINGTON
WEST CROMWELL ROAD
CHESTERTON SQ
LONGRIDGE ROAD
TEMPLETON PLACE
NEVERN ROAD
NEVERN PLACE
SPEAR MS
EARL'S COURT ROAD
EARL'S COURT GARDENS
MORTON MEWS
BARKSTON GDNS
COURTFIELD GARDENS
LAVERTON MEWS
LAVERTON PL
Coll
COLLINGHAM GARDENS
WETHERBY GARDENS
COMMONWEALTH OF DOMINICA / ST LUCIA
CLUNY MEWS
NEVERN SQUARE
NEVERN SQ
NEVERN MANSIONS
Earl's Court
MARY SMITH CT
TREBOVIR ROAD
ORPEN HO
OLD MANOR YD
SIMMONDS CT
SHERIDAN CT
HESPER MEWS
BARKSTON GDNS
BRAMHAM GARDENS
KENSINGTON MANSIONS
WARWICK ROAD
BEACH HO
PHILBEACH GARDENS
PENYWERN ROAD
BOLTON GARDENS
BOLTONS CT
BEATRIX HO
Liby
A3218
BOLTON PL
EARL'S COURT SQUARE
WETHERBY MANSIONS
FARNELL MEWS
WETHERBY MEWS
COLEHERNE MANSIONS
YH
SOUTH BOLTON GARDENS
Bousfield Prim Sch
BOLTON GDNS MEWS
THE LITTLE BOLTONS
THE BOLTONS
Prim Sch
RICHMOND MANSIONS
LANGHAM MANSIONS
RICH LANE
REDCLIFFE CL
OLD BROMPTON ROAD
COLEHERNE COURT
Earl's Court Exhibition Centre
EARDLEY CRESCENT
KEMPSFORD GDNS
SYBIL THORNDIKE CASSON HO
KRAMER MEWS
HUNTER HO
PRINCESS BEATRICE HO
WHARFDALE ST
COLEHERNE ROAD
COLEHERNE MEWS
REDCLIFFE SQUARE
HARCOURT TERRACE
REDCLIFFE MEWS
TREGUNTER ROAD
Tenn
West Brompton
FINBOROUGH ROAD
EMPRESS PL
SHARNBROOK HO
HONEY LANE HO
WESTGATE TER
REDCLIFFE GARDENS
REDCLIFFE ST
LANGTRY PL
RICKETT ST
ROXBY PLACE
LILLIE ROAD
LILLIE YD
Redcliffe Sch
CATHCART RD
West Brompton

245
256
265

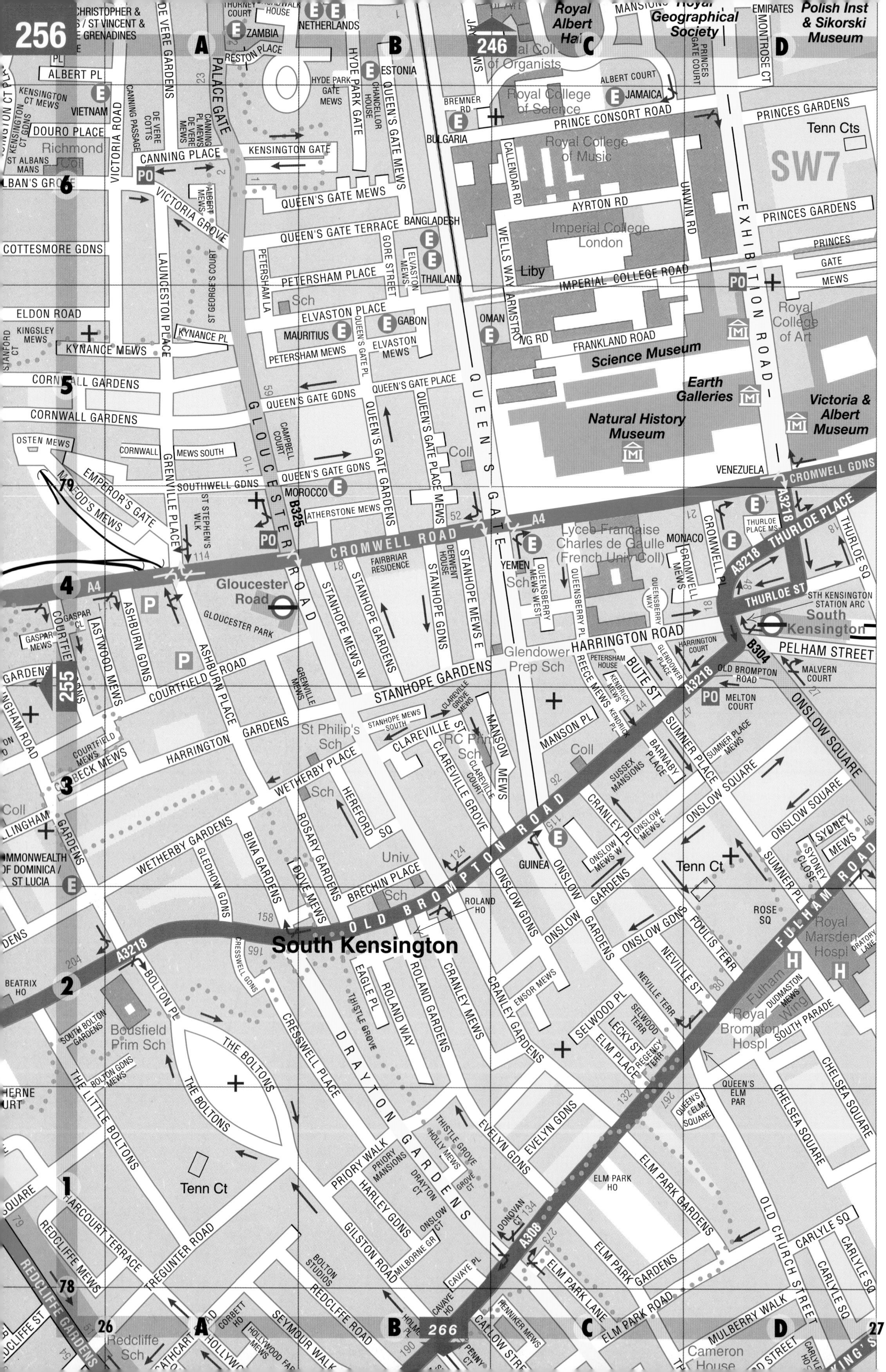

A
B
C
D
246
Royal Albert Hall
Royal Geographical Society
Polish Inst & Sikorski Museum
EMIRATES
MONTROSE CT
PRINCES GATE COURT
CHRISTOPHER & / ST VINCENT & GRENADINES
DE VERE GARDENS
PALACE GATE
ZAMBIA
NETHERLANDS
RESTON PLACE
HYDE PARK GATE
HYDE PARK GATE MEWS
CHANCELLOR HOUSE
QUEEN'S GATE MEWS
ESTONIA
JAY MEWS
Royal College of Organists
ALBERT COURT
JAMAICA
Royal College of Science
BREMNER RD
BULGARIA
PRINCE CONSORT ROAD
PRINCES GARDENS
Tenn Cts
SW7
ALBERT PL
KENSINGTON CT MEWS
VIETNAM
DOURO PLACE
Richmond Coll
ST ALBANS MANS
ALBAN'S GROVE
6
CANNING PASSAGE
DE VERE COTTS
CANNING PL MEWS
DE VERE MEWS
CANNING PLACE
KENSINGTON GATE
PO
VICTORIA ROAD
VICTORIA GROVE
ALBERT MEWS
QUEEN'S GATE MEWS
Royal College of Music
CALLENDAR RD
AYRTON RD
UNWIN RD
EXHIBITION ROAD
PRINCES GARDENS
PRINCES GATE MEWS
COTTESMORE GDNS
LAUNCESTON PLACE
ST GEORGE'S COURT
QUEEN'S GATE TERRACE
BANGLADESH
GORE STREET
ELVASTON MEWS
THAILAND
PETERSHAM LA
PETERSHAM PLACE
Imperial College London
Liby
WELLS WAY
IMPERIAL COLLEGE ROAD
Sch
ELDON ROAD
KINGSLEY MEWS
STANFORD CT
KYNANCE MEWS
KYNANCE PL
ELVASTON PLACE
MAURITIUS
GABON
PETERSHAM MEWS
QUEEN'S GATE PL
ELVASTON MEWS
OMAN
ARMSTRONG RD
FRANKLAND ROAD
Science Museum
Royal College of Art
CORNWALL GARDENS
5
CORNWALL GARDENS
QUEEN'S GATE GDNS
QUEEN'S GATE PLACE
QUEEN'S GATE
Earth Galleries
Natural History Museum
Victoria & Albert Museum
OSTEN MEWS
CORNWALL
MEWS SOUTH
GLOUCESTER ROAD
B325
CAMPBELL COURT
QUEEN'S GATE GARDENS
QUEEN'S GATE PLACE MEWS
Coll
MCLEOD'S MEWS
EMPEROR'S GATE
79
GRENVILLE PLACE
SOUTHWELL GDNS
ST STEPHEN'S WLK
MOROCCO
QUEEN'S GATE GDNS
ATHERSTONE MEWS
VENEZUELA
CROMWELL GDNS
A3218
THURLOE PLACE
THURLOE PLACE MS
CROMWELL ROAD
A4
52
114
110
59
Lycée Français Charles de Gaulle (French Univ Coll)
MONACO
CROMWELL PL
THURLOE SQ
4
A4
Gloucester Road
FAIRBRIAR RESIDENCE
DERWENT HOUSE
STANHOPE GDNS
STANHOPE MEWS E
YEMEN
Sch
QUEENSBERRY MEWS WEST
QUEENSBERRY PL
QUEENSBERRY WAY
CROMWELL MEWS
THURLOE ST
STH KENSINGTON STATION ARC
South Kensington
GASPAR CL
GASPAR MEWS
COURTFIELD
ASTWOOD MEWS
ASHBURN GDNS
P
GLOUCESTER PARK
ASHBURN PLACE
STANHOPE MEWS W
STANHOPE GARDENS
HARRINGTON ROAD
HARRINGTON COURT
GLENDOWER PLACE
B304
PELHAM STREET
GARDENS
255
COURTFIELD ROAD
GRENVILLE MEWS
STANHOPE GARDENS
Glendower Prep Sch
PETERSHAM HOUSE
REECE MEWS
KENDRICK MEWS
BUTE ST
OLD BROMPTON ROAD
MALVERN COURT
MELTON COURT
ONSLOW SQUARE
HARRINGTON GARDENS
St Philip's Sch
STANHOPE MEWS SOUTH
CLAREVILLE GROVE MEWS
CLAREVILLE ST
RC Prim Sch
MANSON MEWS
MANSON PL
SUMNER PLACE
SUMNER PLACE MEWS
COURTFIELD MEWS
COLBECK MEWS
3
WETHERBY PLACE
HEREFORD SQ
CLAREVILLE GROVE
CLAREVILLE COURT
Coll
SUSSEX MANSIONS
BARNABY PLACE
ONSLOW SQUARE
ONSLOW SQUARE
Coll
WETHERBY GARDENS
BINA GARDENS
ROSARY GARDENS
OLD BROMPTON ROAD
92
CRANLEY PL
ONSLOW MEWS E
SYDNEY MEWS
COMMONWEALTH OF DOMINICA / ST LUCIA
GLEDHOW GDNS
DOVE MEWS
Univ
BRECHIN PLACE
124
115
GUINEA
ONSLOW GARDENS
ONSLOW MEWS W
Tenn Ct
SUMNER PL
SYDNEY CLOSE
FULHAM ROAD
ROLAND HO
Sch
158
ONSLOW GDNS
ONSLOW GARDENS
ONSLOW GDNS
FOULIS TERR
ROSE SQ
Royal Marsden Hospl
DRATORY LANE
South Kensington
A3218
204
BEATRIX HO
2
BOLTON PL
CRESSWELL GDNS
165
CRESSWELL PLACE
EAGLE PL
THISTLE GROVE
ROLAND WAY
ROLAND GARDENS
CRANLEY MEWS
CRANLEY GARDENS
ENSOR MEWS
NEVILLE TERR
NEVILLE ST
80
Fulham Wing
DUDMASTON MEWS
SOUTH BOLTON GARDENS
Bousfield Prim Sch
THE BOLTONS
SELWOOD PL
SELWOOD TERR
ELM PLACE
LECKY ST
REGENCY TERR
Royal Brompton Hospl
SOUTH PARADE
BOLTON GDNS MEWS
DRAYTON
QUEEN'S ELM PAR
CHELSEA SQUARE
HERNE URT
THE LITTLE BOLTONS
THE BOLTONS
132
267
QUEEN'S ELM SQUARE
CHELSEA SQUARE
THISTLE GROVE
HOLLY MEWS
EVELYN GDNS
1
Tenn Ct
PRIORY WALK
PRIORY MANSIONS
DRAYTON CT
GROVE CT
DRAYTON GARDENS
ELM PARK HO
ELM PARK GARDENS
SQUARE
HARCOURT TERRACE
HARLEY GDNS
ONSLOW CT
DONOVAN CT
134
A308
273
OLD CHURCH STREET
CARLYLE SQ
79
REDCLIFFE MEWS
TREGUNTER ROAD
GILSTON ROAD
MILBORNE GR
ELM PARK GARDENS
ELM PARK LANE
CARLYLE SQ
78
BOLTON STUDIOS
CAVAYE PL
CAVAYE HO
ELM PARK ROAD
MULBERRY WALK
REDCLIFFE GARDENS
CLIFFE ST
26
CORBETT HO
HOLLYWOOD MEWS
SEYMOUR WALK
REDCLIFFE ROAD
HOLMES PL
266
190
HENNIKER MEWS
CALLOW STREET
PENNY CT
Redcliffe Sch
CATHCART
Cameron House
27

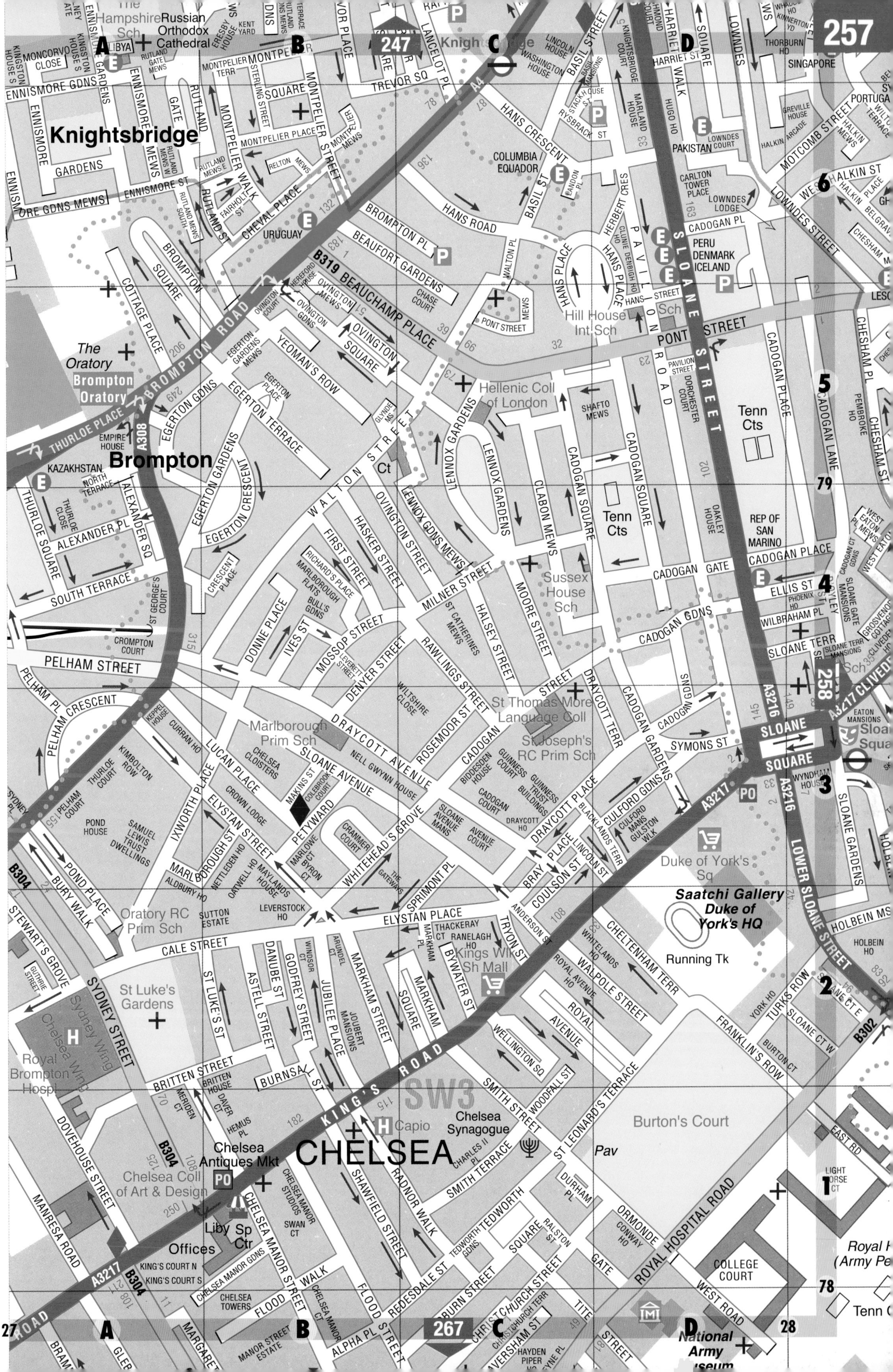

Knightsbridge
Brompton
CHELSEA
SW3
Russian Orthodox Cathedral
LIBYA
Hampshire Sch
ENNISMORE GDNS
ENNISMORE GARDENS
ENNISMORE MEWS
ENNISMORE ST
ENNISMORE GDNS MEWS
MONCORVO CLOSE
MONTPELIER SQUARE
MONTPELIER PLACE
MONTPELIER STREET
MONTPELIER WALK
MONTPELIER TERR
MONTPELIER MEWS
RUTLAND GATE
RUTLAND ST
TREVOR SQ
TREVOR PLACE
LANCELOT PL
Knightsbridge
BASIL STREET
HANS CRESCENT
HANS ROAD
HANS PLACE
HANS STREET
COLUMBIA / EQUADOR
URUGUAY
CHEVAL PLACE
BROMPTON PL
BEAUFORT GARDENS
BEAUCHAMP PLACE
B319
PONT STREET
Hill House Int Sch
WALTON PL
HARRIET ST
HARRIET WALK
LOWNDES SQUARE
LOWNDES STREET
LOWNDES COURT
PAKISTAN
CARLTON TOWER PLACE
CADOGAN PL
PERU
DENMARK
ICELAND
PAVILION ROAD
SLOANE STREET
CADOGAN PLACE
CADOGAN LANE
CHESHAM PL
MOTCOMB STREET
HALKIN ST
SINGAPORE
PORTUGAL
THORBURN HO
Tenn Cts
Hellenic Coll of London
SHAFTO MEWS
LENNOX GARDENS
LENNOX GDNS MEWS
CLABON MEWS
CADOGAN SQUARE
CADOGAN GATE
REP OF SAN MARINO
ELLIS ST
WILBRAHAM PL
SLOANE TERR
Sussex House Sch
The Oratory
Brompton Oratory
BROMPTON ROAD
THURLOE PLACE
THURLOE SQUARE
ALEXANDER PL
ALEXANDER SQ
SOUTH TERRACE
KAZAKHSTAN
EMPIRE HOUSE
A308
EGERTON GDNS
EGERTON GARDENS
EGERTON CRESCENT
EGERTON TERRACE
YEOMAN'S ROW
OVINGTON SQUARE
OVINGTON STREET
WALTON STREET
FIRST STREET
HASKER STREET
MILNER STREET
MOORE STREET
HALSEY STREET
CADOGAN GDNS
PELHAM STREET
PELHAM CRESCENT
CROMPTON COURT
DONNE PLACE
IVES ST
MOSSOP STREET
DENYER STREET
RAWLINGS STREET
DRAYCOTT AVENUE
DRAYCOTT TERR
DRAYCOTT PLACE
ROSEMOOR ST
St Thomas More Language Coll
St Joseph's RC Prim Sch
Marlborough Prim Sch
SLOANE AVENUE
LUCAN PLACE
IXWORTH PLACE
ELYSTAN STREET
ELYSTAN PLACE
PETYWARD
WHITEHEAD'S GROVE
SPRIMONT PL
CULFORD GDNS
BLACKLANDS TERR
SYMONS ST
SLOANE SQUARE
A3216
A3217
LOWER SLOANE STREET
SLOANE GARDENS
HOLBEIN MS
Duke of York's Sq
Saatchi Gallery
Duke of York's HQ
Running Tk
CHELTENHAM TERR
FRANKLIN'S ROW
TURKS ROW
WALPOLE STREET
ROYAL AVENUE
WELLINGTON SQ
SMITH STREET
TRYON ST
BYWATER ST
Kings Wlk Sh Mall
MARKHAM SQUARE
MARKHAM STREET
JUBILEE PLACE
GODFREY STREET
DANUBE ST
ASTELL STREET
ST LUKE'S ST
CALE STREET
St Luke's Gardens
Oratory RC Prim Sch
SYDNEY STREET
POND PLACE
BURY WALK
B304
Royal Brompton Hospl
Chelsea Wing
Sydney Wing
KING'S ROAD
BRITTEN STREET
BURNSALL ST
Chelsea Antiques Mkt
Chelsea Coll of Art & Design
Liby
Sp Ctr
Offices
MANRESA ROAD
DOVEHOUSE STREET
CHELSEA MANOR STREET
CHELSEA MANOR GDNS
FLOOD WALK
FLOOD STREET
SHAWFIELD STREET
RADNOR WALK
Capio
Chelsea Synagogue
SMITH TERRACE
TEDWORTH SQUARE
ST LEONARD'S TERRACE
WOODFALL ST
Burton's Court
Pav
ROYAL HOSPITAL ROAD
ORMONDE GATE
WEST ROAD
COLLEGE COURT
National Army Museum
REDESDALE ST
CHRISTCHURCH STREET
TITE STREET
A B C D
1 2 3 4 5 6
247
258
267
27 28

Buckingham Palace
Queens Gallery
The Royal Mews
SW1
248
A
B
C
D
1
2
3
4
5
6
Belgravia
BELGRAVE SQUARE
TRINIDAD & TOBAGO
Tenn Ct
BELGIUM
SINGAPORE
THORBURN HO
SYRIA
PORTUGAL
MALAYSIA
TURKEY
IVORY COAST
GHANA
AUSTRIA
GERMANY
BAHRAIN
SERBIA/ MONTENEGRO
NORWAY
BRUNEI
SPAIN
FINLAND
LESOTHO
BOLIVIA
HUNGARY
PERU
DENMARK
ICELAND
PAKISTAN
REP OF SAN MARINO
IRELAND
WILTON CRESCENT
BELGRAVE MEWS N
MOTCOMB STREET
HALKIN ARCADE
GREVILLE HOUSE
LOWNDES COURT
WILTON TERRACE
HALKIN MEWS
WEST HALKIN ST
HALKIN PLACE
BELGRAVE MEWS WEST
CHESHAM MEWS
LOWNDES STREET
CARLTON TOWER PLACE
LOWNDES LODGE
CADOGAN PL
SLOANE STREET
CHESHAM PLACE
LOWNDES PLACE
ROBERTS MEWS
LOWNDES CL
BELGRAVE PLACE
BELGRAVE MEWS S
UPPER BELGRAVE STREET
CHAPEL STREET
GROOM PL
CHESTER STREET
CHESTER MEWS
CHESTER CL
WILTON MEWS
LITTLE CHESTER STREET
WILTON STREET
DORSET MEWS
GROSVENOR PLACE A302
HOBART PLACE
LR GROSVENOR PL
GROSVENOR GARDENS
BEESTON PL
VICTORIA SQUARE
LAKE VIEW CT
WARWICK
EATON LANE
ALLINGTON
VICTORIA ARCADE
Victoria
TERMINUS PL A302
Gatwick Express Terminal
Victoria Station
Victoria Place Sh Ctr
ECCLESTON BRIDGE
BRIDGE PL
Passport Office
EATON ROW
GROSVENOR GDNS MEWS NORTH
BELGRAVE YD
LYGON PLACE
LOWER BELGRAVE ST
ECCLESTON MEWS
STREET
CADOGAN PLACE
CADOGAN LANE
CHESHAM PL
CHESHAM ST
PEMBROKE HO
LYALL MEWS
LYALL STREET
CHESHAM CLOSE
EATON PLACE
EATON MEWS NORTH
EATON SQUARE
Eaton Square Gardens
EATON MEWS SOUTH
CHESTER SQ MEWS
EBURY MEWS EAST
BELGRAVIA COURT
ECCLESTON PLACE
Eaton Square Sch
ECCLESTON STREET
BUCKINGHAM PALACE ROAD
Sch
Tenn Cts
DORCHESTER COURT
OAKLEY HOUSE
CADOGAN GATE
ELLIS ST
PHOENIX HO
D'OYLEY ST
SLOANE GATE MANSIONS
SLOANE TERR MANSIONS
WILBRAHAM PL
SLOANE TERR
SEDDING ST
WEST EATON PL MEWS
EATON TERRACE MEWS
GROSVENOR COTTAGES
CLIVEDEN HO
EATON GATE
A3217 CLIVEDEN PLACE
EATON SQ
MINERA MEWS
EATON TERRACE
SOUTH EATON PLACE
CHESTER ROW
ELIZABETH STREET
EATON MEWS WEST
BOSCOBEL PL
GERALD RD
GERALD MEWS
BURTON MEWS
CHESTER SQUARE
EBURY MEWS
HILDRED HOUSE
EBURY STREET
Liby
BULLEID WAY
ROYAL BELGRAVE HO
HUGH STREET
HUGH MEWS
ECCLESTON SQUARE
257
SLOANE SQUARE
Sloane Square
SKINNER PL
EATON MANSIONS
EATON CLOSE
CAROLINE TERR
BOURNE STREET
TARNBROOK COURT
WHITTAKER ST
ST MICHAEL'S MEWS
GRAHAM TERRACE
Francis Holland Sch
PALACE MEWS
KILMUIR HOUSE
Victoria Coach Station
SEMLEY HOUSE
SEMLEY PLACE
JOHNSON HOUSE
CUNDY ST
EBURY SQUARE
LOCHMORE HO
LOXFORD HO
KYLESTROME HO
COLESHILL FLATS
STACK HO
WALDEN HO
AVERY FARM ROW
FOUNTAIN COURT
National Audit Offices
ELIZABETH BRIDGE
ST GEORGE'S DRIVE
TINTERN HOUSE
GLASTONBURY HO
DRYBURGH HO
WARWICK WAY
EBURY BRIDGE
WYNDHAM HOUSE
SLOANE GARDENS
HOLBEIN PLACE
REMBRANDT CL
LUMLEY FLATS
PASSMORE ST
ORMONDE PL
BUNHOUSE PL
PIMLICO ROAD
St Barnabas CE Prim Sch
RANELAGH GR
BLOOMFIELD TERR
ST BARNABAS ST
DOVE WLK
B324
BRIDGE HO
RYE HO
WESTBOURNE HO
PIMLICO HO
MERCER HO
BUCKNILL HO
VICTORIA HO
DALTON HO
WAINWRIGHT HO
EDGSON HO
HILLERSDON HO
FURNESS HO
KIRKSTALL HO
MELROSE HO
FONTHILL HO
EVESHAM HO
SHERBORNE HO
SUTHERLAND ROW
ALDERNEY STREET
CLARENDON STREET
WINCHESTER STREET
CUMBERLAND STREET
SUSSEX ST
SUTHERLAND STREET
WESTMORELAND TERR
WESTMORELAND PL
Duke of York's Sq
Saatchi Gallery
Duke of York's HQ
Running Tk
LOWER SLOANE STREET
HOLBEIN MS
HOLBEIN HO
YORK HO
TURKS ROW
SLOANE CT E
SLOANE CT W
FRANKLIN'S ROW
BURTON CT
A3214
B302
Chelsea Barracks
City of Westminster
Kensington & Chelsea
CHELSEA BRIDGE ROAD
CHEYLESMORE HO
DONERAILE HO
EBURY BRIDGE ROAD
GATLIFF ROAD
GATCLIFF CL
CHELSEA GATE
WELLINGTON BLDGS
CHELSEA GDNS
HEPWORTH CT
Lister Hospl
HIRST CT
CUBITT BLDG
PAVILLION CT
PEABODY AVENUE
TURPENTINE LANE
PEABODY CL
LUPUS STREET
GILBERT HO
NASH HO
CHIPPENDALE HO
ELGAR HO
SULLIVAN HO
SHERATON HO
PAXTON TERR
Churchill Gdns
GROSVENOR RD
Courts Court
EAST RD
LIGHT HORSE CT
HOSPITAL ROAD
Royal Hospital (Army Pensioners)
COLLEGE COURT
Ranelagh Gardens (Site of Chelsea Flower Show)
WEST ROAD
Tenn Cts
National Army Museum
Thames Path
Dock
A3212
268
28
29
78
79

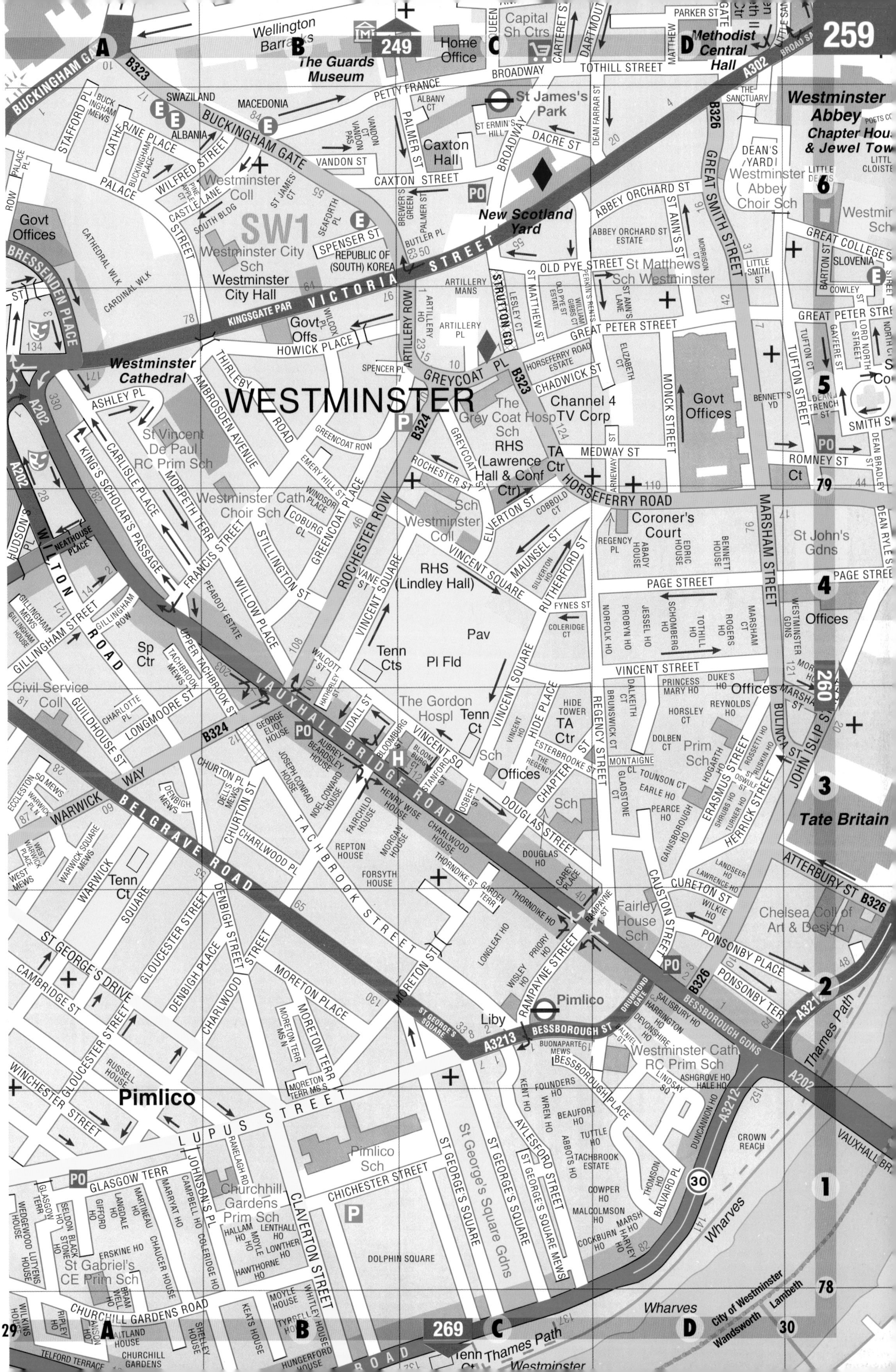

Wellington Barracks
The Guards Museum
249
Home Office
Capital Sh Ctrs
Methodist Central Hall
Tothill Street
Broadway
Petty France
St James's Park
Westminster Abbey
Chapter House & Jewel Tower
Buckingham Gate
Buckingham Palace
Swaziland
Macedonia
Albania
Stafford Pl
Catherine Place
Palace Street
Wilfred Street
Castle Lane
Westminster Coll
SW1
Vandon St
Caxton Street
Caxton Hall
Palmer St
Dacre St
Dean Farrar St
New Scotland Yard
Great Smith Street
Dean's Yard
Westminster Abbey Choir Sch
Abbey Orchard St
Abbey Orchard St Estate
St Ann's St
Spenser St
Republic of (South) Korea
Butler Pl
Westminster City Sch
Westminster City Hall
Govt Offices
Victoria Street
Kingsgate Par
Bressenden Place
Cardinal Wlk
Cathedral Wlk
Old Pye Street
St Matthews Sch Westminster
Great College St
Slovenia
Little Smith St
Artillery Row
Artillery Mans
Artillery Pl
Strutton Gd
Lesley Ct
St Matthew St
Great Peter Street
Tufton St
Lord North Street
Howick Place
Govt Offs
Westminster Cathedral
Spencer Pl
Greycoat Pl
Horseferry Road Estate
Chadwick St
Elizabeth Ct
Monck Street
Govt Offices
Bennett's Yd
Smith Sq
Channel 4 TV Corp
WESTMINSTER
Ashley Pl
Thirleby Road
Ambrosden Avenue
Greencoat Row
The Grey Coat Hosp Sch
RHS (Lawrence Hall & Conf Ctr)
TA Ctr
Medway St
Romney St
St Vincent De Paul RC Prim Sch
Carlisle Place
Morpeth Terr
King's Scholar's Passage
Emery Hill St
Windsor Place
Greencoat Place
Rochester Row
Rochester St
Greycoat St
Horseferry Road
Coroner's Court
Marsham Street
St John's Gdns
Westminster Cath Choir Sch
Coburg Cl
Stillington St
Sch
Westminster Coll
Elverton St
Cobbold Ct
Maunsel St
Rutherford St
Regency Pl
Abady House
Edric House
Bennett House
Neathouse Place
Wilton Road
Hudson's Pl
Francis Street
Vincent Square
RHS (Lindley Hall)
Page Street
Fynes St
Norfolk Ho
Probyn Ho
Jessel Ho
Schomberg Ho
Tothill Ho
Rogers Ho
Marsham Ct
Offices
Gillingham Street
Gillingham Mews
Gillingham Row
Sp Ctr
Peabody Estate
Willow Place
Tenn Cts
Pl Fld
Pav
Coleridge Ct
Vincent Street
Upper Tachbrook St
Walcott St
Hatherley St
Princess Mary Ho
Duke's Ho
Horsley Ct
Reynolds Ho
260
Civil Service Coll
Guildhouse St
Charlotte Pl
Longmoore St
Vauxhall Bridge Road
Udall St
The Gordon Hospl
Tenn Ct
Hide Place
Hide Tower
Regency Street
Dalkeith Ct
Brunswick Ct
Dolben Ct
Prim Sch
Bulinca St
John Islip St
B324
George Eliot House
Aubrey Beardsley House
Bloomburg St
Vincent Sq
Esterbrooke St
Chapter St
Montaigne Cl
Tounson Ct
Earle Ho
Hogarth Ho
Erasmus Street
Rossetti Ho
Ruskin Ho
Warwick Way
Churton Pl
Churton St
Denbigh Mews
Joseph Conrad House
Noel Coward House
Henry Wise House
Fairchild House
Stanford St
Osbert St
Douglas Street
Gladstone Ct
Pearce Ho
Gainsborough Ho
Shrubs Ho
Turner Ho
Herrick Street
Tate Britain
Belgrave Road
Charlwood Pl
Tachbrook Street
Repton House
Morgan House
Charlwood House
Forsyth House
Thorndike St
Garden Terr
Douglas Ho
Carey Place
Landseer Ho
Lawrence Ho
Atterbury St
Eccleston Sq Mews
Warwick Pl N
West Warwick Place
West Mews
Warwick Square Mews
Warwick Square
Tenn Ct
Gloucester Street
Denbigh Street
Thorndike Ho
Rampayne St
Fairley House Sch
Causton Street
Cureton St
Wilkie Ho
Chelsea Coll of Art & Design
Ponsonby Place
Longleat Ho
Priory Ho
Wisley Ho
Rampayne Street
St George's Drive
Cambridge St
Denbigh Place
Charlwood Street
Moreton Place
Moreton St
Moreton Terr
Moreton Terr Ms N
Moreton Terr Ms S
St George's Square
Pimlico
Liby
Bessborough St
Drummond Gate
Salisbury Ho
Harrington Ho
Devonshire Ho
Bessborough Gdns
Ponsonby Ter
Thames Path
A3213
A3212
A202
Winchester Street
Russell House
Buonaparte Mews
Bessborough Place
Westminster Cath RC Prim Sch
Lindsay Sq
Ashgrove Ho
Hale Ho
Kent Ho
Wren Ho
Founders Ho
Beaufort Ho
Abbots Ho
Tuttle Ho
Tachbrook Estate
Aylesford Street
Duncannon Ho
Crown Reach
Vauxhall Br
Lupus Street
Ranelagh Rd
Johnson's Pl
Pimlico Sch
Chichester Street
St George's Square Gdns
St George's Square Mews
Thomson Ho
Balvaird Pl
Cowper Ho
Malcolmson Ho
Marsh Ho
Cockburn Ho
Harvey Ho
Wharves
Glasgow Terr
Churchill Gardens Prim Sch
Campbell Ho
Coleridge Ho
Marryat Ho
Martineau Ho
Chaucer House
Langdale Ho
Gifford Ho
Seldon Ho
Stone Ho
Black Ho
Wedgewood House
Lutyens House
Glasgow Terr
Erskine Ho
St Gabriel's CE Prim Sch
Bramwell Ho
Hallam Ho
Lenthall Ho
Moyle Ho
Lowther Ho
Hawthorne Ho
Claverton Street
Dolphin Square
Churchill Gardens Road
Ripley Ho
Wilkins House
Anson Ho
Aitland House
Shelley House
Keats House
Moyle House
Whitley House
Tyrrell Ho
Hungerford House
Telford Terrace
Churchill Gardens
269
Thames Path
Westminster
City of Westminster
Wandsworth
Lambeth
Wharves
A B C D
29
30
78
79
1 2 3 4 5 6

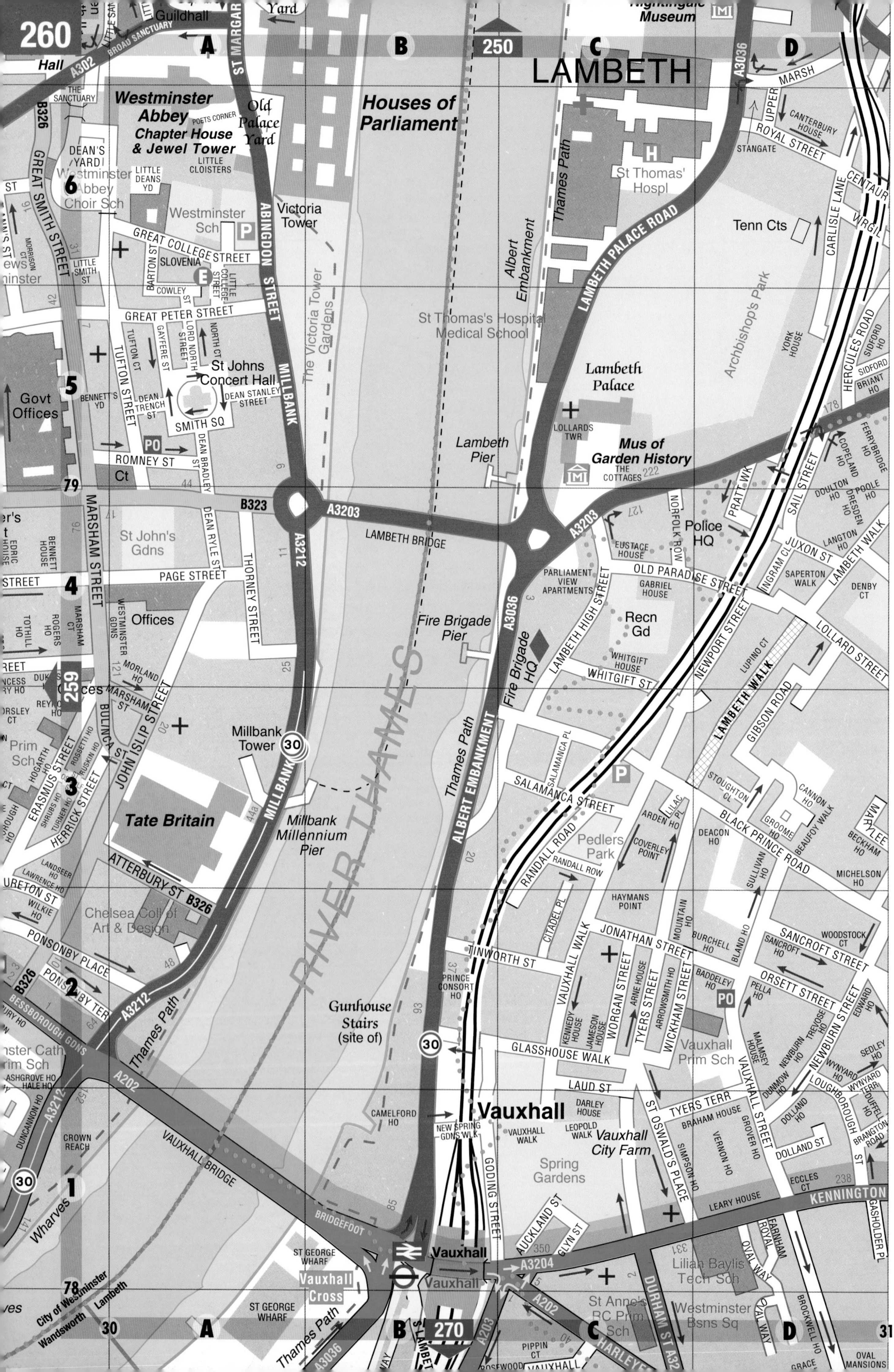
LAMBETH
Houses of Parliament
Westminster Abbey
Chapter House & Jewel Tower
Old Palace Yard
Victoria Tower
Guildhall
Broad Sanctuary
The Sanctuary
Poets Corner
Little Cloisters
Little Deans Yd
Dean's Yard
Westminster Abbey Choir Sch
Westminster Sch
Great College Street
Slovenia
Barton St
Cowley St
Little College Street
Great Peter Street
Tufton Ct
Tufton Street
Gayfere St
Lord North Street
North Ct
St Johns Concert Hall
Dean Trench St
Dean Stanley Street
Smith Sq
Bennett's Yd
Govt Offices
Romney St
Dean Bradley St
Millbank
Abingdon Street
St Margaret
Great Smith Street
Little Smith St
Morrison Ct
Marsham Street
B323
A3203
A3212
Lambeth Bridge
St John's Gdns
Dean Ryle St
Thorney Street
Page Street
Offices
Westminster Gdns
Morland Ho
Marsham St
Bulinga St
John Islip Street
Millbank Tower
Tate Britain
Millbank Millennium Pier
Atterbury St
B326
Chelsea Coll of Art & Design
Ponsonby Place
Ponsonby Ter
Bessborough Gdns
A202
Ashgrove Ho
Hale Ho
Duncannon Ho
Crown Reach
Vauxhall Bridge
Bridgefoot
Wharves
City of Westminster
Lambeth
Wandsworth
Erasmus Street
Herrick Street
Hogarth
Rossetti Ho
Ruskin Ho
Shrubs Ho
Turner Ho
Landseer Ho
Lawrence Ho
Wilkie Ho
Prim Sch
The Victoria Tower Gardens
RIVER THAMES
St Thomas's Hospital Medical School
Thames Path
Albert Embankment
Lambeth Pier
Fire Brigade Pier
Gunhouse Stairs (site of)
St Thomas' Hospl
Lambeth Palace Road
Lambeth Palace
Lollards Twr
Mus of Garden History
The Cottages
Archbishop's Park
Nightingale Museum
A3036
Upper Marsh
Canterbury House
Royal Street
Stangate
Carlisle Lane
Centaur
Virgil
Tenn Cts
York House
Hercules Road
Sidford Ho
Sidford
Briant Ho
Ferrybridge Ho
Copeland Ho
Poole Ho
Doulton Ho
Dresden Ho
Langton Ho
Sail Street
Pratt Wk
Norfolk Row
Police HQ
Eustace House
Parliament View Apartments
Old Paradise Street
Gabriel House
Lambeth High Street
Recn Gd
Whitgift House
Whitgift St
Fire Brigade HQ
Newport Street
Juxon St
Ingram Cl
Saperton Walk
Lambeth Walk
Denby Ct
Lollard Street
Lupino Ct
Gibson Road
Salamanca Pl
Salamanca Street
Stoughton Cl
Cannon Ho
Groome Ho
Beaufoy Walk
Marylee
Beckham Ho
Black Prince Road
Deacon Ho
Arden Ho
Lilac Pl
Coverley Point
Pedlers Park
Randall Road
Randall Row
Haymans Point
Citadel Pl
Mountain Ho
Sullivan Ho
Michelson Ho
Jonathan Street
Burchell Ho
Bland Ho
Sancroft Ho
Sancroft Street
Woodstock Ct
Tinworth St
Vauxhall Walk
Prince Consort Ho
Worgan Street
Tyers Street
Arne House
Arrowsmith Ho
Wickham Street
Baddeley Ho
Pella Ho
Orsett Street
Newburn Street
Edward Ho
Treveose Ho
Kennedy House
Jameson House
Glasshouse Walk
Vauxhall Prim Sch
Malmsey House
Dunmow Ho
Newburn Ho
Sedley Ho
Wynyard Ho
Wynyard Terr
Loughborough St
Duffield Ho
Laud St
Darley House
Tyers Terr
Braham House
Vauxhall Street
Dolland Ho
Dolland St
Brangton Road
Vauxhall
Camelford Ho
New Spring Gdns Wlk
Vauxhall Walk
Leopold Walk
Vauxhall City Farm
Spring Gardens
St Oswald's Place
Simpson Ho
Vernon Ho
Grover Ho
Leary House
Eccles Ct
Kennington
Gasholder Pl
Goding Street
Auckland St
Glyn St
A3204
Royal
Farnham
Oval Way
Lilian Baylis Tech Sch
St Anne's RC Prim Sch
Westminster Bsns Sq
Durham St A3202
Brockwell Ho
Harleyford
St George Wharf
Vauxhall Cross
Vauxhall
Pippin Ct
Oval Mansions
Grace
Rosewood
A203
S Lambeth
A B C D
1 2 3 4 5 6
250
259
270
31

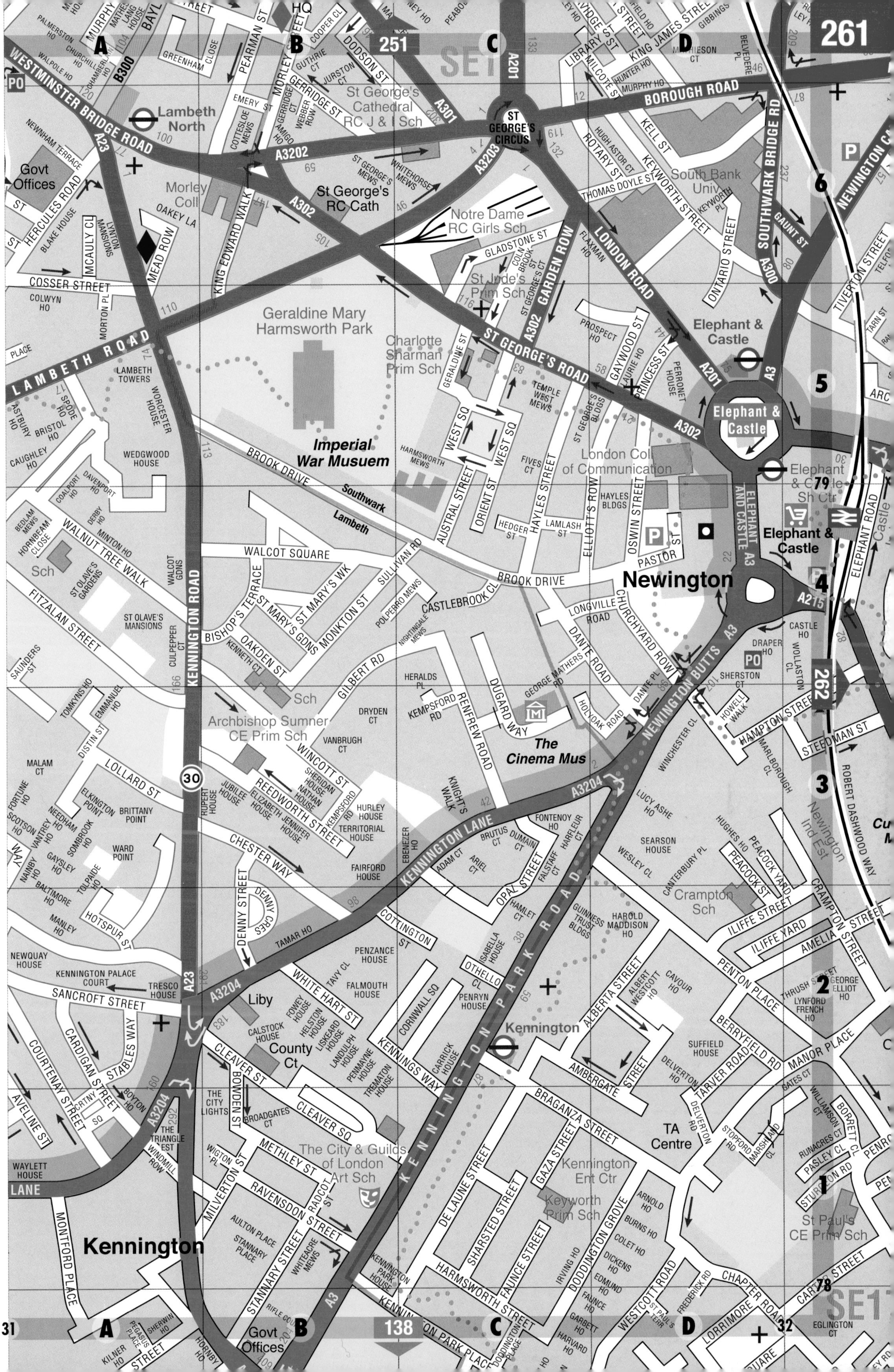

SE1
A
B
C
D
251
Westminster Bridge Road
Lambeth North
Govt Offices
Hercules Road
Morley Coll
Oakey La
Mead Row
King Edward Walk
St George's RC Cath
St George's Cathedral RC J & I Sch
St George's Circus
Borough Road
South Bank Univ
Southwark Bridge Rd
Keyworth Street
London Road
Thomas Doyle St
Notre Dame RC Girls Sch
Gladstone St
Garden Row
St Jude's Prim Sch
Ontario Street
Elephant & Castle
Cosser Street
Lambeth Road
Geraldine Mary Harmsworth Park
Imperial War Musuem
Charlotte Sharman Prim Sch
St George's Road
West Sq
Austral Street
Orient St
Hayles Street
Elliott's Row
Oswin Street
London Coll of Communication
Elephant & Castle Sh Ctr
Brook Drive
Walcot Square
Southwark
Lambeth
Walnut Tree Walk
Fitzalan Street
Kennington Road
Bishop's Terrace
St Mary's Gdns
Monkton St
Sullivan Rd
Castlebrook Cl
Newington
Longville Road
Dante Road
Churchyard Row
Newington Butts
Gilbert Rd
Renfrew Road
Dugard Way
The Cinema Mus
Archbishop Sumner CE Prim Sch
Reedworth Street
Chester Way
Lollard St
Kennington Lane
Kennington Park Road
Hampton Street
Steedman St
Robert Dashwood Way
Newington Ind Est
Crampton Sch
Crampton Street
Iliffe Street
Iliffe Yard
Amelia Street
Penton Place
Manor Place
Berryfield Rd
Liby
County Ct
Kennington
Cleaver Sq
The City & Guilds of London Art Sch
Kennington Ent Ctr
Keyworth Prim Sch
Braganza Street
Ambergate Street
Alberta Street
TA Centre
St Paul's CE Prim Sch
Cardigan Street
Courtenay Street
Aveline St
Montford Place
Milverton St
Ravensdon Street
Methley St
Stannary Street
De Laune Street
Sharsted Street
Faunce Street
Harmsworth Street
Doddington Grove
Westcott Road
Chapter Road
Carter Street
Lorrimore
Kennington Park Place
262
79
78

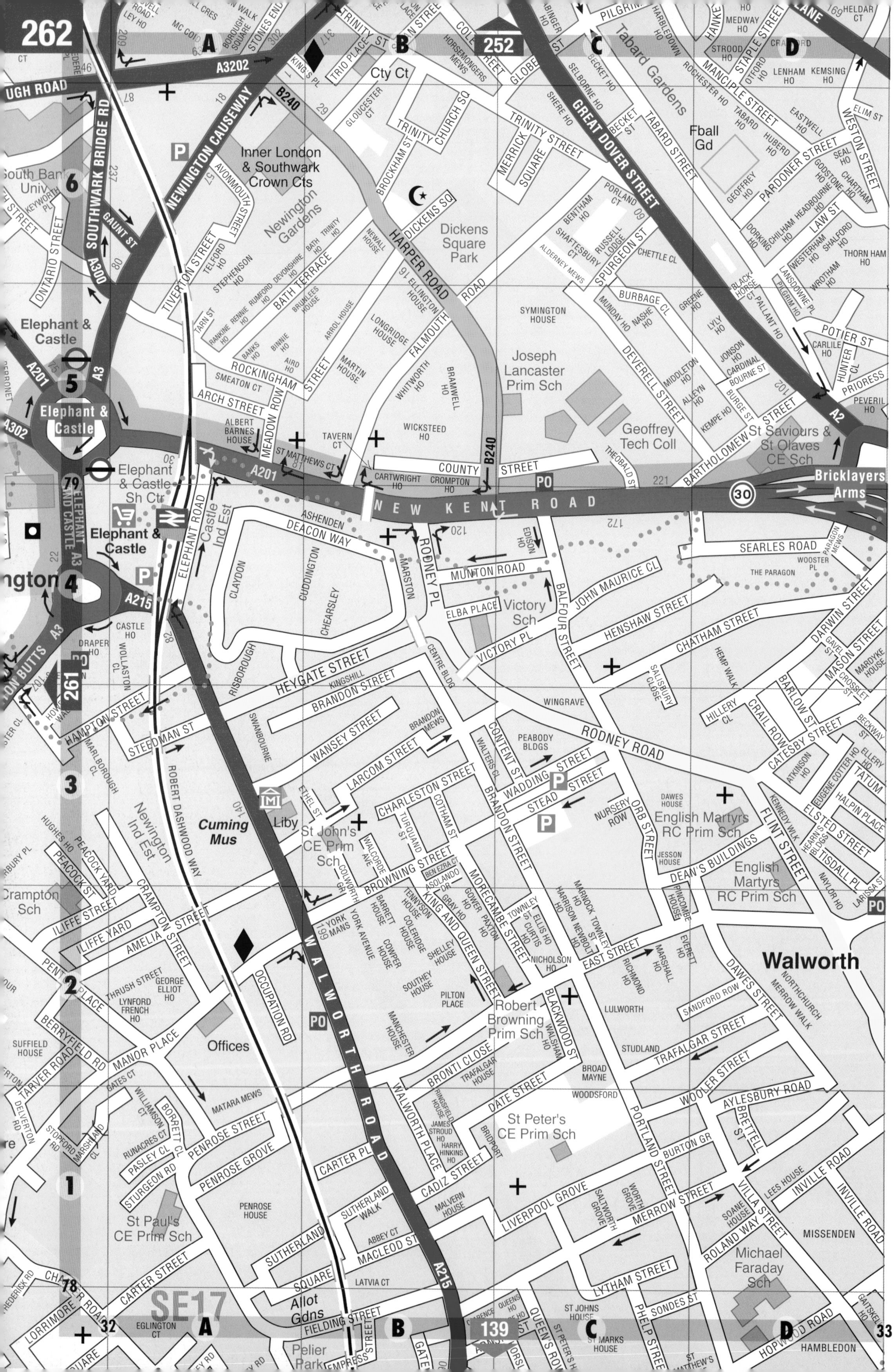
A
B
C
D
252
A3202
B240
NEWINGTON CAUSEWAY
SOUTHWARK BRIDGE RD
A300
GAUNT ST
TRINITY ST
TRIO PLACE
Cty Ct
GLOUCESTER CT
TRINITY CHURCH SQ
HORSEMONGERS MEWS
GLOBE
MERRICK SQUARE
TRINITY STREET
GREAT DOVER STREET
PILGRIM
BECKET HO
SELBORNE HO
SHERE HO
BECKET ST
Tabard Gardens
TABARD STREET
Fball Gd
MANCIPLE STREET
STAPLE STREET
LENHAM HO
KEMSING HO
STROOD HO
MEDWAY HO
HELDAR CT
ROCHESTER HO
TABARD HO
HUBERD HO
EASTWELL HO
WESTON STREET
ELIM ST
PARDONER STREET
GEOFFREY HO
GODSTONE HO
SEAL HO
CHARTHAM
HEADBOURNE HO
CHILHAM HO
DORKING HO
LAW ST
WESTERHAM HO
SHALFORD HO
THORN HAM HO
WROTHAM HO
LANSDOWNE PL
PILGRIM HO
Inner London & Southwark Crown Cts
Newington Gardens
AVONMOUTH STREET
BROCKHAM ST
DICKENS SQ
HARPER ROAD
Dickens Square Park
PORLAND CT
BENTHAM HO
SHAFTESBURY CT
RUSSELL LODGE
SPURGEON ST
CHETTLE CL
ALDERNEY MEWS
BURBAGE CL
GREENE HO
MUNDAY HO
NASHE HO
LYLY HO
BLACK HORSE CT
PALLANT HO
POTIER ST
CARLILE HO
HUNTER CL
PRIORESS
PEVERIL HO
A2
South Bank Univ
KEYWORTH
ONTARIO STREET
TIVERTON STREET
TELFORD HO
STEPHENSON HO
RUMFORD HO
DEVONSHIRE HO
BATH HO
TRINITY HO
BATH TERRACE
NEWALL HOUSE
BRUNLEES HOUSE
TARN ST
RANKINE HO
RENNIE HO
BANKS HO
BINNIE HO
AIRD HO
ARROL HOUSE
ELLINGTON HOUSE
LONGRIDGE HOUSE
FALMOUTH ROAD
SYMINGTON HOUSE
Joseph Lancaster Prim Sch
DEVERELL STREET
MIDDLETON HO
JONSON HO
CARDINAL BOURNE ST
ALLEYN HO
KEMPE HO
BURGE ST
Elephant & Castle
ROCKINGHAM STREET
SMEATON CT
ARCH STREET
MARTIN HOUSE
WHITWORTH HO
BRAMWELL HO
WICKSTEED HO
Geoffrey Tech Coll
St Saviours & St Olaves CE Sch
BARTHOLOMEW STREET
A201
A3
A302
ALBERT BARNES HOUSE
MEADOW ROW
TAVERN CT
ST MATTHEWS CT
COUNTY STREET
CARTWRIGHT HO
CROMPTON HO
THEOBALD ST
PO
Bricklayers Arms
30
NEW KENT ROAD
Elephant & Castle Sh Ctr
ELEPHANT AND CASTLE
Castle Ind Est
ELEPHANT ROAD
ASHENDEN
DEACON WAY
CLAYDON
CUDDINGTON
CHEARSLEY
MARSTON
RODNEY PL
EDISON HO
MUNTON ROAD
SEARLES ROAD
PARAGON MEWS
WOOSTER PL
THE PARAGON
JOHN MAURICE CL
ELBA PLACE
Victory Sch
BALFOUR STREET
HENSHAW STREET
CHATHAM STREET
DARWIN STREET
A215
CASTLE HO
DRAPER HO
WOLLASTON CL
RISBOROUGH
HEYGATE STREET
KINGSHILL
BRANDON STREET
CENTRE BLDG
VICTORY PL
HEMP WALK
SALISBURY CLOSE
BARLOW ST
GAVEL ST
MASON STREET
MARDYKE HOUSE
CROSSLET ST
261
HAMPTON STREET
STEEDMAN ST
MARLBOROUGH CL
SWAMBOURNE
WANSEY STREET
BRANDON MEWS
WINGRAVE
HILLERY CL
CRAIL ROW
CATESBY STREET
BECKWAY ST
RODNEY ROAD
CONTENT ST
WALTERS CL
PEABODY BLDGS
WADDING STREET
STEAD STREET
ATKINSON HO
EUGENE COTTER HO
ELLERY ST
TATUM ST
ROBERT DASHWOOD WAY
LARCOM STREET
CHARLESTON STREET
COTHAM ST
NURSERY ROW
ORB STREET
DAWES HOUSE
English Martyrs RC Prim Sch
KENNEDY WLK
ELSTED STREET
HALPIN PLACE
Newington Ind Est
Cuming Mus
Liby
ETHEL ST
St John's CE Prim Sch
TURQUAND ST
HEARN'S BLDGS
TISDALL PL
NAYLOR HO
LARISSA ST
HUGHES HO
PEACOCK YARD
PEACOCK ST
Crampton Sch
CRAMPTON STREET
ILIFFE STREET
ILIFFE YARD
AMELIA STREET
WALCORDE AVE
COLWORTH GR
BROWNING STREET
BEN EZRA CT
ASOLANDO DR
MORECAMBE STREET
JESSON HOUSE
DEAN'S BUILDINGS
FLINT STREET
PINCOMBE HOUSE
YORK MANS
YORK AVENUE
BARRETT HOUSE
TENNYSON HOUSE
COLERIDGE HOUSE
GRAY HO
GOWER HO
PAXTON HO
KING AND QUEEN STREET
TOWNLEY ST
ELLIS HO
CURTIS HO
HARRISON HO
NEWBOLT HO
MARNOCK HO
TOWNLEY ST
Walworth
COWPER HOUSE
SHELLEY HOUSE
NICHOLSON HO
EAST STREET
MARSHALL HO
EVERETT HO
RICHMOND HO
DAWES STREET
NORTHCHURCH
MERROW WALK
PENTON PLACE
THRUSH STREET
GEORGE ELLIOT HO
LYNFORD FRENCH HO
OCCUPATION RD
WALWORTH ROAD
SOUTHEY HOUSE
PILTON PLACE
Robert Browning Prim Sch
BLACKWOOD ST
WALSHAM
LULWORTH
SANDFORD ROW
SUFFIELD HOUSE
BERRYFIELD RD
TARVER ROAD
MANOR PLACE
Offices
MANCHESTER HOUSE
STUDLAND
TRAFALGAR STREET
BRONTI CLOSE
TRAFALGAR HOUSE
BROAD MAYNE
WOOLER STREET
AYLESBURY ROAD
GATES CT
WILLIAMSON CT
BORRETT CL
MATARA MEWS
WALWORTH PLACE
DATE STREET
WOODSFORD
PORTLAND STREET
BRETTELL ST
DELVERTON RD
STOPFORD RD
MARSHLAND CL
RUNACRES CT
PENROSE STREET
PASLEY CL
PENROSE GROVE
STURGEON RD
RINGSFIELD HOUSE
JAMES STROUD HO
HARRY HINKINS HO
BRIDPORT
St Peter's CE Prim Sch
CARTER PL
CADIZ STREET
BURTON GR
INVILLE ROAD
LEES HOUSE
PENROSE HOUSE
St Paul's CE Prim Sch
SUTHERLAND WALK
MALVERN HOUSE
LIVERPOOL GROVE
SALTWORTH GROVE
WORTH GROVE
MERROW STREET
SOANE HOUSE
VILLA STREET
MISSENDEN
ROLAND WAY
ABBEY CT
MACLEOD ST
SUTHERLAND SQUARE
LATVIA CT
Michael Faraday Sch
CARTER STREET
LYTHAM STREET
78
SE17
Allot Gdns
FIELDING STREET
CLARENCE HO
QUEENS HO
QUEEN'S ROW
ST JOHNS HOUSE
SONDES ST
PHELP STREET
GAITSKELL HO
LORRIMORE ROAD
EGLINGTON CT
Pelier Park
EMPRESS STREET
139
ST MARKS HOUSE
HOPWOOD ROAD
HAMBLEDON
1
2
3
4
5
6

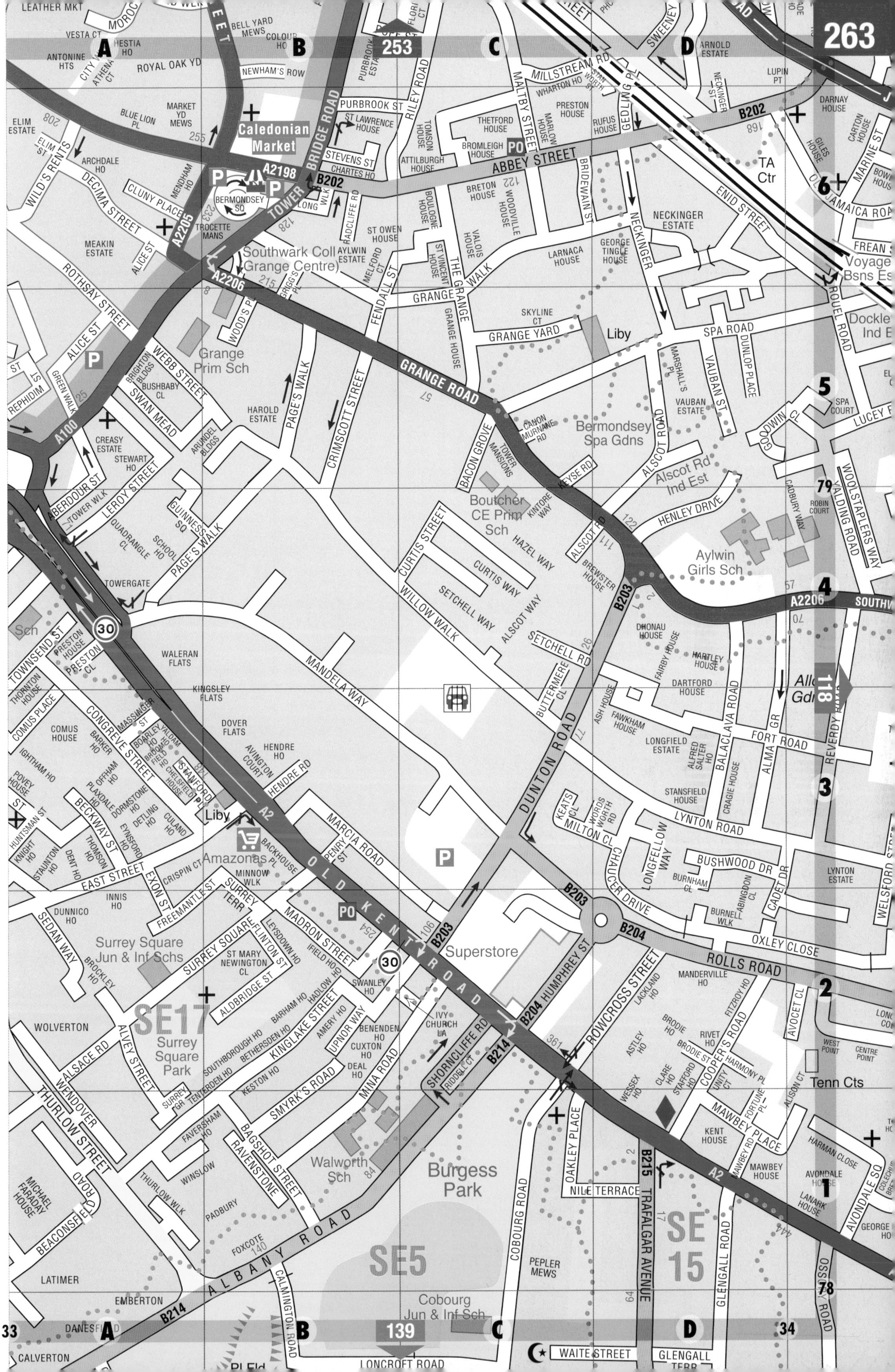

LEATHER MKT
MOROCCO
BELL YARD MEWS
COLOUR HO
VESTA CT
HESTIA HO
ANTONINE HTS
CITY WALK
ATHENA CT
ROYAL OAK YD
NEWHAM'S ROW
253
PURBROOK ESTATE
RILEY ROAD
FLORIS CT
SWEENEY
ARNOLD ESTATE
LUPIN PT
MILLSTREAM RD
WHARTON HO
STANWORTH ST
MALTBY STREET
GEDLING PL
NECKINGER ST
DARNAY HOUSE
B202
CARTON HOUSE
GILES HOUSE
MARINE ST
BLUE LION PL
MARKET YD MEWS
Caledonian Market
PURBROOK ST
ST LAWRENCE HOUSE
THETFORD HOUSE
PRESTON HOUSE
RUFUS HOUSE
MARLOW HOUSE
TOMSON HOUSE
BROMLEIGH HOUSE
PO
ELIM ESTATE
ELIM ST
WILD'S RENTS
ARCHDALE HO
DECIMA STREET
MENDHAM HO
CLUNY PLACE
A2198
STEVENS ST
CHARTES HO
ATTILBURGH HOUSE
ABBEY STREET
BRIDEWAIN ST
TA Ctr
BERMONDSEY SQ
B202
TOWER BRIDGE ROAD
LONG WLK
RADCLIFFE RD
BOULOGNE HOUSE
BRETON HOUSE
WOODVILLE HOUSE
ENID STREET
NECKINGER ESTATE
OLD JAMAICA ROAD
MEAKIN ESTATE
A2205
TROCETTE MANS
ST OWEN HOUSE
VALOIS HOUSE
NECKINGER
FREAN ST
ALICE ST
Southwark Coll (Grange Centre)
AYLWIN ESTATE
MELFORD CT
ST VINCENT HOUSE
THE GRANGE
LARNACA HOUSE
GEORGE TINGLE HOUSE
Voyager Bsns Est
ROTHSAY STREET
A2206
GRIGG'S PL
FENDALL ST
GRANGE WALK
ROUEL ROAD
WOOD'S PL
SKYLINE CT
Dockley Ind E
GRANGE YARD
Liby
SPA ROAD
ALICE ST
Grange Prim Sch
GRANGE HOUSE
MARSHALL'S PL
VAUBAN ST
DUNLOP PLACE
WEBB STREET
GRANGE ROAD
ST
REPHIDIM ST
GREEN WALK
BRIGHTON BLDGS
BUSHBABY CL
SWAN MEAD
HAROLD ESTATE
PAGE'S WALK
CRIMSCOTT STREET
CANON MURNANE RD
Bermondsey Spa Gdns
VAUBAN ESTATE
GOODWIN CL
SPA COURT
LUCEY RD
5
A100
CREASY ESTATE
STEWART HO
ARUNDEL BLDGS
BACON GROVE
TOWER MANSIONS
KEYSE RD
ALSCOT ROAD
Alscot Rd Ind Est
CADBURY WAY
79
ROBIN COURT
WOOLSTAPLERS WAY
YALDING ROAD
ABERDOUR ST
TOWER WLK
LEROY STREET
GUINNESS SQ
Boutcher CE Prim Sch
KINTORE WAY
HENLEY DRIVE
QUADRANGLE CL
SCHOOL HO
PAGE'S WALK
CURTIS STREET
HAZEL WAY
ALSCOT RD
CURTIS WAY
BREWSTER HOUSE
Aylwin Girls Sch
TOWERGATE
SETCHELL WAY
ALSCOT WAY
B203
4
A2206
SOUTHWARK PARK RD
WILLOW WALK
Sch
30
TOWNSEND ST
PRESTON HOUSE
PRESTON CL
WALERAN FLATS
MANDELA WAY
SETCHELL RD
DHONAU HOUSE
FAIRBY HOUSE
HARTLEY HOUSE
THORNTON HOUSE
KINGSLEY FLATS
BUTTERMERE CL
DARTFORD HOUSE
118
COMUS PLACE
COMUS HOUSE
CONGREVE STREET
MASSINGER ST
DOVER FLATS
ASH HOUSE
FAWKHAM HOUSE
BALACLAVA ROAD
ALMA GR
FORT ROAD
REVERDY RD
BARKER HO
BOARLEY HO
VALDAM HO
BROOMFIELD HO
CHELSFIELD HO
HENDRE HO
DUNTON ROAD
LONGFIELD ESTATE
ALFRED SALTER HO
IGHTHAM HO
OFFHAM HO
STAINFORD CL
AVINGTON COURT
HENDRE RD
CRAGIE HOUSE
3
POVEY HOUSE
PLAXDALE HO
DORMSTONE HO
DETLING HO
CULAND HO
A2
KEATS CL
WORDSWORTH RD
STANSFIELD HOUSE
HUNTSMAN ST
BECKWAY ST
EYNSFORD HO
Liby
MARCIA ROAD
MILTON CL
LONGFELLOW WAY
LYNTON ROAD
KNIGHT HO
THOMSON HO
Amazonas
BACKHOUSE PL
PENRY ST
P
BUSHWOOD DR
LYNTON ESTATE
STAUNTON HO
DENT HO
EAST STREET
EXON ST
CRISPIN CT
MINNOW WLK
OLD KENT ROAD
CHAUCER DRIVE
BURNHAM CL
ABINGDON CL
CADET DR
WELSFORD STREET
INNIS HO
FREMANTLE ST
SURREY TERR
B203
BURNELL WLK
DUNNICO HO
SEDAN WAY
PO
MADRON STREET
LEYSDOWN HO
B204
OXLEY CLOSE
Surrey Square Jun & Inf Schs
SURREY SQUARE
FLINTON ST
ST MARY NEWINGTON CL
IFIELD HO
Superstore
ROLLS ROAD
MANDERVILLE HO
BROCKLEY HO
ALDBRIDGE ST
SWANLEY HO
HUMPHREY ST
ROWCROSS STREET
LACKLAND HO
2
SE17
BARHAM HO
HADLOW HO
KINGLAKE STREET
IVY CHURCH LA
B204
FITZROY HO
AVOCET CL
LONG CO
WOLVERTON
Surrey Square Park
BETHERSDEN HO
AMERY HO
UPNOR WAY
BENENDEN HO
SHORNCLIFFE RD
BRODIE HO
RIVET HO
COOPER'S ROAD
ALSACE RD
ALVEY STREET
SOUTHBOROUGH HO
CUXTON HO
361
ASTLEY HO
BRODIE ST
HARMONY PL
WEST POINT
CENTRE POINT
DEAL HO
MINA ROAD
B214
RIDDELL CT
WESSEX HO
CLARE HO
STAFFORD HO
UNITY CT
ALISON CT
Tenn Cts
WENDOVER
SURREY GR
TENTERDEN HO
KESTON HO
SMYRK'S ROAD
FORTUNE PL
THURLOW STREET
FAVERSHAM HO
BAGSHOT STREET
OAKLEY PLACE
MAWBEY PLACE
KENT HOUSE
HARMAN CLOSE
RAVENSTONE
MAWBEY RD
MAWBEY HOUSE
AVONDALE HOUSE
1
MICHAEL FARADAY HOUSE
BEACONSFIELD ROAD
THURLOW WLK
WINSLOW
Walworth Sch
Burgess Park
B215 TRAFALGAR AVENUE
NILE TERRACE
LANARK HOUSE
AVONDALE SQ
COLEGHURST
PADBURY
ALBANY ROAD
COBOURG ROAD
GLENGALL ROAD
GEORGE HO
FOXCOTE
SE5
PEPLER MEWS
SE 15
LATIMER
CALMINGTON ROAD
OSSORY ROAD
78
EMBERTON
Cobourg Jun & Inf Sch
33
DANESFIELD
A
B
139
C
D
34
CALVERTON
WAITE STREET
GLENGALL TERR
LONCROFT ROAD
6
Alls Gdn

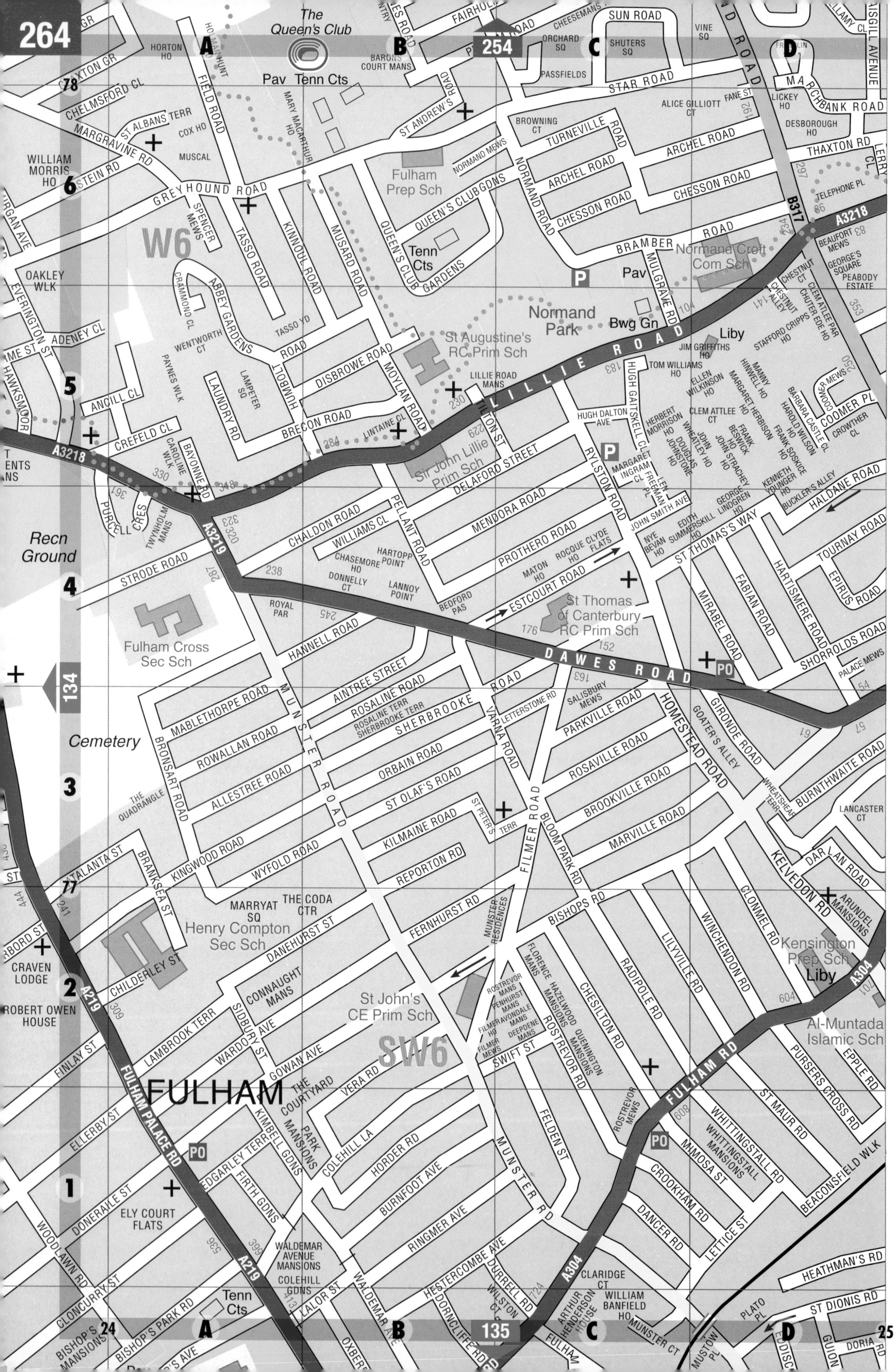
A
B
C
D
254
The Queen's Club
Pav Tenn Cts
HORTON HO
BARONS COURT MANS
SUN ROAD
VINE SQ
ORCHARD SQ
SHUTERS SQ
PASSFIELDS
STAR ROAD
CHEESEMANS
FAIRHOLME
MARCHBANK ROAD
LICKEY HO
DESBOROUGH HO
THAXTON RD
ALICE GILLIOTT CT
FANE ST
78
CHELMSFORD CL
ST ALBANS TERR
COX HO
MARGRAVINE RD
WILLIAM MORRIS HO
STEIN RD
MUSCAL
FIELD ROAD
MARY MACARTHUR HO
ST ANDREW'S ROAD
BROWNING CT
TURNEVILLE ROAD
ARCHEL ROAD
CHESSON ROAD
NORMAND MEWS
NORMAND ROAD
Fulham Prep Sch
QUEEN'S CLUB GDNS
QUEEN'S CLUB GARDENS
Tenn Cts
6
GREYHOUND ROAD
SPENCER MEWS
TASSO ROAD
KINNOUL ROAD
MUSARD ROAD
W6
BRAMBER ROAD
MULGRAVE RD
Normand Croft Com Sch
TELEPHONE PL
A3218
B317
BEAUFORT MEWS
GEORGE'S SQUARE
PEABODY ESTATE
P
Pav
OAKLEY WLK
EVERINGTON ST
CRAMMOND CL
ABBEY GARDENS
TASSO YD
Normand Park
Bwg Gn
CHESTNUT CT
CHESTNUT ALLEY
CHUTER EDE HO
CLEM ATTLEE PAR
ADENEY CL
WENTWORTH CT
PAYNES WLK
HOWBOLT ROAD
DISBROWE ROAD
MOYLAN ROAD
St Augustine's RC Prim Sch
Liby
JIM GRIFFITHS HO
STAFFORD CRIPPS HO
TOM WILLIAMS HO
LILLIE ROAD
HUGH GAITSKELL CL
5
ANGILL CL
LAMPETER SQ
LAUNDRY RD
BRECON ROAD
LILLIE ROAD MANS
ELLEN WILKINSON HO
MARGARET HERBISON HO
MANNY HINWELL HO
BARBARA CASTLE CL
HAROLD WILSON HO
COOMER MEWS
COOMER PL
CREFELD CL
CAROLINE WLK
BAYONNE RD
LINTAINE CL
TILTON ST
HUGH DALTON AVE
HERBERT MORRISON HO
CLEM ATTLEE CT
CROWTHER CL
Sir John Lillie Prim Sch
DELAFORD STREET
RYLSTON ROAD
WHEATLEY HO
DOUGLAS JOHNSTONE HO
JOHN STRACHEY HO
FRANK BESWICK HO
FRANK SOSKICE HO
MARGARET INGRAM CL
LEN FREEMAN PL
JOHN SMITH AVE
GEORGE LINDGREN HO
KENNETH YOUNGER HO
BUCKLER'S ALLEY
HALDANE ROAD
PURCELL CRES
TWYNHOLM MANS
A3219
Recn Ground
CHALDON ROAD
PELLANT ROAD
MENDORA ROAD
WILLIAMS CL
HARTOPP POINT
CHASEMORE HO
PROTHERO ROAD
ROCQUE HO
CLYDE FLATS
NYE BEVAN HO
EDITH SUMMERSKILL HO
ST THOMAS'S WAY
TOURNAY ROAD
4
STRODE ROAD
DONNELLY CT
LANNOY POINT
MATON HO
ESTCOURT ROAD
MIRABEL ROAD
FABIAN ROAD
HARTISMERE ROAD
EPIRUS ROAD
ROYAL PAR
BEDFORD PAS
St Thomas of Canterbury RC Prim Sch
Fulham Cross Sec Sch
HANNELL ROAD
DAWES ROAD
SHORROLDS ROAD
PO
PALACE MEWS
134
AINTREE STREET
ROSALINE ROAD
ROSALINE TERR
SHERBROOKE TERR
SHERBROOKE ROAD
LETTERSTONE RD
SALISBURY MEWS
PARKVILLE ROAD
HOMESTEAD ROAD
GOATER'S ALLEY
GIRONDE ROAD
MABLETHORPE ROAD
MUNSTER ROAD
Cemetery
ROWALLAN ROAD
ORBAIN ROAD
VARNA ROAD
ROSAVILLE ROAD
BURNTHWAITE ROAD
3
BRONSART ROAD
ALLESTREE ROAD
ST OLAF'S ROAD
BROOKVILLE ROAD
WHEATSHEAF TERR
LANCASTER CT
THE QUADRANGLE
ST PETER'S TERR
FILMER ROAD
KILMAINE ROAD
MARVILLE ROAD
ATALANTA ST
BRANKSEA ST
KINGWOOD ROAD
WYFOLD ROAD
REPORTON RD
BLOOM PARK RD
DAR LAN ROAD
KELVEDON RD
77
MARRYAT SQ
THE CODA CTR
FERNHURST RD
BISHOPS RD
ARUNDEL MANSIONS
Henry Compton Sec Sch
DANEHURST ST
MUNSTER RESIDENCES
FLORENCE MANS
CLONMEL RD
WINCHENDON RD
LILLYVILLE RD
RADIPOLE RD
CHESILTON RD
HAZELWOOD MANSIONS
Kensington Prep Sch
CRAVEN LODGE
2
CHILDERLEY ST
CONNAUGHT MANS
St John's CE Prim Sch
ROSTREVOR MANS
PENHURST MANS
AVONDALE MANS
DEEPDENE MANS
QUENINGTON MANSIONS
A304
ROBERT OWEN HOUSE
LAMBROOK TERR
SIDBURY ST
WARDO AVE
GOWAN AVE
SW6
FILMER HO
FILMER MEWS
SWIFT ST
ROSTREVOR RD
Al-Muntada Islamic Sch
FINLAY ST
A219
FULHAM
THE COURTYARD
VERA RD
FELDEN ST
ROSTREVOR MEWS
FULHAM RD
PURSERS CROSS RD
EPPLE RD
ELLERBY ST
FULHAM PALACE RD
KIMBELL GDNS
PARK MANSIONS
COLEHILL LA
HORDER RD
PO
WHITTINGSTALL MANSIONS
WHITTINGSTALL RD
ST MAUR RD
MIMOSA ST
EDGARLEY TERR
FIRTH GDNS
BURNFOOT AVE
MUNSTER RD
CROOKHAM RD
DANCER RD
LETTICE ST
BEACONSFIELD WLK
1
DONERAILE ST
ELY COURT FLATS
WOODLAWN RD
RINGMER AVE
WALDEMAR AVENUE MANSIONS
COLEHILL GDNS
HESTERCOMBE AVE
DURRELL RD
CLARIDGE CT
WILLIAM BANFIELD HO
ARTHUR HENDERSON HOUSE
HEATHMAN'S RD
ST DIONIS RD
PLATO PL
CLONCURRY ST
Tenn Cts
BISHOP'S PARK RD
LALOR ST
WALDEMAR AVE
HEDORNCLIFFE RD
WILSTON CT
MUNSTER CT
MUSTOW PL
DORIA RD
GUION RD
BISHOP'S MANSIONS
24
135
25

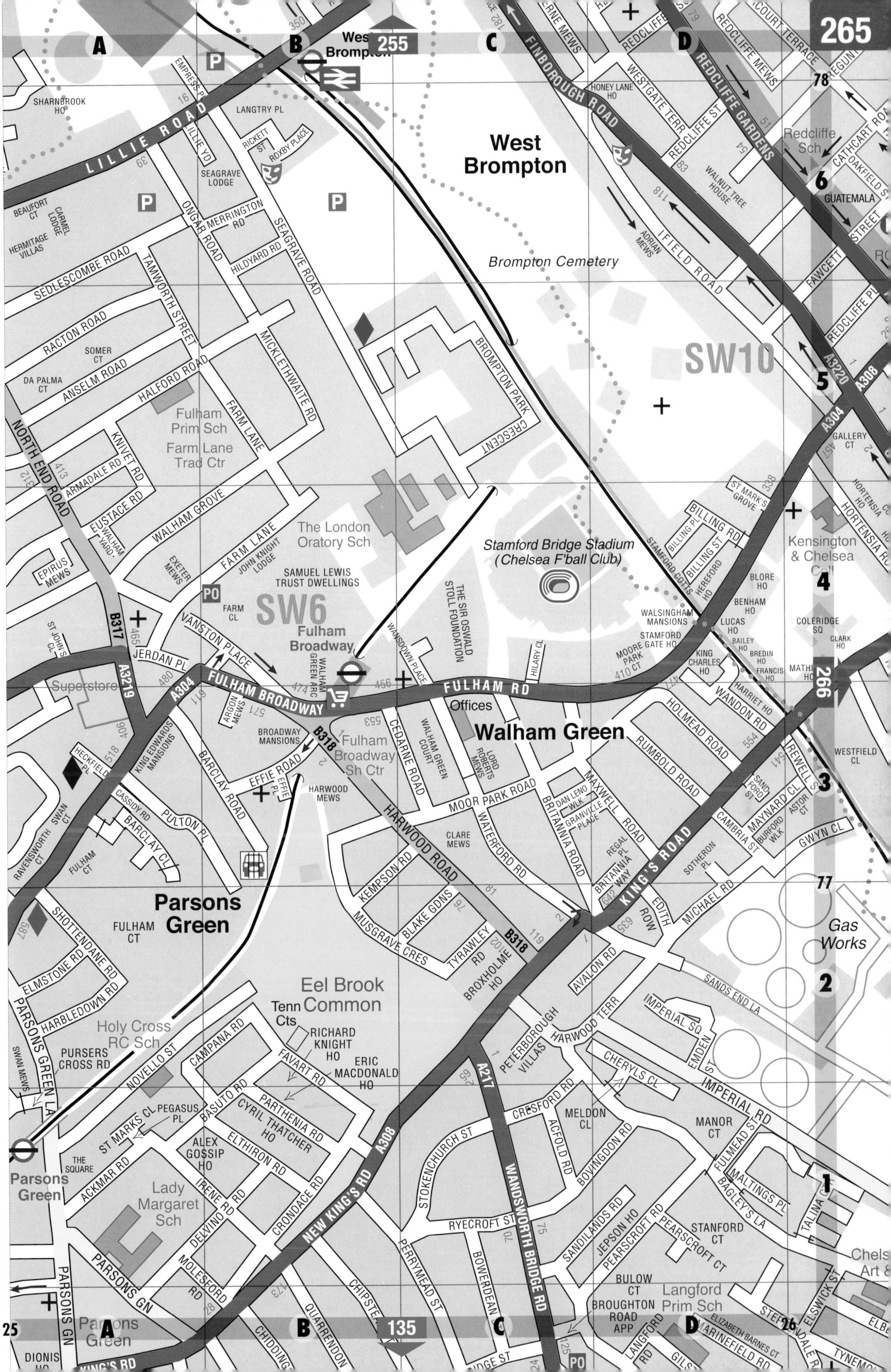
A
B
C
D
255
West Brompton
West Brompton
LILLIE ROAD
EMPRESS PL
LILLIE YD
LANGTRY PL
RICKETT ST
ROXBY PLACE
SHARNBROOK HO
SEAGRAVE LODGE
SEAGRAVE ROAD
MERRINGTON RD
HILDYARD RD
ONGAR ROAD
BEAUFORT CT
CARMEL LODGE
HERMITAGE VILLAS
SEDLESCOMBE ROAD
TAMWORTH STREET
RACTON ROAD
SOMER CT
ANSELM ROAD
DA PALMA CT
HALFORD ROAD
MICKLETHWAITE RD
FARM LANE
NORTH END ROAD
Fulham Prim Sch
Farm Lane Trad Ctr
KNIVET RD
ARMADALE RD
EUSTACE RD
WALHAM YARD
WALHAM GROVE
EPIRUS MEWS
EXETER MEWS
JOHN KNIGHT LODGE
The London Oratory Sch
SAMUEL LEWIS TRUST DWELLINGS
FARM CL
SW6
Fulham Broadway
BROMPTON PARK CRESCENT
FINBOROUGH ROAD
HONEY LANE HO
WESTGATE TERR
REDCLIFFE ST
REDCLIFFE GARDENS
REDCLIFFE MEWS
COURT TERRACE
Redcliffe Sch
CATHCART ROAD
OAKFIELD ST
GUATEMALA
WALNUT TREE HOUSE
ADRIAN MEWS
IFIELD ROAD
Brompton Cemetery
FAWCETT
REDCLIFFE PL
SW10
A3220
A308
A304
GALLERY CT
ST MARK'S GROVE
HORTENSIA HO
HORTENSIA RD
BILLING RD
BILLING PL
BILLING ST
HEREFORD HO
STAMFORD COTTS
Kensington & Chelsea Coll
Stamford Bridge Stadium (Chelsea F'ball Club)
THE SIR OSWALD STOLL FOUNDATION
WALSINGHAM MANSIONS
STAMFORD GATE HO
MOORE PARK CT
BLORE HO
BENHAM HO
LUCAS HO
BAILEY HO
BREDIN HO
FRANCIS HO
COLERIDGE SQ
CLARK HO
KING CHARLES HO
HILARY CL
WANSDOWN PLACE
ST JOHN'S CL
B317
A3219
JERDAN PL
VANSTON PLACE
Superstore
FULHAM BROADWAY
WALHAM GREEN ARC
FULHAM RD
Offices
266
Walham Green
HARRIET HO
WANDON RD
HOLMEAD ROAD
RUMBOLD ROAD
WESTFIELD CL
TREWELL
SANDFORD ST
MAYNARD CL
ASTOR CT
BURFORD WLK
CAMBRIA ST
GWYN CL
ARGON MEWS
BROADWAY MANSIONS
B318
Fulham Broadway Sh Ctr
CEDARNE ROAD
WALHAM GREEN COURT
LORD ROBERTS MEWS
MOOR PARK ROAD
BRITANNIA ROAD
DAN LENO WLK
GRANVILLE PLACE
MAXWELL ROAD
KING EDWARDS MANSIONS
HECKFIELD PL
CASSIDY RD
BARCLAY ROAD
PULTON PL
BARCLAY CL
EFFIE ROAD
EFFIE PL
HARWOOD MEWS
HARWOOD ROAD
CLARE MEWS
WATERFORD RD
REGAL PL
BRITANNIA WAY
KING'S ROAD
SOTHERON PL
MICHAEL RD
EDITH ROW
Gas Works
RAVENSWORTH CT
SWAN CT
FULHAM CT
Parsons Green
FULHAM CT
SHOTTENDANE RD
ELMSTONE RD
HARBLEDOWN RD
KEMPSON RD
BLAKE GDNS
MUSGRAVE CRES
TYRAWLEY RD
BROXHOLME HO
AVALON RD
SANDS END LA
Eel Brook Common
Tenn Cts
RICHARD KNIGHT HO
ERIC MACDONALD HO
FAVART RD
Holy Cross RC Sch
PURSERS CROSS RD
PARSONS GREEN LA
SWAN MEWS
NOVELLO ST
CAMPANA RD
PEGASUS PL
ST MARKS CL
BASUTO RD
CYRIL THATCHER HO
PARTHENIA RD
ELTHIRON RD
ALEX GOSSIP HO
THE SQUARE
ACKMAR RD
Parsons Green
Lady Margaret Sch
IRENE RD
DELVINO RD
CRONDACE RD
NEW KING'S RD
A308
PETERBOROUGH VILLAS
HARWOOD TERR
A217
IMPERIAL SQ
EMDEN ST
CHERYLS CL
IMPERIAL RD
CRESFORD RD
MELDON CL
ACFOLD RD
STOKENCHURCH ST
BOVINGDON RD
MANOR CT
FULMEAD ST
MALTINGS PL
BAGLEY'S LA
TALINA CT
WANDSWORTH BRIDGE RD
RYECROFT ST
SANDILANDS RD
JEPSON HO
PEARSCROFT RD
PEARSCROFT CT
STANFORD CT
PERRYMEAD ST
BOWERDEAN ST
MOLESFORD RD
PARSONS GN
PARSONS GN
CHIPSTEAD
QUARRENDON
CHIDDING
135
BULOW CT
BROUGHTON ROAD APP
LANGFORD RD
Langford Prim Sch
ELIZABETH BARNES CT
MARINEFIELD RD
STEPHENDALE R
ELSWICK ST
TYNEMOUTH
DIONIS HO
KING'S RD
PO
25
26
1
2
3
4
5
6
77
78

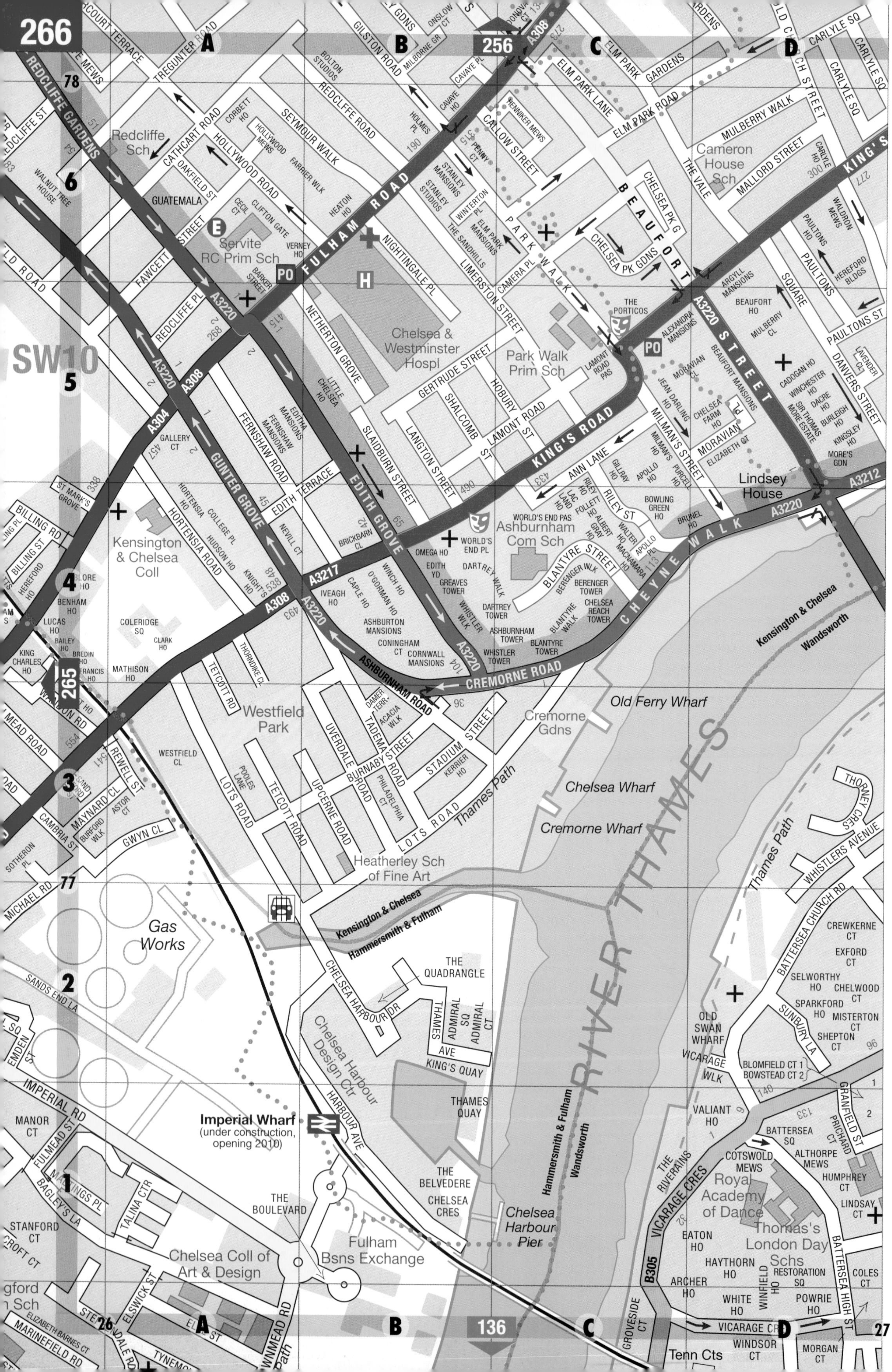

A
B
C
D
256
136
265
SW10
Redcliffe Gardens
Redcliffe Sch
Servite RC Prim Sch
Guatemala
Fulham Road
Chelsea & Westminster Hospl
Park Walk Prim Sch
Cameron House Sch
Beaufort Street
King's Road
Lindsey House
Cheyne Walk
Cremorne Road
Ashburnham Com Sch
Kensington & Chelsea Coll
Gunter Grove
Edith Grove
Westfield Park
Cremorne Gdns
Old Ferry Wharf
Chelsea Wharf
Cremorne Wharf
River Thames
Thames Path
Heatherley Sch of Fine Art
Gas Works
Lots Road
Kensington & Chelsea
Hammersmith & Fulham
Wandsworth
Chelsea Harbour Design Ctr
Imperial Wharf
(under construction, opening 2010)
Chelsea Harbour Pier
Fulham Bsns Exchange
Chelsea Coll of Art & Design
Royal Academy of Dance
Thomas's London Day Schs
Imperial Rd
Sands End La
Battersea Church Rd
Battersea High St
Vicarage Cres
Elm Park Gardens
Elm Park Road
Mulberry Walk
Mallord Street
Old Church Street
Carlyle Sq
Paultons Square
Danvers Street
Milman's Street
Blantyre Street
Ashburnham Road
Tadema Road
Burnaby Street
Uverdale Road
Upcerne Road
Tetcott Road
Stadium Street
Fernshaw Road
Hortensia Road
Slaidburn Street
Langton Street
Hobury St
Lamont Road
Gertrude Street
Limerston Street
Callow Street
Seymour Walk
Hollywood Road
Cathcart Road
Tregunter Road
Gilston Road
Redcliffe Road
Netherton Grove
Edith Terrace
Billing Rd
Maynard Cl
Rewell St
Elswick St
Harbour Ave
Chelsea Harbour Dr
The Quadrangle
Thames Quay
King's Quay
Whistlers Avenue
Thorney Cres
Valiant Ho
Old Swan Wharf
77
78
26
27

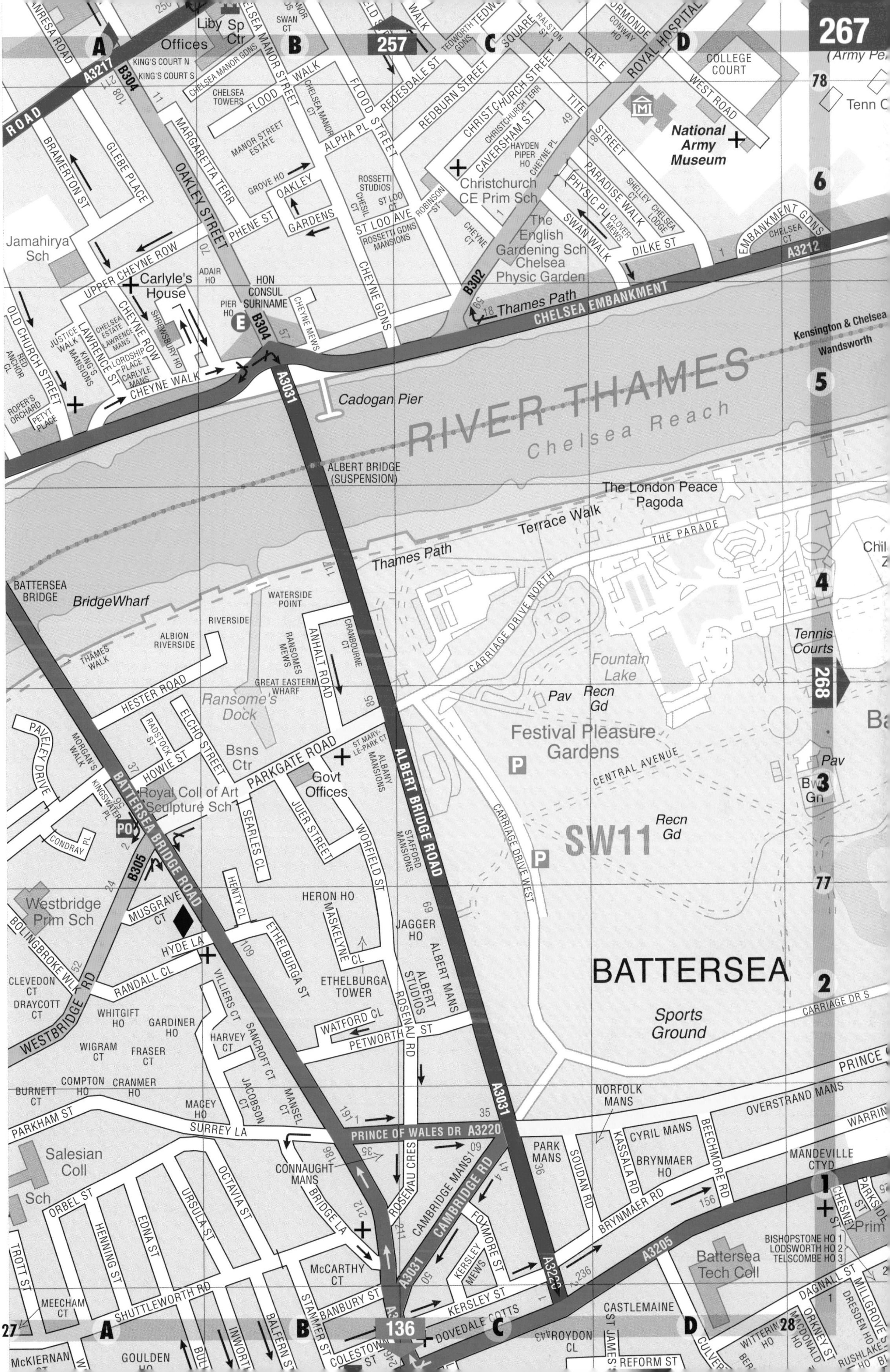
A
B
C
D
257
(Army Pe
78
Tenn C
COLLEGE COURT
National Army Museum
ROYAL HOSPITAL
WEST ROAD
ORMONDE GATE
CONWAY HO
RALSTON ST
TITE STREET
SQUARE
TEDWORTH GDNS
REDESDALE ST
REDBURN STREET
CHRISTCHURCH STREET
CHRISTCHURCH TERR
CAVERSHAM ST
HAYDEN PIPER HO
CHEYNE PL
Christchurch CE Prim Sch
PARADISE WALK
PHYSIC PL
SWAN WALK
SHELLEY CT
CHELSEA LODGE
CLOVER MEWS
DILKE ST
EMBANKMENT GDNS
CHELSEA CT
A3212
The English Gardening Sch
Chelsea Physic Garden
B302
Thames Path
CHELSEA EMBANKMENT
Kensington & Chelsea
Wandsworth
Liby
Sp Ctr
Offices
SWAN CT
A3217
B304
KING'S COURT N
KING'S COURT S
ROAD
CHELSEA MANOR GDNS
CHELSEA MANOR STREET
CHELSEA TOWERS
FLOOD WALK
FLOOD STREET
CHELSEA MANOR CT
ALPHA PL
MANOR STREET ESTATE
BRAMERTON ST
GLEBE PLACE
MARGARETTA TERR
OAKLEY STREET
GROVE HO
OAKLEY GARDENS
ROSSETTI STUDIOS
CHESIL CT
ST LOO CT
ST LOO AVE
ROSSETTI GDNS MANSIONS
ROBINSON ST
CHEYNE CT
PHENE ST
Jamahirya Sch
UPPER CHEYNE ROW
Carlyle's House
ADAIR HO
HON CONSUL SURINAME
PIER HO
CHEYNE MEWS
CHEYNE GDNS
OLD CHURCH STREET
JUSTICE WALK
LAWRENCE ST
CHELSEA ESTATE
LAWRENCE MANS
CHEYNE ROW
KING'S MANSIONS
LORDSHIP PLACE
CARLYLE MANS
SHREWSBURY HO
CHEYNE WALK
RED ANCHOR CL
ROPER'S ORCHARD
PETYT PLACE
A3031
Cadogan Pier
RIVER THAMES
Chelsea Reach
ALBERT BRIDGE (SUSPENSION)
The London Peace Pagoda
Terrace Walk
THE PARADE
Thames Path
Chil
BATTERSEA BRIDGE
BridgeWharf
WATERSIDE POINT
RIVERSIDE
ALBION RIVERSIDE
THAMES WALK
HESTER ROAD
RANSOMES MEWS
ANHALT ROAD
CRANBOURNE CT
GREAT EASTERN WHARF
Ransome's Dock
CARRIAGE DRIVE NORTH
Fountain Lake
Pav
Recn Gd
Tennis Courts
268
Festival Pleasure Gardens
P
CENTRAL AVENUE
Bw Gn
Pav
PAVELEY DRIVE
MORGAN'S WALK
RADSTOCK ST
ELCHO STREET
HOWIE ST
Bsns Ctr
PARKGATE ROAD
ST MARY-LE-PARK CT
ALBANY MANSIONS
Govt Offices
ALBERT BRIDGE ROAD
KINGSWATER PL
Royal Coll of Art Sculpture Sch
BATTERSEA BRIDGE ROAD
PO
CONDRAY PL
SEARLES CL
JUIER STREET
WORFIELD ST
STAFFORD MANSIONS
CARRIAGE DRIVE WEST
SW11
Recn Gd
B305
Westbridge Prim Sch
MUSGRAVE CT
HENTY CL
HERON HO
MASKELYNE CL
JAGGER HO
BOLINGBROKE WLK
HYDE LA
ETHELBURGA ST
ALBERT MANS
ALBERT STUDIOS
BATTERSEA
CLEVEDON CT
DRAYCOTT CT
RANDALL CL
VILLIERS CT
ETHELBURGA TOWER
ROSENAU RD
Sports Ground
CARRIAGE DR S
WESTBRIDGE RD
WHITGIFT HO
GARDINER HO
WIGRAM CT
FRASER CT
HARVEY CT
SANCROFT CT
WATFORD CL
PETWORTH ST
PRINCE
BURNETT CT
COMPTON HO
CRANMER HO
MACEY HO
JACOBSON CT
MANSEL CT
NORFOLK MANS
OVERSTRAND MANS
PARKHAM ST
SURREY LA
PRINCE OF WALES DR A3220
WARRIN
Salesian Coll
CONNAUGHT MANS
ROSENAU CRES
CAMBRIDGE MANS
CAMBRIDGE RD
PARK MANS
SOUDAN RD
KASSALA RD
CYRIL MANS
BRYNMAER HO
BEECHMORE RD
MANDEVILLE CTYD
Sch
ORBEL ST
HENNING ST
EDNA ST
URSULA ST
OCTAVIA ST
BRIDGE LA
FOYMORE ST
BRYNMAER RD
CHESNEY ST
PARKSIDE ST
Prim
A3205
BISHOPSTONE HO
LODSWORTH HO
TELSCOMBE HO
TROTT ST
KERSLEY MEWS
A3220
Battersea Tech Coll
MEECHAM CT
SHUTTLEWORTH RD
McCARTHY CT
BANBURY ST
KERSLEY ST
CASTLEMAINE
DAGNALL ST
MILLGROVE ST
DRESDEN HO
ORKNEY ST
MACDONALD HO
WITTERING HO
136
DOVEDALE COTTS
ROYDON CL
ST JAMES
REFORM ST
STAMMER ST
BALFERN ST
INWORTH
COLESTOWN ST
McKIERNAN
GOULDEN
RUSHLAKE HO
CULVER
27
28
6
5
4
3
77
2
1

Royal Hospital (Army Pensioners)
Ranelagh Gardens (Site of Chelsea Flower Show)
Lister Hospl
HEPWORTH CT
HIRST CT
PAVILLION CT
CUBITT BLDG
CUBITT BLDG
Dock
GILBERT HO
CHIPPENDALE HO
ELGAR HO
SULLIVAN HO
SHERATON HO
PAXTON TERR
PEABODY CL
Churchill Gdns
GROSVENOR RD
A3212
A3216
COLLEGE COURT
WEST ROAD
Tenn Cts
National Army Museum
Thames Path
EMBANKMENT GDNS
CHELSEA CT
CHELSEA BRIDGE
GROSVENOR BRIDGE
Battersea Wharf
Kensington & Chelsea
Wandsworth
CENTURION BLDG
HOWARD BLDG
OSWALD BLDG
EUSTACE BLDG
WARWICK BLDG
QUEENSTOWN ROAD
Battersea Power Station (disused)
CARRIAGE DRIVE NORTH
Peace
PARADE
Tennis Courts
Children's Zoo
Tenn Cts
Millennium Arena (Sports Arena)
Pav
Recn Gd
SOPWITH WAY
War Meml
CARRIAGE DRIVE EAST
CENTRAL AVENUE
Tennis Courts
Battersea Park
Pav
Bwg Gn
Boating Lake
Battersea Dogs Home
Battersea Park
QUEEN'S CIRCUS
PRINCE OF WALES DR
Cloisters Bsns Ctr
A3205
PALMERSTON WAY
HAVELOCK TERR
Newton Prep Sch
LOCKINGTON RD
PAGDEN ST
ST JOSEPH'S ST
GLADSTONE TERR
St Mary's RC Prim Sch
QUEENS CT
MEATH ST
PRINCE OF WALES MANS
ALBERT PALACE MANS
LURLINE GDNS
ELMWOOD CT
TURPIN HO
PATCHAM TERR
Queenstown Road
Abbey Bsns Ctr
CARRIAGE DR S
ERSEA
YORK MANS
MACDUFF RD
CUPAR RD
FORFAR RD
PRIMROSE MANS
PRINCE OF WALES DR
Westminster Kingsway Coll
BANK CT
PARK CT
CONNOR CT
SOUTHOLM ST
INGATE PL
OVERSTRAND MANS
ALEXANDRA AVE
WARRINER GDNS
BATTERSEA PARK RD
RAWSON ST
ALFREDA ST
STRASBURG RD
RAVENET ST
NEWTOWN ST
QUEENSTOWN RD
BEECHMORE RD
MANDEVILLE CTYD
CROMWELL HO
PALMERSTON HO
Liby
ST GEORGE HO
CHARLOTTE DESPARD AVE
ARTHUR CT
YOUNGS CT
Bsns Ctr
LUCAS CT
ROLLO CT
CHESNEY ST
PARKSIDE ST
HARPSDEN ST
PARK S
Prim Sch
AUSTIN RD
BISHOPSTONE HO 1
LODSWORTH HO 2
TELSCOMBE HO 3
Battersea Tech Coll
KENNARD ST
ATKINSON HO
FRANCIS CHICHESTER WAY
RUSSELL CT
LANDSEER HO
QUEENSTOWN MEWS
DAGNALL ST
MILLGROVE ST
WALDEN HO
LANGHURST HO
BOLTON CT
FALKENER CT
KENNARD HO
B224
WITTERING HO
MACDONALD HO
ORKNEY ST
DRESDEN HO
FARNHURST HO
ASTLE ST
VOLTAIRE CT
RUSHLAKE HO
BLONDEL ST
BARLOCH HO
HENLEY ST
LONGHEDGE ST
Street Arches Area
CULVERT

258
267
137

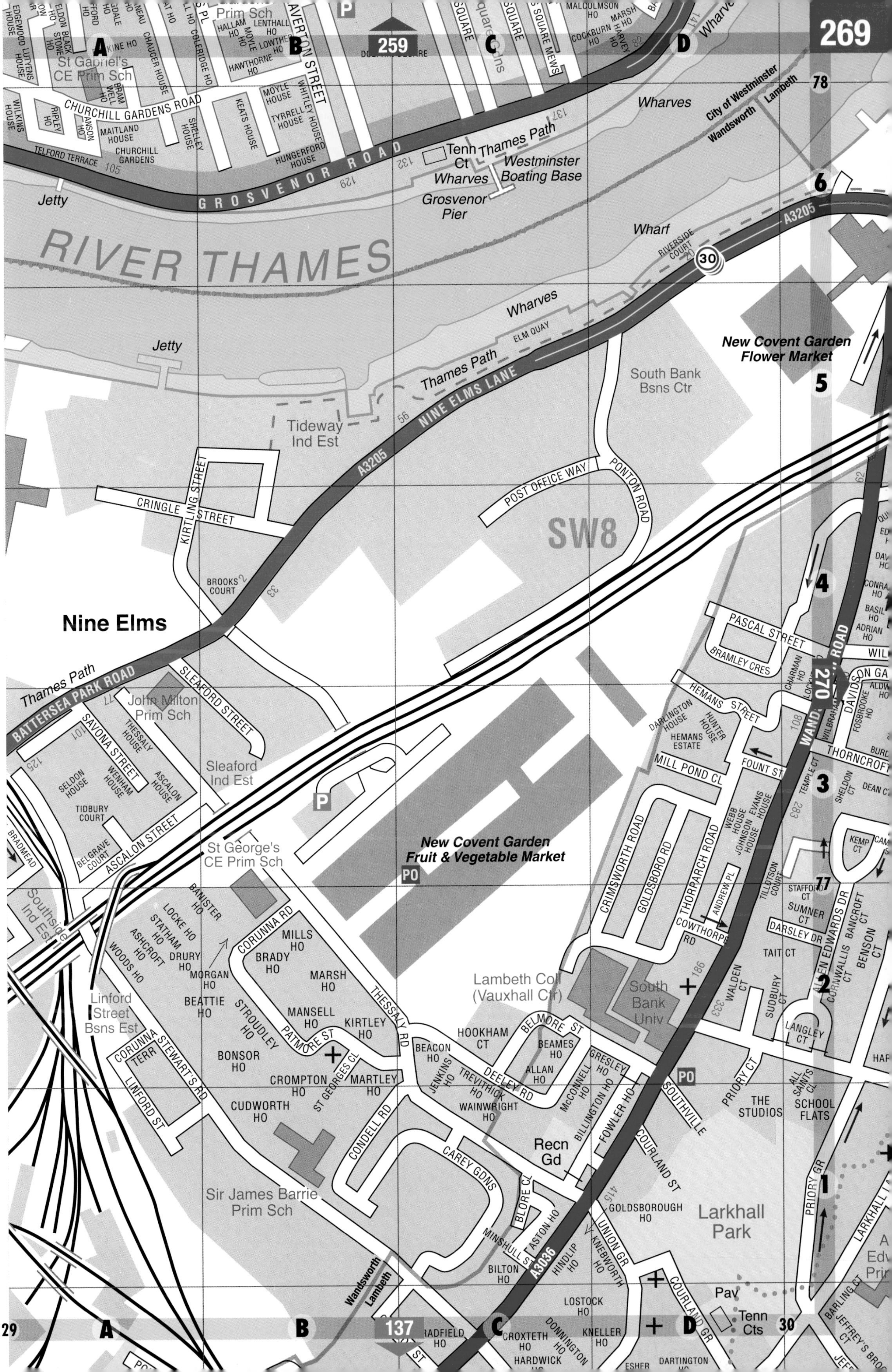
259
137
270
A
B
C
D
1
2
3
4
5
6
77
78
29
30
RIVER THAMES
GROSVENOR ROAD
CHURCHILL GARDENS ROAD
TELFORD TERRACE
CHURCHILL GARDENS
MAITLAND HOUSE
St Gabriel's CE Prim Sch
Prim Sch
CLAVERTON STREET
Jetty
Tenn Ct
Thames Path
Westminster Boating Base
Wharves
Grosvenor Pier
Wharf
City of Westminster
Lambeth
Wandsworth
A3205
RIVERSIDE COURT
ELM QUAY
NINE ELMS LANE
New Covent Garden Flower Market
South Bank Bsns Ctr
Tideway Ind Est
POST OFFICE WAY
PONTON ROAD
SW8
CRINGLE STREET
KIRTLING STREET
BROOKS COURT
Nine Elms
BATTERSEA PARK ROAD
John Milton Prim Sch
SLEAFORD STREET
Sleaford Ind Est
SAVONA STREET
ASCALON STREET
BELGRAVE COURT
TIDBURY COURT
St George's CE Prim Sch
New Covent Garden Fruit & Vegetable Market
PO
PASCAL STREET
BRAMLEY CRES
HEMANS STREET
HEMANS ESTATE
MILL POND CL
FOUNT ST
CRIMSWORTH ROAD
GOLDSBORO RD
THORPARCH ROAD
ANDREW PL
COWTHORPE RD
WANDSWORTH ROAD
THORNCROFT
Southside Ind Est
Linford Street Bsns Est
CORUNNA RD
THESSALY RD
PATMORE ST
ST GEORGES CL
STEWART'S RD
LINFORD ST
CORUNNA TERR
Lambeth Coll (Vauxhall Ctr)
South Bank Univ
BELMORE ST
DEELEY RD
HOOKHAM CT
CONDELL RD
CAREY GDNS
Recn Gd
SOUTHVILLE
PRIORY CT
THE STUDIOS
SCHOOL FLATS
COURLAND ST
Larkhall Park
PRIORY GR
LARKHALL LANE
UNION GR
BLORE CL
MINSHULL ST
A3036
Sir James Barrie Prim Sch
Wandsworth
Lambeth
GOLDSBOROUGH HO
Pav
Tenn Cts
ALLEN EDWARDS DR
LANGLEY CT
KEMP CT
TILLOTSON COURT
SUMNER CT
DARSLEY DR
TAIT CT
WALDEN CT
SUDBURY CT
BENSON CT
CORNWALLIS CT
BANCROFT CT
HEMPLE CT
SHELDON CT
DEAN CT
BARLING CT
JEFFREY'S CT

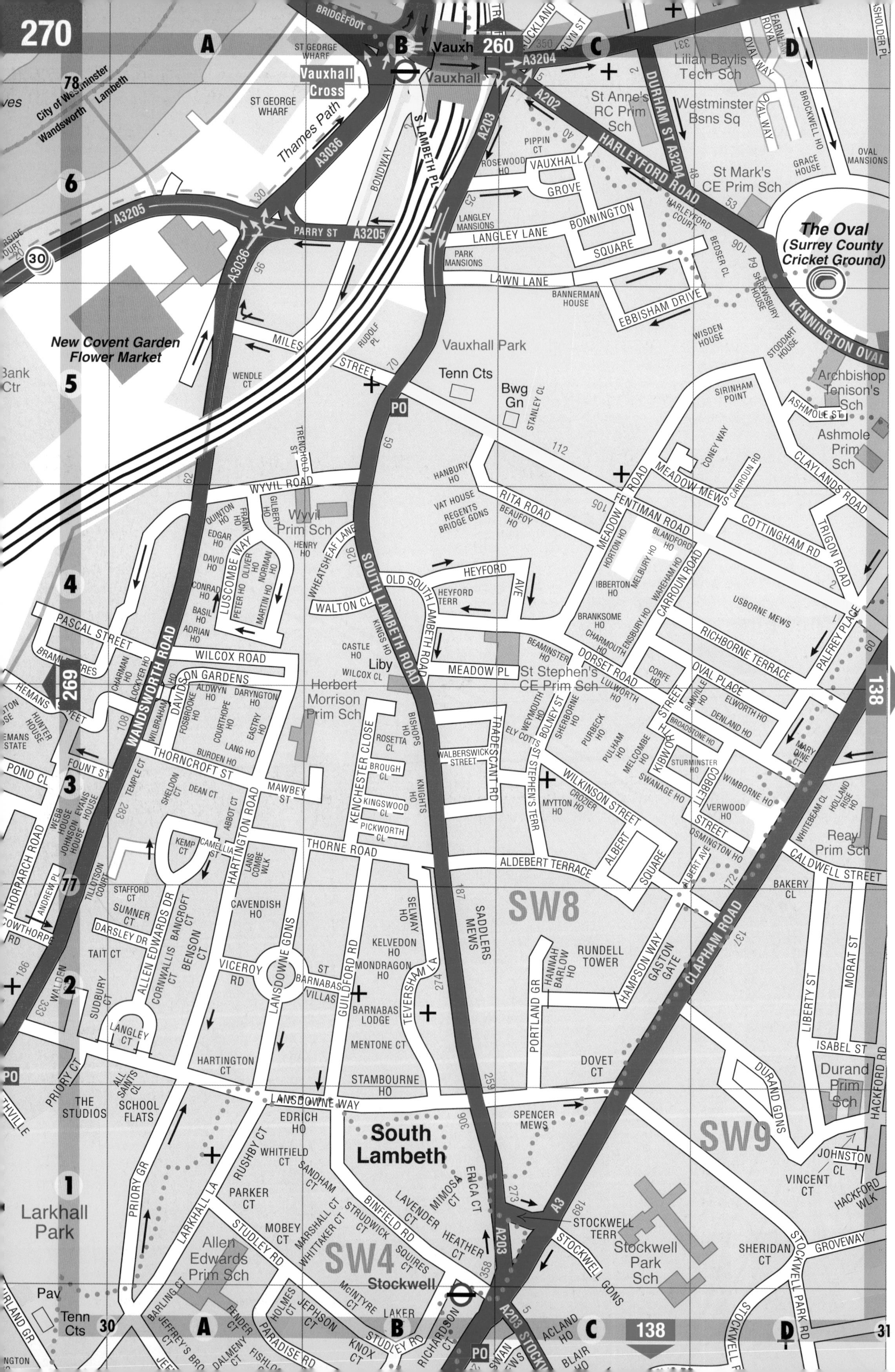

A
B
C
D
260
BRIDGEFOOT
ST GEORGE WHARF
Vauxhall Cross
Vauxhall
A3204
GLYN ST
DURHAM ST A3204
Lilian Baylis Tech Sch
Westminster Bsns Sq
OVAL WAY
BROCKWELL HO
OVAL MANSIONS
City of Westminster
Lambeth
Wandsworth
78
Thames Path
A3036
BONDWAY
S LAMBETH PL
A203
A202
St Anne's RC Prim Sch
HARLEYFORD ROAD
St Mark's CE Prim Sch
GRACE HOUSE
6
A3205
PARRY ST
PIPPIN CT
ROSEWOOD HO
VAUXHALL GROVE
BONNINGTON SQUARE
LANGLEY MANSIONS
LANGLEY LANE
PARK MANSIONS
LAWN LANE
HARLEYFORD COURT
BEDSER CL
SHREWSBURY HOUSE
The Oval (Surrey County Cricket Ground)
BANNERMAN HOUSE
EBBISHAM DRIVE
KENNINGTON OVAL
WISDEN HOUSE
STODDART HOUSE
30
New Covent Garden Flower Market
MILES STREET
RUDOLF PL
Vauxhall Park
Tenn Cts
Bwg Gn
STANLEY CL
5
WENDLE CT
PO
SIRINHAM POINT
Archbishop Tenison's Sch
ASHMOLE ST
Ashmole Prim Sch
CONEY WAY
TRENCHOLD ST
HANBURY HO
MEADOW ROAD
MEADOW MEWS
CARROUN RD
CLAYLANDS ROAD
WYVIL ROAD
VAT HOUSE
REGENTS BRIDGE GDNS
RITA ROAD
BEAUFOY HO
FENTIMAN ROAD
COTTINGHAM RD
TRIGON ROAD
QUINTON HO
FRANK HO
GILBERT HO
Wyvil Prim Sch
EDGAR HO
DAVID HO
LUSCOMBE WAY
OLIVER HO
NORMAN HO
HENRY HO
WHEATSHEAF LANE
SOUTH LAMBETH ROAD
HEYFORD AVE
HORTON HO
BLANDFORD HO
MELBURY HO
IBBERTON HO
WAREHAM HO
CARROUN ROAD
4
CONRAD HO
PETER HO
MARTIN HO
OLD SOUTH LAMBETH ROAD
HEYFORD TERR
WALTON CL
USBORNE MEWS
BASIL HO
ADRIAN HO
BRANKSOME HO
TENSBURY HO
CHARMOUTH HO
PASCAL STREET
WANDSWORTH ROAD
KINGS HO
CASTLE HO
WILCOX CL
Liby
MEADOW PL
BEAMINSTER HO
St Stephen's CE Prim Sch
DORSET ROAD
CORFE HO
RICHBORNE TERRACE
PALFREY PLACE
WILCOX ROAD
DAVIDSON GARDENS
CHARMAN HO
LOCKYER HO
ALDWYN HO
DARYNGTON HO
Herbert Morrison Prim Sch
LULWORTH HO
OVAL PLACE
BANVILLE HO
ELWORTH HO
DENLAND HO
269
138
HEMANS STREET
HUNTER HOUSE
WILBRAHAM HO
FOSBROOKE HO
COURTHOPE HO
EASTRY HO
LANG HO
BURDEN HO
BISHOPS HO
ROSETTA CL
KENCHESTER CLOSE
WALBERSWICK STREET
TRADESCANT RD
WEYMOUTH HO
ELY COTTS
BOLNEY ST
SHERBORNE HO
PURBECK HO
PULHAM HO
MELCOMBE HO
KIBWORTH STREET
BROADSTONE HO
STURMINSTER HO
COBBETT STREET
WIMBORNE HO
MARY DINE CT
FOUNT ST
POND CL
3
THORNCROFT ST
TEMPLE CT
SHELDON CT
DEAN CT
MAWBEY ST
BROUGH CL
KINGSWOOD CL
PICKWORTH CL
KNIGHTS HO
ST STEPHEN'S TERR
WILKINSON STREET
MYTTON HO
CROZIER HO
SWANAGE HO
VERWOOD HO
OSMINGTON HO
WHITEBEAM CL
HOLLAND RISE HO
Reay Prim Sch
THORPARCH ROAD
WEBB HOUSE
JOHNSON HOUSE
EVANS HOUSE
KEMP CT
CAMELLIA ST
ABBOT CT
HARTINGTON ROAD
LANSCOMBE WLK
THORNE ROAD
ALDEBERT TERRACE
ALBERT SQUARE
ALBERT AVE
CALDWELL STREET
TILLOTSON COURT
ANDREW PL
77
STAFFORD CT
SUMNER CT
DARSLEY DR
ALLEN EDWARDS DR
BANCROFT CT
BENSON CT
CAVENDISH HO
SELWAY HO
SADDLERS MEWS
SW8
BAKERY CL
COWTHORPE RD
TAIT CT
CORNWALLIS CT
VICEROY RD
LANSDOWNE GDNS
ST BARNABAS VILLAS
GUILDFORD RD
KELVEDON HO
MONDRAGON HO
TEVERSHAM LA
HANNAH BARLOW HO
RUNDELL TOWER
HAMPSON WAY
GASTON GATE
CLAPHAM ROAD
MORAT ST
LIBERTY ST
2
WALDEN HO
SUDBURY CT
LANGLEY CT
BARNABAS LODGE
MENTONE CT
PORTLAND GR
ISABEL ST
HACKFORD RD
Durand Prim Sch
PRIORY CT
ALL SAINTS CL
HARTINGTON CT
STAMBOURNE HO
DOVET CT
DURAND GDNS
THE STUDIOS
SCHOOL FLATS
LANSDOWNE WAY
EDRICH HO
South Lambeth
SPENCER MEWS
SW9
JOHNSTON CL
WHITFIELD CT
RUSHBY CT
SANDHAM CT
ERICA CT
MIMOSA CT
VINCENT CT
HACKFORD WLK
1
Larkhall Park
PRIORY GR
LARKHALL LA
PARKER CT
BINFIELD RD
LAVENDER CT
A3
STOCKWELL TERR
GROVEWAY
STUDLEY RD
MOBEY CT
MARSHALL CT
WHITTAKER CT
STRUDWICK CT
HEATHER CT
A203
Allen Edwards Prim Sch
SW4
SQUIRES CT
Stockwell
STOCKWELL GDNS
Stockwell Park Sch
SHERIDAN CT
STOCKWELL PARK RD
Pav
BARLING CT
FENDER CT
HOLMES CT
JEPHSON CT
McINTYRE CT
LAKER CT
Tenn Cts
JEFFREY'S RD
DALMENY CT
PARADISE RD
KNOX CT
STUDLEY RD
RICHARDSON CT
ACLAND HO
BLAIR HO
STOCKWELL RD

Index

Place name May be abbreviated on the map

Location number Present when a number indicates the place's position in a crowded area of mapping

Locality, town or village Shown when more than one place has the same name

Postcode district District for the indexed place

Standard-scale reference Page number and grid reference for the standard-scale mapping on pages 1–227

Large-scale reference Page number and grid reference for the large-scale central London mapping on pages 229–270, underlined in red

Example: **Church Rd** [6] Beckenham BR2.....**53** C6 **228** C6

Cities, towns and villages are listed in **CAPITAL LETTERS** **Public and commercial buildings** are highlighted in magenta

Places of interest are highlighted in blue with a star★

Abbreviations used in the index

Acad	**Academy**	Comm	**Common**	Gd	**Ground**	L	**Leisure**	Prom	**Promenade**
App	**Approach**	Cott	**Cottage**	Gdn	**Garden**	La	**Lane**	Rd	**Road**
Arc	**Arcade**	Cres	**Crescent**	Gn	**Green**	Liby	**Library**	Recn	**Recreation**
Ave	**Avenue**	Cswy	**Causeway**	Gr	**Grove**	Mdw	**Meadow**	Ret	**Retail**
Bglw	**Bungalow**	Ct	**Court**	H	**Hall**	Meml	**Memorial**	Sh	**Shopping**
Bldg	**Building**	Ctr	**Centre**	Ho	**House**	Mkt	**Market**	Sq	**Square**
Bsns, Bus	**Business**	Ctry	**Country**	Hospl	**Hospital**	Mus	**Museum**	St	**Street**
Bvd	**Boulevard**	Cty	**County**	HQ	**Headquarters**	Orch	**Orchard**	Sta	**Station**
Cath	**Cathedral**	Dr	**Drive**	Hts	**Heights**	Pal	**Palace**	Terr	**Terrace**
Cir	**Circus**	Dro	**Drove**	Ind	**Industrial**	Par	**Parade**	TH	**Town Hall**
Cl	**Close**	Ed	**Education**	Inst	**Institute**	Pas	**Passage**	Univ	**University**
Cnr	**Corner**	Emb	**Embankment**	Int	**International**	Pk	**Park**	Wk, Wlk	**Walk**
Coll	**College**	Est	**Estate**	Intc	**Interchange**	Pl	**Place**	Wr	**Water**
Com	**Community**	Ex	**Exhibition**	Junc	**Junction**	Prec	**Precinct**	Yd	**Yard**

Index of towns, villages, streets, hospitals, industrial estates, railway stations, schools, shopping centres, universities and places of interest

A

Aaron Ct BR3 .... **207** D6
Aaron Hill Rd E6 ...... **100** C2
Abady Ho SW1 .... **259** D4
Abberley Mews [9]
SW8 .... **137** B2
Abberton IG8 .... **37** C5
Abbess Cl
[11] Newham E6 .... **100** A2
Streatham SW2 .... **160** D3
Abbeville Mews [3]
SW4 .... **137** D1
Abbeville Rd
Clapham Pk SW4 ...... **159** C6
Hornsey N8 .... **49** D5
Abbey Ave HA0 .... **88** A5
Abbey Bsns Ctr
SW8 .... **137** B4 **268** D2
Abbey Cl
Hayes UB3 .... **106** B5
Northolt UB5 .... **85** B4
Pinner HA5 .... **40** C6
Abbey Cres DA17 ...... **125** C2
Abbey Ct
[6] Bedford Pk W12 .... **111** C3
Camberwell SE17 ...... **262** B1
Church End N3 .... **47** C6
[5] Edgware HA8 .... **26** D5
Hampton TW12 .... **173** C3
St John's Wood NW8 ... **229** A4
Twickenham TW2 ...... **152** B2
Abbeydale Rd HA0 ..... **88** C6
Abbey Dr SW17 .... **181** A5
Abbeyfield Cl CR4 ..... **180** C1
Abbeyfield Rd SE16 ... **118** C2
Abbeyfields Cl NW10 ... **88** C5
Abbey Gdns
[10] Bermondsey SE16 ... **118** A2
Chislehurst BR7 .... **188** C2
St John's Wood
NW8 .... **92** A5 **229** B3
West Kensington
W6 .... **135** A6 **264** A5
Abbey Gr SE2 .... **124** B2
Abbeyhill Rd DA15 .... **168** C2
Abbey Ho
Newham E15 .... **98** C5
St John's Wood NW8 ... **229** B2
Abbey Ind Est CR4 ..... **202** D4
Abbey La
Beckenham BR3 .... **185** C3
Mill Meads E15 .... **98** B5
Abbey Lane Commercial
Est [1] E15 .... **98** C5
Abbey Lo
Bromley SE12 .... **187** B6
[1] Ealing W5 .... **109** C6
Lisson Gr NW8 .... **230** B1
Abbey Manufacturing Est
HA0 .... **88** B6
Abbey Mews
Brentford TW7 .... **131** B4
Walthamstow E17 ...... **53** C4
Abbey Mount DA17 .... **125** B1
Abbey Orchard St
SW1 .... **115** D3 **259** D6
Abbey Orchard Street Est
SW1 .... **259** D6
Abbey Par
Ealing NW10 .... **88** B4
Merton SW19 .... **180** A3
Abbey Park Ind Est
IG11 .... **101** A6
Abbey Pk BR3 .... **185** C3
Abbey Prim Sch SM4 .. **201** C2
Abbey Rd
Barking IG11 .... **100** D6
Bexley DA7 .... **147** A1
Croydon CR0 .... **220** D5
Enfield EN1 .... **17** C6
Erith DA17 .... **125** A3
Ilford IG2 .... **57** B4
Lower Halliford TW17 .. **192** C1
Merton SW19 .... **180** A2
Newham E15 .... **98** C5
St John's Wood
NW8 .... **92** A5 **229** A4
Wembley NW10 .... **88** D5
Abbey Rd Motorist Ctr [4]
NW6 .... **91** D6
Abbey St
Bermondsey
SE1 .... **117** D3 **263** C6
Newham E13 .... **99** A3
Abbey Terr SE2 .... **124** C2
Abbey Trad Est SE26 ... **185** B5
Abbey View NW7 .... **11** D1
Abbey Wlk KT8 .... **195** D5
ABBEY WOOD **124** B3
Abbey Wood Rd SE2 .. **124** C2
Abbey Wood Sch SE2 .. **124** A3
Abbey Wood Sta SE2 .. **124** C3
Abbot Cl HA4 .... **62** D5
Abbot Ct SW8 .... **270** A3
Abbot Ho [14] E14 ...... **119** D6
Abbotsbury Cl
Kensington
W14 .... **113** B4 **244** C1
Mill Meads E15 .... **98** A5
Abbotsbury Gdns HA5 .. **40** C3
Abbotsbury Ho W14 ... **244** B2
Abbotsbury Mews
SE15 .... **140** C2
Abbotsbury Prim Sch
SM4 .... **201** D4
Abbotsbury Rd
Coney Hall BR2, BR4 .... **224** D6
Kensington
W14 .... **113** B4 **244** C1
Morden SM4 .... **201** D5
Abbots Cl BR5 .... **211** A1
Abbots Ct SE25 .... **205** C6
Abbots Dr HA2 .... **63** C6
Abbotsfield Sch UB10 .. **82** D5
Abbotsford Ave N15 .... **51** A5
Abbotsford Gdns IG8 .. **37** A3
Abbotsford Rd IG3 ..... **80** B6
Abbots Gdns N2 .... **48** B5
Abbots Gn CR0, CR2 .... **222** D2
Abbots Green CR2 .... **222** D2
Abbotshade Rd [15]
SE16 .... **118** D5
Abbotshall Ave N14 .... **15** C1
Abbotshall Rd SE6 .... **164** B2
Abbots Ho
Kensington W14 .... **254** C5
Pimlico SW1 .... **259** C1
Walthamstow E17 ...... **35** B1
Abbots La SE1 . **117** C5 **253** B3
Abbotsleigh Cl SM2 ... **217** D1
Abbotsleigh Rd
SW16 .... **181** C5
Abbotsmede Cl TW1 .. **152** D2
Abbots Pk SW2 .... **160** C3
Abbot's Pl NW6 .... **91** D6
Abbots Rd
Burnt Oak HA8 .... **27** B3
Cheam SM3 .... **217** A4
Newham E6 .... **99** D6
Abbot St E8 .... **73** D2
Abbots Terr N8 .... **50** A3
Abbotstone Ho [4] E5 ... **74** A6
Abbotstone Rd SW15 .. **134** C2
Abbotsview Ct NW7 .... **12** A1
Abbots Way BR3 ...... **207** A4
Abbotswell Rd SE4 .... **163** B6
Abbotswood Cl [7]
DA17 .... **125** A3
Abbotswood Gdns IG5 . **56** B6
Abbotswood Rd
London SE22 .... **139** C1
Streatham SW16 ...... **159** D1
Abbotswood Way
UB3 .... **106** B5
Abbott Ave SW20 ..... **178** D2
Abbott Cl
Hampton TW12 .... **173** A4
Northolt UB5 .... **63** B2
Abbott Ho SW12 ...... **158** D4
Abbott Rd E14 .... **98** B1
Abbotts Cl
Canonbury N1 .... **73** A2
Romford RM7 .... **59** D6
Woolwich SE28 .... **124** C6
Abbotts Cres
Chingford E4 .... **36** B6
Enfield EN2 .... **4** D3
Abbotts Ct HA2 .... **64** B6
Abbotts Dr HA0 .... **65** B6
Abbotts Park Rd E10 ... **54** A2
Abbotts Rd
Barnet EN5 .... **1** D1
Mitcham CR4 .... **203** C5
Southall UB1 .... **107** A5
Abbotts Wharf [4] E14 .. **97** C1
Abbott's Wlk DA7 ..... **146** D5

Abchurch La EC2,
EC4 .... **117** B6 **252** D6
Abchurch Yd EC4 ..... **252** C6
Abdale Rd W12 .... **112** B5
Abel Ho
[7] Kennington SE11 .... **138** C6
Woolwich SE18 .... **123** A2
Abenglen Ind Est
UB3 .... **105** B4
Aberavon Rd E3 .... **97** A4
Abercairn Rd SW16 ... **181** C3
Aberconway Rd SM4 .. **201** D5
Abercorn Cl
Finchley NW7 .... **29** A3
St John's Wood
NW8 .... **92** A4 **229** A2
Abercorn Cres HA2 .... **41** D1
Abercorn Gdns
Harrow HA3 .... **43** D2
Ilford RM6 .... **58** B3
Abercorn Gr HA4 ...... **39** B5
Abercorn Mans NW8 .. **229** B3
Abercorn Mews [10]
TW10 .... **132** B1
Abercorn Pl
NW8 .... **92** A5 **229** A3
Abercorn Rd
Finchley NW7 .... **29** A3
Stanmore HA7 .... **25** C3
Abercorn Trad Est
HA0 .... **87** D6
Abercorn Way SE1 .... **118** A1
Abercrombie Dr EN1 .... **6** A4
Abercrombie Ho [1]
W12 .... **112** B6

Abercrombie St
SW11 ... 136 C3
Aberdale Ct 22 SE16 ... 118 D4
Aberdare Cl BR4 ... 224 A6
Aberdare Gdns
Finchley NW7 ... 28 D3
South Hampstead NW6 .. 69 D1
Aberdare Rd EN3 ... 6 C1
Aberdeen Cotts HA7 ... 25 C3
Aberdeen Ct
Canonbury N5 ... 73 A3
Paddington W2 ... 236 C5
Aberdeen Ctr N5 ... 73 A3
Aberdeen La N5 ... 73 A3
Aberdeen Mans WC1 .. 240 A6
Aberdeen Par N18 ... 34 B5
Aberdeen Pk N5 ... 73 A3
Aberdeen Pl
NW8 ... 92 B3 236 C6
Aberdeen Rd
Canonbury N5 ... 73 A4
Croydon CR0 ... 221 B4
Dudden Hill NW10 ... 67 D3
Edmonton N18 ... 34 B5
Harrow HA3 ... 24 D1
Aberdeen Terr SE3 ... 142 B3
Aberdour Rd IG3 ... 80 B6
Aberdour St
SE1 ... 117 C2 263 A4
Aberfeldy Ho SE5 ... 138 D5
Aberfeldy St E14 ... 98 A1
Aberford Gdns SE18 ... 144 A4
Aberfoyle Rd SW16 ... 181 D4
Abergeldie Rd SE12 ... 165 B5
Abernethy Rd SE13 ... 142 C1
Abersham Rd E8 ... 73 D3
Abery St SE18 ... 123 C2
Ability Plaza 8 E8 ... 73 D1
Ability Twrs EC1 ... 235 A2
Abingdon W14 ... 254 D3
Abingdon Cl
Fulham SE1 ... 263 D2
Hillingdon UB10 ... 82 B6
Kentish Town NW1 ... 71 D2
Wimbledon SW19 ... 180 A4
Abingdon Ct
Earl's Ct W8 ... 255 B5
Edgware HA8 ... 26 A6
Upper Tooting SW17 ... 180 D4
Abingdon Gdns W8 ... 255 B5
Abingdon Ho
Bromley BR1 ... 187 B3
Spitalfields E2 ... 243 C6
Abingdon Lo
2 Barnet EN5 ... 1 A1
Bromley BR2 ... 186 D1
Abingdon Mans W8 ... 255 A6
Abingdon Rd
Finchley N3 ... 30 A1
Kensington
W8 ... 113 C3 255 B5
Thornton Heath SW16 .. 182 A2
Abingdon St
SW1 ... 116 A3 260 A6
Abingdon Villas
W8 ... 113 C3 255 B5
Abinger Cl
Barking IG11 ... 80 A4
Bickley BR1 ... 210 A6
New Addington CR0 ... 224 A2
Wallington SM6 ... 220 A3
Abinger Ct
3 Ealing W5 ... 109 C6
Thornton Heath CR0 ... 204 D2
Wallington SM6 ... 220 A3
Abinger Gdns TW7 ... 130 C2
Abinger Gr SE8 ... 141 B6
Abinger Ho
Borough The SE1 ... 252 C1
2 Kingston u T KT2 ... 176 D3
Abinger Mews W9 ... 91 C3
Abinger Rd W4 ... 111 C3
Abington Ho NW11 ... 48 A3
Ablett St SE16 ... 118 C1
Abney Gdns 8 N16 ... 73 D6
Abney Park Cemetery*
N16 ... 73 C6
Abney Park Ct N16 ... 73 D6
Aborfield 6 NW5 ... 71 C3
Aboyne Dr SW20 ... 178 A1
Aboyne Rd
Neasden NW10 ... 67 C5
Wandsworth SW17 ... 158 B1
Abraham Cl WD19 ... 22 B6
Abraham Cohen Ct
IG1 ... 56 C3
Abraham Fisher Ho 2
E12 ... 78 C3
Abridge Way IG11 ... 102 B5
Abyssinia Cl SW11 ... 136 C1
Abyssinia Rd SW11 ... 136 C1
Acacia Ave
Brentford TW8 ... 131 B5
East Finchley N2 ... 47 D6
Hayes UB3 ... 83 D1
Littleton TW17 ... 192 C4
Ruislip HA4 ... 40 B2
Tottenham N17 ... 33 B3
Wembley HA9 ... 66 A3
Yiewsley UB7 ... 104 B6
Acacia Bsns Ctr 1
E11 ... 76 C5
Acacia Cl
Penge SE20 ... 184 A1
Petts Wood BR5 ... 211 B4
Rotherhithe SE8 ... 119 A2
Stanmore HA7 ... 24 C4
Acacia Ct
Harrow HA1 ... 41 D3
5 West Norwood
SW16 ... 182 C5
Acacia Dr SM3 ... 201 C1
Acacia Gdns
St John's Wood NW8 ... 229 D4
West Wickham BR4 ... 224 A6
Acacia Gr
Dulwich SE21 ... 161 B2
Kingston u T KT3 ... 199 C6
Acacia Ho
Brockley SE4 ... 141 B1
1 New Malden KT3 ... 199 C5
Stoke Newington N16 ... 73 B6
Wood Green N22 ... 32 C2
Acacia Lo 6 N3 ... 29 B1
Acacia Pl NW8 .. 92 B5 229 D4
Acacia Rd
Acton W3 ... 111 A6
Beckenham BR3 ... 207 B6
Enfield EN2 ... 5 B4
Hampton TW12 ... 173 C4
Leyton E11 ... 76 C6
Mitcham CR4 ... 181 B1
St John's Wood
NW8 ... 92 B5 229 D4
Thornton Heath SW16 .. 182 A2
Walthamstow E17 ... 53 A3
Wood Green N22 ... 32 C2
Acacias Lo EN4 ... 14 B6
Acacias The EN4 ... 14 B6
Acacia Way DA15 ... 167 D3
Acacia Wlk SW10 ... 266 B3
Acad at Peckham The
SE15 ... 139 D4
Academy Ct 13 E2 ... 96 C4
Academy Gdns
Croydon CR0 ... 205 D1
Kensington W8 ... 245 A2
Northolt UB5 ... 84 D5
Academy Pl SE18 ... 144 C4
Academy Rd SE18 ... 144 B5
Academy Sch The
NW3 ... 70 B4
Academy The 2 N19 ... 49 C1
Acad of Live & Recorded
Arts The SW18 ... 158 B5
Acanthus Dr SE1 ... 118 A1
Acanthus Rd SW11 ... 137 A2
Accadia Ct NW9 ... 67 A6
Accommodation Rd
NW11 ... 47 B1
Ace Par KT9 ... 214 A5
Acer Ave UB4 ... 85 A2
Acer Ct
2 Cricklewood NW2 ... 68 D4
3 Enfield EN3 ... 7 A2
Acers BR7 ... 188 A3
Acfold Rd SW6 ... 265 C1
Achilles Cl SE1 ... 118 A1
Achilles Ho 16 E2 ... 96 B5
Achilles Rd NW6 ... 69 C3
Achilles St SE14 ... 141 A5
Achilles Way W1 ... 248 B3
Acklam Rd W10 ... 91 B2
Acklington Dr NW9 ... 27 C2
Ackmar Rd
SW6 ... 135 C4 265 A1
Ackroyd Dr E3 ... 97 C2
Ackroyd Rd SE23 ... 163 A4
Acland Burghley Sch
NW5 ... 71 B4
Acland Cl SE18 ... 145 B5
Acland Cres SE5 ... 139 B2
Acland Ho SW9 ... 138 B3
Acland Rd NW2 ... 68 B2
Acock Gr UB5 ... 64 A4
Acol Cres HA4 ... 62 B3
Acol Ct 3 NW6 ... 69 C1
Acol Rd NW6 ... 69 D1
Aconbury Rd RM9 ... 102 B6
Acorn Cl
Chingford E4 ... 35 D5
Chislehurst BR7 ... 189 A5
Enfield EN2 ... 4 D4
1 Hampton TW12 ... 173 D4
Stanmore HA7 ... 25 B3
Acorn Ct
5 Bow E3 ... 97 C5
Hampton TW12 ... 173 B5
Ilford IG2 ... 57 C4
Upton Pk E6 ... 78 A1
Wood Green N11 ... 31 D4
Acorn Gdns
North Acton W3 ... 89 B2
South Norwood SE19 ... 183 D2
Acorn Gr
Harlington UB3 ... 127 D5
Ruislip HA4 ... 61 D4
Acorn Par 7 SE15 ... 140 B5
Acorn Production Ctr
N7 ... 72 A1
Acorns The 21 SW19 ... 156 D3
Acorns Way KT10 ... 212 A3
Acorn Way
Beckenham BR3 ... 208 A4
Forest Hill SE23 ... 162 D1
Orpington BR6 ... 226 D4
Acorn Wharf SE15 ... 140 A6
Acorn Wlk SE16 ... 119 A5
Acqua Ho TW9 ... 132 D5
Acre Dr SE22 ... 140 A1
Acrefield Ho 4 NW4 ... 46 D5
Acre La
Brixton SW2 ... 138 B1
Wallington SM5 ... 219 A4
Acre Path UB5 ... 63 A2
Acre Rd
Dagenham RM10 ... 81 D1
Kingston u T KT2 ... 176 B2
Mitcham SW19 ... 180 B4
Acre Way HA6 ... 22 A2
Acris St SW18 ... 158 A6
ACS Hillingdon
International Sch
UB10 ... 82 B6
Action Ct TW15 ... 171 A2
ACTON ... 111 B5
Acton Bsns Ctr NW10 ... 89 B3
Acton Central Ind Est 4
W3 ... 110 D5
Acton Central Sta
W3 ... 111 B5
Acton Cl N9 ... 18 A2
ACTON GREEN ... 111 A2
Acton High Sch W3 ... 110 C4
Acton Hill Mews W3 .. 110 D5
Acton Ho
5 Acton W3 ... 89 A1
16 Haggerston E8 ... 95 D6
Acton Hospl W3 ... 110 C4
Acton La
Acton Green W4 ... 111 A2
Acton W3 ... 111 A4
Harlesden NW10 ... 89 B5
Acton Main Line Sta
W3 ... 89 A1
Acton Mews E8 ... 95 D6
Acton Park Ind Est
W3 ... 111 B4
Acton St WC1 ... 94 B4 233 C1
Acton Town Sta W3 ... 110 C4
Acton Vale Ind Pk
W3 ... 111 D5
Acuba Ho SW18 ... 157 D3
Acuba Rd SW18 ... 157 D2
Acworth Cl N9 ... 18 C4
Acworth Ho 1 SE18 ... 144 D6
Ada Ct
Islington N1 ... 235 A5
St John's Wood
W9 ... 92 A4 229 B1
Ada Gdns
Plaistow E15 ... 98 D6
South Bromley E14 ... 98 B1
Ada Ho 23 E2 ... 96 A6
Adair Cl SE25 ... 206 B6
Adair Ho SW3 ... 267 B6
Adair Rd W10 ... 91 A3
Adair Twr 7 W10 ... 91 A3
Ada Kennedy Ct 6
SE10 ... 142 A5
Ada Lewis Ho HA9 ... 66 B4
Adam Cl SE6 ... 185 C6
Adam Ct
Newington SE11 ... 261 C3
15 Sutton SM1 ... 218 A4
Adam & Eve Ct W1 ... 239 B2
Adam & Eve Mews
W8 ... 113 C3 255 B6
Adamfields NW3 ... 70 B1
Adam Lo N21 ... 16 B6
Adam Rd E4 ... 35 B4
Adams Bridge Bsns Ctr
HA9 ... 66 D3
Adams Cl
Finchley N3 ... 29 C3
Surbiton KT5 ... 198 B3
Wembley Pk NW9 ... 66 D6
Adams Ct E17 ... 53 A3
Adams Gardens Est 5
SE16 ... 118 C4
Adams Ho
3 South Bromley E14 ... 98 B1
3 Streatham SW16 ... 181 C5
Adams Mews
Upper Tooting SW17 ... 158 D2
Wood Green N22 ... 32 B3
Adamson Ct N2 ... 48 C6
Adamson Rd
Hampstead NW3 ... 70 B1
Newham E16 ... 99 A1
Adamson Way BR3 ... 208 A4
Adams Pl N7 ... 72 B3
Adams Qtr TW8 ... 131 C6
Adams Rd
Beckenham BR3 ... 207 A4
Tottenham N17 ... 33 B1
Adamsrill Cl EN1 ... 17 B5
Adamsrill Prim Sch
SE26 ... 163 A1
Adamsrill Rd SE26 ... 185 A6
Adam's Row
W1 ... 115 A6 248 B5
Adams Sq DA6 ... 147 A2
Adam St WC2 .. 116 A6 250 B5
Adams Way CR0 ... 206 A3
Adams Wlk 11 KT1 ... 176 A1
Adam Wlk SW6 ... 134 C5
Ada Pl E2 ... 96 A6
Ada Rd
Camberwell SE5 ... 139 C5
Wembley HA0, HA9 ... 65 D5
Adare Ctr The SW16 ... 160 A1
Adare Wlk SW16, SW2 .. 160 B2
Ada St E8 ... 96 B6
Adcot Wlk 6 BR6 ... 227 D4
Adderley Gdns SE9 ... 188 C6
Adderley Gr SW11 ... 159 A6
Adderley Rd HA3 ... 24 D2
Adderley St E14 ... 98 A1
Addey Ho SE8 ... 141 B5
Addey & Stanhope Sch
SE14 ... 141 C4
ADDINGTON ... 223 C3
Addington Ct 7
SW14 ... 133 B2
Addington Dr N12 ... 30 B4
Addington Gr SE26 ... 185 A6
Addington Ho 13
SW9 ... 138 B3
Addington Rd
Bow E3 ... 97 C4
Newham E16 ... 98 C3
Stroud Green N4 ... 50 C3
Thornton Heath CR0 ... 204 C1
West Wickham BR4 ... 224 C6
West Wickham BR4,
CR0 ... 224 B4
Addington Sq SE5 ... 139 B5
Addington St
SE1 ... 116 B4 250 D1
Addington Village Rd
CR0 ... 223 C3
Addington Village Sta
CR0 ... 223 C2
Addis Cl EN3 ... 6 D4
ADDISCOMBE ... 206 A1
Addiscombe Ave CR0 .. 206 A2
Addiscombe Cl HA3 ... 43 C4
Addiscombe Court Rd
CR0 ... 221 C6
Addiscombe Ct UB10 ... 83 A3
Addiscombe Rd CR0 .. 222 B6
Addiscombe Sta CR0 .. 206 A1
Addis Ho 13 E1 ... 96 C2
Addison Ave
Hounslow TW3 ... 130 A4
Notting Hill
W11 ... 113 A5 244 A3
Southgate N14 ... 15 C5
Addison Bridge Pl
W14 ... 113 B2 254 C4
Addison Cl
Northwood HA6 ... 22 A2
Orpington BR5 ... 211 A3
Addison Cres
W14 ... 113 A3 254 B6
Addison Ct
3 Belmont SM2 ... 217 D1
Ealing W5 ... 110 C6
Twickenham TW1 ... 153 A3
Addison Dr SE12 ... 165 B6
Addison Gdns
Hammersmith W14 ... 112 D3
Kingston u T KT5 ... 198 B5
Addison Gr W4 ... 111 C3
Addison Ho
NW8 ... 92 B4 229 C2
Addison Park Mans 12
W14 ... 112 D4
Addison Pl
Notting Hill
W11 ... 113 A5 244 A3
Southall UB1 ... 107 C6
Addison Prim Sch
W14 ... 112 D3
Addison Rd
Bromley BR2 ... 209 D4
Croydon SE25 ... 206 A5
Enfield EN3 ... 6 D4
Kensington
W14 ... 113 B3 254 C6
Teddington TW11 ... 175 B4
Walthamstow E17 ... 54 A4
Wanstead E11 ... 55 A3
Addison's Cl CR0 ... 223 B6
Addison Way
Hampstead Garden Suburb
NW11 ... 47 C5
Hayes UB3 ... 84 A1
Northwood HA6 ... 22 A2
Addle Hill EC4 ... 241 D1
Addle St EC2 ... 242 B3
Addlestone Ho 4
W10 ... 90 C2
Addy Ho SE16 ... 118 C2
Adecroft Way KT8 ... 196 A6
Adela Ave KT3 ... 200 B5
Adela Ho 9 W6 ... 112 C1
Adelaide Ave SE4 ... 141 C1
Adelaide Cl
Brixton SW9 ... 138 C1
Enfield EN1 ... 5 C5
Stanmore HA7 ... 25 A6
Adelaide Ct
15 Beckenham BR3 ... 185 C3
Hackney E5 ... 75 A3
Hanwell W7 ... 108 D4
St John's Wood NW8 ... 229 B3
Adelaide Gdns RM6 ... 59 A4
Adelaide Gr W12 ... 112 A5
Adelaide Ho E17 ... 53 B6
Adelaide Rd
Ashford TW15 ... 170 A6
Chislehurst BR7 ... 188 D5
Ealing W13 ... 109 A4
Heston TW5 ... 129 A4
Ilford IG1 ... 78 D6
Kingston u T KT6 ... 198 A4
Leyton E10 ... 76 A5
Primrose Hill NW3 ... 70 C1
Richmond TW9 ... 132 B1
Southall UB2 ... 107 A2
Teddington TW11 ... 174 D4
2 Wandsworth SW18 .. 157 C6
Adelaide St WC2 ... 250 A5
Adelaide Terr TW8 ... 109 D1
Adela St W10 ... 91 A3
Adelina Gr E1 ... 96 C2
Adelina Mews SW12 .. 159 D3
Adeline Pl WC1 .. 93 D2 239 D3
Adelphi Cres UB4 ... 83 D4
Adelphi Ct
19 Finchley N2 ... 30 B1
20 Rotherhithe SE16 ... 118 D4
Adelphi Terr WC2 ... 250 B5
Adelphi Way UB4 ... 83 D4
Adeney Cl W6 ... 134 D6
Aden Gr N16 ... 73 B4
Aden Ho 15 E1 ... 96 D2
Aden Lo N16 ... 73 B4
Adenmore Rd SE6 ... 163 C4
Aden Rd
Enfield EN3 ... 7 A1
Ilford IG1 ... 57 A2
Adeyfield Ho EC1 ... 235 D1
Adhara Rd HA6 ... 22 A5
Adie Rd W6 ... 112 C3
Adine Rd E13 ... 99 B3
Adisham Ho 4 E5 ... 74 B3
Adler Ind Est UB3 ... 105 B4
Adler St E1 ... 96 A1
Adley St E5 ... 75 A3
Adlington Cl N18 ... 33 C5
Admaston Rd SE18 ... 145 A6
Admiral Ct
Barking IG11 ... 102 C5
Admiral Ct *continued*
Carshalton SM5 ... 202 C1
Chelsea SW10 . 136 A4 266 B2
Hendon NW4 ... 46 A4
Marylebone W1 ... 238 A3
Admiral Ho TW11 ... 175 A6
Admiral Hyson Ind Est
SE16 ... 118 B1
Admiral Mews W10 ... 90 D3
Admiral Pl
Harringay N8 ... 50 D5
Rotherhithe SE16 ... 119 A5
Admirals Cl E18 ... 55 B5
Admirals Ct
Bermondsey SE1 ... 253 C3
3 Newham E6 ... 100 D1
32 Putney SW19 ... 156 D3
Admiral Seymour Rd
SE9 ... 144 B1
Admirals Gate SE10 ... 141 D4
Admiral Sq
SW10 ... 136 A4 266 B2
Admiral St SE8 ... 141 C4
Admirals Way E14 ... 119 C4
Admiral's Wlk NW3 ... 70 A5
Admiralty Arch*
SW1 ... 249 D4
Admiralty Cl 1 SE8 ... 141 C4
Admiralty Rd TW11 ... 174 D4
Admiralty Way TW11 .. 174 D4
Admiral Wlk W9 ... 91 C2
Adolf St SE6 ... 185 D6
Adolphus Rd N4 ... 50 D1
Adolphus St SE8 ... 141 B5
Adomar Rd RM8 ... 81 A5
Adpar St W2 ... 92 B2 236 C4
Adrian Ave NW2 ... 46 B1
Adrian Bolt Ho 2 E2 ... 96 B4
Adrian Cl EN5 ... 12 D5
Adrian Ho
Islington N1 ... 233 D5
South Lambeth SW8 ... 270 A4
Stratford E15 ... 76 B1
Adrian Mews SW10 ... 265 D6
Adriatic Bldg 18 E14 .. 119 A6
Adriatic Ho 18 E1 ... 96 D3
Adrienne Ave UB1 ... 85 B4
Adron Ho 13 SE16 ... 118 C2
Adstock Ho 5 N1 ... 72 D1
ADT Coll SW15 ... 157 B6
Advance Rd SE27 ... 183 A6
Advent Ct IG8 ... 36 D5
Adventurers Ct 17
E14 ... 120 B6
Advent Way N18 ... 34 D5
Adyar Ct 7 SW19 ... 179 A3
Adys Lawn NW2 ... 68 B2
Adys Rd SE15 ... 139 D2
Aegean Apts 7 E16 ... 121 A6
Aegon Ho 3 E14 ... 119 D3
Aerodrome Rd NW4,
NW9 ... 45 D6
Aerodrome Way TW5 . 128 C6
Aeroville NW9 ... 27 C1
Affleck St N1 ... 233 D3
Afghan Rd SW11 ... 136 C3
Africa Ho WC2 ... 240 C2
Afsil Ho EC1 ... 241 B3
Aga Khan Univ WC1 ... 239 D3
Agamemnon Rd NW6 ... 69 B3
Agar Cl KT6 ... 214 B6
Agar Gr NW1 ... 71 D1
Agar Ho 6 KT1 ... 198 A6
Agar Pl NW1 ... 71 C1
Agar St WC2 ... 250 B5
Agate Cl E16 ... 99 D1
Agate Ho
New Malden KT4 ... 199 C1
12 Penge SE26 ... 184 B5
Agate Rd W6 ... 112 C3
Agatha Cl E1 ... 118 C5
Agaton Rd SE9 ... 167 A2
Agave Rd NW2 ... 68 C4
Agdon St EC1 ... 94 D3 241 C6
Agincourt E11 ... 54 D3
Agincourt Rd NW3 ... 70 D4
Agnes Ave IG1 ... 78 D4
Agnes Cl E6 ... 122 C6
Agnes Ct 11 SW18 ... 136 B1
Agnesfield Cl N12 ... 30 C4
Agnes Gdns RM8 ... 80 D4
Agnes Ho 13 W11 ... 112 D6
Agnes Rd W3 ... 111 D4
Agnes St E14 ... 97 B1
Agnew Rd SE23 ... 162 D4
Agricola Pl EN1 ... 17 D6
Aidan Cl RM8 ... 81 A4
Aidans Ct N12 ... 30 C5
Aigburth Mans 5
SW9 ... 138 C5

Ailantus Ct HA8 . . . 26 B5
Aileen Wlk E15 . . . 76 D1
Ailsa Ave TW1 . . . 153 B6
Ailsa Rd TW1 . . . 153 B6
Ailsa St E14 . . . 98 A2
Ainger Rd NW3 . . . 70 D1
Ainsdale NW1 . . . 232 A2
Ainsdale Cl BR6 . . . 211 B1
Ainsdale Cres HA5 . . . 41 C6
Ainsdale Dr SE1 . . . 118 A1
Ainsdale Rd W5 . . . 87 D3
Ainsley Ave RM7 . . . 59 D3
Ainsley Cl N9 . . . 17 C3
Ainsley St E2 . . . 96 B4
Ainslie Ct 2 HA0 . . . 88 A5
Ainslie Ho 1 E4 . . . 35 C5
Ainslie Wlk 8 SW12 . . . 159 B4
Ainslie Wood Cres E4 . . 35 D5
Ainslie Wood Gdns E4 . . 35 D5
Ainslie Wood Prim Sch
E4 . . . 35 D5
Ainslie Wood Rd E4 . . . 35 D5
Ainsty St 20 SE16 . . . 118 C4
Ainsworth Cl
Camberwell SE5 . . . 139 C3
Dollis Hill NW2 . . . 68 A5
Ainsworth Est
NW8 . . . 92 A6 229 A6
Ainsworth Ho NW8 . . . 91 D6
Ainsworth Rd
Croydon CR0 . . . 220 D6
Hackney E9 . . . 74 C1
Ainsworth Way
NW8 . . . 92 A6 229 A6
Aintree Ave E6 . . . 100 A6
Aintree Cl UB8 . . . 82 D2
Aintree Ho SE26 . . . 184 B4
Aintree Rd UB6 . . . 87 B5
Aintree St
SW6 . . . 135 A5 264 B4
Airborne Ho 10 SM6 . . . 219 B4
Aird Ct TW12 . . . 173 D2
Aird Ho SE1 . . . 262 A5
Airdrie Cl
Barnsbury N1 . . . 72 B1
Hayes UB4 . . . 85 A2
Airedale Ave W4 . . . 111 D1
Airedale Ave S W4 . . . 111 D1
Airedale Rd
Balham SW12 . . . 158 D4
Ealing W5 . . . 109 D3
Airlie Gdns
Ilford IG1 . . . 56 D1
Kensington
W8 . . . 113 C5 245 A3
Airlinks Ind Est TW5 . . . 106 C1
Air Park Way TW13 . . . 150 B2
Airport Gate Bsns Ctr
UB7 . . . 126 C5
Airport Ho CR0 . . . 220 C2
Airport Rdbt E16 . . . 121 D5
Air St W1 . . . 249 B5
Airthrie Rd IG3 . . . 80 B6
Aisgill Ave
SW5 . . . 113 B1 254 D1
Aisher Rd SE28 . . . 124 C6
Aislabie Ho N21 . . . 17 B5
Aislibie Rd SE12 . . . 142 C1
Aiten Pl W6 . . . 112 A2
Aithan Ho 15 E14 . . . 97 B1
Aitken Cl
Carshalton CR4 . . . 202 D2
Hackney E8 . . . 96 A6
Aitken Rd
Barnet EN5 . . . 12 C6
Catford SE6 . . . 163 D2
Aits View KT8 . . . 195 D6
Ajax Ave NW9 . . . 45 C6
Ajax Ct NW9 . . . 45 C6
Ajax Ho 15 E2 . . . 96 B5
Ajax Rd NW6 . . . 69 C3
Akabusi Cl SE25 . . . 206 A3
Akbar Ho 7 E14 . . . 119 D2
Akehurst St SW15 . . . 156 A4
Akenside Ct 3 NW3 . . . 70 B3
Akenside Rd NW3 . . . 70 B3
Akerman Rd
Brixton SW9 . . . 138 D4
Kingston u T KT6 . . . 197 C3
Akintaro Ho 7 SE8 . . . 141 B6
Akiva Sch N3 . . . 29 D1
Alabama St SE18 . . . 145 C5
Alacross Rd W5 . . . 109 D4
Aladdin Workspace
UB6 . . . 85 D6
Alamaro Lo 5 SE10 . . . 120 D3
Alandale Dr HA5 . . . 22 B2
Aland Ct SE16 . . . 119 A3
Alander Mews E17 . . . 54 A5
Alan Dr EN5 . . . 13 A5
Alan Gdns RM7 . . . 59 C2
Alan Hocken Way E15 . . 98 C5
Alan Lo N3 . . . 29 C2
Alan Preece Ct NW6 . . . 68 D1
Alan Rd SW19 . . . 179 A5
Alanthus Cl SE12 . . . 165 A5
Alaska Bldg 12 SE13 . . . 141 D4
Alaska St SE1 . . . 251 A3
Alastor Ho 10 E14 . . . 120 A3
Alba Cl UB4 . . . 84 D3
Albacore Cres SE13 . . . 163 D5
Alba Gdns NW11 . . . 47 A3
Albain Cres TW15 . . . 148 A2
Alba Mews SW18,
SW19 . . . 157 C2
Alban Ho
Hampstead NW3 . . . 70 A2
New Cross SE14 . . . 141 B4
Albans Cl SW16 . . . 160 A1
Albany W1 . . . 249 A5
Albany Cl
Bushey WD23 . . . 8 B5
Ickenham UB10 . . . 60 C3
Mortlake SW14 . . . 132 D1
Sidcup DA5 . . . 168 D4
West Green N15 . . . 51 A5
Albany Coll NW4 . . . 46 C4
Albany Coll Hendry Ho
NW4 . . . 46 B4
Albany Cres
Claygate KT10 . . . 212 C2
Edgware HA8 . . . 26 C3
Albany Ct
Ashford TW15 . . . 171 B4
Cheam SM1 . . . 217 B4
Chingford E4 . . . 19 D5
College Pk NW10 . . . 90 B4
Finchley N12 . . . 29 D4
Grahame Pk HA8 . . . 27 B2
Kingston u T KT2 . . . 176 A4
NW8 . . . 229 C3
Richmond TW10 . . . 153 B1
Surbiton KT6 . . . 197 D2
Walthamstow E10 . . . 53 C2
Westminster SW1 . . . 259 C6
8 Whitechapel E1 . . . 96 A1
Albany Ctyd W1 . . . 249 B5
Albany Ho
6 Brentford TW8 . . . 132 A6
Edgware HA8 . . . 26 C3
Upper Clapton E5 . . . 74 C6
Albany Mans SW11 . . . 267 B3
Albany Mews
Camberwell SE5 . . . 139 A6
Islington N1 . . . 72 C1
Kingston u T KT2 . . . 175 D4
Plaistow BR1 . . . 187 A4
Sutton SM1 . . . 217 D3
Albany Par 4 TW8 . . . 132 A6
Albany Park Ave EN3 . . . 6 D4
Albany Park Rd KT2 . . . 176 A4
Albany Park Sta
DA14 . . . 168 D2
Albany Pas 12 TW10 . . . 154 A6
Albany Pl TW8 . . . 131 D6
Albany Rd
Brentford TW8 . . . 131 D6
Camberwell SE5 . . . 139 C6
Chislehurst BR7 . . . 188 D5
Dagenham RM6 . . . 59 B3
Ealing W13 . . . 109 B6
Enfield EN3 . . . 6 D5
Erith DA17 . . . 147 B6
Leyton E10 . . . 53 C2
Manor Pk E12 . . . 77 D4
New Malden KT3 . . . 199 B5
Richmond TW10 . . . 154 A6
Sidcup DA5 . . . 168 C4
Stroud Green N4 . . . 50 C3
Upper Edmonton N18 . . . 34 C5
Walthamstow E17 . . . 53 A3
Wimbledon SW19 . . . 179 D5
Albany Reach KT7 . . . 196 D4
Albany Sch EN3 . . . 6 D5
Albany St NW1 . . 93 B4 231 D2
Albany Terr 6 TW10 . . . 154 B6
Albany The
Kingston u T KT2 . . . 175 D4
Woodford IG8 . . . 36 D6
Albany View IG9 . . . 21 A3
Albany Wlk N15 . . . 50 D5
Alba Pl W11 . . . 91 B1
Albatross 31 NW9 . . . 27 D1
Albatross Cl E6 . . . 100 B3
Albatross St SE18 . . . 145 C5
Albemarle SW19 . . . 156 D2
Albemarle App IG2 . . . 56 D3
Albemarle Ave TW2 . . . 151 B3
Albemarle Gdns
Ilford IG2 . . . 56 D3
Albemarle Gdns *continued*
New Malden KT3 . . . 199 B5
Albemarle Ho
2 Brixton SW9 . . . 138 C2
Rotherhithe SE8 . . . 119 B2
Albemarle Lo SE26 . . . 185 A5
Albemarle Mans NW3 . . 69 D4
Albemarle Pk
Beckenham BR3 . . . 185 D2
Stanmore HA7 . . . 25 C5
Albemarle Prim Sch
SW19 . . . 157 A2
Albemarle Rd
Beckenham BR2, BR3 . . . 186 A2
East Barnet EN4 . . . 14 C4
Albemarle St
W1 . . . 115 C6 249 A5
Albemarle Way EC1 . . . 241 C5
Alberon Gdns NW11 . . . 47 B5
Alberta Ave SM1 . . . 217 B3
Alberta Ct 1 TW10 . . . 154 B6
Alberta Ho
Blackwall E14 . . . 120 A5
Hayes UB4 . . . 84 B4
Alberta Rd EN1 . . . 18 A5
Alberta St
SE17 . . . 116 D1 261 D2
Albert Ave
Chingford E4 . . . 35 C6
South Lambeth SW8 . . . 270 C3
Albert Barnes Ho SE1 . 262 A5
Albert Bigg Point E15 . . 98 A6
Albert Bridge Rd
SW11 . . . 136 D5 267 C3
Albert Carr Gdns
SW16 . . . 182 A5
Albert Cl
11 Hackney E9 . . . 96 B6
Wood Green N22 . . . 31 D2
Albert Cotts 2 E1 . . . 96 A2
Albert Cres E4 . . . 35 C6
Albert Ct
Knightsbridge SW7 . . . 246 C1
9 Putney SW19 . . . 157 A3
Albert Dr SW19 . . . 157 A3
Albert Emb
SE1 . . . 116 A2 260 B3
Albert Gate Ct SW1 . . . 247 C1
Albert Gdns E1 . . . 96 D1
Albert Gr SW20 . . . 178 D2
Albert Gray Ho SW10 . . 266 C4
Albert Hall Mans
SW7 . . . 114 B4 246 C1
Albert Ho
Stanmore HA7 . . . 25 B5
5 Wanstead E18 . . . 55 B6
2 Woolwich SE28 . . . 123 A3
Albert Mans
Battersea SW11 . . . 267 C2
Hornsey N8 . . . 50 A2
Albert Meml*
SW7 . . . 114 B4 246 C1
Albert Mews W8 . . . 256 A6
Albert Palace Mans
SW11 . . . 268 B2
Albert Pl
Finchley N3 . . . 29 C2
Kensington
W8 . . . 113 D4 245 D1
Albert Rd
Ashford TW15 . . . 170 B5
Bromley Comm BR2 . . . 209 D4
Buckhurst Hill IG9 . . . 21 D2
Chislehurst SE9 . . . 166 A1
Croydon SE25 . . . 206 B5
Dagenham RM8 . . . 59 C1
Ealing W5 . . . 87 B3
East Barnet EN4 . . . 2 A1
Erith DA17 . . . 125 B1
Finsbury Pk N4 . . . 50 B2
Hampton TW12 . . . 174 A5
Harrow HA2 . . . 42 A6
Hayes UB3 . . . 105 C3
Hendon NW4 . . . 46 D5
Hounslow TW3 . . . 129 C1
Ilford IG1 . . . 79 A5
Kilburn NW6 . . . 91 B5
Kingston u T KT1 . . . 176 B1
Leyton E10 . . . 54 A1
Mill Hill NW7 . . . 27 D5
Mitcham CR4 . . . 202 D6
Newham E16 . . . 122 B4
New Malden KT3 . . . 199 D5
Penge SE20 . . . 184 D4
Richmond TW10 . . . 154 B6
Sidcup DA5 . . . 169 D4
Southall UB2 . . . 106 D3
South Tottenham N15 . . . 51 C3
Sutton SM1 . . . 218 B3
Teddington TW11 . . . 174 D4
Albert Rd *continued*
Twickenham TW1 . . . 152 D3
Walthamstow E17 . . . 53 C4
4 Wanstead E18 . . . 55 B6
Wood Green N22 . . . 31 C2
Yiewsley UB7 . . . 104 A5
Albert's Ct NW1 . . . 237 B6
Albert Sleet Ct N9 . . . 18 B1
Albert Sq
Leyton E15 . . . 76 C3
South Lambeth
SW8 . . . 138 B5 270 C3
Albert St
Camden Town
NW1 . . . 93 B6 231 D5
North Finchley N12 . . . 30 A5
Albert Starr Ho 7
SE8 . . . 118 D2
Albert Studios SW11 . . . 267 C2
Albert Terr
Buckhurst Hill IG9 . . . 21 D2
Camden Town
NW1 . . . 93 A6 231 A5
Stonebridge NW10 . . . 89 A6
Albert Terr Mews
NW1 . . . 231 A5
Albert Victoria Ho
N22 . . . 32 C2
Albert Way SE15 . . . 140 B5
Albert Westcott Ho
SE17 . . . 261 D2
Albert Whicher Ho 3
E17 . . . 54 A5
Albert Wlk E16 . . . 122 D4
Albion Ave
Clapham SW8 . . . 137 D3
Muswell Hill N10 . . . 31 A2
Albion Cl W2 . . . 247 B6
Albion Coll
WC1 . . . 94 A2 240 B3
Albion Ct
7 Hammersmith W6 . . . 112 B2
Sutton SM2 . . . 218 B1
2 Woolwich SE7 . . . 122 A2
Albion Dr E8 . . . 74 A1
Albion Est SE16 . . . 118 C4
Albion Gate W2 . . . 247 B6
Albion Gdns 1 W6 . . . 112 B2
Albion Gr N16 . . . 73 C4
Albion Hill IG10 . . . 21 D6
Albion Ho
17 Deptford SE8 . . . 141 C5
EC1 . . . 241 C4
Newham E16 . . . 122 D5
Albion Mews
Bayswater
W2 . . . 114 C6 247 B6
6 Hammersmith W6 . . . 112 B2
Islington N1 . . . 234 A6
Albion Pk IG10 . . . 21 D6
Albion Pl
Broadgate EC2 . . . 242 D3
Clerkenwell EC1 . . . 241 C4
Hammersmith W6 . . . 112 B2
South Norwood SE25 . . . 206 A6
Albion Prim Sch
SE16 . . . 118 C4
Albion Rd
Bexley DA6 . . . 147 C1
Dagenham RM10 . . . 81 B3
Hayes UB3 . . . 83 C1
Hounslow TW3 . . . 129 C1
Kingston u T KT2 . . . 177 A2
Stoke Newington N16 . . . 73 B4
Sutton SM2 . . . 218 B1
Tottenham N17 . . . 34 A1
Twickenham TW2 . . . 152 C3
Walthamstow E17 . . . 54 A6
Albion Riverside
SW11 . . . 267 A4
Albion Sq E8 . . . 73 D1
Albion St
Bayswater
W2 . . . 114 C6 247 B6
Rotherhithe SE16 . . . 118 C4
Thornton Heath CR0 . . . 204 D1
Albion Terr
Hackney E8 . . . 73 D1
Sewardstone E4 . . . 7 D1
Albion Villas Rd SE23,
SE26 . . . 162 C1
Albion Way
Barbican EC1 . . . 242 A3
Lewisham SE13 . . . 142 A1
Wembley HA9 . . . 66 C5
Albion Wlk N1 . . . 233 B3
Albion Works Studios 14
E8 . . . 74 A3
Albion Yd N1 . . . 233 B3
Albon Ho SW18 . . . 157 D5
Albrighton Rd SE5,
SE22 . . . 139 C2
Albuhera Cl EN2 . . . 4 C4
Albury Ave
Bexleyheath DA7 . . . 147 A3
Hounslow TW7 . . . 130 D5
Albury Bldgs SE1 . . . 251 D1
Albury Cl TW12 . . . 173 D4
Albury Ct
4 Croydon CR0 . . . 221 A4
Deptford SE8 . . . 141 C6
Mitcham CR4 . . . 180 B1
6 Northolt UB5 . . . 84 C4
Ruislip HA4 . . . 62 C3
Sutton SM1 . . . 218 A4
Albury Dr HA5 . . . 22 D3
Albury Lo 7 SW2 . . . 160 B4
Albury Mews E12 . . . 77 C6
Albury Rd KT9 . . . 214 A3
Albury St SE8 . . . 141 C6
Albyfield BR1 . . . 210 B6
Albyn Rd SE8 . . . 141 C4
Alcester Cres E5 . . . 74 B6
Alcester Ct 4 SM6 . . . 219 B4
Alcester Rd SM6 . . . 219 B4
Alchemea Coll of Audio
Engineering
N1 . . . 94 D6 234 D6
Alcock Cl SM6 . . . 219 D1
Alcock Rd TW5 . . . 128 D5
Alconbury DA6 . . . 169 D6
Alconbury Rd E5 . . . 74 A6
Alcorn Cl SM3 . . . 217 C6
Alcott Cl W7 . . . 86 D2
Aldborough Ct
Chingford E4 . . . 19 D1
Ilford IG2 . . . 57 D4
ALDBOROUGH
HATCH . . . 57 C5
Aldborough Rd IG2 . . . 57 D6
Aldborough Rd N IG2 . . 57 D4
Aldborough Rd S IG3 . . 57 C2
Aldbourne Rd W12 . . . 112 A5
Aldbridge St
SE17 . . . 117 C1 263 B2
Aldburgh Mews W1 . . . 238 B2
Aldbury Ave HA9 . . . 66 D1
Aldbury Ho SW3 . . . 257 A3
Aldbury Mews N9 . . . 17 B4
Aldebert Terr
SW8 . . . 138 B5 270 C3
Aldeburgh Cl 16 E5 . . . 74 B6
Aldeburgh Pl
Greenwich SE10 . . . 121 A2
Woodford IG8 . . . 37 A6
Aldeburgh St SE10 . . . 121 A1
Alden Ave E15 . . . 98 D4
Alden Ct
South Croydon CR0 . . . 221 C5
Wimbledon SW19 . . . 179 C4
Aldenham Ctry Pk WD6 . 9 B6
Aldenham Dr UB8 . . . 82 D3
Aldenham Ho NW1 . . . 232 B3
Aldenham Rd WD6 . . . 9 C6
Aldenham St
NW1 . . . 93 D5 232 C3
Alden Ho E8 . . . 96 B6
Aldensley Rd W6 . . . 112 B3
Alderbrook Prim Sch
SW12 . . . 159 B4
Alderbrook Rd SW12 . . 159 B5
Alderbury Rd SW13 . . . 134 A6
Alder Ct
East Finchley N2 . . . 48 B6
3 West Norwood
SW16 . . . 182 C5
Alder Gr NW2 . . . 68 B6
Aldergrove Gdns
TW4 . . . 129 A3
Aldergrove Ho 3 E5 . . . 74 A6
Alder Ho
Camberwell SE15 . . . 139 D6
1 Maitland Pk NW3 . . . 70 D2
St Johns SE4 . . . 141 C2
Alderley Ho 36 SW8 . . . 137 D3
Alder Lo SW6 . . . 134 D4
Alder Lodge N9 . . . 17 C3
Alderman Ave IG11 . . . 102 A4
Aldermanbury
EC2 . . . 95 A1 242 B2
Aldermanbury Sq EC2 . 242 B3
Alderman Ct 18 N11 . . . 30 D5
Alderman Judge Mall 6
KT1 . . . 176 A1
Alderman's Hill N13 . . . 32 B6
Alderman's Wlk EC2 . . 243 A3
Aldermary Rd BR1 . . . 187 A2
Aldermead 2 TW3 . . . 129 D1
Alder Mews 12 N19 . . . 71 C6
Aldermoor Rd SE6 . . . 163 B1
Alderney Ave TW5 . . . 129 D5
Alderney Gdns UB5 . . . 63 B1
Alderney Ho
20 Canonbury N1 . . . 73 A2
Enfield EN3 . . . 6 D5
Alderney Mews SE1 . . . 262 C6
Alderney Rd E1 . . . 96 D3
Alderney St
SW1 . . . 115 B1 258 D2
Alder Rd
Mortlake SW14 . . . 133 B2
Sidcup DA14 . . . 167 D1
Alders Ave IG8 . . . 36 C4
ALDERSBROOK . . . 77 C6
Aldersbrook Ave EN1 . . . 5 C3
Aldersbrook Dr KT2 . . . 176 B4
Aldersbrook La E12 . . . 78 B5
Aldersbrook Prim Sch
E12 . . . 77 C6
Aldersbrook Rd E11,
E12 . . . 77 C6
Alders Cl
Ealing W5 . . . 109 D3
Edgware HA8 . . . 27 A5
Wanstead E11 . . . 77 B6
Alders Ct N17 . . . 52 B5
Aldersey Gdns IG11 . . . 79 B2
Aldersford Cl SE4 . . . 140 D1
Aldersgate Ct EC1 . . . 242 A3
Aldersgate St
EC1 . . . 95 A2 242 A3
Aldersgrove KT8 . . . 196 B4
Aldersgrove Ave SE9,
SE12 . . . 165 D1
Aldershot Rd NW6 . . . 91 B6
Aldersmead Ave CR0 . . 206 D3
Aldersmead Rd BR3 . . . 185 A3
Alderson Pl UB2 . . . 108 A5
Alderson St W10 . . . 91 A3
Alders Rd HA8 . . . 27 A5
Alders The
Feltham TW13 . . . 173 A6
Heston TW5 . . . 129 B6
Southgate N21 . . . 16 C5
Streatham SW16 . . . 181 C6
West Wickham BR4 . . . 223 D6
Alderton 9 KT2 . . . 176 D2
Alderton Cl NW10 . . . 67 B5
Alderton Cres NW4 . . . 46 B4
Alderton Ct KT8 . . . 195 B5
Alderton Rd
Croydon CR0 . . . 206 A2
Herne Hill SE24 . . . 139 A2
Alderton Way NW4 . . . 46 B4
Alderville Rd SW6 . . . 135 B3
Alderwick Ct N7 . . . 72 B2
Alderwick Dr TW3 . . . 130 B2
Alder Wlk IG11 . . . 79 A2
Alderwood Mews EN4 . . . 2 A5
Alderwood Prim Sch
SE9 . . . 167 C5
Alderwood Rd SE9 . . . 167 B5
Aldford St W1 . . 115 A5 248 B4
Aldgate EC3 . . . 95 C1 243 B1
Aldgate East Sta
E1 . . . 95 D1 243 D2
Aldgate High St
EC3 . . . 95 D1 243 C1
Aldgate Sta
EC3 . . . 95 D1 243 C1
Aldham Hall 1 E11 . . . 55 A3
Aldham Ho SE4 . . . 141 B4
Aldine Ct W12 . . . 112 C5
Aldine St W12 . . . 112 C4
Aldington Cl RM8 . . . 58 C1
Aldington Ct 1 E8 . . . 74 A1
Aldington Rd SE18 . . . 121 D3
Aldis Mews
3 Holdbrook EN3 . . . 7 C6
Upper Tooting SW17 . . . 180 C5
Aldis St SW17 . . . 180 C5
Aldred Rd NW6 . . . 69 C3
Aldren Rd SW17 . . . 158 A1
Aldriche Way E4 . . . 36 A4
Aldrich Gdns SM3 . . . 217 B5
Aldrich Terr SW18 . . . 158 A2
Aldrick Ho N1 . . . 233 D4
Aldridge Ave
Edgware HA8 . . . 10 D1
Holdbrook EN3 . . . 7 C5
Ruislip HA4 . . . 62 D6
Stanmore HA7 . . . 26 A2
Aldridge Ct W11 . . . 91 B2
Aldridge Rd Villas
W11 . . . 91 B2
Aldridge Rise KT3 . . . 199 C3
Aldridge Wlk N14 . . . 16 A4

Aldrington Rd SW16 . . 181 C6
Aldsworth Cl W9 . . 91 D3
Aldwich Ho WC2 . . 240 D1
Aldwick Cl SE9 . . 167 B1
Aldwick Ct N12 . . 30 A6
Aldwick Rd CR0 . . 220 B4
Aldworth Gr SE13 . . 164 A5
Aldworth Rd E15 . . 76 C1
Aldwych WC2 . . 94 B1 240 D1
Aldwych Ave IG6 . . 57 A5
Aldwych Bldgs WC2 . . 240 B2
Aldwyn Ho SW8 . . 270 A3
Alers Rd DA6 . . 168 D6
Alesia Cl N22 . . 32 A3
Alestan Beck Rd E16 . . 99 D1
Alexa Ct 4 SM2 . . 217 C2
Alexander Ave NW10 . . 68 B1
Alexander Cl
Barnet EN4 . . 2 B1
Hayes BR2 . . 209 A1
Sidcup DA15 . . 167 C5
Southall UB2 . . 108 A5
Twickenham TW2 . . 152 D2
Alexander Ct
Beckenham BR3 . . 186 B2
Greenwich SE3 . . 143 B3
Stanmore HA7 . . 44 B6
14 Surbiton KT6 . . 197 D2
Wandsworth SW18 . . 158 A6
Alexander Evans Mews
SE23 . . 162 D2
Alexander Fleming Laboratory Mus*
W2 . . 236 D2
Alexander Ho
8 Kingston u T KT2 . . 176 A2
15 Millwall E14 . . 119 C3
16 Sutton SM2 . . 218 A2
Alexander Lo SM1 . . 217 B3
Alexander McLeod Prim Sch SE2 . . 124 B1
Alexander Mews 2
W2 . . 91 D1
Alexander Pl SW7 . . 257 A4
Alexander Rd
Bexley DA7 . . 146 D3
Chislehurst BR7 . . 188 D5
Upper Holloway N19 . . 72 A6
Alexander Sq
SW3 . . 114 C2 257 A4
Alexander St W2 . . 91 C1
Alexander Terr SE2 . . 124 B1
Alexandra Ave
Battersea SW11 . . 268 A1
Harrow HA2 . . 63 C5
Southall UB1 . . 107 B6
Sutton SM1 . . 217 C5
Wood Green N22 . . 31 D2
Alexandra Bsns Ctr EN3 . 6 D1
Alexandra Cl
Ashford TW15 . . 171 B3
Deptford SE8 . . 141 B6
Harrow HA2 . . 63 D5
Alexandra Cotts
New Cross SE14 . . 141 B4
Penge SE20 . . 184 D4
Alexandra Cres BR1 . . 186 D4
Alexandra Ct
Ashford TW15 . . 171 B4
Ealing W5 . . 87 C2
Greenford UB6 . . 85 D5
Hounslow TW3 . . 129 D3
Paddington W9 . . 236 B6
4 Shacklewell N16 . . 73 D4
5 Shepherd's Bush
W12 . . 112 A4
Southgate N14 . . 15 C6
Wembley HA9 . . 66 B4
Alexandra Dr
Surbiton KT5 . . 198 C2
West Norwood SE19 . . 183 C5
Alexandra Gdns
Chiswick W4 . . 133 C5
Cranley Gdns N10 . . 49 B5
Hounslow TW3 . . 129 D3
Wallington SM5 . . 219 A1
Alexandra Gr
Finchley N12 . . 29 D4
Finsbury Pk N4 . . 50 D1
Alexandra Ho 13 W6 . . 112 C1
Alexandra Inf Sch
Kingston u T KT2 . . 176 C3
Penge BR3 . . 184 D3
Alexandra Jun & Inf Sch
TW3 . . 129 D3
Alexandra Jun Sch
SE26 . . 184 D4
Alexandra Mans
Chelsea SW3 . . 266 C5
Cricklewood NW2 . . 68 D3
6 Hampstead NW6 . . 69 C3
9 Shepherd's Bush
W12 . . 112 C5
Alexandra Mews N2 . . 48 D6
Alexandra National Ho
N4 . . 72 D6
Alexandra Pal* N22 . . 31 D1
Alexandra Palace Sta
N22 . . 32 A1
Alexandra Palace Way
N10 . . 49 C6
Alexandra Park Rd N10,
N22 . . 31 D2
Alexandra Park Sch
N11 . . 31 C2
Alexandra Pl
Croydon CR0 . . 205 C1
South Norwood SE25 . . 205 B4
St John's Wood
NW8 . . 92 A6 229 B6
Alexandra Prim Sch
N22 . . 32 B1
Alexandra Rd
Acton W4 . . 111 B4
Ashford TW15 . . 171 C4
10 Brentford TW8 . . 131 D6
Croydon CR0 . . 205 C2
Dagenham RM6 . . 59 A3
Edmonton N9 . . 18 B4
Enfield EN3 . . 6 D1
Hampstead NW8 . . 70 B1
Hendon NW4 . . 46 D5
Hornsey N8, N22 . . 50 C6
Hounslow TW3 . . 129 D3
Kingston u T KT2 . . 176 C3
Leyton E10 . . 76 A5
Mitcham SW19 . . 180 C3
Mortlake SW14 . . 133 B2
Muswell Hill N10 . . 31 B3
Penge SE26 . . 184 D4
Richmond TW9 . . 132 B3
Thames Ditton KT7 . . 196 D4
Tottenham N15 . . 51 B4
Twickenham TW1 . . 153 C5
Wallend E6 . . 100 C4
Walthamstow E17 . . 53 B2
Wanstead E18 . . 55 B6
Wimbledon SW19 . . 179 C5
Alexandra Sch HA2 . . 63 C6
Alexandra Sq SM4 . . 201 C4
Alexandra St
5 Deptford SE14 . . 141 A5
Newham E16 . . 99 A2
Alexandra Wlk 8
SE19 . . 183 C5
Alexandria Rd W13 . . 109 B6
Alex Gossip Ho SW6 . . 265 A1
Alexis St SE16 . . 118 A2
Alfearn Rd E5 . . 74 C4
Alford Ct
18 Belmont SM2 . . 217 D1
Shoreditch N1 . . 235 B3
Alford Gn CR0 . . 224 B2
Alford Ho
Crouch End N6 . . 49 C3
6 Woolwich SE18 . . 144 D6
Alford Pl N1 . . 235 B3
Alfoxton Ave N8, N15 . . 50 D5
Alfreda Ct SW11 . . 268 C1
Alfreda St
SW11 . . 137 B4 268 C1
Alfred Butt Ho SW17 . . 158 D1
Alfred Cl W4 . . 111 B2
Alfred Findley Ho N22 . . 32 D1
Alfred Gdns UB1 . . 107 A6
Alfred Ho E9 . . 75 A3
Alfred Hurley Ho
SW17 . . 180 A6
Alfred Mews W1, WC1 . . 239 C4
Alfred Nunn Ho NW10 . . 89 D6
Alfred Pl WC1 . . 93 D2 239 C4
Alfred Prior Ho 7 E12 . . 78 C4
Alfred Rd
Acton W3 . . 111 A5
Buckhurst Hill IG9 . . 21 D2
Croydon SE25 . . 206 A4
Erith DA17 . . 125 B1
Feltham TW13 . . 150 C2
Kingston u T KT1 . . 198 B6
Leyton E15 . . 76 D3
Paddington W2 . . 91 C2
Sutton SM1 . . 218 A3
Alfred Salter Ho SE1 . . 263 D3
Alfred Salter Prim Sch
SE16 . . 118 D4
Alfred's Gdns IG11 . . 101 C5
Alfred St E3 . . 97 B4
Alfred's Way (East Ham & Barking By-Pass)
IG11 . . 101 B5
Alfred's Way Ind Est
IG11 . . 102 A6
Alfred Villas 9 E17 . . 54 A5
Alfreton Cl SW19 . . 156 D1
Alfriston KT5 . . 198 B3
Alfriston Ave
Harrow HA2 . . 41 C2
Thornton Heath CR0 . . 204 A2
Alfriston Cl KT5 . . 198 B3
Alfriston Rd SW11 . . 158 D6
Algar Cl
Isleworth TW7 . . 131 A2
Stanmore HA7 . . 24 D5
Algar Ct TW12 . . 173 D2
Algar Ho SE1 . . 251 C1
Algar Rd TW7 . . 131 A2
Algarve Rd SW18 . . 157 D3
Algernon Rd
Hendon NW4 . . 46 A3
Kilburn NW6 . . 91 C6
Lewisham SE13 . . 141 D1
Algers Cl IG10 . . 21 D6
Algers Rd IG10 . . 21 D6
Alghers Mead IG10 . . 21 D6
Algiers Rd SE13 . . 141 C1
Alguin Ct HA7 . . 25 C3
Alibon Gdns RM10 . . 81 C3
Alibon Rd RM10 . . 81 C3
Alice Cl 13 EN5 . . 2 A1
Alice Ct 10 N3 . . 29 C2
Alice Gilliott Ct W14 . . 264 D6
Alice La E3 . . 97 B6
Alice Mews 3 TW11 . . 174 D5
Alice Owen Tech Ctr
EC1 . . 234 C2
Alice Shepherd Ho 12
E14 . . 120 A4
Alice St SE1 . . 117 C3 263 A5
Alice Thompson Cl
SE12 . . 165 C2
Alice Walker Cl 8
SE24 . . 138 D1
Alice Way TW3 . . 129 D1
Alicia Ave HA3 . . 43 C5
Alicia Cl HA3 . . 43 C5
Alicia Gdns HA3 . . 43 C5
Alicia Ho DA16 . . 146 B4
Alie St E1 . . 95 D1 243 D1
Alington Cres NW9 . . 45 A1
Alison Cl
Croydon CR0 . . 206 D1
Newham E6 . . 100 C1
Alison Ct HA8 . . 26 D5
Aliwal Rd SW11 . . 136 C1
Alkerden Rd W4 . . 111 C1
Alkham Rd N16 . . 73 D6
Allam Ho W11 . . 244 A6
Allan Barclay Cl N15 . . 51 D3
Allanbridge N16 . . 51 C2
Allan Cl KT3 . . 199 B4
Allandale Ave N3 . . 47 B6
Allan Ho SW8 . . 269 C2
Allanson Ct E10 . . 75 C6
Allan Way W3 . . 89 A2
Allard Cres WD23 . . 8 A2
Allard Gdns SW4 . . 159 D6
Allardyce St SW4,
SW9 . . 138 B1
Allbrook Cl TW11 . . 174 C5
Allbrook Ho 4 SW15 . . 156 A4
Allcot Cl TW14 . . 149 D3
Allcott Ho TW7 . . 130 D2
Allcroft Rd NW5 . . 71 A2
Allder Way CR2 . . 220 D1
Allenby Cl UB6 . . 85 C4
Allenby Prim Sch UB1 . . 85 C1
Allenby Rd
Forest Hill SE23 . . 163 A1
Southall UB1 . . 85 C3
Woolwich SE28 . . 123 A3
Allen Cl
Streatham CR4 . . 181 C2
Sunbury TW16 . . 172 B2
Allen Ct
Greenford UB6 . . 64 D3
Walthamstow E17 . . 53 C3
Allendale Ave UB1 . . 85 C1
Allendale Cl
Camberwell SE5 . . 139 B4
Forest Hill SE26 . . 184 D5
Allendale Rd UB6 . . 65 B2
Allen Edwards Dr
SW8 . . 138 A4 270 A2
Allen Edwards Prim Sch
SW4 . . 138 A4 270 A1
Allenford Ho SW15 . . 155 D5
All England Lawn Tennis & Croquet Club The
SW19 . . 157 A1
Allen Ho W8 . . 255 B6
Allen Mans W8 . . 255 B6
Allen Rd
Old Ford E3 . . 97 B5
Penge BR3 . . 184 D1
Stoke Newington N16 . . 73 C4
Sunbury TW16 . . 172 B1
Thornton Heath CR0 . . 204 C1
Allensbury Pl
7 Camden Town
NW1 . . 71 D1
Camden Town NW1 . . 72 A1
Allens Rd EN3 . . 18 C6
Allen St W8 . . 113 C3 255 B5
Allenswood 12 SW19 . . 157 A3
Allenswood Rd SE9 . . 144 B3
Allerdale Ho 7 N4 . . 51 B2
Allerford Ct
Catford SE6 . . 163 D1
Harrow HA2 . . 42 A4
Allerford Rd SE6 . . 185 D6
Allerton Ct
5 Hendon NW4 . . 28 D1
North Cheam SM3 . . 216 D6
Allerton Ho
4 Merton SW19 . . 180 A3
Shoreditch N1 . . 235 D3
Allerton Rd N16 . . 73 A6
Allerton St N1 . . 235 D2
Allerton Wlk 11 N7 . . 72 B6
Allestree Rd
SW6 . . 135 A5 264 A3
Alleyn Cres SE21 . . 161 B2
Alleyndale Rd RM8 . . 80 C6
Alleyn Ho
Bermondsey SE1 . . 262 C5
St Luke's EC1 . . 242 B5
Alleyn Pk
Dulwich SE21 . . 161 C1
Southall UB2 . . 107 C1
Alleyn Rd SE21 . . 161 C1
Alleyn's Sch SE22 . . 161 C6
Allfarthing La SW18 . . 158 A5
Allfarthing Prim Sch
SW18 . . 158 A5
Allgood Cl SM4 . . 200 D3
Allgood St 10 E2 . . 95 D5
Allhallows La EC4 . . 252 C5
Allhallows Rd E6 . . 100 A1
All Hallows Rd N17 . . 33 C2
Alliance Cl
Twickenham TW4 . . 151 B6
Wembley HA0 . . 65 D4
Alliance Ct
Acton W3 . . 88 D2
Ashford TW15 . . 171 A6
Alliance Rd
Acton W3 . . 88 D3
East Wickham SE18 . . 146 A5
1 Newham E16 . . 99 C2
Allied Ind Est W3 . . 111 C5
Allied Way W3 . . 111 C4
Allingham Cl W7 . . 108 D6
Allingham Ct NW3 . . 70 C3
Allingham Mews N1 . . 235 A4
Allingham St
N1 . . 95 A5 235 A4
Allington Ave
Tottenham N17 . . 33 C4
Upper Halliford TW17 . . 193 C6
Allington Cl
Greenford UB6 . . 64 A1
3 Wimbledon SW19 . . 178 D5
Allington Ct
6 Clapham SW8 . . 137 C3
Croydon CR0 . . 206 C3
Enfield EN3 . . 18 D6
Allington Rd
Harrow HA2 . . 42 A4
Hendon NW4 . . 46 B3
Kensal Rise W10 . . 91 A5
Orpington BR6 . . 211 C1
Allington St SW1 . . 258 D5
Allison Cl SE10 . . 142 A4
Allison Gr SE21 . . 161 C3
Allison Rd
Acton W3 . . 111 A6
Harringay N8 . . 50 D4
Alliston Ho 27 E2 . . 95 D4
Allitsen Rd
NW8 . . 92 C5 230 A4
All Nations Ho 10 E8 . . 74 B1
Allnutt Way SW4 . . 159 D6
Alloa Ct N14 . . 15 C2
Alloa Rd IG3 . . 80 A6
Allom Ct 11 SW4 . . 138 A3
Allonby Dr HA4 . . 38 D2
Allonby Gdns HA9 . . 43 C1
Allonby Ho E14 . . 97 A2
Alloway Rd E3 . . 97 A4
Allport Ho SE5 . . 139 B2
Allport Mews 44 E1 . . 96 C3
All Saints' Benhilton CE Prim Sch SM1 . . 217 D5
All Saint's CE Jun Sch
SE19 . . 183 C2
All Saints CE Prim Sch
Merton SW19 . . 180 A3
Putney SW15 . . 134 C2
All Saints' CE Prim Sch
Blackheath Vale SE3 . . 142 C3
Child's Hill NW2 . . 69 B5
East Barnet N20 . . 14 B2
Wallington SM5 . . 219 A3
All Saints Church 9
N19 . . 71 D5
All Saints' Cl N9 . . 18 A2
All Saints Ct
Heston TW5 . . 128 D4
Lower Clapton E5 . . 74 C4
10 Shadwell E1 . . 118 C6
All Saints Dr SE3 . . 142 D3
All Saints Ho 2 W11 . . 91 B2
All Saint's Inf Sch
SE19 . . 183 C2
All Saints Mews HA3 . . 24 C4
All Saints Pas SW18 . . 157 C6
All Saints RC Sch
BR4 . . 224 B4
All Saints RC Sch & Tech Coll RM8 . . 59 C1
All Saints Rd
Merton SW19 . . 180 A3
Notting Hill W11 . . 91 B1
Sutton SM1 . . 218 A5
All Saints' Rd W3 . . 111 A3
All Saints St N1 . 94 B5 233 C4
All Saints Sta E14 . . 119 D6
All Saints Twr 19 E10 . . 53 D2
Allsop Pl NW1 . . 92 D3 237 D5
All Souls' Ave NW10 . . 90 B6
All Souls CE Prim Sch
W1 . . 93 C2 239 A4
All Souls Pl W1 . . 238 D3
Allum La WD6 . . 10 A6
Allum Way N20 . . 14 A3
Allwood Cl SE26 . . 184 D6
Alma Ave E4 . . 36 A3
Alma Birk Ho 1 NW6 . . 69 B1
Almack Rd E5 . . 74 C4
Alma Cl N10 . . 31 B2
Alma Cres SM1 . . 217 A3
Alma Gr SE1 . . 117 D2 263 D3
Alma Ho
7 Brentford TW8 . . 132 A6
2 Edmonton N9 . . 34 A6
Alma Pl
College Pk NW10 . . 90 B4
Penge SE19 . . 183 D3
Thornton Heath CR7 . . 204 C4
Alma Prim Sch
Bermondsey SE16 . . 118 A2
Enfield EN3 . . 18 D6
Alma Rd
Carshalton SM5 . . 218 C3
Enfield EN3 . . 7 A1
Muswell Hill N10 . . 31 B3
Sidcup DA14 . . 168 A1
Southall UB1 . . 107 A6
Thames Ditton KT10,
KT7 . . 196 C1
Wandsworth SW18 . . 158 A6
Alma Row HA3 . . 24 B2
Alma Sq NW8 . . 92 A4 229 B2
Alma St
Camden Town NW5 . . 71 B2
Stratford New Town E15 . . 76 B2
Alma Terr
Earl's Ct W8 . . 255 B5
Wandsworth SW18 . . 158 B4
Almeida St 10 N1 . . 72 D1
Almeric Rd SW11 . . 136 D1
Almer Rd SW20 . . 178 A3
Almington St N4 . . 50 B1
Almond Ave
Carshalton SM5 . . 218 D6
Ealing W5 . . 110 A3
Uxbridge UB10 . . 60 D5
West Drayton UB7 . . 104 C3
Almond Cl
Bromley BR2 . . 210 C2
Charlton TW17 . . 171 A1
Feltham TW14 . . 150 A3
Hayes UB3 . . 105 C6
Peckham SE15 . . 140 A3
Ruislip HA4 . . 61 D5
Almond Gr TW8 . . 131 B5
Almond Ho SE4 . . 141 B3
Almond Rd
Bermondsey SE16 . . 118 B2
Tottenham N17 . . 34 A3
Almonds Ave IG9 . . 21 A2
Almond Way
Bromley BR2 . . 210 C2
Harrow HA2 . . 24 A1
Mitcham CR4 . . 203 D5
Almorah Rd
De Beauvoir Town N1 . . 73 B1
Heston TW5 . . 128 D4
Almshouse La EN1 . . 6 B6
Almshouses
Edmonton N9 . . 17 D2
Leyton E10 . . 75 D6
Southall UB1 . . 85 C1
Sunbury TW16 . . 171 D2
Almshouses The IG11 . . 79 A2
Al-Muntada Islamic Sch
SW6 . . 135 B4 264 D2
Alnmouth Ct 10 UB1 . . 86 A1
Al-Noor Muslim Prim Sch
IG3 . . 58 B1
Alnwick 8 N17 . . 34 B3
Alnwick Gr SM4 . . 201 D5
Alnwick Rd
Eltham SE12 . . 165 B4
Newham E16 . . 99 C1
Alonso Ho 4 DA17 . . 125 C1
ALPERTON . . 88 A6
Alperton Com Sch
HA0 . . 66 B1
Alperton La UB6 . . 87 D5
Alperton Lower Sch
HA0 . . 87 D6
Alperton St W10 . . 91 B3
Alperton Sta HA0 . . 88 A6
Alphabet Gdns SM5 . . 202 B3
Alphabet Sq E3 . . 97 C2
Alpha Bsns Ctr E17 . . 53 B4
Alpha Cl NW8 . . 92 C4 230 B1
Alpha Ct 6 NW5 . . 71 B2
Alpha Est The UB3 . . 105 C4
Alpha Gr E14 . . 119 C4
Alpha Ho
19 Brixton SW4 . . 138 B1
Kilburn NW6 . . 91 C5
Lisson Gr NW8 . . 237 B5
Alpha Pl
Chelsea SW3 . . 136 C6 267 B6
Kilburn NW6 . . 91 C5
Alpha Rd
Chingford E4 . . 19 D1
Croydon CR0 . . 205 C1
Edmonton N18 . . 34 A4
Enfield EN3 . . 7 A1
Hillingdon UB10 . . 82 D3
New Cross SE14 . . 141 B4
Surbiton KT5 . . 198 B3
Teddington TW12 . . 174 B5
Alpha St SE15 . . 140 A3
Alphea Cl SW19 . . 180 C3
Alpine Ave KT5 . . 215 A6
Alpine Bsns Ctr E6 . . 100 C2
Alpine Cl CR0 . . 221 C5
Alpine Copse BR1 . . 188 C1
Alpine Ct SE12 . . 142 D1
Alpine Gr 37 E9 . . 74 C1
Alpine Rd
Deptford SE16 . . 118 D1
Leyton E10 . . 75 D6
Walton-on-T KT12 . . 194 A2
Alpine View SM5 . . 218 C3
Alpine Way E6 . . 100 C2
Alpine Wlk HA7 . . 8 C2
Alric Ave
Kingston u T KT3 . . 199 D6
Willesden NW10 . . 67 B1
Alroy Rd N4 . . 50 C2
Alsace Rd
SE17 . . 117 C1 263 A2
Al Sadiq & Al Zahra Schs
NW6 . . 91 A6
Alscot Rd SE1 . . 117 D3 263 D5
Alscot Road Ind Est
SE1 . . 263 D5
Alscot Way SE1 . . 263 C4
Alsike Rd DA18 . . 125 A3
Alsom Ave KT19, KT4 . . 216 A4
Alston Cl KT7 . . 197 B2
Alston Ct 2 EN5 . . 1 A2
Alstone Ct N9 . . 18 A2
Alston Rd
Edmonton N18 . . 34 B5
High Barnet EN5 . . 1 A2
Upper Tooting SW17 . . 180 B6
Altair Cl N17 . . 33 D4
Altair Ct N1 . . 73 B2
Altash Way SE9 . . 166 C2

Altenburg Ave W13 109 B3
Altenburg Gdns SW11 136 D1
Alt Gr SW19 179 B3
Altham Gdns WD19 22 D6
Altham Rd HA5 23 A3
Althea St SW6 135 D2
Althorne Gdns E18 54 D5
Althorne Way RM10 81 C6
Althorp Cl EN5 12 A3
Althorpe Mews SW11 266 D1
Althorpe Rd HA1 42 A4
Althorp Rd SW17 158 D3
Altima Ct SE22 140 A1
Altior Ct N6 49 C3
Altmore Ave E6 100 B6
Altmore Inf Sch E6 100 B6
Alton Ave HA7 24 D3
Alton Cl
Isleworth TW7 130 D3
Sidcup DA5 169 A3
Alton Ct 18 BR3 185 C3
Alton Gdns
Beckenham BR3 185 C3
Twickenham TW2 152 B4
Alton Ho 3 E3 97 D4
Alton Rd
Croydon CR0 220 C5
Richmond TW10, TW9 132 A1
Roehampton SW15 156 A3
Tottenham N17 51 B6
Alton St E14 97 D2
Altyre Cl BR3 207 B4
Altyre Rd CR0 221 B6
Altyre Way BR3 207 B4
Alum Ct KT5 198 B3
Alumni Ct SE1 253 D2
Alvanley Ct NW3 69 D3
Alvanley Gdns NW6 69 D3
Alvanley Ho 14 SW9 138 C4
Alvernia Lo SM1 217 D5
Alverstone Ave
East Barnet EN4 14 C4
Wimbledon SW18, SW19 157 C2
Alverstone Gdns SE9 167 A3
Alverstone Ho 11 SE11 138 C6
Alverstone Rd
Little Ilford E12 78 C4
New Malden KT3 199 D5
Wembley HA9 44 B1
Willesden NW2 68 C1
Alverston Gdns SE25 205 C4
Alverton St SE8 141 B6
Alveston Ave HA3 43 B6
Alveston Sq 5 E18 37 A1
Alvey St SE17 263 A2
Alvia Gdns SM1 218 A4
Alvington Cres E8 73 D3
Alway Ave KT19 215 B3
Alwen Cotts CR0 222 D4
Alwold Cres SE12 165 C5
Alwyn Ave W4 111 B1
Alwyn Cl
Borehamwood WD6 10 B5
New Addington CR0 223 D1
Alwyne La N1 72 D1
Alwyne Mans SW19 179 B4
Alwyne Pl N1 73 A1
Alwyne Rd
Canonbury N1 73 A1
Ealing W7 108 C6
Wimbledon SW19 179 B4
Alwyne Sq N1 73 A2
Alwyne Villas N1 72 D1
Alwyn Gdns
Acton W3 88 D1
Hendon NW9 46 A5
Alyn Ct N8 49 D3
Alyth Gdns NW11 47 C3
Alzette Ho 11 E2 96 D5
Amalgamated Dr TW8 131 B6
Amanda Ct
Ashford TW15 148 B2
Chingford E4 36 C4
Aman Dalvi Ho SW18 157 A4
Amar Ct SE18 123 D2
Amardeep Ct SE18 123 D1
Amazon Apartments N8 50 B6
Amazonas SE1 117 C2 263 B3
Amazon St E1 96 B1
Ambassador Cl TW3 129 A3
Ambassador Ct
9 Hampstead NW6 69 C3
Hendon NW4 46 D4
Ambassador Gdns E6 100 B2
Ambassador Ho
Harrow HA3 42 C6
St John's Wood NW8 229 B5
Ambassador Sq E14 119 D2
Amber Ave E17 35 A2
Amber Ct
Feltham TW13 149 C1
Islington N7 72 C2
Mitcham CR4 202 C5
Southall UB1 107 D5
Amberden Ave N3 47 C6
Amberdene HA7 24 D4
Ambergate St SE17 116 D1 261 D2
Amber Gr NW2 46 D1
Amber Ho HA7 25 D3
Amberley Cl
2 Orpington BR6 227 D3
Pinner HA5 41 B6
Amberley Ct
2 Brixton SW9 138 D2
Sidcup DA14 190 C5
Sutton SM2 218 A1
Amberley Gdns
Enfield EN1 17 C4
Worcester Pk KT19 215 D4
Amberley Gr
Croydon CR0 205 D2
Penge SE26 184 B5
Amberley Ho
8 Barnet EN5 1 D1
7 Ealing W7 108 C5
Amberley Rd
Buckhurst Hill IG9 21 C3
Enfield EN1 17 D5
Palmers Green N13 16 B2
Walthamstow E10 53 D2
Westbourne Green W9 91 C2
West Heath SE2 146 D6
Amberley Way
Heston TW4 150 C6
Morden SM4 201 B2
Romford RM7 59 D5
Uxbridge UB10 82 A5
Amberside Cl TW2 152 B5
Amber Wharf 29 E2 95 D6
Amberwood Cl SM6 220 A3
Amberwood Rise KT3 199 C3
Amblecote Cl SE12 165 B1
Amblecote Mdws SE12 165 B1
Amblecote Rd SE12 165 B1
Ambler Prim Sch N4 72 D6
Ambler Rd N4 72 D5
Ambleside
Catford BR1 186 B4
13 Putney SW19 157 A3
Regent's Pk NW1 231 D3
Ambleside Ave
Beckenham BR3 207 A4
Streatham SW16 181 D6
Walton-on-T KT12 194 C1
Ambleside Cl
Lower Clapton E9 74 C3
5 Tottenham N17 51 D6
Walthamstow E10 53 D2
Ambleside Cres EN3 6 D2
Ambleside Dr TW14 149 D3
Ambleside Gdns
Redbridge IG4 56 A4
Streatham SW16 181 D5
Sutton SM2 218 A2
Wembley HA9 43 D1
Ambleside Ho HA8 27 A5
Ambleside Point 1 SE15 140 C5
Ambleside Rd
Bexleyheath DA7 147 C3
Willesden NW10 67 D1
Ambrook Ct SM1 218 B3
Ambrook Rd DA17 125 C3
Ambrosden Ave SW1 115 C3 259 B5
Ambrose Ave NW11 47 B3
Ambrose Cl
6 Newham E6 100 B2
Orpington BR6 227 D5
Ambrose Ho 9 E14 97 C2
Ambrose Mews 2 SW11 136 D3
Ambrose St SE16 118 B2
Ambrose Wlk E3 97 C5
AMC Bsns Ctr NW10 88 D4
Amelia Cl W3 110 D4
Amelia Ho 5 W6 112 C1
Amelia St SE17 117 A1 262 A2
Amen Cnr
Holborn EC4 241 D1
Amen Cnr *continued*
Streatham SW17 181 A4
Amen Ct EC4 94 D1 241 D1
Amenity Way SM4 200 C2
American Intercontinental Univ W1 93 A2 238 B3
American Sch in London The NW8 92 B5 229 C4
American Univ in London The N7 72 B5
America Sq EC3 253 C6
America St SE1 252 A3
Amerland Rd SW18 157 B5
Amersham Ave N18 33 B4
Amersham Gr SE14 141 B5
Amersham Rd
New Cross SE14 141 B4
Thornton Heath CR0 205 B3
Amersham Vale SE14, SE8 141 B5
Amery Gdns NW10 90 B6
Amery Ho SE17 263 B2
Amery Rd HA1 65 A6
Amesbury Ave SW2 160 B2
Amesbury Cl KT4 200 C1
Amesbury Ct EN2 4 C3
Amesbury Dr E4 19 D5
Amesbury Rd
Bromley BR1 209 D6
Dagenham RM9 80 D1
Feltham TW13 150 D2
Amesbury Twr 4 SW8 137 C3
Ames Cotts 12 E3 97 A2
Ames Ho 10 E2 96 D5
Amethyest Ct 1 EN3 7 A2
Amethyst Cl N11 31 D3
Amethyst Ct BR6 227 C3
Amethyst Rd E15 76 B4
Amherst Ave W13 87 C1
Amherst Dr BR5 211 D5
Amherst Gdns 2 W13 87 C1
Amherst Rd W13 87 C1
Amhurst Ct N4 51 B2
Amhurst Gdns TW7 131 A3
Amhurst Par N16 51 D2
Amhurst Pk N4, N16 51 C2
Amhurst Rd E8, N16 74 A4
Amhurst Terr E8 74 A4
Amhurst Wlk SE28 124 A5
Amias Ho EC1 242 A6
Amidas Gdns RM8 80 B4
Amiel St 15 E1 96 C3
Amies St SW11 136 D2
Amigo Ho SE1 261 B6
Amina Way SE16 118 A3
Amis Ave KT19 214 D3
Amity Gr SW20 178 C2
Amity Rd E15 76 D1
Ammanford Gn NW9 45 C3
Ammonite Ho 3 E15 76 D1
Amner Rd SW11 159 A5
Amora 8 HA7 25 C6
Amor Rd W6 112 C3
Amory Ho N1 233 D4
Amott Rd SE15 140 A2
Amoy Pl E14 119 C6
Ampere Way CR0 204 B1
Ampleforth Rd SE2 124 C4
Ampton Pl WC1 233 C1
Ampton St WC1 94 B4 233 C1
Amroth Cl SE23 162 B3
Amroth Gn NW9 45 C3
Amstel Ct 12 SE15 139 D5
Amsterdam Rd E14 120 A3
Amundsen Ct 7 E14 119 C1
Amundsen Ho 6 NW10 67 B1
Amwell Cl EN2 17 B6
Amwell St EC1 94 C4 234 A2
Amyand Cotts 12 TW1 153 B5
Amyand Park Gdns 2 TW1 153 B4
Amyand Park Rd TW1 153 B4
Amy Cl SM6 220 A1
Amy Johnson Ct HA8 26 D1
Amy Johnson Prim Sch SM6 220 A1
Amyruth Rd SE4 163 C6
Amy Warne Cl E6 100 A3
Anarth Ct KT13 193 C1
Anatola Rd N19 71 C6
Ancaster Cres KT3 200 A3
Ancaster Mews CR0 206 D6
Ancaster Rd BR3 206 D6
Ancaster St SE18 145 C5
Anchorage Cl SW19 179 C5
Anchorage Point 1 E14 119 C4
Anchorage Point Ind Est SE7 121 C3
Anchor Bsns Pk CR0, SM6 220 A5
Anchor Cl IG11 102 B4
Anchor Ct
Bexley DA7 147 A4
5 Enfield EN1 17 C6
Anchor Ho
Ilford IG3 80 A5
Newham E16 99 C1
St Luke's EC1 242 A6
Anchor & Hope La SE7 121 C2
Anchor Mews SW12 159 B5
Anchor Ret Pk E1 96 C3
Anchor St SE16 118 B2
Anchor Terr SE1 252 B4
Anchor Yd EC1 242 B6
Ancill Cl W6 135 A6 264 A5
Ancona Rd
Plumstead SE18 123 B1
Willesden Green NW10 90 A5
Andace Pk BR1 187 C2
Andalus Rd SW9 138 A2
Andaman Ho 3 E1 97 A2
Ander Cl HA0 65 D4
Andersens Wharf 9 E14 97 B1
Anderson Cl
Morden SM3 201 C1
North Acton W3 89 B1
Southgate N21 16 B6
Anderson Ct NW2 46 C2
Anderson Dr TW15 171 A6
Anderson Ho
1 Barking IG11 101 B5
10 Blackwall E14 120 A6
Upper Tooting SW17 180 B5
Anderson Rd
Homerton E9 74 D2
Redbridge IG8 55 D6
Anderson's Pl TW3 129 D1
Andersons Sq N1 234 C5
Anderson St SW3 257 C2
Anderson Way
Erith DA17 125 D4
Erith DA17 125 D4
Anderton Cl SE5 139 B2
Anderton Ct N22 31 D1
Andhurst Ct KT2 176 D2
Andmark Ct UB1 107 B5
Andon Ct BR3 207 A6
Andorra Ct BR1 187 C2
Andover Ave E16 99 D1
Andover Cl
East Bedfont TW14 149 D3
Greenford UB6 85 D3
Andover Ho 5 N7 72 B6
Andover Pl NW6 91 D5
Andover Rd
Finsbury Pk N7 72 B6
Orpington BR6 211 C1
Twickenham TW2 152 B3
Andoversford Ct 2 SE15 139 C6
Andrecht Terr CR4 203 D5
Andreck Ct BR3 186 A1
Andre Malraux Sch W7 86 C2
Andre St E8 74 A3
Andrew Borde St WC2 239 D2
Andrew Ct
Beckenham BR3 207 D6
2 Forest Hill SE23 162 D2
Andrewes Ct 2 W7 108 C5
Andrewes Gdns E6 100 A1
Andrewes Ho
Barbican EC2 242 B3
Sutton SM1 217 C4
Andrew Ewing Jun & Inf Sch TW5 129 B5
Andrew Ho
Enfield EN3 18 C6
New Cross SE4 141 B3
Putney SW15 156 A6
Andrew Logan's Glass Ho* SE1 253 A2
Andrew Marvell Ho 12 N16 73 C4
Andrew Pl SW8 269 D2
Andrew Reed Ho SW18 157 A4
Andrews Cl
Buckhurst Hill IG9 21 C2
Harrow HA1 42 B2
North Cheam KT4 216 D6
Andrews Cl *continued*
Sidcup BR5 190 D1
Andrews Crosse WC2 241 A1
Andrew's Rd E8 96 B6
Andrew St E14 98 A1
Andrews Wharf 14 E8 96 B6
Andrews Wlk SE17 138 D6
Andrew Wells Ho BR1 187 B3
Andrew Wilmot Ct SW18 158 A3
Andridge Ct SW19 179 B2
Andringham Lo 4 BR1 187 B2
Andrula Ct N22 32 D2
Andwell Cl SE2 124 B4
ANERLEY 184 B2
Anerley Ct SE20 184 B3
Anerley Gr SE19 183 D3
Anerley Hill SE19 183 D4
Anerley Park Rd SE20 184 B3
Anerley Pk SE20 184 B3
Anerley Rd SE20 184 B2
Anerley Sta SE20 184 B2
Anerley Station Rd SE20 184 B2
Anerley Vale SE19 184 A3
Aneurin Bevan Ct NW2 68 B6
Aneurin Bevan Ho N11 31 D3
Anfield Cl SW12 159 C4
Angel EC1 94 D5 234 D3
Angela Ct 2 SE23 162 C3
Angela Davis Ind Est 20 SW9 138 D1
Angel Cl N18 34 A6
Angel Corner Par 6 N18 34 A6
Angel Ct
Broadgate EC2 242 D2
St James SW1 249 B3
5 Willesden NW2 68 A2
Angel Edmonton N18 34 A5
Angelfield TW3 151 D6
Angel Gate EC1 234 D2
Angel Hill SM1 217 D5
Angel Hill Dr SM1 217 D5
Angel Ho N1 234 B3
Angelica Cl UB7 82 B1
Angelica Dr E6 100 C2
Angelica Gdns CR0 206 D1
Angelina Ho 2 SE15 140 A4
Angelis Appartments N1 234 D3
Angel La
Hayes UB3 83 B2
Stratford E15 76 B2
Angell Park Gdns 4 SW9 138 C2
Angell Rd SW9 138 D2
Angel Mews
Finsbury N1 234 B3
Putney SW15 156 A4
Stepney E1 118 B6
Angel Pas EC4 117 B6 252 C5
Angel Pl
Borough The SE1 252 C2
1 Edmonton N18 34 A5
Angel Rd
Harrow HA1 42 C3
Thames Ditton KT7 197 A1
Angel Rd (North Circular Rd) N18 34 B5
Angel Rd Works N18 34 C5
Angel Road Sta N18 34 C5
Angel Sq N1 234 B3
Angel St EC1 95 A1 242 A2
Angel Sta EC1 94 C5 234 B3
Angel Wlk W6 112 C2
Angerstein Bsns Pk SE10 121 A2
Angerstein La SE3 142 D4
Anglebury 5 W2 91 C1
Angle Cl UB10 82 C6
Angle Gn RM8 58 C1
Anglers Cl TW10 175 C6
Anglers La NW5 71 B2
Anglers Reach KT6 197 D4
Anglesea Ave 4 SE18 122 D2
Anglesea Ho KT1 197 D5
Anglesea Mews 12 SE18 122 D2
Anglesea Rd
Kingston u T KT1 197 D5
Woolwich SE18 122 D2
Anglesey Cl TW15 148 C1
Anglesey Court Rd SM5 219 A2
Anglesey Ct W7 86 D3
Anglesey Gdns SM5 219 A2
Anglesey Ho 13 E14 97 C1
Anglesey Rd
Enfield EN3 6 B1
South Oxhey WD19 22 C5
Anglesmede Cres HA5 41 C6
Anglesmede Way HA5 41 C6
Angles Rd SW16 182 A6
Anglia Cl N17 34 B3
Anglia Ct RM8 58 D1
Anglia Ho 13 E14 97 A1
Anglian Ind Est IG11 101 D2
Anglian Rd E11 76 B5
Anglia Wlk E6 100 C6
Anglo American Laundry SW17 158 A1
Anglo Rd 16 E3 97 B5
Angrave Ct 4 E8 95 D6
Angrave Pas 5 E8 95 D6
Angus Cl KT9 214 C3
Angus Dr HA4 62 C4
Angus Gdns NW9 27 B2
Angus Ho 12 SW12 159 D4
Angus Rd E13 99 C4
Angus St SE14 141 A5
Anhalt Rd SW11 136 C5 267 B4
Animals in War Meml* W1 247 D6
Ankerdine Cres SE18 144 D4
Anlaby Rd TW11 174 C5
Anley Rd W14 112 D4
Anmersh Gr HA7 25 D2
Annabel Cl E14 97 D1
Anna Cl E8 95 D6
Annadale N22 32 B5
Annandale Gr UB10 61 A5
Annandale Rd
Chiswick W4 111 C1
Croydon CR0 222 A6
Greenwich SE10 120 D1
Sidcup DA15 167 D4
Anna Neagle Cl 2 E7 77 A4
Anne Boleyn's Wlk
Belmont SM3 217 A1
Kingston u T KT2 176 A5
Anne Compton Mews SE12 164 D4
Anne Goodman Ho 3 E1 96 C1
Anne Kerr Ct 18 SW15 156 D5
Annemount Sch N2 48 B3
Anne's Ct NW8 237 B6
Annesley Ave NW9 45 B6
Annesley Cl NW10 67 C5
Annesley Dr CR0 223 B5
Annesley Ho
31 Brixton SW9 138 C4
15 Kennington SW9 138 C5
Annesley Rd SE3 143 B4
Annesley Wlk N19 71 C6
Annesmere Gdns SE3 143 D2
Anne St E13 99 A3
Annett Cl TW17 193 C5
Annette Cl HA3 24 C1
Annette Cres 16 N1 73 A1
Annette Ct N7 72 B5
Annette Rd N7 72 B4
Annette White Lo 20 N2 30 B1
Annett Rd KT12 194 A2
Anne Way KT8 195 D5
Annie Besant Cl E3 97 B6
Annie Taylor Ho 2 E12 78 C4
Anning St E2 243 B6
Annington Rd N2 48 D6
Annis Rd E9 75 A2
Ann La SW10 136 B6 266 C5
Ann Moss Way SE16 118 C3
Ann Parkes Ct TW5 128 D3
Ann's Cl SW1 248 A1
Ann's Pl E1 243 C3
Ann St SE18 123 B2
Ann Stroud Ct SE12 165 A6
Annsworthy Ave CR7 205 B6
Annsworthy Cres CR7 183 B1
Annunciation RC Inf Sch The HA8 27 B2
Annunciation RC Jun Sch The HA8 27 B4
Ansar Gdns E17 53 B4
Ansdell Rd SE15 140 C3

Ansdell St W8 . 113 D3 255 D6
Ansdell Terr
W8 . . . 113 D3 255 D6
Ansell Gr SM5 . . . 203 A1
Ansell Ho E1 . . . 96 C2
Ansell Rd SW17 . . . 158 D1
Anselm Cl CR0 . . . 221 D5
Anselm Rd
Hatch End HA5 . . . 23 B3
West Brompton SW6 . . . 135 C6 265 A5
Ansford Rd BR1, SE6 . . . 186 B6
Ansleigh Pl W11 . . . 112 D6
Anson 30 NW9 . . . 27 D1
Anson Ct TW19 . . . 148 A4
Anson Ho
Pimlico SW1 . . . 269 A6
6 Tower Hamlets E1 . . . 97 A3
Anson Pl SE28 . . . 123 B4
Anson Prim Sch NW2 . . 68 D3
Anson Rd
Cricklewood NW2 . . . 68 C3
Tufnell Pk N7 . . . 71 D4
Anson Terr UB5 . . . 63 D2
Anstey Ct 6 W3 . . . 110 D4
Anstey Ho 7 E9 . . . 96 C6
Anstey Lo EN1 . . . 17 C5
Anstey Rd SE15 . . . 140 A2
Anstey Wlk N15 . . . 51 A5
Anstice Cl W4 . . . 133 C5
Anstridge Rd SE9 . . . 167 B5
Antelope Rd SE18 . . . 122 B3
Antenor Ho 11 E2 . . . 96 B5
Anthony Cl NW7 . . . 27 C6
Anthony Cope Ct N1 . . 235 D2
Anthony Ct
Harrow HA1 . . . 42 B2
Isleworth TW7 . . . 130 D2
Anthony Ho NW8 . . . 237 A5
Anthony Kendal Ho 4
E5 . . . 74 B5
Anthony Rd
Croydon SE25 . . . 206 A3
East Wickham DA16 . . . 146 A4
Greenford UB6 . . . 86 C4
Anthony St E1 . . . 96 B1
Antigua Wlk SE19 . . . 183 B5
Antilles Bay 19 E14 . . . 120 A4
Antilles Ho W3 . . . 89 B1
Antill Rd
Mile End E3 . . . 97 A4
Tottenham Hale N15 . . . 52 A5
Antill Terr 5 E1 . . . 96 D1
Antlers Hill E4 . . . 19 D6
Anton Cres SM1 . . . 217 C5
Antoneys Cl HA5 . . . 22 D1
Antonine Hts SE1 . . . 253 A1
Anton Pl HA9 . . . 66 D5
Anton St E8 . . . 74 A3
Antony Ho
4 Deptford SE14 . . . 140 D5
2 Rotherhithe SE16 . . . 118 C2
Antrim Gr NW3 . . . 70 D2
Antrim Ho SW11 . . . 137 A2
Antrim Mans NW3 . . . 70 D2
Antrim Rd NW3 . . . 70 D2
Antrobus Cl SM1 . . . 217 B3
Antrobus Rd W4 . . . 111 A3
Anvil Cl SW16 . . . 181 C3
Anvil Ho 10 N9 . . . 18 A1
Anvil Rd TW16 . . . 194 A6
Anworth Cl IG8 . . . 37 B4
Apex Cl BR3 . . . 185 D2
Apex Cnr
Edgware NW7 . . . 27 B6
Twickenham TW13 . . . 151 B1
Apex Ct W13 . . . 87 A1
Apex Ind Est NW10 . . . 89 D3
Apex Lo 10 EN5 . . . 14 A6
Apex Ret Pk TW13 . . . 151 B1
Aphrodite Ct 11 E14 . . . 119 C2
Aplin Ct 4 SM1 . . . 217 D2
Aplin Way TW7 . . . 130 C4
Apollo Ave
Bromley BR1 . . . 187 B2
Loughton HA6 . . . 22 A5
Apollo Bldg 2 E14 . . . 119 C2
Apollo Ho
Chelsea SW10 . . . 266 C5
32 Hackney E2 . . . 96 B5
Highgate N6 . . . 48 D2
Apollo Ind Bsns Ctr 29
SE8 . . . 140 D6
Apollo Pl
Chelsea SW10 . . . 266 C4
6 Leyton E11 . . . 76 C5
Apollo Studios 18
NW5 . . . 71 D3
Apollo Way 1 SE18 . . . 123 B3
Apostle Way CR7 . . . 182 D1
Apothecary St EC4 . . . 241 C1
Appach Rd SW2 . . . 160 C5
Appin Ct HA1 . . . 42 C2
Appleby Cl
Chingford E4 . . . 36 A4
Hayes UB3, UB8 . . . 83 A1
Orpington BR5 . . . 211 C2
Twickenham TW2 . . . 152 B2
West Green N15 . . . 51 B4
Appleby Ct W3 . . . 111 A4
Appleby Gdns TW14 . . . 149 D3
Appleby Rd
Hackney E8 . . . 74 A1
Newham E16 . . . 99 A1
Appleby St E2 . . . 95 D5
Appledore Ave HA4 . . . 62 C5
Appledore Cl
Bromley BR2 . . . 209 A4
Edgware HA8 . . . 26 C2
Upper Tooting SW12,
SW17 . . . 158 D2
Appledore Cres DA14 . 167 D1
Appledore Way NW7 . . . 28 D3
Appleford 8 NW5 . . . 71 C3
Appleford Ho 6 W10 . . . 91 A3
Appleford Rd W10 . . . 91 A3
Applegarth
Claygate KT10 . . . 212 D3
New Addington CR0 . . . 223 D1
Apple Garth TW8 . . . 109 D2
Applegarth Dr IG2 . . . 57 D5
Applegarth Ho
Borough The SE1 . . . 251 D2
9 Camberwell SE15 . . . 140 A5
Applegarth Inf Sch
CR0 . . . 223 D2
Applegarth Jun Sch
CR0 . . . 223 D2
Applegarth Rd
Hammersmith W14 . . . 112 D3
Woolwich SE28 . . . 124 C6
Apple Gr
Chessington KT9 . . . 214 A4
Enfield EN1 . . . 5 C2
Apple Lo HA0 . . . 65 C5
Apple Mkt KT1 . . . 175 D1
Apple Mkt WC2 . . . 250 B6
Apple Rd E11 . . . 76 C5
Appleshaw Ho 4
SE5 . . . 139 C2
Appleton Ct 30 E8 . . . 74 B3
Appleton Gdns KT3 . . . 200 A3
Appleton Rd SE9 . . . 144 A2
Appleton Sq CR4 . . . 180 C2
Apple Tree Ave UB7 . . . 82 B1
Appletree Cl 5 SE20 . . . 184 B2
Appletree Ct
Lewisham SE13 . . . 142 B1
Northolt UB5 . . . 85 A4
Appletree Gdns EN4 . . . 2 C1
Apple Tree Yd SW1 . . . 249 B4
Applewood Cl
Dollis Hill NW2 . . . 68 B5
Ickenham UB10 . . . 60 A4
Oakleigh Pk N20 . . . 14 C3
Applewood Dr E13 . . . 99 B3
Appold St EC2 . . 95 C2 243 A4
Appollo Ct 7 SW9 . . . 138 C4
Apprentice Gdns UB5 . . 85 B4
Apprentice Way 5 E5 . . 74 B4
Approach Cl N16 . . . 73 C4
Approach La NW7 . . . 29 A5
Approach Rd
Ashford TW15 . . . 171 A4
Bethnal Green E2 . . . 96 C5
East Molesey KT8 . . . 195 C4
Edgware HA8 . . . 26 C4
Merton SW20 . . . 178 C1
New Barnet EN4, EN5 . . . 2 B1
Approach The
Acton W3 . . . 89 B1
Enfield EN1 . . . 6 B3
Hendon NW4 . . . 46 D4
Orpington BR6 . . . 227 D6
Aprey Gdns NW4 . . . 46 C5
April Cl
Ealing W7 . . . 108 C6
Feltham TW13 . . . 150 A1
Orpington BR6 . . . 227 D3
April Ct 20 E2 . . . 96 A5
April Glen SE23 . . . 162 D1
April St E8 . . . 73 D4
Apsley Cl HA2 . . . 42 A4
Apsley Ct SM2 . . . 218 A2
Apsley Ctr The NW2 . . . 68 A6
Apsley Ho
Enfield EN1 . . . 17 C5
Hounslow TW4 . . . 129 B1
Stepney E1 . . . 96 C2
St John's Wood NW8 . . . 229 C4
Apsley Rd
Croydon SE25 . . . 206 B5
Kingston u T KT3 . . . 199 A6
Apsley Way
Dollis Hill NW2 . . . 68 A6
Mayfair W1 . . . 248 B2
Aquarius TW1 . . . 153 B3
Aquarius Bsns Pk
NW2 . . . 46 A1
Aquarius Way HA6 . . . 22 A6
Aquila St NW8 . . 92 B5 229 D4
Aquinas St
SE1 . . . 116 C5 251 B3
Arabella Ct NW8 . . . 229 B4
Arabella Dr SW15 . . . 133 C1
Arabia Cl E4 . . . 20 B4
Arabian Ho 3 E1 . . . 97 A3
Arabin Rd SE4 . . . 141 B1
Aragon Ave KT7 . . . 196 D4
Aragon Cl
Ashford TW16 . . . 171 D3
Bromley BR2 . . . 210 B1
Enfield EN2 . . . 4 B5
Aragon Ct
Beckenham BR3 . . . 186 A2
East Molesey KT8 . . . 196 A5
Aragon Dr HA4 . . . 40 D1
Aragon Pl SM4 . . . 201 A2
Aragon Prim Sch
SM4 . . . 200 D2
Aragon Rd
Kingston u T KT2 . . . 176 A5
West Barnes SM4 . . . 201 A2
Aragon Twr SE8 . . . 119 B2
Arakan Ho 4 N16 . . . 73 B4
Aral Ho 14 E1 . . . 96 D3
Arandora Cres RM6 . . . 58 B2
Aranya Ct 3 E17 . . . 35 A1
Arapiles Ho 6 E14 . . . 98 B1
Arbery Rd E3 . . . 97 A5
Arbon Ct N1 . . . 235 B5
Arbor Cl BR3 . . . 185 D1
Arbor Ct N16 . . . 73 B6
Arborfield Cl SW2 . . . 160 B3
Arborfield Ho 7 E14 . . . 119 C6
Arbor Rd E4 . . . 20 B1
Arbour Ho 3 E1 . . . 96 D1
Arbour Rd EN3 . . . 6 D2
Arbour Sq E1 . . . 96 D1
Arbroath Rd SE9 . . . 144 A2
Arbrook Chase KT10 . . . 212 A2
Arbrook Ct
Chessington KT9 . . . 213 D3
St Paul's Cray BR5 . . . 190 A2
Arbrook Hall KT10 . . . 212 D2
Arbrook La KT10 . . . 212 B2
Arbury Ho BR1 . . . 188 A3
Arbury Terr 3 SE26 . . . 162 B1
Arbuthnot La DA5 . . . 169 A5
Arbuthnot Rd SE14 . . . 140 D3
Arbutus St E8 . . . 95 D6
Arcade Ho 7 NW11 . . . 47 B4
Arcade The
Broadgate EC2 . . . 243 A3
2 Eltham SE9 . . . 166 C5
1 Tufnell Pk N7 . . . 72 A4
Walthamstow E17 . . . 53 C5
Arcadia Ave N3 . . . 29 C2
Arcadia Centre The
W5 . . . 109 D6
Arcadia Cl SM5 . . . 219 A4
Arcadian Ave DA5 . . . 169 A5
Arcadian Cl DA5 . . . 169 A5
Arcadian Gdns N22 . . . 32 C3
Arcadian Ho SW6 . . . 136 A3
Arcadian Pl SW18 . . . 157 B4
Arcadian Rd DA5 . . . 169 A5
Arcadia St E14 . . . 97 C1
Archangel St SE16 . . . 118 D4
Archbishop Coggan Ho
SE13 . . . 142 B1
Archbishop Lanfranc Sch
The CR0 . . . 204 A3
Archbishop Michael
Ramsey Tech Coll
SE5 . . . 138 D5
Archbishop's Pl 1
SW2 . . . 160 B4
Archbishop Sumner CE
Prim Sch
SE11 . . . 116 C2 261 B3
Archbishop Tenison's CE
High Sch CR0 . . . 221 D5
Archbishop Tenison's Sch
SE11 . . . 138 B6 270 D5
Archdale Bsns Ctr
HA2 . . . 64 A6
Archdale Ct W12 . . . 112 B5
Archdale Ho SE1 . . . 263 A6
Archdale Pl KT3 . . . 198 D6
Archdale Rd SE22 . . . 139 D1
Archdeacon Cambridge's
CE Prim Sch TW2 . . . 152 C2
Archel Rd
W14 . . . 135 B6 264 C6
Archer Cl KT2 . . . 176 A3
Archer Ct TW13 . . . 150 A3
Archer Ho
1 Battersea SW11 . . . 136 B3
Ealing W13 . . . 109 B5
24 Hoxton N1 . . . 95 C6
1 New Cross SE14 . . . 141 A4
Notting Hill W11 . . . 244 D6
Archer Mews TW12 . . . 174 A4
Archer Rd SE25 . . . 206 B5
Archers Ct 3 CR2 . . . 221 A3
Archers Dr EN3 . . . 6 C3
Archers Lo 22 SE16 . . . 118 A1
Archer Sq SE14 . . . 141 A6
Archer St W1 . . . 249 C6
Archer Terr UB7 . . . 104 A6
Archery Cl
Harrow HA3 . . . 42 D6
Paddington W2 . . . 237 B1
Archery Fields Ho
WC1 . . . 234 A2
Archery Rd SE9 . . . 166 B6
Archery Stps W2 . . . 247 B6
Arches Bsns Ctr The
UB2 . . . 107 B4
Arches The
Harrow HA2 . . . 63 D6
Strand WC2 . . . 250 B4
Archgate Bsns Ctr 1
N12 . . . 30 A5
Archibald Mews W1 . . 248 C5
Archibald Rd N7 . . . 71 D4
Archibald St E3 . . . 97 C4
Archie Cl UB7 . . . 104 C4
Archie St SE1 . . . 253 B1
Arch St SE1 . . . 117 A3 262 A5
Archway N19 . . . 71 C6
Archway Bsns Ctr 5
N19 . . . 71 D5
Archway Cl
North Kensington W10 . . . 90 D2
2 Upper Holloway N19 . . 71 C6
Wallington SM6 . . . 220 A5
Wimbledon SW19 . . . 179 D6
Archway Hts 5 N19 . . . 49 C1
Archway Mews SW15 . 135 A1
Archway Rd N6 . . . 49 B2
Archway St SW13,
SW14 . . . 133 C2
Archway Sta N19 . . . 71 C6
Arcola St E8 . . . 73 D3
Arcon Dr UB5 . . . 85 A3
Arctic St NW5 . . . 71 B3
Arcus Rd BR1 . . . 186 C4
Ardbeg Rd SE24 . . . 161 B6
Arden 17 SW19 . . . 156 D3
Arden Cl
Bushey Heath WD23 . . . 8 D4
Erith SE28 . . . 102 D1
Harrow HA1 . . . 64 B5
Arden Court Gdns N2 . . 48 B3
Arden Cres
Dagenham RM9 . . . 80 D1
Millwall E14 . . . 119 C2
Arden Gr BR6 . . . 226 D4
Arden Grange N12 . . . 30 A6
Arden Ho
21 Hoxton N1 . . . 95 C5
29 Stockwell SW9 . . . 138 A3
Vauxhall SE11 . . . 260 C3
Arden Mews E17 . . . 53 D4
Arden Mhor HA5 . . . 40 B5
Arden Rd
Ealing W13 . . . 109 C6
Finchley N3 . . . 47 B6
Ardent Cl SE25 . . . 205 C6
Ardent Ho 30 E3 . . . 97 A5
Ardfern Ave SW16 . . . 204 C6
Ardfillan Rd SE6 . . . 164 B2
Ardgowan Rd SE6 . . . 164 C3
Ardilaun Rd N5 . . . 73 A4
Ardingly Cl CR0 . . . 222 D5
Ardleigh Gdns SM3 . . . 201 C2
Ardleigh Ho 5 IG11 . . . 101 A6
Ardleigh Rd
Kingsland N1 . . . 73 C2
Walthamstow E17 . . . 35 B2
Ardleigh Terr E17 . . . 35 B2
Ardley Cl
Forest Hill SE6 . . . 163 A1
Ardley Cl *continued*
Neasden NW10 . . . 67 C5
Ruislip HA4 . . . 39 A2
Ardlui Rd SE27 . . . 161 A2
Ardmay Gdns KT6 . . . 198 A4
Ardmere Rd SE13 . . . 164 B5
Ardmore La IG9 . . . 21 B4
Ardmore Pl IG9 . . . 21 B4
Ardoch Rd SE6 . . . 164 B2
Ardra Rd N9 . . . 18 D1
Ardrossan Gdns KT4 . . 216 A5
Ardshiel Cl SW15 . . . 134 D2
Ardwell Ave IG6 . . . 57 A4
Ardwell Rd SW2 . . . 160 A2
Ardwick Rd NW2 . . . 69 C4
Arena Bsns Ctr N4 . . . 51 A3
Arena Est N4 . . . 50 D3
Arena Sta SE25 . . . 206 C4
Arena The EN3 . . . 7 B5
Ares Ct 16 E14 . . . 119 C2
Arethusa Ho 8 E14 . . . 119 D2
Argali Ho 3 DA18 . . . 125 A3
Argall Ave E10 . . . 52 D1
Argall Way E10 . . . 53 A1
Argenta Way NW10 . . . 66 D1
Argent Ct KT6 . . . 214 C5
Argent Ctr The UB3 . . . 106 A4
Argent Ho HA5 . . . 23 B4
Argo Bsns Ctr 7 NW6 . . 91 C4
Argon Mews SW6 . . . 265 B3
Argon Rd N18 . . . 34 D5
Argos Ct 5 SW9 . . . 138 C4
Argos Ho 8 E2 . . . 96 B5
Argosy Ho
Fitzrovia W1 . . . 238 D5
Rotherhithe SE8 . . . 119 A2
Argus Way UB5 . . . 85 A4
Argyle Cl W13 . . . 87 A3
Argyle Ho
Cubitt Town E14 . . . 120 A3
Richmond TW10 . . . 153 C2
Sutton SM2 . . . 218 A2
Teddington TW11 . . . 174 C5
Argyle Mans 4 NW2 . . . 68 D4
Argyle Pl W6 . . . 112 B2
Argyle Prim Sch
WC1 . . . 94 A4 233 A2
Argyle Rd
Ealing W13 . . . 87 A2
Edmonton N18 . . . 34 A6
Harrow HA2 . . . 41 D3
Hounslow TW3 . . . 151 D6
Ilford IG1 . . . 78 C6
Leyton E15 . . . 76 C4
Newham E16 . . . 99 B1
Stepney E1 . . . 96 D3
Tottenham N17 . . . 34 A2
Woodside Pk N12 . . . 29 C5
Argyle Sq WC1 . . 94 A4 233 B2
Argyle St WC1 . . 94 A4 233 B2
Argyle Way SE16 . . . 118 A1
Argyle Wlk WC1 . . . 233 B1
Argyll Ave UB1 . . . 107 D5
Argyll Cl SW9 . . . 138 B2
Argyll Ct 15 SW2 . . . 160 A4
Argyll Gdns HA8 . . . 26 D2
Argyll Mans
Chelsea SW3 . . . 266 D6
West Kensington W14 . . 254 B4
Argyll Rd
Kensington
W8 . . . 113 C4 245 B1
Woolwich SE18 . . . 123 A3
Argyll St W1 . . . 93 C1 239 A1
Aria Ct IG2 . . . 57 A3
Arica Ho SE16 . . . 118 B3
Arica Rd SE4 . . . 141 A2
Ariel Ct
5 Belvedere DA17 . . . 125 C1
5 Hammersmith W12 . . 112 A3
Newington SE11 . . . 261 C3
Ariel Rd NW6 . . . 69 C2
Ariel Way
Hounslow TW4 . . . 128 B2
Shepherd's Bush W12 . . 112 C5
Aristotle Rd SW4 . . . 137 D2
Arizona Bldg 10 SE13 . . 141 D4
Arkansas Ho 21 N19 . . . 49 D2
Ark Ct N16 . . . 73 D6
Arkell Gr SW16 . . . 182 D3
Arkindale Rd SE6 . . . 164 A1
Arklay Cl UB8 . . . 82 B3
ARKLEY . . . 12 A6
Arkley Cres E17 . . . 53 B4
Arkley Dr EN5 . . . 12 B6
Arkley Pk EN5 . . . 11 B5
Arkley Rd E17 . . . 53 B4
Arklow Ho SE17 . . . 139 B6
Arklow Mews 4 KT6 . . 214 A6
Arklow Rd SE14 . . . 141 B6
Arklow Road Trad Est
SE14 . . . 141 B6
Arkwright Ho 23
SW2 . . . 160 A4
Arkwright Mans NW3 . . 70 A3
Arkwright Rd NW3 . . . 70 A3
Arlesey Cl SW15 . . . 157 A6
Arlesford Rd SW9 . . . 138 A2
Arless Ho 8 HA1 . . . 42 D4
Arlidge Ho EC1 . . . 241 B4
Arlingford Rd SW2 . . . 160 C5
Arlington N12 . . . 13 C1
Arlington Ave
N1 . . . 95 A6 235 B5
Arlington Cl
Lewisham SE13 . . . 164 B6
Sidcup DA15 . . . 167 C4
Sutton SM1 . . . 217 C6
Twickenham TW1 . . . 153 C5
Arlington Ct
13 Acton W3 . . . 110 D5
Highgate N6 . . . 49 A3
4 Twickenham TW1 . . . 153 C5
Arlington Dr
Carshalton SM5 . . . 218 D6
Ruislip HA4 . . . 39 B3
Arlington Gdns
Acton Green W4 . . . 111 A1
Ilford IG1 . . . 56 C1
Arlington Gn NW7 . . . 28 D3
Arlington Ho
3 Deptford SE8 . . . 141 B6
Finsbury EC1 . . . 234 B2
1 Shepherd's Bush
W12 . . . 112 B5
Arlington Lo SW2 . . . 138 B1
Arlington Park Mans 1
W4 . . . 111 A1
Arlington Pl 7 SE10 . . 142 A5
Arlington Rd
Ashford TW15 . . . 170 B5
Camden Town
NW1 . . . 93 B6 231 D5
Ealing W13 . . . 87 B1
Osidge N14 . . . 15 C3
Richmond TW10 . . . 153 D2
Surbiton KT6 . . . 197 D3
Teddington TW11 . . . 174 D6
Twickenham TW1 . . . 153 C5
Woodford IG8 . . . 37 B3
Arlington Sq
N1 . . . 95 A6 235 B5
Arlington St
SW1 . . . 115 C5 249 A4
Arlington Way
EC1 . . . 94 C4 234 B2
Arliss Way UB5 . . . 84 C6
Arlow Rd N21 . . . 16 C3
Armada Ct 11 SE8 . . . 141 C6
Armadale Cl N17 . . . 52 B5
Armadale Rd
Feltham TW14 . . . 150 A6
West Brompton SW6 . . . 265 A5
Armada St 10 SE8 . . . 141 C6
Armada Way E6 . . . 101 B1
Armagh Rd E3 . . . 97 B6
Armeston KT3 . . . 199 B2
Armfield Cl KT8 . . . 195 B4
Armfield Cotts 3
SW19 . . . 180 D1
Armfield Cres CR4 . . . 180 D1
Armfield Rd EN2 . . . 5 B4
Arminger Rd W12 . . . 112 B5
Armistice Gdns SE25 . . 206 A6
Armitage Ho
NW1 . . . 92 C2 237 B4
Armitage Rd
Golders Green NW11 . . . 47 B1
Greenwich SE10 . . . 120 D1
Armour Cl N7 . . . 72 B2
Armoury Ho E3 . . . 97 A6
Armoury Rd SE8 . . . 141 D3
Armoury Way SW18 . . . 157 C6
Armsby Ho 17 E1 . . . 96 C2
Armstead Wlk RM10 . . . 81 C1
Armstrong Ave IG8 . . . 36 C4
Armstrong Cl
Bickley BR1 . . . 210 A6
Dagenham RM8 . . . 58 D2
Newham E6 . . . 100 B1
Pinner HA5 . . . 40 A3
Walton-on-T KT12 . . . 194 A3
Armstrong Cres EN4 . . . 2 B2
Armstrong Ho 8
SW15 . . . 156 D5
Armstrong Rd
East Acton W3 . . . 111 D5
Feltham TW13 . . . 173 A5
Knightsbridge SW7 . . . 256 C5
Woolwich SE18 . . . 123 A3

Armstrong Way UB2 107 D4
Armytage Rd TW5 128 D5
Arnal Cres SW18 157 A4
Arncliffe NW6 91 D6
Arncliffe Cl N11 31 A4
Arncroft Ct IG11 102 B4
Arndale Wlk 6 SW18 157 D6
Arndell Ho 16 SM1 218 A4
Arne Gr BR6 227 D5
Arne Ho SE11 260 C2
Arne St WC2 94 A1 240 B1
Arnett Sq E4 35 B4
Arneways Ave RM6 58 D6
Arneway St SW1 259 D5
Arne Wlk SE3 142 D1
Arnewood Cl SW15 156 A3
Arney's La CR4 203 A3
Arngask Rd SE6 164 B4
Arnhem Pl E14 119 C3
Arnhem Way 3 SE22 161 C6
Arnhem Wharf E14 119 C3
Arnhem Wharf Prim Sch E14 119 C3
Arnison Rd KT8 196 B5
Arnold Ave E EN3 7 C5
Arnold Ave W EN3 7 B5
Arnold Cir E2 95 D4
Arnold Cl HA3 44 B2
Arnold Cres TW7 152 B6
Arnold Ct E18 36 D2
Arnold Dr KT9 213 D2
Arnold Est SE1 253 D1
Arnold Gdns N13 32 D5
Arnold Ho
Croydon CR0 220 D4
Newington SE17 261 D1
9 Stoke Newington N16 73 C5
Arnold House Sch NW8 92 B5 229 C3
Arnold Rd
Bow E3 97 C4
Dagenham RM10 81 C1
Mitcham SW17 180 D3
Northolt UB5 63 A2
Tottenham N15 51 D6
Arnos Gr N14 15 D1
Arnos Grove Ct 4 N11 31 C5
Arnos Grove Sta N11 31 C6
Arnos Rd N11 31 C6
Arnot Ho 27 SE5 139 A5
Arnott Cl
Acton Green W4 111 B2
Thamesmead SE28 124 C5
Arnould Ave SE5 139 B1
Arnsberg Way DA6, DA7 147 C1
Arnside Gdns HA9 43 D1
Arnside Ho 2 SE17 139 B6
Arnside Rd DA7 147 C4
Arnside St SE17 139 A6
Arnulf St SE6 185 D6
Arnull's Rd SW16 182 D4
Arodene Rd SW2 160 B5
Arosa Rd 8 TW1 153 D5
Arragon Gdns
Streatham SW16 182 A3
West Wickham BR4 223 D5
Arragon Rd
Newham E6 99 D6
4 Twickenham TW1 153 A3
Wandsworth SW18 157 C3
Arran Cl SM6 219 C4
Arran Ct
Edgware HA8 10 D2
32 Hendon NW9 27 D1
Neasden NW10 67 B5
Arrandene Ho 3 BR5 190 B1
Arran Dr
Stanmore HA7 25 C6
Wanstead E12 77 D6
Arran Ho
5 Canary Wharf E14 120 A5
Stoke Newington N16 51 D1
Arran Mews W5 110 B5
Arran Rd SE6 164 A2
Arran Wlk N1 73 A1
Arras Ave SM4 202 A4
Arras Ho SE2 146 D6
Arrol Ho SE1 262 B5
Arrol Rd BR3 206 D6
Arrowe Ct 6 E5 74 B4
Arrow Ho 23 N1 95 C6
Arrow Rd E3 97 D4
Arrow Scout Wlk UB5 85 A4
Arrowsmith Ho SE11 260 C2
Arsenal Rd SE9 144 B2
Arsenal Sta N5 72 C5
Arsenal Way SE18 123 A3
Arta Ho 26 E1 96 C1
Artemis Ct 14 E14 119 C2
Artemis Pl SW18 157 B4
Arterberry Rd SW20, SW19 178 D2
Artesian Cl NW10 67 B1
Artesian Gr EN5 2 A1
Artesian Rd W2 91 C1
Artesian Wlk 4 E11 76 C5
Arthingworth St E15 98 C6
Arthur Ct
Battersea SW11 268 B1
10 North Kensington W10 90 D1
Paddington W2 91 D1
South Croydon CR0 221 B5
Arthur Deakin Ho 1 E1 96 A2
Arthurdon Rd SE4 163 C6
Arthur Gr SE18 123 A2
Arthur Henderson Ho
9 Crouch End N19 49 D2
9 Fulham SW6 135 B3
Arthur Newton Ho 20 SW11 136 B2
Arthur Rd
Dagenham RM6 58 D3
Edmonton N9 17 D2
6 Kingston u T KT2 176 C3
Lower Holloway N7 72 B4
Newham E6 100 B5
West Barnes KT3 200 B4
Wimbledon SW19 179 C6
Arthur Ruxley Est DA14 190 D4
Arthur St EC4 117 B6 252 D6
Arthur Wade Ho 7 E2 95 D4
Arthur Walls Ho 3 E12 78 C5
Artichoke Hill 8 E1 118 B6
Artichoke Mews 5 SE5 139 B4
Artichoke Pl SE5 139 B4
Artillery Cl IG2 57 A3
Artillery Ho
Bow E3 97 A6
Westminster SW1 259 C5
Woolwich SE18 122 C1
Artillery La
Broadgate E1 95 C2 243 B3
North Kensington W12 90 A1
Artillery Pas E1 243 B3
Artillery Pl
Harrow Weald HA3 24 A3
Westminster SW1 259 C5
Woolwich SE18 122 C2
Artillery Row SW1 259 C5
Artington Cl BR6 227 A4
Artisan Cl E16 122 D6
Artisan Ct E8 74 A2
Artisan Mews 9 NW10 90 D4
Artisan Quarter 10 NW10 90 D4
Artizan St E1 243 B2
Arton Wilson Ho 12 SW15 156 A6
Arts Educational Sch The W4 111 C2
Arundale KT1 197 D5
Arundel Ave SM4 201 B5
Arundel Bldgs SE1 263 B5
Arundel Cl
Croydon CR0 220 D5
Hampton TW12 173 D5
Leyton E15 76 C4
Sidcup DA5 169 B5
Wandsworth SW11 158 C6
Arundel Ct
Barnes SW13 134 B6
4 Beckenham BR2 186 C1
2 Bexley DA6 147 A1
Chelsea SW3 257 B2
Colney Hatch N12 30 C4
3 Croydon CR0 220 D5
Harrow HA2 63 C4
Putney SW15 156 D6
Tottenham N17 34 A2
Arundel Dr
Borehamwood WD6 11 A6
Harrow HA2 63 C4
Woodford IG8 37 A3
Arundel Gdns
Burnt Oak HA8 27 B3
Ilford IG3 80 A6
Notting Hill W11 113 B6 244 C6
Southgate N21 16 C3
Arundel Gr N16 73 C3
Arundel Ho
Croydon CR0 221 B3
Islington N1 94 D6 234 D6
Richmond TW10 154 C6
3 South Acton W3 110 D4
Arundel Lo
Church End N3 29 B1
9 Upper Holloway N19 72 A6
Arundel Mans
Barnes SW13 134 B6
Fulham SW6 264 D2
Arundel Pl N1, N7 72 C2
Arundel Rd
Belmont SM2 217 B1
Cockfosters EN4 2 C2
Hounslow TW4 128 C2
Kingston u T KT1 177 A1
Thornton Heath CR0 205 B3
Arundel Sq N7 72 C2
Arundel St WC2 116 B6 250 D6
Arundel Terr SW13 134 B6
Arun Ho 5 KT2 175 D2
Arvon Rd N5 72 C3
Asa Ct UB3 105 D3
Asaph Ho SE14 141 B4
Asbaston Terr IG11 79 A2
Asbury Ct N21 16 A6
Ascalon Ct 16 SW2 160 B4
Ascalon Ho SW8 269 A3
Ascalon St SW8 137 C5 269 A3
Ascham Dr E4 35 C3
Ascham End E17 35 A2
Ascham St NW5 71 C3
Aschurch Rd CR0 205 D2
Ascot Cl
Borehamwood WD6 10 C6
Northolt UB5 63 C3
Ascot Ct
8 Brixton SW4 138 A1
Bromley BR1 188 A1
Old Bexley DA5 169 B4
St John's Wood NW8 229 C1
Ascot Gdns
Enfield EN3 6 C6
Southall UB1 85 C2
Ascot Ho
6 Acton Green W4 111 A1
1 Paddington W9 91 C2
Penge SE26 184 B4
Regent's Pk NW1 231 D2
Ascot Lo
Enfield EN1 17 B6
Paddington NW6 91 D5
Ascot Par 9 SW4 138 A1
Ascot Pl 12 HA7 25 C5
Ascot Rd
East Bedfont TW14 148 D2
Edmonton N18 34 A6
Newham E6 100 B4
Orpington BR5 211 D5
Streatham SW17 181 A4
Tottenham N15 51 B4
Ascott Ave W5 110 A4
Ascott Ct HA5 40 A5
Ashbourne Ave
East Barnet N20 14 D2
Erith DA7 147 A5
Harrow HA2 64 B6
Temple Fortune NW11 47 B4
Wanstead E18 55 B5
Ashbourne Cl
Ealing W5 88 C2
18 Woodside Pk N12 29 D6
Ashbourne Ct
Beckenham BR3 186 A2
Clapton Pk E5 75 A4
13 Woodside Pk N12 29 D6
Ashbourne Gr
Chiswick W4 111 C1
East Dulwich SE22 139 D1
Edgware NW7 27 B5
Ashbourne Ind Sch W8 113 D4 245 C1
Ashbourne Lo 2 N13 32 C6
Ashbourne Par 2 NW11 47 B5
Ashbourne Rd
Ealing W5 88 B3
Mitcham CR4 181 A3
Ashbourne Rise BR6 227 C4
Ashbourne Terr 1 SW19 179 C3
Ashbourne Way NW11 47 B4
Ashbridge Ct 3 W6 112 B3
Ashbridge Rd E11 54 D2
Ashbridge St NW8 92 C3 237 A5
Ashbrook HA8 26 B4
Ashbrook Rd
Dagenham RM10 81 D5
Upper Holloway N19 71 D6
Ashburn Ct BR1 187 A3
Ashburn Gdns SW7 256 A4
Ashburnham Ave HA1 42 D3
Ashburnham Cl N2 48 B5
Ashburnham Com Sch SW10 266 C4
Ashburnham Gdns HA1 42 D3
Ashburnham Gr SE10 141 D5
Ashburnham Pk KT10 212 A4
Ashburnham Pl SE10 141 D5
Ashburnham Rd
Chelsea SW10 136 A5 266 B3
Kensal Rise NW10 90 C5
Richmond TW10 153 B1
Ashburnham Retreat 4 SE10 141 D5
Ashburnham Twr SW10 266 C4
Ashburn Pl SW7 114 A2 256 A3
Ashburton Ave
Croydon CR0 206 B1
Ilford IG3 79 D4
Ashburton Cl CR0 206 A1
Ashburton Ct 1 HA5 40 D6
Ashburton Gdns CR0 222 A6
Ashburton Ho
Enfield EN3 6 D2
2 Wallington SM6 219 D3
Ashburton Jun & Inf Sch CR0 206 B3
Ashburton Learning Village CR9 206 B2
Ashburton Mans SW10 266 B4
Ashburton Rd
Croydon CR0 222 A6
Newham E16 99 A1
Ruislip HA4 62 A6
Ashburton Terr 2 E13 99 A5
Ashbury Dr UB10 60 D5
Ashbury Gdns RM6 58 D4
Ashbury Pl SW19 180 A4
Ashbury Rd SW11 137 A2
Ashby Ave KT19, KT9 214 C2
Ashby Ct NW8 236 D6
Ashby Gr N1 73 A1
Ashby Grange 7 SM6 219 C2
Ashby Ho
6 Brixton SW9 138 D3
17 Islington N1 73 A1
3 Northolt UB5 85 B3
14 Surbiton KT6 198 A3
Ashby Mews
10 Clapham Pk SW2 160 A6
New Cross SE4 141 B3
Ashby Rd
New Cross SE4 141 B3
South Tottenham N15 52 A4
Ashby St EC1 94 D4 234 D1
Ashby Way UB7 126 C5
Ashby Wlk CR0 205 A3
Ashchurch Ct 2 W12 112 A3
Ashchurch Gr W12 112 A3
Ashchurch Park Villas W12 112 A3
Ashchurch Terr W12 112 A3
Ash Cl
Carshalton SM5 218 D6
Edgware HA8 27 A6
Kingston u T KT3 177 B1
Penge SE20 184 C1
Petts Wood BR5 211 B4
Sidcup DA14 168 B1
Stanmore HA7 25 A4
Ashcombe Ave KT6 197 D2
Ashcombe Ct 4 SW15 157 A6
Ashcombe Gdns HA8 26 C6
Ashcombe Ho 33 E3 97 D4
Ashcombe Pk NW2 67 C5
Ashcombe Rd
Wallington SM5 219 A2
Wimbledon SW19 179 C5
Ashcombe Sq KT3 199 A6
Ashcombe St SW6 135 D3
Ashcroft
Hatch End HA5 23 C4
Osidge N14 15 D2
Ashcroft Ave DA15 168 A5
Ashcroft Cres DA15 168 A5
Ashcroft Ct
5 Eltham SE9 166 C5
Ashcroft Ct continued
Wembley HA0 65 A4
3 Whetstone N20 14 B2
Ashcroft Ho SW8 269 A2
Ashcroft Rd
Bow E3 97 A4
Chessington KT9 214 B5
Ashcroft Sq 8 W6 112 C2
Ash Ct
Chingford E4 20 B4
Clapham SW11 159 A6
Lee SE12 165 A4
Marylebone W1 237 C2
Romford RM7 59 D3
6 Rotherhithe SE16 119 A5
Upper Holloway N19 71 C6
West Ewell KT19 215 A4
2 West Norwood SW16 182 C5
9 Wimbledon SW19 179 A3
Woodford E18 37 C2
Ashdale Cl
Stanwell TW19 148 A2
Twickenham TW2 152 A4
Ashdale Gr HA7 24 D4
Ashdale Ho N4 51 B2
Ashdale Rd SE12 165 B3
Ashdale Way TW2 151 D4
Ashdene
6 Deptford SE15 140 B5
Pinner HA5 40 C6
Ashdene Cl TW15 171 A3
Ashdon Cl IG8 37 B4
Ashdon Rd NW10 89 D6
Ashdown
Ealing W13 87 B2
Putney SW15 156 D6
Ashdown Cl 13 BR3 185 D1
Ashdown Cres NW5 71 A3
Ashdown Ct
Dulwich SE22 162 A3
Ilford IG1 78 D2
New Malden KT4 199 D2
Sutton SM2 218 A2
Ashdowne Ct N17 34 A2
Ashdown Ho 7 E5 74 A6
Ashdown Pl
Ewell KT17 215 D1
Thames Ditton KT7 197 A2
Ashdown Rd
Enfield EN3 6 C3
Hillingdon UB10 82 C5
Kingston u T KT1 176 A1
Ashdown Way SW17 159 A2
Ashdown Wlk 20 E14 119 C2
Ashe Ho 9 TW1 153 D5
Ashen E6 100 C1
Ashenden SE17 262 B4
Ashenden Rd E5 75 A3
Ashen Gr SW19 157 C2
Ashentree Ct EC4 241 B1
Asher Loftus Way N11 30 D4
Asher Way E1 118 A6
Ashfield Ave
Bushey WD23 8 A4
Feltham TW13 150 B3
Ashfield Cl
Beckenham BR3 185 C3
Richmond TW10 154 A3
Ashfield Ct SW9 138 A3
Ashfield Ho 5 N5 73 A3
Ashfield La BR7 189 A3
Ashfield Par N14 15 D3
Ashfield Pl BR7 189 B3
Ashfield Rd
East Acton W3 111 D5
New Southgate N14 15 C1
Tottenham N4 51 A3
Ashfield St E1 96 C2
Ashfield Yd 21 E1 96 C2
ASHFORD 170 B4
Ashford Ave
Ashford TW15 170 D4
Hayes UB4 84 D1
Hornsey N8 50 A5
Ashford Bsns Complex TW15 171 A6
Ashford CE Prim Sch TW15 170 D4
Ashford Cl
Ashford TW15 170 A6
Walthamstow E17 53 B3
ASHFORD COMMON 171 B4
Ashford Cres EN3 6 C3
Ashford Ct
Cricklewood NW2 68 D4
Edgware HA8 10 D1
Ashford Gn WD19 22 D5
Ashford Ho
14 Brixton SW9 138 D1
Ashford Ho continued
11 Deptford SE8 141 B6
Ashford Hospl TW15 148 A2
Ashford Ind Est TW15 171 A6
Ashford Mews N17 34 A2
Ashford Rd
Cricklewood NW2 68 D4
Feltham TW13, TW15 171 B6
Littleton TW15, TW17 171 A3
Staines TW18 170 A4
Wallend E6 78 C1
Woodford E18 37 B1
Ashford St N1 95 C4
Ash Gr
Cricklewood NW2 69 A4
Ealing W5 110 A3
East Bedfont TW14 149 C3
Edmonton N13 17 A1
Enfield EN1 17 C4
Hackney E8 96 B6
Hayes UB3 105 B6
Heston TW5 128 D5
Penge SE20 184 C1
Southall UB1 85 C2
Wembley HA0 65 A4
West Wickham BR4 208 A1
Yiewsley UB7 104 B6
Ashgrove SE12 165 A3
Ashgrove Ct 2 W9 91 C2
Ashgrove Ho SW1 259 D2
Ashgrove Rd
Ashford TW15 171 B5
Catford BR1 186 B4
Ashgrove Sch BR1 187 B1
Ash Hill Dr HA5 40 C6
Ash Ho
3 Canary Wharf E14 120 A4
Fulham SE1 263 D3
Kenton NW9 45 A6
Lewisham SE12 165 A3
2 Teddington TW11 175 C3
Ashingdon Cl E4 20 A1
Ashington 1 NW5 71 B2
Ashington Ho 16 E1 96 B3
Ashington Rd SW6 135 B3
Ashlake Rd SW16 182 A6
Ashland Pl W1 238 A4
Ashlar Ct N2 48 C6
Ashlar Pl SE18 122 D2
Ashleigh Commercial Est SE7 121 D3
Ashleigh Ct
Ealing W5 109 D2
Osidge N14 15 C4
Penge SE26 184 B4
Ashleigh Gdns SM1 217 D6
Ashleigh Ho
Mortlake SW14 133 C2
1 Streatham SW16 182 B6
Ashleigh Point 8 SE26 162 D1
Ashleigh Rd
Mortlake SW14 133 C2
Penge SE20 206 B6
Ashley Ave SM4 201 C4
Ashley CE Prim Sch KT12 194 A1
Ashley Cl
Hendon NW4 28 C1
Oatlands Pk KT12, KT13 193 D1
Pinner Green HA5 22 B1
Ashley Cres
Clapham SW11 137 A2
Wood Green N22 32 C1
Ashley Ct
Hampstead NW3 69 D3
Hendon NW4 28 C1
19 Kingsland N16 73 C3
New Barnet EN5 14 A6
Northolt UB5 85 A6
Stanmore HA7 25 B1
Yiewsley UB7 104 A5
Ashley Dr
Borehamwood WD6 11 B6
Hounslow TW7 130 C6
Twickenham TW2 151 D3
Ashley Gdns
Edmonton N13 33 A6
Orpington BR6 227 C3
Richmond TW10 153 D2
Wembley HA9 66 A6
Ashley Ho BR5 190 A1
Ashley La
Croydon CR0 220 D4

Ashley La *continued*
Edgware NW7 28 D3
Hendon NW4 28 C1
Ashley Park Ave KT12 193 D1
Ashley Park Cres KT12 194 A1
Ashley Pl
Walton-on-T KT12 194 A1
Westminster SW1 115 C3 259 A5
Ashley Rd
Chingford E4 35 C4
Enfield EN3 6 C3
Hampton TW12 173 C2
Hornsey N19 50 A2
Richmond TW9 132 A2
Thames Ditton KT7 196 D3
Thornton Heath CR7 204 B5
Tottenham Hale N17 52 A6
Upton E7 77 C1
Walton-on-T KT12 194 A1
Wimbledon SW19 179 D4
Ashleys Alley N15 51 A5
Ashley Wlk NW7 28 D3
Ashling Ho 2 N17 33 D1
Ashling Rd CR0 206 A1
Ashlin Rd E15 76 B4
Ash Lo
2 Ashford TW16 171 D3
Fulham SW6 134 D4
Ashlone Rd SW15 134 D2
Ashlyns Way KT9 213 D2
Ashmead 4 N14 15 C6
Ashmead Bsns Ctr 2 E16 98 B3
Ashmead Gate BR1 187 C2
Ashmead Ho E9 75 A3
Ashmead Prim Sch SE8 141 C3
Ashmead Rd
East Bedfont TW14 150 A3
St Johns SE8 141 C3
Ashmere Ave BR3 186 B1
Ashmere Cl SM3 216 D3
Ashmere Gr 11 SW2, SW4 138 A1
Ashmere Ho 10 SW2 138 A1
Ashmill Ct CR0 205 A3
Ashmill St NW8 92 C2 237 A4
Ashmole Prim Sch SW8 138 B6 270 D5
Ashmole Sch N14 15 C3
Ashmole St SW8 138 B6 270 D5
Ashmoor Lo NW7 27 B4
Ashmore NW1 71 D1
Ashmore Cl SE15 139 D5
Ashmore Ct
Catford SE6 164 C3
Colney Hatch N11 30 D4
Heston TW5 129 C6
Ashmore Gr DA16 145 C2
Ashmore Ho W14 254 B5
Ashmore Rd W9 91 B4
Ashmount Prim Sch N19 49 C2
Ashmount Rd
Crouch End N19 49 D2
South Tottenham N15 51 D4
Ashmount Terr W5 109 D2
Ashneal Gdns HA1 64 B5
Ashness Gdns UB6 65 B2
Ashness Rd SW11 158 D6
Ashpark Ho 4 E14 97 B1
Ash Rd
Cheam SM3 201 B1
Croydon CR0 223 C6
Littleton TW17 192 C5
Orpington BR6 227 D1
Plashet E15 76 D3
Ashridge Cl HA3 43 C3
Ashridge Cres SE18 145 A5
Ashridge Ct
Southall UB1 108 A6
Southgate N14 15 C6
Ashridge Dr WD19 22 C5
Ashridge Gdns
Bowes Pk N13 32 A5
Pinner HA5 41 A5
Ashridge Ho DA14 189 D6
Ashridge Way
Ashford TW16 172 A4
Merton SM4 201 B5
Ash Row BR2 210 C3
Ashtead Ct 15 SW19 156 D3
Ashtead Rd E5 52 A2
AshTech Coll The TW15 148 A1
Ashton Cl SM1 217 C4
Ashton Ct
1 Beckenham BR3 185 B2
Chingford E4 20 C1
Harrow HA1 64 D5
Ashton Gdns
Dagenham RM6 59 A3
Hounslow TW4 129 B1
Ashton Ho
13 Kennington SW9 138 C5
Roehampton SW15 156 B4
Ashton Rd E15 76 B3
Ashton St E14 120 A6
Ashtree Ave CR4 180 B1
Ashtree Cl BR6 226 D4
Ash Tree Cl
Croydon CR0 207 A3
1 Surbiton KT6 198 A1
Ashtree Ct TW15 170 D5
Ash Tree Dell NW9 45 B4
Ash Tree Villas CR0 204 B3
Ash Tree Way CR0 207 A3
Ashurst Cl SE20 184 B2
Ashurst Dr
Ilford IG2, IG6 57 A4
Littleton TW17 192 A4
Ashurst Lo 4 N5 72 D3
Ashurst Rd
Cockfosters EN4 14 D6
Colney Hatch N12 30 C5
Ashurst Wlk CR0 222 B6
Ashvale Rd SW17 180 D5
Ashview Cl TW15 170 A5
Ashview Gdns TW15 170 A5
Ashville Rd E11 76 B6
Ashwater Rd SE12 165 A3
Ashway Ctr 5 KT2 176 A2
Ashwell Cl 8 E6 100 A1
Ashwell Ct TW15 148 A2
Ashwin St E8 73 D2
Ash Wlk HA0 65 C4
Ashwood Ave UB8 82 C1
Ashwood Ct HA9 66 B4
Ashwood Gdns
Hayes UB3 105 D2
New Addington CR0 224 A2
Ashwood Ho 10 NW4 46 C5
Ashwood Lo
9 New Barnet EN5 13 D6
Southgate N21 16 B5
Ashwood Pk 6 SM2 217 C1
Ashwood Rd E4 20 B1
Ashworth Cl SE5 139 B3
Ashworth Mans W9 91 D4
Ashworth Rd W9 91 D4
Aske Ho 2 N1 95 C4
Asker Ho N7 72 A4
Askern Cl DA6 146 D1
Aske St N1 95 C4
Askew Cres W12 112 A4
Askew Mans 14 W12 112 A4
Askew Rd W12 112 A4
Askham Ct W12 112 A5
Askham Lo 5 SE12 165 A4
Askham Rd W12 112 A5
Askill Dr SW15 157 A6
Asland Rd E15 98 B6
Aslett St SW18 158 A4
Asmara Rd NW2 69 A3
Asmuns Hill NW11 47 C4
Asmuns Pl NW11 47 B4
Asolando Dr SE17 262 B3
Aspect Coll WC1 94 A2 240 B3
Aspect Ho 7 E14 120 A4
Aspects SM1 217 D3
Aspen Cl
Ealing W5 110 B4
13 Upper Holloway N19 71 C6
Yiewsley UB7 104 B5
Aspen Copse BR1 188 B1
Aspen Ct
10 Acton W3 89 A1
12 Hackney E8 74 A3
Redbridge IG5 56 A6
Richmond TW9 132 C5
Aspen Dr HA0 65 A5
Aspen Gdns
Ashford TW15 171 A5
2 Hammersmith W6 112 B1
Mitcham CR4 203 A4
Aspen Gn DA18 125 B3
Aspen Gr HA5 39 D6
Aspen Ho
8 Deptford SE15 140 C6
4 Maitland Pk NW3 70 D2
Richmond TW9 132 C5
2 Sidcup DA15 168 A1
Aspen Ho *continued*
Southgate N21 16 B6
Aspen La UB5 85 A4
Aspenlea Rd W6 134 D6
Aspen Lo 1 SW19 179 B4
Aspen Way
Canary Wharf E14 120 A6
Feltham TW13 150 B1
Aspern Gr NW3 70 C3
Aspinall Ho SW12 160 A3
Aspinall Rd SE4 140 D2
Aspinden Rd SE16 118 B2
Aspire Bld 10 SW15 157 B6
Aspley Rd SW18 157 D6
Asplins Rd N17 34 B2
Asprey Ho CR4 202 C6
Asquith Cl RM8 58 C1
Assam SE1 253 D3
Assam St E1 96 A1
Assata Mews N1 72 D2
Assembly Pas E1 96 C2
Assembly Wlk SM5 202 C2
Assheton-Bennett Ho 15 KT6 198 A4
Ass House La HA3 23 D6
Assisi Ct
Upper Tooting SW12 158 D3
Wembley HA0 64 D5
Astall Cl HA3 24 C2
Astbury Bsns Pk 5 SE15 140 C4
Astbury Ho SE11 261 A5
Astbury Rd SE15 140 C4
Astell St SW3 114 C1 257 B2
Aster Ct 3 HA8 27 A6
Aster Ho 3 SE13 142 A3
Aste St E14 120 A4
Astey's Row 1 N1 73 A1
Asthall Gdns IG6 57 A5
Astins Ho 4 E17 53 D5
Astleham Rd TW17 192 A6
Astleham Way TW17 192 A6
Astle St SW11 137 A3
Astley Ave NW2 68 C3
Astley Ho
Fulham SE1 263 D2
39 Paddington W2 91 C2
8 West Norwood SE27 183 A6
Aston Ave HA3 43 C2
Aston Cl
Bushey WD23 8 A5
Sidcup DA14 168 A1
Aston Ct
Stoke Newington N4 73 A6
3 Wimbledon SW19 178 C3
10 Woodford IG8 37 A4
Aston Gn TW5 128 C3
Aston Ho
Notting Hill W11 244 D6
South Lambeth SW8 269 C1
Aston House Sch W5 87 D1
Aston Mews RM6 58 C2
Aston Pl SW16 182 D4
Aston Rd
Claygate KT10 212 C3
Ealing W5 87 D1
Merton SW20 178 C1
Aston St E14 97 A2
Astonville St SW18 157 C3
Astor Ave RM7 59 D3
Astor Cl KT2 176 D4
Astor Ct
Colney Hatch N12 30 C4
Newham E16 99 C1
Walham Green SW6 266 A3
Astoria Mans 18 SW16 160 A1
Astoria Par SW16 160 A1
Astoria Wlk SW9 138 C2
Astra Ct W13 109 A5
Astra Ho
4 Bow E3 97 B4
Hornsey N4 50 B2
Astrid Ho TW13 150 C2
Astrop Mews W6 112 C3
Astrop Terr W6 112 C4
Astwood Mews SW7 256 A4
Asylum Rd SE15 140 B5
Atalanta St SW6 134 D5 264 A3
Atbara Ct TW11 175 B4
Atbara Rd TW11 175 B4
Atcham Rd TW3 130 A1
Atcost Rd IG11 102 A2
Atheldene Rd SW18 158 A3
Athelney Prim Sch SE6 163 C1
Athelney St SE6 163 C1
Athelstan Ct E6 100 C5
Athelstane Gr E3 97 B5
Athelstane Mews N4 50 C1
Athelstan Gdns 8 NW6 69 A1
Athelstan Ho
Hackney Wick E9 75 B3
Kingston u T KT1 198 B5
Stoke Newington N16 73 C4
Athelstan House Sch TW12 173 C2
Athelstan Rd KT1 198 B5
Athelstan Way BR5 190 A2
Athelstone Rd HA3 24 B1
Athena Cl
Harrow HA2 64 C6
Kingston u T KT1 198 B6
Athena Ct
Bermondsey SE1 253 A1
St John's Wood NW8 229 C4
Athenaeum Pl 3 N10 49 B6
Athenaeum Rd N20 14 B3
Athenia Ho 7 E14 98 B1
Athenlay Rd SE15 162 D6
Athenoeum Ct N5 73 A4
Athens Gdns W9 91 C3
Atherden Rd E5 74 C4
Atherfield Ct SW18 157 D5
Atherfold Rd SW9 138 A2
Atherley Way TW4 151 B4
Atherstone Ct W2 91 D2
Atherstone Mews SW7 114 A2 256 B4
Atherton Dr SW19 178 D6
Atherton Ho CR2 221 C2
Atherton Hts HA0 65 C2
Atherton Mews E7 77 A2
Atherton Pl
Harrow HA2 42 B6
Southall UB1 107 C6
Atherton Rd
Barnes SW13 134 A5
Stratford E7 76 D2
Atherton St SW11 136 C3
Athlone KT10 212 C2
Athlone Cl 24 E5 74 B3
Athlone Ct
Lewisham SE6 164 B4
Upper Walthamstow E17 54 B6
Athlone Ho
16 Camden Town NW5 71 A2
9 Stepney E1 96 C1
Athlone House N6 48 D1
Athlone Rd SW2 160 C4
Athlone St NW5 71 A2
Athlon Ind Est HA0 87 D5
Athlon Rd HA0 87 D5
Athol Cl HA5 22 B2
Athol Ct 15 N4 72 B6
Athole Gdns EN1 17 C6
Athole Terr CR7 183 A1
Athol Gdns HA5 22 B2
Atholl Ho W9 229 A1
Atholl Rd IG3 58 A2
Athol Sq E14 98 A1
Athol Way UB10 82 C4
Atkins Ct
13 Old Ford E3 97 B6
Woolwich SE7 122 A2
Atkins Dr BR4 224 B6
Atkins Lo W8 245 A2
Atkinson Ct 3 E10 53 D2
Atkinson Ho
11 Battersea SW11 137 A3
Battersea SW11 268 A1
15 Hackney E2 96 A5
Newham E13 98 D3
Walworth SE17 262 D3
Atkinson Rd E16 99 C2
Atkinson's Almhouses HA8 26 B5
Atkins Rd
Streatham SW4, SW12 159 D4
Walthamstow E10 53 D3
Atlanta Bldg 8 SE13 141 D4
Atlanta Ct CR7 205 A6
Atlantic Ct 19 E14 120 B6
Atlantic Ho
5 Putney SW15 157 B6
4 Tower Hamlets E1 97 A2
Atlantic Rd SW2, SW9, SE24 138 C1
Atlantis Cl IG11 102 B4
Atlas Bsns Ctr NW2 68 B6
Atlas Gdns SE7 121 C2
Atlas Mews
Dalston E8 73 D2
Islington N7 72 B2
Atlas Rd
Friern Barnet N11 31 A4
Atlas Rd *continued*
Newham E13 99 A5
North Acton NW10 89 C4
Wembley HA9 67 A4
Atley Rd E3 97 C6
Atlip Rd HA0 88 A6
Atney Rd SW15 135 A1
Atria Rd HA6 22 A5
Atrium 9 IG9 21 D2
Atterbury Rd N4 50 D3
Atterbury St SW1 116 A2 260 A3
Attewood Ave NW10 67 C5
Attewood Rd UB5 63 A2
Attfield Cl N20 14 B2
Attilburgh Ho SE1 263 C6
Attleborough Ct 4 SE21 162 B2
Attle Cl UB10 82 C5
Attlee Cl
Hayes UB4 84 B4
Thornton Heath CR7 205 A4
Attlee Ct UB4 84 B4
Attlee Ho E1 243 D3
Attlee Rd
Hayes UB4 84 B4
Thamesmead SE28 124 B6
Attlee Terr 3 E17 53 D5
Attneave St WC1 234 A1
Atwater Cl SW2 160 C3
Atwell Cl E10 53 D3
Atwell Pl KT7 197 A1
Atwell Rd 6 SE15 140 A3
Atwood Ave TW9 132 C3
Atwood Ho SE21 161 C1
Atwood Rd W6 112 B2
Aubert Ct N5 72 D4
Aubert Pk N5 72 D4
Aubert Rd N5 72 D4
Aubrey Beardsley Ho SW1 259 B3
Aubrey Mans NW1 237 A4
Aubrey Moore Point E15 98 A5
Aubrey Pl NW8 229 A3
Aubrey Rd
Hornsey N8 50 A4
Kensington W14 113 B5 244 D3
Walthamstow E17 53 D6
Aubrey Wlk W14 113 B5 244 D3
Auburn Cl SE14 141 A5
Aubyn Hill SE27 183 B6
Aubyn Sq SW15 156 A6
Auckland Cl
Enfield EN1 6 B6
South Norwood SE19 183 D2
Auckland Ct UB4 84 C3
Auckland Gdns SE19 183 D2
Auckland Hill SE27 183 A6
Auckland Ho 11 W12 112 B6
Auckland Rd
Clapham SW11 136 C1
Ilford IG1 57 A2
Kingston u T KT1 198 B5
Leyton E10 75 D5
South Norwood SE19 183 D2
Auckland Rise SE19 183 C2
Auckland St SE11 260 C1
Audax 23 NW9 27 D1
Auden Dr WD6 10 C6
Auden Pl NW1 231 A6
Audley Cl
8 Clapham SW11 137 A2
Muswell Hill N10 31 B3
Audley Ct
Ealing W5 88 C2
Mayfair W1 248 C4
Northolt UB5 84 C4
Pinner Green HA5 22 C1
Snaresbrook E11, E18 54 D5
Surbiton KT5 198 B3
Twickenham TW2 152 B1
Audley Dr 8 E16 121 B5
Audley Gdns IG3 79 D6
Audley Ho N8 50 A5
Audley Pl SM2 217 D1
Audley Rd
Ealing W5 88 B2
Enfield EN2 4 D3
Hendon NW4 46 B3
Richmond TW10 154 B6
Audley Sq W1 248 B4
Audrey Cl BR3 207 D3
Audrey Gdns HA0 65 B6
Audrey Ho EC1 241 B3
Audrey Rd IG1 78 D5
Audrey St E2 96 A5
Audric Cl KT2 176 C2
Augurs La 3 E13 99 B4
Augusta Cl KT8 195 B6
Augusta Ct NW4 28 C1
Augusta Rd TW2 152 A2
Augusta St E14 97 D1
Augustine Ho
Broadgate EC2 242 D2
New Cross SE4 141 B4
Augustine Rd
Hammersmith W14 112 D3
Harrow Weald HA3 24 A2
Augustines Ct E9 74 C3
Augustus Cl
Brentford TW8 131 D5
Hammersmith W12 112 B3
Stanmore HA7 9 D1
Augustus Ct
Feltham TW13 173 B6
Isleworth TW3 130 A1
8 Putney SW19 157 A3
South Norwood SE19 183 C3
Streatham SW16 159 D2
Augustus Ho NW1 232 A2
Augustus Rd SW19 157 A3
Augustus St NW1 93 B4 231 D2
Aulay Lawrence Ct N9 18 B1
Aultone Way
Carshalton SM5 218 D5
Sutton SM1 218 A6
Aultone Yd Ind Est SM5 218 D5
Aulton Pl SE11 261 B1
Aura Ho 3 TW9 132 D4
Aurelia Gdns CR0 204 B3
Aurelia Rd CR0 204 B3
Auriga Mews N1 73 B3
Auriol Cl KT4 215 C5
Auriol Dr
Greenford UB6 64 B1
Hillingdon UB10 60 D2
Auriol Jun Sch KT19 215 D4
Auriol Mans W14 254 A3
Auriol Park Rd KT4 215 C5
Auriol Rd W14 113 A2 254 A3
Aurora Bldg 4 E14 120 A5
Aurora Ct IG8 36 D6
Aurora Ho E14 97 D1
Austell Gdns NW7 11 C1
Austell Hts NW7 11 C1
Austen Cl SE28 124 B5
Austen Ho 5 NW6 91 C4
Austen Rd
Erith DA8 147 D5
Harrow HA2 63 D6
Austin Ave BR1, BR2 210 A4
Austin Cl
Forest Hill SE23 163 B4
Twickenham TW1 153 C6
Austin Ct
9 Enfield EN1 17 C6
9 Newham E6 99 C6
Austin Friars EC2 242 D2
Austin Friars Ho EC2 242 D2
Austin Friars Sq EC2 242 D2
Austin Ho
6 Brixton SW2 160 B6
19 Kingston u T KT6 198 A4
1 New Cross SE14 141 B5
Austin Rd
Battersea SW11 137 A4 268 A1
Hayes UB3 105 D4
Austins Ct SE15 140 A2
Austin's La UB10 61 A5
Austin St E2 95 D4
Austral Cl DA15 167 D1
Australia Rd W12 112 B6
Austral St SE11 116 D2 261 C4
Austyn Gdns KT5 198 D1
Autumn Cl
Enfield EN1 6 A4
Wimbledon SW19 180 A4
Autumn Gr BR1 187 B4
Autumn Lo CR2 221 C4
Autumn Rise 9 W4 111 B1
Autumn St E3 97 C6
Avalon BR7 188 C1
Avalon Cl
Ealing W13 87 A2
Enfield EN2 4 C3
Merton SW20 179 A1
Avalon Ct CR0 205 D2
Avalon Rd
Ealing W13 87 A3
Parsons Green SW6 135 D4 265 C2
Avante Ct KT1 197 D6

Avard Gdns BR6 227 A4
Avarn Rd SW17 180 D4
Avebury Ct N1 235 C5
Avebury Rd
Leytonstone E11 54 B1
Merton SW19 179 B2
Orpington BR6 227 B5
Avebury St N1 235 C5
Aveley Ct 15 E5 74 B6
Aveley Mans 1 IG11 78 D1
Aveline St
SE11 116 C1 261 A1
Aveling Ho 12 N19 71 C5
Aveling Park Rd E17 35 C1
Aveling Park Sch E17 35 C1
Ave Maria La EC4 241 D1
Avenell Mans N5 72 D4
Avenell Rd N5 72 D5
Avenfield Ho W1 247 D6
Avening Rd SW18 157 C4
Avening Terr SW18 157 C4
Avenons Rd E13 99 A3
Avenue Cl
Cranford TW5 128 B4
Primrose Hill
NW8 92 C6 230 B5
Southgate N14 15 C5
Avenue Cres
Cranford TW5 128 B5
South Acton W3 110 D4
Avenue Ct
Chelsea SW3 257 C3
Cricklewood NW2 69 A5
Ealing W5 87 D2
Penge SE20 184 C2
Redbridge IG5 56 A6
Southgate N14 15 C5
Avenue Elmers KT6 198 A4
Avenue Gate IG10 21 C5
Avenue Gdns
Cranford TW5 128 B5
Mortlake SW14 133 C2
South Acton W3 110 D4
South Norwood SE25 184 A1
Teddington TW11 174 D4
Avenue Hall N6 49 D3
Avenue Ho
St John's Wood NW8 230 A3
Upper Clapton N16 74 A6
Willesden Green NW10 90 B5
Avenue Ind Est E4 35 B4
Avenue Lo 12 NW8 70 B1
Avenue Mans
Barnet EN5 1 B1
Clapham SW11 137 A1
Hampstead NW3 69 D3
Muswell Hill N10 31 C1
Willesden NW2 68 B2
Avenue Mews N10 49 B6
Avenue Par
Southgate N21 17 B4
Sunbury TW16 194 B6
Avenue Park Rd SE21, SE27 160 D2
Avenue Prim Sch E12 78 A3
Avenue Rd
Bexley DA6, DA7 147 A2
Brentford TW8 109 C1
Crouch End N6 49 D2
Feltham TW13 149 D1
Forest Gate E7 77 B4
Hampton TW12 173 D2
Harlesden NW10 89 D5
Hounslow TW7 130 D4
Ilford RM6 58 C2
Kingston u T KT1 198 A6
Mitcham SW16 181 D1
New Malden KT3 199 C5
North Finchley N12 30 A6
Penge BR3, SE20 184 D2
Pinner HA5 41 A6
Primrose Hill
NW8 92 C6 230 A6
South Acton W3 110 D4
Southall UB1 107 B5
Southgate N14 15 C5
South Norwood SE25 184 A1
Teddington TW11 175 A4
Tottenham N15 51 B4
Wallington SM6 219 C1
Wimbledon SW20 178 B1
Woodford IG8 37 C4
Avenue Road Sta
BR3 184 D1
Avenue S KT5 198 C2
Avenue Sch The NW6 69 A1
Avenue Terr
Ilford IG2 57 C3
Kingston u T KT3 199 A6
Avenue The
Barnet EN5 1 A2
Beckenham BR3 186 A2
Bedford Pk W4 111 C3
Bromley BR1 209 D6
Brondesbury Pk NW6 91 A6
8 Buckhurst Hill IG9 21 C2
Chingford E4 36 B5
Clapham SW4 159 A6
Claygate KT10 212 C3
Cranford TW5 128 A4
Ealing W13 87 B1
Finchley N3 29 C1
Friern Barnet N11 31 B5
Greenwich SE10 142 B5
Hampton TW12 173 B4
Harrow HA3 24 D2
Hatch End HA5 23 B4
Hornsey N8 50 C6
Hounslow TW3 151 D6
Isleworth TW1 153 B6
Keston Mark BR2 225 D5
Loughton IG10 21 D5
Muswell Hill N10 31 C1
4 New Malden KT4 200 A1
Orpington BR6 227 D6
Pinner HA5 41 B3
Richmond TW9 132 B3
Sidcup DA5 168 D4
South Croydon CR0 221 C5
Stoneleigh KT17, SM3 216 C1
St Paul's Cray BR5 190 B3
Sunbury TW16 172 B1
Surbiton KT5 198 B3
Tottenham N17 33 C1
Uxbridge UB10 60 D5
Wallington SM5 219 A1
Wandsworth SW18,
SW12 158 C4
Wanstead E11 55 B4
Wembley HA9 44 B1
West Wickham BR4 208 C2
Worcester Pk KT4 215 D6
Averil Gr SW16 182 D4
Averill St W6 134 D6
Avern Gdns KT8 195 D5
Avern Rd KT8 195 D5
Avery Ct 1 SE20 184 B3
Avery Farm Row SW1 258 C3
Avery Gdns IG2 56 B4
AVERY HILL 167 B5
Avery Hill Coll (Mile End Annexe) E3 97 B3
Avery Hill Rd SE9 167 B3
Avery Row
W1 115 B6 248 D6
Aviary Cl E16 98 D2
Aviemore Cl BR3 207 B4
Aviemore Way BR3 207 A4
Avignon Rd SE4 140 D2
Avingdor Ct 10 W3 111 A5
Avington Ct SE1 263 B3
Avington Gr SE20 184 C3
Avion Cres NW7, NW9 28 A2
Avis Sq E1 96 D1
Avoca Rd SW17 181 A6
Avocet Cl SE1 118 A1
Avocet Mews SE28 123 B3
Avon Cl
Hayes UB4 84 C3
Sutton SM1 218 A4
Worcester Pk KT4 216 A6
Avon Ct
1 Acton W3 89 A1
13 Chingford E4 20 A3
Greenford UB6 85 D3
North Finchley N12 29 D5
11 Putney SW15 157 A6
Wembley HA0 65 A4
Avondale N22 32 A3
Avondale Ave
Barnet EN4 14 D3
Finchley N12 29 D5
Hinchley Wood KT10 213 A5
Neasden NW2 67 C5
New Malden KT4 199 D1
Avondale Cres
Enfield EN3 7 A2
Redbridge IG4 55 D4
Avondale Ct
Canning Town E16 98 C2
Leytonstone E11 54 C1
9 Sutton SM2 218 A1
Woodford E18 37 B2
Avondale Dr UB3 106 B5
Avondale Gdns TW4 151 B6
Avondale Ho
11 Bermondsey SE1 118 A1
6 Mortlake SW14 133 B2
Avondale Mans SW6 264 C2
Avondale Park Gdns
W11 113 A6 244 A5
Avondale Park Prim Sch
W11 113 A6 244 A5
Avondale Park Rd
W11 113 A6 244 A6
Avondale Pavement 7
SE1 118 A1
Avondale Rd
Bexley DA16 146 C3
Bromley BR1 186 D4
Chislehurst SE9 166 A2
Finchley N3 30 A2
Harringay N15 50 D4
Harrow HA3 42 D6
Mortlake SW14 133 B2
Newham E16 98 C2
South Croydon CR2 221 A2
Southgate N13 16 C2
Walthamstow E17 53 C2
Wimbledon SW19 179 D5
Avondale Rise SE15 139 D2
Avondale Sq SE1 118 A1
Avonfield Ct E17 54 B6
Avon Ho
2 Islington N1 72 C1
7 Kingston u T KT2 175 D2
Northolt UB5 85 A3
Southgate N21 16 B6
14 Stoke Newington
N16 73 B4
West Kensington W14 254 D3
Avon House Sch IG8 37 A6
Avonhurst Ho NW6 69 A1
Avonley Rd SE14 140 C5
Avon Mews HA5 23 B2
Avonmore Gdns W14 254 D3
Avonmore Pl W14 254 B4
Avonmore Prim Sch
W14 113 A2 254 B4
Avonmore Rd
W14 113 B2 254 C4
Avonmouth St SE1 262 A6
Avon Path CR0 221 A3
Avon Pl SE1 252 B1
Avon Rd
Ashford TW16 171 D3
Greenford UB6 85 D3
St Johns SE4 141 C2
Upper Walthamstow E17 54 B6
Avonstowe Cl BR6 227 A5
Avon Way E18 55 A6
Avonwick Rd TW3 129 D3
Avril Way E4 36 A5
Avriol Ho W12 112 B5
Avro Ct E9 75 A3
Avro Way SM6 220 A1
Awlfield Ave N17 33 B2
Awliscombe Rd DA16 145 D3
Axeholm Ave HA8 26 D2
Axe St IG11 101 A6
Axford Ho SW2 160 D3
Axiom Apartments 5
BR2 209 B5
Axis Bsns Ctr E15 97 D6
Axis Ct
7 Bermondsey SE16 118 A4
Greenwich SE10 142 C6
Axminster Cres DA16 146 C4
Axminster Rd N7 72 B5
Axon Pl 5 IG1 79 A6
Aybrook St W1 93 A2 238 A3
Aycliffe Cl BR1 210 B5
Aycliffe Rd W12 112 A5
Ayerst Ct 1 E10 54 A2
Aylands Cl HA9 66 A6
Aylesbury Cl E7 76 D2
Aylesbury Ct SM1 218 A5
Aylesbury Ho 13
SE15 140 A6
Aylesbury Rd
Bromley BR2 209 A6
Walworth
SE17 117 B1 262 D1
Aylesbury St
Clerkenwell
EC1 94 D3 241 C5
Neasden NW10 67 B5
Ayles Ct UB4 84 B4
Aylesford Ave BR3 207 A4
Aylesford Ho SE1 252 D1
Aylesford St
SW1 115 D1 259 C1
Aylesham Cl NW7 28 A3
Aylesham Rd BR6 211 D2
Aylesham Sh Ctr
SE15 140 A4
Ayles Rd UB4 84 B4
Aylestone Ave NW6 90 D6
Aylestone Ct 10 HA0 66 A2
Aylett Rd
Croydon SE25 206 B5
Isleworth TW7 130 C3
Ayley Croft EN1 18 A6
Ayliffe Cl KT1 176 C1
Aylmer Cl HA7 25 A6
Aylmer Ct N2 48 D4
Aylmer Dr HA7 25 A6
Aylmer Ho SE10 120 B1
Aylmer Par N2 48 D4
Aylmer Rd
Acton W12 111 D4
Dagenham RM8 81 A5
East Finchley N2 48 C4
Leytonstone E11 54 D1
Ayloffe Rd RM9 81 B2
Aylsham Dr UB10 61 A6
Aylton Est 28 SE16 118 C4
Aylward Fst & Mid Schs
HA7 25 D5
Aylward Rd
Forest Hill SE23 162 D2
Merton SW20 201 B6
Aylward Sch N18 33 B6
Aylwards Rise HA7 25 A6
Aylward St E1 96 D1
Aylwin Est SE1 263 B6
Aylwin Girls Sch
SE1 117 D2 263 D4
Aynhoe Mans W14 112 D2
Aynhoe Rd W14 112 D3
Ayr Ct W3 88 C2
Ayres Cl E13 99 A4
Ayres Cres NW10 67 B1
Ayres St SE1 117 A4 252 B2
Ayrsome Rd N16 73 C5
Ayrton Gould Ho 9
E2 96 D4
Ayrton Ho HA9 65 D6
Ayrton Rd
SW7 114 B3 256 C6
Aysgarth Ct SM1 217 D5
Aysgarth Rd SE21 161 C4
Ayshford Ho E1 96 B4
Ayston Ho 19 SE8 118 D2
Aytoun Ct 17 SW9 138 B3
Aytoun Pl SW9 138 B3
Aytoun Rd SW9 138 B3
Azalea Cl
Ealing W7 108 D5
Ilford IG1 78 D3
Azalea Ct
Chingford IG8 36 C3
Ealing W7 108 D5
Azalea Ho
Feltham TW13 150 B3
New Cross SE14 141 B5
Azalea Wlk HA5 40 B3
Azania Mews NW5 71 B2
Azenby Rd SE15 139 D3
Azhar Acad E7 77 A2
Azof St SE10 120 C2
Azov Ho 10 E1 97 A3
Aztec Ct 8 N16 73 C2
Azure Appartments
HA3 24 B3
Azure Ct TW13 149 D1
Azure Ho 28 E2 96 A4

B

Baalbec Rd N5 72 D3
Babbacombe Cl KT9 213 D3
Babbacombe Gdns
IG4 56 A5
Babbacombe Rd BR1 187 A2
Baber Bridge Par
TW14 150 C5
Baber Dr TW14 150 C5
Babington Ct
Bloomsbury WC1 240 B4
Streatham SW16 181 D5
Babington Ho SE1 252 B2
Babington House Sch
BR7 188 B4
Babington Rd
Dagenham RM8 80 C4
Hendon NW4 46 B5
Streatham SW16 181 D5
Babington Rise HA9 66 C2
Babmaes St SW1 249 C5
Bacchus Wlk 12 N1 95 C5
Bache's St N1 95 B4 235 D1
Back Church La E1 96 A1
Back Hill EC1 241 B5
Backhouse Pl SE1 263 B3
Back La
Brentford TW8 131 D6
Buckhurst Hill IG9 21 D2
Back La continued
Burnt Oak HA8 27 A2
Dagenham RM6 59 A2
Hampstead NW3 70 A4
Hornsey N8 50 A4
Richmond TW10 153 C2
Sidcup DA5 169 C4
Backley Gdns SE25 206 A3
Back Rd
Sidcup DA14 190 A6
Teddington TW11 174 C3
Bacon Gr SE1 117 D3 263 C5
Bacon La
Edgware HA8 26 C2
Queensbury NW9 44 D5
Bacon's Coll SE16 119 A4
Bacon's La N6 49 A1
Bacon St E2 95 D3 243 D6
Bacon Terr RM8 80 B3
Bacton NW5 71 A3
Bacton St E2 96 C4
Baddeley Cl 11 EN3 7 C6
Baddeley Ho
East Molesey KT8 195 C4
Vauxhall SE11 260 D2
Baddow Cl
Dagenham RM10 103 C6
Woodford IG8 37 D4
Baddow Wlk N1 235 A6
Baden Ct N11 31 D3
Baden Pl SE1 252 C2
Baden Powell Cl
Dagenham RM9 103 A6
Surbiton KT6 214 B6
Baden Powell Ho 11
DA17 125 C3
Baden Powell Sch E5 74 B5
Baden Rd
Hornsey N8 49 D5
Ilford IG1 78 D3
Badger Cl
Feltham TW13 150 B1
Hounslow TW4 128 C2
Ilford IG2 57 A2
Badger Ct
Chingford E4 36 B6
Dollis Hill NW2 68 C5
Badgers Cl
Ashford TW15 170 B5
Enfield EN2 4 D2
Harrow HA1 42 B3
Hayes UB3 105 C6
Badgers Copse
Orpington BR6 227 D6
Worcester Pk KT4 215 D6
Badgers Croft
Barnet N20 13 A3
Chislehurst SE9 166 C1
Badgers Hole CR0 222 D4
Badgers Wlk KT3 177 C1
Badlis Rd E17 53 C6
Badma Cl N9 18 C1
Badminton KT2 176 D2
Badminton Cl
Harrow HA1 42 C5
Northolt UB5 63 C2
Badminton Ct 9 N4 51 A2
Badminton Ho SE22 139 C1
Badminton Mews 9
E16 121 A5
Badminton Rd SW12 159 A5
Badric Ct SW11 136 B3
Badsworth Rd 3 SE5 139 A4
Bagley Cl UB7 104 A4
Bagley's La
SW6 135 D4 265 D1
Bagleys Spring RM6 59 A5
Bagnigge Ho WC1 234 A1
Bagshot Ho NW1 231 D2
Bagshot Rd EN1 17 D5
Bagshot St
SE17 117 C1 263 B1
Baildon 27 E2 96 C5
Baildon St SE8 141 B5
Bailey Cl
Chingford E4 36 A6
Wood Green N11 31 D3
Woolwich SE28 123 C5
Bailey Cres KT9 213 D1
Bailey Ct
4 Chingford E4 36 B5
9 Shepherd's Bush
W12 112 A4
Bailey Ho
Mitcham CR4 202 C6
11 Penge SE26 184 B5
Walham Green SW10 265 D4
Bailey Mews
Brixton SW2 160 C6
Chiswick W4 132 D6
Bailey Pl SE26 184 D4
Bainbridge cl KT2 176 A5
Bainbridge Rd RM9 81 B4
Bainbridge St WC1 239 D2
Baines Cl CR2 221 B3
Bain Ho 23 SW9 138 A3
Baird Ave UB1 108 A6
Baird Cl
Kingsbury NW9 45 A3
Walthamstow E10 53 C1
Baird Gdns SE19 183 C6
Baird Ho
12 Belvedere DA17 125 C3
29 Shepherd's Bush
W12 112 B6
Baird Rd EN1 6 B1
Baird St EC1 242 B6
Bairny Wood App IG8 37 B4
Baizdon Rd SE3 142 C3
Baker Beall Ct DA7 147 D2
Baker Ct E11 76 B5
Baker Ho
12 Bromley E3 97 D4
Ealing W7 108 D5
Baker La CR4 203 A6
Baker Rd
Harlesden NW10 89 C6
Kidbrooke SE18 144 A4
Bakers' Almshouses
E10 53 D3
Bakers Ave E17 53 D3
Bakers Ct RM8 59 B2
Bakers Ct SE25 205 C6
Bakers End SW20 179 A1
Bakers Field N7 72 A4
Bakers Gdns SM5 218 C6
Bakers Hall Ct EC3 253 B5
Bakers Hill
Barnet EN5 1 D3
Upper Clapton E5 52 C1
Bakers Ho W5 109 D5
Baker's La N6 48 D3
Bakers Mews 9 BR6 227 D2
Baker's Mews W1 238 A2
Bakers Pas 22 NW3 70 A4
Bakers Rents 18 E2 95 D4
Bakers Row E15 98 C5
Baker's Row
EC1 94 C3 241 A5
Baker St
Enfield EN1 5 B4
Marylebone W1 92 D2 237 D4
Baker Street
W1 92 D2 237 D4
Baker Street Sta
NW1 92 D3 237 D5
Baker's Yd EC1 241 A5
Bakery Cl SW9 270 D3
Bakery Mews KT6 198 C1
Bakewell Way KT3 177 C1
Balaam Ho SM1 217 C4
Balaams La N14 15 D2
Balaam St E13 99 B4
Balaclava Rd
Bermondsey
SE1 117 D2 263 D3
Kingston u T KT6 197 C2
Bala Gn NW9 45 C3
Balcaskie Rd SE9 166 B6
Balchen Rd SE3 143 D3
Balchier Rd SE22 162 B5
Balcombe Cl DA6 146 D1
Balcombe Ho
Lisson Gr NW1 237 C6
3 Streatham SW2 160 B3
Balcombe St
NW1 92 D3 237 C5
Balcon Ct W5 88 B1
Balcorne St E9 74 C1
Balder Rise SE12 165 B2
Balderton Flats W1 238 B1
Balderton St
W1 93 A1 238 B1
Baldewyne Ct N17 34 A2
Baldock Ho 31 SE5 139 A3
Baldock St E3 97 D5
Baldrey Ho 1 SE10 120 D1
Baldry Gdns SW16 182 B4
Baldwin Cres SE5 139 A4
Baldwin Gdns TW3 130 A4
Baldwin Ho
15 Streatham SW2 160 C3
Wallend E12 78 C1
Baldwin's Gdns
EC1 94 C2 241 A4
Baldwin St EC1 235 C1

Baldwin Terr N1 95 A5 235 A4
Baldwyn Gdns W3 111 B6
Balearic Apts 3 E16 121 A6
Bale Rd E1 97 A2
Bales Coll W10 90 D4
Balfern Gr W4 111 C1
Balfern St SW11 136 C3
Balfe St N1 94 A5 233 B3
Balfour Ave W7 108 D5
Balfour Bsns Ctr UB2 106 D3
Balfour Gr N20 14 D1
Balfour Ho W10 90 D2
Balfour Mews
Edmonton N9 18 A1
Mayfair W1 248 B4
Balfour Pl
Mayfair W1 248 B5
Putney SW15 134 B1
Balfour Rd
Bromley Comm BR2 209 D4
Croydon SE25 206 A5
Ealing W13 109 B4
Harrow HA1 42 B4
Highbury N5 73 A4
Hounslow TW3 129 D2
Ilford IG1 57 A1
Merton SW19 179 D3
North Acton W3 89 A2
Southall UB2 106 D3
Wallington SM5 218 D1
Balfour St SE17 117 B2 262 C4
Balfron Twr 4 E14 98 A1
Balgonie Rd E4 20 B3
Balgowan Cl KT3 199 C5
Balgowan Prim Sch BR3 185 A1
Balgowan Rd BR3 185 B1
Balgowan St SE18 123 D2
BALHAM 159 A3
Balham Gr SW12 159 A4
Balham High Rd SW12, SW17 159 A3
Balham Hill SW12 159 B5
Balham New Rd SW12 159 B4
Balham Park Mans SW12 158 D3
Balham Park Rd SW12, SW17 159 A3
Balham Rd N9 18 A2
Balham Sta SW12 159 B3
Balham Station Rd SW12 159 B3
Balin Ho SE1 252 C2
Balkan Wlk E1 118 B6
Balladier Wlk E14 97 D2
Ballamore Rd BR1 165 A1
Ballance Rd E9 75 A2
Ballantine St SW18 136 A1
Ballantrae Ho NW2 69 B4
Ballard Cl KT2 177 B3
Ballard Ho SE10 141 D6
Ballards Cl RM10 103 D6
Ballards Farm Rd CR0, CR2 222 A2
Ballards La N3 29 D3
Ballards Mews HA8 26 C4
Ballards Rd
Dagenham RM10 103 D6
Dollis Hill NW2 68 A6
Ballards Rise CR2 222 A2
Ballards Way CR0, CR2 222 B2
Ballast Quay SE10 120 B1
Ballater Cl WD19 22 C6
Ballater Rd
Brixton SW2, SW4 138 A1
South Croydon CR2 221 D3
Ball Ct EC3 242 D1
Ballentyne Ct N21 16 B6
Ballina St SE23 162 D4
Ballin Ct 14 E14 120 A4
Ballingdon Rd SW11 159 A5
Ballinger Point 18 E3 97 D4
Ballinger Way UB5 85 A3
Balliol Ave E4 36 C6
Balliol Ho 11 SW15 156 D5
Balliol Rd
Bexley DA16 146 B3
North Kensington W10 90 D1
Tottenham N17 33 C2
Balloch Rd SE6 164 B2
Ballogie Ave NW10 67 C4
Ballow Cl 15 SE5 139 C5
Ball's Pond Pl 3 N1 73 B2
Ball's Pond Rd N1 73 C2
Balmain Cl W5 109 D5
Balmain Ct TW3 129 D4
Balman Ho 3 SE16 118 D2
Balmer Rd E3 97 B5
Balmes Rd N1 95 B6 235 D6
Balmoral Ave
Beckenham BR3 207 A5
Friern Barnet N11 31 B5
Balmoral Cl 1 SW15 156 D5
Balmoral Cres KT8 195 C6
Balmoral Ct
18 Belmont SM2 217 C1
Ealing W5 87 D1
Edgware HA8 26 D6
Grove Pk SE12 187 B6
North Cheam KT4 216 B6
21 Rotherhithe SE16 118 D5
St John's Wood NW8 229 C4
Wembley HA9 66 B5
West Norwood SE27 183 A6
Balmoral Dr
Borehamwood WD6 11 B6
Hayes UB4 83 D3
Southall UB1 85 B3
Balmoral Gdns
Ealing W13 109 A3
Ilford IG3 57 D1
Old Bexley DA5 169 B4
Balmoral Gr N7 72 B2
Balmoral Ho
2 Isle Of Dogs E14 119 D3
Stanmore HA7 26 A1
Stoke Newington N4 51 A1
Walthamstow E17 35 B1
West Kensington W14 254 A4
Balmoral Lo BR6 226 C4
Balmoral Mews W12 111 D3
Balmoral Rd
Forest Gate E7 77 C3
Harrow HA2 63 C4
Kingston u T KT1 198 B5
Leyton E10 75 D6
North Cheam KT4 216 B6
Willesden NW2 68 B2
Balmoral Trad Est IG11 101 D2
Balmore Cl E14 98 A1
Balmore Cres EN4 15 A6
Balmore St N19 71 B6
Balmuir Gdns SW15 134 C1
Balnacraig Ave NW10 67 C4
Balniel Gate SW1 259 D2
Balsam Ho 9 E14 119 D6
Baltic Apts 5 E16 121 A6
Baltic Cl SW19 180 B3
Baltic Ho 7 SE5 139 A3
Baltic St E EC1 95 A3 242 A5
Baltic St W EC1 95 A3 242 A5
Baltimore Ho
Clapham SW18 136 A1
Kennington SE11 261 A2
Merton SW19 179 D3
Baltimore Pl DA16 145 D3
Balvaird Pl SW1 259 D1
Balvernie Gr SW18 157 C4
Bamber Ho IG11 101 A6
Bamber Rd 5 SE15 139 D4
Bamborough Gdns 12 W12 112 C4
Bamburgh 9 N17 34 B3
Bamford Ave HA0 88 B5
Bamford Ct E15 75 D3
Bamford Rd
Barking IG11 79 A2
Catford BR1 186 B5
Bampfylde Cl SM6 219 C5
Bampton Ct W5 87 D1
Bampton Dr NW7 28 A3
Bampton Rd SE23 162 D1
Banavie Gdns BR3 186 A2
Banbury Cl EN2 4 D4
Banbury Ct
11 Belmont SM2 217 C1
Ealing W13 109 A3
Strand WC2 250 A6
Banbury Ho 5 E9 74 D1
Banbury Rd
Higham Hill E17 35 A3
Homerton E9 74 D1
Banbury St 3 SW11 136 C3
Banbury Wlk UB5 85 C5
Banchory Rd SE3 143 B5
Bancroft Ave
East Finchley N2 48 C4
Woodford IG9 21 A2
Bancroft Cl TW15 170 C5
Bancroft Ct
Northolt UB5 84 C6
South Lambeth SW8 270 A2
Bancroft Gdns
Harrow Weald HA3 24 A2
Orpington BR6 211 D1
Bancroft Ho 11 E1 96 C3
Bancroft Rd
Bethnal Green E1 96 D3
Harrow Weald HA3 24 A1
Bancrofts Sch IG8 21 A1
Bandon Cl UB10 82 B5
BANDONHILL 219 D3
Bandon Hill Prim Sch SM6 219 D2
Bandon Rise SM6 219 D3
Banff Ho 1 NW3 70 C2
Banfield Rd SE15 140 B2
Banfor Ct SM6 219 C3
Bangabandhu Prim Sch E2 96 C4
Bangalore St SW15 134 D2
Bangor Cl UB5 63 D3
Banim St W6 112 B2
Banister Ho
Hackney E9 74 D3
Nine Elms SW8 269 B2
9 West Kilburn W10 91 A4
Banister Rd W10 90 D4
Bank Ave CR4 180 B1
Bank Bldgs 13 SW16 181 C5
Bank Ct SW11 268 C2
Bank End SE1 252 B4
Bankfoot Rd BR1 186 C6
Bankhurst Rd SE6 163 B4
Bank La
Kingston u T KT2 176 A3
Roehampton SW15 155 C6
Bank Mews SM1 218 A2
Bank of England* EC2 95 B1 242 C1
Bank of England Mus* EC2 95 B1 242 C1
Bank Par N11 31 B5
Banks Ho
Isleworth TW7 130 C3
Newington SE1 262 A5
Banksia Rd N18 34 D5
Bankside
Borough The SE1 117 A6 252 A5
Borough The SE1 252 B4
Enfield EN2 4 D4
Southall UB1 106 D5
South Croydon CR2 221 D2
Bankside Art Gal* SE1 116 D6 251 D5
Bankside Ave
1 Lewisham SE13 142 A2
Northolt UB5 84 A5
Bankside Cl
Carshalton SM5 218 C2
Isleworth TW7 130 D1
Bankside Dr KT7 213 B6
Bankside Ho EC3 243 B1
Bankside Pier SE1 117 A6 252 A5
Bankside Pk IG11 102 A4
Bankside Rd IG1 79 B3
Bankside Way 6 SE19 183 C4
Banks La DA6 147 B1
Bank St E14 119 D5
Bank Sta EC3 95 B1 242 D1
Banks Way E12 78 C4
Bank The N6 49 B1
Bankton Rd SW2 138 C1
Bankwell Rd SE13 142 C1
Banner Ct 5 SE16 118 C2
Banner Ho EC1 242 B5
Bannerman Ho SW8 270 C5
Banner St EC1 95 A3 242 B6
Banning Ho 4 SW19 156 D3
Banning St SE10 120 C1
Bannister Cl
Greenford UB6 64 B3
Streatham SW2 160 C3
Bannister Ho
28 Deptford SE14 140 D6
Harrow HA3 42 C6
Bannister Sports Ctr The HA3 24 A4
Bannockburn Prim Sch SE18 123 D2
Bannockburn Rd SE18 123 D2
Bannow Cl KT19 215 C4
Banqueting Ho* SW1 250 A3
Banstead Ct
Stoke Newington N4 51 A1
Walthamstow E10 53 D1
Banstead Gdns N9 17 C1
Banstead Rd SM5 218 C1
Banstead St SE15 140 C2
Banstead Way SM6 220 A3
Banstock Rd HA8 26 D4
Banting Dr N21 16 B6
Banting Ho 6 NW2 68 A5
Bantock Ct 1 N20 14 D2
Bantock Ho 8 W10 91 A4
Banton Cl EN1 6 B3
Bantry Ho 13 E1 96 D3
Bantry St SE5 139 B5
Banville Ho SW8 270 D3
Banwell Rd DA5 168 D5
Banyan Ho 8 NW3 69 D2
Banyard Rd SE16 118 B3
Baptist Gdns NW5 71 A2
Barandon Wlk 6 W11 112 D6
Barbanel Ho 26 E1 96 C3
Barbara Brosnan Ct NW8 229 C3
Barbara Castle Cl SW6 264 D5
Barbara Cl TW17 192 D4
Barbara Hucklesbury Cl N22 32 D1
Barbara Martin Ho 1 N11 31 C5
Barbara Rudolph Ct 5 N19 50 A2
Barbara Ward Ct 3 E11 76 C6
Barbauld Rd N16 73 C5
Barber Beaumont Ho 21 E1 96 D4
Barber Cl N21 16 C4
Barberry Ct E15 76 C2
Barbers Alley 1 E13 99 B4
Barbers Rd E15 97 D5
BARBICAN 95 A2
Barbican* EC2 95 A2 242 B3
Barbican Arts & Con Ctr* EC2 95 A2 242 B4
Barbican Rd UB1 85 D1
Barbican Sta EC1 95 A2 242 A4
Barb Mews W6 112 C3
Barbon Cl WC1 240 C4
Barbot Cl N9 18 A1
Barbrook Ho E9 74 C2
Barchard St SW18 157 D6
Barchester Cl W7 108 D5
Barchester Lo N12 29 D6
Barchester Rd HA3 24 B1
Barchester St E14 97 D2
Barclay Cl SW6 135 C5 265 A3
Barclay Ct N12 30 A5
Barclay Ho 21 E9 74 C1
Barclay Oval IG8 37 A6
Barclay Prim Sch E10 54 B3
Barclay Rd
Edmonton N18 33 B4
Leyton E11 54 D1
Newham E13 99 C3
Parsons Green SW6 135 C5 265 B3
South Croydon CR0 221 B5
Walthamstow E17 54 A4
Barcombe Ave SW2 160 B2
Barcom Trad Est 1 CR0 204 A2
Bardell Ho 17 SE1 118 A4
Barden St SE18 145 C5
Bardfield Ave RM6 58 D6
Bardney Rd SM4 201 D5
Bardolph Rd
Richmond TW9 132 B2
Tufnell Pk N7 72 A4
Bard Rd W10 112 D6
Bardsey Pl 41 E1 96 C3
Bardsey Wlk 5 N1 73 A2
Bardsley Cl CR0 221 D5
Bardsley Ho 6 SE10 142 A6
Bardsley La SE10 142 A6
Barents Ho 10 E1 96 D3
Barfett St W10 91 B3
Barfield Ave N20 14 D2
Barfield Rd
Bromley BR1, BR7 210 C6
Leytonstone E11 54 D1
Barfleur La SE8 119 B2
Barford Cl NW4 28 A2
Barford Ho 23 E3 97 B5
Barford St N1 94 C6 234 B5
Barforth Rd SE15 140 B2
Barfreston Way SE20 184 B2
Bargate Cl
New Malden KT3 200 A2
Plumstead Comm SE18 123 D1
Bargehouse Rd E16 122 D4
Barge House St SE1 251 B4
Barge La 10 E3 97 B6
Bargery Rd SE6 163 D3
Bargrove Cl 8 SE20 184 A3
Bargrove Cres SE6 163 B2
Barham Cl
Chislehurst BR7 188 D5
Keston Mark BR2 210 A1
Wembley HA0 65 C2
Barham Ct
8 Croydon CR2 221 A4
Keston Mark BR2 210 A1
Wembley HA0 65 C2
Woodside Pk N12 29 B5
Barham Ho SE17 263 B2
Barham Prim Sch HA0 65 C2
Barham Rd
Chislehurst BR7 188 D5
Croydon CR2 221 A3
Wimbledon SW20 178 A3
Baring Cl SE12 165 A2
Baring Ct N1 235 C5
Baring Ho 15 E14 97 C1
Baring Prim Sch SE12 165 A4
Baring Rd
Barnet EN4 2 B2
Croydon CR0 206 A1
Grove Pk SE12 165 A2
Baring St N1 95 B6 235 C5
Barker Cl
Kingston u T KT3 198 D5
Richmond TW9 132 D3
Barker Dr NW1 71 D1
Barker Ho
Dulwich SE21 161 C1
3 Harringay N15 50 D5
Walthamstow E17 53 B2
Walworth SE17 263 A3
Barker Mews SW4 137 B1
Barker St SW10 266 A6
Barker Wlk SW16 159 D1
Barkham Rd N17 33 C3
BARKING 79 B1
Barking Abbey Comp Sch (Sports & Humanities Coll)) IG11 79 C3
Barking Abbey Sch (Sports & Humanities Coll) IG11 79 D2
Barking Bsns Ctr IG11 102 A4
Barking Flyover IG11 78 D1
Barking Hospl IG11 79 D1
Barking Ind Pk IG11 102 A6
Barking Rd
East Ham E6 100 B6
Plaistow E13 99 B4
BARKINGSIDE 57 A6
Barkingside Sta IG6 57 B6
Barking Sta IG11 79 A1
Bark Pl W2 113 D6 245 C6
Barkston Gdns SW5 113 D2 255 C3
Barkway Cl BR6 226 C4
Barkway Ct N4 73 A6
Barkwith Ho 27 SE14 140 D6
Barkworth Rd SE16 118 C1
Barlborough St SE14 140 D5
Barlby Gdns W10 90 D3
Barlby Prim Sch W10 90 D3
Barlby Rd W10 90 D2
Barley Cl WD23 8 A6
Barleycorn Way E14 119 B6
Barley Ct
Ilford IG3 58 B4
Stanwell TW19 148 A3
Barleyfields Cl RM6 58 C2
Barley La IG3 58 B3
Barley Lane Prim Sch RM6 58 B2
Barley Mow Pas
Chiswick W4 111 B1
Clerkenwell EC1 241 D3
Barley Mow Way TW17 192 C5
Barley Shotts Bsns Pk W10 91 B2
Barling 6 NW1 71 B1
Barling Ct 1 SW4 138 A3
Barlings Ho 2 SE4 140 D1
Barloch Ho 14 SW11 137 A3
Barlow Cl SM6 220 A1
Barlow Dr SE18 144 A4
Barlow Ho
14 Bermondsey SE16 118 B2
Notting Hill W11 244 A6
Shoreditch N1 235 C2
Barlow Pl W1 248 D5
Barlow Rd
Acton W3 110 D5
Brondesbury NW6 69 B2
Hampton TW12 173 C3
Barlow St SE17 117 B2 262 D3
Barmeston Rd SE6 163 D2
Barmor Cl HA2 23 D1
Barmouth Ave UB6 86 D5
Barmouth Ho 6 N7 72 B6
Barmouth Rd
Croydon CR0 222 D6
Wandsworth SW18 158 A5
Barnabas Ct N21 16 D6
Barnabas Ho EC1 235 A1
Barnabas Lo SW8 270 B2
Barnabas Rd E9 74 D3
Barnaby Cl HA2 64 A6
Barnaby Ct NW9 45 C6
Barnaby Pl SW7 256 C3
Barnard Cl
Chislehurst BR7 189 B2
Sunbury TW16 172 B3
Wallington SM6 219 D1
Woolwich SE18 122 C3
Barnard Ct SW16 160 B1
Barnard Gdns
Hayes UB4 84 B3
West Barnes KT3 200 A5
Barnard Gr E15 76 D1
Barnard Hill N10 31 B2
Barnard Ho 17 E2 96 B4
Barnard Lo
New Barnet EN5 2 A1
10 Paddington W9 91 C2
Barnard Mews SW11 136 C1
Barnardo Dr IG6 57 A5
Barnardo Gdns 1 E1 118 D6
Barnardo St E1 96 D1
Barnard Rd
Clapham SW11 136 C1
Enfield EN1 6 B3
Mitcham CR4 181 A1
Barnard's Inn EC4 241 B2
Barnbrough NW1 232 A5
Barnby Sq 1 E15 98 C6
Barnby St
Somers Town NW1 93 C4 232 B2
2 West Ham E15 98 C6
Barn Cl
Ashford TW15 170 D5
19 Kentish Town NW5 71 D3
Northolt UB5 84 C5
Barn Cres HA7 25 C4
Barncroft Cl UB8 82 D2
Barn Croft Prim Sch E17 53 A3
Barneby Cl TW2 152 C3
Barnehurst Rd DA7 147 D3
Barnersbury Ho N7 72 A4
BARNES 133 D4
Barnes Ave
Barnes SW13 134 A5
Southall UB2 107 B2
Barnes Bridge Sta SW13 133 C3
Barnes Cl E12 77 D4
Barnes Common* SW13 134 A2
Barnes Ct
Barnet EN5 1 D1
Islington N1 72 C1
3 Newham E16 99 C2
South Norwood CR7 205 A6
Woodford IG8 37 D5
Wood Green N22 32 A3
Barnes End KT3 200 A4
Barnes High St SW13 133 D3
Barnes Ho
8 Barking IG11 101 B6
14 Bethnal Green E2 96 C5
Camden Town NW1 231 D6
26 Deptford SE14 140 D6
Hornsey N19 50 A2
Barnes Hospl SW14 133 C2
Barnes Prim Sch SW13 133 D2
Barnes Qtr 6 TW8 131 C5
Barnes Rd
Edmonton N18 34 C6
Ilford IG1 79 A3
Barnes St E14 97 A1
Barnes Sta SW13 134 A2
Barnes Terr SE8 119 B1
Barnes Wallis Ct HA9 67 A5
BARNET 13 B6
Barnet By-Pass WD6 11 C6
Barnet Coll EN5 1 B1

Barnet Coll (Grahame Park Ctr) NW9 27 D2
Barnet Coll (Montagu Rd) NW4 46 A3
Barnet Dr BR2 226 A6
BARNET GATE 11 C5
Barnet Gate La EN5 11 D4
Barnet Gr E2 96 A4
Barnet Hill EN5 1 C1
Barnet Hill JMI Sch EN5 13 B6
Barnet Ho 35 SE5 139 A3
Barnet La
Barnet EN5, N20 13 B4
Borehamwood WD6 10 B5
Barnet Mus* EN5 1 A1
Barnet Rd
Barnet EN5 1 B5
Edgware EN5 11 C5
Barnett Ho E1 243 C3
Barnett Homestead NW11 47 C5
Barnet Trad Est EN5 1 B2
Barnetts Ct HA2 63 D5
Barnett St 18 E1 96 B1
Barnet Way (Barnet By-Pass) EN5, NW7, WD6 11 B3
Barnet Wood Rd BR2 225 C6
Barney Cl SE7 121 C1
Barnfield KT3 199 C3
Barn Field NW3 70 D3
Barnfield Ave
Croydon CR0 222 C6
Kingston u T KT2 176 A5
Mitcham CR4 203 B6
Barnfield Cl
London N4 50 A2
Wandsworth SW17 158 A1
Barnfield Gdns
Kingston u T KT2 176 A5
Shooters Hill SE18 144 D6
Barnfield Pl E14 119 C2
Barnfield Prim Sch HA8 27 A2
Barnfield Rd
Burnt Oak HA8 27 A2
Ealing W5 87 C3
Erith DA17 147 B6
Shooters Hill SE18 144 D6
Barnfield Wood Cl BR3 208 B3
Barnfield Wood Rd BR3 208 B3
Barnham Dr SE28 123 D5
Barnham Rd UB6 86 A4
Barnham St SE1 253 B2
Barnhill HA5 40 C4
Barn Hill HA9 44 D1
Barnhill Ave BR2 208 D4
Barnhill Com High Sch UB4 84 C4
Barnhill Ct UB4 84 B4
Barnhill La UB4 84 B3
Barnhill Rd
Hayes UB4 84 C3
Wembley HA9 67 A5
Barnhurst Path WD19 22 C5
Barningham Way NW9 45 B3
Barnlea Cl TW13 151 A2
Barnmead Ct RM9 81 B3
Barnmead Gdns RM9 81 B3
Barnmead Rd
Dagenham RM9 81 B3
Penge BR3 185 A2
Barn Rise HA9 66 C6
BARNSBURY 72 A1
Barnsbury Cl KT3 199 A5
Barnsbury Cres KT5 199 A1
Barnsbury Gr N7 72 B1
Barnsbury Ho 12 SW4 159 D5
Barnsbury La KT5 199 A1
Barnsbury Pk N1 72 C1
Barnsbury Rd N1 94 C6 234 A5
Barnsbury Sq N1 72 C1
Barnsbury St N1 72 C1
Barnsbury Terr N1 72 B1
Barnscroft SW20 200 B6
Barnsdale Ave E14 119 C2
Barnsdale Rd W9 91 B3
Barnsley St E1 96 B3
Barn St N16 73 C6
Barnstaple Ho SE12 164 D6
Barnstaple La SE13 142 A1
Barnstaple Rd HA4 62 C5
Barnston Wlk N1 235 A6
Barnview Lo HA3 24 C2
Barn Way HA9 66 C6
Barnwell Ho 1 SE5 139 C4
Barnwell Rd SW2 160 C6
Barnwood Cl
Barnet N20 13 B3
Ruislip HA4 61 B6
Westbourne Green W9 91 D3
Baron Cl
Friern Barnet N11 31 B5
Islington N1 234 A4
Baron Ct
Barnet EN5 1 D1
Mitcham CR4 202 C5
Baroness Rd 5 E2 95 D4
Baronet Gr N17 34 A2
Baronet Rd N17 34 A2
Baron Gdns IG6 57 A6
Baron Gr CR4 202 C5
Baron Ho 6 SW19 180 B2
Baron Rd RM8 58 D1
Barons 14 BR3 185 D1
Barons Court Mans W14 254 B1
Baron's Court Rd W14 113 A1 254 B2
Barons Court Sta W14 113 A1 254 A2
Barons Ct
Ilford IG1 79 B6
Kingsbury NW9 45 B3
Wallington SM6 219 D5
Baronsfield Rd TW1 153 B5
Barons Gate
East Barnet EN4 14 C5
13 South Acton W4 111 A3
Barons Keep W14 113 A1 254 A2
Barons Lo 9 E14 120 A2
Barons Mead HA1 42 C5
Baronsmead Rd SW13 134 A4
Baronsmede W5 110 B4
Baronsmere Ct 9 EN5 1 A1
Baronsmere Rd N2 48 C5
Baron's Pl SE1 116 C4 251 B1
Baron St N1 94 C5 234 A4
Barons The TW1 153 B5
Baron's Wlk CR0 207 A3
Baron Wlk E16 98 D2
Barque Mews SE8 141 C6
Barrack Rd TW4 129 A1
Barradell Ho 15 W14 112 D3
Barra Hall Cir UB3 83 C1
Barra Hall Rd UB3 105 C6
Barrass Cl 7 EN3 7 C6
Barratt Ave N22 32 B1
Barratt Ho 15 N1 72 D1
Barratt Ind Pk
Poplar E3 98 A3
Southall UB1 107 C5
Barratt Way HA3 42 B6
Barr Beacon SE23 162 C4
Barrenger Rd N10 30 D1
Barret Ho NW6 91 C6
Barrett Ct 2 NW10 89 C5
Barrett Rd E17 54 A5
Barrett's Gr N16 73 C3
Barrett's Green Rd NW10 89 B5
Barrett St W1 93 A1 238 B1
Barrhill Rd SW2 160 A2
Barrie Ct EN5 14 A6
Barriedale SE14 141 A3
Barrie Ho
Acton W3 111 A4
Bayswater W2 246 B5
Edmonton N9 18 B4
Primrose Hill NW8 230 B5
8 Stoke Newington N16 73 C5
Barrier Gdns Pier SE18 121 D3
Barrier Point Rd E16 121 C4
Barringers Ct HA4 39 B2
Barringer Sq SW17 181 A6
Barrington N20 14 B3
Barrington Cl NW5 71 A3
Barrington Ct
9 Acton W3 110 D4
Kentish Town NW5 71 A3
4 Muswell Hill N10 31 B1
31 South Lambeth SW9 138 A3
Barrington Prim Sch DA7 146 D3
Barrington Rd
Bexley DA7 146 D3
Brixton SW9 138 D2
Cheam SM3 201 C1
Hornsey N8 49 D4
Little Ilford E12 78 C2
Barrington Villas SE18 144 C4
Barrington Wlk 9 SE19 183 C4
Barrow Ave SM5 218 D1
Barrow Cl N21 16 D2
Barrow Ct 6 SE6 164 D3
Barrowdene Cl HA5 23 A1
Barrowell Gn N21 17 A2
Barrowfield Cl N9 18 C1
Barrowgate Ho W4 111 B1
Barrowgate Rd W4 111 B1
Barrow Hedges Cl SM5 218 C1
Barrow Hedges Prim Sch SM5 218 C1
Barrow Hedges Way SM5 218 C1
Barrow Hill KT4 215 C6
Barrow Hill Cl KT4 215 C6
Barrow Hill Est NW8 92 C5 230 A3
Barrow Hill Jun Sch NW8 92 C5 230 A3
Barrow Hill Rd NW8 230 A3
Barrow Point Ave HA5 23 A1
Barrow Point La HA5 23 A1
Barrow Rd
Croydon CR0 220 C3
Streatham SW16 181 D4
Barrow Wlk TW8 109 C1
Barrs Rd NW10 67 B1
Barry Ave
Erith DA7 147 A5
South Tottenham N15 51 D3
Barry Cl BR6 227 C5
Barry Ct SW4 159 C5
Barrydene N20 14 B2
Barrydene Ct EN2 4 D2
Barry Ho 4 SE16 118 B1
Barry Lo N4 50 B2
Barrymore N12 30 A3
Barry Par SE22 140 A1
Barry Rd
London SE22 162 A6
Newham E6 100 A1
Willesden NW10 67 A1
Barry Terr TW15 148 B2
Barset Rd SE15 140 C2
Barsons Cl SE20 184 C3
Barston Rd SE27 161 A1
Barstow Cres SW2 160 B3
Bartell Ho SW2 160 C5
Barter St WC1 94 A2 240 B3
Barters Wlk HA5 41 A6
Barth Mews SE18 123 C2
Bartholomew Cl
Barbican EC1 242 A3
Wandsworth SW18 136 A1
Bartholomew Ct
16 Blackwall E14 120 B6
Edgware HA8 25 D3
St Luke's EC1 242 B6
Bartholomew Ho
22 Camberwell SE5 139 A3
Enfield EN3 7 A6
Bartholomew La EC2 242 D1
Bartholomew Pas EC1 241 D3
Bartholomew Pl EC1 242 A3
Bartholomew Rd NW5 71 C2
Bartholomew Sq
18 Bethnal Green E1 96 B3
St Luke's EC1 242 B6
Bartholomew St SE1 117 B3 262 D5
Bartholomew Villas NW5 71 C2
Barth Rd SE18 123 C2
Bartle Ave E6 100 A5
Bartle Rd W11 91 A1
Bartlett Cl E14 97 C1
Bartlett Ct EC4 241 B2
Bartletts Cotts 4 EN5 1 A2
Bartletts Ho 10 RM10 81 D2
Bartlett St CR2 221 B3
Bartok Ho W11 244 C5
Barton Ave RM7 59 D1
Barton Cl
Bexley DA6 169 A6
Hackney E9 74 C3
Hendon NW4 46 A5
2 Newham E6 100 B1
Peckham SE15 140 B2
Shepperton TW17 192 D3
Barton Ct
Beckenham BR2 208 B6
10 South Lambeth SW4 138 A3
3 Sutton SM1 217 D2
Barton Ct *continued*
West Kensington W14 254 B2
Barton Gn KT3 177 B1
Barton Ho
8 Bromley E3 97 D4
Islington N1 72 D1
Sands End SW6 135 D2
Barton Mdws IG6 57 A5
Barton Rd
Sidcup DA14 191 A4
West Kensington W14 113 A1 254 B1
Barton St SW1 260 A6
Bartons The WD6 9 D5
Bartonway NW8 229 C4
Bartram Cl UB8 82 D3
Bartram Ct RM9 80 B2
Bartram Rd SE4 163 A5
Bartrams La EN4 2 A5
Bartrip St E9 75 B2
Barts Cl BR3 207 C4
Barts & The London Sch of Medicine & Dentistry EC1 94 D3 241 D5
Barville Cl SE4 141 A1
Barwell Bsns Pk KT9 213 D1
Barwell Ho 7 E2 96 A3
Barwell La KT9 213 C1
Barwick Dr UB8 82 D2
Barwick Ho 7 W3 111 A4
Barwick Rd E7 77 B4
Barwood Ave BR4 207 D1
Bascome St 13 SW2 160 C5
Basden Gr TW13 151 C2
Base Apartments 8 N1 73 A1
Basedale Rd RM9 80 B1
Baseing Cl E6 122 C6
Baseline Business Studios 18 W11 112 D6
Basevi Way SE8 141 D6
Bashley Rd NW10 89 B3
Basil Ave E6 100 A4
Basil Ct 11 EN5 2 A1
Basildene Rd TW4, TW5 128 D2
Basildon Ct W1 238 B4
Basildon Rd SE2 124 A1
Basil Gdns
Croydon CR0 206 D1
West Norwood SE27 183 A5
Basil Ho
South Lambeth SW8 270 A4
22 Whitechapel E1 96 A1
Basil Mans SW1 247 C1
Basilon Rd DA7 147 A3
Basil Spence Ho N22 32 B2
Basil St
Knightsbridge SW1 114 D4 247 C1
Knightsbridge SW1, SW3 114 D3 257 C6
Basin App 20 E14 97 A1
Basing Cl KT7 196 D2
Basing Ct 18 SE15 139 D4
Basingdon Way SE5 139 B1
Basing Dr DA5 169 B5
Basingfield Rd KT7 196 D2
Basinghall Ave EC2 95 B1 242 C2
Basinghall St EC2 95 B1 242 C2
Basing Hill
London NW11 47 B1
Wembley HA9 44 C1
Basing Ho
7 Barking IG11 101 B6
Catford SE6 185 C6
Basing House Yd 22 E2 95 C4
Basing Pl E2 95 C4
Basing St W11 91 B1
Basing Way
London N3 47 D6
Thames Ditton KT7 196 D2
Basire St N1 95 A6 235 B6
Baskerville Ct
South Norwood SE25 205 C4
Wandsworth SW18 158 C4
Baskerville Gdns NW10 67 C4
Baskerville Rd SW18 158 C4
Basket Gdns SE9 166 A6
Basle Ho 3 E15 76 C3
Baslow Cl HA3 24 B2
Baslow Wlk E5 74 D4
Basnett Rd 9 SW11 137 A2
Basque Ct 21 SE16 118 D4
Bassano St SE22 161 D6
Bassant Rd SE18 145 D6
Bassein Park Rd W12 111 D4
Bassett Gdns TW7 130 A5
Bassett Ho RM9 102 B6
Bassett Rd W10 90 D1
Bassetts Cl BR6 226 D4
Bassett St NW5 71 A2
Bassetts Way BR6 226 D4
Bassett Way UB1 85 D1
Bassingbourn Ho 3 N1 72 D1
Bassingham Rd
Wandsworth SW18 158 A4
Wembley HA0 65 D2
Bassishaw Highwalk EC2 242 C3
Basswood Cl 5 SE15 140 B2
Bastable Ave IG11 102 A5
Basterfield Ho EC1 242 A5
Bastion Highwalk EC2 242 A3
Bastion Rd SE18, SE2 124 A1
Baston Manor Rd BR2, BR4 225 B4
Baston Rd BR2 225 B5
Baston Sch BR2 225 B6
Bastwick St EC1 95 A3 242 A6
Basuto Rd SW6 135 C4 265 B1
Batavia Cl TW16 172 C2
Batavia Ho 1 SE14 141 A5
Batavia Mews 3 SE14 141 A5
Batavia Rd
Deptford SE14 141 A5
Sunbury TW16 172 B2
Batchelor St N1 94 C6 234 B5
Bateman Cl IG11 79 A2
Bateman Ho 8 SE17 138 D6
Bateman Rd E4 35 C4
Bateman's Bldgs W1 239 C1
Bateman's Row EC2 95 C3 243 B6
Bateman St W1 93 D1 239 C1
Bates Cres
Croydon CR0 220 C3
Streatham SW16 181 C3
Bateson St 3 SE18 123 C2
Bate St 10 E14 119 B6
Bath Cl SE15 140 B5
Bath Ct
Finsbury EC1 235 C1
3 Forest Hill SE26 162 A1
Holborn EC1 241 A5
Bathgate Ho 8 SW9 138 D4
Bathgate Rd SW19 156 D1
Bath Gr E2 96 A5
Bath Ho
Bethnal Green E2 96 A3
Borough The SE1 262 B6
Bath House Rd CR0 204 A1
Bath Pas KT1 175 D1
Bath Pl
Barnet EN5 1 B2
14 Hammersmith W6 112 C1
11 Shoreditch EC2 95 C4
Bath Rd
Acton W4 111 C2
Cranford TW3, TW4, TW5 128 C4
Dagenham RM6 59 A3
Harlington TW6, UB7, TW5 127 B4
Harmondsworth TW6, UB7 126 B4
Lower Edmonton N9 18 C2
Upton E7 77 D2
Baths Rd BR1, BR2 209 D5
Bath St EC1 95 B4 235 C1
Bath Terr SE1 117 A3 262 A6
Bathurst Ave SW19 179 D2
Bathurst Gdns NW10 90 B5
Bathurst Ho 2 W12 112 B6
Bathurst Mews W2 114 B6 246 D6
Bathurst Rd IG1 56 D1
Bathurst St W2 246 D6
Bathway 11 SE18 122 C2
Batley Cl CR4 202 D2
Batley Pl 3 N16 73 D5
Batley Rd
Enfield EN2 5 B4
Shacklewell N16 73 D5
Batman Cl W12 112 B5
Batoum Gdns W6 112 C3
Batson Ho 29 E1 96 A1
Batson St W12 112 A4
Batsworth Rd CR4 202 B6
Battenburg Wlk 10 SE19 183 C5
Batten Cl E6 100 B1
Batten Ho
7 London SW4 159 C6
8 Walthamstow E17 53 D6
10 West Kilburn W10 91 A4
Batten St SW11 136 C2
Battersby Rd SE6 164 B1
BATTERSEA 136 D4
Battersea Bridge Rd SW11 136 C5 267 A3
Battersea Bsns Ctr SW11 137 A2
Battersea Church Rd SW11 136 B4 266 D2
Battersea Dogs Home SW8 137 B5 268 D3
Battersea High St SW11 136 B3
Battersea Hts SW11 136 D2
Battersea Park* SW11 137 A5 268 A3
Battersea Park Rd SW11, SW8 267 D1
Battersea Park Sta SW8 137 B5 268 C3
Battersea Power Station(dis) SW8 137 B6 268 D6
Battersea Rise SW11 136 C1
Battersea Sq SW11 266 D1
Battery Rd SE28 123 C4
Battishill St 9 N1 72 D1
Battlebridge Ct NW1 233 B4
Battle Bridge La SE1 117 C5 253 A3
Battle Bridge Rd NW1 94 A5 233 A4
Battle Cl SW19 180 A4
Battledean Rd N5 72 D3
Battle Ho 8 SE15 140 A6
Battle House Mews 7 EN5 2 A1
Battle of Britain Mus* NW9 27 D1
Batty St E1 96 A1
Baty Ho SW2 160 B3
Baudwin Rd SE6 164 C2
Baugh Rd DA14 190 C5
Baulk The SW18 157 C4
Bavant Rd SW16 182 B1
Bavaria Rd N19 72 A6
Bavdene Mews NW4 46 B5
Bavent Rd SE5 139 A3
Bawdale Rd SE22 161 D6
Bawdsey Ave IG2 57 D5
Bawtree Rd SE14 141 A5
Bawtry Rd N20 14 D1
Baxendale N20 14 A2
Baxendale St E2 96 A4
Baxter Cl
Bromley BR1 210 D6
Hillingdon UB10 82 D4
Southall UB2 107 D3
Baxter Ho 11 E3 97 D4
Baxter Rd
Edmonton N18 34 B6
Ilford IG1 78 D3
Islington N1 73 B2
Newham E16 99 C1
Bayard Ct DA7 147 D1
Baycliffe Ho 8 E9 74 D2
Baycroft Cl HA5 40 C6
Bay Ct
Ealing W5 110 A3
7 Stepney E1 96 D3
Baydon Ct BR2 208 D6
Bayer Ho EC1 242 A5
Bayes Ct NW3 70 D1
Bayeux Ho 10 SE7 143 C6
Bayfield Ho 3 SE4 140 D1
Bayfield Rd SE9 143 D1
Bayford Lodge HA5 23 B2
Bayford Rd NW10 90 D4
Bayford St Ind Ctr 4 E8 74 B1
Bayford St 5 E8 74 B1
Baygrove Mews KT1 175 C2
Bayham Pl NW1 93 C6 232 B5
Bayham Rd
Acton W4 111 B3
Ealing W13 109 B5
Morden SM4 202 A5
Bayham St NW1 93 C6 232 A5

Bay Ho UB10 60 C4
Bayhurst Ho N4 51 A2
Bayhurst Wood Countryside Park UB9 38 B4
Bayleaf Cl TW12 174 B5
Bayley St WC1 239 C3
Bayley Wlk SE2 125 A1
Baylis Mews TW1 153 A4
Baylis Rd SE1 116 C4 251 A1
Bayliss Ave SE28 124 D6
Bayliss Cl
4 Southall UB1 85 D1
Southgate N21 16 A6
Bayne Cl E6 100 B1
Baynes Cl EN1 6 A4
Baynes Mews 2 NW3 70 B2
Baynes St NW1 71 C1
Baynham Cl DA5 169 B5
Bayon Ho 27 N19 49 D2
Bayonne Rd W6 264 A5
Bays Cl SE26 184 C5
Bays Ct HA8 26 D5
Bayshill Rise UB5 63 D2
Bayston Rd N16 73 D5
BAYSWATER 114 A6
Bayswater Rd W2 114 B6 246 C5
Bayswater Sta W2 113 D6 245 D6
Bayton Ct 2 E8 74 A1
Baytree Cl
Bromley BR1 187 D2
Sidcup DA15 167 D3
Baytree Ho E4 19 D4
Baytree Rd SW2 138 B1
Bazalgette Cl KT3 199 B4
Bazalgette Gdns KT3 199 B4
Bazalgette Ho NW8 236 D6
Bazeley Ho SE1 251 C1
Bazely St E14 120 A6
Bazile Rd N21 16 C5
BBC Television Ctr W12 112 C5
Beacham Cl SE7 143 D6
Beachborough Rd BR1 186 A6
Beachcroft Ave UB1 107 B5
Beachcroft Rd E11 76 C5
Beach Ct SE9 166 A5
Beach Gr TW13 151 C2
Beach Ho SW5 255 A2
Beachy Rd E3 75 C1
Beaconfield Terrace Rd W14 254 A5
Beacon Gate SE14 140 D2
Beacon Gr SM5 219 A4
Beacon Hill N7 72 A3
Beacon Ho
11 Camberwell SE5 139 C5
7 Isle Of Dogs E14 119 D1
10 Penge SE26 184 B5
South Lambeth SW8 269 C2
Beacon House Sch W5 110 B5
Beacon Pl CR0 220 A5
Beacon Rd
Harlington TW19, TW6 148 C5
Hither Green SE13 164 B5
Beacon Rdbt TW6 148 C5
Beacons Cl 10 E6 100 A2
Beaconsfield Cl
Acton Green W4 111 A1
Friern Barnet N11 31 A5
Greenwich SE3 143 A6
Beaconsfield Ct N11 31 A5
Beaconsfield Gdns KT10 212 C1
Beaconsfield Par 1 SE9 188 A6
Beaconsfield Prim Sch UB2 107 A5
Beaconsfield Rd
Acton W4 111 B3
Bromley BR1 209 D6
Claygate KT10 212 C1
Ealing W5 109 D4
Edmonton N9 18 A1
Elmstead SE9 188 A6
Enfield EN3 6 D6
Friern Barnet N11 31 A6
Greenwich SE3 143 A5
Hayes UB4 106 C5
Kingston u T KT3 177 B1
Leyton E10 76 A5
Newham E16 98 D3

Beaconsfield Rd *continued*
Southall UB1 107 A5
South Tottenham N15 51 C5
Surbiton KT5 198 B2
Thornton Heath CR0 205 B3
Twickenham TW1 153 B5
Walthamstow E17 53 B3
Walworth SE17 117 C1 263 A1
Willesden NW10 67 D2
Beaconsfield Wlk SW6 135 B4 264 D1
Beaconshaw BR1 186 C3
Beacontree Ave E17 36 B1
Beacontree Rd E11 54 D2
Beadle Ct CR4 202 C6
Beadlow Cl SM4 202 B3
Beadman Pl SE27 182 D6
Beadman St SE27 182 D6
Beadnell Rd SE23 162 D3
Beadon Rd
Bromley BR2 209 A4
Hammersmith W6 112 C2
Beaford Gr SW20 201 B6
Beagle Cl TW13 172 B6
Beak St W1 115 C6 249 B6
Beal Cl DA16 146 A4
Beale Cl N13 32 D5
Beale Ho 7 SW9 138 B3
Beale Pl E3 97 B5
Beale Rd E3 97 B6
Beal High Sch IG5 56 A5
Beal Rd IG1 78 C6
Beam Ave RM10 103 D6
Beames Ho SW8 269 C2
Beames Rd NW10 89 B6
Beaminster Ct N15 51 B4
Beaminster Gdns IG6 56 D6
Beaminster Ho SW8 270 C4
Beamish Dr WD23 8 A3
Beamish Ho 7 SE16 118 C2
Beamish Rd N9 18 A3
Beanacre Cl E9 75 B2
Bean Rd DA6 146 D1
Beanshaw SE9 188 C6
Beansland Gr RM6 59 A6
Bear Alley EC4 241 C2
Bear Cl RM7 59 D3
Bear Croft Ho 6 SW6 135 B3
Beardell St SE19 183 D4
Beardow Gr N14 15 C5
Beard Rd KT2 176 B5
Beardsfield E13 99 A5
Beard's Hill TW12 173 C2
Beards Hill Cl TW12 173 C2
Beardsley Terr RM8 80 B3
Beardsley Way W3 111 B4
Beard's Rd TW15, TW16 171 C4
Bearfield Rd KT2 176 A3
Bear Gardens Mus* SE1 117 A5 252 A4
Bear Gdns SE1 117 A5 252 A4
Bear La SE1 116 D5 251 D3
Bear Rd TW13 172 D6
Bear St WC2 249 D6
Bearstead Rise SE4 163 B6
Bearsted Terr 7 BR3 185 C2
Beasley's Ait TW17 193 D3
Beasley's Ait La TW16, TW17 193 D3
Beaton Cl SE15 139 D4
Beatrice Ave
Thornton Heath SW16 182 B1
Wembley HA9 66 A3
Beatrice Cl
Newham E13 99 A3
Pinner HA5 40 A5
Beatrice Ct
Buckhurst Hill IG9 21 D2
Hendon NW4 46 C4
Beatrice Ho
1 Brixton SW2 160 B6
Forest Hill SE6 163 C2
4 Hammersmith W6 112 C1
2 Stepney E1 96 D2
Beatrice Lo 3 N12 30 A4
Beatrice Pl W8 255 C5
Beatrice Rd
Bermondsey SE1 118 A2
Edmonton N9 18 C4
Finsbury Pk N4 50 C2
2 Richmond TW10 154 B6
Southall UB1 107 B5
Walthamstow E17 53 C4
Beatrice Tate Sch E2 96 B4

Beatrice Webb Ho 4 E3 97 A5
Beatrix Ho SW5 255 D2
Beatrix Potter Prim Sch SW18 158 A3
Beatson Wlk 23 SE16 118 D5
Beattie Cl TW14 149 D3
Beattie Ho SW8 269 B2
Beattock Rise N10 49 B5
Beatty Ho 16 E14 119 C4
Beatty Rd
Stanmore HA7 25 C4
Stoke Newington N16 73 C4
Beatty St NW1 232 A4
Beattyville Gdns IG6 56 D5
Beauchamp Cl 17 W4 111 A3
Beauchamp Ct HA7 25 C5
Beauchamp Pl SW3 114 C3 257 B5
Beauchamp Rd
Clapham SW11 136 D1
East Molesey KT8 196 A4
South Norwood SE19 183 B2
Sutton SM1 217 C4
Twickenham TW1 153 A4
Upton E7 77 B1
Beauchamp St EC1 241 A3
Beauchamp Terr SW15 134 B2
Beauclerc Inf Sch TW16 194 C6
Beauclerc Rd W6 112 B3
Beauclere Ho 1 SM2 218 A1
Beauclerk Cl TW13 150 B3
Beauclerk Ho 10 SW16 160 A1
Beaudesert Mews UB7 104 A4
Beaufort E6 100 C2
Beaufort Ave HA3 43 B6
Beaufort Cl
Chingford E4 35 D4
Ealing W5 88 B2
Putney SW19 156 B4
Beaufort Ct
Friern Barnet N11 31 B5
Harrow HA3 43 A3
3 New Barnet EN5 14 A6
Richmond TW10 175 C6
West Brompton SW6 265 A6
Beaufort Dr NW11 47 C5
Beaufort Gdns
Hendon NW4 46 C3
Heston TW5 129 A4
Ilford IG1 56 C1
Knightsbridge SW3 114 C3 257 B6
South Norwood SW16 182 B3
Beaufort Ho
Ashford TW15 170 D5
Battersea SW11 136 C3
Chelsea SW3 266 D5
Hampstead Garden Suburb NW11 48 A3
20 Millwall E14 119 C4
Pimlico SW1 259 C1
8 South Tottenham N15 51 D5
1 Wimbledon SW20 178 D2
Beaufort Mans SW3 266 D5
Beaufort Mews SW6 264 D6
Beaufort Pk NW11 47 C5
Beaufort Rd
Ealing W5 88 B2
Kingston u T KT1, KT5, KT6 198 A5
Richmond TW10 175 C6
Ruislip HA4 61 B6
Twickenham TW1 153 C4
Beaufort St SW3 136 B6 266 C6
Beaufort Way KT17 216 A1
Beaufoy Ho
South Lambeth SW8 270 C4
3 West Norwood SE27 160 D1
Beaufoy Rd
11 London SW8 137 B2
Tottenham N17 33 C3
Beaufoy Wlk SE11 116 B2 260 D3
Beaulieu Ave
Forest Hill SE26 184 B6
1 Newham E16 121 B5
Beaulieu Cl
Camberwell SE5 139 B2
Colindale NW9 45 C5
Hounslow TW4 151 B6
Mitcham CR4 181 A2

Beaulieu Cl *continued*
14 Twickenham TW1 153 D5
Beaulieu Ct W5 88 A2
Beaulieu Dr HA5 40 D2
Beaulieu Gdns N21 17 A4
Beaulieu Ho 6 NW4 28 D1
Beaulieu Hts CR7 183 C2
Beaulieu Pl W4 111 A3
Beaumanor Gdns SE9 188 C6
Beaumanor Mans W2 245 D6
Beaumaris 5 N11 32 A4
Beaumaris Dr IG8 37 D3
Beaumaris Gn NW9 45 C3
Beaumaris Twr 2 W3 110 D4
Beaumont SW15 157 A6
Beaumont Ave
Harrow HA2 41 D3
Richmond TW9 132 B2
Wembley HA0 65 C4
West Kensington W14 113 B1 254 C2
Beaumont Bldgs WC2 240 B1
Beaumont Cl KT2 176 C3
Beaumont Cres W14 113 B1 254 C1
Beaumont Ct
10 Acton Green W4 111 A1
16 Hendon NW9 27 D1
Lower Clapton E5 74 B5
Marylebone W1 238 B4
7 Mile End E1 97 A4
6 Mitcham CR4 181 A1
Wembley HA0 65 C3
17 Wimbledon SW19 178 D3
Beaumont Dr
Ashford TW15 171 B5
New Malden KT4 200 B2
Beaumont Gdns NW3 69 C5
Beaumont Gr E1 96 D3
Beaumont Ho
12 Leyton E10 53 D2
1 Streatham SW2 160 A3
West Kensington W14 254 D3
Wimbledon SW19 157 C1
Beaumont Lo E8 74 A2
Beaumont Pl
Barnet EN5 1 B4
Fitzrovia NW1, WC1, W1 93 C3 239 B6
Isleworth TW7 152 D6
Beaumont Rd
Leyton E10 53 D2
Newham E13 99 B4
Orpington BR5 211 B3
Putney SW15, SW19 157 A4
South Acton W4 111 A3
South Norwood SE19 183 A4
Beaumont Rise N19 49 D1
Beaumont Sch The E10 53 D1
Beaumont Sq E1 96 D2
Beaumont St W1 238 B4
Beaumont Terr 1 SE13 164 C4
Beaumont Wlk NW3 70 D1
Beauvais Terr UB5 84 D4
Beauvale 6 NW1 71 A1
Beauval Rd SE22 161 D5
Beaverbank Rd SE9 167 B3
Beaver Cl
Hampton TW12 173 D2
9 Penge SE20 184 A3
West Barnes SM4 200 C2
Beaver Ctr The RM8 59 A2
Beaver Gr UB5 85 A4
Beavers Com Prim Sch TW4 128 C2
Beavers Cres TW4 128 D1
Beavers La TW4 128 C2
Beavers Lo DA14 189 D5
Beaverwood Rd BR7 189 C4
Beaverwood Sch for Girls BR7 189 C4
Beavis Ho N16 73 C5
Beavor La W6 112 A1
Bebbington Rd SE18 123 C2
Beblets Cl 4 BR6 227 D3
Bec Cl HA4 62 D5
Beccles Dr IG11 79 D2
Beccles St E14 119 B6
Bechervaise Ct 2 E10 53 D1
Beck Cl SE13 141 D4
Beck Ct BR3 206 D6
BECKENHAM 185 C1
Beckenham Bsns Ctr BR3 185 A4
Beckenham Ct BR3 185 C2
Beckenham Gdns N9 17 C1

Beckenham Gr BR2 186 B1
Beckenham Hill Rd BR3, SE6 186 A5
Beckenham Hill Sta SE6 186 A5
Beckenham Hospl BR3 185 B1
Beckenham Junction Sta BR3 185 C2
Beckenham La BR1, BR2 186 D1
Beckenham Place Pk BR3 185 D3
Beckenham Rd
Penge BR3 185 A2
West Wickham BR3, BR4 208 A2
Beckenham Rd Sta BR3 185 A2
Beckers The N16 74 A4
Becket Ave E6 100 C4
Becket Cl
Croydon SE25 206 A3
2 Merton SW19 179 D2
Becket Fold 10 HA1 42 D4
Becket Ho SE1 252 C1
Becket Rd N18 34 C6
Becket St SE1 262 C6
Beckett Cl
Abbey Wood DA17 125 B3
Streatham SW16 159 D2
Willesden NW10 67 C2
Beckett Ho
28 London SW9 138 A3
13 Stepney E1 96 C2
Becketts Cl
Feltham TW14 150 B5
Orpington BR6 227 D5
Becketts Pl KT1 175 D2
Beckett Wlk BR3 185 A4
Beckfoot NW1 232 B3
Beckford Cl W14 254 D3
Beckford Dr BR5 211 B2
Beckford Ho 18 N16 73 C3
Beckford Prim Sch NW6 69 B3
Beckford Rd CR0 205 D3
Beckham Ho SE11 260 D3
Beck Ho
4 Edmonton N18 34 A5
Stoke Newington N16 73 C5
Beckington 18 NW5 71 A2
Beck La BR3 206 D6
Beckley Ho E3 97 B3
Becklow Gdns
Chiswick W12 111 D4
1 Shepherd's Bush W12 112 A4
Becklow Mews 7 W12 112 A4
Becklow Rd W12 112 A4
Beckmead Sch BR3 207 C1
Beck Rd E8 96 B6
Beck River Pk 10 BR3 185 C2
Becks Rd DA14 168 A1
BECKTON 100 D2
Beckton Alps E6 100 C3
Beckton Alps Ski Ctr E6 100 C3
Beckton Park Sta E6 122 B6
Beckton Rd E16 98 D2
Beckton Ret Pk E6 100 C2
Beckton Sta E6 100 C2
Beckton Triangle Ret Pk E6 100 D3
Beck Way BR3 207 B6
Beckway Rd SW16 181 D1
Beckway St SE17 117 C2 263 A3
Beckwith Ho 22 E2 96 B5
Beckwith Rd SE24 161 B6
Beclands Rd SW17 181 A4
Becmead Ave
Harrow HA3 43 B4
Streatham SW16 181 D6
Becondale Rd SE19 183 C5
BECONTREE 81 A4
Becontree Ave RM8 80 C5
Becontree Day Hospl RM8 81 A6
Becontree Prim Sch RM8 80 B5
Becontree Sta RM9 80 D2
Bective Pl SW15 135 B1
Bective Rd
Forest Gate E7 77 A4
Putney SW15 135 B1
Becton Pl DA8 147 D5
Bedale Rd EN2 5 A5

Bedale St SE1 252 C3
Beddan Ct HA8 26 C4
BEDDINGTON 220 A6
BEDDINGTON CORNER 203 A2
Beddington Cross CR0 204 A2
Beddington Farm Rd CR0 204 A1
Beddington Gdns SM5, SM6 219 A2
Beddington Gn BR5 189 D2
Beddington Gr SM6 219 D3
Beddington Inf Sch SM6 219 C4
Beddington La
Wallington CR0 203 D2
Wallington CR0 220 A6
Beddington Lane Sta CR0 203 C3
Beddington Manor SM2 218 B2
Beddington Park Cotts SM6 219 D5
Beddington Park Prim Sch CR0 219 D5
Beddington Rd
Ilford IG3 57 D2
St Paul's Cray BR5 189 D2
Beddington Terr CR0 204 B2
Beddington Trad Est CR0 204 A1
Bede Cl HA5 22 D2
Bedefield WC1 233 B1
Bede Ho
London SE14 141 B4
5 Putney SW15 156 D5
Bedelsford Sch KT1 198 A6
Bedens Rd DA14 191 A5
Bede Rd RM6 58 C3
Bedevere Rd N9 18 A1
Bedfont Cl
East Bedfont TW14 149 A5
Mitcham CR4 181 A1
Bedfont Green Cl TW14 149 A3
Bedfont Ind Pk TW15 149 B1
Bedfont Ind Pk N TW15 149 A1
Bedfont Jun & Inf Schs TW14 149 C5
Bedfont La TW14, TW13 149 D4
Bedfont Lakes Ctry Pk TW14 149 A2
Bedfont Rd
East Bedfont TW13, TW14 149 B2
Stanwell TW19 148 B5
Bedford Ave
Barnet EN5 13 B6
Bloomsbury WC1 93 D2 239 D3
Hayes UB4 84 B1
Bedfordbury WC2 116 A6 250 A5
Bedford Cl
Chiswick W4 133 D6
Muswell Hill N10 31 A3
Bedford Cnr 3 W4 111 C2
Bedford Court Mans WC1 239 D3
Bedford Ct
6 Richmond TW9 132 B1
South Norwood SE19 183 D2
St James WC2 250 A5
Wembley HA0 65 D4
Bedford Gardens Ho W8 245 B3
Bedford Gdns W8 113 C5 245 B3
Bedford Hill SW12 159 B2
Bedford Ho
2 Acton W4 111 C2
Edgware HA8 26 B3
7 Stockwell SW4 138 A1
Bedford Mews SE6 163 D2
BEDFORD PARK 111 C3
Bedford Park Cnr 5 W4 111 C2
Bedford Park Mans 4 W4 111 B2
Bedford Pas SW6 264 B4
Bedford Pk CR0 205 A1
Bedford Pl
Bloomsbury WC1 94 A2 240 A4
Croydon CR0 205 B1
Bedford Rd
Acton W4 111 C3

Bedford Rd continued
Barking E6 100 C6
Crouch End N8 49 D3
Ealing W13 109 B6
East Finchley N2 48 C6
Edgware NW7 11 C1
Edmonton N9 18 B4
Harrow HA1 42 A3
Ilford IG1 78 D5
North Cheam KT4 216 C6
Ruislip HA4 61 D4
Sidcup DA15 167 C1
South Tottenham N15 51 C5
Stockwell SW2, SW4 138 A1
Twickenham TW2 152 B1
Walthamstow E17 53 C6
Woodford E18 37 A1
Wood Green N22 32 A1
Bedford Row WC1 94 B2 240 D3
Bedford Sq WC1 93 D2 239 D3
Bedford St WC2 116 A6 250 B5
Bedford Terr SM2 218 A2
Bedford Villas 3 SM5 218 D5
Bedford Way WC1 93 D3 239 D5
Bedgebury Gdns SW19 157 A2
Bedgebury Rd SE9 143 D1
Bedivere Rd BR1 165 A1
Bedlam Mews SE11 261 A4
Bedlow Cl NW8 236 D5
Bedlow Way CR0 220 B4
Bedonwell Inf Sch DA17 147 A6
Bedonwell Jun Sch DA17 147 A6
Bedonwell Rd
Bexley DA17 147 A6
Erith DA7 147 C5
Bedser Cl
Kennington SE11 270 D6
South Norwood CR7 205 A6
Bedser Ct 7 SW4 138 A3
Bedser Dr UB6 64 B3
Bedster Gdns KT8 195 D6
Bedwardine Rd SE19 183 C3
Bedwell Ct 4 RM6 58 D2
Bedwell Gdns UB3 105 C2
Bedwell Ho 18 SW9 138 C3
Bedwell Rd
Belvedere DA17 125 C1
Tottenham N17 33 C2
Beeby Rd E16 99 B2
Beech Ave
Acton W3 111 C5
Brentford TW8 131 B5
4 Chigwell IG9 21 B2
East Barnet N20 14 C3
Ruislip HA4 40 B1
Sidcup DA15 168 A4
Beech Cl
Ashford TW15 171 B5
Carshalton SM5 218 D6
Deptford SE8 141 B6
Enfield N9 18 B5
Putney SW15 156 A4
Sunbury TW16 172 D1
West Drayton UB7 104 C3
Wimbledon SW19 178 C4
Beech Copse
Bickley BR1 188 B1
South Croydon CR2 221 C3
Beechcroft
Chislehurst West BR7 188 C3
3 Kingston u T KT2 176 D2
Beechcroft Ave
Golders Green NW11 47 B2
Harrow HA2 41 C2
Kingston u T KT1, KT3 177 A1
Beechcroft Cl
Heston TW5 129 A5
Orpington BR6 227 B4
Streatham SW16 182 B5
Beechcroft Ct
3 Golders Green NW11 47 B2
Greenwich SE3 143 A4
8 Woodside Pk N12 29 D6
Beech Croft Ct N5 72 D4
Beechcroft Gdns HA9 66 B5
Beechcroft Ho W5 88 A2
Beechcroft Lo 6 SM2 218 A1
Beechcroft Mans SW16 182 B5
Beechcroft Rd
Chessington KT9 214 B5
Mortlake SW14 133 A2
Orpington BR6 227 B4
Upper Tooting SW17 158 C2
Woodford E18 37 B1
Beechcroft Way N19 49 D1
Beech Ct
Beckenham BR3 185 B3
3 Buckhurst Hill IG9 21 D2
Child's Hill NW2 69 B6
Hayes UB3 105 D5
6 Ilford E12 78 C5
Marylebone W1 237 C2
Northolt UB5 85 A6
43 Notting Hill W2 91 C2
7 Rotherhithe SE16 119 A5
Surbiton KT6 198 A2
Teddington TW11 175 C4
Walthamstow E17 54 B6
4 West Norwood SW16 182 C5
Beechdale N21 16 B2
Beechdale Rd SW2 160 B5
Beech Dell BR2, BR6 226 B4
Beechdene 4 SE15 140 B4
Beech Dr N2 48 D6
Beechen Cliff Way TW7 130 D3
Beechengrove HA5 41 B6
Beechen Pl SE23 162 C2
Beeches Ave SM5 218 C1
Beeches Cl SE20 184 C2
Beeches Ct BR1 187 A4
Beeches Prim Ctr The SE2 124 C3
Beeches Rd
Cheam SM3 201 A1
Upper Tooting SW17 158 D1
Beeches The
Ealing W7 108 D4
East Barnet N20 14 C2
East Ham E12 78 B5
Hounslow TW3 129 D4
Mitcham CR4 202 C4
1 Upper Holloway N19 50 A1
Beechey Ho 30 E1 118 B5
Beech Farm Cotts IG8 36 B3
Beechfield Cotts 5 BR1 187 C1
Beechfield Ct 7 CR2 221 A4
Beechfield Rd
Bromley BR1 187 C1
Forest Hill SE6 163 B3
Harringay N4 51 A3
Beech Gdns
Dagenham RM10 81 D1
Ealing W5 110 A3
Beech Gr
Kingston u T KT3 199 B6
Mitcham CR4 203 D5
Beech Hall Cres E4 36 B3
Beech Hall Rd E4 36 B3
Beech Hill EN4 2 C5
Beech Hill Ave EN4 2 B4
Beechhill Rd SE9 166 C6
Beech Ho
Chingford E4 35 C6
Hayes UB4 84 D2
Heston TW5 129 A5
5 Maitland Pk NW3 70 D2
New Addington CR0 223 D2
22 Rotherhithe SE16 118 C4
7 Sidcup DA15 168 A1
5 Stoke Newington N16 73 B6
12 Wallington SM6 219 C2
Beech House Rd CR0 221 B5
Beech La IG9 21 B2
Beech Lawns N12 30 B5
Beechmont Cl BR1 186 C5
Beechmore Gdns SM3 216 D6
Beechmore Rd SW11 136 D4 267 D1
Beechmount Ave W7 86 C2
Beecholme 15 N12 29 D6
Beecholme Ave CR4 181 B2
Beecholme Est E5 74 B5
Beecholme Prim Sch CR4 181 B2
Beech Rd
Bowes Pk N11 32 A4
East Bedfont TW14 149 C4
Thornton Heath SW16 204 B6
Beechrow KT2 176 A6
Beech St EC2 95 A2 242 B4
Beech Tree Cl
Islington N1 72 C1
Stanmore HA7 25 C5
Beech Tree Glade E4 20 D3
Beech Tree Pl SM1 217 D3
Beechvale Cl N12 30 C5
Beechway DA5 168 D5
Beech Way
Twickenham TW2 151 C1
Willesden NW10 67 B1
Beech Wlk NW7 27 C4
Beechwood Ave
Ashford TW16 172 A4
East Finchley N3 47 C6
Greenford UB6 85 D4
Harrow HA2 63 D5
Hayes UB3 105 B6
Hillingdon UB8 82 C1
Orpington BR6 227 C2
Richmond TW9 132 C4
Ruislip HA4 61 D6
Thornton Heath CR7 204 D5
Beechwood Circ HA2 63 D5
Beechwood Cl
Edgware NW7 27 C5
Fortis Green N2 48 D5
Surbiton KT6 197 D2
Beechwood Cres DA7 147 A2
Beechwood Ct
Ashford TW16 172 A5
Carshalton SM5 218 D4
Cheam SM1 217 C3
Chiswick W4 133 B6
Stamford Hill N16 51 C2
Sutton SM2 218 B2
Beechwood Dr
Keston BR2 225 D4
Woodford IG8 36 D5
Beechwood Gdns
Ealing NW10 88 B4
Harrow HA2 63 D5
Ilford IG5 56 C5
Beechwood Gr W3 111 C6
Beechwood Hall N3 47 B6
Beechwood Ho 23 E2 96 A5
Beechwood Mews 2 N9 18 A2
Beechwood Pk E18 55 A6
Beechwood Rd
Dalston E8 73 D2
London N8 50 A5
South Croydon CR2 221 C1
Beechwood Rise BR7 188 D6
Beechwoods Ct 5 SE19 183 D5
Beechworth Cl NW3 69 C6
Beecroft La SE4 163 A6
Beecroft Mews SE4 163 A6
Beecroft Rd SE4 163 A6
Beehive Cl
Dalston E8 73 D1
Elstree WD6 9 D5
Hillingdon UB10 60 B1
Beehive Ct IG1 56 B3
Beehive La IG1 56 B3
Beehive Pl SW9 138 C2
Beehive Prep Sch IG4 56 B4
Beeken Dene BR6 227 A4
Beeleigh Rd SM4 201 D5
Beemans Row 1 SW18 158 A2
Beeston Cl
5 Dalston E8 74 A3
South Oxhey WD19 22 D6
Beeston Pl SW1 258 D6
Beeston Rd EN4 14 B5
Beeston's Ho SE15 140 B2
Beeston Way TW14 150 C5
Beethoven Rd WD6 9 D5
Beethoven St W10 91 A4
Beeton Cl HA5 23 C3
Begbie Ho SW9 138 B3
Begbie Rd SE3 143 C4
Beggars Hill KT17 215 D2
Beggar's Roost La SM1 217 C2
Begonia Cl E6 100 B3
Begonia Pl 1 TW12 173 C4
Begonia Wlk W12 89 D1
Beira St SW12 159 B4
Beis Chinuch Lebonos Girls Sch N4 51 A2
Beis Rochel d'Satmar Girls Sch N16 51 C2
Beis Soroh Schneirer (Sch) NW4 46 A3
Beis Yaakov Prim Sch NW9 45 B6
Bekesbourne St 17 E14 97 A1
Belcroft Cl BR1 186 D3
Beldanes Lo NW10 68 A1
Beldham Gdns KT8 195 D6
Belenoyd Ct SW16 160 B1
Belfairs Dr RM6 58 C2
Belfairs Gn WD19 22 D5
Belfast Rd
Croydon SE25 206 B5
Stoke Newington N16 73 D6
Belfield Rd KT19 215 C1
Belfont Wlk N7 72 A4
Belford Gr SE18 122 C2
Belford Ho 7 E8 95 D6
Belfort Rd SE15 140 C3
Belfry Cl 33 SE16 118 B1
Belgrade Ho N16 73 C4
Belgrade Rd
Hampton TW12 173 D2
Stoke Newington N16 73 C4
Belgrave Cl
1 Acton W3 111 A4
Burnt Oak NW7 27 B5
Southgate N14 15 C6
Belgrave Cres TW16 172 B2
Belgrave Ct
8 Acton Green W4 111 A1
Charlton SE3 143 C5
22 Limehouse E14 119 B6
Newham E13 99 C3
Nine Elms SW8 269 A3
Belgrave Gdns
Kilburn NW8 91 D6
Southgate N14 3 D1
1 Stanmore HA7 25 C5
St John's Wood NW8 229 A5
Belgrave Ho SW9 138 C5
Belgrave Hts E11 55 A1
Belgrave Mans NW8 229 A5
Belgrave Market IG1 78 C6
Belgrave Mews N SW1 248 A1
Belgrave Mews S SW1 115 A3 258 B6
Belgrave Mews W SW1 258 A6
Belgrave Pl SW1 115 A3 258 B5
Belgrave Rd
Barnes SW13 133 D5
Hounslow TW4 129 B2
Leyton E10 54 A1
Mitcham CR4 202 B6
Newham E13 99 C3
Redbridge IG1 56 B1
South Norwood SE25 205 D5
Sunbury TW16 172 B2
Walthamstow E17 53 C3
Wanstead E11 55 A1
Westminster SW1 115 C2 259 A3
Belgrave Sq SW1 115 A3 258 A6
Belgrave St E1 96 D1
Belgrave Terr IG8 21 A1
Belgrave Wlk CR4 202 B6
Belgrave Wlk Sta CR4 202 B5
Belgrave Yd SW1 258 C5
BELGRAVIA 115 B2
Belgravia Cl EN5 1 B2
Belgravia Ct SW1 258 C5
Belgravia Gdns BR1 186 C4
Belgravia Ho
11 London SW4 159 D5
1 Teddington TW11 175 C3
Belgravia Lo N21 16 D6
Belgravia Mews KT1 197 D5
Belgrove St WC1 233 B2
Belham Wlk 13 SE5 139 B4
Belinda Rd 8 SW9 138 D2
Belitha Villas N1 72 C1
Bel La TW13 151 B1
Bellamy Cl
Edgware HA8 11 A1
13 Millwall E14 119 C4
Uxbridge UB10 60 C5
West Kensington SW5 254 D1
Bellamy Ct HA7 25 B2
Bellamy Dr HA7 25 B2
Bellamy Ho
Harrow HA3 44 A2
Heston TW5 129 C6
Upper Tooting SW17 180 B6
Bellamy Rd
Chingford E4 35 D4
Enfield EN2 5 B3
Bellamy's Ct 16 SE16 118 D5
Bellamy St SW12 159 B4
Bellasis Ave SW2 160 A2
Bell Ave UB7 104 B3
Bell Cl
Pinner HA5 40 C6
Bell Cl continued
Ruislip HA4 61 D5
Bellclose Rd UB7 104 A4
Bell Ct
Hendon NW4 46 C5
Ladywell SE13 163 C6
Tolworth KT5 214 D6
Bell Dr SW18 157 A4
Bellefields Rd SW9 138 B2
Bellegrove Cl DA16 145 D3
Bellegrove Par DA16 145 D2
Bellegrove Rd DA16 145 D3
Bellenden Prim Sch SE15 140 A3
Bellenden Rd SE15 139 D3
Bellenden Rd Ret Pk SE15 140 A4
Bellendon Road Bsns Ctr SE15 139 D3
Bellerbys Coll SE8 141 C6
Bellermine Cl SE28 123 D4
Belle Staines Pleasaunce E4 19 C2
Belleville Prim Sch SW11 158 D6
Belleville Rd SW11 158 D6
Belle Vue UB6 86 B6
Belle Vue Gdns SW9 138 A3
Belle Vue La WD23 8 B3
Bellevue Mews N11 31 A5
Bellevue Pk CR7 205 A5
Bellevue Pl E1 96 C3
Bellevue Rd
Barnes SW13 134 A3
Bexley DA6 169 B6
Ealing W13 87 B3
Friern Barnet N11 31 A5
Kingston u T KT1 198 A6
Upper Tooting SW17 158 D3
Belle Vue Rd
Chingford E17 36 B1
8 Hendon NW4 46 C5
Bellew St SW17 158 A1
Bellfield CR0 223 B1
Bellfield Ave HA3 24 B4
Bell Flats 4 NW2 68 A2
Bellflower Cl 2 E6 100 A2
Bellflower Ct SE13 141 D1
Bellgate Mews NW5 71 B5
Bell Gn SE26 185 B6
Bellgrave Lo 9 W4 110 D1
BELL GREEN 163 B1
Bell Green La SE26 185 B6
Bell Ho
6 Dagenham RM10 81 D2
Greenwich SE10 142 A6
15 Streatham SW2 160 C4
Wembley HA9 66 A5
West Heath SE2 124 D1
Bellina Mews NW5 71 C4
Bell Ind Est 2 W4 111 A2
BELLINGHAM 185 C5
Bellingham 10 N17 34 B3
Bellingham Ct IG11 102 B4
Bellingham Gn SE6 163 C1
Bellingham Rd SE6 164 A1
Bellingham Sta SE6 163 D1
Bellingham Trad Est SE6 163 D2
Bell Inn Yd EC3 242 D1
Bell La
Enfield EN3 6 D5
Hendon NW4 46 D5
Newham E16 121 A5
Spitalfields E1 95 D2 243 C3
Twickenham TW1 153 A3
Wembley HA9 65 D6
Bell Lane Prim Sch NW4 46 D5
Bell Language Sch W1 93 C3 239 A5
Bellmaker Ct 13 E3 97 C2
Bell Mdw SE19 183 C6
Bell Moor NW3 70 A5
Bellmore Ct 5 CR0 205 D1
Bello Cl SE24, SW2 160 D3
Bellot Gdns 1 SE10 120 C1
Bellot St SE10 120 C1
Bell Rd
East Molesey KT8 196 B4
Enfield EN1 5 B4
Hounslow TW3 129 D1
Bellring Cl DA17 147 C6
Bell's Coll IG3 58 A1
Bells Hill EN5 12 D6
Bell St
Kidbrooke SE18 144 A4
Paddington NW1 92 C2 237 A4
Bell The E17 53 C6
Bell View BR3 185 B3
Bellview Ct TW3 129 D1
Bell View Manor HA4 39 C2
Bell Water Gate SE18 122 C3
Bell Wharf La EC4 252 B6
Bellwood Rd SE15 140 D1
Bell Yard Mews SE1 253 B1
Bell Yd WC2 94 C1 241 A1
BELMONT 25 B2
Belmont Ave
Bowes Pk N13 32 B5
Cockfosters EN4 14 D6
Edmonton N9 18 A3
Falconwood DA16 145 C2
Southall UB2 107 A3
Tottenham N17 51 A6
Wembley HA0 88 B6
West Barnes KT3 200 A5
Belmont Circ HA3 25 B2
Belmont Cl
Chingford E4 36 B5
Clapham SW4 137 C2
Cockfosters EN4 2 D1
Totteridge N20 13 D3
Uxbridge UB8 60 A2
Woodford IG8 37 B6
Belmont Ct
Highbury N5 73 A4
6 Stamford Hill N16 51 C1
Temple Fortune NW11 47 B4
1 Whetstone N20 14 A1
Wood Green N11 31 D3
Belmont Fst & Mid Schs HA3 24 D1
Belmont Gr
Chiswick W4 111 B2
Lewisham SE13 142 B2
Belmont Hall Ct SE13 142 B2
Belmont Hill SE13 142 B2
Belmont Jun & Inf Schs N22 51 A6
Belmont La
Chislehurst BR7 189 A5
Stanmore HA7 25 C3
Belmont Lo
Harrow HA3 24 B3
Stanmore HA7 25 C6
Belmont Mews SW19 156 D2
Belmont Mill Hill Jun Sch NW7 12 A1
Belmont Par
Chislehurst BR7 189 A5
2 Temple Fortune NW11 47 B4
Belmont Park Cl SE13 142 C1
Belmont Park Rd E10 53 D3
Belmont Pk SE13 142 C1
Belmont Pk Sch E10 54 A3
Belmont Prim Sch
Chiswick W4 111 B2
Erith DA8 147 C5
Belmont Rd
Beckenham BR3 185 B1
Chislehurst BR7 188 D5
Clapham SW4 137 C2
Croydon SE25 206 B4
Erith DA8 147 D4
Harrow HA3 43 A6
Ilford IG1 79 A5
London W4 111 B2
Twickenham TW2 152 B2
Uxbridge UB8 60 A2
Wallington SM6 219 C3
West Green N15, N17 51 A5
Belmont Rise SM1, SM2 217 B1
Belmont St NW1 71 A1
Belmont Terr W4 111 B2
Belmor WD6 10 C5
Belmore Ave UB4 84 A1
Belmore Ho N7 71 D3
Belmore La N7 71 D3
Belmore Prim Sch UB4 84 B4
Belmore St SW8 137 D4 269 C2
Beloe Cl SW15 134 A1
Belper Ct 11 E5 74 D4
Belsham St E9 74 C2
Belsize Ave
Bowes Pk N13 32 B4
Ealing W13 109 B3
Maitland Pk NW3 70 C3
Belsize Court Garages 1 NW3 70 B3
Belsize Cres NW3 70 B2

Belsize Ct NW3 70 B3
Belsize Gdns SM1 217 D4
Belsize Gr NW3 70 C2
Belsize La NW3 70 B3
Belsize Mews NW3 70 B2
Belsize Park Gdns
NW3 70 C2
Belsize Park Mews 1
NW3 70 B2
Belsize Park Sta NW3 70 C3
Belsize Pk NW3 70 B2
Belsize Pl NW3 70 B3
Belsize Rd
Harrow HA3 24 B3
Kilburn NW6 91 D6
Belsize Sq NW3 70 B2
Belsize Terr NW3 70 B2
Belson Rd SE18 122 B2
Beltane Dr SW19 156 D1
Belthorn Cres SW12 159 C4
Belton Rd
Leyton E11 76 C4
Sidcup DA14 190 A6
Tottenham N17 51 C6
Upton E7 77 B1
Willesden NW2 68 A2
Belton Way E3 97 C2
Beltran Rd SW6 135 D3
BELVEDERE 125 D2
Belvedere Ave SW19 179 A5
Belvedere Bldgs SE1 251 D1
Belvedere Cl TW11 174 C5
Belvedere Ct
Abbey Wood DA17 125 B3
Brondesbury NW2 68 D2
7 Clapham Pk SW4 159 D5
East Finchley N2 48 B4
8 Kingston u T KT2 176 C3
Putney SW15 134 C1
33 Shoreditch N1 95 C6
Southall UB1 107 D6
Southgate N21 16 C4
Belvedere Dr SW19 179 A5
Belvedere Gdns KT8 195 C4
Belvedere Gr SW19 179 A5
Belvedere Ho TW14 150 A3
Belvedere Htss NW8 237 A6
Belvedere Jun & Inf Sch
DA17 125 D3
Belvedere Mews
Greenwich SE3 143 B5
Nunhead SE15 140 C2
Belvedere Pl
Brixton SW2 138 B1
Lambeth SE1 251 D1
Belvedere Rd
Bexleyheath DA7 147 B3
Erith SE2, SE28 124 D5
Hanwell W7 108 D3
Lambeth SE1 116 B5 250 D3
Penge SE19 183 D3
Walthamstow E10 53 A1
Belvedere Sq SW19 179 A5
Belvedere Sta DA17 125 D3
Belvedere Strand
NW9 27 D1
Belvedere The SW10 266 B1
Belvedere Way HA3 44 A3
Belvoir Cl SE9 166 A1
Belvoir Ct HA3 43 A3
Belvoir Lo SE22 162 A4
Belvoir Rd SE22 162 A4
Belvue Bsns Ctr UB5 63 D1
Belvue Cl UB5 63 C1
Belvue Rd UB5 63 C1
Belvue Sch UB5 85 C6
Bembridge Cl NW6 69 A1
Bembridge Gdns HA4 61 B6
Bembridge Ho
9 Deptford SE8 119 B2
Wandsworth SW18 157 D5
Bemersyde Point 6
E13 99 B4
Bemerton St
N1 94 B6 233 C6
Bemish Rd SW15 134 D2
Bempton Dr HA4 62 B5
Bemsted Rd E17 53 B6
Benabo Ct 6 E8 74 A3
Benares Rd SE18, SE2 123 D2
Benbow Ct W6 112 B3
Benbow Ho 12 SE8 141 C6
Benbow Rd W6 112 B3
Benbow St SE8 141 C6
Benbury Cl BR1 186 A5
Bence Ho 13 SE8 119 A2
Bench Field CR2 221 D3
Bencroft Rd SW16 181 C3
Bencurtis Pk BR4 224 B6
Bendall Mews NW1 237 B4
Bendemeer Rd SW15 134 D2
Benden Ho SE13 164 A6
Bendish Point SE28 123 A4
Bendish Rd E6 78 A1
Bendmore Ave SE2 124 A2
Bendon Valley SW18 157 D4
Benedict Cl
9 Erith DA17 125 A3
Orpington BR6 227 C5
Benedict Ct
Dagenham RM9 59 B3
Pinner HA5 23 B2
Benedict Dr TW14 149 B4
Benedict House Prep Sch
DA15 168 A1
Benedict Prim Sch
CR4 202 B6
Benedict Rd
London SW9 138 B2
Mitcham CR4 202 B6
Benedict Way N2 48 A6
Benedict Wharf CR4 202 C6
Benenden Gn BR2 209 A4
Benenden Ho SE17 263 B2
Benett Gdns SW16 182 A1
Beney Ct BR3 185 C1
Ben Ezra Ct SE17 262 B3
Benfleet Cl SM1 218 A5
Benfleet Ct 6 E8 95 D6
Benfleet Way N11 15 A2
Bengal Ct EC3 242 D1
Bengal Ho E1 96 D2
Bengal Rd IG1 78 D5
Bengarth Dr HA3 24 B1
Bengarth Rd UB5 85 A6
Bengeo Gdns RM6 58 C3
Bengeworth Rd
Camberwell SE5 139 A2
Harrow HA1 65 A5
Ben Hale Cl HA7 25 B5
Benham Cl
1 Battersea SW11 136 B2
Chessington KT9 213 C2
Benham Gdns TW3,
TW4 151 B6
Benham Ho SW10 265 D4
Benham Rd W7 86 C2
Benham's Pl 11 NW3 70 A4
Benhill Ave SM1 218 A4
Benhill Rd
London SE5 139 B4
Sutton SM1 218 B4
Benhill Wood Rd
SM1 218 A4
BENHILTON 218 A5
Benhilton Ct SM1 218 A5
Benhilton Gdns SM1 217 D5
Benhurst Ct
Ealing W5 110 A6
12 Penge SE20 184 B2
West Norwood SW16 182 C5
Benhurst La SW16 182 C5
Benington Ct N4 73 A6
Benin St SE13 164 B4
Benjafield Cl N18 34 B6
Benjamin Cl E8 96 A6
Benjamin Ct
4 Ealing W7 108 C5
4 Erith DA17 147 B6
Littleton TW15 171 A3
Benjamin Ho 12 W3 110 D5
Benjamin Mews
SW12 159 C4
Benjamin St EC1 241 C4
Ben Jonson Ct 30 N1 95 C5
Ben Jonson Prim Sch
E1 97 A3
Ben Jonson Rd E1 97 A2
Benledi Rd E14 98 B1
Benelong Cl W12 90 B1
Benerley Rd SW11 158 D6
Bennet Cl KT1 175 C2
Bennets Ct SW19 180 A2
Bennetsfield Rd
UB11 104 D5
Bennet's Hill EC4 251 D6
Bennets Lo EN2 5 A2
Bennett Cl
Twickenham TW4 151 A6
Welling DA16 146 A3
Bennett Ct
Hampstead NW6 69 D2
Lower Holloway N7 72 B5
7 South Acton W3 110 D4
Bennett Gr SE13 141 D4
Bennett Ho
2 Streatham SW4 159 D4
Bennett Ho continued
Westminster SW1 259 D4
Bennett Pk SE3 142 D2
Bennett Rd
Brixton SW9 138 C3
Dagenham RM6 59 A2
Newham E13 99 C3
Bennetts Ave
Croydon CR0 223 A6
Greenford UB6 86 C6
Bennett's Castle La
RM8 80 D5
Bennetts Cl
Mitcham CR4, SW16 181 B2
Tottenham N17 33 D4
Bennetts Copse BR7 188 A4
Bennett St
Chiswick W4 111 C1
St James SW1 249 A4
Bennetts Way CR0 223 B6
Bennett's Yd SW1 259 D5
Benn Ho
Bethnal Green E2 96 A4
7 Greenwich SE7 121 C1
Benningholme Rd HA8 27 C4
Bennington Rd
Chingford IG8 36 C3
Tottenham N17 33 C2
Benn St E9 75 A2
Benns Wlk 8 TW9 132 A1
Bensbury Cl SW15 156 C4
Bensham Cl CR7 205 A5
Bensham Gr CR7 183 A1
Bensham La CR0, CR7 204 D3
Bensham Manor Rd
CR7 205 A5
Bensham Manor Sch
CR7 205 A4
Bensington Ct TW14 149 B5
Bensley Cl 7 N11 30 D5
Ben Smith Way 21
SE16 118 A3
Benson Ave E13, E6 99 D5
Benson Cl
Hillingdon UB8 82 A2
Hounslow TW3 129 C1
Benson Ct
Holdbrook EN3 7 C5
South Lambeth SW8 270 A2
1 Tufnell Pk N19 71 C4
Benson Ho
Lambeth SE1 251 B3
1 Richmond TW10 153 C1
Shoreditch E2 243 C6
Benson Prim sch
CR0 223 A5
Benson Quay E1 118 C6
Benson Rd
Croydon CR0 220 C5
Forest Hill SE23 162 C3
Bentall Sh Ctr The 10
KT1 176 A1
Bentfield Gdns SE9 165 D1
Benthal Ct N16 74 A5
Benthal Prim Sch N16 74 A5
Benthal Rd N16 74 A5
Bentham Ct 11 N1 73 A1
Bentham Ho SE1 262 C6
Bentham Rd
Homerton E9 74 D2
Woolwich SE28 124 B5
Bentham Wlk NW10 67 A3
Ben Tillet Cl E16 122 B5
Ben Tillet Ho N15 50 D6
Bentinck Cl NW8 230 B3
Bentinck Ho
4 Richmond TW10 153 C1
4 Shepherd's Bush
W12 112 B6
Bentinck Mans W1 238 B2
Bentinck Mews W1 238 B2
Bentinck Rd UB7 104 A5
Bentinck St W1 93 A1 238 B2
Bentley Cl SW19 157 C1
Bentley Ct SE13 142 A1
Bentley Dr IG2 57 A3
Bentley Ho
6 Bow E3 97 C3
4 Camberwell SE5 139 C4
Bentley Lo WD23 8 C2
Bentley Mews EN1 17 B5
Bentley Rd N1 73 C2
Bentley Way
Stanmore HA7 25 A5
Woodford IG8 21 A1
Bentley Wood High Sch
HA7 24 D5
Benton Rd
Ilford IG1, IG2 57 B1
South Oxhey WD19 22 D5
Benton's La SE27 183 A6
Benton's Rise SE27 183 B5
Bentry Cl RM8 81 A6
Bentry Rd RM8 81 B6
Bentworth Ct 1 E2 96 A3
Bentworth Prim Sch
W12 90 B1
Bentworth Rd W12 90 B1
Benwell Ct TW16 172 A2
Benwell Rd N7 72 C3
Benwick Cl SE16 118 B2
Benwick Ct SE20 184 C2
Benwood Ct SM1 218 A5
Benworth St E3 97 B4
Benyon Ho EC1 234 B2
Benyon Rd N1 95 B6 235 D6
Benyon Wharf 31 E8 95 C6
Beormund Prim Sch
SE1 117 B4 252 D1
Bequerel Ct SE10 120 D3
Berberis Ct IG1 78 D2
Berberis Ho 17 E3 97 C2
Berberis Wlk UB7 104 A2
Berber Pl 2 E14 119 C6
Berber Rd SW11 158 D6
Berberry Cl 5 HA8 27 A6
Bercta Rd SE9 167 A2
Berebinder Ho 21 E3 97 B5
Berengers Pl RM9 80 B2
Berenger Twr SW10 266 C4
Berenger Wlk SW10 266 C4
Berens Ct DA14 189 D6
Berens Rd NW10 90 D4
Berens Way BR5, BR7 211 D6
Beresford Ave
Ealing W7 86 C2
Friern Barnet N20 14 D2
Tolworth KT5 199 A2
Twickenham TW1 153 C5
Wembley HA0 88 C6
Beresford Ct
Homerton E9 75 A3
11 Twickenham TW1 153 C5
Beresford Dr
Bickley BR1 210 A6
Woodford IG8 37 C6
Beresford Gdns
Dagenham RM6 59 A4
Enfield EN1 5 C1
Hounslow TW4 151 B6
Beresford Ho
Dulwich SE21 161 C1
15 Stockwell SW4 138 A1
Beresford Lo N4 73 B3
Beresford Rd
Belmont SM2 217 B1
Canonbury N5 73 B3
Chingford E4 20 C3
East Finchley N2 48 C6
Harringay N8 50 D4
Harrow HA1 42 B4
Kingston u T KT2 176 B2
New Malden KT3 199 A5
Southall UB1 106 D5
Walthamstow E17 35 D2
Beresford Sq 1
SE18 122 D2
Beresford Square Mkt
SE18 122 D2
Beresford St SE18 122 D3
Beresford Terr 3 N5 73 A3
Bere St E1 118 D6
Berestede Rd 4 W6 111 D1
Bergen Ho 1 SE5 139 A3
Bergenia Ho TW13 150 B3
Bergen Sq SE16 119 A3
Berger Cl BR5 211 C3
Berger Prim Sch E9 74 D2
Berger Rd E9 74 D2
Berghem Mews W14 112 D3
Bergholt Ave IG4 56 A4
Bergholt Cres N16 51 C2
Bergholt Mews 4
NW1 71 D1
Berglen Ct E14 119 A6
Berica Ct IG6 57 A6
Bering Sq E14 119 C1
Bering Wlk E16 99 D1
Berisford Mews
SW18 158 A5
Berkeley Ave
Cranford TW4 128 A3
Erith DA16 146 D4
Northolt UB6 64 C2
Berkeley Cl
Borehamwood WD6 10 C6
Broom Hill BR5 211 C2
2 Kingston u T KT2 176 A3
Ruislip HA4 62 A5
Berkeley Cres EN4 14 B6
Berkeley Ct
Ealing W5 109 C6
Edgware HA8 26 D5
Finchley N3 29 D2
1 Golders Green NW11 47 B2
Marylebone NW1 237 D5
Southgate N14 15 C5
Wallington SM6 219 C4
Willesden NW10 67 C4
Berkeley Dr KT8 195 C6
Berkeley Gdns
Claygate KT10 213 A2
Kensington W8 245 B3
Southgate N21 17 B4
Walton-on-T KT12 193 D2
Berkeley Ho
17 Bow E3 97 C4
11 Brentford TW8 131 D6
8 Deptford SE8 119 B1
Berkeley Lo
Enfield EN2 4 C2
New Malden KT3 199 C5
Berkeley Mews
Marylebone W1 237 D1
Sunbury TW16 194 C6
Berkeley Pl SW19 178 D4
Berkeley Prim Sch
TW5 128 D5
Berkeley Rd
Barnes SW13 134 A4
Crouch End N8 49 D3
Hillingdon UB10 61 A1
Manor Pk E12 78 A3
Queensbury NW9 44 C4
Stamford Hill N15 51 B3
Berkeley Sq
W1 115 B6 248 D5
Berkeley St
W1 115 B5 248 D4
Berkeleys The SE25 206 A5
Berkeley The NW11 47 D2
Berkeley Waye TW5 128 D5
Berkeley Wlk 1 N7 72 B6
Berkhampstead Rd
DA17 125 C1
Berkhamsted Ave HA9 66 C2
Berkley Cl TW2 152 C1
Berkley Ct 8 TW1 153 A4
Berkley Gr NW1 71 A1
Berkley Rd NW1 70 D1
Berkshire Ct 1 W7 86 D3
Berkshire Gdns
Bowes Pk N13 32 C4
Upper Edmonton N18 34 B5
Berkshire Ho
Catford SE6 185 C6
St Giles WC2 240 A2
Berkshire Rd E9 75 B2
Berkshire Way CR4 204 A5
Bermans Way NW10 67 D4
BERMONDSEY 118 A4
Bermondsey Leather Mkt
SE1 253 A1
Bermondsey Mkt*
SE1 117 C3 263 B6
Bermondsey Sq SE1 263 B6
Bermondsey St
SE1 117 C4 253 A1
Bermondsey Trad Est
SE16 118 C1
Bermondsey Wall E
SE16 118 B4
Bermondsey Wall W SE1,
SE16 118 A4
Bermuda Ho HA1 64 B5
Bernal Cl SE28 124 D6
Bernard Angell Ho 4
SE10 142 B6
Bernard Ashley Dr
SE7 121 B1
Bernard Ave W13 109 B3
Bernard Cassidy St 2
E16 98 D2
Bernard Gdns SW19 179 B5
Bernard Ho E1 243 C3
Bernard Rd
South Tottenham N15 51 D4
Wallington SM5, SM6 219 B4
Bernard Shaw Ct 5
NW1 71 C1
Bernard Shaw Ho 2
NW10 89 B6
Bernard St
WC1 94 A3 240 B5
Bernays Cl HA7 25 C4
Bernay's Gr SW9 138 B1
Bernel Dr CR0 223 B5
Berne Rd CR7 205 A4
Berners Dr W13 109 A6
Berners Ho N1 234 A4
Bernersmede SE3 143 A2
Berners Mews
W1 93 C2 239 B3
Berners Pl W1 239 B2
Berners Rd
Islington N1 234 C5
Wood Green N22 32 C1
Berners St W1 93 C1 239 B2
Berner Terr 27 E1 96 A1
Berney Ho BR3 207 A4
Berney Rd CR0 205 B2
Bernhard Baron Ho 23
E1 96 A1
Bernhardt Cres NW8 237 A6
Bernhart Cl HA8 27 A3
Bernie Grant Ho 40 E9 74 C1
Bernwell Rd E4 20 C1
Bernwood Ho 6 N4 51 B2
Berridge Gn HA8 26 C3
Berridge Mews NW6 69 C3
Berridge Rd SE19 183 C5
Berriman Rd N7 72 B5
Berrite Works UB7 104 C4
Berriton Rd HA2 41 B1
Berrybank Cl 4 E4 20 A2
Berry Cl
Dagenham RM10 81 C3
Southgate N21 16 D3
Berry Cotts 2 E14 97 A1
Berry Ct TW4 151 B6
Berrydale Rd UB4 85 A3
Berryfield Cl BR1 188 A1
Berry Field Cl 8 E17 53 D5
Berryfield Rd
SE17 116 D1 261 D2
Berryhill SE9 144 D1
Berry Hill HA7 25 D6
Berryhill Gdns SE9 144 D1
Berry Ho
10 Battersea SW11 136 D3
25 Bethnal Green E1 96 B3
Berry La SE21 183 B6
BERRYLANDS 198 C3
Berrylands
Surbiton KT5 198 C3
West Barnes SW20 200 C5
Berrylands Ct 16
SM2 217 D1
Berrylands Rd KT5 198 B3
Berrylands Sta KT5 198 D5
Berryman Cl RM8 80 C5
Berryman's La SE26 184 D6
Berrymead Gdns W3 111 A4
Berrymede Inf Sch
W3 110 D4
Berrymede Jun Sch
W3 110 D4
Berrymede Rd W4 111 B3
Berry Pl EC1 234 D1
Berry St EC1 241 D5
Berry Way W5 110 A3
Bertal Rd SW17 180 B6
Bertha Hollamby Ct
DA14 190 C5
Bertha James Ct BR2 209 B5
Bertha Neubergh Ho 1
SE5 139 A4
Berthan Gdns E17 54 B4
Berthon St SE8 141 C6
Bertie Rd
Penge SE26 184 D4
Willesden NW10 68 A2
Bertram Cotts SW19 179 C3
Bertram Rd
Enfield EN1 6 A1
Hendon NW4 46 A3
Kingston u T KT2 176 C3
Bertram St N19 71 B6
Bertrand Ho 11 SW16 160 A1
Bertrand St SE13 141 D2
Bertrand Way SE28 124 C6
Bert Rd CR7 205 A4
Bert Reilly Ho 1
SE18 123 B1
Bertrum House Sch
SW17 159 A2
Bert Way EN1 5 D1
Berwick Ave UB4 106 D6
Berwick Cl
Harrow HA7 24 D4
Twickenham TW2 151 C3
Berwick Cres DA15 167 C5
Berwick Ct 8 BR3 185 C2
Berwick Gdns SM1 218 A5
Berwick Ho 10 N2 30 B1
Berwick Rd
Newham E16 99 C1
Tottenham N22 32 D2
Welling DA16 146 B4
Berwick St W1 93 C1 239 B1

Berwyn Ave TW3 129 D4
Berwyn Ho 3 N16 51 D1
Berwyn Rd
Mortlake SW14, TW10 132 D1
Streatham SE24 160 D3
Beryl Ave E6 100 A2
Beryl Harding Ho 3 SW19 178 D3
Beryl Ho SE18 123 D1
Beryl Rd W6 112 D1
Berystede KT2 176 D3
Besant Cl NW2 69 A5
Besant Ct
Canonbury N1 73 B3
15 Thamesmead SE28 124 B6
Besant Ho NW8 229 A5
Besant Pl SE22 139 D1
Besant Rd NW2 69 A4
Besant Way NW10 67 A3
Besant Wlk N7 72 B6
Besford Ho 26 E2 96 A5
Besley St SW16 181 C4
Bessant Dr TW9 132 D4
Bessborough Gdns SW1 115 D1 259 D2
Bessborough Pl SW1 115 D1 259 D2
Bessborough Rd
Harrow HA1 42 B1
Roehampton SW15 156 A3
Bessborough St SW1 115 D1 259 C2
Bessborough Wks KT8 195 B4
Bessemer Ct 7 NW1 71 C1
Bessemer Grange Prim Sch SE5 139 C1
Bessemer Park Ind Est 3 SE24 138 D1
Bessemer Rd SE5 139 A3
Bessie Lansbury Cl E6 100 C1
Bessingby Rd HA4 62 B6
Bessingham Wlk SE4 162 D6
Besson St SE14 140 D4
Bessy St E2 96 C4
Bestwood St SE8 118 D2
Beswick Mews 1 NW6 69 D2
Betam Rd UB3 105 B4
Beta Pl 20 SW4 138 B1
Betchworth Cl SM1 218 B3
Betchworth Ho 8 N7 71 D3
Betchworth Rd IG3 79 C5
Betham Rd UB6 86 B4
Bethany Ct 8 DA6 147 A1
Bethany Waye TW14 149 C4
Bethecar Rd HA1 42 C4
Bethel Cl NW4 46 D4
Bethell Ave
Ilford IG1 56 C2
Newham E13, E16 98 D3
Bethel Lo N11 31 C5
Bethel Rd DA16 146 C2
Bethersden Cl BR3 185 B3
Bethersden Ho SE17 263 B2
Bethesda Ct 5 SE20 184 C3
Beth Jacob Gram Sch NW4 46 D5
Bethlehem Ho 13 E14 119 B6
Bethlem Royal Hospl BR3 207 C2
BETHNAL GREEN 96 B4
Bethnal Green Rd
Bethnal Green E2 96 A4
Shoreditch E1, E2 95 D3 243 D6
Bethnal Green Sta
Bethnal Green E1 96 B3
Bethnal Green E2 96 C4
Bethnal Green Tech Coll E2 95 D4
Beths Gram Sch DA5 169 D5
Bethune Ave N11 30 D6
Bethune Rd
North Acton NW10 89 B3
Stamford Hill N16 51 C2
Bethwin Rd SE5 139 A5
Betjeman Cl HA5 41 C5
Betjeman Ct EN4 15 A6
Betony Cl CR0 206 D1
Betoyne Ave E4 36 C6
Betsham Ho SE1 252 C2
Betspath Ho 6 N11 31 C5
Betstyle Circus N11 31 B6
Betstyle Ho 2 N10 31 A3
Betstyle Rd N11 31 B6
Betterton Dr DA14 169 A2
Betterton Ho WC2 240 B1
Betterton St WC2 94 A1 240 B1
Bettons Pk E15 98 C6
Bettridge Rd SW6 135 B3
Betts Cl BR3 185 A1
Betts Ho E1 118 B6
Betts Mews E17 53 B3
Betts Rd E16 121 B6
Betts St E1 118 B6
Betts Way
Long Ditton KT6 197 B1
Penge SE20 184 B2
Bettswood Ct 15 SE20 184 B2
Betty Brooks Ho E11 76 B5
Betty Layward Prim Sch N16 73 B5
Betty May Gray Ho 2 E14 120 A2
Beulah Ave CR7 183 A1
Beulah Cl HA8 10 D1
Beulah Cres CR7 183 A1
Beulah Gr CR0 205 A3
Beulah Hill SE19 183 A3
Beulah Inf Sch CR7 205 A6
Beulah Jun Sch CR7 205 A6
Beulah Rd
Merton SW19 179 B3
South Norwood CR7 205 A6
Sutton SM1 217 C4
Walthamstow E17 53 D4
Beuleigh Ct E17 54 B4
Bevan Ave IG11 80 A1
Bevan Ct
Croydon CR0 220 C3
10 Twickenham TW1 153 D5
Bevan Ho IG11 80 B1
Bevan Rd
Cockfosters EN4 2 D1
Plumstead Comm SE2 124 B1
Bevan St N1 95 A6 235 B5
Bev Callender Cl 4 SW8 137 B2
Bevenden St N1 95 B4 235 D2
Bevercote Wlk 1 DA17 147 B6
Beveridge Ct
Southgate N21 16 A6
1 Thamesmead SE28 124 B6
Beveridge Rd 1 NW10 67 C1
Beverley DA14 190 A5
Beverley Ave
Hounslow TW4 129 B1
Sidcup DA15 167 D4
Wimbledon SW20 177 D2
Beverley Cl
Barnes SW13 134 A3
Chessington KT9 213 C4
Edmonton N21 17 A3
Enfield EN1 5 C1
6 Wandsworth SW11 136 B1
Beverley Cotts SW15 155 C1
Beverley Cres IG8 37 B2
Beverley Ct
9 Acton Green W4 111 A1
5 Acton W12 111 C4
Brockley SE4 141 B2
6 Cheam SM2 217 C2
Chingford Hatch E4 35 B6
Fortis Green N2 48 D5
Harrow HA2 42 B6
Hounslow TW4 129 B1
Islington N5 72 D2
Northolt UB5 84 C5
Oakleigh Pk N20 14 A4
Oakwood N14 15 C4
Sidcup DA14 190 B6
Wimbledon SW20 177 D2
Beverley Dr HA8 44 C6
Beverley Gdns
Barnes SW13 133 D2
Hendon NW11 47 A2
2 New Malden KT4 200 A1
Stanmore HA7 25 A2
Wembley HA9 44 C1
Beverley Ho 5 BR1 186 B5
Beverley Hyrst 10 CR0 221 D6
Beverley La KT2 177 C3
Beverley Lo 6 TW10 154 A6
Beverley Mans TW4 129 B1
Beverley Path 9 SW13 133 D3
Beverley Rd
Barnes SW13 133 D2
Chingford E4 36 B4
Chiswick W4 111 D1
Dagenham RM9 81 A4
Beverley Rd *continued*
Keston Mark BR2 226 A6
Mitcham CR4 203 D5
Newham E6 99 D4
North Cheam KT4 216 C6
Penge SE20 184 B1
Ruislip HA4 62 B6
Southall UB2 107 A3
Sunbury TW16 171 D2
Teddington KT1 175 C2
West Barnes KT3 200 A5
Beverley Trad Est SM4 200 D2
Beverley Way KT3, SW20, KT2 177 D2
Beverley Way (Kingston By Pass) KT3, SW20 200 A6
Beverly Ct HA3 43 C5
Beversbrook Rd N19 71 D5
Beverstone Rd
London SW2 160 B6
Thornton Heath CR7 204 D5
Beverston Mews NW1 237 C3
Bevill Allen Cl SW17 180 D5
Bevill Cl SE25 206 A6
Bevin Cl SE16 119 A5
Bevin Ct WC1 233 D2
Bevington Prim Sch W10 91 A2
Bevington Rd
Beckenham BR3 185 D1
Kensal Town W10 91 A2
Bevington St SE16 118 A4
Bevin Ho
35 Bethnal Green E2 96 C4
8 Bow E3 97 C4
Bevin Rd UB4 84 B4
Bevin Sq SW17 158 D1
Bevin Way WC1 234 A2
Bevis Marks EC3 95 C1 243 B2
Bewcastle Gdns EN2 4 A2
Bew Ct SE21 162 A4
Bewdley Ho N4 51 A2
Bewdley St N1 72 C1
Bewick Mews SE15 140 B5
Bewick St SW8 137 B3
Bewley Ct SW2 160 B5
Bewley Ho 7 E1 118 B6
Bewley St
Stepney E1 118 B6
Wimbledon SW19 180 A4
Bewlys Rd SE27 182 D5
Bexhill Cl TW13 151 A2
Bexhill Rd
Catford SE4 163 B5
Mortlake SW14 133 A2
Wood Green N11 31 D5
Bexhill Wlk 6 E15 98 C6
BEXLEY 146 B1
Bexley Coll (Erith Rd Campus) DA17 125 D1
Bexley Gdns
Edmonton N9 17 B1
Ilford RM6 58 B4
Bexley Gram Sch DA16 146 B1
BEXLEYHEATH 147 B2
Bexleyheath Sch DA8 147 C2
Bexleyheath Sta DA7 147 A3
Bexley High St DA5 169 D3
Bexley Ho SE4 141 A1
Bexley La DA14 168 C1
Bexley Rd SE9 167 A6
Bexley Sta DA5 169 C3
Beynon Rd SM5 218 D3
BFI London Imax Cinema SE1 116 C5 251 A3
Bglws The SM6 219 B3
Bianca Rd SE1, SE15 140 A6
Bibsworth Lo N3 29 B1
Bibsworth Rd N3 29 B1
Bicester Rd TW9 132 D2
Bickenhall Mans W1 237 D4
Bickenhall St W1 92 D2 237 D4
Bickersteth Rd SW17 180 D4
Bickerton Rd N19 71 C6
BICKLEY 188 B1
Bickley Cres BR1 210 A5
Bickley Ct
10 Merton SW19 179 C3
1 Stanmore HA7 25 C6
Bickley Park Rd BR1, BR7 210 B6
Bickley Park Sch BR1 210 A6
Bickley Prim Sch BR1 209 C6
Bickley Rd
Bromley BR1 187 D1
Leyton E10 53 D2
Bickley St SW17 180 D5
Bickley Sta BR1 210 A6
Bicknell Ho 34 E1 96 A1
Bicknell Rd SE5 139 A2
Bicknoller Rd EN1 5 D4
Bicknor Ho 2 E5 74 B3
Bicknor Rd BR6 211 D2
Bidborough Cl 3 BR2 208 D4
Bidborough St N1, WC1 94 A4 233 A1
Biddenden Way SE9 188 C6
Biddenham Ho 18 SE16 118 D2
Bidder St E16 98 C2
Biddesden Ho SW3 257 C3
Biddestone Rd N7 72 B4
Biddulph Ho 22 SE18 122 B2
Biddulph Mans W9 91 D4
Biddulph Rd W9 91 D4
Bideford Ave UB6 87 B5
Bideford Cl
Edgware HA8 26 C2
Twickenham TW13 151 B1
Bideford Gdns EN1 17 C4
Bideford Rd
Catford BR1 164 D1
East Wickham DA16 146 B5
Enfield EN3 7 B5
Ruislip HA4 62 B5
Bidmead Ct KT6 214 A5
Bidwell Gdns N11 31 C3
Bidwell Ho
Southall UB2 107 A2
3 Willesden NW2 68 A5
Bidwell St SE15 140 B4
Big Ben* SW1 250 B1
Bigbury Cl N17 33 C3
Biggerstaff Rd E15 98 A6
Biggerstaff St N4 72 C6
Biggin Ave CR4 180 D2
Biggin Hill SE19 182 D3
Biggin Hill Cl KT2 175 C5
Biggin Way SE19 183 A3
Bigginwood Rd SW16 182 D2
Bigg's Row SW15 134 D2
Big Hill E5 52 B1
Bigland Green Prim Sch E1 96 B1
Bigland St E1 96 B1
Bignell Rd SE18 122 D1
Bignold Rd E7 77 A4
Bigwood Ct NW11 47 D4
Bigwood Rd NW11 47 D3
Biko Ho 1 NW10 67 B1
Bilberry Ho 18 E3 97 C2
Bilberry Manor SM2 218 A1
Billet Rd
Ilford RM6 58 C6
Walthamstow E17 35 B2
Billetts Hart Cl W7 108 C4
Bill Hamling Cl SE9 166 B2
Billie Holiday Ct NW10 89 B5
Billingford Cl SE4 140 D1
Billing Ho 7 E1 96 D1
Billingley NW1 232 A5
Billing Pl SW10 135 D5 265 D4
Billing Rd SW10 135 D5 265 D4
Billings Cl RM9 80 C1
Billingsgate Mkt E14 119 D5
Billing St SW10 135 D5 265 D4
Billington Ho SW8 269 D1
Billington Rd SE14 140 D5
Billinton Hill CR0 221 B6
Billiter Sq EC3 243 B1
Billiter St EC3 95 C1 243 B1
Bill Nicholson Way N17 33 D3
Billockby Cl KT9 214 B2
Billsley Ct SE25 205 C5
Billson St E14 120 A2
Bilsby Gr SE9 187 D6
Bilton Ho SW8 269 C1
Bilton Rd UB6 87 B6
Bilton Twrs W1 237 D1
Bilton Way
Enfield EN3 7 B5
Hayes UB3 106 B4
Bina Gdns SW5 114 A2 256 A3
Binbrook Ho 13 W10 90 C2
Bincote Rd EN2 4 B2
Binden Rd W12 111 D3
Bindon Gn SM4 201 D5
Binfield Ct SE5 139 A3
Binfield Rd
London SW4 138 A4 270 B1
South Croydon CR2 221 D3
Bingfield St N1 94 B6 233 C6
Bingham Cnr CR0 206 A1
Bingham Pl W1 93 A2 238 A4
Bingham Point 11 SE18 122 D2
Bingham Rd CR0 206 B1
Bingham St N1 73 B2
Bingley Rd
Ashford TW16 172 A3
Newham E16 99 C1
Southall UB6 86 A2
Binley Ho SW15 155 D5
Binney St W1 93 A1 238 B1
Binnie Ct SE10 141 D5
Binnie Ho SE1 262 A5
Binns Rd W4 111 C1
Binns Terr 3 W4 111 C1
Binsey Wlk 1 SE2 124 C4
Binstead Cl UB4 85 A2
Binstead Ho SW18 157 D5
Binyon Cres HA7 24 D5
Binyon Ho 8 N16 73 C4
Birbeck Ho 4 N19 49 D1
Birbetts Rd SE9 166 B2
Bircham Path SE4 140 D1
Birchanger Rd SE25 206 A4
Birch Ave
Edmonton N13 17 A1
Hillingdon UB7 82 B1
Birch Cl
Brentford TW8 131 B5
Buckhurst Hill IG9 21 D1
Hounslow TW3 130 B3
Newham E16 98 C2
Peckham SE15 140 A3
Romford RM7 59 D6
Teddington TW11 175 A5
Upper Holloway N19 71 C6
Birch Cres UB10 82 B6
Birch Ct
Chingford E4 35 D4
Forest Gate E7 76 D4
Ilford RM6 58 C3
Sutton SM1 218 A4
9 Wallington SM6 219 B4
7 Woodside Pk N12 29 D6
Birchdale Gdns RM6 58 D2
Birchdale Rd E7 77 C3
Birchdene Dr SE28 124 A5
Birchdown Ho 32 E3 97 D4
Birchen Cl NW9 67 B6
Birchend Cl CR2 221 B2
Birchen Gr NW9 67 B6
Birches Cl
Mitcham CR4 202 D6
Pinner HA5 41 A4
Birches The
2 Beckenham BR2 208 D5
Bushey WD23 8 A6
Camberwell SE5 139 C3
Greenwich SE7 143 B6
Manor Pk E12 78 A4
Orpington BR6 226 C4
Southgate N21 16 B5
South Norwood SE25 183 D1
Twickenham TW4 151 B4
Birchfield Ho 3 E14 119 C6
Birchfield St E14 119 C6
Birch Gn NW9 27 C3
Birch Gr
Acton W3 110 C6
Bexley DA16 146 A1
Lewisham SE12 164 D4
Leyton E11 76 C5
Upper Halliford TW17 171 C1
Birchgrove Ho TW9 132 D5
Birch Hill CR0 222 D3
Birch Ho
New Cross Gate SE14 141 B4
Teddington TW11 175 C3
8 Tulse Hill SW2 160 C5
Birchington Cl DA7 147 D4
Birchington Ct
Crouch End N8 49 D3
2 Kilburn NW6 91 D6
Birchington Ho 1 E5 74 B3
Birchington Rd
Crouch End N8 49 D3
Kilburn NW6 91 C6
Surbiton KT5 198 B2
Birchin La EC3 242 D1
Birchlands Ave SW12 158 D4
Birch Mead BR2, BR6 226 C6
Birchmead Ave HA5 40 C5
Birchmere Bsns Pk SE2 124 A4
Birchmere Lo 18 SE16 118 B1
Birchmere Row SE3 142 D3
Birchmore Wlk N5 73 A5
Birch Pk HA3 24 A3
Birch Rd
Feltham TW13 172 D5
Romford RM7 59 D6
Birch Row BR2 210 C3
Birch Tree Ave BR4 224 D4
Birch Tree Ho 16 SE7 143 C6
Birch Tree Way CR0 222 B6
Birch Vale Ct NW8 236 D6
Birchway UB3 106 A5
Birch Wlk CR4 181 B2
Birchwood Ave
Beckenham BR3 207 B5
Hackbridge SM5, SM6 219 B5
Muswell Hill N10 49 A6
Sidcup DA14 168 C1
Birchwood Cl SM4 201 D5
Birchwood Ct
Burnt Oak HA8 27 A1
Edmonton N13 32 D5
Birchwood Dr NW3 69 D5
Birchwood Gr TW12 173 C4
Birchwood Rd
Orpington BR5 211 C5
Streatham SW17 181 B5
Birdbrook Rd SE3 143 C2
Birdcage Wlk SW1 115 D4 249 C1
Bird Coll DA14 168 A1
Birdham Cl BR1 210 A4
Birdhurst Ave CR2 221 B4
Birdhurst Ct SM6 219 C1
Birdhurst Gdns CR2 221 B4
Birdhurst Rd
London SW18 158 A6
Mitcham SW19 180 C4
South Croydon CR2 221 C3
Birdhurst Rise CR2 221 C3
Bird In Bush Rd SE15 140 A5
Bird-in-Hand La BR1 187 D1
Bird-In-Hand Pas SE23 162 C2
Bird In Hand Yd 24 NW3 70 A4
Birdsall Ho 5 SE5 139 C2
Birdsfield La 12 E3 97 B6
Bird St W1 238 B1
Bird Wlk TW2 151 B3
Birdwood Cl TW11 174 C6
Birkbeck Ave
Acton W3 111 A6
Greenford UB6 86 A6
Birkbeck Coll W1 93 D1 239 C2
Birkbeck Ct W3 111 B5
Birkbeck Gdns IG8 21 A2
Birkbeck Gr W3 111 B4
Birkbeck Hill SE21 160 D3
Birkbeck Mews 5 E8 73 D3
Birkbeck Pl SE21 161 A2
Birkbeck Prim Sch DA14 168 B1
Birkbeck Rd
Acton W3 111 B5
Dalston E8 73 D3
Ealing W5 109 C2
Edgware NW7 27 D5
Enfield EN2 5 B5
Hornsey N8 50 A5
Ilford IG2 57 B4
North Finchley N12 30 A5
Penge BR3 184 D1
Sidcup DA14 168 A1
Tottenham N17 33 D2
Wimbledon SW19 179 D4
Birkbeck St E2 96 B4
Birkbeck Sta SE20 206 C6
Birkbeck Way UB6 86 B6
Birkdale Ave HA5 41 C6
Birkdale Cl
30 Bermondsey SE16 118 B1
Crofton BR6 211 B2
Erith SE28 102 D1
Birkdale Ct 3 UB1 86 A1
Birkdale Gdns CR0 222 D4
Birkdale Rd
Abbey Wood SE2 124 A2
Ealing W5 88 A3
Birkenhead Ave KT2 176 B2
Birkenhead Ho 11 N7 72 C3

Birkenhead St WC1 94 A4 233 B2
Birkhall Rd SE6 164 B2
Birkwood Cl SW12 159 D4
Birley Lo NW8 229 D4
Birley Rd N20 14 A2
Birley St SW11 137 A3
Birnam Rd N4 72 B6
Birnbeck Ct NW11 47 B4
Birnham Ho TW1 153 C4
Birrell Ho 9 SW9 138 B3
Birse Cres NW10 67 C4
Birstal Gn WD19 22 D6
Birstall Rd N15 51 C4
Birtwhistle Ho 5 E3 97 B6
Biscay Ho 11 E1 96 D3
Biscay Rd W6 112 D1
Biscoe Cl TW5 129 C6
Biscoe Ho UB2 107 D2
Biscoe Way SE13 142 B2
Biscott Ho 3 E3 97 D3
Bisenden Rd CR0 221 C6
Bisham Cl CR4 202 D1
Bisham Gdns N6 49 A1
Bishop Butt Cl BR6 227 D5
Bishop Challoner Collegiate Sch E1 96 C1
Bishop Challoner Sch BR2 186 B1
Bishop Ct 20 SW2 160 C5
Bishop Douglass RC High Sch N2 48 A6
Bishop Duppa's Almshouses 7 TW10 154 A6
Bishop Duppas Pk TW17 193 C2
Bishop Fox Way KT8 195 B5
Bishop Gilpins CE Prim Sch SW19 179 B5
Bishop John Robinson CE Prim Sch SE28 124 C6
Bishop Justus CE Sch BR2 210 A2
Bishop Ken Rd HA3 24 D2
Bishop King's Rd W14 113 A2 254 B4
Bishop Perrin CE Prim Sch TW2 151 D3
Bishop Ramsey CE Sch HA4 40 A2
Bishop Ramsey CE Sch (Annexe) HA4 39 D2
Bishop Rd N14 15 B4
Bishop Ridley CE Prim Sch DA16 145 C1
Bishops Ave
Borehamwood WD6 10 B6
Bromley BR1 209 C6
Ilford RM6 58 C3
Newham E13 99 B6
Bishop's Ave SW6 135 A3
Bishops Ave The N2 48 B3
Bishopsbourne Ho BR1 187 B3
Bishop's Bridge Rd W2 92 A1 236 A2
Bishops Cl
Acton Green W4 111 A1
Barnet EN5 12 D5
Enfield EN1 6 B3
New Eltham SE9 167 A2
Richmond TW10 153 D1
Sutton SM1 217 C5
Bishop's Cl
Dartmouth Pk N19 71 C5
Hillingdon UB10 82 C5
Walthamstow E17 53 D5
Bishopscourt 8 CR0 221 D6
Bishops Ct
1 Ashford TW16 171 D3
18 Bayswater W2 91 D1
East Finchley N2 48 C5
Richmond TW9 132 A2
Romford RM7 59 D5
Wembley HA0 65 B4
Bishop's Ct
Holborn EC4 241 C2
Holborn WC2 241 A2
Bishopsdale Ho 8 NW6 91 C6
Bishops Dr
East Bedfont TW14 149 B5
Northolt UB5 85 A6
Bishopsford Com Sch SM4 202 B3
Bishopsford Ho SM4 202 C3
Bishopsford Rd SM4 202 B3
Bishopsgate EC2 95 C1 243 A2
Bishopsgate Arc E1 243 B3
Bishopsgate Churchyard EC2 243 A2
Bishops Gn BR1 187 C2
Bishops Gr
East Finchley N2 48 C3
Feltham TW12 173 B6
Bishopshalt Sch UB8 82 B4
Bishop's Hall KT1 175 D1
Bishops Hill KT12 194 A2
Bishops Ho SW8 270 B3
Bishop's Mans SW6 134 D3
Bishops Mead SE5 139 A5
Bishops Park Rd SW16 182 A2
Bishop's Park Rd SW6 134 D3
Bishop's Pl SM1 218 A3
Bishops Rd
Fulham SW6 135 B4 264 C2
Highgate N6 49 A3
Bishop's Rd
Hanwell W7 108 C4
Hayes UB3 83 A1
Thornton Heath CR0 204 D2
Bishops Sq E1 243 B4
Bishop St N1 95 A6 235 A6
Bishop's Terr SE11 116 C2 261 B4
Bishopsthorpe Rd SE26 184 D6
Bishopstone Ho 4 SW11 137 A3
Bishop Stopford's Sch EN1 6 B3
Bishops View Ct N10 49 B5
Bishop's Way E2 96 C5
Bishops Wlk
Chislehurst BR7 189 A2
South Croydon CR0, CR9 223 A3
Bishopswood Rd N6 48 D2
Bishop Thomas Grant RC Sec Sch SW16 182 B5
Bishop Wand CE Sch The TW16 171 D1
Bishop Way NW10 67 C1
Bishop Wilfred Wood Cl SE15 140 A3
Bishop Wilfred Wood Ct 3 E13 99 C5
Bishop Winnington-Ingram CE Prim Sch HA4 39 B2
Bisley Cl KT4 200 C1
Bisley Ho SW19 156 D2
Bispham Rd NW10 88 B4
Bissextile Ho SE13 141 D3
Bisson Rd E15 98 A5
Bisterne Ave E17 54 B6
Bittacy Bsns Ctr NW7 29 A3
Bittacy Cl NW7 28 D4
Bittacy Ct NW7 29 A3
Bittacy Hill NW7 28 D4
Bittacy Park Ave NW7 28 D5
Bittacy Rd NW7 28 D4
Bittacy Rise NW7 28 D4
Bittern Cl UB4 84 D2
Bittern Ct
Chingford E4 20 B4
7 Deptford SE8 141 C6
Hendon NW9 27 C1
Bittern Ho SE1 252 A1
Bittern St SE1 252 A1
Bittoms The KT1 197 D6
Bixley Cl UB2 107 B2
Blackall St EC2 243 A6
Blackberry Cl TW17 193 C5
Blackberry Farm Cl TW5 129 A5
Blackberry Field BR5 190 A2
Blackbird Ct NW9 67 B5
Blackbird Hill NW9 67 B5
Blackborne Rd RM10 81 D2
Black Boy La N15 51 A4
Blackbrook La BR1, BR2 210 C5
Blackburn 28 NW9 27 D1
Blackburn Ct 21 SW2 160 C5
Blackburne's Mews W1 248 A5
Blackburn Rd NW6 69 D2
Blackburn Trad Est TW19 148 B5
Blackburn Way TW4 151 A6
Blackbush Ave RM6 58 D4
Blackbush Cl SM2 217 D1
Blackcap Ct NW9 27 C1
Blackdown Cl N2 30 A1
Blackdown Ho E8 74 A4
Blackett St SW15 134 D2
Black Fan Cl EN2 5 A4
BLACKFEN 168 A5
Blackfen Par DA15 168 A5
Blackfen Rd DA15 168 B5
Blackfen Sch for Girls DA15 168 B5
Blackford Rd WD19 22 D5
Blackfriars Bridge EC4 251 C5
Blackfriars Ct EC4 251 C6
Black Friars La EC4 94 D1 241 C1
Blackfriars Pas EC4 251 C6
Blackfriars Pier EC4 251 C6
Blackfriars Rd SE1 116 D5 251 C3
Blackfriars Sta EC4 116 D6 251 C6
Blackfriars Underpass EC4 116 C6 251 B6
Blackham Ho SW19 179 A4
BLACKHEATH 142 C2
Blackheath* SE3 142 C4
Blackheath Ave SE3 142 C5
Blackheath Bluecoat CE Sec Sch SE3 143 B5
Blackheath Bsns Est SE10 142 A4
Blackheath Gr SE3 142 D3
Blackheath High Sch
Blackheath SE3 142 D3
Greenwich SE3 143 A5
Blackheath Hill SE10 142 A4
Blackheath Hospl SE3 142 C2
BLACKHEATH PARK 143 A1
Blackheath Pk SE3 143 A2
Blackheath Prep Sch SE3 143 A4
Blackheath Rd SE10 141 D4
Blackheath Rise SE13 142 A3
Blackheath Sta SE3 142 D2
BLACKHEATH VALE 142 D3
Blackheath Vale SE3 142 C3
Blackheath Village SE3 142 D3
Black Horse Ct SE1 262 D6
Blackhorse La
Croydon CR0 206 A2
Higham Hill E17 34 D1
Blackhorse La Sta CR0 206 A2
Blackhorse Mews E17 52 D6
Black Horse Par HA5 40 B4
Blackhorse Rd
Deptford SE8 141 A6
Walthamstow E17 53 A5
Black Horse Rd DA14 190 A6
Blackhorse Road E17 52 D5
Blackhorse Road Sta E17 52 D5
Blacklands Dr UB4 83 A3
Blacklands Rd SE6 186 A6
Blacklands Terr SW3 257 D3
Black Lion La W6 112 A2
Black Lion Mews 4 W6 112 A2
Blackmore Ave UB1 108 B5
Blackmore Dr NW10 66 D1
Blackmore Ho
Forest Hill SE23 163 B3
Islington N1 233 D5
2 Wandsworth SW18 157 D6
Blackmore's Gr TW11 175 A4
Blackmore Twr 1 W3 111 A3
Blackness La BR2 225 D1
Blackpool Gdns UB4 83 C3
Blackpool Rd SE15 140 B3
Black Prince Intc DA6 169 D5
Black Prince Rd SE1, SE11 116 B2 260 D3
Black Rod Cl UB3 105 D3
Black Roof Ho 9 SE5 138 D4
Blackshaw Rd SW17 180 B5
Blacksmith Cl RM6 58 C3
Blacksmiths Ho 7 E17 53 C5
Black's Rd W6 112 C2
Blackstock Ho 2 N5 72 D5
Blackstock Mews N4 72 D5
Blackstock Rd N4, N5 72 D6
Blackstone Ho
Dulwich SE21 161 C1
Pimlico SW1 259 A1
Blackstone Rd NW2 68 C4
Black Swan Yd SE1 253 A2
Blackthorn Ave UB7 104 C3
Blackthorn Ct
20 Camberwell SE15 139 D5
Heston TW5 129 A5
4 Leyton E15 76 B4
6 West Norwood SW16 182 C5
Blackthorne Ave CR0 206 C1
Blackthorne Ct
2 Littleton TW15 171 A3
Southall UB1 107 D5
Blackthorne Dr E4 36 B6
Blackthorn Gr DA7 147 A2
Blackthorn Rd IG1 79 B3
Blackthorn St E3 97 C3
Blacktree Mews 11 SW9 138 C2
BLACKWALL 120 B6
Blackwall Sta E14 120 A6
Blackwall Trad Est E14 98 B2
Blackwall Tunnel E14, SE10 120 B5
Blackwall Tunnel App SE10 120 C4
Blackwall Tunnel Northern Approach E14, E3 98 A3
Blackwall Way E14 120 A6
Blackwater Cl E7 76 D4
Blackwater Ho NW8 236 D4
Blackwater St SE22 161 D6
Blackwell Cl
10 Clapton Pk E5 74 D4
Harrow HA3 24 B3
Blackwell Gdns HA8 10 C1
Blackwell Ho 3 SW4 159 D5
Blackwood Ho 11 E1 96 B3
Blackwood St SE17 117 B1 262 C2
Blade Ho TW1 153 D5
Blade Mews SW15 135 B1
Bladen Ho 4 E1 96 D1
Blades Ct
4 Hammersmith W6 112 B1
Putney SW15 135 B1
Blades Ho 12 SE11 138 C6
Blades Lo 16 SW2 160 C5
Bladindon Dr DA5 168 D4
Bladon Ct
Beckenham BR2 208 C6
Streatham SW16 182 A4
Bladon Gdns HA2 41 D3
Blagden's Cl N14 15 D2
Blagden's La N14 15 D2
Blagdon Ct W7 108 C6
Blagdon Rd
London SE13 163 D5
New Malden KT3 199 D5
Blagdon Wlk TW11 175 C4
Blagrove Rd 1 W10 91 B2
Blair Ave
London NW9 45 C2
Thames Ditton KT10 212 A6
Blair Cl
Avery Hill DA15 167 C6
Canonbury N1 73 A2
Hayes UB3 106 A2
Blair Ct
Beckenham BR3 185 D2
8 Carshalton SM5 218 D5
7 Catford SE6 164 D3
St John's Wood NW8 229 C6
Blairderry Rd SW2 160 A2
Blairgowrie Ct 13 E14 98 B1
Blair Ho SW9 138 B3
Blair Peach Prim Sch UB1 106 D5
Blair St E14 98 B1
Blake Apartments N8 50 B6
Blake Ave IG11 101 D6
Blake Cl
Bexley DA16 145 C4
Carshalton SM5 202 C1
Blake Coll W1 93 C2 239 A4
Blake Ct
8 Bermondsey SE16 118 B1
9 Clapham SW8 137 C3
Croydon CR2 220 D3
Kilburn NW6 91 C4
Southgate N21 16 B6
Blakeden Dr KT10 212 D2
Blake Gdns SW6 135 D4 265 C2
Blake Hall Cres E11 55 A1
Blakehall Rd SM5 218 D2
Blake Hall Rd E11 55 A2
Blake Ho
6 Beckenham BR3 185 D4
2 Deptford SE8 141 C6
Harrow HA1 64 C6
Isle Of Dogs E14 119 D4
1 Kentish Town N19 71 D3
Lambeth SE1 261 A6
14 Stoke Newington N16 73 C4
Blake Lo N3 29 B1
Blake Mews 15 TW9 132 C4
Blakemore Rd
Streatham SW16 160 A1
Thornton Heath CR7 204 B4
Blakemore Way DA17 125 A3
Blakeney Ave BR3 185 B2
Blakeney Cl
5 Camden Town NW1 71 D1
4 Dalston E8 74 A3
Whetstone N20 14 A3
Blakeney Ct EN2 17 B6
Blakeney Rd BR3 185 B2
Blakenham Ct W12 112 A5
Blakenham Rd SW17 180 D6
Blaker Ct SE7 143 C5
Blake Rd
Croydon CR0 221 C6
Mitcham CR4 202 C6
Newham E16 98 D3
Wood Green N11 31 C3
Blaker Rd E15 98 A6
Blakes Ave KT3 199 D3
Blakes Cl W10 90 C2
Blake's Gn BR4 208 A1
Blakes La KT3 199 D4
Blakesley Ave W5 87 C1
Blakesley Ct W5 87 C1
Blakesley Ho 4 E12 78 C5
Blake's Rd SE15 139 C5
Blakes Terr KT3 200 A4
Blakesware Gdns N9 17 B4
Blakewood Cl TW13 172 C6
Blakewood Ct 5 SE20 184 B3
Blanca Ho 16 N1 95 C5
Blanchard Cl SE9 166 A1
Blanchard Gr EN3 7 D5
Blanchard Ho
Chislehurst BR7 189 A4
7 Twickenham TW1 153 D5
Blanchard Way E8 74 A2
Blanch Cl SE15 140 C5
Blanchedowne SE5 139 B1
Blanche Nevile Sch N10 31 A1
Blanche St E16 98 D3
Blanchland Rd SM4 201 D4
Blandfield Rd SW12 159 A4
Blandford Ave
2 Beckenham BR3 185 A1
Twickenham TW2 151 D3
Blandford Cl
London N2 48 A5
Romford RM7 59 D5
Wallington CR0 220 A5
Blandford Cres E4 20 A4
Blandford Ct
Brondesbury Pk NW6 69 A1
6 De Beauvoir Town N1 73 C1
Blandford Ho SW8 270 C4
Blandford Rd
Acton W4 111 C3
Ealing W5 109 D4
Penge BR3 184 D1
Southall UB2 107 C2
Teddington TW11 174 C5
Blandford Sq NW1 237 B5
Blandford St W1 93 A2 238 A3
Blandford Waye UB4 84 C1
Bland Ho SE11 260 D2
Bland St SE9 143 D1
Blaney Cres E6 100 D4
Blanmerle Rd SE9 166 D3
Blann Cl SE9 165 D5
Blantyre St SW10 136 B5 266 C4
Blantyre Twr SW10 266 C4
Blantyre Wlk SW10 136 B5 266 C4
Blashford NW3 70 D1
Blashford St SE13 164 B4
Blasker Wlk 8 E14 119 D1
Blatchford Ct KT12 194 A1
Blatchford Ho 8 RM10 81 C5
Blawith Rd HA1 42 D5
Blaxland Ho 12 W12 112 B6
Blaydon Cl HA4 39 C2
Blaydon Ct 4 UB5 63 C2
Blaydon Wlk N17 34 B3
Blazer Ct NW8 229 D1
Bleak Hill La SE18 145 D6
Blean Gr SE20 184 C3
Bleasdale Ave UB6 87 A5
Blechynden Ho 17 W10 90 D1
Blechynden St W10 112 D6
Bledlow Cl SE28 124 C6
Bledlow Rise UB6 86 A5
Bleeding Heart Yd EC1 241 B3
Blegborough Rd SW16 181 C4
Blemundsbury WC1 240 C4
Blendon Dr DA5 168 D5
Blendon Path 9 BR1 186 D3
Blendon Rd DA5 168 D5
Blendon Terr SE18 145 A6
Blendworth Point 4 SW15 156 B3
Blenheim 26 SW19 156 D3
Blenheim Ave IG2 56 C3
Blenheim Bsns Ctr CR4 180 D1
Blenheim Centre 7 SE20 184 D3
Blenheim Cl
Edmonton N21 17 A3
Eltham SE12 165 B3
Greenford UB6 86 B5
Wallington SM6 219 C1
West Barnes SW20 200 C6
Blenheim Cres
Notting Hill W11 91 A1
Notting Hill W11 244 B6
Ruislip HA4 61 B6
South Croydon CR2 221 A1
Blenheim Ct
Barnsbury N7 72 A2
Beckenham BR2 208 D5
5 Hampton TW12 173 C2
Harrow HA3 43 A3
Hendon NW4 46 D5
Longlands DA14 167 B1
Richmond TW9 132 B2
17 Rotherhithe SE16 118 D5
South Norwood SE19 183 C2
Sutton SM2 218 A2
Upper Holloway N19 72 A6
Woodford IG8 37 B3
Blenheim Ctr TW3 129 D2
Blenheim Dr DA16 145 D4
Blenheim Gdns
Clapham Pk SW2 160 B5
Dollis Hill NW2 68 C3
Kingston u T KT2 176 D3
Wallington SM6 219 C1
Wembley HA9 66 A5
Blenheim Gr SE15 140 A3
Blenheim Ho
6 Edmonton N9 18 A1
Hounslow TW3 129 C2
8 Woolwich SE18 123 A3
Blenheim Par 2 UB10 82 D3
Blenheim Park Rd CR2 221 A1
Blenheim Pas NW8 229 A4
Blenheim Pl TW11 174 D5
Blenheim Rd
Acton W4 111 C3
Bromley BR1, BR2 210 A5
Harrow HA2 41 D3
Leyton E15 76 C4
Newham E6 99 D4
Northolt UB5 63 D2
Penge SE20 184 C3
Sidcup DA15 168 C3
St John's Wood NW8 92 A5 229 B4
Sutton SM1 217 D5
Walthamstow E17 53 A6
West Barnes SW20 200 C6
Blenheim Rise N15 51 D5
Blenheim St W1 238 C1
Blenheim Terr NW8 92 A5 229 A4
Blenheim Way TW7 131 A4
Blenkarne Rd SW11 158 D5
Bleriot 27 NW9 27 D1
Bleriot Rd TW5 128 C5
Blessbury Rd HA8 27 A2
Blessed Dominic RC Sch NW9 27 D1

Blessed Sacrament RC Prim Sch N1 . . . 94 B6 233 C5
Blessington Cl SE13 . . 142 B2
Blessington Rd SE13 . . 142 B1
Blessing Way IG11 . . . . 102 C5
Bletchingley Cl CR7 . . . 204 D5
Bletchington Ct 2 DA17 . . . . 125 C2
Bletchley Ct N1 . . . . 235 C3
Bletchley St N1 . . 95 A5 235 B3
Bletchmore Cl UB3 . . . . 105 B1
Bletsoe Wlk N1 . . . . 235 B4
Blewbury Ho 3 SE2 . . . 124 C4
Blick Ho 1 SE16 . . . . . . 118 C3
Bligh Ho 4 SE27 . . . . . . 183 A6
Blincoe Cl SW19 . . . . . . 156 D2
Blissett St SE10 . . . . . . 142 A4
Blissland Ct 5 N12 . . . . 30 A4
Bliss Mews 14 W10 . . . . . 91 A4
Blisworth Cl UB4 . . . . . . 85 A3
Blisworth Ho 12 E2 . . . . . 96 A6
Blithbury Rd RM9 . . . . . . 80 B2
Blithdale Rd SE2 . . . . . . 124 A2
Blithfield St W8 . . . . . . 255 C5
Blockley Rd HA0 . . . . 65 B6
Bloemfontein Ave W12 . . . . 112 B5
Bloemfontein Rd W12 . . . . 112 B6
Blomfield Ct
Battersea SW11 . . . . 266 D2
Paddington W9 . . . . 236 B6
Blomfield Ho 4 E14 . . 119 D6
Blomfield Mans 3 W12 . . . . 112 C5
Blomfield Rd W9 . . . . 92 A2 236 A4
Blomfield St EC2 . . . . 95 B2 242 D3
Blomfield Villas W9 . . . 236 A4
Blomville Rd RM8 . . . . . . 81 A5
Blondel St SW11 . . . . . . 137 A3
Blondin Ave W5 . . . . . . 109 C3
Blondin St E3 . . . . 97 C5
Bloomburg St SW1 . . . . 259 B3
Bloomfield Cres IG2 . . . 56 D3
Bloomfield Ct N6 . . . . . . 49 A3
Bloomfield Ho 19 E1 . . . 96 A2
Bloomfield Pl W1 . . . . . 248 D6
Bloomfield Rd
Bromley Comm BR2 . . . . 209 D4
Highgate N6 . . . . 49 A3
Kingston u T KT1 . . . . 198 A6
Woolwich SE18 . . . . 122 D1
Bloomfield Terr SW1 . . . . 115 A1 258 B2
Bloom Gr SE27 . . . . 160 D1
Bloomhall Rd SE19 . . . . 183 B5
Bloom Park Rd SW6 . . . 264 C3
BLOOMSBURY 93 D2
Bloomsbury Cl
Ealing W5 . . . . 110 B6
Edgware NW7 . . . . 28 A3
Bloomsbury Ct
Cranford TW5 . . . . 128 B4
Leytonstone E11 . . . . 54 B1
Pinner HA5 . . . . 41 B6
St Giles WC1 . . . . 240 B3
Bloomsbury Ho 10 SW4 . . . . 159 D5
Bloomsbury Pl
London SW18 . . . . 158 A6
St Giles WC1 . . . . 240 B3
Bloomsbury Sq WC1 . . . . 94 A2 240 B3
Bloomsbury St WC1 . . . . 93 D2 239 D3
Bloomsbury Way WC1 . . . . 94 A2 240 B3
Blore Cl SW8 . . . . 269 C1
Blore Ct W1 . . . . 249 C6
Blore Ho SW10 . . . . 265 D4
Blossom Cl
Dagenham RM9 . . . . 103 B6
Ealing W5 . . . . 110 A4
South Croydon CR2 . . . . 221 D3
Blossom La EN2 . . . . 5 A4
Blossom Pl E1 . . . . 243 B5
Blossom St E1 . . 95 C3 243 B5
Blossom Way
Hillingdon UB10 . . . . 60 B1
West Drayton UB7 . . . . . 104 C2
Blossom Waye TW5 . . . 129 A5
Blount St E14 . . . . 97 A1
Bloxam Gdns SE9 . . . . . 166 A6
Bloxhall Rd E10 . . . . 53 B1
Bloxham Cres TW12 . . . 173 B2
Bloxworth Cl SM6 . . . . . 219 C5
Blucher Rd SE5 . . . . 139 A5
Blue Anchor Alley 4 TW9 . . . . 132 A1
Blue Anchor La SE16 . . 118 B2
Blue Anchor Yd E1 . . . . 118 A6
Blue Ball Yd SW1 . . . . . 249 A3
Bluebell Ave E12 . . . . 78 A3
Bluebell Cl
Forest Hill SE26 . . . . 183 D6
Hackbridge SM6 . . . . 203 B1
10 Hackney E9 . . . . 96 C6
Northolt UB5 . . . . 63 B2
Orpington BR6 . . . . 227 A6
Bluebell Ct 4 N12 . . . . . 14 A1
Bluebell Way IG1 . . . . . . 78 D2
Blueberry Cl IG8 . . . . 37 A4
Blueberry Ct
Edgware HA8 . . . . 27 A5
3 Enfield EN2 . . . . 4 D3
Bluebird La RM10 . . . . . . 81 C1
Bluebird Way SE28 . . . . 123 B4
Bluefield Cl TW12 . . . . . 173 C5
Blue Gate Fields Jun & Inf Schs E1 . . . . 118 C6
Bluegate Mews E1 . . . . 118 B6
Bluegates
Stoneleigh KT17 . . . . 216 A1
Wimbledon SW19 . . . . . 179 A5
Bluehouse Rd E4 . . . . . . 20 C1
Blue Lion Pl SE1 . . . . . . 263 A6
Blue Point Ct 2 HA1 . . . 42 D4
Blueprint Apartments 15 SW12 . . . . 159 B4
Blue Sch The TW7 . . . . . . 131 A2
Blundell Cl E8 . . . . 74 A4
Blundell Rd HA8 . . . . 27 C3
Blundell St N7 . . . . 72 A2
Blunden Cl RM8 . . . . 58 C1
Blunt Rd CR0 . . . . 221 B3
Blunts Ave UB7 . . . . 126 C5
Blunts Rd SE9 . . . . 166 C6
Blurton Rd E5 . . . . 74 D4
Blydon Ct N21 . . . . 16 B6
Blyth Cl
4 Cubitt Town E14 . . . . 120 B2
Twickenham TW1 . . . . . . 152 D5
Blythe Cl SE23 . . . . 163 B4
Blythe Hill
Forest Hill SE6 . . . . 163 B4
St Paul's Cray BR5 . . . . . 190 A2
Blythe Hill La SE6 . . . . . 163 B3
Blythe Ho 8 SE11 . . . . . 138 C6
Blythe Mews 2 W14 . . . 112 D3
Blythendale Ho 34 E2 . . 96 A5
Blythe Rd W14 . . . . 113 A3 254 A5
Blythe St E2 . . . . 96 B4
Blytheswood Pl 4 SW16 . . . . 182 B6
Blythe Vale SE6 . . . . 163 B3
Blythewood 5 SM1 . . . 218 B3
Blyth Rd
Bromley BR1 . . . . 186 D2
Hayes UB3 . . . . 105 C4
Walthamstow E17 . . . . . . 53 B2
Woolwich SE28 . . . . 124 C6
Blyth's Wharf E14 . . . . . 119 A6
Blythswood Rd IG3 . . . . 58 A2
Blythwood Pk 10 BR1 . . 186 D2
Blythwood Rd
London N4 . . . . 50 A2
Pinner HA5 . . . . 22 D2
Bnois Jerusalem Sch N16 . . . . 51 B2
Boades Mews 3 NW3 . . 70 B4
Boadicea St N1 . . . . 233 C5
Boardman Ave E4 . . . . . . 19 D6
Boardman Cl EN5 . . . . . . 13 A6
Boardwalk Pl E14 . . . . . 120 A5
Boarhound 25 NW9 . . . . 27 D1
Boarley Ho SE17 . . . . . . 263 A3
Boatemah Wlk 21 SW9 . . . . 138 C3
Boathouse Ctr The W10 . . . . 90 D3
Boathouse Wlk 24 SE15 . . . . 139 D5
Boat Lifter Way 19 SE16 . . . . 119 A2
Bob Anker Cl 1 E13 . . . . 99 A4
Bobbin Cl SW4 . . . . 137 C2
Bobby Moore Bridge The HA9 . . . . 66 C5
Bob Marley Way 11 SE24 . . . . 138 C1
Bob Thompson Ct HA9 . . . . 66 D5
Bockhampton Rd KT2 . . . . 176 B3
Bocking St E8 . . . . 96 B6
Boddicott Cl SW19 . . . . 157 A2
Boddington Gdns W3 . . . . 110 C4
Boddington Ho 2 SE14 . . . . 140 C4
Bodeney Ho 10 SE5 . . . 139 C4
Boden Ho 4 E1 . . . . 96 A2
Bodiam Cl EN1 . . . . 5 C3
Bodiam Ct
Beckenham BR2 . . . . 208 D5
Sutton SM1 . . . . 218 B4
Bodiam Rd SW16 . . . . . . 181 D3
Bodiam Way NW10 . . . . . 88 B4
Bodicea Mews TW4 . . . 151 C5
Bodington Ct 2 W12 . . 112 D4
Bodley Cl KT3 . . . . 199 C4
Bodley Manor Way SE24 . . . . 160 C4
Bodley Rd KT3 . . . . 199 C4
Bodmin 26 NW9 . . . . 27 D1
Bodmin Cl HA2 . . . . 63 B5
Bodmin Gr SM4 . . . . 201 D4
Bodmin St SW18 . . . . . . 157 C3
Bodnant Gdns SW20 . . 200 B6
Bodney Rd E5, E8 . . . . 74 B3
Boeing Way UB2 . . . . . . 106 B3
Boevey Path DA17 . . . . 125 B1
Bogart Ct 13 E14 . . . . . 119 C6
Bognor Gdns WD19 . . . . 22 C5
Bognor Rd DA16 . . . . . . 146 D4
Bohemia Pl 1 E8 . . . . . . 74 B2
Bohn Rd E1 . . . . 97 A2
Bohun Gr EN4 . . . . 14 D5
Boileau Par W5 . . . . 88 B1
Boileau Rd
Barnes SW13 . . . . 134 B6
Ealing W5 . . . . 88 B1
Boilerhouse SE1 . . . . . . 253 C3
Boisseau Ho 31 E1 . . . . . 96 C2
Bolden St SE8 . . . . 141 D3
Boldero Pl NW8 . . . . 237 A5
Bolderwood Way BR4 . . . . 223 D6
Boldmere Rd HA5 . . . . . . 40 C2
Boleyn Ave EN1 . . . . 6 B4
Boleyn Ct
Beckenham BR3 . . . . 186 A2
Buckhurst Hill IG9 . . . . . . 21 B3
East Molesey KT8 . . . . . . 196 B5
Hayes UB3 . . . . 105 D4
Walthamstow E17 . . . . . . 53 C5
Boleyn Dr
East Molesey KT8 . . . . . . 195 B6
Ruislip HA4 . . . . 62 D6
Boleyn Gdns BR4 . . . . . 223 D6
Boleyn Ground (Upton Park) (West Ham Utd FC) E13, E6 . . . . 99 D5
Boleyn Rd
Newham E6 . . . . 99 D5
Stoke Newington N16 . . . . 73 C3
Upton E7 . . . . 77 B1
Boleyn Way EN5 . . . . 2 A2
Bolina Rd SE16 . . . . 118 C1
Bolingbroke Gr SW11 . . . . 158 D5
Bolingbroke Ho
Beckenham BR3 . . . . 207 A4
Catford BR3 . . . . 185 D5
Bolingbroke Hospl The SW11 . . . . 158 C6
Bolingbroke Rd W14 . . 112 D3
Bolingbroke Way UB3, UB11 . . . . 105 B5
Bolingbroke Wlk SW11 . . . . 136 C4 267 A2
Bollo Bridge Rd W3 . . . 111 A4
Bollo Ct 2 W3 . . . . 111 A3
Bollo La W3 . . . . 110 D3
Bolney Ct KT6 . . . . 197 D4
Bolney Gate SW7 . . . . . 247 A1
Bolney St SW8 . . . . 138 B5 270 C3
Bolsover St W1 . . 93 B3 238 D5
Bolstead Rd CR4 . . . . . . 181 B2
Bolster Gr N22 . . . . 31 D2
Bolt Ct EC4 . . . . 241 B1
Boltmore Cl NW4 . . . . . . 46 D6
Bolton Cl
Chessington KT9 . . . . . . 214 A2
Penge SE20 . . . . 184 A1
Bolton Cres SE5 . . . . . . 138 D5
Bolton Ct SW11 . . . . 268 B1
Bolton Dr SM4 . . . . 202 B2
Bolton Gdns
Bromley BR1 . . . . 186 D4
Kensal Rise NW10 . . . . . . 90 D5
South Kensington SW5 . . . . 113 D1 255 D2
Teddington TW11 . . . . . . 175 A4
Bolton Gdns Mews SW10 . . . . 256 A2
Bolton Ho 4 SE10 . . . . 120 C1
Bolton Pl SW5 . . . . 256 A2
Bolton Rd
Chessington KT9 . . . . . . 214 A2
Chiswick W4 . . . . 133 A5
Edmonton N18 . . . . 33 D5
Harlesden NW10 . . . . 89 C6
Harrow HA1 . . . . 42 B5
Kilburn NW8 . . . . 91 D6
Stratford E15 . . . . 76 D2
Boltons Ct SW5 . . . . 255 D2
Bolton's La TW6, UB7 . . 127 A5
Bolton St W1 . . 115 B5 248 D4
Boltons The
Harrow HA1 . . . . 42 A5
South Kensington SW10 . . . . . . 114 A1 256 A2
6 Stratford E15 . . . . 76 D2
Wembley HA0 . . . . 64 D4
Woodford IG8 . . . . 37 A6
Bolton Studios SW10 . . 256 B1
Bolton Wlk N7 . . . . 72 B6
Bombay Ct 8 SE16 . . . . 118 C4
Bombay St SE16 . . . . . . 118 B2
Bomer Cl UB7 . . . . 126 C5
Bomore Rd W11 . . . . 113 A6 244 A6
Bonar Pl BR7 . . . . 188 A3
Bonar Rd SE15 . . . . 140 A5
Bonchester Cl BR7 . . . . 188 C3
Bonchurch Cl SM2 . . . . 217 D1
Bonchurch Rd
Ealing W13 . . . . 109 B5
Kensal Town W10 . . . . 91 A2
Bond Cl UB7 . . . . 82 B1
Bond Ct EC4 . . . . 242 C1
Bondfield Ave UB4 . . . . . 84 A4
Bondfield Rd 4 E6 . . . . 100 B2
Bond Gdns SM6 . . . . 219 C4
Bond Ho 4 NW6 . . . . 91 B5
Bonding Yard Wlk SE16 . . . . 119 A3
Bond Prim Sch CR4 . . . 180 D1
Bond Rd
Mitcham CR4 . . . . 180 D1
Surbiton KT6 . . . . 214 B6
Bond St
Chiswick W4 . . . . 111 B2
Ealing W5 . . . . 109 D6
Stratford E15 . . . . 76 C3
Bond Street Sta W1 . . . . 93 A1 238 B1
Bondway SW8 . . 138 A6 270 B6
Boneta Rd SE18 . . . . 122 B3
Bonfield Rd SE13 . . . . . 142 A1
Bonham Gdns RM8 . . . . . 80 D6
Bonham Ho W11 . . . . . . 244 C4
Bonham Rd
Brixton SW2 . . . . 160 B6
Dagenham RM8 . . . . 80 D5
Bonheur Rd W4 . . . . 111 B4
Bonhill St EC2 . . 95 B3 242 D5
Boniface Gdns HA3 . . . . 23 D3
Boniface Rd UB10 . . . . . . 60 D5
Boniface Wlk HA3 . . . . . . 23 D3
Bonington Ho
Enfield EN1 . . . . 18 A6
Pentonville N1 . . . . 233 C3
Bonita Mews SE15 . . . . 140 D2
Bonne Marche Terr Mews 18 SE27 . . . . 183 C6
Bonner Hill Rd KT1 . . . . 198 C6
Bonner Ho 3 SW15 . . . . 156 A6
Bonner Prim Sch E2 . . . 96 C4
Bonner Rd E2 . . . . 96 C5
Bonnersfield Cl HA1 . . . 43 A3
Bonnersfield La
Greenhill HA1 . . . . 42 D3
Kenton HA1, HA3 . . . . 43 A3
Bonner St E2 . . . . 96 C5
Bonneville Gdns SW4 . 159 C5
Bonneville Prim Sch SW4 . . . . 159 C5
Bonnington Ct 14 UB5 . . 84 D5
Bonnington Ho 9 SM2 . . . . 217 D2
Bonnington Sq SW8 . . . . 138 B6 270 C6
Bonnington Twr BR2 . . 210 A3
Bonny St NW1 . . . . 71 C1
Bonser Rd TW1 . . . . 152 D2
Bonsor Ho SW8 . . . . 269 B2
Bonsor St SE5 . . . . 139 C5
Bonthron Ho SW15 . . . . 134 C3
Bonus Pastor RC Sch BR1 . . . . 186 C6
Bonville Gdns 17 NW4 . . 46 A5
Bonville Rd BR1 . . . . 186 D5
Bookbinder Cotts N20 . . 14 D1
Booker Cl 11 E3 . . . . 97 B2
Booker Rd 5 N18 . . . . . . 34 A5
Bookham Ct CR4 . . . . . . 202 B6
Boone Ct N9 . . . . 18 C1
Boones Rd SE13 . . . . . . 142 C1
Boone St SE13 . . . . 142 C1
Boord St SE10 . . . . 120 C3
Boothby Ct E4 . . . . 20 A1
Boothby Ho 2 SW16 . . 181 C5
Boothby Rd N19 . . . . 71 D6
Booth Cl
10 Hackney E9 . . . . 96 B6
Thamesmead SE28 . . . . . 124 B6
Booth Ho
9 Brentford TW8 . . . . . 131 C5
2 Streatham SW2 . . . . . 160 C4
Booth La EC4 . . . . 252 A6
Boothman Ho HA3 . . . . . 43 D6
Booth Rd
Croydon CR0 . . . . 220 D6
Hendon NW9 . . . . 27 C1
Boothroyd Ho TW7 . . . . 130 D2
Booth's Pl W1 . . . . 239 B3
Boot Par HA8 . . . . 26 C4
Boot St N1 . . . . 95 C4
Bordars Rd W7 . . . . 86 D2
Bordars Wlk W7 . . . . 86 C2
Bordeaux Ho 1 E15 . . . . 76 C3
Borden Ave EN1 . . . . 17 B5
Border Cres SE26 . . . . . 184 B5
Border Gate CR4 . . . . . . 180 D2
Border Gdns CR0 . . . . . 223 D4
Border Rd SE26 . . . . 184 B5
Bordesley Rd SM4 . . . . 201 D5
Bordeston Ct 11 TW8 . . 131 C5
Bordley Ct 4 N20 . . . . . . 14 D2
Bordon Wlk 5 SW15 . . 156 A4
Boreas Wlk N1 . . . . 234 D3
Boreham Ave E16 . . . . . . 99 A1
Boreham Cl E11 . . . . 54 A1
Boreham Rd N22 . . . . 33 A1
BOREHAMWOOD 11 A5
Boreman Ho 11 SE10 . . 142 A6
Borgard Rd SE18 . . . . . . 122 B2
Borkwood Pk BR6 . . . . . 227 D4
Borkwood Way BR6 . . . 227 C4
Borland Rd
London SE15 . . . . 140 C1
Teddington TW11 . . . . . . 175 B3
Borneo St SW15 . . . . . . 134 C2
Borough High St SE1 . . . . 117 B5 252 C4
Borough Hill CR0 . . . . . 220 D5
Borough Mkt* SE1 . . . . 252 C3
Borough Rd
Hounslow TW7 . . . . 130 D4
7 Kingston u T KT2 . . . . 176 C3
Lambeth SE1 . . 116 D3 261 D6
Mitcham CR4 . . . . 180 C1
Borough Sq SE1 . . . . . . 252 A1
Borough Sta SE1 . . . . 117 A4 252 B1
BOROUGH THE 117 A4
Borrett Cl SE17 . . . . 117 A1 262 A1
Borrodaile Rd SW18 . . 157 D5
Borrowdale NW1 . . . . . 232 A1
Borrowdale Ave HA3 . . . 25 A1
Borrowdale Cl IG4 . . . . . 56 A5
Borrowdale Ct EN2 . . . . . 5 A4
Borthwick Mews E15 . . . 76 C4
Borthwick Rd
Leyton E15 . . . . 76 C4
London NW9 . . . . 45 D3
Borthwick St SE8 . . . . . 119 C1
Borwick Ave E17 . . . . 53 B6
Bosbury Rd SE6 . . . . 164 A1
Boscastle Rd NW5 . . . . . 71 B5
Boscobel Cl BR1 . . . . . . 188 B1
Boscobel Ho 4 E8 . . . . . 74 B2
Boscobel Pl SW1 . . . . . . 258 B4
Boscobel St NW8 . . . . 92 B3 236 D5
Boscombe Ave E10 . . . . 54 B2
Boscombe Circus NW9 . 27 B1
Boscombe Cl E5 . . . . 75 A3
Boscombe Gdns SW16 . . . . 182 A4
Boscombe Ho CR0 . . . . 205 B1
Boscombe Rd
Merton SW19 . . . . 179 D2
North Cheam KT4 . . . . . . 200 D1
Shepherd's Bush W12 . . 112 A4
Streatham SW17 . . . . . . 181 A4
Bose Cl N3 . . . . 29 A2
Bosgrove E4 . . . . 20 A2
Boss Ho SE1 . . . . 253 C2
Boss St SE1 . . . . 253 C2
Bostall Hill SE2 . . . . 124 B1
Bostall La SE2 . . . . 124 B1
Bostall Manorway SE2 . . . . 124 B2
Bostall Park Ave DA7 . . 147 A5
Bostall Rd BR5 . . . . 190 B3
Bostock Ho TW5 . . . . . . 129 C6
Boston Bsns Pk W7 . . . 108 C3
Boston Ct
South Norwood SE25 . . . 205 D5
Sutton SM2 . . . . 218 A1
Boston Gdns
Brentford TW8 . . . . 109 B2
Chiswick W4 . . . . 133 C6
Boston Gr HA4 . . . . 39 A3
Boston Ho
24 Camberwell SE5 . . . . 139 A3
Earl's Ct SW5 . . . . 255 D3
Lisson Gr NW1 . . . . 237 C6
Boston Lo W13 . . . . 109 C1
Boston Manor Ho TW8 . . . . 109 B1
Boston Manor Rd TW8 . . . . 109 B1
Boston Manor Sta TW8 . . . . 109 A2
Boston Par W7 . . . . 109 A2
Boston Park Rd TW8 . . 109 C1
Boston Pl NW1 . . 92 D3 237 C5
Boston Rd
Burnt Oak HA8 . . . . 27 A3
Ealing W7 . . . . 109 A3
Newham E6 . . . . 100 A4
Thornton Heath CR0 . . . . 204 C3
Bostonthorpe Rd W7 . . 108 C4
Boston Vale W7 . . . . 109 A2
Bosun Cl 22 E14 . . . . . . 119 C4
Boswell Ct
Bloomsbury WC1 . . . . . . 240 B4
9 Hammersmith W14 . . 112 D3
Kingston u T KT2 . . . . 176 C2
Boswell Ho
Bloomsbury WC1 . . . . . . 240 B4
Bromley Comm BR2 . . . . 209 D4
5 Streatham SW16 . . . . 181 C5
Boswell Rd CR7 . . . . 205 A5
Boswell St WC1 . . 94 A2 240 B4
Boswood Ct TW4 . . . . . 129 B2
Bosworth Cl E17 . . . . 35 B2
Bosworth Ho 4 W10 . . . . 91 A3
Bosworth Rd
Barnet EN5 . . . . 1 C2
Dagenham RM10 . . . . 81 C5
Kensal Town W10 . . . . 91 A3
Wood Green N11 . . . . 31 D4
Botany Bay La BR7 . . . . 189 A1
Botany Cl EN4 . . . . 2 C1
Boteley Cl E4 . . . . 20 B2
Botham Cl 6 HA8 . . . . . . 27 A3
Botha Rd E13 . . . . 99 C2
Bothwell Cl E16 . . . . 98 D2
Bothwell St 4 W6 . . . . . 134 D6
Botolph Alley EC3 . . . . . 253 A6
Botolph La EC3 . . . . 253 A6
Botsford Rd SW20 . . . . 179 A1
Bott's Mews W2 . . . . 91 C1
Botwell Common Rd UB3 . . . . 105 C6
Botwell Cres UB3 . . . . . . 83 C1
Botwell House RC Prim Sch UB3 . . . . 105 D4
Botwell La UB3 . . . . 105 C6
Boucher Cl TW11 . . . . . . 174 D5
Bouchier Ho 6 N2 . . . . . 30 B1
Bough Beech Ct EN3 . . . . 6 D6
Boughton Ave BR2 . . . . 208 D2
Boughton Ho
Borough The SE1 . . . . . . 252 C2
Bromley BR1 . . . . 188 A3
Boughton Rd SE28 . . . . 123 C3
Boulcott St E1 . . . . 96 D1
Boulevard The
Chelsea SW6 . . . . 266 B1
4 Upper Tooting SW17 . . . . 159 A2
Boullen Ct SM1 . . . . 218 A4
Boulogne Ho SE1 . . . . . 263 C6
Boulogne Rd CR0 . . . . . 205 A3
Boulter Ho 4 SE14 . . . . 140 C4
Boulters Ct HA0 . . . . 65 A4
Boulton Ho TW8 . . . . . . 110 A1
Boulton Rd RM8 . . . . 81 B6
Boultwood Rd E6 . . . . . 100 B1
Bounces La N9 . . . . 18 B2
Bounces Rd N9 . . . . 18 C2
Boundaries Mans 3 SW12 . . . . 159 A3

Boundaries Rd
Feltham TW13 150 C3
Upper Tooting SW12 159 A3
Boundary Ave E17 53 B2
Boundary Bsns Ct CR4 202 B6
Boundary Cl
Barnet EN5 1 B4
Ilford IG3 79 C4
Kingston u T KT1 198 D6
Penge SE20 184 A1
Southall UB2 107 C1
Boundary Ct
3 Edmonton N18 33 D4
9 New Southgate N11 31 B6
Boundary Ho
Balham SW12 159 B3
1 Camberwell SE5 139 A5
Edgware HA8 44 B6
Isleworth TW1 153 B6
15 Notting Hill W11 112 D5
Boundary La
Camberwell SE17 139 A6
Newham E13, E6 99 D3
Boundary Pas E2 243 C6
Boundary Rd
Avery Hill DA15 167 C6
Barking IG11 101 A5
London N2 30 B2
Mitcham SW19 180 B4
Newham E13 99 D4
Pinner HA5 40 D2
Ponders End N9 18 C5
St John's Wood NW8 92 A6 229 B6
Tottenham N22 33 A1
Wallington SM5, SM6 219 A1
Walthamstow E17 53 C3
Boundary Road Est NW8 92 A6 229 A5
Boundary Row SE1 251 C2
Boundary St E2 95 D3 243 C6
Boundary Way CR0 223 C3
Boundfield Rd SE6 164 C2
Bounds Green Ct N11 31 D4
Bounds Green Ind Est N11 31 C4
Bounds Green Jun & Inf Schs N11 32 A3
Bounds Green Rd
London N11 31 D4
Wood Green N22 32 A3
Bounds Green Sta N11 31 D3
Bourbon Ho 9 SE6 186 A6
Bourchier St W1 249 C6
Bourdillon Ct 2 SE9 166 A2
Bourdon Pl W1 248 D6
Bourdon Rd SE20 184 C1
Bourdon St W1 115 B6 248 D5
Bourke Cl
London SW4 160 A5
Willesden NW10 67 C2
Bourlet Cl W1 239 A3
Bourn Ave
Hillingdon UB8 82 C3
New Barnet EN4 14 B6
West Green N15 51 B5
Bournbrook Rd SE3, SE9 143 D2
Bourne Ave
Hayes UB3 105 B3
Palmers Green N14 16 A2
Ruislip HA4 62 C3
Bourne Cir UB3 105 A3
Bourne Cl
Hinchley Wood KT7 212 D6
Isleworth TW7 130 C2
Bourne Ct
Chiswick W4 133 A6
Ruislip HA4 62 B3
Wanstead E11 55 A4
Woodford IG8 37 D1
Bourne Dr CR4 180 B1
Bourne Gdns E4 35 D6
Bourne Hill N13 16 B2
Bourne Ho
4 Ashford TW15 170 C5
3 Buckhurst Hill IG9 21 D1
5 Clapham SW4 137 C1
1 Dollis Hill NW2 68 A5
Bourne Mans N13 32 C5
Bournemead Ave UB5 84 A5
Bournemead Cl UB5 84 A4
Bournemead Way UB5 84 B5
Bourne Mews W1 238 B1
Bournemouth Cl SE15 140 A3
Bournemouth Ct 6 SM1 218 A3
Bournemouth Rd
London SE15 140 A3
Merton SW19 179 C2
Bourne Par DA5 169 D4
Bourne Pl W4 111 B1
Bourne Prim Sch HA4 62 C2
Bourne Rd
Bexley DA5 169 D5
Bromley BR2 209 D5
Hornsey N8 50 A3
Leyton E7, E11 76 D5
Bournes Ho 4 N15 51 C3
Bourneside 5 N14 15 D3
Bourneside Cres 6 N14 15 D3
Bourneside Gdns SE6 186 A5
Bourne St
Belgravia SW1 115 A2 258 A3
Croydon CR0 220 D6
Bourne Terr W2 91 D2
Bourne The N14 16 A3
Bourne Vale BR2 209 A2
Bournevale Rd SW16 182 A6
Bourne View UB6 64 D3
Bourne Way
Cheam SM1 217 B3
Coney Hall BR2, BR4 224 D6
West Ewell KT19 215 A4
Bournewood Rd SE18 146 A5
Bournville Rd SE6 163 C4
Bournwell Cl EN4 2 D3
Bourton Cl UB3 106 A5
Bousfield Prim Sch SW10 114 A1 256 A2
Bousfield Rd SE14 140 D3
Boutcher CE Prim Sch SE1 117 D2 263 C4
Boutflower Rd SW11 136 C1
Bouverie Ct 4 SW16 182 A5
Bouverie Gdns HA3 43 D3
Bouverie Mews N16 73 C6
Bouverie Pl W2 236 D2
Bouverie Rd
Harrow HA1 42 A3
Stoke Newington N16 73 C6
Bouverie St EC4 94 C1 241 B1
Bouvier Rd EN3 6 C5
Boveney Rd SE23 162 D4
Bovill Rd SE23 162 D4
Bovingdon Ave HA9 66 C2
Bovingdon Cl 4 N19 71 C6
Bovingdon La NW9 27 C2
Bovingdon Rd SW6 135 D4 265 D1
Bovril Ho EN1 5 C2
BOW 97 B5
Bowater Cl
Clapham Pk SW2 160 A5
Kingsbury NW9 45 B4
Bowater Gdns TW16 172 C2
Bowater Ho EC1 242 B5
Bowater Pl SE3 143 B5
Bowater Rd
Greenwich SE18 121 D3
Wembley HA9 66 D5
Bow Brook The 20 E2 96 D5
Bow Church Sta E3 97 C4
BOW COMMON 97 D2
Bow Common La E3 97 B3
Bowden Cl TW14 149 C3
Bowden Ct HA4 62 C3
Bowden Ho 20 E3 97 D4
Bowden House Hospl (Private) HA1 64 C6
Bowden St SE11 116 C1 261 B1
Bowditch SE8 119 B1
Bowdon Rd E17 53 C2
Bowen Ct 2 N5 72 D4
Bowen Dr SE21 161 C1
Bowen Rd HA1 42 A2
Bowen St E14 97 D1
Bower Ave SE3 142 C5
Bower Cl UB5 84 C5
Bowerdean St SW6 135 D3
Bower Ho SE14 140 D4
Bowerman Ave SE14 141 A6
Bowerman Ct 1 N19 71 D6
Bowers Ho 5 IG11 78 D1
Bower St E1 96 D1
Bowers Wlk 1 E6 100 B1
Bowery Ct 16 RM10 81 D2
Bowes Cl DA15 168 B5
Bowes Ho N13 32 B5
Bowes-Lyon Hall 13 E16 121 A5
Bowes Lyon Ho 2 TW10 153 C1
BOWES PARK 32 A4
Bowes Park Sta N22 32 A3
Bowes Prim Sch N11 31 D5
Bowes Rd
Acton W3 111 C6
Dagenham RM8 80 C4
New Southgate N11 31 C5
Walton-on-T KT12 194 B1
Bowes Rd (North Circular Rd) N13 32 A5
Bowfell Rd W6 134 C6
Bowford Ave DA7 147 A4
Bowhill Cl SW9 138 C5
Bow Ho 1 E3 97 C4
Bowie Cl SW4 159 D4
Bow Ind Pk E15 75 C1
Bow La
Barbican EC2, EC4 95 A1 242 B1
Finchley N12 30 A3
Bowland Ho N4 51 A2
Bowland Rd
London SW4 137 D1
Woodford IG8 37 C4
Bowland Yd SW1 247 D1
Bowl Ct EC2 243 B5
Bowles Ct
Finchley N12 30 C3
Harrow HA3 43 A3
Bowles Rd 1 SE1 140 A6
Bowley Cl SE19 183 D4
Bowley Ho 6 SE16 118 A3
Bowley La SE19 183 D5
Bowling Cl UB10 82 B6
Bowling Green Cl SW19 156 B4
Bowling Green Ct HA9 66 B6
Bowling Green Ho SW10 266 C4
Bowling Green La EC1 94 C3 241 B6
Bowling Green Pl SE1 252 C2
Bowling Green Row 1 SE18 122 B2
Bowling Green St SE11 138 C6
Bowling Green Wlk N1 95 C4
Bowls Cl HA7 25 B5
Bowman Ave E16 120 D6
Bowman Homes W5 109 D4
Bowman Mews
St George in t East E1 118 A6
Wandsworth SW18 157 B3
Bowmans Cl W13 109 B5
Bowmans Lea SE23 162 C4
Bowman's Meadow SM6 219 B5
Bowman's Mews N7 72 A5
Bowman's Pl N7 72 A5
Bowman Trad Est NW9 44 C5
Bowmar Lo 18 EN5 1 D1
Bowmead SE9 166 B2
Bowmore Wlk NW1 71 D1
Bowness Cl 5 E8 73 D2
Bowness Cres KT2, SW15 177 C5
Bowness Dr TW4 129 A1
Bowness Ho SE15 140 C5
Bowness Rd
Catford SE6 163 D4
Erith DA7 147 D3
Bowood Rd
Clapham SW11 159 A6
Enfield EN3 6 D3
Bow Rd E3 97 C4
Bowring Gn WD19 22 C5
Bow Road Sta E3 97 C4
Bowrons Ave HA0 65 D1
Bowry Ho 14 E14 97 B2
Bow Sch E3 97 C4
Bowsley Ct TW13 150 A2
Bowsprit Point 1 E14 119 C3
Bow St
St Giles WC2 94 A1 240 B1
Stratford E15 76 C3
Bowstead Ct SW11 266 D1
Bow Triangle Bsns Ctr 17 E3 97 C3
Bowyer Cl E6 100 B2
Bowyer Ct 4 E4 20 A3
Bowyer Ho
Mitcham CR4 202 C6
27 Shoreditch N1 95 C6
Wandsworth SW18 157 D5
Bowyer Pl SE5 139 A5
Bowyer St 15 SE5 139 A5
Boxall Rd SE21 161 C5
Box Cnr TW2 152 C2
Box Elder Cl HA8 27 A5
Boxgrove Prim Sch SE2 124 C3
Boxgrove Rd SE2 124 C3
Box La IG11 102 C5
Boxley Ho 3 E5 74 B3
Boxley St E16 121 B5
Boxmoor Ho
16 Hackney E2 96 A6
9 Shepherd's Bush W11 112 D5
Boxmoor Rd HA3 43 B5
Boxoll Rd RM9 81 B5
Boxshall Ho 7 SE18 144 D6
Box Tree Ho SE8 119 A1
Boxtree La HA3 24 B3
Boxtree Rd HA3 24 B3
Boxwood Cl UB7 104 B4
Boxworth Cl N12 30 B5
Boxworth Gr N1 94 B6 233 D6
Boyard Rd SE18 122 D1
Boyce Ho
Streatham SW16 181 C5
1 West Kilburn W10 91 B4
Boyce Way E13 99 A3
Boycroft Ave NW9 45 A3
Boyd Ave UB1 107 B5
Boyd Cl KT2 176 C3
Boyd Ct SW15 156 C5
Boydell Ct NW8 70 B1
Boyden Ho 8 E17 54 A6
Boyd Rd SW19 180 B4
Boyd St E1 96 A1
Boyfield St SE1 116 D4 251 D1
Boyland Rd BR1 186 D5
Boyle Ave HA7 25 A4
Boyle Cl UB10 82 B5
Boyle Farm Rd KT7 197 A3
Boyle Ho
13 Belvedere DA17 125 C3
Wembley HA9 66 D5
Boyle St W1 249 A6
Boyne Ave NW4 46 D5
Boyne Ct NW10 68 A1
Boyne Ho 10 E5 74 B6
Boyne Rd
Dagenham RM10 81 C5
Lewisham SE13 142 B2
Boyne Terr Mews W11 113 B5 244 C4
Boyson Rd 10 SE17 139 B6
Boyton Cl
London N8 50 A6
Stepney E1 96 D3
Boyton Ho
Kennington SE11 261 A1
St John's Wood NW8 229 D4
Boyton Rd N8 50 A6
Brabant Ct EC3 253 A6
Brabant Rd N22 32 B1
Brabazon Ave SM6 220 A1
Brabazon Rd
Heston TW5 128 D5
Northolt UB5 85 C5
Brabazon St E14 97 D2
Brabner Ho 3 E2 96 A4
Brabourne Cl 7 SE19 183 C5
Brabourne Cres DA7 147 B6
Brabourne Hts NW7 11 C1
Brabourne Rise BR3 208 B4
Brabourn Gr SE15 140 C3
Brabrook Ct SM6 219 B3
Brabstone Ho 2 UB6 86 D5
Bracer Ho 1 N1 95 C5
Bracewell Ave UB6 65 A2
Bracewell Rd W10 90 C2
Bracewood Gdns CR0 221 D5
Bracey Mews 1 N4 72 A6
Bracey St N4 72 A6
Bracken Ave
Balham SW12 159 A4
Croydon CR0 223 C5
Brackenbridge Dr HA4 62 D5
Brackenbury N4 50 B1
Brackenbury Gdns W6 112 B3
Brackenbury Prim Sch W6 112 B3
Brackenbury Rd
East Finchley N2 48 A6
Hammersmith W6 112 B3
Bracken Cl
Ashford TW16 171 D4
Newham E6 100 B2
Twickenham TW4 151 C4
Brackendale
Kingston u T KT1 176 D1
Southgate N21 16 B2
Brackendale Cl TW5 129 D4
Brackendale Ct 2 BR3 185 C3
Bracken End TW7 152 B6
Brackenfield Cl E5 74 B5
Bracken Gdns SW13 134 A3
Brackenhill HA4 63 A4
Bracken Hill Cl 5 BR1 186 D2
Bracken Hill La BR1 186 D2
Bracken Ho 15 E3 97 C2
Bracken Mews
Chingford E4 20 A3
Romford RM7 59 D3
Brackens BR3 185 C3
Brackens The EN1 17 C4
Bracken The E4 20 A2
Brackenwood TW16 172 A2
Brackenwood Lo EN5 1 C1
Brackley Ave SE15 140 C2
Brackley Cl SM6 220 A1
Brackley Ct NW8 236 D6
Brackley Rd
Beckenham BR3 185 C3
Chiswick W4 111 C1
Brackley Sq IG8 37 D3
Brackley St EC1 242 B4
Brackley Terr 6 W4 111 C1
Bracklyn Ct N1 235 C4
Bracklyn St N1 235 C4
Bracknell Cl N22 32 C2
Bracknell Gate NW3 69 D3
Bracknell Gdns NW3 69 D4
Bracknell Way NW3 69 D4
Bracondale KT10 212 A3
Bracondale Rd SE2 124 A2
Braconhyrst HA1 42 C2
Bradbeer Ho 24 E2 96 C4
Bradbourne Ct 11 SM2 217 D2
Bradbourne Rd DA5 169 C4
Bradbourne St SW6 135 C3
Bradbury Cl UB2 107 B2
Bradbury Ct
4 Barnet EN5 1 D1
2 Greenwich SE3 143 A5
Merton SW20 178 C1
Bradbury Ho E1 243 D2
Bradbury St 28 N16 73 C3
Bradby Ho NW8 91 D5
Braddock Cl TW7 130 D3
Braddon Rd TW9 132 B2
Braddyll St SE10 120 C1
Bradenham 11 SE17 139 B6
Bradenham Ave DA16 146 A1
Bradenham Cl SE17 139 B6
Bradenham Rd
Harrow HA3 43 B5
Hayes UB4 83 C4
Braden St W9 91 D3
Bradfield Ct 14 NW1 71 B1
Bradfield Dr IG11 80 A3
Bradfield Ho 15 SW8 137 D3
Bradfield Rd
Newham E16 121 B4
Ruislip HA4 63 A3
Bradford Cl
Bromley BR2 210 B1
Forest Hill SE26 184 B6
Tottenham N17 33 D4
Bradford Dr KT19 215 D2
Bradford Ho 4 W14 112 D3
Bradford Rd
Acton W3 111 C4
Ilford IG1 57 C1
Bradgate Rd SE6 163 D5
Brading Cres E11 77 B6
Brading Rd
Streatham SW2 160 B4
Thornton Heath CR0 204 B3
Brading Terr W12 112 A3
Bradiston Rd W9 91 B4
Bradley Cl N7 72 B2
Bradley Ct CR0 220 C4
Bradley Gdns W13 87 B1
Bradley Ho
Bermondsey SE16 118 B2
Bradley Ho *continued*
1 Bromley E3 97 D4
Twickenham TW1 152 D3
Woodford IG8 37 A3
Bradley Mews SW12 158 D3
Bradley Rd
Enfield EN3 7 A6
South Norwood SE19 183 A4
Wood Green N22 32 B1
Bradley's Cl N1 234 B4
Bradley Stone Rd E6 100 B2
Bradlord Ho SE21 161 C1
Bradman Row 7 HA8 27 A3
Bradmead SW8 137 C5 269 A3
Bradmore Ct 2 EN3 7 A2
Bradmore Park Rd W6 112 B2
Bradon 24 NW9 27 D1
Bradshaw Cl SW19 179 C4
Bradshaw Dr NW7 28 D3
Bradshawe Waye UB8 82 B2
Bradshaws Cl SE25 206 A6
Bradsole Ho 18 BR3 185 C3
Brad St SE1 116 C5 251 B3
Bradstock Ho E9 75 A1
Bradstock Rd
Homerton E9 74 D2
Stoneleigh KT17 216 B3
Bradwell Ave RM10 81 C6
Bradwell Cl E18 54 D5
Bradwell Ho
8 Kilburn NW6 91 D6
9 Walthamstow E17 53 D6
Bradwell Mews 5 N18 34 A6
Brady Ct RM8 58 D1
Brady Dr BR1 210 C6
Brady Ho
London SW4 159 D6
South Lambeth SW8 269 B2
Bradymead E6 100 D1
Brady St E1 96 B3
Braeburn Ct 1 EN4 2 C1
Brae Ct
2 Kingston u T KT2 176 C2
South Norwood SE25 183 C2
Braefoot Ct SW15 156 D6
Braemar SW15 156 D5
Braemar Ave
Thornton Heath CR7 204 D6
Welsh Harp NW10 67 B6
Wembley HA0 66 A1
Wimbledon SW18, SW19 157 C2
Wood Green N22 32 A2
Braemar Ct
4 Brentford TW8 131 D6
5 Catford SE6 164 D3
Braemar Gdns
Hendon NW9 27 B2
Longlands DA15 167 B1
West Wickham BR4 208 A1
Braemar Ho
Richmond TW11 175 B5
St John's Wood W9 229 A1
Braemar Mans W8 255 D5
Braemar Rd
Brentford TW8 131 D6
Newham E13 98 D3
North Cheam KT4 216 B5
South Tottenham N15 51 C4
Braemore Ct EN4 3 A1
Braeside BR3 185 D5
Braeside Ave SW19 179 A2
Braeside Cl HA5 23 C3
Braeside Rd SW16 181 C3
Braeside Sch
Buckhurst Hill IG9 21 B3
Buckhurst Hill IG9 21 C2
Braes St N1 72 D1
Braesyde Cl DA17 125 B2
Brafferton Rd CR0 221 A4
Braganza St SE17 116 D1 261 C1
Bragg Cl RM8 80 B2
Bragg Rd TW11 174 D4
Braham Ho SE11 260 D1
Braham St E1 243 D2
Brahma Kumaris World Spiritual Univ NW10 68 A1
Braid Ave W3 89 C1
Braid Cl TW13 151 B2
Braid Ho SE10 142 A4
Braidwood Ho 2 CR7 204 D5
Braidwood Rd SE6 164 B3
Braidwood St SE1 117 C5 253 A3
Braikenridge Ho N21 17 B5

Brailsford Cl SW19 180 C3
Brailsford Rd SW2 160 C5
Braintcroft Prim Sch NW2 67 D5
Brainton Ave TW14 150 C4
Braintree Ave IG4 56 A5
Braintree Ho 6 E1 96 C3
Braintree Ind Est HA4 62 B4
Braintree Rd
Dagenham RM10 81 C5
Ruislip HA4 62 B4
Braintree St E2 96 C4
Braithwaite Ave RM7 59 C2
Braithwaite Gdns HA7 25 C2
Braithwaite Ho EC1 242 C6
Braithwaite Rd EN3 7 B2
Braithwaite Twr W2 236 C4
Brake Shear Ho 1 EN5 1 B2
Bramah Gn SW9 138 C4
Bramah Mus of Tea & Coffee* SE1 252 B3
Bramalea Cl N6 49 A3
Bramall Cl E15 76 D3
Bramall Ct N7 72 B2
Bramber WC1 233 A1
Bramber Ct TW8 110 A2
Bramber Ho 9 KT2 176 A2
Bramber Rd
Colney Hatch N12 30 C5
Fulham W14 135 B6 264 C6
Bramble Acres Cl SM2 217 C1
Bramblebury Rd SE18 123 A1
Bramble Cl
Beckenham BR3 208 A4
Croydon CR0 223 D4
Hillingdon UB8 82 B1
South Tottenham N15 52 A5
Stanmore HA7 25 D3
Upper Halliford TW17 193 B6
Brambledown 8 N4 50 A2
Brambledown Cl BR2, BR4 208 C4
Brambledown Rd
South Croydon CR2 221 C1
Wallington SM5, SM6 219 B1
Bramble Gdns W12 111 D6
Bramble Ho 16 E3 97 C2
Bramble La TW12 173 B4
Brambles Cl TW7, TW8 131 B5
Brambles Farm Dr UB10 82 C4
Brambles The
West Drayton UB7 104 A2
8 Wimbledon SW19 179 B5
Bramblewood Cl SM5 202 C1
Brambling Ct
25 Deptford SE8 141 B6
South Norwood SE25 205 D5
Bramblings The E4 36 B6
Bramcote Ave CR4 202 D5
Bramcote Ct CR4 202 D5
Bramcote Gr SE16 118 C1
Bramcote Rd SW15 134 B1
Bramdean Cres SE12 165 A3
Bramdean Gdns SE12 165 A3
Bramerton NW6 68 D1
Bramerton Rd BR3 207 B6
Bramerton St SW3 136 C6 267 A6
Bramfield Ct N4 73 A6
Bramfield Rd SW11 158 D6
Bramford Ct N14 15 D2
Bramford Rd SW18 136 A1
Bramham Gdns
Chessington KT9 213 D4
South Kensington SW5 113 D1 255 D2
Bramham Ho SE22 139 C1
Bramhope La SE7 143 B6
Bramlands Cl SW11 136 C2
Bramley Ave TW17 193 C6
Bramley Cl
Croydon CR2 221 A3
East Barnet N14 15 B6
Hayes UB3 106 A6
Higham Hill E17 35 A1
Orpington BR6 210 D1
Pinner HA5 39 D6
Twickenham TW2 152 A5
Woodford IG8 37 C3
Bramley Cres
Ilford IG2 56 C3
Nine Elms SW8 137 D5 269 D4
Bramley Ct
2 Barnet EN4 2 C1
Bramley Ct *continued*
9 Chingford E4 20 A3
Dollis Hill NW2 68 B5
Feltham TW14 149 C5
Hither Green SE13 164 B6
Mitcham CR4 180 B1
Southall UB1 108 A6
Wallington SM6 219 C3
Welling DA16 146 B4
Bramley Gdns WD19 22 C5
Bramley Hill CR2 221 A4
Bramley Ho
Hounslow TW3 129 B1
Ilford IG2 56 C3
1 Kingston u T KT2 176 D3
19 North Kensington W10 90 D1
Roehampton SW15 155 D5
Bramley House Ct EN2 5 B6
Bramleyhyrst CR2 221 A3
Bramley Lo HA0 65 D4
Bramley Rd
Ealing W5 109 C3
North Kensington W10 90 D1
Southgate N14 15 C6
Sutton SM1 218 B3
Bramley Way
Hounslow TW4 151 B6
West Wickham BR4 223 D6
Brampton WC1 240 C3
Brampton Cl 14 E5 74 B6
Brampton Coll NW4 46 C5
Brampton Ct NW4 46 B5
Brampton Gr
Harrow HA3 43 B5
Hendon NW4 46 C5
Wembley HA9 44 C1
Brampton La 6 NW4 46 C5
Brampton Lo DA7 146 D5
Brampton Manor Sch E6 99 D3
Brampton Park Rd N22 50 C6
Brampton Prim Sch
Bexley DA7 146 D3
Newham E6 100 A4
Brampton Rd
Bexleyheath DA7 147 A4
Croydon CR0 205 D3
Harringay N15 51 A4
Hillingdon UB10 82 D5
Newham E6 99 D4
Queensbury NW9 44 C5
Bramshaw Gdns WD19 22 D5
Bramshaw Rd E9 74 D2
Bramshaw Rise KT3 199 C3
Bramshill Gdns NW5 71 B5
Bramshill Rd NW10 89 D5
Bramshot Ave SE7 143 B6
Bramshott Ct 3 KT6 198 A3
Bramshurst NW8 91 D6
Bramston Rd
Harlesden NW10 90 A5
Wandsworth SW17 158 A1
Bramwell Cl TW16 172 D1
Bramwell Ho
Borough The SE1 262 B5
Chelsea SW1 269 A6
Bramwell Mews N1 233 D6
Brancaster Dr NW7 28 A3
Brancaster Ho
22 Globe Town E1 96 D4
Islington N5 72 D3
Brancaster Rd
Ilford E12 78 B4
Newbury Pk IG2 57 C3
Streatham SW16 160 A1
Brancepeth Gdns IG9 21 A2
Branch Hill NW3 70 A5
Branch Ho 13 SM1 218 A4
Branch Pl N1 95 B6 235 D6
Branch Rd E14 119 A6
Branch St SE15 139 C5
Brancker Rd HA3 43 D6
Brancroft Way EN3 7 B4
Brandan Ho 11 HA1 42 D4
Brand Cl N4 50 D1
Branden Lo 13 W4 111 A1
Brandlehow Rd SW15 135 B1
Brandon Ho BR3 185 D5
Brandon Mews
Barbican EC2 242 C4
Walworth SE17 262 B3
Brandon Pl N8 50 B5
Brandon Rd
Barnsbury N7 72 A1
Southall UB2 107 B1
Sutton SM1 217 D4
Walthamstow E17 54 A6
Brandon St
SE17 117 A2 262 B3
Brandram Rd SE13 142 C1
Brandrams Wharf SE16 118 C4
Brandreth Ct HA1 42 D3
Brandreth Rd
Newham E6 100 B1
Upper Tooting SW17 159 B2
Brandries The SM6 219 D5
Brand St SE10 142 A5
Brandville Gdns IG6 56 D5
Brandville Rd UB7 104 A4
Brandy Way SM2 217 C1
Brangbourne Rd BR1 186 A5
Brangton Rd SE11 260 D1
Brangwyn Cres SW19 180 B1
Brangwyn Ct W14 254 A5
Branham Ho 1 SE18 122 D1
Branksea St SW6 135 A5 264 A3
Branksome Ave N18 33 D5
Branksome Cl
Teddington TW11 174 B6
Walton-on-T KT12 194 D1
Branksome Ct 6 N2 48 A6
Branksome Ho SW8 270 C4
Branksome Rd
London SW2 160 A6
Merton SW19 179 C2
Branksome Way
Harrow HA3 44 B3
Kingston u T KT3 177 B2
Bransby Ct 4 N16 73 C4
Bransby Rd KT9 214 A2
Branscombe NW1 232 B5
Branscombe Ct BR2 208 C4
Branscombe Gdns N21 16 C4
Branscombe St SE13 141 D2
Bransdale Cl NW6 91 C6
Bransgrove Rd HA8 26 B3
Branston Cres BR5 211 B1
Branstone Ct 9 TW9 132 B4
Branstone Rd TW9 132 B4
Branston Ho N7 72 C3
Brants Wlk W7 86 C3
Brantwood Ave
Erith DA8 147 D5
Isleworth TW7 131 A1
Brantwood Cl E17 53 D6
Brantwood Gdns
Enfield EN2 16 A6
Redbridge IG4 56 A5
Brantwood Ho 9 SE5 139 A5
Brantwood Rd
Erith DA7 147 D3
Herne Hill SE24 161 A6
Tottenham N17 34 A4
Brasenose Dr SW13 134 C6
Brasher Cl UB6 64 B3
Brashley Road Cvn Site NW10 89 C4
Brassett Point 3 E15 98 C6
Brassey Cl TW14 150 A3
Brassey Ho
1 Millwall E14 119 D2
Walton-on-T KT12 194 A1
Brassey Rd NW6 69 B2
Brassey Sq SW11 137 A2
Brassie Ave W3 89 C1
Brass Talley Alley 31 SE16 118 D4
Brasted Cl
Bexley DA6 168 D6
Forest Hill SE26 184 C6
Brasted Lo 11 BR3 185 C3
Brathay NW1 232 B3
Brathway Rd SW18 157 C4
Bratley St 11 E1 96 A3
Bratten Ct CR0 205 B3
Braund Ave UB6 85 D3
Braundton Ave DA15 167 D3
Braunston Dr UB4 85 A3
Braunston Ho TW8 131 C6
Bravington Cl TW17 192 B4
Bravington Pl W9 91 B3
Bravington Rd W9 91 B4
Brawne Ho 12 SE17 138 D6
Braxfield Rd SE4 141 B1
Braxted Pk SW16 182 B4
Bray NW3 70 C1
Brayard's Rd SE15 140 B3
Braybourne Dr TW7 130 D5
Braybrooke Gdns SE19 183 C3
Braybrook St W12 89 D1
Brayburne Ave SW4 137 C3
Braycourt Ave KT12 194 C2
Bray Cres SE16 118 D4
Bray Ct
Chessington KT9 214 B3
Streatham SW16 182 A5
Braydon Rd N16 52 A1
Bray Dr E16 120 D6
Brayfield Terr N1 72 C1
Brayford Sq 12 E1 96 C1
Bray Pl SW3 114 D2 257 C3
Bray Rd NW7 28 D4
Brayton Gdns EN2 3 D1
Braywick Ct 9 KT2 176 C3
Braywood Rd SE9 145 B1
Brazier Cres UB5 85 B3
Brazil Cl CR0 204 A2
Breach La RM9 103 C4
Bread St EC2, EC4 242 B1
Breakspeare SE21 161 D1
Breakspear Jun & Inf Schs UB10 60 C6
Breakspear Rd HA4, UB9 38 D3
Breakspear Rd N UB9 38 B5
Breakspear Rd S UB9, UB10 38 C1
Breakspears Dr BR5 190 A2
Breakspears Mews SE4 141 C3
Breakspears Rd SE4 141 C2
Breakwell Ct 16 W10 91 A3
Bream Cl N17 52 B5
Bream Gdns E6 100 C4
Breamore Cl SW15 156 A3
Breamore Ct IG3 80 A6
Breamore Ho 21 SE15 140 A5
Breamore Rd IG3 79 D6
Bream's Bldgs EC4 94 C1 241 A2
Bream St E3 75 C1
Breamwater Gdns TW10 153 B1
Brearley Cl
Burnt Oak HA8 27 A3
Uxbridge UB8 60 A2
Breaside Prep Sch BR1 187 D2
Breasley Cl SW15 134 B1
Brechin Pl SW7 114 A2 256 B3
Brecknock Prim Sch N7 71 D2
Brecknock Rd N19 71 D3
Breckonmead BR1 187 C1
Brecon Cl
Mitcham CR4 204 A6
North Cheam KT4 216 C6
Brecon Ct
7 Eltham SE9 166 C5
Whetstone N12 14 A1
Brecon Gn NW9 45 C3
Brecon Ho
Stamford Hill N16 51 D1
Wandsworth SW18 157 C4
Brecon Rd
Enfield EN3 6 C1
Fulham W6 135 A6 264 B5
Brede Cl E6 100 C4
Bredel Ho 1 E14 97 C2
Bredgar SE13 163 D6
Bredgar Rd N19 71 C6
Bredhurst Cl SE20 184 C4
Bredinghurst SE22 162 A4
Bredinghurst Sch SE15 140 D1
Bredin Ho SW10 265 D4
Bredo Ho IG11 102 B4
Bredon Ct HA8 26 B6
Bredon Rd CR0 205 D2
Breer St SW6 135 D2
Breezer's Ct 22 E1 118 A6
Breezer's Hill E1 118 A6
Brehon Ho NW1 232 A5
Brember Rd HA2 64 A6
Bremer Mews E17 53 D5
Bremner Rd SW7 256 B6
Brenchley Cl
Chislehurst BR7 188 C2
Hayes BR2 208 D3
Brenchley Gdns SE15, SE22, SE23 162 D5
Brenchley Rd BR5 189 D1
Bren Ct 27 EN3 7 C6
Brenda Rd SW17 158 D2
Brende Gdns KT8 195 D5
Brendon Ave NW10 67 C4
Brendon Cl
Esher KT10 212 A2
Harlington UB7 127 A5
Brendon Ct
3 London N20 14 C2
Southall UB2 107 D2
Brendon Dr KT10 212 A2
Brendon Gdns
Harrow HA2 63 D4
Ilford IG2 57 C4
Brendon Gr N2 30 A1
Brendon Ho
Marylebone W1 238 A4
Sutton SM2 218 A2
Brendon Rd
Dagenham RM8 59 C1
New Eltham SE9 167 B2
Brendon St W1 92 C1 237 B2
Brendon Villas N21 17 A3
Brendon Way EN1 17 C4
Brenley Cl CR4 203 A6
Brenley Gdns SE9 143 D1
Brenley Ho SE1 252 C2
Brennands Ct 14 N19 71 C5
Brent Adult Comm Education Service Coll NW10 89 B6
Brent Cl DA5 169 A3
Brentcot Cl W13 87 B3
Brent Cres NW10 88 B5
Brent Cross Flyover NW2, NW4 46 D2
Brent Cross Gdns NW4 46 D3
Brent Cross Interchange NW2, NW4 46 D2
Brent Cross Sh Ctr NW4 46 C2
Brent Cross Sta NW11 46 D2
Brent Ct
5 Acton W12 111 C3
Ealing W7 108 B6
Hendon NW11 46 D2
Brentfield NW10 66 D1
Brentfield Cl NW10 67 B2
Brentfield Gdns NW2 46 D2
Brentfield Ho 7 NW10 67 B1
Brentfield Prim Sch NW10 67 B2
Brentfield Rd NW10 67 B2
BRENTFORD 131 B6
Brentford Bsns Ctr TW8 131 C5
Brentford Cl UB4 84 D3
BRENTFORD END 131 C4
Brentford Fountain L Ctr W4 110 C1
Brentford Ho 6 TW1 153 B4
Brentford Sch for Girls TW8 131 D6
Brentford Sta TW8 131 C6
Brent Gn NW4 46 D4
Brentham Way W5 87 D3
Brent Ho
3 Catford BR1 186 B5
16 Hackney E9 74 C2
Wembley HA9 66 B3
Brenthouse Rd E9 74 C2
Brenthurst Rd NW10 67 D2
Brent Knoll Sch SE26 162 D1
Brent Lea TW8 131 C5
Brent Mans NW4 46 C4
Brentmead Cl W7 108 C6
Brentmead Gdns NW10 88 B5
Brentmead Pl NW11 46 D3
Brent Mus* NW10 68 B2
Brent New Ent Ctr NW10 67 D2
Brenton Ct E9 75 A3
Brenton St E14 97 A1
Brent Park Ind Est UB2 106 C3
Brent Park Rd NW4 46 B2
Brent Pl EN5 13 B6
Brent Rd
Brentford TW8 131 C6
Newham E16 99 A2
Southall UB2 106 C3
Woolwich SE18 144 D5
Brentside TW8 131 C6
Brentside Cl W13 87 A3
Brentside Executive Ctr TW8 131 B6
Brentside High Sch W7 86 C3
Brentside Prim Sch W7 86 C3
Brent St NW4 46 C4
Brent Trad Est NW10 67 C3
Brentvale Ave
Southall UB1 108 B5
Wembley HA0 88 B6
Brent View Rd NW9 46 A2
Brentwaters Bsns Pk TW8 131 C5
Brent Way
Brentford TW8 131 D5
Finchley N3 29 C4
Wembley HA9 66 D2
Brentwick Gdns TW8 110 A2
Brentwood Cl SE9 167 A3
Brentwood Ho 2 SE18 143 D5
Brentwood Lo NW4 46 D4
Brereton Ho 4 SW2 160 C4
Brereton Rd N17 33 D3
Bressenden Pl SW1 115 C3 259 A6
Bressey Ave EN1 6 A4
Bressey Gr E18 36 D1
Bretherton Ct CR2 221 C2
Breton Ho
Bermondsey SE1 263 C6
St Luke's EC2 242 B5
Brett Cl
15 Northolt UB5 84 D4
Stoke Newington N16 73 C6
Brett Cres NW10 89 B6
Brett Ct N9 18 C2
Brettell St SE17 262 D1
Brettenham Ave E17 35 C2
Brettenham Prim Sch N18 34 A6
Brettenham Rd
Edmonton N18 34 A6
Walthamstow E17 35 C2
Brett Ho 1 SW15 156 D4
Brett House Cl 2 SW15 156 D4
Brettinghurst 8 SE1 118 A1
Bretton Ho N19 50 A1
Brett Pas 28 E8 74 B3
Brett Rd
Barnet EN5 12 C6
Hackney E8 74 B3
Brewers Bldgs EC1 234 C2
Brewers Ct W2 236 A2
Brewer's Gn SW1 259 C6
Brewers Hall Gdns EC2 242 B3
Brewers La 11 TW9 153 D6
Brewer St W1 115 C6 249 B6
Brewery Cl HA0 65 A4
Brewery Ind Est The N1 235 B3
Brewery Mews Bsns Ctr 1 TW7 131 A2
Brewery Rd
Islington N7 72 A2
Keston Mark BR2 210 A1
Plumstead SE18 123 B1
Brewery Sq
Bermondsey SE1 253 C3
Clerkenwell EC1 241 D6
Brewhouse La
Putney SW15 135 A2
Wapping E1 118 B5
Brewhouse Rd 3 SE18 122 B2
Brewhouse Wlk SE16 119 A5
Brewhouse Yd EC1 241 C6
Brewood Rd RM8 80 B2
Brewster Gdns W10 90 C2
Brewster Ho
Bermondsey SE1 263 D4
Poplar E14 119 B6
Brewster Rd E10 53 D1
Brian Ct N10 31 B2
Brian Rd RM6 58 C4
Briant Ho SE1 260 D5
Briants Cl HA5 23 B1
Briant St SE14 140 D5
Briar Ave SW16 182 B3
Briarbank Rd W13 87 A1
Briar Cl
Buckhurst Hill IG9 21 D2
Edmonton N13 17 A1
Finchley N2 30 A1
Hampton TW12 173 B5
Isleworth TW7 152 D6
Briar Cres UB5 63 D2
Briar Ct
7 Bow E3 97 C5
Cheam SM3 216 C4
Dalston E8 73 D1
Hampton TW12 173 D5
Leytonstone E11 54 B2
Briardale
Edgware HA8 27 B6

Briardale *continued*
Wandsworth SW19 . . . . 157 B3
Briardale Gdns NW3 . . . 69 C5
Briardale Ho 12 N16. . . . 51 C1
Briarfield Ave N3 . . . . . . 29 D1
Briarfield Cl DA7. . . . . . 147 C3
Briar Gdns BR2 . . . . 208 D1
Briaris Cl 11 N17 . . . . 34 B3
Briar La CR0 . . . . 223 D4
Briar Lo E18 . . . . 37 C2
Briar Rd
Cricklewood NW2 . . . . . . 68 C4
Harrow HA3. . . . . 43 C4
Littleton TW17 . . . . 192 C4
Thornton Heath SW16 . . 204 B6
Twickenham TW2 . . . . . . 152 C3
Briars The WD23. . . . . 8 C4
Briarswood Way BR6. . 227 D3
Briar The 11 SM1. . . . . . 218 A4
Briarview Ct E4. . . . . 36 B4
Briar Way UB7 . . . . 104 C4
Briar Wlk
Burnt Oak HA8 . . . . 27 A3
Putney SW15 . . . . 134 B1
West Kilburn W10 . . . . . . 91 A3
Briarwood Cl
Feltham TW13 . . . . 149 C1
Kingsbury NW9 . . . . 45 A3
Briarwood Ct 5 KT4 . . 200 A1
Briarwood Dr HA6 . . . . . 22 A1
Briarwood Rd
London SW4. . . . . 159 D6
Stoneleigh KT17. . . . . . . 216 A2
Briary Cl NW3 . . . . 70 C1
Briary Ct
10 Canning Town E16. . . . 98 D1
Sidcup DA14. . . . . 190 B5
Briary Gdns BR1 . . . . . . 187 B5
Briary Gr HA8. . . . . 26 D1
Briary La N9. . . . . 17 D1
Briary Lo BR3. . . . . 186 A2
Brickbarn Cl SW10. . . . 266 B4
Brick Ct EC4 . . . . 241 A1
Brickett Cl HA4 . . . . 39 A4
Brick Farm Cl TW9. . . . 132 D4
Brickfield Cl TW8. . . . . . 131 C5
Brickfield Cotts SE18. . 145 D6
Brickfield Farm Gdns
BR6 . . . . 227 A4
Brickfield La
Edgware EN5 . . . . 11 D5
Harlington UB3 . . . . 127 B6
Brickfield Rd
South Norwood CR7,
SW16 . . . . 182 D2
Wimbledon SW19 . . . . . 179 D6
Brickfields HA2. . . . . 64 B6
Brickfields Way UB7 . . 104 B3
Brick La
Enfield EN1. . . . . 6 B3
Northolt UB5 . . . . 85 B4
Shoreditch E2. . . . . 95 D4
Spitalfields E1 . . 95 D3 243 D5
Stanmore HA7 . . . . 25 D3
Bricklayers Arms SE1 . 262 D5
Brick St W1 . . . 115 B5 248 C3
Brickwall La HA4 . . . . . . 39 D1
Brickwood Cl SE26. . . . 162 B1
Brickwood Rd CR0 . . . . 221 C6
Brickworth Ho 26
SW9. . . . . 138 C4
Brideale Cl SE15 . . . . . . 139 D6
Bride Ct EC4. . . . . 241 C1
Bride La EC4. . . . 94 D1 241 C1
Bridel Mews N1 . . . . . . 234 C5
Bride St N7. . . . . 72 B2
Bridewain St SE1 . . . . . 263 C6
Bridewell Pl
Holborn EC4. . . . . 241 C1
20 Wapping E1. . . . . 118 B5
Bridford Mews W1. . . . 238 D4
Bridge App NW3. . . . . . . 71 A1
Bridge Ave
Ealing W7. . . . . 86 B2
Hammersmith W6 . . . . . 112 C1
Bridge Avenue Mans 1
W6. . . . . 112 C1
Bridge Bsns Ctr The
UB2. . . . . 107 C4
Bridge Cl
Enfield EN1. . . . . 6 B3
13 North Kensington
W10. . . . . 90 D1
Teddington TW11 . . . . . . 174 D6
Walton-on-T KT12 . . . . . 193 D1
Bridge Ct
9 Blackwall E14 . . . . . . 120 B6
Bridge Ct *continued*
Leyton E10 . . . . 53 B2
2 Walton-on-T KT12. . . 193 D1
7 Willesden NW10. . . . . 67 C1
Bridge Dr N13 . . . . 32 B6
Bridge End E17 . . . . 36 A2
Bridge Field Ho 7
W2. . . . . 91 D1
Bridgefield Rd SM1 . . . 217 C2
Bridgefoot
SE1. . . . . 116 A1 260 B1
Bridge Gate N21 . . . . 17 A4
Bridge Gdns
Canonbury N16 . . . . 73 B4
East Molesey KT8. . . . . . 196 B5
Littleton TW15 . . . . 171 A3
Bridge Ho
Brockley SE4 . . . . 141 B1
1 Camden Town NW1. . . 71 A1
Ealing TW8. . . . . 109 A2
Homerton E9 . . . . 74 D3
Woolwich SE28 . . . . 123 C5
Bridge Ho S TW8. . . . . . 109 A2
Bridge House Quay
E14. . . . . 120 A5
Bridge La
Battersea
SW11 . . . . . . 136 C4 267 B1
Temple Fortune NW11 . . . 47 B4
Bridgeland Rd E16. . . . 121 A6
Bridgelands Cl BR3 . . . 185 B3
Bridgeman Ho 19 E9 . . . 74 C1
Bridgeman Rd
Islington N1. . . . . 72 B1
Teddington TW11. . . . . . 175 A4
Bridgeman St
NW8. . . . . 92 C5 230 A3
Bridge Meadows
SE14. . . . . 140 D6
Bridgend Rd SW18 . . . . 136 A1
Bridgenhall Rd EN1 . . . . . 5 D4
Bridgen Ho 9 E1 . . . . . . 96 B1
Bridgen Rd DA5. . . . . . . 169 A4
Bridge Par
7 Croydon CR0 . . . . 220 D5
Edmonton N21 . . . . 17 A4
Bridge Pk
7 London SW18 . . . . . . 157 C6
Wembley NW10. . . . . 66 D1
Bridge Pl
Belgravia
SW1 . . . . 115 B2 258 D4
Croydon CR0 . . . . 205 B1
Bridgepoint Lofts 2
E7. . . . . 77 C1
Bridgeport Pl 4 E1 . . . 118 A5
Bridge Rd
Beckenham BR3. . . . . . . 185 B3
Bexleyheath DA7 . . . . . . 147 A3
Chessington KT9 . . . . . . 214 A3
East Ham E6. . . . . 78 B1
East Molesey KT8. . . . . . 196 C5
Isleworth TW3, TW7. . . . 130 B2
Southall UB2 . . . . 107 C4
Stratford Marsh E15 . . . . 98 B6
Sutton SM2 . . . . 217 D2
Twickenham TW1. . . . . . 153 B5
Wallington SM6 . . . . 219 C3
Walthamstow E17 . . . . . . 53 B2
Wembley HA9. . . . . 66 C5
Willesden NW10 . . . . 67 C2
Wood Green N22 . . . . 32 A2
Bridge Row CR0 . . . . . . 205 B1
Bridge Sch The
Clerkenwell
EC1 . . . . 94 D3 241 C6
Shoreditch N1 . . 95 A6 235 B6
Bridges Ct SW11. . . . . . 136 B3
Bridges Ho 15 SE5 . . . . 139 B5
Bridges La CR0 . . . . 220 A4
Bridges Rd
Stanmore HA7 . . . . 24 D5
Wimbledon SW19 . . . . . 179 D4
Bridges Road Mews
SW19. . . . . 179 D4
Bridge St
Chiswick W4. . . . . 111 B2
Pinner HA5. . . . . 41 A6
Richmond TW10. . . . . . . 153 D6
Walton-on-T KT12 . . . . . 193 D2
Westminster
SW1 . . . . 116 A4 250 B1
Bridges The NW4 . . . . . . 46 A6
Bridge Terr E15. . . . . 76 B1
Bridge The HA3. . . . . 42 D5
Bridgetown Cl 5
SE19. . . . . 183 C5
Bridgeview 2 W6 . . . . . 112 C1
Bridgewater Cl BR7 . . . 211 C6
Bridgewater Ct HA0. . . . 65 C2
Bridgewater Gdns HA8 . 26 B1
Bridgewater Ho UB5 . . . 85 A3
Bridgewater Rd
Ruislip HA4. . . . . 62 B4
Stratford Marsh E15 . . . . 98 A6
Wembley HA0. . . . . 65 C1
Bridgewater Sq EC2. . . 242 A4
Bridgewater St EC2 . . . 242 A4
Bridgeway
Barking IG11 . . . . 79 D1
Wembley HA0. . . . . 66 B1
Bridge Way
London NW11 . . . . 47 B4
Twickenham TW2 . . . . . . 152 A4
Uxbridge UB10. . . . . 60 D3
Bridgeway St
NW1. . . . . 93 C5 232 B3
Bridge Wharf 18 E2 . . . . 96 D5
Bridge Wharf Rd
TW7. . . . . 131 B2
Bridgewood Cl SE20 . . 184 B3
Bridgewood Rd
North Cheam KT17,
KT4 . . . . 216 A4
Streatham SW16 . . . . . . 181 D3
Bridge Yd SE1 . . . . 252 D4
Bridgford St SW17,
SW18. . . . . 158 A1
Bridgman Rd W4 . . . . . 111 A3
Bridgnorth Ho 10
SE15. . . . . 140 A6
Bridgwater Ho W2. . . . 236 A2
Bridle Cl
Enfield EN3. . . . . 7 B6
Kingston u T KT1. . . . . . 197 D5
Sunbury TW16 . . . . 194 A6
West Ewell KT19 . . . . . . 215 B3
Bridle La
Marylebone
W1 . . . . 115 C6 249 B6
Twickenham TW1 . . . . . . 153 B5
Bridle Path CR0. . . . . . . 220 A5
Bridle Path The IG8. . . . 36 C3
Bridlepath Way
TW14. . . . . 149 C3
Bridle Rd
Addington CR0 . . . . 223 C4
Claygate KT10 . . . . 213 B2
Croydon CR0 . . . . 223 C6
Pinner HA5. . . . . 40 C4
Bridle Way
Addington CR0 . . . . 223 C3
Orpington BR6 . . . . 227 A4
Bridle Way The SM6. . . 219 C3
Bridlington Ho SW18. . 136 A1
Bridlington Rd N9 . . . . . 18 B4
Bridport SE17 . . . . 262 B1
Bridport Ave RM7 . . . . . . 59 D3
Bridport Ho
6 Edmonton N18 . . . . . . 34 A5
Shoreditch N1 . . . . 235 D5
Bridport Pl N1. . . 95 B6 235 D5
Bridport Rd
Edmonton N18 . . . . 33 D5
Greenford UB6. . . . . 85 D6
Thornton Heath CR7. . . . 204 D6
Bridstow Pl W2. . . . . 91 C1
Brief St SE5 . . . . 138 D4
Brierfield NW1 . . . . 232 A5
Brierley CR0. . . . . 223 D2
Brierley Ave N9. . . . . 18 C3
Brierley Cl SE25. . . . . . . 206 A5
Brierley Ct W7. . . . . 108 C6
Brierley Rd
Leyton E11 . . . . 76 B4
Upper Tooting SW12 . . . 159 C2
Brierly Gdns E2. . . . . 96 C5
Brigade Cl HA2 . . . . 64 B6
Brigade St SE3. . . . . 142 D3
Brigadier Ave EN2 . . . . . . 5 A4
Brigadier Hill EN2. . . . . . . 5 A5
Briggeford Cl 5 E5 . . . . 74 A6
Briggs Cl CR4. . . . . 181 B2
Briggs Ho 20 E2. . . . . 95 D4
Bright Cl DA17 . . . . 124 D2
Bright Ct 8 SE28 . . . . . 124 C5
Brightfield Rd SE12 . . . 164 D6
Brightling Rd SE4. . . . . 163 B5
Brightlingsea Pl 5
E14. . . . . 119 B6
Brightman Rd SW18. . . 158 B3
Brighton Ave E17 . . . . . . 53 B4
Brighton Bldgs SE1 . . . 263 A5
Brighton Cl UB10 . . . . . . 60 D1
Brighton Ct SW15. . . . . 157 B5
Brighton Dr 3 UB5 . . . . 63 C2
Brighton Gr SE14 . . . . . 141 A4
Brighton Ho 7 SE5 . . . 139 B4
Brighton Rd
Belmont SM2 . . . . 217 D1
Brighton Rd *continued*
Finchley N2 . . . . 30 A1
South Croydon CR2 . . . . 221 B2
Stoke Newington N16. . . . 73 C4
Surbiton KT6 . . . . 197 D3
Sutton SM2 . . . . 218 A1
Wallend E6. . . . . 100 C4
Brighton Terr SW9. . . . . 138 B1
Brightside Rd SE13. . . . 164 B5
Brightside The EN3 . . . . . 7 A4
Bright St E14 . . . . 97 D2
Brightwell Cl CR0 . . . . . 204 C1
Brightwell Cres
SW17. . . . . 180 D5
Brightwell Ct N7. . . . . . . 72 B3
Brightwells 1 SW6 . . . 135 D3
Brig Mews SE8 . . . . 141 C6
Brigstock Ho SE5 . . . . . 139 A3
Brigstock Par 1 CR7. . 204 C4
Brigstock Rd
Belvedere DA17 . . . . 125 D2
Thornton Heath CR7. . . . 204 D4
Brill Ho NW10 . . . . 67 B5
Brill Pl NW1 . . . . 93 D5 232 D3
Brim Hill N2. . . . . 48 B5
Brimpsfield Cl SE2. . . . 124 B3
BRIMSDOWN 7 B3
Brimsdown Ave EN3 . . . . 7 A4
Brimsdown Ho E3 . . . . . 98 A3
Brimsdown Jun & Inf Sch
EN3. . . . . 6 D2
Brimsdown Sta EN3. . . . . 7 A3
Brimstone Ho 4 E15. . . . 76 C1
Brindishe Prim Sch
SE12 . . . . 164 D6
Brindle Gate DA15 . . . . 167 C3
Brindley Cl
Bexleyheath DA7 . . . . . . 147 D2
Wembley HA0. . . . . 87 D6
Brindley Ho
Carshalton SM1 . . . . 218 C3
37 Notting Hill W2 . . . . . . 91 C2
22 Streatham SW12. . . . . 160 A4
Brindley St SE14 . . . . . . 141 B4
Brindley Way
Bromley BR1 . . . . 187 B5
Southall UB1 . . . . 107 D6
Brindwood Rd E4 . . . . . . 19 C1
Brine Ct KT6. . . . . 197 D4
Brine Ho 11 E3. . . . . 97 A5
Brinkburn Cl
Abbey Wood SE2. . . . . . . 124 A2
Edgware HA8. . . . . 44 D6
Brinkburn Gdns HA8 . . . 44 C6
Brinkley 18 KT1 . . . . . . 176 C1
Brinkley Rd KT4. . . . . . . 216 B6
Brinklow Cres SE18 . . . 144 D5
Brinklow Ho W2 . . . . 91 D2
Brinkworth Rd IG5. . . . . . 56 A6
Brinkworth Way E9 . . . . 75 B2
Brinsdale Rd NW4 . . . . . 46 D6
Brinsley Ho 17 E1 . . . . . . 96 C1
Brinsley Rd HA3 . . . . 24 B1
Brinsley St 35 E1. . . . . . . 96 B1
Brinsworth Cl TW2. . . . 152 B2
Brinton Wlk SE1 . . . . . . 251 C3
Brion Pl E14 . . . . 98 A2
Brisbane Ave SW19 . . . 179 D2
Brisbane Ct N10 . . . . 31 B3
Brisbane Ho 3 W12. . . 112 B6
Brisbane Rd
Ealing W13. . . . . 109 A4
Ilford IG1. . . . . 57 A1
Leyton E10 . . . . 75 D6
Brisbane St SE5. . . . . . . 139 B5
Briscoe Cl E11 . . . . 76 D6
Briscoe Rd SW19. . . . . . 180 B4
Briset Rd SE9 . . . . 143 D1
Briset St EC1 . . . 94 D3 241 C5
Briset Way N7 . . . . 72 B6
Bristol Cl
Stanwell TW19 . . . . 148 A5
Wallington SM6 . . . . 220 A1
Bristol Ct 11 TW19 . . . . 148 A5
Bristol Gdns
Putney SW15 . . . . 156 C4
Westbourne Green W9. . . 91 D3
Bristol Ho
1 Barking IG11. . . . . 80 A1
SE11. . . . . 261 A5
Bristol Mews W9 . . . . . . 91 D3
Bristol Park Rd 1 E17. . . 53 A5
Bristol Rd
Greenford UB6. . . . . 85 D6
Morden SM4. . . . . 202 A4
Upton E7 . . . . 77 D2
Briston Gr N8. . . . . 50 A3
Briston Mews NW7. . . . . 28 A3
Bristowe Cl 24 SW2 . . . 160 C5
Bristow Rd
Bexleyheath DA7 . . . . . . 147 A4
Hounslow TW3. . . . . 130 A2
Wallington CR0 . . . . 220 A4
West Norwood SE19 . . . 183 C5
Britain at War
Experience*
SE1 . . . . 253 A3
Britannia Building N1 . 235 C2
Britannia Cl
London SW4. . . . . 137 D1
Northolt UB5 . . . . 84 D4
Britannia Gate 11
E16. . . . . 121 A5
Britannia Ho N20 . . . . . . 14 A1
Britannia Junc NW1. . . 231 D6
Britannia La TW2 . . . . . 152 A4
Britannia Rd
Ilford IG1. . . . . 78 D5
23 Millwall E14 . . . . 119 C2
Surbiton KT5 . . . . 198 B2
Walham Green
SW6 . . . . 135 D5 265 C3
Whetstone N12 . . . . 14 A1
Britannia Row
N1 . . . . 95 A6 235 A6
Britannia St
WC1. . . . . 94 B4 233 C2
Britannia Village Prim Sch
E16 . . . . 121 B5
Britannia Way NW10 . . . 88 D3
Britannia Wlk N1 . . . . . 235 C2
British Coll of Osteopathic
Medicine NW3. . . . . 70 A2
British Gr W4. . . . . 111 D1
British Grove Pas 2
W4. . . . . 111 D1
British Grove S 3
W4. . . . . 111 D1
British Home & Hospl for
Incurables SE27 . . . . . 182 D5
British Legion Rd E4 . . . 20 D2
British Library
(Newspaper Library)
NW9 . . . . 45 C6
British Library The*
WC1 . . . . 93 D4 232 D2
British Mus*
WC1 . . . . 94 A2 240 A3
British St E3. . . . . 97 B4
British Wharf Ind Est
SE14 . . . . 140 D6
Britley Ho 16 E14 . . . . . . 97 B1
Brittain Ct SE9. . . . . 166 A3
Brittain Rd RM8. . . . . 81 B5
Brittany Ho SW15 . . . . . 134 C1
Brittany Point SE11 . . . 261 A3
Britten Cl
Elstree WD6. . . . . 9 D5
Golders Green NW11. . . . 47 D1
Brittenden Cl 1 BR6 . . 227 D2
Brittenden Par BR6 . . . 227 D2
Britten Dr UB1. . . . . 85 C1
Britten Ho SW3 . . . . 257 B2
Britten St
SW3. . . . . 114 C1 257 A2
Britton Cl SE6 . . . . 164 B4
Britton St EC1 . . 94 D3 241 C5
Brixham Cres HA4 . . . . . 40 A1
Brixham Gdns IG3 . . . . . 79 C3
Brixham Rd DA16 . . . . . 146 D4
Brixham St E16 . . . . 122 C5
BRIXTON 138 C2
Brixton Day Coll SW9 . 138 A2
Brixton Hill SW2 . . . . . . 160 B5
Brixton Hill Ct 5
SW2. . . . . 160 B6
Brixton Hill Pl SW2. . . . 160 A4
Brixton Mkt SW9. . . . . . 138 C1
Brixton Oval 7 SW2 . . 138 C1
Brixton Rd SW9. . . . . . . 138 C4
Brixton Sta SW9 . . . . . . 138 C1
Brixton Station Rd
SW9. . . . . 138 C2
Brixton Water La
SW2. . . . . 160 B6
Broadacre Cl UB10. . . . . 60 D5
Broadbent Cl N6. . . . . . . 49 B1
Broadbent St W1 . . . . . 248 C6
Broadberry Ct N18 . . . . . 34 B5
Broadbridge Cl SE3 . . . 143 A5
Broad Common Est
N16 . . . . 52 A1
Broadcoombe CR2. . . . 222 D1
Broadcroft Ave HA7. . . . 25 D1
Broadcroft Rd BR5. . . . 211 B2
Broad Ct WC2 . . . . 240 B1
Broadeaves Cl CR2. . . . 221 C3
Broadfield NW6 . . . . 69 D2
Broadfield Cl
Croydon CR0 . . . . 220 B6
Dollis Hill NW2. . . . . 68 C5
Broadfield Ct
Bushey WD23. . . . . 8 C2
Edgware HA8. . . . . 10 D1
Broadfield La NW1 . . . . . 72 A1
Broadfield Rd SE6 . . . . 164 C3
Broadfields
Harrow HA2. . . . . 23 D1
Thames Ditton KT8. . . . . 196 C3
Broadfields Ave
Edgware HA8. . . . . 10 D1
Southgate N21. . . . . 16 C4
Broadfields Hts HA8 . . . 26 D6
Broadfields Prim Sch
HA8. . . . . 10 C2
Broadfield Sq EN1 . . . . . . 6 B3
Broadfields Way
NW10. . . . . 67 D3
Broadfield Way IG9. . . . 21 C1
Broadford Ho 12 E1 . . . . 97 A3
BROADGATE. 95 C2
Broadgate EC2 . . 95 C2 243 A4
Broadgate Circ
EC2. . . . . 95 C2 243 A3
Broadgate Rd E16. . . . . . 99 D1
Broadgates Ave EN4 . . . . 1 D4
Broadgates Ct SE11 . . . 261 B1
Broadgates Rd SW18. . 158 B3
BROAD GREEN. 204 D3
Broad Green Ave
CR0 . . . . 204 D2
Broadhead Strand
NW9. . . . . 27 D2
Broadheath Dr BR7 . . . 188 B5
Broadhinton Rd SW4. . 137 C2
Broadhurst Ave
Edgware HA8. . . . . 26 D6
Ilford IG3. . . . . 79 D4
Broadhurst Cl
Hampstead NW6 . . . . 70 A2
9 Richmond TW10 . . . . 154 B6
Broadhurst Gdns
Hampstead NW6 . . . . 69 D2
Ruislip HA4. . . . . 62 C6
Broadhurst Mans NW6 . 69 D2
Broad La
Broadgate EC2. . . . . 243 A4
Hampton TW12 . . . . 173 C4
Hornsey Vale N8. . . . . 50 B4
South Tottenham N15. . . . 51 D5
South Tottenham N15. . . . 52 A5
Broadlands
Feltham TW13 . . . . 151 C1
Highgate N6. . . . . 49 A2
Broadlands Ave
Enfield EN3. . . . . 6 B2
Shepperton TW17 . . . . . 193 A3
Streatham SW16 . . . . . . 160 A2
Broadlands Cl
Enfield EN3. . . . . 6 C2
Highgate N6. . . . . 49 A2
Streatham SW16 . . . . . . 160 A2
Broadlands Ct TW9 . . . 132 C5
Broadlands Lo N6. . . . . . 48 D2
Broadlands Mans 2
SW16. . . . . 160 A2
Broadlands Rd
Grove Pk BR1 . . . . 187 B6
Highgate N6. . . . . 48 D2
Broadlands Way KT3 . . 199 D3
Broad Lawn SE9 . . . . . . 166 C3
Broadlawns Ct HA3 . . . . 24 D2
Broadley St
NW8. . . . . 92 C2 237 A4
Broadley Terr
NW1. . . . . 92 C3 237 B5
Broadmayne SE17 . . . . 262 C2
Broadmead
Catford SE6 . . . . 163 C1
Hampton TW12 . . . . 173 C4
West Kensington W14 . . 254 A3
Broadmead Ave KT4 . . 200 A2
Broadmead Cl
Hampton TW12 . . . . 173 C4
Pinner HA5. . . . . 23 A3
Broadmead Ct 6 IG8 . . . 37 A4
Broadmead Inf Sch
CR0. . . . . 205 B2
Broadmead Jun Sch
CR0. . . . . 205 B3
Broadmead Rd
Northolt UB5 . . . . 85 A3
Woodford IG8 . . . . 37 B3
Broad Oak
Ashford TW16 . . . . 171 D4
Woodford IG8 . . . . 37 B5
Broad Oak Cl
Chingford E4 . . . . 35 C5

Broad Oak Cl *continued*
St Paul's Cray BR5 ... 190 A1
Broadoak Ct 8 SW9 ... 138 C2
Broadoak Ho 11 NW6 ... 91 D6
Broadoaks BR7 ... 188 D4
Broad Oaks KT6 ... 214 D6
Broadoaks Way BR2 ... 208 D4
Broad St Ave EC2 ... 243 A3
Broad Sanctuary SW1 250 A1
Broad St
Dagenham RM10 ... 81 C1
Teddington TW11 ... 174 D4
Broadstone Ho SW8 ... 270 C3
Broadstone Pl W1 ... 238 A3
Broad Street Health Ctr
RM10 ... 103 C6
Broad Street Pl EC2 ... 242 D3
Broadview NW9 ... 44 C3
Broadview Est TW19 ... 148 C4
Broadview Ho RM8 ... 58 D1
Broadview Rd SW16 ... 181 D3
Broadwalk
Harrow HA2 ... 41 D4
Snaresbrook E18 ... 54 D6
Broadwalk Ho SW7 ... 246 A1
Broadwalk La NW11 ... 47 B2
Broadwalk Sh Ctr The
HA8 ... 26 D4
Broadwall SE1 . 116 C5 251 B4
Broadwater Farm Prim
Sch N17 ... 33 B1
Broadwater Gdns
BR6 ... 227 A4
Broadwater Prim Sch
SW17 ... 180 C6
Broadwater Rd
Plumstead SE18 ... 123 B3
Tottenham N17 ... 33 C1
Upper Tooting SW17 ... 180 C6
Broadway
Barking IG11 ... 101 A6
Bexley DA6 ... 147 C1
Bexleyheath DA6 ... 147 B1
Hanwell W7 ... 108 C5
Stratford E15 ... 76 B1
West Ealing W13 ... 109 A5
Westminster
SW1 ... 115 D3 259 C6
Broadway Arc 3 W6 ... 112 C2
Broadway Ave
Thornton Heath CR0 ... 205 B4
Twickenham TW1 ... 153 B5
Broadway Bldgs 5
W7 ... 108 C5
Broadway Cl IG8 ... 37 B4
Broadway Ct
Beckenham BR3 ... 208 A6
Wimbledon SW19 ... 179 C4
Broadway Ctr The 6
W6 ... 112 C2
Broadway Gdns
Mitcham CR4 ... 202 C5
Woodford IG8 ... 37 B4
Broadway Ho 2 E8 ... 96 B6
Broadway Ho 5
SW19 ... 179 C3
Broadway Lofts
SW17 ... 180 C6
Broadway Mans SW6 ... 265 B3
Broadway Market E8 ... 96 B6
Broadway Market Mews
21 E8 ... 96 A6
Broadway Mews
Bowes Pk N13 ... 32 B5
Southgate N21 ... 16 D3
Stamford Hill E5 ... 51 D2
Broadway Par
Chingford E4 ... 36 A4
Hayes UB3 ... 106 A5
Hornsey N8 ... 50 A3
West Drayton UB7 ... 104 A4
Broadway Pl SW19 ... 179 B4
Broadway Ret Pk NW2 . 68 D4
Broadway Sh Ctr 5
DA6 ... 147 C1
Broadway The
Barnes SW13 ... 133 C3
Cheam SM3 ... 217 A2
Chingford E4 ... 36 B4
Dagenham RM8 ... 81 C6
Ealing W5 ... 109 D6
Edgware NW7 ... 27 D5
Edmonton N9 ... 18 A1
Friern Barnet N11 ... 31 A5
Greenford UB6 ... 86 A3
Harrow HA3 ... 24 D1
Hornsey N8 ... 50 A3
Merton SW19 ... 179 C3
Newham E13 ... 99 B5
Pinner HA5 ... 23 B3

Broadway The *continued*
South Acton W3 ... 110 C4
Southall UB1 ... 107 A6
2 Southgate N14 ... 15 D3
Stanmore HA7 ... 25 C5
Sutton SM1 ... 218 A4
Thames Ditton KT10 ... 196 C1
Tolworth KT6 ... 198 C1
Wallington SM6 ... 220 A4
Wembley HA9 ... 66 A5
Woodford IG8 ... 37 B4
Wood Green N22 ... 32 C1
Broadway Wlk 4
E14 ... 119 C3
Broadwell Ct TW5 ... 128 D4
Broadwick St
W1 ... 93 C1 239 B1
Broad Wlk
Eltham SE3, SE18 ... 144 A3
Heston TW5 ... 129 A4
Mayfair W1 ... 115 A5 248 A4
Regent's Pk
NW1 ... 93 A5 231 B3
Richmond TW9 ... 132 B5
Southgate N21 ... 16 B3
Broad Wlk The
W8 ... 113 D5 245 D3
Broadwood Ave HA4 ... 39 C3
Broadwood Terr W14 . 254 D4
Broad Yd EC1 ... 241 C5
Brocade Ct NW9 ... 45 D5
Brocas Cl NW3 ... 70 C1
Brockbridge Ho
SW15 ... 155 D5
Brockdene Dr BR2 ... 225 D4
Brockdish Ave IG11 ... 79 D3
Brockelbank Lo RM8 ... 80 D6
Brockenhurst KT8 ... 195 B3
Brockenhurst Ave
KT4 ... 199 C1
Brockenhurst Gdns
Edgware NW7 ... 27 C5
Ilford IG1 ... 79 A3
Brockenhurst Mews 9
N18 ... 34 A6
Brockenhurst Rd CR0 . 206 B2
Brockenhurst Way
SW16 ... 181 D1
Brocket Ho 16 SW8 ... 137 D3
Brockham Cl SW19 ... 179 B5
Brockham Cres CR0 ... 224 B1
Brockham Ct
17 Belmont SM2 ... 217 D1
8 South Croydon CR2 .. 221 A3
Brockham Dr
Ilford IG2 ... 57 A4
Streatham SW2 ... 160 B4
Brockham Ho
Camden Town NW1 ... 232 B5
11 Streatham SW2 ... 160 B4
Brockham St SE1 ... 262 B6
Brockhurst Cl HA7 ... 24 D4
Brockhurst Ho N4 ... 51 B2
Brockill Cres SE4 ... 141 A1
Brocklebank Ho 7
E16 ... 122 C5
Brocklebank Rd
Greenwich SE7 ... 121 B2
Wandsworth SW18 ... 158 A4
Brocklebank Road Ind Est
SE7 ... 121 A2
Brocklehurst St SE14 . 140 D5
Brocklesby Rd SE25 ... 206 B5
BROCKLEY ... 141 B1
Brockley Ave HA7 ... 10 A1
Brockley Cl HA7 ... 26 A6
Brockley Cross SE4 ... 141 B2
Brockley Cross Bsns Ctr
SE4 ... 141 A2
Brockley Gdns SE4 ... 141 B3
Brockley Gr SE4 ... 163 B6
Brockley Hall Rd SE4 .. 163 A6
Brockley Hill HA7, HA8 ... 9 D2
Brockley Hill Ho HA7 ... 9 C3
Brockley Ho SE17 ... 263 A2
Brockley Mews SE4 ... 163 A6
Brockley Pk SE23 ... 163 A4
Brockley Prim Sch
SE4 ... 163 B6
Brockley Rd SE4 ... 163 B6
Brockley Rise SE23 ... 163 A4
Brockleyside HA7 ... 26 A6
Brockley Sta SE4 ... 141 A2
Brockley View SE23 ... 163 A4
Brockley Way SE4 ... 163 A6
Brockman Rise BR1 ... 186 B6
Brockmer Ho 5 E1 ... 118 B6
Brock Pl E3 ... 97 D3
Brock Rd E13 ... 99 B2
Brocks Dr SM3 ... 217 A5

Brockshot Cl 1 TW8 ... 131 D6
Brock St SE15 ... 140 C2
Brockway Cl E11 ... 76 C6
Brockweir 28 E2 ... 96 C5
Brockwell Ave BR3 ... 207 D4
Brockwell Cl BR5 ... 211 D4
Brockwell Ct
2 London SW2 ... 160 C6
Thornton Heath CR0 ... 204 D2
Brockwell Ho SE11 ... 270 D6
Brockwell Park*
SE24 160 D5
Brockwell Park Gdns
SE24 ... 160 D4
Brockwell Park Row
SW2 ... 160 C5
Brockworth 8 KT2 ... 176 D2
Broderick Ho SE21 ... 161 C1
Brodia Rd N16 ... 73 C5
Brodick Ho 12 E3 ... 97 B5
Brodie Ct E10 ... 54 B1
Brodie Ho
Bermondsey SE1 ... 263 D2
7 Wallington SM6 ... 219 B4
Brodie Rd
Chingford E4 ... 20 A2
Enfield EN2 ... 5 A5
Brodie St SE1 .. 117 D1 263 D2
Brodlove La E1 ... 118 D6
Brodrick Gr SE2 ... 124 B2
Brodrick Rd SW17 ... 158 C2
Brody Ho E1 ... 243 C3
Brograve Gdns BR3 ... 185 D1
Broken Wharf EC4 ... 252 A6
Brokesley St E3 ... 97 B4
Broke Wlk
Hackney E8 ... 95 D6
1 Hackney E8 ... 96 A6
Bromar Rd SE5 ... 139 C2
Bromborough Gn
WD19 ... 22 C5
Bromefield HA7 ... 25 C2
Bromehead St 8 E1 ... 96 C1
Bromell's Rd SW4 ... 137 C1
Brome Rd SE9 ... 144 B2
Bromfelde Rd SW4 ... 137 D3
Bromfield Ct 20 SE16 . 118 A3
Bromfield St N1 ... 234 B4
Bromhall Rd RM8 ... 80 B2
Bromhedge SE9 ... 166 B1
Bromholm Rd SE2 ... 124 B3
Bromleigh Ct 1 SE21,
SE22 ... 162 B2
Bromleigh Ho SE1 ... 263 C6
BROMLEY
BR1 ... 186 C2
E3 ... 97 D4
Bromley Ave BR1 ... 186 C3
Bromley-by-Bow Sta
E3 ... 98 A4
Bromley Coll BR1 ... 187 A2
Bromley Coll of F & H Ed
BR2 ... 209 D3
Bromley Comm BR2 ... 209 D4
BROMLEY COMMON . 210 A3
Bromley Cres
Beckenham BR2 ... 208 D6
Ruislip HA4 ... 61 D4
Bromley Ct BR1 ... 186 D3
Bromley Gdns BR2 ... 208 D6
Bromley Gr BR2 ... 186 B1
Bromley Hall Rd E14 ... 98 A2
Bromley High Sch
BR1 ... 210 C5
Bromley High St E3 ... 97 D4
Bromley Hill BR1 ... 186 C4
Bromley Ho 5 BR1 ... 187 A2
Bromley Ind Ctr BR1 .. 209 D6
Bromley La BR7 ... 189 B3
Bromley Lo 2 W3 ... 89 A1
Bromley Manor Mans 3
BR1 ... 209 A6
Bromley North Sta
BR1 ... 187 A2
BROMLEY PARK ... 186 D2
Bromley Pk 11 BR1 ... 186 D2
Bromley Pl W1 ... 239 A4
Bromley Rd
Beckenham BR3 ... 185 D2
Bromley BR2, BR3 ... 186 B1
Catford SE6 ... 163 D1
Chislehurst BR7 ... 188 D2
Edmonton N18 ... 17 B1
Leyton E10 ... 53 D3
Tottenham N17 ... 34 A2
Walthamstow E17 ... 53 C6
Bromley Road Inf Sch
BR3 ... 185 D2
Bromley Road Ret Pk
SE6 ... 163 D2

Bromley South Sta
BR2 ... 209 A6
Bromley St E1 ... 96 D1
BROMPTON ... 114 B3
Brompton Arc SW1 ... 247 D1
Brompton Cl
Hounslow TW4 ... 151 B6
Penge SE20 ... 184 A1
Brompton Ct 4 HA7 ... 25 C6
Brompton Gr N2 ... 48 C5
Brompton Ho 3 N9 ... 34 A6
Brompton Oratory
SW3 ... 114 C3 257 A5
Brompton Park Cres
SW6 ... 135 D6 265 C5
Brompton Pl
SW3 ... 114 C3 257 B6
Brompton Rd
SW3 ... 114 C3 257 A5
Brompton Sq
SW3 ... 114 C3 257 A6
Bromstone Ho 19
SW9 ... 138 C4
Bromwich Ave N6 ... 71 A6
Bromwich Ho 3
TW10 ... 154 A5
Bromyard Ave W3 ... 111 C6
Bromyard Ho
Acton W3 ... 111 C5
3 Peckham SE15 ... 140 B5
Bron Ct NW6 ... 91 C6
BRONDESBURY ... 69 A2
Brondesbury Coll for Boys
NW6 ... 69 A1
Brondesbury Ct NW2 .. 68 D2
Brondesbury Mews 11
NW6 ... 69 C1
BRONDESBURY PARK . 90 D6
Brondesbury Park Sta
NW6 ... 91 A6
Brondesbury Pk NW2 .. 68 D1
Brondesbury Rd NW6 .. 91 C5
Brondesbury Sta NW6 .. 69 B1
Brondesbury Villas
NW6 ... 91 C5
Bronhill Terr N17 ... 34 A2
Bronsart Rd
SW6 ... 135 A5 264 A3
Bronson Rd SW20 ... 179 A1
Bronte Cl
Erith DA8 ... 147 D5
1 Forest Gate E7 ... 77 A4
Ilford IG2 ... 56 C5
Bronte Ct 8 W14 ... 112 D3
Bronte Ho
Kilburn NW6 ... 91 C4
6 Stoke Newington
N16 ... 73 C3
Bronti Cl SE17 . 117 A1 262 B2
Bronwen Ct NW8 ... 229 C1
Bronze Age Way
DA17 ... 125 D4
Bronze St SE8 ... 141 C5
Brook Ave
Dagenham RM10 ... 81 D1
Edgware HA8 ... 26 D4
Wembley HA9 ... 66 C5
Brook Bank EN1 ... 6 B6
Brookbank Ave W7 ... 86 B2
Brookbank Rd SE13 ... 141 D2
Brook Cl
Acton W3 ... 110 C5
Finchley N12 ... 29 A3
Ruislip HA4 ... 39 C2
Stanwell TW19 ... 148 B4
Upper Tooting SW17 ... 159 A2
West Barnes SW20 ... 200 B6
Brook Com Prim Sch
E8 ... 74 A3
Brook Cres
Chingford E4 ... 35 D6
Edmonton N9 ... 34 B6
Brook Ct
Barking IG11 ... 101 D6
Beckenham BR3 ... 185 B2
5 Brentford TW8 ... 131 D6
Cheam SM3 ... 216 C4
Edgware HA8 ... 26 D5
2 Leyton E11 ... 76 C5
Mortlake SW14 ... 133 C2
Stratford New Town E15 .. 76 A3
Walthamstow E17 ... 53 A6
Brookdale N11 ... 31 C6
Brookdale Rd
Catford SE6 ... 163 D4
Lewisham SE6 ... 163 D5
Sidcup DA5 ... 169 A5
Walthamstow E17 ... 53 C6
Brookdales The NW4 ... 47 A5
Brookdene N12 ... 29 D6

Brookdene Rd SE18,
SE2 ... 123 D2
Brook Dr
Harrow HA1 ... 42 A5
Newington
SE11 ... 116 D2 261 C4
Ruislip HA4 ... 39 C2
Brooke Ave HA2 ... 64 A5
Brooke Cl WD23 ... 8 A4
Brooke Ct
Kilburn W10 ... 91 A5
7 Kingston u T KT2 ... 175 D6
Brooke Ho
Bushey WD23 ... 8 A4
4 New Cross Gate
SE14 ... 141 A4
Brookehowse Rd SE6 . 163 D1
Brookend Rd DA15 ... 167 C3
Brooke Rd
Shacklewell E5, N16 ... 74 A5
Walthamstow E17 ... 54 A5
Brookes Ct EC1 ... 241 A4
Brooke's Mkt EC1 ... 241 B4
Brooke St EC1 ... 94 C2 241 A3
Brooke Way WD23 ... 8 A4
Brookfield
Dartmouth Pk N6 ... 71 A5
1 Finsbury Pk N4 ... 72 C6
Brookfield Ave
Carshalton SM1, SM5 ... 218 C5
Ealing W5 ... 87 D3
Mill Hill NW7 ... 28 B4
Walthamstow E17 ... 54 A5
Brookfield Cl NW7 ... 28 B4
Brookfield Cres
Harrow HA3 ... 44 A4
Mill Hill NW7 ... 28 B4
Brookfield Ct
Greenford UB6 ... 86 A4
1 London N12 ... 29 D6
Brookfield Gdns
KT10 ... 212 D2
Brookfield Ho 23 E2 ... 96 B5
Brookfield House Sch
IG8 ... 36 C4
Brookfield Path IG8 ... 36 C4
Brookfield Pk NW5 ... 71 B5
Brookfield Prim Sch
Cheam SM3 ... 201 A1
Dartmouth Pk N19 ... 71 B6
Brookfield Rd
Acton W4 ... 111 B4
Edmonton N9 ... 18 B1
Homerton E9 ... 75 A2
Brookfields EN3 ... 6 D1
Brookfields Ave CR4 .. 202 C4
Brookgate N16 ... 73 B6
Brook Gate
W1 ... 114 D6 247 D5
Brook Gdns
Barnes SW13 ... 133 D2
Chingford E4 ... 35 D6
Kingston u T KT2 ... 177 A2
Brook Gn W6 ... 112 D2
BROOK GREEN ... 112 D2
Brook Green Flats 11
W14 ... 112 D3
Brookhill Cl
East Barnet EN4 ... 14 C6
Woolwich SE18 ... 122 D1
Brookhill Ct 2 EN4 ... 14 C5
Brookhill Rd
East Barnet EN4 ... 14 C6
Woolwich SE18 ... 122 D1
Brook Ho
3 Clapham Pk SW4 ... 159 C6
Ealing W3 ... 110 C4
3 Edmonton N9 ... 18 A1
4 Hammersmith W6 ... 112 C2
Marylebone WC1 ... 239 C4
4 Twickenham TW1 ... 153 A4
Brook Hos NW1 ... 232 B3
Brookhouse Gdns E4 ... 36 C6
Brook House Sixth Form
Coll E5 ... 74 B5
Brook Ind Est UB4 ... 106 C5
Brooking Cl RM8 ... 80 C5
Brooking Rd E7 ... 77 A3
Brook La
Bexley DA5 ... 168 D5
Greenwich SE3 ... 143 B3
Plaistow BR1 ... 187 A4
Brook La N 3 TW8 ... 131 D6
Brookland Cl NW11 ... 47 C5
Brookland Garth
NW11 ... 47 D5
Brookland Hill NW11 ... 47 D5
Brookland Jun & Inf Schs
NW11 ... 47 D5
Brookland Rise NW11 . 47 C5

Brooklands Ave
New Eltham DA15 ... 167 B2
Wandsworth SW18 ... 157 D2
Brooklands Cl TW16 .. 171 C2
Brooklands Court
Apartments 3 NW6 .. 69 B1
Brooklands Ct
10 Clapham SW8 ... 137 C3
Enfield N21 ... 17 B6
Kingston u T KT1 ... 197 D5
2 London NW6 ... 69 B1
2 Mitcham CR4 ... 180 B1
Brooklands Dr UB6 ... 87 D6
Brooklands Ho SE3 ... 143 A2
Brooklands Pk SE3 ... 143 A2
Brooklands Pl TW12 .. 173 D5
Brooklands Prim Sch
SE3 ... 143 A2
Brooklands Rd KT7 ... 197 A1
Brooklands The TW7 .. 130 B4
Brook Lane Bns Ctr
TW8 ... 109 D1
Brooklea Cl NW9 ... 27 C2
Brook Lo
Crouch End N8 ... 49 D3
Edgware HA8 ... 26 D4
Hendon NW4 ... 46 D4
Brooklyn SE20 ... 184 A3
Brooklyn Ave SE25 ... 206 B5
Brooklyn Cl SM5 ... 218 C6
Brooklyn Ct
Feltham TW13 ... 150 B2
Shepherd's Bush W12 .. 112 C5
Brooklyn Gr SE25 ... 206 B5
Brooklyn Rd
Bromley BR2 ... 210 A4
Croydon SE25 ... 206 B5
Brookmarsh Ind Est
SE10 ... 141 D5
Brook Mdw N12 ... 13 D1
Brook Mead KT19 ... 215 C2
Brookmead Ave BR1,
BR2 ... 210 B4
Brookmead Ct N20 ... 14 A2
Brookmead Ind Est
CR4 ... 203 C3
Brook Meadow Cl IG8 .. 36 C4
Brookmead Rd CR0 ... 203 C3
Brook Mews N
W2 ... 114 A6 246 B6
Brookmill Rd SE8 ... 141 C4
Brook Park Cl N21 ... 16 D6
Brook Pl EN5 ... 13 C6
Brook Rd
Buckhurst Hill IG9 ... 21 A3
Dollis Hill NW2 ... 68 A6
Finchley N12 ... 30 C3
Hornsey N8 ... 50 A5
Ilford IG2 ... 57 C3
South Norwood CR7 ... 205 A5
Surbiton KT6 ... 214 A6
Twickenham TW1 ... 153 A5
Wood Green N22 ... 50 B6
Brook Rd S TW8 ... 131 D6
Brook Ret Pk HA4 ... 62 D3
Brooks Ave E6 ... 100 B3
Brooksbank Ho 7 E9 .. 74 C2
Brooksbank St 9 E9 .. 74 C2
Brooksby Ho 9 N1 ... 72 C1
Brooksby Mews N1 ... 72 C1
Brooksby St N1 ... 72 C1
Brooksby's Wlk E9 ... 74 D3
Brooks Cl SE9 ... 166 C2
Brookscroft E17 ... 53 D6
Brookscroft Rd E17 ... 35 D2
Brooks Ct
3 London SW4 ... 138 A3
Nine Elms SW8 ... 269 B4
Brookshill HA3 ... 24 B5
Brookshill Ave HA3 ... 24 C5
Brookshill Dr HA3 ... 24 B5
Brookshill Gate HA3 ... 24 B5
Brooks Ho 6 SW2 ... 160 C3
Brookside
Broom Hill BR6 ... 211 D2
East Barnet EN4 ... 14 C5
Hillingdon UB10 ... 60 B1
Southgate N21 ... 16 B5
Wallington SM5 ... 219 A3
Brookside Cl
Barnet EN5 ... 13 A5
Feltham TW13 ... 150 A1
Harrow HA3 ... 43 D4
South Harrow HA2, HA4 .. 63 A4
Brookside Cres 1
KT4 ... 200 A1
Brookside Ct SW16 ... 181 C3

Brookside Gdns EN1 6 C6
Brookside Ho N17 33 C1
Brookside Prim Sch UB4 84 C4
Brookside Rd
Edmonton N9 34 B6
Hayes UB4 106 C6
Temple Fortune NW11 47 B3
Upper Holloway N19 71 C6
Brookside S EN4 15 A4
Brookside Way CR0 206 D3
Brooks La W4 132 C6
Brook's Mans 5 IG3 58 B1
Brook's Mews W1 115 B6 248 C6
Brook's Par 6 IG3 58 B1
Brook Sq SE18 144 A4
Brooks Rd W4 110 C1
Brook's Rd E13 99 A6
Brook St
Bayswater W2 114 B6 246 D6
Erith DA8 147 D5
Kingston u T KT1 176 A1
Mayfair W1 115 B6 248 C6
7 Tottenham N17 33 D1
Brookstone Ct SE15 140 B1
Brooksville Ave NW6 91 A6
Brook Vale DA8 147 D4
Brookview Ct 11 EN1 17 C6
Brookview Rd SW16 181 C5
Brookville Rd SW6 135 B5 264 C3
Brookway SE3 143 A2
Brook Wlk
Burnt Oak HA8 27 B4
Finchley N2 30 B2
Brookwood Ave SW13 133 D3
Brookwood Cl BR2 208 D5
Brookwood Ho SE1 251 D1
Brookwood Rd
Hounslow TW3 129 D4
Wandsworth SW18 157 C3
Broom Ave BR5 190 B1
Broom Cl
Bromley Comm BR2 210 A3
Teddington KT1, TW11 175 D3
Broomcroft Ave UB5 84 C4
Broome Ct 3 TW9 132 C4
Broome Ho 7 E5 74 B3
Broome Rd TW12 173 B2
Broome Way SE5 139 B5
Broom Farm SW6 135 C3
Broomfield
7 Camden Town NW1 71 A1
Sunbury TW16 172 A2
Walthamstow E17 53 B2
Broomfield Ave N13 32 B5
Broomfield Cotts N13 32 A5
Broomfield Ct N13 32 A5
Broomfield Ho
Stanmore HA7 9 A1
4 St Paul's Cray BR5 190 B1
Walworth SE17 263 A3
Broomfield House Sch TW9 132 B4
Broomfield La N13 32 B6
Broomfield Pl W13 109 B5
Broomfield Rd
Beckenham BR3 207 B6
Bexley DA6 169 C6
Bowes Pk N13 32 A5
Dagenham RM6 58 D2
Ealing W13 109 B5
Richmond TW9 132 B4
Surbiton KT5 198 B1
Teddington TW11 175 C4
Broomfields KT10 212 A3
Broomfield Sch N14 31 D5
Broomfield St E14 97 D2
Broom Gdns CR0 223 C5
Broomgrove Gdns HA8 26 C2
Broomgrove Rd SW9 138 B3
BROOM HILL 211 D2
Broomhill Ct 2 IG8 37 A4
Broomhill Rd
Broom Hill BR6 211 D2
Ilford IG3 80 A6
Wandsworth SW18 157 C6
Woodford IG8 37 A4
Broomhill Rise DA6 169 C6
Broomhill Wlk IG8 36 D3
Broomhouse La SW6 135 C2
Broomhouse Rd SW6 135 C3
Broomleigh BR1 187 A2
Broomloan La SM1 217 C6
Broom Lock TW11 175 C4
Broom Mead DA6 169 C6
Broom Pk KT1 175 D3
Broom Rd
Croydon CR0 223 C5
Teddington TW11 175 C4
Broomsleigh Bsns Pk SE26 185 B5
Broomsleigh St NW6 69 B3
Broom Water TW11 175 C5
Broom Water W TW11 175 C5
Broomwood Cl CR0 206 D4
Broomwood Hall Sch SW12 159 A4
Broomwood Rd
London SW11 159 A6
St Paul's Cray BR5 190 B1
Broseley Gr SE26 185 A5
Broster Gdns SE25 205 D6
Brougham Rd
Acton W3 89 A1
Hackney E8 96 A6
Brougham St SW11 136 D3
Brough Cl
Kingston u T KT2 175 D5
South Lambeth SW8 270 B3
Broughton Ave
London N3 47 A6
Richmond TW10 175 C6
Broughton Ct W13 109 B6
Broughton Dr 19 SW9 138 D1
Broughton Gdns N6 49 C3
Broughton Ho 10 SW19 179 A3
Broughton Rd
Ealing W13 109 B6
Orpington BR6 227 B6
Sands End SW6 135 D3
Thornton Heath CR7 204 C3
Broughton Road App 2 SW6 135 D3
Broughton St SW8 137 B3
Brouncker Rd W3 111 A4
Browells La TW13 150 B2
Brown Bear Ct TW13 172 D6
Brown Cl SM6 220 A1
Browne Ho
13 Deptford SE8 141 C5
9 Penge SE26 184 B5
Brownfield St E14 98 A1
Brownflete Ho SE4 141 A1
Browngraves Rd UB7 127 A5
Brown Hart Gdns W1 248 B6
Brownhill Rd SE6 164 A4
Browning Ave
Carshalton SM1 218 C4
Ealing W7 86 D1
North Cheam KT4 200 B1
Browning Cl
Bexley DA16 145 C4
Feltham TW12 173 B6
Paddington W9 236 B5
Walthamstow E17 54 A5
Browning Ct W14 264 C6
Browning Ho
2 London SE14 141 A4
7 Shepherd's Bush W12 90 C1
10 Stoke Newington N16 73 C4
Browning Mews W1 238 B3
Browning Rd
Enfield EN2 5 B5
Leytonstone E11 54 D2
Plashet E12 78 B2
Browning St SE17 117 A2 262 B3
Browning Way TW5 128 D4
Brownlea Gdns IG3 80 A6
Brownlow Cl EN4 14 B6
Brownlow Ct
2 Bowes Pk N11 32 A4
Hampstead Garden Suburb N2 48 A4
Brownlow Ho 10 SE16 118 A4
Brownlow Lo 1 N11 32 A4
Brownlow Mews WC1 94 B3 240 D5
Brownlow Rd
Bowes Pk N11 32 A4
6 Ealing W13 109 A5
Finchley N3 29 D3
3 Forest Gate E7 77 A4
Hackney E8 96 A6
South Croydon CR0 221 D4
Willesden NW10 67 C1
Brownlow St WC1 94 B2 240 D3
Brownrigg Rd TW15 170 C6
Brown's Bldgs EC3 243 B1
Brownsea Wlk NW7 28 D4
Brownspring Dr SE9 166 D1
Brown's Rd
Surbiton KT5, KT6 198 B2
Walthamstow E17 53 C6
Brown St W1 92 D1 237 C2
Brownswell Rd N2 30 B1
Brownswood Rd N4 73 A6
Broxash Rd SW11 159 A5
Broxbourne Ave E18 55 B5
Broxbourne Ho 1 E3 97 D3
Broxbourne Rd
Broom Hill BR6 211 D2
Wanstead E7 77 A5
Broxholme Ho SW6 265 C2
Broxholm Rd SE27, SW16 160 C1
Broxted Rd SE6 163 B2
Broxwood Way NW8 92 C6 230 B5
Bruce Ave TW17 193 A3
Bruce Castle Ct N17 33 C2
Bruce Castle Mus* N17 33 C2
Bruce Castle Rd N17 33 D2
Bruce Cl
North Kensington W10 90 D2
Welling DA16 146 B4
Bruce Ct DA15 189 D6
Bruce Gdns N20 14 D1
Bruce Glasier Ho 13 N19 49 D2
Bruce Gr N17 33 D1
Bruce Grove N17 33 D1
Bruce Grove Prim Sch N17 33 D1
Bruce Grove Sta N17 33 D1
Bruce Hall Mews SW17 181 A6
Bruce Ho
4 Clapham Pk SW4 159 D5
5 Greenhill HA1 42 D4
North Kensington W10 90 D2
Preston HA3 44 A2
Putney SW15 156 B6
Bruce Lawns SW17 181 A6
Bruce Rd
Barnet EN5 1 A2
Bromley E3 97 D4
Harrow HA3 24 C1
Mitcham CR4 181 A3
South Norwood SE25 205 B5
Willesden NW10 67 B1
Bruckner St W10 91 B4
Brudenell Rd SW17 181 A6
Bruffs Meadow UB5 63 A2
Bruges Pl 16 NW1 71 C1
Brumfield Rd KT19 215 A3
Brune Ho E1 243 C3
Brunel Cl
Cranford TW5 128 B5
Northolt UB5 85 B4
Penge SE19 183 D4
Brunel Ct 8 SW13 133 D3
Brunel Engine House Rotherhithe* SE16 118 C4
Brunel Est W2 91 C2
Brunel Ho
Chelsea SW10 266 D4
4 Gospel Oak NW5 71 B4
Hayes UB3 105 D3
Millwall E14 119 D1
New Cross SE8 141 B5
25 Streatham SW2 160 A4
Brunel Mews NW10 90 D4
Brunel Pl 7 UB1 85 D1
Brunel Rd
Acton W3 89 C2
Walthamstow E17 53 A3
Wapping SE16 118 C5
Brunel Science Pk UB8 82 A4
Brunel St E16 98 D1
Brunel Univ UB8 82 A4
Brunel Univ Coll Osterley Campus TW7 130 D5
Brunel Wlk
South Tottenham N15 51 C5
Twickenham TW4 151 C4
Brune St E1 95 D2 243 C3
Brunlees Ho SE1 262 B5
Brunner Cl NW11 48 A4
Brunner Ho 6 SE6 186 A6
Brunner Rd
Ealing W5 87 D3
Walthamstow E17 53 B4
Bruno Ct 5 E8 74 A2
Bruno Pl NW9 67 A6
Brunswick Ave N11 15 A1
Brunswick Cl
Bexley DA6 146 D1
Pinner HA5 41 A3
Thames Ditton KT7 196 D1
Twickenham TW2 152 B1
Brunswick Cres N11 15 A1
Brunswick Ct
Bermondsey SE1 117 C4 253 B2
Finsbury EC1 234 C1
Kingston u T KT2 175 D4
New Barnet EN4 14 B6
2 Penge SE19 184 A3
Westminster SW1 259 D3
2 Wimbledon SW19 179 A3
Brunswick Gdns
Ealing W5 88 A3
Kensington W8 113 C5 245 B3
Brunswick Gr N11 15 A1
Brunswick Ho
Church End N3 29 B2
4 Haggerston E2 95 D5
Lisson Gr NW1 237 C6
Brunswick Lo 6 E4 20 A2
Brunswick Manor SM1 218 A4
Brunswick Mews
Marylebone W1 237 D2
Streatham SW16 181 D4
BRUNSWICK PARK 15 A1
Brunswick Park Gdns N11 15 A2
Brunswick Park Prim Sch
Brunswick Pk N14 15 A2
Camberwell SE5 139 B5
Brunswick Park Rd N11 15 A1
Brunswick Pk SE5 139 C4
Brunswick Pl
Penge SE19 184 A3
Shoreditch N1 95 B4 235 D1
Brunswick Quay SE16 118 D3
Brunswick Rd
Bexley DA6 147 A1
Ealing W5 88 A4
Holdbrook EN3 7 C5
Kingston u T KT2 176 C2
Leyton E10 54 A1
Poplar E14 98 A1
South Tottenham N15 51 C4
South Tottenham N15 51 C5
Sutton SM1 217 D4
Brunswick Sh Ctr WC1 94 A3 240 B6
Brunswick Sq
St Pancras WC1 94 A3 240 B6
Tottenham N17 33 D4
Brunswick St E17 54 A4
Brunswick Terr BR3 185 D2
Brunswick Villas 2 SE5 139 C4
Brunswick Way N11 31 B6
Brunton Pl E14 97 A1
Brushfield St E1 95 D2 243 C4
Brushwood Lo 1 DA17 125 C2
Brussels Ct N18 33 C5
Brussels Rd SW11 136 B1
Bruton Cl BR7 188 B3
Bruton La W1 115 B6 248 D5
Bruton Pl W1 115 B6 248 D5
Bruton Rd SM4 202 A5
Bruton St W1 115 B6 248 D5
Bruton Way W13 87 A2
Brutus Ct SE11 261 C3
Bryan Ave NW10 68 B1
Bryan Cl TW16 172 A3
Bryan Ct W1 237 C2
Bryan Ho SE16 119 B4
Bryan Rd SE16 119 B4
Bryanston Ave TW2 151 D3
Bryanston Cl UB2 107 B2
Bryanston Ct W1 237 C2
Bryanstone Ct SM1 218 A5
Bryanstone Rd N8 49 D4
Bryanston Ho 12 SE15 139 D4
Bryanston Mans W1 237 C4
Bryanston Mews E W1 237 C3
Bryanston Mews W W1 92 D1 237 C2
Bryanston Pl W1 92 D2 237 C3
Bryanston Sq W1 92 D1 237 C2
Bryanston St W1 92 D1 237 D1
Bryant Cl EN5 13 B6
Bryant Ct
Acton W3 111 B5
Haggerston E2 95 D5
Bryant Rd UB5 84 C4
Bryant St E15 76 C1
Bryantwood Rd N5, N7 72 C3
Brycedale Cres N14 15 D1
Bryce Ho 25 SE14 140 D6
Bryce Rd RM8 80 C4
Brydale Ho 2 SE16 118 D2
Bryden Cl SE26 185 A5
Brydges Pl WC2 250 A5
Brydges Rd E15 76 B3
Brydon Wlk N1 233 B6
Bryer Ct EC2 242 A4
Bryett Rd N7 72 A5
Bryher Ho W4 111 A1
Brymay Cl E3 97 C5
Brymon Ct W1 237 D3
Brynmaer Ho SW11 267 D1
Brynmaer Rd SW11 136 D4 267 D1
Bryn-y-Mawr Rd EN1 5 D1
Bryony Cl UB8 82 B2
Bryony Rd W12 112 A6
Bryony Way TW16 172 A4
B Sky B Hq TW7 131 A6
BT Telecom Twr* W1 93 C2 239 A4
Buccleuch Ho E5 52 A2
Buchanan Cl N21 16 B6
Buchanan Ct 16 SE16 118 D2
Buchanan Gdns NW10 90 B5
Buchanan Ho
Dulwich SE21 161 C1
Wandsworth SW18 157 C4
Buchan Ho W3 110 D4
Buchan Rd SE15 140 C2
Bucharest Rd SW18 158 A4
Buckden Cl
Fortis Green N2 48 D5
Lee SE12 165 A5
Buckfast Ct W13 109 A6
Buckfast Ho N14 15 C6
Buckfast Rd SM4 201 D5
Buckfast St E2 96 A4
Buck Hill Wlk W2 114 B6 246 D5
Buckhold Rd SW18 157 C5
Buckhurst Ave CR4, SM5 202 D1
Buckhurst Ct 7 IG9 21 D2
BUCKHURST HILL 21 C2
Buckhurst Hill Ho 3 IG9 21 B2
Buckhurst Hill Sta IG9 21 D2
Buckhurst Ho 15 N7 71 D3
Buckhurst St E1 96 B3
Buckhurst Way IG9 21 D1
Buckingham Ave
East Molesey KT8 173 D1
Falconwood DA16 145 C1
Feltham TW14 150 B5
Oakleigh Pk N20 14 B4
South Norwood CR7 182 C2
Wembley UB6 87 A6
Buckingham Cl
Broom Hill BR5 211 C2
Ealing W5 87 C2
Enfield EN1 5 C3
Hampton TW12 173 B5
Buckingham College Sch HA1 42 C4
Buckingham Ct
2 Ealing W7 86 D3
Hendon NW4 46 A6
Mitcham CR4 204 A4
Northolt UB5 85 A6
Wembley HA0 65 C2
Buckingham Dr BR7 189 A5
Buckingham Gate SW1 115 C3 259 B6
Buckingham Gdns
East Molesey KT8 173 D1
Edgware HA8 26 B3
South Norwood CR7 182 C1
Buckingham Gr UB10 82 C5
Buckingham Ho
1 Acton W3 88 C1
Finsbury Pk N4 51 A1
Richmond TW10 154 C6
Buckingham La SE23 163 A4
Buckingham Lo N10 49 C5
Buckingham Mans NW6 69 D3
Buckingham Mews
Harlesden NW10 89 D5
7 Kingsland N1 73 C2
Westminster SW1 259 A6
Buckingham Pal* SW1 115 C4 249 A1
Buckingham Palace Rd SW1 115 B2 258 D4
Buckingham Par 19 HA7 25 C5
Buckingham Pl SW1 259 A6
Buckingham Prim Sch TW12 173 B5
Buckingham Rd
Edgware HA8 26 B3
Hampton TW12, TW13 173 B5
Harlesden NW10 89 D5
Harrow HA1 42 B4
Ilford IG1 79 B6
Kingsland N1 73 C2
Kingston u T KT1 198 B5
Leyton E10 75 D5
Mitcham CR4 204 A4
Richmond TW10 153 D2
Stratford E15 76 D3
Wanstead E11 55 C4
Woodford E18 36 D2
Wood Green N22 32 A2
Buckingham St WC2 250 B5
Buckingham Way SM6 219 C1
Buckingham Yd NW10 89 D5
Buck La NW9 45 B4
Buckland Cl NW7 28 A6
Buckland Cres NW3 70 B2
Buckland Ct
6 Shoreditch N1 95 C5
Uxbridge UB10 61 A6
Buckland Ho 3 N1 72 C1
Buckland Inf Sch KT9 214 B3
Buckland Rd
Chessington KT9 214 B3
Leyton E10 76 A6
Orpington BR6 227 C4
Buckland Rise HA5 22 D2
Bucklands Rd TW11 175 C4
Buckland St N1 95 B5 235 D3
Buckland Way KT4 200 C1
Buckland Wlk
2 Acton W3 111 A4
Morden SM4 202 A5
Buckle Ct HA8 27 A3
Buckleigh Ave SW20 201 B6
Buckleigh Ho SW17 180 B5
Buckleigh Rd SW16 182 A3
Buckleigh Way SE19 183 D3
Buckler Gdns SE9 166 B1
Buckler's Alley SW6 264 D4
Bucklersbury EC2, EC4 242 C1
Bucklers' Way SM5 218 D5
Buckles Ct DA17 124 D2
Buckle St
15 Whitechapel E1 96 A1
Whitechapel E1 243 D2
Buckley Cl SE23 162 B4
Buckley Ct
5 Brondesbury NW6 69 B1
London N8 49 D4
Buckley Ho W3 110 C5
Buckley Rd NW6 69 B1
Buckmaster Cl 1 SW9 138 C2
Buckmaster Ho 1 N7 72 B4
Buckmaster Rd SW11 136 C1
Bucknall St WC1 240 A2
Bucknall Way BR3 208 A5
Bucknell Cl SW2 138 B1
Buckner Rd SW2 138 B1
Buckrell Rd E4 20 B2
Buckridge Bldg EC1 241 A4
Buckshead Ho 19 W2 91 C2
Buck St NW1 71 B1
Buckstone Cl SE23 162 C5
Buckstone Rd N18 34 A5
Buckters Rents SE16 119 A5
Buckthorne Rd SE4 163 A6
Buckthorn Ho DA15 167 D1
Buckwheat Ct DA18 124 D3
Budd Cl N12 29 D6
Buddings Circ HA9 67 A5
Bude Cl E17 53 B4
Budge La CR4 202 D2
Budge Row EC4 242 C1
Budge's Wlk W2 114 A5 246 B4
Budleigh Cres DA16 146 C4
Budleigh Ho 19 SE15 140 A5
Budoch Ct IG3 80 A6

Budoch Dr IG3 80 A6
Buer Rd SW6 135 A3
Bugsby's Way SE10 120 D2
Buick Ho 4 E3 97 C3
Building 36 7 SE18 123 A3
Building 47 6 SE18 123 A3
Building 48 5 SE18 123 A3
Building 49 4 SE18 123 A3
Building 50 3 SE18 123 A3
Bulbarrow NW8 91 D6
Bulganak Rd CR7 205 A5
Bulinca St
SW1 115 D2 259 D3
Bullace Row SE5 139 B4
Bull Alley DA16 146 B2
Bullard Rd TW11 174 D4
Bullards Pl 13 E2 96 D4
Bull Dog The (Juct)
TW15 148 A2
Bulleid Way
SW1 115 B2 258 D3
Bullen Ho 13 E1 96 B3
Bullen St SW11 136 C3
Buller Cl SE15 140 A5
Buller Rd
Barking IG11 79 C1
Kensal Green NW10 90 D4
South Norwood CR7 205 B6
Tottenham N17 34 A1
Wood Green N22 32 C1
Bullers Cl DA14 191 A5
Bullers Wood Dr BR7 188 B3
Bullers Wood Sch
BR7 188 A2
Bullescroft Rd HA8 10 D1
Bullfinch Ct 4 SE21 161 B2
Bullingham Mans W8 245 B2
Bull Inn Ct WC2 250 B5
Bullivant St 9 E14 120 A6
Bull La
Chislehurst BR7 189 B3
Dagenham RM10 81 D5
Edmonton N18 33 C5
Bull Rd E15 98 D5
Bullrush Cl
Carshalton SM5 218 C6
Thornton Heath CR0 205 C3
Bulls Alley SW14 133 B3
Bulls Bridge Ind Est
UB2 106 B2
Bulls Bridge Rd UB2 106 B2
Bullsbrook Rd UB4 106 C5
Bull's Cross EN1, EN2 6 A6
Bull's Gdns SW3 257 B4
Bulls Head Pas EC3 243 A1
Bull Yd SE15 140 A4
Bulmer Gdns HA3 43 D2
Bulmer Mews
W11 113 C5 245 A4
Bulow Ct 3 SW6 135 D3
Bulstrode Ave TW3 129 C2
Bulstrode Gdns TW3 129 C2
Bulstrode Pl W1 238 B3
Bulstrode Rd TW3 129 C2
Bulstrode St
W1 93 A1 238 B2
Bulwer Court Rd E11 54 B1
Bulwer Ct E11 54 B1
Bulwer Gdns EN5 2 A1
Bulwer Rd
Edmonton N18 33 C6
Leytonstone E11 54 B1
New Barnet EN5 2 A1
Bulwer St W12 112 C5
Bunbury Ho SE15 140 A5
Bunces La IG8 36 D3
Bungalow Rd SE25 205 C5
Bungalows The
Leyton E10 54 A3
Mitcham SW16 181 B3
Bunhill Row
EC1 95 B3 242 C5
Bunhouse Pl SW1 258 B2
Bunkers Hill
London NW11 48 A2
North Cray DA14 169 B1
Bunker's Hill DA17 125 C2
Bunning Ho N7 72 A4
Bunning Way N7 72 B1
Bunn's La NW7 27 D4
Bunsen Ho 2 E3 97 A5
Bunsen St 3 E3 97 A5
Buntingbridge Rd IG2 57 B4
Bunting Cl
London N9 18 D3
Mitcham CR4 202 D4
Bunting Ct NW9 27 C1
Bunton St SE18 122 C3
Bunyan Ct EC2 242 A4
Bunyan Rd E17 53 A6
Buonaparte Mews
SW1 259 C2
BUPA Bushey Hospl
WD23 8 D3
Burbage Cl
Bermondsey
SE1 117 B3 262 C5
Hayes UB3 83 B1
Burbage Ho
16 Deptford SE14 140 D6
Shoreditch N1 235 D5
Burbage Rd SE21,
SE24 161 B4
Burbage Sch N1 95 C5
Burbank KT3 199 D6
Burberry Cl KT3 177 C1
Burberry Ct 8 N3 29 D3
Burbidge Rd TW17 192 C5
Burbridge Way N17 34 A1
Burcham St E14 98 A1
Burcharbro Rd SE2 146 D6
Burchell Ct WD23 8 A4
Burchell Ho SE11 260 D2
Burchell Rd
Leyton E10 53 D1
London SE15 140 B4
Burcher Gale Gr 5
SE15 139 D5
Burchetts Way TW17 192 D3
Burchett Way RM6 59 B3
Burcote Rd SW18 158 B4
Burden Cl TW8 109 C1
Burden Ho SW8 270 A3
Burdenshott Ave
TW10 132 D1
Burden Way E11 77 B6
Burder Cl N1 73 C2
Burder Rd N1 73 C2
Burdett Ave SW20 178 A2
Burdett Cl
2 Ealing W7 108 D5
Sidcup DA14 191 A5
Burdett Coutts &
Townshend CE Prim Sch
SW1 115 D2 259 D3
Burdett Mews 4 W2 91 D1
Burdett Rd
Richmond TW9 132 B2
Thornton Heath CR0 205 B3
Tower Hamlets E3 97 B2
Burdetts Rd RM9 103 B6
Burdock Cl CR0 206 D1
Burdock Rd N17 52 A6
Burdon Ct 3 E8 74 A2
Burdon La SM2 217 A1
Bure Ct 17 EN5 13 D6
Burfield Cl SW17 180 B6
Burford Cl
Dagenham RM8 80 C5
Ickenham UB10 60 A4
Ilford IG6 57 A5
Burford Ct SE8 141 C6
Burford Gdns N13 16 B1
Burford Ho
1 Brentford TW8 110 A1
11 South Lambeth
SW9 138 B3
Burford Rd
Brentford TW8 110 A1
Bromley BR1 210 A5
Forest Hill SE6 163 B2
Newham E6 100 A4
New Malden KT4 200 A2
5 Stratford Marsh E15 98 B6
Sutton SM1 217 C6
Burford Way CR0 224 A2
Burford Wlk SW6 265 D3
Burgate Ct 9 SW9 138 C2
Burges Gr SW13 134 B5
Burges Rd E6 78 B1
Burgess Ave NW9 45 B3
Burgess Cl 4 TW13 173 A6
Burgess Ct
2 London N20 14 D2
3 Southall UB1 85 D1
Wallend E12 78 C1
Burgess Hill NW2 69 C4
Burgess Ho 3 SE5 139 A5
Burgess Ind Pk SE5 139 B5
Burgess Mews SW19 179 D4
Burgess Park Mans
NW6 69 C4
Burgess Rd
Leyton E15 76 C4
Sutton SM1 217 D4
Burgess St E14 97 C2
Burge St SE1 262 D5
Burghill Rd SE26 185 A6
Burghley Ave
Borehamwood WD6 11 A6
Burghley Ave *continued*
Kingston u T KT3 177 B2
Burghley Ct SW19 179 A5
Burghley Hall Cl
SW19 157 A3
Burghley Ho SW19 157 A1
Burghley Pl CR4 202 D5
Burghley Rd
Camden Town NW5 71 B4
Leytonstone E11 54 C1
London N8 50 C6
Wimbledon SW19 179 A6
Burghley Twr W3 111 D6
Burgh St N1 94 D5 234 D4
Burgon St EC4 241 D1
Burgos Cl CR0 220 C2
Burgos Gr SE10 141 D4
Burgoyne Rd
Ashford TW16 171 D4
Brixton SW9 138 B2
Harringay N4 50 D3
South Norwood SE25 205 D5
Burham Cl SE20 184 C3
Burhan Uddin Ho E1 243 C5
Burhill Gr HA5 23 A1
Buriton Ho 9 SW15 156 B3
Burke Cl SW15 133 C1
Burke Ho 1 SW11 136 B1
Burke Lodge E13 99 B4
Burke St E16 98 D2
Burket Cl UB2 107 B2
Burland Rd SW11 158 D6
Burleigh Ave
Bexley DA15 167 D6
Hackbridge SM6 219 B5
Burleigh Ct N17 34 A4
Burleigh Gdns
Ashford TW15 171 A5
Osidge N14 15 C3
Burleigh Ho
Cheam SM3 201 A1
Chelsea SW3 266 D5
North Kensington W10 90 D2
Burleigh Lo 3 SW19 179 D3
Burleigh Par N14 15 D3
Burleigh Pl SW15 156 D6
Burleigh Rd
Cheam SM3 201 A1
Enfield EN1 5 C1
Hillingdon UB10 82 D6
Burleigh St WC2 250 C6
Burleigh Way EN2 5 B2
Burleigh Wlk SE6 164 A3
Burley Cl
Chingford E4 35 C5
Mitcham SW16 181 D1
Burley Ho E1 96 D1
Burley Rd E16 99 C2
Burlington Apartments
SE20 184 B3
Burlington Arc W1 249 A5
Burlington Ave
Richmond TW9 132 C4
Romford RM7 59 D3
Burlington Cl
East Bedfont TW14 149 B4
5 Newham E6 100 A1
Orpington BR6 226 D6
Paddington W9 91 C3
Pinner HA5 40 B6
Burlington Ct
Chiswick W4 133 A5
Highgate N6 49 A1
Burlington Danes Sch
W12 90 B1
Burlington Gate
SW20 179 A1
Burlington Gdns
Acton Green W4 111 A1
Acton W3 111 A5
Dagenham RM6 59 A2
Fulham SW6 135 A3
Marylebone
W1 115 C6 249 A5
Burlington Ho NW3 70 B3
Burlington Inf Sch
KT3 199 D5
Burlington Jun Sch
KT3 199 D5
Burlington La W4 133 B5
Burlington Lo BR7 188 B3
Burlington Mews
Acton W3 111 A5
2 Putney SW15 157 B6
Burlington Park Ho 6
HA7 25 C6
Burlington Pl
Fulham SW6 135 A3
Woodford IG8 21 A1
Burlington Rd
Acton Green W4 111 A1
Enfield EN2 5 B4
Fulham SW6 135 A3
Hounslow TW7 130 B4
Muswell Hill N10 49 A6
New Malden KT3 199 D5
South Norwood CR7 183 B1
Tottenham N17 34 A2
Burlington Rise EN4 14 D4
Burma Rd N16 73 B4
Burmarsh 6 NW5 71 A2
Burmarsh Ct SE20 184 C2
Burma Terr 11 SE19 183 C5
Burmester Ho SW17 158 A1
Burmester Rd SW17 158 A1
Burnaby Cres W4 133 A6
Burnaby Ct 31 SE16 118 A4
Burnaby Gdns W4 132 D6
Burnaby St
SW10 136 A5 266 B3
Burnand Ho 3 W14 112 D3
Burnbrae Cl N12 29 D4
Burnbury Rd SW12 159 C3
Burncroft Ave EN3 6 C3
Burndell Way UB4 84 D2
Burne Jones Ho W14 254 B3
Burnell Ave
Richmond TW10 175 C5
Welling DA16 146 A3
Burnell Gdns HA7 25 D1
Burnell Ho 18 SW2 160 C3
Burnell Rd SM1 217 D4
Burnell Wlk SE1 263 D2
Burnels Ave E6 100 C4
Burness Cl N7 72 B2
Burne St NW1 237 A4
Burnett Cl E9 74 C3
Burnett Ct SW11 267 A1
Burnett Ho 6 SE13 142 A3
Burney Ave KT5 198 B4
Burney Ho 4 SW16 181 C5
Burney St SE10 142 A5
Burnfoot Ave
SW6 135 A4 264 B1
Burnham NW3 70 C1
Burnham Ave UB10 61 A4
Burnham Cl
Bermondsey SE1 263 D3
Enfield EN1 5 C5
Harrow HA3 43 A5
Hendon NW7 28 A3
Burnham Cres E11 55 C5
Burnham Ct
Bayswater W2 245 D6
Hendon NW4 46 C5
15 Stanmore HA7 25 C5
Burnham Dr KT4 216 D6
Burnham Est 8 E2 96 C4
Burnham Gdns
Cranford TW4 128 B4
Croydon CR0 205 D2
Hayes UB3 105 B3
Burnham Rd
Chingford Hatch E4 35 B5
Dagenham RM9 102 B6
Morden SM4 201 D5
Sidcup DA14 169 A2
Burnham St
Bethnal Green E2 96 C4
Kingston u T KT2 176 C2
Burnham Way
Ealing W13 109 B3
Penge SE26 185 B5
Burnhill Ho EC1 235 A1
Burnhill Rd BR3 185 C1
Burnley Cl WD19 22 C5
Burnley Rd
London SW9 138 B3
Willesden NW10 68 A3
Burnsall St
SW3 114 C1 257 B2
Burns Ave
Blackfen DA15 168 B5
Feltham TW14 150 A5
Ilford RM6 58 C2
Southall UB1 107 C6
Burns Cl
Bexley DA16 145 D4
Hayes UB4 84 A2
Mitcham SW17 180 B4
Walthamstow E17 54 A5
Burns Ct
Tottenham N17 34 B3
Wallington SM6 219 B1
Burns Ho
18 Bethnal Green E2 96 C4
Bexley DA16 146 C4
1 Islington N7 72 B2
Kennington SE17 261 D1
Burns Ho *continued*
11 Stoke Newington
N16 73 C4
Burn's Ho NW10 89 C6
Burnside Ave E4 35 B4
Burnside Cl
Barnet EN5 1 C2
Rotherhithe SE16 118 D5
Twickenham TW1 153 A5
Burnside Cres HA0 87 D6
Burnside Ct 1 SM6 219 A5
Burnside Rd RM8 58 D1
Burns Rd
Battersea SW11 136 D3
Ealing W13 109 B4
Wembley HA0 88 A5
Burn's Rd NW10 89 D6
Burns Way TW5 128 D4
Burnt Ash Hill
Lee SE12 164 D5
Lewisham SE12 165 A3
Burnt Ash Hts BR1 187 B5
Burnt Ash La BR1,
SE12 187 B5
Burnt Ash Prim Sch
BR1 187 A5
Burnt Ash Rd SE12 164 D6
Burnthwaite Rd
SW6 135 B5 264 D3
BURNT OAK 27 B3
Burnt Oak Broadway
HA8 26 D2
Burnt Oak Fields HA8 27 A2
Burnt Oak Jun Sch
DA15 168 A3
Burnt Oak La DA15 168 B3
Burnt Oak Sta HA8 27 A2
Burntwood Cl SW18 158 C3
Burntwood Ct SW17 158 A1
Burntwood Grange Rd
SW18 158 C3
Burntwood La SW17 158 B2
Burntwood Sch
SW17 158 B2
Burntwood View 6
SE19 183 D5
Buross St E1 96 B1
Burpham Cl UB4 84 D2
Burrage Ct 17 SE16 118 D2
Burrage Gr SE18 123 A2
Burrage Pl SE18 122 D1
Burrage Rd SE18 123 A1
Burrard Ho 11 E2 96 C5
Burrard Rd
Newham E16 99 B1
West Hampstead NW6 69 C4
Burr Cl
Bexleyheath DA7 147 B2
St George in t East E1 118 A5
Burrell Cl
Croydon CR0 207 A3
Edgware HA8 10 D2
Burrell Ct HA1 42 B2
Burrell Ho 4 TW1 153 B4
Burrell Row BR3 185 C1
Burrells 9 BR3 185 D1
Burrell St SE1 116 D5 251 C4
Burrell's Wharf Sq
E14 119 D1
Burrell Twrs E10 53 C2
Burrhill Ct SE16 118 D3
Burritt Rd KT1 176 C1
Burrmead Ct NW2 67 D5
Burroughs Gdns NW4 46 B5
Burroughs The NW4 46 B5
Burrow Ho 19 SW9 138 B3
Burrow Rd SE22 139 C1
Burrows Mews SE1 251 C2
Burrows Rd NW10 90 C4
Burrow Wlk SE21 161 A4
Burr Rd SW18 157 C4
Bursar St SE1 253 A3
Bursdon Cl DA15 167 D2
Bursland Rd EN3 6 D1
Burslem St E1 96 A1
Bursted Wood Prim Sch
DA7 147 D3
Burstock Rd SW15 135 A1
Burston Rd SW15 156 D6
Burstow Rd SW20 179 A2
Burtenshaw Rd KT7 197 A3
Burtley Cl N4 51 A1
Burton Bank N1 73 B1
Burton Cl
Chessington KT9 213 D1
South Norwood CR7 205 B6
Burton Ct
Chelsea SW3 257 D2
10 Friern Barnet N11 30 D5
Thames Ditton KT7 197 A3
Burton Dr EN3 7 C6
Burton Gdns TW5 129 B4
Burton Gr SE17 262 C1
Burton Ho
8 Bermondsey SE16 118 B4
Brixton SE5 138 D4
Penge SE26 184 B5
Burtonhole Cl NW7 28 D6
Burtonhole La
Finchley NW7 29 A6
Mill Hill NW7 28 D6
Burton La 3 SW9 138 C3
Burton Lo 6 SW15 157 B6
Burton Mews SW1 258 B3
Burton Pl WC1 232 D1
Burton Rd
7 Brixton SW9 138 C3
Brixton SW9 138 D3
Brondesbury NW6 69 B1
Kingston u T KT2 176 A3
Wanstead E18 55 B6
Burtons Ct E15 76 B1
Burtons Rd TW12 174 A6
Burton St WC1 93 D3 239 D6
Burtonwood Ho N4 51 B2
Burt Rd E16 121 C5
Burtt Ho 6 N1 95 C4
Burtwell La SE21,
SE27 183 B6
Burvill Ct SW20 178 C2
Burwash Ho SE1 252 D1
Burwash Rd SE18 123 B1
Burwell 2 KT1 176 C1
Burwell Ave UB6 64 C2
Burwell Cl 27 E1 96 B1
Burwell Rd E10 53 A1
Burwell Wlk 14 E3 97 C3
Burwood Ave
Hayes BR2 225 B6
Pinner HA5 40 C4
Burwood Cl KT6 198 C1
Burwood Ct SE23 162 C4
Burwood Ho 11 SW9 138 D1
Burwood Lo SW19 179 B6
Burwood Pl
Barnet EN4 2 A4
Paddington W2 237 B2
Bury Ave
Hayes UB4 83 C5
Ruislip HA4 39 A3
Bury Cl SE16 118 D5
Bury Ct EC3 243 B2
Buryfield Ct 23 SE8 118 D2
Bury Gr SM4 201 D4
Bury Hall Villas N9 17 D4
Bury Pl WC1 94 A2 240 B3
Bury Rd
Chingford E4 20 C6
Dagenham RM10 81 D3
Hornsey N22 50 C6
Bury St W N9 17 C4
Buryside Cl IG2 57 D5
Bury St
Edmonton N9 18 A3
Ruislip HA4 39 B3
St James SW1 115 C5 249 B4
Whitechapel
EC3 95 C1 243 B2
Bury Wlk SW3 114 C1 257 A2
Burywood Ct EN3 6 C3
Busbridge Ho 24 E14 97 C2
Busby Ho SW16 181 C6
Busby Mews 5 NW1 71 D2
Busby Pl NW5 71 D2
Busch Cl TW7 131 B4
Busch Cnr TW7 131 B4
Bushbaby Cl SE1 263 A5
Bushberry Rd E9 75 A2
Bush Cl IG2 57 B4
Bush Cotts 12 SW18 157 C6
Bush Ct
London N14 15 C3
7 Shepherd's Bush
W12 112 D4
Bushell Cl SW2 160 B2
Bushell Gn WD23 8 B2
Bushell Ho 3 SE27 183 A6
Bushell Way BR7 188 C5
BUSHEY 8 A2
Bushey Ave
Crofton BR5 211 B2
Snaresbrook E18 54 D6
Bushey Cl
Chingford E4 20 A1
Ickenham UB10 60 C6
Bushey Ct SW20 178 B1
Bushey Down SW12 159 B2

Bushey Hall SE5 ... 139 D4
BUSHEY HEATH ... 8 C4
Bushey Heath Prim Sch WD23 ... 8 B3
Bushey Hill Rd SE5 ... 139 D4
Bushey Ho SE12 ... 165 C1
Bushey La SM1 ... 217 C4
Bushey Lees DA15 ... 167 D5
BUSHEY MEAD ... 200 D6
Bushey Meads Sch WD23 ... 8 A6
Bushey Rd
Croydon CR0 ... 223 C6
Hayes UB3 ... 105 C2
Ickenham UB10 ... 60 C6
Newham E13 ... 99 C5
South Tottenham N15 ... 51 C3
Sutton SM1 ... 217 C4
West Barnes SW20 ... 178 D1
Bushey Way BR3 ... 208 B4
Bush Fair Ct N14 ... 15 B5
Bushfield Cl HA8 ... 10 D2
Bushfield Cres HA8 ... 10 D2
Bushfield Ho N5 ... 73 A3
Bush Gr
London NW9 ... 45 A2
Stanmore HA7 ... 25 D2
Bushgrove Rd RM8 ... 80 D5
BUSH HILL ... 17 B5
Bush Hill N21 ... 17 A5
Bush Hill Par EN1 ... 17 B4
BUSH HILL PARK ... 17 C5
Bush Hill Park Prim Sch EN1 ... 18 A6
Bush Hill Park Sta EN1 ... 17 D5
Bush Hill Rd
Enfield N21 ... 17 B5
Harrow HA3 ... 44 B3
Bush Ind Est NW10 ... 89 B3
Bush La EC4 ... 117 B6 252 C6
Bushmead Cl 7 N15 ... 51 D5
Bushmoor Cres SE18 ... 144 D5
Bushnell Rd SW17 ... 159 B1
Bush Rd
Bermondsey SE8 ... 118 D2
Hackney E8 ... 96 B6
Littleton TW17 ... 192 B4
Richmond TW9 ... 132 B6
Wanstead E11 ... 55 A2
Woodford IG9 ... 37 D6
Bushway RM8 ... 80 D5
Bushwood E11 ... 55 A1
Bushwood Dr SE1 ... 117 D2 263 D3
Bushwood Rd TW9 ... 132 C6
Bushy Ct KT1 ... 175 C2
Bushy Park Gdns TW12 ... 174 B5
Bushy Park Rd TW11 ... 175 B3
Bushy Rd TW11 ... 174 D3
Business Acad Bexley The DA18 ... 125 A4
Business Design Ctr* N1 ... 94 C6 234 B5
Buspace Studios 3 W10 ... 91 A3
Butcher Row E1 ... 96 D1
Butchers Rd E16 ... 99 A1
Bute Ave TW10 ... 154 A2
Bute Ct SM6 ... 219 C3
Bute Gardens W SM6 ... 219 C3
Bute Gdns
Hammersmith W6 ... 112 D2
Wallington SM6 ... 219 C3
Bute House Prep Sch W6 ... 112 D2
Bute Mews NW11 ... 48 A4
Bute Rd
Ilford IG6 ... 56 D4
Thornton Heath CR0 ... 204 C1
Wallington SM6 ... 219 C4
Bute St SW7 ... 114 B2 256 C4
Bute Wlk 18 N1 ... 73 B2
Butfield Ho 6 E9 ... 74 C2
Butler Ave HA1 ... 42 B2
Butler Cl HA8 ... 26 D1
Butler Ct
Dagenham RM8 ... 81 C6
Wembley HA0 ... 65 A4
Butler Ho
32 Bethnal Green E2 ... 96 C4
5 Brixton SW9 ... 138 D4
11 Poplar E14 ... 97 B1
Butler Pl SW1 ... 259 C6
Butler Rd
Dagenham RM8 ... 80 B4
Butler Rd *continued*
Harrow HA1 ... 42 A2
Willesden NW10 ... 67 D1
Butlers Cl TW3 ... 129 B1
Butlers & Colonial Wharf SE1 ... 253 D2
Butler's Cotts DA7 ... 147 C3
Butler St
33 Bethnal Green E2 ... 96 C4
Hillingdon UB10 ... 82 D3
Butler's Wharf W SE1 ... 253 C3
Butley Ct 8 E3 ... 97 A5
Butt Ct SM4 ... 202 A3
Buttercup Cl UB5 ... 63 B2
Butterfield Cl
1 Bermondsey SE16 ... 118 B4
Tottenham N17 ... 33 A4
Twickenham TW1 ... 152 D5
Butterfield Ho 4 EN2 ... 4 D3
Butterfields E17 ... 54 A4
Butterfield Sq 10 E6 ... 100 B1
Butterfly Ct E6 ... 100 B4
Butterfly La SE9 ... 166 D5
Butterfly Wlk 2 SE5 ... 139 B4
Butter Hill SM5, SM6 ... 219 A4
Butteridges Cl RM9 ... 103 B6
Buttermere NW1 ... 231 D2
Buttermere Cl
Bermondsey SE1 ... 263 C3
East Bedfont TW14 ... 149 D3
Leyton E11 ... 76 B4
West Barnes SM4 ... 200 D3
Buttermere Ct NW8 ... 229 C6
Buttermere Dr SW15 ... 157 A6
Buttermere Ho
London N12 ... 30 C5
13 Tower Hamlets E3 ... 97 B4
Buttermere Wlk 9 E8 ... 73 D2
Butterwick W6 ... 112 C2
Butterworth Ct SW16 ... 160 A1
Butterworth Gdns IG8 ... 37 A5
Buttesland St N1 ... 95 B4 235 D2
Buttfield Cl RM10 ... 81 D2
Buttmarsh Cl SE18 ... 122 D1
Buttsbury Rd IG1 ... 79 A3
Butts Cotts TW13 ... 151 B1
Butts Cres TW13 ... 151 C1
Butts Ho TW13 ... 151 C1
Butts Piece UB5 ... 84 B5
Butts Rd BR1 ... 186 C5
Butts The TW8 ... 131 D6
Buxhall Cres E9 ... 75 B2
Buxlow Prep Sch HA9 ... 66 A5
Buxted Rd
Camberwell SE22 ... 139 C1
Colney Hatch N12 ... 30 C5
Dalston E8 ... 73 D1
Buxton Cl
London N9 ... 18 C2
Woodford IG8 ... 37 D4
Buxton Cres SM3 ... 217 A4
Buxton Ct
1 Leyton E11 ... 54 D2
Shoreditch N1 ... 235 B2
Buxton Dr
Kingston u T KT3 ... 177 B1
Leytonstone E11 ... 54 C5
Buxton Gdns W3 ... 110 D6
Buxton Ho
Leytonstone E11 ... 54 C5
3 London SW11 ... 136 B1
Buxton Lo E11 ... 77 B6
Buxton Mews SW4 ... 137 D3
Buxton Rd
Chingford E4 ... 20 B4
Ilford IG2 ... 57 C3
Mortlake SW14 ... 133 C2
Newham E6 ... 100 A4
Stratford E15 ... 76 C3
Thornton Heath CR7 ... 204 D4
Upper Holloway N19 ... 49 D1
Walthamstow E17 ... 53 A5
Willesden NW2 ... 68 B2
Buxton St E1 ... 95 D3 243 D5
Buzzard Creek Ind Est IG11 ... 102 A2
Byam Shaw Sch of Art N19 ... 71 D6
Byam St SW6 ... 136 A3
Byards Croft SW16 ... 181 D2
Byards Ct SE16 ... 118 D3
Byas Ho 6 E3 ... 97 B4
Byatt Wlk TW12 ... 173 A4
Bychurch End 11 TW11 ... 174 D5
Bycroft Rd UB1 ... 85 C3
Bycroft St SE20 ... 184 D3
Bycullah Ave EN2 ... 4 D3
Bycullah Ct EN2 ... 4 D2
Bycullah Rd EN2 ... 4 D3
Byefield Cl SE16 ... 119 A4
Byegrove Ct SW19 ... 180 B4
Byegrove Rd SW19 ... 180 B4
Byelands Cl 12 SE16 ... 118 D5
Bye The W3 ... 89 C1
Bye Ways TW2 ... 151 D1
Byeways The KT5 ... 198 D4
Byeway The SW14 ... 133 A2
Bye Way The HA3 ... 24 D2
Byfeld Gdns SW13 ... 134 A4
Byfield Ct KT3 ... 200 A5
Byfield Rd TW7 ... 131 A2
Byford Cl E15 ... 76 C1
Bygrove CR0 ... 223 D1
Bygrove Prim Sch E14 ... 97 D1
Bygrove St E14 ... 97 D1
Byland Cl
Abbey Wood SE2 ... 124 B3
Carshalton SM4 ... 202 B2
Southgate N21 ... 16 B4
Byne Rd
Carshalton SM5 ... 218 C6
Forest Hill SE26 ... 184 C5
Bynes Rd CR2 ... 221 B1
Byng Pl WC1 ... 93 D3 239 C5
Byng St E14 ... 119 C4
Bynon Ave DA7 ... 147 B2
Byre Rd N14 ... 15 B5
Byrne Ho 11 SW2 ... 160 B6
Byrne Rd SW12 ... 159 B2
Byron Ave
Borehamwood WD6 ... 10 C6
Cranford TW4 ... 128 B3
Plashet E12 ... 78 A2
Queensbury NW9 ... 44 D6
Sutton SM1 ... 218 B4
West Barnes KT3 ... 200 A4
Woodford E18 ... 36 D1
Byron Ave E SM1 ... 218 B4
Byron Cl
Feltham TW12 ... 173 B6
Forest Hill SE26 ... 185 A6
Hackney E8 ... 96 A6
Streatham SW16 ... 182 A4
Thamesmead SE28 ... 124 C5
Walton-on-T KT12 ... 195 A1
Byron Court Prim Sch HA0 ... 65 C6
Byron Ct
Chelsea SW3 ... 257 B3
Dulwich SE21 ... 162 A3
Ealing W7 ... 109 A2
Enfield EN2 ... 4 D3
3 Hampstead NW6 ... 70 A1
Harrow HA1 ... 42 C3
4 New Barnet EN5 ... 2 A1
Paddington W9 ... 91 C3
1 Richmond TW10 ... 175 D6
South Norwood CR7 ... 183 A1
St Pancras WC1 ... 240 C6
11 Wanstead E11 ... 55 A5
Woodford E18 ... 37 B2
Byron Dr
East Finchley N2 ... 48 B3
Erith DA8 ... 147 D5
Byron Gdns SM1 ... 218 B4
Byron Hill Rd HA1, HA2 ... 64 C6
Byron Ho 5 BR3 ... 185 D4
Byron Mews
Hampstead NW3 ... 70 C4
2 Maida Vale W9 ... 91 C3
Byron Par UB10 ... 83 A3
Byron Rd
Dollis Hill NW2 ... 68 B6
Ealing W5 ... 110 B5
Edgware NW7 ... 28 A5
Harrow HA1 ... 42 C3
Leyton E10 ... 53 D1
Walthamstow E17 ... 53 C6
Wealdstone HA3 ... 24 D1
Wembley HA0 ... 65 C5
Byron St E14 ... 98 A1
Byron Way
Hayes UB4 ... 83 D3
Northolt UB5 ... 85 A4
West Drayton UB7 ... 104 B2
Bysouth Cl N15 ... 51 B5
Bythorn St SW9 ... 138 B1
Byton Rd SW17 ... 180 D4
Byward Ave TW14 ... 150 C5
Byward St EC3 ... 117 C6 253 B5
Bywater Ho SE18 ... 122 A3
Bywater Pl SE16 ... 119 A5
Bywater St SW3 ... 114 D1 257 C2
Byway The KT19 ... 215 D4
Bywell Pl W1 ... 239 A3
Bywood Ave CR0 ... 206 D3
Bywood Terr CR0 ... 206 C3
Byworth Ho HA7 ... 25 C4
Byworth Wlk N19 ... 50 A1

C

Cabbell St NW1 ... 92 C2 237 A3
Cabinet Off SW1 ... 250 A2
Cabinet War Rooms & Churchill Mus* SW1 ... 115 D4 249 D2
Cabinet Way E4 ... 35 B4
Cable Ho WC1 ... 234 A2
Cable Pl SE10 ... 142 A4
Cable St E1 ... 118 B6
Cabot Ct SE16 ... 118 D3
Cabot Sq E14 ... 119 C5
Cabot Way 3 E6 ... 99 D6
Cabul Rd SW11 ... 136 C3
Cactus Cl SE5 ... 139 C3
Cactus Wlk W12 ... 89 D1
Cadbury Cl
Ashford TW16 ... 171 C3
Isleworth TW7 ... 131 A4
Cadbury Rd TW16 ... 171 C4
Cadbury Way 1 SE16 ... 118 A2
Caddington Cl EN4 ... 14 C6
Caddington Rd NW2 ... 69 A5
Caddis Cl HA7 ... 24 D3
Cadell Cl E2 ... 95 D5
Cadell Ho 12 E2 ... 95 D5
Cade Rd SE10 ... 142 B4
Cader Rd SW18 ... 158 A5
Cadet Dr SE1 ... 117 D1 263 D2
Cade Tyler Ho 10 SE10 ... 142 A4
Cadiz St SE17 ... 117 A1 262 B1
Cadley Terr SE23 ... 162 C2
Cadman Cl SW9 ... 138 D5
Cadmer Cl KT3 ... 199 C5
Cadmore Ho 6 N1 ... 72 D1
Cadmus Cl 9 SW4 ... 137 D2
Cadmus Ct 6 SW9 ... 138 C4
Cadnam Lo E14 ... 120 B3
Cadnam Point 15 SW15 ... 156 B3
Cadogan Cl
Beckenham BR3 ... 186 B1
Hackney Wick E9 ... 75 B1
Harrow HA2 ... 63 D4
Teddington TW11 ... 174 C5
Cadogan Ct
Chelsea SW3 ... 257 C3
New Malden KT3 ... 199 C5
Sutton SM2 ... 217 D2
Cadogan Ct Gdns SW1 ... 258 A4
Cadogan Gate SW1 ... 114 D2 257 D4
Cadogan Gdns
Chelsea SW3 ... 114 D2 257 D3
Finchley N3 ... 29 D2
Southgate N21 ... 16 C6
Wanstead E18 ... 55 B6
Cadogan Ho SW3 ... 266 D5
Cadogan La SW1 ... 115 A3 258 A5
Cadogan Pl SW1 ... 114 D3 257 D5
Cadogan Rd
Kingston u T KT6 ... 197 D4
Woolwich SE18 ... 123 A3
Cadogan Sq SW1 ... 114 D3 257 D5
Cadogan St SW3 ... 114 D2 257 C3
Cadogan Terr E9 ... 75 B1
Cadoxton Ave 3 N15 ... 51 D3
Cadwallon Rd SE9 ... 167 A2
Caedmon Rd N7 ... 72 B4
Caerleon Cl
Claygate KT10 ... 213 B1
Sidcup DA14 ... 190 C5
Caerleon Terr SE2 ... 124 B2
Caernafon Ho HA7 ... 25 A5
Caernarvon Cl CR4 ... 204 A6
Caernarvon Ct 3 KT5 ... 198 B4
Caernarvon Ho W2 ... 236 A2
Caesar Ct 25 E2 ... 96 D5
Caesar's Way TW17 ... 193 B3
Caesars Wlk CR4 ... 202 D4
Cahill St EC1 ... 242 B5
Cahir St E14 ... 119 D2
Cain Ct 2 W5 ... 87 C2
Caine Ho W3 ... 110 D4
Cain's La TW14 ... 149 C6
Caird St W10 ... 91 B4
Cairn Ave W5 ... 109 D5
Cairndale Cl BR1 ... 186 D3
Cairnfield Ave NW2 ... 67 D5
Cairnfield Ct NW2 ... 67 C5
Cairngorm Cl 3 TW11 ... 175 A5
Cairn Ho 3 SW19 ... 180 C3
Cairns Ho 3 N7 ... 72 B4
Cairns Mews SE18 ... 144 A4
Cairns Rd SW11 ... 158 C6
Cairn Way HA7 ... 24 D4
Cairo New Rd CR0 ... 220 D6
Cairo Rd E17 ... 53 C5
Caister Ho N7 ... 72 B2
Caistor Ho
10 Balham SW12 ... 159 B4
5 West Ham E15 ... 98 D6
Caistor Mews SW12 ... 159 B4
Caistor Park Rd E15 ... 98 D6
Caistor Rd SW12 ... 159 B4
Caithness Gdns DA15 ... 167 D5
Caithness Ho N1 ... 233 C6
Caithness Rd
Hammersmith W14 ... 112 D3
Mitcham CR4 ... 181 B3
Calabria Rd N5 ... 72 D3
Calais Gate SE5 ... 138 D4
Calais St SE5 ... 138 D4
Calbourne Rd SW12 ... 159 A4
Calcott Wlk SE9 ... 187 D6
Calcraft Ho 10 E2 ... 96 C5
Caldbeck Ave KT4 ... 200 B1
Caldecot Ct SE5 ... 139 A3
Caldecote 3 KT1 ... 176 C1
Caldecote Gdns WD23 ... 8 C4
Caldecote La WD23 ... 8 D5
Caldecot Rd SE5 ... 139 A3
Caldecott Way E5 ... 74 D5
Calder Ave UB6 ... 86 D5
Calder Cl EN1 ... 5 C2
Calder Ct SE16 ... 119 B5
Calder Gdns HA8 ... 44 C6
Calder Ho UB5 ... 85 A6
Calderon Ho NW8 ... 230 A4
Calderon Pl 20 W10 ... 90 C2
Calderon Rd E11 ... 76 B5
Calder Rd SM4 ... 202 A4
Caldervale Rd SW4 ... 159 D6
Calderwood St SE18 ... 122 C2
Caldew Ct NW7 ... 28 A3
Caldew St SE5 ... 139 B5
Caldicote Gn NW9 ... 45 C3
Caldon Ho 2 UB5 ... 85 B3
Caldwell Rd WD19 ... 22 D6
Caldwell St SW9 ... 138 B5 270 D3
Caldy Rd DA17 ... 125 D3
Caldy Wlk 19 N1 ... 73 A2
Caleb St SE1 ... 252 B2
Caledonia Ct
Barking IG11 ... 102 C5
Hendon NW4 ... 28 C1
Caledonia Ho 15 E14 ... 97 A1
Caledonian Cl 1 IG3 ... 58 B1
Caledonian Ct UB5 ... 85 A3
Caledonian Market SE1 ... 117 C3 263 B6
Caledonian Rd
Islington N1 ... 94 B6 233 C5
Lower Holloway N7 ... 72 B2
Caledonian Road & Barnsbury Sta N7 ... 72 B1
Caledonian Road Sta N7 ... 72 B2
Caledonian Sq 6 NW1 ... 71 D2
Caledonian Wharf Rd E14 ... 120 B2
Caledonia Rd TW19 ... 148 A3
Caledonia St N1 ... 233 B3
Caledon Rd
East Ham E6 ... 78 B1
Hackbridge SM5, SM6 ... 219 A4
Cale St SW3 ... 114 C1 257 A2
Caletock Way SE10 ... 120 D1
Calgarth NW1 ... 232 B3
Calgary Ct 30 SE16 ... 118 C4
Caliban Twr 9 N1 ... 95 C5
Calico Ho 4 SW11 ... 136 A2
Calico Row 5 SW11 ... 136 A2
Calidore Cl SW2 ... 160 B5
California Bldg 2 SE13 ... 141 D4
California La WD23 ... 8 B3
California Rd KT3 ... 199 A6
Callaby Terr 11 N1 ... 73 B2
Callaghan Cl SE13 ... 142 C1
Callahan Cotts 8 E1 ... 96 C2
Callander Rd SE6 ... 164 A2
Callanders The WD23 ... 8 C3
Callan Sch The W1 ... 93 C1 239 B2
Callard Ave N13 ... 32 D6
Callcott Ct NW6 ... 69 B1
Callcott Rd NW6 ... 69 B1
Callcott St W8 ... 245 A4
Callendar Rd SW7 ... 256 C6
Callingham Cl 13 E14 ... 97 B2
Callingham Ho 1 SW4 ... 138 A2
Callis Farm Cl TW19 ... 148 A5
Callis Rd E17 ... 53 B3
Callonfield 3 E17 ... 53 A5
Callow St SW3 ... 136 B6 266 C6
Calmington Rd SE5 ... 139 C6
Calmont Rd BR1 ... 186 C4
Calonne Rd SW19 ... 178 D6
Calshot Ho N1 ... 233 C4
Calshot Rd TW6 ... 126 D3
Calshot St N1 ... 94 B5 233 C3
Calshot Way
Enfield EN2 ... 4 D2
Harlington TW6 ... 126 C3
Calstock NW1 ... 232 C5
Calstock Ho SE11 ... 261 B2
Calthorpe Gdns
Edgware HA8 ... 26 B5
Sutton SM1 ... 218 A5
Calthorpe St WC1 ... 94 B3 240 D6
Calton Ave SE21 ... 161 C5
Calton Rd EN5 ... 14 B5
Calumet Ct SW17 ... 180 C4
Calver 13 NW5 ... 71 B4
Calver Ct E17 ... 54 B6
Calverley Cl BR3 ... 185 D4
Calverley Cres RM10 ... 81 C6
Calverley Gdns HA3 ... 43 D2
Calverley Gr N19 ... 49 D1
Calverley Rd KT17 ... 216 A2
Calvert Ave E2 ... 95 D4
Calvert Cl
Belvedere DA17 ... 125 D2
Sidcup DA14 ... 191 A4
Calvert Ct
1 London N19 ... 49 C1
5 Richmond TW9 ... 132 B1
Calvert Ho 9 W12 ... 112 B6
Calverton SE5 ... 139 C6
Calverton Prim Sch E16 ... 99 D1
Calverton Rd E6 ... 100 C6
Calvert Rd SE10 ... 120 D1
Calvert's Bldgs SE1 ... 252 C3
Calvert St NW1 ... 93 A6 231 A6
Calvin St E1 ... 95 D3 243 C5
Calydon Rd SE7 ... 121 B1
Calypso Cres 6 SE15 ... 139 D5
Calypso Way SE8, SE16 ... 119 B2
Camac Rd TW2 ... 152 B3
Camarthen Gn NW9 ... 45 C3
Cambalt Ho 3 SW15 ... 156 D6
Cambalt Rd SW15 ... 156 D6
Cambay Ho 7 E1 ... 97 A3
Cambell Jun & Inf Schs RM9 ... 80 D1
Camber Ho 4 SE15 ... 140 C6
Camberley Ave
Enfield EN1 ... 5 C1
Wimbledon SW20 ... 178 B1
Camberley Cl SM3 ... 216 D5
Camberley Ct 15 SM2 ... 217 D1
Camberley Ho NW1 ... 231 D3
Camberley Rd TW6 ... 126 C2
Cambert Way SE9 ... 143 B1
CAMBERWELL ... 139 A4
Camberwell Bsns Ctr SE5 ... 139 B5
Camberwell Church St SE5 ... 139 B4
Camberwell Coll of Arts
Camberwell SE5 ... 139 C4
Camberwell SE15 ... 139 D5
Camberwell Glebe SE5 ... 139 C4
Camberwell Gn SE5 ... 139 B4
Camberwell Gr SE5 ... 139 C3
Camberwell Green SE5 ... 139 A4
Camberwell New Rd SW9 ... 138 D5
Camberwell Rd SE5 ... 139 A5
Camberwell Station Rd SE5 ... 139 A4
Camberwell Trad Est SE5 ... 139 A4

Cambeys Rd RM10 81 D3
Cambisgate SW19 179 A5
Camborne Ave W13 109 C4
Camborne Cl TW6 126 C2
Camborne Rd
Belmont SM2 217 D1
Bexley DA16 145 D3
Croydon CR0 206 A2
Harmondsworth TW6 126 C2
Sidcup DA14 168 C1
Wandsworth SW18 157 C4
West Barnes SM4 200 D4
Camborne Way
Harlington TW6 126 C2
Heston TW5 129 C4
Cambourne Ave N9 18 D4
Cambourne Mews 6
W11 91 A1
Cambrai Ct N13 32 A6
Cambray Rd
Broom Hill BR6 211 D2
Streatham SW12 159 C3
Cambria 6 BR3 185 D1
Cambria Cl
Hounslow TW3 129 C1
Sidcup DA15 167 C3
Cambria Ct TW14 150 B4
Cambria Gdns TW19 148 A4
Cambria Ho
Forest Hill SE26 184 A6
14 Limehouse E14 97 A1
Cambria Lo 3 SW15 157 B6
Cambrian Ave IG2 57 C4
Cambrian Cl SE27 160 D1
Cambrian Ct UB2 107 D2
Cambrian Gn NW9 45 C4
Cambrian Rd
Leyton E10 53 C1
Richmond TW10 154 B5
Cambria Rd SE5 139 A2
Cambria St
SW6 135 D5 265 D3
Cambridge Ave
Falconwood DA16 145 D1
Greenford UB6 64 D3
Kilburn NW6 91 C5
Kingston u T KT3,
SW20 177 D1
Cambridge Barracks Rd
11 SE18 122 B2
Cambridge Cir
WC2 93 D1 239 D1
Cambridge Cl
Hounslow TW4 129 A1
Walthamstow E17 53 B3
Willesden NW10 67 A5
Wimbledon SW20 178 B2
Wood Green N22 32 C2
Cambridge Cotts
TW9 132 C6
Cambridge Cres
20 Bethnal Green E2 96 B5
Teddington TW11 175 A5
Cambridge Ct
4 Barnet EN5 1 B2
26 Bethnal Green E2 96 B5
7 Hammersmith W6 112 C2
2 Kilburn NW6 91 C5
Marylebone W2 237 A3
Stamford Hill N16 51 C2
Wembley HA0 65 D4
Wimbledon SW20 178 B2
Cambridge Dr
Lee SE12 165 A6
Ruislip HA4 62 D6
Cambridge Gate NW1 238 C6
Cambridge Gate Mews
NW1 238 D6
Cambridge Gdns
Enfield EN1 6 A3
Kilburn NW6 91 C5
Kingston u T KT1 176 C1
Muswell Hill N10 31 B2
North Kensington W10 91 A1
Southgate N21 17 B4
Tottenham N17 33 B3
Cambridge Gn SE9 166 D3
Cambridge Gr
Hammersmith W6 112 B2
Penge SE20 184 B2
Cambridge Grove Rd
13 Kingston u T KT1 176 C1
Kingston u T KT1 198 C6
Cambridge Heath Rd E1,
E2 96 B4
Cambridge Heath Sta
E2 96 B5
Cambridge Ho
Barking IG11 79 A1
Ealing W13 87 A1
Cambridge Ho *continued*
Fulham SW6 135 A2
2 Teddington TW11 175 A5
8 Woolwich SE18 122 B2
Cambridge Mans
SW11 267 C1
Cambridge Par EN1 6 A4
CAMBRIDGE PARK 153 C4
Cambridge Park Ct
TW1 153 D4
Cambridge Park Rd
E11 55 A2
Cambridge Pas 9 E9 74 C1
Cambridge Pk
Twickenham TW1 153 D5
Wanstead E11 55 A3
Cambridge Pl W8 245 D1
Cambridge Rd
Barking IG11 79 A1
Barnes SW13 133 D3
Battersea
SW11 136 D4 267 C1
Carshalton SM5 218 C3
3 Chingford E4 20 B3
East Molesey KT8 195 B5
Hampton TW12 173 B3
Hanwell W7 108 D4
Harrow HA2 41 C4
Hounslow TW4 129 A1
Ilford IG3 57 C1
Kilburn NW6 91 C4
Kilburn NW6 91 C5
Kingston u T KT1 176 C1
Leytonstone E11 54 D3
Littleton TW15 171 A3
Mitcham CR4 203 C6
New Malden KT3 199 C5
Penge SE20 206 B6
Plaistow BR1 187 A3
Richmond TW9 132 C5
Sidcup DA14 189 C6
Southall UB1 107 B5
Teddington TW11 175 A5
Twickenham TW1 153 D5
Walton-on-T KT12 194 B3
Wimbledon SW20 178 B2
Cambridge Rd N W4 110 D1
Cambridge Rd S 3
W4 110 D1
Cambridge Row
SE18 122 D1
Cambridge Sch W6 112 B2
Cambridge Sq
W2 92 C1 237 A2
Cambridge St
SW1 115 C1 259 A2
Cambridge Terr
Edmonton N9 17 D4
Regent's Pk NW1 231 C1
Cambridge Terr Mews
NW1 231 D1
Cambstone Cl N11 15 A2
Cambus Cl UB4 85 A2
Cambus Rd E16 99 A2
Cam Ct 2 SE15 139 D6
Camdale Rd SE18 145 D5
Camden Ave
Feltham TW13 150 C3
Hayes UB4 106 D6
Camden Cl BR7 189 A2
Camden Coll of English
NW1 71 A1
Camden Ct 9 DA17 125 C1
Camden Gdns
Camden Town NW1 71 B1
Sutton SM1 217 D3
Thornton Heath CR7 204 D6
Camden Gr BR7 188 D4
Camden High St
NW1 93 C6 232 A5
Camden Hill Rd SE19 183 C4
Camden Ho
6 Deptford SE8 119 B1
Wallington CR6 220 A5
Camdenhurst St E14 97 A1
Camden Jun Sch
SM5 218 D4
Camden Lock Pl NW1 71 B1
Camden Mews NW1 71 D2
Camden Mkt*
NW1 93 B6 231 D6
Camden Park Rd
Camden Town NW1 71 D2
Chislehurst West BR7 188 C3
Camden Pas
N1 94 D6 234 C5
Camden Rd
Camden Town
NW1 93 B6 231 D6
Carshalton SM5 218 D4
Camden Rd *continued*
Old Bexley DA5 169 B4
Sutton SM1 217 D3
Walthamstow E17 53 B3
Wanstead E11 55 B3
Camden Road Sta
NW1 71 C1
Camden Row SE3 142 C3
Camden Sch for Girls The
NW5 71 C2
Camden Sq NW1 71 D2
Camden St
NW1 93 C6 232 B5
Camden Studios NW1 232 B5
Camden Terr 17 NW1 71 D2
CAMDEN TOWN 71 B1
Camden Town Sta
NW1 93 B6 231 D6
Camden Way
Chislehurst West
BR7 188 C3
Thornton Heath CR7 204 D6
Camden Wlk N1 234 C5
Cameford Ct 20
SW12 160 A4
Camelford NW1 232 B5
Camelford Ct 15 W11 91 A1
Camelford Ho SE1 260 B1
Camelford Wlk 13
W11 91 A1
Camel Gr KT2 175 D5
Camelia Ct IG8 36 C4
Camellia Ct 20 BR3 185 C3
Camellia Ho
Feltham TW13 150 A3
New Cross SE8 141 B5
Camellia Pl TW2 151 D4
Camellia St SW8 270 A3
Camelot Cl
Plumstead SE18 123 B4
Wimbledon SW19 179 C6
Camelot Ho 15 NW1 71 D2
Camelot Prim Sch
SE15 140 B6
Camel Rd E16 121 D5
Camera Pl SW10 266 C6
Cameret Ct 6 W11 112 D4
Cameron Cl
East Barnet N20 14 C2
Edmonton N18 34 B5
Cameron Ct 3 SW19 157 A3
Cameron Ho
8 Bromley BR1 186 D2
Camberwell SE5 139 A5
St John's Wood NW8 230 A4
Cameron House Sch
SW10 266 D6
Cameron Lo TW3 130 A1
Cameron Pl SW16 160 C2
Cameron Rd
Bromley BR2 209 A4
Forest Hill SE6 163 B2
Ilford IG3 57 C1
Thornton Heath CR0 204 D3
Cameron Sq CR4 180 C2
Camerton Ct 8 E8 73 D2
Camfrey Ct N8 50 A5
Camgate Ctr The
TW19 148 B4
Camilla Cl TW16 171 D4
Camilla Ct 12 SM2 217 C1
Camilla Rd SE16 118 B2
Camille Cl SE25 206 A6
Camlan Rd BR1 186 D6
Camlet St E2 243 C6
Camlet Way EN4 1 D4
Camley St NW1 93 D5 232 D4
Camm 23 NW9 27 D1
Camm Gdns
5 Kingston u T KT1 176 B1
Thames Ditton KT7 196 D2
Camomile Ave CR4 180 D2
Camomile St
EC3 95 C1 243 B2
Camomile Way UB7 82 A1
Campaign Ct W9 91 B3
Campana Rd
SW6 135 C4 265 B2
Campasps Bsns Pk
TW16 193 D4
Campbell Ave IG6 57 A5
Campbell Cl
Ruislip HA4 40 A3
Shooters Hill SE18 144 C4
Streatham SW16 181 D6
Twickenham TW2 152 B3
Campbell Croft HA8 26 C5
Campbell Ct
Dulwich SE21 162 A3
Ealing W7 108 C6
Campbell Ct *continued*
Kingsbury NW9 45 A3
South Kensington SW7 256 A5
Tottenham N17 33 D2
Campbell Gordon Way
NW2 68 B4
Campbell Ho
Paddington W2 236 C5
Pimlico SW1 259 A1
30 Shepherd's Bush
W12 112 B6
6 Wallington SM6 219 B4
Campbell Rd
Bow E3 97 C4
Ealing W7 108 C6
Newham E6 100 A6
Stratford E15 76 D4
Thornton Heath CR0 204 D3
Tottenham N17 34 A2
Twickenham TW2 152 B2
Walthamstow E17 53 B5
Campbell Wlk N1 233 B6
Campdale Rd N7 71 D5
Campden Cres
Dagenham RM8 80 C4
Wembley HA0 65 B5
Campden Gr
W8 113 C4 245 B2
Campden Hill
W8 113 C4 245 A2
Campden Hill Ct W8 245 B2
Campden Hill Gate
W8 245 A2
Campden Hill Gdns
W8 245 A4
Campden Hill Mans
W8 245 B4
Campden Hill Pl W14 244 D4
Campden Hill Rd
W8 113 C4 245 A2
Campden Hill Sq
W14 113 B5 244 D4
Campden Ho 4 NW6 70 B1
Campden Hos W8 245 A3
Campden House Cl
W8 245 B2
Campden Rd
Ickenham UB10 60 B4
South Croydon CR2 221 C3
Campden St
W8 113 C5 245 A3
Campden Way RM8 80 B4
Campe Ho 1 N10 31 A3
Campen Cl SW19 157 A2
Camperdown St E1 243 D1
Campfield Rd SE9 165 D4
Campion Cl
Harrow HA3 44 B3
Hillingdon UB8 82 B2
Newham E6 122 B6
South Croydon CR2 221 C4
Campion Ct
London N12 30 C4
10 Wembley HA0 88 A5
Campion Gdns IG8 37 A5
Campion Ho 15 N16 73 C3
Campion House
(Seminary) TW7 130 B4
Campion Pl SE28 124 B5
Campion Rd
Hounslow TW7 130 D4
Putney SW15 156 C6
Campion Terr NW2 68 D5
Campion Way HA8 27 A6
Camplin Rd HA3 44 A4
Camplin St SE14 140 D5
Camp Rd SW19 178 C5
Campsbourne Ho 3
N8 50 A5
Campsbourne Jun & Inf
Schs N8 50 A6
Campsbourne Rd
Hornsey N8 50 A5
Hornsey N8 50 A6
Campsbourne The N8 50 A5
Campsey Gdns RM9 80 B1
Campsey Rd RM9 80 B1
Campsfield Ho N8 50 A6
Campsfield Rd N8 50 A6
Campshill Pl SE13 164 A6
Campshill Rd SE13 164 A6
Camp Site The BR8 191 C3
Campton Hill Twrs
W8 245 A4
Campus Rd E17 53 B3
Camp View SW19 178 B5
Cam Rd E15 98 B6
Camrose Ave
Edgware HA8 26 B2
Erith DA8 147 D6
Camrose Ave *continued*
Feltham TW13 172 C6
Camrose Cl
Croydon CR0 207 A2
Morden SM4 201 C5
Camrose St SE2 124 A2
Camsey Ho 8 SW2 160 B6
Canada Ave N18 33 A4
Canada Cres W3 89 A3
Canada Gdns SE13 164 A6
Canada Rd W3 89 A2
Canada Sq E14 119 D5
Canada St SE16 118 D4
Canada Water Sta
SE16 118 D3
Canada Way W12 112 B6
Canadian Ave SE6 163 D3
Canal App SE8 141 A6
Canal Bldg N1 235 A4
Canal Bridge SE15 140 A6
Canal Bvd 7 NW1 71 D2
Canal Cl
Mile End E1 97 A3
North Kensington W10 90 D3
Canal Gr SE15 140 B6
Canal Head Public Sq 1
SE15 140 A4
Canal Path 22 E2 95 D6
Canalside Studios 29
N1 95 C6
Canal St SE5 139 B6
Canal Way W10 90 D3
Canal Wlk
Croydon CR0 205 D3
Forest Hill SE26 184 C5
Shoreditch N1 95 B6 235 D6
CANARY WHARF 119 D5
Canary Wharf* E14 119 D5
Canary Wharf Pier (River
Bus) E14 119 B5
Canary Wharf Sta
E14 119 D5
Canary Wharf Sta (DLR)
E14 119 C5
Canberra Cl NW4 46 A6
Canberra Dr UB4 84 C4
Canberra Ho 7 HA4 40 C1
Canberra Prim Sch
W12 112 B6
Canberra Rd
Charlton SE7 143 D6
Ealing W13 109 A5
Erith DA7 146 D6
Harlington TW6 126 C2
Newham E6 100 B6
Canbury Ave KT2 176 B2
Canbury Bsns Pk 3
KT2 176 A2
Canbury Ct 3 KT2 176 A3
Canbury Mews SE26 162 A1
Canbury Park Rd KT2 176 B2
Canbury Sch KT2 176 D4
Cancell Rd SW9 138 C4
Candahar Rd SW11 136 C3
Candida Ct 9 NW1 71 B1
Candishe Ho SE1 253 C2
Candle Gr SE15 140 B2
Candlelight Ct 5 E15 76 D2
Candlemakers 25
SW11 136 B2
Candler Mews TW1 153 A4
Candler St N15 51 B3
Candover St W1 239 A3
Candy St E3 97 B6
Caney Mews NW2 68 D6
Canfield Dr HA4 62 B3
Canfield Gdns NW6 69 D1
Canfield Ho N15 51 C3
Canfield Pl NW6 70 A2
Canford Ave UB5 85 A6
Canford Cl EN2 4 C3
Canford Gdns KT3 199 C3
Canford Pl TW11 175 C4
Canford Rd SW11 159 A6
Canham Rd
Acton W3 111 C4
South Norwood SE25 205 C6
Canmore Gdns SW16 181 C3
Cann Hall Prim Sch
E11 76 D5
Cann Hall Rd E11 76 D4
Cann Ho W14 254 B5
Canning Cres N22 32 B2
Canning Cross SE5 139 C3
Canning Ct N22 32 B2
Canning Ho 23 W12 112 B6
Canning Pas
W8 114 A3 256 A6
Canning Pl
W8 114 A3 256 A6
Canning Pl Mews W8 256 A6
Canning Rd
Croydon CR0 221 D6
Harrow HA3 42 D6
Highbury N5 72 D5
Walthamstow E17 53 A6
West Ham E15 98 C5
Cannington 14 NW5 71 A2
Cannington Rd RM9 80 C2
CANNING TOWN 99 B2
Canning Town E16 98 C1
Canning Town Sta E16 98 C1
Cannizaro Rd SW19 178 D5
Cannock Ho N4 51 B2
Cannock Lo EN1 17 C5
Cannonbury Ave HA5 40 D3
Cannon Cl
Hampton TW12 173 D4
West Barnes SW20 200 C6
Cannon Dr 21 E14 119 C6
Cannon Hill
Palmers Green N14 16 A1
West Hampstead NW6 69 C3
Cannon Hill La SM4,
SW20 201 A5
Cannon Hill Mews
N14 16 A1
Cannon Ho
Lambeth SE11 260 D3
Penge SE26 184 B4
Cannon La
Hampstead NW3 70 B5
Pinner HA5 41 A3
Cannon Lane Fst & Mid
Schs HA5 40 D3
Cannon Pl
Hampstead NW3 70 B5
Woolwich SE7 122 A1
Cannon Rd
Erith DA7 147 B4
Palmers Green N14 16 A1
Cannon St
EC4 117 A6 252 B6
Cannon Street Rd E1 96 B1
Cannon Street Sta
EC4 117 B6 252 C6
Cannon Trad Est HA9 66 D4
Cannon Way KT8 195 D5
Cannon (W End of
General Roy's Base
Line)* TW6 126 D4
Cannon Wharf Bsns Ctr 12
SE8 119 A2
Canon Ave RM6 58 C4
Canon Barnett Prim Sch
E1 95 D1 243 D2
Canon Beck Rd SE16 118 C4
Canonbie Rd SE23 162 C4
CANONBURY 73 A2
Canonbury Bsns Ctr
N1 235 B6
Canonbury Cres N1 73 A1
Canonbury Ct 21 N1 72 D1
Canonbury Gr N1 73 A1
Canonbury Hts 6 N1 73 B2
Canonbury La N1 72 D1
Canonbury Pk N N1 73 A2
Canonbury Pk S N1 73 A2
Canonbury Pl N1 72 D2
Canonbury Prim Sch
N1 72 D2
Canonbury Rd
Enfield EN1 5 C4
Islington N1 72 D1
Canonbury Sq N1 72 D1
Canonbury St N1 73 A1
Canonbury Sta N1, N5 73 A3
Canonbury Villas N1 72 D1
Canon Mohan Cl N14 15 B5
Canon Murnane Rd
SE1 263 C5
Canon Palmer RC Sch
IG3 57 C1
Canon Rd BR1 209 D6
Canon Row
SW1 116 A4 250 A1
Canons Cl
East Finchley N2 48 B2
Edgware HA8 26 B4
Canons Cnr HA8 26 A6
Canons Ct
Edgware HA8 26 B4
Leyton E15 76 C4
Canons Dr HA8 26 B4
Canons High Sch HA8 26 B1
Canons L Ctr The
CR4 202 D5

Canonsleigh Rd RM9 80 B1
CANONS PARK 26 A3
Canons Park Cl HA8 26 A3
Canons Park Sta HA8 26 A3
Canon St N1 95 A6 235 A5
Canon's Wlk CR0 222 D5
Canopus Way
Northwood HA6 22 A6
Stanwell TW19 148 A4
Canrobert St E2 96 B4
Cantelowes Ho EN5 12 D6
Cantelowes Rd NW1 71 D2
Canterbury SE13 164 A6
Canterbury Ave
Redbridge IG1 56 A2
Sidcup DA15 168 C2
Canterbury Cl
Beckenham BR3 185 D2
16 Camberwell SE5 139 A3
7 Newham E6 100 B1
North Cheam KT4 216 D6
Southall UB6 85 D2
Canterbury Cres
SW9 138 C2
Canterbury Ct
Acton W3 111 C5
4 Ashford TW15 170 B6
Eltham SE12 165 B1
15 Hendon NW9 27 D1
Kilburn NW6 91 C5
South Croydon CR2 221 A1
Thornton Heath CR0 204 C2
Canterbury Gr SE27,
SW16 160 C1
Canterbury Hall KT4 200 B2
Canterbury Ho
2 Barking IG11 80 A1
6 Bromley E3 97 D4
Lambeth SE1 260 D6
Canterbury Ind Pk 15
SE15 140 C6
Canterbury Mans NW6 69 D2
Canterbury Pl SE17 261 D3
Canterbury Rd
Feltham TW13 151 A2
Harrow HA1, HA2 42 A4
Kilburn NW6 91 C5
Leyton E10 54 A3
Morden SM4 202 A3
Thornton Heath CR0 204 C2
Canterbury Terr NW6 91 C5
Cantium Ret Pk SE1 140 A6
Cantley Gdns
Ilford IG2 57 A3
South Norwood SE19 183 D2
Cantley Rd W7 109 A3
Canton St E14 97 C1
Cantrell Rd E3 97 C3
Cantwell Ho SE18 144 D5
Cantwell Rd SE18 144 D5
Canute Ct SW16 160 C1
Canute Gdns SE16 118 D2
Canute Ho 1 TW8 131 C5
Canvey St SE1 252 A4
Cape Cl IG11 78 D1
Cape Henry Ct 15
E14 120 B6
Capel KT5 198 B2
Capel Ave SM6 220 B3
Capel Cl
Keston Mark BR2 210 A1
Whetstone N20 14 A1
Capel Ct SE20 184 C2
Capel Gdns
Ilford IG3 79 D4
Pinner HA5 41 B5
Capel Ho
17 Hackney E9 74 C1
South Oxhey WD19 22 D6
Capella Ho 1 SE7 143 B6
Capel Lo
5 Richmond TW9 132 B4
12 Streatham SW2 160 B4
Capel Point E7 77 B4
Capel Rd
East Barnet EN4 14 C5
Forest Gate E7, E12 77 C4
Capener's Cl SW1 248 A1
Cape Rd N17 52 A6
Capern Rd SW18 158 A3
Cape Yd 6 E1 118 A5
Capio Nightingale Hospl
SW3 257 B1
Capital Bsns Ctr
South Croydon CR0 221 B1
Wembley HA0 87 D5
Capital City Acad
NW10 90 B6
Capital East Apts 8
E16 121 A6
Capital Ind Est
Belvedere DA17 125 D3
Mitcham CR4 202 D4
Capital Interchange Way
TW8 110 C1
Capital Sh Ctrs SW1 249 C1
Capital Wharf 15 E1 118 A5
Capitol Ind Pk NW9 45 A6
Capitol Way NW9 45 A6
Capland Ho NW8 236 D6
Capland St
NW8 92 B3 236 D6
Caplan Est CR4 181 C2
Caple Ho SW10 266 B4
Caple Rd NW10 89 D5
Capper St WC1 93 C3 239 B5
Caprea Cl UB4 84 D2
Capricorn Ctr RM8 59 B2
Capri Ho E17 35 B1
Capri Rd CR0 205 D2
Capstan Cl RM6 58 B3
Capstan Ho 6 E14 120 A2
Capstan Rd SE8 119 B2
Capstan Ride EN2 4 C3
Capstan Sq E14 120 A4
Capstan Way SE16 119 A5
Capstone Rd BR1 186 D6
Capthorne Ave HA2 41 B1
Capuchin Cl HA7 25 B4
Capulet Mews 1 E16 121 A5
Capworth St E10 53 D2
Caradoc Cl W2 91 C1
Caradoc Evans Cl N11 31 B5
Caradoc St SE10 120 C1
Caradon Cl 4 E11 76 C6
Caradon Ct 7 TW1 153 C5
Caradon Way N15 51 B5
Cara Ho 10 N1 72 C1
Caranday Villas 5
W11 112 D5
Caravel Cl E14 119 C3
Caravelle Gdns 1
UB5 84 D4
Caravel Mews 14 SE8 141 C6
Caraway Cl E13 99 B2
Caraway Hts E14 120 A6
Caraway Pl SM6 219 B5
Carberry Rd 12 SE19 183 C4
Carbery Ave W3 110 B4
Carbis Cl E4 20 B3
Carbis Rd E14 97 B1
Carbroke Ho 9 E9 96 C6
Carburton St
W1 93 B3 238 D5
Cardale St 1 E14 120 A3
Cardamom Ct 1 E12 78 C4
Carden Rd SE15 140 B2
Cardiff Ho 9 SE15 140 A6
Cardiff Rd
Ealing W7 109 A3
Enfield EN3 6 B1
Cardiff St SE18 145 C5
Cardigan Ct 3 W7 86 D3
Cardigan Gdns IG3 80 A6
Cardigan Rd
Barnes SW13 134 A3
Bow E3 97 B5
Richmond TW10 154 A5
Wimbledon SW19 180 A4
Cardigan St
SE11 116 C1 261 A2
Cardigan Wlk 19 N1 73 A1
Cardinal Ave
Kingston u T KT2 176 A4
West Barnes SM4 201 A3
Cardinal Bourne St
SE1 262 D5
Cardinal Cap Alley
SE1 252 A5
Cardinal Cl
Burnt Oak HA8 27 B3
Chislehurst BR7 189 B2
West Barnes SM4 201 A3
Worcester Pk KT19,
KT4 216 A4
Cardinal Cres KT3 177 A1
Cardinal Ct KT8 196 B5
Cardinal Dr KT12 194 D1
Cardinal Hinsey Cl
NW10 90 A5
Cardinal Hinsley RC High
Sch (Boys) NW10 90 A6
Cardinal Pl SW15 134 D1
Cardinal Pole RC Sch
London E9 74 D1
London E9 75 A3
Cardinal Rd
Feltham TW13 150 B3
Ruislip HA4 40 D1
Cardinal Road Inf Sch
TW13 150 B3
Cardinals Way N19 49 D1
Cardinal's Wlk
Ashford TW16 171 C4
Hampton TW12 174 A3
Cardinal Vaughan Meml
Sch The W14 244 A2
Cardinal Way HA3 42 C6
Cardinal Wiseman RC Sch
The UB6 86 A2
Cardinal Wlk SW1 259 A5
Cardine Mews SE15 140 B5
Cardington Sq TW4 128 D1
Cardington St
NW1 93 C4 232 B1
Cardozo Rd N7 72 A3
Cardrew Ave N12 30 B5
Cardrew Cl N12 30 B5
Cardrew Ct 8 N12 30 B5
Cardross St W6 112 B3
Cardwell Prim Sch
SE18 122 B2
Cardwell Rd 3 N7 72 A4
Career Ct 11 SE16 118 D4
Carew Cl N7 72 B6
Carew Ct
15 Deptford SE14 140 D6
Ilford RM6 58 B3
Carew Ho
West Norwood SW16 160 C1
23 Woolwich SE18 122 B2
Carew Manor Sch
SM6 219 D5
Carew Rd
Ashford TW15 171 A4
Ealing W13 109 C4
Mitcham CR4 181 A1
Thornton Heath CR7 204 D5
Tottenham N17 34 A1
Wallington SM6 219 C2
Carew St SE5 139 A3
Carey Ct
Bexley DA6 169 D6
20 Camberwell SE5 139 A5
Carey Gdns
SW8 137 D4 269 C1
Carey Ho E5 74 B5
Carey La EC2 242 A2
Carey Pl SW1 259 C3
Carey Rd RM9 81 A4
Carey St WC2 94 B1 240 D1
Carey Way HA9 66 D4
Carfax Pl SW4 137 D1
Carfax Rd UB3 106 A2
Carfree Cl 5 N1 72 C1
Cargill Rd SW18 158 A3
Cargreen Pl SE25 205 D5
Cargreen Rd SE25 205 D5
Cargrey Ho 9 HA7 25 C5
Carholme Rd SE23 163 B3
Carillon Ct W5 109 D6
Carinthia Ct 5 SE8 119 A2
Carisbrook 2 N10 31 B1
Carisbrook Cl EN1 5 D4
Carisbrooke Ave DA5 168 D3
Carisbrooke Cl
Stanmore HA7 25 D1
Twickenham TW4 151 A4
Carisbrooke Ct
Acton W3 111 A4
Belmont SM2 217 B1
Northolt UB5 85 B6
1 Streatham SW16 160 B1
Carisbrooke Gdns
SE15 139 D5
Carisbrooke Ho
10 Kingston u T KT2 176 A2
Richmond TW10 154 C6
Carisbrooke Rd
Bromley BR2 209 C5
Mitcham CR4 204 A5
Walthamstow E17 53 A4
Carleton Ave SM6 219 D1
Carleton Cl KT10 196 B1
Carleton Gdns N19 71 C3
Carleton Ho 4 N8 50 A4
Carleton Rd N7 71 D4
Carley Ct 6 N12 30 B5
Carlile Cl E3 97 B5
Carlile Ho SE1 262 D5
Carlina Gdns IG8 37 B5
Carling Ct TW1 152 D4
Carlingford DA14 190 A5
Carlingford Gdns
CR4 181 A3
Carlingford Rd
Hampstead NW3 70 B4
London N15 50 D6
West Barnes SM4 200 D3
Carlisle Ave
Acton W3 89 C1
Whitechapel EC3 243 C1
Carlisle Cl
Kingston u T KT2 176 C2
Pinner HA5 41 A2
Carlisle Gdns
Harrow HA3 43 D2
Redbridge IG1 56 A3
Carlisle Ho
6 Dartmouth Pk NW5 71 C5
Redbridge IG1 56 A3
Carlisle Inf Sch
TW12 173 D4
Carlisle La
SE1 116 B3 260 D6
Carlisle Lo 1 N3 29 B1
Carlisle Pl
London N11 31 B6
Westminster
SW1 115 C3 259 A5
Carlisle Rd
Cheam SM1 217 B2
Finsbury Pk N4 50 C2
Hampton TW12 173 D3
Hendon NW9 45 A6
Kilburn NW6 91 A6
Leyton E10 53 C1
Carlisle St W1 93 D1 239 C1
Carlisle Way SW17 181 A5
Carlisle Wlk 6 E8 73 D2
Carlos Pl W1 115 B6 248 C5
Carlow St NW1 232 A4
Carlson Ct SW15 135 B1
Carlton Ave
Feltham TW14 150 C5
Harrow HA3 43 B4
Hayes UB3 105 C2
South Croydon CR2 221 C1
Southgate N14 15 D6
Carlton Ave E HA9 65 D6
Carlton Ave W HA0 65 B6
Carlton Cl
Chessington KT9 213 D2
Child's Hill NW3 69 C6
Edgware HA8 26 C5
Northolt UB5 64 A3
Carlton Cres SM3 217 A4
Carlton Ct
Brixton SW9 138 D4
Ealing W7 108 D4
Finchley N3 29 C3
Ilford IG6 57 B6
Kilburn NW6 91 D5
11 Penge SE20 184 B2
South Norwood SE19 183 D2
8 Willesden NW2 68 C2
Carlton Dr
Ilford IG6 57 B6
Putney SW15 157 A6
Carlton Gdns
Ealing W5 109 C6
St James SW1 115 D5 249 C3
Carlton Gn DA14 189 D6
Carlton Gr SE15 140 B4
Carlton Hill
NW8 92 A5 229 A4
Carlton Ho
Cheam SM1 217 B2
Edmonton N21 17 A3
Feltham TW14 149 D5
Hounslow TW4 151 C5
8 Kilburn NW6 91 B5
Kilburn NW6 91 C5
Marylebone W1 237 D2
Carlton House Terr
SW1 115 D5 249 D4
Carlton Lo N4 50 C2
Carlton Mans
Brixton SW9 138 C1
Cricklewood NW2 68 D3
Kensington W14 244 B2
Maida Vale W9 91 D4
7 South Hampstead
NW6 69 C1
Stamford Hill N16 51 D1
Carlton Par HA9 44 A1
Carlton Park Ave
SW20 178 D1
Carlton Prim Sch NW5 71 A3
Carlton Rd
Acton W4 111 B4
Ashford TW16 171 D3
Ealing W5 87 C1
Erith DA8 147 D6
Finsbury Pk N4 50 C2
Carlton Rd *continued*
Friern Barnet N11 31 A5
Higham Hill E17 35 A2
Kingston u T KT3 177 C1
Leytonstone E11 54 D1
Manor Pk E12 77 D4
Mortlake SW14 133 A1
Sidcup DA14 189 D6
South Croydon CR2 221 B1
Walton-on-T KT12 194 B2
Welling DA16 146 B2
Carlton Sq E1 96 D3
Carlton St SW1 249 C5
Carltons The 5
SW15 157 A6
Carlton Terr
Edmonton N18 33 B6
Forest Hill SE26 162 C1
Upton E7 77 C1
Wanstead E11 55 B4
Carlton Tower Pl
SW1 257 D6
Carlton Twrs SM5 218 D5
Carlton Vale NW6 91 C5
Carlton Vale Inf Sch
NW6 91 B4
Carlwell St SW17 180 C5
Carlyle Ave
Bromley BR1 209 D6
Southall UB1 107 B6
Carlyle Cl
East Molesey KT8 173 D1
Hampstead Garden Suburb
N2 48 A3
Carlyle Gdns UB1 107 B6
Carlyle Ho
4 Camberwell SE5 139 A5
Chelsea SW3 266 D6
Ealing W5 109 D2
East Molesey KT8 195 C4
12 Stoke Newington
N16 73 C5
Carlyle Lo 6 EN5 14 A6
Carlyle Mans SW3 267 A5
Carlyle Mews 24 E1 96 D3
Carlyle Pl SW15 134 D1
Carlyle Rd
Croydon CR0 222 A6
Ealing W5 109 C2
Manor Pk E12 78 A4
1 Stonebridge NW10 89 B6
Woolwich SE28 124 C6
Carlyle's Ho* SW3 267 A5
Carlyle Sq
SW3 114 B1 256 D1
Carlyon Ave HA2 63 C4
Carlyon Cl HA0 88 A6
Carlyon Ct HA0 88 B6
Carlyon Mans 1 HA0 88 A5
Carlyon Rd
Hayes UB4 84 C2
Wembley HA0 88 A6
Carlys Cl BR3 184 D1
Carmalt Gdns SW15 134 C1
Carmarthen Ct 4 W7 86 D3
Carmarthen Ho 8
SW15 156 C4
Carmarthen Pl SE1 253 A2
Carmel Ct
Kensington W8 245 C2
Wembley Pk HA9 66 D6
Carmelite Cl HA3 24 A2
Carmelite Rd HA3 24 A1
Carmelite St
EC4 116 C6 251 B6
Carmelite Way HA3 24 A1
Carmelite Wlk HA3 24 A2
Carmel Lo SW6 265 A6
Carmen St E14 97 D1
Carmichael Cl
9 London SW11 136 B2
Ruislip HA4 62 A4
Carmichael Ct 5
SW13 133 D3
Carmichael Ho
17 Dulwich SE21 183 C6
6 Poplar E14 120 A6
Carmichael Mews
SW18 158 B4
Carmichael Rd SE25 206 A5
Carminia Rd SW17 159 B2
Carnaby St*
W1 93 C1 239 A1
Carnac St SE21, SE27 161 B1
Carna Ct TW9 132 A2
Carnanton Rd E17 36 B2
Carnarvon Ave EN1 5 D3
Carnarvon Dr UB3 105 A3
Carnarvon Rd
Barnet EN5 1 A2
Carnarvon Rd *continued*
Leyton E10 54 A4
Stratford E15 76 D2
Woodford E18 36 D2
Carnation St SE2 124 B1
Carnbrook Rd SE3 143 D2
Carnecke Gdns SE9 166 A6
Carnegie Cl
Holdbrook EN3 7 D5
Surbiton KT6 214 B6
Carnegie Ho NW3 70 B5
Carnegie Pl SW19 156 D1
Carnegie St N1 94 B6 233 D5
Carnforth Cl KT19 214 D2
Carnforth Rd SW16 181 D3
Carnicot Ho 9 SE15 140 B4
Carnoustie Cl SE28 102 D1
Carnoustie Dr N1 72 B1
Carnwath Ho SW6 135 D2
Carnwath Rd SW6 135 D2
Caroe Ct N9 18 B3
Carol Cl NW4 46 D5
Carole Ho 18 SE20 184 B2
Carolina Cl E15 76 C3
Carolina Rd CR7 183 A2
Caroline Cl
Bayswater W2 245 D5
Hounslow TW7 130 C5
Muswell Hill N10 31 B1
South Croydon CR0 221 C4
Streatham SW16 160 B1
Caroline Ct
Ashford TW15 170 D4
Catford SE6 186 B6
Stanmore HA7 25 A4
17 Surbiton KT6 197 D2
23 Woodside Pk N12 29 D6
Caroline Gdns E2 95 C4
Caroline Ho
Bayswater W2 245 D5
20 Hammersmith W6 112 C1
Caroline Martyn Ho 8
N19 49 D2
Caroline Pl
Bayswater W2 245 D5
Clapham SW11 137 A3
Harlington UB3 127 C5
Caroline Pl Mews W2 245 D5
Caroline Rd SW19 179 B3
Caroline St E1 96 D1
Caroline Terr
SW1 115 A2 258 A3
Caroline Wlk W6 264 A5
Carol St NW1 93 C6 232 A6
Carolyn Ho IG3 58 A1
Caronia Ct 4 SE16 119 A2
Carpenter Gdns N21 16 D2
Carpenter Ho
London NW11 48 A3
11 Tower Hamlets E14 97 C2
5 Tufnell Pk N19 71 D4
Carpenters Bsns Pk
E15 75 D1
Carpenters Cl EN5 13 D5
Carpenters Ct
Camden Town NW1 232 A6
5 Dagenham RM10 81 D2
Twickenham TW2 152 C2
Carpenter's Pl SW4 137 D1
Carpenters Prim Sch
E15 98 A6
Carpenter's Rd E15 75 D1
Carpenter St W1 248 C5
Carradale Ho 2 E14 98 A1
Carrara Cl 18 SW9 138 D1
Carrara Wharf SW6 135 A2
Carr Cl HA7 25 A4
Carr Gr SE18 122 A2
Carriage Dr E
SW11 137 A5 268 B4
Carriage Drive E
SW11 137 A5 268 B4
Carriage Drive N SW11,
SW8 137 A6 268 B5
Carriage Drive N
Battersea SW8,
SW11 136 D5 267 C4
Battersea SW8,
SW11 137 A6 268 B5
Carriage Dr S
SW11 137 A4 268 A2
Carriage Dr W
SW11 136 D5 267 C3
Carriage Mews IG1 79 A6
Carriage Pl 14 SW16 181 C5
Carrick Cl TW7 131 A2
Carrick Gate KT10 212 A5
Carrick Gdns N17 33 C3
Carrick Ho
Islington N7 72 B2

Carrick Ho *continued*
Kennington SE11 261 C2
Carrick Mews SE8 141 C6
Carrill Way DA17 124 D3
Carrington Ave
Borehamwood WD6 10 D6
Hounslow TW3 151 D6
Carrington Cl
Barnet EN5 12 A6
Borehamwood WD6 11 A6
Croydon CR0 207 A2
Carrington Ct
London SW11 136 C1
3 New Malden KT3 199 C5
Southgate N21 16 D5
Carrington Gdns 4
E7 77 A4
Carrington Ho
Mayfair W1 248 C3
7 Merton SW19 179 C3
Carrington Lo
3 Richmond TW10 154 A6
Wembley HA9 66 B5
Carrington Pl KT10 212 A4
Carrington Rd TW10 132 C1
Carrington Sq HA3 24 C3
Carrington St W1 248 C3
Carrol Cl NW5 71 B4
Carroll Cl E15 76 D3
Carroll Ct
Acton W3 110 D3
4 Shacklewell E5 74 A5
Carroll Ho W2 246 C6
Carronade Pl SE18 123 B3
Carron Cl E14 97 D1
Carroun Rd
SW8 138 B5 270 C4
Carroway La UB6 86 B4
Carrow Rd RM9 80 B1
Carr Rd
Northolt UB5 64 A1
Walthamstow E17 35 C1
Carrs La N21 17 B6
Carr St 5 E14 97 A1
CARSHALTON 218 C4
Carshalton, Beddington & Wallington War Meml Hospl SM5 218 D2
Carshalton Beeches Sta SM5 218 D2
Carshalton Boys Sports Coll SM5 218 C6
Carshalton Coll SM5 218 D5
Carshalton Gr SM1 218 B3
Carshalton High Sch for Girls SM5 218 C5
CARSHALTON ON THE HILL 219 B1
Carshalton Park Rd
SM5 218 D3
Carshalton Pl SM5 219 A3
Carshalton Rd
Mitcham CR4 203 A4
Sutton SM1, SM5 218 B3
Carshalton Sta SM5 218 D4
Carslake Rd SW15 156 C5
Carson Rd
Cockfosters EN4 2 D1
Dulwich SE21 161 B2
Newham E16 99 A2
Carstairs Rd SE6 164 A1
Carston Cl SE12 164 D6
Carswell Cl IG4 55 D5
Carswell Rd SE6 164 A4
Carter Cl
Kenton NW9 45 B3
Wallington SM6 219 D1
Carter Ct EC4 241 D1
Carteret Ho 8 W12 112 B6
Carteret St SW1 249 C1
Carteret Way SE8 119 A2
Carterhatch Jun & Inf Schs EN1 6 B4
Carterhatch La EN1 6 A4
Carterhatch Rd EN3 6 D4
Carter Ho
11 London SW2 160 C6
Spitalfields E1 243 C3
Carter La EC4 94 D1 241 D1
Carter Pl SE17 117 A1 262 B1
Carter Rd
Mitcham SW19 180 B4
Newham E13 99 B6
Carters Cl
10 Kentish Town NW5 71 D2
North Cheam KT4 200 D1
Carters Hill Cl SE9 165 C3
Carters La SE23 163 B1
Carters Rd N2 30 C3
Carter St SE17 117 A1 262 A1
Carter's Yd SW18 157 C6
Carthew Rd W6 112 B3
Carthew Villas W6 112 B3
Carthusian St EC1 242 A4
Cartier Circ E14 120 A5
Carting La
WC2 116 A6 250 B5
Cart La E4 20 C3
Cartmel NW1 232 A2
Cartmel Cl N17 34 B3
Cartmel Ct
Beckenham BR2 186 C1
Northolt UB5 63 A2
Cartmel Gdns SM4 202 A4
Cartmel Rd DA7 147 C4
Carton Ho
4 Bermondsey SE16 118 A3
2 Dollis Hill NW2 68 A5
12 Shepherd's Bush W11 112 D6
Cartoon Mus The* WC1 94 A2 240 A3
Cartwright Gdns
WC1 94 A4 233 A1
Cartwright Ho SE1 262 B5
Cartwright Rd RM9 81 B1
Cartwright St
E1 117 D6 253 D5
Cartwright Way
SW13 134 B5
Carvel Ho E14 120 A1
Carver Cl 15 W4 111 A3
Carver Rd SE24 161 A5
Carville Cres TW8 110 A2
Caryl Ho 6 SW19 156 D3
Cary Rd E11 76 C5
Carysfort Rd
Canonbury N16 73 B4
London N8 49 D4
Casby Ho 7 SE16 118 A3
Cascade Ave N10 49 C5
Cascade Cl IG9 21 D2
Cascade Rd IG9 21 D2
Cascadia Ho 22 KT1 176 C1
Casella Rd SE14 140 D5
Casewick Rd SE27 182 D6
Casey Cl NW8 92 C4 230 B1
Casimir Rd E5 74 C5
Casino Ave SE24 161 B6
Caspian Ho 10 E1 96 D2
Caspian St SE5 139 B5
Caspian Wlk E16 99 D1
Cassandra Cl UB5 64 B4
Cassandra Ct 7 NW2 68 C2
Cass Bsns Ctr
EC1 95 B3 242 C5
Casselden Rd NW10 67 B1
Cassel Hospl TW10 175 D6
Cassell Ho 21 SW9 138 A3
Casserley Ho W4 111 B3
Cass Ho 23 E9 74 D2
Cassidy Rd SW6 265 A3
Cassilda Rd SE2 124 A2
Cassilis Rd
Millwall E14 119 C4
Twickenham TW1 153 B5
Cassinghurst SE24 161 B6
Cassiobury Ave
TW14 149 D4
Cassiobury Rd E17 53 A4
Cassland Rd
Homerton E9 74 D2
South Norwood CR7 205 B5
Casslee Rd SE6 163 B4
Cassocks Sq TW17 193 B2
Casson Ho 11 E1 96 A2
Casson St E1 96 A2
Castalia Sq 6 E14 120 A4
Castellain Mans W9 91 D3
Castellain Rd W9 91 D3
Castellane Cl HA7 24 D3
Castell Ho 11 SE8 141 C5
Castello Ave SW15 156 C6
Castelnau SW13 134 B5
Castelnau Gdns
SW13 134 B6
Castelnau Mans
SW13 134 B6
Castelnau Row SW13 134 B6
Casterbridge
Kilburn NW6 91 D6
3 Notting Hill W11 91 C1
Casterbridge Rd SE3 143 A2
Casterton St E8 74 B2
Castile Rd SE18 122 C2
Castilion Prim Sch
SE28 102 C1
Castillon Rd SE6 164 C2
Castlands Rd SE6 163 B2
Castleacre W2 237 A1
Castle Ave
Chingford E4 36 B5
Yiewsley UB7 104 B6
Castlebar Ct 5 W5 87 C2
Castlebar Hill W5 87 C2
Castlebar Mews W5 87 C2
Castle Bar Park Sta
W7 86 D2
Castlebar Pk W5 87 B2
Castlebar Rd W5 87 C1
Castlebar Sch W13 87 A2
Castle Baynard St
EC4 117 A6 252 A6
Castlebrook Cl
SE11 116 D2 261 C4
Castle Bsns Village
TW12 173 D2
Castle Cl
12 Acton W3 111 A4
Ashford TW16 171 C3
Beckenham BR2 208 C6
Homerton E9 75 A3
South Acton W3 110 D4
Wimbledon SW19 156 D1
Castlecombe Dr
SW19 156 D4
Castlecombe Prim Sch
SE9 188 A5
Castlecombe Rd SE9 188 A6
Castle Ct
Belmont SM2 217 C2
City of London EC3 242 D1
Dagenham RM9 103 A6
Forest Hill SE26 185 A6
Morden SM4 202 B4
Castleden Ho NW6 70 B1
Castledine Rd SE20 184 B3
Castle Dr IG4 56 A3
Castleford Ave SE9 166 D3
Castleford Cl N17 33 D4
Castleford Ct NW8 236 D6
Castlefrank Ho 20 N1 95 C4
Castlegate TW9 132 B2
CASTLE GREEN 102 C6
Castleham Ct HA8 26 C4
Castlehaven Rd NW1 71 B1
Castle Hill Ave CR0 224 A1
Castle Hill Prim Sch
CR0 224 A2
Castle Ho
17 Belmont SM2 217 C1
3 Chingford E4 36 B5
Newington SE1 262 A4
South Lambeth SW8 270 B4
Castle Hts RM9 102 B6
Castle Ind Est SE17 262 A4
Castle La SW1 115 C3 259 A6
Castleleigh Ct EN2 17 B6
Castlemaine 8
SW11 136 D3
Castlemaine Ave CR2 221 D3
Castlemaine St 2 E1 96 B2
Castle Mead SE5 139 A5
Castle Mews
Camden Town NW1 71 B2
North Finchley N12 30 A5
Castle Par KT17 216 A1
Castle Pl
8 Acton W4 111 C2
Camden Town NW1 71 B2
Castle Point 4 E13 99 C5
Castle Rd
Camden Town NW1 71 B2
Dagenham RM9 102 B6
Enfield EN3 7 A5
Isleworth TW7 130 D3
North Finchley N12 30 B5
Northolt UB5 63 D1
Southall UB2 107 B3
Castlereagh Ho HA7 25 B4
Castlereagh St W1 237 C2
Castle St
Kingston u T KT2 176 A1
Newham E6 99 C5
Castleton Ave HA9 66 A4
Castleton Cl CR0 207 A3
Castleton Ct KT5 198 B4
Castleton Gdns HA9 66 A5
Castleton Ho 3 E14 120 A2
Castleton Rd
Chingford E17 36 B1
Ilford IG3 58 B1
Mitcham CR4 203 D5
Mottingham SE12, SE9 187 D6
Ruislip HA4 40 D1
Castletown Rd
W14 113 A1 254 B1
Castleview Cl N4 73 A6
Castleview Gdns IG1 56 B3
Castle Way
Feltham TW13 172 C6
Wimbledon SW19 156 D1
Castle Wlk TW16 194 C6
Castlewood Day Hospl
SE18 144 C4
Castlewood Dr SE9 144 B3
Castlewood Ho WC1 239 D2
Castlewood Rd
Barnet EN4 2 B2
Stamford Hill N16 52 A3
Castle Yd
Highgate N6 49 A2
Lambeth SE1 251 D4
18 Richmond TW10 153 D6
Castor La E14 119 D6
Catalina Rd TW6 126 C2
Catalpa Ct SE13 164 B5
Caterham Rd SE13 142 B2
Catesby Ho 25 E9 74 C1
Catesby St
SE17 117 B2 262 D3
CATFORD 163 C3
Catford Br SE6 163 C4
Catford Bridge Sta
SE6 163 C4
Catford Broadway
SE6 163 D4
Catford Gyratory SE6 163 D4
Catford High Sch
SE6 164 A1
Catford Hill SE6 163 C3
Catford Rd SE6 163 C4
Catford Sh Ctr SE6 163 D4
Catford Sta SE6 163 C4
Cathall Rd E11 76 B5
Cathay Ho SE16 118 B4
Cathay St 12 SE16 118 B4
Cathay Wlk UB5 85 C5
Cathcart Dr BR6 211 C1
Cathcart Hill N19 71 C5
Cathcart Rd
SW10 136 A6 266 A6
Cathcart St NW5 71 B2
Cathedral Ct EC4 241 D1
Cathedral Lo EC1 242 A4
Cathedral Sch of St Saviour & St Mary Overie Prim Sch
SE1 117 A4 252 B2
Cathedral St
SE1 117 B5 252 C4
Cathedral Wlk SW1 259 A6
Catherall Rd N5, N16 73 A5
Catherine Baird Ct 12
SW12 159 B4
Catherine Ct
Barnet EN5 1 D2
1 Ilford IG2 57 A3
2 Southgate N14 15 C6
3 Wimbledon SW19 179 B5
Catherine Dr
Ashford TW16 171 D4
Richmond TW9 132 A1
Catherine Gdns TW3 130 B1
Catherine Godfrey Ho
RM9 103 B6
Catherine Gr SE10 141 D4
Catherine Griffiths Ct
EC1 241 B6
Catherine Ho
Isleworth TW7 131 B4
16 Shoreditch N1 95 C6
Catherine Lo E18 37 C2
Catherine Pl
Harrow HA1 42 D4
Westminster
SW1 115 C3 259 A6
Catherine Rd
Enfield EN3 7 A6
Kingston u T KT6 197 D4
Catherine St
WC2 116 B6 250 C6
Catherine Wheel Alley
E1 243 B3
Catherine Wheel Rd
TW8 131 D5
Catherine Wheel Yd
SW1 249 A3
Catherwood Ct N1 235 C3
Cat Hill EN4 14 D6
Cathles Rd SW12 159 B5
Cathnor Rd W12 112 B4
Catisfield Rd EN3 7 A6
Catlin Cres TW17 193 B4
Catling Cl SE23 162 D1
Catlin's La HA5 40 B5
Catlin St SE16 118 B1
Catman Ho N4 50 B1
Caton Ct BR2 186 C1
Cato Rd SW4 137 D1
Cator La BR3 185 B2
Cator Park Sch BR3 185 A3
Cator Rd
Penge SE20, SE26 184 D5
Wallington SM5 218 D3
Cator St
Camberwell SE15 139 D5
Camberwell SE15 139 D6
Cato St W1 92 C1 237 B2
Catsey La WD23 8 A4
Catsey Wood WD23 8 A4
Catterick Cl N11 31 A4
Cattistock Rd SE9 188 B5
Cattley Cl EN5 1 A1
Catton St WC1 240 C3
Caughley Ho SE11 261 A5
Caulfield Ct 15 NW1 71 C1
Caulfield Rd
East Ham E6 78 B1
London SE15 140 B3
Causeway TW14, TW4 128 B1
Causeway The
Carshalton SM5 219 A6
Chessington KT9 214 A4
Claygate KT10 212 D1
East Finchley N2 48 C5
Teddington TW11 174 D4
Wandsworth SW18 157 D6
Wimbledon SW19 178 C5
Causeyware Rd N9 18 C4
Causton Cotts 3 E14 97 A1
Causton Ho SE5 139 A5
Causton Rd N6 49 B2
Causton Sq RM10 81 C1
Causton St
SW1 115 D1 259 D2
Cautley Ave SW4 159 C6
Cavalier Cl RM6 58 D5
Cavalier Gdns UB3 83 B1
Cavalier Ho W5 109 C6
Cavalry Cres TW4 128 D1
Cavalry Gdns SW15 157 B6
Cavan Pl HA5 23 B2
Cavaye Ho SW10 266 B6
Cavaye Pl SW10 256 B1
Cavell Ct 5 N19 71 C6
Cavell Dr EN2 4 C3
Cavell Ho 8 N1 95 C6
Cavell Rd N17 33 B3
Cavell St E1 96 B2
Cavendish Ave
Ealing W13 87 A1
Falconwood DA16 145 D2
Finchley N3 29 C1
Harrow HA1 64 C4
Ruislip HA4 62 B3
Sidcup DA15 168 A4
St John's Wood
NW8 92 B5 229 D3
West Barnes KT3 200 B5
Woodford IG8 37 B3
Cavendish Cl
Ashford TW16 171 D4
Brondesbury NW6 69 B2
Edmonton N18 34 B5
Hayes UB4 83 C2
3 Putney SW15 157 A6
St John's Wood
NW8 92 B4 229 D2
Cavendish Coll
WC1 93 D2 239 C4
Cavendish Cres WD6 10 C6
Cavendish Ct
Ashford TW16 171 D4
Catford SE6 163 D3
5 Chingford E4 20 C4
Wallington SM6 219 B2
Wembley HA0 65 D3
Whitechapel EC2 243 B2
Cavendish Dr
Claygate KT10 212 C3
Edgware HA8 26 B4
Leytonstone E11 54 B1
Cavendish Gdns
Barking IG11 79 D3
Clapham Pk SW4 159 C5
Dagenham RM6 59 A4
Ilford IG1 56 C1
Cavendish Ho
London N12 30 A6
5 Muswell Hill N10 31 A3
3 Richmond TW10 153 C1
South Lambeth SW8 270 A2
St John's Wood NW8 229 D3
Twickenham TW1 153 A5
Cavendish Mans
2 Clapham Pk
SW12 159 C5
Hackney E5 74 C3
Cavendish Mans *continued*
Holborn EC1 241 A5
8 West Hampstead
NW6 69 C3
Cavendish Mews N
W1 238 D4
Cavendish Mews S
W1 238 D3
Cavendish Par
Balham SW12 159 B5
Hounslow TW4 129 A3
Cavendish Pl
Balham SW4 159 B5
Bromley BR1 210 B6
Brondesbury NW2 68 D2
Marylebone W1 238 D2
Cavendish Prim Sch
W4 133 C5
Cavendish Rd
Ashford TW16 171 D4
Brondesbury NW6 69 B1
Chingford E4 36 A4
Chiswick W4 133 A4
Clapham Pk SW12 159 C5
Edmonton N18 34 B5
Harringay N4 50 D3
Mitcham SW19 180 C3
New Malden KT3 199 D5
Sutton SM2 218 A1
Thornton Heath CR0 204 D1
Cavendish Sch The
NW1 93 B6 231 D6
Cavendish Sq
W1 93 B1 238 D2
Cavendish St
N1 95 B5 235 C3
Cavendish Terr
Feltham TW13 150 A2
11 Tower Hamlets E3 97 B4
Cavendish The NW11 47 D2
Cavendish Way BR4 207 D1
Cavenham Gdns IG1 79 B5
Cave Rd
Newham E13 99 B4
Richmond TW10 175 C6
Caverleigh Way KT4 200 B2
Caversham Ave
Cheam SM3 217 A6
Palmers Green N13 16 C1
Caversham Ct N11 15 A1
Caversham Ho
8 Kingston u T KT1 176 A1
7 Peckham SE15 140 A6
Wallington CR0 220 A5
West Green N15 51 A5
Caversham Lo N10 31 C1
Caversham Rd
Kentish Town NW5 71 C2
Kingston u T KT1 176 B1
West Green N15 51 A5
Caversham St
SW3 136 D6 267 C6
Caverswall St W12 90 C1
Caveside Cl BR7 188 C2
Cavour Ho SE17 261 D2
Cawdor Cres W7 109 A2
Cawnpore St SE19 183 C5
Cawston Ct 8 BR1 186 D3
Caxton Gr E3 97 C4
Caxton Hall* SW1 259 C6
Caxton Rd
Shepherd's Bush
W12 112 D4
Southall UB2 106 D3
Wimbledon SW19 180 A5
Wood Green N22 32 B1
Caxton St N E16 98 D1
Caxton St
SW1 115 D3 259 C6
Caxton Trad Est UB3 105 C5
Caxton Wlk WC2 239 D1
Cayford Ho 1 NW3 70 D3
Caygill Cl BR2 208 D5
Cayley Cl SM6 220 A1
Cayley Prim Sch E14 97 A1
Cayley Rd UB2 107 D3
Cayton Pl EC1 235 C1
Cayton Rd UB6 86 C5
Cayton St EC1 235 C1
Cazenove Mans 1
N16 74 A6
Cazenove Rd
Stoke Newington N16 74 A6
Walthamstow E17 35 C2
Cearns Ho E6 99 D6
Ceasors Ct TW1 152 D2

Cecil Ave
Barking IG11 79 B1
Enfield EN1 5 D1
Wembley HA9 66 B3
Cecil Cl
Chessington KT9 213 D4
Ealing W5 87 D2
Littleton TW15 171 A3
Cecil Ct
Chelsea SW10 266 A6
12 Croydon CR0 221 D6
Ealing W5 87 D2
South Hampstead NW6 69 D1
St James WC2 250 A5
Cecile Pk N8 50 A3
Cecil Ho E17 35 C2
Cecilia Cl N2 48 A6
Cecilia Rd E8 74 A3
Cecil Lo KT9 213 D4
Cecil Mans 2 SW17 159 A2
Cecil Pk HA5 41 A5
Cecil Pl CR4 202 D4
Cecil Rd
Acton W3 89 A2
Ashford TW15 171 A4
Cheam SM1, SM2 217 B2
Colindale NW9 45 C6
Dagenham RM6 58 D2
Enfield EN2 5 B1
Harlesden NW10 89 C6
Harrow HA3 42 C6
Hounslow TW3 130 A3
Ilford IG1 78 D4
Leyton E11 76 C5
Merton SW19 179 D3
Muswell Hill N10 31 B1
Newham E13 99 A6
Osidge N14 15 C3
Thornton Heath CR0 204 B3
Walthamstow E17 35 C2
Cecil Rhodes Ho NW1 232 C4
Cecil Rosen Ct HA0 65 B5
Cecil Way BR2 209 A1
Cedar Ave
Dagenham RM6 59 A4
East Barnet EN4 14 C4
Enfield EN3 6 C3
Hayes UB3 84 A1
Ruislip HA4 62 C3
Sidcup DA15 168 A4
Twickenham TW2 152 A5
Yiewsley UB7 104 B6
Cedar Cl
Buckhurst Hill IG9 21 D2
East Molesey KT8 196 C5
Keston Mark BR2 226 A5
Kingston u T KT2 177 B6
Old Ford E3 97 B6
Wallington SM5 218 D2
West Norwood SE21 161 A2
Cedar Copse BR1 188 B1
Cedar Cres BR2 226 A5
Cedarcroft Rd KT9 214 B4
Cedar Ct
7 Brentford TW8 131 D6
19 Charlton SE7 143 C6
Edgware HA8 11 A1
Eltham SE9 166 A5
Finchley N3 29 C3
Islington N1 73 A1
Marylebone W1 237 B2
Mortlake SW14 133 A1
1 Muswell Hill N10 31 B1
5 New Southgate N11 31 C5
Oakleigh Pk N20 14 B3
Stoneleigh KT17 216 A1
3 Sutton SM2 218 A2
6 Wanstead E11 55 B4
Wembley HA0 65 B4
Wimbledon SW19 156 D1
5 Woodford E18 37 A2
Cedar Dr
London N2 48 C5
Pinner HA5 23 C4
Cedar Gdns SM2 218 A2
Cedar Gr
Ealing W5 110 A3
Sidcup DA5 168 D5
Southall UB1 85 C2
Cedar Grange 10 EN1 17 C6
Cedar Ho
Ashford TW16 171 D3
5 Cubitt Town E14 120 A4
Hayes UB4 84 C3
Kensington W8 255 C6
New Addington CR0 223 D2
New Cross Gate SE14 140 D4
Cedar Ho *continued*
5 Richmond TW9 132 D4
16 Rotherhithe SE16 118 D4
Wood Green N22 32 C2
Cedar Hts TW10 154 A3
Cedarhurst BR1 186 C3
Cedarhurst Dr SE9 165 C6
Cedar Lawn Ave EN5 13 A6
Cedar Lo
Brondesbury NW2 69 B2
Fulham SW6 134 D4
Cedarmore Ct BR7 189 A2
Cedar Mount SE9 165 D3
Cedarne Rd
SW6 135 D5 265 C3
Cedar Park Gdns RM6 58 D2
Cedar Park Rd EN2 5 A5
Cedar Pl 3 SE7 121 C1
Cedar Rd
Bromley BR1 187 C1
Cranford TW5 128 C3
Cricklewood NW2 68 C4
Croydon CR0 221 C6
East Bedfont TW14 149 B3
East Molesey KT8 196 C5
Enfield EN2 5 A5
Sutton SM2 218 A2
Teddington TW11 175 A5
Tottenham N17 33 D2
Cedar Rise N14 15 A4
Cedars Ave
Mitcham CR4 203 A6
Walthamstow E17 53 C4
Cedars Cl
Hendon NW4 46 D6
Lewisham SE13 142 B2
Cedars Ct
Edmonton N9 17 D2
Putney SW15 156 A5
Cedars Dr UB10 82 C5
Cedars Fst & Mid Schs
HA3 24 A2
Cedars Ho
21 London SW2 138 B1
15 Walthamstow E17 53 D6
5 West Norwood
SW27 182 D5
Cedars Mews SW4 137 B1
Cedars Prim Sch The
TW5 128 A5
Cedars Rd
Barnes SW13 134 A3
Beckenham BR3 185 B1
Clapham SW4 137 B1
4 Lower Edmonton N9 18 A2
Morden SM4 201 C5
Stratford E15 76 C2
Teddington KT8 175 C2
Wallington CR0 220 A4
Winchmore Hill N21 16 D2
Cedars The
Buckhurst Hill IG9 21 A3
Ealing W13 87 C1
Hackney E9 74 D1
4 Kingston u T KT2 176 D2
Teddington TW11 174 D4
Wallington SM6 219 C4
Cedar Terr
9 Dagenham RM8 58 D2
Richmond TW9 132 A1
Cedar Tree Gr SE27 182 D5
Cedarville Gdns
SW16 182 B4
Cedar Way
Ashford TW16 171 C3
Camden Town
NW1 93 D6 232 C6
Cedar Wlk KT10 212 D2
Cedarwood BR3 185 B3
Cedarwood Ho EN2 4 D3
Cedarwood Lo HA8 26 B5
Cedra Ct N16 52 A1
Cedric Chambers
NW8 236 C6
Cedric Rd SE9 167 A1
Celadon Cl EN3 7 A2
Celandine Cl E3, E14 97 C2
Celandine Ct E4 19 D1
Celandine Dr
Dalston E8 73 D1
Woolwich SE28 124 B5
Celandine Gr N14 15 C6
Celandine Way E15 98 C4
Celbridge Mews W2 91 D1
Celestial Gdns SE13 142 B1
Celia Blairman Ho E1 243 C4
Celia Ct 7 TW9 132 B4
Celia Ho 10 N1 95 C5
Celia Rd N19 71 C4
Celtic Ave BR2 208 C6
Celtic St E14 97 D2
Cemetery La
Lower Halliford
TW17 192 D2
Woolwich SE7 144 A6
Cemetery Rd
East Wickham SE2 146 B5
Forest Gate E7 76 D4
Tottenham N17 33 C3
Cenacle Cl NW3 69 C5
Cenotaph* SW1 250 A2
Centaur Ct 3 TW8 110 A1
Centaurs Bsns Pk
TW7 131 A6
Centaur St
SE1 116 B3 260 D6
Centenary Rd EN3 7 B1
Centennial Ave WD6 9 C4
Centennial Ct WD6 9 C4
Centennial Pk HA7, WD6 9 C4
Central Ave
Battersea
SW11 136 D5 267 D3
East Finchley N2 47 D6
East Molesey KT8 195 B4
Edmonton N9 17 D1
Enfield EN1 6 B3
Finchley N2 30 B1
Hayes UB3 106 A6
Isleworth TW3, TW7 130 A1
Leyton E11 76 B6
Pinner HA5 41 B2
Wallington SM6 220 A3
Welling DA16 146 A3
Central Bsns Ctr
NW10 67 C3
Central Chambers
W5 109 D6
Central Cir NW4 46 B4
Central Criminal Court
(Old Bailey)*
EC4 94 D1 241 D2
Central Ct 2 SE18 122 D2
Centrale Ctr CR0 221 A6
Central Foundation Boys'
Sch EC2 95 B3 242 D6
Central Foundation Lower
Girls Sch The E3 97 A4
Central Foundation Upper
Girls Sch The E3 97 B4
Central Gdns SM4 201 D4
Central Hill SE19 183 B4
Central Ho
Barking IG11 79 A1
Mill Meads E15 98 A5
Central Mans
8 London NW4 46 B4
1 Streatham SW16 182 A6
Central Middlesex Hospl
NW10 89 A4
Central Par
Croydon CR0 220 C4
Ealing UB6 87 A4
Enfield EN3 6 C3
Feltham TW14 150 C4
Harrow HA1 42 D4
Heston TW5 129 C5
Ilford IG2 57 B3
Penge SE20 184 D3
South Acton W3 110 D4
2 Streatham SW16 182 A6
Surbiton KT6 198 A3
8 Walthamstow E17 53 C5
Central Park Ave
RM10 81 D5
Central Park Prim Sch
E6 99 D5
Central Park Rd E6 99 D5
Central Par Villas
BR5 190 C1
Central Pk Est TW4 128 D1
Central Public Health
Laboratories NW9 45 C6
Central Rd
Morden SM4 201 D4
Wembley HA0 65 B3
Worcester Pk KT4 216 A6
Central St Martins Coll
EC1 94 C3 241 B5
Central St Martin's Coll of
Art & Design
W1 93 D1 239 D1
Central St Martins Coll of
Art & Design (The
London Inst)
WC1 94 B2 240 C3
Central Sch of Ballet
EC1 94 C3 241 B5
Central Sch of Speech &
Drama The NW3 70 B1
Central Sq
East Molesey KT8 195 B5
Hampstead Garden Suburb
NW11 47 D3
4 Wembley HA9 66 A3
Central St EC1 95 A4 235 A1
Central Terr BR3 206 D6
Central Way
Feltham TW14 150 B6
Lower Place NW10 89 A4
Sutton SM5 218 C1
Thamesmead SE28 124 B6
Centre Ave
Acton W3 111 B5
Finchley N2 30 C1
Centre Bldg SE17 262 B4
Centre Common Rd
BR7 189 A3
Centre Court Sh Ctr 3
SW19 179 B4
Centre Ct N20 14 B2
Centre Dr E7 77 C4
Centre Hts 5 NW3 70 B1
Centre Point 3 SE1 118 A1
Centre Point Ho WC2 239 D2
Centre Rd
Dagenham RM10 103 D5
Wanstead E7, E11 77 A6
Centre St E2 96 B5
Centre The TW13 150 B3
Centreway 4 IG1 79 A6
Centre Way N9 18 D2
Centro Ct E11 54 C1
Centurian Way DA18 125 C3
Centurion Bldg SW8 268 C5
Centurion Cl N7 72 B1
Centurion Ct
Hackbridge SM6 219 B6
7 Woolwich SE18 122 B2
Centurion La E3 97 B5
Centurion Lodge 2
RM10 81 D2
Century Cl NW4 46 D4
Century Ho
Edgware HA8 26 C3
Harrow HA3 42 C6
Lewisham SE13 141 D3
Wembley HA9 66 B6
Century Rd E17 53 A6
Century Yd SE23 162 C2
Cephas Ave E1 96 C3
Cephas Ho 9 E1 96 C3
Cephas St E1 96 C3
Ceres Ct 12 KT1 176 A1
Ceres Rd SE18 123 D2
Cerise Rd SE15 140 A4
Cerne Cl UB4 106 C6
Cerne Rd SM4 202 A3
Cerney Mews W2 246 C6
Cervantes Ct 12 W2 91 D1
Cester St E2 96 A6
Ceylon Rd
6 Hammersmith
W14 112 D3
Kensington W14 254 A5
Chabot Dr SE15 140 B2
Chace Com Sch EN1 5 C4
Chadacre Ave IG5 56 B6
Chadacre Ct E15 99 A6
Chadacre Ho 10 SW9 138 D1
Chadacre Rd KT17 216 B3
Chadbourn St E14 97 D2
Chadbury Ct NW7 28 A2
Chad Cres N9 18 C1
Chadd Dr BR1 210 A6
Chadd Gn E13 99 A6
Chaddlewood EN4 3 A1
Chadston Ho 17 N1 72 D1
Chadswell WC1 233 B1
Chadview Ct 2 RM6 58 D2
Chadville Gdns RM6 58 D4
Chadway RM8 58 C1
Chadwell Ave RM6 58 B2
CHADWELL HEATH 58 D4
Chadwell Heath
Foundation Sch The
RM6 58 B3
Chadwell Heath Hospl
RM6 58 B4
Chadwell Heath Ind Pk
RM8 58 D1
Chadwell Heath La
RM6 58 C3
Chadwell Heath Sta
RM6 58 D2
Chadwell Prim Sch
RM6 58 C2
Chadwell St
EC1 94 C4 234 B2
Chadwick Ave
Chingford E4 36 B6
Enfield N21 4 B1
Wimbledon SW19 179 C4
Chadwick Cl
12 Ealing W7 86 D2
Roehampton SW15 155 D4
Teddington TW11 175 A4
Chadwick Ct 4 SE28 124 B5
Chadwick Pl KT6 197 C3
Chadwick Rd
Harlesden NW10 89 D6
Ilford IG1 78 D5
Leytonstone E11 54 D3
Peckham SE15 139 D3
Chadwick St
SW1 115 D3 259 C5
Chadwick Way SE28 124 D6
Chadwin Rd E13 99 B2
Chadworth Ho
Finsbury EC1 235 A1
Finsbury Pk N4 51 A1
Chadworth Way KT10 212 B3
Chaffey Ho 6 SE7 121 C1
Chaffinch Ave CR0 206 D3
Chaffinch Bsns Pk
CR0 206 D5
Chaffinch Cl
Croydon CR0 206 D3
Edmonton N9 18 D3
Tolworth KT6 214 C5
Chaffinch Rd BR3 185 A2
Chafford Way RM6 58 C5
Chagford Ct SW19 180 C3
Chagford Ho
38 Bromley E3 97 D4
Marylebone NW1 237 C5
Chagford St
NW1 92 D3 237 D5
Chailey Ave EN1 5 D3
Chailey Cl TW5 128 D4
Chailey Ind Est UB3 106 A4
Chailey St E5 74 C5
Chalbury Ho 8 SW9 138 B1
Chalbury Wlk N1 234 A4
Chalcombe Rd SE2 124 B3
Chalcot Cl SM2 217 C1
Chalcot Cres
NW1 92 D6 230 D6
Chalcot Gdns NW3 70 D2
Chalcot Mews SW16 160 A1
Chalcot Rd
NW1 93 A6 231 A6
Chalcot Sch NW1 71 B1
Chalcot Sq NW1 71 A1
Chalcott Gdns KT6 197 C1
Chalcroft Rd SE13 164 C6
Chaldon Rd
SW6 135 A5 264 B4
Chale Rd SW2 160 A5
Chalfont Ave HA9 66 D2
Chalfont Ct
3 Belvedere DA17 125 C1
12 Harrow HA1 42 D3
Hendon NW9 45 D6
Marylebone NW1 237 D5
Chalfont Gn N9 17 C1
Chalfont Ho
2 Bermondsey SE16 118 B3
Willesden NW10 67 B5
Chalfont Rd
Edmonton N9 17 D1
Hayes UB3 106 A4
South Norwood SE25 205 D6
Chalfont Way W13 109 B3
Chalfont Wlk 5 HA5 22 C1
Chalford 7 NW3 70 A2
Chalford Cl KT8 195 C5
Chalford Ct
Ilford IG2 56 D4
15 Putney SW15 156 D5
Surbiton KT6 198 B2
Chalford Rd SE21 183 B6
Chalford Wlk IG8 37 D3
Chalgrove Ave SM4 201 C4
Chalgrove Gdns N3 47 A6
Chalgrove Prim Sch
N3 47 A6
Chalgrove Rd
Sutton SM2 218 B1
Tottenham N17 34 B2
Chalice Cl SM6 219 D2
Chalice Ct N2 48 C5
Chalkenden Cl SE20 184 B3
Chalkers Cnr TW9 132 D2
Chalk Farm Rd NW1 71 A1
Chalk Farm Sta NW3 71 A1
Chalkhill Prim Sch
HA9 66 D5
Chalkhill Rd HA9 67 A5
Chalk Hill Rd W6 112 D2
Chalk La EN4 2 D1
Chalklands HA9 67 A5
Chalkley Cl CR4 181 A1
Chalkmill Dr EN1 6 B2
Chalk Pit Ave BR5 190 C1
Chalk Pit Way SM1 218 A3
Chalk Rd E13 99 C2
Chalkstone Cl DA16 146 A4
Chalkwell Ho 10 E1 96 D1
Chalkwell Park Ave EN1 5 C1
Challenge Cl NW10 89 C6
Challenge Ct TW2 152 C4
Challenge Rd TW15 149 B1
Challenger Ho 7
E14 119 A6
Challice Way SW2 160 B3
Challiner Ct HA1 43 A4
Challin St 1 SE20 184 C2
Challis Rd TW8 109 D1
Challoner Cl N2 30 B1
Challoner Cres W14 254 C1
Challoner Ct BR2 186 B1
Challoner Mans W14 254 C1
Challoners Cl KT8 196 B5
Challoner St
W14 113 B1 254 C1
Chalmers Ho
13 London SW11 136 A2
Walthamstow E17 53 D4
Chalmers Rd TW15 170 D5
Chalmers Rd E TW15 171 A5
Chalmers Way TW14 150 B6
Chalmer's Wlk 14
SE17 138 D6
Chalner Ho SW2 160 C3
Chaloner Ct SE1 252 C2
Chalsey Lodge SE4 141 B1
Chalsey Rd SE4 141 B1
Chalton Dr N2 48 B3
Chalton St
NW1 93 D5 232 C3
Chamberlain Cl
Ilford IG1 79 A5
Plumstead SE18 123 B3
Chamberlain Cotts
SE5 139 B4
Chamberlain Cres
BR4 207 D1
Chamberlain Gdns
TW3 130 A4
Chamberlain Ho 6
E1 118 C6
Chamberlain La HA5 40 A5
Chamberlain Pl E17 53 A6
Chamberlain Rd
Ealing W13 109 A4
Finchley N2 30 A1
Chamberlain St 7
NW1 70 D1
Chamberlain Way
Pinner HA5 40 B6
Surbiton KT6 198 A2
Chamberlain Wlk 5
TW13 173 A6
Chamberlayne Ave
HA9 66 A6
Chamberlayne Mans 3
NW10 90 D4
Chamberlayne Rd
NW10 90 C6
Chambers Gdns N2 30 B2
Chambers Ho 2
SW16 181 C6
Chambers La NW10 68 C1
Chambers Pl CR2 221 B1
Chambers Rd N7 72 A4
Chambers St SE16 118 A4
Chamber St
E1 117 D6 253 D6
Chambers Walk HA7 25 B5
Chambon Pl 7 W6 112 A2
Chambord Ho 24 E2 95 D4
Chambord St E2 95 D4
Chamomile Ct E17 53 C3
Champa Cl N17 33 D1
Champion Cres SE26 185 A6
Champion Gr SE5 139 B2
Champion Hill SE5 139 B2
Champion Pk SE5 139 B3
Champion Rd SE26 185 A6
Champlain Ho 26
W12 112 B6
Champness Cl 9
SE27 183 B6
Champness Rd IG11 79 D1
Champneys Cl SM2 217 B1
Champneys Ct N21 16 A6
Chancel Ct W1 249 C6
Chancellor Gr SE21 161 A1

Chancellor Ho
South Kensington SW7 256 B6
29 Wapping E1 118 B5
Chancellor Pas E14 119 C5
Chancellor Pl NW9 27 D1
Chancellors' Ct WC1 240 C4
Chancellors Loft N8 50 A3
Chancellor's Rd W6 112 C1
Chancellors St W6 112 C1
Chancellors Wharf 21 W6 112 C1
Chancelot Rd SE2 124 B2
Chancel St SE1 116 D5 251 C3
Chancery Bldgs 14 E1 118 C6
Chancerygate Bsns Ctr HA4 63 A3
Chancery Gate Bsns Ctr CR4 202 D4
Chancery Ho WC2 241 A3
Chancery La
Beckenham BR3 185 D1
Holborn EC4 94 C1 241 A2
Chancery Lane Sta WC1 94 C2 241 A3
Chancery Mews SW17 158 C2
Chance St E2 243 C6
Chanctonbury Cl SE9 166 D1
Chanctonbury Gdns SM2 217 D1
Chanctonbury Way N12 29 C6
Chanderia Ct 5 CR0 221 A5
Chand Ho 7 N12 30 A5
Chandler Ave E16 99 A2
Chandler Cl TW12 173 C2
Chandler Ct
Feltham TW14 150 A5
Thornton Heath CR7 204 D4
2 Tolworth KT5 198 D1
8 Wallington SM6 219 B2
Chandlers Cl TW14 149 D4
Chandlers Field Prim Sch KT8 195 C4
Chandlers Mews E14 119 C4
Chandler St E1 118 B5
Chandlers Way 11 SE24 160 C4
Chandler Way SE15 139 D5
Chandlery Ho 26 E1 96 A1
Chandon Lo SM2 218 A1
Chandos Ave
Ealing W5 109 D2
New Southgate N14 15 C1
Oakleigh Pk N20 14 B3
Walthamstow E17 35 C1
Chandos Bsns Ctr 11 SM6 219 C2
Chandos Cl IG9 21 B2
Chandos Cres HA8 26 C3
Chandos Ct
Edgware HA8 26 B3
Palmers Green N14 15 D2
Stanmore HA7 25 B4
Chandos Pl WC2 116 A6 250 A5
Chandos Rd
Cricklewood NW2 68 C3
Finchley N2 30 C1
Harrow HA1 42 A4
Old Oak Comm NW10 89 C3
Pinner HA5 40 D2
Stratford New Town E15 76 B3
Tottenham N17 33 C1
Chandos St W1 93 B2 238 D3
Chandos Way NW11 47 D1
Change Alley EC3 242 D1
Channel Cl TW5 129 C4
Channel Gate Rd NW10 89 C4
Channel Ho E14 97 A2
Channelsea Bsns Ctr E15 98 B5
Channelsea Rd E15 98 B6
Channing Sch N6 49 B1
Channon Ct 3 KT6 198 A4
Chantrey Rd SW9 138 B2
Chantries The HA7 25 A5
Chantry Cl
2 Abbey Wood SE2 124 C3
Edgware NW7 11 D4
Enfield EN2 5 A5
Harrow HA3 44 B4
Sidcup DA14 191 A5
Sunbury TW16 172 A3
West Kilburn W9 91 B3
Chantry Cres NW10 67 D2
Chantry Ct SM5 218 C5
Chantry Ct SW6 135 A2
Chantry La BR2 209 D4
Chantry Pl HA3 23 D2
Chantry Rd
Chessington KT9 214 C3
Harrow HA3 23 D2
Chantry Sch UB7 104 A6
Chantry Sq W8 113 D3 255 C5
Chantry St N1 94 D6 234 D5
Chantry The
3 Chingford E4 20 A3
Hillingdon UB8 82 B4
Chantry Way CR4 202 B6
Chant Sq E15 76 B1
Chant St E15 76 B1
Chapel Cl NW10 67 D2
Chapel Ct
Borough The SE1 252 C2
East Finchley N2 48 C6
Hayes UB3 105 D6
Chapel End Ho E17 35 D2
Chapel End Inf Sch E17 35 D2
Chapel End Jun Sch E17 35 D2
Chapel Farm Rd SE9 166 B2
Chapel Hill N2 30 C1
Chapel House St E14 119 D2
Chapel La
5 Dagenham RM6 58 D2
Hillingdon UB8 82 C1
Pinner HA5 40 D6
Chapel Market N1 94 C5 234 A4
Chapel Mill Rd KT1 198 B6
Chapel Pl
Islington N1 234 B4
Marylebone W1 238 C1
12 Shoreditch EC2 95 C4
Tottenham N17 33 D3
Chapel Rd
Bexleyheath DA7 147 C1
Ealing W13 109 B5
Hounslow TW3 129 D2
Ilford IG1 78 D5
Twickenham TW1 153 B4
West Norwood SE27 182 D6
Chapel Side W2 113 D6 245 C5
Chapel St
Enfield EN2 5 B2
Paddington NW1 92 C2 237 A3
Westminster SW1 115 A4 248 B1
Chapel View CR2 222 C1
Chapel Wlk NW4 46 C5
Chapleton Ho SW2 160 C6
Chaplin Cl
Lambeth SE1 251 C2
Wembley HA0 65 D2
Chaplin Cres TW16 171 C4
Chaplin Ho
6 London SW9 138 C1
Sidcup DA14 190 A6
Chaplin Rd
Dagenham RM9 81 A1
3 Tottenham N17 51 D6
Wembley HA0 65 D2
West Ham E15 98 D6
Willesden NW2 68 A2
Chaplow Cl SW6 136 A3
Chapman Cl UB7 104 B3
Chapman Cres HA3 44 B4
Chapman Gn N22 32 C2
Chapman Ho
26 Stepney E1 96 B1
2 West Norwood SE27 160 D1
Chapman Rd
Belvedere DA17 125 D1
Hackney Wick E9 75 B2
Thornton Heath CR0 204 C1
Chapmans End BR5 191 A1
Chapman's La BR5 190 D1
Chapmans Park Ind Est NW10 67 D2
Chapman Sq SW19 156 D2
Chapman St E1 118 B6
Chapone Pl W1 239 C1
Chapter Cl
Hillingdon UB10 60 B1
16 South Acton W4 111 A3
Chapter House & Jewel Twr* SW1 260 A6
Chapter Rd
Kennington SE17 116 D1 261 D1
Chapter Rd *continued*
Willesden NW2 68 A3
Chapter St SW1 259 C3
Chapter Way
Hampton TW12 173 C6
Mitcham SW19 180 B2
Chara Pl W4 133 B6
Charcot Ho SW15 155 D5
Charcroft Ct 11 W14 112 D4
Charcroft Gdns EN3 6 D1
Chard Ho 7 N7 72 B6
Chardin Ho 30 SW9 138 C4
Chardin Rd 11 W4 111 C2
Chardmore Rd N16 52 A1
Chardwell Cl E6 100 B1
Charecroft Way W12 112 D4
Charfield Ct W9 91 D3
Charford Rd E16 99 A2
Chargeable La E13 99 A3
Chargeable St E16 98 D3
Chargrove Cl 24 SE16 118 D4
Charing Cl BR6 227 D4
Charing Cross SW1 116 A5 250 A4
Charing Cross Hospl W6 112 D1
Charing Cross Rd WC2 93 D1 239 D1
Charing Cross Sta WC2 116 A5 250 B4
Charing Ct BR2 186 C1
Charing Ho SE1 251 B2
Chariot Cl 3 E3 97 C6
Charlbert Ct NW8 230 A4
Charlbert St NW8 92 C5 230 A4
Charlbury Ave HA7 25 D5
Charlbury Gdns IG3 79 D6
Charlbury Gr W5 87 C1
Charlbury Ho 1 E12 78 C5
Charlbury Rd UB10 60 B5
Charldane Rd SE9 166 D1
Charlecote Gr SE26 162 B1
Charlecote Rd RM8 81 A5
Charlemont Rd E6 100 C4
Charles Allen Ho EC1 234 A2
Charles Auffray Ho 30 E1 96 C2
Charles Babbage Cl KT9 213 C1
Charles Barry Cl SW4 137 C2
Charles Bradlaugh Ho 2 N17 34 B3
Charles Burton Ct E5 75 A4
Charles Cl DA14 190 B6
Charles Cobb Gdns CR0 220 C3
Charles Coveney Rd 4 SE15 139 D4
Charles Cres HA1 42 B2
Charles Ct 5 TW11 174 C5
Charles Darwin Ho
8 Bethnal Green E2 96 B4
Bromley BR1 187 B3
Charles Dickens Ct SE25 206 A5
Charles Dickens Ho 1 E2 96 B4
Charles Dickens Prim Sch SE1 117 A4 252 A1
Charles Edward Brooke Sch SW9 138 D4
Charles Edward Brooke Sch (Dennen Site) SE5 138 D4
Charlesfield SE12 165 C1
Charles Flemwell Mews 7 E16 121 A5
Charles Goddard Ho 3 HA0 65 D3
Charles Gr N14 15 C3
Charles Grinling Wlk SE18 122 C2
Charles Haller St 25 SW2 160 C4
Charles Harrod Ct SW13 134 C6
Charles Ho
Southall UB2 107 C4
1 Tottenham N17 33 D3
Charles Hobson Ho 4 NW10 67 C1
Charles Hocking Ho 8 W3 111 A4
Charles II Pl SW3 114 D1 257 C1
Charles II St SW1 115 D5 249 C4
Charles La NW8 92 C5 230 A4
Charles Lamb Ct N1 234 D4
Charles Lamb Prim Sch N1 95 A6 235 A6
Charles Lesser KT9 213 D3
Charles Mackenzie Ho 7 SE16 118 A2
Charlesmere Gdns SE28 123 C4
Charles Mills Ct SW16 182 A4
Charles Pl NW1 232 B1
Charles Rd
Dagenham RM6 58 D3
Ealing W13 87 A1
Merton SW19 179 C2
Upton E7 77 C1
Charles Rowan Ho WC1 234 A1
Charles Sevright Dr NW7 28 D5
Charles Sq N1 95 B4 235 D1
Charles St
Barnes SW13 133 C3
Croydon CR0 221 A5
Enfield EN1 17 D6
Hillingdon UB10 82 D3
Hounslow TW3 129 B3
Mayfair W1 115 B5 248 C4
Newham E16 121 C5
Charles Staunton Ho 3 SE27 183 B6
Charleston Cl TW13 150 A1
Charleston St SE17 262 B3
Charles Townsend Ho EC1 241 C6
Charles Utton Ct E8 74 A4
Charles Whincup Rd 2 E16 121 B5
Charlesworth Ho 6 E14 97 C1
Charleville Cir SE26 184 A5
Charleville Ct SW5 254 C1
Charleville Mans W14 254 B1
Charleville Mews TW7 131 B1
Charleville Rd W14 113 B1 254 C1
Charlie Browns Rdbt E18 37 C1
Charlmont Rd SW17 180 D4
Charlotte Cl DA6 169 A6
Charlotte Ct
Crouch End N8 49 D3
Esher KT10 212 A3
10 Hammersmith W6 112 A2
Ilford IG2 56 C3
11 Wembley HA0 66 A2
Charlotte Despard Ave SW11 137 A4 268 B1
Charlotte Ho 12 W6 112 C1
Charlotte Mews
Marylebone W1 239 B4
North Kensington W10 90 D1
West Kensington W14 254 A4
Charlotte Par SE23 163 A2
Charlotte Park Ave BR1 210 A6
Charlotte Pl
Kenton NW9 45 A4
Marylebone W1 239 B3
Westminster SW1 259 A3
Charlotte Rd
Barnes SW13 133 D4
Dagenham RM10 81 D2
Shoreditch EC2 95 C3 243 A6
Wallington SM6 219 C2
Charlotte Row SW4 137 C2
Charlotte Sharman Prim Sch SE11 116 D3 261 C5
Charlotte Sq 5 TW10 154 B5
Charlotte St W1 93 C2 239 B4
Charlotte Terr N1 94 B6 233 D5
CHARLTON
143 D6
171 B1
Charlton Church La SE7 121 C1
Charlton Cl UB10 60 D6
Charlton Cres IG11 101 D5
Charlton Ct
Finchley N3 29 A1
25 Hackney E2 95 D6
17 Kentish Town N7 71 D3
Newham E6 100 B4
Charlton Dene SE7 143 D5
Charlton Gate Bsns Pk SE7 121 C2
Charlton Ho
5 Brentford TW8 132 A6
Charlton TW17 171 A1
Somers Town NW1 232 C2
Charlton King's Rd NW5 71 D3
Charlton La
Greenwich SE7 121 D1
Upper Halliford TW17 193 B5
Upper Halliford TW17 193 C5
Charlton Lo 1 NW11 47 B3
Charlton Manor Prim Sch SE7 143 D5
Charlton Park La SE7 144 A6
Charlton Park Rd SE7 143 D6
Charlton Pl N1 94 D5 234 C4
Charlton Rd
Charlton TW17 171 A1
Edmonton N9 18 D4
Greenwich SE3, SE7 143 B6
Harlesden NW10 89 C6
Harrow HA3 43 D5
Wembley HA9 44 B1
Charlton Sch SE7 144 A6
Charlton Way SE10, SE3 142 C4
Charlwood Cl HA3 24 C4
Charlwood Ho
Richmond TW9 132 D5
1 Streatham SW2 160 B3
Westminster SW1 259 C3
Charlwood Pl SW1 115 C2 259 B3
Charlwood Rd SW15 134 D1
Charlwood St SW1 115 C1 259 B2
Charlwood Terr 5 SW15 134 D1
Charman Ho
18 London SW2 160 C5
South Lambeth SW8 270 A4
Charmian Ave HA7 25 D1
Charmian Ho 19 N1 95 C5
Charminster Ave SW19 179 D1
Charminster Ct 3 KT6 197 D2
Charminster Rd
Mottingham SE12, SE9 187 D6
North Cheam KT4 200 D1
Charmouth Ct TW10 154 B6
Charmouth Ho SW8 270 C4
Charmouth Rd DA16 146 C4
Charnock Ho 22 W12 112 B6
Charnock Rd E5 74 B5
Charnwood Ave SW19 179 D1
Charnwood Cl KT3 199 C5
Charnwood Dr E18 55 B5
Charnwood Gdns E14 119 C2
Charnwood Ho 9 E5 74 B6
Charnwood Pl N20 14 A1
Charnwood Rd
Hillingdon UB10 82 C5
South Norwood SE25 205 B5
Charnwood St E5 74 B6
Charolais Ho UB4 83 B2
Charrington Ho 42 E1 96 C3
Charrington Rd 2 CR0 221 A6
Charrington St NW1 93 D5 232 C4
Charsley Rd SE6 163 D2
Chart Cl
Bromley BR2 186 C2
Croydon CR0 206 C3
Mitcham CR4 202 D5
Charter Ave IG2 57 B2
Charter Bldgs 14 SE10 141 D4
Charter Cres TW4 129 A1
Charter Ct
Finsbury Pk N4 50 C1
Kingston u T KT3 199 C6
Marylebone W1 237 B3
Southall UB1 107 C5
Wood Green N22 31 D2
Charter Dr DA5 169 A4
Charter Ho WC2 240 B1
Charterhouse Ave HA0 65 C3
Charterhouse Bldgs EC1 242 A5
Charterhouse Mews EC1 241 D4
Charterhouse Rd E8 74 A3
Charterhouse Sq EC1 94 D2 241 D4
Charterhouse Square Sch EC1 94 D2 241 D4
Charterhouse St EC1 241 C3
Charterhouse Works SW18 136 A1
Charteris Rd
Finsbury Pk N4 50 C1
Kilburn NW6 91 B6
Woodford IG8 37 B4
Charter Nightingale Hospl The NW1 92 C2 237 B4
Charter Rd KT1 198 D6
Charter Rd The IG8 36 D4
Charter Sch The SE24 161 B6
Charters Cl SE19 183 C5
Charter Sq KT1 176 D1
Charter Way
London NW3 47 B5
Southgate N14 15 D5
Chartes Ho SE1 263 B6
Chartfield Ave SW15 156 C6
Chartfield Sch SW15 156 B6
Chartfield Sq SW15 156 D6
Chartham Ct 12 SW9 138 C2
Chartham Gr SE27 160 D1
Chartham Ho SE1 262 D6
Chartham Rd SE25 206 B6
Chart Hills Cl SE28 103 A1
Chart Ho 7 SW19 180 D1
Chart House The 5 E14 119 D1
Chartley Ave
Harrow HA7 24 D4
Neasden NW2 67 C5
Charton Cl 5 DA17 147 B6
Chartres Ct UB6 86 B5
Chartridge SE17 139 B6
Chartridge Cl
Barnet EN5 12 A6
Bushey WD23 8 A5
Chartridge Ct 6 HA7 25 C5
Chart St N1 95 B4 235 D2
Chartwell 25 SW19 156 D3
Chartwell Bsns Ctr BR1 209 D6
Chartwell Cl
2 Croydon CR0 205 B1
Greenford UB6 85 D6
Sidcup SE9 167 B2
Chartwell Ct
10 Barnet EN5 1 A1
Dollis Hill NW2 68 A5
2 Woodford IG8 37 A3
Chartwell Dr BR6 227 B3
Chartwell Gdns SM3 217 A4
Chartwell Lo 5 BR3 185 C3
Chartwell Pl
Cheam SM3 217 B4
Harrow HA2 64 B6
Chartwell Way 3 SE20 184 B2
Charville Ct 8 HA1 42 D3
Charville La UB4 83 C5
Charville La W UB10 82 D4
Charville Prim Sch UB4 83 C5
Charwood SW16 182 C6
Chase Bridge Prim Sch TW2 152 C5
Chase Court Gdns EN2 5 A2
Chase Ct
Chelsea SW3 257 C5
Isleworth TW7 131 A3
Merton SW20 179 A1
Southgate N14 15 C5
Wembley HA0 65 D2
Chase Ctr The NW10 89 B4
Chase Farm Hospl EN2 4 C5
Chasefield Rd SW17 180 D6
Chase Gdns
Chingford E4 35 C6
Twickenham TW2 152 B4
Chase Gn EN2 5 A2
Chase Green Ave EN2 5 A3
Chase Hill EN2 5 A2
Chase La IG6 57 B4
Chase Lane Inf Sch E4 35 B6
Chase Lane Jun Sch E4 35 B6
Chaseley Ct
Gunnersbury W4 110 D1
Oatlands Pk KT13 193 C1
Chaseley St E14 97 A1
Chasemore Cl CR4 202 D2

Chasemore Gdns
CR0 . . . . . 220 C3
Chasemore Ho SW6 . . . 264 B4
Chase Rd
North Acton NW10 . . . . . 89 B3
Southgate N14 . . . . . 15 D5
Chase Ridings EN2 . . . . . 4 C3
Chase Road Trad Est
NW10 . . . . . 89 B3
Chase Side
East Barnet N14 . . . . . 15 B4
Enfield EN2 . . . . . 5 A3
Chase Side Ave
Enfield EN2 . . . . . 5 A3
Merton SW20 . . . . . 179 A1
Chase Side Cres EN2 . . . . 5 A4
Chase Side Pl EN2 . . . . . 5 A3
Chase Side Prim Sch
EN2 . . . . . 5 A3
Chase Side Works
N14 . . . . . 15 D4
Chase The
Bromley BR1 . . . . . 209 B6
Clapham SW4 . . . . . 137 B2
Dagenham RM6 . . . . . 59 A3
Eastcote HA5 . . . . . 40 C3
Edgware HA8 . . . . . 26 D2
Erith DA7 . . . . . 147 D2
Ickenham UB10 . . . . . 60 C3
Loughton IG10 . . . . . 21 D4
Manor Pk E12 . . . . . 77 D4
Pinner HA5 . . . . . 41 B5
South Norwood SW16 . . 182 C3
Stanmore HA7 . . . . . 25 A4
Sunbury TW16 . . . . . 172 B2
Wallington CR0, SM6 . . . 220 B3
Chaseville Par N21 . . . . 16 B6
Chaseville Park Rd
N21 . . . . . 16 B6
Chase Way N14 . . . . . 15 C3
Chasewood Ave EN2 . . . . 4 D3
Chasewood Ct 4 NW7 . 27 B5
Chasewood Pk HA1 . . . . 64 C5
Chateau The 4 SM5 . . 218 D5
Chatelain Ho NW7 . . . . 28 C6
Chater Ho 6 E2 . . . . . 96 D4
Chatfield Rd
London SW11 . . . . . 136 A2
Thornton Heath CR0 . . . . 204 D1
Chatham Ave BR2 . . . . 209 A2
Chatham Cl
Cheam SM3 . . . . . 201 B2
Hampstead Garden Suburb
NW11 . . . . . 47 C4
Chatham Ct SW11 . . . . 158 D6
Chatham Ho
7 London SE5 . . . . . 139 C3
6 Wallington SM6 . . . . 219 B3
21 Woolwich SE18 . . . . 122 B2
Chatham Pl E9 . . . . . 74 C2
Chatham Rd
Clapham SW11 . . . . . 158 D6
Kingston u T KT1, KT2 . . . 176 C1
Walthamstow E17 . . . . . 53 A6
1 Woodford E18 . . . . . 36 D1
Chatham St
SE17 . . . . . 117 B2 262 D4
Chatsfield Pl W5 . . . . . 88 A1
Chatsworth Ave
Grove Pk BR1 . . . . . 187 B6
Hendon NW4 . . . . . 28 C1
Merton SW20 . . . . . 179 A1
Sidcup DA15 . . . . . 168 A3
Wembley HA9 . . . . . 66 B3
Chatsworth Cl
Coney Hall BR2, BR4 . . . 224 D6
Hendon NW4 . . . . . 28 C1
Chatsworth Cres TW3,
TW7 . . . . . 130 B2
Chatsworth Ct
Brondesbury NW2 . . . . . 68 D2
Clapton Pk E5 . . . . . 74 D4
Earl's Ct W8 . . . . . 255 A4
5 Stanmore HA7 . . . . . 25 C5
Thornton Heath SW16 . . 204 B6
Chatsworth Dr EN1 . . . . 18 A5
Chatsworth Est E5 . . . . 74 D4
Chatsworth Gdns
Acton W3 . . . . . 110 D5
Harrow HA2 . . . . . 41 D1
New Malden KT3 . . . . . 199 D4
Chatsworth Ho
2 Bromley BR2 . . . . . 209 A5
Kingston u T KT6 . . . . . 197 D4
Chatsworth Inf Sch
Isleworth TW3 . . . . . 130 A1
Sidcup DA15 . . . . . 168 A3
Chatsworth Jun Sch
TW3 . . . . . 130 A1
Chatsworth Lo
1 Chiswick W4 . . . . . 111 B1
West Wickham BR4 . . . . 224 A6
Chatsworth Par BR5 . . 211 A4
Chatsworth Pl
Mitcham CR4 . . . . . 202 D6
Teddington TW11 . . . . . 175 A6
Chatsworth Rd
Brondesbury NW2 . . . . . 68 D2
Cheam SM3 . . . . . 217 A4
Chiswick W4 . . . . . 133 A6
Clapton Pk E5 . . . . . 74 D4
Ealing W5 . . . . . 88 B3
Hayes UB4 . . . . . 84 B3
South Croydon CR0 . . . . 221 B5
Stratford E15 . . . . . 76 D3
Chatsworth Rise W5 . . . 88 B3
Chatsworth Way
SE27 . . . . . 161 A1
Chattenden Ho 8 N4 . . 51 B2
Chatteris Ct NW4 . . . . . 46 D6
CHATTERN HILL 170 D6
Chattern Hill TW15 . . . . 170 D6
Chattern Rd TW15 . . . . 171 A6
Chatterton Ct TW9 . . . . 132 B3
Chatterton Rd
Bromley Comm BR2 . . . . 209 D4
Highbury N4 . . . . . 72 D5
Chatton Ct 5 NW9 . . . . 46 A5
Chatto Rd SW11 . . . . . 158 D6
Chaucer Ave
Cranford TW4 . . . . . 128 B3
Hayes UB4 . . . . . 84 A2
Richmond TW9 . . . . . 132 C3
Chaucer Cl N11 . . . . . 31 D5
Chaucer Ct
14 New Barnet EN5 . . . . 13 D6
17 Stoke Newington
N16 . . . . . 73 C4
Chaucer Dr
SE1 . . . . . 117 D2 263 D3
Chaucer Gdns SM1 . . . . 217 C5
Chaucer Gn CR0 . . . . . 206 C2
Chaucer Ho
Harrow HA2 . . . . . 41 D4
Pimlico SW1 . . . . . 259 A1
Sutton SM1 . . . . . 217 C5
2 West Norwood
SE27 . . . . . 183 A6
Chaucer Rd
Acton W3 . . . . . 111 A5
Ashford TW15 . . . . . 170 B6
Bexley DA16 . . . . . 145 D4
Chingford E17 . . . . . 36 A1
Herne Hill SE24 . . . . . 160 D6
Sidcup DA15 . . . . . 168 C3
Sutton SM1 . . . . . 217 C4
Upton E7 . . . . . 77 A2
Wanstead E11 . . . . . 55 A3
Chaucer Way SW17 . . . 180 B5
Chaulden Ho EC1 . . . . 235 D1
Chauncey Cl N9 . . . . . 18 A1
Chaundrye Cl SE9 . . . . 166 B5
Chauntler Cl E16 . . . . . 121 B6
Chaville Ct N11 . . . . . 31 A6
Cheadle Ct NW8 . . . . . 236 D6
Cheadle Ho 17 E14 . . . . 97 B1
CHEAM 217 B3
Cheam Common Inf Sch
KT4 . . . . . 216 B6
Cheam Common Jun Sch
KT4 . . . . . 216 B6
Cheam Common Rd
KT4 . . . . . 216 C5
Cheam Court Flats 1
SM3 . . . . . 217 A2
Cheam Fields Prim Sch
SM3 . . . . . 217 A3
Cheam High Sch
SM3 . . . . . 217 A4
Cheam Mans SM3 . . . . 217 A1
Cheam Park Farm Inf Sch
SM3 . . . . . 217 A5
Cheam Park Farm Jun
Sch SM3 . . . . . 217 A5
Cheam Park Way
SM3 . . . . . 217 A2
Cheam Rd
Belmont SM2, SM3 . . . . 216 D1
Cheam SM1 . . . . . 217 C2
Cheam St 6 SE15 . . . . 140 B2
Cheam Sta SM2 . . . . . 217 A1
Cheam Village SM3 . . . 217 A2
Cheapside
Barbican EC2 . . . . 95 A1 242 B1
Edmonton N13 . . . . . 33 A6
Chearsley SE17 . . . . . 262 B4
Cheddar Cl 1 N11 . . . . . 31 A4
Cheddar Rd TW6 . . . . . 126 C3
Cheddar Waye UB4 . . . . 84 B1
Cheddington Ho 9 E2 . 96 A6
Cheddington Rd N18 . . . 33 C6
Chedworth Cl E16 . . . . . 98 D1
Chedworth Ho
London N15 . . . . . 51 B5
2 Stoke Newington E5 . . 74 A6
Cheeseman Cl TW12 . . 173 A4
Cheeseman Ct UB1 . . . 107 D6
Cheesemans Terr
W14 . . . . . 254 C1
Cheffrey Ct TW15 . . . . 170 D4
Cheldon Ave NW7 . . . . . 28 D3
Chelford Rd BR1 . . . . . 186 B5
Chelmer Cres IG11 . . . . 102 B5
Chelmer Ct E18 . . . . . 37 B2
Chelmer Rd E9 . . . . . 74 D3
Chelmsford Cl
Fulham W6 . . . . . 134 D6
Newham E6 . . . . . 100 B1
Chelmsford Ct N14 . . . . 15 D4
Chelmsford Gdns IG1 . . 56 B2
Chelmsford Ho 5 N7 . . 72 B4
Chelmsford Rd
Leytonstone E11 . . . . . 54 B1
London N14 . . . . . 15 C4
Walthamstow E17 . . . . . 53 C3
Woodford E18 . . . . . 36 D2
Chelmsford Sq NW10 . . 90 C6
CHELSEA 114 C1
Chelsea Barracks*
SW1 . . . . . 115 A1 258 B1
Chelsea Bridge
SW1 . . . . . 137 B6 268 C6
Chelsea Bridge Rd
SW1 . . . . . 115 A1 258 B1
Chelsea Cl
Edgware HA8 . . . . . 26 C1
Hampton TW12 . . . . . 174 A5
New Malden KT4 . . . . . 200 A2
Stonebridge NW10 . . . . 89 B6
Chelsea Cloisters
SW3 . . . . . 257 B3
Chelsea Coll of Art &
Design
Chelsea
SW3 . . . . . 114 C1 257 A1
Pimlico SW1 . . . 116 A1 260 A2
Chelsea Cres
Brondesbury NW2 . . . . . 69 B2
Chelsea SW10 . . . . . 266 B1
Chelsea Ct
Chelsea SW3 . . . . . 268 A6
8 Chingford E4 . . . . . 20 A3
Sutton SM2 . . . . . 217 D2
Chelsea Emb
SW3 . . . . . 136 D6 267 C5
Chelsea Est SW3 . . . . . 267 A5
Chelsea Farm Ho
SW10 . . . . . 266 D5
Chelsea Fields SW19 . . 180 B2
Chelsea Gate SW1 . . . . 258 B1
Chelsea Gdns
Cheam SM3 . . . . . 217 A4
Chelsea SW1 . . . . . 258 B1
Ealing W13 . . . . . 86 D2
**Chelsea Harbour Design
Ctr** SW10 . . . . . 266 B2
Chelsea Harbour Dr
SW10 . . . . . 136 A4 266 B2
Chelsea Harbour Pier
SW10 . . . . . 266 C1
Chelsea Lo SW3 . . . . . 267 D6
Chelsea Manor Ct
SW3 . . . . . 267 B6
Chelsea Manor Gdns
SW3 . . . . . 257 B1
Chelsea Manor St
SW3 . . . . . 114 C1 257 B1
Chelsea Manor Studios
SW3 . . . . . 257 B1
Chelsea Park Gdns
SW3 . . . . . 136 B6 266 C6
Chelsea Physic Gdn*
SW1 . . . . . 267 C6
Chelsea Reach Twr
SW10 . . . . . 266 C4
Chelsea Sq
SW3 . . . . . 114 B1 256 D1
Chelsea Twrs SW3 . . . . 267 B6
Chelsea & Westminster
Hospl SW10 . . 136 A6 266 B5
Chelsfield Ave N9 . . . . . 18 D4
Chelsfield Gdns SE26 . . 162 C1
Chelsfield Gn N9 . . . . . 18 D4
Chelsfield Ho SE17 . . . . 263 A3
Chelsfield Point 3 E9 . . 74 D1
Chelsham Ho 1 SW4 . . 137 D2
Chelsham Rd
London SW4 . . . . . 137 D2
South Croydon CR2 . . . . 221 B2
Chelsiter Ct DA14 . . . . 189 D6
Chelston App HA4 . . . . . 62 A6
Chelston Ct 2 E11 . . . . 55 B4
Chelston Rd HA4 . . . . . 40 A1
Chelsworth Dr SE18 . . 145 B6
Cheltenham Ave 10
TW1 . . . . . 153 A4
Cheltenham Cl
Kingston u T KT3 . . . . . 199 A6
Northolt UB5 . . . . . 63 D2
Cheltenham Ct 8 HA7 . 25 C5
Cheltenham Gdns E6 . . 100 A5
Cheltenham Ho UB3 . . 105 A3
Cheltenham Pl
10 Acton W3 . . . . . 110 D5
Acton W3 . . . . . 111 A4
Harrow HA3 . . . . . 44 A5
1 South Acton W3 . . . . 110 D4
Cheltenham Rd
Leyton E10 . . . . . 54 A3
London SE15 . . . . . 162 C6
Cheltenham Terr
SW3 . . . . . 114 D1 257 D2
Cheltenham Villas
CR7 . . . . . 204 C3
Chelverton Ct SW15 . . . 134 D1
Chelverton Rd SW15 . . 134 D1
Chelwood
Gospel Oak NW5 . . . . . 71 A3
London N20 . . . . . 14 B2
Chelwood Cl E4 . . . . . 19 D5
Chelwood Ct
Battersea SW11 . . . . . 266 D2
9 South Croydon CR2 . . 221 A3
Chelwood Gdns TW9 . . 132 C3
Chelwood Ho W2 . . . . . 236 D1
Chelwood Lo N12 . . . . . 30 A4
Chenappa Cl E13 . . . . . 99 A4
Chenduit Way HA7 . . . . 24 D5
Chene Colline Ct KT6 . . 198 A3
Cheney Ct SE23 . . . . . 162 D3
Cheney Row E17 . . . . . 35 B2
Cheneys Rd E11 . . . . . 76 C5
Cheney St HA5 . . . . . 40 C4
Chenies Ho W2 . . . . . 245 C6
Chenies Mews WC1 . . . 239 C5
Chenies Pl NW1 . . . . . 232 D4
Chenies St
WC1 . . . . . 93 D2 239 C4
Chenies The
Orpington BR6 . . . . . 211 C3
Somers Town NW1 . . . . 232 D4
Cheniston Gdns W8 . . . 255 C6
Chennestone Prim Sch
TW16 . . . . . 172 B1
Chepstow Cl SW15 . . . . 157 A6
Chepstow Cres
Ilford IG3 . . . . . 57 C3
Notting Hill
W11 . . . . . 113 C6 245 A6
Chepstow Ct W11 . . . . . 245 A6
Chepstow Gdns UB1 . . . 85 B1
Chepstow Pl
W2 . . . . . 113 C6 245 B6
Chepstow Rd
Croydon CR0 . . . . . 221 D6
Ealing W7 . . . . . 109 A3
Paddington W2 . . . . . 91 C1
Chepstow Rise CR0 . . . 221 C5
Chepstow Villas
W11 . . . . . 113 C6 245 A6
Chequers IG9 . . . . . 21 B3
Chequers Cl
London NW9 . . . . . 45 C6
Orpington BR5 . . . . . 211 D5
Chequers Ct
7 Croydon CR0 . . . . . 205 D1
St Luke's EC1 . . . . . 242 C5
Chequers Ho NW8 . . . . 237 A6
Chequers La RM9 . . . . . 103 C5
Chequers Par
Dagenham RM9 . . . . . 103 C6
Edmonton N13 . . . . . 33 A5
Chequer St EC1 . 95 A3 242 B5
Chequers The HA5 . . . . 40 D6
Chequers Way N13 . . . . 32 D5
Cherbury Cl SE28 . . . . . 102 D1
Cherbury Ct N1 . . . . . 235 D3
Cherbury St N1 . 95 B5 235 D3
Cherchefells Mews
HA7 . . . . . 25 B5
Cherimoya Gdns KT8 . . 195 D6
Cherington Rd W7 . . . . 108 D5
Cheriton Ave BR2 . . . . . 209 A4
Cheriton Cl
Cockfosters EN4 . . . . . 2 D1
10 Ealing W5 . . . . . 87 C2
Cheriton Ct
4 Lee SE12 . . . . . 165 A4
South Norwood SE25 . . . 205 C4
Walton-on-T KT12 . . . . . 194 C1
Cheriton Dr SE18 . . . . . 145 B6
Cheriton Ho 9 E5 . . . . . 74 B3
Cheriton Sq SW17 . . . . 159 A2
Cherry Ave UB1 . . . . . 106 D5
Cherry Blossom Cl
N13 . . . . . 32 D5
Cherry Cl
Carshalton SM5 . . . . . 218 D6
Ealing W5 . . . . . 109 D3
Merton SM4 . . . . . 201 A5
Ruislip HA4 . . . . . 61 D5
7 Streatham SW2 . . . . . 160 C4
Walthamstow E17 . . . . . 53 D4
Cherrycot Hill BR6 . . . . 227 B4
Cherrycot Rise BR6 . . . 227 A4
Cherry Cres TW8 . . . . . 131 B5
Cherry Croft Gdns 3
HA5 . . . . . 23 B3
Cherry Ct
Acton W3 . . . . . 111 C5
Hackbridge CR4 . . . . . 203 A1
Ilford IG6 . . . . . 56 D6
Pinner HA5 . . . . . 22 D2
5 Rotherhithe SE16 . . . 119 A5
Sidcup DA14 . . . . . 168 B1
Cherrydeal Ct E11 . . . . 54 B2
Cherrydown Ave E4 . . . . 19 C1
Cherrydown Cl E4 . . . . . 19 C1
Cherrydown Rd DA14 . 168 D2
Cherry Garden Ho 7
SE16 . . . . . 118 B4
Cherry Garden Sch
SE16 . . . . . 118 A2
Cherry Garden St
SE16 . . . . . 118 B4
Cherry Garth TW8 . . . . 109 D1
Cherry Gdns
Dagenham RM9 . . . . . 81 B3
Northolt UB5 . . . . . 63 D1
Cherry Gr
Hayes UB3 . . . . . 106 B5
Hillingdon UB8 . . . . . 83 A2
Cherry Hill
New Barnet EN5 . . . . . 13 D5
Stanmore HA3 . . . . . 24 C4
Cherry Hill Gdns CR0 . . 220 B4
Cherry Hills WD19 . . . . 23 A5
Cherry La UB7 . . . . . 104 C2
Cherrylands Cl NW9 . . . 67 A6
Cherry Lane Prim Sch
UB7 . . . . . 104 B2
Cherry Laurel Wlk
SW2 . . . . . 160 B5
Cherry Orch
Charlton SE7 . . . . . 143 C6
West Drayton UB7 . . . . . 104 A4
Cherry Orchard Gdns
7 Croydon CR0 . . . . . 205 B1
East Molesey KT8 . . . . . 195 B6
5 South Croydon CR0 . . 221 B6
Cherry Orchard Prim Sch
SE7 . . . . . 143 C5
Cherry Orchard Rd
Croydon CR0 . . . . . 205 C1
East Molesey KT8 . . . . . 195 C6
Keston Mark BR2 . . . . . 226 A6
Cherry Rd EN3 . . . . . 6 C5
Cherry Tree Ave UB7 . . . 82 B1
Cherry Tree Cl
11 Hackney E9 . . . . . 96 C6
Wembley HA0 . . . . . 65 A4
Cherry Tree Ct
1 Camden Town NW1 . . . 71 C1
17 Charlton SE7 . . . . . 143 C6
Kingsbury NW9 . . . . . 45 A5
11 Peckham SE15 . . . . . 140 B4
3 Woodford E18 . . . . . 36 D1
Cherry Tree Dr SW16 . . 160 A1
Cherry Tree Hill N6 . . . . 48 D4
Cherrytree Ho 8 W10 . . 90 D4
Cherry Tree Ho
London SE14 . . . . . 141 B3
Ruislip HA4 . . . . . 39 C1
Twickenham TW2 . . . . . 152 B2
Wood Green N22 . . . . . 32 A3
Cherry Tree Rd
London N2 . . . . . 48 D5
Stratford E15 . . . . . 76 C3
Cherry Tree Rise IG9 . . . 37 D6
Cherry Trees Sch The
E3 . . . . . 97 C4
Cherry Tree Terr SE1 . . 253 B2
Cherry Tree Way HA7 . . 25 B4
Cherry Tree Wlk
Beckenham BR3 . . . . . 207 B5
Coney Hall BR4 . . . . . 224 D4
Cherry Tree Wlk *continued*
St Luke's EC1 . . . . . 242 B5
Cherry Way
Upper Halliford
TW17 . . . . . 193 C5
West Ewell KT19 . . . . . 215 B2
Cherry Wlk BR2 . . . . . 209 A1
Cherrywood Cl
Bow E3 . . . . . 97 A4
Kingston u T KT2 . . . . . 176 C3
Cherrywood Ct 1
TW11 . . . . . 175 A5
Cherrywood Dr
SW15 . . . . . 156 D6
Cherrywood La SM4,
SW20 . . . . . 201 A5
Cherry Wood Way W5 . . 88 C2
Chertsey Ct SW14 . . . . . 132 D2
Chertsey Dr SM3 . . . . . 217 A6
Chertsey Ho
Feltham TW13 . . . . . 151 C1
37 Shoreditch E2 . . . . . 95 D4
Chertsey Rd
Ashford TW15, TW16 . . . 171 B4
Feltham TW13, TW16 . . . 171 C6
Ilford IG1 . . . . . 79 B4
Leyton E11 . . . . . 76 B6
Lower Halliford TW17 . . 192 C2
Shepperton TW17 . . . . . 192 A2
Twickenham TW2 . . . . . 152 B4
Chertsey St SW17 . . . . . 181 A5
Chervil Cl TW13 . . . . . 150 A1
Chervil Mews SE28 . . . . 124 B5
Cherwell Ct
Teddington KT1 . . . . . 175 D3
West Ewell KT19 . . . . . 215 A4
Cherwell Ho NW8 . . . . . 236 D5
Cherwell Way HA4 . . . . . 39 A3
Cheryls Cl
SW6 . . . . . 135 D4 265 D2
Cheseman St SE26 . . . . 162 B1
Chesfield Rd KT2 . . . . . 176 A3
Chesham Ave BR2,
BR5 . . . . . 210 D3
Chesham Cl SW1 . . . . . 258 A5
Chesham Cres SE20 . . . 184 C2
Chesham Ct SW18 . . . . 158 B4
Chesham Flats W1 . . . . 248 B6
Chesham Ho SW1 . . . . . 258 A5
Chesham Mews SW1 . . 258 A6
Chesham Pl
SW1 . . . . . 115 A3 258 A5
Chesham Rd
Kingston u T KT1,
KT2 . . . . . 176 C1
Mitcham SW19 . . . . . 180 B4
Penge SE20 . . . . . 184 C2
Chesham St
Westminster
SW1 . . . . . 115 A3 258 A5
Willesden NW10 . . . . . 67 B5
Chesham Terr W13 . . . . 109 B4
Cheshire Cl
Chingford E17 . . . . . 35 D2
Mitcham CR4, SW16 . . . 204 A6
Cheshire Gdns KT9 . . . . 213 D2
Cheshire Ho SM4 . . . . . 201 D2
Cheshire Rd N22 . . . . . 32 B4
Cheshire St E2 . . 95 D3 243 D6
Cheshir Ho NW4 . . . . . 46 C5
Chesholm Rd N16 . . . . . 73 C5
Cheshunt Ho
Hendon NW4 . . . . . 46 C6
9 Kilburn NW6 . . . . . 91 D6
Cheshunt Rd
Belvedere DA17 . . . . . 125 C1
Upton E7 . . . . . 77 B2
Chesil Ct
17 Bethnal Green E2 . . . . 96 C5
Chelsea SW3 . . . . . 267 B6
Chesil Ho BR7 . . . . . 189 B2
Chesilton Rd
SW6 . . . . . 135 B4 264 C2
Chesil Way UB4 . . . . . 83 D4
Chesley Gdns E6 . . . . . 100 A4
Chesney Cres CR0 . . . . . 224 A1
Chesney Ct W9 . . . . . 91 C3
Chesney Ho SE13 . . . . . 142 B1
Chesney St SW11 . . . . . 268 A1
Chesnut Gr N17 . . . . . 51 D6
Chesnut Rd N17 . . . . . 51 D6
Chessell Cl CR7 . . . . . 204 D5
Chessholme Ct TW16 . . 171 C3
Chessholme Rd
TW15 . . . . . 171 A4
Chessing Ct N2 . . . . . 48 D6
CHESSINGTON 214 A2
Chessington Ave
Church End N3 . . . . . 47 B6
Erith DA7 . . . . . 147 A5

Chessington Cl KT19 215 A2
Chessington Com Coll
KT9 213 D1
Chessington Ct
London N3 47 B6
Pinner HA5 41 B5
Chessington Hall Gdns
KT9 213 D1
Chessington Hill Pk
KT9 214 C3
Chessington Ho 19
SW8 137 D3
Chessington Lo N3 47 B6
Chessington Mans
Leyton E10 53 C2
Leytonstone E11 54 C2
Chessington North Sta
KT9 214 A3
Chessington Par KT9 213 D3
Chessington Pk KT9 214 C4
Chessington Rd KT19 215 B1
Chessington South Sta
KT9 213 D1
Chessington Trade Pk
KT9 214 C4
Chessington Way
BR4 223 D6
Chesson Rd
W14 135 B6 264 D6
Chessum Ho E8 74 A2
Chesswood Way HA5 22 D1
Chestbrook Ct 12 EN1 17 C6
Chester Ave
Richmond TW10 154 B5
Twickenham TW2 151 B3
Chester Cl
Ashford TW15 171 B5
Barnes SW13 134 B2
Hayes UB8 82 D1
Knightsbridge SW1 248 C1
1 Richmond TW10 154 B5
Sutton SM1 217 C6
Chester Close N NW1 231 D2
Chester Close S NW1 231 D1
Chester Cres E8 73 D3
Chester Ct
2 Acton W3 88 C1
Bermondsey SE8 118 D1
4 Camberwell SE5 139 B5
Gospel Oak NW5 71 A4
Harrow HA1 42 D3
Regent's Pk NW1 231 D1
Chester Dr HA2 41 C3
Chesterfield Ct
Ashford TW15 170 A6
Kingston u T KT6 198 A4
Lewisham SE13 142 A2
Chesterfield Dr KT10 213 A6
Chesterfield Flats EN5 12 D6
Chesterfield Gdns
Greenwich SE10 142 B5
Harringay N4 50 D4
Mayfair W1 248 C4
Chesterfield Gr SE22 161 D6
Chesterfield Hill
W1 115 B5 248 C4
Chesterfield Ho
Highgate N6 49 A1
Mayfair W1 248 B4
6 Streatham SW16 181 C5
Chesterfield Lo N21 16 B4
Chesterfield Mews
Ashford TW15 170 A6
Harringay N4 50 D4
Chesterfield Rd
Ashford TW15 170 A5
Barnet EN5 12 D6
Chiswick W4 133 A6
Enfield EN3 7 A6
Finchley N3 29 C4
Leyton E10 54 A3
West Ewell KT19 215 B1
Chesterfield Sch EN3 7 A6
Chesterfield St W1 248 C4
Chesterfield Way
Hayes UB3 106 A4
Peckham SE15 140 C5
Chesterford Gdns
NW3 69 D4
Chesterford Ho 4
SE18 143 D5
Chesterford Rd E12 78 B3
Chester Gate NW1 231 D1
Chester Gdns
Ealing W13 87 B1
Enfield EN3 18 B5
Morden SM4 202 A3
Chester Ho
5 Barnet EN5 1 D1
Dartmouth Pk N19 71 B6
Chester Ho *continued*
1 Deptford SE8 141 B6
Kingston u T KT1 176 D1
Chesterman Ct W4 133 C5
Chester Mews
Belgravia SW1 258 C6
Walthamstow E17 35 C1
Chester Pl NW1 231 C2
Chester Rd
Avery Hill DA15 167 C6
Dartmouth Pk N19 71 B6
Edmonton N9 18 B3
Harlington TW6 126 C2
Hounslow TW4 128 B2
Ilford IG3 57 D2
Newham E16 98 C3
Regent's Pk
NW1 93 B4 231 C2
Tottenham N17 51 C6
Upton E7 77 D1
Walthamstow E17 52 D4
Wanstead E11 55 B3
Wimbledon SW19,
SW20 178 C4
Chester Row
SW1 115 A2 258 B4
Chester Sq
SW1 115 B2 258 C4
Chester Sq Mews
SW1 258 C5
Chester St
Bethnal Green E2 96 A3
Westminster
SW1 115 A3 258 B6
Chesters The KT3 177 C2
Chester Terr
NW1 93 B4 231 C2
Chesterton Cl
Greenford UB6 85 D5
Wandsworth SW18 157 C6
Chesterton Ct W3 110 D3
Chesterton Dr TW19 148 B3
Chesterton Ho
21 Battersea SW11 136 B2
3 Kensal Town W10 91 A2
3 Sutton SM1 218 A4
Chesterton Prim Sch
SW11 137 A4 268 A1
Chesterton Rd
Kensal Town W10 91 A2
Newham E13 99 A4
Chesterton Sq W8 255 A3
Chesterton Terr
6 Kingston u T KT1 176 C1
Newham E13 99 A4
Chester Way
SE11 116 C2 261 B3
Chesthunte Rd N17 33 A2
Chestnut Alley SW6 264 D5
Chestnut Ave
Brentford TW8 109 D2
Buckhurst Hill IG9 21 D1
Coney Hall BR4 224 C4
Edgware HA8 26 B4
Forest Gate E7 77 B4
Hampton TW12 173 C3
Hornsey N8 50 A4
Kingston u T KT8, KT11 174 D2
11 Mortlake SW14 133 B2
Thames Ditton KT10 196 B1
Wembley HA0 65 B3
Worcester Pk KT19 215 C4
Yiewsley UB7 104 B6
Chestnut Ave N E17 54 B5
Chestnut Ave S E17 54 B4
Chestnut Cl
Buckhurst Hill IG9 21 D2
Carshalton SM5 202 D1
Catford SE6 186 A6
Chattern Hill TW15 170 D6
Harlington UB7 126 D5
Hayes UB3 105 C6
New Cross Gate SE14 141 B4
Sidcup DA15 168 A2
Southgate N14 15 D6
1 Stoke Newington
N16 73 B6
Sunbury Comm TW16 171 D4
West Norwood SW16 182 C6
Chestnut Ct
Beckenham BR3 185 C3
7 Cheam SM2 217 C2
5 Croydon CR0 221 A4
Feltham TW13 172 D5
Harrow HA1 42 C2
Hornsey N8 50 A4
Hounslow TW3 129 C2
Kingston u T KT3 199 C6
Surbiton KT6 198 A2
Wembley HA0 65 B3
Chestnut Ct *continued*
West Brompton SW6 264 D6
Chestnut Dr
Bexley DA7 147 A2
Harrow HA3 24 D2
Pinner HA5 41 A3
Wanstead E11 55 A3
Chestnut Gr
Cockfosters EN4 14 D6
Ealing W5 109 D3
Isleworth TW7 131 A1
Kingston u T KT3 199 B6
Mitcham CR4 203 D5
Penge SE20 184 C3
South Croydon CR2 222 B1
Upper Tooting SW12 159 A3
Wembley HA0 65 B3
Chestnut Grove Sch
SW12 159 A3
Chestnut Ho
1 Acton W4 111 C2
Brockley SE4 141 B2
7 Maitland Pk NW3 70 D2
West Norwood SE27 161 A1
Chestnut La N20 13 A3
Chestnut Pl SE19 183 D6
Chestnut Rd
Ashford TW15 170 D6
Kingston u T KT2 176 A3
Twickenham TW2 152 C2
West Barnes SW20 178 D1
West Norwood SE21,
SE27 161 A1
Chestnut Rise SE18 123 C1
Chestnut Row N3 29 C3
Chestnuts Ct 3 E17 54 A6
Chestnuts Prim Sch
N15 51 A4
Chestnuts Royal BR7 189 B3
Chestnuts The
Chislehurst BR7 189 B3
Colindale NW9 45 C6
East Finchley N2 48 D4
7 Erith DA17 125 B1
1 Highbury N5 72 D4
Penge BR3 206 D6
8 Pinner HA5 23 B3
Shooters Hill SE18 144 D4
Uxbridge UB10 60 A1
Walton-on-T KT12 194 B1
Chestnut Way TW13 150 B1
Chestnut Wlk
Upper Halliford
TW17 193 C5
Woodford IG8 37 A5
Cheston Ave CR0 207 B1
Chestwood Gr UB10 60 B1
Chettle Cl SE1 262 C6
Chettle Ct N8 50 C3
Chetwode Ho NW8 237 A6
Chetwode Rd SW17 158 D1
Chetwood Wlk 13 E6 100 A2
Chetwynd Ave EN4 14 D3
Chetwynd Dr UB10 82 B5
Chetwynd Rd NW5 71 B5
Cheval Ct SW15 134 B1
Chevalier Cl HA7 26 A6
Cheval Pl SW7 114 C3 257 B6
Cheval St E14 119 C3
Chevender BR7 188 D3
Cheveney Wlk 2
BR2 209 A6
Chevening Ho BR5 190 A2
Chevening Rd
Cubitt Town SE10 120 D1
Kilburn NW6 91 A6
South Norwood SE19 183 B4
Chevenings The
DA14 168 C1
Cheverell Ho 25 E2 96 A5
Cheverton Rd N19 49 D1
Chevet St E9 75 A3
Chevington NW2 69 B2
Cheviot 4 N17 34 B3
Cheviot Cl
Bushey WD23 8 A5
Enfield EN1 5 B3
Harlington UB3 127 B5
Cheviot Ct
16 Deptford SE14 140 C5
Enfield EN2 5 B3
Southall UB2 107 D2
Cheviot Gate NW2 69 A6
Cheviot Gdns
Cricklewood NW2 69 A6
West Norwood SE27 182 D6
Cheviot Ho N16 51 D1
Cheviot Rd SE27 182 D5
Cheviots Hostel EN1 5 B3
Cheviot Way IG2 57 C5
Chevron Cl E16 99 A1
Chevy Rd UB2 108 A4
Chewton Rd E17 53 A5
Cheylesmore Ho SW1 258 C2
Cheyne Ave
Snaresbrook E18 54 D6
Twickenham TW2 151 B3
Cheyne Cl
6 Hendon NW4 46 B4
Keston Mark BR2 226 A5
Cheyne Ct
Chelsea SW3 267 C6
1 Croydon CR0 221 D6
Ruislip HA4 39 C1
4 Wallington SM6 219 B2
Cheyne Gdns
SW3 136 C6 267 B5
Cheyne Hill KT5 198 B5
Cheyne Mews
SW3 136 C6 267 B5
Cheyne Park Dr BR4 224 A5
Cheyne Path W7 86 D1
Cheyne Pl SW3 267 C6
Cheyne Rd TW15 171 B4
Cheyne Row
SW3 136 C6 267 A5
Cheyne Wlk
Chelsea
SW10 136 B5 266 C4
Croydon CR0 222 A6
Hendon NW4 46 C3
Southgate N21 16 D6
Cheyney Ho 2 E9 74 D2
Cheyneys Ave HA8 25 D4
Chichele Gdns CR0 221 C4
Chichele Ho HA8 26 B6
Chichele Mans NW2 68 D3
Chichele Rd NW2 68 D3
Chicheley Gdns HA3 24 A3
Chicheley Rd HA3 24 A3
Chicheley St SE1 250 D2
Chichester Ave HA4 61 B6
Chichester Cl
Hampton TW12 173 B4
Kidbrooke SE3 143 C4
Newham E6 100 A1
Chichester Ct
Barnet EN4 2 B1
2 Camden Town NW1 71 C1
Edgware HA8 26 C4
Harrow HA2 41 B1
Northolt UB5 85 A6
3 Sidcup DA5 169 C4
Stanmore HA7 44 A6
Stanwell TW19 148 A3
Chichester Gdns IG1 56 B2
Chichester Ho
Kilburn NW6 91 C5
2 Kingston u T KT2 176 D2
Chichester Mews
SE27 182 C6
Chichester Rd
Bayswater W2 91 D2
Edmonton N9 18 A3
Kilburn NW6 91 C5
Leyton E11 76 C5
South Croydon CR0 221 C5
Chichester Rents
WC2 241 A2
Chichester St
SW1 115 C1 259 B1
Chichester Way
Cubitt Town E14 120 B2
Feltham TW14 150 C4
Chicksand Ho 14 E1 96 A2
Chicksand St
E1 95 D2 243 D3
Chicksand Street E1 96 A2
Chiddingfold N12 13 C1
Chiddingstone SE13 164 A6
Chiddingstone Ave
DA7 147 B5
Chiddingstone St
SW6 135 C3
Chieveley Par DA7 147 D2
Chieveley Rd DA7 147 D1
Chignell Pl 7 W13 109 A5
Chigwell Ct 1 E9 75 A2
Chigwell Hill E1 118 B6
Chigwell Hurst Ct HA5 40 D6
Chigwell Rd
Wanstead E18 55 B6
Woodford IG8 37 D3
Chiham Ho 5 SE15 140 C6
Chilchester Ct 3
BR3 207 D6
Chilcombe Ho 6
SW15 156 A4
Chilcot Cl 13 E14 97 D1
Chilcott Cl HA0 65 C4
Child Ct E11 54 B2
Childebert Rd SW17 159 B2
Childeric Prim Sch
SE14 141 A5
Childeric Rd SE14 141 A5
Childerley St
SW6 135 A4 264 A2
Childerly KT1 198 C6
Childers St SE8 141 B6
Child La SE10 120 D3
Childs Ct UB3 106 A6
CHILD'S HILL 69 C6
Child's Hill Prim Sch
NW2 69 A5
Childs La 11 SE19 183 C4
Child's Mews SW5 255 B3
Child's Pl SW5 255 B3
Child's St SW5 255 B3
Childs Way NW11 47 B4
Child's Wlk SW5 255 B3
Chilham Cl
Old Bexley DA5 169 B4
Wembley UB6 87 A5
Chilham Ct 18 SW9 138 C2
Chilham Ho SE1 262 D6
Chilham Rd SE9 188 A6
Chilham Way BR2 209 A2
Chillerton Rd SW17 181 B5
Chillingford Ho
SW17 180 A6
Chillington Dr SW11 136 B1
Chillingworth Gdns
TW1 152 D1
Chillingworth Rd N7 72 C3
Chilmark Gdns KT3 200 A3
Chilmark Rd SW16 181 D2
Chiltern Ave
Bushey WD23 8 A5
Twickenham TW2 151 C3
Chiltern Cl
Bus WD23 8 A5
Ickenham UB10 60 C6
North Cheam KT4 216 C6
South Croydon CR0 221 C5
Chiltern Ct
15 Deptford SE14 140 C5
6 East Barnet N20 14 C2
11 Eltham SE9 166 C5
Harrow HA1 42 B4
Hillingdon UB8 82 D3
Marylebone NW1 237 D5
Muswell Hill N10 31 A1
1 New Barnet EN5 14 A6
Chiltern Dene EN2 4 B1
Chiltern Dr KT5 198 D4
Chiltern Gdns
Beckenham BR2 208 D5
Cricklewood NW2 68 D5
Chiltern Ho
Camberwell SE17 139 B6
Ealing W5 88 A2
5 Edmonton N9 18 A1
Harrow HA1 42 C1
4 Kensal Town W10 91 A2
5 Stamford Hill N16 51 D1
Chiltern Rd
Bow E3 97 C3
Ilford IG2 57 C4
Pinner HA5 40 C4
Chiltern St W1 93 A2 238 A4
Chilterns The BR1 187 B1
Chiltern Way IG8 21 A1
Chilthorne Cl SE6 163 B4
Chilton Ave W5 109 D2
Chilton Gr SE8 119 A2
Chiltonian Ind Est
SE12 164 D5
Chilton Rd
Edgware HA8 26 C4
Richmond TW9 132 C2
Chilton St E2 95 D3 243 D6
Chiltons The 1 E18 37 A1
Chilvers Cl TW2 152 C2
Chilver St SE10 120 D1
Chilwell Gdns WD19 22 C6
Chilworth Ct 8
SW19 156 D3
Chilworth Gdns SM1 218 A5
Chilworth Mews
W2 92 B1 236 C1
Chilworth St
W2 92 A1 236 B1
Chimes Ave N13 32 D6
Chimney Ct 23 E1 118 B5
Chimneys Ct 2
SW19 178 C3
China Ct 1 E1 118 B5
China Hall Mews 16
SE16 118 C3
China Mews 17 SW2 160 B4
Chinbrook Cres SE12 165 B1
Chinbrook Rd SE12 165 B1
Chinchilla Dr TW4 128 C3
Chindit Ho 11 N16 73 B4
Chine The
London N10 49 C5
Southgate N21 16 D6
Wembley HA0 65 B3
Ching Ct
Chingford E4 20 C1
St Giles WC2 240 A1
Chingdale Rd E4 20 C1
CHINGFORD 20 C3
Chingford Ave E4 19 D2
Chingford CE Inf Sch
E4 20 B3
Chingford CE Jun Sch
E4 20 B3
Chingford Foundation Sch
E4 19 D3
CHINGFORD GREEN 20 A4
Chingford Hall Com Prim
Sch E4 35 B4
CHINGFORD HATCH 36 B6
Chingford Hospl E4 20 A1
Chingford Ind Ctr E4 35 A5
Chingford La IG8 36 D5
Chingford Mount Rd
E4 35 C5
Chingford Rd
Highams Pk E4 35 C3
Walthamstow E17 35 D1
Chingford Sta E4 20 C4
Chingley Cl BR1 186 C4
Ching Way E4 35 B4
Chinnery Cl EN1 5 D4
Chinnocks Wharf
E14 119 A6
Chinnor Cres UB6 86 A5
Chipka St E14 120 A4
Chipley St SE14 141 A6
Chipmunk Gr UB5 85 A4
Chippendale Ho SW1 258 D1
Chippendale St E5 74 D5
Chippenham 4 KT1 176 B1
Chippenham Ave HA9 66 D3
Chippenham Cl HA5 39 D5
Chippenham Gdns
NW6 91 C4
Chippenham Mews
W9 91 C3
Chippenham Rd W9 91 C3
Chipperfield Rd BR5 190 A1
CHIPPING BARNET 1 B1
Chipping Cl EN5 1 A2
Chip St SW4 137 D1
Chipstead Ave CR7 204 D5
Chipstead Cl SE19 183 D3
Chipstead Gdns NW2 68 B6
Chipstead Ho 4
SW2 160 A3
Chipstead St SW6 135 C3
Chirk Cl UB4 85 A3
Chirk Ct SE4 141 B3
Chisenhale Prim Sch
E3 97 A5
Chisenhale Rd E3 97 A5
Chisholm Ct 1 W6 112 A1
Chisholm Rd
Croydon CR0 221 C6
13 Richmond TW10 154 B5
Chisledon Wlk E9 75 B2
CHISLEHURST 189 C3
Chislehurst Ave N12 30 A3
Chislehurst High St
BR7 188 D4
Chislehurst Rd
Bromley BR1, BR7 188 A2
Broom Hill BR6 211 D2
Orpington BR5, BR6,
BR7 211 C4
Richmond TW10 154 A6
Sidcup DA14 190 A5
Chislehurst St Nicholas
CE Prim Sch BR7 189 A3
Chislehurst & Sidcup
Gram Sch DA15 168 B2
Chislehurst Sta BR7 188 C1
CHISLEHURST
WEST 188 C4
Chislet 5 NW5 71 A2
Chislet Cl BR3 185 C3
Chisley Rd 5 N15 51 C3
Chiswell Sq SE3 143 B3
Chiswell St
Barbican EC1 95 B2 242 C4
Camberwell SE5 139 B5

CHISWICK ... 111 D1
Chiswick & Bedford Park Prep Sch W4 ... 111 C2
Chiswick Cl CR0 ... 220 B5
Chiswick Common Rd W4 ... 111 B2
Chiswick Com Sch W4 ... 133 B5
Chiswick Ct HA5 ... 41 B6
Chiswick Green Studios 1 W4 ... 111 A2
Chiswick High Rd W4 ... 111 C2
Chiswick High Road (North Circular Rd) W4 ... 110 C1
Chiswick Ho* W4 133 B6
Chiswick La W4 ... 111 C1
Chiswick La S W4 ... 133 D6
Chiswick Mall W4 ... 111 D1
Chiswick Maternity Hospl W4 ... 111 D1
Chiswick Park Sta W4 ... 111 A2
Chiswick Pier W4 ... 133 D5
Chiswick Pk W4 ... 110 D2
Chiswick Plaza W4 ... 133 A6
Chiswick Quay W4 ... 133 A4
Chiswick Rd
Acton W4 ... 111 A2
Edmonton N9 ... 18 A2
Chiswick Rdbt W4 ... 110 C1
Chiswick Sq W4 ... 133 C6
Chiswick Sta W4 ... 133 A5
Chiswick Staithe W4 ... 133 A4
Chiswick Terr 6 W4 ... 111 A2
Chiswick Village W4 ... 132 D6
Chiswick Wharf W4 ... 133 D6
Chitterfield Gate UB7 ... 126 C5
Chitty's La RM8 ... 80 D6
Chitty St W1 ... 93 C2 239 B4
Chivalry Rd SW11 ... 158 C6
Chivelston 27 SW19 ... 156 D3
Chivenor Gr KT2 ... 175 D5
Chivers Rd E4 ... 35 D6
Chivins Ct N3 ... 29 C3
Choats Manor Way RM9 ... 103 B4
Choats Rd IG11 ... 102 D4
Chobham Gdns SW19 ... 156 D2
Chobham Rd E15 ... 76 B3
Cholmeley Cres N6 ... 49 B2
Cholmeley Ct N12 ... 30 A6
Cholmeley Lo N6 ... 49 B1
Cholmeley Pk N6 ... 49 B2
Cholmley Gdns NW6 ... 69 C3
Cholmley Rd KT7 ... 197 B3
Cholmondeley Ave NW10 ... 90 A5
Cholmondeley Wlk TW9 ... 153 C6
Chopin's Ct 13 E1 ... 118 B5
Chopwell Cl E15 ... 76 B1
Chorleywood Cres BR5 ... 190 A1
Choumert Gr SE15 ... 140 A3
Choumert Mews SE15 ... 140 A3
Choumert Rd SE15 ... 139 D3
Choumert Sq 4 SE15 ... 140 A3
Chow Sq 2 E8 ... 73 D3
Chrisp Ho SE10 ... 142 C6
Chrisp St E14 ... 97 D1
Christabel Cl TW7 ... 130 C2
Christ Church TW9 ... 132 A2
Christchurch Ave
Brondesbury Pk NW6 ... 69 A1
Finchley N12 ... 30 A4
Harrow HA3 ... 42 D5
Harrow HA3 ... 43 A5
5 Teddington TW11 ... 175 A5
Wembley HA0 ... 66 A2
Christ Church Bentinck CE Prim Sch NW1 ... 92 C2 237 B4
Christ Church CE Mid Sch W5 ... 109 D6
Christchurch CE Prim Sch SW3 ... 136 D6 267 C6
Christ Church CE Prim Sch
Battersea SW11 ... 136 C2
Brondesbury NW6 ... 69 B1
Camberwell SW9 ... 138 C4
Cubitt Town SE10 ... 120 C1
Christ Church CE Prim Sch *continued*
Forest Hill SE23 ... 162 D2
Shooters Hill SE18 ... 144 C4
Surbiton KT5 ... 198 C3
Christchurch CE Sch E1 ... 95 D2 243 D3
Christchurch Cl
Enfield EN2 ... 5 A3
Finchley N12 ... 30 B3
Mitcham SW19 ... 180 B3
Christchurch Ct UB4 ... 84 C3
Christ Church Ct
1 Brondesbury Pk NW6 ... 69 A1
Harlesden NW10 ... 89 C6
Christchurch Gdns HA3 ... 43 A5
Christchurch Gn HA0 ... 66 A2
Christchurch Hill NW3 ... 70 B4
Christchurch Ho 2 SW2 ... 160 A3
Christ Church La EN5 ... 1 A3
Christchurch Lo EN4 ... 2 D1
Christ Church New Malden CE Prim Sch KT3 ... 199 C6
Christchurch Pas NW3 ... 70 A5
Christchurch Pk SM2 ... 218 A1
Christchurch Prim Sch IG1 ... 57 A1
Christ Church Prim Sch, Hampstead NW3 ... 70 B5
Christchurch Rd
Ilford IG1 ... 57 A1
Mitcham SW19 ... 180 B3
Mortlake SW14 ... 155 A6
Sidcup DA15 ... 167 D1
Streatham SW2 ... 160 C3
Christ Church Rd
1 Beckenham BR3 ... 185 C1
Hornsey N8 ... 50 A3
Surbiton KT5 ... 198 B3
Christ Church Sch NW1 ... 93 B4 231 D2
Christchurch Sq 2 E9 ... 96 C6
Christchurch St SW3 ... 136 D6 267 C6
Christ Church Streatham CE Prim Sch SW2 ... 160 B3
Christchurch Terr SW3 ... 267 C6
Christchurch Way SE10 ... 120 C1
Christian Ct SE16 ... 119 B5
Christian Fields SW16 ... 182 C3
Christian St E1 ... 96 A1
Christie Ct
Maitland Pk NW3 ... 70 C3
2 Upper Holloway N19 ... 72 A6
Christie Dr SE25 ... 206 A4
Christie Gdns RM6 ... 58 B2
Christie Ho
Bexley DA6 ... 169 D6
2 Cubitt Town SE10 ... 120 D1
Harrow HA3 ... 42 D6
4 West Wickham BR4 ... 207 D1
Christie Rd E9 ... 75 A2
Christina Sq N4 ... 50 D1
Christina St EC2 ... 243 A6
Christine Worsley Cl N21 ... 16 D3
Christopher Ave W7 ... 109 A3
Christopher Boone's Almshouses SE13 ... 142 B1
Christopher Cl
Bexley DA15 ... 167 D6
Rotherhithe SE16 ... 118 D4
Christopher Ct
Ashford TW15 ... 170 A5
12 Barnet EN5 ... 1 D1
6 Croydon CR0 ... 206 A1
Hendon NW4 ... 28 C1
23 Surbiton KT6 ... 198 A4
Sutton SM1 ... 217 C3
Christopher France Ho 6 E1 ... 97 A4
Christopher Gdns RM9 ... 80 D3
Christopher Hatton Prim Sch EC1 ... 94 C3 241 A5
Christopher Lo 2 N6 ... 49 D2
Christopher Pl NW1 ... 232 D1
Christopher Rd UB2 ... 106 B2
Christopher St EC2 ... 95 B3 242 D5
Christ's Coll Finchley NW11 ... 47 D6
Christ's Coll Upper Sch N3 ... 29 B1
Christ's Sch TW10 ... 154 C6
Christ the King RC Fst Sch TW19 ... 148 A5
Christ the King RC Prim Sch N4 ... 72 B6
Christ the King Sixth Form Coll SE13 ... 142 B2
Chryssell Rd SW9 ... 138 C5
Chubworthy St 5 SE14 ... 141 A6
Chudleigh 1 DA14 ... 190 B6
Chudleigh Cres IG3 ... 79 C4
Chudleigh Gdns SM1 ... 218 A5
Chudleigh Rd
Hampstead NW6 ... 68 D1
London SE4 ... 163 C6
Twickenham TW1, TW2 ... 152 D4
Chudleigh St E1 ... 96 D1
Chudleigh Way HA4 ... 40 A1
Chulsa Rd SE26 ... 184 B5
Chumleigh Gdns SE5 ... 139 C6
Chumleigh St SE5 ... 139 C6
Chumleigh Wlk KT5 ... 198 B5
Church App SE21 ... 161 B1
Church Ave
Beckenham BR3 ... 185 C2
Camden Town NW1 ... 71 B2
Chingford E4 ... 36 B4
Finchley N2 ... 30 B2
Mortlake SW14 ... 133 B2
Northolt UB5 ... 63 B1
Pinner HA5 ... 41 B3
Ruislip HA4 ... 39 B1
Sidcup DA14 ... 190 B5
Southall UB2 ... 107 A3
Churchbank E17 ... 53 C5
Churchbury Cl EN1 ... 5 C3
Churchbury La EN1 ... 5 C3
Churchbury Rd
Eltham SE9 ... 165 D4
Enfield EN1 ... 5 C3
Church Cl
Edgware HA8 ... 27 A5
Friern Barnet N20 ... 14 C1
Hayes UB4 ... 83 B2
Hounslow TW4 ... 129 B3
Kensington W8 ... 245 C2
West Drayton UB7 ... 104 A3
Church Cres
Church End N3 ... 29 B2
Cranley Gdns N10 ... 49 B5
Friern Barnet N20 ... 14 C1
Hackney E9 ... 74 D1
Churchcroft Cl SW12 ... 159 A4
Church Ct
East Finchley N2 ... 48 B6
Forest Hill SE26 ... 185 A5
Harmondsworth UB7 ... 126 C6
Holborn EC4 ... 241 B1
16 Richmond TW10 ... 153 D6
Rotherhithe SE16 ... 119 B4
Ruislip HA4 ... 62 D5
5 West Norwood SE27 ... 182 D6
Churchdale Ct 1 W4 ... 110 D1
Churchdown BR1 ... 186 C6
Church Dr
Coney Hall BR4 ... 224 C5
Harrow HA2 ... 41 C3
Welsh Harp NW9 ... 45 B1
Church Elm La RM10 ... 81 C2
Church End NW4 ... 46 B6
CHURCH END
N3 ... 29 C1
NW10 ... 67 D3
Church End E17 ... 53 D5
Church Entry EC4 ... 241 D1
Church Estate Almshouses 8 TW9 ... 132 B1
Church Farm House Mus* NW4 46 B6
Church Farm La SM3 ... 217 A2
Churchfield Ave N12 ... 30 B4
Churchfield Cl
Harrow HA2 ... 42 A5
Hayes UB3 ... 105 D6
Churchfield Ho W2 ... 236 C5
Churchfield Mans 5 SW6 ... 135 B3
Churchfield Pl TW17 ... 192 D2
Churchfield Prim Sch N9 ... 17 D3
Churchfield Rd
Acton W3 ... 111 A5
Ealing W13 ... 109 C5
Hanwell W7 ... 108 C4
Walton-on-T KT12 ... 194 A1
Welling DA16 ... 146 A2
Churchfields
East Molesey KT8 ... 195 C6
Greenwich SE10 ... 142 A6
Woodford E18 ... 37 A2
Churchfields Ave TW13 ... 151 C1
Churchfields Jun & Inf Sch E18 ... 37 A2
Churchfields Prim Sch BR3 ... 206 D6
Churchfields Rd BR3 ... 185 A1
Churchfield Way N12 ... 30 A4
Church Garth 4 N19 ... 71 D6
Church Gate SW6 ... 135 A2
Church Gdns
Ealing W5 ... 109 D4
Wembley HA0 ... 65 A4
Church Gn
4 Brixton SW9 ... 138 C3
Hayes UB3 ... 83 D1
Church Gr
London SE13 ... 163 D6
Teddington KT1 ... 175 C1
Church Hill
Harrow HA1 ... 42 C1
Southgate N21 ... 16 C4
Wallington SM5 ... 218 D3
Walthamstow E17 ... 53 D5
Wimbledon SW19 ... 179 B5
Woolwich SE18 ... 122 B3
Churchhill Gardens Prim Sch SW1 ... 115 C1 259 B1
Church Hill Rd
Cheam SM1, SM3 ... 217 A4
East Barnet EN4 ... 14 D4
Kingston u T KT6 ... 198 A4
Walthamstow E17 ... 53 D5
Church Hill Sch EN4 ... 14 D4
Church Hill Wood BR5 ... 211 D4
Church Ho EC1 ... 241 D6
Church Hyde SE18 ... 145 C6
Churchill Ave
Harrow HA3 ... 43 B3
Hillingdon UB10 ... 82 D4
Churchill Cl
East Bedfont TW14 ... 149 D3
Hillingdon UB10 ... 82 D4
Churchill Ct
Ealing W5 ... 88 B3
Edmonton N9 ... 17 B3
4 Farnborough BR6 ... 227 A3
Finsbury Pk N4 ... 50 C2
Harrow HA2 ... 41 D4
7 Ilford IG1 ... 78 D5
Northolt UB5 ... 63 C3
Peckham SE15 ... 140 A3
Willesden NW2 ... 68 B3
9 Woolwich SE18 ... 122 B2
Churchill Gdns
Acton W3 ... 88 C1
Pimlico SW1 ... 137 C6 269 A6
Churchill Gdns Rd SW1 ... 137 C6 269 A6
Churchill Ho
Brentford TW8 ... 109 C1
Mitcham CR4 ... 180 D2
Churchill Lo
Streatham SW16 ... 181 D5
Woodford IG8 ... 36 D4
Churchill Lodge IG6 ... 57 A5
Churchill Mews IG8 ... 36 D4
Churchill Pl
Canary Wharf E14 ... 119 D5
Harrow HA1 ... 42 C5
Churchill Rd
Edgware HA8 ... 26 C4
Gospel Oak NW5 ... 71 B4
Newham E16 ... 99 C1
South Croydon CR2 ... 221 A1
Willesden NW2 ... 68 B2
Churchill Terr E4 ... 19 C1
Churchill Way
Ashford TW16 ... 172 A4
Bromley BR1 ... 187 A1
Churchill Wlk E9 ... 74 C3
Church La
Chessington KT9 ... 214 B2
Chislehurst BR7 ... 189 A2
Dagenham RM10 ... 81 D1
Ealing W5 ... 109 D4
East Finchley N2 ... 48 B6
Edmonton N9 ... 18 A2
Enfield EN1 ... 5 B2
Harrow HA3 ... 24 D2
Hornsey N8 ... 50 B5
Keston Mark BR2 ... 210 A1
Kingsbury NW9 ... 45 B2
Leytonstone E11 ... 54 C1
Merton SW19 ... 179 C2
Church La *continued*
Pinner HA5 ... 41 B6
Teddington TW11 ... 174 D5
Thames Ditton KT7 ... 197 A3
Tottenham N17 ... 33 C2
Twickenham TW1 ... 153 A3
Upper Tooting SW17 ... 181 A5
Wallington SM6 ... 219 D5
Walthamstow E17 ... 53 D5
Churchley Rd SE26 ... 184 B6
Churchley Villas SE26 ... 184 B6
Church Lo UB5 ... 63 B1
Church Manor Way SE18, SE2 ... 124 A2
Church Mdw KT6 ... 213 C6
Church Mead SE5 ... 139 A5
Churchmead Cl EN4 ... 14 C5
Church Mead Inf Sch E10 ... 53 C1
Churchmead Rd NW10 ... 68 A2
Churchmore Rd SW16 ... 181 D2
Church Mount N2 ... 48 B4
Church Paddock Ct SM6 ... 219 D5
Church Par
5 Ashford TW15 ... 170 B6
Harrow HA3 ... 42 C6
Church Path
Merton SW19 ... 179 C1
Mitcham CR4 ... 202 C6
South Acton W4 ... 111 A3
Walthamstow E17 ... 53 D5
Wanstead E11 ... 55 A4
Church Pl
Ealing W5 ... 109 D4
Mitcham CR4 ... 202 C6
St James SW1 ... 249 B5
Uxbridge UB10 ... 61 A5
Church Rd
Acton W3 ... 111 A4
Ashford TW15 ... 170 B6
Barking IG11 ... 79 A2
Barnes SW13 ... 134 A4
Beckenham BR2 ... 208 C6
Bexleyheath DA7 ... 147 B2
Bromley BR1, BR2 ... 187 A1
Buckhurst Hill IG9 ... 21 B3
24 Canonbury N1 ... 73 A2
Cheam SM3 ... 217 A2
Claygate KT10 ... 212 D1
Cranford TW5 ... 128 B6
Croydon CR0 ... 221 A5
Ealing W7 ... 108 C6
East Molesey KT8 ... 196 B6
Enfield EN3 ... 18 C6
Farnborough BR6 ... 227 B3
Feltham TW13 ... 172 D5
Hayes UB3 ... 105 D6
Hendon NW4 ... 46 C5
Heston TW5 ... 129 C5
Higham Hill E17 ... 35 A1
Highgate N6 ... 49 A3
Hillingdon UB8 ... 82 A3
Hounslow TW7 ... 130 C5
Ilford IG2 ... 57 C3
Keston BR2 ... 225 D1
Kingston u T KT1 ... 176 B1
Leyton E10 ... 75 C6
Long Ditton KT6 ... 197 C1
Lower Halliford TW17 ... 192 D2
Manor Pk E12 ... 78 A3
Mitcham CR4 ... 202 C6
Mitcham CR4, SW19 ... 180 B1
New Malden KT4 ... 199 C1
Northolt UB5 ... 85 A6
Richmond TW10 ... 176 A6
Richmond TW10, TW9 ... 154 A6
Sidcup DA14 ... 190 A6
Southall UB2 ... 107 B3
South Norwood SE19 ... 183 C3
Stanmore HA7 ... 25 B5
Teddington TW11 ... 174 D5
Tottenham N17 ... 33 D3
Wallington SM6 ... 219 D5
Welling DA16 ... 146 B3
West Drayton UB7 ... 104 A3
West Ewell KT19 ... 215 B1
Willesden NW10 ... 67 C1
Wimbledon SW19 ... 179 A6
Church Rd N N2 ... 30 B2
Church Rd S N2 ... 30 B2
Church Rise
Chessington KT9 ... 214 B2
Forest Hill SE23 ... 162 D2
Church Row
Chislehurst BR7 ... 189 A2
Hampstead NW3 ... 70 A4
Church Row Mews BR7 ... 189 A3
Church St N E15 ... 98 C6
Church St Sta CR0 ... 221 A6
Church Sq TW17 ... 192 D2
Church St
Chiswick W4 ... 133 D6
Croydon CR0 ... 220 D6
Croydon CR0 ... 221 A6
Dagenham RM10 ... 81 D2
Edmonton N9 ... 17 C2
Enfield EN2 ... 5 B2
Hampton TW12 ... 174 A2
Isleworth TW7 ... 131 B3
Kingston u T KT1 ... 175 D1
Lisson Gr NW8 ... 92 C3 237 A5
Newham E16 ... 122 D5
Sunbury TW16 ... 194 B6
Twickenham TW1 ... 153 A3
Walton-on-T KT12 ... 194 A2
West Ham E15 ... 98 D6
Church Street Est NW8 ... 236 D5
Church Stretton Rd TW3 ... 152 A6
Church Studios 16 NW1 ... 71 D2
Church Terr
Hendon NW4 ... 46 B6
Lewisham SE13 ... 142 C2
21 Richmond TW10 ... 153 D6
Church Vale
Forest Hill SE23 ... 162 D2
Muswell Hill N2 ... 48 D6
Churchview Rd TW2 ... 152 B2
Church Villa TW16 ... 194 B6
Churchward Ho
Camberwell SE17 ... 138 D6
West Kensington SW5 ... 254 D1
Churchway NW1 ... 232 D2
Church Way
Cockfosters EN4 ... 2 D1
Friern Barnet N20 ... 14 C1
Church Wlk
Barnes SW13 ... 134 A4
Brentford TW8 ... 131 C6
Canonbury N16 ... 73 B4
Child's Hill NW2 ... 69 B5
Dartmouth Pk N6 ... 71 A5
Hayes UB3 ... 83 D1
Mitcham SW16 ... 181 C1
15 Richmond TW10 ... 153 D6
Thames Ditton KT7 ... 196 D3
Walton-on-T KT12 ... 194 A1
Welsh Harp NW9 ... 67 B6
West Barnes SW20 ... 200 C6
Churchwood Gdns IG8 ... 37 A6
Churchyard Row SE11 ... 116 D2 261 D4
Churnfield 2 N4 ... 72 C6
Churston Ave E13 ... 99 B6
Churston Cl 16 SW2 ... 160 C3
Churston Dr SM4 ... 201 A4
Churston Gdns N11 ... 31 C4
Churston Mans WC1 ... 240 D5
Churton Pl
Brentford W4 ... 132 D6
Pimlico SW1 ... 259 B3
Churton St SW1 ... 115 C2 259 B3
Chute Ho 17 SW9 ... 138 C3
Chuter Ede Ho SW6 ... 264 D5
Chyngton Cl DA15 ... 167 D1
Chyngton Ct HA1 ... 64 C6
Cibber Rd SE23 ... 162 D2
Cicada Rd SW18 ... 158 A6
Cicely Ho NW8 ... 229 D3
Cicely Rd SE15 ... 140 A4
Cinderford Way BR1 ... 186 C6
Cinema Mus The* SE11 261 C3
Cinema Par RM8 ... 81 B6
Cinnabar Wharf Central 17 E1 ... 118 A5
Cinnabar Wharf East 16 E1 ... 118 A5
Cinnabar Wharf West 18 E1 ... 118 A5
Cinnamon Cl
8 Camberwell SE15 ... 139 D5
Thornton Heath CR0 ... 204 A2
Cinnamon Row 3 SW11 ... 136 A2
Cinnamon St E1 ... 118 B5
Cinnamon Wharf SE1 ... 253 D2
Cinque Cotts SW19 ... 178 C4
Cintra Ct SE19 ... 183 D4
Cintra Pk SE19 ... 183 D3
Circle Ct HA0 ... 65 D4

Circle Gdns SW19 179 C1
Circle Ho 14 E14 98 B1
Circle The
Bermondsey SE1 253 D2
Burnt Oak NW7 27 B4
Neasden NW2 67 C5
Circuits The HA5 40 C5
Circular Rd
London N2 30 B2
Tottenham N17 51 D6
Circular Way SE18 144 C6
Circus Lo NW8 229 C2
Circus Mews W1 237 C4
Circus Pl EC2 242 D3
Circus Rd NW8 92 B5 229 C3
Circus St SE10 142 A5
Cirencester St W2 91 D2
Cirrus 17 NW9 27 D1
Cirrus Cl 4 SM6 220 A1
Cissbury Ho 6 SE26 162 A1
Cissbury Rd N15 51 B4
Cissbury Ring N N12 29 C5
Cissbury Ring S N12 29 B5
Citadel Pl SE11 260 C2
Citizen Ho N7 72 C4
Citizen Rd N7 72 C4
Citron Terr 4 SE15 140 B2
Citrus Ho 14 SE8 119 B1
City Banking Coll
SE1 117 B4 252 D2
City Bsns Ctr 33 SE16 118 C4
City Central Est EC1 235 A1
City Coll N1 235 C2
City Coll of London The
WC1 240 D3
City Forum EC1 95 A4 235 A2
City Garden Row
N1 94 D5 234 D3
City Gate E1 96 C3
City & Guilds of London
Art Sch The
SE11 116 C1 261 B1
City Harbour E14 119 D3
City & Islington 6th Form
Coll EC1 94 D4 234 C2
City & Islington Coll
Finsbury Pk N4 72 D6
Lower Holloway N7 72 A4
Lower Holloway N7 72 B4
Shoreditch EC1 95 A4 235 B1
Shoreditch N1 95 B6 235 C6
City Lights The SE11 261 B1
CITY OF LONDON 117 A6
City of London Sch
EC4 117 A6 252 A6
City of London Sch for
Girls EC2 95 A2 242 B4
City of Westminster Coll
Paddington
NW1 92 C2 237 B4
Paddington W2 92 B2 236 C4
City of Westminster Coll,
Maida Vale Ctr W9 91 D4
City of Westminster Coll,
Queens Park Ctr W9 91 C4
City Prospect 5
SE19 183 C4
City Rd EC1 95 A4 235 B2
City Thameslink Sta
EC4 94 D1 241 C1
City University
EC1 94 D4 234 C1
City View 3 IG1 79 A6
City Wharf Ho KT7 197 B3
City Wlk SE1 253 A1
Civic Way
Ilford IG6 57 A5
Ruislip HA4 62 D3
Civil Service Coll
SW1 115 C2 259 A3
Clabon Mews
SW1 114 D2 257 C4
Clack St SE16 118 C4
Clacton Rd
Newham E6 99 D4
Tottenham N17 33 D1
Walthamstow E17 53 A3
Claigmar Gdns N3 29 D2
Claire Ct
Brondesbury NW2 69 A2
Bushey WD23 8 B3
4 Pinner HA5 23 B3
Whetstone N12 14 A1
Claire Gdns HA7 25 C5
Claire Pl E14 119 C3
Clairvale Rd TW5 129 A4
Clairview Rd SW16 181 B5
Clairville Gdns W7 108 C5
Clairville Point 12
SE23 162 D1
Clamp Hill HA7 24 C5
Clancarty Rd SW6 135 C3
Clandon Cl
South Acton W3 110 D4
Stoneleigh KT17 216 A2
Clandon Ct
Plaistow BR1 187 A4
Sutton SM2 218 B2
Clandon Gdns N3 47 C6
Clandon Ho
East Finchley N3 47 C6
12 Kingston u T KT2 176 D4
Clandon Rd IG3 79 C6
Clandon St SE8 141 C3
Clanfield Ho 12
SW15 156 A3
Clanricarde Gdns
W2 113 C6 245 B5
CLAPHAM 137 B2
Clapham Common*
SW4 137 B1
Clapham Common North
Side SW4 137 A1
Clapham Common South
Side SW4 159 C6
Clapham Common Sta
SW4 137 C1
Clapham Common West
Side
Clapham SW4, SW11 136 D1
Clapham SW11 159 A6
Clapham Computer &
Secretarial Coll
SW11 158 D6
Clapham Court Terr 2
SW4 160 A6
Clapham Cres SW4 137 D1
Clapham Ct 3 SW4 160 A6
Clapham High St
SW4 137 D1
Clapham High Street Sta
SW4 137 D2
Clapham Junction Est
SW11 136 C1
Clapham Junction Sta
SW11 136 C1
Clapham Manor Ct 1
SW4 137 C2
Clapham Manor Prim Sch
SW4 137 C2
Clapham Manor St
SW4 137 D2
Clapham Mans SW4 159 B5
Clapham North Bsns Ctr
10 SW4 137 D2
Clapham North Sta
SW4 138 A2
CLAPHAM PARK 159 D6
Clapham Park Rd
SW4 137 D1
Clapham Park Terr 4
SW2 160 A6
Clapham Rd
SW9 138 B5 270 D4
Clapham South Sta
SW4 159 B5
Claps Gate La E6 100 D3
Clapton Comm E5 52 A2
Clapton Girls Tec Coll
E5 74 C4
CLAPTON PARK 74 D4
Clapton Pas E5 74 C3
Clapton Sq E5 74 C3
Clapton Sta E5 74 B6
Clapton Terr E5 52 A1
Clapton Way E5 74 A4
Clara Grant Ho 10
E14 119 C3
Clara Grant Prim Sch The
E3 97 C3
Clara Pl SE18 122 C2
Clare Cl
Borehamwood WD6 10 B5
East Finchley N2 48 A6
Clare Cnr SE9 166 D4
Clare Ct
Chislehurst BR7 188 B2
St Pancras WC1 233 B1
Wimbledon SW19 179 A4
Claredale Ct SM2 218 A1
Claredale Ho 3 E2 96 B5
Claredale St E2 96 A5
Clare Gdns
Barking IG11 80 A1
Forest Gate E7 77 A4
Notting Hill W11 91 A1
Clare Ho
Bermondsey SE1 263 D2
4 Burnt Oak HA8 27 A1
5 Ealing W7 108 D5
Clare Ho *continued*
6 Old Ford E3 97 B6
Clare House Prim Sch
BR3 186 A1
Clare La N1 73 A1
Clare Lawn Ave
SW14 155 B6
Clare Mews SW6 265 C3
Clare Mkt WC2 240 D1
Claremont
1 Putney SW15 157 A6
Shepperton TW17 192 D3
Claremont Ave
Harrow HA3 44 A4
Sunbury TW16 172 B2
West Barnes KT3 200 B4
Claremont Cl
Finsbury N1 94 C5 234 B3
Newham E16 122 C5
Orpington BR6 226 C4
4 Streatham SW2 160 B3
Claremont Ct 1 W9 91 B5
Claremont Dr TW17 192 D3
Claremont Gdns
Ilford IG3 79 C6
Kingston u T KT6 198 A4
Claremont Gr
Chiswick W4 133 C5
Woodford IG8 37 C4
Claremont High Sch
HA3 44 A4
Claremont Ho 15
SM2 217 C1
Claremont Hts EN2 4 D1
Claremont La KT10 212 A3
Claremont Lo 12
SW19 178 D3
Claremont Pk N3 29 A2
Claremont Pl KT10 212 D2
Claremont Prim Sch
NW2 68 D6
Claremont Rd
Bromley BR1 210 B5
Claygate KT10 212 C1
Croydon CR0 206 A1
Ealing W13 87 A2
Forest Gate E7 77 C3
Hadley Wood EN4 2 B6
Harrow HA3 24 C1
Hendon NW2 68 D6
Higham Hill E17 35 A1
Highgate N6 49 C2
Kingston u T KT6 198 A4
Leyton E7 76 B5
Teddington TW11 174 D6
Twickenham TW1 153 C5
West Kilburn W9 91 B5
Claremont Sq
N1 94 C5 234 A3
Claremont St
Edmonton N18 34 A4
Greenwich SE10 141 D6
Newham E16 122 C4
Claremont Terr KT7 197 B2
Claremont Way NW2 46 C1
Claremont Way Ind Est
NW2 46 C1
Clarence Ave
Bromley BR1, BR2 210 A5
Clapham Pk SW4 159 D5
Ilford IG2 56 C3
Kingston u T KT3 177 B1
Clarence Cl
Bushey WD23 8 D4
New Barnet EN4 14 B6
Clarence Cres
Clapham Pk SW4 159 D5
Sidcup DA14 168 B1
Clarence Ct
Edgware NW7 27 D5
10 Hammersmith W6 112 B2
5 North Finchley N12 30 B5
Clarence Gate NW1 237 D6
Clarence Gate Gdns
NW1 237 D5
Clarence Gdns
NW1 93 B4 231 D1
Clarence Ho SE17 139 A6
Clarence Ho*
SW1 115 C5 249 B3
Clarence La SW15 155 D5
Clarence Mews
Balham SW12 159 B4
Hackney E5 74 B3
1 Rotherhithe SE16 118 D5
Clarence Pl 25 E5 74 B3
Clarence Rd
Bexley DA6 147 A1
Brentford W4 110 C1
Bromley BR1, BR2 210 A6
Clarence Rd *continued*
Brondesbury NW6 69 B1
Chislehurst SE9 166 A2
Enfield EN3 18 C6
Harringay N15 51 A4
Higham Hill E17 34 D1
Lower Clapton E5 74 B4
Manor Pk E12 77 D3
Newham E16 98 C3
Richmond TW9 132 C4
Sidcup DA14 168 B1
Sutton SM1 217 D3
Teddington TW11 175 A4
Thornton Heath CR0 205 B2
Wallington SM6 219 B3
Wimbledon SW19 179 D4
Wood Green N22 32 A3
Clarence St
Kingston u T KT1,
KT2 176 A1
5 Richmond TW9 132 A1
Southall UB2 106 D3
Clarence Terr
Hounslow TW3 129 D1
Lisson Gr NW1 237 D6
Clarence Way NW1 71 B1
Clarence Wlk 9
SW4 138 A3
Clarendon Cl
Bayswater W2 247 A6
38 Hackney E9 74 C1
Clarendon Cres TW2 152 B1
Clarendon Cross W11 244 B5
Clarendon Ct
London NW11 47 B5
Mitcham SM4 202 C4
Paddington W9 236 B6
1 Richmond TW9 132 C4
Willesden NW2 68 C1
Clarendon Dr SW15 134 C1
Clarendon Flats W1 238 B1
Clarendon Gdns
Hendon NW4 46 B6
Paddington W9 92 A3 236 B5
Redbridge IG1 56 B2
Wembley HA9 66 A4
Clarendon Gr
Mitcham CR4 202 D6
Somers Town NW1 232 C2
Clarendon Ho
Harrow HA2 42 B6
North Finchley N12 30 A5
Somers Town NW1 232 B3
South Oxhey WD19 22 D5
Clarendon Mews
Bayswater W2 247 A6
Old Bexley DA5 169 D3
Clarendon Pl
W2 114 C6 247 A6
Clarendon Prim Sch
TW15 170 B6
Clarendon Rd
Ashford TW15 170 B6
Croydon CR0 220 D6
Ealing W5 88 A3
Edmonton N18 34 A5
Harrow HA1 42 C3
Hayes UB3 105 D4
Hornsey N8 50 B6
Leytonstone E11 54 B1
Mitcham SW19 180 C3
Notting Hill
W11 113 A6 244 B5
Wallington SM6 219 C2
Walthamstow E17 53 D3
Wanstead E18 55 A6
West Green N15 51 A5
Wood Green N22 32 B1
Clarendon Rise SE13 142 A1
Clarendon Sch TW12 173 D4
Clarendon St
SW1 115 B1 258 D2
Clarendon Terr W9 236 B6
Clarendon Way
Enfield N21 17 A5
Orpington BR5, BR7 211 D6
Clarendon Wlk 11
W11 91 A1
Clarens St SE6 163 B2
Clare Pl SW15 155 D4
Clare Point NW2 46 D1
Clare Rd
Hounslow TW4 129 B2
Leytonstone E11 54 B3
New Cross Gate SE14 141 B4
Northolt UB6 64 B2
Stanwell TW19 148 A4
Willesden NW10 68 A1
Clare St E2 96 B5
Claret Gdns SE25 205 C5
Clareville Ct SW7 256 B3
Clareville Gr
SW7 114 A2 256 B3
Clareville Grove Mews
SW7 256 B3
Clareville Rd BR5 227 A6
Clareville St
SW7 114 A2 256 B3
Clare Way DA7 147 A4
Clarewood Ct W1 237 C3
Clarewood Wlk SW9 138 C1
Clarges Ho W1 248 D4
Clarges Mews
W1 115 B5 248 C4
Clarges St W1 115 B5 248 D4
Clariat Ct W3 110 C4
Claribel Rd SW9 138 D3
Clarice Ct NW4 46 B6
Claridge Ct SW6 264 C1
Claridge Rd RM8 58 D1
Clarinet Ct HA8 26 D3
Clarissa Ho 7 E14 97 D1
Clarissa Rd RM6 58 D2
Clarissa St E8 95 D6
Clark Ct 17 NW10 67 B1
Clarke Ho
2 London SW4 137 C2
5 Richmond TW10 153 C1
Clarke Mans 9 IG11 79 D1
Clarke Mews N9 18 B1
Clarke Path N16 52 A1
Clarke's Ave KT4, SM3 216 D6
Clarkes Dr UB8 82 A2
Clarkes Mews W1 238 B4
Clark Ho SW10 266 A4
Clark Lawrence Ct 11
SW11 136 B2
Clarks Mead WD23 8 B4
Clarkson Rd E16 98 D1
Clarkson Row NW1 232 A3
Clarkson St E2 96 B4
Clarksons The IG11 101 A5
Clark's Pl EC2 243 A2
Clark's Rd IG1 79 B6
Clark St E1 96 C2
Clark Way TW5 128 D5
Classic Mans 33 E9 74 C1
Classinghall Ho 14
SW15 156 D5
Classon Cl UB7 104 A4
Claude Rd
Leyton E10 54 A1
London SE15 140 B3
Newham E13 99 B6
Claude St E14 119 C2
Claudia Jones Way
SW2 160 A5
Claudia Pl SW19 157 A3
Claudius Cl HA7 9 D1
Claughton Rd E13 99 C5
Clauson Ave UB5 64 A3
Clavell St 8 SE10 142 A6
Claverdale Rd SW2 160 C4
Clavering Ave SW13 134 B6
Clavering Cl TW1 175 A6
Clavering Ho SE13 142 B1
Clavering Rd E12 77 D6
Claverings Ind Est N9 18 C2
Claverley Gr N3 29 D2
Claverley Villas N3 29 D3
Claverton St
SW1 115 C1 259 B1
Clave St E1 118 C5
Claxton Gr
W6 112 D1 254 A1
Clay Ave CR4 181 B1
Claybank Gr SE13 141 D2
Claybee Ct N22 32 B5
Claybourne Mews 2
SE19 183 D3
Claybridge Rd SE12 187 C6
Claybrook Cl N2 48 B6
Claybrook Rd W6 134 D6
Claybury Broadway
IG5 56 A6
Clay Ct E17 54 B6
Claydon SE17 262 A4
Claydon Dr CR0 220 A4
Claydon Ho NW4 28 D1
Claydown Mews
SE18 122 C1
Clayfarm Rd SE9 167 A2
CLAYGATE 212 D1
Claygate Cres CR0 224 B2
Claygate Ct SM1 218 A5
Claygate La
Hinchley Wood KT10 213 A6
Thames Ditton KT7 197 A1
Claygate Lodge Cl
KT10 212 C1
Claygate Prim Sch
KT10 212 C1
Claygate Rd W13 109 B3
Claygate Sta KT10 212 C2
CLAYHALL 56 B6
Clayhall Ct 20 E3 97 B5
CLAY HILL 5 A6
Clay Hill EN2 5 B6
Clayhill Cres SE12,
SE9 187 D6
Clay La
Bushey WD23 8 C4
Stanwell TW19 148 B4
Claylands Ct SE19 183 B5
Claylands Pl SW8 138 C5
Claylands Rd
SW8 138 B6 270 D5
Claymill Ho 2 SE18 123 A1
Claymore Cl SM3,
SM4 201 C2
Claymore Ct 4 E17 35 A2
Claypole Ct E17 53 C4
Claypole Dr TW5 129 A4
Claypole Rd E15 98 A5
Clayponds Ave TW8 110 A2
Clayponds Gdns W5 109 D2
Clayponds Hospl & Day
Treatment Ctr TW8 110 A2
Clayponds La TW8 110 A1
Clays Ct N16 51 D1
Clays La E15 75 D3
Clays Lane Cl E15 75 D3
Clays Lane Cvn Site
E15 76 A3
Clay St W1 92 D2 237 D3
Clayton 22 NW9 27 D1
Clayton Ave HA0 66 A1
Clayton Bsns Ctr UB3 105 C4
Clayton Cl 3 E6 100 B1
Clayton Cres
Brentford TW8 109 D1
Islington N1 233 C5
Clayton Ct
1 Higham Hill E17 35 A1
Stamford Hill N16 52 A2
Clayton Field NW9 27 C2
Clayton Ho
22 Hackney E9 74 C1
Long Ditton KT7 197 B1
Clayton Mews SE10 142 B4
Clayton Rd
Chessington KT10,
KT9 213 D4
Hayes UB3 105 C4
Isleworth TW7 130 C2
Peckham SE15 140 A4
Clayton St SE11 138 C6
Clayton Terr UB4 84 D2
Claytonville Terr
DA17 125 D4
Clay Wood Cl BR6 211 C2
Clayworth Cl DA15 168 B5
Cleanthus Cl SE18 144 D4
Cleanthus Rd SE18 144 D4
Clearbrook Way 13 E1 96 C1
Clearmont Ho UB2 107 C3
Clearwater Ho BR3 207 D4
Clear Water Ho 9
TW10 154 A6
Clearwater Pl KT6 197 C3
Clearwater Terr 4
W11 112 D4
Clearwell Dr W9 91 D3
Cleave Ave
Hayes UB3 105 C2
Orpington BR6 227 C2
Cleaveland Rd KT6 197 D4
Cleaver Ho 6 NW3 70 D1
Cleaverholme Cl
SE25 206 B3
Cleaver Sq
SE11 116 C1 261 B1
Cleaver St
SE11 116 C1 261 B2
Cleave's Almshos 1
KT2 176 A1
Cleeve Ct
East Bedfont TW14 149 C3
Muswell Hill N10 31 B3
Cleeve Hill SE23 162 B3
Cleeve Ho 15 E2 95 C4
Cleeve Park Gdns
DA14 168 B2
Cleeve Park Sch
DA14 168 C1
Cleeve Way
Cheam SM1 201 D1

Cleeve Way *continued*
Roehampton SW15 ... 155 D4
Cleeve Workshops 14
E2 ... 95 C4
Clegg Ho SE3 ... 143 B1
Clegg St
Newham E13 ... 99 A5
16 Wapping E1 ... 118 B5
Cleland Ho 19 E2 ... 96 C5
Clematis Gdns IG8 ... 37 A5
Clematis St W12 ... 112 A6
Clem Atlee Par SW6 ... 264 D5
Clem Attlee Ct
SW6 ... 135 B6 264 D5
Clemence St E14 ... 97 B2
Clement Attlee Ho
NW10 ... 67 D1
Clement Ave SW4 ... 137 D1
Clement Cl
Acton W4 ... 111 B2
Hampstead NW6 ... 68 C1
Clement Danes Ho 2
W12 ... 90 B1
Clement Gdns UB3 ... 105 C2
Clement Ho
14 Deptford SE8 ... 119 A2
17 North Kensington
W10 ... 90 C2
Clementhorpe Rd RM9 . 80 C2
Clementina Rd E10 ... 53 B1
Clementine Churchill
Hospl The HA1 ... 64 D5
Clementine Cl W13 ... 109 B4
Clementine Wlk 4
IG8 ... 37 A3
Clement Rd
Penge BR3 ... 184 D1
Wimbledon SW19 ... 179 A5
Clements Ave 1 E16 .. 121 A6
Clements Cl 19 N12 ... 29 D6
Clements Ct
Hounslow TW4 ... 128 D1
5 Ilford IG1 ... 78 D5
Clements Ho N17 ... 34 A2
Clements Inn
WC2 ... 94 B1 240 D1
Clements Inn Pas
WC2 ... 240 D1
Clements La IG1 ... 78 D5
Clement's La EC2,
EC4 ... 117 B6 252 D6
Clements Pl TW8 ... 109 D1
Clements Rd
East Ham E6 ... 78 B1
Ilford IG1 ... 78 D5
Clement's Rd SE16 ... 118 B3
Cleminson Ct DA14 ... 190 D4
Clemson Ho 9 E8 ... 95 D6
Clendon Way SE18 ... 123 B2
Clennam St SE1 ... 252 B2
Clensham Ct SM3 ... 217 C6
Clensham La SM1 ... 217 C6
Clenston Mews W1 ... 237 C2
Clent Ho 4 N16 ... 51 D1
Cleopatra's Needle*
WC2 116 B6 250 C5
Clephane Rd 13 N1 ... 73 A2
Clephane Rd N N1 ... 73 A2
Clephane Rd S N1 ... 73 B2
Clere Pl EC2 ... 242 D6
Clere St EC2 ... 95 B3 242 D6
Clerics Wlk TW17 ... 193 B3
CLERKENWELL ... 94 D3
Clerkenwell Cl
EC1 ... 94 C3 241 B5
Clerkenwell Gn
EC1 ... 94 D3 241 C5
Clerkenwell Parochial CE
Prim Sch EC1 .. 94 C4 234 A1
Clerkenwell Rd
EC1 ... 94 D3 241 C5
Clermont Rd E9 ... 96 C6
Cleveden Ct CR2 ... 221 C3
Cleveden Ho BR1 ... 188 A3
Clevedon Ct
Battersea SW11 ... 267 A2
Dulwich SE21 ... 161 B1
Clevedon Gdns
Cranford TW5 ... 128 B4
Hayes UB3 ... 105 B3
Clevedon Ho 4 SM1 .. 218 A4
Clevedon Mans NW5 ... 71 A4
Clevedon Rd
Kingston u T KT1 ... 176 C1
Penge SE20 ... 184 D2
Twickenham TW1 ... 153 D5
Cleve Ho NW6 ... 69 D1
Cleveland Ave
Chiswick W4 ... 111 D2
Hampton TW12 ... 173 B3
Merton SW20 ... 179 B1
Cleveland Cres WD6 ... 11 A6
Cleveland Ct
Ealing W13 ... 87 B2
Marylebone W1 ... 239 B5
Southall UB2 ... 107 D2
Cleveland Gdns
Barnes SW13 ... 133 D3
Harringay N4, N15 ... 51 A4
Hendon NW2 ... 68 D6
Paddington W2 .. 92 A1 236 A1
Worcester Pk KT4 ... 215 D6
Cleveland Gr 39 E1 ... 96 C3
Cleveland Ho 7 N2 ... 30 B1
Cleveland Inf Sch IG1 .. 78 D5
Cleveland Jun Sch
IG1 ... 78 D5
Cleveland Mans
8 Brixton SW9 ... 138 C5
4 Brondesbury NW6 ... 69 B1
Paddington W9 ... 91 C3
Cleveland Mews W1 .. 239 A4
Cleveland Park Ave
E17 ... 53 C5
Cleveland Park Cres
E17 ... 53 C5
Cleveland Pk TW19 ... 148 A5
Cleveland Pl SW1 ... 249 B4
Cleveland Rd
Barnes SW13 ... 133 D3
Bexley DA16 ... 145 D3
Ealing W13 ... 87 B2
Edmonton N9 ... 18 B4
Ilford IG1 ... 78 D5
Isleworth TW7 ... 131 A1
Islington N1 ... 73 B1
New Malden KT3 ... 199 C5
14 South Acton W4 ... 111 A3
Wanstead E18 ... 55 A6
Worcester Pk KT4 ... 215 C6
Cleveland Rise SM4 ... 200 D2
Cleveland Row
SW1 ... 115 C5 249 B3
Cleveland Sq
W2 ... 92 A1 236 A1
Cleveland St
W1 ... 93 C3 239 A5
Cleveland Terr
W2 ... 92 A1 236 B2
Cleveland Way E1 ... 96 C3
Cleveley Cres W5 ... 88 B5
Cleveleys Rd E5 ... 74 B5
Clevely Cl SE7 ... 121 D2
Clevendon Cl N16 ... 73 D5
Cleve Rd
Sidcup DA14 ... 168 D1
South Hampstead NW6 .. 69 D1
Cleverly Cotts W12 ... 111 D5
Cleverly Est W12 ... 112 A6
Cleves Ct KT6 ... 198 A3
Cleves Prim Sch E6 ... 99 D6
Cleves Rd
Newham E6 ... 99 D5
Richmond TW10 ... 153 C1
Cleves Way
Ashford TW16 ... 171 D4
Hampton TW12 ... 173 B3
Ruislip HA4 ... 40 D1
Clewer Cres HA3 ... 24 B2
Clewer Ct 2 E10 ... 53 C1
Clewer Ho 6 SE2 ... 124 D4
Cley Ho SE4 ... 140 D1
Clichy Ho 32 E1 ... 96 C2
Clifden Centre (Richmond
Adult & Com Coll)
TW1 ... 152 D3
Clifden Ho 6 TW8 ... 131 D6
Clifden Mews E5 ... 74 D3
Clifden Rd
Brentford TW8 ... 131 D6
Homerton E5 ... 74 D3
Twickenham TW1 ... 152 D3
Cliff Ct 14 NW1 ... 71 D2
Cliffe Ho 4 SE10 ... 120 D1
Cliffe Rd CR2 ... 221 B3
Cliffe Wlk 2 SM1 ... 218 A3
Clifford Ave
Elmstead BR7 ... 188 B4
Mortlake SW14 ... 133 A3
Mortlake SW14, TW9 ... 132 D2
Wallington SM6 ... 219 C4
Clifford Cl UB5 ... 85 A6
Clifford Ct
Bayswater W2 ... 91 D2
Wandsworth SW18 ... 158 B4
Willesden NW10 ... 67 C4
Clifford Dr SW9 ... 138 D1
Clifford Gdns
Hayes UB3 ... 105 B2
Kensal Green NW10 ... 90 C5
Clifford Gr TW15 ... 170 C6
Clifford Haigh Ho
SW6 ... 134 D5
Clifford Ho
2 Beckenham BR3 ... 185 D4
West Kensington W14 .. 254 C3
Clifford Lo 5 N3 ... 29 B1
Clifford Rd
Barnet EN5 ... 1 D2
Chingford E17 ... 36 A1
Croydon SE25 ... 206 A5
Hounslow TW4 ... 128 D2
Newham E16 ... 98 D3
Ponders End N9 ... 18 C5
Richmond TW10 ... 153 D2
Wembley HA0 ... 87 D6
Clifford's Inn Pas EC4 . 241 A1
Clifford St W1 . 115 C6 249 A5
Clifford Way NW10 ... 67 D4
Cliff Rd NW1 ... 71 D2
Cliff Road Studios 13
NW1 ... 71 D2
Cliffsend Ho 23 SW9 .. 138 C4
Cliff Terr SE8 ... 141 C3
Cliffview Rd SE13 ... 141 C2
Cliff Villas NW1 ... 71 D2
Cliff Wlk E16 ... 98 D2
Clifton Ave
Church End N3 ... 29 B2
Feltham TW13 ... 150 C1
Shepherd's Bush W12 .. 111 D5
Stanmore HA7 ... 25 B1
Walthamstow E17 ... 52 D6
Wembley HA9 ... 66 B2
Clifton Cl 8 BR6 ... 227 A3
Clifton Cres SE15 ... 140 B5
Clifton Ct
1 Beckenham BR3 ... 185 D2
Finsbury Pk N4 ... 72 C6
Paddington NW8 ... 236 C6
Peckham SE15 ... 140 B5
Putney SW15 ... 156 D6
South Norwood SE25 ... 205 C4
9 Stanwell TW19 ... 148 A5
Surbiton KT5 ... 198 B2
3 Woodford IG8 ... 37 A4
Clifton Gate SW10 ... 266 A6
Clifton Gdns
Chiswick W4 ... 111 B2
Enfield EN2 ... 16 A6
Hillingdon UB10 ... 82 D5
Paddington W9 .. 92 A3 236 A5
South Tottenham N15 ... 51 D3
2 Temple Fortune
NW11 ... 47 B3
Clifton Gr E8 ... 74 A2
Clifton Hill
NW8 ... 92 A6 229 A5
Clifton Ho
Leyton E11 ... 76 C6
Shoreditch E2 ... 243 C6
Clifton Mans 4 SW9 .. 138 C1
Clifton Mews SE25 ... 205 C5
Clifton Par TW13 ... 172 C6
Clifton Park Ave
SW20 ... 178 C1
Clifton Pl
Paddington W2 ... 236 D1
Rotherhithe SE16 ... 118 C4
Clifton Prim Sch UB2 .. 107 A2
Clifton Rd
Bexley DA16 ... 146 C2
Crouch End N8 ... 49 D3
Finchley N3 ... 30 A2
Greenford UB6 ... 86 B3
Harlesden NW10 ... 90 A5
Harlington TW6 ... 126 D2
Harrow HA3 ... 44 B4
Ilford IG2 ... 57 B3
Isleworth TW7 ... 130 C3
Kingston u T KT2 ... 176 B3
Newham E16 ... 98 C2
Paddington W9 .. 92 A3 236 B6
Sidcup DA14 ... 189 C6
Southall UB2 ... 107 A2
South Norwood SE25 ... 205 C5
Teddington TW11 ... 174 C6
Upton E7 ... 77 D2
Wallington SM6 ... 219 B3
Wimbledon SW19 ... 178 D4
Wood Green N22 ... 31 C2
Clifton Rise SE14 ... 141 A5
Cliftons Roundabout SE9,
SE12 ... 165 C5
Clifton St EC2 ... 95 C3 243 A5
Clifton Terr N4 ... 72 C6
Clifton The KT6 ... 214 A6
Clifton Villas
W9 ... 92 A2 236 A4
Cliftonville Ct SE12 ... 165 A3
Clifton Way
Peckham SE15 ... 140 C5
Wembley HA0 ... 88 A6
Climsland Ho SE1 ... 251 B4
Clinch Ct 11 E16 ... 99 A2
Cline Ho SW15 ... 156 A6
Cline Rd N11 ... 31 C4
Clinger Ct N1 ... 95 C6
Clink St SE1 ... 117 B5 252 C4
Clinton Ave
Bexley DA16 ... 146 A1
East Molesey KT8 ... 196 A5
Clinton Ho
New Malden KT3 ... 199 B1
6 Surbiton KT6 ... 197 D2
Clinton Rd
Bow E3 ... 97 A4
Forest Gate E7 ... 77 A4
West Green N15 ... 51 B5
Clipper Appts 12
SE10 ... 142 A6
Clipper Cl 3 SE16 ... 118 D4
Clipper Ho E14 ... 120 A1
Clipper Way SE13 ... 142 A1
Clippesby Cl KT9 ... 214 B2
Clipstone Ho 10
SW15 ... 156 A6
Clipstone Mews W1 .. 239 A4
Clipstone Rd TW3 ... 129 C2
Clipstone St
W1 ... 93 C2 239 A4
Clissold Cl N2 ... 48 D6
Clissold Cres N16 ... 73 B4
Clissold Ct N4 ... 73 A6
Clissold Ho 4 N16 ... 73 B6
Clissold Rd N16 ... 73 B5
Clitheroe Ave HA2 ... 41 C1
Clitheroe Rd SW9 ... 138 A3
Clitherow Ave W7 ... 109 A3
Clitherow Rd TW8 ... 109 C1
Clitterhouse Cres
NW2 ... 46 C1
Clitterhouse Rd NW2 .. 46 C1
Clive Ave N18 ... 34 A4
Clive Ct
Paddington W9 ... 236 B6
Streatham SW16 ... 181 D5
Tolworth KT6 ... 214 C6
Cliveden Cl N12 ... 30 A6
Cliveden Ho SW1 ... 258 A4
Cliveden Pl
Belgravia
SW1 ... 115 A2 258 A4
Shepperton TW17 ... 193 A3
Cliveden Rd SW19 ... 179 B2
Clivedon Ct
Ealing W13 ... 87 B2
6 New Barnet EN5 ... 2 A1
Clivedon Rd E4 ... 36 C5
Clive Ho
18 Clapham SW8 ... 137 D3
3 Croydon CR0 ... 205 D1
Greenwich SE10 ... 142 A6
Clive Lloyd Ho N15 ... 51 A4
Clive Lo NW4 ... 46 D3
Clive Rd
Belvedere DA17 ... 125 C2
Enfield EN1 ... 6 A1
Feltham TW14 ... 150 A5
Mitcham SW19 ... 180 C4
Teddington TW1 ... 175 A6
West Norwood SE21,
SE27 ... 161 B1
Clivesdale Dr UB3 ... 106 B5
Clive Way EN1 ... 6 A1
Cloak La EC4 .. 117 B6 252 C6
Clochar Ct NW10 ... 89 D6
Clock Ct 2 E11 ... 55 B5
Clock Ho
Stamford Hill N16 ... 51 D2
Walthamstow E17 ... 54 B5
Clock Ho The EN2 ... 5 D6
Clockhouse Ave IG11 . 101 A6
Clockhouse Cl SW19 .. 156 C2
Clock House Ct 1
BR3 ... 185 A1
Clockhouse Junc N13 .. 32 C5
Clockhouse La TW14,
TW15 ... 148 D2
Clockhouse Mans N13 . 32 C5
Clockhouse Par N13 ... 32 C5
Clock House Par E11 ... 55 B3
Clockhouse Pl SW15 .. 157 A5
Clock House Rd BR3 .. 185 A1
Clockhouse Rdbt
TW14 ... 149 A3
Clock House Sta BR3 .. 185 A2
Clockhouse The
SW19 ... 156 C1
Clock Mus*
EC2 95 A1 242 B2
Clocktower Mews 6
W7 ... 108 C5
Clock Tower Mews
Islington N1 ... 235 B5
Thamesmead SE28 ... 124 B6
Clock Tower Pl N7 ... 72 A2
Clock Tower Rd TW7 .. 130 D2
Cloister Cl TW11 ... 175 B5
Cloister Gdns
Croydon SE25 ... 206 B3
Edgware HA8 ... 27 A5
Cloister Rd
Acton W3 ... 89 A2
Child's Hill NW2 ... 69 B6
Cloisters Ave BR1,
BR2 ... 210 B4
Cloisters Ct
Erith DA7 ... 147 D2
Highgate N6 ... 49 B1
Cloisters Ho 8 SW19 .. 179 C3
Cloisters The 3 SW9 .. 138 C4
Clonard Way HA5 ... 23 C4
Clonbrock Rd N16 ... 73 C4
Cloncurry St SW6 ... 134 D3
Clone Ct 4 W12 ... 111 C3
Clone The 5 KT2 ... 176 D3
Clonmel Cl HA2 ... 42 B1
Clonmell Rd N17 ... 51 B6
Clonmel Rd
Fulham SW6 .. 135 B4 264 D2
Teddington TW11 ... 174 B6
Clonmore St SW18 ... 157 B3
Cloonmore Ave BR6 .. 227 D4
Clorane Gdns NW3 ... 69 C5
Close The
Beckenham BR3 ... 207 A5
Cheam SM3 ... 201 B2
Chingford E4 ... 36 A3
Cockfosters EN4 ... 14 D6
Croydon SE25 ... 206 A3
Dagenham RM6 ... 59 A3
Eastcote HA5 ... 40 C2
Harrow HA2 ... 24 A1
Hillingdon UB10 ... 82 C6
Hounslow TW7 ... 130 B3
Ilford IG2 ... 57 C3
Kingston u T KT3 ... 177 A1
Lewisham SE3 ... 142 B3
Mitcham CR4 ... 202 D5
Mortlake TW9 ... 132 D2
Muswell Hill N10 ... 31 B1
1 Old Bexley DA5 ... 169 C4
Palmers Green N14 ... 15 D2
Petts Wood BR5 ... 211 C3
Rayners La HA5 ... 41 B2
Sidcup DA14 ... 190 B5
Surbiton KT6 ... 198 A3
Totteridge N20 ... 13 B2
Wembley HA0 ... 66 A2
Wembley Pk HA9 ... 67 A5
Cloth Ct EC1 ... 241 D3
Cloth Fair EC1 .. 94 D2 241 D3
Clothier Ho SE7 ... 122 A1
Clothier St EC3 ... 243 B2
Cloth St EC1 ... 95 A2 242 A4
Clothworkers Rd
SE18 ... 145 B5
Cloudesdale Rd
SW17 ... 159 B2
Cloudesley Mans N1 .. 234 B5
Cloudesley Pl
N1 ... 94 C6 234 B5
Cloudesley Rd
Erith DA7 ... 147 B4
Islington N1 ... 94 C6 234 A5
Cloudesley Sq
N1 ... 94 C6 234 B6
Cloudesley St
N1 ... 94 C6 234 B5
Clouston Cl SM6 ... 220 A3
Clova Rd E7 ... 77 A3
Clove Cres E14 ... 120 B6
Clovelly Ave
London NW9 ... 45 D5
Uxbridge UB10 ... 61 A4
Clovelly Cl
Pinner HA5 ... 40 C6
Uxbridge UB10 ... 61 A4
Clovelly Ct NW2 ... 68 C3
Clovelly Gdns
Enfield EN1 ... 17 C4
South Norwood SE19 ... 183 D2
Clovelly Ho W2 ... 236 A2
Clovelly Rd
Acton W4 ... 111 B4
Ealing W5 ... 109 C4
Clovelly Rd *continued*
Erith DA7 ... 147 A6
Hornsey N8 ... 49 D5
Hounslow TW3 ... 129 C3
Clovelly Way
Harrow HA2 ... 63 B6
Orpington BR6 ... 211 D3
Stepney E1 ... 96 C1
Clover Cl E11 ... 76 B6
Clover Ct
Enfield EN3 ... 7 A1
Sutton SM2 ... 217 D2
Cloverdale Gdns
DA15 ... 167 D5
Clover Ho
Hounslow TW3 ... 130 A4
Southgate N21 ... 16 B6
Cloverleys IG10 ... 21 D6
Clover Mews SW3 ... 267 D6
Clover Way SM6 ... 203 A1
Clove St 9 E13 ... 99 A3
Clowders Rd SE6 ... 163 B1
Clowes Ho 3 SW4 ... 138 A1
Clowser Cl 4 SM1 ... 218 A3
Cloysters Gn E1 ... 118 A5
Cloyster Wood HA8 ... 25 D4
Club Gardens Rd BR2 . 209 A2
Club Row E2 ... 95 D3 243 C6
Clumps The TW15 ... 171 B6
Clunbury Ave UB2 ... 107 B1
Clunbury St N1 ... 235 D3
Clunie Ho SW1 ... 257 D6
Cluny Mews SW5 ... 255 A3
Cluny Pl SE1 ... 117 C3 263 A6
Cluse Ct N1 ... 235 A4
Clutton St E14 ... 97 D2
Clydach Rd EN1 ... 5 D1
Clyde Cir N15 ... 51 C5
Clyde Ct NW1 ... 232 D4
Clyde Flats SW6 ... 264 C4
Clyde Ho 9 KT2 ... 175 D2
Clyde Pl E10 ... 53 D2
Clyde Rd
Croydon CR0 ... 221 D6
South Tottenham N15 ... 51 C5
Stanwell TW19 ... 148 A3
Sutton SM1 ... 217 C3
Wallington SM6 ... 219 C2
Wood Green N22 ... 31 D2
Clydesdale EN3 ... 6 D1
Clydesdale Ave HA7 ... 43 D6
Clydesdale Cl
Borehamwood WD6 ... 11 B6
Isleworth TW7 ... 130 D2
Clydesdale Ct N20 ... 14 B3
Clydesdale Gdns
TW10 ... 132 D1
Clydesdale Ho
Abbey Wood DA18 ... 125 A4
4 Notting Hill W11 ... 91 B1
Clydesdale Path WD6 .. 11 B6
Clydesdale Rd W11 ... 91 B1
Clyde St SE8 ... 141 B6
Clyde Terr SE23 ... 162 C2
Clyde Vale SE23 ... 162 C2
Clyde Works 10 SM6 .. 219 C2
Clyfford Rd HA4 ... 61 D4
Clymping Dene TW14 . 150 B4
Clynes Ho
6 Dagenham RM10 ... 81 C5
3 Globe Town E2 ... 96 D4
Hayes UB4 ... 84 A4
Clyro Ct N4 ... 50 B1
Clyston St SW8 ... 137 C3
Clytha Ct SE27 ... 183 A6
Coach Ho NW10 ... 67 A1
Coach & Horses Yd
W1 ... 249 A6
Coach House La
Highbury N5 ... 72 D4
Wimbledon SW19 ... 156 D1
Coach House Mews
SE23 ... 162 D5
Coach House Yd 5
NW3 ... 70 B4
Coachmaker Mews 5
SW9 ... 138 A2
Coachman Lo N12 ... 30 A5
Coalbrook Mans 3
SW12 ... 159 B3
Coaldale Wlk SE21 ... 161 A4
Coalecroft Rd SW15 ... 156 C6
Coalport Ho SE11 ... 261 A4
Coal Post Cl BR6 ... 227 D2
Coatbridge Ho 8 N1 ... 72 B1
Coates Ave SW18 ... 158 C5
Coates Cl CR7 ... 205 A6
Coates Ct NW3 ... 70 C3
Coates Hill Rd BR1 ... 188 C1
Coates Rd WD6 ... 9 D4

Coate St E2 96 A5
Coates Wlk TW8 110 A1
Cobalt SE2 124 A4
Cobalt Cl CR0 206 D5
Cobb Cl WD6 11 A6
Cobbett Rd
Kidbrooke SE9 144 A2
Twickenham TW2 151 C3
Cobbetts Ave IG4 55 D4
Cobbett St
SW8 138 B5 270 D3
Cobble La N1 72 D1
Cobble Mews N4, N5 73 A5
Cobbler's Wlk TW11 174 D3
Cobblestone Pl CR0 205 A1
Cobbold Ct SW1 259 C4
Cobbold Ind Est NW10 67 D2
Cobbold Mews W12 111 D4
Cobbold Rd
Bedford Pk W12 111 D4
Leyton E11 76 D5
Willesden NW10 67 D2
Cobb's Hall 1 SW6 134 D6
Cobbs Rd TW4 129 B1
Cobb St E1 243 C3
Cobden Bldgs WC1 233 C2
Cobden Ct
Bromley BR2 209 C5
9 Thamesmead SE28 124 C5
Cobden Ho
11 Bethnal Green E2 96 A4
Regent's Pk NW1 232 A4
Cobden Mews SE26 184 B5
Cobden Rd
Croydon SE25 206 A4
Leyton E11 76 C6
Orpington BR6 227 B4
Cobham 21 NW9 27 D1
Cobham Ave KT3 200 A4
Cobham Cl
2 Blackfen DA15 168 B5
Bromley BR2 210 A2
Clapham SW11 158 C5
Edgware HA8 26 D1
Enfield EN1 6 A2
Wallington SM6 220 A2
Cobham Ct CR4 180 B1
Cobham Ho IG11 101 A6
Cobham Mews 3
NW1 71 D1
Cobham Pl DA6 168 D6
Cobham Rd
Chingford E17 36 A2
Harringay N22 50 D6
Heston TW5 128 C5
Ilford IG3 79 C5
Kingston u T KT1, KT2 176 C1
Cobland Rd SE12 187 C6
Coborn Mews 9 E3 97 B4
Coborn Rd E3 97 B4
Coborn St E3 97 B4
Cobourg Prim Sch
SE5 139 D6
Cobourg Rd SE5 139 D6
Cobourg St
NW1 93 C4 232 B1
Coburg Cl SW1 259 B4
Coburg Cres SW2 160 C3
Coburg Dwellings 11
E1 118 C6
Coburg Gdns IG5 37 D1
Coburg Rd N22 32 B1
Cochrane Cl NW8 229 D3
Cochrane Ct 3 E10 53 C1
Cochrane Ho 15 E14 119 C4
Cochrane Mews
NW8 92 B5 229 D3
Cochrane Rd SW19 179 B3
Cochrane St
NW8 92 B5 229 D3
Coci Ho W14 254 D3
Cockburn Ho SW1 259 D1
Cockerell Rd E17 53 A3
COCKFOSTERS 2 D1
Cockfosters Par EN4 3 A1
Cockfosters Rd EN4 2 D3
Cockfosters Sta EN4 3 A1
Cock Hill E1 243 B3
Cock La EC1 94 D2 241 D3
Cockpit Yd WC1 240 D4
Cocks Cres KT3 199 D5
Cocksett Ave BR6 227 C2
Cockspur Ct SW1 249 D4
Cockspur St
SW1 115 D5 249 D4
Cocksure La DA14 191 C6
Coda Ctr The
SW6 135 A4 264 B2
Code St E1 95 D3 243 D5
Codicote Ho 22 SE8 118 D2
Codicote Terr N4 73 A6
Codling Cl 13 E1 118 A5
Codling Way HA0 65 D4
Codrington Ct 3
SE16 119 A5
Codrington Hill SE23 163 A4
Codrington Ho 7 E1 96 B3
Codrington Mews
W11 91 A1
Cody Cl
Harrow HA3 43 D6
Wallington SM6 219 D1
Cody Rd E16 98 B3
Coe Ave SE25 206 A3
Coe's Alley EN5 1 A1
Coffey St SE8 141 C5
Cogan Ave E17 35 A2
Cohen Ho NW7 28 A6
Cohen Lo E5 75 A3
Coin St SE1 116 C5 251 A4
Coity Rd NW5 71 A2
Cokers La SE21 161 B3
Coke St E1 96 A1
Colab Ct N22 32 C2
Colas Mews 7 NW6 91 C6
Colbeck Mews
SW5 113 D2 255 D3
Colbeck Rd HA1 42 A2
Colberg Pl N16 51 D2
Colbert 1 SE5 139 D4
Colborne Ct 8 SW19 179 D2
Colborne Ho 8 E14 119 C6
Colborne Way KT4 216 C6
Colbrook Ave UB3 105 B3
Colbrook Cl UB3 105 B3
Colburn Ave HA5 23 A4
Colburn Way SM1 218 B5
Colby Rd
Walton-on-T KT12 194 A1
West Norwood SE19 183 C5
Colchester Ave E12 78 B5
Colchester Dr HA5 40 D4
Colchester Ho 17
SW8 137 D3
Colchester Rd
Burnt Oak HA8 27 A3
Leyton E10 54 A2
Pinner HA6 22 A1
Walthamstow E17 53 C3
Colchester St E1 243 D2
Colchester Villas
CR7 204 C3
Coldbath Sq EC1 241 A6
Coldbath St SE13 141 D3
Cold Blow La SE14 140 D6
Coldershaw Rd W13 109 A4
Coldfall Ave N10 31 A1
Coldfall Prim Sch N10 30 D1
Coldham Ct N22 32 D2
Coldham Gr EN3 7 A6
Coldharbour E14 120 A5
Coldharbour Crest
SE9 166 C1
Coldharbour Ind Est
SE5 139 A3
Coldharbour La
Brixton SW9 138 D2
Bushey WD23 8 A6
Hayes UB3 106 A5
Coldharbour Lane Ho
UB3 106 A5
Coldharbour Pl SE5 139 B3
Coldharbour Rd CR0 220 C3
Coldharbour Sports Ctr
SE9 166 C2
Coldharbour Way
CR0 220 C3
Coldstream Gdns
SW18 157 B5
Colebeck Mews N1 72 D2
Colebert Ave E1 96 C3
Colebert Ho 21 E1 96 C3
Colebrook Cl
Edgware NW7 28 D3
Putney SW19 156 D4
Colebrook Ct SW3 257 B3
Colebrooke Ave W13 87 B1
Colebrooke Ct DA14 190 B6
Colebrooke Dr E11 55 C2
Colebrooke Pl N1 234 D5
Colebrooke Row
Islington N1 94 D5 234 C4
Islington N1 234 D5
Colebrook Ho 1 E14 97 D1
Colebrook Rd SW16 182 A2
Colebrook Rise BR2 186 C1
Colebrook Way N11 31 B5
Coleby Path 21 SE5 139 B5
Colechurch Ho 9
SE1 118 A1
Cole Cl SE28 124 B5
Cole Court Lo 9
TW1 153 A4
Coledale Dr HA7 25 C2
Colefax Bldg 12 E1 96 A1
Coleford Rd SW18 158 A6
Cole Gdns TW5 128 A5
Colegrave Prim Sch
E15 76 B3
Colegrave Rd E15 76 B3
Colegrove Rd SE15 139 D6
Coleherne Ct
SW10 113 D1 255 D1
Coleherne Mans SW5 255 D2
Coleherne Mews
SW10 113 D1 255 C1
Coleherne Rd
SW10 113 D1 255 C1
Colehill Gdns SW6 264 A1
Colehill La
SW6 135 A4 264 B1
Cole Ho SE1 251 B1
Coleman Cl SE25 184 A1
Coleman Ct SW18 157 C4
Coleman Fields
N1 95 A6 235 B6
Coleman Mans N19 50 A2
Coleman Rd
Belvedere DA17 125 C2
Camberwell SE5 139 C5
Dagenham RM9 81 A2
Colemans Heath SE9 166 D1
Coleman St
EC2 95 B1 242 C2
Coleman Street Bldgs
EC2 242 C2
Colenso Dr NW7 28 A3
Colenso Rd
Ilford IG2 57 C2
Lower Clapton E5 74 C4
Cole Park Gdns TW1 153 A5
Cole Park Rd TW1 153 A5
Cole Park View 2
TW1 153 A5
Colepits Wood Rd
SE9 167 B6
Coleraine Park Prim Sch
N17 34 B2
Coleraine Rd
Greenwich SE3 142 D6
Hornsey N8, N22 50 C6
Cole Rd TW1 153 A5
Coleridge Ave
Carshalton SM1 218 C4
Plashet E12 78 A2
Coleridge Cl SW8 137 B3
Coleridge Ct
Hammersmith W14 112 D3
15 New Barnet EN5 13 D6
2 Richmond TW10 175 D6
Coleridge Gdns NW6 70 A1
Coleridge Ho
Pimlico SW1 259 B1
Walworth SE17 262 B2
Wembley HA9 65 D6
Coleridge Prim Sch
N8 49 D2
Coleridge Rd
Ashford TW15 170 B6
Crouch End N8 49 D3
Croydon CR0 206 C2
Finsbury Pk N4, N7 72 C6
North Finchley N12 30 A5
Walthamstow E17 53 B5
Coleridge Sq
Chelsea SW10 266 A4
Ealing W13 87 A1
Coleridge Way
Borehamwood WD6 10 C6
Hayes UB4 84 A1
West Drayton UB7 104 B2
Coleridge Wlk NW11 47 C5
Colerne Ct NW4 29 A1
Colesburg Rd BR3 185 B1
Coles Cres HA2 63 D6
Coles Ct SW11 266 D1
Coles Gn WD23 8 A3
Coles Green Ct NW2 68 A6
Coles Green Rd NW2 68 B6
Coleshill Flats SW1 258 B3
Coleshill Rd TW11 174 C4
Cole St SE1 117 A4 252 B1
Colestown St 4
SW11 136 C3
Coleswood N20 14 C3
Colesworth Ho 1 HA8 27 A1
Colet Cl N13 32 D4
Colet Gdns W14 112 D2
Colet Ho SE17 261 D1
Colette Ct 5 SE16 118 D4
Coley St WC1 94 B3 240 D5
Colfe & Hatchcliffe's
Glebe SE13 163 D6
Colfe Rd SE23 163 A3
Colfe's Sch SE12 165 A5
Colgate Ct EN5 13 A6
Colgate Ho SE13 141 D3
Colgate Pl 10 EN3 7 C6
Colham Ave UB7 104 A5
COLHAM GREEN 82 C2
Colham Green Rd UB8 82 C2
Colham Manor Prim Sch
UB8 82 C1
Colham Rd UB8 82 B3
Colina Mews N8, N15 50 D5
Colina Rd N8, N15 50 D4
Colin Blanchard Ho
SE4 141 C3
Colin Cl
Colindale NW9 45 C5
Coney Hall BR4 224 D5
Croydon CR0 223 B5
Colin Cres NW9 45 D5
Colin Ct
Forest Hill SE6 163 B4
Hendon NW9 45 D5
Streatham SW16 159 D2
COLINDALE 45 C6
Colindale Ave NW9 45 C6
Colindale Bsns Pk
NW9 45 A6
Colindale Hospl NW9 45 C6
Colindale Prim Sch
NW9 45 D5
Colindale Sta NW9 45 C6
Colindeep Gdns NW4 46 A5
Colindeep La NW9,
NW4 45 D5
Colin Dr NW9 45 D4
Colinette Rd SW15 134 C1
Colin Gdns NW9 45 D5
Colin Par NW9 45 C5
Colin Park Rd NW9 45 C5
Colin Pond Ct RM6 58 D6
Colin Rd NW10 68 A2
Colinsdale N1 234 C5
Colinton Rd IG3 80 B6
Colin Winter Ho 45 E1 96 C3
Coliseum Apartments
N8 50 D4
Coliston Pas SW18 157 C4
Coliston Rd SW18 157 C4
Collamore Ave SW18 158 C3
Collapit Cl HA1 41 D3
Collard Pl NW1 71 B1
Collard's Almshouses 1
E17 54 A4
Collcutt Lo SW4 138 A1
Collection Point N8 50 A3
College App SE10 142 A6
College Ave HA3 24 C2
College Cl
Edmonton N18 33 D5
Hackney E5 74 C3
Harrow HA3 24 C3
Twickenham TW2 152 B3
College Cres NW3 70 B2
College Cross N1 72 C1
College Ct
Chelsea
SW3 114 D1 257 D1
Croydon CR0 222 A6
Ealing W5 110 A6
Enfield EN3 18 C6
3 Hammersmith W6 112 C1
Hampstead NW3 70 B2
College Dr
Ruislip HA4 40 A2
Thames Ditton KT7 196 C2
College Fields Bsns Ctr
SW19 180 B2
College Gdns
Chingford E4 20 A3
Dulwich SE21 161 C3
Edmonton N18 34 A5
Enfield EN2 5 B4
New Malden KT3 199 D4
Redbridge IG4 56 A4
Upper Tooting SW17 158 C2
College Gn SE19 183 C3
College Gr NW1 232 C6
College Green Ct
SW9 138 D2
College Hill EC4 252 B6
College Hill Rd HA3 24 C3
College La NW5 71 B4
College Mews 5
SW18 157 D6
COLLEGE PARK 90 B4
College Park Cl SE13 142 B1
College Park Rd N17 33 D4
College Park Sch W2 91 D1
College Pl
Camden Town
NW1 93 C6 232 B5
Chelsea SW10 266 A4
Walthamstow E17 54 C5
College Pt 3 E15 76 D2
College Rd
Dulwich SE19, SE21 161 C2
Ealing W13 87 B1
Enfield EN2 5 B3
Harrow HA1 42 C3
Harrow Weald HA3 24 C2
Hounslow TW7 130 D4
Kensal Green NW10 90 C5
Mitcham SW19 180 B4
Plaistow BR1 187 A3
South Croydon CR0 221 B6
Southgate N21 16 C2
Tottenham N17 33 D4
Walthamstow E17 54 A4
Wembley HA9 43 D1
College Rdbt 1 KT1 198 A6
College St
EC4 117 A6 252 B6
College Terr
Bow E3 97 B4
Church End N3 29 B1
College View SE9 165 D3
College Way
Ashford TW15 170 B6
Hayes UB3 106 A6
College Wlk 10 KT1 198 A6
Collent Ho 12 E9 74 C2
Collent St E9 74 C2
Collerston Ho SE10 120 D1
Colless Rd N15 51 D4
Collette Ct SE25 205 C4
Collette Ho N16 51 D1
Collett Ho SE13 141 D2
Collett Rd SE16 118 A3
Collett Way UB2 107 D4
Colley Ho 12 N7 71 D3
Collier Cl
Newham E16 122 D6
West Ewell KT19 214 D2
Collier Dr HA8 26 C1
Colliers Shaw BR2 225 D3
Collier St N1 94 B5 233 C3
Colliers Water La
CR7 204 C4
Colliers Wood SW19 180 B3
COLLIER'S WOOD 180 C4
Collier's Wood Sta
SW19 180 B3
Collindale Ave
Erith DA8 147 D6
Sidcup DA15 168 A3
Collingbourne Rd
W12 112 B5
Collingham Gdns
SW5 113 D2 255 D3
Collingham Pl
SW5 113 D2 255 D4
Collingham Rd
SW5 113 D2 255 D3
Collingham Sixth Form
Coll SW5 113 D2 255 D3
Collings Cl N22 32 B4
Collington Ho 2 SE7 143 B6
Collington St SE10 120 B1
Collingtree Rd SE26 184 C6
Collingwood Ave
London N10 49 A5
Tolworth KT5 199 A1
Collingwood Cl
2 Penge SE20 184 B2
Twickenham TW2,
TW4 151 C4
Collingwood Ct
London NW4 46 C4
New Barnet EN5 13 D6
Sutton SM1 217 C4
Collingwood Ho
27 Bethnal Green E1 96 B3
Marylebone W1 239 A4
Collingwood Rd
Hillingdon UB8 82 D3
Mitcham CR4 202 C6
South Tottenham N15 51 C5
Sutton SM1 217 C4
Collingwood Sch
SM6 219 B3
Collingwood St E1 96 B3
Collins Ave HA7 26 A1
Collins Ct
Dalston E8 74 A2
3 Loughton IG10 21 D6
Collins Dr HA4 62 C6
Collins Ho
8 Barking IG11 78 D1
6 Cubitt Town SE10 120 D1
4 Poplar E14 120 A6
Collinson Ct
Borough The SE1 252 A1
Edgware HA8 26 B6
Collinson Ho 14 SE15 140 A5
Collinson St SE1 252 A1
Collinson Wlk SE1 252 A1
Collins Rd N5, N16 73 A4
Collins Sq SE3 142 D3
Collins St SE3 142 C3
Collins Yd N1 234 C5
Collinwood Ave EN3 6 C2
Collinwood Gdns IG5 56 C5
Collison Pl N16 51 C1
Collis Prim Sch TW11 175 B4
Coll of Arms*
EC4 117 A6 252 A6
Coll of Central London
The EC2 243 A6
Coll of Law The
EC1 95 B3 242 C5
Coll of North East London
The N15 51 D5
Coll of NW London
NW6 91 C6
Coll of NW London
(Willesden Centre)
NW10 67 D3
Coll of Optometrists The
SW1 250 A4
Coll Sharp Ct 42 E2 95 D4
Coll's Rd SE15 140 C4
Collyer Ave CR0 220 A4
Collyer Pl SE15 140 A4
Collyer Rd CR0 220 A4
Colman Ct
London N12 30 A4
Stanmore HA7 25 B4
Colman Rd E16 99 C2
Colmans Wharf 5
E14 97 D2
Colmar Cl 3 E1 96 D3
Colmer Pl HA3 24 B3
Colmer Rd SW16 182 A3
Colmore Ct NW4 46 A6
Colmore Mews SE15 140 B4
Colmore Rd EN3 6 C1
Colnbrook Ct SW17 180 B6
Colnbrook St SE1 261 C6
Colne Ct
Ealing W7 86 B1
West Ewell KT19 215 A4
Colne Ho
Barking IG11 78 D2
Paddington NW8 236 D5
Colne Rd
Clapton Pk E5 75 A4
Southgate N21 17 B4
Twickenham TW1,
TW2 152 C3
Colne St E13 99 A4
COLNEY HATCH 30 C4
Colney Hatch N10 31 A3
Colney Hatch La N10 31 A3
Cologne Rd SW11 136 B1
Coloma Convent Girls Sch
CR0 222 D5
Colombo Rd IG1 57 A2
Colombo St SE1 251 C3
Colomb St SE10 120 C1
Colonades The 4
SE5 139 B4
Colonels Wlk EN2 4 D2
Colonial Ave TW2 152 A5
Colonial Dr W4 111 A2
Colonial Rd TW14 149 C4
Colonnade WC1 240 B5
Colonnade Ho SE3 142 D3
Colonnades The
Croydon CR0 220 C2
6 Hackney E8 74 B2
Colonnade The 12
SE8 119 B2
Colorado Bldg 9
SE13 141 D4
Colosseum Ct N3 29 B1
Colosseum Ret Pk EN1 6 A1
Colosseum Terr NW1 238 D6
Colour Ho SE1 253 B1
Colroy Ct NW4 47 A4
Colson Rd CR0 221 C6
Colson Way SW16 181 C6
Colstead Ho 22 E1 96 B1
Colsterworth Rd N15 51 D5

Colston Ave SM1,
SM5 ... 218 C4
Colston Ct SM5 ... 218 D4
Colston Rd
Mortlake SW14 ... 133 A1
Upton E7 ... 77 D2
Colthurst Cres N4 ... 73 A6
Colthurst Dr N9 ... 18 B1
Coltman Ho SE10 ... 142 A6
Coltman St E14 ... 97 A2
Colt Mews 5 EN3 ... 7 C6
Coltness Cres SE2 ... 124 B1
Colton Gdns N17 ... 51 A6
Colton Rd HA1 ... 42 C4
Coltsfoot Dr UB7 ... 82 A1
Coltswood Ct N14 ... 15 D3
Colts Yd E11 ... 54 D2
Columba Ho SE14 ... 141 B4
Columbas Dr NW3 ... 48 B1
Columbia Ave
Edgware HA8 ... 26 D2
New Malden KT4 ... 199 D2
Ruislip HA4 ... 40 B1
Columbia Ct
Edgware HA8 ... 26 D2
New Malden KT3 ... 199 D2
Columbia Ho 18 E3 ... 97 C4
Columbia Point 7
SE16 ... 118 C3
Columbia Prim Sch
E2 ... 95 D4
Columbia Rd
9 Hackney E2 ... 96 A5
Newham E13 ... 98 D3
Shoreditch E2 ... 95 D4
Columbia Road Mkt
E2 ... 95 D4
Columbine Ave
Croydon CR2 ... 220 D1
Newham E6 ... 100 A2
Columbus Gdns HA6 ... 22 A2
Colveiw Ct SE9 ... 165 D3
Colverson Ho 14 E1 ... 96 C2
Colvestone Cres E8 ... 73 D3
Colvestone Prim Sch
E8 ... 73 D3
Colville Gdns W11 ... 91 B1
Colville Ho
32 Bethnal Green E2 ... 96 C5
Notting Hill W11 ... 91 B1
Colville Mews W11 ... 91 B1
Colville Pl W1 ... 239 B3
Colville Prim Sch W11 .. 91 B1
Colville Rd
Edmonton N9 ... 18 B3
Higham Hill E17 ... 35 A1
Leyton E11 ... 76 A5
Notting Hill W11 ... 91 B1
South Acton W3 ... 110 D3
Colville Sq W11 ... 91 B1
Colville Terr W11 ... 91 B1
Colvin Cl SE26 ... 184 C5
Colvin Gdns
Chingford E4 ... 20 A1
Wanstead E11 ... 55 B5
Colvin Rd
Thornton Heath CR7 ... 204 C4
Upton Pk E6 ... 78 A1
Colwall Gdns IG8 ... 37 A5
Colwall Ho 18 SW9 ... 138 B3
Colwell Rd SE22 ... 161 D6
Colwick Cl N6 ... 49 D2
Colwith Rd W6 ... 134 C6
Colwood Gdns SW19 .. 180 B3
Colworth Gr SE17 ... 262 B3
Colworth Rd
Croydon CR0 ... 206 A1
Leytonstone E11 ... 54 C2
Colwyn Ave UB6 ... 86 D5
Colwyn Cl SW16 ... 181 C5
Colwyn Cres TW3 ... 130 A4
Colwyn Gn NW9 ... 45 C3
Colwyn Ho SE1 ... 261 A5
Colwyn Rd NW2 ... 68 B5
Colyer Cl SE9 ... 166 D2
Colyer Ho SE2 ... 124 D1
Colyton Cl
Erith DA16 ... 146 D4
Wembley HA0 ... 65 C2
Colyton La 14 SW16 ... 182 C5
Colyton Rd SE22 ... 162 B6
Colyton Way N18 ... 34 A5
Combe Ave SE3 ... 142 D5
Combedale Rd SE10 ... 121 A1
Combe Ho
Mortlake SW14 ... 133 A3
20 Paddington W2 ... 91 C2
Combe Lane Sta CR0 .. 222 C3
Combemartin Rd
SW18 ... 157 A3
Combe Mews 4 SE3 ... 142 D5
Comber Cl NW2 ... 68 B6
Comber Gr SE5 ... 139 A5
Comber Grove Prim Sch
SE5 ... 139 A5
Comber Ho SE5 ... 139 A5
Combermere Rd
London SW9 ... 138 B2
Morden SM4 ... 201 D4
Comberton 10 KT1 ... 176 C1
Comberton Rd E5 ... 74 B6
Combeside SE18 ... 145 D5
Combes Rd RM9 ... 81 B1
Combe The NW1 ... 231 D1
Combwell Cres SE2 ... 124 A3
Com Coll Hackney The
E8 ... 96 B6
Comely Bank Rd E17 ... 54 A4
Comeragh Mews W14 254 B1
Comeragh Rd
W14 ... 113 A1 254 B1
Comer Cres UB2 ... 108 A4
Comerford Rd SE4 ... 141 B1
Comer Ho 10 EN5 ... 2 A1
Comet Cl E12 ... 77 D4
Comet Pl SE8 ... 141 C5
Comet St SE8 ... 141 C5
Comins Ho SW4 ... 159 C6
Commerce Est E18 ... 37 C1
Commerce Pk CR0 ... 220 B6
Commerce Rd
Brentford TW8 ... 131 C5
Wood Green N22 ... 32 B2
Commerce Way CR0 ... 220 B6
Commercial Rd
Edmonton N18 ... 33 C4
Stepney E1 ... 96 C1
Whitechapel E1 ... 96 A1
Commercial St
E1 ... 95 D2 243 C4
Commercial Way
Peckham SE15 ... 140 A5
Wembley NW10 ... 88 D5
Commerell Pl SE10 ... 120 D1
Commerell St SE10 ... 120 C1
Commodity Quay E1 .. 253 D5
Commodore Ct SE8 ... 141 C4
Commodore Ho 7
E14 ... 120 A6
Commodore St E1 ... 97 A3
Commondale SW15 ... 134 C2
Common La KT10 ... 213 A1
Common Rd
Barnes SW13 ... 134 A2
Claygate KT10 ... 213 A1
Stanmore HA7 ... 8 C1
Commonside BR2 ... 225 C4
Commonside Ct
SW16 ... 182 A4
Commonside E CR4 ... 203 B6
Commonside W CR4 ... 203 A6
Common The
Ealing W5 ... 110 A5
Southall UB2 ... 106 D2
Stanmore HA7 ... 8 D2
1 Stratford E15 ... 76 D2
Common View SW15 .. 134 C2
Commonwealth Ave
Hayes UB3 ... 83 B1
21 Shepherd's Bush
W12 ... 112 B6
25 Shepherd's Bush
W12 ... 112 B6
Commonwealth Ho
WC1 ... 240 B2
Commonwealth Rd
N17 ... 34 A3
Commonwealth Way
SE2 ... 124 C1
Community Cl
Cranford TW5 ... 128 B4
Uxbridge UB10 ... 61 A5
Community Rd
Greenford UB6 ... 86 A6
Stratford New Town E15 .. 76 B3
Comodore Ho SW18 ... 136 A1
Como Rd SE23 ... 163 A2
Compania Bldg 12
E1 ... 118 D6
Compass Cl
Edgware HA8 ... 26 B6
Littleton TW15 ... 171 A3
Compass Ct SE1 ... 253 C3
Compass Hill TW10 ... 153 D5
Compass Ho
Bayswater W2 ... 91 D1
London SE8 ... 141 D3
Compass Point 10
E14 ... 119 C6
Compayne Gdns NW6 .. 69 D1
Compton Ave
Islington N1 ... 72 D2
London N6 ... 48 C2
Newham E6 ... 99 D5
Wembley HA0 ... 65 C4
Compton Cl
5 Burnt Oak HA8 ... 27 A3
Camberwell SE15 ... 139 D5
Cricklewood NW11 ... 68 D5
Ealing W13 ... 87 A1
Esher KT10 ... 212 B3
Regent's Pk NW1 ... 231 D1
Compton Cres
Chessington KT9 ... 214 A2
Chiswick W4 ... 133 A6
Northolt UB5 ... 84 D6
Tottenham N17 ... 33 A3
Compton Ct
London N12 ... 30 A2
Sutton SM1 ... 218 A4
9 West Norwood
SE19 ... 183 C5
Compton Ho SW11 ... 267 A2
Compton Lo N21 ... 16 D3
Compton Pas EC1 ... 241 D6
Compton Pl
Bloomsbury WC1 ... 240 A6
South Oxhey WD19 ... 23 A6
Compton Rd
Croydon CR0 ... 206 B1
Hayes UB3 ... 105 D6
Islington N1 ... 72 D2
Kensal Green NW10 ... 90 D4
Southgate N21 ... 16 D3
Wimbledon SW19 ... 179 B4
Compton Rise HA5 ... 41 B4
Compton Sch The N12 .. 30 C4
Compton St
EC1 ... 94 D3 241 D6
Compton Terr
Islington N1 ... 72 D2
Southgate N21 ... 16 C3
Comreddy Cl EN2 ... 4 D4
Comus Ho SE17 ... 263 A3
Comus Pl
SE17 ... 117 C2 263 A3
Comyn Rd SW11 ... 136 C1
Comyns Cl E16 ... 98 D2
Comyns Rd RM9 ... 81 C1
Comyns The WD23 ... 8 A3
Conal Ct SW16 ... 181 D5
Conant Ho SE11 ... 138 D6
Conant Mews 1 E1 ... 118 A6
Concanon Rd SW2,
SW4 ... 138 B1
Concert Hall App
SE1 ... 116 B5 250 D3
Concord Bsns Ctr W3 .. 88 D2
Concord Cl UB5 ... 85 A4
Concord Ct KT1 ... 198 B6
Concorde Cl
Hounslow TW3 ... 129 D3
Uxbridge UB10 ... 82 A5
Concorde Dr E6 ... 100 B2
Concorde Way SE16 ... 118 D2
Concord Ho
Kingston u T KT3 ... 199 C6
5 Tottenham N17 ... 33 D3
Concordia Wharf 10
E14 ... 120 A5
Concord Rd
Acton W3 ... 88 D3
Enfield EN3 ... 18 C6
Concord Terr HA2 ... 63 D6
Concourse The
32 Edgware NW9 ... 27 D2
7 Edmonton N9 ... 18 A2
Condell Rd
SW8 ... 137 C4 269 B1
Conder St E14 ... 97 A1
Condor Path UB5 ... 85 C5
Condover Cres SE18 .. 144 D5
Condray Pl SW11 ... 267 A3
Conduit Ct WC2 ... 250 A6
Conduit Ho SE10 ... 142 B4
Conduit La
London N18 ... 34 C5
South Croydon CR0 ... 222 A3
Conduit Mews
W2 ... 92 B1 236 C1
Conduit Pas W2 ... 236 C1
Conduit Pl W2 ... 236 C1
Conduit Rd SE18 ... 122 D1
Conduit St
W1 ... 115 C6 249 A6
Conduit Way NW10 ... 67 A1
Conewood St N5 ... 72 D5
Coney Acre SE21 ... 161 A3
Coney Burrows E4 ... 20 C2
Coney Gr UB8 ... 82 C4
Coneygrove Path UB5 .. 63 A2
CONEY HALL ... 224 D5
Coney Hall Par BR4 ... 224 C5
Coney Hall Rdbt BR4 .. 224 C5
Coney Hill Rd BR4 ... 224 D6
Coney Way SW8 ... 270 D5
Conference Cl 3 E4 ... 20 A2
Conference Ho UB8 ... 83 A1
Conference Rd SE2 ... 124 C2
Congers Ho SE8 ... 141 C5
Congleton Gr SE18 ... 123 A1
Congo Dr N9 ... 18 C1
Congo Rd SE18 ... 123 B1
Congress Ho WC1 ... 239 D2
Congress Rd SE2 ... 124 C2
Congreve Ho 10 N16 ... 73 C3
Congreve Rd SE9 ... 144 B2
Congreve St
SE17 ... 117 C2 263 A3
Congreve Wlk 6 E16 ... 99 D2
Conical Cnr EN2 ... 5 A3
Conifer Cl BR6 ... 227 B4
Conifer Ct
Ashford TW15 ... 170 B5
Hendon NW4 ... 28 C1
Ilford IG1 ... 78 D2
23 Putney SW19 ... 156 D3
Sutton SM2 ... 218 B2
Conifer Gdns
Enfield EN1 ... 17 C5
Streatham SW16 ... 160 B1
Sutton SM1 ... 217 D6
Conifer Ho SE4 ... 141 B1
Conifers Cl TW11 ... 175 C3
Conifer Way
Hayes UB3 ... 106 A6
Wembley HA0 ... 65 C5
Coniger Rd SW6 ... 135 C3
Coningham Ct SW10 ... 266 B4
Coningham Mews
W12 ... 112 A5
Coningham Rd W12 ... 112 B4
Coningsby Ave NW9 ... 27 C1
Coningsby Cotts W5 .. 109 D4
Coningsby Ct 4 CR4 ... 181 A1
Coningsby Gdns E4 ... 35 D4
Coningsby Rd
Ealing W5 ... 109 D4
Harringay N4 ... 50 D2
Conington Rd SE13 ... 142 A3
Conisbee Ct 3 N14 ... 15 C6
Conisborough Cres
SE6 ... 164 A1
Conisbrough NW1 ... 232 A5
Coniscliffe Cl BR7 ... 188 C2
Coniscliffe Rd N13 ... 17 A1
Coniston NW1 ... 232 A2
Coniston Ave
Barking IG11 ... 79 C1
Ealing UB6 ... 87 B4
Falconwood DA16 ... 145 C2
Coniston Cl
Barking IG11 ... 79 C1
Barnes SW13 ... 133 D5
Chiswick W4 ... 133 A5
West Barnes SM4 ... 200 D3
Whetstone N20 ... 14 A1
Coniston Ct
Beckenham BR3 ... 186 A2
Chessington KT9 ... 214 A5
Edgware HA8 ... 26 B5
4 Finchley NW7 ... 29 A3
Marylebone W2 ... 237 B1
Penge SE26 ... 184 B4
6 Rotherhithe SE16 ... 118 D4
3 Wallington SM6 ... 219 B4
Conistone Way N7 ... 72 A1
Coniston Gdns
Edmonton N9 ... 18 C3
Kingsbury NW9 ... 45 B4
Pinner HA5 ... 40 A5
Redbridge IG4 ... 56 A5
Sutton SM2 ... 218 B2
Wembley HA9 ... 43 C1
Coniston Ho
14 Bow E3 ... 97 B4
18 Camberwell SE5 ... 139 A5
Coniston Rd
Catford BR1 ... 186 C4
Croydon CR0 ... 206 A2
Muswell Hill N10 ... 31 B1
Tottenham N17 ... 34 A4
Twickenham TW2 ... 151 D5
Coniston Way KT9 ... 214 A5
Coniston Wlk E9 ... 74 C3
Conlan St W10 ... 91 A3
Conley Rd NW10 ... 67 C2
Conley St SE10 ... 120 C1
Connaught Ave
Ashford TW15 ... 170 A6
Barnet EN4 ... 14 D3
Chingford E4 ... 20 B4
Enfield EN1 ... 5 C3
Hounslow TW4 ... 129 A1
Mortlake SW14 ... 133 A1
Connaught Bridge
E16 ... 121 D6
Connaught Bsns Ctr
London NW9 ... 45 D4
Mitcham CR4 ... 202 D4
Wallington CR0 ... 220 B2
Connaught Cl
Carshalton SM1 ... 218 B6
Enfield EN1 ... 5 C3
Hillingdon UB8 ... 83 A3
Lea Bridge E10 ... 75 A6
Marylebone W2 ... 237 B1
Connaught Ct
1 Chingford E4 ... 20 C4
9 Walthamstow E17 ... 53 D5
Connaught Day Hospl
E11 ... 54 C3
Connaught Dr NW11 ... 47 C5
Connaught Gdns
Cranley Gdns N10 ... 49 B4
Edmonton N13 ... 32 D6
Morden SM4 ... 202 A5
Connaught Grange
N13 ... 32 D6
Connaught Ho
College Pk NW10 ... 90 B4
London N10 ... 49 B4
Mayfair W1 ... 248 C5
Connaught Hts UB10 ... 83 A3
Connaught La IG1 ... 79 B6
Connaught Lo N4 ... 50 C2
Connaught Mans
Battersea SW11 ... 267 B1
3 Brixton SW9 ... 138 C1
15 Canonbury N16 ... 73 B4
Fulham SW6 ... 264 A2
Connaught Mews
Ilford IG1 ... 79 B6
Woolwich SE18 ... 122 C1
Connaught Pl W2 ... 237 C1
Connaught Rd
Barnet EN5 ... 12 D5
Carshalton SM1 ... 218 B6
Chingford E4 ... 20 C3
Ealing W13 ... 109 B6
Finsbury Pk N4 ... 50 C2
Harlesden NW10 ... 89 C5
Harrow HA3 ... 24 D2
Ilford IG1 ... 79 B6
Leytonstone E11 ... 54 B1
Newham E16 ... 121 D5
New Malden KT3 ... 199 C5
5 Richmond TW10 ... 154 B6
Teddington TW11,
TW12 ... 174 B5
Walthamstow E17 ... 53 C4
Woolwich SE18 ... 122 D1
Connaught Sch for Girls
E11 ... 54 C1
Connaught Sch for Girls
(Annexe) E11 ... 76 C6
Connaught Sq
W2 ... 92 D1 237 C1
Connaught St
W2 ... 92 C1 237 B1
Connaught Way N13 ... 32 D6
Connaught Works E3 ... 97 A6
Connections Ho N2 ... 30 B2
Connell Cres W5 ... 88 B3
Connell Ct 6 SE14 ... 140 D6
Connell Ho 6 SM6 ... 219 C2
Connemara Cl WD6 ... 11 B5
Conniffe Ct SE9 ... 166 D6
Connington 5 KT1 ... 176 C1
Connington Cres E4 ... 20 B1
Connolly Ho SW19 ... 180 A4
Connoly Ct NW2 ... 68 B5
Connop Rd EN3 ... 6 D5
Connor Cl E11 ... 54 C2
Connor Ct SW11 ... 268 C1
Connor Rd RM9 ... 81 B4
Connor St E9 ... 96 D6
Conolly Rd W7 ... 108 C5
Conrad Dr KT4 ... 200 D1
Conrad Ho
8 Limehouse SE16 ... 119 A6
South Lambeth SW8 ... 270 A4
12 Stoke Newington
N16 ... 73 C3
Conrad Twr W3 ... 110 D3
Conroy Ct 6 DA14 ... 190 A6
Conservatory Ct SE19 . 183 C3
Consfield Ave KT3 ... 200 A4
Consort Ho
Bayswater W2 ... 245 D5
Edgware NW7 ... 27 D5
Consort Lo NW8 ... 230 C5
Consort Mews TW7 ... 152 B6
Consort Rd SE15 ... 140 B3
Cons St SE1 ... 251 B2
Constable Ave E16 ... 121 B5
Constable Cl
12 Friern Barnet N11 ... 30 D5
Hampstead Garden Suburb
NW11 ... 47 D3
Hayes UB4 ... 83 A5
Constable Cres N15 ... 52 A4
Constable Ct 11 SE16 .. 118 B1
Constable Gdns
Edgware HA8 ... 26 C1
Isleworth TW7 ... 152 B6
Constable Ho
Enfield EN1 ... 18 A6
25 Millwall E14 ... 119 C4
13 Northolt UB5 ... 84 D5
Primrose Hill NW3 ... 70 D1
Constable Mews RM8 .. 80 B4
Constable Wlk SE21 ... 161 C1
Constance Cres BR2 .. 208 D1
Constance Ct N10 ... 31 B3
Constance Rd
Enfield EN1 ... 17 C5
Sutton SM1 ... 218 A4
Thornton Heath CR0 ... 204 D2
Twickenham TW2 ... 151 D4
Constance St E16 ... 122 A5
Constant Ho 26 E14 ... 119 D6
Constantine Ho SW2 .. 160 D3
Constantine Pl UB10 ... 82 B6
Constantine Rd NW3 ... 70 C4
Constitution Hill SW1,
W1 ... 115 B4 248 D2
Constitution Rise
SE18 ... 144 C4
Consul Ho 5 E3 ... 97 C3
Content St
SE17 ... 117 B2 262 C3
Contessa Cl BR6 ... 227 C3
Control Tower Rd
TW6 ... 126 D2
Convair Wlk 11 UB5 ... 84 D4
Convent Cl BR3 ... 186 A3
Convent Gdns
Ealing W5 ... 109 C2
Notting Hill W11 ... 91 B1
Convent Hill SE19 ... 183 A4
Convent Lo TW15 ... 170 D5
Convent of Jesus & Mary
Language Coll NW10 .. 89 D6
Convent of Jesus & Mary
RC Inf Sch NW2 ... 68 C2
Convent Rd TW15 ... 170 D5
Convent Way UB2 ... 106 D2
Conway Cl HA7 ... 25 A4
Conway Cres
Dagenham RM6 ... 58 C3
Greenford UB6 ... 86 C5
Conway Dr
Ashford TW15 ... 171 A4
Hayes UB3 ... 105 A3
Sutton SM2 ... 217 D2
Conway Gdns
Enfield EN2 ... 5 C5
Mitcham CR4 ... 204 A5
Wembley HA9 ... 43 C2
Conway Gr W3 ... 89 B2
Conway Ho
Chelsea SW3 ... 257 D1
5 Millwall E14 ... 119 D2
6 Streatham SW2 ... 160 A3
Conway Mews W1 ... 239 A5
Conway Prim Sch
SE18 ... 123 C2
Conway Rd
Dollis Hill NW2 ... 68 C6
Feltham TW13 ... 172 D5
Harlington TW6 ... 126 D2
Harringay N15 ... 51 A4
Palmers Green N14 ... 16 A1
Plumstead SE18 ... 123 C2
Twickenham TW4 ... 151 C4
Wimbledon SW20 ... 178 C2
Conway St W1 .. 93 C3 239 A5
Conway Wlk TW12 ... 173 B4
Conybeare NW3 ... 70 C1
Conyers Cl IG8 ... 36 C4
Conyer's Rd SW16 ... 181 D5
Conyer St 21 E3 ... 97 A5
Cooden Cl BR1 ... 187 B3
Cookes Cl E11 ... 76 D6
Cookes La SM3 ... 217 A2
Cooke St 3 IG11 ... 101 A6

Cookham Cl UB2 107 D4
Cookham Cres SE16 118 D4
Cookham Dene Cl BR7 189 B2
Cookham Ho E2 243 C6
Cookham Rd BR8, DA14 191 C2
Cookhill Rd SE2 124 B3
Cooks Ferry N18 34 D5
Cook's Hole Rd EN2 5 A5
Cookson Gr DA8 147 D5
Cook's Rd
  Camberwell SE17 138 D6
  Stratford Marsh E15 97 D5
Coolfin Rd E16 99 B1
Coolgardie Ave E4 36 B5
Coolgardie Rd TW15 171 A5
Coolhurst Rd N8 49 D3
Cool Oak La NW9 45 D2
Coomassie Rd W9 91 B3
COOMBE 177 B3
Coombe Ave CR0 221 C4
Coombe Bank KT2, KT3 177 C2
Coombe Boys' Sch KT3 200 A4
Coombe Cl
  Edgware HA8 26 B1
  Hounslow TW3 129 C1
Coombe Cnr N21 16 D3
Coombe Cres TW12 173 A3
Coombe Ct 2 BR3 185 B2
Coombe Dr HA4 40 B1
Coombe End KT2 177 B3
Coombefield Cl KT3 199 C4
Coombe Gdns
  New Malden KT3 199 D5
  Wimbledon SW20 178 A2
Coombe Girls Sch KT3 177 B1
Coombe Hill Glade KT2 177 C3
Coombe Hill Inf Sch KT2 177 B2
Coombe Hill Jun Sch KT2 177 B2
Coombe Hill Rd KT2 177 C3
Coombe Ho 13 N7 71 D3
Coombe House Chase KT3 177 B2
Coombehurst Cl EN4 2 D3
Coombehurst (Kingston University) KT2 177 A5
Coombe La CR0 222 B3
Coombe Lane Flyover SW20 177 D2
Coombe La W KT2 177 B2
Coombe Lea BR1 210 A6
Coombe Lo SE7 143 C6
Coombe Neville KT2 177 B3
Coombe Pk KT2 177 B5
Coombe Pl KT2 177 A5
Coombe Rd
  Bushey WD23 8 B4
  Chiswick W4 111 C1
  Ealing W13 109 B3
  Forest Hill SE26 184 B6
  Hampton TW12 173 B4
  New Malden KT3 199 C6
  Norbiton KT2 176 C2
  South Croydon CR0, CR2 221 C4
  Willesden NW10 67 B5
  Wood Green N22 32 C2
Coomber Ho SW6 135 D2
Coombe Ridings KT2 177 A5
Coombe Rise KT2 177 A2
Coomber Way CR0 203 D3
Coombes Rd RM9 103 B6
Coombe Wlk SM1 217 D5
Coombewood Dr RM6 59 B3
Coombe Wood Rd KT2 177 A5
Coombs St N1 234 D3
Coomer Mews SW6 264 D5
Coomer Pl SW6 135 B6 264 D5
Cooms Wlk HA8 27 A2
Cooperage Cl 5 N17 33 D4
Cooperage The SE1 253 C3
Cooper Ave E17 35 A2
Cooper Cl SE1 251 B1
Cooper Cres SM5 218 D5
Cooper Ct
  Shooters Hill SE18 144 D6
  Stratford New Town E15 76 A3
Cooper Ho
  Hounslow TW4 129 B2
  Paddington NW8 236 C5
  Upper Tooting SW17 180 B6
Cooper Ho *continued*
  7 West Norwood SW27 182 D5
Cooper Rd
  Croydon CR0, CR9 220 D4
  Hendon NW4 46 D3
  Willesden NW10 68 A3
Coopersale Cl 3 IG8 37 C3
Coopersale Rd E9 74 D3
Coopers Cl
  Bethnal Green E1 96 C3
  Dagenham RM10 81 D2
Coopers Ct
  9 Acton W3 111 A5
  4 Friern Barnet N20 14 D1
  Isleworth TW7 130 D3
  Tower Hamlets E3 97 B3
Coopers La
  Grove Pk SE12 165 B2
  Somers Town NW1 232 D3
Cooper's La E10 54 A1
Cooper's Lane Prim Sch SE12 165 B2
Coopers Lo SE1 253 C2
Coopers Mews BR3 185 C1
Cooper's Rd SE1 117 D1 263 D2
Cooper's Row EC3 117 D6 253 C6
Cooper St 10 E16 98 D2
Coopers Tech Sch BR7 189 A2
Coopers Yd N1 72 D1
Cooper's Yd SE19 183 C4
Coote Gdns RM8 81 B5
Coote Rd
  Dagenham RM8 81 B5
  Erith DA7 147 B4
Cope Ho EC1 235 B1
Copeland Dr E14 119 C2
Copeland Ho
  Lambeth SE11 260 D5
  Upper Tooting SW17 180 B6
Copeland Rd
  London SE15 140 B3
  Walthamstow E17 53 D3
Copelands BR3 185 B3
Copeman Cl SE26 184 C5
Copenhagen Gdns W4 111 B4
Copenhagen Ho N1 234 A5
Copenhagen Pl E14 97 B1
Copenhagen Prim Sch N1 94 B6 233 C5
Copenhagen St N1 94 B6 233 C5
Cope Pl W8 113 C3 255 A5
Copers Cope Rd BR3 185 B3
Cope St SE16 118 D2
Copeswood Ct UB7 126 C5
Copford Wlk N1 235 A6
Copgate Path SW16 182 C4
Copinger Wlk HA8 26 D2
Copland Ave HA0 65 D3
Copland Cl HA0 65 C3
Copland Com Sch & Tech Ctr HA9 66 B3
Copland Ho UB1 107 B4
Copland Mews 8 HA0 66 A2
Copland Rd HA0 66 A2
Copleston Rd SE15 139 D2
Copley Cl
  15 Camberwell SE17 138 D6
  Ealing W7 86 D2
Copley Dene BR1 187 D2
Copley Pk SW16 182 B4
Copley Rd HA7 25 C5
Coppard Gdns KT9 213 C2
Coppedhall 2 SE21 161 B2
Coppelia Rd SE3 142 D1
Coppen Rd RM8 59 B2
Copperas St SE8 141 D6
Copper Beech N6 49 A2
Copperbeech Cl NW3 70 B3
Copper Beech Ct N20 14 A1
Copper Beeches TW7 130 B4
Copper Cl
  Penge SE19 183 D3
  Tottenham N17 34 B3
Copperdale Rd UB3 106 A4
Copperfield Ave UB8 82 C3
Copperfield Ct
  Blackheath SE3 142 D2
  Ilford IG6 57 A6
Copperfield Dr N15 51 D5
Copperfield Ho 12 SE1 118 A4
Copperfield Mews N18 33 C5
Copperfield Rd
  Stepney E3 97 A2
  Thamesmead SE28 102 C1
Copperfields
  5 Beckenham BR3 186 A2
  Harrow HA1 42 C2
Copperfields Ct W3 110 C4
Copperfield St SE1 117 A4 252 A2
Copperfield Way
  Chislehurst BR7 189 A4
  Pinner HA5 41 B5
Coppergate Cl BR1 187 B2
Coppermead Cl NW2 68 C5
Copper Mews 19 W4 111 A3
Copper Mill Dr TW7 130 D3
Coppermill La E17 52 D4
Copper Mill La SW17 180 A6
Coppermill Prim Sch E17 52 D4
Copper Row SE1 253 C3
Copperwood Lo EN2 4 D3
Coppetts Cl N12 30 D3
Coppetts Ctr N12 30 D3
Coppetts Rd N10 30 D2
Coppetts Wood Hospl N10 30 D2
Coppetts Wood Prim Sch N10 31 A2
Coppice Cl
  Beckenham BR3 207 D5
  Harrow HA7 24 D4
  Ruislip HA4 39 B3
  West Barnes SW20 200 C6
Coppice Dr SW15 156 B5
Coppice The
  Ashford TW15 170 D4
  Enfield EN2 4 D1
  Hillingdon UB7 82 A1
  New Barnet EN5 13 D5
Coppice Way E18 54 D6
Coppice Wlk N20 13 C1
Coppies Gr N11 31 B6
Copping Cl CR0 221 C4
Coppin Ho SW2 160 D3
Coppins The
  2 Ilford RM6 58 B2
  New Addington CR0 223 D2
  Stanmore HA3 24 C4
Coppock Cl SW11 136 C3
Coppsfield KT8 195 C6
Copse Ave BR4 223 D5
Copse Cl SE7 143 B6
Copse Ct SW15 157 A6
Copse Glade KT6 197 D1
COPSE HILL 178 B3
Copse Hill
  Belmont SM2 217 D1
  Wimbledon SW20 178 B3
Copsem Dr KT10 212 A2
Copsem La KT10 212 A1
Copsem Way KT10 212 A2
Copse The
  Chingford E4 20 D3
  Muswell Hill N2 48 D6
Copse View CR2 223 A1
Copsewood Cl DA15 167 C5
Coptefield Dr DA17 125 A3
Copthall Ave EC2 95 B1 242 D2
Copthall Bldgs EC2 242 D2
Copthall Cl EC2 242 C2
Copthall Dr NW7 28 A4
Copthall Gdns
  Hendon NW7 28 A3
  Twickenham TW1 152 D3
Copthall Rd E UB10 60 C5
Copthall Rd W UB10 60 C6
Copthall Sch NW7 28 B3
Copthall Sports Ctr NW4 28 B2
Copthorne Ave
  Bromley BR2 226 B6
  Streatham SW12 159 D4
Copthorne Chase 3 TW15 170 B6
Copthorne Cl TW17 193 A3
Copthorne Ct SM1 218 A5
Copthorne Mews UB3 105 C2
Coptic St WC1 94 A2 240 A3
Copton Cl E3 97 C2
Copwood Cl N12 30 B6
Coral Apts 6 E16 121 A6
Coral Cl RM6 58 C6
Coral Ho 5 E1 97 A3
Coraline Cl UB1 85 B4
Coralline Wlk 4 SE2 124 C4
Coral Row 14 SW11 136 A2
Coral St SE1 116 C4 251 B1
Coram Ho
  Bloomsbury WC1 240 A6
  9 Chiswick W4 111 C1
Coram Mans WC1 240 C5
Coram St WC1 94 A3 240 A5
Coran Cl N9 18 D4
Corban Rd TW3 129 C2
Corbar Cl EN4 2 B4
Corbden Cl SE15 139 D4
Corbet Cl CR4, SM6 219 A6
Corbet Ct EC3 242 D1
Corbet Ho N1 234 A5
Corbet Pl E1 95 D2 243 C4
Corbett Ct SE26 185 B6
Corbett Gr N22 32 A3
Corbett Ho SW10 266 A6
Corbett Rd
  Walthamstow E17 54 A6
  Wanstead E11 55 C3
Corbett's La SE16 118 C2
Corbetts Pas 8 SE16 118 C2
Corbett Villas RM8 58 C1
Corbicum E11 54 C2
Corbidge Ct SE8 141 D6
Corbiere Ct SW19 178 D4
Corbiere Ho 5 N1 95 C6
Corbin Ho 7 E3 97 D4
Corbin's La HA2 63 D5
Corbridge 5 N17 34 B3
Corbridge Cres E2 96 B5
Corbridge Ho SE2 124 C3
Corby Cres EN2 4 A1
Corbylands Rd DA15 167 C3
Corbyn St N4, N19 50 A1
Corby Rd NW10 89 B5
Corby Way E3 97 C3
Cordelia Cl SE24 138 D1
Cordelia Gdns TW19 148 A4
Cordelia Ho 26 N1 95 C5
Cordelia Rd TW19 148 A4
Cordelia St E14 97 D1
Cordell Ho N15 51 D4
Cordingley Rd HA4 61 B6
Cording St E14 97 D2
Cordwainers Ct 18 E9 74 C1
Cordwainers Wlk 9 E13 99 A5
Cordwain Ho 7 N18 34 A5
Cordwell Rd SE13 164 C6
Corefield Cl N11 15 A2
Corelli Rd SE3 144 A4
Corfe Ave HA2 63 C4
Corfe Cl
  Hayes UB4 84 C1
  Twickenham TW4 151 A3
Corfe Ho SW8 270 C4
Corfe Lodge 15 SE21 161 B2
Corfe Twr 6 W3 111 A4
Corfield Rd N21 16 B6
Corfield St E2 96 B4
Corfton Lo W5 88 A2
Corfton Rd W5 88 A2
Coriander Ave E14 98 B1
Coriander Ct SE1 253 D2
Cories Cl RM8 80 D6
Corigan Ct 6 E11 76 C6
Corinium Cl HA9 66 B4
Corinne Rd N19 71 C4
Corinth Ho IG3 58 A2
Cork St Mews W1 249 A5
Corkscrew Hill BR4 224 B5
Cork Sq E1 118 B5
Cork St W1 115 C6 249 A5
Cork Tree Ho 3 SW27 182 D5
Cork Tree Ret Pk N18 35 A4
Cork Tree Way E4 35 A5
Corlett St NW1 237 A4
Cormont Rd SE5 138 D4
Cormorant Cl E17 35 A3
Cormorant Ct
  36 Deptford SE8 141 B6
  13 Dulwich SE21 161 B2
Cormorant Ho EN3 18 D6
Cormorant Pl SM1 217 B3
Cormorant Rd E7 76 D3
Cornbury Ho 5 SE8 141 B6
Cornbury Rd HA8 25 D3
Cornel Ho 4 DA15 168 A1
Cornelia Dr UB4 84 C3
Cornelia St N7 72 B2
Cornelion Cotts 1 SM6 219 B3
Cornelius Ct 4 N12 30 A5
Cornell Bldg 9 E1 96 A1
Cornell Cl DA14 191 A4
Cornell Ct 4 EN3 7 A2
Cornell Ho HA2 63 B5
Corner Fielde SW2 160 B3
Corner Gn SE3 143 A3
Corner House St WC2 250 A4
Corner Mead NW9 27 D2
Cornerside TW15 171 A3
Cornerstone Ct 13 E1 96 A3
Cornerways
  Harrow HA1 65 A5
  Putney SW15 134 A1
Corney Rd W4 133 C6
Corney Reach Way W4 133 C5
Cornflower La CR0 206 D1
Cornflower Terr SE22 162 B5
Cornford Cl BR2 209 A4
Cornford Gr SW12 159 B2
Cornhill EC3 95 B1 242 D1
Cornhill Dr EN3 7 A6
Cornick Ho 7 SE16 118 B3
Cornish Ct N9 18 B4
Cornish Gr SE20 184 B2
Cornish Ho
  Brentford TW8 110 B1
  7 Camberwell SE17 138 D6
Cornmill La SE13 142 A2
Cornmow Dr NW10 68 A3
Cornshaw Rd RM8 58 D1
Cornthwaite Rd E5 74 C5
Cornwall Ave
  Bethnal Green E2 96 C4
  Claygate KT10 212 D1
  Falconwood DA16 145 D2
  Finchley N3 29 C3
  Southall UB1 85 C2
  Wood Green N22 32 A2
Cornwall Cl IG11 79 D2
Cornwall Cres W11 91 A1
Cornwall Ct
  5 Ealing W7 86 D3
  5 Pinner HA5 23 B3
  Upper Tooting SW17 180 C6
Cornwall Dr BR5 190 C3
Cornwall Flats SE1 251 B2
Cornwall Gdns
  Kensington SW7 113 D3 255 D5
  Willesden NW10 68 B2
Cornwall Gdns Wlk SW7 255 D5
Cornwall Gr W4 111 C1
Cornwall Ho
  Marylebone NW1 237 D5
  3 Putney SW15 156 C4
Cornwallis Ave
  London N9 18 C2
  New Eltham SE9 167 B2
Cornwallis Ct SW8 270 A2
Cornwallis Gr N9 18 C2
Cornwallis Ho 24 W12 112 B6
Cornwallis Rd
  Dagenham RM9 81 A4
  Edmonton N9 18 B2
  Upper Holloway N19 72 A6
  Walthamstow E17 52 D5
  Woolwich SE18 122 D3
  Woolwich SE18 123 A3
Cornwallis Sq N19 72 A6
Cornwallis Wlk SE9 144 B2
Cornwall Mans
  Chelsea SW10 266 B4
  Marylebone NW1 237 D5
Cornwall Mews S SW7 256 A5
Cornwall Mews W SW7 255 D5
Cornwall Rd
  Belmont SM2 217 B1
  Croydon CR0 220 D6
  Edmonton N18 34 A5
  Finsbury Pk N4 50 C2
  Harrow HA1 42 A3
  Lambeth SE1 116 C4 251 B2
  Pinner HA5 23 B3
  Ruislip HA4 61 D6
  Twickenham TW1 153 A3
  West Green N15 51 B4
Cornwall Sq SE11 261 C2
Cornwall St 4 E1 118 B6
Cornwall Terr NW1 237 D5
Cornwall Terrace Mews NW1 237 D5
Corn Way E11 76 C5
Cornwood Cl N2 48 B5
Cornwood Dr E1 96 C1
Cornworthy Rd RM8 80 C3
Corona Rd SE12 165 A4
Coronation Ave 1 N16 73 D4
Coronation Cl
  Bexley DA5 168 D5
  Ilford IG6 57 A5
Coronation Ct
  19 North Kensington W10 90 C2
  Stratford E15 76 D2
Coronation Rd
  Acton NW10 88 C3
  Hayes UB3 105 D2
  Newham E13 99 C4
Coronet Ho HA7 24 D4
Coronet Par 9 HA0 66 A2
Coronet St N1 95 C4
Corporation Ave TW4 129 A1
Corporation Row EC1 241 B6
Corporation St
  Lower Holloway N7 72 A3
  West Ham E15 98 D5
Corpus Christi RC Prim Sch
  Brixton SW2 160 B6
  Kingston u T KT3 199 A6
Corrance Rd SW2, SW4 138 A1
Corri Ave N14 31 D6
Corrib Ct N13 16 B1
Corrib Dr SM1 218 C3
Corrib Hts N8 49 D3
Corrigan Cl NW4 46 C6
Corringham Ct NW11 47 C2
Corringham Ho 11 E1 96 D1
Corringham Rd
  London NW11 47 C2
  Wembley HA9 66 C6
Corringway
  Ealing W5 88 C2
  Golders Green NW11 47 D2
Corris Gn NW9 45 C3
Corry Dr SW9 138 D1
Corry Ho 2 E14 119 D6
Corsair Cl TW19 148 A4
Corsair Rd TW19 148 A4
Corscombe Cl KT2 177 A5
Corsehill St SW16 181 C4
Corsell Ho 5 TW8 131 C5
Corsham Ho HA9 66 C2
Corsham St N1 95 B4 235 D1
Corsica St N5 72 D2
Corsley Way E9 75 B2
Cortayne Ct TW2 152 C2
Cortayne Rd SW6 135 B3
Cortis Rd SW15 156 B5
Cortis Terr SW15 156 B5
Corunna Rd SW8 137 C4 269 B2
Corunna Terr SW8 269 A2
Corvette Sq 5 SE10 142 B6
Corwell Gdns UB8 83 A1
Corwell La UB8 83 A1
Coryton Path W9 91 B3
Cosbycote Ave SE24 161 A6
Cosdach Ave SM6 219 D1
Cosedge Cres CR0, CR9 220 D3
Cosgrove Cl
  Edmonton N21 17 A2
  Hayes UB4 84 D3
Cosgrove Ho 11 E2 96 A6
Cosmo Pl WC1 240 B4
Cosmur Cl W12 111 D3
Cossall Wlk SE15 140 B4
Cossar Mews 10 SW2 160 C6
Cosser St SE1 116 C3 261 A6
Costa St SE15 140 A3
Coston Prim Sch UB6 86 A4
Costons Ave UB6 86 B4
Costons La UB6 86 B4
Coston Wlk 4 SE4 140 D1
Cosway Ho NW11 48 A3
Cosway Mans NW1 237 B4
Cosway St NW1 92 C2 237 B4
Cotall St E14 97 C2
Coteford Cl HA5 40 A4
Coteford Inf Sch HA5 40 A3
Coteford Jun Sch HA5 39 D4
Coteford St SW17 181 A6
Cotelands CR0 221 C5
Cotesbach Rd E5 74 C5
Cotes Ho NW8 237 A5
Cotesmore Gdns RM8 80 C4
Cotford Rd CR7 205 A5
Cotham St SE17 262 B3
Cotherstone Rd SW2 160 B3
Cotleigh Ave DA5 168 D2
Cotleigh Rd NW6 69 C1
Cotman Cl
  London NW11 48 A3
  Putney SW15 156 D6

Cotman Ct BR3 .... 185 B2
Cotmandene Cres
BR5 .... 190 A1
Cotman Gdns HA8 ..... 26 C1
Cotman Ho
5 Northolt UB5........ 84 D5
St John's Wood NW8 ... 230 A4
Cotman Mews RM8 .... 80 C3
Cotmans Cl UB3 ...... 106 A5
Coton Rd DA16........ 146 A2
Cotrill Gdns E8 .... 74 B2
Cotsford Ave KT3 ..... 199 B4
Cotswold Ave WD23..... 8 A5
Cotswold Cl
Hinchley Wood KT10.... 212 D6
Kingston u T KT2....... 177 A4
Cotswold Ct
London N11 .... 31 A6
St Luke's EC1 .... 242 A6
3 Wembley UB6 .... 86 D5
Cotswold Gate NW2.... 47 A1
Cotswold Gdns
Hendon NW2 .... 68 D6
Ilford IG2............. 57 B2
Newham E6 .... 99 D5
Cotswold Gn EN2 ....4 B1
Cotswold Ho N16 ...... 51 D1
Cotswold Mews SW11 266 D1
Cotswold Rd TW12..... 173 C4
Cotswold Rise BR6.... 211 D3
Cotswold St SE27 ..... 182 D6
Cotswold Way
Enfield EN2..............4 B2
North Cheam KT4...... 216 C6
Cottage Ave BR2...... 210 A1
Cottage Cl
Harrow HA2........... 64 C6
Ruislip HA4............ 39 B1
Cottage Field Cl
DA14 .... 168 C3
Cottage Gn SE5....... 139 B5
Cottage Gr
London SW9.......... 138 A2
Surbiton KT6 .... 197 D3
Cottage Pl
SW3......... 114 C3 257 A5
Cottage Rd KT19...... 215 B1
Cottage St E14........ 119 D6
Cottages The
Ickenham UB10 .... 60 A6
Lambeth SE1 .... 260 C5
Uxbridge UB10......... 60 D5
Cottage Wlk 2 N16.... 73 D5
Cottenham Dr
London NW9 .... 45 D6
Wimbledon SW20 ..... 178 B3
Cottenham Ho 5 N19.. 72 A6
Cottenham Par SW20 . 178 B1
COTTENHAM PARK .. 178 B2
Cottenham Park Rd
SW20............... 178 C3
Cottenham Pl SW20... 178 B3
Cottenham Rd E17..... 53 B5
Cotterill Rd KT6....... 198 B1
Cottesbrook St 9
SE14................ 141 A5
Cottesloe Ho NW8 .... 237 A6
Cottesloe Mews SE1 .. 261 B6
Cottesmore Ct W8 .... 255 D6
Cottesmore Gdns
W8.......... 113 D3 255 D6
Cottimore Ave KT12... 194 B1
Cottimore Cres KT12.. 194 B2
Cottimore La KT12.... 194 B2
Cottimore Terr KT12 .. 194 B2
Cottingham Chase
HA4 .... 62 A5
Cottingham Rd
Penge SE20 .... 184 D3
South Lambeth
SW8 .... 138 B5 270 D4
Cottington Rd TW13... 172 D6
Cottington St SE11.... 261 C2
Cotton Ave W3 .... 89 B1
Cotton Cl
Dagenham RM9 .... 80 C1
12 Leyton E11 .... 76 C6
Cottongrass Cl 1
CR0 .... 206 D1
Cotton Hill BR1 .... 186 B6
Cotton Ho
Bedford Pk W12....... 111 D4
18 Streatham SW12.... 160 A4
Cotton Row SW11..... 136 B2
Cotton's Gdns E2 ...... 95 C4
Cottons La SE1 .... 252 D4
Cotton St E14......... 120 A6
Cottrell Ct SE10....... 120 D2
Cotts Cl 13 W7........ 86 D2
Couchman Ho 8
SW4................. 159 C5
Couchmore Ave KT10 . 212 C6
Coulgate St SE4 ...... 141 A2
Coulsdon Ct 4 N8 ..... 49 D4
Coulsdon Ho 5 SW2 .. 160 A3
Coulson Cl RM8........ 58 C1
Coulson St
SW3......... 114 D1 257 C2
Coulter Cl UB4......... 85 A3
Coulter Rd W6........ 112 B3
Coulthurst Ct SW16 ... 182 A3
Coults Cres NW5....... 71 A5
Councillor St SE5 ..... 139 A5
Counters Ct W14...... 254 B6
Counter St SE1 .... 253 A3
Countess Rd NW5....... 71 C3
Countisbury Ave EN1... 17 D4
Countisbury Ho SE26.. 162 A1
Country Way TW13,
TW16............... 172 C5
County Gate
Longlands SE9 .... 167 A1
New Barnet EN5........ 13 D5
County Gr SE5 .... 139 A4
County Ho
22 Herne Hill SE24..... 138 D1
9 South Lambeth
SW9 .... 138 C4
County Par TW8 ...... 131 D5
County Rd
Newham E6 .... 100 D2
South Norwood CR7.... 182 D1
County St SE1 . 117 A3 262 B5
Coupland Pl SE18..... 123 A1
Courcy Rd N8, N22 ..... 50 C6
Courier Ho 17 SW2.... 160 C4
Courland Gr SW8 ..... 137 D3
Courland St
SW8......... 137 D4 269 D1
Course The SE9....... 166 C1
Courtauld Ho 12 E2 .... 96 A5
Courtauld Inst of Art*
Marylebone W1 .... 237 D2
Strand WC2 .... 250 C6
Courtauld Rd N19...... 50 A1
Courtaulds Cl SE28.... 124 A5
Court Ave DA17 .... 125 B1
Court Cl
Harrow HA3........... 44 A6
Twickenham TW13,
TW2............... 151 D1
Wallington SM6 .... 219 D1
Court Close Ave TW13,
TW2................ 151 D1
Court Cres KT9 .... 213 D2
Court Downs Rd BR3 .. 185 D1
Court Dr
Carshalton SM1 .... 218 C4
Edgware HA7.......... 26 A6
Hillingdon UB10........ 82 C6
Wallington CR0 .... 220 B4
Courtenay Ave
Harrow HA3........... 24 A2
Highgate N6........... 48 C2
Courtenay Dr BR3..... 186 B1
Courtenay Gdns HA3 ... 24 A1
Courtenay Mews E17... 53 A4
Courtenay Pl E17 ...... 53 A4
Courtenay Rd
Leyton E11 .... 76 D5
North Cheam KT4, SM3 . 216 C5
Penge BR3, SE20 ...... 184 D4
Walthamstow E17 ...... 52 D5
Courtenay Rd HA9 ..... 65 D5
Courtenay Sq SE11.... 261 A1
Courtenay St
SE11........ 116 C1 261 A2
Courtens Mews HA7 ... 25 C3
Court Farm Ave KT19.. 215 B3
Court Farm Ind Est
TW19 .... 148 B5
Court Farm Rd
Chislehurst SE9 .... 166 A1
Northolt UB5 .... 63 C1
Courtfield W13 .... 87 C2
Courtfield Ave HA1 .... 42 D4
Courtfield Cres HA1.... 42 D4
Courtfield Gdns
Ealing W13............ 87 A1
Ruislip HA4............ 61 D6
South Kensington
SW5 .... 113 D2 255 D3
Courtfield Ho EC1..... 241 A4
Courtfield Mews SW7 255 D3
Courtfield Rd
Ashford TW15 .... 170 D4
Courtfield Rd *continued*
South Kensington
SW7 .... 114 A2 256 A3
Courtfield Rise BR4 ... 224 B5
Courtgate Cl NW7...... 27 D4
Court Gdns N7......... 72 C2
Courthill Rd SE13 ..... 142 A1
Courthope Ho
14 Rotherhithe SE16 ... 118 C3
South Lambeth SW8.... 270 A3
Courthope Rd
Gospel Oak NW3 .... 70 D4
Greenford UB6......... 86 B5
Wimbledon SW19 ..... 179 A5
Courthope Villas
SW19................ 179 A3
Court House Gdns N3 .. 29 C4
Court House Rd N12 ... 29 D4
Court La SE21......... 161 D4
Courtland Ave
Chingford E4 .... 20 D2
Edgware NW7 .... 11 C1
Redbridge IG1 .... 78 B6
South Norwood SW16 .. 182 B3
Courtland Gr SE28 .... 124 D6
Courtland Rd E6 ...... 100 A6
Courtlands
11 Beckenham BR3 .... 185 D1
8 Belmont SM2........ 217 D1
Ealing W5............. 87 C2
Richmond TW10....... 154 C6
5 Upper Clapton E5 .... 52 B1
Walton-on-T KT12 ..... 194 A2
Courtlands Ave
Hampton TW12 .... 173 B4
Hayes BR2 .... 208 D1
Lee SE12 .... 165 B6
Richmond TW9......... 132 D3
Courtland Sch NW7 .... 11 C2
Courtlands Cl HA4 ..... 39 D2
Courtlands Dr KT19 ... 215 D2
Courtlands Rd KT5 .... 198 C2
Court Lane Gdns
SE21................. 161 C4
Courtleet Dr DA8 ..... 147 D4
Courtleigh 6 NW11.... 47 B4
Courtleigh Ave EN4 ......2 B5
Courtleigh Gdns NW11 . 47 A5
Court Lo 11 DA17 ..... 125 C1
Courtman Rd N17...... 33 A3
Court Mans 8 W6 .... 112 A2
Court Mead UB5 .... 85 B4
Courtmead Cl SE24 ... 161 A5
Courtnell St W2 .... 91 C1
Courtney Cl SE19 ..... 183 C4
Courtney Cres SM5 ... 218 D1
Courtney Ct N7 .... 72 C3
Courtney Ho
1 Hendon NW4........ 46 C5
Kensington W14....... 254 B6
Courtney Pl CR0 ...... 220 C5
Courtney Rd
Croydon CR0 .... 220 C5
Islington N7........... 72 C3
Mitcham SW19........ 180 C3
Courtney Twrs IG2..... 57 B3
Courtney Way TW6.... 126 C2
Court One TW15 ...... 149 A1
Court Par HA0 .... 65 B5
Courtrai Rd SE23...... 163 A5
Court Rd
Eltham SE9........... 166 B4
Southall UB2 .... 107 B1
South Norwood SE25 ... 205 D6
Uxbridge UB10......... 60 D4
Court Royal SW15..... 157 A6
Courtside
Crouch End N8 .... 49 D3
Forest Hill SE23 ...... 162 C1
Court St
Bromley BR1 .... 187 A1
3 Stepney E1 .... 96 B2
Court The
London N10 .... 49 C5
Ruislip HA4........... 63 A4
Court Three TW15..... 149 A1
Court Two TW15...... 149 A1
Courtville Ho 12 W10... 91 A4
Courtway IG8 .... 37 C5
Court Way
Acton W3 .... 89 A2
Colindale NW9......... 45 C5
Ilford IG6............. 57 A6
Twickenham TW1,
TW2................ 152 D4
Courtyard Apartments
TW11............... 174 B5
Courtyard Mews BR5.. 190 A3
Courtyard The
Fulham SW6... 135 A4 264 A1
Courtyard The *continued*
Islington N1........... 72 B1
Keston BR2 .... 226 A2
Thornton Heath CR0.... 204 B3
13 Wandsworth SW18 .. 136 B1
Court Yd SE9 .... 166 B5
Cousin La EC4 . 117 B6 252 C5
Cousins Cl 2 UB7..... 104 A6
Cousins Ct 2 NW9..... 46 A5
Couthurst Rd SE3 ..... 143 B5
Coutts Ave KT9 .... 214 A3
Couzens Ho 8 E3...... 97 B2
Coval Gdns SW14 ..... 132 D1
Coval La SW14........ 132 D1
Coval Pas SW14....... 133 A1
Coval Rd SW14........ 133 A1
Covardale Ct EN3 .... 7 A6
Covelees Wall E6 ..... 100 C1
Covell Ct 16 SE8 ..... 141 C5
Covent Garden Sta
WC2 .... 94 A1 240 B1
Covent Gdn*
WC2 116 A6 250 B6
Coventry Cl
Kilburn NW6........... 91 C6
9 Newham E6......... 100 B1
Coventry Rd
Bethnal Green E1 .... 96 B3
Croydon SE25......... 206 A5
Ilford IG1............. 56 D1
Coventry St W1 .... 249 C5
Coverack Cl
Croydon CR0 .... 207 A2
Southgate N14 .... 15 C5
Coverdale Cl HA7 ...... 25 B5
Coverdale Gdns CR0 .. 221 D5
Coverdale Rd
Brondesbury NW2 ...... 69 A2
Friern Barnet N11 ...... 31 A4
Hammersmith W12 .... 112 B4
Hampstead NW6 .... 68 D1
Coverdales The IG11.. 101 B5
Coverham Ho 5 SE4 .. 140 D1
Coverley Cl E1 .... 96 A2
Coverley Point SE11... 260 C3
Coverton Rd SW17 .... 180 C5
Coverts Rd KT10 ...... 212 D1
Covert The BR6 .... 211 C3
Covert Way EN4 .... 2 A3
Covet Wood Cl BR5 ... 211 D3
Covey Cl SW19........ 179 D1
Covington Gdns
SW16 .... 182 D3
Covington Way
South Norwood
SW16 .... 182 C3
South Norwood SW16 .. 182 D3
Cowan Cl E6.......... 100 A2
Cowan Ct 14 NW10..... 67 B1
Cowan Lo 6 IG8....... 37 C4
Cowbridge La IG11 .... 78 D1
Cowbridge Rd HA3..... 44 B5
Cowcross St
EC1.......... 94 D2 241 C4
Cowdenbeath Path
N1 .... 233 C6
Cowden Rd BR6....... 211 D2
Cowden St SE6 .... 185 C6
Cowdray Hall Royal Coll
of Nursing
W1 .... 93 B1 238 C2
Cowdray Ho 22 SE22 .. 139 C2
Cowdray Rd UB10...... 83 A6
Cowdrey Cl EN1 .... 5 C3
Cowdrey Rd SW19 .... 180 A5
Cowdry Rd E9 .... 75 B2
Cowell Lo E4 .... 36 D5
Cowen Ave HA2........ 64 B6
Cowen Ho 4 SE18 .... 144 D6
Cowgate Rd UB6....... 86 B4
Cowick Rd SW17 ..... 180 D6
Cowings Mead UB5 .... 63 A2
Cowland Ave EN3 .... 6 C1
Cow Leaze E6 .... 100 C1
Cowleaze Rd KT2 ..... 176 A2
Cowley Ct 8 E18 ...... 37 A1
Cowley La E11 .... 76 C5
COWLEY PEACHY 82 A2
Cowley Pl NW4 .... 46 C4
Cowley Rd
Brixton SW9.......... 138 C4
East Acton W3 .... 111 D5
16 Kennington SW9.... 138 C5
Mortlake SW14 .... 133 C2
Redbridge IG1 .... 56 B2
Wanstead E11 .... 55 B4
Cowley St SW1 .... 260 A5
Cowling Cl W11....... 244 A4
Cowper Ave
Sutton SM1 .... 218 B4
Cowper Ave *continued*
Upton Pk E6 .... 78 A1
Cowper Cl
Bexley DA16.......... 168 A6
Bromley BR2 .... 209 D5
Cowper Gdns
Southgate N14......... 15 C5
Wallington SM6 .... 219 C2
Cowper Ho
Pimlico SW1.......... 259 D1
Walworth SE17 .... 262 B2
Cowper Rd
Acton W3 .... 111 B5
6 Belvedere DA17 .... 125 C2
Bromley BR2 .... 209 D5
Ealing W7............ 108 D6
East Barnet N14........ 15 B3
Edmonton N18 .... 34 A5
Kingston u T KT2....... 176 B5
Stoke Newington N16.... 73 C4
Wimbledon SW19 ..... 180 A4
Cowper's Ct EC3 ..... 242 D1
Cowper St EC1,
EC2.......... 95 B3 242 D6
Cowper Terr W10...... 90 D2
Cowslip Cl UB10 .... 60 A1
Cowslip Rd E18 .... 37 B1
Cowthorpe Rd SW8 ... 269 D2
Cox Ct 3 EN4........... 2 C1
Coxe Pl HA3 .... 43 A5
Cox Ho W6 .... 264 A6
Cox La
Chessington KT9 ...... 214 B4
West Ewell KT19 ...... 215 A3
Coxmount Rd SE7..... 121 D1
Coxs Ave TW17 .... 193 C6
Coxson Way SE1 ...... 253 C1
Coxwell Rd
Plumstead SE18....... 123 B1
South Norwood SE19 ... 183 C3
Coxwold Path KT9 .... 214 A1
Coysh Ct 8 SW15..... 157 A6
Crabbs Croft Cl 7
BR6 .... 227 A3
Crab Hill BR3 .... 186 B3
Crabtree Ave
Dagenham RM6 .... 58 D5
Wembley HA0.......... 88 B5
Crabtree Cl E2......... 95 D5
Crabtree Ct
Barnet EN5............. 1 D1
Temple Mills E15 .... 75 D3
Crabtree Hall SW6 .... 134 C5
Crabtree La SW6...... 134 D5
Cracknell Cl EN1.........6 B6
Craddock Rd EN1 .... 5 D2
Craddock St NW5....... 71 A2
Cradley Rd SE9 .... 167 B3
Cragie Ho SE1 .... 263 D3
Craig Dr UB8 .... 82 D1
Craigen Ave CR0...... 206 B1
Craigerne Rd SE3 ..... 143 B5
Craig Gdns E18 .... 36 D1
Craig Ho
Ealing W13........... 109 B6
Greenwich SE3........ 143 B5
Craigholm SE18 ...... 144 C4
Craigie Lea N10........ 31 B1
Craigleith SW15 ...... 156 D5
Craigmuir Pk HA0...... 88 B6
Craignair Rd SW2..... 160 C4
Craignish Ave SW16... 182 B1
Craig Park Rd N18 ..... 34 B6
Craig Rd TW10........ 175 C6
Craig's Ct SW1........ 250 A4
Craigside KT2 .... 176 D2
Craigton Rd SE9 ...... 144 B1
Craigweil Cl HA7....... 25 D5
Craigweil Dr HA7 ...... 25 D5
Craigwell Ave TW13... 150 A1
Craik Ct NW6 .... 91 B5
Crail Row
SE17......... 117 B2 262 D3
Crales Ho SE18 .... 122 A3
Cramer Ct KT3........ 199 A6
Cramer St W1 .. 93 A2 238 B3
Cramhurst Ho 3
SM1 .... 218 B3
Crammond Cl W6...... 264 A5
Cramond Ct TW14 .... 149 C3
Cramonde Ct DA16.... 146 A3
Crampton Rd SE20 .... 184 C4
Crampton Sch
SE17 .... 116 D1 261 D2
Crampton St
SE17......... 117 A1 262 A2
Cranberry Cl 2 UB5.... 84 D5
Cranberry La E16 ...... 98 C3
Cranborne Ave
Southall UB2 .... 107 C2
Cranborne Ave *continued*
Tolworth KT6, KT9 ..... 214 C5
Cranborne Rd IG11 ... 101 B6
Cranborne Waye
Hayes UB4............ 84 B1
Hayes UB4 .... 106 C6
Cranbourn Alley WC2 . 249 D6
Cranbourne Cl SW16.. 204 A6
Cranbourne Ct
East Finchley N2........ 47 D6
2 Edgware HA8 .... 26 D5
Finchley NW7.......... 29 A3
SW11............... 267 B4
Walton-on-T KT12 ..... 194 B2
Wanstead E18 .... 55 B5
Cranbourne Dr HA5.... 40 D4
Cranbourne Gdns
Ilford IG6............. 57 A6
Temple Fortune NW11 ... 47 B4
Cranbourne Rd
Leyton E15............ 76 A4
London N10 .... 31 B1
Manor Pk E12.......... 78 A3
Northwood HA6 .... 39 D6
Cranbourn Ho 6
SE16................ 118 B4
Cranbourn Pas 5
SE16................ 118 B4
Cranbourn St
WC2......... 115 D6 249 D6
CRANBROOK 56 C1
Cranbrook NW1 ...... 232 B5
Cranbrook Cl BR2..... 209 A3
Cranbrook Coll (Boys)
IG1 .... 78 C6
Cranbrook Ct
8 Brentford TW8 ..... 131 D6
South Croydon CR2 ... 221 C3
Cranbrook Dr
Thames Ditton KT10.... 196 A1
Twickenham TW2...... 151 D3
Cranbrook Ho
5 Hackney E5 .... 74 B3
South Norwood SE19 ... 183 B2
Cranbrook La N11 ..... 31 B6
Cranbrook Mews E17 .. 53 B4
Cranbrook Pk N22 ..... 32 C2
Cranbrook Rd
Chiswick W4........... 111 C1
Erith DA7 .... 147 B4
Hounslow TW4........ 129 B1
Ilford IG1, IG2 .... 56 C3
New Barnet EN4........ 14 B5
South Norwood CR7.... 183 A1
St Johns SE8 .... 141 C4
Wimbledon SW19 ..... 179 A3
Cranbrook Rise IG1.... 56 B2
Cranbrook St E2....... 96 D5
Cranbury Rd SW6..... 135 D3
Crandale Ho 8 E5 ..... 74 B3
Crandley Ct SE8 ...... 119 A2
Crane Ave
Acton W3 .... 111 A6
Isleworth TW7........ 153 A6
Cranebank TW4....... 128 B2
Cranebank Mews
TW1 .... 131 A1
Cranebrook TW2 ..... 152 A2
Crane Cl
Dagenham RM10 .... 81 C2
Harrow HA2........... 64 A5
Crane Ct
7 Acton W12......... 111 C4
Holborn EC4.......... 241 B1
West Ewell KT19 ...... 215 A4
Craneford Cl TW2..... 152 D4
Craneford Way TW2... 152 D4
Crane Gdns UB3 ...... 105 D2
Crane Gr N7 .... 72 C2
Crane Ho
24 Bow E3 .... 97 A5
9 Catford BR1 .... 186 B5
Feltham TW13 .... 151 C1
10 Peckham SE15 ..... 139 D4
Crane Lodge Rd TW5.. 128 B6
Crane Mead SE16 ..... 118 D2
Crane Mead Ct TW1... 152 D4
Crane Park Prim Sch
TW13 .... 151 B2
Crane Park Rd TW2 ... 151 D2
Crane Rd
Stanwell TW19........ 148 C5
Twickenham TW2...... 152 C3
Cranesbill Cl NW9 ..... 45 B6
Cranes Dr KT5 .... 198 B5
Cranes Park Ave KT5,
KT6................. 198 B5
Cranes Park Cres
KT5................. 198 B5
Cranes Pk KT5, KT6.... 198 A4

Crane St
Greenwich SE10 120 B1
6 Peckham SE15 139 D4
Craneswater TW6 127 D5
Craneswater Pk UB2 107 B1
Cranes Way WD6 11 A6
Crane Way TW2 152 A4
Cranfield Ct
Marylebone NW1 237 B3
2 Woodford IG8 37 A6
Cranfield Dr NW9 27 C3
Cranfield Ho WC1 240 B4
Cranfield Rd SE4 141 B2
CRANFORD 128 C4
Cranford Ave
Bowes Pk N13 32 A5
Stanwell TW19 148 B4
Cranford Cl
Stanwell TW19 148 A4
Wimbledon SW20 178 B3
Cranford Com Coll
TW5 128 B6
Cranford Cotts 8 E1 118 D6
Cranford Ct SM1 218 A4
Cranford Dr UB3 105 D2
Cranford Jun & Inf Schs
TW4 128 B3
Cranford La
Harlington TW6 127 D4
Harlington UB3 127 C5
Hatton TW6 127 D2
Heston TW5 128 C5
Cranford Lo SW19 156 D2
Cranford Park Prim Sch
UB3 105 D2
Cranford Park Rd
UB3 105 D2
Cranford Rise KT10 212 A3
Cranford St E1 118 D6
Cranford Way N8 50 C4
Cranhurst Rd NW2 68 C3
Cranleigh W11 244 C4
Cranleigh Cl
Bexley DA5 169 D5
Penge SE20 184 B1
Cranleigh Ct
1 Barnet EN5 1 D1
Mitcham CR4 202 B6
Richmond TW9 132 C2
Southall UB1 85 B1
4 Stamford Hill N16 51 C1
Cranleigh Gardens Ind Est
UB1 85 B2
Cranleigh Gdns
Barking IG11 79 B2
Harrow HA3 44 A4
Kingston u T KT2 176 B4
Southall UB1 85 B1
Southgate N21 16 C6
South Norwood SE25 205 C6
Sutton SM1 217 D6
Cranleigh Ho SW20 178 B1
Cranleigh Hos NW1 232 B3
Cranleigh Mews
SW11 136 D3
Cranleigh Rd
Feltham TW13 171 D6
Harringay N15 51 A4
Merton SW19 201 C6
Thames Ditton KT10 196 A1
Cranleigh St
NW1 93 C5 232 B3
Cranley Dene Ct N10 49 B5
Cranley Dr
Ilford IG2 57 A2
Ruislip HA4 61 D6
CRANLEY GARDENS 49 B5
Cranley Gdns
London N10 49 B5
Palmers Green N13 16 B1
South Kensington
SW7 114 B1 256 C2
Wallington SM6 219 C1
Cranley Mews
SW7 114 A1 256 B2
Cranley Par 2 SE9 188 A6
Cranley Pl
SW7 114 B2 256 C3
Cranley Rd
Ilford IG2 57 A2
Newham E13 99 B2
Cranmer Ave W13 109 B3
Cranmer Cl
Ruislip HA4 40 D1
Stanmore HA7 25 C3
West Barnes SM4 200 D3
Cranmer Ct
Chelsea SW3 257 B3
Church End N3 29 A1
Hampton TW12 173 D5
Cranmer Ct *continued*
Kingston u T KT2 175 D6
Cranmere Prim Sch
KT10 196 A1
Cranmer Farm Cl
CR4 202 D5
Cranmer Ho SW11 267 A2
Cranmer Prim Sch
CR4 202 D5
Cranmer Rd
Brixton SW9 138 C5
Croydon CR0 221 A5
Edgware HA8 10 D1
Forest Gate E7 77 B4
Hampton TW12 173 D5
Hayes UB3 83 B1
Kingston u T KT2 176 A5
Mitcham CR4 202 D5
Cranmer Terr SW17 180 B5
Cranmore Ave TW7 130 A5
Cranmore Rd
Catford BR1 164 D1
Elmstead BR7 188 B5
Cranmore Way N10 49 C5
Cranston Cl
Hounslow TW3, TW4 129 A3
Uxbridge UB10 61 B6
Cranston Ct 6 N20 14 D2
Cranston Gdns E4 35 D4
Cranston Rd SE23 163 A2
Cranswick Rd SE16 118 B1
Crantock Rd SE6 164 A2
Cranwell Cl E3 97 D3
Cranwell Ct
Croydon CR0 222 D6
6 Hendon NW9 27 D3
Cranwell Gr TW17 192 B5
Cranwell Rd TW6 126 D3
Cranwich Ave N21 17 B4
Cranwich Rd N16 51 C2
Cranwood Ct EC1 235 D1
Cranwood St
EC1 95 B4 235 D1
Cranworth Cres 7 E4 20 B3
Cranworth Gdns SW9 138 C4
Cranworth Ho 6 N7 72 B4
Craster Rd SW2 160 B4
Craston Ho 2 SE5 139 C3
Crathie Rd SE12 165 B5
Crathorne Ho N2 30 B1
Cravan Ave TW13 150 A2
Craven Ave
Ealing W5 109 C6
Southall UB1 85 B2
Craven Cl
Hayes UB4 84 A1
Stamford Hill N16 52 A2
Craven Cottage (Fulham FC) SW6 134 D4
Craven Ct
Dagenham RM6 59 A3
Edgware HA8 26 B6
Harlesden NW10 89 C6
Southall UB1 107 D5
Craven Gdns
Barking IG11 101 C5
Ilford IG6 57 B6
Wimbledon SW19 179 D5
Craven Hill
W2 114 A6 246 B6
Craven Hill Gdns
W2 114 A6 246 A6
Craven Hill Mews W2 246 B6
Craven Ho
Ealing W5 109 C6
16 Finchley N2 30 B1
2 Mortlake SW14 133 B2
Craven Lo
Bayswater W2 246 B6
Fulham SW6 134 D4
Craven Mews 6
SW11 137 A2
Craven Park Mews
NW10 89 C6
Craven Park Rd
Harlesden NW10 89 C6
South Tottenham N15 52 A3
Craven Pas WC2 250 A4
Craven Pk NW10 89 C6
Craven Rd
Croydon CR0 206 B1
Ealing W5 109 C6
Kingston u T KT2 176 B2
Paddington W2 92 A1 236 B1
Stonebridge NW10 89 B6
Craven St
WC2 116 A5 250 A4
Craven Terr
W2 114 A6 246 B6
Craven Wlk E5, N16 52 A2
Crawford Ave HA0 65 D3
Crawford Bldgs NW1 237 B3
Crawford Cl TW7 130 C3
Crawford Ct SE18 146 A6
Crawford Gdns
Edmonton N13 16 D1
Northolt UB5 85 B4
Crawford Mews W1 237 C3
Crawford Pas EC1 241 B5
Crawford Pl
W1 92 C2 237 B3
Crawford Place Dwellings
NW1 237 B3
Crawford Point 4 E16 98 D1
Crawford Prim Sch
SE5 139 A4
Crawford Rd SE5 139 A3
Crawford St
Marylebone
W1 92 D2 237 C3
16 Willesden NW10 67 B1
Crawley Rd
Enfield EN1 17 D4
Leyton E10 53 D1
Tottenham N22 33 A1
Crawshay Ct SW9 138 C4
Crawshay Ho 13 N16 73 B4
Crawthew Gr SE22 139 D1
Cray Bldgs DA14 190 C4
Craybrooke Rd DA14 190 B6
Craybury End SE9 167 A2
Crayfields Bsns Pk
BR5 190 C2
Crayfields Ind Pk
BR5 190 C1
Crayford Cl E6 100 A1
Crayford Ho
Bermondsey SE1 252 D1
5 Lower Holloway N7 72 A4
Crayford Rd N7 72 A4
Crayke Hill KT9 214 A1
Crayle Ho EC1 241 D6
Crayleigh Terr DA14 190 C4
Crayonne Cl TW16 171 C2
Cray Rd
Erith DA17 147 C6
Sidcup DA14 190 C4
Crays Par The BR5 190 C1
Crealock Gr IG8 36 D5
Crealock St SW18 157 D5
Creasy Est SE1 263 A5
Crebor St SE22 162 A5
Credenhall Dr BR2 210 B1
Credenhill Ho 2
SE15 140 B5
Credenhill St SW16 181 C4
Crediton Hill NW6 69 D3
Crediton Ho EN3 6 D2
Crediton Rd
Brondesbury Pk NW10 90 D6
Newham E16 99 A1
Crediton Way KT10 213 A3
Credon Rd
Bermondsey SE16 118 B1
Newham E13 99 C5
Creechurch La EC3 243 B1
Creechurch Pl EC3 243 B1
Creed Ct 5 E1 97 A4
Creed Ho SE15 140 B2
Creed La EC4 241 D1
Creek Ho W14 254 B6
CREEKMOUTH 101 D2
Creekmouth Ind Pk
IG11 101 D3
Creek Rd
Barking IG11 101 D4
East Molesey KT8 196 C5
Greenwich SE10, SE8 141 D6
Creek Road Ind Est
SE8 141 D6
Creekside SE8 141 D5
Creekside Foyer SE8 141 D6
Creek The TW16 194 A4
Creeland Gr SE6 163 B3
Crefeld Cl W6 135 A6 264 A5
Creffield Rd W3, W5 110 C6
Creighton Ave
London N2, N10 30 D1
Newham E6 99 D5
Creighton Cl W12 112 B6
Creighton Ho N2 48 C6
Creighton Rd
Ealing W5 109 D3
Kensal Rise NW6 90 D5
Tottenham N17 33 C3
Cremer Bsns Ctr 8
E2 95 D5
Cremer Ho 9 SE8 141 C5
Cremer St E2 95 D5
Cremorne Rd
SW10 136 B5 266 C4
Creon Ct 3 SW9 138 C4
Crescent EC3 253 C6
Crescent Arc 1 SE10 142 A6
Crescent Court Bsns Ctr
1 E16 98 B3
Crescent Ct
Clapham Pk SW4 159 D6
Crouch End N8 49 D3
Kingston u T KT6 197 D4
14 Sidcup DA15 168 A1
Crescent Dr BR5 211 A3
Crescent E EN4 2 A5
Crescent Gdns
Ruislip HA4 40 B2
Wimbledon SW19 157 C1
Crescent Gr
London SW4 137 C1
Mitcham CR4 202 C5
Crescent Ho
London SE13 141 D3
5 Wimbledon SW20 178 D2
Crescent La SW4 159 D6
Crescent Mans
Islington N5 72 D3
Notting Hill W11 244 B6
Crescent Par UB10 82 C4
Crescent Pl SW3 257 B4
Crescent Rd
Beckenham BR3 185 D1
Chingford E4 20 C4
Church End N3 29 B2
Crouch End N8 49 D3
Dagenham RM10 81 D5
East Barnet EN4 14 C6
Edmonton N9 18 A3
Enfield EN2 4 D1
Friern Barnet N11 30 D6
Harringay N15 50 D6
Kingston u T KT2 176 D3
Leyton E10 75 D6
Plaistow BR1 187 A3
Shepperton TW17 193 A4
Sidcup DA15 167 D1
Upton Pk E6 99 C6
West Ham E13 99 A6
Wimbledon SW20 178 D2
Woodford E18 37 C2
Wood Green N22 31 D2
Woolwich SE18 122 D2
Crescent Rise
East Barnet EN4 14 C6
3 Finchley N3 29 C2
Wood Green N22 31 D2
Crescent Row EC1 242 A5
Crescent St N1 72 B1
Crescent Stables
SW15 157 A6
Crescent The
Acton W3 89 C1
Ashford TW15 170 B5
Barnes SW13 134 A3
Barnet EN5 1 D3
Beckenham BR3 185 C2
Bexley DA5 168 C4
Coombe KT3 177 A1
Dollis Hill NW2 68 B5
East Finchley N2 47 D6
East Molesey KT8 195 C5
Friern Barnet N11 31 A6
Harlington UB7 127 B5
Harrow HA2 42 A1
Ilford IG2 56 C3
Loughton IG10 21 D5
Lower Halliford TW17 193 D2
Sidcup DA14 189 D6
Southall UB1 107 A4
Surbiton KT6 198 A4
Sutton SM1 218 B3
Thornton Heath CR0 205 B3
Walthamstow E17 53 A4
Wembley HA0 65 B6
West Wickham BR4 208 C3
Wimbledon SW19 157 C1
Crescent View IG10 21 D6
Crescent W EN4 2 A5
Crescentway N12 30 C4
Crescent Way
London SE4 141 C2
Orpington BR6 227 C3
South Norwood SW16 182 C3
Crescent Wood Rd SE21,
SE26 162 A1
Cresford Rd
SW6 135 D4 265 C1
Crespigny Rd NW4 46 B3
Cressage Cl UB1 85 C3
Cressage Ho 9 TW8 132 A6
Cressall Ho 14 E14 119 C3
Cresset Ho 8 E9 74 C2
Cresset Rd E9 74 C2
Cresset St SW4 137 D2
Cressfield Cl NW5 71 A3
Cressida Rd N19 49 D1
Cressingham Ct 1
DA17 125 C3
Cressingham Gr SM1 218 A4
Cressingham Rd
Burnt Oak HA8 27 B3
Lewisham SE13 142 A2
Cressington Cl 4 N16 73 C3
Cress Mews BR1 186 B5
Cresswell Gdns SW5 256 A2
Cresswell Ho HA9 66 A5
Cresswell Pk SE3 142 D2
Cresswell Pl
SW10 114 A1 256 B2
Cresswell Rd
Croydon SE25 206 A5
Feltham TW13 173 A6
Twickenham TW1 153 D5
Cresswell Way N21 16 C4
Cressy Ct
Hammersmith W6 112 B3
6 Stepney E1 96 C2
Cressy Ho SW13 134 B2
Cressy Hos 7 E1 96 C2
Cressy Pl E1 96 C2
Cressy Rd NW3 70 D4
Cresta Ct W5 88 B3
Cresta Ho
7 Bow E3 97 C3
Hampstead NW6 70 B1
Crestbrook Ave N13 16 D1
Crestbrook Pl N13 16 D1
Crest Ct NW4 46 C4
Crest Dr EN3 6 C5
Crestfield St N1, WC1 233 B2
Crest Gdns HA4 62 C5
Crest Ho 3 TW15 170 C5
Creston Way KT4 200 D1
Crest Rd
Dollis Hill NW2 68 A6
Hayes BR2 208 D2
South Croydon CR2 222 B1
Crest The
Edmonton N13 32 C6
Finchley N12 29 D4
Hendon NW4 46 C4
Surbiton KT5 198 C4
10 West Norwood
SW27 182 D5
Crestview NW5 71 B5
Crest View HA5 40 D5
Crest View Dr BR5 211 A4
Crestway SW15 156 B5
Crestwood Way TW4 151 A6
Creswell Dr BR3 207 D4
Creswick Ct W3 110 D6
Creswick Rd W3 110 D6
Creswick Wlk
7 Bow E3 97 C4
Temple Fortune NW11 47 B5
Creton St SE18 122 C3
Crewdson Rd SW9 138 C5
Crewe Pl NW10 89 D4
Crewkerne Ct SW11 266 D2
Crews St E14 119 C2
Crewys Rd
Child's Hill NW2 69 B6
London SE15 140 B3
Crichton Ave SM6 219 D4
Crichton Rd SM5 218 D1
Crichton St SW8 137 C3
Cricket Ct E6 100 B4
Cricketers Arms Rd
EN2 5 A3
Cricketers Cl
Chessington KT9 213 D4
Oakwood N14 15 C4
Cricketers Mews 4
SW18 157 D6
Cricketers Terr SM5 218 C5
Cricketers Wlk SE26 184 C5
Cricketfield Rd E5 74 B4
Cricket Gn CR4 202 D5
Cricket Green Sch
CR4 202 C6
Cricket Ground Rd
BR7 188 D2
Cricket La BR3 185 A4
Cricket Row N2 48 B6
Cricklade Ave SW2 160 B2
CRICKLEWOOD 68 D4
Cricklewood Broadway
NW2 68 D4
Cricklewood La NW2 69 B5
Cricklewood Sta NW2 68 D4
Cridland St E15 98 D6
Crieff Ct 3 TW11 175 C3
Crieff Rd SW18 158 A5
Criffel Ave SW2 159 D3
Crimscott St
SE1 117 C3 263 B5
Crimsworth Rd
SW8 137 D5 269 D3
Crinan St N1 94 A5 233 B4
Cringle St
SW8 137 C5 269 A4
Cripplegate St EC1 242 B4
Cripps Gn UB4 84 B3
Crispe Ho
4 Barking IG11 101 B5
Islington N1 233 D5
Crispen Rd TW13 173 A6
Crispian Cl NW10 67 C4
Crispin Cl SM6 220 A6
Crispin Cres SM6 219 D6
Crispin Ct SE17 263 A3
Crispin Pl E1 243 C4
Crispin Rd HA8 27 A4
Crispin St E1 95 D2 243 C3
Crispin Way UB8 82 B3
Crisp Rd W6 112 C1
Cristowe Rd SW6 135 B3
Criterion Bldgs KT7 197 B2
Criterion Mews N19 71 D6
Crittall's Cnr DA14 190 C3
Crittenden Lo BR4 207 C1
Crockerton Rd SW17 158 D2
Crockham Way SE9 188 C6
Crocus Cl CR0 206 D1
Crocus Field EN5 13 B5
Croft Ave BR4 208 A1
Croft Cl
Edgware NW7 11 C1
Elmstead BR7 188 B5
Erith DA17 125 B1
Harlington UB7 127 A5
Hillingdon UB10 60 C1
Croft Ct
London SE13 164 A5
Ruislip HA4 39 D1
Croftdown Rd NW5 71 B5
Croft End Cl KT9 214 B5
Crofters Cl TW7 152 B6
Crofters Ct 9 SE8 119 A2
Crofters Way
NW1 93 D6 232 C6
Croft Gdns
Ealing W7 109 A4
Ruislip HA4 39 D1
Croft Ho
Putney SW15 157 A5
11 West Kilburn W10 91 A4
Croft Lodge Cl IG8 37 B4
Croft Mews 3 N12 14 A1
CROFTON 227 B6
Crofton Ave
Chiswick W4 133 B5
Orpington BR6 227 A6
Sidcup DA5 168 D4
Crofton Gate Way
SE4 163 A6
Crofton Gr E4 36 B6
Crofton Inf Sch BR5 211 B2
Crofton Jun Sch BR5 211 B2
Crofton La BR5, BR6 211 B2
Crofton L Ctr SE4 163 C5
Crofton Park Rd SE4 163 B5
Crofton Park Sta SE4 163 A6
Crofton Rd
Camberwell SE5 139 C3
Locksbottom BR6 226 C5
Newham E13 99 B3
Crofton Roman Villa*
BR6 227 C6
Crofton Sch SE4 163 C5
Crofton Terr
Homerton E5 75 A3
Richmond TW9 132 B1
Crofton Way
Enfield EN2 4 C3
New Barnet EN5 13 D5
Croft Rd
Carshalton SM1 218 C3
Enfield EN3 7 A4
Merton SW19 180 A3
Plaistow BR1 187 A4
South Norwood SW16 182 C3
Crofts Ho 21 E2 96 A5
Croftside The 3
SE25 206 A6
Crofts La N22 32 C3
Crofts Rd HA1 43 A4
Crofts St E1 118 A6

Croft St SE8 119 A2
Crofts The TW17 193 C5
Croft The
Barnet EN5 1 A1
Chingford E4 20 C2
Ealing W5 88 A2
Edgware HA8 26 D3
Harlesden NW10 89 D5
Heston TW5 129 A5
New Malden KT3 199 C4
Pinner HA5 41 B2
Ruislip HA4 62 C4
Wembley HA0 65 C3
Croft Villas HA1 43 A3
Croft Way
Richmond TW10 153 B1
Sidcup DA15 167 C1
Crogsland Rd NW1 71 A1
Croham Cl CR2 221 C1
Croham Hurst Sch
CR2 221 D3
Croham Manor Rd
CR2 221 C2
Croham Mount CR2 221 C1
Croham Park Ave
CR2 221 D3
Croham Rd CR2 221 C3
Croham Valley Rd
CR2 222 B1
Croindene Rd SW16 182 A2
Crokesley Ho 2 HA8 27 A1
Cromartie Rd N19 49 D2
Cromarty Ct 7 BR1 187 C1
Cromarty Ho 8 E1 97 A2
Cromarty Rd HA8 10 D2
Cromberdale Ct N17 34 A2
Crombie Cl IG4 56 B4
Crombie Mews 5
SW11 136 C3
Crombie Rd DA15 167 B3
Cromdale Ct N16 51 D2
Crome Ho UB5 85 A5
Cromer Cl UB8 83 A1
Cromer Ct
Streatham SW16 160 A1
Wandsworth SW18 157 B5
Crome Rd NW10 67 C2
Cromer Mans 6
SM1 217 D3
Cromer Pl 5 BR6 211 B1
Cromer Rd
Barnet EN5 2 A2
Croydon SE25 206 B6
Dagenham RM6 59 A3
Harlington TW6 126 C3
Leyton E10 54 B2
Streatham SW17 181 A4
Tottenham N17 34 A1
Woodford IG8 37 A6
Cromer Road Prim Sch
EN5 2 A2
Cromer St WC1 94 A4 233 B1
Cromer Terr
Dalston E8 74 A3
3 Ilford RM6 58 B4
Cromer Villas Rd
SW18 157 B5
Cromford Cl BR6 227 C5
Cromford Path 1 E5 74 D4
Cromford Rd SW18 157 C6
Cromford Way KT3 177 B2
Cromlix Cl BR7 188 D1
Crompton Ct SW3 257 A4
Crompton Ho
Borough The SE1 262 B5
Paddington W2 236 C5
South Lambeth SW8 269 B1
Crompton Pl EN3 7 C5
Crompton St
W2 92 B3 236 C5
Cromwell Ave
Bromley BR2 209 B5
Hammersmith W6 112 B2
Highgate N6 49 B1
New Malden KT3 199 D4
Cromwell Cl
Acton W3 111 A5
Bromley BR2 209 B5
East Finchley N2 48 B5
2 Gunnersbury W4 110 D1
Walton-on-T KT12 194 B1
Cromwell Cres
SW5 113 C2 255 A4
Cromwell Ct
Enfield EN3 18 D6
15 Kingston u T KT2 176 C3
Wembley HA0 88 A5
Cromwell Ctr
Barking IG11 102 A4
North Acton NW10 89 B4
Cromwell Ctr The RM8 59 B2
Cromwell Est E10 53 A1
Cromwell Gdns
SW7 114 B3 256 D5
Cromwell Gr W6 112 C3
Cromwell Ho
Battersea SW11 268 B1
2 Croydon CR0 220 D5
Muswell Hill N10 31 B3
Putney SW15 134 A1
Cromwell Hospl
SW5 113 D2 255 C4
Cromwell Lo
Barking IG11 79 C3
40 Bethnal Green E1 96 C3
Cromwell Mans SW5 255 B4
Cromwell Mews SW7 256 D4
Cromwell Pl
5 Acton W3 111 A5
Highgate N6 49 B1
Mortlake SW14 133 A2
South Kensington
SW7 114 B2 256 D4
Cromwell Rd
Beckenham BR3 207 A6
Brixton SW9 138 D4
Feltham TW13 150 B3
Finchley N3 30 A2
Hayes UB3 83 B1
Hounslow TW3 129 C1
Kingston u T KT2 176 A2
Muswell Hill N10 31 A3
South Kensington SW7 256 B4
Teddington TW11 175 A4
Thornton Heath CR0 205 B2
Upton E7 77 C1
Walthamstow E17 54 A4
Walton-on-T KT12 194 B1
Wembley HA0 88 A5
Wimbledon SW19 179 D5
Worcester Pk KT4 215 C5
Cromwell St TW3 129 C1
Cromwell Trad Ctr
IG11 101 C4
Cromwell Twr EC2 242 B4
Crondace Rd
SW6 135 C4 265 B1
Crondall Ct 7 N1 95 C5
Crondall Ho SW15 156 A3
Crondall Pl 15 N1 95 C5
Crondall St N1 95 C5
Crone Ct 5 NW6 91 B5
Cronin St SE15 139 D5
CROOKED BILLET 178 C4
Crooked Billet
Chingford E4 35 C3
Wimbledon SW19 178 C4
Crooked Billet Yd 18
E2 95 C4
Crooked Usage N3 47 A6
Crooke Rd SE8 119 A1
Crookham Rd
SW6 135 B4 264 C1
Crook Log DA6 146 D1
Crook Log L Ctr DA7 146 D2
Crook Log Prim Sch
DA6 146 D1
Crookston Rd SE9 144 C2
Croombs Rd E16 99 C2
Croom's Hill SE10 142 B5
Croom's Hill Gr SE10 142 A5
Cropley Ct N1 235 C4
Cropley St N1 95 B5 235 C4
Croppath Rd RM10 81 C4
Cropthorne Ct W9 229 B1
Crosbie 10 NW9 27 D1
Crosbie Ho 20 E17 53 D6
Crosby Cl TW13 173 A6
Crosby Ct
Borough The SE1 252 C2
East Finchley N2 48 A5
7 New Southgate N11 31 B6
Crosby Ho
18 Cubitt Town E14 120 A3
Forest Gate E7 77 A2
Crosby Rd
Dagenham RM10 103 D6
Upton E7 77 A2
Crosby Row
SE1 117 B4 252 C2
Crosby Sq EC3 243 A2
Crosby Wlk
3 Dalston E8 73 D2
Streatham SE24 160 C4
Crosfield Ct 3 W10 90 D1
Crosfield Ho W11 244 A5
Crosier Cl SE3 144 A3
Crosier Rd UB10 61 A4
Crosier Way HA4 61 C5
Crosland Pl 5 SW11 137 A2
Crossbow Ho
Ealing W13 109 B5
15 Shoreditch N1 95 C6
Crossbrook Rd SE3 144 A2
Cross Cl SE15 140 B3
Cross Ct
London SE5 139 B2
11 Thamesmead SE28 124 B6
Cross Deep TW1 153 A2
Cross Deep Gdns
TW1 152 D2
Crossfield Rd
Hampstead NW3 70 B2
London N17 51 A6
Crossfield St SE8 141 C5
Crossford St SW9 138 B3
Crossgate
Edgware HA8 10 C1
Wembley UB6 65 B2
Crossharbour Sta
E14 119 D3
Cross Ho N8 50 B5
Cross Keys Cl
5 Edmonton N9 18 A2
Marylebone W1 238 B3
Cross La
City of London EC3 253 A5
Hornsey N8 50 B5
Old Bexley DA5 169 B4
Cross Lances Rd
TW3 129 D1
Crossland Rd CR7 204 D3
Crosslands Ave
Ealing W5 110 B5
Southall UB2 107 B1
Crosslands Rd KT19 215 B2
Crossleigh Ct
3 New Cross SE14 141 B5
Streatham SW16 181 B6
Crosslet St SE17 262 D4
Crosslet Vale SE10 141 D4
Crossley St N7 72 C2
Crossman Hos 19
SW12 160 A4
Crossmead SE9 166 B3
Crossmead Ave UB6 85 C4
Crossmount Ho 13
SE5 139 A5
Crossness Rd IG11 101 D4
Cross Rd
Belmont HA3 25 A1
Camberwell SE5 139 C3
Chingford E4 20 C3
Croydon CR0 205 B1
Enfield EN1 5 C1
Feltham TW13 173 A6
Finchley N2 30 C1
Friern Barnet N11 31 B5
Harrow HA1 42 B4
Ilford RM6 58 C2
Keston Mark BR2 226 A6
Kingston u T KT2 176 B3
Merton SW19 179 C3
Romford RM7 59 C6
Sidcup DA14 190 B6
South Harrow HA2 63 D5
Sutton SM1 218 B3
Wood Green N22 32 C3
Cross St
2 Edmonton N18 34 A5
Hampton TW12 174 A5
Islington N1 94 D6 234 D6
Mortlake SW13 133 C2
Crossthwaite Ave SE5,
SE24 139 B1
Crosstrees Ho 7 E14 119 C3
Crosswall EC3 117 D6 253 C6
Crossway
Dagenham RM8 80 C5
Ealing W13 87 A3
Enfield EN1 17 C4
Finchley N12 30 B4
Hayes UB3 106 A5
Hendon NW9 45 D5
Kingsland E8, N16 73 C3
Petts Wood BR5 211 B4
Pinner HA5 22 B1
Ruislip HA4 62 C4
Thamesmead SE28 102 D1
West Barnes KT3,
SW20 200 C5
Woodford IG8 37 C6
Crossway Ct SE4 141 A3
Crossway Par N22 32 D3
Crossways
Ashford TW16 171 D3
South Croydon CR2 223 B1
Crossways *continued*
Sutton SM2 218 B1
Crossways Acad SE4 141 A3
Crossways Par CR2 223 B1
Crossways Rd
Beckenham BR3 207 C5
Mitcham CR4 203 B6
Crossways The
Heston TW5 129 B5
Wembley HA9 66 C6
Crossway The
Chislehurst SE9 165 D2
Hillingdon UB10 82 B5
Tottenham N22 32 D3
Cross Way The HA3 24 C1
Crosswell Cl TW17 171 A1
Croston St E8 96 A6
Crothall Cl N13 16 B1
Crouch Ave IG11 102 B5
Crouch Cl BR3 185 C4
Crouch Croft SE9 166 C1
CROUCH END 49 D3
Crouch End Hill N8 49 D2
Crouch Hall Ct N19 50 A1
Crouch Hall Rd N8 49 D3
Crouch Hill N4, N8, N19 50 A2
Crouch Hill Sta N4 50 B2
Crouchmans Cl SE21,
SE26 162 A1
Crouch Rd NW10 67 B1
Crowborough Ct
W13 109 C6
Crowborough Path
WD19 22 D6
Crowborough Rd
SW17 181 A5
Crowden Way SE28 124 C6
Crowder Cl N12 30 A3
Crowder St E1 118 B6
Crowfield Ho N5 73 A4
Crowfoot Cl
Hackney Wick E9 75 B3
Woolwich SE28 123 C5
Crowhurst SE25 206 A6
Crowhurst Cl SW9 138 C3
Crowhurst Ct N17 34 B2
Crowhurst Ho 21
SW9 138 B3
Crow La RM7, RM8 59 D2
Crowland Ave UB3 105 D2
Crowland Gdns N14 16 A4
Crowland Ho NW8 229 A5
Crowland Prim Sch
N15 52 A4
Crowland Rd
South Norwood CR7 205 B5
South Tottenham N15 51 D4
Crowlands Ave RM7 59 D3
Crowland Terr N1 73 B1
Crowland Wlk SM4 202 A3
Crowley Cres CR0 220 C3
Crowline Wlk 1 N1 73 A2
Crowmarsh Gdns
SE23 162 C4
Crown Arc KT1 175 D1
Crown Bldgs 4 E4 20 B3
Crownbourne Ct
SM1 217 D4
Crown Cl
Bow E3 97 C6
Edgware NW7 11 D2
Hampstead NW6 69 D2
Hayes UB3 105 D4
Walton-on-T KT12 194 C2
Wood Green N22 32 C2
Crown Close Bsns Ctr 12
E3 97 C6
Crown Ct
Bromley BR1 209 D4
City of London EC4 242 B1
Harrow HA2 42 C1
Lee SE12 165 B5
11 Muswell Hill N10 31 A3
4 Putney SW15 134 D1
St Giles WC2 240 B1
St John's Wood NW8 230 B1
3 Twickenham TW1 153 B4
Crown Dale SE19 183 A5
Crowndale Ct NW1 232 C4
Crowndale Rd
NW1 93 C5 232 B4
Crowne Ho SE1 252 B3
Crownfield Ave IG2 57 C4
Crownfield Rd E15 76 B4
Crowngate Ho 33 E3 97 B5
Crown Hill CR0 221 A5
Crownhill Rd NW10 89 D6
Crown Ho
Ruislip HA4 40 A1
Wembley HA9 66 B3
Crown Ho *continued*
Woolwich SE18 123 A2
Crown La
Bromley Comm BR2 209 D4
Chislehurst BR7 189 A2
Merton SM4 201 C6
Osidge N14 15 C3
South Norwood SE19,
SW16 182 C5
Crown Lane Gdns
SE27 182 C5
Crown Lane Prim Sch
SE27 182 D5
Crown Lane Spur
BR2 209 D3
Crownleigh Ct SW2 160 C6
Crown Lo
Chelsea SW3 257 B3
Finchley N3 29 B1
Crownmead Way RM7 59 D5
Crown Mews
2 Newham E13 99 C6
9 Stepney E1 96 D2
Crown Mill CR4 202 C4
Crown Office Row
EC4 251 A6
Crown Par
London N14 15 C3
Morden SM4 201 D5
Crown Pas
Kingston u T KT1 175 D1
St James SW1 249 B3
Crown Pl
Broadgate EC2 243 A4
Kentish Town NW5 71 B2
Crown Point Par
SE19 182 D4
Crown Rd
Enfield EN1 6 B2
Ilford IG6 57 B5
Kingston u T KT3 177 A2
Morden SM4 201 D5
Muswell Hill N10 31 A3
Ruislip HA4 62 D3
Sutton SM1 217 D4
Twickenham TW1 153 B5
Crown Reach SW1 259 D1
Crown St
Acton W3 110 D5
Camberwell SE5 139 A5
Dagenham RM10 81 D2
Harrow HA2 42 C1
Crownstone Ct 1
SW2 160 C6
Crownstone Rd SW2 160 C6
Crown Terr TW9 132 B1
Crown Trad Ctr UB3 105 C4
Crowntree Cl TW7 130 D6
Crown Way UB7 104 B5
Crown Wlk HA9 66 B5
Crown Wood La SE18 144 D3
Crown Woods Sch
SE9 167 A6
Crown Woods Way
SE9 167 B6
Crown Yard TW3 130 A2
Crowshott Ave HA7 25 D2
Crows Rd
Barking IG11 78 D2
Mill Meads E15 98 B4
Crowther Ave TW8 110 A2
Crowther Cl
SW6 135 B6 264 D5
Crowther Rd SE25 206 A5
Crowthorne Cl SW18 157 B3
Crowthorne Rd W10 90 D1
Croxall Ho KT12 194 C3
Croxden Cl HA8 44 C6
Croxden Wlk SM4 202 A3
Croxford Gdns N22 32 D3
Croxley Cl BR5 190 B1
Croxley Gn BR5 190 B2
Croxley Rd W9 91 B4
Croxted Cl SE21 161 A4
Croxted Rd SE21,
SE24 161 B3
Croxteth Ho 11 SW8 137 D3
Croxton 17 KT1 176 C1
Croyde Ave
Greenford UB6 86 A4
Hayes UB3 105 C2
Croyde Cl DA15 167 B4
Croyden Ct HA0 65 D2
CROYDON 221 B5
Croydon N17 33 B1
Croydon Airport Ind Est
CR0 220 B2
Croydon Coll CR0 221 B6
Croydon Coll Annexe
CR0 205 B1
Croydon Coll (Selhurst
Tertiary Ctr) SE25 205 B4
Croydon Flyover The
CR0 221 A5
Croydon Gr CR0 204 D1
Croydon Ho
Lambeth SE1 251 B2
Thornton Heath CR0 204 B3
Croydon Rd
Bandonhill CR0, SM5,
SM6 219 C5
Beckenham BR3 207 A6
Coney Hall BR2, BR4 224 D5
Harlington TW6 126 D2
Keston Mark BR2, BR4,
BR6 225 C5
Mitcham CR0, CR4 203 C4
Newham E13 98 D3
Penge SE20 184 C2
Waddon CR0 220 B4
Croydon Rd Ind Est
BR3 206 D5
Croydon Valley Trade Pk
2 CR0 204 A2
Croyland Rd N9 18 A3
Croylands Dr KT6 198 A2
Croysdale Ave TW16 194 A6
Crozier Ho
Blackheath Pk SE3 143 B2
South Lambeth SW8 270 C3
Crozier Terr E9 74 D3
Crucible Cl RM6 58 B3
Crucifix La
SE1 117 C4 253 A2
Cruden Ho
15 Bow E3 97 B5
11 Camberwell SE17 138 D6
Cruden St N1 94 D6 234 D5
Cruickshank St WC1 234 A2
Cruikshank Ho NW8 230 B4
Cruikshank Rd E15 76 C3
Crummock Gdns NW9 45 C4
Crumpsall St SE2 124 C2
Crundale Ave NW9 44 C4
Crunden Rd CR2 221 B1
Crusader Gdns CR0 221 C5
Crusader Ho EC1 241 C5
Crusader Ind Est N4 51 A3
Crusoe Ct E11 76 D5
Crusoe House Sch
N1 95 B4 235 C2
Crusoe Mews N16 73 B6
Crusoe Rd CR4 180 D3
Crutched Friars
EC3 117 C6 253 B6
Crutchfield La KT12 194 B1
Crutchley Rd SE6 164 C2
Crystal Ct SE19 183 D5
Crystal Ctr The 1
HA1 42 D4
Crystal Ho SE18 123 D1
CRYSTAL PALACE 184 A5
Crystal Palace Mus*
SE19 183 D4
Crystal Palace National
Sports Ctr SE20 184 A4
Crystal Palace Par
SE19 183 D5
Crystal Palace Park Rd
SE26 184 B5
Crystal Palace Rd
SE22 162 A6
Crystal Palace Sta
SE19 184 A4
Crystal Palace Station Rd
SE19 184 A4
Crystal Terr SE19 183 B4
Crystal View Ct BR1 186 B6
Crystal Way
Dagenham RM8 58 C1
Harrow HA1 42 D4
Crystal Wharf N1 234 D3
Cuba Dr EN3 6 C3
Cuba St E14 119 C4
Cubitt Bldg SW1 258 C1
Cubitt Ho 4 SW4 159 C5
Cubitt Sq UB2 108 A5
Cubitt St WC1 94 B4 233 D1
Cubitt Terr SW4 137 C2
CUBITT TOWN 120 A2
Cubitt Town Jun & Inf Sch
E14 120 A3
Cuckoo Ave W7 86 C3
Cuckoo Dene W7 86 B2
Cuckoo Hall La N9 18 D4
Cuckoo Hall Prim Sch
N9 18 C4
Cuckoo Hill HA5 40 C6
Cuckoo Hill Dr HA5 40 C6
Cuckoo Hill Rd HA5 40 D5

Cuckoo La W7 108 C6
Cuda's Cl KT19 215 D4
Cuddington SE17 262 B4
Cuddington Ave KT19, KT4 215 D5
Cuddington Com Prim Sch KT4 215 D5
Cudham La N BR6 227 C1
Cudham St SE6 164 A4
Cudworth Ho SW8 269 B1
Cudworth St E1 96 B3
Cuff Cres SE9 165 D5
Cuffley Ho 3 W10 90 C2
Cuff Point 12 E2 95 D4
Culand Ho SE17 263 A3
Culford Gdns SW3 114 D2 257 D3
Culford Gr N1 73 C2
Culford Mans SW3 257 D3
Culford Mews N1 73 C2
Culford Rd
Kingsland N1 73 C2
Shoreditch N1 95 C6
Culgaith Gdns EN2 4 A1
Culham Ho
21 Paddington W2 91 C2
33 Shoreditch E2 95 D4
Cullen Ho W9 91 B5
Cullen Way NW10 89 A3
Culling Rd SE16 118 C3
Cullington Cl HA3 43 A5
Cullingworth Rd NW10 68 B3
Culloden Cl 21 SE16 118 A1
Culloden Prim Sch E14 98 A1
Culloden Rd EN2 4 D3
Cullum St EC3 253 A6
Culmington Mans W13 109 C6
Culmington Par W13 109 C6
Culmington Rd
Ealing W13, W5 109 C5
South Croydon CR2 221 A1
Culmore Rd SE15 140 C5
Culmstock Rd SW11 159 A6
Culpepper Cl N18 34 B5
Culpepper Ct SE11 261 A4
Culross Bldgs NW1 233 A4
Culross Cl N15 51 A5
Culross St W1 115 A6 248 A5
Culsac Rd KT6 214 A6
Culver Ct SW18 157 D5
Culverden Rd SW12 159 C2
Culver Gr HA7 25 C1
Culverhouse WC1 240 C3
Culverhouse Gdns SW16 160 B1
Culverin Ct 1 N7 72 B3
Culverlands Cl HA7 25 B6
Culverlands Ct N20 14 B3
Culverley Rd SE6 164 A3
Culvers Ave SM5 218 D6
Culvers House Prim Sch CR4 203 A1
Culvers Retreat SM5 218 D6
Culverstone Cl BR2 208 D4
Culvers Way SM5 218 D6
Culvert Ct SW11 137 A3
Culverton Ct 8 DA14 190 A6
Culvert Pl SW11 137 A3
Culvert Rd
London SW11 136 D3
South Tottenham N15 51 C4
Culworth Ho NW8 230 A4
Culworth St NW8 230 A3
Cumber Ho SW18 157 C3
Cumberland Ave
Falconwood DA16 145 D1
Wembley NW10 88 D4
Cumberland Bsns Pk NW10 88 D4
Cumberland Cl
Dalston E8 73 D2
2 Twickenham TW1 153 B5
8 Wimbledon SW20 178 D3
Cumberland Cres W14 254 B4
Cumberland Ct
4 Croydon CR0 205 B1
7 Finchley N3 29 B1
Harrow HA1 42 C6
Marylebone W1 237 D1
Woodford IG8 37 B3
Cumberland Dr
Chessington KT9 214 B5
Erith DA7 147 A5
Hinchley Wood KT10 213 A6
Cumberland Gate W1 114 D6 247 D6
Cumberland Gdns
Church End NW4 29 A1
Finsbury WC1 234 A2
Cumberland Ho
Edmonton N9 18 C3
Kingston u T KT2 176 D3
Paddington W9 236 A5
1 Putney SW15 156 C4
Woolwich SE28 123 B4
Cumberland Mans
Marylebone W1 237 C2
7 West Hampstead NW6 69 C3
Cumberland Market NW1 93 B4 231 D2
Cumberland Mills Sq E14 120 B1
Cumberland Park Ind Est NW10 90 A4
Cumberland Pk W3 111 A6
Cumberland Pl
Catford SE6 164 D3
Regent's Pk NW1 231 C2
Sunbury TW16 194 A5
Cumberland Rd
Acton W3 111 A6
Ashford TW15 148 A1
Barnes SW13 134 A4
Beckenham BR2 208 D6
Croydon SE25 206 B3
Edmonton N9 18 C3
Hanwell W7 108 D4
Harrow HA1 41 D4
Higham Hill E17 35 A1
Manor Pk E12 77 D4
Newham E13 99 B3
Richmond TW9 132 C5
Stanmore HA7, HA8 44 B6
Wood Green N22 32 B1
Cumberland Sch E13 99 C3
Cumberland St SW1 115 B1 258 D2
Cumberland Terr NW1 231 C3
Cumberland Terrace Mews NW1 231 C3
Cumberland Villas W3 111 A6
Cumberland Wharf 12 SE16 118 C4
Cumberlow Ave SE25 206 A6
Cumbernauld Gdns TW16 171 D5
Cumberton Rd N17 33 B2
Cumbrae Gdns KT6 213 D6
Cumbrian Gdns NW2 69 A6
Cuming Mus* SE17 262 A3
Cumming St N1 233 D3
Cumnor Cl 23 SW9 138 B3
Cumnor Gdns KT17 216 A2
Cumnor Rd SM2 218 A2
Cunard Cres N21 17 B5
Cunard Pl EC3 243 B1
Cunard Rd NW10 89 B4
Cunard Wlk 3 SE16 119 A2
Cundy Rd E16 121 D6
Cundy St SW1 115 A2 258 B3
Cunliffe Rd KT19 215 D4
Cunliffe St SW16 181 C4
Cunningham Cl
Dagenham RM6 58 C4
West Wickham BR4 223 D6
Cunningham Ct
Harrow HA1 42 B4
Paddington W2 236 C5
Cunningham Ho 16 SE5 139 B5
Cunningham Pk HA1 42 B4
Cunningham Pl NW8 92 B3 236 C6
Cunningham Rd N15 52 A5
Cunnington St W4 111 A2
Cupar Rd SW11 268 B2
Cupola Cl BR1 187 B5
Cureton St SW1 115 D2 259 D3
Curie Gdns NW9 27 C1
Curie Ho 1 HA9 67 A5
Curlew Cl SE28 124 D6
Curlew Ct KT6 214 C5
Curlew Ho
Brockley SE4 141 A1
Enfield EN3 18 D6
7 Peckham SE15 139 D4
Curlew St SE1 117 D4 253 D2
Curlew Way UB4 84 D2
Curness St SE13 142 A1
Curnick's La SE27 183 A6
Curran Ave
Bexley DA15 167 D6
Curran Ave *continued*
Hackbridge SM6 219 A5
Curran Ho SW3 257 A3
Currey Rd UB6 64 B2
Curricle St W3 111 C5
Currie Hill Cl SW19 179 B6
Currie Ho 13 SW12 159 D4
Curry Rise NW7 28 D4
Cursitor St EC4 94 C1 241 A2
Curtain Pl EC2 243 B6
Curtain Rd EC2 95 C3 243 B6
Curthwaite Gdns EN2 15 D6
Curtis Dr W3 89 B1
Curtis Field Rd SW16 182 C6
Curtis Ho
7 London N11 31 C5
Walworth SE17 262 C2
Curtis La HA0 66 A3
Curtis Rd
Twickenham TW4 151 B4
West Ewell KT19 215 A4
Curtis St SE1 117 D2 263 C4
Curtis Way
Bermondsey SE1 263 C4
7 Thamesmead SE28 124 B6
Curtlington Ho 3 HA8 27 A1
Curve Bldg The SE4 163 B6
Curve The
Ealing W5 109 D4
Shepherd's Bush W12 112 A6
Curwen Ave E7 77 B4
Curwen & New Acad Gall* W1 239 C3
Curwen Prim Sch E13 99 A5
Curwen Rd W12 112 A4
Curzon Ave
Enfield EN3 18 D6
Stanmore HA7 25 A2
Curzon Cl BR6 227 B4
Curzon Cres
Barking IG11 101 D4
Willesden NW10 67 C1
Curzon Ct SE9 167 A1
Curzon Gate W1 248 B3
Curzon Ho W5 87 B3
Curzon Pl HA5 40 C4
Curzon Rd
Ealing W5 87 B3
Muswell Hill N10 31 B1
Thornton Heath CR7 204 C3
Curzon Sq W1 248 B3
Curzon St W1 115 B5 248 C4
Cusack Cl TW1 174 D6
Custance Ho N1 235 C3
Custance St N1 235 C2
CUSTOM HOUSE 121 C6
Custom House EC3 117 C6 253 A5
Custom House for ExCeL Sta E16 121 B6
Custom House Reach SE16 119 B3
Cutbush Ho N7 71 D3
Cutcombe Rd SE5 139 A3
Cuthberga Cl IG11 79 A1
Cuthbert Gdns SE25 205 C6
Cuthbert Harrowing Ho EC1 242 A5
Cuthbert Ho W2 236 C4
Cuthbert Rd
Croydon CR0 220 D6
8 Edmonton N18 34 A6
Walthamstow E17 54 A6
Cuthbert St W2 236 C5
Cuthill Wlk 3 SE5 139 B4
Cutlers Gdns EC2 243 B2
Cutlers Gdns Arc EC2 243 B2
Cutlers Sq E14 119 C2
Cutler St EC2 243 B2
Cut The SE1 116 C4 251 B2
Cutty Sark* SE10 142 A6
Cutty Sark Ho 10 E14 119 D2
Cutty Sark Ret Development SE10 142 A6
Cutty Sark Sta SE10 142 A6
Cuxton BR5 211 A4
Cuxton Cl DA6 169 A6
Cuxton Ho SE17 263 B2
Cyclamen Cl 4 TW12 173 C4
Cyclamen Way KT19 215 A3
Cyclops Mews 12 E14 119 C2
Cygnet Ave TW14 150 D4
Cygnet Cl NW10 67 B3
Cygnet Ct EN3 7 A4
Cygnet Ho
Harrow HA7 24 D4
St John's Wood NW8 229 A6
Cygnet House N 18 E14 97 D1
Cygnet House S 19 E14 97 D1
Cygnet St E1 243 D6
Cygnets The TW13 173 A6
Cygnet Way UB4 84 D2
Cygnus Bsns Ctr NW10 67 D2
Cymbeline Ct 6 HA1 42 D3
Cyna Ct 5 E11 55 A3
Cynthia St N1 233 D3
Cyntra Pl 8 E8 74 B1
Cypress Ave
London N2 47 D6
Twickenham TW2 152 A4
Cypress Cl 9 E5 74 A6
Cypress Ct
Cheam SM1 217 C2
5 Leyton E11 76 B4
7 West Norwood SW16 182 C5
Cypress Gdns SE4 163 A6
Cypress Ho SE14 140 D4
Cypress Inf Sch SE25 183 C1
Cypress Jun Sch SE25 183 C1
Cypress Lo SE25 183 C1
Cypress Pl W1 239 B5
Cypress Rd
Harrow HA3 24 B1
South Norwood SE25 183 C1
Cypress Tree Cl DA15 167 D3
CYPRUS 122 C6
Cyprus Ave N3 29 A1
Cyprus Cl N4 50 C3
Cyprus Ct 9 N3 29 B1
Cyprus Gdns N3 29 A1
Cyprus Ho 10 N3 29 B1
Cyprus Pl
23 Bethnal Green E2 96 C5
Newham E6 122 C6
Cyprus Rd
Church End N3 29 B1
Edmonton N9 17 D2
Cyprus St E2 96 C5
Cyprus Sta E6 122 C6
Cyrena Rd SE22 161 D6
Cyril Jackson Prim Sch (North Bldg) E14 119 B6
Cyril Jackson Prim Sch (South Bldg) E14 119 B6
Cyril Lo 2 DA14 190 A6
Cyril Mans SW11 267 D1
Cyril Rd DA7 147 A3
Cyril Smith Ho N13 32 B5
Cyril Thatcher Ho SW6 265 B1
Cyrus Ho EC1 241 D6
Cyrus St EC1 94 D3 241 D6
Czar St SE8 141 C6

D

Dabbs Hill La UB5 63 C3
Dabb's La EC1 241 B5
Dabin Cres SE10 142 A4
Dacca St SE8 141 B6
Dace Rd E3 97 C6
Dacre Cl UB6 85 D5
Dacre Gdns
Borehamwood WD6 11 B6
Lewisham SE13 142 C1
Dacre Ho SW3 266 D5
Dacre Pk SE13 142 C1
Dacre Pl SE13 142 C2
Dacre Rd
Leytonstone E11 54 D1
Newham E13 99 B6
Thornton Heath CR0 204 A2
Dacres Rd SE23 162 D1
Dacre St SW1 115 D3 259 C6
Dade Way UB2 107 B1
Daerwood Cl BR2 210 B1
Daffodil Cl CR0 206 D1
Daffodil Gdns IG1 78 D3
Daffodil Pl 7 TW12 173 C4
Daffodil St W12 111 D6
Dafforne Rd SW17 159 A1
DAGENHAM 81 D1
Dagenham Ave
Dagenham RM9 81 B1
Dagenham RM9 103 A6
Dagenham Dock Sta RM9 103 B5
Dagenham East Sta RM10 81 D3
Dagenham Heathway Sta RM9 81 B2
Dagenham Park Com Sch RM10 103 D6
Dagenham Rd
Dagenham RM10 81 D4
London E10 53 B1
Dagger La WD23 9 A6
Dagmar Ave HA9 66 B4
Dagmar Ct
Cubitt Town E14 120 A3
South Tottenham N15 51 B5
Dagmar Gdns NW10 90 D5
Dagmar Mews UB2 107 A3
Dagmar Pas N1 234 D6
Dagmar Rd
Camberwell SE5 139 C4
Finsbury Pk N4 50 C2
4 Kingston u T KT2 176 C3
Southall UB2 107 A3
South Norwood SE25 205 C4
West Green N15 51 B5
Wood Green N22 31 D2
Dagmar Terr N1 94 D6 234 D6
Dagnall Pk SE25 205 C4
Dagnall Rd SE25 205 C4
Dagnall St SW11 137 A4 268 A1
Dagnan Rd SW12 159 C4
Dagobert Ho 27 E1 96 C2
Dagonet Gdns BR1 165 A1
Dagonet Rd BR1 165 A1
Dahlia Gdns
Ilford IG1 78 D2
Mitcham CR4 203 D5
Dahlia Rd SE2 124 B2
Dahomey Rd SW16 181 C4
Daiglen Sch The IG9 21 C2
Daimler Ho 8 E3 97 C3
Daimler Way SM6 220 A1
Daines Cl E12 78 B5
Dainford Cl BR1 186 B5
Dainton Cl 1 BR1 187 B2
Dainton Ho 22 W2 91 C2
Daintry Cl HA3 43 A5
Daintry Way E9 75 B2
Dairsie Ct 3 BR1 187 C1
Dairsie Rd SE9 144 C2
Dairy Cl
Bromley BR1 187 B3
South Norwood CR7 183 A1
Willesden NW10 90 A6
Dairy La SE18 122 B2
Dairyman Cl NW2 69 A5
Dairy Meadow Prim Sch UB2 107 B3
Daisy Cl CR0 206 D1
Daisy Dormer Ct 11 SW9 138 B1
Daisy Ho IG3 58 A1
Daisy La SW6 135 C2
Daisy Rd
Newham E16 98 C3
Woodford E18 37 B1
Dakin Pl 9 E1 97 A2
Dakota bldg 6 SE13 141 D4
Dakota Cl SM6 220 B1
Dakota Gdns
Newham E6 100 A3
Northolt UB5 85 A4
Dalberg Rd SW2 160 C6
Dalberg Way SE2 124 D3
Dalbury Ho 6 SW9 138 B1
Dalby Rd SW18 136 A1
Dalbys Cres N17 33 C4
Dalby St NW5 71 B2
Dalcross Rd TW4, TW5 129 A3
Dale Ave
Edgware HA8 26 B1
Hounslow TW4 129 A2
Dalebury Rd SW17 158 D2
Dale Cl
Blackheath Pk SE3 143 A2
New Barnet EN5 13 D5
Pinner HA5 22 B2
Dale Croft N4 73 A5
Dale Ct
Cranley Gdns N8 49 C5
3 Kingston u T KT2 176 B3
Northolt UB5 63 B1
Wembley HA0 65 D4
Woodford E18 37 A1
Dale Dr UB4 83 D4
Dalefield IG9 21 D3
Dale Gdns IG8 37 B6
Dale Gr N12 30 A5
Dale Green Rd N11 15 B1
Dalehaed NW1 232 A3
Daleham Dr UB8 82 D1
Daleham Gdns NW3 70 B2
Daleham Mews NW3 70 B2
Dale Ho
London SE4 141 A1
St John's Wood NW8 229 A6
Dale Lo N6 49 C3
Dalemain Ho 5 SW8 137 D3
Dalemain Mews 12 E16 121 A5
Dale Park Ave SM5 218 D6
Dale Park Rd SE19 183 B2
Dale Rd
Ashford TW16 171 D3
Camberwell SE17 138 D6
Cheam SM1 217 B4
Gospel Oak NW5 71 A3
Southall UB6 85 D2
Walton-on-T KT12 193 D2
Dale Row W11 91 A1
Daleside Rd
Streatham SW17 181 B5
West Ewell KT19 215 B2
Dales Path WD6 11 B6
Dales Rd WD6 11 B6
Dale St W4 111 C1
Dale The BR2 225 D4
Dale View Ave E4 20 A2
Dale View Cres E4 20 A1
Dale View Gdns E4 20 B1
Daleview Rd N15 51 C3
Dalewood Gdns KT4 216 B6
Dale Wood Rd BR6 211 C1
Daley Ho 6 W12 90 B1
Daley St E9 74 D2
Daley Thompson Way 7 SW8 137 B2
Dalgarno Gdns W10 90 C2
Dalgarno Way W10 90 C3
Daling Way E3 97 A5
Dalkeith Ct SW1 259 D3
Dalkeith Gr HA7 26 A5
Dalkeith Ho 6 SW9 138 D4
Dalkeith Rd
Ilford IG1 79 A5
West Norwood SE21 161 A4
Dallas Ct SM3 217 A2
Dallas Rd
Cheam SM3 217 A2
Ealing W5 88 B2
Forest Hill SE26 162 B1
Hendon NW4 46 A2
Dallas Terr UB3 105 D3
Dallega Cl UB3 105 B6
Dallinger Rd SE12 164 D5
Dalling Rd W6 112 B2
Dallington Sch EC1 94 D3 241 D6
Dallington St EC1 94 D3 241 D6
Dallin Rd
Bexley DA6 146 D1
Woolwich SE18 144 D5
Dalmain Prim Sch SE23 163 A3
Dalmain Rd SE23 162 D3
Dalmally Pas CR0 205 D2
Dalmally Passage CR0 205 D3
Dalmally Rd CR0 206 A2
Dalmeny Ave
Thornton Heath SW16 182 C1
Tufnell Pk N7 71 D4
Dalmeny Avenue Est 3 N7 71 D4
Dalmeny Cl HA0 65 C2
Dalmeny Cres TW3 130 B1
Dalmeny Ct 4 SW4 138 A3
Dalmeny Rd
Erith DA8 147 D4
New Barnet EN5 14 A5
North Cheam KT4 216 B5
Tufnell Pk N7 71 D4
Wallington SM5 219 A1
Dalmeyer Rd NW10 67 D2
Dalmore Ave KT10 212 D2
Dalmore Rd SE21 161 A2
Dalrymple Cl N14 15 D4
Dalrymple Rd SE4 141 A1
DALSTON 74 A2
Dalston Gdns HA7 26 A1
Dalston Jct E8 73 D2
Dalston Kingsland Sta E8 73 D3
Dalston La E8 74 A3
Dalton Ave CR4 180 C1

Dalton Cl
Hayes UB4 ... 83 B3
Orpington BR6 ... 227 C5
Dalton Ho
7 Balham SW12 ... 159 B4
10 Bow E3 ... 97 A5
19 Deptford SE14 ... 140 D6
Merton SW19 ... 180 A2
Stanmore HA7 ... 25 B5
Dalton St SE27 ... 160 D1
Daltry Ho HA1 ... 42 D5
Dalwood St SE5 ... 139 C4
Daly Ct E15 ... 76 A3
Daly Dr BR1 ... 210 C6
Dalyell Rd SW9 ... 138 B2
Damascene Wlk SE21 ... 161 A3
Damask Cres E16 ... 98 C3
Damask Ct SM1 ... 201 D1
Damer Ho 9 TW10 ... 154 B5
Damer Terr SW10 ... 266 B3
Dames Rd E7 ... 77 A5
Dame St N1 ... 95 A5 235 A4
Damien Ct 12 E1 ... 96 B1
Damien St E1 ... 96 B1
Damon Cl DA14 ... 168 B1
Damon Ct DA14 ... 168 B1
Damon Ho 2 N12 ... 30 B5
Damory Ho 1 SE16 ... 118 C2
Damson Dr UB3 ... 106 A6
Damsonwood Rd UB2 ... 107 C3
Danbrook Rd SW16 ... 182 A3
Dan Bryant Ho 5 SW12 ... 159 C4
Danbury Cl RM6 ... 58 D6
Danbury Mans 3 IG11 ... 78 D1
Danbury Mews SM5, SM6 ... 219 B4
Danbury St N1 ... 94 D5 234 D4
Danbury Way IG8 ... 37 C4
Danby Ct EN2 ... 5 A2
Danby Ho
23 Hackney E9 ... 74 C1
3 West Kilburn W10 ... 91 B4
Danby St SE15 ... 139 D2
Dancastle Ct 7 N3 ... 29 C2
Dancer Rd
Fulham SW6 ... 135 B4 264 C1
Richmond TW9 ... 132 C2
Dando Cres SE3 ... 143 B2
Dandridge Cl SE10 ... 120 D1
Dandridge Ho E1 ... 243 C4
Danebury
New Addington CR0 ... 223 D2
18 North Kensington W10 ... 90 C2
Danebury Ave SW15 ... 155 D5
Daneby Rd SE6 ... 164 A2
Dane Cl
Farnborough BR6 ... 227 B3
Sidcup DA5 ... 169 C4
Danecourt Gdns CR0 ... 221 D5
Danecroft Rd SE24 ... 161 B6
Daneglen Ct 18 HA7 ... 25 C5
Danegrove Prim Sch EN4 ... 14 C5
Danegrove Sch EN4 ... 14 D5
Danehill Wlk DA14 ... 168 A1
Dane Ho
15 London SE5 ... 139 A3
Upper Tooting SW17 ... 180 A6
Danehurst TW8 ... 131 C5
Danehurst Gdns IG4 ... 56 B4
Danehurst St SW6 ... 135 A4 264 A2
Daneland EN4 ... 14 D5
Danemead Gr UB5 ... 63 D3
Danemere St SW15 ... 134 C2
Dane Pl E3 ... 97 B5
Dane Rd
Ashford TW15 ... 171 B4
Ealing W13 ... 109 C5
Ilford IG1 ... 79 A3
Lower Edmonton N18 ... 18 C1
Merton SW19 ... 180 A2
Southall UB1 ... 107 A6
Danesbury Rd TW13 ... 150 B3
Danescombe SE12 ... 165 A3
Danescourt Cres SM1 ... 218 A6
Danescroft
Hendon NW4 ... 46 D4
3 North Finchley N12 ... 30 A5
Danescroft Ave NW4 ... 46 D4
Danescroft Gdns NW4 ... 46 D4
Danes Ct
Primrose Hill NW8 ... 230 C5
Wembley HA9 ... 66 D5
Danesdale Rd E9 ... 75 A2
Danesfield SE5 ... 139 C6
Danes Gate HA1 ... 42 C6
Danes Ho 10 W10 ... 90 C2
Dane St WC1 ... 240 C3
Daneswood Ave SE6 ... 164 A1
Danethorpe Rd HA0 ... 65 D2
Danetree Cl KT19 ... 215 A1
Danetree Jun Sch KT19 ... 215 A1
Danetree Rd KT19 ... 215 A1
Danette Gdns RM8 ... 81 B6
Daneville Rd SE5 ... 139 B4
Danford Ho 9 N11 ... 31 C5
Dangan Rd E11 ... 55 A3
Daniel Almshouse NW4 ... 46 B5
Daniel Bolt Cl E14 ... 97 D2
Daniel Cl
London N18 ... 34 C6
Twickenham TW4 ... 151 B4
Upper Tooting SW17 ... 180 C4
Daniel Ct
Acton W3 ... 111 C6
3 Beckenham BR3 ... 185 C3
7 Edgware HA8 ... 26 D5
10 Hendon NW9 ... 27 C2
Daniel Gdns SE15 ... 139 D5
Daniel Ho 1 HA5 ... 22 C1
Daniell Ho N1 ... 235 D4
Daniell Way CR0 ... 204 B1
Daniel Pl NW4 ... 46 B2
Daniel Rd W5 ... 110 B6
Daniel's Rd SE15 ... 140 C2
Dan Leno Wlk SW6 ... 265 C3
Dansey Pl W1 ... 249 C6
Dansington Rd DA16 ... 146 A1
Danson Cres DA16 ... 146 B2
Danson House* DA6 146 C1
Danson Intc DA5 ... 168 C5
Danson La DA16 ... 146 B1
Danson Mead DA16 ... 146 C2
Danson Prim Sch DA16 ... 146 A1
Danson Rd DA5 ... 168 D6
Danson Underpass DA5 ... 168 C5
Dante Pl SE11 ... 261 D3
Dante Rd SE11 ... 116 D2 261 C4
Danube Ct 13 SE15 ... 139 D5
Danube St SW3 ... 114 C1 257 B2
Danvers Ho 35 E1 ... 96 A1
Danvers Rd N8 ... 49 D5
Danvers St SW3 ... 136 B6 266 D5
Da Palma Ct SW6 ... 265 A5
Daphne Ct
Ealing W5 ... 87 C1
Wembley HA0 ... 65 D3
Worcester Pk KT4 ... 215 C6
Daphne Gdns E4 ... 20 A1
Daphne Ho N22 ... 32 C2
Daphne St SW18 ... 158 A5
Daplyn St 6 E1 ... 96 A2
D'arblay St W1 ... 93 C1 239 B1
Darby Cres TW16 ... 172 C1
Darby Gdns TW16 ... 172 C1
Darcy Ave SM6 ... 219 C4
Darcy Cl N20 ... 14 B2
D'arcy Dr HA3 ... 43 D5
D'arcy Gdns
Dagenham RM9 ... 103 B6
Harrow HA3 ... 44 A5
Darcy Ho E8 ... 96 B6
D'arcy Pl BR2 ... 209 A5
Darcy Rd
Isleworth TW7 ... 131 A4
Thornton Heath SW16 ... 182 A1
D'arcy Rd SM3 ... 216 D4
Dare Ct 2 E10 ... 54 A2
Dare Gdns RM8 ... 81 A5
Darell Prim Sch TW9 ... 132 C2
Darell Rd TW9 ... 132 C2
Daren Ct N7 ... 72 A4
Darent Ho
4 Catford BR1 ... 186 B5
Lisson Gr NW8 ... 236 D4
Darenth Rd
Stamford Hill N16 ... 51 D1
Welling DA16 ... 146 A4
Darfield NW1 ... 232 A5
Darfield Rd SE4 ... 163 B6
Darfield Way W10 ... 90 D1
Darfur St SW15 ... 134 D2
Dargate Cl SE19 ... 183 D3
Darien Ho
17 London SW11 ... 136 B2
11 Stepney E1 ... 96 D2
Darien Rd SW11 ... 136 B2
Daring Ho 23 E3 ... 97 A5
Darland Ho SE9 ... 167 B5
Darlands Dr EN5 ... 12 D6
Darlan Rd SW6 ... 135 B5 264 D3
Darlaston Rd SW19 ... 179 A3
Darley Cl CR0 ... 207 A3
Darley Dr KT3 ... 177 B1
Darley Gdns SM4 ... 201 D3
Darley Ho SE11 ... 260 C1
Darley Rd
Clapham SW11 ... 158 D5
Edmonton N9 ... 17 D3
Darling Ho 12 TW1 ... 153 D5
Darling Rd SE4 ... 141 C2
Darling Row E1 ... 96 B3
Darlington Ct 8 SE6 ... 164 D3
Darlington Ho
South Lambeth SW8 ... 269 D3
2 Surbiton KT6 ... 197 D2
Darlington Rd SE27 ... 182 D5
Darmaine Cl CR2 ... 221 A1
Darnall Ho 4 SE10 ... 142 A4
Darnay Ho 3 SE16 ... 118 A3
Darndale Cl E17 ... 35 B1
Darnell Ho 9 SE10 ... 142 A5
Darnley Ho 7 E14 ... 97 A1
Darnley Rd
Hackney E9 ... 74 C2
Woodford IG8 ... 37 B2
Darnley Terr 12 W11 ... 112 D5
Darrell Ct BR2 ... 208 C6
Darrell Rd SE22 ... 162 A6
Darren Cl N4 ... 50 B2
Darrick Wood Ho BR6 ... 227 A5
Darrick Wood Inf Sch BR6 ... 226 D5
Darrick Wood Jun Sch BR6 ... 226 D4
Darrick Wood Rd BR6 ... 227 B6
Darrick Wood Sch BR6 ... 226 D5
Darrick Wood Sports Ctr BR6 ... 227 A5
Darris Cl UB4 ... 85 A3
Darsley Dr SW8 ... 138 A4 270 A2
Dartford Ave N9 ... 18 D5
Dartford Gdns RM6 ... 58 B4
Dartford Ho SE1 ... 263 D4
Dartford St SE17 ... 139 A6
Dartington NW1 ... 232 B5
Dartington Ho
Bayswater W2 ... 91 D2
7 London SW8 ... 137 D3
Dartle Ct 29 SE16 ... 118 A4
Dartmoor Wlk 18 E14 ... 119 C2
Dartmouth Cl W11 ... 91 C1
Dartmouth Ct SE10 ... 142 A4
Dartmouth Gr SE10 ... 142 A4
Dartmouth Hill SE10 ... 142 A4
Dartmouth Ho
Dartmouth Pk N19 ... 71 B6
11 Kingston u T KT2 ... 176 A2
Lewisham SE10 ... 142 A3
Thornton Heath CR0 ... 204 D2
DARTMOUTH PARK ... 71 B5
Dartmouth Park Ave NW5 ... 71 B5
Dartmouth Park Hill N19 ... 71 B6
Dartmouth Park Rd NW5 ... 71 B5
Dartmouth Pl
Chiswick W4 ... 133 C6
Forest Hill SE23 ... 162 C2
Dartmouth Rd
Brondesbury NW2 ... 68 D2
Forest Hill SE23, SE26 ... 162 C1
Hayes BR2 ... 209 A2
Hendon NW4 ... 46 A3
Ruislip HA4 ... 62 A5
Dartmouth Row SE10 ... 142 A4
Dartmouth St SW1 ... 115 D4 249 D1
Dartmouth Terr SE10 ... 142 B4
Dartnell Rd CR0 ... 205 D2
Darton Ct W3 ... 111 A5
Dartrey Twr SW10 ... 266 C4
Dartrey Wlk SW10 ... 136 A5 266 B4
Dart St W10 ... 91 B4
Darville Rd N16 ... 73 D5
Darwell Cl E6 ... 100 C5
Darwen Pl E2 ... 96 B6
Darwin Cl
Farnborough BR6 ... 227 B3
New Southgate N11 ... 15 B1
Darwin Ct
Eltham SE9 ... 166 C5
Newham E13 ... 99 B4
Primrose Hill NW1 ... 231 B6
Darwin Dr UB1 ... 85 D1
Darwin Gdns WD19 ... 22 C5
Darwin Ho
8 London SE13 ... 142 A3
2 Wembley HA9 ... 67 A5
Darwin Rd
Ealing W5 ... 109 C2
Falconwood DA16 ... 145 D2
Tottenham N22 ... 32 D1
Darwin St SE17 ... 117 B2 262 D4
Daryngton Dr UB6 ... 86 C5
Daryngton Ho SW8 ... 270 A3
Dashwood Cl DA6 ... 169 C6
Dashwood Ct TW3 ... 130 A1
Dashwood Ho SE21 ... 161 D1
Dashwood Rd N8 ... 50 B3
Dassett Rd SE27 ... 182 D5
Data Point Bsns Ctr E16 ... 98 B3
Datchelor Pl 14 SE5 ... 139 B4
Datchet Ho NW1 ... 231 D2
Datchet Rd SE6 ... 163 B2
Datchett Ho 40 E2 ... 95 D4
Datchwood Ct N4 ... 73 A5
Datchworth Ct 7 EN1 ... 17 C6
Datchworth Ho 8 N1 ... 72 D1
Date St SE17 ... 117 B1 262 C1
Daubeney Gdns N17 ... 33 A3
Daubeney Pl TW12 ... 173 D1
Daubeney Prim Sch E5 ... 75 A4
Daubeney Rd
Clapton Pk E5 ... 75 A4
Tottenham N17 ... 33 A3
Daubeney Twr 2 SE8 ... 119 B1
Dault Rd SW18 ... 158 A5
Dauney Ho SE1 ... 251 C1
Dauphine Ct HA3 ... 24 C1
Dave Adams Ho 8 E3 ... 97 B5
Davenant Ho 20 E1 ... 96 A2
Davenant Rd
Croydon CR0, CR9 ... 220 D4
Upper Holloway N19 ... 71 D6
Davenant St E1 ... 96 A2
Davenport Cl TW11 ... 175 A4
Davenport Ctr IG11 ... 102 B5
Davenport Ho SE11 ... 261 A5
Davenport Lo TW3 ... 129 A5
Davenport Mews 6 W12 ... 112 B5
Davenport Rd
London SE6 ... 164 A5
Sidcup DA14 ... 169 A2
Daventer Dr HA7 ... 24 D3
Daventry Ave E17 ... 53 C3
Daventry St NW1 ... 92 C2 237 A4
Dave Porter Hts SW19 ... 157 A4
Dave Ramsey Ho SE18 ... 123 B2
Daver Ct
Chelsea SW3 ... 257 B1
Ealing W5 ... 87 D3
Davern Cl SE10 ... 120 D2
Davey Cl
Bowes Pk N13 ... 32 B5
Islington N7 ... 72 B2
Davey Ho HA9 ... 67 A6
Davey Rd E9 ... 75 C1
Davey's Ct WC2 ... 250 A6
Davey St SE15 ... 139 D6
David Ave UB6 ... 86 C5
David Beckham Acad The SE10 ... 120 D4
David Cl UB3 ... 127 C5
David Coffer Ct DA17 ... 125 D2
David Ct N20 ... 14 A1
David Devine Ho 7 E8 ... 74 A3
David Game Coll SW7 ... 256 C3
Davidge Ho SE1 ... 251 B1
Davidge St SE1 ... 116 D4 251 D1
David Henry Waring Ct TW14 ... 149 A3
David Hewitt Ho 2 E3 ... 97 D2
David Ho
8 Putney SW15 ... 156 A6
South Lambeth SW8 ... 270 A4
David Ho *continued*
South Norwood SE25 ... 206 A6
David Lee Point 4 E15 ... 98 C6
David Livingstone Prim Sch CR7 ... 183 A2
David Mews W1 ... 237 D4
David Rd RM8 ... 81 A6
Davidson Gdns SW8 ... 138 A5 270 A4
Davidson Ho 7 N19 ... 71 C4
Davidson Lo CR0 ... 205 C2
Davidson Prim Sch CR0 ... 205 D2
Davidson Rd CR0 ... 205 D3
Davidson Terrs E7 ... 77 B3
David's Rd SE23 ... 162 C3
David St E15 ... 76 B3
David Twigg Cl KT2 ... 176 A2
Davies Cl CR0 ... 206 A3
Davies La E11 ... 76 D6
Davies Laing & Dick Coll W1 ... 93 A1 238 B2
Davies Lane Prim Sch E11 ... 76 D6
Davies Mews W1 ... 248 C6
Davies St W1 ... 115 B6 248 C6
Davies Walk TW7 ... 130 B4
Davina Ho
Brondesbury NW2 ... 69 B2
14 Hackney E5 ... 74 B3
Da Vinci Ct 12 SE16 ... 118 B1
Davington Ct 19 SM2 ... 217 C1
Davington Gdns RM8 ... 80 B3
Davington Rd RM8 ... 80 B3
Davis Ct 1 N20 ... 14 B2
Davis Ho 35 W12 ... 112 B6
Davis Rd
Bedford Pk W3 ... 111 D4
Chessington KT9 ... 214 C4
Davis Sch The E10 ... 53 D1
Davis St E13 ... 99 B5
Davisville Rd W12 ... 112 A4
Davmor Ct TW8 ... 109 C1
Dawes Ave TW7 ... 131 A1
Dawe's Cl UB10 ... 82 A5
Dawes Ho SE17 ... 262 C3
Dawes Rd SW6 ... 135 B5 264 C4
Dawe's Rd UB10 ... 82 A5
Dawes St SE17 ... 117 B1 262 D2
Dawley Ave UB8 ... 83 A1
Dawley Par UB3 ... 105 A6
Dawley Rd
Harlington UB3 ... 105 C2
Hayes UB3 ... 105 B6
Dawlish Ave
Bowes Pk N13 ... 32 A5
Wandsworth SW18 ... 157 D2
Wembley UB6 ... 87 A5
Dawlish Dr
Ilford IG3 ... 79 D4
Pinner HA5 ... 41 A3
Ruislip HA4 ... 62 B6
Dawlish Prim Sch E10 ... 54 A1
Dawlish Rd
Brondesbury NW2 ... 68 D2
Leyton E10 ... 76 A6
Tottenham Hale N17 ... 52 A6
Dawnay Gdns SW18 ... 158 B2
Dawnay Rd SW17, SW18 ... 158 B2
Dawn Cl TW4 ... 129 A2
Dawn Cres E15 ... 98 B6
Dawn Wlk BR2 ... 186 B1
Dawpool Rd NW2 ... 67 D6
Daws La NW7 ... 28 A5
Dawson Ave
Barking IG11 ... 79 D1
St Paul's Cray BR5 ... 190 B1
Dawson Cl
Hayes UB3 ... 83 B2
Woolwich SE18 ... 123 A2
Dawson Gdns 10 IG11 ... 79 D1
Dawson Ho
23 Bethnal Green E2 ... 96 C4
5 Camberwell SE5 ... 139 C4
Dawson Pl W2 ... 113 C6 245 B6
Dawson Rd
Cricklewood NW2 ... 68 C4
Kingston u T KT1 ... 198 B6
Dawson St E2 ... 95 D5
Dawson Terr N9 ... 18 C4
Dax Ct TW16 ... 194 C6
Daybrook Rd SW19 ... 201 D6
Day Ho 2 SE5 ... 139 A5
Daylesford Ave SW15 ... 134 A1
Daymer Gdns HA5 ... 40 C5
Daynor Ho 4 NW6 ... 91 C6
Day's Armhouses HA8 ... 26 B5
Daysbrook Rd SW2 ... 160 B3
Days La DA15 ... 167 C4
Days Lane Prim Sch DA15 ... 167 D5
Daytone Ho SW20 ... 178 D2
Dayton Gr SE15 ... 140 C4
Deaconess Ct 5 N15 ... 51 D5
Deacon Ho SE11 ... 260 D3
Deacon Mews N1 ... 73 B1
Deacon Rd
Kingston u T KT2 ... 176 B2
Willesden NW2 ... 68 A2
Deacons Cl HA5 ... 22 B1
DEACONS HILL ... 10 C5
Deacon's Hill Rd WD6 ... 10 C6
Deacons Hts WD6 ... 10 C5
Deacons Leas BR6 ... 227 B4
Deacons Rise N2 ... 48 B4
Deacons Wlk TW12 ... 173 C6
Deacon Way SE17 ... 117 A2 262 B4
Deal Ct
13 Hendon NW9 ... 27 D1
7 Southall UB1 ... 86 A1
Deal Ho
Deptford SE15 ... 140 D6
Walworth SE17 ... 263 B2
Deal Porters Way SE16 ... 118 D3
Deal Rd SW17 ... 181 A4
Deal St E1 ... 96 A2
Dealtry Rd SW15 ... 134 C1
Deal Wlk 3 SW9 ... 138 C5
Dean Bradley St SW1 ... 260 A5
Dean Cl
Hackney E9 ... 74 C3
Hillingdon UB10 ... 60 B1
Rotherhithe SE16 ... 118 D5
Dean Coll of London N7 ... 72 B5
Deancross St E1 ... 96 C1
Dean Ct
Acton W3 ... 89 B1
Ealing W13 ... 109 B5
10 Kingston u T KT2 ... 176 C3
South Lambeth SW8 ... 270 A3
Wembley HA0 ... 65 B5
Dean Dr HA7 ... 26 A1
Deane Ave HA4 ... 62 C3
Deane Croft Rd HA5 ... 40 C3
Deanery Cl N2 ... 48 C5
Deanery Mews W1 ... 248 B4
Deanery Rd E15 ... 76 C2
Deanery St W1 ... 115 A5 248 B4
Deanesfield Prim HA4 ... 62 D4
Deane Way HA4 ... 40 B3
Dean Farrar St SW1 ... 259 D6
Deanfield Gdns CR0 ... 221 B4
Dean Gdns E17 ... 54 B5
Deanhill Ct 2 SW14 ... 132 D1
Deanhill Rd SW14 ... 132 D1
Dean Ho
London N4 ... 51 A2
New Cross SE14 ... 141 B5
Ruislip HA4 ... 39 B1
Stamford Hill N16 ... 51 D1
18 Stepney E1 ... 96 C1
Dean Rd
Croydon CR0 ... 221 B4
Hampton TW12 ... 173 C5
Hounslow TW3 ... 151 D6
Thamesmead SE28 ... 124 A6
Willesden NW2 ... 68 C2
Dean Ryle St SW1 ... 260 A4
Dean's Bldgs SE17 ... 117 B2 262 D3
Deansbrook Cl HA8 ... 27 A3
Deansbrook Jun & Inf Schs NW7 ... 27 A4
Deansbrook Rd
Burnt Oak HA8 ... 27 B4
Edgware HA8 ... 26 D3
Deans Cl
Burnt Oak HA8 ... 27 A4
Chiswick W4 ... 132 D6
South Croydon CR0 ... 221 D5
Deanscroft Ave NW9 ... 45 A1
Deans Ct HA8 ... 26 D4
Dean's Ct EC4 ... 241 D1
Deans Dr N13 ... 32 D4
Dean's Dr HA8 ... 27 B5
Deansfield Prim Sch
Eltham SE9 ... 144 C2
Ruislip HA4 ... 62 D4
Deans Gate Cl SE23 ... 162 D1
Deanshanger Ho 21 SE8 ... 118 D2

Dean's La HA8 27 A4
Dean's Mews W1 238 D2
Deans Rd SM1 217 D5
Dean's Rd W7 108 D4
Dean St
Forest Gate E7 77 A3
Soho W1 93 D1 239 C1
Dean Stanley St SW1 260 A5
Deansway
East Finchley N2 48 B5
Edmonton N9 17 C1
Deans Way HA8 27 A5
Deanswood N11 31 D4
Dean's Yd SW1 259 D6
Dean Trench St SW1 260 A5
Dean Way UB2 107 D4
Dean Wlk HA8 27 B3
Deanwood Ct N14 15 C3
Dearmer Ho 6 SW2 160 C4
Dearne Cl HA7 25 A5
De'arn Gdns CR4 202 C6
Dearsley Rd EN1 6 A2
Deason St E15 98 A6
Deauville Ct
14 London SW4 159 C5
4 Rotherhithe SE16 118 D4
Deauville Mans 13
SW4 159 C5
De Barowe Mews 1
N5 72 D3
Debdale Ho 20 E2 96 A6
Debden N17 33 B1
Debden Cl
7 Edgware NW9 27 C2
Kingston u T KT2 175 D5
Woodford IG8 37 D3
De Beauvoir Cres N1 95 C6
De Beauvoir Ct N1 73 B1
De Beauvoir Pl 5 N1 73 C2
De Beauvoir Prim Sch
N1 73 C2
De Beauvoir Rd N1 73 C1
De Beauvoir Sq N1 73 C1
DE BEAUVOIR TOWN 73 C1
Debenham Ct
Barnet EN5 12 C6
Hackney E8 96 A6
Debham Ct NW2 68 C5
Debnams Rd SE16 118 C2
De Bohun Ave N14 15 B5
De Bohun Prim Sch
N14 15 B6
Deborah Cl TW7 130 C4
Deborah Cres HA4 39 B2
Deborah Ct 7 E18 55 B6
Deborah Lo HA8 26 D2
De Broome Rd TW13 150 C3
De Burgh Ho 10
SW19 180 A3
Deburgh Rd SW19 180 A3
Debussy 9 NW9 27 D1
Decimal Ctr UB2 107 C4
Decima St
SE1 117 C3 263 A6
Decimus Cl CR7 205 B5
Deck Cl SE16 118 D5
Decoy Ave NW11 47 A5
De Crespigny Pk SE5 139 B3
Dedham Ho 1 SE6 186 A6
Dee Ct W7 86 B1
Deeley Rd
SW8 137 D4 269 C2
Deena Cl W3 88 B1
Deepdale
Highbury N4 72 D5
Wimbledon SW19 178 D6
Deepdale Ave BR2 208 D5
Deepdale Cl N11 31 A4
Deepdene N12 30 C6
Deepdene Ave CR0 221 D5
Deepdene Cl E11 55 A5
Deepdene Ct
Beckenham BR2 208 C6
Southgate N21 16 D5
Deepdene Gdns SW2 160 B4
Deepdene Ho N16 51 B1
Deepdene Lo 5 SW2 160 B4
Deepdene Mans SW6 264 C2
Deepdene Point 9
SE26 162 D1
Deepdene Rd
London SE5, SE24 139 B1
Welling DA16 146 A2
Deepwell Cl TW7 131 A4
Deepwood La UB6 86 B4
Deerbrook Rd SE24,
SW2 160 D3
Dee Rd TW9 132 B1
Deerdale Rd SE24 139 A1
Deerfield Cl NW9 45 D4
Deerhurst
7 Kingston u T KT2 176 D2
5 Streatham SW16 182 A5
Deerhurst Cl TW13 172 B6
Deerhurst Cres TW12 174 A5
Deerhurst Ct CR0 204 D1
Deerhurst Ho 6
SE15 140 A6
Deerhurst Rd
Brondesbury NW2 68 D2
Streatham SW16 182 B5
Deerings Ct 2 N20 14 B2
Deerings Dr HA5 40 A4
Deerleap Gr E4 19 D6
Deer Lo SW6 135 A2
Deer Park Cl KT2 176 D3
Deer Park Gdns CR4 202 B5
Deer Park Rd SW19 180 A1
Deer Park Way BR4 224 D6
Deesdale Ct CR2 221 B4
Deeside Rd SW17 158 B1
Dee St E14 98 A1
Defence Cl SE28 123 C5
Defiance Wlk SE18 122 B3
Defiant 18 NW9 27 D1
Defiant Way SM6 220 A1
Defoe Ave TW9 132 C5
Defoe Cl SW17 180 C4
Defoe Ho
Barbican EC2 242 A4
5 Stoke Newington
N16 73 C5
Defoe Pl
Barbican EC2 242 A4
Upper Tooting SW17 180 D6
Defoe Rd
Rotherhithe SE16 119 B4
Stoke Newington N16 73 C5
De Frene Rd SE26 163 A1
De Gama Pl 3 E14 119 C1
Degema Rd BR7 188 D5
Dehar Cres NW9 46 A2
De Haviland Dr 8
SE18 122 D1
Dehavilland Cl UB5 84 D4
De Havilland Rd
Edgware HA8 26 D1
Heston TW5 128 C5
De Havilland Sq IG1 57 B1
Dehavilland Studios
E5 74 C6
De Havilland Way
TW19 148 A5
Dekker Ho 19 SE5 139 B5
Dekker Rd SE21 161 C5
Delacourt Rd SE3 143 B5
Delafield Ho 25 E1 96 A1
Delafield Rd SE7 121 C1
Delaford Rd SE16 118 B1
Delaford St
SW6 135 A6 264 B5
Delamare Cres CR0 206 C3
Delamere Gdns NW7 27 B4
Delamere Ho 4 N4 51 B2
Delamere Rd
Ealing W5 110 A4
Hayes UB4 106 D6
Wimbledon SW20 178 D2
Delamere St W2 236 A3
Delamere Terr W2 91 D2
Delancey Pas NW1 231 D5
Delancey St
NW1 93 B6 231 D5
Delancey Studios
NW1 231 D5
Delany Ho SE10 142 A6
Delarch Ho SE1 251 C1
De Laune St
SE17 116 D1 261 C1
Delaware Rd W9 91 D3
Delawyk Cres SE24 161 B5
Delcombe Ave KT4 200 C1
Delft Ho 8 KT2 176 B3
Delft Way 2 SE22 161 C6
Delhi Rd EN1 17 D4
Delhi St N1 94 A6 233 B5
Delia St SW18 157 D4
Delisle Rd SE28 123 C5
Delius Gr E15 98 A5
Dellafield N4 72 C6
Della Path E5 74 B5
Dellbow Rd TW14 150 B6
Dell Cl
Stratford Marsh E15 98 B6
Wallington SM6 219 D4
Woodford IG8 21 B1
Dellfield Cl BR3 186 A2
Dell La KT17 216 A3
Dellors Cl EN5 12 D6
Dellow Cl IG2 57 B2
Dellow Ho 6 E1 118 B6
Dellow St E1 118 B6
Dell Rd
Enfield EN3 6 C5
Stoneleigh KT17 216 A2
West Drayton UB7 104 B3
Dells Cl
Chingford E4 19 D4
Teddington TW11 174 D4
Dell's Mews SW1 259 B3
Dell The
Brentford TW8 131 C6
Feltham TW14 150 B4
Pinner HA5 22 D1
Plumstead Comm SE2 124 A1
South Norwood SE19 183 D2
Wembley HA0 65 B3
Woodford IG8 21 B1
Dell Way W13 87 C1
Dell Wlk KT3 177 C1
Dellwood Gdns IG5 56 C6
Delme Cres SE3 143 B3
Delmey Cl CR0 221 D5
Deloraine Ho SE8 141 C4
Deloraine St SE8 141 C4
Delorme St W6 134 D6
Delphian Ct 5 SW16 182 C6
Delroy Ct N20 14 A4
Delta Bldg 7 E14 98 A1
Delta Cl KT4 215 D5
Delta Ct NW2 68 A6
Delta Gr UB5 84 D4
Delta Ho N1 235 C2
Delta Pk SW18 135 D1
Delta Pk Ind Est EN3 7 B3
Delta Point 5 E2 96 A4
Delta Rd KT4 215 C5
Delta St 4 E2 96 A4
De Lucy Prim Sch
SE2 124 B4
De Lucy St SE2 124 B2
Delvan Cl SE18 144 C5
Delverton Ho SE17 261 D2
Delverton Rd SE17 261 D1
Delvino Rd
SW6 135 C4 265 B1
De Mandeville Gate
EN1 6 B1
Demesne Rd SM6 219 D4
Demeta Cl HA9 67 A5
De Montfort Ct 1
SW16 160 A1
De Montfort Rd
SW16 160 A2
De Morgan Rd SW6 135 D2
Dempster Cl KT6 197 C1
Dempster Rd SW18 158 A6
Denberry Dr DA14 168 B1
Denbigh Cl
Cheam SM1 217 B3
Elmstead BR7 188 B4
Notting Hill
W11 113 B6 244 D6
Ruislip HA4 61 D6
Southall UB1 85 B1
Willesden NW10 67 C1
Denbigh Ct
1 Ealing W7 86 D2
Newham E6 99 D4
Denbigh Dr UB3 105 A4
Denbigh Gdns TW10 154 B6
Denbigh Ho
Knightsbridge SW1 257 D6
7 Notting Hill W11 91 B1
Notting Hill W11 244 D6
Denbigh Mews SW1 259 A3
Denbigh Pl
SW1 115 C1 259 A2
Denbigh Rd
Ealing W13 87 B1
Hounslow TW3 129 D3
Newham E6 99 D4
Notting Hill
W11 113 B6 244 D6
Southall UB1 85 B1
Denbigh St
SW1 115 C1 259 B2
Denbigh Terr
W11 113 B6 244 D6
Denbridge Rd BR1,
BR7 188 B1
Denbury Ho 48 E3 97 D4
Denby Ct
Barnet EN5 1 D2
Lambeth SE11 260 D4
Dence Ho 15 E2 96 A4
Denchworth Ho 14
SW9 138 C3
Den Cl BR2, BR3 208 B6
Dencliffe 2 TW15 170 C5
Dencora Centre The
EN3 7 A2
Dendridge Cl EN1 6 B6
Dene Ave
Blackfen DA15 168 B4
Hounslow TW3 129 B2
Dene Cl
Brockley SE4 141 A1
Hayes BR2 208 D1
Worcester Pk KT4 215 D6
Denecroft Cres UB10 82 D6
Dene Ct
Ealing W5 87 C2
Hanwell W7 108 D4
Dene Gdns
Hinchley Wood KT7 213 A6
Stanmore HA7 25 C5
Dene Ho N14 15 D4
Denehole Ho SE18 124 A1
Denehurst Gdns
Acton W3 110 D5
Hendon NW4 46 C3
Richmond TW10 132 C1
Twickenham TW2 152 B4
Woodford IG8 37 B6
Dene Mans 1 NW6 69 C2
Dene Rd
Buckhurst Hill IG9 21 D3
Friern Barnet N11 14 D2
Denesmead SE24 161 A6
Dene The
Ealing W13 87 B2
East Molesey KT12,
KT8 195 B4
South Croydon CR0 222 D4
Wembley HA9 66 A4
Denewood EN5 14 A6
Denewood Ho 6
SM1 218 A4
Denewood Rd N6 48 D2
Dengie Wlk N1 235 A6
Denham Cl DA16 146 C2
Denham Cres CR4 202 D5
Denham Ct
Forest Hill SE26 162 B1
Southall UB1 108 A6
Denham Dr IG2 57 A3
Denham Ho 32 W12 112 B6
Denham Lo W5 88 A1
Denham Rd
Feltham TW14 150 C4
Friern Barnet N20 14 D1
Denham St SE10 121 A1
Denham Way IG11 101 D6
Denholme Rd W9 91 B4
Deniel Lo TW9 153 C6
Denise Ct HA0 65 C4
Denison Cl N2 48 A6
Denison Rd
Ealing W5 87 C3
Feltham TW13 171 D6
Mitcham SW19 180 B4
Deniston Ave DA5 169 A3
Denland Ho SW8 270 D3
Denleigh Ct N14 15 D4
Denleigh Gdns
Southgate N21 16 C4
Thames Ditton KT7 196 C3
Denman Dr
Ashford TW15 170 D4
Claygate KT10 213 A3
Hampstead Garden Suburb
NW11 47 C4
Denman Dr N NW11 47 C4
Denman Dr S NW11 47 C4
Denman Ho N16 73 C6
Denman Rd SE15 139 D3
Denman St W1 249 C5
Denmark Ave SW19 179 A3
Denmark Ct SM4 201 C4
Denmark Gdns SM5 218 D5
Denmark Gr N1 234 A4
Denmark Hill SE5 139 B3
Denmark Hill Dr NW9 46 A6
Denmark Hill Sta SE5 139 B3
Denmark Ho 9 SE7 122 A2
Denmark Mans 14
SE5 139 A3
Denmark Pl
2 Bromley E3 97 C4
Soho WC2 239 D2
Denmark Rd
Bromley BR1 187 B2
Camberwell SE5 139 A3
Carshalton SM5 218 D5
Croydon SE25 206 B4
Ealing W13 109 B6
Hornsey N8 50 C5
Kilburn NW6 91 B5
Denmark Rd continued
Kingston u T KT1 198 A6
Twickenham TW2 152 B1
Wimbledon SW19 178 D4
Denmark St
8 Leyton E11 76 C5
Newham E13 99 B2
Soho WC2 239 D2
Tottenham N17 34 B3
Denmark Terr NW2 48 D6
Denmead Ho SW15 155 D5
Denmead Rd CR0 204 D1
Denmead Sch TW12 173 D3
Denmead Upper Sch
TW12 173 D3
Denmore Ct SM6 219 B3
Dennan Rd KT6 198 B1
Dennard Way BR6 226 C4
Denner Rd E4 19 C2
Denne Terr E8 95 D6
Dennett Rd CR0 204 C2
Dennett's Gr SE14 140 D3
Dennett's Rd SE14 140 C4
Denning Ave CR0 220 C3
Denning Cl
Hampton TW12 173 B5
St John's Wood
NW8 92 A4 229 B1
Denning Point E1 243 D2
Denning Rd NW3 70 B4
Dennington Cl 17 E5 74 B6
Dennington Park
Mansions 12 NW6 69 C3
Dennington Park Rd
NW6 69 C2
Denningtons The
KT4 215 C6
Dennis Ave HA9 66 B3
Dennis Cl TW15 171 B3
Dennis Ct
Chingford E17 36 B1
Greenford UB6 86 A1
Lewisham SE10 142 A4
Dennis Gdns HA7 25 C5
Dennis Ho
4 Bow E3 97 B5
Sutton SM1 217 C4
Dennis La HA7 25 B6
Dennison Point E15 76 A1
Dennis Par 1 N14 15 D3
Dennis Park Cres
SW20 179 A2
Dennis Rd KT8 196 A5
Dennis Reeve Cl CR4 180 D2
Dennis Way SW4 137 D2
Denny Cl 15 E6 100 A2
Denny Cres SE11 261 B2
Denny Gdns RM9 80 B1
Denny Rd N9 18 B3
Denny St SE11 116 C1 261 B2
Den Rd BR2 208 B6
Densham Ho NW8 229 D3
Densham Rd E15 98 C6
Densole Cl BR3 185 A2
Denstone Ho 5 SE15 140 A6
Densworth Gr N9 18 C2
Dent Ho SE17 263 A3
Denton NW1 71 A2
Denton Cl EN5 12 C6
Denton Ct BR2 210 C2
Denton Ho N1 72 D1
Denton Rd
Bexley DA16 146 C5
Edmonton N18 33 C6
Hornsey N8 50 B3
Twickenham TW1 153 D5
Denton St SW18 157 D5
Denton Way E5 74 D5
Dents Rd SW11 158 D5
Denvale Trade Pk
CR4 202 B5
Denver Cl BR6 211 C3
Denver Ct UB1 107 B5
Denver Rd N16 51 C2
Denwood SE23 162 D1
Denyer Ho 1 NW5 71 B4
Denyer St
SW3 114 C2 257 B4
Denys Bldg EC1 241 A4
Denziloe Ave UB10 82 D4
Denzil Rd NW10 67 D3
Deodar Rd SW15 135 A1
Deodora Cl N20 14 D1
Depot App NW2 68 D4
Depot Rd
Isleworth TW3, TW7 130 B2
Shepherd's Bush W12 112 C6
Depot St SE5 139 B6
DEPTFORD 140 D6
Deptford Bridge SE8 141 C4
Deptford Bridge Sta
SE8 141 C4
Deptford Broadway SE8,
SE14 141 C4
Deptford Church St
SE8 141 C5
Deptford Ferry Rd 24
E14 119 C2
Deptford Gn SE8 141 C6
Deptford Green Sch
SE14 141 B5
Deptford Green Sch
(Annex) SE14 141 A5
Deptford High St SE8 141 C5
Deptford Park Prim Sch
SE8 119 A1
Deptford Sta SE8 141 C5
Deptford Trad Est
SE8 141 A6
Deptford Wharf SE8 119 B2
Dept of Transport &
Environment SW1 259 D5
De Quincey Mews 3
E16 121 A5
De Quincey Rd N17 33 B2
Derby Ave
Harrow HA3 24 B2
North Finchley N12 30 A5
Romford RM7 59 D3
Derby Ct
8 Clapton Pk E5 74 D4
Woodford E18 36 D2
Derby Gate SW1 250 A2
Derby Hill SE23 162 C2
Derby Hill Cres SE23 162 C2
Derby Ho
Hendon NW4 46 C6
Lambeth SE11 261 A4
Pinner HA5 22 D1
4 Wallington SM6 219 B3
Derby Lo N3 29 B1
Derby Rd
Cheam SM1, SM2 217 B2
Edmonton N18 34 C5
Enfield EN3 18 C6
Greenford UB6 85 D6
Hounslow TW3 129 D1
Merton SW19 179 C3
Mortlake SW14 132 D1
South Hackney E9 96 D6
Surbiton KT5, KT6 198 C1
Thornton Heath CR0 204 D1
Upton E7 77 D1
Woodford E18 36 D2
Derbyshire St E2 96 A4
Derby St W1 248 B3
Dereham Ho 7 SE4 140 D1
Dereham Pl EC2 243 B6
Dereham Rd IG11 79 D3
Derek Ave
Chessington KT19 214 D3
Wallington SM6 219 B4
Wembley HA9 66 D1
Derek Cl KT19 214 D3
Derek Walcott Cl
SE24 160 D6
Dericote St E8 96 B6
Deri Dene Cl 2
TW19 148 A5
Derifall Cl E6 100 B2
Dering Pl CR0 221 A4
Dering Rd CR0 221 A4
Dering St W1 238 D1
Derinton Rd SW17 181 A6
Derley Rd UB2 106 D3
Dermody Gdns SE13 164 B6
Dermody Rd SE13 164 B6
Deronda Rd SE24,
SW2 160 D3
Deroy Cl SM5 218 D2
Derrick Gdns SE7 121 C2
Derrick Ho 13 SW2 160 C3
Derrick Rd BR3 207 B5
Derrycombe Ho 18
W2 91 C2
Derry Rd CR0, SM6 220 A5
Derry St W8 113 D4 245 C1
Dersingham Ave E12 78 C4
Dersingham Inf Sch
E12 78 C3
Dersingham Rd NW2 69 A5
Derwent NW1 232 A1
Derwent Ave
Barnet EN4 14 D3
Burnt Oak NW7 27 B4
Edmonton N18 33 B5
Hyde The NW9 45 C4

Derwent Ave *continued*
Kingston u T SW15 ... 177 C6
Pinner HA5 ... 23 A4
Uxbridge UB10 ... 60 C5
Derwent Cl
Claygate KT10 ... 212 D2
East Bedfont TW14 ... 149 D3
Derwent Cres
Bexleyheath DA7 ... 147 C3
Stanmore HA7 ... 25 C1
Whetstone N20 ... 14 A1
Derwent Ct
2 Hammersmith W6 ... 112 A2
Hornsey N8 ... 50 A3
8 Rotherhithe SE16 ... 118 D4
Derwent Dr
Crofton BR5 ... 211 B2
Hayes UB4 ... 83 C2
Derwent Gdns
Redbridge IG4 ... 56 A5
Wembley HA9 ... 43 C2
Derwent Gr SE22 ... 139 D1
Derwent Ho
Penge SE20 ... 184 B1
South Kensington SW7 ... 256 B4
Tower Hamlets E3 ... 97 B3
Derwent Lo
Hounslow TW7 ... 130 B3
North Cheam KT4 ... 216 B6
Derwent Rd
Ealing W5 ... 109 C3
Palmers Green N13 ... 16 B1
Penge SE20 ... 184 B1
Southall UB1 ... 85 B1
Twickenham TW2 ... 151 D5
West Barnes SM4 ... 200 D3
Derwent Rise NW9 ... 45 C3
Derwent St SE10 ... 120 C1
Derwentwater Mans 2
W3 ... 111 A5
Derwentwater Prim Sch
W3 ... 111 A5
Derwentwater Rd
W3 ... 111 A5
Derwent Wlk SM6 ... 219 B1
Derwent Yd W5 ... 109 C3
De Salis Rd UB10 ... 83 A3
Desborough Cl
Bayswater W2 ... 91 D2
Lower Halliford TW17 ... 192 C2
Desborough Ct SE25 ... 206 B5
Desborough Ho W14 ... 264 D6
Desenfans Rd SE21 ... 161 C5
Deseret Ho 6 CR4 ... 202 D6
Desford Rd E16 ... 98 C3
Desford Way TW15 ... 148 B2
Desmond Ho 4 EN4 ... 14 C5
Desmond St SE14 ... 141 A6
Desmond Tutu Dr
SE23 ... 163 A3
Despard Ho SW2 ... 160 C2
Despard Rd N19 ... 49 C1
Dessouter 19 NW9 ... 27 D1
Desvignes Dr SE13 ... 164 B5
Detherick Ct TW3 ... 130 A1
Dethick Ct E3 ... 97 A6
Detling Ho SE17 ... 263 A3
Detling Rd BR1 ... 187 A5
Detmold Rd E5 ... 74 C6
Devalls Cl E6 ... 122 C6
Devana End SM5 ... 218 D5
Devas Rd SW20 ... 178 C2
Devas St E3 ... 97 D3
Devema Cl BR7 ... 188 C2
Devenay Rd E15 ... 76 D1
Devenish Rd SE2 ... 124 A4
Deventer Cres 8
SE22 ... 161 C6
Deveraux Cl BR3 ... 208 A4
De Vere Cotts W8 ... 256 A6
De Vere Ct 1 E5 ... 74 B5
De Vere Gdns
Kensington
W8 ... 114 A4 246 A1
Redbridge IG1 ... 56 B1
Deverell St
SE1 ... 117 B3 262 C5
De Vere Mews W8 ... 256 A6
Devereux Ct WC2 ... 241 A1
Devereux Ho 7
SW15 ... 156 A6
Devereux La SW13 ... 134 B5
Devereux Rd SW11 ... 158 D5
Deverill Ct SE20 ... 184 C2
Devey Cl KT2 ... 177 B5
Devitt Ho 5 E14 ... 119 D6
Devizes St N1 ... 235 D5
Devon Ave TW2 ... 152 A3
Devon Cl
Chigwell IG9 ... 21 B2
Tottenham N17 ... 51 D6
Wembley UB6 ... 87 C6
Devoncroft Gdns
TW1 ... 153 A4
Devon Ct
3 Acton W3 ... 88 C1
2 Ealing W7 ... 86 D2
Hampton TW12 ... 173 C3
Devon Gdns N4 ... 50 D3
Devon Ho
9 Penge SE20 ... 184 B3
Walthamstow E17 ... 35 B1
6 Wanstead E11 ... 55 A4
Devonhurst Pl 4 W4 ... 111 B1
Devonia Gdns N18 ... 33 A4
Devonia Rd N1 ... 94 D5 234 D4
Devon Mans SE1 ... 253 B2
Devon Par HA3 ... 43 C4
Devonport W2 ... 237 A2
Devonport Gdns IG1 ... 56 B3
Devonport Ho
Greenwich SE10 ... 142 A6
23 Paddington W2 ... 91 C2
Devonport Rd W12 ... 112 B4
Devonport St E1 ... 96 D1
Devon Rd IG11 ... 101 C6
Devon Rise N2 ... 48 B5
Devonshire Ave SM2 ... 218 A1
Devonshire Cl
Edmonton N13 ... 32 C6
Leyton E15 ... 76 C4
Marylebone W1 ... 238 C4
Devonshire Cres NW7 ... 28 D3
Devonshire Ct
14 Balham SW12 ... 159 B4
Croydon CR0 ... 207 C1
Feltham TW13 ... 150 B2
Pinner HA5 ... 23 B2
6 Richmond TW9 ... 132 B4
Tottenham N17 ... 33 A4
Devonshire Dr
London SE10 ... 141 D4
Long Ditton KT6 ... 213 D6
Devonshire Gdns
Chiswick W4 ... 133 A5
Edmonton N21 ... 17 A4
Tottenham N17 ... 33 A4
Devonshire Gr SE15 ... 140 B6
Devonshire Hall 15 E9 ... 74 C2
Devonshire Hill La
N17 ... 33 A4
Devonshire Hill Prim Sch
N17 ... 33 B4
Devonshire Ho
Brondesbury NW6 ... 69 B2
Hounslow TW3 ... 130 A2
Newington SE1 ... 262 A6
Paddington W2 ... 236 D4
2 Putney SW15 ... 156 C4
10 Sutton SM2 ... 218 A1
Westminster SW1 ... 259 D2
Whetstone N12 ... 14 A1
Devonshire Hospl
W1 ... 93 A2 238 B4
Devonshire House Prep
Sch NW3 ... 70 B3
Devonshire House Sch
NW3 ... 70 A3
Devonshire Mews 2
W4 ... 111 C1
Devonshire Mews N
W1 ... 238 C4
Devonshire Mews S
W1 ... 238 C4
Devonshire Mews W
W1 ... 238 B4
Devonshire Pl
Child's Hill NW2 ... 69 C5
Kensington W8 ... 255 C5
Marylebone W1 ... 93 A2 238 B4
Devonshire Place Mews
W1 ... 238 B4
Devonshire Prim Sch
SM2 ... 218 A1
Devonshire Rd
Bexley DA6 ... 147 A1
Chislehurst SE9 ... 166 A2
Chiswick W4 ... 111 C1
Ealing W5 ... 109 C3
Eastcote HA5 ... 40 C2
Edmonton N9 ... 18 C3
Feltham TW13 ... 173 A6
Forest Hill SE23 ... 162 C4
Hackbridge SM5, SM6 ... 219 A4
Harrow HA1 ... 42 B3
Hatch End HA5 ... 23 B2
Ilford IG2 ... 57 C2
Devonshire Rd *continued*
Mill Hill NW7 ... 28 D3
Mitcham SW19 ... 180 C3
Newham E16 ... 99 B1
Palmers Green N13 ... 32 C6
Southall UB1 ... 85 C2
Sutton SM2 ... 218 A1
Thornton Heath CR0 ... 205 B2
Tottenham N17 ... 33 A4
Walthamstow E17 ... 53 C3
Devonshire Row EC2 ... 243 B3
Devonshire Row Mews
W1 ... 238 D5
Devonshire Sq
Bromley BR2 ... 209 B5
Whitechapel
EC2 ... 95 C1 243 B2
Devonshire St
Chiswick W4 ... 111 C1
Marylebone W1 ... 93 B2 238 C4
Devonshire Terr
W2 ... 92 A1 236 B1
Devonshire Way
Croydon CR0, CR9 ... 223 B6
Hayes UB4 ... 84 B1
Devons Rd E3 ... 97 D3
Devons Road Sta E3 ... 97 D3
Devon St SE15 ... 140 B6
Devon Way
Chessington KT9 ... 213 C3
Ewell KT19 ... 214 D3
Hillingdon UB10 ... 82 B5
Devon Waye TW5 ... 129 B5
De Walden Ho NW8 ... 230 A4
De Walden St W1 ... 238 B3
Dewar Ho 2 SW17 ... 180 C5
Dewar St SE15 ... 140 A2
Dewberry Gdns E6 ... 100 A2
Dewberry St E14 ... 98 A2
Dewey Rd
Dagenham RM10 ... 81 D2
Islington N1 ... 94 C5 234 A4
Dewey St SW17 ... 180 D5
Dewhurst Rd W14 ... 112 D3
Dewlands Ct 7 NW4 ... 28 D1
Dewsbury Cl HA5 ... 41 A3
Dewsbury Ct 5 W4 ... 111 A2
Dewsbury Gdns KT4 ... 216 A5
Dewsbury Rd NW10 ... 68 A3
Dewsbury Terr NW1 ... 231 D6
Dexter Ho 2 DA18 ... 125 A3
Dexter Rd EN5 ... 12 D5
Deyncourt Rd N17 ... 33 A2
Deynecourt Gdns E11 ... 55 C5
D'eynsford Rd SE5 ... 139 B4
Dhonau Ho SE16 ... 263 D4
Diadem Ct W1 ... 239 C2
Dial Wlk The
W8 ... 113 D4 245 D2
Diameter Rd BR5 ... 211 A3
Diamond Cl RM8 ... 58 C1
Diamond Ct 8 W7 ... 108 C5
Diamond Est SW17 ... 158 C1
Diamond Ho 22 E3 ... 97 A5
Diamond Rd HA4 ... 63 A4
Diamond St
18 London NW10 ... 67 B1
SE15 ... 139 C5
Diamond Terr SE10 ... 142 A4
Diana Cl
27 Deptford SE8 ... 141 B6
Sidcup DA14 ... 169 A2
Woodford E18 ... 37 B2
Diana Ct SM5 ... 219 A1
Diana Gdns KT6 ... 214 B6
Diana Ho
Barnes SW13 ... 133 D4
4 Brixton SW2 ... 160 B6
Diana, Princess of Wales
Mml Wlk W2 ... 114 A5 246 A3
Diana Rd E17 ... 53 B6
Dianne Ct SE12 ... 165 A3
Dianne Way EN4 ... 2 C1
Dianthus Cl SE2 ... 124 B1
Dias Ho UB5 ... 85 A6
Dibden Ho 8 SE5 ... 139 C5
Dibden St N1 ... 95 A6 235 A6
Dibdin Cl SM1 ... 217 C5
Dibdin Ho W9 ... 91 D5
Dibdin Rd SM1 ... 217 C6
Dicey Ave NW2 ... 68 C4
Dickens Ave
Finchley N3 ... 30 A2
Hayes UB8 ... 82 D1
Dickens Cl
Erith DA8 ... 147 D5
Hayes UB3 ... 105 C2
Richmond TW10 ... 154 A2
Dickens Ct
Clerkenwell EC1 ... 241 C5
Dickens Ct *continued*
10 Wanstead E11 ... 55 A5
Wembley HA0 ... 65 C5
Dickens Dr BR7 ... 189 A4
Dickens Ho
Bloomsbury WC1 ... 240 A6
3 Erith DA17 ... 125 B1
Hayes UB3 ... 105 C2
Kennington SE17 ... 261 D1
Kilburn NW6 ... 91 C4
Paddington NW8 ... 236 D6
Dickens House Mus*
WC1 ... 94 B3 240 D5
Dickens La N18 ... 33 C5
Dickenson Cl N9 ... 18 A3
Dickenson Ho N8 ... 50 B3
Dickenson Rd
Feltham TW13 ... 172 D5
Hornsey N8 ... 50 A2
Dickenson's La SE25 ... 206 A3
Dickenson's Pl SE25 ... 206 A3
Dickens Rd E6 ... 99 D5
Dickens Sq
SE1 ... 117 A3 262 B6
Dickens St SW8 ... 137 B3
Dickenswood Cl
SE19 ... 182 D3
Dickerage Hill
Kingston u T KT3 ... 177 A1
Kingston u T KT3 ... 199 A6
Dickerage La KT3 ... 199 A6
Dickerage Rd KT1, KT2,
KT3 ... 177 A1
Dickinson Ho 18 E2 ... 96 A4
Dicksee Ho NW8 ... 236 C5
Dick Shepherd Ct 17
SW2 ... 160 C5
Dickson Fold HA5 ... 40 D5
Dickson Ho
3 Charlton SE18 ... 144 A4
4 Stepney E1 ... 96 B1
Dickson Rd SE9 ... 144 A2
Dick Turpin Way
TW14 ... 127 D1
Didbin Ho N7 ... 72 B6
Didsbury Cl E6 ... 100 B6
Digby Bsns Ctr E9 ... 74 D2
Digby Cres N4 ... 73 A6
Digby Gdns RM10 ... 103 C6
Digby Mans W6 ... 112 C1
Digby Pl CR0 ... 221 D5
Digby Rd
Barking IG11 ... 79 D1
Homerton E9 ... 74 D2
Digby St E2 ... 96 C4
Diggon St E1 ... 96 D2
Dighton Ct SE17 ... 139 A6
Dighton Rd SW18 ... 136 A1
Dignum St N1 ... 234 A4
Digswell St N7 ... 72 C2
Dilhorne Cl SE12 ... 165 B1
Dilke St SW3 ... 136 D6 267 D6
Dilloway Yd UB2 ... 107 A4
Dillwyn Cl SE26 ... 185 A6
Dilston Cl 1 UB5 ... 84 C4
Dilston Gr SE16 ... 118 C2
Dilton Gdns SW15 ... 156 B3
Dilwyn Ct E17 ... 35 A1
Dimes Pl 9 W6 ... 112 B2
Dimmock Dr UB6 ... 64 B3
Dimond Cl E7 ... 77 A4
Dimsdale Dr
Enfield EN1 ... 18 A5
Welsh Harp NW9 ... 45 A1
Dimsdale Wlk 4 E13 ... 99 A5
Dimson Cres E3 ... 97 C4
Dinerman Ct NW8 ... 229 B6
Dingle Cl EN5 ... 11 D5
Dingle Ct 16 HA7 ... 25 C5
Dingle Gdns E14 ... 119 C6
Dingle Rd TW15 ... 170 D5
Dingles Ct HA5 ... 22 D1
Dingle The UB10 ... 82 D4
Dingley La SW16 ... 159 D2
Dingley Pl EC1 ... 95 A4 235 B1
Dingley Rd EC1 ... 95 A4 235 A1
Dingwall Ave CR0 ... 221 A6
Dingwall Gdns NW11 ... 47 C3
Dingwall Rd
South Croydon CR0 ... 221 B6
Wandsworth SW18 ... 158 A4
Dinmont Ho 27 E2 ... 96 A5
Dinmont St 1 E2 ... 96 B5
Dinmore Ho 6 E9 ... 96 C6
Dinnington Ho 17 E1 ... 96 B3
Dinorben SM6 ... 219 C1
Dinsdale Ct EN5 ... 13 D6
Dinsdale Gdns
New Barnet EN5 ... 13 D6
South Norwood SE25 ... 205 C4
Dinsdale Rd SE3 ... 142 D6
Dinsmore Rd SW12 ... 159 B4
Dinton Ho NW8 ... 237 A6
Dinton Rd
Kingston u T KT2 ... 176 B3
Mitcham SW19 ... 180 B4
Dinwiddy Ho N1 ... 233 C3
Dionis Ho SW6 ... 135 C3
Diploma Ave N2 ... 48 C5
Diploma Ct N2 ... 48 C5
Diprose Lo SW17 ... 180 B6
Dirleton Rd E15 ... 98 D6
Disbrowe Rd
W6 ... 135 A6 264 B5
Discovery Bsns Pk 13
SE16 ... 118 A3
Discovery Dock E
E14 ... 119 D4
Discovery Ho 1 E14 ... 120 A6
Dishforth La NW9 ... 27 C2
Disley Ct 2 UB1 ... 85 D1
Disney Pl SE1 ... 252 B2
Disney St SE1 ... 252 B2
Dison Cl EN3 ... 6 D4
Disraeli Cl
1 Acton W4 ... 111 B2
Thamesmead SE28 ... 124 C5
Disraeli Gdns SW15 ... 135 B1
Disraeli Rd
Acton NW10 ... 89 B5
Ealing W5 ... 109 D5
Putney SW15 ... 135 A1
Upton E7 ... 77 A2
Diss St E2 ... 95 D4
Distaff La EC4 ... 252 A6
Distillery La W6 ... 112 C1
Distillery Rd W6 ... 112 C1
Distillery Wlk 14
TW8 ... 132 A6
Distin Ct 3 SM1 ... 217 D3
Distin St SE11 ... 116 C2 261 A3
District Rd HA0 ... 65 B3
Ditchburn St E14 ... 120 A6
Ditchfield Rd UB4 ... 85 A3
Ditchley Ct W7 ... 86 D2
Dittisham Rd SE9 ... 188 A6
Ditton Cl KT7 ... 197 A2
Dittoncroft Cl CR0 ... 221 C4
Ditton Grange Cl KT6 ... 197 D1
Ditton Grange Dr
KT6 ... 197 D1
Ditton Hill KT6 ... 213 D6
Ditton Hill Rd KT6 ... 197 C1
Ditton Ho 10 E5 ... 74 B3
Ditton Lawn KT7 ... 197 A1
Ditton Pl 6 SE20 ... 184 B2
Ditton Rd
Bexley DA6 ... 169 A6
Southall UB2 ... 107 B1
Surbiton KT6 ... 198 B1
Ditton Reach KT7 ... 197 B3
Divis Way SW15 ... 156 B5
Dixon Cl 4 E6 ... 100 B1
Dixon Clark Ct N1 ... 72 D2
Dixon Ct N4 ... 50 C3
Dixon Ho
20 North Kensington
NW10 ... 90 D1
West Heath SE2 ... 124 C1
Dixon Pl BR4 ... 207 D1
Dixon Rd
London SE14 ... 141 A4
South Norwood SE25 ... 205 D6
Dixon's Alley 10 SE16 ... 118 B4
Dobbin Cl HA3 ... 25 A1
Dobell Rd SE9 ... 166 B6
Dobree Ave NW10 ... 68 B1
Dobson Cl NW6 ... 70 B1
Dobson Ho 18 SE14 ... 140 D6
Doby Ct EC4 ... 252 B6
Dockers Tanner Rd 26
E14 ... 119 C2
Dockett Eddy La KT16,
TW17 ... 192 B1
Dockett Moorings
KT16 ... 192 B1
Dockhead
SE1 ... 117 D4 253 D1
Dockhead Wharf SE1 ... 253 D2
Dock Hill Ave SE16 ... 118 D4
Docklands Ct 20 E14 ... 97 B1
Docklands Heritage Mus*
SE16 ... 119 B5
Dockland St E16 ... 122 C5
Dockley Rd SE16 ... 118 A3
Dockley Road Ind Est 11
SE16 ... 118 A3
Dock Offices 12 SE16 ... 118 C3
Dock Rd
Brentford TW8 ... 131 D5
Dock Rd *continued*
Canning Town E16 ... 120 D6
Dockside Rd E16 ... 121 D6
Dock St E1 ... 118 A6
Dockwell Cl TW14 ... 128 A1
Dockwell's Ind Est
TW14 ... 150 B6
Doctor Johnson Ho 2
SW16 ... 181 D6
Doctors Cl SE26 ... 184 C5
Doctor Spurstowe
Almshouses 9 E8 ... 74 B2
Docura Ho N7 ... 72 B6
Docwras Bldgs N1 ... 73 C2
Dodbrooke Rd SE27 ... 160 D1
Dodd Ho 18 SE16 ... 118 B2
Doddington Gr
SE17 ... 116 D1 261 D1
Doddington Pl 4
SE17 ... 138 D6
Dodsley Pl N9 ... 18 C1
Dodson St
SE1 ... 116 C4 251 B1
Dod St E14 ... 97 C1
Doebury Wlk SE18 ... 146 A6
Doel Cl SW19 ... 180 A3
Doggett Rd SE6 ... 163 C4
Doggetts Ct EN4 ... 14 C6
Doghurst Ave UB3 ... 126 D5
Doghurst Dr UB7 ... 126 D5
Dog Kennel Hill SE22 ... 139 C2
Dog Kennel Hill Sch
SE22 ... 139 C2
Dog La NW10 ... 67 C4
Dogrose Ct 14 NW9 ... 46 A5
Doherty Rd E13 ... 99 A3
Dokal Ind Est UB2 ... 107 A4
Doland Ct SW17 ... 180 D4
Dolben Ct SW1 ... 259 D3
Dolben St SE1 ... 116 D5 251 D3
Dolby Rd SW6 ... 135 B3
Doleman Ho 19 SE10 ... 141 D4
Dolland Ho SE11 ... 260 D1
Dolland St SE11 ... 260 D1
Dollar Bay E14 ... 120 A4
Dollary Ct KT3 ... 198 D6
Dolliffe Cl CR4 ... 180 D1
Dollis Ave N3 ... 29 B2
Dollis Brook Wlk EN5 ... 13 A5
Dollis Cres HA4 ... 40 C1
Dolliscroft NW7 ... 29 A3
Dollis Ct N3 ... 29 B2
DOLLIS HILL ... 68 B5
Dollis Hill Ave NW2 ... 68 B5
Dollis Hill Est NW2 ... 68 A5
Dollis Hill La NW2 ... 68 A5
Dollis Hill Sta NW2 ... 68 A3
Dollis Hts NW2 ... 68 B5
Dollis Jun & Inf Schs
NW7 ... 28 C3
Dollis Mews N3 ... 29 C2
Dollis Pk N3 ... 29 B2
Dollis Rd N3, NW7 ... 29 B3
Dollis Valley Dr EN5 ... 13 B6
Dollis Valley Way EN5 ... 13 B5
Dolman Cl N3 ... 30 A1
Dolman Rd W4 ... 111 B2
Dolman St SW4 ... 138 B1
Dolphin Cl
Kingston u T KT6 ... 197 D4
2 Rotherhithe SE16 ... 118 D4
Thamesmead SE28 ... 102 D1
Dolphin Ct
London NW11 ... 47 A3
Merton SW19 ... 179 C3
Tufnell Pk N7 ... 71 D4
2 Wallington SM6 ... 219 B2
Dolphin Est The
TW16 ... 171 B2
Dolphin La E14 ... 119 D6
Dolphin Rd
Charlton TW16 ... 171 C2
Northolt UB5 ... 85 B5
Dolphin Rd N TW16 ... 171 C2
Dolphin Rd S TW16 ... 171 C2
Dolphin Rd W TW16 ... 171 C2
Dolphin Sch SW11 ... 158 D6
Dolphin Sq
SW1 ... 115 C1 259 B1
Dolphin St KT2 ... 176 A2
Dolphin Twr 21 SE8 ... 141 B6
Dombey Ho
13 Bermondsey SE1 ... 118 A4
4 Shepherd's Bush
W11 ... 112 D5
Dombey St WC1 ... 240 C4
Dome Hill Pk SE26 ... 183 D6
Domelton Ho SW18 ... 157 D5
Domett Cl SE5 ... 139 B1
Domfe Pl E5 ... 74 C4

Domingo St EC1 242 A5
Dominica Cl 6 E6 99 D5
Dominion Bsns Pk N9 18 D2
Dominion Cl TW3 130 B3
Dominion Ind Est UB2 107 A4
Dominion Par HA1 42 D4
Dominion Rd
  Croydon CR0 205 D2
  Southall UB2 107 A3
Dominion St EC2 95 B2 242 D4
Dominion Wks RM8 59 A1
Domonic Dr SE9 166 D1
Domville Cl N20 14 B2
Donaghue Cotts 11 E14 97 A2
Donald Dr RM6 58 C4
Donald Lynch Ho CR4 180 D1
Donald Rd
  Newham E13 99 B6
  Thornton Heath CR0 204 B2
Donaldson Rd
  Kilburn NW6 91 B6
  Shooters Hill SE18 144 C4
Donald Woods Gdns KT5 215 A6
Doncaster Dr UB5 63 B3
Doncaster Gdns
  London N4 51 A3
  Northolt UB5 63 B3
Doncaster Gn WD19 22 C5
Doncaster Rd N9 18 B4
Doncel Ct E4 20 B4
Donegal Ho 2 E1 96 C3
Donegal St N1 94 B5 233 D3
Doneraile Ho SW1 258 C1
Doneraile St SW6 134 D4
Dongola Rd
  Newham E13 99 B4
  Tottenham N17 51 C6
  Tower Hamlets E1 97 A2
Dongola Rd W 5 E13 99 B4
Don Gratton Ho 23 E1 96 A2
Donington Ave IG6 57 A4
Donkey Alley SE22 162 A5
Donkey La EN1 6 A3
Donkin Ho 15 SE16 118 B2
Donne Ct SE24 161 A5
Donnefield Ave HA8 26 A3
Donne Ho
  18 Canonbury N16 73 B4
  14 Deptford SE14 140 D6
  11 Poplar E14 97 C1
Donnelly Ct SW6 264 B4
Donne Pl
  Chelsea SW3 114 C2 257 B4
  Mitcham CR4 203 B5
Donne Rd RM8 80 C6
Donnington Ct
  11 Camden Town NW1 71 B1
  Willesden NW10 68 B1
Donnington Ho 12 SW8 137 D3
Donnington Prim Sch NW10 90 B6
Donnington Rd
  Harrow HA3 43 D3
  Willesden Green NW10 90 B6
  Worcester Pk KT4 216 A6
Donnybrook Rd SW16 181 D3
Donoghue Bsns Pk NW2 68 D5
Donovan Ave N10 31 C1
Donovan Ct SW7 256 C1
Donovan Ho 4 E1 118 C6
Donovan Pl N21 16 B6
Don Phelan Cl SE5 139 B4
Doone Cl TW11 175 A4
Doon St SE1 116 C5 251 A4
Doradus Ct 20 SW19 156 D3
Dora Ho
  11 Shepherd's Bush W11 112 D6
  1 Tower Hamlets E14 97 B1
Doral Way SM5 218 D3
Doran Ct E6 100 B5
Dorando Cl W12 112 B6
Doran Gr SE18 145 C5
Doran Manor N2 48 D4
Doran Wlk
  Stratford E15 76 A1
  Stratford Marsh E15 98 A6
Dora Rd SW19 179 C6
Dora St E14 97 B1
Dora Way SW9 138 C3
Dorcas Ct 9 SW18 136 B1
Dorchester Ave
  Edmonton N13 33 A6
  Harrow HA2 42 A3
  Sidcup DA5 168 D4
Dorchester Cl
  Northolt UB5 63 D3
  St Paul's Cray BR5 190 B3
Dorchester Ct
  Cricklewood NW2 68 D5
  1 De Beauvoir Town N1 73 C1
  East Barnet N14 15 B4
  Herne Hill SE24 161 A6
  Knightsbridge SW1 257 D5
  1 Muswell Hill N10 49 B6
  5 Streatham SW16 160 A2
  2 Woodford E18 36 D2
Dorchester Dr
  Feltham TW14 149 C5
  Herne Hill SE24 161 A6
Dorchester Gdns
  Chingford E4 35 C6
  East Finchley NW11 47 C5
Dorchester Gr W4 111 D1
Dorchester Ho
  Richmond TW9 132 D5
  Wallington SM5 218 D3
Dorchester Mews
  New Malden KT3 199 B5
  Twickenham TW1 153 C5
Dorchester Prim Sch KT4 200 C1
Dorchester Rd
  Cheam SM4 202 A2
  North Cheam KT4 200 C1
  Northolt UB5 63 D3
Dorchester Way HA3 44 B3
Dorchester Waye
  Hayes UB4 84 B1
  Hayes UB4 84 C1
Dorcis Ave DA7 147 A3
Dordrecht Rd W3 111 C5
Dore Ave E12 78 C3
Doreen Ave NW9 45 B1
Doreen Capstan Ho 5 E11 76 C5
Dore Gdns SM4 201 D2
Dorell Cl UB1 85 B2
Dorey Ho 7 TW8 131 C5
Doria Rd SW6 135 B3
Doric Ho 7 E2 96 D5
Doric Way NW1 93 D4 232 C2
Dorie Mews N12 29 D6
Dorien Rd SW20 178 D1
Doris Emmerton Ct SW18 136 A1
Doris Rd
  Ashford TW15 171 B4
  Upton E7 77 A1
Dorking Cl
  Deptford SE8 141 B6
  North Cheam KT4 216 D6
Dorking Ct N17 34 A2
Dorking Ho SE1 262 D6
Dorland Ct SW15 157 B5
Dorlcote Rd SW18 158 C4
Dorleston Ct N1 235 D6
Dorly Cl TW17 193 C4
Dorman Pl 6 N9 18 A2
Dorman Way NW8 92 B6 229 C6
Dorman Wlk NW10 67 B2
Dorma Trad Pk E10 52 D1
Dormay St SW18 157 D6
Dormer Cl
  Barnet EN5 12 D6
  Stratford E15 76 D2
Dormer's Ave UB1 85 C1
Dormers Lo EN4 2 D3
Dormers Rise UB1 85 D1
DORMER'S WELLS 107 C6
Dormer's Wells High Sch UB1 85 C1
Dormers Wells Ho UB4 84 C2
Dormer's Wells Inf Sch UB1 107 D6
Dormer's Wells Jun Sch UB1 107 D6
Dormer's Wells La UB1 107 C5
Dormstone Ho SE17 263 A3
Dormywood HA4 39 D4
Dornberg Cl SE3 143 A5
Dornberg Rd SE3 143 B5
Dorncliffe Rd SW6 135 A3
Dorney NW3 70 C1
Dorney Ct SW6 135 A2
Dorney Rise BR5 211 D5
Dorney Way TW4 151 A6
Dornfell St NW6 69 B3
Dornoch Ho 26 E3 97 B5
Dornton Rd
  South Croydon CR2 221 C3
  Upper Tooting SW12, SW17 159 C2
Dorothy Ave HA0 66 A1
Dorothy Barley Schs RM8 80 B3
Dorothy Charrington Ho 1 SE22 162 A6
Dorothy Evans Cl DA7 147 D1
Dorothy Gdns RM8 80 B4
Dorothy Pettingel Ho 1 SM1 217 D5
Dorothy Rd SW11 136 D2
Dorothy Villas UB1 107 C5
Dorrien Wlk SW16 159 D2
Dorrington Ct SE25 183 C1
Dorrington Point 20 E3 97 D4
Dorrington St EC1 241 A4
Dorrington Way BR3 208 A4
Dorrit Ho 2 W11 112 D5
Dorrit Mews N18 33 C5
Dorrit St SE1 252 B2
Dorrit Way BR7 189 A4
Dorryn Ct SE26 184 D5
Dors Cl NW9 45 B1
Dorset Ave
  Falconwood DA16 145 D1
  Hayes UB4 83 C4
  Southall UB2 107 C2
Dorset Bldgs EC4 241 C1
Dorset Cl
  Hayes UB4 83 C4
  Marylebone NW1 237 C4
Dorset Ct
  3 Ealing W7 86 D2
  3 London N1 73 C1
  4 Northolt UB5 85 B4
Dorset Dr HA8 26 B4
Dorset Gdns SW16 204 B5
Dorset Hall SW19 179 C2
Dorset Ho 1 SE20 184 B2
Dorset Mans 2 W6 134 D6
Dorset Mews
  Belgravia SW1 258 C6
  Finchley N3 29 C2
Dorset Pl E15 76 B2
Dorset Rd
  Ashford TW15 148 A1
  Chislehurst SE9 166 A2
  Ealing W5 109 D3
  Harrow HA1 42 A3
  Merton SW19 179 C1
  Mitcham CR4 180 C1
  Penge BR3 206 D6
  South Lambeth SW8 138 B5 270 C4
  Upton E7 77 C1
  West Green N15 51 B5
  Wood Green N22 32 A2
Dorset Rise EC4 94 D1 241 C1
Dorset Road Inf Sch SE9 166 A2
Dorset Sq NW1 92 D3 237 C5
Dorset St W1 92 D2 237 D3
Dorset Way
  Hillingdon UB10 82 B5
  Twickenham TW2 152 B3
Dorset Waye TW5 129 B5
Dorton Cl 6 SE15 139 C5
Dorton Villas UB7 126 C4
Dorville Cres W6 112 B3
Dorville Rd SE12 165 A6
Dothill Rd SE18 145 A5
Douai Gr TW12 174 A2
Douay Martyrs RC Sch (Annexe) The UB10 60 D3
Douay Martyrs RC Sch The UB10 60 D4
Doughty Ct 11 E1 118 B5
Doughty Mews WC1 94 B3 240 C5
Doughty St WC1 94 B3 240 C5
Douglas 20 NW9 27 D1
Douglas Ave
  Walthamstow E17 35 C2
  Wembley HA0 66 A1
  West Barnes KT3 200 B5
Douglas Bader Ho N3 29 D4
Douglas Bldgs SE1 252 B2
Douglas Cl
  Stanmore HA7 25 A5
  Wallington SM6 220 A2
Douglas Cres UB4 84 D3
Douglas Ct
  London N3 29 D1
  5 South Hampstead NW6 69 C1
  1 Upper Tooting SW17 180 C4
Douglas Dr CR0 223 C5
Douglas Gracey Ho SW18 157 A4
Douglas Ho
  Isleworth TW1 153 B6
  Putney SW15 156 A5
  Westminster SW1 259 C3
Douglas Johnstone Ho SW6 264 C5
Douglas Mews NW2 69 A5
Douglas Path E14 120 A1
Douglas Rd
  Chingford E4 20 C3
  Hounslow TW3 129 D2
  Ilford IG3 58 A3
  Islington N1 73 A1
  Kilburn NW6 91 B6
  Kingston u T KT1 176 D1
  5 Newham E16 99 A2
  Stanwell TW19 148 A5
  Surbiton KT6 198 B1
  Thames Ditton KT10 212 A6
  Welling DA16 146 B4
  Wood Green N22 32 C2
Douglas Rd N N1 73 A2
Douglas Rd S N1 73 A2
Douglas Robinson Ct SW16 182 A3
Douglas Sq SM4 201 C3
Douglas St SW1 115 D2 259 C3
Douglas Terr E17 35 B2
Douglas Waite Ho NW6 69 D1
Douglas Way SE8 141 B5
Doulton Ho SE11 260 D4
Doulton Mews 4 NW6 69 D2
Dounesforth Gdns SW18 157 D3
Douro Pl W8 113 D3 255 D6
Douro St E3 97 C5
Douthwaite Sq 12 E1 118 A5
Dove App E6 100 A2
Dove Cl
  Hendon NW7 27 D3
  Northolt UB5 84 D3
  Wallington SM6 220 B1
Dovecot Cl HA5 40 C4
Dovecote Gdns 8 SW14 133 B2
Dove Ct
  City of London EC2 242 C1
  Enfield EN3 18 D6
  Stanwell TW19 148 A4
Dovedale Ave HA3 43 C3
Dovedale Cl DA16 146 A3
Dovedale Cotts 6 SW11 136 D3
Dovedale Ho N16 51 B2
Dovedale Rd SE22 162 B5
Dovedale Rise CR4 180 D3
Dovedon Cl N14 16 A2
Dove House Gdns E4 19 C2
Dovehouse Mead IG11 101 B5
Dovehouse St SW3 114 C1 257 A1
Dove Mews SW7 114 A1 256 B2
Dove Pk HA5 23 C3
Dover Cl NW2 68 D6
Dovercourt Ave CR7 204 C5
Dovercourt Gdns HA7 26 A5
Dovercourt La SM1 218 A5
Dovercourt Rd SE22 161 D5
Dover Ct
  Clerkenwell EC1 241 C6
  17 Greenwich SE10 141 D4
  Sutton SM1 218 B4
Dove Rd N1 73 B2
Doverfield Rd SW2 160 A4
Dover Flats SE1 263 B3
Dover Gdns SM5 218 D5
Dover Ho
  7 Beckenham BR3 185 C3
  Brixton SE5 138 D4
  11 Deptford SE15 140 C6
  Edgware HA8 26 B3
  14 Penge SE20 184 B2
Dover House Rd SW15 156 B6
Doveridge Gdns N13 32 D6
Dover Mans 16 SW9 138 C2
Dove Row E2 96 A6
Dover Park Dr SW15 156 B5
Dover Patrol SE3 143 C3
Dover Rd
  Dagenham RM6 59 A3
  Lower Edmonton N9 18 C2
  South Norwood SE19 183 B4
  Wanstead E12 77 C6
  Woolwich SE18 145 A3
Dover St W1 115 C5 249 A4
Dover Terr TW9 132 C3
Dover Yd W1 249 A4
Doves Cl BR2 226 A6
Doves Yd N1 94 C6 234 A5
Dovet Ct SW8 270 C2
Doveton Ho 7 E1 96 C3
Doveton Rd CR2 221 B3
Doveton St 8 E1 96 C3
Dove Wlk SW1 258 A2
Dovey Lo 4 N1 72 C1
Dowanhill Rd SE6 164 B3
Dowd Cl N11 15 A2
Dowdeny Cl 12 NW5 71 C3
Dowdeswell Cl SW15 133 C1
Dowding Ho N6 49 A2
Dowding Pl HA7 25 A4
Dowding Rd UB10 60 B1
Dowe Ho SE3 142 C2
Dowell Ho SE21 161 D1
Dower Ho The DA14 169 B1
Dowes Ho 13 SW16 160 A1
Dowgate Hill EC4 252 C6
Dowland Ho EN1 5 D5
Dowland St W10 91 A4
Dowlas St SE5 139 C5
Dowlen Ct 14 E14 119 C4
Dowler Ct 2 KT2 176 B2
Dowler Ho 32 E1 96 A1
Dowlerville Rd BR6 227 D2
Dowling Ho DA17 125 B3
Dowman Cl 2 SW19 179 D3
Downage NW4 46 C6
Downalong WD23 8 B3
Down Barns Rd HA4 62 D5
Downbarton Ho 11 SW9 138 C4
Downbury Mews 13 SW18 157 C6
Down Cl UB5 84 B5
Downderry Prim Sch BR1 186 C6
Downderry Rd BR1 186 C6
Downe Cl DA16 146 C5
Downe Ho 9 SE7 143 C6
Downe Manor Prim Sch UB5 84 B4
Downend SE18 144 D5
Downend Ct 1 SE15 139 C6
Downe Rd CR4 180 D1
Downer's Cotts SW4 137 C1
Downes Cl TW1 153 B5
Downes Ct N21 16 C3
Downes Ho CR0 220 D4
Downey Ho 6 E1 96 D3
Downfield KT4 200 A1
Downfield Cl W9 91 D3
Downfield Ho KT3 199 B1
Down Hall Rd KT2 175 D2
DOWNHAM 186 C5
Downham Ct 1 N1 73 B1
Downham Ent Ctr SE6 164 D2
Downham La BR1 186 B5
Downham Rd N1 73 B1
Downham Way BR1 186 C6
Downhills Ave N17 51 B6
Downhills Park Rd N17 51 A6
Downhills Prim Sch N15 51 B5
Downhills Way N17 33 A1
Downhurst Ave NW7 27 B5
Downhurst Ct NW4 46 C6
Downing Cl HA2 42 A6
Downing Ct N12 29 D5
Downing Dr UB6 86 C6
Downing Ho
  9 Merton SW19 179 C3
  2 North Kensington W10 90 D1
  4 Putney SW15 156 A6
Downing Rd RM9 81 B1
Downings E6 100 C1
Downing St* SW1 116 A4 250 A2
Downland Cl N20 14 A3
Downland Ct E11 76 C6
Downleys Cl SE9 166 B2
Downman Rd SE9 144 A2
Down Pl W6 112 B1
Down Rd TW11 175 B4
Down St Mews W1 248 C3
Downs Ave
  Elmstead BR7 188 B5
  Pinner HA5 41 B2
Downs Bridge Rd BR3 186 B2
Downs Ct
  16 Hackney E8 74 B3
  13 Wimbledon SW19 178 D3
Downsell Prim Sch E15 76 B4
Downsell Rd E15 76 B4
Downsfield Rd E17 53 A3
Downshall Ave IG3 57 C3
Downshall Ct IG3 57 C3
Downshall Prim Sch IG3 57 C2
Downs Hill BR2, BR3 186 B2
Downshire Hill NW3 70 B4
Downside
  2 Putney SW15 157 A6
  Sunbury TW16 172 A2
  Twickenham TW1 152 D1
Downside Cl SW19 180 A4
Downside Cres
  Ealing W13 87 A3
  Maitland Pk NW3 70 C3
Downside Rd SM2 218 C2
Downside Wlk UB5 85 B4
Downs La 2 E5 74 B4
Downs Park Rd E5, E8 74 A3
Downs Rd
  Beckenham BR3 185 D1
  Enfield EN1 5 C1
  Shacklewell E5, N16 74 A4
  South Norwood CR7 183 A2
Down St
  East Molesey KT8 195 C4
  Mayfair W1 115 B5 248 C3
Downs The SW19, SW20 178 D3
Downs View TW7 131 A4
Downsview Gdns SE19 183 A3
Downs View Lo 9 KT6 198 A3
Downsview Prim Sch SE19 183 A3
Downsview Rd SE19 183 A3
Downsview Sch E5 74 B4
Downsway BR6 227 C3
Downton Ave SW2 160 B2
Downtown Rd SE16 119 A4
Downway N12 30 C3
Down Way UB5 84 B4
Dowrey St N1 234 A6
Dowsett Rd N17 34 A1
Dowson Cl SE5 139 B1
Dowson Ct SE13 142 B2
Dowson Ho 8 E1 96 D1
Doyce St SE1 252 A2
Doyle Gdns NW10 90 B6
Doyle Ho W3 110 D4
Doyle Rd SE25 206 A5
D'Oyley St SW1 258 A4
Doynton St N19 71 B6
Draco St SE17 139 A6
Dragon Ct WC2 240 B2
Dragonfly Cl E13 99 B4
Dragon Rd SE15 139 C6
Dragon Yd WC1 240 B2
Dragoon Rd SE8 119 B1
Dragor Rd NW10 89 A3
Drake Cl 30 SE16 118 D4
Drake Cres SE28 102 C1
Drake Croft N16 73 B6
Drake Ct
  Dulwich SE19 183 D5
  5 Hammersmith W12 112 B4
  Kingston u T KT5 198 B5
Drakefell Rd SE4, SE14 140 D2
Drakefield Rd SW17 159 A1
Drake Hall 13 E16 121 B5
Drake Ho
  2 Limehouse E14 119 A6
  20 Stepney E1 96 C2
Drakeley Ct N5 72 D4
Drake Mews BR2 209 C5
Drake Rd
  Brockley SE4 141 C2
  Chessington KT9 214 C3
  Harrow HA2 63 B6
  Mitcham CR4 203 A3
  Thornton Heath CR0 204 B2

Drakes Ct SE23 162 C3
Drakes Ctyd NW6 69 B1
Drake St
Enfield EN2 5 B4
Holborn WC1 240 C3
Drakes Wlk E6 100 B6
Drakewood Rd SW16 181 D3
Draper Cl
Belvedere DA17 125 B2
Hounslow TW7 130 B3
Draper Ct BR1 210 A5
Draper Ho SE1 261 D4
Draper Pl N1 234 D6
Drapers Almhouses 5
E3 97 C4
Draper's Cottage Homes
NW7 28 A6
Drapers Gdns EC2 242 D2
Drapers Rd
Enfield EN2 4 D4
Leyton E15 76 B4
Tottenham N17 51 D6
Drappers Way 8
SE16 118 A2
Draven Cl BR2 208 D2
Drawell Cl SE18 123 C1
Drax Ave SW20 178 A3
Draxmont SW19 179 A4
Draycot Rd
Tolworth KT6 198 C1
Wanstead E11 55 B2
Draycott Ave
Chelsea SW3 114 C2 257 B3
Harrow HA3 43 C3
Draycott Cl
Camberwell SE5 139 B5
Cricklewood NW2 68 D5
Harrow HA3 43 B3
Draycott Ct SW11 267 A2
Draycott Ho SW3 257 C3
Draycott Pl
SW3 114 D2 257 C3
Draycott Terr
SW3 114 D2 257 D3
Drayford Cl W9 91 B3
Dray Gdns SW2 160 B6
Draymans Ct 4 SW9 138 B2
Draymans Way TW7 130 D2
Drayside Mews UB2 107 B4
Drayson Mews
W8 113 C4 245 B1
Drayton Ave
Ealing W13 109 A6
Orpington BR6 210 D1
Drayton Bridge Rd
Ealing W7, W13 108 D6
Ealing W13 87 A1
Drayton Cl
Hounslow TW4 151 B6
Ilford IG1 57 B1
Drayton Ct
South Kensington
SW10 256 B1
Tolworth KT5 214 D6
West Drayton UB7 104 B2
Drayton Gdns
Ealing W13 109 A6
Southgate N21 16 D4
South Kensington
SW10 114 A1 256 B1
West Drayton UB7 104 A4
Drayton Gn W13 109 A6
Drayton Gr W13 109 A6
Drayton Green Prim Sch
W13 109 A6
Drayton Green Rd
W13 109 B6
Drayton Green Sta W7 86 D1
Drayton Ho
14 Camberwell SE5 139 B5
Leytonstone E11 54 B1
Drayton Lo E17 35 D1
Drayton Manor High Sch
W7 86 D1
Drayton Park Mews 12
N5 72 C3
Drayton Park Prim Sch
N5 72 C3
Drayton Park Sta N5 72 C3
Drayton Pk N5, N7 72 C4
Drayton Rd
Croydon CR0 220 D6
Ealing W13 109 B6
Harlesden NW10 89 D6
Leytonstone E11 54 B1
Tottenham N17 33 C1
Drayton Waye HA3 43 B3
Dreadnought Cl
SW19 180 B1
Dreadnought St SE10 120 C3
Drenon Sq UB3 105 D6
Dresden Cl NW6 69 D2
Dresden Ho
5 Clapham SW11 137 A3
Lambeth SE11 260 D4
Dresden Rd N19 49 D1
Dressington Ave SE4 163 C5
Drew Ave NW7 29 A4
Drewery Ct SE3 142 C2
Drewett Ho 31 E1 96 A1
Drew Gdns UB6 64 D2
Drew Ho 12 SW16 160 A1
Drew Prim Sch E16 122 A5
Drew Rd E16 122 A5
Drewstead La SW16 159 D2
Drewstead Rd SW16 159 D2
Driberg Ct RM9 80 B2
Driffield Ct 4 NW9 27 C2
Driffield Rd E3 97 A5
Drift The BR2 225 D5
Driftway Ho 19 E3 97 B5
Driftway The CR4 181 A2
Drinkwater Ho 11
SE5 139 B5
Drinkwater Rd HA2 63 D6
Drive Ct HA8 26 C5
Drive Ho CR4 202 C5
Drive Mans SW6 135 A3
Drive The
Acton W3 89 A1
Ashford TW15 171 B3
Barking IG11 79 D1
Barking IG11 80 A2
Barnet EN5 1 A2
Beckenham BR3 185 C2
Bexley DA5 168 D4
Buckhurst Hill IG9 21 C4
Chingford E4 20 B4
Chislehurst BR7 189 D2
Edgware HA8 26 C5
Enfield EN2 5 B4
Erith DA8 147 D6
Feltham TW14 150 C4
Finchley N3 29 C3
Fortis Green N6 48 D4
Harlesden NW10 89 D6
Harrow HA2 41 C2
Hendon NW11 47 A2
Hounslow TW3, TW7 130 B3
Ickenham UB10 60 A5
Islington N7 72 B2
Kingston u T KT2 177 A3
Morden SM4 202 B4
New Barnet EN5 14 A5
Orpington BR6 227 D6
Redbridge IG1 56 B2
Sidcup DA14 190 B6
South Norwood CR7 205 B5
St Paul's Cray BR7 211 D6
Surbiton KT6 198 A2
Thames Ditton KT10 196 A1
Walthamstow E17 53 D6
Wanstead E18 55 A6
Wembley Pk HA9 67 A6
West Ewell KT19 215 D2
West Wickham BR4 208 B2
Wimbledon SW19,
SW20 178 C3
Wood Green N11 31 D4
Dr Johnson Ave
SW17 159 B1
Dr Johnson's House Mus*
EC4 241 B1
Droitwich Cl SE26 162 A1
Dromey Gdns HA3 24 D3
Dromore Rd SW15 157 A5
Dronfield Gdns RM8 80 C3
Dron Ho E1 96 C2
Droop St W10 91 A3
Drovers Ct
3 Kingston u T KT1 176 A1
Lewisham SE13 142 A2
Drovers Pl SE15 140 B5
Drovers Rd CR2 221 B3
Dr Triplett's CE Prim Sch
UB3 83 D1
Druce Rd SE21 161 C5
Druid St SE1 117 D4 253 C1
Druids Way BR2 208 B5
Drumaline Ridge KT4 215 C6
Drummer Lo N7 72 B5
Drummond Castle Ct
E7 76 D4
Drummond Cres
NW1 93 D4 232 C2
Drummond Ct
Finchley N12 30 C3
Drummond Ct *continued*
Harrow HA1 42 C2
Drummond Ctr CR0 221 A6
Drummond Dr HA7 24 D3
Drummond Gate SW1 259 D2
Drummond Ho
13 Bethnal Green E2 96 A5
Finchley N2 30 A1
Drummond Rd
Bermondsey SE16 118 B3
Croydon CR0 221 A6
Wanstead E11 55 C3
Drummonds Pl TW9 132 A1
Drummond St
NW1 93 C3 239 A6
Drummonds The IG9 21 B2
Drum St E1 243 D2
Drury Cres CR0 220 C6
Drury Ho SW8 269 A2
Drury La WC2 94 A1 240 B1
Drury Rd HA1 42 A2
Drury Way NW10 67 B3
Drury Way Ind Est
NW10 67 B3
Dryad St SW15 134 D2
Dryburgh Gdns NW9 44 C6
Dryburgh Ho SW1 258 D2
Dryburgh Mans
SW15 134 C2
Dryburgh Rd SW15 134 C2
Dryden Ave W7 86 D1
Dryden Bldg 10 E1 96 A1
Dryden Ct
Lambeth SE11 261 B3
11 Richmond TW10 175 D6
Dryden Ho
Bromley Comm BR2 209 D4
6 Camberwell SE5 139 C4
16 Stoke Newington
N16 73 C5
Dryden Rd
Bexley DA16 145 D4
Enfield EN1 17 D5
Harrow HA3 24 D2
Wimbledon SW19 180 A4
Dryden St WC2 240 B1
Dryer Ct 21 EN3 7 C6
Dryfield Cl NW10 67 A2
Dryfield Rd HA8 27 A4
Dryfield Wlk 1 SE8 141 C6
Dryhill Rd DA17 147 B6
Dryland Ave 5 BR6 227 D4
Drylands Rd N8 50 A3
Drysdale Ave E4 19 D5
Drysdale Flats 3 E8 73 D3
Drysdale Ho 19 E2 95 C4
Drysdale Pl N1 95 C4
Drysdale St N1 95 C4
Dublin Ave E8 96 A6
Du Burstow Terr W7 108 C4
Ducal St 25 E2 95 D4
Ducane Cl 6 W12 90 C1
Du Cane Ct SW12 159 A3
Du Cane Rd W12 90 A1
Ducavel Ho SW2 160 B3
Duchess Cl
London N11 31 B5
Sutton SM1 218 A4
Duchess Gr IG9 21 B2
Duchess Mews W1 238 D3
Duchess of Bedford Ho
W8 245 A2
Duchess of Bedford's Wlk
W8 113 C4 245 A1
Duchess St W1 93 B2 238 D3
Duchy Rd EN4 2 B5
Duchy St SE1 116 C5 251 B4
Ducie Ho
8 Charlton SE7 143 C6
2 Putney SW15 156 C6
Ducie St SW4 138 B1
Duckett Mews N4 50 D3
Duckett Rd N4 50 D3
Duckett St E1 97 A2
Duck La W1 239 C1
Duck Lees La EN3 7 A1
Ducks Hill Rd HA4, HA6 39 A5
DUCKS ISLAND 12 D5
Duck's Wlk TW1 153 C6
Du Cros Dr HA7 25 D4
Du Cros Rd W3 111 C5
DUDDEN HILL 68 A3
Dudden Hill La NW10 67 D3
Duddington Cl SE9 187 D6
Dudley Ave HA3 43 C6
Dudley Ct
Colney Hatch N12 30 C5
Marylebone W1 237 C1
St Giles WC2 240 A2
Temple Fortune NW11 47 B5
Dudley Ct *continued*
14 Wanstead E11 55 A4
Wembley HA0 65 D3
Dudley Dr
Ruislip HA4 62 B3
West Barnes SM4 201 A2
Dudley Gdns
Ealing W13 109 B4
Harrow HA2 42 B1
Dudley Ho
13 Brixton SW9 138 C3
Edgware HA8 26 B3
Paddington W2 236 C3
Dudley Mews 14
SW2 160 C5
Dudley Pl UB3 105 B2
Dudley Rd
Ashford TW15 170 B6
East Bedfont TW14 149 B3
Finchley N3 29 D1
Harrow HA2 64 A6
Ilford IG1 78 D4
Kilburn NW6 91 B5
Kingston u T KT1 198 B6
Richmond TW9 132 B3
Southall UB2 106 D3
Walthamstow E17 35 C1
Walton-on-T KT12 194 A2
Wimbledon SW19 179 C4
Dudley St W2 236 C3
Dudlington Rd E5 74 C6
Dudmaston Mews
SW3 256 D2
Dudsbury Rd DA14 190 B4
Dudset La TW5 128 A4
Duett Ct TW3 129 A5
Duffell Ho SE11 260 D1
Dufferin Ave EC1 242 C5
Dufferin Ct EC1 242 C5
Dufferin St EC1 95 A3 242 B5
Duffield Cl HA1 42 D4
Duffield Dr N15 51 D5
Duffield Ho N4 51 A2
Duff St E14 97 D1
Dufour's Pl W1 239 B1
Dugard Way
SE11 116 D2 261 C3
Dugdale Ho 10 N7 71 D3
Duggan Dr BR7 188 A4
Dugolly Ave HA9 66 D5
Duke Gdns IG6 57 B5
Duke Humphrey Rd
SE3 142 C3
Duke Of Cambridge Cl
TW2 152 B5
Duke Of Edinburgh Rd
SM1 218 B6
Duke Of Wellington Ave
SE18 123 A3
Duke of Wellington Pl SW1,
W1 248 B2
Duke of York's Sq
SW3 114 D2 257 D3
Duke of York St SW1 249 B4
Duke Rd
Chiswick W4 111 B1
Ilford IG6 57 B5
Duke St Hill SE1 252 D4
Duke St St James's
SW1 115 C5 249 B4
Dukes Ave
Edgware HA8 26 B5
Finchley N3 29 D2
Hornsey N10 49 C6
Hounslow TW4 129 A1
Kingston u T KT3 199 D6
Northolt UB5 63 A1
Rayners La HA2, HA5 41 B3
Richmond KT2, TW10 175 D6
Wealdstone HA1 42 C5
Duke's Ave W4 111 B1
Dukes Cl
Ashford TW15 171 A6
Hampton TW12 173 B5
Dukes Ct
Barking E6 100 C6
Beckenham BR3 207 A6
Dulwich SE22 162 A3
Ealing W13 87 B2
East Dulwich SE22 162 B6
Lewisham SE13 142 A3
Mortlake SW14 133 B3
Dukes Gate 4 W4 111 A2
Dukes Green Ave
TW14 150 A6
Dukes Head Yd N6 49 B1
Duke's Ho SW1 259 D4
Duke Shore Wharf
E14 119 B6
Dukes La W8 113 D4 245 C2
Dukes Mews N10 49 B6
Duke's Mews W1 238 B2
Duke's Pl EC3 95 C1 243 B1
Dukes Point N6 49 B1
Dukes Rd
Acton W3 88 C3
Barking E6 100 C6
Duke's Rd WC1 93 D4 232 D1
Dukes Ride UB10 60 A4
Duke St
Marylebone
W1 93 A1 238 B1
Richmond TW10, TW9 153 D6
Sutton SM1 218 B4
Dukesthorpe Rd
SE26 184 D6
Duke Street Mans W1 238 B1
Dukes Way BR4 224 C5
Duke's Yd W1 248 B6
Dulas St N4 50 B1
Dulford St
W11 113 A6 244 A6
Dulka Rd SW11 158 D6
Dulverton NW1 232 B5
Dulverton Ct 12 KT6 198 A4
Dulverton Mans WC1 240 D5
Dulverton Prim Sch
SE9 167 B2
Dulverton Rd
New Eltham SE9 167 B2
Ruislip HA4 62 A6
DULWICH 161 C1
Dulwich Bsns Ctr
SE23 162 D3
Dulwich Coll SE21 161 C2
Dulwich Coll Picture
Gall* SE21 161 C4
Dulwich Coll Prep Sch
SE21 161 C1
Dulwich Comm SE21 161 C3
Dulwich Ct SE22 162 B3
Dulwich Hamlet Jun Sch
SE21 161 B5
Dulwich Hospl SE22 139 C1
Dulwich Lawn Cl
SE22 161 D6
Dulwich Mead SE24 161 A5
Dulwich Mews
1 East Dulwich
SE22 139 D1
East Dulwich SE22 161 D6
Dulwich Oaks The
SE21 161 D1
Dulwich Rd SE24 160 D5
DULWICH VILLAGE 161 C4
Dulwich Village SE21 161 C5
Dulwich Village CE Inf
Sch SE21 161 C5
Dulwich Wood Ave
SE19 183 C5
Dulwich Wood Pk
SE19 183 C6
Dumain Ct SE11 261 C3
Du Maurier Ho 2
NW3 70 D3
Dumbarton Ct 16
SW2 160 A4
Dumbarton Rd SW2 160 A5
Dumbleton Cl KT2 176 D2
Dumbreck Rd SE9 144 C2
Dumont Rd N16 73 C5
Dumphreys Ho 5
SW4 159 D4
Dumpton Pl NW1 71 A1
Dunally Pk TW17 193 B2
Dunbar Ave
Beckenham BR3 207 A5
Dagenham RM10 81 C5
Thornton Heath SW16 182 C1
Dunbar Cl UB4 84 A2
Dunbar Ct
3 London N12 29 D6
Sutton SM1 218 B3
Walton-on-T KT12 194 C1
Dunbar Gdns RM10 81 D3
Dunbar Rd
New Malden KT3 199 A5
Tottenham N22 32 D2
Upton E7 77 A2
Dunbar St SE27 161 A1
Dunbar Wharf 20 E14 119 B6
Dunblane Cl HA8 10 D2
Dunblane Rd SE9 144 A3
Dunboe Pl TW17 193 A2
Dunboyne Rd NW3 70 D3
Dunbridge Ho SW15 155 D5
Dunbridge St
Bethnal Green E2 ....
Bethnal Green E2 96 B3
Duncan Cl EN5 2 A1
Duncan Ct
5 London N12 29 D5
3 Poplar E14 98 A2
Southgate N21 16 D3
Duncan Gr W3 89 C1
Duncan Ho
Harrow HA2 64 A5
3 Primrose Hill NW3 70 D1
Duncannon Ho SW1 259 D1
Duncannon St WC2 250 A5
Duncan Rd
Hackney E8 96 B6
Richmond TW9 132 A1
Duncan St N1 94 D5 234 C4
Duncan Terr
N1 94 D5 234 C4
Dunch St 33 E1 96 B1
Dunchurch Ho RM10 81 C1
Duncombe Hill SE23 163 A4
Duncombe Ho 7
SW19 156 D3
Duncombe Prim Sch
N19 50 A1
Duncombe Rd N19 49 D1
Duncrievie Rd SE13 164 B5
Duncroft SE18 145 C5
Dundalk Ho 2 E1 96 C1
Dundalk Rd SE4 141 A2
Dundas Gdns KT8 195 D6
Dundas Ho 12 E2 96 C5
Dundas Mews 4 EN3 7 C6
Dundas Rd SE15 140 C3
Dundee Ct 36 E1 118 B5
Dundee Ho W9 229 A2
Dundee Rd
Croydon SE25 206 B4
Newham E13 99 B5
Dundee St E1 118 B5
Dundee Way EN3 7 A2
Dundee Wharf E14 119 B6
Dundela Gdns KT17,
KT4 216 B4
Dundonald Cl 6 E6 100 A1
Dundonald Prim Sch
SW19 179 B3
Dundonald Rd
Brondesbury Pk NW10 90 D6
Merton SW19 179 B3
Dundonald Road Sta
SW19 179 B3
Dundry Ho 8 SE26 162 A1
Duneaves HA1 64 C5
Dunedin Ho E16 122 B5
Dunedin Rd
Ilford IG1 57 A1
Leyton E10 75 D5
Dunedin Way UB4 84 C3
Dunelm Gr SE27 161 A1
Dunelm St E1 96 D1
Dunfield Gdns SE6 185 D5
Dunfield Rd SE6 185 D5
Dunford Ct 9 HA5 23 B3
Dunford Rd N7 72 B4
Dungarvan Ave SW15 134 A1
Dungeness Ho SW18 136 A1
Dunheved Cl CR7 204 C3
Dunheved Ct 2 CR7 204 C3
Dunheved Rd N CR7 204 C3
Dunheved Rd S CR7 204 C3
Dunheved Rd W CR7 204 C3
Dunhill Point 12
SW15 156 B3
Dunholme Gn N9 17 D1
Dunholme La N9 17 D1
Dunholme Rd N9 17 D1
Dunkeld Ho 15 E14 98 B1
Dunkeld Rd
Dagenham RM8 80 C6
South Norwood SE25 205 B5
Dunkery Rd SE9 166 A1
Dunkirk St 12 SE27 183 A6
Dunlace Rd E5 74 D4
Dunleary Cl TW4 151 B4
Dunley Dr CR0 224 A2
Dunlin Ct 12 SE21 161 B2
Dunlin Ho 13 SE16 118 D2
Dunloe Ave N17 51 B6
Dunloe Ct 7 E2 95 D5
Dunloe St E2 95 D5
Dunlop Pl
SE16 117 D3 263 D5
Dunmore Point 15 E2 95 D4
Dunmore Rd
Kilburn NW6 91 A6
Wimbledon SW20 178 D2
Dunmow Cl
Dagenham RM6 58 C4
3 Feltham TW13 173 A6
Dunmow Ho
Dagenham RM9 102 B6

Dunmow Ho *continued*
Vauxhall SE11 260 D2
Dunmow Rd E15 76 B4
Dunmow Wlk N1 235 A6
Dunnage Cres SE16 119 A2
Dunne Mews 11 NW5 71 C3
Dunnet Ho 27 E3 97 B5
Dunnico Ho SE17 263 A2
Dunn Mead NW9 27 D3
Dunnock Cl N9 18 D3
Dunnock Ct 11 SE21 161 B2
Dunnock Rd E6 100 A1
Dunn's Pas WC1 240 B2
Dunn St E8 73 D3
Dunollie Pl NW5 71 C3
Dunollie Rd NW5 71 C3
Dunoon Gdns SE23 162 D4
Dunoon Ho N1 233 C5
Dunoon Rd SE23 162 C4
Dunraven Dr EN2 4 C3
Dunraven Ho 12 TW9 132 B4
Dunraven Rd W12 112 A5
Dunraven Sch SW16 160 B1
Dunraven St
W1 114 D6 247 D6
Dunrobin Ct NW3 69 D3
Dunsany Rd W14 112 D3
Dunsfold Ct 14 SM2 217 D1
Dunsfold Ho
10 Kingston u T KT2 176 D4
4 Streatham SW2 160 B4
Dunsfold Way CR0 223 D1
Dunsford Way SW15 156 B5
Dunsmore Cl
Bushey WD23 8 B5
Hayes UB4 85 A3
Dunsmore Rd KT12 194 B3
Dunsmore Way WD23 8 B5
Dunsmure Rd N16 51 C1
Dunstable Ct 3 SE3 143 A5
Dunstable Mews W1 238 B4
Dunstable Rd
East Molesey KT8 195 B5
Richmond TW10, TW9 132 A1
Dunstall Ho 9 SE15 140 A4
Dunstall Rd SW19,
SW20 178 C4
Dunstall Way KT8 195 D6
Dunstall Welling Est
DA16 146 B3
Dunstan Cl 2 N2 48 A6
Dunstan Glade BR5 211 B3
Dunstan Ho SE4 141 B3
Dunstan Hos 5 E1 96 C2
Dunstan Rd NW11 47 C1
Dunstan's Gr SE22 162 B5
Dunstan's Rd SE22 162 A5
Dunster Ave SM4 200 D1
Dunster Ct EC3 253 B6
Dunster Dr NW9 45 A1
Dunster Gdns NW6 69 B1
Dunster Ho SE6 163 D1
Dunsterville Way SE1 252 D1
Dunster Way
Carshalton CR4 203 A1
Harrow HA2 63 A5
Dunston Rd
Clapham SW11 137 A3
Hackney E8 95 D6
Dunston St E8 95 D6
Dunton Cl KT6 198 A1
Dunton Ct 5 SE26 162 B2
Dunton Ho 14 SW16 160 A1
Dunton Rd
Bermondsey
SE1 117 D2 263 C3
Leyton E10 53 D2
Duntshill Rd SW18 157 D3
Dunvegan Cl KT8 195 D5
Dunvegan Rd SE9 144 B1
Dunwich Ct 2 RM6 58 B4
Dunwich Rd DA7 147 B4
Dunworth Mews W11 91 B1
Duplex Ride SW1 247 D1
Dupont Rd SW20 178 D1
Duppas Ave CR0 220 D4
Duppas Cl TW17 193 B4
Duppas Ct CR0 220 D5
Duppas Hill La CR0 220 D4
Duppas Hill Rd CR0 220 D4
Duppas Hill Terr CR0 220 D5
Duppas Jun Sch CR0 220 D3
Duppas Rd CR0 220 D5
Dupree Rd SE7 121 B1
Dura Den Cl BR3 185 D3
Durand Cl SM5 202 D1
Durand Gdns
SW9 138 B4 270 D1
Durand Prim Sch
SW9 138 B4 270 D2
Durand Way NW10 67 A1
Durants Lo EN3 6 D2
Durants Park Ave EN3 6 D1
Durants Rd EN3 6 D1
Durants Sch EN3 6 C4
Durant St E2 96 A4
Durban Ct E7 77 D1
Durban Ho 28 W12 112 B6
Durban Rd
Beckenham BR3 185 B1
Ilford IG2 57 C1
Newham E15 98 C4
Tottenham N17 33 D4
Walthamstow E17 35 B2
West Norwood SE27 183 B6
Durbin Ho 18 N9 18 A1
Durbin Rd KT9 214 B4
Durdan Cotts UB5 85 B1
Durdans Ho 3 NW1 71 C1
Durdans Park Prim Sch
UB1 85 B2
Durdans Rd UB1 85 B1
Durell Gdns RM9 80 D3
Durell Rd RM9 80 D3
Durfey Pl SE5 139 B5
Durford Cres SW15 156 B3
Durham Ave
Beckenham BR2 208 D5
Hounslow TW5 107 B1
Woodford IG8 37 D5
Durham Cl SW20 178 B1
Durham Ct
2 Barnet EN5 1 B2
Brockley SE4 141 C2
4 Kilburn NW6 91 C5
Teddington TW11 174 C6
Durham Hill BR1 186 D6
Durham Ho
3 Barking IG11 80 A1
7 Dartmouth Pk NW5 71 C5
Edgware HA8 26 B3
Lisson Gr NW8 230 B1
Durham House St
WC2 250 B5
Durham Pl
Chelsea SW3 257 C1
Ilford IG1 79 A4
Durham Rd
Beckenham BR2 208 D6
Ealing W5 109 D3
Edmonton N9 18 A2
Feltham TW14 150 C4
Harrow HA1 41 D4
Lower Holloway N4, N7 72 B6
Manor Pk E12 77 D4
Muswell Hill N2 48 D6
Newham E16 98 C3
Sidcup DA14 190 B5
Wimbledon SW20 178 B2
Durham Rise SE18 123 B1
Durham Row E1 97 A2
Durham St
SE11 138 B6 270 C6
Durham Terr W2 91 D1
Durham Wharf Dr
TW8 131 C5
Durley Ave HA5 41 A3
Durley Rd N16 51 C2
Durlock Ho 16 SW9 138 C4
Durlston Rd
Kingston u T KT2 176 A4
Stoke Newington E5 74 A6
Durnford Ho SE6 163 D1
Durnford St
4 Greenwich SE10 142 A6
South Tottenham N15 51 C4
Durning Rd SE19 183 B5
Durnsford Ave SW18,
SW19 157 C2
Durnsford Ct 5 EN3 7 A2
Durnsford Rd
London N11 31 D3
Wimbledon SW18,
SW19 157 C1
Durnston Ct 2 SM1 217 D2
Durrant Ct HA3 24 C2
Durrant Way BR6 227 B3
Durrell Rd SW6 264 C1
Durrell Way TW17 193 B3
Durrels Ho W14 254 D4
Durrington Ave
SW20 178 C3
Durrington Park Rd
SW20 178 C2
Durrington Rd E5 75 A4
Durrington Twr 3
SW8 137 C3
Durrisdeer Ho NW2 69 B4
Dursley Cl SE3 143 C3
Dursley Gdns SE3 143 D4
Dursley Rd SE3 143 C3
Durston NW5 71 A3
Durston House
Middleton's Sch W5 87 D1
Durston House Prep Sch
W5 87 D1
Durward St E1 96 B2
Durweston Mews W1 237 D4
Durweston St W1 237 D3
Dury Rd EN5 1 B3
Dutch Gdns KT2 176 D4
Dutch Yd SW18 157 C6
Dutton Ho SW2 160 D3
Dutton St SE10 142 A4
Duxberry Cl BR2 210 A4
Duxford 21 KT1 176 C1
Duxford Ho 10 SE2 124 D4
Dwight Ct SW6 135 A3
Dycer Ho 19 E9 74 D2
Dye House La E3 97 C6
Dyer Ho
Hampton TW12 173 D2
New Cross SE4 141 A3
Dyer's Bldgs EC1 241 A3
Dyers Hall Rd
Leyton E11 76 B6
Leytonstone E11 54 C1
Dyer's La SW15 134 B1
Dykes Ct 11 SW2 160 B3
Dykes Way BR2 208 D6
Dylan Cl WD6 9 D4
Dylan Rd
Belvedere DA17 125 C3
2 Brixton SE24 138 D1
Dylways SE5 139 B1
Dymchurch Cl
Ilford IG5 56 C6
Orpington BR6 227 C4
Dymchurch Ho 12 E5 74 B3
Dymes Path SW19 156 D2
Dymock St SW6 135 D2
Dyneley Rd SE12 165 C1
Dyne Rd NW6 69 B1
Dynevor Rd
Richmond TW10 154 A6
Shacklewell N16 73 D5
Dynham Rd NW6 69 C1
Dyott St
Soho WC1 239 D2
St Giles WC1,
WC2 94 A1 240 A2
Dysart Ave KT2, TW10 175 C6
Dysart Sch KT6 198 B2
Dysart St EC2 95 C3 243 A5
Dyson Ct
London NW2 46 C2
Wembley HA0 65 A4
Dyson Ho 3 SE10 120 D1
Dyson Rd
Leytonstone E11 54 C3
Stratford E15 76 D2
Dyson's Rd N18 34 B4

E

Eade Rd N4 51 A2
Eagans Cl N2 48 B6
Eagle Ave RM6 59 A3
Eagle Cl
Bermondsey SE16 118 C1
Enfield EN3 6 C1
Wallington SM6 220 A2
Eagle Ct
10 Dulwich SE21 161 B2
Edmonton N18 33 D4
Holborn EC1 241 C4
6 Wanstead E11 55 A5
Eagle Dr NW9 27 C1
Eagle Dwellings EC1 235 B2
Eagle Hill SE19 183 B4
Eagle Ho
22 Bethnal Green E1 96 B3
Finsbury Pk N7 72 B5
Eagle House Sch
CR4 180 D1
Eagle Hts 10 SW11 136 C2
Eagle La E11 55 A5
Eagle Lo
Leytonstone E11 54 D5
London NW11 47 B2
Eagle Mans N16 73 D3
Eagle Mews N1 73 C2
Eagle Pl
South Kensington
SW7 114 A1 256 B2
St James SW1 249 B5
Eagle Rd
Hatton TW6 127 D2
Wembley HA0 65 D1
Eaglesfield Rd SE18 144 D4
Eagle St WC1 94 B2 240 C3
Eagle Star Ho SM1 217 D4
Eagle Terr IG8 37 B3
Eagle Trad Est CR4 202 D3
Eagle Wharf SE1 253 C3
Eagle Wharf Rd
N1 95 A5 235 B4
Eagle Works E1 243 D5
Eagling Cl E3 97 C4
Ealcom Ct W5 110 B5
Ealdham Prim Sch
SE9 143 C1
Ealdham Sq SE9 143 C1
EALING 109 D6
Ealing Broadway Ctr
W5 109 D6
Ealing Broadway Sta
W5 109 D6
Ealing Coll W13 87 B1
Ealing Coll of Higher Ed
W5 109 D5
Ealing Common W5 110 B6
Ealing Common Sta
W5 110 B5
Ealing Court Man
W5 109 D4
Ealing Gateway W5 109 C6
Ealing Gn W5 109 D5
Ealing, Hammersmith &
West London Coll
W14 113 A1 254 A2
Ealing Hospl UB1,
UB2 108 B4
Ealing Park Gdns W5 109 C2
Ealing Park Lo UB6 87 A5
Ealing Park Mans
W5 109 D3
Ealing Rd
Brentford TW8 109 D2
Northolt UB5 63 C1
Wembley HA0 66 A1
Ealing Road Trad Est
TW8 109 D1
Ealing Tertiary Coll
W3 110 D5
Ealing Village W5 88 A1
Ealing & West London
Coll W5 109 D5
Eamann Casey Ho 34
SW9 138 C4
Eamont Cl HA4 38 D2
Eamont Ct NW8 230 B4
Eamont St NW8 92 C5 230 B4
Eardley Cres
SW5 113 C1 255 B1
Eardley Point 9
SE18 122 D2
Eardley Rd
Belvedere DA17 125 C1
Streatham SW16 181 C4
Eardley Sch SW16 181 C4
Earl Cl N11 31 B5
Earldom Rd SW15 134 C1
Earle Gdns KT2 176 A3
Earle Ho SW1 259 D3
Earlham Gr
Forest Gate E7 77 A3
Wood Green N22 32 B3
Earlham Prim Sch
Stratford E7 76 D3
Wood Green N22 32 C3
Earlham St
WC2 94 A1 240 A1
Earl Ho NW1 237 B5
Earlom Ho WC1 234 A1
Earl Rd SW14 133 A1
Earl Rise SE18 123 B2
EARL'S COURT 113 C1
Earl's Court Ex Ctr*
SW5 113 C1 255 A1
Earl's Court Gdns
SW5 113 D2 255 C3
Earl's Court Rd SW5,
W8 113 C2 255 B4
Earl's Court Sq
SW5 113 D1 255 C2
Earl's Court Sta
SW5 113 C2 255 B3
Earls Cres HA1 42 C5
Earlsdown Ho 6
IG11 101 B5
Earlsferry Way N1 72 A1
EARLSFIELD 158 A3
Earlsfield Ho 16 KT2 175 D2
Earlsfield Prim Sch
SW18 158 A2
Earlsfield Rd SW18 158 A4
Earlsfield Sta SW18 158 A3
Earlshall Rd SE9 144 C1
Earlsmead HA2 63 B4
Earlsmead Fst & Mid Sch
HA2 63 B4
Earlsmead Prim Sch
N15 51 D5
Earlsmead Rd
Kensal Green NW10 90 C4
South Tottenham N15 51 D4
Earl St EC2 95 C2 243 A4
Earls Terr W8 254 D5
Earlsthorpe Mews 3
SW12 159 A5
Earlsthorpe Rd SE26 184 D6
Earlstoke St EC1 234 C2
Earlston Gr E9 96 B6
Earls Wlk
Dagenham RM8 80 B4
Kensington
W8 113 C3 255 A5
Earlswood Ave CR7 204 C4
Earlswood Cl 10
SE10 120 C1
Earlswood Gdns IG5 56 C6
Earlswood Ho 2
SW2 160 B3
Earlswood St SE10 120 C1
Early Mews NW1 231 D6
Earnshaw Ho EC1 234 D1
Earnshaw St WC1,
WC2 239 D2
Earsby St W14 254 B4
Earth Galleries*
SW7 114 B3 256 D5
Easby Cres SM4 201 D3
Easebourne Rd RM8 80 C3
Easedale Ho TW7 152 D6
Eashing Point 5
SW15 156 B3
Easleys Mews W1 238 B2
East 10 Ent Pk E10 53 A1
EAST ACTON 111 C5
East Acton Arc W3 89 D1
East Acton Ct W3 111 C6
East Acton La W3 111 C6
East Acton Prim Sch
W3 111 C6
East Acton Sta W12 89 D1
East Arbour St E1 96 D1
East Ave
Croydon CR0 220 B3
East Finchley NW2 48 A6
Hayes UB3 106 A5
Plashet E12 78 A1
Southall UB1 107 B6
Walthamstow E17 53 D5
East Bank N16 51 C2
Eastbank Rd TW12 174 A5
EAST BARNET 14 D4
East Barnet Rd EN4 2 B1
East Barnet Sch
Barnet EN4 2 B2
East Barnet EN4 14 D5
East Beckton District Ctr
E6 100 B2
EAST BEDFONT 149 C3
East Block 5 E1 118 D6
Eastbourne Ave W3 89 B1
Eastbourne Gdns
SW14 133 A2
Eastbourne Mews
W2 92 A1 236 B2
Eastbourne Rd
Brentford TW8 109 D1
Chiswick W4 133 A6
Feltham TW13 150 D2
South Tottenham N15 51 C3
Streatham SW17 181 A4
Wallend E6 100 C4
West Ham E15 98 C6
Eastbourne Terr
W2 92 A1 236 B2
Eastbournia Ave N9 18 B1
Eastbrook Ave N9 18 C4
Eastbrook Rd SE3 143 B4
EASTBURY 22 A5
Eastbury Ave
Barking IG11 101 C6
Enfield EN1 5 D4
Mo Pk HA6 22 A5
Eastbury Comp Sch
IG11 79 C2
Eastbury Ct
Barking IG11 101 C6
New Barnet EN5 14 A6
Eastbury Gr W4 111 C1
Eastbury Inf Sch IG11 79 D1
Eastbury Rd
Kingston u T KT2 176 A3
Newham E6 100 C3
Orpington BR5 211 B3
Eastbury Sq IG11 101 D6
Eastbury Terr E1 96 D3
Eastcastle St
W1 93 C1 239 B2
Eastcheap
EC3 117 C6 253 A6
East Churchfield Rd
W3 111 B5
Eastchurch Rd TW6 127 C2
Eastchurch Road Rdbt
TW6 127 C3
East Cl
Cockfosters EN4 3 A1
Ealing W5 88 C3
Greenford UB6 86 A5
Eastcombe Ave SE7 143 B6
EASTCOTE 40 C3
Eastcote BR6 211 D1
Eastcote Ave
East Molesey KT8 195 C4
Harrow HA2 64 A6
Wembley UB6 65 A3
Eastcote Ind Est HA4 40 C2
Eastcote La
Harrow HA2 63 C5
Northolt UB5 63 B2
Eastcote La N UB5 63 C2
Eastcote Pl HA5 40 B3
Eastcote Prim Sch
DA16 145 B2
Eastcote Rd
Bexley DA16 145 B3
Harrow HA2 64 A5
Pinner HA5 40 D4
Ruislip HA4 40 A3
Eastcote St SW9 138 B3
Eastcote Sta HA5 40 C2
Eastcote View HA5 40 C5
EASTCOTE VILLAGE 40 B4
Eastcourt Ind Sch IG3 58 A1
East Cres
Enfield EN1 17 D6
Friern Barnet N11 30 D6
Eastcroft Rd KT19 215 C1
East Cross Ctr E15 75 C2
East Cross Route
Bow E3 97 C6
Hackney Wick E9 75 B3
East Croydon Sta
CR0 221 B6
East Ct
Sunbury TW16 172 C1
Wembley HA0 65 C6
Eastdown Ho E8 74 A4
Eastdown Pk SE13 142 B1
East Duck Lees La EN3 7 B1
EAST DULWICH 162 A6
East Dulwich Gr SE22 161 C6
East Dulwich Rd SE15,
SE22 140 A1
East Dulwich Sta
SE22 139 C1
East End Rd
East Finchley N2, N3 48 A6
Finchley N3 29 C1
East End Way HA5 41 A6
East Entrance RM10 103 D5
Eastern Ave
Gants Hill IG1, IG2,
IG4 56 C3
Newbury Pk IG2 57 B3
Pinner HA5 40 D2
Wanstead E11 55 C3
Eastern Avenue W
RM7 59 C5
Eastern Bsns Pk
TW16 127 D3
Eastern Perimeter Rd
TW14 127 D3
Eastern Quay 15 E16 121 B5
Eastern Rd
Brockley SE4 141 C1
Fortis Green N2 48 D5
Newham E13 99 B5
Walthamstow E17 54 A4
Wood Green N22 32 A2
Easternville Gdns IG2 57 A3
Eastern Way SE28 124 B4
East Ferry Rd E14 119 D2
Eastfield Gdns RM10 81 C4
Eastfield Prim Sch EN3 6 D5
Eastfield Rd
Dagenham RM9 81 B4
Dagenham RM10 81 C4
Enfield EN3 6 D5
Hornsey N8 50 A6
Walthamstow E17 53 C5

Eastfields HA5 40 C4
Eastfields Ave SW18 135 C1
Eastfields Rd
Acton W3 89 A2
Mitcham CR4 181 A1
Eastfield St E14 97 A2
EAST FINCHLEY 48 B5
East Finchley Sta N2 48 C5
Eastgate Bsns Pk E10 53 A1
Eastgate Cl SE28 102 D1
Eastgate Ct N3 29 C1
East Gdns SW17 180 C4
Eastglade HA5 41 B6
EAST HAM 100 A5
Eastham Cl EN5 13 B6
East Ham Ind Est E6 100 A2
East Ham Manor Way E6 100 C1
East Ham Meml Hospl E7 77 D1
East Ham Sta E6 78 A1
East Harding St EC4 241 B2
East Heath Rd NW3 70 B5
East Hill
London SW18 158 A6
Wembley HA9 44 C1
Eastholm NW11 47 D5
Eastholme UB3 106 A5
East India Bldgs 9 E14 119 C6
East India Ct 7 SE16 118 C4
East India Dock Basin* E14 120 C6
East India Dock Rd E14 119 D6
East India Dock Road Tunnel 18 E14 98 B1
East India Sta E14 120 B6
East India Way CR0 205 D1
East La
5 Bermondsey SE16 118 A4
Bermondsey SE16 118 A4
Kingston u T KT1 197 D6
Wembley HA0, HA9 65 D5
Eastlake Ho NW8 236 D5
Eastlake Rd SE5 139 A3
Eastland Ct 2 BR1 187 C1
Eastlands Cres SE21 161 D5
East Lane Bsns Pk HA9 65 D5
Eastlea Com Sch E16 98 C3
Eastlea Mews E16 98 C3
Eastleigh Ave HA2 63 D6
Eastleigh Cl
Belmont SM2 217 D1
Neasden NW2 67 C5
Eastleigh Rd E17 35 B1
Eastleigh Way TW14 150 A3
Eastleigh Wlk 9 SW15 156 A4
East London Coll E11 76 C6
East London Coll & Toynbee Theatre E1 95 D2 243 D3
East London Stad E3 97 B2
Eastman Dental Hospl WC1 94 B3 240 C6
Eastman Ho 7 SW4 159 C5
Eastman Rd W3 111 B4
East Mascalls 15 SE7 143 C6
Eastmead IG3 58 A2
East Mead HA4 62 D5
Eastmead Ave UB6 85 D4
Eastmead Cl BR1 188 A1
Eastmearn Rd SE21, SE27 161 A2
EAST MOLESEY 196 A4
Eastmont Rd KT10 212 D6
Eastmoor Pl SE7 121 D3
Eastmoor St SE7 121 D3
East Mount St E1 96 B2
Eastney Rd CR0 204 D1
Eastney St SE10 120 B1
Eastnor Rd SE9 167 A3
Easton Ho 8 SE27 160 D1
Easton St WC1 241 A6
East Park Cl RM6 59 A4
East Parkside SE10 120 D4
East Pas EC1 242 A4
East Pl SE27 183 A6
East Plaza E14 119 D5
East Point 4 SE1 118 A1
Eastpole Cotts N14 3 D1
East Poultry Ave EC1 241 C3
East Putney Sta SW15 157 A6
East Ramp TW6 126 D4
East Rd
Burnt Oak HA8 27 A2
Chelsea SW1 115 A1 258 A1
Dagenham RM6 59 A4
East Barnet EN4 15 A3
East Bedfont TW14 149 B4
Enfield EN3 6 C5
Finchley N2 30 C2
Kingston u T KT2 176 A2
Newham E15 99 A6
Shoreditch N1 95 B4 235 D2
Welling DA16 146 B3
West Drayton UB7 104 C2
Wimbledon SW19 180 A4
East Rochester Way DA5, DA15, SE9 168 C5
East Row
Kensal Town W10 91 A3
Wanstead E11 55 A3
Eastry Ave BR2 208 D3
Eastry Ho SW8 270 A3
Eastry Rd DA8 147 C5
EAST SHEEN 133 B1
East Sheen Ave SW14 133 B1
East Sheen Prim Sch SW14 133 C1
Eastside Rd NW11 47 B5
East Smithfield E1 117 D6 253 D5
East St
Barking IG11 79 A1
Bexleyheath DA7 147 C1
Brentford TW8 131 C5
Bromley BR1 187 A1
Walworth SE17 117 B1 262 C2
East Surrey Gr SE15 139 D5
East Tenter St E1 95 D1 243 D1
East Terr DA15 167 C3
East Thamesmead Bsns Pk DA18 125 B4
East Towers HA5 40 D3
Eastvale W3 111 D5
East View
Barnet EN5 1 B2
Chingford E4 36 A5
Hampstead NW3 70 B6
Eastview Ave SE18 145 C5
East View Ho 18 N2 30 B1
Eastville Ave NW11 47 B3
Eastway
Hayes BR2 209 A2
Merton SM4, SW20 201 A5
South Hackney E3, E9 97 A6
Temple Mills E9, E10 75 C4
Wallington SM6 219 C4
Wanstead E11 55 B4
East Way
Croydon CR0 223 A5
Hayes UB3 106 A5
Ruislip HA4 40 A1
Eastway Cres HA2 63 D6
Eastwell Cl BR3 185 A2
Eastwell Ho SE1 262 D6
Eastwick Ct 2 SW19 156 D3
EAST WICKHAM 146 A5
East Wickham Inf Sch DA16 145 D4
East Wickham Jun Sch DA16 146 A4
East Wlk
East Barnet EN4 15 A3
Hayes UB3 106 A5
Eastwood Cl
2 Islington N7 72 C3
7 Tottenham N17 34 B3
Woodford E18 37 A1
Eastwood Rd
Ilford IG3 58 A2
Muswell Hill N10 31 A1
West Drayton UB7 104 C4
Woodford E18 37 A1
East Woodside DA5 169 A3
Eastwood St SW16 181 C4
Eatington Rd E10 54 B4
Eaton Cl
Belgravia SW1 258 A3
Stanmore HA7 25 B6
Eaton Ct
Chislehurst BR7 189 A4
Ealing W5 87 D1
Edgware HA8 26 C6
Southall UB1 107 B6
Sutton SM2 218 B2
6 Woodford E18 37 A1
Eaton Dr
Brixton SW9 138 D1
Kingston u T KT2 176 C3
Eaton Gate SW1 115 A2 258 A4
Eaton Gdns RM9 81 A1
Eaton Ho
Battersea SW11 266 D1
Ealing W5 87 D1
23 Limehouse E14 119 B6
Eaton House Sch SW1 115 A2 258 A4
Eaton House The Manor Sch SW4 137 B1
Eaton La SW1 115 B3 258 D5
Eaton Lo SM2 218 B2
Eaton Mans SW1 258 A3
Eaton Mews N SW1 115 A3 258 B5
Eaton Mews S SW1 115 B3 258 C5
Eaton Mews W SW1 258 B4
Eaton Park Rd N13 16 D2
Eaton Pl SW1 115 A3 258 B5
Eaton Rd
Enfield EN1 5 C1
Hendon NW4 46 C4
Isleworth TW3, TW7 130 B1
Sidcup DA14 168 D2
Sutton SM2 218 B2
Eaton Rise
Ealing W5 87 D1
Wanstead E11 55 C4
Eaton Row SW1 115 B3 258 C5
Eatons Mead E4 19 C2
Eaton Sq SW1 115 A3 258 B5
Eaton Square Sch SW1 115 B2 258 C4
Eaton Terr
Belgravia SW1 115 A2 258 B4
Bow E3 97 A4
Eaton Terr Mews SW1 258 A4
Eatonville Rd SW17 158 D2
Eatonville Villas SW17 158 D2
Ebb Ct E16 123 A6
Ebbisham Dr SW8 138 B6 270 C5
Ebbisham Rd KT4 216 C6
Ebbsfleet Rd NW2 69 A4
Ebdon Way SE3 143 B2
Ebenezer Ho SE11 261 C3
Ebenezer Mussel Ho 5 E2 96 C5
Ebenezer St N1 235 C2
Ebenezer Wlk CR4 181 C2
Ebley Cl SE15 139 D6
Ebner St SW18 157 D6
Ebony Ct NW10 67 D2
Ebony Ho
27 Bethnal Green E2 96 A4
10 West Hampstead NW3 69 D2
Ebor Cotts SW15 155 C1
Ebor St E1, E2 243 C6
Ebrington Rd HA3 43 D3
Ebsworth St SE23 162 D4
Eburne Rd N7 72 A5
Ebury Bridge Rd SW1 115 A1 258 B1
Ebury Cl BR2 226 A5
Ebury Mews
Belgravia SW1 115 B2 258 C4
West Norwood SE27 160 D1
Ebury Mews E SW1 258 C5
Ebury Sq SW1 258 B3
Ebury St SW1 115 B2 258 C4
Ecclesbourne Cl N13 32 C5
Ecclesbourne Gdns N13 32 C5
Ecclesbourne Inf Sch CR7 205 A4
Ecclesbourne Jun Sch CR7 205 A4
Ecclesbourne Rd
Islington N1 73 A1
Thornton Heath CR7 205 A4
Eccles Ct SE11 260 D1
Eccleshill 3 BR2 208 D5
Eccles Rd SW11 136 D1
Eccleston Cl
Cockfosters EN4 2 D1
Crofton BR6 211 B1
Eccleston Cres RM6 58 B2
Ecclestone Ct HA9 66 A3
Ecclestone Mews HA9 66 A3
Ecclestone Pl HA9 66 B3
Eccleston Ho 1 SW2 160 C5
Eccleston Mews SW1 115 A3 258 B5
Eccleston Pl SW1 115 B2 258 C4
Eccleston Rd W13 109 A5
Eccleston Sq SW1 115 B2 258 D3
Eccleston Sq Mews SW1 259 A3
Eccleston St SW1 115 B2 258 C4
Echelforde Dr TW15 170 C6
Echelford Prim Sch The TW15 170 D5
Echo Hts E4 19 D3
Eckford St N1 234 A4
Eckington Ho N15 51 B3
Eckstein Rd SW11 136 C1
Eclipse Ho N22 32 B1
Eclipse Rd E13 99 B2
Ector Rd SE6 164 C2
Edam Ct 11 DA14 168 A1
Edans Ct W12 111 D4
Edbrooke Rd W9 91 C3
Eddisbury Ho 7 SE26 162 A1
Eddiscombe Rd SW6 135 B3
Eddison Ct N19 72 A6
Eddy Cl RM7 59 D3
Eddystone Rd SE4 163 A6
Eddystone Twr SE8 119 A1
Eddystone Wlk TW19 148 A4
Ede Cl TW4 129 B2
Edenbridge Cl 29 SE16 118 B1
Edenbridge Rd
Enfield EN1 17 C5
Hackney E9 74 D1
Eden Cl
Child's Hill NW3 69 C6
Enfield EN3 7 C5
Kensington W8 255 B6
Wembley HA0 87 D6
Edencourt W5 88 B1
Edencourt Rd SW16 181 B4
Eden Ct 3 N3 29 B1
Edendale W3 110 D6
Edenfield Gdns KT4 215 D5
Eden Gr
Islington N7 72 B3
Walthamstow E17 53 D4
Edenham High Sch CR0 207 B2
Edenham Way W10 91 B2
Eden Ho
15 Battersea SW11 136 C2
Lisson Gr NW8 237 A5
Edenhurst Ave SW6 135 B2
Eden Lodge NW6 68 D1
Eden Mews SW17 158 A1
EDEN PARK 207 C5
Eden Park Ave BR3 207 C4
Eden Park Sta BR3 207 C4
Eden Rd
Croydon CR0 221 B4
Penge BR3 185 A2
Walthamstow E17 53 D4
West Norwood SE27 182 D5
Edensmuir Ct SE3 143 A5
Edensor Gdns W4 133 C5
Edensor Rd W4 133 C5
Eden St KT1, KT2 176 A1
Edenvale Cl CR4 181 A3
Edenvale Rd CR4 181 A3
Edenvale St SW6 136 A3
Eden Way
Beckenham BR3 207 C3
Bow E3 97 B6
Eden Wlk 5 KT1 176 A1
Ederline Ave SW16 182 C1
Edgar Ct KT3 199 C6
Edgar Ho
Homerton E9 75 A3
South Lambeth SW8 270 A4
Wanstead E11 55 A2
Edgar Kail Way SE22 139 C1
Edgarley Terr SW6 264 A1
Edgar Rd
Bromley E3 97 D4
Dagenham RM6 58 D2
Twickenham TW4 151 B4
Yiewsley UB7 104 A5
Edgar Wallace Cl 4 SE15 139 C5
Edgbury Ct NW9 45 A5
Edgcott Ho 2 W10 90 C2
Edgeborough Way BR1 187 D2
Edge Bsns Ctr The NW2 68 B6
Edgebury BR7, SE9 188 D6
Edgebury Prim Sch BR7 189 A6
Edgebury Wlk BR7 167 A1
Edgecombe Ho
4 London SE5 139 C3
Putney SW19 157 A4
Edgecoombe CR2 222 C1
Edgecoombe Cl KT2 177 B3
Edgecote Cl 7 W3 111 A5
Edgecot Gr N15 51 C4
Edgecumbe Ct 2 CR0 206 A1
Edgefield Ave IG11 79 D1
Edgefield Ct 8 IG11 79 D1
Edge Hill
Shooters Hill SE18 144 D6
Wimbledon SW19 178 D3
Edge Hill Ave N3 47 C5
Edgehill Ct KT12 194 C1
Edge Hill Ct
Sidcup DA14 189 D6
Wimbledon SW19 178 D3
Edgehill Gdns RM10 81 C4
Edgehill Ho 4 SW9 138 D3
Edgehill Rd
Ealing W13 87 C2
Longlands BR7 189 A6
Mitcham CR4 181 B2
Edgeley La SW4 137 D2
Edgeley Rd SW4 137 D2
Edgel St SW18 135 D1
Edge Point Cl SE27 182 D5
Edge St W8 113 C5 245 B4
Edgewood Dr BR6 227 D3
Edgewood Gn CR0 206 D1
Edgeworth Ave NW4 46 A4
Edgeworth Cl NW4 46 A4
Edgeworth Cres NW4 46 A4
Edgeworth Ct 10 EN4 2 C1
Edgeworth Ho NW8 229 A6
Edgeworth Rd
Barnet EN4 2 C1
Eltham SE9 143 D1
Edgington Rd SW16 181 D4
Edgington Way DA14 190 D3
Edgson Ho SW1 258 C2
EDGWARE 26 C6
Edgware Acad WC2 240 B1
EDGWARE BURY 10 B3
Edgwarebury Ct HA8 26 C5
Edgwarebury Gdns HA8 26 C5
Edgwarebury La
Edgware Bury HA8 10 C2
Edgware HA8 26 C5
Edgware Community Hospl HA8 26 D3
Edgware Ct HA8 26 C4
Edgware Jun & Inf Schs HA8 26 C4
Edgware Rd
Dollis Hill NW2 68 C6
Paddington W1, W2, NW1, NW8 92 C2 237 A3
Edgware Rd Burnt Oak Broadway HA8 26 D3
Edgware Rd High St HA8 26 C4
Edgware Road Sta (Bakerloo) NW1 92 C2 237 A3
Edgware Road Sta (Met, Distr, Circle) NW1 237 B3
Edgware Road The Hyde NW9 45 C5
Edgware Road West Hendon Broadway NW9 46 A2
Edgware Sta HA8 26 D4
Edgware Way (Watford By-Pass) HA8 27 A6
Edinburgh Cl
7 Bethnal Green E2 96 C5
Pinner HA5 41 A2
Uxbridge UB10 60 D4
Edinburgh Ct
1 Catford SE6 164 D3
2 Kingston u T KT1 198 A6
Newham E13 99 B5
10 Rotherhithe SE16 118 D5
West Barnes SM4 200 D4
Edinburgh Dr UB10 60 D4
Edinburgh Ho
3 Acton W3 89 B1
Carshalton SM1 218 B6
Hendon NW4 46 C6
Maida Vale W9 91 D4
Edinburgh Prim Sch E17 53 B4
Edinburgh Rd
Carshalton SM1 218 B6
Edmonton N18 34 A5
Hanwell W7 108 D4
Newham E13 99 B5
Walthamstow E17 53 C4
Edington 20 NW5 71 A2
Edington Rd
Abbey Wood SE2 124 B3
Enfield EN3 6 C3
Edison Bldg 7 E14 119 C4
Edison Cl
Walthamstow E17 53 C4
West Drayton UB7 104 B4
Edison Ct SE10 120 D3
Edison Dr
Southall UB1 85 D1
Wembley HA9 66 A6
Edison Gr SE18 145 D5
Edison Ho
Walworth SE1 262 C4
7 Wembley HA9 67 A5
Edison Rd
Bexley DA16 145 D4
Brimsdown EN3 7 B3
Bromley BR2 187 A1
Crouch End N8 49 D3
Edis St NW1 93 A6 231 B6
Editha Mans SW10 266 A5
Edith Cavell Cl 2 N19 50 A2
Edith Cavell Way SE18 144 A4
Edith Ct TW14 149 B5
Edith Gdns KT5 198 D3
Edith Gr SW10 136 A5 266 B4
Edith Ho 6 W6 112 C1
Edithna St SW9 138 A2
Edith Neville Cotts NW1 232 C2
Edith Neville Prim Sch NW1 93 D5 232 C3
Edith Pond Ct SE9 166 D2
Edith Ramsay Ho 2 E1 97 A2
Edith Rd
Dagenham RM6 58 D2
South Norwood SE25 205 B4
Stratford New Town E15 76 B3
Upton Pk E6 77 D1
West Kensington W14 113 A2 254 B3
Wimbledon SW19 179 D4
Wood Green N11 31 D3
Edith Row SW6 265 D2
Edith St E2 96 A5
Edith Summerskill Ho SW6 264 C4
Edith Terr SW10 136 A5 266 A4
Edith Villas W14 113 B1 254 C2
Edith Yd SW10 266 B4
Edmansons' Cl N17 33 D2
Edmeston Cl E9 75 A2
Edmond Ct SE14 140 C4
Edmonscote W13 87 A2
EDMONTON 33 D6
Edmonton Ct 5 SE16 118 C3
Edmonton Cty Lower Sch N9 17 C3
Edmonton Cty Upper Sch EN1 17 D4
Edmonton Green Sh Ctr N9 18 B2
Edmonton Green Sta N9 18 A2
Edmonton Wharf N18 34 D4
Edmund Gr TW13 151 B2
Edmund Halley Way SE10 120 C4
Edmund Ho
Kennington SE17 261 D1
New Cross Gate SE14 141 B4
Edmund Hurst Dr E6 100 D2
Edmund Rd
Mitcham CR4 202 C6
Welling DA16 146 A2
Edmundsbury Ct Est 16 SW9 138 B1
Edmunds Cl UB4 84 C2
Edmund St SE5 139 B5
Edmunds Wlk N2 48 C5
Edmund Waller Prim Sch SE14 140 D3
Ednam Ho SE15 140 A6
Edna Rd SW20 178 D1
Edna St SW11 136 C4 267 A1
Edred Ho E9 75 A4
Edrich Ho SW4 270 A1
Edric Ho SW1 259 D4

Edrick Rd HA8 27 A4
Edrick Wlk HA8 27 A4
Edric Rd SE14 140 D5
Edridge Cl WD23 8 A6
Edridge Ho 9 SE27 160 D1
Edridge Rd CR0 221 B5
Edward Alleyn Ho SE21 161 C4
Edward Ave
Chingford E4 35 D4
Morden SM4 202 B4
Edward Betham CE Prim Sch UB6 86 A5
Edward Cl
Edmonton N9 17 D4
Hampton TW12 174 A5
Edward Ct
2 Ealing W5 87 B3
Harrow HA1 64 C6
2 Newham E16 99 A2
Edward Dodd Ct N1 235 D2
Edward Edward's Ho SE1 251 C3
Edwardes Pl W8 254 D5
Edwardes Sq W8 113 B3 254 D5
Edward Friend Ho 6 N16 73 C5
Edward Gr EN4 14 B6
Edward Harvey Ct DA17 125 B1
Edward Ho
Paddington W2 236 C5
Vauxhall SE11 260 D2
Edward Kennedy Ho 18 W10 91 A3
Edward Mann Cl 13 E1 96 D1
Edward Mans 8 IG11 79 D1
Edward Mews NW1 231 D3
Edward Pauling Ho TW14 149 D4
Edward Pauling Prim Sch TW13 149 C2
Edward Pinner Ct 5 KT6 214 A6
Edward Pl SE8 141 B6
Edward Rd
Bromley BR1 187 C3
Chislehurst BR7 188 D5
Croydon CR0 205 C2
Dagenham RM6 59 A3
Hampton TW12 174 A5
Harrow HA2 42 A6
Hatton TW14 149 C6
New Barnet EN4 14 B6
Northolt UB5 84 C5
Penge SE20 184 D4
Walthamstow E17 52 D4
Edward Robinson Ho 3 SE14 140 D5
Edward's Ave HA4 62 C2
Edwards Cl KT4 216 D6
Edward's Cotts 11 N1 72 D1
Edwards Dr N11 31 D3
Edwards Ho 7 TW10 153 C1
Edward's La N16 73 C6
Edwards Language Sch W5 110 A6
Edwards Mews
Islington N1 72 C1
Marylebone W1 93 A1 238 A1
Edward Sq
Islington N1 233 C5
1 Rotherhithe SE16 119 A5
Edwards Rd DA17 125 C2
Edward St
New Cross SE14 141 B5
10 Newham E16 99 A3
Edward Temme Ave E15 76 D1
Edward Tyler Rd SE12 165 C2
Edward VII Mans NW10 90 D4
Edward Way TW15 148 B2
Edward Wilson Prim Sch W2 91 D2
Edwina Ct SM1 217 D4
Edwina Gdns IG4 56 A4
Edwin Arnold Ct DA15 189 D6
Edwin Ave E6 100 C5
Edwin Cl DA7 147 B6
Edwin Ho SE15 140 A5
Edwin Rd
Burnt Oak HA8 27 B4
Twickenham TW1, TW2 152 C3
Edwin's Mead E9 75 A4
Edwin St
Bethnal Green E1 96 C3
Newham E16 99 A2
Edwin Stray Ho TW13 151 C1
Edwin Ware Ct 4 HA5 22 C1
Edwy Ho E9 75 B4
Edwyn Cl EN5 12 D5
Edwyn Ho SW18 157 D5
Eel Pie Island* TW1 153 A3
Effie Pl SW6 265 B3
Effie Rd SW6 135 C5 265 B3
Effingham Cl SM2 217 D1
Effingham Ct SW19 180 C3
Effingham Ho
37 Clapham SW8 137 D3
9 Kingston u T KT2 176 D4
Effingham Lo 1 KT6 198 A4
Effingham Rd
Hornsey N8 50 C5
Lewisham SE12 164 D6
Thames Ditton KT6, KT7 197 C2
Thornton Heath CR0 204 B2
Effort St SW17 180 C5
Effra Cl SW19 179 D4
Effra Ct
London SW2 160 B6
South Norwood SE19 183 C3
Effra Mans SW2 160 C6
Effra Par SW2 160 C6
Effra Rd
London SW2 160 C6
Wimbledon SW19 179 D4
Effra Road Ret Pk SW2 160 C6
EF International Language Sch SE1 251 B3
Egan Way UB3 105 C6
Egbert Ho E9 75 A3
Egbert St NW1 93 A6 231 A6
Egbury Ho SW15 155 D5
Egerton Cl HA5 40 A5
Egerton Cres SW3 114 C2 257 B4
Egerton Ct
Leytonstone E11 54 B2
5 Richmond TW10 154 A6
Egerton Dr SE10 141 D4
Egerton Gdns
Ealing W13 87 B1
Hendon NW4 46 B5
Ilford IG3 79 D5
Knightsbridge SW3 114 C3 257 A5
Willesden NW10 90 C6
Egerton Gdns Mews SW3 257 B5
Egerton Ho W4 133 A6
Egerton Pl SW3 257 B5
Egerton Rd
New Malden KT3 199 D5
South Norwood SE25 205 C6
Stamford Hill N16 51 D2
Twickenham TW2 152 C4
Wembley HA0 66 B1
Egerton Terr SW3 114 C3 257 B5
Egerton Way UB3 126 D5
Eggardon Ct UB5 64 A2
Egham Cl
Cheam SM3 217 A6
Putney SW19 157 A2
Egham Cres SM3 217 A6
Egham Ct KT6 197 D4
Egham Rd E13 99 B2
Eglantine Rd SW18 158 A6
Egleston Rd SM4 201 D3
Eglington Ct SE17 139 A6
Eglington Rd E4 20 B4
Eglinton Hill SE18 144 D5
Eglinton Prim Sch SE18 144 C6
Eglinton Rd SE18 144 D6
Egliston Mews SW15 134 C2
Egliston Rd SW15 134 C2
Egmont Ave KT6 198 B1
Egmont Rd
New Malden KT3 199 D5
Sutton SM2 218 A1
Tolworth KT6 198 C1
Walton-on-T KT12 194 B2
Egmont St SE14 140 D5
Egremont Ho SE13 141 D3
Egremont Rd SE27 160 C1
Egret Ho 11 SE16 118 D2
Egret Way UB4 84 D2
Eider Cl
Hayes UB4 84 D2
Stratford E7 76 D3
Eider Ct 38 SE8 141 B6
Eighteenth Rd CR4 204 A5
Eighth Ave
Hayes UB3 106 A5
Ilford E12 78 B4
Eileen Ct BR7 188 C5
Eileen Rd SE25 205 B4
Eindhoven Cl SM5 203 A1
Einstein Ho HA9 67 A5
Eisenhower Dr E6 100 A2
Eisenhower Ho KT8 175 C2
Elaine Ct 13 NW3 70 D2
Elaine Gr NW5 71 A3
Elaine Ho N4 50 A1
Elam Cl SE5 138 D3
Elam St SE5 138 D3
Elan Ct E1 96 B2
Eland Pl CR0 220 D5
Eland Rd
Clapham SW11 136 D2
Croydon CR0 220 D5
Elba Pl SE17 117 A2 262 B4
Elberon Ave CR0 203 C3
Elbe St SW6 136 A3
Elborough Rd SE25 206 A4
Elborough St SW18 157 C3
Elbourne Trad Est DA17 125 D3
Elbury Dr E16 99 A1
Elcho St SW11 136 C5 267 B3
Elcot Ave SE15 140 B5
Elder Ave N8 50 A4
Elderberry Ct 2 EN2 4 D3
Elderberry Gr 10 SE27 183 A6
Elderberry Rd W5 110 A4
Elderberry Way E6 100 B4
Elder Cl
Barnet N20 13 D3
Sidcup DA15 167 D3
Yiewsley UB7 104 A6
Elder Ct WD23 8 C2
Elderfield Ho 4 E14 119 C6
Elderfield Pl SW17 181 B6
Elderfield Rd E5 74 C4
Elderfield Wlk E11 55 B4
Elderflower Way E15 76 C1
Elder Gdns 9 SE27 183 A6
Elder Oak Cl SE20 184 B2
Elder Rd SE27 183 A5
Elderslie Cl BR3 207 D3
Elderslie Rd SE9 166 C6
Elder St E1 95 D3 243 C5
Elderton Rd SE26 185 A6
Eldertree Pl CR4 181 C2
Eldertree Way CR4 181 C2
Elder Wlk
Islington N1 234 D6
2 Lewisham SE13 142 A2
Elderwood Pl SE27 183 A5
Eldon Ave
Croydon CR0 222 C6
Heston TW5 129 C5
Eldon Ct NW6 91 C6
Eldon Gr NW3 70 B3
Eldon Ho SW9 138 D2
Eldon Jun & Inf Schs N9 18 C3
Eldon Pk SE25 206 B5
Eldon Rd
Edmonton N9 18 C3
Kensington W8 113 D3 255 D5
Tottenham N22 32 D2
Walthamstow E17 53 B5
Eldon St EC2 95 B2 242 D3
Eldonwall Est RM8 59 B1
Eldon Way NW10 88 D5
Eldred Rd IG11 101 C6
Eldrick Ct TW14 149 B3
Eldridge Cl TW14 150 A3
Eldridge Ct
Bermondsey SE16 118 A3
14 Dagenham RM10 81 D2
Eleanor Cl
Rotherhithe SE16 118 D4
South Tottenham N15 51 D6
Eleanor Cres NW7 28 D6
Eleanor Ct 13 E2 96 A6
Eleanor Gdns
Barnet EN5 12 D6
Dagenham RM8 81 B6
Eleanor Gr
Mortlake SW13 133 C2
Uxbridge UB10 60 D5
Eleanor Ho
18 Hammersmith W6 112 C1
1 Kentish Town NW5 71 C3
6 Merton SW19 179 D2
Eleanor Palmer Prim Sch NW5 71 C4
Eleanor Rathbone Ho 1 N6 49 D2
Eleanor Rd
Bowes Pk N11 32 A4
Hackney E8 74 B1
Stratford E15 76 D2
Eleanor Smith Sch E13 99 B5
Eleanor Smith Sch (West Beckton Site) E16 99 C2
Eleanor St E3 97 C4
Eleanor Wlk 24 SE18 122 B2
Electra Ave TW6 127 D2
Electra Ct 6 NW2 68 C2
Electric Ave SW9 138 C1
Electric Ho
13 Bow E3 97 C4
Walthamstow E17 53 C5
Electric La 2 SW9 138 C1
Electric Mans 1 SW9 138 C1
Electric Par
Ilford IG3 57 D1
Surbiton KT6 197 D3
Woodford E18 37 A1
Elenmore Ct BR1 210 A5
Elephant & Castle
Newington SE1 116 D3 261 D5
Newington SE1 261 D4
Elephant & Castle Sh Ctr SE1 117 A2 262 A4
Elephant & Castle Sta
Lambeth SE1 116 D3 261 D5
Newington SE17 117 A2 262 A4
Elephant La SE16 118 C4
Elephant Rd SE17 117 A2 262 A4
Elers Rd
Ealing W13 109 C4
Hayes UB3 105 B2
Eley Rd N18 34 D5
Eley's Est N18 34 D6
Elfindale Rd SE24 161 A6
Elfin Gr TW11 174 D5
Elford Cl SE9 143 C1
Elfort Rd N5 72 C4
Elfrida Cres SE6 185 C6
Elfrida Prim Sch SE6 185 C6
Elf Row E1 118 C6
Elfwine Rd W7 86 C2
Elgal Cl BR6 226 D3
Elgar N8 50 A6
Elgar Ave
Ealing W5 110 A4
Thornton Heath SW16 204 A6
Tolworth KT5, KT6 198 D2
Willesden NW10 67 B2
Elgar Cl
Buckhurst Hill IG9 21 D2
Deptford SE8 141 C5
Elstree WD6 9 D4
Ickenham UB10 60 C6
Newham E13 99 C5
Elgar Ct W14 254 A5
Elgar Ho
Hayes UB4 84 C2
Isleworth TW2 152 B5
Pimlico SW1 258 D1
Southall UB1 85 C1
South Hampstead NW6 70 A1
Elgar St SE16 119 A3
Elgin Ave
Ashford TW15 171 A4
Hammersmith W12 112 B3
Harrow HA3 25 B1
Westbourne Green W9 91 D3
Elgin Cl W12 112 B4
Elgin Cres
Hatton TW6 127 C3
Notting Hill W11 113 A6 244 B6
Elgin Ct
6 Croydon CR0 221 A4
Westbourne Green W9 91 D3
Elgin Ho
Northolt UB5 84 B5
8 Poplar E14 97 D1
Elgin Mans W9 91 D4
Elgin Mews W11 91 A1
Elgin Mews N W9 91 D4
Elgin Mews S W9 91 D4
Elgin Rd
Croydon CR0 221 D6
Ilford IG3 57 C2
Sutton SM1 218 A5
Elgin Rd *continued*
Wallington SM6 219 C2
Wood Green N22 31 C1
Elgood Ave HA6 22 A3
Elgood Cl W11 244 A3
Elgood Ho NW8 229 D3
Elham Cl BR1 187 D3
Elham Ho 13 E5 74 B3
Elia Mews N1 94 D5 234 C3
Elias Pl SW8 138 C6
Elia St N1 94 D5 234 C3
Elibank Rd SE9 144 C1
Elim Est SE1 263 A6
Elim St SE1 263 A6
Elim Way E13 98 D4
Eliot Bank SE23, SE26 162 B2
Eliot Bank Prim Sch SE26 162 B2
Eliot Cotts SE3 142 C3
Eliot Ct SW18 157 D5
Eliot Dr HA2 63 D6
Eliot Gdns SW15 134 A1
Eliot Hill SE13 142 A3
Eliot Ho 10 TW10 154 B5
Eliot Mews NW8 229 A3
Eliot Pk SE13 142 A3
Eliot Pl SE3 142 C3
Eliot Rd RM9 80 D4
Eliot Vale SE3 142 B3
Elis David Almshouses CR0 220 D4
Elizabethan Ct N3 47 A6
Elizabeth Ave
Enfield EN2 4 D2
Ilford IG1 79 B6
Islington N1 73 B1
Shoreditch N1 95 A6 235 B6
Elizabeth Barnes Ct 5 SW6 135 D3
Elizabeth Blackwell Ho N22 32 C2
Elizabeth Blount Ct 4 E14 97 A1
Elizabeth Cl
Cheam SM1 217 B4
Paddington W9 236 B5
12 Poplar E14 97 D1
Elizabeth Clyde Cl N15 51 C5
Elizabeth Cooper Lo SW12 159 A5
Elizabeth Cotts 5 TW9 132 C4
Elizabeth Ct
Buckhurst Hill IG9 21 B3
Chelsea SW10 266 D5
East Dulwich SE22 140 A1
Kingston u T KT2 176 A2
Marylebone NW8 237 B6
South Croydon CR0 221 C5
Sunbury TW16 194 C6
3 Teddington TW11 174 C5
Upper Tooting SW17 181 A5
West Barnes SM4 201 A2
Westminster SW1 259 D5
6 Woodford Green E18 37 A2
2 Woodford Green IG8 37 C3
10 Woolwich SE18 122 B2
Elizabeth Finn Ho 1 W12 112 A3
Elizabeth Fry Ho UB3 105 D2
Elizabeth Fry Pl SE18 144 A4
Elizabeth Garrett Anderson Ho 9 DA17 125 C3
Elizabeth Garrett Anderson Hospl NW1 93 C3 239 B5
Elizabeth Garrett Anderson Language Coll N1 94 B5 233 D3
Elizabeth Gdns
East Acton W3 111 D5
Isleworth TW7 131 A1
Stanmore HA7 25 C5
Sunbury TW16 194 C6
Elizabeth Ho
Cheam SM3 217 A2
Friern Barnet N20 14 D1
15 Hammersmith W6 112 C1
Lambeth SE11 261 B3
Stanmore HA7 26 A1
Wembley HA9 66 B3
Elizabeth Ind Est SE14 140 D6
Elizabeth Kenny Ho N1 73 A2
Elizabeth Mews
28 Hackney E2 96 A5
Maitland Pk NW3 70 D2
Elizabeth Pl N15 51 B5
Elizabeth Rd
Newham E6 99 D6
South Tottenham N15 51 C4
Elizabeth Ride N9 18 B4
Elizabeth Selby Inf Sch E2 96 A4
Elizabeth Sq 13 SE16 119 A6
Elizabeth St SW1 115 A2 258 B4
Elizabeth Terr SE9 166 B5
Elizabeth Way
Feltham TW13 172 C6
South Norwood SE19 183 B3
Elkanette Mews N20 14 A2
Elkington Point SE11 261 A3
Elkington Rd E13 99 B3
Elkstone Rd W10 91 B2
Ella Cl BR3 185 C1
Ellacombe Ho 1 SW2 160 C4
Ellaline Rd W6 134 D6
Ella Mews NW3 70 D4
Ellanby Cres N18 34 B5
Elland Ho 18 E14 97 B1
Elland Rd SE15 140 C1
Ella Rd N4, N8 50 A2
Ellard Ct DA16 146 C2
Elle Ct N12 29 D5
Ellement Cl HA5 40 D4
Ellena Ct N14 16 A1
Ellenborough Ct N22 32 D2
Ellenborough Ho 5 W12 112 B6
Ellenborough Pl SW15 134 A1
Ellenborough Rd
Sidcup DA14 191 A5
Tottenham N22 33 A2
Ellen Cl BR1 209 D6
Ellen Ct
6 Chingford E4 20 A3
Lower Edmonton N9 18 C2
Ellen Miller Ho 2 E17 54 A4
Ellen St E1 96 A1
Ellen Webb Dr HA3 42 C6
Ellen Wilkinson Ho
12 Dagenham RM10 81 C5
7 Globe Town E2 96 D4
West Brompton SW6 264 D5
Ellen Wilkinson Prim Sch E6 100 A2
Ellen Wilkinson Sch for Girls W3 88 B1
Elleray Rd TW11 174 D4
Ellerby St SW6 134 D4
Ellerdale Cl 15 NW3 70 A4
Ellerdale Rd NW3 70 A3
Ellerdale St SE13 141 D2
Ellerdine Rd TW3 130 B1
Ellerker Gdns TW10 154 A5
Ellerman Ave TW2, TW4 151 B3
Ellerslie Ct 6 SM6 219 B2
Ellerslie Gdns NW10 90 A6
Ellerslie Ind Est SW2 160 A6
Ellerslie Rd W12 112 B5
Ellerton Ct W3 110 D4
Ellerton Gdns RM9 80 C1
Ellerton Lo N3 29 C1
Ellerton Rd
Barnes SW13 134 A4
Dagenham RM9 80 C1
Surbiton KT6 198 B1
Wandsworth SW17, SW18 158 B3
Wimbledon SW20 178 A3
Ellery Cl 5 NW10 89 D5
Ellery Ho SE17 262 D3
Ellery Rd SE19 183 B3
Ellery St SE15 140 B3
Ellesborough Cl WD19 22 C5
Ellesmere Ave
Beckenham BR3 185 D1
Edgware NW7 11 B1
Ellesmere Cl
Leytonstone E11 54 D4
Ruislip HA4 39 A2
Ellesmere Ct
Chiswick W4 133 B6
Lewisham SE12 165 A3
Penge SE20 184 B1
Ellesmere Gdns IG4 56 A3
Ellesmere Gr EN5 13 B6
Ellesmere Rd
Bow E3 97 A5
Chiswick W4 133 B6

Ellesmere Rd *continued*
Greenford UB6 . . . . 86 A3
Twickenham TW1 . . . . . . 153 C5
Willesden NW10 . . . . 68 A3
Ellesmere St E14 . . . . 97 D1
Ellies Mews TW15 . . . . . 148 A2
Ellingfort Rd E8 . . . . 74 B1
Ellingham Prim Sch
KT9 . . . . 213 D1
Ellingham Rd
Chessington KT9 . . . . . . 213 D2
Leyton E15 . . . . 76 B4
Shepherd's Bush W12 . . 112 A4
Ellington Ct N14 . . . . 15 D2
Ellington Ho SE1 . . . . . . 262 B5
Ellington Rd
Cranley Gdns N10 . . . . . 49 B5
Feltham TW13 . . . . 171 D6
Hounslow TW3 . . . . 129 D3
Ellington St N7 . . . . 72 C2
Elliot Cl
Stratford E15 . . . . 76 C1
Wembley HA9 . . . . 66 C5
Woodford IG8 . . . . 37 D4
Elliot Ct 6 N15 . . . . 51 D5
Elliot Rd NW4 . . . . 46 B3
Elliott Ave HA4 . . . . 62 B6
Elliott Gdns TW17 . . . . . 192 C5
Elliott Ho 3 CR7 . . . . . . 204 D5
Elliott Rd
Acton W4 . . . . 111 C2
Brixton SW9 . . . . 138 D4
Bromley BR2 . . . . 209 D5
Camberwell SW9 . . . . . . 138 D4
Stanmore HA7 . . . . 25 A4
Thornton Heath CR7 . . . . 204 D5
Elliott Sch SW15 . . . . . . 156 C5
Elliott's Pl N1 . . . . 234 D5
Elliott Sq NW3 . . . . 70 C1
Elliott's Row
SE11 . . . . 116 D2 261 D4
Ellis Cl
Burnt Oak HA8 . . . . 27 C4
New Eltham SE9 . . . . 167 A2
Willesden NW10 . . . . 68 C2
Elliscombe Mount 11
SE7 . . . . 143 C6
Elliscombe Rd SE7 . . . . 143 C6
Ellis Ct W7 . . . . 86 D2
Ellisfield Dr SW15 . . . . . 156 A4
Ellis Franklin Ct NW8 . . 229 A4
Ellis Ho
Walthamstow E17 . . . . . . 54 A4
Walworth SE17 . . . . 262 C2
Ellison Gdns UB2 . . . . . 107 B2
Ellison Ho 1 SE13 . . . . 142 A3
Ellison Rd
Barnes SW13 . . . . 133 D3
New Eltham DA15 . . . . . 167 B3
Streatham SW16 . . . . . . 182 A3
Ellis Rd
Mitcham CR4 . . . . 202 D3
Southall UB2 . . . . 108 A5
Ellis St SW1 . . . 115 A2 258 A4
Elliston Ho 8 SE18 . . . . 122 C2
Ellora Rd SW16 . . . . 181 D5
Ellswood Ct 18 KT6 . . . . 197 D2
Ellsworth St E2 . . . . 96 B4
Ellwood Ct 1 W9 . . . . 91 D3
Elmar Ct SW6 . . . . 135 A3
Elmar Rd N15 . . . . 51 B5
Elm Ave
Ealing W5 . . . . 110 B5
Ruislip HA4 . . . . 40 B2
Elmbank N14 . . . . 16 A4
Elm Bank BR1 . . . . 187 D1
Elm Bank Gdns SW13 . . 133 C3
Elm Bank Mans
SW13 . . . . 133 C3
Elmbank Way W7 . . . . . . 86 B2
Elmbourne Dr DA17 . . . . 125 D2
Elmbourne Rd SW17 . . . 159 B1
Elmbridge Ave KT5 . . . . 199 A3
Elmbridge Cl HA4 . . . . . . 40 A3
Elmbridge Dr HA4 . . . . . . 40 A3
Elmbridge Wlk E8 . . . . . . 74 A1
Elmbrook 3 E18 . . . . 55 A6
Elmbrook Cl TW16 . . . . . 172 B2
Elmbrook Gdns SE9 . . . . 144 A1
Elmbrook Rd SM1 . . . . . 217 B4
Elm Cl
Buckhurst Hill IG9 . . . . . . 21 D2
Carshalton SM5 . . . . 202 D1
Harrow HA2 . . . . 41 D3
Hayes UB3 . . . . 84 A1
Hendon NW4 . . . . 46 D4
South Croydon CR2 . . . . 221 C2

Elm Cl *continued*
Tolworth KT5 . . . . 199 A2
Twickenham TW13,
TW2 . . . . 151 D2
Upper Holloway N19 . . . . 71 C6
Wanstead E11 . . . . 55 B3
West Barnes SW20 . . . . 200 C5
Elmcote HA5 . . . . 22 D1
Elmcourt Rd SE21,
SE27 . . . . 160 D2
Elm Court Sch SE27 . . . 161 A2
Elm Cres
Ealing W5 . . . . 110 A4
Kingston u T KT2 . . . . . . 176 A2
Elmcroft
Highgate N6 . . . . 49 C2
Hornsey Vale N8 . . . . 50 B4
Elmcroft Ave
Blackfen DA15 . . . . 168 A5
Enfield N9 . . . . 18 B5
Golders Green NW11 . . . . 47 B2
Wanstead E11 . . . . 55 B5
Elmcroft Cl
Chessington KT9 . . . . . . 214 A5
Ealing W5 . . . . 87 D1
Feltham TW14 . . . . 149 D5
Wanstead E11 . . . . 55 B5
Elmcroft Cres
Harrow HA2 . . . . 41 C6
Hendon NW11 . . . . 47 A2
Elmcroft Dr
Ashford TW15 . . . . 170 C5
Chessington KT9 . . . . . . 214 A5
Elmcroft Gdns NW9 . . . . 44 C4
Elmcroft St E5 . . . . 74 C4
Elmcroft Terr UB8 . . . . . 82 C1
Elm Ct
5 Ashford TW16 . . . . . . 171 D3
Brixton SW9 . . . . 138 C4
Catford SE6 . . . . 163 D3
Chingford E4 . . . . 36 A4
4 Finchley N3 . . . . 29 C2
Lewisham SE13 . . . . 142 B2
Mitcham CR4 . . . . 180 D1
42 Notting Hill W2 . . . . . . 91 C2
Strand EC4 . . . . 251 A6
Elmdale Rd N13 . . . . 32 B5
Elmdene KT5 . . . . 199 A1
Elmdene Cl BR3 . . . . . . 207 B4
Elmdene Rd SE18 . . . . . 122 D1
Elmdon Rd
Hatton TW6 . . . . 127 D2
Hounslow TW5 . . . . 129 A3
Elm Dr
Harrow HA2 . . . . 41 D3
Sunbury TW16 . . . . 172 C1
Elmer Cl EN2 . . . . 4 B2
Elmer Ct HA1 . . . . 42 D3
Elmer Gdns
Edgware HA8 . . . . 26 D3
Isleworth TW7 . . . . 130 B2
Elmer Ho NW1 . . . . 237 A4
Elmer Rd SE6 . . . . 164 A4
Elmer's Dr TW11 . . . . . . 175 B4
ELMERS END 206 D6
Elmers End Rd BR3,
SE20 . . . . 206 C6
Elmers End Sta BR3 . . . 206 D5
Elmerside Rd BR3 . . . . . 207 A5
Elmers Rd SE25 . . . . 206 A2
Elmfield Ave
London N8 . . . . 50 A4
Mitcham CR4 . . . . 181 A2
Teddington TW11 . . . . . . 174 D5
Elmfield Cl HA1 . . . . 64 C6
Elmfield Ct DA16 . . . . . . 146 B4
Elmfield Ho
6 Canonbury N5 . . . . 73 A3
22 London N2 . . . . 30 B1
Paddington W9 . . . . 91 C3
Elmfield Mans 5
SW17 . . . . 159 A2
Elmfield Pk BR1 . . . . 209 A6
Elmfield Rd
Bromley BR1 . . . . 209 A6
Chingford E4 . . . . 20 B2
East Finchley N2 . . . . 48 B6
Southall UB2 . . . . 107 A3
Upper Tooting SW17 . . . 159 B2
Walthamstow E17 . . . . . . 52 D3
Elmfield Way
Paddington W9 . . . . 91 C2
South Croydon CR2 . . . . 221 D1
Elm Friars Wlk NW1 . . . . 71 D1
Elmgate Ave TW13 . . . . 150 C1
Elmgate Ct HA8 . . . . 27 A5
Elmgate Gdns HA8 . . . . . 27 B6
Elm Gdns
Claygate KT10 . . . . 212 D2
East Finchley N2 . . . . 48 A6

Elm Gdns *continued*
Enfield EN2 . . . . 5 B5
Mitcham CR4 . . . . 203 D5
Elm Gn W3 . . . . 89 C1
Elm Gr
Cricklewood NW2 . . . . . . 68 D4
Harrow HA2 . . . . 41 C2
Hornsey N8 . . . . 50 A3
Kingston u T KT2 . . . . . . 176 A2
Orpington BR6 . . . . 211 D1
Peckham SE15 . . . . 140 A3
Sutton SM1 . . . . 217 D4
Wimbledon SW19 . . . . . 179 A3
Woodford IG8 . . . . 36 D5
Yiewsley UB7 . . . . 104 B6
Elmgreen Cl 8 E15 . . . . . 98 C6
Elmgrove Cres HA1 . . . . 43 A4
Elmgrove Fst & Mid Schs
HA3 . . . . 43 A5
Elmgrove Gdns HA1 . . . . 43 A4
Elm Grove Par SM6 . . . 219 A5
Elmgrove Rd
Croydon CR0 . . . . 206 B2
Harrow HA1 . . . . 42 D4
Elm Grove Rd
Barnes SW13 . . . . 134 A3
Ealing W5 . . . . 110 A4
Elm Hall Gdns E11 . . . . . 55 B3
Elm Hatch HA5 . . . . 23 B3
Elm Ho
4 Cubitt Town E14 . . . . 120 A4
2 Kingston u T KT2 . . . . 176 B3
Teddington TW11 . . . . . . 175 C3
Elmhurst DA17 . . . . 147 A6
Elmhurst Ave
London N2 . . . . 48 B6
Mitcham CR4 . . . . 181 B3
Elmhurst Cres N2 . . . . . . 48 B5
Elmhurst Ct
Carshalton SM5 . . . . 218 B6
Croydon CR0 . . . . 221 B3
Elmhurst Dr E18 . . . . 37 A1
Elmhurst Lo 3 SM2 . . . . 218 A1
Elmhurst Mans SW4 . . . 137 D2
Elmhurst Prim Sch E7 . . 77 B1
Elmhurst Rd
Chislehurst SE9 . . . . 166 A1
Enfield EN3 . . . . 6 C6
Tottenham N17 . . . . 33 D1
Upton E7 . . . . 77 B1
Elmhurst Sch CR2 . . . . . 221 B3
Elmhurst St SW4 . . . . . . 137 D2
Elmhurst Villas SE15 . . 140 C1
Elmington Cl DA5 . . . . . 169 D5
Elmington Rd SE5 . . . . . 139 B5
Elmira St SE13 . . . . 141 D2
Elm La SE6 . . . . 163 B2
Elm Lawn Cl UB8 . . . . . . 60 A1
Elmlea Dr UB3 . . . . 83 D2
Elm Lea Trad Est N17 . . . 34 B4
Elmlee Cl BR7 . . . . 188 B4
Elmley Cl 12 E6 . . . . 100 A2
Elmley St SE18 . . . . 123 B2
Elm Lo SW6 . . . . 134 D4
Elmore Cl HA0 . . . . 88 A5
Elmore Ho SW9 . . . . 138 D3
Elmore Rd
Enfield EN3 . . . . 6 D5
Leyton E11 . . . . 76 B5
Elmore St N1 . . . . 73 B1
Elm Park Ave N15 . . . . . . 52 A3
Elm Park Ct HA5 . . . . 40 C6
Elm Park Gdns
Chelsea
SW10 . . . . . . 114 B1 256 C1
Hendon NW4 . . . . 46 D4
Elm Park Ho SW10 . . . . 256 C1
Elm Park La
SW3 . . . . 114 B1 256 C1
Elm Park Mans SW10 . . 266 B6
Elm Park Rd
Chelsea SW3 . . 136 B6 266 C6
Edmonton N21 . . . . 17 A4
Finchley N3 . . . . 29 B3
Pinner HA5 . . . . 40 D6
South Norwood SE25 . . . 205 D6
Walthamstow E10 . . . . . . 53 A1
Elm Pk
Stanmore HA7 . . . . 25 C5
Streatham SW2 . . . . 160 B4
Elm Pl SW7 . . . . 114 B1 256 C2
Elm Quay SW8 . . . . 269 C5
Elm Rd
Barnet EN5 . . . . 1 B1
Beckenham BR3 . . . . 185 B1
Chessington KT9 . . . . . . 214 A4
Claygate KT10 . . . . 212 D2
East Bedfont TW14 . . . . . 149 B4
Hackbridge SM6 . . . . 203 A1
Kingston u T KT2 . . . . . . 176 B2

Elm Rd *continued*
Leyton E11 . . . . 76 B6
Mortlake SW14 . . . . 133 A1
New Malden KT3 . . . . . . 199 B6
Sidcup DA14 . . . . 190 A6
South Norwood CR7 . . . . 205 B5
Stoneleigh KT17 . . . . . . 215 D2
Stratford E7 . . . . 76 D2
Tottenham N22 . . . . 32 D2
Walthamstow E17 . . . . . . 54 A4
Wembley HA9 . . . . 66 A3
Elm Rd W SM4 . . . . 201 B2
Elm Row NW3 . . . . 70 A5
Elms Ave
Hendon NW4 . . . . 46 D4
Muswell Hill N10 . . . . 49 B6
Elmscott Gdns N21 . . . . . 17 A5
Elmscott Rd BR1 . . . . . . 186 D5
Elms Cotts 1 CR4 . . . . . 180 D1
Elms Cres SW4 . . . . 159 D5
Elms Ct
Merton SW19 . . . . 179 D3
Wembley HA0 . . . . 65 A4
Elmsdale Rd E17 . . . . 53 B5
Elms Gdns
Dagenham RM9 . . . . 81 B4
Wembley HA0 . . . . 65 A4
Elmshaw Rd SW15 . . . . 156 A6
Elmside CR0 . . . . 223 D2
Elmside Rd HA9 . . . . 66 C5
Elms La HA0 . . . . 65 A5
Elmsleigh Ave HA3 . . . . . 43 C5
Elmsleigh Ct SM1 . . . . . 217 D5
Elmsleigh Ho TW2 . . . . 152 B2
Elmsleigh Rd TW2 . . . . 152 B2
Elmslie Ct SE9 . . . . 166 C5
Elmslie Point 2 E3 . . . . . 97 B2
Elms Mews W2 . . . . 246 C6
Elms Park Ave HA0 . . . . 65 A4
Elms Rd
Clapham Pk SW4 . . . . . . 159 C6
Harrow HA3 . . . . 24 C3
Elm St WC1 . . . . . 94 B3 240 D5
ELMSTEAD 188 A5
Elmstead Ave
Elmstead BR7 . . . . 188 B5
Wembley HA9 . . . . 66 B6
Elmstead Cl
Totteridge N20 . . . . 13 C2
West Ewell KT19 . . . . . . 215 C3
Elmstead Ct HA9 . . . . 44 B1
Elmstead Gdns KT4 . . . 216 A5
Elmstead Glade BR7 . . . 188 B4
Elmstead La BR7 . . . . . . 188 B5
Elmstead Rd IG3 . . . . 79 D6
Elmstead Woods Sta
BR7 . . . . 188 A4
Elmsted Cres DA16 . . . . 146 C6
Elms The
5 Ashford TW15 . . . . . . 170 C5
Barnes SW13 . . . . 133 D2
Claygate KT10 . . . . 212 D1
Croydon CR0 . . . . 205 A1
3 Harlesden NW10 . . . . . 89 C5
Kingsbury NW9 . . . . 45 A3
Plashet E12 . . . . 78 A2
Wallington SM6 . . . . 219 C4
Elmstone Rd SW6 . . . . . 265 A2
Elmsway TW15 . . . . 170 C5
Elmsworth Ave TW3 . . . 129 D3
Elm Terr
Child's Hill NW2 . . . . 69 C5
3 Eltham SE9 . . . . 166 C5
Harrow HA3 . . . . 24 B2
Elmton Ct NW8 . . . . 236 C6
Elm Tree Ave KT10 . . . . 196 C2
Elm Tree Cl
Ashford TW15 . . . . 170 D5
Northolt UB5 . . . . 85 B5
St John's Wood
NW8 . . . . 92 B4 229 C2
Elmtree Ct HA4 . . . . 40 A1
Elm Tree Ct
5 Camberwell SE5 . . . . 139 A4
18 Charlton SE7 . . . . . . 143 C6
St John's Wood NW8 . . . 229 C2
Elmtree Rd TW11 . . . . . 174 C5
Elm Tree Rd
NW8 . . . . 92 B4 229 C2
Elm View Ct UB2 . . . . . . 107 C2
Elm Way
London N11 . . . . 31 A4
North Cheam KT4 . . . . . 216 C5
West Ewell KT19 . . . . . . 215 B3
Willesden NW10 . . . . 67 C4
Elm Wlk
Child's Hill NW3 . . . . 69 C6
Orpington BR6 . . . . 226 B5
West Barnes SW20 . . . . 200 D5

Elmwood Ave
Bowes Pk N13 . . . . 32 A5
Feltham TW13 . . . . 150 B1
Harrow HA3 . . . . 43 B3
Elmwood Cl
Hackbridge SM6 . . . . 219 B6
Stoneleigh KT17 . . . . . . 216 A1
Elmwood Cres NW9 . . . . 45 A5
Elmwood Ct
Battersea SW11 . . . . 268 C2
Walthamstow E10 . . . . . . 53 C1
Wembley HA0 . . . . 65 A5
Elmwood Dr
Sidcup DA5 . . . . 169 A4
Stoneleigh KT17 . . . . . . 216 A1
Elmwood Gdns W7 . . . . . 86 C1
Elmwood Ho
Enfield EN2 . . . . 4 D1
Feltham TW13 . . . . 150 B1
Elmwood Inf Sch
CR0 . . . . 204 D3
Elmwood Jun Sch
CR0 . . . . 204 D2
Elm Wood Prim Sch
SE27 . . . . 161 B1
Elmwood Rd
Chiswick W4 . . . . 133 A6
Herne Hill SE24 . . . . 161 B6
Mitcham CR4 . . . . 202 D6
Thornton Heath CR0 . . . . 204 D2
Elmworth Gr SE21 . . . . . 161 B2
Elnathan Mews W9 . . . . . 91 D3
Elphinstone Ct SW16 . . 182 A4
Elphinstone Rd E17 . . . . 35 B1
Elphinstone St N5 . . . . . 72 D4
Elrington Rd
Dalston E8 . . . . 74 A2
Woodford IG8 . . . . 37 A5
Elsa Ct BR3 . . . . 185 B2
Elsa Rd DA16 . . . . 146 C3
Elsa St E1 . . . . 97 A2
Elsdale Ho 14 E9 . . . . 74 C2
Elsdale St E9 . . . . 74 C1
Elsden Mews E2 . . . . 96 C5
Elsden Rd N17 . . . . 33 D2
Elsenham Rd E12 . . . . . . 78 C3
Elsenham St SW18,
SW19 . . . . 157 B2
Elsfield NW5 . . . . 71 B3
Elsham Rd
Kensington
W14 . . . . 113 A4 244 A1
Leyton E11 . . . . 76 C4
Elsham Terr W14 . . . . . 244 A1
Elsiedene Rd N21 . . . . . . 17 A4
Elsie Lane Ct W2 . . . . . . 91 D2
Elsiemaud Rd SE4 . . . . . 163 B6
Elsie Rd SE22 . . . . 139 D1
Elsinge Rd EN1 . . . . 6 B6
Elsinore Ave TW19 . . . . 148 A4
Elsinore Gdns NW2 . . . . 69 A5
Elsinore Ho
12 Camberwell SE5 . . . . 139 A3
Islington N1 . . . . 234 A5
7 Woolwich SE7 . . . . . . 122 A2
Elsinore Rd SE23 . . . . . 163 A3
Elsinore Way TW9 . . . . 132 D2
Elsley Ct HA9 . . . . 66 D2
Elsley Prim Sch HA9 . . . . 66 B2
Elsley Rd SW11 . . . . 137 A2
Elsley Sch SW11 . . . . . . 137 A2
Elspeth Rd
London SW11 . . . . 136 D1
Wembley HA0 . . . . 66 A3
Elsrick Ave SM4 . . . . 201 C4
Elstan Way CR0 . . . . 207 A2
Elstead Ct SM3 . . . . 201 A1
Elstead Ho 9 SW2 . . . . 160 B4
Elsted St SE17 . 117 B2 262 D3
Elstow Cl
Eltham SE9 . . . . 166 B6
Ruislip HA4 . . . . 40 D2
Elstow Gdns RM9 . . . . . 103 A6
Elstow Grange NW6 . . . . 68 D1
Elstow Rd RM9 . . . . 103 A6
ELSTREE 10 A5
Elstree Gdns
Abbey Wood DA17 . . . . . 125 A2
Edmonton N9 . . . . 18 B3
Ilford IG1 . . . . 79 A3
Elstree Hill BR1 . . . . 186 C3
Elstree Hill N WD6 . . . . . . 9 D6
Elstree Hill S WD6 . . . . . . 9 D4
Elstree Ho 3 HA7 . . . . . . 25 C6
Elstree Pk WD6 . . . . 11 B5
Elstree Rd
Bushey WD23 . . . . 8 C4
Elstree WD6 . . . . 9 A5
Elswick Rd SE13 . . . . . . 141 D3
Elswick St SW6 . . . . 136 A3

Elsworth Cl TW14 . . . . . 149 C3
Elsworthy KT7 . . . . 196 C3
Elsworthy Rd
NW3 . . . . 92 C6 230 A6
Elsworthy Rise NW3 . . . . 70 C1
Elsworthy Terr NW3 . . . . 70 C1
Elsynge Rd SW18 . . . . . 158 B6
Elsynge Road Mans
SW18 . . . . 158 B6
ELTHAM 166 B6
Eltham CE Prim Sch
SE9 . . . . 166 B6
Eltham Coll SE9 . . . . 165 D2
Eltham Coll Jun Sch
SE9 . . . . 165 D3
Eltham Green Rd SE9 . 165 C6
Eltham Green Specialist
Sports Coll SE9 . . . . . . 165 D5
Eltham High St SE9 . . . 166 B5
Eltham Hill SE9 . . . . 166 A6
Eltham Hill Tech Coll for
Girls SE9 . . . . 166 A5
Eltham Pal* SE9 . . . . . . 166 A4
Eltham Palace Rd
SE9 . . . . 165 D5
Eltham Park Gdns
SE9 . . . . 144 C1
Eltham Rd SE9, SE12 . . . 165 B6
Eltham Sta SE9 . . . . 166 B6
Elthiron Rd
SW6 . . . . 135 C4 265 B1
Elthorne Ave W7 . . . . . . 109 A4
Elthorne Ct
Feltham TW13 . . . . 150 C3
Kingsbury NW9 . . . . 45 B3
Elthorne Park High Sch
W7 . . . . 108 D3
Elthorne Park Rd W7 . . 109 A4
Elthorne Rd
London NW9 . . . . 45 B2
Upper Holloway N19 . . . . 71 D6
Elthorne Way NW9 . . . . . 45 B3
Elthruda Rd SE13 . . . . . 164 B5
Eltisley Rd IG1 . . . . 78 D4
Elton Ave
Barnet EN5 . . . . 13 B6
Wembley HA0 . . . . 65 B3
Wembley UB6 . . . . 64 D2
Elton Cl KT1 . . . . 175 C3
Elton Ho 3 E3 . . . . 97 B6
Elton Lo 4 W5 . . . . 110 A6
Elton Pl N16 . . . . 73 C3
Elton Rd KT2 . . . . 176 C2
Elton St 11 N16 . . . . 73 C3
Eltringham St SW18 . . . 136 A1
Elvaston Ct EN5 . . . . 12 C6
Elvaston Mews SW7 . . . 256 B6
Elvaston Pl
SW7 . . . . 114 A3 256 B5
Elveden Ho 17 SW9 . . . 138 D1
Elveden Pl NW10 . . . . . . 88 C5
Elveden Rd NW10 . . . . . 88 C5
Elvedon Rd TW13 . . . . . 149 D1
Elvendon Rd N13 . . . . . . 32 A4
Elver Gdns 10 E2 . . . . . . 96 A4
Elverson Rd SE8 . . . . . . 141 D3
Elverson Rd Sta SE8 . . . 141 D3
Elverton St
SW1 . . . . 115 D2 259 C4
Elvin Ct NW9 . . . . 45 A2
Elvington Gn BR2 . . . . . 208 D4
Elvington La NW9 . . . . . . 27 C2
Elvin Ho 2 E9 . . . . 74 C2
Elvino Rd SE26 . . . . 185 A5
Elvis Rd NW2 . . . . 68 C2
Elwill Way BR3 . . . . 208 B5
Elwin St E2 . . . . 96 A4
Elwood Ho N5 . . . . 72 D5
Elwood St N4, N5 . . . . . . 72 D5
Elworth Ho SW8 . . . . . . 270 D3
Elwyn Gdns SE12 . . . . . 165 A4
Ely Cl SW20 . . . . 177 D1
Ely Cotts SW8 . . . . 270 C3
Ely Court Flats SW6 . . . 264 A1
Ely Ct
Holborn EC1 . . . . 241 B3
3 Maida Vale NW6 . . . . . 91 C5
Ely Gdns
Borehamwood WD6 . . . . . 11 B6
Redbridge IG1 . . . . 56 A2
Ely Ho
Barnet EN4 . . . . 2 C1
Northolt UB5 . . . . 85 A6
22 Peckham SE15 . . . . . 140 A5
Elyne Rd N4 . . . . 50 C3
Ely Pl EC1 . . . . . . 94 C2 241 B3
Ely Rd
Hatton TW6 . . . . 127 D3
Hounslow TW4 . . . . 128 C2
Leyton E10 . . . . 54 A2

Ely Rd *continued*
Thornton Heath CR0 ... 205 B4
Elysian Ave BR5 ... 211 D3
Elysium Gate 7 SW6 ... 135 B3
Elysium Pl SW6 ... 135 B3
Elysium St SW6 ... 135 B3
Elystan Bsns Ctr UB4 ... 106 C6
Elystan Ct SW15 ... 156 B6
Elystan Pl
SW3 ... 114 D1 257 C2
Elystan St
SW3 ... 114 C2 257 B3
Elystan Wlk N1 ... 234 A5
Emanuel Ave W3 ... 89 A1
Emanuel Ct
Acton W3 ... 89 B1
10 Leyton E10 ... 53 D2
Emanuel Dr TW12 ... 173 B5
Emanuel Sch SW11 ... 158 C6
Embankment SW15 ... 134 D3
Embankment Gdns
SW3 ... 136 D6 267 D6
Embankment Pier
WC2 ... 116 A5 250 B4
Embankment Pl WC2 ... 250 B4
Embankment Sta
WC2 ... 116 A5 250 B4
Embankment The
TW1 ... 153 A3
Embassy Ct
Ealing W5 ... 110 B6
Kingston u T KT6 ... 197 D4
Sidcup DA14 ... 168 B1
St John's Wood NW8 ... 229 D3
7 Wallington SM6 ... 219 B2
8 Wanstead E18 ... 55 A6
Welling DA16 ... 146 B2
Wood Green N11 ... 31 D4
Embassy Gdns BR3 ... 185 B2
Embassy Ho 2 NW6 ... 69 C1
Embassy Lo N3 ... 29 B1
Emba St SE16 ... 118 A4
Ember Cl BR5 ... 211 A2
Embercourt Rd KT10, KT7,
KT8 ... 196 C3
Ember Ct
2 Acton W12 ... 111 C3
14 Hendon NW9 ... 27 D1
Ember Farm Ave KT8 ... 196 B3
Ember Farm Way
KT8 ... 196 B4
Ember Gdns KT10,
KT8 ... 196 C2
Ember Ho 8 BR1 ... 186 B5
Ember La KT10, KT8 ... 196 B2
Emberson Ho 7 E17 ... 54 A5
Emberton SE5 ... 139 C6
Emberton Ct EC1 ... 234 C1
Embleton Rd SE13 ... 141 D1
Embleton Wlk TW12 ... 173 B5
Embry Cl HA7 ... 25 A6
Embry Dr HA7 ... 25 A4
Embry Way HA7 ... 25 A6
Emden Cl UB7 ... 104 C4
Emden St SW6 ... 265 D2
Emerald Cl E16 ... 100 A1
Emerald Ct N12 ... 30 A6
Emerald Gdns RM8 ... 59 C1
Emerald Rd NW10 ... 89 B6
Emerald Sq UB2 ... 106 D3
Emerald St
WC1 ... 94 B2 240 C4
Emerson Apartments
N8 ... 50 B6
Emerson Ct 8 SW19 ... 179 A4
Emerson Gdns HA3 ... 44 B3
Emerson Ho N16 ... 73 C3
Emerson Rd IG1 ... 56 C2
Emerson St
SE1 ... 117 A5 252 A4
Emerton Cl DA6 ... 147 A1
Emery Hill St SW1 ... 259 B5
Emery St SE1 ... 116 C3 261 B6
Emilia Cl EN3 ... 18 B6
Emily St 7 E16 ... 98 D1
Emirates Stad (Arsenal
FC) N7 ... 72 C4
Emlyn Gdns 3 W12 ... 111 C3
Emlyn Rd W12 ... 111 D3
Emmanual Ho SE18 ... 123 B1
Emmanuel CE Prim Sch
NW6 ... 69 C3
Emmanuel Ct 3 EN4 ... 14 D3
Emmanuel Ho
Dulwich SE21 ... 161 B1
Lambeth SE11 ... 261 A3
Emmanuel Rd
Northwood HA6 ... 22 A3
Streatham SW12 ... 159 D3
Emma Rd E13 ... 98 D5
Emma St E2 ... 96 B5
Emmeline Ct KT12 ... 194 C2
Emminster NW6 ... 91 D6
Emmott Ave IG6 ... 57 A4
Emmott Cl
London NW11 ... 48 A3
Mile End E1 ... 97 A3
Emperor's Gate
SW7 ... 114 A2 256 A4
Empingham Ho 20
SE8 ... 118 D2
Empire Ave N18 ... 33 A4
Empire Ct HA9 ... 66 D5
Empire Ho
Brompton SW3 ... 257 A5
Edmonton N18 ... 33 B4
Empire Par
Edmonton N18 ... 33 B4
Wembley HA9 ... 66 C5
Empire Rd UB6 ... 65 C1
Empire Sq N19 ... 72 A5
Empire Way HA9 ... 66 C4
Empire Wharf E3 ... 97 A6
Empire Wharf Rd
E14 ... 120 B2
Empress Ave
Chingford E4 ... 35 D3
Ilford IG1 ... 78 C6
Wanstead E12 ... 77 D6
Woodford IG8 ... 36 D3
Empress Dr BR7 ... 188 D4
Empress Mews 36
SE5 ... 139 A3
Empress Par E4 ... 35 C3
Empress Pl
SW5 ... 113 C1 255 A1
Empress St SE17 ... 139 A6
Empson St E3 ... 97 D3
Emsworth Cl N9 ... 18 C3
Emsworth St SW2 ... 160 B2
Emu Rd SW8 ... 137 B3
Ena Rd SW16 ... 204 A6
Enard Ho 28 E3 ... 97 B5
Enbrook St W10 ... 91 A4
Enclave Ct EC1 ... 241 D6
Endale Cl SM5 ... 218 D6
Endeavour Way
Barking IG11 ... 102 A5
Thornton Heath CR0 ... 204 A2
Wimbledon SW19 ... 179 D6
Endell St WC2 ... 94 A1 240 B1
Enderby St SE10 ... 120 C1
Enderfield Ct BR7 ... 188 C2
Enderley Cl HA3 ... 24 C2
Enderley Ho SE19 ... 183 D2
Enderley Rd HA3 ... 24 C2
Endersby Rd EN5 ... 12 C6
Endersleigh Gdns
NW4 ... 46 A5
Endlebury Ct E4 ... 20 B2
Endlebury Rd E4 ... 20 A2
Endlesham Ct 2
SW12 ... 159 A4
Endlesham Rd SW12 ... 159 A4
Endsleigh Gdns
Bloomsbury
WC1 ... 93 D3 239 C6
Ilford IG1 ... 56 D1
Kingston u T KT6 ... 197 C3
Endsleigh Ind Est
UB2 ... 107 B2
Endsleigh Mans 4
SW16 ... 160 A1
Endsleigh Pl WC1 ... 239 D6
Endsleigh Rd
Ealing W13 ... 109 A6
Southall UB2 ... 107 A2
Endsleigh St
WC1 ... 93 D3 239 D6
Endway KT5 ... 198 D2
Endwell Rd SE4 ... 141 A3
Endymion Rd
Harringay N4 ... 50 D2
Tulse Hill SW2 ... 160 B5
Energen Cl NW10 ... 67 C2
ENFIELD ... 6 B2
Enfield Chase Sta EN2 ... 5 A2
Enfield Cloisters 7
N1 ... 95 C4
Enfield Coll EN3 ... 6 C2
Enfield Gram Sch EN2 ... 5 B2
Enfield Gram Sch Lower
EN1 ... 5 B3
ENFIELD HIGHWAY ... 6 C3
Enfield Ho 24 SW9 ... 138 A3
ENFIELD LOCK ... 7 B6
Enfield Lock Sta EN3 ... 7 A6
Enfield Rd
Brentford TW8 ... 109 D1
Enfield Rd *continued*
De Beauvoir Town E8,
N1 ... 73 C1
Enfield EN2 ... 4 A2
Hatton TW6 ... 127 C3
South Acton W3 ... 110 D4
Enfield Ret Pk EN1 ... 6 A2
Enfield Road Rdbt
TW6 ... 127 C3
Enfield Sec Tuition Ctr
PRU N9 ... 18 C3
ENFIELD TOWN ... 5 B1
Enfield Town Sta EN1 ... 5 B2
ENFIELD WASH ... 6 D5
Enfield Wlk TW8 ... 109 D1
Enford St W1 ... 92 D2 237 C4
Engadine Cl CR0 ... 221 D5
Engadine St SW18 ... 157 C3
Engate St SE13 ... 142 A1
Engel Pk NW7 ... 28 C4
Engineer Cl SE18 ... 144 C6
Engineers Way HA9 ... 66 C4
England's La NW3 ... 70 D2
England Way KT3 ... 199 A5
Englefield
Bromley BR1 ... 188 A1
Regent's Pk NW1 ... 232 A1
Englefield Cl
Enfield EN2 ... 4 C3
Orpington BR5 ... 211 D5
Thornton Heath CR0 ... 205 A3
Englefield Path BR5 ... 211 D5
Englefield Rd N1 ... 73 C1
Engleheart Dr TW14 ... 149 D5
Engleheart Rd SE6 ... 164 A4
Englewood Rd SW12 ... 159 C5
English Gardening Sch
The SW3 ... 136 D6 267 C6
English Grounds SE1 ... 253 A3
English Martyrs RC Prim
Sch E1 ... 95 D1 243 D1
English St E3 ... 97 B3
Enid St SE16 ... 117 D3 263 D6
Enid Stacy Ho 11 N19 ... 49 D2
Enmore Ave SE25 ... 206 A4
Enmore Ct SW14 ... 155 B6
Enmore Gdns SW14 ... 155 B6
Enmore Rd
Croydon SE25 ... 206 A4
Putney SW15 ... 156 C6
Southall UB1 ... 85 C3
Ennerdale Ave HA3,
HA7 ... 43 C6
Ennerdale Cl
Cheam SM1 ... 217 B4
East Bedfont TW14 ... 149 D3
Ennerdale Ct E11 ... 55 A2
Ennerdale Dr NW9 ... 45 C4
Ennerdale Gdns HA9 ... 43 C1
Ennerdale Ho 3 N4 ... 51 B2
Ennerdale Rd
Erith DA7 ... 147 C4
Richmond TW9 ... 132 B3
Ennersdale Rd SE13 ... 164 B6
Ennis Ho 16 E14 ... 97 D1
Ennismore Ave
Chiswick W4 ... 111 D2
Greenford UB6 ... 64 C3
Ennismore Gdns
Knightsbridge
SW7 ... 114 C3 257 A6
Thames Ditton KT7 ... 196 C3
Ennismore Gdns Mews
SW7 ... 114 C3 257 A6
Ennismore Mews
SW7 ... 114 C3 257 A6
Ennismore St
SW7 ... 114 C3 257 A6
Ennis Rd
London N4 ... 50 C1
Shooters Hill SE18 ... 145 A6
Ennor Ct KT4 ... 216 C4
Ensbury Ho SW8 ... 270 C4
Ensign Cl TW19 ... 148 A3
Ensign Ct 12 E1 ... 118 A6
Ensign Dr N13 ... 17 A1
Ensign Ho 19 E14 ... 119 C4
Ensign St E1 ... 118 A6
Ensign Way
Stanwell TW19 ... 148 A3
2 Wallington SM6 ... 220 A1
Enslin Rd SE9 ... 166 C4
Ensor Mews SW7 ... 256 C2
Enstone Rd
Enfield EN3 ... 7 A2
Ickenham UB10 ... 60 B5
Enterprise Cl CR0 ... 204 C1
Enterprise Ho IG11 ... 101 D4
Enterprise Ho E4 ... 20 A4
Enterprise Ho
36 Hackney E9 ... 74 C1
Walton-on-T KT12 ... 194 B2
Enterprise Row N15 ... 51 D4
Enterprise Way
College Pk NW10 ... 90 A4
Teddington TW11 ... 174 D4
Wandsworth SW18 ... 135 C1
Enterprise Works EN3 ... 7 B4
Enterprize Way SE8 ... 119 B2
Enthoven Ho SE18 ... 122 D2
Enton Pl TW3 ... 129 D1
Enversham Ct SE23 ... 163 A1
Epirus Mews SW6 ... 265 A4
Epirus Rd
SW6 ... 135 B5 264 D4
Epping Cl
Millwall E14 ... 119 C2
Romford RM7 ... 59 D6
Epping Forest* IG10 ... 21 B6
Epping Glade E4 ... 20 A5
Epping Ho 8 E5 ... 74 A6
Epping New Rd IG9 ... 21 B5
Epping Pl N1 ... 72 C2
Epping Way E4 ... 19 D5
Epple Rd SW6 ... 135 B4 264 D2
Epsom Cl
Erith DA7 ... 147 D2
Northolt UB5 ... 63 B3
Epsom & Ewell High Sch
KT19 ... 215 A3
Epsom Ho SM1 ... 217 D4
Epsom Rd
Croydon CR0 ... 220 C4
Ilford IG3 ... 57 D3
Leyton E10 ... 54 A3
Morden SM3, SM4 ... 201 B2
Epsom Sq TW6 ... 127 D3
Epstein Ct N1 ... 234 D5
Epstein Rd SE28 ... 124 B5
Epworth Rd TW7,
TW8 ... 131 B5
Epworth St EC2 ... 95 B3 242 D5
Equity Sq 29 E2 ... 95 D4
Erasmus St
SW1 ... 115 D2 259 D3
Erconwald St W12 ... 89 D1
Erebus Dr SE28 ... 123 B4
Eresby Dr BR3 ... 207 C1
Eresby Ho SW7 ... 247 B1
Eresby Pl NW6 ... 69 C1
Erica Ct SW4 ... 270 B1
Erica Gdns CR0 ... 223 D5
Erica Ho
London SE4 ... 141 B2
6 Wimbledon SW19 ... 179 A3
Wood Green N22 ... 32 C2
Erica St W12 ... 112 A6
Eric Cl E7 ... 77 A4
Eric Clarke La IG11 ... 101 A4
Ericcson Cl SW18 ... 157 C6
Eric Fletcher Ct 15 N1 ... 73 A1
Eric Macdonald Ho
SW6 ... 265 B1
Eric Rd
Dagenham RM6 ... 58 D2
Forest Gate E7 ... 77 A4
Willesden NW10 ... 67 D2
Eric Shipman Terr 2
E13 ... 99 A3
Ericson Ho
London SE13 ... 142 B1
Stamford Hill N16 ... 51 D1
Eric St E3 ... 97 B3
Eric Wilkins Ho 14
SE1 ... 118 A1
Eridge Ho SE22 ... 139 D2
Eridge Rd W4 ... 111 B3
Erin Cl
Bromley BR1 ... 186 C3
Ilford IG3 ... 58 A3
Erin Ct NW2 ... 68 C2
Erindale SE18 ... 145 B6
Erindale Ct 1 BR3 ... 185 C2
Erindale Terr SE18 ... 145 B6
ERITH ... 147 D6
Erith Rd
Belvedere DA17 ... 125 D1
Erith DA7 ... 147 D2
Erlanger Rd SE14 ... 140 D3
Erlesmere Gdns W13 ... 109 A3
Ermine Cl TW4 ... 128 C3
Ermine Ho 3 N17 ... 33 D3
Ermine Rd
London SE13 ... 141 D1
South Tottenham N15 ... 51 D3
Ermine Side EN1 ... 18 A6
Ermington Rd SE9 ... 167 A2
Ernald Ave E6 ... 100 A5
Erncroft Way TW1 ... 152 D5
Ernest Ave SE27 ... 182 D6
Ernest Bevin Coll
SW17 ... 158 C2
Ernest Cl BR3 ... 207 C4
Ernest Cotts KT17 ... 215 D1
Ernest Gdns W4 ... 132 D6
Ernest Gr BR3 ... 207 B4
Ernest Rd KT1 ... 176 D1
Ernest Richards Twr
E17 ... 53 B3
Ernest Simmonds Ho
SE14 ... 140 C3
Ernest Sq KT1 ... 176 D1
Ernest St E1 ... 96 D3
Ernle Rd SW20 ... 178 C3
Ernshaw Pl SW15 ... 157 A6
Eros Ho SE6 ... 163 D4
Eros (Shaftesbury
Meml)*
W1 ... 115 D6 249 C5
Erpingham Rd SW15 ... 134 C2
Erridge Rd SW19 ... 179 C1
Errington Manor 6
SM5 ... 218 D5
Errington Rd W9 ... 91 B3
Errol Gdns
Hayes UB4 ... 84 B3
West Barnes KT3 ... 200 A5
Errol St EC1 ... 95 A3 242 B5
Erskine Cl SM1 ... 218 C5
Erskine Cres N17 ... 52 B5
Erskine Hill NW11 ... 47 C4
Erskine Ho
7 Charlton SE7 ... 143 C6
Pimlico SW1 ... 259 A1
Erskine Rd
Carshalton SM1 ... 218 B5
Primrose Hill NW3 ... 70 D1
Walthamstow E17 ... 53 B5
Erwood Rd SE7 ... 122 A1
Esam Way SW16 ... 182 C5
Escot Rd TW16 ... 171 C3
Escott Gdns SE9 ... 188 A6
Escot Way EN5 ... 12 C6
Escreet Gr SE18 ... 122 C2
Escuan Lo N5 ... 73 A3
ESHER ... 212 A4
Esher Ave
Cheam SM3 ... 216 D5
Walton-on-T KT12 ... 194 A1
Esher CE Prim Sch
KT10 ... 212 A3
Esher Cl DA5 ... 169 A3
Esher Coll KT7 ... 196 C2
Esher Cres TW6 ... 127 D3
Esher Gdns SW19 ... 156 D2
Esher Ho 8 SW8 ... 137 D3
Esher Mews 4 CR4 ... 202 D6
Esher Park Ave KT10 ... 212 A3
Esher Rd
East Molesey KT8 ... 196 B4
Ilford IG3 ... 79 C5
Esher Sta KT10 ... 212 B6
Eskdale
Enfield EN1 ... 17 C6
Regent's Pk NW1 ... 232 A3
Eskdale Ave UB5 ... 85 B6
Eskdale Cl HA9 ... 65 D6
Eskdale Rd DA7 ... 147 C4
Esk Ho E3 ... 97 B3
Eskmont Ridge SE19 ... 183 C3
Esk Rd E13 ... 99 B3
Esmar Cres NW9 ... 46 A2
Esme Ho SW15 ... 133 D1
Esmeralda Rd SE1 ... 118 A2
Esmond Ct
Barnet EN5 ... 1 C1
Kensington W8 ... 255 D6
Esmond Gdns W4 ... 111 B2
Esmond Rd
Acton W4 ... 111 B3
Kilburn NW6 ... 91 B6
Esmond St SW15 ... 135 A1
Esparto St SW18 ... 157 D4
Espirit Ct E1 ... 243 C3
Espirit Ho 6 SW15 ... 157 A6
Essan Ho W13 ... 87 B2
Essence Ct HA9 ... 66 B6
Essenden Rd
Belvedere DA17 ... 125 C1
South Croydon CR2 ... 221 C1
Essendine Mans W9 ... 91 C4
Essendine Prim Sch
W9 ... 91 C4
Essendine Rd W9 ... 91 C4
Essex Ave TW7 ... 130 C2
Essex Cl
Romford RM7 ... 59 D5
Ruislip HA4 ... 40 D1
Walthamstow E17 ... 53 A5
Essex Cl *continued*
West Barnes SM4 ... 200 D2
Essex Ct
Barnes SW13 ... 133 D3
Hammersmith W6 ... 112 C3
Holborn EC4 ... 241 A1
South Norwood SE19 ... 183 B4
Essex Gdns N4 ... 50 D3
Essex Gr SE19 ... 183 B4
Essex Ho
4 Acton W3 ... 88 C1
2 Poplar E14 ... 97 D1
Essex Lo 5 N10 ... 31 B1
Essex Mans E11 ... 54 B2
Essex Park Mews W3 ... 111 C5
Essex Pk N3 ... 29 D4
Essex Pl W4 ... 111 A2
Essex Place Sq 5
W4 ... 111 B2
Essex Prim Sch E12 ... 78 A3
Essex Rd
Acton W3 ... 111 A6
Barking IG11 ... 79 B1
Chingford E4 ... 20 C3
Chiswick W4 ... 111 B2
Enfield EN2 ... 5 B1
Ilford RM6 ... 58 C2
Islington N1 ... 94 D6 234 D6
Leyton E10 ... 54 A3
Plashet E12 ... 78 A2
Romford RM7 ... 59 D5
Walthamstow E17 ... 53 A3
Willesden NW10 ... 67 C1
Woodford E18 ... 37 B1
Essex Rd S E11 ... 54 B2
Essex Road Sta N1 ... 73 A1
Essex St
Forest Gate E7 ... 77 A3
Strand WC2 ... 116 C6 251 A6
Essex Twr 4 SE20 ... 184 B2
Essex Villas
W8 ... 113 C4 245 A1
Essian St E1 ... 97 A2
Essington SW15 ... 157 A5
Essoldo Way HA8 ... 44 B6
Estate Way E10 ... 53 B1
Estcourt Rd
Croydon SE25 ... 206 B3
Fulham SW6 ... 135 B5 264 C4
Estella Ave KT3 ... 200 B5
Estella Ho 15 W11 ... 112 D6
Estelle Rd NW3 ... 70 D4
Esterbrooke St SW1 ... 259 C3
Este Rd SW11 ... 136 C2
Esther Cl N21 ... 16 C4
Esther Doe Lo N21 ... 16 C4
Esther Rd E11 ... 54 C2
Estoria Cl 22 SW2 ... 160 C4
Estreham Rd SW16 ... 181 D4
Estridge Cl TW3 ... 129 C1
Estuary Cl IG11 ... 102 B4
Eswyn Rd SW17 ... 180 D5
Etal Ho N1 ... 72 D1
Etchingham Ct N12 ... 30 A3
Etchingham Park Rd
N3 ... 29 D3
Etchingham Rd E15 ... 76 A4
Eternit Wlk SW6 ... 134 D4
Etfield Gr DA14 ... 190 B5
Ethelbert Cl BR1 ... 209 A6
Ethelbert Gdns IG2 ... 56 C4
Ethelbert Ho E9 ... 75 A4
Ethelbert Rd
Bromley BR1, BR2 ... 209 A6
Wimbledon SW20 ... 178 D2
Ethelbert St SW12 ... 159 B3
Ethel Brooks Ho
SE18 ... 144 D6
Ethelburga St
SW11 ... 136 C4 267 B2
Ethelburga Twr SW11 ... 267 B2
Ethel Cotts RM6 ... 58 D6
Etheldene Ave N10 ... 49 C5
Ethelden Rd W12 ... 112 B5
Ethel Rankin Ct 8
SW6 ... 135 B3
Ethel Rd
Ashford TW15 ... 170 A5
Newham E16 ... 99 B1
Ethel St SE17 ... 262 B3
Ethelworth Ct 4
SW2 ... 160 C3
Etheridge Rd NW2 ... 46 C2
Etherley Rd N15 ... 51 A4
Etherow St SE22 ... 162 A4
Etherstone Gn SW16 ... 182 C6
Etherstone Rd SW16 ... 182 C6

Ethnard Rd SE15 140 B6
Ethronvi Rd DA7 147 A2
Etienne Ho NW7 28 C6
Etloe Ho E10 53 C1
Etloe Rd E10 75 C6
Eton Ave
East Barnet EN4 14 C5
Finchley N12 30 A3
Heston TW5 129 C6
New Malden KT3 199 B5
Primrose Hill NW3 70 C1
Wembley HA0 65 C4
Eton Cl SW18 157 D4
Eton College Rd NW3 70 D2
Eton Ct
Hampstead NW3 70 B1
Highgate N6 49 B3
Wembley HA0 65 C4
Eton Garages 11 NW3 70 C2
Eton Gr
Lewisham SE13 142 C2
Queensbury NW9 44 C5
Eton Hall NW3 70 D2
Eton Ho
Hackney E9 75 B2
Highbury N5 72 D4
Eton Manor Ct E10 75 C6
Eton Pl NW1 71 A1
Eton Rd
Harlington UB3 127 D5
Ilford IG1 79 B4
Maitland Pk NW3 70 D2
Eton Rise NW3 70 D2
Eton St TW10 154 A6
Eton Villas NW3 70 D2
Etta St SE8 141 A6
Ettrick Ho 8 E5 74 B6
Ettrick St E14 98 A1
Etwell Pl KT5 198 B3
Euesden Cl N9 18 B1
Eugene Cotter Ho
SE17 262 D3
Eugenia Rd SE16 118 C2
Eugenie Mews BR7 188 D2
Eureka Rd 8 KT1 176 C1
Euro Bsns Ctr 3 E15 98 D6
Euro Cl NW10 68 A2
Eurolink Bsns Ctr
SW2 160 C6
Europa Pl EC1 235 A1
Europe Rd SE18 122 B3
Eustace Bldg SW8 268 C5
Eustace Ho SE11 260 C4
Eustace Pl SE18 122 B2
Eustace Rd
Dagenham RM6 58 D2
Newham E6 100 A4
Walham Green
SW6 135 C5 265 A4
Euston Ct 5 HA0 66 A2
Euston Rd
Fitzrovia NW1 93 C3 239 B6
Thornton Heath CR0 204 C1
Euston Sq NW1 232 C1
Euston Square Sta
WC1 93 C3 239 B6
Euston St NW1 93 C4 232 B1
Euston Sta
NW1 93 D4 232 C1
Euston Underpass
NW1 239 A6
Evandale Rd SW9 138 C3
Evangelist Rd NW5 71 B4
Evans Cl E8 73 D2
Evans Gr TW13 151 C2
Evans Ho
34 Shepherd's Bush
W12 112 B6
South Lambeth SW8 269 D3
Evans Rd SE6 164 C2
Evanston Ave E4 36 A3
Evanston Gdns IG4 56 A3
Eva Rd RM6 58 D2
Eve Ct CR4 181 A1
Evelina Mans 9 SE5 139 B5
Evelina Rd
London SE15 140 C3
Penge SE20 184 D3
Eveline Ct N10 49 B4
Eveline Lowe Prim Sch
SE1 118 A1
Eveline Rd CR4 180 D2
Evelyn Ave
London NW9 45 B5
Ruislip HA4 39 D2
Evelyn Cl TW2 151 D4
Evelyn Cres TW16 171 D2
Evelyn Ct
Chislehurst SE9 166 A2
Marylebone W1 237 C1
Shacklewell E8 74 A4
Shoreditch N1 235 C3
Evelyn Denington Ct 2
N1 72 D1
Evelyn Denington Rd
E6 100 A3
Evelyn Dr HA5 22 D3
Evelyn Fox Ct W10 90 C2
Evelyn Gdns
Richmond TW9 132 A1
South Kensington
SW7 114 B1 256 C1
Evelyn Gr
Ealing W5 110 B5
Southall UB1 85 B1
Evelyn Ho
Bedford Pk W12 111 D4
3 Brixton SW2 160 B6
Harrow HA1 42 B4
18 Spitalfields E1 96 A2
Evelyn Rd
Acton W4 111 B3
Cockfosters EN4 2 D1
Ham TW10 153 C1
Newham E16 121 B5
Richmond TW9 132 A2
Walthamstow E17 54 A5
Wimbledon SW19 179 D4
Evelyns Cl UB8 82 C1
Evelyn St SE8 119 A1
Evelyn Terr TW9 132 A2
Evelyn Way
Sunbury TW16 171 D2
Wallington SM6 219 D4
Evelyn Wlk N1 95 B5 235 C3
Evelyn Yd W1 239 C2
Evening Hill BR3 186 A3
Evenlode Ho 5 SE2 124 C4
Evenwood Cl SW15 157 A6
Everard Ave BR2 209 A1
Everard Ct N13 16 B1
Everard Ho 33 E1 96 A1
Everard Way HA9 66 A5
Everatt Cl SW18 157 B6
Eve Rd
Isleworth TW7 131 A1
Leyton E11 76 C4
Tottenham N17 51 C6
West Ham E15 98 C5
Everdale Ct N2 48 C5
Everdon Rd SW13 134 A6
Everest Ct
6 Chislehurst SE9 166 A2
South Norwood SE19 183 C2
Everest Pl E14 98 A2
Everest Rd
Eltham SE9 166 B6
Stanwell TW19 148 A4
Everett Cl
Bushey WD23 8 C3
Pinner HA5 39 D6
Everett Ho
Islington N7 72 C4
Walworth SE17 262 C2
Everett Wlk DA17 125 B1
Everglade Ho E17 35 B1
Everglades
Beckenham BR2 208 C6
Hounslow TW3 130 A2
Everglade Strand
NW9 27 D2
Evergreen Cl SE20 184 C3
Evergreen Ct 6 SM2 218 A2
Evergreen Sq 3 E8 73 D1
Evergreen Way UB3 105 D6
Everilda St N1 233 D5
Evering Rd E5, N16 74 A5
Everington Rd N10 30 D1
Everington St W6 134 D6
Everitt Rd NW10 89 B4
Everleigh St N4 50 B1
Eversfield Ct SE12 165 B2
Eversfield Gdns HA8,
NW7 27 C3
Eversfield Rd TW9 132 B3
Evershed Ho E1 243 D2
Evershed Wlk W4 111 B2
Eversholt Ct EN5 14 A6
Eversholt St
NW1 93 D4 232 C2
Evershot Rd N4 50 B1
Eversleigh Ct N3 29 C3
Eversleigh Rd
Clapham SW11 137 A3
Finchley N3 29 B3
New Barnet EN5 14 A6
Newham E6 99 D6
Eversley Ave HA9 66 C6
Eversley Cl N21 16 B5
Eversley Cres
Hounslow TW7 130 B4
Ruislip HA4 61 D6
Southgate N21 16 C5
Eversley Ho 12 E2 96 A4
Eversley Mount N21 16 B5
Eversley Park Rd N21 16 B5
Eversley Pk SW19 178 B5
Eversley Prim Sch N21 16 B5
Eversley Rd
Greenwich SE7 143 B6
Kingston u T KT5 198 B4
South Norwood SE19 183 B3
Eversley Way CR0 223 C5
Everthorpe Rd SE15 139 D2
Everton Bldgs NW1 232 A1
Everton Ct HA0 65 D4
Everton Dr HA7 44 A6
Everton Rd CR0 206 A1
Evesham Ave E17 35 C1
Evesham Cl
Belmont SM2 217 C1
Greenford UB6 85 D5
Evesham Ct
2 Ealing W13 109 A5
2 Richmond TW10 154 B5
Evesham Gn SM4 201 D3
Evesham Ho
1 Bethnal Green E2 96 C5
Pimlico SW1 258 D2
St John's Wood NW8 229 A5
Evesham Rd
London N11 31 D5
Morden SM4 201 D3
Stratford E15 76 D1
Evesham St W11 112 D6
Evesham Way
Clapham SW11 137 A2
Ilford IG5 56 C6
Evesham Wlk
Brixton SW9 138 C3
Camberwell SE5 139 B3
Evry Rd DA14 190 C4
Ewald Rd SW6 135 B3
Ewanrigg Terr IG8 37 C5
Ewart Gr N22 32 C2
Ewart Pl 18 E3 97 B5
Ewart Rd SE23 162 D4
Ewe Cl N7 72 A2
EWELL 215 C1
Ewell By-Pass KT17 216 A1
EWELL COURT 215 C2
Ewell Court Ave KT19 215 C3
Ewell Park Gdns
KT17 216 A1
Ewell Park Way KT17 216 A1
Ewell Rd
Cheam SM2, SM3 216 D2
Surbiton KT6 198 B2
Thames Ditton KT6,
KT7 197 B2
Tolworth KT6 198 D1
Ewelme Rd SE23 162 C3
Ewen Cres SW2 160 C4
Ewen Henderson Ct 10
SE14 141 A5
Ewen Ho N1 233 C5
Ewer St SE1 117 A5 252 A3
Ewhurst 19 SW15 156 D5
Ewhurst Cl E1 96 C2
Ewhurst Ct CR4 202 B6
Ewhurst Rd SE4 163 B5
Exbury Ho
Hackney E9 74 C2
4 London SW9 138 B1
Exbury Rd SE6 163 C2
Excel Ct WC2 249 D5
Excel Ex Ctr E16 121 B6
Excelsior Cl KT1 176 C1
Excelsior Gdns SE13 142 A3
Excelsior Ind Est
SE16 140 C6
Exchange Apartments 4
BR2 209 B5
Exchange Arc EC2 243 B4
Exchange Cl N11 15 A2
Exchange Ct WC2 250 B5
Exchange Mans 2
NW11 47 B2
Exchange Pl EC2 243 A4
Exchange The IG1 78 D6
Exchange Wlk HA5 41 A2
Exeforde Ave TW15 170 C6
Exeter Cl E6 100 B1
Exeter Ct
Kilburn NW6 91 C5
Kingston u T KT6 198 A4
Mitcham SW19 180 C3
Exeter Gdns IG1 56 B1
Exeter Ho
7 Barking IG11 80 A1
Feltham TW13 151 C2
Paddington W2 236 A2
11 Peckham SE15 140 A6
Putney SW15 156 C5
Exeter Mans NW2 69 A2
Exeter Mews
Fulham SW6 265 A4
12 Hampstead NW6 69 D2
Exeter Rd
Bexley DA16 145 D3
Brondesbury NW2 69 A2
Croydon CR0 205 D2
Dagenham RM10 81 D2
East Barnet N14 15 B4
Enfield EN3 6 D2
Harrow HA2 63 A6
Hatton TW6 127 C2
Lower Edmonton N9 18 C2
Newham E16 99 A2
Twickenham TW13 151 B1
Walthamstow E17 53 C4
Exeter St WC2 116 B6 250 C6
Exeter Way
Hatton TW6 127 C3
2 New Cross SE14 141 B5
Exford Ct SW11 266 D2
Exford Gdns SE12 165 B3
Exford Rd SE12 165 B3
Exhibition Cl W12 112 C6
Exhibition Rd
SW7 114 B3 256 D6
Exit Rd N2 30 B1
Exmoor Ho 25 E3 97 A5
Exmoor St W10 90 D2
Exmouth Ho
Clerkenwell EC1 241 B6
6 Millwall E14 119 D2
Exmouth Market
EC1 94 C3 241 B6
Exmouth Mews NW1 232 B1
Exmouth Pl E8 74 B1
Exmouth Rd
Bexley DA16 146 C5
Hayes UB4 83 C4
Ruislip HA4 62 C5
Walthamstow E17 53 B4
Exmouth St E1 96 C1
Exning Rd E16 98 D3
Exonbury NW8 91 D6
Exon St SE17 117 C2 263 A3
Explorer Ave TW19 148 A3
Explorers Ct 6 E14 120 B6
Express Dr IG3 58 B1
Express Wharf 10
E14 119 C4
Exton Cres NW10 67 A1
Exton Gdns RM8 80 C3
Exton Rd NW10 67 A1
Exton St SE1 116 C5 251 A3
Eyebright Cl 3 CR0 206 D1
Eyhurst Cl NW2 68 A6
Eylewood Rd SE27 183 A5
Eynella Rd SE21 161 D4
Eynham Rd W12 90 C1
Eynsford Cl BR5 211 A3
Eynsford Cres DA5 168 D3
Eynsford Ho
Borough The SE1 252 C2
12 Deptford SE15 140 C6
Walworth SE17 263 A3
Eynsford Rd IG3 79 C6
Eynsford Terr UB7 82 B1
Eynsham Dr SE2 124 B3
Eynswood Dr DA14 190 C5
Eyot Gdns W6 111 D1
Eyot Gn W4 111 D1
Eyre Ct NW8 229 C4
Eyre St Hill EC1 94 C3 241 A5
Eysham Ct 12 EN5 13 D6
Eythorne Rd SW9 138 C4
Ezra St E2 95 D4

F

Faber Gdns NW4 46 A4
Fabian Rd
SW6 135 B5 264 D4
Fabian St E6 100 B3
Fabyc Ho TW9 132 C5
Factory La
Croydon CR0 220 D6
Tottenham N17 33 D1
Factory Rd E16 122 A5
Factory Yd W7 108 C5
Fagg's Rd TW14 150 A6
Fairacre
Hounslow TW7 130 B4
Kingston u T KT3 199 C6
Pinner HA5 40 A5
Fairacres
Putney SW15 134 A1
Ruislip HA4 39 D2
Fair Acres BR2 209 A4
Fairbairn Gn 1 SW9 138 D4
Fairbairn Hall E13 99 A3
Fairbank Ave BR6 226 D6
Fairbanks Rd N17 52 A6
Fairbourne Ho UB3 105 A3
Fairbourne Rd N17 51 C6
Fairbriar Residence
SW7 256 B4
Fairbridge Rd N19 71 D6
Fairbrook Cl N13 32 C5
Fairbrook Rd N13 32 C4
Fairburn Ct SW15 157 A6
Fairburn Ho
9 Stamford Hill N16 51 C1
West Kensington SW5 254 D1
Fairby Ho SE1 263 D4
Fairby Rd SE12 165 B6
Faircharm Trad Est
SE8 141 D5
Fairchild Cl 6 SW11 136 B3
Fairchild Ho
13 Hackney E9 74 C1
Pimlico SW1 259 B3
5 Shoreditch N1 95 C4
Fairchild Pl EC2 243 B5
Fairchild St EC2 243 B5
Fairclough Cl UB5 85 B3
Fairclough St E1 96 A1
Faircourt 14 NW3 70 D2
Faircroft
6 Forest Hill SE26 184 C6
Stoke Newington N16 51 B1
FAIR CROSS 79 D3
Fair Cross IG11 79 C3
Faircross Ave IG11 79 A2
Faircross Par IG11 79 C3
Fairdale Gdns
Hayes UB3 106 A4
Putney SW15 134 B1
Fairdene Ct N7 72 A3
Fairey Ave UB3 105 D3
Fairfax Cl KT12 194 B1
Fairfax Gdns SE3 143 C4
Fairfax Ho
11 Brixton SW9 138 C3
5 Ealing W5 88 A4
6 Putney SW15 156 A6
Fairfax Mews
London N8 50 D5
Newham E16 121 B5
Putney SW15 134 C1
Fairfax Pl
Kensington W14 254 B5
South Hampstead NW6 70 A1
Fairfax Rd
Acton W4 111 C3
Hornsey N8 50 C5
South Hampstead NW6 70 A1
Teddington TW11 175 B3
Fairfax Way N10 31 A3
Fairfield
Camden Town NW1 232 A5
Oakleigh Pk N20 14 B4
Pinner HA6 22 A1
4 Stepney E1 96 C2
Fairfield Ave
Edgware HA8 26 D3
Hendon NW4 46 B3
Ruislip HA4 39 A2
Twickenham TW2 151 D3
Fairfield Cl
Blackfen DA15 167 D5
Enfield EN3 7 A1
Mitcham SW19 180 C3
North Finchley N12 30 A6
West Ewell KT19 215 C3
Fairfield Cres HA8 26 D4
Fairfield Ct
Harlesden NW10 90 A6
1 London SW18 157 D6
Ruislip HA4 39 B1
8 Woodford IG8 37 A4
Fairfield Dr
Harrow HA2 42 A6
Wandsworth SW18 157 D6
Wembley UB6 87 C6
Fairfield E KT1 176 A1
Fairfield Gdns N8 50 A4
Fairfield Gr SE7 143 D6
Fairfield Ind Est KT1 198 B6
Fairfield N KT1, KT2 176 A1
Fairfield Path CR0 221 B5
Fairfield Pl KT1 198 A6
Fairfield Rd
Beckenham BR3 185 C1
Bexleyheath DA7 147 B3
Bow E3 97 C5
Edmonton N18 34 A6
Higham Hill E17 35 A1
Hornsey N8 50 A4
Ilford IG1 78 D2
Kingston u T KT1 176 A1
Petts Wood BR5 211 B3
Plaistow BR1 187 A3
Southall UB1 85 B1
South Croydon CR0 221 C5
Woodford IG8 37 A4
Yiewsley UB7 104 A6
Fairfields SE6 163 D4
Fairfield S KT1 176 B1
Fairfields Cl NW9 45 A4
Fairfields Cres NW9 45 A4
Fairfields Rd TW3 130 A2
Fairfield St SW18 157 D6
Fairfield W KT1 176 A1
Fairfield Way
Barnet EN5 13 C6
West Ewell KT19 215 C3
Fairfoot Rd E3 97 C3
Fairford SE6 163 C3
Fairford Ave CR0 206 D4
Fairford Cl CR0 207 A4
Fairford Ct SM2 217 D1
Fairford Gdns KT4 215 D5
Fairford Ho SE11 261 B3
Fairgreen EN4 2 D2
Fairgreen Ct EN4 2 D2
Fair Green Ct 1 CR4 202 D6
Fairgreen E EN4 2 D2
Fairgreen Rd CR7 204 D4
Fairhall Ct KT6 198 B2
Fairhaven Ave CR0 206 D3
Fairhaven Ct 7 CR2 221 A3
Fairhazel Gdns NW6 70 A1
Fairheathe SW15 156 D5
Fairholme TW14 149 C4
Fairholme Cl N3 47 A5
Fairholme Cres UB4 84 A3
Fairholme Gdns N3 47 A5
Fairholme Ho 4 KT3 199 C5
Fairholme Prim Sch
TW14 149 B3
Fairholme Rd
Ashford TW15 170 B5
Cheam SM1 217 B2
Harrow HA1 42 D4
Ilford IG1 56 C2
Thornton Heath CR0 204 C2
West Kensington
W14 113 A1 254 B1
Fairholt Cl N16 51 C1
Fairholt Rd N16 51 B1
Fairholt St SW7 257 B6
Fairhurst 4 NW6 70 A2
Fairland Ho BR2 209 B5
Fairland Rd E15 76 D1
Fairlands Ave
Sutton SM1 217 C6
Thornton Heath CR7 204 C4
Woodford IG9 21 A2
Fairlands Ct 6 SE9 166 C5
Fairlawn SE7 143 C6
Fairlawn Ave
Acton W4 111 A2
Bexley DA7 146 D3
East Finchley N2 48 C5
Fairlawn Cl
Claygate KT10 212 D2
Feltham TW13 173 B6
Kingston u T KT2 177 A4
Southgate N14 15 D5
Fairlawn Ct
3 Acton W4 111 A2
Charlton SE7 143 C5
Fairlawn Dr IG8 37 A3
Fairlawnes SM6 219 B3
Fairlawn Gdns UB1 107 B6
Fairlawn Gr W4 111 A2
Fairlawn Mans SE14 140 D4
Fairlawn Pk SE26 185 A5
Fairlawn Prim Sch
SE23 162 C4
Fairlawn Prim Sch
(Annexe) SE23 162 C3
Fairlawn Rd SW19 179 B3
Fairlawns
4 Bowes Pk N11 32 A4
10 Chingford E4 20 A2
Pinner HA5 22 D1
Putney SW15 156 D6
Sunbury TW16 194 A6
Twickenham TW1 153 C5

Fairlead Ho 6 E14 119 C3
Fairlea Pl W5 87 D3
Fair Lea Pl W5 87 C2
Fairleas 12 BR3 185 D1
Fairley Ct HA0 65 D3
Fairley House Sch
SW1 259 D2
Fairlie Ct
22 Bromley E3 97 D4
1 Tufnell Pk N7 71 D4
Fairlie Gdns SE23 162 C4
Fairlight TW12 173 D5
Fairlight Ave
Chingford E4 20 B2
Harlesden NW10 89 C5
Woodford IG8 37 A4
Fairlight Cl
Cheam KT4 216 C4
Chingford E4 20 B2
Fairlight Ct
Greenford UB6 86 B5
4 Harlesden NW10 89 C5
Fairlight Rd SW17 180 B6
Fairline Ct BR3 186 A1
Fairlop Ct E11 54 C1
Fairlop Pl NW8 229 D1
Fairlop Rd E11 54 B2
Fairmark Cl UB10 60 C2
Fairmead
Bromley BR1 210 B5
Tolworth KT5, KT6 198 D1
Fairmead Cl
Bromley BR1 210 B5
Heston TW5 128 D5
Kingston u T KT3 199 B6
Fairmead Cres HA8 11 A1
Fairmead Ct
3 Chingford E4 20 C4
Oakleigh Pk N20 14 A4
Fairmead Gdns IG4 56 A4
Fairmead Ho E9 75 A4
Fairmead Rd
Lower Holloway N7,
N19 72 A5
Thornton Heath CR0 204 C2
Fairmeadside IG10 21 C6
Fairmile Ave SW16 181 D5
Fairmile Ho
St Paul's Cray BR5 190 A1
Teddington TW11 175 A6
Fairmont Ave E14 120 B5
Fairmont Cl DA17 125 B1
Fairmont Ho 1 E3 97 C3
Fairmount Rd SW2 160 B5
Fairoak Cl BR5 210 D2
Fairoak Dr SE9 167 B6
Fairoaks Gr EN3 6 D6
Fairseat Cl WD23 8 C2
Fair St
Bermondsey
SE1 117 D4 253 C2
Hounslow TW3 130 A2
Fairstead Lo 4 IG8 37 A4
Fairstead Wlk N1 235 A6
Fairthorn Rd SE7,
SE10 121 A1
Fairview Ave HA0 65 D2
Fairview Cl SE26 185 A5
Fair View Cl E17 35 A2
Fairview Cres HA2 41 C1
Fairview Ct
Ashford TW15 170 C5
Hendon NW4 28 D1
Kingston u T KT2 176 D2
Fairview Dr
Littleton TW17 192 B4
Orpington BR6 227 B4
Fairview Gdns IG8 37 B2
Fairview Ho 14 SW2 160 B4
Fairview Pl SW2 160 B4
Fairview Rd
Carshalton SM1, SM5 218 C3
Enfield EN2 4 C4
South Tottenham N15 51 D3
Thornton Heath SW16 182 B2
Fairview Way HA8 26 C6
Fairwall Ho 9 SE5 139 C4
Fairwater Ave DA16 146 A1
Fairwater Ho TW11 175 A6
Fairway
Bexley DA6 169 A6
Petts Wood BR5 211 B4
West Barnes SW20 200 C6
Woodford IG8 37 C5
Fairway Ave NW9 44 D6
Fairway Cl
Croydon CR0 207 A4
Heston TW4 150 C6
Hounslow TW4 150 D6
North End NW11 48 A2
Fairway Cl *continued*
West Ewell KT19 215 A4
Fairway Ct
Edgware NW7 11 B1
12 Eltham SE9 166 C5
New Barnet EN5 13 D5
13 Rotherhithe SE16 118 D4
Fairway Dr
Erith SE28 103 A1
Greenford UB6 63 D1
Fairway Est TW4 150 C6
Fairway Gdns
Ilford IG1 79 A3
West Wickham BR3 208 B3
Fairway Prim Sch
NW7 11 B2
Fairways
Ashford TW15 170 D4
12 Chingford E4 20 A3
4 Hounslow TW7 130 C4
Stanmore HA7 26 A1
Teddington TW11 175 D3
Walthamstow E17 54 A5
Fairways Bsns Pk E10 75 A6
Fairway The
Acton W3 89 C1
Bromley BR1, BR2 210 B4
East Molesey KT8 195 D6
Edgware NW7 11 B1
Edmonton N13 17 B1
Hillingdon UB10 82 B5
Kingston u T KT3 177 B2
New Barnet EN5 13 D5
Northolt UB5 64 A2
Ruislip HA4 62 D5
Southgate N14 15 C5
Wembley HA0 65 B6
Fairweather Cl N15 51 C5
Fairweather Ct N13 32 B6
Fairweather Ho N7 72 A4
Fairweather Rd N16 52 A3
Fairwood Ct E11 54 B2
Fairwyn Rd SE26 185 A6
Faith Ct NW2 68 B2
Faithfull Ho N5 73 A3
Fakenham Cl
Hendon NW7 28 A3
5 Northolt UB5 63 C2
Fakruddin St E1 96 A3
Falcon Ave BR1 210 A5
Falconberg Ct W1 239 D2
Falconberg Mews W1 239 D2
Falconbrook Prim Sch
SW11 136 B2
Falcon Cl
Chiswick W4 133 A6
Lambeth SE1 251 D4
Falcon Cres EN3 18 D6
Falcon Ct
9 Dulwich SE21 161 B2
Holborn EC4 241 A1
Islington N1 234 D3
New Barnet EN5 2 A1
Ruislip HA4 61 C6
6 Wanstead E18 55 B6
Falcon Dr TW19 148 A5
Falconer Ct N17 33 A3
Falconer Wlk 12 N7 72 B6
Falcon Gr SW11 136 C2
Falcon Ho
11 London SE15 139 D4
9 Merton SW19 179 D2
Falconhurst 4 KT6 198 A4
Falcon La SW11 136 C2
Falcon Lo
11 Paddington W9 91 C2
West Hampstead NW3 69 D4
Falcon Pk Ind Est
NW10 67 C3
Falcon Point SE1 251 D5
Falcon Rd
Battersea SW11 136 C2
Enfield EN3 18 D6
Hampton TW12 173 B3
Falconry Ct KT1 198 A6
Falcon St E13 99 A3
Falcon Terr SW11 136 C2
Falcon Way
Feltham TW14 150 B6
Harrow HA3 44 A3
Hendon NW9 27 C1
Millwall E14 119 D2
Sunbury TW16 171 C1
Wanstead E11 55 A5
FALCONWOOD 145 C1
Falconwood Ave
DA16 145 C3
Falconwood Ct SE3 142 D3
Falconwood Par
DA16 145 D1
Falconwood Rd CR0 223 C1
Falconwood Sta SE9 145 B1
Falcourt Cl SM1 217 D3
Falkener Ct SW11 268 B1
Falkirk Ct 11 SE16 118 D5
Falkirk Gdns WD19 22 D5
Falkirk Ho W9 91 D4
Falkirk St N1 95 C5
Falkland Ave
Finchley N3 29 C3
Friern Barnet N11 31 B6
Falkland Ho
Catford SE6 186 A6
Kensington W8 255 C5
West Kensington W14 254 C2
Falkland Park Ave
SE25 183 C1
Falkland Pl 2 NW5 71 C3
Falkland Rd
Barnet EN5 1 A3
Hornsey N8 50 C5
Kentish Town NW5 71 C3
Falkner House Sch
SW7 256 B2
Fallaize Ave IG1 78 D4
Falling La UB7 104 A6
Falloden Ct NW11 47 C5
Falloden Way NW11 47 C5
Fallodon Ho
6 London SW8 137 D3
Paddington W11 91 B2
Fallow Court Ave N12 30 A4
Fallow Ct 20 SE16 118 A1
Fallowfield
Lower Holloway N4 72 B6
Stanmore HA7 9 A1
Fallowfield Ct HA7 9 A1
Fallow Fields IG10 21 C4
Fallowfields Dr N12 30 C4
Fallows Cl N2 30 B1
Fallsbrook Rd SW16 181 C4
Falman Cl N9 18 A3
Falmer Rd
Enfield EN1 5 C1
Walthamstow E17 53 D6
West Green N15 51 B4
Falmouth Ave E4 36 C5
Falmouth Cl
London SE12 164 D6
Wood Green N22 32 B3
Falmouth Gdns IG4 55 D5
Falmouth Ho
Bayswater W2 247 A6
Kennington SE11 261 B2
15 Kingston u T KT2 175 D2
6 Pinner HA5 23 B3
Falmouth Rd
SE1 117 A3 262 B5
Falmouth St E15 76 B3
Falmouth Way E17 53 B4
Falstaff Ct SE11 261 C3
Falstaff Ho 18 N1 95 C5
Fambridge Cl SE26 185 B6
Fambridge Rd RM8 59 C1
Fane St W14 264 D6
Fann St EC1 95 A3 242 B5
Fanshawe Ave IG11 79 A2
Fanshawe Cres RM9 81 B3
Fanshawe Rd TW10 175 C6
Fanshaw Ho 6 E17 53 D6
Fanshaw St N1 95 C4
Fantail Cl SE28 102 C1
Fantail The BR6 226 B5
Fanthorpe St SW15 134 C2
Faraday Ave DA14 168 B2
Faraday Cl N7 72 B2
Faraday Ho
2 Balham SW12 159 B4
4 Belvedere DA17 125 C3
6 Gospel Oak NW5 71 B4
5 Hampton TW12 173 D4
Kensal Town W10 91 A2
6 Poplar E14 119 B6
Wembley HA9 67 A5
Faraday Lo SE10 120 D3
Faraday Pl KT8 195 C5
Faraday Rd
Acton W3 111 A6
East Molesey KT8 195 C5
Kensal Town W10 91 A2
Southall UB1 107 D6
Stratford E15 76 D2
Welling DA16 146 A2
Wimbledon SW19 179 D4
Faraday Way
Greenwich SE18 121 D3
Thornton Heath CR0 204 B1
Fareham Ho 13 SW15 156 A3
Fareham Rd TW14 150 C4
Fareham St W1 239 C2
Farendon Ho 15 SM2 218 A2
Farewell Pl CR4 180 C2
Faringdon Ave BR2 210 C3
Faringford Rd E15 76 C1
Farjeon Ho NW6 70 B1
Farjeon Rd SE3 143 D4
Farleigh Ave BR2 209 A2
Farleigh Ct CR2 221 A3
Farleigh Ho 7 KT2 176 D4
Farleigh Pl N16 73 D4
Farleigh Rd N16 73 D4
Farleycroft 1 CR0 206 A1
Farley Croft BR2 186 C1
Farley Ct
Kensington W14 254 C6
Marylebone NW1 238 A5
Farley Dr IG3 57 C1
Farley Ho SE26 162 B1
Farley Mews SE6 164 A4
Farley Pl SE25 206 A5
Farley Rd
Catford SE6 164 A4
South Croydon CR2 222 B1
Farlington Pl SW15 156 B4
Farlow Rd SW15 134 D2
Farlton Rd SW18 157 D4
Farman Gr 2 UB5 84 D4
Farman Terr HA3 43 D5
Farm Ave
Child's Hill NW2 69 B5
Harrow HA2, HA5 41 C3
Streatham SW16 182 A6
Wembley HA0 65 C2
Farmborough Cl HA1 42 B2
Farm Cl
Barnet EN5 12 C6
Buckhurst Hill IG9 21 C1
Coney Hall BR4 224 D5
Lower Halliford TW17 192 C2
Southall UB1 107 D6
Sutton SM2 218 B1
Uxbridge UB10 60 D6
Walham Green SW6 265 B4
Farmcote Rd SE12 165 A3
Farm Cotts E17 53 A3
Farm Ct NW4 46 A6
Farmdale Rd
Greenwich SE10 121 A1
Sutton SM5 218 C1
Farm Dr CR0 223 B6
Farm End E4 20 C6
Farmer Ho 4 SE16 118 B3
Farmer Rd E10 53 D1
Farmers Rd SE5 138 D5
Farmer St W8 245 A4
Farmfield Rd BR1 186 C5
Farm House Ct NW7 28 A3
Farmhouse Rd SW16 181 C3
Farmilo Rd E17 53 C2
Farmington Ave SM1 218 B5
Farm La
Croydon CR0 223 B6
East Barnet N14 15 B5
Walham Green
SW6 135 C5 265 B4
Farmlands
Enfield EN2 4 C4
Pinner HA5 40 A5
Farmlands The UB5 63 C2
Farmland Wlk BR7 188 D5
Farm Lane Trad Ctr
SW6 135 C6 265 B5
Farmleigh N14 15 C4
Farmleigh Ho SW9 160 D6
Farm Pl W8 245 A4
Farm Rd
Edgware HA8 27 A5
Edmonton N21 17 A3
Morden SM4 201 D4
Stonebridge NW10 89 B6
Sutton SM2 218 B1
Thames Ditton KT10 195 C1
Twickenham TW4 151 A3
Farm St W1 115 B6 248 C5
Farmstead Ct 3 SM6 219 B3
Farmstead Rd
Catford SE6 185 D6
Harrow HA3 24 B1
Farm Vale DA5 169 D5
Farm View N3 47 B6
Farmway RM8 80 C5
Farm Way
Buckhurst Hill IG9 37 C6
North Cheam KT4 216 C5
Farm Wlk NW11 47 C4
Farnaby Ho 2 W10 91 B4
Farnaby Rd
Bromley BR1, BR2 186 C2
Kidbrooke SE9 143 C1
Farnan Ave E17 53 D6
Farnan Hall 6 SW16 182 A5
Farnan Rd SW16 182 A5
FARNBOROUGH 227 B3
Farnborough Ave
South Croydon CR2 223 A1
Walthamstow E17 53 A6
Farnborough Cl HA9 66 D6
Farnborough Comm
Keston Mark BR2,
BR6 226 B5
Orpington BR6 226 C4
Farnborough Cres
3 Hayes BR2 208 D1
South Croydon CR2 223 A1
Farnborough Ct 2
BR6 227 A3
Farnborough Hill
BR6 227 C3
Farnborough Ho 1
SW15 156 A3
Farnborough Prim Sch
BR6 227 A3
Farnborough Way
BR6 227 B3
Farncombe St SE16 118 A4
Farndale Ave N13 17 A1
Farndale Cres UB6 86 A4
Farndale Ho 3 NW6 91 D6
Farnell Mews SW5 255 C2
Farnell Pl W3 110 D6
Farnell Rd TW7 130 B2
Farnell's Almshouses
TW7 130 D3
Farnfield Ho 12 SW2 160 B6
Farnham Cl N20 14 A4
Farnham Ct
2 Cheam SM3 217 A2
1 Southall UB1 86 A1
2 Stamford Hill N16 51 C1
Farnham Gdns SW20 178 B1
Farnham Green Prim Sch
IG3 58 A3
Farnham Ho
Borough The SE1 252 A3
Marylebone NW1 237 B5
Farnham Pl SE1 251 D3
Farnham Rd
Bexley DA16 146 C3
Ilford IG3 57 D2
Farnham Royal
SE11 116 B1 260 D1
Farnhurst Ho 7
SW11 137 A3
Farningham Ct SW16 181 D3
Farningham Ho 9 N4 51 B2
Farningham Rd N17 34 A3
Farnley Ho 13 SW8 137 D3
Farnley Rd
Chingford E4 20 C4
South Norwood SE25 205 B5
Farnsworth Ct SE10 120 D3
Farnsworth Ho 8
SW27 182 D5
Farnworth Ho 5 E14 120 B2
Faro Cl BR1 188 C1
Faroe Rd W14 112 D3
Farorna Wlk EN2 4 C4
Farquhar Rd
Dulwich SE19 183 D5
Wimbledon SW19 157 C1
Farquharson Rd CR0 205 A1
Farrance Rd RM6 59 A2
Farrance St E14 97 C1
Farrans Ct HA3 43 B2
Farrant Ave N22 32 D1
Farrant Cl BR6 227 D1
Farrant Ho 15 SW11 136 B2
Farrants Ct BR1 188 B1
Farr Ave IG11 102 A5
Farrell Ho E1 96 C1
Farren Rd SE23 163 A2
Farrer Ho SE8 141 C5
Farrer Mews N8 49 C5
Farrer Rd
Harrow HA3 44 A5
Hornsey N8 49 D5
Farrer's Pl CR0 222 D4
Farrier Cl
Bromley BR1 209 D6
Hillingdon UB8 82 C1
Sunbury TW16 194 A5
Farrier Pl SM1 217 D6
Farrier Rd UB5 85 C5
Farriers Ct
Belmont SM2 217 A1
Wimbledon SW19 179 A3
Farriers Mews SE15 140 C2
Farrier St NW1 71 C1
Farriers Way WD6 11 B6
Farrier Wlk
SW10 136 A6 266 A6
Farringdon La
EC1 94 C3 241 B5
Farringdon Rd
EC1 94 C3 241 B5
Farringdon St
EC4 94 D1 241 C2
Farringdon Sta
EC1 94 D2 241 C4
Farrington Pl BR7 189 B3
Farrington & Stratford
House Sch BR7 189 B3
Farrins Rents SE16 119 A5
Farrow La SE14 140 C5
Farrow Pl SE16 119 A3
Farr Rd EN2 5 B4
Farthingale Wlk E15 76 B1
Farthing Alley 8 SE1 118 A4
Farthing Ct 3 NW7 29 A3
Farthing Fields 8 E1 118 B5
Farthings Cl
Chingford E4 20 C1
Pinner HA5 40 B3
Farthing St BR6 226 B1
Farthings The 1 KT2 176 C2
FARTHING STREET 226 B1
Farwell Rd DA14 190 C6
Farwig La BR1 187 A2
Fashion & Design Mus
The* SE1 253 A2
Fashion Retail Acad The
W1 239 C2
Fashion St E1 95 D2 243 D3
Fashoda Rd BR2 209 D5
Fassett Rd
Dalston E8 74 A2
Kingston u T KT1 198 A5
Fassett Sq E8 74 A2
Fauconberg Ct W4 133 A6
Fauconberg Rd W4 133 A6
Faulkner Cl 6 RM8 58 D2
Faulkner Ho SW15 134 C3
Faulkner's Alley EC1 241 C4
Faulkner St SE14 140 C4
Fauna Cl
Dagenham RM6 58 C3
Stanmore HA7 25 D6
Faunce Ho 1 SE17 138 D6
Faunce St
SE17 116 D1 261 C1
Favart Rd
SW6 135 C4 265 B2
F Ave SE18 122 D3
Faversham Ave
Chingford E4 20 D3
Enfield EN1 17 B5
Faversham Ct SE6 163 B3
Faversham Ho
Camden Town NW1 232 B5
Walworth SE17 263 A1
Faversham Rd
Beckenham BR3 185 B1
Forest Hill SE6 163 B3
Morden SM4 201 D3
Fawcett Cl
London SW11 136 B3
West Norwood SW16 182 C6
Fawcett Est E5 52 A1
Fawcett Ho 25 SW9 138 A3
Fawcett Rd
Croydon CR0 221 A5
Willesden NW10 67 D1
Fawcett St
SW10 136 A6 266 A6
Fawcus Cl KT10 212 C2
Fawe Park Rd SW15 135 B1
Fawe St E14 97 D2
Fawkham Ho SE1 263 D3
Fawley Ct SE27 160 D2
Fawley Lo 2 E14 120 B2
Fawley Rd NW6 69 D3
Fawnbrake Ave SE24 161 A6
Fawn Rd E13 99 C5
Fawns Manor Cl
TW14 149 A3
Fawns Manor Rd
TW14 149 B3
Fawood Ave NW10 67 B1
Fayetteville Ho 26 N19 49 D2
Faygate Cres DA6 169 C6
Faygate Ct CR2 220 D1
Faygate Rd SW2 160 B2
Fayland Ave SW16 181 C5
Fazal Laj IG1 79 A6
Fazerley Ct 49 W2 91 C2
Fearnley Cres TW12 173 B4

Fearnley Ho SE5 139 C3
Fearon St SE10 121 A1
Featherbed La CR0 223 B1
Feathers Pl SE10 142 B6
Featherstone Ave 4 SE23 162 C2
Featherstone Ct NW7 28 A3
Featherstone High Sch UB2 107 A3
Featherstone Ho UB4 84 C2
Featherstone Ind Est UB2 107 A3
Featherstone Prim Sch UB2 106 C2
Featherstone Rd
Mill Hill NW7 28 B4
Southall UB2 107 A3
Featherstone St EC1 95 B3 242 C6
Featherstone Terr UB2 107 A3
Featley Rd SW9 138 D2
Federal Rd UB6 87 C5
Federation Rd SE2 124 C2
Fee Farm Rd KT10 212 D1
Felbridge Ave HA7 25 B2
Felbridge Cl SW16 182 C6
Felbridge Ct
Croydon CR2 221 A1
Feltham TW13 150 B3
Harlington UB3 127 B6
Felbridge Ho 21 SE22 139 C2
Felbrigge Rd IG3 57 D1
Felday Rd SE13 163 D5
Felden Cl HA5 23 A3
Felden St SW6 135 B4 264 C1
Feldman Cl N16 52 A1
Feldspar Ct 6 EN3 7 A2
Felgate Mews 4 W6 112 B2
Felhampton Rd SE9 166 D1
Felhurst Cres RM10 81 D4
Feline Ct 1 EN4 14 C5
Felix Ave N8 50 A3
Felix Ct E17 53 D4
Felix La TW17 193 D3
Felix Manor BR7 189 C4
Felix Neubergh Ct EN1 5 C1
Felix Rd
Ealing W13 109 A6
Walton-on-T KT12 194 A3
Felix St 19 E2 96 B5
Felixstowe Ct E16 122 D5
Felixstowe Rd
Abbey Wood SE2 124 B3
College Pk NW10 90 B4
Edmonton N9 34 A6
Tottenham N17 51 D6
Fellbrigg Rd SE22 161 D6
Fellbrigg St 21 E1 96 B3
Fellbrook TW10 153 B1
Fell Ho 11 N19 71 C5
Fellmongers Yd 1 CR0 221 A5
Fellowes Cl UB4 84 D3
Fellowes Ct UB3 127 B6
Fellowes Rd SM5 218 C6
Fellows Ct E2 95 D5
Fellows Rd NW3 70 C1
Fell Rd CR0 221 A5
Fells Haugh 6 W3 89 A1
Felltram Way SE7 121 A1
Fell Wlk HA8 26 D2
Felmersham Cl 2 SW4 137 D1
Felmingham Rd SE20 184 C1
Felnex Trad Est SM6 219 A6
Felpham Ct HA9 65 D4
Felsberg Rd SW2 160 A4
Fels Cl RM10 81 D5
Felsham Ho SW15 134 D2
Felsham Mews SW15 134 D2
Felsham Rd SW15 134 D2
Felspar Cl SE18 123 D1
Felstead Cl N13 32 C5
Felstead Rd E11 55 A2
Felstead St E9 75 B2
Felstead Wharf E14 120 A1
Felsted Rd E16 99 D1
FELTHAM 150 B2
Feltham Ave KT8 196 C5
Felthambrook Ind Est TW13 150 B1
Felthambrook Way TW13 172 B6
Feltham Bsns Complex TW13 150 B2
Feltham Com Sch TW13 150 C2
Feltham Corporate Ctr TW13 150 B1
FELTHAMHILL 171 D5
Feltham Hill Jun & Inf Schs TW13 149 D1
Feltham Hill Rd
Ashford TW15 171 A4
Feltham TW13 172 C5
Feltham Rd
Ashford TW15 171 A6
Mitcham CR4 181 A1
Feltham Sta TW13 150 B3
Felton Cl BR5 210 D3
Felton Gdns IG11 101 C5
Felton Ho
Kidbrooke SE9 143 C1
Shoreditch N1 235 D5
Felton Lea DA14 189 D5
Felton Rd
Barking IG11 101 C5
Ealing W13 109 C4
Felton St N1 95 B6 235 D5
Fenchurch Ave EC3 95 C1 243 A1
Fenchurch Bldgs EC3 243 B1
Fenchurch Pl EC3 253 B6
Fenchurch St EC3 117 C6 253 B6
Fenchurch Street Sta EC3 117 C6 253 B6
Fen Ct EC3 253 A6
Fendall Rd KT19 215 A3
Fendall St SE1 117 C3 263 B5
Fender Ct 5 SW4 138 A3
Fendt Cl 8 E16 98 D1
Fendyke Rd SE2, DA17 124 D3
Fenelon Pl W14 113 B2 254 D3
Fen Gr DA15 167 D5
Fenham Rd SE15 140 B5
Fenman Ct N17 34 B2
Fenman Gdns IG3 58 B1
Fenn Cl BR1 187 A4
Fenn Ct HA1 43 A4
Fennel Cl
Croydon CR0 206 D1
Newham E16 98 C3
Fennell St SE18 144 C6
Fenner Cl SE16 118 B2
Fenner Ho 25 E1 118 B5
Fenner Sq 10 SW11 136 B2
Fenn Ho TW7 131 B4
Fenning Ct CR4 202 C5
Fenning St SE1 253 A2
Fenn St E9 74 C3
Fen St E16 120 D6
Fenstanton 3 N4 50 B1
Fenstanton Ave N12 30 B5
Fenstanton Prim Sch SW2 160 C3
Fenswood Cl DA5 169 C5
Fentiman Rd SW8 138 B5 270 C4
Fentiman Way HA2 63 D6
Fenton Cl
Dalston E8 73 D2
Elmstead BR7 188 B5
South Lambeth SW9 138 B3
Fenton Ct TW3 129 A5
Fenton Ho
Deptford SE14 141 A5
Heston TW5 129 C6
Fenton House* NW3 70 A5
Fenton Rd N17 33 A3
Fentons SE3 142 D5
Fenton's Ave E13 99 B5
Fenton St E1 96 B1
Fenwick Cl 16 SE18 144 C6
Fenwick Gr SE15 140 A2
Fenwick Pl
Croydon CR2 220 D1
Stockwell SW9 138 A2
Fenwick Rd SE15 140 A2
Ferby Ct DA15 189 D6
Ferdinand Ho 1 NW1 71 B1
Ferdinand Pl NW1 71 A1
Ferdinand St NW1 71 A1
Ferguson Ave KT5 198 B4
Ferguson Cl BR2, BR3 208 B6
Ferguson Dr W3 89 B1
Ferguson Ho SE10 142 A4
Ferguson's Cl E14 119 C2
Fergus Rd N5 72 D3
Fermain Ct E N1 95 C6
Fermain Ct N N1 95 C6
Fermain Ct W N1 95 C6
Ferme Park Rd N4, N8 50 B3
Fermor Rd SE23 163 A3
Fermoy Rd
Greenford UB6 85 D3
West Kilburn W9 91 B3
Fern Ave CR4 203 D5
Fernbank IG9 21 B3
Fernbank Ave
Walton-on-T KT12 195 A2
Wembley HA0 64 D3
Fernbank Mews SW12 159 C5
Fernbrook Cres SE13 164 C5
Fernbrook Dr HA2 41 D2
Fernbrook Rd SE13 164 C5
Fern Cl 3 N1 95 C5
Ferncliff Rd E8 74 A3
Ferncroft Ave
London N12 30 D4
Ruislip HA4 62 C6
West Hampstead NW3 69 C4
Fern Ct
Bexleyheath DA7 147 C1
Chingford E4 36 A4
New Cross Gate SE14 140 D3
Ferndale BR1 187 C1
Ferndale Ave
Hounslow TW4 129 A2
Walthamstow E17 54 B4
Ferndale Cl DA7 147 A4
Ferndale Ct 3 SE3 142 D5
Ferndale Ho N16 51 B1
Ferndale Rd
Ashford TW15 170 A5
Brixton SW4, SW9 138 B1
Croydon SE25 206 B4
Enfield EN3 7 A6
Leyton E11 76 D6
South Tottenham N15 51 D4
Upton E7 77 B1
Ferndale St E6 100 D1
Ferndale Way BR6 227 B3
Ferndene NW9 45 A4
Fern Dene W13 87 B2
Ferndene Rd SE24 139 A1
Fernden Way RM7 59 D3
Ferndown
5 Kingston u T KT6 198 A4
Pinner HA6 22 A1
7 Wanstead E18 55 A6
Ferndown Ave BR6 211 B1
Ferndown Cl
Pinner HA5 23 A3
Sutton SM2 218 B2
Ferndown Ct 6 UB1 86 A1
Ferndown Lo 17 E14 120 A3
Ferndown Rd
Eltham SE9 165 D4
South Oxhey WD19 22 C6
Ferney Meade Way TW7 131 A3
Ferney Rd EN4 15 A3
Fern Gr TW14 150 B4
Fernhall N12 30 C5
Fernhall Dr IG4 55 D4
Fernham Rd CR7 205 A6
Fernhead 12 SM1 218 A4
Fernhead Rd W9 91 B4
Fernhill Ct
Chingford E17 36 B1
Kingston u T KT2 175 D5
Fernhill Gdns KT2 176 A5
Fernhill Ho E5 74 A6
Fern Hill Pl 3 BR6 227 A3
Fern Hill Prim Sch KT2 176 A4
Fernhill St E16 122 B5
Fern Ho HA7 24 D4
Fernholme Rd SE15 162 D6
Fernhurst Gdns HA8 26 C4
Fernhurst Rd
Ashford TW15 171 A6
Croydon CR0 206 B1
Fulham SW6 135 A4 264 B2
Fernie Ho SE22 139 D2
Fern La TW5 107 B1
Fernlea Ho NW10 88 B4
Fernlea Rd
Balham SW12 159 B3
Mitcham CR4 181 A2
Fernleigh Cl
Croydon CR0 220 C4
West Kilburn W9 91 B4
Fernleigh Ct
Harrow HA2 23 D1
Wembley HA9 44 A1
Fernleigh Rd N21 16 D2
Fern Lo 13 SW16 182 C5
Fernly Cl HA5 40 A5
Fernsbury St WC1 234 A1
Fernshaw Mans SW10 266 A5
Fernshaw Rd SW10 136 A6 266 A5
Fernside
Buckhurst Hill IG9 21 B3
Golders Green NW11 47 C1
Fernside Ave
Edgware NW7 11 B1
Feltham TW13 172 B6
Fernside Ct NW4 28 D1
Fernside Rd SW12 159 A4
Ferns Rd E15 76 D2
Fern St E3 97 C3
Fernthorpe Rd SW16 181 C4
Ferntower Rd N5 73 B3
Fernways IG1 78 D4
Fern Wlk 18 SE16 118 A1
Fernwood
Wandsworth SW19 157 B3
Wood Green N22 32 A3
Fernwood Ave
Streatham SW16 181 D6
Wembley HA0 65 C2
Fernwood Cl BR1 187 C1
Fernwood Cres N20 14 D1
Fernwood Ct N14 15 D3
Ferny Hill EN4 3 A5
Ferranti Cl SE18 121 D3
Ferraro Cl TW5 129 C6
Ferrers Ave
Wallington SM6 219 D4
West Drayton UB7 104 A4
Ferrers Rd SW16 181 D5
Ferrestone Rd N8 50 B5
Ferrey Mews 19 SW9 138 C3
Ferriby Cl N1 72 C1
Ferrier Ind Est SW18 135 D1
Ferrier Point 6 E16 99 A2
Ferrier St SW18 135 D1
Ferring Cl HA2 42 A1
Ferrings SE21 161 C1
Ferris Ave CR0 223 B5
Ferris Rd SE22 140 A1
Ferron Rd E5 74 B5
Ferrour Ct N2 48 B6
Ferrybridge Ho SE11 260 D5
Ferrydale Lo 4 NW4 46 C5
Ferry Ho E5 52 B1
Ferry Island Ret Pk N17 52 A6
Ferry La
Barnes SW13 133 D6
Brentford TW8 132 A6
Lower Halliford TW17 192 C1
Richmond TW9 132 B6
Tottenham Hale N17 52 B5
Ferry Lane Ind Est E17 52 D5
Ferry Lane Prim Sch N17 52 B5
Ferrymead Ave UB6 85 C5
Ferrymead Dr UB6 85 C5
Ferrymead Gdns UB6 86 A5
Ferrymoor TW10 153 B1
Ferry Quays Ctyd 13 TW8 131 D6
Ferry Rd
Barnes SW13 134 A4
East Molesey KT8 195 C6
Richmond TW11 175 B5
Thames Ditton KT7 197 B3
Twickenham TW1 153 B3
Ferry Sq
1 Brentford TW8 132 A6
Lower Halliford TW17 192 D2
Ferry St E14 120 A1
Ferry Wks TW17 192 C1
Festing Rd SW15 134 D2
Festival Cl
Hillingdon UB10 82 D6
Sidcup DA5 168 D3
Festival Ct
Cheam SM1 201 D1
5 Dalston E8 73 D1
Festival Pier SE1 116 B5 250 C4
Festival Pleasure Gdns SW11 136 D5 267 C3
Festoon Way E16 121 D6
Fetherston Ct RM6 59 B3
Fetter La EC4 94 C1 241 B2
Fettes Ho NW8 229 D3
Fews Lodge RM6 58 D5
Ffinch St SE8 141 C5
Fidgeon Cl BR1 210 C6
Field Cl
Bromley BR1 187 C1
Buckhurst Hill IG9 21 C1
Chessington KT9 213 C3
Chingford E4 35 D4
Cranford TW4 128 B4
East Molesey KT8 195 D4
Field Cl *continued*
Harlington UB7 127 A5
Ruislip HA4 39 A1
Uxbridge UB10 60 D6
Willesden NW2 68 A6
Fieldcommon La KT12 195 B1
Field Ct
Hampstead NW3 70 A3
Holborn WC1 240 D3
Lower Holloway N7 72 A3
Wimbledon SW19 157 C1
Fieldend TW11 174 D6
Field End HA4 62 C2
Field End Jun & Inf Schs HA4 62 D6
Fieldend Rd SW16 181 C2
Field End Rd HA5, HA4 40 C1
Fielders Cl
2 Enfield EN1 5 C1
Harrow HA2 42 A1
Fieldfare Rd SE28 124 C6
Fieldgate Mans 25 E1 96 A2
Fieldgate St E1 96 A2
Field Ho
4 Edmonton N9 34 A6
Kensal Green NW10 90 D4
8 Richmond TW10 153 C1
Fieldhouse Cl E18 37 B2
Fieldhouse Rd SW12 159 C3
Fielding Ave TW2 152 A1
Fielding Ho
Chiswick W4 133 C6
6 Kilburn NW6 91 C4
St John's Wood NW8 229 A6
Fielding Mews SW13 134 B6
Fielding Prim Sch W13 109 B3
Fielding Rd
Acton W4 111 C3
Hammersmith W14 112 D3
Fielding St SE17 139 A6
Fieldings The SE23 162 C3
Fielding Terr W5 110 B6
Field La
Brentford TW8 131 C5
Teddington TW11 175 A5
Field Lo NW10 67 D2
Field Mead NW9, NW7 27 D3
Fieldpark Gdns CR0 207 A1
Field Pl KT3 199 D3
Field Point E7 77 A4
Field Rd
Feltham TW14 150 B5
Forest Gate E7 77 A4
Fulham W6 135 A6 264 A6
Tottenham N17 51 C6
Fieldsend Rd SM3 217 A3
Fields Est E8 74 A1
Fieldside Cl BR6 227 A4
Fieldside Rd BR1 186 B5
Fields Park Cres RM6 58 D4
Field St WC1 233 C2
Fieldsway Ho N5 72 C3
Fieldview SW17, SW18 158 B3
Field View TW13 171 B6
Field View Cl RM7 59 C6
Fieldview Ct
2 Islington N5 72 D3
London NW9 44 C3
Fieldway
Dagenham RM8 80 C4
Petts Wood BR5 211 B3
Field Way
Greenford UB6 85 D6
New Addington CR0 223 D2
Ruislip HA4 39 A1
Willesden NW10 67 A1
Fieldway Cres N5, N7 72 C3
Fieldway Sta CR0 223 D1
Fieldwick Ho 14 E9 74 D2
Fiennes Cl RM8 58 C1
Fife Ct 5 W3 88 C1
Fifehead Cl TW15 170 A4
Fife Rd
Kingston u T KT2 176 A1
Mortlake SW14 155 A6
Newham E16 99 A2
Tottenham N22 32 D3
Fife Terr N1 233 D4
Fifield Path SE23 162 D1
Fifteenpenny Fields SE9 166 C6
Fifth Ave
Hayes UB3 105 D5
Ilford E12 78 B4
West Kilburn W10 91 A4
Fifth Cross Rd TW2 152 B2
Fifth Way HA9 66 D4
Figge's Rd CR4 181 A3
Fig Tree Cl NW10 89 C6
Filanco Ct W7 108 D5
Filby Rd KT9 214 B2
Filey Ave N16 52 A1
Filey Cl SM2 218 A1
Filey Ho SW18 136 A1
Filey Waye HA4 62 B6
Filigree Ct SE16 119 B5
Fillebrook Ave EN1 5 D3
Fillebrook Rd E11 54 C1
Filmer Ho SW6 264 B2
Filmer Mews SW6 264 B2
Filmer Rd SW6 135 B5 264 C3
Filston Rd DA8 125 D1
Filton Cl NW9 27 C1
Filton Ct 14 SE14 140 C5
Finborough Rd
Upper Tooting SW17 180 D4
West Brompton SW10 135 D6 265 D6
Finchale Rd SE2 124 A3
Fincham Cl UB10 61 A5
Finch Ave SE27 183 B6
Finch Cl
Barnet EN5 13 C6
Willesden NW10 67 B2
Finch Ct DA14 168 B1
Finchdean Ho SW15 155 D4
Finch Dr TW14 150 D4
Finch Gdns E4 35 C5
Finch Ho 1 SE8 141 D5
Finchingfield Ave IG8 37 C3
Finch La EC2, EC3 242 D1
FINCHLEY 29 D3
Finchley Cath High Sch N12 13 D1
Finchley Central Sta N3 29 C2
Finchley Ct N3 29 D4
Finchley La NW4 46 D5
Finchley Lo N12 29 D5
Finchley Meml Hospl N12 30 A3
Finchley Pk N12 30 B6
Finchley Pl NW8 229 C4
Finchley Rd
Hampstead NW3 70 A2
London NW11 47 B3
St John's Wood NW8 229 C4
Finchley Road & Frognal Sta NW3 70 A3
Finchley Road Sta NW3 70 A2
Finchley Way N3 29 C3
Finch Lo 15 W9 91 C2
Finch Mews 3 SE15 139 D4
Finch's Ct 10 E14 119 D6
Finden Rd E7 77 C3
Findhorn Ave UB4 84 B2
Findhorn St 8 E14 98 A1
Findon Cl
Harrow HA2 63 D5
Wandsworth SW18 157 C5
Findon Rd
Edmonton N9 18 B3
Shepherd's Bush W12 112 A4
Fine Bush La HA4 38 D3
Fineran Ct 16 SW11 136 B1
Fingal St SE10 120 D1
Fingest Ho NW8 237 A6
Finians Cl UB10 60 B1
Finland Rd SE4 141 A2
Finland St SE16 119 A3
Finlays Cl KT9 214 C3
Finlay St SW6 134 D4
Finley Ct 21 SE5 139 A5
Finmere Ho 1 N4 51 A2
Finnemore Ho N1 235 A6
Finney La TW7 131 A4
Finn Ho N1 235 D2
Finnis St E2 96 B3
Finnymore Rd RM9 81 A1
FINSBURY 94 C4
Finsbury Ave EC2 242 D3
Finsbury Cir EC2 95 B2 242 D3
Finsbury Coll N4 72 C6
Finsbury Cotts N22 32 A3
Finsbury Ct EC2 242 C4
Finsbury Ho N22 32 A2
Finsbury Market EC2 243 A4
Finsbury Mkt EC2 243 A5
FINSBURY PARK 72 C6
Finsbury Park Ave N4 51 A3
Finsbury Park Rd N4, N5 72 D6
Finsbury Park Sta N4 72 C6

Finsbury Pavement
EC2 95 B2 242 D4
Finsbury Rd N22 32 B2
Finsbury Sq
EC2 95 B2 242 D4
Finsbury St EC2 242 C4
Finsbury Way DA5 169 B5
Finsen Rd SE5 139 A2
Finstock Rd W10 90 D1
Finton House Sch
SW17 158 D2
Finucane Ct TW9 132 B2
Finucane Rise WD23 8 A2
Finwhale Ho E14 119 D3
Fiona Ct
Enfield EN2 4 D2
9 Kilburn NW6 91 B5
Firbank Cl
Enfield EN2 5 A1
Newham E16 99 D2
Firbank Rd SE15 140 B3
Fir Cl KT12 194 A2
Fircroft N1 94 D6 234 D6
Fircroft Gdns HA1 64 C5
Fircroft Prim Sch
SW17 158 D1
Fircroft Rd
Chessington KT9 214 B4
Upper Tooting SW17 158 D1
Firdene KT5 199 A1
Fir Dene BR6 226 C5
Fire Bell Alley KT6 198 A3
Firebell Mews KT6 198 A3
Fire Brigade Cotts
HA5 41 C5
Fire Brigade Pier SE1 260 B4
Firecrest Dr NW3 69 D5
Firefly 7 NW9 27 D1
Firefly Gdns E6 100 A3
Firemans Cotts N10 49 A6
Fireman's Flats N22 32 A2
Firepower (The Royal
Artillery Mus)*
SE18 122 D3
Fire Station Alley EN5 1 A3
Fire Station Flats
TW7 130 C3
Fire Station Mews 4
BR3 185 D2
Firethorn Cl 4 HA8 27 A6
Fir Gr KT3 199 D3
Fir Grove Rd 25 SW9 138 C3
Firhill Rd SE6 163 C1
Fir Island NW7 28 C5
Firle Ho 7 W10 90 C2
Fir Lo SW15 134 B1
Firmans Ct E17 54 B5
Firmston Ho 9 SW14 133 B2
Fir Rd
Cheam SM3 201 B1
Feltham TW13 172 D5
Firs Ave
Fortis Green N10 49 A5
Friern Barnet N11 31 A4
Mortlake SW14 133 A1
Firsby Ave CR0 207 A1
Firsby Rd N16 52 A1
Firs Cl
Claygate KT10 212 C2
Forest Hill SE23 163 A4
Mitcham CR4 181 B2
Muswell Hill N10 49 A6
Firscroft N13 17 A1
Firs Dr TW5 128 B5
Firs Farm Prim Sch
N13 17 B1
Firs Ho N22 32 C2
Firside Gr DA15 167 D3
Firs La N21, N13 17 A2
Firs Park Ave N21 17 B3
Firs Park Gdns N21 17 B3
First Ave
Bexley DA7 146 C5
Chadwell Heath RM6 58 C4
Dagenham RM10 103 D5
East Acton W3 111 D5
East Molesey KT8 195 C5
Edmonton N18 34 C6
Enfield EN1 17 D6
Hayes UB3 105 D5
Hendon NW4 46 C5
Manor Pk E12 78 A3
Mortlake SW14 133 C2
Newham E13 99 A4
Walthamstow E17 53 D4
Walton-on-T KT12 194 B3
Wembley HA9 65 D6
West Kilburn W10 91 B3
First Cl KT8 196 A6
First Cross Rd TW2 152 C2
First Dr NW10 67 A1
Firs The
Belmont SM2 217 D1
Claygate KT10 212 C2
Ealing W5 87 D2
Forest Hill SE26 184 C5
Oakleigh Pk N20 14 B3
2 Penge SE26 184 B5
Sidcup DA15 167 D1
Upton Pk E6 78 A1
Wimbledon SW20 178 A3
Woodford IG8 37 C3
First St SW3 114 C2 257 B4
Firstway SW20 178 C1
First Way HA9 66 D4
Firs Wlk IG8 37 A5
Firswood Ave KT19 215 D3
Firth Gdns
SW6 135 A4 264 A1
Firtree Ave CR4 181 A1
Fir Tree Ave UB7 104 C3
Fir Tree Cl
Ealing W5 88 A1
Esher KT10 212 A3
5 Orpington BR6 227 D3
Streatham SW16 181 C5
Worcester Pk KT19 215 D4
Firtree Ct BR2 208 D6
Fir Tree Gdns CR0 223 C4
Fir Tree Gr SM5 218 D1
Firtree Ho SE13 164 B4
Fir Tree Ho 11 SE14 140 C5
Firtree Lodge N21 17 A2
Fir Tree Rd TW4 129 A1
Fir Trees Cl SE16 119 A5
Fir Tree Wlk EN1 5 B2
Fir Wlk KT17, SM3 216 D2
Fisher Cl
Croydon CR0 205 D1
Holdbrook EN3 7 C6
Southall UB6 85 C4
Fisherdene KT10 213 A1
Fisher Ho
Islington N1 234 A5
9 Shadwell E1 118 C6
2 Tufnell Pk N19 71 C5
Fisherman Cl TW10 175 C6
Fishermans Dr SE16 118 D4
Fishermans Wlk
SE28 123 C4
Fisherman's Wlk E14 119 C5
Fisher Rd HA3 24 D1
Fishers Cl SW16 159 D1
Fishers Ct
London SE14 140 D4
6 Teddington TW11 174 D5
Fisher's La W4 111 B2
Fisher St
Holborn WC1 240 C3
Newham E16 99 A2
Fisherton St
NW8 92 B3 236 D6
Fisherton Street Est
NW8 92 B3 236 D5
Fishguard Way E16 122 D5
Fishlock Ct 6 SW4 138 A3
Fishponds Rd
Keston BR2 225 D3
Upper Tooting SW17 180 C6
Fish St Hill EC3 252 D5
Fisk Cl TW16 171 D4
Fiske Ct
Barking IG11 101 B5
1 Merton SW19 180 A3
Sutton SM2 218 A1
Tottenham N17 34 A2
Fitch Ct
London SW2 160 C6
8 Mitcham CR4 181 A1
Fitzalan Rd
Church End N3 47 B6
Claygate KT10 212 C1
Fitzalan St
SE11 116 C2 261 A4
Fitzclarence Ho W11 244 A2
Fitzgeorge Ave KT2,
KT3 177 B2
Fitz-George Ave W14 254 A3
Fitzgerald Ave SW14 133 C2
Fitzgerald Ct 1 E10 53 D1
Fitzgerald Ho
15 Brixton SW9 138 C3
Hayes UB3 106 B5
14 Poplar E14 97 D1
Fitzgerald Rd
Mortlake SW14 133 B2
Thames Ditton KT7 197 A3
Wanstead E11 55 A4
Fitzhardinge Ho
Beckenham BR3 185 D1
Fitzhardinge Ho *continued*
Marylebone W1 238 A2
Fitzhardinge St W1 238 A2
Fitzherbert Ho 11
TW10 154 B5
Fitzhugh Gr SW18 158 B5
Fitzjames Ave
Croydon CR0 222 A6
West Kensington W14 254 B3
Fitzjohn Ave EN5 1 B1
Fitzjohn's Ave NW3 70 B3
Fitzjohns Mans NW3 70 A2
Fitzjohns Prim Sch
NW3 70 B3
Fitzmaurice Ho 17
SE16 118 B2
Fitzmaurice Pl W1 248 D4
Fitzneal St W12 89 D1
FITZROVIA 93 C2
Fitzroy Cl N6 48 D1
Fitzroy Cres W4 133 B5
Fitzroy Ct
London N6 49 C3
Marylebone W1 239 B5
Fitzroy Gdns SE19 183 C3
Fitzroy Ho
Bermondsey SE1 263 D2
12 Tower Hamlets E14 97 B1
Fitzroy Lo N21 16 D6
Fitzroy Mews W1 239 A5
Fitzroy Pk N6 48 D1
Fitzroy Rd NW1 93 A6 231 A6
Fitzroy Sq W1 239 A5
Fitzroy St W1 93 C3 239 A5
Fitzroy Yd NW1 231 A6
Fitzstephen Rd RM8 80 C3
Fitzwarren Gdns N19 49 C1
Fitzwilliam Ave TW9 132 B3
Fitzwilliam Ho
4 Higham Hill E17 35 A1
Richmond TW9 131 D1
Fitzwilliam Hts 1
SE23 162 C2
Fitzwilliam Mews
E16 121 A5
Fitzwilliam Rd SW4 137 C2
Fitzwygram Cl TW12 174 A5
Five Acre NW9 27 D1
Fiveacre Cl CR7 204 C3
Five Arch Bridge
DA14 191 A6
Five Arches Bsns Pk
DA14 190 D4
Five Elms Prim Sch
RM8 81 B5
Five Elms Rd
Dagenham RM9 81 B5
Keston Mark BR2 225 C5
Five Oaks Mews BR1 165 A1
Fives Ct SE11 261 C5
Fiveways
Chislehurst SE9 166 D2
Croydon CR0 220 C4
Ruislip HA4 39 B1
Five Ways Cnr NW4 28 A2
Fiveways Rd SW9 138 C3
Flack Ct 15 E10 53 D2
Fladbury Rd N15 51 B3
Fladgate Rd E11 54 C3
Flag Cl CR0 206 D1
Flag Wlk HA5 40 A3
Flambard Rd HA1, HA3 43 A3
Flamborough Ho 12
SE15 140 A4
Flamborough Rd HA4 62 A5
Flamborough St E14 97 A1
Flamingo Ct 2 SE8 141 C5
Flamingo Gdns UB5 85 A4
Flamstead Gdns RM9 80 C1
Flamstead Rd RM9 80 C1
Flamsted Ave HA9 66 C2
Flamsteed Ct 15
SE13 141 D4
Flamsteed Ho* SE10 142 B5
Flamsteed Rd SE7 122 A1
Flanchford Rd W12 111 D3
Flanders Cres SW17 180 D4
Flanders Ct E17 53 A3
Flanders Ho N16 73 C5
Flanders Mans 1
W4 111 D2
Flanders Rd
Acton W4 111 C2
Wallend E6 100 C5
Flanders Way E9 74 D2
Flandrian Cl EN3 7 D5
Flank St 9 E1 118 A6
Flansham Ho 2 E14 97 B1
Flash La EN2 5 A6
Flask Cotts 4 NW3 70 B4
Flask Wlk NW3 70 B4
Flatford Ho 2 SE6 186 A6
Flather Cl 12 SW16 181 C5
Flatiron Sq SE1 252 B3
Flatiron Yd SE1 252 B3
Flavell Mews SE10 120 C1
Flaxen Cl E4 19 D1
Flaxen Rd E4 19 D1
Flaxley Rd SM4 201 D2
Flaxman Ct
12 Belvedere DA17 125 C1
Soho W1 239 C1
Flaxman Ho
10 Chiswick W4 111 C1
Newington SE1 261 D6
Flaxman Rd SE5 138 D3
Flaxman Terr
WC1 93 D4 232 D1
Flaxman Villas N2 48 A6
Flaxmore Ct
Erith DA7 147 D2
South Norwood CR7 183 B1
Flaxton Rd SE18 145 C5
Flecker Cl HA7 24 D5
Flecker Ho 6 SE5 139 B5
Fleece Dr N9 34 A6
Fleecefield Prim Sch
N18 34 A6
Fleece Rd KT6 197 C1
Fleece Wlk N7 72 A2
Fleeming Cl E17 35 B1
Fleeming Rd E17 35 B1
Fleet Cl
East Molesey KT8 195 B4
Ruislip HA4 39 A3
Fleet Ct 1 W12 111 C3
Fleetfield WC1 233 B2
Fleet Ho
6 Brixton SW2 160 C6
1 Limehouse E14 119 A6
Fleet Pl EC4 241 C2
Fleet Prim Sch NW3 70 D3
Fleet Rd NW3 70 D3
Fleetside KT8 195 C4
Fleet Sq WC1 233 D1
Fleet St EC4 94 C1 241 B1
Fleet Street Hill 10 E1 96 A3
Fleet Terr SE6 164 A4
Fleetway WC1 233 B2
Fleetway West Bsns Pk
UB6 87 B5
Fleet Wood 6 N16 73 D6
Fleetwood Cl
Chessington KT9 213 D1
Newham E16 99 D2
South Croydon CR0 221 D5
Fleetwood Ct
1 Newham E6 100 B2
Orpington BR6 226 C4
8 Stanwell TW19 148 A5
Fleetwood Rd
Kingston u T KT3 198 D6
Willesden NW10 68 A3
Fleetwood Sq KT3 198 D6
Fleetwood St N16 73 C6
Fleetwood Way WD19 22 C6
Fleming Cl 4 W9 91 C3
Fleming Ct
Croydon CR0 220 C3
Paddington W2 236 C4
Fleming Dr N21 16 B6
Fleming Ho
14 Bermondsey SE16 118 A4
Finsbury Pk N4 51 A1
5 Wembley HA9 67 A5
Fleming Mead CR4 180 D3
Fleming Rd
Camberwell SE17 138 D6
Southall UB1 86 A1
Fleming Way
Isleworth TW7 130 D1
Thamesmead SE28 124 D6
Fleming Wlk NW9 27 C1
Flemming Ave HA4 62 B6
Flempton Rd E10 53 A1
Fletcher Bldgs WC2 240 B1
Fletcher Cl E16 122 D6
Fletcher Ct 9 NW5 71 B4
Fletcher Ho 16 N16 73 C4
Fletcher La E10 54 A2
Fletcher Path 7 SE8 141 C5
Fletcher Rd W4 111 A3
Fletchers Cl BR2 209 B5
Fletcher St 16 E1 118 A6
Fletching Rd
Charlton SE7 143 D6
Lower Clapton E5 74 C5
Fletton Rd N11 32 A3
Fleur De Lis St E1 243 C5
Fleur Gates 7 SW19 156 D4
Flexmere Rd N17 33 C2
Flimwell Cl BR1 186 C5
Flinders Ho 28 E1 118 B5
Flint Cl
8 Green Street Green
BR6 227 D2
1 Stratford E15 76 D1
Flint Ct CR0 204 B3
Flint Down Cl BR5 190 A2
Flintmill Cres SE3,
SE9 144 A3
Flinton St
SE17 117 C1 263 B2
Flint St SE17 117 B2 262 D3
Flitcroft St WC2 239 D1
Flitton Ho 7 N1 72 D1
Floathaven Cl SE28 124 A5
Flock Mill Pl SW18 157 D3
Flockton St
20 Bermondsey SE16 118 A4
3 Bermondsey SE16 118 A4
Flodden Rd SE5 139 A4
Flood La 5 TW1 153 A3
Flood St SW3 136 C6 267 B6
Flood Wlk
SW3 136 C6 267 B6
Flora Cl E14 97 D1
Flora Gardens Prim Sch
W6 112 B2
Flora Gdns
Dagenham RM6 58 C3
2 Hammersmith W6 112 B2
Floral St WC2 116 A6 250 A6
Flora St DA17 125 B1
Florence Ave
Enfield EN2 5 A2
Morden SM4 202 A4
Florence Cl KT12 194 B2
Florence Ct
18 New Barnet EN5 13 D6
St John's Wood W9 229 B1
Wanstead E11 55 C5
5 Wimbledon SW19 179 A4
Florence Dr EN2 5 A2
Florence Elson Cl E12 78 C4
Florence Gdns
Chiswick W4 133 A6
Ilford RM6 58 C2
Florence Ho
20 Bermondsey SE16 118 B1
2 Brixton SW2 160 B6
Kidbrooke SE18 144 B4
5 Kingston u T KT2 176 B3
10 Shepherd's Bush
W11 112 D6
7 Wandsworth SW18 136 B1
Florence Mans
Fulham SW6 264 C2
4 Hendon NW4 46 B4
Florence Nightingale Ho
14 N1 73 A2
Florence Nightingale
Mus* SE1 250 D1
Florence Rd
Abbey Wood SE2 124 C2
Acton W4 111 B3
5 Beckenham BR3 185 A1
Bromley BR1 187 A2
Ealing W5 110 A6
Feltham TW13 150 B3
Finsbury Pk N4 50 C2
6 Kingston u T KT2 176 B3
New Cross Gate SE14 141 B4
Southall UB2 106 D3
7 Upton Pk E6 99 C6
Walton-on-T KT12 194 B2
West Ham E13 99 A5
Wimbledon SW19 179 D4
Florence Root Ho 3
IG4 56 B4
Florence St
Islington N1 72 D1
London NW4 46 C5
Newham E16 98 D3
Florence Terr
Kingston u T SW15 155 C1
New Cross Gate SE14 141 B4
Florence Way SW12 158 D3
Florence White Ct N9 18 B1
Florentine Ho 3 IG1 78 D6
Flores Ho 13 E1 96 D2
Florey Sq N21 16 B6
Florfield Rd E8 74 B2
Florian SE5 139 C4
Florian Ave SM1 218 B4
Florian Rd SW15 135 A1
Florida Cl WD23 8 B2
Florida Ct BR2 208 D5
Florida Rd CR7 182 D2
Florida St E2 96 A4
Florida State Univ
WC1 93 D2 239 D3
Florin Ct
Bermondsey SE1 253 C1
Edmonton N18 33 C6
8 St George in t East
SE1 118 A6
Floris Pl 7 SW4 137 C2
Floriston Ave UB10 61 A1
Floriston Cl HA7 25 B2
Floriston Ct UB5 63 D3
Floriston Gdns HA7 25 B2
Florys Ct 7 SW19 157 A3
Floss St SW15 134 C3
Flower & Dean Wlk
E1 243 D3
Flower La NW7 27 D4
Flower Mews NW11 47 A3
Flower Pot Cl N15 51 D3
Flowers Cl NW2 68 A5
Flowersmead SW17 159 A2
Flowers Mews 1 N19 71 C6
Flower Wlk The
SW7 114 A4 246 B2
Floyd Rd SE7 121 C1
Floyer Cl TW10 154 B6
Fludyer St SE13 142 C1
Flynn Ct 19 E14 119 C6
Fogerty Cl EN3 7 D6
Foley Cotts KT10 212 D2
Foley Ct N12 30 A5
Foley Ho 19 E1 96 C1
Foley Mews KT10 212 C2
Foley Rd KT10 212 C1
Foley St W1 93 C2 239 A3
Folgate St E1 95 D2 243 C4
Foliot Ho N1 233 C4
Foliot St W12 89 D1
Folkestone Ct UB5 63 D3
Folkestone Rd
Edmonton N18 34 A6
Wallend E6 100 C4
Walthamstow E17 53 D5
Folkingham La 6
NW9 27 C2
Folkington Cnr N12 29 B5
Folland 6 NW9 27 D1
Follett Ho SW10 266 C4
Follett St E14 98 A1
Folly La
Higham Hill E17 35 A2
Walthamstow E4 35 B3
Folly Wall E14 120 A4
Fonda Ct 14 E14 119 C6
Fontaine Ct
3 Beckenham BR3 185 B2
Southgate N14 15 D2
Fontaine Rd SW16 182 B3
Fontarabia Rd SW11 137 A1
Fontenelle SE5 139 C4
Fontenoy Ho SE11 261 C3
Fontenoy Rd SW12,
SW17 159 C2
Fonteyne Gdns IG8 37 D1
Fonthill Cl SE20 184 A1
Fonthill Ct SE23 162 C4
Fonthill Ho
Kensington W14 254 B6
Pimlico SW1 258 D2
Fonthill Mews N4 72 B6
Fonthill Rd N4 72 C6
Font Hills N2 30 A1
Fontley Way SW15 156 A4
Fontmell Cl TW15 170 C5
Fontmell Pk TW15 170 C5
Fontwell Cl
Harrow HA3 24 C3
Northolt UB5 63 C2
Fontwell Dr BR2 210 C4
Football La HA1 42 C1
Footpath The SW15 156 A6
FOOTS CRAY 190 B4
Foots Cray High St
DA14 190 D4
Foots Cray La DA14 168 C3
Footscray Rd SE9 166 D3
Forber Ho 25 E2 96 C4
Forbes Cl NW2 68 A5
Forbes Ct SE19 183 C5
Forbes Ho 2 W4 110 C1
Forbes St E1 96 A1
Forbes Way HA4 62 B6
Forburg Rd N16 52 A1
Fordbridge Ct TW15 170 A4
Fordbridge Rd
Ashford TW15 170 B5

Fordbridge Rd *continued*
Lower Halliford TW16,
TW17 193 D3
Sunbury TW16 194 A5
Fordbridge Rdbt
TW15 170 A4
Ford Cl
Ashford TW15 170 A4
12 Bow E3 97 A5
Harrow HA1 42 B2
Littleton TW17 192 C4
Thornton Heath CR7 204 D4
Fordcombe 13 NW5 71 A2
Forde Ave BR1 209 C6
Fordel Rd SE6 164 B3
Ford End IG8 37 B4
Fordham 4 KT1 176 C1
Fordham Cl EN4 2 C2
Fordham Ho 11 SE14 141 A5
Fordham Rd EN4 2 C2
Fordham St 13 E1 96 A1
Ford Ho
2 New Barnet EN5 13 D6
2 Woolwich SE18 122 D1
Fordhook Ave W5 110 C6
Fordingley Rd W9 91 B4
Fordington Ho 2
SE26 162 B1
Fordington Rd N6 48 D5
Fordmill Rd SE6 163 C2
Ford Rd
Ashford TW15 170 B6
Bow E3 97 B5
Dagenham RM10 81 C1
Ford's Gr N21 17 A3
Fords Park Rd E16 99 A1
Ford Sq E1 96 B2
Ford St
Bow E3 97 A5
Canning Town E16 98 D1
Fordwich Cl BR6 211 D2
Fordwych Ct NW2 69 A2
Fordwych Rd NW2 69 A3
Fordyce Ho 3 SW16 181 C6
Fordyce Rd SE13 164 A6
Fordyke Rd RM8 81 B6
Forecastle Ct E14 119 C4
Foreign, Commonwealth & Home Offices
SW1 250 A2
Foreland Ct NW4 29 A2
Foreland Ho W11 244 A6
Foreland St SE18 123 B2
Foreshore SE8 119 B2
Fore St
Barbican EC2 95 A2 242 B3
Edmonton N18 34 A6
Pinner HA5 40 A4
Forest App
Chingford E4 20 C4
Woodford IG8 37 A3
Forest Ave E4 20 C4
Forest Bsns Pk E17 52 D2
Forest Cl
Brondesbury NW6 69 A1
Chislehurst BR7 188 C2
Wanstead E11 55 A4
Woodford IG8 37 B6
Forest Croft SE23 162 B2
Forest Ct
Chingford E4 20 D3
Leytonstone E11 54 C5
14 Woodside Pk N12 29 D6
Forestdale N14 31 D6
Forestdale Ctr The
CR0 223 B1
Forest Dene Ct 2
SM2 218 A2
Forest Dr
Ashford TW16 171 D3
Chingford IG8 36 C3
Keston Mark BR2 226 A4
Wanstead E12 77 D5
Forest Dr E E11 54 B3
Forest Dr W E11 54 B2
Forest Edge IG9 21 D1
Forester Rd SE15 140 B2
Foresters Cl SM6 219 D1
Foresters Cres DA7 147 D1
Foresters Dr
Wallington SM6 219 D1
Walthamstow E17 54 B5
Foresters Homes The
DA7 147 D1
Foresters Prim Sch
SM6 219 D1
FOREST GATE 77 A3
Forest Gate NW9 45 C4
Forest Gate Com Sch
E7 77 A3
Forest Gate Sta E7 77 A3
Forest Gdns N17 33 D1
Forest Glade
Chingford E4 36 C5
Leytonstone E11 54 C3
Forest Gr E8 73 D2
FOREST HILL 163 A3
Forest Hill SE23 162 C3
Forest Hill Bsns Ctr
SE23 162 C2
Forest Hill Ct 6
SE26 162 B1
Forest Hill Ind Est
SE23 162 C2
Forest Hill Rd SE22 162 B5
Forest Hill Sec Sch
SE23 162 D1
Forest Hill Sta SE23 162 C2
Forest Ho 9 E4 20 C4
Forestholme Cl SE23 162 C2
Forest Ho The SE23 163 A3
Forest Hts IG9 21 A2
Forest La E7, E15 76 D3
Forest Lawns BR1 187 C2
Forest Lea 3 E11 54 D2
Forest Lo 1 SE23 162 C1
Forest Mount Rd IG8 36 B3
Forest Point E7 77 B3
Forest Rd
Dalston E8 73 D2
Edmonton N9 18 B3
Feltham TW13 150 C1
Forest Gate E7 77 A4
Leytonstone E11 54 B2
Morden SM3, SM4 201 C2
Richmond TW9 132 C5
Romford RM7 59 D6
Walthamstow E17 53 C6
Woodford IG8 21 A1
Fore Street Ave EC2 242 C3
Forest Ridge
Beckenham BR3 207 C6
Bromley BR2 226 B4
Forest Rise E17 54 B5
Forest Sch E17 54 C5
Forest Side
Buckhurst Hill IG9 21 C3
Chingford E4 20 D3
Forest Gate E7 77 B4
New Malden KT4 199 D1
Forest St E7 77 A3
Forest The E11 54 C5
Forest Trad Est E17 52 D6
Forest View
Chingford E4 20 B4
Leytonstone E11 54 D2
Forest View Ave E10 54 B4
Forest View Rd
Chingford E17 36 A2
Manor Pk E12 78 A4
Forest Way
Orpington BR5 211 D4
Sidcup DA15 167 B4
9 Upper Holloway N19 71 C6
Woodford IG8 37 B6
Forest Wlk N10 31 B2
Forfar Rd
London
SW11 137 A4 268 B2
Tottenham N22 32 D2
Forge Cl
Harlington UB3 127 B6
Hayes BR2 209 A1
Forge Cotts W5 109 D5
Forge Dr KT10 213 A1
Forge La
Belmont SM3 217 A1
Feltham TW13 173 A5
Richmond TW10 154 A3
Sunbury TW16 194 A6
Forge Lane Prim Sch
TW13 173 A5
Forge Lo 2 TW7 131 A2
Forge Mews
Addington CR0 223 C3
Sunbury TW16 194 A6
Forge Pl NW1 71 A2
Forlong Path UB5 63 A2
Forman Ct TW1 152 D3
Forman Ho SE4 140 D1
Forman Pl N16 73 D4
Formby Ave HA3, HA7 43 C6
Formby Ct 9 N7 72 C3
Formosa Ho 1 E1 97 A3
Formosa St W9 91 D3
Formunt Cl E16 98 D2
Forres Gdns NW11 47 C3
Forrest Ct N7 72 C2
Forrester Path SE26 184 C6
Forresters The HA5 40 B3
Forrest Gdns SW16 204 B6
Forrest Ho SW15 134 C3
Forris Ave UB3 105 D5
Forset Ct W1 237 B2
Forset St W1 92 C1 237 B2
Forstal Cl BR2 209 A6
Forster Cl IG8 36 B3
Forster Ho SE6 164 B1
Forster Park Prim Sch
SE6 164 C1
Forster Rd
Beckenham BR3 207 A6
Streatham SW2 160 A4
Thornton Heath CR0 205 A2
Tottenham N17 51 D6
Walthamstow E17 53 A3
Forsters Cl RM6 59 B3
Forsters Way UB4 84 B1
Forston St N1 95 A5 235 B4
Forsyte Cres SE19 183 C2
Forsyte Ct KT2 176 D2
Forsyth Ct
13 Dagenham RM10 81 D2
Harrow HA1 42 B3
Kingston u T KT3 177 C1
Forsythe Shades BR3 186 A2
Forsyth Gdns SE17 138 D6
Forsyth Ho
14 Hackney E9 74 C1
Pimlico SW1 259 B3
Forsythia Cl IG1 78 D3
Forsythia Ho SE4 141 A2
Forsyth Pl EN1 17 C6
Forterie Gdns IG3 80 A4
Fortescue Ave
1 Hackney E8 74 B1
Twickenham TW2 152 A1
Fortescue Rd
Burnt Oak HA8 27 B3
Mitcham SW19 180 B3
Fortess Gr NW5 71 C3
Fortess Rd NW5 71 C4
Fortess Wlk NW5 71 B3
Forthbridge Rd SW11 137 A1
Forth Ho 30 E3 97 B5
Forties The 9 NW5 71 C3
Fortior Ct N6 49 C2
Fortis Cl E16 99 C1
Fortis Ct N10 49 A6
Fortis Gn N2, N10 48 D6
FORTIS GREEN 48 D5
Fortis Green Ave N2 48 D5
Fortis Green Cotts N2 48 D6
Fortismere Ave N10 49 A6
Fortismere Sch N10 30 D1
Fortismere Sch (South Wing) N10 49 A6
Fortnam Rd N19 71 D6
Fortnums Acre HA7 24 D4
Fort Rd
Bermondsey
SE1 117 D2 263 D3
Northolt UB5 63 C1
Fortrose Cl E14 98 B1
Fortrose Gdns SW12,
SW2 160 A3
Fort St
Broadgate E1 243 B3
Newham E16 121 B5
Fortuna Cl N7 72 B2
Fortune Ct
Barking IG11 102 B5
6 Dalston E8 73 D1
Fortune Gate Rd
NW10 89 C6
Fortune Green Rd
NW6 69 C4
Fortune Ho
Lambeth SE11 261 A3
St Luke's EC1 242 B5
Fortune La WD6 9 D5
Fortunes Mead UB5 63 A2
Fortune St EC1 95 A3 242 B5
Fortune Way NW10 90 A4
Fortune Wlk 4 SE28 123 B3
Forty Acre La E16 99 A2
Forty Ave HA9 66 B6
Forty Cl HA9 66 B5
Forty Hall* EN2 5 D6
FORTY HILL 5 D4
Forty Hill EN2 5 D5
Forty Hill CE Prim Sch
EN2 6 A6
Forty Hill Ho EN1 5 D5
Forty La HA9 66 D6
Forum Cl 7 E3 97 C6
Forumside HA8 26 C4
Forum The KT8 195 D5
Forum Way HA8 26 C4
Forval Cl CR4 202 D4
Forward Bsns Ctr The 3
E16 98 B3
Forward Dr HA3 42 D5
Fosbrooke Ho SW8 270 A3
Fosbury Ho 7 SW9 138 B1
Fosbury Mews W2 245 D5
Foscote Mews W9 91 C2
Foscote Rd NW4 46 B3
Foskett Ho 21 N2 30 B1
Foskett Rd SW6 135 B3
Foss Ave CR0, CR9 220 C3
Fossdene Prim Sch
SE7 121 B1
Fossdene Rd SE7 121 B1
Fossdyke Cl UB4 85 A2
Fosse Way W13 87 A2
Fossil Rd SE13 141 C2
Fossington Rd DA17 124 D2
Foss Rd SW17 180 B6
Fossway RM8 80 C6
Foster Ct
6 Camden Town NW1 71 C1
Canning Town E16 120 D6
Hendon NW4 46 C5
Foster Ho SE14 141 B4
Foster La EC2 95 A1 242 A2
Foster Rd
Acton W3 111 C6
Chiswick W4 111 B1
Newham E13 99 A3
Fosters Cl
Elmstead BR7 188 B5
Woodford E18 37 B2
Fosters Old Sch DA16 146 B3
Foster's Prim Sch
DA16 146 C2
Foster St NW4 46 C5
Foster Wlk NW4 46 C5
Fothergill Cl E13 99 A5
Fothergill Dr N21 16 A6
Fotheringham Ct EN1 5 D1
Fotheringham Rd EN1 5 D1
Foubert's Pl W1 239 A1
Foulden Rd N16 73 D4
Foulden Terr N16 73 D4
Foulis Terr
SW7 114 B1 256 D2
Foulser Rd SW17 159 A1
Foulsham Rd CR7 205 B6
Foundary Ho 6 E14 97 D2
Founder Cl 2 E6 100 D1
Founders Cl UB5 85 B4
Founders Ct EC2 242 C2
Founders Gdns SE19 183 A3
Founders Ho SW1 259 C2
Foundling Ct WC1 240 A6
Foundling Mus The*
WC1 94 A3 240 B6
Foundry Cl SE16 119 A5
Foundry Mews NW1 239 B6
Foundry Pl
Stepney E1 96 C2
Wandsworth SW18 157 D4
Fountain Cl UB8 83 A2
Fountain Ct
Belgravia SW1 258 C3
Blackfen DA15 168 B5
New Malden KT3 199 A5
5 Penge SE26 184 C4
14 Shepherd's Bush
W11 112 D4
Strand EC4 251 A6
Fountain Dr
Dulwich SE19 183 D6
Wallington SM5 218 D1
Fountain Green Sq 34
SE16 118 A4
Fountain Ho
33 Bermondsey SE16 118 A4
3 Brondesbury Pk NW6 69 A1
Mayfair W1 248 A4
5 Mitcham SW19 180 D1
Fountain Mews
1 Highbury N5 73 A4
Maitland Pk NW3 70 D2
Fountain Pl SW9 138 C4
Fountain Rd
South Norwood CR7 183 A1
Upper Tooting SW17 180 B6
Fountains Ave TW13 151 B1
Fountains Cl TW13 151 B1
Fountains Cres N14 16 A4
Fountains The
London N3 29 D3
Loughton IG10 21 D4
Fountayne Bsns Ctr
N15 52 A5
Fountayne Rd
South Tottenham N15 52 A5
Stoke Newington N16 74 A6
Fount St SW8 137 D5 269 D3
Fouracres EN3 7 A4
Four Acres N12 29 D6
Fourland Wlk HA8 27 A4
Fournier St E1 95 D2 243 D4
Fourscore Mans E8 74 A1
Four Seasons Cl E3 97 C5
Four Seasons Cres
SM3 217 B6
Four Square Ct TW4 151 C5
Fourth Ave
Hayes UB3 105 D5
Ilford E12 78 B4
West Kilburn W10 91 A4
Fourth Cross Rd TW2 152 B2
Fourth Way
Wembley HA9 66 D4
Wembley HA9 67 A4
Four Tubs The WD23 8 B4
Fourways 2 CR0 221 D6
Four Wents The E4 20 B2
Fovant Ct 5 SW8 137 C3
Fowey Ave IG4 55 D4
Fowey Cl E1 118 B5
Fowey Ho SE11 261 B2
Fowler Cl
London SW11 136 B2
Sidcup DA14 191 A5
Fowler Ho
5 Camberwell SE5 139 C3
Islington N1 94 D6 234 D6
South Lambeth SW8 269 D1
West Green N15 51 B4
Fowler Rd
Forest Gate E7 77 A4
Islington N1 94 D6 234 D6
Mitcham CR4 181 A1
Fowler's Wlk W5 87 D3
Fownes St SW11 136 C2
Fox and Knot St EC1 241 D4
Foxberry Ct SE4 141 B1
Foxberry Rd SE4 141 A2
Foxborough Gdns
SE4 163 C6
Foxbourne Rd SW17 159 A2
Foxbury Ave BR7 189 B4
Foxbury Cl BR1 187 B4
Foxbury Rd BR1 187 B4
Fox Cl
Bethnal Green E1 96 C3
Elstree WD6 9 D5
Newham E16 99 A2
Foxcombe CR0 223 D2
Foxcombe Cl 1 E6 99 D5
Foxcombe Rd 6
SW15 156 A3
Foxcote SE5 263 B1
Foxcroft N1 233 D3
Foxcroft Rd SE18 144 D4
Foxes Dale
Beckenham BR2 208 B6
Blackheath Pk SE3 143 A2
Foxfield NW1 231 D5
Foxfield Prim Sch
SE18 123 A1
Foxfield Rd BR6 227 B6
Foxglove Cl
Bexley DA15 168 A5
Edmonton N9 18 C3
Southall UB1 107 A6
Foxglove Ct 11 HA0 88 A5
Foxglove Gdns E11 55 C5
Foxglove La KT9 214 C4
Foxglove Path SE28 123 C5
Foxglove St W12 111 D6
Foxglove Way SM6 203 B1
Fox Gr KT12 194 B2
Foxgrove N14 16 A1
Foxgrove Ave BR3 185 D3
Foxgrove Path WD19 22 D5
Foxgrove Rd BR3 186 A3
Foxham Rd N19 71 D5
Fox Hill SE19 183 D3
Fox Hill Gdns SE19 183 D3
Fox Ho
2 London SW11 136 B1
Northolt UB5 85 A6
Foxhole Rd 2 SE9 166 A6
Fox Hollow Cl 1
SE18 123 C1
Fox Hollow Dr DA7 146 D2
Foxholt Gdns NW10 67 A1
Foxhome Cl BR7 188 C4
Fox House Rd DA17 125 D1
Fox La
Ealing W5 88 A3
Keston BR2 225 C3
Fox La *continued*
Palmers Green N13 16 B1
Foxlees HA0 65 A4
Foxley Cl E8 74 A3
Foxley Ct SM2 218 A1
Foxley Ho 4 E3 97 D4
Foxley Rd
Camberwell SW9 138 D5
Thornton Heath CR7 204 D5
Foxley Sq 3 SW9 138 D4
Foxmead Cl EN2 4 B2
Foxmore St SW11 267 C1
Fox Prim Sch
W8 113 C5 245 A3
Fox Rd E16 98 D2
Foxs Path CR4 180 C1
Fox's Yd E2 243 D6
Foxtail Ho TW3 130 A4
Foxton KT1 198 C6
Foxton Gr CR4 180 B1
Foxton Ho E16 122 C4
Foxwarren KT10 212 D1
Foxwell Mews SE4 141 A2
Foxwell St SE4 141 A2
Foxwood Cl
Edgware NW7 27 C6
Feltham TW13 150 B1
Foxwood Green Cl
EN1 17 C5
Foxwood Rd SE3 142 D1
Foyle Rd
Greenwich SE3 142 D6
Tottenham N17 34 A2
Fradel Lo N16 51 B1
Framfield Cl N12 13 C1
Framfield Ct EN1 17 C5
Framfield Rd
Ealing W7 86 D1
Islington N5 72 D3
Mitcham CR4 181 A3
Framlingham Cl 2 E5 74 C6
Framlingham Cres
SE9 188 B6
Framlingham Ct 5
RM6 58 B4
Frampton NW1 71 D1
Frampton Cl SM2 217 C1
Frampton Ct 3 W3 111 A4
Frampton Ho NW8 236 D5
Frampton Park Rd E9 74 C1
Frampton Rd TW4 151 A6
Frampton St
NW8 92 B3 236 D5
Francemary Rd SE4 163 C6
Frances Ct
South Norwood SE25 183 D1
Walthamstow E17 53 C3
Frances & Dick James Ct
2 NW7 29 A3
Frances Rd E4 35 C4
Frances St SE18 122 B2
Franche Court Rd
SW17 158 A1
Francis Ave
Bexleyheath DA7 147 C3
Feltham TW13 150 A1
Ilford IG1 79 B6
Francis Barber Cl
SW16 182 B6
Franciscan Prim Sch
SW17 181 A5
Franciscan Rd SW17 181 A6
Francis Chichester Way
SW11 137 A4 268 B1
Francis Cl
6 Cubitt Town E14 120 B2
Littleton TW17 192 C5
West Ewell KT19 215 B4
Francis Ct
12 Deptford SE14 140 D6
Ealing W5 110 B6
Edgware NW7 27 D5
Kingston u T KT5 198 A5
Francis Gr SW19 179 B4
Francis Ho
Harlesden NW10 89 D6
11 Shoreditch N1 95 C6
Walham Green SW10 265 D4
Francis Holland Sch
Belgravia
SW1 115 A2 258 B3
Marylebone
NW1 92 D3 237 C6
Francis Rd
Fortis Green N2 48 D5
Harrow HA1 43 A4
Hounslow TW4 128 D3
Ilford IG1 79 B6
Leyton E10 76 A6
Pinner HA5 40 C4

Francis Rd *continued*
Thornton Heath CR0 204 D2
Wallington SM6 219 C2
Wembley UB6 87 C6
Francis Snary Lo 11 SW18 157 C6
Francis St
Ilford IG1 79 B6
Stratford E15 76 C3
Westminster SW1 115 C2 259 B4
Francis Terr N19 71 C5
Francis Terrace Mews 16 N19 71 C5
Francis Wlk N1 233 C6
Francklyn Gdns HA8 10 C1
Franconia Rd SW4 159 D6
Frank Bailey Wlk E12 78 C2
Frank Barnes Sch NW3 70 B1
Frank Beswick Ho SW6 264 D5
Frank Burton Cl 4 SE7 121 B1
Frank Dixon Cl SE21 161 C3
Frank Dixon Way SE21 161 C3
Frankfurt Rd SE24 161 A6
Frank Godley Ct DA14 190 B5
Frankham Ho 8 SE8 141 C5
Frankham St SE8 141 C5
Frank Ho SW8 270 A4
Frankland Cl
Bermondsey SE16 118 B2
Woodford IG8 37 C5
Frankland Ho 4 SW12 159 B4
Frankland Rd
Brompton SW7 114 B3 256 C5
Chingford E4 35 C5
Franklin Bldg 5 E14 119 C4
Franklin Cl
Greenwich SE13 141 D4
Kingston u T KT1 198 C6
Oakleigh Pk N20 14 A4
West Norwood SE27 160 D1
Franklin Cres CR4 203 C5
Franklin Ho
Beckenham BR2 208 C6
New Cross SE4 141 A3
26 Wapping E1 118 B5
West Hendon NW9 45 D2
Franklin Ind Est SE20 184 C2
Franklin Pas SE9 144 A2
Franklin Pl SE13 141 D4
Franklin Rd
Bexleyheath DA7 147 A4
Penge SE20 184 C3
Walton-on-T KT12 194 A3
Franklins Mews HA2 64 A6
Franklin Sq SW5 254 D1
Franklin's Row SW3 114 D1 257 D2
Franklin St
43 Bromley E3 97 D4
South Tottenham N15 51 C3
Franklin Way CR0 204 A2
Franklyn Rd
Walton-on-T KT12 194 B3
Willesden NW10 67 D2
Franks Ave KT3 199 A5
Franks Ho TW7 131 B1
Frank Slater Ho 4 IG3 58 B1
Frank Soskice Ho SW6 264 D5
Frank St 5 E13 99 A3
Frankswood Ave
Hillingdon UB7 82 B1
Petts Wood BR2, BR5 211 A4
Frank Towell Ct TW14 150 A3
Frank Welch Ct HA5 40 C5
Frank Whymark Ho 4 SE16 118 C4
Franlaw Cres N13 33 A6
Frans Ct HA4 40 A1
Fransfield Gr SE26 162 B1
Frans Hals Ct E14 120 B3
Franshams WD23 8 C2
Frant Cl SE20 184 C3
Franthorne Way SE6 163 D1
Frant Rd CR7 204 D4
Fraserburgh Ho 29 E3 97 B5
Fraser Cl 3 E6 100 A1
Fraser Ct
Battersea SW11 267 A2
Heston TW3 129 A5
Fraser Ho
Brentford TW8 110 B1
40 Clapham SW8 137 D3
3 Woolwich SE18 122 C2
Fraser Rd
Edmonton N9 18 B1
Walthamstow E17 53 D3
Wembley UB6 87 C6
Fraser Regnart Ct 12 NW5 70 D3
Fraser St W4 111 C1
Frating Cres IG8 37 B4
Frazer Ave HA4 62 C3
Frazier St SE1 116 C4 251 A1
Freame Ho N21 17 B5
Frean St SE16 118 A3
Frearson Ho WC1 233 D2
Freda Corbett Cl 10 SE15 140 A5
Frederica Rd E4 20 B4
Frederica St 4 N7 72 B1
Frederick Blg N1 73 C2
Frederick Charrington Ho 4 E1 96 C3
Frederick Cl
Cheam SM1 217 B3
Marylebone W2 114 D6 247 C6
Frederick Cres
Camberwell SW9 138 D5
Enfield EN3 6 C3
Frederick Ct SW6 135 A2
Frederick Gdns
Cheam SM1 217 B3
Thornton Heath CR0 204 D3
Frederick Ho
Ashford TW15 170 A6
Southall UB1 107 B6
Woolwich SE7 122 A3
Frederick Pl SE18 122 D1
Frederick Rd SM1 217 B3
Frederick's Pl
City of London EC2 242 C1
North Finchley N12 30 A6
Frederick Sq 11 SE16 119 A6
Frederick's Row EC1 234 C2
Frederick St WC1 94 B4 233 C1
Frederick Terr E8 73 D1
Frederic Mews SW1 248 A1
Frederic St E17 53 A4
Fredora Ave UB4 83 D3
Fred Styles Ho SE7 143 C6
Fred Tibble Ct RM9 81 A4
Fred Wigg Twr E11 76 D6
Freedom Cl E17 53 A5
Freedom St SW11 136 D3
Freegrove Rd N7 72 A3
Freehold Ind Ctr TW4 150 C6
Freeland Ct
Ealing W5 110 B6
15 Sidcup DA14 168 A1
Freeland Pk N3 29 A1
Freeland Rd W5 110 B6
Freelands Ave CR2 222 D1
Freelands Gr BR1 187 B2
Freelands Rd BR1 187 B2
Freeling Ho NW8 229 C6
Freeling St 7 N1 72 B1
Freeman Cl
Northolt UB5 63 A1
Upper Halliford TW17 193 C5
Freeman Ct SW16 182 A1
Freeman Dr KT8 195 B5
Freeman Ho 13 SW2 160 A4
Freeman Rd SM4 202 B4
Freemans La UB3 105 C6
Freemantle Ave EN3 18 D6
Freemantle St SE17 117 C1 263 A2
Freemasons Rd E16 99 B1
Freemason's Rd CR0 205 C1
Freemens Hos 1 SW9 138 B1
Freesia Cl BR6 227 D3
Freethorpe Cl SE19 183 C2
Freezeland Way UB10 60 D2
Freke Rd SW11 137 A2
Fremantle Ho 14 E1 96 B3
Fremantle Rd
Belvedere DA17 125 C2
Ilford IG6 57 A6
Fremont St E9 96 C6
French Gdns KT12 195 B1
French Pl E1 243 B6
French St TW16 172 C1
Frendsbury Rd SE4 141 A1
Frensham Cl UB1 85 B4
Frensham Ct
Canonbury N5 73 A3
4 London NW9 46 A5
Mitcham CR4 202 B6
Frensham Dr
New Addington CR0 224 A1
Roehampton SW15 156 A2
Frensham Ho 7 KT6 198 A4
Frensham Rd SE9 167 B2
Frensham St SE15 140 A6
Frere St 6 SW11 136 C3
Fresham Ho BR2 208 D6
Freshfield Ave E8 73 D1
Freshfield Cl SE13 142 B1
Freshfield Dr N14 15 B4
Freshfields CR0 207 B1
Freshford St SW17, SW18 158 A1
Freshwater Cl SW17 181 A4
Freshwater Ct UB1 85 C4
Freshwater Rd
Dagenham RM8 59 A1
Streatham SW17 181 A4
Freshwell Ave RM6 58 C5
Fresh Wharf Est IG11 100 D6
Fresh Wharf Rd IG11 100 D5
Freshwood Cl BR3 185 D2
Freston Gdns EN4 15 A6
Freston Pk N3 29 B1
Freston Rd W10, W11 112 D6
Freswick Ho 6 SE8 119 A2
Freta Rd DA6 169 B6
Freud Mus The* NW3 70 A2
Frewell Bldg EC1 241 A4
Frewing Cl BR7 188 C5
Frewin Rd SW18 158 B3
Friar Mews SE27 160 D1
Friar Rd UB4 84 D3
Friars Ave
London N20 30 C6
Roehampton SW15 155 D1
Friars Cl
Chingford E4 20 A1
Ilford IG1 57 B1
Lambeth SE1 251 D3
13 Northolt UB5 84 D4
Friars Ct
5 Wallington SM6 219 B4
Walthamstow E17 35 B2
Friars Gate Cl IG8 37 A6
Friars Gdns W3 89 B1
Friars La TW9 153 D6
Friars Mead E14 120 A3
Friars Mews SE9 166 C6
Friars Place La W3 111 B6
Friars Prim Sch SE1 116 D4 251 D1
Friar's Rd E6 99 D6
Friars Stile Pl 9 TW10 154 A5
Friars Stile Rd TW10 154 A5
Friar St EC4 241 D1
Friars Way W3 89 B1
Friars Wlk
London N14 15 B4
West Heath SE2 124 D1
Friary Cl N12 30 C5
Friary La IG8 37 A6
Friary Park Ct 12 W3 89 A1
Friary Rd
Acton W3 89 B1
London N12 30 C6
Peckham SE15 140 A5
Friary Way N12 30 C6
Friday Grove Mews 11 SW12 159 C4
FRIDAY HILL 20 C1
Friday Hill E4 20 C1
Friday Hill E E4 20 C1
Friday Hill W E4 20 C2
Friday Rd CR4 180 D3
Friday St EC4 117 A6 252 A6
Frideswide Pl NW5 71 C3
Friendly Pl 16 SE13 141 D4
Friendly St SE8 141 C4
Friendly Street Mews SE8 141 C3
Friendship Way E15 98 A6
Friendship Wlk UB5 84 D4
Friends' Rd CR0 221 B5
Friend St EC1 94 D4 234 C2
FRIERN BARNET 31 A6
Friern Barnet La N20 30 C6
Friern Barnet Rd N11 31 A5
Friern Barnet Sch N11 30 D5
Friern Bridge Ret Pk N11 31 B4
Friern Ct N20 14 B1
Friern Mount Dr N20 14 A4
Friern Pk N12 30 B5
Friern Rd SE22 162 A5
Friern Watch Ave N12 30 B6
Frigate Ho 7 E14 120 A2
Frigate Mews SE8 141 C6
Frimley Ave SM6 220 B3
Frimley Cl
New Addington CR0 224 A1
Putney SW19 157 A2
Frimley Cres CR0 224 A1
Frimley Ct DA14 190 C5
Frimley Gdns CR4 202 C6
Frimley Ho CR4 202 C6
Frimley Rd
Chessington KT9 214 A3
Ilford IG3 79 C5
Frimley Way E1 96 D3
Frinstead Ho 1 W10 112 D6
Frinton Ct W13 87 B2
Frinton Dr IG8 36 B3
Frinton Mews IG2 56 C3
Frinton Rd
Newham E6 99 D4
Sidcup DA14 169 A2
South Tottenham N15 51 C3
Streatham SW17 181 A4
Friston St SW6 135 D3
Friswell Pl 1 DA6 147 C1
Fritham Cl KT3 199 C3
Frith Ct NW7 29 A3
Frith Ho
Bethnal Green E2 96 A4
Paddington NW8 236 D5
Frith La NW7 29 A4
Frith Manor Cotts N12 29 B5
Frith Manor Prim Sch N12 29 B5
Frith Rd
Croydon CR0 221 A6
Leyton E11 76 B4
Frith St W1 93 D1 239 C1
Frithville Ct 2 W12 112 C5
Frithville Gdns W12 112 C5
Frizlands La RM10 81 D5
Frobisher Cl HA5 40 D2
Frobisher Cres TW19 148 A4
Frobisher Ct
Belmont SM2 217 B1
6 Forest Hill SE23 162 B2
1 Greenwich SE10 142 B6
Hendon NW9 27 C1
3 Shepherd's Bush W12 112 C4
Frobisher Gdns TW19 148 A4
Frobisher Ho
3 Ealing W5 88 A4
27 Wapping E1 118 B5
Frobisher Mews EN2 5 B1
Frobisher Pas E14 119 C5
Frobisher Pl SE14 140 C4
Frobisher Rd
London N8 50 C5
Newham E6 100 B1
Frobisher St SE10 142 C6
Froghall Cotts EN5 11 B5
Frogley Rd SE22 139 D1
Frogmore SW18 157 C6
Frogmore Ave UB4 83 C3
Frogmore Cl SM3 217 A5
Frogmore Ct UB2 107 B2
Frogmore Est NW10 89 A4
Frogmore Gdns
Cheam SM3 217 A4
Hayes UB4 83 C3
Frogmore Ind Est
Hayes UB3 105 D4
Highbury N5 73 A4
Frognal NW3 70 A3
Frognal Ave
Harrow HA1 42 D5
Sidcup DA14 190 A4
Frognal Cl NW3 70 A3
Frognal Cnr BR7 189 D4
Frognal Ct NW3 70 A2
Frognal Gdns NW3 70 A4
Frognal La NW3 69 D3
Frognal Par NW3 70 A2
Frognal Pl DA14 190 A5
Frognal Rise NW3 70 A4
Frognal Way NW3 70 A4
Froissart Rd SE9 166 A6
Frome Ho SE15 140 C1
Frome Rd N22 50 D6
Frome St N1 95 A5 235 A4
Fromondes Rd SM3 217 A3
Fromow's Cnr 14 W4 111 A1
Frontenac NW10 68 B1
Frontier Works N17 33 C4
Frosbery Ct 23 EN3 7 C6
Frostic Wlk E1 243 D3
Froude St SW8 137 B3
Fruen Rd TW14 149 D4
Fryatt Rd N17 33 B3
Frye Ct 5 E3 97 B4
Fryent Cl NW9 44 C3
Fryent Cres NW9 45 C3
Fryent Ctry Park HA3, HA9, NW9 44 C2
Fryent Fields NW9 45 C3
Fryent Gr NW9 45 C3
Fryent Prim Sch NW9 45 A2
Fryent Way HA9, NW9 44 D2
Fry Ho E6 77 C1
Frying Pan Alley E1 243 C3
Fry Rd
Harlesden NW10 89 D6
Upton Pk E6 77 D1
Fryston Ave CR0 222 A6
Fuchsia St SE2 124 B1
Fulbeck Dr NW9 27 C2
Fulbeck Ho N7 72 B2
Fulbeck Way HA2 24 A1
Fulbourn 9 KT1 176 C1
Fulbourne Rd E17 36 A1
Fulbourne St E1 96 B2
Fulbrook Rd N19 71 C4
Fulcher Ct SE8 141 B6
Fulcher Ho
13 Deptford SE8 119 B1
10 Shoreditch N1 95 C6
Fulford Mans 3 N19 72 A5
Fulford Rd KT19 215 B1
Fulford St SE16 118 B4
FULHAM 134 D3
Fulham Broadway SW6 135 C5 265 B3
Fulham Broadway Sh Ctr SW6 265 B3
Fulham Broadway Sta SW6 135 C5 265 B4
Fulham Bsns Exchange SW6 266 B1
Fulham Cl UB10 83 A3
Fulham Cross Sec Sch SW6 135 A5 264 A3
Fulham Ct SW6 135 C4 265 A2
Fulham High St SW6 135 A3
Fulham Pal* SW6 135 A3
Fulham Palace Rd SW6, W6 134 D6
Fulham Park Gdns SW6 135 B3
Fulham Park Rd SW6 135 B3
Fulham Prep Sch
Fulham SW6 135 A3
Fulham W14 135 A6 264 B6
Fulham Prim Sch SW6 135 C6 265 A5
Fulham Rd
Chelsea SW10 136 A6 266 B6
Fulham SW6 135 B4 264 D2
Fulke Ho E5 74 B5
Fullbrooks Ave KT4 199 D1
Fuller Cl
4 Bethnal Green E2 96 A3
Bushey WD23 8 B4
Orpington BR6 227 D3
Fuller Rd RM8 80 C4
Fullers Ave KT6 214 B6
Fuller's Ave IG8 36 D3
Fullers Ho 6 SW18 157 C6
Fuller's Rd E18 36 D3
Fuller St NW4 46 C5
Fullers Way N KT6 214 B5
Fullers Way S KT9 214 A5
Fuller's Wood CR0 223 C3
Fuller Terr IG1 79 B3
Fullerton Ct TW11 175 A4
Fullerton Rd
Croydon CR0 205 D2
Wandsworth SW18 158 A6
Fuller Way UB3 105 D1
Fullwood Prim Sch IG6 57 A5
Fullwood's Mews N1 235 D2
Fulmar Ct
6 Dulwich SE21 161 B2
10 Ealing W13 86 D3
Surbiton KT5 198 B3
Fulmar Ho
12 Bermondsey SE16 118 D2
Marylebone NW8 237 B5
Fulmead St SW6 265 D1
Fulmer Cl TW12 173 A5
Fulmer Rd E16 99 D2
Fulmer Way W13 109 B3
Fulneck 1 E1 96 C2
Fulready Rd E10 54 B4
Fulstone Cl TW4 129 B1
Fulthorp Rd SE3 143 A3
Fulton Ct EN3 7 C5
Fulton Mews W2 246 A6
Fulton Rd HA9 66 C5
Fulwell Ct
Southall UB1 108 A6
Teddington TW11 174 C6
Fulwell Park Ave TW2 152 A2
Fulwell Rd TW11, TW12 174 B6
Fulwell Sta TW11 174 B6
Fulwood Ave HA0 88 B5
Fulwood Cl UB3 83 D1
Fulwood Ct
Harrow HA3 43 A3
Stanwell TW19 148 B5
Fulwood Gdns TW1 153 A5
Fulwood Pl WC1 240 D3
Fulwood Wlk SW19 157 A3
Furber St W6 112 B3
Furham Field HA5 23 C3
Furley Ho 7 SE15 140 A5
Furley Rd SE15 140 A5
Furlong Cl SM6 203 B1
Furlong Rd N7 72 C2
Furmage St SW18 157 D4
Furneaux Ave SE27 182 D5
Furness Ho SW1 258 C2
Furness Lo 4 SW14 132 D1
Furness Prim Sch The NW10 90 A5
Furness Rd
Harlesden NW10 90 A5
Harrow HA2 41 D1
Morden SM4 201 D3
Sands End SW6 135 D3
Furnival St EC4 94 C1 241 A2
Furrow La E9 74 C3
Furrows The KT12 194 C1
Fursby Ave N3 29 C4
Fursecroft W1 237 C2
Further Acre NW9 27 D1
Furtherfield Cl CR0 204 C3
Further Green Rd SE6 164 C3
Furze Cl WD19 22 C5
Furze Ct CR0 222 A6
FURZEDOWN 181 B6
Furzedown Dr SW17 181 B5
Furzedown Prim Sch SW17 181 A4
Furzedown Rd SW17 181 B5
Furzefield Cl BR7 188 D4
Furzefield Rd SE3 143 B5
Furzeground Way UB11 105 A5
Furzeham Rd UB7 104 A4
Furzehill Rd WD6 11 A6
Furze Inf Sch RM6 59 A3
Furzeland Ho 2 KT3 199 C2
Furze Rd CR7 205 A6
Furze St E3 97 C2
Furzewood TW16 172 A2
Fuschia Ct IG8 36 C4
Fuscia Ct TW13 149 D1
Fusion Ct SW15 155 C1
Futters Ct 1 NW10 89 C5
Fyfe Way BR1 187 A1
Fyfield N4 72 C6
Fyfield Cl BR2, BR3 208 B5
Fyfield Ct E7 77 A2
Fyfield Ho RM9 80 B1
Fyfield Rd
5 Brixton SW9 138 C2
Enfield EN1 5 C2
Walthamstow E17 54 B6
Woodford IG8 37 C3
Fynes St SW1 259 C4

G

Gable Cl HA5 23 C3
Gable Ct SE26 184 B6
Gable Ho 12 W4 111 C2
Gable Lo
Hadley Wood EN4 2 A5
5 North Finchley N12 30 A5
West Wickham BR4 208 A1
Gables Ave TW15 170 B5
Gables Cl
Camberwell SE5 139 C4
Lewisham SE12 165 A3

Gables The
Barking IG11 79 A2
Bromley BR1 187 B3
3 Clapham SW4 137 C2
Ealing W13 87 B1
Hampstead NW3 70 B6
Heston TW5 129 C6
Mitcham CR4 203 B6
Muswell Hill N10 49 A6
North Finchley N12 29 D5
Wembley HA9 66 B5
Gabriel Cl 1 TW13 173 A6
Gabriel Ho SE11 260 C4
Gabrielle Cl HA9 66 B5
Gabrielle Ct NW3 70 B2
Gabriel Mews NW2 69 B6
Gabriel St SE23 163 A4
Gabriel's Wharf SE1 251 A4
Gad Cl E13 99 B4
Gaddesden Ave HA9 66 B2
Gaddesden Ho EC1 235 D1
Gade Cl UB3 106 B5
Gadesden Rd KT19 215 A2
Gadsbury Cl NW9 45 D3
Gadsden Ho
6 Homerton E9 74 D2
8 Kensal Town W10 91 A3
Gadwall Cl E16 99 B1
Gadwall Way SE28 123 B4
Gagarin Ho SW11 136 B2
Gage Rd E16 98 C2
Gage St WC1 240 B4
Gainford Ho 18 E2 96 B4
Gainford St N1 94 C6 234 A6
Gainsboro Gdns UB6 64 C3
Gainsborough Ave
E12 78 C3
Gainsborough Cl
Beckenham BR3 185 C3
Thames Ditton KT10 196 C1
Gainsborough Ct
11 Barnet EN5 1 D1
6 Bermondsey SE16 118 B1
Bromley BR2 209 C5
Dulwich SE21 161 C2
North Finchley N12 29 D5
Shepherd's Bush W12 112 C4
Gainsborough Gdns
Edgware HA8 26 C1
Golders Green NW11 47 B2
Hampstead NW3 70 B5
Isleworth TW7 152 B6
Gainsborough Ho
Dagenham RM8 80 B4
Enfield EN1 18 A6
Finsbury Pk N4 50 B1
3 Hampstead NW3 70 A4
5 Limehouse E14 119 A6
Westminster SW1 259 D3
Gainsborough Lodge
HA1 42 C4
Gainsborough Mews 5
SE26 162 B1
Gainsborough Prim Sch
Hackney Wick E9 75 C2
Newham E15 98 C4
Gainsborough Rd
Bedford Pk W4 111 D2
Dagenham RM8 80 B5
Hayes UB4 83 B5
Leytonstone E11 54 C2
Newham E15 98 C4
New Malden KT3 199 B2
North Finchley N12 29 D5
Richmond TW9 132 B2
Gainsborough Sq
DA6 146 D2
Gainsborough St 3
E9 75 B2
Gainsborough Studios
N1 235 C5
Gainsborough Twr 7
UB5 84 D5
Gainsfield Ct 3 E11 76 C5
Gainsford Rd E17 53 B5
Gainsford St
SE1 117 D4 253 D2
Gairloch Ho 2 NW1 71 D1
Gairloch Rd SE5 139 C3
Gaisford St NW5 71 C2
Gaitskell Ct SW11 136 C3
Gaitskell Ho
Camberwell SE17 139 B6
2 Newham E6 99 D6
3 Walthamstow E17 53 D6
Gaitskell Rd SE9 167 A3
Gaitskell Way SE1 252 A2
Galahad Rd
Edmonton N9 18 A1
Grove Pk BR1 187 A6
Galata Rd SW13 134 A5
Galatea Sq SE15 140 B2
Galaxy Bldg 6 E14 119 C2
Galaxy Ho EC2 242 D6
Galba Ct 1 TW8 131 D5
Galbraith St E14 120 A3
Galdana Ave EN5 2 A2
Galeborough Ave IG8 36 B3
Gale Cl
Hampton TW12 173 A4
Mitcham CR4 202 B6
Gale Ho
10 Brixton SW2 160 B6
Carshalton SM5 218 C3
Galena Ho
5 Hammersmith W6 112 B2
Plumstead Comm SE18 123 D1
Galena Rd W6 112 B2
Galen Pl WC1 240 B3
Galesbury Rd SW18 158 A5
Gales Gdns E2 96 B4
Gale St
Dagenham RM9 80 D1
Tower Hamlets E3 97 C2
Galgate Cl 4 SW19 157 A3
Gallants Farm Rd EN4 14 C3
Galleon Cl SE16 118 D4
Galleon Ho 8 E14 120 A2
Galleons Dr IG11 102 A4
Gallery Ct SW10 266 A5
Gallery Gdns UB5 84 D5
Gallery Rd SE21 161 B3
Galleywall Rd SE16 118 B2
Galleywall Road Trad Est
12 SE16 118 B2
Galleywood Ho 1
W10 90 C2
Gallia Rd N5 72 D3
Galliard Cl N9 18 C5
Galliard Ct N9 18 A5
Galliard Prim Sch N9 18 A4
Galliard Rd N9 18 A5
Gallica Ct SM1 201 D1
Gallions Cl IG11 102 A4
Gallions Mount Prim Sch
SE18 123 D1
Gallions Prim Sch E6 100 D1
Gallions Rd E16 122 D6
Gallions Reach Shp Pk
IG11 101 A2
Gallions Reach Sta
E16 122 D6
Gallions View Rd
SE28 123 C4
Gallon Cl SE7 121 C2
Gallop The
South Croydon CR2 222 B1
Sutton SM2 218 A1
Gallosson Rd SE18 123 C2
Galloway Rd W12 112 A5
Gallus Cl N21 16 B5
Gallus Sq SE3 143 B2
Galpin's Rd CR4, CR7 204 B5
Galsworthy Ave
Ilford RM6 58 B2
Tower Hamlets E14 97 A2
Galsworthy Cl SE28 124 B5
Galsworthy Cres SE3 143 C4
Galsworthy Ct W3 110 D3
Galsworthy Ho 4 W11 91 A1
Galsworthy Rd
Cricklewood NW2 69 A4
Kingston u T KT2 176 D2
Galton Ho SE18 144 B4
Galton St W10 91 A4
Galva Cl EN4 3 A1
Galvani Way CR0 204 B1
Galveston Ho 2 E1 97 A3
Galveston Rd SW15 157 B6
Galway Cl 28 SE16 118 B1
Galway Ho
Finsbury EC1 235 B1
7 Stepney E1 96 D2
Galway St EC1 95 A4 235 B1
Galy 5 NW9 27 D1
Gambetta St 3 SW8 137 B3
Gambia St
SE1 116 D5 251 D3
Gambler Ho EC1 235 B1
Gambole Rd SW17 180 C6
Games Ho 6 SE7 143 C6
Games Rd EN4 2 D2
Gamlen Rd SW15 134 D1
Gamma Ct 9 CR0 205 B1
Gamuel Cl E17 53 C3
Gander Green Cres
TW12 173 C2
Gander Green La KT4, SM1,
SM3 217 B5
Gandhi Cl E17 53 C3
Gandolfi St 5 SE15 139 C6
Ganley Ct 19 SW11 136 B2
Gannet Ct 5 SE21 161 B2
Gannet Ho SE15 139 D4
Ganton St W1 239 B1
Ganton Wlk WD19 22 D6
GANTS HILL 56 C3
Gants Hill IG2 56 C3
Gantshill Cres IG2 56 C4
Gants Hill Sta IG2 56 C3
Gap Rd SW19 179 D5
Garage Rd W3 88 C1
Garand Ct 2 N7 72 B3
Garbett Ho 2 SE17 138 D6
Garbutt Pl W1 238 B3
Garden Ave
Bexleyheath DA7 147 C2
Mitcham CR4 181 B3
Garden City HA8 26 C4
Garden Cl
Ashford TW15 171 A4
Chingford E4 35 C5
Grove Pk SE12 165 B1
Hampton TW12 173 B5
Northolt UB5 85 A6
Roehampton SW15 156 B4
Ruislip HA4 61 D6
Wallington SM6 220 A3
Garden Cotts BR5 190 C1
Garden Ct
5 Belmont SM2 217 C1
10 Eltham SE9 166 C5
Hampton TW12 173 B5
North Finchley N12 29 D5
4 Richmond TW9 132 B4
12 South Acton W4 111 A3
South Croydon CR0 221 D5
4 Stanmore HA7 25 C5
St John's Wood NW8 229 C2
Strand EC4 251 A6
Wembley HA0 65 C5
Wimbledon SW20 178 D2
Gardeners Cl SE9 166 A1
Gardeners Rd CR0 204 D1
Garden Flats SW16 160 A1
Garden Ho
2 Finchley N2 30 B1
12 South Lambeth
SW9 138 A3
Garden Hospl The
NW4 46 C6
Gardenia Ct 1 BR3 185 C3
Gardenia Rd
Bromley BR1 210 C6
Enfield EN1 17 C5
Gardenia Way IG8 37 A5
Garden La
Bromley BR1 187 B4
Streatham SW2 160 B3
Garden Lodge Ct N2 48 B6
Garden Mews W2 245 B5
Garden Pl 28 E2 95 D6
Garden Prim Sch
CR4 203 D6
Garden Rd
Bromley BR1 187 B4
Penge SE20 184 C2
Richmond TW9 132 C2
St John's Wood
NW8 92 A4 229 B2
Walton-on-T KT12 194 B2
Garden Row
SE1 116 D3 261 C6
Garden Royal 16
SW15 156 D5
Garden St E1 96 D2
Gardens The
Beckenham BR3 186 A2
East Bedfont TW14 149 B5
East Dulwich SE22 140 A1
Harrow HA1, HA2 42 A3
Pinner HA5 41 B3
Stamford Hill N16 51 D2
Garden Suburb Jun & Inf
Schs NW11 47 B4
Garden Terr
Knightsbridge SW7 247 B1
Pimlico SW1 259 C2
Garden Way NW10 67 A2
Garden Wlk
Beckenham BR3 185 B2
Shoreditch EC2 95 C3 243 A6
Gardiner Ave NW2 68 C3
Gardiner Cl
Chislehurst BR5 190 C1
Dagenham RM8 80 D4
Enfield EN3 18 D5
Gardiner Ct NW10 89 B6
Gardiner Ho SW11 267 A2
Gardner Cl E11 55 B3
Gardner Ct
Highbury N5 73 A4
Hounslow TW3 129 C2
Tottenham N22 32 D1
Gardner Ho
Feltham TW13 151 B2
Southall UB1 106 D6
Gardner Ind Est SE26 185 B5
Gardner Pl TW14 150 B5
Gardner Rd E13 99 B3
Gardners Cl N11 15 A2
Gardners La EC4 252 A6
Gardnor Mans 14 NW3 70 A4
Gardnor Rd NW3 70 B4
Gard St EC1 234 D2
Garendon Gdns SM4 201 D2
Garendon Rd SM4 201 D2
Garenne Ct 10 E4 20 A3
Gareth Cl KT4 216 D6
Gareth Ct SW16 159 D1
Gareth Gr BR1 187 A6
Garfield
Edmonton N9 18 B3
Enfield EN2 17 B6
Garfield Ho W2 237 C1
Garfield Mews 7
SW11 137 A2
Garfield Prim Sch
London N11 31 C5
Wimbledon SW19 180 A4
Garfield Rd
Chingford E4 20 B3
Clapham SW11 137 A2
Enfield EN3 6 C1
Newham E13 98 D3
3 Twickenham TW1 153 A3
Wimbledon SW19 180 A4
Garford St E14 119 C6
Garganey Ct NW10 67 B2
Garganey Wlk SE28 124 C6
Garibaldi St SE18 123 C2
Garland Ct 12 E14 119 C6
Garland Dr TW3 130 A3
Garland Ho
12 Kingston u T KT2 176 A2
Stoke Newington N16 73 B5
Garland Rd
Plumstead Comm
SE18 145 B5
Stanmore HA7 26 A2
Garlands Ct CR0 221 B4
Garlands Ho NW8 91 D5
Garlands La HA1 42 D1
Garlands The HA1 42 D2
Garlick Hill
EC4 117 A6 252 B6
Garlies Rd SE23 163 A1
Garlinge Ho 12 SW9 138 C4
Garlinge Rd NW2 69 B2
Garman Cl N18 33 B5
Garman Rd N17 34 C3
Garnault Mews EC1 234 B1
Garnault Pl EC1 234 B1
Garnault Rd EN1 5 D5
Garner Cl RM8 58 D1
Garner Rd E17 36 A2
Garner St E2 96 A5
Garnet Ct TW13 149 C1
Garnet Ho KT4 199 B1
Garnet Rd
South Norwood CR7 205 B5
Willesden NW10 67 C2
Garnet St E1 118 C6
Garnett Cl SE9 144 B2
Garnett Ho 5 NW3 70 D3
Garnett Rd NW3 70 D3
Garnett Way 3 E17 35 A2
Garnet Wlk 3 E6 100 A2
Garnham Cl 2 N16 73 D6
Garnham St 1 N16 73 D6
Garnies Cl SE15 139 D5
Garrad's Rd SW16 159 D1
Garrard Cl
Bexleyheath DA7 147 C2
Chislehurst BR7 188 D5
Garrard Ho BR2 209 C5
Garrard Wlk NW10 67 C2
Garratt Cl CR0 220 A4
Garratt Ho 8 N16 51 C1
Garratt La
Upper Tooting SW17,
SW18 180 C6
Wandsworth SW18 157 D3
Garratt Park Sch
SW18 158 A1
Garratt Rd HA8 26 C3
Garratts Rd WD23 8 A4
Garratt Terr SW17 180 C6
Garraway Ct SW13 134 C5
Garraway Ho SE21 161 D1
Garrett Cl W3 89 B2
Garrett Ho
8 Shepherd's Bush
W12 90 B1
Teddington TW11 175 B4
Garrett St EC1 95 A3 242 B6
Garrick Ave NW11 47 A3
Garrick Cl
Ealing W5 88 A3
1 Richmond TW9 153 D6
Wandsworth SW18 136 A1
Garrick Cres CR0 221 C6
Garrick Ct HA8 26 B6
Garrick Dr
Hendon NW4 28 C1
Plumstead SE18 123 B3
Garrick Gdns KT8 195 C6
Garrick Ho
Chiswick W4 133 C6
2 Kingston u T KT1 198 A5
Mayfair W1 248 C3
7 Streatham SW16 181 C5
Garrick Ind Ctr NW9 45 D4
Garrick Pk NW4 28 D1
Garrick Rd
Greenford UB6 85 D3
Richmond TW9 132 C3
West Hendon NW9 45 D3
Garrick's Ait KT8 174 A1
Garricks Ho KT1 175 D1
Garrick St
WC2 116 A6 250 A6
Garrick's Villa TW12 174 A1
Garrick Way NW4 46 D5
Garrick Yd WC2 250 A6
Garrison Cl
Hounslow TW4 151 B6
Shooters Hill SE18 144 C5
Garrison La KT9 214 A1
Garrowsfield EN5 13 B6
Garsdale Cl N11 31 A4
Garsdale Terr SW5 254 D2
Garside Cl
Hampton TW12 173 D4
Plumstead SE28 123 B3
Garside Ct 5 N20 14 D2
Garsington Mews
SE4 141 B2
Garson Ho W2 246 C6
Garston Ho 6 N1 72 D1
Garter Way SE16 118 D4
Garth Cl
Kingston u T KT2 176 B5
Ruislip HA4 40 D1
West Barnes SM4 200 D2
Garth Ct
Chiswick W4 133 B6
11 Harrow HA1 42 D3
Garth Dr N9 18 A2
Garth Ho NW2 69 B6
Garthland Dr EN5 12 C6
Garth Mews W5 88 A3
Garthorne Rd SE23 162 D4
Garth Rd
Child's Hill NW2 69 B6
8 Chiswick W4 111 B1
Kingston u T KT2 176 B5
West Barnes SM4 200 D2
Garth Road Ind Ctr The
SM4 200 D1
Garthside TW10 176 A5
Garth The
Hampton TW12 173 D4
Harrow HA3 44 B3
North Finchley N12 29 D5
Garthway N12 30 C4
Gartmoor Gdns SW19 157 B3
Gartmore Rd IG3 79 D6
Garton Ho 6 N6 49 D2
Garton Pl SW18 158 A5
Gartons Cl EN3 6 C1
Gartons Way SW11 136 A2
Garvary Rd E16 99 B1
Garvens SE19 183 C5
Garway Rd W2 91 D1
Garwood Cl N17 34 B2
Garwood Lo N22 32 B3
Gascoigne Gdns IG8 36 C3
Gascoigne Pl 17 E2 95 D4
Gascoigne Prim Sch
IG11 101 A6
Gascoigne Rd IG11 101 A5
Gascony Ave NW6 69 C1
Gascoyne Ho 2 E9 74 D1
Gascoyne Rd E9 74 D1
Gaselee St E14 120 A6
Gasholder Pl
SE11 116 B1 260 D1
Gaskarth Rd
Balham SW12 159 B5
Burnt Oak HA8 27 A1
Gaskell Rd N6 48 D3
Gaskell St SW4 138 A3
Gaskin Ho N16 73 B5
Gaskin St N1 94 D6 234 C6
Gaspar Cl SW7 255 D4
Gaspar Mews SW5 255 D4
Gassiot Rd SW17 180 D6
Gassiot Way SM1 218 B5
Gasson Ho 24 SE14 140 D6
Gastein Rd W6 134 D6
Gastigny Ho EC1 235 B1
Gaston Bell Cl TW9 132 B2
Gaston Bridge Rd
TW17 193 B3
Gaston Gate SW8 270 C2
Gaston Rd CR4 203 A6
Gaston Way TW17 193 B4
Gataker Ho 5 SE16 118 B3
Gataker St 6 SE16 118 B3
Gatcliff Cl SW1 258 B1
Gatcombe Ct BR3 185 C3
Gatcombe Ho 20
SE22 139 C2
Gatcombe Mews W5 110 B6
Gatcombe Rd
8 Newham E16 121 A5
Tufnell Pk N19 71 D5
Gatcombe Way EN4 2 D2
Gateacre Ct DA14 190 B6
Gate End HA6 22 A3
Gatefield Ct SE15 140 A2
Gateforth St NW8 237 A5
Gate Hill Ct W11 244 D4
Gatehill Rd HA6 22 A3
Gate Ho 4 KT6 198 A1
Gatehouse Cl KT2 177 A3
Gatehouse Sch E2 96 D5
Gatehouse Sq SE1 252 B4
Gateley Ho 6 SE4 140 D1
Gateley Rd SW9 138 B2
Gate Mews
SW7 114 C4 247 B1
Gater Dr EN2 5 B4
Gates 4 NW9 27 D1
Gatesborough St EC2 243 A6
Gates Ct SE17 262 A2
Gatesden WC1 233 B1
Gates Green Rd BR2,
BR4 225 A4
Gateside Rd SW17 158 D1
Gate St WC2 94 B1 240 C2
Gatestone Ct 10 SE19 183 C4
Gatestone Rd SE19 183 C4
Gateway SE17 139 A6
Gateway Arc N1 234 C4
Gateway Bsns Ctr
SE28 123 B3
Gateway Ho
Balham SW12 159 B5
4 Barking IG11 101 A6
3 Upper Tooting
SW17 180 C4
Gateway Mews 4 E8 73 D3
Gateway Prim Sch
NW8 92 B3 236 D6
Gateway Ret Pk E6 100 D3
Gateways KT6 198 A4
Gateways Ct SM6 219 B3
Gateways The
Chelsea SW3 257 B3
Richmond TW9 131 D1
Gateway Trad Est
NW10 89 D4
Gatfield Gr TW13 151 C2
Gatfield Ho TW13 151 C2
Gathorne Rd N22 32 C2
Gathorne St 19 E2 96 D5
Gatley Ave KT19 214 D3
Gatliff Rd
SW1 115 B1 258 C1
Gatling Rd SE18, SE2 124 A1
Gatonby St SE15 139 D4
Gatting Cl HA8 27 A3
Gatting Way UB8 60 A2
Gatton Prim Sch
SW17 180 C6
Gatton Rd SW17 180 C6
Gattons Way DA14 191 B6
Gatward Cl N21 16 D5
Gatward Gn N9 17 D2
Gatwick Ho 3 E14 97 B1
Gatwick Rd SW18 157 B4
Gauden Cl SW4 137 D2
Gauden Rd SW4 137 D2
Gaugin Ct 18 SE16 118 B1

Gauntlet 1 NW9 27 D1
Gauntlet Cl UB5 63 A1
Gauntlett Ct HA0 65 B3
Gauntlett Rd SM1 218 B3
Gaunt St SE1 262 A6
Gautrey Rd SE15 140 C3
Gautrey Sq 5 E6 100 B1
Gavel St SE17 262 D4
Gaven Ho N17 33 C1
Gaverick Mews 3
E14 119 C2
Gavestone Cres SE12 165 B4
Gavestone Rd SE12 165 B4
Gavestone Terr SE12 165 B4
Gaviller Pl 3 E5 74 B4
Gavina Cl SM4 202 C4
Gavin Ho 1 SE18 123 C2
Gawain Wlk N9 18 A1
Gawber St E2 96 C4
Gawsworth Cl E15 76 D3
Gawthorne Ave NW7 29 A5
Gawthorne Ct E3 97 C5
Gay Cl NW2 68 B3
Gaydon Ho W2 91 D2
Gaydon La NW9 27 C2
Gayfere Rd
Redbridge IG5 56 B6
Stoneleigh KT17 216 A3
Gayfere St
SW1 116 A3 260 A5
Gayford Rd W12 111 D4
Gay Ho N16 73 C3
Gayhurst SE17 139 B6
Gayhurst Ct 9 UB5 84 C4
Gayhurst Ho NW8 237 B6
Gayhurst Prim Sch E8 74 A1
Gayhurst Rd E8 74 A1
Gaylor Rd UB5 63 B3
Gaymead NW8 91 D6
Gaynesford Rd
Forest Hill SE23 162 D2
Wallington SM5 218 D1
Gay Rd E15 98 B5
Gaysham Ave IG2 56 D4
Gaysham Hall IG5 56 D6
Gaysley Ho SE11 261 A3
Gay St SW15 134 D2
Gayton Cres NW3 70 B4
Gayton Ct
3 Harrow HA1 42 D3
New Malden KT3 199 D4
Gayton Ho E3 97 C3
Gayton Rd
Abbey Wood SE2 124 C3
Hampstead NW3 70 B4
Harrow HA1 43 A3
Gayville Rd SW11 158 D5
Gaywood Cl SW2 160 C3
Gaywood Rd E17 53 C6
Gaywood St SE1 261 D5
Gaza St SE17 116 D1 261 C1
Gaze Ho 11 E14 98 B1
Gean Ct 3 E11 76 B4
Gearies Inf Sch IG2 56 D4
Gearies Jun Sch IG2 56 D4
Geariesville Gdns IG6 56 D5
Gearing Cl SW17 181 A6
Geary Ho N7 72 B3
Geary Rd NW10 68 A3
Geary St N7 72 B3
GEC Est HA9 65 D6
Geddes Pl 3 DA6 147 C1
Gedeney Rd N17 33 A2
Gedge Ct CR4 202 C5
Gedling Ho SE22 139 D2
Gedling Pl SE1 263 D6
Geere Rd E15 98 D6
Gees Ct W1 238 B1
Gee St EC1 95 A3 242 A6
Geffrey's Ct SE9 166 A1
Geffrye Ct N1 95 C5
Geffrye Mus* E2 95 D5
Geffrye St E2 95 D5
Geldart Rd SE15 140 B5
Geldeston Rd E5 74 A6
Gellatly Rd SE14 140 D3
Gell Cl UB10 60 B5
Gemima Ct SM1 217 C3
Gemini Bsns Ctr E16 98 B3
Gemini Gr UB5 85 A4
Gemini Ho 11 E3 97 C6
Gemma Ct BR3 185 B1
General Gordon Pl
SE18 122 D2
Generals Wlk The EN3 7 A6
General Wolfe Rd
SE10 142 B4
Genesis Bsns Pk
NW10 88 D5
Genesis Cl TW19 148 B3
Genesis Ho KT6 197 D1
Genesta Rd SE18 145 A6
Geneva Cl TW17 171 C1
Geneva Ct
Hendon NW9 45 D4
1 Putney SW15 156 D6
Stoke Newington N16 51 B1
Geneva Dr SW9 138 C1
Geneva Gdns RM6 59 A4
Geneva Rd
Kingston u T KT1 198 A5
Thornton Heath CR7 205 A4
Genever Cl E4 35 C5
Genista Rd N18 34 B5
Genoa Ave SW15 156 C6
Genoa Ho 19 E1 96 D3
Genoa Rd SE20 184 C2
Genotin Rd EN1 5 B2
Genotin Terr EN1 5 B2
Gentleman's Row EN2 5 A2
Gentry Gdns E13 99 A4
Geoffrey Chaucer Tech
Coll SE1 117 B3 262 D5
Geoffrey Cl SE5 139 A3
Geoffrey Ct SE4 141 B2
Geoffrey Gdns E6 100 A5
Geoffrey Ho SE1 262 D6
Geoffrey Jones Ct
NW10 90 A6
Geoffrey Rd SE4 141 B2
George Akass Ho 5
SE18 123 A1
George Beard Rd 11
SE8 119 B2
George Beare Lo 9
SW4 159 C6
George Belt Ho 8 E2 96 D4
George Carver Ho E7 77 A3
George Comberton Wlk 4
E12 78 C3
George Cres N10 31 A3
George Ct
Buckhurst Hill IG9 21 D2
St James WC2 250 B5
George Davies Lodge
IG6 57 A4
George Downing Est
N16 73 D6
George Eliot Ho SW1 259 B3
George Eliot Jun & Inf
Schs NW8 92 B6 229 C6
George Elliot Ho SE17 262 A2
George Elliston Ho 13
SE1 118 A1
George Eyre Ho NW8 229 D3
George Gange Way
HA3 42 D6
George Green's Sec Sch
E14 120 A1
George Groves Rd
SE20 184 A2
George Ho 8 SE26 184 B5
George Inn Yd SE1 252 C3
George La
Hayes BR2 209 B1
Lewisham SE13 164 A5
Wanstead E18 55 B6
Woodford E18 37 A1
George Lansbury Ho
7 Bow E3 97 B4
3 Willesden NW10 67 C1
Wood Green N22 32 C2
George Lashwood Ct 12
SW9 138 B1
George Leybourne Ho 15
E1 118 A6
George Lindgren Ho
SW6 264 D4
George Loveless Ho 4
E2 95 D4
George Lovell Dr EN3 7 C6
George Mathers Rd
SE11 261 C4
George Mews NW1 232 A1
George Mitchell Sch
E10 53 D1
George Parr Ho N21 16 D4
George Peabody Ct
NW1 237 A4
George Rd
Chingford E4 35 C4
Kingston u T KT2 177 A3
New Malden KT3 199 D4
George Row SE16 118 A4
Georges Mead WD6 10 A5
George Spicer Prim Sch
EN1 5 D2
George Sq SW19 201 C6
George's Rd N7 72 B3
George's Sq SW6 264 D6
George St
Barking IG11 79 A1
6 Canning Town E16 98 D1
Ealing W7 108 C5
Hounslow TW3, TW5 129 B3
Marylebone W1 92 D1 237 D2
Richmond TW10 153 D6
Southall UB2 107 A2
South Croydon CR0 221 B6
George Street Sta
CR0 221 A6
George Taylor Ct N9 18 B1
George Tingle Ho
SE1 263 D6
George Tomlinson Prim
Sch E11 54 C1
Georgetown Cl 4
SE19 183 C5
Georgette Pl SE10 142 A5
George Vale Ho 35 E2 96 A5
George V Ave HA2,
HA5 41 C6
Georgeville Gdns IG6 56 D5
George V Way UB6 87 B6
George Walter Ho 11
SE16 118 C2
George Wyver Cl
SW18 157 A4
George Yd
City of London EC3 242 D1
Mayfair W1 115 A6 248 B6
Georgiana St
NW1 93 C6 232 B6
Georgian Cl
Hayes BR2 209 B1
Ickenham UB10 60 A4
Stanmore HA7 25 A3
Georgian Ct
Croydon CR0 205 B1
12 Hackney E9 96 C6
3 Hendon NW4 46 B4
Wembley HA9 66 D2
Georgian Ho HA0 65 A5
Georgian Lo HA5 40 B4
Georgian Village The
E17 54 A6
Georgian Way HA1 64 B6
Georgia Rd
New Malden KT3 199 A5
South Norwood CR7 182 D2
Georgina Ct 5 TW1 153 C5
Georgina Gdns 10 E2 95 D4
Geraint Rd BR1 187 A6
Geraldine Ct 6 NW9 46 A5
Geraldine Rd
Brentford W4 132 C6
Wandsworth SW18 158 A6
Geraldine St SE11 261 C5
Gerald Mews SW1 258 B4
Gerald Rd
Belgravia
SW1 115 A2 258 B4
Dagenham RM8 59 B1
Newham E16 98 D3
Gerard Ave TW4 151 C4
Gerard Ct NW2 68 D3
Gerard Rd
Barnes SW13 133 D4
Harrow HA1 43 A3
Gerards Cl SE16 118 C1
Gerboa Ct 6 E4 36 B5
Gerda Rd SE9 167 A2
Germander Way E15 98 C4
German Sch The
TW10 153 D3
Gernigan Ho SW18 158 B5
Gernon Rd E3 97 A5
Geron Way NW2 68 C6
Gerrard Gdns HA5 40 A4
Gerrard Ho 5 SE14 140 D5
Gerrard Pl W1 249 D6
Gerrard Rd N1 94 D5 234 D4
Gerrards Cl N14 15 C6
Gerrard's Ct W5 109 D3
Gerrard St
W1 115 D6 249 D6
Gerridge Ct SE1 261 B6
Gerridge St
SE1 116 C3 261 B6
Gerry Raffles Sq E15 76 B2
Gertrude Rd DA17 125 C2
Gertrude St
SW10 136 A6 266 B5
Gervase Cl HA9 67 A5
Gervase Rd HA8 27 B2
Gervase St SE15 140 B5
Getters Talmud Torah
N16 51 B2
Ghent St SE6 163 C2
Ghent Way E8 73 D2
Giant Arches Rd
SE24 161 A5
Giant Tree Hill WD23 8 B3
Gibbards Cott 1 IG11 79 D1
Gibbfield Cl RM6 59 A6
Gibbings Ho SE1 251 D1
Gibbins Rd E15 76 A1
Gibbon Ho NW8 236 D5
Gibbon Rd
Acton W3 111 C6
Kingston u T KT2 176 A3
Nunhead SE15 140 C3
Gibbons Mews NW11 47 B4
Gibbons Rd NW10 67 C2
Gibbon's Rents SE1 253 A3
Gibbon Wlk SW15 134 A1
Gibbs Ave SE19 183 B5
Gibbs Cl SE19 183 B5
Gibbs Gn
Edgware HA8 27 A6
West Kensington
W14 113 B1 254 D2
Gibbs Green Rd
W14 113 B1 254 C2
Gibbs Green Sch
W14 113 B1 254 D2
Gibbs Ho
6 Balham SW12 159 B4
2 Bromley BR1 186 D2
Gibbs Rd N18 34 C6
Gibbs Sq SE19 183 B5
Gibraltar Ho NW10 89 C5
Gibraltar Wlk 28 E2 95 D4
Gibson Bsns Ctr 10
N17 33 D3
Gibson Cl
Bethnal Green E1 96 C3
Chessington KT9 213 C3
Isleworth TW7 130 B2
Southgate N21 16 C5
Gibson Ct
9 Friern Barnet N11 30 D5
Hinchley Wood KT10 212 D5
Gibson Gdns N16 73 D6
Gibson Ho
South Croydon CR2 221 A2
Sutton SM1 217 C4
Gibson Rd
Dagenham RM8 58 C1
Ickenham UB10 60 B4
Lambeth SE11 260 D3
Sutton SM1 217 D3
Gibson's Hill SW16 182 C3
Gibson Sq N1 94 C6 234 B6
Gibson St SE10 120 C1
Gideon Cl DA17 125 D2
Gideon Mews W5 109 D4
Gideon Rd SW11 137 A2
Giesbach Rd N19 71 D6
Giffard Rd N18 33 C4
Giffen Square Mkt
SE8 141 C5
Giffin St SE8 141 C5
Gifford Gdns W7 86 C2
Gifford Ho
5 Clapham SW4 137 D1
Greenwich SE10 120 B1
Pimlico SW1 259 A1
Gifford Prim Sch UB5 85 B5
Gifford St N1 72 A1
Gift La E15 98 D6
Giggs Hill BR5 190 A2
Giggs Hill Gdns KT7 197 A1
Giggs Hill Rd KT7 197 A2
Gilbert Cl
Kidbrooke SE18 144 B4
1 Merton SW19 179 D2
Gilbert Ct W5 88 B1
Gilbert Gr HA8 27 B2
Gilbert Ho
Barbican EC2 242 B3
Deptford SE8 141 C6
5 Globe Town E2 96 D4
Pimlico SW1 258 D1
South Lambeth SW8 270 A4
5 Walthamstow E17 54 A6
Gilbert Pl WC1 94 A2 240 A3
Gilbert Rd
Belvedere DA17 125 C3
Lambeth SE11 116 C2 261 B4
Merton SW19 180 A3
Pinner HA5 40 D5
Plaistow BR1 187 A3
Gilbert Scott Inf Com Sch
CR2 223 A1
Gilbert Scott Jun Com
Sch CR2 223 A1
Gilbert Sheldon Ho
W2 236 D4
Gilbertson Ho 11 E14 119 C3
Gilbert St
Enfield EN3 6 C6
Hounslow TW3 130 A2
Leyton E15 76 C4
Marylebone W1 93 A1 238 B1
Gilbey Cl UB10 60 D4
Gilbey Rd SW17 180 C5
Gilbeys Yd NW1 71 A1
Gilbourne Rd SE18 145 D6
Gilby Ho 5 E9 74 D2
Gilda Ave EN3 19 A6
Gilda Cres N16 52 A1
Gilda Ct NW7 28 A2
Gildea Cl HA5 23 C3
Gildea St W1 238 D3
Gilden Cres NW5 71 A3
Gildersome St SE18 144 C6
Gilders Rd KT9 214 B2
Giles Coppice SE19 183 D6
Giles Ho
5 Bermondsey SE16 118 A3
Notting Hill W11 91 C1
Gilesmead SE5 139 B4
Gilfrid Cl UB8 82 D1
Gilkes Cres SE21 161 C5
Gilkes Pl SE21 161 C5
Gillam Ho 9 SE16 118 C2
Gillan Ct SE12 165 B1
Gillan Gn WD23 8 A2
Gillards Mews 6 E17 53 C5
Gillards Way E17 53 C5
Gill Ave E16 99 A1
Gill Ct SE18 123 A2
Gillender St E3 98 A3
Gillespie Prim Sch N5 72 D5
Gillespie Rd N4, N5 72 D5
Gillett Ave E6 100 A5
Gillette Cnr TW7 131 A5
Gillett Ho N8 50 A6
Gillett Pl 27 E8 73 C3
Gillett Rd CR7 205 B5
Gillett St E8, N16 73 C3
Gillfoot NW1 232 A3
Gillham Terr N17 34 A3
Gillian Ho HA3 24 C4
Gillian Park Rd SM3 201 B1
Gillian St SE13 163 D6
Gillies Ct
Sidcup DA14 189 C6
Southgate N21 16 B6
Gillies St NW5 71 A3
Gilling Ct 5 NW3 70 C2
Gillingham Ho SW1 259 A4
Gillingham Mews
SW1 259 A4
Gillingham Rd NW2 69 A5
Gillingham Row SW1 259 A4
Gillingham St
SW1 115 C2 259 A4
Gillings Ct EN5 1 A1
Gillison Wlk 19 SE16 118 A3
Gillman Dr E15 98 D6
Gillman Ho 24 E2 96 A5
Gillray Ho
Chelsea SW10 266 C5
2 Sutton SM1 218 B3
Gills Ct 2 EN5 14 A6
Gill St E14 119 B6
Gillum Cl EN4 14 D3
Gilmore Cl UB10 60 C5
Gilmore Cres TW15 170 C4
Gilmore Ct N11 30 D5
Gilmore Ho SW4 136 D1
Gilmore Rd SE13 142 B1
Gilpin Ave SW14 133 B1
Gilpin Cl
Mitcham CR4 180 C1
Paddington W2 236 B4
Gilpin Cres
Edmonton N18 33 D5
Twickenham TW2 151 D4
Gilpin Ho
9 Edmonton N9 18 A1
New Malden KT3 199 C4
Gilpin Rd E5 75 A4
Gilpin Way UB3 127 B5
Gilray Ho W2 246 C6
Gilsland Rd CR7 205 B5
Gilstead Ho IG11 102 B5
Gilstead Rd SW6 135 D3
Gilston Rd
SW10 114 A1 256 B1
Gilton Rd SE6 164 C1
Giltspur St EC1 94 D1 241 D2
Gilwell Cl E4 7 D1
Gilwell Ct 7 E5 74 B4
Gippeswyck Cl HA5 22 D2
Gipsy Cnr W3 89 B2
Gipsy Hill SE19 183 C5
Gipsy Hill Sta SE19 183 C5
Gipsy La SW15 134 B2
Gipsy Moth IV* SE10 142 A6
Gipsy Rd
Bexley DA16 146 D3
West Norwood SE27 183 B6
Gipsy Road Gdns
SE27 183 A6
Giralda Cl E16 99 D2
Giraud St E14 97 D1
Girdlers Rd W14 112 D2
Girdlestone Wlk N19 71 C6
Girdwood Rd SW18,
SW19 157 A4
Girling Ho 9 N1 95 C6
Girling Way TW14 128 A2
Gironde Rd
SW6 135 B5 264 D3
Girtin Ho
6 Belmont SM2 217 D1
4 Northolt UB5 84 D5
Girton Ave NW9 44 C6
Girton Cl UB5 64 A2
Girton Gdns CR0 223 C5
Girton Ho SW15 156 D5
Girton Rd
Forest Hill SE26 184 D5
Northolt UB5 64 A2
Girton Villas 6 W10 90 D1
Gisbourne Cl SM6 219 D5
Gisburn Ho 23 SE15 140 A5
Gisburn Mans N8 50 B5
Gisburn Rd N8 50 B5
Gissing Wlk N1 72 C1
Gittens Cl BR1 186 D6
Given-Wilson Wlk E13 98 D5
Glacier Way HA0 87 D5
Gladbeck Way EN2 4 D1
Gladding Rd E12 77 D4
Gladebury Ct 2
SW19 179 B4
Glade Cl KT6 213 D6
Glade Gdns CR0 207 A2
Glade La UB2 107 D4
Gladeside
Croydon CR0 206 D3
Southgate N21 16 B4
Gladeside Cl KT9 213 D1
Gladesmore Com Sch
N15 52 A4
Gladesmore Rd N15 51 D3
Glades Sh Ctr The
BR1 187 A1
Gladeswood Rd DA17 125 D2
Glade The
Bromley BR1 187 D1
Charlton SE7 143 C5
Croydon CR0 206 D3
Enfield EN2 4 C3
Hammersmith W12 112 B4
Southgate N21 16 B4
Stoneleigh KT17 216 A2
West Wickham BR4 223 D5
Woodford IG8 21 B1
Gladiator St SE23 163 A4
Glading Terr N16 73 D5
Gladioli Cl 6 TW12 173 C4
Gladsdale Dr HA5 40 B5
Gladsmuir Rd
Barnet EN5 1 A3
Upper Holloway N19 49 C1
Gladstone Ave
Feltham TW14 150 B5
Plashet E12 78 A1
Tottenham N22 32 D1
Twickenham TW2 152 B4
Gladstone Ct
12 Merton SW19 179 C3
Ruislip HA4 61 C6
Westminster SW1 259 D3
Willesden NW2 68 B3
Gladstone Gdns TW3 130 A4
Gladstone Ho
6 Mitcham SW19 180 D1
16 Poplar E14 97 C1
Gladstone Mews
3 Penge SE20 184 C3
Wood Green N22 32 C1
Gladstone Par NW2 68 C5
Gladstone Park Gdns
NW2 68 B5
Gladstone Park Sch
NW10 68 B3
Gladstone Pl KT8 196 C4
Gladstone Rd
Acton W4 111 B3
Buckhurst Hill IG9 21 C3
Farnborough BR6 227 A3

Gladstone Rd *continued*
Kingston u T KT1 . . . . 198 C6
Merton SW19 . . . . 179 C3
Southall UB2 . . . . 107 A4
Surbiton KT6 . . . . 214 A6
Thornton Heath CR0 . . . . 205 B2
Gladstone St SE1 . . . . . 261 C6
Gladstone Terr
SW8 . . . . 137 B4 268 D2
Gladstone Way HA3 . . . . 42 C6
Gladwell Rd
London N8 . . . . 50 B3
Plaistow BR1 . . . . 187 A4
Gladwin Ho NW1 . . . . . . 232 B3
Gladwyn Rd SW15 . . . . . 134 D2
Gladys Dimson Ho E7 . . 76 D3
Gladys Rd NW6 . . . . 69 C1
Glaisdale Sch SM2 . . . . . 217 B1
Glaisher St SE8 . . . . 141 D6
Glamis Cres UB3 . . . . . . 105 A3
Glamis Ct W3 . . . . 110 D4
Glamis Est 3 E1 . . . . . . 118 D6
Glamis Pl E1 . . . . 118 C6
Glamis Rd E1 . . . . 118 C6
Glamis Way UB5 . . . . 64 A2
Glamorgan Cl CR4,
SW16 . . . . 204 A6
Glamorgan Ct 4 W7 . . . 86 D2
Glamorgan Rd KT1 . . . . 175 C3
Glandford Way RM6 . . . . 58 B4
Glanfield Rd BR3 . . . . . . 207 B5
Glanleam Rd HA7 . . . . . . 25 D6
Glanville Ho 4 SW12 . . 159 C4
Glanville Mews HA7 . . . . 25 A5
Glanville Rd
Bromley BR2 . . . . 209 B6
Clapham Pk SW2 . . . . . . 160 A6
Glasbrook Ave TW2 . . . . 151 B3
Glasbrook Rd SE9 . . . . . 165 D4
Glasbury Ho 5 SW9 . . . . 138 B1
Glaserton Rd N16 . . . . . . 51 C2
Glasford St SW17 . . . . . 180 D4
Glasfryn Ct HA2 . . . . 64 B6
Glasgow Ho W9 . . . . 91 D5
Glasgow Rd
Edmonton N18 . . . . 34 B5
Newham E13 . . . . 99 B5
Glasgow Terr
SW1 . . . . 115 C1 259 A1
Glasier Ct 6 E15 . . . . . . 76 C1
Glasse Cl W13 . . . . 109 A6
Glasshill St
SE1 . . . . 116 D4 251 D2
Glasshouse Cl UB8 . . . . . 82 D2
Glasshouse Fields E1 . 118 D6
Glasshouse St
W1 . . . . 115 C6 249 B5
Glasshouse The SE13 . . 142 A1
Glasshouse Wlk
SE11 . . . . 116 B1 260 C2
Glasshouse Yd EC1 . . . . 242 A5
Glasslyn Rd N8 . . . . 49 D4
Glassmill La BR2 . . . . . . 186 D1
Glass St 4 E2 . . . . 96 B3
Glass Yd SE18 . . . . 122 C3
Glastonbury Ave IG8 . . . 37 D4
Glastonbury Ct
12 Deptford SE14 . . . . . . 140 C5
1 Ealing W13 . . . . 109 A5
Glastonbury Ho
London SE12 . . . . 164 D6
Pimlico SW1 . . . . 258 C2
Glastonbury Pl 22 E1 . . . 96 C1
Glastonbury Rd
Edmonton N9 . . . . 18 A3
Morden SM4 . . . . 201 C2
Glastonbury St NW6 . . . . 69 B3
Glaston Ct W5 . . . . 109 D5
Glaucus St E3 . . . . 97 D2
Glazbury Rd
W14 . . . . 113 A1 254 B2
Glazebrook Cl SE21 . . . 161 B2
Glazebrook Rd TW11 . . 174 D3
Gleave Ct 7 N20 . . . . 14 D2
Glebe Ave
Enfield EN2 . . . . 4 D2
Harrow HA3 . . . . 44 A6
Mitcham CR4 . . . . 180 C1
Ruislip HA4 . . . . 62 B2
Uxbridge UB10 . . . . 61 A4
Woodford IG8 . . . . 37 A4
Glebe Cl
1 Chiswick W4 . . . . 111 C1
Uxbridge UB10 . . . . 61 A4
Glebe Cotts
Feltham TW13 . . . . 151 C1
Sutton SM1 . . . . 217 D4
Glebe Cres
Harrow HA3 . . . . 44 A6
Hendon NW4 . . . . 46 C5
Glebe Ct
15 Bromley E3 . . . . 97 D4
Ealing W5 . . . . 109 D5
Hanwell W7 . . . . 108 B6
Lewisham SE3 . . . . 142 C2
Mitcham CR4 . . . . 202 D6
Palmers Green N13 . . . . . 16 C1
Ruislip HA4 . . . . 39 B2
Stanmore HA7 . . . . 25 C5
Glebe Fst & Mid Sch
HA3 . . . . 44 A5
Glebe Gdns KT3 . . . . . . 199 C2
Glebe Ho
8 Bermondsey SE16 . . . 118 B3
Feltham TW13 . . . . 151 C1
7 Woolwich SE18 . . . . . 122 C2
Glebe House Dr BR2 . . 209 B1
Glebehyrst SE19 . . . . . . 183 C6
Glebe La
Barnet EN5 . . . . 12 A5
Harrow HA3 . . . . 44 A5
Glebeland Gdns
TW17 . . . . 193 A3
Glebelands
East Molesey KT8 . . . . . . 195 D5
Leyton E10 . . . . 75 D6
Mitcham CR4 . . . . 202 C6
Glebelands Ave
Ilford IG2 . . . . 57 B2
Woodford E18 . . . . 37 A1
Glebelands Cl
Camberwell SE5 . . . . 139 C2
Finchley N2 . . . . 30 B2
Glebelands Rd TW14 . . 150 A4
Glebe Path CR4 . . . . 202 D6
Glebe Pl SW3 . . 136 C6 267 A6
Glebe Prim Sch UB10 . . . 61 B4
Glebe Rd
Barnes SW13 . . . . 134 A3
Belmont SM2 . . . . 217 A1
Bromley BR1 . . . . 187 A2
Dagenham RM10 . . . . 81 D2
Dalston E8 . . . . 73 D1
Finchley N3 . . . . 30 A2
Hayes UB3 . . . . 105 D5
Hornsey N8 . . . . 50 B5
Stanmore HA7 . . . . 25 C5
Wallington SM5 . . . . 218 D2
Willesden NW10 . . . . 68 A2
Glebe Sch BR4 . . . . 224 B6
Glebe Side TW1 . . . . 152 D5
Glebe Sq CR4 . . . . 202 D6
Glebe St W4 . . . . 111 C1
Glebe The
Chislehurst BR7 . . . . 189 A2
Lewisham SE3 . . . . 142 C2
New Malden KT4 . . . . . . 199 D1
Streatham SW16 . . . . . . 181 D6
West Drayton UB7 . . . . . 104 B2
Glebeway IG8 . . . . 37 C5
Glebe Way
Feltham TW13 . . . . 151 C1
West Wickham BR4 . . . . 224 B6
Gledhow Gdns SW5 . . . 256 A3
Gledstanes Rd
W14 . . . . 113 A1 254 B1
Gledwood Ave UB4 . . . . . 84 A2
Gledwood Cres UB4 . . . . 83 D2
Gledwood Ct UB4 . . . . . . 83 D2
Gledwood Dr UB4 . . . . . . 83 D2
Gledwood Gdns UB4 . . . . 84 A2
Gleed Ave WD23 . . . . 8 B2
Gleeson Dr BR6 . . . . . . 227 D4
Glegg Pl 3 SW15 . . . . . 134 D1
Glenaffric Ave E14 . . . . 120 B2
Glen Albyn Rd SW19 . . . 156 D2
Glenalla Rd HA4 . . . . 39 D2
Glenalmond Ho
Ashford TW15 . . . . 148 A1
2 Putney SW15 . . . . . . 156 D5
Glenalmond Rd HA3 . . . . 44 A5
Glenalvon Way 5
SE7 . . . . 122 A2
Glena Mount SM1 . . . . . 218 A4
Glenarm Coll IG1 . . . . . . 78 D6
Glenarm Rd E5 . . . . 74 D4
Glen Ave TW15 . . . . 170 C6
Glenavon Cl KT10 . . . . . 213 A1
Glenavon Ct KT4 . . . . . . 216 B6
Glenavon Lo 5 E18 . . . . . 55 A6
Glenavon Rd E15 . . . . 76 C1
Glenbarr Cl SE9 . . . . . . 144 D2
Glenbow Rd BR1 . . . . . . 186 C5
Glenbrook N EN2 . . . . 4 B1
Glenbrook Prim Sch
SW4 . . . . 159 D5
Glenbrook Rd NW6 . . . . 69 C3
Glenbrook S EN2 . . . . 4 B1
Glenbuck Ct 6 KT6 . . . . 198 A3
Glenbuck Rd KT6 . . . . . 198 A3
Glenburnie Rd SW17 . . 158 D1
Glencairn Dr W5 . . . . 87 C3
Glencairne Cl E16 . . . . . . 99 D2
Glencairn Rd SW16 . . . 182 A3
Glen Cl TW17 . . . . 192 C5
Glencoe Ave IG2 . . . . 57 C2
Glencoe Dr RM10 . . . . . . 81 C4
Glencoe Mans 6
SW9 . . . . 138 C5
Glencoe Rd UB4 . . . . 84 D3
Glencorse Gn WD19 . . . . 22 D6
Glen Cres IG8 . . . . 37 B4
Glencroft Ct SM1 . . . . . 217 C3
Glen Ct
6 Bromley BR1 . . . . 186 D3
9 Penge SE20 . . . . 184 B2
Sidcup DA14 . . . . 190 A6
Glendale Ave
Edgware HA8 . . . . 26 C6
Ilford RM6 . . . . 58 C2
Wood Green N22 . . . . 32 C3
Glendale Cl SE9 . . . . . . 144 C2
Glendale Dr SW19 . . . . 179 B5
Glendale Gdns HA9 . . . . 44 A1
Glendale Mews BR3 . . . 185 D2
Glendale Way SE28 . . . 124 C6
Glendall St SW9 . . . . . . 138 B1
Glendarvon St SW15 . . 134 D2
Glendevon Cl HA8 . . . . . . 10 D1
Glendish Rd N17 . . . . 34 B2
Glendor Gdns NW7 . . . . . 27 B6
Glendower Gdns 10
SW14 . . . . 133 B2
Glendower Pl SW7 . . . . 256 C4
Glendower Prep Sch
SW7 . . . . 114 B2 256 C4
Glendower Rd
Chingford E4 . . . . 20 B3
Mortlake SW14 . . . . 133 B2
Glendown Ho 2 E8 . . . . . 74 A3
Glendown Rd SE2 . . . . . 124 A1
Glendun Ct W3 . . . . 111 C6
Glendun Rd W3 . . . . 111 C6
Gleneagle Lo BR3 . . . . . 185 C2
Gleneagle Mews
SW16 . . . . 181 D5
Gleneagle Rd SW16 . . . 181 D5
Gleneagles
Ealing W13 . . . . 87 B2
Stanmore HA7 . . . . 25 B4
Gleneagles Cl
21 Bermondsey SE16 . . . 118 B1
Crofton BR6 . . . . 211 B1
South Oxhey WD19 . . . . . . 22 D6
Gleneagles Ct 4
TW11 . . . . 175 A5
Gleneagles Gn 1
BR6 . . . . 211 B1
Gleneagles Twr 2
UB1 . . . . 86 A1
Gleneldon Mews
SW16 . . . . 182 A6
Gleneldon Rd SW16 . . . 182 A6
Glenelg Rd SW2 . . . . . . 160 A6
Glenesk Rd SE9 . . . . . . 144 D1
Glenfarg Rd SE6 . . . . . . 164 B3
Glenfield Cres HA4 . . . . . 39 B2
Glenfield Rd
Ashford TW15 . . . . 171 A4
Ealing W13 . . . . 109 B4
Streatham SW12 . . . . . . 159 C3
Glenfield Terr W13 . . . . 109 B5
Glenfinlas Way SE5 . . . 138 D5
Glenforth St SE10 . . . . 120 D1
Glengall Ct SE23 . . . . . 163 A4
Glengall Gr E14 . . . . . . 120 A3
Glengall Pass 2 NW6 . . . 91 C6
Glengall Rd
Bexley DA7 . . . . 147 A2
Camberwell SE15 . . . . . . 139 D6
Edgware HA8 . . . . 10 D1
Kilburn NW6 . . . . 91 B6
Woodford IG8 . . . . 37 B4
Glengall Terr SE15 . . . . 139 D6
Glengarnock Ave E14 . . 120 A2
Glengarry Rd SE22 . . . . 161 D6
Glen Gdns CR0 . . . . 220 C4
Glenham Dr IG2 . . . . 56 D4
Glenhead Cl SE9 . . . . . . 144 D2
Glenhill Cl N3 . . . . 29 C1
Glen Ho
6 Newham E16 . . . . 122 C5
Wallington SM6 . . . . 219 C4
Glenhouse Rd SE9 . . . . 166 C6
Glenhurst 4 BR3 . . . . . 186 A2
Glenhurst Ave
Gospel Oak NW5 . . . . 71 A4
Glenhurst Ave *continued*
Ruislip HA4 . . . . 39 A1
Sidcup DA5 . . . . 169 B3
Glenhurst Ct 1 SE19 . . 183 D5
Glenhurst Rd
Brentford TW8 . . . . 109 C1
North Finchley N12 . . . . . 30 B5
Glenhurst Rise SE19 . . . 183 A3
Glenilla Rd NW3 . . . . 70 C2
Glenister Ho UB3 . . . . . 106 B5
Glenister Park Rd
SW16 . . . . 181 D3
Glenister Rd SE10 . . . . . 120 D1
Glenister St E16 . . . . . . 122 C5
Glenkerry Ho 1 E14 . . . 98 A1
Glenlea Rd SE9 . . . . 166 C6
Glenloch Ct 2 NW3 . . . . 70 C2
Glenloch Rd
Enfield EN3 . . . . 6 C3
Maitland Pk NW3 . . . . 70 C3
Glenluce Rd SE3 . . . . . . 143 A6
Glenlyon Rd SE9 . . . . . . 166 C6
Glenmead IG9 . . . . 21 C3
Glenmere Ave NW7 . . . . 28 A4
Glen Mews E17 . . . . 53 B4
Glenmill TW12 . . . . 173 B5
Glenmore SW15 . . . . . . 156 D5
Glenmore Ho 6
TW10 . . . . 154 A5
Glenmore Lawns W13 . . 87 A1
Glenmore Rd
Bexley DA16 . . . . 145 D4
Maitland Pk NW3 . . . . 70 C2
Glenmore Way IG11 . . . 102 A5
Glenmount Path 1
SE18 . . . . 123 A1
Glennie Ct SE21 . . . . . . 162 A3
Glennie Ho SE10 . . . . . . 142 A4
Glennie Rd SE27,
SW16 . . . . 160 C1
Glenny Rd IG11 . . . . 79 A2
Glenorchy Cl UB4 . . . . . 85 A2
Glenpark Ct W13 . . . . . 109 A6
Glenparke Rd E7 . . . . . . 77 B2
Glen Rd
Chessington KT9 . . . . . . 214 A5
Newham E13 . . . . 99 C3
Walthamstow E17 . . . . . . 53 B4
Glenridding NW1 . . . . . 232 B3
Glen Rise IG8 . . . . 37 B4
Glenrosa St SW6 . . . . . 136 A3
Glenrose Ct DA14 . . . . . 190 B5
Glenrose Ho 9 SM1 . . . 218 A4
Glenroy St W12 . . . . 90 C1
Glensdale Rd SE4 . . . . . 141 B2
Glenshaw Mans 7
SW9 . . . . 138 C5
Glenshiel Rd SE9 . . . . . 166 C6
Glentanner Way
SW17 . . . . 158 B1
Glen Terr E14 . . . . 120 A4
Glentham Gdns SW13 . . 134 B6
Glentham Rd SW13 . . . . 134 B6
Glen The
Beckenham BR2 . . . . 186 C1
Eastcote Village HA5 . . . . 40 B4
Enfield EN2 . . . . 4 D1
Locksbottom BR6 . . . . . . 226 C5
Rayners La HA5 . . . . 41 A2
Southall UB2 . . . . 107 B1
South Croydon CR0 . . . . 222 D5
Wembley HA9 . . . . 65 D4
Glenthorne Ave CR0 . . 206 C1
Glenthorne Cl SM3 . . . . 201 C1
Glenthorne Gdns
Cheam SM3 . . . . 201 C1
Ilford IG6 . . . . 56 D5
Glenthorne High Sch
SM3 . . . . 201 C1
Glenthorne Mews
W6 . . . . 112 B2
Glenthorne Rd
Friern Barnet N11 . . . . . . 31 A5
Hammersmith W6 . . . . . . 112 B2
Kingston u T KT1 . . . . 198 B5
Walthamstow E17 . . . . . . 53 A4
Glenthorpe SW15 . . . . . 134 A1
Glenthorpe Rd SM4 . . . 200 D4
Glenton Rd SE13 . . . . . . 142 C1
Glentrammon Ave
BR6 . . . . 227 D2
Glentrammon Cl BR6 . . 227 D3
Glentrammon Gdns
BR6 . . . . 227 D2
Glentrammon Rd
BR6 . . . . 227 D2
Glentworth Ct HA8 . . . . . 26 B5
Glentworth St
NW1 . . . . 92 D3 237 D5
Glenure Rd SE9 . . . . 166 C6
Glenview SE2 . . . . 146 D6
Glen View Rd BR1 . . . . . 187 D1
Glenville Ave EN2 . . . . 5 A5
Glenville Gr SE8 . . . . . . 141 B5
Glenville Mews SW18 . 157 C4
Glenville Rd KT2 . . . . . . 176 C2
Glen Wlk TW7 . . . . 152 B6
Glenwood Ave NW9 . . . . 45 C1
Glenwood Cl HA1 . . . . . . 42 D4
Glenwood Ct
7 Sidcup DA14 . . . . 190 A6
6 Wanstead E18 . . . . 55 A6
Glenwood Gdns IG2 . . . . 56 C4
Glenwood Gr NW9 . . . . . 45 A1
Glenwood Ho 3 EN5 . . . 13 D6
Glenwood Rd
Edgware NW7 . . . . 11 C1
Forest Hill SE6 . . . . 163 C3
Harringay N15 . . . . 50 D4
Hounslow TW3 . . . . 130 B2
Stoneleigh KT17 . . . . 216 A2
Glenwood Way CR0 . . . . 206 D3
Glenworth Ave E14 . . . . 120 B2
Gliddon Dr E5 . . . . 74 B4
Gliddon Rd
W14 . . . . 113 A1 254 A2
Glimpsing Gn DA18 . . . . 125 A3
Glisson Rd UB10 . . . . 82 C5
Globe Ct SE18 . . . . 145 A6
Globe Pond Rd SE16 . . . 119 A5
Globe Prim Sch E2 . . . . . 96 C4
Globe Rd
Bethnal Green E1, E2 . . . . 96 C3
Stratford E15 . . . . 76 D3
Woodford IG8 . . . . 37 C4
Globe St SE1 . . 117 B4 252 C1
Globe Terr 9 E2 . . . . 96 C4
Globe Theatre The*
SE1 . . . . 252 A5
GLOBE TOWN 96 D4
Globe View EC4 . . . . 252 A6
Globe Yd W1 . . . . 238 C1
Glossop Ho TW7 . . . . . . 131 A1
Gloster Rd KT3 . . . . 199 C5
Gloucester W14 . . . . . . 254 D3
Gloucester Ave
Camden Town
NW1 . . . . 93 A6 231 B6
Falconwood DA16 . . . . . 145 D1
Sidcup DA15 . . . . 167 C2
Gloucester Cir SE10 . . . 142 A5
Gloucester Cl
Thames Ditton KT7 . . . . . 197 A1
Willesden NW10 . . . . 67 B1
Gloucester Cres
Camden Town
NW1 . . . . 93 B6 231 C6
Staines TW18 . . . . 170 A4
Gloucester Ct
6 Acton W3 . . . . 88 C1
10 Belmont SM2 . . . . . . 217 C1
Borough The SE1 . . . . . . 262 B6
City of London EC3 . . . . 253 B5
Dulwich SE22 . . . . 162 A3
5 Ealing W7 . . . . 86 D2
Golders Green NW11 . . . . 47 B2
Harrow HA1 . . . . 42 C6
Redbridge IG1 . . . . 56 B2
Richmond TW9 . . . . 132 C5
8 Surbiton KT6 . . . . 197 D2
Gloucester Dr
Finsbury Pk N4 . . . . 72 D6
London NW11 . . . . 47 C5
Gloucester Gate NW1 . 231 C4
Gloucester Gate Mews
NW1 . . . . 231 C4
Gloucester Gdns
Cockfosters EN4 . . . . 15 A6
Golders Green NW11 . . . . 47 B2
Paddington W2 . . . . 236 A2
Redbridge IG1 . . . . 56 A2
Sutton SM1 . . . . 217 D6
Gloucester Gr HA8 . . . . . 27 B2
Gloucester Ho
Kilburn NW6 . . . . 91 C5
Richmond TW10 . . . . 154 C6
Gloucester Lo 9
CR0 . . . . 221 D6
Gloucester Mews
Paddington W2 . . . . 236 B1
Walthamstow E17 . . . . . . 53 C2
Gloucester Mews W
W2 . . . . 236 B1
Gloucester Par
Bexley DA15 . . . . 168 A6
Hayes UB3 . . . . 105 A3
Gloucester Pk SW7 . . . . 256 A4
Gloucester Pl
W1 . . . . 92 D2 237 D4
Gloucester Pl Mews
W1 . . . . 92 D2 237 D3
Gloucester Prim Sch
SE15 . . . . 139 C5
Gloucester Rd
Acton W3 . . . . 111 A4
Croydon CR0 . . . . 205 C2
Ealing W5 . . . . 109 C4
Edmonton N18 . . . . 33 D5
Enfield EN2 . . . . 5 A5
Erith DA17 . . . . 125 B1
Feltham TW13 . . . . 150 C3
Hampton TW12 . . . . 173 D3
Harrow HA1 . . . . 41 D4
Higham Hill E17 . . . . 34 D1
Hounslow TW4 . . . . 129 A1
Ilford E12 . . . . 78 B4
Kingston u T KT1, KT2 . . . 176 D1
Leyton E10 . . . . 53 C2
New Barnet EN5 . . . . 14 A6
Richmond TW9 . . . . 132 C5
South Kensington
SW7 . . . . 114 A2 256 A4
Teddington TW11 . . . . . . 174 C5
Tottenham N17 . . . . 51 B6
Twickenham TW2 . . . . . . 152 A3
Wanstead E11 . . . . 55 C4
Gloucester Road Sta
SW7 . . . . 114 A2 256 A4
Gloucester Sq
6 Hackney E2 . . . . 96 A6
Paddington W2 . . 92 C1 237 A1
Gloucester St
SW1 . . . . 115 C1 259 A2
Gloucester Terr
W2 . . . . 92 A1 236 B1
Gloucester Way EC1 . . 234 B1
Gloucester Wlk
W8 . . . . 113 C4 245 B2
Glover Cl SE2 . . . . 124 C2
Glover Dr N18 . . . . 34 C4
Glover Ho
London SE15 . . . . 140 B1
2 South Hampstead
NW6 . . . . 70 A1
Glover Rd HA5 . . . . 40 D3
Glovers Gr HA4 . . . . 38 D2
Glovers Lo 24 TW10 . . . 153 D6
Glowhill Ct N12 . . . . 30 A3
Gloxinia Wlk TW12 . . . . 173 C4
Glycena Rd SW11 . . . . . 136 D2
Glyn Ave EN4 . . . . 2 B1
Glyn Cl SE25 . . . . 183 C2
Glyn Ct
Stanmore HA7 . . . . 25 B4
West Norwood SE27 . . . 160 C1
Glyndale Grange
SM2 . . . . 217 D2
Glyndebourne Ct 5
UB5 . . . . 84 C4
Glyndebourne Pk
BR6 . . . . 226 D6
Glynde Mews SW3 . . . . 257 B5
Glynde Rd DA7 . . . . 147 A2
Glynde Reach WC1 . . . . 233 B1
Glynde St SE4 . . . . 163 B5
Glyndon Rd SE18 . . . . . 123 B2
Glyn Dr DA14 . . . . 190 B6
Glynfield Rd NW10 . . . . . 67 C1
Glyn Mans W14 . . . . 254 B4
Glynne Rd N22 . . . . 32 C1
Glyn Rd
Clapton Pk E5 . . . . 74 D4
Enfield EN3 . . . . 6 C1
North Cheam KT4,
SM3 . . . . 216 D6
Glyn St SE11 . . . . 260 C1
Glynwood Ct 7 SE23 . . 162 C2
Goater's Alley SW6 . . . 264 D3
Goat La EN1 . . . . 5 D5
Goat Rd CR4 . . . . 202 D2
Goat Wharf TW8 . . . . . . 132 A6
Godalming Ave SM6 . . . 220 B3
Godalming Rd E14 . . . . . 97 D2
Godbold Rd E15 . . . . 98 C4
Goddard Cl TW17 . . . . . 192 B6
Goddard Ct HA3 . . . . 25 A1
Goddard Ho SW19 . . . . 156 D2
Goddard Pl N19 . . . . 71 C5
Goddard Rd BR3 . . . . . . 207 A5
Goddards Way IG1 . . . . . 57 B1
Goddarts Ho E17 . . . . . . 53 C6
Godfrey Ave
Northolt UB5 . . . . 85 A6
Twickenham TW2 . . . . . . 152 B4
Godfrey Hill SE18 . . . . . 122 A2
Godfrey Ho EC1 . . . . . . 235 C1
Godfrey Rd SE18 . . . . . . 122 B2
Godfrey St
Chelsea SW3 . . 114 C1 257 B2

Godfrey St *continued*
Mill Meads E15 98 A5
Godfrey Way TW4 151 B4
Goding St
SE11 116 A1 260 B1
Godley Rd SW18 158 B3
Godliman St EC4 252 A6
Godman Rd SE15 140 B3
Godolphin Cl N13 32 D4
Godolphin Ho
Primrose Hill NW3 70 C1
7 Streatham SW2 160 C3
Godolphin & Latymer Sch
W6 112 B2
Godolphin Pl W3 111 B6
Godolphin Rd W12 112 B4
Godson Rd CR0 220 C5
Godson St N1 234 A4
Godstone Ct 1 N16 51 C1
Godstone Ho
Borough The SE1 262 D6
1 Kingston u T KT2 176 D4
Godstone Rd
Sutton SM1 218 A4
Twickenham TW1 153 B5
Godstow Rd SE2 124 C4
Godwin Cl
Shoreditch N1 235 B4
West Ewell KT19 215 A2
Godwin Ct NW1 232 B4
Godwin Ho
2 Haggerston E2 95 D5
Kidbrooke SE18 144 B4
Kilburn NW6 91 D5
Godwin Jun Sch E7 77 B4
Godwin Prim Sch RM9 81 A1
Godwin Rd
Bromley BR1, BR2 209 C6
Forest Gate E7 77 B4
Godwyn Ho 13 KT6 198 A3
Goffers Ho SE3 142 C3
Goffers Rd SE3, SE13 142 C3
Goffs Rd TW15 171 B4
Goffton Ho 14 SW9 138 B3
Goidel Cl SM6 219 D4
Golborne Gdns
5 Kensal Town W10 91 A3
West Kilburn W10 91 B3
Golborne Mews 9
W10 91 A2
Golborne Rd W10 91 A2
Golda Cl EN5 12 D5
Golda Ct N3 29 B1
Goldbeaters Gr HA8 27 C3
Goldbeaters Prim Sch
HA8 27 B2
Goldcliff Cl SM4 201 C2
Goldcrest Cl
Newham E16 99 D2
Woolwich SE28 124 C6
Goldcrest Mews W5 87 D2
Goldcrest Way
Bushey WD23 8 A3
New Addington CR0 224 B1
Golden Cres UB3 105 D5
Golden Cross Mews 2
W11 91 B1
Golden Ct
4 Barnet EN4 2 C1
Ealing W7 108 C6
Hounslow TW3 130 B3
10 Richmond TW9 153 D6
Golden Hinde The*
SE1 252 C4
Golden Hind Pl 5
SE8 119 B2
Golden La EC1 95 A3 242 B5
Golden Manor W7 108 C6
Golden Mews SE20 184 C2
Golden Par 2 E17 54 A6
Golden Plover Cl E16 99 A1
Golden Sq W1 115 C6 249 B6
Golders Cl HA8 26 D5
Golders Ct NW11 47 B2
Golders Gdns NW11 47 B2
GOLDERS GREEN 47 B2
Golders Green Coll
NW11 47 C1
Golders Green Cres
NW11 47 C2
Golders Green Rd
NW11 47 A2
Golders Green Sta
NW11 47 C1
Golders Hill Sch NW11 47 C2
Golderslea NW11 47 C1
Golders Manor Dr
NW11 47 A3
Golders Park Cl NW11 47 C1
Golders Rise NW4 46 D4
Golders Way NW11 47 B2
Golderton 2 NW4 46 C5
Goldfinch Rd SE28 123 B3
Goldhawk Ind Est The
W6 112 B3
Goldhawk Mews 2
W12 112 B4
Goldhawk Rd W12 112 A3
Goldhawk Road Sta
W12 112 C4
Goldhaze Cl IG8 37 D3
Gold Hill HA8 27 B4
Goldhurst Terr NW6 70 A1
Goldie Ho N19 49 D2
Goldie Leigh Hospl
SE2 146 C6
Golding Cl KT9 213 C2
Golding Ct 7 IG1 78 C5
Golding St E1 96 A1
Goldington Cres NW1 232 C4
Goldington Ct NW1 232 C5
Goldington St
NW1 93 D5 232 C4
Gold La HA8 27 B4
Goldman Cl E2 96 A3
Goldmark Ho SE3 143 B2
Goldney Rd W9 91 C3
Goldrill Dr N11 15 A2
Goldsboro Rd
SW8 137 D5 269 D3
Goldsborough Cres E4 20 A2
Goldsborough Ho
SW8 269 D1
Goldsdown Cl EN3 7 A3
Goldsdown Rd EN3 7 A3
Goldsmid St 2 SE18 123 C1
Goldsmith Ave
Acton W3 111 B6
Dagenham RM7 59 C2
Hyde The NW9 45 C3
Plashet E12 78 A2
Goldsmith Cl HA2 41 D1
Goldsmith Ct
Edgware HA8 26 B6
St Giles WC1 240 B2
Goldsmith Ho W3 111 B6
Goldsmith La NW9 45 A5
Goldsmith Rd
Acton W3 111 B5
Friern Barnet N11 30 D5
Higham Hill E17 34 D1
Leyton E10 53 D1
Peckham SE15 140 A4
Goldsmiths Bldgs
W3 111 B5
Goldsmiths Cl W3 111 B5
Goldsmiths Coll, Univ of
London SE14 141 A4
Goldsmith's Ct N6 49 B3
Goldsmith's Pl 6 NW6 91 D6
Goldsmith's Row E2 96 A5
Goldsmith's Sq 17 E2 96 A5
Goldsmith St EC2 242 B2
Goldthorpe NW1 232 A5
Goldwell Ho SE22 139 C1
Goldwell Rd CR7 204 B5
Goldwin Cl SE14 140 C4
Goldwing Cl E16 99 A1
Golf Cl
South Norwood
SW16 182 C2
Stanmore HA7 25 C3
Golf Club Dr KT2 177 B3
Golfe Ho IG1 79 B5
Golfe Rd IG1 79 B5
Golfers View N12 30 B6
Golf Rd
Bromley BR1 210 C6
Ealing W5 88 B1
Golf Side TW2 152 B1
Golfside Cl N20 14 C1
Golf Side Cl KT3 177 C1
Gollogly Terr 9 SE7 121 C1
Gomer Gdns TW11 175 A4
Gomer Pl TW11 175 A4
Gomm Rd SE16 118 C3
Gomshall Ave SM6 220 A3
Gondar Gdns NW6 69 B3
Gondar Mans NW6 69 B3
Gonson St SE8 141 D6
Gonston Cl SW19 157 A2
Gonville Cres UB5 63 D2
Gonville Ct 6 EN4 14 D3
Gonville Ho 6 SW15 156 D5
Gonville Prim Sch
CR7 204 B4
Gonville Rd CR7 204 B4
Gonville St SW6 135 A2
Gooch Ho
Holborn EC1 241 A4
Gooch Ho *continued*
Lower Clapton E5 74 B5
Goodall Ho 10 SE4 140 D1
Goodall Rd E11 76 A5
Goodbehere Ho 7
SE27 183 A6
Gooden Ct HA1 64 C5
Goodenough Coll
WC1 94 B3 240 C6
Goodenough Rd
SW19 179 B3
Goodey Rd IG11 79 D1
Goodfaith Ho 18 E14 119 D6
Goodge Pl W1 239 B3
Goodge St W1 93 C2 239 B3
Goodge Street Sta
W1 93 D2 239 C4
Goodhall Cl HA7 25 B4
Goodhall St NW10 89 D4
Good Hart Pl E14 119 A6
Goodhart Way BR4 208 C3
Goodhew Rd CR0 206 A3
Goodhope Ho 17 E14 119 D6
Gooding Cl KT3 199 A4
Goodinge Cl N7 72 A2
Goodinge Rd N7 72 A2
Gooding Ho 4 SE7 121 C1
Goodison Cl WD23 8 A6
Goodland Ho 1 KT3 199 C2
Goodman Cres SW2 159 D2
Goodman Rd E10 54 A2
Goodmans Ct HA0 65 D4
Goodman's Stile 17 E1 96 A1
Goodman's Yd E1,
EC3 117 D6 253 C6
GOODMAYES 58 B1
Goodmayes Ave IG3 58 A1
Goodmayes Hospl IG3 58 A4
Goodmayes La IG3 80 A5
Goodmayes Lodge
RM8 80 A4
Goodmayes Prim Sch
IG3 58 B1
Goodmayes Rd IG3 58 A1
Goodmayes Ret Pk
RM6 58 B2
Goodmayes Sta IG3 58 A1
Goodrich Com Sch
SE22 162 A5
Goodrich Ct 9 W10 90 D1
Goodrich Ho
20 Bethnal Green E2 96 C5
Stamford Hill N16 51 C2
Goodrich Rd SE22 162 A5
Goodridge Ho E17 36 A3
Good Shepherd RC Prim
Sch
Catford BR1 186 D6
New Addington CR0 223 D1
Good Shepherd RC Prim
Sch The W12 111 D4
Goodson Ho SM4 202 A2
Goodson Rd NW10 67 C1
Goodspeed Ho 20
E14 119 D6
Goodsway NW1 94 A5 233 A4
Goodway Gdns E14 98 B1
Goodwill Ho 22 E14 119 D6
Goodwin Cl
Bermondsey
SE16 117 D3 263 D5
Mitcham CR4 202 B6
Goodwin Ct
East Barnet EN4 14 C5
Hornsey N8 50 A6
2 Mitcham SW19 180 C3
Goodwin Dr DA14 168 D2
Goodwin Gdns CR0,
CR2 220 D2
Goodwin Ho
Edmonton N9 18 C3
2 Peckham SE15 140 B2
Goodwin Rd
Croydon CR0 220 D3
Edmonton N9 18 D3
Shepherd's Bush W12 112 A4
Goodwins Ct WC2 250 A6
Goodwin St N4 72 C6
Goodwood Ave EN3 6 C6
Goodwood Cl
Morden SM4 201 C5
11 Stanmore HA7 25 C5
Goodwood Ct W1 238 D4
Goodwood Dr UB5 63 C2
Goodwood Ho
3 Acton Green W4 111 A1
Penge SE26 184 B4
Goodwood Lo 1
SM6 219 D5
Goodwood Mans 3
SW9 138 C2
Goodwood Par BR3 207 A5
Goodwood Rd SE14 141 A5
Goodwyn Ave NW7 27 C5
Goodwyn Sch NW7 28 A5
Goodwyn's Vale N10 31 B2
Goodyear Ho 8 N2 30 B1
Goodyers Gdns NW4 46 D4
Goosander Ct 34 NW9 27 D1
Goosander Way SE18,
SE28 123 B3
Gooseacre La HA3 43 D4
Goose Green Cl BR5 190 A1
Goose Green Prim Sch
SE22 139 D1
Goose Green Trad Est
SE22 140 A1
Gooseley La E6 100 C4
Goose Sq 8 E6 100 B1
Goossens Cl 1 SM1 218 A3
Gophir La EC4 252 C6
Gopsall St N1 95 B6 235 D5
Gordon Ave
Chingford E4 36 C4
Isleworth TW1 153 B6
Mortlake SW14 133 C1
Stanmore HA7 25 A4
Gordonbrock Prim Sch
SE4 163 C6
Gordonbrock Rd SE4 163 C6
Gordon Cl E17 53 C3
Gordon Cres
Croydon CR0 205 D1
Hayes UB3 106 A2
Gordon Ct
Edgware HA8 26 B5
Hampton TW12 174 A5
5 Shepherd's Bush
W12 90 C1
18 Wimbledon SW20 178 D3
Gordondale Rd SW18,
SW19 157 C2
Gordon Dr TW17 193 B2
Gordon Gdns HA8 26 D1
Gordon Gr SE5 138 D3
Gordon Hill EN2 5 A4
Gordon Hill Sta EN2 4 D4
Gordon Ho
2 Ealing W5 88 A4
Lee SE12 165 A4
17 Shadwell E1 118 C6
Gordon Hospl The
SW1 115 D2 259 C3
Gordon House Rd
NW5 71 A4
Gordon Inf Sch IG1 79 B5
Gordon Lo N16 51 B1
Gordon Mans
3 Barnet EN5 1 B1
Marylebone WC1 239 C5
Gordon Pl W8 113 C4 245 B2
Gordon Prim Sch
SE9 144 B1
Gordon Rd
Ashford TW15 148 A1
Avery Hill DA15 167 C6
Barking IG11 101 C6
Beckenham BR3 207 B6
Chingford E4 20 C4
Chiswick W4 132 D6
Claygate KT10 212 C1
Dagenham RM6 59 B3
Ealing W13 109 C6
Edmonton N9 18 B2
Enfield EN2 5 B3
Finchley N3 29 B3
Harrow HA3 42 C6
Ilford IG1 79 B5
Isleworth TW3 130 A1
Kingston u T KT2 176 B2
Leyton E15 76 A4
Peckham SE15 140 B3
Richmond TW9 132 B3
Shepperton TW17 193 B3
Southall UB2 107 A2
Surbiton KT5 198 B2
Wallington SM5 218 D2
Wanstead E11 55 A3
Woodford E18 37 B2
Wood Green N11 31 D3
Yiewsley UB7 104 A6
Gordon Sq
WC1 93 D3 239 D6
Gordon St
Bloomsbury
WC1 93 D3 239 C6
Newham E13 99 A4
Gordon Way
Barnet EN5 1 B1
Gordon Way *continued*
Bromley BR1 187 A2
Gore Ct NW9 44 C4
Gorefield Ho NW6 91 C5
Gorefield Pl NW6 91 C5
Gore Rd
Hackney E9 96 C6
Merton SW20 178 C1
Goresbrook Rd RM9 102 D6
Gore St SW7 114 A3 256 B6
Gorham Ho 12 SW4 159 C5
Gorham Pl W11 244 A5
Goring Gdns RM8 80 C4
Goring Rd N11 32 A4
Goring St EC3 243 B2
Goring Way UB6 86 A5
Gorleston Rd N15 51 B4
Gorleston St
W14 113 A2 254 B4
Gorman Rd SE18 122 B2
Gorringe Park Ave
CR4 181 A3
Gorringe Park Prim Sch
CR4 181 A2
Gorse Cl E16 99 A1
Gorsefield Ho 6 E14 119 C6
Gorse Rd CR0 223 C5
Gorse Rise SW17 181 A5
Gorse Wlk UB7 82 A1
Gorst Rd
London SW11 158 D5
North Acton NW10 89 B3
Gorsuch Pl 1 E2 95 D4
Gorsuch St E2 95 D4
Gosberton Rd SW12 159 A3
Gosbury Hill KT9 214 A4
Gosfield Rd RM8 59 C1
Gosfield St W1 93 C2 239 A3
Gosford Gdns IG4 56 B4
Gosford Ho 25 E3 97 B5
Goshawk Gdns UB4 83 C5
Goslett Yd WC2 239 D2
Gosling Cl UB6 85 C4
Gosling Ho 2 E1 118 C6
Gosling Way SW9 138 C4
Gosmore Ct N9 18 B2
Gospatric Home Ho
SW14 133 C2
Gospatrick Rd N17 33 A2
GOSPEL OAK 71 A4
Gospel Oak Prim Sch
NW5 71 A4
Gospel Oak Sta NW5 71 A4
Gosport Ho 9 SW15 156 A3
Gosport Rd E17 53 B4
Gosport Wlk N17 52 B5
Gossage Rd
Hillingdon UB10 60 B1
Plumstead SE18 123 B1
Gosset St E2 96 A4
Gosshill Rd BR7 188 C1
Gossington Cl BR7 188 D6
Gosterwood St SE8 141 A6
Gostling Rd TW2 151 C3
Goston Gdns CR7 204 C6
Goswell Pl EC1 234 D1
Goswell Rd
EC1 94 D4 234 D2
Gothic Ct
17 Camberwell SE5 139 A5
Harlington UB3 127 B6
Gothic Rd TW2 152 B2
Gottfried Mews NW5 71 C4
Goudhurst Ho 7
SE20 184 C3
Goudhurst Rd BR1 186 D5
Gough Ho
Islington N1 234 D6
4 Kingston u T KT1 176 A1
Gough Rd
Enfield EN1 6 B3
Stratford E15 76 D4
Gough Sq EC4 94 C1 241 B2
Gough St WC1 94 B3 240 D5
Gough Wlk 14 E14 97 C1
Gould Ct SE19 183 C5
Goulden Ho SW11 136 C3
Goulding Gdns CR7 183 A1
Gouldman Ho 33 E1 96 C3
Gould Rd
East Bedfont TW14 149 C4
Twickenham TW2 152 C3
Gould's Gn UB8 104 D6
Gould Terr 26 E8 74 B3
Goulston St E1 95 D1 243 C2
Goulton Rd E5 74 B4
Gourley Pl N15 51 C4
Gourley St N15 51 C4
Gourock Rd SE9 166 C6
Govan St E2 96 A6
Gover Ct 8 SW4 138 A3
Government Row EN3 7 C6
Govett Ave TW17 193 A4
Govier Cl E15 76 C1
Gowan Ave
SW6 135 A4 264 A2
Gowan Ho 22 E2 95 D4
Gowan Lea 4 E18 55 A5
Gowan Rd NW10 68 B2
Gower Cl SW4 159 C5
Gower Ct WC1 239 C6
Gower Ho
Barking IG11 79 A1
Hayes UB3 105 C6
Upper Tooting SW17 180 B4
12 Walthamstow E17 53 D6
Walworth SE17 262 B2
Gower House Sch
NW9 67 A6
Gower Mews WC1 239 D4
Gower Pl NW1,
WC1 93 D3 239 C6
Gower Rd
Hounslow TW7 130 D6
Upton E7 77 A2
Gower Sch The N7 72 A2
Gower St WC1 93 D3 239 C5
Gower's Wlk E1 96 A1
Gowland Pl BR3 185 B1
Gowlett Rd SE15 140 A2
Gowlland Cl CR0 206 A2
Gowrie Rd SW11 137 A2
Graburn Way KT8 196 B6
Grace Ave DA7 147 B3
Grace Bsns Ctr CR4 202 D3
Gracechurch St EC2,
EC4 252 D6
Grace Cl
Burnt Oak HA8 27 A3
Mottingham SE9 165 D1
Grace Ct
5 Croydon CR0 220 D5
Twickenham TW2 152 C2
Gracedale Rd SW16 181 B5
Gracedyer Ho N22 32 A3
Gracefield Gdns
SW16 160 A1
Gracehill 2 E1 96 C2
Grace Ho
Kennington SE11 270 D6
Penge SE26 184 B5
Grace Jones Cl E8 74 A2
Grace Path 2 SE26 184 C6
Grace Pl E3 97 D4
Grace Rd CR0 205 A3
Graces Alley 14 SE1 118 A6
Graces Mews NW8 229 B3
Grace's Mews SE5 139 C3
Grace's Rd SE5 139 C3
Grace St E3 97 D4
Gradient The SE26 184 A6
Graeme Ct UB6 85 D4
Graeme Rd EN1 5 C3
Graemesdyke Ave
SW14 132 D1
Grafton Cl
Ealing W13 87 A1
Twickenham TW4 151 B3
Worcester Pk KT4 215 C5
Grafton Cres NW1 71 B2
Grafton Ct
10 Dalston E8 74 A3
East Bedfont TW14 149 B3
Grafton Gdns
Dagenham RM8 81 A6
Harringay N4 51 A3
Grafton Ho
16 Bow E3 97 C4
12 Deptford SE8 119 B1
Grafton Jun & Inf Schs
RM8 81 B6
Grafton Mans SW4 137 C1
Grafton Mews W1 239 A5
Grafton Park Rd KT4 215 C6
Grafton Pl
NW1 93 D4 232 D1
Grafton Prim Sch N7 72 A5
Grafton Rd
Acton W3 111 A6
Dagenham RM8 81 A6
Enfield EN2 4 B2
Gospel Oak NW5 71 A3
Harrow HA1 42 A4
Kingston u T KT3 199 C6
Thornton Heath CR0 204 C1
Worcester Pk KT4 215 C5
Grafton Sq SW4 137 C2

Grafton St W1 115 B6 248 D5
Grafton Terr NW5 71 A3
Grafton Way
East Molesey KT8 195 B5
Marylebone W1 239 B5
Grafton Yd NW5 71 B2
Graham Ave
Ealing W13 109 B4
Mitcham CR4 181 A2
Graham Cl CR0 223 C6
Graham Ct
Bromley BR1 187 B3
5 Deptford SE14 140 D6
Northolt UB5 63 B3
GRAHAME PARK 27 C2
Grahame Park Way NW7, NW9 27 D2
Grahame White Ho HA3 43 D6
Graham Gdns KT6 198 A1
Graham Ho
5 Balham SW12 159 B4
6 Barnet EN5 1 D1
Edmonton N9 18 C3
6 Tufnell Pk N19 71 D4
Woolwich SE18 144 D5
Graham Lo
Edgware HA8 26 B4
Hendon NW4 46 B3
Graham Mans
11 Barking IG11 80 A1
2 Hackney E8 74 B2
Graham Rd
Acton W4 111 B3
Bexleyheath DA6 147 C1
Dalston E8 74 A2
Hampton TW12 173 C6
Harringay N15 50 D6
Harrow HA3 42 C6
Hendon NW4 46 B3
Merton SW19 179 B3
Mitcham CR4 181 A2
Newham E13 99 A3
Graham St N1 94 D5 234 D3
Graham Terr SW1 115 A2 258 B3
Graham Twr W3 110 D3
Grainger Cl UB5 64 A3
Grainger Ct 22 SE5 139 A5
Grainger Rd
Isleworth TW7 130 D3
Tottenham N22 33 A2
Gramer Cl E11 76 B6
Grampian Cl
Harlington UB3 127 B5
Orpington BR6 211 D3
15 Sutton SM2 218 A1
Grampian Gdns NW2 47 A1
Grampians The 10 W14 112 D4
Gramsci Way SE6 163 D1
Granada St SW17 180 D5
Granard Ave SW15 156 B6
Granard Bsns Ctr NW7 27 C4
Granard Ho 20 E9 74 D2
Granard Prim Sch SW15 156 B5
Granard Rd SW11, SW12 158 D4
Granary Cl N9 18 C4
Granary Ct 3 RM6 58 D2
Granary Mans SE28 123 A4
Granary Rd E1 96 B3
Granary Sq N1 72 C2
Granary St NW1 93 D6 232 C5
Granary The SE8 141 C5
Granby Ho 13 SE18 122 B2
Granby Pl SE1 251 A1
Granby Rd
Eltham SE9 144 B2
Woolwich SE18 122 D3
Granby St
Bethnal Green E2 96 A3
Shoreditch E2 243 D6
Granby Terr NW1 93 C5 232 A3
Grand Arc N12 30 A5
Grand Ave
Clerkenwell EC1 241 D4
Fortis Green N10 49 A5
Tolworth KT5 198 D3
Wembley HA9 66 C3
Grand Ave E HA9 66 D3
Grand Avenue Prim Sch KT5 199 A3
Grand Ct RM8 81 A5
Grand Depot Rd SE18 122 C1
Grand Dr
Southall UB2 108 A4
West Barnes SM4, SW20 200 C5
Granden Rd SW16 182 A1
Grandfield Ct W4 133 B6
Grandison Rd
London SW11 158 D6
North Cheam KT4 216 C5
Grand Junction Wharf N1 235 A3
Grand Par
London N4 50 D3
Mortlake SW14 133 A1
Tolworth KT6 198 C1
Wembley HA9 66 C6
Grand Union Cl W9 91 B2
Grand Union Cres E8 96 A6
Grand Union Ind Est NW10 88 D5
Grand Union Way UB2 107 C4
Grand Vitesse Ind Est SE1 251 D3
Granfield St SW11 266 D1
Grange Ave
East Barnet EN4 14 D3
North Finchley N12 30 A5
South Norwood SE25 183 C1
Stanmore HA7 25 C1
Totteridge N20 13 A4
Twickenham TW2 152 C2
Woodford IG8 37 A3
Grange Cl
East Molesey KT8 195 D5
Edgware HA8 27 A5
Hayes UB3 83 C2
Heston TW5 129 B6
Sidcup DA15 168 A1
Woodford IG8 37 A3
Grangecliffe Gdns SE25 183 C1
Grangecourt Rd N16 51 C1
Grange Cres SE28 102 C1
Grange Ct
Belmont SM2 217 D1
4 Finchley N12 30 A4
Hackbridge SM6 219 B5
Harrow HA1 64 D5
Ilford IG6 57 A6
Littleton TW17 192 C5
Loughton IG10 21 D6
Northolt UB5 84 C5
Peckham SE15 139 D3
Pinner HA5 41 A6
Strand WC2 240 D1
Wembley HA0 65 C3
1 Willesden NW10 67 C4
Grange Dr BR7 188 B4
Grange Farm Cl HA2 64 A6
Grange Farm Est TW17 193 C6
Grangefield NW1 72 A1
Grange Fst & Mid Schs HA2 41 D1
Grange Gdns
London N14 15 D3
Pinner HA5 41 A5
South Norwood SE25 183 C1
West Hampstead NW3 69 D5
Grange Gr N1 73 A2
Grange Hill
Edgware HA8 27 A5
South Norwood SE25 183 C1
Grangehill Pl SE9 144 B2
Grangehill Rd SE9 144 B1
Grange Ho
6 Barking IG11 101 B6
Bermondsey SE1 263 C5
Willesden NW10 68 B1
Grange La SE21 161 D2
Grange Lo SW19 178 D4
Grange Mans KT17 215 D1
Grangemill 11 NW5 71 B4
Grangemill Rd SE6 163 C2
GRANGE MILLS 113 C3
Grange Mills SW12 159 C3
Grangemill Way SE6 163 C2
GRANGE PARK 16 C6
Grange Park Ave N21 17 A5
Grange Park Jun & Inf Schs UB4 83 D3
Grange Park Pl SW20 178 B3
Grange Park Prep Sch N21 16 D5
Grange Park Prim Sch N21 4 C1
Grange Park Rd
Leyton E10 53 D1
South Norwood CR7 205 B6
Grange Park Sta N21 16 D5
Grange Pk W5 110 A5
Grange Pl NW6 69 C1
Grange Prim Sch
Bermondsey SE1 117 C3 263 A5
Ealing W5 109 D4
Newham E13 98 D4
Grange Rd
Barnes SW13 134 A4
Belmont SM2 217 C1
Bermondsey SE1 117 D3 263 C5
Borehamwood WD6 10 B6
Burnt Oak HA8 27 B4
Chessington KT9 214 A4
Ealing W5 110 A5
East Molesey KT8 195 D5
Greenhill HA1 43 A4
Gunnersbury W4 110 D1
Hayes UB3 83 C1
Highgate N6 49 A3
Ilford IG1 79 A4
Kingston u T KT1 198 A6
Leyton E10 53 C1
Newham E13 98 D4
Orpington BR6 227 A6
Roxeth HA2 64 B6
Southall UB1 107 A4
South Norwood SE19, SE25 183 B1
Tottenham N17 34 A4
Walthamstow E17 53 A4
Willesden NW10 68 B2
Grange St N1 235 D5
Grange The
Bermondsey SE1 117 D3 263 C5
Cockfosters EN4 2 D2
Croydon CR0 223 B6
Ealing W13 87 C2
7 Gunnersbury W4 110 D1
Hammersmith W12 112 B3
19 Maitland Pk NW3 70 D2
South Acton W3 110 D4
3 Walthamstow E17 53 A4
4 Wanstead E18 55 A6
Wembley HA0 66 C1
West Barnes KT3 200 A4
West Ewell KT19 215 B4
West Kensington W14 113 B2 254 C3
Wimbledon SW19 178 D4
Grange Vale SM2 217 D1
Grange View Rd N20 14 A3
Grangeway
London N12 29 D6
South Hampstead NW6 69 C1
Woodford IG8 37 C6
Grangeway Gdns IG4 56 A4
Grangeway The N21 16 D5
Grange Wlk SE1 117 D3 263 C5
Grangewood DA5 169 B3
Grangewood Cl HA5 40 A4
Grangewood Ind Sch E7 77 D1
Grangewood La BR3 185 B4
Grangewood Sch HA5 39 D4
Grangewood St E6 99 D6
Grange Yd SE1 117 D3 263 C5
Granham Gdns N9 17 D2
Granite Apts E15 76 B2
Granite St SE18 123 D1
Granleigh Rd E11 76 C6
Grannary The 10 SE16 118 C4
Gransden Ave E8 74 B1
Gransden Ho 1 SE8 119 B1
Gransden Rd W12 111 D4
Grantbridge St N1 94 D5 234 D4
Grantchester 12 KT1 176 C1
Grantchester Cl HA1 64 D5
Grant Cl
London N14 15 C4
Shepperton TW17 192 D3
Tottenham N17 33 C1
Grant Ct
2 Chingford E4 20 A3
11 Hendon NW9 27 D1
Grantham Cl HA8 10 A1
Grantham Ct
Dagenham RM6 59 B2
Kingston u T KT2 175 D5
9 Rotherhithe SE16 118 D4
Grantham Gdns RM6 59 B2
Grantham Gn WD6 11 A6
Grantham Ho
Ashford TW16 171 C3
12 Peckham SE15 140 A6
Grantham Pl W1 248 C3
Grantham Rd
Chiswick W4 133 C5
Little Ilford E12 78 C4
South Lambeth SW9 138 A3
Grant Ho
38 Clapham SW8 137 D3
Clerkenwell EC1 241 D4
Grantley Ho
2 Deptford SE14 140 D6
5 Putney SW19 156 D3
Grantley Pl KT10 212 A3
Grantley Rd TW4, TW5 128 C3
Grantley St E1 96 D3
Grant Mus of Zoology & Comparative Anatomy* WC1 93 D3 239 C5
Grantock Rd E17 36 B2
Granton Prim Sch SW16 181 C3
Granton Rd
Ilford IG3 58 A1
Sidcup DA14 190 C4
Streatham SW16 181 C2
Grant Pl 2 CR0 205 D1
Grant Rd
Battersea SW11 136 C2
Croydon CR0 205 D1
Harrow HA3 42 D6
Grants Cl NW7 28 D3
Grants Cotts KT10 212 B6
Grant St
Islington N1 234 A4
Newham E13 99 A4
Grantully Rd W9 91 D4
Grant Way TW7 131 A6
Granville Ave
Feltham TW13 150 A2
Hounslow TW3, TW4 151 C6
Lower Edmonton N9 18 C1
Granville Cl CR0 221 C6
Granville Ct
8 Deptford SE14 141 A5
Hornsey N4 50 B3
Shoreditch N1 235 D6
Granville Gdns
Ealing W5 110 B5
South Norwood SW16 182 B3
Granville Gr SE13 142 A2
Granville Ho 18 E14 97 C1
Granville Ind Est NW2 69 B6
Granville Mans 8 W12 112 C4
Granville Mews DA14 190 A6
Granville Pk SE13 142 B2
Granville Pl
London N12 30 A3
Marylebone W1 93 A1 238 A1
Pinner HA5 40 D6
Walham Green SW6 265 C3
Granville Point NW2 69 B6
Granville Rd
Bexley DA16 146 C2
Bowes Pk N13 32 B4
Child's Hill NW2 69 B6
Finchley N12 30 A3
Hayes UB3 105 D2
Hillingdon UB10 60 D2
Hornsey N4, N8 50 B3
Ilford IG1 78 D6
Kilburn NW6 91 C5
Merton SW19 179 C3
Sidcup DA14 190 B6
Tottenham N22 32 D2
Walthamstow E17 53 D3
Wandsworth SW18 157 B4
Woodford E18 37 B1
Granville Sq
3 Camberwell SE15 139 C5
Finsbury WC1 94 B4 233 D1
Granville St WC1 233 D1
Granwood Ct 5 TW7 130 C4
Grape St WC2 240 A2
Grapsome Cl KT9 213 C1
Grasdene Rd SE18 146 A5
Grasgarth Cl W3 111 A6
Grasmere NW1 231 D1
Grasmere Ave
Acton W3 111 B6
Kingston u T SW15 177 C6
Locksbottom BR6 226 D5
Merton SW19 201 C6
Ruislip HA4 39 A2
Twickenham TW3 151 D5
Grasmere Ave *continued*
Wembley HA9 43 D1
Grasmere Cl TW14 149 D3
Grasmere Ct
Barnes SW13 134 A6
Bowes Pk N22 32 B4
Forest Hill SE26 184 A5
7 Sutton SM2 218 A2
Grasmere Gdns
Harrow HA3 25 A1
Locksbottom BR6 226 D5
Redbridge IG4 56 B4
Grasmere Ho 20 N16 73 B4
Grasmere Point 2 SE15 140 C5
Grasmere Prim Sch N16 73 B4
Grasmere Rd
Bromley BR1 186 D3
Croydon SE25 206 B4
Locksbottom BR6 226 D5
Muswell Hill N10 31 B2
3 Newham E13 99 A5
Streatham SW16 182 B5
Tottenham N17 34 A4
Grasshaven Way SE28 123 D5
Grassington Cl N11 31 A4
Grassington Rd DA14 190 A6
Grassmere Ct 6 EN1 17 C6
Grassmount SE23 162 B2
Grass Pk N3 29 B2
Grassway SM6 219 C4
Grasvenor Ave EN5 13 C5
Grasvenor Avenue Inf Sch EN5 13 C5
Grateley Ho 10 SW15 156 B3
Gratton Rd W14 113 A3 254 A5
Gratton Terr NW2 68 D5
Graveley 16 KT1 176 C1
Graveley Ave WD6 11 A6
Graveley Ho 7 SE8 119 A2
Gravel Hill
Bexley DA6 169 D6
Church End N3 29 B1
South Croydon CR0, CR2 223 B1
Gravel Hill Cl DA6 169 D5
Gravel Hill Prim Sch DA6 169 D6
Gravel Hill Sta CR0 223 A2
Gravel La E1 95 D1 243 C2
Gravel Rd
Keston Mark BR2 226 A6
Twickenham TW2 152 C3
Gravelwood Cl BR7 167 A1
Gravenel Gdns 5 SW17 180 C5
Graveney Gr SE20 184 C3
Graveney Rd SW17 180 C6
Graveney Sch SW17 181 B5
Gravesend Rd W12 112 A6
Graves Est DA16 146 B3
Gray Ave RM8 59 B1
Gray Ct 8 KT2 175 D6
Grayfriars Pas EC1 241 D2
Grayham Cres KT3 199 B5
Grayham Rd KT3 199 B5
Gray Ho SE17 262 B2
Grayland Cl BR1 187 D2
Grayland Ct WC1 233 C1
Grayling Cl E16 98 C3
Grayling Ct
Ealing W5 109 D5
Tottenham Hale N17 52 B5
Grayling Rd N16 73 B6
Grayling Sq E2 96 A4
Grays Cotts UB9 38 C1
Grays Court Hospl RM10 81 D1
Grayscroft Rd SW16 181 D3
Grays Farm Prim Sch BR5 190 B2
Grays Farm Production Village BR5 190 B2
Grays Farm Rd BR5 190 B2
Grayshott Ct 10 SM2 217 D1
Grayshott Rd SW11 137 A2
Gray's Inn* WC1 94 B2 240 D4
Gray's Inn Pl WC1 240 D3
Gray's Inn Rd WC1 94 B3 240 D6
Gray's Inn Sq WC1 94 C2 241 A4
Grays La TW15 170 D6
Grayson Ho EC1 235 B1
Gray's Rd UB10 60 A1
Gray St SE1 116 C4 251 B1
Grayswood Gdns SW20 178 B1
Grayswood Point 14 SW15 156 A3
Gray's Yd W1 238 B2
Graywood Ct N12 30 A3
Grazebrook Prim Sch N16 73 C6
Grazebrook Rd N16 73 B6
Grazeley Ct SE19 183 C5
Great Arthur Ho EC1 242 A5
Great Bell Alley EC2 242 C2
Great Benty UB7 104 A2
Great Brownings SE21 183 D6
Great Bushey Dr N20 13 D3
Great Cambridge Ind Est EN1 18 B6
Great Cambridge Junction N13, N18 33 B6
Great Cambridge Rd
Edmonton N9, N18 17 C3
Enfield EN1 6 A3
Great Castle St W1 239 A2
Great Central Ave HA4 62 C3
Great Central St NW1 92 D2 237 C4
Great Central Way NW10 67 B4
Great Chapel St W1 93 D1 239 C2
Great Chart St SW11 136 A1
Great Chertsey Rd
Chiswick SW14, W4 133 B4
Feltham TW13, TW2 151 C1
Great Church La W6 112 D1
Great College St SW1 116 A3 260 A6
Great Croft WC1 233 B1
Great Cross Ave SE3 142 C5
Great Cumberland Mews W1 237 C1
Great Cumberland Pl W1 92 D1 237 D1
Great Dover St SE1 117 B3 262 C6
Greatdown Rd W7 86 D2
Great Eastern Bldgs 10 E8 74 B2
Great Eastern Ent Ctr E14 119 D4
Great Eastern Pier E14 119 C1
Great Eastern Rd E15 76 B2
Great Eastern St EC2 95 C3 243 A6
Great Eastern Wharf SW11 267 B3
Great Elms Rd BR2 209 C5
Great Field
Hendon NW9 27 D2
7 Kentish Town NW5 71 C3
Greatfield Ave E6 100 B3
Greatfield Cl
London SE4 141 C1
4 Tufnell Pk N19 71 C4
Greatfields Dr UB8 82 C2
Greatfields Rd IG11 101 B5
Great Fleete Way IG11 102 C5
Great Galley Cl IG11 102 C4
Great Gatton Cl CR0 207 A2
Great George St SW1 116 A4 250 A1
Great Guildford Bsns Sq SE1 252 A3
Great Guildford St SE1 117 A5 252 A3
Great Hall The 1 E11 55 B5
Greatham Wlk 8 SW15 156 A3
Great Harry Dr SE9 166 C1
Great James St WC1 240 C4
Great Marlborough St W1 93 C1 239 A1
Great Maze Pond SE1 117 B4 252 D2
Great Newport St WC2 250 A6
Great North Rd
Barnet EN5 1 A2
East Finchley N2 48 C5
New Barnet EN5 13 D6
Great North Way (Barnet By-Pass) NW4 46 D6
Greatorex Ho 13 E1 96 A2
Greatorex St E1 96 A2
Great Ormond St Hospl for Children WC1 94 B3 240 C5

Great Ormond St WC1 94 B3 240 C5
Great Percy St WC1 94 C4 234 A2
Great Peter St SW1 115 D3 259 D5
Great Portland St W1 93 B2 238 D4
Great Portland Street Sta W1 93 B3 238 D5
Great Pulteney St W1 249 B6
Great Queen St WC2 94 A1 240 B2
Great Russell Mans WC1 240 A3
Great Russell St WC1 94 A2 240 A3
Great St Helen's EC3 243 A2
Great St Thomas Apostle EC4 252 B6
Great Scotland Yd SW1, WC2 116 A5 250 A4
Great Smith St SW1 115 D3 259 D6
Great South West Rd TW6, TW14, TW4 148 B6
Great South-West Rd TW5 128 B2
Great Spilmans SE22 161 C6
Greatstone Ho 10 SE20 184 C3
Great Strand NW9 27 D1
Great Suffolk St SE1 116 D5 251 D3
Great Sutton St EC1 94 D3 241 D5
Great Swan Alley EC2 242 C2
Great Thrift BR5 211 A5
Great Titchfield St W1 93 C2 239 A3
Great Tower St EC3 117 C6 253 A6
Great Trinity La EC4 252 B6
Great Turnstile WC2 240 D3
Great Western Ind Pk UB2 108 A4
Great Western Rd W2, W9 91 B2
Great West Ho TW8 131 C6
Great West Rd
Brentford TW7, TW8 131 B6
Chiswick W4, W6 133 B6
Heston TW5, TW7 129 B4
Hounslow TW5, TW7 130 B5
Great West Road Cedars Rd W4 133 A6
Great West Road Hogarth La W4 133 C6
Great West Trad Est TW8 131 B6
Great Winchester St EC2 95 B1 242 D2
Great Windmill St W1 115 D6 249 C6
Greatwood BR7 188 C3
Great Yd SE1 253 B2
Greaves Cl IG11 79 C1
Greaves Cotts 10 E14 97 A2
Greaves Ct N8 50 C5
Greaves Pl SW17 180 C6
Greaves Twr SW10 266 B4
Grebe 3 NW9 27 D1
Grebe Ave UB4 84 D1
Grebe Cl
Barking IG11 102 A3
Higham Hill E17 35 A3
Stratford E7 76 D3
Grebe Ct
Cheam SM1 217 B3
16 Cubitt Town E14 120 A4
Grebe Terr 4 KT1 198 A6
Grecian Cres SE19 182 D4
Greek Ct W1 239 D1
Greek St W1 93 D1 239 D1
Greenacre Cl
Barnet EN5 1 B5
Northolt UB5 63 B3
Greenacre Ct E8 74 A3
Greenacre Gdns E17 54 A5
Greenacre Pl SM6 219 B6
Greenacres
Bushey WD23 8 B2
Church End N3 29 A1
Eltham SE9 166 C5
Green Acres
Hayes UB4 84 B3
Sidcup DA14 189 D6
South Croydon CR0 221 D5
Greenacres Ave UB10 60 C5
Greenacres Cl BR6 227 A4
Greenacres Dr HA7 25 B3
Greenacres Prim Sch SE9 166 C2
Greenacre Sq 26 SE16 118 D4
Greenacre Wlk N14 15 D1
Green Arbour Ct EC1 241 C2
Green Ave
Ealing W13 109 B3
Edgware NW7 27 C6
Greenaway Gdns NW3 69 D4
Greenaway Ho
Finsbury WC1 234 A1
St John's Wood NW8 229 A6
Greenaway Terr TW19 148 A3
Green Bank
London N12 29 D6
Wapping E1 118 B5
Greenbank Ave HA0 65 A3
Greenbank Cl E4 20 A2
Greenbank Cres NW4 47 A5
Greenbank Lo 2 BR7 188 C2
Greenbanks HA1 64 C4
Greenbay Rd SE7 143 D5
Greenberry St NW8 230 A3
Greenbrook Ave EN4 2 A4
Green CE Prim Sch The N17 51 D6
Green CE Sch Holy Trinity (Inf Annexe) The N15 51 D5
Green Cl
Beckenham BR2 208 C6
Carshalton SM5 218 D6
Feltham TW13 173 A5
Kingsbury NW9 45 A3
North End NW11 48 A2
Greencoat Pl SW1 115 C2 259 B4
Greencoat Row SW1 259 B5
Greencourt Ave HA8 26 D2
Green Court Ave CR0 222 B6
Green Court Gdns CR0 222 B6
Greencourt Ho 25 E1 96 D3
Greencourt Rd BR5 211 C4
Greencroft HA8 27 A5
Greencroft Ave HA4 62 C6
Greencroft Cl E16 99 D2
Greencroft Gdns
Enfield EN1 5 C2
South Hampstead NW6 70 A1
Greencroft Rd TW5 129 B4
Green Ct
Ashford TW16 171 D4
2 Willesden NW10 67 C4
Greendale NW7 27 C6
Green Dale SE22 161 C6
Greendale Cl SE22 161 C6
Greendale Ct CR2 221 A2
Green Dr UB1 107 C5
Green Dragon Ct SE1 252 C3
Green Dragon Ho WC1 240 B2
Green Dragon La
Brentford TW8 110 B1
Southgate N21 16 D5
Green Dragon Prim Sch TW8 132 A6
Green Dragon Yd 24 E1 96 A2
Greene Ct 20 SE14 140 D6
Greene Ho SE1 262 C5
Green Elms IG6 57 A6
Green End
Chessington KT9 214 A4
Edmonton N21 16 D2
Greenend Rd W4 111 C4
Greener Ct 26 EN3 7 C6
Greener Ho 3 SW4 137 D2
Green Farm Cl BR6 227 D3
Greenfell Mans SE8 141 D6
Greenfield Ave KT5 198 D3
Greenfield Ct SE9 166 A1
Greenfield Dr
Bromley BR1 187 C1
Fortis Green N2 48 D5
Greenfield Gdns
Cricklewood NW2 69 A5
Crofton BR5 211 B2
Dagenham RM9 102 D6
Greenfield Ho 28 SW19 156 D3
Greenfield Rd
Dagenham RM9 102 C6
South Tottenham N15 51 C4
Whitechapel E1 96 A1
Greenfields UB1 85 C1
Greenfields Prim Sch WD19 22 C5
Greenfield Way HA2 41 D6
GREENFORD 86 A4
Greenford Ave
Ealing W7 86 C1
Southall UB1 107 B6
Greenford Gdns UB6 86 A4
Greenford High Sch UB6 85 C4
Greenford Rd
Greenford UB6 86 A3
Sudbury HA1, UB6 64 C3
Sutton SM1 217 D4
Greenford Rdbt UB6 86 B5
Greenford Sta UB6 86 B6
Greengate UB6 65 B2
Greengate St E13 99 B4
Green Gdns BR6 227 A3
Greenhalgh Wlk N2 48 A5
Greenham Cl SE1 251 A1
Greenham Cres E4 35 B4
Greenham Ho
5 Hackney E9 96 C6
Isleworth TW7 130 B2
Greenham Rd N10 31 A1
Greenhaven Dr SE28 102 B1
Greenheath Bsns Ctr 3 E2 96 B3
Green Hedges 8 TW1 153 C5
Greenheys Dr E18 54 D6
GREENHILL 42 D4
Greenhill
Buckhurst Hill IG9 21 C3
Hampstead NW3 70 B4
Sutton SM1 218 A6
Wembley HA9 66 D6
Green Hill SE18 122 B1
Greenhill Cts SE7 122 B1
Greenhill Gdns UB5 85 B5
Greenhill Gr E12 78 A4
Greenhill Par EN5 13 D6
Greenhill Pk
Harlesden NW10 89 C6
New Barnet EN5 13 D6
Greenhill Rd
Harlesden NW10 89 C6
Harrow HA1 42 C3
Greenhill's Rents EC1 241 C4
Greenhills Terr 16 N1 73 B2
Greenhill Terr
Northolt UB5 85 B5
Woolwich SE18 122 B1
Greenhill Way
Harrow HA1 42 C3
Wembley Pk HA9 66 D6
Greenhithe Cl DA15 167 C4
Green Ho TW7 130 D3
Greenholm Rd SE9 166 D6
Green Ho The 5 SW19 157 A3
Green Hundred Rd SE15 140 A6
Greenhurst Rd SE27 182 C5
Greening Ho SE13 142 B1
Greening St SE2 124 C2
Green La
Ashford TW16 171 D4
Chessington KT9 214 A1
Chislehurst SE9 166 D1
Dagenham RM8 81 B6
East Molesey KT8 195 D4
Edgware HA8 26 C5
Feltham TW13 173 A5
Hanwell W7 108 C4
Hendon NW4 46 D4
Hillingdon UB8 83 A2
Hounslow TW4 128 C1
Ilford IG1, IG3 79 C6
Morden SM4 201 D3
New Malden KT3 199 A4
New Malden KT4 200 A1
Penge SE20 184 D3
Shepperton TW17 193 A4
South Norwood CR7, SW16 182 C2
Stanmore HA7 25 B5
Greenland Cres UB2 106 D3
Greenland Ho
Bermondsey SE8 118 D1
4 Mile End E1 97 A3
Greenland Mews SE8 118 D1
Greenland Pl NW1 231 D6
Greenland Quay SE16 118 D2
Greenland Rd
Barnet EN5 12 C5
Camden Town NW1 93 C6 232 A6
Greenlands
Borehamwood WD6 11 B5
Chessington KT19 214 D3
Greenland St NW1 231 D6
Greenland Way CR0 203 D2
Green Lane Bsns Pk SE9 166 C2
Green Lane Cotts HA7 25 B6
Green Lane Gdns CR7 183 A1
Green Lane Mews SM4 201 D3
Green Lane Prim Sch KT4 200 B2
Green Lanes
London N4, N8, N15 50 D2
Palmers Green N13 16 C1
West Ewell KT19 215 C1
Greenlaw Ct W5 87 D1
Greenlaw Gdns KT3 199 D2
Greenlawn La TW8 109 D2
Greenlawns N12 29 D4
Green Lawns
Ruislip HA4 40 C1
8 Woolwich SE18 122 D2
Greenlaw St SE18 122 C3
Green Leaf Ave SM6 219 D4
Greenleaf Cl 8 SW2 160 C4
Greenleaf Ct N20 14 B3
Greenleafe Dr IG6 56 D6
Greenleaf Prim Sch E17 53 B6
Greenleaf Rd
5 Newham E6 99 C6
Walthamstow E17 53 B6
Greenleaf Way HA3 42 D6
Greenlea Pk SW19 180 C2
Green Leas
Ashford TW16 171 D4
Kingston u T KT1 198 A6
Green Leas Cl TW16 171 D4
Greenleaves Ct TW15 170 D4
Green Link Wlk TW9 132 D4
Green Man Gdns W13 109 A6
Green Man Intc E11 54 D2
Green Man La
Ealing W13 109 A5
Hatton TW14 128 A1
Greenman St N1 95 A6 235 A6
Greenmead Cl SE25 206 A4
Greenmead Sch SW15 156 B6
Green Moor Link N21 16 D4
Greenmoor Rd EN3 6 C3
Greenoak Pl EN4 2 D3
Green Oaks UB2 106 D2
Greenoak Way SW19 178 D6
Greenock Rd
Mitcham SW16 181 D2
11 South Acton W3 111 A3
Greeno Cres TW17 192 C4
Green Park* SW1, W1 115 B4 248 D2
Greenpark Ct HA0 65 C1
Green Park Sta W1 115 C5 249 A4
Green Park Way UB6 86 C6
Green Pond Cl E17 53 B6
Green Pond Rd E17 53 A6
Green Pt E15 76 C2
Green Rd
East Barnet N14 15 B5
Whetstone N20 14 A1
Green Ride IG10, E4 21 A6
Greenroof Way SE10 120 D3
Green Sch (Girls) The TW7 131 A4
Greens Ct
Soho W1 249 C6
Wembley HA9 65 D5
Green's Ct W11 244 C3
Greens End SE18 122 D2
Greenshank Cl E17 35 A3
Greenshaw High Sch SM1 218 A6
Greenshields Ind Est E16 121 B5
Greenside
Dagenham RM8 58 C1
Sidcup DA5 169 A3
Greenside Cl
Catford SE6 164 B2
Whetstone N20 14 B2
Greenside Prim Sch W12 112 A4
Greenside Rd
Shepherd's Bush W12 112 A4
Greenside Rd *continued*
Thornton Heath CR0 204 C2
Greenslade Prim Sch SE18 145 B6
Greenslade Rd IG11 79 B1
Greensleeves Ho UB2 107 D2
Greensleeves Manor SM2 217 D2
Green St
Enfield EN3 6 D3
Mayfair W1 115 A6 248 A6
Newham E13 99 C6
Sunbury TW16 172 A1
Upton E7 77 C1
Greenstead Ave IG8 37 C4
Greenstead Cl IG8 37 C4
Greenstead Gdns
Putney SW15 156 B6
Woodford IG8 37 C4
Greenstone Mews E11 55 A3
GREEN STREET GREEN 227 C2
Green Street Green Prim Sch BR6 227 D2
Greenstreet Hill SE4 140 D2
Greensward Ho SW6 136 A3
Green Terr EC1 234 B1
Green The
Acton W3 89 C1
Buckhurst Hill IG9 21 B3
Chingford E4 20 B3
Claygate KT10 212 D2
Ealing W5 109 D6
Edmonton N9 18 A2
Erith DA7 147 C4
Falconwood DA16 145 C1
Feltham TW13 150 B2
Grove Pk BR1 165 A1
Hackbridge SM6 219 A6
Hayes BR2 209 A2
Heston TW5 129 C6
Kingston u T KT3 177 A1
Merton SM4 201 A5
Palmers Green N14 15 D1
Richmond TW9 131 D1
7 Richmond TW9 153 D6
Sidcup DA14 190 A5
Southall UB2 107 B4
Southgate N21 16 C4
St Paul's Cray BR5 190 B3
Stratford E15 76 D2
Sutton SM1 217 D5
Tottenham N17 33 A4
Twickenham TW2 152 C2
Upper Halliford TW17 193 C5
Uxbridge UB10 61 A6
Wallington SM5 219 A4
Wanstead E11 55 B3
Wembley HA0 65 A6
Wimbledon SW19 178 D5
Woodford IG8 37 A5
Green Vale
Bexley DA6 168 D6
Ealing W5 88 B1
Greenvale Rd SE9 144 C1
Greenvale Sch SE23 163 A1
Green Verges HA7 25 D3
Green View KT9 214 B1
Greenview Ave CR0 207 A3
Greenview Cl W3 111 C5
Greenview Ct
Ashford TW15 170 B6
East Dulwich SE22 140 A1
Oakleigh Pk N20 14 A4
Wandsworth SW18 158 C4
Greenway
Chislehurst BR7 188 D5
Dagenham RM8 58 C1
Harrow HA3 44 A4
Hayes UB4 84 B3
Palmers Green N14 16 A2
Pinner HA5 22 B1
Totteridge N20 13 C2
Wallington SM6 219 C4
West Barnes SW20 200 C5
Woodford IG8 37 C5
Green Way
Bromley Comm BR2 210 A3
Eltham SE9 165 D6
Sunbury TW16 194 A5
Greenway Ave E17 54 B5
Greenway Cl
Finsbury Pk N4 73 A6
Friern Barnet N11 31 A4
Hendon NW9 27 B1
2 South Tottenham N15 51 D5
Totteridge N20 13 C2
Greenway Ct
Hayes UB4 84 B3
Ilford IG1 56 D1
2 Newham E15 98 C5
Greenway Gdns
Croydon CR0 223 B5
Greenford UB6 85 D4
Hendon NW9 27 B1
Green Way Gdns HA3 24 C1
Greenways
Beckenham BR3 185 C1
5 Forest Hill SE26 184 C6
Hinchley Wood KT10 212 C4
Greenways The 1 TW1 153 A5
Greenway The
Harrow HA3 24 C2
Hendon NW9 27 B1
Hounslow TW4 129 B1
Pinner HA5 41 B3
Uxbridge UB8 82 A5
West Ruislip UB10 61 A6
Greenwell St W1 238 D5
GREENWICH 142 C6
Greenwich Acad SE10 141 D4
Greenwich Borough Mus* SE18 123 D1
Greenwich Bsns Ctr SE10 141 D5
Greenwich Bsns Pk SE10 141 D5
Greenwich Church St SE10 142 A6
Greenwich Coll SE10 142 A5
Greenwich Com Coll Plumstead Ctr SE18 123 A2
Greenwich Cres E6 100 A2
Greenwich Ct 11 E1 96 B1
Greenwich High Rd SE10 141 D5
Greenwich Ho SE13 164 B5
Greenwich Hts SE18 144 A5
Greenwich Ind Est SE10 141 D5
Greenwich London Coll SE18 122 D2
Greenwich Mkt 2 SE10 142 A6
Greenwich Mkt SE10 142 A6
Greenwich Park* SE10 142 C5
Greenwich Park St SE10 142 B6
Greenwich Quay SE8 141 D6
Greenwich Sh Pk SE7 121 B2
Greenwich South St SE10 142 A4
Greenwich Sta SE10 141 D5
Greenwich View Pl E14 119 D3
Green Wlk
Bermondsey SE1 263 A5
Hampton TW12 173 B4
Hendon NW4 46 D4
Ruislip HA4 39 D1
Southall UB2 107 C1
Green Wlk The E4 20 B3
Greenwood
8 Putney SW19 156 D4
3 Woodford IG8 37 A3
Green Wood NW5 71 C3
Greenwood Ave
Dagenham RM10 81 D4
Enfield EN3 7 A4
Greenwood Cl
Bushey WD23 8 C3
Merton SM4 201 A5
Orpington BR5 211 C3
Sidcup DA15 168 A2
Thames Ditton KT7 197 A1
Greenwood Dr E4 36 B5
Greenwood Gdns N13 16 D1
Greenwood Ho
Finsbury WC1 234 A1
8 Nunhead SE4 140 D1
Wood Green N22 32 C2
Greenwood La TW12 173 D5
Greenwood Mans 9 IG11 80 A1
Greenwood Pk KT2 177 C3
Greenwood Pl NW5 71 B3
Greenwood Prim Sch UB5 64 A3
Greenwood Rd
Dalston E8 74 A2

Greenwood Rd *continued*
Hinchley Wood KT7 213 A6
Isleworth TW7 130 D2
Mitcham CR4 203 D6
Thornton Heath CR0 205 A2
West Ham E13 98 D5
Greenwoods The HA2 64 A5
Greenwood Terr NW10 89 B5
Green Wrythe Cres
SM5 202 C1
Green Wrythe La
SM5 202 C2
Green Wrythe Prim Sch
SM5 202 B3
Green Yd WC1 240 D6
Greer Rd HA3 24 A2
Greet Ho SE1 251 B1
Greet St SE1 116 C5 251 B3
Greg Cl E10 54 A3
Gregor Mews SE3 143 A5
Gregory Cres SE9 165 D4
Gregory Ho SE3 143 B3
Gregory Pl W8 245 C2
Gregory Rd
Dagenham RM6 58 D5
Southall UB2 107 C3
Greig City Acad N8 50 A5
Greig Cl N8 50 A4
Greig Ho 9 TW10 153 C1
Greig Terr SE17 138 D6
Grenaby Ave CR0 205 B2
Grenaby Rd CR0 205 B2
Grenada Ho 18 E14 119 B6
Grenada Rd SE7 143 C5
Grenade St E14 119 B6
Grenadier St E16 122 C5
Grena Gdns TW9 132 B1
Grena Rd TW10, TW9 132 B1
Grenard Cl SE15 140 A5
Grendon Gdns HA9 66 C6
Grendon Ho
29 Hackney E9 74 C1
Pentonville N1 233 C3
Grendon St
NW8 92 C3 237 A6
Grenfell Ct NW7 28 B4
Grenfell Gdns
Harrow HA3 44 A2
Ilford IG2 57 D4
Grenfell Ho SE5 139 A5
Grenfell Rd
Mitcham CR4, SW17 180 D4
Shepherd's Bush W11 112 D6
Grenfell Twr 5 W11 112 D6
Grenfell Wlk 4 W11 112 D6
Grengate Lodge 2
E13 99 B4
Grenier Apartments 11
SE15 140 B5
Grennell Cl SM1 218 B6
Grennell Rd SM1 218 A6
Grenoble Gdns N13 32 C4
Grenville Cl
Church End N3 29 B2
Tolworth KT5 199 A1
Grenville Ct
3 Dulwich SE19 183 D5
Ealing W13 87 B2
Edgware HA8 26 D6
Grenville Gdns IG8 37 C3
Grenville Ho
26 Bow E3 97 A5
4 Deptford SE8 141 C6
Grenville Lo N6 49 C2
Grenville Mans WC1 240 A6
Grenville Mews
Hampton TW12 173 D5
South Kensington SW7 256 A3
Grenville Pl
Burnt Oak NW7 27 B5
South Kensington
SW7 114 A2 256 A4
Grenville Rd N19 50 A1
Grenville St WC1 240 B5
Gresham Almshouses 3
SW9 138 B1
Gresham Ave N20 30 D6
Gresham Cl
Enfield EN2 5 A2
Sidcup DA5 169 B5
Gresham Coll
EC1 94 C2 241 B3
Gresham Ct TW3 130 A4
Gresham Dr RM6 58 B3
Gresham Gdns NW11 47 A1
Gresham Ho
4 Teddington TW11 174 D5

Gresham Ho *continued*
3 Thames Ditton KT7 197 A2
West Barnes KT3 200 B5
Gresham Lo E17 53 D4
Gresham Pl 2 N19 71 D6
Gresham Rd
Beckenham BR3 185 A1
Brixton SW9 138 C2
Canning Town E16 99 B1
Croydon SE25 206 A5
East Ham E6 100 B5
Edgware HA8 26 B4
Hampton TW12 173 C4
Hillingdon UB10 82 C5
Hounslow TW3, TW5 130 A4
Willesden NW10 67 B3
Gresham St
EC2 95 A1 242 B2
Gresham Way SW19 157 C1
Gresham Way Est
SW19 157 D1
Gresley Cl
London N15 51 B5
Walthamstow E17 53 A3
Gresley Ho SW8 269 D2
Gresley Rd N19 49 C2
Gressenhall Rd SW18 157 B4
Gressenham Ct 7
HA7 25 C6
Gresse St W1 93 D1 239 C2
Gresswell Cl DA14 168 A1
Greswell St SW6 134 D4
Greta Ho SE3 142 D6
Gretton Ho 2 E2 96 C4
Gretton Rd N17 33 D3
Greville Cl TW1 153 B4
Greville Ct
Harrow HA1 64 C4
3 Lower Clapton E5 74 B5
Greville Hall NW6 91 D5
Greville Ho
Harrow HA2 42 B1
Knightsbridge SW1 258 A6
Putney SW15 134 D2
Greville Lo
5 Bayswater W2 91 D1
16 London N12 29 D6
Greville Mews 5 NW6 91 D6
Greville Pl W9 91 D5
Greville Rd
Kilburn NW6 91 D5
Richmond TW10 154 B5
Walthamstow E17 54 A5
Greville St EC1 94 C2 241 B4
Grey Cl NW11 48 A3
Grey Coat Hospital Sch
(St Michaels) The
SW1 115 D2 259 C3
Grey Coat Hospital Sch
The SW1 115 D3 259 C5
Greycoat Pl
SW1 115 D3 259 C5
Greycoat St
SW1 115 D3 259 C5
Greycot Rd BR3 185 C5
Grey Court Sch TW10 153 C1
Grey Eagle St
E1 95 D3 243 D5
Greyfell Cl HA7 25 B5
Greyfriars 16 SE26 162 A1
Greyfriars Ho SE3 142 D6
Grey Ho 27 W12 112 B6
Greyhound Ct WC2 251 A6
Greyhound Hill NW4 46 B6
Greyhound La SW16 181 D4
Greyhound Rd
College Pk NW10 90 B4
Fulham W6 135 A6 264 A6
Sutton SM1 218 A3
Tottenham N17 51 C6
Greyhound Terr
SW16 181 C2
Greyladies Gdns
SE10 142 A3
Greys Park Cl BR2 225 D3
Greystead Rd SE23 162 C4
Greystoke Ave HA5 41 C6
Greystoke Ct W5 88 B3
Greystoke Dr HA4 38 D3
Greystoke Gdns
Ealing W5 88 B3
Enfield EN2 3 D1
Greystoke Ho
Ealing W5 88 A3
Peckham SE15 140 A6
Greystoke Lo W5 88 B3
Greystoke Park Terr
W5 88 A4
Greystoke Pl EC4 241 B2
Greystone Gdns HA3 43 C3

Greystones TW2 152 A2
Greyswood St SW16 181 B4
Greytiles TW11 174 D4
Grey Turner Ho W12 90 A1
Grice Ct N1 73 A2
Grierson Ho SW16 181 C6
Grierson Rd
Forest Hill SE23 162 D4
Forest Hill SE23 163 A5
Griffin Cl NW10 68 B3
Griffin Ct
8 Brentford TW8 132 A6
Chiswick W4 111 D1
Shepherd's Bush W12 112 B5
Griffin Ctr TW14 150 B5
Griffin Ctr The KT1 175 D1
Griffin Gate SW15 134 D2
Griffin Lo N12 30 A6
Griffin Manor Way
SE28 123 B3
Griffin Park (Brentford
FC) TW8 131 D6
Griffin Rd
Plumstead SE18 123 B1
Tottenham N17 33 C1
Griffins Cl N21 17 B4
Griffin Way
Sunbury TW16 172 A1
Woolwich SE28 123 C3
Griffith Cl RM8 58 C1
Griffiths Cl KT4 216 B6
Griffiths Ho 2 SE18 144 D6
Griffiths Rd SW19 179 D3
Griffon Ho 3 SW11 136 C2
Griggs App IG1 79 A6
Grigg's Pl SE1 263 B5
Griggs Rd E10 54 A3
Grilse Cl N9 34 B6
Grimaldi Ho N1 233 C4
Grimsby Gr E16 122 D5
Grimsby St
8 Bethnal Green E2 96 A3
Shoreditch E2 243 D6
Grimsdyke Fst & Mid Sch
HA5 23 B4
Grimsdyke Rd HA5 23 A3
Grimsel Path SE5 138 D5
Grimshaw Cl N6 49 A2
Grimston Rd SW6 135 B3
Grimthorpe Ho EC1 241 C6
Grimwade Ave CR0 222 A5
Grimwade Cl SE15 140 C2
Grimwood Rd TW1 152 D4
Grindall Cl CR0 220 D4
Grindall Ho 25 E1 96 B3
Grindal St SE1 251 A1
Grindleford Ave N11 15 A2
Grindley Gdns CR0 205 D3
Grindley Ho 8 E3 97 B2
Grinling Gibbons Prim
Sch SE8 141 B6
Grinling Ho 6 SE18 122 C2
Grinling Pl SE8 141 C6
Grinstead Rd SE8 119 A1
Grisedale NW1 232 A2
Grittleton Ave HA9 66 D2
Grittleton Rd W9 91 C3
Grizedale Terr 8
SE23 162 B2
Grogan Cl TW12 173 B4
Groombridge Cl
DA16 168 A6
Groombridge Ho 1
SE20 184 D3
Groombridge Rd E9 74 D1
Groom Cl BR2 209 B5
Groom Cres SW18 158 B4
Groome Ho SE11 260 D3
Groomfield Cl SW17 181 A6
Groom Pl
SW1 115 A3 258 B6
Grooms Dr HA5 40 A4
Grosmont Rd SE18 123 D1
Grosse Way SW15 156 B5
Grosslea SM4 202 B4
Grosvenor Ave
Canonbury N5 73 A3
Harrow HA2 41 D3
Hayes UB4 83 D5
Mortlake SW14 133 C2
Richmond TW10 154 A6
Wallington SM5, SM6 219 A2
Grosvenor Bridge
SW1 137 B6 268 D6
Grosvenor Cotts SW1 258 A4
Grosvenor Court Mans
W2 237 C1
Grosvenor Cres
Hillingdon UB10 82 D6
Queensbury NW9 44 C5

Grosvenor Cres *continued*
Westminster
SW1 115 A4 248 B1
Grosvenor Cres Mews
SW1 248 A1
Grosvenor Ct
4 Acton W3 110 C5
Brondesbury Pk NW6 90 D6
3 Ealing W5 110 A6
3 Edgware NW7 27 B5
Gunnersbury W4 110 D1
Leyton E10 53 D1
Morden SM4 201 C5
Oakwood N14 15 C4
Penge SE19 183 D4
22 Poplar E14 97 B1
Putney SW15 157 A6
1 Sutton SM2 218 A2
Teddington TW11 175 A4
3 Wanstead E11 55 B4
2 Wimbledon SW19 179 A5
Grosvenor Gdns
Cricklewood NW2 68 C3
Hornsey N10 49 C6
Kingston u T KT2 175 D4
Mortlake SW14 133 C2
Newham E6 99 D4
Southgate N14 15 D6
Temple Fortune NW11 47 B4
Wallington SM6 219 C1
Westminster
SW1 115 B3 258 D5
Woodford IG8 37 B4
Grosvenor Gdns Mews E
SW1 258 D6
Grosvenor Gdns Mews N
SW1 258 C5
Grosvenor Gdns Mews S
SW1 258 D5
Grosvenor Hill
Mayfair W1 115 B6 248 C6
Wimbledon SW19 179 A4
Grosvenor Hill Ct W1 248 C6
Grosvenor Ho
5 Sutton SM1 217 D3
Upper Clapton E5 52 A1
Grosvenor Hts E4 20 C4
Grosvenor Lo
London N20 14 A1
4 Woodford E18 36 D1
Grosvenor Par 1
W5 110 C5
Grosvenor Park SE5 139 A5
Grosvenor Park Rd
E17 53 D4
Grosvenor Pier SW1 269 C6
Grosvenor Pk SE5 139 A6
Grosvenor Pl
SW1 115 B4 248 C1
Grosvenor Rd
Acton Green W4 111 A1
Bexley DA6 169 A6
Brentford TW8 131 D6
Croydon SE25 206 A5
Dagenham RM8 59 B1
Ealing W7 109 A5
Edmonton N9 18 B3
Erith DA17 147 C6
Finchley N3 29 C3
Hounslow TW3, TW4 129 B2
Ilford IG1 79 A5
Leyton E10 54 A1
Muswell Hill N10 31 B2
Newham E6 99 D6
Orpington BR6 211 C3
Pimlico SW1 137 C6 269 B6
Richmond TW10 154 A6
Southall UB2 107 B3
Twickenham TW1 153 A3
Upton E7 77 B2
Wallington SM6 219 B3
Wanstead E11 55 B4
West Wickham BR4 223 D6
Grosvenor Residences 1
W14 112 D3
Grosvenor Rise E E17 53 D4
Grosvenor Sq
W1 115 A6 248 B6
Grosvenor St
W1 115 B6 248 C6
Grosvenor Terr SE5 139 A6
Grosvenor The NW11 47 D2
Grosvenor Vale HA4 61 D6
Grosvenor Way E5 74 C6
Grosvernor Wharf Rd
E14 120 B2
Grote's Bldgs SE3 142 C3
Grote's Pl SE3 142 C3
Groton Rd SW18 157 D2
Grotto Ct SE1 252 A2

Grotto Pas W1 238 A4
Grotto Rd TW1 152 D2
Grove Ave
Cheam SM1 217 C2
Ealing W7 86 C1
Finchley N3 29 C3
Pinner HA5 41 A5
Twickenham TW1 152 D3
Wood Green N10 31 C1
Grovebury Ct
Bexley DA6 169 D6
Southgate N14 15 D4
Grovebury Rd SE2 124 B4
Grove Cl
East Barnet N14 15 B4
Forest Hill SE23 163 A3
Hayes BR2 225 A6
Ickenham UB10 60 C3
Kingston u T KT1 198 B5
Grove Cres
Feltham TW13 173 A6
Kingsbury NW9 45 B5
Kingston u T KT1 198 A6
Walton-on-T KT12 194 B2
Woodford E18 36 D1
Grove Crescent Rd
E15 76 B2
Grove Ct
Barnet EN5 1 B2
Camberwell SE5 139 C3
Clapham SW4 137 C2
Ealing W5 110 A5
East Molesey KT8 196 B4
3 Forest Hill SE26 185 A6
Hounslow TW3 129 C1
8 Kingston u T KT1 198 A6
New Malden KT3 199 C6
Penge SE20 184 B3
Seething Wells KT6 197 D4
South Kensington SW10 256 B1
St John's Wood NW8 229 C2
Grovedale Rd N19 71 D6
Grove Dwellings E1 96 C2
Grove End
Gospel Oak NW5 71 B4
Woodford E18 36 D1
Grove End Gdns NW8 229 B3
Grove End Ho NW8 229 C1
Grove End La KT10 196 B1
Grove End Rd
NW8 92 B4 229 C1
Grove Farm Ct CR4 202 D4
Grovefield 1 N11 31 B6
Grove Footpath KT5 198 A5
Grove Gdns
Enfield EN3 6 D5
Hendon NW4 46 A5
Lisson Gr NW8 92 C4 230 B1
Teddington TW11 175 A6
Grove Glade Shop Hall
W13 109 A5
Grove Green Rd E11 76 B6
Grove Hall Ct
Bow E3 97 C5
St John's Wood
NW8 92 A4 229 B2
Grove Hill
Harrow HA1 42 C2
Woodford E18 36 D1
Grovehill Ct BR1 186 D4
Grove Hill Rd
Camberwell SE5 139 C2
Harrow HA1 42 D2
Grove Ho
Blackheath SE3 142 D3
Chelsea SW3 267 B6
Hendon N3 46 D6
Grove House Rd N8 50 A5
Grove La
Camberwell SE5 139 C2
Hillingdon UB8 82 B3
Kingston u T KT1 198 A5
Groveland Ave SW16 182 B3
Groveland Ct EC4 242 B1
Groveland Rd BR3 207 B6
Grovelands
East Molesey KT8 195 C5
Kingston u T KT1 197 D5
Grovelands Cl
Camberwell SE5 139 C3
Harrow HA2 63 D5
Grovelands Ct N14 15 D4
Grovelands Inf Sch
KT12 194 B3
Grovelands Priory
(Private Hospl) N14 16 A3
Grovelands Rd
Palmers Green N13 16 B1
South Tottenham N15 52 A3
St Paul's Cray BR5 190 A3

Groveland Way KT3 199 B4
Grove Lane Terr SE5 139 B3
Groveley Ho 7 N4 51 A2
Groveley Rd TW13,
TW16 171 D5
Grove Lo
Clapham SW4 137 C1
Cranley Gdns N10 49 C5
Grove Mans
London SW4 136 D1
2 Shepherd's Bush
W6 112 C4
3 Stamford Hill N16 52 A1
Grove Market Pl SE9 166 B5
Grove Mews W6 112 C3
Grove Mill CR4 202 C4
Grove Mill Pl SM5 219 A5
GROVE PARK
SE9 165 B1
W4 133 A4
Grove Park Ave E4 35 D3
Grove Park Bridge
W4 133 A5
Grove Park Gdns W4 133 A5
Grove Park Mews
W4 133 A5
Grove Park Prim Sch
W4 133 A6
Grove Park Rd
Chiswick W4 132 D5
Mottingham SE9, SE12 165 D2
South Tottenham N15 51 C5
Grove Park Sch NW9 45 A5
Grove Park Sta SE12 165 B1
Grove Park Terr W4 132 D6
Grove Pk
Camberwell SE5 139 C3
Kingsbury NW9 45 B5
Wanstead E11 55 B4
Grove Pl
Acton W3 111 A5
Balham SW12 159 B5
Hampstead NW3 70 B5
Grove Prim Sch RM6 58 C4
Grover Ct SE13 141 D3
Grove Rd
Acton W3 111 A5
Barnes SW13 133 D3
Belmont SM2 217 C2
Bow E3 97 A5
Brentford TW8 109 C1
Chingford E4 20 A1
Cockfosters EN4 2 C2
Dagenham RM6 58 C3
Ealing W5 109 D6
East Molesey KT8 196 B5
Edgware HA8 26 C4
8 Erith DA17 147 B6
Friern Barnet N11 31 B5
Hounslow TW3 129 C1
Kingston u T KT6 197 D4
Leytonstone E11 54 D2
Merton SW19 180 A3
Mitcham CR4 181 B1
North Finchley N12 30 B5
Pinner HA5 41 B4
Richmond TW10 154 B5
Shepperton TW17 193 A3
South Tottenham N15 51 C4
Spring Gr TW7 130 C4
Thornton Heath CR7 204 C5
Twickenham TW2 152 B1
Uxbridge UB8 60 A1
Walthamstow E17 53 D4
Willesden NW2 68 C2
Woodford E18 36 D1
Grove Rd Prim Sch
TW3 129 C1
Grove Rd W EN3 6 C6
Grover Ho
4 London SW4 159 C6
Vauxhall SE11 260 D1
Groves Ho UB4 84 B4
Groveside Cl
Acton W3 88 C1
Carshalton SM5 218 C6
Groveside Ct SW11 136 B3
Groveside Rd E4 20 C1
Grove St
Deptford SE8 119 B1
Edmonton N18 33 D4
Grovestile Waye
TW14 149 B4
Grove Terr
Gospel Oak NW5 71 B4
Southall UB1 107 C6
Teddington TW11 175 A6
Grove Terrace Mews
NW5 71 B5

Grove The
Bexley DA6 146 D1
Dulwich SE21 162 A3
Ealing W5 110 A5
Edgware HA8 26 D6
Edmonton N13 32 C6
Enfield EN2 4 C3
Finchley N3 29 C3
Hendon NW11 47 A2
Highgate N6 49 A1
Hornsey N8 49 D4
Hounslow TW7 130 C4
Ickenham UB10 60 C3
Kingsbury NW9 45 B4
Sidcup DA14 191 A6
Southall UB6 86 A1
Stratford E15 76 C2
Stroud Green N4 50 B2
Teddington TW11 175 A6
1 Twickenham TW1 153 B5
Walton-on-T KT12 194 B2
West Wickham BR4 224 A6
Grove Vale
Chislehurst West BR7 188 C4
East Dulwich SE22 139 D1
Groveway
Dagenham RM8 80 D4
South Lambeth SW9 138 B4 270 D1
Grove Way
Thames Ditton KT10 196 A1
Wembley HA9 67 A3
Grovewood 9 TW9 132 C4
Grovewood Ct 6 TW7 130 C4
Grovewood Ho NW2 69 B6
Grummant Rd SE15 139 D4
Grundy St E14 97 D1
Gruneisen Rd N3 29 D3
Guardian Angels RC Prim Sch E3 97 A4
Guardian Ct SE12 164 C6
Guards Mus The* SW1 115 C4 249 B1
Gubyon Ave SE24 160 D6
Guerin Sq E3 97 B4
Guernsey Cl TW5 129 C5
Guernsey Gr SE24 161 A4
Guernsey Ho
10 Canonbury N1 73 A2
Enfield EN3 6 D5
Guernsey Rd
11 Canonbury N1 73 A2
Leytonstone E11 54 B1
Guibal Rd SE12 165 B3
Guildersfield Rd SW16 182 A3
Guildford Ave TW13 150 A2
Guildford Gr SE10 141 D4
Guildford Ho 23 SE5 139 A3
Guildford Rd
Chingford E17 36 A2
Ilford IG3 79 C6
Newham E6 100 B1
South Lambeth SW8 138 A4 270 B2
Thornton Heath CR0 205 B3
Guildford Way SM6 220 A3
Guild Hall* EC2 95 A1 242 B2
Guildhall Bldgs EC2 242 C2
Guildhall Ho EC2 242 C2
Guildhall Sch Music & Drama EC2 95 A2 242 B4
Guildhall Yd EC2 242 B2
Guild Ho SW19 179 B4
Guildhouse St SW1 115 C2 259 A3
Guildown Ave N12 29 D6
Guild Rd SE7 143 D6
Guildsway E17 35 B2
Guilford Ave KT5 198 B4
Guilford Pl WC1 240 C5
Guilford St WC1 94 A3 240 B5
Guilfoyle 2 NW9 27 D1
Guillemot Ct 28 SE8 141 B6
Guilsborough Cl NW10 67 C1
Guinness Cl
Hayes UB3 105 B3
Homerton E9 75 A1
Guinness Ct
Chelsea SW3 257 C3
6 Croydon CR0 221 D6
Finsbury EC1 235 B1
Primrose Hill NW8 230 B5
Whitechapel E1 243 D1
Guinness Sq SE1 263 A4
Guinness Trust Bldgs
Bermondsey SE1 253 A2
7 Bethnal Green E2 96 A5
Chelsea SW3 257 C3
Hammersmith W6 112 C1
Kennington SE11 261 C2
Guion Rd SW6 135 B3
Gujarat Ho 1 N16 73 C5
Gulland Cl WD23 8 A6
Gulland Wlk 21 N1 73 A2
Gullane Ho 24 E3 97 B5
Gull Cl SM6 220 A1
Gulliver Cl UB5 85 B6
Gulliver Ct CR2 220 D1
Gulliver Rd DA15 167 C2
Gulliver St SE16 119 B3
Gulston Wlk SW3 257 D3
Gumleigh Rd W5 109 C2
Gumley Gdns TW7 131 A2
Gumley House RC Convent Sch (Girls) TW7 131 A2
Gumping Rd BR5 227 A6
Gundulph Rd BR2 209 C6
Gunmakers La E3 97 A6
Gunnel Cl SE20 184 A6
Gunnell Cl SE25 206 A3
Gunnell Ct 3 CR4 180 C2
Gunnels Ct & Hastingwood Ct 6 IG9 21 C2
Gunner Dr 9 EN3 7 C6
Gunner La SE18 122 C1
GUNNERSBURY 110 D2
Gunnersbury Avenue (North Circular Rd) W3 110 C3
Gunnersbury Cl 8 W4 110 D1
Gunnersbury Cres W3 110 C4
Gunnersbury Ct 8 W3 110 D4
Gunnersbury Dr W5 110 B4
Gunnersbury Gdns W3 110 C4
Gunnersbury La W3 110 C4
Gunnersbury Manor W5 110 B5
Gunnersbury Mews 6 W4 110 D1
Gunnersbury Park W3 110 C3
Gunnersbury Park Mus* W3 110 C3
Gunnersbury RC Sch TW8 109 C1
Gunnersbury Sta W4 110 D1
Gunners Gr E4 20 A1
Gunners Rd SW18 158 B2
Gunnery Terr SE18 123 A3
Gunning St SE18 123 C2
Gunpowder Sq EC4 241 B2
Gun St E1 243 C3
Gunstor Rd N16 73 C4
Gunter Gr
Chelsea SW6 136 A5 266 A4
Hendon HA8 27 B2
Gunterstone Rd W14 113 A1 254 B2
Gunthorpe St E1 95 D1 243 D2
Gunton Rd
Streatham SW17 181 A4
Upper Clapton E5 74 B6
Gunwhale Cl SE16 118 D5
Gun Wharf
Old Ford E3 97 A6
Wapping E1 118 C5
Gurdon Ho 7 E14 97 C1
Gurdon Rd SE7 121 A1
Gurnell Gr W13 86 D3
Gurney Cl
Barking IG11 78 D2
Higham Hill E17 34 D2
Stratford E15 76 C3
Gurney Cres CR0 204 B1
Gurney Dr N2 48 A5
Gurney Ho
3 Bayswater W2 91 D1
14 Bethnal Green E2 96 A5
Hayes UB3 105 C2
Gurney Rd
London SW6 136 A2
Northolt UB5 84 C4
Stratford E15 76 C3
Wallington SM5 219 A4
Guru Nanak Sikh Prim & Sec Schs UB4 106 C5
Guthrie Ct SE1 251 B1
Guthrie St SW3 257 A2
Gutter La EC2 95 A1 242 A2
Guyatt Gdns CR4 181 A1
Guy Barnett Gr SE3 143 A2
Guy Rd SM6 219 D5
Guyscliff Rd SE13 164 A6
Guy's Hospl SE1 117 B4 252 D2
Guy's Hospl Sch SE1 117 B5 252 D3
Guy's Retreat IG9 21 C4
Guy St SE1 117 B4 252 D2
Gwalior Ho N14 15 C5
Gwalior Rd SW15 134 D2
Gwendolen Ave SW15 156 D6
Gwendolen Cl SW15 156 D6
Gwendolen Ho TW19 148 A3
Gwendoline Ave E13 99 B6
Gwendoline Ct TW15 170 A6
Gwendwr Rd W14 113 A1 254 B2
Gwent Ct 13 SE16 118 D5
Gwillim Cl DA15 168 A6
Gwilym Maries Ho 11 E2 96 B4
Gwydor Rd BR3 206 D6
Gwydyr Rd BR2 208 D6
Gwyn Cl SW6 136 A5 266 A3
Gwyn Jones Prim Sch E11 54 B2
Gwynne Ave CR0 206 D2
Gwynne Cl W4 133 D6
Gwynne Ho
Finsbury WC1 234 A1
6 Streatham SW2 160 B3
3 Wanstead E11 55 A4
Whitechapel E1 96 B2
Gwynne Pl WC1 233 D1
Gwynne Rd SW11 136 B3
Gye Ho 2 SW4 138 A1
Gylcote Cl SE5 139 B1
Gyles Pk HA7 25 C2
Gyllyngdune Gdns IG3 79 D5

H

Haarlem Rd 12 W14 112 D3
Haberdasher Pl 4 N1 95 C4
Haberdashers' Aske's Hatcham Coll SE4 141 A3
Haberdashers' Aske's Knights Acad BR1 187 A6
Haberdasher St N1 95 B4 235 D2
Haccombe Rd SW19 180 A4
HACKBRIDGE 219 B6
Hackbridge Park Gdns SM5 218 D6
Hackbridge Prim Sch SM5 203 A1
Hackbridge Rd SM5, SM6 219 A6
Hackbridge Sta SM6 219 B6
Hackford Rd SW9 138 B4 270 D2
Hackford Wlk SW9 138 C4
Hackforth Cl EN5 12 B6
Hackington Cres BR3 185 C4
HACKNEY 74 B2
Hackney Central Sta E8 74 B2
Hackney Cl WD6 11 B6
Hackney Coll (Poplar Ctr) E3 97 D3
Hackney Com Coll N1 95 C4
Hackney Downs Sta E8 74 B3
Hackney Free & Parochial CE Sec Sch E9 74 C2
Hackney Gr E8 74 B2
Hackney Hospl E9 75 A3
Hackney Rd E2 96 A5
Hackney Stadium Mkt* E15 75 C2
HACKNEY WICK 75 C2
Hackney Wick E9 75 B2
Hackney Wick Sta E9 75 C2
Hackworth Point 24 E3 97 D4
Hacon Sq 12 E8 74 B1
Hadar Cl N20 13 D3
Haddenham Ct SW17 180 B6
Hadden Rd SE28 123 C3
Hadden Way UB6 64 B2
Haddington Rd BR1 186 B6
Haddo Ho
Gospel Oak NW5 71 B4
Haddo Ho *continued*
Greenwich SE10 141 D6
Haddon Cl
Enfield EN1 18 A5
New Malden KT3 199 D4
Haddon Ct
East Acton W3 111 D6
Hendon NW4 46 C6
Haddon Gr DA15 168 A4
Haddon Rd SM1 217 D4
Haddo St SE10 142 A6
Haden Ct N4 72 C6
Hadfield Cl UB1 85 B4
Hadfield Ho
Edgware NW7 28 C6
37 Whitechapel E1 96 A1
Hadleigh Cl
17 Bethnal Green E1 96 C3
Merton SW20 179 B1
Hadleigh Ct 8 E4 20 C4
Hadleigh Ho 16 E1 96 C3
Hadleigh Lo 5 IG8 37 A4
Hadleigh Rd N9 18 B4
Hadleigh St E2 96 C4
Hadleigh Wlk 1 E6 100 A1
HADLEY 1 B2
Hadley Cl
Borehamwood WD6 10 B5
Southgate N21 16 C5
Hadley Ct
1 London N3 29 D3
Stamford Hill N16 52 A1
Hadley Gdns
Chiswick W4 111 B1
Southall UB2 107 B1
Hadley Gn EN5 1 B3
Hadley Gn W EN5 1 B3
Hadley Gr EN5 1 A3
Hadley Green Rd EN5 1 B3
Hadley Hall N21 16 C3
Hadley Highstone EN5 1 B4
Hadley Ho BR5 189 D1
Hadley Hts EN5 1 D3
Hadley Rd
Barnet EN5 1 D2
Belvedere DA17 125 B2
Enfield EN2 4 A5
Mitcham CR4 203 D5
Hadley Ridge EN5 1 B2
Hadley St NW1 71 B2
Hadleyvale Ct EN5 1 D2
Hadley View 9 EN5 1 D1
Hadley Way N21 16 C5
HADLEY WOOD 2 B5
Hadley Wood Prim Sch EN4 2 A5
Hadley Wood Rd
Barnet EN4 2 A3
Barnet EN5 1 C3
Hadley Wood Sta EN4 2 A5
Hadlow Coll (Mottingham Ctr) SE12 165 C3
Hadlow Coll Nature Reserve* SE12 165 C3
Hadlow Ho SE17 263 B2
Hadlow Pl SE19 184 A3
Hadlow Rd
Bexley DA16 146 C5
Sidcup DA14 190 A6
Hadrian Cl
5 Old Ford E3 97 C6
Stanwell TW19 148 A4
Hadrian Ct
Barnet EN5 1 D1
11 Belmont SM2 217 D1
Brockley SE4 141 C2
Hadrian Est 33 E2 96 A5
Hadrian's Ride EN1 17 D6
Hadrian St SE10 120 C1
Hadrian Way TW19 148 A4
Hadstock Ho NW1 232 D2
Hadyn Park Ct 13 W12 112 A4
Hadyn Park Rd W12 112 A4
Hafer Rd SW11 136 D1
Hafton Rd SE6 164 C2
Haggard Rd TW1 153 B4
Hagger Ct E17 54 B6
HAGGERSTON 95 D5
Haggerston Rd E8 95 D6
Haggerston Sch E2 95 D5
Haggerston Studios 30 E8 95 D6
Hague Prim Sch E2 96 B3
Hague St 30 E2 96 A4
Ha-Ha Rd SE7, SE18 144 B6
Haig Ct BR7 188 D5
Haig Ho 4 E2 96 A5
Haig Pl SM4 201 C3
Haig Rd
Hillingdon UB8 83 A2
Stanmore HA7 25 C5
Haig Rd E E13 99 C5
Haig Rd W E13 99 C4
Haigville Gdns IG6 56 D5
Hailes Cl SW19 180 A4
Haileybury Ave EN1 17 D5
Hailey Rd DA18 125 C4
Hailey Rd Bsns Pk DA18 125 C4
Hailing Mews BR2 209 B6
Hailsham Ave SW2 160 B2
Hailsham Cl KT6 197 D2
Hailsham Dr HA1 42 B6
Hailsham Rd SW17 181 A4
Hailsham Terr N18 33 B5
Haimo Prim Sch SE9 165 D6
Haimo Rd SE9 165 D6
Hainault Bldgs E10 54 A1
Hainault Bridge Par 5 IG1 78 D6
Hainault Ct E17 54 B5
Hainault Gore RM6 59 A4
Hainault Rd
Dagenham RM6 59 B3
Ilford RM6 58 B6
Leytonstone E11 54 B2
Hainault St
Ilford IG1 78 D6
New Eltham SE9 166 D3
Haines Wlk SM4 201 D2
Hainford Cl SE4 140 D1
Haining Cl 3 W4 110 C1
Hainthorpe Rd SE27 182 D6
Hainton Cl E1 96 B1
Halberd Mews E5 74 B6
Halbutt Gdns RM9 81 B5
Halbutt St RM9 81 B4
Halcomb St N1 95 C6
Halcot Ave DA6 169 D6
Halcroft Ct SM1 218 B4
Halcrow St E1 96 B2
Halcyon Ho 3 EN1 17 C6
Halcyon Wharf 19 E1 118 A5
Haldane Cl
Holdbrook EN3 7 D5
Muswell Hill N10 31 B3
Haldane Pl SW18 157 D3
Haldane Rd
Fulham SW6 135 B6 264 D5
Newham E6 100 A4
Southall UB1 86 A1
Thamesmead SE28 124 D6
Haldan Rd E4 36 A4
Haldon Rd SW18 157 B5
Hale Cl
Chingford E4 20 A1
Edgware HA8 27 A5
Orpington BR6 227 A4
Hale Ct HA8 27 A5
Hale Dr NW7 27 B4
HALE END 36 C4
Hale End Cl HA4 40 A3
Hale End Rd E17 36 B2
Halefield Rd N17 34 B2
Hale Gdns
Acton W3 110 C5
Tottenham Hale N17 52 A6
Hale Grove Gdns NW7 27 C5
Hale Ho
Enfield EN3 6 D6
Westminster SW1 259 D2
Hale La NW7, HA8 27 B5
Hale Lo HA1 42 C2
Hale Rd
Newham E6 100 A3
Tottenham Hale N17 52 A6
Hales Ct 6 TW11 175 A5
Hales Ho 3 SW12 159 B4
Halesowen Rd SM4 201 D2
Hales Prior N1 233 C3
Hales St SE8 141 C5
Hale St E14 119 D6
Halesworth Cl 3 E5 74 C6
Halesworth Rd SE13 141 D2
Hale The
Chingford E4 36 B3
Tottenham Hale N17 52 A6
Hale Wlk W7 86 C2
Haley Rd NW4 46 C3
Halfacre 14 HA7 25 C5
Half Acre
Brentford TW8 131 D6
2 Wanstead E18 55 A6
Half Acre Mews TW8 131 D6
Half Acre Rd W7 108 C5
Half Moon Cres N1 233 D4
Half Moon Ct EC1 242 A3
Half Moon La SE24 161 A5
Halfmoon Pas E1 243 D1
Half Moon St
W1 115 B5 248 D3
Halford Cl HA8 26 D1
Halford Ct KT9 214 A1
Halford Ho 9 SW15 156 D6
Halford Rd
Ickenham UB10 60 C3
Leyton E10 54 B4
Richmond TW10 154 A6
West Brompton SW6 135 C6 265 A5
Halfway St DA15 167 C3
Haliburton Rd TW1, TW7 131 A1
Haliday Ho N1 73 B2
Haliday Wlk 4 N1 73 B2
Halidon Cl E9 74 C3
Halifax 8 NW9 27 D1
Halifax Cl TW11 174 C4
Halifax Rd
Enfield EN2 5 B3
Greenford UB6 85 D6
Halifax St SE26 162 B1
Halifield Dr DA17 125 A3
Haling Gr CR2 221 A1
Haling Manor High Sch CR2 220 D1
Haling Park Gdns CR2 220 D2
Haling Park Rd
Croydon CR2 220 D3
South Croydon CR2 221 A2
Haling Rd CR2 221 B2
Haliwell Ho 10 NW6 91 D6
Halkett Ho 1 E2 96 C6
Halkin Arc SW1 114 D3 257 D6
Halkin Mews SW1 258 A6
Halkin Pl SW1 258 A6
Halkin St SW1 115 A4 248 B1
Hallam Cl BR7 188 B5
Hallam Ct W1 238 D4
Hallam Gdns HA5 23 A3
Hallam Ho
17 London SW9 138 C4
Pimlico SW1 259 B1
Hallam Mews W1 238 D4
Hallam Rd
Barnes SW13 134 B2
Harringay N15 50 D5
Hallam St W1 93 B2 238 D4
Hallane Ho SE27 183 A5
Hall Cl W5 88 A2
Hall Ct TW11 174 D5
Hall Dr
Ealing W7 86 C1
Forest Hill SE26 184 C5
Halley Gdns SE13 142 B1
Halley Ho
16 Bethnal Green E2 96 A5
8 Cubitt Town SE10 120 D1
Halley Prim Sch E14 97 A2
Halley Rd E7, E12 77 D2
Halley St E14 97 A2
Hall Farm Cl HA7 25 B6
Hall Farm Dr TW2 152 B4
Hallfield Jun & Inf Schs W2 91 D1
Hallgate SE3 143 A2
Hall Gate NW8 92 A4 229 B2
Hall Gdns E4 35 B6
Halliards The KT12 194 A3
Halliday Ho 40 E1 96 A1
Halliday Sq UB2 108 B5
Halliford Cl TW17 193 C6
Halliford Rd
Sunbury TW16 194 A5
Upper Halliford TW16, TW17 193 D5
Halliford Sch TW17 193 A2
Halliford St N1 73 B1
Hallingbury Ct 1 E17 53 D6
Halling Ho SE1 252 D1
Hallings Wharf Studios 2 E15 98 B6
Halliwell Ct 4 SE22 162 A6
Halliwell Rd SW2 160 B5
Halliwick Court Par 2 N12 30 D5
Halliwick Ct 1 N12 30 D5
Halliwick Ho N21 17 B5
Halliwick Rd N10 31 A2
Hall La
Chingford Hatch E4 35 B5
Harlington UB3 127 B5
Hendon NW4 28 A1

Hall Lane E4 . . . . 35 A5
Hallmark Trad Ctr
HA9 . . . . 67 A4
Hallmead Rd SM1 . . . . . 217 D5
Hall Oak Wlk NW6 . . . . . 69 B2
Hallowell Ave CR0 . . . . 220 A4
Hallowell Cl CR4 . . . . . . 203 A6
Hallowfield Way CR4 . . 202 C6
Hallows Gr TW16 . . . . . 171 D5
Hall Pl W2 . . . . . . 92 B3 236 C5
Hall Rd
Dagenham RM6 . . . . 58 D3
Isleworth TW7 . . . . 152 B6
Leyton E15 . . . . 76 B4
Newham E6 . . . . 100 B6
St John's Wood
NW8 . . . . 92 A4 229 B2
Halls Bsns Ctr UB3 . . . . 106 A3
Hall Sch SW20 . . . . 178 D2
Hall Sch The NW3 . . . . . . 70 B2
Hall Sch Wimbledon
SW15 . . . . 156 A1
Hallside Rd EN1 . . . . 5 D5
Hall St
Finsbury EC1 . . . 94 D4 234 D2
North Finchley N12 . . . . . . 30 A5
Halls Terr UB10 . . . . 82 D3
Hallsville Prim Sch
E16 . . . . 99 A1
Hallsville Rd E16 . . . . 98 D1
Hallswelle Par 1
NW11 . . . . 47 B4
Hallswelle Rd NW11 . . . . 47 B4
Hall The SE3 . . . . 143 A2
Hall Twr W2 . . . . 236 D4
Hall View SE9 . . . . 165 D2
Hallywell Cres E6 . . . . . 100 B2
Halons Rd SE9 . . . . 166 C4
Halpin Pl
SE17 . . . . 117 B2 262 D3
Halsbrook Rd SE3 . . . . . 143 D2
Halsbury Cl HA7 . . . . 25 B6
Halsbury Ct HA7 . . . . 25 B6
Halsbury Ho 4 N7 . . . . . . 72 B4
Halsbury Rd W12 . . . . . . 112 B5
Halsbury Rd E UB5 . . . . . 64 A4
Halsbury Rd W UB5 . . . . 63 D3
Halsend UB3 . . . . 106 B5
Halsey St
SW3 . . . . 114 D2 257 C4
Halsham Cres IG11 . . . . 79 D3
Halsmere Rd SE5 . . . . . 138 D4
Halstead Cl 2 CR0 . . . . . 221 A5
Halstead Ct
Shoreditch N1 . . . . 235 D3
Walthamstow E17 . . . . . . 53 B2
Halstead Gdns N21 . . . . . 17 B3
Halstead Rd
Edmonton N21 . . . . 17 B3
Enfield EN1 . . . . 5 C1
Wanstead E11 . . . . 55 B4
Halston Cl SW11 . . . . . . 158 D5
Halstow 12 NW5 . . . . 71 A2
Halstow Prim Sch
SE10 . . . . 121 A1
Halstow Rd
Greenwich SE3, SE10 . . . 121 A1
Kensal Green NW10 . . . . . 90 D4
Halsway UB3 . . . . 106 A5
Halter Cl WD6 . . . . 11 B6
Halton Cl N11 . . . . 30 D4
Halton Cross St
N1 . . . . 94 D6 234 D6
Haltone Ho 1 SW4 . . . . 137 D3
Halton Ho 22 N1 . . . . 72 D1
Halton Mans N1 . . . . 72 D1
Halton Pl N1 . . . . 235 A6
Halton Rd N1 . . . 94 D6 234 D6
Halt Robin La DA17 . . . . 125 D2
Halt Robin Rd DA17 . . . 125 D2
Halyard Ho E14 . . . . 120 A3
HAM 153 C1
Hamara Ghar 4 E13 . . . 99 C6
Hambalt Rd SW4 . . . . . . 159 C6
Hamble Cl HA4 . . . . 61 C6
Hamble Ct KT1 . . . . 175 D3
Hambledon SE17 . . . . . . 139 B6
Hambledon Chase N4 . . 50 A2
Hambledon Cl UB8 . . . . . 82 D3
Hambledon Ct
5 Ealing W5 . . . . 110 A6
9 Wallington SM6 . . . . . 219 B2
Hambledon Gdns
SE25 . . . . 205 D6
Hambledon Ho
2 Kingston u T KT2 . . . . 176 D4
Lower Clapton E5 . . . . 74 B4
Hambledon Pl SE21 . . . 161 D3
Hambledon Rd SW18 . . 157 B4
Hambledown Rd
DA15 . . . . 167 C4
Hamble St SW6 . . . . 135 D2
Hambleton Cl KT4 . . . . . 216 C6
Hamble Wlk UB5 . . . . 85 C5
Hambley Ho 5 SE16 . . . 118 B2
Hamblin Ho UB1 . . . . . . 107 A6
Hambly Mans SW16 . . . 182 A4
Hamblyn Ct N16 . . . . 51 D2
Hambridge Way SW2 . 160 C4
Hambro Ave BR2 . . . . . . 209 A1
Hambrook Ct 12 NW5 . . 71 B4
Hambrook Rd SE25 . . . 206 B6
Hambro Rd SW16 . . . . . 181 D5
Hambrough Ho UB4 . . . 84 C2
Hambrough Prim Sch
UB1 . . . . 107 B5
Hambrough Rd UB1 . . . 107 A5
Ham Cl TW10 . . . . 153 C1
Ham Comm TW10 . . . . . 153 D1
Ham Croft Cl TW13 . . . . 150 A1
Ham Ct 12 NW9 . . . . 27 D1
Hamden Cres RM10 . . . . 81 D5
Hamel Cl HA3 . . . . 43 D5
Hamers Ho 19 SW2 . . . 160 C4
Hameway E6 . . . . 100 C3
Ham Farm Rd KT2,
TW10 . . . . 176 A6
Hamfrith Rd E15 . . . . 76 D2
Ham Gate Ave TW10 . . . 176 A6
Ham Ho* TW10 153 C2
Hamilton Ave
Cheam SM3 . . . . 217 A6
Edmonton N9 . . . . 18 A4
Ilford IG6 . . . . 57 A4
Tolworth KT6, SM3 . . . . 214 C6
Hamilton Cl
Ashford TW13 . . . . 171 D5
Cockfosters EN4 . . . . 2 D1
Rotherhithe SE16 . . . . . . 119 A4
St John's Wood
NW8 . . . . 92 B4 229 C1
Teddington TW11 . . . . . . 175 B4
Tottenham N17 . . . . 51 D6
Hamilton Cres
Edmonton N13 . . . . 32 C6
Harrow HA2 . . . . 63 B5
Hounslow TW3 . . . . 151 D6
Hamilton Ct
9 Catford SE6 . . . . 164 D3
Croydon CR0 . . . . 206 A1
Ealing W5 . . . . 110 B6
St John's Wood W9 . . . . 229 A2
Hamilton Gdns
NW8 . . . . 92 A4 229 B2
Hamilton Hall
NW8 . . . . 92 A5 229 A3
Hamilton Ho
23 Bow E3 . . . . 97 B4
Chiswick W4 . . . . 133 C6
Kensington W8 . . . . 245 C2
Oakleigh Pk N20 . . . . 14 A4
1 Poplar E14 . . . . 119 B6
Putney SW15 . . . . 156 A6
10 Richmond TW9 . . . . . 132 C4
St John's Wood NW8 . . . 229 C2
Hamilton La N5 . . . . 72 D4
Hamilton Lo 37 E1 . . . . . . 96 C3
Hamilton Mews W1 . . . 248 C2
Hamilton Par TW13 . . . 172 A6
Hamilton Pk N5 . . . . 72 D4
Hamilton Pk W N5 . . . . . 72 D4
Hamilton Pl
Mayfair W1 . . . . 115 A5 248 B3
Sunbury TW16 . . . . 172 B3
Tottenham N17 . . . . 33 D1
Hamilton Rd
Acton W4 . . . . 111 C4
Barnet EN4 . . . . 2 C1
Bexleyheath DA7 . . . . . . 147 A3
Brentford TW8 . . . . 131 D6
Ealing W5 . . . . 110 A6
East Finchley N2 . . . . 48 A6
Edmonton N9 . . . . 18 A4
Feltham TW13 . . . . 171 D6
Harrow HA1 . . . . 42 C4
Hayes UB3 . . . . 106 B6
Hendon NW11 . . . . 47 A2
Higham Hill E17 . . . . 35 A1
Ilford IG1 . . . . 78 D4
Merton SW19 . . . . 179 D3
Newham E15 . . . . 98 C4
Sidcup DA15 . . . . 190 A6
Southall UB1 . . . . 107 B5
South Norwood CR7 . . . . 205 B6
Twickenham TW2 . . . . . . 152 C3
West Norwood SE27 . . . 183 B6
Willesden NW10 . . . . 68 A3
Hamilton Road Ind Est
SE27 . . . . 183 B6
Hamilton Road Mews 1
SW19 . . . . 179 D3
Hamilton Sq
Bermondsey SE1 . . . . . . 252 D2
Finchley N12 . . . . 30 A4
Hamilton St SE8 . . . . . . 141 C6
Hamilton Terr
NW8 . . . . 92 A4 229 B2
Hamilton Way
Edmonton N13 . . . . 32 D6
Finchley N3 . . . . 29 C4
Hamlea Cl SE12 . . . . . . 165 A6
Hamlet Cl SE13 . . . . 142 C1
Hamlet Ct
14 Enfield EN1 . . . . 17 C6
1 Hammersmith W6 . . . 112 A2
Kennington SE11 . . . . . . 261 C2
Hamlet Gdns W6 . . . . . . 112 A2
Hamlet Ho SE9 . . . . 166 C6
Hamlet Ind Est E9 . . . . . . 75 C1
Hamleton Terr RM9 . . . . 80 C1
Hamlet Rd SE19 . . . . 184 A3
Hamlet Sq NW2 . . . . 69 A5
Hamlets Way E3 . . . . 97 B3
Hamlet The SE5 . . . . 139 B2
Hamlet Way SE1 . . . . . . 252 D2
Hamlin Cres HA5 . . . . 40 C4
Hamlyn Cl HA8 . . . . 10 A1
Hamlyn Gdns SE19 . . . . 183 C3
Hamlyn Ho TW13 . . . . . 150 B3
Hammelton Ct 4
BR1 . . . . 186 D2
Hammelton Gn 2
SW9 . . . . 138 D4
Hammelton Rd BR1 . . . 187 A2
Hammers La NW7 . . . . . . 28 A6
Hammersley Ho 8
SE14 . . . . 140 C5
HAMMERSMITH 112 C2
Hammersmith Bridge Rd
W6, SW13 . . . . 112 C1
Hammersmith Broadway
Hammersmith W6 . . . . . 112 C1
5 Hammersmith W6 . . . 112 C2
Hammersmith Flyover
W6 . . . . 112 C1
Hammersmith Gr W6 . 112 C3
Hammersmith Hospl
W12 . . . . 90 B1
Hammersmith Rd
Hammersmith W6 . . . . . 112 D2
Kensington W14 . . . . . . 254 B4
Hammersmith Sta
W6 . . . . 112 C2
Hammersmith Terr 6
W6 . . . . 112 A1
Hammet Cl UB4 . . . . 84 D2
Hammett St EC3 . . . . . . 253 C6
Hammond Ave CR4 . . . 181 B1
Hammond Cl
Barnet EN5 . . . . 13 B6
Greenford UB6 . . . . 64 B3
Hampton TW12 . . . . 173 C2
Hammond Ct
1 Leyton E10 . . . . 75 D6
1 Walthamstow E17 . . . . 53 A4
Hammond Ho
10 Deptford SE14 . . . . . 140 C5
Millwall E14 . . . . 119 D3
Hammond Lo 6 W9 . . . . 91 C2
Hammond Rd
Enfield EN1 . . . . 6 B3
Southall UB2 . . . . 107 A3
Hammonds Cl RM8 . . . . 80 C5
Hammonds Ho TW19 . . 148 B3
Hammond St NW5 . . . . . 71 C2
Hammond Way 2
SE28 . . . . 124 B6
Hamonde Cl HA8 . . . . 10 D2
Hamond Sq N1 . . . . 95 C5
Ham Park Rd E15 . . . . . . 76 D1
Hampden Ave BR3 . . . . 185 A1
Hampden Cl NW1 . . . . . 232 D4
Hampden Ct
Harrow HA1 . . . . 42 A5
10 Muswell Hill N10 . . . . 31 A3
Hampden Gurney CE Prim
Sch W1 . . . . 92 C1 237 B2
Hampden Gurney St
W1 . . . . 237 C1
Hampden La N17 . . . . . . 34 A2
Hampden Rd
Beckenham BR3 . . . . . . 185 A1
Harrow HA3 . . . . 24 A1
Hornsey N8 . . . . 50 C5
Kingston u T KT1 . . . . . . 198 C6
Muswell Hill N10 . . . . 31 A3
Tottenham N17 . . . . 34 A2
Hampden Rd *continued*
Upper Holloway N19 . . . . 71 D6
Hampden Sq N14 . . . . . . 15 B3
Hampden Way N14 . . . . . 15 B2
Hampshire Cl N18 . . . . . 34 B5
Hampshire Ct
6 Barnes SW13 . . . . . . 133 D3
Hendon NW4 . . . . 46 D4
Hampshire Ho HA8 . . . . . 26 B3
Hampshire Hog La
3 Hammersmith W6 . . . 112 B1
11 Hammersmith W6 . . . 112 B2
Hampshire Rd N22 . . . . . 32 B3
Hampshire Sch The
SW7 . . . . 114 C4 247 A1
Hampshire St NW5 . . . . . 71 D2
Hampson Way
SW8 . . . . 138 B4 270 C2
HAMPSTEAD 70 A3
Hampstead Cl SE28 . . . 124 B5
Hampstead Coll of Fine
Arts & Humanities
NW3 . . . . 70 C2
HAMPSTEAD GARDEN
SUBURB 47 D4
Hampstead Garden
Suburb Inst NW11 . . . . . 47 D4
Hampstead Gate NW3 . . 70 A3
Hampstead Gdns
NW11 . . . . 47 C3
Hampstead Gn NW3 . . . . 70 C3
Hampstead Gr NW3 . . . . 70 A5
Hampstead Heath*
NW3 70 B6
Hampstead Heath Sta
NW3 . . . . 70 C4
Hampstead High St
NW3 . . . . 70 B4
Hampstead Hill Gdns
NW3 . . . . 70 C4
Hampstead Hill Sch
NW3 . . . . 70 C3
Hampstead Hts N2 . . . . . 48 A6
Hampstead La N6 . . . . . . 48 C2
Hampstead Parochial CE
Prim Sch NW3 . . . . 70 A4
Hampstead Rd
NW1 . . . . 93 C4 232 A2
Hampstead Sch NW2 . . . 69 A4
Hampstead Sq 1
NW3 . . . . 70 A5
Hampstead Sta NW3 . . . 70 A4
Hampstead Way NW11 . 47 A3
Hampstead West 4
NW6 . . . . 69 C2
Hampstead Wlk 1 E3 . . 97 B6
HAMPTON 173 C1
Hampton Cl
Borehamwood WD6 . . . . . 11 A6
Friern Barnet N11 . . . . . . 31 B5
Kilburn NW6 . . . . 91 C4
Wimbledon SW20 . . . . . 178 C3
Hampton Com Coll
TW12 . . . . 173 C5
Hampton Court Ave
KT8 . . . . 196 C3
Hampton Court Cres
KT8 . . . . 196 B6
Hampton Court Landing
Stage KT8 . . . . 196 C6
Hampton Court Pal*
KT8 196 D6
Hampton Court Par
KT8 . . . . 196 C5
Hampton Court Rd KT1,
KT8 . . . . 197 B6
Hampton Court Sta
KT8 . . . . 196 C5
Hampton Court Way KT10,
KT7, KT8 . . . . 196 C3
Hampton Ct
Hampton KT8 . . . . 196 C6
1 Islington N1 . . . . 72 D2
19 Rotherhithe SE16 . . . 118 D5
Wood Green N22 . . . . 31 C2
Hampton Farm Ind Est
TW13 . . . . 151 A1
HAMPTON HILL 174 A5
Hampton Hill Bsns Pk
TW12 . . . . 174 A5
Hampton Hill Jun Sch
TW12 . . . . 174 A5
Hampton Ho DA7 . . . . . 147 D3
Hampton Inf Sch
TW12 . . . . 173 C3
Hampton Jun Sch
TW12 . . . . 173 C2
Hampton La TW13 . . . . 173 A6
Hampton Rd
Chingford Hatch E4 . . . . . 35 B5
Hampton Rd *continued*
Forest Gate E7 . . . . 77 C3
Ilford IG1 . . . . 79 A4
Leytonstone E11 . . . . 54 B1
North Cheam KT4 . . . . . 216 B6
Teddington TW11,
TW12 . . . . 174 C5
Thornton Heath CR0 . . . . 205 A3
Twickenham TW2 . . . . . . 152 B1
Hampton Rd E TW13 . . 151 B1
Hampton Rd W TW13 . . 151 A1
Hampton Rise HA3 . . . . . 44 A3
Hampton Road Ind Pk
CR0 . . . . 205 A3
Hampton Sch TW12 . . . 173 C5
Hampton St
SE1 . . . . 116 D2 261 D3
Hampton Sta TW12 . . . . 173 C2
HAMPTON WICK 175 D3
Hampton Wick Inf Sch
TW11 . . . . 175 D3
Hampton Wick Sta
KT1 . . . . 175 C2
Ham Ridings TW10 . . . . 176 B5
Ham Shades Cl 1
DA15 . . . . 168 A1
Hamson Ct HA2 . . . . 64 B6
Ham St TW10 . . . . 153 C1
Hamstead Gates 11
NW5 . . . . 71 B2
Ham The TW8 . . . . 131 C5
Ham View CR0 . . . . 207 A3
Ham Yd W1 . . . . 249 C6
Hanameel St E16 . . . . . . 121 B5
Hana Mews E5 . . . . 74 B4
Hanbury Cl NW4 . . . . 46 C6
Hanbury Ct HA1 . . . . 42 D3
Hanbury Dr
2 Leyton E11 . . . . 54 D2
Southgate N21 . . . . 16 B6
Hanbury Ho
8 Bethnal Green E1 . . . . 96 A2
South Lambeth SW8 . . . . 270 B5
Hanbury Mews N1 . . . . 235 B5
Hanbury Rd
South Acton W3 . . . . 110 D4
Tottenham N17 . . . . 34 B1
Hanbury St E1 . . 95 D2 243 D4
Hancocke Ho 4 E17 . . . 53 D6
Hancock Nunn Ho 1
NW3 . . . . 70 D1
Hancock Rd
Bromley E3 . . . . 98 A4
South Norwood SE19 . . . 183 B4
Handa Wlk 3 N1 . . . . 73 A2
Handcroft Rd CR0 . . . . . 204 D1
Hand Ct WC1 . . . . 240 D3
Handel Cl HA8 . . . . 26 B4
Handel Ho TW2 . . . . 152 B5
Handel House Museum*
W1 115 B6 248 D6
Handel Mans
Barnes SW13 . . . . 134 C5
Bloomsbury WC1 . . . . . . 240 B6
Handel Par HA8 . . . . 26 C3
Handel Pl NW10 . . . . 67 B2
Handel St WC1 . . 94 A3 240 B6
Handel Way HA8 . . . . 26 C3
Handen Rd SE12 . . . . . . 164 D6
Handforth Rd
Brixton SW9 . . . . 138 C5
6 Ilford IG1 . . . . 78 D5
Handley Gr NW2 . . . . 68 D5
Handley Page Rd
SM6 . . . . 220 B1
Handley Rd E9 . . . . 96 C6
Handowe Cl NW4 . . . . . . 46 A5
Handside Cl KT4 . . . . . . 200 D1
Hands Wlk E16 . . . . 99 A1
Handsworth Ave E4 . . . . 36 B4
Handsworth Prim Sch
E4 . . . . 36 B4
Handsworth Rd N17 . . . . 51 B6
Handtrough Way
IG11 . . . . 100 D5
Hanford Cl SW18 . . . . . . 157 C3
Hanford Row SW19 . . . 178 C4
Hanger Ct W5 . . . . 88 C3
Hanger Gn W5 . . . . 88 C3
Hanger Lane Sta W5 . . . 88 A4
Hanger La (North Circular
Rd) W5 . . . . 88 B2
Hanger Vale La W5 . . . . 88 B1
Hanger View Way W3 . . 88 C2
Hangmans Cnr BR7 . . . 188 D2
Hankey Pl SE1 . 117 B4 252 D1
Hankins La NW7 . . . . 11 C1
Hanley Ct N4 . . . . 50 B1
Hanley Gdns N4 . . . . 50 B1
Hanley Pl BR3 . . . . 185 C3
Hanley Rd N4, N19 . . . . . . 50 A1
Hanmer Wlk N7 . . . . 72 B6
Hannah Cl
Beckenham BR3 . . . . . . 208 A6
Wembley NW10 . . . . 67 A4
Hannah Ct
Palmers Green N13 . . . . . 16 B2
5 Sutton SM1 . . . . 217 D2
Wimbledon SW19 . . . . . 178 D3
Hannah Mary Way 17
SE1 . . . . 118 A2
Hannah Mews SM6 . . . . 219 C1
Hannay La N8 . . . . 49 D2
Hannay Wlk SW16 . . . . 159 D2
Hannell Rd
SW6 . . . . 135 A5 264 B4
Hannen Ho SE5 . . . . 139 B2
Hannen Rd SE27 . . . . . . 160 D1
Hannibal Rd
Stanwell TW19 . . . . 148 A4
Stepney E1 . . . . 96 C2
Hannibal Way CR0 . . . . 220 B2
Hanning Lo TW3 . . . . . . 130 A1
Hannington Rd SW4 . . 137 B2
Hanover Ave
Feltham TW13 . . . . 150 A2
Newham E16 . . . . 121 A5
Hanover Circ UB3 . . . . . . 83 B1
Hanover Cl
Cheam SM3 . . . . 217 B4
Richmond TW9 . . . . 132 C5
Hanover Ct
Colindale NW9 . . . . 45 C6
Harrow HA1 . . . . 42 B2
1 Penge SE19 . . . . 184 A3
11 Pinner HA5 . . . . 23 B3
Shepherd's Bush W12 . . 112 A5
Stamford Hill N16 . . . . 51 D2
Hanover Dr BR7 . . . . . . 189 A6
Hanover Gate Mans
NW1 . . . . 237 B6
Hanover Gdns SE11 . . . 138 C6
Hanover Ho
1 New Barnet EN5 . . . . . . 2 A1
St John's Wood NW8 . . . 230 A3
Tolworth KT6 . . . . 198 C1
Hanover Lo N21 . . . . 16 D6
Hanover Mans 5
SW2 . . . . 160 C6
Hanover Mead NW11 . . . 47 A3
Hanover Pk SE15 . . . . . . 140 A4
Hanover Pl
16 Bow E3 . . . . 97 B4
St Giles WC2 . . . . 240 B1
Hanover Prim Sch
N1 . . . . 95 A5 235 A4
Hanover Rd
Merton SW19 . . . . 180 A3
South Tottenham N15 . . . . 51 D5
Willesden NW10 . . . . 90 C6
Hanover Sq W1 . 93 B1 238 D1
Hanover St
Croydon CR0 . . . . 220 D5
Marylebone W1 . 93 B1 238 D1
Hanover Stps W2 . . . . . 237 B1
Hanover Terr
Isleworth TW7 . . . . 131 A4
Lisson Gr NW1 . . 92 D4 230 C1
Hanover Terrace Mews
NW1 . . . . 92 C4 230 B1
Hanover Way DA6 . . . . . 146 D2
Hanover West Ind Est
NW10 . . . . 89 B4
Hanover Yd N1 . . . . 235 A4
Hansard Mews W14 . . . 112 D4
Hansart Way EN2 . . . . 4 C4
Hanscomb Mews
SW4 . . . . 137 C1
Hans Cres
SW1 . . . . 114 D3 257 C6
Hanselin Cl HA7 . . . . 24 D5
Hansen Dr N21 . . . . 16 B6
Hanshaw Dr HA8 . . . . 27 B2
Hansler Ct 14 SW19 . . . 157 A3
Hansler Gr KT8 . . . . 196 B5
Hansler Rd SE22 . . . . . . 161 D6
Hansol Rd DA6 . . . . 169 A6
Hanson Cl
Balham SW12 . . . . 159 B4
Beckenham BR3 . . . . 185 D4
Mortlake SW14 . . . . 133 A2
West Drayton UB7 . . . . . 104 B3
Hanson Ct E17 . . . . 53 D3
Hanson Gdns UB1 . . . . . 107 A4
Hanson Ho 2 E1 . . . . 118 A6
Hanson St W1 . . 93 C2 239 A4
Hans Pl SW1 . . . 114 D3 257 C6
Hans Rd SW3 . . . 114 D3 257 C6
Hans St SW1 . . . 114 D3 257 D5
Hanway Ho 25 SW9 . . . 138 C4

Hanway Pl W1 .... 239 C2
Hanway Rd W7 .... 86 C1
Hanway St W1 .... 239 C2
HANWELL 108 D5
Hanwell Sta W7 .... 108 C6
HANWORTH 172 D6
Hanworth Ho SE5 .... 138 D5
Hanworth Rd
Ashford TW16 .... 172 A3
Feltham TW13 .... 150 B3
Hampton TW12 .... 173 C5
Hounslow TW3, TW4 .... 129 D1
Twickenham TW4 .... 151 B4
Hanworth Terr TW3 .... 129 D1
Hanworth Trad Est
TW13 .... 151 A1
Hapgood Cl UB6 .... 64 B3
Harben Rd NW6 .... 70 A1
Harberson Rd
Balham SW12 .... 159 B3
West Ham E15 .... 98 D6
Harberton Rd N19 .... 49 C1
Harbet Rd
Highams Pk N18 .... 35 A4
Paddington W2 .. 92 B2 236 D3
Harbex Cl DA5 .... 169 D4
Harbinger Prim Sch
E14 .... 119 D2
Harbinger Rd E14 .... 119 D2
Harbin Ho 5 SW2 .... 160 C3
Harbledown Ho SE1 .... 252 C1
Harbledown Rd SW6 .... 265 A2
Harbord Cl SE5 .... 139 B3
Harbord Ho 5 SE16 .... 118 D2
Harbord St SW6 .... 134 D4
Harborne Cl WD19 .... 22 C5
Harborough Ave
DA15 .... 167 D4
Harborough Rd SW16 .... 182 B6
Harborough Sch N19 .... 71 D6
Harbour Ave
SW10 .... 136 A4 266 B1
Harbour Exchange Sq
E14 .... 119 D4
Harbour Rd SE5 .... 139 A2
Harbridge Ave SW15 .... 156 A4
Harbury Rd SM5 .... 218 C1
Harbut Rd SW11 .... 136 B1
Harcombe Rd N16 .... 73 C5
Harcourt Ave
Edgware HA8 .... 11 A1
Little Ilford E12 .... 78 B3
Sidcup DA15 .... 168 C4
Wallington SM6 .... 219 B4
Harcourt Cl TW7 .... 131 A2
Harcourt Field SM6 .... 219 B4
Harcourt Ho
5 Chingford E4 .... 36 B5
27 Clapham SW8 .... 137 D3
Marylebone W1 .... 238 C2
4 Willesden NW10 .... 68 C2
Harcourt Lo 2 SM6 .... 219 B4
Harcourt Rd
Bexley DA6 .... 147 A1
Brockley SE4 .... 141 B2
Bushey WD23 .... 8 A6
Merton SW19 .... 179 C3
Thornton Heath CR7 .... 204 C3
Wallington SM6 .... 219 B4
West Ham E15 .... 98 D5
Wood Green N22 .... 31 D2
Harcourt St W1 .. 92 C2 237 B3
Harcourt Terr
SW10 .... 113 D1 255 D1
Hardcastle Cl SE25 .... 206 A3
Hardcastle Ho
3 New Cross Gate
SE14 .... 141 A4
8 Peckham SE15 .... 140 A4
Hardcourts Cl BR4 .... 223 D5
Hard Ct IG8 .... 37 C4
Hardel Rise SW2 .... 160 D3
Hardel Wlk SE24, SW2 .... 160 C4
Harden Ct 1 SE7 .... 122 A2
Harden Ho SE5 .... 139 C3
Harders Rd SE15 .... 140 B3
Hardess St SE24 .... 139 A2
Hardham Ho 5 SW2 .... 160 C5
Hardie Cl NW10 .... 67 B3
Harding Cl
Camberwell SE17 .... 139 A6
South Croydon CR0 .... 221 D5
Harding Ct SE25 .... 183 D1
Hardinge Cl UB8 .... 82 D1
Hardinge Cres SE18 .... 123 A3
Hardinge Rd
Edmonton N18 .... 33 C4
Willesden NW10 .... 90 C6
Hardinge St
Stepney E1 .... 96 C1
Hardinge St *continued*
Woolwich SE18 .... 122 D3
Harding Ho
Barnes SW13 .... 134 B6
Hayes UB3 .... 84 B1
14 Woolwich SE18 .... 122 B2
Harding Pl SE23 .... 163 A4
Harding Rd DA7 .... 147 B3
Hardings Cl KT2 .... 176 B2
Hardings La SE20 .... 184 D4
Hardington 2 NW1 .... 71 A1
Hardman Rd
Greenwich SE7 .... 121 B1
Kingston u T KT2 .... 176 A1
Hardwick Cl 7 HA7 .... 25 C5
Hardwick Ct 8 E11 .... 55 A3
Hardwicke Ave TW5 .... 129 C4
Hardwicke Ho 14 E3 .... 97 D4
Hardwicke Mews
WC1 .... 233 D1
Hardwicke Rd
Acton W4 .... 111 B2
Bowes Pk N13 .... 32 A4
Richmond TW10 .... 175 C6
Hardwicke St IG11 .... 101 A6
Hardwick Gn W13 .... 87 B2
Hardwick Ho
14 London SW8 .... 137 D3
Marylebone NW8 .... 237 B6
Hardwick St
EC1 .... 94 C4 234 B1
Hardwick's Way
SW18 .... 157 C6
Hardwidge St SE1 .... 253 A2
Hardy Ave
4 Newham E16 .... 121 A5
Ruislip HA4 .... 62 B3
Hardy Cl
Barnet EN5 .... 13 A6
Pinner HA5 .... 40 D2
Rotherhithe SE16 .... 118 D4
Hardy Cotts 2 SE10 .... 142 B6
Hardy Ct
Greenwich SE3 .... 142 D6
9 Wanstead E11 .... 55 A5
Hardyng Ho 4 E17 .... 53 A5
Hardy Pas N22 .... 32 C1
Hardy Rd
Greenwich SE3 .... 142 D6
Merton SW19 .... 179 D3
Walthamstow E4 .... 35 B4
Hardys Mews KT8 .... 196 C5
Hardy Way EN2 .... 4 C4
Hare and Billet Rd
SE3 .... 142 B3
Harebell Dr E6 .... 100 C2
Harecastle Cl UB4 .... 85 A3
Harecourt Rd N1 .... 73 A2
Hare Ct EC4 .... 241 A1
Haredale Ho 24 SE16 .... 118 A4
Haredale Rd SE24 .... 139 A1
Haredon Cl SE23 .... 162 D4
Harefield KT10 .... 212 C5
Harefield Cl EN2 .... 4 C4
Harefield Ct 4 SW19 .... 179 C3
Harefield Mews SE4 .... 141 B2
Harefield Rd
Brockley SE4 .... 141 B2
Hornsey N8 .... 49 D4
Sidcup DA14 .... 168 D1
South Norwood SW16 .... 182 B3
Uxbridge UB8 .... 60 A3
Hare La KT10 .... 212 C2
Hare Marsh E2 .... 96 A3
Harenc Sch Trust
DA14 .... 190 C5
Hare Pl EC4 .... 241 B1
Hare Row E2 .... 96 B5
Haresfield Rd RM10 .... 81 C2
Hare St SE18 .... 122 C3
Harestone Ct CR2 .... 221 C2
Hare Wlk N1 .... 95 C5
Harewood Ave
Lisson Gr
NW1 .... 92 C3 237 B5
Northolt UB5 .... 63 B1
Harewood Cl UB5 .... 63 B1
Harewood Ct HA3 .... 24 C2
Harewood Pl W1 .... 238 D1
Harewood Rd
Hounslow TW7 .... 130 D4
Mitcham SW19 .... 180 C4
South Croydon CR2 .... 221 C2
Harewood Row NW1 .... 237 B4
Harewood Terr UB2 .... 107 B2
Harfield Gdns 1 SE5 .... 139 C2
Harfield Rd TW16 .... 172 D1
Harfleur Ct SE11 .... 261 C3
Harford Cl E4 .... 19 D4
Harford Ho
Camberwell SE5 .... 139 A6
Notting Hill W11 .... 91 B2
Harford Mews 6 N19 .... 71 D5
Harford Rd E4 .... 19 D4
Harford St E1 .... 97 A3
Harford Wlk N2 .... 48 B5
Hargood Cl HA3 .... 44 A3
Hargood Rd SE3 .... 143 C4
Hargrave Mans 3
N19 .... 71 D6
Hargrave Park Prim Sch
N19 .... 71 C6
Hargrave Pk N19 .... 71 C6
Hargrave Pl N7 .... 71 D3
Hargrave Rd N19 .... 71 C6
Hargraves Ho 14
W12 .... 112 B6
Hargwyne St SW9 .... 138 B2
Haringey Pk N8 .... 50 A3
Haringey Rd N8 .... 50 A5
Harington Terr N18 .... 17 B1
Harkett Cl HA3 .... 24 D1
Harkett Ct HA3 .... 24 D1
Harkness Ct SM1 .... 201 D1
Harkness Ho 30 E1 .... 96 A1
Harland Ave
Sidcup DA15 .... 167 C2
South Croydon CR0 .... 222 A5
Harland Cl SW19 .... 201 D6
Harland Rd SE12 .... 165 A3
Harlands Gr BR6 .... 226 D4
Harlech Ct 1 SE23 .... 162 C3
Harlech Gdns TW5 .... 128 C5
Harlech Rd N14 .... 16 A1
Harlech Twr 5 W3 .... 111 A4
Harlequin Ave TW8 .... 131 A6
Harlequin Cl
Hayes UB4 .... 84 D2
Isleworth TW7 .... 152 C6
Harlequin Ct
Croydon CR2 .... 221 A1
Ealing W5 .... 109 C6
Willesden NW10 .... 67 B2
Harlequin Ho 1
DA18 .... 125 A3
Harlequin Rd TW11 .... 175 B3
Harlescott Rd SE15 .... 140 D1
HARLESDEN 89 D6
Harlesden Gdns NW10 .... 89 D6
Harlesden Plaza 2
NW10 .... 89 D5
Harlesden Prim Sch
NW10 .... 89 C5
Harlesden Rd NW10 .... 90 A6
Harlesden Sta NW10 .... 89 B5
Harleston Cl 4 E5 .... 74 C6
Harley BR7 .... 189 B2
Harley Cl HA0 .... 65 D2
Harley Cres HA1 .... 42 B5
Harley Ct
Harrow HA1 .... 42 B5
Wanstead E11 .... 55 A2
Whetstone N20 .... 14 A1
Harleyford BR1 .... 187 C2
Harleyford Ct
Kennington SW8 .... 270 C6
Wembley HA0 .... 65 A4
Harleyford Manor 8
W3 .... 111 A5
Harleyford Rd
SE11 .... 138 B6 270 C6
Harleyford St SE11 .... 138 C6
Harley Gdns
Orpington BR6 .... 227 C4
South Kensington
SW10 .... 114 A1 256 B1
Harley Gr E3 .... 97 B4
Harley Ho
Leytonstone E11 .... 54 B2
Marylebone NW1 .... 238 B5
Harley Pl W1 .. 93 B2 238 C3
Harley Rd
Hampstead NW3 .... 70 B1
Harlesden NW10 .... 89 C5
Harrow HA1 .... 42 B5
Harley St W1 .. 93 B2 238 C3
Harley Villas NW10 .... 89 C5
Harling Ct 3 SW11 .... 136 D3
Harlinger St SE18 .... 122 A3
HARLINGTON 127 A6
Harlington Cl UB7 .... 127 A5
Harlington Cnr UB3 .... 127 B4
Harlington Com Sch
UB3 .... 105 B2
Harlington Rd
Bexley DA7 .... 147 A2
Hillingdon UB8 .... 82 C3
Harlington Rd E TW13,
TW14 .... 150 C3
Harlington Rd W
TW14 .... 150 B5
Harlowe Ho 13 E8 .... 95 D6
Harlow Mans 2 IG11 .... 78 D1
Harlow Rd N13 .... 17 B1
Harlyn Dr HA5 .... 40 B6
Harlyn Prim Sch HA5 .... 40 B6
Harlynwood 19 SE5 .... 139 A5
Harman Ave IG8 .... 36 D4
Harman Cl
10 Bermondsey SE1 .... 118 A1
Chingford E4 .... 36 B6
Cricklewood NW2 .... 69 A5
Harman Dr
Blackfen DA15 .... 167 D5
Cricklewood NW2 .... 69 A4
Harman Rd EN1 .... 17 D6
HARMONDSWORTH 126 A6
Harmondsworth La
UB7 .... 126 B6
Harmondsworth Rd
UB7 .... 104 A2
Harmon Ho 7 SE8 .... 119 B2
Harmony Cl NW11 .... 47 A4
Harmony Way
Bromley BR1 .... 187 A1
Hendon NW4 .... 46 C5
Harmood Gr NW1 .... 71 B1
Harmood Ho 2 NW1 .... 71 B1
Harmood St NW1 .... 71 B1
Harmsworth St
SE17 .... 116 D1 261 C1
Harmsworth Way N20 .... 13 C3
Harnage Ho TW8 .... 110 A1
Harness Rd SE28 .... 124 A4
Harney Ct SE14 .... 141 A4
Harold Ave
Erith DA17 .... 125 B1
Hayes UB3 .... 105 D3
Harold Ct
14 Rotherhithe SE16 .... 118 D4
6 Teddington TW11 .... 174 C5
Harold Est SE1 .... 263 B5
Harold Gibbons Ct 12
SE7 .... 143 C6
Harold Ho 16 E2 .... 96 D5
Harold Laski Ho EC1 .... 234 D1
Harold Maddison Ho
SE17 .... 261 D2
Harold Rd
Chingford E4 .... 20 A1
Hornsey N8 .... 50 B5
Leytonstone E11 .... 54 C1
Newham E13 .... 99 B6
North Acton NW10 .... 89 B4
South Norwood SE19 .... 183 B3
South Tottenham N15 .... 51 D4
Sutton SM1 .... 218 B4
Woodford IG8 .... 37 A2
Haroldstone Rd E17 .... 53 A4
Harold Wilson Ho
SW6 .... 264 D5
Haronton Ct E10 .... 76 A6
Harp Alley EC4 .... 241 C2
Harp Bsns Ctr The
NW2 .... 68 A6
Harpenden Rd
Wanstead E12 .... 77 C6
West Norwood SE27,
SW16 .... 160 D2
Harpenmead Point
NW2 .... 69 B6
Harper Cl N14 .... 15 C6
Harper Ho 3 SW9 .... 138 D2
Harper Mews SW17 .... 158 A1
Harper Rd
Bermondsey
SE1 .... 117 A3 262 B6
Newham E6 .... 100 B1
Harper's Yd N17 .... 33 D2
Harp Island Cl NW10 .... 67 B6
Harp La EC3 .... 253 A5
Harpley Sq E1 .... 96 D3
Harpour Rd IG11 .... 79 A2
Harp Rd W7 .... 86 D3
Harpsden St SW11 .... 268 A1
Harpur Mews WC1 .... 240 C4
Harpur St WC1 .. 94 B2 240 C4
Harraden Rd SE3 .... 143 C4
Harrier Ave E11 .... 55 B3
Harrier Ct TW4 .... 129 A3
Harrier Ho 9 SW11 .... 136 C2
Harrier Mews SE28 .... 123 B4
Harrier Rd NW9 .... 27 C1
Harriers Cl W5 .... 110 A6
Harrier Way E6 .... 100 B2
Harries Rd UB4 .... 84 C3
Harriet Cl E8 .... 96 A6
Harriet Gdns CR0 .... 222 A6
Harriet Ho
Walham Green SW6 .... 265 D3
Walthamstow E17 .... 53 D4
Harriet St
SW1 .... 114 D4 247 D1
Harriet Tubman Cl 21
SW2 .... 160 C4
Harriet Way WD23 .... 8 B4
Harriet Wlk
SW1 .... 114 D4 247 D1
HARRINGAY 50 D4
Harringay Gdns N8 .... 50 D5
Harringay Green Lanes
Sta N4 .... 50 D3
Harringay Rd N15 .... 50 D5
Harringay Sta N4 .... 50 C3
Harrington Cl
Wallington CR0 .... 220 A6
Willesden NW10 .... 67 B5
Harrington Ct
6 South Croydon
CR0 .... 221 B6
South Kensington SW7 .... 256 D4
9 West Kilburn W9 .... 91 B4
Harrington Gdns
SW7 .... 114 A2 256 A3
Harrington Hill E5 .... 52 B1
Harrington Hill Prim Sch
E5 .... 52 B1
Harrington Ho
2 Bromley BR1 .... 187 A2
Regent's Pk NW1 .... 232 A2
Upper Clapton E5 .... 52 C1
Westminster SW1 .... 259 D2
Harrington Rd
Croydon SE25 .... 206 B5
Leytonstone E11 .... 54 C1
South Kensington
SW7 .... 114 B2 256 C4
Harrington Road Sta
SE25 .... 206 C6
Harrington Sq
NW1 .... 93 C5 232 A3
Harrington St
NW1 .... 93 C4 232 A2
Harrington Way SE18 .... 121 D3
Harriott Cl SE10 .... 120 D2
Harriott Ho 11 E1 .... 96 C1
Harris Acad CR4 .... 203 D6
Harris City Tech Coll
SE19 .... 183 D2
Harris Cl
Enfield EN2 .... 4 D4
Heston TW5 .... 129 C4
Harris Cotts 1 E15 .... 98 D6
Harris Ct HA9 .... 66 B5
Harris Girl's Acad
SE15 .... 162 C6
Harris Ho
11 Bow E3 .... 97 C4
7 Brixton SW9 .... 138 C2
Harris Lo SE6 .... 164 A3
Harrison Cl N20 .... 14 C3
Harrison Ho SE17 .... 262 C2
Harrison Rd
Dagenham RM10 .... 81 D2
Stonebridge NW10 .... 89 B6
Harrisons Ct 1 SE14 .... 140 D6
Harrison's Rise CR0 .... 220 D5
Harrison St
WC1 .... 94 A4 233 B1
Harrison Way TW17 .... 192 D4
Harris Rd
Dagenham RM9 .... 81 B3
Erith DA7 .... 147 B4
Harris St
Camberwell SE5 .... 139 B5
Walthamstow E17 .... 53 B2
Harris Way TW16 .... 171 C2
Harrodian Sch The
SW13 .... 133 D5
Harrogate Ct
2 Forest Hill SE26 .... 162 A1
9 New Southgate N11 .... 31 A4
Harrold Ho 1 NW3 .... 70 A1
Harrold Rd RM8 .... 80 B3
HARROW 42 B3
Harrow Ave EN1 .... 17 D5
Harroway Rd SW11 .... 136 B3
Harrowby St
W1 .... 92 C1 237 B2
Harrow Cl KT9 .... 213 D1
Harrow Coll HA1 .... 42 C2
Harrow Coll (Harrow
Weald Campus) HA3 .... 24 C4
Harrowdene Cl HA0 .... 65 D4
Harrowdene Ct SW19 .... 179 A5
Harrowdene Gdns
TW11 .... 175 A3
Harrowdene Rd HA0 .... 65 D4
Harrow Dr N9 .... 17 D3
Harrowes Meade HA8 .... 10 C1
Harrow Fields Gdns
HA1 .... 64 C5
Harrowgate Ho 22 E9 .... 74 D2
Harrowgate Rd E9 .... 75 A1
Harrow Gn E11 .... 76 C5
Harrow High Sch & Sports
Coll HA1 .... 43 A3
Harrow La E14 .... 120 A6
Harrow Lo SM2 .... 218 B2
Harrow Manor Way
SE2 .... 124 C3
Harrow Mus & Her Ctr*
HA2 .... 42 A6
HARROW ON THE
HILL 42 C1
Harrow-on-the-Hill Sta
HA1 .... 42 C3
Harrow Pk HA1 .... 64 C6
Harrow Pl E1 .. 95 C1 243 B2
Harrow Rd
Ashford TW15 .... 148 C2
Barking IG11 .... 101 C6
Carshalton SM5 .... 218 C2
Ilford IG1 .... 79 A4
Leyton E11 .... 76 D5
Little Venice W2 .. 92 A2 236 B3
2 Newham E6 .... 100 A6
Sudbury HA0 .... 65 A4
Tokyngton HA9 .... 66 C2
Wembley HA0 .... 65 D3
Westbourne Green W2,
W9 .... 91 C3
Harrow Sch HA1 .... 42 C1
Harrow St NW1 .... 237 A4
Harrow View
Harrow HA1, HA2 .... 42 B5
Hayes UB3 .... 84 A1
Hillingdon UB10 .... 83 A4
Harrow View Rd W5 .... 87 B3
Harrow Way
Charlton TW17 .... 171 A1
South Oxhey WD19 .... 23 A6
HARROW WEALD 24 B2
Harrow Weald Pk HA3 .... 24 B4
Harrow & Wealdstone Sta
HA1 .... 42 C5
Harry Ct 15 NW9 .... 46 A5
Harry Gosling Prim Sch
E1 .... 96 A1
Harry Hinkins Ho
SE17 .... 262 B1
Harry Lambourn Ho 10
SE15 .... 140 B5
Harston 15 KT1 .... 176 C1
Harston Dr EN3 .... 7 C5
Hart Ct E12 .... 78 C1
Harte Rd TW3 .... 129 B3
Hartfield Ave
Borehamwood WD6 .... 10 C6
Northolt UB5 .... 84 B5
Hartfield Cl WD6 .... 10 C6
Hartfield Cres
Coney Hall BR4 .... 225 A5
Merton SW19 .... 179 B3
Hartfield Ct CR2 .... 220 D1
Hartfield Gr SE20 .... 184 C2
Hartfield Ho UB5 .... 84 B5
Hartfield Rd
Chessington KT9 .... 213 D3
Hayes BR4 .... 225 A4
Merton SW19 .... 179 C3
Hartfield Terr E3 .... 97 C5
Hartford Ave HA3 .... 43 B6
Hartford Rd
Old Bexley DA5 .... 169 C5
West Ewell KT19 .... 214 D2
Hart Gr
Ealing W5 .... 110 C5
Southall UB1 .... 85 C2
Hartgrove Ct NW9 .... 45 A5
Hart Grove Ct 3 W5 .... 110 C5
Hartham Cl
Isleworth TW7 .... 131 A4
Lower Holloway N7 .... 72 A3
Hartham Rd
Isleworth TW7 .... 131 A4
Lower Holloway N7 .... 72 A3
Tottenham N17 .... 33 D1
Hart Ho
Hayes UB4 .... 83 B2
Streatham SW2 .... 160 C3
Harting Rd SE9 .... 166 A1
Hartington Cl
Farnborough BR6 .... 227 A3
Harrow HA1 .... 64 C4

Hartington Ct
Chiswick W4 132 D5
South Lambeth SW8 270 A2
Hartington Rd
Chiswick W4 133 A4
Ealing W13 109 B6
Newham E16 99 B1
Southall UB2 107 A3
South Lambeth SW8 138 A5 270 A3
Twickenham TW1 153 B5
Walthamstow E17 53 A3
Hartismere Rd SW6 135 B5 264 D4
Hartlake Rd E9 75 A2
Hartland NW1 232 B5
Hartland Cl
Edgware HA8 10 C2
Enfield N21 17 A5
Hartland Ct 5 N11 30 D5
Hartland Dr
Edgware HA8 10 C2
Ruislip HA4 62 B4
Hartland Rd
Camden Town NW1 71 B1
Cheam SM4 201 D2
Friern Barnet N11 30 D5
Hampton TW12 173 D6
Isleworth TW7 131 A2
Kilburn NW6 91 B6
Stratford E15 76 D1
Hartlands Cl DA5 169 B5
Hartlands The TW5 128 B6
Hartland Way
Croydon CR0 223 A6
Morden SM4 201 B2
Hartlepool Ct E16 122 D5
Hartley Ave
Edgware NW7 27 D5
Newham E6 100 A6
Hartley Cl
Bickley BR1 188 B1
Edgware NW7 27 D5
Hartley Ct
Ealing W5 110 C5
5 Mitcham CR4 180 C2
Hartley Ho
Bermondsey SE1 263 D4
Finchley N3 29 D4
Putney SW15 156 A6
Hartley Prim Sch E6 100 A6
Hartley Rd
Bexley DA16 146 C5
Leytonstone E11 54 D1
Thornton Heath CR0 205 A2
Hartley St E2 96 C4
Hart Lo EN5 1 A2
Hartmann Rd E16 122 A5
Hartmoor Mews EN3 6 D6
Hartnoll Ho 4 N7 72 C3
Hartnoll St N7 72 B3
Harton Cl BR1 187 D2
Harton Lodge 2 SE8 141 C4
Harton Rd N9 18 B2
Harton St SE8 141 C4
Hartopp Ct 20 N16 73 C5
Hartopp Point SW6 264 B4
Hartsbourne Ave WD23 8 B2
Hartsbourne Cl WD23 8 B2
Hartsbourne Ct 5 UB1 86 A1
Hartsbourne Pk WD23 8 C2
Hartsbourne Prim Sch WD23 8 B2
Hartsbourne Rd WD23 8 B2
Harts Gr IG8 37 A5
Hartshill Cl UB10 60 D2
Hartshorn Alley EC3 243 B1
Hartshorn Gdns E6 100 C3
Harts La IG11 78 D2
Hart's La SE14 141 A4
Hartslock Dr SE2 124 D4
Hartsmead Rd SE9 166 B2
Hart Sq SM4 201 C3
Hart St EC3 253 B6
Hartsway EN3 6 C1
Hartswood Gn WD23 8 B2
Hartswood Ho 10 SW2 160 A3
Hartswood Rd W12 111 D3
Hartsworth Cl E13 98 D5
Hartville Rd SE18 123 C2
Hartwell Ct SE22 140 A1
Hartwell Dr E4 36 A4
Hartwell Ho 2 SE7 121 B1
Hartwell St E8 73 D2
Harvard Ct
9 Eltham SE9 166 C5
West Hampstead NW6 69 D3
Harvard Hill W4 132 D6
Harvard Ho
3 Camberwell SE17 138 D6
Putney SW15 156 D5
Harvard Mans 18 SW11 136 B1
Harvard Rd
11 Acton Green W4 111 A1
Gunnersbury W4 110 D1
Hounslow TW7 130 C4
Lewisham SE13 164 A6
Harvel Cres SE2 124 D1
Harvel Ct SE2 125 A1
Harvest Bank Rd BR4 225 A5
Harvest Ct
Beckenham BR3 185 C3
Littleton TW17 192 C5
Harvesters Cl TW7 152 B6
Harvest La
Loughton IG10 21 D4
Thames Ditton KT7 197 A3
Harvest Rd TW13 150 A1
Harvey Ct
Battersea SW11 267 B2
Walthamstow E17 53 C4
Harvey Dr TW12 173 C2
Harvey Gdns
Greenwich SE7 121 C1
Leytonstone E11 54 D1
Harvey Ho
Barking IG11 79 A1
10 Bethnal Green E1 96 B3
Brentford TW8 110 A1
Dagenham RM6 58 D5
Hornsey N8 50 A6
Pimlico SW1 259 D1
Shoreditch N1 235 D5
Wembley Pk HA9 66 D6
Harvey Lo 8 W9 91 C2
Harvey Mews N8 50 B4
Harvey Point 7 E16 99 A2
Harvey Rd
15 Camberwell SE5 139 B4
Hillingdon UB10 82 C5
Hornsey Vale N8 50 B4
Ilford IG1 78 D3
Leytonstone E11 54 D1
Ruislip UB5 62 C1
Twickenham TW4 151 B4
Walton-on-T KT12 194 A2
Harvey St N1 235 D5
Harvill Rd
Newyears Green UB9 38 A2
Sidcup DA14 191 A5
Harvil Rd UB9, UB10 38 A2
Harvington Sch W5 87 D1
Harvington Wlk E8 74 A1
Harvist Rd NW6 91 A5
Harwell Cl HA4 39 B1
Harwood Ave
Bromley BR1 187 B1
Mitcham CR4 202 C6
Harwood Cl
London N12 30 C4
Wembley HA0 65 D4
Harwood Ct
Putney SW15 134 C1
Shoreditch N1 235 D5
Harwood Dr UB10 82 B6
Harwood Point SE16 119 B4
Harwood Rd SW6 135 D5 265 C3
Harwoods Yd N21 16 C4
Harwood Terr SW6 135 D4 265 C2
Hascombe Ho 11 SW15 156 B3
Hascombe Terr 2 SE5 139 B3
Haselbury Rd N9 17 C1
Haseley End SE23 162 C4
Haselrigge Rd SW4 137 D1
Haseltine Prim Sch SE26 185 B6
Haseltine Rd SE26 185 B6
Haselwood Dr EN2 4 D1
Haskard Rd RM9 80 D4
Hasker St SW3 114 C2 257 B4
Haslam Ave SM3 201 A1
Haslam Cl
Islington N1 72 C1
Uxbridge UB10 61 A6
Haslam Ct N11 31 B6
Haslam Ho 18 N1 73 A1
Haslam St SE15 139 D4
Haslemere Ave
Barnet EN4 14 D3
Cranford TW5 128 C3
Ealing W13 109 A3
Hendon NW4 46 D3
Mitcham CR4, SW19 180 B1
Wandsworth SW18 157 D2
Haslemere Bsns Ctr EN1 18 B6
Haslemere Cl
Hampton TW12 173 B5
Wallington SM6 220 A3
Haslemere Ct 5 N16 51 C1
Haslemere Gdns N3 47 B5
Haslemere & Heathrow Est The TW4 128 B3
Haslemere Ind Est
Feltham TW14 150 A6
Wandsworth SW18 157 D2
Haslemere Prim Sch CR4 180 B1
Haslemere Rd
Bexleyheath DA7 147 C3
Hornsey N8 50 A2
Ilford IG3 79 D6
Southgate N21 16 D3
Thornton Heath CR7 204 D4
Hasler Cl SE28 124 C6
Hasler Ct E12 78 A4
Haslett Rd TW17 171 C1
Hasluck Gdns EN5 14 A5
Hasmonean High Sch (Boys) NW4 28 D1
Hasmonean High Sch (Girls) NW7 28 A2
Hasmonean Prim Sch NW4 46 D4
Hassard St E2 95 D5
Hassendean Rd SE3 143 B5
Hassett Rd E9 75 A2
Hassocks Cl SE23, SE26 162 B1
Hassocks Rd SW16 181 D2
Hassock Wood BR2 225 D4
Hassop Rd NW2 68 D4
Hassop Wlk SE9 188 A6
Hasted Rd SE7 121 D1
Hasting Ct TW11 174 B5
Hastings Ave IG6 57 A5
Hastings Cl
New Barnet EN5 2 A1
17 Peckham SE15 140 A5
Wembley HA0 65 C4
Hastings Dr KT6 197 C3
Hastings Ho
Ealing W13 109 B6
Enfield EN3 6 C3
18 Shepherd's Bush W12 112 B6
Tottenham N17 34 A2
6 Woolwich SE18 122 B2
Hastings Hos WC1 233 A1
Hastings Pl 1 CR0 205 D1
Hastings Rd
Croydon CR0 205 D1
Ealing W13 109 B6
Keston Mark BR2 226 A6
Tottenham N17 51 B6
Wood Green N11 31 D5
Hastings St
St Pancras WC1 94 A4 233 A1
Woolwich SE18 123 A3
Hastingwood Ct
Newham E6 100 B5
Walthamstow E17 53 D4
Hastingwood Trad Est N18 35 A4
Hastoe Cl UB4 85 A3
Hasty Cl CR4 181 A2
Hatcham Mews Bsns Ctr SE14 140 D4
Hatcham Park Mews SE14 140 D4
Hatcham Park Rd SE14 140 D4
Hatcham Rd SE15 140 C6
Hatchard Rd N19 72 A6
Hatchcroft NW4 46 B6
HATCH END 23 A3
Hatch End High Sch HA3 23 D2
Hatch End Sta HA5 23 C3
Hatchers Mews SE1 253 B1
Hatchett Rd TW14 149 A3
Hatchfield Ho 8 N15 51 C3
Hatch Gr RM6 59 A5
Hatch Ho
8 Muswell Hill N10 31 A3
14 Richmond TW10 153 C1
Hatch La E4 20 C1
Hatch Pl KT2 176 B5
Hatch Rd SW16 182 A1
Hatch The EN3 6 D4
Hatchwoods IG8 36 D6
Hatcliffe Almshouses 8 SE10 120 C1
Hatcliffe Cl SE3 142 D2
Hatcliffe St SE10 120 D1
Hatfield Cl
Deptford SE14 140 D5
Ilford IG6 56 D6
Mitcham CR4 202 B5
Hatfield Ct
Greenwich SE3 143 A5
8 Northolt UB5 84 C4
Hatfield Ho
16 Kingston u T KT6 198 A4
Leytonstone E11 54 D2
St Luke's EC1 242 A5
Hatfield Mead SM4 201 C4
Hatfield Mews RM9 81 A1
Hatfield Prim Sch SM4 201 A3
Hatfield Rd
Acton W4 111 B4
Dagenham RM9 81 A1
10 Ealing W13, W7 109 A5
Stratford E15 76 C3
Hatfields SE1 116 C5 251 B4
Hathaway Cl
Bromley BR2 210 B1
Ruislip HA4 61 D4
Stanmore HA7 25 A5
Hathaway Cres E12 78 C2
Hathaway Gdns
Ealing W13 87 A2
Ilford RM6 58 D4
Hathaway Ho 3 N1 95 C4
Hathaway Prim Sch W13 86 D2
Hathaway Rd CR0 204 D2
Hatherleigh Cl
Barnet EN4 1 D4
Chessington KT9 213 D3
Edgware NW7 28 D3
Morden SM4 201 C5
Hatherleigh Ho SM4 201 C5
Hatherleigh Rd HA4 62 A6
Hatherley Cres DA14 168 A2
Hatherley Ct 6 W2 91 D1
Hatherley Gdns
London N8 50 A3
Newham E6 99 D4
Hatherley Gr W2 91 D1
Hatherley Ho 2 E17 53 C5
Hatherley Mews E17 53 C5
Hatherley Rd
Richmond TW9 132 B4
Sidcup DA14 168 A1
Walthamstow E17 53 C5
Hatherley St SW1 259 B3
Hathern Gdns SE9 188 C6
Hatherop Rd TW12 173 B3
Hathersage Ct N1 73 B3
Hathersley Ho 3 SW2 160 C4
Hathorne Cl 3 SE15 140 B3
Hathway Ho 3 SE15 140 C3
Hathway St 4 SE15 140 C3
Hatley Ave IG6 57 A5
Hatley Cl N11 30 D5
Hatley Rd N4, N7 72 B6
Hat & Mitre Ct EC1 241 D5
Hatstone Ct NW3 70 A3
Hatteraick St 6 SE16 118 C4
Hattersfield Cl DA17 125 B2
HATTON 127 D1
Hatton Cl SE18 145 B5
Hatton Cross Rdbt TW6 127 D2
Hatton Cross Sta TW6 127 D1
Hatton Ct BR7 188 B3
Hatton Gdn EC1 94 C2 241 B4
Hatton Gdns CR4 202 D4
Hatton Gn TW14 128 A1
Hatton Ho 17 E1 118 A6
Hatton Pl EC1 241 B4
Hatton Rd
Hatton TW14, TW6 149 C6
Thornton Heath CR0 204 C1
Hatton Rd N TW6 127 B4
Hatton Row NW8 236 D5
Hatton Sch IG8 55 D6
Hatton St NW8 236 D5
Hatton Wall EC1 94 C2 241 B4
Haughmond 4 N12 29 D6
Haunch of Venison Yd W1 238 C1
Hauteville Court Gdns 2 W6 111 D3
Havana Rd SW18, SW19 157 C2
Havannah St E14 119 C4
Havant Rd E17 54 A6
Havelock Cl 13 W12 112 B6
Havelock Ct
8 Peckham SE15 140 B5
Southall UB2 107 B3
Havelock Hall 8 CR0 205 D1
Havelock Ho
4 Croydon CR0 205 D1
Forest Hill SE23 162 C3
Havelock Pl HA1 42 C3
Havelock Prim Sch UB2 107 B3
Havelock Rd
Belvedere DA17 125 B2
Bromley BR2 209 C5
Croydon CR0 221 D6
Harrow HA3 42 C6
Southall UB2 107 C3
Tottenham N17 34 A1
Wimbledon SW19 180 A5
Havelock St
Ilford IG1 78 D6
Islington N1 94 A6 233 B6
Havelock Terr SW8 137 B5 268 D3
Havelock Wlk SE23 162 C2
Haven Cl
Chislehurst SE9 166 B1
Hayes UB4 83 C3
Hinchley Wood KT10 212 C6
Sidcup DA14 190 C4
Wimbledon SW19 156 D1
Haven Ct
Beckenham BR3 186 A1
Hinchley Wood KT10 212 C6
Thornton Heath CR7 204 C6
Haven Gn W5 87 D1
Haven Green Ct W5 87 D1
Havenhurst Rise EN2 4 C3
Haven La W5 88 A1
Haven Lo
15 Enfield EN1 17 C6
Temple Fortune NW11 47 B4
7 Woolwich SE18 122 D2
Haven Pl
Ealing W5 109 D6
Hinchley Wood KT10 212 C6
Havenpool NW8 91 D6
Haven Rd TW15 148 D1
Haven St 18 NW1 71 B1
Haven The
Ashford TW16 172 A3
East Barnet N14 15 B5
Richmond TW9 132 C2
Havenwood HA9 66 D5
Havercourt 3 NW3 70 C2
Haverfield Gdns TW9 132 C5
Haverfield Rd E3 97 A4
Haverford Way HA8 26 B2
Havergal Villas N15 50 D6
Haverhill Rd
Chingford E4 20 A3
Streatham SW12 159 C3
Havering 8 NW1 71 B1
Havering Gdns RM6 58 D4
Havering Ho N4 51 A2
Havering St E1 96 D1
Havering Way IG11 102 B4
Haverley 15 SW20 178 D3
Haversham Cl TW1 153 D5
Haversham Ct UB6 64 D2
Haversham Lo NW2 68 D3
Haversham Pl N6 70 D6
Haverstock Ct 2 BR5 190 B1
Haverstock Hill NW3 70 D2
Haverstock Rd NW5 71 A3
Haverstock Sch NW1 71 A2
Haverstock St N1 94 D5 234 D3
Haverthwaite Rd BR6 227 B5
Havilland Ct HA8 26 B6
Havil St SE5 139 C4
Havisham Ho 25 SE16 118 A4
Havisham Pl SW16 182 D3
Hawarden Gr SE24 161 A4
Hawarden Hill NW2 68 A5
Hawarden Rd E17 52 D5
Hawberry Lo N7 72 A2
Hawbridge Rd E11 54 B1
Hawes Down Inf Sch BR4 208 B1
Hawes Down Jun Sch BR4 208 B1
Hawes La BR4 224 C6
Hawes Rd
Bromley BR1 187 B2
Edmonton N18 34 B4
Hawes St N1 72 D1
Haweswater Ho TW1 152 D6
Hawfinch 23 NW9 27 D2
Hawgood St E3 97 C2
Hawkdene E4 20 A5
Hawke Ct UB4 84 C3
Hawkedale Inf Sch TW16 193 D6
Hawke Ho 20 E1 96 D3
Hawke Park Rd N22 50 D6
Hawke Pl 29 SE16 118 D4
Hawker 28 NW9 27 D2
Hawker Ct 14 KT2 176 C3
Hawke Rd SE19 183 C4
Hawkesbury Rd SW15 156 B6
Hawkesfield Rd SE23 163 B2
Hawkesley Cl TW1 175 A6
Hawkes Rd
Feltham TW14 150 A4
Mitcham CR4 180 D2
Hawkesworth Ho 5 SW4 159 C5
Hawke Twr 4 SE14 141 A6
Hawkewood Rd TW16 194 A6
Hawkfield Ct TW7 130 C3
Hawk Ho 7 SW11 136 C2
Hawkhurst Gdns KT9 214 A4
Hawkhurst Rd SW16 181 D2
Hawkhurst Way
New Malden KT3 199 B4
West Wickham BR4 223 D6
Hawkinge N17 33 B1
Hawkins Cl
Burnt Oak NW7 27 B5
Harrow HA1 42 B2
Hawkins Ho
3 Deptford SE8 141 C6
10 Richmond TW10 153 C1
Hawkins Rd
Teddington TW11 175 B4
Willesden NW10 67 C1
Hawkins Way SE6 185 C5
Hawkley Gdns SE27 160 D2
Hawkridge 19 NW5 71 A2
Hawkridge Cl RM6 58 C3
Hawksbrook La BR3 208 A3
Hawkshaw Cl 28 SW2 160 A4
Hawkshead NW1 232 A2
Hawkshead Cl BR1 186 C3
Hawkshead Rd
Acton W4 111 C4
Willesden NW10 67 D1
Hawkslade Rd SE15 162 D6
Hawksley Rd N16 73 C5
Hawks Mews 10 SE10 142 A5
Hawksmoor Cl
2 Newham E6 100 A1
Plumstead Comm SE18 123 C1
Hawksmoor Mews E1 118 B6
Hawksmoor Pl 2 E2 96 A3
Hawksmoor Sch SE28 124 B6
Hawksmoor St 5 W6 134 D6
Hawksmouth E4 20 A4
Hawks Rd KT1 176 B1
Hawkstone Rd SE16 118 C2
Hawkwell Ct E4 20 A1
Hawkwell Ho RM8 81 C6
Hawkwell Wlk N1 235 B6
Hawkwood Cres E4 19 D5
Hawkwood La BR7 189 A2
Hawkwood Mount 1 E5 52 B1
Hawlands Dr HA5 41 A2
Hawley Cl TW12 173 B4
Hawley Cres NW1 71 B1
Hawley Inf Sch NW1 71 B1
Hawley Mews 4 NW1 71 B1
Hawley Rd
3 Camden Town NW1 71 B1
London N18 34 D5
Hawley St NW1 71 B1
Hawley Way TW15 170 D5
Haworth Ho 7 SW2 160 C5
Hawstead Rd SE6 163 D5
Hawsted IG9 21 B4
Hawthorn Ave
Bowes Pk N13 32 A5
Old Ford E3 97 B6
South Norwood CR7 182 D2

Hawthorn Cl
Cranford TW5 . . . 128 B5
Hampton TW12 . . . 173 C5
Petts Wood BR5 . . . 211 B3
Hawthorn Cres SW17 . . 181 A5
Hawthorn Ct
Littleton TW15 . . . 171 A3
2 Pinner HA5 . . . 22 C1
Putney SW15 . . . 134 B2
Redbridge IG5 . . . 56 B6
Richmond TW9 . . . 132 D4
Sutton SM1 . . . 217 C4
8 West Norwood SW16 . . . 182 C5
Hawthorn Ctr HA1 . . . 43 A4
Hawthornden Cl N12 . . . 30 C4
Hawthorndene Cl BR2 . . . 225 A6
Hawthorndene Rd BR2 . . . 225 A6
Hawthorn Dr
Coney Hall BR4 . . . 224 C4
Harrow HA2 . . . 41 C3
Hawthorne Ave
Harrow HA3 . . . 43 A3
Mitcham CR4 . . . 180 B1
Ruislip HA4 . . . 40 B2
Wallington SM5 . . . 219 A1
Hawthorne Cl
Bickley BR1 . . . 210 B6
Kingsland N1 . . . 73 C2
Sutton SM1 . . . 218 A6
Hawthorne Cres UB7 . . 104 B4
Hawthorne Ct
Chingford E4 . . . 35 D4
Ealing W5 . . . 110 A5
Pinner HA6 . . . 22 A1
Hawthorne Gr NW9 . . . 45 A2
Hawthorne Ho SW1 . . . 259 B1
Hawthorne Mews UB6 . . 86 A1
Hawthorne Rd
Bickley BR1 . . . 210 B6
Edmonton N18 . . . 33 D5
Walthamstow E17 . . . 53 C6
Hawthorne Way N9 . . . 17 D2
Hawthorn Farm Ave UB5 . . . 85 A6
Hawthorn Gdns W5 . . . 109 D3
Hawthorn Gr
Edgware EN5 . . . 11 D5
Enfield EN2 . . . 5 B5
Penge SE20 . . . 184 B2
Hawthorn Hatch TW8 . . 131 B5
Hawthorn Ho SE14 . . . 141 B4
Hawthorn Mews NW7 . . 29 A2
Hawthorn Pl UB3 . . . 105 D6
Hawthorn Rd
Bexleyheath DA6 . . . 147 B1
Brentford TW8 . . . 131 B5
Carshalton SM1 . . . 218 C2
Feltham TW14 . . . 150 A3
Hornsey N8 . . . 50 A6
Wallington SM5, SM6 . . 219 B1
Willesden NW10 . . . 68 A1
Woodford IG9 . . . 37 D6
Hawthorns IG8 . . . 21 A1
Hawthorns The
2 Cheam SM2 . . . 217 C2
Edgware NW7 . . . 27 B4
Stoneleigh KT17 . . . 216 A1
Hawthorn Terr DA15 . . 167 D6
Hawthorn Way TW17 . . 193 B5
Hawthorn Wlk W10 . . . 91 A3
Hawtrey Ave UB5 . . . 84 D5
Hawtrey Dr HA4 . . . 40 A2
Hawtrey Rd NW3 . . . 70 C1
Haxted Rd BR1 . . . 187 B2
Haybridge Ho 1 E5 . . . 74 C6
Hay Cl E15 . . . 76 D1
Haycroft Gdns NW10 . . . 90 B6
Haycroft Mans NW10 . . 90 A6
Haycroft Rd
London SW2 . . . 160 A6
Surbiton KT6 . . . 214 A6
Hay Currie St E14 . . . 97 D1
Hayday Rd E16 . . . 99 A2
Hayden Piper Ho SW3 267 C6
Hayden's Pl W11 . . . 91 B1
Haydock Ave UB5 . . . 63 C2
Haydock Gn UB5 . . . 63 C2
Haydock Green Flats 2
UB5 . . . 63 C2
Haydock Lo 2 SM6 . . . 219 D5
Haydon Cl
Enfield EN1 . . . 17 C6
Kingsbury NW9 . . . 45 A5
Haydon Ct NW9 . . . 45 A5
Haydon Dr HA5 . . . 40 A5
Haydon Ho W7 . . . 108 D5

Haydon Park Rd
SW19 . . . 179 D5
Haydon Rd RM8 . . . 80 C6
Haydon Sch HA5 . . . 39 D6
Haydon's Rd SW19 . . . 180 A4
Haydons Road Sta
SW19 . . . 180 A5
Haydon St E1,
EC3 . . . 117 D6 253 C6
Haydon Way SW11 . . . 136 B1
Haydon Wlk E1 . . . 243 D1
HAYES
BR2 . . . 209 A2
UB3 . . . 83 C1
Hayes Bridge Ret Pk
UB4 . . . 106 D6
Hayes Chase BR4 . . . 208 C3
Hayes Cl BR2 . . . 225 A6
Hayes Cres
Cheam SM3 . . . 216 D4
Temple Fortune NW11 . . . 47 B4
Hayes Ct
23 Camberwell SE5 . . . 139 A5
Streatham SW12 . . . 160 A3
Wimbledon SW19 . . . 179 A4
HAYES END . . . 83 B3
Hayes End Cl UB4 . . . 83 B2
Hayes End Dr UB4 . . . 83 B3
Hayesend Ho SW17 . . . 180 A6
Hayes End Rd UB4 . . . 83 B3
Hayesford Park Dr
BR2 . . . 208 D4
Hayes Gdn BR2 . . . 209 A1
Hayes Gr SE15, SE22 . . . 139 D1
Hayes & Harlington Sta
UB3 . . . 105 D3
Hayes Hill BR2 . . . 208 C1
Hayes Hill Rd BR2 . . . 208 D1
Hayes La
Beckenham BR2, BR3 . . . 208 B5
Hayes BR2 . . . 209 A4
Hayes Mead Rd BR2 . . . 208 C1
Hayes Park Sch UB4 . . . 83 D3
Hayes Pl NW1 . . . 237 B5
Hayes Prim Sch BR2 . . 209 B1
Hayes Rd
Bromley BR2 . . . 209 A5
Southall UB2 . . . 106 B2
Hayes Sch BR2 . . . 225 B6
Hayes St BR2 . . . 209 B1
Hayes Sta BR2 . . . 208 D1
HAYES TOWN . . . 106 B5
Hayes Way BR3 . . . 208 B5
Hayes Wood Ave BR2 . . 209 B1
Hayfield Pas E1 . . . 96 C3
Hayfield Yd 43 E1 . . . 96 C3
Hayford Ct NW2 . . . 68 D5
Haygarth Pl 2 SW19 . . 178 D5
Haygreen Cl KT2 . . . 176 D4
Hay Hill W1 . . . 115 B6 248 D5
Hayhurst N1 . . . 234 D6
Hay La NW9 . . . 45 B5
Hayland Cl NW9 . . . 45 B5
Hay Lane Sch NW9 . . . 45 A5
Hayles Bldgs SE11 . . . 261 D4
Hayles St
SE11 . . . 116 D2 261 C4
Haylett Gdns KT1 . . . 197 D5
Hayley Ho DA17 . . . 147 C6
Hayling Ave TW13 . . . 150 A1
Hayling Cl 20 N16 . . . 73 C3
Hayling Ct SM3 . . . 216 C4
Haymaker Cl UB10 . . . 60 B1
Hayman Cres UB4 . . . 83 B5
Haymans Point SE11 . . 260 C2
Haymarket
SW1 . . . 115 D6 249 C5
Haymeads Dr KT10 . . . 212 A2
Haymer Gdns KT4 . . . 216 A5
Haymerle Ho 6 SE15 . . 140 A5
Haymerle Rd SE15 . . . 140 A6
Haymerle Sch SE15 . . . 140 A6
Haymill Cl UB6 . . . 86 D4
Haymills Ct W5 . . . 88 B3
Hayne Ho W11 . . . 244 A4
Hayne Rd BR3 . . . 185 B2
Haynes Cl
Friern Barnet N11 . . . 15 A1
Lewisham SE3 . . . 142 C2
Tottenham N17 . . . 34 B3
Haynes Dr N9 . . . 18 B1
Haynes Ho 3 E9 . . . 74 D2
Haynes La SE19 . . . 183 C4
Haynes Rd HA0 . . . 66 A1
Hayne St EC1 . . . 94 D2 241 D4
Haynt Wlk SW20 . . . 201 A6
Hay's Galleria* SE1 . . 253 A4
Hay's La SE1 . . . 253 A4
Haysleigh Gdns SE20 . . 184 A1
Haysleigh Ho SE20 . . . 184 B1

Hay's Mews
W1 . . . 115 B5 248 C4
Hay St E2 . . . 96 A6
Haystall Cl UB4 . . . 83 C5
Hayter Ct E11 . . . 77 B6
Hayter Ho W12 . . . 112 A6
Hayter Rd SW2 . . . 160 B6
Haythorn Ho
SW11 . . . 136 B4 266 D1
Hayton Cl 11 E8 . . . 73 D2
Hayward Cl SW19 . . . 179 D2
Hayward Ct
14 London SW4 . . . 138 A3
Mitcham CR4 . . . 180 B1
Hayward Gallery*
SE1 . . . 116 B5 250 D4
Hayward Gdns SW15 . . 156 C5
Hayward Ho
Islington N1 . . . 234 A4
Lower Clapton E5 . . . 74 B5
Hayward Rd
London N20 . . . 14 A2
Thames Ditton KT7 . . . 196 D1
Haywards Cl RM6 . . . 58 C4
Haywards Pl EC1 . . . 241 C6
Hayward's Pl EC1 . . . 241 C6
Haywood Cl HA5 . . . 22 D1
Haywood Ct N11 . . . 31 D4
Haywood Lo 23 N7 . . . 71 D3
Haywood Rd BR2 . . . 209 D5
Haywood Rise BR6 . . . 227 C3
Hazel Ave UB7 . . . 104 C3
Hazelbank KT5 . . . 199 A1
Hazel Bank SE25 . . . 183 C1
Hazelbank Rd SE6 . . . 164 C2
Hazelbourne Rd
SW12 . . . 159 B5
Hazelbury Cl SW19 . . . 179 C1
Hazelbury Gn N9 . . . 17 C1
Hazelbury Inf Sch N9 . . 17 C1
Hazelbury Jun Sch N9 . . 17 C1
Hazelbury La N9 . . . 17 C1
Hazel Cl
Brentford TW8 . . . 131 B5
Croydon CR0 . . . 206 D1
Edmonton N13 . . . 17 B1
Hendon NW9 . . . 27 D1
Mitcham CR4 . . . 203 D5
Peckham SE15 . . . 140 A3
Twickenham TW2 . . . 152 A4
Upper Holloway N19 . . . 71 C6
Hazelcroft HA5 . . . 23 D4
Hazelcroft Cl UB10 . . . 60 B1
Hazel Ct
Ealing W5 . . . 110 A6
8 Rotherhithe SE16 . . . 119 A5
9 West Norwood
SW16 . . . 182 C5
Hazeldean Rd NW10 . . . 67 B1
Hazeldene Dr HA5 . . . 40 C6
Hazeldene Gdns UB10 . . 83 A6
Hazeldene Rd
Bexley DA16 . . . 146 C3
Ilford IG3 . . . 80 B6
Hazeldon Rd SE4 . . . 163 A6
Hazel Gdns HA8 . . . 26 D6
Hazel Gr
Dagenham RM6 . . . 59 A6
Enfield EN1 . . . 18 A5
Feltham TW14 . . . 150 A3
Forest Hill SE26 . . . 184 D6
Orpington BR6 . . . 226 D6
Wembley HA0 . . . 88 A6
Hazelgreen Cl N21 . . . 16 D3
Hazel Ho
London SE4 . . . 141 B2
12 Maitland Pk NW3 . . . 70 D2
Hazelhurst BR3 . . . 186 B2
Hazelhurst Ct SE6 . . . 186 A5
Hazelhurst Rd SW17 . . 180 B6
Hazellville Rd N19 . . . 49 D1
Hazel Mead EN5 . . . 12 B6
Hazelmere Cl
Feltham TW14 . . . 149 C5
Northolt UB5 . . . 85 B5
Hazelmere Ct 10
SW2 . . . 160 B3
Hazelmere Dr UB5 . . . 85 B5
Hazelmere Rd
Kilburn NW6 . . . 91 B6
Northolt UB5 . . . 85 B5
Petts Wood BR5 . . . 211 B5
Hazelmere Way BR2 . . 209 A3
Hazelmere Wlk UB5 . . . 85 B5
Hazel Rd
Kensal Green NW10 . . . 90 C4
Stratford E15 . . . 76 C3
Hazeltree La UB5 . . . 85 A4
Hazel Way
Bermondsey SE1 . . . 263 C4

Hazel Way *continued*
Walthamstow E4 . . . 35 B4
Hazel Wlk BR2 . . . 210 C3
Hazelwood IG10 . . . 21 D6
Hazelwood Ave SM4 . . 201 D5
Hazelwood Cl
Clapton Pk E5 . . . 75 A5
Ealing W5 . . . 110 A4
Harrow HA2 . . . 41 D5
Hazelwood Cres N13 . . . 32 C6
Hazelwood Ct
1 Edmonton N13 . . . 32 C6
Surbiton KT6 . . . 198 A3
1 Willesden NW10 . . . 67 C5
Hazelwood Dr HA5 . . . 22 B1
Hazelwood Ho
Beckenham BR2 . . . 208 C6
Chingford E4 . . . 20 B4
11 Deptford SE8 . . . 119 A2
Edmonton N13 . . . 32 D6
2 Sutton SM1 . . . 218 A4
Hazelwood Jun & Inf Schs
N13 . . . 32 C6
Hazelwood La N13 . . . 32 C6
Hazelwood Lo BR4 . . . 208 A2
Hazelwood Mans
SW6 . . . 264 C2
Hazelwood Rd
Enfield EN1 . . . 17 D5
Walthamstow E17 . . . 53 A4
Hazlebury Rd SW6 . . . 135 D3
Hazledean Rd CR0 . . . 221 B6
Hazledene Rd W4 . . . 133 A6
Hazlemere 3 DA14 . . . 190 A6
Hazlemere Gdns KT4 . . 200 A1
Hazlewell Rd SW15 . . . 156 C6
Hazlewood Cres W10 . . 91 A3
Hazlewood Twr W10 . . . 91 B3
Hazlitt Cl TW13 . . . 173 A6
Hazlitt Ct 4 SE28 . . . 124 C5
Hazlitt Mews W14 . . . 254 A5
Hazlitt Rd
W14 . . . 113 A3 254 A5
Heacham Ave UB10 . . . 61 A5
Headbourne Ho SE1 . . 262 D6
Headcorn 10 NW5 . . . 71 A2
Headcorn Pl CR7 . . . 204 B5
Headcorn Rd
Plaistow BR1 . . . 187 A5
Thornton Heath CR7 . . . 204 B5
Tottenham N17 . . . 33 D3
Headfort Pl
SW1 . . . 115 A4 248 B1
Headington Rd SW18 . . 158 A2
Headlam Rd SW4 . . . 159 D4
Headlam St E1 . . . 96 B3
Headley App IG2 . . . 56 D4
Headley Ave CR0, SM6 . . 220 B3
Headley Cl KT19 . . . 214 C2
Headley Ct SE26 . . . 184 C5
Headley Dr
Ilford IG2 . . . 56 D3
New Addington CR0 . . . 224 A1
Headley Ho 5 BR5 . . . 190 B1
Heads Mews W11 . . . 91 C1
Head St E1 . . . 96 D1
Headstart Montessori Sch
SW17 . . . 180 A6
HEADSTONE . . . 41 D5
Headstone Dr HA1,
HA3 . . . 42 C6
Headstone Gdns HA2 . . 42 A5
Headstone La
Harrow HA2, HA3 . . . 23 D2
Headstone HA2 . . . 41 D5
Headstone Lane Sta
HA3 . . . 23 D2
Headstone Rd HA1 . . . 42 C3
Headway Cl TW10 . . . 175 C6
Heald St SE8, SE14 . . . 141 C4
Healey Ho RM6 . . . 59 A5
Healey St NW1 . . . 71 B2
Healy Ct EN5 . . . 12 D5
Healy Dr 1 BR6 . . . 227 D4
Healy Ho
12 Kennington SW9 . . . 138 C5
2 Tower Hamlets E3 . . . 97 C3
Heanor Ct 4 E5 . . . 74 D4
Hearne Rd W4 . . . 132 C6
Hearn Rise UB5 . . . 84 D6
Hearn's Bldgs SE17 . . . 262 D3
Hearnshaw St 1 E14 . . . 97 A1
Hearn St EC2 . . . 95 C3 243 B5
Hearnville Rd SW12 . . . 159 A3
Heart Hospl The
W1 . . . 93 A2 238 B3
Heart Raido W11 . . . 112 D6
Heart The KT12 . . . 193 D1
Heatham Pk TW2 . . . 152 D4
Heath Ave DA7 . . . 146 D6

Heathbourne Rd WD23 . . 8 D3
Heathbrook Prim Sch
SW4 . . . 137 C3
Heath Brow NW3 . . . 70 A5
Heath Bsns Ctr The
TW3 . . . 130 A1
Heath Cl
Croydon CR2 . . . 220 D2
Ealing W5 . . . 88 B3
Golders Green NW11 . . . 47 D2
Harlington UB3 . . . 127 B5
Heathcote Gr E4 . . . 20 A2
Heathcote Point 25 E9 . 74 D2
Heathcote Rd TW1 . . . 153 B6
Heathcote Sch E4 . . . 20 C2
Heathcote St
WC1 . . . 94 B4 233 C1
Heathcroft
Ealing W5 . . . 88 B3
Golders Green NW11 . . . 47 D1
Heathcroft Ave TW16 . 171 D3
Heathcroft Gdns E4 . . . 36 B2
Heath Ct
Carshalton SM5 . . . 218 B6
Eltham SE9 . . . 167 A3
2 Hampstead NW3 . . . 70 A2
Leytonstone E11 . . . 54 D3
Stoke Newington N16 . . . 51 B1
Uxbridge UB8 . . . 60 A1
Heathdale Ave TW4 . . 129 A2
Heathdene N14 . . . 15 C4
Heathdene Dr DA17 . . . 125 D2
Heathdene Rd
South Norwood
SW16 . . . 182 B3
Wallington SM5, SM6 . . . 219 B1
Heath Dr
West Barnes SW20 . . . 200 C5
West Hampstead NW3 . . . 69 D4
Heathedge SE23, SE26 . 162 B2
Heath End Ct WD23 . . . 8 C2
Heatherbank
Chislehurst BR7 . . . 188 C1
Eltham SE9 . . . 144 B3
Heather Cl
Clapham SW8 . . . 137 B2
Hampton TW12 . . . 173 B2
Hillingdon UB8 . . . 82 B2
Hither Green SE13 . . . 164 B4
Isleworth TW7 . . . 152 B6
Newham E6 . . . 100 C1
Heather Ct
South Lambeth SW4 . . . 270 B1
6 West Norwood
SW16 . . . 182 C6
Heatherdale Cl KT2 . . 176 D3
Heatherdene Cl
London N12 . . . 30 A2
Mitcham CR4 . . . 202 C5
Heatherdene Ct CR4 . . 202 B5
Heatherdene Mans 2
TW1 . . . 153 D5
Heather Dr EN2 . . . 4 D3
Heatherfold Way HA5,
HA6 . . . 39 D6
Heather Gdns
Belmont SM2 . . . 217 C2
Hendon NW11 . . . 47 A3
Heather Ho 11 E14 . . . 98 A1
Heather La UB7 . . . 82 A1
Heatherlands TW16 . . 172 A4
Heatherley Ct N16 . . . 74 A5
Heatherley Dr IG5 . . . 56 B6
Heatherley Sch of Fine
Art SW10 . . . 266 B3
Heather Lo N16 . . . 51 C1
Heather Park Dr HA0 . . 66 C1
Heather Park Par HA0 . . 66 B1
Heather Rd
Dollis Hill NW2 . . . 67 D6
Lewisham SE12 . . . 165 A3
Walthamstow E4 . . . 35 B4
Heatherset Cl KT10 . . . 212 A3
Heatherset Gdns
SW16 . . . 182 B3
Heatherside Rd
Sidcup DA14 . . . 168 C1
West Ewell KT19 . . . 215 B1
Heathers The TW19 . . 148 B4
Heather Way HA7 . . . 24 D4
Heather Wlk
Edgware HA8 . . . 26 D5
Twickenham TW4 . . . 151 C4
West Kilburn W10 . . . 91 A3
Heatherwood Cl E12 . . . 77 C6
Heatherwood Dr UB4 . . 83 B5
Heathfield
Chingford E4 . . . 20 A1
Chislehurst BR7 . . . 189 A4
Heathfield Ave SW18 . . 158 B4

Heathfield Cl
Keston BR2 . . . 225 C3
Newham E16 . . . 99 D2
Heathfield Ct
Ashford TW15 . . . 148 A1
3 Bow E3 . . . 97 C5
5 Chiswick W4 . . . 111 B1
Penge SE20 . . . 184 C3
Sidcup DA14 . . . 190 B5
8 Sutton SM2 . . . 218 A2
Wandsworth SW18 . . . 158 B4
Heathfield Dr CR4 . . . 180 C2
Heathfielde N2 . . . 48 A4
Heathfield Gdns
Acton Green W4 . . . 111 A1
Blackheath SE3 . . . 142 C3
Croydon CR0 . . . 221 B4
Hendon NW11 . . . 46 D3
Wandsworth SW18 . . . 158 B5
Heathfield Ho SE3 . . . 142 C3
Heathfield Inf Sch
TW2 . . . 151 C3
Heathfield Jun Sch
TW2 . . . 151 C3
Heathfield La BR7 . . . 189 A4
Heathfield N TW1,
TW2 . . . 152 D4
Heathfield Park Dr
RM6 . . . 58 B4
Heathfield Pk NW2 . . . 68 C2
Heathfield Rd
Bexleyheath DA6 . . . 147 B1
Bromley BR1 . . . 186 D3
Croydon CR0 . . . 221 B4
Keston BR2 . . . 225 D3
South Acton W3 . . . 110 D4
Wandsworth SW18 . . . 158 B5
Heathfield Rise HA4 . . . 39 A2
Heathfield S TW1,
TW2 . . . 152 D4
Heathfield Sch HA5 . . . 40 D2
Heathfield Sq SW18 . . . 158 B4
Heathfield Terr
Chiswick W4 . . . 111 B1
Plumstead Comm SE18 . 145 D6
Heathfield Vale CR2 . . 223 A1
Heathgate NW11 . . . 47 D3
Heathgate Pl NW3 . . . 70 D4
Heath Gdns TW1 . . . 152 D2
Heath Gr
Ashford TW16 . . . 171 D3
Penge SE20 . . . 184 C3
Heath Ho
Sidcup DA15 . . . 189 D6
Thornton Heath CR7 . . . 204 C4
Uxbridge UB10 . . . 60 D4
Heath Hurst Rd NW3 . . . 70 C4
Heath La SE3 . . . 142 B3
Heathland Rd N16 . . . 51 C1
Heathland Sch The
TW4 . . . 151 B5
Heathlands Cl
Sunbury TW16 . . . 172 A1
Twickenham TW1 . . . 152 D3
Heathlands Ct
Hounslow TW4 . . . 151 A6
Mitcham CR4 . . . 203 A6
Heathlands Way TW4 . 151 A6
Heathlee Rd SE3 . . . 142 D1
Heathley End BR7 . . . 189 A4
Heath Lo WD23 . . . 8 B3
Heath Mans
5 Hampstead NW3 . . . 70 A4
Putney SW15 . . . 156 D5
Heathman's Rd
SW6 . . . 135 B4 264 D1
Heath Mead SW19 . . . 156 D1
Heathmere Prim Sch
SW15 . . . 156 A3
Heath Park Dr BR1 . . . 210 A6
Heath Park Gdns NW3 . . 69 D5
Heath Park Ind Est
RM8 . . . 59 A1
Heathpool Ct 8 E1 . . . 96 B3
Heath Rd
Clapham SW8 . . . 137 B3
Dagenham RM6 . . . 59 A2
Harrow HA1 . . . 42 A2
Hillingdon UB10 . . . 83 A3
Isleworth TW3, TW7 . . . 130 A1
South Norwood CR7 . . . 205 A6
Twickenham TW1 . . . 152 D3
Heath Rise
Hayes BR2 . . . 209 A3
Putney SW15 . . . 156 D5
Heathrow Airport London
TW6 . . . 126 D3

Heathrow Bvd UB7 126 B5
Heathrow Causeway Est TW4 128 B2
Heathrow International Trad Est TW4 128 B2
Heathrow Prim Sch UB7 126 B6
Heathrow Terminal 4 Sta TW6 149 A5
Heathrow Terminals 1, 2, 3 TW6 126 D2
Heath Royal SW15 156 D5
Heath's Cl EN1 5 C3
Heathshott 8 TW10 154 A5
Heathside
Hampstead NW3 70 B4
Hinchley Wood KT10 212 C5
Twickenham TW4 151 B4
Heath Side BR5 211 A2
Heathside Ave DA7 147 A3
Heathside Cl
Hinchley Wood KT10 212 C5
Ilford IG2 57 B4
Heathside Prep Sch NW3 70 A4
Heath St NW3 70 A5
Heathstan Rd W12 90 A1
Heath Terr RM6 58 D2
Heath The W7 108 C5
Heath View
Gospel Oak NW5 71 A4
London N2 48 A5
Heath View Cl N2 48 A5
Heathview Ct SW19 156 D2
Heath View Dr SE2 146 D6
Heathview Gdns SW15 156 C4
Heathview Rd CR7 204 C5
Heath Villas
Hampstead NW3 70 B5
Plumstead Comm SE18 123 D1
Heathville Rd N4, N19 50 A2
Heathwall St SW11 136 D2
Heathway
Croydon CR0 223 B5
Dagenham RM10 81 C2
Dagenham RM10 103 C6
Greenwich SE3 143 A5
Woodford IG8 37 C5
Heathway Ct NW3 69 C6
Heathway Ind Est RM10 81 D4
Heathwood Ct
1 Hounslow TW3 129 D1
Streatham SW12 159 C3
Heathwood Gdns SE7 122 A1
Heathwood Point 7 SE26 162 D1
Heaton Cl E4 20 A1
Heaton Ct 3 N20 14 D2
Heaton Ho
Chelsea SW10 266 B6
6 Peckham SE15 140 B3
Heaton Rd
London SE15 140 B3
Mitcham CR4 181 A3
Heaven Tree Cl N1 73 A3
Heaver Rd 24 SW11 136 B2
Heavers Farm Prim Sch SE25 205 D4
Heavitree Cl SE18 123 B1
Heavitree Ct E17 35 D2
Heavitree Rd SE18 123 B1
Hebble Ho UB5 85 A6
Hebden Ct 24 E2 95 D6
Hebden Terr N17 33 C4
Hebdon Rd SW17 158 C1
Hebe Ct SM1 218 A4
Heber Prim Sch SE22 161 D5
Heber Rd
Cricklewood NW2 68 D4
East Dulwich SE22 161 D5
Hebron Rd W6 112 B3
Hecham Cl E17 35 A2
Heckfield Pl SW6 135 C5 265 A3
Heckford Ho E14 97 D1
Heckford St E1 118 D6
Hector 31 NW9 27 D2
Hector Ct
1 London SW9 138 C4
Putney SW15 156 D6
Hector Ho 16 E2 96 B5
Hector St SE18 123 C2
Heddington Gr N7 72 B3
Heddon Cl TW7 131 A1
Heddon Court Ave EN4 14 D6
Heddon Court Par EN4 15 A6
Heddon Ct EN4 15 A6
Heddon Rd EN4 14 D6
Heddon St W1 249 A6
Hedge Hill EN2 4 D4
Hedge La N13 17 A1
Hedgeley IG4 56 B5
Hedgemans Rd RM9 81 A1
Hedgemans Way RM9 81 A2
Hedgemoor Ct 1 E4 36 B5
Hedgerley Gdns UB6 86 A5
Hedgerow La EN5 12 B6
Hedger's Gr E9 75 A2
Hedger St SE11 261 C4
Hedge Wlk SE6 185 D6
Hedgewood Gdns IG5 56 C4
Hedgewood Specl Sch UB4 83 C4
Hedgley Mews SE12 164 D6
Hedgley St SE12 164 D6
Hedingham Cl 6 N1 73 A1
Hedingham Ho 7 KT2 176 A2
Hedingham Rd RM8 80 B3
Hedley Ct SW15 156 D5
Hedley Ho E14 120 A3
Hedley Rd TW4 151 C4
Hedley Row N5, N16 73 B3
Hedsor Ho E2 243 C6
Heenan Cl IG11 79 A2
Heene Rd EN2 5 B4
Heidegger Cres SW13 134 B5
Heigham Rd E6 78 A1
Heighton Gdns CR0 220 D3
Heights Cl SW20 178 B3
Heights The
Beckenham BR3 186 A3
Greenwich SE7 121 C1
Hampstead NW3 70 A4
Northolt UB5 63 C3
Stroud Green N4 50 C3
Heiron St SE17 138 D6
Helby Rd SW4 159 D5
Heldar Ct SE1 252 D1
Helder Gr SE12 164 D4
Helder St CR2 221 B2
Heldmann Cl TW7 130 B1
Helegan Cl BR6 227 D4
Helena Cl EN4 2 B5
Helena Ct W5 87 D2
Helena Pl 3 E9 96 C6
Helena Rd
Ealing W5 87 D2
Newham E13 99 A5
Walthamstow E17 53 C4
Willesden NW10 68 B3
Helena Sq 12 SE16 119 A6
Helen Ave TW14 150 B4
Helen Cl
East Finchley N2 48 A6
East Molesey KT8 195 D5
Helen Clare Ct EN2 4 D2
Helen Ct N3 47 A6
Helen Gladstone Ho SE1 251 C2
Helen Ho 9 E2 96 B5
Helen Mackay Ho 10 E14 98 B1
Helen Peele Cotts 10 SE16 118 C3
Helenslea Ave NW11 47 C1
Helen's Pl E2 96 C4
Helen St SE18 122 D2
Helen Taylor Ho 5 SE16 118 A2
Helford Cl HA4 61 C6
Helgiford Gdns TW16 171 C3
Helios Rd CR4 203 A1
Heliport Est The SW11 136 B3
Helix Ct 17 W11 112 D5
Helix Gdns SW2 160 B5
Helix Ho TW7 131 B3
Helix Rd SW2 160 B5
Helix The SW19 156 D2
Hellenic Coll of London SW1 114 D3 257 C5
Hellen Way WD19 22 D6
Hellings St E1 118 A5
Helme Cl SW19 179 B5
Helmet Row EC1 242 B6
Helmore Rd IG11 79 D1
Helmsdale Cl UB4 85 A3
Helmsdale Ho NW6 91 D5
Helmsdale Rd SW16 181 D2
Helmsley 11 E18 55 A6
Helmsley Pl E8 74 B1
Helmsley St 7 E8 74 B1
Helperby Rd NW10 67 C1
Helsby Ct NW8 236 C6
Helsinki Sq SE16 119 A3
Helston NW1 232 B4
Helston Cl HA5 23 B3
Helston Ct N15 51 C4
Helston Ho SE11 261 B2
Helvetia St SE6 163 B2
Helwys Ct E4 36 A4
Hemans Est SW8 137 D5 269 D3
Hemans St SW8 137 D5 269 D3
Hemberton Rd SW9 138 A2
Hemery Rd UB6 64 B3
Hemingford Cl N12 30 B5
Hemingford Rd
Cheam SM3 216 C4
Islington N1 94 B6 233 D6
Heming Rd HA8 26 D3
Hemington Ave N11 30 D5
Hemlock Rd W12 111 D6
Hemmen La UB3 83 D1
Hemming Cl 6 TW12 173 C2
Hemmings Cl DA14 168 B2
Hemmings Ct HA8 27 A3
Hemmings Mead KT19 215 A2
Hemming St E1 96 A3
Hemmingway Cl NW5 71 A4
Hempstead Cl IG9 21 A2
Hempstead Rd E17 36 B1
Hemp Wlk SE17 262 D4
Hemsby Rd KT9 214 B2
Hemstal Rd NW6 69 C1
Hemswell Dr NW9 27 C2
Hemsworth Ct N1 95 C5
Hemsworth St N1 95 C5
Hemus Pl SW3 257 B1
Henchman St W12 89 D1
Hendale Ave NW4 46 B6
Hendale Ho 13 E5 74 B6
Henderson Cl NW10 67 A2
Henderson Ct
8 Deptford SE14 140 D6
Hampstead NW3 70 B3
Wandsworth SW18 158 C4
Woodside Pk N12 29 D6
Henderson Dr NW8 92 B3 236 C6
Henderson Ho 7 RM10 81 C5
Henderson Rd
Edmonton N9 18 B3
Forest Gate E7 77 C2
Hayes UB4 84 A4
Thornton Heath CR0 205 B3
Wandsworth SW18 158 C4
Hendfield Ct 5 SM6 219 B2
Hendham Rd SW17 158 D2
HENDON 46 C3
Hendon Ave N3 29 A2
Hendon Central NW4 46 B4
Hendon Central Sta NW4 46 B4
Hendon Hall Ct NW4 46 D6
Hendon Ho NW4 46 D4
Hendon La N3 29 B1
Hendon Lo NW4 46 B6
Hendon Park Mans NW4 46 C4
Hendon Park Row NW11 47 B3
Hendon Pk Cotts NW7 11 D2
Hendon Prep Sch NW4 46 D6
Hendon Rd N9 18 A2
Hendon Sch NW4 46 D4
Hendon Sta NW4 46 A3
Hendon Terr TW15 171 B4
Hendon Way NW2, NW4 46 C3
Hendon Wood La NW7 12 A3
Hendre Ho SE1 263 B3
Hendren Cl UB6 64 B3
Hendre Rd SE1 117 C2 263 B3
Hendrick Ave SW12 158 D4
Heneage La EC3 243 B1
Heneage Pl EC3 243 B1
Heneage St E1 95 D2 243 D4
Henfield Cl
London N19 49 C1
Old Bexley DA5 169 C5
Henfield Rd SW19 179 B2
Hengelo Gdns CR4 202 B5
Hengist Rd
Eltham SE12 165 B4
Hengist Rd *continued*
Erith DA8 147 D5
Hengist Way BR2, BR3 208 C5
Hengrave Rd SE23 162 D4
Hengrove Ct DA5 169 A3
Henley Ave SM3 217 A5
Henley Cl
Greenford UB6 86 A5
Hounslow TW7 130 D4
Rotherhithe SE16 118 C4
Henley Ct
Brondesbury NW2 68 D2
Hendon NW4 46 A6
Ilford IG1 78 D4
Mitcham CR4 203 A6
Oakwood N14 15 C4
Peckham SE15 140 A2
Sidcup DA5 169 B4
Henley Dr
Bermondsey SE1 117 D2 263 D4
Kingston u T KT2 177 D3
Henley Gdns
Dagenham RM6 59 A4
Pinner HA5 40 B6
Henley Ho
London N12 30 B5
Shoreditch E2 243 D6
Henley Lo
South Norwood SE25 205 D5
Walthamstow E17 53 B4
Henley Prior N1 233 C3
Henley Rd
Edmonton N18 33 C6
Ilford IG1 79 B4
Newham E16 122 B4
Willesden NW10 90 C6
Henleys Cnr NW11 47 B5
Henleys Rdbt TW5 128 C3
Henley St SW11 137 A3
Henley Way TW13 172 D5
Henlow Pl TW10 153 D2
Hennel Cl SE23 162 C1
Hennessy Rd N9 18 C2
Henniker Gdns E6 100 A4
Henniker Mews SW3 266 C6
Henniker Point E15 76 C3
Henniker Rd E15 76 B3
Henningham Rd N17 33 B2
Henning St SW11 136 C4 267 A1
Henrietta Barnett Sch NW11 47 D3
Henrietta Cl SE8 141 C6
Henrietta Ho
11 Hammersmith W6 112 C1
3 New Barnet EN5 2 A1
3 South Tottenham N15 51 C3
Henrietta Mews WC1 240 B6
Henrietta Pl W1 93 B1 238 C2
Henrietta St
Strand WC2 116 A6 250 B6
Stratford New Town E15 76 A3
Henriques St E1 96 A1
Henry Addlington Cl E6 100 D2
Henry Cavendish Prim Sch SW12 159 C3
Henry Cl EN2 5 C5
Henry Compton Sec Sch SW6 135 A4 264 A2
Henry Cooper Way SE12 187 D6
Henry Darlot Dr NW7 29 A5
Henry Dent Cl SE5 139 B2
Henry Dickens Ct W11 244 A4
Henry Doulton Dr SW17 181 B6
Henry Fawcett Prim Sch SE11 138 C6
Henry Green Prim Sch RM8 80 D6
Henry Hatch Ct SM2 218 A1
Henry Ho
Lambeth SE1 251 B3
South Lambeth SW8 270 A4
St John's Wood NW8 230 A4
Henry Jackson Ho SW15 134 D2
Henry Jackson Rd SW15 134 D2
Henry Macaulay Ave 13 KT2 175 D2
Henry Maynard Inf Sch E17 54 A4
Henry Maynard Jun Sch E17 54 A4
Henry Peters Dr TW11 174 C5
Henry Rd
London N4 51 A1
New Barnet EN4 14 B6
Newham E6 100 A5
Henry's Ave IG8 36 D5
Henryson Rd SE4 163 C6
Henry St BR1 187 B2
Henry Tate Mews SW16 182 C5
Henry Wise Ho SW1 259 B3
Hensford Gdns SE26 184 B6
Henshall Point 19 E3 97 D4
Henshall St N1 73 B2
Henshawe Rd RM8 80 D5
Henshaw St SE17 117 B2 262 C4
Hensley Point 28 E9 74 D2
Henslowe Rd SE22 162 A6
Henslow Ho 12 SE15 140 A5
Henson Ave NW2 68 C3
Henson Cl BR6 226 D6
Henson Ct 3 N5 73 A4
Henson Path HA3 43 D6
Henson Pl UB5 84 C6
Henstridge Pl NW8 230 A5
Henty Cl SW11 136 C4 267 B2
Henty Wlk SW15 156 B6
Henville Rd BR1 187 B2
Henwick Prim Sch SE9 144 A2
Henwick Rd SE9 144 A2
Hepburn Gdns BR2 208 D1
Hepburn Mews SW11 158 D6
Hepple Cl TW7 131 B3
Hepplestone Cl SW15 156 B5
Hepscott Rd E9 75 C1
Hepworth Ct
Barking IG11 80 A3
Cheam SM3 201 C1
Chelsea SW1 258 C1
Islington N1 234 C6
Hepworth Gdns IG11 80 A3
Hepworth Ho IG8 21 A1
Hepworth Rd SW16 182 A3
Hepworth Way KT12 193 D1
Heracles 30 NW9 27 D2
Heracles Cl SM6 220 A1
Hera Ct 15 E14 119 C2
Herald Gdns SM6 219 B5
Heralds Pl SE11 261 C4
Herald St 5 E2 96 B3
Herbal Hill EC1 241 B5
Herbert Chapman Ct N5 72 D4
Herbert Cres SW1 257 D6
Herbert Ct 4 KT5 198 B3
Herbert Gdns
Chiswick W4 132 D6
Dagenham RM6 58 D2
Willesden Green NW10 90 B5
Herbert Ho E1 243 C2
Herbert Mews 15 SW2 160 C5
Herbert Morrison Ho SW6 264 C5
Herbert Morrison Prim Sch SW8 138 A5 270 A3
Herbert Pl
Hounslow TW3 130 B3
Shooters Hill SE18 144 D6
Herbert Rd
Bexleyheath DA7 147 A3
Bromley BR2 210 A4
Hendon NW9 46 A3
Ilford IG3 79 C6
Kingston u T KT1 198 B6
Manor Pk E12 78 A4
Merton SW19 179 B3
Shooters Hill SE18 144 D6
Southall UB1 107 B5
South Tottenham N15 51 D4
Walthamstow E17 53 B2
Wood Green N11 32 A3
Herbert St
Camden Town NW5 71 A2
Newham E13 99 A5
Herbrand Est WC1 94 A3 240 A6
Herbrand St WC1 94 A3 240 A6
Hercies Rd UB10 60 C2
Hercules Ct 7 SE14 141 A6
Hercules Pl N7 72 A5
Hercules Rd SE1 116 B3 260 D5
Hercules St N7 72 A5
Hereford Ave EN4 14 D3
Hereford Bldgs SW3 266 D6
Hereford Ct
20 Belmont SM2 217 C1
6 Croydon CR0 205 D1
6 Ealing W7 86 D2
Harrow HA1 42 C6
Hereford Gdns
London SE13 164 C6
Pinner HA5 41 A4
Redbridge IG1 56 A2
Twickenham TW2 152 A3
Hereford Ho
7 Acton W3 88 C1
5 Brixton SW2 138 C1
25 Camberwell SE5 139 A3
Edgware HA8 26 B3
Knightsbridge SW3 257 B6
Walham Green SW10 265 D4
Hereford Mans 10 W2 91 C1
Hereford Mews 11 W2 91 C1
Hereford Pl SE14 141 B5
Hereford Rd
Acton W3 111 A6
Bayswater W2 113 C6 245 B6
Ealing W5 109 C3
Feltham TW13 150 C3
Wanstead E11 55 B4
Hereford Retreat 5 SE15 140 A5
Hereford Sq SW7 114 A2 256 B3
Hereford St E2 96 A3
Hereford Way KT9 213 D3
Herent Dr IG5 56 B6
Hereward Gdns N13 32 C5
Hereward House Sch NW3 70 B2
Hereward Rd SW17 180 D6
Herga Ct HA1 64 C6
Herga Rd HA3 42 D5
Heriot Ave E4 19 C2
Heriot Rd NW4 46 C4
Heriots Cl HA7 25 A6
Heritage Cl
London SW9 138 D2
Sunbury TW16 172 A2
Heritage Ct SE8 118 D1
Heritage Hill BR2 225 C3
Heritage Ho
22 Putney SW19 156 D3
3 Twickenham TW1 153 A4
Heritage View HA1 64 D5
Herlwyn Ave HA4 61 C5
Herlwyn Gdns SW17 180 D6
Herm Cl TW7 130 A5
Hermes Cl 5 W9 91 C3
Hermes Ct 4 SW9 138 C4
Hermes Ho BR3 185 A2
Hermes St N1 234 A3
Hermes Way SM6 219 D1
Hermes Wlk UB5 85 C5
Herm Ho EN3 6 D5
Hermiston Ave N8 50 A4
Hermiston Ct
3 Hornsey N8 50 A4
7 North Finchley N12 30 B5
Hermitage Cl
1 Abbey Wood SE2 124 C3
Claygate KT10 213 A2
Enfield EN2 4 D3
Littleton TW17 192 C5
Snaresbrook E18 54 D5
Hermitage Ct
2 Child's Hill NW2 69 C5
Colney Hatch N11 30 D4
3 Wanstead E18 55 A5
14 Wapping E1 118 A5
Hermitage Gdns
Child's Hill NW2 69 C5
South Norwood SE19 183 A3
Hermitage La
Child's Hill NW2 69 C5
Croydon CR0 206 A3
South Norwood SW16 182 B3
Hermitage Prim Sch E1 118 A5
Hermitage Rd
London N4, N15 51 A3
South Norwood SE19 183 B4
Hermitage Row 9 E8 74 A3
Hermitage St W2 236 C3
Hermitage The
Barnes SW13 133 D4
Feltham TW13 149 D1
Forest Hill SE23 162 C3
Kingston u T KT1 197 D5
Richmond TW10 154 A6
Uxbridge UB8 60 A2

Hermitage Villas SW6 265 A6
Hermitage Wall E1 118 A5
Hermitage Way HA7 25 A2
Hermitage Wlk E18 54 D5
Hermit Pl NW6 91 D6
Hermit Rd E16 98 D3
Hermit St EC1 234 C2
Hermon Gr UB3 106 A5
Hermon Hill E11 55 A5
Herndon Rd SW18 158 A6
Herne Cl
Hayes UB3 83 D1
Willesden NW10 67 B3
Herne Ct WD23 8 A4
HERNE HILL 161 A6
Herne Hill SE24 139 A1
Herne Hill Ho SE24 160 D5
Herne Hill Mans
SE24 161 A5
Herne Hill Rd SE24 139 A1
Herne Hill Sch SE24 161 A6
Herne Hill Sta SE24 160 D5
Herne Hill Stad SE24 161 B5
Herne Mews N18 34 A6
Herne Pl SE24 160 D6
Herne Rd KT6 214 A6
Heron Cl
Buckhurst Hill IG9 21 A3
Cheam SM1 217 B3
Walthamstow E17 35 B1
Willesden NW10 67 C2
Heron Cres DA14 189 C6
Heron Ct
Bromley BR2 209 C5
16 Cubitt Town E14 120 A3
7 Dulwich SE21 161 B2
9 Forest Hill SE23 162 C3
Ilford IG1 78 D6
5 Kingston u T KT1 198 A6
Merton SW20 178 C1
Mitcham CR4 180 C2
Ruislip HA4 61 B6
Stanwell TW19 148 A3
Herondale Ave SW18 158 C3
Heron Dr N4 73 A6
Herongate N1 235 B6
Herongate Rd E12 77 C6
Heron Hill DA17 125 B2
Heron Ho
Battersea SW11 267 B2
Ealing W13 87 A3
Peckham SE15 139 D4
Sidcup DA14 168 B1
St John's Wood NW8 230 A3
Teddington KT1 175 C2
Heron Ind Est E15 97 D5
Heron Mead EN3 7 C5
Heron Mews IG1 78 D6
Heron Pl
Marylebone W1 238 B2
Rotherhithe SE16 119 A5
Heron Quays E14 119 C5
Heron Quays Sta E14 119 C5
Heron Rd
Croydon CR0 221 C6
Herne Hill SE24 139 A1
Isleworth TW1 131 B1
Heronsforde W13 87 C1
Heronsgate HA8 26 C5
Heronsgate Prim Sch
SE28 123 B3
Heron's Lea N6 48 D3
Heronslea Dr HA7 26 A5
Herons Pl TW7 131 B2
Heron Sq 27 TW10 153 D6
Herons Rise EN4 2 C1
Herons The E11 54 D3
Heron Trad Est W3 88 D2
Heronway IG8 37 C6
Heron Way TW14 128 A1
Herrick Ct 4 TW10 175 D6
Herrick Ho
18 Camberwell SE5 139 B5
17 Canonbury N16 73 B4
Herrick Rd N5 73 A5
Herrick St
SW1 115 D2 259 D3
Herries St W10 91 A5
Herringham Rd SE7 121 C3
Herrongate Cl EN1 5 D3
Hersant Cl NW10 90 A6
Herschell Rd SE23 163 A4
Herschell's Mews
SE5 139 A2
Hersham Cl SW15 156 A4
Hersham Rd KT12 194 A1
Hershell Ct 1 SW14 132 D1
Hertford Ave SW14 133 C1
Hertford Cl EN4 2 B2
Hertford Ct
16 London SW11 136 C2
Newham E6 100 B4
Palmers Green N13 16 C1
Hertford Ho 5 UB5 85 B3
Hertford Lo 10 SW19 157 A3
Hertford Pl W1 239 B5
Hertford Rd
Barking IG11 78 D1
Barnet EN4 2 A2
East Finchley N2 48 C6
Edmonton N9 18 B3
Enfield EN3 6 C5
Ilford IG2 57 C3
Shoreditch N1 95 C6
Hertford Rd High St
EN3 18 C6
Hertford St
W1 115 B5 248 C3
Hertford Way CR4 204 A5
Hertford Wlk 13
DA17 125 C1
Hertmitage The 5
SE13 142 A3
Hertslet Rd N7 72 B5
Hertsmere Rd E14 119 C6
Hertswood Ct 1 EN5 1 A1
Hervey Cl N3 29 C2
Hervey Park Rd E17 53 A5
Hervey Rd SE3 143 B4
Hesa Rd UB3 106 A6
Hesewall Cl SW4 137 C3
Hesketh Pl W11 244 A5
Hesketh Rd E7 77 A5
Heslop Ct 1 SW12 159 A3
Heslop Rd SW12 158 D3
Hesper Mews
SW5 113 D2 255 C3
Hesperus Cres E14 119 D2
Hessel Rd W13 109 B4
Hessel St E1 96 B1
Hestercombe Ave
SW6 135 A4 264 B1
Hester Ct SW16 181 C5
Hesterman Way CR0 204 B1
Hester Rd
Battersea
SW11 136 C5 267 A3
Edmonton N18 34 A5
Hester Terr TW9 132 C2
Hestia Ho SE1 253 A1
HESTON 129 B5
Heston Ave TW5 129 A5
Heston Com Sch
TW5 129 C5
Heston Ctr The TW5 106 C1
Heston Grange TW5 129 B6
Heston Grange La
TW5 129 B6
Heston Ho
Gunnersbury W4 110 D1
5 St Johns SE8 141 C4
Heston Ind Mall TW5 129 B5
Heston Inf Sch TW5 129 C5
Heston Jun Sch TW5 129 C5
Heston Phoenix
Distribution Pk
TW5 128 C6
Heston Rd TW5 129 C5
Heston St SE14 141 C4
Hetherington Rd
Charlton TW17 171 A1
Stockwell SW2, SW4 138 A1
Hetherington Way
UB10 60 A4
Hethpool Ho W2 236 C5
Hetley Gdns 1 SE19 183 D3
Hetley Rd W12 112 B4
Heton Gdns NW4 46 A5
Hetty Rees Ct 6 N19 50 A2
Hevelius Cl SE10 120 D1
Hever Croft SE9 188 C6
Heverfield Ct CR4 180 D3
Hever Gdns BR1 188 C1
Heverham Rd SE18 123 C2
Hever Ho SE15 140 D6
Heversham Ho SE15 140 C6
Heversham Rd DA7 147 C4
Hevingham Dr RM6 58 C4
Heward Ct SE13 142 A3
Hewens Rd UB4 83 A3
Hewer Ho 6 SW4 159 C6
Hewer St W10 90 D2
Hewes Ho E17 52 D5
Hewett Cl HA7 25 B6
Hewett Ho
Putney SW15 134 C3
7 Woolwich SE18 122 D1
Hewett Rd RM8 80 D4
Hewetts Quay 7
IG11 101 A6
Hewett St EC2 95 C3 243 B5
Hewish Rd N18 33 C6
Hewison St E3 97 B5
Hewitt Ave N22 32 D1
Hewitt Cl CR0 223 C5
Hewitt Ho 2 E4 36 B5
Hewitt Rd N8 50 D4
Hewlett Rd E3 97 A5
Hewling Ho 1 N16 73 C3
Hexagon Bsns Ctr
UB4 106 C6
Hexagon The N6 48 D1
Hexal Rd SE6 164 C1
Hexham Gdns TW7 131 A5
Hexham Rd
Barnet EN5 1 D1
Cheam SM4 201 D1
West Norwood SE27 161 A2
Hexton Ct N4 73 A6
Heybourne Rd N17 34 B3
Heybridge 9 NW1 71 B2
Heybridge Ave SW16 182 B4
Heybridge Dr IG6 57 B6
Heybridge Way E10 53 B1
Heydon Ct BR4 224 C6
Heydon Ho 3 SE14 140 C4
Heyford Ave
Merton SW20 201 B6
South Lambeth
SW8 138 A5 270 B4
Heyford Rd CR4 180 C1
Heyford Terr SW8 270 B4
Heygate St
SE17 117 A2 262 B4
Heylyn Sq E3 97 B4
Heynes Rd RM8 80 C4
Heysham Dr WD19 22 D5
Heysham La NW3 69 D5
Heysham Rd N15 51 B3
Heythorp St SW18 157 B2
Heythrop Dr UB10 60 B4
Heyward Ct SM2 217 C2
Heywood Ave NW9 27 C2
Heywood Ct 2 HA7 25 C5
Heywood Ho
11 Deptford SE14 140 D6
6 Tulse Hill SW2 160 C5
Heyworth Rd
Lower Clapton E5 74 B4
Stratford E15 76 D4
Hibbert Ho 13 E14 119 C3
Hibbert Rd
Harrow HA3 24 D1
Walthamstow E17 53 B2
Hibbert St SW11 136 B2
Hibernia Gdns TW3 151 C6
Hibernia Point 9
SE2 124 D4
Hibernia Rd TW3 129 C1
Hibiscus Cl 6 HA8 27 A6
Hibiscus Lo 5 E15 76 C1
Hichisson Rd SE15 162 C6
Hickes Ho 6 NW6 70 B1
Hickey's Almshouses 7
TW9 132 B1
Hickin Cl SE7 121 D2
Hickin St 2 E14 120 A3
Hickleton NW1 232 B5
Hickling Ho 10 SE16 118 B3
Hickling Rd IG1 78 D3
Hickman Ave E4 36 A4
Hickman Cl E16 99 D2
Hickman Rd RM6 58 C2
Hickmore Wlk SW4 137 C2
Hickory Cl N9 18 A4
Hicks Ave UB6 86 C4
Hicks Cl SW11 136 C2
Hicks Ct RM10 81 D5
Hicks St SE8 119 A1
Hidaburn Ct 7 SW16 181 C6
Hidcote Gdns SW20 200 B6
Hidcote Ho 11 SM2 218 A1
Hide E6 100 C1
Hide Pl SW1 115 D2 259 C3
Hider Ct SE3 143 C5
Hide Rd HA1 42 B5
Hide Twr SW1 259 C3
Hieover SE21 161 A2
Higgins Ho 7 N1 95 C6
Higginson Ho 2 NW3 70 D1
Higgins Wlk TW12 173 A4
Higgs Ind Est 9
SE24 138 D2
High Acre EN2 4 D2
Higham Ct 9 IG8 37 A4
HIGHAM HILL 35 A2
Higham Hill Ho E17 34 D2
Higham Hill Rd E17 35 A1
Higham Ho E4 35 C4
Higham Mews UB5 85 B3
Higham Pl E17 53 A6
Higham Rd
Tottenham N17 51 B6
Woodford IG8 37 A4
Highams Lodge Bsns Ctr
E17 52 D6
HIGHAMS PARK 36 A3
Highams Park Sch E4 36 B4
Highams Park Sta E4 36 B4
Higham St E17 53 A6
Higham Station Ave
E4 35 D4
Highams The E17 36 A2
High Ashton 11 KT2 176 D3
Highbanks Cl DA16 146 B5
Highbanks Rd HA5 23 D4
Highbank Way N8 50 C3
HIGH BARNET 1 B2
High Barnet Sta EN5 1 C1
Highbarrow Rd CR0 206 A1
High Beech
South Croydon CR2 221 C1
Southgate N21 16 B5
High Beeches DA14 191 A5
High Birch Ct 7 EN4 2 C1
Highbridge Ct 13
SE14 140 C5
Highbridge Rd IG11 100 D6
High Bridge Wharf
SE10 120 B1
Highbrook Rd SE3 143 D2
High Broom Cres
BR4 207 D2
Highburty Mans 24 N1 72 D1
HIGHBURY 72 D4
Highbury Ave CR7 182 D1
Highbury Cl
New Malden KT3 199 A4
West Wickham BR4 223 D6
Highbury Cnr N5 72 D2
Highbury Corner N5 72 D2
Highbury Cres N5 72 C3
Highbury Fields Sch
N5 72 D3
Highbury Gdns IG3 79 C6
Highbury Gr N5 72 D3
Highbury Grange N5 73 A4
Highbury Grove Ct N5 72 D2
Highbury Grove Sch
N5 73 A3
Highbury Hill N5 72 D4
Highbury & Islington Sta
N1 72 D2
Highbury New Pk N5 73 A4
Highbury Pk N5 72 D4
Highbury Pl N5 72 D3
Highbury Quadrant
N5 73 A5
Highbury Quadrant Prim
Sch N5 73 A4
Highbury Rd SW19 179 A5
Highbury Sq N14 15 C3
Highbury Station Rd
N1 72 C2
Highbury Terr N5 72 D3
Highbury Terrace Mews
N5 72 D3
High Cedar Dr SW20 178 B3
Highclears 6 IG9 21 B2
Highclere Rd KT3 199 B6
Highclere St SE26 185 A6
Highcliffe
Beckenham BR3 185 D2
Ealing W13 87 B2
Highcliffe Dr SW15 155 D5
Highcliffe Gdns IG4 56 A4
Highcombe SE7 143 B6
Highcombe Cl SE9 166 A3
High Coombe Pl KT2 177 B3
Highcroft
Highgate N6 49 A3
Hyde The NW9 45 C4
2 Kingston u T KT5 198 B4
Highcroft Ave HA0 88 C6
Highcroft Gdns NW11 47 B3
Highcroft Point E17 35 D2
Highcroft Rd N19 50 A2
High Cross Ctr The
N15 52 A5
High Cross Rd N17 52 A6
Highcross Way 4
SW15 156 A3
Highdaun Dr SW16 204 B5
High Dene EN2 4 D2
Highdown KT4 215 D6
Highdown Rd SW15 156 B5
High Dr KT2, KT3 177 A1
High Elms IG8 37 A5
High Elms Ctry Pk*
BR6 227 A1
High Elms Rd BR6 227 A1
Highfield WD23 8 C2
Highfield Ave
Erith DA8 147 D6
Greenford UB6 64 D3
Hendon NW11 47 A2
Kingsbury NW9 45 A4
Orpington BR6 227 D3
Pinner HA5 41 B4
Wembley HA9 66 B5
Highfield Cl
Hither Green SE13 164 B5
Kingsbury NW9 45 A4
Long Ditton KT6 197 C1
Wood Green N22 32 C2
Highfield Ct
7 Barnet EN5 1 D1
Hendon NW11 47 A3
Mitcham CR4 202 C5
Southgate N14 15 C5
Wanstead E12 77 C6
Highfield Dr
Beckenham BR2 208 D5
Ickenham UB10 60 A5
West Ewell KT19 215 D2
West Wickham BR4 224 A5
Highfield Gdns NW11 47 A3
Highfield Hill SE19 183 C3
Highfield Ho N21 16 D3
Highfield Inf Sch
BR2 208 C5
Highfield Jun Sch
BR2 208 C5
Highfield Mews NW6 69 D1
Highfield Prim Sch
Edmonton N21 17 A3
Hillingdon UB10 82 D4
Highfield Rd
Acton W3 89 A2
Bexley DA6 169 B6
Bromley BR1 210 B5
Carshalton SM1 218 C3
Edmonton N21 16 D2
Feltham TW13 150 A2
Hendon NW11 47 A3
Hounslow TW7 130 D4
Orpington BR5, BR7 211 D6
St Paul's Cray BR5,
BR7 211 D6
Tolworth KT5 199 A2
Upper Halliford TW16 193 D4
Walton-on-T KT12 194 A1
Highfields SM1 217 C6
Highfield Sch SW18 158 C4
Highfields Gr N6 48 D1
High Foleys KT10 213 B1
High Gables
Beckenham BR2 186 C1
Loughton IG10 21 D6
High Garth KT10 212 A2
HIGHGATE 49 A2
Highgate Archway N6 49 C1
Highgate Ave N6 49 B2
Highgate Ballet Sch
NW11 47 D5
Highgate Cemetery*
N19 71 B6
Highgate Cl N6 49 A2
High Gate Edge N2 48 C4
Highgate High St N6 49 B1
Highgate Hill N19 49 C1
Highgate Ho 11 SE26 162 A1
Highgate Hts N6 49 C3
Highgate Prim Sch N6 48 D3
Highgate Private Hospl
N6 48 D3
Highgate Rd NW5 71 B4
Highgate Sch
Highgate N6 48 D2
Highgate N6 49 A2
Highgate Spinney N8 49 D3
Highgate Sta N6 49 B3
Highgate West Hill N6 71 A6
Highgate Wlk SE23 162 C2
Highgate Wood Sec Sch
N8 49 C4
High Gr
Bromley BR1 187 D2
Woolwich SE18 145 B4
Highgrove Cl
London N11 31 A5
Widmore BR7 188 A2
Highgrove Ct BR3 185 C3
Highgrove Ho HA4 40 A3
Highgrove Mews
SM5 218 D5
Highgrove Point 2
NW3 70 A4
Highgrove Rd RM8 80 C4
Highgrove Way HA4 40 A2
High Hill Ferry 3 E5 52 B1
High Holborn
WC1 94 B2 240 C3
High Holborn Ho
WC1 240 D3
High La W7 86 B1
Highland Ave W7 86 C1
Highland Cotts SM6 219 C4
Highland Croft BR3 185 D4
Highland Dr WD23 8 A4
Highland Lo 3 SE19 183 D3
Highland Pk TW13 171 D6
Highland Rd
Bexley DA6 147 C1
Bromley BR1 186 D2
Pinner HA6 22 A1
West Norwood SE19 183 C4
Highlands N20 14 B2
Highlands Ave
Acton W3 111 A6
Southgate N21 16 B6
Highlands Cl
Hornsey N4 50 A2
Hounslow TW3 129 D4
Highlands Ct SE19 183 C4
Highlands Gdns IG1 56 B1
Highlands Heath
SW15 156 C4
Highlands Prim Sch
IG1 56 B1
Highlands Rd EN5 13 C6
Highlands Sch N21 4 C1
Highlands The
Barnet EN5 1 D1
Edgware HA8 26 D1
Highlawn Hall HA1 64 C5
Highlea Cl NW9 27 C2
High Level Dr SE26 184 A6
Highlever Rd W10 90 C2
High Limes 2 SE19 183 C4
High London 5 N6 49 D2
Highmead
9 Edmonton N18 34 A5
Plumstead Comm SE18 145 D5
High Mead
Harrow HA1 42 D4
West Wickham BR4 224 C6
Highmead Cres HA0 66 B1
High Meadow Cl HA5 40 C5
High Meadow Cres
NW9 45 B4
High Meads Rd E16 99 D1
Highmore Rd SE3 142 C5
High Mount
Hendon NW4 46 A3
11 Hornsey N4 50 A2
High Oaks EN2 4 B5
High Oaks Lo 9 E18 37 A1
High Park Ave TW9 132 C4
High Park Rd TW9 132 C4
High Par The SW16 160 A1
High Path SW19 180 A2
Highpoint EN5 14 A6
High Point
Chislehurst SE9 166 D1
Highgate N6 49 A2
High Range SW20 178 C3
High Rd
Buckhurst Hill IG9,
IG10 21 C5
Bushey WD23 8 B3
Chadwell Heath RM6 58 C2
East Finchley N2 48 C6
Finchley N2, N12 30 A3
Friern Barnet N11 31 B5
Harrow HA3 24 C3
Ilford IG1 78 D6
Leyton E10 53 D3
Oakleigh Pk N20 14 A4
Seven Kings IG1, IG3 79 C6
South Tottenham N15,
N17 51 D5
Tottenham N17 33 D2
Wembley HA0, HA9 66 A3
Willesden NW10 68 A2
Woodford E18 37 A2
Wood Green N22 32 B3
High Ridge N10 31 B2
Highridge Pl EN2 4 B5
High Road Buckhurst Hill
5 IG9 21 B2
High Road Eastcote
HA5 40 B4

High Road, Ickenham
UB10 . . . . 61 A6
High Road Leyton E10 . . 75 D6
High Road Leytonstone
E11 . . . . 76 C6
High Road Woodford Gn
IG8 . . . . 37 A6
High St Mews SW19 . . . 179 A5
High St N
Newham E6 . . . . 100 A6
Plashet E12 . . . . 78 A2
High St S E6 . . . . 100 B4
High Sheldon N6 . . . . . . 48 D3
Highshore Rd SE15 . . . . 139 D3
Highshore Sch SE15 . . . 139 D4
High Silver IG10 . . . . 21 D6
High St
Acton W3 . . . . 110 D5
Barnet EN5 . . . . 1 B1
Beckenham BR3 . . . . 185 C1
Brentford TW8 . . . . 132 A6
Bromley BR1 . . . . 187 A1
Cheam SM1, KT17 . . . . . 217 A2
Claygate KT10 . . . . 212 D2
Cranford TW5 . . . . 128 B5
Croydon CR0 . . . . 221 A5
Ealing W5 . . . . 109 D6
East Molesey KT8 . . . . . . 195 C5
Elstree WD6 . . . . 9 D5
Farnborough BR6 . . . . . . 227 A3
Feltham TW13 . . . . 150 A2
Green Street Green
BR6 . . . . 227 D2
Hampton TW12 . . . . 174 A4
Harlington UB3 . . . . 127 B6
Harrow on t H HA1 . . . . . . 42 C1
Hornsey N8 . . . . 50 B5
Hounslow TW3 . . . . 129 D2
Ilford IG6 . . . . 57 A6
Kingston u T KT1 . . . . 175 D2
Kingston u T KT1 . . . . 197 D6
Mill Hill NW7 . . . . 28 B5
Newham E13 . . . . 99 A5
New Malden KT3 . . . . . . 199 C5
Palmers Green N14 . . . . . 15 D2
Penge SE20 . . . . 184 D3
Pinner HA5 . . . . 41 A6
Ruislip HA4 . . . . 39 C1
Shepperton TW17 . . . . . 193 A3
Sidcup DA14 . . . . 190 A6
Southall UB1 . . . . 107 B5
South Norwood CR7 . . . . 205 B5
South Norwood SE25 . . . 206 A5
Stratford Marsh E15 . . . . 98 A6
Sutton SM1 . . . . 217 D4
Sutton SM1, SM2 . . . . . . 217 D3
Teddington TW11 . . . . . . 175 A5
Thames Ditton KT7 . . . . . 197 A3
Twickenham TW2 . . . . . . 152 A4
Wallington SM5 . . . . 219 A4
Walthamstow E17 . . . . . . 53 B5
Walton-on-T KT12 . . . . . . 194 A1
Wanstead E11 . . . . 55 A4
Wealdstone HA3 . . . . 24 C1
Wealdstone HA3 . . . . 42 C6
Wembley HA9 . . . . 66 B4
West Wickham BR4 . . . . 207 D1
Wimbledon SW19 . . . . . . 178 D5
Yiewsley UB7 . . . . 104 A6
Highstone Ave E11 . . . . . 55 A3
Highstone Ct E11 . . . . . . 54 D3
High Street Collier's
Wood SW17, SW19 . . . 180 B4
High Street Harlesden
NW10 . . . . 89 D5
High Street Harlington
TW6 . . . . 127 B5
High Street Kensington
Sta W8 . . . . . . 113 D4 245 C1
High The SW16 . . . . 160 A1
High Timber St EC4 . . . . 252 A6
High Tor Cl BR1 . . . . 187 B3
High Tor View SE28 . . . 123 C5
High Trees
Cheam SM3 . . . . 201 B2
Croydon CR0 . . . . 207 A1
East Barnet EN4 . . . . 14 C6
Streatham SW2 . . . . 160 C3
Uxbridge UB10 . . . . 61 A6
Whetstone N20 . . . . 14 A1
Hightrees Ct W7 . . . . 108 C6
Hightrees Ho SW12 . . . 159 A5
Highview
Crouch End N6 . . . . 49 C3
Hornsey N8 . . . . 50 A2
Northolt UB5 . . . . 85 A4
Woolwich SE18 . . . . 144 D5
High View
6 Penge SE19 . . . . 183 D3
Pinner HA5 . . . . 40 C6
Highview Ave HA8 . . . . . 27 A6
High View Ave CR0,
SM6 . . . . 220 B3
High View Cl
Loughton IG10 . . . . 21 C6
South Norwood SE19 . . . 183 D1
Highview Ct
2 Loughton IG10 . . . . . . 21 D6
2 Putney SW19 . . . . . . 157 A3
High View Ct HA3 . . . . . . 24 C3
Highview Gdns
Edgware HA8 . . . . 27 A6
Hendon N3 . . . . 47 A6
New Southgate N11 . . . . . 31 C5
Highview Ho
1 Buckhurst Hill IG9 . . . . 21 D1
2 Buckhurst Hill IG9 . . . . 21 D1
High View Ho RM6 . . . . . 59 A5
High View Par 1 IG4 . . 56 B4
High View Prim Sch
London SW11 . . . . 136 B1
Wallington SM6 . . . . 220 A3
Highview Rd
Ealing W13 . . . . 87 A1
Sidcup DA14 . . . . 190 B6
High View Rd
London N10 . . . . 30 D2
Snaresbrook E18 . . . . 54 D6
South Norwood SE19 . . . 183 B4
Highway Bsns Pk The 7
E1 . . . . 118 D6
Highway The
Shadwell E1 . . . . 118 C6
Stanmore HA7 . . . . 25 A3
Highway Trad Ctr The 6
E1 . . . . 118 D6
High Wigsell TW11 . . . . 175 A5
Highwood IG8 . . . . 36 D6
Highwood Ave N12 . . . . . 30 A6
Highwood Cl
Dulwich SE22 . . . . 162 A3
Orpington BR6 . . . . 227 A6
Highwood Ct
Barnet EN5 . . . . 13 C6
Whetstone N12 . . . . 14 A1
Highwood Dr BR6 . . . . . 227 A6
Highwood Gdns IG5 . . . 56 B5
Highwood Gr NW7 . . . . . . 27 B5
Highwood Hill NW7 . . . . . 11 D2
Highwood Rd N19 . . . . . 72 A5
High Worple HA2 . . . . . . 41 B1
Highworth Rd N11 . . . . . 31 D5
Highworth St NW1 . . . . 237 B4
Hilary Ave CR4 . . . . 203 A6
Hilary Cl
Bexley DA8 . . . . 147 D4
Walham Green SW6 . . . . 265 C4
Hilary Ct N9 . . . . 18 D3
Hilary Rd W12 . . . . 111 D6
Hilbert Rd SM3 . . . . 216 D5
Hilborough Cl SW19 . . . 180 A3
Hilborough Ct 1 E8 . . . . 95 D6
Hilborough Rd 1 E8 . . . . 73 D1
Hilborough Way BR6 . . 227 B3
Hilda Lockert Wlk
SW9 . . . . 138 D3
Hilda Rd
Newham E16 . . . . 98 C3
Upton Pk E6 . . . . 77 D1
Hilda Terr 2 SW9 . . . . . 138 C3
Hilda Vale Cl BR6 . . . . . 226 D4
Hilda Vale Rd BR6 . . . . . 226 D4
Hildenborough Gdns
BR1 . . . . 186 D4
Hildenbrough Ho
BR3 . . . . 185 B3
Hildenlea Pl BR2 . . . . . . 186 C1
Hilditch Ho 7 TW10 . . . 154 B5
Hildred Ho SW1 . . . . 258 C4
Hildreth St SW12 . . . . . 159 B3
Hildreth Street Mews 2
SW12 . . . . 159 B3
Hildyard Rd SW6 . . . . . . 265 B6
Hiley Rd NW10 . . . . 90 C4
Hilfield La WD23 . . . . 8 C6
Hilgrove Rd NW6 . . . . . . 70 A1
Hiliary Gdns HA7 . . . . . . 25 C1
Hillary Cres KT12 . . . . . 194 C1
Hillary Ct
3 Chislehurst SE9 . . . . . 166 A2
13 Shepherd's Bush
W12 . . . . 112 C4
Stanwell TW19 . . . . 148 A3
Hillary Dr TW7 . . . . 152 D6
Hillary Rd UB2 . . . . 107 C3
Hillary Rise EN5 . . . . 1 C1
Hillbeck Cl
Deptford SE15 . . . . 140 C5
Deptford SE15 . . . . 140 C6
Hillbeck Way UB6 . . . . . . 86 B6
Hillborne Cl UB3 . . . . . . 106 A1
Hillboro Ct
Leytonstone E11 . . . . 54 B3
1 Woodford E18 . . . . 36 D2
Hillborough Ct HA1 . . . . 42 C2
Hillbrook Rd SW17 . . . . 181 A6
Hillbrook Sch SW17 . . . 181 A6
Hillbrow
Kingston u T KT3 . . . . 199 D6
7 Richmond TW10 . . . . . 154 A5
Hill Brow BR1 . . . . 187 D2
Hillbrow Ct KT10 . . . . . . 212 A4
Hillbrow Rd
Catford BR1 . . . . 186 C4
Esher KT10 . . . . 212 A4
Hill Bunker's DA17 . . . . 125 C2
Hillbury Ave HA3 . . . . 43 B4
Hillbury Rd SW17 . . . . . 159 B1
Hill Cl
Barnet EN5 . . . . 12 C6
Chislehurst BR7 . . . . 188 D5
Dollis Hill NW2 . . . . 68 B5
Hampstead Garden Suburb
NW11 . . . . 47 C3
Harrow HA1 . . . . 64 C5
Stanmore HA7 . . . . 25 B6
Hillcote Ave SW16 . . . . 182 C3
Hillcourt N6 . . . . 49 C3
Hillcourt Ave N12 . . . . . . 29 D4
Hillcourt Rd SE22 . . . . . 162 B5
Hill Cres
Harrow HA1 . . . . 43 A4
Kingston u T KT5 . . . . 198 B4
North Cheam KT4 . . . . . . 216 C6
Totteridge N20 . . . . 13 D2
Hillcrest
Camberwell SE24 . . . . . . 139 B1
Highgate N6 . . . . 49 A2
Notting Hill W11 . . . . 244 C5
Southgate N21 . . . . 16 C4
Hill Crest DA15 . . . . 168 B4
Hillcrest Ave
Edgware HA8 . . . . 26 D6
Pinner HA5 . . . . 40 D5
Temple Fortune NW11 . . . 47 B4
Hillcrest Cl
Beckenham BR3 . . . . 207 B3
Forest Hill SE26 . . . . 184 A6
Hillcrest Ct
Brondesbury NW2 . . . . . . 69 A3
8 Edgware HA8 . . . . 26 D5
Lewisham SE6 . . . . 164 B4
Sutton SM2 . . . . 218 B2
Hillcrest Gdns
Dollis Hill NW2 . . . . 68 A5
Hendon N3 . . . . 47 A5
Hinchley Wood KT10 . . . 212 D5
Hillcrest Hts W5 . . . . 88 A3
Hillcrest Rd
Acton W3 . . . . 110 D5
Chingford E17 . . . . 36 B1
Ealing W5 . . . . 88 A2
Grove Pk BR1 . . . . 187 A6
Loughton IG10 . . . . 21 D5
Woodford E18 . . . . 37 A1
Hillcrest View BR3 . . . . 207 B3
Hillcroft Ave HA5 . . . . . . 41 B3
Hillcroft Coll KT6 . . . . . 198 A3
Hillcroft Cres
Ealing W5 . . . . 87 D1
Ruislip HA4 . . . . 62 D5
Wembley HA9 . . . . 66 B4
Hillcroft Rd E6 . . . . 100 D2
Hillcroome Rd SM2 . . . 218 B2
Hillcross Ave SM4 . . . . . 201 A4
Hillcross Prim Sch
SM4 . . . . 201 B5
Hill Ct
Barnet EN4 . . . . 2 C1
Ealing W5 . . . . 88 B3
Hampstead NW3 . . . . 70 C4
8 Norbiton KT2 . . . . 176 D3
Northolt UB5 . . . . 63 C3
Putney SW15 . . . . 156 D6
14 Surbiton KT6 . . . . 198 A4
Wembley HA0 . . . . 65 A4
9 Wimbledon SW19 . . . 179 A4
Hilldale Rd SM1 . . . . 217 B4
Hilldown Ct SW16 . . . . . 182 A3
Hilldown Rd
Hayes BR2 . . . . 208 D1
South Norwood SW16 . . 182 B3
Hill Dr
London NW9 . . . . 45 A1
Thornton Heath SW16 . . 204 B6
Hilldrop Cres N7 . . . . 71 D3
Hilldrop La N7 . . . . 71 D3
Hilldrop Rd
Bromley BR1 . . . . 187 B4
Kentish Town N7 . . . . 71 D3
Hill End
Orpington BR6 . . . . 227 D6
Shooters Hill SE18 . . . . . 144 C4
Hillersdon Ave
Barnes SW13 . . . . 134 A3
Edgware HA8 . . . . 26 B5
Hillersdon Ho SW1 . . . . 258 C2
Hillery Cl SE17 . . . . 262 D3
Hill Farm Rd W10 . . . . . . 90 D2
Hillfield Ave
Colindale NW9 . . . . 45 C5
Hornsey N8 . . . . 50 A5
Mitcham SM4 . . . . 202 C4
Wembley HA0 . . . . 66 B1
Hillfield Cl HA2 . . . . 42 A5
Hillfield Ct NW3 . . . . 70 C3
Hillfield Ho N5 . . . . 73 A3
Hillfield La S WD23 . . . . . . 8 D5
Hillfield Lo SW17 . . . . . 180 D5
Hillfield Mans NW3 . . . . 70 C3
Hillfield Par SM4 . . . . . . 202 B3
Hillfield Park Mews
N10 . . . . 49 B5
Hillfield Pk
London N10 . . . . 49 B5
Southgate N21 . . . . 16 C2
Hillfield Rd
Hampton TW12 . . . . 173 B2
West Hampstead NW6 . . . 69 C3
Hillgate Pl
Balham SW12 . . . . 159 B4
Kensington
W8 . . . . 113 C5 245 A4
Hillgate St W8 . . . . 245 A4
Hill Gate Wlk N6 . . . . 49 C3
Hill Gr TW13 . . . . 151 B2
Hill Ho
Southall UB1 . . . . 85 C1
Stanmore HA7 . . . . 9 A1
Upper Clapton E5 . . . . 52 B1
Woolwich SE28 . . . . 123 C5
Hill House Ave HA7 . . . . 24 D3
Hill House Cl N21 . . . . . . 16 C4
Hill House Dr TW12 . . . 173 C2
Hill House Rd SW16 . . . 182 B5
Hill House Sch
SW1 . . . . 114 D3 257 D5
Hilliard Ct SM6 . . . . 219 D2
Hilliard Ho 15 E1 . . . . . . 118 B5
Hilliard's Ct E1 . . . . 118 C5
Hillier Cl EN5 . . . . 13 D5
Hillier Gdns CR0 . . . . . . 220 C3
Hillier Ho 1 NW1 . . . . . . 71 D1
Hillier Lo TW12 . . . . 174 B5
Hillier Pl KT9 . . . . 213 D2
Hillier Rd SW11 . . . . 158 D5
Hilliers Ave UB8 . . . . 82 C4
Hillier's La CR0, SM6 . . . 220 A5
HILLINGDON 82 D5
Hillingdon Ave TW19 . . 148 A3
Hillingdon Circus
UB10 . . . . 60 D2
HILLINGDON HEATH . . . 82 D2
Hillingdon Hill UB10 . . . 82 B4
Hillingdon Hospl UB8 . . . 82 B2
Hillingdon Manor Sch
UB8 . . . . 82 D2
Hillingdon Par 6
UB10 . . . . 82 D3
Hillingdon Prim Sch
UB10 . . . . 82 D4
Hillingdon Rd UB10 . . . . 82 A5
Hillingdon St SE17 . . . . 138 D6
Hillingdon Sta UB10 . . . . 60 D3
Hillington Gdns IG8 . . . . 37 D1
Hill La HA4 . . . . 39 A1
Hill Lo SW11 . . . . 136 B1
Hillman Cl UB8 . . . . 60 A3
Hillman Dr 12 NW10 . . . . 90 C3
Hillman St E8 . . . . 74 B2
Hillmarton Rd N7 . . . . . . 72 A3
Hillmead Dr SW9 . . . . . 138 D1
Hill Mead Prim Sch
SW9 . . . . 138 D1
Hillmont Rd KT10 . . . . . 212 C5
Hillmore Ct SE13 . . . . . . 142 B2
Hillmore Gr SE26 . . . . . 185 A5
Hill Rd
Carshalton SM5 . . . . 218 C2
Finchley N10 . . . . 30 D2
Harrow HA1 . . . . 43 A4
Mitcham CR4 . . . . 181 B3
Pinner HA5 . . . . 41 A3
St John's Wood
NW8 . . . . 92 A5 229 B3
Sutton SM1 . . . . 217 D3
Hill Rd continued
Wembley HA0 . . . . 65 B5
Hillreach SE7, SE18 . . . . 122 B1
Hillrise KT12 . . . . 193 D2
Hill Rise
East Finchley NW11 . . . . . 47 D5
Enfield N9 . . . . 18 B5
Forest Hill SE23 . . . . 162 B3
Greenford UB6 . . . . 86 A6
Hinchley Wood KT10 . . . . 213 B6
Richmond TW10 . . . . 153 D6
Ruislip HA4 . . . . 39 B1
Hillrise Mans N19 . . . . . . 50 A2
Hillrise Rd N19 . . . . 50 A2
Hillsboro Rd SE22 . . . . . 161 C6
Hillsborough Ct 13
NW6 . . . . 91 D6
Hillsde 6 SM1 . . . . 218 B3
Hillsgrove Cl DA16 . . . . 146 C5
Hillsgrove Prim Sch
DA16 . . . . 146 C5
Hillside
Barnet EN5 . . . . 14 A6
Crouch End N8 . . . . 49 D3
Greenwich SE10 . . . . 142 B5
Kingsbury NW9 . . . . 45 B5
Stonebridge NW10 . . . . . . 89 B6
Wimbledon SW19 . . . . . 178 D4
Hill Side EN5 . . . . 14 A6
Hillside Ave
London N11 . . . . 30 D4
Wembley HA9 . . . . 66 B4
Woodford IG8 . . . . 37 C5
Hillside Cl
Merton SM4 . . . . 201 A5
St John's Wood NW8 . . . . 91 D5
Woodford IG8 . . . . 37 C5
Hillside Cres
Enfield EN2 . . . . 5 B5
Harrow HA2 . . . . 42 A1
Northwood HA6 . . . . 22 A2
Hillside Ct
Hampstead NW3 . . . . 69 D3
7 Kingston u T KT2 . . . . 176 D3
Hillside Dr HA8 . . . . 26 C5
Hillside Gdns
Chipping Barnet EN5 . . . . . 1 A1
Edgware HA8 . . . . 26 B6
Friern Barnet N11 . . . . . . 31 C4
Harrow HA3 . . . . 44 A2
Highgate N6 . . . . 49 B3
Northwood HA6 . . . . 22 B2
Streatham SW2 . . . . 160 C2
Wallington SM6 . . . . 219 C1
Walthamstow E17 . . . . . . 54 B6
Hillside Glen CR0 . . . . . 220 D4
Hillside Gr
Hendon NW7 . . . . 28 A3
Southgate N14 . . . . 15 D4
Hillside Ho CR0 . . . . 220 D4
Hillside Jun & Inf Schs
HA6 . . . . 22 A3
Hillside La BR2 . . . . 224 D6
Hillside Mans EN5 . . . . 1 B1
Hillside Rd
Beckenham BR2 . . . . 208 D6
Belmont SM2 . . . . 217 B1
Croydon CR0 . . . . 220 D4
Ealing W5 . . . . 88 A2
Northwood HA6, HA5 . . . . 22 B3
Southall UB1 . . . . 85 C3
South Tottenham N15 . . . . 51 C3
Streatham SW2 . . . . 160 C2
Surbiton KT5 . . . . 198 C4
Hillside Rise HA6 . . . . . . 22 A3
Hillsleigh Rd
W14 . . . . 113 B5 244 D4
Hillsley DA14 . . . . 190 A6
Hills Mews 2 W5 . . . . . . 110 A6
Hills Pl W1 . . . . 239 A1
Hill's Rd IG9 . . . . 21 B3
Hill St
Mayfair W1 . . . . 115 B5 248 C4
Richmond TW10 . . . . 153 D6
Hillstone Ct 5 E3 . . . . . . 97 D3
Hillstowe St E5 . . . . 74 C5
Hilltop 7 E17 . . . . 53 D6
Hill Top
Cheam SM3 . . . . 201 B2
East Finchley NW11 . . . . . 47 D5
Hilltop Ave NW10 . . . . . . 67 A1
Hilltop Ct
12 London SW18 . . . . . . 136 B1
South Hampstead NW8 . . 70 A1
South Norwood SE19 . . . 183 B2
Hilltop Gdns
Hendon NW4 . . . . 28 B1
Orpington BR6 . . . . 227 C6
Hilltop Ho 7 N6 . . . . 49 D2
Hilltop Rd NW6 . . . . 69 C1
Hilltop Way HA7 . . . . 9 A1
Hillview SW20 . . . . 178 B3
Hill View
Mitcham CR4 . . . . 204 A5
Primrose Hill NW1 . . . . . 230 D6
Hillview Ave HA3 . . . . . . 44 A4
Hillview Cl
Pinner HA5 . . . . 23 B4
Wembley HA9 . . . . 66 B6
Hillview Cres
Orpington BR6 . . . . 211 D1
Redbridge IG1 . . . . 56 B3
Hillview Ct SE19 . . . . . . 183 C6
Hill View Dr
Bexley DA16 . . . . 145 C3
Woolwich SE28 . . . . 123 C5
Hillview Gdns
Harrow HA2 . . . . 41 C5
Hendon NW4 . . . . 46 D5
Hill View Gdns NW9 . . . . 45 B4
Hillview Rd
Carshalton SM1 . . . . 218 B5
Chislehurst BR7 . . . . 188 D6
Mill Hill NW7 . . . . 28 D6
Pinner HA5 . . . . 23 B4
Hill View Rd
Claygate KT10 . . . . 213 A1
Orpington BR6 . . . . 227 D6
Twickenham TW1 . . . . . . 153 A5
Hillway
Highgate N6 . . . . 71 A6
London NW9 . . . . 45 C1
Hill Wood Ho NW1 . . . . 232 C3
Hillworth 7 BR3 . . . . . . 185 D1
Hillworth Rd SW2 . . . . . 160 C4
Hillyard Rd W7 . . . . 86 C2
Hillyard St SW9 . . . . 138 C4
Hillyfield E17 . . . . 35 A1
Hillyfield Cl E9 . . . . 75 A3
Hillyfield Prim Sch
E17 . . . . 53 A6
Hilly Fields Cres SE4 . . 141 C2
Hilly Mead SW19 . . . . . 179 A3
Hilsea Point 7 SW15 . . 156 B3
Hilsea St E5 . . . . 74 C4
Hilton Ave N12 . . . . 30 B5
Hilton Ho
4 Ealing W13 . . . . 87 C1
12 Finchley N2 . . . . 30 B1
Lower Holloway N7 . . . . . 72 A4
9 Nunhead SE4 . . . . 140 D1
Hilversum Cres 10
SE22 . . . . 161 C6
Himley Rd SW17 . . . . . . 180 D4
Hinchlay Manor KT10 . 212 D5
Hinchley Cl KT10 . . . . . . 212 D5
Hinchley Dr KT10 . . . . . 212 D5
Hinchley Way KT10 . . . . 213 A5
HINCHLEY WOOD 212 D6
Hinchley Wood Prim Sch
KT10 . . . . 213 A6
Hinchley Wood Sch &
Sixth Form Ctr
KT10 . . . . 213 A6
Hinchley Wood Sta
KT10 . . . . 212 D5
Hinckley Rd SE15 . . . . . 140 A1
Hind Ct EC4 . . . . 241 B1
Hinde Mews W1 . . . . . . 238 B2
Hindes Rd HA1 . . . . 42 C4
Hinde St W1 . . . . . . 93 A1 238 B2
Hind Gr E14 . . . . 97 C1
Hindhead Cl UB8 . . . . 82 D2
Hindhead Gdns UB5 . . . . 85 A6
Hindhead Gn WD19 . . . . 22 C5
Hindhead Point 6
SW15 . . . . 156 B3
Hindhead Way SM6 . . . 220 A3
Hind Ho
13 Deptford SE14 . . . . . 140 D6
Islington N7 . . . . 72 C4
Hindhurst Ct NW9 . . . . . . 45 A5
Hindle Ho E8 . . . . 73 D3
Hindley Ho N7 . . . . 72 B5
Hindlip Ho SW8 . . . . 269 C1
Hindmans Rd SE22 . . . . 162 A6
Hindmans Way RM9 . . . 103 B3
Hindmarsh Cl E1 . . . . . . 118 A6
Hindrey Rd E5 . . . . 74 B3
Hindsley's Pl SE23 . . . . 162 C2
Hines Ct HA1 . . . . 43 A4
Hinkler Rd HA3 . . . . 43 D6
Hinksey Path SE2 . . . . . 124 D3
Hinstock NW6 . . . . 91 D6
Hinstock Rd SE18 . . . . . 145 A5
Hinton Ave TW4 . . . . . . 128 D1
Hinton Cl SE9 . . . . 166 A3
Hinton Ct 3 E10 . . . . 75 D6
Hinton Rd
Brixton SE24 . . . . 138 D2

Hinton Rd *continued*
Edmonton N18 33 C6
Wallington SM6 219 C2
Hippisley Ct TW7 130 D2
Hippodrome Mews
W11 244 A5
Hippodrome Pl W11 244 B5
Hirst Cres HA9 66 A5
Hirst Ct SW1 258 C1
Hispano Mews 17 EN3 7 C6
Hitcham Rd E17 53 B2
Hitchcock Cl TW17 192 B6
Hitchin Sq E3 97 A5
Hithe Gr 15 SE16 118 C3
Hitherbroom Rd UB3 106 A6
Hither Farm Rd SE3 143 C2
Hitherfield Prim Sch
SW16 160 C2
Hitherfield Rd
Dagenham RM8 81 A6
Streatham SW16,
SW27 160 C1
HITHER GREEN 164 C5
Hither Green La SE13 164 B5
Hither Green Prim Sch
SE13 164 B5
Hither Green Sta
SE13 164 C5
Hitherlands SW12 159 B2
Hitherwell Dr HA3 24 B2
Hitherwood Ct SE21 183 D6
Hitherwood Dr SE19 183 D6
Hive Cl WD23 8 B2
Hive Rd WD23 8 C2
Hive Wood Ho E7 77 A2
HM Prison Wormwood
Scrubs W12 90 A1
HMS Belfast* SE1 253 B4
Hoadly Rd SW16 159 D2
Hobart Cl
East Barnet N20 14 C2
Hayes UB4 84 D3
Hobart Ct
Harrow HA1 42 C2
Woodford IG8 36 D6
Hobart Dr UB4 84 D3
Hobart Gdns CR7 205 B6
Hobart Ho 24 KT6 198 A4
Hobart La UB4 84 D3
Hobart Pl
Richmond TW10 154 B4
Westminster
SW1 115 B3 258 C6
Hobart Rd
Dagenham RM9 80 D4
Hayes UB4 84 D3
North Cheam KT4 216 B5
Hobbayne Prim Sch
W7 86 D1
Hobbayne Rd W7 86 B1
Hobbes Wlk SW15 156 B6
Hobb's Ct SE1 253 D2
Hobbs Gn N2 48 A6
Hobbs Mews IG3 79 D6
Hobbs' Pl N1 95 C6
Hobbs Rd 5 SE27 183 A6
Hobby St EN3 18 D6
Hobday St E14 97 D1
Hobhouse Ct SW1 249 D5
Hobill Wlk KT5 198 B3
Hoblands End BR7 189 C4
Hobsons Pl 7 E1 96 A2
Hobury St
SW10 136 B6 266 C5
Hockenden La BR5,
BR8 191 D1
Hocker St 41 E2 95 D4
Hockett Cl SE8 119 B2
Hockington Ct 7 EN5 13 D6
Hockley Ave E6 100 A5
Hockley Ct 2 E18 37 A2
Hockley Ho 4 E9 74 C2
Hockley Mews IG11 101 C5
Hockliffe Ho 5 W10 90 C2
Hockney Ct 1 SE16 118 B1
Hockworth Ho 7 N16 51 C1
Hocroft Ave NW2 69 B5
Hocroft Ct NW2 69 B5
Hocroft Rd NW2 69 B5
Hocroft Wlk NW2 69 B5
Hodder Dr UB6 86 D5
Hoddesdon Rd DA17 125 C1
Hodford Lo NW11 69 C6
Hodford Rd NW11 47 B1
Hodgkins Cl SE28 124 D6
Hodgkins Mews HA7 25 B5
Hodister Cl 26 SE5 139 A5
Hodson Cl HA2 63 B5
Hodson Pl EN3 7 C5
Hoecroft Ct EN3 6 C5
Hoe La EN1 6 B5
Hoe St E17 53 C4
Hoffman Gdns CR2 222 B1
Hoffman Sq N1 235 D2
Hofland Rd
W14 113 A3 254 A6
Hogan Mews W2 236 C4
Hogan Way E5 74 A6
Hogarth Ave TW15 171 A4
Hogarth Bsns Pk W4 133 C6
Hogarth Cl
Ealing W5 88 A2
Newham E16 99 D2
Hogarth Cres
Mitcham SW19 180 B2
Thornton Heath CR0 205 A2
Hogarth Ct
8 Camden Town NW1 71 C1
City of London EC3 253 B6
Dulwich SE19 183 D6
Heston TW5 129 A5
24 Whitechapel E1 96 A1
Hogarth Gdns TW5 129 C5
Hogarth Hill NW11 47 B5
Hogarth Ho
Enfield EN1 18 A6
12 Northolt UB5 84 D5
1 Sutton SM1 218 B3
Westminster SW1 259 D3
6 West Norwood
SE27 183 A6
Hogarth Ind Est NW10 90 A3
Hogarth La W4 133 C6
Hogarth Pl SW5 255 C3
Hogarth Rd
Barking RM8 80 B3
Earl's Ct SW5 113 D2 255 C3
Edgware HA8 26 C1
Hogarth Roundabout
W4 133 C6
Hogarth's House*
W4 133 C6
Hogarth Way TW12 174 A2
Hogsmill Way KT19 215 A4
Holbeach Cl 8 NW9 27 C2
Holbeach Gdns DA15 167 D5
Holbeach Mews 1
SW12 159 B3
Holbeach Prim Sch
SE6 163 C4
Holbeach Rd SE6 163 D4
Holbeck Row SE15 140 A5
Holbein Ho
Chelsea SW1 258 A2
10 Stanmore HA7 25 C5
Holbein Mews
SW1 115 A1 258 A2
Holbein Pl
SW1 115 A2 258 A3
Holberry Ho 5 SE21 183 C6
Holberton Gdns NW10 90 B4
HOLBORN 94 C2
Holborn EC1 94 C2 241 B3
Holborn Cir
EC1 94 C2 241 B3
Holborn Ho 1 W12 90 B1
Holborn Pl WC1 240 C3
Holborn Rd E13 99 B3
Holborn Sta
WC1 94 B2 240 C3
Holborn Viaduct
EC1 94 D2 241 C3
Holborn Way CR4 180 D1
Holbrook Cl
Enfield EN1 6 A5
Highgate N19 49 B1
Holbrook Ct W7 108 C6
Holbrooke Ct N7 72 A4
Holbrooke Pl 25
TW10 153 D6
Holbrook Ho
Acton W3 89 B2
Chislehurst BR7 189 B2
5 Streatham SW2 160 B3
Holbrook La BR7 189 B3
Holbrook Rd E15 98 D5
Holbrook Way BR2 210 B4
Holburne Cl SE3 143 C4
Holburne Gdns SE3 143 D4
Holburne Rd SE3 143 D4
Holcombe Hill NW7 12 A1
Holcombe Ho SW9 138 A2
Holcombe Pl SE4 141 A2
Holcombe Rd
Ilford IG1 56 C2
Tottenham Hale N17 52 A6
1 Tottenham N17 51 D6
Holcombe St W6 112 B2
Holcote Cl DA17 125 A3
Holcroft Ct W1 239 A4
Holcroft Ho
Battersea SW11 136 B2
Lewisham SE10 142 A4
Holcroft Rd E9 74 C1
Holden Ave
North Finchley N12 29 D5
Welsh Harp NW9 45 A1
Holdenby Rd SE4 163 A6
Holden Cl RM8 80 B5
Holden Ho
12 Deptford SE8 141 C5
Islington N1 235 A5
Holden Hts N12 13 D1
Holdenhurst Ave N12 30 A3
Holden Lo N11 31 C5
Holden Point E15 76 B2
Holden Rd N12 29 D6
Holden St SW11 137 A3
Holdernesse Rd
Isleworth TW7 131 A4
6 Upper Tooting
SW17 159 A2
Holderness Ho SE5 139 C2
Holderness Way
SE27 182 D5
Holders Hill Ave NW4 46 D6
Holders Hill Cres NW4 28 D1
Holders Hill Dr NW4 28 D1
Holders Hill Gdns
NW4 29 A1
Holders Hill Par NW7 29 A2
Holders Hill Rd
Church End NW4, NW7 29 A2
Hendon NW4 28 D1
Holdsworth Ho 5
SW2 160 C4
Holford Ho
6 Bermondsey SE16 118 B2
Finsbury WC1 233 D2
Holford Pl WC1 233 D2
Holford Rd NW3 70 A5
Holford St WC1 234 A2
Holford Yd WC1 234 A3
Holgate Ave SW11 136 B2
Holgate Ct HA8 26 B6
Holgate Gdns RM10 81 C2
Holgate Rd RM10 81 C3
Holgate St SE7 121 D3
Holkham Ho 6 EN5 1 A2
Hollam Ho N8 50 B5
Holland Ave
Belmont SM2 217 C1
Wimbledon SW20 177 D2
Holland Cl
Coney Hall BR2 224 D6
New Barnet EN5 14 B4
Stanmore HA7 25 B5
Holland Ct
Ashford TW15 170 B4
Hendon NW7 28 A4
6 Walthamstow E17 54 A5
Holland Dr SE23 163 A1
Holland Gdns
Brentford TW8 132 A6
Kensington W14 254 B6
Holland Gr SW9 138 C5
Holland Ho E4 36 A6
Holland House Sch
HA8 26 D6
Holland Park
W11 113 B5 244 C3
Holland Park Ave
Ilford IG3 57 D4
Notting Hill
W11 113 A5 244 B3
Holland Park Ct W14 244 B2
Holland Park Gdns
W14 113 A4 244 A2
Holland Park Mews
W11 113 B5 244 C3
Holland Park Rd
W14 113 B3 254 D5
Holland Park Rdbt
W12 112 D4
Holland Park Sch
W8 113 B4 244 D2
Holland Park Sta
W11 113 B5 244 C3
Holland Pas N1 235 A6
Holland Pl W8 245 C2
Holland Rd
Croydon SE25 206 A4
Newham E15 98 C4
Wallend E6 78 C1
Wembley HA0 65 D2
West Kensington
W14 113 A3 254 B6
Willesden Green NW10 90 B5
Holland Rise Ho SW9 270 D3
Holland St
Kensington
W8 113 C4 245 B2
Lambeth SE1 116 D5 251 D4
Hollands The
Feltham TW13 172 D6
New Malden KT4 199 D1
Holland Villas Rd
W14 113 A4 244 A1
Holland Way BR2 224 D6
Holland Wlk
Kensington
W14 113 B4 244 D1
Stanmore HA7 25 A5
Upper Holloway N19 49 D1
Hollar Rd N16 73 D5
Hollen St W1 239 C2
Holles Cl TW12 173 C5
Holles Ho 8 SW9 138 C3
Holles St W1 93 B1 238 D2
Holley Rd W3 111 C4
Hollickwood Ave N12 30 D4
Hollickwood Prim Sch
N10 31 B3
Holliday Sq 7 SW11 136 B2
Hollidge Way RM10 81 D1
Hollies Ave DA15 167 D3
Hollies Cl
South Norwood
SW16 182 C4
Twickenham TW1 152 D2
Hollies End NW7 28 B5
Hollies Rd W5 109 C2
Hollies The
Harrow HA3 43 A5
Oakleigh Pk N20 14 B3
Upper Tooting SW12 159 C2
9 Wanstead E11 55 A4
Wood Green N11 31 D4
Hollies Way 1 SW12 159 A4
Holligrave Rd BR1 187 A2
Hollingbourne Ave
DA7 147 B4
Hollingbourne Gdns
W13 87 B2
Hollingbourne Rd
SE24 161 A6
Hollingsworth Ct 7
KT6 197 D2
Hollingsworth Rd
CR0 222 B2
Hollington Cres KT3 199 D3
Hollington Ct BR7 188 D4
Hollington Rd
Newham E6 100 B4
Tottenham N17 34 A1
Hollingworth Cl KT8 195 B5
Hollingworth Rd BR2,
BR5 210 D2
Hollins Ho N7 72 A4
Hollisfield WC1 233 B1
Hollman Gdns SW16 182 D4
Holloway Cl UB7 104 A1
Holloway La UB7 104 B1
Holloway Rd
Leyton E11 76 B5
Lower Holloway N7 72 B4
Newham E6 100 B4
Upper Holloway N19 71 D6
Holloway Road Sta N7 72 B3
Holloway Sch N7 71 D3
Holloway St TW3 129 D2
Hollow Combe SE20 184 B6
Hollowfield Wlk UB5 63 A2
Hollow The IG8 36 D6
Holly Ave
London N2 47 D6
Stanmore HA7 26 A1
Walton-on-T KT12 194 D1
Hollybank Cl TW12 173 C5
Holly Berry La 8 NW3 70 A4
Hollybrake Cl BR7 189 B3
Hollybush Cl
Harrow HA3 24 C2
Wanstead E11 55 A4
Hollybush Gdns E2 96 B4
Hollybush Hill E11 54 D3
Holly Bush Hill 4
NW3 70 A4
Hollybush Ho 23 E2 96 B4
Holly Bush La TW12 173 C3
Hollybush Pl E2 96 B4
Hollybush Rd KT2 176 A4
Hollybush St E13 99 B4
Holly Bush Steps 6
NW3 70 A4
Holly Bush Vale 10
NW3 70 A4
Holly Cl
Beckenham BR3 208 A5
Holly Cl *continued*
Buckhurst Hill IG9 21 D1
Feltham TW13 173 A5
Wallington SM6 219 B1
Holly Cottage Mews
UB8 82 C2
Holly Cotts KT7 197 A1
Holly Cres
Beckenham BR3 207 B4
Chingford IG8 36 B3
Hollycroft Ave
Child's Hill NW3 69 C5
Wembley HA9 66 B5
Hollycroft Cl
Harmondsworth UB7 126 C6
South Croydon CR2 221 C3
Hollycroft Gdns UB7 126 C6
Holly Ct
16 Belmont SM2 217 C1
Catford SE6 164 A1
4 Sidcup DA14 190 B6
South Tottenham N15 51 C5
Hollydale Cl UB5 63 D4
Hollydale Dr BR2 226 B5
Hollydale Prim Sch
SE15 140 C3
Hollydale Rd SE15 140 C3
Hollydene
Bromley BR1 186 D2
Hither Green SE13 164 B5
5 Peckham SE15 140 B4
Hollydown Way E11 76 B5
Holly Dr E4 19 D4
Holly Farm Rd UB2 107 A1
Hollyfield Ave N11 30 D5
Hollyfield Rd KT5 198 B2
Hollyfield Sch & Sixth
Form Ctr The KT6 198 A4
Holly Gdns UB7 104 B4
Holly Gr
Kingsbury NW9 45 A2
Peckham SE15 140 A3
Pinner HA5 23 A2
Hollygrove WD23 8 B4
Hollygrove Cl TW3 129 B1
Hollyhedge Ho SE3 142 B3
Holly Hedge Terr
SE13 164 B6
Holly Hill
Hampstead NW3 70 A4
Southgate N21 16 B5
Holly Hill Rd DA8,
DA17 125 D1
Holly Ho
Brentford TW8 131 C6
Ilford IG3 58 A1
Holly House Hospl IG9 21 B2
Holly Lo
Cottenham Pk SW20 178 B1
Harrow HA1 42 B4
Kensington W8 245 A2
Southgate N21 16 C3
4 Wimbledon SW19 179 A4
Holly Lodge
Lewisham SE13 142 B1
Southall UB2 107 B2
Holly Lodge Gdns N6 49 A1
Holly Lodge Mans N6 71 A6
Hollymead SM5 218 D5
Holly Mews SW10 256 B1
Holly Mount NW3 70 A4
Hollymount Cl 9
SE10 142 A4
Hollymount Sch
SW20 178 C2
Holly Park Est N4 50 B2
Holly Park Gdns N3 47 C6
Holly Park Prim Sch
N11 31 A5
Holly Park Rd
Ealing W7 108 D5
Friern Barnet N11 31 A5
Holly Pk
East Finchley N3 47 C6
Hornsey N4 50 B2
Holly Pl NW3 70 A4
Holly Rd
6 Chiswick W4 111 B2
Hampton TW12 174 A4
Hounslow TW3 129 D1
Leytonstone E11 54 D2
Twickenham TW1 153 A3
Holly St E8 73 D1
Holly Terr N6 49 A1
Hollytree Cl SW19 156 D3
Holly Tree Ho SE4 141 B2
Holly Tree Lo EN2 4 D3
Hollyview Cl NW4 46 A3
Holly Village N6 71 B6
Holly Way CR4 203 D6
Holly Wlk
Enfield EN2 5 B2
Hampstead NW3 70 A4
Hollywood Ct W5 110 B6
Hollywood Gdns UB4 84 B1
Hollywood Lofts E1 243 C5
Hollywood Mews
SW10 266 A6
Hollywood Rd
Chelsea
SW10 136 A6 266 A6
Highams Pk E4 35 A5
Hollywood Way IG8 36 B4
Holman Ho 2 E2 96 D4
Holman Hunt Ho W14 254 A1
Holman Rd
London SW11 136 B3
West Ewell KT19 215 A3
Holmbank Dr TW17 193 C5
Holmbridge Gdns EN3 6 D1
Holmbrook NW1 232 B3
Holmbrook Dr NW4 46 D4
Holmbury Cl WD23 8 C2
Holmbury Ct
Mitcham SW19 180 C3
Upper Tooting SW17 158 D1
Holmbury Gdns UB3 105 D5
Holmbury Gr CR0 223 B1
Holmbury Ho SW9 160 D6
Holmbury Manor 9
DA14 190 A6
Holmbury Pk BR7 188 A3
Holmbury View 2 E5 52 B1
Holmbush Ct NW4 46 D4
Holmbush Rd SW15 157 A5
Holmcote Gdns N5 73 A3
Holmcroft Ho 10 E17 53 D5
Holmcroft Way BR2 210 B4
Holm Ct SE12 165 B1
Holmdale Gdns NW4 46 D4
Holmdale Rd
Chislehurst BR7 189 A5
South Hampstead NW6 69 C3
Holmdale Terr N15 51 C3
Holmdene N12 29 D5
Holmdene Ave
Harrow HA2 41 D6
Hendon NW7 28 A4
Herne Hill SE24 161 A6
Holmdene Cl BR3 186 A1
Holmdene Ct BR1 210 A6
Holmead Rd
SW6 135 D5 265 D3
Holme Ct 12 TW7 131 A2
Holmefield Ct 4 NW3 70 C2
Holmefield Ho W10 91 A3
Holme Lacey Rd
SE12 164 D5
Holmeleigh Ct EN3 6 C1
Holme Rd E6 100 A6
Holmes Ave
Mill Hill NW7 29 A5
Walthamstow E17 53 B6
Holmes Cl SE22 140 A1
Holmes Ct
Chingford E4 20 B2
18 South Acton W4 111 A3
18 South Lambeth
SW4 138 A3
Holmesdale Ave
SW14 132 D1
Holmesdale Cl SE25 205 D6
Holmesdale Ho 12
NW6 91 C6
Holmesdale Rd
Bexley DA7 146 D3
Highgate N6 49 B2
Richmond TW9 132 B4
South Norwood SE25 205 C5
Teddington TW11 175 C4
Thornton Heath CR0 205 B4
Holmesley Rd SE23 163 A5
Holmes Pl SW10 266 B6
Holmes Rd
Kentish Town NW5 71 B3
Merton SW19 180 A3
Twickenham TW1 152 D2
Holmes Terr SE1 251 A2
Holmeswood 1 SM2 217 D1
Holmeswood Ct 3
N22 32 C1
Holme Way HA7 24 D4
Holmewood Gdns
SW2 160 B4
Holmewood Rd
South Norwood SE25 205 C6
Streatham SW2 160 B4

Holmfield Ave NW4 46 D4
Holmfield Ho E17 54 B5
Holm Gr UB10 60 C1
Holmhurst
 London SE13 164 B5
 Wimbledon SW19 178 C3
Holmhurst Rd DA17 125 D1
Holmlea Ct CR0 221 B4
Holmleigh Prim Sch N16 51 C1
Holmleigh Rd N16 51 C1
Holm Oak Cl SW15 157 B5
Holmoaks Ho BR3 186 A1
Holmsbury Ho 6 N7 71 D3
Holmsdale Ho
 6 London N11 31 B6
 24 Poplar E14 119 D6
Holmshaw Cl SE26 185 A6
Holmside Ct SW12 159 A5
Holmside Rd SW12 159 A5
Holmsley Cl KT3 199 D2
Holmsley Ho SW15 155 D4
Holmstall Ave HA8 27 A1
Holmstall Par HA8 27 A1
Holm Wlk SE3 143 A3
Holmwood 2 KT5 198 B3
Holmwood Cl
 Cheam SM2 216 D1
 Harrow HA2 42 A6
 Northolt UB5 63 D2
Holmwood Ct
 Kingston u T KT3 199 B6
 Sidcup DA14 189 D5
 3 Stamford Hill N16 51 D2
Holmwood Gdns
 London N3 29 C1
 Wallington SM6 219 B2
Holmwood Gr NW7 27 B5
Holmwood Mans W3 110 C5
Holmwood Rd
 Chessington KT9 214 A3
 Ilford IG3 79 C6
Holne Chase
 London N2 48 A3
 Morden SM4 201 C3
Holne Lo N6 49 C3
Holness Rd E15 76 D2
Holocaust Meml Gdn* W2 114 D4 247 D2
Holroyd Rd SW15 156 C6
Holsgrove Ct W3 111 C5
Holstein Way 6 DA18 125 A3
Holst Mans SW13 134 C5
Holstock Rd IG1 79 A6
Holsworth Cl HA2 42 A4
Holsworthy Ho 49 E3 97 D4
Holsworthy Sq WC1 240 D5
Holsworthy Way KT9 213 C3
Holt Cl
 London N10 49 A5
 Woolwich SE28 124 C6
Holt Ct
 Greenwich SE10 142 A6
 Stratford New Town E15 76 A3
Holt Ho SW2 160 C5
Holtoake Ct 1 W5 87 C3
Holtoake Ho 3 W5 87 C3
Holton St E1 96 D3
Holt Rd
 Newham E16 122 A5
 Wembley HA0 65 C5
Holt The
 Morden SM4 201 C5
 Wallington SM6 219 C4
Holtwhite Ave EN2 5 A3
Holtwhite's Hill EN2 4 D4
Holwell Pl HA5 41 A5
Holwood Park Ave BR2, BR6 226 B4
Holwood Pl 7 SW4 137 D1
Holybourne Ave SW15 156 A4
Holy Cross Prep Sch KT2 177 A3
Holy Cross RC Prim Sch SE6 164 A3
Holy Cross RC Sch SW6 135 C4 265 A2
Holy Cross Sch The KT3 199 C4
Holy Family RC Coll The
 Walthamstow E17 54 A5
 Walthamstow E17 54 A6
Holy Family RC Prim Sch
 Kidbrooke SE9 143 C1
 Poplar E14 119 C6
Holy Ghost RC Prim Sch SW12 159 A4
Holyhead Cl
 Bow E3 97 C4
 3 Newham E6 100 B2
Holyhead Ct KT1 197 D5
Holy Innocents RC Prim Sch BR6 227 D5
Holyoake Ct SE16 119 B4
Holyoake Wlk
 Ealing W5 87 C3
 East Finchley N2 48 A6
Holyoak Rd SE11 116 D2 261 D3
Holyport Rd SW6 134 D5
Holyrood Ave HA2 63 B4
Holyrood Gdns HA8 26 D1
Holyrood Ho N4 51 A1
Holyrood Mews 10 E16 121 A5
Holyrood Rd EN5 14 B5
Holyrood St SE1 117 C5 253 A3
Holy Trinity CE Jun Sch SM6 219 C4
Holy Trinity CE Prim Sch
 Belgravia SW1 115 A2 258 A4
 Dalston E8 73 D2
 East Finchley N2 48 B6
 Forest Hill SE26 162 C2
 Hampstead NW3 70 A2
 Richmond TW10 132 C1
 Streatham SW2 160 B4
 Wimbledon SW19 179 D4
Holy Trinity Coll Prep Sch BR1 187 C2
Holy Trinity Lamorbey CE Prim Sch DA15 168 A3
Holy Trinity & Saint Silas CE Prim Sch NW1 71 B1
Holywell Cl
 35 Bermondsey SE16 118 B1
 2 Greenwich SE3 143 A6
 Stanwell TW19 148 A3
Holywell La EC2 243 B6
Holywell Lo EN2 4 B5
Holywell Row EC2 95 C3 243 A5
Holywell Way TW19 148 A3
Homan Ct N12 30 A6
Homan Ho 6 SW4 159 D4
Homebush Ho E4 19 D4
Homecedars Ho WD23 8 B3
Homecherry Ho 5 IG10 21 D6
Home Cl
 Carshalton SM5 218 D6
 Northolt UB5 85 B4
Homecoppice Ho 1 BR1 186 D3
Homecroft Rd
 Forest Hill SE26 184 C5
 Tottenham N22 33 A2
Homecross Ho 7 W4 111 B2
Home Ct KT6 197 D4
Homedale Ho SM1 217 D4
Home Farm Cl
 Thames Ditton KT7 196 D2
 Upper Halliford TW17 193 C5
Home Farm Cotts BR5 190 D2
Homefarm Rd W7 86 D1
Homefield SM4 201 C5
Home Field EN5 13 B6
Homefield Ave IG2 57 C4
Homefield Cl
 Hayes UB4 84 D3
 Willesden NW10 67 A2
Homefield Ct NW4 46 C5
Homefield Gdns
 London N2 48 B6
 Mitcham CR4, SW19 180 B1
Homefield Ho SE23 162 D1
Homefield Pk SM1, SM2 217 D2
Homefield Pl 4 SW19 178 D5
Homefield Prep Sch SM1 217 C3
Homefield Rd
 Bromley BR1 187 C2
 Burnt Oak HA8 27 B4
 Chiswick W4 111 D1
 Walton-on-T KT12 195 A2
 Wembley HA0 65 B4
 Wimbledon SW19 179 A4
Homefield St 14 N1 95 C5
Homefirs Ho HA9 66 B5
Homeheather Ho 5 IG4 56 B4
Homelands Dr SE19 183 C3
Home Lea BR6 227 D3
Homeleigh Ct 8 SW16 160 A1
Homeleigh Rd SE15 162 D6
Homemead SW12 159 B2
Home Mead HA7 25 C2
Homemead Rd
 Bromley BR2 210 B4
 Wallington CR0 203 C3
Home Office SW1 249 C1
Home Park Rd SW19 157 B1
Home Park Terr KT1 175 D1
Home Park Wlk KT1 197 D5
Home Rd SW11 136 C3
Homer Dr E14 119 C2
Homer Rd
 Croydon CR0 206 D3
 Homerton E9 75 A2
Homer Row W1 237 B3
Homersham Rd KT1 176 D1
Homer St W1 92 C2 237 B3
HOMERTON 74 D1
Homerton Coll of Technology E9 74 C3
Homerton Ct 2 EN4 14 D3
Homerton Gr E9 74 D3
Homerton High St E9 74 D3
Homerton Rd E9 75 B3
Homerton Row E9 74 C3
Homerton Sta E9 74 D2
Homerton Terr E9 74 C2
Homerton University Hospl E9 74 D3
Homesdale Cl E11 55 A4
Homesdale Rd
 Bromley BR1, BR2 209 C6
 Orpington BR5 211 C2
Homesfield NW11 47 C4
Homes Of Rest (CE Temperance Society) IG1 79 B5
Homestall Rd SE22 162 C6
Homestead Ct EN5 13 C6
Homestead Gdns KT10 212 C3
Homestead Paddock N14 15 B6
Homestead Pk NW2 67 D5
Homestead Rd
 Dagenham RM8 81 B6
 Fulham SW6 135 B5 264 D3
Homesteads The BR3 185 D4
Homestead The N11 31 B6
Homewalk Ho 1 SE26 184 C6
Homewaters Ave TW16 171 D2
Homewillow Cl N21 16 D5
Homewood Cl TW12 173 B4
Homewood Cres BR7 189 C4
Homewood Gdns SE25 205 C4
Homewoods 2 SW12 159 C4
Homildon Ho 10 SE26 162 A1
Homington Ct KT2 176 A3
Honduras St EC1 242 A6
Honeybourne Rd NW6 69 D3
Honeybourne Way BR5 211 B1
Honeybrook Rd SW12, SW4 159 C4
Honey Cl RM10 81 D2
Honeycroft Hill UB10 60 A1
Honeyden Rd DA14 191 A4
Honeyfield N4 72 C6
Honey Hill UB10 60 B1
Honey La EC2 242 B1
Honey Lane Ho SW10 265 D6
Honeyman Cl NW6 68 D1
Honeypot Bsns Ctr HA7 26 A2
Honeypot Cl NW9 44 B5
Honeypot La HA3, HA7, NW9 44 B6
Honeysett Rd 3 N17 33 D1
Honeysuckle Cl UB1 107 A6
Honeysuckle Ct
 Ilford IG1 78 D2
 2 Lee SE12 165 A4
 6 Sutton SM2 217 D2
Honeysuckle Gdns CR0 206 D1
Honeywell Jun & Inf Schs SW11 158 D5
Honeywell Rd SW11 158 D5
Honeywood Heritage Ctr* SM5 218 D4
Honeywood Ho 5 SE15 140 A4
Honeywood Rd
 Harlesden NW10 89 D5
 Isleworth TW7 131 A1
Honeywood Wlk SM5 218 D4
Honister Cl HA7 25 B2
Honister Gdns HA7 25 B2
Honister Pl HA7 25 B2
Honiton Gdns
 Edgware NW7 28 D3
 1 Nunhead SE15 140 C3
Honiton Ho 29 SE5 139 A3
Honiton Rd
 Bexley DA16 145 D3
 Kilburn NW6 91 B5
Honley Rd SE6 163 D4
Honnor Gdns TW7 130 B3
HONOR OAK 162 C6
Honor Oak Park Sta SE23 162 D5
Honor Oak Pk SE23 162 D5
Honor Oak Rd SE23 162 C4
Honor Oak Rise SE23 162 C5
Honwell Ho 24 W2 91 C2
Hood Ave
 East Barnet N14 15 B5
 Mortlake SW14 155 A6
Hood Cl CR0 204 D1
Hoodcote Gdns N21 16 D4
Hood Ct N7 72 B5
Hood Ho 17 SE5 139 B5
Hood Lo E11 77 B6
Hood Rd SW20 177 D3
HOOK 214 A4
Hook KT6 214 A5
Hooke Ct SE10 142 A4
Hooke Ho 32 E3 97 A5
Hooker's Rd E17 52 D6
Hook Farm Rd BR2 209 D4
Hookham Ct SW8 269 C2
Hook Ho 9 SW27 182 D5
Hooking Gn HA2 41 D4
Hook La DA16 146 A1
Hook Lane Prim Sch DA16 146 A2
Hook Rd KT19, KT17 215 A1
Hook Rise N
 Surbiton KT6 214 A5
 Tolworth KT6 214 D6
Hook Rise S KT6, KT9 214 D6
Hook Rise South KT6 214 A5
Hook Rise South Ind Pk KT6 214 C5
Hooks Cl SE15 140 B4
Hookstone Way IG8 37 D3
Hook The EN5 14 B5
Hook Underpass KT6 214 A5
Hook Wlk HA8 27 A4
Hooper Dr UB8 82 D2
Hooper Ho 9 SW18 157 B6
Hooper Rd E16 99 A1
Hooper's Ct SW1 247 C1
Hooper's Mews 4 W3 111 A5
Hooper St E1 96 A1
Hoop La NW11 47 C2
Hoover Ho 5 SE6 186 A6
Hope Cl
 2 Brentford TW8 110 A1
 Canonbury N1 73 A2
 Dagenham RM6 58 D5
 Grove Pk SE12 165 B1
 Sutton SM1 218 A3
 1 Woodford IG8 37 C4
Hope Ct 1 SE1 118 A1
Hopedale Rd SE7 143 B6
Hopefield 3 W7 108 D5
Hopefield Ave NW6 91 A5
Hope Gdns 10 W3 110 D4
Hope Pk BR1 186 D3
Hopes Cl TW5 129 C6
Hope St SW11 136 B2
Hopetown St E1 243 D3
Hopewell St SE5 139 B5
Hop Gdns WC2 250 A5
Hopgood St 5 W12 112 C5
Hopkins Cl N10 31 A3
Hopkins Ho 17 E14 97 C1
Hopkins Mews E15 98 D6
Hopkinson Ho 1 SW11 137 A3
Hopkinson's Pl NW1 231 A6
Hopkins St W1 93 D1 239 C1
Hopley Ho W13 109 B6
Hoppers Rd N21 16 C2
Hoppett Rd E4 20 C2
Hopping La N1 72 D2
Hoppingwood Ave KT3 199 C6
Hoppner Rd UB4 83 B5
Hop St SE10 120 D2
Hopton Ct BR2 209 A1
Hopton Gdns KT3 200 A3
Hopton Ho 5 SW9 138 D3
Hopton Par 2 SW16 182 A5
Hopton Rd
 Streatham SW16 182 A5
 Woolwich SE18 122 D3
Hopton's Gdns SE1 251 D4
Hopton St SE1 116 D5 251 D4
Hoptree Cl N12 29 D6
Hopwood Cl SW17 158 A1
Hopwood Rd SE17 139 B6
Hopwood Wlk E8 74 A1
Horace Rd
 Forest Gate E7 77 B4
 Ilford IG6 57 A6
 Kingston u T KT1 198 B6
Horatio Ho
 13 Haggerston E2 95 D5
 4 Merton SW19 179 D3
Horatio Pl
 9 Canary Wharf E14 120 A5
 Merton SW19 179 C2
Horatio St 11 E2 95 D5
Horatius Way CR0 220 B2
Horbury Cres W11 113 C6 245 A5
Horbury Lo TW12 173 C3
Horbury Mews W11 113 B6 244 D5
Horder Rd SW6 135 A4 264 B1
Hordle Prom E 15 SE15 139 D5
Hordle Prom N 4 SE15 139 D5
Hordle Prom S 7 SE15 139 D5
Horizon Bldg 22 E14 119 C6
Horizon Sch N16 73 C4
Horle Wlk SE5 138 D3
Horley Cl DA6 169 C6
Horley Rd SE9 188 A6
Hormead Rd W9 91 B3
Hornbeam Cl
 Barking IG11 102 B3
 Buckhurst Hill IG9 21 D1
 Edgware NW7 11 D1
 Ilford IG1 79 B3
 Lambeth SE11 261 A4
 Northolt UB5 63 B3
Hornbeam Cres TW8 131 B5
Hornbeam Gdns KT3 200 A3
Hornbeam Gr E4 20 D1
Hornbeam Ho
 1 Buckhurst Hill IG9 21 D1
 2 Maitland Pk NW3 70 D2
 6 Penge SE20 184 D3
 6 Sidcup DA15 168 A1
Hornbeam La E4 20 C6
Hornbeam Rd
 Buckhurst Hill IG9 21 D1
 Hayes UB4 84 C2
Hornbeam Sq 8 E3 97 B6
Hornbeams Rise N11 31 A4
Hornbeam Terr SM5 202 C1
Hornbeam Way BR2 210 C3
Hornblower Cl 2 SE16 119 A2
Hornbuckle Cl HA2 64 B6
Hornby Cl NW3 70 B1
Hornby Ho
 6 Kennington SE11 138 C6
 13 Richmond TW10 153 C1
Horncastle Cl SE12 165 A4
Horncastle Rd SE12 165 A4
Hornchurch N17 33 B1
Hornchurch Cl KT2 175 D6
Horndean Cl 3 SW15 156 A3
Horne Ho 4 SE18 144 A4
Horner Ct E11 76 B5
Horne Rd TW17 192 C5
Horner Hos 18 N1 95 C6
Horner La 3 CR4 180 B1
Horne Way SW15 134 C3
Hornfair Rd SE7 143 D5
Horniman Dr SE23 162 C4
Horniman Grange 7 SE23 162 C3
Horniman Mus & Gdns* SE23 162 B3
Horniman Sch SE23 162 B3
Horning Cl SE9 188 A6
Horn La
 Acton W3 89 A1
 Greenwich SE10 121 A2
 Woodford IG8 37 A3
Horn Link Way SE10 121 A2
Horn Park Cl SE12 165 B6
Horn Park La SE12 165 B5
Horn Park Prim Sch SE12 165 B4
Hornsby House Sch SW12 159 A3
Horns Croft IG11 79 C1
Horns End Pl HA5 40 C4
HORNSEY 50 A5
Hornsey Central Hospl N8 49 D4
Hornsey La N6 49 C2
Hornsey Lane Gdns N6 49 C2
Hornsey Park Rd N8 50 B6
Hornsey Rd N7, N19 72 B6
Hornsey Rise Gdns N19 50 A2
Hornsey Sch for Girls N8 50 B4
Hornsey St N7 72 B3
Hornsey Sta N8 50 B5
HORNSEY VALE 50 B4
Hornshay St SE15 140 C6
Horns Rd IG2, IG6 57 A4
Hornton Ct W8 245 B1
Hornton Pl W8 245 B1
Hornton St W8 113 C4 245 B2
Horrocks Ho SW15 156 B6
Horsa Rd
 Eltham SE12 165 C4
 Erith DA8 147 D5
Horsebridge Cl RM9 103 A6
Horsecroft Rd HA8 27 B3
Horse & Dolphin Yd W1 249 D6
Horse Fair KT1 175 D1
Horseferry Pl SE10 142 A6
Horseferry Rd
 Limehouse E14 119 A6
 Westminster SW1 115 D2 259 D4
Horseferry Rd Est SW1 259 C5
Horse Guards Ave SW1 116 A5 250 A3
Horse Guards Par* SW1 115 D5 249 D3
Horse Guards Rd SW1 115 D4 249 D2
Horse Leaze E6 100 C1
Horsell Rd
 Islington N5 72 C3
 St Paul's Cray BR5 190 B2
Horselydown La SE1 117 D5 253 C3
Horselydown Mans SE1 253 C2
Horsemongers Mews SE1 252 B1
Horsenden Ave UB6 64 D3
Horsenden Cres UB6 64 D3
Horsenden La N UB6 64 D1
Horsenden La S UB6 87 A6
Horsenden Prim Sch UB6 64 C2
Horsendon Ho 11 N7 71 D3
Horseshoe Cl
 Cubitt Town E14 120 A1
 Dollis Hill NW2 68 B6
Horse Shoe Cres UB5 85 C5
Horseshoe Dr UB8 82 C1
Horse Shoe Gn SM1 217 D6
Horseshoe La
 Barnet N20 12 D3
 Enfield EN2 5 A2
Horse Yd N1 234 D6
Horsfeld Gdns 1 SE9 166 A6
Horsfeld Rd SE9 165 D6
Horsfield Ho 18 N1 73 A1
Horsford Rd SW2 160 B6
Horsham Ave N12 30 C5
Horsham Ct N17 34 A2
Horsham Rd
 Bexley DA6 169 C6
 East Bedfont TW14 149 A5
Horsley Ct SW1 259 D3
Horsley Dr
 Kingston u T KT2 175 D5
 New Addington CR0 224 A1
Horsley Ho 11 SE4 140 D1
Horsley Rd
 Bromley BR1 187 B2

Horsley Rd *continued*
Chingford E4 .... 20 A2
Horsley St 3 SE17 .... 139 B6
Horsman Ho SE5 .... 139 A6
Horsman St SE5 .... 139 A6
Horsmonden Cl BR6 .... 211 D2
Horsmonden Rd SE4 .... 163 B5
Horston Ho N4 .... 51 A2
Hortensia Ho SW10 .... 266 A4
Hortensia Rd SW10 .... 136 A5 266 A4
Horticultural Pl 6 W4 .... 111 B1
Horton Ave NW2 .... 69 A4
Horton Bridge Rd UB7 .... 104 B5
Horton Cl UB7 .... 104 B5
Horton Ctry Pk KT19 .... 214 C1
Horton Ho
13 Deptford SE15 .... 140 C6
South Lambeth SW8 .... 270 C4
West Kensington W14 .... 254 A1
Horton Ind Pk UB7 .... 104 B5
Horton La KT19 .... 215 A1
Horton Par UB7 .... 104 A5
Horton Rd
Hackney E8 .... 74 B2
Yiewsley UB7 .... 104 B5
Horton Road Ind Est UB7 .... 104 B5
Horton St SE13 .... 141 D2
Horton Way CR0 .... 206 D4
Hortus Rd
Chingford E4 .... 20 A2
Southall UB2 .... 107 B4
Horwood Ho
24 Bethnal Green E2 .... 96 B4
Marylebone NW8 .... 237 B6
Hosack Rd SW12, SW17 .... 159 A2
Hoser Ave SE12 .... 165 A2
Hosier La EC1 .... 94 D2 241 D3
Hoskins Cl UB3 .... 105 D1
Hoskin's Cl E16 .... 99 C1
Hoskins St SE10 .... 120 B1
Hospital Bridge Rd TW2 .... 151 D3
Hospital Bridge Rdbt TW2 .... 151 D2
Hospital of the Holy Trinity (Almshouses) 5 CR0 .... 221 A6
Hospital Rd TW3 .... 129 C2
Hospital Way SE13 .... 164 B4
Hospl for Tropical Diseases
Fitzrovia WC1 .... 93 C3 239 B5
Somers Town NW1 .... 232 D5
Hospl of St John & St Elizabeth NW8 .... 92 B5 229 C3
Hotham Cl KT8 .... 195 C6
Hotham Prim Sch SW15 .... 134 D1
Hotham Rd
Merton SW19 .... 180 A3
Putney SW15 .... 134 C2
Hotham Road Mews 12 SW19 .... 180 A3
Hotham St E15 .... 98 C6
Hothfield Pl SE16 .... 118 C3
Hotspur Ind Est N17 .... 34 B4
Hotspur Rd UB5 .... 85 C5
Hotspur St SE11 .... 116 C1 261 A2
Houblon Rd TW10 .... 154 A6
Houghton Cl
10 Dalston E8 .... 73 D2
Hampton TW12 .... 173 A4
Houghton Rd N15 .... 51 D5
Houghton Sq SW9 .... 138 A2
Houghton St WC2 .... 240 D1
Houlder Cres CR0 .... 220 D2
Houndsden Rd N21 .... 16 C5
Houndsditch EC3 .... 95 C1 243 B2
Houndsfield Prim Sch N9 .... 18 B4
Houndsfield Rd N9 .... 18 B4
HOUNSLOW 129 C3
Hounslow Ave TW3 .... 151 D6
Hounslow Bsns Pk TW3 .... 129 D1
Hounslow Central Sta TW3 .... 129 D2
Hounslow Ctr The TW3 .... 129 D2
Hounslow East Sta TW3 .... 130 A3
Hounslow Gdns TW3 .... 151 D6
Hounslow Heath Jun & Inf Schs TW4 .... 129 A2
Hounslow Heath Nature Reserve TW4 .... 151 A5
Hounslow Manor Sch TW3 .... 130 A2
Hounslow Rd
Feltham TW14 .... 150 B4
Hanworth TW13 .... 151 A2
Twickenham TW2, TW3 .... 152 A5
Hounslow Sta TW3 .... 151 D6
Hounslow Town Prim Sch TW3 .... 130 B2
HOUNSLOW WEST 128 D2
Hounslow West Sta TW3 .... 129 A3
Houseman Way 20 SE5 .... 139 B5
House of Detention* EC1 .... 94 C3 241 B6
Houses of Parliament* SW1 .... 116 A3 260 B6
Houston Ct 3 CR0 .... 205 C1
Houston Pl KT10 .... 196 C1
Houston Rd
Forest Hill SE23 .... 163 A1
Thames Ditton KT6 .... 197 B3
Houstoun Ct TW5 .... 129 B5
Hove Ave E17 .... 53 B4
Hoveden Rd NW2 .... 69 A3
Hove Gdns SM1 .... 201 D1
Hovenden Ho 6 SE21 .... 183 C6
Hoveton Rd SE28 .... 102 C1
Howard Ave DA5 .... 168 C4
Howard Bldg SW8 .... 268 C5
Howard Cl
Acton W3 .... 88 D1
Ashford TW16 .... 171 D4
Brunswick Pk N11 .... 15 A2
Bushey WD23 .... 8 C4
Cricklewood NW2 .... 69 A4
Hampton TW12 .... 174 A4
Howard Ct
12 Barking IG11 .... 101 B6
Beckenham BR3 .... 186 A1
Lewisham SE10 .... 142 A4
Peckham SE15 .... 140 A2
Howard Ho
6 Brixton SW9 .... 138 C2
14 Deptford SE8 .... 141 B6
Fitzrovia W1 .... 238 D5
Penge SE20 .... 184 C2
6 Upper Clapton E5 .... 74 C6
Howard Mans E17 .... 53 D6
Howard Mews N5 .... 72 D4
Howard Prim Sch CR0 .... 221 A4
Howard Rd
Barking IG11 .... 101 B6
Canonbury N16 .... 73 B4
Cricklewood NW2 .... 68 D4
Croydon SE25 .... 206 A3
Ilford IG1 .... 78 D4
Isleworth TW7 .... 130 D2
Leyton E11 .... 76 C5
Newham E6 .... 100 B5
New Malden KT3 .... 199 D5
Penge SE20 .... 184 C2
Plaistow BR1 .... 187 A3
Southall UB1 .... 85 D1
South Tottenham N15 .... 51 C3
Surbiton KT5 .... 198 B3
Walthamstow E17 .... 53 D6
Howards Cl HA5 .... 22 B1
Howards Crest Cl BR3 .... 186 A1
Howard's La SW15 .... 134 C1
Howard's Rd E13 .... 99 A4
Howard St KT7 .... 197 B3
Howard Way EN5 .... 12 D6
Howard Wlk N2 .... 48 B5
Howarth Ct E15 .... 76 A3
Howarth Rd SE2 .... 124 A2
Howberry Cl HA8 .... 25 D4
Howberry Rd
South Norwood CR7 .... 183 B1
Stanmore HA7, H8 .... 25 D4
Howbury Rd SE15 .... 140 C2
Howcroft Cres N3 .... 29 C3
Howcroft Ho 3 E3 .... 97 B4
Howcroft La UB6 .... 86 B4
Howden Cl SE28 .... 124 D6
Howden Ct SE25 .... 183 D1
Howden Rd SE25 .... 183 D1
Howden St SE15 .... 140 A2
Howell Cl RM6 .... 58 D4
Howell Ct 2 E10 .... 53 D2
Howell Ho 5 N7 .... 71 D3
Howell Wlk SE1 .... 261 D3
Howe Lo TW1 .... 153 A4
Howerd Way SE18 .... 144 A4
Howes Cl N3 .... 47 C6
Howeth Ct 7 N11 .... 31 A4
Howfield Pl N17 .... 51 D6
Howgate Rd SW14 .... 133 B2
Howick Mans SE18 .... 122 A3
Howick Pl SW1 .... 115 C3 259 B5
Howie St SW11 .... 136 C5 267 A3
Howitt Cl
6 Maitland Pk NW3 .... 70 C2
Stoke Newington N16 .... 73 C4
Howitt Rd NW3 .... 70 C2
Howland Ho 9 SW16 .... 160 A1
Howland Mews E W1 .... 239 B4
Howland St W1 .... 93 C2 239 B4
Howland Way SE16 .... 119 A4
Howletts La HA4 .... 39 A3
Howletts Rd SE24 .... 161 A5
Howley Pl W2 .... 92 A2 236 B4
Howley Rd CR0 .... 221 A5
Howmic Ct 1 TW1 .... 153 C5
Howsman Rd SW13 .... 134 A6
Howson Rd SE4 .... 141 A1
Howson Terr TW10 .... 154 A5
How's St E2 .... 95 D5
Howton Pl WD23 .... 8 B3
HOXTON 95 C5
Hoxton Mkt 10 N1 .... 95 C4
Hoxton Point EC1 .... 95 C4
Hoxton Sq N1 .... 95 C4
Hoxton St N1 .... 95 C5
Hoylake Cres UB10 .... 60 D6
Hoylake Gdns
Mitcham CR4 .... 203 C6
Ruislip HA4 .... 40 B1
South Oxhey WD19 .... 22 D6
Hoylake Rd W3 .... 89 C1
Hoyland Cl 4 SE15 .... 140 B5
Hoyle Rd SW17 .... 180 C5
Hoy St E16 .... 98 D1
Hubbard Dr KT9 .... 213 D2
Hubbard Rd SE27 .... 183 A6
Hubbards Cl UB8 .... 82 D1
Hubbard St E15 .... 98 C6
Hub Buildings The 4 SW12 .... 159 B3
Huberd Ho SE1 .... 262 D6
Hubert Gr SW9 .... 138 A2
Hubert Ho NW8 .... 237 A5
Hubert Rd E6 .... 99 D4
Hucknall Ct NW8 .... 236 C6
Huddart St 6 E3 .... 97 B2
Huddlestone Cl E2 .... 96 C5
Huddlestone Rd
Forest Gate E7 .... 76 D4
Willesden NW2 .... 68 B2
Huddleston Rd N7 .... 71 C4
Hudson 27 NW9 .... 27 D2
Hudson Cl
Newham E15 .... 99 A6
15 Shepherd's Bush W12 .... 112 B6
Hudson Ct
Croydon SE25 .... 206 A5
1 Isle Of Dogs E14 .... 119 C1
4 Merton SW19 .... 179 D2
Hudson Ho
Chelsea SW10 .... 266 A4
5 Notting Hill W11 .... 91 A1
Hudson Pl SE18 .... 123 A1
Hudson Rd
Erith DA7 .... 147 B4
Harlington UB7 .... 127 B6
Hudsons Ho N1 .... 235 D1
Hudson's Pl SW1 .... 115 C2 259 A4
Hudson Way N9 .... 18 C2
Huggin Ct EC4 .... 252 B6
Huggin Hill EC4 .... 252 B6
Huggins Ho 9 E3 .... 97 C4
Huggins Pl SW2 .... 160 B3
Hughan Rd E15 .... 76 B3
Hugh Astor Ct SE1 .... 261 D6
Hugh Clark Ho 13 W13 .... 109 A5
Hugh Dalton Ave SW6 .... 264 C5
Hughenden Ave HA3 .... 43 B4
Hughenden Gdns UB5 .... 84 C4
Hughenden Ho NW8 .... 237 A6
Hughenden Rd KT4 .... 200 A2
Hughendon EN5 .... 1 D1
Hughendon Terr E15 .... 76 A4
Hughes Cl N12 .... 30 A5
Hughes Ho
26 Bethnal Green E2 .... 96 C4
Camberwell SE5 .... 139 A4
Hughes Ho *continued*
15 Deptford SE8 .... 141 C6
Newington SE17 .... 261 D3
Hughes Mans E1 .... 96 A3
Hughes Rd
Ashford TW15 .... 171 A4
Hayes UB3 .... 106 B6
Hughes Terr 6 E16 .... 98 D2
Hughes Wlk CR0 .... 205 A2
Hugh Gaitskell Cl SW6 .... 264 C5
Hugh Gaitskell Ho
Stoke Newington N16 .... 73 D6
Willesden NW10 .... 67 D1
Hugh Herland KT1 .... 198 A6
Hugh Mews SW1 .... 258 D3
Hugh Morgan Ho 5 SW4 .... 137 D2
Hugh Myddelton Prim Sch EC1 .... 94 C4 234 B1
Hugh Platt Ho 29 E2 .... 96 B5
Hugh St SW1 .... 115 B2 258 D3
Hugo Ho SW1 .... 257 D6
Hugon Rd SW6 .... 135 D2
Hugo Rd N19 .... 71 C4
Huguenot Ct 9 E1 .... 96 A2
Huguenot Pl
London SW18 .... 158 A6
Spitalfields E1 .... 243 D4
Huguenot Sq SE15 .... 140 B2
Hullbridge Mews N1 .... 235 C6
Hull Cl SE16 .... 118 D5
Hull Ct SE5 .... 139 B3
Hull Pl E16 .... 123 A5
Hull St EC1 .... 235 A1
Hulme Pl SE1 .... 252 B1
Hulse Ave IG11 .... 79 C2
Humber Ct W7 .... 86 B1
Humber Dr W10 .... 90 D3
Humber Rd
Dollis Hill NW2 .... 68 B6
Greenwich SE3 .... 142 D6
Humberstone Rd E13 .... 99 C4
Humberton Cl E9 .... 75 A3
Humber Trad Est NW2 .... 68 B6
Humbolt Rd W6 .... 135 A6 264 A5
Hume Ct N1 .... 72 D1
Hume Ho 14 W11 .... 112 D5
Humes Ave W7 .... 108 D4
Hume Terr E16 .... 99 B1
Hume Way HA4 .... 40 A3
Humphrey Ct SW11 .... 266 D1
Humphrey St SE1 .... 117 D1 263 C2
Humphries Cl RM9 .... 81 B4
Humphry Ho 10 SW15 .... 156 D6
Hundred Acre NW9 .... 27 D1
Hungerdown E4 .... 20 A3
Hungerford Bridge WC2 .... 250 C4
Hungerford Ho SW1 .... 269 B6
Hungerford La WC2 .... 250 B4
Hungerford Prim Sch N7 .... 71 D2
Hungerford Rd
12 Camden Town N7 .... 71 D2
Lower Holloway N7 .... 72 A3
Hungerford St 21 E1 .... 96 B1
Hunsdon Cl RM9 .... 81 A2
Hunsdon Ho E5 .... 74 B5
Hunsdon Rd SE14 .... 140 D5
Hunslett St 26 E2 .... 96 C5
Hunstanton Ho NW1 .... 237 B4
Hunston Rd SM4 .... 201 D1
Hunt Cl W11 .... 112 D5
Hunt Ct
London N14 .... 15 B4
10 Northolt UB5 .... 84 D5
Hunter Cl
Borehamwood WD6 .... 11 A6
Borough The SE1 .... 262 D5
Upper Tooting SW12 .... 159 A3
3 Wallington SM6 .... 220 A1
Huntercombe Roehampton Hospl The SW15 .... 156 A4
Huntercrombe Gdns WD19 .... 22 C5
Hunter Ct
8 London SE5 .... 139 B1
27 Streatham SW2 .... 160 C4
11 Wanstead E11 .... 55 A4
Hunter Ho
Bloomsbury WC1 .... 240 B6
Feltham TW14 .... 150 A3
Lambeth SE1 .... 251 D1
South Lambeth SW8 .... 269 D3
1 Tufnell Pk N19 .... 71 C5
Hunter Ho *continued*
West Brompton SW5 .... 255 B1
Hunterian Mus* WC2 .... 94 B1 240 D2
Hunter Lo 9 W9 .... 91 C2
Hunter Rd
South Norwood CR7 .... 205 B6
Wimbledon SW20 .... 178 C2
Hunters Ct 5 TW9 .... 153 D6
Hunters Gr
Harrow HA3 .... 43 C5
Hayes UB3 .... 106 A4
Hunter's Gr BR6 .... 227 A4
Hunters Hall Prim Sch RM10 .... 81 D3
Hunters Hall Rd RM10 .... 81 C3
Hunters Hill HA4 .... 62 D5
Hunters Lo
9 Edgware HA8 .... 26 D5
10 Sidcup DA15 .... 168 A1
Hunters Mdw SE19 .... 183 C6
Hunters Rd
Chessington KT9 .... 214 A4
Ilford IG1 .... 78 D3
Hunters Sq RM10 .... 81 C4
Hunter St WC1 .... 94 A3 240 B6
Hunters The 2 BR3 .... 186 A2
Hunters Way
Enfield EN2 .... 4 C4
South Croydon CR0 .... 221 C4
Hunter Wlk
Borehamwood WD6 .... 11 B6
Newham E13 .... 99 A5
Huntingdon Cl
Mitcham CR4, SW16 .... 204 A5
Northolt UB5 .... 63 C2
Huntingdon Ct
3 Barnet EN5 .... 1 B2
Mortlake SW14 .... 133 A2
Huntingdon Gdns
Chiswick W4 .... 133 A5
North Cheam KT4 .... 216 C5
Huntingdon Ho SW5 .... 255 B4
Huntingdon Rd
East Finchley N2 .... 48 C6
Edmonton N9 .... 18 C3
Huntingdon St
Canning Town E16 .... 98 D1
Islington N1 .... 72 B1
Huntingfield CR0 .... 223 B1
Huntingfield Rd SW15 .... 156 A6
Huntingford Ho SW15 .... 134 C3
Hunting Gate Cl EN2 .... 4 C2
Hunting Gate Dr KT9 .... 214 A1
Hunting Gate Mews
Sutton SM1 .... 217 D5
Twickenham TW2 .... 152 C3
Huntings Farm IG1 .... 79 C6
Huntings Rd RM10 .... 81 C2
Huntington Ho NW2 .... 68 C2
Huntley Cl TW19 .... 148 A4
Huntley Ho 7 SE21 .... 183 C6
Huntley St WC1 .... 93 D3 239 C5
Huntley Way SW20 .... 178 A1
Huntly Dr N3 .... 29 C4
Huntly Rd SE25 .... 205 C5
Hunton St E1 .... 96 A2
Hunt Rd UB2 .... 107 C3
Hunts Cl SE3 .... 143 A3
Hunt's Ct WC2 .... 249 D5
Huntshaw Ho 37 E3 .... 97 D4
Hunt's La E15 .... 98 A5
Huntsmans Cl TW13 .... 172 B6
Huntsman St SE17 .... 263 A3
Hunts Mead EN3 .... 6 D2
Hunts Mead Cl BR7 .... 188 B3
Huntsmoor Rd KT19 .... 215 B3
Huntspill St SW17 .... 158 A1
Hunts Slip Rd SE21 .... 161 C2
Huntsworth Ct SE6 .... 163 C3
Huntsworth Mews NW1 .... 92 D3 237 C5
Huon Ct N20 .... 14 C2
Hurdwick Ho NW1 .... 232 A4
Hurdwick Pl NW1 .... 232 A4
Hurleston Ho 11 SE8 .... 119 B1
Hurley Cres SE16 .... 118 D4
Hurley Ct 1 W5 .... 87 C1
Hurley Ho
Lambeth SE11 .... 261 B3
34 Shoreditch E2 .... 95 D4
Hurley Lo SE22 .... 162 C5
Hurley Rd UB6 .... 85 D2
Hurlingham Bsns Pk SW6 .... 135 C2
Hurlingham & Chelsea Sec Sch SW6 .... 135 C2
Hurlingham Court Mans SW6 .... 135 C3
Hurlingham Ct SW6 .... 135 B2
Hurlingham Gdns SW6 .... 135 B2
Hurlingham Rd
Erith DA7 .... 147 B5
Fulham SW6 .... 135 B3
Hurlingham Sch SW15 .... 135 B1
Hurlingham Sq SW6 .... 135 D2
Hurlock Ho 1 N5 .... 72 D5
Hurlock St N5 .... 72 D5
Hurlstone Rd SE25 .... 205 C4
Hurn Court Rd TW5 .... 128 D3
Hurn Ct TW5 .... 128 D3
Huron Cl 5 BR6 .... 227 D2
Huron Rd SW17 .... 159 A2
Huron Univ WC1 .... 94 A2 240 A4
Hurren Cl SE3 .... 142 C2
Hurricane Rd SM6 .... 220 B1
Hurricane Trad Ctr NW9 .... 28 A2
Hurry Cl E15 .... 76 C1
Hursley Ct 11 KT6 .... 197 D2
Hurst Ave
Chingford E4 .... 19 C1
Highgate N6 .... 49 C3
Hurstbourne KT10 .... 212 D2
Hurstbourne Cotts DA5 .... 169 D4
Hurstbourne Gdns IG11 .... 79 C2
Hurstbourne Ho SW15 .... 155 D5
Hurstbourne Priors CR2 .... 221 C2
Hurstbourne Rd SE23 .... 163 A3
Hurst Cl
Chessington KT9 .... 214 C3
Chingford E4 .... 19 C1
Hampstead Garden Suburb NW11 .... 47 D3
Hayes BR2 .... 208 D1
Northolt UB5 .... 63 B3
Hurstcombe IG9 .... 21 A2
Hurstcourt Rd SM1 .... 217 D6
Hurst Ct
Beckenham BR3 .... 185 C3
Newham E6 .... 99 D2
South Norwood SE25 .... 205 D5
Woodford IG8 .... 37 B4
Hurstdene Ave BR2 .... 208 D1
Hurstdene Gdns N15 .... 51 C2
Hurstfield BR2 .... 209 A4
Hurstfield Cres UB4 .... 83 C2
Hurstfield Rd KT8 .... 195 C6
Hurst Gr KT12 .... 193 D1
Hurst Ho
7 Penge SE26 .... 184 B5
Pentonville N1 .... 233 D3
West Heath SE2 .... 124 D1
Hurst La
East Molesey KT8 .... 196 A6
West Heath SE2 .... 124 D1
Hurst Lo
London N8 .... 49 D3
Wembley HA0 .... 66 B1
Hurstmead Ct HA8 .... 26 D6
Hurstmere Foundation Sch for Boys DA15 .... 168 C3
HURST PARK 174 A1
Hurst Park Prim Sch KT8 .... 195 C6
Hurst Pl
Erith SE2 .... 146 D6
Woolwich SE2 .... 124 C1
Hurst Prim Sch DA5 .... 168 D3
Hurst Rd
Buckhurst Hill IG9 .... 21 D3
Croydon CR0 .... 221 B3
East Molesey KT8, KT12 .... 195 C6
Sidcup DA5, DA15 .... 168 C3
Southgate N21 .... 16 C3
Walthamstow E17 .... 53 D6
Walton-on-T KT8&KT12 .... 194 D5
Hurst Rise EN5 .... 1 C2
Hurst Springs DA5 .... 169 A3
Hurst St SE24 .... 160 B3
Hurst View Grange CR2 .... 220 D1
Hurst View Rd CR2 .... 221 C1
Hurst Way CR2 .... 221 C2

Hurstway Wlk 2 W11 112 D6
Hurstwood Ave
Sidcup DA5 169 A3
Wanstead E18 55 B5
Hurstwood Ct
Colney Hatch N12 30 C4
Temple Fortune NW11 47 B5
Hurstwood Dr BR1 210 B6
Hurstwood Rd NW11 47 B5
Hurtwood Rd KT12 195 B2
Husbourne Ho 8 SE8 119 A2
Huson Cl NW3 70 C1
Hussain Cl HA1 64 D4
Hussars Cl TW4 129 A2
Husseywell Cres BR2 209 A1
Hutching's St E14 119 C4
Hutching's Wharf 11 E14 119 C4
Hutchings Wlk NW11 47 D5
Hutchins Cl E15 76 A1
Hutchins Ho 8 SW4 159 D4
Hutchinson Ct RM6 58 D5
Hutchinson Ho 9 SE14 140 C5
Hutchinson Terr HA9 65 D5
Hutchins Rd SE28 124 A5
Hutton Cl
Greenford UB6 64 B3
Woodford IG8 37 B4
Hutton Ct
1 Ealing W5 87 C2
Edmonton N9 18 C4
4 Finsbury Pk N4 50 B1
Hutton Gdns HA3 24 A3
Hutton Gr N12 29 D5
Hutton Ho 19 E2 96 A4
Hutton La HA3 24 A3
Hutton Row 4 HA8 27 A3
Hutton St EC4 241 B1
Hutton Wlk HA3 24 A3
Huxbear St SE4 163 B6
Huxley Cl UB5 85 A6
Huxley Dr RM6 58 B2
Huxley Gdns NW10 88 B5
Huxley Ho
4 London SW9 138 B3
Paddington NW8 236 D5
West Heath SE2 124 D1
Huxley Par N18 33 B5
Huxley Pl N13 16 D1
Huxley Rd
Edmonton N18 33 C6
Falconwood DA16 145 D2
Leyton E10 76 A6
Huxley Sayze N18 33 B5
Huxley South N18 33 B5
Huxley St W10 91 A4
Hyacinth Cl
3 Hampton TW12 173 C4
Ilford IG1 78 D2
Hyacinth Ct 2 HA5 40 C6
Hyacinth Dr UB10 60 A1
Hyacinth Rd SW15 156 A3
Hyde Cl
Ashford TW16 171 C4
Barnet EN5 1 B2
Newham E13 99 A5
Hyde Cres NW9 45 C4
Hyde Ct
Forest Hill SE23 163 A2
Hounslow TW4 151 B6
Kingsbury NW9 45 B2
Whetstone N20 14 B1
Hyde Estate Rd NW9 45 D4
Hyde Farm Mews SW12 159 D3
Hydefield Cl N21 17 B3
Hydefield Ct N9 17 C2
Hyde Ho
12 Ealing W13 109 A5
Hounslow TW3 130 A2
Hyde Ind Est The NW9 45 D4
Hyde La SW11 136 C4 267 A2
Hyde Park* W2 114 D5 247 C3
Hyde Park Ave N21 17 B3
Hyde Park Cnr SW1 248 B2
Hyde Park Corner Sta SW1 115 A4 248 B2
Hyde Park Cres W2 92 C1 237 A1
Hyde Park Gate Mews SW7 246 B1
Hyde Park Gdns
Bayswater W2 114 B6 246 D6
Edmonton N21 17 A3
Hyde Park Gdns Mews W2 114 C6 247 A6
Hyde Park Mans NW1 237 A3
Hyde Park Pl W2 247 B6
Hyde Park Sq W2 92 C1 237 A1
Hyde Park Square Mews W2 237 A1
Hyde Park St W2 92 C1 237 A1
Hyde Park Twrs W2 246 A5
Hyderabad Way E15 76 C1
Hyde Rd
Bexleyheath DA7 147 B3
Richmond TW10 154 B6
Shoreditch N1 95 C6
Hyde Sch The NW9 45 D4
Hydeside Gdns N9 17 D2
Hyde's Pl 12 N1 72 D1
Hyde St SE8 141 C6
Hyde Terr TW15, TW16 171 C4
HYDE THE 45 D4
Hydethorpe Ave N9 17 D2
Hydethorpe Rd SW12 159 C3
Hyde Vale SE10 142 A5
Hyde Way
Edmonton N9 17 D2
Hayes UB3 105 D2
Hyde Wlk SM4 201 C2
Hydon Ct N11 30 D5
Hyh Ho E17 35 D2
Hyland House Sch E17 36 B1
Hylands Rd E17 36 B1
Hylda Ct NW5 71 A5
Hylton St SE18 123 D2
Hyndewood 14 SE23 162 D1
Hyndman Ho
5 Dagenham RM10 81 C5
4 Tufnell Pk N19 71 D4
Hyndman St SE15 140 B6
Hynton Rd RM8 80 C6
Hyperion Ho
27 Bow E3 97 A5
Streatham SW2 160 B4
Hyrstdene CR0 220 D4
Hyrst The CR0 207 A1
Hyson Rd SE16 118 B1
Hythe Ave DA7 147 B5
Hythe Cl N18 34 A6
Hythe Ho 14 SE16 118 C4
Hythe Rd
College Pk NW10 90 A3
South Norwood CR7 183 B1
Hythe Road Ind Est NW10 90 A3
Hyver Hill NW7 11 B4

I

Ian Ct SE23 162 C2
Ian Hamilton Ho NW1 232 C2
Ian Mikardo Sch E3 97 D4
Ian Sq EN3 6 D4
Ibberton Ho
Kensington W14 254 B5
South Lambeth SW8 270 C4
Ibbotson Ave E16 98 D1
Ibbott St 22 E1 96 C3
Iberia Ho 17 N19 49 D2
Iberian Ave CR0, SM6 220 A4
Ibex Ho E15 76 C3
Ibis Ct 16 SE8 141 B6
Ibis Ho E12 78 B4
Ibis La W4 133 A4
Ibis Way UB4 84 D1
Ibrox Ct 3 IG9 21 C2
Ibsley Gdns SW15 156 A3
Ibsley Way EN4 2 C1
Ibstock Place Sch SW15 155 C5
Icarus Ho 21 E3 97 B4
Iceland Rd E3 97 C6
Iceland Wharf SE16 119 A2
Iceni Ct
23 Bow E3 97 B6
Buckhurst Hill IG9 21 B3
Ice Wharf NW1 233 B4
Ickburgh Est E5 74 B6
Ickburgh Rd E5 74 B5
Ickburgh Sch E5 74 B5
ICKENHAM 60 C4
Ickenham Cl HA4 61 B6
Ickenham Rd HA4 39 B1
Ickenham Sta UB10 61 A4
Ickleton Rd SE9 188 A6
Icknield Dr IG2 56 D4
Ickworth Park Rd E17 53 A5
Icough Ct SE3 143 B5
Idaho Bldg 7 SE13 141 D4
Ida Rd N15 51 B5
Ida St E14 98 A1
Iden Cl BR2 208 C6
Idlecombe Rd SW17 181 A4
Idmiston Rd
New Malden KT4 199 D2
Stratford E15 76 D3
West Norwood SE21, SE27 161 A2
Idmiston Sq KT4 199 D2
Idol La EC3 117 C6 253 A5
Idonia St SE8 141 C5
Iffley Ho 47 E2 95 D4
Iffley Rd W6 112 B3
Ifield Ho SE17 263 B2
Ifield Rd SW10 135 D6 265 D6
Ifor Evans Pl E1 96 D3
Ightham Ho
Beckenham BR3 185 B3
Walworth SE17 263 A3
Ightham Rd DA8 147 C5
Ikon Ho 21 E1 118 C6
Ikra Prim Sch N16 73 D4
Ilbert St W10 91 A4
Ilchester Gdns W2 245 C6
Ilchester Mans W8 255 A6
Ilchester Pl W14 113 B3 254 D6
Ilchester Rd RM8 80 C3
Ildersly Gr SE21 161 B2
Ilderton Prim Sch SE16 118 C1
Ilderton Rd SE15, SE16 140 C6
Ilex Cl TW16 172 C1
Ilex Rd NW10 67 D2
Ilex Way SW16 182 C5
ILFORD 78 D6
Ilford Chambers 10 IG1 78 D5
Ilford Hill IG1 78 C5
Ilford Ho 14 N1 73 B2
Ilford Interchange IG1 78 C5
Ilford Jewish Prim Sch IG6 57 B6
Ilford La IG1 78 D4
Ilford Prep Sch IG3 58 A1
Ilford Ret Pk IG1 79 A6
Ilford Sta IG1 78 D6
Ilford Ursuline High Sch IG1 78 D6
Ilfracombe Flats SE1 252 B2
Ilfracombe Gdns RM6 58 B2
Ilfracombe Rd BR1 164 D1
Iliffe St SE17 116 D1 261 D2
Iliffe Yd SE17 116 D1 261 D2
Ilkeston Ct 7 E5 74 D4
Ilkley Cl SE19 183 B4
Ilkley Ct N11 31 A4
Ilkley Rd
Newham E16 99 C2
South Oxhey WD19 22 D5
Illingworth Cl CR4 202 B6
Illingworth Way EN1 17 C6
Ilmington Rd HA3 43 D3
Ilminster Gdns SW11 136 C1
Ilsley Ct 8 SW8 137 C3
Imber Cl
London N14 15 C4
Thames Ditton KT7 196 B1
Imber Court Trad Est KT8 196 B3
Imber Cross KT7 196 D3
Imber Ct 4 SE9 166 C5
Imber Gr KT10 196 B2
Imber Park Rd KT10 196 B1
Imber St N1 235 C5
Immanuel Coll WD23 8 C4
Immanuel & St Andrew CE Prim Sch SW16 182 A4
Impact Ct SE20 184 B1
Imperial Ave 5 N16 73 C4
Imperial Cl HA2 41 C3
Imperial College London SW7 114 B3 256 C6
Imperial College Rd SW7 114 B3 256 C6
Imperial Cres SW6 136 A3
Imperial Ct
Chislehurst BR7 188 D4
Harrow HA2 41 C2
St John's Wood NW8 230 B4
Wembley HA9 66 C5
Whetstone N20 14 A1
Imperial Dr HA2 41 C3
Imperial Gdns CR4 203 B6
Imperial Ho
1 Bow E3 97 A4
2 Poplar E14 119 B6
Strand WC2 240 C1
Imperial Mews 5 E6 99 D5
Imperial Pl BR7 188 C2
Imperial Rd
East Bedfont TW14 149 C4
Walham Green SW6 265 D1
Wood Green N22 32 A2
Imperial Sq SW6 265 D2
Imperial St E3 98 A4
Imperial Twrs 8 NW3 70 A2
Imperial War Mus* SE1, SE11 116 C3 261 B5
Imperial Way
Croydon CR0, CR9 220 C2
Harrow HA3 44 A3
Longlands BR7 167 A1
Imperial Wharf Sta SW10 136 A4 266 B1
Impington 19 KT1 176 C1
Imre Cl W12 112 B5
Inca Dr SE9 166 D4
Ince Terr 3 N15 50 D6
Inchmery Rd SE6 164 A3
Inchwood BR4, CR0 223 D4
Independant Jewish Day Sch NW4 46 D4
Independence Ho 4 SW19 180 B2
Independent Ind Est UB7 104 C5
Independent Pl E8 73 D3
Independents Rd SE3 142 D2
Inderwick Rd N8 50 B4
Indescon Ct E14 119 D4
Indiana Bldg 7 SE8 141 C4
India St EC3 243 C1
India Way W12 112 B6
Indigo Ct TW13 149 D1
Indigo Mews N16 73 B5
Indus Ct 16 SE15 139 D5
Indus Rd SE7 143 C5
Ingal Rd E13 99 A3
Ingate Pl SW8 137 B4 268 D1
Ingatestone Rd
Croydon SE25 206 B5
Wanstead E12 55 C1
Woodford IG8 37 B3
Ingelow Ho W8 245 C2
Ingelow Rd SW8 137 B3
Ingersoll Rd
Enfield EN3 6 C5
Shepherd's Bush W12 112 B5
Ingestre Pl W1 239 B1
Ingestre Rd
Forest Gate E7 77 A4
Gospel Oak NW5 71 B4
Ingham Rd NW6 69 C4
Inglebert St EC1 94 C4 234 A2
Ingleborough EN2 4 C3
Ingleborough St SW9 138 C3
Ingleby Ct N21 16 D3
Ingleby Dr HA1 64 B5
Ingleby Rd
Dagenham RM10 81 D2
Ilford IG1 56 D1
Lower Holloway N7 72 A5
Ingleby Way
Chislehurst West BR7 188 C5
Wallington SM6 219 D1
Ingle Cl HA5 41 B6
Ingledew Rd SE18 123 B1
Inglefield Sq 12 E1 118 B5
Ingle Ho 3 SW12 159 D3
Inglehurst Gdns IG4 56 B4
Inglemere Ct CR4, SW17 180 D3
Inglemere Rd
Forest Hill SE23 162 D1
Mitcham CR4, SW17 180 D3
Inglesham Wlk E9 75 B2
Ingleside Cl BR3 185 C3
Ingleside Gr SE3 142 D6
Inglethorpe Ho 6 E5 74 A6
Inglethorpe St SW6 134 D4
Ingleton Ave DA16 168 A6
Ingleton Rd N18 34 A4
Ingleton St SW9 138 C3
Ingleway N12 30 C4
Inglewood BR7 189 B4
Inglewood Cl E14 119 C2
Inglewood Copse BR1 188 B1
Inglewood Ct 4 BR1 186 D3
Inglewood Mans 11 NW6 69 C3
Inglewood Rd NW6 69 C3
Inglis Ct W5 110 B6
Inglis Ho 1 SW15 156 C6
Inglis Rd
Croydon CR0 205 D1
Ealing W5 110 B6
Inglis St SE5 138 D4
Ingram Ave NW11 48 A2
Ingram Cl
Lambeth SE11 260 D4
Stanmore HA7 25 C5
Ingram Ct EN1 17 D5
Ingram Ho
7 Harrow HA1 42 D4
Old Ford E3 97 A6
Teddington KT8 175 C2
Ingram Lo 8 SW4 159 D5
Ingram Rd
London N2 48 C5
South Norwood CR7 183 A2
Ingram Way UB6 86 B6
Ingrave Ho RM9 102 B6
Ingrave St SW11 136 C2
Ingrebourne Ct E4 19 D2
Ingrebourne Ho
2 Catford BR1 186 B5
Lisson Gr NW8 236 D4
Ingress St 4 W4 111 C1
Inigo Jones Rd SE7 144 A5
Inigo Pl WC2 250 A6
Inkerman Rd NW5 71 B2
Inkerman Terr W8 255 B5
Inks Gn E4 36 A5
Inkster Ho 8 SW11 136 C2
Inkwell Cl N12 14 A1
Inman Rd
Harlesden NW10 89 C6
Wandsworth SW18 158 A4
Inmans Row IG8 37 A6
Inner Circ NW1 93 A4 231 A2
Inner Park Rd SW19 156 D2
Inner Ring E TW6 126 D2
Inner Ring W TW6 126 C2
Inner Temple* EC4 251 A6
Inner Temple La EC4 241 A1
Innes Cl SW20 179 A1
Innes Gdns SW15 156 B5
Innes Lo SE23 162 D1
Innes Yd CR0 221 A5
Innisfree Ho NW2 68 D2
Innis Ho SE17 263 A2
Inniskilling Rd E13 99 C5
Innova Bsns Pk EN3 7 B3
Innovation Cl HA0 88 A6
Inskip Cl E10 75 D6
Inskip Rd RM8 58 D1
Insley Ho 13 E3 97 D4
Inst for Child Health WC1 94 B3 240 C5
Institute Pl E8 74 B3
Instituto Espanol Vicente Canada Blanch W10 91 A2
Inst of Neurology
Bloomsbury WC1 94 A2 240 B4
St Pancras WC1 94 A3 240 B5
Int Coll of Accountancy The SW17 158 D1
Integer Gdns E11 54 B2
Interchange The
Kentish Town NW5 71 B3
Thornton Heath CR0 204 D2
International Ave TW5 106 C1
International House Language Sch WC2 94 A1 240 B2
International Sch of London W3 110 C2
International Trad Est UB2 106 B3
International Way TW16 171 C2
Inverary Pl SE18 145 B6
Inver Cl E5 74 C6
Inverclyde Gdns RM6 58 D5
Inver Ct
11 Bayswater W2 91 D1
4 Hammersmith W6 112 A3
Inveresk Gdns KT4 216 A5
Inverey Ho 2 N12 29 D5
Inverforth Cl NW3 70 A6
Inverforth Ho NW3 70 A6
Inverforth Rd N11 31 B5
Invergarry Ct 11 EN5 13 D6
Invergarry Ho NW6 91 D5
Inverine Rd SE7 121 B1
Invermead Cl W6 112 A2
Invermore Pl SE18 123 A2
Inverness Ave EN1 5 C4
Inverness Ct
8 Acton W3 88 C1
10 Catford SE6 164 D3
Inverness Gdns W8 245 C3
Inverness Mews
Bayswater W2 245 D6
Newham E16 122 D5
North Woolwich E16 123 A5
Inverness Pl W2 245 D6
Inverness Rd
Edmonton N18 34 B5
Hounslow TW3 129 C1
North Cheam KT4 200 D1
Southall UB2 107 A2
Inverness St NW1 231 D6
Inverness Terr W2 113 D6 245 D6
Inverton Rd SE15 140 D1
Invicta Cl
Chislehurst West BR7 188 C5
East Bedfont TW14 149 D3
21 Tower Hamlets E3 97 C2
Invicta Ct KT9 214 B3
Invicta Ctr The IG11 102 A6
Invicta Gr UB5 85 B4
Invicta Plaza SE1 251 C4
Invicta Prim Sch SE3 143 A5
Invicta Rd SE3, SE7 143 A6
Inville Rd SE17 117 B1 262 D1
Inwen Ct SE8 119 A1
Inwood Ave TW3 130 A2
Inwood Bsns Pk TW3 129 D1
Inwood Cl CR0 223 A6
Inwood Ct 12 NW1 71 C1
Inwood Ho 19 SE22 139 C2
Inwood Rd TW3 130 A1
Inworth St SW11 136 C3
Inworth Wlk N1 235 A6
Io Ctr
Barking IG11 101 D3
Woolwich SE18 123 A3
Iona Cl
Catford SE6 163 C4
Morden SM4 201 D2
Ion Ct 8 E2 96 A5
Ionian Bldg 19 E14 119 A6
Ionian Ho 22 E1 96 D3
Ipsden Bldgs SE1 251 B2
Ipswich Ho SE4 162 D6
Ipswich Rd SW17 181 A4
Irby Ho SW2 160 C5
Ireland Cl E6 100 B2
Ireland Pl N22 32 A3
Ireland Yd EC4 241 D1
Irene Rd
Broom Hill BR6 211 D2
Parsons Green SW6 135 C4 265 B1
Ireton Cl N10 31 A3
Ireton Ho 22 SW9 138 C3
Ireton St 12 E3 97 C3
Iris Ave DA5 169 A5
Iris Cl
Croydon CR0 206 D1
Newham E6 100 A3
Surbiton KT6 198 B2
Iris Cres DA7 147 B6
Iris Ct
Dagenham IG11 80 B1
8 Peckham SE15 140 B3
4 Pinner HA5 40 C6
Iris Rd KT19 214 D3
Iris Way E4 35 B4
Iris Wlk 1 HA8 27 A6
Irkdale Ave EN1 5 D4
Iroko Ho 4 NW3 69 D2
Iron Bridge Cl
Southall UB2 108 A5
Willesden NW10 67 C3
Iron Bridge Ho NW3 70 D1
Iron Bridge Rd N UB11 104 C5
Iron Bridge Rd S UB7 104 C4
Irongate Ho EC3 243 B2
Iron Mill Pl SW18 157 D5
Iron Mill Rd SW18 157 D5
Ironmonger La EC2 95 B1 242 C1
Ironmonger Pas EC1 235 B1
Ironmonger Row EC1 95 A4 235 B1
Ironmonger's Pl 22 E14 119 C2
Ironside Cl SE16 118 D4
Ironside Ho E9 75 A4
Ironworks 1 E3 97 C6

Irvine Ave HA3 43 B6
Irvine Cl N20 14 C2
Irvine Ct
Marylebone W1 239 B5
Thornton Heath CR7 204 C3
Irvine Ho N7 72 B2
Irvine Way BR6 211 D2
Irving Ave UB5 84 D6
Irving Ct N22 32 D2
Irving Gr SW9 138 B3
Irving Ho SE17 261 C1
Irving Mews N1 73 A2
Irving Rd W14 112 D3
Irving St WC2 249 D5
Irwell Ct W7 86 B1
Irwell Est 31 SE16 118 C4
Irwin Ave SE18 145 C5
Irwin Cl UB10 60 C5
Irwin Gdns NW10 90 B6
Isabel Hill Cl TW12 173 C2
Isabella Cl N14 15 C4
Isabella Ct 8 TW10 154 B5
Isabella Dr BR6 227 A4
Isabella Ho
19 Hammersmith W6 112 C1
Kennington SE11 261 C2
Isabella Pl KT2 176 B5
Isabella Rd E9 74 C3
Isabella St SE1 251 C3
Isabel St SW9 270 D2
Isambard Mews E14 120 A3
Isambard Pl SE16 118 C5
Iseldon Ct N7 72 A4
Isel Way 4 SE22 161 C6
Isham Rd SW16 182 A1
Isis Cl
Putney SW15 134 C1
Ruislip HA4 39 A3
Isis Ct W4 132 D5
Isis Ho
2 Edmonton N18 33 D4
Paddington NW8 236 D5
Isis St SW18 158 A2
Islamia Girls' High Sch NW6 91 A6
Islamia Prim Sch NW6 91 A6
Islamic Coll for Advanced Studies NW10 68 B2
Island Centre Way 16 EN3 7 C6
Island Farm Ave KT8 195 B4
Island Farm Rd KT8 195 C4
Island Gardens Sta E14 120 A1
Island Ho
Bromley E14 98 A4
Morden SW19 202 A5
Island Rd
Deptford SE16 118 D2
Mitcham CR4 180 D3
Island Row E14 97 B1
Isla Rd SE18 145 A6
Islay Gdns TW4 150 D6
Islay Wlk 17 N1 73 A2
Isleden Ho N1 235 A6
Isledon Rd N4, N7 72 C5
Islehurst Cl BR7 188 C2
ISLE OF DOGS 120 A2
ISLEWORTH 131 B2
Isleworth Bsns Complex TW7 130 D3
Isleworth Sta TW7 130 D3
Isleworth & Syon Sch for Boys TW7 130 C5
Isleworth Town Prim Sch TW7 131 A3
ISLINGTON 72 D2
Islington Arts & Media Sch N4 50 B1
Islington Bsns Ctr N1 235 B6
Islington Est N1 95 A6 235 A6
Islington Gn N1 94 D6 234 C5
Islington Green Sch N1 95 A6 235 A5
Islington High St N1 94 D5 234 C4
Islington Park Mews 1 N1 72 D1
Islington Park St N1 72 D1
Islington Sixth Form Ctr N7 72 C4
Islip Gdns
Burnt Oak HA8 27 B3
Northolt UB5 63 A1
Islip Manor Rd UB5 63 A1
Islip St NW5 71 C3
Ismailia Rd E7 77 B1
Isobel Ho
10 Ashford TW16 171 D3
Harrow HA1 42 D4
Isokon Flats 3 NW3 70 D3
Isom Cl E13 99 B4
Issac Way SE1 252 B2
Italia Conti Acad of Theatre Arts EC1 242 A5
Ithell Ct HA0 65 D3
Ivanhoe Dr HA3 25 B1
Ivanhoe Ho
11 Balham SW12 159 B4
34 Bow E3 97 A5
Ivanhoe Rd
Hounslow TW4 128 D2
Peckham SE5 139 D2
Ivatt Pl W14 113 B1 254 D1
Ivatt Way N17 50 D6
Iveagh Ave NW10 88 C5
Iveagh Cl
Ealing NW10 88 C5
South Hackney E9 96 D6
Iveagh Ct
4 Beckenham BR3 207 D6
Whitechapel EC3 243 C1
Iveagh Ho
2 Brixton SW9 138 D3
Chelsea SW10 266 B4
Ivebury Ct 9 W10 90 C1
Ivedon Rd DA16 146 C3
Ive Farm Cl E10 75 C6
Ive Farm La E10 75 C6
Iveley Rd SW4 137 C3
Iver Ct N1 73 A2
Ivere Dr EN5 13 D5
Iverhurst Cl DA6 168 D6
Iverna Ct W8 255 B6
Iverna Gdns
Hatton TW14 149 B6
Kensington W8 113 C3 255 B6
Iverson Rd NW6 69 C2
Ivers Way CR0 223 D1
Ives Rd E16 98 C2
Ives St SW3 114 C2 257 B4
Ivestor Terr SE23 162 C4
Ivimey St E2 96 A4
Ivinghoe Cl EN1 5 C4
Ivinghoe Ho 14 N7 71 D3
Ivinghoe Rd
Barking RM8 80 B3
Bushey WD23 8 B4
Ivor Ct
Hendon N3 47 A6
Hornsey N8 50 A3
Lisson Gr NW1 237 C6
Ivor Gr SE9 166 D3
Ivor Ho DA14 190 C5
Ivories The N1 73 A1
Ivor Mayor Lo SW12 159 A5
Ivor Pl NW1 92 D3 237 C5
Ivor St NW1 71 C1
Ivory Ct TW13 150 A3
Ivorydown BR1 187 A6
Ivory Ho
9 London SW11 136 A2
St George in t East E1 253 D4
Ivory Sq 15 SW18 136 A2
Ivybridge Cl
2 Twickenham TW1 153 A4
Uxbridge UB8 82 A4
Ivybridge Ct 1 BR7 188 C2
Ivybridge Ho 18 SE22 139 C2
Ivybridge La WC2 250 B5
Ivybridge Prim Sch TW1 152 D5
Ivybridge Ret Pk TW7 152 D6
Ivychurch Cl SE20 184 C3
Ivy Church La SE1, SE17 263 C2
Ivy Cl
Harrow HA2 63 B4
Pinner HA5 40 C2
Sunbury TW16 172 C1
Ivy Cotts UB10 82 C4
Ivy Cres W4 111 A2
Ivy Ct
19 Bermondsey SE16 118 A1
Lewisham SE3 142 D1
Ivydale Prim Sch SE15 140 D1
Ivydale Rd
Carshalton SM5 218 D6
Nunhead SE15 140 D1
Ivyday Gr SW16 160 B1
Ivydene KT12, KT8 195 B4
Ivydene Cl SM1 218 A4
Ivy Gdns
London N8 50 A3
Ivy Gdns *continued*
Mitcham CR4 203 D6
Ivy Ho
Croydon CR0 206 D1
6 Upper Clapton E5 52 B1
Ivyhouse Rd RM9 81 A2
Ivy House Rd UB10 60 D5
Ivy La TW4 129 B1
Ivy Lo W8 245 A4
Ivymount Rd SE27 160 C1
Ivy Rd
Brockley SE4 141 C1
Cricklewood NW2 68 C4
Hounslow TW3 129 D1
Newham E16 99 A1
Southgate N14 15 D4
Tolworth KT6 198 C1
Upper Tooting SW17 180 C5
Walthamstow E17 53 C3
Ivy St N1 95 C5
Ivy Terr 3 IG2 57 A3
Ivy Wlk RM9 81 A2
Ixworth Pl SW3 114 C2 257 A3
Izane Rd DA6 147 B1

J

Jacaranda Cl KT3 199 C6
Jacaranda Gr E8 73 D1
Jack Ashley Ct 5 NW9 27 C2
Jackass La BR2 225 C2
Jack Barnett Way N22 32 B1
Jack Clow Rd E15 98 C5
Jack Cook Ho 9 IG11 78 D1
Jack Cornwell St E12 78 C4
Jack Goodchild Way KT3 198 D6
Jack & Jill Sch TW12 173 C4
Jacklin Gn IG8 37 A6
Jackman Ho 24 E1 118 B5
Jackman Mews NW2 67 C5
Jackman St E8 96 B6
Jackson Cl
Hackney E9 74 D1
Uxbridge UB10 60 A1
Jackson Ct
Forest Gate E7 77 B2
Wanstead E11 55 B1
Jackson Ho
16 London SW11 136 B2
13 New Southgate N11 31 C5
Jackson Rd
Barking IG11 101 B6
Bromley BR2 226 B6
East Barnet EN4 14 C5
Lower Holloway N7 72 B4
Uxbridge UB10 60 A1
Jackson's La N6 49 B2
Jackson's Pl CR0 205 C1
Jackson St SE18 144 C6
Jackson's Way CR0 223 C5
Jackson Way UB2 107 D4
Jack Taylor Sch NW8 92 A6 229 A6
Jack Tizard Sch W12 112 B5
Jack Walker Ct N5 72 D4
Jacob Ct 24 EN3 7 C6
Jacob Ho 14 DA18 124 D4
Jacobin Lo N7 72 A3
Jacob Mans 15 E1 96 B1
Jacobs Cl RM10 81 D4
Jacobs Ho E13 99 C4
Jacobson Ct SW11 267 B1
Jacobson Ho E1 243 C2
Jacob St SE1 118 A4
Jacob's Well Mews W1 238 B2
Jacotts Ho W10 90 C3
Jacqueline Cl UB5 85 A6
Jacqueline Ho 8 E1 96 D2
Jade Cl
Dagenham RM8 58 C1
Hendon NW2 46 D2
Newham E16 99 D1
Jaffe Rd IG1 57 B1
Jaffray Rd BR2 209 D5
Jaggard Way SW12 158 D4
Jagger Ho SW11 267 C2
Jago Cl SE18 145 A6
Jago Wlk SE5 139 B5
Jamahiriya Sch SW3 136 C6 267 A6
Jamaica Rd
Bermondsey SE1 253 D1
Bermondsey SE16 118 B3
Thornton Heath CR7 204 D3
Jamaica St E1 96 C2
James Allen's Girls' Sch SE22 161 C6
James Allens Pre-Prep Sch SE21 161 B5
James Anderson Ct 29 E2 95 C5
James Ave
Cricklewood NW2 68 C3
Dagenham RM8 59 B1
James Bedford Cl HA5 22 C1
James Boswell Cl 1 SW16 182 C6
James Brine Ho 6 E2 95 D4
James Campbell Ho 2 E2 96 C5
James Cl
London NW11 47 A3
8 Newham E13 99 A5
James Collins Cl W9 91 B3
James Ct
Chingford E4 20 B2
Finchley N12 30 C3
Hendon NW9 27 C1
Northolt UB5 85 A5
3 Woodford E18 37 B1
James Dixon Prim Sch SE20 184 B3
James Docherty Ho 4 E2 96 C5
James Dudson Ct NW10 67 A1
James Est CR4 180 D1
James Gdns N22 32 D3
James Hammett Ho 9 E2 95 D5
James Ho
Mile End E1 97 A3
33 Rotherhithe SE16 118 D4
James Joyce Wlk 7 SE24 138 D1
James La E10, E11 54 B3
James Lee Sq EN3 7 C5
James Leicester Hall of Residence N7 72 A2
James Lind Ho 6 SE8 119 B2
James Middleton Ho 20 E2 96 B4
James Newman Ct SE9 166 C1
Jameson Ct 6 E2 96 C5
Jameson Ho SE11 260 C2
Jameson Lo N6 49 C3
Jameson Pl 11 W3 111 A4
Jameson St W8 245 B4
James Pl N17 33 D2
James's Cotts TW9 132 C5
James St
Barking IG11 79 A1
Enfield EN1 17 D6
Hounslow TW3 130 B2
Marylebone W1 93 A1 238 B1
Strand WC2 116 A6 250 B6
James Stewart Ho NW6 69 B1
James Stroud Ho SE17 262 B1
Jamestown Rd NW1 93 B6 231 C6
Jamestown Way E14 120 B6
James Way WD19 22 D6
James Wolfe Prim Sch SE10 142 A5
Jamieson Ho TW4 151 B5
Jamuna Cl E14 97 A2
Jane Austen Hall 14 E16 121 B5
Jane St E1 96 B1
Janet Ct
4 Bexleyheath DA7 147 C1
Wood Green N22 32 B2
Janet St E14 119 C3
Janeway Pl 2 SE16 118 B4
Janeway St SE16 118 A4
Janice Mews 3 IG1 78 D5
Jansen Ho 5 SW15 156 A6
Jansen Wlk SW11 136 B1
Janson Cl
Stratford E15 76 C3
Willesden NW10 67 C5
Janson Rd E15 76 C3
Jansons Rd N15 51 C6
Japan Cres N4 50 B1
Japanese Sch The W3 110 C6
Japan Rd RM6 58 D3
Jaquets Ct DA5 169 C2
Jardine Ho HA1 42 C2
Jardine Rd E1 118 D6
Jarman Ho
Bermondsey SE16 118 D2
16 Stepney E1 96 C2
Jarrett Cl SW2 160 D3
Jarrow Cl SM4 201 D4
Jarrow Rd
Bermondsey SE16 118 C1
Dagenham RM6 58 C3
Tottenham Hale N17 52 B5
Jarrow Way E9 75 A4
Jarvis Cl
1 Barking IG11 101 B6
Barnet EN5 12 D6
Jarvis Ho 3 SE15 140 A4
Jarvis Rd
London SE22 139 C1
South Croydon CR2 221 B2
Jasmin SE1 253 D3
Jasmine Cl
Ilford IG1 78 D3
Orpington BR6 226 D6
Southall UB1 107 A6
Jasmine Ct
Lee SE12 165 A5
11 Wallington SM6 219 B2
Wimbledon SW19 179 C5
Jasmine Gdns
Harrow HA2 63 C6
West Wickham CR0 223 D5
Jasmine Gr SE20 184 B2
Jasmine Sq 15 E3 97 B6
Jasmine Terr UB7 104 C4
Jasmine Way KT7 196 C5
Jasmin Ho SE4 141 B2
Jasmin Lo 17 SE16 118 B1
Jasmin Rd KT19 214 D3
Jason Ct
2 London SW9 138 C4
Marylebone W1 238 B2
Jason Ho UB5 84 B4
Jason Wlk SE9 188 C6
Jasper Cl EN3 6 C5
Jasper Ho KT4 199 B1
Jasper Rd
Newham E16 99 D1
Penge SE19 183 D4
Jasper Wlk N1 235 C2
Java Wharf SE1 253 D2
Javelin Ct HA7 25 B5
Javelin Way UB5 84 D4
Jawahar Bagh SW16 182 D4
Jaycroft EN2 4 C4
Jay Gdns BR7 188 B6
Jay Ho SW15 134 C3
Jay Mews SW7 114 A4 246 B1
Jayson Ct 7 CR0 206 A1
Jazzfern Terr HA0 65 A3
Jean Batten Cl SM6 220 B1
Jean Darling Ho SW10 266 C5
Jean Ho 3 SW17 180 C5
Jean Humbert Ho 2 SE27 183 B6
Jean Pardies Ho 23 E1 96 C2
Jebb Ave SW2 160 A5
Jebb St E3 97 C5
Jedburgh Rd E13 99 C4
Jedburgh St SW11 137 A1
Jeddo Mews W12 111 D4
Jeddo Rd W12 111 D4
Jefferies Ho 13 NW10 67 B1
Jefferson Bldg 3 E14 119 C4
Jefferson Cl
Ealing W13 109 B3
Ilford IG2 56 D4
Jefferson Wlk 13 SE18 144 C6
Jeffrey Row SE12 165 B6
Jeffrey's Ct 2 SW4 138 A3
Jeffrey's Pl NW1 71 C1
Jeffreys Rd EN3 7 B1
Jeffrey's Rd SW4 138 A3
Jeffrey's St NW1 71 C1
Jeffs Cl TW12 173 D4
Jeffs Rd SM1 217 B4
Jeff Wooller Coll WC1 94 A2 240 B4
Jefton Ct SM6 219 C3
Jeger Ave E2 95 D6
Jeken Rd SE9 143 C1
Jelf Rd SW2 160 C6
Jellicoe Ct E4 36 B4
Jellicoe Gdns HA7 25 A4
Jellicoe Ho
5 Bethnal Green E2 96 A5
Fitzrovia NW1 238 D5
11 Putney SW15 156 D6
Jellicoe Rd
4 Newham E13 99 A3
Tottenham N17 33 B3
Jemmett Cl KT2 176 D2
Jemotts Ct 9 SE14 140 D6
Jem Paterson Ct HA1 64 C4
Jengar Cl SM1 217 D4
Jenkins Ho SW8 269 C2
Jenkins La IG11 101 A4
Jenkinson Ho 12 E2 96 D4
Jenkins Rd E13 99 B3
Jenner Ave W3 89 B2
Jenner Cl DA14 190 A6
Jenner Ct N21 16 A6
Jenner Ho
5 Belvedere DA17 125 C3
Greenwich SE3 142 C6
Jenner Pl SW13 134 B6
Jenner Rd N16 73 D5
Jennett Rd CR0 220 C5
Jennifer Ho SE11 261 B3
Jennifer Rd BR1 164 D1
Jennings Cl KT6 197 C2
Jennings Ho SE10 120 B1
Jennings Rd SE22 161 D5
Jenny Hammond Cl E11 76 D5
Jenny Hammond Prim Sch E11 76 C4
Jensen Ho 10 E3 97 C3
Jenson Way SE19 183 D3
Jenton Ave DA7 147 A3
Jephson Ct 17 SW4 138 A3
Jephson Ho 6 SE17 138 D6
Jephson Rd E7 77 C1
Jephson St SE5 139 B4
Jephtha Rd SW18 157 C5
Jeppo's La CR4 202 D5
Jerdan Pl SW6 265 A4
Jeremiah St 11 E14 97 D1
Jeremy Bentham Ho 24 E2 96 A4
Jeremy's Gn N18 34 C6
Jermyn St SW1 115 C5 249 B4
Jerningham Ct SE14 141 A4
Jerningham Rd SE14 141 A4
Jerome Cres NW8 92 C3 237 A6
Jerome Ct 2 N11 31 C5
Jerome Ho
Kingston u T KT1 175 D1
Lisson Gr NW1 237 B4
Jerome Pl KT1 175 D1
Jerome St E1 95 D3 243 C5
Jerome Twr 5 W3 110 D4
Jerrard St SE13 141 D2
Jerrold Lo SW15 134 C2
Jerrold St 24 N1 95 C5
Jersey Ave HA7 25 C1
Jersey Ct UB2 107 B3
Jersey Dr BR5 211 B3
Jersey Ho
15 Canonbury N1 73 A2
Enfield EN3 6 D5
Jersey Rd
Canonbury N1 73 A2
Ealing W7 109 A4
Hounslow TW5, TW7 130 B5
Ilford IG1 78 D4
Leytonstone E11 54 B1
Mitcham SW17 181 B4
Newham E16 99 C1
Jersey St E2 96 B4
Jerusalem Pas EC1 241 C5
Jervis Bay Ho 9 E14 98 B1
Jervis Ct
9 Dagenham RM10 81 D2
2 Greenwich SE10 142 A4
Marylebone W1 238 D1
Jerviston Gdns SW16 182 C4
Jesmond Ave HA9 66 B2
Jesmond Cl CR4 203 B6
Jesmond Ct HA9 66 C2
Jesmond Rd CR0 205 D2
Jesmond Way HA7 26 A5
Jessam Ave E5 52 B1
Jessamine Rd W7 108 D5
Jessel Ho
St Pancras WC1 233 A1
Westminster SW1 259 D4
Jesse Rd E10 54 A1
Jessica Rd SW18 158 A6
Jessie Blythe La 4 N19 50 A2
Jessie Duffett Ho 11 SE5 139 A5

Jessie's Cotts E17 53 A3
Jessiman Terr TW17 192 C4
Jesson Ho SE17 262 C3
Jessop Ave UB2 107 B2
Jessop Ct N1 234 D3
Jessop Ho 9 W4 111 B2
Jessop Pl CR4 202 C5
Jessop Prim Sch SE24 139 A1
Jessop Sq E14 119 C5
Jessops Way CR0 203 C3
Jessops Wharf 4 TW8 131 C5
Jessup Cl SE18 123 A2
Jeston Ho 10 SE27 160 D1
Jethou Ho 16 N1 73 A2
Jetstar Way UB5 85 A4
Jevington Way SE12 165 B3
Jevons Ho 9 NW8 70 B1
Jewell Ho 3 SW12 159 C4
Jewel Rd E17 53 C6
Jewish Mus The*
  Camden Town NW1 93 B6 231 D5
  Finchley N3 29 D1
Jewry St EC3 95 D1 243 C1
Jews Row SW18 136 A1
Jews Wlk SE26 184 B6
Jeymer Ave NW2 68 C3
Jeymer Dr UB6 86 A6
Jeypore Rd SW18 158 A5
JFS Sch HA3 44 C3
Jillian Cl TW12 173 C3
Jim Bradley Cl 10 SE18 122 C2
Jim Griffiths Ho SW6 264 D5
Joan Cres SE9 165 D4
Joan Gdns RM8 81 A6
Joanna Ho 7 W6 112 C1
Joanne Ct EN1 17 C5
Joan Player Ho EN3 6 D6
Joan Rd RM8 81 A6
Joan St SE1 116 D5 251 C3
Joan Villas IG2 57 A2
Jocelin Ho N1 233 D5
Jocelyn Rd TW9 132 A2
Jocelyn St SE15 140 A4
Jockey's Fields WC1 94 B2 240 D4
Jodane Rd SE8 119 B2
Jodrell Cl TW7 131 A4
Jodrell Rd E3 75 B1
Joe Hunte Ct 2 SW27 182 D5
Joel St HA5, HA6 40 A5
Johanna Prim Sch SE1 116 C4 251 A1
Johanna St SE1 251 A1
John Adam St WC2 116 A6 250 B5
John Aird Ct W2 92 A2 236 B4
John Aldis Ho N22 32 B1
John Archer Way SW18 158 B5
John Ashby Cl SW2 160 A5
John Austin Cl KT2 176 B2
John Baird Ct SE26 184 D6
John Baird Ho 11 SE20 184 C3
John Ball Prim Sch SE3 142 C3
John Barker Ct NW6 69 A1
John Barker Ho IG1 79 B6
John Barnes Wlk E15 76 D2
John Barter Ho TW3 129 B3
John Betts' Ho W12 112 A3
John Betts Prim Sch W6 112 B3
John Bond Ho 2 E3 97 B5
John Bradshaw Rd N14 15 D3
John Brent Ho 8 SE8 118 D2
John Buck Ho NW10 89 D6
John Burns Dr IG11 79 C1
John Burns Prim Sch SW11 137 A3
Johnby Cl EN3 7 A6
John Campbell Rd 26 N16 73 C3
John Carpenter St EC4 251 C6
John Cartwright Ho 7 E2 96 B4
John Chilton Sch UB5 63 A1
John Clifford Ho N8 50 A3
John Clynes Ct SW15 134 B1
John Conwey Ho 23 SW2 160 C5
John Cornwell VC Ho 6 E12 78 C4
John Day Ho TW7 131 B2
John Dee Ho 3 SW14 133 B2
John Donne Prim Sch SE15 140 B4
John Drinkwater Cl E11 54 D2
John Dwight Ho SW6 135 D2
John Fearon Wlk 5 W10 91 A4
John Felton Rd 19 SE16 118 A4
John Fielden Ho 10 E2 96 B4
John Fisher St E1 118 A6
John F. Kennedy Specl Sch E15 98 B6
John Gooch Dr EN2 4 D4
John Harris Ho SE15 140 A2
John Harrison Way SE10 120 D3
John Hunt Ct 5 SE9 166 A2
John Islip St SW1 116 A2 260 A3
John Kaye Ct TW17 192 C4
John Keall Ho SW15 134 D2
John Keats Ho N22 32 B2
John Keats Lo EN2 5 B4
John Keble CE Prim Sch NW10 89 D6
John Kelly Tech Colls NW2 67 D5
John Kennedy Ct 1 N1 73 B2
John Kennedy Ho 1 SE16 118 D2
John Kennedy Lo 2 N1 73 B2
John King Ct 5 N19 71 D6
John Kirk Ho
  22 Battersea SW11 136 B2
  Beckenham BR3 207 A5
  5 Streatham SW16 160 A1
John Knight Lo SW6 265 B4
John Lamb Ct HA3 24 C2
John Loughborough Sch N17 33 D1
John Lyon Sch The HA2 42 B1
John McDonald Ho 3 E14 120 A3
John McKenna Wlk 17 SE16 118 A3
John & Mary Sch NW5 71 D3
John Masefield Ho N15 51 B3
John Maurice Cl SE17 117 B2 262 C4
John Milton Prim Sch SW8 137 C5 269 A3
John Nettleford Ho 14 E2 96 B4
John Newton Ct DA16 146 B2
John Orwell Sports Ctr E1 118 B5
John Parker Cl RM10 81 D1
John Parker Sq 8 SW11 136 B2
John Parry Ct 28 N1 95 C5
John Paul II Sch SW19 156 D4
John Penn Ho SE8 141 B5
John Penn St SE13 141 D4
John Perrin Pl HA3 44 A2
John Perryn Prim Sch W3 89 C1
John Prince's St W1 238 D2
John Pritchard Ho 16 E1 96 A3
John Ratcliffe Ho 8 NW6 91 C4
John Rennie Wlk 1 E1 118 C5
John Roan Sch The SE3 142 C5
John Roll Way SE16 118 A3
John Ruskin Coll CR2 223 A1
John Ruskin Prim Sch SE5 139 A6
John Ruskin St SE5 139 A6
John's Ave NW4 46 C5
Johns Cl TW15 171 A6
John Scurr Ho 18 E14 97 A1
John Scurr Prim Sch E1 96 C3
John Silkin La SE8 118 D1
Johns La SM4 202 A4
John's Mews WC1 94 B3 240 D5
John Smith Ave SW6 135 B5 264 C4
John Smith Mews E14 120 B6
Johnson Cl E8 96 A6
Johnson Ct
  Hendon NW4 46 A6
  10 Wandsworth SW18 136 B1
Johnson Ho
  Belgravia SW1 258 B3
  23 Bethnal Green E2 96 A4
  Somers Town NW1 232 B3
  South Lambeth SW8 269 D3
Johnson Lo 12 W9 91 C2
Johnson Rd
  Bromley Comm BR2 209 D4
  Heston TW5 128 C5
  Stonebridge NW10 89 B6
  Thornton Heath CR0 205 B2
Johnson's Cl SM5 218 D5
Johnsons Ct EC4 241 B1
Johnsons Dr TW12 174 A2
Johnson's Ind Est UB3 106 A3
Johnson's Pl SW1 115 C1 259 A1
Johnson St
  Southall UB2 106 D3
  Stepney E1 96 C1
Johnsons Way NW10 88 D3
John Spencer Sq N1 72 D2
John's Pl E1 96 B1
John St
  Croydon SE25 206 A5
  Enfield EN1 17 D6
  Finsbury WC1 94 B3 240 D5
  Hounslow TW3, TW5 129 A3
  West Ham E15 98 D6
John Stainer Com Prim Sch SE4 141 A2
John's Terr CR0 205 C1
Johnston Cl SW9 270 D1
Johnstone Ho SE13 142 B2
Johnstone Rd E6 100 B4
Johnston Rd IG8 37 A5
Johnston Terr NW2 68 D5
John Strachey Ho SW6 264 D5
John Strype Ct E10 53 D1
John Trundle Ct EC2 242 A4
John Tucker Ho 3 E14 119 C3
John Walsh Twr E11 76 D6
John Wesley Ct 6 TW1 153 A3
John Wesley's House & Mus* EC1 242 D6
John Wheatley Ho
  14 London N19 49 D2
  West Brompton SW6 264 D5
John William Cl 12 KT2 175 D2
John Williams Cl SE14 140 D6
John Wilson St SE18 122 C2
John Wooley Cl SE13 142 C1
Joiners Arms Yd 1 SE5 139 B4
Joiners Ct 5 N20 14 D1
Joiner St SE1 252 D3
Joiners Yd N1 233 B3
Joint Rd N10 30 C2
Jolles Ho 9 E3 97 D4
Jollys La
  Harrow HA2 42 B1
  Hayes UB4 84 D2
Jonathan Ct 9 W4 111 C2
Jonathan St SE11 116 B1 260 C2
Jones Ho
  4 South Bromley E14 98 B1
  Stamford Hill N16 51 C1
Jones Rd E13 99 B3
Jones St W1 248 C5
Jones Wlk 6 TW10 154 B5
Jonquil Gdns 5 TW12 173 C4
Jonson Cl
  Hayes UB4 84 A2
  Mitcham CR4 203 B6
Jonson Ho
  Borough The SE1 262 D5
  16 Canonbury N16 73 B4
Jordan Cl HA2 63 B5
Jordan Ct SW15 134 D1
Jordan Hill N10 30 C2
Jordan Ho
  12 London SE4 140 D1
  Shoreditch N1 235 D5
Jordan Lo SW17 180 C5
Jordan Rd UB6 87 C6
Jordans Cl
  Dagenham RM10 81 D4
  Hounslow TW7 130 C4
Jordans Ho NW8 237 A5
Jordans Mews TW11 152 C2
Jo Richardson Comm Sch RM9 102 D6
Jo Richardson Com Sch RM9 80 C2
Joscoyne Ho 5 E1 96 B1
Josef Perrin Ho 1 SE27 183 B6
Joseph Ave W3 89 B1
Joseph Clarke Sch E4 36 B4
Joseph Conrad Ho SW1 259 B3
Joseph Ct N16 51 C2
Joseph Hardcastle Cl SE14 140 D5
Joseph Hood Prim Sch SW20 201 A6
Josephine Ave SW2 160 B6
Joseph Irwin Ho 11 E14 119 B6
Joseph Lancaster Prim Sch SE1 117 B3 262 C5
Joseph Lister Ct E7 77 A1
Joseph Lister Lo E11 55 B1
Joseph Powell Cl 1 SW12 159 C5
Joseph Priestley Ho 12 E2 96 B4
Joseph Ray Rd E11 76 C6
Joseph St E3 97 B3
Joseph Trotter Cl EC1 234 B1
Joshua Cl
  Croydon CR2 220 D1
  Muswell Hill N10 31 B3
Joshua St E14 98 A1
Joslings Cl W12 112 A6
Joslyn Cl EN3 7 C5
Josseline Ct 9 E3 97 A5
Joubert Mans SW3 257 B2
Joubert St SW11 136 D3
Jowett Ho 27 SW9 138 A3
Jowett St SE15 139 D5
Joyce Ave N18 33 D5
Joyce Butler Ho N22 32 B2
Joyce Dawson Way SE28 124 A6
Joyce Lattimore Ct N9 18 B1
Joyce Page Cl SE7 143 D6
Joy Ct NW2 68 D5
Joydon Dr RM6 58 B3
Joyner Ct UB1 107 B6
Joyners Cl RM9 81 B4
Joystone Ct 8 EN4 2 C1
Jubb Powell Ho N15 51 C3
Jubet Ho 9 N16 73 B4
Jubilee Ave
  Chingford E4 36 A4
  Romford RM7 59 D4
  Twickenham TW2 152 A3
Jubilee Bldgs NW8 229 C4
Jubilee Cl
  4 Harlesden NW10 89 D5
  Kingsbury NW9 45 B3
  Pinner HA5 22 C1
  Romford RM7 59 D4
  Teddington KT1 175 C2
Jubilee Cres
  Cubitt Town E14 120 A3
  Edmonton N9 18 A3
Jubilee Ct
  Harrow HA3 44 A2
  Hounslow TW3 129 D2
  Islington N1 233 B6
  Muswell Hill N10 49 A6
  12 Sutton SM2 218 A2
  Thornton Heath CR7 204 C5
Jubilee Dr HA4 63 A4
Jubilee Gdns UB1 85 C1
Jubilee Ho
  3 Hampton TW12 173 C2
  Lambeth SE11 261 B3
Jubilee Hts NW2 69 B2
Jubilee Lo HA7 25 A5
Jubilee Mans 10 E1 96 C1
Jubilee Mkt WC2 250 B6
Jubilee Par IG8 37 C4
Jubilee Park Ctry Pk BR2 210 C4
Jubilee Pl SW3 114 C1 257 B2
Jubilee Prim Sch
  London SW2 160 C5
  Stamford Hill N16 52 A1
  Woolwich SE28 124 C6
Jubilee Rd
  Cheam SM3 216 D1
  Wembley UB6 87 B6
Jubilee St E1 96 C2
Jubilee The 2 SE10 141 D5
Jubilee Villas KT10 196 C1
Jubilee Way
  East Bedfont TW14 150 A3
  Merton SW19 179 D2
  Sidcup DA14 168 A2
  Tolworth KT4, KT9 214 D5
Jubilee Wks SW19 180 A1
Jubilee Wlk WD19 22 B6
Jubilee Yd SE1 253 C2
Judd St WC1 94 A4 233 A1
Jude St E16 98 D1
Judge Heath La UB3 83 B1
Judges' Wlk NW3 70 A5
Judge Wlk KT10 212 C2
Juer St SW11 136 C5 267 B3
Jules Thorn Ave EN1 6 A1
Julia Ct E17 53 D4
Julia Garfield Mews 4 E16 121 B5
Julia Gdns IG11 102 D5
Juliana Cl N2 48 A6
Julian Ave W3 110 D6
Julian Cl EN5 1 D2
Julian Ct SW13 133 D4
Julian Hill HA1 64 C6
Julian Ho SE21 183 C6
Julian Pl E14 119 D1
Julian's Prim Sch SW16 182 C6
Julian Taylor Path 7 SE23 162 B2
Julia St NW5 71 A3
Julien Rd W5 109 C3
Juliet Ho 11 N1 95 C5
Juliette Rd E13 99 A5
Julius Caesar Way HA7 9 D1
Julius Ct TW8 132 A5
Julius Ho 8 E14 98 B1
Julius Nyerere Cl N1 233 C5
Junction App
  Battersea SW11 136 C2
  Lewisham SE13 142 A2
Junction Mews W2 237 A2
Junction Pl W2 236 D2
Junction Rd
  Ashford TW15 171 B5
  Brentford TW8 109 D2
  Croydon CR2 221 B3
  Dartmouth Pk N19 71 C5
  Edmonton N9 18 A3
  Harrow HA1 42 C3
  Newham E13 99 B5
  Tottenham Hale N17 52 A6
Junction Rd E RM6 59 A2
Junction Rd W RM6 59 A2
Junction Wembley Ret Pk The HA9 66 D4
Juniper Cl
  Barnet EN5 12 D6
  Chessington KT9 214 B3
  Wembley HA9 66 C3
Juniper Cres NW1 71 A1
Juniper Ct
  Dagenham RM6 58 C3
  Harrow HA3 24 D2
  Hounslow TW3 129 D1
  Stoke Newington N16 73 B6
  Thornton Heath CR0 204 C3
Juniper Dr SW18 136 A1
Juniper Gdns
  Ashford TW16 171 D4
  Streatham CR4 181 C2
Juniper Ho
  12 Ealing W5 87 C2
  6 Peckham SE14, SE15 140 C5
  9 Richmond TW9 132 D4
Juniper La E6 100 A2
Juniper Rd IG1 78 D4
Juniper St 16 E1 118 C6
Juniper Way UB3 105 C6
Juno Ct 11 SW9 138 C5
Juno Ho 2 E3 97 C6
Juno Way SE14 140 D6
Juno Way Ind Est SE14 140 D6
Jupiter Ct
  10 Brixton SW9 138 C5
  8 Northolt UB5 84 D4
Jupiter Hts UB10 82 B6
Jupiter Way N7 72 B2
Jupp Rd E15 76 B1
Jupp Rd W E15 98 B6
Jura Ho SE16 119 A2
Jurston Ct SE1 251 B1
Justice Wlk SW3 267 A5
Justin Cl TW8 131 D5
Justin Ct 3 CR7 204 C4
Justines Pl E2 96 D4
Justin Plaza CR4 202 C5
Justin Rd E4 35 B4
Jute La EN3 7 A2
Jutland Cl N19 50 A1
Jutland Ho
  4 London SE5 139 A3
  10 Woolwich SE7 122 A2
Jutland Rd
  Catford SE6 164 A4
  Newham E13 99 A3
Jutsums Ave RM7 59 D3
Jutsums Ct RM7 59 D3
Jutsums La RM7 59 D2
Juxon Cl HA3 23 D2
Juxon St SE11 116 B2 260 D4
JVC Bsns Pk NW2 46 A1

K

Kaduna Cl HA5 40 B4
Kaizen Prim Sch E13 99 B3
Kale Rd DA18 125 A4
Kambala Rd SW11 136 B2
Kangley Bridge Ctr SE26 185 B5
Kangley Bridge Rd SE26 185 B5
Kaplan Dr N21 16 B6
Karachi Ho E15 76 C2
Kara Way NW2 68 D4
Karen Ct
  Bromley BR1 186 D2
  2 Camberwell SE5 139 C2
  Forest Hill SE23 163 A5
Karen Ho 7 N16 73 B4
Karens Ct EN3 6 D6
Karen Terr
  Ilford IG2 57 B4
  Leyton E11 76 D6
Karenza Ct HA9 43 C2
Kariba Cl N9 18 C1
Karman Ct HA3 42 C6
Karma Way HA2 41 C1
Karoline Gdns UB6 86 B5
Karyatis Ct EN1 17 D6
Kashgar Rd SE18 123 D2
Kashmir Rd SE7 143 D5
Kasmin Ct NW10 68 A1
Kassala Rd SW11 136 D4 267 D1
Katella Trad Est IG11 101 C4
Kates Cl EN5 12 A6
Katharine Rd 1 TW1 153 A3
Katharine St CR0 221 A5
Katherine Cl 3 SE16 118 D5
Katherine Ct
  10 Forest Hill SE23 162 C3
  Penge SE20 184 C2
Katherine Gdns SE9 143 D1
Katherine Ho
  11 Kensal Town W10 91 A3
  6 South Croydon CR0 221 A5
  South Norwood SE19 183 C4
Katherine Rd E6, E7 77 C1
Katherine Sq W11 244 A4
Kathleen Ave
  Acton W3 89 A2
  Wembley HA0 66 A1
Kathleen Ferrier Ct 4 N17 33 D3
Kathleen Godfree Ct SW19 179 C5
Kathleen Moore Ct BR4 224 A6
Kathleen Rd SW11 136 D2
Katrine Ct NW2 68 C5
Kayemoor Rd SM2 218 C2
Kays Rd SW9 138 B3
Kays Ct EN3 6 D1
Kay St
  Bethnal Green E2 96 A5
  Welling DA16 146 B4
Keadby Ho 2 UB5 85 B4
Kean Ho 5 SE17 138 D6
Kean St WC2 94 B1 240 C1
Keates Est N16 73 D6
Keatley Gn E4 35 B4
Keats Ave E16 121 B5

Keats Cl
Bermondsey SE1 263 C3
Enfield EN3 18 D6
Hampstead NW3 70 C4
Hayes UB4 84 A2
Mitcham SW19 180 B4
Wanstead E11 55 B4
Keats Ct HA0 65 C5
Keats Gr NW3 70 C4
Keats Ho
7 Beckenham BR3 185 D4
22 Bethnal Green E2 96 C4
30 Camberwell SE5 139 A5
Chelsea SW1 269 B6
Harrow HA2 64 C6
Keats House Mus* NW3 70 C4
Keats Par 3 N9 18 A2
Keats Pl EC2 242 C3
Keats Rd DA16 145 D4
Keats Way
Croydon CR0 206 C3
Southall UB6 85 D2
West Drayton UB7 104 B2
Kebbell Terr E7 77 B3
Keble Cl
New Malden KT4 199 D1
Northolt UB5 64 A3
Keble Ct SW19 179 C4
Keble Ho 4 SW15 156 D5
Keble Pl SW13 134 B6
Keble Prep Sch N21 16 C4
Keble St SW17 180 A6
Kechill Gdns BR2 209 A2
Kedelston Ct E5 75 A4
Kedeston Ct SM1 201 D1
Kedge Ho 16 E14 119 C3
Kedleston Dr BR5 211 D4
Kedleston Wlk 21 E2 96 B4
Kedyngton Ho 5 HA8 27 A1
Keeble Cl SE18 144 D6
Keedonwood Rd BR1 186 D5
Keel Cl
Barking IG11 102 C5
Rotherhithe SE16 118 D5
Keel Ct 8 E14 120 B6
Keeley Rd CR0 221 A6
Keeley St WC2 94 B1 240 C1
Keeling 2 TW11 174 C5
Keeling Ct CR0 220 D4
Keeling Ho 4 E2 96 B5
Keeling Rd SE9 165 D6
Keelson Ho 9 E14 119 C3
Keely Cl EN4 14 C6
Keemor Cl SE18 144 C5
Keens Cl SW16 181 D5
Keen's Rd CR0 221 A4
Keen's Yd N1 72 D2
Keepers Ct 4 CR2 221 A3
Keepers Mews TW11 175 C4
Keeper Wharf E1 118 D6
Keepier Wharf 15 E1 118 D6
Keep The
Forest Hill SE6 163 C3
Kidbrooke SE3 143 A3
Kingston u T KT2 176 B3
Keeton's Rd SE16 118 B3
Keevil Dr SW19 157 A4
Keighley Cl N7 72 A4
Keightley Dr SE9 167 A3
Keilder Cl UB10 82 C5
Keildon Rd SW11 136 D1
Keir Hardie Est E5 52 B1
Keir Hardie Ho
6 Belvedere DA17 125 C3
Fulham W6 134 D6
15 Upper Holloway N19 49 D2
Willesden NW10 67 D1
Keir Hardie Way
Barking IG11 80 A1
Hayes UB4 84 A4
Keir Hardy Prim Sch E16 99 A2
Keir The SW19 178 C5
Keith Connor Cl 5 SW8 137 B2
Keith Gr W12 112 A5
Keith Ho NW6 91 D5
Keith Park Rd UB10 60 B1
Keith Rd
Barking IG11 101 B5
Hayes UB3 105 C3
Walthamstow E17 35 B2
Keith Sutton Ho 3 SE9 167 A2
Kelbrook Rd SE3 144 A2
Kelby Ho N7 72 B2
Kelceda Cl NW2 68 A6
Kelf Gr UB3 83 D1
Kelfield Ct 1 W10 90 D1
Kelfield Gdns W10 90 D1
Kelfield Mews W10 90 D1
Kelham Ho 10 SE18 144 D6
Kelland Cl 1 N8 49 D4
Kelland Rd E13 99 A3
Kellaway Rd SE3 143 D3
Keller Cres E12 77 D4
Kellerton Rd SE13 164 C6
Kellett Ho N1 235 D5
Kellett Rd SW2 138 C1
Kelling Gdns CR0 204 D2
Kellino St SW17 180 D6
Kellner Rd SE28 123 D3
Kellow Ho SE1 252 C2
Kell St SE1 116 D3 261 D6
Kelly Ave SE15 139 D4
Kelly Cl
Upper Halliford TW17 171 C1
Willesden NW10 67 B5
Kelly Ct 18 E14 119 C6
Kelly Mews 4 W9 91 B3
Kelly Rd NW7 29 A4
Kelly St NW1 71 B2
Kelly Way RM6 59 A3
Kelman Cl SW4 137 D3
Kelmore Gr SE22 140 A1
Kelmscott 5 SE23 162 D1
Kelmscott Cl E17 35 B2
Kelmscott Ct 2 HA7 25 C6
Kelmscott Gdns W12 112 A3
Kelmscott L Ctr E17 53 B3
Kelmscott Rd SW11 158 D6
Kelmscott Sch E17 53 B3
Kelross Rd N5 73 A4
Kelsall Cl SE3 143 B3
Kelsall Mews TW9 132 D4
Kelsey Gate 8 BR3 185 D1
Kelsey La BR3 207 C6
Kelsey Park Ave BR3 185 D1
Kelsey Park Man BR3 207 D6
Kelsey Park Rd BR3 185 C1
Kelsey Park Sp Coll BR3 207 C6
Kelsey Rd BR5 190 B1
Kelsey Sq BR3 185 C1
Kelsey St E2 96 A3
Kelsey Way BR3 207 C6
Kelshall Ct N4 73 A6
Kelso Ct SE20 184 B3
Kelso Lo E18 37 B1
Kelson Ho E14 120 A3
Kelso Pl W8 113 D3 255 D6
Kelso Rd SM5 202 A2
Kelvedon Cl KT2 176 C4
Kelvedon Ct HA4 62 C4
Kelvedon Ho SW8 270 B2
Kelvedon Rd SW6 135 B5 264 D3
Kelvin Ave N13 32 B4
Kelvinbrook KT8 195 D6
Kelvin Cl KT19 214 C2
Kelvin Cres HA3 24 C3
Kelvin Ct
Chiswick W4 133 A5
Harrow HA2 42 A1
Isleworth TW7 130 C3
Notting Hill W11 245 A5
7 Penge SE20 184 B2
8 Twickenham TW1 153 B5
Kelvin Dr TW1 153 B5
Kelvin Gdns
Southall UB1 85 C1
Thornton Heath CR0 204 A2
Kelvin Gr
Forest Hill SE26 162 B1
Surbiton KT6 214 A5
Kelvin Grove Prim Sch SE26 162 B1
Kelvington Cl CR0 207 A2
Kelvington Rd SE15 162 D6
Kelvin Ho 3 DA17 125 C3
Kelvin Par BR6 211 C1
Kelvin Rd
Highbury N5 73 A4
Welling DA16 146 A2
Kelyway Ho 20 SW2 160 C4
Kember St N1 72 B1
Kemble Dr BR2 226 A5
Kemble Ho
London SW9 138 D2
Stanmore HA7 24 D5
Kemble Rd
Croydon CR0 220 D5
Forest Hill SE23 162 D3
Tottenham N17 34 A2
Kemble St WC2 94 B1 240 C1
Kemerton Rd
Beckenham BR3 185 D1
Kemerton Rd *continued*
Camberwell SE5 139 A2
Croydon CR0 205 D2
Kemey's St E9 75 A3
Kemnal Rd BR7 189 B5
Kemnal Tech Coll DA14 190 B3
Kemnal Warren BR7 189 B4
Kemp 24 NW9 27 D2
Kemp Ct SW8 270 A3
Kempe Ho SE1 262 D5
Kempe Rd NW6 90 D5
Kemp Gdns CR0 205 A3
Kemp Ho
Finsbury EC1 235 C1
1 Globe Town E2 96 D5
Wallend E6 78 C2
Kempis Way 5 SE22 161 C6
Kemplay Rd NW3 70 B4
Kemp Rd RM8 58 D1
Kemps Ct NW2 68 D5
Kemp's Ct W1 239 C1
Kemps Dr E14 119 C6
Kempsford Gdns SW5 113 C1 255 B1
Kempsford Rd
Lambeth SE11 261 B3
Newington SE11 261 C3
Kemps Gdns SE13 164 A6
Kempshott Rd SW16 182 A3
Kempson Rd SW6 135 C5 265 B3
Kempthorne Rd SE8 119 B2
Kempton Ave
Northolt UB5 63 C3
Sunbury TW16 172 B2
Kempton Cl UB10 61 A4
Kempton Ct
Stepney E1 96 B2
Sunbury TW16 172 B2
Kempton Ho 13 N1 95 C6
Kempton Lo 3 SM6 219 D5
Kempton Park Race Course TW16 172 C3
Kempton Park Sta TW16 172 B3
Kempton Rd E6 100 B6
Kempton Wlk CR0 207 A3
Kempt St SE18 144 C6
Kemsing Cl
Coney Hall BR2 224 D6
Sidcup DA5 169 A4
South Norwood CR7 205 A5
Kemsing Ho SE1 252 D1
Kemsing Rd SE10 121 A1
Kemsley SE13 163 D6
Kemsley Ct
Ealing W13 109 C5
St Paul's Cray BR5 190 B2
Kenbrook Ho
Kensington W14 254 D5
5 Kentish Town NW5 71 C3
Kenbury Cl UB10 60 C5
Kenbury Gdns 10 SE5 139 A3
Kenbury Mans 18 SE5 139 A3
Kenbury St SE5 139 A3
Kenchester Cl SW8 138 A5 270 B3
Kencot Cl DA18 125 B4
Kendal NW1 231 D2
Kendal Ave
Acton W3 88 D2
Barking IG11 101 C6
Edmonton N18 33 B6
Kendal Cl
Camberwell SE5 138 D5
East Bedfont TW14 149 D3
Hayes UB4 83 C5
Woodford IG8 20 D2
Kendal Ct
Acton W3 88 C2
Brondesbury NW2 69 A3
11 Chingford E4 20 A3
Kendale Rd BR1 186 C5
Kendal Gdns
Edmonton N18 33 B6
Sutton SM1 218 A6
Kendal Ho
Edgware HA8 27 A6
Forest Hill SE23 163 B3
32 Hackney E9 74 C1
Islington N1 233 D4
Penge SE20 184 B1
Kendall Ave BR3 185 A1
Kendall Ct
3 London SE22 162 A6
Mitcham SW19 180 B4
5 Penge SE19 183 D3
Sidcup DA15 168 A1
Kendall Ho SE12 164 D4
Kendall Lo 5 BR1 187 B2
Kendall Pl W1 238 A3
Kendall Rd
Beckenham BR3 185 A1
Isleworth TW7 131 A3
Kidbrooke SE18 144 A4
Kendalmere Cl N10 31 B2
Kendal Par N18 33 B6
Kendal Pl SW15 157 B6
Kendal Rd NW10 68 A4
Kendal St W2 92 C1 237 B1
Kendal Stps W2 237 B1
Kender Prim Sch SE14 140 C4
Kender St SE14 140 C4
Kendoa Rd 1 SW4 137 D1
Kendon Cl E11 55 B4
Kendon Ho E15 76 B1
Kendra Ct CR2 220 D1
Kendra Hall Rd CR2 220 D1
Kendrey Gdns TW2 152 C4
Kendrick Ct 12 SE15 140 B4
Kendrick Mews SW7 256 C3
Kendrick Pl SW7 256 C3
Kenelm Cl HA1 65 A5
Kenerne Dr EN5 13 A6
Kenilford Rd SW12 159 B4
Kenilworth Ave
Harrow HA2 63 B4
Walthamstow E17 53 C6
Wimbledon SW19 179 C6
Kenilworth Cres EN1 5 C4
Kenilworth Ct
7 Chingford E4 20 A2
Fulham SW6 135 A2
Twickenham TW2 152 C2
Kenilworth Gdns
Hayes UB4 83 D2
Ilford IG3 79 D6
Southall UB1 85 B4
South Oxhey WD19 22 C5
Woolwich SE18 144 D3
Kenilworth Ho HA7 25 B3
Kenilworth Rd
Ashford TW15,TW19 148 A1
Bow E3 97 A5
Ealing W5 110 A5
Edgware HA8 11 A1
Kilburn NW6 91 B6
Orpington BR5 211 A3
Penge SE20 184 D2
Stoneleigh KT17 216 A3
Kenilworth Terr 3 SM2 217 C1
Kenley N17 33 B1
Kenley Ave NW9 27 C2
Kenley Cl
Barnet EN4 2 C1
Sidcup DA5 169 C4
St Paul's Cray BR7 211 C6
Kenley Gdns CR7 204 D5
Kenley Ho
5 Croydon CR0 206 A1
6 St Paul's Cray BR5 190 B1
Kenley Rd
Kingston u T KT1, KT3 176 D1
Merton SW19 201 C6
Twickenham TW1 153 B5
Kenley Wlk
Cheam SM3 216 D4
Notting Hill W11 244 A5
Kenlor Ct 6 HA8 26 D5
Kenlor Rd SW17 180 B5
Kenmare Ct 5 HA7 25 C6
Kenmare Dr
Mitcham CR4 180 D3
1 Tottenham N17 33 D1
Kenmare Gdns N13 33 A6
Kenmare Rd CR7 204 C3
Kenmere Gdns HA0 88 C6
Kenmere Rd DA16 146 C3
Kenmont Gdns NW10 90 B4
Kenmont Prim Sch NW10 90 B4
Kenmore Ave HA3 43 A6
Kenmore Cl TW9 132 C5
Kenmore Cres UB4 83 D4
Kenmore Ct NW6 69 C1
Kenmore Gdns HA8 26 D1
Kenmore Park Fst & Mid Schs HA3 44 A6
Kenmore Rd HA3 43 D5
Kenmure Mans W5 87 C3
Kenmure Rd E8 74 B3
Kenmure Yd E8 74 B3
Kennacraig Cl 6 E16 121 A5
Kennard Ho 12 SW11 137 A3
Kennard Mans 6 N11 30 D5
Kennard Rd
London N11 30 D5
Stratford E15 76 B1
Kennard St
9 London SW11 137 A3
Newham E16 122 B5
Kennedy Ave EN3 18 C5
Kennedy Cl
Crofton BR5 211 B1
1 Mitcham CR4 181 A1
Newham E13 99 A5
Pinner HA5 23 B4
Kennedy Cox Ho 9 E16 98 D2
Kennedy Ct
Ashford TW15 171 A5
Bushey WD23 8 B2
Kennedy Ho SE11 260 C2
Kennedy Path W7 86 D3
Kennedy Rd
Barking IG11 101 C6
Ealing W7 86 C2
Kennedy Wlk SE17 262 D3
Kennet Cl SW11 136 B1
Kennet Ct 47 W2 91 C2
Kennet Dr UB4 85 A2
Kenneth Ave IG1 78 D4
Kenneth Campbell Ho NW8 236 D6
Kenneth Cres NW2 68 B3
Kenneth Ct SE11 261 B4
Kenneth Gdns HA7 25 A4
Kenneth More Rd 4 IG1 78 D5
Kennet Ho NW8 236 D5
Kenneth Rd RM6 59 A2
Kenneth Robbins Ho 1 N17 34 B3
Kenneth Younger Ho SW6 264 D5
Kennet Rd
Isleworth TW7 130 D2
West Kilburn W9 91 B3
Kennet Sq CR4 180 C2
Kennet St E1 118 A5
Kennett Ho HA1 64 D6
Kennett Wharf La EC4 252 B6
Kenninghall N18 34 C5
Kenninghall Rd
London N18 34 C5
Lower Clapton E5 74 B5
Kenning Ho 6 N1 95 C6
Kenning St 18 SE16 118 C4
Kennings Way SE11 116 C1 261 B2
KENNINGTON 116 C1
Kennington Ent Ctr SE17 261 C1
Kennington La SE11 116 B1 260 D1
Kennington Oval SE11 138 B6 270 D5
Kennington Palace Ct SE11 261 A2
Kennington Park Gdns SE17 138 D6
Kennington Park Ho SE11 261 B1
Kennington Park Pl SE11 138 D6
Kennington Park Rd SE11 116 D1 261 C2
Kennington Rd SE11 116 C2 261 A3
Kennington Sta SE17 116 D1 261 C2
Kennoldes SE21 161 B2
Kennyland Ct NW4 46 B3
Kenny Rd NW7 29 A5
Kenrick Pl W1 238 A3
KENSAL GREEN 90 C4
Kensal Green Cemy (All Souls)* NW10 90 C4
Kensal Green Sta NW10 90 C4
Kensal Ho W10 90 D3
Kensal Rd W10 91 A3
KENSAL RISE 90 D5
Kensal Rise Prim Sch NW6 90 D5
Kensal Rise Sta NW10 90 D5
KENSAL TOWN 91 A3
KENSINGTON 113 C4
Kensington Ave
Plashet E12 78 B2
South Norwood CR7 182 C2
Kensington Avenue Prim Sch CR7 182 C2
Kensington & Chelsea Coll
Chelsea SW10 136 A5 266 A4
Kensal Town W10 91 A2
Kensington Church Ct W8 245 C1
Kensington Church St W8 113 C5 245 B3
Kensington Church Wlk W8 245 C1
Kensington Cl N11 31 A4
Kensington Court Mans W8 245 D1
Kensington Court Mews W8 255 D6
Kensington Court Pl W8 113 D3 255 D6
Kensington Ct
2 Burnt Oak NW7 27 B5
Enfield EN2 5 C5
Hendon NW4 28 C1
Kensington W8 113 D4 245 D1
Kensington Ct Gdns W8 255 D6
Kensington Dr IG8 37 D1
Kensington Gardens* W2 114 A5 246 B3
Kensington Gate W8 114 A3 256 A6
Kensington Gdns
Kingston u T KT1 197 D6
Redbridge IG1 56 B1
Kensington Gdns Sq W2 91 D1
Kensington Gore SW7 114 B4 246 C1
Kensington Hall Gdns W14 254 C2
Kensington High St W8 113 C3 255 B6
Kensington Ho 3 NW5 71 C3
Kensington Hts
Harrow HA1 42 D3
Kensington W8 245 A3
Kensington Lodge UB5 85 C5
Kensington Mall W8 245 B4
Kensington Mans SW5 255 B2
Kensington Olympia Sta W14 113 A3 254 A6
Kensington Pal* W8 113 D5 245 D3
Kensington Palace Gdns W8 113 D5 245 C4
Kensington Park Gdns W11 113 B6 244 D5
Kensington Park Mews W11 91 B1
Kensington Park Rd W11 113 B6 244 D6
Kensington Pl W8 113 C5 245 A4
Kensington Prep Sch SW6 135 B4 264 D2
Kensington Prim Sch E12 78 B2
Kensington Rd
Kensington SW7 114 A4 246 B1
Northolt UB5 85 C5
Kensington Sports Ctr W11 244 A6
Kensington Sq W8 113 D4 245 C1
Kensington Terr CR2 221 B1
Kensington Village W14 113 B2 254 D3
Kensington W W14 254 A4
Kensit Meml Coll N3 29 A1
Kensworth Ho EC1 235 D1
Kent Ave
Bexley DA16 167 D6
Dagenham RM9 103 C3
Ealing W13 87 B2
Kent Cl
Mitcham CR4, SW16 204 A5
Orpington BR6 227 C2
Kent Ct
Acton W3 88 B1
3 Haggerston E2 95 D5
Hendon NW9 27 C1
Kent Dr
Cockfosters EN4 15 A6

Kent Dr *continued*
Teddington TW11 174 C5
Kentford Way UB5 85 A6
Kent Gate Way CR0 223 D3
Kent Gdns
Ealing W13 87 B2
Ruislip HA4 40 B3
Kent Ho
Camberwell SE1 263 D1
13 Chiswick W4 111 C1
Edgware HA8 26 B3
Marylebone W1 239 A2
Pimlico SW1 259 C1
Richmond TW10 154 C6
Kent House La BR3 185 A5
Kent House Rd BR3 185 A4
Kent House Sta BR3 185 A2
Kent House Station App BR3 184 D2
Kentish Bldgs SE1 252 C3
Kentish Rd DA17 125 C2
KENTISH TOWN 71 C3
Kentish Town CE Prim Sch NW5 71 C3
Kentish Town Rd NW1 71 B2
Kentish Town Sta NW5 71 C3
Kentish Town West Sta NW5 71 B2
Kentish Way BR1, BR2 209 B6
Kentlea Rd SE28 123 C4
Kent Lo 9 SW19 156 D3
Kentmere Ho SE15 140 C6
Kentmere Rd SE18 123 C2
KENTON 43 C3
Kenton Ave
Harrow HA1 42 D2
Southall UB1 107 C6
Sunbury TW16 173 A1
Kenton Ct
2 Forest Hill SE26 185 A6
Harrow HA3 43 B3
3 Richmond TW10 153 D5
West Kensington W14 254 C5
Kenton Gdns HA3 43 C4
Kenton Grove Ho HA3 44 B4
Kenton Ho
20 Globe Town E1 96 C3
Highbury N5 72 C5
Kenton La
Harrow HA3 24 D3
Kenton HA3 43 C6
Kenton Park Ave HA3 43 D5
Kenton Park Cl HA3 43 C4
Kenton Park Cres HA3 43 D5
Kenton Park Mans HA3 43 C4
Kenton Park Par HA3 43 D4
Kenton Park Rd HA3 43 C5
Kenton Rd
Harrow HA3 43 C4
Homerton E9 74 D2
Kenton St WC1 240 A6
Kenton Sta HA3 43 B3
Kenton Way UB4 83 C4
Kent Pas NW1 237 C6
Kent Pk Ind Est SE15 140 B6
Kent Rd
Dagenham RM10 81 D3
East Molesey KT8 196 A5
Kingston u T KT1 197 D6
Richmond TW9 132 C5
South Acton W4 111 A3
Southgate N21 17 B4
West Wickham BR4 207 D1
Kent St
Haggerston E2 95 D5
Newham E13 99 B4
Kent Terr NW1 92 C4 230 B1
Kent Twr SE20 184 B3
Kent View Gdns IG3 79 C6
Kent Way KT6 214 B6
Kentwell Cl SE4 141 A1
Kentwins N14 15 B6
Kentwode Gn SW13 134 A5
Kent Yard SW7 247 B1
Kenver Ave N12 30 B4
Kenward Rd SE9 165 D6
Ken Way HA9 67 A5
Kenway Rd SW5 113 D2 255 C3
Ken Wilson Ho 19 E2 96 A5
Kenwood Ave N14 15 D6
Kenwood Cl
North End NW3 48 B1
Sipson UB7 126 C6
Kenwood Ct NW9 45 A5
Kenwood Dr BR3 208 A6
Kenwood Gdns
Ilford IG2 56 C4
2 Wanstead E18 55 B6
Kenwood Ho
15 Brixton SW9 138 D1
Enfield EN1 17 C5
Kenwood Ho* NW3 48 C1
Kenwood Rd
Edmonton N9 18 A3
Highgate N6 48 D3
Kenworthy Rd E9 75 A2
Kenwrick Ho N1 233 D5
Kenwyn Dr NW2 67 D5
Kenwyn Rd
Clapham SW4 137 D1
Wimbledon SW20 178 C2
Kenya Rd SE7 143 D5
Kenyngton Dr TW16 172 A5
Kenyngton Manor Prim Sch TW16 172 A4
Kenyngton Pl HA3 43 C4
Kenyon Ho 31 SE5 139 A5
Kenyon St SW6 134 D4
Keogh Rd E15 76 D2
Kepler Ho 9 SE10 120 D1
Kepler Rd SW2, SW4 138 A1
Keppel Ho
Brompton SW3 257 A3
5 Deptford SE8 119 B1
Keppel Rd
Dagenham RM9 81 A4
Newham E6 100 B6
Keppel Row SE1 252 A3
Keppel St WC1 239 D4
Kerala Ct N17 33 D2
Kerbela St 3 E2 96 A3
Kerbey St E14 97 D1
Kerem Sch N2 48 B4
Kerfield Cres SE5 139 B4
Kerfield Pl SE5 139 B4
Kerridge Ct N1 73 C2
Kerrier Ho SW10 266 B3
Kerrington Ct 7 W12 112 C4
Kerrison Pl W5 109 D5
Kerrison Rd
Battersea SW11 136 C2
Ealing W5 109 D5
Mill Meads E15 98 B6
Kerrison Villas W5 109 D5
Kerry N7 72 A2
Kerry Ave HA7 25 D6
Kerry Cl
Newham E16 99 B1
Palmers Green N13 16 B2
Kerry Ct HA7 25 D6
Kerry Ho 5 E1 96 C1
Kerry Path SE8 141 B6
Kerry Rd SE8 141 B6
Kerscott Ho 30 E3 97 D4
Kersey Gdns SE9 188 A6
Kersfield Ho SW15 156 D5
Kersfield Rd SW15 156 D5
Kershaw Cl SW18 158 B5
Kershaw Ho 7 SE27 160 D1
Kershaw Rd RM10 81 C5
Kersley Mews SW11 267 C1
Kersley Rd N16 73 C5
Kersley St SW11 136 D3
Kerstin Cl UB3 105 D6
Kerswell Cl N15 51 C4
Kerwick Cl 1 N7 72 B1
Keslake Mans NW10 90 D5
Keslake Rd NW6 90 D5
Kessock Cl N17 52 B4
Kestlake Rd DA5 168 C5
KESTON 225 D4
Keston Ave BR2 225 C3
Keston CE Prim Sch BR2 225 D3
Keston Cl
Bexley DA16 146 C5
Edmonton N18 17 B1
Keston Ct DA5 169 B4
Keston Gdns BR2 225 C4
Keston Ho SE17 263 B2
KESTON MARK 225 D6
Keston Mark BR2 226 A5
Keston Park Cl BR2 226 B5
Keston Rd
East Dulwich SE15 140 A2
Thornton Heath CR7 204 C3
West Green N17 51 B5
Kestrel Ave
East Ham E6 100 A2
Herne Hill SE24 161 A6
Kestrel Cl
Grahame Pk NW9 27 C1
Kingston u T KT2 175 D6
Kestrel Cl *continued*
Neasden NW10 67 B3
Kestrel Ct
Higham Hill E17 34 D1
Ruislip HA4 61 B6
South Croydon CR2 221 A2
Wallington SM6 219 C3
Kestrel Ho
4 Battersea SW11 136 C2
Enfield EN3 19 A6
Finsbury EC1 235 A2
Kestrel Pl SE14 141 A6
Kestrel Way UB3 105 B4
Keswick Apartments 4 N17 51 D6
Keswick Ave
Kingston u T KT2, SW15 177 C5
Merton SW19 179 C1
Upper Halliford TW17 193 C6
Keswick Broadway 1 SW15 157 B6
Keswick Cl SM1 218 A4
Keswick Ct
13 Catford SE6 164 D3
2 East Dulwich SE22 162 A6
Keswick Dr EN3 6 C6
Keswick Gdns
Redbridge IG4 56 A5
Ruislip HA4 39 B3
Wembley HA9 66 A4
Keswick Ho 8 SE5 139 A4
Keswick Hts 9 SW15 157 A6
Keswick Lo E8 73 D2
Keswick Mews W5 110 A5
Keswick Rd
Bexleyheath DA7 147 C4
Broom Hill BR6 211 D1
Putney SW15 157 A6
Twickenham TW2 152 A5
West Wickham BR4 224 C6
Kettering Ct CR7 205 A5
Kettering Rd EN3 6 D6
Kettering St SW16 181 C4
Kett Gdns SW2 160 B6
Kettlebaston Rd E10 53 B1
Kettleby Ho SW9 138 D2
Kettlewell Cl N11 31 A4
Ketton Ho 11 W10 90 C3
Kevan Ct 6 E17 53 D5
Kevan Ho SE5 139 A5
Kevelioc Rd N17 33 A2
Kevin Cl TW4 128 D3
Kevington Cl BR5 211 D5
Kevington Dr BR5, BR7 211 D5
KEW 132 C6
Kew Bridge TW8 110 B1
Kew Bridge Ct 8 W4 110 C1
Kew Bridge Distribution Ctr TW8 110 B1
Kew Bridge Rd TW8 110 B1
Kew Bridge Sta TW8 110 B1
Kew Bridge Steam Mus* TW8 110 B1
Kew Coll TW9 132 C5
Kew Cres SM3 217 B5
Kew Ct KT2 176 A2
Kew Foot Rd TW9 132 A2
Kew Gardens Rd TW9 132 C4
Kew Gardens (Royal Botanic)* TW9 132 A4
Kew Gardens Sta TW9 132 C4
Kew Gn TW9 132 B6
Kew Green TW9 132 C6
Kew Green Prep Sch TW9 132 B6
Kew Lo 11 TW9 132 B4
Kew Montessori Sch TW9 132 C4
Kew Obsy* TW9 131 C2
Kew Pal* TW9 132 A5
Kew Pier TW9 132 C6
Kew Rd
Finchley N2 30 C2
Richmond TW9, W4 132 B4
Kew Ret Pk TW9 132 D4
Kew Riverside Prim Sch TW9 132 D3
Key Cl E1 96 B3
Keyes Ct SE22 162 A6
Keyes Rd NW2 68 D3
Keyham Ho 31 W2 91 C2
Key Ho 9 SE11 138 C6
Keymer Rd SW2 160 B2
Keynes Cl N2 48 D6
Keynes Ct 9 SE28 124 B6
Keynsham Ave IG8 36 C6
Keynsham Gdns SE9 166 A6
Keynsham Ho 2 N4 51 A2
Keynsham Rd
Cheam SM4 201 D1
Eltham SE9 166 A6
Keynsham Wlk SM4 201 D1
Keyse Rd SE1 117 D3 263 C5
Keysham Ave TW5 128 A4
Keysham Ct HA9 66 A6
Keystone Cres N1 233 B3
Keywood Dr TW16 172 A4
Keyworth Cl E5 75 A4
Keyworth Pl SE1 261 D6
Keyworth Prim Sch SE17 116 D1 261 C2
Keyworth St SE1 116 D3 261 D6
Kezia St SE8 119 A1
Khalsa Ct N22 32 D2
Khama Rd SW17 180 C6
Khartoum Rd
Ilford IG1 78 D3
Newham E13 99 B4
Upper Tooting SW17 180 B6
Khyber Rd SW11 136 C3
Kibworth St SW8 138 B5 270 C3
KIDBROOKE 143 C3
Kidbrooke Gdns SE3 143 A4
Kidbrooke Gr SE3 143 B4
Kidbrooke Interchange SE3 143 C2
Kidbrooke La SE9 144 A1
Kidbrooke Park Cl SE3 143 B4
Kidbrooke Park Prim Sch SE3 143 C4
Kidbrooke Park Rd SE12, SE3 143 B2
Kidbrooke Sch SE3 143 D3
Kidbrooke Sta SE3 143 B2
Kidbrooke Way SE3 143 B3
Kiddens BR8 191 D1
Kidderminster Pl CR0 204 D1
Kidderminster Rd CR0 205 A2
Kidderpore Ave NW3 69 C4
Kidderpore Gdns NW3 69 C4
Kidd Ho RM9 81 B4
Kidd Pl SE7 122 A1
Kidlington Way NW9 27 C2
Kierbeck Bsns Complex E16 121 B4
Kiffen St EC2 242 D6
Kilberry Cl TW7 130 B4
Kilbrennan Ho 9 E14 98 A1
KILBURN 91 C6
Kilburn Bridge 14 NW6 91 C6
Kilburn Gate NW6 91 D5
Kilburn High Rd NW6 91 C6
Kilburn High Road Sta NW6 91 D6
Kilburn Ho 11 W9 91 B4
Kilburn La W10 91 A5
Kilburn Park Foundation Sch The NW6 91 B5
Kilburn Park Rd NW6 91 C4
Kilburn Park Sta NW6 91 C5
Kilburn Pl NW6 91 C6
Kilburn Priory NW6 91 D6
Kilburn Sq NW6 91 C6
Kilburn Sta NW2 69 B2
Kilburn Vale NW6 91 D6
Kilburn Vale Est 13 NW6 91 C6
Kilby Ct SE10 120 D3
Kildare Cl HA4 40 C1
Kildare Ct W2 91 C1
Kildare Gdns W2 91 C1
Kildare Rd E16 99 A2
Kildare Terr W2 91 C1
Kildare Wlk E14 97 C1
Kildoran Rd SW2 160 A6
Kildowan Rd IG3 58 A1
Kilgour Rd SE23 163 A5
Kilkie St SW6 136 A3
Killarney Rd SW18 158 A5
Killburns Mill Cl SM6 219 B6
Killearn Rd SE6 164 B3
Killester Gdns KT17, KT4 216 B4
Killick Ho SM1 217 D4
Killick St N1 94 B5 233 C3
Killieser Ave SW2 160 A2
Killigrew Ho TW16 171 C3
Killip Cl E16 98 D1
Killoran Ho 9 E14 120 A3
Killowen Ave UB5 64 A3
Killowen Rd E9 74 D2
Killyon Rd SW8 137 C3
Kilmaine Rd SW6 135 A5 264 B3
Kilmarnock Gdns RM8 80 C5
Kilmarnock Rd WD19 22 D6
Kilmarsh Rd W6 112 C2
Kilmartin Ave SW16 204 C6
Kilmartin Rd IG3 80 A6
Kilmington Rd SW13 134 A6
Kilmiston Ave TW17 193 A3
Kilmiston Ho TW17 193 A3
Kilmore Ho 17 E14 97 D1
Kilmorey Gdns TW1 131 B1
Kilmorey Rd TW1 131 B1
Kilmorie Prim Sch SE23 163 A2
Kilmorie Rd SE23 163 A2
Kilmuir Ho SW1 258 B3
Kiln Cl UB3 127 B6
Kiln Ct E14 119 B6
Kilner Ho 3 SE11 138 C6
Kilner St E14 97 C2
Kiln Mews SW17 180 B5
Kiln Pl NW5 71 A3
Kilnsey Ct 8 N11 31 A4
Kilnside KT10 213 A1
Kiloh Ct 1 SW11 136 C2
Kilpatrick Ct N16 51 D1
Kilpatrick Way UB4 85 A2
Kilpeck Ho 3 N4 51 A2
Kilravock Ho SE25 205 C6
Kilravock St W10 91 A4
Kilronan 5 W3 89 B1
Kilross Rd TW14 149 C3
Kilsby Wlk RM9 80 B2
Kilsha Rd KT12 194 C3
Kilvinton Dr EN2 5 B5
Kimbell Gdns SW6 135 A4 264 A1
Kimbell Pl SE9 143 C1
Kimber Ctr The SW18 157 C4
Kimber Ho 11 SE18 144 D6
Kimberley Ave
Ilford IG2 57 C2
Newham E6 100 A5
Nunhead SE15 140 C2
Kimberley Ct
Belvedere DA17 125 B2
Kilburn NW6 91 A6
Kimberley Dr DA14 168 D2
Kimberley Gate 3 BR1 186 D3
Kimberley Gdns
Enfield EN1 5 D2
Harringay N4 50 D4
Kimberley Ho 7 E14 120 A3
Kimberley Ind Est E17 35 B2
Kimberley Rd
Chingford E4 20 C3
Edmonton N18 34 B4
Kilburn NW6 91 A6
Leyton E11 76 B6
Newham E16 98 D3
Penge BR3 184 D1
Stockwell SW9 138 A2
Thornton Heath CR0 204 D3
Tottenham N17 34 A1
Walthamstow E17 35 B2
Kimberley Way E4 20 C3
Kimberley Wlk KT12 194 B2
Kimber Rd SW18 157 D4
Kimble Cres WD23 8 A4
Kimble Ho
Lisson Gr NW8 237 B6
1 Lower Holloway N7 72 A3
Kimble Rd SW17 180 B4
Kimbolton Cl SE12 164 D5
Kimbolton Row SW3 257 A3
Kimmeridge Gdns 3 SE9 188 A6
Kimmeridge Rd SE9 188 A6
Kimm Ho 10 E17 53 D6
Kimpton Ct 12 SE5 139 B4
Kimpton Ho SW15 156 A4
Kimpton Link Bsns Ctr SM3 217 B6
Kimpton Park Way SM3 217 B6
Kimpton Rd
Camberwell SE5 139 B4
Cheam SM3 217 B6
Kimpton Trade & Bsns Ctr SM3 217 B6
Kinburn St SE16 118 D4
Kincaid Rd SE15 140 B5
Kincardine Gdns W9 91 C3
Kinch Gr HA3, HA9 44 B2
Kincraig BR7 188 C2
Kindell Ho 4 SW14 133 B2
Kinder Cl SE28 124 D6
Kinder Ho N1 235 D4
Kindersley Ho 33 E1 96 A1
Kinder St 19 E1 96 B1
Kinderton Cl N14 15 C3
Kinefold Ho N7 72 A2
Kinfauns Rd
Ilford IG3 58 B1
Streatham SW2 160 C2
King Alfred Ave
Catford SE6 163 C1
Catford SE6 185 C6
King Alfred Sch NW11 47 D1
King Arthur Cl SE15 140 C5
King Athelstan Prim Sch KT1 198 B6
King Charles Cres KT5 198 B2
King Charles Ct 16 SE17 138 D6
King Charles Ho SW6 265 D4
King Charles' Rd KT5, KT6 198 B3
King Charles St SW1 116 A4 250 A2
King Charles Terr 11 E1 118 B6
King Charles Wlk 6 SW19 157 A3
King Ct 16 E10 53 D2
Kingcup Cl CR0 206 D1
King David La E1 118 C6
Kingdon Ho 8 E14 120 A3
Kingdon Rd NW6 69 C2
Kingdown Cl W10 90 D1
King Edward Dr KT6 214 A5
King Edward Mans 12 E8 96 B6
King Edward Mews SW13 134 A4
King Edward Rd
Barnet EN5 1 D1
Leytonstone E10 54 A1
Walthamstow E17 53 A6
King Edward's Gdns W3 110 C5
King Edward's Gr TW11 175 C4
King Edwards Mans SW6 265 A3
King Edward's Rd
Barking IG11 101 B5
Edmonton N9 18 B4
Enfield EN3 6 D1
Ruislip HA4 39 B1
South Hackney E9 96 C6
King Edward St EC1 242 A2
King Edward The Third Mews 11 SE16 118 B4
King Edward VII Hospl-Sister Agnes W1 93 A2 238 B4
King Edward Wlk SE1 116 C3 261 B6
King Fahad Acad The W5 109 C2
King Fahed Acad W3 111 D6
Kingfield Rd W5 87 D3
Kingfield St E14 120 A2
Kingfisher Ave E11 55 B3
Kingfisher Cl
Harrow HA3 24 D3
Woolwich SE28 124 C6
Kingfisher Ct
11 Battersea SW11 136 C2
Cheam SM1 217 B3
17 Cubitt Town E14 120 A4
East Molesey KT8 196 C5
Enfield EN2 4 B5
Hounslow TW3 151 D6
Merton SW19 179 B3
Putney SW19 157 A2
Spring Gr TW3 130 B3
Kingfisher Dr TW10 175 B6
Kingfisher Ho
16 Battersea SW18 136 A2
Peckham SE15 139 D4
West Kensington W14 254 C6
Kingfisher Lo TW11 175 A6
Kingfisher Mews SE13 163 D6
Kingfisher Sq 19 SE8 141 B6
Kingfisher St E6 100 A2
Kingfisher Way
Croydon CR0 206 D4
Neasden NW10 67 B3
Kingfisher Wlk NW9 27 C1
King Frederick IX Twr SE16 119 B3

King Garth Mews SE23 162 C2
King Gdns CR0 220 D3
King George Ave
Ilford IG2 57 B3
Newham E16 99 D1
Walton-on-T KT12 194 D1
King George Cl TW16 171 C5
King George Hospl IG3 58 A4
King George Sq TW10 154 B5
King George St SE10 142 A5
King George's Trad Est KT9 214 C4
King George VI Ave CR4 202 D5
King George V Sta E16 122 C5
Kingham Cl
3 Shepherd's Bush W11 112 D4
Wandsworth SW18 158 A4
Kingham Ind Est NW10 89 B4
King Harolds Way DA7 147 A5
King Henry Mews
Harrow HA2 42 C1
7 Orpington BR6 227 D3
King Henry's Mews EN3 7 C6
King Henry's Rd
Kingston u T KT1, KT3 198 D6
Primrose Hill NW3 70 C1
King Henry's Reach W6 134 C6
King Henry St N16 73 C3
King Henry's Wlk N1 73 C2
King Henry's Yd 5 N16 73 C3
King Henry Terr 10 E1 118 B6
King Ho 5 W12 90 B1
Kinghorn St EC1 242 A3
King James St SE1 116 D4 251 D1
King John Ct EC2 243 B6
King John St E1 96 D2
King John's Wlk SE9 166 A5
Kinglake St SE17 117 C1 263 B2
Kinglet Cl E7 77 A2
Kingly Ct W1 249 B6
Kingly St W1 115 C6 249 A6
King & Queen Cl 4 SE9 188 A6
King & Queen St SE17 117 A1 262 B2
Kingsand Rd SE12 165 A2
Kings Arbour UB2 107 A1
King's Arms Ct E1 96 A2
King's Arms Yd EC2 242 C2
Kingsash Dr UB4 85 A3
Kings Ave
Bromley BR1 186 D4
Clapham Pk SW4 160 A5
Dagenham RM6 59 B3
Ealing W5 87 D1
Muswell Hill N10 49 A6
New Malden KT3 199 D5
Wallington SM5 218 D1
King's Ave
Ashford TW16 171 D4
Buckhurst Hill IG9 21 D2
Hounslow TW3, TW5 129 D4
Southall UB1 85 D1
Southgate N21 16 D3
Woodford IG8 37 C5
Kings Avenue Sch SW4 160 A6
King's Bench St SE1 116 D4 251 D2
King's Bench Wlk EC4 241 B1
Kingsbridge N16 51 B1
Kingsbridge Ave W3 110 B4
Kingsbridge Cres UB1 85 B2
Kingsbridge Ct
Edmonton N21 16 D2
Millwall E14 119 C2
Kingsbridge Dr NW7 28 D3
Kingsbridge Ho 10 SE20 184 B2
Kingsbridge Ind Est IG11 101 C4
Kingsbridge Rd
Barking IG11 101 B5
North Kensington W10 90 C1
Southall UB2 107 B2
Walton-on-T KT12 194 B2
West Barnes SM4 200 D2
Kingsbridge Way UB4 83 C4
KINGSBURY 45 B3
Kingsbury Green Prim Sch NW9 44 D4
Kingsbury High Sch (Lower Sch) NW9 45 A5
Kingsbury High Sch (Upper Sch) NW9 44 D5
Kingsbury Hospl NW9 44 C5
Kingsbury Rd
Kingsbury NW9 44 D4
Kingsland N1 73 C2
Kingsbury Sta NW9 44 C4
Kingsbury Terr N1 73 C2
Kingsbury Trad Est NW9 45 B3
Kings Chase KT8 196 A6
Kings Chase View EN2 4 C3
Kings Cl
Hendon NW4 46 D5
Walton-on-T KT12 194 B1
King's Cl
Thames Ditton KT7 197 A2
Walthamstow E10 53 D2
Kingsclere Cl SW15 156 A4
Kingsclere Ct
Colney Hatch N12 30 C5
New Barnet EN5 14 A6
Kingsclere Pl EN2 5 A3
Kingscliffe Gdns SW19 157 B3
King's Coll
Dulwich Village SE24 161 B5
Strand WC2 116 B6 250 D6
Kings College Ct NW3 70 C1
King's College Hospl SE5 139 B3
Kings College Rd
Primrose Hill NW3 70 B1
Ruislip HA4 39 D3
King's Coll London (Hampstead) NW3 69 C4
King's Coll Sch SW19 178 D4
King's Coll Univ SE1 116 C5 251 A3
Kingscote NW11 47 B1
Kingscote Rd
Bedford Pk W4 111 B3
Croydon CR0 206 B2
Kingston u T KT3 199 B6
Kingscote St EC4 251 C6
Kings Court Mews KT8 196 B4
King's Court N SW3 257 A1
Kingscourt Rd SW16 160 A1
King's Court S SW3 257 A1
King's Cres N4, N5 73 A5
Kingscroft SW4 160 A5
Kingscroft Rd NW2 69 B2
KING'S CROSS 94 A5
King's Cross WC1 94 A4 233 B2
King's Cross Bridge WC1 233 B2
King's Cross Rd WC1 94 B4 233 D1
King's Cross, St Pancras N1 94 A4 233 A2
King's Cross Sta N1 94 A5 233 B3
Kings Ct
6 Barnsbury N7 72 B1
2 Buckhurst Hill IG9 21 D2
Chiswick W6 112 A2
East Dulwich SE22 140 A1
16 Kingston u T KT2 176 C3
Newham E13 99 B6
Primrose Hill NW8 230 C5
10 Putney SW15 156 A4
3 Wallington SM6 219 B2
Wembley Pk HA9 66 D6
King's Ct
Beckenham BR3 207 D6
9 Ealing W5 87 C2
Wimbledon SW19 179 C4
Kingsdale Ct EN4 2 D3
Kingsdale Gdns W11 112 D5
Kingsdale Rd
Penge SE20 184 D3
Plumstead Comm SE18 145 D6
Kingsdale Sec Sch SE21 161 C1
Kingsdown SW19 178 D3
Kingsdown Ave
East Acton W3 111 C6
West Ealing W13 109 B4
Kingsdown Cl
26 Deptford SE16 118 B1
8 Notting Hill W11 91 A1
Kingsdown Ct SW11 158 C5
Kingsdowne Rd KT6 198 B2
Kingsdown Ho 1 E8 74 A3
Kingsdown Rd
Cheam SM3 217 A3
Leyton E11 76 C5
4 Upper Holloway N19 72 A6
Kingsdown Way BR2 209 A3
Kings Dr
Edgware HA8 26 B6
Surbiton KT5 198 C3
Wembley Pk HA9 66 D6
King's Dr KT7 197 B2
Kingsend HA4 39 C1
Kingsend Ct HA4 39 C1
Kings Farm E17 35 D2
Kings Farm Ave TW10 132 C1
Kingsfield Ave HA1, HA2 42 A4
Kingsfield Ct HA1 42 B2
Kingsfield Ho
Mottingham SE9 165 D1
7 Muswell Hill N10 31 A3
18 Stoke Newington N16 73 C5
Kingsfield Rd HA1 42 B2
Kingsford Com Sch E6 100 B1
Kingsford St NW5 70 D3
Kingsford Way E6 100 B2
Kingsgate HA9 67 A5
Kingsgate Ave N3 47 C6
Kingsgate Bsns Ctr KT2 176 A2
Kingsgate Cl
Erith DA7 147 A4
Sidcup BR5 190 C1
Kingsgate Est N1 73 C2
Kingsgate Ho 29 SW9 138 C4
Kingsgate Par SW1 259 B5
Kingsgate Pl NW6 69 C1
Kingsgate Prim Sch NW6 69 C1
Kingsgate Rd
Hampstead NW6 69 C1
Kingston u T KT2 176 A2
Kings Gdns IG1 57 B1
King's Gdns 6 NW6 69 C1
King's Gr
Peckham SE15 140 B4
Peckham SE15 140 B5
Kings Grange HA4 39 D1
Kingsground SE9 166 A5
Kingshall Mews SE13 142 A2
Kings Hall Rd BR3 185 A2
Kings Head Hill E4 19 D4
King's Head Yd SE1 252 C3
King's Highway SE18 145 D6
Kingshill SE17 262 B4
Kingshill Ave
Harrow HA3 43 B5
Hayes UB4 83 D4
New Malden KT4 200 B2
Northolt UB5 84 B4
Kingshill Cl UB4, UB5 84 A4
Kingshill Ct 8 EN5 1 A1
Kingshill Dr HA3 43 B6
Kings Ho
19 Limehouse E14 119 B6
South Lambeth SW8 270 B4
Kingshold Rd E9 74 C1
Kingsholm Gdns SE9 144 A1
King's House Sch TW10 154 B6
King's House Sch (Jun) TW10 154 B6
Kingshurst Rd SE12 165 A4
Kings Keep KT6 198 A5
King's Keep 6 SW15 156 D6
King's La SM1 218 B3
KINGSLAND 73 C2
Kingsland NW8 92 C6 230 B5
Kingsland Gn 1 E8, N1 73 C2
Kingsland High St E8 73 D3
Kingsland Pas 2 E8 73 C2
Kingsland Rd
Hoxton E2 95 C5
Newham E13 99 C4
Kingsland Sh Ctr 12 E8 73 D2
Kingslawn Cl SW15 156 B6
Kingslee Ct 4 SM2 217 D1
Kingsleigh Cl TW8 131 D6
Kingsleigh Pl CR4 202 D6
Kingsleigh Wlk BR2 208 D5
Kingsley Ave
Ealing W13 87 A1
Hounslow TW3 130 A3
Kingsley Ave *continued*
Southall UB1 107 C6
Sutton SM1 218 B4
Kingsley Cl
Dagenham RM10 81 D4
East Finchley N2 48 A4
Kingsley Ct
Bexley DA6 147 C1
Edgware HA8 10 D2
Snaresbrook E11 54 D3
1 Thamesmead SE28 124 C5
Willesden NW2 68 B2
Wood Green N22 32 B3
Worcester Pk KT4 215 D6
Kingsley Dr KT4 215 D6
Kingsley Flats SE1 263 B3
Kingsley Gdns E4 35 C5
Kingsley Grange 1 E11 55 A4
Kingsley High Sch HA3 24 A3
Kingsley Ho
Chelsea SW3 266 D5
3 Clapham SW4 137 D3
East Finchley NW11 48 A3
8 Kingston u T KT6 198 A4
Kingsley Mews
Chislehurst West BR7 188 D4
Dagenham RM9 80 D4
4 Ilford IG1 78 D6
Kensington W8 255 D5
15 St George in t East E1 118 B6
Kingsley Pl N6 49 A2
Kingsley Prim Sch CR9 204 C1
Kingsley Rd
Chingford E17 36 A1
Edmonton N13 32 D6
Harrow HA2 64 A5
Hounslow TW3 130 A3
Kilburn NW6 91 B6
Orpington BR6 227 D1
Pinner HA5 41 B5
Thornton Heath CR0 204 C1
Upton E7 77 A1
Wimbledon SW19 179 D5
Kingsley St SW11 136 D2
Kingsley Way N2 48 A4
Kingsley Wood Dr SE9 166 B1
Kings Lo HA4 39 C1
Kingslyn Cres SE19 183 C2
Kings Mall Sh Ctr W6 112 C2
Kingsman Par SE18 122 B3
King's Mans SW3 267 A5
Kingsman St SE18 122 B2
Kingsmead
Barnet EN5 1 C1
Richmond TW10 154 B5
Kingsmead Ave
Edmonton N9 18 B3
Kingsbury NW9 45 B2
Mitcham CR4 203 C6
North Cheam KT4 216 B5
Sunbury TW16 172 C1
Tolworth KT6 214 C6
Kingsmead Cl
Sidcup DA15 168 A2
Teddington TW11 175 B4
West Ewell KT19 215 B1
Kingsmead Cotts BR2 210 A1
Kingsmead Ct
Bromley BR1 186 D3
Crouch End N6 49 D2
Kingsmead Dr UB5 63 B1
Kingsmead Ho E9 75 A4
Kingsmead Lo
9 Chingford E4 20 A2
Sutton SM2 218 B2
Kings Mead Pk KT10 212 C1
Kingsmead Prim Sch E9 75 A4
Kingsmead Rd SW2 160 C2
Kingsmead Sch EN1 6 A2
King's Mead Way E5, E9 75 A4
Kingsmere
Catford SE6 163 D3
Widmore BR7 188 A2
Kingsmere Cl SW15 134 D2
Kingsmere Ct NW9 44 D1
Kingsmere Pk NW9 45 A1
Kingsmere Pl N16 51 B1
Kingsmere Rd SW19 156 D2
King's Mews
1 Clapham Pk SW4 160 A6
King's Mews *continued*
Gray's Inn WC1 94 B3 240 D5
Kingsmill NW8 92 B5 229 D4
Kingsmill Bsns Pk KT1 198 B6
Kingsmill Gdns RM9 81 B3
Kingsmill Rd RM9 81 B3
Kingsmill Terr NW8 92 B5 229 D4
Kingsmount Ct SM1 217 D4
Kingsnorth Ho 12 W10 90 D1
Kingsnympton Pk KT2 176 D4
Kings Oak RM7 59 C6
Kings Oak Hospl (Private) The EN2 4 C5
King's Orch SE9 166 A5
King's Paddock TW12 174 A2
King's Par
3 Hammersmith W12 112 A3
Willesden NW10 90 C6
Kingspark Bsns Ctr KT3 199 A6
Kingspark Ct E18 55 A6
King's Pas KT2 175 D2
King's Penny Ho 4 KT2 176 A3
Kings Pl
Acton Green W4 111 A2
Buckhurst Hill IG9 21 D2
Loughton IG10 21 D4
King's Pl SE1 252 A1
King Sq EC1 95 A4 235 A1
King's Quay SW10 266 B2
Kings Rd
Ealing W5 87 D2
Feltham TW13 150 C3
Harrow HA2 63 B6
Mitcham CR4 203 A6
Orpington BR6 227 D4
Richmond TW10, TW9 154 B6
Walton-on-T KT12 194 B1
West Drayton UB7 104 B4
Willesden NW10 68 B1
Wood Green N22 32 B2
King's Rd
Barking IG11 79 A1
Chelsea SW3 257 B1
Chelsea SW10 136 B6 266 C5
Chingford E4 20 B3
Edmonton N18 34 A6
Kingston u T KT2 176 B3
Leytonstone E11 54 C2
Long Ditton KT6 197 C1
Mortlake SW14 133 B2
Newham E6 99 C6
South Norwood SE25 206 A6
Teddington TW11, TW12 174 B5
Tottenham N17 33 D2
Twickenham TW1 153 B5
Wimbledon SW19 179 C4
Kings Ride Gate TW10 132 C1
Kingsridge SW19 157 A2
Kings Road Bglws HA2 63 B5
King's Scholars' Pas SW1 259 A4
King St
Acton W3 111 A5
East Finchley N2 48 B6
Hammersmith W6 112 A2
Newham E13 98 D3
Newham E13 99 A3
Richmond TW9 153 D6
Southall UB2 107 A3
St James SW1 115 C5 249 B4
Strand WC2 250 A6
Tottenham N17 33 D2
Twickenham TW1 153 A3
Whitechapel EC2 95 A1 242 B1
King Stairs Cl SE16 118 B4
King's Terr
Camden Town NW1 93 C6 232 A5
10 Isleworth TW7 131 A2
Kingsthorpe Rd SE26 184 D6
Kingston Ave
Cheam SM3 217 A5
Feltham TW14 149 D5
Yiewsley UB7 104 B6
Kingston Bsns Ctr KT9 214 B5
Kingston By-Pass KT6, KT7, KT9 213 C5
Kingston By - Pass KT6 214 C5
Kingston Cl
Dagenham RM6 59 A6
Northolt UB5 85 B6
Teddington TW11 175 B4
Kingston Coll of F Ed KT1 197 D6
Kingston Coll of F Ed (M V Annex) KT2 176 A2
Kingston Cres BR3 185 B2
Kingston Ct HA3 44 B4
Kingston Gdns CR0 220 A5
Kingston Gram Sch KT2 176 B1
Kingston Hall Rd KT1 197 D6
Kingston Hill KT2 177 A5
Kingston Hill Ave RM6 59 A6
Kingston Hill Pl KT2, TW10 177 A6
Kingston Ho 4 NW6 69 A1
Kingston Ho E SW7 247 A1
Kingston Ho N SW7 247 A1
Kingston Ho S SW7 247 A1
Kingston Hospl KT2 176 D2
Kingston House Est KT6 197 B3
Kingston La
Teddington TW11 175 B4
Uxbridge UB8 82 A4
West Drayton UB7 104 B4
Kingston Lo 2 KT3 199 C5
Kingston Mus* KT1 176 A1
Kingston Pl HA3 24 D3
Kingston Rd
Ashford TW15 170 A4
Ashford TW15 170 B4
Edmonton N9 18 A2
Ewell KT17 215 D1
Ilford IG1 79 A4
Kingston u T KT1, KT3 199 A5
Merton SW19, SW20 179 B1
New Barnet EN4 14 B6
Roehampton SW15, SW19 156 B3
Southall UB2 107 B4
Teddington TW11 175 B4
Kingston Sq SE19 183 B5
Kingston Sta KT2 176 A2
Kingston Univ
Kingston u T KT1 198 A6
Kingston Vale KT2 177 B5
Kingston Univ Annex KT1 176 B1
Kingston Univ Roehampton Vale Campus SW15 155 D1
KINGSTON UPON THAMES 197 C6
KINGSTON VALE 177 B6
Kingston Vale SW15 155 C1
Kingstown St NW1 93 A6 231 A6
King Street Cloisters 8 W6 112 B2
King Street Coll W12 112 C4
King Street Par 7 TW1 153 A3
Kings View Ct 1 SW20 178 D3
Kingswater Pl SW11 267 A3
Kingsway
Coney Hall BR4 224 D5
Enfield EN3 18 B6
Hayes UB3 83 A2
Mortlake SW14, TW9 132 D2
North Finchley N12 30 A4
Petts Wood BR5 211 B4
Stanwell TW19 148 A3
St Giles WC2 94 B1 240 C2
Wembley HA9 66 A4
West Barnes KT3 200 C4
Woodford IG8 37 C5
Kings Way
Croydon CR0 220 B3
Harrow HA1 42 C5
Kingsway Bsns Pk TW12 173 B2
Kingsway Coll NW5 71 B2
Kingsway Cres HA2 42 A5
Kingsway Est N18 34 D4
Kingsway Mans WC1 240 C4
Kingsway Pl EC1 241 C6
Kingsway Rd SM3 217 A1
Kingswear Ho 5 SE23 162 C2
Kingswear Rd
Dartmouth Pk NW5 71 B5
Ruislip HA4 62 A6

Kings Well 25 NW3 70 A4
Kings Wlk Sh Mall
SW3 114 D1 257 C2
Kingswood 31 E2 96 C5
Kingswood Ave
Beckenham BR2, BR3 208 C5
Belvedere DA17 125 B2
Hampton TW12 173 D4
Hounslow TW3, TW5 129 B3
Kensal Rise NW6 91 A5
Thornton Heath CR7 204 C4
Kingswood Cl
Ashford TW15 171 B5
Crofton BR6 211 B2
East Barnet N20 14 A4
Enfield EN1 17 D6
New Malden KT3 199 D3
South Lambeth SW8 270 B3
Surbiton KT6 198 A2
Kingswood Ct
Chingford E4 35 C5
Hither Green SE13 164 B5
7 Richmond TW10 154 B6
Kings Wood Ct 4
NW6 69 C1
Kingswood Dr
Carshalton SM5 202 D1
Dulwich SE19, SE21 183 D6
Kingswood Ho 3
KT2 176 D4
Kingswood Mans 14
SM2 217 C1
Kingswood Pk N3 29 B1
Kingswood Pl SE13 142 C1
Kingswood Prim Sch
SE27 183 B5
Kingswood Rd
Beckenham BR2 208 C6
Ilford IG3 58 A2
Leytonstone E11 54 C2
Merton SW19 179 B2
Penge SE20 184 C4
South Acton W4 111 A3
Streatham SW2 160 A4
Wembley HA9 66 C5
Kingswood Terr W4 111 A3
Kingswood Way SM6 220 A3
Kingsworth Cl BR3 207 A4
Kingsworthy Cl KT1 198 B6
Kings Yd E15 75 C2
Kingthorpe Rd NW10 67 B1
Kingthorpe Terr 2
NW10 67 B1
Kington Ho 18 NW6 91 D6
Kingward Ho E1 96 A2
Kingwell Rd EN4 2 B5
Kingweston Cl NW2 69 A5
King William IV Gdns
SE20 184 C4
King William La 3
SE10 120 C1
King William St
EC4 117 B6 252 D6
King William Wlk
SE10 142 A6
Kingwood Rd
SW6 135 A5 264 A3
Kinlet Rd SE18 145 A4
Kinloch Dr NW9 45 C2
Kinloch St N7 72 B5
Kinloss Ct NW3 47 B5
Kinloss Gdns NW3 47 B5
Kinloss Rd SM5 202 A2
Kinnaird Ave
Bromley BR1 186 D4
Chiswick W4 133 A5
Kinnaird Cl BR1 186 D4
Kinnear Ct 2 SW20 178 D2
Kinnear Rd W12 111 D4
Kinnerton Pl N SW1 247 D1
Kinnerton Pl S SW1 247 D1
Kinnerton St
SW1 115 A4 248 A1
Kinnerton Yd SW1 248 A1
Kinnoull Mans 10 E5 74 B4
Kinnoul Rd
W6 135 A6 264 A6
Kinross Ave KT4 216 A6
Kinross Cl
Ashford TW16 171 D5
Edgware HA8 10 D2
Harrow HA3 44 B4
Kinross Ct 1 SE6 164 D2
Kinross Dr TW16 171 D5
Kinross Ho N1 233 C6
Kinross Terr E17 35 B1
Kinsale Grange 10
SM2 218 A2
Kinsale Rd SE15 140 A2
Kinsella Gdns SW19 178 B5
Kinsey Ho SE21 183 C6
Kinsham Ho 5 E2 96 A3
Kintore Way SE1 263 C4
Kintyre Cl SW16 204 B6
Kintyre Ct 17 SW2 160 A4
Kintyre Ho 6 E14 120 A5
Kinveachy Gdns SE7 122 A1
Kinver Ho N4 51 B2
Kinver Rd SE26 184 C6
Kipling Ct W7 108 D6
Kipling Dr SW17 180 B4
Kipling Ho 29 SE5 139 A5
Kipling Pl HA7 24 D4
Kipling Rd DA7 147 A4
Kipling St SE1 117 B4 252 D2
Kipling Terr N9 17 B2
Kipling Twr 3 W3 111 A3
Kippington Dr SE9 165 D3
Kirby Cl KT19 215 D3
Kirby Est SE16 118 B3
Kirby Gr SE1 117 C4 253 A2
Kirby St EC1 94 C2 241 B4
Kirby Way
Hillingdon UB8 82 B3
Walton-on-T KT12 194 C3
Kirchen Rd W13 109 B6
Kirkby Cl N11 31 A4
Kirkdale SE26 162 B1
Kirkdale Rd E11 54 C2
Kirkeby Bldg EC1 241 A4
Kirkfield Cl W13 109 B5
Kirkham Rd E6 100 A1
Kirkham St SE18 145 C6
Kirk Ho HA9 66 A5
Kirk La SE18 145 A6
Kirkland Cl DA15 167 C5
Kirkland Dr EN2 5 A4
Kirkland Terr BR3 185 C4
Kirkland Wlk 4 E8 73 D2
Kirkleas Rd KT6 198 A1
Kirklees Rd
Dagenham RM8 80 C3
Thornton Heath CR7 204 C4
Kirkley Ho N16 51 C1
Kirkley Rd SW19 179 C2
Kirkman Ho W1 239 C3
Kirkman Pl W1 239 C3
Kirkmichael Rd E14 98 A1
Kirk Rd E17 53 B3
Kirk Rise SM1 217 D5
Kirkside Rd SE3 143 A6
Kirkstall Ave N17 51 B5
Kirkstall Gdns SW2 160 A3
Kirkstall Ho SW1 258 C2
Kirkstall Rd SW2 160 A3
Kirkstead Ct E5 75 A4
Kirksted Rd SM4 201 D1
Kirkstone NW1 232 A2
Kirkstone Way BR1 186 C3
Kirkton Rd N15 51 C5
Kirkwall Pl E2 96 C4
Kirkwood Rd SE15 140 B3
Kirn Rd W13 109 B6
Kirrane Cl KT3 199 D4
Kirtley Ho SW8 269 B2
Kirtley Rd SE26 185 A6
Kirtling St
SW8 137 C5 269 A4
Kirton Cl W4 111 B2
Kirton Gdns 23 E2 95 D4
Kirton Rd E13 99 C5
Kirton Wlk HA8 27 A3
Kirwin Way SE5 138 D5
Kisharon Day Sch
NW11 47 B3
Kitcat Terr E3 97 C4
Kitchener Rd
Dagenham RM10 81 D2
East Finchley N2 48 C6
South Norwood CR7 205 B6
Tottenham N17 51 C6
Upton E7 77 B2
Walthamstow E17 35 D2
Kite Ho 5 SW11 136 C2
Kite Pl 9 E2 96 A4
Kitley Gdns SE19 183 D2
Kitson Rd
Barnes SW13 134 A4
Camberwell SE5 139 A5
Kittiwake Ct 26 SE8 141 B6
Kittiwake Pl SM1 217 B3
Kittiwake Rd UB5 84 D4
Kittiwake Way UB4 84 D2
Kitto Rd SE14 140 D3
KITTS END 1 A5
Kitt's End Rd EN5 1 A6
Kiver Rd N19 72 A6
Klea Ave SW4 159 C5
Kleffens Ct 2 SE3 142 D5
Kleine Wharf 30 N1 95 C6
Knaggs Ho 1 TW11 174 C5
Knapdale Cl SE23 162 B2
Knapmill Rd SE6 163 D2
Knapmill Way SE6 163 D2
Knapp Cl NW10 67 C2
Knapp Rd
Ashford TW15 170 B6
Bow E3 97 C3
Knapton Mews SW17 181 A4
Knaresborough Dr
SW18 157 D3
Knaresborough Ho 4
N4 51 A2
Knaresborough Pl
SW5 113 D2 255 C4
Knatchbull Rd
Brixton SE5 138 D4
Stonebridge NW10 89 B6
Knebworth Ave E17 35 C2
Knebworth Ho
South Lambeth SW8 269 D1
2 Stoke Newington
N16 73 C4
Walthamstow E17 35 C2
Knebworth Rd 3 N16 73 C4
Knee Hill SE2 124 C1
Knee Hill Cres SE2 124 C2
Kneller Gdns TW7 152 B5
Kneller Ho 9 SW8 137 D3
Kneller Rd
Brockley SE4 141 A1
Isleworth TW2 152 B5
New Malden KT3 199 C2
Knevett Terr TW3 129 C1
Knight Cl RM8 80 C6
Knight Ct
1 Chingford E4 20 A3
Stamford Hill N15 51 C4
Knighten St E1 118 B5
Knighthead Point 26
E14 119 C4
Knight Ho
Walworth SE17 263 A3
Worcester Pk KT4 216 A6
Knightland Ho E5 74 B6
Knightland Rd E5 74 B6
Knightleas Ct NW2 68 C2
Knightleys Ct E10 53 A1
Knighton Cl
Croydon CR2 220 D1
Woodford IG8 37 B6
Knighton Dr IG8 37 B6
Knighton Gn IG9 21 B2
Knighton La IG9 21 B2
Knighton Park Rd
SE26 184 D5
Knighton Rd E7 77 A4
Knightrider Ct EC4 252 A6
Knightrider St EC4 251 D6
Knights Arc SW1 247 C1
Knight's Ave W5 110 A4
KNIGHTSBRIDGE 114 C4
Knightsbridge SW1,
SW7 114 D4 247 C1
Knightsbridge Ct
SW1 247 D1
Knightsbridge Gn
SW1 247 C1
Knightsbridge Mews
BR7 188 B3
Knightsbridge Under Sch
SW7 256 B3
Knights Cl
East Molesey KT8 195 B4
Lower Clapton E9 74 C3
Knights Ct
Bushey WD23 8 B3
11 Friern Barnet N11 30 D5
Kingston u T KT1 198 A6
Penge BR3 185 A2
Knight's Ct BR1 164 D1
Knightshayes Ho 8
NW4 28 D1
Knight's Hill SE19,
SE27 182 D6
Knight's Hill Sq SE27 182 D6
Knights Ho
Bermondsey SE1 253 C2
South Lambeth SW8 270 B3
West Kensington SW5 254 C2
Knight's Ho SW10 266 A4
Knight's Pk KT1 198 A6
Knight's Pl TW2 152 C3
Knights Rd
Newham E16 121 A4
Stanmore HA7 25 C6
Knight's Wlk SE11 261 C3
Knightswood Cl HA8 11 A2
Knightswood Ct N6 49 D2
Knightswood Ho N12 30 A4
Knightwood Cres
KT3 199 C3
Knivet Rd
SW6 135 C6 265 A5
Knobs Hill Rd E15 97 D6
Knockholt Rd SE9 165 D6
Knole Cl CR0 206 C3
Knole Ct UB5 84 C4
Knole Gate DA15 167 C1
Knole The SE9 188 C6
Knoll Ct
Dulwich SE19 183 D5
Orpington BR6 227 D6
Knoll Dr N14 15 A4
Knoll Ho NW8 229 A4
Knoll Lo EN5 14 A6
Knollmead KT4, KT5 199 A1
Knollmead Prim Sch
KT5 215 A6
Knoll Rd
Bexley DA5 169 C5
Sidcup DA14 190 B6
Wandsworth SW18 158 A6
Knoll Rise BR6 211 D1
Knolls Cl KT4 216 B5
Knoll The
Beckenham BR3 185 D2
Ealing W13 87 C2
Hayes BR2 209 A1
Knolly's Cl SE27,
SW16 160 C1
Knolly's Rd SE27,
SW16 160 C1
Knot Ho SE1 253 C3
Knottisford St E2 96 C4
Knotts Green Mews
E10 54 A3
Knotts Green Rd E10 54 A3
Knowlden Ho 5 E1 118 C6
Knowle Ave DA7 147 B5
Knowle Cl SW9 138 C2
Knowledge Point Sch
N7 72 B2
Knowle Lo BR7 188 B4
Knowle Rd
Bromley BR2 226 A6
Twickenham TW2 152 C3
Knowles Cl UB7 104 A5
Knowles Ct 7 HA1 42 D3
Knowles Hill Cres
SE13 164 B6
Knowles Ho
Wandsworth SW18 157 D5
Willesden Green NW10 90 A6
Knowles Wlk SW4 137 C2
Knowl Pk WD6 10 A6
Knowlton Gn 1 BR2 208 D4
Knowlton Ho 32 SW9 138 C4
Knowl Way WD6 10 B6
Knowsley Ave UB1 107 D5
Knowsley Rd SW11 136 D3
Knox Ct 16 SW4 138 A3
Knox Ho SW15 134 C3
Knox Rd E7 77 A2
Knox St W1 92 D2 237 C4
Knoyle Ho W14 254 B6
Knoyle St SE14 141 A6
Kobi Nazrul Prim Sch
E1 96 A1
Koblenz Ho N8 50 A6
Kohat Rd SW19 179 D5
Korda Cl TW17 192 B6
Kossuth St SE10 120 C1
Kotree Way 16 SE1 118 A2
Kramer Mews SW5 255 C1
Kreedman Wlk 8 E8 74 A3
Kreisel Wlk TW9 132 B6
Kristina Ct 5 SM2 217 C2
Kuala Gdns SW16 182 B2
Kubrick Bsns Est E7 77 B4
Kuhn Way E7 77 A3
Kwesi Johnson Ct 4
N22 32 C1
Kydbrook Cl BR5 211 A2
Kyle Ho TW12 174 A2
Kylemore Cl 3 E6 99 D5
Kylemore Ct 4 W12 112 A4
Kylemore Rd NW6 69 C1
Kylestrome Ho SW1 258 B3
Kymberley Rd HA1 42 C3
Kynance Gdns HA7 25 C2
Kynance Mews
SW7 113 D3 255 D5
Kynance Pl SW7 256 A5
Kynaston Ave CR7 205 A4
Kynaston Cl HA3 24 B3
Kynaston Cres CR7 205 A4
Kynaston Ho 7 SW2 160 B3
Kynaston Rd
Enfield EN2 5 B4
Plaistow BR1 187 A5
Stoke Newington N16 73 C5
Thornton Heath CR7 205 A4
Kynaston Wood HA3 24 B3
Kynersley Cl 1 SM5 218 D5
Kynoch Rd N18 34 D6
Kyrle Rd SW11 159 A5
Kyverdale Rd N16 51 D1

L

Laburnam Ct 12
SW16 182 C5
Laburnham Cl HA0 88 C6
Laburnham Ct
Child's Hill NW2 69 B6
Sutton SM1 217 C3
Laburnham Pl SE9 166 C6
Laburnum Ave
Carshalton SM1 218 C5
Edmonton N9 17 D2
Tottenham N17 33 B3
Yiewsley UB7 104 B6
Laburnum Cl
Friern Barnet N11 31 A4
5 Nunhead SE15 140 C5
Walthamstow E4 35 B4
Laburnum Cres TW16 172 B2
Laburnum Ct
26 Haggerston E2 95 D6
Harrow HA1 41 D3
5 Mitcham CR4 181 A1
Stanmore HA7 25 C6
Laburnum Gdns
Croydon CR0 206 D1
Edmonton N21 17 A2
Laburnum Gr
Edmonton N21 17 A2
Hounslow TW3 129 B1
Kingsbury NW9 45 A2
Kingston u T KT3 177 B1
Ruislip HA4 39 B3
Southall UB1 85 B3
Laburnum Ho
Dagenham RM10 81 C6
New Cross SE4 141 B3
6 Stoke Newington
N16 73 B6
Laburnum JMI Sch E2 95 D6
Laburnum Lo 2 N3 29 B1
Laburnum Rd
Hayes UB3 105 D2
Merton SW19 180 A3
Mitcham CR4 181 A1
Laburnum St E2 95 D6
Laburnums The E6 100 A3
Laburnum Way
Southborough BR2 210 D2
Stanwell TW19 148 B3
Lacebark Cl DA15 167 D4
Lacewing Cl E13 99 A4
Lacey Cl N9 18 A2
Lacey Dr
Dagenham RM8 80 C5
Edgware HA8 26 B6
Hampton TW12 173 B2
Lacey Ho 7 SE13 142 A3
Lacine Ct 12 SE16 118 D4
Lackington St EC2 242 D4
Lackland Ho SE1 263 D2
Lacland Ho SW10 266 C4
Lacock Cl SW19 180 A4
Lacock Ct 3 W13 109 A5
Lacon Rd SE22 140 A1
Lacrosse Way SW16 181 D2
Lacy Rd SW15 134 D1
Ladas Rd SE27 183 A5
Ladbroke Cres W11 91 A1
Ladbroke Gdns
W11 113 B6 244 C6
Ladbroke Gr
Kensal Town W10 91 A2
Notting Hill
W11 113 B6 244 C6
Ladbroke Grove Ho
W11 244 C6
Ladbroke Grove Sta
W10 91 A1
Ladbroke Ho E1 243 D3
Ladbroke Mews W11 244 B3
Ladbroke Rd
Enfield EN1 17 D5
Notting Hill
W11 113 B5 244 C4
Ladbroke Sq
W11 113 B6 244 D5
Ladbroke Terr
W11 113 B5 244 D4
Ladbroke Wlk
W11 113 B5 244 D4
Ladbrook Cl HA5 41 B4
Ladbrooke Cres
DA14 168 D1
Ladbrook Rd SE25 205 B5
Ladderstile Ride KT2,
TW10 176 D5
Ladderswood Way
N11 31 C5
Ladlands SE22 162 A4
Lady Alesford Ave HA7 25 B5
Lady Bankes Jun & Inf
Schs HA4 62 A6
Lady Booth Rd 7
KT1 176 A1
Ladybower Ct 6 E5 74 D4
Ladycroft Gdns 6
BR6 227 A3
Ladycroft Rd SE13 141 D2
Ladycroft Way BR6 227 A3
Ladycroft Wlk HA7 25 D1
Lady Eleanor Holles Sch
The (Jun Girls)
TW12 173 D5
Lady Eleanor Holles Sch
The (Senior Girls)
TW12 173 D5
Lady Elizabeth Ho
SW14 133 A2
Ladyfern Ho 19 E3 97 C2
Lady Florence Ctyd 15
SE8 141 C5
Ladygate La HA4 39 A3
Lady Hay KT4 215 D6
Lady Helen Seymour Ho
14 E13 99 A5
Lady Margaret Prim Sch
UB1 85 B2
Lady Margaret Rd
Kentish Town NW5 71 C3
Southall UB1 85 B2
Lady Margaret Sch
SW6 135 C4 265 A1
Lady Shaw Ct N13 16 B1
Ladysmith Ave
Ilford IG2 57 C2
Newham E6 100 A5
Ladysmith Cl NW7 28 A3
Ladysmith Rd
Edmonton N18 34 B5
Eltham SE9 166 C5
Enfield EN1 5 D3
Harrow HA3 24 C1
Newham E16 98 D4
Tottenham N17 34 A1
Lady Somerset Rd
NW5 71 B4
LADYWELL 163 C6
Ladywell Cl SE4 141 C1
Ladywell Ho 7 BR5 190 B1
Ladywell Hts SE4 163 B5
Ladywell Rd SE13 163 D6
Ladywell St 4 E15 98 D6
Ladywell Sta SE13 163 D6
Ladywell Water Twr
SE4 163 C6
Ladywood Ave BR5 211 C4
Ladywood Rd KT6 214 C6
Lafitte Ho 22 N19 49 D2
Lafone Ave TW13 150 C2
Lafone Ho 11 SW2 160 A4
Lafone St SE1 117 D4 253 C2
Lagado Mews SE16 118 D5
Lagonda Ho 11 E3 97 C3
Lagonier Ho EC1 235 B1
Laidlaw Dr N21 16 B6
Laindon Ho 6 N16 51 D1
Laing Dean UB5 84 C6
Laing Ho SE5 139 A5
Laings Ave CR4 180 D1
Laings Cnr CR4 180 D2
Lainlock Pl TW3 129 D4
Lainson St SW18 157 C4
Lairdale Cl SE21 161 A4
Laird Ho SE5 139 A5
Lairs Cl N7 72 A2
Lait Ho 3 BR3 185 D2
Laitwood Rd SW12 159 B3
Lakanal 14 SE5 139 C4
Lake Ave BR1 187 A4
Lake Bsns Ctr N17 34 A3
Lake Cl
Dagenham RM8 80 D5
6 Wimbledon SW19 179 B5
Lakedale Ct IG11 102 A3

Lakedale Rd SE18 123 C1
Lake Dr WD23 8 B2
Lake Farm Ctry Pk
UB3 105 C5
Lakefield Cl SE20 184 B3
Lakefield Rd N22 32 D1
Lake Gdns
Dagenham RM10 81 C3
Hackbridge SM6 219 B5
Richmond TW10 153 B2
Lakehall Gdns CR7 204 D4
Lakehall Rd CR7 204 D4
Lake Ho
Borough The SE1 252 A1
[4] West Norwood SW27 182 D5
Lake House Rd E11 77 A6
Lakehurst Rd KT19 215 C3
Lakeland Cl HA3 24 B4
Lakeman Ct CR7 183 A1
Lakenheath N14 15 D6
Laker Ct SW4 138 A3
Lake Rd
Croydon CR0 223 B6
Dagenham RM6 58 D5
Wimbledon SW19 179 B5
Laker Pl SW15 157 A5
Lakeside
Beckenham BR3 207 D6
Deacons Hill WD6 10 C6
Ealing W13 87 C1
Enfield EN2 3 D1
Finchley N3 29 D1
[10] Kingston u T KT2 176 D3
Wallington SM6 219 B4
West Ewell KT19 215 C2
Lakeside Ave
Redbridge IG4 55 D5
Thamesmead SE28 124 A5
Lakeside Cl
Ruislip HA4 39 B5
Sidcup DA15 168 C6
South Norwood SE25 184 A1
Lakeside Complex The
SE2 124 D5
Lakeside Cres EN4 14 D6
Lakeside Ct N4 51 A1
Lakeside Dr
Acton NW10 88 B4
Esher KT10 212 A2
Keston Mark BR2 226 A5
Lakeside Lo NW4 47 A5
Lakeside Rd
Brook Green W14 112 D3
Palmers Green N13 16 B1
Lakeside Way HA9 66 C4
Lakes Rd BR2 225 C3
Lakeswood Rd BR5 211 A3
Lake The WD23 8 B3
Lakeview [23] E3 96 D5
Lake View HA8 26 B5
Lakeview Ct E4 36 B4
Lake View Ct SW1 258 D6
Lakeview Rd
Bexley DA16 146 B1
West Norwood SE27 182 D5
Lake View Terr N18 33 D6
Lakis Cl NW3 70 A4
Laleham Ave NW7 11 B1
Laleham Ho E2 243 C6
Laleham Rd
Catford SE6 164 A4
Littleton TW17 192 C4
Lalor St SW6 135 A3
Lambarde Ave SE9 188 C6
Lambard Ho [4] SE10 142 A5
Lamb Cl UB5 85 A4
Lamb Ct [16] E14 119 A6
Lamberhurst Ho [14]
SE15 140 C6
Lamberhurst Rd
Dagenham RM8 59 B1
West Norwood SE27 182 C5
Lambert Ave TW9 132 D2
Lambert Ho
[16] Brixton SW9 138 C3
[19] Crouch End N19 49 D2
Lambert Lo TW8 109 D1
Lambert Rd
Clapham Pk SW2 160 B6
Newham E16 99 B1
North Finchley N12 30 B5
Lambert's Pl CR0 205 B1
Lambert's Rd KT6 198 B4
Lambert St N1 72 C1
Lambert Way N12 30 A5
Lambert Wlk HA9 65 D5
LAMBETH 116 B4
Lambeth Acad SW4 159 C6
Lambeth Coll (Brixton
Ctr) SW2 160 B6
Lambeth Coll (Clapham
Ctr) SW4 159 C6
Lambeth Coll (Tower
Bridge Ctr)
SE1 117 C5 253 B3
Lambeth Coll (Vauxhall
Ctr) SW8 137 D4 269 C2
Lambeth Ct [8] SW18 157 C6
Lambeth High St
SE1 116 B2 260 C4
Lambeth Hill EC4 252 A6
Lambeth Hospl SW9 138 B2
Lambeth North Sta
SE1 116 C3 261 A6
Lambeth Pal*
SE1 116 B3 260 C5
Lambeth Palace Rd
SE1 116 B3 260 C6
Lambeth Pier SE1 260 B5
Lambeth Prospect
SE19 183 B4
Lambeth Rd
Lambeth SE1 116 C3 261 B5
Thornton Heath CR0 204 D1
Lambeth Twrs SE11 261 A5
Lambeth Wlk
SE11 116 B2 260 D4
Lambfold Ho N7 72 A2
Lamb Ho
[28] Camberwell SE5 139 A5
[11] Camberwell SE5 139 B4
Greenwich SE10 142 A6
Lamb La E8 74 B1
Lamble St NW5 71 A4
Lambley Rd RM9 80 B2
Lambolle Pl NW3 70 C2
Lambolle Rd NW3 70 C2
Lambourn Cl
Hanwell W7 108 D4
[9] Kentish Town NW5 71 C4
Lambourne Ave
SW19 179 B6
Lambourne Ct [5] IG8 37 C3
Lambourne Gdns
[5] Barking IG11 79 D1
Chingford E4 19 C2
Enfield EN1 5 D3
Lambourne Gr
Deptford SE16 118 D1
Kingston u T KT1 176 D1
Lambourne Ho NW8 236 D4
Lambourne Pl SE3 143 B4
Lambourne Rd
Barking IG11 79 D1
Ilford IG3 79 C6
Leytonstone E11 54 A2
Lambourn Ho BR1 188 A3
Lambourn Rd SW4 137 B2
Lambrook Ho [13]
SE15 140 A4
Lambrook Terr
SW6 135 A4 264 A2
Lamb's Bldgs EC1 242 C5
Lamb's Cl N9 18 A2
Lamb's Conduit Pas
WC1 240 C4
Lamb's Conduit St
WC1 94 B3 240 C5
Lambscroft Ave SE9,
SE12 165 D1
Lambs Mdw IG8 37 D1
Lamb's Mews N1 234 C5
Lamb's Pas EC1 95 B3 242 C5
Lamb St E1 95 D2 243 C4
Lamb's Terr N9 17 B2
Lambs Wlk EN2 5 A3
Lambton Ct [2] N19 50 A1
Lambton Mews [4]
N19 50 A1
Lambton Pl W11 244 D6
Lambton Rd
Finsbury Pk N19 50 A1
Wimbledon SW20 178 C2
Lamb Wlk SE1 253 A1
Lamerock Rd BR1 186 D6
Lamerton Lo [10] TW9 132 B4
Lamerton St [8] SE8 141 C6
Lamford Cl N17 33 B3
Lamington St [3] W6 112 B2
Lamlash St SE11 261 C4
Lamley Ho SE10 141 D5
Lammas Ave CR4 181 A1
Lammas Gn SE26 162 B1
Lammas Park Gdns
W5 109 C5
Lammas Park Rd W5 109 D4
Lammas Rd
Homerton E9 74 D1
Lammas Rd continued
Richmond TW10 175 C6
Walthamstow E10 53 A1
Lammas Sch The E10 53 B1
Lammermoor Rd
SW12 159 B4
Lamont Rd
SW10 136 B6 266 C5
Lamont Rd Pas SW10 266 C5
Lamorbey Cl DA15 167 D2
Lamorna Cl E17 36 A2
Lamorna Gr HA7 25 D1
Lampard Gr N16 51 D1
Lampern Sq [8] E2 96 A4
Lampeter Cl NW9 45 C3
Lampeter Sq W6 264 A5
Lamplighter Cl [34] E1 96 C3
Lampmead Rd SE12 142 D1
Lamport Cl SE18 122 B2
Lampson Ho [6] N19 71 C4
LAMPTON 129 D4
Lampton Ave TW5 129 D4
Lampton Ct TW5 129 D4
Lampton House Cl
SW19 178 D6
Lampton Park Rd
TW3 129 D3
Lampton Rd TW3,
TW5 129 D3
Lampton Sch TW5 129 C4
Lanacre Ave NW9 27 C2
Lanain Ct SE12 164 D4
Lanark Cl W5 87 C2
Lanark Ct UB5 63 C3
Lanark Ho [12] SE1 118 A1
Lanark Mans
Paddington W9 236 B6
[15] Shepherd's Bush
W12 112 C4
Lanark Mews NW8 229 B1
Lanark Pl W9 92 A3 236 B6
Lanark Rd W9 92 A4 229 A1
Lanark Sq E14 119 D3
Lanata Wlk UB4 84 D3
Lanbury Rd SE15 140 D1
Lancashire Ct W1 248 D6
Lancaster Ave
Barking IG11 101 C6
Croydon CR4 204 A5
Hadley Wood EN4 2 B5
Wanstead E18 55 B5
West Norwood SE21,
SE27 161 A2
Wimbledon SW19 178 D5
Lancaster Cl
Ashford TW15 170 A6
Beckenham BR2 208 D5
[10] De Beauvoir Town
N1 73 C1
Grahame Pk NW9 27 D3
Kensington W2 245 C5
Kingston u T KT2 175 D5
New Malden KT4 200 B2
Stanwell TW19 148 A5
Tottenham N17 34 A3
Lancaster Cotts [1]
TW10 154 A5
Lancaster Ct
Bayswater W2 246 B6
[1] Belmont SM2 217 C1
Parsons Green SW6 264 D3
Stanwell TW19 148 A3
Walton-on-T KT12 194 B2
West Norwood SE27 160 D2
Lancaster Dr
Canary Wharf E14 120 A5
Maitland Pk NW3 70 C2
Lancaster Gate
W2 114 A6 246 B6
Lancaster Gate Sta
W2 114 B6 246 C6
Lancaster Gdns
Bromley BR1 210 A4
Kingston u T KT2 175 D5
West Ealing W13 109 B4
Wimbledon SW19 179 A5
Lancaster Gr NW3 70 C2
Lancaster hall [14] E16 121 A5
Lancaster Ho
Enfield EN2 5 B4
Putney SW15 134 C3
Stanmore HA7 9 A1
Lancaster Ho SW1 249 A2
Lancaster Ho SW18 157 D4
Lancasterian Prim Sch
N17 33 D2
Lancaster Lo [2] W11 91 A1
Lancaster Mews
Bayswater
W2 114 A6 246 B6
Lancaster Mews continued
[2] Richmond TW10 154 A5
[3] Wandsworth SW18 157 D6
Lancaster Pk TW10 154 A6
Lancaster Pl
Hounslow TW5 128 D3
Ilford IG1 79 A4
Strand WC2 116 B6 250 C5
Twickenham TW1 153 A4
[1] Wimbledon SW19 178 D5
Lancaster Rd
Bowes Pk N11 31 D4
Dudden Hill NW10 68 A3
Edmonton N18 33 D5
Enfield EN2 5 B4
Finsbury Pk N4 50 C2
Harrow HA2 41 C4
Higham Hill E17 34 D1
Leytonstone E11 76 C6
New Barnet EN4 14 B6
Northolt UB5 64 A2
Notting Hill W11 91 A1
Southall UB1 107 A6
South Norwood SE25 206 A6
Upton E7 77 A1
Wimbledon SW19 178 D5
Lancaster Road Ind Est [2]
EN4 14 B6
Lancaster St
SE1 116 D4 251 D1
Lancaster Stables [10]
NW3 70 C2
Lancaster Terr
W2 114 B6 246 C6
Lancaster Wlk
Hayes UB3 83 A1
Knightsbridge
W2 114 A5 246 B4
Lancastrian Rd SM6 220 B1
Lancefield Ho SE15 140 B2
Lancefield St W10 91 B4
Lancell St N16 73 C6
Lancelot Ave HA0 65 D4
Lancelot Cres HA0 65 D4
Lancelot Gdns EN4 15 A4
Lancelot Ho SM5 202 C1
Lancelot Pl
SW7 114 D4 247 C1
Lancelot Rd
Welling DA16 146 A2
Wembley HA0 65 D3
Lance Rd HA1 42 A2
Lancer Sq W8 245 C2
Lancey Cl SE7 122 A2
Lanchester Ct W2 237 C1
Lanchester Rd N6 48 D4
Lanchester Way
SE14 140 D4
Lancing Gdns N9 17 D3
Lancing Rd
Ealing W13 109 B6
Feltham TW13 149 D2
Ilford IG2 57 B2
Thornton Heath CR0 204 B2
Lancing St NW1 232 C1
Lancresse Ct N1 95 C6
Landale Ct SE10 142 A4
Landale Ho [18] SE16 118 C3
Landau Ct [11] CR2 221 A3
Landcroft Rd SE22 161 D5
Landells Rd SE22 162 A5
Lander Ct EN5 14 A6
Landford Rd SW15 134 C2
Landgrove Rd SW19 179 C5
Landin Ho [1] E14 97 C1
Landleys Field [27] N7 71 D3
Landmann Ho [16]
SE16 118 B2
Landmann Way SE14 118 D1
Landmark Commercial Ctr
N18 33 C4
Landmark Hts E5 75 A4
Landon Pl SW1 257 C6
Landons Cl E14 120 A5
Landon Way TW15 170 D4
Landon Wlk [16] E14 119 D6
Landor Ct N16 73 C3
Landor Ho [7] SE5 139 B5
Landor Rd SW9 138 A2
Landor Wlk [11] W12 112 A4
Landra Gdns N21 16 D5
Landrake NW1 232 B5
Landridge Dr EN1 6 B5
Landridge Rd SW6 135 B3
Landrock Rd N8 50 B3
Landscape Rd IG8 37 B3
Landsdown Cl [9] EN5 2 A1
Landseer Ave E12 78 C3
Landseer Cl
Edgware HA8 26 C1
Landseer Cl continued
Mitcham SW19 180 B2
Landseer Ct
Hayes UB4 83 B5
[10] Upper Holloway N19 72 A6
Landseer Ho
Battersea SW11 268 B1
[16] Northolt UB5 84 D5
Paddington NW8 236 D6
Westminster SW1 259 D3
Landseer Rd
Cheam SM1 217 C2
Enfield EN1 18 A6
New Malden KT3 199 B2
Upper Holloway N19 72 A6
Lands' End WD6 9 D5
Landstead Rd SE18 145 B5
Landulph Ho SE11 261 B2
Landward Ct W1 237 B2
Lane Cl NW2 68 B5
Lane Ct SW11 158 D4
Lane End DA7 147 D2
Lane Gdns
Bushey Heath WD23 8 C4
Claygate KT10 212 D1
Lane Mews E12 78 B5
Lanercost Cl SW2 160 C2
Lanercost Gdns N14 16 A4
Lanercost Rd SW2 160 C2
Laneside
Chislehurst BR7 189 A5
Edgware HA8 27 A5
Laneside Ave RM8 59 B2
Lane The
Blackheath Pk SE3 143 A2
St John's Wood
NW8 92 A5 229 A3
Laneway SW15 156 B6
Laney Bldg EC1 241 A4
Lanfranc Ct HA1 64 D5
Lanfranc Rd E3 97 A5
Lanfrey Pl W14 254 C1
Langbourn Ct E17 53 A3
Langbourne Ave N6 71 A6
Langbourne Ho [7]
SW2 160 C6
Langbourne Mans N6 71 A6
Langbourne Pl E14 119 D1
Langbourne Prim Sch
SE21 161 C1
Langbourne Way
KT10 213 A2
Langbrook Rd SE3 143 D3
Langcroft Cl SM5 218 D5
Langdale NW1 232 A2
Langdale Ave CR4 202 D6
Langdale Cl
Camberwell SE17 139 A6
Dagenham RM8 58 C1
Locksbottom BR6 226 D5
Mortlake SW14 132 D1
Langdale Cres DA7 147 C4
Langdale Ct
[3] Ealing W5 87 C2
[9] Ilford IG1 78 D5
Ruislip HA4 62 B3
Langdale Dr UB4 83 C5
Langdale Gdns UB6 87 B4
Langdale Ho SW1 259 A1
Langdale Par [8] CR4 202 D6
Langdale Rd
Greenwich SE10 142 A5
Thornton Heath CR7 204 C5
Langdale St [25] E1 96 B1
Langdon Cres E6 100 C5
Langdon Ct
Finsbury EC1 234 D3
Harlesden NW10 89 C6
Langdon Dr NW9 45 A1
Langdon Ho [3] E14 98 A1
Langdon Park Rd N6 49 C2
Langdon Park Sec Sch
E14 98 A1
Langdon Park Sta E14 97 D1
Langdon Pk TW11 175 C3
Langdon Pl SW14 133 A2
Langdon Rd
Barking E6 100 C6
Bromley BR2 209 B6
Morden SM4 202 A4
Langdon Sch E6 100 D6
Langdons Ct UB2 107 C3
Langdon Shaw DA14 189 D5
Langdon Way [18] SE1 118 A2
Langdon Wlk SM4 202 A4
Langford Cl
Shacklewell E8 74 A3
[7] South Tottenham
N15 51 C3
St John's Wood NW8 229 B4
Langford Cres EN4 2 D1
Langford Ct NW8 229 B3
Langford Gn SE5 139 C2
Langford Ho [5] SE8 141 C6
Langford Pl
Sidcup DA14 168 A1
St John's Wood
NW8 92 A5 229 B4
Langford Prim Sch
SW6 135 D3
Langford Rd
Cockfosters EN4 2 D1
[4] Sands End SW6 135 D3
Woodford IG8 37 C4
Langfords IG9 21 D2
Langham Cl [1] N15 50 D6
Langham Ct
Hendon NW4 46 D4
Merton SW20 178 C1
[4] Putney SW15 156 D6
Ruislip HA4 62 B3
[12] Twickenham TW1 153 C5
Langham Dr RM6 58 B3
Langham Gdns
Burnt Oak HA8 27 A3
Ealing W13 109 B6
Richmond TW10 175 C6
Southgate N21 16 D6
Wembley HA0 65 C6
Langham Ho
Clapham Pk SW4 159 C6
[3] Wanstead E11 55 B5
Langham House Cl
TW10 175 D6
Langham Mans SW5 255 C1
Langham Park Pl
BR2 208 D5
Langham Pl
Chiswick W4 133 C6
Fitzrovia W1 93 B2 238 D3
Noel Pk N15 50 D6
Langham Rd
Burnt Oak HA8 27 A4
Teddington TW11 175 B4
West Green N15 51 A6
Wimbledon SW20 178 C2
Langham St
W1 93 B2 238 D3
Langhedge Cl N18 33 D4
Langhedge La N18 33 D4
Langhedge Lane Ind Est
N18 33 D4
Lang Ho
South Lambeth SW8 270 A3
Stanwell TW19 148 A3
[3] Tufnell Pk N19 71 C5
Langholm Cl SW12 159 D4
Langholme WD23 8 A3
Langhorn Dr TW2 152 C4
Langhorne Ct [10] NW8 70 B1
Langhorne Ho [5]
SE7 143 C6
Langhorne Rd RM10 81 C1
Langhurst Ho [10]
SW11 137 A3
Langland Cres HA7 25 D1
Langland Dr HA5 23 A3
Langland Gdns
Croydon CR0 223 B6
West Hampstead NW3 69 D3
Langland Ho
[10] SE5 139 B5
Upper Tooting SW17 180 B5
Langland Mans NW3 69 D3
Langler Rd NW10 90 C5
Langley Ave
North Cheam KT4,
SM3 216 D6
Ruislip HA4 62 B6
Surbiton KT6 198 A1
Langley Cres
Dagenham RM9 80 D1
Edgware HA8 11 A1
Harlington UB3 127 D5
Wanstead E11 55 C2
Langley Ct
South Lambeth SW8 270 A2
Strand WC2 250 A6
[13] Sutton SM2 218 A2
Langley Dr
South Acton W3 110 D4
Wanstead E11 55 B2
Langley Gdns
Bromley BR2 209 C5
Dagenham RM9 80 D1
Southborough BR5 210 D3
Langley Gr KT3 177 C1

Langley Ho
11 Lower Clapton E5 74 B3
36 Paddington W2 91 C2
Langley La
SW8 138 A6 270 B6
Langley Lawns SM2 218 B1
Langley Manor BR3 208 A4
Langley Mans SW8 270 B6
Langley Park Rd SM1,
SM2 218 A1
Langley Park Sch for Boys
BR3 207 D3
Langley Park Sch for Girls
BR3 208 A3
Langley Pk NW7 27 C4
Langley Rd
Beckenham BR3 207 A5
Isleworth TW7 130 D3
Merton SW19 179 C2
Surbiton KT6 198 A2
West Heath DA16 146 C6
Langley Row EN5 1 B4
Langley St WC2 94 A1 240 A1
Langley Way BR4 208 C2
Langmead Dr WD23 8 B3
Langmead Ho 34 E3 97 D4
Langmead St SE27 183 A6
Langmore Ct DA6 146 D2
Langmore Ho 39 E1 96 A1
Langport Ct KT12 194 C1
Langport Ho 1 SW9 138 D3
Langridge 15 NW5 71 A2
Langridge Mews
TW12 173 B4
Langroyd Rd SW17 158 D2
Langside Ave SW15 134 A1
Langside Cres N14 15 D1
Lang St E1 96 C3
Langstone Way NW7 28 D3
Langston Hughes Cl 5
SE24 138 D1
Langthorn Ct EC2 242 D2
Langthorne Ct 3
SE6 186 A6
Langthorne Ho UB3 105 C2
Langthorne Hospl E11 76 B5
Langthorne Lo 30
SW2 160 C4
Langthorne Rd E11 76 B5
Langthorne St SW6 134 D5
Langton Ave
Oakleigh Pk N20 14 B4
Wallend E6 100 C4
Langton Cl
WC1 94 B3 240 D6
Langton Ct SW15 157 B5
Langton Ho
Harrow HA2 64 C6
Lambeth SE11 260 D4
5 Streatham SW16 181 C6
Langton Pl SW18 157 C3
Langton Rd
Camberwell SW9 138 D5
Cricklewood NW2 68 C5
East Molesey KT8 196 A5
Harrow Weald HA3 24 A3
Langton Rise SE22,
SE23 162 B4
Langton St
SW10 136 A6 266 B5
Langton Way
Greenwich SE3 143 A5
South Croydon CR0 221 C4
Langtry Ho BR1 187 B3
Langtry Pl SW6 265 B6
Langtry Rd
Northolt UB5 84 D5
Paddington NW8 91 D6
Langtry Wlk
NW8 92 A6 229 A6
Langwood Chase
TW11 175 C4
Langworth Dr UB4 84 B1
Langworthy HA5 23 C4
Lanherne Ho 7
SW19 178 D3
Lanhill Rd W9 91 C3
Lanier Rd SE13 164 B5
Lanigan Dr TW3 151 D6
Lankaster Gdns N2 30 B2
Lankers Dr HA2 41 B3
Lankton Cl BR3 186 A2
Lanner Ho 2 SW11 136 C2
Lannock Ct 2 SW17 180 C4
Lannock Rd UB3 105 D5
Lannoy Point SW6 264 B4
Lannoy Rd SE9 167 A3
Lanrick Rd E14 98 C1
Lanridge Rd SE2 124 D3
Lansan Ct E11 76 D6
Lansbury Ave
Barking IG11 80 A1
Dagenham RM6 59 A4
Edmonton N18 33 C5
Feltham TW14 150 B5
Lansbury Cl NW10 67 A3
Lansbury Ct 4 SE28 124 B6
Lansbury Dr UB4 83 D3
Lansbury Gdns 1 E14 98 B1
Lansbury Ho 5 DA17 125 B1
Lansbury Lawrence Prim
Sch E14 97 D1
Lansbury Rd EN3 6 D4
Lansbury Way N18 33 C5
Lanscombe Wlk SW8 270 A3
Lansdell Ho 9 SW2 160 C5
Lansdell Rd CR4 181 A1
Lansdown Cl KT12 194 C1
Lansdowne Ave
Orpington BR6 210 D1
West Heath DA7 146 D5
Lansdowne Cl
Tolworth KT5 214 D6
Twickenham TW1 152 D3
Wimbledon SW20 178 D3
Lansdowne Coll W2 245 C5
Lansdowne Copse 1
KT4 216 A6
Lansdowne Cres
W11 113 A6 244 B5
Lansdowne Ct
Redbridge IG5 56 A6
2 Worcester Pk KT4 216 A6
Lansdowne Dr E8 74 A1
Lansdowne Gdns
SW8 138 A4 270 A2
Lansdowne Gr NW10 67 C4
Lansdowne Hill SE27 160 D1
Lansdowne Ho
19 Belmont SM2 217 D1
Enfield EN2 4 C3
Notting Hill W11 244 C4
Lansdowne Int Coll Ltd
SW7 256 B5
Lansdowne La SE7 121 D1
Lansdowne Mews
Greenwich SE7 121 D1
Notting Hill W11 244 C4
Lansdowne Pl
Borough The SE1 262 D6
Penge SE19 183 D3
Lansdowne Rd
Chingford E4 19 C2
Croydon CR0 205 B1
Finchley N3 29 C3
Harrow HA1 42 C2
Hayes UB8 83 A1
Hounslow TW3 129 D2
Ilford IG3 57 D2
Leytonstone E11 76 D6
Muswell Hill N10 31 C1
Notting Hill
W11 113 A6 244 B5
Stanmore HA7 25 C4
Sundridge BR1 187 B3
Tottenham N17 34 A2
Walthamstow E17 53 C3
Wanstead E18 55 A6
West Ewell KT19 215 B1
Wimbledon SW19,
SW20 178 C3
Lansdowne Rise
W11 113 A6 244 B5
Lansdowne Row W1 248 D4
Lansdowne Sch SW9 138 B2
Lansdowne Terr WC1 240 B5
Lansdowne Way SW4,
SW8 138 A4 270 B1
Lansdowne Wlk
W11 113 B5 244 C4
Lansdowne Wood Cl 11
SE27 160 D1
Lansdowne Workshops
SE7 121 D1
Lansdown Ho 28 SE5 139 A3
Lansdown Rd
Sidcup DA14 168 B1
Upton E7 77 C1
Lansfield Ave N18 34 A6
Lanson Ho HA8 26 C4
Lantern Cl
Orpington BR6 226 D4
Putney SW15 134 A1
Wembley HA0 65 D3
Lantern Ct
Southgate N14 15 D3
4 Wimbledon SW20 178 D2
Lantern Ho
Millwall E14 119 C4
Woolwich SE18 122 C1
Lanterns Ct E14 119 C3
Lanterns The N12 29 D4
Lantern Way UB7 104 B4
Lant Ho SE1 252 A1
Lantry Ct 1 W3 110 D5
Lant St SE1 117 A4 252 B1
Lanvanor Rd SE15 140 C3
Lanyard Ho 4 SE8 119 B2
Lapford Cl W9 91 B3
Lapponum Wlk UB4 84 D2
Lapsang SE1 253 D3
Lapse Wood Wlk
SE22 162 B3
Lapstone Gdns HA3 43 C3
Lapwing Ct
Grahame Pk NW9 27 C1
Tolworth KT6 214 C5
Lapwing Terr E7 77 D3
Lapwing Twr 31 SE8 141 B6
Lapwing Way UB4 84 D1
Lapworth 2 N11 31 B6
Lapworth Ct W2 91 D2
Lara Cl
Chessington KT9 214 A1
Lewisham SE13 164 A5
Lara Lo SM1 217 C3
Larbert Rd SW16 181 C3
Larch Ave W3 111 C5
Larch Cl
Balham SW12 159 B2
Colney Hatch N11 31 A3
15 Deptford SE8 141 B6
Newham E13 99 C3
10 Upper Holloway N19 71 C6
Larch Cres
Hayes UB4 84 D2
West Ewell KT19 214 D2
Larch Ct 41 W2 91 C2
Larch Dene BR6 226 C6
Larches Ave SW14 133 B1
Larches The
Edmonton N13 17 A1
Hillingdon UB10 82 D5
Larchfield Ho 2 N5 73 A3
Larch Gn NW9 27 C2
Larch Gr DA15 167 D3
Larch Ho
Hayes UB4 84 C2
23 Rotherhithe SE16 118 C4
Larchmont HA4 39 B2
Larchmore Ct N19 72 A6
Larch Rd
Cricklewood NW2 68 C4
Leyton E10 75 C6
Larch Tree Way CR0 223 C5
Larchvale Ct 20 SM2 217 D1
Larch Way BR2 210 C2
Larchwood Rd SE9 166 D2
Larcombe Cl CR0 221 D4
Larcom St
SE17 117 A2 262 B3
Larden Rd W3 111 C4
La Retraite RC Girls Sch
SW12 159 C4
Largewood Ave KT6 214 C6
Larissa St SE17 262 D3
Larix Ct NW10 90 A6
Larkbere Rd SE26 185 A6
Larken Cl WD23 8 A3
Larken Dr WD23 8 A3
Larkfield Ave HA3 43 B6
Larkfield Cl BR2 225 A6
Larkfield Rd
Longlands DA14 167 D1
Richmond TW9 132 A1
Larkhall La
SW4 138 A4 270 A1
Lark Hall Prim Sch
SW4 137 D3
Larkhall Rise SW4 137 D3
Larkham Cl TW13 149 C1
Lark Row E2 96 C6
Larksfield Gr EN1 6 B4
Larks Gr IG11 79 C1
Larkshall Bsns Ctr E4 20 B2
Larkshall Cres E4 36 A6
Larkshall Ct E4 36 A5
Larkshall Rd E4 36 B6
Larkspur Cl
Kingsbury NW9 44 D4
4 Newham E6 100 A2
Ruislip HA4 39 A2
Tottenham N17 33 B3
Larkspur Ct SM6 219 B1
Larkspur Gr HA8 27 A6
Larkspur Way KT19 215 A3
Larkswood Ct E4 36 B5
Larkswood Prim Sch
E4 35 D6
Larkswood Rd E4 35 D6
Larkswood Rise HA5 40 C5
Lark Way SM5 202 C2
Larkway Cl NW9 45 B5
Larmenier & Sacred Heart
RC Prim Sch W6 112 D2
Larnaca Ho SE1 263 C6
Larnach Rd W6 134 D6
Larne Rd HA4 39 D2
Larpent Ave SW15 156 C6
Larwood Cl UB6 64 B3
La Saint Union RC Sec
Sch NW5 71 A5
Lascelles Ave HA1 42 B2
Lascelles Cl E11 76 B6
Lascelles Ho NW1 237 B5
Lascott's Rd N22 32 B4
Laseron Ho 1 N15 51 D5
Lashford Ho HA8 27 A4
Lassa Rd SE9 166 B6
Lassell St SE10 120 B1
Lasseter Pl SE3 142 D6
Latchett Rd E18 37 B2
Latchingdon Ct E17 52 D5
Latchmere Cl KT2,
TW10 176 A5
Latchmere Jun & Inf Schs
KT2 176 B4
Latchmere La KT2,
TW10 176 B5
Latchmere Rd
Battersea SW11 136 D3
Kingston u T KT2 176 B4
Latchmere St 5
SW11 136 D3
Lateward Rd TW8 131 D6
Latham Cl
Newham E6 100 A1
Putney SW15 156 D6
6 Twickenham TW1 153 A4
Latham Ct
3 Bowes Pk N11 32 A4
7 Northolt UB5 84 D4
Latham Ho
Stepney E1 96 D1
18 Walthamstow E17 53 D6
Latham Rd
Bexleyheath DA6 169 C6
Twickenham TW1 152 D4
Latham's Way CR0 220 B6
Lathkill Cl EN1 18 A4
Lathkill Ct BR3 185 B2
Lathom Jun Sch E6 78 A1
Lathom Rd E6 78 B1
Lathwood Ho 6
SE26 184 B5
Latimer SE17 263 A1
Latimer Ave E6 100 B6
Latimer Cl
North Cheam KT4 216 B4
Pinner Green HA5 22 C2
Latimer Gdns HA5 22 C2
Latimer Ho
11 Homerton E9 74 D2
Notting Hill W11 244 D5
Latimer Ind Est 1
NW10 90 C1
Latimer Pl W10 90 C1
Latimer Rd
Barnet EN5 1 D2
1 Croydon CR0 220 D5
Forest Gate E7 77 B4
North Kensington W10 90 C1
South Tottenham N15 51 C3
Teddington TW11 174 D5
Wimbledon SW19 179 D4
Latimer Road Sta
W10 112 D6
Latitude Ho NW1 231 C5
Latona Rd SE15 140 A6
La Tourne Gdns BR6 227 A5
Lattimer Pl W4 133 C6
Latton Cl KT12 195 A2
Latvia Ct SE17 262 B1
Latymer All Saints CE
Prim Sch N9 17 D2
Latymer Ct W6 112 D2
Latymer Rd N9 17 D3
Latymer Sch The N9 17 C2
Latymer Upper Sch
W6 112 A1
Latymer Way N9 17 C2
Laubin Cl TW1 131 B1
Lauder Cl UB5 84 D5
Lauder Ct N14 16 A4
Lauderdale Dr TW10 153 D1
Lauderdale Mans W9 91 D4
Lauderdale Rd W9 91 D4
Lauderdale Twr EC2 242 A4
Laud St
Croydon CR0 221 A5
Vauxhall SE11 116 B1 260 C2
Laughton Ho 11 SW2 160 C5
Laughton Rd UB5 84 D6
Launcelot Prim Sch
BR1 187 A6
Launcelot Rd BR1,
SE12 187 A6
Launcelot St SE1 251 A1
Launceston Ct CR7 204 C3
Launceston Gdns UB6 65 C1
Launceston Pl
W8 114 A3 256 A5
Launceston Rd UB6 87 C6
Launch St E14 120 A3
Laundress La N16 74 A5
Laundry La 7 N1 73 A1
Laundry Mews SE23 162 D4
Laundry Rd
W6 135 A6 264 A5
Launton Dr DA6 146 D1
Laura Cl
Enfield EN1 17 C6
Wanstead E11 55 C4
Laura Ct HA2 24 A1
Lauradale Rd N2 48 D5
Laura Pl E5 74 C4
Laurel Ave TW1 152 D3
Laurel Bank Gdns 3
SW6 135 B3
Laurel Bank Rd EN2 5 B4
Laurel Cl
Sidcup DA14 168 A1
8 Upper Holloway N19 71 C6
Upper Tooting SW17 180 C5
Laurel Cres CR0 223 C5
Laurel Ct
Dalston E8 73 D1
2 Putney SW15 156 D6
9 Rotherhithe SE16 119 A5
South Norwood SE25 205 C4
8 Wembley HA0 88 A5
Laurel Dr N21 16 C4
Laurel Gdns
Bromley BR1 210 A5
Chingford E4 19 D4
Ealing W7 108 C5
Edgware NW7 11 B1
Hounslow TW4 129 A1
Laurel Gr
Forest Hill SE26 185 A6
Penge SE20 184 C3
Laurel Ho
Brentford W5 109 C2
9 Deptford SE8 141 B6
5 Hamstead NW3 69 D2
Morden SM4 201 D4
Laurel La UB7 104 A2
Laurel Manor SM2 218 A1
Laurel Mead Ct 8 E18 37 A2
Laurel Pk HA3 24 D3
Laurel Rd
Barnes SW13 134 A3
Teddington TW12 174 B5
Wimbledon SW20 178 B2
Laurel St E8 73 D2
Laurels The
8 Belvedere DA17 125 C1
2 Buckhurst Hill IG9 21 C3
Bushey WD23 8 C2
Finchley N3 29 D4
Shortlands BR2 209 A5
9 Sundridge BR1 187 B2
Laurel View N12 13 D1
Laurel Way
Snaresbrook E18 54 D5
Woodside Pk N20 13 C1
Laurence Ct E10 53 D2
Laurence Mews 12
W12 112 A4
Laurence Pountney Hill
EC4 252 C6
Laurence Pountney La
EC4 252 D6
Laurie Gr SE14 141 A4
Laurie Ho
Newington SE1 261 D5
Notting Hill
W8 113 C5 245 A3
Laurie Rd W7 86 C2
Laurier Rd
Croydon CR0 205 D2
Dartmouth Pk NW5 71 B5
Laurimel Cl HA7 25 B4
Laurino Pl WD23 8 A2
Lauriston Apartments 6
N17 51 D6
Lauriston Ho 6 E9 74 D1
Lauriston Lo NW6 69 B2
Lauriston Rd
Homerton E9 74 D1
Wimbledon SW19 178 D4
Lauriston Sch E9 96 D6
Lausanne Rd
Hornsey N8 50 C5
St Johns SE15 140 C4
Lavehham Ho E17 35 D2
Lavell St N16 73 B4
Lavender Ave
Mitcham CR4 180 D2
North Cheam KT4, SM3 216 C5
Welsh Harp NW9 45 A1
Lavender Cl
Bromley Comm BR2 210 A3
South Kensington SW3 266 D5
Wallington SM5 219 B4
Lavender Ct
Colney Hatch N12 30 C4
East Molesey KT8 195 D6
Edgware HA8 27 A5
Feltham TW14 150 B5
South Lambeth SW4 270 B1
Sutton SM2 218 A1
Lavender Gdns
Clapham SW11 136 D1
Enfield EN2 4 D4
Stanmore HA3 24 C4
Lavender Gr
Dalston E8 74 A1
Mitcham CR4 180 C2
Lavender Hill
Clapham SW11 137 A2
Enfield EN2 4 D4
Lavender Ho
8 Richmond TW9 132 D4
14 Rotherhithe SE16 118 D5
Lavender Pl IG1 78 D3
Lavender Prim Sch EN2 5 C5
Lavender Rd
Battersea SW11 136 B2
Enfield EN2 5 B4
Hillingdon UB8 82 B2
Rotherhithe SE16 119 A5
Sutton SM1 218 B4
Thornton Heath CR0 204 B3
Wallington SM5 219 A4
West Ewell KT19 214 D2
Lavender Rise UB7 104 C4
Lavender St E15 76 C2
Lavender Sweep
SW11 136 D1
Lavender Terr 12
SW11 136 C2
Lavender Vale SM6 219 D2
Lavender Way CR0 206 D3
Lavender Wlk SW11 136 D1
Lavendon Ho NW8 237 B6
Lavengro Rd SE27 161 A2
Lavenham Rd SW18 157 C3
Lavernock Rd DA7 147 C3
Lavers Rd N16 73 C5
Laverstoke Gdns
SW15 156 A4
Laverton Mews SW5 255 D3
Laverton Pl SW5 255 D3
Lavidge Rd SE9 166 B2
Lavina Gr N1 233 C4
Lavington Cl E9 75 B2
Lavington Rd
Ealing W13 109 B5
Wallington CR0 220 B4
Lavington St
SE1 116 D5 251 D3
Lavinia Ct BR1 186 C3
Lavisham Ho BR1 187 B5
Lawdale Jun Sch E2 96 A4
Lawdon Gdns CR0 220 D4
Lawford Rd
Chiswick W4 133 A5
De Beauvoir Town N1 73 C1
Kentish Town NW5 71 C2
Lawfords Wharf 18
NW1 71 C1
Law Ho IG11 102 A5
Lawless Ho 5 E14 120 A6
Lawless St 12 E14 119 D6
Lawley Ho 11 TW1 153 D5
Lawley Rd N14 15 B4
Lawley St E5 74 C4
Lawman Ct 2 TW9 132 B4
Lawn Cl
Edmonton N9 17 D4
Kingston u T KT3 177 C1
Ruislip HA4 61 D5
Sundridge BR1 187 B3
Lawn Cres TW9 132 C3
Lawn Farm Gr RM6 59 A5
Lawnfield Ct NW6 68 D1
Lawn Gdns W7 108 C5

Lawn House Cl E14 ... 120 A4
Lawn La SW8 .. 138 B6 270 C6
Lawn Mans EN5 ... 1 B1
Lawn Rd
Beckenham BR3 ... 185 B3
Maitland Pk NW3 ... 70 D3
Lawns Ct HA9 ... 66 C6
Lawnside SE3 ... 142 D1
Lawns The
Belmont SM2 ... 217 A1
Blackheath SE3 ... 142 D2
Chingford E4 ... 35 C5
Harrow HA5 ... 23 D3
Sidcup DA14 ... 190 B6
South Norwood SE19 ... 183 B2
Stoke Newington N16 ... 73 C3
1 Wimbledon SW19 ... 179 B5
Lawn Terr SE3 ... 142 C2
Lawn The UB2 ... 107 C1
Lawn Vale HA5 ... 23 A1
Lawrence Ave
Edmonton N13 ... 32 D6
Higham Hill E17 ... 34 D2
Little Ilford E12 ... 78 C4
Mill Hill NW7 ... 27 D6
New Malden KT3 ... 199 C2
Stonebridge NW10 ... 89 B6
Lawrence Bldgs 1 N16 ... 73 D5
Lawrence Camp Cl N20 ... 14 B1
Lawrence Cl
Bow E3 ... 97 C5
6 Shepherd's Bush W12 ... 112 B6
West Green N15 ... 51 C5
Lawrence Cres
Dagenham RM10 ... 81 D5
Edgware HA8 ... 26 C1
Lawrence Ct
Hornsey N10 ... 49 C6
Mill Hill NW7 ... 27 C5
4 South Acton W3 ... 111 A3
Stoke Newington N16 ... 73 D5
5 Woodford IG8 ... 37 C4
Lawrence Dr UB10 ... 61 A4
Lawrence Est TW4 ... 128 C1
Lawrence Gdns NW7 ... 11 D1
Lawrence Hall E13 ... 99 B3
Lawrence Hill E4 ... 19 C2
Lawrence Ho
Bowes Pk N22 ... 32 B4
20 Camden Town NW1 ... 71 B1
Westminster SW1 ... 259 D3
Lawrence La EC2 ... 242 B2
Lawrence Mans SW3 .. 267 A5
Lawrence Pl N1 ... 233 B6
Lawrence Rd
Coney Hall BR4 ... 225 A4
Ealing W5 ... 109 D2
Edmonton N18 ... 34 B6
Erith DA8 ... 147 D5
Hampton TW12 ... 173 B3
Hillingdon UB4 ... 83 A5
Hounslow TW4 ... 128 C1
Pinner HA5 ... 40 D4
Richmond TW10 ... 175 C6
South Norwood SE25 ... 205 D5
Tottenham N15 ... 51 C5
Upton Pk E6 ... 100 A6
West Ham E13 ... 99 B6
Lawrence St
Canning Town E16 ... 98 D2
Chelsea SW3 .. 136 C6 267 A5
Mill Hill NW7 ... 27 D6
Lawrence Trad Est SE10 ... 120 C2
Lawrence Univ SW7 ... 256 B3
Lawrence Way NW10 ... 67 B5
Lawrence Weaver Cl SM4 ... 201 C3
Lawrence Yd N15 ... 51 C5
Lawrie Ct HA3 ... 24 D3
Lawrie Park Ave SE26 ... 184 B5
Lawrie Park Cres SE26 ... 184 B5
Lawrie Park Gdns SE26 ... 184 B5
Lawrie Park Rd SE26 .. 184 C5
Laws Cl SE25 ... 205 B5
Lawson Cl
Ilford IG1 ... 79 B3
Newham E16 ... 99 C2
Wimbledon SW19 ... 156 D1
Lawson Ct
1 Finsbury Pk N4 ... 50 B1
13 Surbiton KT6 ... 197 D2
Lawson Gdns HA5 ... 40 B6
Lawson Ho
17 Shepherd's Bush W12 ... 112 B6
1 Woolwich SE18 ... 144 C6
Lawson Rd
Enfield EN3 ... 6 C4
Southall UB1 ... 85 C3
Law St SE1 ... 117 B3 262 D6
Lawton Rd
Barnet EN4 ... 2 B2
Bow E3 ... 97 A4
Leytonstone E10 ... 54 A1
Laxcon Cl NW10 ... 67 B3
Laxey Rd BR6 ... 227 D2
Laxfield Ct E8 ... 96 A6
Laxley Cl SE5 ... 138 D5
Laxmi Ct N3 ... 29 B2
Laxton Ct CR7 ... 205 A5
Laxton Path 1 SE4 ... 140 D1
Laxton Pl NW1 ... 238 D6
Layard Rd
Enfield EN1 ... 5 D4
Rotherhithe SE16 ... 118 B2
South Norwood CR7 ... 183 B1
Layard Sq SE16 ... 118 B2
Laybourne Ho 18 E14 ... 119 C4
Laycock Prim Sch N1 .. 72 D2
Laycock St N1 ... 72 C2
Layer Gdns W3 ... 110 C6
Layfield Cl NW4 ... 46 B2
Layfield Cres NW4 ... 46 B2
Layfield Ho 1 SE10 ... 121 A1
Layfield Rd NW4 ... 46 B2
Laymarsh Cl DA17 ... 125 B3
Laymead Cl UB5 ... 63 A2
Laystall Ct EC1 ... 241 A5
Laystall St EC1 ... 241 A5
Layton Cres CR0 ... 220 D3
Layton Ct TW8 ... 109 D1
Layton Pl TW9 ... 132 C4
Layton Rd
Brentford TW8 ... 109 D1
Hounslow TW3 ... 129 D1
Layton's La TW16 ... 171 D1
Layzell Wlk SE9 ... 165 D3
Lazar Wlk 2 N7 ... 72 B6
Leabank Cl HA1 ... 64 C5
Leabank Sq E9 ... 75 C2
Leabank View N15 ... 52 A3
Leabourne Rd N16 ... 52 A2
LEA BRIDGE ... 74 D5
Lea Bridge Rd E10 ... 53 C2
Lea Cl TW2 ... 151 B4
Lea Cotts 10 CR4 ... 181 A1
Lea Cres HA4 ... 61 D4
Leacroft Ave SW12 ... 158 D4
Leacroft Cl
Southgate N21 ... 16 D2
3 Yiewsley UB7 ... 104 A6
Lea Ct
3 Bedford Pk W12 ... 111 C4
1 Chingford E4 ... 20 A2
3 Hillingdon UB10 ... 82 D3
2 Newham E13 ... 99 A4
Leadale Ave E4 ... 19 C2
Leadale Rd N16 ... 52 A3
Leadbeaters Cl 8 N11 ... 30 D5
Leadbetter Ct 12 NW10 ... 67 B1
Leadenhall Mkt EC3 ... 243 A1
Leadenhall Pl EC3 ... 243 A1
Leadenhall St EC3 ... 95 C1 243 A1
Leadenham Ct 15 E3 ... 97 C3
Leader Ave E12 ... 78 C3
Leadings The HA9 ... 67 A5
Leaf Cl KT7, KT8 ... 196 C4
Leaf Gr SE27 ... 182 C5
Leaf Ho
Barnet EN5 ... 1 D1
9 Harrow HA1 ... 42 D4
Leafield Cl SW16 ... 182 D4
Leafield La DA14 ... 169 B1
Leafield Rd
Merton SW19, SW20 ... 201 B6
Sutton SM1 ... 217 C6
Leafy Gr BR2 ... 225 C3
Leafy Oak Rd SE12 ... 165 C1
Leafy Way CR0 ... 221 D6
Lea Gdns HA9 ... 66 B4
Leagrave St E5 ... 74 C5
Lea Hall Gdns E10 ... 53 C1
Lea Hall Rd E10 ... 53 C1
Lea Ho
2 Edmonton N9 ... 18 A1
Lisson Gr NW8 ... 237 A5
Upper Clapton E5 ... 52 C1
Leaholme Way HA4 ... 39 A3
Leahurst Rd SE13 ... 164 B6
Lea Int E9 ... 75 C3
Leake St
Lambeth SE1 ... 251 A1
South Bank SE1 ... 116 B4 250 D2
Lealand Rd N15 ... 51 D3
Leamington Ave
Bromley BR1 ... 187 C5
Farnborough BR6 ... 227 C4
Merton SM4 ... 201 B5
Walthamstow E17 ... 53 C4
Leamington Cl
Bromley BR1 ... 187 C5
Hounslow TW3 ... 152 A6
Plashet E12 ... 78 A3
Leamington Cres HA2 .. 63 B5
Leamington Ct
4 Forest Hill SE26 ... 162 A1
North Acton W3 ... 89 B2
Leamington Gdns IG3 .. 79 D6
Leamington Ho
Edgware HA8 ... 26 B5
4 Kensal Town W11 ... 91 B2
Leamington Pk W3 ... 89 B2
Leamington Pl UB4 ... 83 D3
Leamington Rd UB2 ... 106 D2
Leamington Rd Villas W11 ... 91 B2
Leamington Villas SE13 ... 164 C6
Leamore St W6 ... 112 C2
Leamouth Rd
Newham E6 ... 100 A2
South Bromley E14 ... 98 B1
Leander Ct
11 Edgware NW9 ... 27 C2
27 Hackney E9 ... 74 C1
St Johns SE8 ... 141 C4
5 Surbiton KT6 ... 197 D2
Leander Rd
Northolt UB5 ... 85 C5
Thornton Heath CR7 ... 204 B5
Tulse Hill SW2 ... 160 C5
Lea Park Trad Est E10 .. 53 B1
Lea Rd
2 Beckenham BR3 ... 185 C1
Enfield EN2 ... 5 B4
Southall UB2 ... 107 A2
Learner Dr HA2 ... 63 C6
Learoyd Gdns E6 ... 122 C6
Leary Ho SE11 ... 260 D1
Leas Cl KT9 ... 214 B1
Leas Dale SE9 ... 166 C1
Leas Gn BR7 ... 189 D4
Leaside Ave N10 ... 49 A5
Leaside Bsns Ctr EN3 ... 7 B3
Leaside Ct UB10 ... 82 D4
Leaside Ho 4 E5 ... 52 B1
Leaside Mans N10 ... 49 A6
Leaside Rd E5 ... 52 C1
Leasowes Rd E10 ... 53 C1
Lea Sq 22 E3 ... 97 B6
Leas The SE18 ... 144 D4
Leatherbottle Gn DA18 ... 125 B3
Leather Cl CR4 ... 181 A1
Leatherdale St
32 Bethnal Green E1 ... 96 C3
19 Globe Town E1 ... 96 D4
Leather Gdns E15 ... 98 C6
Leatherhead Cl N16 ... 51 D1
Leatherhead Rd KT9 .. 213 D1
Leather La EC1 .. 94 C2 241 B4
Leathermarket Ct SE1 .. 253 A1
Leathermarket St SE1 ... 117 C4 253 A1
Leather Rd SE16 ... 118 D2
Leathersellers Cl 5 EN5 ... 1 A2
Leathsale Rd HA2 ... 63 D5
Leathwaite Rd SW11 .. 158 D6
Leathwell Rd SE8 ... 141 D3
Lea Valley Prim Sch N17 ... 34 A3
Lea Valley Rd EN3 ... 19 B5
Lea Valley Technopark N17 ... 52 A6
Lea Valley Trad Est N18 ... 34 D5
Leaveland Cl BR3 ... 207 C5
Leaver Gdns UB6 ... 86 C5
Leavesden Rd HA7 ... 25 A4
Lea View Ho E5 ... 52 B1
Lebanon Ave TW13 ... 172 D5
Lebanon Ct 10 TW1 ... 153 B4
Lebanon Gdns SW18 .. 157 C5
Lebanon Park Mans TW1 ... 153 B4
Lebanon Pk TW1 ... 153 B4
Lebanon Rd
Croydon CR0 ... 205 C1
Lebanon Rd *continued*
Wandsworth SW18 ... 157 C6
Lebanon Road Sta CR0 ... 221 C6
Lebrun Sq SE3 ... 143 B2
Lebus Ho NW8 ... 230 A3
Le Chateau CR0 ... 221 B5
Lechmere App IG8 ... 37 D1
Lechmere Ave IG8 ... 37 D1
Lechmere Rd NW2 ... 68 B2
Leckford Rd SW18 ... 158 A3
Leckhampton Pl 23 SW2 ... 160 C4
Leckwith Ave DA7 ... 147 A6
Lecky Ho NW2 ... 68 B4
Lecky St SW7 .. 114 B1 256 C2
Leclair Ho SE3 ... 143 B2
L'Ecole des Petits Sch SW6 ... 135 D3
Leconfield Ave SW13, SW15 ... 133 D2
Leconfield Ho SE5 ... 139 C2
Leconfield Rd N5 ... 73 B4
Lector Ct EC1 ... 241 B5
Leda Ave EN3 ... 6 D5
Leda Ct 9 SW9 ... 138 C5
Ledalle Ho NW2 ... 68 B5
Ledam Bldg EC1 ... 241 A4
Leda Rd SE18 ... 122 B3
Ledbury Ho 12 SE22 ... 139 C2
Ledbury Mews N W11 .. 91 C1
Ledbury Mews W W11 ... 245 A6
Ledbury Pl 10 CR0 ... 221 A4
Ledbury Rd
Croydon CR0 ... 221 B4
Kensington W11 ... 91 C1
Ledbury St SE15 ... 140 A5
Ledo Ho 1 N16 ... 73 B4
Ledrington Rd SE19 ... 184 A4
Ledway Dr HA9 ... 44 B2
LEE ... 164 D5
Lee Ave RM6 ... 59 A3
Leechcroft Ave DA15 ... 167 D6
Leechcroft Rd SM6 ... 219 A5
Lee Church St SE13 ... 142 C1
Lee Cl
Higham Hill E17 ... 34 D2
New Barnet EN5 ... 2 A1
Lee Conservancy Rd E9 ... 75 B3
Leecroft Rd EN5 ... 1 A1
Lee Ct SE13 ... 142 B1
Leeds Ct
7 Carshalton SM5 ... 218 D5
Catford SE6 ... 163 D1
Clerkenwell EC1 ... 241 C6
Leeds Rd IG1 ... 57 B1
Leeds St N18 ... 34 A5
Leegate SE12 ... 164 D6
Lee Green SE12 ... 142 D1
Lee High Rd SE12, SE13 ... 142 C1
Lee Ho
3 Kentish Town N19 ... 71 D3
Wimbledon SW19 ... 179 D4
Leeke St WC1 ... 94 B4 233 C2
Leeland Mans 15 W13 ... 109 A5
Leeland Rd W13 ... 109 A5
Leeland Terr W13 ... 109 A5
Leeland Way NW10 ... 67 D4
Lee Manor Sch SE13 ... 164 C5
Lee Mews BR3 ... 207 A6
Lee Park Way N9, N18 .. 19 A1
Lee Pk SE3 ... 142 D2
Lee Rd
Enfield EN1 ... 18 A5
Lewisham SE3 ... 142 D1
Merton SW19 ... 179 D2
Mill Hill NW7 ... 28 D3
Wembley UB6 ... 87 C6
Leerdam Dr E14 ... 120 A3
Lees Ct W1 ... 248 A6
Lees Ho SE17 ... 262 D1
Leeside EN5 ... 13 A5
Leeside Cres NW11 ... 47 C3
Leeside Ind Est N17 ... 34 B3
Leeside Rd N17 ... 34 B4
Leeside Trad Est N17 ... 34 C3
Leeside Works N17 ... 34 C3
Leeson Ho 7 TW1 ... 153 B4
Leeson Rd 12 SE24 ... 138 C1
Leesons Hill BR5, BR7 .. 211 D6
Leesons Way BR5 ... 189 D1
Lees Par UB10 ... 82 D3
Lees Pl W1 ... 115 A6 248 A6
Lees Rd UB8 ... 82 D3
Lee St E8 ... 95 D6
Lee Sta SE12 ... 165 A5
Lees The CR0 ... 223 B6
Leet Ct N16 ... 73 B4
Lee Terr SE3 ... 142 C2
Lee Valley Country Pk EN3 ... 7 C4
Lee Valley L Ctr N9 ... 19 A3
Lee Valley Riding Ctr E10 ... 52 D1
Lee Valley Sp Ctr E10 ... 75 D4
Leeve Ho 7 W9 ... 91 B4
Lee View EN2 ... 4 D4
Leeview Ct 7 E4 ... 20 A3
Leeward Ct 3 E1 ... 118 A5
Leeward Gdns SW19 ... 179 B5
Leeway SE8 ... 119 B1
Leeway Cl HA5 ... 23 B3
Leewood Cl SE12 ... 165 A5
Lefevre Wlk E3 ... 97 C6
Leffern Rd W12 ... 112 A4
Leff Ho 9 NW6 ... 69 A1
Lefroy Ho SE1 ... 252 A1
Lefroy Rd W12 ... 111 D4
Legard Rd N5 ... 72 D5
Legat Ct N4 ... 51 A4
Legatt Rd SE9 ... 165 D6
Leggatt Rd E15 ... 98 A5
Legge St SE13 ... 164 A6
Leghorn Rd
Plumstead SE18 ... 123 B1
Willesden Green NW10 .. 90 A5
Legion Cl N1 ... 72 C1
Legion Ct SM4 ... 201 C3
Legion Rd UB6 ... 86 A5
Legion Terr E3 ... 97 C6
Legion Way N12 ... 30 C3
Legrace Ave TW4, TW5 ... 128 D3
Leicester Ave CR4 ... 204 A5
Leicester Cl KT4 ... 216 C4
Leicester Ct
46 Paddington W2 ... 91 C2
St James WC2 ... 249 D6
5 Twickenham TW1 ... 153 D5
Leicester Gdns IG3 ... 57 C2
Leicester Ho
4 Brixton SW9 ... 138 D2
Carshalton SM5 ... 218 C5
5 Putney SW15 ... 156 C4
2 Thames Ditton KT7 .. 197 A2
Leicester Mews N2 ... 48 C6
Leicester Pl WC2 ... 249 D6
Leicester Rd
Barnet EN5 ... 1 D1
Croydon CR0 ... 205 C2
East Finchley N2 ... 48 C6
Stonebridge NW10 ... 67 B1
Wanstead E11 ... 55 B4
Leicester Sq* WC2 ... 115 D6 249 D5
Leicester Square Sta WC2 ... 115 D6 249 D6
Leicester St WC2 ... 249 D6
Leigham Ave SW16 ... 160 A1
Leigham Cl
Streatham SW16 ... 182 B6
9 Wallington SM6 ... 219 C2
Leigham Court Rd SW16 ... 182 C6
Leigham Dr TW7 ... 130 C5
Leigham Hall 3 SW16 ... 160 A1
Leigham Hall Par 2 SW16 ... 160 A1
Leigham Vale SE27, SW16, SW2 ... 160 C2
Leigh Ave IG4 ... 55 D5
Leigh Cl KT3 ... 199 B5
Leigh Close Ind Est KT3 ... 199 B5
Leigh Cres CR0 ... 223 D1
Leigh Ct
Harrow HA2 ... 42 C1
22 Tulse Hill SW2 ... 160 C5
3 Woodford E18 ... 37 A1
Leighfield Ho 5 N4 ... 51 A2
Leigh Gdns NW10 ... 90 C5
Leigh Ho
4 Kingston u T KT2 ... 176 D4
9 Putney SW15 ... 156 A6
Leigh Hunt Dr N14 ... 15 D3
Leigh Orchard Cl SW16 ... 160 B1
Leigh Pl
Feltham TW13 ... 150 C3
Holborn EC1 ... 241 A4
Welling DA16 ... 146 A3
Leigh Rd
Highbury N5 ... 72 D4
Isleworth TW3 ... 130 B1
Leytonstone E10 ... 54 A2
Leigh Rd *continued*
Wallend E6 ... 78 C2
Leigh St WC1 ... 94 A4 233 A1
Leigh The KT2 ... 177 C3
Leighton Ave
Little Ilford E12 ... 78 C3
Pinner HA5 ... 41 A6
Leighton Cl HA8 ... 26 C1
Leighton Cres NW5 ... 71 C3
Leighton Ct NW7 ... 28 D3
Leighton Gdns
Thornton Heath CR0 ... 204 D1
Willesden Green NW10 ... 90 C5
Leighton Gr NW5 ... 71 C3
Leighton Ho 7 KT6 ... 198 A3
Leighton House (Art Gall & Mus)* W14 ... 254 D6
Leighton Pl NW5 ... 71 C3
Leighton Rd
Ealing W13 ... 109 A4
Enfield EN1 ... 18 A6
Harrow HA3 ... 24 B1
Kentish Town NW5 ... 71 C3
Leighton St CR0 ... 204 D1
Leila Parnell Pl 14 SE7 ... 143 C6
Leinster Ave SW14 ... 133 A1
Leinster Gdns W2 ... 114 A6 246 A6
Leinster Mews
7 Barnet EN5 ... 1 A2
Bayswater W2 ... 246 A6
Leinster Pl W2 ... 236 A1
Leinster Rd N10 ... 49 B5
Leinster Sq W2 ... 91 D1
Leinster Terr W2 ... 246 A6
Leisure Way N12 ... 30 B3
Leitch Ho 8 NW8 ... 70 B1
Leith Cl NW9 ... 45 B1
Leithcote Gdns SW16 .. 182 B6
Leithcote Path SW16 .. 160 B1
Leith Hill BR5 ... 190 A2
Leith Hill Gn BR5 ... 190 A2
Leith Ho
7 Kentish Town N7 ... 71 D3
13 Streatham SW2 ... 160 B4
Leith Mans W9 ... 91 D4
Leith Rd N22 ... 32 D2
Leith Towers 7 SM2 .. 217 D1
Leith Yd 3 NW6 ... 91 C6
Lela Ave TW4, TW5 ... 128 C3
Lelitia Cl E8 ... 96 A6
Lely Ho 3 UB5 ... 84 D5
Leman St E1 ... 96 A1
Lemark Cl HA7 ... 25 C4
Le May Ave SE12 ... 165 B1
Lemmon Rd SE10 ... 142 C6
Lemna Ct E11 ... 54 C2
Lemna Rd E11 ... 54 C2
Le Moal Ho 28 E1 ... 96 C2
Lemon Gr TW14 ... 150 A3
Lemonwell Ct SE9 ... 167 A6
Lemonwell Dr SE9 ... 167 A6
Lemsford Cl N15 ... 52 A4
Lemsford Ct N4 ... 73 A6
Lena Cres N9 ... 18 C2
Lena Gardens Prim Sch W6 ... 112 C3
Lena Gdns W6 ... 112 C3
Lena Kennedy Cl E4 ... 36 A4
Lenan Ct W13 ... 109 C5
Len Clifton Ho 12 SE18 ... 122 B2
Lendal Terr 7 SW4 ... 137 D2
Lenelby Rd KT6 ... 198 C1
Len Freeman Pl SW6 .. 264 C5
Lenham 11 NW5 ... 71 A2
Lenham Ho SE1 ... 252 D1
Lenham Rd
Erith DA7 ... 147 B6
Lewisham SE12 ... 142 D1
South Norwood CR7 ... 183 B1
Sutton SM1 ... 218 A3
Lennard Ave BR4 ... 224 C6
Lennard Cl BR4 ... 224 C6
Lennard Rd
Bromley BR2 ... 210 B1
Croydon CR0 ... 205 A1
Penge BR3 ... 185 A4
Lennon Rd NW2 ... 68 C2
Lennox Gdns
Croydon CR0 ... 220 D4
Knightsbridge SW1 ... 114 D3 257 C5
Redbridge IG1 ... 56 B1
Willesden NW10 ... 67 D4

Lennox Gdns Mews SW1 257 C4
Lennox Ho
7 Belvedere DA17 125 C3
10 Hackney E9 74 C2
4 Twickenham TW1 153 D5
Lennox Rd
Finsbury Pk N4, N7 72 C6
Walthamstow E17 53 C3
Lenor Cl DA6 147 A1
Lensbury Way SE2 124 D3
Lens Rd E7 77 C1
Lenthall Ho SW1 259 B1
Lenthall Rd E8 74 A1
Lenthorp Rd SE10 120 D2
Lentmead Rd BR1 164 D1
Lenton Rise TW9 132 A2
Lenton St SE18 123 B2
Len Williams Ct NW6 91 C5
Leo Ct 4 TW8 131 D5
Leof Cres SE6 185 D5
Leominster Rd SM4 202 A3
Leominster Wlk SM4 202 A3
Leonard Ave SM4 202 A4
Leonard Ct
Bloomsbury WC1 240 A6
Harrow HA3 24 C3
Kensington W8 255 A6
Leonard Day Ho 3
NW5 71 B2
Leonard Ho 10 E17 54 A5
Leonard Pl 6 N16 73 C4
Leonard Rd
Chingford E4 35 C4
Edmonton N9 18 A1
Forest Gate E7 77 A4
Mitcham CR4, SW16 181 C2
Southall UB2 106 D2
Leonard Robbins Path 3
SE28 124 B6
Leonard St
Broadgate
EC2 95 B3 242 D6
Newham E16 122 A5
Leonora Ho W9 236 A6
Leontine Cl SE15 140 A5
Leopards Ct EC1 241 A4
Leopold Ave SW19 179 B5
Leopold Bldgs 14 E2 95 D4
Leopold Ct 12 SW19 179 B5
Leopold Mews E9 96 C6
Leopold Prim Sch
NW10 67 D1
Leopold Rd
Ealing W5 110 B5
East Finchley N2 48 B6
Edmonton N18 34 B5
Walthamstow E17 53 C4
Willesden NW10 67 C1
Wimbledon SW19 179 B5
Leopold St E3 97 B2
Leopold Terr SW19 179 C5
Leopold Wlk SE11 260 C1
Leo St SE15 140 B5
Leo Yd EC1 241 D5
Leppoc Rd SW4 159 D6
Leroy St SE1 117 C2 263 A4
Lerry Cl W14 264 D6
Lerwick Ct 4 EN1 17 C6
Lerwick Ho SW18 136 A1
Lescombe Cl SE23 163 A1
Lescombe Rd SE23,
SE6 163 A1
Lesley Cl DA5 169 D4
Lesley Ct
8 Wallington SM6 219 B4
Westminster SW1 259 C5
Leslie Gdns SM2 217 C1
Leslie Gr CR0 205 C1
Leslie Grove Pl CR0 205 C1
Leslie Park Rd CR0 205 C1
Leslie Prince Ct 8
SE5 139 B5
Leslie Rd
East Finchley N2 48 B6
Leyton E11 76 B4
Newham E16 99 B1
Leslie Smith Sq 7
SE18 144 C6
Lessar Ave SW4 159 C5
Lessar Ct SW4 159 C5
Lessingham Ave
Ilford IG5 56 C6
Upper Tooting SW17 181 A6
Lessing St SE23 163 A4
Lessness Ave DA7 146 D5
LESSNESS HEATH 125 D1
Lessness Heath Prim Sch
DA17 125 C1
Lessness Pk DA17 125 C1
Lessness Rd
Belvedere DA17 125 C1
Morden SM4 202 A4
Lester Ave E16 98 C3
Lester Ct 42 E3 97 D4
Lester Ho IG8 36 B3
Lestock Cl 2 SE25 206 A6
Lestock Ho SE3 143 D4
Lestor Ct TW7 130 D2
Leswin Pl N16 73 D5
Leswin Rd N16 73 D5
Letchford Gdns NW10 90 A4
Letchford Mews NW10 90 A4
Letchmore Ho 7 W10 90 C3
Letchworth Ave
TW14 149 D4
Letchworth Cl
Bromley BR2 209 A4
South Oxhey WD19 22 D5
Letchworth Dr BR2 209 A4
Letchworth St SW17 180 D6
Lethaby Ho 15 SW4 138 B1
Lethbridge Cl SE13 142 A3
Letterstone Rd SW6 264 C3
Lettice St
SW6 135 B4 264 D1
Lett Rd E15 76 B1
Lettsom St SE5 139 C3
Lettsom Wlk 1 E13 99 A5
Leucha Rd E17 53 A4
Levana Cl SW19 157 A3
Levant Ho 17 E1 96 D3
Levehurst Ho SE27 183 A5
Levehurst Way SW4,
SW9 138 A3
Leven Cl WD19 22 D5
Levendale Rd SE23 163 B2
Leven Rd E14 98 B1
Leven Way UB3 83 C1
Lever Ct 15 E9 74 D2
Leverett St SW3 257 B4
Leverholme Gdns
SE9 188 C6
Leverington Pl N1 235 D1
Leverson St SW16 181 C4
Lever St EC1 95 A4 235 A1
Leverstock Ho SW3 257 B2
Leverton Pl NW5 71 C3
Leverton St NW5 71 C3
Levett Gdns IG3 80 A5
Levett Ho 8 SW16 181 C5
Levett Rd IG11 79 C2
Levine Gdns IG11 102 D5
Levison Way 2 N19 49 D1
Levita Ho NW1 232 D2
Levyne Ct EC1 241 A6
Lewes Cl UB5 63 C2
Lewes Ct 3 CR4 202 D6
Lewesdon Cl 13
SW19 156 D3
Lewes Ho
Bermondsey SE1 253 B2
Peckham SE15 140 A6
Lewes Rd
Bromley BR1 187 D1
Colney Hatch N12 30 C5
Leweston Pl N16 51 D2
Lewey Ho E3 97 B3
Lewgars Ave NW9 45 A3
Lewin Ct
4 Plumstead SE18 123 C2
Streatham SW16 182 A4
Lewing Cl BR6 211 C1
Lewington Ct EN3 6 D6
Lewin Rd
Bexley DA6 147 A1
Mortlake SW14 133 B2
Streatham SW16 181 D4
Lewin Terr TW14 149 B4
Lewis Ave E17 35 C2
Lewis Cl N14 15 C4
Lewis Cres NW10 67 B3
Lewis Ct 5 SE16 118 B1
Lewis Gdns N2 30 B1
Lewis Gr SE13 142 A2
LEWISHAM 142 A1
Lewisham Bridge Prim
Sch SE13 141 D2
Lewisham Bsns Ctr
SE14 140 D6
Lewisham Coll SE4 141 C3
Lewisham Ct EN3 7 C5
Lewisham Ctr SE13 142 A2
Lewisham High St
SE13 163 D6
Lewisham Hill SE13 142 A3
Lewisham Hospl
SE13 163 D6
Lewisham Pk SE13 164 A5
Lewisham Rd SE13 142 A3
Lewisham St SW1 249 D1
Lewisham Sta SE13 142 A2
Lewisham Way SE4,
SE14 141 B4
Lewis Ho 2 E4 35 C5
Lewis King Ho BR1 187 B3
Lewis Pl E8 74 A3
Lewis Rd
Bexley DA16 146 C2
Mitcham CR4 180 C1
19 Richmond TW10 153 D6
Sidcup DA14 168 C1
Southall UB1 107 A4
Sutton SM1 217 D4
Lewis Silkin Ho 9
SE15 140 C6
Lewis Sports & L Ctr
SE19 183 D2
Lewis St NW1 71 B2
Lewiston Cl KT4 200 B2
Lewis Way RM10 81 D2
Lexden Dr RM6 58 B3
Lexden Rd
Acton W3 110 D5
Mitcham CR4 203 D5
Lexdon Ct RM6 58 B3
Lexfield Ho N5 73 A4
Lexham Ct UB6 86 B6
Lexham Gardens Mews
W8 255 D5
Lexham Gdns
W8 113 D2 255 C4
Lexham Ho 9 IG11 101 B6
Lexham Mews
W8 113 C2 255 B4
Lexham Wlk W8 255 D5
Lexington Pl KT1 175 D2
Lexington St
W1 115 C6 249 B6
Lexton Gdns SW12 159 D3
Leyborne Ave W13 109 C4
Leyborne Pk TW9 132 C4
Leybourne Cl BR2 209 A3
Leybourne Ct 1
SE25 206 A6
Leybourne Ho 20
SE15 140 C6
Leybourne Rd
17 Camden Town NW1 71 B1
Hillingdon UB10 83 A6
Leytonstone E11 54 D1
Queensbury NW9 44 C4
Leybourne St 5 NW1 71 B1
Leybridge Ct SE12 165 A6
Leyburn Cl E17 53 D5
Leyburn Gdns CR0 221 C6
Leyburn Gr N18 34 A4
Leyburn Ho SE18 144 A5
Leyburn Rd N18 34 B4
Leyden Mans 7 N19 50 A2
Leyden St E1 95 D2 243 C3
Leydon Cl SE16 118 D5
Leyes Rd E16 99 D1
Leyfield KT4 199 D1
Ley Ho SE1 252 A1
Leyland Ave EN3 7 A3
Leyland Ct 8 N11 31 B6
Leyland Gdns IG8 37 C5
Leyland Ho
6 Canary Wharf
E14 119 D6
12 Richmond TW10 153 C1
Leyland Rd SE12 165 A6
Leylands SW18 157 B5
Leylang Rd SE14 140 D5
Leys Cl
Finchley N12 30 C3
Harrow HA1 42 B4
Leys Ct 9 SW9 138 C3
Leysdown 9 NW5 71 A2
Leysdown Ho SE17 263 B2
Leysdown Rd SE9 166 B2
Leysfield Rd W12 112 A4
Leys Gdns EN4 15 A6
Leyspring Rd E11 54 D1
Leys Rd E EN3 7 A4
Leys Rd W EN3 7 A4
Ley St
Ilford IG1 78 D6
Newbury Pk IG1, IG2 57 B1
Leys The
East Finchley N2 48 A5
Harrow HA3 44 B3
Leyswood Dr IG2 57 C4
Leythe Rd W3 111 A4
LEYTON 76 B5
Leyton Bsns Ctr E10 75 C6
Leyton Ct SE23 162 C3
Leyton Grange E10 53 C1
Leyton Green Rd E10 54 A3
Leyton Green Twrs
E10 54 A3
Leyton Ind Village E10 52 D2
Leyton Link Est E10 53 A2
Leyton Midland Road Sta
E10 54 A1
Leyton Mills E10 76 A4
Leyton Park Rd E10 76 A5
Leyton Rd
Merton SW19 180 A3
Stratford E15 76 B2
Leyton Sixth Form Coll
E10 54 B3
Leyton Sta E11 76 A5
Leyton Stadium (Leyton
Orient FC) E10 75 D5
LEYTONSTONE 54 D1
Leytonstone Bsns & Spec
Sch E11 54 C3
Leytonstone High Road
Sta E11 76 C6
Leytonstone Rd E15 76 C3
Leytonstone Sta E11 54 C1
Leyton Town Ctr E10 76 A5
Leywick St E15 98 C5
Lezayre Rd BR6 227 D2
Liardet St SE14 141 A6
Liberia Rd N5 72 D2
Libert Cl N18 33 D6
Liberty Ave SW19 180 B2
Liberty Ct IG11 102 C5
Liberty Ctr HA0 88 B6
Liberty Ho 11 E1 118 A6
Liberty Mews
Balham SW12 159 B5
Orpington BR6 227 D6
Liberty Sch CR4 180 C1
Liberty St
SW9 138 B4 270 D2
Libra Rd
7 Bow E3 97 B5
Newham E13 99 A5
Library Ct N17 51 D6
Library Mans 4 W12 112 C4
Library Par NW10 89 C6
Library Pl E1 118 B6
Library St SE1 116 D4 251 D1
Libro Ct E4 35 C6
Lichen Ct IG6 56 D6
Lichfield Cl EN4 2 D2
Lichfield Ct
Kingston u T KT6 198 A4
Richmond TW9 132 A1
Lichfield Gdns TW10,
TW9 154 A6
Lichfield Gr N3 29 C1
Lichfield Ho 27 SE5 139 A3
Lichfield Rd
Dagenham RM8 80 C5
Edmonton N9 18 A2
Hounslow TW4 128 C2
Mile End E3 97 A4
Newham E6 99 D4
Northwood HA6 40 A6
Richmond TW9 132 B4
West Hampstead NW2 69 A4
Woodford IG8 36 C6
Lichfield Terr 1
TW9 154 A6
Lichlade Cl 7 BR6 227 D4
Lichport Ct N4 50 D1
Lickey Ho W14 264 D6
Lidbury Rd NW7 29 A4
Lidcote Gdns 22 SW9 138 B3
Liddall Way UB7 104 B5
Liddell Cl HA3 43 D6
Liddell Gdns NW10 90 C5
Liddell Rd NW6 69 C2
Lidding Rd HA3 43 D4
Liddington Rd E15 98 D6
Liddlesdale Ho E 6
KT2 176 D2
Liddlesdale Ho W 5
KT2 176 D2
Liddon Rd
Bromley BR1 209 D6
Newham E13 99 B4
Liden Cl E10, E17 53 B1
Lidfield Rd N16 73 B4
Lidgate Rd 22 SE15 139 D5
Lidiard Rd SW18 158 A2
Lidlington Pl NW1 232 B3
Lido Sq N17 33 B1
Lidyard Rd N19 49 C1
Liffey Ct
Edmonton N9 18 C1
Liffey Ct *continued*
Willesden NW10 68 A1
Liffler Rd SE18 123 C1
Liffords Pl SW13 133 D3
Lifford St SW15 134 D1
Lightcliffe Rd N13 16 C1
Lighter Cl 16 SE16 119 A2
Lighterman Mews 15
E1 96 D1
Lighterman's Rd E14 119 D4
Lightermans Wlk
SW18 135 C1
Lightfoot Rd N8 50 A4
Light Horse Ct SW1 258 A1
Lightley Cl HA0 88 B6
Ligonier St E2 243 C6
Lilac Cl E4 35 B4
Lilac Ct
Colney Hatch N12 30 C4
3 Newham E13 99 C6
Teddington TW11 174 D6
Lilac Gdns
Croydon CR0 223 C5
Ealing W5 109 D3
Hayes UB3 83 C1
Lilac Ho SE4 141 B2
Lilac Pl
Vauxhall
SE11 116 B2 260 C3
Yiewsley UB7 104 B6
Lilac St W12 112 A6
Lilah Mews BR2 186 D1
Lilburne Gdns SE9 166 A6
Lilburne Rd SE9 166 A6
Lilburne Wlk NW10 67 A2
Lile Cres W7 86 C2
Lilestone Est NW8 236 D5
Lilestone Ho NW8 236 D6
Lilestone St
NW8 92 C3 237 A6
Lilford Ho 21 SE5 139 A3
Lilford Rd SE5 138 D3
Lilian Barker Cl SE12 165 A6
Lilian Baylis Ho N1 73 A2
Lilian Baylis Tech Sch
SE11 116 B1 260 D1
Lilian Board Way UB6 64 B3
Lilian Gdns IG8 37 B2
Lilian Rd SW16 181 C2
Lilian Rolfe Ho 5
SE27 183 B6
Lillechurch Rd RM8 80 C2
Lilleshall Rd SM4 202 B3
Lilley Cl E1 118 A5
Lillian Ave W3 110 C4
Lillian Cl 14 N16 73 C5
Lillian Rd SW13 134 B6
Lillie Ho N5 72 C3
Lillie Rd SW6 135 B6 264 C5
Lillie Road Mans SW6 264 B5
Lillieshall Rd SW4 137 C2
Lillie Yd SW6 135 C6 265 A6
Lillington Ho N7 72 C4
Lilliput Ave UB5 85 B6
Lillywhite 21 NW9 27 D2
Lily Albon Ct RM9 81 B4
Lily Cl W14 112 D2
Lily Gdns HA0 87 C5
Lily Ho 7 HA9 66 A3
Lily Pl EC1 241 B4
Lily Rd E17 53 C3
Lilyville Rd
SW6 135 B4 264 C2
Limavady Ho 12 SE18 122 C2
Limborough Ho 5
E14 97 C2
Limbourne Ave RM8 59 B2
Limburg Rd SW11 136 C1
Lime Ave UB7 104 B6
Limeburner La
EC4 94 D1 241 C2
Lime Cl
Bromley BR1 210 A5
Buckhurst Hill IG9 21 D2
Carshalton SM5 218 D6
Harrow HA3 25 A1
Pinner HA5 39 D6
Wapping E1 118 A5
Lime Cres TW16 172 C1
Limecroft Cl KT19 215 B1
Lime Ct
9 Harrow HA1 42 D3
Hendon NW4 28 C1
Kingston u T KT3 198 D6
9 Leyton E11 76 C6
Mitcham CR4 180 B1
Putney SW15 134 B2
Limedene Cl HA5 22 D2
Lime Gr
Barnet N20 13 B3
Lime Gr *continued*
Blackfen DA15 167 D5
Hayes UB3 105 B6
Kingston u T KT3 199 C6
Orpington BR6 226 D6
Ruislip HA4 40 B2
Shepherd's Bush W12 112 C4
Twickenham TW1 153 A5
Walthamstow E4 35 B4
Limeharbour E14 119 D4
Lime Ho 7 TW9 132 D4
LIMEHOUSE 119 A6
Limehouse Cswy E14 119 B6
Limehouse Ct 5 E14 97 C1
Lime House Ct 23 E14 97 B1
Limehouse Cut 4 E14 97 D2
Limehouse Fields Est 14
E14 97 A2
Limehouse Link (Tunnel)
E14 119 B6
Limehouse Sta E14 97 A1
Lime Kiln Dr SE7 143 B6
Limekiln Pl SE19 183 D3
Limekiln Wharf 21
E14 119 B6
Limeleaf Ct HA8 27 A6
Lime Lo 3 TW16 171 D3
Limerick Cl SW12 159 C4
Limerick Ct 1 SW12 159 C4
Lime Row DA18 125 B3
Limerston St
SW10 136 A6 266 B5
Lime St Pas EC3 253 A6
Limes Ave
Barnes SW13 133 D3
Carshalton SM5 202 D1
Croydon CR0 220 C5
Edgware NW7 27 C4
Golders Green NW11 47 A2
North Finchley N12 30 A6
Penge SE20 184 B3
Wanstead E11 55 B5
Limes Ave The N11 31 C5
Limes Cl
Ashford TW15 170 C5
3 Friern Barnet N11 31 C5
Limes Ct
Beckenham BR3 185 D1
Willesden NW6 68 D1
Limesdale Gdns HA8 27 A1
Limes Field Rd SW14 133 C2
Limesford Rd SE15 140 D1
Limes Gdns SW18 157 C5
Limes Gr SE13 142 A1
Limes Rd
Beckenham BR3 185 D1
Thornton Heath CR0 205 B2
Limes Row BR6 226 D3
Lime St
Walthamstow E17 53 A5
Whitechapel
EC3 95 C1 243 A1
Limes The
Camberwell SE5 139 C2
3 Cheam SM2 217 C2
East Molesey KT8 195 D5
Kensington W2 245 B5
Keston Mark BR2 226 A6
Stanmore HA7 9 B2
Limestone Wlk 12
DA18 124 D4
Limes Wlk
Ealing W5 109 D4
Nunhead SE15 140 C1
Lime Terr W7 108 C6
Lime Tree Ave KT10,
KT7 196 C1
Limetree Cl SW2 160 B3
Lime Tree Cl E11 55 C5
Limetree Ct HA5 23 C3
Lime Tree Ct
East Barnet EN4 14 C6
East Finchley N2 47 D6
14 Poplar E3 97 C2
South Croydon CR2 221 A2
Lime Tree Gr CR0 223 B5
Limetree Pl CR4 181 B2
Lime Tree Rd TW5 129 D4
Limetree Wlk 2
SW17 181 A5
Lime Tree Wlk
Bushey WD23 8 C2
Coney Hall BR4 224 D4
Enfield EN2 5 A5
Lime Wlk 11 E15 98 C6
Limewood Cl
Beckenham BR3 208 A4
Ealing W13 87 B1
Walthamstow E17 53 B5
Limewood Ct IG4 56 B4

Limpsfield Ave
Putney SW19 156 D2
Thornton Heath CR7 204 B4
Limscott Ho 35 E3 97 D4
Linacre Cl SE15 140 B2
Linacre Ct W6 112 D1
Linacre Rd NW2 68 B2
Linale Ho N1 235 C3
Linberry Wlk 3 SE8 119 B2
Linchmere Rd SE12 164 D4
Lincoln Ave
Osidge N14 15 C2
Twickenham TW2 152 A2
Wimbledon SW19 156 D1
Lincoln Cl
Croydon SE25 206 B3
Greenford UB6 86 A6
Harrow HA2 41 B4
Lincoln Cres EN1 17 D6
Lincoln Ct
Borehamwood WD6 11 B6
Enfield EN2 5 B1
Grove Pk SE12 165 C1
Hampton TW12 173 B5
Hendon NW4 46 B5
2 Ilford IG2 57 A3
Mitcham CR4 204 A4
Redbridge IG1 56 B2
5 South Croydon CR2 221 A3
Stoke Newington N16 51 B2
Lincoln Gdns IG1 56 A2
Lincoln Green Rd
BR5 211 D4
Lincoln Ho
Bloomsbury WC1 240 D3
9 Dartmouth Pk NW5 71 C5
2 Islington N1 73 A1
Knightsbridge SW1 247 C1
10 Putney SW15 157 A6
Lincoln Lo 10 BR3 185 D1
Lincoln Mews NW6 91 B6
Lincoln Rd
Croydon SE25 206 B6
East Finchley N2 48 C6
Enfield EN1, EN3 18 B6
Harrow HA2, HA5 41 B4
Kingston u T KT3 199 A6
Mitcham CR4 204 A4
Newham E13 99 B3
North Cheam KT4 200 B1
Northwood HA6 39 D6
Plashet E7 77 D2
Sidcup DA14 190 B5
Twickenham TW13 151 B1
Wembley HA0 65 D2
Woodford E18 37 A2
Lincoln's Inn*
WC2 94 B1 240 D2
Lincoln's Inn Fields
WC2 94 B1 240 D2
Lincoln St
Chelsea SW3 257 C3
Leyton E11 76 C6
Lincolns The NW7 11 D1
Lincoln Terr 4 SM2 217 C1
Lincoln Way
Charlton TW16 171 C2
Enfield EN1 18 B6
Lincombe Rd BR1 164 D1
Linda Ct KT9 213 D4
Lindal Cres EN2 4 B1
Lindal Ct 1 E18 37 A2
Lindale SW19 157 A2
Lindales The N17 33 D4
Lindal Rd SE4 163 B6
Lindbergh Rd SM6 220 A1
Linden Ave
Enfield EN1 6 A4
Hounslow TW3 151 D6
Kensal Rise NW10 90 D5
Ruislip HA4 40 A1
Thornton Heath CR7 204 D5
Wembley HA9 66 B3
Linden Bridge Sch
KT4 215 C5
Linden Cl
Ruislip HA4 40 A1
Southgate N14 15 C5
Stanmore HA7 25 B5
Thames Ditton KT7 197 A2
Linden Cotts 6
SW19 179 A4
Linden Cres
Kingston u T KT1 176 B1
Wembley UB6 64 D2
Woodford IG8 37 B4
Linden Ct
8 Battersea SW18 136 B1
1 Beckenham BR3 207 D6
2 Bromley BR1 186 D3
Linden Ct *continued*
Edgware NW7 27 B5
Penge SE20 184 B3
1 Shepherd's Bush
W12 112 C5
Sidcup DA14 189 C6
11 Sutton SM2 218 A2
Lindenfield BR7 188 D1
Linden Gate SW20 200 C6
Linden Gdns
Chiswick W4 111 B1
Enfield EN1 6 A4
Notting Hill
W2 113 C6 245 B5
Linden Gr
Kingston u T KT3 199 C6
Nunhead SE15 140 C2
Penge SE20 184 C4
Teddington TW11 174 D5
Linden Ho
Bromley BR1 187 B3
10 Deptford SE8 141 B6
Hampton TW12 173 D4
Walthamstow E17 35 B1
Linden Lawns HA9 66 B4
Linden Lea N2 48 A4
Lindenlea Ct E17 53 B5
Linden Leas BR4 224 B6
Linden Lo N21 16 B4
Linden Lodge Sch
SW19 157 A3
Linden Mans N6 49 B1
Linden Mews
Kensington W2 245 B5
Stoke Newington N1 73 B3
Linden Pl CR4 202 C5
Linden Rd
Brunswick Pk N11 15 A2
Cranley Gdns N10 49 B5
Hampton TW12 173 C2
Tottenham N15 51 A5
Lindens The
Chiswick W4 133 A4
New Addington CR0 224 A2
North Finchley N12 30 B5
5 Walthamstow E17 53 D5
Linden Way
Shepperton TW17 193 A4
Southgate N14 15 C5
Lindeth Cl HA7 25 B4
Lindfield Gdns NW3 70 A3
Lindfield Hts NW3 70 A3
Lindfield Rd
Croydon CR0 205 D3
Ealing W5 87 C3
Lindfield St E14 97 C1
Lindford Christie Stadium
The W12 90 B2
Lindhill Cl EN3 6 D3
Lindholme Ct 3 NW9 27 C2
Lindisfarne Rd
Dagenham RM8 80 C5
Wimbledon SW20 178 A3
Lindisfarne Way E9 75 A4
Lindley Ct KT1 175 C2
Lindley Ho
13 Peckham SE15 140 A5
9 Stepney E1 96 C2
Lindley Pl TW9 132 C4
Lindley Rd E10 76 A6
Lindley St E1 96 C2
Lindon Bennett Sch
TW13 172 D5
Lindop Ho 8 E1 97 A3
Lindore Rd SW11 136 D1
Lindores Rd SM5 202 A1
Lindo St SE15 140 C3
Lind Rd SM1 218 A3
Lindrop St SW6 136 A3
Lindsay Cl KT9 214 A1
Lindsay Ct
Battersea SW11 266 D1
Sutton SM1 217 C3
Lindsay Dr
Harrow HA3 44 B4
Shepperton TW17 193 B3
Lindsay Ho 2 SE18 122 C2
Lindsay Rd
Hampton TW12 173 D6
North Cheam KT4 216 B6
Lindsay Sq
SW1 115 D1 259 D2
Lindsell St 6 SE10 142 A4
Lindsey Cl
Bickley BR1 210 A6
Mitcham CR4, SW16 204 A5
Lindsey Ct N13 16 C1
Lindsey Gdns TW14 149 B4
Lindsey Ho W5 109 D2
Lindsey Ho* SW10 266 D4
Lindsey Mews 18 N1 73 A1
Lindsey Rd RM8 80 C5
Lindsey St EC1 94 D2 241 D4
Lind St SE8 141 D3
Lindum Rd TW11 175 C3
Lindums The BR3 185 B4
Lindway SE27 182 D5
Lindwood Cl 8 E6 100 B2
Linear View HA9 66 D6
Linfield WC1 233 C1
Linfield Cl NW4 46 C5
Linford Ct 1 CR4 180 C2
Linford Ho 17 E2 96 A6
Linford Rd E17 54 A6
Linford St
SW8 137 C4 269 A1
Linford Street Bsns Est
SW8 269 A2
Lingard Ho 11 E14 120 A3
Lingards Rd SE13 142 A1
Lingey Cl DA15 167 D2
Lingfield Ave KT1,
KT5 198 B5
Lingfield Cl EN1 17 C5
Lingfield Cres SE9 145 B1
Lingfield Ct
Northolt UB5 85 C5
Wimbledon SW19 178 D4
Lingfield Gdns N9 18 B4
Lingfield Ho
5 Acton Green W4 111 A1
Lambeth SE1 251 D1
Penge SE26 184 B4
Lingfield Rd
North Cheam KT4 216 C5
Wimbledon SW19 178 D4
Lingham St SW9 138 B3
Lingholm Way EN5 12 D6
Ling Rd E16 99 A2
Lingrove Gdns IG9 21 B2
Ling's Coppice SE21 161 B2
Lingwell Rd SW17 158 C1
Lingwood DA7 147 D3
Lingwood Gdns TW7 130 C5
Lingwood Rd E5 52 A2
Linhope St
NW1 92 D3 237 C5
Linkenholt Mans 3
W6 111 D2
Linkfield KT8 195 D6
Link Field BR2 209 A3
Linkfield Rd TW7 130 D3
Link La SM6 220 A2
Linklea Cl NW9 27 C3
Link Prim Sch CR0 220 A4
Link Rd
Dagenham RM9 103 D5
East Bedfont TW14 149 D4
Friern Barnet N11 31 A6
Hackbridge SM6 203 A1
Links Ave SM4 201 C5
Linkscroft Ave TW15 170 D4
Links Ct N20 14 B1
Links Dr N20 13 D3
Link Sec Sch CR0 220 B4
Links Gdns SW16 182 C3
Linkside
Finchley N12 29 C4
Kingston u T KT3 177 C1
Linkside Cl EN2 4 C2
Linkside Gdns EN2 4 B2
Links Ind Est TW13 151 A1
Links Prim Sch SW17 181 A4
Links Rd
Acton W3 88 C1
Ashford TW15 170 A5
Mitcham SW16, SW17 181 A4
West Wickham BR4 208 A1
Willesden NW2 67 D6
Woodford IG8 37 A5
Links Side EN2 4 C2
Link St E9 74 C3
Links The E17 53 A5
Linksview N2 48 D4
Links View
Finchley N3 29 B3
Shooters Hill SE18 144 D4
Links View Cl HA7 25 A4
Links View Rd
Croydon CR0 223 C5
Hampton TW12 174 A6
Linksway NW4 28 D1
Links Way
Beckenham BR3 207 C3
Streatham SW17 181 A4
Links Yd
10 Spitalfields E1 96 A2
Spitalfields E1 243 D4
Link The
Acton W3 88 D1
Link The *continued*
Chislehurst SE9 166 C1
Enfield EN3 7 A4
Hendon NW2 46 A1
Northolt UB5 63 B3
Pinner HA5 40 C2
Teddington TW11 174 D4
Wembley HA0 43 C1
Linkway
Dagenham RM8 80 C4
Pinner HA5 22 D2
Stoke Newington N4 51 A2
West Barnes SW20 200 B5
Link Way
Bromley BR2 210 A2
Richmond TW10 153 B2
Linkway The EN5 13 D5
Linkwood Wlk NW1 71 D1
Linley Cres RM7 59 D6
Linley Ct
1 Dulwich SE21 183 C6
Sutton SM1 218 A4
Linley Rd N17 33 C1
Linnell Cl NW11 47 D3
Linnell Dr NW11 47 D3
Linnell Ho
Spitalfields E1 243 C4
St John's Wood NW8 229 A6
Linnell Rd
Camberwell SE5 139 C3
Edmonton N18 34 A5
Linnet Cl
Bushey WD23 8 A3
Lower Edmonton N9 18 D3
Woolwich SE28 124 C6
Linnet Ct CR4 180 C2
Linnet Mews SW12 159 A4
Linnett Cl E4 36 A6
Linom Rd SW4 138 A1
Linscott Rd E5 74 C4
Linsdell Rd IG11 101 A6
Linsey St
Bermondsey SE16 118 A2
Bermondsey SE16 118 A3
Linslade Cl
Hounslow TW4 151 A6
Pinner HA5 40 B6
Linslade Ho
10 Hackney E2 96 A6
Marylebone NW8 237 B6
Linstead St 1 NW6 69 C1
Linstead Way SW18,
SW19 157 A4
Linsted Ct SE9 167 C5
Linster Gr WD6 11 A6
Lintaine Cl W6 264 B5
Linthorpe Ave HA0 65 C2
Linthorpe Rd
Cockfosters EN4 2 C2
Stamford Hill N16 51 C2
Linton Cl
Carshalton CR4 202 D2
2 Greenwich SE7 121 C1
Welling DA16 146 B4
Linton Gdns E6 100 A1
Linton Gr SE27 183 A5
Linton Ho
Lower Holloway N7 72 B4
2 Tower Hamlets E3 97 C2
Linton Mead Prim Sch
SE28 124 B6
Linton Rd IG11 79 A1
Linton St N1 95 A6 235 B5
Lintons The
Barking IG11 79 A1
Finchley N3 29 B2
Linver Rd SW6 135 C3
Linwood Cl SE5 139 D3
Linwood Cres EN1 6 A4
Linzee Rd N8 50 A5
Lion Ave TW1 152 D3
Lion Cl
Ladywell SE4 163 C5
Littleton TW17 192 A6
Lion Ct 12 NW9 46 A5
Lion Ctr The TW13 151 A1
Lionel Gdns SE9 165 D6
Lionel Ho
Bowes Pk N22 32 B4
5 Kensal Town W10 91 A2
Lionel Mans 14 W14 112 D3
Lionel Mews 13 W10 91 A2
Lionel Rd SE9 165 D6
Lionel Road N TW8 110 A2
Lionel Road Prim Sch
TW8 110 A2
Lionel Road S TW8 110 B1
Lion Gate Gdns TW9 132 B2
Lion Gate Mews
SW18 157 C4
Lion House Sch
SW15 134 D1
Lion Mills 36 E2 96 A5
Lion Park Ave KT9 214 C4
Lion Rd
Bexleyheath DA6 147 B1
Edmonton N9 18 A2
Newham E6 100 B2
Thornton Heath CR0 205 A4
Twickenham TW1,
TW2 152 D3
Lions Cl SE12 165 D1
Lion Way TW8 131 D5
Lion Wharf Rd TW7 131 B2
Lion Yd SW4 137 D1
Liphook Cres SE23 162 C4
Liphook Rd WD19 22 D6
Lipton Cl SE28 124 C6
Lipton Ct N14 15 C4
Lipton Rd 9 E1 96 D1
Lisa Lo 5 EN5 13 D6
Lisbon Ave TW2 152 A2
Lisbon Cl E17 35 B1
Lisburne Rd NW3 70 D4
Lisford St SE15 139 D4
Lisgar Terr
W14 113 B2 254 C4
Liskeard Cl BR7 189 A4
Liskeard Gdns SE3 143 A4
Liskeard Ho SE11 261 B2
Lisle Cl SW17 181 B6
Lisle Ct NW2 69 A5
Lisle St WC2 115 D6 249 D6
Lismirrane Ind Pk WD6 9 B5
Lismore 9 SW19 179 B5
Lismore Cir NW5 71 A3
Lismore Cl TW7 131 A3
Lismore Rd
South Croydon CR2 221 C2
Tottenham N17 51 B6
Lismore Wlk 4 N1 73 A2
Lissant Cl KT6 197 D2
Lisselton Ho 8 NW4 46 D5
Lissenden Gdns NW5 71 A4
Lissenden Mans NW5 71 A4
Lisson Cotts NW1 237 B4
Lisson Gr NW1,
NW8 92 C3 237 A6
LISSON GROVE 92 B3
Lisson Ho NW1 237 A4
Lisson St NW1 92 C2 237 A4
Lister Cl
Dagenham W3 89 B2
Mitcham SW19 180 C2
Lister Com Sch E13 99 B5
Lister Cotts WD6 9 A6
Lister Ct
Hendon NW9 27 C1
Stoke Newington N16 73 C6
Lister Gdns N18 33 A5
Lister Ho
Greenwich SE3 142 C6
Hayes UB3 105 C2
Marylebone W1 238 C2
Spitalfields E1 96 A2
6 Wembley HA9 67 A5
West Heath SE2 124 D1
Lister Hospl
SW1 115 B1 258 C1
Lister Mews N7 72 B4
Lister Rd E11 54 D1
Lister Wlk SE28 124 D6
Liston Ho N21 16 B6
Liston Rd
Clapham SW4 137 C2
Tottenham N17 34 A2
Liston Way 1 IG8 37 C3
Listowel Cl 2 SW9 138 C5
Listowel Rd RM10 81 C5
Listria Lo N16 73 D6
Listria Pk N16 73 D6
Litcham Ho 23 E1 96 D4
Litchfield Ave
Morden SM4 201 B2
Stratford E15 76 C2
Litchfield Ct E17 53 C3
Litchfield Gdns NW10 68 A2
Litchfield Rd SM1 218 A4
Litchfield St WC2 249 D6
Litchfield Way NW11 48 A4
Lithgow's Rd TW14,
TW6 127 D1
Lithos Rd NW3 70 A2
Little Acre BR3 207 C6
Little Albany St NW1 238 D6
Little Argyll St W1 239 A1
Littleberry Ct NW7 28 C6
Little Birches DA15 167 C2
Little Boltons The
SW10 255 D1
Little Bornes SE21 183 C6
Littlebourne 2 SE13 164 C4
Little Britain EC1 242 A3
Littlebrook Cl CR0 206 D3
Little Brownings
SE23 162 B2
Littlebury Rd SW4 137 D2
Little Bury St N9 17 C4
Little Bushey La WD23 8 B5
Little Cedars N12 30 A6
Little Chelsea Ho
SW10 266 B5
Little Chester St SW1 258 C6
Little Cloisters SW1 260 A6
Little College St SW1 260 A6
Littlecombe SE7 143 B6
Little Combe Cl 13
SW15 156 D5
Little Common HA7 9 A1
Littlecote Cl SW19 157 A4
Littlecote Pl HA5 23 B2
Little Cottage Pl
SE10 141 D5
Littlecroft SE9 144 C2
Little Ct
Harrow HA1 42 C2
West Wickham BR4 224 C6
Littledale SE2 146 A6
Little Deans Yd SW1 260 A6
Little Dell Lo 8 N3 29 B1
Little Dimocks SW12 159 B2
Little Dorrit Ct SE1 252 B2
Little Ealing La W5 109 C2
Little Ealing Prim Sch
W5 109 C3
Little Edward St NW1 231 D2
Little Elms UB3 127 B5
Little Essex St WC2 251 A6
Little Ferry Rd TW1 153 B3
Littlefield Cl
9 Kingston u T KT1 176 A1
Tufnell Pk N19 71 C4
Littlefield Ct UB7 126 A5
Littlefield Ho KT1 176 A1
Littlefield Rd HA8 27 A3
Little Friday Rd E4 20 C2
Little Gearies IG6 56 D5
Little George St SW1 250 A1
Little Gn TW9 131 D1
Little Grange UB6 87 A4
Little Green St NW5 71 B4
Littlegrove EN4 14 C5
Littlegrove Ct 3 EN4 14 C5
Little Halliards KT12 194 A3
LITTLE HEATH 58 B5
Little Heath
Ilford RM6 58 B5
Woolwich SE7 122 A1
Littleheath Rd CR2 222 B1
Little Heath Rd DA7 147 B5
Little Heath Sch RM6 58 B5
Little Holt 10 E11 55 A4
LITTLE ILFORD 78 C3
Little Ilford La E12 78 B4
Little Ilford Sch E12 78 B3
Littlejohn Rd W7 86 D1
Little Larkins EN5 13 A5
Little London Cl UB8 82 D2
Little Marlborough St
W1 239 A1
Littlemead KT10 212 B4
Littlemede SE9 166 B1
Littlemoor Rd IG1 79 B5
Littlemore Rd SE2 124 A4
Little Moss La HA5 23 A1
Little Newport St
WC2 249 D6
Little New St EC4 241 B2
Little Oak Cl TW17 192 B5
Little Orchard Cl HA5 23 A1
Little Oxhey La WD19 23 A6
Little Park Dr TW13 151 A2
Little Park Gdns EN2 5 B2
Little Pluckett's Way
IG9 21 D3
Little Portland St W1 239 A2
Little Potters WD23 8 C4
Little Queens Rd
TW11 174 D4
Little Rd UB3 105 D4
Little Redlands BR1 188 A1
Littlers Cl SW19 180 B2
Little Russell St WC1 240 A3
Little St James's St
SW1 249 A3
Little St Leonards
SW14 133 A2

Little Sanctuary SW1 .. 250 A1
Little Smith St SW1 ... 259 D6
Little Somerset St E1 . 243 C1
LITTLE STANMORE 26 B2
Littlestone Cl BR3 .... 185 C4
Little Strand NW9 ...... 27 D1
Little Thrift BR5 .... 211 A5
Little Titchfield St
W1 .... 239 A3
LITTLETON 192 C6
Littleton Ave E4 .... 20 D3
Littleton CE Inf Sch
TW17 .... 192 C6
LITTLETON
COMMON 171 B3
Littleton Cres HA1 ...... 64 D6
Littleton Ho TW15 ..... 171 A3
Littleton La TW17,
TW18 .... 192 A4
Littleton Rd
Harrow HA1 .... 64 D6
Littleton TW15, TW17 ... 171 A3
Littleton St SW18 ..... 158 A2
Little Trinity La EC4 ... 252 B6
Little Turnstile WC1 ... 240 C3
LITTLE VENICE 92 A2
Little Venice*
W9 92 A2 236 A4
Littlewood SE13 ...... 164 A5
Littlewood Cl W13 .... 109 B3
Little Wood Cl BR5 .... 190 A2
Littleworth Ave KT10 .. 212 B3
Littleworth Common Rd
KT10 .... 212 B5
Littleworth La KT10 ... 212 B4
Littleworth Pl KT10 ... 212 B4
Littleworth Rd KT10 ... 212 C5
Livermere Ct 3 E8 ..... 95 D6
Livermere Rd E8 .... 95 D6
Liverpool Gr
SE17 .... 117 B1 262 C1
Liverpool Ho N7 .... 72 C2
Liverpool Rd
Ealing W5 .... 109 D4
Islington N1 .... 234 B5
Islington N1, N7 .... 72 C1
Kingston u T KT2 .... 176 C3
Leytonstone E10 .... 54 A3
Newham E16 .... 98 C2
South Norwood CR7 ... 205 A6
Liverpool St
EC2 .... 95 C2 243 A3
Liverpool Street Sta
EC2 .... 95 C2 243 A3
Livesey Cl
Kingston u T KT1 .... 198 B6
Woolwich SE28 .... 123 A3
Livesey Mus* SE15 140 B6
Livesey Pl SE15 .... 140 A6
Livingstone Ct
Barnet EN5 .... 1 A3
Leytonstone E10 .... 54 A3
Stanwell TW19 .... 148 A3
Livingstone Ho 16
SE5 .... 139 A5
Livingstone Lo
13 Paddington W9 ...... 91 C2
Walthamstow E17 ...... 35 C1
Livingstone Pl E14 .... 120 A1
Livingstone Prim Sch
EN4 .... 2 B2
Livingstone Rd
14 Battersea SW11 .... 136 B2
Bowes Pk N13 .... 32 A5
Isleworth TW3 .... 130 A1
Mill Meads E15 .... 98 A6
Southall UB1 .... 106 D6
South Norwood CR7 .... 183 B1
Walthamstow E17 ...... 53 D3
Livity Sch The SW2 .... 160 A6
Livonia St W1 .... 239 B1
Lizard St EC1 ... 95 A4 235 B1
Lizban St SE3 .... 143 B5
Llandovery Ho 1
E14 .... 120 A4
Llanelly Rd NW2 .... 69 B6
Llanover Rd
Shooters Hill SE18 ..... 144 C5
Wembley HA9 .... 65 D4
Llanthony Rd SM4 ..... 202 B4
Llanvanor Rd NW2 ...... 69 B6
Llewellyn Ct SE20 ..... 184 C2
Llewellyn Ho 10 N19 ... 71 C5
Llewellyn St SE16 ..... 118 A4
Lloyd Ave SW16 .... 182 A2
Lloyd Baker St
WC1 .... 94 C4 234 A1
Lloyd Ct
Ladywell SE13 .... 163 D6
Pinner HA5 .... 40 D4
6 West Norwood
SE27 .... 160 D1
Lloyd Ho
3 Beckenham BR3 .... 185 D4
Bromley BR1 .... 187 B5
Stoke Newington N16 ... 73 B5
Lloyd Mews EN3 .... 7 C5
Lloyd Park Ave CR0 ... 221 D4
Lloyd Park Ho E17 ..... 53 C6
Lloyd Park Sta CR0 ... 221 D4
Lloyd Rd
Dagenham RM9 .... 81 B1
Newham E6 .... 100 B6
North Cheam KT4,
SM3 .... 216 D5
Walthamstow E17 ...... 52 D5
Lloyd's Ave EC3 .... 243 B1
Lloyd's Bldg*
EC3 95 C1 243 A1
Lloyd's Pl SE3 .... 142 C3
Lloyd Sq WC1 ... 94 C4 234 A2
Lloyd's Row
EC1 .... 94 D4 234 C1
Lloyd St WC1 ... 94 C4 234 A2
Lloyds Way BR3 .... 207 B4
Lloyd Villas SE4 .... 141 C3
Loampit Hill SE13 ..... 141 D3
Loampit Vale SE13 .... 142 A2
Loanda Cl 17 E8 .... 95 D6
Loats Rd SW2 .... 160 A5
Lobelia Cl 5 E6 ...... 100 A2
Locarno Cl 15 SW16 ... 181 C5
Locarno Rd
6 Acton W3 .... 111 A5
Greenford UB6 .... 86 B3
Lochaber Rd SE13 ..... 142 C1
Lochaline St W6 ...... 134 C6
Lochan Cl UB4 .... 85 A3
Lochbie 9 N4 .... 50 A2
Lochinvar St SW12 .... 159 B4
Lochleven Ho 9 N2 .... 30 B1
Lochmere Cl DA8 ..... 147 D6
Lochmore Ho SW1 .... 258 B3
Lochnagar St E14 ...... 98 A2
Lockbridge Ct 3 W9 ... 91 C2
Lock Chase SE3 .... 142 C2
Lock Cl UB2 .... 108 A4
Locke Ho
Nine Elms SW8 .... 269 A2
Stamford Hill N16 ...... 51 D1
Lockesfield Pl E14 .... 119 D1
Lockesley Dr BR5 ..... 211 D3
Lockesley Sq KT6 ..... 197 D3
Locket Rd HA3 .... 24 D1
Lockfield Ave EN3 .... 7 B4
Lockgate Cl E9 .... 75 B3
Lockhart Cl
Barnsbury N7 .... 72 B2
Enfield EN3 .... 18 B6
Lockhart Lo 4 E4 ...... 20 C4
Lockhart St E3 .... 97 B3
Lockhurst St E5 .... 74 D4
Lockier Wlk HA9 .... 65 D5
Lockington Rd
SW8 .... 137 B4 268 D2
Lockmead Rd
Lewisham SE13 .... 142 A2
South Tottenham N15 ... 52 A3
Lock Mews 9 NW1 ..... 71 D2
Lock Rd TW10 .... 175 C6
LOCKSBOTTOM 226 D5
Lockside 17 E14 ...... 119 A6
Lock's La CR4 .... 181 A1
Locksley St E14 .... 97 B2
Locksmeade Rd
TW10 .... 175 C6
Lock View Ct 9 E14 ... 119 A6
Lockwell Rd RM10 ..... 81 C5
Lockwood Cl SE26 .... 184 D6
Lockwood Ct KT3 ..... 199 A5
Lockwood Ho 10
SE11 .... 138 C6
Lockwood Ind Pk N17 .. 52 B6
Lockwood Pl E4 .... 35 C4
Lockwood Sq SE16 .... 118 B3
Lockwood Way
Chessington KT9 ...... 214 C3
Higham Hill E17 .... 34 D1
Lockyer Cl EN3 .... 7 D5
Lockyer Est SE1 .... 252 D1
Lockyer Ho
7 Greenwich SE10 .... 120 D1
Putney SW15 .... 134 D2
South Lambeth SW8 ... 270 A4
Lockyer St SE1 .... 252 D1
Locomotive Dr TW14 .. 150 A3
Locton Gn 4 E3 .... 97 B6
Lodden Lo 13 SM2 .... 218 A1
Loddiges Ho 5 E9 ..... 74 C1
Loddiges Rd E9 .... 74 C1
Loddon Ho NW8 ...... 236 D5
Loder St SE15 .... 140 C5
Lodge Ave
Borehamwood WD6 ..... 10 B6
Croydon CR0 .... 220 C5
Dagenham RM8, RM9,
IG11 .... 80 B3
Harrow HA3 .... 44 A5
Mortlake SW14 .... 133 C2
Lodge Cl
Edgware HA8 .... 26 C4
Edmonton N18 .... 33 A5
Hackbridge SM6 ...... 203 A1
Isleworth TW7 .... 131 B4
Lodge Ct 3 HA0 .... 66 A3
Lodge Dr N13 .... 32 C6
Lodge Gdns BR3 ...... 207 B4
Lodge Hill
East Wickham DA16 .... 146 B5
Redbridge IG4 .... 56 A5
Lodgehill Park Cl HA2 .. 63 D6
Lodge La
Bexley DA5 .... 168 D5
New Addington CR0 .... 223 D1
North Finchley N12 ...... 30 A5
Lodge Mead Ct 5 N3 ... 29 D3
Lodge Pl SM1 .... 217 D3
Lodge Rd
Bromley BR1 .... 187 C3
Hendon NW4 .... 46 C5
Lisson Gr NW8 .. 92 C4 230 A1
Sutton SM1 .... 217 D3
Thornton Heath CR0 .... 204 D2
Wallington SM6 .... 219 B3
Lodge The
9 Chiswick W4 .... 111 C3
1 Sutton SM1 .... 218 A4
Lodge Villas IG8 .... 36 D4
Lodge Way
Charlton TW17 .... 171 A1
Stanwell TW15 .... 148 A2
Lodore Gdns NW9 ..... 45 C4
Lodore Gn UB10 .... 60 A5
Lodore St E14 .... 98 A1
Lodsworth Ho SW11 .. 268 A1
Lofthouse Pl KT9 ..... 213 C2
Loftie St SE16 .... 118 A4
Lofting Ho 8 N1 .... 72 C1
Lofting Rd N1 .... 72 C1
Lofts on the Park 24
E9 .... 74 D2
Loftus Rd
Barking IG11 .... 79 A2
Shepherd's Bush W12 .. 112 B5
Loftus Rd (Queens Park
Rangers FC) W12 .... 112 B5
Logan Cl
Enfield EN3 .... 6 D4
Hounslow TW4 .... 129 B2
Logan Mews W8 ...... 255 A4
Logan Pl W8 ... 113 C2 255 A4
Logan Rd
Edmonton N9 .... 18 B2
Wembley HA9 .... 66 A6
Loggetts SE21 .... 161 C2
Logs Hill BR1, BR7 ..... 188 A2
Logs Hill Cl BR7 ...... 188 A2
Lohmann Ho 5 SE11 .. 138 C6
Lois Dr TW17 .... 192 D4
Lolesworth Cl E1 ..... 243 D3
Lolland Ho 8 SE7 ..... 122 A2
Lollard St
SE11 .... 116 C2 261 A3
Lollards Twr SE1 ...... 260 C5
Loman St SE1 .. 116 D4 251 D2
Lomas Cl CR0 .... 224 A1
Lomas St E1 .... 96 A2
Lombard Ave
Enfield EN3 .... 6 C4
Ilford IG3 .... 57 C1
Lombard Bsns Pk
Merton SW19 .... 179 D1
Thornton Heath CR0 .... 204 B2
Lombard Ct
14 Acton W3 .... 110 D5
City of London EC3 .... 252 D6
Lombard La EC4 ...... 241 B1
Lombard Rd
Battersea SW11 ...... 136 B3
Friern Barnet N11 ...... 31 B5
Merton SW19 .... 179 D1
Lombard Rdbt CR0 .... 204 B2
Lombard St
EC3 .... 95 B1 242 D1
Lombard Trad Est
SE7 .... 121 B2
Lombard Wall SE7 .... 121 B2
Lombardy Pl W2 ...... 245 D5
Lombardy Ret Pk
UB3 .... 106 B6
Lomley Ho 10 SW2 .... 160 C5
Lomond Cl
Tottenham N15 .... 51 C4
Wembley HA0 .... 66 B1
Lomond Ct HA3 .... 42 D6
Lomond Gdns CR2 .... 223 A1
Lomond Gr SE5 .... 139 B5
Lomond Ho 10 SE5 .... 139 B4
Loncroft Rd SE5 ...... 139 C6
Londesborough Ho 1
N16 .... 73 C4
Londesborough Rd
N16 .... 73 C4
London Academy HA8 .. 26 B6
London Acad of
Computing & Electronics
SW17 .... 158 D1
London Aquarium*
SE1 250 C1
London Bridge EC4,
SE1 .... 117 B6 252 D5
London Bridge City Pier
SE1 .... 117 C5 253 A4
London Bridge Hospl
SE1 .... 117 B5 252 D4
London Bridge St
SE1 .... 117 B5 252 D3
London Bridge Sta
SE1 .... 117 B5 252 D3
London Bridge Wlk
SE1 .... 252 D4
London Britannia Coll
N1 .... 95 B4 235 C2
London Business Sch
NW1 .... 92 D3 237 C6
London Butterfly Ho*
TW8 131 B4
London Canal Mus*
N1 94 A5 233 B4
London Central Mosque*
NW8 92 C4 230 B1
London Chest Hospl
E2 .... 96 C5
London City Airport
E16 .... 122 B5
London City Airport Sta
E16 .... 122 A5
London Clinic
NW1 .... 93 A3 238 B5
London Coll of Advanced
Studies SE1 .... 252 C3
London Coll of Beauty
Therapy W1 ... 93 C1 239 B1
London Coll of Bsns &
Computer Studies
SW4 .... 137 D1
London Coll of
Communication (Sch of
Printing & Publishing)
SE11 .... 116 D3 261 D5
London Coll of Economics
& Science NW10 ...... 89 A3
London Coll of Fashion
Broadgate
EC2 .... 95 C3 243 B6
Marylebone W1 .... 238 D2
Marylebone W1 .... 238 B1
Marylebone W1 .... 238 C1
St Luke's EC1 ... 95 A3 242 A5
London Coll of Fashion
(Mare St) E8 .... 74 B1
London Coll of
International Business
Studies WC1 .... 240 B3
London Ct 3 SW18 ... 157 C6
London Docklands Visitor
Ctr* E14 120 A4
London Dungeon The*
SE1 117 B5 252 D4
London Electronics Coll
SW5 .... 113 D1 255 C2
London Eye (Millennium
Wheel)*
SE1 116 B4 250 C2
London Fields East Side
E8 .... 74 B1
London Fields Prim Sch
E8 .... 96 B6
London Fields Sta E8 .. 74 B1
London Fields West Side
E8 .... 74 A1
London Fire Brigade
Mus* SE1 252 A2
London Gas Mus The* E3,
E16 98 B3
London Group Bsns Pk
NW2 .... 46 A1
London Ho
Edgware HA8 .... 26 A6
13 Hammersmith W6 ... 112 A2
London Ho TW9 .... 132 B2
London Ho NW8 ...... 230 B4
London Hospital Dental
Inst E1 .... 96 B2
London Independent
Hospl The E1 .... 96 D2
London Inst The
SW17 .... 181 B5
London Int Coll N7 ..... 72 B5
London International Film
Sch WC2 ...... 94 A1 240 A1
London IT Coll IG2 ..... 56 C3
London La
Bromley BR1 .... 186 D3
Hackney E8 .... 74 B1
London Metropolitan Univ
Islington N7 .... 72 C3
Whitechapel E1 . 95 D1 243 C1
Whitechapel E1 . 95 D1 243 C2
Whitechapel
EC3 .... 117 D6 253 C6
London Metropolitan Univ
(Central Ho) E1 .... 96 A1
London Metropolitan Univ
(Commercial Rd) E1 .. 96 A1
London Metropolitan Univ
(Ladbrook Ho) N5 .... 72 D3
London Metropolitan Univ
(Moorgate)
EC2 .... 95 B2 242 D3
London Metropolitan
Univ (Spring Ho) N7 .. 72 C2
London Mews W2 ..... 236 D2
London Motorcycle Mus*
UB6 86 A4
London Nautical Sch The
SE1 .... 116 C5 251 B4
London Oratory Sch The
SW6 .... 135 C5 265 B4
London Pavilion SW1 . 249 C5
London Peace Pagoda*
SW3 267 D4
London Rd
Ashford TW15, TW18, TW19,
TW14 .... 148 B2
Brentford TW7, TW8 .... 131 B4
Bromley BR1 .... 186 D3
Carshalton CR4 .... 203 A2
Enfield EN2 .... 5 B1
Forest Hill SE22, SE23 .. 162 C3
Hackbridge SM6, CR4 ... 219 B6
Harrow HA1 .... 64 C6
Hounslow TW3, TW7, TW1,
TW8 .... 130 B3
Kingston u T KT1, KT2 ... 176 B1
Lambeth SE1 .. 116 D3 261 D6
Mitcham CR4 .... 180 D2
Morden SM4 .... 201 C5
Newham E13 .... 99 A5
Romford RM7, RM8 ..... 59 C5
Stanmore HA7 .... 25 D6
Stoneleigh KT17, KT4,
SM3 .... 216 B3
Thornton Heath CR0, CR7,
SW16 .... 204 C3
Twickenham TW1 ...... 153 A4
Wembley HA9 .... 66 A2
London Road Rdbt
TW1 .... 153 A5
London Sch of Economics
& Political Science
WC2 .... 94 B1 240 D1
London Sch of Jewish
Studies NW4 .... 46 D5
London St
City of London EC3 .... 253 B6
Paddington W2 .. 92 B1 236 C1
London Stile 5 W4 ... 110 C1
London Stock Exchange*
EC2 242 A2
London Stone Bsns Est 15
SW11 .... 137 A3
London Terr 1 E2 ..... 96 A5
London Tottenham Coll
N17 .... 33 D3
London Transport Mus*
WC2 250 B6
London Wall
EC2 .... 95 B2 242 D3
London Wall Bldgs
EC2 .... 242 D3
London Wetland Ctr*
SW13 134 B5
London Wetland Visitor
Ctr* SW13 134 B4
London Wharf 4 E2 ... 96 B6
London Xtra Tuition Coll
N4 .... 72 D6
London Zoo*
NW1 93 A5 231 A4
Lonesome Prim Sch
CR4 .... 181 B1
Lonesome Way CR4 ... 181 C2
Long Acre WC2 . 94 A1 240 B1
Long Acre Ct W13 ...... 87 A2
Longacre Pl SM5 ...... 219 A2
Longacre Rd E17 .... 36 B2
Longbeach Rd SW11 .. 136 D2
Longberrys NW2 .... 69 B5
Longboat Row UB1 .... 85 B1
Longbridge Ho RM8 .... 80 B4
Longbridge Rd
Barking IG11 .... 79 C3
Dagenham RM8 .... 80 B4
Longbridge Way
SE13 .... 164 A6
Longbury Dr BR5 ..... 190 B1
Longchamp Ct 13 HA7 .. 25 C5
Longcliffe Ho SW18 ... 157 D6
Longcroft SE9 .... 166 C1
Longcrofte Rd HA8 ..... 25 D3
Long Deacon Rd E4 .... 20 C3
LONG DITTON 197 C1
Long Ditton Inf Sch
KT6 .... 197 C1
Longdon Wood BR2 ... 226 A4
Longdown Rd SE6 .... 185 C6
Long Dr
Dagenham W3 .... 89 C1
Greenford UB6 .... 85 D6
Ruislip HA4 .... 62 D4
Long Elmes HA3 .... 24 A2
Longfellow Rd
North Cheam KT4 ...... 200 B1
Walthamstow E17 ...... 53 B3
Longfellow Way SE1 .. 263 D3
Longfield
3 Bromley BR1 .... 186 D2
Loughton IG10 .... 21 C6
Long Field NW9 .... 27 D3
Longfield Ave
Ealing W5 .... 109 C6
Enfield EN3 .... 6 C5
Hackbridge SM6 ...... 203 A1
Hendon NW7 .... 28 A3
Walthamstow E17 ...... 53 A5
Wembley HA9 .... 44 A1
Longfield Cres SE23,
SE26 .... 162 C1
Longfield Ct 4 N2 ..... 48 A6
Longfield Dr
Mitcham SW19 .... 180 C2
Mortlake SW14 .... 154 D6
Longfield Est SE1 ..... 263 D3
Longfield Fst & Mid Schs
HA2 .... 41 C3
Longfield Ho
Ealing W5 .... 109 C6
Walthamstow E17 ...... 53 B4
Longfield Rd W5 .... 87 C1
Longfield St SW18 .... 157 C4
Longford Ave
Feltham TW14 .... 149 D5
Southall UB1 .... 107 D6
Stanwell TW19 .... 148 A3
Longford Cl
Feltham TW13 .... 151 A1
Hampton TW12 .... 173 C6
Hayes UB4 .... 106 D6
Longford Com Sch
TW14 .... 149 D4
Longford Ct
1 Bedford Pk W12 .... 111 C4
2 Clapton Pk E5 .... 74 D4
Hampton TW12 .... 173 D4
9 Hendon NW4 .... 46 C5
Southall UB1 .... 107 C5
West Ewell KT19 ...... 215 A4
Longford Gdns
Hayes UB4 .... 106 D6
Sutton SM1 .... 218 A6
Longford Ho
1 Catford BR1 .... 186 B5
Hampton TW12 .... 173 C6
7 Stepney E1 .... 96 C1
Longford Ind Est
TW12 .... 173 D4
Longford Rd TW2 ..... 151 D3
Longford St
NW1 .... 93 B3 238 D6
Longford Way TW19 .. 148 A3
Longford Wlk 9
SW2 .... 160 C4
Longhayes Ave RM6 ... 58 D5
Longhayes Ct RM6 ..... 58 D5
Longheath Gdns CR0 .. 206 C4

Longhedge Ho SE26 184 A6
Longhedge St SW11 137 A3
Longhill Rd SE6 164 B1
Long Ho SM5 218 C6
Longhook Gdns UB5 84 B4
Longhope Cl SE15 139 D6
Longhurst Ho 8 W9 91 B4
Longhurst Rd
Croydon CR0 206 B3
Lewisham SE13 164 C6
Long La
Bermondsey SE1 117 B4 252 D1
Croydon CR0 206 C3
East Finchley N2 48 B6
Erith DA7 147 B4
Finchley N3 29 D2
Hillingdon UB10 82 D6
Holborn EC1 94 D2 241 D4
Stanwell TW15,TW19 148 B3
Longland Ct
Bermondsey SE1 118 A1
Hackney E9 75 A3
Longland Dr N20 13 D2
LONGLANDS 167 B1
Longlands Ct
Higham Hill E17 35 A2
Mitcham CR4 181 A2
Notting Hill W11 244 D6
Sidcup DA15 167 D1
Longlands Park Cres DA15 167 C2
Longlands Prim Sch DA15 167 C1
Longlands Rd DA15 167 D1
Longleat Ct 3 DA6 147 A1
Longleat Ho SW1 259 C2
Longleat Rd EN1 17 C6
Longleat Way TW14 149 B4
Longleigh Ho 8 SE5 139 C4
Longleigh La SE2, DA7 146 C6
Longlents Ho 3 NW10 89 B6
Longley Ave HA0 88 B6
Longley Ho 5 N19 71 C4
Longley Rd
Harrow HA1 42 B5
Thornton Heath CR0 204 D2
Upper Tooting SW17 180 D4
Long Leys E4 36 A4
Longley St SE1 118 A2
Longley Way NW2 68 C5
Longman Ho
9 Globe Town E2 96 D5
10 Shoreditch E8 95 D6
Long Mark Rd 5 E16 99 D2
Longmarsh La SE28 123 C5
Longmead BR7 188 C1
Long Mead NW9 27 D2
Longmead Dr DA14 168 D2
Longmead Ho SE27 183 A5
Long Meadow 20 N7 71 D3
Long Meadow Cl BR3, BR4 208 A2
Longmeadow Rd DA15 167 C3
Longmead Prim Sch UB7 104 A2
Longmead Rd
Hayes UB3 105 D6
Thames Ditton KT7 196 D2
Upper Tooting SW17 180 D5
Longmoor Point 14 SW15 156 B3
Longmore Ave EN4, EN5 14 B5
Longmore St SW1 115 C2 259 A3
Longnor Rd E1 96 D4
Long Pond Rd SE3 142 C4
Long Rd SW4 137 C1
Longreach Ct IG11 101 B5
Long Reach Rd IG11 101 D3
Longridge Ho SE1 262 B5
Longridge La UB1 85 D1
Longridge Rd SW5 113 C2 255 B3
Long Ridges N2 49 A6
Longs Ct 2 TW9 132 B1
Long's Ct W1 249 D5
Longshaw Prim Sch E4 20 B1
Longshaw Rd E4 20 B1
Longshore SE8 119 B2
Long St E2 95 D4
Longstaff Cres SW18 157 C4
Longstaff Rd SW18 157 C5
Longstone Ave NW10 89 D6
Longstone Rd SW17 181 B5
Longthorne Ho 18 E3 97 B4
Longthornton Rd SW16 181 D1
Longthorpe Ct 9 W6 112 A2
Longton Ave SE26 184 A6
Longton Gr SE26 184 B6
Longville Rd SE11 261 D4
Longwalk Rd UB11 104 D5
Long Wlk
Bermondsey SE1 263 B6
Kingston u T KT3 199 A6
Shooters Hill SE18 144 D6
Longwood Bsns Pk TW16 193 D4
Longwood Dr SW15 156 A5
Longwood Gdns IG2, IG6, IG5 56 C6
Longwood Par IG6 56 D6
Longworth Cl SE28 102 D1
Long Yd WC1 94 B3 240 C5
Loning The
Enfield EN3 6 C5
Hyde The NW9 45 D5
Lonsdale Ave
Newham E6 100 A3
Wembley HA9 66 A3
Lonsdale Cl
Edgware HA8 26 B5
Hillingdon UB8 83 A2
Mottingham SE12 165 D1
Newham E6 100 A3
Pinner HA5 23 A2
Lonsdale Cres IG2 56 D3
Lonsdale Dr EN2 16 A6
Lonsdale Dr N EN2 4 A1
Lonsdale Gdns CR7, SW16 204 B5
Lonsdale Ho
Fulham SW6 135 C2
6 Stoke Newington N4 51 A2
Lonsdale Mews
Notting Hill W11 91 B1
4 Richmond TW9 132 C4
Lonsdale Pl N1 72 C1
Lonsdale Rd
Barnes SW13 133 D5
Bexley DA7 147 B3
Chiswick W4 111 D2
Croydon SE25 206 B5
Kilburn NW6 91 B6
Leytonstone E11 54 D2
Notting Hill W11 91 B1
Southall UB2 106 D3
Lonsdale Sq
Islington N1 72 C1
Islington N1 234 B6
Loobert Rd N15 51 C6
Looe Gdns IG6 56 D6
Loop Rd BR7 189 A4
Lopen Rd N18 33 C6
Lopen Works N18 33 C6
Lopez Ho 4 SW9 138 A2
Lorac Ct 13 SM2 217 C1
Loraine Cl EN3 18 C6
Loraine Ct BR7 188 D5
Loraine Ho 1 SM5 219 B4
Loraine Rd
Chiswick W4 132 D6
Islington N7 72 B4
Lord Ave IG5 56 B6
Lord Chancellor Wlk KT2 177 A2
Lord David Pitt Ho 8 SE24 138 C1
Lordell Pl SW19 178 C4
Lorden Wlk 13 E2 96 A4
Lord Gdns IG5 56 B5
Lord Hills Rd W2 91 D2
Lord Holland La 5 SW9 138 C3
Lord Knyvetts Ct 3 TW19 148 A5
Lord Napier Pl W6 112 A1
Lord North St SW1 260 A5
Lord Roberts Mews SW6 265 C3
Lord Roberts Terr SE18 122 C1
Lords Cl
Feltham TW13 151 A2
West Norwood SE21 161 A2
Lord's Cricket Mus* NW8 92 B4 229 D1
Lords Ct 3 HA8 27 A3
Lordship Gr N16 73 B6
Lordship Ho 3 N16 73 B6
Lordship La
Dulwich Village SE22 161 D5
Tottenham N22 33 B2
Lordship Lane Prim Sch N22 33 A2
Lordship Park Mews N16 73 A6
Lordship Pk N16 73 B6
Lordship Pl SW3 267 A5
Lordship Rd
Northolt UB5 63 A1
Stoke Newington N16 73 B6
Lordship Terr N16 73 B6
Lord's Indoor Cricket Sch NW8 230 A2
Lord's (MCC & Middlesex Cty Cricket Ground)* NW8 92 B4 229 D2
Lordsmead Rd N17 33 C1
Lord St E16 122 A5
Lord's View NW8 229 D1
Lord Warwick St SE18 122 B3
Loreburn Ho 2 N7 72 B4
Lorenzo St N1, WC1 233 C2
Loretto Gdns HA3 44 A5
Lorian Cl N12 29 D6
Loring Rd
East Barnet N20 14 C2
Isleworth TW7 130 D3
Loris Rd W6 112 C3
Lorn Ct SW9 138 C3
Lorne Ave CR0 206 D2
Lorne Cl NW8 92 C4 230 B1
Lorne Ct
Harrow HA1 42 C2
Putney SW15 156 D5
Lorne Gdns
Croydon CR0 206 D2
5 Hammersmith W11 112 D4
Wanstead E11 55 C5
Lorne Ho
Friern Barnet N11 31 B5
Hornsey N4 50 B2
7 Tower Hamlets E1 97 A2
Lorne Rd
Finsbury Pk N4 50 B1
Forest Gate E7 77 C4
Harrow HA3 24 D1
3 Richmond TW10 154 B6
Walthamstow E17 53 C4
Lorn Rd SW9 138 C3
Lorraine Ct
Beckenham BR3 186 A2
9 Belmont SM2 217 C1
10 Camden Town NW1 71 B1
Lorraine Pk HA3 24 C3
Lorrimore Rd SE17 138 D6
Lorrimore Sq SE17 138 D6
Lorton Ho 9 NW6 91 C6
Loseberry Rd KT10 212 B3
Lostock Ho 10 SW8 137 D3
Lothair Rd W5 109 D4
Lothair Rd N N4 50 D3
Lothair Rd S N4 50 D2
Lothbury EC2 95 B1 242 C2
Lothian Ave UB4 84 B2
Lothian Cl HA0 65 A5
Lothian Rd SW9 138 D4
Lothrop St W10 91 A4
Lots Rd SW10 136 A5 266 B3
Loubet St SW17 180 D4
Loudoun Ave IG6 56 D4
Loudoun Rd NW8 92 A6 229 B5
Loudwater Cl TW16 194 A5
Loudwater Rd TW16 194 A5
Loughborough Ct 7 SW9 138 D2
Loughborough Junction Sta SW9 138 D2
Loughborough Pk SW9 138 D1
Loughborough Prim Sch SW9 138 D3
Loughborough Rd SE5, SW9 138 D3
Loughborough St SE11 116 B1 260 D1
Lough Rd N7 72 B2
LOUGHTON 21 D5
Loughton Way IG9 21 D3
Louie Black Ho 4 SW19 179 A3
Louisa Cl E9 96 D6
Louisa Ct
Twickenham TW2 152 C2
Wood Green N11 31 D3
Louisa Gdns E1 96 D3
Louisa Ho SW15 133 D1
Louisa St E1 96 D3
Louis Ct 3 RM10 81 D2
Louise Bennett Cl 9 SE24 138 D1
Louise Ct
7 Bexley DA6 147 A1
4 Wanstead E11 55 B4
Wood Green N22 32 C2
Louise De Marillac Ho 26 E1 96 C2
Louise Graham Ho 5 IG11 101 B6
Louise Rd E15 76 C2
Louise White Ho 1 N19 49 D1
Louis Gdns BR7 188 B6
Louis Mews N10 31 B2
Louisville Rd SW17 159 A1
Lousada Lo N14 15 C5
Louvaine Rd SW11 136 B1
Lovage App E6 100 A2
Lovat Cl NW2 67 D5
Lovat La EC3 253 A5
Lovatt Cl HA8 26 D4
Lovatt Ct SW12 159 B3
Lovatt Dr HA4 39 D4
Lovat Wlk TW5 129 A5
Loveday Ho 2 SW2 160 C3
Loveday Rd W13 109 B5
Lovegrove St SE1 140 A6
Lovegrove Wlk E14 120 A5
Lovekyn Cl KT2 176 B1
Love La
Cheam SM3 217 A2
City of London EC2 95 A1 242 B2
Croydon SE25 206 B6
Long Ditton KT6 213 D6
Mitcham CR4 202 C6
Morden SM4 201 D2
Old Bexley DA5 169 C5
Pinner HA5 41 A6
Tottenham N17 33 D3
Woolwich SE18 122 D2
Lovelace Ave BR2 210 C3
Lovelace Gdns
Barking IG11 80 A4
Surbiton KT6 197 D2
Lovelace Gn SE9 144 B2
Lovelace Ho 12 E8 95 D6
Lovelace Prim Sch KT9 213 C3
Lovelace Rd
East Barnet EN4 14 C4
Surbiton KT6 197 D2
West Norwood SE21 161 A3
Loveland Mans 7 IG11 79 D1
Lovel Ave DA16 146 A3
Lovelinch Cl SE15 140 C6
Lovell Ho
Hackney E8 96 A6
4 Merton SW19 180 A2
Lovell Pl SE16 119 A3
Lovell Rd
Richmond TW10 153 C1
Southall UB1 85 D1
Loveridge Mews NW6 69 B2
Loveridge Rd NW6 69 B2
Lover's Wlk W1 115 A5 248 A3
Lovett Dr SM5 202 B2
Lovette Ho 4 E3 97 C4
Lovetts Pl SW18 135 D1
Lovett Way NW10 67 A3
Love Wlk SE5 139 B3
Lovibonds Ave
Hillingdon UB7 82 B1
Locksbottom BR6 226 D5
Lowbrook Rd IG1 78 D4
Lowdell Cl UB7 82 A1
Lowden Rd
Edmonton N9 18 B3
Herne Hill SE24 139 A1
Southall UB1 107 A6
Lowder Ho 6 E1 118 B5
Lowe Ave E16 99 A2
Lowell Ho 10 SE5 139 A5
Lowell St E14 97 A1
Lower Addiscombe Rd CR0 205 C1
Lower Addison Gdns W14 113 A4 244 A1
Lower Belgrave St SW1 115 B3 258 C5
Lower Boston Rd W7 108 C4
Lower Broad St RM10 103 C6
Lower Camden BR7 188 B2
Lower Church St CR0 220 D6
LOWER CLAPTON 74 C4
Lower Clapton Rd E5 74 C4
Lower Clarendon Wlk 9 W11 91 A1
Lower Comm S SW15 134 B2
Lower Coombe St CR0 221 A4
Lower Downs Rd SW20 178 D2
LOWER EDMONTON 18 B1
LOWER FELTHAM 149 D1
Lower Fosters NW4 46 C4
Lower George St 13 TW10 153 D6
Lower Gn W CR4 202 C6
Lower Gravel Rd BR2 210 B1
LOWER GREEN 195 C1
Lower Green Gdns KT4 200 A1
Lower Green Rd KT10 212 A6
Lower Grosvenor Pl SW1 115 B3 258 D6
Lower Grove Rd TW10 154 B6
LOWER HALLIFORD 193 C3
Lower Hall La E4 35 A6
Lower Hampton Rd TW12, TW16 172 D1
Lower Ham Rd KT2 175 D4
LOWER HOLLOWAY 72 A3
Lower James St W1 249 B6
Lower John St W1 249 B6
Lower Kenwood Ave EN2 16 A6
Lower Kings Rd KT2 176 A3
Lower Lea Crossing E14, E16 120 C6
Lower Maidstone Rd N11 31 C4
Lower Mall W6 112 B1
Lower Marsh SE1 116 C4 251 A1
Lower Marsh La KT1, KT5 198 C5
Lower Merton Rise NW3 70 C1
LOWER MORDEN 201 A2
Lower Morden La SM4 201 A3
Lower Mortlake Rd TW9 132 B2
Lower Park Rd
Belvedere DA17 125 C2
Friern Barnet N11 31 C5
4 Loughton IG10 21 D6
Lower Pk
Acton W3 89 A3
5 Putney SW15 156 D6
LOWER PLACE 89 A5
Lower Place Bsns Ctr NW10 89 A5
Lower Queen's Rd IG9 21 D2
Lower Rd
Belvedere DA17 125 D3
Finchley N2 30 B2
Harrow HA2 42 B1
Rotherhithe SE16 118 C4
Sutton SM1 218 A4
Lower Richmond Rd
Mortlake SW14,TW9 132 D2
Putney SW15 134 C2
Lower Robert St WC2 250 B5
Lower Sand Hills KT6 197 C2
Lower Sloane St SW1 115 A1 258 A2
Lower Sq TW7 131 B2
Lower Strand NW9 27 D1
Lower Sunbury Rd TW12 173 C1
LOWER SYDENHAM 185 A6
Lower Sydenham Sta SE26 185 B5
Lower Teddington Rd KT1 175 D2
Lower Terr NW3 70 A5
Lower Thames St EC3 117 C6 253 A5
Lower Tub WD23 8 B4
Lowerwood Ct W11 91 A1
Lower Wood Rd KT10 213 B2
Lowestoft Cl 5 E5 74 C6
Lowestoft Mews E16 122 D4
Loweswater Cl HA9 65 D6
Loweswater Ho E3 97 B3
Lowfield Rd
Dagenham W3 89 A1
Hampstead NW6 69 C1
Low Hall Cl E4 19 D4
Low Hall La E17 53 A3
Lowick Rd HA1 42 C4
Lowland Gdns RM7 59 D3
Lowlands NW3 70 C2
Lowlands Ct NW7 27 D5
Lowlands Rd
Harrow HA1 42 C2
Pinner HA5 40 C3
Lowman Rd N7 72 B4
Lowndes Cl SW1 258 B5
Lowndes Ct
Knightsbridge SW1 257 D6
Marylebone W1 239 A1
Lowndes Lo
Barnet EN5 1 D2
SW1 257 D6
Lowndes Pl SW1 115 A3 258 A5
Lowndes Sq SW1 114 D4 247 D1
Lowndes St SW1 115 A3 258 A6
Lownds Ct BR1 187 A1
Lowood Ct SE19 183 D5
Lowood Ho 12 E1 118 C6
Lowood St E1 118 B6
Lowry Cres CR4 180 C1
Lowry Ct 3 SE16 118 B1
Lowry Ho N17 33 D2
Lowry Lo 1 HA0 65 D3
Lowry Rd RM8 80 B3
Lowther Cl WD6 10 B6
Lowther Dr EN2 4 A1
Lowther Hill SE23 163 A4
Lowther Ho
Pimlico SW1 259 B1
11 Shoreditch E8 95 D6
Lowther Prim Sch SW13 134 A6
Lowther Rd
Barnes SW13 133 D4
Higham Hill E17 35 A1
Islington N7 72 C3
Kingston u T KT2 176 B2
Stanmore HA7 44 B6
Lowth Rd SE5 139 A3
Lowton Lo E17 53 A6
LOXFORD 79 A3
Loxford Ave E6 99 D5
Loxford Ho SW1 258 B3
Loxford La IG1 79 B3
Loxford Rd IG11 78 D2
Loxford Sch of Science & Tech IG1 79 B3
Loxham Rd E4 35 D3
Loxham St WC1 233 B1
Loxley Cl SE26 184 D5
Loxley Hall E11 54 C2
Loxley Ho HA9 66 A5
Loxley Rd
Feltham TW12 173 B6
Wandsworth SW18 158 B3
Loxton Rd SE23 163 A3
Loxwood Cl TW14 149 B3
Loxwood Rd N17 51 C6
Loyola Prep Sch IG9 21 C3
LTC Coll London W1 239 A2
Lubavitch House Sch (Jun Boys) E5 51 D2
Lubbock Ct BR7 188 B3
Lubbock Ho
21 Canary Wharf E14 119 D6
Orpington BR6 227 C6
Lubbock Rd BR7 188 B3
Lubbock St SE14 140 C5
Lucan Ho N1 235 D5
Lucan Pl SW3 114 C2 257 B3
Lucan Rd EN5 1 A2
Lucas Ave
Harrow HA2 63 C6
Newham E13 99 B6
Lucas Ct
Battersea SW11 268 B1
Forest Hill SE26 185 A5
Lucas Gdns N2 30 A1
Lucas Ho
2 Clapham SW8 137 C3
Walham Green SW10 265 D4
Lucas Rd SE20 184 C4
Lucas Sq NW11 47 C3
Lucas St SE4, SE8 141 C4
Lucas Vale Prim Sch SE8 141 C4
Lucerne Cl N14 16 A1
Lucerne Ct
5 Abbey Wood DA18 125 A3
8 Beckenham BR3 185 C3
Lucerne Gr E17 54 B5
Lucerne Mews W8 245 B4

Lucerne Rd
Highbury N5 72 D4
Orpington BR6 211 D1
South Norwood CR7 205 A5
Lucey Rd SE16 118 A3
Lucey Way SE16 118 A2
Lucie Ave TW15 170 D4
Lucien Rd
Upper Tooting SW17 181 A6
Wandsworth SW18 157 D2
Lucille Ho SE26 184 B4
Lucknow St SE18 145 C5
Lucorn Cl SE12 164 D5
Lucraft Ho 12 SW2 160 A4
Luctons Ave IG9 21 C3
Lucy Ashe Ho SE17 261 D3
Lucy Brown Ho SE1 252 B3
Lucy Cres W3 89 A3
Lucy Gdns RM8 81 A5
Luddesdon Rd DA8 147 C5
Ludford Cl
Croydon CR0 220 D4
Edgware NW9 27 C1
Ludgate Broadway
EC4 241 D1
Ludgate Cir
EC4 94 D1 241 C1
Ludgate Hill
EC4 94 D1 241 D1
Ludgate Ho EC4 241 C1
Ludgate Sq EC4 241 D1
Ludgrove Ct EN4 2 C1
Ludgrove Hall EN4 2 C2
Ludham NW5 70 D3
Ludham Cl SE28 102 C1
Lud Lo TW15 148 A2
Ludlow Cl
Bromley BR2 209 A6
Harrow HA2 63 B4
Ludlow Ct
Acton W3 111 A4
East Barnet EN4 14 C6
Ludlow Rd
Ealing W5 87 C3
Feltham TW13 172 A6
Ludlow St EC1 242 A6
Ludlow Way N2 48 A5
Ludovick Wlk SW15 133 C1
Ludwell Ho W14 254 B6
Ludwick Mews SE14 141 A5
Luffield Rd SE2 124 B3
Luffman Rd SE12 165 B1
Lugard Ho 2 W12 112 B5
Lugard Rd SE15 140 B4
Lugg App E12 78 C5
Luke Ho 32 E1 96 B1
Lukes Ct N3 47 C6
Luke St EC2 95 C3 243 A6
Lukin Cres E4 20 B1
Lukin St E1 96 C1
Lullingstone Cl BR5 190 B3
Lullingstone Cres
BR5 190 B3
Lullingstone Ho 21
SE15 140 C6
Lullingstone La SE13 164 B5
Lullingstone Rd 3
DA17 147 B6
Lullington Garth
Borehamwood WD6 10 D6
Bromley BR1 186 C3
Finchley N12 29 B5
Lullington Rd
Dagenham RM9 81 A1
Penge SE20 184 A3
Lulot Gdns N19 71 B6
Lulworth
Camden Town NW1 71 D1
Walworth SE17 262 C2
Lulworth Ave
Hounslow TW5,TW7 130 A5
Wembley HA9 43 C2
Lulworth Cl HA2 63 B5
Lulworth Cres CR4 180 C1
Lulworth Ct N14 16 A1
Lulworth Dr HA5 41 A2
Lulworth Gdns HA2 63 B6
Lulworth Ho SW8 270 C3
Lulworth Rd
Bexley DA16 145 D3
Chislehurst SE9 166 A2
Peckham SE15 140 B3
Lulworth Waye UB4 84 B1
Lumen Rd HA9 65 D6
Lumiere Bldg The E7 77 D3
Lumiere Ct 7 SW17 159 A2
Lumina Bldg 1 E14 120 A5
Lumley Cl DA17 125 C1
Lumley Ct WC2 250 B5
Lumley Flats SW1 258 A2
Lumley Gdns SM3 217 A3
Lumley Ho KT3 199 B1
Lumley Rd SM1, SM3 217 A3
Lumley St W1 238 B1
Lumsdon NW8 91 D6
Luna Ho 6 SE16 118 A4
Lunan Ho 14 E3 97 B5
Luna Rd CR7 205 A6
Lundin Wlk WD19 22 D6
Lund Point E15 98 A6
Lundy Dr UB3 105 C2
Lunham Rd SE19 183 C4
Luntley Pl E1 96 A2
Lupin Cl
Croydon CR0 206 D1
Streatham SW2 160 D2
Lupin Cres IG11 78 D2
Lupino Ct SE11 260 D4
Lupin Point SE1 253 D1
Lupton Cl SE12 187 B6
Lupton St NW5 71 C4
Lupus Ct SE19 183 B2
Lupus St SW1 115 C1 259 B1
Luralda Gdns E14 120 B1
Lurgan Ave W6 134 D6
Lurline Gdns
SW11 137 A4 268 B2
Luscombe Ct BR2 186 C1
Luscombe Ho SW18 157 B6
Luscombe Way
SW8 138 A5 270 A4
Lusher Ho SW15 156 D5
Lushington Ho KT12 194 C3
Lushington Rd
Catford SE6 185 D5
Willesden Green NW10 90 B5
Lushington Terr 11 E8 74 A3
Lutea Ho SM2 218 A1
Luther Cl HA8 11 A2
Luther King Cl E17 53 A3
Luther Mews 2
TW11 174 D5
Luther Rd TW11 174 D5
Luton Pl SE10 142 A5
Luton Rd
Newham E13 99 A3
Sidcup DA14 168 C1
Walthamstow E17 53 B6
Luton St NW8 92 B3 236 D5
Luttrell Ave SW15 156 B6
Lutwyche Rd SE6 163 B2
Lutyens Ho SW1 259 A1
Luxborough Ho W1 238 A4
Luxborough St
W1 93 A2 238 A4
Luxborough Twr W1 238 A4
Luxembourg Mews 2
E15 76 C3
Luxemburg Gdns W6 112 D2
Luxfield Rd SE9 166 A3
Luxford St SE16 118 D2
Luxmore St SE4 141 B4
Luxor St SE5 139 A2
Lyall Ave SE21 183 D6
Lyall Mews
SW1 115 A3 258 A5
Lyall Mews W SW1 258 A5
Lyall St SW1 115 A3 258 A5
Lyal Rd E3 97 A5
Lyce e Francais Charles
de Gaulle (French Univ
Coll) SW7 114 B2 256 C4
Lycee The
SE11 116 C1 261 B1
Lycett Ho 10 SW2 160 A4
Lycett Pl 3 W12 112 A4
Lychgate Ct 4 N12 30 B5
Lychgate Manor HA1 42 C2
Lych Gate Wlk UB3 105 D6
Lyconby Gdns CR0 207 A2
Lydd Cl DA14 167 C1
Lydden Ct SE9 167 C5
Lydden Gr SW18 157 D4
Lydden Rd SW18 157 D4
Lydd Rd DA7 147 B5
Lydeard Rd E6 78 B1
Lydford NW1 232 B5
Lydford Cl 22 N16 73 C3
Lydford Rd
Brondesbury NW2 68 D2
Paddington W9 91 B3
Tottenham N15 51 B4
Lydgate Ho 8 N16 73 C3
Lydhurst Ave SW2 160 B2
Lydia Ct 2 N12 30 A4
Lydia Lodge HA1 64 C4
Lydney Cl
Camberwell SE15 139 C5
Putney SW19 157 A2
Lydon Rd SW4 137 C2
Lydstep Rd BR7 188 C6
Lydwell Ho 29 SW8 137 D3
Lyford Rd SW18 158 C3
Lyford St SE7 122 A2
Lygoe Ho 18 N6 49 D2
Lygoe Rd N2 30 B2
Lygon Ho 2 E2 96 A4
Lygon Pl SW1 258 C5
Lyham Cl SW2 160 A5
Lyham Rd SW2 160 A5
Lyle Cl CR4 203 A2
Lyle Ct SM4 202 B3
Lyle Pk SW15 156 D5
Lyly Ho SE1 262 D5
Lyme Farm Rd SE12 143 B1
Lyme Gr E9 74 C1
Lyme Grove Ho 2 E9 74 C1
Lymer Ave SE19 183 D5
Lyme Rd DA16 146 B4
Lymescote Gdns SM1 217 C6
Lyme St NW1 93 C6 232 A6
Lyminge Cl DA14 189 D6
Lyminge Gdns SW17,
SW18 158 C3
Lymington Ave N22 32 D1
Lymington Cl
Mitcham SW16 181 D1
2 Newham E6 100 B2
Lymington Ct SM1 218 A5
Lymington Dr HA4 61 B6
Lymington Gdns
KT19 215 D3
Lymington Mans NW6 69 D2
Lymington Rd
Dagenham RM8 58 D1
Hampstead NW6 69 D2
Lyminster Cl UB4 85 A2
Lympne N17 33 B1
Lympstone Gdns
SE15 140 A5
Lynbridge Gdns N13 32 D6
Lynbrook Gr SE15 139 C5
Lynchen Cl TW5 128 B4
Lynch Wlk 2 SE8 141 B6
Lyncott Cres SW4 137 B1
Lyncourt SE3 142 B3
Lyncroft Ave HA5 41 A4
Lyncroft Gdns
Ealing W13 109 C5
Hampstead NW6 69 C3
Hounslow TW3 152 A6
Lyncroft Mans 4 NW6 69 C3
Lyndale NW2 69 B5
Lyndale Ave NW2 69 B5
Lyndale Cl SE3 142 D6
Lyndean Ind Est SE2 124 C3
Lynde Ho
2 Clapham SW4 137 D2
Walton-on-T KT12 194 C3
Lynden Gate SW15 156 B4
Lyndenhurst SE3 142 D2
Lynden Hyrst CR0 221 D6
Lyndhurst BR7 188 D4
Lyndhurst Ave
Colney Hatch N12 30 D4
Edgware NW7 27 C4
Mitcham SW16 181 D1
Pinner HA5 22 B2
Southall UB1 107 D5
Sunbury TW16 194 A6
Tolworth KT5 198 D1
Twickenham TW2,
TW4 151 C3
Lyndhurst Cl
Bexleyheath DA7 147 D2
Neasden NW10 67 B5
Orpington BR6 226 D4
South Croydon CR0 221 D5
Lyndhurst Ct
8 Belmont SM2 217 C1
11 Woodford E18 37 A2
Lyndhurst Dr
Leytonstone E10 54 A2
New Malden KT3 199 D2
Lyndhurst Gdns
Barking IG11 79 C2
Enfield EN1 5 C1
Hampstead NW3 70 B3
Hendon N3 29 A2
Ilford IG2 57 B3
Pinner HA5 22 B2
Lyndhurst Gr SE5,
SE15 139 D3
Lyndhurst Ho 2
SW15 156 A4
Lyndhurst House Prep Sch
NW3 70 B3
Lyndhurst Lo 3 E14 120 B2
Lyndhurst Rd
Bexleyheath DA7 147 D2
Chingford E4 36 A3
Edmonton N18 34 A6
Greenford UB6 85 D3
Hampstead NW3 70 B3
Thornton Heath CR7 204 C5
Tottenham N22 32 C4
Lyndhurst Sch SE5 139 B3
Lyndhurst Sq SE15 139 D4
Lyndhurst Terr NW3 70 B3
Lyndhurst Way
Belmont SM2 217 C1
Camberwell SE15 139 D3
Lyndon Ave
Bexley DA15 167 D6
Hackbridge SM6 219 A5
Pinner HA5 23 A4
Lyndon Rd DA17 125 C2
Lyndon Yd SW17 179 D6
Lyndum Ct N22 32 C2
Lyne Cres E17 35 B2
Lyne Ct NW9 45 B2
Lynegrove Ave TW15 171 A5
Lyneham Wlk
Hackney E5 75 A3
Pinner HA5 39 D6
Lynette Ave SW4 159 C5
Lynfield Ct SE23 162 D4
Lynford Cl
Barnet Gate EN5 11 D6
Burnt Oak HA8 27 A2
Lynford French Ho
SE17 262 A2
Lynford Gdns
Edgware HA8 10 D1
Ilford IG3 79 D6
Lynford Terr N9 17 D3
Lyngham Ct 10 N4 50 A2
Lynhurst Cres UB10 61 B1
Lynhurst Ct NW8 229 C5
Lynhurst Rd UB10 61 A1
Lynmere Rd DA16 146 B3
Lyn Mews 12 E3 97 B4
Lynmouth Ave
Enfield EN1 17 D5
West Barnes SM4 200 D2
Lynmouth Dr HA4 62 B5
Lynmouth Gdns
Heston TW5 128 D4
Wembley UB6 65 B1
Lynmouth Rd
Fortis Green N2 48 D5
Stamford Hill N16 51 D1
Walthamstow E17 53 A4
Wembley UB6 87 B6
Lynn Cl
Ashford TW15 171 B5
Harrow HA3 24 B1
Lynn Ct SW16 181 D5
Lynne Cl 7 BR6 227 D2
Lynne Ct
Forest Hill SE23 163 B4
Hampstead NW6 69 D1
South Croydon CR2 221 C4
Wimbledon SW20 178 B2
Lynnett Ct E9 75 A2
Lynnett Rd RM8 58 D1
Lynne Way UB5 84 D5
Lynne Wlk KT10 212 A3
Lynn Ho SE15 140 A6
Lynn Mews E11 76 C6
Lynn Rd
Balham SW12 159 B4
Ilford IG2 57 B2
Leyton E11 76 C5
Lynn St EN2 5 B4
Lynsted Cl
Bexley DA6 169 D6
Bromley BR1 187 C1
Lynsted Ct 4 BR3 185 A1
Lynsted Gdns SE9 143 D2
Lynton KT7 197 A2
Lynton Ave
Ealing W13 87 A1
Hyde The NW9 45 D5
North Finchley N12 30 B6
Lynton Cl
Chessington KT9 214 A4
Isleworth TW7 130 D1
Willesden NW10 67 D3
Lynton Cres IG2 56 D3
Lynton Ct
Bowes Pk N13 32 A5
9 Dagenham W3 89 A1
Penge SE20 184 B2
Sutton SM2 218 A2
Lynton Est SE1 118 A2
Lynton Gdns
Enfield EN1 17 C4
Friern Barnet N11 31 D4
Lynton Grange N2 48 D6
Lynton Ho 16 W2 91 D1
Lynton Lo N5 72 D3
Lynton Mans SE1 261 A6
Lynton Mead N20 13 D2
Lynton Rd
Acton W3 110 D6
Bermondsey SE1 117 D2
Chingford E4 35 D5
Harrow HA2 63 A6
Hornsey N8 50 A4
New Malden KT3 199 B4
Paddington NW6 91 B5
Thornton Heath CR0 204 C3
Lynton Terr 4 W3 89 A1
Lynton Wlk UB4 83 C4
Lynwood Cl
Harrow HA2 63 A5
Woodford E18 37 C2
Lynwood Ct TW15 170 B5
Lynwood Dr KT4 216 A6
Lynwood Gdns
Southall UB1 85 B1
Wallington CR0 220 B4
Lynwood Gr
Orpington BR6 211 C1
Southgate N21 16 C3
Lynwood Rd
Ealing W5 88 A3
Thames Ditton KT7 196 D1
Upper Tooting SW17 180 D6
Lynx Terr SW19 157 C1
Lynx Way E16 121 D6
Lyon Bsns Pk IG11 101 C5
Lyon Ct HA4 39 D1
Lyon Ho NW8 237 A5
Lyon Meade HA7 25 C2
Lyon Park Ave HA0 66 B2
Lyon Park Jun & Inf Schs
HA0 66 B1
Lyon Rd
Harrow HA1 42 D3
Merton SW19 180 A2
Lyonsdown Ave EN5 14 A5
Lyonsdown Ct EN5 14 A6
Lyonsdown Rd EN5 14 A6
Lyonsdown Sch EN5 14 A6
Lyons Pl NW8 92 B3 236 C5
Lyon St N1 72 B1
Lyons Wlk W14 254 A4
Lyon Way UB6 86 C6
Lyoth Rd BR5 227 A6
Lyric Dr UB6 85 D3
Lyric Mews SE26 184 C6
Lyric Rd SW13 133 D4
Lysander 20 NW9 27 D2
Lysander Ct 8 EN5 13 D6
Lysander Gdns KT5 198 B3
Lysander Gr N19 49 D1
Lysander Ho 10 E2 96 B5
Lysander Rd
Ruislip HA4 61 B6
Wallington CR0 220 B2
Lysander Way BR6 227 A5
Lysia Ct SW6 134 D5
Lysias Rd SW12 159 B5
Lysia St SW6 134 D5
Lysons Wlk SW15 156 A6
Lytchet Rd BR1 187 B3
Lytchet Way EN3 6 C4
Lytchgate Cl CR2 221 C1
Lytcott Dr KT8 195 B6
Lytcott Gr SE22 161 D6
Lytham Ave WD19 22 D5
Lytham Cl SE28 103 A1
Lytham Ct 5 UB1 85 D1
Lytham Gr W5 88 B4
Lytham St
SE17 117 B1 262 C1
Lyttelton Cl NW3 70 C1
Lyttelton Ct N2 48 A4
Lyttelton Rd
Hampstead Garden Suburb
N2 48 A4
Leyton E10 76 A5
Lytten Ct 6 W12 112 A4
Lyttleton Ct UB4 84 C3
Lyttleton Ho 10 E9 74 C1
Lyttleton Rd N8 50 C6
Lytton Ave
Enfield EN3 7 A5
Southgate N13 16 C2
Lytton Cl
Hampstead Garden Suburb
N2 48 B4
Northolt UB5 63 B1
Lytton Ct WC1 240 B3
Lytton Gdns SM6 219 D4
Lytton Gr SW15 157 A5
Lytton Ho 8 TW12 173 D4
Lytton Rd
Leytonstone E11 54 C2
New Barnet EN5 2 A1
Pinner HA5 23 A3
Lytton Strachey Path 8
SE28 124 B6
Lyveden Rd
Greenwich SE3 143 B5
Mitcham SW17, SW19 180 D4

M

Mabbett Ho 2 SE18 144 C6
Mabel Crout Ct SE9 145 B1
Mabel Evetts Ct UB3 106 B6
Mabel Thornton Ho 12
N16 73 B4
Maberley Cres SE19 184 A3
Maberley Ct SE19 184 A3
Maberley Rd SE19 182 C2
Mabledon Pl NW1,
WC1 232 D1
Mablethorpe Rd SW6 264 A3
Mabley St E9 75 A3
Mablin Lo 3 IG9 21 C3
Mcadam Dr EN2 4 D3
Macallister Ho 8
SE18 144 D6
Macaret Cl N20 14 A4
Macarthur Cl E7 77 A2
MacArthur Ho 4
SW2 160 A4
Macartney Ho SE10 142 B5
Macaulay Ave KT10 212 C6
Macaulay CE Prim Sch
SW4 137 B1
Macaulay Ct SW4 137 B2
Macaulay Ho
2 Kensal Town W10 91 A2
10 Stoke Newington
N16 73 C5
Macaulay Rd
Clapham SW4 137 B2
Newham E6 99 D5
Macaulay Sq SW4 137 B1
Macaulay Way 2
SE28 124 B5
McAuley Cl
Eltham SE9 166 C6
Lambeth SE1 116 C3 261 A6
Macauley Mews SE13 142 A3
McAusland Ho 5 E3 97 B5
Macbean St SE18 122 D3
Macbeth Ho 4 N1 95 C5
Macbeth St W6 112 B1
McBride Ho 6 E3 97 B5
McCall Cl SW4 138 A3
McCall Cres SE7 122 A1
McCall Ho N7 72 A4
Mccarthy Ct SW11 267 B1
McCarthy Rd TW13 172 D5
Macclesfield Rd
Croydon SE25 206 C4
Shoreditch EC1 95 A4 235 A2
Macclesfield St W1 249 D6
McClintock Pl EN3 7 D6
McCoid Way SE1 252 A1
Mcconnell Ho SW8 269 C1
McCormick Ho 9
SW2 160 C3
McCrone Mews 3
NW3 70 B2
McCullum Rd E3 97 B6
McDermott Cl SW11 136 C2
McDermott Rd SE15 140 A2
Macdonald Ave RM10 81 D5
Macdonald Ct TW3 130 A1
McDonald Ho 1 KT2 176 B3
Macdonald Ho 2
SW11 137 A3
Macdonald Rd
Chingford E17 36 A1
Dartmouth Pk N19 71 C6
Forest Gate E7 77 A4
Friern Barnet N11 30 D5
McDonough Cl KT9 214 A4
McDougall Ct TW9 132 C3
Mcdougall Rd E3 96 A4
McDowall Cl E16 98 D2
McDowall Rd SE5 139 A4
Macduff Rd
SW11 137 A4 268 B2
Mace Cl E1 118 B5
Mace Ho 2 E17 53 D6
McEntee Ave E17 35 A2

Mace St E2 96 D5
McEwan Way E15 98 B6
Macey Ho
Battersea SW11 267 A1
10 Greenwich SE10 142 A6
Macfarlane La TW7 131 A6
Macfarlane Rd W12 112 C5
Macfarren Ho 7 W10 91 A4
MacFarren Pl NW1 238 B5
McGlashon Ho 15 E1 96 A3
McGrath Rd E15 76 D2
McGregor Ct 8 N1 95 C4
MacGregor Ho 2
SW12 159 D3
McGregor Rd W11 91 B2
Macgregor Rd E16 99 C2
Mcguffie Ct E17 53 B6
Machell Rd SE15 140 C2
McIndoe Ct N1 235 C6
McIntosh Cl SM6 220 A1
McIntosh Ho 14 SE16 118 C2
McIntyre Ct 19 SW4 138 A3
Mackay Ho 33 W12 112 B6
McKay Rd SW20 178 C4
Mackay Rd SW4 137 B2
McKellar Cl WD23 8 A2
McKenna Ho 3 E3 97 B5
Mackennal St
NW8 92 C5 230 B4
Mackenzie Cl 7 W12 112 B6
Mackenzie Ho
5 Dollis Hill NW2 68 A5
1 Hornsey N8 50 A5
Mackenzie Rd
Barnsbury N7 72 B2
Penge BR3 184 D1
Mackenzie Wlk E14 119 C5
McKerrell Rd SE15 140 A4
Mackeson Rd NW3 70 D4
Mackie Ho 18 SW2 160 C4
Mackie Rd SW2 160 C4
McKiernan Ct 2
SW11 136 C3
Mc Killop Way DA14 190 C3
McKinlay Ct
Beckenham BR3 185 B1
Bexley DA16 146 C2
McKinnon Wood Ho 16
E2 96 A4
Mackintosh La E9 74 D3
Macklin Ho SE23 162 B2
Macklin St WC2 94 A1 240 B2
Mackonochie Ho EC1 241 A4
Mackrow Wlk 11 E14 120 A6
Macks Rd SE16 118 A2
Mackworth Ho NW1 232 A2
Mackworth St NW1 232 A2
Mac Laren Mews
SW15 134 C1
Maclean Rd SE23 163 A5
Mcleod Ct SE21 162 A3
McLeod Ho 3 SE23 162 C2
McLeod Rd SE2 124 B2
Macleod Rd N21 16 A6
McLeod's Mews
SW7 113 D2 255 D4
Macleod St
SE17 117 A1 262 B1
Maclise Rd
W14 113 A3 254 A5
McManus Ho 3
SW11 136 B2
McMillan Ct 2 SE6 164 D3
Macmillan Ct HA2 41 C1
Mcmillan Ho SE4 141 A2
Macmillan Ho
Cricklewood NW4 68 B4
Lisson Gr NW8 230 B1
McMillan St SE8 141 C6
Macmillan Way SW17 181 B6
Mcmorran Ho 4 N7 72 A4
McNair Rd UB2 107 D3
Macnamara Ho SW10 266 C4
Mcneil Rd SE5 139 C3
McNicol Dr NW10 89 A5
Macoma Rd SE18 145 B6
Macoma Terr SE18 145 B6
Maconochies Rd 9
E14 119 D1
Macquarie Way E14 119 D2
McRae La CR4 202 D2
Macready Ho W1 237 B3
Macready Pl 2 N7 72 A4
Macroom Ho W9 91 B4
Macroom Rd W9 91 B4
Mac's Pl EC4 241 B2
Madame Tussaud's*
NW1 93 A3 238 A5
Mada Rd BR6 226 D5
Maddams St E3 97 D3
Madderfields Ct N11 31 D2
Maddison Cl
Finchley N2 30 A1
Teddington TW11 174 D4
Maddison Ct NW4 28 C1
Maddocks Cl DA14 191 A5
Maddocks Ho 3 E1 118 B6
Maddock Way SE17 138 D6
Maddox Ct 1 E4 20 B3
Maddox St W1 248 D6
Madeira Ave BR1 186 C3
Madeira Gr IG8 37 C4
Madeira Rd
Edmonton N13 16 D1
Leytonstone E11 54 C1
Mitcham CR4 202 D5
Streatham SW16 182 A5
Madeleine Cl RM6 58 C3
Madeley Ct W5 88 A1
Madeley Rd W5 88 A1
Madeline Gr IG1 79 B3
Madeline Rd SE20 184 A3
Madge Gill Way 4
E6 100 A6
Madge Hill W7 108 C6
Madinah Rd E8 74 A3
Madingley 11 KT1 176 C1
Madingley Ct TW1 153 C6
Madison Apartments
N11 31 D3
Madison Cres DA7 146 C5
Madison Ct 15 RM10 81 D2
Madison Gdns
Beckenham BR2 208 D6
Bexley DA7 146 C5
Madison Ho E3 98 A4
Madras Ho IG1 78 D4
Madras Pl N7 72 C2
Madras Rd IG1 78 D4
Madrid Rd SW13 134 A5
Madron St
SE17 117 C1 263 B2
Mafeking Ave
Brentford TW8 132 A6
Ilford IG2 57 B2
Newham E6 100 A5
Mafeking Rd
Enfield EN1 5 D2
Newham E16 98 D3
Tottenham N17 34 A1
Magdala Ave N19 71 C6
Magdala Rd
Isleworth TW7 131 A2
South Croydon CR2 221 B1
Magdalen Ct SE25 206 A4
Magdalene Cl 7
SE15 140 B3
Magdalene Gdns E6 100 C3
Magdalene Ho 7
SW15 156 D5
Magdalene Rd TW17 192 B6
Magdalen Pas E1 253 D6
Magdalen Rd SW18 158 B3
Magdalen St SE1 253 A3
Magee St SE11 138 C6
Magellan Ct 11 NW10 67 B1
Magellan Ho 16 E1 96 D3
Magellan Pl 25 E14 119 C2
Magna Ct UB6 86 B4
Magnaville Rd WD23 8 D4
Magnet Rd HA9 65 D6
Magnin Cl 5 E8 96 A6
Magnolia Cl
Kingston u T KT2 176 D4
Leyton E10 75 C6
Magnolia Ct
13 Belmont SM2 217 D1
Feltham TW14 150 A3
2 Finchley N12 29 D6
Forest Hill SE26 184 C5
Harrow HA3 44 B2
Hillingdon UB10 60 D2
Northolt UB5 85 A3
Richmond TW9 132 D4
Wallington SM6 219 B3
Wandsworth SW11 158 D5
Magnolia Gdns HA8 27 A6
Magnolia Ho 13 SE8 141 B6
Magnolia Lo E4 19 D1
Magnolia Pl
Clapham Pk SW4 160 A6
Ealing W5 87 D2
Magnolia Rd W4 132 D6
Magnolia Way KT19 215 A3
Magnolia Wharf W4 132 D6
Magpie Cl
Edgware NW9 27 C1
Enfield EN1 6 A4
Forest Gate E7 76 D3
Magpie Hall Cl BR2 210 A3
Magpie Hall La BR2 210 B3
Magpie Hall Rd WD23 8 C2
Magpie Ho 7 E3 97 B6
Magpie Pl SE14 141 A6
Magri Wlk 22 E1 96 C2
Maguire Dr TW10 175 C6
Maguire St
SE1 117 D4 253 D2
Mahatma Gandhi Ind Est
1 SE24 138 D1
Mahlon Ave HA4 62 B2
Mahogany Cl SE16 119 A5
Mahon Cl EN1 5 D4
Mahoney Ho SE14 141 B4
Maida Ave
Chingford E4 19 D4
Little Venice W2 92 A3 236 B5
Maida Rd DA17 125 C3
MAIDA VALE 91 D4
Maida Vale W9 92 A4 229 A1
Maida Vale Sta W9 91 D4
Maida Way E4 19 D4
Maiden Erlegh Ave
DA5 169 A3
Maiden La
Borough The
SE1 117 A5 252 B4
Camden Town NW1 71 D1
Strand WC2 116 A6 250 B6
Maiden Rd E15 76 C1
Maidenstone Hill
SE10 142 A4
Maids of Honour Row 4
TW9 153 D6
Maidstone Bldgs SE1 252 C3
Maidstone Ct N11 31 D4
Maidstone Ho 4 E14 97 D1
Maidstone Rd
Friern Barnet N11 31 D4
Ruxley DA14 191 C3
Mail Coach Yd 23 E2 95 C4
Main Ave EN1 17 D6
Main Dr HA9 65 D5
Main Rd
Chislehurst BR5 190 C1
Sidcup DA14 167 C1
Mainridge Rd BR7,
SE9 188 C6
Main St TW13 172 D5
Mainwaring Ct 3
CR4 181 A1
Main Yd E9 75 C2
Mais Ho SE26 162 B2
Maismore St SE15 140 A6
Maison Alfort HA3 24 C2
Maisonettes The SM1 217 B3
Maitland Cl
3 Greenwich SE10 141 D5
Hounslow TW4 129 B2
Maitland Ct W2 246 C6
Maitland Ho
Chelsea SW1 269 A6
16 South Hackney E2 96 C5
MAITLAND PARK 70 D2
Maitland Park Rd
NW3 70 D2
Maitland Park Villas
NW3 70 D2
Maitland Pl E5 74 C4
Maitland Rd
Penge SE26 184 D4
Stratford E15 76 D2
Majendie Rd SE18 123 B1
Majestic Ct N4 50 D1
Majestic Way CR4 180 D1
Major Cl SW9 138 D2
Majorie Mews 6 E1 96 D1
Major Rd
22 Bermondsey SE16 118 A3
Stratford New Town E15 76 B3
Makepeace Ave N6 71 A6
Makepeace Mans N6 71 A6
Makepeace Rd
Northolt UB5 85 A6
Wanstead E11 55 A5
Makinen Ho 5 IG9 21 C3
Makins St SW3 257 B3
Malabar Ct 20 W12 112 B6
Malabar St E14 119 C4
Malam Ct SE11 261 A3
Malam Gdns 3 E14 119 D6
Malatia CR2 221 A2
Malay Ho 2 E1 118 C5
Malborough Ho 3
N20 14 D1
Malbrook Rd SW15 134 B1
Malbury Ct N22 32 A3
Malcolm Cl SE20 184 C3
Malcolm Cres NW4 46 A3
Malcolm Ct
Ealing W5 88 B3
Hendon NW4 46 A3
Stanmore HA7 25 C5
Stratford E7 76 D2
Malcolm Dr KT6 198 A1
Malcolm Ho 13 N1 95 C5
Malcolm Pl E2 96 C3
Malcolm Prim Sch
SE20 184 C3
Malcolm Rd
Bethnal Green E1 96 C3
Croydon SE25 206 A3
Ickenham UB10 60 B4
Penge SE20 184 C3
Wimbledon SW19 179 A4
Malcolmson Ho SW1 259 D1
Malcolms Way N14 15 C6
Malcolm Way E11 55 A5
Malden Ave
Croydon SE25 206 B6
Northolt UB6 64 C2
Malden CE Prim Sch
KT4 199 C1
Malden Cres NW1 71 A2
Malden Ct
Stoke Newington N4 51 A3
West Barnes KT3 200 B6
Malden Green Ave
KT4 200 A1
Malden Hill KT3 199 D6
Malden Hill Gdns
KT3 199 D6
Malden Junc KT3 199 D4
Malden Manor Prim Sch
KT3 199 C2
Malden Manor Sta
KT3 199 C2
Malden Pk KT3 199 D3
Malden Pl NW5 71 A3
Malden Rd
Camden Town NW5 71 A2
Cheam KT4, SM3 216 D4
New Malden KT3, KT4 199 D2
Malden Way KT3 200 A5
Malden Way (Kingston By
Pass) KT3, KT5 199 C4
Maldon Cl
Camberwell SE5 139 C2
Shoreditch N1 235 B6
Stratford New Town E15 76 B3
Maldon Ct
Barking E6 100 C6
Wallington SM6 219 C3
Maldon Rd
Acton W3 111 A6
Edmonton N9 17 D1
Wallington SM6 219 B3
Maldon Wlk IG8 37 C4
Malet Pl WC1 239 C5
Malet St WC1 93 D2 239 D4
Maley Ave SE27 160 D2
Malford Ct E18 37 A1
Malford Gr E18 54 D6
Malfort Rd SE5 139 C2
Malham Cl N11 31 A4
Malham Rd SE23 162 D3
Malham Road Ind Est
SE23 162 D3
Malindi Ct N8 49 D4
Malins Cl EN5 12 C6
Malins Ct SW12 159 A5
Mallaig Ct HA8 10 D2
Mallams Mews 1
SW9 138 D2
Mallard Cl
1 Hackney E9 75 B2
Hanwell W7 108 C4
Kilburn NW6 91 C6
New Barnet EN5 14 B5
Twickenham TW4 151 C4
Mallard Ct
Chingford E4 20 B4
Ilford IG1 79 A6
Kingsbury NW9 45 A2
Little Ilford E12 78 B3
16 Richmond TW10 153 D5
Walthamstow E17 54 B6
Mallard Ho
8 Camberwell SE15 139 D4
St John's Wood NW8 230 A3
Mallard Path 3 SE28 123 B3
Mallard Pl TW1 153 A1
Mallard Point 6 E3 97 C4
Mallards E11 55 A2
Mallards Rd
Barking IG11 102 A3
Woodford IG8 37 B3
Mallard Way NW9 45 A2
Mallard Wlk
Beckenham BR3 206 D4
Sidcup DA14 190 C4
Mall Ct W5 110 A6
Mallet Dr UB5 63 B3
Mallet Ho 1 SW15 156 A6
Mallet Rd SE13 164 B5
Malling SE13 163 D6
Malling Cl CR0 206 C3
Malling Gdns SM4 202 A3
Malling Ho 9 BR3 185 C3
Malling Way BR2 208 D2
Mallinson Ct 2 E11 76 C6
Mallinson Rd
Wallington SM6 219 D5
Wandsworth SW11 158 D6
Mallon Gdns E1 243 D3
Mallord St
SW3 136 B6 266 D6
Mallory Bldgs EC1 241 C5
Mallory Cl SE4 141 A1
Mallory Gdns EN4 15 A4
Mallory St NW8 92 C3 237 B6
Mallow Cl CR0 206 D1
Mallow Ct
Colney Hatch N12 30 C4
Lewisham SE13 142 A3
Mallow Mead NW7 29 A3
Mallow St EC1 242 C6
Mallows The UB10 60 D5
Mall Rd W6 112 B1
Mall Studios 9 NW3 70 D3
Mall The
6 Bexley DA6 147 C1
Brentford TW8 131 D6
4 Bromley BR1 209 A6
Ealing W5 110 A6
Harrow HA3 44 B3
Kingston u T KT6 197 D4
Mortlake SW14 155 A6
Palmers Green N14 16 A1
St James SW1 115 D5 249 C3
Mall The (Prep Sch)
TW2 152 B1
Malmains Cl BR3 208 B5
Malmains Way BR3 208 B5
Malmesbury 30 E2 96 C5
Malmesbury Cl HA5 40 A5
Malmesbury Prim Sch
Morden SM4 202 A3
Tower Hamlets E3 97 B4
Malmesbury Rd
Bow E3 97 B5
Morden SM4 202 A3
Newham E16 98 C2
Woodford E18 36 D2
Malmesbury Terr E16 98 D2
Malmsey Ho SE11 260 D2
Malmsmead Ho E9 75 A3
Malorees Jun & Inf Schs
NW6 68 D1
Malory Cl BR3 185 A1
Malpas Dr HA5 40 D4
Malpas Rd
Dagenham RM9 80 D2
Hackney E8 74 B2
New Cross SE4 141 B3
Malta Rd E10 53 C2
Malta St EC1 241 D6
Maltby Dr EN1 6 B5
Maltby Rd KT9 214 C2
Maltby St SE1 117 D3 263 C6
Maltham Terr N18 34 B4
Malthouse Dr
Chiswick W4 133 D6
Feltham TW13 172 D5
Malthouse Pas SW13 133 C3
Malthus Path 7
SE28 124 C5
Malting Ho E14 119 B6
Maltings W4 110 C1
Maltings Cl SW13 133 C3
Maltings Lo W4 133 C5
Maltings Pl
Bermondsey SE1 253 B2
Parsons Green SW6 265 D1
Maltings The BR6 211 D1
Malting Way TW7 130 D2
Malt Mill SE1 253 C3
Malton Ho SE25 205 C5
Malton Mews
1 Notting Hill W10 91 A1
Plumstead Comm SE18 145 C6
Malton Rd W10 91 A1
Malton St SE18 145 C6
Maltravers St WC2 251 A6
Malt St SE1 140 A6
Malva Cl SW18 157 D6
Malvern Ave
Chingford E4 36 B3
Malvern Ave *continued*
Erith DA7 147 A5
Harrow HA2 63 B5
Malvern Cl
Bushey WD23 8 A5
Ickenham UB10 60 C6
Mitcham CR4 203 C6
Notting Hill W10 91 B2
Penge SE20 184 A1
Surbiton KT6 198 A1
Malvern Ct
Belmont SM2 217 C1
5 East Barnet N20 14 C2
15 Shepherd's Bush
W12 112 A4
South Kensington SW7 256 D4
3 Surbiton KT6 198 A1
Malvern Dr
Feltham TW13 172 D5
Ilford IG3 79 D4
Woodford IG8 37 C6
Malvern Gdns
Cricklewood NW2 69 A6
Harrow HA3 44 A5
Malvern Ho
London N16 51 D1
SE17 262 B1
Malvern Lo N12 30 B6
Malvern Mews NW6 91 C4
Malvern Pl NW6 91 B4
Malvern Rd
Dalston E8 74 A1
Enfield EN3 7 A6
Hampton TW12 173 C3
Harlington UB3 127 C5
Hornsey N8 50 C6
Leytonstone E11 76 D6
Maida Vale NW6 91 C4
Newham E6 100 A6
Surbiton KT6 198 A1
Thornton Heath CR7 204 C5
Tottenham Hale N17 52 A6
Upper Holloway N19 49 D1
Malvern Terr
Edmonton N9 17 D3
Islington N1 234 A6
Malvern Way W13 87 B2
Malwood Rd SW12 159 B5
Malyons Rd SE13 163 D6
Malyons Terr SE13 163 D6
Malyons The TW17 193 B3
Managers St 8 E14 120 A5
Manatee Pl SM6 219 D5
Manaton Cl SE15 140 B2
Manaton Cres UB1 85 C1
Manbey Gr E15 76 C2
Manbey Park Rd E15 76 C2
Manbey Rd E15 76 C2
Manbey St E15 76 C2
Manbre Rd W6 134 C6
Manbrough Ave E6 100 C4
Manchester Ct E16 99 B1
Manchester Dr W10 91 A3
Manchester Gr E14 120 A1
Manchester Ho SE17 262 B2
Manchester Mans N19 49 D2
Manchester Mews
W1 238 A3
Manchester Rd
Cubitt Town E14 120 A3
South Norwood CR7 205 A6
Tottenham N15 51 B3
Manchester Sq
W1 93 A1 238 B2
Manchester St
W1 93 A2 238 A3
Manchester Way
RM10 81 D4
Manchuria Rd SW11 159 A5
Manciple St
SE1 117 B3 262 D6
Mandalay Ho 6 N16 73 B4
Mandalay Rd SW4 159 C6
Mandarin Ct
6 Deptford SE8 141 C6
Willesden NW10 67 B2
Mandarin Way UB4 84 D1
Mandela Cl
36 Shepherd's Bush
W12 112 B6
Stonebridge NW10 67 A1
Mandela Ho
Plumstead Comm
SE18 145 B6
18 Spitalfields E2 95 D4
Mandela Rd E16 99 A1

Mandela St
Camden Town NW1 . . . 93 C6 232 B6
Kennington SW9 . . . 138 C5
Mandela Way SE1 . . . 117 C2 263 B4
Manderville Ho SE1 . . . 263 D2
Mandeville Cl
5 Greenwich SE3 . . . 142 D5
Merton SW19 . . . 179 A2
Mandeville Ct
Hampstead NW3 . . . 69 D3
Highams Pk E4 . . . 35 A6
Mandeville Ctyd SW11 . . . 268 A1
Mandeville Dr KT6 . . . 197 D1
Mandeville Ho 8 SW4 . . . 159 C6
Mandeville Pl W1 . . . 238 B2
Mandeville Prim Sch E5 . . . 74 D5
Mandeville Rd
Enfield EN3 . . . 7 A6
Isleworth TW7 . . . 131 A3
Littleton TW17 . . . 192 C4
Northolt UB5 . . . 63 C1
Osidge N14 . . . 15 C2
Mandeville Sch UB5 . . . 63 B2
Mandeville St E5 . . . 75 A5
Mandrake Rd SW17 . . . 158 D1
Mandrake Way 3 E15 . . . 76 C1
Mandrell Rd SW2 . . . 160 A6
Manesty Ct N14 . . . 15 D4
Manette St W1 . . . 239 D1
Manfred Ct 7 SW15 . . . 157 B6
Manfred Rd SW15 . . . 157 B6
Manger Rd N7 . . . 72 A2
Mangold Way 4 DA18 . . . 125 A3
Manilla Ct RM6 . . . 58 B3
Manilla St E14 . . . 119 C4
Manister Rd SE2 . . . 124 A3
Manitoba Ct 29 SE16 . . . 118 C4
Manitoba Gdns 6 BR6 . . . 227 D2
Manley Ct N16 . . . 73 D5
Manley Ho SE11 . . . 261 A2
Manley St NW1 . . . 231 A6
Manly Dixon Dr EN3 . . . 7 A6
Mann Cl 3 CR0 . . . 221 A5
Manneby Prior N1 . . . 233 D3
Mannering Ho 16 SW2 . . . 160 B6
Manning Ct 3 SE28 . . . 124 B5
Manningford Cl EC1 . . . 234 C2
Manning Gdns HA3 . . . 43 D2
Manning Ho
3 Notting Hill W11 . . . 91 A1
6 Walthamstow E17 . . . 54 A6
Manning Pl TW10 . . . 154 B5
Manning Rd
Dagenham RM10 . . . 81 C1
Walthamstow E17 . . . 53 A4
Manningtree Cl SW19 . . . 157 A3
Manningtree Rd HA4 . . . 62 B4
Manningtree St 2 E1 . . . 96 A1
Mannin Rd RM6 . . . 58 B2
Mannock Mews IG8 . . . 37 B2
Mannock Rd N22 . . . 50 D6
Mann's Cl TW7 . . . 152 D6
Manns Rd HA8 . . . 26 C4
Manny Shinwell Ho SW6 . . . 264 D5
Manoel Rd TW2 . . . 152 A2
Manor Ave
Hounslow TW4 . . . 128 D3
New Cross SE4 . . . 141 B3
Northolt UB5 . . . 63 B1
Manorbrook SE12, SE3 . . . 143 A1
Manor Circus TW9 . . . 132 C2
Manor Cl
Barnet EN5 . . . 1 A1
Edgware NW7 . . . 27 B5
Higham Hill E17 . . . 35 A1
Kingsbury NW9 . . . 44 D4
New Malden KT4 . . . 199 C1
Ruislip HA4 . . . 39 D1
Thamesmead SE28 . . . 102 C1
Manor Cottages App N2 . . . 30 A1
Manor Cotts N2 . . . 30 A1
Manor Court Lo 12 E18 . . . 37 A2
Manor Court Rd W7 . . . 108 C6
Manor Cres KT5 . . . 198 C3
Manor Croft HA8 . . . 26 C4
Manor Ct
4 Barking IG11 . . . 79 D1
7 Brixton SW2 . . . 160 B6
Camberwell SE15 . . . 139 D4
Chingford E4 . . . 20 C3
Fortis Green N2 . . . 48 D4
Friern Barnet N20 . . . 14 D1
Gunnersbury W3 . . . 110 C2
5 Hackbridge SM6 . . . 219 A5
Harrow HA1 . . . 42 D3
Kingston u T KT2 . . . 176 C2
Osidge N14 . . . 15 D2
Parsons Green SW6 . . . 265 D1
Streatham SW16 . . . 160 A1
Surbiton KT5 . . . 198 C3
8 Sutton SM1 . . . 218 A4
Twickenham TW2 . . . 152 A2
Walthamstow E10 . . . 53 D1
5 Wembley HA9 . . . 66 A3
Manordene Cl KT7 . . . 197 A1
Manordene Rd SE28 . . . 102 D1
Manor Dr
East Barnet N14 . . . 15 B3
Edgware NW7 . . . 27 B5
Feltham TW13 . . . 172 D5
Friern Barnet N20 . . . 14 D1
Hinchley Wood KT10 . . . 213 A5
Sunbury TW16 . . . 172 A1
Surbiton KT5 . . . 198 C3
Wembley HA9 . . . 66 B4
West Ewell KT19 . . . 215 C2
Manor Dr N KT3, KT4 . . . 199 B2
Manor Dr The KT4 . . . 199 D1
Manor Farm Ave TW17 . . . 192 D3
Manor Farm Cl KT4 . . . 199 C1
Manor Farm Ct E6 . . . 100 B4
Manor Farm Dr E4 . . . 20 C1
Manor Farm Rd
Thornton Heath CR7, SW16 . . . 182 C1
Wembley HA0 . . . 87 D5
Manorfield Cl 3 N19 . . . 71 C4
Manorfield Prim Sch E14 . . . 97 D2
Manorfields Cl BR7 . . . 211 D6
Manor Gate UB5 . . . 63 A1
Manorgate Rd KT2 . . . 176 C2
Manor Gdns
8 Chiswick W4 . . . 111 C1
Clapham SW4 . . . 137 C3
Gunnersbury W3 . . . 110 C2
Hampton TW12 . . . 174 A3
Merton SW20 . . . 179 B1
Richmond TW10, TW9 . . . 132 B1
Ruislip HA4 . . . 62 C3
South Croydon CR2 . . . 221 D2
Sunbury TW16 . . . 172 A1
Upper Holloway N7 . . . 72 A5
Manor Gr
Beckenham BR3 . . . 185 D1
Deptford SE15 . . . 140 C6
Richmond TW9 . . . 132 C2
Manor Gt SW15 . . . 157 A6
Manor Hall Ave NW4 . . . 28 D1
Manor Hall Dr NW4 . . . 28 D1
Manor Hall Gdns E10 . . . 53 C1
Manor Ho
Brentford TW8 . . . 109 C1
Manor Pk E12 . . . 77 D4
Osidge N14 . . . 15 D3
Paddington NW1 . . . 237 B4
Twickenham TW2 . . . 152 C2
Wallington SM6 . . . 219 B3
Manor Ho The
Bexley DA5 . . . 169 D3
Chislehurst SE9 . . . 188 A5
Manor House Ct
Lower Halliford TW17 . . . 192 D2
Paddington W9 . . . 236 A5
Manor House Dr NW6 . . . 68 D1
Manor House Est HA7 . . . 25 B5
Manor House Gdns E11 . . . 55 B3
Manor House Sta N4 . . . 50 D1
Manor House Way TW7 . . . 131 B2
Manor Jun & Inf Schs IG11 . . . 79 D2
Manor La
Feltham TW13 . . . 150 A2
Harlington UB3 . . . 127 B6
Hither Green SE12 . . . 164 C5
Sunbury TW16 . . . 172 B1
Sutton SM1 . . . 218 A3
Manor Lane Terr SE13 . . . 164 C6
Manor Lo NW2 . . . 68 D2
Manor Mans
7 Hampstead NW3 . . . 70 C2
Tufnell Pk N7 . . . 72 A5
Manor Mead Sch TW17 . . . 192 D4
Manor Mews
New Cross SE4 . . . 141 B3
Paddington NW6 . . . 91 C5
Manor Mount SE23 . . . 162 C3
Manor Oak Mans SE22 . . . 162 B5
Manor Par
Harrow HA1 . . . 42 D3
Stoke Newington N16 . . . 73 D6
MANOR PARK . . . 78 A4
Manor Park Cl BR4 . . . 207 D1
Manor Park Cres HA8 . . . 26 C4
Manor Park Dr HA2 . . . 41 D6
Manor Park Gdns HA8 . . . 26 C4
Manor Park Par SE13 . . . 142 B1
Manor Park Prim Sch SM1 . . . 218 A3
Manor Park Rd
Chislehurst BR7 . . . 189 B2
Dagenham NW10 . . . 89 D6
East Finchley N2 . . . 48 B6
Manor Pk E12 . . . 77 D4
Sutton SM1 . . . 218 A3
West Wickham BR4 . . . 207 D1
Manor Park Sta E12 . . . 77 D4
Manor Pk
Chislehurst BR7 . . . 189 B2
Lewisham SE13 . . . 164 C6
Richmond TW9 . . . 132 B1
Manor Pl
Chislehurst BR7 . . . 189 B1
East Bedfont TW14 . . . 150 A3
Mitcham CR4 . . . 203 C6
Newington SE17 . . . 117 A1 262 A2
Sutton SM1 . . . 217 D4
Walton-on-T KT12 . . . 194 A2
Manor Prim Sch E15 . . . 98 C5
Manor Rd
Ashford TW15 . . . 170 C5
Barking IG11 . . . 79 D2
Barnet EN5 . . . 1 A1
Beckenham BR3 . . . 185 D1
Belmont SM2 . . . 217 B1
Bowes Pk N22 . . . 32 A4
Dagenham RM6 . . . 58 D3
Ealing W13 . . . 109 A6
East Molesey KT8 . . . 196 B5
Enfield EN2 . . . 5 B3
Harrow HA1 . . . 43 A3
Hayes UB3 . . . 84 A1
Higham Hill E17 . . . 35 A1
Loughton IG10 . . . 21 B5
Merton SW20 . . . 179 B1
Mitcham CR4 . . . 203 C6
Newham E15, E16 . . . 98 C4
Old Bexley DA5 . . . 169 D3
Richmond TW10, TW9 . . . 132 B1
Ruislip HA4 . . . 39 B1
Sidcup DA15 . . . 168 A1
South Norwood SE25 . . . 206 A6
Stamford Hill N16 . . . 51 C1
Teddington TW11 . . . 175 B5
Tottenham N17 . . . 34 B2
Twickenham TW2 . . . 152 B2
Wallington SM5, SM6 . . . 219 B3
Walthamstow E10 . . . 53 C2
Walton-on-T KT12 . . . 193 D2
West Wickham BR4 . . . 223 D6
Manor Rd N
Hinchley Wood KT7 . . . 213 A6
Wallington SM5, SM6 . . . 219 B4
Manor Rd S KT10 . . . 212 C4
Manor Road Ho HA1 . . . 43 A3
Manor Sch NW10 . . . 90 C6
Manorside EN5 . . . 1 A1
Manorside Cl SE2 . . . 124 D2
Manorside Prim Sch N3 . . . 30 A2
Manor Sq RM8 . . . 80 C6
Manor Street Est SW3 . . . 267 B6
Manor The
Dulwich SE23 . . . 162 C4
Mayfair W1 . . . 248 C5
Manor Vale TW8 . . . 109 C1
Manor View N3 . . . 29 D1
Manorway
Enfield EN1 . . . 17 C4
Woodford IG8 . . . 37 C5
Manor Way
Beckenham BR3 . . . 207 C6
Bromley BR2 . . . 210 A3
Chingford E4 . . . 36 B6
Colindale NW9 . . . 45 C5
Manor Way *continued*
Greenwich SE3 . . . 143 A1
Gunnersbury W3 . . . 110 C2
Harrow HA2 . . . 41 D5
Mitcham CR4 . . . 203 C6
New Malden KT4 . . . 199 D1
Orpington BR5 . . . 211 A5
Ruislip HA4 . . . 39 D1
Sidcup DA5 . . . 169 C3
Southall UB2 . . . 106 D2
South Croydon CR2 . . . 221 D2
Manor Waye UB8 . . . 82 A6
Manor Way The SM6 . . . 219 B4
Manpreet Ct E12 . . . 78 B3
Manray Ct 2 N8 . . . 50 A4
Manresa Rd SW3 . . . 114 C1 257 A1
Mansard Beeches SW17 . . . 181 A5
Mansard Cl HA5 . . . 40 D6
Mansard Manor 4 SM2 . . . 218 A1
Manse Cl UB3 . . . 127 B6
Manse Ct DA14 . . . 190 C5
Mansel Ct SW11 . . . 267 B1
Mansel Gr E17 . . . 35 C2
Mansell Ho SW8 . . . 269 B2
Mansell Rd
Acton W3 . . . 111 B4
Southall UB6 . . . 85 D2
Mansell St E1 . . . 95 D1 243 D1
Mansel Rd SW19 . . . 179 B4
Manse Rd N16 . . . 73 D5
Mansergh Cl SE18 . . . 144 A5
Mansfield Ave
East Barnet EN4 . . . 15 A5
Ruislip HA4 . . . 40 B1
Tottenham N15 . . . 51 B5
Mansfield Cl N9 . . . 18 A5
Mansfield Ct 27 E2 . . . 95 D6
Mansfield Dr UB4 . . . 83 C3
Mansfield Hill E4 . . . 19 D3
Mansfield Ho SW15 . . . 156 D5
Mansfield Hts N2 . . . 48 D4
Mansfield Mews W1 . . . 238 C3
Mansfield Pl 28 NW3 . . . 70 A4
Mansfield Rd
Acton W3 . . . 88 D3
Chessington KT9 . . . 213 D3
Ilford IG1 . . . 78 C6
Maitland Pk NW3 . . . 70 D4
South Croydon CR2 . . . 221 B2
Walthamstow E17 . . . 53 B5
Wanstead E11 . . . 55 B3
Mansfield St W1 . . . 93 B2 238 C3
Mansford St E2 . . . 96 A5
Manship Rd CR4 . . . 181 A2
Mansion Cl SW9 . . . 138 C4
Mansion Gdns NW3 . . . 69 D5
Mansion Ho* EC4 . . . 242 C1
Mansion House Pl EC3, EC4 . . . 242 C1
Mansion House St EC2 . . . 242 C1
Mansion House Sta EC4 . . . 117 A6 252 B6
Mansions The NW6 . . . 69 B3
Manson Mews SW7 . . . 114 B2 256 C3
Manson Pl SW7 . . . 114 B2 256 C3
Manstead Gdns RM6 . . . 58 C2
Manston
Camden Town NW1 . . . 71 C1
Tottenham N17 . . . 33 B1
Manston Ave UB2 . . . 107 C2
Manston Cl SE20 . . . 184 C2
Manstone Rd NW2 . . . 69 A3
Manston Gr KT2 . . . 175 D5
Manston Ho W14 . . . 254 B5
Mantell Ho SW4 . . . 159 C6
Manthorpe Rd SE18 . . . 123 A1
Mantilla Rd SW17 . . . 181 A6
Mantle Rd SE4 . . . 141 A2
Mantlet Cl SW16 . . . 181 C3
Mantle Way E15 . . . 76 C1
Manton Ave W7 . . . 109 A4
Manton Cl UB3 . . . 105 C6
Manton Ho N16 . . . 73 B5
Manton Rd
Holdbrook EN3 . . . 7 C5
Plumstead SE2 . . . 124 A2
Mantua St 23 SW11 . . . 136 B2
Mantus Cl
Bethnal Green E1 . . . 96 C3
19 Stepney E1 . . . 96 C3
Mantus Rd E1 . . . 96 C3
Manus Way N20 . . . 14 A3
Manville Gdns SW17 . . . 159 B1
Manville Rd SW17 . . . 159 B1
Manwood Rd SE4 . . . 163 B5
Manwood St E16 . . . 122 B5
Manygate La TW17 . . . 193 A3
Many Gates SW12 . . . 159 B2
Mapesbury Ct NW2 . . . 69 A3
Mapesbury Mews 1 NW9 . . . 46 A3
Mapesbury Rd NW2 . . . 69 A2
Mapeshill Pl NW2 . . . 68 C2
Mapes Ho 7 NW6 . . . 69 A1
Mape St E2 . . . 96 B3
Maple Ave
East Acton W3 . . . 111 C5
Harrow HA2 . . . 63 D6
Walthamstow E4 . . . 35 B4
Yiewsley UB7 . . . 104 B6
Maple Cl
Buckhurst Hill IG9 . . . 21 D1
Clapham Pk SW4 . . . 159 D5
Finchley N3 . . . 29 C4
Hampton TW12 . . . 173 B4
Hayes UB4 . . . 84 D4
Mitcham CR4 . . . 181 B2
Petts Wood BR5 . . . 211 B4
Ruislip HA4 . . . 40 B3
South Tottenham N16 . . . 52 A3
Maple Cres DA15 . . . 168 A5
Maplecroft Cl E6 . . . 100 A1
Maple Ct
Ashford TW15 . . . 171 B3
Catford SE6 . . . 163 D3
2 Croydon CR0 . . . 221 A4
7 Dagenham RM8 . . . 58 D2
Kingston u T KT3 . . . 199 B6
Newham E6 . . . 100 C2
6 Pinner HA5 . . . 22 C1
Sidcup DA14 . . . 190 B5
11 West Norwood SW16 . . . 182 C5
3 Willesden NW2 . . . 68 D4
Mapledale Ave CR0 . . . 222 A5
Mapledene BR7 . . . 189 A5
Mapledene Est E8 . . . 74 A1
Mapledene Rd E8 . . . 74 A1
Mapledown Sch NW2 . . . 46 C2
Mapledurham Ct 3 N13 . . . 32 C6
Maple Gdns
Grahame Pk HA8 . . . 27 C3
Stanwell TW19 . . . 148 A2
Maple Gr
Brentford TW8 . . . 131 B5
Ealing W5 . . . 109 D3
Kingsbury NW9 . . . 45 A2
Southall UB1 . . . 85 B2
Maple Gr Bsns Ctr TW4 . . . 128 C1
Maple Ho
2 Kingston u T KT6 . . . 198 A4
11 Maitland Pk NW3 . . . 70 D2
5 New Cross SE8 . . . 141 B5
4 Richmond TW9 . . . 132 D4
Teddington KT1 . . . 175 C3
13 Walthamstow E17 . . . 53 D6
Maplehurst 2 BR2 . . . 186 C1
Maplehurst Cl KT1 . . . 198 A5
Maple Ind Est TW13 . . . 150 A1
Maple Inf Sch KT6 . . . 197 D4
Maple Leaf Dr DA15 . . . 167 D3
Mapleleafe Gdns IG6 . . . 56 D6
Maple Leaf Sq 27 SE16 . . . 118 D4
Maple Lo
Buckhurst Hill IG9 . . . 21 D3
Putney SW15 . . . 157 A5
Welsh Harp NW9 . . . 67 B6
Maple Mews
Paddington NW6 . . . 91 D5
Streatham SW16 . . . 182 B5
Maple Pl
Marylebone W1 . . . 239 B5
Tottenham N17 . . . 34 A3
Yiewsley UB7 . . . 104 B6
Maple Rd
Hayes UB4 . . . 84 D4
Kingston u T KT6 . . . 197 D4
Leytonstone E11 . . . 54 C3
Penge SE20 . . . 184 C2
Maples Pl E1 . . . 96 B2
Maple St
5 Bethnal Green E2 . . . 96 B5
Fitzrovia W1 . . . 93 C3 239 B5
Maplestead Rd
Dagenham RM9 . . . 102 B6
Streatham SW2 . . . 160 B4
Maples The 4 KT1 . . . 175 C3
Maplethorpe Rd CR7 . . . 204 D5
Mapleton Cl BR2 . . . 209 A3
Mapleton Cres
Enfield EN3 . . . 6 C5
Wandsworth SW18 . . . 157 D5
Mapleton Rd
Chingford E4 . . . 20 A1
Enfield EN1 . . . 6 B3
Wandsworth SW18 . . . 157 D5
Maple Tree Pl 7 SE3 . . . 144 A4
Maple Way TW13 . . . 150 B1
Maple Wlk W10 . . . 90 D3
Maplin Cl N21 . . . 16 B5
Maplin Ho 7 SE2 . . . 124 D4
Maplin Rd E16 . . . 99 B1
Maplin St E3 . . . 97 B4
Mapperley Cl 3 E11 . . . 55 A3
Mapperley Dr IG8 . . . 36 C3
Marabou Cl E12 . . . 78 A3
Marada Ho NW6 . . . 69 A1
Marais W4 . . . 133 A5
Maran Way DA18 . . . 124 D3
Marathon Way SE28 . . . 123 D4
Marban Rd W9 . . . 91 B4
Marble Arch* W1 . . . 114 D6 247 D6
Marble Arch Sta W1 . . . 92 D1 237 D1
Marble Cl W3 . . . 110 D5
Marble Dr NW2 . . . 46 D2
Marbleford Ct 4 N6 . . . 49 D2
Marble Hill* TW1 . . . 153 C4
Marble Hill Cl TW1 . . . 153 B4
Marble Hill Gdns TW1 . . . 153 B4
Marble Ho
Paddington W9 . . . 91 B3
Plumstead Comm SE18 . . . 123 D1
Marble Quay SE1 . . . 118 A5
Marbrook Ct SE12 . . . 165 C1
Marcella Rd SW9 . . . 138 C3
Marcellina Way BR6 . . . 227 D5
March 23 NW9 . . . 27 D2
Marchant Ho 13 SW2 . . . 160 B6
Marchant Rd E11 . . . 76 B6
Marchant St SE14 . . . 141 A6
Marchbank Rd W14 . . . 135 B6 264 D6
March Ct SW15 . . . 134 B1
Marchmont Ho 10 SW16 . . . 181 C5
Marchmont Rd
Richmond TW10 . . . 154 B6
Wallington SM6 . . . 219 C1
Marchmont St WC1 . . . 94 A3 240 A6
March Rd 7 TW1 . . . 153 A4
Marchside Cl TW5 . . . 128 D4
Marchwood Cl 9 SE5 . . . 139 C5
Marchwood Cres W5 . . . 87 D1
Marcia Rd SE1 . . . 117 C2 263 B3
Marcilly Rd SW18 . . . 158 B6
Marcol Ho W1 . . . 238 D2
Marcon Ct 29 E8 . . . 74 B3
Marconi Pl N11 . . . 31 B6
Marconi Rd E10 . . . 53 C1
Marconi Way UB1 . . . 85 D1
Marcon Pl E8 . . . 74 B3
Marco Rd W6 . . . 112 C3
Marcourt Lawns W5 . . . 88 A3
Marcus Ct
Brentford TW8 . . . 132 A5
Newham E15 . . . 98 C6
Marcus Garvey Mews SE22 . . . 162 B6
Marcus Garvey Way 9 SE24 . . . 138 C1
Marcus Ho 14 SE15 . . . 139 D4
Marcus St
Wandsworth SW18 . . . 157 D5
West Ham E15 . . . 98 D6
Marcus Terr SW18 . . . 157 D5
Mardale Ct NW7 . . . 28 A3
Mardale Dr NW9 . . . 45 B4
Mardell Rd CR0 . . . 206 D4
Marden Ave BR2 . . . 209 A3
Marden Cres CR0 . . . 204 B3
Marden Ho 6 E8 . . . 74 B3
Marden Rd
Thornton Heath CR0 . . . 204 B3
Tottenham N17 . . . 33 C1
Marden Sq SE16 . . . 118 B3
Marder Rd W13 . . . 109 A4
Mardon HA5 . . . 23 B3
Mardyke Ho SE17 . . . 262 D4
Marechal Niel Ave DA15 . . . 167 B1
Marechal Niel Par DA15 . . . 167 B1
Maresby Ho E4 . . . 19 D2

Maresfield CR0 221 C5
Maresfield Gdns NW3 70 A2
Mare St E8 74 B1
Marey Ct 10 CR2 221 A3
Marfleet Cl SM5 218 C6
Margaret Ave E4 19 D5
Margaret Bondfield Ave IG11 80 A1
Margaret Bondfield Ho
5 Bow E3 97 A5
22 Kentish Town N7 71 D3
Margaret Ct
Barnet EN4 2 B1
Marylebone W1 239 A2
Margaret Gardner Dr SE9 166 B2
Margaret Herbison Ho SW6 264 D5
Margaret Hill Ho 1 N8 50 A4
Margaret Ho
16 Hammersmith W6 112 C1
2 Sutton SM1 217 D5
Margaret Ingram Cl SW6 264 C5
Margaret Lockwood Cl KT5 198 B5
Margaret Mcmillan Ho 10 N19 49 D2
Margaret Rd
Barnet EN4 2 B1
Bexley DA5 168 D5
Stamford Hill N16 51 D1
Margarets Ct HA8 26 D5
Margaret's Ct E11 54 B2
Margaret St W1 93 C1 239 A2
Margaretta Terr SW3 136 C6 267 B6
Margaretting Rd E12 55 C1
Margaret Way IG4 56 A3
Margaret White Ho NW1 232 C2
Margate Rd SW2 160 A6
Margery Fry Ct N7 72 A5
Margery Park Rd E7 77 A2
Margery Rd RM8 80 D5
Margery St WC1 94 C4 234 A1
Margin Dr SW19 178 D6
Margravine Gdns
Hammersmith W6 112 D1
West Kensington W14 254 A2
Margravine Rd W6 135 A6 264 A6
Marham Gdns
Morden SM4 202 A3
Wandsworth SW17, SW18 158 C3
Mar Ho 4 SE7 143 C6
Maria Cl 13 SE1 118 A2
Maria Fidelis Convent Sch (Lower) NW1 93 C4 232 B1
Maria Fidelis Convent Sch (Upper) NW1 93 D4 232 C2
Marian Cl UB4 84 D3
Marian Ct
Hackney E9 74 C3
1 Sutton SM1 217 D3
Marian Lo 5 SW20 178 D3
Marian Pl E2 96 B5
Marian Rd SW16 181 C2
Marian Sq E2 96 B5
Marian St 2 E2 96 B5
Marian Vian Prim Sch BR3 207 A4
Marian Way NW10 67 D1
Maria Terr E1 96 D3
Maria Theresa Cl KT3 199 B4
Maribor 13 SE10 142 A5
Maricas Ave HA3 24 B2
Marie Curie SE5 139 C4
Marie Lloyd Ct 13 SW9 138 B1
Marie Lloyd Gdns 1 N19 50 A2
Marie Lloyd Ho N1 235 C3
Marien Ct E4 36 B5
Marie Stopes Ct 3 N19 50 A2
Marigold Cl UB1 107 A6
Marigold Rd N17 34 C3
Marigold St SE16 118 B4
Marigold Way CR0 206 D1
Marilea Ct W5 109 D4
Marillic Ho NW7 28 C6
Marina App UB4 85 A2
Marina Ave KT3 200 B4
Marina Cl 1 BR2 209 A6
Marina Ct
12 Bow E3 97 C4
Greenford UB6 85 D5
Marina Dr DA16 145 C3
Marina Gdns RM7 59 D4
Marina Pl KT1 175 D2
Marina Point 4 E14 119 D3
Marina Way TW11 175 D3
Marine Dr
Barking IG11 102 B4
5 Woolwich SE18 122 B2
Marinefield Rd SW6 135 D3
Marinel Ho 25 SE5 139 A5
Mariner Gdns TW10 153 C1
Mariner Rd E12 78 C4
Mariners Mews E14 120 B2
Marine St SE16 118 A3
Marine Twr 29 SE8 141 B6
Marion Ave TW17 192 D4
Marion Ct 4 SW17 180 C5
Marion Gr IG8 36 C6
Marion Rd
Mill Hill NW7 28 A5
Thornton Heath CR0 205 B4
Marion Richardson Prim Sch E1 96 D1
Marischal Rd SE13 142 B2
Maritime Ho
5 Clapham SW4 137 C2
14 Woolwich SE18 122 D2
Maritime Ind Est SE7 121 B2
Maritime Quay 5 E14 119 C1
Maritime St E3 97 B3
Marius Mans 3 SW17 159 A2
Marius Rd SW17 159 A2
Marjorie Gr SW11 136 D1
Marjorie McClure Sch BR7 189 A2
Marjory Kinnon Sch TW14 149 C6
Markab Rd HA6 22 A5
Mark Ave E4 19 D5
Mark Cl
Bexleyheath DA7 147 A4
Keston Mark BR2 226 A4
Southall UB1 107 D5
Markeston Gn WD19 22 D6
Market Ct W1 239 A2
Market Ctr The UB2 106 B2
Market La
Burnt Oak HA8 27 A2
Shepherd's Bush W12 112 C4
Market Mews W1 115 B5 248 C3
Market Par
Croydon SE25 206 A5
1 Edmonton N9 18 A2
Feltham TW13 151 A2
Leyton E10 53 D3
Walthamstow E17 53 B6
Market Pavilion E10 75 C5
Market Pl
3 Acton W3 111 A5
1 Bermondsey SE16 118 B2
2 Bexleyheath DA6 147 C1
Brentford TW8 131 C5
East Finchley N2 48 C6
Enfield EN2 5 B2
Kingston u T KT1 175 D1
Marylebone W1 239 A2
Market Pl The NW11 47 D5
Market Rd
Barnsbury N7 72 A2
Richmond TW9 132 C2
Market Sq
Bromley BR1 187 A1
Poplar E14 97 D1
Market Sq The N9 18 B2
Market St
Spitalfields E1 243 C4
Wallend E6 100 C5
Woolwich SE18 122 C2
Market Studios 14 W12 112 C4
Market The SM1, SM5 202 A1
Market Way
Poplar E14 97 D1
2 Wembley HA0 66 A3
Market Yd Mews SE1 263 A6
Markfield Beam Engine & Mus* N15 52 A4
Markfield Gdns E4 19 D4
Markfield Ho N15 52 A4
Markfield Rd N15 52 A4
Markham Ct NW4 46 C6
Markham Ho
1 Dagenham RM10 81 C5
9 Dulwich SE21 183 C6
Markham Pl SW3 257 C2
Markham Sq SW3 114 D1 257 C2
Markham St SW3 114 C1 257 B2
Mark Ho 3 E2 96 D5
Markhole Cl TW12 173 B3
Markhouse Ave E17 53 A3
Markhouse Pas E17 53 B3
Markhouse Rd E17 53 B3
Mark La EC3 117 C6 253 B6
Markland Ho W10 112 D6
Mark Lo 9 EN4 2 C1
Markmanor Ave E17 53 B2
Mark Mans W12 112 A4
Mark Rd N22 32 D1
Marksbury Ave TW9 132 C2
Marks Gate Jun & Inf Schs RM6 59 A6
Mark Sq EC2 243 A6
Mark St
Broadgate EC2 243 A6
Stratford E15 76 C1
Markstone Ho SE1 251 C1
Mark Wade Cl E12 55 D1
Markway The TW16 172 C1
Markwell Cl SE26 184 B6
Markyate Ho 6 W10 90 C3
Markyate Rd RM8 80 B3
Marland Ho SW1 257 D6
Marlands Rd IG5 56 B6
Marlang Ct BR3 186 B2
Marlborough
11 Putney SW19 156 D3
St John's Wood W9 229 A2
Marlborough Ave
Edgware HA8 10 D1
3 Hackney E8 96 A6
New Southgate N14 15 C1
Ruislip HA4 39 B3
Marlborough Cl
Broom Hill BR6 211 D3
Friern Barnet N20 14 D1
Mitcham SW19 180 C4
Newington SE17 261 D3
Marlborough Cres
Bedford Pk W4 111 C3
Harlington UB3 127 B5
Marlborough Ct
6 Beckenham BR3 185 C2
7 Bromley BR1 186 D3
7 Buckhurst Hill IG9 21 C2
Harrow HA1 42 B5
Kensington W8 255 A4
Marylebone W1 239 A1
Wallington SM6 219 C1
Marlborough Day Hospl NW8 92 A5 229 A4
Marlborough Dr IG5 56 A6
Marlborough Flats SW3 257 B4
Marlborough Fst & Mid Sch HA1 42 C5
Marlborough Gdns
Friern Barnet N20 14 D1
Surbiton KT6 197 D2
Marlborough Gr SE1 118 A1
Marlborough Hill
Harrow HA1 42 C5
St John's Wood NW8 92 A6 229 B5
Marlborough Ho
Marylebone NW1 238 D6
Richmond TW10 154 C6
Stoke Newington N4 51 A1
Marlborough Ho SW1 249 B3
Marlborough Ho SW19 156 D1
Marlborough La SE7 143 C5
Marlborough Lo
36 Stepney E1 96 C3
St John's Wood NW8 229 A3
Marlborough Mans 5 NW6 69 C3
Marlborough Mews 18 SW2 138 B1
Marlborough Par 1 UB10 82 D3
Marlborough Park Ave DA15 168 A3
Marlborough Pl NW8 92 A5 229 B4
Marlborough Prim Sch
Chelsea SW3 114 C2 257 B3
Isleworth TW7 131 A4
Marlborough Rd
Acton Green W4 111 A1
Ashford TW15 170 A5
Bexley DA7 146 D2
Bowes Pk N22 32 B4
Marlborough Rd *continued*
Brentford TW7 131 B5
Bromley BR2 209 C5
Chingford E4 35 D4
Dagenham RM8 80 C4
Ealing W5 109 D4
Edmonton N9 18 A3
Feltham TW13 150 D2
Hampton TW12 173 C4
Hillingdon UB10 82 D4
Leyton E15 76 C4
Mitcham SW19 180 C4
Richmond TW10 154 B5
Romford RM7 59 D5
Southall UB2 106 C3
South Croydon CR2 221 A1
St James SW1 115 C5 249 B3
Sutton SM1 217 C6
Upper Holloway N19 72 A6
Upton E7 77 C1
Wanstead E18 55 A6
Woolwich SE18 123 A3
Marlborough Sch DA15 168 A4
Marlborough St SW3 114 C2 257 B3
Marlborough Trad Est TW9 132 D4
Marlborough Yd N19 71 D6
Marlbury NW8 91 D6
Marler Rd SE23 163 B3
Marlesford Ct SM6 219 C4
Marlex Lo N3 29 D2
Marley Ave DA7 146 D6
Marley Cl
Harringay N15 50 D5
Southall UB6 85 C4
Marley Ho 14 W11 112 D6
Marley Wlk NW2 68 C3
Marl Field Cl KT4 200 A1
Marlfield Ct KT3 199 D2
Marlin Cl TW16 171 C4
Marlin Ct 5 DA14 190 A6
Marling Ct TW12 173 B4
Marlingdene Cl TW12 173 C4
Marlings Cl BR7 211 C5
Marlings Park Ave BR7 211 C6
Marlin Ho SW15 157 A6
Marlins Cl 3 SM1 218 A3
Marloes Cl HA0 65 D4
Marloes Rd W8 113 D3 255 C5
Marlow Cl SE20 206 B6
Marlow Cres TW1 152 D5
Marlow Ct
Colindale NW9 45 D6
1 Ealing W7 108 C5
6 Finchley N3 29 C2
Harrow HA1 42 A3
Osidge N14 15 C4
Willesden NW6 68 D1
Marlow Dr SM3 216 D5
Marlowe Bsns Ctr 2 SE14 141 A5
Marlowe Cl BR7 189 B4
Marlowe Ct
Chelsea SW3 257 B3
2 Dulwich SE19 183 D5
6 Kingston u T KT2 175 D6
Marlowe Gdns SE9 166 C5
Marlowe Ho
Kingston u T KT1 197 D5
15 Stoke Newington N16 73 C4
Marlowe Lo CR0 223 A6
Marlowe Rd E17 54 A5
Marlowe Sq CR4 203 C5
Marlowes The NW8 92 B6 229 C6
Marlowe Way CR0 220 A6
Marlow Gdns UB3 105 B3
Marlow Ho
Bermondsey SE1 263 C6
15 Kensington W2 91 D1
44 Spitalfields E2 95 D4
Teddington TW11 175 A6
Wallington CR0 220 A5
Marlow Rd
Newham E6 100 B4
Penge SE20 184 B1
Southall UB2 107 B3
Marlow Studio Workshops 43 E2 95 D4
Marlow Way SE16 118 D4
Marl Rd SW18 136 A1
Marlston NW1 231 D1
Marlton St SE10 120 D1
Marlwood Cl DA15 167 C2
Marmadon Rd SE18, SE2 123 D2
Marmara Apts 4 E16 121 A6
Marmion App E4 35 C6
Marmion Ave E4 35 B6
Marmion Cl E4 35 B6
Marmion Ho 13 SW12 159 B4
Marmion Mews 4 SW11 137 A2
Marmion Rd SW11 137 A1
Marmont Rd SE15 140 A5
Marmora Ho E1 97 A2
Marmora Rd SE22 162 C5
Marmot Rd TW4 128 D2
Marncrest Ct KT5 198 B4
Marne Ave
Friern Barnet N11 31 B6
Welling DA16 146 A2
Marnell Way TW4 128 D2
Marner Prim Sch E3 97 D3
Marne St W10 91 A4
Marney Rd SW11 137 A1
Marnfield Cres SW2 160 B3
Marnham Ave NW2 69 A4
Marnham Cres UB6 85 D5
Marnham Ct HA0 65 C3
Marnie Ct 11 E11 76 C6
Marnock Ho SE17 262 C2
Marnock Rd SE4 163 B6
Maroon St E14 97 A2
Maroons Way SE6 185 C5
Marqueen Twrs 1 SW16 182 B3
Marquess Rd N1 73 B2
Marquess Rd N N1 73 B2
Marquess Rd S 22 N1 73 A2
Marquis Cl HA0 66 B1
Marquis Ct
Barking IG11 79 C3
Finsbury Pk N4 50 B1
1 Kingston u T KT1 198 A5
Stanwell TW19 148 A3
Marquis Rd
Bowes Pk N22 32 B4
Finsbury Pk N4 50 C1
Kentish Town NW1 71 D2
Marrabon Cl DA15 168 A3
Marrick Cl SW15 134 A1
Marrick Ho 19 NW6 91 D6
Marrilyne Ave EN3 7 B5
Marriner Ct UB3 105 C6
Marriott Cl TW14 149 B5
Marriott Ho 8 SE6 186 A6
Marriott Rd
Finsbury Pk N4 50 B1
Muswell Hill N10 30 D2
Newham E15 98 C6
Marriotts Cl NW9 45 D3
Marryat Cl TW3 129 B1
Marryat Ct 12 W6 112 B2
Marryat Ho SW1 259 A1
Marryat Pl SW19 179 A6
Marryat Rd SW19 179 A6
Marryat Sq SW6 264 A2
Marryatt Ct W5 88 B1
Marsala Rd SE13 141 D1
Marsalis Ho 3 E3 97 C4
Marsden Rd
Camberwell SE15 139 D2
Edmonton N9 18 B2
Marsden St NW5 71 A2
Marsden Way 2 BR6 227 D4
Marshall Cl
Brunswick Pk N11 15 B1
Harrow HA1 42 B2
Hounslow TW4 151 B6
Wandsworth SW18 158 A5
Marshall Ct SW4 270 B1
Marshall Dr UB4 83 D2
Marshall Ho
5 New Malden KT3 199 C5
Paddington NW6 91 B5
Shoreditch N1 235 D4
Walworth SE17 262 C2
Marshall Path 10 SE28 124 B6
Marshall Rd
Leyton E10 75 D4
Tottenham N17 33 B2
Marshalls Gr SE18 122 A2
Marshall's Pl SE16 263 D5
Marshall's Rd SM1 217 D4
Marshall St W1 93 C1 239 B1
Marshalsea Rd SE1 117 A4 252 B2
Marsham Cl BR7 188 D5
Marsham Ct
19 Putney SW19 156 D3
Westminster SW1 259 D4
Marsham St SW1 115 D2 259 D4
Marsh Ave CR4 181 A1
Marshbrook Cl SE3 143 D2
Marsh Cl NW7 11 D1
Marsh Ct
Dalston E8 74 A2
3 Merton SW19 180 A2
Marsh Dr NW9 45 D3
Marsh Farm Rd TW2 152 D3
Marshfield St E14 120 A3
Marsh Gate Bsns Ctr E15 98 A5
Marshgate Ctr The E15 97 D6
Marshgate La E15 75 D1
Marshgate Prim Sch TW10 154 B6
Marsh Green Prim Sch RM10 103 C5
Marsh Green Rd RM10 103 C6
Marsh Hall HA9 66 B5
Marsh Hill E9 75 A3
Marsh Ho
Nine Elms SW8 269 B2
Pimlico SW1 259 D1
Marsh La
Edgware NW7 11 C1
Leyton E10 75 C6
Stanmore HA7 25 C4
Tottenham N17 34 B2
Marsh Point HA5 41 B5
Marsh Rd
Pinner HA5 41 A5
Wembley HA0 87 D5
Marshside Cl N9 18 C3
Marsh St E14 119 D2
Marsh Wall E14 119 D4
Marshwood Ho 10 NW6 91 C6
Marsland Cl SE17 261 D1
Marsom Ho N1 235 C3
Marston SE17 262 B4
Marston Ave
Chessington KT9 214 A2
Dagenham RM10 81 C5
Marston Cl
Dagenham RM10 81 C5
South Hampstead NW6 70 A1
Marston Ct
Barnet EN5 13 C6
Sidcup DA14 189 D6
Walton-on-T KT12 194 C1
Marston Ho 23 SW9 138 C3
Marston Rd TW11 175 B5
Marston Way SE19 183 A3
Marsworth Ave HA5 22 D2
Marsworth Cl UB4 85 A2
Marsworth Ho 8 E2 96 A6
Martaban Rd N16 73 D6
Martello St E8 74 B1
Martello Terr E8 74 B1
Martell Rd SE21 161 B1
Martel Pl E8 73 D2
Marten Rd E17 35 C1
Martens Ave DA7 147 D1
Martham Cl SE28 124 D6
Martha Rd E15 76 C2
Martha's Bldgs EC1 242 C6
Martha St E1 96 C1
Marthorne Cres HA3 24 B1
Martin Bowes Rd SE9 144 B2
Martinbridge Trad Est EN1 18 A6
Martin Cl
Lower Edmonton N9 18 D3
Uxbridge UB10 82 A5
Martin Cres CR0 204 C1
Martin Ct
15 Cubitt Town E14 120 A4
Lewisham SE12 164 D4
Merton SW19 179 C3
Southall UB2 107 B4
Martindale SW14 155 A6
Martindale Ave 2 E16 121 A6
Martindale Ho 23 E14 119 D6
Martindale Rd
Balham SW12 159 B4
Hounslow TW4 129 A2
Martin Dene DA6 169 B6
Martin Dr UB5 63 B3
Martineau Cl KT10 212 B4
Martineau Dr TW1 131 B1
Martineau Ho SW1 259 A1

Martineau Mews N5 . . . 72 D4
Martineau Rd N5 . . . . . . 72 D4
Martingale Cl TW16 . . . 194 A5
Martingales Cl TW10 . . 153 D1
Martin Gdns RM8 . . . . . . 80 D4
Martin Gr SM4 . . . . 201 C6
Martin Ho
Newington SE1. . . . . 262 B5
7 New Malden KT3 . . . . 199 C5
South Lambeth SW8. . . . 270 A4
Martini Dr EN3. . . . . 7 C6
Martin Jun & Inf Schs
N2. . . . . 30 C1
Martin La EC4 . . . . 252 D6
Martin Rd RM8. . . . . 80 D4
Martin Rise DA6 . . . . . . 169 B6
Martins Cl BR4. . . . . 224 B6
Martins Mount EN5 . . . . . 1 D1
Martins Pl SE28. . . . . . . 123 C5
Martin's Rd BR2 . . . . . . 186 D1
Martin St SE28. . . . . 123 C5
Martins The
Penge SE26 . . . . 184 B5
Wembley HA9. . . . . 66 B5
Martins Wlk
Muswell Hill N10 . . . . 31 A2
Woolwich SE28 . . . . 123 C5
Martin Way SW20,
SM4 . . . . 201 B6
Martlesham N17. . . . . . . 33 C1
Martlesham Wlk NW9 . . 27 C2
Martlet Gr 5 UB5. . . . . . 84 D4
Martlett Ct WC2 . . . . . . 240 B1
Martlett Lo NW3 . . . . 69 D4
Martley Dr IG2. . . . . 56 D4
Martley Ho SW8 . . . . . . 269 B2
Martock Cl HA3 . . . . 43 A5
Martock Ct 10 SE15 . . . 140 B4
Martock Gdns N11 . . . . . 31 A5
Marton Cl SE6 . . . . 163 C1
Marton Rd 2 N16. . . . . . . 73 C5
Martyn Ct HA8 . . . . 26 B6
Martyn Ho SE2. . . . . 146 D6
Martynside 22 NW9 . . . . 27 D2
Marvel Ho 5 SE5 . . . . . 139 B5
Marvell Ave UB4 . . . . 84 A2
Marvels Cl SE12. . . . . . . 165 B2
Marvels La SE12 . . . . . . 165 C1
Marvels Lane Prim Sch
SE12 . . . . 187 C6
Marville Rd
SW6. . . . . 135 B5 264 C3
Marvin Ho 9 SE18 . . . . 144 D6
Marvin St 3 E8. . . . . 74 B2
Marwell Cl BR4 . . . . 224 D6
Marwell Ct SE3 . . . . 142 B3
Marwick Rd UB7 . . . . . . 104 B4
Marwood Cl DA16. . . . . . 146 B2
Marwood Ct N3. . . . . 29 D3
Marwood Dr NW7. . . . . . . 28 D3
Mary Adelaide Cl
Kingston u T SW15 . . . . . 155 C1
Kingston u T SW15 . . . . . 177 C6
Mary Adelaide Ho W2 236 D4
Mary Ann Bldgs SE8. . . 141 C6
Maryatt Ave HA2. . . . . . . 63 D6
Marybank SE18 . . . . 122 B2
Mary Cl HA7 . . . . 44 B5
Mary Datchelor Cl
SE5. . . . . 139 B4
Mary Dine Ct SW8. . . . . 270 D3
Mary Gn NW8. . . . . 91 D6
Marygold Ho TW3. . . . . 130 A4
Mary Ho
8 Hammersmith W6. . . . 112 C1
6 Stockwell SW9 . . . . . 138 B3
Mary James Ho 32 E2 . . 96 A5
Mary Jones Ho 20
E14. . . . . 119 C6
Maryland Ct KT1 . . . . . . 176 D1
Maryland Pk E15. . . . . . . 76 C3
Maryland Point E15 . . . . 76 C2
Maryland Prim Sch
E15 . . . . 76 C3
Maryland Rd
Paddington W9. . . . . 91 C3
South Norwood CR7 . . . . 182 D2
Stratford New Town E15. . 76 B3
Tottenham N22. . . . . 32 C4
Marylands Ind Est E15. . 76 C3
Maryland Sq E15. . . . . . . 76 C3
Marylands Rd W9. . . . . . 91 D3
Maryland St E15 . . . . 76 C3
Maryland Sta E15 . . . . . . 76 C2
Maryland Way TW16 . . 172 A1
Maryland Wlk N1 . . . . . 235 A6
Mary Lawrenson Pl 1
SE3. . . . . 143 A5
MARYLEBONE 93 B1
Marylebone Ct 3 HA0. . 66 A2
Marylebone Flyover
NW1. . . . . 92 C2 237 A3
Marylebone High St
W1. . . . . 93 A2 238 B4
Marylebone La
W1. . . . . 93 A1 238 B2
Marylebone Mews
W1. . . . . 238 C3
Marylebone Pas W1 . . 239 B2
Marylebone Rd
NW1. . . . . 92 D2 237 D4
Marylebone St
W1. . . . . 93 A2 238 B3
Marylebone Sta
NW1 . . . . 92 D3 237 C5
Marylee Way
SE11. . . . . 116 B2 260 D3
Mary McArthur Ho 12
N19 . . . . 49 D2
Mary Macarthur Ho
8 Belvedere DA17 . . . . 125 C3
11 Dagenham RM10. . . . . 81 C5
15 Globe Town E2. . . . . . . 96 D4
W14. . . . . 264 A6
Marymount International
Sch KT2 . . . . 177 A3
Maryon Gr SE7. . . . . . . 122 A2
Maryon Mews NW3 . . . . 70 C4
Maryon Rd SE7 . . . . 122 A2
Mary Peters Dr UB6 . . . . 64 B3
Mary Pl W11. . . 113 A6 244 A5
Mary Rose Cl TW12 . . . 173 C2
Mary Rose Mall E6 . . . . 100 B2
Maryrose Way N20. . . . . 14 B3
Mary's Ct NW8. . . . . . . 237 B6
Mary Seacole Villas 19
NW10. . . . . 67 B1
Mary Secole Cl 21 E8. . . 95 D6
Mary Smith Ct SW5 . . . 255 B3
Mary St
5 Canning Town E16. . . . 98 D2
Shoreditch N1 . . 95 A6 235 B5
Mary's Terr TW1. . . . . . 153 A4
Mary Tates Cotts
CR4 . . . . 202 D5
Mary Terr NW1 . . . . 232 A5
Maryville DA16 . . . . 145 D3
Mary Way WD19 . . . . 22 C6
Mary Wharrie Ho 4
NW3. . . . . 70 D1
Marzena Ct TW2 . . . . . . 152 A6
Masbro' Rd W14 . . . . . . 112 D3
Mascalls Ct 13 SE7 . . . . 143 C6
Mascalls Rd SE7 . . . . . . 143 C6
Mascotte Rd 2
SW15 . . . . 134 D1
Mascotts Cl NW2 . . . . . . 68 B5
Masefield Ave
Borehamwood WD6. . . . . 10 D6
Southall UB1 . . . . 107 C6
Stanmore HA7 . . . . 24 D5
Masefield Cres N14 . . . . 15 C5
Masefield Ct
New Barnet EN5. . . . . 2 A1
Stoke Newington N5 . . . . 73 B3
19 Surbiton KT6. . . . . . . 197 D2
Masefield Gdns E6. . . . 100 C3
Masefield Ho 4 NW6 . . . 91 C4
Masefield La UB4 . . . . . . 84 C3
Masefield Rd TW13 . . . 173 B6
Masefield View BR6. . . . 227 A5
Masefield Way TW19. . 148 B3
Masham Ho 13 DA18 . . 124 D4
Mashie Rd W3. . . . . 89 C1
Maskall Cl SW2. . . . . . . 160 C3
Maskani Wlk SW16. . . . 181 C3
Maskell Rd SW17 . . . . . 158 A1
Maskelyne Cl
SW11. . . . . 136 C4 267 B2
Mason Cl
Bermondsey SE16 . . . . . 118 A1
Bexleyheath DA7 . . . . . . 147 D2
Hampton TW12 . . . . 173 B2
Newham E16 . . . . 121 A6
Wimbledon SW20 . . . . . 178 D2
Mason Ct
4 Penge SE19. . . . . 183 D3
Wembley HA9. . . . . 66 C6
Mason Ho
15 Bermondsey SE1. . . . 118 A2
8 Friern Barnet N11. . . . 31 C5
16 Hackney E9 . . . . 74 C1
Mason Rd
Sutton SM1 . . . . 217 D3
Woodford IG8 . . . . 36 C6
Mason's Arms Mews
W1. . . . . 248 D6
Masons Ave HA3 . . . . 42 D5
Mason's Ave
City of London EC2 . . . . . 242 C2
Croydon CR0 . . . . 221 A5
Masons Hill
Bromley BR2 . . . . 209 B5
13 Woolwich SE18 . . . . . 122 D2
Masons Ho NW9 . . . . 44 D4
Mason's Pl
Finsbury EC1 . . . . 235 A2
Mitcham CR4 . . . . 180 D2
Mason St
SE17. . . . . 117 B2 262 D4
Mason's Yd
Finsbury EC1 . . . . 234 D2
St James SW1 . . . . 249 B4
Wimbledon SW19 . . . . . 178 D5
Massey Cl N11. . . . . 31 B5
Massey Ct 6 E6 . . . . 99 C6
Massie Rd E8. . . . . 74 A2
Massingberd Way
SW17 . . . . 181 B6
Massinger St SE1,
SE17. . . . . 263 A3
Massingham St E1 . . . . . 96 D3
Masson Ave HA4 . . . . 62 C2
Mast Ct 17 SE16. . . . . . 119 A2
Master Gunner's Pl 1
SE18. . . . . 144 A4
Masterman Ho 1
SE5. . . . . 139 B5
Masterman Rd E6. . . . . 100 A4
Masters Cl SW16. . . . . . 181 C4
Masters Ct HA4 . . . . 61 C6
Masters Dr SE16 . . . . . . 118 B1
Masters Lo 24 E1 . . . . . . 96 C1
Master's St 16 E1 . . . . . . 96 D2
Mast House Terr E14 . . 119 C2
Mastin Ho SW18 . . . . . . 157 C3
Mastmaker Rd E14. . . . 119 C4
Maswell Park Cres
TW3. . . . . 152 A6
Maswell Park Rd
TW3. . . . . 130 A1
Matara Mews SE17. . . . 262 A1
Matcham Rd E11. . . . . . . 76 D5
Matching Ct 14 E3 . . . . . 97 C4
Matchless Dr SE18 . . . . 144 C5
Matfield Cl BR2. . . . . . . 209 A4
Matfield Rd DA17 . . . . . 147 C6
Matham Gr SE22 . . . . . . 139 D1
Matham Rd KT8. . . . . . . 196 B4
Mathart Ct E4 . . . . 36 B4
Matheson Lang Ho
SE1. . . . . 251 A1
Matheson Rd
W14. . . . . 113 B2 254 C3
Mathews Ave E6 . . . . . . 100 C5
Mathews Park Ave
E15. . . . . 76 D2
Mathews Yd WC2 . . . . . 240 A1
Mathieson Ct SE1 . . . . . 251 D1
Mathieson Ho 10 E4. . . . 20 C4
Mathilda Marks-Kennedy
Jewish Prim Sch
NW7 . . . . 27 B5
Mathison Ho SW10. . . . 266 A4
Matilda Cl SE19. . . . . . . 183 B3
Matilda Ho E1. . . . . 118 A5
Matilda St N1. . . 94 B6 233 D6
Matlock Cl
Barnet EN5. . . . . 12 D6
Herne Hill SE24 . . . . 139 A1
Matlock Cres SM3 . . . . 217 A4
Matlock Ct
7 Herne Hill SE5. . . . . . 139 B1
St John's Wood NW8 . . . 229 A4
Woodford IG8 . . . . 36 D2
Matlock Gdns SM1,
SM3 . . . . 217 A4
Matlock Pl SM1, SM3 . . 217 A4
Matlock Rd E10. . . . . 54 A3
Matlock St E14 . . . . 97 A1
Matlock Way KT3 . . . . . 177 B2
Maton Ho SW6. . . . . 264 C4
Matson Ct IG8 . . . . 36 C3
Matson Ho
9 Bermondsey SE16. . . 118 B3
16 Homerton E9. . . . . 74 D2
Matthew Cl W10 . . . . 90 D3
Matthew Ct
Mitcham CR4 . . . . 203 D4
4 Walthamstow E17 . . . . 54 A6
Matthew Parker St
SW1. . . . . 249 D1
Matthews Ct N5 . . . . 73 A4
Matthews Ho 3 E14 . . . 97 C2
Matthews Rd UB6 . . . . . . 64 B3
Matthews St SW11 . . . . 136 D3
Matthias Ct 12 TW10 . . 154 A5
Matthias Ho 2 N16 . . . . 73 C3
Matthias Rd N16 . . . . 73 C3
Mattingly Way 3
SE15. . . . . 139 D5
Mattison Rd N4. . . . . 50 D3
Mattock La W5, W13. . . 109 C5
Maud Cashmore Way
SE18. . . . . 122 B3
Maude Ho 3 E2 . . . . 96 A5
Maude Rd
Camberwell SE5. . . . . . . 139 C4
Walthamstow E17 . . . . . . 53 A4
Maudesville Cotts
W7 . . . . 108 C5
Maude Terr E17 . . . . 53 A5
Maud Gdns
Barking IG11 . . . . 101 D5
Newham E13 . . . . 98 D5
Maudlins Gn E1. . . . . . . 118 A5
Maud Rd
Leyton E10 . . . . 76 A5
Newham E13 . . . . 98 D5
Maudslay Rd SE9 . . . . . 144 B2
Maudsley Ho TW8. . . . . 110 A1
Maudsley Hospl The
SE5 . . . . 139 B3
Maud St E16. . . . . 98 D2
Maud Wilkes Cl 10
NW5. . . . . 71 C3
Maugham Ct 5 W3 . . . 111 A3
Mauleverer Rd SW2. . . 160 A6
Maultway Ct KT19. . . . . 215 B3
Maundeby Wlk NW10 . . 67 C2
Maunder Rd 4 W7. . . . 108 D5
Maunsel St
SW1. . . . . 115 D2 259 C4
Maureen Campbell Ct
TW17 . . . . 192 D4
Maurer Ct 2 SE10 . . . . 120 D3
Mauretania Bldg 11
E1. . . . . 118 D6
Maurice Ave N22 . . . . . . 32 D1
Maurice Browne Cl
NW7. . . . . 28 D4
Maurice Ct
3 Brentford TW8 . . . . . 131 D5
4 Mile End E1. . . . . 97 A4
Wood Green N22 . . . . 32 C2
Maurice Ho
Hither Green SE12 . . . . 164 D5
1 Stockwell SW9 . . . . . 138 B3
Maurice St W12 . . . . 90 B1
Maurice Wlk NW11. . . . . 48 A5
Maurier Cl UB5 . . . . 84 C6
Mauritius Rd SE10 . . . . 120 C2
Maury Rd N16 . . . . 74 A5
Mauveine Gdns TW3 . . 129 C1
Mavelstone Cl BR1. . . . 188 A2
Mavelstone Rd BR1 . . . 188 A2
Maverton Rd E3 . . . . 97 C6
Mavery Ct 5 BR1 . . . . . 186 D3
Mavis Ave KT19 . . . . . . 215 C3
Mavis Cl KT19. . . . . 215 C3
Mavis Ct 33 NW9. . . . . . . 27 D1
Mavis Wlk 9 E6 . . . . . . 100 A2
Mavor Ho N1 . . . . 233 D5
Mawbey Ho SE1 . . . . . . 263 D1
Mawbey Pl
SE1. . . . . 117 D1 263 D1
Mawbey Rd SE1. . . . . . . 263 D1
Mawbey St SW8 . . . . . . 270 A3
Mawdley Ho SE1. . . . . . 251 B1
Mawney Cl RM7. . . . . 59 D6
Mawney Rd RM7 . . . . 59 D6
Mawson Cl SW20 . . . . . 179 A1
Mawson Ct N1. . . . . 235 D5
Mawson Ho EC1 . . . . . . 241 A4
Mawson La W4 . . . . 133 D6
Maxden Ct SE15 . . . . . . 140 A2
Maxey Gdns RM9 . . . . . . 81 A4
Maxey Rd
Dagenham RM9 . . . . 81 A4
Plumstead SE18. . . . . . . 123 A2
Maxfield Cl N20. . . . . 14 A4
Maxim Apartments 3
BR2 . . . . 209 B5
Maxim Rd N21. . . . . 16 C5
Maxted Pk HA1 . . . . 42 C2
Maxted Rd SE15 . . . . . . 139 D2
Maxwell Cl
Croydon CR0 . . . . 204 A1
Hayes UB3 . . . . 106 A6
Maxwell Ct SE21 . . . . . 162 A3
Maxwell Gdns BR6 . . . . 227 D5
Maxwell Ho
Bowes Pk N22 . . . . 32 B4
Chislehurst BR7 . . . . 188 D3
12 Shooters Hill SE18 . . 144 D6
Maxwell Rd
Ashford TW15 . . . . 171 A4
Fulham SW6. . . 135 D5 265 D3
Welling DA16 . . . . 146 A2
West Drayton UB7 . . . . . 104 B2
Maxwelton Ave NW7 . . . 27 B5
Maxwelton Cl NW7. . . . . 27 B5
Maya Angelou Ct E4 . . . 36 A6
Maya Cl SE15 . . . . 140 B3
Mayall Cl EN3. . . . . 7 C5
Mayall Rd SE24 . . . . . . 160 D6
Maya Pl N11. . . . . 31 D3
Maya Rd N2 . . . . 48 A5
Maybank Ave
Wembley HA0. . . . . 65 A3
Woodford E18 . . . . 37 B1
Maybank Gdns HA5 . . . . 40 A4
Maybank Rd E18. . . . . . . 37 C2
May Bate Ave KT2. . . . . 175 D2
Maybells Commercial Est
IG11 . . . . 102 D5
Mayberry Pl KT5 . . . . . . 198 B2
Maybourne Cl SE26 . . . 184 B5
Maybourne Grange
CR0 . . . . 221 C6
Maybrook Ct E11 . . . . . . 77 B6
Maybury Cl
Enfield EN1. . . . . 6 B5
Petts Wood BR5 . . . . 210 D4
Maybury Ct
Beckenham BR3. . . . . . . 185 B3
Croydon CR2 . . . . 220 D3
Harrow HA1. . . . . 42 B3
Marylebone W1 . . . . 238 B3
Maybury Gdns NW10 . . . 68 B2
Maybury Mews N6 . . . . . 49 C2
Maybury Rd
Barking IG11 . . . . 102 A5
Newham E13 . . . . 99 C3
Maybury St SW17 . . . . . 180 C5
Maychurch Cl HA7 . . . . . 25 D3
May Cl KT9 . . . . 214 B2
Maycroft
2 Hayes BR2. . . . . 208 D1
Pinner HA5. . . . . 22 B1
Maycross Ave SM4 . . . . 201 C5
May Ct 2 SW19. . . . . . . 180 A2
Mayday Gdns SE3 . . . . . 144 A3
Mayday Rd CR0, CR7 . . 204 D3
Mayday University Hospl
CR7. . . . . 204 D3
Maydeb Ct RM6. . . . . 59 B3
Maydew Ho SE16 . . . . . 118 C2
Maydwell Ho 6 E14. . . . 97 C2
Mayerne Rd SE9 . . . . . . 165 D6
Mayesbrook Rd
Barking IG11 . . . . 101 D6
Dagenham RM8, IG3 . . . . 80 B5
Mayesford Rd RM6. . . . . 58 C2
Mayespark Prim Sch
IG3 . . . . 80 A5
Mayes Rd N22 . . . . 32 B1
Mayeswood Rd SE12 . . 187 C6
MAYFAIR 115 B6
Mayfair Ave
Bexley DA7. . . . . 146 D4
Dagenham RM6 . . . . 58 D3
Ilford IG1. . . . . 56 C1
New Malden KT4 . . . . . . 200 A1
Twickenham TW2 . . . . . . 152 A4
Mayfair Cl
Beckenham BR3. . . . . . . 185 D2
Surbiton KT6 . . . . 198 A1
Mayfair Ct
2 Beckenham BR3 . . . . 185 D2
7 Croydon CR0 . . . . 221 D6
Edgware HA8. . . . . 26 B5
13 Wimbledon SW19 . . . 179 A3
Mayfair Gdns
Tottenham N17. . . . . 33 B4
Woodford IG8 . . . . 37 A3
Mayfair Ho 11 SE1 . . . . 118 A2
Mayfair Pl W1 . . . . 248 D4
Mayfair Terr N14 . . . . . . 15 D4
Mayfield DA7 . . . . 147 B2
Mayfield Ave
Broom Hill BR6. . . . . 211 D2
Chiswick W4. . . . . 111 C2
Harrow HA3. . . . . 43 B4
North Finchley N12. . . . . . 30 B6
Osidge N14 . . . . 15 D2
West Ealing W13 . . . . . . 109 B4
Woodford IG8 . . . . 37 A4
Mayfield Cl
Ashford TW15 . . . . 170 D4
Clapham Pk SW4 . . . . . . 159 D6
Dalston E8 . . . . 73 D2
Hillingdon UB10. . . . . 82 D4
Long Ditton KT7 . . . . 197 B1
Penge SE20 . . . . 184 B2
Mayfield Cres
Enfield N9. . . . . 18 B5
Thornton Heath CR7. . . . 204 B4
Mayfield Ct SM2 . . . . . . 218 A1
Mayfield Dr HA5 . . . . 41 B5
Mayfield Gdns
Ealing W7. . . . . 86 C2
Hendon NW4 . . . . 46 D3
Mayfield Ho
31 Bethnal Green E2 . . . . 96 B5
Stamford Hill N16. . . . . . . 51 C2
Mayfield Mans SW15. . 157 B6
Mayfield Prim Sch W7. . 86 B1
Mayfield Rd
Acton W3 . . . . 110 D6
Bedford Pk W12 . . . . 111 C4
Bromley BR1 . . . . 210 A4
Chingford E4 . . . . 20 B2
Dagenham RM8 . . . . 58 C1
Dalston E8 . . . . 73 D1
Enfield EN3. . . . . 6 D3
Higham Hill E17 . . . . 35 A1
Hornsey Vale N8. . . . . 50 B3
Merton SW19. . . . . 179 B2
Newham E13 . . . . 98 D3
South Croydon CR2 . . . . 221 B1
Sutton SM2 . . . . 218 B2
Thornton Heath CR7. . . . 204 B4
Mayfields HA9 . . . . 66 C6
Mayfield Sch & Coll
RM8 . . . . 58 C1
Mayfields Cl HA9 . . . . . . 66 C6
Mayfield Villas DA14 . . 190 C4
Mayflower Cl
Bermondsey SE16 . . . . . 118 D2
Ruislip HA4. . . . . 39 A3
Mayflower Ho 2
IG11. . . . . 101 B6
Mayflower Lo
Hendon N3. . . . . 47 B6
Muswell Hill N10 . . . . 31 A2
Mayflower Prim Sch
E14 . . . . 97 D1
Mayflower Rd SW9. . . . 138 A2
Mayflower St 1
SE16. . . . . 118 C4
Mayfly Cl HA5 . . . . 40 C2
Mayfly Gdns 12 UB5. . . . 84 D4
Mayford NW1. . . . . 232 B4
Mayford Cl
Balham SW12. . . . . 158 D4
Penge BR3 . . . . 206 D6
Mayford Rd SW12. . . . . 159 A4
May Gdns
Elstree WD6. . . . . 9 D5
Wembley HA0. . . . . 87 C4
Maygood Ho N1 . . . . . . 234 A4
Maygood St N1 . 94 C5 234 A4
Maygrove Rd NW6 . . . . . 69 B2
Mayhew Cl E4 . . . . 19 C1
Mayhew Ct 2 SE5 . . . . 139 B1
Mayhill Rd
Barnet EN5. . . . . 13 A5
Greenwich SE7. . . . . 143 B6
Mayland Mans 4
IG11. . . . . 78 D1
Maylands Dr DA14 . . . . 168 D1
Maylands Ho SW3. . . . . 257 B3
Maylands Rd WD19 . . . . 22 C6
Maylie Ho 4 SE16 . . . . 118 B4
Maynard Cl
Fulham SW6. . . 135 D5 265 D3
Tottenham N15. . . . . 51 C4
Maynard Ct EN3 . . . . 7 C5
Maynard Ho
Mile End E1. . . . . 97 A4
Plumstead SE18. . . . . . . 123 A2
Maynard Rd E17 . . . . 54 A4
Maynards Quay E1 . . . . 118 C6
Mayne Ct E8. . . . . 74 A4
Maynooth Gdns CR4 . . 202 D2
Mayo Ct W13 . . . . 109 B3
Mayo Ho 10 E1. . . . . 96 C2
Mayola Rd E5. . . . . 74 C4
Mayo Rd
Thornton Heath CR0. . . . 205 B4
Walton-on-T KT12 . . . . . 194 A2
Willesden NW10 . . . . 67 C2
Mayow Rd SE23, SE26 . . 184 D6
Mayplace Cl DA7. . . . . . 147 D2
Mayplace La SE18. . . . . 144 D6
Mayplace Rd W DA7. . . 147 C1
Maypole Ct UB2. . . . . . . 107 B4
May Rd
Chingford E4 . . . . 35 C4
Newham E13 . . . . 99 A5
Twickenham TW2 . . . . . . 152 C3
Mayroyd Ave KT6 . . . . . 214 C6
May's Buildings Mews
SE10. . . . . 142 B5

Mays Ct WC2 250 A5
May's Ct SE10 142 B5
May's Hill Rd BR2 208 C6
Mays La EN5 12 C5
Maysoule Rd SW11 136 B1
Mays Rd TW11, TW12 174 B5
May St W14 254 D1
Maystocks E18 55 C6
Mayston Mews 3
SE10 121 A1
May Terr IG1 78 D4
Maythorne Cotts
SE13 164 B5
Maytime Prep Sch IG1 78 C5
Mayton St N7 72 B5
Maytree Cl HA8 11 A1
Maytree Ct
Mitcham CR4 203 A6
Northolt UB5 85 A4
May Tree Ho SE4 141 B2
Maytree La HA7 24 D3
Maytree Wlk SW2 160 C2
Mayville Prim Sch E11 76 C6
Mayville Rd
Ilford IG1 78 D3
Leyton E11 76 C6
Mayward Ho 7 SE5 139 C4
May Wlk E13 99 B5
Maywood Cl BR3 185 D3
May Wynne Ho E16 99 B1
Maze Hill SE10, SE3 142 C6
Maze Hill Lodge 7
SE10 142 B6
Maze Hill Sta SE10 142 C6
Mazenod Ave NW6 69 C1
Maze Rd TW9 132 C5
Mead Cl
3 Camden Town NW1 71 A1
Harrow HA3 24 B2
Mead Cres
Carshalton SM1 218 C4
Chingford E4 36 A6
Meadcroft Ho 4 KT3 199 C2
Meadcroft Rd SE17 138 D6
Mead Ct NW9 45 B4
Meade Cl W4 132 C6
Meader Ct SE14 140 D5
Meadfield HA8 10 D2
Mead Field HA2 63 B5
Meadfield Gn HA8 10 D2
Meadfoot Rd SW16 181 C2
Mead Gr RM6 58 D6
Mead Ho W11 244 C4
Mead House La UB4 83 B3
Meadhurst Pk TW16 171 C4
Mead Inf Sch The
KT19 215 D4
Meadlands Dr TW10 153 D2
Meadlands Prim Sch
TW10 175 C6
Mead Lo W4 111 B4
Meadow Ave CR0 206 D3
Meadowbank
Lewisham SE3 142 D2
Primrose Hill NW3 70 D1
Southgate N21 16 B5
Surbiton KT5 198 B3
Meadow Bank 8
SW15 157 B6
Meadowbank Cl SW6 134 C5
Meadowbank Gdns
TW5 128 B4
Meadowbank Rd NW9 45 B2
Meadowbanks EN5 12 A6
Meadowbrook Ct
TW7 130 D2
Meadow Cl
Barnet EN5 13 B5
Bexley DA6 169 B6
Catford SE6 185 C5
Chingford E4 19 D3
Chislehurst BR7 188 D5
Enfield EN3 7 A5
Hackney E9 75 B3
Hinchley Wood KT10 212 D5
Hounslow TW4 151 C5
Northolt UB5 85 C5
Richmond TW10 154 A3
Ruislip HA4 39 D3
Sutton SM1 218 A6
West Barnes SW20 200 C5
Meadowcourt Rd
SE3 142 D1
Meadowcroft 9 W4 110 C1
Meadow Croft BR1 210 B6
Meadowcroft Rd N13 16 C2
Meadow Dr
Hendon NW4 28 C1
Muswell Hill N10 49 B6
Meadowford Cl SE28 124 A6
Meadow Garth NW10 67 B2
Meadow Gate HA2 63 D5
Meadowgate Cl NW7 27 D5
Meadowgate Sch
SE4 141 A2
Meadow Gdns HA8 27 A4
Meadow High Sch
UB8 82 A2
Meadow Hill KT3 199 C3
Meadow La SE12 165 B1
Meadow Mews SW8 270 C5
Meadow Pl
Chiswick W4 133 C5
South Lambeth
SW8 138 A5 270 B4
Meadow Rd
Ashford TW15 171 B5
Barking IG11 80 A1
Beckenham BR2 186 C1
Carshalton SM1 218 C3
Claygate KT10 212 C2
Dagenham RM9 81 B2
Feltham TW13 151 A2
Merton SW19 180 A3
Pinner HA5 41 A5
Southall UB1 107 B6
South Lambeth
SW8 138 B5 270 C4
Meadow Row SE1 262 A5
Meadows Cl E10 75 C6
Meadows Ct DA14 190 B4
Meadows End TW16 172 A2
Meadowside
Eltham SE9 143 C1
Twickenham TW1 153 D4
Meadow Stile CR0 221 A5
Meadowsweet Cl
3 Newham E16 99 D2
West Barnes KT3 200 C5
Meadow The BR7 189 A4
Meadowview TW17 193 A2
Meadow View
Blackfen DA15 168 B4
Harrow HA1 42 C1
Meadowview Rd
Catford SE6 185 C5
Sidcup DA5 169 B5
West Ewell KT19 215 C1
Meadow View Rd
Hayes UB4 83 B3
Thornton Heath CR7 204 D4
Meadow Way
Kingsbury NW9 45 B4
Locksbottom BR6 226 C5
Ruislip HA4 40 B3
Wembley HA9 65 D4
Meadow Waye TW5 129 A5
Meadow Way The HA3 24 C2
Meadow Wlk
Dagenham RM9 81 B2
Hackbridge SM6 219 B5
Wanstead E18 55 A5
West Ewell KT17, KT19 215 D1
Meadow Wood Sch
WD23 8 A6
Mead Pl
Croydon CR0 205 A1
Hackney E9 74 C2
Mead Plat NW10 67 A2
Mead Rd
Chislehurst BR7 189 A4
Edgware HA8 26 C4
Richmond TW10 153 C1
Mead Road Inf Sch
BR7 189 A4
Mead Row
SE1 116 C3 261 A6
Meads Ct E15 76 D2
Meadside Cl BR3 185 A2
Meads La IG3 57 D2
Meads Rd
Enfield EN3 7 A4
Tottenham N22 32 D1
Meads The
Cheam SM3 217 A5
Edgware HA8 27 B4
Hillingdon UB8 82 A3
Mead The
Beckenham BR3 186 A2
Ealing W13 87 B2
Finchley N2 30 A1
Ickenham UB10 60 C6
Wallington SM6 219 D2
West Wickham BR4 208 B1
Meadvale Rd
Croydon CR0 206 A3
Ealing W5 87 C3
Meadway
Ashford TW15 170 C6
Barnet EN5 1 C1
Meadway *continued*
Beckenham BR3 186 A2
Enfield EN3 6 D6
Esher KT10 212 A1
Hampstead Garden Suburb
NW11 47 D3
Ilford IG3 79 C4
Palmers Green N14 16 A2
Tolworth KT5 199 A1
Twickenham TW2 152 B3
West Barnes SW20 200 C5
Woodford IG8 37 C5
Mead Way
Croydon CR0 223 A6
Hayes BR2 209 A3
Ruislip HA4 39 B3
Meadway Cl
Barnet EN5 1 C1
Hampstead Garden Suburb
NW11 47 D3
Pinner HA5 23 D4
Meadway Ct
Dagenham RM8 81 B6
Ealing W5 88 B2
Hampstead Garden Suburb
NW11 47 D3
Meadway Gate NW11 47 C3
Meadway Gdns HA4 39 B3
Meadway The
Buckhurst Hill IG9 21 D3
Lewisham SE3 142 B3
Meaford Way SE20 184 B3
Meakin Est SE1 263 A6
Meakin Ho N7 72 B3
Meanley Rd E12 78 A3
Meard St W1 239 C1
Meath Ho SE24 160 D5
Meath Rd
Ilford IG1 79 A5
Newham E15 98 D5
Meath St
SW11 137 B4 268 C2
Mecklenburgh Pl
WC1 240 C6
Mecklenburgh Sq
WC1 94 B3 240 C6
Mecklenburgh St
WC1 240 C6
Medburn St NW1 232 C4
Medcalf Rd EN3 7 B6
Medcroft Gdns SW14 133 A1
Medebourne Cl SE3 143 A2
Mede Ho BR1 187 B5
Medesenge Way N13 32 D4
Medfield St SW15 156 B4
Medhurst Cl 19 E3 97 A5
Median Rd E5 74 C3
Medina Ave KT10 212 C5
Medina Ct N7 72 C5
Medina Gr N7 72 C5
Medina Ho SE15 140 C1
Medina Rd N7 72 C5
Medland Cl CR4 203 A1
Medlar Cl 1 UB5 84 D5
Medlar Ho 3 DA15 168 A1
Medlar St SE5 139 A4
Medley Rd NW6 69 C2
Medora Rd SW2 160 B4
Medresco Ho NW3 70 B3
Medusa Rd SE6, SE13 163 D5
Medway Bldgs E3 97 A5
Medway Cl
Croydon CR0 206 C3
Ilford IG1 79 A3
Medway Ct
South Norwood SE25 205 C4
St Pancras WC1 233 A1
Medway Dr UB6 86 D5
Medway Gdns HA0 65 A4
Medway Ho
Bermondsey SE1 252 D1
6 Kingston u T KT2 175 D2
Paddington NW8 237 A4
Stoke Newington N16 73 B4
Medway Mews 35 E3 97 A5
Medway Par 1 UB6 86 D5
Medway Rd E3 97 A5
Medway St
SW1 115 D3 259 D5
Medwin St SW4 138 B1
Meecham Ct 1
SW11 136 C3
Meerbrook Rd SE3 143 C2
Meers Ct SW20 178 C2
Meeson Rd E15 76 D1
Meeson St E5 75 A4
Meeting House Alley 7
E1 118 B5
Meeting House La
SE15 140 B5
Mehetabel Rd E9 74 C3
Meister Cl IG1 57 B1
Melanda Cl BR7 188 B5
Melanie Cl DA7 147 A4
Melba Way SE13 141 D4
Melbourne Ave
Bowes Pk N13 32 B4
Ealing W13 109 A5
Pinner HA2, HA5 41 D6
Melbourne Cl
Broom Hill BR6 211 C2
Ickenham UB10 60 C4
Wallington SM6 219 C3
Melbourne Ct
Hackney E5 75 A4
Muswell Hill N10 31 B3
Paddington W9 236 B6
Penge SE20 184 A3
Twickenham TW2 152 B3
Melbourne Gdns RM6 59 A4
Melbourne Gr SE22 139 D1
Melbourne Ho
Hayes UB4 84 C3
Kensington W8 245 A3
South Norwood SE25 205 D5
Melbourne Mews
Brixton SW9 138 C4
Catford SE6 164 A4
Melbourne Pl WC2 240 D1
Melbourne Rd
Ilford IG1 56 D1
Leyton E10 53 D2
Merton SW19 179 C2
Newham E6 100 B5
Teddington TW11 175 C4
Wallington SM6 219 C3
Walthamstow E17 53 A5
Melbourne Sq 21
SW9 138 C4
Melbourne Way EN1 17 D5
Melbray Mews 11
SW6 135 B3
Melbreak Ho 11 SE22 139 C2
Melbury Ave UB2 107 D3
Melbury Cl
Claygate KT10 213 B2
Elmstead BR7 188 B4
Melbury Ct
W8 113 B3 254 D6
Melbury Dr SE5 139 C5
Melbury Gdns SW20 178 B2
Melbury Grange BR1 188 A2
Melbury Ho
South Lambeth SW8 270 C4
Twickenham TW2 152 B2
Melbury Rd
Harrow HA3 44 B4
Kensington
W14 113 B3 254 D6
Melchester 5 W11 91 B1
Melchester Ho 1 N19 71 D5
Melcombe Ct NW1 237 C4
Melcombe Gdns HA3 44 B3
Melcombe Ho SW8 270 C3
Melcombe Pl NW1 237 C4
Melcombe Prim Sch
W6 134 D6
Melcombe St
NW1 92 D3 237 D5
Meldex Cl NW7 28 C4
Meldon Cl SW6 265 D2
Meldone KT3 199 B1
Meldone Cl KT5 198 D3
Meldrum Rd IG3 80 A6
Melfield Gdns SE6 186 A5
Melford Ave IG11 79 D2
Melford Cl KT9 214 B3
Melford Ct
Bermondsey SE1 263 B6
Dulwich SE22 162 A4
Hackney E5 74 B5
2 Sutton SM2 218 A1
Melford Rd
Dulwich SE21, SE22 162 A3
Ilford IG1 79 B6
Leyton E11 76 C6
Newham E6 100 B4
Walthamstow E17 53 B5
Melfort Ave CR7 204 D6
Melfort Rd CR7 204 D6
Melgund Rd N5 72 C3
Melina Cl UB3 83 B2
Melina Ct
Putney SW15 134 A2
St John's Wood NW8 229 C1
Melina Pl NW8 92 B4 229 C1
Melina Rd W12 112 B4
Melior Ct N6 49 C3
Melior Pl SE1 253 A2
Melior St SE1 117 C4 253 A2
Meliot Rd SE6 164 B2
Melisa Ct N6 49 D2
Meller Cl SM6 220 A5
Melling Dr EN1 6 A4
Melling St SE18 145 C6
Mellington Ct 2 N16 74 A5
Mellis Ave TW9 132 D4
Mellish Cl IG11 101 D6
Mellish Ct KT6 198 A3
Mellish Flats E10 53 C2
Mellish Gdns IG8 37 A5
Mellish Ho 2 E1 96 B1
Mellish Ind Est SE18 121 D3
Mellish St E14 119 C3
Mellison Rd SW17 180 C5
Mellitus St W12 89 D1
Mellor Cl KT12 195 B2
Mellor Ct 2 SW19 180 A3
Mellor Ho 2 SE21 183 C6
Mellow La E UB4 83 A3
Mellow Lane Sch UB4 83 A3
Mellow La W UB10 83 A4
Mellows Rd
Redbridge IG5 56 B6
Wallington SM6 219 D3
Mells Cres SE9 188 B6
Mell St 6 SE10 120 C1
Melody La N5 73 A3
Melody Rd SW18 158 A6
Melon Pl W8 245 B2
Melon Rd
Leyton E11 76 C5
Peckham SE15 140 A4
Melrose Ave
Borehamwood WD6 10 D6
Cricklewood NW2 68 C3
Greenford UB6 85 D5
Mitcham CR4 181 B3
Thornton Heath SW16 204 C6
Tottenham N22 32 D2
Twickenham TW2 151 D4
Wimbledon SW19 157 C1
Melrose Cl
Greenford UB6 85 D5
Grove Pk SE12 165 B3
Hayes UB4 84 A2
Melrose Cres BR6 227 B3
Melrose Ct
5 Ealing W13 109 A5
Wandsworth SW18 157 B5
Melrose Dr UB1 107 C5
Melrose Gdns
Edgware HA8 26 D1
Hammersmith W6 112 C3
Kingston u T KT3 199 B6
Melrose Ho
Maida Vale NW6 91 C4
Pimlico SW1 258 D2
Melrose Rd
1 Barnes SW13 133 D3
Merton SW19 179 C2
Pinner HA5 41 B5
Wandsworth SW18 157 B5
Melrose Sch CR4 202 C6
Melrose Terr W6 112 C3
Melrose Tudor SM6 220 A3
Melsa Rd SM4 202 A3
Melthorne Dr HA4 62 C5
Melthorpe Gdns SE3 144 A4
Melton Cl HA4 40 C1
Melton Ct
11 Croydon CR0 221 D6
South Kensington SW7 256 D3
Sutton SM2 218 A1
1 Twickenham TW1 153 B4
Melton Ho E5 74 A6
Melton St NW1 93 D4 232 C1
Melville Ave
Greenford UB6 64 D3
South Croydon CR2 221 D3
Wimbledon SW20 178 A3
Melville Cl UB10 61 B5
Melville Court Flats 8
W12 112 B4
Melville Ct
4 Brentford W4 110 C1
Rotherhithe SE8 119 A2
Melville Gdns N13 32 D5
Melville Ho
Lewisham SE10 142 A4
New Barnet EN5 14 B5
Melville Pl 4 N1 73 A1
Melville Rd
Barnes SW13 134 A4
Sidcup DA14 168 C2
Stonebridge NW10 67 B1
Walthamstow E17 53 B6
Melville Villas Rd W3 111 B5
Melvin Ct 11 TW9 132 C4
Melvin Rd SE20 184 C2
Melwood Ho 23 E1 96 B1
Melyn Cl N7 71 C4
Memel Ct EC1 242 A5
Memel St EC1 242 A5
Memess Path 4
SE18 144 C6
Memorial Ave E15 98 C4
Memorial Cl TW5 129 B6
Memorial Hospl SE18 144 C3
Memorial Hts IG2 57 B3
Menai Pl 2 E3 97 C5
Menard Ct EC1 235 B1
Mendham Ho SE1 263 A6
Mendip Cl
Forest Hill SE26 184 C6
Harlington UB3 127 B5
North Cheam KT4 216 C6
Mendip Ct
12 Battersea SW11 136 A2
Deptford SE14 140 C6
1 East Barnet N20 14 C2
Mendip Dr NW2, NW11 69 A6
Mendip Ho
Harrow HA3 43 A3
2 Stoke Newington N4 51 B2
Mendip Hos 12 E2 96 C4
Mendip Rd
Battersea SW11 136 A2
Bushey WD23 8 A5
Ilford IG2 57 C4
Mendora Rd
SW6 135 B5 264 C4
Menelik Rd NW2 69 B4
Menin Wks CR4 180 D1
Menlo Gdns SE19 183 B3
Mennie Ho SE18 144 B4
Mennis Ho SM5 218 C6
Menon Dr N9 18 B1
Menorah Foundation Sch
HA8 27 A3
Menorah Prim Sch
NW11 47 A2
Menotti St 6 E2 96 A3
Menteath Ho 9 E14 97 C1
Mentmore Cl HA3 43 C3
Mentmore Terr E8 74 B1
Mentone Ct SW8 270 B2
Meon Ct TW7 130 C3
Meon Rd W3 111 A4
Meopham Rd CR4,
SW16 181 C2
Mepham Cres HA3 24 A3
Mepham Gdns HA3 24 A3
Mepham St
SE1 116 C5 251 A3
Mera Dr DA7 147 D1
Merantun Way SW19 180 A2
Merbury Cl
Lewisham SE13 164 B6
Woolwich SE28 123 B5
Merbury Rd SE28 123 C4
Mercator Pl 4 E14 119 C1
Mercator Rd SE13 142 B1
Mercer Cl KT7 196 D2
Merceron Ho 3 E2 96 C4
Merceron St E1 96 B3
Mercer Pl HA5 22 C1
Mercers Cl SE10 120 D2
Mercer's Cotts 8 E3 97 A1
Mercers Mews N7 71 D4
Mercers Pl W6 112 D2
Mercers Rd N19 71 D5
Mercer St WC2 94 A1 240 A1
Merchant Ct E1 118 C5
Merchants Cl SE25 206 A5
Merchants Ho SE10 120 B1
Merchants Lo 5 E17 53 C5
Merchant St E3 97 B4
Merchant Taylors'
Almshouses SE13 142 C1
Merchant Taylors Hall*
EC3 242 D1
Merchiston Rd SE6 164 B2
Merchland Rd SE9 167 A3
Merchon Ho N7 71 C4
Mercia Gr SE13 142 A1
Mercia Ho
9 Camberwell SE5 139 A3
Charlton TW15 171 A2
Mercie Ct SE22 162 A3
Mercier Rd SW15 157 A6
Mercury 25 NW9 27 D2
Mercury Ct
8 Brixton SW9 138 C4
10 Millwall E14 119 C2
Mercury Ctr TW14 150 A6

Mercury Ho
Brentford TW8 109 D1
6 Old Ford E3 97 C6
Mercury Rd TW8 109 C1
Mercury Way SE14 140 D6
Mercy Terr SE13 163 D6
Merebank La CR0, SM6 220 B3
Mere Cl
Orpington BR6 226 D6
Putney SW15, SW19 156 D4
Meredith Ave NW2 68 C3
Meredith Cl HA5 22 D3
Meredith Ho 17 N16 73 C3
Meredith Mews SE4 141 B1
Meredith St
Finsbury EC1 234 C1
Newham E13 99 A4
Meredith Twr W3 110 D3
Meredyth Rd SW13 134 A3
Mere End CR0 206 D2
Mere Rd TW17 192 D3
Mereside BR6 226 C6
Mereside Pk TW15 171 A6
Meretone Cl SE4 141 A1
Mereton Mans 6 SE8 141 C4
Meretune Ct SM4 201 B6
Merevale Cres SM4 202 A3
Mereway Industry TW2 152 C4
Mereway Rd TW2 152 C3
Merewood Cl BR1 188 C1
Merewood Gdns CR0 206 D2
Mereworth Cl BR2 208 D4
Mereworth Dr SE18 145 A5
Mereworth Ho 3 SE15 140 C6
Merganser Ct 17 SE8 141 B6
Merganser Gdns SE28 123 B3
Meridan Ct SE13 142 B1
Meriden Cl BR1 187 D3
Meriden Ct SW3 257 A1
Meriden Ho
4 Barnet EN5 1 A1
25 Hoxton N1 95 C6
Meridian Building* SE10 142 B5
Meridian Ct
4 Bermondsey SE16 118 A4
4 Catford SE6 164 D3
Croydon CR0 220 C4
Meridian Ho SE10 120 C2
Meridian Pl E14 120 A4
Meridian Prim Sch SE10 142 B6
Meridian Rd SE7 143 D5
Meridian Sq E15 76 B1
Meridian Trad Est SE7 121 B2
Meridian Way
Enfield EN3 19 A5
Lower Edmonton N9, N18 18 D1
Meridian Wlk N17 33 C4
Merifield Rd SE9 143 C1
Merino Cl E11 55 C5
Merino Pl DA15 168 A6
Merioneth Ct 7 W7 86 D2
Merivale Rd
Harrow HA1 42 A2
Putney SW15 135 A1
Merlewood Dr BR7 188 B2
Merley Ct NW9 45 A1
Merlin 26 NW9 27 D2
Merlin Cl
Mitcham CR4 202 C6
4 Northolt UB5 84 C4
South Croydon CR0 221 C4
Wallington SM6 220 B2
Merlin Cres HA8 26 B2
Merlin Ct
Beckenham BR2 208 D5
6 Ealing W7 86 D3
Mitcham CR4 180 C2
Ruislip HA4 61 B6
Stanmore HA7 25 B5
Wood Green N22 32 C2
Merling Cl KT9 213 D3
Merlin Gdns BR1 165 A1
Merlin Gr BR3 207 C4
Merlin Ho
7 Chiswick W4 111 B1
Enfield EN3 18 D6
West Hampstead NW3 69 D4
Merlin Prim Sch BR1 165 A1
Merlin Rd
Bexley DA16 146 A1
Wanstead E12 77 D6
Merlin Rd N DA16 146 A1
Merlins Ave HA2 63 B5
Merlin Sch SW15 157 A6
Merlins Ct WC1 234 A1
Merlin St EC1 94 C4 234 A1
Mermaid Ct
Bermondsey SE1 117 B4 252 C2
Rotherhithe SE16 119 B5
Stroud Green N4 50 C3
Mermaid Ho 8 E14 120 A6
Mermaid Twr 22 SE8 141 B6
Meroe Ct N16 73 C6
Merredene St SW2 160 B5
Merriam Ave 2 E9 75 B2
Merriam Cl E4 36 A5
Merrick Rd UB2 107 B3
Merricks Ct 5 SW14 132 D1
Merrick Sq SE1 117 B3 262 C6
Merridale SE12 164 D6
Merridene N21 16 D5
Merrielands Cres RM9 103 B5
Merrielands Ret Pk RM9 103 B5
Merrilands Rd KT4 200 C1
Merrilees Rd DA15 167 C4
Merrilyn Cl KT10 213 A2
Merriman Rd SE3 143 C4
Merrington Rd SW6 265 B6
Merrion Ave HA7 25 D5
Merritt Gdns KT9 213 C2
Merritt Rd SE4 163 B6
Merrivale
Camden Town NW1 232 B5
Southgate N14 15 D6
Merrivale Ave IG4 55 D5
Merrow Ct CR4 180 B1
Merrow St SE17 117 B1 262 C1
Merrow Way CR0 224 A2
Merrow Wlk SE17 262 D2
Merrydown Way BR7 188 B2
Merry Fiddlers RM8 81 B6
Merryfield SE3 142 D3
Merryfield Gdns HA7 25 C5
Merryfield Ho SE12 165 C1
Merryhill Cl E4 19 D4
Merry Hill Rd WD23 8 A3
Merryhills Ct N14 15 C6
Merryhills Dr EN2 4 A1
Merryhills Prim Sch EN2 4 B1
Merryweather Ct
13 Dartmouth Pk N19 71 C5
1 New Malden KT3 199 C4
Mersea Ho IG11 78 D2
Mersey Ct 10 KT2 175 D2
Mersey Ho 10 N7 72 C3
Mersey Rd E17 53 B6
Mersey Wlk UB5 85 C5
Mersham Dr NW9 44 D4
Mersham Pl
Penge SE20 184 B2
South Norwood CR7 183 B1
Mersham Rd CR7 183 B1
Merstone Ho SW18 157 D5
Merten Rd RM6 59 A2
Merthyr Terr SW13 134 B6
MERTON 179 C2
Merton Abbey Mills SW19 180 A2
Merton Abbey Prim Sch SW19 179 D2
Merton Ave
Chiswick W4 111 D2
Hillingdon UB10 60 D1
Northolt UB5 64 A3
Merton Coll SM4 201 B4
Merton Court Sch DA14 190 C6
Merton Ct
Barnet EN5 1 D1
Welling DA16 146 B3
Merton Gdns BR5 210 D4
Merton Hall Gdns SW20 179 A2
Merton Hall Rd SW19 179 A2
Merton High St SW19 180 A3
Merton Ho SW18 157 C3
Merton Ind Pk SW19 180 A2
Merton La N6 70 D6
Merton Lo
New Barnet EN5 14 A6
3 Streatham SW16 182 A5
Merton Mans SW20 178 D1
MERTON PARK 179 C1
Merton Park Par SW19 179 B2
Merton Park Prim Sch SW19 179 C1
Merton Park Sta SW19 179 C2
Merton Pl 9 SW19 180 A3
Merton Rd
Barking IG11 79 D1
Croydon SE25 206 A4
Enfield EN2 5 B5
Harrow HA2 42 A1
Ilford IG3 57 D2
Leytonstone E17 54 A3
Merton SW19 179 D3
Wandsworth SW18 157 C4
Merton Rise NW3 70 C1
Merton Road Ind Est SW18 157 C4
Merton Way
East Molesey KT8 196 A6
Hillingdon UB10 60 D1
Merttins Rd SE15 162 D6
Meru Cl NW5 71 A3
Mervan Rd SW2 138 C1
Mervyn Ave SE9 167 A2
Mervyn Ct SE18 145 C6
Mervyn Rd
Brentford W13 109 A3
Shepperton TW17 193 A2
Meryvn Stockwood Ho 1 SE9 167 A2
Messaline Ave W3 89 A1
Messent Rd SE9 165 D6
Messer Ct CR0 220 D4
Messeter Pl SE9 166 C5
Messina Ave NW6 69 C1
Messiter Ho N1 233 D5
Met Appts The SE12 164 D6
Metcalfe Ho 28 SW8 137 D3
Metcalfe Wlk 2 TW13 173 A6
Metcalf Rd TW15 170 D5
Meteor St SW11 137 A1
Meteor Way SM6 220 A1
Metford Cres EN3 7 C5
Metherell Ho N21 17 B5
Metheringham Way NW9 27 C2
Methley Ho 8 N7 72 B6
Methley St SE11 116 C1 261 B1
Methodist Central Hall* SW1 115 D4 249 D1
Methuen Cl HA8 26 C3
Methuen Pk N10 49 B6
Methuen Rd
Belvedere DA17 125 D2
Bexleyheath DA6 147 B1
Edgware HA8 26 C3
Methwold Rd W10 90 D2
Metro Bsns Ctr The SE26 185 B5
Metro Ctr UB4 106 C6
Metro Ho E7 77 B2
Metro Ind Ctr TW7 130 C3
Metropolis Apartments 5 SW12 159 B3
Metropolitan Benefit Societies Almshouses 3 N1 73 C2
Metropolitan Bsns Ctr 9 N1 73 C1
Metropolitan Cl 23 E14 97 C2
Metropolitan Ctr The UB6 85 D6
Metro Trad Ctr HA9 66 D4
Meudon Ct KT6 197 D4
Mews Pl IG8 37 A6
Mews St E1 118 A5
Mews The
Beckenham BR3 185 C2
Hampton TW12 174 A4
Hornsey N8 50 C5
Redbridge IG4 55 D4
Shoreditch N1 235 B6
Thornton Heath SW16 182 B2
Tottenham N15 51 C5
5 Upper Holloway N19 50 A1
Woolwich SE18 122 D1
Mexborough NW1 232 A5
Mexfield Rd SW15 157 B6
Meyer Gn EN1 6 A5
Meyer Ho 1 SW12 159 B4
Meymott St SE1 116 D5 251 C3
Meynell Cres E9 74 D1
Meynell Gdns E9 74 D1
Meynell Rd E9 74 D1
Meyrick Ct CR7 204 C3
Meyrick Ho 8 E14 97 C2
Meyrick Rd
Battersea SW11 136 C2
Willesden NW10 68 A2
Miah Terr 10 E1 118 A5
Miall Wlk SE26 185 A6
Micawber Ave UB8 82 C3
Micawber Ct N1 235 B2
Micawber Ho 27 SE16 118 A4
Micawber St N1 95 A4 235 B2
Michael Cliffe Ho EC1 234 B1
Michael Faraday Ho SE17 262 D1
Michael Faraday Sch SE17 117 B1 262 D1
Michael Gaynor Cl W7 108 D5
Michael Marshall Ho 2 SE9 167 A2
Michaelmas Cl SW20 200 C6
Michael Rd
Leytonstone E11 54 D1
Parsons Green SW6 135 D4 265 D2
South Norwood SE25 205 C6
Michaels Cl SE13 142 C1
Michael Sobell Sinai Sch HA3 44 C3
Michaelson Ho 4 SE21 183 C6
Michael Tippet Sch SE27 161 A2
Michael Tippett Sch The SE11 116 C2 261 B3
Michelangelo Ct 14 SE16 118 B1
Micheldever Rd SE12 164 D5
Michelham Gdns TW1 152 D1
Michelle Ct
Acton W3 111 B6
North Finchley N12 30 A5
Michell Ho TW1 152 D3
Michels Almshouses 11 TW10 154 A6
Michelsdale Dr 3 TW9 132 A1
Michelson Ho SE11 260 D3
Michel's Row 2 TW9 132 A1
Michel Wlk SE18 122 D1
Michigan Ave E12 78 B4
Michigan Ho E14 119 C3
Michleham Down N12 29 B6
Mickledore NW1 232 B3
Micklefield Ct CR0 204 D3
Mickleham Cl BR5 190 A1
Mickleham Gdns SM3 217 A2
Mickleham Rd BR5 190 A1
Mickleham Way CR0 224 B1
Micklethwaite Rd SW6 135 C6 265 B5
Mickleton Ho 30 W2 91 C2
Midas Bsns Ctr RM10 81 D4
Midas Metro Ctr SM4 200 D2
Midcroft HA4 39 C1
Middle Dene NW7 11 B1
Middlefield NW8 92 B6 229 C6
Middlefielde W13 87 B2
Middlefield Gdns IG2 56 D3
Middle Green Cl 3 KT5 198 B3
Middleham Gdns N18 34 A4
Middleham Rd N18 34 A4
Middle La
Hornsey N8 50 A4
Teddington TW11 174 D4
Middle Lane Mews N8 50 A4
Middle Mill KT5 198 B6
Middle Park Ave SE9 165 D4
Middle Park Prim Sch SE9 165 D4
Middle Rd
East Barnet EN4 14 C5
Finchley N10 30 C2
Harrow HA2 42 B1
Mitcham SW16 181 D1
12 Newham E13 99 A5
Middle Row W10 91 A3
Middle Row Prim Sch W10 91 A3
Middlesborough Rd N18 34 A4
Middlesex Bsns Ctr UB2 107 B4
Middlesex Cl UB6 85 D3
Middlesex Coll of Computing & Tech HA0 66 A3
Middlesex Ct
5 Chiswick W4 111 D2
6 Harrow HA1 42 D4
Middlesex Cty Cricket Sch N3 29 D1
Middlesex Ho
Marylebone W1 239 B4
4 Penge SE20 184 C3
Wembley HA0 87 D6
Middlesex Pas EC1 241 D3
Middlesex Pl 18 E9 74 C2
Middlesex Rd CR4 204 A4
Middlesex St E1 95 D1 243 C2
Middlesex Univ N17 33 D4
Middlesex Univ (Cat Hill) EN4 15 A6
Middlesex Univ (Enfield Campus) EN3 18 C6
Middlesex Univ (Hendon Campus) NW4 46 B5
Middlesex Univ Trent Park EN4 3 C3
Middle St
Croydon CR0 221 A5
Holborn EC1 242 A4
Middle Temple* EC4 116 C6 251 A6
Middle Temple La EC4 116 C6 251 A6
Middleton Ave
Chingford Green E4 19 B1
Greenford UB5 86 B5
Sidcup DA14 190 C5
Middleton Cl E4 19 B1
Middleton Ct
Bromley BR1 187 B3
New Barnet EN5 2 A1
Middleton Dr
Bermondsey SE16 118 D4
Pinner HA5 40 A6
Middleton Gdns IG2 56 D3
Middleton Gr N7 72 A3
Middleton Ho
Dalston E8 73 D1
Newington SE1 262 C5
Middleton Mews N7 72 A3
Middleton Pl W1 239 A3
Middleton Rd
Carshalton CR4, SM5 202 B2
Dalston E8 73 D1
Golders Green NW11 47 C2
Hayes UB3 83 B2
Middleton St E2 96 B4
Middleton Way SE13 142 B1
Middleway NW11 47 D4
Middle Way
Hayes UB4 84 C3
Mitcham SW16 181 D1
Middle Way The HA3 24 D1
Middlewich Ho 7 UB5 85 B3
Midfield Prim Sch BR5 190 A3
Midfield Way BR5 190 B2
Midford Ho 1 NW4 46 D5
Midford Pl W1 239 B5
Midholm
East Finchley NW11 47 D5
Wembley HA9 44 C1
Midholm Cl NW11 47 D5
Midholm Rd CR0 223 A6
Midhope Ho WC1 233 B1
Midhope St WC1 233 B1
Midhurst 1 SE26 184 C4
Midhurst Ave
Muswell Hill N10 49 A6
Thornton Heath CR0 204 C2
Midhurst Ct N8 50 A2
Midhurst Gdns UB10 61 A1
Midhurst Hill DA6 169 C6
Midhurst Ho 6 E14 97 B1
Midhurst Par N10 49 A6
Midhurst Rd W13 109 A3
Midhurst Way E5 74 A4
Midland Mainline Terminal NW1 93 D5 232 D3
Midland Pl E14 120 A1
Midland Rd
Leytonstone E10 54 A2
St Pancras NW1 94 A4 233 A2
Midland Terr
Cricklewood NW2 68 D5
Dagenham NW10 89 C3
Midlea Ho EN3 6 C4
Midleton Rd KT3 177 A1
Midlothian Ho NW2 68 B4
Midlothian Rd E3 97 B3
Midmoor Rd
Merton SW19 179 A2
Streatham SW12 159 C3
Midship Cl SE16 118 D5
Midship Point E14 119 C4
Midstrath Rd NW10 67 C4
Midsummer Apartments 7 SM2 217 C1
Midsummer Ave TW4 129 B1
Midsummer Ct
Blackheath Pk SE12 143 A1
Edgware HA8 10 D1
Harrow HA1 42 B4
Midway SM3 201 B2
Midway Ho EC1 234 D2
Midwinter Cl 3 DA16 146 A2
Midwood Cl NW2 68 B5
Mighell Ave IG4 55 D4
Milan Ct N11 31 D2
Milan Rd UB1 107 B4
Milborne Gr SW10 256 B1
Milborne Ho 11 E9 74 C2
Milborne St E9 74 C2
Milborough Cres SE12 164 C5
Milbourne La KT10 212 A3
Milbourne Lodge Jun Sch KT10 212 A2
Milbourne Lodge Sen Sch KT10 212 B2
Milbrook KT10 212 A2
Milbrook Ct NW3 48 A1
Milburn Dr 1 UB7 104 A6
Milburn Ho SW20 178 B1
Milcote St SE1 251 D1
Mildenhall Rd E5 74 C5
Mildmay Ave N1 73 B2
Mildmay Ct N1 73 B3
Mildmay Gr N N1 73 B3
Mildmay Gr S N1 73 B3
Mildmay Ho 6 SW15 156 C6
Mildmay Mission Hospl E2 95 D4
Mildmay Pk N1 73 B3
Mildmay Rd
Ilford IG1 78 D5
Stoke Newington N1 73 C3
Mildmay St N1 73 B2
Mildon Ho EN3 6 C3
Mildred Ave
Hayes UB3 105 B3
Northolt UB5 63 D3
Mildura Ct N8 50 B5
MILE END 97 A3
Mile End Pl E1 96 D3
Mile End Rd E1, E3 96 D3
Mile End Sta E3 97 B4
Mile End The E17 34 D2
Mile Rd
Hackbridge SM6 203 A1
Wallington CR0, CR4, CR9 203 D1
Miles Bldgs NW1 237 A4
Miles Cl SE28 123 B5
Miles Coverdale Prim Sch W12 112 C4
Miles Ct
Croydon CR0 220 D6
Stepney E1 96 B1
Miles Dr SE28 123 C5
Miles Ho 5 SE10 120 C1
Miles Lo
Harrow HA1 42 B4
Stratford New Town E15 76 B3
Milespit Hill NW7 28 C5
Miles Pl NW8 236 D4
Miles Rd
Hornsey N8 50 A6
Mitcham CR4 202 C6
Miles St SW8 138 A6 270 B5
Milestone Cl
Edmonton N9 18 A2
Sutton SM2 218 B1
Milestone Ct TW7 131 A4
Milestone Green SW14 133 B1
Milestone Ho KT1 197 D5
Milestone Rd SE19 183 D4
Miles Way N20 14 C2
Milfoil St W12 112 A6
Milford Cl SE2 147 A6
Milford Ct
Southall UB1 107 C5
3 Stamford Hill N16 51 C1

Milford Gdns
Croydon CR0 206 D4
Edgware HA8 26 C3
Wembley HA0 65 D3
Milford Gr SM1 218 A4
Milford La
WC2 116 C6 251 A6
Milford Mews SW16 160 B1
Milford Rd
Ealing W13 109 B5
Southall UB1 107 C6
Milk St
Bromley BR1 187 B4
City of London
EC2 95 A1 242 B2
Newham E16 122 D5
Milkwell Gdns IG8 37 B3
Milkwell Yd 7 SE5 139 A4
Milkwood Rd SE24 138 D1
Milk Yd E1 118 C6
Millais Ave E12 78 C3
Millais Cres KT19 215 C3
Millais Ct 9 UB5 84 D5
Millais Gdns HA8 26 C1
Millais Rd
Enfield EN1 17 D6
Leyton E11 76 B4
New Malden KT3 199 C2
Millais Way KT19 215 A4
Milland Ho 11 SW15 156 A3
Millard Cl 21 N16 73 C3
Millard Terr RM10 81 C2
Millars Meadow Cl
SE12 165 A6
Millbank
Wallington SM6 219 D3
Westminster
SW1 116 A2 260 A3
Millbank Ho KT6 198 B2
Millbank Prim Sch
SW1 115 D2 259 D3
Millbank Way SE12 165 A6
Millbourne Rd TW13 173 A6
Mill Bridge EN5 13 B5
Millbrook 1 E18 55 A6
Millbrook Ave DA16 145 B1
Millbrooke Ct 7
SW15 157 A6
Millbrook Gdns RM6 59 A3
Millbrook Ho 4 SE15 140 A6
Millbrook Pl NW1 232 A4
Millbrook Rd
Brixton SW9 138 D2
Edmonton N9 18 B3
Mill Cl SM5 219 A6
Mill Cnr EN5 1 B4
Millcroft Ho SE6 185 D6
Mill Ct
Hendon NW7 29 A2
Leyton E10 76 A5
14 Thamesmead SE28 124 B6
Millender Wlk SE16 118 C2
Millennium Bridge* SE1,
EC4 252 A5
Millennium Bsns Ctr
NW2 68 B6
Millennium City Acad
W1 238 D3
Millennium Cl E16 99 B1
Millennium Dr E14 120 B2
Millennium Harbour
E14 119 C4
Millennium Ho E17 52 D4
Millennium Pl 27 E2 96 B5
Millennium Prim Sch
SE10 120 D3
Millennium Sq SE1 253 D2
Millennium Way
SE10 120 C3
Miller Ave EN3 7 C5
Miller Cl
Bromley BR1 187 B5
Carshalton CR4 202 D2
Pinner HA5 22 C1
Miller Ct
Bexleyheath DA7 147 D2
8 Hendon NW9 46 A5
Miller Ho
Harringay N15 50 D5
9 Streatham SW2 160 A4
Miller Rd
Mitcham SW19 180 B4
Thornton Heath CR0 204 C1
Miller's Ave E8, N16 73 D3
Millers Cl NW7 28 A6
Millers Ct 3 HA0 88 A5
Miller's Ct 1 W4 111 D1
Millers Green Cl EN2 4 D2
Miller's House Visitor
Ctr* 1 E3 98 A4
Millers Mead Ct
SW19 180 B3
Miller St NW1 232 A4
Miller's Terr 1 E8 73 D3
Miller's Way W6 112 C4
Millers Wharf Ho E1 118 A5
Millers Yd N3 29 D3
Miller Wlk SE1 251 B3
Millet Rd UB6 85 D5
Mill Farm Ave TW16 171 C3
Millfarm Bsns Pk
TW4 151 A4
Mill Farm Cl HA5 22 C1
Mill Farm Cres TW4 151 A3
Millfield
Charlton TW16 171 B2
Finsbury Pk N4 72 C6
Kingston u T KT1 198 B6
Millfield Ave E17 35 B2
Millfield La N6 70 D6
Millfield Pl N6 71 A6
Millfield Rd
Hendon HA8 27 A1
Twickenham TW4 151 B3
Millfields Com Sch E5 74 C4
Millfields Rd E5 74 C5
Mill Gdns SE26 162 B1
Mill Gn CR4 203 A2
Mill Green Bsns Pk
CR4 203 A2
Mill Green Rd CR4 203 A2
Millgrove St 6 SW11 137 A3
Millharbour E14 119 D4
Millhaven Cl RM6 58 B3
MILL HILL 28 B5
Mill Hill SW13 134 A2
Mill Hill Broadway Sta
NW7 27 C4
Mill Hill Circus NW7 27 D5
Mill Hill Cty High Sch
NW7 11 C2
Mill Hill East Sta NW7 29 A3
Mill Hill Gr 11 W3 110 D5
Mill Hill Ind Est NW7 27 D4
Mill Hill Rd
Barnes SW13 134 A3
South Acton W3 110 D4
Mill Hill Sch NW7 28 B6
Mill Hill Terr 9 W3 110 D5
Mill Ho
4 Lewisham SE13 142 A2
Morden SM4 202 A5
Woodford IG8 36 D5
Millhouse Pl SE27 182 D6
Millicent Fawcett Ct
N17 33 D2
Millicent Preston Ho 4
IG11 101 B6
Millicent Rd E10 53 B1
Milligan Ho SE23 163 B3
Milligan St E14 119 B6
Milliners Ho SW18 135 C1
Milling Rd HA8 27 B3
Millington Ho N16 73 B5
Millington Rd UB3 105 C3
Mill La
Brondesbury NW6 69 B3
Carshalton SM5 219 A5
Croydon CR0 220 C5
Dagenham RM6 59 A3
Sewardstone E4 7 D2
Woodford IG8 36 D5
Woolwich SE18 122 C1
Mill Lane Trad Est
CR0 220 B5
Millman Ct
Bloomsbury WC1 240 C5
Greenwich SE3 143 B5
Millman Mews WC1 240 C5
Millman Pl WC1 240 D5
Millman St
WC1 94 B3 240 C5
Millmark Gr SE14 141 A3
Millmarsh La EN3 7 B3
Millmead Bsns Ctr
N17 52 B6
Millmead Ind Ctr N17 52 B6
Mill Mead Rd N17 52 B6
MILL MEADS 98 B5
Millner Ct SE4 141 B3
Mill Pl
Chislehurst BR7 188 D2
Kingston u T KT1 198 B6
Limehouse E14 97 A1
Mill Plat TW7 131 A3
Mill Plat Ave TW7 131 A3
Mill Pond Cl
SW8 137 D5 269 D3
Millpond Est SE16 118 B4
Millpond Pl 2 SM6 219 A5
Mill Rd
Ilford IG1 78 C5
Merton SW19 180 A3
Newham E16 121 B5
Twickenham TW2 152 A2
Mill Ridge HA8 26 C5
Mill River Trad Est EN3 7 A1
Mill Row N1 95 C6
Mills Cl UB10 82 C5
Mills Ct
9 Leyton E11 76 C5
Shoreditch EC2 95 C4
Mills Gr
Hendon NW4 46 D6
1 South Bromley E14 98 A2
Mills Ho
Nine Elms SW8 269 B2
Walthamstow E17 54 B6
Millshott Cl SW6 134 C4
Millside SM5 218 D6
Millside Pl TW7 131 B3
Millson Cl N20 14 B2
Mills Row W4 111 B2
Mill St
Bermondsey
SE1 117 D4 253 D2
Kingston u T KT1 198 A6
Mayfair W1 249 A6
Millstream Cl N13 32 C5
Millstream Ho 14
SE16 118 B4
Millstream Rd
SE1 117 D4 253 C1
Mill Trad Est The
NW10 89 A4
Mill Vale BR2 186 D1
Mill View Cl KT17 215 D1
Mill View Gdns CR0 222 D5
MILLWALL 119 C3
Millwall Dock Rd E14 119 C3
Mill Way
Edgware NW7 27 C5
Feltham TW14 150 B6
Millway Gdns UB5 63 B2
Millwood Rd TW3,
TW7 152 A6
Millwood St 10 W10 91 A2
Mill Yd E1 118 A6
Milman Cl HA5 40 D6
Milman Rd NW6 91 A5
Milman's Ho SW10 266 C5
Milman's St
SW10 136 B6 266 C5
Milne Ct
Enfield EN2 4 C3
4 Woodford E18 37 A2
Milne Field HA5 23 C3
Milne Gdns SE9 166 A6
Milne Ho 18 SE18 122 B2
Milner Bldg N16 73 B5
Milner Dr TW2 152 B4
Milner Ho
2 Battersea SW11 136 B2
Hayes UB4 84 B4
Milner Pl N1 94 C6 234 B6
Milner Rd
Dagenham RM8 80 C6
Kingston u T KT1 197 D6
Merton SW19 179 D2
Morden SM4 202 B4
Newham E15 98 C4
South Norwood CR7 205 B6
Milner Sq N1 72 D1
Milner St
SW3 114 D2 257 C4
Milner Wlk SE9 167 B3
Milnthorpe Rd W4 133 B6
Milo Rd SE22 161 D5
Milrood Ho 5 E1 96 D2
Milroy Wlk SE1 251 C4
Milson Rd
W14 113 A3 254 A6
Milsted Ho 23 E5 74 B3
Milton Ave
Barnet EN5 13 B6
Becontree NW10 89 B6
Carshalton SM1 218 C4
Crouch End N6 49 C2
Kingsbury NW9 45 A6
Plashet E6 78 A1
Thornton Heath CR0 205 B2
Milton Cl
Bermondsey
SE1 117 D2 263 C3
Carshalton SM1 218 B5
Hampstead Garden Suburb
N2 48 A3
Hayes UB4 84 A1
Milton Court Rd SE14 141 A6
Milton Cres IG2 57 A3
Milton Ct
Fulham SW6 135 A2
Ilford RM6 58 C2
Kingston u T KT2 176 A6
St Luke's EC2 242 C4
Twickenham TW2 152 C1
Uxbridge UB10 60 D5
9 Wandsworth SW18 157 C6
Milton Dr
Borehamwood WD6 10 D6
Littleton TW17 192 A5
Milton Gdns TW19 148 B3
Milton Gr
Friern Barnet N11 31 D5
Stoke Newington N16 73 C4
Milton Ho
12 Beckenham BR3 185 C3
19 Bethnal Green E2 96 C4
2 Camberwell SE5 139 B5
5 Kingston u T KT2 176 D4
Sutton SM1 217 C5
Milton House Mans
E8 73 D4
Milton Lo
4 Sidcup DA14 190 A6
Southgate N21 16 D3
Twickenham TW1 152 D4
Milton Pk N6 49 C2
Milton Pl 3 N7 72 C3
Milton Rd
Acton W3 111 B5
Belvedere DA17 125 C2
Bexley DA16 145 D4
Crouch End N6 49 C2
Ealing W7 108 D6
Hampton TW12 173 C3
Harrow HA1 42 C5
1 Hendon NW9 46 A2
Mill Hill NW7 28 A5
Mitcham CR4 181 A3
Mortlake SW14 133 B2
Sutton SM1 217 C4
Thornton Heath CR0 205 B2
Tottenham N15 50 D6
Tulse Hill SE24 160 D6
Uxbridge UB10 60 D4
Wallington SM6 219 D2
Walthamstow E17 53 C5
Wimbledon SW19 180 A4
Milton St EC1,
EC2 95 B2 242 C4
Milton Way UB7 104 B2
Milverton NW5 71 A3
Milverton Dr UB10 61 A4
Milverton Gdns IG3 79 D6
Milverton Ho SE23 163 A1
Milverton Rd NW6 68 C1
Milverton St
SE11 116 C1 261 B1
Milverton Way SE9 188 C6
Milward St E1 96 B2
Milward Wlk 14 SE18 144 C6
Mimosa N15 51 B4
Mimosa Ct
Colney Hatch N12 30 C4
South Lambeth SW4 270 B1
Mimosa Ho UB4 84 C2
Mimosa Rd UB4 84 C2
Mimosa St
SW6 135 B4 264 D1
Mina Rd
Merton SW19 179 C2
Walworth
SE17 117 C1 263 B2
Minard Rd SE6 164 C3
Minchenden Cres N14 15 D1
Minchenden Ct N14 15 D2
Minchin Ho 10 E14 97 C1
Mincing La
EC3 117 C6 253 A6
Minden Rd
Cheam SM3 217 B6
Penge SE20 184 B2
Minehead Ct HA2 63 C6
Minehead Rd
Harrow HA2 63 C5
Streatham SW16 182 B5
Mineral Cl EN5 12 C6
Mineral St SE18 123 C2
Minera Mews SW1 258 B4
Minerva Cl
Kennington SW9 138 C5
Sidcup DA14 189 C6
Minerva Rd
Becontree NW10 89 B4
Chingford E4 35 D3
Kingston u T KT1 176 B1
Minerva St E2 96 B5
Minerva Wlk EC1 241 D2
Minet Ave NW10 89 C5
Minet Ctry Pk UB2, UB3,
UB4 106 C4
Minet Dr UB3 106 A5
Minet Gdns
Dagenham NW10 89 C5
Hayes UB3 106 B5
Minet Ho 20 E1 96 A1
Minet Jun & Inf Schs
UB3 106 B5
Minet Rd SE5, SW9 138 D3
Minetta Ct 19 EN5 13 D6
Minford Gdns W14 112 D4
Mingard Wlk N7 72 B5
Ming St E14 119 C6
Minimax Cl TW14 150 A5
Ministry Way SE9 166 B2
Mink Ct TW4 128 C3
Minnie Bennett Ho
SE3 143 C5
Minniedale KT5 198 B4
Minnow Wlk SE17 263 B3
Minories EC3 117 D6 253 C6
Minshaw Ct DA14 189 D6
Minshull Pl 23 BR3 185 C3
Minshull St SW8 269 C1
Minson Rd E9 96 D6
Minstead Gdns SW15 155 D4
Minstead Way KT3 199 C3
Minster Ave SM1 217 C6
Minster Ct EC3 253 B6
Minster Dr CR0 221 C4
Minster Gdns KT8 195 B5
Minsterley Ave TW16,
TW17 193 C5
Minster Rd
Bromley BR1 187 B3
Brondesbury NW2 69 A3
Minster Wlk N8 50 A5
Minstrel Ct HA3 24 C1
Minstrel Gdns KT5 198 B5
Mint Bsns Pk 12 E16 99 A2
Mint Cl UB10 82 D4
Mintern Cl N13 16 D1
Minterne Ave UB2 107 C2
Minterne Rd HA3 44 B4
Minterne Waye UB4 84 C1
Mintern St N1 95 B5 235 D4
Minton Ho SE11 261 A4
Minton Mews 3 NW6 69 D2
Mint Rd SM5, SM6 219 B4
Mint St SE1 252 B2
Mint Wlk CR0 221 A5
Mirabel Rd
SW6 135 B5 264 D4
Mirage Ctr The HA9 66 D4
Miranda Cl 19 E1 96 C2
Miranda Ct W3 88 B1
Miranda Ho
6 Belvedere DA17 125 C1
17 Hoxton N1 95 C5
Miranda Rd N19 49 C1
Mirfield Ct SE20 184 A1
Mirfield St SE7 121 D3
Miriam Ct DA14 190 B6
Miriam Rd SE18 123 C1
Miravale Ct 11 IG9 21 C2
Mirravale Trad Est
RM8 59 A2
Mirren Cl HA2 63 B5
Mirror Path SE12 165 C1
Misbourne Rd UB10 82 C6
Missenden SE17 262 D1
Missenden Cl TW14 149 D3
Missenden Gdns SM4 202 A3
Missenden Ho NW8 237 A6
Mission Gr E17 53 A4
Mission Grove Prim Sch
E17 53 B5
Mission Pl SE15 140 A4
Mission Sq 18 TW8 132 A6
Mission The
13 Bermondsey SE16 118 B4
14 Poplar E14 97 B1
Missouri Ct HA5 40 C3
Misterton Ct SW11 266 D2
Mistletoe Cl CR0 206 D1
Mistley Thorn IG1 56 C2
Mistral SE5 139 C4
Mistral Ct E4 19 D1
Mistys Field KT12 194 C1
Mitali Pas 21 E1 96 A1
MITCHAM 202 D5
Mitcham Eastfields Sta
CR4 181 A1
Mitcham Garden Village
CR4 203 A4
Mitcham Ho 9 SE5 139 A4
Mitcham Ind Est CR4 181 A2
Mitcham Junction Sta
CR4 203 A4
Mitcham La SW16 181 C5
Mitcham Pk CR4 202 C5
Mitcham Rd
Ilford IG3 57 D2
Newham E6 100 A4
Upper Tooting SW17 180 D5
Mitcham Sta CR4 202 C5
Mitchell 19 NW9 27 D2
Mitchell Brook Prim Sch
NW10 67 C2
Mitchellbrook Way
NW10 67 B2
Mitchell Cl
Abbey Wood SE2 124 C2
Belvedere DA17 125 D3
Mitchell Ct SW14 133 C1
Mitchell Ho
Gunnersbury W4 110 D1
6 Islington N1 72 C1
31 Shepherd's Bush
W12 112 B6
Mitchell Rd
Edmonton N13 33 A5
Orpington BR6 227 D4
Mitchell's Pl SE21 161 C4
Mitchell St EC1 95 A3 242 B6
Mitchell Way
1 Bromley BR1 187 A2
Tokyngton NW10 67 A2
Mitchell Wlk E6 100 B2
Mitchison Rd N1 73 B2
Mitchley Rd N17 52 A6
Mitford Cl KT9 213 C2
Mitford Rd N19 72 A6
Mitre Bridge Ind Pk
W10 90 B3
Mitre Cl
Shepperton TW17 193 B3
Sutton SM2 218 B1
Mitre Ct
Belvedere DA17 125 C1
1 Ilford RM6 58 B2
9 Woodford E18 37 A2
Mitre Ho RM7 59 D5
Mitre Rd
Lambeth SE1 116 C4 251 B2
Newham E15 98 C5
Mitre Sq EC3 243 B1
Mitre St EC3 95 C1 243 B1
Mitre The 9 E14 119 B6
Mitre Way W10 90 B2
Mizzen Ct E14 119 C4
Moatbridge Sch SE9 165 D5
Moat Cl BR6 227 D2
Moat Cres N3 47 D6
Moat Croft DA16 146 C2
Moat Ct
Eltham SE9 166 B5
Sidcup DA15 167 D1
Moat Dr
Harrow HA1 42 B5
5 Newham E13 99 C5
Ruislip HA4 39 C2
Moat Farm Rd UB5 63 B1
Moatfield NW6 69 A1
Moat Lodge The HA1 64 C6
Moat Pl
Acton W3 88 D1
Stockwell SW9 138 B2
Moat Sch The SW6 135 A3
Moat Side
Enfield EN3 6 D1
Feltham TW13 172 C6
Moat The KT3 177 C2
Moberly Rd SW4 159 D4
Mobey Ct SW4 270 A1
Moby Dick RM6 59 B5
Mocatta Ho 9 E1 96 B3
Modbury Gdns NW5 71 A2
Modder Pl SW15 134 D1
Model Cotts SW14 133 A2
Model Farm Cl SE9 166 A1
Modling Ho 8 E2 96 D5
Modoc Ho EN3 18 D6
Moelwyn Hughes Ct
N7 71 D3
Moelyn Mews HA1 43 A4
Moffat Ct
Upper Tooting SW17 180 C6
Wimbledon SW19 179 C5
Moffat Ho 24 SE5 139 A5
Moffat Rd
Bowes Pk N13 32 A4
South Norwood CR7 183 B1
Upper Tooting SW17 180 D6
Mogden La TW7 152 D6

Mohammedi Pk Complex UB5 85 C6
Mohawk Ho 33 E3 97 A5
Mohmmad Khan Rd E11 54 D1
Mohr Ct N22 32 B3
Moidart Ct HA8 10 D2
Moineau 18 NW9 27 D2
Moira Cl N17 33 C1
Moira Ct SW17 159 A2
Moira Ho 13 SW9 138 C4
Moira Rd SE9 144 B1
Molasses Ho 1 SW11 136 A2
Molasses Row 2 SW11 136 A2
Mole Abbey Gdns KT8 195 D6
Mole Ct
2 Bedford Pk W12 111 C4
West Ewell KT19 215 A4
Mole Ho NW8 236 D5
Molember Ct KT7 196 C5
Molember Rd KT8 196 C4
Molescroft SE9 167 A1
Molesey Ave KT12, KT8 195 B4
Molesey Bsns Ctr KT8 195 B4
Molesey Dr SM3 217 A5
Molesey Ho E2 243 C6
Molesey Hospl KT8 195 C4
Molesey Park Ave KT8 195 D4
Molesey Park Cl KT8 196 A4
Molesey Park Rd KT8 196 A4
Molesey Rd KT12 195 A2
Molesford Rd SW6 265 A1
Molesham Cl KT8 195 D6
Molesham Way KT8 195 D6
Molesworth Ho 9 SE17 138 D6
Molesworth St SE13 142 A2
Moliner Ct 4 BR3 185 C3
Mollie Davis Ct SE19 183 D4
Mollison Ave EN3 7 B5
Mollison Dr SM6 220 A1
Mollison Sq SM6 219 D1
Mollison Way HA8 26 C1
Molly Huggins Cl SW12 159 C4
Molton Ho N1 233 D5
Molvic Ct BR3 185 B1
Molyneux Dr SW17 181 B6
Molyneux Ho W1 237 B2
Molyneux St W1 92 C2 237 B3
Monarch Cl
Coney Hall BR4 224 D4
East Bedfont TW14 149 C4
Monarch Ct
Ealing W5 87 C2
Hampstead Garden Suburb N2 48 A4
Monarch Dr E16 99 D2
Monarch Mews
Walthamstow E17 53 D3
West Norwood SW16 182 C5
Monarch Par CR4 180 D1
Monarch Pl
Buckhurst Hill IG9 21 C2
Sutton SM1 218 B3
Monarch Rd DA17 125 C3
Monarchs Ct
1 Edgware NW7 27 B5
Harrow HA2 41 C2
Monarch's Way HA4 39 C1
Monarch Way IG2 57 B3
Mona Rd SE15 140 C3
Mona St E16 98 D2
Monastery Gdns EN2 5 B3
Monaveen Gdns KT8 195 D6
Monck's Row SW18 157 B5
Monck St SW1 115 D3 259 D5
Monckton Ct W14 254 C6
Monclar Rd SE5 139 B1
Moncorvo Cl SW7 114 C4 247 A1
Moncrieff Cl 4 E6 100 A1
Moncrieff St SE15 140 A3
Mondial Way UB7 127 A5
Mondragon Ho SW8 270 B2
Monega Prim Sch E12 77 D2
Monega Rd E7, E12 77 D2
Monet Ct 15 SE16 118 B1
Moneyer Ho N1 235 C2
Monica Ct SW16 181 D4
Monica James Ho 12 DA14 168 A1
Monica Shaw Ct NW1 232 D3
Monier Rd E3 75 C1
Monivea Rd BR3 185 B3
Monkbretton Ho E2 96 A4
Monk Ct W12 112 A5
Monk Dr E16 121 A6
MONKEN HADLEY 1 A3
Monken Hadley CE Prim Sch EN4 1 C4
Monkfrith Ave N14 15 B5
Monkfrith Cl N14 15 B4
Monkfrith Prim Sch N14 15 A4
Monkfrith Way N14 15 B4
Monkham's Ave IG8 37 B5
Monkham's Dr IG8 37 B5
Monkham's La IG8 37 B6
Monkleigh Rd SM4, SW20 201 A5
Monkridge 3 N8 49 D2
Monks Ave
East Molesey KT8 195 B4
New Barnet EN5 14 A5
Monks Cl
Abbey Wood SE2 124 D2
Enfield EN2 5 A3
Harrow HA2 63 D6
Ruislip HA4 62 D4
Monks Cres KT12 194 B1
Monksdene Gdns SM1 217 D5
Monks Dr W3 88 C1
Monksfield N4 72 C6
MONKS ORCHARD 207 A3
Monks Orchard Rd BR3, CR0 207 C2
Monks Orchard Sch CR0 206 D4
Monks Park Gdns HA9 66 D1
Monks Pk HA9 67 A2
Monks Rd EN2 5 A3
Monk St SE18 122 C2
Monks Way
Beckenham BR3 207 C3
Crofton BR5 211 B1
Harmondsworth UB7 126 A6
Temple Fortune NW11 47 B5
Monkswell Ct N10 31 A2
Monkswell Ho E2 96 A4
Monkswood Gdns
Borehamwood WD6 11 B6
Ilford IG5 56 C6
Monk Terr SE23 163 B2
Monkton Ho
32 Bermondsey SE16 118 D4
22 Hackney E5 74 B3
Monkton Rd DA16 145 D3
Monkton St SE11 116 C2 261 B4
Monkville Ave NW11 47 B5
Monkville Par 1 NW11 47 B5
Monkwell Sq EC2 242 B3
Monmouth Ave
Teddington KT1 175 C3
Wanstead E18 55 B6
Monmouth Cl
Bedford Pk W4 111 B3
Bexley DA16 146 A1
Mitcham CR4, SW16 204 A5
Monmouth Ct 9 W7 86 D2
Monmouth Gr TW8 110 A2
Monmouth Ho
5 Camden Town NW5 71 B2
Wandsworth SW18 157 C5
Monmouth Pl W2 91 D1
Monmouth Rd
Dagenham RM9 81 B3
Hayes UB3 105 D2
Lower Edmonton N9 18 C2
Newham E6 100 B4
Notting Hill W2 91 C1
Monmouth St WC2 94 A1 240 A1
Monnery Rd N19 71 C5
Monnow Rd SE1 118 A2
Mono La TW13 150 B2
Monoux Almshouses E17 53 D5
Monoux Gr E17 35 C2
Monroe Cres EN1 6 B4
Monroe Dr SW14 154 D6
Monroe Ho
16 Crouch End N19 49 D2
Lisson Gr NW8 230 B1
Monro Gdns HA3 24 C3
Monro Ho
16 Hampstead NW3 70 A4
Putney SW15 156 B6
Monro Way E5 74 A4
Monsal Ct E5 75 A4
Monsell Ct 4 N4 72 D5
Monsell Rd N4, N5 72 D5
Monson Prim Sch SE14 140 D5
Monson Rd
Deptford SE14 140 D5
Willesden Green NW10 90 B5
Mons Way BR2 210 A3
Montacute Rd
Bushey WD23 8 C4
Carshalton SM4 202 B3
Forest Hill SE6 163 B4
Montagu Cres N18 34 B6
Montagu Ct W1 237 D3
Montague Ave
Brockley SE4 141 C1
Ealing W7 108 D5
Montague Cl
Borough The SE1 252 C4
Walton-on-T KT12 194 A2
Montague Ct 16 DA14 168 A1
Montague Fell HA0 64 D4
Montague Gdns W3 110 C6
Montague Pl WC1 93 D2 239 D4
Montague Rd
Ealing W13 87 B1
Hanwell W7 108 D4
Hornsey Vale N8 50 B4
Hounslow TW3 129 D2
Leytonstone E11 76 D6
Merton SW19 179 D3
Richmond TW10 154 A5
Shacklewell E8 74 A3
Southall UB2 107 A2
Thornton Heath CR0 204 D1
Tottenham Hale N15 52 A5
Uxbridge UB8 60 A1
Montague Sq SE15 140 C5
Montague St
Bloomsbury WC1 94 A2 240 A4
City of London EC1 242 A3
Montague Terr 1 BR2 209 A5
Montague Waye UB2 107 A3
Montague Works HA0 88 B5
Montagu Gdns
Edmonton N18 34 B6
Wallington SM6 219 C4
Montagu Ind Est N18 34 C6
Montagu Mans W1 92 D2 237 D3
Montagu Mews N W1 237 D3
Montagu Mews S W1 237 D2
Montagu Mews W W1 237 D2
Montagu Pl W1 92 D2 237 D3
Montagu Rd
Hendon NW4 46 A3
Lower Edmonton N9, N18 18 C1
Montagu Row W1 237 D3
Montagu Sq W1 92 D1 237 D2
Montagu St W1 92 D1 237 D2
Montaigne Cl SW1 259 D3
Montalt Ho IG8 36 D6
Montalt Rd IG8 36 D5
Montana Bldg 4 SE13 141 D4
Montana Gdns
Penge SE26 185 B5
5 Sutton SM1 218 A3
Montana Rd
Upper Tooting SW17 159 A1
Wimbledon SW20 178 C2
Montbelle Prim Sch SE9 188 C6
Montbelle Rd SE9 166 D1
Montcalm Cl
Hayes BR2 209 A3
Yeading UB4 84 B4
Montcalm Ho E14 119 C3
Montcalm Rd SE7 143 D5
Montclair Ct 21 N12 29 D6
Montclare St E2 95 D3 243 C6
Monteagle Ave IG11 79 A2
Monteagle Ct
Barking IG11 79 A1
27 Hoxton N1 95 C5
Monteagle Prim Sch RM9 102 B6
Monteagle Way
Nunhead SE15 140 B2
Shacklewell E5 74 A5
Montefiore Ct 2 N16 51 D1
Montefiore St 2 SW8 137 B3
Montego Cl 10 SW2 138 C1
Montem Prim Sch N7 72 B5
Montem Rd
Forest Hill SE23 163 B4
New Malden KT3 199 C5
Montem St N4 50 B1
Montenotte Rd N8 49 C4
Monteray Studios W10 91 A5
Monterey Cl NW7 27 C5
Montesole Ct 7 HA5 22 C1
Montesquieu Terr 3 E16 98 D1
Montford Pl
Kennington SE11 138 C6
Kennington SE11 261 A1
Montford Rd TW16 194 A5
Montfort Ho
4 Bethnal Green E2 96 C4
Cubitt Town E14 120 A3
Montfort Pl SW19 156 D3
Montgolfier Wlk UB5 85 A4
Montgomerie Ct 2 BR3 185 C2
Montgomery Ave KT10 212 C6
Montgomery Cl
Blackfen DA15 167 D5
Mitcham CR4 204 A5
Montgomery Ct W4 133 A6
Montgomery Gdns SM2 218 B1
Montgomery Ho 5 SW14 133 B2
Montgomery Lo 38 E1 96 C3
Montgomery Rd
Acton W4 111 A2
Edgware HA8 26 B4
Montholme Rd SW11 158 D5
Monthope Rd 17 E1 96 A2
Montolieu Gdns SW15 156 B6
Montpelier Ave
Ealing W5 87 C2
Sidcup DA5 168 D4
Montpelier Cl UB10 82 C6
Montpelier Ct
5 Beckenham BR2 208 D5
Ealing W5 87 D2
Montpelier Gdns
Ilford RM6 58 C2
Newham E6 99 D4
Montpelier Gr NW5 71 C3
Montpelier Mews SW7 257 B6
Montpelier Pl
Knightsbridge SW7 257 B6
21 Stepney E1 96 C1
Montpelier Prim Sch W5 87 D2
Montpelier Rd
Ealing W5 87 D2
Finchley N3 30 A2
Peckham SE15 140 B4
Sutton SM1 218 A4
Montpelier Rise
Golders Green NW11 47 A2
Wembley HA9 43 D1
Montpelier Row
Blackheath Vale SE3 142 D3
Twickenham TW1 153 C4
Montpelier Sq SW7 114 C4 247 B1
Montpelier St SW7 114 C3 257 B6
Montpelier Terr SW7 247 B1
Montpelier Vale SE3 142 D3
Montpelier Way NW11 47 A2
Montpelier Wlk SW7 114 C3 257 B6
Montpellier Ct KT12 194 B3
Montrave Rd SE20 184 C3
Montreal Ho
Catford SE6 163 D3
Hayes UB4 84 B4
Montreal Pl WC2 250 C6
Montreal Rd IG1 57 A2
Montrell Rd SW2 160 A3
Montrose Ave
Falconwood DA16 145 C2
Hendon HA8 27 B2
Kensal Rise NW6 91 A5
Montrose Ave *continued*
Sidcup DA15 168 A4
Twickenham TW2 151 D4
Montrose Cl
Ashford TW15 171 A5
Falconwood DA16 145 D2
Woodford IG8 37 A6
Montrose Cres
Finchley N12 30 A4
1 Wembley HA0 66 A2
Montrose Ct
2 Catford SE6 164 D2
Hendon NW9 27 A1
Knightsbridge SW7 114 B4 246 D1
Temple Fortune NW11 47 B5
Montrose Gdns
Mitcham CR4 180 D1
Sutton SM1 217 D6
Montrose Ho
Belgravia SW1 248 B1
Millwall E14 119 C3
Twickenham TW2 151 D4
Montrose Pl SW1 115 A4 248 B1
Montrose Rd
East Bedfont TW14 149 B5
Harrow HA3 24 D1
Montrose Villas 5 W6 112 A1
Montrose Way SE23 162 D3
Montserrat Ave IG8 36 B3
Montserrat Cl SE19 183 B5
Montserrat Rd SW15 135 A1
Montway Hts SW19 179 D3
Monument Gdns SE13 164 A6
Monument St EC3 117 B6 252 D6
Monument Sta EC3 117 B6 252 D6
Monument The* EC3 252 D6
Monument Way N17 51 D6
Monza Bldg The E1 118 C6
Monza St E1 118 C6
Moodkee St SE16 118 C3
Moody Rd SE15 139 D4
Moody St E1 96 D4
Moon Ct SE12 143 A1
Moon Ho HA1 42 D5
Moon La EN5 1 B2
Moon St N1 94 D6 234 C6
Moorcroft HA8 26 D2
Moorcroft Ct 4 N3 29 B1
Moorcroft Gdns BR1 210 A4
Moorcroft La UB8 82 C2
Moorcroft Rd SW16 160 A1
Moorcroft Sch UB8 82 B1
Moorcroft Way HA5 41 A4
Moordown SE18 144 D4
Moore Cl
Mitcham CR4 181 B1
Mortlake SW14 133 A2
Wallington SM6 220 A1
Moore Cres RM9 102 B6
Moore Ct N1 234 C5
Moorefield Rd N17 33 D1
Moore Ho
16 Bethnal Green E2 96 C4
5 Greenwich SE10 120 D1
Hornsey N8 50 A5
7 Shadwell E1 118 C6
Wandsworth SW17 158 B1
1 West Norwood SE27 183 A6
Mooreland Rd BR1 187 A2
Moore Park Ct SW6 265 D4
Moore Park Rd SW6 135 D5 265 C3
Moore Rd SE19 183 A4
Moore St SW3 114 D2 257 C4
Moore Wlk E7 77 A4
Moorey Cl 2 E15 98 D6
Moorfield Ave W5 87 D3
Moorfield Rd
Chessington KT9 214 A3
Enfield EN3 6 C4
Moorfields EC2 95 B2 242 C3
Moorfields Ct 6 SW16 181 C6
Moorfields Eye Hospl EC1 95 B4 235 C1
Moorfields Highwalk EC2 242 C3
Moorgate EC2 95 B2 242 C3
Moorgate Pl EC2 242 C2
Moorgate Sta EC2 95 B2 242 C3
Moorgreen Ho EC1 234 C2
Moorhead Way SE3 143 B2
Moorhouse 17 NW9 27 D2
Moorhouse Rd
Harrow HA3 43 D6
Notting Hill W2 91 C1
Moorings Ho 3 TW8 131 C5
Moorings The 5 E16 99 C2
Moor La
Broadgate EC2 95 B2 242 C3
Chessington KT9 214 A3
Moorland Cl TW4 151 C4
Moorland Ct N21 16 B5
Moorland Rd SW9 138 D1
Moorlands
Chislehurst BR7 188 D3
Northolt UB5 85 A6
17 Wallington SM6 219 B2
Moorlands Ave NW7 28 B4
Moor Lane Jun Sch KT9 214 B3
Moormead Dr KT19 215 C3
Moor Mead Rd TW1 153 A5
Moor Park Gdns KT2 177 C3
Moor Park Ho N21 16 D4
Moor Pl EC2 242 C3
Moorside Ct W13 109 C5
Moorside Rd BR1 186 D6
Moor St W1 239 D1
Moortown Rd WD19 22 C6
Moot Ct NW9 44 C4
Morant Ho SW9 138 B3
Morant Pl N22 32 B2
Morant St E14 119 C6
Mora Prim Sch NW2 68 C4
Mora Rd NW2 68 C4
Mora St EC1 95 A4 235 B1
Morat St SW9 138 B4 270 D2
Moravian Cl SW3 266 D5
Moravian Pl SW10 136 B6 266 D5
Moravian St 10 E2 96 C4
Moray Ave UB3 105 D5
Moray Cl HA8 10 D2
Moray Ho
11 Kingston u T KT6 198 A4
9 Mile End E1 97 A3
Moray Mews N4, N7 72 B6
Moray Rd N4, N7 72 B6
Mordaunt Gdns RM9 81 A1
Mordaunt Ho
4 Becontree NW10 89 B6
34 Clapham SW8 137 D3
Mordaunt Rd NW10 89 B6
Mordaunt St SW9 138 B2
MORDEN 201 D3
Morden Court Par SM4 201 D5
Morden Ct SM4 201 D5
Morden Gdns
Greenford UB6 64 D3
Mitcham CR4 202 B5
Morden Hall SW19 201 D6
Morden Hall Rd SM4 202 A5
Morden Hill SE13 142 A3
Morden Ho
Morden SM4 201 C5
19 Tulse Hill SW2 160 C5
Morden La SE13 142 A4
Morden Lo BR2 186 B1
Morden Mount Prim Sch SE13 141 D3
MORDEN PARK 201 A3
Morden Park Sch Sports Ctr SM4 201 B4
Morden Prim Sch SM4 201 C4
Morden Rd
Dagenham RM6 59 A2
Kidbrooke SE3 143 A3
Merton SW19 179 D1
Mitcham CR4, SM4 202 B5
Morden Road Mews SE3 143 A3
Morden Road Sta SW19 179 D1
Morden South Sta SM4 201 C4
Morden St SE13 141 D4
Morden Sta SW19 201 D6
Morden Way SM3 201 C2
Morden Wharf Rd SE10 120 C3
Mordern Ho NW1 237 B5
Mordon Rd IG3 57 D2
Mordred Rd SE6 164 C2
Morecambe Cl 3 E1 96 D2
Morecambe Gdns HA7 25 D6
Morecambe St SE17 117 A1 262 B2

Morecambe Terr N18 ... 33 B6
More Cl
Canning Town E16 ... 98 D1
West Kensington W14 ... 113 A2 254 A3
Morecoombe Cl KT2 ... 176 D3
Morecroft TW2 ... 152 A2
Moredown Ho 3 E8 ... 74 A3
Moree Way N18 ... 34 A6
More House Sch SW1 ... 114 D3 257 D5
Moreland Ct 3 NW2 ... 69 C5
Moreland Prim Sch EC1 ... 94 D4 234 D1
Moreland St EC1 ... 94 D4 234 D2
Moreland Way E4 ... 20 A1
Morella Rd SW11, SW12 ... 158 D4
Morell Ho 5 SW9 ... 138 B3
Morello Ave UB8 ... 82 D2
Morello Ct HA9 ... 66 B5
Moremead Rd SE6 ... 185 C6
Morena St SE6 ... 163 D4
Moresby Ave KT5 ... 198 D2
Moresby Rd E5 ... 52 B1
Moresby Wlk 6 SW8 ... 137 B3
More's Gdn SW3 ... 266 D5
Moreton Ave TW7 ... 130 C4
Moreton Cl
Mill Hill NW7 ... 28 C4
Tottenham N15 ... 51 B3
Upper Clapton E5 ... 52 C1
Moreton Ho
Bermondsey SE16 ... 118 B3
Upper Tooting SW17 ... 180 B6
Moreton Pl SW1 ... 115 C1 259 B2
Moreton Rd
Croydon CR2 ... 221 B3
North Cheam KT4 ... 216 B6
Tottenham N15 ... 51 B3
Moreton St SW1 ... 115 D1 259 C2
Moreton Terr SW1 ... 115 C1 259 B2
Moreton Terr Mews N SW1 ... 259 B2
Moreton Terr Mews S SW1 ... 259 B2
Moreton Twr 3 W3 ... 110 D5
Morford Cl HA4 ... 40 B2
Morford Way HA4 ... 40 B2
Morgan Ave E17 ... 54 B5
Morgan Cl RM10 ... 81 C1
Morgan Ct
Ashford TW15 ... 170 D5
5 Battersea SW11 ... 136 B3
Carshalton SM5 ... 218 D4
Morgan Ho
Nine Elms SW8 ... 269 B2
Pimlico SW1 ... 259 B3
Morgan Rd
Islington N7 ... 72 C3
Notting Hill W10 ... 91 B2
Plaistow BR1 ... 187 A3
Morgan's La UB3 ... 83 B2
Morgan St
Canning Town E16 ... 98 D2
Globe Town E3 ... 96 D4
Morgan's Wlk SW11 ... 267 A3
Morgan Terr RM6 ... 58 C4
Moriah Jewish Day Sch The HA5 ... 41 A1
Moriatry Cl N7 ... 72 A4
Morie St SW18 ... 157 D6
Morieux Rd E10 ... 53 B1
Moring Rd SW17 ... 181 A6
Morkyns Wlk SE21 ... 161 C1
Morland Ave CR0 ... 205 C1
Morland Cl
Golders Green NW11 ... 47 D1
Hampton TW12 ... 173 B5
Mitcham CR4 ... 202 C6
Morland Ct W12 ... 112 B4
Morland Est E8 ... 74 A1
Morland Gdns
Southall UB1 ... 107 D5
Stonebridge NW10 ... 67 B1
Morland Ho
Kilburn NW6 ... 91 C6
Notting Hill W11 ... 91 A1
Somers Town NW1 ... 232 B3
Westminster SW1 ... 260 A4
Morland Mews N1 ... 72 C1
Morland Rd
Croydon CR0 ... 205 D2
Dagenham RM10 ... 81 C1
Harrow HA3 ... 44 A5
Ilford IG1 ... 78 D6

Morland Rd *continued*
Penge SE20 ... 184 D4
Sutton SM1 ... 218 A3
Walthamstow E17 ... 52 D4
Morley Ave
Chingford E4 ... 36 B3
Edmonton N18 ... 34 A6
Tottenham N22 ... 32 D1
Morley Cl BR6 ... 226 D6
Morley Coll SE1 ... 116 C3 261 B6
Morley Cres
Edgware HA8 ... 11 A2
Ruislip HA4 ... 62 C6
Morley Cres E HA7 ... 43 D6
Morley Cres W HA7 ... 43 C6
Morley Ct
Bromley BR3 ... 186 B2
Chingford Hatch E4 ... 35 B5
Lewisham SE13 ... 142 A1
Shortlands BR2 ... 208 D5
Morley Hill EN2 ... 5 B5
Morley Ho
Stoke Newington N16 ... 74 A6
Streatham SW2 ... 160 A4
W1 ... 238 D2
Morley Rd
Barking IG11 ... 101 B6
Cheam SM3 ... 201 B1
Chislehurst BR7 ... 189 A2
Dagenham RM6 ... 59 A4
Lewisham SE13 ... 142 A1
Leytonstone E10 ... 54 A1
Newham E15 ... 98 D5
Twickenham TW1 ... 153 D5
Morley St SE1 ... 116 C4 251 B1
Morna Rd SE5 ... 139 A3
Morning La E9 ... 74 C2
Morningside Prim Sch E9 ... 74 C2
Morningside Rd KT4 ... 216 C6
Mornington Ave
Bromley BR1 ... 209 D6
Ilford IG1 ... 56 C2
West Kensington W14 ... 113 B2 254 C3
Mornington Avenue Mans W14 ... 254 C3
Mornington Cl IG8 ... 37 A6
Mornington Cres
Camden Town NW1 ... 93 C5 232 A4
Cranford TW5 ... 128 B4
Mornington Crescent Sta NW1 ... 93 C5 232 A4
Mornington Ct NW1 ... 232 A4
Mornington Gr E3 ... 97 C4
Mornington Lo EN1 ... 17 C6
Mornington Mews 2 SE5 ... 139 A4
Mornington Pl
4 New Cross SE8 ... 141 B5
Regent's Pk NW1 ... 232 A4
Mornington Rd
Ashford TW15 ... 171 A5
Chingford E4 ... 20 B4
Greenford UB6 ... 85 D3
Leytonstone E11 ... 54 D1
New Cross SE14, SE8 ... 141 B5
Woodford IG8 ... 36 D6
Mornington St NW1 ... 93 B5 231 D4
Mornington Terr NW1 ... 93 B5 231 D4
Mornington Wlk TW10 ... 175 C6
Morocco St SE1 ... 117 C4 253 A1
Morpeth Gr E9 ... 96 D6
Morpeth Rd E9 ... 96 D6
Morpeth Sec Sch E2 ... 96 C4
Morpeth St E2 ... 96 D4
Morpeth Terr SW1 ... 115 C2 259 A4
Morpeth Wlk N17 ... 34 B3
Morrab Gdns IG3 ... 79 D5
Morrel Cl EN5 ... 2 A2
Morrel Ct 11 E2 ... 96 A5
Morris Ave E12 ... 78 B3
Morris Blitz Ct 2 N16 ... 73 D4
Morris Cl
Croydon CR0 ... 207 A4
Orpington BR6 ... 227 C5
Morris Ct
Chingford E4 ... 19 D1
Croydon CR0 ... 220 D4
3 Herne Hill SE5 ... 139 B1
Morris Gdns SW18 ... 157 C4
Morris Ho
17 Bethnal Green E2 ... 96 C4

Morris Ho *continued*
Lisson Gr NW8 ... 237 A5
1 Stockwell SW4 ... 138 A1
10 Tufnell Pk N19 ... 71 C4
Morrish Rd SW2 ... 160 A4
Morrison Ave
Chingford E4 ... 35 C4
Tottenham N17 ... 51 C6
Morrison Bldgs 5 E1 ... 96 A1
Morrison Ct
7 Barnet EN5 ... 1 A1
Finchley N12 ... 30 C3
Morrison Ho SW2 ... 160 C3
Morrison Rd
Barking IG11 ... 103 A5
24 Brixton SW9 ... 138 C3
Hayes UB4 ... 84 B4
Morrison St SW11 ... 137 A2
Morrison Yd N17 ... 33 D1
Morris Pl N4 ... 72 C6
Morris Rd
Bow Comm E14 ... 97 D2
Dagenham RM8 ... 81 B6
Isleworth TW7 ... 130 D2
Leyton E15 ... 76 C4
Morriss Ho
9 Bermondsey SE16 ... 118 B4
5 Upper Clapton E5 ... 74 B6
Morris St E1 ... 96 B1
Morris Stephany Ho 4 SE27 ... 182 D6
Morriston Cl WD19 ... 22 C5
Morritt Ho 2 HA0 ... 65 D3
Morse Cl E13 ... 99 A4
Morshead Mans W9 ... 91 C4
Morshead Rd W9 ... 91 C4
Morson Rd EN3 ... 19 A5
Morston Gdns SE9 ... 188 B6
Mortain Ho 9 SE16 ... 118 B2
Morten Cl SW4 ... 159 D5
Morteyne Rd N17 ... 33 B2
Mortgramit Sq SE18 ... 122 C3
Mortham St E15 ... 98 C6
Mortimer Cl
1 Child's Hill NW2 ... 69 B5
Streatham SW16 ... 159 D2
Mortimer Cres
Paddington NW6 ... 91 D6
Worcester Pk KT4 ... 215 B5
Mortimer Ct
St John's Wood NW8 ... 229 B3
4 Whetstone N20 ... 14 A2
Mortimer Dr EN1 ... 17 C6
Mortimer Est NW6 ... 91 D6
Mortimer Ho
6 Shepherd's Bush W11 ... 112 D5
West Kensington W14 ... 254 B3
Mortimer Lo 11 SW19 ... 157 A3
Mortimer Market WC1 ... 239 B5
Mortimer Pl NW6 ... 91 D6
Mortimer Rd
De Beauvoir Town N1 ... 73 C1
Ealing W13 ... 87 C1
Kensal Green NW10 ... 90 C4
Mitcham CR4 ... 180 D2
Newham E6 ... 100 B4
Mortimer Sq W11 ... 112 D6
Mortimer St W1 ... 93 C2 239 B3
Mortimer Terr NW5 ... 71 B4
MORTLAKE ... 133 A2
Mortlake Cl CR0 ... 220 A5
Mortlake Dr CR4 ... 180 C2
Mortlake High St SW14 ... 133 B2
Mortlake Ho 7 W4 ... 111 A2
Mortlake Rd
Ilford IG1 ... 79 B4
Newham E16 ... 99 B1
Richmond SW14, TW9 ... 132 C4
Mortlake Sta SW14 ... 133 A2
Mortlake Terr TW9 ... 132 C5
Mortlock Cl SE15 ... 140 B4
Mortlock Ct E12 ... 77 D4
Morton Cl
Hillingdon UB8 ... 82 B3
Stepney E1 ... 96 C1
Wallington SM6 ... 220 B1
Morton Cres N14 ... 31 D6
Morton Ct UB5 ... 64 A3
Morton Gdns SM6 ... 219 C3
Morton Ho
Kennington SE17 ... 138 D6
West Norwood SE27 ... 183 B5
Morton Mews SW5 ... 255 C3
Morton Pl SE1 ... 261 A5

Morton Rd
Islington N1 ... 73 A1
Morden SM4 ... 202 B4
Stratford E15 ... 76 D1
Morton Way N14 ... 31 D6
Morvale Cl DA17 ... 125 B2
Morval Rd SW2 ... 160 C6
Morven Rd SW17 ... 158 D1
Morville Ho SW18 ... 158 B5
Morville St E3 ... 97 C5
Morwell St WC1 ... 239 D3
Moscow Pl W2 ... 245 C6
Moscow Rd W2 ... 113 D6 245 C6
Mosedale NW1 ... 231 D1
Moseley Row SE10 ... 120 D2
Moselle Ave N22 ... 32 C1
Moselle Cl N8 ... 50 B6
Moselle Ct N9 ... 18 C1
Moselle Ho 2 N17 ... 33 D3
Moselle Pl N17 ... 33 D3
Moselle Sch (main site) N17 ... 33 C1
Moselle Sch (Upper) N17 ... 51 A6
Moselle St N17 ... 33 D3
Mosque Tower 26 E1 ... 96 A2
Mossborough Cl N12 ... 29 D4
Mossbourne Com Acad E8 ... 74 A3
Mossbury Rd SW11 ... 136 C2
Moss Cl
Pinner HA5 ... 23 A1
Spitalfields E1 ... 96 A2
Mossdown Cl DA17 ... 125 C2
Mossford Ct IG6 ... 56 D6
Mossford Gn IG6 ... 57 A6
Mossford St E3 ... 97 B3
Moss Gdns
Feltham TW13 ... 150 A2
South Croydon CR2 ... 222 D1
Moss Hall Cres N12 ... 30 A4
Moss Hall Ct N12 ... 29 D4
Moss Hall Gr N12 ... 29 D4
Moss Hall Inf Sch N12 ... 29 D4
Moss Hall Jun Sch N3 ... 29 D4
Mossington Gdns SE16 ... 118 C2
Moss La HA5 ... 23 A1
Mosslea Rd
Bromley Comm BR2 ... 209 D4
Orpington BR6 ... 227 A5
Penge SE20 ... 184 C4
Mossop St SW3 ... 114 C2 257 B4
Moss Rd RM10 ... 81 C1
Mossville Gdns SM4 ... 201 B5
Mosswell Ho 4 N10 ... 31 A3
Moston Cl UB3 ... 105 D1
Mostyn Ave HA9 ... 66 B3
Mostyn Gdns NW10 ... 90 D5
Mostyn Gr E3 ... 97 C5
Mostyn Lo N5 ... 73 A4
Mostyn Rd
Brixton SW9 ... 138 C4
Bushey WD23 ... 8 A6
Grahame Pk HA8 ... 27 C3
Merton SW19 ... 179 B1
Mosul Way BR2 ... 210 A3
Motcomb St SW1 ... 115 A3 258 A6
Moth Cl SM6 ... 220 A1
Mothers Sq The 13 E5 ... 74 B4
Motley Ave EC2 ... 243 A6
Motley St SW8 ... 137 C3
MOTSPUR PARK ... 200 A3
Motspur Park Sta KT3 ... 200 B4
Motspur Pk KT3 ... 200 A3
MOTTINGHAM ... 165 D2
Mottingham Ct SE9 ... 166 B3
Mottingham Gdns SE9 ... 165 D3
Mottingham La SE9 ... 165 C3
Mottingham Prim Sch SE9 ... 166 B1
Mottingham Rd
Chislehurst SE9 ... 166 B1
Ponders End N9 ... 18 D4
Mottingham Sta SE9 ... 166 B3
Mottisfont Rd SE2 ... 124 B2
Moules Ct SE5 ... 139 A5
Moulins Rd E9 ... 74 C1
Moulsford Ho
5 Lower Holloway N7 ... 72 A3
32 Paddington W2 ... 91 C2
Moulton Ave TW3, TW5 ... 129 B3
Moundfield Rd N16 ... 52 A3
Mound The SE9 ... 166 C1

Mounsey Ho 13 W10 ... 91 A4
Mountacre Cl SE26 ... 183 D6
Mount Adon Pk SE21, SE22 ... 162 A4
Mountague Pl 2 E14 ... 120 A6
Mountain Ho SE11 ... 260 C2
Mountaire Ct NW9 ... 45 B4
Mount Angelus Rd SW15 ... 155 D4
Mount Ararat Rd TW10 ... 154 A6
Mount Arlington 3 BR2 ... 186 C1
Mount Ash Rd SE26 ... 162 B1
Mount Ave
Chingford E4 ... 19 D1
Ealing W5 ... 87 D2
Southall UB1 ... 85 C1
Mountbatten Cl
Plumstead Comm SE18 ... 145 C6
6 West Norwood SE19 ... 183 C5
Mountbatten Ct 8 IG9 ... 21 D2
Mountbatten Gdns BR3 ... 207 A5
Mountbatten Ho N6 ... 49 A2
Mountbatten Mews SW18 ... 158 A3
Mountbel Rd HA7 ... 25 A1
Mount Carmel 3 N7 ... 72 B3
Mount Carmel RC Tech Coll for Girls N19 ... 49 D1
Mount Cl
Bromley BR1 ... 188 A2
Cockfosters EN4 ... 3 A1
Ealing W5 ... 87 C2
Mountcombe Cl KT6 ... 198 A2
Mountcombe Ho SW17 ... 180 B5
Mount Ct
6 Kingston u T KT2 ... 176 D3
West Wickham BR4 ... 224 C6
Mount Culver Ave DA14 ... 190 D4
Mount Dr
Bexley DA6 ... 169 A6
Harrow HA2, HA5 ... 41 B4
Welsh Harp HA9 ... 67 A6
Mountearl Gdns SW16, SW2 ... 160 B1
Mount Eaton Ct W5 ... 87 C2
Mount Echo Ave E4 ... 19 D3
Mount Echo Dr E4 ... 19 D3
Mount Ephraim La SW16 ... 159 D1
Mount Ephraim Rd SW16 ... 159 D1
Mount Felix KT12 ... 193 D1
Mountfield NW2 ... 69 B6
Mountfield Cl SE6 ... 164 B4
Mountfield Ct SE13 ... 164 B5
Mountfield Rd
Ealing W5 ... 88 A1
East Finchley N3 ... 47 C6
Wallend E6 ... 100 C4
Mountford Ho EN2 ... 4 D1
Mount Ford St E1 ... 96 A1
Mountfort Cres N1 ... 72 C1
Mountfort Terr 1 N1 ... 72 C1
Mount Gdns SE26 ... 162 B1
Mount Gr HA8 ... 27 B6
Mountgrove Rd N5 ... 73 A5
Mounthurst Rd BR2 ... 208 D2
Mountier Ct 12 E11 ... 55 A4
Mountington Park Cl HA3 ... 43 D3
Mountjoy Cl SE2 ... 124 B4
Mountjoy Ho EC2 ... 242 A3
Mount Lo N6 ... 49 C3
Mount Lodge SW4 ... 137 D1
Mount Mews TW12 ... 173 D2
Mount Mills EC1 ... 234 D1
Mount Nod Rd SW16, SW2 ... 160 B1
Mount Olive Ct W7 ... 108 C4
Mount Par EN4 ... 2 C1
Mount Park Ave HA1 ... 64 C6
Mount Park Cres W5 ... 87 D1
Mount Park Rd
Ealing W5 ... 87 D1
Harrow HA1 ... 64 B5
Pinner HA5 ... 40 A4
Mount Pk SM5 ... 219 A1
Mount Pl 7 W3 ... 110 D5
Mount Pleasant
Cockfosters EN4 ... 2 D1
Finsbury WC1 ... 94 C3 241 A5
Ilford IG1 ... 79 A3

Mount Pleasant *continued*
Ruislip HA4 ... 62 D6
Wembley HA0 ... 88 B6
West Norwood SE27 ... 183 A6
Mount Pleasant Cotts
Osidge N14 ... 15 D4
Southall UB1 ... 85 C1
Mount Pleasant Cres N4 ... 50 B2
Mount Pleasant Hill E5 ... 74 C6
Mount Pleasant La E5 ... 52 B1
Mount Pleasant Pl SE18 ... 123 B2
Mount Pleasant Rd
Ealing W5 ... 87 C3
Higham Hill E17 ... 35 A1
Kingston u T KT3 ... 199 A6
Lewisham SE13 ... 164 A5
Tottenham N17 ... 33 C1
Willesden NW10 ... 90 C6
Mount Pleasant Villas N4 ... 50 B2
Mount Prim Sch The KT3 ... 199 A6
Mount Rd
Bexley DA6 ... 169 A6
Chessington KT9 ... 214 B3
Dagenham RM8 ... 59 B1
Dollis Hill NW2 ... 68 C5
East Barnet EN4 ... 14 C6
Feltham TW13 ... 151 A1
Hayes UB3 ... 106 A4
Hendon NW4 ... 46 A3
Kingston u T KT3 ... 199 B6
Mitcham CR4 ... 180 C1
South Norwood SE19 ... 183 B4
Wimbledon SW18, SW19 ... 157 D2
Mount Row W1 ... 115 B6 248 C5
Mount Sch NW7 ... 28 C5
Mountside HA7 ... 25 A2
Mounts Pond Rd SE3, SE13 ... 142 B3
Mount Sq The 3 NW3 ... 70 A5
Mount St W1 ... 115 A6 248 B5
Mount Stewart Ave HA3 ... 43 D2
Mount Stewart Jun & Inf Schs HA3 ... 43 D2
Mount Terr E1 ... 96 B2
Mount The
Bexley DA6 ... 169 D6
Cheam SM1 ... 217 C2
Chislehurst BR7 ... 188 C2
Finchley N2 ... 30 C1
Hampstead NW3 ... 70 A5
Harrow HA1 ... 64 C6
Kensington W8 ... 245 A3
Kingston u T KT3 ... 199 D6
North Cheam KT4 ... 216 B4
Northolt UB5 ... 63 D3
6 South Croydon CR2 ... 221 A3
Upper Clapton E5 ... 74 B6
Welsh Harp HA9 ... 67 A6
Whetstone N20 ... 14 A2
Mount Tyndal NW3 ... 48 B1
Mount Vernon NW3 ... 70 A4
Mountview
Edgware NW7 ... 11 B1
Northwood HA6 ... 22 A4
5 Streatham SW16 ... 160 B1
Mount View
Ealing W5 ... 87 D3
Enfield EN2 ... 4 B5
Southall UB2 ... 106 D2
Mountview Cl NW11 ... 48 A1
Mountview Cotts EN5 ... 11 D5
Mountview Ct
Harringay N8 ... 50 D5
3 Whetstone N20 ... 14 A2
Mount View Rd
Chingford E4 ... 20 B4
Claygate KT10 ... 213 B1
Hornsey Vale N4 ... 50 B3
Kingsbury NW9 ... 45 B4
Mount Villas SE27 ... 160 D1
Mountwood KT8 ... 195 D6
Mountwood Ho W5 ... 87 D3
Mourne Ho NW3 ... 70 A2
Movers La IG11 ... 101 C6
Movers Lane (Flyover) IG11 ... 101 C5
Mowat Ct KT4 ... 215 D6
Mowatt Cl N19 ... 49 D1

Mowbray Ct
South Norwood SE19 183 D2
Wood Green N22 32 C2
Mowbray Gdns UB5 85 C6
Mowbray Ho 5 N2 30 B1
Mowbray Rd
Brondesbury NW6 69 A1
Edgware HA8 26 C6
New Barnet EN5 14 A6
Richmond TW10 153 C1
South Norwood SE19 183 D2
Mowlem Prim Sch E2 96 C5
Mowlem St E2 96 B5
Mowlem Trad Est N17 34 C3
Mowll St SW9 138 C5
Moxon Cl 10 E13 98 D5
Moxon St
Barnet EN5 1 B2
Marylebone W1 93 A2 238 A3
Moye Cl 10 E2 96 A5
Moyers Rd E10 54 A2
Moylan Rd
W6 135 A6 264 B5
Moyle Ho SW1 269 B6
Moyne Ho 16 SW9 138 D1
Moyne Pl NW10 88 C5
Moynihan Dr N21 16 A6
Moys Cl CR0 204 A3
Moyser Rd SW16 181 B5
Mozart St W10 91 B4
Mt Carmel RC Prim Sch
W5 109 C3
Muchelney Rd SM4 202 A3
Mudchute Sta E14 119 D2
Mudie Ho 8 SW2 160 A4
Mudlarks Blvd 3
SE10 120 D3
Muggeridge Cl CR2 221 B3
Muggeridge Rd RM10 81 D4
Muirdown Ave SW14 133 B1
Muir Dr SW18 158 C5
Muirfield W3 89 C1
Muirfield Cl
23 Bermondsey SE16 118 B1
South Oxhey WD19 22 C6
Muirfield Cres E14 119 D3
Muirfield Gn WD19 22 C6
Muirfield Rd WD19 22 C6
Muirhead Quay IG11 101 A5
Muirkirk Rd SE6 164 A3
Muir Rd E5 74 A5
Muir St E16 122 A5
Mulbarton Ct BR7 189 B4
Mulberry Ave TW19 148 A3
Mulberry Bsns Ctr
SE16 118 D4
Mulberry Cl
Barnet EN4 2 B1
Charlton SE7 143 D6
Chelsea SW3 266 D5
Chingford E4 19 C2
East Dulwich SE22 162 A5
Hampstead NW3 70 B4
Hendon NW4 46 C6
Hornsey N8 50 A4
Northolt UB5 85 A5
Streatham SW16 181 C6
Mulberry Cres
Brentford TW8 131 C5
West Drayton UB7 104 C4
Mulberry Ct
Barking IG11 79 D1
Bexley DA16 145 D3
Finchley N2 48 C6
Finsbury EC1 234 D1
Islington N5 72 D3
1 Leyton E11 76 B4
10 Paddington W9 91 B4
4 Surbiton KT6 197 D2
Twickenham TW1 152 D1
Willesden NW10 67 B2
Mulberry Ho
1 Bethnal Green E2 96 C4
8 Deptford SE8 141 B6
Mulberry House Sch The
NW2 69 A3
Mulberry La CR0 205 D1
Mulberry Mews
New Cross SE14 141 B4
2 Wallington SM6 219 C2
Mulberry Par UB7 104 C4
Mulberry Pl
Chiswick W6 112 A1
Greenwich SE9 143 D1
Mulberry Prim Sch
N17 34 A1
Mulberry Rd E8 73 D1
Mulberry Sch for Girls
Stepney E1 96 B1
St George in t East E1 118 B6
Mulberry St 7 E1 96 A1
Mulberry Trees TW17 193 B2
Mulberry Way
Ilford IG6 57 A5
Woodford E18 37 B1
Mulberry Wlk
SW3 136 B6 266 D6
Mulgrave Chambers
SM2 217 D2
Mulgrave Hall SM2 217 D2
Mulgrave Ho 19 SE18 122 B2
Mulgrave Manor
SM2 217 D2
Mulgrave Prim Sch
SE18 122 C2
Mulgrave Rd
Belmont SM2 217 C2
Ealing W5 87 D3
Harrow HA1 65 A6
South Croydon CR0 221 B5
West Kensington W14 264 C6
Willesden NW10 67 D4
Woolwich SE18 122 C2
Mulholland Cl CR4 181 B1
Mulkern Rd N19 49 D1
Mullard Ho WC1 239 C4
Mullards Cl CR4 202 D1
Mullens Ho 7 SW15 156 C6
Mullen Twr EC1 241 A5
Muller Ho SE18 122 C1
Muller Rd SW4 159 D5
Mullet Gdns 7 E2 96 A4
Mulletsfield WC1 233 B1
Mull Ho 17 E3 97 B5
Mullins Path SW14 133 B2
Mullion Cl HA3 23 D2
Mullion Wlk WD19 22 D6
Mulready St NW8 237 A5
Multi Way W3 111 C4
Multon Ho E9 74 C1
Multon Rd SW18 158 B4
Mulvaney Way SE1 252 D1
Mumford Rd SE24 160 D6
Muncaster Cl TW15 170 C6
Muncaster Rd
Ashford TW15 170 D5
Balham SW11 159 A6
Muncies Mews SE6 164 A2
Mundania Ct SE22 162 B5
Mundania Rd SE22 162 C5
Munday Ho SE1 262 C5
Munday Rd E16 121 A6
Munden Ho 5 E3 97 D4
Munden St
W14 113 A2 254 A4
Mundesley Cl WD19 22 C6
Mundford Rd E5 74 C6
Mundon Gdns IG1 57 B1
Mund St W14 113 B1 254 D1
Mundy Ho 6 W10 91 A4
Mundy St N1 95 C4
Mungo-Park Cl WD23 8 A2
Munnery Way BR6 226 D6
Munning Ho 12 E16 121 B5
Munnings Gdns TW7 152 B6
Munro Ho
Bermondsey SE1 252 D1
Lambeth SE1 251 A1
Munro Mews W10 91 A2
Munro Rd WD23 8 A6
Munslow Gdns SM1 218 B4
Munstead Ct 12 SM2 218 A1
Munster Ave TW4 151 A6
Munster Ct
Fulham SW6 135 B3
Teddington TW11 175 C4
Munster Gdns N13 33 A6
Munster Ho N17 33 D2
Munster Rd
Fulham SW6 135 A5 264 B4
Teddington TW11 175 C4
Munster Residences
SW6 264 B2
Munster Sq
NW1 93 B3 238 D6
Munton Rd SE1,
SE17 117 A2 262 B4
Murchison Ave DA5 169 A3
Murchison Ho 1 W10 91 A2
Murchison Rd E10 76 A6
Murdoch Ho 4 SE16 118 C3
Murdock Cl E16 98 D1
Murdock St SE15 140 B6
Murfett Cl SW19 157 A2
Muriel Ct 18 E10 53 D2
Muriel St N1 94 B6 233 D6
Murillo Rd SE13 142 C1
Murley Ct N21 17 A4
Murphy Ho SE1 261 D6
Murphy St
SE1 116 C4 251 A1
Murray Ave
Bromley BR1 187 B1
Hounslow TW3 151 D6
Murray Cl SE28 123 C5
Murray Cres HA5 22 D2
Murray Ct
5 Harrow HA1 42 D3
Southall TW7 108 C3
Twickenham TW2 152 A2
Murray Gr N1 95 B5 235 C3
Murray Grey Ho UB4 83 B2
Murray Ho
1 North Finchley N12 30 B5
20 Woolwich SE18 122 B2
Murray Mews NW1 71 D1
Murray Rd
Brentford W5 109 C2
Richmond TW10 153 C2
Wimbledon SW19 178 D4
Murray Sq E16 121 B6
Murray St NW1 71 D1
Murray Terr NW3 70 B4
Musard Rd
W6 135 A6 264 B6
Musbury St E1 96 C1
Muscal W6 264 A6
Muscatel Pl SE5 139 C4
Muschamp Prim Sch
SM5 218 C6
Muschamp Rd
Camberwell SE15 139 D2
Carshalton SM5 218 C6
Muscott Ho 15 E2 96 A6
Muscovy Ho DA18 125 A4
Muscovy St EC3 253 B6
Museum Ho 7 E2 96 C4
Museum in Docklands*
E14 119 C6
Museum Mans WC1 240 A3
Museum of Brands*
W11 91 B1
Museum of Domestic
Design & Architecture*
EN4 15 A6
Museum St
WC1 94 A1 240 A2
Musgrave Cl EN4 2 A4
Musgrave Cres
SW6 135 C4 265 B2
Musgrave Ct SW11 267 A2
Musgrave Rd TW7 130 D4
Musgrove Ho 1 E9 74 D2
Musgrove Rd SE14 141 A4
Musical Mus The*
TW8 132 A6
Musjid Rd 7 SW11 136 B3
Muslim Coll The W5 110 C6
Mus of Childhood (V&A)*
E2 96 C4
Mus of Culinary History &
Alimentation* NW1 232 B4
Mus of Garden History*
SE1 260 C5
Mus of London*
EC2 95 A2 242 A3
Mus of Richmond*
TW10 153 D6
Mus of the Great Eastern
Rly* E16 122 C4
Mus of the Order of St
John* EC1 94 D3 241 C5
Musquash Way TW4 128 C3
Muston Rd E5 74 B6
Mustow Pl 2 SW6 135 B3
Muswell Ave N10 31 B1
MUSWELL HILL 49 A6
Muswell Hill N10 49 C6
Muswell Hill Broadway
N10 49 B6
Muswell Hill Pl N10 49 B5
Muswell Hill Prim Sch
N10 49 B6
Muswell Hill Rd N10 49 A4
Muswell Mews N10 49 B6
Muswell Rd N10 31 B1
Mutrix Rd NW6 91 C6
Mutton Pl NW1 71 A2
Muybridge Rd KT3 177 A1
Myatt Garden Prim Sch
SE4 141 B3
Myatt Ho SE5 138 D3
Myatt Rd SW9 138 D4
Myatts Field Ct SE5 139 A4
Mycenae Rd SE3 143 A6
Mychell Ho 8 SW19 180 A3
Myddelton Ave EN1 5 C5
Myddelton Cl EN1 5 D4
Myddelton Gdns N21 17 A4
Myddelton Ho N8 50 A6
Myddelton Pas
EC1 94 C4 234 B2
Myddelton Pk N20 14 B2
Myddelton Rd N8 50 A5
Myddelton Sq
EC1 94 C4 234 B2
Myddelton St
EC1 94 C4 234 B1
Myddleton Ave N4 73 A6
Myddleton Ho 14 N2 30 B1
Myddleton Mews N22 32 A3
Myddleton Rd N22 32 B3
Myers Ho 5 SE5 139 A5
Myers La SE14 140 D6
Myherin Ct SE23 163 B2
Mylis Cl SE26 184 B6
Mylius Cl SE14 140 C4
Mylne Cl W6 112 A1
Mylne Ho N21 17 B5
Mylne St EC1 234 A3
Mynterne Ct 16
SW19 156 D3
Myra St SE2 124 A2
Myrdle Ct 14 E1 96 A1
Myrdle St E1 96 A1
Myrna Cl SW19 180 C3
Myron Pl SE13 142 A2
Myrtle Alley SE18 122 C3
Myrtle Ave
Hatton TW14 149 C6
Ruislip HA4 40 B2
Myrtle Cl
Barnet EN4 14 D3
Hillingdon UB8 82 B2
West Drayton UB7 104 B3
Myrtledene Rd SE2 124 A1
Myrtle Gdns W7 108 C5
Myrtle Gr
Enfield EN2 5 B5
Kingston u T KT3 177 A1
Myrtle Ho SE14 140 D4
Myrtle Rd
Acton W3 111 A5
Croydon CR0 223 C5
Edmonton N13 17 B1
Hampton TW12 174 A4
Hounslow TW3 130 A3
Ilford IG1 78 D6
Newham E6 100 A6
Sutton SM1 218 A3
Walthamstow E17 53 A3
Myrtle Wlk 20 N1 95 C5
Mysore Rd SW11 136 D1
Myton Rd SE21 161 B1
Mytton Ho SW8 270 C3

N

N1 Shopping Ctr
N1 94 C5 234 B4
Nacton Ct 2 RM6 58 C4
Nadine St SE7 121 C1
Nadir Ct E11 55 A2
Naffenton Rise IG10 21 D6
Nagle Cl E17 36 B1
Nags Head N7 72 B4
Nags Head Ct EC1 242 B5
Nag's Head La DA16 146 B2
Nags Head Rd EN3 6 D1
Nags Head Sh Ctr The
N7 72 B4
Naima Jewish Prep Sch
NW6 91 D5
Nainby Ho SE11 261 A3
Nairn Ct
3 Wallington SM6 219 C2
Wimbledon SW19 179 D4
Nairne Gr SE5, SE24 139 B1
Nairn Rd HA4 62 C2
Nairn St E14 98 A2
Naish Ct N1 233 B6
Naish Ho SW19 201 D6
Naldera Gdns SE3 143 A6
Nallhead Rd TW13 172 C5
Nalton Ho 4 NW6 70 A1
Namba Roy Cl SW16 182 B6
Namton Dr CR7, SW16 204 B5
Nan Clark's La NW7 11 D2
Nankin St E14 97 C1
Nansen Ct 1 E11 76 C6
Nansen Ho 8 NW10 67 B1
Nansen Rd SW11 137 A2
Nansen Village 5 N12 29 D6
Nant Ct NW2 69 B6
Nantes Cl SW18 136 A1
Nant Rd NW2 69 B6
Nant St E2 96 B4
Naomi Watts Ho 11
SW19 179 A3
Naoroji St WC1 234 A1
Napier 15 NW9 27 D2
Napier Ave
Deptford E14 119 C1
Fulham SW6 135 B2
Napier Cl
New Cross SE14, SE8 141 B5
West Drayton UB7 104 B3
West Kensington W14 254 C6
Napier Ct
13 Croydon CR0 221 D6
Fulham SW6 135 B2
Grove Pk SE12 165 B1
Hayes UB4 84 C3
Shoreditch N1 235 C4
1 Surbiton KT6 197 D2
12 Wallington SM6 219 B2
Wembley HA0 65 D2
Napier Gr N1 95 A5 235 B4
Napier Ho
Eltham SE12 165 B1
Kennington SE17 138 D6
Napier Lo TW15 171 B4
Napier Pl W14 113 B3 254 C5
Napier Rd
Ashford TW15 171 B3
Belvedere DA17 125 B2
Bromley BR2 209 B5
College Pk NW10 90 B4
Croydon SE25 206 B5
Enfield EN3 18 D6
Isleworth TW7 131 A1
Kensington
W14 113 B3 254 C5
Leyton E11 76 C5
Newham E15 98 C5
South Croydon CR2 221 B1
Tottenham N17 51 C6
Wallend E6 100 C5
Wembley HA0 65 D2
Napier Terr N1 72 D1
Napier Wlk TW15 171 B3
Napoleon Rd
Hackney E5 74 B5
Twickenham TW1 153 B4
Napton Cl UB4 85 A3
Narbonne Ave SW4 159 C6
Narborough Cl UB10 61 A6
Narborough St SW6 135 D3
Narcissus Rd NW6 69 C3
Nardini 12 NW9 27 D2
Naresby Fold HA7 25 C4
Narford Rd E5 74 A6
Narrow Boat Cl SE28 123 B4
Narrow St
6 Acton W3 110 D5
Limehouse E14 119 A6
Narrow Way BR2 210 A3
Nascot St W12 90 C1
Naseby Cl
Hounslow TW7 130 C4
South Hampstead NW6 70 A1
Naseby Ct DA14 189 D6
Naseby Rd
Dagenham RM10 81 C5
South Norwood SE19 183 B4
NASH 225 A2
Nash Cl SM1 218 B5
Nash Ct HA3 43 B3
Nashe Ho SE1 262 C5
Nash Gn BR1 187 A4
Nash Ho
5 Millwall E14 119 C3
Pimlico SW1 258 D1
1 Walthamstow E17 53 D5
Nash La BR2 225 A2
Nash Rd
Brockley SE4 163 A6
Dagenham RM6 58 D5
Lower Edmonton N9 18 C2
Nash St NW1 231 D2
Nash Way HA3 43 B3
Nasmyth St W6 112 B3
Nassau Path 6 SE28 124 C5
Nassau Rd SW13 133 D4
Nassau St W1 239 A3
Nassington Rd NW3 70 D4
Natalie Cl TW14 149 B4
Natalie Mews TW2 152 B1
Natal Rd
Bowes Pk N11 32 A4
Ilford IG1 78 D4
South Norwood CR7 205 B6
Streatham SW16 181 D4
Nathan Ct N9 18 C4
Nathan Ho SE11 261 B3
Nathaniel Cl E1 243 D3
Nathaniel Ct E17 53 A3
Nathans Rd HA0 65 C6
Nathan Way SE28,
SE18 123 D3
National Army Mus*
SW3 136 D6 267 D6
National Fan Mus*
SE10 142 A5
National Film Theatre*
SE1 250 D4
National Gallery*
W1 115 D6 249 D5
National Hospl The
WC1 94 A3 240 B5
National Maritime Mus*
SE10 142 B6
National Physical
Laboratory TW11 174 C4
National Portrait Gallery*
W1 115 D6 249 D5
National Portrait Gallery
(Annexe)*
SW1 115 D5 249 D4
National Theatre*
SE1 116 B5 250 D4
National Wks TW4 129 B2
Nation Way E4 20 A3
Natural History Mus*
SW7 114 B3 256 C5
Nat West Twr* EC2 243 A2
Nautilus Bldg The
EC1 234 B2
Naval Row E14 120 A6
Navarino Gr E8 74 A2
Navarino Mans E8 74 A2
Navarino Rd E8 74 A2
Navarre Rd E6 100 A5
Navarre St E2 243 C6
Navenby Wlk 13 E3 97 C3
Navestock Cl E4 20 A1
Navestock Cres IG8 37 C3
Navestock Ho IG11 102 B5
Navigation Ct E16 123 A6
Navigator Dr UB2 108 A4
Navy St SW4 137 D2
Naxos Bldg 9 E14 119 C4
Nayland Ho SE6 186 A6
Naylor Bldg W 4 E1 96 A1
Naylor Gr EN3 18 D6
Naylor Ho
33 Clapham SW8 137 D3
Walworth SE17 262 D2
5 West Kilburn W10 91 B4
Naylor Rd
Peckham SE15 140 B5
Whetstone N20 14 A2
Nayor Bldg E 6 E1 96 A1
Nazareth Cl SE15 140 B3
Nazrul St E2 95 D4
Neal Ave UB1 85 B3
Neal Cl HA6 22 A2
Nealden St SW9 138 B2
Neale Cl N2 48 A6
Neale Ct
Dagenham RM9 80 B2
Muswell Hill N10 31 B3
Neal St WC2 94 A1 240 A1
Neal's Yd WC2 240 A1
Near Acre NW9 27 D2
NEASDEN 67 B4
Neasden Cl NW10 67 C3
Neasden Junc NW10 67 C4
Neasden La
Church End NW10 67 C3
Neasden NW10 67 B5
Neasden La N NW10 67 C5
Neasden Sta NW10 67 C3
Neasham Rd RM8 80 B3
Neate St SE5 139 D6
Neath Gdns SM4 202 A3
Neathouse Pl SW1 259 A4
Neats Acre HA4 39 B2
Neatscourt Rd E16 99 D2
Nebraska Bldg 11
SE13 141 D4
Nebraska St
SE1 117 B4 252 C1
Neckinger
SE16 117 D3 263 D6
Neckinger Est SE16 263 D6
Neckinger St SE1 263 D6
Nectarine Way SE13 141 D3
Nedahall Ct 4 NW11 47 B2
Needham Ct 20 EN3 7 C6
Needham Ho SE11 261 A3
Needham Rd W11 91 C1
Needham Terr NW2 68 D5
Needleman St SE16 118 D4
Needwood Ho N4 51 A1
Neela Cl UB10 60 D4

Neeld Cres
Hendon NW4 46 B4
Wembley HA9 66 C3
Neeld Ct HA9 66 C3
Neeld Par HA9 66 B3
Neil Cl TW15 171 A5
Neilson-Terry Ct 9 SW9 138 B1
Neil Wates Cres 17 SW2 160 C3
Nelgarde Rd SE6 163 C4
Nella Rd W6 134 D6
Nelldale Rd SE16 118 C2
Nellgrove Rd UB10 82 D3
Nell Gwynn Ave TW17 193 B3
Nell Gwynn Ho SW3 257 B3
Nello James Gdns SE27 183 B6
Nelson Cl
East Bedfont TW14 149 D3
Hillingdon UB10 82 D4
2 Paddington NW6 91 C4
Thornton Heath CR0 204 D1
Walton-on-T KT12 194 B1
Nelson Ct
5 Carshalton SM5 218 D5
Rotherhithe SE16 119 B5
Nelson Dock Pier SE16 119 B5
Nelson Gdns
Bethnal Green E2 96 A4
Twickenham TW3, TW4 151 C5
Nelson Grove Rd SW19 180 A2
Nelson Ho 1 W5 88 A4
Nelson Hospl SW20 179 B1
Nelson La UB10 82 D4
Nelson Mandela Cl N10 31 A1
Nelson Mandela Rd SE3 143 C2
Nelson Pas EC1 235 B2
Nelson Pl N1 234 D3
Nelson Prim Sch
Twickenham TW2 151 D5
Wallend E6 100 C5
Nelson Rd
Ashford TW15 170 A5
Bromley BR2 209 C5
Chingford E4 35 D4
Edmonton N9 18 B2
Enfield EN3 18 D5
Erith DA17 125 B1
Greenwich SE10 142 A6
Harmondsworth TW6 126 B4
Harrow HA1 42 C1
Hillingdon UB10 82 D4
Hornsey Vale N8 50 B3
Merton SW19 180 A3
New Malden KT3 199 B4
Sidcup DA14 190 A6
Stanmore HA7 25 C4
Tottenham N15 51 C5
Twickenham TW2, TW4 151 C5
Wanstead E11 55 B5
Nelson's Monument* WC2 250 A4
Nelson Sq SE1 116 D4 251 C2
Nelsons Row SW4 137 D1
Nelson St
Barking E6 100 C6
Canning Town E16 120 D6
Newham E6 100 B5
Stepney E1 96 B1
Nelsons Yd NW1 232 A4
Nelson Terr N1 234 D3
Nelson Trad Est SW19 179 D2
Nemoure Rd W3 111 A6
Nene Gdns TW13 151 B2
Nene Rd TW6, UB7 126 D4
Nene Road Rdbt TW6 126 D4
Nepaul Rd 17 SW11 136 C2
Nepean St SW15 156 A4
Neptune Ct
Dagenham IG11 102 B4
13 Millwall E14 119 C2
Neptune Ho
2 Rotherhithe SE16 118 C3
14 Stoke Newington N16 73 C3
Neptune Rd
Harlington TW6 127 A4
Harrow HA1 42 B3
Neptune St SE16 118 C3
Nero Ct 6 TW8 131 D5
Nesbit Cl SE3 142 C2
Nesbit Rd SE9 143 D1
Nesbitt Ho DA6 169 D6
Nesbitt Sq SE19 183 C3
Nesham Ho 14 N1 95 C6
Nesham St E1 118 A5
Ness St 9 SE16 118 A3
Nesta Rd IG8 36 D4
Nestle's Ave UB3 105 D3
Nestor Ave N21 16 D5
Nestor Ho 13 E2 96 B5
Netheravon Rd
Chiswick W4 111 D1
Ealing W7 108 D5
Netheravon Rd S W4 111 D1
Netherbury Rd W5 109 D3
Netherby Gdns EN2 4 A1
Netherby Ho 23 SW8 137 D3
Netherby Rd SE23 162 C4
Nether Cl N3 29 C3
Nethercombe Ho 1 SE3 143 A6
Nethercott Ho 27 E3 97 D4
Nethercourt Ave N3 29 C4
Netherfield Gdns IG11 79 B1
Netherfield Rd
Finchley N12 29 D5
Upper Tooting SW17 159 A1
Netherford Rd SW4 137 C3
Netherhall Gdns NW3 70 A3
Netherhall Way NW3 70 A3
Netherlands Rd EN5 14 B5
Netherleigh Cl N6 49 B1
Nether St
Finchley N3 29 D4
North Finchley N12 30 A5
Netherton Gr SW10 136 A6 266 B5
Netherton Ho 1 UB5 85 B4
Netherton Rd
Isleworth TW1 153 B6
Tottenham N15 51 B3
Netherwood 24 N2 30 B1
Netherwood Rd W14 112 D4
Netherwood St NW6 69 C2
Nethewode Ct DA17 125 D3
Netley 13 SE5 139 C4
Netley Cl
Cheam SM3 216 D3
New Addington CR0 224 A1
Netley Ct IG2 57 B4
Netley Dr KT12 195 B2
Netley Gdns SM4 202 A2
Netley Prim Sch NW1 93 C4 232 A1
Netley Rd
Brentford TW8 132 A6
Cheam SM4 202 A2
Ilford IG2 57 B4
Walthamstow E17 53 B4
Netley St NW1 93 C4 232 A1
Nettlecombe NW1 71 D1
Nettleden Ave HA9 66 C2
Nettleden Ho SW3 257 B3
Nettlefold Pl SE27 160 D1
Nettlestead Cl 16 BR3 185 C3
Nettleton Rd
Harlington TW6 126 D4
Ickenham UB10 60 B4
New Cross Gate SE14 140 D4
Nettlewood Rd SW16 181 D3
Neuchatel Rd SE6 163 B2
Nevada Cl KT3 199 A5
Nevada St SE10 142 A6
Nevena Ct 3 SW2 160 C6
Nevern Mans SW5 255 A2
Nevern Pl SW5 113 C2 255 B3
Nevern Rd SW5 255 A3
Nevern Sq SW5 113 C2 255 B3
Nevil Ho 7 SW9 138 D3
Nevill Ct SW10 266 A4
Neville Ave KT3 177 B2
Neville Cl
Acton W3 111 A4
Hounslow TW3 129 D3
Leyton E11 76 D5
Paddington NW6 91 B5
Peckham SE15 140 A4
Sidcup DA15 189 D6
Somers Town NW1 232 D3
Neville Ct 10 SW12 159 C4
Neville Dr N2 48 A3
Neville Gdns RM8 80 D5
Neville Gill Cl SW18 157 D5
Neville Ho
Friern Barnet N11 31 A6
Neville Ho *continued*
5 Twickenham TW1 153 A4
Neville Pl N22 32 B2
Neville Rd
Dagenham RM8 80 D5
Ealing W5 87 D3
Forest Gate E7 77 B1
Kingston u T KT1 176 C1
Paddington NW6 91 B5
Richmond TW10 153 C2
Thornton Heath CR0 205 B2
Neville's Ct NW2 68 A5
Neville St SW7 114 B1 256 C2
Neville Terr SW7 256 C2
Neville Wlk SM5 202 C2
Nevill Rd N16 73 C5
Nevin Dr E4 19 D3
Nevin Ho UB3 105 A3
Nevinson Cl SW18 158 B5
Nevis Rd SW17 159 A2
Nevitt Ho N1 235 D3
New Acres Rd SE28 123 C5
NEW ADDINGTON 224 B1
Newall Ho SE1 262 B6
Newall Rd TW6 127 A4
Newark Cres NW10 89 B4
Newark Ct KT12 194 C1
Newark Ho 3 SW9 138 D3
Newark Knok E6 100 C2
Newark Rd CR2 221 B2
Newark St E1 96 B2
Newark Way NW4 46 A6
New Ash Cl N2 48 B6
New Atlas Wharf E14 119 C3
New Barn Cl SM6 220 B2
NEW BARNET 14 A6
New Barnet Sta EN5 14 B6
New Barns Ave CR4 203 D5
New Barn St E13 99 B3
NEW BECKENHAM 185 A4
New Beckenham Sta BR3 185 B3
New Belmont Ho 4 SE23 162 C3
New Bentham Ct 10 N1 73 A1
Newbery Ho N1 73 A1
Newbiggin Path WD19 22 C6
Newbold Cotts 4 E1 96 C1
Newbolt Ave SM3 216 D3
Newbolt Ho SE17 262 C2
Newbolt Rd HA7 24 D5
New Bond St W1 115 B6 248 D6
Newborough Gn KT3 199 B5
Newborough Ho SW19 180 B3
New Brent St NW4 46 C4
Newbridge Ct SW17 180 A6
Newbridge Point 3 SE23 162 D1
Newbridge Sch RM6 58 B4
New Bridge St EC4 94 D1 241 C1
New Broad St EC2 95 C2 243 A3
New Broadway
Ealing W5 109 D6
7 Hillingdon UB10 82 D3
Teddington TW12 174 B5
New Bsns Ctr The NW10 89 D4
Newburgh Rd W3 111 A5
Newburgh St W1 239 B1
New Burlington Mews W1 249 A6
New Burlington Pl W1 249 A6
New Burlington St W1 249 A6
Newburn Ct N12 30 A3
Newburn Ho SE11 260 D2
Newburn St SE11 116 B1 260 D2
Newbury Ave EN3 7 B6
Newbury Cl UB5 63 B2
Newbury Cotts 4 IG2 57 A3
Newbury Ct
Hackney E5 75 A3
Sidcup DA14 189 D6
7 Wanstead E11 55 A5
Newbury Gdns KT19 215 D4
Newbury Ho
Barnet EN4 2 B1
Brixton SW9 138 D3
14 Kensington W2 91 D1
Wood Green N22 32 A2
Newbury Mews NW5 71 A2
NEWBURY PARK 57 B3
Newbury Park Prim Sch IG2 57 B3
Newbury Park Sta IG2 57 B3
Newbury Rd
Bromley BR2 209 A6
Chingford E4 36 A4
Harmondsworth TW6 126 B4
Ilford IG2 57 C3
Newbury St EC1 242 A4
Newbury Way UB5 63 B2
New Butt La SE8 141 C5
Newby NW1 232 A2
Newby Cl EN1 5 C3
Newby Pl E14 120 A6
Newby St SW8 137 B2
New Caledonian Wharf SE16 119 B3
New Campden Ct 9 NW3 70 A4
Newcastle Cl EC4 241 C2
Newcastle Ct EC4 252 B6
Newcastle Ho W1 238 A4
Newcastle Pl W2 92 B2 236 D4
Newcastle Row EC1 241 B5
New Cavendish St W1 93 B2 238 C3
New Change EC4 95 A1 242 A1
New Chapel Sq TW13 150 B3
New Charles St EC1 234 D2
NEW CHARLTON 121 C2
New Church Ct 3 SE19 184 A3
New Church Rd
32 Camberwell SE5 139 A5
Camberwell SE5 139 B6
New City Prim Sch E13 99 C4
New City Rd E13 99 C4
New Cl
Feltham TW13 173 A5
Morden SW19 202 A6
New Colebrooke Ct SM5 219 A1
New College Ct 6 NW3 70 A2
New College Mews 7 N1 72 C1
New College Par 1 NW3 70 B1
Newcombe Gdns TW3 129 B1
Newcombe Ho N5 73 A3
Newcombe Pk
Edgware NW7 27 C5
Wembley HA0 88 B6
Newcombe Rise UB7 82 A1
Newcombe St W8 245 B4
Newcome Gdns SW16 182 A6
Newcome Ho E5 74 B5
Newcomen Ho 5 NW5 71 B4
Newcomen Rd
Battersea SW11 136 B2
Leyton E11 76 D5
Newcomen St SE1 117 B4 252 C2
New Compton St WC2 94 A1 240 A1
New Concordia Wharf SE1 253 D2
Newcourt Ho 26 E2 96 B4
Newcourt St NW8 92 C5 230 A3
New Covent Garden Flower Market SW8 138 A6 270 A5
New Covent Garden Fruit & Vegetable Mkt SW8 137 D5 269 C3
New Crane Pl E1 118 C5
New Crescent Yd 1 NW10 89 D5
Newcroft Cl UB8 82 B2
Newcroft Ho 10 NW10 67 B1
NEW CROSS 141 B4
New Cross SE14 141 B5
NEW CROSS GATE 140 D4
New Cross Gate SE14 140 D4
New Cross Gate Sta SE14 141 A5
New Cross Hospl SE14 140 C5
New Cross Rd SE14 141 A4
New Cross Sta SE14 141 B5
New Ct
City of London EC4 241 A1
26 Hampstead NW3 70 A4
New Ct *continued*
Northolt UB5 63 D3
Stoke Newington N16 51 B1
Newdales Cl N9 18 A2
Newdene Ave UB5 84 D5
New Den (Millwall FC) The SE16 118 C1
Newdigate Ho
6 Kingston u T KT2 176 D4
5 Poplar E14 97 B1
Newell St E14 97 B1
NEW ELTHAM 167 A2
New Eltham Sta SE9 166 D3
New End NW3 70 A5
New End Prim Sch NW3 70 A4
New End Sq NW3 70 B4
New England Est IG11 101 A5
Newent Cl
Camberwell SE15 139 C5
Carshalton SM5 202 D1
New Farm Ave BR2 209 A5
New Ferry App SE18 122 C3
New Fetter La EC4 94 C1 241 B2
Newfield Cl TW12 173 C2
Newfield Prim Sch NW10 67 D1
Newfield Rise NW2 68 B5
Newgale Gdns HA8 26 B2
New Garden Dr UB7 104 A4
Newgate CR0 205 A1
Newgate Cl TW13 151 A1
Newgate St
Chingford E4 20 C1
Holborn EC1 94 D1 241 D2
New Globe Wlk SE1 252 A4
New Goulston St E1 243 C2
New Green Pl SE19 183 C4
NEWHAM 98 D4
Newham Acad of Music E6 100 A6
Newham Coll of FE E6 100 B5
Newham Coll (Stratford Campus) E15 76 C1
Newham Ctr for Mental Health E16 99 D3
Newham General Hospl E13 99 C3
Newham Gn N22 32 C2
Newham Sch of Nursing E3 97 D3
Newham Sixth Form Coll E13 99 B3
Newham Sixth Form Coll (Stratford Ctr) E15 76 B1
Newham's Row SE1 253 B1
Newham Way
Beckton E6 100 B3
Canning Town E13 99 B2
Newhaven Cl UB3 105 D2
Newhaven Cres TW15 171 B5
Newhaven Gdns SE9 143 D1
Newhaven La 3 E16 99 A2
Newhaven Rd SE25 205 B4
New Heston Rd TW5 129 B5
New Horizons Ct TW8 131 A6
Newhouse 5 KT3 199 C2
Newhouse Ave RM6 58 D6
Newhouse Cl KT3 199 C2
Newhouse Wlk SM4 202 A2
Newick Cl DA5 169 D5
Newick Rd E5 74 C5
Newing Gn BR1 187 D3
NEWINGTON 116 D2
Newington Barrow Way N7 72 B5
Newington Butts SE1, SE11 116 D2 261 D3
Newington Cswy SE1 117 A3 262 A6
Newington Gn N16 73 B3
Newington Green Mans N16 73 B3
Newington Green Prim Sch N16 73 B3
Newington Green Rd N1 73 B3
Newington Ind Est SE17 262 A3
New Inn Broadway EC2 243 B6
New Inn Ct The KT8 196 B4
New Inn Sq EC2 243 B6
New Inn St EC2 243 B6
New Inn Yd EC2 95 C3 243 B6
New James Ct SE15 140 B2
New Jubilee Ct 1 IG8 37 A3
New Kelvin Ave TW11 174 C4
New Kent Rd SE1 117 A2 262 B4
New King's Prim Sch SW6 135 B3
New King's Rd SW6 135 C4 265 B1
New King St SE8 141 C6
Newland Cl HA5 23 B4
Newland Ct
St Luke's EC1 242 C6
Wembley HA9 66 C6
Newland Dr EN1 6 B4
Newland Gdns W13 109 A4
Newland Ho
17 Deptford SE14 140 D6
Hornsey N8 50 A6
Newland House Sch TW1 174 D6
Newland House Sch Annex TW1 174 D6
Newland Rd N8 50 A6
Newlands NW1 232 A2
Newlands Ave KT7 196 C1
Newlands Cl
Edgware HA8 10 A1
Southall UB2 107 A1
Wembley HA0 65 C2
Newlands Croft SE20 184 D4
Newlands Ct
8 Eltham SE9 166 C5
6 Penge SE26 184 C4
Streatham SW16 182 A5
Newlands Pk SE26 184 D5
Newlands Pl EN5 12 D6
Newlands Quay E1 118 C6
Newlands Rd
Thornton Heath SW16 182 A1
Woodford IG8 20 D2
Newland St E16 122 B5
Newlands The
Thames Ditton KT7 196 C1
Wallington SM6 219 D1
Newlands Way KT9 213 C3
Newling Cl E6 100 B1
New London St EC3 253 B6
New Lydenburg Commercial Est SE7 121 C3
New Lydenburg St SE7 121 C3
Newlyn NW1 232 B5
Newlyn Cl
Hillingdon UB8 82 C2
Orpington BR6 227 D4
Newlyn Gdns HA2 41 B2
Newlyn Ho
7 Pinner HA5 23 B3
7 Sutton SM1 218 A4
Newlyn Rd
Barnet EN5 1 B1
Bexley DA16 145 D3
Tottenham N17 33 D2
NEW MALDEN 199 D5
New Malden Sta KT3 199 C6
Newman Ct
3 Bromley BR1 187 A2
8 Finchley N3 29 C2
Newman Ho 11 TW10 153 C1
Newman Pas W1 239 B3
Newman Rd
Bromley BR1 187 A2
Hayes UB3 106 B6
Newham E13 99 B4
Thornton Heath CR0 204 B1
Walthamstow E17 52 D4
Newman's Ct EC3 242 D1
Newman's Row WC2 240 D3
Newman St W1 93 C2 239 B3
Newman's Way EN4 2 A4
Newman Terr 9 CR4 202 D6
Newmarket Ave UB5 63 D3
Newmarket Gn SE9 165 D4
Newmarsh Rd SE28 123 D5
Newmill Ho E3 98 A3
New Mill Rd BR5 190 C2
Newminster Rd SM4 202 A3
Newmount NW3 70 B3
New Mount St E15 76 B1
Newnes Path SW15 134 B1
Newnham Ave HA4 40 C1

Newnham Cl
Loughton IG10 21 D5
Northolt UB5 64 A2
South Norwood CR7 183 A1
Newnham Gdns UB5 64 A2
Newnham Ho
Catford SE6 164 A1
Loughton IG10 21 D5
9 Putney SW15 156 D5
Newnham Jun & Inf Schs HA4 40 C1
Newnham Lo 10 DA17 125 C1
Newnham Mews N22 32 C2
Newnham Rd N22 32 C2
Newnhams Cl BR1 210 B6
Newnham Terr SE1 261 A6
Newnham Way HA3 44 A4
New North Com Sch The N1 73 B1
New North Pl EC2 243 A6
New North Rd N1 95 B6 235 C5
New North Road Bridge N1 235 C5
New North St WC1 94 B2 240 C4
Newnton Cl N4 51 B2
New Oak Rd N2 30 A1
New Oxford St WC1 94 A1 240 A2
New Palace Yd SW1 116 A4 250 A1
New Par
Ashford TW15 170 B6
Yiewsley UB7 104 A5
New Park Ave N13 17 B1
New Park Cl UB5 63 A2
New Park Ct 26 SW2 160 A4
New Park Est N18 34 C5
New Park Ho N13 32 B6
New Park Par 14 SW2 160 A4
New Park Rd
Ashford TW15 171 A5
Streatham SW2 160 A4
New Pl CR0 223 C2
New Place Sq SE16 118 B3
New Plaistow Rd E15 98 C6
New Pond Par HA4 62 A5
Newport Ave
Blackwall E14 120 B6
Newham E13 99 B3
Newport Cl EN3 7 A6
Newport Ct WC2 249 D6
Newport Ho 2 E3 97 A4
Newport Lo 2 EN1 17 C6
Newport Mead WD19 22 D6
Newport Pl WC2 249 D6
Newport Rd
Barnes SW13 134 A4
Harmondsworth TW6 126 C4
Hayes UB4 83 B2
Leyton E10 76 B6
Walthamstow E17 53 A5
Newport Sch E10, E11 76 A6
Newport St SE11 116 B2 260 D4
New Priory Ct 9 NW6 69 C1
New Providence Wharf E14 120 B5
Newquay Cres HA2 63 A6
Newquay Ho SE11 261 A2
Newquay Rd SE6 164 A2
New Quebec St W1 237 D1
New Rd
Brentford TW8 109 D1
Carshalton CR4 203 A1
Chingford E4 36 A6
Dagenham RM10 103 D5
East Bedfont TW14 149 B5
East Molesey KT8 195 C6
Edmonton N9 18 B2
Elstree WD6 9 D5
Esher KT10 212 A4
feltham TW14 150 B3
Finchley N10 30 C2
Hanworth TW13 173 A5
Harlington TW6, UB7 127 A5
Harrow HA1 64 D4
Hendon NW7 29 A3
Hillingdon UB8 83 A2
Hornsey N8 50 A4
Hounslow TW3 129 D1
Ilford IG3 79 C6
Kingston u T KT2 176 C3
Littleton TW17 192 D6
New Rd *continued*
Richmond TW10 175 C6
Stepney E1 96 B2
Tottenham N22 33 A2
Welling DA16 146 B3
West Heath SE2 124 D1
New River Cres N13 32 D6
New River Ct N5 73 B4
New River Sports & Recreation Ctr N22 32 D3
New River Way N4 51 B2
New Row WC2 116 A6 250 A6
New Rush Hall Sch IG1 79 A6
Newry Rd TW1 153 A6
New St Sq EC4 94 C1 241 B2
Newsam Ave N15 51 B4
New Scotland Yard* SW1 115 D3 259 C6
New Shepherd's Bush Mkt* 6 W12 112 C4
Newsholme Dr N21 16 B6
NEW SOUTHGATE 31 C6
New Southgate Ind Est 10 N11 31 C5
New Southgate Sta N11 31 B5
New Spitalfields Mkt E10 75 C5
New Spring Gdns Wlk SE11 260 B1
New Sq
East Bedfont TW14 149 A3
St Giles WC2 94 B1 240 D2
New Square Pas WC2 241 A2
New St EC2 95 C2 243 B3
Newstead Ave BR6 227 C6
Newstead Cl N12 30 C4
Newstead Ct UB5 85 A4
Newstead Ho
Edmonton N9 17 D1
Islington N1 234 B4
Newstead Rd SE12 164 D4
Newstead Way SW19 178 D6
Newstead Wlk SM5 202 A2
Newstead Wood Sch for Girls BR6 227 B5
New Street Hill BR1 187 C5
Newton Ave
Acton W3 111 A4
Muswell Hill N10 31 B2
Newton Cl
Harrow HA2 63 C6
Walthamstow E17 53 A3
Newton Farm Fst & Mid Sch HA2 63 B6
Newton Gr W4 111 C2
Newton Ho
22 Clapham SW8 137 D3
Paddington NW8 91 D6
1 Stepney E1 118 B6
10 Walthamstow E17 54 A6
Newton Ind Est RM6 58 D5
Newton Pl E14 119 C2
Newton Point 1 E16 98 D1
Newton Prep Sch SW8 137 B4 268 D2
Newton Rd
Acton W3 111 A4
Cricklewood NW2 68 C5
Harrow HA3 24 C1
Isleworth TW7 130 D3
Kensington W2 91 D1
South Tottenham N15 52 A4
Stratford New Town E15 76 B3
Welling DA16 146 A2
Wembley HA0 66 B1
Wimbledon SW19 179 A3
Newton St WC2 94 A1 240 B2
Newton's Yd 14 SW18 157 C6
Newton Terr BR2 209 D3
Newton Way N18 33 A5
Newton Wlk HA8 26 D2
New Tower Bldgs 21 E1 118 B5
Newtown Ct
Battersea SW11 268 C1
Clapham SW4 159 B6
New Trinity Rd 1 N2 30 B1
New Union Cl E14 120 A3
New Union St EC2 242 C3
New Victoria Hospl KT3 177 C2
New Wanstead E11 55 A3
New Way Rd NW9 45 C5
New Wharf Rd N1 94 A5 233 B4
New Woodlands Sch BR1 186 C6
NEWYEARS GREEN 38 B3
Newyears Green La UB9 38 B3
New Zealand Ave KT12 193 D1
Nexus Ct E11 54 C2
Niagara Ave W5 109 C2
Niagara Cl N1 235 B4
Niagara Ct 6 SE16 118 C3
Niagara Ho W5 109 C2
Nibthwaite Rd HA1 42 C4
Nicholas Cl UB6 85 D5
Nicholas Ct
Chiswick W4 133 C5
Golders Green NW11 47 C2
Lewisham SE12 165 A3
Newham E13 99 B4
Nicholas Gdns W5 109 D4
Nicholas Ho
Ealing W13 87 C1
Penge SE26 184 B4
2 Putney SW15 156 A6
Nicholas La EC2, EC4 252 D6
Nicholas Pas EC3 252 D6
Nicholas Rd
Bethnal Green E1 96 C3
Borehamwood WD6 10 B6
Dagenham RM8 81 B5
Wallington CR0 220 A4
Nicholas Stacey Ho 3 SE7 121 B1
Nicholay Rd N19 49 D1
Nichol Cl N14 15 D3
Nicholes Rd TW3 129 C1
Nichol La BR1 187 A3
Nicholl Ho N4 51 A1
Nicholls Almshouses NW7 28 B5
Nicholls Ave UB8 82 C3
Nicholls Point E15 99 A6
Nicholl St E2 96 A6
Nichols Cl
Chessington KT9 213 C2
Finsbury Pk N4 50 C1
Nichols Ct E2 95 D5
Nichols Gn W5 88 A2
Nicholson Ct 9 N17 51 D6
Nicholson Ho SE17 262 C2
Nicholson Mews KT1 198 A5
Nicholson Rd CR0 205 D1
Nicholson St SE1 251 C3
Nickelby Cl SE28 102 C1
Nickleby Cl UB8 82 D1
Nickleby Ho
18 Bermondsey SE1 118 A4
7 Shepherd's Bush W11 112 D5
Nickols Wlk SW18 135 D1
Nicola Cl
Harrow HA3 24 B1
South Croydon CR2 221 A2
Nicola Terr DA7 147 A4
Nicol Cl 6 TW1 153 B5
Nicole Ho SE25 206 A6
Nicoll Ct
Dagenham NW10 89 C6
Muswell Hill N10 31 B3
Nicoll Pl NW4 46 B2
Nicoll Rd NW10 89 C6
Nicoll Way WD6 11 B6
Nicolson 14 NW9 27 D2
Nicolson Dr WD23 8 A2
Nicosia Rd SW18 158 C4
Niederwald Rd SE26 185 A6
Nield Rd UB3 105 D4
Nigel Bldg EC1 241 A4
Nigel Cl UB5 85 A6
Nigel Ct N3 29 D3
Nigel Fisher Way KT9 213 D1
Nigel Mews IG1 78 D4
Nigel Playfair Ave W6 112 B1
Nigel Rd
Forest Gate E7 77 C3
Peckham SE15 140 A2
Nigeria Rd SE7 143 D5
Nighthawk 16 NW9 27 D2
Nightingale Ave
Chingford E4 36 C5
Harrow HA1 43 B1
Nightingale Cl
Carshalton SM5 219 A6
Chingford E4 36 C6
Chiswick W4 133 A6
Pinner HA5 40 C4
Nightingale Ct
14 Cubitt Town E14 120 A3
Nightingale Ct *continued*
Finsbury Pk N4 72 B6
1 Harrow HA1 42 D3
Penge SE19 183 D4
Sutton SM1 218 A3
1 Wanstead E11 55 B4
Nightingale Dr KT19 214 D2
Nightingale Gr SE13 164 B6
Nightingale Ho
Hayes UB3 105 D2
21 Hoxton E1 95 C6
4 North Kensington W12 90 C1
7 St George in t East E1 118 A5
Woolwich SE18 122 C1
Nightingale La
Balham SW11, SW12 159 A5
Bromley BR1 187 D1
Hornsey N8 50 A6
Richmond TW10 154 A4
Wanstead E11 55 B4
Nightingale Lo
Edgware HA8 27 A4
5 Paddington W9 91 C2
Nightingale Mans 4 SW12 159 A5
Nightingale Mews
1 Bow E3 97 A5
Newington SE11 261 C4
8 Wanstead E11 55 B4
Nightingale Pl
Shooters Hill SE18 144 D6
West Brompton SW10 136 A6 266 B6
Nightingale Prim Sch
Shacklewell E5 74 A4
Wanstead E18 55 C5
Wood Green N22 32 B2
Woolwich SE18 122 D1
Nightingale Rd
Carshalton SM5 219 A6
Dagenham NW10 89 D5
Ealing W7 108 D5
East Molesey KT8 195 D4
Hackney E5 74 B5
Hampton TW12 173 C4
Orpington BR5 211 A3
Ponders End N9 18 C4
Walton-on-T KT12 194 B2
Wood Green N22 32 B3
Nightingale Sch SW17 158 C2
Nightingale Sq SW12 159 A4
Nightingales The TW19 148 B3
Nightingale Vale SE18 144 C6
Nightingale Way E6 100 A2
Nightingale Wlk SW18, SW4 159 B5
Nile Cl N16 73 D5
Nile Ct N12 30 C4
Nile Dr N9 18 C2
Nile Ho N1 235 C2
Nile Path 6 SE18 144 C6
Nile Rd E13 99 C5
Nile St N1 95 B4 235 C2
Nile Terr SE1, SE15 117 D1 263 D1
Nimegen Way 9 SE22 161 C6
Nimmo Dr WD23 8 B4
Nimrod 12 NW9 27 C2
Nimrod Cl UB5 84 D4
Nimrod Pas 4 N1 73 C2
Nimrod Rd SW16 181 B5
Nina Mackay Cl 10 E15 98 C6
Nine Acres Cl E12 78 A3
NINE ELMS 137 C5
Nine Elms Cl TW14 149 D3
Nine Elms La SW8 137 D6 269 C5
Nineteenth Rd CR4 204 A5
Ninhams Wood BR6 226 C4
Ninth Ave UB3 106 A6
Nisbet 13 NW9 27 C2
Nisbet Ho E9 74 D3
Nisbett Wlk DA14 190 A6
Nita Ct SE12 165 A3
Nithdale Rd SE18 145 A5
Nithsdale Gr UB10 61 A5
Niton Cl EN5 12 D5
Niton Rd TW9 132 C2
Niton St SW6 134 D5
No 1 St SE18 122 D3
No 2 Willow Rd* NW3 70 C4
Noam Prim Sch N12 29 D6
Nobel Dr TW6 127 C5
Nobel Ho 8 SE5 139 A3
Nobel Rd N18 34 C6
Noble Cnr TW5 129 C4
Noble Ct
Mitcham CR4 180 B1
Stepney E1 118 B6
Noblefield Hts N2 48 D4
Noble Ho 18 E1 118 A6
Noble St EC2 95 A1 242 A2
Noel 13 NW9 27 D2
Noel Baker Ct 5 E11 76 C6
Noel Coward Ho SW1 259 B3
Noel Ct TW4 129 B2
Noel Dene W5 109 C1
Noel Ho 3 NW3 70 B1
NOEL PARK 32 D1
Noel Park Prim Sch N22 32 C1
Noel Park Rd N22 32 C1
Noel Rd
Acton W3 88 D1
Islington N1 94 D5 234 D4
Newham E6 100 A3
Noel Sq RM8 80 C4
Noel St W1 93 C1 239 B1
Noel Terr
Forest Hill SE23 162 C2
Sidcup DA14 190 B6
Noko NW10 90 D4
Nolan Way E5 74 A4
Noll Ho N7 72 B6
Nolton Pl HA8 26 B2
Nonsuch Ct SM3 217 A2
Nonsuch High Sch for Girls SM3 216 D1
Nonsuch Ho 5 SW19 180 B2
Nonsuch Prim Sch KT17 216 B3
Nook The SW19 180 A1
Noor Ul Islam Prim Sch E10 76 A6
Nora Gdns NW4 46 D5
NORBITON 176 C1
Norbiton Ave KT1, KT2 176 C1
Norbiton Common Rd KT1, KT3 198 D6
Norbiton Hall KT2 176 B1
Norbiton Rd E14 97 B1
Norbiton Sta KT1 176 C2
Norbreck Gdns NW10 88 B4
Norbreck Par NW10 88 B4
Norbroke St W12 111 D6
Norburn St W10 91 A2
NORBURY 182 C2
Norbury Ave
Isleworth TW3 130 B1
Thornton Heath CR7, SW16 182 C1
Norbury Cl SW16 182 D2
Norbury Court Rd SW16 182 A1
Norbury Cres SW16 182 C1
Norbury Cross SW16 204 A6
Norbury Ct N12 30 A6
Norbury Gdns RM6 58 D4
Norbury Gr NW7 11 C1
Norbury Hill SW16 182 D3
Norbury Manor Bsns & Enterprise Coll For Girls CR7 182 C2
Norbury Manor Prim Sch SW16 182 A2
Norbury Rd
Chingford E4 35 C5
Feltham TW13 149 D1
South Norwood CR7 205 A6
Norbury Rise SW16 204 A6
Norbury Sch HA1 42 C4
Norbury Sta SW16 182 B2
Norbury Trad Est SW16 182 B1
Norcombe Gdns HA3 43 C4
Norcombe Ho 2 N19 71 D5
Norcott Cl UB4 84 C3
Norcott Rd N16 74 A5
Norcroft Gdns SE22 162 A4
Norcutt Rd TW2 152 C3
Norden Ho 25 E2 96 B4
Norden Point NW2 46 C1
Nore Ct NW10 68 A1
Norfolk Ave
Edmonton N13 32 D4
South Tottenham N15 51 D3
Norfolk Cl
Cockfosters EN4 3 A1
East Finchley N2 48 C6
Edmonton N13 32 D4
5 Twickenham TW1 153 B5
Norfolk Cres
Paddington W2 92 C1 237 B2
Sidcup DA15 167 C4
Norfolk Ct
5 Barnet EN5 1 A1
4 Ilford RM6 58 B4
Surbiton KT5 198 B3
Wembley HA0 65 C2
Norfolk Gdns DA7 147 B4
Norfolk Ho
13 Acton W3 88 C1
Beckenham BR2 208 D5
City of London EC4 252 A6
Edgware HA8 26 B3
Greenwich SE3 142 C6
11 Merton SW19 180 A3
Penge SE20 184 C2
4 Putney SW15 156 C4
Richmond TW10 154 C6
Shacklewell E8 73 D4
2 South Croydon CR0 221 B6
3 Stanmore HA7 25 C5
St Johns SE8 141 C4
Westminster SW1 259 D4
Norfolk House Rd SW16 160 A1
Norfolk House Sch N10 31 B1
Norfolk Mans
Battersea SW11 267 D1
10 Wandsworth SW18 157 C6
Norfolk Mews 12 W10 91 A2
Norfolk Pl
Paddington W2 92 B1 236 D2
Welling DA16 146 A3
Norfolk Rd
Barking IG11 79 C1
Barnet EN5 1 C2
Claygate KT10 212 C3
Dagenham RM10 81 D3
Enfield EN3 18 B6
Feltham TW13 150 C3
Harrow HA1 41 D4
Higham Hill E17 34 D1
Ilford IG3 57 C2
Mitcham SW19 180 C4
Newham E6 100 B6
South Norwood CR7 205 A6
St John's Wood NW8 92 B6 229 D5
Willesden NW10 67 C1
Norfolk Row SE1, SE11 116 B2 260 C4
Norfolk Sq W2 92 B1 236 D2
Norfolk Sq Mews W2 236 D1
Norfolk St E7 77 A3
Norgrove St SW12 159 A4
Norhyrst Ave SE25 205 D6
Norland Ho 18 W11 112 D5
Norland Pl W11 113 A5 244 B3
Norland Place Sch W11 113 A5 244 A3
Norland Rd 16 W11 112 D5
Norlands Cres BR7 188 D2
Norland Sq W11 113 A5 244 B3
Norley Vale SW15 156 A3
Norlington Rd E10, E11 54 B1
Norlington Sch for Boys E10 54 B1
Norman Ave
Feltham TW13 151 B2
Southall UB1 107 A6
Tottenham N22 33 A2
Twickenham TW1 153 C4
Norman Butler Ho 10 W10 91 A3
Normanby Cl SW15 157 B6
Normanby Rd NW10 67 D4
Norman Cl
Orpington BR6 227 A5
Tottenham N22 33 A2
Norman Cres
Heston TW5 128 D5
Pinner HA5 22 C2
Norman Ct
Dulwich SE22 162 A4
5 Finchley N3 29 C2
Finsbury Pk N4 50 C2
8 Hampton TW12 173 C2
Ilford IG2 57 B2
West Norwood SW16 182 C5
Willesden NW10 68 A1
Woodford IG8 37 B5
Normand Croft Com Sch W14 135 B6 264 D6
Normand Mews W14 264 B6

Normand Rd
W14 135 B6 264 C6
Normandy Ave EN5 1 B1
Normandy Cl SE26 163 A1
Normandy Dr UB3 83 A1
Normandy Ho
8 Cubitt Town E14 120 A4
4 Hendon NW4 28 D1
Normandy Rd SW9 138 C4
Normandy Terr E16 99 B1
Norman Gr E3 97 A5
Norman Ho
1 Cheam SM1 217 C2
Feltham TW13 151 B2
7 Leyton E11 76 C6
Lower Halliford TW17 192 C2
South Lambeth SW8 270 A4
Normanhurst TW15 170 C5
Normanhurst Ave
DA7 146 D4
Normanhurst Dr TW1 153 B6
Normanhurst Rd
St Paul's Cray BR5 190 B1
Streatham SW2 160 B2
Walton-on-T KT12 194 D1
Normanhurst Sch E4 20 B4
Norman Par DA14 168 D2
Norman Rd
Ashford TW15 171 B4
Belvedere DA17 125 D3
Greenwich SE10 141 D5
Ilford IG1 78 D3
Leyton E11 76 C6
Merton SW19 180 A3
Newham E6 100 B3
South Tottenham N15 51 D4
Sutton SM1 217 C3
Thornton Heath CR7 204 D4
Normans Cl
Hillingdon UB8 82 A2
Willesden NW10 67 B2
Normansfield Ave KT1,
KT8 175 C3
Normanshire Dr E4 35 D6
Normans Mead NW10 67 B2
Norman St EC1 95 A4 235 B1
Normanton Ave SW18,
SW19 157 C2
Normanton Ct CR2 221 C3
Normanton Ho 6
SW4 159 C5
Normanton Pk E4 20 C2
Normanton Rd CR2 221 C2
Normanton St SE23 162 D2
Norman Way
Acton W3 88 D1
Palmers Green N14 16 A2
Normington Cl SW16 182 C5
Norrice Lea N2 48 B4
Norris 11 NW9 27 D2
Norris Ho
12 Hoxton N1 95 C6
15 South Hackney E9 96 C6
Norris St SW1 249 C5
Norroy Rd SW15 134 D1
Norrys Cl EN4 2 D1
Norrys Rd EN4 2 D1
Norse Ho 13 SE5 139 A3
Norseman Cl 3 IG3 58 B1
Norseman Way UB6 85 D6
Norstead Pl SW15 156 A2
North Access Rd E17 52 D3
North Acre NW9 27 C2
NORTH ACTON 89 B4
North Acton Rd NW10 89 B4
North Acton Sta W3 89 B4
Northampton Gr N1 73 B3
Northampton Pk N1 73 B2
Northampton Rd
Croydon CR0 222 A6
Enfield EN3 7 A1
Finsbury EC1 94 C3 241 B6
Northampton Sq
EC1 94 D4 234 C1
Northampton St N1 73 A1
Northanger Rd SW16 182 A4
North Audley St
W1 115 A6 248 A6
North Ave
Ealing W13 87 B2
Edmonton N18 34 A6
Harrow HA2 41 D3
Hayes UB3 106 A6
8 Richmond TW9 132 C4
Southall UB1 107 B6
Wallington SM5 219 A1
Northaw Ho 4 W10 90 C3
North Bank
NW8 92 C4 230 A1
Northbank Rd E17 36 A1
North Beckton Prim Sch
E6 100 B2
North Birkbeck Rd
E11 76 B5
North Block 19 E1 118 C6
Northborough Rd
SW16 182 A1
Northbourne BR2 209 A2
Northbourne Ho
21 Hackney E5 74 B3
Osidge N14 15 D4
Northbourne Rd SW4 159 D6
North Bridge House Sch
NW3 70 A2
North Bridge House
Senior Sch
NW1 93 B6 231 C5
Northbrook CE Sch
SE12 164 D6
Northbrook Rd
Barnet EN5 13 A5
Ilford IG1 78 C6
Lewisham SE13 164 C6
Thornton Heath CR0 205 B4
Wood Green N22 32 A3
Northburgh St
EC1 94 D3 241 D6
Northbury Jun & Inf Schs
IG11 79 A2
North Carriage Dr
W2 114 C6 247 B6
NORTH CHEAM 216 C6
Northchurch SE17 262 D2
Northchurch Ho 19 E2 96 A6
Northchurch Rd
De Beauvoir Town N1 73 B1
Wembley HA9 66 C2
Northchurch Terr N1 73 C1
North Circular Rd
Edmonton N13 32 C5
Finchley N2 30 B2
Highams Pk E17 35 D2
Ilford IG1, E12 78 C4
Neasden NW2, NW10 67 C3
Temple Fortune N3, NW2,
NW4 47 A4
Woodford E18 37 C1
North Cl
Barnet EN5 12 C6
Bexley DA6 146 D1
Dagenham RM10 103 C6
East Bedfont TW14 149 B5
Merton SM4 201 A5
Northcliffe Cl KT4 215 C5
Northcliffe Dr N20 13 B3
North Colonnade The
E14 119 D5
North Common Rd
Ealing W5 110 A6
Uxbridge UB8 60 A3
Northcote 3 HA5 22 C1
Northcote Ave
Ealing W5 110 A6
Isleworth TW7 153 A6
Southall UB1 107 A6
Tolworth KT5 198 D2
Northcote Ho UB4 84 D2
Northcote Lodge Sch
SW11 158 D5
Northcote Rd
Isleworth TW7 153 A6
Kingston u T KT3 199 B6
Sidcup DA14 189 C6
Thornton Heath CR0 205 B3
Walthamstow E17 53 A5
Wandsworth SW11 158 D6
Willesden NW10 67 C1
Northcott Ave N22 32 A2
North Countess Rd
E17 35 B2
Northcourt W1 239 B4
NORTH CRAY 169 B1
North Cray Rd DA14 191 A5
North Cres
Finchley N3 29 B1
Marylebone WC1 239 C4
Newham E16 98 B3
Northcroft Ct 8 W12 112 A4
Northcroft Rd
Brentford W13 109 B3
West Ewell KT19 215 C1
North Crofts SE21 162 B3
North Cross Rd
East Dulwich SE22 162 A6
Ilford IG6 57 A5
North Ct SW1 260 A5
North Dene
Edgware NW7 11 B1
Hounslow TW5 129 D4
Northdene Gdns N15 51 D3
Northdown Cl HA4 61 D5
Northdown Gdns IG2 57 C4
Northdown Rd DA16 146 C3
Northdown St
N1 94 B5 233 C3
North Dr
Beckenham BR3 207 D5
Hounslow TW3, TW7 130 A3
Orpington BR6 227 C4
Ruislip HA4 39 C2
Streatham SW16 181 C6
North Dulwich Sta
SE21 161 B6
North Ealing Prim Sch
W5 87 B3
North Ealing Sta W3 88 B1
NORTH END 70 A6
North End
Buckhurst Hill IG9 21 C4
Croydon CR0 221 A6
North End NW3 70 A6
North End Ave NW3 70 A6
North End Cres
W14 113 B2 254 C3
North End Ho
W14 113 A2 254 B3
North End La BR6 226 D1
Northend Lodge 2
HA5 40 D6
North End Par W14 254 B3
North End Rd
Golders Green NW11 47 D1
Wembley HA9 66 D5
West Kensington
W14 113 B1 254 D1
North End Way NW3 70 A6
Northern Ave N9 17 D2
Northernhay Wlk
SM4 201 A5
Northern Hts N8 49 D2
Northern Perimeter Rd
TW6 127 C4
Northern Perimeter Rd
(W) TW6 126 B4
Northern Rd E13 99 B5
Northern Relief Rd
IG11 79 A2
Northern Star Ho N11 31 B5
Northesk Ho 6 E1 96 B3
North Eyot Gdns 5
W6 111 D1
Northey St E14 119 A6
NORTH FELTHAM 150 B6
North Feltham Trad Est
TW14 128 B1
Northfield IG10 21 D6
Northfield Ave
Pinner HA5 40 D5
West Ealing W13, W5 109 B4
Northfield Cl
Bromley BR1 188 A2
Hayes UB3 105 D3
Northfield Cres SM3 217 A4
Northfield Gdns RM9 81 B4
Northfield Hall N6 49 A2
Northfield Ho
2 Newham E13 99 C5
3 Peckham SE15 140 A6
Northfield Ind Est HA0 88 C6
Northfield Par UB3 105 D3
Northfield Path RM9 81 B4
Northfield Pk UB3 105 D3
Northfield Rd
Cockfosters EN4 2 C2
Dagenham RM9 81 B4
Enfield EN3 18 B6
Heston TW5 128 D5
Plashet E6 78 B1
Stamford Hill N16 51 C2
West Ealing W13 109 B4
Northfields SW18 135 C1
Northfields Prospect
SW18 135 C1
Northfields Rd W3 89 A2
Northfields Sta W5 109 C3
NORTH FINCHLEY 30 A6
Northfleet Ho SE1 252 C2
North Flower Wlk
W2 114 B6 246 C5
North Gate
NW8 92 C5 230 A3
Northgate Bsns Ctr EN1 6 B1
Northgate Ct 14 SW9 138 C2
Northgate Dr NW9 45 C3
North Gates N12 30 A2
North Gdns SW19 180 B3
North Glade The DA5 169 B3
North Gn NW9 27 C3
North Gower St
NW1 93 C4 232 B1
North Gr
Highgate N6 49 A2
Tottenham N15 51 B4
North Greenwich Sta
SE10 120 C4
North Harringay Prim Sch
N8 50 C5
NORTH HARROW 41 D2
North Harrow Sta HA2 41 D4
North Hill N6 49 A3
North Hill Ave N6 48 D3
North Hill Ct N6 49 A2
NORTH HILLINGDON 61 A2
North Ho 3 SE8 119 B1
NORTH HYDE 107 A1
North Hyde Gdns UB2,
UB3 106 A3
North Hyde La UB2 107 A1
North Hyde Rd UB3 105 D3
Northiam
Finchley N12 29 C6
St Pancras WC1 233 B1
Northiam St E9 96 B6
Northington St
WC1 94 B3 240 D5
NORTH KENSINGTON 90 D2
North La TW11 174 D4
Northlands 4 BR1 187 C1
Northlands Ave BR6 227 C4
Northlands St SE5 139 A3
Northleigh Ho 36 E3 97 D4
North Lo
Clapham SW4 137 B1
Muswell Hill N22 31 D1
New Barnet EN5 14 A6
North Lodge Cl SW15 156 D6
North London Bsns Pk
N11 15 A1
North London Collegiate
Sch The HA7, HA8 26 A5
North London Nuffield
Hospl EN2 4 C3
North Mall The N9 18 B2
North Mews
WC1 94 B3 240 D5
North Middlesex
University Hospl N18 33 C5
Northmoor 4 SE23 162 D1
North Mount N20 14 A2
Northolm HA8 27 B6
Northolme Gdns HA8 26 C2
Northolme Rd N5 73 A4
Northolme Rise BR6 227 C6
NORTHOLT 63 C1
Northolt N17 33 C1
Northolt Ave HA4 62 B3
Northolt Gdns UB6 64 D3
Northolt High Sch UB5 63 B2
Northolt Park Inf Sch
UB5 63 D3
Northolt Park Sta HA2 63 D4
Northolt Rd HA2 64 A5
Northolt Sta UB5 63 C2
Northolt Trad Est UB5 63 D1
Northover BR1 164 D1
North Par
Chessington KT9 214 B3
Edgware HA8 26 C1
Southall UB1 85 C1
North Pas SW18 157 C6
North Pk SE9 166 C5
North Pl
Mitcham SW19 180 D3
Teddington TW11 174 D4
Northpoint BR1 187 A2
North Point UB7 104 A5
Northpoint Cl SM1 218 A5
Northpoint Sq 8 NW1 71 D2
North Pole La BR2 225 A2
North Pole Rd W10 90 C2
Northport St N1 235 D5
North Prim Sch UB1 107 B6
North Rd
Barnsbury N7 72 A2
Brentford TW8 132 A6
Bromley BR1 187 B2
Dagenham RM6 59 A4
Ealing W5 109 D3
East Bedfont TW14 149 B5
Edgware HA8 26 D2
Edmonton N9 18 B3
Erith DA17 125 D4
Finchley N2 30 C2
Hayes UB3 83 B2
Heston TW5 128 C6
Highgate N6 49 A2
Ilford IG3 79 C6
Plumstead SE18 123 C2
Richmond TW9 132 C3
Southall UB1 107 C6
North Rd *continued*
Surbiton KT6 197 D3
West Drayton UB7 104 B3
1 West Wickham BR4 207 D1
Wimbledon SW19 180 A4
North Residence IG3 58 B4
North Ride
W2 114 C6 247 A5
North Rise W2 237 B1
Northrop Rd TW6 127 C4
North Row
W1 115 A6 248 A6
NORTH SHEEN 132 C3
North Sheen Sta
TW10 132 C1
Northside Prim Sch
N12 30 A5
Northside Rd BR1 187 A2
North Side Wandsworth
Comm SW18 158 B6
Northspur Rd SM1 217 C5
North Sq
Edmonton N9 18 B2
Hampstead Garden Suburb
NW11 47 C4
North St
Barking IG11 79 A1
Bexleyheath DA7 147 C1
Bromley BR1 187 A2
Carshalton SM5 218 D4
Clapham SW4 137 C2
Hendon NW4 46 C4
Isleworth TW7 131 A2
Newham E13 99 B5
Northstead Rd SW2 160 C2
North Tenter St E1 243 D1
North Terr SW3 257 A5
Northumberland Alley
EC3 243 B1
Northumberland Ave
Enfield EN1 6 B4
Falconwood DA16 145 C2
Hounslow TW7 130 D4
Wanstead E12 55 C1
Westminster
WC2 116 A5 250 A4
Northumberland Cl
TW19 148 A5
Northumberland Cres
TW14 149 C5
Northumberland Ct
3 Hounslow TW3 129 D1
South Croydon CR2 221 C3
Northumberland Gdns
Brentford TW7 131 A5
Bromley BR1 210 C5
Edmonton N9 17 D1
Mitcham CR4 203 D4
Northumberland Gr
N17 34 B3
Northumberland Heath
Prim Sch DA8 147 D5
Northumberland Ho
Finchley N12 29 D4
Kentish Town NW5 71 C2
Northumberland Mans
E5 74 C4
Northumberland Park
Com Sch N17 34 A3
Northumberland Park Ind
Est N17 34 B3
Northumberland Park
Sports Ctr N17 34 A3
Northumberland Park Sta
N17 34 B3
Northumberland Pk
Erith DA8 147 D5
Tottenham N17 34 A3
Northumberland Pl
Notting Hill W2 91 C1
26 Richmond TW10 153 D6
Northumberland Rd
Harrow HA2 41 C4
New Barnet EN5 14 A4
Newham E6 100 A1
Walthamstow E17 53 C2
Northumberland St
WC2 250 A4
Northumbria Ct 10
TW9 132 A1
Northumbria St E14 97 C1
North Verbena Gdns 2
W6 112 A1
Northview 1 N7 72 A5
North View
Ealing W5 87 C3
Pinner HA5 40 C2
Wimbledon SW19 178 C5
Northview Cres NW10 67 D4
Northview Dr IG8 37 D1
Northview Prim Sch
NW10 67 D4
North View Rd N8 49 D6
North Villas NW1 71 D2
Northway
Hampstead Garden Suburb
NW11 47 D4
Merton SM4 201 A5
Wallington SM6 219 C4
North Way
Friern Barnet N11 31 C4
Lower Edmonton N9 18 D2
Pinner HA5 40 D5
Queensbury NW9 44 D6
Uxbridge UB10 60 A1
Northway Cir NW7 27 B6
Northway Cres NW7 27 C6
Northway Ct NW7 27 B6
Northway Rd
Camberwell SE5 139 A2
Croydon CR0 205 D2
Northway Sch NW7 11 B1
Northways Par 2
NW3 70 B1
Northweald La KT2 175 D5
NORTH WEMBLEY 65 C6
North Wembley Sta HA0,
HA9 65 D5
North Western Ave (Tylers
Way) WD23 8 C6
North Western Ave
(Watford By-Pass)
WD6 9 B4
Northwest Pl N1 234 B4
North Wharf Rd
W2 92 B2 236 C3
Northwick Ave HA3 43 B3
Northwick Circ HA3 43 C3
Northwick Cl
Harrow HA1 43 B1
Lisson Gr NW8 92 B3 236 C6
Northwick Ho NW8 236 B6
Northwick Park Hospl
HA1 43 A2
Northwick Park Rd
HA1 42 D3
Northwick Park Sta
HA3 43 B2
Northwick Rd
South Oxhey WD19 22 C6
Wembley HA0 87 D6
Northwick Terr
NW8 92 B3 236 C6
North Wlk
Bayswater
W2 114 A6 246 A5
New Addington CR0 224 A3
Northwold Dr HA5 40 C6
Northwold Prim Sch
E5 74 A6
Northwold Rd E5, N16 74 A6
NORTHWOOD 22 A3
Northwood Gdns
Greenford UB6 64 D3
Ilford IG5 56 C5
North Finchley N12 30 B5
NORTHWOOD HILLS 22 A1
Northwood Hills Cir
HA6 22 A2
Northwood Hills Sta
HA6 22 A1
North Wood Lo NW3 69 D4
Northwood & Pinner Com
Hospl HA6 22 A2
Northwood Pl DA18 125 B3
Northwood Prim Sch
DA18 125 B3
Northwood Rd
Forest Hill SE23 163 B3
Highgate N6 49 B2
South Norwood CR7 183 A1
Wallington SM5 219 A2
Northwood Sch HA6 22 A2
Northwood Twr 1
E17 54 A5
Northwood Way
Northwood HA6 22 A3
1 West Norwood
SE19 183 C4
NORTH WOOLWICH 122 D4
North Woolwich Rd
E16 121 B5
North Woolwich Rdbt
E16 121 D5
North Worple Way
SW14 133 B2
Norton Ave KT5 198 D2

Norton Cl
Chingford E4 35 C5
Enfield EN1 6 B3
Norton Ct
Beckenham BR3 185 B2
Ilford IG2 57 B3
Norton Folgate E1 243 B4
Norton Gdns SW16 182 A1
Norton Ho
14 Globe Town E2 96 D5
6 New Malden KT3 199 C5
30 Stepney E1 96 B1
16 Stockwell SW9 138 B3
Norton Rd
Walthamstow E10 53 B1
Wembley HA0 65 D2
Norval Gn 1 SW9 138 C3
Norval Rd HA0 43 B1
Norvic Ho 5 SE5 139 A3
Norway Gate SE16 119 A3
Norway Pl E14 97 B1
Norway St SE10 141 D6
Norwegian Sch The SW20 178 C3
Norwich Cres RM6 58 B4
Norwich Ho 6 E14 97 D1
Norwich Mews IG3 58 A1
Norwich Pl 7 DA6 147 C1
Norwich Rd
Forest Gate E7 77 A3
Greenford UB6 85 D6
Northwood HA6 39 D6
South Norwood CR7 205 A6
Norwich St EC4 94 C1 241 A2
Norwich Wlk HA8 27 A3
Norwood Ave HA0 88 B5
Norwood Cl
Cricklewood NW2 69 A5
Southall UB2 107 C2
Twickenham TW2 152 B2
Norwood Dr HA2 41 C3
Norwood Gdns
Hayes UB4 84 C3
Southall UB2 107 B2
NORWOOD GREEN 107 C2
Norwood Green Inf Sch UB2 107 B1
Norwood Green Jun Sch UB2 107 A1
Norwood Green Rd UB2 107 C2
Norwood Heights Sh Ctr 13 SE19 183 C4
Norwood High St SE27 183 A6
Norwood Ho 25 E14 119 D6
Norwood Hospl SE19 183 B4
Norwood Junction Sta SE25 206 A5
NORWOOD NEW TOWN 183 A4
Norwood Park Rd SE27 183 A5
Norwood Rd
Southall UB2 107 C2
West Norwood SE24, SE27 160 D3
Norwood Sch SE19 183 A5
Norwood Terr UB2 107 D2
Notley St SE5 139 B5
Notre Dame RC Girls Sch SE1 116 D3 261 D5
Notre Dame RC Prim Sch SE18 144 D6
Notson Rd SE25 206 B5
Notting Barn Rd W10 90 D3
Nottingdale Sq W11 244 A4
Nottingham Ave E16 99 C1
Nottingham Ct WC2 240 A1
Nottingham Ho
33 Camberwell SE5 139 A3
Stoke Newington N4 51 A1
Nottingham Pl W1 93 A2 238 A4
Nottingham Rd
Croydon CR2 221 A3
Isleworth TW7 130 D3
Leytonstone E10 54 A3
Upper Tooting SW17 158 D3
Nottingham St W1 238 A4
Nottingham Terr NW1 238 A5
NOTTING HILL 113 B6
Notting Hill & Ealing High Sch W13 87 B2
Notting Hill Gate W11 113 C5 245 A4
Notting Hill Gate Sta W11 113 C5 245 A4
Nottingwood Ho W11 244 A6
Nova Bldg 1 E14 119 C2
Nova Ct E 3 E14 120 A5
Nova Ct W 2 E14 120 A5
Nova Mews SM4 201 A2
Novar Cl BR6 211 D2
Nova Rd CR0 205 A2
Novar Rd SE9 167 A3
Novello St SW6 135 C4 265 A2
Nowell Rd SW13 134 A6
Nower Ct HA5 41 B5
NOWER HILL 41 B6
Nower Hill HA5 41 B5
Nower Hill High Sch HA5 41 C5
Noyna Rd SW17 158 D1
Nubia Way SE6 164 C1
Nucleus NW10 89 A4
Nuding Cl SE13 141 C2
Nuffield Ct TW5 129 B5
Nuffield Lo 14 W9 91 C2
Nugent Ct
Streatham SW16 181 C6
3 Upper Holloway N19 50 A1
Nugent Rd
Finsbury Pk N19 50 A1
South Norwood SE25 205 D6
Nugents Ct HA5 23 A2
Nugent's Pk HA5 23 B2
Nugent Terr NW8 92 A5 229 B3
Numa Ct TW8 131 D5
Nun Ct EC2 242 C2
Nuneaton Rd RM9 81 A1
Nuneham SW16 181 D6
NUNHEAD 140 C1
Nunhead Cres SE15 140 B2
Nunhead Gn SE15 140 B2
Nunhead Gr SE15 140 C2
Nunhead La SE15 140 B2
Nunhead Sta SE15 140 C3
Nunnington Cl SE9 166 A1
Nunn's Rd EN2 5 A3
Nupton Dr EN5 12 C5
Nurse Cl HA8 27 A2
Nursery Ave
Bexleyheath DA7 147 B2
Croydon CR0 222 D6
Finchley N3 30 A1
Nursery Cl
Broom Hill BR6 211 D2
Croydon CR0 222 D6
Dagenham RM6 58 D3
Enfield EN3 6 D4
Feltham TW14 150 B4
New Cross SE4 141 B3
Putney SW15 134 D1
Woodford IG8 37 B5
Nursery Ct
Ealing W13 87 A2
8 Tottenham N17 33 D3
Nursery Gdns
Chislehurst BR7 188 D4
Enfield EN3 6 D4
Hampton TW13 173 B6
Hounslow TW4 151 B6
Sunbury TW16 171 D1
Nursery La
Forest Gate E7 77 A2
Hillingdon UB8 82 A3
North Kensington W10 90 C2
Shoreditch E2 95 D6
Nurserymans Rd N11 15 A2
Nursery Rd
Finchley N2 30 B2
Hackney E9 74 C2
Loughton IG10 21 C6
Merton SW19 179 D1
Mitcham CR4 202 C6
Osidge N14 15 C4
Pinner HA5 40 C6
South Norwood CR7 205 B5
Stockwell SW9 138 B1
Sunbury TW16 171 D1
Sutton SM1 218 A4
Wimbledon SW19 179 A3
Nursery Row SE17 262 C3
Nursery St N17 33 D3
Nursery Walk Ct NW4 46 B6
Nursery Wlk NW4 46 C6
Nurstead Rd DA8 147 C5
Nutborn Ho SW19 178 D4
Nutbourne St W10 91 A4
Nutbrook St SE15 140 A2
Nutbrowne Rd RM9 103 B6
Nutchford EN1 17 C5
Nutcroft Rd SE15 140 B5
Nutfield Cl
Carshalton SM5 218 C5
Edmonton N18 34 A4
Nutfield Gdns
Ilford IG3 80 A6
Northolt UB5 84 C5
Nutfield Pl 1 CR7 204 D5
Nutfield Rd
Dollis Hill NW2 68 A5
East Dulwich SE22 139 D1
Leyton E15 76 A4
Thornton Heath CR7 204 D5
Nutfield Way BR6 226 D6
Nutford Pl W1 92 D1 237 C2
Nuthatch Cl TW19 148 B3
Nuthatch Gdns SE28 123 B4
Nuthurst Ave SW2 160 B2
Nutkin Wlk UB8 60 A1
Nutley Terr NW3 70 B2
Nutmeg Cl E16 98 C3
Nutmeg La E14 98 B1
Nuttall St N1 95 C5
Nutter La E11 55 C4
Nutt Gr HA8 9 D2
Nutt St SE15 139 D5
Nutty La TW17 193 A6
Nutwell St SW17 180 C5
Nuxley Rd DA17 125 C1
NW London Jewish Day Sch NW6 69 A1
Nyanza St SE18 145 B6
Nye Bevan Est E5 74 D5
Nye Bevan Ho SW6 264 C4
Nye's Wharf SE1, SE15 140 A6
Nylands Ave TW9 132 C3
Nymans Gdns SW20 200 B6
Nynehead St SE14 141 A5
Nyon Gr SE6 163 B2
Nyton Cl N19 50 A1

O

O2 Millennium Dome The* SE10 120 C5
Oak Apple Ct SE12 165 A3
Oak Ave
Croydon CR0 223 D6
Enfield EN2 4 B5
Hampton TW12, TW13 173 A4
Heston TW5 129 A5
Hornsey N8 50 A5
Muswell Hill N10 31 B3
Tottenham N17 33 C3
Uxbridge UB10 60 D6
West Drayton UB7 104 C3
Oak Bank CR0 224 A2
Oakbank Ave KT12 195 B2
Oakbank Gr SE24 139 A1
Oakbark Ho 10 TW8 131 C5
Oakbrook 3 BR3 185 D1
Oakbrook Cl BR1 187 B6
Oakbury Rd SW6 135 D3
Oak Cl
East Barnet N14 15 B4
Sutton SM1 218 A6
Oakcombe Cl KT3 177 C2
Oak Cottage Cl 11 SE6 164 D3
Oak Cotts W7 108 C4
Oakcourt 17 SE15 139 D5
Oak Cres E16 98 C2
Oakcroft SE12 165 B1
Oakcroft Bsns Ctr KT9 214 B4
Oakcroft Cl HA5 22 B1
Oakcroft Ct SE3 143 A4
Oakcroft Ho 3 KT3 199 C2
Oakcroft Rd
Chessington KT9 214 B4
Lewisham SE13 142 B3
Oakcroft Villas KT9 214 B4
Oak Ct
Bickley BR1 188 B1
Chingford E4 35 D4
Oakdale
Beckenham BR3 186 A1
East Barnet N14 15 B3
Oakdale Ave
Harrow HA3 44 A4
Pinner HA6 22 A1
Oakdale Cl WD19 22 C6
Oakdale Ct
Chingford E4 36 A5
Upper Holloway N19 72 A6
Oakdale Gdns E4 36 A5
Oakdale Inf Sch E18 37 B1
Oakdale Jun Sch E18 37 B1
Oakdale Lo NW4 29 A2
Oakdale Rd
Leyton E11 76 B6
Nunhead SE15 140 C2
South Oxhey WD19 22 C6
Streatham SW16 182 A5
Tottenham N4 51 B3
Upton E7 77 B1
Woodford E18 37 B1
Oakdale Way CR4 203 A2
Oakdene
3 Peckham SE15 140 B4
1 West Norwood SE19 183 C5
Oak Dene W13 87 B2
Oakdene Ave
Chislehurst West BR7 188 C5
Thames Ditton KT7 197 A1
Oakdene Cl HA5 23 B3
Oakdene Ct
Feltham TW12 173 B6
1 Streatham SW16 182 A5
Oakdene Dr KT5 199 A1
Oakdene Ho
Enfield EN2 4 D2
11 Stamford Hill N16 51 C1
Oakdene Lo 3 SE20 184 B3
Oakdene Mews SM3 201 B1
Oakdene Pk N3 29 B3
Oakdene Rd
Hillingdon UB10 82 D5
Orpington BR5 211 D4
Oakden St SE11 116 C2 261 B4
Oake Ct SW15 157 A6
Oakeford Ho W14 254 B5
Oakend Ho 10 N4 51 B2
Oaken Dr KT10 212 D2
Oakenholt Ho 1 SE2 124 D4
Oaken La KT10 212 C3
Oakenshaw Cl KT6 198 A2
Oakes Cl E6 100 B1
Oakeshott Ave N6 71 A6
Oakey La SE1 261 A6
Oak Farm WD6 11 A6
Oak Farm Jun & Inf Schs UB10 82 D6
Oakfield E4 35 D5
Oakfield Ave HA3 43 B6
Oakfield Cl
New Malden KT3 199 D4
Ruislip HA4 39 D3
Oakfield Ct
Clapham Pk SW4 160 A5
2 Ealing W5 110 C5
Finchley N3 29 D2
Finsbury Pk N8 50 A2
Hendon NW2 46 D2
South Croydon CR2 221 A2
Oakfield Gdns
Beckenham BR3 207 C4
Carshalton SM5 202 D1
Edmonton N18 33 C6
Greenford UB6 86 B4
3 West Norwood SE19 183 C5
Oakfield Ho 2 IG1 78 D5
Oakfield La BR2 225 C4
Oakfield Lo 8 IG1 78 D5
Oakfield Prep Sch SE21 161 B3
Oakfield Rd
Ashford TW15 170 D5
Croydon CR0 205 A1
Finchley N3 29 D2
Finsbury Pk N4 50 C2
Higham Hill E17 35 A1
Ilford IG1 78 D5
Newham E6 100 A6
Palmers Green N14 16 A2
Penge SE20 184 B3
Wimbledon SW19 156 D1
Oakfield Road Ind Est 11 SE20 184 B3
Oakfields KT12 194 A1
Oakfields Rd NW11 47 A3
Oakfield St SW10 136 A6 266 A6
Oakford Rd NW5 71 C4
Oak Gdns
Croydon CR0 223 C6
Hendon HA8 27 A1
Oak Gr
Ruislip HA4 40 B1
Sunbury TW16 172 B3
West Hampstead NW2 69 A4
West Wickham BR4 208 A1
Oak Grove Rd SE20 184 C1
Oakhall Ct
Ashford TW16 171 D5
Oakhall Ct *continued*
Wanstead E11 55 B3
Oakhall Dr TW16 171 D5
Oak Hall Rd E11 55 B3
Oakham Cl
Cockfosters EN4 2 D2
Forest Hill SE6 163 B2
Oakham Dr BR2 208 D5
Oakham Ho 5 W10 90 C3
Oakhampton Rd NW7 28 D3
Oakhill KT10 213 A2
Oak Hill
Chingford IG8 36 C3
Surbiton KT6 198 A2
Oakhill Ave
Pinner HA5 23 A1
West Hampstead NW3 69 D4
Oak Hill Cl IG8 36 B3
Oakhill Coll N14 15 A5
Oak Hill Cres
Chingford IG8 36 C3
Surbiton KT6 198 A2
Oakhill Ct
Honor Oak SE23 162 C5
Putney SW15 157 B6
8 Surbiton KT6 198 A3
Wimbledon SW19 178 D3
Oak Hill Ct IG8 36 C3
Oak Hill Gdns E4 36 C2
Oak Hill Gr KT6 198 A3
Oakhill Ho BR5 190 A2
Oak Hill Lo NW3 69 D4
Oakhill Mans EN4 14 C5
Oak Hill Park Mews NW3 70 A4
Oak Hill Pk NW3 69 D4
Oakhill Pl SW15 157 C6
Oakhill Prim Sch IG8 36 C4
Oakhill Rd
Beckenham BR3 186 A1
Orpington BR6 227 D6
Putney SW15 157 B6
Sutton SM1 218 A5
Thornton Heath SW16 182 B2
Oak Hill Rd KT6 198 A3
Oak Hill Way NW3 70 A4
Oak Ho
13 Cubitt Town E14 120 A4
11 Finchley N2 30 B1
8 Maitland Pk NW3 70 D2
Penge SE20 184 B1
2 Richmond TW9 132 D4
13 Sidcup DA15 168 A1
9 Stoke Newington N16 73 B6
Teddington TW11 175 C4
Wood Green N22 32 A3
Oakhouse Rd DA6 169 C6
Oakhurst Ave
East Barnet EN4 14 C4
Erith DA7 147 A5
Oakhurst Cl
Chislehurst BR7 188 B2
Snaresbrook E17 54 C5
4 Teddington TW11 174 C5
Oakhurst Ct E17 54 C5
Oakhurst Gdns
Chingford E4 20 D3
Erith DA7 147 A5
Snaresbrook E11, E17 54 C5
Oakhurst Gr SE22 140 A1
Oakhurst Rd KT19 215 B2
Oakington 14 KT1 176 C1
Oakington Ave
Harrow HA2 41 C2
Hayes UB3 105 B2
Wembley HA9 66 B5
Oakington Cl TW16 172 C1
Oakington Ct 1 EN2 4 D3
Oakington Dr TW16 172 C1
Oakington Manor Dr HA9 66 C3
Oakington Manor Prim Sch HA9 66 D3
Oakington Rd W9 91 C3
Oakington Way N8 50 A2
Oak La
Finchley N2 30 B1
Friern Barnet N11 31 D4
Isleworth TW7 130 C1
Limehouse E14 119 B6
Twickenham TW1 153 A4
Woodford IG8 36 D6
Oakland Pl IG9 21 A2
Oakland Rd E15 76 C4
Oaklands
Chislehurst BR7 189 B4
Croydon CR0 220 D3
Ealing W13 87 A2
Southgate N21 16 B2
Oaklands *continued*
Twickenham TW2 152 A4
Oaklands Ave
Enfield N9 18 B5
Hounslow TW7 130 D6
Sidcup DA15 167 D4
Thames Ditton KT10 196 B1
Thornton Heath CR7 204 C5
West Wickham BR4 223 D5
Oaklands Cl
Bexley DA6 169 B6
Chessington KT9 213 C4
Orpington BR5 211 C3
Oaklands Ct
Beckenham BR3 186 A1
Dagenham NW10 89 C6
Orpington BR6 227 A6
5 Shepherd's Bush W12 112 B5
Wembley HA0 65 D3
Oaklands Dr TW2 152 A4
Oaklands Gr W12 112 A5
Oaklands Ho SE4 141 B2
Oaklands Mews 1 NW2 68 D4
Oaklands Park Ave IG1 79 A6
Oaklands Pas NW2 68 D4
Oaklands Pl 8 SW4 137 D1
Oaklands Prim Sch W7 108 D4
Oaklands Rd
Barnet N20 13 B4
Bexley DA6 169 B6
Bromley BR1 186 C3
Cricklewood NW2 68 D4
Ealing W7 108 D4
Mortlake SW14 133 B2
West Ealing W7, W13 109 A4
Oaklands Sch
Hounslow TW3 130 B2
Loughton IG10 21 D6
Oaklands Sec Sch E2 96 B4
Oaklands Way SM6 219 D1
Oakland Way KT19 215 C2
Oaklawn Ct HA7 25 B4
Oakleafe Gdns IG6 56 D6
Oaklea Pas KT1 197 D6
Oakleigh Ave
East Barnet N20 14 C3
Edgware HA8 26 D2
Tolworth KT6 214 D6
Oakleigh Cl N20 14 D1
Oakleigh Cres N20 14 C1
Oakleigh Ct
East Barnet EN4 14 C5
Hendon HA8 27 A1
7 Penge SE20 184 B3
Southall UB1 107 B5
Surbiton KT6 214 B6
Oakleigh Gdns
Edgware HA8 26 B5
Oakleigh Pk N20 14 B3
Orpington BR6 227 C4
Oakleigh Lodge IG3 80 A5
Oakleigh Mews 2 N20 14 A2
OAKLEIGH PARK 14 B3
Oakleigh Park Ave BR7 188 C2
Oakleigh Park Sta EN4 14 C4
Oakleigh Pk N N20 14 B3
Oakleigh Pk S N20 14 C3
Oakleigh Rd
Hillingdon UB10 61 A1
Pinner HA5 23 B4
Oakleigh Rd N N20 14 C2
Oakleigh Rd S N11 31 A6
Oakleigh Sch N20 14 D1
Oakleigh Way
Mitcham CR4 181 B2
1 Tolworth KT6 198 D1
Oakley Ave
Barking IG11 79 D1
Ealing W5 110 C6
Wallington CR0 220 A4
Oakley Cl
Chingford E4 20 A1
Ealing W7 108 C6
Hounslow TW7 130 B4
7 Newham E6 100 A1
Oakley Cres EC1 234 D3
Oakley Ct
Carshalton CR4 203 A2
Harlington UB7 127 A5
Wembley HA0 65 A4
Oakley Dr
Keston Mark BR2 226 A5
Lewisham SE13 164 B5
New Eltham SE9 167 B3

Oakley Gdns
Chelsea SW3 .. 136 C6 267 B6
Hornsey Vale N8 ... 50 B4
Oakley Ho
Chelsea SW1 ... 257 D4
Ealing W5 ... 110 C6
Oakley Pk DA5 ... 168 C4
Oakley Pl SE1 .. 117 D1 263 C1
Oakley Rd
Croydon SE25 ... 206 B4
De Beauvoir Town N1 ... 73 B1
Harrow HA1 ... 42 C3
Keston Mark BR2 ... 226 A6
Oakley Sq NW1 . 93 C5 232 B4
Oakley St
SW3 ... 136 C6 267 A6
Oakley Wlk W6 ... 134 D6
Oak Lo
4 Ashford TW16 ... 171 D3
Southgate N21 ... 16 B5
10 Sutton SM1 ... 218 A4
Wanstead E11 ... 55 A2
6 Wembley HA0 ... 65 D3
Oak Lodge 14 SE21 ... 161 B2
Oak Lodge Cl HA7 ... 25 C5
Oak Lodge Dr BR4 ... 207 D2
Oak Lodge Sch
Balham SW12 ... 159 A4
East Finchley N2 ... 48 A5
Oaklodge Way NW7 ... 27 D4
Oakman Ho 29 SW19 .. 156 D3
Oakmead HA1 ... 64 B5
Oakmead Ave BR2 ... 209 A3
Oakmead Ct HA7 ... 25 C6
Oakmeade HA5 ... 23 C4
Oakmead Gdns HA8 ... 27 B6
Oakmead Pl CR4 ... 180 C2
Oakmead Rd
Balham SW12 ... 159 B3
Wallington CR0 ... 203 D3
Oakmere Rd SE2 ... 146 A6
Oakmont Pl 6 BR6 ... 211 B1
Oak Park Gdns SW19 .. 156 D3
Oak Park Mews N16 ... 73 D5
Oak Rd
Ealing W5 ... 109 D6
Kingston u T KT3 ... 177 B1
Oakridge Dr N2 ... 48 B6
Oakridge La BR1 ... 186 B5
Oakridge Rd BR1 ... 186 C6
Oak Rise IG9 ... 21 D1
Oak Row CR4 ... 181 C1
Oaks Ave
Feltham TW13 ... 151 A2
North Cheam KT4 ... 216 B4
West Norwood SE19 ... 183 C5
Oaksford Ave SE26 ... 162 B1
Oaks Gr E4 ... 20 C2
Oakshade Rd BR1 ... 186 B6
Oakshaw Rd SW18 ... 157 D4
Oakshott Ct NW1 ... 232 C3
Oaks La
Ilford IG2 ... 57 C5
South Croydon CR0 ... 222 C5
Oaks Park High Sch
IG2 ... 57 C4
Oaks Rd CR0 ... 222 C4
Oaks Sh Ctr The W3 ... 111 A5
Oaks The
Brondesbury Pk NW6 ... 68 D1
Chingford IG8 ... 36 C3
Enfield EN2 ... 4 D2
Finchley N12 ... 29 D6
Hayes UB4 ... 83 A5
Long Ditton KT6 ... 213 C5
Ruislip HA4 ... 39 C2
Southborough BR2 ... 210 C3
Wallington SM6 ... 219 C4
Willesden NW10 ... 68 B1
Wimbledon SW19 ... 179 A4
Woolwich SE18 ... 123 A1
Oaks Way
Surbiton KT6 ... 197 D1
Wallington SM5 ... 218 D1
Oakthorpe Ct N13 ... 33 A5
Oakthorpe Prim Sch
N13 ... 33 A5
Oakthorpe Rd N13 ... 32 C5
Oaktree Ave N13 ... 16 D1
Oak Tree Ave N2 ... 47 D6
Oak Tree Cl
Ealing W5 ... 87 C1
Stanmore HA7 ... 25 C3
Oak Tree Ct
Acton W3 ... 110 D6
8 Clapham Pk SW4 ... 160 A6
Elstree WD6 ... 9 D5
Oak Tree Dell NW9 ... 45 B4
Oak Tree Dr N20 ... 13 D3
Oak Tree Gdns BR1 ... 187 B5
Oaktree Gr IG1 ... 79 B3
Oak Tree Ho W9 ... 91 D3
Oak Tree Rd
NW8 ... 92 C4 230 A1
Oaktree Sch EN4 ... 15 A5
Oaktrees Hostel HA8 ... 11 A2
Oakview Gdns N2 ... 48 B5
Oakview Gr CR0 ... 207 A1
Oakview Lo NW11 ... 47 B2
Oakview Rd SE6 ... 185 D5
Oak Village NW5 ... 71 A4
Oakway
Beckenham BR2 ... 186 B1
West Barnes SW20 ... 200 C5
Oak Way
Croydon CR0 ... 206 D3
East Acton W3 ... 111 C5
East Barnet N14 ... 15 B4
East Bedfont TW14 ... 149 C3
Oakway Cl DA5 ... 169 A5
Oakways SE9 ... 166 D5
Oakwell Ho 24 SW8 ... 137 D3
Oak Wlk CR4 ... 203 A1
OAKWOOD ... 15 D6
Oakwood Ave
Beckenham BR2, BR3 ... 186 A1
Bromley BR2 ... 209 B6
Mitcham CR4 ... 180 B1
Osidge N14 ... 15 D4
Southall UB1 ... 107 C6
Oakwood Cl
Chislehurst West
BR7 ... 188 C4
Lewisham SE13 ... 164 B5
Southgate N14 ... 15 C5
Oakwood Cres
Southgate N21 ... 16 B5
Wembley UB6 ... 65 B2
Oakwood Ct
Beckenham BR3 ... 186 A1
6 Chingford E4 ... 20 C4
Kensington
W14 ... 113 B3 254 C6
1 Newham E6 ... 100 A6
17 Sutton SM1 ... 218 A4
Oakwood Dr
Burnt Oak HA8 ... 27 A4
West Norwood SE19 ... 183 C4
Oakwood Gdns
Ilford IG3 ... 79 D6
Orpington BR6 ... 227 A6
Sutton SM1 ... 217 C6
Oakwood La
W14 ... 113 B3 254 C6
Oakwood Park Rd N14 . 16 A5
Oakwood Pl CR0 ... 204 C3
Oakwood Rd
Hampstead Garden Suburb
NW11 ... 47 D4
Orpington BR6 ... 227 A6
Pinner HA5 ... 22 B1
Thornton Heath CR0 ... 204 C3
Wimbledon SW20 ... 178 A2
Oakwood Sta N14 ... 15 C6
Oakwood View N14 ... 15 D4
Oakworth Rd W10 ... 90 D2
Oarsman Pl KT8 ... 196 C5
Oasis The 6 BR1 ... 187 C1
Oast Ct 8 E14 ... 119 B6
Oast Lo W4 ... 133 C5
Oates Cl BR2 ... 208 B6
Oatfield Ho 1 N15 ... 51 C3
Oatfield Rd BR6 ... 211 D1
Oat La EC2 ... 95 A1 242 B2
Oatland Rise E17 ... 35 A1
Oatlands Ct 3 SW19 .. 156 D3
Oatlands Dr KT13 ... 193 C1
Oatlands Rd EN3 ... 6 C4
Oatwell Ho SW3 ... 257 B3
Oban Cl E13 ... 99 C3
Oban Ct HA8 ... 10 D2
Oban Ho
5 Barking IG11 ... 101 B5
South Bromley E14 ... 98 B1
Oban Rd
Newham E13 ... 99 C4
South Norwood SE25 ... 205 B5
Oban St E14 ... 98 B1
Oberon Ho 5 N1 ... 95 C5
Oberon Way TW17 ... 192 A6
Oberstein Rd 15
SW11 ... 136 B1
Oborne Cl SE24 ... 160 D6
O'Brian Ho 10 E1 ... 96 D4
Observatory Gdns W8 245 B2
Observatory Mews
E14 ... 120 B2
Observatory Rd
SW14 ... 133 A1
Occupation La
Brentford W5 ... 109 D2
Shooters Hill SE18 ... 144 D4
Occupation Rd
Newington
SE17 ... 117 A1 262 A2
West Ealing W13 ... 109 B4
Ocean St E1 ... 96 D2
Ocean Wharf E14 ... 119 C4
Ochre Ct TW13 ... 149 D1
Ockbrook 3 E1 ... 96 C2
Ockendon Rd N1 ... 73 B2
Ockham Dr BR5 ... 190 A3
Ockley Ct
Sidcup DA14 ... 167 C1
Sutton SM1 ... 218 A4
Ockley Ho 8 KT2 ... 176 D4
Ockley Rd
Streatham SW16 ... 160 A1
Thornton Heath CR0 ... 204 B2
Octagon Arc EC2 ... 243 A3
Octagon The NW3 ... 69 C4
Octavia Cl CR4 ... 202 C4
Octavia Ho
Catford SE6 ... 163 D4
Kensal Town W10 ... 91 A3
Octavia Mews 1 W9 ... 91 B3
Octavia Rd TW7 ... 130 D2
Octavia St
SW11 ... 136 C4 267 B1
Octavia Way 12 SE28 .. 124 B6
Octavius St SE8 ... 141 C5
October Ct BR2 ... 208 D6
October Pl NW4 ... 46 D6
Odard Rd KT8 ... 195 C5
Odell Cl IG11 ... 79 D1
Odell Wlk SE13 ... 142 A2
Odeon Ct
Dagenham NW10 ... 89 C6
1 Newham E16 ... 99 A2
Odeon Par
Eltham SE9 ... 144 A1
Wembley UB6 ... 65 B2
Odeon The IG11 ... 79 B1
Odessa Inf Sch E7 ... 77 A3
Odessa Rd
Leyton E7 ... 76 D4
Willesden Green NW10 ... 90 A5
Odessa St SE16 ... 119 B3
Odette Ct N20 ... 14 A1
Odette Duval Ho 29
E1 ... 96 C2
Odette Ho 6 SE27 ... 183 B6
Odger St SW11 ... 136 D3
Odhams Wlk WC2 ... 240 B1
Odin Ho 6 SE5 ... 139 A3
O'Donnell Ct WC1 ... 240 B6
O'Driscoll Ho 4 W12 ... 90 B1
Odyssey Bsns Pk HA4 .. 62 B3
Offa's Mead E9 ... 75 A4
Offenbach Ho 12 E2 ... 96 D5
Offenham Rd BR7,
SE9 ... 188 B6
Offers Ct KT1 ... 198 B6
Offerton Rd SW4 ... 137 C2
Offham Ho SE17 ... 263 A3
Offham Slope N12 ... 29 B5
Offley Ho 10 E9 ... 74 D2
Offley Pl TW7 ... 130 B3
Offley Rd SW9 ... 138 C5
Offord Cl N17 ... 34 A4
Offord Rd N1 ... 72 B1
Offord St N1 ... 72 B1
Ogden Ho TW13 ... 173 A6
Ogilby St SE18 ... 122 B2
Ogilvie Ho 12 E1 ... 96 D1
Oglander Rd SE15 ... 139 D2
Ogle St W1 ... 93 C2 239 A4
Oglethorpe Rd RM10 ... 81 C5
O'Gorman Ho SW10 ... 266 B4
O'Grady Ct 17 W13 ... 109 A5
O'Grady Ho 17 E17 ... 53 D6
Ohio Bldg 13 SE13 ... 141 D4
Ohio Rd E13 ... 98 D3
Oil Mill La W6 ... 112 A1
Okeburn Rd SW17 ... 181 A5
Okehampton Cl N12 ... 30 B5
Okehampton Cres
DA16 ... 146 C4
Okehampton Rd NW10 . 90 D6
Okeover Manor SW4 .. 137 B1
Olaf Palme Ho TW13 .. 150 B1
Olaf St W11 ... 112 D6
Old Bailey EC4 .. 94 D1 241 D1
Old Barn Cl SM2 ... 217 A1
Old Barrack Yd SW1 .. 248 A1
Old Barrowfield 7
E15 ... 98 C6
Old Bellgate Wharf
E14 ... 119 C3
Oldberry Rd HA8 ... 27 B4
Old Bethnal Green Rd
E2 ... 96 B4
OLD BEXLEY ... 169 D4
Old Bexley Bsns Pk
DA5 ... 169 D4
Old Bexley CE Prim Sch
DA5 ... 169 B3
Old Billingsgate Wlk
EC3 ... 253 A5
Old Bldgs WC2 ... 241 A2
Old Bond St
W1 ... 115 C6 249 A5
Oldborough Rd HA0 ... 65 C5
Old Brewery Mews
NW3 ... 70 B4
Old Bridge Cl UB5 ... 85 C5
Old Bridge St KT1 ... 175 D1
Old Broad St
EC2 ... 95 B1 242 D2
Old Bromley Rd BR1 .. 186 B5
Old Brompton Rd SW5,
SW7 ... 114 A2 256 B3
Old Burlington St
W1 ... 115 C6 249 A5
Oldbury Ct E9 ... 75 A3
Oldbury Pl W1 .. 93 A2 238 B4
Oldbury Rd EN1 ... 6 A3
Old Castle St
E1 ... 95 D1 243 D2
Old Cavendish St W1 .. 238 C1
Old Change Ct EC4 ... 242 A1
Old Chapel Pl 2 N10 ... 49 B6
Old Charlton Rd
TW17 ... 193 A4
Old Chiswick Yd W4 .. 133 C6
Old Church Ct N11 ... 31 B5
Old Church La
Ealing UB6 ... 87 A4
Stanmore HA7 ... 25 C4
Welsh Harp NW9 ... 67 B6
Old Church Path
KT10 ... 212 A4
Old Church Rd
Chingford E4 ... 19 C1
Stepney E1 ... 96 D1
Old Church St SW3 ... 256 D1
Old Claygate La KT10 .. 213 A3
Old Clem Sq 12 SE18 .. 144 C6
Old College Ct DA17 ... 125 D1
Old Compton St
W1 ... 93 D1 239 C1
Old Cote Dr TW5 ... 129 C6
Old Court Ho W8 ... 245 C1
Old Court (Mus & Liby)*
HA0 ... 65 C3
Old Court Pl
W8 ... 113 D4 245 C1
Old Covent Gdn*
WC2 ... 250 B6
Old Ctyd The BR1 ... 187 B2
Old Cty H* SE1 ... 250 C2
Old Dairy Mews
5 Balham SW12 ... 159 A3
4 Camden Town NW5 ... 71 B2
Old Dairy Sq The N21 .. 16 C4
Old Deer Park Gdns
TW9 ... 132 A2
Old Devonshire Rd
SW12 ... 159 B4
Old Dock Cl TW9 ... 132 C6
Old Dover Rd SE3 ... 143 B5
Oldegate Ho 1 E6 ... 99 D6
Old Farm Ave
Osidge N14 ... 15 C4
Sidcup DA15 ... 167 C2
Old Farm Cl TW4 ... 129 B1
Old Farm Ct UB2 ... 107 D2
Old Farm Rd
Hampton TW12 ... 173 C4
London N2 ... 30 B2
Old Farm Rd E DA15 ... 168 A2
Old Farm Rd W DA15 .. 167 D2
Oldfield Cl
Bromley BR1 ... 210 B5
Greenford UB6 ... 64 C2
Stanmore HA7 ... 25 A5
Oldfield Farm Gdns
UB6 ... 86 B6
Oldfield Gr SE16 ... 118 D2
Oldfield Ho
14 Chiswick W4 ... 111 C1
Streatham SW16 ... 181 B6
Oldfield House Unit
TW12 ... 173 B2
Oldfield La N UB6 ... 64 B1
Oldfield La S UB6 ... 86 A4
Oldfield Mews N6 ... 49 C2
Oldfield Prim Sch UB6 . 86 B5
Oldfield Rd
Bedford Pk W3, W12 ... 111 D4
Bexleyheath DA7 ... 147 A3
Bromley BR1 ... 210 B5
Hampton TW12 ... 173 B2
Stoke Newington N16 ... 73 C5
Willesden NW10 ... 67 D1
Wimbledon SW19 ... 179 A4
Oldfields Cir UB5 ... 64 A2
Oldfields Rd SM1,
SM3 ... 217 C6
Oldfields Trad Est
SM1 ... 217 C5
Old Fire Station The
SE18 ... 144 D5
Old Fish St Hill EC4 ... 252 A6
Old Fleet La EC4 ... 241 C2
Old Fold Cl EN5 ... 1 B4
Old Fold La EN5 ... 1 B4
OLD FORD ... 97 B6
Old Ford Ho CR0 ... 220 A5
Old Ford Prim Sch E3 .. 97 B5
Old Ford Rd E2, E3 ... 96 D5
Old Ford Trad Ctr 13
E3 ... 97 C6
Old Forge Cl HA7 ... 25 A6
Old Forge Cres TW17 .. 192 D3
Old Forge Mews W12 .. 112 B4
Old Forge Rd
Enfield EN1 ... 5 D5
Upper Holloway N19 ... 71 D6
Old Forge Way DA14 ... 190 B6
Old Gloucester St
WC1 ... 94 A2 240 B4
Old Hall Cl HA5 ... 23 A2
Old Hall Dr HA5 ... 23 A2
Oldham Ho 10 SE21 ... 183 C6
Oldham Terr W3 ... 111 A5
Old Hatch Manor HA4 .. 40 A2
Old Hill
Chislehurst BR7 ... 188 C2
Orpington BR6 ... 227 C2
Oldhill St N16 ... 52 A1
Old Homesdale Rd
BR2 ... 209 C5
Old Hospital Cl SW12,
SW17 ... 158 D3
Old Ho The BR7 ... 189 B2
Old House Cl SW19 ... 179 A5
Old House Gdns 9
TW1 ... 153 C5
Old Howlett's La HA4 ... 39 B3
Olding Ho 6 SW12 ... 159 C4
Old Jamaica Bsns Est 23
SE16 ... 118 A3
Old Jamaica Rd SE16 .. 118 A3
Old James St SE15 ... 140 B2
Old Jewry EC2 .. 95 B1 242 C1
Old Kenton La NW9 ... 44 D4
Old Kent Rd
Deptford SE1, SE15 ... 140 B6
Walworth SE1 .. 117 C1 263 B2
Old Kingston Rd KT4 .. 215 A5
Old Laundry The 14
SW18 ... 136 B1
Old Lodge Pl 7 TW1 ... 153 B5
Old Lodge Way HA7 ... 25 A5
Old London Rd KT2 ... 176 A1
Old Maidstone Rd BR8,
DA14 ... 191 B3
OLD MALDEN ... 199 C1
Old Malden La KT4 ... 215 C6
Oldman Ct SE12 ... 165 B2
Old Manor Ct NW8 ... 229 B4
Old Manor Dr TW7 ... 152 A5
Old Manor House Mews
TW17 ... 192 C6
Old Manor Rd UB2 ... 106 D2
Old Manor Way BR7,
SE9 ... 188 B5
Old Manor Yd SW5 ... 255 C3
Old Market Ct SM1 ... 217 D4
Old Market Sq 11 E2 ... 95 D4
Old Marylebone Rd
NW1 ... 92 C2 237 B3
Oldmead Ho 8 RM10 ... 81 D2
Old Mill Ct E18 ... 55 C6
Old Mill Rd SE18 ... 145 B6
Old Mitre Ct EC4 ... 241 B1
Old Montague St E1 ... 96 A2
Old Nichol St
E2 ... 95 D3 243 C6
Old North St WC1 ... 240 C4
Old Nursery Pl TW15 .. 170 D5
OLD OAK COMMON ... 89 D3
Old Oak Common La
NW10 ... 89 C3
Old Oak La NW10 ... 89 D4
Old Oak Prim Sch
W12 ... 89 D1
Old Oak Rd W3 ... 111 D6
Old Orch TW16 ... 172 C1
Old Orchard Cl
Hadley Wood EN4 ... 2 B5
Hillingdon UB8 ... 82 C1
Old Orch The NW3 ... 70 D4
Old Palace La TW9 ... 153 C6
Old Palace Prim Sch
E3 ... 97 D4
Old Palace Rd CR0 ... 221 A5
Old Palace Sch of John
Whitgift CR9 ... 220 D5
Old Palace Terr 8
TW9 ... 153 D6
Old Palace Yd 2
TW9 ... 153 D6
Old Paradise St
SE11 ... 116 B2 260 C4
Old Park Ave
Balham SW12 ... 159 A5
Enfield EN2 ... 5 A1
Old Park Gr EN2 ... 5 A1
Old Park Ho N13 ... 32 B6
Old Park La
W1 ... 115 B5 248 C3
Old Park Mews TW5 ... 129 B5
Old Park Rd
Enfield EN2 ... 4 D2
Palmers Green N13 ... 32 B6
Plumstead Comm SE2 .. 124 A1
Old Park Rd S EN2 ... 4 D1
Old Park Ridings N21 .. 17 A6
Old Park View EN2 ... 4 D2
Old Perry St BR7 ... 189 C3
Old Post Office La
SE3 ... 143 B2
Old Pound Cl TW7 ... 131 A4
Old Priory UB9 ... 38 D2
Old Pye St SW1 ... 259 C6
Old Pye Street Est
SW1 ... 259 C5
Old Quebec St W1 ... 237 D1
Old Queen St
SW1 ... 115 D4 249 D1
Old Rd
Enfield EN3 ... 6 C4
Lewisham SE13 ... 142 C1
Old Rectory Gdns HA8 .. 26 C4
Old Redding HA3 ... 24 A6
Oldridge Rd SW12 ... 159 B4
Old Royal Free Pl N1 .. 234 B5
Old Royal Free Sq
N1 ... 94 C6 234 B5
Old Ruislip Rd UB5 ... 84 C5
Old St Andrews Mans
NW9 ... 67 B6
Old School Cl
3 Beckenham BR3 ... 185 A1
Merton SW19 ... 179 C1
Old School Cres E7 ... 77 A2
Old School Ct 8 N17 ... 51 D6
Old School Ho CR4 ... 202 C6
Old School Ho The EN2 .. 4 D2
Old School Pl CR0 ... 220 C4
Old School Rd UB8 ... 82 B3
Old School Sq
12 Poplar E14 ... 97 C1
Thames Ditton KT7 ... 196 D3
Old School The
Bloomsbury WC1 ... 240 D4
Merton SW19 ... 179 C1
Old Seacoal La EC4 ... 241 C1
Old South Cl HA5 ... 22 D2
Old South Lambeth Rd
SW8 ... 138 A5 270 B4
Old Spitalfields Mkt
E1 ... 95 D2 243 D4
Old Sq WC2 ... 241 A2
Old St
Broadgate
EC1 ... 95 B3 242 D6
Newham E13 ... 99 B5
Old Stable Mews N5 ... 73 A5
Old Station Rd UB3 ... 105 D3
Old Station Yard The 11
E17 ... 54 A5
Oldstead Rd BR1 ... 186 B6
Old Street Sta
EC1 ... 95 B3 242 D6
Old Studio Cl CR0 ... 205 B2
Old Sun Wharf E14 ... 119 A6
Old Swan Wharf
SW11 ... 266 D2
Old Swan Yd SM5 ... 218 D4
Old Theatre Ct SE1 ... 252 B4
Old Town
Clapham SW4 ... 137 C2

Old Town continued
Croydon CR0 220 D5
Old Tramyard SE18 123 C2
Old Twelve Cl W7 86 C3
Old Vicarage Sch
TW10 154 A5
Old Vicarage The
CR4 202 C6
Old Woolwich Rd
SE10 120 B1
Old York Rd SW18 157 D6
Oleander Cl BR6 227 B3
O'Leary Sq E1 96 C2
Oleastor Ct IG5 56 A6
Olga Prim Sch E3 97 A5
Olga St 20 E3 97 A5
Olinda Rd N16 51 D3
Oliphant St W10 91 A4
Olive Blythe Ho 14
W10 91 A3
Oliver Ave SE25 205 D6
Oliver Bsns Pk NW10 89 A5
Oliver Cl W4 132 D6
Oliver Ct
Isleworth TW7 130 D2
2 Penge SE26 184 C4
Plumstead SE18 123 A2
Olive Rd
Cricklewood NW2 68 C4
Ealing W5 109 D3
3 Merton SW19 180 A3
Newham E13 99 C4
Oliver Gdns E6 100 A2
Oliver Goldsmith Prim
Sch
Camberwell SE5 139 D4
Kingsbury NW9 45 B4
Oliver Gr SE25 205 D5
Oliver Ho
22 Bermondsey SE16 118 A4
Notting Hill W11 244 A5
South Lambeth SW8 270 A4
Oliver House Prep Sch
SW4 159 B5
Oliver Mews SE15 140 A3
Oliver Rd
Kingston u T KT3 177 A1
Leyton E10 75 D5
Sutton SM1 218 B4
Walthamstow E17 54 A4
Oliver's Yd EC1 242 D6
Olive Tree Ho
7 Deptford SE15 140 C6
Stroud Green N4 50 C3
Olive Tree Sch The
SE13 163 D5
Olivette St 1 SW15 134 D1
Olive Waite Ho NW6 69 D1
Olivia Ct 1 EN5 1 B1
Ollard's Gr IG10 21 D6
Ollerton Gn E3 97 B6
Ollerton Rd N11 31 D5
Olley Cl SM6 220 A2
Ollgar Cl W12 111 D5
Olliffe St E14 120 A3
Olmar St SE1 140 A6
Olney Ho NW8 237 B6
Olney Rd SE17 139 A6
Olron Cres DA6 169 A6
Olven Rd SE18 145 A6
Olveston Wlk SM5 202 B3
Olwen Mews HA5 22 D1
Olyffe Ave DA16 146 A3
Olyffe Dr BR3 186 A2
Olympia Ex Ctr*
W14 113 A3 254 B5
Olympia Ind Est N22 50 B6
Olympian Ct 8 E14 119 C2
Olympia Way
W14 113 A3 254 B5
Olympia Yd W2 245 D5
Olympic Ho 10 W10 90 C1
Olympic Ret Pk HA9 66 D4
Olympic Way
Greenford UB6 85 D6
Wembley HA9 66 C4
Olympus Gr N22 32 C2
Olympus Sq E5 74 A5
Oman Ave NW2 68 C4
Oman Ct NW10 68 B4
Ombersley Ho N4 51 A2
Omeara St SE1 252 B3
Omega Cl E14 119 D3
Omega Ho SW10 266 B4
Omega Pl N1 233 B3
Omega St SE14 141 C4
Omega Works E3 75 C1
Ommaney Rd SE14 141 A4
Omnibus Bsns Ctr N7 72 A3
Omnibus Way E17 35 C1
Ondine Rd SE15 139 D1
Onedin Point 10 E1 118 A6
Onega Gate SE16 119 A3
O'Neill Ho NW8 229 D3
O'Neill Path 11 SE18 144 C6
One Tree Cl SE23 162 C5
Ongar Cl RM6 58 C4
Ongar Ho 15 N1 73 B2
Ongar Rd SW6 135 C6 265 B6
Onra Rd E17 53 C2
Onslow Ave TW10 154 A6
Onslow Avenue Mans 10
TW10 154 A6
Onslow Cl
Chingford E4 20 B2
Notting Hill W9 91 B4
Thames Ditton KT7 196 C1
Onslow Cres BR7 188 D2
Onslow Ct SW10 256 B1
Onslow Dr DA14 168 D2
Onslow Gdns
Chelsea SW7 114 B1 256 C2
Cranley Gdns N10 49 B4
Southgate N21 16 C6
Thames Ditton KT7 196 C1
Wallington SM6 219 C1
Wanstead E18 55 C6
Onslow Ho 1 KT2 176 B2
Onslow Lo 28 SW2 160 C4
Onslow Mews E SW7 256 C3
Onslow Mews W SW7 256 C3
Onslow Par N14 15 B3
Onslow Rd
Richmond TW10 154 A5
Thornton Heath CR0 204 C1
West Barnes KT3 200 A5
Onslow Sq
SW7 114 B2 256 D3
Onslow St EC1 241 B5
Onslow Way KT7 196 C1
Ontario St
SE1 116 D3 261 D6
Ontario Way E14 119 C6
Onyx Ct N11 31 D3
Onyx Ho KT4 199 B1
Onyx Mews 4 E15 76 D2
Opal Cl E16 99 D1
Opal Ct N11 31 D3
Opal Ho KT4 199 B1
Opal Mews 2 IG1 78 D6
Opal St SE11 116 D1 261 C2
Open Air Theatre,
Regent's Pk* NW1 231 A1
Openshaw Rd SE2 124 B2
Openview SW17,
SW18 158 B2
Opera Ct 7 N19 71 D5
Operating Theatre Mus &
Herb Garret*
SE1 117 B5 252 D3
Ophelia Gdns NW2 69 A5
Ophir Terr SE15 140 A4
Opie Ho NW8 230 B4
Opossum Way TW4 128 C2
Oppenheim Rd SE13 142 A3
Oppidan Apartments
NW6 69 C2
Oppidans Rd NW3 70 D1
Opus Studios E13 99 A5
Orange Gr E11 76 C5
Orange Hill Rd HA8 27 A3
Orange Pl SE16 118 C3
Orangery Gallery The*
W8 113 B4 244 C1
Orangery La SE9 166 B6
Orangery The TW10 153 C2
Orange St
WC2 115 D6 249 D5
Orange Yd WC2 239 D1
Oransay Rd 25 N1 73 A2
Oratory La SW3 256 D2
Oratory RC Prim Sch
SW3 114 C1 257 A2
Oratory The*
SW7 114 C3 257 A5
Orbain Rd
SW6 135 A5 264 B3
Orbel St SW11 136 C4 267 A1
Orb St SE17 117 B2 262 C3
Orchard Ave
Ashford TW15 171 A4
Carshalton CR4 203 A1
Croydon CR0 207 A1
East Finchley N3 47 C6
Erith DA17 147 B6
Hatton TW14 149 B6
Heston TW5 129 A5
Orchard Ave continued
Hinchley Wood KT7 213 A6
Kingston u T KT3 199 C6
Osidge N14 15 C4
Southall UB1 107 B5
Whetstone N20 14 B2
Orchard Bsns Ctr
SE26 185 B5
Orchard Cl
Ashford TW15 171 A4
Bexleyheath DA7 147 A4
Bushey WD23 8 B3
Chingford E4 35 C6
Dollis Hill NW2 68 A5
Edgware HA8 26 A4
Honor Oak SE23 162 C5
Islington N1 73 A1
Kensal Town W10 91 A2
Northolt UB5 64 A2
Ruislip HA4 39 A2
Thames Ditton KT7 197 B2
Walton-on-T KT12 194 B2
Wanstead E11 55 B5
Wembley HA0 88 A6
West Barnes SW20 200 C5
West Ewell KT19 214 D2
Orchard Cotts
Chislehurst BR7 189 C4
Hayes UB3 105 C4
Orchard Cres
Edgware HA8 27 A5
Enfield EN1 5 D4
Orchard Ct
Barnes SW13 133 D2
Barnet EN5 1 D2
Croydon BR3 207 C1
Edgware HA8 26 B5
Hounslow TW7 130 B5
Marylebone W1 238 A2
New Malden KT4 200 A1
Penge SE26 184 D5
Southgate N14 15 C5
Wallington SM6 219 B3
Walthamstow E10 53 D1
1 Walton-on-T KT12 193 D1
Wood Green N22 32 A3
Orchard Dr
Blackheath Vale SE3 142 C3
Edgware HA8 26 B5
Upper Halliford TW17 193 C6
Orchard Gate
Colindale NW9 45 C5
Thames Ditton KT10 196 B1
Wembley UB6 65 B2
Orchard Gdns
Chessington KT9 214 A4
Sutton SM1 217 C3
Orchard Gn
Bromley BR1 187 C2
Orpington BR6 227 C6
Orchard Gr
BR6 227 D6
Croydon CR0 207 A2
Edgware HA8 26 D2
Harrow HA3 44 B4
Orpington BR6 211 D1
Penge SE20 184 A3
Orchard Hill SE13 141 D4
Orchard Hill Coll
SM6 219 B2
Orchard Ho
Camberwell SE5 139 A4
11 Rotherhithe SE16 118 C3
Shepherd's Bush W12 112 A5
Orchard Inf Sch The
KT8 196 B5
Orchard Jun & Inf Sch
The TW3 151 C6
Orchard La
Thames Ditton KT8 196 B3
Wimbledon SW20 178 B2
Woodford IG8 37 C6
Orchardleigh Ave EN3 6 C3
Orchard Lo N12 14 A1
Orchard Mead Ho
NW11 69 C6
Orchardmede N21 17 B5
Orchard Mews N1 73 B1
Orchard Pl
Canning Town E14 120 C6
Tottenham N17 33 D3
Orchard Prim Sch E9 74 C1
Orchard Rd
Barnet EN5 1 B1
Belvedere DA17 125 C2
Brentford TW8 131 C6
Bromley BR1 187 C2
Carshalton CR4 203 A1
Chessington KT9 214 A4
Dagenham RM10 103 C6
Orchard Rd continued
Enfield EN3 18 C6
Farnborough BR6 226 D3
Feltham TW14 150 A3
Hampton TW12 173 B3
Hayes UB3 106 A6
Highgate N6 49 B2
Hounslow TW4 151 C6
Isleworth TW1 153 B6
Kingston u T KT1 176 A1
Richmond TW9 132 C2
Sidcup DA14 189 C6
Sunbury TW16 172 B3
Sutton SM1 217 C4
Welling DA16 146 B2
Orchard Rise
Croydon CR0 207 B1
Kingston u T KT2 177 A2
Mortlake TW10 132 D1
Pinner HA5 39 D6
Orchard Rise E DA15 167 D6
Orchard Rise W DA15 167 C6
Orchard Sch DA14 190 B5
Orchard School Sports Ctr
SE20 184 A2
Orchardson Ho NW8 236 D5
Orchardson St
NW8 92 B3 236 D5
Orchard Sq W14 254 C1
Orchard St
Marylebone W1 238 B2
Walthamstow E17 53 A5
Orchard Terr EN1 18 A5
Orchard The
Acton Green W4 111 B2
Ealing W5 87 D2
East Barnet N14 15 B6
Edgware HA8 26 C5
Enfield N21 17 B5
Ewell KT17 215 D1
Hampstead Garden Suburb
NW11 47 C4
Hounslow TW3 130 A3
Lewisham SE3 142 B3
Totteridge N20 13 D3
Orchard Villas BR7 189 C4
Orchard Way
Ashford TW15 148 B2
Croydon BR3, CR0 207 A3
Enfield EN1 5 C2
Esher KT10 212 A2
Sutton SM1 218 B4
Orchard Way Prim Sch
CR0 207 A2
Orchestra Ct HA8 26 D3
Orchid Cl
Chessington KT9 213 C1
1 Newham E6 100 A2
Southall UB1 85 A1
Orchid Ct
Catford BR1 164 B1
Harrow HA3 24 C2
Wembley HA9 66 A6
Orchid Gdns TW3 129 B1
Orchid Grange N14 15 C4
Orchid Lo N14 15 C4
Orchid Rd N14 15 C4
Orchid St W12 112 A6
Orde 6 NW9 27 D2
Orde Hall St
WC1 94 B2 240 C4
Orde Ho 10 N16 73 B4
Ordell Ct 36 E3 97 B5
Ordell Rd E3 97 B5
Ordnance Cl TW13 150 A2
Ordnance Cres SE10 120 C4
Ordnance Hill
NW8 92 B6 229 D5
Ordnance Mews NW8 229 D4
Ordnance Rd
Canning Town E16 98 D2
Enfield EN3 7 B6
Shooters Hill SE18 144 C6
Oregano Cl UB7 104 B6
Oregano Dr E14 98 B1
Oregon Ave E12 78 B4
Oregon Bldg 5 SE13 141 D4
Oregon Cl KT3 199 A5
Oregon Sq BR6 211 B1
Orestes Ct 9 E18 55 A6
Orestes Mews 1 NW6 69 C3
Orford Ct
Stanmore HA7 25 C4
Wallington SM6 219 C3
West Norwood SE27 160 D2
Orford Gdns TW1 152 D2
Orford Rd
Catford SE6 163 D1
Walthamstow E17 53 D4
Wanstead E18 55 B6
Organ Crossroads
KT17 216 A1
Oriana Ct CR0 221 B1
Oriana Ho 3 E14 119 B6
Oriel Cl CR4 203 D6
Oriel Ct
6 Croydon CR0 205 B1
Hampstead NW3 70 A4
Oriel Dr SW13 134 C6
Oriel Gdns IG5 56 B6
Oriel Jun & Inf Sch
TW13 151 A1
Oriel Rd
Hackney E9 75 A2
Homerton E9 74 D2
Oriel Way UB5 63 D1
Oriental City NW9 45 B6
Oriental Rd E16 121 D5
Orient Ind Pk E10 75 C6
Orient St
SE11 116 D2 261 C4
Orient Way
Lea Bridge E5 74 D5
Leyton E10 75 B6
Oriole Way SE28 124 B6
Orion Bsns Ctr SE14 118 D1
Orion Ct 10 HA8 26 D5
Orion Ctr The CR0 220 A6
Orion Ho 20 E1 96 B3
Orion Mews SM4 201 C5
Orion Point 5 E14 119 C2
Orion Prim Sch The
NW9 27 D2
Orion Rd N11 31 A4
Orion Way HA6 22 A6
Orissa Rd SE18 123 C1
Orkney Ho N1 233 C6
Orkney St SW11 137 A3
Orlando Rd SW4 137 C2
Orleans Cl KT10 212 B6
Orleans Ct 9 TW1 153 B4
Orleans House Gallery*
TW1 153 B3
Orleans Inf Sch TW1 153 B4
Orleans Park Sch
TW1 153 B4
Orleans Rd
South Norwood SE19 183 B4
Twickenham TW1 153 C4
Orleston Mews N7 72 C2
Orleston Rd N7 72 C2
Orley Farm Rd HA1 64 C5
Orley Farm Sch HA1 64 B5
Orlop St SE10 120 C1
Ormanton Rd SE26 184 A6
Orme Ct W2 113 D6 245 C5
Orme Ct Mews W2 245 D5
Orme Ho 8 E8 95 D6
Orme La W2 113 D6 245 C5
Ormeley Rd SW12 159 B3
Orme Rd
Kingston u T KT1,
KT3 176 D1
Sutton SM1 217 D2
Ormerod Gdns CR4 181 A2
Ormerod Ho 3 SW9 138 A2
Ormesby Cl SE28 124 D6
Ormesby Way HA3 44 B4
Orme Sq W2 245 C5
Ormiston Gr W12 112 B5
Ormiston Rd SE10 121 A1
Ormond Ave
Hampton TW12 173 D2
23 Richmond TW10 153 D6
Ormond Cl WC1 240 B4
Ormond Cres TW12 173 D2
Ormond Dr TW12 173 D3
Ormonde Ave BR6 227 A6
Ormonde Ct
Hendon NW4 46 D6
Putney SW15 134 C1
Ormonde Gate
SW3 114 D1 257 D1
Ormonde Mans WC1 240 B4
Ormonde Pl SW1 258 B3
Ormonde Rd SW14 133 A2
Ormonde Rise IG9 21 C3
Ormonde Terr
NW8 92 D6 230 C5
Ormond Ho 7 N16 73 B6
Ormond Mans WC1 240 C5
Ormond Mews WC1 240 B5
Ormond Rd
Finsbury Pk N4, N19 50 A1
Richmond TW10 153 D6
Ormond Yd SW1 249 B4
Ormrod Ct W11 91 B1
Ormsby SM2 217 D1
Ormsby Gdns UB6 86 A5
Ormsby Lo 7 W4 111 C3
Ormsby Pl N16 73 D5
Ormsby Point 6
SE18 122 D2
Ormsby St E2 95 D5
Ormside St SE15 140 C6
Ormskirk Rd WD19 22 D5
Ornan Rd NW3 70 C3
Orpen Ho SW5 255 B3
Orpen Wlk N16 73 C5
Orpheus Ho 25 N19 49 D2
Orpheus St SE5 139 B4
ORPINGTON 227 D6
Orpington Gdns N18 17 C1
Orpington Hospl BR6 227 D4
Orpington Mans N21 16 C3
Orpington Rd
Southgate N21 16 D3
St Paul's Cray BR7 211 C6
Orpington Sta BR6 227 C6
Orpwood Cl TW12 173 B4
Orsett Mews
W2 92 A1 236 A2
Orsett St SE11 116 B1 260 D2
Orsett Terr
Bayswater
W2 92 A1 236 A2
Woodford IG8 37 C3
Orsman Rd N1 95 C6
Orton Gr EN1 6 A4
Orton St E1 118 A5
Orville Rd SW11 136 B3
Orwell Cl UB3 105 C6
Orwell Ct
Hackney E8 96 A6
Highbury N5 73 A4
Northolt UB5 85 A6
Orwell Ho W12 112 A6
Orwell Lo 2 E18 55 A5
Orwell Rd E13 99 C6
Osbaldeston Rd N16 52 A1
Osberton Rd SE12 165 A6
Osbert St SW1 259 C3
Osborn Cl E8 96 A6
Osborne Ave TW19 148 B3
Osborne Cl
Beckenham BR3 207 A5
Cockfosters EN4 2 D2
Feltham TW13 172 D5
Osborne Ct
Ealing W5 88 A2
10 Surbiton KT6 198 A3
17 Walthamstow E10 53 D2
Osborne Gdns CR7 183 A1
Osborne Gr E17 53 B5
Osborne Mews E17 53 B5
Osborne Pl SM1 218 B3
Osborne Rd
Buckhurst Hill IG9 21 B3
Dagenham RM9 81 B3
Enfield EN3 7 A3
Erith DA17 147 B6
Finsbury Pk N4 50 C1
Forest Gate E7 77 B3
Hackney E9 75 B2
Hounslow TW3, TW4 129 B2
Kingston u T KT2 176 A3
Leyton E10 75 D6
Palmers Green N13 16 C1
South Acton W3 110 D4
Southall UB1 86 A1
South Norwood CR7 183 A1
Walton-on-T KT12 194 A1
Willesden NW2 68 B2
Osborne Sq RM9 81 B4
Osborne Terr 1
SW17 181 A5
Osborne Way KT9 214 B3
Osborn Gdns NW7 28 D3
Osborn La SE23 163 A4
Osborn St E1 95 D2 243 D4
Osborn Terr SE3 142 D1
Osbourne Ct HA2 41 D5
Osbourne Ho
Richmond TW10 154 C6
Twickenham TW2 152 A2
Oscar Faber Pl 8 N1 73 C1
Oscar St SE8 141 C3
Oseney Cres NW5 71 D2
Osgood Ave BR6 227 D3
Osgood Gdns 1 BR6 227 D3
OSIDGE 15 B2
Osidge Ct N14 15 B3
Osidge La N14 15 B3
Osidge Prim Sch N14 15 C3
Osier Cres N10 30 D2
Osier Ct E1 96 D3
Osier La SE10 120 D3
Osier Mews W4 133 D6
Osiers Ct 3 KT1 175 D2
Osiers Rd SW18 135 C1

Osier St E1 96 C3
Osier Way
Leyton E10 75 D5
Mitcham CR4 202 D4
Oslac Rd SE6 185 D5
Oslo Ct
Mitcham SW19 180 B3
St John's Wood NW8 230 A3
Oslo Ho 2 SE5 139 A3
Oslo Sq SE16 119 A3
Osman Cl N15 51 B3
Osmani Prim Sch E1 96 A2
Osman Rd
Edmonton N9 18 A1
Hammersmith W6 112 C3
Osmington Ho SW8 270 D3
Osmond Cl HA2 64 A6
Osmond Gdns SM6 219 C3
Osmund St W12 89 D2
Osnaburgh St
NW1 93 B3 238 D6
Osnaburgh Terr NW1 238 D6
Osney Ho 4 SE2 124 D4
Osney Wlk SM5 202 B3
Osprey 7 NW9 27 D2
Osprey Cl
Cheam SM1 217 B3
Higham Hill E17 35 A3
Keston Mark BR2 210 A1
Newham E6 100 A2
Wanstead E11 55 A5
West Drayton UB7 104 A4
Osprey Ct
7 Ealing W7 86 D3
Hampstead NW3 69 D3
Thornton Heath SW16 182 B1
Osprey Ho
Camberwell SE15 139 D4
Isleworth TW7 131 B2
3 Limehouse E14 119 A6
Walthamstow E4 35 B4
Osprey Mews EN3 18 B6
Ospringe Cl 6 SE20 184 C3
Ospringe Ct SE9 167 B5
Ospringe Ho SE1 251 B3
Ospringe Rd NW5 71 C4
Osram Ct W6 112 C3
Osram Rd HA9 65 D5
Osric Path 8 N1 95 C5
Ossian Mews N4 50 B2
Ossian Rd N4 50 B2
Ossie Garvin Rdbt
UB4 106 C6
Ossington Bldgs W1 238 A3
Ossington Cl W2 245 B5
Ossington St
W2 113 D6 245 C5
Ossory Rd SE1 140 A6
Ossulston St
NW1 93 D5 232 D4
Ossultan Pl N2 48 A6
Ossulton Way N2 48 A5
Ostade Rd SW2 160 B4
Ostell Cres EN3 7 C5
Osten Mews
SW7 113 D3 255 D5
OSTERLEY 130 B5
Osterley Ave TW7 130 B5
Osterley Cl BR5 190 A2
Osterley Cres TW7 130 D4
Osterley Ct
Hounslow TW7 130 B4
7 Northolt UB5 84 C4
Osterley Gdns
Southall UB2 108 A4
South Norwood CR7 183 A1
Osterley Ho 5 E14 97 D1
Osterley La
Isleworth TW7 108 C1
Southall UB2, TW7 107 D1
Osterley Lo 1 TW7 130 C4
Osterley Park* TW7 108 B1
Osterley Park Rd UB2 107 B3
Osterley Park View Rd
W7 108 C4
Osterley Rd
Hounslow TW7 130 C4
Stoke Newington N16 73 C4
Osterley Sta TW7 130 B5
Osterley Views UB2 108 B4
Osterly Lodge UB2 107 B3
Oster Terr E17 52 D4
Ostlers Dr TW15 171 A5
Ostliffe Rd N13 33 A5
Oswald Bldg SW8 268 C5
Oswald Rd UB1 107 A5
Oswald's Mead E9 75 A4
Oswald St E5 74 D5
Oswald Terr NW2 68 C5
Osward Pl N9 18 B2
Osward Rd SW12,
SW17 158 D2
Oswell Ho 9 E1 118 B5
Oswin St SE11 116 D2 261 D4
Oswyth Rd SE5 139 C3
Otford Cl
Bexley DA5 169 D5
Bromley BR1 210 C6
Penge SE20 184 C2
Otford Cres SE4 163 B5
Otford Ho
Bermondsey SE1 252 D1
6 Deptford SE15 140 C6
Otha Ho 13 SW9 138 A3
Othello Cl SE11 261 C2
Otho Ct 5 TW8 131 D5
Otis St E3 98 A4
Otley App IG2 56 D3
Otley Ct N11 31 A4
Otley Dr IG2 56 D3
Otley Ho N5 72 D5
Otley Rd E16 99 C1
Otley Terr E5 74 D5
Ottawa Ho 4 HA4 40 C1
Ottaway Ct E5 74 A5
Ottaway St E5 74 A5
Otterbourne Rd
Chingford E4 20 B1
1 Croydon CR0 221 A6
Otterburn Gdns TW7 131 A5
Otterburn Ho 12 SE5 139 A5
Otterburn St SW17 180 D4
Otter Cl E15 98 A6
Otterden Cl BR6 227 C4
Otterden St SE6 185 C6
Otterfield Rd UB7 104 A6
Otter Rd UB6 86 A3
Ottershaw Ho BR5 190 B2
Otto Cl SE26 162 B1
Ottoman Ct W5 109 D2
Otto St SE17 138 D6
Otway Ct N4 50 B3
Otway Gdns WD23 8 C4
Oulton Cl
Erith SE28 102 C1
Upper Clapton E5 74 C6
Oulton Cres IG11 79 D3
Oulton Rd N15 51 B4
Oulton Way WD19 23 B6
Oundle Ave WD23 8 A5
Our Lady Immaculate RC
Prim Sch KT6 198 D1
Our Lady of Dolours RC
Prim Sch W2 91 D2
Our Lady of Grace RC Inf
Sch NW2 68 C6
Our Lady of Grace RC Jun
Sch NW2 68 B5
Our Lady of Grace RC
Prim Sch SE7 143 B6
Our Lady of Lourdes RC
Prim Sch
Finchley N12 30 A2
Friern Barnet N11 31 C5
Lewisham SE13 142 B2
Our Lady of Lourdes RC
Sch NW10 89 A6
Our Lady of Lourds RC
Prim Sch E11 55 A3
Our Lady of Muswell Prim
Sch N10 49 A6
Our Lady of Muswell RC
Prim Sch N10 31 A1
Our Lady of the Rosary RC
Prim Sch DA15 167 C5
Our Lady of the Visitation
RC Prim Sch UB6 86 A3
Our Lady of Victories RC
Prim Sch
Putney SW15 134 D1
South Kensington
SW7 114 A2 256 B3
Our Lady Queen of
Heaven RC Sch
SW19 156 D4
Our Lady RC Prim Sch
Camden Town
NW1 93 C6 232 B6
Poplar E14 97 B1
Our Lady & St John's RC
Jun & Inf Sch TW8 109 C1
Our Lady & St Joseph RC
Prim Sch N1 73 C2
Our Lady & St Philip Neri
RC Prim Sch SE26 185 A6
Our Lady's Convent RC
High Sch N15 51 C2
Ouseley Rd SW12 158 D3
Outer Circ
NW8 92 D5 230 D3
Outgate Rd NW10 67 D1
Outram Pl N1 94 A6 233 B6
Outram Rd
Croydon CR0 221 D6
Muswell Hill N22 31 D2
Newham E6 100 A6
Outwich St EC3 243 B2
Outwood Ct CR2 221 A1
Outwood Ho 3 SW2 160 B4
Oval Ct
Burnt Oak HA8 27 A3
8 Teddington TW11 174 D5
Oval Mans SE11 270 D6
Oval Pl SW8 138 B5 270 D4
Oval Prim Sch CR0 205 C1
Oval Rd
Camden Town
NW1 93 B6 231 C6
Croydon CR0 205 C1
Oval Rd N RM10 103 D6
Oval Rd S RM10 103 D5
Oval Sta SE11 138 C6
Oval The
Hackney E2 96 B5
Sidcup DA15 168 A4
Oval The (Surrey Cnty
Crkt Gd) SE11 138 C6
Oval Way
SE11 116 B1 260 D1
Overbrae BR3 185 C5
Overbrook Wlk HA8 26 C3
Overbury 1 BR3 208 A6
Overbury Ave BR3 208 A6
Overbury Ho 3 E5 74 D4
Overbury Rd N4, N15 51 B3
Overbury St E5 74 D4
Overcliff Rd SE13 141 C2
Overcourt Cl DA15 168 B5
Overdale Ave KT3 177 B1
Overdale Rd W5 109 C3
Overdown Rd SE6 185 D6
Overhill Rd SE21,
SE22 162 A4
Overhill Way BR3 208 B4
Overlea Rd E5 52 A2
Overmead DA15 167 B4
Oversley Ho 17 W2 91 C2
Overstand Cl BR3 207 C4
Overstone Gdns CR0 207 B2
Overstone Ho 19 E14 97 C1
Overstone Rd W6 112 C2
Overstrand Mans
SW11 268 A1
Overton Cl
Hounslow TW7 130 D4
Tokyngton NW10 67 A2
Overton Ct E11 55 A2
Overton Dr
Ilford RM6 58 C2
Wanstead E11 55 B2
Overton Grange Sch
SM2 217 D1
Overton Ho SW15 155 D4
Overton Rd
Abbey Wood SE2 124 D3
Belmont SM2 217 C1
Brixton SW9 138 C3
Southgate N14 16 A6
Walthamstow E10 53 A1
Overton's Yd CR0 221 A5
Overy Ho SE1 251 C1
Ovesdon Ave HA2 41 B1
Ovett Cl SE19 183 C4
Ovex Cl E14 120 A4
Ovington Ct SW3 257 B5
Ovington Gdns SW3 257 B5
Ovington Mews SW3 257 B5
Ovington Sq
SW3 114 C3 257 B5
Ovington St
SW3 114 C2 257 B4
Owen Cl
Hayes UB4 84 B4
Northolt UB5 63 A2
Thamesmead SE28 124 C5
Thornton Heath CR0 205 B3
Owen Ct UB4 84 B4
Owen Ho
Feltham TW14 150 A4
11 Tufnell Pk N19 71 C4
5 Twickenham TW1 153 B4
Owenite St SE2 124 B2
Owen Rd
Edmonton N13 33 A5
Hayes UB4 84 B4
Owen's Ct EC1 234 C2
Owens Mews 10 E11 76 C6
Owen's Row EC1 234 C2
Owen St EC1 234 C3
Owens Way SE23 163 A4
Owen Way NW10 67 A3
Owen Wlk 7 SE20 184 A3
Owgan Cl SE5 139 B5
Oxberry Ave SW6 135 A3
Oxbridge Ct 4 W4 110 D1
Oxendon St SW1,
W1 115 D6 249 C5
Oxenford St SE15 139 D2
Oxenham Ho 13 SE8 141 C6
Oxenholme NW1 232 B3
Oxenpark Ave HA9 44 A2
Oxestalls Rd SE8 119 A1
Oxford Ave
Harlington TW6 127 D5
Hounslow TW5 107 C1
Merton SW20 179 A1
Southgate N14 15 C3
Oxford & Cambridge Mans
NW1 237 B3
Oxford Cir W1 93 C1 239 A1
Oxford Circus Ave
W1 239 A1
Oxford Circus Sta
W1 93 C1 239 A1
Oxford Cl
Edmonton N9 18 B2
Littleton TW15, TW17 171 A3
Mitcham CR4 203 C6
Oxford Cres KT3 199 B3
Oxford Ct
16 Acton W3 88 C1
City of London EC4 252 C6
8 Ealing W7 86 D2
Gunnersbury W4 110 D1
17 Kingston u T KT6 198 A4
48 Paddington W2 91 C2
Sidcup DA14 189 D6
Oxford Dr
Bermondsey SE1 253 A3
Ruislip HA4 62 C6
Oxford Gardens Prim Sch
W10 90 D1
Oxford Gate W6 112 D2
Oxford Gdns
Brentford W4 132 C6
Edmonton N21 17 A4
North Kensington W10 90 D1
Oakleigh Pk N20 14 B3
Oxford Ho N4 50 C1
Oxford Mews DA5 169 C4
Oxford Rd
Carshalton SM5 218 C3
Ealing W5 109 D6
Edmonton N9 18 B2
Enfield EN3 18 B6
Finsbury Pk N4 50 C1
Harrow HA1 42 A3
Ilford IG1 79 A3
Paddington NW6 91 C5
Putney SW15 135 A1
Sidcup DA14 190 B5
South Norwood SE19 183 B4
Stratford E15 76 B2
Teddington TW11,
TW12 174 B5
Wallington SM6 219 C3
Wealdstone HA3 42 D6
Woodford IG8 37 D5
Oxford Rd N W4 110 D1
Oxford Rd S W4 110 D1
Oxford Sq W2 92 C1 237 B1
Oxford St W1 93 B1 238 D1
Oxford Way TW13 172 D6
Oxford Wlk UB1 107 B5
Oxgate Ct NW2 68 A6
Oxgate Ct Par NW2 68 A6
Oxgate Ctr NW2 68 B6
Oxgate Gdns NW2 68 B6
Oxgate La NW2 68 B6
Oxhawth Cres BR2 210 D3
Oxhey Dr WD19 22 B6
Oxhey Dr S HA6 22 B5
Oxhey La HA5 23 C5
Oxhey Ridge Cl HA6 22 B5
Oxhey Wood Prim Sch
WD19 22 C6
Oxleas E6 100 D1
Oxleas Cl DA16 145 B3
Oxleay Rd HA2 41 C1
Oxleigh Cl KT3 199 C4
Oxley Cl SE1 118 A1
Oxleys Rd NW2 68 B5
Oxlip Cl 2 CR0 206 D1
Oxlow La RM10 81 C4
Oxonian St SE22 139 D1
Oxo Tower Wharf SE1 251 B5
Oxo Twr* SE1 251 B5
Oxted Cl CR4 202 B6
Oxted Ct N16 51 C1
Oxtoby Way SW16 181 D2
OYH Prim Sch NW4 46 D5
Oyster Catchers Cl
E16 99 B1
Oyster Catcher Terr
IG5 56 C6
Oyster Row E1 96 C1
Ozolins Way E16 99 A1

P

Pablo Neruda Cl 4
SE24 138 D1
Pace Pl E1 96 B1
Pacific Cl TW14 149 D3
Pacific Ho 15 E1 96 D3
Pacific Hts BR3 185 C3
Pacific Rd E16 99 A1
Pacific Wharf IG11 78 D1
Pacific Wharf SE16 118 D5
Packenham Ho
24 Crouch End N19 49 D2
21 Spitalfields E2 95 D4
Packham Ct KT4 216 C5
Packington Sq
N1 95 A6 235 A6
Packington St
N1 94 D6 234 D5
Packmores Rd SE9 167 B6
Padbury SE17 263 B1
Padbury Cl TW14 149 B3
Padbury Ct E2 95 D4
Padbury Ho NW8 237 B6
Padden Ct NW7 28 D3
Paddenswick Ct 2
W6 112 B3
Paddenswick Rd W6 112 A3
PADDINGTON 92 A2
Paddington Acad
Paddington
W2 92 B2 236 C3
Paddington W9 91 C3
Paddington Cl UB4 84 D3
Paddington Com Hospl
W9 91 C2
Paddington Ct
10 Ealing W7 86 D2
7 Wembley HA0 66 A2
Paddington Gn
W2 92 B2 236 C4
Paddington Green Prim
Sch NW8 92 B3 236 C5
Paddington St W1 238 A4
Paddington Sta
W2 92 B1 236 C2
Paddock Cl
Forest Hill SE26 184 D6
Kidbrooke SE3 143 A3
New Malden KT4 199 C1
Northolt UB5 85 C5
Orpington BR6 226 D4
Paddock Ct SW20 200 C5
Paddock Gdns SE19 183 C4
Paddock Lo 13 EN1 17 C6
Paddock Rd
Bexley DA6 147 A1
Dollis Hill NW2 68 A6
Ruislip HA4 62 D5
Paddock Sch SW15 133 D1
Paddocks Cl HA2 63 D4
Paddocks Gn NW9 44 D1
Paddocks The
Addington CR0 223 C2
Cockfosters EN4 2 D2
Preston HA9 66 D6
Paddock The
Muswell Hill N10 49 B6
Uxbridge UB10 60 D4
Paddock Way
Chislehurst BR7 189 B3
11 Putney SW15 156 C4
Padfield Ct HA9 66 B5
Padfield Rd SE5 139 A2
Padley Cl KT9 214 B3
Padnall Ct RM6 58 D6
Padnall Rd RM6 58 D5
Padstone Ho 50 E3 97 D4
Padstow Cl BR6 227 D4
Padstow Ho 12 E14 119 B6
Padstow Rd EN2 4 D4
Padstow Wlk TW14 149 D3
Padua Rd SE20 184 C2
Pagden St SW8 268 D2
Pageant Ave NW9 27 C2
Pageant Cres SE16 119 B5
Pageantmaster Ct
EC4 241 C1
Pageant Wlk CR0 221 C5
Page Cl
Dagenham RM9 81 A3
Page Cl *continued*
Hampton TW12 173 A4
Harrow HA3 44 B3
Page Cres CR0 220 D3
Page Ct NW7 28 A3
Page Green Rd N15 52 A4
Page Green Terr N15 51 D4
Page Heath La BR1 209 D6
Page Heath Villas
BR1 209 D6
Page High N22 50 C6
Page Ho SE10 142 A6
Pagehurst Rd CR0 206 B2
Page Mdw NW7 28 A3
Page Rd TW14 149 B5
Page's Ct N10 31 A1
Page's Hill N10 31 A1
Page's La N10 31 A1
Page St
Hendon NW7 28 A3
Westminster
SW1 115 D2 259 D4
Page's Wlk
SE1 117 C3 263 B5
Page's Yd W4 133 C6
Paget Ave SM1 218 B5
Paget Cl TW12 174 B6
Paget Ct UB7 104 A4
Paget Gdns BR7 188 D2
Paget Ho 15 E2 96 C5
Paget La TW7 130 C2
Paget Pl
Kingston u T KT2 177 A4
Thames Ditton KT7 196 D1
Paget Rd
Hillingdon UB10 83 A3
Ilford IG1 78 D4
Stoke Newington N16 51 B1
Paget Rise SE18 144 C5
Paget St EC1 234 C2
Paget Terr SE18 144 D6
Pagham Ho 8 W10 90 C3
Pagin Ho N15 51 C4
Pagitts Gr EN4 1 D4
Pagnell St SE14 141 B5
Pagoda Ave TW9 132 B2
Pagoda Gdns SE3 142 B3
Pagoda Gr SE27 161 A2
Paignton Rd
Ruislip HA4 62 A5
Tottenham N15 51 C3
Paine Ct SE3 142 D6
Paines Cl HA5 41 A6
Paine's La HA5 23 A1
Pain's Cl CR4 181 B1
Painsthorpe Rd 3
N16 73 C5
Painswick Ct 1 SE15 139 D5
Painters Mews SE16 118 A2
Painters Rd IG2, RM6 58 A6
Paisley Rd
Carshalton SM5 202 B1
Tottenham N22 32 D2
Paisley Terr SM5 202 B2
Pakeman Ho SE1 251 D2
Pakeman Prim Sch N7 72 B5
Pakeman St N7 72 B5
Pakenham Cl SW12 159 A3
Pakenham St
WC1 94 B3 240 D6
Pakington Ho 22
SW9 138 A3
Palace Ave
W8 113 D4 245 D2
Palace Court Gdns
N10 49 C6
Palace Ct
Bromley BR1 187 B2
Eltham SE9 166 B5
Hampstead NW3 69 D3
Harrow HA3 44 A3
Kensington
W2 113 D6 245 C5
South Norwood CR7 205 B5
Streatham SW2 160 C2
Palace Garden Mews
W8 245 B4
Palace Gate
Hampton KT8 196 C6
Knightsbridge
W8 114 A4 246 A1
Palace Gate Mews 4
N8 50 A5
Palace Gates Rd N22 31 D2
Palace Gdns IG9 21 D3
Palace Gdns Mews
W8 113 D5 245 D3

Palace Gdns Sh Ctr EN2 ... 5 B1
Palace Gn
Kensington W8 ... 113 D5 245 C3
New Addington CR0 ... 223 B1
Palace Gr
Bromley BR1 ... 187 B2
Penge SE19 ... 183 D3
Palace Mans W14 ... 254 B4
Palace Mews
Belgravia SW1 ... 258 B3
Fulham SW6 ... 264 D4
Walthamstow E17 ... 53 B5
Palace of Ind HA9 ... 66 C4
Palace Par E17 ... 53 C5
Palace Pl SW1 ... 259 A6
Palace Rd
Bromley BR1 ... 187 B2
East Molesey KT8 ... 196 B6
Hornsey N8 ... 49 D4
Kingston u T KT1 ... 197 D5
Penge SE19 ... 183 D3
Ruislip HA4 ... 63 A4
Streatham SE27, SW16, SW2 ... 160 C2
Wood Green N11 ... 32 A3
Palace Sq SE19 ... 183 D3
Palace St SW1 ... 115 C3 259 A6
Palace View
Bromley BR1 ... 209 B6
Croydon CR0 ... 223 B4
Grove Pk SE12 ... 165 A2
Palace View Rd E4 ... 35 D5
Palamos Rd E10 ... 53 C1
Palatine Ave N16 ... 73 C4
Palatine Rd N16 ... 73 C4
Palazzo Apartments 11 N1 ... 73 C1
Palemead Cl SW6 ... 134 D4
Palermo Rd NW10 ... 90 A5
Palestine Gr SW19 ... 180 B2
Palewell Cl BR5 ... 190 B1
Palewell Common Dr SW14 ... 155 B6
Palewell Pk SW14 ... 133 B1
Palfrey Pl SW8 ... 138 B5 270 D4
Palgrave Ave UB1 ... 107 C6
Palgrave Gdns NW1 ... 92 C3 237 B6
Palgrave Ho
7 Camberwell SE5 ... 139 A5
4 Maitland Pk NW3 ... 70 D3
Twickenham TW2 ... 152 A4
Palgrave Rd W12 ... 111 D3
Palissy St 35 E2 ... 95 D4
Palladino Ho 6 SW17 ... 180 C5
Pallant Ho SE1 ... 262 D5
Pallant Way BR6 ... 226 C5
Pallester Ct NW11 ... 47 A1
Pallet Way SE18 ... 144 A4
Palliser Ct W14 ... 254 A1
Palliser Ho
3 Greenwich SE10 ... 142 B6
21 Stepney E1 ... 96 D3
Palliser Rd W14 ... 113 A1 254 A1
Pallister Terr SW15 ... 155 D2
Pall Mall SW1 ... 115 D5 249 C3
Pall Mall E SW1 ... 115 D5 249 D4
Pall Mall Pl SW1 ... 249 B3
Palmar Cres DA7 ... 147 C3
Palmar Rd DA7 ... 147 C3
Palm Ave DA14 ... 190 D4
Palm Cl E10 ... 75 D5
Palm Ct
Beckenham BR3 ... 207 B6
18 Camberwell SE15 ... 139 D5
Stoke Newington N16 ... 73 B6
Wood Green N22 ... 32 B3
Palmeira Rd DA7 ... 146 D2
Palmer Ave KT4, SM3 ... 216 C4
Palmer Cl
Heston TW5 ... 129 C4
Northolt UB5 ... 63 A2
West Wickham BR4 ... 224 B6
Palmer Cres KT1 ... 198 A6
Palmer Gdns EN5 ... 12 D6
Palmer Ho
6 Deptford SE14 ... 140 D5
8 Kentish Town NW5 ... 71 C4
5 Tufnell Pk N19 ... 71 C5
Palmer Pl N7 ... 72 C3
Palmer Rd
Dagenham RM8 ... 58 D1
Newham E13 ... 99 B3
Palmer's Ct 11 N11 ... 31 C5
Palmers Gr KT8 ... 195 C5
PALMERS GREEN ... 16 A1
Palmers Green High Sch N21 ... 16 C2
Palmers Green Sta N13 ... 32 B6
Palmers La EN3 ... 6 C4
Palmers Rd
Globe Town E2 ... 96 D5
Mortlake SW14 ... 133 A2
Thornton Heath SW16 ... 182 B1
Palmer's Rd N11 ... 31 C5
Palmer St SW1 ... 259 C6
Palmerston Cres
Bowes Pk N13 ... 32 B5
Woolwich SE18 ... 145 A6
Palmerston Ct
2 Buckhurst Hill IG9 ... 21 C2
22 Globe Town E3 ... 96 D5
9 Surbiton KT6 ... 197 D2
7 Sutton SM1 ... 218 A3
Walthamstow E17 ... 53 B5
Palmerston Ctr HA3 ... 42 D6
Palmerston Gr 11 SW19 ... 179 C3
Palmerston Ho
Battersea SW11 ... 268 B1
Kensington W8 ... 245 A3
Palmerston Rd
Acton Green W3 ... 111 A3
Bowes Pk N22 ... 32 B4
Brondesbury NW6 ... 69 B1
Buckhurst Hill IG9 ... 21 C3
Farnborough BR6 ... 227 A3
Hampstead NW6 ... 69 C1
Harrow HA3 ... 42 D6
Hounslow TW3 ... 130 A4
Merton SW19 ... 179 C3
Mortlake SW14 ... 133 A1
Sutton SM1 ... 218 A3
Thornton Heath CR0 ... 205 B4
Twickenham TW2 ... 152 C5
Upton E7 ... 77 B2
Wallington SM5 ... 219 A4
Walthamstow E17 ... 53 B5
Palmerston Way SW8 ... 268 D3
Palm Gr W5 ... 110 A3
Palm Tree Ct 5 N17 ... 33 D1
Palm Tree Ho 2 SE14 ... 140 D5
Pamela Ct
Finchley N12 ... 29 D4
Willesden NW10 ... 68 A1
Pamela Gdns HA5 ... 40 B4
Pamela Ho 14 E8 ... 95 D6
Pamir Ct 10 SM2 ... 217 D2
Pamlion Ct N4 ... 50 A2
Pams Way KT19 ... 215 B3
Panama Ho 6 E1 ... 96 D2
Panbro Ho SE18 ... 144 B4
Pancras La EC2 ... 242 C1
Pancras Rd NW1 ... 93 D5 232 D4
Pandian Way 4 NW5 ... 71 D2
Pandora Ct 4 KT6 ... 198 A3
Pandora Rd NW6 ... 69 C2
Panfield Mews IG2 ... 56 C3
Panfield Rd SE2 ... 124 A3
Pangbourne NW1 ... 232 A1
Pangbourne Ave W10 ... 90 C2
Pangbourne Ct
Oakleigh Pk N20 ... 14 A4
Upper Tooting SW17 ... 180 A6
Pangbourne Dr HA7 ... 26 A5
Pangbourne Ho 4 N7 ... 72 A3
Panhard Pl UB1 ... 107 D6
Pank Ave EN5 ... 14 A6
Pankhurst Ave 8 E16 ... 121 B5
Pankhurst Cl
7 Deptford SE14 ... 140 D5
Isleworth TW7 ... 130 D2
Pankhurst Ho
2 Kensington NW10 ... 90 C1
Streatham SW16 ... 181 D5
Pankhurst Rd KT12 ... 194 C2
Panmuir Rd SW20 ... 178 B2
Panmure Cl N5 ... 72 D4
Panmure Ct 11 UB1 ... 86 A1
Panmure Rd SE26 ... 162 B1
Panorama Ct N6 ... 49 C3
Pansy Gdns W12 ... 112 A6
Panther Dr NW10 ... 67 B3
Pantiles Cl N13 ... 32 D5
Pantiles The
Bickley BR1 ... 210 A6
Pantiles The *continued*
Bushey WD23 ... 8 B3
Erith DA7 ... 147 B5
Temple Fortune NW11 ... 47 B4
Panton Cl CR0 ... 204 D1
Panton St SW1 ... 249 C5
Panyer Alley EC2 ... 242 A2
Papermill Cl SM5 ... 219 A4
Paper Mill Wharf E14 ... 119 A6
Papillons Wlk SE3 ... 143 A2
Papworth Gdns N7 ... 72 B3
Papworth Way SW2 ... 160 C4
Parade Mans
19 Camberwell SE5 ... 139 A3
2 Hendon NW4 ... 46 B4
Parade Mews SE27, SW2 ... 160 D2
Parade The
Ashford TW16 ... 171 D3
Battersea SW11 ... 136 D5 267 D4
Claygate KT10 ... 212 C2
Ilford IG2 ... 57 B3
Thornton Heath CR0 ... 204 A3
Thornton Heath CR7 ... 204 C6
Waddon CR0 ... 220 B3
Wembley UB6 ... 65 B3
Paradise Pas N7 ... 72 C3
Paradise Pl 15 SE7 ... 122 A2
Paradise Rd
Richmond TW10 ... 154 A6
South Lambeth SW4 ... 138 A3
Paradise Row E2 ... 96 B4
Paradise St SE16 ... 118 B4
Paradise Wlk SW3 ... 136 D6 267 D6
Paragon N8 ... 50 A5
Paragon Cl E16 ... 99 A1
Paragon Ct NW4 ... 29 A2
Paragon Gr KT5 ... 198 B3
Paragon Ho SE3 ... 142 D3
Paragon Mews SE1 ... 262 D4
Paragon Pl
Blackheath Vale SE3 ... 142 D3
Surbiton KT5 ... 198 B3
Paragon Rd E9 ... 74 C2
Paragon The
Kidbrooke SE3 ... 143 A3
Walworth SE17 ... 262 D4
Paramount Bldg EC1 ... 241 C6
Paramount Ct WC1 ... 239 B5
Paramount Ho 10 E11 ... 76 C5
Parbury Rd SE23 ... 163 A5
Parbury Rise KT9 ... 214 A2
Parchmore Rd CR7 ... 205 A6
Parchmore Way CR7 ... 182 D1
Pardes House Gram N3 ... 29 B1
Pardes House Prim N3 ... 29 B1
Pardoner St SE1 ... 117 B3 262 D6
Pardon St EC1 ... 241 D6
Parfett St E1 ... 96 A1
Parfew Ct 2 SE22 ... 162 B2
Parfitt Cl NW11 ... 48 A1
Parfrey St W6 ... 134 C6
Pargraves Ct HA9 ... 66 C6
Parham Dr IG2 ... 56 D4
Paris Gdn SE1 ... 116 D5 251 C4
Parish CE Prim Sch BR1 ... 187 A3
Parish Church CE Inf Sch CR0 ... 220 D5
Parish Church CE Jun Sch CR0 ... 220 D5
Parish Ct KT6 ... 198 A3
Parish Gate Dr DA15 ... 167 C5
Parish La SE20 ... 184 D3
Paris Ho 12 E2 ... 96 B5
Parish Wharf 6 SE7 ... 122 A2
Park App DA16 ... 146 B1
Park Ave
Barking IG11 ... 79 A2
Bromley BR6 ... 226 C6
Edmonton N18 ... 34 A6
Enfield EN1 ... 17 C5
Finchley N3 ... 29 D2
Golders Green NW11 ... 47 D1
Ilford IG1 ... 56 C1
Mitcham CR4 ... 181 B3
Mortlake SW14 ... 133 B1
Palmers Green N13 ... 16 C1
Plaistow BR1 ... 187 A4
Ruislip HA4 ... 39 C3
Southall UB1 ... 107 C5
Stratford E15 ... 76 C2
Twickenham TW3 ... 151 D5
Upper Halliford TW17 ... 193 C6
Park Ave *continued*
Wallend E6 ... 100 C5
Wallington SM5 ... 219 A2
West Wickham BR4 ... 224 A6
Willesden NW2 ... 68 C2
Woodford IG8 ... 37 B5
Wood Green N22 ... 32 B2
Park Ave E KT17 ... 216 A2
Park Ave N
Dudden Hill NW10 ... 68 B3
Hornsey N8 ... 49 D5
Park Avenue Mews CR4 ... 181 B3
Park Avenue Rd N17 ... 34 B3
Park Ave S N8 ... 49 D5
Park Ave W KT17 ... 216 A2
Park Chase HA9 ... 66 B4
Park Cl
Dollis Hill NW2 ... 68 B5
Ealing NW10 ... 88 B4
Hampton TW12 ... 174 A2
Harrow HA3 ... 24 C2
Isleworth TW3, TW7 ... 152 A6
Kensington W14 ... 113 B3 254 D6
Kingston u T KT2 ... 176 C2
Knightsbridge SW1 ... 247 C1
North Finchley N12 ... 30 B6
13 South Hackney E9 ... 96 C6
Wallington SM5 ... 218 D2
Park Cotts 10 TW1 ... 153 B5
Park Cres
Enfield EN2 ... 5 B1
Finchley N3 ... 30 A3
Harrow HA3 ... 24 C2
Regent's Pk W1 ... 93 B3 238 C5
Twickenham TW2 ... 152 B3
Park Crescent Mews E W1 ... 238 D5
Park Crescent Mews W W1 ... 238 C5
Park Croft HA8 ... 27 A2
Parkcroft Rd SE12 ... 164 D4
Park Ct
Battersea SW11 ... 268 C2
2 Beckenham BR3 ... 207 D6
2 Chingford E4 ... 20 A2
Clapham Pk SW4 ... 159 D6
Dulwich SE21 ... 161 B1
12 Hammersmith W6 ... 112 A2
New Barnet EN5 ... 14 B4
New Malden KT3 ... 199 B5
North Finchley N12 ... 30 B5
Teddington KT1 ... 175 C2
Twickenham TW4 ... 151 D6
Upper Tooting SW12 ... 159 A3
Wallington SM6 ... 220 A3
Walthamstow E17 ... 53 D4
Wembley HA9 ... 66 A3
Wood Green N11 ... 31 D3
Parkdale N11 ... 31 D4
Parkdale Cres KT4 ... 215 B5
Parkdale Rd SE18 ... 123 C1
Park Dr
Acton W3 ... 110 C3
Enfield N21 ... 17 A5
Golders Green NW11 ... 47 D1
Harrow HA2 ... 41 C2
Mortlake SW14 ... 133 B1
Stanmore HA3 ... 24 C4
Woolwich SE7 ... 144 A6
Park Dwellings 7 NW3 ... 70 D3
Park End
Bromley BR1 ... 186 D2
Hampstead NW3 ... 70 C4
Parker Cl
Newham E16 ... 122 A5
Wallington SM5 ... 218 D2
Parker Ct
Shoreditch N1 ... 235 B6
South Lambeth SW4 ... 270 A1
Wimbledon SW19 ... 179 A3
Parke Rd
Barnes SW13 ... 134 A4
Sunbury TW16 ... 194 A5
Parker Ho 4 SE18 ... 122 D1
Parker Mews WC2 ... 240 B2
Parker Rd CR0 ... 221 A4
Parkers Rd N10 ... 30 C2
Parkers Row 15 SE16 ... 118 A4
Parker's Row SE1 ... 253 D1
Parker St
Newham E16 ... 122 A5
St Giles WC2 ... 94 A1 240 B2
Park Farm Cl
East Finchley N2 ... 48 A6
Pinner HA5 ... 40 B4
Park Farm Ct UB3 ... 105 C6
Park Farm Rd
Bromley BR1 ... 187 D2
Kingston u T KT2 ... 176 A3
Parkfield 3 TW7 ... 130 C4
Parkfield Ave
Feltham TW13 ... 150 A1
Harrow HA2 ... 24 A1
Hillingdon UB10 ... 82 D4
Mortlake SW14 ... 133 C1
Northolt UB5 ... 84 D5
Parkfield Cl
Edgware HA8 ... 26 D4
Northolt UB5 ... 85 A5
Parkfield Cres
Feltham TW13 ... 150 A1
Harrow HA2 ... 24 A1
Ruislip HA4 ... 63 A5
Parkfield Ct SE14 ... 141 B4
Parkfield Dr UB5 ... 84 D5
Parkfield Gdns HA2 ... 41 D6
Parkfield Ho HA2 ... 23 D2
Parkfield Ind Est SW11 ... 137 A3
Parkfield Par TW13 ... 150 A1
Parkfield Prim Sch NW4 ... 46 B2
Parkfield Rd
Feltham TW13 ... 150 A1
Harrow HA2 ... 64 A5
New Cross SE14 ... 141 B4
Northolt UB5 ... 85 A5
Uxbridge UB10 ... 60 D6
Willesden NW10 ... 68 B1
Parkfields
Croydon CR0 ... 207 B1
Putney SW15 ... 134 C1
Parkfields Ave
Welsh Harp NW9 ... 45 B1
Wimbledon SW20 ... 178 B1
Parkfields Cl SM5 ... 219 A4
Parkfields Rd KT2 ... 176 B5
Parkfield St N1 ... 94 C5 234 B4
Parkfield Way BR2 ... 210 B4
Park Flats N6 ... 48 C2
Parkgate SE3 ... 142 D2
Park Gate
Ealing W5 ... 87 D2
East Finchley N2 ... 48 B6
Southgate N21 ... 16 B4
Parkgate Ave EN4 ... 2 A4
Parkgate Cl KT2 ... 176 D4
Parkgate Cres EN4 ... 2 A4
Park Gate Ct TW12 ... 174 A5
Parkgate Gdns SW14 ... 155 B6
Parkgate House Sch SW11 ... 137 A1
Parkgate Mews N6 ... 49 C2
Parkgate Rd
Battersea SW11 ... 136 C5 267 B3
Wallington SM5, SM6 ... 219 B3
Park Gates HA2 ... 63 C4
Park Gdns
Kingston u T KT2 ... 176 B5
Queensbury NW9 ... 44 D6
Park Gr
Bromley BR1 ... 187 B2
Edgware HA8 ... 26 B5
Newham E15 ... 99 A6
Wood Green N11 ... 31 D3
Park Grove Rd E11 ... 76 C6
Park Hall SE10 ... 142 B5
Park Hall Rd
Dulwich SE21 ... 161 B1
East Finchley N2 ... 48 C5
Park Hall Road Trad Est SE21 ... 161 B1
Parkham Ct BR2 ... 186 C1
Parkham St SW11 ... 136 C4 267 A1
Parkham Way N10 ... 31 C1
Park Heights Ct 21 E14 ... 97 B1
Park High Sch HA7 ... 25 D1
Park Hill
Bromley BR1 ... 210 B5
Clapham Pk SW4 ... 159 D6
Ealing W5 ... 87 D2
Forest Hill SE23 ... 162 C3
Loughton IG10 ... 21 D6
Richmond TW10 ... 154 B5
Wallington SM5 ... 218 D2
Park Hill Cl SM5 ... 218 C3
Park Hill Ct
Croydon CR0 ... 221 C6
Ealing W5 ... 87 D2
Upper Tooting SW17 ... 158 D1
Parkhill Ho 1 SW16 ... 182 C5
Parkhill Inf Sch IG5 ... 56 C6
Park Hill Inf Sch CR0 ... 221 C5
Parkhill Jun Sch IG5 ... 56 C6
Park Hill Jun Sch CR0 ... 221 C5
Parkhill Rd
Chingford E4 ... 20 A4
Maitland Pk NW3 ... 70 D3
Old Bexley DA5 ... 169 B4
Sidcup DA15 ... 167 C1
Park Hill Rd
Beckenham BR2 ... 186 C1
South Croydon CR0 ... 221 C5
Wallington SM6 ... 219 B1
Park Hill Rise CR0 ... 221 D5
Park Hill Sch KT2 ... 176 C3
Park Hill Wlk 10 NW3 ... 70 D3
Park Ho
8 Camberwell SE5 ... 139 B4
Finsbury Pk N4 ... 72 D6
Forest Hill SE26 ... 184 A5
35 Hackney E9 ... 74 C1
Richmond TW10 ... 154 A5
Sidcup DA14 ... 190 A5
Southgate N21 ... 16 B4
Parkholme Rd E8 ... 74 A2
Park House Gdns TW1 ... 153 C6
Parkhouse St SE5 ... 139 B5
Park Hts NW4 ... 46 B6
Parkhurst Ct N7 ... 72 A4
Parkhurst Gdns 2 DA5 ... 169 C4
Parkhurst Rd
Bowes Pk N22 ... 32 B4
Friern Barnet N11 ... 31 A5
Little Ilford E12 ... 78 C4
Lower Holloway N7 ... 72 A4
Sidcup DA5 ... 169 C4
Sutton SM1 ... 218 B4
Tottenham N17 ... 34 A1
Walthamstow E17 ... 53 A5
Parkin Ho SE20 ... 184 D3
Parkinson Ct
Finsbury N1 ... 235 C1
Shoreditch EC1 ... 235 D2
Parkinson Ho 6 E9 ... 74 C1
Park La
Cheam SM3 ... 217 A2
Cranford TW5 ... 128 A5
Dagenham RM6 ... 58 D3
Edmonton N9 ... 17 D1
Harrow HA2 ... 63 D5
Hayes UB4 ... 83 C3
Mayfair W1 ... 115 A6 248 A5
Mill Meads E15 ... 98 B6
Richmond TW9 ... 131 D1
South Croydon CR0 ... 221 B5
Stanmore HA7 ... 9 A1
Teddington TW11 ... 174 D4
Tottenham N17 ... 34 A3
Wallington SM5, SM6 ... 219 A3
Wembley HA9 ... 66 A4
Parkland Ct
Kensington W14 ... 244 A2
Stratford E15 ... 76 C3
Parkland Gdns 12 SW19 ... 156 D3
Parkland Gr
Ashford TW15 ... 170 C6
Hounslow TW7 ... 130 D4
Parkland Mead BR1 ... 210 D6
Parkland Rd
Ashford TW15 ... 170 C6
Woodford IG8 ... 37 B3
Wood Green N22 ... 32 B1
Parklands
Bushey WD23 ... 8 A5
East Dulwich SE22 ... 162 B6
Highgate N6 ... 49 B2
Kingston u T KT5 ... 198 B4
5 Whetstone N20 ... 14 A2
Parklands Cl
Hadley Wood EN4 ... 2 B5
Ilford IG2 ... 57 A2
Mortlake SW14 ... 155 A6
Parklands Ct TW5 ... 128 D3
Parklands Dr N3 ... 47 A6
Parklands Par TW5 ... 128 D3
Parklands Pl HA8 ... 26 B6
Parklands Rd SW16 ... 181 B5
Parklands Way KT4 ... 215 C6
Park Lane Cl N17 ... 34 A3
Park Lane Mans CR0 ... 221 B5
Park Lane Prim Sch HA9 ... 66 A4
PARK LANGLEY ... 208 B4
Park Lawn CR7 ... 183 A1
Parklea Cl NW9 ... 27 C2
Park Lea Ct N16 ... 51 C2
Parkleigh Ct SW19 ... 179 D1
Parkleigh Rd SW19 ... 179 D1

Parkleys KT2, TW10 175 D6
Park Lo
[3] Ealing W5 87 B3
North Finchley N12 30 A5
[11] South Hampstead NW8 70 B1
[10] Wapping E1 118 B5
Willesden NW2 68 C4
Park Lofts [9] SW4 160 A6
Park Lorne NW8 230 B1
Park Mans
Battersea SW11 267 C1
Bedford Pk W6 111 D3
Forest Hill SE26 162 C1
Fulham SW6 264 B1
[5] Hendon NW4 46 B4
Knightsbridge SW1 247 C1
St John's Wood NW8 230 A3
Vauxhall SW8 270 B6
Parkmead SW15 156 B5
Park Mead
Blackfen DA15 168 B5
Harrow HA2 63 D5
Parkmead Gdns NW7 27 D4
Park Mews
Chislehurst BR7 188 D4
Greenwich SE10 120 D1
Kensal Rise W10 91 A5
Stanwell TW19 148 B4
Parkmore BR7 188 D3
Parkmore Cl IG8 37 A6
Park Nook Gdns EN2 5 B6
Park Par
Acton W3 110 C3
Dagenham NW10 89 D5
Hayes UB3 83 C1
Kingsbury NW9 45 B6
Park Pl
Canary Wharf E14 119 C5
Ealing W5 109 D5
Gunnersbury W3 110 C2
Hampton TW12 174 A4
Shoreditch N1 235 D6
St James SW1 115 C5 249 A4
Wembley HA9 66 B4
Park Place Dr W3 110 C3
Park Place Ho [8] SE10 142 B6
Park Place Villas W2 236 B4
Park Prim Sch E15 76 D1
Park Rd
Ashford TW15 170 D5
Beckenham BR3 185 C3
Bromley BR1 187 B2
Cheam SM3 217 A2
Chipping Barnet EN5 1 B1
Chislehurst BR7 188 D4
Chiswick W4 133 B6
Cockfosters EN4 2 C1
Dagenham NW10 89 C6
Ealing W7 108 D6
East Finchley N2 48 B6
East Molesey KT8 196 A5
Edmonton N18 34 A6
Feltham TW13 172 D6
Hackbridge SM6 219 B6
Hampton TW12 174 A5
Hampton Wick KT1 175 C2
Harringay N8, N15 50 D5
Hayes UB4 83 C2
Hendon NW4 46 B3
Hornsey N8 49 D4
Hounslow TW3, TW7 152 A6
Ilford IG1 79 B5
Isleworth TW7 131 B3
Kingsbury NW9 45 B2
Kingston u T KT2, TW10 176 C3
Leyton E10 53 C1
Lisson Gr NW1, NW8 92 C3 237 B6
Lower Halliford TW17 192 C1
Mitcham SW19 180 C4
Newham E15 99 A6
New Malden KT3 199 B5
Osidge N14 15 D4
Richmond TW10 154 B5
South Norwood SE25 205 C5
Sunbury TW16 172 B3
Teddington TW11 174 D4
Twickenham TW1 153 C5
Upton Pk E6 99 C6
Uxbridge UB8 60 A2
Wallington SM6 219 B3
Walthamstow E17 53 B4
Wanstead E12 77 B6
Wembley HA0 66 A2
Wood Green N11 31 D3
Park Rd E
Acton W3 111 A4
Park Rd E *continued*
Uxbridge UB10 82 A5
Park Rd N
Chiswick W4 111 B1
South Acton W3 110 D4
Park Ridings N8 50 C6
Park Rise
Forest Hill SE23 163 A3
Harrow HA3 24 C2
Park Rise Rd SE23 163 A3
Park Road E [11] W3 110 D4
Park Road Ho [3] KT2 176 C3
Park Row SE10 142 B6
PARK ROYAL 88 D4
Park Royal NW10 88 D6
Park Royal Bsns Ctr NW10 89 A3
Park Royal Metro Ctr NW10 88 D3
Park Royal Rd NW10, W3 89 A3
Park Royal Sta W5 88 C3
Park S SW11 268 A1
Park St James NW8 230 C5
Park Sch IG1 56 D1
Park Sheen [3] SW14 132 D1
Parkshot TW9 132 A1
Parkside
[1] Beckenham BR3 185 D1
Cheam SM3 217 A2
Ealing W5 110 A6
East Acton W3 111 C5
Finchley N3 29 D3
Greenwich SE3 142 D5
Hampton TW12 174 A5
Hayes UB3 105 C6
Hendon NW7 28 A4
Sidcup DA14 168 B2
Wimbledon SW19 178 D6
Park Side
Chigwell IG9 21 B2
Dollis Hill NW2 68 B4
Parkside Ave
Bromley BR1 210 A5
Wimbledon SW19 178 D5
Parkside Bsns Est SE8 141 A6
Parkside Cl SE20 184 C3
Parkside Cres
Highbury N7 72 C5
Tolworth KT5 199 A3
Parkside Ct
Bowes Pk N22 32 B4
[2] Wanstead E11 55 A3
Parkside Dr HA8 10 C1
Parkside Est E9 96 D6
Parkside Gdns
East Barnet EN4 15 A4
Wimbledon SW19 178 D6
Parkside Lo DA17 125 D1
Parkside Prep Sch N17 33 C2
Parkside (private) Hospl SW19 156 D1
Parkside Rd
Belvedere DA17 125 D2
Hounslow TW3 151 D6
Parkside St SW11 268 A1
Parkside Terr N18 33 B6
Parkside Way HA2 42 A5
Park Sq E NW1 93 B3 238 D6
Park Square Mews NW1 238 C5
Park Sq W NW1 93 B3 238 C5
Park St
Borough The SE1 117 A5 252 B4
Croydon CR0 221 A6
Mayfair W1 115 A6 248 A5
Teddington TW11 174 C4
Parkstead Rd SW15 156 B6
Parkstone Ave N18 33 D5
Parkstone Rd
[5] Peckham SE15 140 A3
Walthamstow E17 54 A6
Park Stps W2 247 B6
Park Terr
Carshalton SM5 218 C5
Enfield EN3 7 A5
New Malden KT4 200 A1
Park The
Ealing W5 109 D5
Forest Hill SE23 162 C3
Golders Green NW11 47 D1
Highgate N6 49 A3
Sidcup DA14 190 A5
Wallington SM5 218 D3
Parkthorne Cl HA2 41 D3
Parkthorne Dr HA2 41 D3
Parkthorne Rd SW12 159 D4
Park Twrs W1 248 C3
Parkview UB6 87 A4
Park View
Dagenham W3 89 A2
Highbury N5 73 A4
Kingston u T KT3 199 D6
Morden SM4 202 B4
Pinner HA5 23 B2
Southgate N21 16 B4
Wembley HA9 66 D3
Willesden NW2 68 C4
Yiewsley UB7 104 A6
Park View Acad N15 51 A5
Park View Cres N11 31 B6
Parkview Ct
Fulham SW6 135 A3
Harrow HA3 24 C3
Ilford IG2 57 C3
Penge SE20 184 B2
Twickenham TW1 153 C4
Park View Ct
Colney Hatch N12 30 C6
Kingsbury NW9 45 A5
Wandsworth SW18 157 C5
Park View Dr CR4 180 B1
Park View Gdns
Hendon NW4 46 D4
Redbridge IG4 56 B5
Wood Green N22 32 C2
Park View Ho
Chingford E4 35 C5
Hampton TW12 174 A5
Streatham SE24 160 D5
Parkview Lo BR3 207 D6
Park View Mans N4 50 D2
Park View Mews [24] SW9 138 B3
Parkview Rd
Chislehurst SE9 166 D2
Croydon CR0 206 A1
Park View Rd
Bexley DA16 146 C2
Ealing W5 88 A2
Finchley N3 29 D2
Hillingdon UB8 82 C1
Pinner HA5 22 B3
Southall UB1 107 C5
Tottenham N17 34 A1
Willesden NW10 67 D4
Park Village E NW1 93 B5 231 D3
Park Village W NW1 93 B5 231 C4
Park Villas RM6 58 D3
Parkville Rd SW6 135 B5 264 C3
Park Vista SE10 142 B6
Park Vista Apartments E13 98 D4
Park Walk Prim Sch SW10 136 B6 266 C5
Parkway
Abbey Wood DA18 125 A3
Camden Town NW1 93 B6 231 C5
Hillingdon UB10 60 D1
Ilford IG3 79 D5
Palmers Green N14 16 A2
West Barnes SW20 200 D5
Woodford IG8 37 C5
Park Way
East Molesey KT8 195 D6
Edgware HA8 26 D2
Enfield EN2 4 C3
Feltham TW14 150 B4
Friern Barnet N20 30 D6
Gunnersbury W3 110 C2
Ruislip HA4 40 A1
Temple Fortune NW11 47 A4
Park Way Ct HA4 39 D1
Parkway Ho SW14 133 B1
Parkway Prim Sch DA18 125 A3
Parkway The
Cranford TW5 128 B5
Hayes UB2, UB3, UB4, TW5 106 B3
Yeading UB4 84 D2
Parkway Trad Est TW5 128 C6
Park West W2 92 C1 237 B1
Park West Pl W1, W2 92 C1 237 B2
Park Wlk
Chelsea SW10 136 B6 266 C6
Highgate N6 49 A2
Parkwood
Beckenham BR3 185 C3
Parkwood *continued*
Primrose Hill NW8 230 C5
Parkwood Ave KT10 196 A1
Parkwood Gr TW16 194 A6
Parkwood Mews N6 49 B3
Parkwood Prim Sch N4 72 D6
Parkwood Rd
Hounslow TW7 130 D4
Old Bexley DA5 169 B4
Wimbledon SW19 179 B5
Parliament Ct NW3 70 C4
Parliament Hill NW3 70 C4
Parliament Hill Mans NW5 71 A4
Parliament Hill Sch NW5 71 A4
Parliament Mews SW14 133 A3
Parliament Sq* SW1 116 A4 250 A1
Parliament St SW1 116 A4 250 A2
Parliament View Apartments SE11 260 C4
Parma Cres SW11 136 D1
Parminter Ind Est [24] E2 96 B5
Parmiter St E2 96 B5
Parmoor Ct EC1 242 A6
Parnall Ho [11] SE19 183 C6
Parnell Cl
Edgware HA8 27 A6
Hammersmith W12 112 B3
Parnell Ho WC1 239 D2
Parnell Rd E3 97 B6
Parnham Cl BR1 210 D6
Parnham St E14 97 A1
Parolles Rd N19 49 C1
Paroma Rd DA17 125 C3
Parr Cl N9 34 B6
Parr Ct
Feltham TW13 172 C6
Shoreditch N1 235 C4
Parrington Ho [1] SW4 159 D5
Parr Pl W4 111 D2
Parr Rd
Newham E6 99 D6
Stanmore HA7 26 A2
Parr's Pl TW12 173 C3
Parr St N1 95 B5 235 C4
Parry Ave E6 100 B1
Parry Cl KT17 216 A1
Parry Ho [32] E1 118 B5
Parry Pl SE18 122 D2
Parry Rd
South Norwood SE25 205 C6
West Kilburn W10 91 A4
Parry St SW8 138 A6 270 B6
Parsifal Coll NW3 69 C4
Parsifal Ho NW3 69 C4
Parsifal Rd NW6 69 C3
Parsley Gdns CR0 206 D1
Parsloes Ave RM9 81 A3
Parsloes Prim Sch RM9 81 B2
Parsonage Cl UB3 83 D1
Parsonage Ct WD6 11 A6
Parsonage Gdns EN2 5 A3
Parsonage La
Enfield EN2 5 B3
Sidcup DA14 191 B6
Parsonage Manorway DA17 147 C6
Parsonage St E14 120 A2
Parsons Cl SM1 217 D5
Parsons Cres HA8 10 C1
Parsons Gn SW6 135 C4 265 A1
PARSONS GREEN 135 C4
Parsons Green La SW6 135 C4 265 A2
Parsons Green Sta SW6 135 C4 265 A1
Parsons Hill SE18 122 C3
Parsons Ho
Paddington W2 236 C5
[21] Streatham SW12 160 A4
Parsons Lo NW6 69 D1
Parsons Mead KT8 196 A6
Parson's Mead CR0 204 D1
Parsons Rd
Edgware HA8 10 C1
Newham E13 99 C5
Parson St NW4 46 C6
Parthenia Rd SW6 135 C4 265 B1
Partingdale La NW7 28 D5
Partington Cl N19 49 D1
Parton Lo [14] E8 73 D2
Partridge Cl
Barnet EN5 12 C5
Bushey WD23 8 A3
[1] Newham E16 99 D2
Stanmore HA7 26 A6
Partridge Ct EC1 241 C6
Partridge Dr BR6 227 A5
Partridge Gn SE9 166 C1
Partridge Ho [22] E3 97 B5
Partridge Rd
[8] Hampton TW12 173 C4
Sidcup DA14 189 C6
Partridge Sq [3] E6 100 A2
Partridge Way N22 32 A2
Pasadena Cl UB3 106 B4
Pascall Ho SE17 139 A6
Pascal St SW8 137 D5 269 D4
Pascoe Rd SE13 164 B6
Pasley Cl SE17 262 A1
Pasquier Rd E17 53 A6
Passey Pl SE9 166 B5
Passfield Dr E14 97 D2
Passfield Ho SE18 123 B2
Passfield Path [13] SE28 124 B6
Passfields
Catford SE6 164 A1
West Kensington W14 254 C1
Passing Alley EC1 241 D5
Passingham Ho TW5 129 C6
Passmore Edwards Ho N11 31 D3
Passmore Gdns N11 31 D4
Passmore Ho [12] N9 18 A1
Passmore St SW1 115 A1 258 A2
Pasters Ct EN1 17 D5
Pasteur Cl NW9 27 C1
Pasteur Gdns N18 33 A5
Paston Cl SM6 219 C5
Paston Cres SE12 165 B4
Pastor Ct N6 49 C3
Pastor St SE1, SE11 116 D2 261 D4
Pasture Cl
Bushey WD23 8 A4
Wembley HA0 65 B5
Pasture Rd
Catford SE6 164 D3
Dagenham RM9 81 B3
Wembley HA0 65 B5
Pastures Mead UB10 60 C2
Pastures The N20 13 B3
Patcham Terr SW8 268 D2
Patch Cl UB10 82 B6
Patching Way UB4 85 A2
Pat Drew Ho BR1 187 C2
Patent Ho E14 97 D2
Paternoster La EC4 94 D1 241 D2
Paternoster Row EC2, EC4 95 A1 242 A1
Paternoster Sq EC4 94 D1 241 D2
Pater St W8 113 C3 255 A5
Pates Manor Dr TW14 149 B4
Pathfield Rd SW16 181 D4
Path The SW19 179 D2
Pathway Ho SW17 180 D4
Pathway Lo CR4 180 D2
Patience Rd SW11 136 C3
Patience Villas SE13 142 B2
Patio Cl SW4 159 D5
Patmore Ho [9] N16 73 C3
Patmore St SW8 137 C4 269 B2
Patmos Rd SW9 138 D4
Paton Cl E3 97 C4
Paton Ho [3] SW9 138 B3
Paton St EC1 235 A1
Patricia Ct
Chislehurst BR7 189 B2
Woolwich DA16 146 B5
Patrick Coman Ho EC1 234 C1
Patrick Connolly Gdns [41] E3 97 D4
Patrick Rd E13 99 C4
Patriot Sq E2 96 B5
Patrol Pl SE6 163 D5
Pat Shaw Ho [2] E1 96 D3
Patshull Pl NW5 71 C2
Patshull Rd NW5 71 C2
Patson Cl E5 74 D5
Pattenden Rd SE6 163 B3
Patten Ho N4 51 A1
Patten Rd SW18 158 C4
Patterdale NW1 231 D1
Patterdale Cl BR1 186 C4
Patterdale Rd SE15 140 C5
Patterson Ct SE19 183 D4
Patterson Rd SE19 183 D4
Pattina Wlk SE16 119 A5
Pattinson Point [10] E16 99 A2
Pattison Ho
Borough The SE1 252 B2
[1] Stepney E1 96 D1
Pattison Rd NW2 69 C5
Pattison Wlk SE18 123 A1
Pat Williams Ho SE27 161 A1
Paul Byrne Ho [3] N2 48 A6
Paul Cl E15 76 C1
Paul Ct
[7] Edmonton N18 34 A6
Hendon N3 29 A1
Paul Daisley Ct [2] NW6 69 A1
Paulet Rd SE5 138 D4
Paul Gdns CR0 221 D6
Paulhan Rd HA3 43 D5
Paul Ho [13] W10 91 A3
Paulin Dr N21 16 C4
Pauline Cres TW2 152 A3
Pauline Ho [21] E1 96 A2
Paulinus Cl BR5 190 C1
Paul Julius Cl E14 120 B6
Paul Robeson Cl E6 100 C4
Paulson Ho [7] IG11 78 D1
Paul St
Broadgate EC2 95 C3 243 A6
Newham E15 98 C6
Paultons Ho SW3 266 D6
Paultons Sq SW3 136 B6 266 D6
Paultons St SW3 136 B6 266 D5
Pauntley Ho [6] N19 49 C1
Pauntley St [4] N19 49 C1
Pavan Ct [29] E2 96 C4
Paved Ct [9] TW9 153 D6
Paveley Ct NW7 28 D3
Paveley Dr SW11 136 C5 267 A3
Paveley Ho N1 233 C3
Paveley St NW8 92 C3 237 B6
Pavement Mews [1] RM6 58 D2
Pavement Sq CR0 206 A1
Pavement The
Brentford W5 110 A3
Clapham SW4 137 C1
Leytonstone E11 54 A1
[11] West Norwood SE27 183 A6
Pavet Cl RM10 81 D2
Pavilion Ct
Dagenham RM9 103 A6
[7] Hampstead NW3 70 A4
Hampstead NW3 70 B3
[3] Paddington NW6 91 C4
[5] South Norwood SW16 182 B3
[3] Wimbledon SW19 179 A3
Pavilion L Ctr The BR1 187 A1
Pavilion Lo HA2 42 B1
Pavilion Mans [10] SW9 138 B1
Pavilion Mews N3 29 C1
Pavilion Rd
Knightsbridge SW1 114 D3 257 D5
Redbridge IG1 56 B2
Pavilion Sq SW17 158 D1
Pavilion St SW1 257 D5
Pavilions The BR3 185 C4
Pavilion Terr
Ilford IG2 57 C4
[8] North Kensington W12 90 C1
Pavilion Way
Burnt Oak HA8 27 A3
Ruislip HA4 62 C6
Pavillion Ct SW1 268 C6
Pavitt Ct NW10 68 A1
Pawleyne Cl SE20 184 C3
Pawsey Cl E13 99 A6
Pawson's Rd CR0 205 A4
Paxford Rd HA0 65 B6
Paxton Cl
Richmond TW9 132 B3

Paxton Cl *continued*
Walton-on-T KT12 ... 194 C2
Paxton Ct
1 Forest Hill SE26 ... 185 A6
Grove Pk SE9 ... 165 C1
Mitcham CR4 ... 180 D1
Paxton Ho SE17 ... 262 B2
Paxton Pl SE27 ... 183 C6
Paxton Prim Sch
SE19 ... 183 C4
Paxton Rd
Chiswick W4 ... 133 C6
Forest Hill SE23 ... 163 A1
Plaistow BR1 ... 187 A3
Tottenham N17 ... 34 A3
Paxton Terr SW1 ... 268 D6
Paymal Ho 33 E1 ... 96 C2
Payne Cl IG11 ... 79 D1
Payne Ho N1 ... 233 D5
Paynell Ct SE3 ... 142 C2
Payne Rd E3 ... 97 D5
Paynesfield Ave
SW14 ... 133 B2
Paynesfield Rd WD23 ... 8 D4
Payne St SE8 ... 141 B6
Paynes Wlk
W6 ... 135 A6 264 A5
Payzes Gdns IG8 ... 36 D5
Peabody Ave
SW1 ... 115 B1 258 D1
Peabody Bldgs
6 Camberwell SE5 ... 139 B4
Walworth SE17 ... 262 C3
Peabody Cl
Croydon CR0 ... 206 C1
SW1 ... 268 D6
Peabody Cotts N17 ... 33 C2
Peabody Ct
9 Camberwell SE5 ... 139 B4
25 Enfield EN3 ... 7 C6
St Luke's EC1 ... 242 B5
Peabody Est
18 Bethnal Green E2 ... 96 B5
Borough The SE1 ... 252 A3
Fulham SW6 ... 135 B6 264 D6
17 Hammersmith W6 ... 112 C1
Holborn EC1 ... 241 B5
Lambeth SE1 ... 251 B3
North Kensington W10 ... 90 C2
4 Ratcliff E1 ... 118 D6
7 St George in t East
E1 ... 118 A6
St Luke's EC1 ... 242 B5
Strand WC2 ... 240 C1
Streatham SE24 ... 161 A4
Westminster SW1 ... 259 B4
Peabody Hill SE21 ... 161 A3
Peabody Sq SE1 ... 251 C1
Peabody Twr EC1 ... 242 B5
Peabody Yd N1 ... 235 A6
Peace Cl
East Barnet N14 ... 15 B6
Greenford UB6 ... 86 B6
South Norwood SE25 ... 205 C5
Peace Ct 10 NW9 ... 46 A5
Peace Gr HA9 ... 66 D5
Peacehaven Ct 8 N10 ... 31 A3
Peace St SE18 ... 144 C6
Peach Ct E4 ... 35 C6
Peaches Cl SM2 ... 217 A1
Peaches Ct SM2 ... 217 A1
Peach Gr E11 ... 76 B5
Peach Rd
Feltham TW14 ... 150 A3
London W10 ... 91 A4
Peach Tree Ave UB7 ... 82 B1
Peachum Rd SE3 ... 142 D6
Peach Walk Mews 24
E3 ... 96 D5
Peacock Ave TW14 ... 149 B3
Peacock Cl
Dagenham RM8 ... 80 C6
Walthamstow E4 ... 35 B3
Peacock Ct EN1 ... 17 C5
Peacock Ind Est N17 ... 33 D3
Peacock St
SE17 ... 116 D2 261 D3
Peacock Wlk E16 ... 99 B1
Peacock Yd SE17 ... 261 D3
Peaketon Ave IG4 ... 55 D4
Peak Hill SE26 ... 184 C6
Peak Hill Ave SE26 ... 184 C6
Peak Hill Gdns SE26 ... 184 C6
Peak Ho N4 ... 51 A1
Peak The SE26 ... 162 C1
Peal Gdns W13 ... 87 A3
Peall Rd CR0 ... 204 B3
Peall Rd Ind Est CR0 ... 204 B3
Pear Ave TW17 ... 193 C6
Pearce Cl 2 CR4 ... 181 A1
Pearcefield Ave 5
SE23 ... 162 C3
Pearce Ho
Camden Town N19 ... 71 C5
7 Streatham SW2 ... 160 A4
Westminster SW1 ... 259 D3
Pear Cl
Kingsbury NW9 ... 45 B5
New Cross Gate SE14 ... 141 A5
Pearcroft Rd E11 ... 76 B6
Pear Ct 21 SE15 ... 139 D5
Peardon St SW8 ... 137 B3
Peareswood Gdns
HA7 ... 25 D2
Pearfield Ho 1 N5 ... 73 A3
Pearfield Rd SE23 ... 163 A1
Pearl Cl
Hendon NW2 ... 46 D2
Newham E6 ... 100 C1
Pearl Ct 18 NW9 ... 46 A5
Pearl Rd E17 ... 53 C6
Pearl St E1 ... 118 B5
Pearlstones Ct RM10 ... 103 C6
Pearmain Cl TW17 ... 192 D4
Pearman Ho 9 SE13 ... 142 A3
Pearman St
SE1 ... 116 C4 251 B1
Pear Pl SE1 ... 251 A2
Pear Rd E11 ... 76 C5
Pearscroft Ct
SW6 ... 135 D4 265 D1
Pearscroft Rd
SW6 ... 135 D4 265 D1
Pearse St 3 SE15 ... 139 C6
Pearson Cl
Barnet EN5 ... 1 D2
4 Camberwell SE5 ... 139 A4
Pearson Ct SM4 ... 201 D4
Pearson Ho SW15 ... 134 C3
Pearson's Ave SE8,
SE14 ... 141 C4
Pearson St E2 ... 95 D5
Pearson Way CR4 ... 181 A2
Pears Rd TW3 ... 130 A2
Peartree Ave SW17 ... 158 A1
Pear Tree Ave UB7 ... 82 B1
Pear Tree Cl
Bromley BR2 ... 209 D4
Chessington KT9 ... 214 C3
Mitcham CR4 ... 180 C1
23 Shoreditch E2 ... 95 D6
Pear Tree Ct
Holborn EC1 ... 241 B5
Putney SW15 ... 134 B1
Woodford IG8 ... 37 B2
Peartree Gdns RM8 ... 80 B4
Pear Tree Ho
Brockley SE4 ... 141 B1
Hayes UB8 ... 83 A1
Peartree La E1 ... 118 C6
Peartree Rd EN1 ... 5 C2
Pear Tree Rd TW15 ... 171 A5
Peartree St
EC1 ... 95 A3 242 A6
Peartree Way SE10 ... 121 A2
Peary Ho 4 NW10 ... 67 B1
Peary Pl E2 ... 96 C4
Peaslake Ct SM2 ... 218 A1
Peas Mead Terr E4 ... 36 A6
Peatfield Cl DA15 ... 167 C1
Pebworth Lo
2 Belmont SM2 ... 217 D1
South Norwood SE25 ... 205 D5
Pebworth Rd HA1 ... 65 A6
Peckarmans Wood SE21,
SE26 ... 162 A1
Peckett Sq 3 N5 ... 72 D4
Peckford Pl SW9 ... 138 C3
PECKHAM ... 140 A4
Peckham Gr SE15 ... 139 C5
Peckham High St
SE15 ... 140 A4
Peckham Hill St SE15 ... 140 A5
Peckham Park Prim Sch
SE15 ... 140 A5
Peckham Park Rd
SE15 ... 140 A5
Peckham Rd SE5 ... 139 C4
Peckham Rye
East Dulwich SE22 ... 140 A1
Peckham SE15, SE22 ... 140 B1
Peckham Rye Sta
SE15 ... 140 A3
Peckwater Ho 2 NW5 ... 71 D2
Peckwater St NW5 ... 71 C3
Pedlars Wlk N7 ... 72 A3
Pedley Rd RM8 ... 58 C1
Pedley St E1 ... 95 D3 243 D5
Pedro St E5 ... 74 D4
Pedworth Gdns 4
SE16 ... 118 C2
Peebles Ct UB1 ... 86 A1
Peek Cres SW19 ... 178 D5
Peel Centre (Metropolitan
Police Training
Establishment) NW9 ... 45 D6
Peel Cl
Chingford E4 ... 19 D2
Edmonton N9 ... 18 A1
Peel Ct UB6 ... 86 A4
Peel Dr
Colindale NW9 ... 45 D6
Redbridge IG5 ... 56 A6
Peel Gr E2 ... 96 C5
Peel Pass W8 ... 245 A3
Peel Pl IG5 ... 37 D1
Peel Prec NW6 ... 91 C5
Peel Rd
Farnborough BR6 ... 227 A3
Harrow HA3 ... 42 D6
Wembley HA0, HA9 ... 65 D5
Woodford E18 ... 36 D2
Peel St W8 ... 113 C5 245 A3
Peel Way UB8 ... 82 A2
Peel Yates Ho 13 SE7 ... 122 A2
Peerglow Est EN3 ... 18 C6
Peerless St EC1 ... 95 B4 235 C1
Pegamoid Rd N18 ... 18 C1
Pegasus Cl N16 ... 73 B4
Pegasus Ct
11 Acton W3 ... 89 A1
Brentford TW8 ... 110 B1
6 Buckhurst Hill IG9 ... 21 D2
College Pk NW10 ... 90 B4
Edmonton N21 ... 17 A4
Harrow HA3 ... 43 D4
Kingston u T KT1 ... 197 D6
Sutton SM1 ... 217 D6
Pegasus Ho 9 E1 ... 96 D3
Pegasus Lo N21 ... 17 A4
Pegasus Pl 2 SE11 ... 138 C6
Pegasus Rd CR0, CR9 ... 220 C2
Pegasus Way N11 ... 31 B4
Peggotty Way UB8 ... 82 D1
Pegg Rd TW5 ... 128 D5
Peggy Quirke Ct 2
HA0 ... 66 A2
Pegley Gdns SE12 ... 165 A2
Pegwell Ho 19 E5 ... 74 B3
Pegwell St SE18 ... 145 C5
Pekin St E14 ... 97 C1
Pekoe SE1 ... 253 D3
Peldon Ct TW10 ... 154 B6
Pele Ct N17 ... 33 B3
Pelham Ave IG11 ... 101 D6
Pelham Cl SE5 ... 139 C2
Pelham Cotts DA5 ... 169 D3
Pelham Cres SW7 ... 257 A3
Pelham Ct SW3 ... 257 A3
Pelham Ho W14 ... 254 C3
Pelham Pl
Chelsea SW7 ... 257 A3
8 Ealing W7 ... 86 D3
Pelham Prim Sch
Bexleyheath DA7 ... 147 C2
Merton SW19 ... 179 C3
Pelham Rd
Bexleyheath DA7 ... 147 C2
Ilford IG1 ... 79 B6
Merton SW19 ... 179 C3
Penge BR3, SE20 ... 184 C1
Tottenham N15 ... 51 D5
Wanstead E18 ... 55 B6
Wood Green N22 ... 32 C1
Pelham St
SW7 ... 114 B2 256 D4
Pelican Ho 8 SE8 ... 119 B2
Pelican Pas 3 E1 ... 96 C3
Pelier St SE17 ... 139 A6
Pelinore Rd SE6 ... 164 C2
Pella Ho SE11 ... 260 D2
Pellant Rd
SW6 ... 135 A5 264 B4
Pellatt Gr N22 ... 32 C2
Pellatt Rd
East Dulwich SE22 ... 161 D6
Wembley HA9 ... 66 A6
Pellerin Rd N16 ... 73 C3
Pellew Ho 15 E1 ... 96 B3
Pellings Cl BR2 ... 208 C6
Pelling St E14 ... 97 C1
Pellipar Cl N13 ... 16 C1
Pellipar Gdns SE18 ... 122 B1
Pellipar Rd SE18 ... 122 B1
Pelly Ct 4 E17 ... 54 A5
Pelly Rd E13 ... 99 A5
Pelter St E2 ... 95 D4
Pelton Ct CR2 ... 221 A2
Pelton Rd SE10 ... 120 C1
Pembar Ave E17 ... 53 A6
Pemberley Chase
KT19 ... 214 D3
Pemberley Cl KT19 ... 214 D3
Pemberley Ho KT19 ... 214 D3
Pember Rd NW10 ... 90 D4
Pemberton Ct 18 E1 ... 96 D4
Pemberton Gdns
Camden Town N19 ... 71 C5
Dagenham RM6 ... 59 A4
Pemberton Ho SE26 ... 184 A6
Pemberton Pl
Esher KT10 ... 212 A5
2 Hackney E8 ... 74 B1
Pemberton Rd
East Molesey KT8 ... 196 A5
Harringay N4 ... 50 D4
Pemberton Row EC4 ... 241 B2
Pemberton Terr N19 ... 71 C5
Pembridge Ave TW4 ... 151 B3
Pembridge Cres
W11 ... 113 C6 245 A6
Pembridge Gdns
W2 ... 113 C6 245 A5
Pembridge Hall Sch
W2 ... 113 C6 245 B5
Pembridge Mews
W11 ... 113 C6 245 A6
Pembridge Pl
Notting Hill
W2 ... 113 C6 245 B6
1 Wandsworth SW15 ... 157 C6
Pembridge Rd
W11 ... 113 C6 245 A5
Pembridge Sq
W2 ... 113 C6 245 B5
Pembridge Villas
W11 ... 113 C6 245 A6
Pembroke W14 ... 254 D3
Pembroke Ave
Enfield EN1 ... 6 B4
Harrow HA3 ... 43 B6
Islington N1 ... 94 A6 233 B6
Surbiton KT5 ... 198 D4
Pembroke Bldgs
NW10 ... 90 A4
Pembroke Cl SW1 ... 248 B1
Pembroke Ct 11 W7 ... 86 D2
Pembroke Gdns
Dagenham RM10 ... 81 D5
West Kensington
W8 ... 113 B2 254 D4
Pembroke Gdns Cl
W8 ... 255 A5
Pembroke Hall NW4 ... 46 C6
Pembroke Ho
Acton W3 ... 111 A4
Chelsea SW1 ... 258 A5
5 Clapham Pk SW2 ... 160 A6
17 Kensington W2 ... 91 D1
Putney SW15 ... 156 A6
Upper Tooting SW17 ... 180 B5
Pembroke Lo 2
SW16 ... 160 B1
Pembroke Mews
8 Bow E3 ... 97 A4
Bromley BR1 ... 187 D1
Kensington W8 ... 255 A5
Muswell Hill N10 ... 31 A2
Pembroke Pl
Edgware HA8 ... 26 C3
Isleworth TW7 ... 130 C3
Kensington W8 ... 255 A5
Pembroke Rd
Bromley BR1 ... 187 D1
Edmonton N13 ... 17 A1
Greenford UB6 ... 85 D3
Hornsey N8 ... 50 A5
Ilford IG3 ... 57 D2
Kensington
W8 ... 113 C2 255 A4
Mitcham CR4 ... 181 A1
Muswell Hill N10 ... 31 A3
Newham E6 ... 100 B2
Ruislip HA4 ... 39 D1
South Norwood SE25 ... 205 C5
South Tottenham N15 ... 51 D4
Walthamstow E17 ... 53 D4
Wembley HA9 ... 65 D5
Pembroke Sq
W8 ... 113 C3 255 A5
Pembroke St
N1 ... 94 A6 233 B6
Pembroke Studios
W8 ... 254 D5
Pembroke Terr NW8 ... 229 C5
Pembroke Villas
Kensington W8 ... 255 A4
Pembroke Villas *continued*
Richmond TW9 ... 131 D1
Pembroke Way UB3 ... 105 A3
Pembroke Wlk W8 ... 255 A4
Pembry Cl SW9 ... 138 C4
Pembury Ave KT4 ... 200 A2
Pembury Cl
Hackney E5 ... 74 B3
Hayes BR2 ... 208 D2
Pembury Cres DA14 ... 169 A2
Pembury Ct UB3 ... 127 B6
Pembury Ho
Camberwell SE5 ... 139 C3
Keston Mark BR2 ... 210 A1
Pembury Pl 15 E5, E8 ... 74 B3
Pembury Rd
Croydon SE25 ... 206 A5
Erith DA7 ... 147 A6
Hackney E5 ... 74 B3
Tottenham N17 ... 33 D1
Pemdevon Rd CR0 ... 204 C2
Pemell Cl 30 E1 ... 96 C3
Pemell Ho 31 E1 ... 96 C3
Pemerich Cl UB3 ... 105 D1
Pempath Pl HA9 ... 65 D6
Penair Lodge HA1 ... 64 C5
Penally Pl N1 ... 235 D6
Penang St E1 ... 118 B5
Penard Rd UB2 ... 107 D3
Penarth Ct SM2 ... 218 A1
Penarth Ctr The SE15 ... 140 C6
Penarth St SE15 ... 140 C6
Penates KT10 ... 212 B4
Penberth Rd SE6 ... 164 A3
Penbury Rd UB2 ... 107 B1
Penceat Ct SE20 ... 184 C1
Pencombe Mews
W11 ... 244 D6
Pencraig Way SE15 ... 140 B6
Pendall Cl EN4 ... 2 C1
Penda Rd DA8 ... 147 D5
Pendarves Rd SW20 ... 178 C2
Penda's Mead E9 ... 75 A4
Pendell Ave UB3 ... 127 D5
Pendennis Ho 15 SE8 ... 119 A2
Pendennis Rd
Streatham SW16 ... 182 A6
Tottenham N17 ... 51 B6
Penderel Rd TW3 ... 151 C6
Penderry Rise SE6 ... 164 B2
Penderyn Way N7 ... 71 D4
Pendlebury Ho 5
SE18 ... 144 A4
Pendle Ho 13 SE26 ... 162 A1
Pendle Rd SW16 ... 181 B5
Pendlestone Rd E17 ... 53 D4
Pendley Ho 18 E2 ... 96 A6
Pendolino Way NW10 ... 66 D1
Pendragon Rd BR1 ... 165 A1
Pendragon Sch BR1 ... 165 A1
Pendragon Wlk NW9 ... 45 C3
Pendrell Ho WC2 ... 239 D1
Pendrell Rd SE4 ... 141 A3
Pendrell St SE18 ... 145 B6
Pendula Dr UB4 ... 84 D3
Penelope Ho 20 SW9 ... 138 C4
Penerley Rd SE6 ... 163 D3
Penfield Lo 7 W9 ... 91 C2
Penfields Ho N7 ... 72 A2
Penfold Cl CR0 ... 220 C5
Penfold Ct 7 CR4 ... 181 A1
Penfold Ho 14 SE18 ... 144 D6
Penfold La DA5 ... 168 D3
Penfold Pl
NW1 ... 92 C2 237 A4
Penfold Rd N9 ... 18 D3
Penfold St
NW8 ... 92 B3 236 D5
Penford Gdns SE9 ... 143 D2
Penford St SE5 ... 138 D3
Pengarth Rd DA5 ... 168 D5
PENGE ... 184 D4
Penge East Sta SE20 ... 184 C4
Penge La SE20 ... 184 D3
Penge Rd
Newham E13 ... 99 C6
South Norwood SE25 ... 206 A6
Penge West Sta SE20 ... 184 B4
Penhall Rd SE7 ... 121 D2
Penhill Rd DA5 ... 168 C4
Penhurst Mans SW6 ... 264 C2
Penifather La UB6 ... 86 B4
Peninsula Ct E14 ... 119 D3
Peninsular Cl TW14 ... 149 C5
Peninsular Park Rd
SE7 ... 121 A2
Penistone Rd SW16 ... 182 A3
Penketh Dr HA1 ... 64 B5
Penmayne Ho SE11 ... 261 B2
Penmon Rd SE2 ... 124 A3
Pennack Rd SE15 ... 139 D6
Penn Almshouses 1
SE10 ... 142 A4
Pennant Mews
W8 ... 113 D2 255 C4
Pennant Terr E17 ... 35 B1
Pennard Mans 5
W12 ... 112 C4
Pennard Rd W12 ... 112 C4
Pennards The TW16 ... 194 C6
Penn Cl
Greenford UB6 ... 85 D5
Harrow HA3 ... 43 C5
Penn Ct NW9 ... 45 B6
Pennefather Ho N1 ... 73 B2
Pennells Ct TW5 ... 129 C6
Penner Cl SW19 ... 157 A2
Penners Gdns KT6 ... 198 A2
Pennethorne Cl E9 ... 96 C6
Pennethorne Ho
SW11 ... 136 B2
Pennethorne Rd
SE15 ... 140 B5
Penn Gdns BR7 ... 188 D1
Penn Ho
7 Edmonton N9 ... 18 A1
Lisson Gr NW8 ... 237 A5
Pennine Dr NW2 ... 68 D6
Pennine La NW2 ... 69 A6
Pennine Mans NW2 ... 69 A6
Pennine Par NW2 ... 69 A6
Pennine Way UB7 ... 127 B5
Pennington Cl 10
SE27 ... 183 B6
Pennington Ct
4 Rotherhithe SE16 ... 119 A5
23 St George in t East
E1 ... 118 A6
Pennington Dr N21 ... 16 A6
Pennington Lo 18
KT5 ... 198 A4
Pennington St E1 ... 118 B6
Pennington Way
SE12 ... 165 B2
Penniston Cl N17 ... 33 A1
Penn La
Bexley DA5 ... 168 D5
Sidcup DA5 ... 169 A5
Penn Rd N7 ... 72 A4
Penn St N1 ... 95 B6 235 D5
Penny Ct SW10 ... 266 B6
Pennyfields E14 ... 119 C6
Pennyford Ct NW8 ... 236 C6
Penny La TW17 ... 193 C2
Penny Mews SW12 ... 159 B4
Pennymore Wlk W9 ... 91 B3
Penny Rd NW10 ... 88 D4
Penny Royal SM6 ... 219 D2
Pennyroyal Ave E6 ... 100 C1
Penpoll Rd E8 ... 74 B2
Penpool La DA16 ... 146 B2
Penray EN5 ... 1 A2
Penrhyn Ave E17 ... 35 C2
Penrhyn Cres
Mortlake SW14 ... 133 A1
Walthamstow E17 ... 35 C2
Penrhyn Gdns KT1 ... 197 D5
Penrhyn Gr E17 ... 35 C2
Penrhyn Rd KT1 ... 198 A6
Penrith Cl
Beckenham BR3 ... 185 D2
Putney SW15 ... 157 A6
Penrith Pl SE27 ... 160 D2
Penrith Rd
New Malden KT3 ... 199 B5
South Norwood CR7 ... 183 A1
Tottenham N15 ... 51 B4
Penrith St SW16 ... 181 C4
Penrose Gr
SE17 ... 117 A1 262 A1
Penrose Ho
Camberwell SE17 ... 262 A1
Southgate N21 ... 16 B6
Penrose St
SE17 ... 117 A1 262 A1
Penryn Ho SE11 ... 261 C2
Penryn St NW1 ... 93 D5 232 C4
Penry St SE1 ... 263 B3
Pensbury Pl SW8 ... 137 C3
Pensbury St SW8 ... 137 C3
Pensford Ave TW9 ... 132 C3
Penshurst 2 NW5 ... 71 A2
Penshurst Ave DA15 ... 168 A5
Penshurst Ct
Croydon CR2 ... 220 D1
1 Edgware HA8 ... 26 D5
Penshurst Gdns HA8 ... 26 D5
Penshurst Gn BR2 ... 208 D4
Penshurst Ho 1
SE15 ... 140 C6

Penshurst Rd
Erith DA7 147 B4
Homerton E9 74 D1
Thornton Heath CR7 204 D4
Tottenham N17 33 D3
Penshurst Way SM2 217 C1
Penshurst Wlk 4
BR2 208 D4
Pensilver Cl EN4 2 C1
Penstemon Cl N3 29 C4
Pentavia Retail Pk
NW7 27 D3
Pentelow Gdns TW14 150 A5
Pentire Rd E17 36 B2
Pentland Ave
Edgware HA8 10 D2
Littleton TW17 192 C4
Pentland Cl
Cricklewood NW11 69 A6
Lower Edmonton N9 18 C2
Pentland Gdns SW18 158 A5
Pentland Ho
17 Camden Town NW5 71 A2
7 Stamford Hill N16 51 D1
Pentland Pl UB5 85 A6
Pentland Rd
Bushey WD23 8 A5
1 Maida Vale NW6 91 C4
Pentlands BR3 186 A2
Pentlands Cl CR4 203 B6
Pentland St SW18 158 A5
Pentland Way UB10 61 A5
Pentlow St SW15 134 C2
Pentney Rd
5 Chingford E4 20 B3
Merton SW19, SW20 179 A2
Streatham SW12 159 C3
Penton Gr N1 234 A3
Penton Ho
3 Abbey Wood SE2 124 D4
Islington N1 234 A3
Sutton SM2 218 A1
Penton Pl
SE17 116 D1 261 D2
Penton Rise
WC1 94 B4 233 D2
Penton St N1 94 C5 234 A3
PENTONVILLE 94 B5
Pentonville Rd
N1 94 B5 233 C3
Pentrich Ave EN1 6 A5
Pentridge St SE15 139 D5
Pentyre Ave N18 33 B5
Penwerris Ave TW5,
TW7 130 A5
Penwerris Ct TW7 130 A5
Penwith Rd SW18 157 D2
Penwood Ct HA5 41 B5
Penwood Ho SW15 155 D5
Penwortham Ct 1
N22 32 C1
Penwortham Prim Sch
SW17 181 B4
Penwortham Rd
SW16 181 C4
Penylan Pl HA8 26 C3
Penywern Rd
SW5 113 C1 255 B2
Penzance Ho SE11 261 B2
Penzance Pl
W11 113 A5 244 B4
Penzance St
W11 113 A5 244 A4
Peony Ct IG8 36 C3
Peony Gdns W12 112 A6
Peperfield WC1 233 C1
Pepler Ho 17 W10 91 A3
Pepler Mews SE1 263 C1
Peploe Rd NW6 90 D5
Pepper Cl E6 100 B2
Peppercorn Cl CR7 183 B1
Peppermead Sq SE13 163 C6
Peppermint Cl CR0 204 A2
Peppermint Pl 7 E11 76 C5
Pepper St
Borough The SE1 252 A2
Millwall E14 119 D3
Peppie Cl N16 73 C6
Pepsi Trocadero*
W1 249 C5
Pepys Cl UB10 60 D4
Pepys Cres
Barnet EN5 12 C6
2 Newham E16 121 A5
Pepys Ct SW20 178 C1
Pepys Ent Ctr 13 SE8 119 B2
Pepys Ho
14 Bethnal Green E2 96 C4
Clapham Pk SW4 159 D6
Pepys Rd
New Cross Gate
SE14 140 D3
Wimbledon SW20 178 C2
Pepys Rise BR6 211 D1
Pepys St EC3 117 C6 253 B6
Perak Ct KT5 199 A2
Peralte Terr CR4 204 A5
Perceval Ave NW3 70 C3
Perceval Ct UB5 63 C3
Percheron Cl TW7 130 D2
Percheron Ct 3 SW9 138 B2
Percheron Rd WD6 11 B5
Perch St E8 73 D4
Percival Ct N17 33 D3
Percival Gdns RM6 58 C3
Percival Ho 3 IG8 37 A6
Percival Rd
Enfield EN1 5 D1
Feltham TW13 149 D2
Mortlake SW14 133 A1
Orpington BR6 226 D6
Percival St EC1 94 D4 234 D1
Percival Way KT19 215 B4
Percy Ave TW15 170 C5
Percy Bilton Ct TW5 129 D4
Percy Bryant Rd
TW16 171 C3
Percy Bush Rd UB7 104 B3
Percy Cir WC1 94 B4 233 D2
Percy Ct 1 KT5 198 B3
Percy Gdns
Enfield EN3 18 D6
Hayes UB4 83 C4
5 Isleworth TW7 131 A2
New Malden KT4 199 C1
Percy Ho 4 SW16 181 C6
Percy Laurie Ho 6
SW15 134 D1
Percy Mews W1 239 C3
Percy Pas W1 239 C3
Percy Rd
Bexleyheath DA7 147 A3
Carshalton CR4 203 A2
Croydon SE25 206 A4
Edmonton N21 17 A4
Hampton TW12 173 C3
Ilford IG3 58 A2
Isleworth TW7 131 A1
Leytonstone E11 54 C2
Newham E16 98 C2
North Finchley N12 30 A5
Penge SE20 184 D2
Romford RM7 59 D6
Shepherd's Bush W12 112 A4
Twickenham TW2 152 A3
Percy St W1 93 D2 239 C3
Percy Terr BR1 210 D6
Percy Way TW2 152 A3
Peregrine Cl NW10 67 B3
Peregrine Ct
Bexley DA16 145 D4
Streatham SW16 182 B6
Peregrine Gdns CR0 223 A6
Peregrine Ho
6 Battersea SW11 136 C2
Finsbury EC1 234 D2
Peregrine Rd
Sunbury TW16 171 D1
Tottenham N17 33 B3
Peregrine Way SW19,
SW20 178 C3
Performing Arts & Tech
Sch SE25 205 B3
Perham Rd
W14 113 A1 254 B1
Peridot St E6 100 A2
Perifield SE21 161 A3
Perimeade Rd UB6 87 C5
Period Wks E10 53 A1
Periton Rd SE9 143 D1
PERIVALE 87 B5
Perivale UB6 86 D5
Perivale Gdns W13 87 B3
Perivale Grange UB6 87 A4
Perivale Ind Pk UB6 87 B5
Perivale La UB6 87 A4
Perivale Lo UB6 87 A4
Perivale New Bsns Ctr
UB6 87 C5
Perivale Prim Sch UB6 87 C5
Perivale Sta UB6 87 A5
Perkin Cl
Hounslow TW3 129 D1
Wembley HA0 65 B3
Perkins Ct TW15 170 B5
Perkins Ho 15 E14 97 B2
Perkins Rd IG2 57 B4
Perkins Rents SW1 259 C5
Perkins Sq SE1 252 B4
Perks Cl SE3 142 C2
Perley Ho 9 E3 97 B2
Perotti Ho SW6 135 D2
Perpins Rd SE9 167 C5
Perran Rd SE24, SW2 160 D2
Perren St NW5 71 B2
Perrers Rd W6 112 B2
Perrin Cl TW15 170 B5
Perrin Ct TW15 170 C6
Perring Est E3 97 C2
Perrin Grange HA9 66 B6
Perrin Rd HA0 65 B4
Perrins Ct HA3 44 B2
Perrin's Ct 20 NW3 70 A4
Perrin's La NW3 70 A4
Perrin's Wlk NW3 70 A4
Perronet Ho SE1 261 D5
Perry Ave W3 89 B1
Perry Cl UB8 82 D1
Perry Ct
6 Isle of Dogs E14 119 C1
2 Kingston u T KT2 176 A1
Sutton SM1 217 C3
2 Tottenham N15 51 C3
Perryfield Way
Richmond TW10 153 B2
West Hendon NW9 45 D3
Perry Garth UB5 84 C6
Perry Gdns N9 17 C1
Perry Hall Prim Sch
BR6 211 D3
Perry Hill SE6 163 B1
Perry Ho 24 SW2 160 A4
Perry How KT4 199 D1
Perryman Ho
Barking IG11 101 A6
Tottenham N17 34 B3
Perrymans Farm Rd
IG2 57 B4
Perry Mead
Bushey WD23 8 A5
Enfield EN2 4 D3
Perrymead St
SW6 135 D4 265 C1
Perrymount Prim Sch
SE23 162 D2
Perryn Ct 1 TW1 153 A4
Perryn Ho W3 111 C6
Perryn Rd
Acton W3 111 B6
1 Bermondsey SE16 118 B3
Perry Rise SE23 163 A1
Perry's Pl W1 239 C2
Perry St BR7 189 C4
Perry Street Gdns
BR7 189 C4
Perry Vale SE23 162 D2
Perrywood Ho 17 E5 74 B3
Persant Rd SE6 164 C2
Perseverance Pl
SW9 138 C5
Perseverance Works 17
E2 95 C4
Pershore Cl IG2 56 D4
Pershore Gr SM5 202 B3
Pershore Ho 11 W13 109 A5
Pert Cl N10 31 B4
Perth Ave
Hayes UB4 84 C3
Kingsbury NW9 45 B2
Perth Cl
Northolt UB5 63 C3
Wimbledon SW20 178 A1
Perth Ct 5 SE5 139 B1
Perth Ho
12 Acton W3 88 C1
Barnsbury N1 72 B1
Perth Rd
Barking IG11 101 B6
Beckenham BR3 186 A1
Finsbury Pk N4 50 C1
Ilford IG2 56 D3
Newham E13 99 B5
Tottenham N22 32 D2
Walthamstow E10 53 B1
Perth Terr IG2 57 A2
Perwell Ave HA2 41 B1
Perystreete SE23 162 C2
Petavel Rd TW11 174 C4
Petchey Acad The E8 73 D3
Peter Ave NW10 68 B1
Peter Best Ho 1 E1 96 B1
Peterboat Cl SE10 120 C2
Peterborough Ct EC4 241 B1
Peterborough Gdns
IG1 56 A2
Peterborough Mews
SW6 135 C3
Peterborough Prim Sch
SW6 135 C3
Peterborough Rd
Carshalton SM5 202 C3
Fulham SW6 135 C2
Harrow HA1 42 D2
Leytonstone E10 54 B3
Peterborough Villas
SW6 265 C2
Peter Bradley Ct RM9 81 B1
Peter Butler Ho 9
SE1 118 A4
Peterchurch Ho SE15 140 B6
Peter Fagan Ho UB3 105 C3
Petergate SW11 136 A1
Peterhead Ct 12 UB1 86 A1
Peter Heathfield Ho 4
E15 98 B6
Peter Hills Ho 6
SE16 118 A2
Peter Hills with St Mary's
& St Paul's CE Prim Sch
SE16 118 D5
Peter Ho SW8 270 A4
Peter James Bsns Ctr
UB3 106 A4
Peter James Ent Ctr
NW10 89 A4
Peter Kennedy Ct
CR0 207 B3
Peterley Bsns Ctr 21
E2 96 B5
Peter Lyell Ct HA4 62 B6
Peters Cl
Bexley DA16 145 C3
Dagenham RM8 58 D1
Stanmore HA7 25 D4
Peters Ct 9 W2 91 D1
Peter's Ct SW4 160 A5
Petersfield Cl N18 33 A5
Petersfield Rd W3 111 A4
Petersfield Rise
SW15 156 B3
PETERSHAM 154 A3
Petersham Cl
Richmond TW10 153 D2
Sutton SM1 217 C3
Petersham Dr BR5 190 A1
Petersham Gdns BR5 189 D1
Petersham Ho SW7 256 C4
Petersham La SW7 256 A6
Petersham Mews
SW7 114 A3 256 B5
Petersham Pl
SW7 114 A3 256 B6
Petersham Rd TW10 154 A3
Petersham Terr CR0 220 A5
Peter's La EC1 241 D4
Peter's Lo HA8 26 B4
Peter's Path SE26 184 B6
Peter St W1 115 D6 249 C6
Peterstone Rd SE2 124 B4
Peterstow Cl SW19 157 A2
Peterwood Pk CR9 220 B6
Peterwood Way CR0 220 B6
Petherton Ct
Brondesbury Pk NW10 90 D6
10 Harrow HA1 42 D3
Petherton Ho N4 51 A1
Petherton Rd N5 73 A3
Petiver Cl 26 E9 74 C1
Petley Rd W6 134 D5
Peto Pl NW1 238 D6
Peto St N E16 98 D1
Petrel Ct 8 SE21 161 B2
Petrie Cl NW2 69 A2
Petrie Ho 8 SE18 144 C6
Petrie Mus of Egyptian
Archaeology*
WC1 93 D3 239 C5
Petros Gdns 1 NW3 70 A2
Pettacre Cl SE28 123 A3
Petticoat Lane Mkt*
EC2 95 D2 243 C3
Petticoat Sq E1 243 C2
Petticoat Twr E1 243 C2
Pettit's Pl RM10 81 C3
Pettit's Rd RM10 81 C3
Pettiward Cl SW15 134 C1
Pettman Cres SE18,
SE28 123 B3
Pettsgrove Ave HA0 65 C3
Pett's Hill UB5 63 D3
Petts La TW17 192 C5
Pett St SE7 122 A2
PETTS WOOD 211 B5
Petts Wood Rd BR5 211 B4
Petts Wood Sta BR5 211 A4
Petty France
SW1 115 D3 259 C6
Petty Wales EC3 253 B5
Petworth Cl UB5 63 B1
Petworth Gdns
Hillingdon UB10 83 A6
West Barnes SW20 200 B6
Petworth Ho 16 SE22 139 C2
Petworth Rd
Bexley DA6 169 C6
Colney Hatch N12 30 C5
Petworth St
SW11 136 C4 267 B2
Petyt Pl SW3 136 C6 267 A5
Petyward SW3 114 C2 257 B3
Pevensey Ave
Enfield EN1 5 C3
Friern Barnet N11 31 D5
Pevensey Cl TW7 130 A5
Pevensey Ct
4 South Acton W3 110 D4
West Norwood SW16 160 C1
10 Woodford E18 37 A2
Pevensey Ho 5 E1 97 A2
Pevensey Rd
Feltham TW13 151 A3
Forest Gate E7 77 A4
Upper Tooting SW17 180 B6
Peverel E6 100 C1
Peverel Ho RM10 81 C6
Peverett Cl N11 31 B5
Peveril Dr TW11 174 B5
Peveril Ho SE1 262 D5
Pewsey Cl E4 35 C5
Pewsham Ho N4 51 A1
Pewterers Ct N3 29 B2
Peyton Ho N11 31 A6
Peyton Pl SE10 142 A5
Pharamond NW2 68 D2
Pharaoh Cl CR4 202 D2
Pheasant Cl E16 99 B1
Phelps Ho SW15 134 D2
Phelp St SE17 139 B6
Phelps Way UB3 105 D2
Phene St SW3 136 C6 267 B6
Philadelphia Ct SW10 266 B3
Philbeach Gdns
SW5 113 C1 255 A2
Phil Brown Pl 3
SW8 137 B2
Philchurch Pl 36 E1 96 A1
Philia Ho 4 NW1 71 C1
Philimore Cl SE18 123 C1
Philip Blairman Ho
E1 243 C5
Philip Ct
Enfield EN2 5 B4
Paddington W2 236 C4
Philip Gdns CR0 223 B6
Philip Ho
East Barnet N20 14 D2
12 Paddington NW6 91 D6
Philip La N15 51 C6
Philipot Almshouse
SE9 166 B5
Philipot Path SE9 166 B5
Philippa Gdns SE9 165 D6
Philips Cl CR4 203 A1
Philip St E13 99 A3
Philip Turner Est 28
E9 74 C1
Philip Wlk SE15 140 A2
Phillimore Ct W8 245 B1
Phillimore Gardens Cl
W8 113 C3 255 A6
Phillimore Gdns
Kensington
W8 113 C4 245 A1
Willesden NW10 90 C6
Phillimore Pl
W8 113 C4 245 A1
Phillimore Terr W8 255 B6
Phillimore Wlk
W8 113 C3 255 B6
Phillip Ho E1 243 D3
Phillipp St N1 95 C6
Phillips Ct
Edgware HA8 26 C4
Hayes UB4 84 B4
Phillipson Ho 6 N12 29 D5
Philpot La EC3 253 A6
Philpot Sq SW6 135 D2
Philpot St E1 96 B1
Philson Mans 13 E1 96 B1
Phineas Pett Rd SE9 144 A2
Phipp's Bridge Rd CR4,
SW19 202 B6
Phipps Bridge Sta
CR4 202 B6
Phipps Hatch La EN2 5 A5
Phipps Ho
1 Greenwich SE7 121 B1
16 Shepherd's Bush
W12 112 B6
Phipp St EC2 95 C3 243 A6
Phoebeth Rd SE4 163 C6
Phoenix Bsns Ctr 22
E3 97 C2
Phoenix Cl
18 Shoreditch E8 95 D6
Walthamstow E17 35 B1
West Wickham BR4 224 C6
Phoenix Ct
4 Brentford TW8 110 A1
Chingford E4 19 D1
Croydon SE25 206 A4
2 Deptford SE14 141 A6
Enfield EN3 6 C5
Feltham TW13 171 C6
Millwall E14 119 C2
8 New Barnet EN5 2 A1
Phoenix Ctr The 1
SM6 220 A1
Phoenix Dr BR2 225 D5
Phoenix High Sch
W12 112 A6
Phoenix Ho
Chelsea SW1 258 A4
Kingston u T KT3 199 D6
Phoenix Ind Est HA1 42 D5
Phoenix Lodge Mans 1
W6 112 C2
Phoenix Pk NW2 68 A6
Phoenix Pl
WC1 94 B3 240 D6
Phoenix Rd
Penge SE20 184 C4
Somers Town
NW1 93 D4 232 C2
Phoenix Sch E3 97 B4
Phoenix Sch The NW3 70 A2
Phoenix St WC2 239 D1
Phoenix Trad Est UB6 87 D6
Phoenix Trad Pk
TW8 109 D1
Phoenix Way TW5 128 D6
Phoenix Wharf Rd
SE1 253 D1
Phyllis Ave KT3 200 B4
Phyllis Ho CR0 220 D4
Phyllis Hodges Ho
NW1 93 D5 232 C3
Physic Pl SW3 136 D6 267 C6
Picador Ho 1 RM10 81 D2
Picardy Manorway
DA17 125 D4
Picardy Rd DA17 125 C2
Picardy St DA17 125 C3
Piccadilly W1 115 C5 249 A4
Piccadilly Arc SW1 249 A4
Piccadilly Cir*
W1 115 D6 249 C5
Piccadilly Circus Sta
SW1 115 D6 249 C5
Piccadilly Ct 5 N7 72 B2
Piccadilly Pl W1 249 B5
Pickard Cl N14 15 D3
Pickard St EC1 234 D2
Pickering Ave E6 100 C4
Pickering Cl E9 74 D1
Pickering Ct N22 32 D2
Pickering Gdns
Croydon SE25 205 D3
Friern Barnet N11 31 A4
Pickering Ho
Brentford W5 109 C2
18 Kensington W2 91 D1
Stoke Newington N4 51 B2
4 Woolwich SE18 122 C2
Pickering Mews 9
W2 91 D1
Pickering Pl SW1 249 B3
Pickering St N1 234 D6
Pickets Cl WD23 8 C3
Pickets St SW12 159 B4
Pickett Croft HA7 25 D2
Pickett's Lock La N9 18 D2
Pickford Cl DA7 147 A3
Pickford La DA7 147 A3
Pickford Rd DA7 147 A2
Pickfords Wharf N1 235 A3
Pickhurst Gn BR2 208 D2
Pickhurst Inf Sch
BR2 208 D3
Pickhurst Jun Sch
BR2 208 D3
Pickhurst La BR2, BR3,
BR4 208 C2
Pickhurst Mead BR2 208 D2
Pickhurst Pk BR2 208 D4
Pickhurst Rise BR4 208 B1

Pickwick Cl TW4 ... 151 A6
Pickwick Ct SE9 ... 166 B3
Pickwick Ho
21 Bermondsey SE16 ... 118 A4
3 Shepherd's Bush W11 ... 112 D5
Pickwick Mews N18 ... 33 C5
Pickwick Pl HA1 ... 42 C2
Pickwick Rd SE21 ... 161 C4
Pickwick St SE1 ... 252 A1
Pickwick Way BR7 ... 189 A4
Pickworth Cl SW8 ... 270 B3
Picton Ho 1 SW4 ... 160 A4
Picton Pl
Marylebone W1 ... 238 B1
Tolworth KT6 ... 198 C1
Picton St SE5 ... 139 B5
Picture Ho 6 SW16 ... 160 A2
Pied Bull Ct WC1 ... 240 B3
Pied Bull Yd WC1 ... 240 B3
Piedmont Rd SE18 ... 123 B1
Pield Heath Ave UB8 ... 82 C3
Pield Heath House Sch UB8 ... 82 A3
Pield Heath Rd UB8 ... 82 B3
Pier Head E1 ... 118 B5
Pierhead Wharf 37 E1 ... 118 B5
Pier Ho SW3 ... 267 B5
Piermont Pl BR1 ... 188 A1
Piermont Rd SE22 ... 162 B6
Pier Par 3 E16 ... 122 C5
Pierpoint Bldg 4 E14 ... 119 C4
Pier Rd
Feltham TW14 ... 150 B6
Newham E16 ... 122 C4
Pierrepoint SE25 ... 205 C6
Pierrepoint Rd W3 ... 110 D6
Pierrepoint Row N1 ... 234 C4
Pierson Ho 12 SE19 ... 183 C6
Pier St E14 ... 120 A2
Pier Terr SW18 ... 136 A1
Pier Way SE18 ... 123 B3
Pigeon Ct E4 ... 36 A4
Pigeon La TW12 ... 173 C6
Piggott Ho 2 E2 ... 96 D5
Pigott St E14 ... 97 C1
Pike Cl
Bromley BR1 ... 187 B5
Hillingdon UB10 ... 82 B6
Pike Rd NW7 ... 27 B6
Pike's End HA5 ... 40 B5
Pikestone Cl UB4 ... 85 A3
Pikethorne 1 SE23 ... 162 D2
Pilgrimage St SE1 ... 117 B4 252 C1
Pilgrim Cl SM4 ... 201 D2
Pilgrim Hill SE27 ... 183 A6
Pilgrim Ho SE1 ... 262 D5
Pilgrims Cl
Northolt UB5 ... 64 A3
Palmers Green N13 ... 32 B6
Pilgrims Cloisters 10 SE5 ... 139 C5
Pilgrims Ct
Enfield EN1 ... 5 B3
Greenwich SE3 ... 143 A4
Pilgrim's La NW3 ... 70 B4
Pilgrims Mews 12 E14 ... 120 B6
Pilgrim's Pl 6 NW3 ... 70 B4
Pilgrim's Rise EN4 ... 14 C6
Pilgrim St EC4 ... 241 C1
Pilgrims Way
5 Newham E6 ... 100 A6
Upper Holloway N19 ... 49 D1
Wembley HA9 ... 44 D1
Pilgrim's Way CR2 ... 221 D3
Pilgrims Way Prim Sch SE15 ... 140 C6
Pilkington Ct 1 NW9 ... 46 A5
Pilkington Rd
Orpington BR6 ... 227 A6
4 Peckham SE15 ... 140 B3
Pillions La UB4 ... 83 B3
Pilot Ind Ctr NW10 ... 89 C3
Pilsden Cl SW19 ... 156 D3
Piltdown Rd WD19 ... 22 D6
Pilton Est The CR0 ... 220 D6
Pilton Pl SE17 ... 262 B2
Pimento Ct W5 ... 109 D3
Pimilico Sta SW1 ... 115 D1 259 C2
PIMLICO ... 115 C1
Pimlico Rd SW1 ... 115 A1 258 B2
Pimlico Sch SW1 ... 115 C1 259 B1
Pimlico Wlk 1 N1 ... 95 C4
Pinchbeck Rd BR6 ... 227 D2
Pinchin St E1 ... 118 A6
Pincombe Ho SE17 ... 262 C2
Pincott Pl SE4 ... 140 D2
Pincott Rd
8 Bexley DA6 ... 147 C1
Merton SW19 ... 180 A2
Pindar St EC2 ... 95 C2 243 A4
Pindock Mews W9 ... 91 D3
Pine Apple Ct SW1 ... 259 A6
Pine Ave
Stratford New Town E15 ... 76 B3
West Wickham BR4 ... 207 D1
Pine Cl
11 Dartmouth Pk N19 ... 71 C6
London E10 ... 75 D6
Osidge N14 ... 15 C4
3 Penge SE20 ... 184 C2
Stanmore HA7 ... 25 B6
Pine Coombe CR0 ... 222 D4
Pinecrest Gdns BR6 ... 226 D4
Pinecroft
East Wickham DA16 ... 146 A5
Harrow HA3 ... 44 B4
Pinecroft Cres EN5 ... 1 A1
Pine Ct UB5 ... 85 A4
Pinedene 2 SE15 ... 140 B4
Pinefield Cl E14 ... 119 C6
Pine Gdns
Ruislip HA4 ... 62 B6
Surbiton KT5 ... 198 C3
Pine Glade BR6 ... 226 B4
Pine Gr
Finsbury Pk N4, N19 ... 72 B6
Totteridge N20 ... 13 C3
Wimbledon SW19 ... 179 B5
Pine Ho
Bow E3 ... 97 A6
21 Rotherhithe SE16 ... 118 C4
Pinehurst
Chislehurst BR7 ... 188 D4
Stanmore HA7 ... 25 A5
Pinehurst Ct 6 W11 ... 91 B1
Pinehurst Wlk 4 BR6 ... 211 B1
Pinelands Cl 7 SE3 ... 142 D5
Pine Lo SW15 ... 157 A5
Pinemartin Cl NW2 ... 68 C5
Pine Pl UB4 ... 83 D3
Pine Rd
Brunswick Pk N11 ... 15 A2
Cricklewood NW2 ... 68 D4
Pine Ridge SM5 ... 219 A1
Pines Ct 14 SW19 ... 156 D3
Pines Rd BR1 ... 188 A1
Pine St EC1 ... 94 C3 241 A6
Pines The
Southgate N14 ... 15 C6
South Norwood SE19 ... 182 D4
Sunbury TW16 ... 194 A6
Surbiton KT6 ... 214 A5
Woodford IG8 ... 21 A1
Pine Tree Cl TW5 ... 128 B4
Pine Tree Ho SE14 ... 140 D5
Pine Tree Lo BR2 ... 208 D5
Pine Trees Dr UB10 ... 60 A4
Pineview Ct 5 E4 ... 20 A3
Pine Wlk KT5 ... 198 C3
Pinewood BR7 ... 188 C4
Pine Wood TW16 ... 172 A2
Pinewood Ave
Hillingdon UB8 ... 82 B1
Pinner HA5 ... 23 D4
Sidcup DA15 ... 167 C3
Pinewood Cl
Crofton BR6 ... 211 B1
Croydon CR0 ... 223 A5
Pinner HA5 ... 23 D4
South Oxhey HA6 ... 22 B5
Pinewood Ct
Clapham Pk SW4 ... 159 D5
Enfield EN2 ... 4 D2
Merton SW19 ... 179 D3
Pinewood Dr BR6 ... 227 C3
Pinewood Gr W5 ... 87 C1
Pinewood Lo WD23 ... 8 B3
Pinewood Pl KT19 ... 215 B4
Pinewood Rd
Bromley BR2 ... 209 A5
Feltham TW13 ... 150 B1
West Heath SE2 ... 146 D6
Pinfold Rd SW16 ... 182 A6
Pinglestone Cl UB7 ... 126 A5
Pinkcoat Cl TW13 ... 150 B1
Pinkerton Ct KT2 ... 176 D1
Pinkerton Pl SW16 ... 181 D6
Pinkham Mans W4 ... 110 C1
Pinkham Way (North Circular Rd) N12 ... 31 A4
Pinkwell Ave UB3 ... 105 B2
Pinkwell La UB3 ... 105 B2
Pinkwell Prim Sch UB3 ... 105 A2
Pinley Gdns RM9 ... 102 B6
Pinnace Ho E14 ... 120 A3
Pinnacle Hill DA7 ... 147 D1
Pinnacle Hill N DA7 ... 147 D1
Pinnacle Ho EC3 ... 253 A5
Pinnacle The
Dagenham RM6 ... 59 A3
7 Kingsland N1 ... 73 B2
Pinnell Rd SE9 ... 143 D1
PINNER ... 41 A6
Pinner Ct
Paddington NW8 ... 236 C6
Pinner HA5 ... 41 C5
Pinner Gn HA5 ... 22 C1
Pinner Gr HA5 ... 41 A4
PINNER GREEN ... 22 C1
Pinner Hill HA5 ... 22 B3
Pinner Hill Rd HA5 ... 22 C1
Pinner Ho
30 Camberwell SE5 ... 139 A3
Pinner HA5 ... 41 A6
Pinner Park Ave HA2 ... 24 A1
Pinner Park Fst & Mid Schs HA5 ... 41 D6
Pinner Park Gdns HA2 ... 24 A1
Pinner Rd
Harrow HA1, HA2 ... 42 A3
Northwood HA6 ... 22 A1
Pinner HA2, HA5 ... 41 C5
Pinner Sta HA5 ... 41 A5
Pinner View HA1, HA2 ... 42 A4
PINNERWOOD PARK ... 22 C3
Pinner Wood Sch HA5 ... 22 C2
Pinn Way HA4 ... 39 C2
Pintail Cl E6 ... 100 A2
Pintail Ct 39 SE8 ... 141 B6
Pintail Rd IG8 ... 37 B3
Pintail Way UB4 ... 84 D2
Pinter Ho 30 SW9 ... 138 A3
Pinto Cl WD6 ... 11 B5
Pinto Way SE3 ... 143 B1
Pioneer Cl W12 ... 90 B1
Pioneers Ind Pk CR0 ... 204 A1
Pioneer St SE15 ... 140 A4
Pioneer Way W12 ... 90 C1
Piper Cl N7 ... 72 B3
Piper Rd KT1 ... 198 C6
Pipers Gdns CR0 ... 207 A2
Pipers Gn NW9 ... 45 A4
Pipers Green La HA8 ... 10 A1
Pipers Ho SE10 ... 120 B1
Piper Way IG1 ... 57 B1
Pipewell Rd SM5 ... 202 C3
Pippenhall SE9 ... 166 D5
Pippin Cl
Croydon CR0 ... 207 B1
Dollis Hill NW2 ... 68 B5
Pippin Ct 5 EN4 ... 2 C1
Pippin Ho 10 W10 ... 112 D6
Pippins Ct TW15 ... 170 D4
Piquet Rd SE20 ... 184 C1
Pirbright Cres CR0 ... 224 A2
Pirbright Ho 11 KT2 ... 176 D4
Pirbright Rd SW18 ... 157 C3
Pirie St 6 E16 ... 121 B5
Pitcairn Cl RM7 ... 59 C5
Pitcairn Ct CR4 ... 180 D3
Pitcairne Ct N21 ... 16 B6
Pitcairn Ho 1 E9 ... 74 C1
Pitcairn Rd CR4 ... 180 D3
Pitchford St E15 ... 76 C1
Pitfield Cres SE28 ... 124 A5
Pitfield Ho N5 ... 73 A3
Pitfield St N1 ... 95 C5
Pitfield Way
Enfield EN3 ... 6 C4
Tokyngton NW10 ... 67 A2
Pitfold Cl SE12 ... 165 B5
Pitfold Rd SE12 ... 165 A4
Pit Ho NW10 ... 67 B5
Pitlake CR0 ... 220 D6
Pitman Ho
Southgate N21 ... 16 B6
4 St Johns SE8 ... 141 C4
Pitman St SE5 ... 139 A5
Pitmaston Ho 2 SE13 ... 142 A3
Pitsea Pl E1 ... 96 D1
Pitsea St E1 ... 96 D1
Pitshanger Ct 2 W5 ... 87 C3
Pitshanger La W5 ... 87 C3
Pitshanger Manor Mus & Art Gallery* W5 ... 109 D5
Pitt Cres SW19 ... 179 D6
Pitt Ho 4 SW11 ... 136 B1
Pittman Gdns IG1 ... 79 A3
Pitt Rd
Harrow HA2 ... 64 A6
Orpington BR6 ... 227 A4
Thornton Heath CR0, CR7 ... 205 A4
Pitt's Head Mews W1 ... 248 B3
Pittsmead Ave BR2 ... 209 A2
Pitt St W8 ... 113 C4 245 B2
Pittville Gdns SE25 ... 206 A6
Pixfield Ct BR2 ... 186 D1
Pixham Ct 5 SW19 ... 179 B5
Pixley St E14 ... 97 B1
Pixton 14 NW9 ... 27 C2
Pixton Way CR2 ... 223 B1
Place Farm Ave BR5, BR6 ... 211 B1
Plains The 7 E4 ... 20 C4
PLAISTOW
BR1 ... 187 A4
E13 ... 99 B4
Plaistow Gr
Bromley BR1 ... 187 B3
West Ham E15 ... 98 D6
Plaistow Hospl E13 ... 99 C5
Plaistow La BR1 ... 187 C2
Plaistow Park Rd E13 ... 99 B5
Plaistow Prim Sch E13 ... 99 B5
Plaistow Rd E13, E15 ... 98 D5
Plaistow Sta E13 ... 98 D5
Plane St SE26 ... 162 B1
Plane Tree Cres TW13 ... 150 B1
Planetree Ct W6 ... 112 D2
Plane Tree Ho
Deptford SE8 ... 141 A6
Greenwich SE7 ... 121 D1
Plane Tree Wlk 4 SE19 ... 183 C4
Plantagenet Cl KT19 ... 215 B4
Plantagenet Gdns RM6 ... 58 D2
Plantagenet Ho SE18 ... 122 B3
Plantagenet Pl RM6 ... 58 D2
Plantagenet Rd EN5 ... 2 A1
Plantain Gdns E11 ... 76 B5
Plantain Pl SE1 ... 252 C2
Plantation La EC3 ... 253 A6
Plantation The SE3 ... 143 A3
Plasel Ct E13 ... 99 B6
PLASHET ... 78 A2
Plashet Gr E6 ... 77 D1
Plashet Rd E13 ... 77 B1
Plashet Sch E6 ... 78 A1
Plassy Rd SE6 ... 163 D4
Platehouse The 3 E14 ... 119 D1
Platina St EC2 ... 242 D6
Platinum Ct RM7 ... 59 D6
Plato Pl 1 SW6 ... 135 B3
Plato Rd SW2 ... 138 A1
Platt Halls (a) 35 NW9 ... 27 D1
Platt Halls (b) 37 NW9 ... 27 D1
Platt Halls (c) 38 NW9 ... 27 D1
Platt's Eyot TW12 ... 173 C1
Platt's La NW3 ... 69 C5
Platts Rd EN3 ... 6 C4
Platt St NW1 ... 232 C4
Plaxdale Ho SE17 ... 263 A3
Plaxtol Cl BR1 ... 187 C2
Plaxtol Rd DA8 ... 147 C5
Plaxton Ct E11 ... 76 D5
Playfair St W6 ... 112 C1
Playfield Cres SE22 ... 161 D6
Playfield Rd HA8 ... 27 A1
Playford Rd
Finsbury Pk N4 ... 72 B6
Finsbury Pk N4 ... 72 C6
Playgreen Way SE6 ... 185 C6
Playground Cl BR3 ... 184 D1
Playhouse Yd EC4 ... 241 C1
Plaza Bsns Ctr EN3 ... 7 B3
Plaza Hts E10 ... 76 A5
Plaza Sh Ctr W1 ... 93 C1 239 B2
Plaza Wlk NW9 ... 45 A6
Pleasance Rd
Putney SW15 ... 156 B6
St Paul's Cray BR5 ... 190 B1
Pleasance The SW15 ... 134 B1
Pleasant Gr CR0 ... 223 B5
Pleasant Pl N1 ... 72 D1
Pleasant Row NW1 ... 231 D5
Pleasant View BR6 ... 227 A3
Pleasant View Pl BR6 ... 227 A3
Pleasant Way HA0 ... 87 C5
Pleasaunce Ct SE9 ... 144 B1
Plender Ct NW1 ... 232 B5
Plender St NW1 ... 93 C6 232 B5
Pleshey Rd N7 ... 71 D4
Plevna Cres N15 ... 51 C3
Plevna Ho 1 N9 ... 18 A1
Plevna Rd
Edmonton N9 ... 18 B1
Hampton TW12 ... 173 D2
Plevna St E14 ... 120 A3
Pleydell Ave
Chiswick W6 ... 111 D2
Penge SE19 ... 183 D3
Pleydell Ct EC4 ... 241 B1
Pleydell Gdns SE19 ... 183 D4
Pleydell St EC4 ... 241 B1
Plimsoll Cl E14 ... 97 D1
Plimsoll Rd N4 ... 72 D5
Plough Ct EC3 ... 252 D6
Plough Farm Cl HA4 ... 39 B3
Plough La
Dulwich Village SE22 ... 161 D5
7 Teddington TW11 ... 175 A5
Wallington CR0, SM6 ... 220 A3
Wimbledon SW17, SW19 ... 180 A6
Plough Lane Cl CR0, SM6 ... 220 A3
Ploughmans Cl NW1 ... 232 C6
Ploughmans End TW7 ... 152 B6
Plough Mews 19 SW11 ... 136 B1
Plough Pl EC4 ... 241 B2
Plough Rd
Battersea SW11 ... 136 B1
West Ewell KT19 ... 215 B1
Plough St 16 E1 ... 96 A1
Plough Terr SW11 ... 136 B1
Plough Way SE16 ... 119 A2
Plough Yd EC2 ... 243 B5
Plover Ho 4 SW9 ... 138 C5
Plover Way
Hayes UB4 ... 84 D2
Rotherhithe SE16 ... 119 A3
Plowman Cl N18 ... 33 B5
Plowman Ho SW19 ... 156 D2
Plowman Way RM8 ... 58 C1
Plumbers Row E1 ... 96 A1
Plumbridge St 7 SE10 ... 142 A4
Plum Cl TW14 ... 150 A3
Plumcroft Prim Sch SE18 ... 145 A6
Plume Ho SE10 ... 141 D6
Plum Garth TW8 ... 109 D2
Plum La SE18 ... 145 A5
Plummer Ct SE13 ... 163 D5
Plummer La CR4 ... 180 D1
Plummer Rd SW4 ... 159 D4
Plumpton Cl UB5 ... 63 C2
Plumpton Ct SE23 ... 163 A4
Plumpton Lo E5 ... 74 D5
Plumpton Way SM5 ... 218 C5
PLUMSTEAD ... 123 C2
PLUMSTEAD COMMON ... 145 D6
Plumstead Common Rd SE18 ... 145 A6
Plumstead High St SE18, SE2 ... 123 C2
Plumstead Manor/Negus Sch SE18 ... 145 B6
Plumstead Rd SE18, SE28 ... 123 A2
Plumstead Road Covered Mkt SE18 ... 122 D2
Plumstead Sta SE18 ... 123 B2
Plumtree Cl
Dagenham RM10 ... 81 D2
Wallington SM6 ... 219 D1
Plumtree Ct EC4 ... 241 C2
Plymen Ho KT8 ... 195 C4
Plymouth Ho
10 Barking IG11 ... 80 A1
20 Lewisham SE10 ... 141 D4
Plymouth Rd
Bromley BR1 ... 187 B2
Newham E16 ... 99 A2
Plymouth Wharf E14 ... 120 B2
Plympton Ave NW6 ... 69 B1
Plympton Cl 8 DA17 ... 125 A3
Plympton Pl NW1 ... 237 A5
Plympton Rd NW6 ... 69 B1
Plympton St NW8 ... 237 A5
Plymstock Rd DA16 ... 146 C5
Pocklington Cl NW9 ... 27 C1
Pocklington Ct SW15 ... 156 A3
Pocklington Lo 6 W12 ... 112 A3
Pocock Ave UB7 ... 104 B3
Pocock St SE1 ... 116 D4 251 D2
Podmore Rd SW18 ... 136 A1
Poets Cnr* SW1 ... 260 A6
Poet's Rd N5 ... 73 B3
Poets Way HA1 ... 42 C5
Pointalls Cl N3 ... 30 A1
Point Cl SE10 ... 142 A4
Pointer Cl SE28 ... 102 D1
Pointer Sch The SE3 ... 143 A5
Pointers Cl E14 ... 119 D1
Point Hill SE10 ... 142 A4
Point Ho SE10 ... 142 A4
Point Pl HA9 ... 66 D1
Point Pleasant SW18 ... 135 C1
Point Terr E7 ... 77 B3
Point The HA4 ... 62 A4
Point Wharf La TW8 ... 132 A5
Poland Ho 3 E15 ... 98 B6
Poland St W1 ... 93 C1 239 B1
Polaris Ct EN4 ... 14 B6
Polebrook Rd SE3 ... 143 C2
Polecroft La SE6 ... 163 B2
Polehamptons The TW12 ... 174 A2
Pole Hill Rd
Chingford E4 ... 20 A4
Hillingdon UB4 ... 83 A4
Polesden Gdns SW20 ... 178 B1
Polesworth Ho 16 W2 ... 91 C2
Polesworth Rd RM9 ... 80 D1
Polish Inst & Sikorski Mus* SW7 ... 246 D1
Polish Univ Abroad W6 ... 112 A2
Polish War Meml HA4 ... 62 C2
Pollard Cl
Islington N7 ... 72 B4
Newham E16 ... 121 A6
Pollard Ct SM4 ... 202 C4
Pollard Ho
Cheam KT4 ... 216 C4
Islington N1 ... 233 C3
Pollard Rd
East Barnet N20 ... 14 C2
Morden SM4 ... 202 B4
Pollard Row E2 ... 96 A4
Pollards Cl IG10 ... 21 C6
Pollards Cres SW16 ... 204 A6
Pollards Hill E SW16 ... 204 B6
Pollards Hill N SW16 ... 204 B6
Pollards Hill S SW16 ... 204 B6
Pollards Hill W SW16 ... 204 B6
Pollard St E2 ... 96 A4
Pollards Wood Rd SW16 ... 204 A6
Pollard Wlk DA14 ... 190 C4
Pollen St W1 ... 238 D1
Pollitt Dr NW8 ... 92 B3 236 D6
Pollock Ho W10 ... 91 A3
Polperro Cl BR6 ... 211 D3
Polperro Mans 3 NW6 ... 69 C3
Polperro Mews SE11 ... 261 C4
Polsted Rd SE6 ... 163 B4
Polsten Mews 2 EN3 ... 7 C6
Polthorne Gr SE18 ... 123 B2
Polworth Rd SW16 ... 182 A5
Polygon Rd NW1 ... 93 D5 232 C3
Polygon The
1 Clapham SW4 ... 137 C1
St John's Wood NW8 ... 229 D6
Polytechnic St SE18 ... 122 C2
Pomell Way E1 ... 243 D2
Pomeroy Cl TW1 ... 131 B1
Pomeroy Ct W11 ... 91 A1
Pomeroy Ho 5 E2 ... 96 D5
Pomeroy St SE14 ... 140 C4
Pomfret Rd SE5 ... 138 D2
Pomoja La N19 ... 72 A6
Pomona Ho 10 SE8 ... 119 A2
Pond Cl
Colney Hatch N12 ... 30 C4
Kidbrooke SE3 ... 143 A3
Pond Cottage La BR3, BR4 ... 207 C1
Pond Cotts SE21 ... 161 C3
PONDERS END ... 18 D6
Ponders End Ind Est EN3 ... 19 A6
Ponders End Sta EN3 ... 19 A6
Ponder St 5 N7 ... 72 B1
Pond Farm Est E5 ... 74 C5
Pondfield End IG10 ... 21 C4
Pondfield Ho
4 Islington N5 ... 73 A3
West Norwood SE27 ... 183 A5
Pondfield Rd
Dagenham RM10 ... 81 D3

Pondfield Rd *continued*
Locksbottom BR6 . . . . . . 226 D5
West Wickham BR2 . . . . 208 C1
Pond Gn HA4 . . . . 61 C6
Pond Hill Gdns SM3 . . . 217 A2
Pond Ho
Chelsea SW3 . . . . 257 A3
Stanmore HA7 . . . . 25 B4
Pond Mead SE21 . . . . . . 161 B5
Pond Path BR7 . . . . 188 D4
Pond Pl SW3 . . 114 C2 257 A3
Pond Rd
Blackheath Vale SE3 . . . . 142 D3
Newham E15 . . . . 98 C5
Pondside Cl UB3 . . . . . . 127 B6
Pond Sq N6 . . . . 49 A1
Pond St NW3 . . . . 70 C3
Pond Way TW11 . . . . . . 175 C4
Pondwood Rise BR6 . . 211 C2
Ponler St E1 . . . . 96 B1
Ponsard Rd NW10 . . . . . . 90 B4
Ponsford St E9 . . . . 74 C2
Ponsonby Ho 13 E2 . . . . 96 C5
Ponsonby Pl
SW1 . . . . 115 D1 259 D2
Ponsonby Rd SW15 . . . 156 B4
Ponsonby Terr SW1 . . . 259 D2
Pontefract Ct UB5 . . . . . 63 D3
Pontefract Rd BR1 . . . . 186 D5
Ponton Ho SW2 . . . . 160 C3
Ponton Rd
SW8 . . . . 137 D6 269 D5
Pontoon Dock Sta
E16 . . . . 121 C5
Pont St Mews SW1 . . . . 257 C5
Pont St SW1 . . . 114 D3 257 D5
Pontypool Pl SE1 . . . . . 251 C2
Pool Cl
Beckenham BR3 . . . . 185 C5
East Molesey KT8 . . . . . . 195 B4
Pool Ct SE6 . . . . 163 C2
Poole Cl HA4 . . . . 61 C6
Poole Court Rd TW5 . . 129 A3
Poole Ct
De Beauvoir Town N1 . . . . 73 C1
Hounslow TW5 . . . . 129 A3
Poole Ho SE11 . . . . 260 D5
Pool End Cl TW17 . . . . . 192 C4
Poole Rd
Homerton E9 . . . . 74 D2
West Ewell KT19 . . . . . . 215 B2
Pooles Bldgs EC1 . . . . . 241 A5
Pooles Ct IG3 . . . . 80 A5
Pooles La SW10 . . . . 266 A3
Pooles Park Prim Sch
N4 . . . . 72 B6
Pooles Pk N4 . . . . 72 C6
Poole St N1 . . . . 95 B6 235 C5
Poole Way UB4 . . . . 83 C4
Pooley Ho E1 . . . . 96 D4
Pool Ho NW8 . . . . 236 D4
Poolmans St SE16 . . . . . 118 D4
Pool Rd
East Molesey KT12,
KT8 . . . . 195 B4
Harrow HA1 . . . . 42 B2
Poolsford Rd NW9 . . . . . 45 C5
Poonah St E1 . . . . 96 C1
Pope Cl
East Bedfont TW14 . . . . . 149 D3
Mitcham SW17, SW19 . . 180 B4
Pope Ct 10 KT2 . . . . 175 D6
Pope Ho
7 Bermondsey SE16 . . . 118 B2
3 Camberwell SE5 . . . . 139 B5
Pope John RC Prim Sch
W12 . . . . 112 B6
Pope Rd BR2 . . . . 209 D4
Pope's Ave TW2 . . . . 152 C2
Popes Ct TW2 . . . . 152 C2
Popes Dr N3 . . . . 29 C2
Popes Gr CR0 . . . . 223 B5
Pope's Gr TW1, TW2 . . . 152 D2
Pope's Head Alley
EC3 . . . . 242 D1
Pope's La W5 . . . . 110 A3
Pope's Rd SW9 . . . . 138 C2
Pope St SE1 . . . . 253 B1
Pope Street Ct SE9 . . . . 166 B3
Popham Cl TW13 . . . . . . 151 B1
Popham Ct N16 . . . . 73 C5
Popham Gdns TW9 . . . . 132 D2
Popham Rd N1 . . 95 A6 235 A6
Popham St
Islington N1 . . . . 234 D6
Shoreditch N1 . . 95 A6 235 A6
Pop In Bsns Ctr HA9 . . . . 66 D3
POPLAR 97 C1
Poplar Ave
Mitcham CR4 . . . . 180 D2
Poplar Ave *continued*
Orpington BR6 . . . . 226 D6
Southall UB2 . . . . 107 D3
Yiewsley UB7 . . . . 104 B6
Poplar Bath St 11
E14 . . . . 119 D6
Poplar Bsns Pk E14 . . . 120 A6
Poplar Cl
Hackney E9 . . . . 75 B3
Pinner HA5 . . . . 22 D2
Poplar Cres KT19 . . . . . 215 A2
Poplar Ct
Chingford E4 . . . . 35 D4
Northolt UB5 . . . . 84 C5
4 Streatham SW16 . . . . 160 B1
13 Twickenham TW1 . . . . 153 C5
Wimbledon SW19 . . . . . 179 C5
Poplar Farm Cl KT19 . . 215 A2
Poplar Gdns KT3 . . . . . . 177 B1
Poplar Gr
Friern Barnet N11 . . . . . . 31 A4
Hammersmith W6 . . . . . 112 C4
Kingston u T KT3 . . . . . . 199 B6
Wembley HA9 . . . . 67 A5
Poplar High St E14 . . . . 119 D6
Poplar Ho
Brockley SE4 . . . . 141 B1
19 Rotherhithe SE16 . . . 118 D4
Poplar Mews 4 W12 . . 112 C5
Poplar Mount DA17 . . . 125 D2
Poplar Pl
Hayes UB3 . . . . 106 A6
Kensington
W2 . . . . 113 D6 245 D6
Woolwich SE28 . . . . 124 C6
Poplar Prim Sch
SW19 . . . . 201 C6
Poplar Rd
Ashford TW15 . . . . 171 A5
Cheam SM3 . . . . 201 B1
Herne Hill SE24 . . . . 139 A1
Merton SW19 . . . . 179 C1
Poplar Rd S SW19 . . . . . 201 C6
Poplars Cl HA4 . . . . 39 C1
Poplars Ho 14 E17 . . . . . 53 D6
Poplars Rd E17 . . . . 53 D3
Poplar Sta E14 . . . . 119 D6
Poplars The
East Barnet N14 . . . . 15 B6
Kentish Town NW5 . . . . . . 71 C3
Poplar View HA9 . . . . 65 D6
Poplar Way
Feltham TW13 . . . . 150 B1
Ilford IG6 . . . . 57 A5
Poplar Wlk
Croydon CR0 . . . . 205 A1
Herne Hill SE24 . . . . 139 A1
Poppins Ct EC4 . . . . 241 C1
Poppleton Rd E11 . . . . . . 54 C3
Poppy Cl
Belvedere DA17 . . . . 125 D4
Hackbridge SM6 . . . . 203 A1
Northolt UB5 . . . . 63 B2
Poppy Ct HA3 . . . . 42 C6
Poppy La CR0 . . . . 206 C1
Porchester Ct W2 . . . . . . 91 D1
Porchester Gate W2 . . 246 A5
Porchester Gdn Mews
W2 . . . . 91 D1
Porchester Gdns
W2 . . . . 113 D6 245 D6
Porchester Ho 3 E1 . . . 96 B1
Porchester Mead
BR3 . . . . 185 D4
Porchester Mews W2 . . 91 D1
Porchester Pl W2 . . . . . 237 B1
Porchester Rd
Kensington W2 . . . . 91 D1
Kingston u T KT1 . . . . . . 176 D1
Porchester Sq W2 . . . . . 91 D1
Porchester Terr
W2 . . . . 114 A6 246 A6
Porchester Terr N W2 . . 91 D1
Porch Way N20 . . . . 14 D1
Porcupine Cl SE9 . . . . . 166 A2
Porden Rd SW2 . . . . 138 B1
Porland Ct SE1 . . . . 262 C6
Porlock Ave HA1, HA2 . . . 42 A1
Porlock Ho 5 SE26 . . . 162 A1
Porlock Rd EN1 . . . . 17 D4
Porlock St
SE1 . . . . 117 B4 252 D2
Porrington Cl BR7 . . . . 188 C2
Porson Ct SE13 . . . . 141 D2
Portal Cl
Hillingdon UB10 . . . . 60 B1
Ruislip HA4 . . . . 62 B4
West Norwood SE27 . . . 160 C1
Portal Way W3 . . . . 89 B2
Portbury Cl 17 SE15 . . . 140 A4
Portchester Cl SE24 . . . 139 B1
Port Cres E13 . . . . 99 B3
Portcullis Lodge Rd
EN1 . . . . 5 B2
Porte 10 NW9 . . . . 27 D2
Portelet Ct 1 N1 . . . . . . 95 C6
Portelet Rd E1 . . . . 96 D4
Porten Hos W14 . . . . . . 254 A5
Porten Rd W14 . . . . 254 A5
Porter Rd E6 . . . . 100 B1
Porters Ave RM8, RM9 . . 80 C3
Porter Sq N19 . . . . 50 A1
Porter St
Borough The
SE1 . . . . 117 A5 252 B4
Marylebone W1 . . . . 237 D4
Porters & Walters
Almshouses N22 . . . . . 32 B3
Porters Way UB7 . . . . . . 104 B4
Porteus Rd W2 . . . . 236 B4
Portfleet Pl 34 N1 . . . . . 95 C6
Portgate Cl W9 . . . . 91 B3
Porthallow Cl BR6 . . . . 227 D4
Porthcawe Rd SE26 . . . 185 B6
Porthkerry Ave DA16 . . 146 A1
Port Ho 6 SW11 . . . . . . 136 A2
Port House The 6
E14 . . . . 119 D1
Portia Ct 12 IG11 . . . . . . 80 A1
Portia Way E3 . . . . 97 B3
Porticos The SW3 . . . . . 266 C5
Portinscale Rd SW15 . . 157 B6
Portishead Ho 29 W2 . . . 91 C2
Portland Ave
Blackfen DA15 . . . . 168 A5
New Malden KT3 . . . . . . 199 D2
Stamford Hill N16 . . . . 51 D2
Portland Cl
Dagenham RM6 . . . . 59 A4
New Malden KT4 . . . . . . 200 B2
Portland Commercial Est
IG11 . . . . 102 C5
Portland Cotts
Feltham TW13 . . . . 173 A5
Wallington CR0 . . . . 203 D2
Portland Cres
1 Chislehurst SE9 . . . . . 166 A2
Feltham TW13 . . . . 171 B6
Southall UB6 . . . . 86 A2
Stanmore HA7 . . . . 25 D1
Portland Cres W HA7 . . . 43 D6
Portland Ct
7 De Beauvoir Town
N1 . . . . 73 C1
1 Deptford SE14 . . . . . . 141 A6
1 Sutton SM2 . . . . 217 D2
Portland Dr EN2 . . . . 5 C5
Portland Gdns
Harringay N4 . . . . 50 D3
Ilford RM6 . . . . 58 D4
Portland Gr
SW8 . . . . 138 B4 270 C2
Portland Ho 19 SW2 . . . 160 C3
Portland Hospl for
Women & Children The
W1 . . . . 238 D5
Portland Mans SE25 . . . 206 B4
Portland Mews W1 . . . 239 B1
Portland Pl
Croydon SE25 . . . . 206 A5
Marylebone W1 . 93 B2 238 D3
Portland Place Sch
W1 . . . . 93 B2 238 D3
Portland Place Schs
W1 . . . . 93 B2 238 D4
Portland Rd
Ashford TW15 . . . . 148 A1
Bromley BR1 . . . . 187 C5
Chislehurst SE9 . . . . 166 A2
Croydon SE25 . . . . 206 B4
Hayes UB4 . . . . 83 C4
Kingston u T KT1 . . . . . . 198 B6
Mitcham CR4 . . . . 180 C1
Notting Hill
W11 . . . . 113 A5 244 B4
Notting Hill
W11 . . . . 113 A6 244 A5
Southall UB2 . . . . 107 B3
Tottenham N15 . . . . 51 D5
Portland Rise N4 . . . . 51 A1
Portland Sq 4 E1 . . . . . 118 B5
Portland St
SE17 . . . . 117 B1 262 C1
Portland Terr
Edgware HA8 . . . . 26 C3
Richmond TW9 . . . . 131 D1
Portland Village W6 . . 112 C3
Portman Ave SW14 . . . . 133 B2
Portman Cl
Bexley DA7 . . . . 147 A2
Portman Cl *continued*
Marylebone W1 . 93 A1 238 A2
Portman Dr IG8 . . . . 37 D1
Portman Gate NW1 . . . 237 B5
Portman Gdns
Hendon NW9 . . . . 27 B1
Hillingdon UB10 . . . . 60 C1
Portman Hall HA3 . . . . . . 24 B5
Portman Hts 1 NW3 . . . 69 C5
Portman Lo N21 . . . . 16 D6
Portman Mews S W1 . . 238 A1
Portman Pl E2 . . . . 96 C4
Portman Rd KT1 . . . . . . 176 B1
Portman Sq
W1 . . . . 93 A1 238 A2
Portman St W1 . 93 A1 238 A1
Portman The NW11 . . . . 47 C2
Portman Twrs W1 . . . . 237 D2
Portmeadow Wlk
SE2 . . . . 124 D4
Portmeers Cl E17 . . . . . . 53 C3
Portnall Rd W9 . . . . 91 B4
Portobello Ct Est W11 . . 91 B1
Portobello Ho 6
SW27 . . . . 182 D5
Portobello Mews
W11 . . . . 245 A5
Portobello Rd
W11 . . . . 113 B6 244 D6
Portobello Road Mkt*
W10 91 A2
Porton Ct KT6 . . . . 197 C3
Portpool La
EC1 . . . . 94 C2 241 A4
Portree Cl N22 . . . . 32 B3
Portree St E14 . . . . 98 B1
Port Royal Pl 3 N16 . . . 73 C3
Portrush Ct 9 UB1 . . . . . 86 A1
Portsdown HA8 . . . . 26 C5
Portsdown Ave NW11 . . 47 B3
Portsdown Mews
NW11 . . . . 47 B3
Portsea Hall W2 . . . . . . 237 B1
Portsea Ho 3 SW15 . . . 156 B3
Portsea Mews W2 . . . . 237 B1
Portsea Pl W2 . . . . 237 B1
Portslade Rd SW8 . . . . . 137 C3
Portsmouth Ave KT7 . . 197 A2
Portsmouth Rd
Esher KT10 . . . . 212 A5
Putney SW15 . . . . 156 C4
Thames Ditton KT6,
KT7 . . . . 197 C3
Portsmouth St WC2 . . . 240 D1
Portsoken St E1, EC3 . . 253 C6
Portswood Pl SW15 . . . 155 D5
Portugal Gdns TW2 . . . 152 A2
Portugal St
WC2 . . . . 94 B1 240 D1
Portway E15 . . . . 98 D6
Portway Gdns SE18 . . . 143 D5
Portway Prim Sch E13 . 98 D6
Poseidon Ct
Dagenham IG11 . . . . 102 B4
9 Millwall E14 . . . . 119 C2
Postern Gn EN2 . . . . 4 C2
Postern The EC2 . . . . . . 242 B3
Post La TW2 . . . . 152 B3
Postmasters Lodge
HA5 . . . . 41 A2
Postmill Cl CR0 . . . . 222 D5
Post Office App E7 . . . . . 77 B3
Post Office Way
SW8 . . . . 137 D5 269 C4
Post Rd UB2 . . . . 107 D3
Postway Mews 1 IG1 . . 78 D5
Potier St SE1 . . . . 262 D5
Potter Cl CR4 . . . . 181 B1
Potteries The EN5 . . . . . 13 C6
Potterill Ct TW11 . . . . . 175 B3
Potterne Cl 5 SW19 . . 156 D4
Potters Cl
5 Camberwell SE15 . . . 139 C5
Croydon CR0 . . . . 207 A1
Pottersfield EN1 . . . . 5 C1
Potters Fields
SE1 . . . . 117 C5 253 B3
Potters Gr KT3 . . . . 199 A5
Potters Heights Cl
HA5 . . . . 22 B3
Potter's La
Barnet EN5 . . . . 1 C1
Streatham SW16 . . . . . . 181 D4
Potters Lo E14 . . . . 120 A1
Potters Mews 4 WD6 . . . 9 D5
Potters Rd SW6 . . . . 136 A3
Potter's Rd EN5 . . . . 1 D1
Potter St HA5 . . . . 22 B2
Potter Street Hill HA5 . . 22 B3
Pottery La
W11 . . . . 113 A5 244 B4
Pottery Rd TW8 . . . . 132 A6
Pottery St SE16 . . . . 118 B4
Pott St E2 . . . . 96 B4
Poulett Gdns TW1 . . . . 153 A3
Poulett Rd E6 . . . . 100 B5
Poullett Ho SW2 . . . . . . 160 D3
Poulters Wood BR2 . . . 225 D3
Poulton Ave SM1 . . . . . 218 B5
Poulton Cl E8 . . . . 74 B2
Poultry EC2 . . . . . 95 B1 242 C1
Pound Cl
Long Ditton KT6 . . . . 197 C1
Orpington BR6 . . . . 227 B6
Pound Court Dr BR6 . . 227 B6
Pound Farm Cl KT10 . . 196 B1
Pound Green Ct 4
DA5 . . . . 169 C4
Pound La NW10 . . . . 68 A2
Pound Park Rd SE7 . . . 121 D2
Pound Pl SE9 . . . . 166 C5
Pound St SM5 . . . . 218 D3
Pountney Rd SW11 . . . . 137 A2
Poverest Rd BR5 . . . . . . 211 D4
Povey Ho
Tulse Hill SW2 . . . . 160 C5
Walworth SE17 . . . . 263 A3
Powder Mill La TW2,
TW4 . . . . 151 C3
Powell Cl
Chessington KT9 . . . . . . 213 D3
Edgware HA8 . . . . 26 B4
Wallington SM6 . . . . 220 A1
Powell Ct
Croydon CR2 . . . . 221 A4
19 Walthamstow E17 . . . . 53 D6
Powell Gdns RM10 . . . . . 81 C4
Powell Ho 10 SW19 . . . 179 A4
Powell Rd
Buckhurst Hill IG9 . . . . . . 21 C4
Hackney E5 . . . . 74 B5
Powell's Wlk W4 . . . . . 133 D6
Powell Terr CR4 . . . . . . 204 A5
Powergate Bsns Pk
NW10 . . . . 89 B4
Power Ho 13 TW9 . . . . . 132 C4
Power Ho The W4 . . . . . 111 D2
Power Rd W4 . . . . 110 C2
Powerscroft Rd
Lower Clapton E5 . . . . 74 C4
Sidcup DA14 . . . . 190 C4
Powers Ct TW1 . . . . 153 D4
Powis Ct
Bushey WD23 . . . . 8 B3
Edgware HA8 . . . . 26 B6
Powis Gdns
Golders Green NW11 . . . . 47 B2
Notting Hill W11 . . . . 91 B1
Powis Ho WC2 . . . . 240 B2
Powis Mews W11 . . . . . . 91 B1
Powis Pl WC1 . . . 94 A3 240 B5
Powis Rd E3 . . . . 97 D4
Powis Sq W11 . . . . 91 B1
Powis St SE18 . . . . 122 D2
Powis Terr W11 . . . . 91 B1
Powlesland Ct 21 E14 . . 97 A1
Powle Terr IG1 . . . . 79 B3
Powlett Ho NW1 . . . . 71 B2
Powlett Pl NW1 . . . . 71 B1
Pownall Gdns TW3 . . . . 129 D1
Pownall Rd
Hackney E8 . . . . 96 A6
Hounslow TW3 . . . . 129 D1
Pownsett Terr IG1 . . . . . 79 A3
Powrie Ho 4 SW11 . . . 136 B3
Powster Rd BR1 . . . . . . 187 B5
Powys Cl DA7 . . . . 146 D6
Powys Ct N11 . . . . 32 A5
Powys La
Bowes Pk N13 . . . . 32 A5
Palmers Green N14 . . . . . 32 A6
Poynder Ct 3 N7 . . . . . . 72 A3
Poynder Lo TW7 . . . . . . 131 A4
Poynders Ct 9 SW4 . . . 159 C5
Poynders Gdns SW12 . 159 C4
Poynders Rd SW12,
SW4 . . . . 159 D4
Poynings Rd N19 . . . . . . 71 C5
Poynings Way N12 . . . . . 29 C5
Poyntell Cres BR7 . . . . 189 B2
Poynter Ct 11 UB5 . . . . . 84 D5
Poynter Ho
Paddington NW8 . . . . . . 236 C6
10 Shepherd's Bush
W11 . . . . 112 D5
Poynter Rd EN1 . . . . 18 A6
Poynton Rd N17 . . . . 34 A1
Poyntz Rd SW11 . . . . . . 136 D3
Poyser St E2 . . . . 96 B5
Praed Mews W2 . . . . . . 236 D2
Praed St W2 . . . . 92 B1 236 D2
Pragel St E13 . . . . 99 C5
Pragnell Rd SE12 . . . . . 165 B2
Prague Pl SW2 . . . . 160 A6
Prah Rd N4 . . . . 72 C6
Prairie St SW8 . . . . 137 B3
Pratt Mews NW1 . . . . . . 232 A5
Pratt St NW1 . . . 93 C6 232 A6
Pratt Wlk SE1,
SE11 . . . . 116 B2 260 D4
Prayle Gr NW2 . . . . 46 D1
Preachers Ct EC1 . . . . . 241 D5
Prebend Gdns W4,
W6 . . . . 111 D2
Prebend Mans 4
W4 . . . . 111 D2
Prebend St N1 . . 95 A6 235 A6
Precinct Rd UB3 . . . . . . 106 A6
Precincts The SM4 . . . . 201 C3
Precinct The
Islington N1 . . . . 235 A5
Islington N5 . . . . 72 D3
Premier Corner NW6 . . . 91 B5
Premier Ct EN3 . . . . 6 D5
Premier Ho 25 N1 . . . . . . 72 D1
Premier League Hall of
Fame* SE1 250 C2
Premier Lo N3 . . . . 29 C2
Premier Park Rd
NW10 . . . . 88 D5
Premier Pk NW10 . . . . . . 88 D5
Premier Pl 17 E14 . . . . 119 C6
Prendergast Ho 7
SW4 . . . . 159 D4
Prendergast Rd SE3 . . . 142 C2
Prendergast Sch SE4 . . 141 C1
Prentice Ct 2 SW19 . . . 179 B5
Prentis Rd SW16 . . . . . . 181 D6
Prentiss Ct SE7 . . . . 121 D2
Presburg Rd KT3 . . . . . . 199 C4
Prescelly Pl HA8 . . . . 26 B2
Prescot St E1 . . 117 D6 253 D6
Prescott Ave BR5 . . . . . 210 D3
Prescott Ho
Croydon CR0 . . . . 220 C5
13 Kennington SE17 . . . . 138 D6
Prescott Pl
Clapham SW4 . . . . 137 D1
Streatham SW16 . . . . . . 182 A3
Presentation Mews
SW2 . . . . 160 B3
Preshaw Cres CR4 . . . . 202 C6
President Dr E1 . . . . . . 118 B5
President Ho EC1 . . . . . 234 D1
President St EC1 . . . . . 235 A2
Prespa Cl N9 . . . . 18 C2
Press Ho NW10 . . . . 67 B5
Press Rd NW10 . . . . 67 B5
Prestage Way 13 E14 . . 120 A6
Prestbury Rd E7 . . . . 77 C1
Prestbury Sq SE9 . . . . . 188 B6
Prested Rd SW11 . . . . . 136 C1
PRESTON 44 A1
Preston Ave E4 . . . . 36 B4
Preston Cl
Twickenham TW2 . . . . . . 152 C1
Walworth SE1 . . . . 263 A4
Preston Ct
5 New Barnet EN5 . . . . . . 2 A1
Northwood Hills HA6 . . . . 22 A1
Sidcup DA14 . . . . 189 D6
Walton-on-T KT12 . . . . . 194 C1
Preston Dr
Bexley DA7 . . . . 146 D4
Wanstead E11 . . . . 55 C4
West Ewell KT19 . . . . . . 215 D2
Preston Gdns
Enfield EN3 . . . . 7 A6
Redbridge IG1 . . . . 56 A3
Willesden NW10 . . . . 67 C2
Preston Hill HA3 . . . . 44 B3
Preston Ho
Bermondsey SE1 . . . . . . 263 C6
3 Dagenham RM10 . . . . . 81 C5
Walworth SE1 . . . . 263 A4
1 Woolwich SE18 . . . . . 122 C2
Preston Manor High Sch
HA9 . . . . 66 B6
Preston Park Prim Sch
HA9 . . . . 43 D1
Preston Pl
Richmond TW10 . . . . 154 A6
Willesden NW2 . . . . 68 A2
Preston Rd
Leytonstone E11 . . . . 54 C3
Littleton TW17 . . . . 192 C4

Preston Rd *continued*
South Norwood SE19 182 D4
Wembley HA3, HA9 66 A6
Wimbledon SW20 177 D3
Preston Road Sta HA3 44 A1
Prestons Rd BR2 225 A6
Preston's Rd E14 120 A5
Preston Waye HA3 44 A1
Prestwich Terr SW4 159 D6
Prestwick Cl UB2 107 A1
Prestwick Ct
Southall UB1 108 A6
Tottenham N17 34 A3
Prestwick Rd WD19 22 D6
Prestwood Ave HA3 43 B5
Prestwood Cl
East Wickham SE18 146 A6
Harrow HA3 43 B5
Prestwood Gdns CR0 205 A2
Prestwood Ho 3
SE16 118 B3
Prestwood St N1 235 B3
Pretoria Ave E17 53 A5
Pretoria Cres E4 20 A3
Pretoria Ho 3 HA4 40 C1
Pretoria Rd
Chingford E4 20 B3
Ilford IG1 78 D3
Leytonstone E11 54 B1
Newham E16 98 D3
Streatham SW16 181 C5
Tottenham N17 33 D4
Pretoria Rd N N18 33 D4
Pretty Cnr HA6 22 A5
Prevost Rd N11 15 A2
Priam Ho 17 E2 96 B5
Price Cl
Finchley NW7 29 A4
Upper Tooting SW17 158 D1
Price Ct HA1 43 A4
Price Ho N1 235 A5
Price Rd CR0 220 D3
Prices Ct SW11 136 B2
Price's St SE1 251 D4
Price's Yd N1 233 D5
Price Way TW12 173 A4
Prichard Ct
Battersea SW11 266 D1
Islington N7 72 B3
Pricklers Hill EN5 13 D5
Prickley Wood BR2 208 D1
Priddy's Yd 4 CR0 221 A6
Prideaux Ho WC1 233 D2
Prideaux Pl
Acton W3 111 B6
St Pancras WC1 94 B4 233 D2
Prideaux Rd SW9 138 A2
Pride Ct N1 234 B4
Pridham Rd CR7 205 B5
Priestfield Rd SE23 163 A1
Priestlands Park Rd
DA15 167 D1
Priestley Cl N16 51 D2
Priestley Gdns RM6 58 B3
Priestley Ho
2 Camden Town NW5 71 B2
St Luke's EC1 242 B6
3 Wembley HA9 67 A5
Priestley Rd CR4 181 A1
Priestley Way
Hendon NW2 46 A1
Walthamstow E17 52 D6
Priestman Point 25 E3 97 D4
Priestmead Fst & Mid Schs HA3 43 B6
Priest Park Ave HA2 63 C6
Priests Bridge SW14 133 C2
Priest's Ct EC2 242 A2
Prima Rd SW9 138 C5
Primrose Ave
Enfield EN2 5 C4
Ilford RM6 58 B2
Primrose Cl
6 Bow E3 97 C5
Catford SE6 186 A5
Finchley N3 29 D1
Hackbridge SM6 203 B1
Harrow HA2 63 B5
Primrose Ct
2 Child's Hill NW2 69 B5
New Malden KT4 200 A2
Primrose Hill NW8 230 C5
11 Streatham SW12 159 D4
Primrose Gdns
Hampstead NW3 70 C2
Ruislip HA4 62 C3
PRIMROSE HILL 70 D1
Primrose Hill EC4 241 B1
Primrose Hill Ct NW3 70 D1
Primrose Hill Rd
Primrose Hill NW1, NW3 70 D1
Primrose Hill NW1, NW3 230 C6
Primrose Hill Sch
NW1 93 A6 231 B6
Primrose Hill Studios
NW1 231 A6
Primrose Ho
7 Peckham SE15 140 A4
1 Richmond TW9 132 B4
Primrose La CR0 206 D1
Primrose Mans SW11 268 A2
Primrose Mews 9
NW1 70 D1
Primrose Pl TW7 130 D3
Primrose Rd
Walthamstow E10 53 D1
Woodford E18 37 B1
Primrose Sq E9 96 C6
Primrose St
EC2 95 C2 243 B4
Primrose Way HA0 87 D5
Primrose Wlk
Ewell KT17 215 D1
6 New Cross Gate SE14 141 A5
Primula St W12 90 A1
Prince Albert Ct
Primrose Hill NW8 230 C5
Sunbury TW16 171 C3
Prince Albert Rd
NW8 92 D6 230 C5
Prince Arthur Ct 18
NW3 70 A4
Prince Arthur Mews 17
NW3 70 A4
Prince Arthur Rd NW3 70 A3
Prince Charles Dr
NW2 46 C2
Prince Charles Rd
SE3 142 D4
Prince Charles Way
SM6 219 B5
Prince Consort Dr
BR7 189 B2
Prince Consort Ho
SE1 260 B2
Prince Consort Rd
SW7 114 B3 256 C6
Princedale Rd
W11 113 A5 244 B4
Prince Edward Mans
W2 245 B6
Prince Edward Rd E9 75 B2
Prince George Ave
N14 15 D6
Prince George Rd N16 73 C4
Prince George's Ave
SW20 178 C1
Prince Georges Rd
SW19 180 B2
Prince Henry Rd SE7 143 D5
Prince Imperial Rd
Chislehurst BR7 188 D3
Kidbrooke SE18 144 B4
Prince John Rd SE9 166 A6
Princelet St E1 95 D2 243 D4
Prince of Orange La 3
SE10 142 A5
Prince Of Wales Cl
NW4 46 B5
Prince of Wales Dr
SW11 137 A4 268 A2
Prince of Wales Mans
Battersea SW11 268 B2
Clapham SW4 159 B6
Prince of Wales Pas
NW1 232 A1
Prince of Wales Prim Sch
EN3 7 B6
Prince of Wales Rd
Blackheath Vale SE3 142 D4
Camden Town NW5 71 A2
Newham E16 99 C1
Prince Of Wales' Rd
SM1 218 B6
Prince Of Wales Terr
Chiswick W4 111 C1
Kensington W8 245 D1
Prince Rd SE25 205 C4
Prince Regent E16 99 C2
Prince Regent Ct 2
SE16 119 A5
Prince Regent La E13 99 C3
Prince Regent Mews
NW1 232 A1
Prince Regent Rd
TW3 130 A2
Prince Regent Sta
E16 121 C6
Prince Rupert Rd
SE9 144 B1
Princes Arc SW1 249 B4
Princes Ave
Acton W3 110 C3
Edmonton N13 32 C5
Finchley N3 29 D2
Muswell Hill N10 49 B6
Orpington BR5 211 C4
Queensbury NW9 44 D5
Tolworth KT6 214 C6
Wallington SM5 218 D1
Woodford IG8 37 C6
Wood Green N22 31 D2
Prince's Ave UB1 85 D1
Princes Cir
WC2 94 A1 240 A2
Princes Cl
Edgware HA8 26 C5
Finsbury Pk N4 50 D1
Queensbury NW9 44 C5
Sidcup DA14 168 D1
Prince's Cl TW11, TW12 174 B6
Princes Coll WC1 240 A2
Princes Court Bsns Ctr 14
E1 118 B6
Princes Ct
Brondesbury NW2 69 A3
Hampstead NW3 70 B4
Kingston u T KT3 199 D6
Stepney E1 118 B6
Wembley HA9 66 A3
Prince's Ct SE16 119 B3
Princes Dr HA1 42 C6
Princes Gate
SW7 114 B4 246 D1
Prince's Gate
SW7 114 C4 247 A1
Princes Gate Ct SW7 246 D1
Princes Gate Mews
SW7 114 B3 256 D6
Princes Gdns
Acton W3 88 C2
Brompton SW7 114 B3 256 D6
Ealing W5 87 C3
Princes Ho W11 245 A5
Princes La N10 49 B6
Princes Mews TW3 129 C1
Prince's Mews
1 Hammersmith W6 112 B1
Kensington W2 113 D6 245 C6
Princes Par NW11 47 A3
Princes Park Ave
Hayes UB3 105 B6
Temple Fortune NW11 47 A4
Princes Park Circ
UB3 105 B6
Princes Park Cl UB3 105 B6
Princes Park La UB3 105 B6
Princes Park Par
UB3 105 B6
Princes Pl
Notting Hill W11 113 A5 244 A4
St James SW1 249 B4
Prince's Plain BR2 210 A1
Princes Plain Prim Sch
BR2 210 A2
Princes Rd
Ashford TW15 170 B5
Buckhurst Hill IG9 21 C2
Ealing W13 109 B5
Edmonton N18 34 C6
Feltham TW13 149 D1
Ilford IG6 57 B5
Kew TW9 132 B4
Kingston u T KT2 176 C3
Penge SE20 184 D4
Richmond TW10 154 B6
Prince's Rd
Mortlake SW14 133 B2
Teddington TW11, TW12 174 B6
Wimbledon SW19 179 C4
Princes Rise SE13 142 A3
Princes Riverside Rd 7
SE16 118 D5
Princessa Ct EN2 17 B6
Princess Alexandra School of Nursing The
E1 96 B2
Princess Alice Ho 1
W10 90 C3
Princess Alice Way
SE28 123 B4
Princess Ave HA9 66 A6
Princess Beatrice Ho
SW10 255 C1
Princess Cl SE28 102 D1
Princess Cres N4 72 D6
Princess Ct
Catford BR1 186 C4
3 Croydon CR0 221 D6
Hampstead NW6 69 D1
Hounslow TW4 128 C2
Kensington W2 245 D6
Marylebone W1 237 C3
11 Wimbledon SW19 178 D3
Princess Frederica CE Prim Sch NW10 90 C5
Princess Grace Hospl The
W1 93 A3 238 A5
Princess La HA4 39 C1
Princess Louise Cl
W2 236 D4
Princess Louise Hospl
W10 90 C2
Princess Mary Ho
SW1 259 D3
Princess May Prim Sch
N16 73 D4
Princess May Rd N16 73 C4
Princess Mews
Hampstead NW3 70 B2
Kingston u T KT1 198 B6
Princess Par
Dagenham RM10 103 C5
Locksbottom BR6 226 C5
Princess Park Manor
N11 31 A5
Prince's Sq
W2 113 D6 245 C6
Princess Rd
Camden Town NW1 93 A6 231 B6
Paddington NW6 91 C5
Thornton Heath CR0 205 A3
Princess Royal University Hospl BR6 226 C5
Princess St
Bexley DA7 147 B2
Newington SE1 261 D5
Princes St
Bexleyheath DA7 147 B1
Marylebone W1 238 D1
Sutton SM1 218 B4
Tottenham N17 33 C4
Prince's St
City of London EC2 95 B1 242 C1
Richmond TW10, TW9 154 A6
Prince St SE8 141 B6
Prince's Terr E13 99 B6
Princes Way
Acton W3 110 C3
Buckhurst Hill IG9 21 C2
Coney Hall BR4 224 D5
Croydon CR0 220 B3
Putney SW15, SW19 157 A3
Ruislip HA4 63 A4
Princes Yd W11 244 B3
Princethorpe Ho W2 91 D2
Princethorpe Rd
SE26 184 D6
Princeton Ct SW15 134 D2
Princeton Mans WC1 240 C3
Princeton Mews 3
KT2 176 C2
Princeton St
WC1 94 B2 240 C4
Prince William Ct
TW15 170 B5
Principal Cl N14 15 C3
Principal Sq E9 74 D3
Pringle Gdns SW16 181 C6
Pringle Ho N21 16 B6
Printers Mews E3 97 A6
Printer St EC4 241 B2
Printinghouse La
UB3 105 C4
Printing House Yd 16
E2 95 C4
Printon Ho 16 E3 97 B2
Print Village Ind Est
SE15 139 D3
Priolo Rd SE7 121 C1
Prior Ave SM2, SM5 218 C1
Prior Bolton St N1 72 D2
Prioress Ho 2 E3 97 D4
Prioress Rd SE27 160 D1
Prioress St SE1 262 D5
Prior Rd IG1 78 C5
Priors Croft E17 35 B1
Priors Field UB5 63 A2
Priors Gdns HA4 62 C3
Priors Lo 4 TW10 154 A5
Priors Mead EN1 5 C4
Prior St SE10 142 A5
Priors Wood KT10 212 D6
Prior Weston Prim Sch
Broadgate EC1 95 B3 242 C6
St Luke's EC1 95 A3 242 B5
Priory Ave
Bedford Pk W4 111 C3
Cheam SM3 216 D4
Chingford E4 19 C1
Hornsey N8 49 D5
Petts Wood BR5 211 B3
Walthamstow E17 53 C4
Wembley HA0 64 D4
Priory CE Prim Sch
SW19 179 D5
Priory Cl
Ashford TW16 172 A3
Barnet N20 13 B4
Beckenham BR3 207 A6
Chingford Green E4 19 B1
Chislehurst BR7 188 B2
East Barnet N14 15 B6
Finchley N3 29 B2
Hampton TW12 173 B2
Hayes UB3 106 B6
3 Merton SW19 179 D2
Ruislip HA4 39 D1
Stanmore HA7 8 D1
Wembley HA0 64 D4
Woodford E18 37 A2
Priory Cres
Cheam SM3 216 D4
South Norwood SE19 183 A3
Wembley HA0 65 A5
Priory Ct
Bushey WD23 8 A3
Cheam SM3 217 A4
City of London EC4 241 D1
Hampton TW12 173 C3
Highgate N6 49 B3
Homerton E9 74 D3
Hounslow TW3 129 D2
Ilford RM6 58 B3
Newham E6 99 D6
Nunhead SE15 140 C1
Roehampton SW15 133 D1
South Lambeth SW8 137 D4 269 D2
Walthamstow E17 35 B1
4 Wembley HA0 88 A5
Priory Dr
Stanmore HA7 8 D1
West Heath SE2 124 D1
Priory Field Dr HA8 26 D6
Priory Gdns
Ashford TW15 171 B5
Barnes SW13 133 D2
6 Chiswick W4 111 C2
Ealing W5 88 A4
Hampton TW12 173 B2
Highgate N6 49 B3
South Norwood SE25 205 D5
Wembley HA0 65 A4
Priory Gn N1 233 C4
Priory Gr
Barnet EN5 13 C6
South Lambeth SW8 138 A4 270 A1
Priory Grange N2 48 D6
Priory Hill HA0 65 A4
Priory Ho
3 Charlton SE7 143 C6
Clerkenwell EC1 241 C6
Pimlico SW1 259 C2
Spitalfields E1 243 C4
Priory Hospl Hayes Grove The BR2 225 A6
Priory Hospl The
SW15 133 D1
Priory House Ct SE6 163 D3
Priory Htss N1 233 D4
Priory La
East Molesey KT8 195 D5
Roehampton SW15 155 D6
Priory Leas SE9 166 A3
Priory Lo
7 Brentford W4 110 C1
Coney Hall BR4 224 C5
Ealing W5 87 C1
Priory Mans
17 Maitland Pk NW3 70 D2
South Kensington SW10 256 B1
Priory Park Rd
Kilburn NW6 91 B6
Wembley HA0 65 A4
Priory Pk SE3 142 D2
Priory Rd
Barking IG11 79 B1
Bedford Pk W4 111 B3
Cheam SM3 216 D4
Chessington KT9 214 A5
Hampstead NW6 69 D1
Hampton TW12 173 C3
Hornsey N8 49 D5
Hounslow TW3 152 A6
Mitcham SW19 180 B3
Newham E6 99 D5
Richmond TW9 132 C5
Thornton Heath CR0 204 C2
Priory Ret Pk SW19 180 B3
Priory Sch SE25 205 D5
Priory St 16 E3 97 D4
Priory Terr NW6 91 D6
Priory The
Croydon CR0 220 C5
Hornsey N8 49 D5
21 Kingston u T KT6 198 A4
Lambeth SE1 251 C1
Lewisham SE3 142 D1
Priory View WD23 8 C4
Priory Villas N11 30 D5
Priory Way
Harmondsworth UB7 126 A6
Harrow HA2 41 D5
Southall UB2 106 D3
Priory Wlk
South Kensington SW10 114 A1 256 B1
Sunbury TW16 172 A3
Priscilla Cl N15 51 A4
Priscilla Ho 8 TW16 171 D3
Pritchard Ho 38 E2 96 A5
Pritchard's Rd E2 96 A5
Pritchett Cl 13 EN3 7 C6
Priter Rd SE16 118 A3
Priter Road Hostel 14
SE16 118 A3
Private Rd EN1 17 C6
Probert Rd SW2 160 C6
Probyn Ho SW1 259 D4
Probyn Rd SW2 160 D2
Procter Ho 12 SE5 139 B5
Procter St WC1 94 B2 240 C3
Proctor Cl CR4 181 A2
Proctor Ho 5 SE1 118 A1
Proctors Cl TW14 150 A3
Prodger 8 NW9 27 D2
Progress Bsns Pk
CR9 220 B6
Progress Way
Croydon CR0 220 B6
Enfield EN1 18 A6
Wood Green N22 32 C2
Prologis Pk
Hounslow TW4 128 C1
Wallington CR0 203 D2
Prome Ho 3 N16 73 B4
Promenade Approach Rd
W4 133 C5
Promenade Mans HA8 26 C5
Promenade The W4 133 C4
Pronto Trad Est UB4 83 C2
Prospect Cl
Belvedere DA17 125 C2
Forest Hill SE26 184 B6
Hounslow TW5 129 B4
Ruislip HA4 40 D2
Prospect Cotts SW18 135 C1
Prospect Cres TW2 152 A5
Prospect Hill E17 53 D5
Prospect Ho
1 Dalston E8 73 D2
Islington N1 234 A3
3 Mitcham SW19 180 B2
Newington SE1 261 D5
14 North Kensington W10 90 D1
9 Walthamstow E17 54 A6
Prospect House Sch
SW15 156 D4
Prospect Pl
Bromley BR2 209 B6
5 Child's Hill NW2 69 B5
2 Chiswick W4 111 B1
6 Deptford SE8 141 B6
East Finchley N2 48 B5
12 Hampstead NW3 70 A4
7 Lower Holloway N7 72 A4
Tottenham N17 33 C3
Wapping E1 118 C5
Wimbledon SW20 178 B3
Prospect Quay SW18 135 C1
Prospect Rd
Barnet EN5 1 D1
Child's Hill NW2 69 C5

Prospect Rd *continued*
Kingston u T KT6 197 C3
Woodford IG8 37 C5
Prospect Ring N2 48 B6
Prospect St SE16 118 B4
Prospect Vale SE7, SE18 122 A2
Prospect Wharf E1 118 C6
Prospero Ho 7 DA17 125 C1
Prospero Rd N19 49 D1
Protea Cl E16 98 D3
Protheroe Ho 11 N17 51 D6
Prothero Gdns NW4 46 B4
Prothero Ho 15 NW10 67 B1
Prothero Rd SW6 135 B5 264 C4
Proud Ho 16 E1 96 B1
Prout Gr NW10 67 D4
Prout Rd E5 74 B5
Provence St N1 235 A4
Providence 1 SE16 118 A4
Providence Ave HA2 41 C1
Providence Cl E9 96 D6
Providence Ct
Harlington UB3 127 B5
Islington N1 234 C5
Mayfair W1 248 B6
Providence La UB3 127 B5
Providence Pl N1 234 C5
Providence Rd UB7 104 B5
Providence Row N1 233 C3
Providence Row Cl 30 E1 96 B4
Providence Sq 36 SE1 118 A4
Providence Yd 1 E2 96 A4
Provident Ind Est UB3 106 A4
Provincial Terr 2 SE20 184 D3
Provost Ct NW3 70 D2
Provost Rd NW3 70 D1
Provost St N1 95 B4 235 C2
Prowse Ave WD23 8 A2
Prowse Pl NW1 71 C1
Prudence La BR6 226 C4
Pruden Cl N14 15 C2
Prudent Pas EC2 242 B1
Prusom's Island 8 E1 118 C5
Prusom St E1 118 B5
Pryors The NW3 70 B5
Public Record Office TW9 132 D5
Puccinia Ct TW19 148 A3
Pudding La EC3 252 D6
Pudding Mill La E15 97 D6
Pudding Mill Lane Sta E15 97 D6
Puddle Dock EC4 116 D6 251 D6
Puffin Cl
Barking IG11 102 B4
Beckenham BR3 206 D4
Puffin Ct 9 W13 86 D3
Puffin Terr IG5 56 C6
Puget Ct N12 30 A5
Pugin Ct N1 72 C1
Pulborough Rd SW18 157 B4
Pulborough Way TW4 128 C1
Pulford Rd N15 51 B3
Pulham Ave N2 48 B5
Pulham Ho SW8 270 C3
Puller Rd EN5 1 A3
Pulleyns Ave E6 100 A4
Pullman Ct SW2 160 B3
Pullman Gdns SW15 156 C5
Pullman Mews SE12 165 B1
Pullman Pl SE9 166 A6
Pulross Rd SW9 138 B2
Pulteney Cl
3 Isleworth TW7 131 A2
20 Old Ford E3 97 B6
Pulteney Gdns 9 E18 55 B6
Pulteney Rd E18 55 B6
Pulteney Terr N1 94 B6 233 D6
Pulton Ho SE4 141 A1
Pulton Pl SW6 135 C5 265 A3
Puma Ct E1 243 C4
Puma Trade Pk CR4 202 B5
Pump Alley 8 TW8 131 D5
Pump Cl UB5 85 C5
Pump Ct EC4 241 A1
Pump House Cl
Bromley BR2 186 D1
Rotherhithe SE16 118 C4
Pumphouse Educational Mus The* SE16 119 A5
Pumping Ho 3 E14 120 B6
Pumping Station Rd W4 133 C6
Pump La
Deptford SE14 140 C5
Hayes UB3 106 A4
Pump Pail N CR0 221 A5
Pump Pail S CR0 221 A5
Punchard Cres EN3 7 D5
Punderson's Gdns E2 96 B4
Puran Ho E13 99 C5
Purbeck Ave KT3 199 D3
Purbeck Ct 2 N20 14 C2
Purbeck Dr NW2 68 D6
Purbeck Ho SW8 270 C3
Purbrook Est SE1 253 B1
Purbrook Ho 2 SW15 156 B3
Purbrook St SE1 263 B6
Purcell Cres SW6 135 A5 264 A4
Purcell Ho
Chelsea SW10 266 C5
Isleworth TW2 152 B5
Southall UB1 85 C1
Purcell Mews 2 NW10 67 C1
Purcell Rd UB6 85 D2
Purcells Ave HA8 26 C5
Purcell St N1 95 C5
Purchese St NW1 93 D5 232 D3
Purday Ho 4 W10 91 B4
Purdey Ct 3 KT4 200 A1
Purdon Ho 11 SE15 140 A4
Purdy St E3 97 D3
Purkis Cl UB3 105 A6
Purland Cl RM8 59 B1
Purland Rd SE28, SE18 123 D4
Purley Ave NW2 69 A6
Purley Oaks Prim Sch CR2 221 B1
Purley Pl N1 72 D1
Purley Rd
Edmonton N9 17 C1
South Croydon CR2 221 B1
Purley View Terr CR2 221 B1
Purley Way
Croydon CR0, CR9 220 C3
Thornton Heath CR0 204 B1
Purley Way Cres CR0 204 B2
Purneys Rd SE9 143 D1
Purrett Rd SE18 123 D1
Purser Ho 3 SW2 160 C5
Pursers Cross Rd SW6 135 B4 264 D2
Pursewardens Cl W13 109 C5
Pursley Rd NW7 28 B3
Purves Rd NW10 90 C5
Purvis Ho CR0 205 B2
Pusey Ho 20 E14 97 C1
Puteaux Ho 6 E2 96 D5
PUTNEY 156 C6
Putney Bridge App SW6 135 A2
Putney Bridge Rd SW15 135 B1
Putney Bridge Sta SW6 135 B2
Putney Comm SW15 134 C2
Putney Exchange Shopping Ctr SW15 134 D1
Putney Gdns RM6 58 B4
PUTNEY HEATH 156 C4
Putney Heath SW15 156 C5
Putney Heath La SW15 156 D5
Putney High Sch SW15 156 D6
Putney High St SW15 135 A1
Putney Hill SW15 156 D6
Putney Park Ave SW15 134 A1
Putney Park La SW15 156 B6
Putney Park Sch SW15 134 B1
Putney Pier SW15 135 A2
Putney School of Art & Design SW15 135 A1
Putney Sta SW15 135 A1
PUTNEY VALE 156 A1
Putney Wharf Twr SW15 135 A2
Pycombe Cnr N12 29 B6
Pycroft Way N9 34 A6
Pykewell Lo 13 E8 74 A3
Pylbrook Rd SM1 217 D5
Pylon Trad Est E16 98 B2
Pylon Way CR0 204 A1
Pym Cl EN4 14 B6
Pymers Mead SE21 161 A3
Pymmes Brook Dr EN4 2 C1
Pymmes Brook Ho 3 N10 31 A3
Pymmes Cl
Bowes Pk N13 32 B5
Tottenham N17 34 B2
Pymmes Gdns N N9 17 D1
Pymmes Gdns S N9 17 D1
Pymmes Green Rd N11 15 C1
Pymmes Mews N13 32 A5
Pymmes Rd N13 32 A5
Pynchester Cl UB10 60 C6
Pyne Rd KT6 198 C1
Pynfolds SE16 118 B4
Pynham Cl SE2 124 B3
Pynnacles Cl HA7 25 B5
Pynnersmead SE24 161 A6
Pyramid Ho N12 30 A6
Pyrford Ho 12 SW9 138 D1
Pyrland Rd
Richmond TW10 154 B5
Stoke Newington N5 73 B3
Pyrmont Gr SE27 160 D1
Pyrmont Rd W4 132 C6
Pytchley Cres SE19 183 A4
Pytchley Rd SE22 139 C2

Q

Quadrangle Cl SE1 263 A4
Quadrangle Ho The E15 76 C2
Quadrangle Lo SW19 179 C4
Quadrangle The
Chelsea SW10 266 B2
Fulham SW6 264 A3
Herne Hill SE24 161 A6
3 North Kensington W12 90 C1
Paddington W2 237 A2
Stanmore HA7 25 C3
Walthamstow E17 35 B1
Quadrant Arc W1 249 B5
Quadrant Bsns Ctr NW6 91 A6
Quadrant Cl NW4 46 B4
Quadrant Gr NW5 70 D3
Quadrant Ho E15 98 C4
Quadrant Rd
Richmond TW9 131 D1
Thornton Heath CR7 204 D5
Quadrant The
4 Kensal Green W10 90 D4
Richmond TW9 132 A1
Sutton SM2 218 A2
West Heath DA7 146 D5
Wimbledon SW20 179 A2
Quad Rd HA9 65 D5
Quaggy Wlk SE3 143 A1
Quainton Hall Sch HA1 42 C4
Quainton St NW10 67 B5
Quaker Ct EC1 242 B6
Quaker La UB2 107 C3
Quakers Course NW9 27 D2
Quaker's Pl E7 77 D3
Quaker St E1 95 D3 243 C5
Quakers Wlk N21 17 B5
Quality Ct WC2 241 A2
Quantock Cl UB3 127 B5
Quantock Ct
4 East Barnet N20 14 C2
Greenford UB6 64 C3
Quantock Dr KT4 216 C6
Quantock Gdns NW2 68 D6
Quantock Ho N16 51 D1
Quantock Mews 3 SE15 140 A3
Quarles Park Rd RM6 58 C3
Quarrendon St SW6 135 C3
Quarr Rd SM5 202 C3
Quarry Park Rd SM1 217 B2
Quarry Rd SW18 158 A5
Quarry Rise SM1 217 B2
Quarterdeck The E14 119 C4
Quartermain Ho SM4 202 A4
Quartermile La E10, E15 75 D4
Quayside Ct 6 SE16 118 D5
Quay West Ct TW11 175 B5
Quebec & Crown Wharves E14 97 B1
Quebec Ind Est SE16 119 A3
Quebec Mews W1 237 D1
Quebec Rd
Hayes UB4 84 C1
Ilford IG1 57 A2
Quebec Way SE16 119 A4
Quebec Wharf 32 E8 95 C6
Quedgeley Ct 3 SE15 139 D6
Queen Adelaide Ct SE20 184 C4
Queen Adelaide Rd SE20 184 C3
Queen Alexandra Mans WC1 233 A1
Queen Alexandra's Ct SW19 179 B5
Queen Anne Ave BR2 208 D6
Queen Anne Dr KT10 212 C1
Queen Anne Gate DA7 146 D2
Queen Anne Mews W1 238 D3
Queen Anne Rd E9 74 D2
Queen Annes Cl TW2 152 B1
Queen Anne's Gate SW1 115 D4 249 C1
Queen Anne's Gdns
Bedford Pk W4 111 C3
Ealing W5 110 A4
Enfield EN1 17 C5
Mitcham CR4 202 D6
Queen Anne's Gr
Bedford Pk W4 111 C3
Ealing W5 110 A4
Enfield EN1 17 C5
Queen Anne's Pl EN1 17 C5
Queen Anne St W1 93 B2 238 C3
Queen Anne Terr 9 E1 118 B6
Queenborough Gdns
Chislehurst BR7 189 B4
Ilford IG2 56 C5
Queen Caroline St W6 112 C1
Queen Charlottes & Chelsea Hospl W12 90 A1
Queen Ct WC1 240 B5
Queen Elizabeth Ct
Barnet EN5 1 B1
5 Kingsland N1 73 B2
Queen Elizabeth Gdns SM4 201 C5
Queen Elizabeth Hall & Purcell Room* SE1 250 D4
Queen Elizabeth Ho SW12 159 A4
Queen Elizabeth Hospl SE18 144 A5
Queen Elizabeth II Con Ctr SW1 249 D1
Queen Elizabeth II Jubilee Sch W9 91 B3
Queen Elizabeth II Pier SE10 120 D5
Queen Elizabeth Rd
Kingston u T KT2 176 B1
Walthamstow E17 53 A6
Queen Elizabeth's Cl N16 73 B6
Queen Elizabeth's Coll 15 SE10 142 A5
Queen Elizabeth's Dr N14 16 A3
Queen Elizabeth's Girls Sch EN5 1 B1
Queen Elizabeth's Hunting Lodge Mus* E4 20 D4
Queen Elizabeth St SE1 117 D4 253 C2
Queen Elizabeth's Wlk
Stoke Newington N16 73 B6
Wallington SM6 219 D4
Queen Elizabeth Wlk SW13 134 B4
Queenhithe EC4 252 B6
Queen Margaret Flats 22 E2 96 B4
Queen Margarets Ct N1 73 C3
Queen Margaret's Gr N1 73 C3
Queen Mary Ave SM4 200 D4
Queen Mary Cl KT9 214 C5
Queen Mary Ct TW19 148 A3
Queen Mary Rd
Charlton TW17 171 A1
South Norwood SE19 182 D4
Queen Mary's Ave SM5 218 D1
Queen Mary's Gdns* NW1 231 A1
Queen Mary's Hospl
Hampstead NW3 70 A5
Sidcup DA14 190 A4
Queen Mary's Univ Hospl SW15 156 A5
Queen Mary, Univ of London E1 97 A3
Queen of Denmark Ct SE16 119 B3
Queens Acre SM3 217 A1
Queen St Pl EC4 252 B6
Queens Ave
Feltham TW13 172 C6
Muswell Hill N10 49 B6
Stanmore HA7 25 C1
Whetstone N20 14 B2
Queen's Ave
Finchley N3 30 A2
Southall UB1 86 A1
Southgate N21 16 D3
Woodford IG8 37 B5
Queensberry Ho 6 TW9 153 D6
Queensberry Mews W SW7 256 C4
Queensberry Pl
Chelsea SW7 114 B2 256 C4
Plashet E12 78 A3
Queensberry Way SW7 256 C4
Queensborough Ct N3 47 B5
Queensborough Mews W2 246 A6
Queensborough Pas W2 246 A6
Queensborough Terr W2 113 D6 245 D6
Queensbridge Ct 1 E2 95 D5
Queensbridge Inf Sch E8 73 D1
Queensbridge Pk TW7 152 C6
Queensbridge Rd
Dalston E8 73 D1
Shoreditch E2, E8 95 D6
QUEENSBURY 44 B6
Queensbury IG9 21 B3
Queensbury Circ Par HA3 44 A6
Queensbury Ct CR7 183 A1
Queensbury Rd
Kingsbury NW9 45 B2
Wembley HA0 88 B5
Queensbury St N1 73 A1
Queensbury Sta HA7, HA8 44 B6
Queensbury Station Par HA8 44 B6
Queen's CE Prim Sch The TW9 132 C5
Queen's Cir SW11 137 B5 268 C3
Queen's Cl
Edgware HA8 26 C5
Wallington SM6 219 B3
Queen's Club Gdns W14 135 A6 264 B6
Queen's Club The W14 113 A1 254 B1
Queen's Coll W1 93 B2 238 C3
Queenscourt HA9 66 A4
Queens Cres TW10 154 B6
Queen's Cres NW5 71 A2
Queenscroft Rd SE9 165 D5
Queens Ct
Battersea SW11 268 C2
Beckenham BR3 185 D3
Camberwell SE5 139 C3
Leyton E10 53 C2
4 Limehouse E14 119 B6
Sidcup DA14 190 A6
Stanmore HA7 25 B1
8 Temple Fortune NW11 47 B4
Walthamstow E17 53 C4
Queen's Ct
Barnes SW13 134 A2
Beckenham BR3 185 C2
Croydon CR2 221 A3
8 Ealing W5 87 C2
Hampstead Garden Suburb NW11 47 C4
Kensington W2 245 D5
1 Kingston u T KT2 176 C3
Leytonstone E11 54 C2
3 Richmond TW10 154 B5
Queen's Ct *continued*
St John's Wood NW8 229 C4
Thornton Heath CR7 204 C4
Queensdale W11 112 D5
Queensdale Cres W11 112 D5
Queensdale Pl W11 244 A3
Queensdale Rd
Notting Hill W11 112 D5
Notting Hill W11 113 A5 244 A3
Queensdale Wlk W11 244 A3
Queensdown Rd E5 74 B4
Queens Dr
Surbiton KT5 198 C3
Walthamstow E10 53 C2
Queen's Dr
Acton W3 88 C1
Finsbury Pk N4 72 D6
Thames Ditton KT7 197 A3
Queen's Elm Par SW3 256 D2
Queen's Elm Sq SW3 256 D1
Queensferry Wlk N17 52 B5
Queensfield Ct SM3 216 C4
Queen's Gallery* SW1 115 B4 248 D1
Queens Gate IG4 56 B5
Queen's Gate SW7 114 A3 256 B5
Queensgate Ct N12 29 D5
Queensgate Gdns SW15 134 B1
Queens Gate Gdns BR7 189 B2
Queen's Gate Gdns SW7 114 A3 256 B5
Queensgate Ho 34 E3 97 B5
Queen's Gate Mews SW7 114 A3 256 B6
Queensgate Pl 10 NW6 69 C1
Queen's Gate Pl SW7 114 A3 256 B5
Queen's Gate Pl Mews SW7 114 A3 256 B5
Queen's Gate Sch SW7 256 C4
Queen's Gate Terr SW7 114 A3 256 B6
Queens Gate Villas E9 75 A1
Queens Gdns NW4 46 C4
Queen's Gdns
Bayswater W2 114 A6 246 A6
Ealing W5 87 C3
Heston TW5 129 A4
Queen's Gr NW8 92 B6 229 D5
Queen's Grove Rd E4 20 B3
Queen's Head Pas EC2 242 A2
Queen's Head St N1 94 D6 234 D5
Queen's Head Yd SE1 252 C3
Queens Ho 1 SE17 139 B6
Queen's Ho TW11 174 D4
Queen's House The* SE10 142 B6
Queens Keep 10 TW1 153 C5
Queens La
2 Ashford TW15 170 B6
Muswell Hill N10 49 B6
Queensland Ave
Edmonton N18 33 A4
Merton SW19 179 D2
Queensland Cl E17 35 B1
Queensland Ct N10 31 B3
Queensland Ho 2 E16 122 C5
Queensland Rd N7 72 C4
Queens Lo HA7 25 A5
Queens Manor Sch SW6 134 D5
Queens Mans
Hampstead NW6 69 D3
Hendon NW4 46 B4
Queen's Mans
Brook Green W6 112 D2
Muswell Hill N10 49 A6
Queensmead
Ashford TW15 170 B5
St John's Wood NW8 92 B6 229 D6
Queens Mead HA8 26 B4
Queen's Mead Rd BR2 186 D1
Queensmead Sch HA4 62 D4

Queensmere 4 SM1 217 D3
Queensmere Cl SW19 156 D2
Queensmere Ct SW13 134 A6
Queensmere Rd SW19 156 D2
Queens Mews 5 IG9 21 C2
Queen's Mews W2 113 D6 245 C6
Queensmill Rd SW6 134 D5
Queensmill Sch SW6 135 C3
Queen's Mkt E13 99 C6
Queens Par
Ealing W5 88 B1
7 Hendon NW4 46 B4
3 Willesden NW2 68 C2
Queen's Par
3 Friern Barnet N11 30 D5
Wood Green N11 32 A3
Queens Parade Cl N11 30 D5
Queens Park Com Sch NW6 90 D6
Queens Park Ct 5 W10 90 D4
Queens Park Gdns TW13 149 D1
Queen's Park Prim Sch W10 91 A3
Queen's Park Sta NW6 91 B5
Queen's Pas BR7 188 D4
Queen's Pl SM4 201 C5
Queen Sq WC1 94 A2 240 B4
Queen's Quay EC4 252 B6
Queens Rd
Hayes UB3 83 C1
Morden SM4 201 C5
Twickenham TW1 153 A3
West Drayton UB7 104 B4
Queen's Rd
Barking IG11 79 A2
Beckenham BR3 185 A1
Bowes Pk N11 32 A4
Bromley BR1 187 A1
Buckhurst Hill IG9 21 C2
Chislehurst BR7 188 D4
Ealing W5 88 A1
Edmonton N9 18 B2
Enfield EN1 5 C1
Feltham TW13 150 B3
Finchley N3 30 A2
Hampton TW12 173 D6
Hendon NW4 46 C4
Hounslow TW3 129 D2
Kingston u T KT2 176 C3
Leytonstone E11 54 C2
Mitcham CR4 202 B6
Mortlake SW14 133 B2
New Cross Gate SE14, SE15 140 C4
Newham E13 99 C6
New Malden KT3 199 D4
Richmond KT2,TW10 176 C5
Richmond TW10 154 B5
Southall UB2 107 A4
Teddington TW11 174 D4
Thames Ditton KT7 196 D4
Thornton Heath CR0 205 A3
Wallington SM6 219 B3
Walthamstow E17 53 C3
Welling DA16 146 B3
Wimbledon SW19 179 C4
Queen's Rd W E13 99 B5
Queens Reach KT8 196 C5
Queen's Ride SW13 134 B2
Queen's Rise TW10 154 B5
Queen's Road Sta SE15 140 C4
Queen's Row SE17 139 B6
Queen St
Bexleyheath DA7 147 B2
City of London EC4 117 A6 252 B6
Croydon CR0 221 A4
Mayfair W1 115 B5 248 C4
Tottenham N17 33 C4
Queens Terr
Harrow HA3 24 C1
Newham E13 99 B6
St John's Wood NW8 92 B5 229 C4
Queen's Terr TW7 131 A1
Queens Terr Cotts W7 108 C4
Queensthorpe Rd SE26 184 D6
Queenstown Mews SW8 268 C1
Queenstown Rd SW8 137 B5 268 C4
Queenstown Road Sta SW8 137 B4 268 D2
Queensville Rd SW12, SW4 159 D4
Queens Walk Ho W5 87 C2
Queensway
Coney Hall BR4 224 D4
Croydon CR0 220 B3
Enfield EN3 6 C1
Kensington W2 113 D6 245 D6
Orpington BR5 211 A3
Sunbury TW16 172 B1
Queens Way
Feltham TW13 172 C6
Hendon NW4 46 C4
Queensway Bsns Ctr EN3 6 C1
Queensway Sta W2 113 D6 245 D5
Queens Well Ave N20 30 C6
Queenswell Jun & Inf Schs N20 14 B2
Queens Wlk
Ashford TW15 170 A6
Chingford E4 20 B3
Harrow HA1 42 C5
Ruislip HA4 62 C5
Welsh Harp NW9 67 A6
Queen's Wlk
Ealing W5 87 C2
St James SW1 115 C5 249 A3
Queenswood Ave
Chingford E17 36 A2
Hampton TW12 173 D4
Hounslow TW3,TW5 129 B3
Thornton Heath CR7 204 C4
Wallington CR0, SM6 219 D4
Queenswood Ct
7 Clapham Pk SW4 160 A6
11 West Norwood SE27 183 B6
Queenswood Gdns E11 55 B1
Queenswood Pk N3 29 A2
Queenswood Rd
Blackfen DA15 167 D5
Forest Hill SE23 163 A1
Queen's Wood Rd N6 49 B3
Queens Yd E9 75 C2
Queen's Yd W1 239 B5
Queen Victoria Ave HA0 65 D1
Queen Victoria Meml* SW1 249 A2
Queen Victoria St EC4 117 A6 252 A6
Queen Victoria Terr 12 E1 118 B6
Quelch Ho 2 N19 71 D3
Quemerford Rd N7 72 B3
Quendon Ho 9 W10 90 C3
Quenington Ct 5 SE15 139 D6
Quenington Mans SW6 264 C2
Quennel Ho 7 SW12 159 C4
Quentin Pl SE13 142 C2
Quentin Rd SE13 142 C2
Quernmore Cl BR1 187 A4
Quernmore Rd
Plaistow BR1 187 A4
Stroud Green N4 50 C3
Querrin St SW6 136 A3
Quested Ct 27 E8 74 B3
Quex Mews NW6 91 C6
Quex Rd NW6 91 C6
Quick Rd W4 111 C1
Quicks Rd SW19 179 D3
Quick St N1 94 D5 234 D3
Quick Street Mews N1 234 C3
Quickswood NW3 70 C1
Quiet Nook BR2 225 D5
Quill La SW15 134 D1
Quill St
Ealing W5 88 A5
Highbury N4 72 C5
Quilp St SE1 252 A2
Quilter St
Bethnal Green E2 96 A4
Plumstead Comm SE18 123 D1
Quilting Ct 23 SE16 118 D4
Quince Ho TW13 150 A3
Quince Rd SE13 141 D3
Quinta Dr EN5 12 C6
Quintin Ave SW20 179 B2
Quintin Cl HA5 40 B4
Quintin Ct W4 133 A5
Quintin Kynaston Sch NW8 92 B6 229 C5
Quintock Ho 2 TW9 132 C4
Quinton Cl
Beckenham BR3 208 A6
Cranford TW5 128 B5
Wallington SM6 219 B4
Quinton Ho SW8 270 A4
Quinton Rd KT7 197 A1
Quinton St SW18 158 A2
Quixley St 1 E14 120 B6
Quorn Rd SE22 139 C2
Quwwat-Ul-Islam Girls Sch E7 77 B2

R

Rabbit Row W8 245 B4
Rabbits Rd E12 78 A4
Rabbs Farm Prim Sch UB7 104 A6
Rabinal Ho EN3 18 D6
Rabournmead Dr UB5 63 A3
Raby Rd KT3 199 B5
Raby St E14 97 A1
Raccoon Way TW4 128 C3
Rachel Cl IG6 57 B6
Rachel Ct SM2 218 B1
Racine 15 SE5 139 C4
Rackham Cl DA16 146 B3
Rackham Mews SW16 181 C4
Racs Flats 9 SE1 118 A2
Racton Rd SW6 135 C6 265 A5
Radbourne Ave W5 109 C2
Radbourne Cl E5 74 D4
Radbourne Cres E17 36 B1
Radbourne Ct HA3 43 B3
Radbourne Rd SW12 159 D3
Radcliff Bldg EC1 241 A4
Radcliffe Ave
Enfield EN2 5 A4
Willesden Green NW10 90 A5
Radcliffe Coll
Marylebone W1 93 C1 239 B1
Soho W1 93 D1 239 C2
Radcliffe Gdns SM5 218 C1
Radcliffe Ho 10 SE16 118 B2
Radcliffe Path 5 SW8 137 B3
Radcliffe Rd
Bermondsey SE1 263 B6
Harrow HA3 25 A1
South Croydon CR0 221 D5
Southgate N21 16 D3
Radcliffe Sq SW15 156 D5
Radcliffe Way UB5 84 D4
Radcliff Mews TW12 174 A5
Radcot Point 2 SE23 162 D1
Radcot St SE11 261 B1
Raddington Rd W10 91 A2
Radfield Way DA15 167 B4
Radford Ho
7 Bow Comm E14 97 D2
Islington N7 72 B3
Radford Rd SE13 164 A5
Radford Way IG11 101 D4
Radipole Rd SW6 135 B4 264 C2
Radius Pk TW6 127 D1
Radland Rd E16 99 A1
Radlet Ave SE23 162 B2
Radlett Cl E7 76 D2
Radlett Pl NW8 92 C6 230 A6
Radley Ave IG3 80 A4
Radley Cl TW14 149 D3
Radley Ct
4 Catford BR1 186 A6
25 Rotherhithe SE16 118 D4
Radley Gdns HA3 44 A5
Radley Ho
11 Abbey Wood SE2 124 D4
Marylebone NW1 237 C6
Radley Lo 10 SW19 156 D3
Radley Mews W8 255 B5
Radley Rd N17 33 C1
Radley's La E18 37 A1
Radleys Mead RM10 81 D2
Radley Sq E5 74 C6
Radley Terr 1 E16 98 D2
Radlix Rd E10 53 C1
Radnor Ave
Bexley DA16 168 B6
Harrow HA1 42 C4
Radnor Cl
Chislehurst BR7 189 C4
Mitcham CR4 204 A5
Radnor Cres
Redbridge IG4 56 B4
Woolwich SE18 146 A5
Radnor Ct
Ealing W7 86 D1
6 Forest Hill SE23 162 D1
Harrow HA3 24 D2
Radnor Gdns
Enfield EN1 5 C4
Twickenham TW1 152 D2
Radnor Gr UB10 82 C5
Radnor Ho
East Molesey KT8 196 B5
Thornton Heath SW16 182 B1
Radnor Lo W2 236 D1
Radnor Mews W2 92 B1 236 D1
Radnor Pl W2 92 C1 237 A1
Radnor Rd
Harrow HA1 42 C4
Kensal Rise NW6 91 A6
Peckham SE15 140 A5
Twickenham TW1 152 D2
Radnor St EC1 95 A4 235 B1
Radnor Terr W14 113 B2 254 C4
Radnor Way NW10 88 D3
Radnor Wlk
Chelsea SW3 114 D1 257 C1
Croydon CR0 207 A3
21 Millwall E14 119 C2
Radstock Ave HA3 43 B6
Radstock Cl N11 31 A4
Radstock St SW11 267 A3
Radway Ho 38 W2 91 C2
Radwell Ho SW2 160 C6
Raebarn Ct 6 SW16 160 A1
Raebarn Gdns EN5 12 B6
Raeburn Ave KT5 198 D3
Raeburn Cl
Hampstead Garden Suburb NW11 48 A3
Teddington KT1 175 D3
Raeburn Ho
5 Belmont SM2 217 D1
6 Northolt UB5 84 D5
Raeburn Rd
Edgware HA8 26 C2
Hayes UB4 83 B5
Sidcup DA15 167 C5
Raeburn St SW2 138 A1
Raffles Ct HA8 26 B6
Raffles Ho NW4 46 B5
Rafford Way BR1 209 B6
RAF Mus* NW9 28 A1
Ragged School Mus The* E3 97 A2
Raggleswood BR7 188 C2
Raglan Cl TW4 151 B6
Raglan Ct
Brixton SW9 138 C2
Croydon CR0, CR2 220 D3
Lee SE12 165 A6
Wembley HA9 66 C5
Raglan Jun & Inf Schs EN1 17 C4
Raglan Prim Sch BR2 209 D5
Raglan Rd
Belvedere DA17 125 B2
Bromley BR2 209 C5
Enfield EN1 17 D4
Walthamstow E17 54 B4
Woolwich SE18 123 A1
Raglan St NW5 71 B2
Raglan Terr HA2 63 D4
Raglan Way UB5 64 A2
Ragley Cl W3 111 A4
Ragwort Ct 1 SE26 184 B5
Rahere Ho EC1 235 A2
Railey Mews NW5 71 C3
Railshead Rd TW1, TW7 131 B1
Railton Rd SE24 160 D6
Railway App
Bermondsey SE1 252 D4
Harrow HA1, HA3 42 D5
Stroud Green N4 50 C3
11 Twickenham TW1 153 A4
Wallington SM6 219 B3
Railway Ave SE16 118 C4
Railway Cotts
Hammersmith W6 112 C4
Ilford IG6 57 B6
Railway Gr SE14 141 B5
Railway Pl DA17 125 C3
Railway Rd TW11 174 D6
Railway Rise SE22 139 C1
Railway Side SW13 133 C2
Railway St
Ilford RM6 58 C2
King's Cross N1 233 B3
Railway Terr
Chingford E17 36 A2
Feltham TW13, TW14 150 A3
Ladywell SE13 163 D6
Rainborough Cl NW10 67 A2
Rainbow Ave E14 119 D1
Rainbow Ct 3 SE14 141 A6
Rainbow Ind Est SW20 178 B1
Rainbow Quay SE16 119 A3
Rainbow Sch The SW17 158 A2
Rainbow St SE5 139 C5
Rainbow Works N15 52 A4
Raine Gdns 4 IG8 37 A6
Raines Ct N16 73 D6
Raine's Foundation Lower Sch E2 96 B5
Raine's Foundation Sch E2 96 C5
Raine St E1 118 B5
Rainford Ho 9 N7 72 B6
Rainham Cl
Sidcup SE9 167 C5
Wandsworth SW11 158 C5
Rainham Ho NW1 232 B5
Rainham Rd NW10 90 C4
Rainham Rd N RM10 81 D6
Rainham Rd S RM10 81 D4
Rainhill Way E3 97 C4
Rainsborough Ave SE8 119 A2
Rainsford Cl HA7 25 C5
Rainsford Ct NW10 88 D5
Rainsford Ho 14 SW2 160 B6
Rainsford Rd NW10 88 D5
Rainsford St W2 237 A2
Rainstar Est N18 34 C6
Rainton Rd SE7 121 A1
Rainville Rd W6 134 C6
Raisins Hill HA5 40 C6
Raith Ave N14 15 D1
Raleigh Ave
Hayes UB4 84 B2
Wallington SM6 219 D4
Raleigh Cl
Hendon NW4 46 C4
Pinner HA5 40 D2
Ruislip HA4 61 D6
Raleigh Ct
Beckenham BR3 185 D2
4 Dulwich SE19 183 D5
Ealing W13 87 B2
7 Hammersmith W12 112 B4
2 Rotherhithe SE16 118 D5
Wallington SM6 219 B2
Raleigh Dr
East Barnet N20 14 C1
Esher KT10 212 B3
Tolworth KT5 199 A1
Raleigh Gdns
Mitcham CR4 202 D6
Tulse Hill SW2 160 B5
Raleigh Ho
30 Clapham SW8 137 D3
Isle of Dogs E14 119 D4
1 Thames Ditton KT7 197 A2
Raleigh Mews
Islington N1 234 D5
6 Orpington BR6 227 D3
Raleigh Rd
Enfield EN2 5 B1
Feltham TW13 149 D2
Finchley N10 30 C2
Hornsey N8 50 C5
Penge SE20 184 D3
Richmond TW9 132 B2
Southall UB2 107 A1
Raleigh St N1 94 D6 234 D5
Raleigh Way
Feltham TW13 172 C5
Southgate N14 16 A3
Ralph Ct 8 W2 91 D1
Ralph Perring Ct BR3 207 C5
Ralston St SW3 257 C1
Ramac Ind Est SE7 121 B1
Rama Cl SW16 182 A3
Rama Ct HA1 64 C6
Ramac Way SE7 121 B1
Rama La SE19 183 D3
Ramar Ho 12 E1 96 A2
Rambler Cl SW16 181 C6
Rambler Ct 11 NW9 46 A5
Rame Cl SW17 181 A5
Ramilles Cl SW2 160 A5
Ramilles Ho W1 239 B1
Ramillies Pl W1 93 C1 239 A1
Ramillies Rd
Bedford Pk W4 111 B3
Blackfen DA15 168 B5
Edgware NW7 11 C2
Ramillies St W1 239 A1
Ramney Dr EN3 7 A6
Rampart St E1 96 B1
Ram Pas KT1 175 D1
Rampayne St SW1 259 C2
Rampton Cl E4 19 C1
Ramsay Ho NW8 230 A4
Ramsay Rd
Acton W3 111 A4
Leyton E7 76 D4
Ramscroft Cl N9 17 C4
Ramsdale Rd SW17 181 A5
Ramsdean Ho 1 SW15 156 B3
Ramsden Rd
Balham SW12 159 A4
Friern Barnet N11 30 D5
Ramsey Cl
Greenford UB6 64 B3
West Hendon NW9 45 D3
Ramsey Ct
Croydon CR0 220 D6
Hornsey N8 49 D4
Putney SW15 156 C5
6 Upper Holloway N19 71 D6
Ramsey Ho
5 Battersea SW11 136 B1
14 Kennington SW9 138 C5
7 Merton SW19 179 D2
Ramsey Rd CR7 204 B3
Ramsey St E2 96 A3
Ramsey Way N14 15 C4
Ramsfort Ho 4 SE16 118 B2
Ramsgate Cl 10 E16 121 B5
Ramsgate St E8 73 D2
Ramsgill App IG2 57 D5
Ramsgill Dr IG2 57 D5
Rams Gr RM6 59 A5
Ram St SW18 157 D6
Ramulis Dr UB4 84 D3
Ramus Wood Ave BR6 227 C3
Rance Ho 12 SE7 122 A2
Rancliffe Gdns SE9 144 A1
Rancliffe Rd E6 100 A5
Randal Cremer JMI Sch E2 95 D5
Randall 9 NW9 27 D2
Randall Ave NW2 67 D5
Randall Cl SW11 136 C4 267 A2
Randall Ct NW7 28 A3
Randall Pl SE10 142 A5
Randall Rd SE11 116 B2 260 C3
Randall Row SE11 260 C3
Randell's Rd N1 94 A6 233 B6
Randisbourne Gdns SE6 163 D1
Randle Rd TW10 175 C6
Randlesdown Rd SE6 163 D1
Randmore Ct 6 BR3 185 C3
Randolf Ct
Paddington NW6 91 D5
St John's Wood NW8 229 A5
Randolph App E16 99 C1
Randolph Ave W9 92 A4 229 A1
Randolph Cl KT2 177 A5
Randolph Cres W9 92 A3 236 A6
Randolph Ct HA5 23 C3
Randolph Gdns NW6 91 D5
Randolph Gr RM6 58 C4
Randolph Mews W9 92 A3 236 B5
Randolph Rd
Bromley BR2 210 B1
Paddington W9 92 A3 236 B5
Southall UB1 107 B4
Walthamstow E17 53 D4
Randolph St NW1 71 C1
Randon Cl HA2 23 D1
Ranelagh Ave
Barnes SW13 134 A3
Fulham SW6 135 B2
Ranelagh Cl HA8 26 C6
Ranelagh Ct HA8 26 C6
Ranelagh Dr
Edgware HA8 26 C6
Twickenham TW1 153 C6

Ranelagh Gardens Mans SW6 135 A2
Ranelagh Gardens (site of Chelsea Flower Show)* SW1 115 A1 258 B1
Ranelagh Gdns
3 Bedford Pk W6 111 D3
Chiswick W4 133 A5
Fulham SW6 135 B2
Ilford IG1 56 C1
Wanstead E11 55 C4
Ranelagh Gr SW1 115 A1 258 B2
Ranelagh Ho SW3 257 C2
Ranelagh Mans 4 SW6 135 B3
Ranelagh Pl KT3 199 C4
Ranelagh Prim Sch E15 98 C5
Ranelagh Rd
Dagenham NW10 89 D5
Ealing W5 109 D4
Leyton E11 76 C4
Newham E15 98 C5
Pimlico SW1 115 C1 259 B1
Southall UB1 106 D5
Tottenham N17 51 C6
Wallend E6 100 C5
Wembley HA0 65 D2
Wood Green N22 32 B2
Ranfurly Rd SM1 217 C6
Rangdon St EC3 243 C1
Rangefield Prim Sch BR1 186 C5
Rangefield Rd BR1 186 D5
Rangemoor Rd N15 51 D4
Ranger's House (The Wernher Collection)* SE10 142 B4
Ranger's Rd
Buckhurst Hill IG9, IG10 21 A4
Chingford E4 20 D4
Rangers Sq SE10 142 B4
Range Villas TW17 192 A2
Range Way TW17 192 C2
Rangeworth Pl DA15 167 D1
Rangoon Ho 5 N16 73 B4
Rankin Cl NW9 45 C6
Rankine Ho SE1 262 A5
Ranleigh Gdns DA7 147 B5
Ranmere St SW12 159 B3
Ranmoor Cl HA1 42 B5
Ranmoor Gdns HA1 42 C5
Ranmore Ave CR0 221 D5
Ranmore Ct
Kingston u T KT6 197 D4
3 Wimbledon SW20 178 D2
Rann Ho 1 SW14 133 B2
Rannoch Cl HA8 10 D2
Rannoch Ct 9 KT6 198 A4
Rannoch Rd W6 134 D6
Rannock Ave NW9 45 C2
Ransford Ho 16 SE21 183 C6
Ransomes Dock Bsns Ctr SW11 267 B3
Ransomes Mews SW11 267 B4
Ransom Rd 1 SE7 121 C1
Ranston St NW1 237 A4
Ranulf Rd NW2 69 B4
Ranwell Cl 18 E3 97 B6
Ranwell Ho 17 E3 97 B6
Ranworth Rd N9 18 C2
Ranyard Cl KT9 214 B5
Raphael Ct 9 SE16 118 B1
Raphael Dr KT7 196 D2
Raphael St SW7 247 C1
Rapide 15 NW9 27 C2
Rapley Ho 14 E2 96 A4
Rashleigh Ct 8 SW8 137 B2
Rashleigh Ho WC1 233 A1
Rasper Rd N20 14 A2
Rastell Ave SW12 159 D3
RATCLIFF 118 D6
Ratcliffe Cl SE12 165 A4
Ratcliffe Cross St E1 96 D1
Ratcliffe Ho 10 E14 97 A1
Ratcliffe La 16 E14 97 A1
Ratcliffe Orch 9 E1 118 D6
Ratcliff Rd E7 77 C3
Rathbone Ho
5 Canning Town E16 98 D1
Kilburn NW6 91 C6
10 Wimbledon SW19 178 D3
Rathbone Mkt 3 E16 98 D2
Rathbone Pl W1 93 D1 239 C2
Rathbone St
Canning Town E16 98 D1
Rathbone St *continued*
Fitzrovia W1 93 C2 239 B3
Rathcoole Ave N8 50 B4
Rathcoole Gdns N8 50 B4
Rathfern Prim Sch SE6 163 B3
Rathfern Rd SE6 163 B3
Rathgar Ave W13 109 C5
Rathgar Cl N3 29 B1
Rathgar Rd SW9 138 D2
Rathmell Dr SW4 159 D5
Rathmore Rd SE7 121 B1
Ratier 16 NW9 27 C2
Rattray Ct 3 SE6 164 D2
Rattray Rd SW2 160 C6
Raul Rd SE15 140 A4
Raveley St NW5 71 C4
Raven Cl NW9 27 C1
Ravendale Rd TW16 171 D1
Ravenet Ct
Battersea SW11 268 C1
Clapham SW4 159 B6
Ravenet St SW11 137 B4 268 C1
Ravenfield Rd SW17 158 D1
Ravenhill Rd E13 99 C5
Raven Ho 10 SE16 118 D2
Ravenings Par IG3 58 A1
Ravenna Rd SW15 156 D6
Ravenor Ct UB6 85 D3
Ravenor Park Rd UB6 86 A4
Ravenor Prim Sch UB6 85 C4
Raven Rd E18 37 C1
Raven Row E1 96 B2
Ravensbourne Ave
Bromley BR2, BR3 186 C2
Catford BR2 186 B3
Stanwell TW19 148 A3
Ravensbourne Bsns Ctr BR2 225 D4
Ravensbourne Coll of Design & Communication BR7 188 B5
Ravensbourne Ct SE6 163 C4
Ravensbourne Gdns W13 87 B2
Ravensbourne Ho
10 Catford BR1 186 B5
Paddington NW8 237 A4
3 Twickenham TW1 153 C5
Ravensbourne Mans 9 SE8 141 C6
Ravensbourne Park Cres SE6 163 B4
Ravensbourne Pk SE6 163 C4
Ravensbourne Pl SE13 141 D3
Ravensbourne Rd
Bromley BR1, BR2 209 A6
Forest Hill SE23 163 B3
Twickenham TW1 153 C5
Ravensbourne Sch The BR2 209 B5
Ravensbourne Sta BR3 186 B3
Ravensbury Ave SM4 202 A4
Ravensbury Ct CR4 202 B5
Ravensbury Gr CR4 202 B5
Ravensbury La CR4 202 B5
Ravensbury Rd
Orpington BR5 211 D5
Wandsworth SW18 157 D2
Ravensbury Terr SW18 157 D2
Ravenscar NW1 232 A5
Ravenscar Lo 14 SW19 178 D3
Ravenscar Rd
Catford BR1 186 C6
Surbiton KT6 214 B6
Ravens Cl
Bromley BR2 186 D1
Enfield EN1 5 C3
Kingston u T KT6 197 D3
Ravenscourt
1 Shacklewell N16 74 A5
Sunbury TW16 171 D2
Ravenscourt Ave W6 112 A2
Ravenscourt Cl HA4 39 A2
Ravenscourt Gdns W6 112 A2
Ravenscourt Ho 13 W6 112 B2
Ravenscourt Park Mans 1 W6 112 B3
Ravenscourt Park Prep Sch W6 112 A2
Ravenscourt Park Sta W6 112 B2
Ravenscourt Pk W6 112 A2
Ravenscourt Pl W6 112 B2
Ravenscourt Rd
Hammersmith W6 112 B2
St Paul's Cray BR5 190 B1
Ravenscourt Sq W6 112 A3
Ravenscourt Theatre Sch W6 112 B2
Ravenscraig Rd N11 31 C6
Ravenscroft Ave
Golders Green NW11 47 B2
Wembley HA9 44 B2
Ravenscroft Cl 4 E16 99 A2
Ravenscroft Cres SE9 166 B1
Ravenscroft Ct NW11 47 B2
Ravenscroft Pk EN5 1 A1
Ravenscroft Point 26 E9 74 D2
Ravenscroft Prim Sch E16 99 A3
Ravenscroft Rd
Acton W4 111 A2
Newham E16 99 A2
Penge BR3 184 D1
Ravenscroft Sch a Tech Coll The N20 13 B4
Ravenscroft St E2 95 D4
Ravensdale Ave N12 30 B6
Ravensdale Commercial Est N16 52 A3
Ravensdale Gdns
Hounslow TW4 129 A2
South Norwood SE19 183 B3
Ravensdale Mans N8 50 A3
Ravensdale Rd
Hounslow TW4 129 A2
South Tottenham N16 51 D3
Ravensdon St SE11 116 C1 261 B1
Ravensfield Cl RM9 80 D4
Ravensfield Gdns KT19 215 C4
Ravenshaw St NW6 69 B3
Ravenshill BR7 188 D2
Ravens Ho KT1 175 D1
Ravenshurst Ave NW4 46 C5
Ravenside KT6 197 D4
Ravenside Cl N18 34 D5
Ravenside Ret Pk N18 34 D5
Ravenslea Rd SW11, SW12 158 D4
Ravensleigh Gdns BR1 187 B5
Ravensmead Rd BR2 186 B3
Ravensmede Way W4 111 D2
Ravensroost SE19 183 B2
Ravenstone SE17 117 C1 263 B1
Ravenstone Prim Sch SW12 159 A2
Ravenstone Rd
Hornsey N8 50 C6
West Hendon NW9 45 D3
Ravenstone St SW12 159 A3
Ravensview Ct KT6 197 D4
Ravens Way SE3, SE12 165 A6
Ravenswood
Bowes Pk N22 32 B4
Sidcup DA5 169 A3
Ravenswood Ave
Tolworth KT6 214 C6
West Wickham BR4 208 A1
Ravenswood Cres
Harrow HA2 63 B6
West Wickham BR4 208 A1
Ravenswood Gdns TW7 130 C4
Ravenswood Ind Est 5 E17 54 A5
Ravenswood Pk HA6 22 A4
Ravenswood Rd
Balham SW12 159 B4
Croydon CR0 220 D5
Walthamstow E17 54 A5
Ravens Wood Sch BR2 225 D5
Ravensworth Ct SW6 265 A3
Ravensworth Rd
Chislehurst SE9 188 B6
College Pk NW10 90 B4
Raven Wharf SE1 253 C2
Ravey St EC2 95 C3 243 A6
Ravine Gr SE18 145 C6
Rav Pinter Cl N16 51 C2
Rawlings Cl
Beckenham BR3 208 A4
3 Orpington BR6 227 D3
Rawlings Cres HA9 66 D5
Rawlings St SW3 114 D2 257 C4
Rawlins Cl
Hendon N3 47 A6
South Croydon CR2 223 B1
Rawlinson Ct NW2 46 C2
Rawlinson Ho SE13 142 B1
Rawlinson Point 8 E16 98 D2
Rawnsley Ave CR4 202 C4
Rawreth Wlk N1 235 B6
Rawson Ct SW11 268 B1
Rawson St SW11 137 B4 268 C1
Rawsthorne Cl E16 122 B5
Rawstone Wlk 5 E13 99 A5
Rawstorne Pl EC1 234 C2
Rawstorne St EC1 94 D4 234 C2
Raybell Ct TW7 130 D3
Rayburne Ct
1 Buckhurst Hill IG9 21 C3
West Kensington W14 254 A6
Ray Cl KT9 213 C2
Ray Ct
Ealing W13 109 B5
Stanmore HA7 25 B5
Woodford IG8 37 D4
Raydean Rd EN5 13 D6
Raydons Gdns RM9 81 A3
Raydons Rd RM9 81 A3
Raydon St N19 71 B6
Rayfield Cl BR2 210 A3
Rayford Ave SE12 164 D4
Ray Gdns
Barking IG11 102 A5
Stanmore HA7 25 B5
Ray Ho
7 North Kensington W10 90 D1
Shoreditch N1 235 D5
Rayleas Cl SE18 144 D4
Rayleigh Ave TW11 174 C4
Rayleigh Cl N13 17 B1
Rayleigh Ct
2 Kingston u T KT1 176 B1
Tottenham N22 33 A2
Rayleigh Rd
Edmonton N13 17 B1
Merton SW19 179 B2
5 Newham E16 121 B5
Woodford IG8 37 C3
Rayleigh Rise CR2 221 C2
Ray Lodge Prim Sch IG8 37 D4
Ray Lodge Rd IG8 37 D4
Ray Massey Way 3 E6 100 A6
Raymead Ave CR7 204 C4
Raymede Twr W10 90 D2
Raymere Gdns SE18 145 C5
Raymond Ave
Brentford W13 109 A3
Woodford E18 36 D1
Raymond Bldgs WC1 240 D4
Raymond Cl SE26 184 C5
Raymond Ct N10 31 A3
Raymond Postgate Ct 5 SE28 124 B6
Raymond Rd
Beckenham BR3 207 A5
Ilford IG2 57 B2
Newham E13 99 C6
Wimbledon SW19 179 A4
Raymond Way KT10 213 A2
Raymouth Rd SE16 118 B2
Raynald Ho 15 SW16 160 A1
Rayne Ct
Bermondsey SE1 253 C2
Snaresbrook E18 54 D5
Rayne Ho
1 Balham SW12 159 A5
Paddington W9 91 D3
Rayner Ct 10 W12 112 C4
Rayners Cl HA0 65 D3
Rayners Cres UB5 84 B4
Rayners Gdns UB5 84 B4
Rayners La
Harrow HA2 63 D6
Pinner HA5 41 B3
RAYNERS LANE 41 B1
Rayners Lane Sta HA5 41 B2
Rayner's Rd SW15 157 A6
Rayner Twrs E10 53 C2
Raynes Ave E11 55 C2
Raynes Ct NW2 69 A4
Raynesfield SW20 200 C6
RAYNES PARK 200 C6
Raynes Park High Sch SW20 200 B6
Raynes Park Sta SW20 178 C1
Raynham W2 237 A2
Raynham Ave N18 34 A5
Raynham Ho 1 E1 96 D3
Raynham Prim Sch N18 34 A5
Raynham Rd
Edmonton N18 34 A5
Hammersmith W6 112 B2
Raynham Terr N18 34 A5
Raynor Cl UB1 107 B5
Raynor Pl N1 235 B6
Raynton Cl
Harrow HA2 41 A2
Hayes UB4 83 D3
Raynton Dr
Hayes UB4 83 C5
Hayes UB4 83 D3
Raynton Rd EN3 6 D6
Ray Rd KT8 195 D4
Rays Ave N18 34 C6
Rays Rd
Edmonton N18 34 C6
West Wickham BR4 208 A2
Ray St EC1 241 B5
Ray Wlk N7 72 B6
Raywood Cl UB7 127 A5
Reachview Cl 17 NW1 71 C1
Read Cl KT7 197 A2
Read Ct E17 53 D3
Reade Ct 6 W3 111 A3
Reade Wlk 5 NW10 67 C1
Read Ho
Friern Barnet N11 30 D6
4 Kennington SE11 138 C6
Reading Ho
Paddington W2 236 A1
Peckham SE15 140 A6
Reading La E8 74 B2
Reading Rd
Northolt UB5 64 A3
Sutton SM1 218 A3
Reading Way NW7 29 A5
Readman Ct 8 SE20 184 B2
Reads Cl IG1 78 D5
Reapers Cl NW1 232 C6
Reapers Way TW7 152 B6
Reardon Ho 5 E1 118 B5
Reardon Path 31 E1 118 B5
Reardon St E1 118 B5
Reaston St SE14 140 D5
Reay Prim Sch SW9 138 B5 270 D3
Rebecca Ct
3 Beckenham BR3 185 C2
Sidcup DA14 190 B6
Rebecca Ho 12 N12 29 D6
Reckitt Rd W4 111 C1
Record St SE16 140 C6
Recovery St SW17 180 C5
Recreation Rd
Bromley BR2 186 D1
Forest Hill SE26 184 D6
Southall UB2 107 A2
Recreation Way CR4, SW16 204 A6
Rector St N1 95 A6 235 A5
Rectory Bsns Ctr 5 DA14 190 B6
Rectory Cl
Chingford E4 19 C1
Finchley N3 29 B2
Littleton TW17 192 C6
Long Ditton KT6 197 C1
Sidcup DA14 190 B6
Stanmore HA7 25 B5
West Barnes SW20 200 C6
Rectory Cres E11 55 C3
Rectory Ct
Cranford TW5 128 C3
Feltham TW13 172 C6
Leyton E11 76 D5
Wallington SM6 219 C4
West Drayton UB7 104 A4
Woodford E18 36 D2
Rectory Field Cres SE7 143 C5
Rectory Gdns
Beckenham BR3 185 C2
6 Clapham SW4 137 C2
Hornsey N8 50 A5
Northolt UB5 85 B6
Rectory Gn BR3 185 B2
Rectory Gr
Clapham SW4 137 C2
Rectory Gr *continued*
Croydon CR0 220 D6
Hampton TW12, TW13 173 B6
Rectory La
Edgware HA8 26 C4
Long Ditton KT6 197 C1
Sidcup DA14 190 C6
Stanmore HA7 25 B5
Upper Tooting SW17 181 A5
Wallington SM6 219 C4
Rectory Orch SW19 179 A6
Rectory Paddock Sch BR5 190 C1
Rectory Park Ave UB5 85 B4
Rectory Pl SE18 122 C2
Rectory Rd
Barnes SW13 134 A3
Beckenham BR3 185 C2
Cranford TW5 128 C3
Dagenham RM10 81 D1
Hayes UB3 84 A1
Keston BR2 225 D1
Little Ilford E12 78 B3
1 London W3 111 A5
Shacklewell N16 73 D5
Southall UB2 107 B3
Sutton SM1 217 D5
Walthamstow E17 53 D5
Rectory Road Sta N16 73 D5
Rectory Sq E1 96 D2
Rectory Way UB10 60 D5
Reculver Ho 2 SE15 140 C6
Reculver Mews N18 34 A6
Reculver Rd SE16 118 D1
Red Anchor Cl SW3 267 A5
Redan Pl W2 91 D1
Redan St W14 112 D3
Redan Terr SE5 138 D3
Red Barracks Rd 4 SE18 122 B2
Redberry Gr SE23, SE26 162 C1
Redbourne Ave N3 29 C2
Redbourne Dr SE28 102 D1
Redbourne Ho
Finchley N3 29 C2
7 Poplar E14 97 B1
Redbourn Ho 10 W10 90 C3
REDBRIDGE 55 C3
Redbridge Coll RM6 58 B4
Redbridge Ct IG1 55 D3
Redbridge Ent Ctr IG1 79 A6
Redbridge Foyer IG1 79 A6
Redbridge Gdns SE5 139 C5
Redbridge La E IG4 56 A4
Redbridge La W E11 55 C3
Redbridge Prim Sch IG4 56 A4
Redbridge Rdbt IG4 55 D3
Redbridge Sta IG4 55 D3
Redburn St SW3 136 D6 267 C6
Redburn Trad Est EN3 18 D5
Redcar Cl UB5 63 D2
Redcar Ho SE26 184 B4
Redcar St SE5 139 A5
Redcastle Cl E1 118 C6
Red Cedars Rd BR6 211 C2
Redchurch St E2 95 D3 243 C6
Redcliffe Cl SW5 255 C1
Redcliffe Ct 2 E5 74 B5
Redcliffe Gdns
Chiswick W4 132 D5
Fulham SW10 135 D6 265 D6
Ilford IG1 56 C1
Redcliffe Mews SW10 255 D1
Redcliffe Pl SW10 266 A5
Redcliffe Rd SW10 136 A6 266 B6
Redcliffe Sch SW10 136 A6 266 A6
Redcliffe Sq SW10 113 D1 255 D1
Redcliffe St SW10 265 D6
Redclose Ave SM4 201 C4
Redclyffe Rd E6 99 C6
Redclyffe Terr 2 SM2 217 C1
Redclyf Ho 13 E1 96 C3
Redcroft 5 NW6 69 C3
Redcroft Rd UB1 86 A1
Red Cross Cotts SE1 252 B2
Redcross Way SE1 117 A5 252 B3
Redding Ho SE18 122 A3
Reddings Ave WD23 8 A6

Reddings Cl NW7 27 D6
Reddings The NW7 11 D1
Reddins Rd SE15 140 A6
Reddons Rd BR3 185 A3
Rede Pl W2 113 C6 245 B6
Redesdale Gdns TW7 131 A5
Redesdale St SW3 267 C6
Redfern Ave TW2, TW4 151 C4
Redfern Ho 6 E13 98 D6
Redfern Rd
 Catford SE6 164 A4
 Willesden NW10 67 C1
Redfield La SW5 113 D2 255 C4
Redfield Mews SW5 255 B4
Rediff Est SE16 119 B3
Redford Ave
 Thornton Heath CR7 204 B5
 Wallington SM6 220 A2
Redford Cl TW13 149 D2
Redford Wlk N1 235 A6
Redgate Dr BR2 225 B6
Red Gates Sch CR9 220 C3
Redgate Terr SW15 156 D5
Redgrave Cl SE25 205 D3
Redgrave Rd SW15 134 D2
Red Hill BR7 188 D5
Redhill Ct SW2 160 C2
Redhill Dr HA8 27 A1
Red Hill Prim Sch BR7 188 D5
Redhill St NW1 93 B4 231 D2
Red House* DA6 147 A1
Red House La DA6 147 A1
Red House Rd CR0 203 D3
Red House Sq 20 N1 73 A1
Redif Ho RM10 81 D4
Redington Gdns NW3 69 D4
Redington Ho N1 233 D4
Redington Rd NW3 69 D4
Redknap Ho TW10 153 C1
Red La KT10 213 A2
Redland Gdns KT8 195 B5
Redlands
 Teddington TW11 175 A4
 Tottenham N15 51 B5
Redlands Ct BR1 186 D3
Redlands Prim Sch E1 96 C2
Redlands Rd EN3 7 A4
Redlands The 5 BR3 185 D1
Redlands Way SW2 160 B4
Redleaf Cl DA17 147 C6
Redleaves Ave TW15 170 D4
Redlees Cl TW7 131 A1
Red Leys UB8 60 A1
Red Lion Bsns Ctr KT6 214 B5
Red Lion Cl 9 SE17 139 B6
Red Lion Ct
 Holborn EC4 241 B1
 Hounslow TW3 129 D2
Red Lion Hill N2 30 B1
Red Lion La SE18 144 C4
Red Lion Pl SE18 144 C4
Red Lion Rd KT6 214 C6
Red Lion Row SE17 139 A6
Red Lion Sq WC1 94 B2 240 C3
Red Lion St
 Gray's Inn WC1 94 B2 240 C3
 Richmond TW10 153 D6
Red Lion Yd W1 248 B4
Red Lo
 Ealing W5 88 A2
 West Wickham BR4 208 A2
Red Lodge Rd BR3, BR4 208 B2
Redlynch Ct W14 113 A4 244 B1
Redlynch Ho 27 SW9 138 C4
Redman Bldg EC1 241 A4
Redman Cl UB5 84 C5
Redman Ho SE1 252 B1
Redman's Rd E1 96 C2
Redmayne Ho 15 SW9 138 B3
Redmead La E1 118 A5
Redmead Rd UB3 105 C2
Redmill Ho 24 E1 96 B3
Redmond Ho N1 233 D5
Redmore Rd W6 112 B2
Red Oak Cl BR6 226 D6
Redo Ho 3 E12 78 C3
Red Pl W1 248 A6
Redpoll Way DA18 124 D3
Red Post Hill SE21, SE24 161 B6
Red Post Ho E6 77 D1
Redriffe Rd E13 98 D6
Redriff Prim Sch SE16 119 A4
Redriff Rd SE16 119 A3
Redroofs Cl BR3 185 D2
Redrose Trad Ctr 1 EN4 14 B6
Red Rover SW13 134 A2
Redrup Ho 21 SE14 140 D6
Redruth Cl N22 32 B3
Redruth Gdns KT10 212 D1
Redruth Ho SM2 217 D1
Redruth Rd E9 96 C6
Red Sq The N16 73 B5
Redstart Cl
 New Cross Gate SE14 141 A5
 Newham E6 100 A2
Redston Rd N8 49 D5
Redvers Rd N22 32 C1
Redvers St E2 95 C4
Redwald Rd E5 74 D4
Redway Dr TW2 152 A4
Redwing Path SE28 123 B4
Redwing Rd SM6 220 B1
Redwood Cl
 4 Bow E3 97 C5
 Chigwell IG9 21 B2
 Hillingdon UB10 82 D5
 Osidge N14 15 D4
 Rotherhithe SE16 119 A5
 Sidcup DA15 168 A3
 South Oxhey WD19 22 D6
Redwood Ct
 Brondesbury NW6 69 A1
 Crouch End N19 49 D2
 Northolt UB5 85 A4
 10 Surbiton KT6 197 D2
Redwood Est TW5 128 B6
Redwood Gdns E4 19 D5
Redwood Gr W5 109 B2
Redwood Mews
 Ashford TW15 171 B3
 2 Clapham SW4 137 B2
Redwoods SW15 156 A3
Redwood Way EN5 12 D6
Redwood Wlk KT6 197 D1
Reece Mews SW7 256 C4
Reed Ave BR6 227 C5
Reed Cl
 Lee SE12 165 A6
 Newham E16 99 A2
Reede Gdns RM10 81 D3
Reede Rd RM10 81 D2
Reede Way RM10 81 D2
Reedham Cl N17 52 B5
Reedham St SE15 140 A2
Reed Ho SW15 156 A5
Reedholm Villas N16 73 B4
Reed Mans 6 E11 55 A3
Reed Pl
 Clapham SW4 137 D1
 Lower Halliford TW17 192 B1
Reed Rd N17 33 D1
Reedsfield Cl TW15 148 D1
Reedsfield Rd TW15 170 D6
Reed's Pl NW1 71 C1
Reedworth St SE11 116 C2 261 B3
Reef Ho E14 120 A3
Reenglass Rd HA7 25 D6
Rees Dr HA7 26 A6
Rees Gdns CR0 205 D3
Rees Ho 6 N17 33 D3
Reesland Cl E12 78 C2
Rees St N1 95 A6 235 B5
Reets Farm Cl NW9 45 C3
Reeves Ave NW9 45 B2
Reeves Cnr CR0 220 D6
Reeves Cnr Sta CR0 220 D6
Reeves Ho
 Lambeth SE1 251 A1
 Mayfair W1 248 A5
Reeves Mews W1 115 A6 248 B5
Reeves Rd
 Bromley E3 97 D3
 Shooters Hill SE18 144 D6
Reflection Ho 9 E2 96 A3
Reflection The E16 122 D4
Reflex Apartments 1 BR2 209 B5
Reform Row N17 33 D1
Reform St SW11 136 D3
Regal Cl
 Ealing W5 87 D2
 Spitalfields E1 96 A2
Regal Cres SM6 219 B5
Regal Ct
 Edmonton N18 33 D5
 2 Mitcham CR4 202 D6
 Wembley HA0 65 D4
Regal Dr N11 31 B5
Regal Ho IG2 57 B3
Regal La NW1 231 B5
Regal Pl
 8 Tower Hamlets E3 97 B4
 Walham Green SW6 265 D3
Regal Way HA3 44 A3
Regan Ho 1 N18 33 D4
Regan Way N1 95 C5
Regatta Ho TW11 175 A6
Regatta Point TW8 132 B6
Regel Ct NW7 29 A2
Regency Cl
 Ealing W5 88 A1
 Hampton TW12 173 B5
Regency Cres 3 NW4 28 D1
Regency Ct
 9 Bow E3 97 B5
 Enfield EN1 17 B6
 4 Kingston u T KT5 198 B4
 4 Penge SE19 184 A3
 14 South Hackney E9 96 C6
 Sutton SM1 217 D5
 Wimbledon SW19 179 B3
 7 Woodford E18 37 A1
Regency Dr HA4 39 C1
Regency Gdns KT12 194 C1
Regency Ho
 Finchley N3 29 B1
 Marylebone NW1 238 D6
Regency Lo
 1 Buckhurst Hill IG9 21 D2
 Harrow HA3 42 C6
 South Hampstead NW3 70 B1
Regency Mews
 Beckenham BR3 186 A2
 Camberwell SW9 138 D5
 Isleworth TW7 152 C6
 1 Willesden NW10 68 A2
Regency Pl SW1 259 D4
Regency St SW1 115 D2 259 D3
Regency Terr SW7 256 C2
Regency Way DA6 147 A2
Regency Wlk
 Croydon CR0 207 B3
 8 Richmond TW10 154 A6
Regeneration Rd SE16 118 D1
Regent Ave UB10 60 D1
Regent Bsns Ctr UB3 106 A4
Regent Cl
 Cranford TW4 128 B4
 Harrow HA3 44 A3
 North Finchley N12 30 A5
Regent Ct
 4 Finchley N3 29 D3
 Lisson Gr NW8 230 A1
 South Norwood SE19 182 D4
 1 Stamford Hill N16 51 D2
Regent Gdns IG3 58 A2
Regent Ho W14 254 A4
Regent Pl
 Croydon CR0 205 D1
 St James W1 249 B6
 Wimbledon SW19 180 A5
Regent Rd
 Surbiton KT5 198 C4
 Tulse Hill SE24 160 D6
Regents Ave N13 32 C5
Regents Bridge Gdns SW8 270 B4
Regents Canal Ho 19 E14 97 A1
Regents Cl
 Hayes UB4 83 C2
 South Croydon CR2 221 C2
Regent's Coll NW1 93 A3 238 A6
Regents Ct
 22 Beckenham BR3 185 C3
 Bromley BR1 186 D3
 Edgware HA8 26 A6
 Hackney E8 96 A6
 1 Kingston u T KT2 176 A2
Regent's Ct HA5 22 D1
Regents Dr BR2 225 D3
Regents Gate Ho 20 E14 119 A6
Regents Lo 9 SW2 160 B3
Regents Mews NW8 92 A5 229 B4
REGENT'S PARK 93 B4
Regent's Park* NW1 93 A5 231 A3
Regent's Park Barracks NW1 231 D3
Regent's Park Rd
 Camden Town NW1 93 A6 231 A6
 Hendon N3 47 B6
 Primrose Hill NW3 71 A1
Regent's Park Sta NW1 93 B3 238 C5
Regent's Park Terr NW1 231 C6
Regents Pl IG10 21 D4
Regent's Pl SE3 143 A3
Regents Plaza 2 NW6 91 D5
Regent Sq
 Belvedere DA17 125 D2
 23 Bromley E3 97 D4
 St Pancras WC1 94 A4 233 B1
Regent's Row E8 96 A6
Regent St
 Brentford W4 110 C1
 7 Kensal Green NW10 90 D4
 Mayfair W1 115 C6 249 A6
Regents Wharf
 3 Hackney E2 96 B6
 Islington N1 233 C4
Regina Coeli RC Prim Sch CR2 220 D1
Regina Ct TW11 174 C5
Reginald Ct BR3 186 A2
Reginald Pl 6 SE8 141 C5
Reginald Rd
 Deptford SE8 141 C5
 Forest Gate E7 77 A2
Reginald Sorenson Ho E11 54 B2
Reginald Sq SE8 141 C5
Regina Point SE16 118 C3
Regina Rd
 Ealing W13 109 A5
 Finsbury Pk N4 50 B1
 Southall UB2 107 A2
 South Norwood SE25 206 A6
Regina Terr W13 109 B5
Regis Ct
 East Bedfont TW14 149 B5
 Hornsey N8 50 B5
 Marylebone NW1 237 C4
 Mitcham SW19 180 C2
Regis Pl 17 SW2 138 B1
Regis Rd NW5 71 B3
Regnart Bldgs NW1 232 B1
Regnolruf Ct KT12 194 A2
Reid Cl
 Hayes UB3 83 C1
 Pinner HA5 40 A5
Reid Ct SW14 133 A3
Reidhaven Rd SE18 123 C2
Reigate Ave SM1 201 D1
Reigate Rd
 Catford BR1 164 D1
 Grove Pk BR1, SE12 165 A2
 Ilford IG3 79 D6
Reigate Way SM6 220 A3
Reighton Rd E5 74 A6
Reizel Cl N16 51 D1
Relay Rd W12 112 C5
Relf Rd SE15 140 A2
Reliance Sq E2 243 B6
Relko Gdns SM1 218 B3
Relton Ct W3 110 C4
Relton Mews SW7 257 B6
Rembrandt Cl E14 120 B3
Rembrandt Ct
 10 Bermondsey SE16 118 B1
 Harrow HA3 43 A3
 West Ewell KT19 215 D2
Rembrandt Rd
 Edgware HA8 26 C1
 Lewisham SE13 142 C1
Rembrant Cl SW1 258 A3
Remembrance Ave N2 47 D6
Remington Rd
 Newham E6 100 A1
 Tottenham N15 51 B3
Remington St N1 94 D5 234 D3
Remnant St WC2 240 C2
Remsted Ho 7 NW6 91 D6
Remus Rd E3 75 C1
Renaissance Ct SM1 202 A1
Renaissance Wlk 4 SE10 120 D3
Renbold Ho 5 SE10 142 A4
Rendlebury Ho 17 SE18 122 B2
Rendle Cl CR0 206 A4
Rendlesham Ho 3 E5, N16 74 A5
Rendlesham Rd
 Enfield EN2 4 D4
 Shacklewell E5 74 A5
Renforth St SE16 118 C4
Renfree Way TW17 192 C2
Renfrew Cl E6 122 C6
Renfrew Ct TW5 129 A3
Renfrew Ho
 Paddington NW6 91 D5
 Walthamstow E17 35 B1
Renfrew Rd
 Hounslow TW5 129 A3
 Kingston u T KT2 177 A3
 Newington SE11 116 D2 261 C3
Renmuir St SW17 180 D4
Rennell Ho 18 E9 74 D2
Rennell St SE13 142 A2
Renness Rd E17 53 A6
Rennets Cl SE9 167 C6
Rennets Wood Ho SE9 167 B6
Rennets Wood Rd SE9 167 B6
Rennie Cotts 20 E1 96 C3
Rennie Ct
 Holdbrook EN3 7 C5
 Lambeth SE1 251 C4
Rennie Ho SE1 262 A5
Rennie St SE1 116 D5 251 C4
Renoir Ct 7 SE16 118 B1
Renovation The E16 122 D4
Renown Cl CR0 204 D1
Rensburg Rd E17 52 D3
Rensburg Villas E17 52 D4
Renshaw Cl 7 DA17 147 B6
Renshaw Cnr CR4 181 A2
Renshaw Ct SW19 179 A6
Renshaw Ho 11 SW27 182 D5
Renters Ave NW4 46 C3
Renton Cl SW2 160 B5
Renwick Rd IG11 102 B4
Repens Way UB4 84 D3
Rephidim St SE1 263 A5
Replingham Rd SW18 157 C3
Reporton Rd SW6 135 A5 264 B3
Repository Rd SE7, SE18 122 B1
Repton Ave
 Hayes UB3 105 B2
 Wembley HA0 65 C4
Repton Cl SM5 218 C3
Repton Ct
 Beckenham BR3 185 D2
 Southgate N21 16 C3
Repton Ho SW1 259 B3
Repton Rd
 Harrow HA3 44 B5
 Orpington BR6 227 D5
Repton St E14 97 A1
Reservoir Cl CR7 205 B5
Reservoir Rd
 New Cross Gate SE4 141 A3
 Ruislip HA4 39 B5
 Southgate N14 15 C6
Reservoir Studios 14 E1 96 D1
Resham Cl UB2 106 C3
Resolution Way 14 SE8 141 C5
Resolution Wlk SE18 122 B3
Restell Cl SE3 142 C6
Restmor Way SM5, SM6 219 A6
Reston Pl SW7 246 A1
Restons Cres DA15, SE9 167 C5
Restoration Sq SW11 266 D1
Restormel Cl TW3 151 C6
Retcar Pl N19 71 B6
Retford St E2 95 C5
Retingham Way E4 19 D2
Retlas Ct HA1 42 B2
Retreat Cl HA3 43 C4
Retreat Cvn Site The IG9 21 A3
Retreat Ho 5 E9 74 C2
Retreat Pl E9 74 C2
Retreat Rd TW9 153 D6
Retreat The
 Harrow HA2 41 C2
 Kingsbury NW9 45 B4
 Mortlake SW14 133 C2
 North Cheam KT4 216 B6
 South Norwood CR7 205 B5
 Surbiton KT5 198 B3
Reunion Row E1 118 B6
Reveley Sq SE16 119 A4
Revell Rd
 Cheam SM1 217 B2
 Kingston u T KT1 176 D2
Revell Rise SE18 145 D6
Revelon Rd SE4 141 A2
Revelstoke Rd SW18, SW19 157 C2
Reventlow Rd SE9 167 A3
Reverdy Rd SE1 118 A2
Reverend Cl HA2 63 D5
Revesby Rd SM5 202 C3
Review Lo RM10 103 D5
Review Rd
 Dagenham RM10 103 D6
 Willesden NW2 67 D6
Rewell St SW6 136 A5 266 A3
Rewley Rd SM4 202 B3
Rew Lo 25 N2 30 B1
Rex Ave TW15 170 C5
Rex Ho TW13 151 A1
Rex Par 2 IG8 37 C4
Rex Pl W1 115 A5 248 B4
Reydon Ave E11 55 C3
Reygate Ct N4 51 A3
Reynard Cl
 Brockley SE4 141 A2
 Bromley BR1 210 C6
Reynard Dr SE19 183 D3
Reynard Mills Trad Est TW8 109 C1
Reynard Pl SE14 141 A6
Reynardson Rd N17 33 A3
Reynardson's Ct 10 N17 51 D6
Reynolah Gdns SE7 121 B1
Reynolds Ave
 Chessington KT9 214 A1
 Ilford RM6 58 C2
 Little Ilford E12 78 C3
Reynolds Cl
 Carshalton SM5 202 D1
 Golders Green NW11 47 D2
 Mitcham SW19 180 B2
Reynolds Ct
 Ilford RM6 58 D6
 Leyton E11 76 D5
Reynolds Dr HA8 44 B6
Reynolds Ho
 Enfield EN1 18 A6
 Finsbury Pk N4 50 A1
 18 South Hackney E2 96 C5
 St John's Wood NW8 229 D3
 Westminster SW1 259 D3
Reynolds Pl
 Greenwich SE3 143 B5
 12 Richmond TW10 154 B5
Reynolds Rd
 Acton Green W4 111 A3
 Hayes UB4 84 C3
 New Malden KT3 199 B2
 Nunhead SE15 140 C1
Reynolds Way CR0 221 C4
Rheidol Mews N1 235 A4
Rheidol Terr N1 95 A6 235 A5
Rhein Ho N8 50 A6
Rheola Cl N17 33 D2
Rhoda St E2 95 D3 243 D6
Rhodes Ave N22 31 C2
Rhodes Avenue Prim Sch N22 31 C2
Rhodes Ho
 Shepherd's Bush W12 112 B5
 Shoreditch N1 235 C2
Rhodesia Rd
 Leyton E11 76 B6
 Stockwell SW9 138 A3
Rhodes-Moorhouse Ct SM4 201 C3
Rhodes St N7 72 B3
Rhodeswell Rd E14 97 B1
Rhodrons Ave KT9 214 A3
Rhondda Gr E3 97 B4
Rhyl Prim Sch NW5 71 A2
Rhyl Rd UB6 86 D5
Rhyl St NW5 71 A2
Rhys Ave N11 31 D3
Rialto Rd CR4 181 A1
Ribble Cl IG8 37 C4
Ribblesdale Ave
 Friern Barnet N11 31 A4
 Northolt UB5 63 D2
Ribblesdale Ho 11 NW6 91 C6
Ribblesdale Rd
 Hornsey N8 50 B5
 Streatham SW16 181 B5

Ribbon Dance Mews SE5 139 B4
Ribchester Ave UB6 86 D4
Ribston Cl BR2 210 B1
Ribstone Ho 12 E9 74 D2
Ricardo Path 5 SE28 124 C5
Ricardo St E14 97 D1
Ricards Lodge High Sch SW19 179 B5
Ricards Rd SW19 179 B5
Riccall Ct 2 NW9 27 C2
Riceyman Ho WC1 234 A1
Richard Alibon Prim Sch RM10 81 C3
Richard Anderson Ct 1 SE14 140 D5
Richard Atkins Prim Sch SW2 160 A4
Richard Burbidge Mans SW13 134 C6
Richard Burton Ct 4 IG9 21 C2
Richard Challoner Sch KT3 199 B2
Richard Cl SE18 122 A2
Richard Cloudesley Sch EC1 95 A3 242 A5
Richard Cobden Prim Sch NW1 93 C6 232 B5
Richard Ct
Ashford TW15 170 B5
1 Barnet EN5 1 A2
Richard Fell Ho 3 E12 78 C4
Richard Fox Ho N4 73 A5
Richard Ho 10 SE16 118 C2
Richard House Dr E16 100 A1
Richard Knight Ho SW6 265 B2
Richard Neale Ho 2 E1 118 B6
Richard Neve Ho 2 SE18 123 C2
Richards Cl
Bushey WD23 8 B4
Harlington UB3 127 B6
Harrow HA1 43 A4
Hillingdon UB10 82 C6
Richards Ct BR3 184 D2
Richard Sharples Ct 16 SM2 218 A1
Richardson Cl 19 E8 95 D6
Richardson Ct 20 SW4 138 A3
Richardson Gdns 12 RM10 81 D2
Richardson Ho
Isleworth TW7 130 D2
10 Poplar E14 97 C2
Richardson Rd E15 98 C5
Richardson's Mews W1 239 A5
Richards Pl E17 53 C6
Richard's Pl SW3 257 B4
Richard St 20 E1 96 B1
Richbell WC1 240 B4
Richbell Pl WC1 240 C4
Richborne Terr SW8 138 B5 270 D4
Richborough Ho
10 Deptford SE15 140 C6
14 Hackney E5 74 B4
Richborough Rd NW2 69 A4
Richbourne Ct W1 237 B2
Richens Cl TW3 130 B3
Riches Rd IG1 79 A6
Richfield Ct
4 Beckenham BR3 185 B2
Wembley HA0 66 A2
Richfield Rd WD23 8 A4
Richford Gate W6 112 C3
Richford Rd E15 98 D6
Richford St W6 112 C3
Richings Ho BR5 190 A2
Rich La SW5 255 C2
Richland Ho 4 SE15 140 A4
Richlands Ave KT17 216 A4
Richman Ho 10 SE8 119 B1
RICHMOND 131 C1
Richmond Adult Com Coll TW9 131 D1
Richmond Ave
Chingford E4 36 B5
Feltham TW14 149 C5
Hillingdon UB10 60 D2
Islington N1 94 B6 233 D6
Willesden NW10 68 C2
Wimbledon SW20 179 A2
Richmond Bldgs W1 239 C1
Richmond Bridge TW1 153 D5
Richmond Bridge Mans 1 TW1 153 D5
Richmond Circus TW9 132 A1
Richmond Cl
Borehamwood WD6 11 B6
Walthamstow E17 53 B3
Richmond Coll
Kensington W8 113 D3 255 D6
Richmond TW10 154 A4
Richmond Cres
Chingford E4 36 B5
Edmonton N9 18 A3
Islington N1 94 C6 234 A6
Richmond Ct
Bromley BR1 187 B3
12 Kingston u T KT2 176 C3
Knightsbridge SW1 247 D1
1 Loughton IG10 21 D6
Mitcham CR4 202 B6
4 New Southgate N11 31 A4
Wembley HA9 66 B6
Wimbledon SW20 178 B1
Richmond Dr TW17 193 B3
Richmond Gate TW10 154 B4
Richmond Gdns
Harrow HA3 24 D3
Hendon NW4 46 A4
Richmond Gn CR0 220 A5
Richmond Gr
Islington N1 72 D1
Surbiton KT5 198 B3
Richmond Healthcare Hamlet Hospl TW9 132 A2
RICHMOND HILL 154 A5
Richmond Hill TW10 154 A5
Richmond Hill Ct 5 TW10 154 A5
Richmond Ho
12 Forest Hill SE26 162 A1
Regent's Pk NW1 231 D3
Walworth SE17 262 C2
Richmond Ho (Hampton Com Coll) TW12 173 B5
Richmond International Bsns Ctr 9 TW9 132 B1
Richmond Mans
Earl's Ct SW5 255 C2
Putney SW15 135 A2
13 Twickenham TW1 153 D5
Richmond Mews W1 239 C1
Richmond Park* TW10 155 A3
Richmond Park Rd
Kingston u T KT2 176 A3
Mortlake SW14 133 B1
Richmond Pk IG10 21 D4
Richmond Pl SE18 123 A2
Richmond Rd
Bowes Pk N11 32 A4
Chingford E4 20 B3
Dalston E8 74 A1
Ealing W5 110 A4
Finchley N2 30 A1
Forest Gate E7 77 B3
Ilford IG1 79 A5
Isleworth TW7 131 A2
Kingston u T KT2 176 A4
Leyton E11 76 B6
New Barnet EN5 14 A6
Thornton Heath CR7 204 D5
Tottenham N15 51 C3
Twickenham TW1 153 C4
Wallington CR0 220 A5
Wimbledon SW20 178 B2
Richmond St E13 99 A5
Richmond Sta TW9 132 A1
Richmond Terr SW1 116 A4 250 A2
Richmond upon Thames Coll TW2 152 C4
Richmond Way
Hammersmith W12, W14 112 D4
Wanstead E11 77 A6
Richmount Gdns SE3 143 A2
Rich St E14 119 B6
Rickard Cl
Hendon NW4 46 A5
Streatham SW2 160 C3
Rickards Cl KT6 214 A6
Rickett St SW6 265 B6
Rickman Ho 23 E2 96 C3
Rickman St 24 E1 96 C3
Rickmansworth Rd HA5 22 C1
Rick Roberts Way E15 98 B5
Rickthorne Rd 7 N19 72 A6
Rickyard Path SE9 144 A1
Riddell Ct SE1 263 C2
Riddell Lo EN2 4 D3
Ridding La UB6 64 D3
Riddons Rd SE12 187 C6
Rideout St SE18 122 B2
Rider Cl DA15 167 C5
Ride The
Brentford TW8 109 C1
Enfield EN3 6 D2
Ridgdale St E3 97 D5
Ridge Ave N21 17 B4
Ridgebrook Rd SE3, SE9 143 D2
Ridge Cl
Hendon NW4 28 D1
Kingsbury NW9 45 B5
Plumstead SE28 123 B4
Ridge Crest EN2 4 B4
Ridge Hill NW11 47 A1
Ridge Ho 4 KT2 176 D3
Ridgeleigh Ct 3 EN5 1 A2
Ridgemead Cl N13, N14 16 A2
Ridgemont Gdns HA8 27 A6
Ridgemount Ave CR0 222 D6
Ridgemount Cl 4 SE20 184 B3
Ridgemount Gdns EN2 4 D3
Ridgeon Ct N22 32 B4
Ridge Rd
Cheam SM3 201 B1
Child's Hill NW2 69 B5
Edmonton N21 17 B3
Hornsey Vale N8 50 B3
Mitcham CR4 181 B3
Ridges The E4 35 C6
Ridge Terr N21 17 A4
Ridge The
Barnet EN5 13 B6
Old Bexley DA5 169 B4
Orpington BR6 227 B6
Surbiton KT5 198 C4
Twickenham TW2 152 B4
Ridgeview Cl EN5 12 D5
Ridgeview Ct EN4 15 C6
Ridgeview Rd N20 14 A1
Ridgeway
Hayes BR2 225 A6
11 Richmond TW10 154 A5
Walton-on-T KT12 193 D1
Woodford IG8 37 C6
Ridge Way
Feltham TW13 151 A1
7 West Norwood SE19 183 C4
Ridgeway Ave EN4 14 D5
Ridgeway Cres BR6 227 C5
Ridgeway Crescent Gdns BR6 227 C5
Ridgeway Ct HA5 23 C3
Ridgeway Dr
Acton W3 110 C3
Grove Pk BR1 187 B6
Ridgeway E DA15 167 D6
Ridgeway Gdns
Crouch End N6 49 C2
Redbridge IG4 56 A4
Ridgeway Rd TW7 130 C4
Ridgeway Rd N TW7 130 C5
Ridgeway The
Acton W3 110 C3
Chingford E4 20 A3
Enfield EN2 4 B5
Finchley N3 29 D3
Friern Barnet N11 30 D6
Golders Green NW11 47 B1
Kenton HA3 43 C3
Kingsbury NW9 45 B5
Mill Hill NW7 28 B6
North Harrow HA2 41 D3
Palmers Green N14 16 A2
Pinner HA2 41 B4
Ruislip HA4 40 A2
Stanmore HA7 25 C4
Wallington CR0 220 B5
Ridgeway W DA15 167 C6
Ridgeway Wlk UB5 63 A2
Ridgewell Cl
Dagenham RM10 103 D6
Forest Hill SE26 185 B6
Shoreditch N1 235 B6
Ridgmount Gdns WC1 93 D2 239 C4
Ridgmount Pl WC1 239 C4
Ridgmount Rd SW18 157 D6
Ridgmount St WC1 93 D2 239 C4
Ridgway SW19, SW20 178 D4
Ridgway Ct SW19 178 D4
Ridgway Gdns SW19 178 D3
Ridgway Pl SW19 179 A4
Ridgway Rd SW9 138 D2
Ridgway The SM2 218 B1
Ridgwell Rd E16 99 C2
Riding House St W1 93 C2 239 A3
Ridings Ave N21 17 A6
Ridings Cl N6 49 C2
Ridings The
Ealing W5 88 B3
Oakleigh Pk EN4 14 B4
Sunbury TW16 172 A2
Surbiton KT5 198 C4
Riding The NW11 47 B2
Ridler Rd EN1 5 C5
Ridley Ave W13 109 B3
Ridley Cl IG11 79 D1
Ridley Ct
Orpington BR6 227 A4
Streatham SW16 182 A4
Ridley Ho 14 SW11 136 C2
Ridley Rd
Beckenham BR2 208 D6
Dalston E8 73 D3
Forest Gate E7 77 C4
Merton SW19 179 D3
Welling DA16 146 B4
Willesden Green NW10 90 A5
Ridley Road Mkt E8 73 D3
Ridsdale Rd SE20 184 B2
Riefield Rd SE9 167 A6
Riesco Dr CR0 222 C2
Riffel Rd NW2 68 C3
Rifle Ct SE11 138 C6
Rifle Pl W11 112 D5
Rifle St E14 97 D2
Riga Ho 12 E1 96 D2
Rigault Rd SW6 135 A3
Rigby Cl CR0 220 C5
Rigby Ho 2 N17 51 D6
Rigby La UB3 105 A4
Rigby Mews IG1 78 C6
Rigby Pl 8 EN3 7 C6
Rigden St E14 97 D1
Rigeley Rd NW10 90 A4
Rigg App E10 53 A1
Rigge Pl SW4 137 D1
Rigg Ho 2 SW4 160 A4
Riggindale Rd SW16 181 D6
Rignold Ho 6 SE5 139 C3
Riley Ho
9 Bow E3 97 C3
Chelsea SW10 266 C5
1 Streatham SW4 159 D4
Riley Rd
Bermondsey SE1 117 D3 263 C6
Enfield EN3 6 C5
Riley St SW10 136 B5 266 C4
Rill Ho 16 SE5 139 C5
Rimini Ct SW12 158 D3
Rinaldo Rd SW12 159 B4
Ring Cl BR1 187 B3
Ringcroft St N7 72 C3
Ringer's Rd BR1 209 A6
Ringford Ho SW18 157 B6
Ringford Rd SW18 157 C5
Ring Ho 15 E1 118 C6
Ringlet Cl E16 99 B2
Ringlewell Cl EN1 6 B3
Ringmer Ave SW6 135 A4 264 B1
Ringmer Gdns 3 N19 72 A6
Ringmer Ho 15 SE22 139 C2
Ringmer Pl N21 17 B6
Ringmer Way BR1 210 B4
Ringmore Rise SE23 162 B4
Ring Rd W12 112 C5
Ringsfield Ho SE17 262 B1
Ringslade Rd N22 32 B1
Ringstead Bldgs SE6 163 D4
Ringstead Ct SM1 218 B3
Ringstead Rd
Catford SE6 163 D4
Sutton SM1 218 B3
Ringway UB2 107 A1
Ring Way N11 31 C4
Ringwold Cl BR3 185 A3
Ringwood Ave
Muswell Hill N2 48 D6
Thornton Heath CR0 204 A2
Ringwood Cl HA5 40 C6
Ringwood Gdns
17 Millwall E14 119 C2
Roehampton SW15 156 A3
Ringwood Rd E17 53 B3
Ringwood Way
Hampton TW12 173 C6
Ringwood Way *continued*
Southgate N21 16 D4
Ripley Cl
Bromley BR1 210 B4
New Addington CR0 224 A2
Ripley Ct 1 CR4 180 B1
Ripley Gdns
Mortlake SW14 133 B2
Sutton SM1 218 A4
Ripley Ho
13 Kingston u T KT2 176 D4
Mortlake SW14 133 C2
Nine Elms SW1 269 A6
5 Penge SE26 184 B5
Ripley Mews E11 54 C3
Ripley Rd
Belvedere DA17 125 C2
Enfield EN2 5 A4
Hampton TW12 173 C3
Ilford IG3 79 D6
Newham E16 99 C1
Riplington Ct SW15 156 B4
Ripon Cl UB5 63 C2
Ripon Ct 10 N11 31 A4
Ripon Gdns
Chessington KT9 213 D3
Redbridge IG1 56 A2
Ripon Rd
Edmonton N9 18 B4
Shooters Hill SE18 144 D6
Tottenham N17 51 B6
Ripon Way WD6 11 B6
Rippersley Rd DA16 146 A4
Ripple Ct 10 IG11 101 B6
Ripple Jun & Inf Schs IG11 79 C1
Ripple Rd
Barking IG11 79 A1
Barking IG11 101 C6
Castle Green RM9 102 A6
Rippleside Commercial Est IG11 102 C5
Ripplevale Gr N1 72 B1
Rippolson Rd SE18 123 D1
Ripston Rd TW15 171 B5
Risborough SE17 262 A4
Risborough Cl 4 N10 49 B6
Risborough Ct 5 N10 49 B6
Risborough Dr KT4 200 A2
Risborough Ho NW8 237 B6
Risborough St SE1 251 D2
Risdon Ho 26 SE16 118 C4
Risdon St 27 SE16 118 C4
Risedale Rd DA7 147 D2
Riseholme Ct E9 75 B2
Riseholme Ho 14 SE22 139 C2
Riseldine Rd SE23 163 A5
Rise The
Borehamwood WD6 10 B6
Buckhurst Hill IG9 21 D4
Chingford E4 20 C3
Edgware HA8 26 D5
Edmonton N13 32 C6
Harrow HA2 24 A1
Hendon NW7 27 D4
Hillingdon UB10 82 B5
Neasden NW10 67 B5
Sidcup DA5 168 C4
Wanstead E11 55 A4
Wembley HA0, UB6 65 A3
Risinghill St N1 234 A4
Risingholme Cl HA3 24 C2
Risingholme Rd HA3 24 C1
Risings The E17 54 B5
Rising Sun Ct EC1 241 D3
Risley Ave N17 33 B2
Risley Avenue Prim Sch N17 33 C2
Risley Ho 7 E9 74 D2
Rita Rd SW8 138 B5 270 C4
Ritches Rd N15 51 A4
Ritchie Ho
Crouch End N19 49 D2
8 Rotherhithe SE16 118 C3
12 South Bromley E14 98 B1
Ritchie Rd CR0 206 B3
Ritchie St N1 94 C5 234 B4
Ritchings Ave E17 53 A5
Ritherdon Rd SW17 159 B2
Ritson Ho N1 233 C5
Ritson Rd E8 74 A2
Ritter St SE18 144 C6
Ritz Par W5 88 B3
Rivaz Pl E9 74 C2
Riven Ct 10 W2 91 D1
Rivenhall Gdns E11, E18 54 D5
Riverains The SW11 266 C1
River Ave
Southgate N13 16 D1
Thames Ditton KT7 197 A2
Riverbank KT8 196 C5
River Bank
Edmonton N21 17 A4
Thames Ditton KT7 196 D4
Riverbank Rd BR1 165 A1
Riverbank Way TW8 131 C6
River Barge Cl E14 120 A4
River Brent Bsns Pk W7 108 C3
River Cl
Ruislip HA4 39 D3
Southall UB2 108 A4
Wanstead E11 55 C3
River Cotts BR5 190 C1
Rivercourt Rd W6 112 B1
River Crane Way TW13 151 B2
River Ct
Kingston u T KT6 197 D4
Lambeth SE1 251 C5
Shepperton TW17 193 A2
Wanstead E11 55 C3
Riverdale Cl IG11 102 B3
Riverdale Ct N21 17 B6
Riverdale Dr SW18 157 D3
Riverdale Gdns TW1 153 C6
Riverdale Rd
Erith DA8 125 D1
Feltham TW13 173 B6
Plumstead Comm SE18 123 D1
Sidcup DA5 169 B5
Twickenham TW1 153 C5
Riverdene HA8 11 A1
Riverdene Rd IG1 78 D5
Riverfleet WC1 233 B2
Riverford Ho 28 W2 91 C2
River Front EN1 5 C2
River Gdns
Carshalton SM5 219 A5
Feltham TW14 150 B6
River Gdns Bsns Ctr TW14 128 B1
River Grove Pk BR3 185 B2
Riverhead Cl E17 34 D1
River Ho
Barnes SW13 133 C3
1 Forest Hill SE26 162 B1
Riverholme KT8 196 C6
Riverhope Mans SE18 122 A3
Riverine Lo HA7 25 A5
River La TW10 153 D3
Riverleigh Ct E4 35 A5
Rivermead
East Molesey KT8 196 A6
Kingston u T KT6 197 D4
Rivermead Cl TW11 175 B5
Rivermead Ct
Ealing UB6 87 A4
Fulham SW6 135 B2
Rivermead Ho
Hackney E9 75 A3
Sunbury TW16 194 C6
River Meads Ave TW13, TW2 151 D1
River Mount KT12 193 D2
Rivernook Cl KT12 194 C4
River Park Gdns BR2 186 B3
River Park Rd N22 32 B1
River Pl N1 73 A1
River Plate Ho EC2 242 D3
River Rd
Barking IG11 101 D3
Buckhurst Hill IG9 21 D3
River Reach TW11 175 C5
River Road Bsns Pk IG11 101 D4
Riversdale Gdns N22 32 C2
Riversdale Prim Sch SW18 157 C3
Riversdale Rd
Highbury N5 73 A5
Thames Ditton KT7 197 A3
Riversdene N5 73 A5
Riversfield Rd EN1 5 C2
Rivers Ho 11 TW8 110 C1
Riverside
Battersea SW11 267 B4
Forest Hill SE6 185 B6
Greenwich SE7 121 B3
Hendon NW4 46 B2
Oatlands Pk TW17 193 C2
11 Rotherhithe SE16 118 C4
St Pancras WC1 233 B2

Riverside *continued*
Sunbury TW16 172 D1
Twickenham TW1 153 B3
Riverside Apartments
N13 32 B5
Riverside Ave KT8 196 B4
Riverside Bsns Ctr
SW18 157 D3
Riverside Bsns Pk
SW19 180 A2
Riverside Cl
Chislehurst BR5 190 C1
Ealing W7 86 C3
Hackbridge SM6 219 B5
Kingston u T KT1 197 D5
Upper Clapton E5 74 C6
Riverside Ct
Chingford E4 19 D5
Lewisham SE12 142 D1
Nine Elms SW8 269 D6
Richmond TW11 175 C5
Riverside Dr
Chiswick W4 133 C4
Mitcham CR4 202 C4
Richmond TW10 153 B1
Temple Fortune NW11 47 A3
Riverside Est EN3 19 A5
Riverside Gdns
Enfield EN2 5 A3
Hammersmith W6 112 B1
Hendon N3 47 A6
Wembley HA0 88 A5
Riverside Ho
Finchley N12 29 D6
14 Islington N1 73 A1
Morden SW19 202 A5
30 Richmond TW10 153 D6
Riverside Ind Est
IG11 102 A4
Riverside Mans 4
E1 118 C5
Riverside Pl
New Southgate N11 15 C1
Stanwell TW19 148 A5
Riverside Prim Sch
SE16 118 A4
Riverside Rd
Mill Meads E15 98 A5
Sidcup DA14 169 A2
South Tottenham N15 52 A3
Stanwell TW19 148 A5
Wandsworth SW17,
SW19 158 A1
Riverside The KT8 196 B6
Riverside Wlk
Isleworth TW7 130 C2
3 West Wickham BR4 207 D1
Riverside Works IG11 78 D1
Riverside Workshops
SE1 252 B4
River St EC1 94 C4 234 A2
Riverstone Cl HA2 64 B6
Riverstone Ct KT2 176 B2
Riverston Sch SE12 165 A6
River Terr W6 112 C1
Riverton Cl W9 91 B4
Riverview TW17 193 B2
River View EN2 5 A2
Riverview CE Prim Sch
KT19 215 B4
Riverview Ct 14 DA17 125 C1
Riverview Gdns
SW13 134 B6
River View Gdns
TW1 152 D2
Riverview Gr W4 132 D6
Riverview Hts SE18 144 D5
Riverview Lo NW9 67 B6
Riverview Pk SE6 163 C2
Riverview Rd
Chiswick W4 132 D6
West Ewell KT19 215 B4
Riverway N13 32 C6
River Way
Canning Town SE10 120 D3
Twickenham TW13,
TW2 151 D2
West Ewell KT19 215 C3
River Wlk KT12 194 A3
Riverwood La BR7 189 B2
Rivet Ho SE1 263 D2
Rivington Ave IG8 37 D1
Rivington Cres NW7 27 D3
Rivington Ct
17 Dagenham RM10 81 D2
Willesden Green NW10 90 A6
Rivington Pl EC2 95 C4
Rivington St EC2 95 C4
Rivington Wlk 4 E8 96 A6
Rivulet Rd N17 33 A3
Rixon Ho SE18 144 D6
Rixon St N7 72 C5
Rixsen Rd E12 78 A3
Roach Rd E3 75 C1
Roads Pl N19 72 A6
Roan Ind Est CR4 180 D2
Roan St SE10 142 A6
Robart Ho 2 N12 30 A5
Robarts Cl HA5 40 B4
Robbins Hall EN3 18 D5
Robb Rd HA7 25 A4
Robert Adam St W1 238 A2
Roberta St E2 96 A4
Robert Bell Ho 2
SE16 118 A2
Robert Blair Prim Sch
N7 72 A2
Robert Browning Prim
Sch SE17 117 B1 262 C2
Robert Burns Ho N17 34 B3
Robert Cl
Barking IG11 79 A2
Paddington W9 236 B5
Robert Clack Lower Sch
RM8 81 B6
Robert Clack Upper Sch
RM8 59 C1
Robert Dashwood Way
SE17 262 A3
Robert Gentry Ho
W14 254 B1
Robert Gerard Ho 7
SE27 183 B6
Robert Ho 12 HA1 42 D4
Robert Jones Ho 3
SE16 118 A2
Robert Keen Cl 18
SE15 140 A4
Robert Lowe Cl SE14 140 D5
Roberton Dr BR1 187 C2
Robert Owen Ho
Fulham SW6 134 D4
8 Spitalfields E2 95 D4
Robert Owen Lo 4 E5 74 B4
Robertsbridge Rd
SM5 202 B2
Roberts Cl
Cheam SM3 216 D1
New Eltham SE9 167 B3
South Norwood CR7 205 B6
Yiewsley UB7 104 A5
Roberts Ct
Chessington KT9 213 D3
Ealing W5 88 A1
Islington N1 234 D5
Penge SE20 184 C2
Willesden NW10 67 C2
Roberts Ho
Dagenham RM10 81 D1
Friern Barnet N11 31 B5
6 Kidbrooke SE18 144 A4
5 West Norwood
SE27 160 D1
Roberts Mews SW1 258 A5
Robertson Ho
Kidbrooke SE18 144 B4
11 Lewisham SE10 142 A4
1 Upper Tooting
SW17 180 C5
Robertson Rd E15 98 A6
Robertson St SW8 137 B3
Roberts Pl RM10 81 C2
Robert's Pl EC1 241 B6
Roberts Rd
Belvedere DA17 125 C1
Finchley NW7 29 A4
Highams Pk E17 35 D2
Robert St
Croydon CR0 221 A5
Newham E16 122 D5
Plumstead SE18 123 B2
Regent's Pk
NW1 93 B4 231 D1
Strand WC2 250 B5
Robert Sutton Ho 20
E1 96 C1
Robeson St 7 E3 97 B2
Robina Cl
DA6 146 D1
Northwood HA6 22 A2
Robin Cl
Edgware NW7 11 C1
Hampton TW12 173 A5
Robin Cres E16 99 D2
Robin Ct
15 Cubitt Town E14 120 A3
Wallington SM6 219 C2
Robin Ct *continued*
Wood Green N22 32 B3
Robin Gr
Brentford TW8 131 C6
Dartmouth Pk N6 71 A6
Harrow HA3 44 B3
Robin Hill Dr BR7 188 A4
Robin Ho NW8 230 A3
Robin Hood SW15 155 C1
Robinhood Cl CR4 203 C6
Robin Hood Ct 2
SM1 217 D3
Robin Hood Dr HA3 24 D3
Robin Hood Gdns 12
E14 120 A6
Robin Hood Inf Sch
SM1 217 C3
Robin Hood Jun Sch
SM1 217 D3
Robinhood La CR4 203 C6
Robin Hood La
Bexley DA6 169 A6
Blackwall E14 120 A6
Kingston u T SW15 177 C6
Sutton SM1 217 D3
Robin Hood Prim Sch
SW15 177 C5
Robin Hood Way UB6 64 D2
Robin Hood Way
(Kingston By Pass) KT2,
SW15, SW20 177 C5
Robinia Cl SE20 184 A2
Robinia Cres E10 75 D6
Robin La NW4 46 D6
Robinscroft Mews 18
SE10 141 D4
Robins Ct
Grove Pk SE12 165 C1
Richmond TW10 154 A5
South Croydon CR2 221 C4
Robin's Ct
Beckenham BR3 186 B1
Clapham Pk SW4 160 A5
Robinsfield Inf Sch
NW8 92 C5 230 A4
Robins Gr BR4 225 A5
Robinson Cl
Enfield EN2 5 A2
11 Leyton E11 76 C5
Robinson Cres WD23 8 A3
Robinson Ct
5 Barnet EN4 14 D3
Islington N1 234 D6
4 Richmond TW9 132 B1
Thornton Heath CR0 204 D3
Robinson Ho
4 North Kensington
W10 90 D1
12 Tower Hamlets E14 97 C2
Robinson Rd
Dagenham RM10 81 C4
Mitcham SW19 180 C4
South Hackney E2 96 C5
Robinson's Cl W13 87 A2
Robinson St SW3 267 C6
Robinwood Gr UB8 82 B3
Robinwood Pl SW15 177 B6
Robsart St SW9 138 C3
Robson Ave NW10 68 A1
Robson Cl
Enfield EN2 4 D3
Newham E6 100 A1
Robson Ct N12 30 A5
Robson Rd SE21, SE27 161 A1
Roby Ho EC1 242 A6
Roch Ave HA8 26 B1
Rochdale 8 SE19 183 C4
Rochdale Rd
Abbey Wood SE2 124 B2
Walthamstow E17 53 C2
Rochdale Way 4
SE8 141 C5
Roche Ho 15 E14 119 B6
Rochelle Cl SW11 136 B1
Rochelle Ct
Beckenham BR3 185 D3
14 Stepney E1 96 C1
Rochelle St 31 E2 95 D4
Rochemont Wlk 2 E8 96 A6
Roche Rd SW16 182 B2
Roche Sch The SW18 157 C6
Rochester Ave
Bromley BR1 187 B1
Feltham TW13 149 D2
Newham E13 99 C6
Rochester Cl
1 Blackfen DA15 168 B5
Enfield EN1 5 C4
Streatham SW16 182 A3
Rochester Ct
1 Bethnal Green E2 96 B3
9 Camden Town NW1 71 C1
Finchley N3 29 A1
Kingsbury NW9 45 B4
South Norwood SE25 184 A1
Rochester Dr
Old Bexley DA5 169 C5
Pinner HA5 40 D4
Rochester Gdns
Redbridge IG1 56 B2
South Croydon CR0 221 C5
Rochester Ho
Bermondsey SE1 252 D1
18 Deptford SE15 140 C6
Rochester Mews NW1 71 C1
Rochester Par TW13 150 A1
Rochester Pl NW1 71 C1
Rochester Rd
Carshalton SM5 218 D4
Kentish Town NW1 71 C2
Northwood HA6 39 D6
Rochester Row
SW1 115 C2 259 B4
Rochester Sq NW1 71 C1
Rochester St SW1 259 C5
Rochester Terr NW1 71 C2
Rochester Way
Eltham SE9 144 C2
Kidbrooke SE3, SE9 143 D2
Rochester Wlk SE1 252 C4
Roche Wlk SM5 202 B3
Rochford N17 33 C1
Rochford Ave RM6 58 C4
Rochford Cl 2 E6 99 D5
Rochford Way CR0 204 A3
Rochford Wlk 3 E8 74 A1
Rochfort Ho 4 SE8 119 B1
Rock Ave 13 SW14 133 B2
Rockbourne Rd SE23 162 D3
Rock Cl CR4 180 B1
Rockell's Pl SE22 162 B5
Rockfield Ho
Greenwich SE10 142 A6
2 Hendon NW4 46 D5
Rockford Ave UB6 87 B5
Rock Gdns RM10 81 D3
Rock Grove Way
SE16 118 A2
Rockhall Rd NW2 68 D4
Rockhampton Cl 4
SE27 182 C6
Rockhampton Rd
South Croydon CR2 221 C2
West Norwood SE27,
SW16 182 C6
Rock Hill SE19 183 D6
Rockingham Cl SW15 133 D1
Rockingham Ct 19
BR3 185 C3
Rockingham Gate
WD23 8 A5
Rockingham St
SE1 117 A3 262 A5
Rockland Rd SW15 135 A1
Rocklands N3 29 B3
Rocklands Dr HA7 25 C1
Rockley Ct 9 W14 112 D4
Rockley Rd W14 112 D4
Rockliffe Manor Prim Sch
SE18 145 D6
Rockmount Prim Sch
SE19 183 B4
Rockmount Rd
Plumstead Comm SE18,
SE2 123 D1
South Norwood SE19 183 B4
Rocks La SW13 134 A2
Rock St N4 72 C6
Rockstraw Ho 5 NW3 70 D1
Rockware Ave UB6 86 C6
Rockware Bsns Ctr
UB6 86 B6
Rockways EN5 11 D5
Rockwell Gdns SE19 183 C6
Rockwell Rd RM10 81 D3
Rockwood Ct N16 52 A2
Rocliffe St N1 94 D5 234 D3
Rocombe Cres SE23 162 C4
Rocque Ho SW6 264 C4
Rocque La SE3 142 D2
Rodborough Rd NW11 47 C1
Rodd Est TW17 193 B4
Roden Gdns CR0 205 C3
Rodenhurst Ct SW4 159 D6
Rodenhurst Rd SW4 159 D5
Roden St
Ilford IG1 78 C5
Upper Holloway N7 72 B5
Roderick Ho 3 SE16 118 C2
Roderick Rd NW3 70 D4
Rodgers Cl WD6 9 D5
Rodgers Ho 4 SW4 159 D4
Rodin Ct N1 234 C5
Roding Ct 6 W12 111 C4
Roding Ho N1 234 A5
Roding Hospl IG4 55 D6
Roding La IG9 21 D3
Roding La N IG8 37 D1
Roding La S IG4 55 D5
Roding Lo IG1 55 D3
Roding Mews E1 118 A5
Roding Prim Sch RM8 80 C3
Roding Rd
Hackney E5 75 A3
Newham E6 100 D2
Rodings Ct E4 36 B5
Rodings Row EN5 1 A1
Rodings The 4 IG8 37 C4
Roding Valley Sta IG9 37 D6
Roding View IG9 21 D3
Rodmarton St
W1 92 D2 237 D3
Rodmell WC1 233 B1
Rodmell Cl UB4 85 A3
Rodmell Slope N12 29 B5
Rodmere St SE10 120 C1
Rodmill La SW2 160 A4
Rodney Ct
New Malden KT3 199 C4
Pinner HA5 41 A2
Thornton Heath CR0 204 D1
Walton-on-T KT12 194 C1
Rodney Ct NW8 236 B6
Rodney Gdns
Hayes BR4 225 A4
Pinner HA5 40 C4
Rodney Ho
4 Cubitt Town E14 119 D2
Islington N1 233 D3
Notting Hill W11 245 A6
Rodney Pl
Merton SW19 180 A2
Newington
SE17 117 A2 262 B4
Walthamstow E17 35 B1
Rodney Rd
Mitcham CR4 202 C6
New Malden KT3 199 C4
Twickenham TW4 151 C4
Walton-on-T KT12 194 C1
Walworth
SE17 117 B2 262 C3
Wanstead E11 55 B5
Rodney St N1 94 B5 233 D3
Rodwall Pl HA8 26 C3
Rodway Rd
Bromley BR1 187 B2
Putney SW15 156 A4
Rodwell Cl 2 HA4 40 C1
Rodwell Rd SE22 161 D5
Roe 5 NW9 27 D2
Roebourne Way E16 122 C4
Roebuck Cl
Feltham TW13 172 B6
Tottenham N17 33 D4
Roebuck Ct
Chingford E4 36 A3
2 New Malden KT3 199 C4
Roebuck Hts IG10 21 C4
Roebuck La IG9 21 C3
Roebuck Rd KT9 214 C3
Roedean Ave EN3 6 C5
Roedean Cl EN3 6 C4
Roedean Cres SW15 155 C6
Roe End NW9 45 A5
Roe Gn NW9 45 A4
Roe Green Jun & Inf Schs
NW9 44 D5
ROEHAMPTON 155 C4
Roehampton CE Prim Sch
SW15 156 B4
Roehampton Cl
SW15 134 A1
Roehampton Ct
SW13 134 A2
Roehampton Dr BR7 189 A4
Roehampton Gate
SW15 155 C5
Roehampton High St
SW15 156 A4
Roehampton La
Putney SW15 156 A5
Roehampton SW15 156 B3
Roehampton Univ (Digby
Stuart Coll) SW15 156 A6
Roehampton Univ
(Froebel Coll)
SW15 155 D5
Roehampton Univ
(Southlands Coll)
SW15 156 A6
Roehampton Univ
(Whitelands Coll)
SW15 156 A4
Roehampton Vale
SW15 155 D2
Roe La NW9 45 A5
Roe Way SM6 220 A2
Roffey Ct 9 NW9 46 A5
Roffey St E14 120 A4
Rogate Ho E5 74 A5
Roger Ascham Prim Sch
E17 35 B2
Roger Dowley Ct 8
E2 96 C5
Roger's Almshouses 2
SW9 138 B1
Rogers Ct 16 E14 119 C6
Rogers Est 28 E2 96 C4
Rogers Gdns RM10 81 C3
Rogers Ho
9 Dagenham RM10 81 C5
Westminster SW1 259 D4
Rogers Rd
Canning Town E16 98 D1
Dagenham RM10 81 C3
Upper Tooting SW17 180 C6
Roger St WC1 94 B3 240 D5
Roger Stone Ct NW10 67 B6
Rogers Wlk N12 13 D1
Rohan Pl 4 IG4 56 B4
Rojack Rd SE23 162 D3
Rokeby Gdns IG8 37 A2
Rokeby Ho
9 Balham SW12 159 B4
Bloomsbury WC1 240 C5
Rokeby Pl SW20 178 B3
Rokeby Rd SE4 141 B3
Rokeby Sch
Kingston u T KT2 177 A3
Stratford E15 76 B1
Rokeby St E15 98 C6
Rokeland Ho SE4 141 A1
Rokell Ho BR3 185 D5
Roker Park Ave UB10 60 A4
Rokesby Cl DA16 145 B3
Rokesby Pl HA0 65 D3
Rokesly Ave N8 50 A4
Rokesly Jun & Inf Schs
N8 50 A4
Roland Ct SE19 183 D2
Roland Gdns
SW7 114 A1 256 B2
Roland Ho SW7 256 B2
Roland Mews 1 E1 96 D2
Roland Rd E17 54 B5
Roland Way
South Kensington
SW7 114 A1 256 B2
Walworth SE17 262 D1
Worcester Pk KT4 215 D6
Roles Gr RM6 59 A5
Rolfe Cl EN4 2 C1
Rolfe Ho N11 30 D6
Rolinsden Way BR2 225 D4
Rolland Ho W7 86 C2
Rollesby Rd KT19, KT9 214 C2
Rollesby Way SE28 102 C1
Rolleston Ave BR5 210 D3
Rolleston Cl BR5 210 D2
Rolleston Rd CR2 221 B1
Roll Gdns IG2 56 C4
Rollins St SE15 140 C6
Rollit Cres TW3 151 C6
Rollit Ho N7 72 C3
Rollit St N7 72 C3
Rollo Ct SW11 268 C1
Rolls Bldgs EC4 241 B2
Rollscourt Ave SE24 161 A6
Rolls Ct The E4 36 A5
Rolls Park Ave E4 35 D5
Rolls Park Rd E4 35 D5
Rolls Pas EC4 241 A2
Rolls Rd SE1 117 D1 263 D2
Rolt St SE8 141 A6
Rolvenden Gdns BR1 187 D3
Rolvenden Pl N17 34 A2
Roman Cl
Feltham TW14 150 C6
South Acton W3 110 D4
Roman Ct 4 N7 72 B2
Romanfield Rd SW2 160 B4
Romanhurst Ave BR2 208 C5
Romanhurst Gdns BR2,
BR3 208 C5
Roman Ind Est CR0 205 C2
Roman Lo 6 IG9 21 C3

Roman Rd
Chiswick W4 111 D2
Finchley N12 30 C2
Globe Town E2, E3 96 D5
Ilford IG1 78 D2
Muswell Hill N10 31 B3
Newham E6 100 A3
25 Old Ford E3 97 B6
Willesden NW2 68 C5
Roman Rise SE19 183 B4
Roman Road Prim Sch E6 99 D3
Roman Sq SE28 124 A5
Roman Square Mkt 1 E3 97 B5
Roman Way
Barnsbury N7 72 B2
Croydon CR0 220 D6
4 Deptford SE15 140 C5
Enfield EN1 17 D6
Romany Gdns
Cheam SM3 201 C2
1 Higham Hill E17 35 A2
Romany Ho 8 N9 18 A1
Romany Prospect SE19 183 B4
Romany Rise BR5 211 A1
Roma Rd E17 53 A6
Roma Read Cl SW15 156 B4
Romayne Ho SW4 137 D2
Romberg Rd SW17 159 A1
Romborough Gdns SE13 164 A6
Romborough Way SE13 164 A6
Romeland WD6 9 D5
Romeland Ct WD6 9 D5
Romer Ho 9 SW2 160 B6
Romero Cl SW9 138 B2
Romero Sq SE9 143 C1
Romeyn Rd SW16 160 B1
ROMFORD 59 D4
Romford Ho 17 N1 73 B2
Romford Rd
Forest Gate E7, E12 77 C3
Stratford E15 76 D2
Romford St E1 96 B2
Romilly Dr WD19 23 A6
Romilly Rd N4 72 D6
Romilly St W1 249 D6
Romily Ct SW6 135 A3
Rommany Ct SE27 183 B6
Rommany Rd SE27 183 B6
Romney Cl
Ashford TW15 171 A5
Chessington KT9 214 A4
7 Deptford SE14 140 C5
Harrow HA2 41 C2
North End NW11 48 A1
Tottenham N17 34 B2
Romney Ct
9 Hammersmith W12 112 C4
9 Hampstead NW3 70 C2
15 Northolt UB5 84 D5
Romney Dr
Bromley BR1 187 D3
Harrow HA2 41 C2
Romney Gdns DA7 147 B4
Romney Ho
2 Blackwall E14 120 B6
Enfield EN1 18 A6
Sutton SM2 217 D2
Romney Mews W1 238 A4
Romney Par UB4 83 B5
Romney Rd
Greenwich SE10 142 B6
Hayes UB4 83 B5
New Malden KT3 199 B3
Romney Row NW2 68 D6
Romney St SW1 116 A3 260 A5
Romola Rd SE24, SW2 160 D3
Romsey Cl BR6 226 D4
Romsey Gdns RM9 102 D6
Romsey Rd
Dagenham RM9 102 D6
Ealing W13 109 A6
Romulus Ct 7 TW8 131 D5
Ronald Ave E15 98 C4
Ronald Cl BR3 207 B4
Ronald Ct EN5 1 D2
Ronald Ho
Eltham SE9 143 C1
4 Sutton SM1 218 B3
Ronald Ross Prim Sch SW19 157 A4
Ronaldshay N4 50 C1
Ronalds Rd
Bromley BR1 187 A2
Ronalds Rd *continued*
Islington N5 72 C3
Ronald St E1 96 C1
Ronaldstone Rd DA15 167 C5
Rona Rd NW3 71 A4
Ronart St HA3 42 D6
Rona Wlk 20 N1 73 B2
Rondu Rd NW2 69 A3
Ronelean Rd KT6 214 B5
Ron Leighton Way E6 100 A6
Ronnie La E12 78 C4
Ron Todd Cl RM10 103 C6
Ronver Lo E4 20 C1
Ronver Rd SE12 164 D3
Rood La EC3 117 C6 253 A6
Rookby Ct N21 16 D2
Rook Cl HA9 66 D5
Rookeries Cl TW13 150 C1
Rookery Cl NW9 45 D4
Rookery Cotts EN4 3 B2
Rookery Cres RM10 81 D1
Rookery Dr BR7 188 C2
Rookery La BR2 209 D3
Rookery Rd SW4 137 C1
Rookery Way NW9 45 D4
Rooke Way SE10 120 D1
Rookfield Ave N10 49 C5
Rookfield Cl N10 49 C5
Rook Lo IG1 55 D3
Rooks Heath High Sch HA2 63 C5
Rooksmead Rd TW16 172 A1
Rooks Terr UB7 104 A4
Rookstone Rd SW17 180 D5
Rook Wlk E6 100 A1
Rookwood Ave
Wallington SM6 219 D4
West Barnes KT3 200 A5
Rookwood Gdns E4 20 D2
Rookwood Ho 2 IG11 101 B5
Rookwood Rd N16 52 A2
Roosevelt Ct 15 SW19 157 A3
Rootes Dr W10 90 D2
Ropemaker Rd SE16 119 A3
Ropemaker's Fields 7 E14 119 B6
Ropemaker St EC2 95 B2 242 C4
Roper Ho 13 SE21 183 C6
Roper La SE1 117 C4 253 B1
Ropers Ave E4 36 A5
Roper's Orch SW3 267 A5
Roper St 1 SE9 166 C5
Ropers Wlk 13 SE24 160 C4
Roper Way CR4 181 A1
Ropery Bsns Pk SE7 121 C2
Ropery St E3 97 B3
Rope St SE16 119 A3
Ropewalk Gdns 18 E1 96 A1
Rope Yard Rails SE18 122 D3
Ropley St 6 E2 96 A5
Rosa Alba Mews N5 73 A4
Rosa Ave TW15 170 C6
Rosa Freedman Ctr NW2 46 C1
Rosalind Ct 6 IG11 80 A1
Rosalind Ho 25 N1 95 C5
Rosaline Rd SW6 135 A5 264 B3
Rosaline Terr SW6 264 B3
Rosamond St SE26 162 B1
Rosamund Cl CR2 221 B4
Rosamun St UB2 107 A2
Rosa Parks Ho 8 SW9 138 B3
Rosary Cl TW3, TW5 129 A3
Rosary Ct 17 E1 96 D2
Rosary Gdns
Ashford TW15 170 D6
Bushey WD23 8 C4
South Kensington SW7 114 A2 256 B3
Rosary RC Inf Sch TW5 129 C6
Rosary RC Jun Sch TW5 129 C6
Rosary RC Prim Sch NW3 70 C3
Rosaville Rd SW6 135 B5 264 C3
Rosbury SW15 157 A5
Roscastle Rd SE4 163 A6
Roscoe St EC1 95 A3 242 B5
Roscoff Cl HA8 27 A2
Roscommon Ho 2 NW3 70 B3
Roseacre Cl
Ealing W13 87 B2
Littleton TW17 192 C4
Roseacre Lo EN3 6 C1
Roseacre Rd DA16 146 B2
Rose Alley
Borough The SE1 252 B4
Broadgate EC2 243 B3
Rose Ave
Mitcham CR4 180 D2
Morden SM4 202 A4
Woodford E18 37 B1
Rosebank
2 Dagenham W3 89 B1
Fulham SW6 134 C5
Penge SE20 184 B3
Rosebank Ave HA0 64 D4
Rosebank Cl
Colney Hatch N12 30 C5
Teddington TW11 175 A4
Rosebank Gdns
Bow E3 97 B5
1 Dagenham W3 89 B1
Rosebank Gr E17 53 B6
Rosebank Rd
Hanwell W7 108 C4
Walthamstow E17 53 D3
Rosebank Villas E17 53 C5
Rosebank Way W3 89 B1
Rosebank Wlk
Camden Town NW1 71 D1
14 Woolwich SE7 122 A2
Rose Bates Dr NW9 44 C5
Rosebay Ho 20 E3 97 C2
Roseberry Gdns
Harringay N4 50 D3
Orpington BR6 227 C5
Roseberry Pl E8 73 D2
Roseberry St SE16 118 B2
Rosebery Ave
Finsbury EC1 94 C4 234 B1
Harrow HA2 63 B4
Kingston u T KT3 199 D6
Plashet E12 78 B2
Sidcup DA15 167 C4
South Norwood CR7 183 A1
Tottenham N17 34 A1
Rosebery Cl SM4 200 D3
Rosebery Ct
Chessington KT9 214 B3
Holborn EC1 241 A6
Mayfair W1 248 C4
Rosebery Gdns
Ealing W13 87 A1
Hornsey N8 50 A4
Sutton SM1 217 D4
Rosebery Ho 21 E2 96 C5
Rosebery Ind Pk N17 34 B1
Rosebery Mews N10 31 C1
Rosebery Rd
Cheam SM1, SM2 217 B2
Clapham Pk SW2 160 A5
Isleworth TW3, TW7 152 A6
Kingston u T KT1 176 D1
Muswell Hill N10 31 C1
Rosebery Sq
Holborn EC1 241 A5
Kingston u T KT1 176 D1
Rosebine Ave TW2 152 B4
Rosebriars KT10 212 A3
Rose Bruford Coll DA15 168 B3
Rosebury Ct SW16 182 B2
Rosebury Rd SW6 135 D3
Rosebury Vale HA4 62 A6
Rose Bush Ct NW3 70 D3
Rose Cotts KT10 212 B3
Rosecourt Rd CR0 204 B3
Rosecroft N22 32 B2
Rosecroft Ave NW3 69 C5
Rosecroft Gdns
Dollis Hill NW2 68 A5
Twickenham TW2 152 B3
Rosecroft Rd UB1 85 C3
Rosecroft Wlk
Pinner HA5 40 D4
Wembley HA0 65 D3
Rose & Crown Ct EC2 242 A2
Rose & Crown Yd SW1 249 B3
Rose Ct
7 Dalston E8 73 D1
Harrow HA2 64 A6
Ilford IG1 78 D2
Islington N1 234 C5
Muswell Hill N10 31 B3
3 Pinner HA5 40 C6
Spitalfields E1 243 D3
Rose Ct *continued*
7 Wembley HA0 88 A5
10 Wimbledon SW19 179 B5
Rose Dale BR6 226 D6
Rosedale Ave UB3 83 B2
Rosedale Cl
Abbey Wood SE2 124 B3
Hanwell W7 108 D4
Stanmore HA7 25 B4
Rosedale Cnr BR7 188 B2
Rosedale Coll UB3 83 C1
Rosedale Ct N5 72 D4
Rosedale Dr RM9 80 B1
Rosedale Gdns RM9 80 B1
Rosedale Ho N16 51 B1
Rosedale Lo N14 15 B4
Rosedale Pl CR0 206 D2
Rosedale Rd
Dagenham RM9 80 B1
Forest Gate E7 77 C3
Richmond TW9 132 A1
Stoneleigh KT17 216 A3
Rosedale Terr W6 112 B3
Rosedene NW6 90 D6
Rosedene Ave
Morden SM4 201 C4
Southall UB6 85 C4
Streatham SW16 160 B1
Thornton Heath CR0 204 A2
Rosedene Ct HA4 39 C1
Rosedene Gdns IG2 56 C5
Rosedene Terr E10 75 D6
Rosedew Rd W6 134 D6
Rose End KT4 200 D1
Rosefield Cl SM5 218 C3
Rosefield Ct EN4 2 D1
Rosefield Gdns E14 119 C6
Roseford Ct 16 W12 112 D4
Rose Garden Cl HA8 26 A4
Rosegate Ho 32 E3 97 B5
Rose Gdns
Ealing W5 109 D3
Feltham TW13 150 A2
Southall UB1 85 C3
Rose Glen NW9 45 B5
Rosehart Mews 8 W11 91 C1
Rosehatch Ave RM6 58 D6
Roseheath Rd TW4 151 B6
ROSEHILL 202 A1
Rosehill
Claygate KT10 213 A2
Hampton TW12 173 C2
Rose Hill
Carshalton SM4, SM5 202 A2
Cheam SM1 201 D1
Rosehill Ave SM1, SM5 202 A1
Rosehill Ct SM4 202 A2
Rosehill Gdns
Greenford UB6 64 D3
Sutton SM1 218 A6
Rose Hill Park W SM1 218 A6
Rosehill Rd SW18 158 A6
Rose La RM6 59 A5
Roseland Cl N17 33 B3
Roseland Ho SW6 135 A2
Rose Lawn WD23 8 A3
Roseleigh Ave N5 72 D4
Roseleigh Cl 15 TW1 153 D5
Roselle Ct W5 88 A1
Rosemary Ave
East Finchley NW2 47 D5
East Molesey KT8 195 C5
Edmonton N9 18 B3
Enfield EN2 5 C4
Finchley N3 29 D1
Hounslow TW4 128 D3
Rosemary Branch Bridge N1 235 D6
Rosemary Cl
Hillingdon UB8 82 C2
Thornton Heath CR0 204 A3
Rosemary Cotts 4 SW19 178 C3
Rosemary Ct 35 SE8 141 B6
Rosemary Dr
Redbridge IG4 55 D4
16 South Bromley E14 98 B1
Rosemary Gdns
Chessington KT9 214 A4
Dagenham RM8 59 B1
Mortlake SW14 133 A2
Rosemary Ho
Shoreditch N1 235 D5
Willesden NW10 90 B6
Rosemary La SW14 133 A2
Rosemary Rd
Bexley DA16 145 D4
Rosemary Rd *continued*
Camberwell SE15 139 D5
Wandsworth SW17 158 A1
Rosemary St N1 235 D6
Rosemary Works Sch N1 95 B6 235 D5
Rosemead NW9 46 A2
Rosemead Ave
Feltham TW13 149 D2
Mitcham CR4 181 C1
Wembley HA9 66 A3
Rosemead Prep Sch SE27 161 A2
Rose Mews N18 34 B6
Rosemont Ave N12 30 A4
Rosemont Mans 11 NW3 69 D2
Rosemont Rd
Acton W3 110 D6
Kingston u T KT3 199 A6
Richmond TW10 154 A5
South Hampstead NW3 70 A2
Wembley HA0 88 A6
Rosemoor Ho 14 W13 109 A5
Rosemoor St SW3 114 D2 257 C3
Rosemount Ct
2 Acton W3 110 D5
South Norwood SE25 205 C6
Rosemount Dr BR1 210 B5
Rosemount Lo W3 110 D6
Rosemount Point 10 SE23 162 D1
Rosemount Rd W13 87 A1
Rosemount Twrs 5 SM6 219 C2
Rosenau Cres SW11 267 C1
Rosenau Rd SW11 136 D4 267 C2
Rosendale Prim Sch SE21 161 A4
Rosendale Rd SE21, SE24 161 A3
Roseneath Ave N21 16 D3
Roseneath Pl 2 SW16 182 B6
Roseneath Rd SW11 159 A5
Roseneath Wlk EN1 5 C1
Rosens Wlk HA8 10 D1
Rosenthal Ho SE6 163 D5
Rosenthal Rd SE6 164 A5
Rosenthorpe Rd SE15 162 D6
Roserton St E14 120 A4
Rosery The CR0 206 D3
Rose Sq SW7 256 D2
Rose St
Holborn EC4 241 D2
Strand WC2 116 A6 250 A6
Roses The IG8 36 D3
Rosethorn Cl SW12 159 D4
Rosetta Cl SW8 270 B3
Rosetta Ct SE19 183 C3
Rosetta Prim Sch E16 99 B2
Rosetti Terr RM8 80 B4
Roseveare Rd SE12 187 C6
Roseville N21 16 C3
Roseville Ave TW3, TW4 151 C6
Roseville Rd UB3 106 A2
Rosevine Rd SW20 178 C2
Rosewall Ct SW19 179 D5
Roseway SE21 161 B5
Rose Way
Edgware HA8 27 A6
Lee SE12 165 A6
Rosewell Cl SE20 184 B3
Rose Wlk
Surbiton KT5 198 D4
West Wickham BR4 224 B6
Rosewood Ave UB6 65 A2
Rosewood Cl DA14 168 C1
Rosewood Ct
Bromley BR1 187 D2
Dagenham RM6 58 C4
Kingston u T KT2 176 C3
2 Leyton E11 76 B4
Rosewood Dr TW17 192 B4
Rosewood Gdns SE13 142 A3
Rosewood Gr SM1 218 A6
Rosewood Ho 9 NW3 69 D2
Rosewood Sq W12 90 A1
Rosher Cl E15 76 B1
Roshni Ho SW17 180 C4
Rosh Pinah Prim Sch
Edgware HA8 10 D1
Edgware HA8 26 C6
Rosina Ct SW17 180 C5
Rosina St E9 74 D2
Roskeen Ct 1 SW19 178 C3
Roskell Rd SW15 134 D2
Roskild Ct HA9 66 B4
Roslin Ho 2 E1 118 D6
Roslin Rd W3 110 D3
Roslin Way BR1 187 A5
Roslyn Cl CR4 180 B1
Roslyn Rd N15 51 C4
Rosmead Rd W11 113 A6 244 B6
Rosoman Pl EC1 241 B6
Rosoman St EC1 234 B1
Rossal Ct 2 SE20 184 B3
Rossall Cres NW10 88 B4
Rossanne Ho N3 29 D3
Ross Ave
Dagenham RM8 59 B1
Finchley NW7 29 A5
Ross Cl
Harrow HA3 24 A3
Hayes UB3 105 B2
Northolt UB5 64 B4
Ross Ct
Chislehurst BR7 188 B3
Colindale NW9 45 C6
Ealing W13 87 B2
Edgware HA8 10 D2
1 Hackney E5 74 B4
4 Putney SW15 156 D4
South Croydon CR2 221 A2
Rossdale SM1 218 C3
Rossdale Dr
Ponders End N9 18 C5
Welsh Harp NW9 45 A1
Rossdale Rd SW15 134 C1
Rosse Gdns SE13 164 B5
Rosse Mews SE3 143 B4
Rossendale Cl EN2 4 D6
Rossendale Ho 7 E5 74 B6
Rossendale St E5 74 B6
Rossendale Way NW1 93 C6 232 B6
Rossendon Ct 1 SM6 219 C2
Rossetti Ct WC1 239 C4
Rossetti Gdns Mans SW3 267 C6
Rossetti Ho SW1 259 D3
Rossetti Mews NW8 229 D5
Rossetti Rd SE16 118 B1
Rossetti Studios SW3 267 B6
Ross Ho
2 Kidbrooke SE18 144 A4
Twickenham TW2 151 D2
18 Wapping E1 118 B5
Rossignol Gdns SM5 219 A6
Rossindel Rd TW3 151 C6
Rossington Cl EN1 6 B5
Rossington St E5 74 A6
Rossiter Fields EN5 13 B5
Rossiter Rd SW12 159 B3
Rossland Cl DA6 169 D6
Rosslyn Ave
Barnes SW13 133 D2
Chingford E4 20 D2
Dagenham RM8 59 C2
East Barnet EN4 14 C5
Feltham TW14 150 A5
Rosslyn Cl
Ashford TW16 171 C4
Coney Hall BR4 224 D5
Hayes UB3 83 B2
Rosslyn Cres
Harrow HA1 42 D5
Wembley HA9 66 A4
Rosslyn Ct NW3 70 C3
Rosslyn Hill NW3 70 B3
Rosslyn Ho 8 TW9 132 B4
Rosslyn Mans
8 Hampstead NW3 70 A2
South Hampstead NW6 70 A2
Rosslyn Mews 7 NW3 70 B4
Rosslyn Park Mews NW3 70 B3
Rosslyn Rd
Barking IG11 79 B1
Twickenham TW1 153 C5
Walthamstow E17 54 A5
Rossmore Cl EN3 6 D1
Rossmore Ct NW1 237 C6
Rossmore Rd NW1 92 C3 237 B6
Ross Par SM6 219 B2
Ross Rd
South Norwood SE25 205 C6
Twickenham TW2 152 A3

Ross Rd continued
Wallington SM6 219 C3
Ross Way SE9 144 A2
Rossway Dr WD23 8 B6
Rosswood Gdns SM6 219 C2
Rosswood Ho 13 SM6 219 B2
Rosswood Lo CR0 222 D6
Rostella Rd SW17 180 B6
Rostrever Gdns UB3 105 C5
Rostrevor Ave N15 51 D3
Rostrevor Gdns UB2 107 A1
Rostrevor Mans SW6 264 C2
Rostrevor Mews SW6 264 C1
Rostrevor Rd
Fulham SW6 135 B4 264 C2
Wimbledon SW19 179 C5
Rotary Ct KT8 196 C6
Rotary Lo 12 SE27 160 D1
Rotary St SE1 261 D6
Rothay NW1 231 D2
Rothbury Gdns TW7 131 A5
Rothbury Rd E9 75 C1
Rothbury Wlk N17 34 A3
Rotheley Ho 39 E9 74 C1
Rotherfield Ct
De Beauvoir Town N1 73 B1
Shoreditch N1 95 B6 235 C6
Rotherfield Prim Sch
N1 95 A6 235 B6
Rotherfield Rd
Enfield EN3 6 D6
Wallington SM5 219 A3
Rotherfield St
Islington N1 73 A1
Shoreditch N1 95 A6 235 B6
Rotherham Wlk SE1 251 C3
Rotherhill Ave SW16 181 D4
ROTHERHITHE 118 D3
Rotherhithe Bsns Est 6
SE16 118 C2
Rotherhithe New Rd
SE16 118 B1
Rotherhithe Old Rd
SE16 118 D2
Rotherhithe Prim Sch
SE16 118 D2
Rotherhithe St SE16 118 C4
Rotherhithe Sta SE16 118 C4
Rotherhithe Tunnel
SE16 118 D5
Rother Ho SE15 140 B1
Rotherwick Hill W5 88 B3
Rotherwick Rd NW11 47 C2
Rotherwood Cl SW20 179 A2
Rotherwood Rd
SW15 134 D2
Rothery St N1 234 D6
Rothesay Ave
Merton SW20 179 A1
Mortlake SW14, TW10 132 D1
Northolt UB6 64 B2
Rothesay Ct
4 Catford SE6 164 D2
Grove Pk SE12 165 B1
13 Kennington SE11 138 C6
Rothesay Rd SE25 205 C5
Rothley Ct NW8 236 C6
Rothsay Rd E7 77 C2
Rothsay St
SE1 117 C3 263 A5
Rothsay Wlk 19 E14 119 C2
Rothschild Rd W4 111 A3
Rothschild St SE27 182 D6
Rothwell Ct
2 Bromley BR1 187 B2
4 Harrow HA1 42 D4
Rothwell Gdns RM9 102 C6
Rothwell Ho TW5 129 C6
Rothwell Rd RM9 102 C6
Rothwell St
10 Hampstead NW1 70 D1
Primrose Hill NW1 230 D6
Roth Wlk N7 72 B6
Rotten Row
SW1 114 D4 247 C2
Rotterdam Dr E14 120 A3
Rouel Rd
Bermondsey SE16 118 A2
Bermondsey SE16 118 A3
Rougemont Ave SM4 201 C3
Roundabout Ho HA6 22 A2
Roundacre SW19 156 D2
Roundel Cl SE4 141 B1
Roundell Ho 14 SE21 183 C6
Rounders Ct 7 RM10 81 D2
Round Gr CR0 206 D2
Roundhay Cl SE23 162 D2
Roundhedge Way EN2 4 B5
Round Hill SE23 162 C1
Roundhill Dr EN2 4 B1
ROUNDSHAW 220 B1
Roundshaw Ctr SM6 220 A1
Roundtable Rd BR1 164 D1
Roundtree Rd HA0 65 B3
Roundways HA4 61 D5
Roundway The
Claygate KT10 212 D2
Tottenham N17 33 B2
Roundwood BR7 188 D1
Roundwood Ave
UB11 105 A5
Roundwood Cl HA4 39 B2
Roundwood Rd NW10 67 D1
Rounton Rd E3 97 C3
Rountree Ct 9 UB1 85 D1
Roupell Ho 7 KT2 176 B3
Roupell Rd SW2 160 B3
Roupell St
SE1 116 C5 251 B3
Rousden St NW1 71 C1
Rouse Gdns SE21 183 C6
Routemaster Cl E13 99 B4
Routh Ct TW14 149 B3
Routh Rd SW18 158 C4
Routh St E6 100 B2
Rover Ho 26 N1 95 C6
Rowallan Ct 3 SE6 164 D3
Rowallan Rd
SW6 135 A5 264 A3
Rowallen Par RM8 58 C1
Rowan N10 31 B1
Rowan Ave E4 35 B4
Rowan Cl
Ealing W5 110 A4
Harrow HA7 24 D4
Ilford IG1 79 B3
Kingston u T KT3 177 C1
Streatham SW16 181 C2
Wembley HA0 65 A5
Rowan Cres SW16 181 C2
Rowan Ct
19 Camberwell SE15 139 D5
Forest Hill SE26 184 C6
11 Kingston u T KT2 176 C3
Newham E13 99 B5
Twickenham TW4 151 D6
Wandsworth SW11 158 D5
Wimbledon SW20 178 B1
Rowan Dr NW9 46 A6
Rowan Gdns CR0 221 D5
Rowan Ho
9 Bow E3 97 B6
Dagenham NW10 89 C3
East Bedfont TW14 149 B5
Ilford IG1 79 B3
5 Maitland Pk NW3 70 D2
Sidcup DA14 167 D1
Rowan Pl UB3 105 D6
Rowan Rd
Brentford TW8 131 B5
Brook Green W6 112 D2
DA7 147 A2
Mitcham SW16 181 C1
West Drayton UB7 104 A2
Rowans The
Ashford TW16 171 D5
Edmonton N13 17 A1
7 Sutton SM2 217 D2
Rowan Terr W6 112 D2
Rowantree Cl N21 17 B3
Rowantree Rd
Edmonton N21 17 B3
Enfield EN2 4 D3
Rowan Way RM6 58 C6
Rowan Wlk
BR2 226 B5
7 Dartmouth Pk N19 71 C6
Hampstead Garden Suburb
N2 48 A4
Kensal Town W10 91 A3
1 New Barnet EN5 13 D6
Rowanwood Ave
DA15 168 A3
Rowanwood Mews EN2 4 D3
Rowben Cl N20 13 D3
Rowberry Cl SW6 134 C5
Rowcross St
SE1 117 D1 263 D2
Rowdell Rd UB5 85 C6
Rowden Par E4 35 C4
Rowden Park Gdns E4 35 C4
Rowden Rd
Beckenham BR3 185 B2
Chingford E4 35 D4
West Ewell KT19 215 A4
Rowditch La SW11 137 A3
Rowdon Ave NW10 68 B1
Rowdowns Rd RM9 81 B1
Rowe Gdns IG11 102 A5
Rowe Ho E9 74 C2
Rowe La E9 74 C3
Rowena Cres SW11 136 C3
Rowe Wlk HA2 63 C5
Rowfant Rd SW12,
SW17 159 A2
Rowhill Mans 11 E5 74 B4
Rowhill Rd E5 74 B4
Rowington Cl W2 91 D2
Rowland Ave HA3 43 C6
Rowland Ct
E16 98 D3
South Croydon CR0 221 C6
Rowland Gr SE26 162 B1
Rowland Hill Almshouses
7 TW15 170 C5
Rowland Hill Ave N17 33 B4
Rowland Hill Ho SE1 251 C2
Rowland Hill St NW3 70 C3
Rowlands Ave HA5 23 D4
Rowlands Cl
Hendon NW7 28 A3
Highgate N6 49 A3
Rowlands Rd RM8 81 B6
Rowland Way
Ashford TW15 171 B3
Merton SW19 179 D2
Rowley Ave DA15 168 B4
Rowley Cl HA0 66 B1
Rowley Ct EN1 17 C6
Rowley Gdns N4 51 A2
Rowley Green Rd EN5 12 A6
Rowley Ho SE8 141 C6
Rowley Ind Pk W3 110 D3
Rowley La EN5 11 D6
Rowley Rd N15 51 A4
Rowley Way NW8 229 A6
Rowlheys Pl UB7 104 A3
Rowlls Rd KT1 198 B6
Rowney Gdns RM9 80 C2
Rowney Rd RM9 80 B2
Rowntree Cl NW6 69 C2
Rowntree Clifford Cl 7
E13 99 B4
Rowntree Path 1
SE28 124 B5
Rowntree Rd TW2 152 C3
Rowse Cl E15 98 A6
Rowsham Ct HA1 64 C5
Rowsley Ave NW4 46 C6
Rowstock 1 NW5 71 D2
Rowstock Gdns N7 71 D3
Rowton Rd SE18 145 A5
Roxborough Ave
Harrow HA1 42 C2
Hounslow TW7 130 D5
Roxborough Pk HA1 42 C2
Roxborough Rd HA1 42 B3
Roxbourne Cl UB5 62 D2
Roxbourne Fst & Mid Schs
HA2 63 A6
Roxburgh Rd SE27 182 D5
Roxburn Way HA4 61 D5
Roxby Pl SW6 135 C6 265 B6
ROXETH 64 A6
Roxeth Ct 6 TW15 170 C5
Roxeth Fst & Mid Sch
HA2 64 B6
Roxeth Gr HA2 63 D4
Roxeth Green Ave
HA2 63 D6
Roxeth Hill HA2 64 C6
Roxeth Manor Fst & Mid
Schs HA2 63 C5
Roxeth Mead Sch HA2 64 B6
Roxford Cl TW17 193 C4
Roxford Ho 2 E3 97 D3
Roxley Rd SE13 163 D5
Roxton Gdns CR0 223 C3
Roxwell 10 NW1 71 B2
Roxwell Rd
Barking IG11 102 A5
Shepherd's Bush W12 112 A4
Roxwell Trad Pk E10 53 A2
Roxwell Way IG8 37 C3
Roxy Ave RM6 58 C2
Royal Academy of
Dramatic Art*
WC1 93 D2 239 C4
Royal Acad of Arts*
W1 115 C6 249 A5
Royal Acad of Dance
SW11 266 D1
Royal Acad of Music
NW1 238 B5
Royal Albert Hall*
SW7 114 B4 246 C1
Royal Albert Sta E16 122 A6
Royal Albert Way E6 122 B6
Royal Arc W1 249 A5
Royal Armouries The*
E1 253 C5
Royal Ave
SW3 114 D1 257 C2
Worcester Pk KT4 215 C6
Royal Avenue Ho
SW3 257 C2
Royal Ballet Sch The
Hammersmith W14 112 D1
St Giles WC2 94 A1 240 B1
Royal Ballet Sch (White
Lodge) The TW10 155 B3
Royal Brompton Hospl
Chelsea SW3 114 B1 256 C2
Chelsea SW3 114 C1 257 A2
Royal Cir SE27 160 D1
Royal Cl
Deptford SE8 141 B6
Hillingdon UB7 82 B1
Ilford IG3 58 A2
Locksbottom BR6 226 D4
Putney SW19 156 D2
Stamford Hill N16 51 C1
Worcester Pk KT4 215 C6
Royal College of
Physicians Liby
NW1 93 B3 238 D6
Royal College St
NW1 93 C6 232 B6
Royal Coll of
Anaesthetists WC1 240 C3
Royal Coll of Art
SW7 114 B4 246 C1
Royal Coll of Art
Sculpture Sch
SW11 136 C5 267 A3
Royal Coll of Midwives
W1 93 B2 238 C3
Royal Coll of Music
SW7 114 B3 256 C6
Royal Coll of
Obstetricians &
Gynaecologists
NW1 92 D3 237 C6
Royal Coll of
Ophthalmologists
NW1 238 A5
Royal Coll of Paediatrics
& Child Health W1 238 D4
Royal Coll of Pathologists
SW1 115 D5 249 C3
Royal Coll of Physicians
NW1 93 B3 238 D6
Royal Coll of Radiologists
W1 238 D4
Royal Coll of Science
SW7 114 B3 256 C6
Royal Coll of Speech
Language Therapists
SE1 252 C3
Royal Coll of Surgeons
WC2 94 B1 240 D2
Royal Connaught Apts
E16 121 D5
Royal Courts of Justice
WC2 94 C1 241 A1
Royal Cres
Ilford IG2 57 B3
Ruislip HA4 63 A5
W11 113 A5 244 A3
Royal Crescent Mews
W11 112 D5
Royal Crest Ho SM2 217 A1
Royal Ct
City of London EC3 242 D1
Enfield EN1 17 C5
9 Kingston u T KT2 176 D3
Mottingham SE9 166 B3
Rotherhithe SE16 119 B3
Ruislip HA4 40 A2
Royal Docks Com Sch The
E16 99 C1
Royal Docks Rd E6 100 D2
Royal Dr N11 31 A5
Royal Duchess Mews
SW12 159 B4
Royal Exchange*
EC3 242 D1
Royal Exchange Bldgs
EC3 242 D1
Royal Festival Hall*
SE1 116 B5 250 D3
Royal Free Hospl NW3 70 C3
Royal Fusiliers Mus*
E1 253 C5
Royal Gdns W7 109 A3
Royal Geographical
Society SW7 246 D1
Royal Hill SE10 142 A5
Royal Hill Ct 2 SE10 142 A5
Royal Horticultural
Society (Lawrence Hall
& Conf Ctr) SW1 259 C5
Royal Horticultural
Society (Lindley Hall)
SW1 259 C4
Royal Hospital (Army
Pensioners)*
SW1 115 A1 258 A1
Royal Hospital Rd
SW3 114 D1 257 D1
Royal Hospl and Home
SW15 157 A5
Royal La
Hillingdon UB7 82 B1
Hillingdon UB8 82 B3
Royal Langford
Apartments 3 NW6 91 D5
Royal London Est N17 34 B4
Royal London Est The
NW10 89 B5
Royal London
Homeopathic Hospl The
WC1 94 A2 240 B4
Royal London Hospl
Archives & Mus* E1 96 B2
Royal London Hospl (Mile
End) The E2 96 D4
Royal London Hospl (St
Clements) The E3 97 B4
Royal London Hospl
(Whitechapel) The
E1 96 B2
Royal Marsden Hospl
SW3 114 B1 256 D2
Royal Mews KT8 196 C6
Royal Mews The*
SW1 115 B3 258 D6
Royal Military Sch of
Music (Kneller Hall)
TW2 152 B5
Royal Mint Pl 6 E1 118 A6
Royal Mint St
E1 117 D6 253 D6
Royal National
Orthopaedic Hospl
Regent's Pk
W1 93 B3 238 D5
Stanmore HA7 9 C2
Royal National TNE Hospl
The WC1 94 B4 233 C2
Royal Nat TN&E Hospl The
W5 87 C2
Royal Naval Pl SE14 141 B5
Royal Oak Ct
Dagenham RM8 80 C6
9 Shoreditch N1 95 C4
Royal Oak Mews 9
TW11 175 A5
Royal Oak Pl SE22 162 B5
Royal Oak Rd
Bexley DA6 147 C1
DA6 169 B6
5 Hackney E8 74 B2
Royal Oak Sta W2 91 D2
Royal Oak Yd SE1 253 A1
Royal Observatory The*
SE10 142 B5
Royal Opera Arc SW1 249 C4
Royal Orchard Cl
SW18 157 A4
Royal Par
Blackheath Vale SE3 142 D3
Chislehurst BR7 189 A3
11 Dagenham RM10 81 D2
Ealing W5 88 A4
Fulham SW6 264 A4
12 Richmond TW9 132 C4
Royal Park Prim Sch
DA14 169 A1
Royal Pl 11 SE10 142 A5
Royal Rd
Kennington SE17 138 D6
Newham E16 99 D1
Sidcup DA14 168 D1
Teddington TW11 174 B5
Royal Route HA9 66 B4
Royal Russell Sch
CR0 222 B3
Royal Sch Hampstead The
NW3 70 B4
Royal St SE1 116 B3 260 D6
Royal Tower Lo 3
SE1 118 A6
Royalty Ho W1 239 C1
Royalty Mews W1 239 C1
Royalty Studios W11 91 A1
Royal United Services
Mus* SW1 250 A3
Royal Veterinary Coll
NW1 93 D6 232 C5
Royal Victoria Pl 7
E16 121 B5
Royal Victoria Sq
E16 121 B6
Royal Victoria Sta
E16 121 A6
Royal Victor Pl E3 96 D5
Royal Wlk SM6 219 B5
Roycraft Ave IG11 101 D5
Roycroft Cl
Streatham SW2 160 C3
Woodford E18 37 B2
Roydene Rd SE18 123 C1
Roydon Cl 7 SW11 136 D3
Roy Gdns IG2 57 D4
Roy Gr TW12 173 D4
Royle Cres W13 87 A3
Roymount Ct TW2 152 C1
Roy Ridley Ho 6
SW4 137 D2
Roy Sq E14 119 A6
Royston Ave
Carshalton SM1 218 B5
Chingford E4 35 D5
Wallington SM6 219 D4
Royston Cl
Cranford TW5 128 B4
Walton-on-T KT12 194 A1
Royston Ct
Hinchley Wood KT10 212 D6
New Cross SE4 141 B3
1 Newham E13 99 A6
Redbridge IG1 55 D3
3 Richmond TW9 132 B4
Ruislip HA5 40 C2
Tolworth KT6 214 C6
Royston Gdns IG1 55 D3
Royston Gr HA5 23 C4
Royston Ho
Friern Barnet N11 31 A6
14 SE15 140 A6
Royston Lo SW19 180 A4
Royston Par IG1 55 D3
Royston Park Rd HA5 23 C5
Royston Prim Sch
SE20 184 D2
Royston Rd
Penge SE20 184 D2
Richmond TW10 154 A6
Royston St 24 E2 96 C5
Roystons The KT5 198 D4
Rozel Ct 3 N1 95 C6
Rozelle Ct 1 CR7 204 C3
Rozel Rd SW4 137 C2
Rubastic Rd UB2 106 C3
Rubens Rd UB5 84 D5
Rubens St SE6 163 B2
Rubin Pl 14 EN3 7 C6
Ruby Ct TW13 149 D1
Ruby Rd E17 53 C6
Ruby St
SE15 140 B6
Stonebridge NW10 67 A1
Ruby Triangle SE15 140 B6
Ruckholt Cl E10 75 D5
Ruckholt Rd E10 75 D5
Rucklidge Ave NW10 90 A5
Rudall Cres NW3 70 B4
Rudbeck Ho 11 SE15 140 A5
Ruddlngton Cl E5 75 A4
Ruddock Cl HA8 27 A3
Ruddstreet Cl SE18 123 A2
Rudge Ho 1 SE16 118 A3
Rudgwick Terr
NW8 92 C6 230 B5
Rudhall Ho 4 SW2 160 C5
Rudland Rd DA7 147 D2
Rudloe Rd SW12 159 C4
Rudolf Pl SW8 270 B5
Rudolph Ct SE22 162 B4
Rudolph Rd
E13 98 D5
Paddington NW6 91 C5
Rudstone Ho 10 E3 97 D4
Rudyard Ct SE1 252 D1
Rudyard Gr NW7 27 A4
Ruegg Ho 5 SE18 144 C6
Ruffetts Cl CR2 222 B1
Ruffetts The CR2 222 B1
Ruffle Cl UB7 104 B4
Rufford Cl HA3 43 A3
Rufford St N1 94 A6 233 B6
Rufford Street Mews
N1 72 A1
Rufford Twr 5 W3 110 D5
Rufforth Ct 1 NW9 27 C2

Rufus Bsns Ctr SW18 157 D2
Rufus Cl HA4 63 A5
Rufus Ho SE1 263 D6
Rufus St N1 95 C4
Rugby Ave
  Edmonton N9 17 D3
  Northolt UB6 64 B2
  Wembley HA0 65 C4
Rugby Cl HA1 42 C5
Rugby Gdns RM9 80 C2
Rugby Mans W14 254 B4
Rugby Rd
  Bedford Pk W4 111 C4
  Dagenham RM9 80 C2
  Queensbury NW9 44 D5
  Twickenham TW1, TW2, TW7 152 C5
Rugby St WC1 94 B3 240 C5
Rugg St E14 119 C6
Rugless Ho 2 E14 120 A4
Rugmere 4 NW1 71 A1
RUISLIP 39 B2
Ruislip Cl UB6 85 D3
RUISLIP COMMON 39 B4
Ruislip Ct HA4 61 D6
RUISLIP GARDENS 61 D5
Ruislip Gardens Prim Sch HA4 61 D4
Ruislip Gardens Sta HA4 62 A4
Ruislip Lido* HA4, HA5 39 B5
Ruislip Lido Rly* HA4 39 B5
RUISLIP MANOR 40 A1
Ruislip Manor Sta HA4 40 A1
Ruislip Rd UB6, UB5 85 C4
Ruislip Rd E
  Ealing UB6, W7 86 D3
  Greenford UB6 86 B3
Ruislip St SW17 180 D6
Ruislip Sta HA4 39 D1
Rumball Ho 14 SE5 139 C5
Rumbold Rd SW6 135 D5 265 D3
Rum Cl E1 118 C6
Rumford Ho SE1 262 A5
Rumsey Cl TW12 173 B4
Rumsey Rd SW9 138 B2
Runacres Ct SE17 262 A1
Runbury Circ NW9 67 B6
Runcorn Cl N17 52 B5
Runcorn Pl W11 244 A6
Rundell Cres NW4 46 B4
Rundell Twr SW8 270 C2
Runes Cl CR4 202 C5
Runnelfield HA1 64 C5
Running Horse Yd 12 TW8 132 A6
Runnymede SW19 180 B2
Runnymede Cl TW2 151 D4
Runnymede Cres SW16 182 A2
Runnymede Ct
  Roehampton SW15 156 A3
  1 Wallington SM6 219 B2
Runnymede Gdns
  Greenford UB6 86 C5
  Twickenham TW2 151 D4
Runnymede Ho
  Hackney E9 75 A4
  Richmond TW10 154 C6
Runnymede Rd TW2 151 D5
Runway The HA4 62 C3
Rupack St 3 SE16 118 C4
Rupert Ave 6 HA9 66 A3
Rupert Ct W1 249 C6
Rupert Gdns SW9 138 D3
Rupert Ho
  SE11 261 B3
  8 Upper Holloway N19 71 D5
Rupert Rd
  Bedford Pk W4 111 C3
  Paddington NW6 91 B5
  Upper Holloway N19 71 D6
Rupert St W1 115 D6 249 C6
Rural Way SW16 181 B3
Rusbridge Cl E8 74 A3
Ruscoe Ho 12 SW27 182 D5
Ruscoe Rd E16 98 D1
Ruscombe Way TW14 149 D4
Rusham Rd SW12 158 D4
Rushbrook Cres E17 35 B2
Rushbrook Ho 20 SW8 137 D3
Rushbrook Rd SE9 167 A2
Rushbury Ct 4 TW12 173 C2
Rushby Ct SW4 270 A1
Rush Common Mews 18 SW2 160 B4
Rushcroft Rd
  Brixton SW2, SW9 138 C1
  Chingford E4 35 D3
Rush Croft Sch E4 35 D3
Rushcutters Ct 18 SE16 119 A2
Rushden Cl SE19 183 B3
Rushdene SE2 124 D3
Rushdene Ave EN4 14 C4
Rushdene Cl UB5 84 C5
Rushdene Cres UB5 84 C4
Rushdene Rd HA5 40 D3
Rushden Gdns
  Ilford IG5 56 C6
  Mill Hill NW7 28 C4
Rushen Wlk SM5 202 B1
Rushet Rd BR5 190 A1
Rushett Cl KT7 197 B1
Rushett Rd KT7 197 B2
Rushey Cl KT3 199 B5
Rushey Gn SE6 163 D4
Rushey Green Prim Sch SE6 163 D3
Rushey Hill EN2 4 B1
Rushey Mead SE4 163 C6
Rushford Rd SE4 163 B5
Rush Green Rd RM7, RM8, RM10 59 D1
Rushgrove Ave NW9 45 D5
Rushgrove Ct NW9 45 C4
Rushgrove St SE18 122 B2
Rush Hill Mews 3 SW11 137 A2
Rush Hill Rd SW11 137 A2
Rushlake Ho 3 SW11 137 A3
Rushley Cl BR2 226 A4
Rushman Villas KT3 199 D5
Rushmead
  5 Bethnal Green E2 96 B4
  Richmond TW10 153 B1
Rushmead Cl CR0 221 D4
Rushmere Ct KT4 216 A6
Rushmere Ho 2 SW15 156 A3
Rushmere Pl SW19 178 D5
Rushmon Pl SM3 217 A2
Rushmoor Cl HA5 40 B5
Rushmore Cl BR1 210 A6
Rushmore Cres 9 E5 74 D4
Rushmore Ho
  9 Kentish Town N7 71 D3
  W14 254 B5
Rushmore Prim Sch E5 74 D4
Rushmore Rd
  Clapton Pk E5 74 D4
  Hackney E5 75 A4
Rusholme Ave RM10 81 C5
Rusholme Gr SE19 183 C5
Rusholme Rd SW15 157 A5
Rushout Ave HA3 43 B3
Rush The SW20 179 B2
Rushton Ho 26 SW8 137 D3
Rushton St N1 95 B5 235 D4
Rushworth St SE1 116 D4 251 D1
Rushy Meadow La SM5 218 C5
Rushy Meadow Prim Sch SM5 218 C5
Ruskin Ave
  DA16 146 A3
  Feltham TW14 149 D5
  Plashet E12 78 A2
  Richmond TW9 132 C5
Ruskin Cl NW11 47 D3
Ruskin Ct
  Herne Hill SE5 139 B2
  SE9 166 B5
  Southgate N21 16 B4
Ruskin Dr
  North Cheam KT4 216 C6
  Orpington BR6 227 C5
  Welling DA16 146 A2
Ruskin Gdns
  Ealing W5 87 D3
  Harrow HA3 44 B5
Ruskin Gr DA16 146 A3
Ruskin Ho SW1 259 D3
Ruskin Par CR0 221 B3
Ruskin Park Ho SE5 139 B2
Ruskin Rd
  Belvedere DA17 125 C2
  Croydon CR0 220 D6
  Isleworth TW7 130 D2
  Southall UB1 107 A6
  Tottenham N17 33 D2
  Wallington SM5 219 A3
Ruskin Way SW19 180 B2
Ruskin Wlk
  BR2 210 B3
  Edmonton N9 18 A2
  Herne Hill SE24 161 A6
Rusland Ave BR6 227 B5
Rusland Hts HA1 42 C5
Rusland Park Rd HA1 42 C5
Rusper Cl
  Cricklewood NW2 68 C5
  Stanmore HA7 25 C6
Rusper Ct SW9 138 A3
Rusper Rd
  Dagenham RM9 80 C2
  Tottenham N17, N22 51 A6
Russel Cl BR3 208 A6
Russel Ct N14 15 D6
Russell Ave N22 32 D1
Russell Cl
  Bexleyheath DA7 147 C1
  Chiswick W4 133 D6
  Greenwich SE7 143 C5
  Ruislip HA4 62 C6
  Stonebridge NW10 67 A1
Russell Ct
  Battersea SW11 268 B1
  Bloomsbury WC1 240 A5
  Bromley BR1 186 D3
  12 New Barnet EN5 2 A1
  5 Peckham SE15 140 B3
  St James SW1 249 B3
  Streatham SW16 182 B5
  Surbiton KT6 198 A2
  Wallington SM6 219 C3
  4 Walthamstow E10 53 D2
  Wembley HA0 66 A1
Russell Gdns
  East Barnet N20 14 C2
  Ilford IG2 57 B2
  Richmond TW10 153 C2
  Temple Fortune NW11 47 A3
  W14 113 A3 254 A6
  West Drayton UB7 104 C1
Russell Gdns Mews W14 113 A3 254 A6
Russell Gr
  33 Brixton SW9 138 C4
  Edgware NW7 27 C6
Russell Ho
  21 Poplar E14 97 C1
  SW1 259 A2
Russell Kerr Cl W4 133 A5
Russell La N20 14 D2
Russell Lo
  5 Chingford E4 20 A2
  SE1 262 C6
Russell Mans WC1 240 B4
Russell Mead HA3 24 D2
Russell Par NW11 47 A3
Russell Pickering Ho 2 SW4 138 A2
Russell Pl
  Hampstead NW3 70 C3
  Rotherhithe SE16 119 A3
Russell Rd
  Bowes Pk N13 32 B4
  Buckhurst Hill IG9 21 C3
  Chingford Hatch E4 35 B6
  Crouch End N8 49 D3
  East Barnet N20 14 C2
  Enfield EN1 5 D5
  Leyton E10 53 D3
  Merton SW19 179 C3
  Mitcham CR4 202 C6
  Newham E16 99 B1
  Northolt UB5 64 A3
  Shepperton TW17 193 A2
  Tottenham N15 51 C4
  Twickenham TW1, TW2 152 D5
  W14 113 A3 254 B5
  Walthamstow E17 53 B6
  Walton-on-T KT12 194 A3
  West Hendon NW9 45 D3
Russell Sch The TW10 153 D3
Russell Sq WC1 94 A3 240 A5
Russell Square Ho WC1 240 A5
Russell Square Mans WC1 240 B4
Russell Square Sta WC1 94 A3 240 A5
Russell St WC2 116 A6 250 B6
Russell's Wharf 2 W9 91 B3
Russell Way SM1 217 D3
Russell Wlk 4 TW10 154 B5
Russet Ave TW16, TW17 193 C6
Russet Cl UB10 83 A3
Russet Cres N7 72 B3
Russet Ct
  6 Barnet EN4 2 C1
  Dollis Hill NW2 68 B5
  Feltham TW13 149 C1
Russet Dr CR0 207 A1
Russet Ho TW3 129 B1
Russet House Sch EN1 6 B4
Russets Cl E4 36 B6
Russettings 1 HA5 23 B3
Russett Way SE13 141 D3
Russia Dock Rd SE16 119 A5
Russia La E2 96 C5
Russia Row EC2 242 B1
Russington Rd TW17 193 B3
Rusthall Ave W4 111 B3
Rusthall Cl CR0 206 C3
Rusthall Mans 3 W4 111 B2
Rustic Ave SW16 181 B3
Rustic Pl HA0 65 D4
Rustic Wlk E16 99 B1
Rustington Wlk SM4 201 B2
Ruston Ave KT5 198 D2
Ruston Gdns N14 15 A5
Ruston Mews W11 91 A1
Ruston Rd SE18 122 A3
Ruston St E3 97 B6
Rust Sq SE5 139 B5
Rutford Rd SW16 182 A5
Ruth Cl HA7 44 B5
Ruth Ct 16 E3 97 A5
Rutherford Cl
  Hillingdon UB8 82 B3
  Sutton SM2 218 B2
Rutherford Ct
  Mitcham SW19 180 B3
  Southgate N21 16 B6
Rutherford Ho
  12 Bethnal Green E1 96 B3
  Teddington TW11 174 D5
  4 Wembley HA9 67 A5
Rutherford St SW1 115 D2 259 C4
Rutherford Twr 8 UB1 85 D1
Rutherford Way
  Bushey WD23 8 C3
  Wembley HA9 66 C4
Rutherglen Rd SE2 146 A6
Rutherwyke Cl KT17 216 A2
Ruth Ho W10 91 A3
Ruthin Cl NW9 45 C3
Ruthin Rd SE3 143 A6
Ruthven St E9 96 D6
Rutland Ave DA15 168 A4
Rutland Cl
  Chessington KT9 214 B2
  DA5 168 D3
  Mitcham SW19 180 C3
  Mortlake SW14 133 A2
Rutland Ct
  15 Acton W3 88 C1
  Chislehurst BR7 188 C2
  Enfield EN3 18 B6
  Herne Hill SE5 139 B1
  Sidcup SE9 167 A2
  SW7 247 B1
  Twickenham TW2 152 C1
Rutland Dr
  Morden SM4 201 C2
  Richmond TW10 154 A3
Rutland Gate
  Beckenham BR2 208 D5
  Belvedere DA17 125 D1
  SW7 114 C4 247 B1
Rutland Gate Mews SW7 247 A1
Rutland Gdns
  Dagenham RM8 80 C3
  Ealing W13 87 A2
  South Croydon CR0 221 C4
  Stoke Newington N4 51 A3
  SW7 114 C4 247 B1
Rutland Gdns Mews SW7 247 B1
Rutland Gr W6 112 B1
Rutland Ho
  Edgware HA8 26 B4
  6 Northolt UB5 63 C2
  2 Penge SE20 184 C2
  10 Putney SW15 156 C4
  Tolworth KT6 198 C1
  W8 255 C5
  15 Woolwich SE18 122 B2
Rutland Lo
  Forest Hill SE6 163 B2
  Teddington TW11 174 C5
Rutland Mews E SW7 257 B6
Rutland Mews S SW7 257 A6
Rutland Mews W SW7 257 A6
Rutland Park Gdns 1 NW2 68 C2
Rutland Park Mans 2 NW2 68 C2
Rutland Pk
  Forest Hill SE6 163 B2
  Willesden NW2 68 C2
Rutland Pl
  Bushey WD23 8 B3
  EC1 241 D4
Rutland Rd
  Forest Gate E7 77 D1
  Harrow HA1 42 A3
  Hayes UB3 105 B2
  Ilford IG1 78 D5
  Mitcham SW19 180 C3
  Southall UB1 85 C2
  South Hackney E9 96 D6
  Twickenham TW2 152 B2
  Walthamstow E17 53 C3
  Wanstead E11 55 B4
Rutland St SW7 257 B6
Rutland Studios NW10 90 A4
Rutland Wlk SE6 163 B2
Rutley Cl SE11 138 D6
Rutlish Rd SW19 179 C2
Rutlish Sch SW20 179 B1
Rutter Gdns CR4 202 B5
Rutters Cl UB7 104 C4
Rutt's Terr SE14 140 D4
Rutts The WD23 8 B3
Ruvigny Gdns SW15 134 D2
Ruvigny Mans SW15 134 D2
Ruxbury Ct TW15 148 A1
RUXLEY 191 A3
Ruxley Cl
  Chessington KT19 214 D3
  Sidcup DA14 191 A4
Ruxley Cnr DA14 191 A4
Ruxley Corner Ind Est DA14 190 D4
Ruxley Cres KT10 213 B1
Ruxley Ct KT19 215 A3
Ruxley Gdns TW17 193 A4
Ruxley La KT19 215 B3
Ruxley Mews KT19 214 D3
Ruxley Ridge KT10 213 A1
Ryall's Ct N20 14 D1
Ryan Cl
  Ruislip HA4 40 B1
  SE9 143 C1
Ryan Ct SW16 182 A3
Ryan Dr TW8 131 A6
Ryan Ho 3 HA1 42 D4
Ryarsh Cres BR6 227 C4
Rycott Path SE22 162 A4
Rycroft Way N17 51 D6
Ryculff Sq SE3 142 D3
Rydal Cl NW4 29 A2
Rydal Cres UB6 87 C5
Rydal Ct
  Edgware HA8 26 B5
  Wembley HA9 44 A2
Rydal Dr
  DA7 147 C4
  West Wickham BR4 224 C6
Rydal Gdns
  Kingsbury NW9 45 C4
  Kingston u T SW15 177 C5
  Twickenham TW2, TW3 151 D5
  Wembley HA9 43 C1
Rydal Ho 25 SW8 137 D3
Rydal Lo N17 34 A3
Rydal Rd SW16 181 D6
Rydal Water NW1 232 A1
Rydal Way
  Enfield EN3 18 C5
  Ruislip HA4 62 C4
Ryde Ho 1 NW6 91 C6
Rydens Ho SE9 165 C1
Rydens Rd KT12 194 D1
Ryde Pl TW1 153 D5
Ryder Cl BR1 187 B5
Ryder Ct
  Leyton E10 75 D6
  SW1 249 B4
Ryder Dr SE16 118 B1
Ryder Ho
  18 Bethnal Green E1 96 C3
  5 Merton SW19 179 D2
Ryder St SW1 249 B4
Ryder's Terr NW8 92 A5 229 A4
Ryder Yd SW1 249 B4
Ryde Vale Rd SW12 159 C2
Rydon Mews SW19 178 C3
Rydons Cl SE9 144 A2
Rydon St N1 235 B6
Rydston Cl 2 N7 72 B1
Rye Cl DA5 169 D5
Ryecotes Mead SE21 161 C3
Ryecroft Ave TW2 151 D3
Ryecroft Cres EN5 12 B6
Ryecroft Rd
  BR5 211 B3
  Lewisham SE13 164 A6
  South Norwood SW16 182 C4
Ryecroft St SW6 135 D4 265 C1
Rye Ct BR3 185 B2
Ryedale SE22 162 B5
Ryedale Ct 7 TW12 173 C2
Ryefield Ave UB10 60 D1
Ryefield Cres HA5, HA6 22 A1
Ryefield Ct HA6 22 A1
Ryefield Path 7 SW15 156 A3
Ryefield Prim Sch UB10 83 B6
Ryefield Rd SE19 183 A4
Ryegates 2 SE15 140 B3
Ryehill Ct KT3 199 D2
Rye Hill Pk SE15 140 C1
Rye Ho 17 SE16 118 C4
Rye La SE15 140 A3
Ryeland Cl UB7 82 A1
Ryelands Cres SE12 165 C5
Ryelands Prim Sch SE25 206 B4
Rye Lane Mkt SE15 140 A3
Rye Oak Sch SE15 140 B2
Rye Rd SE15 140 D1
Rye The N14 15 C4
Rye Way HA8 26 B4
Rye Wlk SW15 156 D6
Ryfold Rd SW19 157 C1
Ryhope Rd N11 31 B6
Ryland Cl TW13 171 D6
Rylandes Rd NW2 68 A5
Ryland Ho 11 SW16 181 C5
Ryland Rd NW5 71 B2
Rylett Cres W12 111 D3
Rylett Rd W12 111 D3
Rylston Rd
  Edmonton N13 17 B1
  SW6 135 B6 264 C5
Rylton Ho KT12 194 A1
Rymer Rd CR0 205 C2
Rymer St SE24 160 D5
Rymill St E16 122 C5
Rysbrack St SW1 257 C6
Rythe Cl KT9 213 C1
Rythe Ct KT7 197 A2
Rythe Ho 7 BR1 186 B5
Rythe Rd KT10 212 C3

S

Saatchi Gallery Duke of York's HQ* SW3 114 D1 257 D2
Sabah Ct TW15 170 C6
Sabbarton St 9 E16 98 D1
Sabella Ct E3 97 B5
Sabine Rd SW11 137 A2
Sable Cl TW4 128 C2
Sable Ct 3 KT3 199 C4
Sable St N1 72 D1
Sach Rd E5 74 B6
Sackets Ho 24 SW9 138 C4
Sackville Ave BR2 209 A1
Sackville Cl HA2 64 B5
Sackville Gdns IG1 56 B1
Sackville Ho
  Hornsey N8 50 A5
  16 Streatham SW16 160 A1
Sackville Rd SM2 217 C1
Sackville St W1 115 C6 249 B5
Sacred Heart High Sch W6 112 C2
Sacred Heart Jun Sch W6 112 D2
Sacred Heart Language Coll The HA3 24 C1
Sacred Heart Prim Sch, Battersea SW11 136 C3
Sacred Heart RC Prim Sch
  East Barnet N20 14 C2
  Islington N7 72 B3
  Putney SW15 156 A6
  Ruislip HA4 61 C6
  Teddington TW11 175 B3
  West Barnes KT3 200 A5

Sacred Heart RC Sec Sch SE5 139 A4
Saddlebrook Pk TW16 171 C3
Saddlers Cl
Barnet EN5 12 B6
Borehamwood WD6 11 B5
Pinner HA5 23 C5
Saddlers Mews SW8 270 B2
Teddington KT1 175 C2
Wembley HA0 64 D4
Saddlers Path WD6 11 B6
Saddlescombe Way N12 29 C5
Sadler Cl CR4 180 D1
Sadler Ho
17 Bromley E3 97 D4
EC1 234 C2
Sadlers Ho EN1 17 C6
Sadlers Ride KT8 174 A1
Saffron Ave E14 120 B6
Saffron Cl
Temple Fortune NW11 47 B3
Thornton Heath CR0 204 A3
Saffron Ct
East Bedfont TW14 149 A4
10 Kingsland N1 73 B2
Stratford E15 76 C3
Saffron Hill
EC1 94 C2 241 B4
Saffron Ho 6 TW9 132 D4
Saffron St EC1 241 B4
Saffron Way KT6 197 D1
Saffron Wharf SE1 253 D2
Sage Cl 7 E6 100 B2
Sage Mews SE22 161 D6
Sage St E1 118 C6
Sage Way WC1 233 C1
Sage Yd KT6 198 B1
Sahara Ct UB1 107 A6
Saigasso Cl E16 99 D1
Sailacre Ho 10 SE10 120 D1
Sail Ct 10 E14 120 B6
Sailmakers Ct SW6 136 A2
Sail St SE11 116 B2 260 D4
Saimet 3 NW9 27 D2
Sainfoin Rd SW17 159 A2
Sainsbury Rd SE19 183 C5
St Agatha's Dr KT2 176 B4
St Agatha's Gr SM5 202 D1
St Agatha's RC Prim Sch
KT2 176 B4
St Agnes Cl E9 96 C6
St Agnes Pl SE11 138 D6
St Agnes RC Prim Sch
E3 97 D4
St Agnes RC Sch NW2 69 A5
St Aidans Ct IG11 102 B5
St Aidan's Prim Sch
N4 50 C2
St Aidan's RC Prim Sch
IG1 57 B1
St Aidan's Rd
East Dulwich SE22 162 B6
West Ealing W13 109 B4
St Aiden's Ct W13 109 C4
St Albans Ave
Bedford Pk W4 111 B3
Feltham TW13 172 D5
St Alban's Ave E6 100 C4
St Alban's CE Prim Sch
EC1 94 C2 241 A4
St Alban's Cl NW11 47 C1
St Albans Cres N22 32 C2
St Alban's Cres IG8 37 A2
St Alban's Gdns
TW11 175 A5
St Alban's Gr
Carshalton SM5 202 C2
W8 113 D3 255 D6
St Albans Ho 2
SW16 182 C6
St Albans La NW11 47 C1
St Albans Mans W8 255 D6
St Alban's Pl
N1 94 D6 234 C5
St Alban's RC Prim Sch
KT8 196 A4
St Albans Rd
Barnet EN5 1 A3
Cheam SM1 217 B4
Ilford IG3 57 D2
Kingston u T KT2 176 A4
St Alban's Rd
Dagenham NW10 89 C6
Dartmouth Pk NW5 71 B5
St Alban's Rd *continued*
Woodford IG8 37 A3
St Alban's St SW1 249 C5
St Albans Studios W8 255 D6
St Albans Terr W6 264 A6
St Alban's Villas NW5 71 A5
St Alfege Pas SE10 142 A6
St Alfege Rd SE7 143 D6
St Alfege with St Peter's
CE Prim Sch SE10 142 A6
St Aloysius RC Coll
N19 49 C1
St Aloysius RC Inf Sch
NW1 93 D4 232 C2
St Aloysius RC Jun Sch
NW1 93 D5 232 C3
St Alphage Ct NW9 45 B6
St Alphage Gdn EC2 242 B3
St Alphage Highwalk
EC2 242 B3
St Alphage Wlk HA8 27 A1
St Alphege Rd N9 18 C4
St Alphonsus Rd
SW4 137 D1
St Amunds Cl SE6 185 C6
St Andrew & St Francis CE
Prim Sch NW2 68 A2
St Andrews Ave HA0 65 A4
St Andrew's (Barnsbury)
CE Prim Sch
N1 94 B6 233 D6
St Andrew's CE Prim Sch
Enfield EN1 5 C3
Osidge N14 15 D3
Stockwell SW9 138 A3
St Andrew's CE Sch
N20 13 B2
St Andrews Chambers
W1 239 B2
St Andrews Cl
25 Bermondsey SE16 118 B1
Erith SE28 102 D1
Long Ditton KT7 197 B1
Ruislip HA4 62 D6
Stanmore HA7 25 C1
Wimbledon SW19 179 D4
St Andrew's Cl
Dollis Hill NW2 68 B5
2 Hounslow TW7 130 C4
North Finchley N12 30 A6
Upper Halliford TW17 193 B5
St Andrews Ct W4 133 A4
St Andrew's Ct
Carshalton SM5 218 C5
2 Higham Hill E17 35 A1
Kingston u T KT3 199 D6
2 Wandsworth SW18 158 A2
St Andrews Dr HA7 25 C2
St Andrew's Gr N16 51 B1
St Andrew's Greek Sch
NW1 71 C2
St Andrew's High Sch
CR0 220 D4
St Andrew's Hill
EC4 94 D1 241 D1
St Andrews Ho
11 Bermondsey SE16 118 B3
Bromley BR1 187 B4
St Andrew's Hospl E3 97 D3
St Andrews Mans 9
E5 74 B4
St Andrew's Mans W1 238 A3
St Andrews Mews
Greenwich SE3 143 A5
4 Streatham SW12 159 D3
St Andrew's Mews
N16 51 C1
St Andrew's Pl NW1 238 D6
St Andrews RC Prim Sch
SW16 182 A5
St Andrews Rd
Carshalton SM5 218 C5
DA14 168 D1
Higham Hill E17 35 A1
Ponders End N9 18 C4
Uxbridge UB10 60 B1
Welsh Harp NW9 45 B1
St Andrew's Rd
3 Croydon CR0 221 A4
Dagenham W3 89 C1
Enfield EN1 5 B2
Hanwell W7 108 C4
Hillingdon UB10 82 B6
Leytonstone E11 54 C3
Newham E13 99 B4
Redbridge IG1 56 B2
Surbiton KT6 197 D3
Temple Fortune NW11 47 B3
W14 264 B6
Willesden NW2 68 B2
St Andrew's & St Mark's
CE Jun Sch KT6 197 D4
St Andrew's Sq
Notting Hill W11 91 A1
Surbiton KT6 197 D3
St Andrew St EC4 241 B3
St Andrews Terr WD19 22 C5
St Andrew's Twr UB1 108 A6
St Andrews Way E3 97 D3
St Andrew's Wharf
SE1 253 D2
St Angela's Ursuline
Convent Sch E7 77 B2
St Anna Rd EN5 12 D6
St Anne RC Prim Sch
E1 96 A3
St Annes Catholic High
Sch for Girls (Upper)
N13 32 C6
St Anne's CE Prim Sch
SW18 157 D6
St Annes Cl WD19 22 C6
St Anne's Cl N6 71 A5
St Anne's Ct 8 SM2 217 D2
St Anne's Ct
Kensal Rise NW6 91 A6
W1 239 C1
St Anne's Flats NW1 232 C2
St Annes Gdns NW10 88 B4
St Anne's Pas E14 97 B1
St Anne's RC High Sch for
Girls EN2 5 B1
St Anne's RC Prim Sch
SE11 138 B6 270 C6
St Anne's Rd
Leyton E11 76 B6
Wembley HA0 65 D3
St Anne's Row E14 97 B1
St Anne St E14 97 B1
St Anne's Trad Est 25
E14 97 B1
St Ann's IG11 101 A6
St Ann's CE Prim Sch
N15 51 B4
St Ann's Cres SW18 158 A5
St Ann's Ct NW4 46 B6
St Ann's Ctr HA1 42 C3
St Ann's Gdns NW5 71 A2
St Ann's General Hospl N4,
N15 51 A4
St Ann's Hill SW18 158 A5
St Ann's Ho WC1 234 A1
St Ann's La SW1 259 D5
St Ann's Park Rd
SW18 158 A5
St Anns Rd SW13 133 D4
St Ann's Rd
2 Barking IG11 101 A6
Edmonton N9 17 D3
Harrow HA1 42 C3
Shepherd's Bush W11 112 D6
Tottenham N15 51 B4
St Ann's Sch
Ealing W7 108 C5
Morden SM4 201 D4
St Ann's St
SW1 115 D3 259 D6
St Ann's Terr
NW8 92 B5 229 D4
St Ann's Villas
W11 113 A5 244 A3
St Ann's Way CR2 220 D2
St Anselm RC Prim Sch
UB2 107 B3
St Anselm's Ct SW16 182 A5
St Anselm's Pl W1 248 C6
St Anselm's RC Prim Sch
Harrow HA1 42 C2
Upper Tooting SW17 159 A1
St Anselms Rd UB3 105 D4
St Anthony's Ave IG8 37 C3
St Anthonys Cl SW17 158 C2
St Anthony's Cl 8 E1 118 A5
St Anthony's Ct
2 Balham SW12 159 A5
Orpington BR6 226 D6
Upper Tooting SW17 159 A2
St Anthony's Flats
NW1 232 C3
St Anthony's Hospl
KT4 200 D1
St Anthony's RC Prim Sch
East Dulwich SE22 162 A5
Penge SE20 184 B2
Upton E7 77 B1
St Anthony's Way
TW14 127 D1
St Antony's RC Prim Sch
IG8 37 A6
St Antony's Rd E7 77 B1
St Arvans Cl CR0 221 C5
St Asaph Ct SE4 140 D2
St Asaph Rd SE4 140 D2
St Aubins Ct N1 235 D6
St Aubyns E18 54 D5
St Aubyn's Ave
Hounslow TW3, TW4 151 C6
Wimbledon SW19 179 B5
St Aubyns Cl BR6 227 D5
St Aubyn's Ct SW19 179 A4
St Aubyns Gdns BR6 227 D6
St Aubyn's Rd SE19 183 D4
St Aubyn's Sch IG8 36 D3
St Audrey Ave DA7 147 C3
St Augustine of
Canterbury CE Prim Sch
DA17 125 B2
St Augustine's Ave
BR1, BR2 210 A4
Ealing W5 88 A4
South Croydon CR2 221 A1
Wembley HA9 66 A5
St Augustine's CE High
Sch NW6 91 C5
St Augustine's CE Prim
Sch NW6 91 D5
St Augustines Ct
Beckenham BR3 185 A1
4 New Barnet EN5 14 A6
St Augustine's Ct E11 54 D1
St Augustine's Ho
NW1 232 C2
Upper Tooting SW17 180 D6
St Augustine's RC Prim
Sch
Ilford IG2 56 D4
W6 135 A6 264 B5
St Augustine's Rd
Camden Town NW1 71 D1
DA17 125 B2
St Augustines's RC Prim
Sch SE6 186 A5
St Austell Cl HA8 26 D3
St Austell Rd SE13 142 B3
St Awdry's Rd IG11 79 B1
St Barnabas CE Prim Sch
SW1 115 A1 258 B2
St Barnabas Cl
Beckenham BR3 186 A1
11 Dulwich Village
SE22 161 C6
St Barnabas Ct HA3 24 A2
St Barnabas' Gdns
KT8 195 C4
St Barnabas Ho CR4 181 A3
St Barnabas Rd
Mitcham CR4 181 A3
Sutton SM1 218 B3
Walthamstow E17 53 C3
Woodford IG8 37 C3
St Barnabas & St Philip's
CE Prim Sch
W8 113 C3 255 A5
St Barnabas St SW1 258 B2
St Barnabas Terr E9 74 D3
St Barnabas Villas
SW8 138 A4 270 B2
St Bartholomews CE Prim
Sch SE26 162 C1
St Bartholomew's CE Prim
Sch SE26 184 C6
St Bartholomew's Cl
SE26 184 C6
St Bartholomews Ct 6
E6 100 A6
St Bartholomew's Hospl
EC1 94 D2 241 D3
St Bartholomew's Rd
E6 100 B5
St Bede's RC Inf Sch
SW12 159 D3
St Bede's RC Prim Sch
RM6 58 C4
St Benedict's Cl
SW17 181 A5
St Benedict's Jun Sch
W5 87 C2
St Benedict's Sch W5 87 D2
St Benets Cl SW17 158 C2
St Benet's Gr SM5 202 A2
St Benet's Pl EC3 252 D6
St Bernadette RC Jun Sch
SW12 159 C4
St Bernadette's Prim Sch
HA3 44 B5
St Bernadette's RC Prim
Sch UB10 82 D6
St Bernard Ho 6
E14 120 A3
St Bernards CR0 221 C5
St Bernards Cl 8
SE27 183 B6
St Bernards Ho 1
KT6 214 A6
St Bernard's Rd E6 99 D6
St Blaise Ave BR1 187 B1
St Bonaventure's RC Sch
E7 77 A1
St Boniface RC Prim Sch
SW17 180 D5
St Botolph St E1,
EC3 95 D1 243 C2
St Brelades Ct N1 235 D6
St Bride's Ave
EC4 241 C1
Edgware HA8 26 B2
St Brides Cl DA18 124 D4
St Bride's Pas EC4 241 C1
St Bride St EC4 94 D1 241 C2
St Catherines Cl
Chessington KT9 213 D2
Upper Tooting SW17 158 C2
St Catherines Ct
TW13 150 A3
St Catherine's Ct 8
W4 111 C3
St Catherine's Dr
SE14 140 D3
St Catherines Farm Ct
HA4 39 A3
St Catherines Mews
SW3 257 C4
St Catherine's RC Sch
EN5 1 C1
St Catherine's RC Sch for
Girls DA6 169 D6
St Catherines Rd
Chingford E4 19 C2
Ruislip HA4 39 B3
St Catherine's Sch
TW1 153 A2
St Catherines Twr 5
E10 53 D2
St Cecilia's CE Sch
SW18 157 B3
St Cecilia's Cl SM3 201 A1
St Cecilia's RC Prim Sch
SM3 216 D6
St Chads Cl KT6 197 C2
St Chad's Gdns RM6 59 A2
St Chad's Pl WC1 233 C2
St Chad's RC Prim Sch
SE25 205 C4
St Chad's Rd RM6 59 A2
St Chad's St WC1 233 B2
St Charles' Hospl W10 90 D2
St Charles Pl W10 91 A2
St Charles RC Prim Sch
W10 90 D2
St Charles RC Sixth Form
Coll W10 90 D2
St Charles Sq W10 90 D2
St Christina's Sch
NW8 92 C5 230 B4
St Christopher's Cl
TW7 130 C4
St Christophers Ct 15
N19 71 C5
St Christophers Dr
UB3 106 B6
St Christophers Gdns
CR7 204 C6
St Christopher's Ho
NW1 232 C3
St Christopher's Mews
SM6 219 C3
St Christopher's Pl
W1 238 B2
St Christopher's Sch
Beckenham BR3 186 A1
Hampstead NW3 70 B3
Wembley HA9 66 B5
St Clair Dr KT4 216 B4
St Clair Ho 17 E3 97 B4
St Clair Rd E13 99 B5
St Clair's Rd CR0 221 C6
St Clare Bsns Pk
TW12 174 A4
St Clare St EC3 243 C1
St Clement Danes CE
Prim Sch WC2 94 B1 240 C1
St Clement & St James CE
Prim Sch
W11 113 A5 244 A4
St Clements Ct
Barnsbury N7 72 B2
7 SE14 140 D6
8 Shepherd's Bush
W11 112 D6
St Clement's Ct EC3 252 D6
St Clements Ho
E1 243 C3
Walton-on-T KT12 194 A2
St Clement's Hts
SE26 184 A6
St Clement's La WC2 240 D1
St Clements Mans 3
SW6 134 D6
St Clements St N7 72 C1
St Cloud Rd SE27 183 B6
St Columba's Ct E15 76 C4
St Columbas Ho 2
E17 53 D5
St Columba's RC Boys Sch
DA6 169 D6
St Columb's Ho 11
W10 91 A2
St Crispins Cl NW3 70 C4
St Crispin's Cl UB1 85 B1
St Crispins Ct 1 UB1 85 B1
St Cross St EC1 94 C2 241 B4
St Cuthberts Gdns 2
HA5 23 B3
St Cuthberts Rd N13 32 C4
St Cuthbert's Rd NW2 69 B2
St Cuthbert with St
Matthias Prim Sch
SW5 113 D1 255 C2
St Cyprian's Greek
Orthodox Prim Sch
CR7 183 A2
St Cyprian's St SW17 180 D6
St Davids Cl
27 Bermondsey SE16 118 B1
Wembley HA9 67 A5
St David's Cl BR4 207 D2
St David's Coll BR4 207 D2
St Davids Ct 5 E11 55 B4
St David's Ct
Bromley BR1 210 D6
8 Southall UB1 86 A1
1 Walthamstow E17 54 A6
St David's Dr HA8 26 B2
St David's Pl NW4 46 B2
St David's Sch TW15 148 B1
St David's Sq E14 119 D1
St Denis Rd SE27 183 B6
St Dionis Rd SW6 135 B3
St Domingo Ho SE18 122 B3
St Dominic RC Prim Sch
NW5 70 D3
St Dominics RC Prim Sch
E9 75 A2
St Dominic's Sixth Form
Coll (RC) HA1 64 C6
St Donatt's Rd SE14 141 B4
St Dunstans SM1 217 B2
St Dunstan's Alley
EC3 253 A5
St Dunstan's Ave W3 111 B6
St Dunstan's CE Prim Sch
SM3 217 A1
St Dunstans Cl UB3 105 D2
St Dunstan's Coll SE6 163 C3
St Dunstan's Ct EC4 241 B1
St Dunstan's Gdns
W3 111 B6
St Dunstan's Hill
Cheam SM1, SM3 217 A3
EC3 253 A5
St Dunstan's La
Beckenham BR3 208 A4
EC3 253 A5
St Dunstans Rd E7 77 C2
St Dunstan's Rd
Cranford TW5 128 B3
Feltham TW13 149 D1
Hammersmith W6 112 D1
Hanwell W7 108 C4
South Norwood SE25 205 D5
St Edmund RC Sch
E14 119 C2
St Edmunds Ave HA4 39 B3
St Edmunds Cl
DA18 124 D4
Upper Tooting SW17 158 C2
St Edmund's Cl NW8 230 C5
St Edmund's Ct NW8 230 C5
St Edmunds Dr HA7 25 A2
St Edmund's La TW2 151 D4
St Edmund's RC Prim Sch
Edmonton N9 18 B3
Twickenham TW2 151 D4
St Edmunds Rd N9 18 A4
St Edmund's Rd IG1 56 B3
St Edmund's Sq
SW13 134 C6
St Edmund's Terr
NW8 92 D6 230 C5

St Edward's CE Comp Sch RM7 ... 59 C3
St Edward's Cl NW11 ... 47 C3
St Edwards Ct 3 E10 ... 54 A2
St Edward's Ct NW11 ... 47 C3
St Edwards RC Prim Sch E6 ... 99 C6
St Edward's RC Prim Sch NW1 ... 92 C3 237 B5
St Egberts Way E4 ... 20 A3
St Elizabeth Ct
 North Finchley N12 ... 30 A6
 9 Walthamstow E10 ... 53 D2
St Elizabeth RC Prim Sch E2 ... 96 C5
St Elizabeth's RC Prim Sch TW10 ... 154 B5
St Elmo Rd W12 ... 111 D4
St Elmos Rd SE16 ... 119 A4
St Elphege's RC Inf Sch SM6 ... 220 A2
St Elphege's RC Jun Sch SM6 ... 220 A2
SS Peter & Paul's RC Prim Sch
 Ilford IG1 ... 79 B5
 Mitcham CR4 ... 202 D5
St Erkenwald Mews IG11 ... 101 B6
St Erkenwald Rd IG11 ... 101 B6
St Ermin's Hill SW1 ... 259 C6
St Ervan's Rd W10 ... 91 B2
St Eugene de Mazenod Rc Prim Sch NW6 ... 69 C1
St Faith's CE Prim Sch SW18 ... 158 A6
St Faith's Cl EN2 ... 5 A4
St Faith's Rd SE24 ... 160 D3
St Fillans Rd SE6 ... 164 A4
St Francesca Cabrini Prim Sch SE23 ... 162 C5
St Francis Cl BR5 ... 211 C3
St Francis de Sales RC Jun & Inf Sch N17 ... 33 D3
St Francis' Ho NW1 ... 232 C3
St Francis Lodge HA0 ... 64 D5
St Francis of Assisi RC Prim Sch W11 ... 112 D6
St Francis Pl SW12 ... 159 B5
St Francis RC Prim Sch
 SE15 ... 140 A5
 Stratford E15 ... 76 C3
St Francis Rd SE22 ... 139 C1
St Francis Way IG1 ... 79 B4
St Francis Xavier Sixth Form Coll SW12 ... 159 B5
St Frideswides Mews 5 E14 ... 98 A1
St Gabriel's CE Prim Sch SW1 ... 115 C1 259 A1
St Gabriels Cl 3 E14 ... 97 D2
St Gabriel's Cl E11 ... 55 B1
St Gabriels Ct N11 ... 31 D3
St Gabriel's Rd NW2 ... 68 D3
St George Ho SW11 ... 268 B1
ST GEORGE IN THE EAST ... 118 A6
St George's Ave
 Ealing W5 ... 109 D4
 Kingsbury NW9 ... 45 B5
 Southall UB1 ... 107 B6
 Tufnell Pk N7 ... 71 D4
 Upton E7 ... 77 B1
St George's Battersea CE Prim Sch SW8 ... 137 C5 269 B3
St George's Bickley CE Prim Sch BR1 ... 187 D1
St George's Bldgs SE11 ... 261 D5
St George's Cath NW1 ... 231 D2
St George's Cath RC Jun & Inf Sch SE1 ... 116 D3 261 C6
St George's CE Prim Sch SE5 ... 139 C5
St George's Circ SE1 ... 116 D3 261 C6
St Georges Cl
 Erith SE28 ... 102 D1
 Nine Elms SW8 ... 269 B2
 Wembley HA0 ... 65 A5
St George's Cl NW11 ... 47 B3
St Georges Coll N7 ... 72 C5
St Georges Ct
 Harrow HA3 ... 43 A3
 Newham E6 ... 100 B3
 Penge SE20 ... 184 B2
St Georges Ct *continued*
 Putney SW15 ... 135 B1
 Walthamstow E17 ... 54 B4
St George's Ct
 Brompton SW3 ... 257 A4
 Kensington SW7 ... 256 A5
 Newington SE1 ... 261 C5
St George's Dr
 Ickenham UB10 ... 60 B6
 South Oxhey WD19 ... 23 A6
 SW1 ... 115 C1 259 A2
St George's Field W2 ... 92 C1 237 B1
St George's Gdns KT6 ... 214 D6
St George's Gr SW17 ... 158 B1
St Georges Hanover Sq Sch W1 ... 115 A6 248 B5
St George's Ho NW1 ... 232 B3
St George's Hospl SW17 ... 180 B5
St Georges Ind Est N22 ... 32 D3
St George's Ind Est KT2 ... 175 D5
St George's La EC3 ... 253 A6
St Georges Lo N10 ... 49 C5
St Georges Mews 11 NW1 ... 70 D1
St George's Mews
 2 Rotherhithe SE8 ... 119 B2
 SE1 ... 261 B6
St Georges Pl N7 ... 71 D4
St George's RC Cath SE1 ... 116 C3 261 B6
St George's RC Prim Sch
 Enfield EN2 ... 5 B3
 Harrow HA1 ... 64 D5
St George's RC Sec Sch W9 ... 91 D5
St Georges Rd
 Acton W4 ... 111 B4
 Bickley BR1 ... 210 B6
 Dagenham RM9 ... 81 A4
 Petts Wood BR5 ... 211 B3
St George's Rd
 Beckenham BR3 ... 185 D2
 Ealing W7 ... 108 D5
 Enfield EN1 ... 5 D5
 Feltham TW13 ... 172 D6
 Isleworth TW1 ... 153 B6
 2 Kingston u T KT2 ... 176 C3
 Leyton E10 ... 76 A5
 Mitcham CR4 ... 203 B6
 Newington SE1 ... 116 D3 261 C5
 Palmers Green N13 ... 16 B2
 Redbridge IG1 ... 56 B2
 Richmond TW9 ... 132 B2
 Sidcup DA14 ... 190 D4
 Temple Fortune NW11 ... 47 B3
 Upton E7 ... 77 B2
 Wallington SM6 ... 219 B3
 Wimbledon SW19 ... 179 B4
St Georges Rd Ctr RM9 ... 81 B4
St Georges Rd W BR1 ... 188 A1
St George's Residences 4 SW2 ... 160 C6
St Georges's Ct EC4 ... 241 C2
St Georges Sh & L Ctr HA1 ... 42 C3
St Georges Sq 1 E14 ... 119 A6
St George's Sq
 Kingston u T KT3 ... 199 C6
 Rotherhithe SE8 ... 119 B2
 SW1 ... 115 D1 259 C1
 Upton E7 ... 77 B1
St George's Square Mews SW1 ... 259 C1
St George St W1 ... 115 B6 248 D6
St Georges Terr
 Hampstead NW1 ... 70 D1
 NW1 ... 230 D6
St George's Way SE15 ... 139 C6
St George's Wlk CR0 ... 221 A5
St George the Martyr CE Prim Sch WC1 ... 94 B3 240 D5
St George Wharf SW8 ... 270 A6
St Gerards Cl SW4 ... 159 C6
St German's Pl SE3 ... 143 A4
St German's Rd SE23 ... 163 A3
St Gildas' RC Jun Sch N8 ... 50 A2
ST GILES ... 94 A1
St Giles Ave
 Dagenham RM10 ... 81 D1
 Uxbridge UB10 ... 61 A4
St Giles Cir WC1 ... 93 D1 239 D2
St Giles Cl
 BR6 ... 227 B3
 Dagenham RM10 ... 81 D1
 Heston TW3 ... 129 A5
St Giles Coll WC1 ... 94 A2 240 B4
St Giles Ct
 Ealing W13 ... 109 C5
 WC2 ... 240 A2
St Giles High St WC2 ... 93 D1 239 D2
St Giles Ho
 2 New Barnet EN5 ... 2 A1
 Streatham SW16 ... 160 A1
St Giles Hospl SE5 ... 139 C4
St Giles Pas WC2 ... 239 D1
St Giles Rd SE5 ... 139 C4
St Giles' Sch CR2 ... 220 D2
St Giles Twr 3 SE5 ... 139 C4
St Gilles Ho 15 E2 ... 96 D5
St Gothard Rd SE21, SE27 ... 183 B6
St Gregory Cl HA4 ... 62 C4
St Gregory RC High Sch HA3 ... 43 D4
St Gregory's RC Prim Sch W5 ... 87 D2
St Helena Ho WC1 ... 234 A1
St Helena Pier TW9 ... 153 D6
St Helena Rd SE16 ... 118 D2
St Helena St WC1 ... 234 A1
St Helena Terr 31 TW9 ... 153 D6
St Helens KT7 ... 196 D2
St Helens Coll UB10 ... 60 C1
St Helen's Cres SW16 ... 182 B2
St Helen's Gdns W10 ... 90 D1
St Helen's Pl EC3 ... 243 A2
St Helen's RC Inf Sch E17 ... 54 A4
St Helen's RC Prim Sch E13 ... 99 A3
St Helen's RC Sch SW9 ... 138 C2
St Helens Rd 5 DA18 ... 124 D4
St Helen's Rd
 Ealing W13 ... 109 C5
 Redbridge IG1 ... 56 B3
 Thornton Heath SW16 ... 182 B2
ST HELIER ... 202 B2
St Helier Ave SM4 ... 202 A3
St Helier Ct 4 N1 ... 95 C6
St Helier Hospl SM5 ... 202 A1
St Heliers Ave TW3, TW4 ... 151 C6
St Helier's Rd E10 ... 54 A3
St Helier Sta SM4 ... 201 C3
St Hilary's Ct BR1 ... 210 D6
St Hilda's Ave TW15 ... 170 A5
St Hildas Cl SW17 ... 158 C2
St Hilda's Cl NW6 ... 68 D1
St Hilda's Rd SW13 ... 134 B6
St Hildas Wharf E1 ... 118 C5
St Hubert's Ho 2 E14 ... 119 C3
St Hughes Cl SW17 ... 158 C2
St Hugh's Rd SE20 ... 184 B3
St Ignatius Coll EN1 ... 6 B6
St Ignatius RC Prim Sch TW16 ... 172 A2
St Ignatius' RC Prim Sch N15 ... 51 D3
St Ives Ct NW2 ... 69 A2
St Ivian Ct 3 N10 ... 31 B1
ST JAMES ... 115 C5
St James Apartments 2 E17 ... 53 A4
St James Ave
 East Barnet N20 ... 14 C1
 Sutton SM1 ... 217 C3
St James' Ave W13 ... 109 A5
St James CE Jun Sch E7 ... 77 A3
St James CE Prim Sch EN3 ... 6 C3
St James' CE Prim Sch SE16 ... 118 A3
St James Cl
 Barnet EN4 ... 2 B1
 East Barnet N20 ... 14 C1
St James' Cl
 New Malden KT3 ... 199 D4
 Ruislip HA4 ... 62 C6
St James Ct
 26 Bethnal Green E2 ... 96 A4
 10 Brentford W4 ... 110 C1
 1 Bromley BR2 ... 187 A1
 Forest Hill SE23 ... 163 A3
 SE3 ... 143 B4
 Thornton Heath CR0 ... 204 D2
 Wanstead E12 ... 77 C6
St James' Ct
 Bedford Pk W4 ... 111 B3
 7 Kingston u T KT1 ... 198 A6
 SW1 ... 259 B6
St James Gate IG9 ... 21 B3
St James Gdns IG6 ... 58 B5
St James' Gdns HA0 ... 66 A1
St James Ho N5 ... 72 C3
St James Hts 3 SE18 ... 123 A1
St James Independent Schs W14 ... 113 A2 254 B4
St James Ind Mews 16 SE1 ... 118 A1
St James Ind Sch for Boys TW1 ... 153 A2
St James' Mans NW6 ... 69 C1
St James Mews E14 ... 120 A3
St James' RC High Sch NW9 ... 27 D2
St James RC Prim Sch BR5 ... 210 D4
St James Rd
 Carshalton SM5 ... 218 C5
 Kingston u T KT1 ... 175 D1
 Sutton SM1, SM2 ... 217 C3
St James' Rd
 Edmonton N9 ... 18 B2
 Forest Gate E15 ... 76 D3
 Mitcham CR4 ... 181 A3
 Surbiton KT6 ... 197 D3
St James's SE14 ... 141 A4
St James's App EC2 ... 243 A5
St James's Ave
 Beckenham BR3 ... 207 A6
 Hampton TW12 ... 174 A5
 South Hackney E2 ... 96 C5
St James's CE Prim Sch N10 ... 49 A5
St James School Flats 5 N7 ... 72 C3
St James's Cl
 NW8 ... 230 C5
 Upper Tooting SW17 ... 158 D2
 Woolwich SE18 ... 123 A1
St James's Cloisters 2 SE22 ... 139 D1
St James's Cotts 14 TW10 ... 153 D6
St James's Cres SW9 ... 138 C2
St James's Ct
 8 Edmonton N18 ... 34 A5
 Harrow HA1 ... 43 A3
St James's Dr
 Balham SW12, SW17 ... 158 D4
 Upper Tooting SW17 ... 158 D3
St James's Gdns W11 ... 113 A5 244 A4
St James's Gr SW11 ... 136 D3
St James's Hatcham CE Prim Sch SE14 ... 141 A4
St James's La N10 ... 49 B5
St James's Market SW1 ... 249 C5
St James's Mews E17 ... 53 A4
St James's Pal* SW1 ... 115 C5 249 B3
St James's Park Sta SW1 ... 115 D3 259 C6
St James's Pas EC3 ... 243 B1
St James's Pk* SW1 ... 249 C2
St James's Pk CR0 ... 205 A2
St James's Pl SW1 ... 115 C5 249 A3
St James's RC Prim Sch TW2 ... 152 C1
St James's Rd
 Bermondsey SE1, SE16 ... 118 A2
 Hampton TW12 ... 173 D5
 Peckham SE1 ... 140 A6
 Thornton Heath CR0 ... 205 B2
St James's & St Michael's CE Prim Sch W2 ... 114 A6 246 B6
St James's Sq SW1 ... 115 C5 249 B4
St James's St
 SW1 ... 115 C5 249 A4
 Walthamstow E17 ... 53 A4
St James St W6 ... 112 C1
St James's Terr NW8 ... 230 C6
St James's Terr *continued*
 2 Upper Tooting SW12 ... 159 A3
St James's Terrace Mews NW8 ... 230 C5
St James Street Sta E17 ... 53 A4
St James The Great RC Prim Sch
 Camberwell SE15 ... 139 D4
 South Norwood CR7 ... 182 D1
St James Way DA14 ... 191 A5
St James Wlk EC1 ... 241 C6
St Jerome's Gr UB3 ... 83 A1
St Joachim's RC Prim Sch E16 ... 99 C1
St Joan of Arc RC Prim Sch N5 ... 73 A4
St Joan's Rd N9 ... 17 D2
St John Baptist CE Prim Sch BR1 ... 186 A6
St John Evangelist RC Prim Sch N1 ... 94 D5 234 C4
St John Fisher RC Fst & Mid Sch HA5 ... 41 C5
St John Fisher RC Prim Sch
 DA18 ... 125 A3
 Wembley UB6 ... 87 C4
 West Barnes SW20 ... 200 D4
St John of Jerusalem CE Prim Sch E9 ... 74 C1
ST JOHNS ... 141 C3
St John & St James CE Prim Sch
 Edmonton N18 ... 33 D5
 Hackney E9 ... 74 C3
St John's Angell Town CE Prim Sch SW9 ... 138 C3
St John's Ave
 Dagenham NW10 ... 89 D6
 Friern Barnet N11 ... 30 D5
 Putney SW15 ... 156 D6
St John's CE First Sch HA7 ... 25 A6
St John's CE JMI Sch N11 ... 30 D6
St John's CE Prim Sch
 Buckhurst Hill IG9 ... 21 B3
 Croydon CR0 ... 222 D5
 Enfield EN2 ... 4 D6
 Fulham SW6 ... 135 A4 264 B2
 Kingston u T KT1 ... 198 A6
 Penge SE20 ... 184 C3
 SE17 ... 117 A2 262 B3
 South Hackney E2 ... 96 C5
 Whetstone N20 ... 14 A2
St John's CE Sch Stanmore HA7 ... 25 A6
St John's Church Rd E9 ... 74 C3
St Johns Cl N14 ... 15 C5
St John's Cl
 SW6 ... 265 A4
 Wembley HA9 ... 66 A3
St John's Concert Hall* SW1 ... 260 A5
St John's Cotts 2 SE20 ... 184 C3
St John's Cres SW9 ... 138 C2
St Johns Ct 39 E1 ... 118 B5
St John's Ct
 Buckhurst Hill IG9 ... 21 B3
 Finsbury Pk N4 ... 72 D6
 Hammersmith W6 ... 112 B2
 2 Harrow HA1 ... 42 D3
 Isleworth TW7 ... 130 D3
 Kingston u T KT1 ... 198 A5
 Lewisham SE13 ... 142 A3
 Leytonstone E11 ... 54 D1
 5 South Hampstead NW3 ... 70 A2
Saint John's Ct N5 ... 72 D4
St Johns Dr KT12 ... 194 C1
St John's Dr SW18 ... 157 D3
St John's Est SE1 ... 253 C1
St John's Gdns W11 ... 113 B6 244 C5
St John's Gr
 3 Barnes SW13 ... 133 D3
 1 Richmond TW9 ... 132 A1
 Upper Holloway N19 ... 71 C6
St John's Highbury Vale CE Prim Sch N5 ... 72 D5
St John's Hill SW11 ... 136 B1
St John's Hill Gr SW11 ... 136 B1
St Johns Ho
 5 SE17 ... 139 B6
 Streatham SW16 ... 182 A4
St John's Ho 1 E14 ... 120 A2
St John's La EC1 ... 94 D2 241 D4
St John's Lodge 8 SE8 ... 141 C4
St John's Mans E5 ... 74 C3
St John's Par
 Ealing W13 ... 109 B5
 3 Sidcup DA14 ... 190 B6
St John's Park Mans N19 ... 71 C5
St John's Path EC1 ... 241 C5
St John's Pk SE3 ... 143 A5
St John's Pl EC1 ... 241 C5
St John's Prim Sch W13 ... 109 A6
St John's RC Prim Sch SE16 ... 119 A4
St Johns Rd
 Ilford IG2 ... 57 C2
 Kingston u T KT3 ... 199 A6
St John's Rd
 Barking IG11 ... 101 C6
 Battersea SW11 ... 136 C1
 Canning Town E16 ... 99 A1
 Carshalton SM5 ... 218 C5
 Chingford E4 ... 35 D6
 Croydon CR0 ... 220 D5
 DA16 ... 146 B2
 East Ham E6 ... 100 A6
 East Molesey KT8 ... 196 B5
 Feltham TW13 ... 173 B6
 Harrow HA1 ... 42 D3
 Isleworth TW7 ... 130 D3
 Orpington BR5 ... 211 C3
 Penge SE20 ... 184 C4
 Richmond TW9 ... 132 A1
 Sidcup DA14 ... 190 B6
 Southall UB2 ... 107 A3
 Sutton SM1 ... 217 D6
 Teddington KT1 ... 175 C1
 Temple Fortune NW11 ... 47 B3
 Tottenham N15 ... 51 C3
 Walthamstow E17 ... 36 A1
 Wembley HA9 ... 66 A3
 Wimbledon SW19 ... 179 A4
St John's & St Clements CE Prim Sch SE15 ... 140 A2
St John's Sch HA6 ... 22 B4
St John's Sq EC1 ... 94 D3 241 C5
St Johns Sta SE8 ... 141 C3
St John St EC1 ... 94 D3 241 C6
St John's Terr
 Enfield EN2 ... 5 B6
 North Kensington W10 ... 90 D3
 SE18 ... 145 B6
 Upton E7 ... 77 B2
St Johnstone Ho 17 N12 ... 29 D6
St John's Upper Holloway CE Prim Sch N19 ... 71 D6
St John's Vale SE8 ... 141 C3
St John's Villas
 4 Friern Barnet N11 ... 30 D5
 Upper Holloway N19 ... 71 D6
 W8 ... 255 D5
St John's Way N19 ... 49 D1
ST JOHN'S WOOD ... 92 B5
St John's Wood Ct NW8 ... 229 D1
St John's Wood High St NW8 ... 92 C5 230 A3
St John's Wood Park NW8 ... 92 B6 229 C6
St John's Wood Pre-Prep Sch NW8 ... 92 C4 230 A2
St John's Wood Rd NW8 ... 92 B4 229 D1
St John's Wood Sta NW8 ... 92 B5 229 C4
St John's Wood Terr NW8 ... 92 C5 230 A4
St John the Baptist CE Jun Sch KT1 ... 175 D3
St John the Baptist CE Prim Sch N1 ... 95 B5 235 D3
St John the Divine CE Jun & Inf Sch SE5 ... 138 D5
St John Vianney RC Prim Sch N8 ... 50 D5
St Joseph RC Prim Sch W7 ... 108 C5
St Joseph's Acad SE3 ... 142 C2
St Josephs Cl BR6 ... 227 D4
St Joseph's Cl W10 ... 91 A2

St Joseph's Coll Mill Hill Missionaries NW7 27 D6
St Joseph's Convent Sch E11 55 A3
St Josephs Ct
3 Dagenham NW10 89 D5
20 Walthamstow E10 53 D2
St Joseph's Ct E4 20 B4
St Joseph's Dr UB1 107 B5
St Joseph's Flats NW1 232 C2
St Josephs Gr NW4 46 B5
St Joseph's Ho W6 112 D2
St Joseph's Hospice E9, E8 96 B6
St Joseph's RC Coll SW16 182 D4
St Joseph's RC Fst & Mid Sch HA3 25 A1
St Joseph's RC Inf & Jun Schs
Hendon NW4 46 B5
SE5 139 A5
St Joseph's RC Inf Sch
Leyton E10 75 C6
South Norwood SE19 183 A4
St Joseph's RC Jun & Inf Schs HA9 66 B3
St Joseph's RC Jun Sch
South Norwood SE19 183 A4
Walthamstow E10 53 D1
St Joseph's RC Prim Sch
Barking IG11 101 A6
Bermondsey SE16 118 A4
Bromley BR1 187 B3
Chelsea SW3 114 D2 257 C3
Dagenham RM9 81 B4
Deptford SE8 141 C5
Greenwich SE10 120 C1
Kingston u T KT1 176 B1
Paddington W9 92 A4 229 A1
Rotherhithe SE16 118 C3
St Giles WC2 94 A1 240 B2
Upper Holloway N19 49 B1
Wandsworth SW18 157 C6
Willesden NW10 67 C1
St Joseph's Rd N9 18 C3
St Joseph's St SW8 268 D2
St Joseph's Vale SE3 142 B2
St Jude & St Paul's CE Prim Sch N1 73 C2
St Jude's CE Prim Sch SE24 160 D6
St Judes Ho 6 W10 91 B4
St Jude's Prim Sch SE1 116 D3 261 C5
St Jude's Rd E2 96 B5
St Jude St N16 73 C3
St Julian's Cl SW16 182 C6
St Julian's Farm Rd SE27, SW16 182 D6
St Julian's Rd NW6 91 C6
St Katharine's Ho N1 234 A4
St Katharine's Prec NW1 231 C4
St Katharine's Way E1 117 D5 253 D4
St Katherines Rd DA18 124 D4
St Katherine's Row EC3 243 B1
St Katherine's Wlk 1 W11 112 D5
St Keverne Rd SE9 188 A6
St Kilda Rd
BR6 211 D1
Ealing W13 109 A4
St Kilda's Rd
Harrow HA1 42 C3
Stamford Hill N16 51 C1
St Kitts Terr SE19 183 C5
St Laurence's Cl NW6 90 D6
St Lawrence CE Jun Sch KT8 196 B5
St Lawrence Cl HA8 26 B3
St Lawrence Ct N1 235 D6
St Lawrence Dr HA5 40 B4
St Lawrence Ho SE1 263 B6
St Lawrence RC Prim Sch TW13 150 B2
St Lawrence St E14 120 A5
St Lawrence Terr W10 91 A2
St Lawrence Way SW9 138 C3
St Leonards Ave HA3 43 C4
St Leonard's Ave E4 36 B4
St Leonard's CE Prim Sch SW16 181 D5
St Leonards Cl 4 DA16 146 A2
St Leonards Ct SW14 133 A2
St Leonard's Ct N1 235 D2
St Leonards Gdns IG1 79 A3
St Leonard's Gdns TW5 129 A4
St Leonard's Hospl N1 95 C5
St Leonards Rd SW14 133 A2
St Leonard's Rd
Becontree NW10 89 B3
Claygate KT10 212 D2
Croydon CR0 220 D5
Ealing W13 109 C6
Kingston u T KT6 197 D4
South Bromley E14 98 A2
Thames Ditton KT7 197 A2
St Leonards Rise BR6 227 C4
St Leonard's Sq
Camden Town NW5 71 A2
Kingston u T KT6 197 D4
St Leonard's St E3 97 D4
St Leonard's Terr SW3 114 D1 257 D1
St Leonard's Wlk SW16 182 B3
St Loo Ave SW3 136 C6 267 B6
St Loo Ct SW3 267 C6
St Louis Rd SE27 183 B6
St Loy's Rd N17 51 D6
St Lucia Dr E15 98 D6
St Luke Prim Sch E16 98 D1
ST LUKE'S 95 A3
St Luke's Ave
Clapham SW4 137 D1
Enfield EN2 5 B5
Ilford IG1 78 D3
St Luke's CE Prim Sch
Cubitt Town E14 120 B2
Kingston u T KT2 176 B2
Paddington W9 91 B4
Shoreditch EC1 95 A3 235 B1
West Norwood SE27 183 A5
St Luke's Cl
Croydon SE25 206 B3
St Luke's EC1 95 A3 242 B6
St Lukes Ct 6 E10 53 D2
St Luke's Ct W11 91 B1
St Luke's Hospl W1 93 C3 239 A5
St Luke's Mews W11 91 B1
St Luke's Path 1 IG1 78 D3
St Luke's RC Sixth Form Coll DA14 189 D5
St Luke's Rd
Notting Hill W11 91 B2
Uxbridge UB10 60 A1
St Luke's Sq E16 98 D1
St Luke's St SW3 257 B2
St Luke's Woodside Hospl N10 49 A5
St Malo Ave N9 18 C1
St Margaret Clitherow RC Prim Sch
Neasden NW10 67 B4
Woolwich SE28 124 B5
ST MARGARETS 153 A5
St Margarets IG11 101 B6
St Margarets Ave
Ashford TW15 170 D5
DA15 167 B1
Hillingdon UB8 82 C3
Whetstone N20 14 A3
St Margaret's Ave
Cheam SM3 217 A5
Harringay N8, N15 50 D5
Harrow HA2 64 A5
St Margarets Bsns Ctr 11 TW1 153 B5
St Margaret's CE Prim Sch
Barking IG11 79 A1
Woolwich SE18 123 A1
St Margaret's Cres SW15 156 B6
St Margaret's Ct
Leyton E15 76 C4
Putney SW15 134 B1
SE1 252 C3
9 Twickenham TW1 153 B5
St Margaret's Dr TW1 153 B6
St Margaret's Gr
Leyton E11 76 D5
SE18 145 A6
Twickenham TW1 153 A5
St Margaret's La W8 113 D3 255 C5
St Margaret's Lee CE Prim Sch SE13 142 C1
St Margarets Lo W3 110 D4
St Margaret's Pass SE13 142 C2
St Margaret's Path 4 SE18 123 A1
St Margarets Rd
Edgware HA8 26 D5
Ruislip HA4 39 B3
St Margaret's Rd
Brockley SE4 141 B1
Hanwell W7 108 C4
Isleworth TW1 153 B6
Kensal Green NW10 90 C4
Tottenham N17 51 C6
Wanstead E12 77 C6
St Margarets Rdbt TW1 153 B6
St Margaret's Sch NW3 69 D4
St Margaret's Sta TW1 153 B5
St Margaret St SW1 250 A1
St Margaret's Terr SE18 123 A1
St Margret's Ct N11 31 A6
St Mark's CE Acad CR4 181 B1
St Mark's CE Prim Sch
Bromley BR2 209 A6
Croydon SE25 206 A5
Kennington SE11 138 B6 270 D6
St Marks Cl 5 SE10 142 A5
St Mark's Cl
Barnet EN5 1 D2
Harrow HA1 43 B1
St Mark's Cres NW1 93 A6 231 B6
St Mark's Ct
Hanwell W7 108 C4
8 Walthamstow E10 53 D2
St Marks Gate E9 75 B1
St Mark's Gr SW10 135 D5 265 D4
St Mark's Hill KT6 198 A3
St Marks Ho 6 SE17 139 B6
St Mark's Ho 8 E17 54 A5
St Mark's Hospl EC1 94 D4 234 D2
St Mark's Hts 25 KT6 198 A4
St Marks Ind Est E16 121 D5
St Mark's Mans 14 N4 72 B6
St Mark's Pl
Notting Hill W11 91 A1
Wimbledon SW19 179 B4
St Mark's Prim Sch
Hanwell W7 108 C4
Mitcham CR4 180 D1
Upper Holloway N19 72 A6
St Mark's RC Sch TW3 129 C2
St Marks Rd 15 NW10 90 D1
St Mark's Rd
Bromley BR2 209 B6
Croydon SE25 206 A5
Ealing W5 110 A5
Enfield EN1 17 D6
Hanwell W7 108 C4
Mitcham CR4 181 A1
North Kensington W10 90 D2
Notting Hill W11 91 A1
Teddington TW11 175 B3
St Mark's Rise E8 73 D3
St Mark's Sq NW1 231 A5
St Mark St E1 95 D1 243 D1
St Martha's Convent Jun Sch EN5 1 A1
St Martha's Senior Sch EN4 1 C4
St Martin-in-the-Fields High Sch for Girls SW2 160 C3
St Martin of Porres RC Prim Sch N11 31 C4
St Martin's Almshouses NW1 232 A6
St Martin's App HA4 39 C2
St Martin's Ave E6 99 D5
St Martins Cl
DA18 124 D4
South Oxhey WD19 22 C6
St Martin's Cl
Enfield EN1 6 B4
NW1 232 A6
St Martins Ct N1 95 C6
St Martin's Ct
WC2 250 A6
West Norwood SE27 160 D2
St Martins La BR3 207 D4
St Martin's La WC2 116 A6 250 A5
St Martin's Le Grand EC1 242 A2
St Martin's Pl WC2 250 A5
St Martin's Rd
Edmonton N9 18 B2
Finchley N2 30 B2
Stockwell SW9 138 B3
St Martin's Sch NW7 27 B5
St Martin's St WC2 249 D5
St Martin's Way SW17 158 A1
St Mary Abbots CE Prim Sch W8 113 D4 245 C1
St Mary Abbot's Ct W14 254 C5
St Mary Abbot's Pl W8 254 D5
St Mary Abbots Terr W14 254 D5
St Mary at Hill EC3 117 C6 253 A5
St Mary Ave SM6 219 B5
St Mary Axe EC3 95 C1 243 B2
St Marychurch St SE16 118 C4
St Mary Graces Ct E1 253 D5
St Marylebone CE Sch The W1 93 A2 238 B4
St Mary le Bow Church* EC2 242 B1
St Mary- le-Park Ct SW11 267 B3
St Mary Magdalene CE Prim Sch
Islington N7 72 C2
Paddington W2 91 D2
Peckham SE15 140 B3
Woolwich SE18 122 C2
St Mary Magdalen's RC Prim Sch
Brockley SE4 141 A1
Mortlake SW14 133 B2
St Mary Magdelen's RC Jun Sch NW2 68 B2
St Mary Newington Cl SE17 263 B2
St Mary of the Angels RC Prim Sch W2 91 C1
St Mary RC Prim Sch W10 91 A3
St Mary Rd E17 53 D5
St Marys IG11 101 B6
St Mary & St Joseph's RC Sch DA14 189 D5
St Mary & St Michael Prim Sch E1 96 C1
St Mary & St Pancras CE Prim Sch NW1 93 D5 232 C3
St Mary's App E12 78 B3
St Marys Ave UB2 107 D2
St Mary's Ave
Beckenham BR2 208 C6
Finchley N3 29 B1
Teddington TW11 174 D4
Wanstead E11 55 B2
St Mary's Bryanston Square CE Sch W1 92 D2 237 C4
St Mary's CE High Sch (Lower & Upper) NW4 46 C6
St Mary's CE High Sch (Middle) NW4 46 C6
St Mary's CE Inf Sch N8 50 B5
St Mary's CE Jun Sch N8 50 A5
St Mary's CE Prim Sch
Chessington KT9 214 B2
East Barnet EN4 14 C5
Finchley N3 29 B3
Islington N1 94 D6 234 D6
Long Ditton KT7 197 B1
Putney SW15 134 D2
Walthamstow E17 53 D5
Willesden NW10 67 C2
St Mary's CE Prim Sch (Inf) TW1 153 A4
St Mary's CE Prim Sch (Jun) TW1 153 B4
St Mary's Church Ho 11 E17 53 D5
St Mary's Cl
BR5 190 B1
Chessington KT9 214 B1
St Mary's Cl *continued*
Ewell KT17 215 D1
Sunbury TW16 194 A5
Tottenham N17 34 A2
St Mary's Coll TW1 152 D1
St Mary's Cottage Hospl TW12 173 B2
St Mary's Cres
Hayes UB3 105 D6
Hendon NW4 46 B6
Hounslow TW7 130 C5
St Marys Ct
Abbey Wood SE2 124 D2
Newham E6 100 B3
SE7 143 D5
St Mary's Ct
Bedford Pk W6 111 D3
Ealing W5 109 D4
Finchley N12 30 A3
Kingston u T KT3 199 C6
Leytonstone E11 54 D1
Wallington SM6 219 C4
St Mary's Dr TW14 149 A4
St Mary's Est 2 SE16 118 C4
St Mary's Flats NW1 232 C2
St Mary's Gate W8 255 C5
St Mary's Gdns SE11 261 B4
St Mary's Gn 1 N2 48 A6
St Mary's Gr
Barnes SW13 134 B2
Chiswick W4 132 D6
Islington N1 72 D2
Richmond TW10, TW9 132 B1
St Mary's Ho
Ealing W5 109 D3
N1 234 D6
St Mary's Hospl W2 92 B1 236 D2
St Mary's Hospl Medical Sch W2 92 B1 236 D2
St Mary's Kilburn CE Prim Sch NW6 91 C6
St Mary's Lewisham CE Prim Sch SE13 163 D6
St Mary's Lo E11 55 B3
St Mary's Mans
Dagenham NW10 89 C6
Paddington W2 92 B2 236 C4
St Mary's Mews NW6 69 D1
St Mary's Path N1 234 D6
St Mary's Pl
Ealing W5 109 D4
Eltham SE9 166 C5
Kensington W8 113 D3 255 C5
St Mary's RC High Sch CR0 205 A1
St Mary's RC Inf Sch
Carshalton SM5 218 D4
Croydon CR0 205 B1
St Mary's RC Jun & Inf Schs N15 51 B4
St Mary's RC Jun Sch
Croydon CR0 205 B1
Wallington SM5 218 D3
Walthamstow E17 54 A6
St Mary's RC Prim Sch
Beckenham BR3 186 A3
Chingford E4 20 B3
Chiswick W4 133 C6
Clapham Pk SW4 159 C6
Clapham SW8 137 B4 268 D2
Enfield EN3 6 D1
Hammersmith W14 112 D3
Isleworth TW7 131 A2
Merton SW19 179 C3
Paddington NW6 91 C5
SE9 166 C6
St Marys Rd IG1 79 B6
St Mary's Rd
Dagenham NW10 89 C6
Ealing W5 109 D5
East Barnet EN4 14 D4
East Molesey KT8 196 B4
Finchley N2 30 B2
Golders Green NW11 47 A2
Hayes UB3 105 D6
Hornsey N8 50 A5
Leyton E10 76 A6
Long Ditton KT6 197 C1
Lower Edmonton N9 18 C3
Newham E13 99 B5
Nunhead SE15 140 C3
South Norwood SE25 205 C6
Surbiton KT6 197 D3
Wimbledon SW19 179 B5
Worcester Pk KT4 215 C6
St Mary's & St John's CE Prim Sch NW4 46 B4
St Mary's & St Peter's CE Prim Sch TW11 174 D5
St Mary's Sch Hampstead NW3 70 B3
St Mary's Sq
Ealing W5 109 D4
W2 236 C4
St Mary's Stoke Newington CE Prim Sch N16 73 C6
St Mary St SE18 122 C2
St Mary's Terr W2 236 C4
St Mary's Twr EC1 242 B5
St Marys View HA3 43 C4
St Mary's Wlk
Hayes UB3 105 D6
SE11 261 B4
St Matthew's Ave KT6 198 B1
St Matthew's CE Prim Sch
Enfield EN3 18 C6
Surbiton KT6 198 A2
Wimbledon SW20 178 A2
Yiewsley UB7 104 A5
St Matthews Ct
Muswell Hill N10 31 A1
SE1 262 A5
2 Stratford E15 76 D1
7 Walthamstow E10 53 D2
St Matthew's Ct 1 TW15 170 C5
St Matthews Dr BR1 210 B6
St Matthew's Ho 8 SE17 139 B6
St Matthew's Lo NW1 232 B4
St Matthew's Rd
Clapham Pk SW2 160 B6
Ealing W5 110 A5
St Matthew's Row E2 96 A3
St Matthews Sch Westminster SW1 115 D3 259 D6
St Matthew St SW1 259 C5
St Matthias CE Prim Sch E2 95 D3 243 D6
St Matthias Cl NW9 45 D4
St Matthias's CE Prim Sch N16 73 C4
St Mauritius Ho SE13 164 A6
St Maur Rd SW6 135 B4 264 D1
St Mellion Cl SE28 102 D1
St Merryn Cl SE18 145 B5
St Merryn Ct BR3 185 C3
St Michael-at-Bowes CE Jun Sch N13 32 C4
St Michael RC Prim Sch TW15 170 C5
St Michael & St Martin RC Prim Sch TW4 129 B2
St Michael's Alley EC3 242 D1
St Michaels Ave N9 18 C4
St Michael's Ave HA9 66 C2
St Michael's CE Prim Sch
Camden Town NW1 93 C6 232 A6
Enfield EN2 5 A4
Forest Hill SE26 185 A6
Highgate N6 49 A2
Wandsworth SW18 157 B4
Wood Green N22 32 B2
St Michaels Cl
BR1 210 A6
4 Newham E16 99 D2
Worcester Pk KT4 215 D6
St Michael's Cl
Colney Hatch N12 30 C5
DA18 124 D4
Finchley N3 29 B1
St Michael's Cres HA5 41 A3
St Michaels Ct 2 E14 98 A2
St Michael's Ct
Brunswick Pk N11 15 A1
Golders Green NW11 47 B2
St Michael's East Wickham CE Prim Sch DA16 146 C4
St Michael's Flats NW1 232 C3
St Michael's Gdns W10 91 A2
St Michaels Ho SE26 185 B6
St Michael's Hospl EN2 5 B4
St Michael's RC Gram Sch N12 30 A5
St Michael's RC Prim Sch E6 100 B5
St Michael's RC Sch SE16 118 A4

St Michaels Rd TW15 ... 170 C5
St Michael's Rd
Cricklewood NW2 ... 68 C4
Croydon CR0 ... 205 A1
DA16 ... 146 B2
Stockwell SW9 ... 138 B3
Wallington SM6 ... 219 C2
St Michael's Rise
DA16 ... 146 B4
St Michael's St
W2 ... 92 C1 237 A2
St Michael Steiner Sch
The SW18 ... 157 C6
St Michael's Terr N22 ... 32 A2
St Mildred's Ct EC2 ... 242 C1
St Mildreds Rd SE12,
SE6 ... 164 D4
St Mirren Ct 8 EN5 ... 14 A6
St Monica's RC Prim Sch
Palmers Green N14 ... 16 A1
Shoreditch N1 ... 95 C4
St Nicholas CE Prim Sch
TW17 ... 192 D3
St Nicholas Cl WD6 ... 9 D5
St Nicholas Ct E4 ... 36 A4
St Nicholas Ctr 7
SM1 ... 217 D3
St Nicholas Dr TW17 ... 192 C2
St Nicholas Elstree CE
Prim Sch WD6 ... 9 D5
St Nicholas' Flats
NW1 ... 232 C3
St Nicholas Glebe
SW17 ... 181 A4
St Nicholas Ho SE8 ... 141 C6
St Nicholas Mans
SW17 ... 158 D2
St Nicholas Rd
Plumstead SE18 ... 123 D2
Sutton SM1 ... 217 D3
Thames Ditton KT7 ... 196 D3
St Nicholas Sch NW9 ... 67 A6
St Nicholas St SE8 ... 141 C4
St Nicholas Way SM1 ... 217 D3
St Nicolas La BR7 ... 188 A2
St Ninian's Ct N20 ... 14 D1
St Norbert Gn SE4 ... 141 A1
St Norbert Rd SE4 ... 141 A1
St Olaf's Rd
SW6 ... 135 A5 264 B3
St Olaves Ct W2 ... 245 C5
St Olave's Ct EC2 ... 242 C1
St Olave's Est SE1 ... 253 B2
St Olave's Gdns SE11 ... 261 A4
St Olave's Mans SE11 ... 261 A4
St Olaves Prep Sch
SE9 ... 166 D2
St Olave's Rd E6 ... 100 C6
St Olave's Wlk SW16 ... 181 D1
St Olav's Sq 32 SE16 ... 118 C4
St Osmund's RC Prim Sch
SW13 ... 133 D4
St Oswald's Pl
SE11 ... 116 B1 260 C1
St Oswald's Rd SW16 ... 182 D2
St Oswulf St SW1 ... 259 D3
St Owen Ho SE1 ... 263 B6
ST PANCRAS ... 94 A4
St Pancras Almshouses 13
NW5 ... 70 D3
St Pancras Commercial
Ctr NW1 ... 232 B6
St Pancras Ct
Finchley N2 ... 30 B1
6 Wembley HA0 ... 66 A2
St Pancras Hospl
NW1 ... 93 D6 232 C5
St Pancras International
Sta WC1 ... 94 A4 233 A2
St Pancras Way
NW1 ... 93 D6 232 C6
St Patrick's Coll
W1 ... 93 D1 239 C2
St Patricks Ct IG8 ... 36 C3
St Patrick's RC Prim Sch
Camden Town NW5 ... 71 B3
Plumstead SE18 ... 123 B2
Walthamstow E17 ... 53 A5
St Paul's Acad SE2 ... 146 A6
St Paul's & All Hallows CE
Jun & Inf Schs N17 ... 34 A3
St Paul's Ave
Harrow HA3 ... 44 B5
Rotherhithe SE16 ... 118 D5
Willesden NW2 ... 68 C2
St Paul's Cath*
EC4 95 A1 242 A1
St Paul's Cath Sch
EC4 ... 95 A1 242 A1
St Paul's CE Jun Sch
KT2 ... 176 C3
St Pauls CE Prim Sch
TW8 ... 131 D6
St Paul's CE Prim Sch
Chessington KT9 ... 214 A4
Friern Barnet N11 ... 31 B5
Hammersmith W6 ... 112 C1
Hampstead NW3 ... 70 D1
Mill Hill NW7 ... 28 B6
SE17 ... 117 A1 262 A2
Southgate N21 ... 16 D4
St Paul's Church Yd
EC4 ... 95 A1 242 A1
St Pauls Cl
Ealing W5 ... 110 B4
Hayes UB3 ... 105 B1
St Paul's Cl
Ashford TW15 ... 171 A5
Borehamwood WD6 ... 11 A6
Carshalton SM5 ... 202 C1
Chessington KT9 ... 213 D4
Greenwich SE7 ... 121 D1
Hounslow TW3,TW4 ... 129 A3
ST PAUL'S CRAY ... 190 A1
St Paul's Cray Rd
BR7 ... 189 B2
St Pauls Cres NW1 ... 71 D1
St Paul's Ct
Clapham SW4 ... 137 D1
Hounslow TW4 ... 129 A2
6 Upper Holloway N19 ... 72 A6
St Paul's Dr E15 ... 76 B3
St Paul's Girls' Sch
W6 ... 112 D2
St Pauls Ho N17 ... 34 A3
St Pauls Mews NW1 ... 71 D1
St Paul's Pl N1 ... 73 B2
St Paul's RC Coll
TW16 ... 172 A2
St Paul's RC Prim Sch
Thames Ditton KT7 ... 196 C2
Wood Green N22 ... 32 B1
St Pauls Rd
Barking IG11 ... 101 A6
Richmond TW9 ... 132 B2
St Paul's Rd
Brentford TW8 ... 131 D6
Canonbury N1 ... 73 A2
South Norwood CR7 ... 205 A6
Tottenham N17 ... 34 A2
St Pauls Rise N13 ... 32 D4
St Paul's Sch SW13 ... 112 A1
St Paul's Sq BR2 ... 187 A1
St Paul's Sta
EC2 ... 95 A1 242 A2
St Paul St N1 ... 235 B5
St Paul's Terr SE17 ... 138 D6
St Paul's Twr 14 E10 ... 53 D2
St Pauls View WC1 ... 234 A1
St Paul's Way
Finchley N3 ... 29 D3
Tower Hamlets E3 ... 97 C2
St Paul's Way Com Sch
E3 ... 97 C2
St Paul's Whitechapel CE
Prim Sch E1 ... 118 A6
St Paul's with St Michael's
Prim Sch E8 ... 96 A6
St Paul's Wood Hill
BR5 ... 189 D1
St Paul with St Luke CE
Prim Sch E3 ... 97 B2
St Peter Chanel RC Prim
Sch DA14 ... 190 C5
St Peter in Chains RC Inf
Sch N8 ... 50 A3
St Peter & Paul RC Prim
Sch BR5 ... 189 C1
St Peter & St Paul RC
Prim Sch EC1 ... 94 D3 241 D6
St Peter's Alley EC3 ... 242 D1
St Peters Ave N12 ... 30 C3
St Peter's Ave
Edmonton N18 ... 34 A6
37 Hackney E2 ... 96 A5
Walthamstow E17 ... 54 C5
St Petersburgh Mews
W2 ... 245 C6
St Petersburgh Pl
W2 ... 113 D6 245 C5
St Peter's CE Prim Sch
Chiswick W6 ... 112 A1
Paddington W9 ... 91 C3
SE17 ... 117 B1 262 C1
St Peter's Church Ct
N1 ... 234 D5
St Peters Cl
BR7 ... 189 B3
Ilford IG2 ... 57 D5
St Peters Cl *continued*
Upper Tooting SW17 ... 158 C2
St Peter's Cl
Barnet EN5 ... 12 B6
Bushey WD23 ... 8 B3
Hackney E2 ... 96 A5
Ruislip HA4 ... 62 D6
St Peters Ct
East Molesey KT8 ... 195 C5
New Cross SE4 ... 141 B3
28 Stepney E1 ... 96 C3
St Peter's Ct
Hendon NW4 ... 46 C4
Lewisham SE12 ... 164 D6
St Peter's Eaton Square
Prim Sch
SW1 ... 115 B3 258 D5
St Peter's Gdns SE27 ... 160 C1
St Peter's Gr W6 ... 112 A2
St Peters Ho
Tottenham Hale N15 ... 52 A5
WC1 ... 233 B1
St Peter's Ho
4 SE17 ... 139 B6
Stamford Hill N16 ... 51 C2
St Peters La BR5 ... 190 A1
St Peter's London Docks
CE Prim Sch E1 ... 118 C5
St Peters Mews N4 ... 50 D4
St Peter's Pl W9 ... 91 D3
St Peter's Prim Sch
CR2 ... 221 C2
St Peter's RC Prim Sch
Dagenham RM9 ... 103 B6
Woolwich SE18 ... 122 D2
St Peters Rd KT1 ... 176 C1
St Peter's Rd
Chiswick W6 ... 112 A1
Croydon CR0 ... 221 B4
East Molesey KT8 ... 195 C5
Edmonton N9 ... 18 B3
Isleworth TW1 ... 153 B6
Southall UB1 ... 85 C2
St Peter's Sq
Chiswick W6 ... 111 D1
Hackney E2 ... 96 A5
St Peter's St
Croydon CR2 ... 221 B3
Islington N1 ... 94 D6 234 D5
St Peter's Street Mews
N1 ... 234 D4
St Peter's Terr SW6 ... 264 B3
St Peter's Villas 5
W6 ... 112 A2
St Peters Way UB3 ... 105 B1
St Peter's Way
De Beauvoir Town N1 ... 73 C1
Ealing W5 ... 87 D2
St Peter's Wharf 8
W6 ... 112 A1
St Philip Ho WC1 ... 234 A1
St Philip's Ave KT4 ... 216 B6
St Philips Gate KT4 ... 216 B6
St Philip Sq 1 SW8 ... 137 B3
St Philip's Rd
Dalston E8 ... 74 A2
Surbiton KT6 ... 197 D3
St Philip's Sch
Chessington KT9 ... 213 D2
SW7 ... 114 A2 256 B3
St Philip St SW8 ... 137 B3
St Philip's Way N1 ... 235 B5
St Philomena's Sch
SM5 ... 218 C3
St Quentin Ho SW18 ... 158 B5
St Quentin Rd DA16 ... 145 D2
St Quintin Ave W10 ... 90 D2
St Quintin Gdns 21
W10 ... 90 C2
St Quintin Rd E13 ... 99 B5
St Raphaels Ho W13 ... 109 C5
St Raphael's RC Prim Sch
UB5 ... 84 B5
St Raphael's Way
NW10 ... 67 A3
St Regis Cl N10 ... 31 B1
St Regis Hts NW3 ... 69 D5
St Richards Ct TW10 ... 153 B1
St Richard's Ho NW1 ... 232 C2
St Richard's with St
Andrew's CE Prim Sch
TW10 ... 153 B1
St Robert Southwell RC
Prim Sch NW9 ... 45 A3
St Ronan's 2 N3 ... 29 C2
St Ronans Cl EN4 ... 2 B5
St Ronans Cres IG8 ... 37 A3
St Rule St SW8 ... 137 C3
St Savior's CE Inf Sch
W5 ... 109 D6
St Saviours SW4 ... 137 B1
St Saviour's CE Prim Sch
Bow Comm E14 ... 97 D2
Camberwell SE24 ... 139 A2
Paddington W9 ... 91 D3
Walthamstow E17 ... 53 B2
St Saviour's Coll
SE27 ... 183 B6
St Saviours Ct
Harrow HA1 ... 42 C4
Muswell Hill N22 ... 31 D1
St Saviours Ho 35
SE1 ... 118 A4
St Saviour's RC Prim Sch
SE13 ... 142 A1
St Saviour's Rd
Clapham Pk SW2 ... 160 B6
Thornton Heath CR0 ... 205 A3
St Saviours & St Olaves
CE Sch SE1 ... 117 B3 262 D5
St Saviour's Wharf
SE1 ... 253 D2
St Scholastica's RC Prim
Sch E5 ... 74 A5
Saints Cl SE27 ... 182 D6
Saints Dr E7 ... 77 D3
St Silas Pl NW5 ... 71 A2
St Simon's Ave SW15 ... 156 C6
St Stephen's Ave
Ealing W13 ... 87 B1
Shepherd's Bush W12 ... 112 B4
Walthamstow E17 ... 54 A4
St Stephen's CE Jun Sch
TW1 ... 153 B5
St Stephen's CE Prim Sch
Paddington W2 ... 91 C2
Shepherd's Bush W12 ... 112 C4
St Johns SE8 ... 141 C3
SW8 ... 138 B5 270 C4
St Stephen's Cl
Maitland Pk NW5 ... 70 D3
NW8 ... 230 B5
Southall UB1 ... 85 C2
Walthamstow E17 ... 53 D4
St Stephen's Cres
Notting Hill W2 ... 91 C1
Thornton Heath CR7 ... 204 C6
St Stephens Ct
Ealing W13 ... 87 B1
Enfield EN1 ... 17 C5
Hornsey Vale N8 ... 50 B3
St Stephen's Gdns
Notting Hill W2 ... 91 C1
4 Putney SW15 ... 157 B6
Twickenham TW1 ... 153 C5
St Stephen's Gr SE13 ... 142 A2
St Stephens Ho 7
SE17 ... 139 B6
St Stephen's Mews 34
W2 ... 91 C2
St Stephens Par E6 ... 77 C1
St Stephens Prim Sch
E6 ... 77 C1
St Stephen's RC Prim Sch
DA16 ... 146 A3
St Stephens Rd
Barnet EN5 ... 12 D6
Upton E6 ... 77 C1
St Stephen's Rd
Bow E3 ... 97 B5
Ealing W13 ... 87 C1
Enfield EN3 ... 6 D6
Hounslow TW3,TW4 ... 151 C6
Walthamstow E17 ... 53 D4
Yiewsley UB7 ... 104 A5
St Stephen's Row EC4 242 C1
St Stephen's Terr
SW8 ... 270 C3
St Stephen's Wlk SW7 256 A4
St Swithin's La
EC4 ... 117 B6 252 C6
St Swithun's Rd SE13 ... 164 B6
St Swithun Wells RC Prim
Sch HA4 ... 62 D5
St Teresa's RC Fst & Mid
Sch HA3 ... 24 A2
St Teresa's RC Prim Sch
SM4 ... 202 B3
St Teresa's RC Prim Sch
The RM8 ... 80 C4
St Theresa Ct E4 ... 20 B4
St Theresa's RC Sch
N3 ... 47 D6
St Theresa's Rd
TW14 ... 127 D1
St Thomas a Beckett RC
Prim Sch SE2 ... 124 A3
St Thomas Becket RC
Prim Sch SE25 ... 206 A3
St Thomas' CE Prim Sch
W10 ... 91 A3
St Thomas' Cl KT6 ... 198 B1
St Thomas Ct
14 Camden Town NW1 ... 71 C1
Sidcup DA5 ... 169 C4
11 Walthamstow E10 ... 53 D2
St Thomas' Ct HA5 ... 23 A2
St Thomas' Dr
BR5 ... 211 A1
Pinner HA5 ... 23 A2
St Thomas Gdns IG1 ... 79 A2
St Thomas Ho 2 E1 ... 96 D1
St Thomas More
Language Coll
SW3 ... 114 D2 257 C3
St Thomas More RC Comp
Sch SE9 ... 166 C5
St Thomas More RC Prim
Sch
Bexley DA7 ... 147 B3
SE9 ... 144 A2
St Thomas More Sch
N22 ... 32 C3
St Thomas of Canterbury
RC Prim Sch
Mitcham CR4 ... 203 A6
SW6 ... 135 B5 264 C4
St Thomas Rd
Newham E16 ... 99 A1
Osidge N14 ... 15 D4
St Thomas' Rd W4 ... 133 A6
St Thomas's Gdns
NW5 ... 71 A2
St Thomas's Hospl
SE1 ... 116 B3 260 C6
St Thomas's Hospl
Medical Sch
SE1 ... 116 B3 260 C5
St Thomas's Pl 20 E9 ... 74 C1
St Thomas's Rd
Dagenham NW10 ... 89 C6
Highbury N4, N5 ... 72 C5
St Thomas's Sq E9 ... 74 C1
St Thomas St
SE1 ... 117 B5 252 D3
St Thomas's Way
SW6 ... 135 B5 264 D4
St Thomas the Apostle
Coll The SE15 ... 140 C4
St Timothy's Mews 3
BR1 ... 187 B2
St Ursula Gr HA5 ... 41 A4
St Ursula Rd UB1 ... 85 C1
St Ursula's Convent Sch
SE10 ... 142 B5
St Vincent Cl SE27 ... 182 D5
St Vincent De Paul Ho 24
E1 ... 96 C2
St Vincent De Paul RC
Prim Sch
SW1 ... 115 C3 259 B6
St Vincent Ho SE1 ... 263 C6
St Vincent Rd TW2 ... 152 A5
St Vincent's Hospl
HA5 ... 39 D6
St Vincents La NW7 ... 28 C6
St Vincents RC Prim Sch
SE9 ... 188 A6
St Vincent's RC Prim Sch
Acton W3 ... 110 D6
Dagenham RM8 ... 80 C6
Marylebone W1 ... 93 A2 238 B3
St Vincent's RC Sch
NW7 ... 28 C5
St Vincent St W1 ... 238 B3
St Wilfrid's Cl EN4 ... 14 C6
St Wilfrid's Rd EN4 ... 14 C6
St William of York RC
Prim Sch SE23 ... 163 A3
St Winefride's Ave E12 ... 78 B3
St Winefride's RC Prim
Sch E12 ... 78 B3
St Winifred's RC Inf Sch
SE12 ... 164 C6
St Winifred's RC Jun Sch
SE12 ... 164 D4
St Winifred's Rd
TW11 ... 175 B4
Sakura Dr N22 ... 31 D2
Sala Ho SE3 ... 143 B1
Salamanca Pl SE1 ... 260 C3
Salamanca St SE1,
SE11 ... 116 B2 260 C3
Salamander Cl KT2 ... 175 C5
Salamander Quay
KT1 ... 175 D2
Salcombe Dr
Dagenham RM6 ... 59 B3
North Cheam SM4 ... 200 D1
Salcombe Gdns
Clapham SW4 ... 137 B1
Mill Hill NW7 ... 28 C4
Salcombe Ho 6
SE23 ... 162 C2
Salcombe Lo NW5 ... 71 A4
Salcombe Pk IG10 ... 21 D6
Salcombe Rd
Ashford TW15 ... 148 A1
23 Stoke Newington
N16 ... 73 C3
Walthamstow E17 ... 53 B2
Salcombe Sch N14 ... 15 B4
Salcombe Villas 13
TW10 ... 154 A6
Salcombe Way
Hayes UB4 ... 83 C4
Ruislip HA4 ... 62 A6
Salcot N4 ... 72 B6
Salcott Rd
Wallington CR0 ... 220 B4
Wandsworth SW11 ... 158 D6
Salehurst Cl HA3 ... 44 A4
Salehurst Rd SE4 ... 163 B5
Salem Ho 18 E9 ... 74 D2
Salem Pl CR0 ... 221 A5
Salem Rd W2 ... 113 D6 245 D6
Sale Pl W2 ... 92 C1 237 A2
Salesian Coll
SW11 ... 136 C4 267 A1
Sale St E2 ... 96 A3
Salford Ho 5 E14 ... 120 A2
Salford Rd SW12,
SW2 ... 159 D3
Salhouse Cl SE28 ... 102 C1
Salisbury Ave
Barking IG11 ... 79 C1
Cheam SM1, SM2 ... 217 B2
Hendon N3 ... 47 B6
Salisbury Cl
SE17 ... 262 C4
Worcester Pk KT4 ... 215 D5
Salisbury Ct
15 Bermondsey SE16 ... 118 A3
Chiswick W4 ... 111 C2
EC4 ... 241 C1
Edgware HA8 ... 26 B6
Enfield EN2 ... 5 B1
Finchley N3 ... 29 B1
Hackney E9 ... 75 A3
Northolt UB5 ... 63 D3
Salisbury Gdns
5 Buckhurst Hill IG9 ... 21 D2
Wimbledon SW19 ... 179 A3
Salisbury Hall Gdns
E4 ... 35 C4
Salisbury Ho
2 Islington N1 ... 72 D2
Islington N1 ... 234 C6
3 Poplar E14 ... 97 D1
1 Ruislip HA4 ... 40 C1
Stanmore HA7 ... 25 A4
5 Wallington SM6 ... 219 B3
Westminster SW1 ... 259 D2
Wimbledon SW19 ... 156 D1
Salisbury Lower Sch
N9 ... 18 C4
Salisbury Mans
Edmonton N9 ... 18 A1
Harringay N4, N15 ... 50 D4
Salisbury Mews
Bromley Comm BR2 ... 210 A4
Fulham SW6 ... 264 C3
Salisbury Pl
Camberwell SW9 ... 138 D5
Marylebone W1 ... 237 C4
Salisbury Prim Sch
E12 ... 78 A3
Salisbury Rd
Barnet EN5 ... 1 A2
Bromley Comm BR2 ... 210 A4
Chingford E4 ... 19 C1
Croydon SE25 ... 206 A3
Dagenham RM10 ... 81 D2
East Bedfont TW6 ... 149 A5
Enfield EN3 ... 7 B6
Feltham TW13 ... 150 C3
Forest Gate E7 ... 77 A2
Harringay N4 ... 50 D4
Harrow HA1 ... 42 B4
Hounslow TW4 ... 128 C2
Ilford IG3 ... 79 C6
Kingston u T KT3 ... 199 B6
Leyton E10 ... 76 A6
Old Bexley DA5 ... 169 C3
Pinner HA5 ... 40 A5
Plashet E12 ... 77 D3

Salisbury Rd *continued*
Richmond TW9 . . . . 132 A1
Southall UB2 . . . . 107 A2
Tottenham N22 . . . . 32 D1
Wallington SM5 . . . . 218 D2
Walthamstow E17 . . . . . . 54 A4
West Ealing W13 . . . . . . 109 B4
Wimbledon SW19 . . . . . 179 A3
Worcester Pk KT4 . . . . . 215 C5
Salisbury Sq EC4 . . . . . 241 B1
Salisbury St
10 Acton W3 . . . . 111 A4
NW8 . . . . 237 A5
Salisbury Terr SE15 . . . 140 C2
Salisbury Upper Sch
N9 . . . . 18 C4
Salisbury Wlk N19 . . . . . 71 C6
Salix Cl TW16 . . . . 172 B3
Salix Ct N3 . . . . 29 C4
Salliesfield TW2 . . . . . . 152 B5
Sally Murray Cl E12 . . . . 78 C4
Salmen Rd E13 . . . . 98 D5
Salmond Cl HA7 . . . . 25 A4
Salmon La E14 . . . . 97 A1
Salmon Rd DA17 . . . . . . 125 C1
Salmons Brook Ho EN2 . . 4 D2
Salmons Rd
Chessington KT9 . . . . . . 214 A2
Edmonton N9 . . . . 18 A3
Salmon St
Kingsbury NW9 . . . . 45 A2
13 Poplar E14 . . . . 97 B1
Salomons Rd 2 E13 . . . 99 C2
Salop Rd E17 . . . . 52 D3
Saltash Cl SM1 . . . . 217 B4
Saltash Rd DA16 . . . . . . 146 C4
Saltcoats Rd W4 . . . . . . 111 C4
Saltcroft Cl HA9 . . . . 44 D1
Saltdene N4 . . . . 50 B1
Salter Cl HA2 . . . . 63 B4
Salterford Rd SW17 . . . 181 A4
Salter Ho 8 SW16 . . . . 181 C6
Saltern Ct IG11 . . . . 102 B4
Salter Rd SE16 . . . . 119 A5
Salters' Hall Ct EC4 . . . 252 C6
Salter's Hill SE19 . . . . . 183 B5
Salters Rd
North Kensington W10 . . . 90 D3
Walthamstow E17 . . . . . . 54 B5
Salter St
College Pk NW10 . . . . 90 A4
11 Poplar E14 . . . . 119 C6
Salterton Rd N7 . . . . 72 B5
Salt Hill Cl UB8 . . . . 60 A3
Saltley Cl E6 . . . . 100 A1
Saltoun Rd SW2, SW9 . . 138 C1
Saltram Cl N15 . . . . 51 D5
Saltram Cres W9 . . . . . . 91 C4
Saltwell St E14 . . . . 119 C6
Saltwood Gr SE17 . . . . . 262 C1
Saltwood Ho 19 SE15 . . 140 C6
Salusbury Prim Sch
NW6 . . . . 91 B6
Salusbury Rd NW6 . . . . . 91 A6
Salutation Rd SE10 . . . . 120 C2
Salvador SW17 . . . . 180 D5
Salvatorian RC Coll
HA3 . . . . 24 C1
Salvia Gdns UB6 . . . . 87 A5
Salvin Rd SW15 . . . . 134 D2
Salway Cl IG8 . . . . 37 A3
Salway Ho E10 . . . . 75 D6
Salway Pl E15 . . . . 76 C2
Salway Rd E15 . . . . 76 B2
Salween Ho 2 N16 . . . . 73 B4
Samantha Cl E17 . . . . 53 B2
Samantha Ct E11 . . . . 54 C2
Samaritan Hospl for
Women NW1 . . . . 237 C4
Sam Bartram Cl SE7 . . . 121 C1
Sambrooke Ct EN1 . . . . . 17 D6
Sambrook Ho 25 E1 . . . . 96 C2
Sambruck Mews SE6 . . 163 D3
Samels Ct W6 . . . . 112 A1
Samford Ho N1 . . . . 234 A5
Samford St NW8 . . . . . . 237 A5
Samira Cl E17 . . . . 53 C3
Sam Manners Ho 7
SE10 . . . . 120 C1
Sam March Ho 5 E14 . . . 98 B1
Samos Rd SE20 . . . . 184 B1
Sampson Ave EN5 . . . . . 12 D6
Sampson Cl DA17 . . . . . 125 A3
Sampson Ct TW17 . . . . 193 A4
Sampson St E1 . . . . 118 A5
Samson Ct 5 DA17 . . . 125 C2
Samson Ho SE18 . . . . . . 123 A2
Samson St E13 . . . . 99 C5
Samuel Cl
SE14 . . . . 140 D6
Shoreditch E8 . . . . 95 D6
Woolwich SE18 . . . . 122 A2
Samuel Ct
Beckenham BR3 . . . . 207 D6
Shoreditch N1 . . . . 95 C4
Samuel Gray Gdns
KT2 . . . . 175 D2
Samuel Ho
15 Shoreditch E8 . . . . 95 D6
3 West Norwood
SE27 . . . . 182 D6
Samuel Johnson Cl
SW16 . . . . 182 B6
Samuel Jones Ind Est 7
SE15 . . . . 139 C5
Samuel Lewis Bldgs
N1 . . . . 72 C2
**Samuel Lewis Trust
Dwellings**
6 Camberwell SE5 . . . . 139 A4
Chelsea SW3 . . . . 257 A3
Walham Green
SW6 . . . . 135 C5 265 B4
West Kensington W14 . . 254 B4
Samuel Lewis Trust Est
N15 . . . . 51 C3
Samuel Lo N3 . . . . 29 B1
Samuel Rhodes Sch
N1 . . . . 94 C6 234 A6
Samuel Richardson Ho
W14 . . . . 254 C3
Samuel's Cl 2 W6 . . . . 112 C2
Samuel St
SE15 . . . . 139 D5
Woolwich SE18 . . . . 122 B2
Sancroft Cl NW2 . . . . . . 68 B5
Sancroft Ct SW11 . . . . . 267 B2
Sancroft Ho SE11 . . . . . 260 D2
Sancroft Rd HA3 . . . . 25 A1
Sancroft St
SE11 . . . . 116 B1 260 D2
Sanctuary Mews 15
E8 . . . . 73 D2
Sanctuary Rd TW19,
TW6 . . . . 148 C5
Sanctuary St SE1 . . . . . 252 B2
Sanctuary The
Morden SM4 . . . . 201 C3
Sidcup DA5 . . . . 168 D5
35 Wapping E1 . . . . 118 B5
Westminster
SW1 . . . . 115 D3 259 D6
Sandale Cl N16 . . . . 73 B5
Sandall Cl W5 . . . . 88 A3
Sandall Ho 7 E3 . . . . 97 A5
Sandall Rd
Ealing W5 . . . . 88 A3
Kentish Town NW5 . . . . . . 71 C2
Sandal Rd
Edmonton N18 . . . . 34 A5
New Malden KT3 . . . . . . 199 C5
Sandal St E15 . . . . 98 C6
Sandalwood Cl 11 E1 . . . 97 A3
Sandalwood Dr HA4 . . . . 39 A2
Sandalwood Ho
DA15 . . . . 167 D1
6 Hampstead NW3 . . . . . 69 D2
Sandalwood Rd
TW13 . . . . 150 B1
Sandbach Pl SE18 . . . . . 123 A1
Sandbourne
4 Kensington W11 . . . . . 91 C1
14 Paddington NW8 . . . . 91 D6
Sandbourne Ave
SW19 . . . . 179 D1
Sandbourne Rd SE4 . . . 141 A3
Sandbrook Cl NW7 . . . . . 27 B4
Sandbrook Rd N16 . . . . . 73 C5
Sandby Ct BR3 . . . . 185 B2
Sandby Gn SE9 . . . . 144 A2
Sandby Ho
11 Camberwell SE5 . . . . 139 C4
6 Kilburn NW6 . . . . 91 C6
Sandcroft Cl N13 . . . . . . 32 D4
Sandells Ave
Ashford TW15 . . . . 171 A6
Ashford TW15 . . . . 171 A6
Sandell St SE1 . . . . 251 A2
Sanderling Ct
20 SE8 . . . . 141 B6
Woolwich SE28 . . . . 124 C6
Sanders Cl TW12 . . . . . 174 A5
Sanders Ho
Streatham SW16 . . . . . . 182 A4
WC1 . . . . 234 A2
Sanders La NW7 . . . . 28 C3
Sanderson Cl NW5 . . . . . 71 B4
Sanderson Ho 7 SE8 . . 119 B1
Sanderson Sq BR1 . . . . 210 C6
Sanderstead Ave NW2 . . 69 A6
Sanderstead Cl SW12 . 159 C4
Sanderstead Rd
South Croydon CR2 . . . . 221 B1
Walthamstow E10 . . . . . . 53 A1
Sanders Way 3 N19 . . . 49 D1
Sandfield WC1 . . . . 233 B1
Sandfield Gdns CR7 . . . 204 D6
Sandfield Pl CR7 . . . . . . 205 A6
Sandfield Rd CR7 . . . . . 204 D6
Sandford Ave N22 . . . . . 33 A2
Sandford Cl E6 . . . . 100 B3
Sandford Ct
Barnet EN5 . . . . 1 D2
Stamford Hill N16 . . . . 51 C1
Sandford Rd
Bexley DA7 . . . . 147 A2
BR2 . . . . 209 A5
Newham E6 . . . . 100 B4
Sandford Row SE17 . . . 262 D2
Sandford St SW6 . . . . . . 265 D3
Sandgate Ho
14 Beckenham BR3 . . . . 185 C3
Ealing W5 . . . . 87 C2
15 Hackney E5 . . . . 74 B4
Sandgate La SW17,
SW18 . . . . 158 C3
Sandgate Rd DA16 . . . . 146 C5
Sandgate St SE15 . . . . . 140 B6
Sandgate Trad Est
SE15 . . . . 140 B6
Sandham Ct SW4 . . . . . 270 B1
Sandham Point 10
SE18 . . . . 122 D2
Sandhills CR0, SM6 . . . . 219 D4
Sandhills Mdw TW17 . . 193 A2
Sandhills The SW10 . . . 266 B6
Sandhurst Ave
Harrow HA2 . . . . 41 D3
Tolworth KT5 . . . . 198 D2
Sandhurst Cl
Queensbury NW9 . . . . 44 C6
South Croydon CR2 . . . . 221 C1
Sandhurst Ct SW2 . . . . 138 A1
Sandhurst Dr IG3 . . . . . . 79 D4
Sandhurst Ho 12 E1 . . . . 96 C2
Sandhurst Jun & Inf Schs
SE6 . . . . 164 C3
Sandhurst Mkt SE6 . . . . 164 A3
Sandhurst Rd
Bexley DA5 . . . . 168 D6
Catford SE6 . . . . 164 B3
DA15 . . . . 168 A1
Ponders End N9 . . . . 18 D5
Queensbury HA8, NW9 . . 44 C6
Sandhurst Way CR2 . . . 221 C1
Sandifer Dr NW2 . . . . 68 D5
Sandiford Rd SM3 . . . . . 217 B6
Sandiland Cres BR2 . . . 224 D6
Sandilands CR0 . . . . 222 A5
Sandilands Rd
SW6 . . . . 135 D4 265 C1
Sandilands Sta CR0 . . . 221 D6
Sandison St SE15 . . . . . 140 A2
Sandland St WC1 . . . . . . 240 D3
Sandling Rise SE9 . . . . 166 C1
Sandlings Cl SE15 . . . . . 140 B3
Sandlings The
Tottenham N22 . . . . 50 D6
5 Wood Green N22 . . . . . 32 C1
Sandmartin Way CR4 . . 203 A1
Sandmere Rd SW4 . . . . 138 A1
Sandon Cl KT10 . . . . 196 B1
Sandon Ct IG3 . . . . 80 A5
Sandon Ho 5 SW2 . . . . 160 A4
Sandow Commercial Est
UB3 . . . . 105 D3
Sandow Cres UB3 . . . . . 105 D3
Sandown Ave KT10 . . . . 212 A3
Sandown Cl TW5 . . . . . . 128 A4
Sandown Ct 12 SM2 . . . 217 D1
Sandown Gate KT10 . . . 212 B5
Sandown Ho
2 Acton Green W4 . . . . 111 A1
Esher KT10 . . . . 212 A4
Penge SE26 . . . . 184 B4
Sandown Park KT10 . . . 212 A6
Sandown Rd
Croydon SE25 . . . . 206 B4
Esher KT10 . . . . 212 A4
Sandown Way UB5 . . . . . 63 B3
Sandpiper Cl
Higham Hill E17 . . . . 34 D3
Rotherhithe SE16 . . . . . . 119 B4
Sandpiper Ct
13 Cubitt Town E14 . . . . 120 A3
1 SE8 . . . . 141 C5
Sandpiper Rd SM1 . . . . 217 B3
Sandpiper Terr IG5 . . . . 56 D6
Sandpit Pl SE7 . . . . 122 A1
Sandpit Rd BR1 . . . . 186 C5
Sandpits Rd
Richmond TW10 . . . . 153 D2
South Croydon CR0 . . . . 222 D4
Sandra Cl
Hounslow TW3 . . . . 151 D6
Tottenham N17 . . . . 33 A2
Sandra Ho KT8 . . . . 196 B4
Sandridge Cl
Hadley Wood EN4 . . . . 2 C6
Harrow HA1 . . . . 42 C5
Sandridge St 3 N19 . . . . 71 C6
Sandringham Ave
SW20 . . . . 179 A1
Sandringham Cl
Enfield EN1 . . . . 5 C3
Ilford IG6 . . . . 57 A6
1 Putney SW19 . . . . 156 D3
Sandringham Cres
HA2 . . . . 63 D6
Sandringham Ct
3 Beckenham BR3 . . . . 186 A2
Edgware HA8 . . . . 26 D6
Hillingdon UB10 . . . . 83 A3
Kingston u T KT2 . . . . . . 176 A2
Marylebone W1 . . . . 239 B1
Putney SW15 . . . . 156 D5
18 Rotherhithe SE16 . . . 118 D5
St John's Wood W9 . . . . 229 B1
2 Twickenham TW1 . . . . 153 A3
Sandringham Dr
Ashford TW15 . . . . 170 A6
DA16 . . . . 145 C3
Sandringham Flats
WC2 . . . . 249 D6
Sandringham Gdns
Cranford TW5 . . . . 128 A4
East Molesey KT8 . . . . . 195 C5
Finchley N12 . . . . 30 B4
Hornsey Vale N8 . . . . 50 A3
Ilford IG6 . . . . 57 A6
Sandringham Ho
Richmond TW10 . . . . 154 C6
W14 . . . . 254 A4
Sandringham Lo BR6 . . 226 C4
Sandringham Mews
TW12 . . . . 173 B2
Sandringham Prim Sch
E7 . . . . 77 C3
Sandringham Rd
Barking IG11 . . . . 79 D2
BR1 . . . . 187 A5
Dalston E8 . . . . 73 D3
Forest Gate E7 . . . . 77 C3
Golders Green NW11 . . . . 47 A2
Leytonstone E10 . . . . 54 B3
Northolt UB5 . . . . 63 C1
Stanwell TW19, TW6 . . . 148 A6
Thornton Heath CR0 . . . . 205 A4
Tottenham N22 . . . . 33 A1
Willesden NW2 . . . . 68 B2
Worcester Pk KT4 . . . . . 216 A5
Sandrock Pl CR0 . . . . . . 222 D4
Sandrock Rd SE13 . . . . 141 C2
SANDS END 136 A2
Sands End La
SW6 . . . . 135 D4 265 D2
Sandstone TW9 . . . . 132 C5
Sandstone La E16 . . . . . 121 B6
Sandstone Pl N19 . . . . . . 71 B6
Sandstone Rd SE12 . . . 165 B2
Sandtoft Rd SE7 . . . . . . 143 B6
Sandways 6 TW9 . . . . . 132 C4
Sandwell Cres 2 NW6 . . 69 C2
Sandwell Mans 3
NW6 . . . . 69 C2
Sandwich Ho
15 Rotherhithe SE16 . . . 118 C4
WC1 . . . . 233 A1
Sandwich St
WC1 . . . . 94 A4 233 A1
Sandwick Cl NW7 . . . . . . 28 A3
Sandy Bury BR6 . . . . 227 B5
Sandycombe Ctr
TW9 . . . . 132 C2
Sandycombe Rd
East Bedfont TW14 . . . . 150 A3
Richmond TW9 . . . . 132 C3
Sandycoombe Rd
TW1 . . . . 153 C5
Sandycroft SE2 . . . . 146 A6
Sandy Dr TW14 . . . . 149 C3
Sandy Hill Ave SE18 . . . 122 D1
Sandy Hill La SE18 . . . . 122 D2
Sandyhill Rd IG1 . . . . 78 D4
Sandy Hill Rd SE18 . . . . 122 D1
Sandy La
Belmont SM2 . . . . 217 A1
Sandy La *continued*
BR5 . . . . 190 D2
Eastbury HA6 . . . . 22 A6
Harrow HA3 . . . . 44 C3
Mitcham CR4 . . . . 181 A2
Richmond TW10 . . . . 153 D2
Teddington KT8, TW11 . . 175 B3
Walton-on-T KT12 . . . . . 194 C3
Sandy Lane N SM6 . . . . 219 D3
Sandy Lane S SM6 . . . . 219 C1
Sandy Lo N6 . . . . 49 C2
Sandymount Ave HA7 . . 25 D5
Sandy Rd NW3 . . . . 69 D6
Sandy Ridge BR7 . . . . . 188 C4
Sandy's Row E1 . . . . . . 243 B3
Sandy Way
Croydon CR0 . . . . 223 B5
Walton-on-T KT12 . . . . . 193 D1
Sanford La 3 N16 . . . . . 73 D6
Sanford St SE14, SE8 . . 141 A6
Sanford Terr N16 . . . . . . 73 D5
Sanford Wlk
SE14 . . . . 141 A6
4 Stoke Newington
N16 . . . . 73 D6
Sangam Cl UB2 . . . . 107 A3
Sanger Ave KT9 . . . . 214 B4
Sangley Rd
Catford SE6 . . . . 164 A3
South Norwood SE25 . . . 205 C5
Sangora Rd 17 SW11 . . 136 B1
San Ho 29 E9 . . . . 74 D2
Sankey Ho 22 E2 . . . . 96 C5
Sansom Rd E11 . . . . 76 D6
Sansom St
Camberwell SE5 . . . . 139 B4
SE5 . . . . 139 B5
Sans Wlk EC1 . . . 94 D3 241 C6
Santana SE18 . . . . 144 D5
Santley Ho SE1 . . . . 251 B1
Santley St SW4 . . . . 138 B1
Santos Rd SW18 . . . . . . 157 C6
Sapcote Trad Ctr
NW10 . . . . 67 D2
Saperton Wlk SE11 . . . . 260 D4
Saphora Cl BR6 . . . . 227 B3
Sapperton Ct EC1 . . . . . 242 A6
Sapphire Cl
Dagenham RM8 . . . . 58 C1
Newham E6 . . . . 100 C1
Sapphire Ct 13 E1 . . . . . 118 A6
Sapphire Rd
Rotherhithe SE8 . . . . . . 119 A2
Willesden NW10 . . . . 67 A1
Saracen Cl CR0 . . . . 205 B3
Saracen St E14 . . . . 97 C1
Sarah Bonnell Sch
E15 . . . . 76 C2
Sarah Ct UB5 . . . . 85 B6
Sarah Ho
Roehampton SW15 . . . . 133 D1
8 Stepney E1 . . . . 96 B1
Sarah Swift Ho SE1 . . . 252 D2
Sarah Turnbull Ho 2
SE18 . . . . 122 B2
Sara Lane Ct 31 N1 . . . . . 95 C5
Saratoga Rd E5 . . . . 74 C4
Sardeson Ho 13
SW27 . . . . 182 D5
Sardinia Ho WC2 . . . . . . 240 C1
Sardinia St WC2 . . . . . . 240 C2
Sargents Hill N2 . . . . 30 C2
Sarita Cl HA3 . . . . 24 B1
Sarjant Path SW19 . . . . 156 D2
Sark Cl TW5 . . . . 129 C5
Sark Ho
9 Canonbury N1 . . . . 73 A2
Enfield EN3 . . . . 6 D5
Sark Twr SE28 . . . . 123 A4
Sark Wlk E16 . . . . 99 B1
Sarnersfield Ho SE15 . . 140 B6
Sarnes Ct 4 N11 . . . . 31 B6
Sarnesfield Rd EN2 . . . . . 5 B2
Sarratt Ho 6 W10 . . . . . . 90 C2
Sarre Rd NW2 . . . . 69 B3
Sarsden Bldgs W1 . . . . . 238 B1
Sarsen Ave TW3 . . . . . . 129 C3
Sarsfeld Rd SW12,
SW17 . . . . 158 D3
Sarsfield Rd UB6 . . . . 87 C5
Sartor Rd SE15 . . . . 140 D1
Sarum Hall Sch NW3 . . . 70 C1
Sarum Ho W11 . . . . 244 D5
Sarwan Ho 1 E7 . . . . 77 C1
Sassoon 4 NW9 . . . . 27 D2
Sassoon Ho SE15 . . . . . 140 C3
Satanita Cl E16 . . . . 99 D1
Satchell Mead NW9 . . . . 27 D2
Satchwell Rd 17 E2 . . . . . 96 A4
Satin Ct NW9 . . . . 45 D5
Saturn Ho 4 E3 . . . . 97 C6
Saul Ct 4 SE15 . . . . 139 D6
Sauls Gn E11 . . . . 76 C5
Saunders Cl
Ilford IG1 . . . . 57 B1
14 Limehouse E14 . . . . . 119 B6
Saunders Ho 11 SW2 . . 160 C3
Saunders Ness Rd
E14 . . . . 120 B2
Saunders Rd
Hillingdon UB10 . . . . 82 B6
Plumstead Comm SE18 . 123 D1
Saunders St SE11 . . . . . 261 A4
Saunders Way SE28 . . . 124 B6
Saunderton Rd HA0 . . . . 65 B3
Saunton Ave UB3 . . . . . 127 D5
Saunton Ct UB1 . . . . 108 A6
Savage Gdns
EC3 . . . . 253 B6
Newham E6 . . . . 100 B1
Savana N16 . . . . 73 C6
Savannah Cl 9 SE15 . . 139 D5
Savernake Ct HA7 . . . . . . 25 B4
Savernake Ho N4 . . . . . . 51 B2
Savernake Rd
Enfield N9 . . . . 18 A5
Maitland Pk NW3 . . . . 70 D4
Savery Dr KT6 . . . . 197 C2
Savile Cl
New Malden KT3 . . . . . . 199 C4
Thames Ditton KT7 . . . . 197 A1
Savile Gdns CR0 . . . . . . 221 D6
Savill Ct IG8 . . . . 36 D4
Saville Cres TW15 . . . . . 171 B4
Saville Ho E16 . . . . 122 D5
Saville Rd
Bedford Pk W4 . . . . 111 B3
Dagenham RM6 . . . . 59 B2
Newham E16 . . . . 122 A5
Twickenham TW1 . . . . . . 152 D3
Saville Row
Enfield EN3 . . . . 6 D3
Hayes BR2 . . . . 208 D1
W1 . . . . 115 C6 249 A6
Savill Gdns SW20 . . . . . 200 A6
Savill Ho 2 SW4 . . . . . . 159 D5
Savill Row IG8 . . . . 36 D4
Savin Lo 7 SM2 . . . . 218 A1
Savona Cl 16 SW19 . . . . 178 D3
Savona Ct SW20 . . . . . . 178 D2
Savona St
SW8 . . . . 137 C5 269 A3
Savoy Ave UB3 . . . . 105 C1
Savoy Circus W3 . . . . . . 111 D6
Savoy Cl
Edgware HA8 . . . . 26 C5
Newham E15 . . . . 98 C6
Savoy Ct
Earl's Ct SW5 . . . . 255 B4
Strand WC2 . . . . 250 B5
Savoy Hill WC2 . . . . 250 C5
Savoy Mews SW9 . . . . . 138 A2
Savoy Par EN1 . . . . 5 C2
Savoy Pier WC2 . . . . 250 C5
Savoy Pl WC2 . . 116 B6 250 C5
Savoy Row WC2 . . . . 250 C6
Savoy St WC2 . . 116 B6 250 C5
Savoy Stps WC2 . . . . . . 250 C5
Savoy Way WC2 . . . . 250 C5
Sawbill Cl UB4 . . . . 84 D2
Sawkins Cl SW19 . . . . . 157 A2
Sawley Rd W12 . . . . 112 A5
Sawmill Yd E3 . . . . 97 A6
Sawtry Cl SM5 . . . . 202 C2
Sawyer Cl N9 . . . . 18 A2
Sawyer Ho 15 SE21 . . . . 183 C6
Sawyer's Hill TW10 . . . 154 B4
Sawyers Lawn W13 . . . . 87 A1
Sawyer St SE1 . . 117 A4 252 A2
Saxby Rd SW2 . . . . 160 A4
Saxham Rd IG11 . . . . . . 101 D5
Saxlingham Rd E4 . . . . . 20 B1
Saxon Ave TW13 . . . . . . 151 B2
Saxon Bsns Ctr SW19 . . 180 A2
Saxonbury Ave TW16 . . 172 B1
Saxonbury Cl CR4 . . . . . 202 B6
Saxonbury Ct
16 Kentish Town N7 . . . . . 71 D3
2 Lower Holloway N7 . . . 72 A3
Saxonbury Gdns KT6 . . 197 C1
Saxon Cl
Hillingdon UB8 . . . . 82 A2
Surbiton KT6 . . . . 197 D3
Walthamstow E17 . . . . 53 C2
Saxoncroft Ho SW16 . . 159 D1
Saxon Ct
Colney Hatch N12 . . . . . . 30 C5
4 Edgware HA8 . . . . 26 D5
Saxon Dr W3 . . . . 88 D2
Saxonfield Cl SW2 . . . . 160 B4

Saxon Gdns UB1 107 A6
Saxon Hall W2 245 C5
Saxon Ho
4 Clapham SW4 137 D1
Feltham TW13 151 B2
Saxon Prim Sch TW17 192 C4
Saxon Rd
Ashford TW15 171 B4
Bow E3 97 B5
Bromley BR1 186 D3
Ilford IG1 78 D3
Kingston u T KT2 176 A2
Newham E6 100 B3
Southall UB1 107 A6
South Norwood SE25 205 B4
Tottenham N22 32 D2
Wembley HA9 67 A5
Saxon Terr SE6 163 B2
Saxon Way N14 15 D5
Saxon Wlk DA14 190 C4
Saxony Par UB3 83 A2
Saxton Cl SE13 142 B2
Saxville Rd BR5 190 B1
Sayer Ho SE4 141 A1
Sayers Ho 4 N2 30 B1
Sayer's Wlk TW10 154 B4
Sayesbury La N18 34 A5
Sayes Court St SE8 141 B6
Sayes Ct SE8 141 B6
Sayline Ct CR0 221 B5
Scadbury Gdns BR5 190 A1
Scadbury Park Nature Reserve* BR7 189 D4
Scads Hill Cl BR6 211 D3
Scafell NW1 232 A2
Scala St W1 239 B4
Scales Rd N17 52 A6
Scampston Mews 5 W10 90 D1
Scandrett St 38 E1 118 B5
Scarba Wlk N1 73 B2
Scarborough Rd
East Bedfont TW6 149 A5
Finsbury Pk N4 50 C1
Leytonstone E11 54 B1
Ponders End N9 18 C4
Scarborough St E1 243 D1
Scarbrook Rd CR0 221 A5
Scardale Ho 12 E5 74 B6
Scarle Rd HA0 65 D2
Scarlet Rd SE6 164 C1
Scarlette Manor Wlk 10 SE24 160 C4
Scarsbrook Ho 2 SW2 160 C5
Scarsbrook Rd SE3 143 D2
Scarsdale Pl W8 255 C6
Scarsdale Rd HA2 64 A5
Scarsdale Villas W8 113 C3 255 B5
Scarth Rd SW13 133 D2
Scawen Cl SM5 219 A4
Scawen Rd SE8 119 A1
Scawfell St E2 95 D5
Scaynes Link N12 29 C6
Sceptre Ho 10 E1 96 C3
Sceptre Rd E2 96 C4
Schiller International Univ SE1 116 C5 251 A3
Schofield Wlk SE3 143 A5
Sch of Pharmacy WC1 94 A3 240 B6
Scholars Cl EN5 1 A1
Scholars Ct 5 N19 49 D1
Scholars Ho 6 E4 20 B3
Scholars Rd
Chingford E4 20 B3
Streatham SW12 159 C3
Scholefield Rd N19 71 D6
Scholey Ho SW11 136 C2
Schomberg Ho SW1 259 D4
Schonfeld Sq N16 51 B1
School App 21 E2 95 C4
Schoolbank Rd SE10 120 D2
School Bell Cloisters 17 E3 97 A5
Schoolbell Mews 18 E3 97 A5
School Cotts
Bromley BR1 187 A3
Sidcup DA14 190 C5
School Flats SW8 270 A1
School Ho SE1 263 A4
Schoolhouse La E1 118 D6
School House La TW11 175 C3
Schoolhouse Yd 9 SE18 122 D1
School La
DA16 146 B2
Lower Halliford TW17 192 D2
Pinner HA5 41 A5
Surbiton KT6 198 B1
Teddington KT1 175 C2
School Pas
3 Kingston u T KT1 176 B1
Southall UB1 107 B6
School Rd
Ashford TW15 170 D4
Becontree NW10 89 B3
BR7 189 A3
Dagenham RM10 103 D6
East Molesey KT8 196 B5
Hampton TW12 174 A4
Hounslow TW3 130 A2
Ilford E12 78 B4
Littleton TW15 170 D3
Teddington KT1 175 C2
School Road Ave TW12 174 A4
School Sq SE10 120 D3
Schoolway N12 30 B4
School Way RM8 80 C5
School Wlk TW16 193 D6
Schooner Cl
Barking IG11 102 B4
Cubitt Town E14 120 B3
1 Rotherhithe SE16 118 D4
Schubert Rd
Elstree WD6 9 D5
Putney SW15 157 B6
Science Mus* SW7 114 B3 256 C5
Scilly Isles KT10 212 C6
Sclater St E1 243 D6
Scoles Cres SW2 160 C3
Scope Way KT1 198 A5
Scoresby St SE1 251 C3
Scoresdale SE19 183 C2
Scorton Ave UB6 87 A5
Scorton Ho 2 N1 95 C5
Scotch Comm W13 87 B2
Scotch Ho SW1 114 D4 247 C1
Scoter Cl IG8 37 B3
Scoter Ct 23 SE8 141 B6
Scot Gr HA5 22 D3
Scotia Bldg 10 E1 118 D6
Scotia Ct 3 SE16 118 C3
Scotia Rd 24 SW2 160 C4
Scotland Gn N17 33 D1
Scotland Green Rd EN3 18 D6
Scotland Green Rd N EN3 7 A1
Scotland Pl SW1 250 A3
Scotland Rd IG9 21 C3
Scotney Cl BR6 226 C4
Scotney Ho E9 74 C2
Scots Cl TW19 148 A3
Scotsdale Cl
Belmont SM3 217 A1
BR5 211 C5
Scotsdale Rd SE12 165 B6
Scotson Ho SE11 261 A3
Scotswood St EC1 94 C3 241 B6
Scotswood Wlk N17 34 A3
Scott Cl
Thornton Heath SW16 182 B2
West Drayton UB7 104 B2
West Ewell KT19 215 A3
Scott Ct
Acton W4 111 B4
4 Clapham SW11 137 B3
17 Stoke Newington N16 73 C5
Scott Ellis Gdns NW8 92 B4 229 C1
Scottes La RM8 58 D1
Scott Farm Cl KT7 197 B1
Scott Gdns TW5 128 D5
Scott Ho
2 Barnsbury N7 72 B2
3 Edmonton N18 34 A5
4 Erith DA17 125 B1
Islington N1 235 C6
Lisson Gr NW8 237 A5
17 Millwall E14 119 C4
6 Newham E13 99 A5
Richmond TW10 153 C2
3 Stonebridge NW10 67 B1
Scott Lidgett Cres SE16 118 A4
Scott Rd HA8 26 D1
Scott's Ave
Ashford TW16 171 C3
Scott's Ave *continued*
Beckenham BR2 186 B1
Scotts Ct 6 W12 112 B4
Scotts Dr TW12 173 D3
Scotts Farm Rd KT19 215 A2
Scotts Ho DA16 146 C4
Scott's La BR2, BR3 186 B1
Scotts Park Prim Sch BR1 187 C2
Scotts Rd
BR1 187 A3
Southall UB2 106 D3
Scott's Rd
Leytonstone E10 54 A1
Shepherd's Bush W12 112 B4
Scott's Sufferance Wharf SE1 253 D1
Scott St E1 96 B3
Scott's Way TW16 171 C3
Scott's Yd EC4 252 C6
Scott Trimmer Way TW3 129 A3
Scottwell Dr NW9 45 D4
Scott Wilkie Prim Sch E16 99 C1
Scoulding Ho 12 E14 119 C3
Scoulding Rd E16 99 A1
Scouler St E14 120 B6
Scout App NW10 67 C4
Scout La SW4 137 C2
Scout Way NW7 27 B6
Scovell Cres SE1 252 A1
Scovell Rd SE1 252 A1
Scratchwood Nature Trail* NW7 11 B4
Scrattons Terr IG11 103 A5
Scriven Ct 2 E8 95 D6
Scriven St E8 95 D6
Scrooby St SE6 163 D5
Scrope Bldg EC1 241 A4
Scrubs La NW10, W10, W12 90 B3
Scrutton Cl SW12 159 D4
Scrutton St EC2 95 C3 243 A5
Scudamore La NW9 45 A5
Scutari Rd SE22 162 C6
Scylla Cres TW6&TW14 148 D4
Scylla Rd
East Bedfont TW14, TW6 148 D5
Nunhead SE15 140 B2
Seabright St 27 E2 96 B4
Seabrook Dr BR4 224 C6
Seabrook Gdns RM7 59 C2
Seabrook Rd RM8 80 D5
Seacole Cl W3 89 B2
Seacole Ct N15 51 D4
Seacole Lo N21 16 B6
Seacon Twr 8 E14 119 C4
Seacourt Rd SE2 124 D4
Seacroft Gdns WD19 22 D6
Seafield Rd N11 31 D6
Seaford Cl HA4 61 B6
Seaford Ho 13 SE16 118 C4
Seaford Rd
Ealing W13 109 B5
Enfield EN1 5 C1
Tottenham N15 51 C4
Walthamstow E17 53 D6
Seaford St WC1 233 B1
Seaforth Ave KT3 200 B5
Seaforth Cres N5 73 A3
Seaforth Gdns
Southgate N21 16 C3
Woodford IG8 37 C5
Worcester Pk KT19 215 D3
Seaforth Lo 2 SW13 133 D3
Seaforth Pl SW1 259 B6
Seagrave Lo SW6 265 B6
Seagrave Rd SW6 135 C6 265 B6
Seagrove Cl E1 96 D2
Seagry Rd E11 55 B2
Seagull Cl IG11 102 A4
Seagull La E16 121 A6
Sealand Rd TW6 148 C5
Sealand Wlk UB5 85 A4
Seal Ho SE1 262 D6
Seal St E8 73 D4
Searle Ct 2 CR4 180 C2
Searle Pl N4 50 B1
Searles Cl SW11 136 C5 267 B3
Searles Dr E6 100 D2
Searles Rd SE1 262 D4
Searson Ho SE17 261 D3
Sears Ret Pk UB6 86 C6
Sears St SE5 139 B5
Seasalter Ho 10 SW9 138 C4
Seasprite Cl 10 UB5 84 D4
Seath Ho 4 SE26 184 B5
Seaton Ave IG3 79 D3
Seaton Cl
Isleworth TW2 152 B5
6 Newham E13 99 A3
Roehampton SW15 156 B4
Seaton Dr TW15 148 A2
Seaton Gdns HA4 62 A6
Seaton Point E5 74 A4
Seaton Rd
Bexley DA16 146 C5
Hayes UB3 105 B3
Mitcham CR4 180 C1
Twickenham TW2 152 A5
Wembley HA0 88 A5
Seaton Sq NW7 28 D3
Seaton St N18 34 A5
Seavington Ho 3 SE5 139 C2
Sebastian Ct 11 IG11 79 D1
Sebastian Ho 22 N1 95 C5
Sebastian St EC1 94 D4 234 D1
Sebastopol Rd N9 34 A6
Sebbon St N1 72 D1
Sebergham Gr NW7 28 A3
Sebert Rd E7 77 B4
Sebright Ho 22 E2 96 A5
Sebright Pas 29 E2 96 A5
Sebright Rd EN5 1 A2
Sebright Sch E2 96 A5
Secker Cres HA3 24 A2
Secker Ho SW9 138 D3
Secker St SE1 251 A3
Second Ave
Chadwell Heath RM6 58 C4
Dagenham RM10 103 D5
East Acton W3 111 D5
Edmonton N18 34 C6
Enfield EN1 17 D6
Hayes UB3 105 D5
Hendon NW4 46 D5
Kensal Town W10 91 A3
Manor Pk E12 78 A3
Mortlake SW14 133 C2
Newham E13 99 A4
Walthamstow E17 53 C4
Walton-on-T KT12 194 B3
Wembley HA9 65 D6
Second Cl KT8 196 A5
Second Cross Rd TW2 152 C2
Second Way HA9 66 D4
Secrett Ho 6 TW10 153 C1
Sedan Way SE17 117 C1 263 A2
Sedcombe Cl DA14 190 C6
Sedcote Rd EN3 18 D6
Sedding St SW1 258 A4
Seddon Ho EC2 242 A4
Seddon Rd SM4 202 B4
Seddon St WC1 94 B4 233 D1
Sedgebrook Rd SE3 143 D2
Sedgecombe Ave HA3 43 C4
Sedgefield Ct UB5 63 D3
Sedgeford Rd W12 111 D5
Sedgehill Rd SE6 185 D5
Sedgehill Sch SE6 185 D5
Sedgemere Ave N2 48 A6
Sedgemere Rd SE2 124 C3
Sedgemoor Dr RM10 81 C4
Sedge Rd N17 34 C3
Sedgeway SE6 164 D3
Sedgewick Ho SW19 156 D2
Sedgewood Cl BR2 208 D2
Sedgley Ho N4 72 B6
Sedgmoor Pl SE5 139 C5
Sedgwick Ave UB10 60 D1
Sedgwick Rd E10 76 A6
Sedgwick St E9 74 D3
Sedleigh Rd SW18 157 B5
Sedlescombe Rd SW6 135 C6 265 A6
Sedley Cl EN1 6 B5
Sedley Ct SE26 162 B2
Sedley Ho SE11 260 D2
Sedley Pl W1 238 C1
Sedum Cl NW9 44 D4
Seeley Dr SE21 183 C6
Seelig Ave NW9 46 A2
Seely Rd SW17 181 A4
Seething La EC3 117 C6 253 B6
SEETHING WELLS 197 D3
Seething Wells Halls of Residence KT6 197 C3
Seething Wells La KT6 197 C3
Sefton Ave
Edgware NW7 27 B5
Harrow HA3 24 B2
Sefton Cl BR5 211 D5
Sefton Ct TW5 129 D4
Sefton Lo 2 TW1 153 C5
Sefton Rd
Croydon CR0 206 A1
Orpington BR5 211 D5
Sefton St SW15 134 C2
Segal Cl SE23 163 A4
Sekforde St EC1 94 D3 241 C6
Sekhon Terr TW13 151 C1
Selan Gdns UB4 84 B2
Selbie Ave NW10 67 D3
Selborne 2 SW11 137 A2
Selborne Ave
DA5 169 A3
Little Ilford E12 78 C4
Walthamstow E17 53 B5
Selborne Gdns
Hendon NW4 46 A5
Wembley UB6 87 A5
Selborne Ho SE1 252 C1
Selborne Prim Sch UB6 86 D5
Selborne Rd
1 Camberwell SE5 139 B3
Ilford IG1 78 C6
Kingston u T KT3 177 C1
Palmers Green N14 16 A1
Sidcup DA14 190 B6
South Croydon CR0 221 D5
Walthamstow E17 53 C4
Wood Green N22 32 B2
Selborne Wlk E17 53 B5
Selborne Wlk Sh Ctr E17 53 B5
Selbourne Ave KT6 214 C5
Selbridge Ct SW19 179 C4
Selby Chase HA4 62 B6
Selby Cl
BR7 188 C4
Chessington KT9 214 A1
14 Newham E6 100 A2
Selby Ct TW2 152 B2
Selby Gdns UB1 85 C3
Selby Gn SM5 202 C2
Selby Ho 10 SW4 159 C5
Selby Rd
Ashford TW15 171 A4
Carshalton SM5 202 C2
Ealing W5 87 C3
Leyton E11 76 C5
Newham E13 99 B2
Penge SE20 184 A1
Tottenham N17 33 C4
Selby Sq 1 W10 91 A4
Selby St E1 96 A3
Selden Ho 2 SE15 140 C3
Selden Rd SE15 140 C3
Selden Wlk N7 72 B6
Seldon Ho
Nine Elms SW8 269 A3
Pimlico SW1 259 A1
Selena Ct N20 14 D1
SELHURST 205 B4
Selhurst Cl SW19 156 D3
Selhurst New Ct SE25 205 C3
Selhurst New Rd SE25 205 C3
Selhurst Park (Crystal Palace FC) SE25 205 C5
Selhurst Pl SE25 205 C3
Selhurst Rd
Edmonton N9 17 C1
South Norwood SE25 205 C4
Selhurst Sta SE25 205 C4
Selina Ho NW8 236 D6
Selinas La RM8 59 B2
Selkirk Ct N17 33 C1
Selkirk Ho
N1 233 C6
4 Stoke Newington N16 73 C5
Selkirk Rd
Twickenham TW2 152 A3
Upper Tooting SW17 180 C6
Sellers Hall Cl N3 29 C3
Sellincourt Prim Sch SW17 180 C4
Sellincourt Rd SW17 180 C4
Sellindge Cl BR3 185 B3
Sellons Ave NW10 89 D6
Sellsby Ct N11 31 B5
Sellwood Dr EN5 12 D6
Selma Ho 7 W12 90 B1
Selman Ho 3 E9 75 A2
SELSDON 223 A1
Selsdon Ave CR2 221 B2
Selsdon Cl KT6 198 A4
Selsdon High Sch CR2 222 D1
Selsdon Park Rd CR0, CR2 223 B1
Selsdon Rd
Newham E13 99 C5
South Croydon CR2 221 B2
Wanstead E11 55 A2
West Norwood SE27 182 D6
Willesden NW2 67 D6
Selsdon Road Ind Est CR2 221 B2
Selsdon Way E14 119 D3
Selsea Pl N16 73 C3
Selsey Cres DA16 146 D4
Selsey St E14 97 C2
Selvage La NW7 27 B6
Selway Cl HA5 40 B6
Selway Ho SW8 270 B2
Selwood Ho
Chislehurst BR7 189 A4
1 Stoke Newington N4 51 B2
Selwood Pl SW7 114 B1 256 C2
Selwood Rd
Cheam SM3 201 B1
Chessington KT9 213 D4
Croydon CR0 206 B1
Selwood Terr SW7 256 C2
Selworthy Cl E11 55 A4
Selworthy Ho SW11 266 D2
Selworthy Rd SE6 163 B1
Selwyn Ave
Chingford E4 36 A4
Ilford IG3 57 D3
Richmond TW9 132 B2
Selwyn Cl TW4 129 A1
Selwyn Cres DA16 146 B1
Selwyn Ct
Edgware HA8 26 D3
Lewisham SE3 142 D2
8 Richmond TW10 154 B6
Walthamstow E17 53 C4
Wembley HA9 67 A5
Selwyn Ho 3 SW15 156 D5
Selwyn Inf Sch E4 36 A4
Selwyn Jun Sch E4 36 A4
Selwyn Prim Sch E13 99 A6
Selwyn Rd
Bow E3 97 B5
Newham E13 99 B6
New Malden KT3 199 B4
Willesden NW10 67 C1
Semley Gate E9 75 B2
Semley Ho SW1 258 C3
Semley Pl
SW1 115 B2 258 C3
Thornton Heath SW16 182 B1
Semley Rd SW16 182 A1
Senate St SE15 140 C3
Senators Lo 31 E3 97 A5
Senator Wlk 2 SE28 123 B3
Sencler Ho SE2 146 D6
Sendall Ct 18 SW11 136 B2
Seneca Rd CR7 205 A5
Senga Rd SM6 203 A1
Senhouse Rd SM3 216 D5
Senior St W2 91 D2
Senlac Rd SE12 165 B3
Sennen Rd EN1 17 D4
Sennen Wlk SE9 166 A1
Senrab St E1 96 D1
Sentinel Cl UB5 85 A3
Sentinel Ho NW4 46 C5
Sentinel Sq NW4 46 C5
September Ct UB1 107 D5
September Way HA7 25 B4
Sequoia Cl WD23 8 B3
Sequoia Gdns BR6 211 D2
Sequoia Pk HA5 23 D4
Seraph Ct EC1 95 A4 235 A2
Serbin Cl E10 54 A2
Serenaders Rd 20 SW9 138 C3
Sergeant Ind Est The SW18 157 D5
Serica Ct 14 SE10 142 A5
Serjeants' Inn EC4 241 B1
Serlby Ct W14 254 C6
Serle St WC2 94 B1 240 D2
Sermon La EC4 242 A1
Serpentine Ct 10 SE16 118 D4

Serpentine Gallery* W2 114 B4 246 D2
Serpentine Rd W2 114 D5 247 C3
Serpentine The* W2 114 C5 247 B3
Service Route No 1 E15 76 B1
Service Route No 2 1 E15 76 B1
Service Route No 3 2 E15 76 B1
Serviden Dr BR1 187 D2
Servite Ho
Beckenham BR3 185 B2
Bromley BR1 188 B1
East Barnet N14 15 B6
Lewisham SE13 141 D4
Penge SE26 184 C4
Worcester Pk KT4 215 D6
Servite RC Prim Sch SW10 136 A6 266 A6
Servius Ct 2 TW8 131 D5
Sessions Terr CR4 180 D2
Setchell Rd SE1 117 D2 263 C4
Setchell Way SE1 263 C4
Seth St 25 SE16 118 C4
Seton Ct 3 NW9 46 A5
Seton Gdns RM9 80 C1
Settle Point 11 E13 99 A5
Settlers Ct 11 E14 120 B6
Settles St E1 96 A1
Settrington Rd SW6 135 D3
Seven Acres
Carshalton SM5 218 C6
Northwood HA6 22 A4
Seven Dials WC2 94 A1 240 A1
SEVEN KINGS 57 D2
Seven Kings High Sch IG2 57 B2
Seven Kings Rd IG3 79 D6
Seven Kings Sta IG3 57 C1
Seven Kings Way KT2 176 A2
Seven Mills Prim Sch E14 119 C4
Sevenoaks Rd
BR6 227 D4
Catford SE4 163 B5
Sevenoaks Way BR5 190 C1
Seven Sisters N15 51 D4
Seven Sisters Prim Sch N15 51 B4
Seven Sisters Rd
Finsbury Pk N4 72 D6
Stoke Newington N4, N7, N15 51 A2
Seven Sisters Sta N15 51 C4
Seven Stars Cnr W12 112 A3
Seven Stars Yd E1 243 D4
Seventh Ave
Hayes UB3 106 A5
Ilford E12 78 B4
Seven Ways Par IG2 56 C4
Severnake Cl E14 119 C2
Severn Ave 2 W10 91 A4
Severn Ct 11 KT2 175 D2
Severn Dr
Enfield EN1 6 A5
Hinchley Wood KT10 213 A6
Severn Way NW10 67 D3
Severus Rd SW11 136 C1
Seville Ho 11 E1 118 A5
Seville Mews N1 73 C1
Seville St SW1 247 D1
Sevington Rd NW4 46 B3
Sevington St W9 91 D3
Seward Rd
Penge BR3 184 D1
West Ealing W7 109 A4
Seward St EC1 95 A4 235 A1
SEWARDSTONEBURY 20 C6
Sewardstone Gdns E4 19 D6
Sewardstone Rd
Chingford E4 19 D6
South Hackney E2 96 C5
Sewdley St E5 74 D5
Sewell Ho 7 N16 73 C3
Sewell Rd SE2 124 B4
Sewell St E13 99 A4
Sextant Ave E14 120 B2
Sexton Ct 7 E14 120 B6
Sexton's Ho 5 SE13 142 A6
Seychelle Ct BR3 185 D3
Seymour Ave
Tottenham N17 34 A1
West Barnes SM4 200 D2
Seymour Cl
East Molesey KT8 196 A4
Pinner HA5 23 B2
Seymour Ct
Chingford E4 20 D2
Dollis Hill NW2 68 B6
Muswell Hill N10 31 A1
Putney SW15 134 B1
Southgate N21 16 B5
Upper Clapton N16 52 A1
Seymour Dr BR2 210 B1
Seymour Gdns
Brockley SE4 141 A2
Feltham TW13 172 C6
Kingston u T KT5 198 B4
Redbridge IG1 56 B1
Ruislip HA4 40 D1
Twickenham TW1 153 B4
Seymour Ho
Bloomsbury WC1 240 A6
1 Clapham SW8 137 C3
Ruislip HA4 40 A5
Somers Town NW1 232 D1
Seymour Lo 14 KT1 175 D2
Seymour Mews W1 238 A2
Seymour Pl
Croydon SE25 206 B5
Paddington W1 92 D1 237 C2
Seymour Rd
Acton W4 111 A2
Carshalton CR4 203 A2
Chingford E4 19 D3
East Molesey KT8 196 A4
Edmonton N9 18 B2
Finchley N3 29 D3
Hampton TW12 174 A5
Harringay N8 50 D4
Newham E6 99 D6
Teddington KT1 175 D2
Wallington SM5 219 A3
Walthamstow E10 53 B1
Wandsworth SW18 157 B5
Wimbledon SW19 156 D1
Seymour St
Paddington W1 92 D1 237 D1
Woolwich SE18 123 A3
Seymour Terr SE20 184 B2
Seymour Villas SE20 184 A2
Seymour Way TW16 171 C3
Seymour Wlk SW10 136 A6 266 A6
Seyssel St E14 120 A2
Shaa Rd W3 111 B6
Shabana Ct 3 W12 112 B5
Shacklegate La TW11 174 C6
Shackleton Cl SE23 162 B2
Shackleton Ct
3 Dulwich SE21 161 B2
2 Isle of Dogs E14 119 C1
4 Shepherd's Bush W12 112 B4
7 Stanwell TW19 148 A5
Shackleton Ho
5 Stonebridge NW10 67 B1
5 Wapping E1 118 C5
Shackleton Lo SW16 181 D5
Shackleton Rd UB1 107 B6
SHACKLEWELL 73 D4
Shacklewell Ho 3 E8 73 D4
Shacklewell La E8 73 D3
Shacklewell Prim Sch E8 73 D4
Shacklewell Rd N16 73 D4
Shacklewell Row E8 73 D4
Shacklewell St 30 E2 95 D4
Shadbolt Ave E4 35 A5
Shadbolt Cl KT4 215 D6
Shad Thames SE1 117 D4 253 D2
SHADWELL 118 C6
Shadwell Ct UB5 85 B5
Shadwell Dr UB5 85 B4
Shadwell Gdns E1 118 C6
Shadwell Pierhead E1 118 C6
Shadwell Pl 1 E1 118 C6
Shadwell Sta E1 118 B6
Shady Bush Cl WD23 8 A4
Shaef Way TW11 175 A3
Shaftesbury Ave
Enfield EN3 6 D3
Feltham TW14 150 A5
Kenton HA3 44 A3
New Barnet EN5 2 A1
Southall UB2 107 C3
W1 115 D6 249 D6
Shaftesbury Ave continued
West Harrow HA1, HA2 42 A1
Shaftesbury Circ HA2 42 A1
Shaftesbury Ct
Borough The SE1 262 C6
1 Herne Hill SE5 139 B1
Ilford RM6 58 C2
Newham E6 100 C1
Shoreditch N1 235 C3
Streatham SW16 159 D1
3 Thamesmead SE28 124 C5
Shaftesbury Ctr NW10 90 D3
Shaftesbury Gdns NW10 89 C3
Shaftesbury High Sch HA3 23 D2
Shaftesbury Ho
11 Canning Town E16 98 D1
Croydon SE25 206 A3
13 Stoke Newington N16 73 C5
Upper Tooting SW17 180 B6
W2 245 D6
Shaftesbury Lo 9 E14 97 D1
Shaftesbury Mews
2 Clapham Pk SW4 159 C6
W8 255 B5
Shaftesbury Park Chambers 1 SW11 137 A2
Shaftesbury Point E13 99 B5
Shaftesbury Prim Sch E7 77 C1
Shaftesbury Rd
Beckenham BR3 185 B1
Carshalton SM5 202 C2
Chingford E4 20 B3
Edmonton N18 33 D4
Finsbury Pk N4, N19 50 A1
Leyton E10 53 C1
Richmond TW9 132 A2
Upton E7 77 C1
Walthamstow E17 53 D3
Shaftesbury St N1 235 C3
Shaftesburys The IG11 101 A5
Shaftesbury Way TW2 152 B1
Shaftesbury Waye UB4 84 C1
Shafteswood Ct SW17 158 D1
Shafto Mews SW1 257 D5
Shafton Rd E9 96 D6
Shaftsbury Park Prim Sch SW11 137 A3
Shafts Ct EC3 243 A1
Shahjalal Ho 18 E2 96 A5
Shakespeare Ave
7 Becontree NW10 89 B6
Feltham TW14 150 A5
Friern Barnet N11 31 C5
Hayes UB4 84 B2
Shakespeare Cl HA3 44 C2
Shakespeare Cres E12 78 B2
Shakespeare Ct EN5 1 D2
Shakespeare Dr HA3 44 B3
Shakespeare Gdns N2 48 D5
Shakespeare Ho
1 Erith DA17 125 B1
3 Hackney E9 74 C1
Osidge N14 15 D2
Shakespeare Rd
Acton W3 111 A5
Brixton SE24 138 D1
DA7 147 A4
Ealing W7 108 D6
Finchley N3 29 C2
Higham Hill E17 34 D1
Mill Hill NW7 28 A6
Shakespeare's Globe Theatre (site of)* SE1 252 B4
Shakespeare Twr EC2 242 B4
Shakespeare Way TW13 172 C6
Shakspeare Mews 7 N16 73 C4
Shakspeare Wlk N16 73 C4
Shalbourne Sq E9 75 B2
Shalcomb St SW10 136 A6 266 B5
Shalden Ho SW15 155 D5
Shaldon Dr
Ruislip HA4 62 C5
West Barnes SM4 201 A4
Shaldon Rd HA8 26 B1
Shalfleet Dr W10 112 D6
Shalford
Willesden Green NW10 90 A6
Shalford continued
3 Woodford IG8 37 C4
Shalford Cl BR6 227 A4
Shalford Ct N1 234 C4
Shalford Ho SE1 262 D6
Shalimar Gdns W3 111 A6
Shalimar Lo W3 111 A6
Shalimar Rd W3 111 A6
Shallons Rd SE9 188 D6
Shalstone Rd SW14, TW9 132 D2
Shalston Villas KT5, KT6 198 B3
Shamrock Ct E7 77 D3
Shamrock Ho
East Barnet N14 15 B4
Forest Hill SE26 184 A6
Shamrock Rd CR0 204 B3
Shamrock St SW4 137 D2
Shamrock Way N14 15 B3
Shandon Ct SE4 141 A3
Shandon Rd SW4 159 C5
Shand St SE1 117 C4 253 B2
Shandy St E1 96 D3
Shane Ct EN2 5 A3
Shan Ho WC1 240 C5
Shanklin Gdns WD19 22 C6
Shanklin Ho E17 35 B1
Shanklin Rd
Hornsey N8 49 D4
Tottenham Hale N15 52 A5
Shannon Cl
Cricklewood NW2 68 D5
Southall UB2 106 D1
Shannon Cnr KT3 200 A5
Shannon Cnr Ret Pk KT3 200 A5
Shannon Commercial Ctr KT3 200 A5
Shannon Ct
Croydon CR0 205 A1
11 Peckham SE15 139 D5
Stoke Newington N16 73 C5
Willesden NW10 68 A2
Shannon Gr SW9 138 B1
Shannon Pl NW8 92 C5 230 B4
Shannon Way BR3 185 D4
Shanti Ct SW18 157 C3
Shap Cres SM5 202 D1
Shapland Way N13 32 B5
Shapla Prim Sch E1 118 A6
Shapwick Cl N11 30 D5
Shardcroft Ave SE24 160 D6
Shardeloes Rd SE14 141 B3
Shard's Sq SE15 140 A6
Sharebourne Ho SW2 160 C6
Sharland Cl CR7 204 C3
Sharman Ct DA14 190 A6
Sharman Ho 13 E14 98 A1
Sharnbrooke Cl DA16 146 C2
Sharnbrook Ho W6 265 A6
Sharon Cl KT6 197 C1
Sharon Ct 1 N12 30 A4
Sharon Gdns E9 96 C6
Sharon Rd
Chiswick W4 111 B1
Enfield EN3 7 A3
Sharpe Cl W7 86 D2
Sharp Ho SW8 137 B2
Sharples Hall St 8 NW1 70 D1
Sharpness Cl UB4 85 A2
Sharpness Ct 2 SE15 139 D5
Sharps La HA4 39 B2
Sharratt St SE15 140 C6
Sharsted St SE17 116 D1 261 C1
Sharvel La UB5 84 B6
Sharwood WC1 233 D3
Shaver's Pl SW1 249 C5
Shaw Ave IG11 103 A5
Shawbrooke Rd SE9 143 D1
Shawbury Cl 9 NW9 27 C2
Shawbury Ct SE22 161 D6
Shawbury Rd SE22 161 D6
Shaw Cl
Bushey WD23 8 C2
Woolwich SE28 124 B5
Shaw Cotts SE23 163 A1
Shaw Cres 6 E14 97 A1
Shaw Ct
8 Acton Green W3 111 A3
12 Battersea SW11 136 B2
Cheam SM4 202 A2
Upper Holloway N19 72 A6
Shaw Dr KT12 194 C2
Shawfield Ct UB7 104 A3
Shawfield Pk BR1 187 D1
Shawfield St SW3 114 C1 257 B1
Shawford Ct 8 SW15 156 A4
Shawford Rd KT19 215 B2
Shaw Gdns IG11 103 A5
Shaw Ho
6 Erith DA17 125 B1
5 Newham E16 122 C5
Shaw Path BR1 164 D1
Shaw Rd
Camberwell SE22 139 C1
Catford BR1 164 D1
Enfield EN3 6 D4
Shaw Sq E17 35 A2
Shaws Wood Cotts EN4 3 C3
Shaw Way SM6 220 A1
Shearing Dr SM4 202 A2
Shearling Way N7 72 A2
Shearman Rd SE3 142 D2
Shears Ct TW16 171 C3
Shearsmith Ho 19 E1 118 A6
Shears The TW16 171 C3
Shears Way TW16 171 C2
Shearwater Cl IG11 102 A4
Shearwater Ct 24 SE8 141 B6
Shearwater Rd SM1 217 B3
Shearwater Way UB4 84 D1
Sheaveshill Ave NW9 45 C5
Sheaveshill Ct NW9 45 C5
Sheaveshill Par NW9 45 C5
Sheba Ct N17 34 A4
Sheba Pl E1 243 D5
Sheen Common Dr SW14, TW10 154 C6
Sheen Court Rd TW10 132 C1
Sheen Ct TW10 132 C1
Sheendale Rd TW9 132 B1
Sheenewood SE26 184 B6
Sheen Gate Gdns SW14 133 A1
Sheengate Mans SW14 133 B1
Sheen Gr N1 94 C6 234 A6
Sheen La SW14 133 A1
Sheen Mount Prim Sch SW14 154 D6
Sheen Pk TW10, TW9 132 A1
Sheen Rd
Orpington BR5 211 D5
Richmond TW10, TW9 132 B1
Sheen Way SM6 220 B3
Sheen Wood SW14 155 A6
Sheepcote Cl TW5 128 A5
Sheepcote La SW11 136 D3
Sheepcote Rd HA1 42 D3
Sheepcotes Rd RM6 59 A5
Sheephouse Way KT3 199 C2
Sheep La E8 96 B6
Sheepwalk TW17 192 B3
Sheep Walk Mews 7 SW19 179 A4
Sheerness Mews E16 122 D4
Sheerwater Rd E16 99 D2
Sheffield Ho 15 SE15 139 D4
Sheffield Rd TW14, TW6 149 A6
Sheffield Sq 2 E3 97 B4
Sheffield St WC2 240 C1
Sheffield Terr W8 113 C5 245 B3
Sheffield Way TW14, TW6 149 B6
Shefton Rise HA6 22 A3
Shelbey Ct BR1 186 D2
Shelbourne Cl HA5 41 B6
Shelbourne Ho 20 N19 49 D2
Shelbourne Rd N17 34 B2
Shelburne Ct SW15 156 D6
Shelburne Dr TW4 151 C5
Shelburne Ho 9 SW16 181 C5
Shelburne Rd N7 72 B4
Shelbury Cl DA14 168 A1
Shelbury Rd SE22 162 B6
Sheldon Ave N6 48 D3
Sheldon Cl
Penge SE20 184 B2
SE12 165 B6
Sheldon Ct
Barnet EN5 1 D1
SW8 270 A3
Sheldon Ho
Chingford E4 36 C4
9 Homerton E9 74 D2
Teddington TW11 175 A4
Sheldon Pl E2 96 B5
Sheldon Rd
Cricklewood NW2 68 D4
DA7 147 B4
Dagenham RM9 81 A1
Edmonton N18 33 C6
Sheldon Sq W2 236 B3
Sheldon St CR0 221 A5
Sheldrake Cl E16 122 B5
Sheldrake Ho 15 SE16 118 D2
Sheldrake Pl W8 113 C4 245 A2
Sheldrick Cl CR4 180 B1
Shelduck Cl E15 76 D3
Shelduck Ct 37 SE8 141 B6
Sheldwich Terr BR2 210 A3
Shelford 20 KT1 176 C1
Shelford Ct 7 E5 52 B1
Shelford Pl N16 73 B5
Shelford Rd EN5 12 C5
Shelford Rise SE19 183 D3
Shelgate Rd SW11 158 D6
Shell Cl BR2 210 A3
Shell Ctr SE1 250 D3
Shellduck Cl NW9 27 C1
Shelley N8 50 A6
Shelley Ave
Greenford UB6 86 B4
Plashet E12 78 A2
Shelley Cl
BR6 227 C5
Edgware HA8 26 C6
Greenford UB6 86 B4
Hayes UB4 84 A2
Peckham SE15 140 B3
Shelley Cres
Heston TW5 128 D4
Southall UB1 85 B1
Shelley Ct
Finsbury Pk N4 50 B1
9 Kingston u T KT2 175 D6
SW3 267 D6
13 Walthamstow E10 53 D2
8 Wanstead E11 55 A5
Wembley HA0 65 C4
West Barnes KT3 200 A4
Shelley Dr DA16 145 C4
Shelley Gdns HA0 65 C6
Shelley Ho
21 Bethnal Green E2 96 C4
Chelsea SW1 269 A6
9 Stoke Newington N16 73 C4
Walworth SE17 262 B2
Shelley Rd NW10 89 B6
Shelley Way SW17 180 B4
Shellgrove Rd N16 73 C3
Shellness Rd E5 74 B3
Shell Rd SE13 141 D2
Shellwood Rd SW11 136 D3
Shelly Lo EN2 5 B4
Shelmerdine Cl E3 97 C2
Shelson Ave TW13 171 D6
Shelton Ct N21 16 C4
Shelton Rd SW19 179 C2
Shelton St WC2 94 A1 240 A1
Shene Bldg EC1 241 A4
Shene Sch SW14 133 C1
Shenfield Ho 3 SE18 143 D5
Shenfield Rd IG8 37 B3
Shenfield St N1 95 C5
Shenley Ave HA4 39 D1
Shenley Ho 3 SW16 182 B6
Shenley Rd
Camberwell SE5 139 C4
Heston TW5 129 A4
Shenstone W13 109 C5
Shenstone Gdns IG2 57 D4
Shenstone Ho SW16 181 C5
Shepard Ho 18 SW11 136 B2
Sheperdess Pl N1 235 B2
Shepherd Cl
Feltham TW13 173 A6
W1 248 A6
Shepherdess Wlk N1 95 A5 235 B3
Shepherd Ho
Barnsbury N7 72 A2
10 Poplar E14 97 D1
Shepherd Mkt W1 248 C3
SHEPHERD'S BUSH 112 B5
Shepherd's Bush Gn W12 112 C4
Shepherd's Bush Market W12 112 C4
Shepherd's Bush Mkt Sta W12 112 C5
Shepherd's Bush Pl W12 112 D4

Shepherd's Bush Rd
W6 112 C3
Shepherd's Bush Sta
W12 112 D4
Shepherds Cl
Dagenham RM6 58 D5
Orpington BR6 227 D5
Shepperton TW17 192 D3
Stanmore HA7 25 A5
Shepherd's Cl N6 49 B3
Shepherds Ct
8 Hammersmith
W12 112 D4
13 Harrow HA1 42 D3
Shepherds Gn BR7 189 B3
Shepherd's Hill N6 49 C3
Shepherds La SE28 123 C5
Shepherd's La E9 74 D2
Shepherds Leas SE9 145 B1
Shepherds Path UB5 63 A2
Shepherds Pl W1 248 A6
Shepherd St
W1 115 B5 248 C3
Shepherds Way CR2 222 D1
Shepherds Wlk
Bushey WD23 8 B2
Dollis Hill NW2 68 A6
Shepherd's Wlk NW3 70 B4
Shepiston La UB3 105 A1
Shepley Cl SM5 219 A5
Shepley Ct SW16 181 C6
Shepley Mews EN3 7 C6
Sheppard Cl
Enfield EN1 6 B5
Kingston u T KT6 198 A5
Sheppard Dr SE16 118 B1
Sheppard Ho
31 Hackney E2 96 A5
8 Streatham SW2 160 C3
Sheppard's Ct
Harrow HA1 42 C2
Wembley UB6 64 D2
Sheppard St E16 98 D3
SHEPPERTON 193 A3
Shepperton Bsns Park
TW17 193 A4
Shepperton Court Dr
TW17 192 D4
Shepperton Ct TW17 192 D3
SHEPPERTON
GREEN 192 D5
Shepperton Rd
Littleton TW17,
TW18 192 A5
Orpington BR5 211 A3
Shoreditch N1 95 B6 235 C6
Shepperton Sta
TW17 193 A4
Shepperton Studios
TW17 192 B6
Sheppey Gdns RM9 80 C1
Sheppey Ho 16 E5 74 B4
Sheppey Rd RM9 80 C1
Shepton Ct SW11 266 D2
Shepton Hos 11 E2 96 C4
Sherard Ct N19 72 A5
Sherard Ho 24 E9 74 C1
Sherard Rd SE9 166 A6
Sheraton Bsns Ctr
UB6 87 C5
Sheraton Cl WD6 10 B6
Sheraton Ho SW1 268 D6
Sheraton Lo HA3 42 C6
Sheraton St W1 239 C1
Sheraton The 22 KT6 198 A4
Sherborne Ave
Enfield EN3 6 C3
Southall UB2 107 C2
Sherborne Cl UB4 84 C1
Sherborne Cres SM5 202 C2
Sherborne Ct SE20 184 C1
Sherborne Gdns
Ealing W13 87 B2
Queensbury NW9 44 C6
Sherborne Ho
Pimlico SW1 258 D2
South Lambeth SW8 270 C3
Sherborne La EC4 252 D6
Sherborne Rd
BR5 211 D4
Cheam SM3 201 C1
Chessington KT9 214 A3
East Bedfont TW14 149 B3
Sherborne St
N1 95 B6 235 C6
Sherboro Rd 1 N15 51 D3
Sherbourne Ct
1 Hampton TW12 173 C2
9 Sutton SM2 218 A2
SW5 255 C4
Sherbourne Gdns
TW17 193 C2
Sherbourne Pl HA7 25 A4
Sherbrooke Cl DA7 147 C1
Sherbrooke Ho 9 E2 96 C5
Sherbrooke Rd
SW6 135 A5 264 B3
Sherbrooke Terr SW6 264 B3
Sherbrooke Way KT4 200 B2
Sherbrook Gdns N21 16 D4
Sherbrook Ho 2 N3 29 D3
Shere Cl KT9 213 D3
Sheredan Rd E4 36 C5
Shere Ho SE1 262 C6
Shere Lo 1 SW19 180 C3
Shere Rd IG2 56 C4
Sherfield Cl KT3 198 D5
Sherfield Gdns SW15 155 D5
Sheridan N8 50 C5
Sheridan Bldgs WC2 240 B1
Sheridan Cl UB10 83 A3
Sheridan Cres BR7 188 D1
Sheridan Ct
Ealing W7 108 D6
Earl's Ct SW5 255 C3
Harrow HA1 42 B3
Hounslow TW4 151 A6
South Hampstead NW6 70 A1
South Lambeth SW9 270 D1
Sheridan Gdns HA3 43 D3
Sheridan Ho
SE11 261 B3
7 Stoke Newington
N16 73 C5
Sheridan Lo
Barnet EN5 1 D1
Bromley BR2 209 C5
East Barnet N14 15 B4
Sheridan Mews E11 55 B3
Sheridan Pl
Barnes SW13 133 D2
Hampton TW12 174 A2
Harrow HA1 42 C2
Sheridan Rd
Belvedere DA17 125 C2
DA7 147 A2
Leyton E7 76 D5
Little Ilford E12 78 B3
Merton SW19 179 B2
Richmond TW10 153 C1
Sheridan St 34 E1 96 B1
Sheridan Terr UB5 63 D3
Sheridan Way 5 BR3 185 B2
Sheridan Wlk
Golders Green NW11 47 C3
Wallington SM5 218 D3
Sheringdale Prim Sch
SW18 157 B3
Sheringham NW8 229 D6
Sheringham Ave
Feltham TW13 150 A1
Little Ilford E12 78 B3
Southgate N14 15 D5
Twickenham TW2 151 C3
Sheringham Ct 1 N3 29 C2
Sheringham Dr IG11 80 A3
Sheringham Ho NW1 237 B4
Sheringham Jun Sch
E12 78 B4
Sheringham Mews 4
SW18 158 A2
Sheringham Rd
Islington N7 72 C2
Penge SE20 206 C6
Sheringham Twr
UB1 107 D6
Sherington Ave HA5 23 C3
Sherington Prim Sch
SE7 143 B6
Sherington Rd SE7 143 B6
Sheriton Ct SM1 217 C5
Sherland Rd TW1 152 D3
Sherleys Ct HA4 61 C6
Sherlies Ave BR6 227 C6
Sherlock Ct NW8 229 C6
Sherlock Holmes Mus*
NW1 92 D3 237 D5
Sherlock Mews W1 238 A4
Sherman Gdns RM6 58 C3
Sherman Rd BR1 187 A2
Shernhall St E17 54 A5
Shernwood Ho 1 E18 55 A5
Sherrard Rd E7, E12 77 D2
Sherrards Way EN5 13 D5
Sherren Ho 35 E1 96 C3
Sherrick Green Rd
NW10 68 B3
Sherriff Ct NW6 69 C2
Sherriff Rd NW6 69 C2
Sherringham Ave N17 34 A1
Sherrin Rd E10 75 D4
Sherrock Gdns NW4 46 A5
Sherry Mews IG11 79 B1
Sherston Ct
Finsbury WC1 234 A1
Newington SE1 261 D4
Sherwin Ho 1 SE11 138 C6
Sherwin Rd SE14 140 D4
Sherwood
3 Barnet EN5 1 D1
Brondesbury NW6 69 A1
Long Ditton KT6 213 D6
Sherwood Ave
Greenford UB6 64 C3
Hayes UB4 84 B3
Mitcham SW16 181 D2
Ruislip HA4 39 C3
Wanstead E18 55 B6
Sherwood Cl
Barnes SW13 134 B2
DA5 168 C5
Ealing W13 109 B5
Walthamstow E17 35 B1
Sherwood Ct
11 Battersea SW11 136 A2
Colney Hatch N12 30 C5
2 South Croydon CR2 221 A3
St Johns SE13 141 D3
Sutton SM1 217 C3
W1 237 C3
6 West Wickham BR4 207 D1
Sherwood Gdns
Barking IG11 79 B1
Bermondsey SE16 118 B1
Millwall E14 119 C2
Sherwood Hall 7 N2 48 A6
Sherwood Ho N4 51 A2
Sherwood Park Ave
DA15 168 B5
Sherwood Park Prim Sch
DA15 168 B5
Sherwood Park Rd
Mitcham CR4 203 D5
Sutton SM1 217 C3
Sherwood Park Sch
SM6 219 D5
Sherwood Rd
Croydon CR0 206 B1
DA16 145 C2
Hampton TW12 174 A5
Harrow HA2 64 A6
Hendon NW4 46 C6
Ilford IG6 57 B5
Merton SW19 179 B3
Sherwood Sch The
CR4 203 C5
Sherwood St
W1 249 B6
Whetstone N20 14 B1
Sherwood Terr N20 14 B1
Sherwood Way BR4 224 A6
Shetland Cl WD6 11 B5
Shetland Rd
Bow E3 97 B5
East Bedfont TW6 149 A5
Shield Dr TW8 131 A6
Shieldhall St SE2 124 C2
Shield Rd TW15 171 B6
Shifford Path SE23 162 D1
Shillaker Ct W3 111 D5
Shillibeer Ct N18 34 B5
Shillibeer Pl W1 237 B3
Shillingford Cl NW7 28 D3
Shillingford Ho 40 E3 97 D4
Shillingford St 23 N1 72 D1
Shilling Pl TW8 109 A5
Shillingstone Ho W14 254 B5
Shine Ho 3 N3 29 D3
Shinfield St W12 90 C1
Shinglewell Rd DA8 147 C5
Shinners Cl SE25 206 A4
Shipka Rd SW12 159 B3
Ship La SW14 133 A3
Shiplake Ct SW17 180 B6
Shiplake Ho 45 E2 95 D4
Shipley Ct SE20 184 A1
Shipley Ho 32 SW8 137 D3
Shipman Rd
Forest Hill SE23 162 D2
Newham E16 99 C1
Ship & Mermaid Row
SE1 253 A2
Ship St SE8 141 C4
Ship Tavern Pas EC3 253 A6
Shipton Cl RM8 80 D5
Shipton Ho
7 Camden Town NW5 71 A2
14 Haggerston E2 95 D5
Shipton Rd UB8 60 B4
Shipton St E2 95 D4
Shipwright Rd SE16 119 A4
Shipwright Yd SE1 253 A3
Shirburn Cl SE23 162 C4
Shirbutt St E14 119 D6
Shirebrook Rd SE3 143 D2
Shire Ct
DA18 124 D3
Ewell KT17 215 D1
Shirehall Cl NW4 46 D3
Shirehall Gdns NW4 46 D3
Shirehall La NW4 46 D3
Shirehall Pk NW4 46 D3
Shire Ho E11 76 D5
Shire Horse Way
TW7 130 D2
Shire La BR6 227 B2
Shiremeade WD6 10 B6
Shire Mews TW2 152 A5
Shire Pl
12 Brentford TW8 131 C5
Wandsworth SW18 158 A4
Shires The TW10 176 A6
Shirland Mews W9 91 B4
Shirland Rd W9 91 C3
SHIRLEY 206 C1
Shirley Ave
Carshalton SM1 218 C4
Croydon CR0 206 D1
DA5 168 D3
Shirley Church Rd
CR0 223 A5
Shirley Cl
Hounslow TW3 152 A6
Walthamstow E17 53 D4
Shirley Cres BR3 207 A5
Shirley Ct
8 Ealing W13 109 A5
Ilford IG2 57 B4
Kingsbury NW9 45 B4
2 South Norwood
SW16 182 B3
Thornton Heath SW16 204 B6
Shirley Dr TW3 152 A6
Shirley Gdns
Barking IG11 79 C2
Ealing W7 108 D5
Shirley Gr
Clapham SW11 137 A2
Ponders End N9 18 D4
Shirley High Sch
Performing Arts Coll
CR0 222 D5
Shirley Hills Rd CR0 222 D3
Shirley Ho 18 SE5 139 B5
Shirley House Dr SE7 143 C5
Shirley Hts 6 DA6 147 A1
Shirley Lo 4 SE26 185 A6
SHIRLEY OAKS 207 A1
Shirley Oaks Hospl
CR0 206 C2
Shirley Oaks Rd CR0 222 D6
Shirley Park Rd CR0 206 C1
Shirley Rd
Acton W4 111 B4
Croydon CR0 206 B1
Enfield EN2 5 A2
Sidcup DA15 167 C1
Stratford E15 76 C1
Shirley St E16 98 D1
Shirley Way CR0 223 B5
Shirlock Rd NW3 70 D4
Shirwell Cl NW7 28 D3
Shobden Rd N17 33 B2
Shobroke Cl NW2 68 C5
Shoebury Rd E6 78 B1
Shoe La EC4 94 C1 241 B2
Shoelands Ct NW9 45 B6
Shona Ho E16 99 C2
Shooters Ave HA3 43 C5
SHOOTERS HILL 145 A4
Shooters Hill SE18 144 C4
Shooters Hill Rd
Blackheath Vale SE3,
SE10 142 C4
SE18, SE3, SE7 143 D5
Shooters Rd EN2 4 D4
Shoot-Up Hill NW2 69 A2
Shopstop SW11 136 C1
Shore Bsns Ctr 31 E9 74 C1
Shore Cl
Feltham TW14 150 A4
Hampton TW12 173 A5
Shorediche Cl UB10 60 B5
SHOREDITCH 95 B5
Shoreditch Ct 2 E8 73 D1
Shoreditch High St
E2 95 C3 243 B6
Shoreditch Ho N1 235 D1
Shore Gr TW13 151 C2
Shoreham Cl
Croydon CR0 206 C3
DA5 168 D3
Wandsworth SW18 157 D6
Shoreham Rd BR5 190 B1
Shoreham Rd (E)
TW6 148 A6
Shoreham Rd (W)
TW6 148 A6
Shoreham Way BR2 209 A3
Shore Ho SW8 137 B2
Shore Mews 30 E9 74 C1
Shore Pl E9 74 C1
Shore Point 2 IG9 21 B2
Shore Rd E9 74 C1
Shore Way 26 SW9 138 C3
Shorncliffe Rd
SE1 117 D1 263 C2
Shorndean St SE6 164 A3
Shorne Cl 3 DA15 168 B5
Shornefield Cl BR1 210 C6
Shornells Way SE2 124 C1
Shorrolds Rd
SW6 135 B5 264 D4
Shortcroft Mead Ct
NW10 68 A3
Shortcroft Rd KT17 215 D1
Shortcrofts Rd RM9 81 B2
Shorter St
EC3 117 D6 253 D6
Shortgate N12 29 B6
Short La TW15, TW19 148 B3
SHORTLANDS 208 C6
Shortlands
Brook Green W6 112 D2
Harlington UB3 127 B6
Shortlands Cl
DA17 125 B3
Edmonton N18 17 B1
Shortlands Gdns BR2 186 C1
Shortlands Gr BR2 208 B6
Shortlands Rd
Beckenham BR2, BR3 208 C6
Kingston u T KT2 176 B3
Walthamstow E10 53 D2
Shortlands Sta BR2 186 C1
Short Path SE18 144 D6
Short Rd
Chiswick W4 133 C6
Leyton E11 76 C6
Stanwell TW19 148 A5
Shorts Croft NW9 44 D5
Shorts Gdns
WC2 94 A1 240 A1
Shorts Rd SM5 218 C3
Short St
7 Hendon NW4 46 C5
SE1 251 B2
Shortway SE9 144 A2
Short Way
Colney Hatch N12 30 C4
Twickenham TW2 152 A4
Shotfield SM6 219 B2
Shott Cl SM1 218 A3
Shottendane Rd
SW6 135 C4 265 A2
Shottery Cl SE9 166 A1
Shottfield Ave SW14 133 C1
Shottsford 1 W11 91 C1
Shoulder of Mutton Alley
10 E14 119 A6
Shouldham St
W1 92 C2 237 B3
Showers Way UB3 106 A5
Shrapnel Cl SE18 144 A5
Shrapnel Rd SE9 144 B2
Shreveport Ho 23 N19 49 D2
Shrewsbury Ave
Harrow HA3 44 A5
Mortlake SW14 133 B1
Shrewsbury Cl KT6 214 A6
Shrewsbury Ho
Chelsea SW3 267 A5
Kennington SE11 270 D5
Shrewsbury House Sch
KT6 214 A6
Shrewsbury La SE18 144 D4
Shrewsbury Mews 33
W2 91 C2
Shrewsbury Rd
Beckenham BR3 207 A6
Carshalton SM5 202 C2
Friern Barnet N11 31 D4
Harlington TW14, TW6 149 B5
Notting Hill W2 91 C1
Plashet E7 77 D2
Shrewsbury St W10 90 C3
Shrewsbury Wlk 9
TW7 131 A2
Shrewton Rd SW17 180 D3
Shri Swaminarayan
Mandir* NW10 67 B2
Shroffold Rd BR1 164 D1
Shropshire Cl CR4 204 A5
Shropshire Ct W7 86 D1
Shropshire Ho WC1 239 B5
Shropshire Rd N22 32 B3
Shroton St
NW1 92 C2 237 B4
Shrubberies The
Ilford IG2 57 D4
Woodford E18 37 A1
Shrubbery Cl N1 235 B5
Shrubbery Gdns N21 16 D4
Shrubbery Rd
Edmonton N9 18 A1
Southall UB1 107 C5
Streatham SW16 182 A6
Shrubbery The
2 Surbiton KT6 198 A1
7 Wanstead E11 55 B4
Shrub Ct 5 SM2 218 A2
Shrubland Gr KT4 216 C5
Shrubland Rd
Hackney E8 96 A6
Leyton E10 53 C2
Walthamstow E17 53 C4
Shrublands Ave CR0 223 C4
Shrublands Cl
Forest Hill SE26 162 C1
Whetstone N20 14 B2
Shrubsall Cl SE9 166 A3
Shrubs Ho SW1 259 D3
Shurland Ave EN4 14 B5
Shurland Gdns SE15 139 D5
Shurlock Dr BR6 227 A4
Shuters Sq W14 254 C1
Shuttle Cl DA15 167 D4
Shuttlemead DA5 169 B4
Shuttle St E1 96 A3
Shuttleworth Rd
SW11 136 C3
Sibella Rd SW4 137 D3
Sibford Ct 5 CR4 202 D6
Sibley Cl
Bexley DA6 169 A6
Bromley BR1 210 A4
Sibley Ct
Beckenham BR3 186 C1
Hillingdon UB8 83 A2
Sibley Gr E12 78 A1
Sibthorpe Rd SE12 165 C4
Sibthorp Rd 2 CR4 180 D1
Sibton Rd SM5 202 C2
Sicilian Ave WC1 240 B3
Sidbury St
SW6 135 A4 264 A2
SIDCUP 190 A5
Sidcup By Pass Rd
Sidcup DA14 189 C6
St Paul's Cray BR5,
BR7 190 B3
Sidcup Hill DA14 190 B5
Sidcup Hill Gdns
DA14 190 C5
Sidcup Pl DA14 190 A5
Sidcup Rd SE9 166 A3
Sidcup Sta DA15 168 A2
Sidcup Tech Ctr
DA14 190 D4
Siddeley Dr TW4 129 A3
Siddons Ct WC2 240 C1
Siddons Ho 8 NW3 70 D3
Siddons La
NW1 92 D3 237 D5
Siddons Rd
Croydon CR0 220 D5
Forest Hill SE23 163 A2
Tottenham N17 34 A2
Side Rd E17 53 B4
Sidewood Rd SE9 167 B3
Sidford Ho SE1 260 D5
Sidford Pl SE1 116 B3 260 D5
Sidgwick Ho 26 SW9 138 A3
Sidi Ct 2 N15 50 D6
Sidings Mews N7 72 C4
Sidings The E11 54 A1
Sidlaw Ho N16 51 D1
Sidmouth Ave TW7 130 C3
Sidmouth Dr HA4 62 A5
Sidmouth Ho
18 Camberwell SE15 140 A5
Marylebone W1 237 B2
26 Streatham SW2 160 C4
Sidmouth Mews WC1 233 C1
Sidmouth Par NW2 68 C1

Sidmouth Rd
Bexley DA16 146 C5
Leyton E10 76 A5
Willesden NW2 68 C1
Sidmouth St
WC1 94 B4 233 C1
Sidney Ave N13 32 B5
Sidney Boyd Ct NW6 69 C1
Sidney Elson Way E6 100 C5
Sidney Gdns TW8 131 D6
Sidney Godley (VC) Ho 31
E2 96 C4
Sidney Gr EC1 234 C3
Sidney Ho
4 Globe Town E2 96 D5
SE18 144 B4
Sidney Miller Ct 8
W3 110 D5
Sidney Rd
Beckenham BR3 185 A1
Croydon SE25 206 A4
Harrow HA2 42 A6
Stockwell SW9 138 B3
Twickenham TW1 153 B5
Walton-on-T KT12 194 B1
Wanstead E7 77 A5
Wood Green N22 32 B3
Sidney Sq E1 96 C2
Sidney St E1 96 C2
Sidworth St 6 E8 74 B1
Siebert Rd SE3 143 A6
Siedle Ho 9 SE18 144 C6
Siege Ho 14 E1 96 B1
Siemens Rd SE18 121 D3
Sienna SE28 123 D3
Sienna Ct TW13 149 D1
Sierra Dr RM9 103 D5
Sigdon Rd E8 74 A3
Sigers The HA5 40 B3
Signal Ho
9 London E8 74 B1
SE1 252 A1
Signmakers Yd NW1 231 D5
Sigrist Sq 4 KT2 176 A2
Silbury Ave CR4 180 C2
Silbury Ho 9 SE26 162 A1
Silbury St N1 235 C2
Silchester Ct
Stanwell TW15 148 A2
Thornton Heath CR7 204 C5
Silchester Rd W10 90 D1
Silecroft Rd DA7 147 C4
Silesia Bldgs E8 74 B1
Silex St SE1 116 D4 251 D1
Silicone Bsns Ctr UB6 87 C5
Silk Cl SE12 165 A5
Silkfield Rd NW9 45 C4
Silk Ho NW9 45 B6
Silk Mills Path SE13 142 A2
Silk Mills Sq E9 75 B2
Silks Ct E11 54 C1
Silk St EC2 95 A2 242 B4
Silkstream Par HA8 27 A2
Silkstream Rd HA8 27 A2
Sillitoe Ho N1 235 D5
Silsoe Ho NW1 231 D3
Silsoe Rd N22 50 B6
Silverbell Ct 1 N12 29 D5
Silver Birch Ave E4 35 B4
Silver Birch Cl
Forest Hill SE6 163 B1
Friern Barnet N11 31 A4
Ickenham UB10 60 A4
SE28 124 A5
Silver Birch Ct EN3 18 D6
Silver Birch Gdns E6 100 B3
Silverbirch Wlk 1
NW3 71 A2
Silverburn Ho 4
SW9 138 D4
Silver Cl
Harrow HA3 24 B3
SE14 141 A5
Silvercliffe Gdns EN4 2 C1
Silver Cres W4 110 D2
Silver Ct N19 71 C5
Silverdale
Enfield EN2 4 A1
Forest Hill SE26 184 C6
NW1 232 A2
Silverdale Ave IG3 57 D4
Silverdale Cl
Cheam SM1 217 B4
1 Ealing W7 108 D5
Northolt UB5 63 B3
Silverdale Ct EC1 241 D6
Silverdale Dr
Chislehurst SE9 166 A2
Sunbury TW16 172 B1
Silverdale Factory Ctr
UB3 106 A3
Silverdale Gdns UB3 106 A4
Silverdale Ind Est
UB3 106 A4
Silverdale Par IG3 57 D4
Silverdale Rd
Bexleyheath DA7 147 D3
Chingford E4 36 B4
Hayes UB3 106 A4
Petts Wood BR5 211 A5
Silverhall St TW7 131 A2
Silverholme Cl HA3 44 A2
Silver Ind Est N17 33 D1
Silver Jubilee Way
TW4 128 B3
Silver La BR4 224 B6
Silverland St E16 122 B5
Silverleigh Rd CR7 204 B4
Silvermead 7 E18 37 A2
Silvermere Rd SE6 163 D5
Silver Pl W1 249 B6
Silver Rd
Shepherd's Bush
W12 112 D6
St Johns SE13 141 D2
Silvers 4 IG9 21 C3
Silver Spring Cl DA8 147 D6
Silver St
Edmonton N18 33 C6
Enfield EN1 5 B2
Silverstone Ct 8
BR1 187 C1
Silverston Way HA7 25 C4
Silver Street Sta N18 33 D5
Silverthorn 17 NW6 91 D6
Silverthorne Lo EN1 17 C6
Silverthorne Rd SW8 137 B3
Silverthorn Gdns E4 19 C2
Silverton Lo SE19 183 C3
Silverton Rd W6 134 D6
SILVERTOWN 121 B4
Silvertown Way E16 121 A5
Silvertree La UB6 86 B4
Silver Way
Hillingdon UB10 82 D5
Romford RM7 59 D6
Silver Wing Ind Est
CR0 220 B2
Silver Wlk SE16 119 B5
Silverwood Cl BR3 185 C3
Silvester Ho
27 Bethnal Green E2 96 C4
1 Notting Hill W11 91 B1
Pinner HA5 40 A5
6 Stepney E1 96 B1
Silvester Rd SE22 161 D6
Silvester St SE1 252 C1
Silwex Ho E1 243 C5
Silwood St SE16 118 C1
Simba Ct TW1 152 D3
Simla Ho SE1 252 D1
Simmil Rd KT10 212 C3
Simmonds Ct SW5 255 C3
Simmons Cl
Chessington KT9 213 C2
East Barnet N20 14 C3
Simmons Dr RM8 81 A5
Simmons Gate KT10 212 A3
Simmons Ho
20 Bethnal Green E2 96 A4
Finsbury Pk N7 72 B6
Simmons La E4 20 B2
Simmons Rd SE18 122 D1
Simmons' Way N20 14 C2
Simms Cl SM5 218 C6
Simms Ct SW6 135 A2
Simms Gdns N2 30 A1
Simms Rd SE1 118 A2
Simnel Rd SE12 165 B4
Simon Cl W11 113 B6 244 D6
Simon Ct
Paddington W9 91 C4
5 Woolwich SE28 124 B5
Simonds Rd E10 75 C6
Simone Ct BR1 187 D2
Simon Lo 31 SW19 156 D3
Simon Marks Jewish Prim
Sch N16 73 D6
Simons Wlk E15 76 B3
Simpson Cl N21 16 B6
Simpson Dr W3 89 B1
Simpson Ho
Lisson Gr NW8 230 A1
Vauxhall SE11 260 C1
Wembley HA9 65 D6
Simpson Rd
Hounslow TW4 151 B5
Richmond TW10 175 C6
Simpson's Rd
BR2 209 A6
Poplar E14 119 D6
Simpson St SW11 136 C3
Simpson Way KT6 197 C3
Sim's Cotts KT10 212 D2
Sims Wlk SE3 142 D1
Sinclair Ct
21 Beckenham BR3 185 C3
Canonbury N5 73 A2
5 Croydon CR0 221 D6
Sinclair Gdns W14 112 D4
Sinclair Gr NW11 46 D3
Sinclair Ho
Harrow HA7 24 D4
3 South Norwood
SW16 182 B3
1 Streatham SW12 159 D3
Sinclair Mans 13
W12 112 D4
Sinclair Pl SE4 163 C5
Sinclair Rd
Chingford Hatch E4 35 B5
W14 113 A3 254 A6
Sinclairs Ho 18 E3 97 B5
Sinclare Cl EN1 5 D4
Singapore Rd W13 109 A5
Singer St EC2 235 D1
Singlegate Prim Sch
SW19 180 B3
Singleton Cl
Mitcham SW17 180 D3
Thornton Heath CR0 205 A2
Singleton Rd RM9 81 B3
Singleton Scarp N12 29 C5
Sinnott Rd E17 34 D2
Sion Ct TW1 153 B3
Sion Ho SE13 142 A1
Sion-Manning RC Sch for
Girls
Kensal Town W10 91 A2
North Kensington W10 90 D2
Sion Rd TW1 153 B3
Sippetts Ct IG1 57 B1
SIPSON 126 C6
Sipson Cl UB7 126 C6
Sipson La UB3, UB7 126 D6
Sipson Rd
Harmondsworth UB7 126 C6
West Drayton UB7 104 B2
West Drayton UB7 104 C1
Sipson Way UB7 126 C5
Sir Abraham Dawes Cotts
SW15 135 A1
Sir Alexander Cl W3 111 D5
Sir Alexander Rd W3 111 D5
Sir Arthur Bliss Ct 4
SW19 180 D1
Sir Cyril Black Way 2
SW19 179 C3
Sirdar Rd
Mitcham CR4 181 A4
Tottenham N22 33 A1
W11 113 A6 244 A5
Sir Francis Drake Prim
Sch SE8 119 A1
Sir George Monoux Sixth
Form Coll E17 35 D1
Sir Henry Floyd Ct HA7 9 B2
Sirinham Point SW8 270 D5
Sirius Bldg 13 E1 118 D6
Sir James Barrie Prim Sch
SW8 137 C4 269 B1
Sir John Cass Foundation
& Redcoat CE Sec Sch
E1 96 D2
Sir John Cass's
Foundation Prim Sch
EC3 95 C1 243 B1
Sir John Heron Prim Sch
E12 78 B4
Sir John Kirk Cl 33
SE5 139 A5
Sir John Lillie Prim Sch
SW6 135 A6 264 B5
Sir Martin Bowes Ho 9
SE18 122 C2
Sir Oswald Stoll
Foundation The
SW6 265 C4
Sir Thomas Abney Sch
N16 51 B1
Sir Thomas More Est
SW3 136 B6 266 D5
Sirus Rd HA6 22 A5
Sir William Burrough
Prim Sch E14 97 A1
Sir William Powell's
Almshos SW6 135 A2
Sise La EC4 242 C1
Siskin Ho
Edmonton N9 18 D3
14 Rotherhithe SE16 118 D2
Sisley Rd IG11 101 D6
Sispara Gdns SW18 157 B5
Sissinghurst Cl BR1 186 C5
Sissinghurst Ho 17
SE15 140 C6
Sissinghurst Rd CR0 206 A2
Sissulu Ct 8 E6 99 C6
Sister Mabel's Way 15
SE15 140 A5
Sisters Ave SW11 136 D1
Sistova Rd SW12 159 B3
Sisulu Pl SW9 138 C2
Sitarey Ct 4 W12 112 B5
Site of Changing of the
Guard* SW1 249 A1
Sittingbourne Ave EN1 17 B5
Sitwell Gr HA7 24 D5
Siverst Cl UB5 63 D2
Sivill Ho 9 E2 95 D4
Siviter Way RM10 81 D1
Siward Rd
Bromley BR2 209 C6
Tottenham N17 33 B2
Wandsworth SW17 158 A1
Six Bridges Ind Est 15
SE1 118 A1
Sixpenny Ct IG11 79 A2
Sixth Ave
Hayes UB3 105 D5
Ilford E12 78 B4
West Kilburn W10 91 A4
Sixth Cross Rd TW2 152 A1
Skardu Rd NW2 69 A3
Skeena Hill SW18,
SW19 157 A4
Skeffington Rd E6 100 B6
Skeffington St SE18 123 A3
Skeggs Ho 5 E14 120 A3
Skegness Ho 3 N7 72 B1
Skelbrook St SW18 158 A2
Skelgill Rd SW15 135 B1
Skelley Rd E15 76 D1
Skelton Cl 7 E8 73 D2
Skelton Ho N16 73 C3
Skelton Rd E7 77 A2
Skelton's La E10 53 D2
Skelwith Rd W6 134 C6
Skenfrith Ho SE15 140 B6
Skerne Rd KT2 175 D2
Skerne Wlk KT2 175 D2
Sketchley Gdns SE16 118 D1
Sketty Rd EN1 5 D2
Skiers St E15 98 C6
Skiffington Cl SW2 160 C3
Skillen Lodge HA5 22 D2
Skinner Ct E17 53 C4
Skinner Pl SW1 258 A3
Skinners Almshouses
N13 16 C1
Skinners Company Sch
(Upper) N16 51 D2
Skinner's Company's
Lower Sch E5 52 B1
Skinners La
EC4 252 B6
Hounslow TW5 129 D4
Skinner St EC1 94 C3 241 B6
Skipper Ct 6 IG11 101 A6
Skipsea Ho SW18 158 B5
Skipsey Ave E6 100 B4
Skipton Cl N11 31 A4
Skipton Dr UB3 105 A3
Skipton Ho SE4 141 A1
Skipwith Bldg EC1 241 A4
Skipworth Rd E9 96 C6
Skua Ct 33 SE8 141 B6
Skyline Ct SE1 263 C5
Skyline Plaza Bldg 19
E1 96 A1
Skylines E14 120 A4
Sky Peals Rd IG8 36 B3
Sky Studios E16 122 C4
Sladebrook Rd SE3 143 D2
Slade Ct
Barnet EN5 1 D2
Brondesbury NW2 69 A3
Muswell Hill N10 31 B3
Sladedale Rd SE18 123 C1
Slade Ho TW4 151 B5
Sladen Pl 12 E5 74 B4
Slades Cl EN2 4 C2
Slades Dr BR7 189 A6
Slades Gdns EN2 4 C2
Slades Hill EN2 4 C2
Slades Rise EN2 4 C2
Slade The SE18 145 C6
Slade Twr E10 75 C6
Slade Way CR4 181 A2
Slagrove Pl SE13 163 D6
Slaidburn St
SW10 136 A6 266 B5
Slaithwaite Rd SE13 142 A1
Slaney Ct NW10 68 C1
Slaney Pl 1 N7 72 C3
Slater Cl 13 SE18 122 C2
Slatter 1 NW9 27 D2
Slattery Rd TW13 150 C3
Sleaford Ho 16 E3 97 C3
Sleaford Ind Est
SW8 137 C5 269 B3
Sleaford St
SW8 137 C5 269 B3
Sleat Ho 11 E3 97 B5
Sledmere Ct TW14 149 C3
Slievemore Cl 8
SW4 137 D2
Sligo Ho 8 E1 96 D3
Slingsby Pl WC2 250 A6
Slippers Pl SE16 118 B3
Slipway Ho 1 E14 119 D1
Sloane Ave
SW3 114 C2 257 B3
Sloane Avenue Mans
SW3 257 C3
Sloane Ct E SW3 258 A2
Sloane Ct W SW3 258 A2
Sloane Gate Mans
SW1 258 A4
Sloane Gdns
Belgravia
SW1 115 A2 258 A3
Orpington BR6 227 A5
Sloane Ho 7 E9 74 C1
Sloane Hospl BR3 186 B2
Sloane Sq SW1 257 D3
Sloane Square Sta
SW1 115 A2 258 A3
Sloane St
SW1 114 D3 257 D5
Sloane Terr SW1 258 A4
Sloane Terr Mans
SW1 258 A4
Sloane Wlk CR0 207 B3
Sloan Ho RM10 81 D1
Slocum Cl SE28 124 C6
Slough La NW9 45 A3
Sly St 17 E1 96 B1
Smaldon Cl UB7 104 C3
Smallberry Ave TW7 130 D3
Smallberry Green Prim
Sch The TW7 131 A4
Smallbrook Mews W2 236 C1
Smallbugh Mans HA0 65 B4
Smalley Cl N16 73 D5
Smallwood Prim Sch
SW17 180 B6
Smallwood Rd SW17 180 B6
Smarden Cl DA17 125 C1
Smarden Gr SE9 188 B6
Smart's Pl
Edmonton N18 34 A5
WC1, WC2 240 B2
13 Shadwell E1 118 C6
Stepney E1 118 B6
Smart St E2 96 D4
Smeaton Cl KT9 213 D2
Smeaton Ct SE1 262 A5
Smeaton Rd
Holdbrook EN3 7 C6
Wandsworth SW18 157 C4
Smeaton St E1 118 B5
Smedley St SW4 137 D3
Smeed Rd E3 75 C1
Smiles Pl SE13 142 A3
Smith Cl SE16 118 D5
Smithers Ho 3 SE20 184 D3
Smithfield Mkt EC1 241 D3
Smithfield St
EC1 94 D2 241 C3
Smithies Ct E15 76 A3
Smithies Rd SE2 124 B2
Smith's Ct W1 249 C6
Smithson Rd N17 33 B2
Smiths Point E13 99 A6
Smith Sq SW1 116 A3 260 A5
Smith St
Surbiton KT5 198 B3
SW3 114 D1 257 C1
Smith's Yd SW18 158 A2
Smith Terr
SW3 114 D1 257 C1
Smithwood Cl SW19 157 A2
Smithy St E1 96 C2
Smithy Street Sch E1 96 C2
Smock Wlk CR0 205 A3
Smoothfield TW3 129 C1
Smugglers Way
SW18 135 D1
Smyrk's Rd
SE17 117 C1 263 B1
Smyrna Mans 8 NW6 69 C1
Smyrna Rd NW6 69 C1
Smythe St E14 119 D6
Snakes La EN4, N14 3 C1
Snakes La E IG8 37 C4
Snakes La W IG8 37 B4
Snakey La TW13 172 B6
SNARESBROOK 54 D6
Snaresbrook Coll E18 37 A1
Snaresbrook Dr HA7 26 A6
Snaresbrook Hall 12
E18 55 A6
Snaresbrook Ho E18 54 D5
Snaresbrook Prim Sch
E18 55 A5
Snaresbrook Rd E11 54 D5
Snaresbrook Sta E11 55 A4
Snarsgate St W10 90 C2
Sneath Ave NW11 47 B2
Snell's Pk N18 33 D4
Sneyd Rd NW2 68 C4
Snowberry Cl E11 76 B4
Snowbury Rd 6 SW6 135 D3
Snow Ct 4 HA0 65 D3
Snowden Ave UB10 82 D5
Snowden St
EC2 95 C3 243 A5
Snowdon Cres UB3 105 A3
Snowdon Dr NW9 45 C3
Snowdon Rd TW6 149 A5
Snowdown Cl SE20 184 D2
Snowdrop Cl 2
TW12 173 C4
Snowe Ho SE27 160 D1
Snow Hill EC1 94 D2 241 C3
Snowman Ho NW6 91 D6
Snowsfields
SE1 117 B4 252 D2
Snowsfields Prim Sch
SE1 117 C4 253 A2
Snowshill Rd E12 78 A3
Snowy Fielder Waye
TW7 131 B3
Soames St SE15 139 D2
Soames Wlk KT3 177 C2
Soane Cl W5 109 D4
Soane Ct 10 NW1 71 C1
Soane Ho SE17 262 D1
Soane Mus The*
WC2 94 B1 240 C2
Soaphouse La TW8 132 A5
Soham Rd EN3 7 B6
SOHO 93 D1
Soho* W1 93 D1 239 C2
Soho Mills SM6 203 B1
Soho Parish CE Prim Sch
W1 115 D6 249 C6
Soho Sq W1 93 D1 239 C2
Soho St W1 239 C2
Sojourner-Truth Cl 11
E8 74 B2
Sola Ct 8 CR0 205 B1
Solander Gdns
13 Shadwell E1 118 C6
Stepney E1 118 B6
Solar Ct N3 29 D3
Soldene Ct N7 72 B2
Solebay St E1 97 A3
Solent Ct SW16 182 B1
Solent Ho 6 E1 97 A2
Solent Rd NW6 69 C3
Solent Rise E13 99 A4
Soley Mews WC1 234 A2
Solidarity Ho 5 NW10 68 C2
Solna Ave SW15 156 C6
Solna Rd N21 17 B4
Solomon Ave N9 34 A6
Solomons Ct N12 30 A3
Solomon's Pas SE15 140 B1
Solon New Rd SW4 138 A1
Solon Rd SW2 138 A1
Solway Cl TW4 129 A2
Solway Ho 12 E1 96 D3
Solway Rd
East Dulwich SE22 140 A1
Tottenham N22 32 D2
Somaford Gr EN4 14 B5
Somali Rd NW2 69 B3
Somborne Ho 11
SW15 156 A4
Sombrook Ho SE11 261 A3
Somerby Rd IG11 79 B1
Somercoates Cl EN4 2 C2
Somer Ct SW6 265 A5
Somerfield Rd N4 72 D6
Somerfield St SE16 118 D1

Somerford Cl HA5 ... 40 A5
Somerford Gr
Shacklewell N16 ... 73 D4
Tottenham N17 ... 34 A3
Somerford Grove Est
N16 ... 73 D4
Somerford St E1 ... 96 B3
Somerford Way SE16 ... 119 A4
Somerhill Ave DA15 ... 168 B4
Somerhill Rd DA16 ... 146 B3
Somerleyton Rd SW9 ... 138 C1
Somersby Est SE20 ... 184 C3
Somersby Gdns IG4 ... 56 B4
Somers Cl NW1 ... 232 C4
Somers Cres W2 ... 237 A1
Somerset Ave
Chessington KT9 ... 213 D4
DA16 ... 145 D1
Wimbledon SW20 ... 178 B1
Somerset Cl
New Malden KT3 ... 199 C3
Tottenham N17 ... 33 B1
Woodford IG8 ... 37 A2
Somerset Ct
10 Buckhurst Hill IG9 ... 21 C2
Ealing W7 ... 86 D1
2 Hampton TW12 ... 173 C2
Somerset Gdns
Highgate N6 ... 49 A2
St Johns SE13 ... 141 D3
Teddington TW11 ... 174 C5
Thornton Heath SW16 ... 204 B6
Tottenham N17 ... 33 C3
Somerset Hall N17 ... 33 C3
Somerset Ho
WC2 ... 116 B6 250 D6
Somerset Ho SW19 ... 157 A1
Somerset Lo
9 Brentford TW8 ... 131 D6
5 New Barnet EN5 ... 14 A6
Putney SW15 ... 134 B1
Somerset Rd
Bedford Pk W4 ... 111 B3
Brentford TW8 ... 131 C6
Ealing W13 ... 109 C5
Edmonton N18 ... 33 D5
Harrow HA1 ... 42 A4
Hendon NW4 ... 46 C5
Holdbrook EN3 ... 7 C5
Kingston u T KT1 ... 176 B1
New Barnet EN5 ... 14 A6
Southall UB1 ... 85 C2
Teddington TW11 ... 174 C5
Tottenham N17 ... 51 D6
Walthamstow E17 ... 53 C3
Wimbledon SW19 ... 157 A1
Somerset Sq
W14 ... 113 B4 244 C1
Somerset Waye TW5 ... 129 A5
Somersham Rd DA7 ... 147 A3
Somers Pl SW2 ... 160 B4
Somers Rd
Tulse Hill SW2 ... 160 B5
Walthamstow E17 ... 53 B5
SOMERS TOWN ... 93 D4
Somers Town Est
NW1 ... 93 C5 232 B3
Somers Way WD23 ... 8 A4
Somerton Ave TW9 ... 132 D2
Somerton Rd
Cricklewood NW2 ... 69 A5
Nunhead SE15 ... 140 B1
Somertrees Ave SE12 ... 165 B2
Somervell Rd HA2 ... 63 C3
Somerville Ave SW13 ... 134 C6
Somerville Ct SW16 ... 181 D4
Somerville Ho 10
SW15 ... 156 D5
Somerville Point
SE16 ... 119 B4
Somerville Rd
Dagenham RM6 ... 58 C4
Penge SE20 ... 184 D3
Sonderburg Rd 13 N7 ... 72 B6
Sondes St SE17 ... 139 B6
Songhurst Cl CR0 ... 204 B3
Sonia Ct
Edgware HA8 ... 26 B3
North Finchley N12 ... 30 A6
Sonia Gdns
Heston TW5 ... 129 C5
North Finchley N12 ... 30 A6
Willesden NW10 ... 67 D4
Sonning Ct CR0 ... 222 A6
Sonning Gdns TW12 ... 173 A4
Sonning Ho 22 E2 ... 95 D4
Sonning Rd CR0 ... 206 A3
Soper Cl
Chingford Hatch E4 ... 35 B5
4 Forest Hill SE23 ... 162 D2
Soper Mews EN3 ... 7 C5
Sophia Cl N7 ... 72 B2
Sophia Ho
10 Hammersmith
W6 ... 112 C1
Tottenham N15 ... 51 D5
Sophia Rd
Newham E13 ... 99 B2
Walthamstow E10 ... 53 D1
Sophia Sq 14 SE16 ... 119 A6
Sopwith 2 NW9 ... 27 D2
Sopwith Ave KT9 ... 214 A3
Sopwith Cl KT2 ... 176 B5
Sopwith Rd TW5 ... 128 C5
Sopwith Way
Battersea
SW8 ... 137 B5 268 C4
Kingston u T KT2 ... 176 A2
Sorbus Ct EN2 ... 4 D3
Sorensen Ct 2 E10 ... 75 D6
Sorrel Cl SE28 ... 124 A5
Sorrel Gdns E6 ... 100 A2
Sorrel Ho TW3 ... 130 A4
Sorrel La 17 E14 ... 98 B1
Sorrell Cl
6 Brixton SW9 ... 138 C3
SE14 ... 141 A5
Sorrento Rd SM1 ... 217 D5
Soseki Mus* SW4 ... 137 B2
Sotheby Rd N5 ... 73 A4
Sotheran Cl E8 ... 96 A6
Sotheron Pl SW6 ... 265 D3
Soudan Rd
SW11 ... 136 D4 267 C1
Souldern Rd 10 W14 ... 112 D3
South Access Rd E17 ... 53 A3
South Acre NW9 ... 27 D1
Southacre Way HA5 ... 22 C2
SOUTH ACTON ... 110 D3
South Acton Sta W3,
W4 ... 111 A3
South Africa Rd W12 ... 112 B6
SOUTHALL ... 107 A5
Southall Ct UB1 ... 107 B6
Southall Ent Ctr UB2 ... 107 C4
Southall La TW5 ... 106 B1
Southall Norwood Hospl
UB2 ... 107 B3
Southall Pl SE1 ... 252 C1
Southall Sta UB1 ... 107 B4
Southall & West London
Coll UB1 ... 107 A5
Southam Ho 9 W10 ... 91 A3
Southampton Bldgs
WC2 ... 241 A3
Southampton Gdns
CR4 ... 204 A4
Southampton Mews
E16 ... 121 B5
Southampton Pl WC1 ... 240 B3
Southampton Rd
Maitland Pk NW5 ... 70 D3
Stanwell TW19, TW6 ... 148 B5
Southampton Row
WC1 ... 94 A2 240 B4
Southampton St WC2 ... 250 B6
Southampton Way
SE5 ... 139 C5
Southam St W10 ... 91 A3
South Audley St
W1 ... 115 A5 248 B4
South Ave
Chingford E4 ... 20 A4
East Finchley NW11 ... 47 D5
Richmond TW9 ... 132 C3
Southall UB1 ... 107 B6
Wallington SM5 ... 219 A1
South Avenue Gdns
UB1 ... 107 B6
Southbank KT7 ... 197 B2
SOUTH BANK ... 116 B4
South Bank KT6 ... 198 A3
South Bank Bsns Ctr
SW8 ... 137 D6 269 D5
Southbank International
Sch NW3 ... 70 A2
Southbank International
Sch (Westminster
Campus) W1 ... 93 B2 238 C4
Southbank Int Sch
W11 ... 113 C6 245 A5
South Bank Lo 2
KT6 ... 198 A3
South Bank Terr KT6 ... 198 A3
South Bank Univ
London SW8 ... 137 D4 269 D2
SE1 ... 116 D3 261 D6
SOUTH
BEDDINGTON ... 219 C2
South Bermondsey Sta
SE16 ... 118 C1
South Birkbeck Rd
E11 ... 76 B5
South Black Lion La 7
W6 ... 112 A1
South Bldg SW1 ... 259 B6
South Block 20 E1 ... 118 C6
South Bolton Gdns
SW10 ... 255 D2
SOUTHBOROUGH
BR2 ... 210 B3
KT6 ... 197 D1
Southborough Cl
KT6 ... 197 D1
Southborough High Sch
KT6 ... 214 A5
Southborough Ho
SE17 ... 263 B2
Southborough La BR1,
BR2 ... 210 B4
Southborough Prim Sch
BR2 ... 210 C4
Southborough Rd
Bromley BR1, BR2 ... 210 A5
South Hackney E9 ... 96 D6
Surbiton KT6 ... 198 A1
Southborough Rd (The
Lane) KT6 ... 198 A1
Southbourne BR2 ... 209 A2
Southbourne Ave NW9 ... 27 B1
Southbourne Cl HA5 ... 41 A2
Southbourne Cres
NW4 ... 47 A5
Southbourne Ct NW9 ... 27 A1
Southbourne Gdns
Ilford IG1 ... 79 A3
Ruislip HA4 ... 40 B1
SE12 ... 165 B6
Southbridge Pl CR0 ... 221 A4
Southbridge Rd CR0 ... 221 A4
Southbridge Way
UB2 ... 107 A4
SOUTH BROMLEY ... 98 B2
Southbrook Mews
SE12 ... 164 D5
Southbrook Rd
Hither Green SE12 ... 164 D5
Thornton Heath SW16 ... 182 A2
South Building*
SE10 ... 142 B5
Southbury NW8 ... 229 B6
Southbury Ave EN1 ... 6 A1
Southbury Prim Sch
EN3 ... 6 C1
Southbury Rd
Enfield EN1 ... 5 D2
Enfield EN1, EN3 ... 6 B1
Southbury Sta EN3 ... 6 B1
South Camden Com Sch
NW1 ... 93 D5 232 C4
South Carriage Dr SW1,
SW7 ... 114 D4 247 C2
South Chelsea Coll
SW9 ... 138 B1
Southchurch Ct
Bowes Pk N13 ... 32 B5
Newham E6 ... 100 B5
Southchurch Rd E6 ... 100 B5
South Cl
Barnet EN5 ... 1 B2
DA6 ... 146 D1
Dagenham RM10 ... 103 C6
Highgate N6 ... 49 B3
Morden SM4 ... 201 C3
Pinner HA5 ... 41 B2
Twickenham TW2 ... 151 C1
West Drayton UB7 ... 104 C3
South Colonnade The
E14 ... 119 D5
Southcombe St W14 ... 254 A4
South Common Rd
UB8 ... 60 A2
Southcote Ave
Feltham TW13 ... 150 A2
Tolworth KT5 ... 198 D2
Southcote Rd
Croydon SE25 ... 206 B3
Tufnell Pk N19 ... 71 C4
Walthamstow E17 ... 53 A4
Southcote Rise HA4 ... 39 B2
Southcott Ho
31 Bromley E3 ... 97 D4
W9 ... 236 B5
South Countess Rd
E17 ... 53 B6
South Cres
Newham E16 ... 98 B3
WC1 ... 239 C3
Southcroft SM1 ... 218 C3
Southcroft Ave
DA16 ... 145 C2
West Wickham BR4 ... 224 A6
Southcroft Rd
BR6 ... 227 C5
Streatham SW17 ... 181 A4
South Cross Rd IG6 ... 57 A4
South Croxted Rd
SE21 ... 183 B6
SOUTH CROYDON ... 221 B1
South Croydon Sta
CR2 ... 221 B3
South Ct 17 SW15 ... 156 D5
Southdean Gdns
SW19 ... 157 B2
South Dene NW7 ... 11 B1
Southdene Ct N11 ... 15 C1
Southdown N7 ... 72 A2
Southdown Ave W7 ... 109 A3
Southdown Cres
Harrow HA2 ... 42 A1
Ilford IG2 ... 57 C4
Southdown Dr SW20 ... 178 D3
Southdown Rd SW20 ... 178 D2
South Dr
Orpington BR6 ... 227 C3
Ruislip HA4 ... 39 C1
South Ealing Cemy
W5 ... 109 D2
South Ealing Rd W5 ... 109 D3
South Ealing Sta W5 ... 109 D3
South Eastern Ave N9 ... 17 D1
South Eastern Univ N7 ... 72 B5
South Eaton Pl
SW1 ... 115 A2 258 B4
South Eden Park Rd
BR3 ... 207 D4
South Edwardes Sq
W8 ... 255 A5
SOUTHEND ... 186 B6
South End
Croydon CR0 ... 221 A4
W8 ... 113 D3 255 D6
Southend Cl SE9 ... 166 D5
South End Cl NW3 ... 70 C4
Southend Cres SE9 ... 166 D5
South End Gn NW3 ... 70 C4
Southend Ho SE9 ... 166 C4
Southend La SE6 ... 185 C6
Southend Rd
Beckenham BR3 ... 185 C2
Plashet E6 ... 78 B1
Woodford IG8 ... 37 D1
South End Rd NW3 ... 70 C4
Southend Road (North
Circular Rd) E17, E18 ... 36 C2
South End Row
W8 ... 113 D3 255 D6
Southern Ave
East Bedfont TW14 ... 150 A3
South Norwood SE25 ... 205 D6
Southerngate Way
SE14 ... 141 A5
Southern Gr E3 ... 97 B3
Southernhay IG10 ... 21 D6
Southern Perimeter Rd
Hatton TW14, TW6 ... 149 B6
West Bedfont TW19,
TW6 ... 148 C5
Southern Rd
Fortis Green N2 ... 48 D5
Newham E13 ... 99 B5
Southern Road Prim Sch
E13 ... 99 B5
Southern Row W10 ... 91 A3
Southern St N1 ... 233 C4
Southern Way
Greenwich SE10 ... 120 D3
Romford RM7 ... 59 C3
Southerton Rd W6 ... 112 C2
South Esk Rd E7 ... 77 C2
Southey Ho SE17 ... 262 B2
Southey Mews E16 ... 121 A5
Southey Rd
Brixton SW9 ... 138 C4
Merton SW19 ... 179 C3
Tottenham N15 ... 51 C4
Southey St SE20 ... 184 D3
Southfield EN5 ... 12 D5
Southfield Cl UB8 ... 82 C4
Southfield Cotts W7 ... 108 D4
Southfield Ct E11 ... 76 D5
Southfield Gdns TW1,
TW2 ... 174 D6
Southfield Lo W4 ... 111 B4
Southfield Pk HA2 ... 41 D5
Southfield Prim Sch
W4 ... 111 C4
Southfield Rd
Acton W4 ... 111 B4
Southfield Rd *continued*
Enfield EN3 ... 18 C5
St Paul's Cray BR7 ... 211 D6
SOUTHFIELDS ... 157 D3
Southfields
Hendon NW4 ... 46 B6
Thames Ditton KT8 ... 196 C3
Southfields Ave
TW15 ... 170 D4
Southfields Com Coll
SW18 ... 157 C3
Southfields Ct SM3 ... 217 C6
Southfields Rd SW18 ... 157 C5
Southfields Sta SW18 ... 157 B3
Southfleet Rd BR6 ... 227 C4
SOUTHGATE ... 16 B4
South Gate Ave TW13 ... 171 B6
Southgate Cir 3 N14 ... 15 D3
Southgate Coll N14 ... 15 D2
Southgate Ct N1 ... 73 B1
Southgate Gr N1 ... 73 B1
Southgate Ho 7 E17 ... 54 A6
Southgate Rd
N1 ... 95 B6 235 D6
Southgate Sch EN4 ... 15 B6
Southgate Sta N14 ... 15 D3
Southgate Way N2 ... 30 C2
South Gdns
Mitcham SW19 ... 180 B3
Wembley HA9 ... 66 C6
South Gipsy Rd DA16 ... 146 D2
South Glade The DA5 ... 169 B3
South Gn NW9 ... 27 C2
South Gr
Highgate N6 ... 49 A1
Tottenham N15 ... 51 B4
Walthamstow E17 ... 53 B4
South Greenford Sta
UB6 ... 86 C4
South Grove Ho N6 ... 49 A1
South Grove Prim Sch
E17 ... 53 B3
SOUTH HACKNEY ... 96 C6
SOUTH HAMPSTEAD ... 70 A1
South Hampstead High
Sch NW3 ... 70 B2
South Hampstead High
Sch Jun Dept NW3 ... 70 A2
South Hampstead Sta
NW8 ... 70 A1
South Harringay Jun & Inf
Schs N4 ... 50 D4
SOUTH HARROW ... 63 D5
South Harrow Sta HA2 ... 64 A5
South Hill BR7 ... 188 B4
South Hill Ave HA1,
HA2 ... 64 B5
South Hill Gr HA1 ... 64 C4
South Hill Pk NW3 ... 70 C4
South Hill Pk Gdns
NW3 ... 70 C4
South Hill Rd BR2 ... 208 C5
Southholme Cl SE19 ... 183 C2
Southill La HA5 ... 40 B5
Southill Rd BR7 ... 188 B3
Southill St E14 ... 97 D1
South Island Pl SW9 ... 138 C5
SOUTH
KENSINGTON ... 114 A1
South Kensington Sta
SW7 ... 114 B2 256 D4
South Kensington Station
Arc SW7 ... 256 D4
South Kenton Sta HA9 ... 43 C1
South La
Kingston u T KT1 ... 197 D6
New Malden KT3 ... 199 B3
SOUTH LAMBETH ... 138 A4
South Lambeth Pl
SW8 ... 270 B6
South Lambeth Rd
SW8 ... 138 A5 270 B4
Southland Rd SE18 ... 145 D5
Southlands Ave BR6 ... 227 C3
Southlands Ct BR2 ... 209 D5
Southlands Dr SW19 ... 156 D2
Southlands Gr BR1 ... 210 A6
Southlands Rd BR1,
BR2 ... 209 D5
Southland Way TW7 ... 152 B6
South La W KT3 ... 199 B5
South Lo
6 New Barnet EN5 ... 13 D6
NW8 ... 229 C2
Twickenham TW2 ... 152 A5
South Lodge Ave CR4, CR7,
SW16 ... 204 A5
South Lodge Cres EN2 ... 3 D1
South Lodge Dr N14 ... 15 D6
South London Montessori
Sch SW11 ... 267 A1
South Mall The N9 ... 18 A1
South Mead
Grahame Pk NW9 ... 27 D2
West Ewell KT19 ... 215 D1
Southmead Prim Sch
SW19 ... 157 A3
Southmead Rd SW19 ... 157 A3
South Merton Sta
SW20 ... 201 B6
South Molton La
W1 ... 93 B1 238 C1
South Molton Rd E16 ... 99 A1
South Molton St
W1 ... 93 B1 238 C1
Southmont Rd KT10 ... 212 C5
Southmoor Way E9 ... 75 B3
South Mount N20 ... 14 A2
SOUTH NORWOOD ... 205 C6
South Norwood Ctry Pk*
SE25 ... 206 C5
South Norwood Hill SE19,
SE25 ... 183 D1
South Norwood Prim Sch
SE25 ... 206 A5
South Oak Rd SW16 ... 182 B6
Southold Rise SE9 ... 166 B1
Southolm St
SW11 ... 137 B4 268 D1
South Ordnance Rd
EN3 ... 7 C5
Southover
BR1 ... 187 A5
Finchley N12 ... 29 C6
SOUTH OXHEY ... 22 B6
South Par
Acton Green W4 ... 111 B2
Edgware HA8 ... 26 C1
Wallington SM6 ... 219 C2
South Parade
SW3 ... 114 B1 256 D2
South Park Bsns Ctr
IG3 ... 79 C6
South Park Cres
Catford SE6 ... 164 D3
Ilford IG1 ... 79 C5
Southpark Ct SW19 ... 179 C4
South Park Ct 24
BR3 ... 185 C3
South Park Dr IG3 ... 79 C4
South Park Gr KT3 ... 199 A5
South Park Hill Rd
CR2 ... 221 B4
South Park Mews
SW6 ... 135 D2
South Park Prim Sch
IG3 ... 79 C5
South Park Rd
Ilford IG1 ... 79 B5
Wimbledon SW19 ... 179 D4
South Park Terr IG1 ... 79 C5
South Park Villas IG3 ... 79 C4
South Park Way HA4 ... 62 C3
South Pl
Broadgate
EC2 ... 95 B2 242 D3
Enfield EN3 ... 18 C6
Surbiton KT5 ... 198 B2
South Pl Mews EC2 ... 242 D3
Southport Rd SE18 ... 123 B2
South Quay Plaza
E14 ... 119 D4
South Quay Sta E14 ... 119 D4
South Rd
Brentford W5 ... 109 D2
Edgware HA8 ... 26 D2
Edmonton N9 ... 18 A3
Feltham TW13 ... 172 D5
Forest Hill SE23 ... 162 D2
Hampton TW12 ... 173 B4
Heston TW5 ... 128 D6
Mitcham SW19 ... 180 B4
Southall UB1 ... 107 B5
Twickenham TW2 ... 152 B1
West Drayton UB7 ... 104 C3
South Residence IG3 ... 58 B4
South Ridge BR2 ... 209 C5
Southridge Pl SW20 ... 178 D3
South Rise W2 ... 247 B6
South Rise Prim Sch
SE18 ... 123 B1
South Rise Way SE18 ... 123 B2
South Row SE3 ... 142 D3
SOUTH RUISLIP ... 62 D4
South Ruislip Sta HA4 ... 62 C3
Southsea Rd KT1 ... 198 A5

South Sea St SE16 119 B3
Southside N7 71 D4
South Side W6 111 D3
Southside Comm
SW19 178 D4
Southside Ind Est
SW8 269 A2
Southside Quarter 4
SW11 136 D3
Southside Sh Ctr
SW18 157 D5
Southspring DA15 167 B4
South Sq
Hampstead Garden Suburb
NW11 47 D3
WC1 241 A3
South St
Bromley BR1 187 A1
Enfield EN3 18 D6
Isleworth TW7 131 A2
Mayfair W1 115 A5 248 B4
South Tenter St
E1 95 D1 243 D1
South Terr
Muswell Hill N22 31 D1
Surbiton KT6 198 A3
SW7 114 C2 257 A4
South Thames Coll (Battersea Ctr)
SW11 136 D4 267 D1
South Thames Coll (Putney Ctr) SW15 156 D6
South Thames Coll (Roehampton Ctr)
SW15 156 A5
South Thames Coll (Tooting Ctr) SW17 180 C5
South Thames Coll (Wandsworth Ctr)
SW18 157 D6
SOUTH TOTTENHAM 51 D3
South Tottenham Sta
N15 51 D4
South Vale
Harrow HA1 64 C4
West Norwood SE19 183 C4
Southvale Rd SE3 142 C3
South View
BR1 187 C1
Wimbledon SW19 178 D4
Southview Ave NW10 67 D3
Southview Cl SW17 181 A5
South View Cl DA5 169 B5
South View Cres IG2 56 D3
South View Ct
8 Forest Hill SE23 162 C3
South Norwood SE19 183 A3
Southview Dr E18 55 B6
Southview Gdns SM6 219 C1
Southview Rd BR1 186 B6
South View Rd
Hornsey N8 50 A6
Pinner HA5 22 B4
South Villas NW1 71 D2
Southville
SW8 137 D4 269 D1
Southville Cl
East Bedfont TW14 149 C3
West Ewell KT19 215 B1
Southville Cres TW14 149 C3
Southville Jun & Inf Schs
TW14 149 D3
Southville Rd
East Bedfont TW14 149 C4
Thames Ditton KT7 197 B2
SOUTHWARK 117 B5
Southwark Bridge SE1,
EC4 117 A6 252 B5
Southwark Bridge Rd
SE1 117 A5 252 B3
Southwark Cath*
SE1 117 B5 252 C4
Southwark Coll
SE1 116 D4 251 C2
Southwark Coll (Blackfriars Ctr)
SE1 251 C3
Southwark Coll (Camberwell Ctr)
SE5 139 C5
Southwark Coll (Grange Ctr) SE1 263 B5
Southwark Coll (Surrey Docks Ctr) SE16 118 B3
Southwark Park Est 11
SE16 118 B2
Southwark Park Prim Sch
SE16 118 B3
Southwark Park Rd
SE16 118 A2
Southwark Pl BR1 210 B6
Southwark St
SE1 117 A5 252 A3
Southwater Cl
Beckenham BR3 185 D3
8 Poplar E14 97 B1
Southway
Hampstead Garden Suburb
NW11 47 D4
Hayes BR2 209 A2
Totteridge N20 13 C2
Wallington SM6 219 C4
West Barnes SW20 200 D5
South Way
Croydon CR0 223 A5
Friern Barnet N11 31 C4
Harrow HA2 41 C5
Lower Edmonton N9 18 C2
Wembley HA9 66 C3
Southway Cl 9 W12 112 B4
Southwell Ave UB5 63 C2
Southwell Gdns SW7 256 A3
Southwell Grove Rd
E11 76 C6
Southwell Ho
8 Bermondsey SE16 118 B2
13 Stoke Newington
N16 73 C3
Southwell Rd
Camberwell SE5 139 A2
Harrow HA3 43 D3
Thornton Heath CR0 204 C3
South Western Rd
TW1 153 B5
Southwest Rd E11 54 B1
South Wharf Rd
W2 92 B1 236 D2
Southwick Mews W2 236 D2
Southwick Pl W2 237 A1
Southwick St
W2 92 C1 237 A2
Southwick Yd W2 237 A1
SOUTH WIMBLEDON 179 D4
South Wimbledon Sta
SW19 179 D3
South Wlk
Coney Hall BR4 224 C5
Hayes UB3 83 B2
Southwold Dr IG11 80 A3
Southwold Mans W9 91 C4
Southwold Prim Sch
E5 74 B6
Southwold Rd
DA5 169 D5
Upper Clapton E5 74 C6
Southwood Ave
Highgate N6 49 B2
Kingston u T KT2, KT3 177 A2
Southwood Cl
BR1 210 B5
North Cheam KT4 200 D1
Southwood Ct
EC1 234 C1
Hampstead Garden Suburb
NW11 47 D4
Southwood Dr KT5 199 A1
South Woodford Sta
E18 37 B1
Southwood Gdns
Hinchley Wood KT10 213 A5
Ilford IG2 56 D5
Southwood Hall N6 49 B3
Southwood Ho
New Eltham SE9 166 D2
Notting Hill W11 244 A6
Southwood Hospl (Geriatric) N6 49 A2
Southwood Hts N6 49 B2
Southwood La N6 49 A2
Southwood Lawn Rd
N6 49 B2
Southwood Mans N6 49 B3
Southwood Park N6 49 A2
Southwood Prim Sch
RM9 81 A4
Southwood Rd
SE9 166 D2
Woolwich SE28 124 B5
Southwood Smith Ho 4
E2 96 B4
Southwood Smith St
N1 234 C5
South Worple Ave
SW14 133 C2
Southwyck Ho SW9 138 C1
South Yd EC1 242 C4
Sovereign Bsns Ctr EN3 7 B2
Sovereign Cl
Ealing W5 87 C2
Ruislip HA4 39 C1
Stepney E1 118 B6
Sovereign Cres SE16 119 A6
Sovereign Ct
BR2 210 B3
East Molesey KT8 195 B5
Harlington UB7 126 D5
3 Richmond TW9 132 B1
13 Stepney E1 118 B6
Sovereign Gr HA0 65 D5
Sovereign Ho
Ashford TW15 170 A6
23 Bethnal Green E1 96 B3
Chislehurst BR7 189 B3
Edgware NW7 27 B6
3 Wimbledon SW19 179 A4
Woolwich SE18 122 B3
Sovereign Mews
Barnet EN4 2 D2
6 Haggerston E2 95 D5
Sovereign Pk NW10 88 D3
Sovereign Pl HA1 42 D4
Sovereign Rd IG11 102 C4
Sovreign Ct HA6 22 A2
Sowerby Cl SE9 166 B6
Space Apartments
N22 32 B3
Space Bsns Pk NW10 88 D4
Spa Central 1 SW16 182 A3
Space Waye TW14 150 B6
Spa Cl SE19 183 C2
Spa Ct
12 Bermondsey SE16 118 A3
Streatham SW16 182 B6
Spafield St EC1 241 A6
Spa Hill CR7, SE19 183 B2
Spalding Cl HA8 27 C3
Spalding Ct HA8 26 B6
Spalding Ho SE4 163 A6
Spalding Rd
Hendon NW4 46 C3
Streatham SW17 181 B5
Spanby Rd E3 97 C3
Spangate SE3 142 D2
Spaniards Cl NW11 48 B1
Spaniards End NW3 48 B1
Spaniards Rd NW3 70 A6
Spanish Pl W1 238 B2
Spanish Rd SW18 158 A6
Spanswick Lo 2 N15 50 D5
Spa Rd SE16 117 D3 263 D5
Sparkbridge Rd HA1 42 C5
Sparkes Cl BR2 209 B5
Sparke Terr 2 E16 98 D1
Sparkford Gdns N11 31 A5
Sparkford Ho SW11 266 D2
Sparks Cl
Acton W3 89 B1
Dagenham RM8 80 D6
Hampton TW12 173 A4
Sparrow Cl TW12 173 A4
Sparrow Ct E4 36 A4
Sparrow Dr BR5 211 B1
Sparrow Farm Com Jun Sch KT17 216 B4
Sparrow Farm Dr
TW14 150 D4
Sparrow Farm Inf Sch
TW14 150 C4
Sparrow Farm Jun Sch
TW14 150 C4
Sparrow Farm Rd KT17,
KT4 216 B4
Sparrow Gn RM10 81 D5
Sparrow's Farm L Ctr
SE9 167 A4
Sparrows Herne WD23 8 A4
Sparrows La SE9 167 A3
Sparrows Way WD23 8 A4
Sparsholt Rd
Barking IG11 101 C6
Finsbury Pk N19 50 B1
Sparta St SE10 142 A4
Spa Sch SE1 118 A2
Spa View 6 SW16 160 B1
Speakers' Corner*
W1 114 D6 247 D6
Speaker's Ct 3 CR0 205 B1
Speakman Ho SE4 141 A2
Spearman St 8 SE18 144 C6
Spear Mews
SW5 113 C2 255 B3
Spearpoint Gdns IG2 57 D5
Spears Rd N19 50 A1
Speart La TW5 129 A5
Spectacle Works E13 99 C4
Spectrum Ho NW5 71 A4
Spectrum Twr 1 IG1 79 A6
Spedan Cl NW3 70 A5
Speechly Mews E8 73 D3
Speed Ho EC2 242 C4
Speedwell Ct 9 N12 29 D6
Speedwell Ho 11 N12 29 D6
Speedwell St 5 SE8 141 C5
Speedy Pl WC1 233 A1
Speer Rd KT7 196 D3
Speirs Cl KT3 199 D3
Spekehill SE9 166 B1
Speke Rd CR7 183 B1
Speldhurst Cl 2 BR2 208 D4
Speldhurst Rd
Bedford Pk W4 111 B3
Homerton E9 74 D1
Spellbrook Wlk N1 235 B6
Spelman Ho 15 E1 96 A2
Spelman St E1 96 A2
Spelthorne Coll
TW15 170 B6
Spelthorne Gr TW16 171 D3
Spelthorne Inf Sch
TW15 171 B4
Spelthorne Jun Sch
TW15 171 B4
Spelthorne La TW15,
TW17 171 A2
Spence Cl SE16 119 B4
Spencer Ave
Bowes Pk N13 32 B4
Hayes UB4 84 A2
Spencer Cl
BR6 227 D6
Church End N3 29 C1
Ealing NW10 88 B4
Woodford IG8 37 C5
Spencer Ct
5 BR6 227 A3
6 Finchley N3 29 D3
Wimbledon SW20 178 B2
Spencer Dr N2 48 A3
Spencer Gdns SW14 155 A6
Spencer Hill SW19 179 A3
Spencer Hill Rd
SW19 179 A3
Spencer Ho
31 Clapham SW8 137 D3
Hendon NW4 46 B4
24 Putney SW19 156 D3
Vale of Health NW3 70 B5
Wimbledon SW19 156 D1
Spencer House Mus*
SW1 115 C5 249 A3
Spencer Mews
Fulham W6 264 A6
South Lambeth SW9 270 C1
Spencer Park Ct
SW18 158 B6
Spencer Pk
East Molesey KT8 196 A4
Wandsworth SW18 158 B6
Spencer Pl
16 Islington N1 72 D1
SW1 259 B5
Thornton Heath CR0 205 B2
Spencer Rd
Acton W3 111 A5
Bromley BR1 186 D3
Carshalton CR4 203 A2
Chingford E17 36 A1
Chiswick W4 133 A5
East Molesey KT8 196 A4
Friern Barnet N11 31 B6
Harrow HA3 24 C1
Hornsey Vale N8 50 B4
Hounslow TW3, TW5,
TW7 130 A4
Ilford IG3 57 D1
Mitcham CR4 203 A6
Newham E6 99 D6
South Croydon CR2 221 C3
Tottenham N17 34 A2
Twickenham TW2 152 C2
Wandsworth SW18 158 B6
Wembley HA0 65 C6
Wimbledon SW20 178 B2
Spencer Rise NW5 71 B5
Spencer St
Finsbury EC1 94 D4 234 C1
Southall UB2 106 D4
Spencer Wlk
23 Hampstead NW3 70 A4
Putney SW15 134 D1
Spencer Yd SE3 142 D3
Spenlow Ho 2 SE16 118 A3
Spenser Ct 5 TW10 175 D6
Spenser Gr N16 73 C4
Spenser Mews SE21 161 B3
Spenser Rd SE24 160 D6
Spenser St SW1 259 B6
Spens Ho WC1 240 C5
Spensley Wlk N16 73 B5
Speranza St SE18 123 D1
Sperling Rd N17 33 C1
Spert St E14 119 A6
Speyside N14 15 C5
Spey St E14 98 A2
Spezia Rd NW10 90 A5
Spice Ct
10 Battersea SW11 136 A2
2 St George in t East
E1 118 A5
Spice Quay Htss SE1 253 D3
Spicer Cl
Brixton SE5, SW9 138 D3
Walton-on-T KT12 194 C3
Spicer Ct EN1 5 C2
Spicer Ho E2 96 A4
Spices Yd CR0 221 A4
Spigurnell Rd N17 33 B2
Spikes Bridge Rd
UB1 107 A6
Spilsby Cl NW9 27 C1
Spindle Cl SE18 122 A3
Spindle Ho 8 DA15 168 A1
Spindlewood Gdns
CR0 221 C4
Spindrift Ave E14 119 D2
Spinel Cl SE18 123 D1
Spinnaker Cl IG11 102 B4
Spinnaker Ct 2 KT1 175 D2
Spinnaker Ho 21 E14 119 C4
Spinnells Rd HA2 41 B1
Spinney Cl
Beckenham BR3 207 D5
New Malden KT3 199 C4
Worcester Pk KT4 215 D6
Yiewsley UB7 104 A6
Spinney Dr TW14 149 A4
Spinney Gdns
Dagenham RM9 81 A3
Dulwich SE19 183 D5
Spinney Oak BR1 188 A1
Spinneys The BR1 188 B1
Spinney The
Barnes SW13 134 B6
Barnet EN5 1 D3
Cheam SM3 216 C4
DA14 191 A5
Edgware HA7 26 A6
Southgate N21 16 C4
Streatham SW16 159 D1
Sunbury TW16 172 A2
Wembley HA0 65 A5
Spire Ct 10 TW10 154 A5
Spire Ho W2 246 B6
Spires The EN5 1 A2
Spirit Quay E1 118 B5
SPITALFIELDS 95 D2
Spital Sq E1 95 C2 243 B4
Spital St E1 96 A2
Spital Yd E1 243 B4
Spitfire Bsns Pk CR0 220 C2
Spitfire Est The TW5 106 C1
Spitfire Rd SM6 220 A1
Spitfire Way TW5 106 C1
Splendour Wlk SE16 118 C1
Spode Ho SE11 261 A5
Spode Wlk NW3 69 D3
Spondon Rd N15 52 A5
Spoonbill Way UB4 84 D2
Spooner 8 NW9 27 D3
Spooner Ho TW5 129 C6
Spooner Wlk SM6 219 D3
Sporle Ct 6 SW11 136 B2
Sportsbank St SE6 164 A4
Spottons Gr N17 33 A2
Spout Hill CR0 223 C3
Spratt Hall Rd E11 55 A3
Spray St SE18 122 D2
Spreighton Rd KT8 195 D5
Sprewell SW15 157 A5
Spriggs Ho 14 N1 72 D1
Sprimont Pl
SW3 114 D1 257 C2
Springall St 9 SE15 140 B5
Springalls Wharf 2
SE16 118 A4
Springbank N21 16 B5
Springbank Rd SE13 164 C5
Springbank Wlk NW1 71 D1
Springbourne Ct BR3 186 A2
Spring Bridge Rd W5 109 D6
Spring Cl
Barnet EN5 12 D6
Dagenham RM8 58 D1
Springclose La SM3 217 A2
Spring Cnr TW13 149 D1
Spring Cott 10 W12 112 A4
Spring Cotts KT6 197 D4
Spring Court Rd EN2 4 C5
Springcroft Ave N2 48 D5
Spring Ct
Brondesbury NW2 69 B2
Ealing W7 108 B6
Edgware HA8 26 B5
10 Wanstead E18 55 B6
Springdale Rd N16 73 B4
Spring Dr HA5 40 A3
Springett Ho 15 SW2 160 B6
Springfield
Bushey WD23 8 B3
South Norwood SE25 206 A6
Upper Clapton E5 52 B1
Springfield Ave
Hampton TW12 173 D4
Hornsey N10 49 C6
Merton SW20 201 B6
Springfield Cl
Finchley N12 29 D5
Stanmore HA7 9 A1
Springfield Com Prim Sch
N16 52 A3
Springfield Ct
7 Dagenham W3 89 A1
1 Friern Barnet N20 14 D1
Hampstead NW3 70 C1
2 Ilford IG1 78 D3
9 Kingston u T KT1 198 A6
Upper Clapton E5 52 B1
Wallington SM6 219 B3
Springfield Dr IG2 57 A3
Springfield Gdns
BR1 210 B5
Kingsbury NW9 45 B4
Ruislip HA4 40 B1
Upper Clapton E5 52 B1
West Wickham BR4 223 D6
Woodford IG8 37 C3
Springfield Gr
SE7 143 C6
Sunbury TW16 172 A2
Springfield Ho
Acton W3 111 A5
1 Camberwell SE5 139 C3
8 Dalston E8 73 D2
Springfield Hospl
SW17 158 C1
Springfield La NW6 91 D6
Springfield Mount
NW9 45 C4
Springfield Pl KT3 199 A5
Springfield Prim Sch
TW16 171 D1
Springfield Rd
Ashford TW15 170 B5
Bexleyheath DA7 147 D1
Bromley BR1 210 B5
Chingford E4 20 C4
Ealing W7 108 C5
Friern Barnet N11 31 C5
Harrow HA1 42 C3
Hayes UB4 106 C5
Kingston u T KT1 198 A6
Newham E15 98 C4
Penge SE26 184 B5
Plashet E6 78 B1
South Norwood CR7 183 A2
St John's Wood
NW8 92 A6 229 B5
8 Teddington TW11 175 A5
Tottenham Hale N15 52 A5
Twickenham TW2 151 C3
Wallington SM6 219 B3
Walthamstow E17 53 B3
Welling DA16 146 B2
Wimbledon SW19 179 B5
Springfield Rise SE26 162 B1
Springfields 16 EN5 13 D6
Springfield Wlk
3 BR6 211 B1
Paddington NW6 91 D6
Spring Gdns
East Molesey KT8 196 A5
Islington N5 73 A3
SW1 116 A5 250 A4
Wallington SM6 219 C3
Woodford IG8 37 C3
Spring Gr
Brentford W4 132 C6
Hampton TW12 173 D2
Loughton IG10 21 D5
Mitcham CR4 181 A2
SPRING GROVE 130 C3
Spring Grove Cres TW3,
TW5 130 A4
Spring Grove Prim Sch
TW7 130 B3

Spring Grove Rd
Hounslow TW3, TW5,
TW7 130 A4
Richmond TW10 154 B6
Springhallow Sch
W13 87 A1
Spring Hill
Forest Hill SE26 184 C6
Upper Clapton E5 52 A2
Springhill Cl SE5 139 B2
Spring Ho
Merton SW19 179 B2
WC1 234 A1
Springhurst Cl CR0 223 B4
Spring La
Croydon SE25 206 B3
Muswell Hill N10 49 A6
Upper Clapton E5 52 B1
Spring Lake HA7 25 B6
Spring Mews W1 237 D4
SPRING PARK 223 B5
Spring Park Ave CR0 222 D6
Springpark Dr
Beckenham BR3 208 A6
Stoke Newington N4 51 A1
Spring Park Prim Sch
CR0 223 C5
Spring Park Rd CR0 222 D6
Spring Pl
Camden Town NW5 71 B3
Church End N3 29 C1
Springpond Rd RM9 81 A3
Spring Rd TW13 149 D1
Springrice Rd SE13 164 B5
Spring Shaw Rd BR5 190 A2
Spring St W2 92 B1 236 C1
Spring Terr TW10 154 A6
Springtide Cl 10
SE15 140 A4
Spring Vale DA7 147 D1
Springvale Ave TW8 110 A1
Springvale Ct SE12 143 A1
Springvale Terr 5
W14 112 D3
Spring Villa Rd HA8 26 C3
Springwater WC1 240 C4
Springwater Cl SE18 144 C4
Springway HA1 42 B2
Springwell Ave NW10 89 D6
Springwell Cl SW16 182 B6
Springwell Ct TW5 128 D3
Springwell Jun & Inf Schs
TW5 129 A5
Springwell Rd
Heston TW5 128 D4
West Norwood SW16 182 C5
Spring Wlk E1 96 A2
Springwood Cl 8 E3 97 C5
Springwood Cres HA8 11 A2
Springwood Ct CR2 221 C4
Sprowston Mews E7 77 A3
Sprowston Rd E7 77 A3
Spruce Ct W5 110 A3
Sprucedale Gdns
CR0 222 D4
Spruce Hills Rd E17 36 A1
Spruce Ho
2 Brentford TW8 131 C5
15 Rotherhithe SE16 118 D4
Spruce Pk BR2 208 D5
Sprules Rd SE4 141 A3
Spurfield KT8 195 D6
Spurgeon Ave SE19 183 B2
Spurgeon Rd SE19 183 B3
Spurgeon's Coll SE25 183 C1
Spurgeon St
SE1 117 B3 262 C6
Spur Ho 10 SW19 179 D2
Spurling Rd
Dagenham RM9 81 B2
East Dulwich SE22 139 D1
Spur Rd
Brentford TW7 131 B5
Edgware HA8 26 A6
Feltham TW14 128 B1
SE1 116 C4 251 A2
Tottenham N15 51 B5
Wallend IG11 101 A4
Spurstowe Rd E8 74 B2
Spurstowe Terr E8 74 B3
Spurway Par 2 IG2 56 B4
Square Rigger Row 7
SW11 136 A2
Square The
Hammersmith W6 112 C1
Hayes UB11 105 B5
Ilford IG1 56 C2
Leyton E10 76 A5
12 Richmond TW10 153 D6
SW6 265 A1
Square The *continued*
Wallington SM5 219 A3
Woodford IG8 37 A5
Squarey St SW17 158 A1
Squire Ct 2 CR0 205 C1
Squire Gdns NW8 229 C1
Squire's Almshouses 7
E17 53 D5
Squires Bridge Rd
KT17 192 B5
Squires Ct
Finchley N3 30 A2
SW4 270 B1
Wimbledon SW19 179 C6
Squires Ho 3 SE18 144 D6
Squires La N3 30 A2
Squire's Mount NW3 70 B5
Squire's Rd TW17 192 C5
Squires The RM7 59 D3
Squires Wlk TW15 171 B3
Squires Wood Dr
BR7 188 B3
Squirrel Cl TW4 128 C2
Squirrel Mews W13 109 A6
Squirrels Cl
Hillingdon UB10 60 C1
North Finchley N12 30 A6
Orpington BR6 211 C1
Squirrels Ct KT4 215 D6
Squirrels Gn KT4 216 A6
Squirrel's La IG9 21 D1
Squirrels The
Bushey WD23 8 B5
Lewisham SE13 142 B2
Pinner HA5 41 B6
Squirrels Trad Est
UB3 105 D3
Squirries St E2 96 A4
Stable Cl
Kingston u T KT2 176 B4
Northolt UB5 85 C5
Stable Ct 4 SM6 219 A5
Stable Ho 9 SE16 118 C4
Stable Mews
Twickenham TW1 152 D3
West Norwood SE27 183 A5
Stables End BR6 227 A5
Stables The IG9 21 C4
Stables Way
SE11 116 C1 261 A2
Stable Way W10 90 C1
Stable Wlk N2 30 B2
Stable Yd Rd
SW1 115 C4 249 B2
Staburn Ct HA8 27 A1
Stacey Ave N18 34 C6
Stacey Cl E10 54 B4
Stacey St
Highbury N7 72 C5
Soho WC2 93 D1 239 D1
Stack Ho SW1 258 B3
Stackhouse St SW1 257 C6
Stacy Path 13 SE5 139 C5
Staddon Cl BR3 207 A5
Stadium Bsns Ctr HA9 66 D5
Stadium Rd
Hendon NW2 46 C2
SE7, SE18 144 B6
Stadium Rd E NW2 46 C2
Stadium Ret Pk HA9 66 C5
Stadium St
SW10 136 A5 266 B3
Stadium Way HA9 66 C4
Staffa Rd E10 53 A1
Stafford Cl
Cheam SM3 217 A2
Maida Vale NW6 91 C4
Southgate N14 15 C6
Walthamstow E17 53 B3
Stafford Cripps Ho
30 Bethnal Green E2 96 C4
SW6 264 D5
Stafford Cross CR0 220 B3
Stafford Cross Bsns Pk
CR0 220 B3
Stafford Ct
Croydon CR0 220 C4
Ealing W7 86 D1
Kensington W8 255 B6
South Lambeth SW8 270 A2
Stafford Gdns CR0 220 B3
Stafford Ho SE1 263 D2
Stafford Mans
13 Hammersmith
W14 112 D3
14 Stockwell SW4 138 A1
SW11 267 C3
Stafford Morris Ho 9
E15 98 C6
Stafford Pl
Richmond TW10 154 B4
SW1 115 C3 259 A6
Stafford Rd
Bow E3 97 B5
Harrow HA3 24 A3
Kingston u T KT3 199 A6
Maida Vale NW6 91 C4
Plashet E7 77 D2
Ruislip HA4 61 D4
Sidcup DA14 189 C6
Wallington CR0, SM6 220 A3
Staffordshire Ho N3 47 A6
Staffordshire St
Peckham SE15 140 A4
Peckham SE15 140 B4
Stafford St W1 249 A4
Stafford Terr
W8 113 C3 255 A6
Stag Cl HA8 27 A1
Stag Ct 16 SM6 219 B2
Stagg Hill EN4 2 C6
Stag Hts 1 IG9 21 B2
Stag La
Chigwell IG9 21 B2
Edgware HA8, NW9 45 A6
Roehampton SW15 155 D2
Stag Lane Fst & Mid Schs
HA8 26 C1
Stags Ct KT7 197 A2
Stagshaw Ho 17 SE22 139 C2
Stags Way TW7 130 D6
Stainbank Rd CR4 203 B6
Stainby Cl UB7 104 A3
Stainby Rd N15 51 D5
Staincliffe Ho 5
SM1 218 A4
Stainer Ho SE9 143 C1
Stainer St SE1 252 D3
Staines Ave SM3 216 D6
Staines By-Pass
TW15 170 A4
Staines Rd
East Bedfont TW14 149 B4
Feltham TW14, TW3 150 C6
Hounslow TW3 129 C1
Ilford IG1 79 B4
Twickenham TW2 152 A1
Twickenham TW13,
TW2 151 D1
Staines Rd E TW12,
TW16 172 C2
Staines Rd W TW15 171 B3
Staines Wlk DA14 190 C4
Stainford Cl TW15 171 B5
Stainforth Rd
Ilford IG2 57 B2
Walthamstow E17 53 C5
Staining La EC2 242 B2
Stainmore Cl BR7 189 B2
Stainsbury St 25 E2 96 C5
Stainsby Rd E14 97 C1
Stainton Rd
Enfield EN3 6 C4
Lewisham SE13 164 B4
Stalbridge Flats W1 238 B1
Stalbridge Ho NW1 232 A3
Stalbridge St NW1 237 B4
Stalham St SE16 118 B3
Stambourne Ho SW8 270 B2
Stambourne Way
Penge SE19 183 D3
West Wickham BR4 224 A5
Stamford Bridge Stadium
(Chelsea FC)
SW6 135 D5 265 C4
Stamford Brook Ave
W6 111 D3
Stamford Brook Gdns 1
W6 111 D3
Stamford Brook Mans 2
W6 111 D2
Stamford Brook Rd
W6 111 D3
Stamford Brook Sta
W6 111 D2
Stamford Cl
Harrow HA3 24 C3
2 London NW3 70 A5
Southall UB1 107 C6
Tottenham Hale N15 52 A5
Stamford Cotts SW10 265 D4
Stamford Ct
Chiswick W6 112 A2
Edgware HA8 26 B6
Stamford Dr BR2 208 D5
Stamford Gdns RM9 80 C1
Stamford Gr E 1 N16 52 A1
Stamford Gr W 4 N16 52 A1
STAMFORD HILL 51 C1
Stamford Hill N16 51 D1
Stamford Hill Mans 1
N16 51 D1
Stamford Hill Prim Sch
N15 51 B3
Stamford Hill Sta N16 51 C2
Stamford Ho N15 52 A4
Stamford Hospl W6 112 A2
Stamford Lo 2 N16 51 D2
Stamford Mans 2
N16 52 A1
Stamford Rd
Dagenham RM9 80 C1
Kingsland N1 73 C2
Newham E6 100 A6
South Tottenham N15 52 A4
Stamford St
SE1 116 C5 251 B4
Stamp Pl E2 95 D4
Stanard Cl N16 51 C2
Stanborough Cl
TW12 173 B4
Stanborough Ho 4
E3 97 D3
Stanborough Pas E8 73 D2
Stanborough Rd TW3,
TW7 130 B2
Stanbridge Mans
SW15 134 C2
Stanbridge Pl N21 16 D2
Stanbridge Rd SW15 134 C2
Stanbrook Ct W1 249 A4
Stanbrook Rd SE2 124 B4
Stanburn Fst & Mid Schs
HA7 25 C3
Stanbury Ct 16 NW3 70 D2
Stanbury Rd
Nunhead SE15 140 C3
Peckham SE15 140 B3
Stancroft NW9 45 C4
Standale Gr HA4 39 A4
Standard Ind Est E16 122 B4
Standard Pl 13 EC2 95 C4
Standard Rd
Becontree NW10 89 B3
Belvedere DA17 125 C1
DA6 147 A1
Enfield EN3 7 A6
Hounslow TW4 129 A2
Standen Rd SW18 157 C4
Standfield Gdns RM10 81 C2
Standfield Rd RM10 81 C3
Standish Ho
6 Chiswick W6 112 A2
SE9 143 B1
Standish Rd W6 112 A2
Standlake Point 1
SE23 162 D1
Standor Ho 7 CR4 202 D6
Stane Cl SW19 179 D3
Stanedge Ct SW16 182 A5
Stane Gr SW4 138 A3
Stanesgate Ho 20
SE15 140 A5
Stanetta Ct 3 RM6 58 B2
Stane Way SE18 144 A5
Stanfield Ho
8 Northolt UB5 84 D5
NW8 236 D6
Stanfield Rd 14 E3 97 A5
Stanford Cl
Hampton TW12 173 B4
Romford RM7 59 D3
Ruislip HA4 39 A3
Stanford Ct
Friern Barnet N11 31 A5
Kensington W8 255 D5
Walham Green SW6 265 D1
Stanford Ho IG11 102 B5
Stanford Pl
SE1 117 C2 263 A3
Stanford Prim Sch
SW16 181 D2
Stanford Rd
Friern Barnet N11 30 D5
Thornton Heath SW16 182 A1
W8 113 D3 255 D6
Stanford St SW1 259 C3
Stanford Way SW16 181 D1
Stangate SE1 260 D6
Stangate Cres WD6 11 C6
Stangate Gdns HA7 25 B6
Stangate Lo N21 16 B4
Stangate Mansi TW1 152 D1
Stanger Rd SE25 206 A5
Stanhope Ave
Harrow HA3 24 B2
Hayes BR2 209 A1
Hendon N3 47 B6
Stanhope Cl 28 SE16 118 D4
Stanhope Ct N3 29 B1
Stanhope Gate W1 248 B4
Stanhope Gdns
Crouch End N6 49 C3
Dagenham RM8 81 B5
Edgware NW7 27 D5
Redbridge IG1 56 B1
Stoke Newington N4 51 A3
SW7 114 A2 256 B4
Stanhope Gr BR3 207 B5
Stanhope Ho
Crouch End N6 49 C3
5 Friern Barnet N11 31 B6
4 Putney SW15 156 C6
SE8 141 B5
Stanhope Mews E
SW7 114 A2 256 B4
Stanhope Mews S
SW7 256 B3
Stanhope Mews W
SW7 114 A2 256 B4
Stanhope Par NW1 232 A2
Stanhope Park Rd
UB6 86 A3
Stanhope Pl W2 237 C1
Stanhope Prim Sch
UB6 86 A3
Stanhope Rd
Barnet EN5 12 D5
Crouch End N6 49 C2
DA7 147 A3
Dagenham RM8 81 B5
North Finchley N12 30 A5
Sidcup DA15 190 A6
Southall UB6 86 A2
South Croydon CR0 221 C5
Wallington SM5 219 A1
Walthamstow E17 53 D4
Stanhope Row W1 248 C3
Stanhope St
NW1 93 C4 232 A1
Stanhope Terr
W2 114 B6 246 D6
Stanier Cl SW5 254 D1
Stanlake Mews 7
W12 112 C5
Stanlake Rd W12 112 C5
Stanlake Villas 8
W12 112 C5
Stanley Ave
Barking IG11 101 D5
Beckenham BR2, BR3 208 A6
Dagenham RM8 59 B2
Greenford UB6 86 A6
Wembley HA0 66 A1
West Barnes KT3 200 A4
Stanley Bldgs NW1 233 A3
Stanley Cl
Eltham SE9 167 A3
SW8 270 C5
Wembley HA0 66 A1
Stanley Cohen Ho
EC1 242 A5
Stanley Cres
W11 113 B6 244 C6
Stanleycroft Cl TW7 130 C4
Stanley Ct
Belmont SM2 217 D1
11 Ealing W5 87 C2
Wallington SM5 219 A1
Wimbledon SW19 179 C4
Stanley Gardens Rd
TW11 174 C5
Stanley Gdns
Bedford Pk W3 111 C4
Cricklewood NW2 68 C3
Mitcham CR4 181 A4
W11 244 C6
Wallington SM6 219 C2
Stanley Glynn Ct BR7 188 C5
Stanley Gr
Clapham SW11 137 A3
Thornton Heath CR0 204 C3
Stanley Ho
35 Clapham SW8 137 D3
Leytonstone E11 54 C3
22 Poplar E14 97 C1
Wembley HA0 66 A1
Stanley Holloway Ct
E16 99 A1
Stanley Inf Sch KT11 174 C6
Stanley Jun Sch
KT11 174 C6
Stanley Mans
SW10 266 B6
Upper Tooting SW17 158 D2
Stanley Park Dr HA0 88 B6
Stanley Park High Sch
SM5 219 A2
Stanley Park Inf Sch
SM5 218 D1
Stanley Park Jun Sch
SM5 218 D1
Stanley Park Rd SM5,
SM6 219 A1
Stanley Rd
Acton Green W3 111 A3
Ashford TW15 170 A5
Belmont SM2 217 D1
BR6 211 D1
Bromley BR2 209 C5
Chingford E4 20 B3
East Finchley N2 48 B6
Edmonton N9 17 D2
Enfield EN1 5 C2
Friern Barnet N11 31 D5
Harringay N15 50 D5
Harrow HA2 64 A6
2 Hendon NW9 46 A2
Ilford IG1 79 B6
Isleworth TW3 130 A1
Mill Meads E15 98 B6
Mitcham CR4 181 A3
Morden SM4 201 C5
Mortlake SW14 132 D1
Muswell Hill N10 31 B3
Northwood HA6 22 A2
Plashet E12 78 A3
Sidcup DA14 168 A1
Southall UB1 107 A6
Teddington TW11,
TW2 174 C5
Thornton Heath CR0 204 C3
Twickenham TW2 152 B1
Wallington SM5 219 A1
Walthamstow E10 53 D3
Wembley HA9 66 B2
Wimbledon SW19 179 C4
Woodford E18 36 D2
Stanley St SE14, SE8 141 B5
Stanley Studios SW10 266 B6
Stanley Tech High Sch for
Boys SE25 205 D6
Stanley Terr 8 N19 72 A6
Stanliff Ho 8 E14 119 C3
Stanmer St SW11 136 C3
STANMORE 25 A5
Stanmore Coll HA7 25 C4
Stanmore Gdns
Richmond TW9 132 B2
Sutton SM1 218 A5
Stanmore Hill HA7 25 A6
Stanmore Ho 21 SW8 137 D3
Stanmore Lo HA7 25 B6
Stanmore Pl NW1 231 D6
Stanmore Rd
Harringay N15 50 D5
Leytonstone E11 54 D1
Richmond TW9 132 B2
Stanmore St
N1 94 B6 233 C6
Stanmore Sta HA7 25 D6
Stanmore Terr 3
BR3 185 C1
Stanmuir Lo NW9 45 A4
Stannard Cotts 27 E1 96 C3
Stannard Ct SE6 163 D3
Stannard Mews E8 74 A2
Stannard Rd E8 74 A2
Stannary Pl SE11 261 B1
Stannary St
SE11 116 C1 261 B1
Stannet Way SM6 219 C4
Stansbury Sq 3 W10 91 A4
Stansfeld Ho SE1 263 D3
Stansfeld Rd E6 99 D1
Stansfield Rd
Cranford TW4, TW5 128 B3
Stockwell SW9 138 B2
Stansgate Rd RM10 81 C5
Stanstead Cl BR2 208 D3
Stanstead Gr SE23 163 B3
Stanstead Ho E3 98 A3
Stanstead Manor
SM1 217 C2
Stanstead Rd
Forest Hill SE23, SE6 163 A3
Wanstead E11 55 B4
Stansted Cres DA5 168 D3
Stansted Express
Terminal EC2 243 A4
Stansted Rd TW6 148 B5
Stanswood Gdns SE5 139 C5
Stanthorpe Cl SW16 182 A5
Stanthorpe Rd SW16 182 A5
Stanton Ave TW11 174 C4

Stanton Cl
Chessington KT19 214 D3
North Cheam KT4 200 D1
Stanton Ct
5 DA15 168 A1
Finchley N3 29 C2
Stoke Newington N16 51 B2
Stanton Ho 9 SE10 142 A6
Stanton Rd
Barnes SW13 133 D3
Thornton Heath CR0 205 A2
Wimbledon SW20 178 D2
Stanton Sq SE26 185 B6
Stanton Way SE26 185 B6
Stanway Ct 23 N1 95 C5
Stanway Gdns
Acton W3 110 C5
Edgware HA8 27 A5
Stanway St N1 95 C5
STANWELL 148 A3
Stanwell Fields CE Prim Sch TW19 148 A4
Stanwell Rd
Ashford TW15 170 A6
East Bedfont TW14, TW19, TW6 148 D4
Stanwell TW15 148 A1
Stanwick Rd W14 113 B2 254 C3
Stanworth Ct TW5 129 C5
Stanworth St SE1 253 D1
Stanyhurst SE23 163 A3
Stapenhill Rd HA0 65 B5
Staplefield Cl
Pinner HA5 23 A3
3 Streatham SW2 160 A3
Stapleford N17 33 C1
Stapleford Ave IG2 57 C4
Stapleford Cl
Chingford E4 20 A1
Kingston u T KT1 198 C6
Putney SW19 157 A4
Stapleford Rd HA0 65 D1
Stapleford Way IG11 102 B4
Staplehurst Ct SW11 158 D5
Staplehurst Ho 18 E5 74 B3
Staplehurst Rd
Lewisham SE13 164 C6
Sutton SM5 218 C1
Staple Inn WC2 241 A3
Staple Inn Bldgs WC2 241 A3
Staples Cl SE16 119 A5
Staples Corner Bsns Pk NW2 46 B1
Staples Corner (East) NW2 46 B1
Staples Corner Ret Pk NW2 46 B1
Staples Corner (West) NW2 46 B1
Staple St SE1 117 B4 252 D1
Stapleton Gdns CR0 220 C3
Stapleton Hall N4 50 B2
Stapleton Hall Rd N4 50 B2
Stapleton Ho 19 E2 96 B4
Stapleton Rd
DA7 147 B6
Orpington BR6 227 D5
Upper Tooting SW17 159 A1
Stapley Rd DA17 125 C1
Stapylton Rd EN5 1 A2
Star Alley EC3 253 B6
Star and Garter Hill TW10 154 A4
Starboard Way E14 119 C3
Starbuck Cl SE9 166 C4
Star Cl EN3 18 C5
Starcross St NW1 93 C4 232 B1
Star Ct UB10 83 A3
Stardome* NW1 238 A5
Starfield Rd W12 112 A4
Star & Garter Mans SW15 134 D2
Star La E16 98 C3
Starliner Ct N7 72 C2
Starling Cl
Beckenham BR3 207 A3
Buckhurst Hill IG9 21 A3
Pinner HA5 40 C6
Starling Ct E13 99 B6
Starling Ho NW8 230 A4
Starling Wlk TW12 173 A5
Starmans Cl RM9 103 A6
Star Path UB5 85 C5
Star Pl E1 118 A6
Star Prim Sch E16 98 C3
Star Rd
Hillingdon UB10 83 A3
Hounslow TW7 130 B3
W14 113 B1 254 C1
Star St W2 92 C1 237 A2
Starts Cl BR6 226 C5
Starts Hill Ave BR6 226 D4
Starts Hill Rd BR6 226 D4
Starveall Cl UB7 104 B3
Star Works NW10 90 A4
Star Yd WC2 94 C1 241 A2
State Farm Ave BR6 227 A4
Stateland Ct 10 N11 31 B6
Staten Gdns TW1 152 D3
Statham Ct N7 72 A5
Statham Gr
Edmonton N18 33 C5
Stoke Newington N16 73 B5
Statham Ho SW8 269 A2
Station App
Ashford TW15 170 B6
Belmont SM2 217 A1
Bexleyheath DA7 147 A3
Chislehurst BR7 188 C1
Dagenham NW10 89 D4
Elmstead BR7 188 A4
20 Finchley N12 29 D6
Forest Gate E7 77 B4
Friern Barnet N11 31 B5
Fulham SW6 135 A2
Greenford UB6 64 B1
Hampton TW12 173 C2
Hayes BR2 209 A1
Hayes Town UB3 105 D3
Hinchley Wood KT10 212 D5
4 Kingston u T KT1, KT2 176 C2
Lewisham SE3 143 B2
Mottingham SE9 166 B3
New Barnet EN5 2 A1
6 New Malden KT4 200 A1
Orpington BR6 227 D6
Penge SE26 185 B5
Pinner HA5 41 A6
Richmond TW9 132 C4
Ruislip HA4 39 D1
Shepperton TW17 193 A4
3 South Croydon CR0 221 B6
South Ruislip HA4 62 B3
Streatham SW16 181 D5
Sunbury TW16 172 A2
1 Surbiton KT6 198 A3
Walthamstow E17 53 C4
Wanstead E11 55 A4
Welling DA16 146 A3
Wembley HA0 65 B2
2 Woodford E18 37 B1
Woodford IG8 37 B4
Woodford IG9 37 D6
Worcester Pk KT19 216 A3
Yiewsley UB7 104 A5
Station Approach Rd W4 133 A5
Station Ave
5 Brixton SW9 138 D2
Kingston u T KT3 199 C6
14 Richmond TW9 132 C4
West Ewell KT19 215 D1
Station Bldgs
Catford SE6 163 C4
Merton SW20 178 C1
Station Blgs W5 110 B5
Station Cl
Finchley N3 29 C2
Hampton TW12 173 D2
Station Cres
Ashford TW15 170 A6
Greenwich SE3 121 A1
Tottenham N15 51 B5
Wembley HA0 65 B2
Station Ct
Mitcham CR4 202 C5
5 Nunhead SE15 140 C3
South Tottenham N15 51 D4
Wembley HA9 43 C1
Stationers Hall Ct EC4 241 D1
Station Est BR3 206 D5
Station Est 1 E18 37 B1
Station Estate Rd TW14 150 B3
Station Gdns W4 133 A5
Station Gr HA0 66 A2
Station Hill BR2 225 A6
Station House Mews N9 34 A6
Station Mans 9 N3 29 C2
Station Mews Terr 4 SE3 121 A1
Station Par
Acton W3 88 C1
1 Ashford TW15 170 B6
Barking IG11 79 A1
Belmont HA3 25 A1
Cockfosters EN4 3 A1
Cricklewood NW2 68 C2
Dagenham RM10 81 C2
Ealing W5 110 B5
Edgware HA8 26 A3
Feltham TW14 150 B4
Northolt UB5 63 D4
4 Osidge N14 15 D3
Richmond TW9 132 C4
Ruislip HA4 61 B6
South Harrow HA2 63 D4
4 Upper Tooting SW12 159 A3
2 Wanstead E11 55 A4
Woodford IG9 37 D6
Station Pas
New Cross Gate SE15 140 C4
Woodford E18 37 B1
Station Pl N4 72 C6
Station Rd
Ashford TW15 170 B6
Barkingside IG6 57 B6
Barnes SW13 133 D3
Beckenham BR2 186 C1
Belvedere DA17 125 C3
Bexleyheath DA7 147 A2
Bromley BR1 187 A2
Camden Town N19 71 C5
Carshalton SM5 218 D4
Chadwell Heath RM6 58 D2
Chessington KT9 214 A3
Chingford E4 20 B3
Church End N3 29 C1
Claygate KT10 212 C3
Croydon CR0 205 A1
Edgware HA8 26 C4
Edgware NW7 27 C4
Esher KT10 212 B6
Forest Gate E7 77 A4
Friern Barnet N11 31 B5
Greenhill HA1 42 D4
Hampton TW12 173 D2
Hampton Wick KT1 175 D2
Hanwell W7 108 C5
Harlesden NW10 89 D5
Hayes UB3 105 C2
Hendon NW4 46 A4
Hounslow TW3 129 D1
Ilford IG1 78 D5
Kingston u T KT2 176 C2
Lewisham SE13 142 A2
Leyton E10 76 A5
Manor Pk E12 78 A4
Merton SW19 180 A2
New Barnet EN5 13 D6
North Harrow HA1, HA2 41 D4
Orpington BR6 227 D6
Penge SE20 184 C4
Shepperton TW17 193 A4
Sidcup DA14, DA15 168 A1
Southgate N21 16 D3
South Norwood SE25 205 D5
Sunbury TW16 172 A3
Teddington TW11 175 A4
Thames Ditton KT7 196 D2
Tottenham Hale N17 52 A6
Twickenham TW1 152 D4
Walthamstow E17 53 A4
West Acton W5 88 B1
West Barnes KT3 200 B4
West Drayton UB7 104 A4
West Wickham BR4 208 A1
Wood Green N22 32 B1
Station Rd N DA17 125 D3
Station Rise SE27 160 D2
Station Sq BR5 211 A4
Station St
Newham E16 122 D5
Stratford E15 76 B1
Station Terr
Camberwell SE5 139 A4
Kensal Rise NW10 90 D5
Station View UB6 86 B6
Station Way
Cheam SM2, SM3 217 A1
Claygate KT10 212 C2
Woodford IG9 37 D6
Station Yd TW1 153 A4
Staton Ct 1 E10 53 D2
Staunton Ho SE17 263 A3
Staunton Rd KT2 176 B3
Staunton St SE8 141 B6
Staveley NW1 232 A2
Staveley Cl
Hackney E9 74 C3
Lower Holloway N7 72 A4
New Cross Gate SE15 140 C4
8 Peckham SE15 140 B4
Staveley Ct 4 E11 55 A4
Staveley Gdns W4 133 B4
Staveley Ho SE4 163 A6
Staveley Rd
Ashford TW15 171 B4
Chiswick W4 133 B5
Stavers Ho 31 E3 97 B5
Staverton Rd NW2 68 C1
Stave Yard Rd SE16 119 A5
Stavordale Lo W14 254 D6
Stavordale Rd
Carshalton SM5 202 A2
Highbury N5 72 D4
Stayner's Rd E1 96 D3
Stayton Rd SM1 217 C5
Steadfast Rd KT1 175 D2
Steadman Ct EC1 242 B6
Steadman Ho 4 RM10 81 C5
Stead St SE17 117 B2 262 C3
Steam Farm La TW14 127 D1
Stean St E8 95 D6
Stebbing Ho 8 W11 112 D5
Stebbing Way IG11 102 A5
Stebondale St E14 120 A2
Stebon Prim Sch E14 97 C2
Stedham Pl WC1 240 A2
Stedman Cl UB10 60 C5
Steedman St
SE17 117 A2 262 A3
Steeds Rd N10 30 D2
Steel App IG11 102 B5
Steele Rd
Acton Green W4 111 A3
Becontree NW10 89 A5
Isleworth TW7 131 A1
Leyton E11 76 C4
Tottenham N17 51 C6
Steele's Mews N NW3 70 D2
Steele's Mews S NW3 70 D2
Steele's Rd NW3 70 D2
Steele Wlk DA8 147 D5
Steel's La 23 E1 96 C1
Steen Way 7 SE22 161 C6
Steep Cl BR6 227 D2
Steep Hill
South Croydon CR0 221 C4
Streatham SW16 159 D1
Steeple Cl
Fulham SW6 135 A3
Wimbledon SW19 179 A5
Steeple Ct
19 Bethnal Green E1 96 B3
Wimbledon SW19 179 A5
Steeplestone Cl N18 33 A5
Steepleton Ct E11 54 A1
Steeple Wlk N1 235 B6
Steerforth St SW18 158 A2
Steering Cl N9 18 C3
Steers Mead CR4 180 D2
Steers Way SE16 119 A4
Steetley Ct 14 SM2 218 A1
Steinman Ct TW7 130 D2
Stelfax Ho WC1 233 D2
Stella Cl UB8 82 D2
Stella Rd SW17 180 D4
Stellar Ho 4 N17 33 D4
Stellman Cl E5 74 A5
Stembridge Rd SE20 184 B1
Sten Cl 12 EN3 7 C6
Stephan Cl E8 96 A6
Stephen Cl BR6 227 D5
Stephen Ct 18 SW19 156 D3
Stephendale Rd SW6 136 A3
Stephen Fox Ho 7 W4 111 C1
Stephen Hawking Sch E14 97 A1
Stephen Mews W1 239 C3
Stephen Pl SW4 137 C2
Stephen Saunders Ct SW11 158 C6
Stephens Ct
Brockley SE4 141 A2
E16 98 D3
Stephens Lo N12 14 A1
Stephenson Ct SM2 217 B1
Stephenson Ho
2 Gospel Oak NW5 71 B4
6 Maitland Pk NW3 70 D3
Newington SE1 262 A6
West Heath SE2 124 D1
Stephenson Rd
Ealing W7 86 D1
Twickenham TW4 151 C4
Walthamstow E17 53 A4
Stephenson St
Dagenham NW10 89 D4
Newham E16 98 C2
Stephenson Way
NW1 93 C3 239 B6
Stephen's Rd E15 98 C6
Stephen St W1 239 C3
STEPNEY 96 D2
Stepney City E1 96 C2
Stepney Cswy E1 96 D1
Stepney Gn E1 96 D2
Stepney Greencoat CE Prim Sch The E14 97 B1
Stepney Green Ct 4 E1 96 D2
Stepney Green Sch E1 96 D2
Stepney Green Sta E1 96 D3
Stepney High St E1 96 D2
Stepney Way
Mitcham CR4 181 A2
Stepney E1 96 C2
Sterling Ave HA8 26 B6
Sterling Cl NW10 68 A1
Sterling Gdns SE14 141 A6
Sterling Ho SE9 143 B1
Sterling Ind Est RM10 81 D4
Sterling Pl W5 110 A2
Sterling Rd EN2 5 B5
Sterling St SW7 257 B6
Sterling Way (North Circular Rd) N18 33 C5
Stern Cl IG11 102 C5
Sterndale Rd W14 112 D3
Sterne St W12 112 D4
Sternhall La SE15 140 A2
Sternhold Ave SW12, SW2 159 D2
Sterry Cres RM10 81 C3
Sterry Dr
Thames Ditton KT7 196 C3
Worcester Pk KT19 215 C4
Sterry Gdns RM10 81 C2
Sterry Rd
Barking IG11 101 D6
Dagenham RM10 81 C3
Sterry St SE1 252 C1
Steucers La SE23 163 A3
Stevanne Ct 1 DA17 125 C1
Steve Biko Ct W10 90 D3
Steve Biko La SE6 185 C6
Steve Biko Lodge 13 E13 99 A5
Steve Biko Rd N7 72 C5
Steve Biko Way TW3 129 C2
Stevedale Rd DA16 146 C3
Stevedore St 3 E1 118 B5
Stevenage Rd
Fulham SW6 134 D4
Wallend E6 78 C2
Stevens Ave E9 74 C2
Stevens Cl
Beckenham BR3 185 C4
Hampton TW12 173 B4
Pinner HA5 40 C4
Stevens Ct BR3 185 C4
Stevens Gn WD23 8 A3
Stevens Ho KT1 175 D1
Stevens' La KT10 213 A2
Stevenson Cl EN5 14 B4
Stevenson Cres SE16 118 B1
Stevenson Ho
1 Battersea SW11 136 D3
6 Clapham Pk SW2 160 A6
NW8 229 A6
Wembley HA9 65 D6
Stevens Rd RM8 80 C5
Stevens St SE1 263 B6
Steventon Rd W12 111 D6
Stewards Holte Wlk 3 N11 31 B6
Stewart Ave TW17 192 C5
Stewart Cl
BR7 188 D6
Hampton TW12 173 A4
Kingsbury NW9 45 A3
Stewart Fleming Prim Sch SE20 206 C6
Stewart Headlam Prim Sch E1 96 B3
Stewart Ho
SE1 263 A5
Stanmore HA7 25 B5
Stewart Quay UB3 105 C4
Stewart Rainbird Ho 1 E12 78 C3
Stewart Rd E15 76 B4
Stewartsby Cl N18 33 A5
Stewart's Gr SW3 114 C1 257 A2
Stewart's Rd SW8 137 C4 269 A2
Stewart St E14 120 A4
Stew La EC4 252 A6
Steyne Ho
15 Acton W3 110 D5
11 Acton W3 111 A5
Steyne Rd W3 110 D5
Steyning Gr SE9 188 B6
Steynings Way N12 29 C5
Steyning Way TW4 128 C1
Steynton Ave DA5 168 D2
Stickland Rd DA17 125 C2
Stickleton Cl UB6 85 D4
Stifford Ho E1 96 C2
Stilecroft Gdns HA0 65 B5
Stile Hall Gdns W4 110 C1
Stile Hall Par 6 W4 110 C1
Stileman Ho 4 E3 97 B2
Stile Path TW16 194 A5
Stiles Cl
BR2 210 B3
Erith DA8 125 D1
Stillingfleet Rd SW13 134 A6
Stillington St SW1 115 C2 259 B4
Stillness Jun & Inf Schs SE23 163 A5
Stillness Rd SE23 163 B5
Stilwell Dr UB8 82 B3
Stilwell Rdbt UB8 104 D6
Stipularis Dr UB4 84 D3
Stirling Ave
Pinner HA5 41 A2
Upper Halliford TW17 193 C6
Wallington SM6 220 A1
Stirling Cl
Sidcup DA14 189 D6
Streatham SW16 181 C2
Stirling Cnr EN5, WD6 11 B5
Stirling Ct
Clerkenwell EC1 241 C6
Ealing W13 109 B6
Strand WC2 240 C1
Stirling Gr TW3 130 A3
Stirling Ho 5 SE18 122 D1
Stirling Ind Ctr WD6 11 B6
Stirling Lo 7 EN5 14 A6
Stirling Mans NW6 70 A2
Stirling Rd
Harrow HA3 42 D6
Hayes UB3 106 B6
Newham E13 99 B5
South Acton W3 110 D3
Stanwell TW19, TW6 148 B5
Stockwell SW9 138 A3
Tottenham N17 34 A2
Twickenham TW2 151 D4
Walthamstow E17 53 A6
Wood Green N22 32 D2
Stirling Ret Pk WD6 11 B5
Stirling Way
Borehamwood WD6 11 B6
Thornton Heath CR0 204 A2
Stiven Cres HA2 63 B5
Stoatley Ho 10 SW15 156 A3
Stockbeck NW1 232 B3
Stockbridge Ho EN2 4 D3
Stockbury Rd CR0 206 C3
Stockdale Rd RM8 81 B6
Stockdove Way UB6 86 D4
Stocker Gdns RM9 80 C1
Stockfield Rd
Claygate KT10 212 C3
Streatham SW16 160 B1
Stockford Ave NW7 28 D3
Stockholm Ho E1 118 A6
Stockholm Rd SE16 118 C1
Stockholm Way 9 E1 118 A5
Stockhurst Cl SW15 134 D3
Stockingswater La EN3 7 B2
Stockleigh Hall NW8 230 B4
Stockley Acad UB8 82 B1
Stockley Cl UB7 104 D4
Stockley Ctry Pk UB7 104 C6
Stockley Farm Rd UB7 104 D3
Stockley Park Bsns Pk UB11 105 A5
Stockley Rd UB7, UB8, UB11 104 D4
Stock Orchard Cres N7 72 B3
Stock Orchard St N7 72 B3
Stockport Rd SW16 181 D2
Stocks Ct 5 E1 96 D3
Stocksfield Rd E17 54 A6
Stocks Pl
Hillingdon UB10 82 C6

Stocks Pl *continued*
16 Limehouse E14 119 B6
Stock St E13 99 A5
Stockton Cl EN5 2 A1
Stockton Gdns
Edgware NW7 11 C1
Tottenham N17 33 A3
Stockton Ho
16 E2 96 B4
Harrow HA2 41 C1
Stockton Rd
Edmonton N18 34 B4
Tottenham N17 33 A3
STOCKWELL 138 A2
Stockwell Ave SW9 138 B2
Stockwell Cl BR1 187 B1
Stockwell Gdns
SW9 138 B4 270 C1
Stockwell Gn SW9 138 B3
Stockwell La SW9 138 B3
Stockwell Park Cres
SW9 138 B3
Stockwell Park Rd
SW9 138 B4 270 D1
Stockwell Park Sch
SW9 138 B4 270 C1
Stockwell Park Wlk
SW9 138 C2
Stockwell Prim Sch
SW9 138 B2
Stockwell Rd SW9 138 B3
Stockwell St SE10 142 A6
Stockwell Sta SW4 138 A3
Stockwell Terr SW9 270 C1
Stodart Rd SE20 184 C2
Stoddart Ho SW8 270 D5
Stodmarsh Ho 28
SW9 138 C4
Stofield Gdns SE9 165 D1
Stoford Cl SW19 157 A4
Stokenchurch St
SW6 135 D4 265 C1
STOKE NEWINGTON 73 C6
Stoke Newington Church
St N16 73 C6
Stoke Newington Comm
N16 73 D6
Stoke Newington High St
N16 73 D5
Stoke Newington Rd
N16 73 D4
Stoke Newington Sch
N16 73 B5
Stoke Newington Sta
N16 73 D6
Stoke Pl NW10 89 D4
Stoke Rd KT2 177 A3
Stokesby Rd KT9 214 B2
Stokes Ct N2 48 C5
Stokesley St W12 89 D1
Stokes Rd
Croydon CR0 206 D3
Newham E6 100 A3
Stokley Ct N8 50 A5
Stoll Cl NW2 68 C5
Stoms Path SE6 185 C5
Stonard Rd
Dagenham RM8 80 B4
Palmers Green N13 16 C1
Stondon Pk SE23 163 A5
Stondon Wlk 4 E6 99 D5
Stonebanks KT12 194 A2
Stone Bldgs
WC2 94 B2 240 D3
STONEBRIDGE 89 A6
Stonebridge Ct 9
NW10 67 B1
Stonebridge Ctr 6
NW10 89 B6
Stonebridge Ctr The
N15 52 A4
Stonebridge Park HA9 66 D1
Stonebridge Park Sta
NW10 66 D1
Stonebridge Pk NW10 67 B1
Stonebridge Rd N15 51 D4
Stonebridge Sch The
NW10 89 B6
Stonebridge Way HA9 66 D2
Stonechat Sq 6 E6 100 A2
Stone Cl
Clapham SW4 137 C3
Dagenham RM8 81 B6
Yiewsley UB7 104 B5
Stonecot Cl SM3 201 A1
Stonecot Hill SM3 201 A1
Stone Cres TW14 149 D4
Stonecroft Way CR0 204 A2
Stonecrop Cl NW9 45 B6
Stone Ct
Southgate N21 16 B6
4 Stratford E15 76 D1
Stonecutter St EC4 241 C2
Stonefield N4 72 B6
Stonefield Cl
DA7 147 C2
Ruislip HA4 63 A3
Stonefield Mans N1 234 A5
Stonefield St
N1 94 C6 234 B6
Stonefield Way
Ruislip HA4 63 A3
SE7 143 D5
Stonegate 8 NW5 71 A2
Stone Gr HA8 26 B5
Stone Grove Ct HA8 26 B5
Stonegrove Gdns HA8 26 A5
Stonegrove Ho HA8 26 B5
Stonehall Ave IG1 56 A3
Stone Hall Rd N21 16 C4
Stoneham Rd N11 31 C5
Stonehaven BR3 185 D1
Stonehill Bsns Pk N18 34 D5
Stonehill Cl SW14 155 B6
Stonehill Ct E4 19 D4
Stonehill Rd
Brentford W4 110 C1
Mortlake SW14 155 B6
Stonehills Ct SE21 161 C1
Stonehill's Mans 3
SW16 160 A2
Stonehill Woods Pk
DA14 191 D4
Stonehorse Rd EN3 18 C6
Stonehouse NW1 232 B5
Stonehouse Ct EC2 243 B2
Stonehouse Ho 27 W2 91 C2
Stone Lake Ind Pk
SE7 121 C2
Stone Lake Ret Pk
SE7 121 C2
STONELEIGH 216 A3
Stoneleigh Ave
Enfield EN1 6 B4
North Cheam KT17,
KT4 216 A5
Stoneleigh Broadway
KT17 216 A3
Stoneleigh Cres
KT19 215 D3
Stoneleigh Ct
Redbridge IG5 56 A6
6 Tottenham N17 33 D1
Stoneleigh Fst Sch
KT17 216 B4
Stoneleigh Lo 13
TW9 132 B4
Stoneleigh Mews 15
E3 97 A5
Stoneleigh Park Ave
CR0 206 D3
Stoneleigh Park Rd KT19,
KT4 216 A3
Stoneleigh Pl W11 112 D6
Stoneleigh Rd
Bromley BR1 210 D6
Carshalton SM5 202 C2
Redbridge IG5 56 B6
Tottenham N17 33 D1
Stoneleigh St W11 112 D6
Stoneleigh Sta KT19 216 A3
Stoneleigh Terr N19 71 B6
Stonell's Rd SW11 158 D6
Stonemasons Cl N15 51 B5
Stonenest St N4 50 B1
Stone Park Ave BR3 207 D5
Stone Pl KT4 216 A6
Stone Rd BR2 208 D4
Stones End St SE1 252 A1
Stonewall E6 100 C2
Stoneworth Ct SE25 206 A3
Stoney Alley SE18 144 C3
Stoneyard La E14 119 D6
Stoneycroft Cl SE12 164 D4
Stoney Deep TW11 175 A6
Stoneydown E17 53 A5
Stoneydown Ave E17 53 A5
Stoneydown Ho 2
E17 53 A5
Stoneydown Park Sch
E17 53 A5
Stoneyfields Gdns
HA8 27 A6
Stoneyfields La HA8 27 A6
Stoney La
E1 243 B2
Penge SE19 183 D4
Stoney St SE1 117 B5 252 C4
Stonhouse St SW4 137 D1
Stonor Rd
W14 113 B2 254 C3
Stonycroft Cl EN3 7 A3
Stopes St SE15 139 D5
Stopford Rd
Newham E13 99 A6
SE17 261 D1
Stopher Ho SE1 251 D1
Storace Ho 6 SW4 138 A1
Store Rd E16 122 C4
Storers Quay E14 120 B2
Store St
Bloomsbury
WC1 93 D2 239 C4
Stratford New Town E15 76 B3
Storey Ct NW8 229 C1
Storey Ho 13 E14 119 D6
Storey Prim Sch E16 122 D5
Storey Rd
Highgate N6 48 D3
Walthamstow E17 53 B5
Storey's Gate
SW1 115 D4 249 D1
Storey St E16 122 C4
Stories Rd SE5 139 C2
Stork Rd E7 77 A2
Storksmead Rd HA8 27 C3
Storks Rd SE16 118 A3
Stormont House Sch
E5 74 B4
Stormont Rd
Clapham SW11 137 A1
Highgate N6 48 D2
Stormont Way KT9 213 C3
Stormount Dr UB3 105 A4
Storrington WC1 233 B1
Storrington Rd CR0 205 D1
Story St N1 72 B1
Stotfold BR1 188 A2
Stothard Ho 25 E1 96 C3
Stothard Pl E1 243 B4
Stothard St 12 E1 96 C3
Stott Cl SW18 158 B5
Stoughton Ave SM3 217 A3
Stoughton Cl
Roehampton SW15 156 A3
SE11 260 D3
Stour Ave UB2 107 C3
Stourbridge Ho 8
UB5 85 B3
Stour Cl BR2 225 C4
Stourcliffe Cl W1 237 C2
Stourcliffe St W1 237 C1
Stour Ct UB1 86 B1
Stourhead Cl 6
SW19 156 D4
Stourhead Gdns
SW20 200 A6
Stour Rd
Dagenham RM10 81 C6
Hackney Wick E3 75 C1
Stourton Ave TW13 173 B6
Stowage SE8 141 D6
Stow Cres E17 35 A3
Stowe Cres HA4 39 A3
Stowe Gdns N9 17 D3
Stowe Ho
Hampstead Garden Suburb
NW11 48 A3
11 Stoke Newington
N16 73 C5
Stowell Ho 2 N8 50 A5
Stowe Pl N15 51 C6
Stowe Rd W12 112 B4
Stowford Coll SM2 218 A1
Stowting Rd BR6 227 C4
Stox Mead HA3 24 B2
Stracey Rd
Becontree NW10 89 B6
Forest Gate E7 77 A4
Strachan Pl SW19,
SW20 178 C4
Stradbroke Gr
Buckhurst Hill IG9 21 D3
Redbridge IG5 56 C6
Stradbroke Rd N5 73 A4
Stradbrook Cl HA2 63 B5
Stradella Rd SE24 161 A5
Straffan Lo 8 NW3 70 C2
Strafford Ho 9 SE8 119 B1
Strafford Rd
Acton W3 111 A4
Barnet EN5 1 A2
Hounslow TW3 129 B2
Twickenham TW1 153 A4
Strafford St E14 119 C4
Strahan Rd E3 97 A4
Straightsmouth SE10 142 A5
Straight The UB2 107 A4
Strait Rd E6 122 B6
Straker's Rd SE15 140 B1
Strale Ho 17 N1 95 C6
STRAND 116 B6
Strand
Strand WC2 116 B6 250 C6
Strand WC2 240 D1
Strand Ct SE18 123 D1
Strand Dr TW9 132 D5
Strandfield Cl SE18 123 C1
Strand Ho SE28 123 B5
Strand La WC2 250 D6
STRAND ON THE
GREEN 132 C6
Strand-on-the-Green
W4 132 C6
Strand-on-the-Green
Schs W4 132 C6
Strand Pl N18 33 C6
Strang Ho N1 235 A5
Strangways Terr W14 254 C5
Stranraer Way
Barnsbury N1 72 A1
1 Stanwell TW6 148 A5
Strasburg Rd
SW11 137 B4 268 C1
Stratfield Ho SE12 165 A2
Stratfield Park Cl N21 16 D4
STRATFORD 76 A2
Stratford Ave UB10 82 B5
Stratford Bus Sta E15 76 B1
Stratford Cir (Newham
6th Form Coll) E15 76 B2
Stratford Cl IG11 80 A1
Stratford Ct KT3 199 B5
Stratford Gr SW15 134 D1
Stratford House Ave
BR1 210 A6
Stratford International Sta
E15 76 A2
STRATFORD MARSH 97 D6
STRATFORD NEW
TOWN 76 A3
Stratford Office Village
The 1 E15 76 C1
Stratford Pl W1 238 C1
Stratford Rd
Harlington TW6 149 A6
Hayes UB4 84 B3
Hendon NW4 46 D5
Newham E13 99 A6
Southall UB2 107 A2
Thornton Heath CR7 204 D6
W8 113 C3 255 B5
Stratford Sch E7 77 A1
Stratford Sch (Annexe)
E7 77 B2
Stratford Sh Ctr E15 76 B1
Stratford Sta E15 76 B1
Stratford Studios W8 255 C5
Stratford Villas NW1 71 D1
Stratford Workshops
E15 98 B6
Strathan Cl SW18 157 A5
Strathaven Rd SE12 165 B5
Strathblaine Rd
SW11 136 B1
Strathbrook Rd SW16 182 B3
Strathcona Rd HA9 65 D6
Strathdale SW16 182 B5
Strathdon Dr SW17 158 B1
Strathearn Ave
Harlington UB3 127 D5
Twickenham TW2 152 A3
Strathearn Ho W2 247 A6
Strathearn Pl
W2 114 C6 247 A6
Strathearn Rd
Sutton SM1 217 C3
Wimbledon SW19 179 C6
Stratheden Par SE3 143 A5
Stratheden Rd SE3 143 A5
Strathfield Gdns IG11 79 B2
Strathleven Rd SW2 160 A6
Strathmore Ct NW8 230 A2
Strathmore Gdns
Edgware HA8 26 D1
Finchley N3 29 D2
W8 245 B4
Strathmore Rd
Teddington TW11,
TW2 174 C6
Thornton Heath CR0 205 B2
Wimbledon SW19 157 C1
Strathmore Sch
TW10 153 D2
Strathnairn St SE1 118 A2
Strathray Gdns NW3 70 C2
Strath Terr SW11 136 C1
Strathville Rd SW18 157 D2
Strathyre Ave SW16 204 C6
Stratton Ave EN2 5 B6
Stratton Cl
DA7 147 A2
Edgware HA8 26 B4
Heston TW5 129 C4
Merton SW19 179 C1
Walton-on-T KT12 194 C1
Stratton Ct
4 De Beauvoir Town
N1 73 C1
10 Kingston u T KT6 198 A4
10 Pinner HA5 23 B3
Strattondale St E14 120 A3
Stratton Dr IG11 79 D2
Stratton Gdns UB1 85 C1
Stratton Ho HA8 26 B6
Stratton Lo 10 EN5 1 D1
Stratton Rd
DA7 147 A2
Merton SW19 179 C1
Sunbury TW16 171 D1
Stratton St
W1 115 B5 248 D4
Strauss Rd W4 111 B4
Strawberry Fields
BR6 226 D3
STRAWBERRY HILL 152 D1
Strawberry Hill Cl
TW1 152 D1
Strawberry Hill Rd
TW1 152 D1
Strawberry Hill Sta
TW2 152 D1
Strawberry La SM5 219 A5
Strawberry Terr N10 30 D2
Strawberry Vale
Finchley N2 30 B2
Twickenham TW1 153 A1
Strayfield Rd EN2 4 D6
Streakes Field Rd
NW2 68 A6
Streamdale SE2 146 B6
Stream La HA8 26 D5
Streamline Mews
SE22 162 A3
Streamside Cl
BR2 209 A5
Edmonton N9 17 D3
Stream Way DA17 147 C6
Streatfeild Ave E6 100 B6
Streatfield Rd HA3,
HA7 43 D6
STREATHAM 182 A4
Streatham Cl SW16 160 A2
Streatham & Clapham
High Sch SW16 159 D1
Streatham Common N
SW16 182 B5
Streatham Common S
SW16 182 B4
Streatham Common Sta
SW16 181 D3
Streatham Ct SW16 160 A1
Streatham High Rd SW16,
SW2 182 A5
STREATHAM HILL 160 A3
Streatham Hill SW2 160 A3
Streatham Hill & Clapham
High Sch SW2 160 B3
Streatham Hill Sta
SW2 160 A2
STREATHAM PARK 181 C6
Streatham Pl SW2 160 A4
Streatham Rd CR4 181 A2
Streatham St WC1 240 A2
Streatham Sta SW16 181 D5
STREATHAM VALE 181 D3
Streatham Vale
SW16 181 D3
Streathbourne Rd
SW17 159 A1
Streathem Wells Prim Sch
SW2 160 C2
Streatleigh Par 4
SW16 160 A2
Streatley Pl
27 Hampstead NW3 70 A4
Hampstead NW3 70 B4
Streatley Rd NW6 69 B1
Streeters La SM6 219 D5
Streetfield Mews
SE3 143 A2
Streimer Rd E15 98 A5
Strelley Way W3 111 C6
Stretford Ct 1 SW19 179 A3
Stretton Lo W13 109 B6
Stretton Mans 16
SE8 141 C6
Stretton Rd
Croydon CR0 205 C2
Stretton Rd *continued*
Richmond TW10 153 C2
Strickland Ct SE15 140 A2
Strickland Ho 26 E2 95 D4
Strickland Row SW18 158 B4
Strickland St SE8 141 C4
Strickland Way 4
BR6 227 D4
Stride Rd E13 98 D5
Strimon Cl N9 18 C2
Stringer Hos 19 N1 95 C6
Strode Cl N10 31 A3
Strode Ho 3 SW2 160 C3
Strode Rd
Forest Gate E7 77 A4
SW6 135 A5 264 A4
Tottenham N17 33 C1
Willesden NW10 68 A2
Strome Ho NW6 91 D5
Strone Rd E7, E12 77 D2
Strone Way UB4 85 A3
Strongbow Cres SE9 166 B6
Strongbow Rd SE9 166 B6
Strongbridge Cl HA2 41 C1
Stronsa Rd W12 111 D4
Strood Ho
9 Penge SE20 184 C3
SE1 252 D1
Stroud Cres SW15 156 A1
Stroudes Cl KT4 199 D2
Stroud Field UB5 63 A2
Stroud Gate HA2 63 D4
STROUD GREEN 50 C3
Stroud Green Gdns
CR0 206 C2
Stroud Green Prim Sch
N4 50 C1
Stroud Green Rd N4 50 C1
Stroud Green Way
CR0 206 C3
Stroudley Ho SW8 269 B2
Stroudley Wlk E3 97 D4
Stroud Rd
Croydon SE25 206 A3
Wimbledon SW19 157 C1
Strouds Cl RM6 58 B4
Stroud Way TW15 171 A4
Strout's Pl 2 E2 95 D4
Struan Ho 15 E11 55 A4
Strudwick Ct SW4 270 B1
Strutton Ground
SW1 115 D3 259 C5
Strype St E1 243 C3
Stuart Ave
Ealing W5 110 B4
Harrow HA2 63 B5
Hayes BR2 209 A1
Hendon NW9 46 A2
Walton-on-T KT12 194 B1
Stuart Cl UB10 60 C2
Stuart Cres
Croydon CR0 223 B5
Hayes UB3 83 A1
Wood Green N22 32 B2
Stuart Ct
Chingford E4 20 D2
6 Croydon CR0 220 D5
2 Elstree WD6 9 D5
Stuart Evans Cl DA16 146 C2
Stuart Gr TW11 174 C5
Stuart Ho
Hammersmith W6 112 C3
1 Homerton E9 74 D1
Queensbury NW9 44 C5
5 Stockwell SW4 138 A1
W14 254 A4
Stuart Lo SE25 183 C1
Stuart Mill Ho N1 233 C3
Stuart Pl CR4 180 D2
Stuart Rd
Acton W3 111 A5
Barking IG11 79 D1
DA16 146 B4
East Barnet EN4 14 D4
Harrow HA3 42 D6
Maida Vale NW6 91 C4
Nunhead SE15 140 C1
Richmond TW10 153 B1
South Norwood CR7 205 A5
Wimbledon SW19 157 C1
Stubbs Cl NW9 45 A4
Stubbs Dr SE16 118 B1
Stubbs Ho
Finsbury Pk N4 50 B1
1 Globe Town E2 96 D4
Stubbs Mews RM8 80 B4
Stubbs Point E13 89 B3

Stubbs Way SW19 180 B2
Stucley Pl 19 NW1 71 B1
Stucley Rd TW5, TW7 130 A5
Studdridge St SW6 135 C3
Studd St N1 94 D6 234 C6
Studholme Ct NW3 69 C4
Studholme St SE15 140 B5
Studio Mews 5 NW4 46 C5
Studio Pl SW1 247 D1
Studios NW8 229 A4
Studios Rd TW17 192 B6
Studios The
4 Clapham SW4 137 C1
SW8 269 D1
Studland SE17 262 C2
Studland Cl DA15 167 D1
Studland Ho E14 97 A1
Studland Rd
Ealing W7 86 C1
Forest Hill SE26 184 D5
Kingston u T KT2 176 A4
Studland St W6 112 B2
Studley Ave E4 36 B3
Studley Cl E5 75 A3
Studley Ct
13 Blackwall E14 120 B6
DA14 190 B5
Redbridge IG4 55 D3
Studley Dr IG4 55 D3
Studley Grange Rd
W7 108 D4
Studley Rd
Dagenham RM9 80 D1
South Lambeth SW4 138 A3
Upton E7 77 B2
Study Prep Sch The
SW19 178 C5
Study Sch The KT3 199 C4
Stukeley Rd E7 77 B1
Stukeley St
WC2 94 A1 240 B2
Stumps Hill La BR3 185 C4
Stunell Ho 23 SE14 140 D6
Sturdee Ho 2 E2 96 A5
Sturdy Ho 28 E3 97 A5
Sturdy Rd SE15 140 B3
Sturge Ave E17 35 D1
Sturgeon Rd
SE17 117 A1 262 A1
Sturges Field BR7 189 B4
Sturgess Ave NW4 46 B2
Sturge St SE1 117 A4 252 A2
Sturmer Way N7 72 B3
Sturminster Cl UB4 84 C1
Sturminster Ho SW8 270 D3
Sturrock Cl N15 51 B5
Sturry St E14 97 D1
Sturt St N1 235 B3
Stutfield St E1 96 A1
Stuttle Ho 14 E1 96 A3
Styles Gdns SW9 138 D2
Styles Ho SE1 251 C3
Styles Way BR3 208 A5
Stylus Apartments 25
E1 96 C1
Sudbourne Prim Sch
SW2 160 B6
Sudbourne Rd SW2 160 B6
Sudbrooke Rd SW12 159 A5
Sudbrook Gdns
TW10 154 A1
Sudbrook La TW10 154 A2
SUDBURY 65 A4
Sudbury E6 100 C1
Sudbury Ave HA0 65 D4
Sudbury Court Dr HA1 65 A5
Sudbury Court Rd HA1 65 A5
Sudbury Cres
BR1 187 A5
Wembley HA0 65 B3
Sudbury Croft HA0 64 D4
Sudbury Ct
1 Ilford RM6 58 B4
SW8 269 D2
Sudbury Gdns CR0 221 C4
Sudbury & Harrow Road
Sta HA0 65 B3
Sudbury Heights Ave
UB6 65 A3
Sudbury Hill HA1 64 C5
Sudbury Hill Cl HA0 64 D5
Sudbury Hill Harrow Sta
HA1 64 C4
Sudbury Hill Sta HA1 64 C4
Sudbury Ho SW18 157 D6
Sudbury Prim Sch
HA0 65 B4
Sudbury Rd IG11 79 D3
Sudbury Town Sta
UB6 65 B2
Sudeley St N1 94 D5 234 D3
Sudlow Rd SW18 157 C6
Sudrey St SE1 252 A1
Suez Ave UB6 86 D5
Suez Rd EN3 7 A2
Suffield Ho SE17 261 D2
Suffield Rd
Chingford E4 35 D6
Penge SE20 184 C1
2 South Tottenham
N15 51 D4
Suffolk Cl WD6 11 B6
Suffolk Ct
3 Dagenham RM6 58 C4
Ilford IG3 57 C3
Walthamstow E17 53 C2
3 West Norwood
SW16 182 C6
Suffolk Ho
11 Acton W3 88 C1
Beckenham BR2 208 D5
8 Dartmouth Pk NW5 71 C5
Edgware HA8 26 B4
Penge SE20 184 C2
4 South Croydon CR0 221 B6
Suffolk La EC4 252 C6
Suffolk Park Rd E17 53 A5
Suffolk Pl SW1 249 D4
Suffolk Rd
Barking IG11 79 B1
Barnes SW13 134 A5
Dagenham RM10 81 D3
Enfield EN3 18 B6
Harrow HA2 41 C4
Ilford IG3 57 C3
4 Newham E13 99 A4
Sidcup DA14 190 C4
South Norwood SE25 205 D5
Tottenham N15 51 B3
Willesden NW10 67 C1
Worcester Pk KT4 215 D6
Suffolks Prim Sch EN1 6 B3
Suffolk St
Forest Gate E7 77 A4
SW1 115 D5 249 D4
Sugar House La E15 98 A5
Sugar Loaf Wlk 6 E2 96 C4
Sugden Rd
Clapham SW11 137 A1
Long Ditton KT7 197 B1
Sugden Way IG11 101 D5
Sulby Ho SE4 141 A1
Sulgrave Gdns 11
W6 112 C4
Sulgrave Rd W6 112 C3
Sulina Rd SW2 160 A4
Sulivan Ct SW6 135 C3
Sulivan Ent Ctr SW6 135 C2
Sulivan Prim Sch
SW6 135 C3
Sulivan Rd SW6 135 C2
Sulkin Ho 11 E2 96 D4
Sullivan Ave E16 99 D2
Sullivan Cl
Battersea SW11 136 C2
Hayes UB4 84 C2
Sullivan Ct
4 Croydon CR0 206 A1
Stamford Hill N16 51 D1
SW5 255 B4
Sullivan Ho
Chelsea SW1 268 D6
Isleworth TW2 152 B5
Vauxhall SE11 260 D3
Sullivan Rd
SE11 116 C2 261 B4
Sullivans Reach KT12 193 D2
Sullivan Way WD6 9 C5
Sultan Ho SE1 118 A1
Sultan Rd E11 55 B5
Sultan St
Penge BR3 184 D1
SE5 139 A5
Sumal Ct E9 76 B6
Sumatra Rd NW6 69 C2
Sumburgh Rd SW12 159 A5
Summer Ave KT8 196 C4
Summercourt Rd E1 96 C1
Summer Crossing
KT7 196 C4
Summerene Cl SW16 181 C3
Summerfield 6 BR1 187 B2
Summerfield Ave
Colney Hatch N12 30 C4
Kensal Rise NW6 91 A5
Summerfield Ho RM9 80 D4
Summerfield La KT6 213 D6
Summerfield Rd
Ealing W5 87 B3
Loughton IG10 21 D5
Summerfield St SE12 164 D4
Summer Gdns KT8 196 C4
Summer Gr WD6 9 D5
Summer Hill
Borehamwood WD6 10 C6
BR7 188 C1
Summerhill Cl BR6 227 C5
Summerhill Gr EN1 17 C5
Summerhill Rd N15 51 B5
Summerhill Villas
BR7 188 D2
Summerhill Way CR4 181 A2
Summer Ho SE13 142 B1
Summerhouse Ave
TW5 129 A4
Summerhouse Rd N16 73 C6
Summerland Gdns
N10 49 B6
Summerland Grange
N10 49 B6
Summerlands Ave
W3 111 A6
Summerlands Lo
BR6 226 C4
Summerlee Ave N2 48 D5
Summerlee Gdns N2 48 D5
Summerley St SW18 157 D2
Summer Rd
East Molesey KT8 196 B4
Thames Ditton KT7,
KT8 196 D4
Summersby Rd N6 49 B3
Summers Cl
Belmont SM2 217 C1
Wembley HA9 44 D1
Summersell Ho SE27 183 B5
Summerside Prim Sch
N12 30 B4
Summerskille Cl N9 18 B2
Summers La N12 30 B3
Summers Row N12 30 C4
Summers St EC1 241 A5
SUMMERSTOWN 158 A1
Summerstown SW17 180 A6
Summerton Way
SE28 102 D1
Summer Trees TW16 172 B2
Summerville Gdns
SM1 217 B2
Summerwood Rd TW1,
TW7 152 D5
Summit Ave NW9 45 B4
Summit Bsns Pk The
TW16 172 A3
Summit Cl
Edgware HA8 26 C3
Kingsbury NW9 45 B5
Osidge N14 15 C2
Summit Ct
5 Barnet EN5 1 B2
Brondesbury NW2 69 A3
Summit Dr IG8 37 D1
Summit Est N16 52 A2
Summit Rd
Northolt UB5 63 C1
Walthamstow E17 53 D5
Summit Way
Brunswick Pk N14 15 B2
South Norwood SE19 183 C3
Sumner Ave SE15 139 D4
Sumner Bldgs SE1 252 A4
Sumner Cl BR6 227 A4
Sumner Ct SW8 270 A2
Sumner Gdns CR0 204 C1
Sumner Ho 1 E3 97 D2
Sumner Pl
SW7 114 B2 256 D3
Sumner Place Mews
SW7 256 D3
Sumner Rd
Harrow HA1 42 A2
SE15 139 D5
Thornton Heath CR0 204 D1
Sumner Rd S CR0 204 C1
Sumner St
SE1 117 A5 252 A4
Sumpter Cl NW3 70 A2
Sun Alley 6 TW9 132 A1
Sun Alliance Ho WC2 241 A2
Sunbeam Cres W10 90 C3
Sunbeam Rd NW10 89 B3
SUNBURY 194 B6
Sunbury Ave
Edgware NW7 27 B6
Mortlake SW14 133 B1
Sunbury Cl KT12 194 A3
SUNBURY COMMON 171 D3
Sunbury Court Island
TW16 194 D6
Sunbury Court Mews
TW16 172 D1
Sunbury Court Rd
TW16 172 C1
Sunbury Cres TW13 171 D6
Sunbury Cross TW16 172 A3
Sunbury Cross Ctr 9
TW16 171 D3
Sunbury Ct
3 Barnet EN5 1 A1
3 SE14 140 D6
Sunbury TW16 172 D1
Sunbury Ct (Con Ctr)
TW16 172 D1
Sunbury Gdns NW7 27 B5
Sunbury Ho 38 E2 95 D4
Sunbury Int Bsns Ctr
TW16 171 C2
Sunbury La
Battersea
SW11 136 B4 266 D2
Walton-on-T KT12 194 A3
Sunbury Manor Sch
TW16 171 D2
Sunbury Rd
Cheam SM3 217 A5
Feltham TW13 171 D6
Sunbury St SE18 122 B3
Sunbury Sta TW16 172 A2
Sunbury Way TW13 172 C5
Sunbury Workshops 39
E2 95 D4
Suncroft Pl SE26 162 C1
Sun Ct EC3 242 D1
Sunderland Ct
Dulwich SE22 162 A4
12 Stanwell TW19 148 A5
Sunderland Ho 26 W2 91 C2
Sunderland Mount
SE23 162 D2
Sunderland Point
E16 123 A5
Sunderland Rd
Ealing W5 109 D3
Forest Hill SE23 162 D2
Sunderland Terr W2 91 D1
Sunderland Way E12 77 D6
Sundew Ave W12 112 A6
Sundew Ct 9 HA0 88 A5
Sundial Ave SE25 205 D6
Sundial Ct KT5 214 D6
Sundorne Rd SE7 121 C1
Sundown Rd TW15 171 A5
Sundra Wlk 26 E1 96 D3
SUNDRIDGE 187 C4
Sundridge Ave
Bromley BR1, BR7 188 A3
DA16 145 B2
Sundridge Ho
Bromley BR1 187 B5
4 Homerton E9 74 D1
Sundridge Par BR1 187 B3
Sundridge Park Sta
BR1 187 B3
Sundridge Rd CR0 206 A1
Sunfields Pl SE3 143 B5
Sun in the Sands SE3 143 B5
Sunken Rd CR0 222 C3
Sun La SE3 143 B5
Sunland Ave DA6 147 A1
Sunleigh Ct HA0 88 A6
Sunleigh Rd HA0 88 A6
Sunley Gdns UB6 87 A6
Sunley Ho E1 243 D3
Sun Life Trad Est
TW14 128 A2
Sunlight Cl SW19 180 A4
Sunlight Sq 29 E2 96 B4
Sunmead Rd TW16 194 A6
Sunna Gdns TW16 172 B1
Sunna Lo TW16 171 D3
Sunniholme Ct CR2 221 A3
Sunningdale
Ealing W13 87 B2
Friern Barnet N14 31 D5
Sunningdale Ave
Barking IG11 79 B1
East Acton W3 111 C6
Feltham TW13 151 A2
Ruislip HA4 40 C1
Sunningdale Cl
22 Bermondsey SE16 118 B1
Erith SE28 103 A1
Newham E6 100 B4
Stanmore HA7 25 A3
3 Surbiton KT6 214 A6
Sunningdale Ct
13 Kingston u T KT2 176 C3
Sunningdale Ct *continued*
13 Southall UB1 86 A1
Sunningdale Gdns
Kingsbury NW9 45 A4
W8 255 B5
Sunningdale Lo HA8 26 B5
Sunningdale Rd
BR1, BR2 210 A4
Cheam SM1 217 B4
Sunningfields Cres
NW4 28 B1
Sunningfields Rd NW4 46 B6
Sunninghill Ct 9 W3 111 A4
Sunninghill Gdns IG2 57 D4
Sunninghill Rd SE13 141 D3
Sunny Bank SE25 206 A6
Sunny Cres NW10 67 A1
Sunnycroft Rd
Hounslow TW3 129 D3
Southall UB1 85 C2
South Norwood SE25 206 A6
Sunnydale BR6 226 C6
Sunnydale Gdns NW7 27 C4
Sunnydale Rd SE12 165 B6
Sunnydene Ave
Chingford E4 36 B5
Ruislip HA4 62 A6
Sunnydene Gdns HA0 65 C2
Sunnydene St SE26 185 A6
Sunnyfield NW7 27 D6
Sunnyfields Prim Sch
NW4 46 B6
Sunny Gardens Par
NW4 28 B1
Sunny Gardens Rd
NW4 46 C6
Sunny Hill NW4 46 B6
Sunnyhill Cl E5 75 A4
Sunny Hill Ct NW4 28 B1
Sunnyhill Prim Sch
SW16 182 B6
Sunnyhill Rd SW16 182 A6
Sunnyhurst Cl SM1 217 C5
Sunnymead Ave CR4 203 D6
Sunnymead Ct W5 109 D6
Sunnymead Rd
Kingsbury NW9 45 B2
Putney SW15 156 B6
Sunnymede Ave
KT19 215 C1
Sunnymede Dr IG6 56 D5
Sunny Nook Gdns
CR2 221 B2
Sunny Pl NW4 46 C5
Sunny Rd The EN3 6 D4
Sunnyside
4 Child's Hill NW2 69 B5
Walton-on-T KT12 194 C4
Wimbledon SW19 179 A4
Sunnyside Dr E4 20 A4
Sunnyside Ho 3 NW2 69 B5
Sunnyside Pl SW19 179 A4
Sunnyside Rd
Crouch End N19 49 D2
Ealing W5 109 D5
Ilford IG1 79 B5
Teddington TW11 174 B6
Walthamstow E10 53 C1
Sunnyside Rd E N9 18 A1
Sunnyside Rd N N9 18 A1
Sunnyside Rd S N9 18 A1
Sunny View NW9 45 B4
Sunny Way N12 30 C3
Sun Pas 8 SE16 118 A3
Sunray Ave
BR2 210 B3
Herne Hill SE5, SE24 139 B1
Tolworth KT5 214 D6
Sun Rd W14 113 B1 254 C1
Sunrise Cl TW13 151 B1
Sunrise View NW7 27 D4
Sun St Pas EC2 95 C2 243 A3
Sunset Ave
Chingford E4 19 D3
Woodford IG8 36 D6
Sunset Ct 4 IG8 37 C3
Sunset Gdns SE25 183 D1
Sunset Ho HA3 42 C6
Sunset Rd
Herne Hill SE5 139 B1
SE28 124 A5
Wimbledon SW19 178 B5
Sunset View EN5 1 A3
Sunshine Way CR4 180 D1
Sun St EC2 95 B2 242 D4
Sunwell Cl SE15 140 B4
Superior Dr 4 BR6 227 D2
Suraj Ho 6 N22 32 C1
SURBITON 198 A2
Surbiton Boys Prep Sch
KT6 198 A4
Surbiton Cres KT1,
KT6 198 A5
Surbiton Ct KT6 197 D3
Surbiton Hall Cl KT1 198 A5
Surbiton High Sch
KT1 198 A5
Surbiton High Sch Jun
Girls Sch KT1 198 A5
Surbiton Hill Pk KT5 198 C4
Surbiton Hill Rd KT6 198 A4
Surbiton Hospl KT6 198 A3
Surbiton Par 11 KT6 198 A3
Surbiton Rd KT1 198 A5
Surbiton Sta KT6 198 A3
Surcot Ho 2 SW4 137 D3
Surlingham Cl SE28 124 D6
Surma Cl E1 96 A3
Surmans Cl RM9 102 C6
Surrendale Pl W9 91 C3
Surrey Canal Rd SE14, SE16,
SE8 140 D6
Surrey Cl N3 47 A6
Surrey Cres 1 W4 110 C1
Surrey Ct 15 SM6 219 B2
Surrey Gdns N4 51 A3
Surrey Gr
Carshalton SM1 218 B5
SE17 263 A1
Surrey Ho
Edgware HA8 26 B4
8 Rotherhithe SE16 118 D5
Surrey La
SW11 136 C4 267 B1
Surrey Lo SW20 178 C1
Surrey Mews SE27 183 C6
Surrey Mount SE23 162 B3
Surrey Quays Rd
SE16 118 D4
Surrey Quays Sh Ctr
SE16 118 D3
Surrey Quays Sta
SE16 118 D2
Surrey Rd
Barking IG11 79 C1
Dagenham RM10 81 D3
Harrow HA1 42 A4
Honor Oak SE15 162 D6
West Wickham BR4 207 D1
Surrey Row
SE1 116 D4 251 D2
Surrey Sq
SE17 117 C1 263 B2
Surrey Square Inf Sch
SE17 117 C1 263 A2
Surrey Square Jun Sch
SE17 117 C1 263 A2
Surrey St
Croydon CR0 221 A5
4 Newham E13 99 B4
WC2 116 B6 250 D6
Surrey Terr SE17 263 B2
Surrey Water Rd
SE16 118 D5
Surrey Wharf SE1 140 A6
Surridge Ct 15 SW9 138 A3
Surridge Gdns SE19 183 B4
Surr St N7 72 A3
Sury Basin KT2 176 A2
Susan Constant Ct 18
E14 120 B6
Susan Lawrence Ho 4
E12 78 C4
Susannah St E14 98 A1
Susan Rd SE3 143 B3
Susan Wood BR7 188 C2
Sussex Ave TW7 130 C2
Sussex Cl
New Malden KT3 199 C5
Redbridge IG4 56 B4
4 Twickenham TW1 153 B5
Upper Holloway N19 72 A6
Sussex Cres UB5 63 C2
Sussex Ct
4 Barnes SW13 133 D3
Greenwich SE10 142 A6
Mitcham CR4 204 A4
Paddington W2 236 C1
Sussex Gate N6 48 D4
Sussex Gdns
Chessington KT9 213 D2
Fortis Green N6 48 D4
Harringay N4 51 A4
Paddington W2 92 B1 236 D1
Sussex Ho
Edgware HA8 26 B4
Hampstead NW3 70 C2
Richmond TW9 132 B3

Sussex House Sch SW3 114 D2 257 C4
Sussex Lo W2 236 D1
Sussex Mans
South Kensington SW7 256 C3
Strand WC2 250 B6
Sussex Mews SE6 163 C3
Sussex Mews E W2 236 D1
Sussex Mews W W2 246 D6
Sussex Pl
22 Hammersmith W6 112 C1
Lisson Gr NW1 92 D3 237 C6
New Malden KT3 199 C5
Paddington W2 92 B1 236 D1
Sussex Rd
Barking E6 100 C6
Erith DA8 147 D5
Harrow HA1 42 A4
Mitcham CR4 204 A4
New Malden KT3 199 C5
Sidcup DA14 190 B5
Southall UB2 106 D3
South Croydon CR2 221 B2
Uxbridge UB10 61 A3
Wallington SM5 218 D2
2 West Wickham BR4 207 D1
Sussex Ring N12 29 C5
Sussex Sq W2 114 B6 246 D6
Sussex St
Newham E13 99 B4
SW1 258 D2
Sussex Way
Cockfosters EN4 15 B6
Upper Holloway N7 72 B5
Upper Holloway N7, N19 72 A6
Upper Holloway N19 49 D1
Sutcliffe Cl NW11 47 D4
Sutcliffe Ho UB3 84 A1
Sutcliffe Rd
Bexley DA16 146 C3
SE18 145 C6
Sutherland Ave
Ealing W13 87 B1
Falconwood DA16 145 C1
Hayes UB3 106 A2
Orpington BR5 211 D4
Paddington W9 92 A3 236 A6
Sunbury TW16 171 D1
Sutherland Cl EN5 1 A1
Sutherland Ct
Kingsbury NW9 44 D4
3 Paddington W9 91 C3
Stoke Newington N16 73 B5
Sutherland Dr SW19 180 B2
Sutherland Gdns
Mortlake SW14 133 C2
North Cheam KT4 200 B1
Sunbury TW16 171 D1
Sutherland Gr
Putney SW18, SW19 157 B4
Teddington TW11 174 C5
Sutherland Ho
Ealing W13 109 A6
Kensington W8 255 C5
Kidbrooke SE18 144 B4
7 Putney SW15 156 C4
Richmond TW10 153 C2
9 South Hampstead NW6 70 A2
Sutherland Pl W2 91 C1
Sutherland Rd
Belvedere DA17 125 C3
Chiswick W4 133 C6
Ealing W13 87 A1
Edmonton N9 18 B3
Enfield EN3 18 D6
Southall UB1 85 B1
Thornton Heath CR0 204 C2
Tottenham N17 34 A2
Walthamstow E17 53 A6
Sutherland Row SW1 258 D2
Sutherland Sq SE17 117 A1 262 A1
Sutherland St SW1 115 B1 258 D2
Sutherland Wlk SE17 262 B1
Sutlej Rd SE7 143 C5
Sutterton St N7 72 B2
SUTTON 218 A2
Sutton Cl
Beckenham BR3 185 D2
Pinner HA5 40 A4
Sutton Coll of Liberal Arts SM1 217 D3
Sutton Common Rd
Cheam SM3 201 C1
Sutton SM1, SM3 217 D6
Sutton Common Sta SM1 217 D6
Sutton Courtenay Ho SW17 180 B6
Sutton Court Mans W4 133 A6
Sutton Court Rd
Chiswick W4 133 A6
Hillingdon UB10 82 D6
Newham E13 99 C4
Sutton SM1 218 A2
Sutton Cres EN5 12 D6
Sutton Ct
Chiswick W4 133 A6
Ealing W5 110 A5
East Molesey KT8 195 B4
8 Hackney E5 74 B4
Penge SE19 183 D3
Sutton SM2 218 A2
Sutton Dene TW3 129 D4
Sutton Est
SW3 114 C1 257 B2
Sutton Est The 8
W10 90 C2
Sutton Gdns
Barking IG11 101 C5
Croydon CR0 205 D4
Sutton Gn IG11 101 C6
Sutton Gr SM1 218 B3
Sutton Gram Sch For Boys SM1 218 A3
Sutton Hall Rd TW5 129 C5
Sutton High Sch SM1 217 D2
Sutton Ho N21 16 B6
Sutton House* E9 74 C3
Sutton Hts SM2 218 B1
Sutton La
EC1 241 D5
Hounslow TW3, TW4, TW5 129 B3
Sutton La N W4 111 A1
Sutton La S W4 133 A6
Sutton Par NW4 46 C5
Sutton Park Rd SM1, SM2 217 D2
Sutton Pl E9 74 C3
Sutton Rd
Barking IG11 101 C6
E13 98 D3
Heston TW5 129 C4
Higham Hill E17 34 D2
Muswell Hill N10 31 A2
Sutton Row W1 239 D2
Sutton Sq
Hackney E9 74 C3
Hounslow TW5 129 B4
Sutton St E1 96 C1
Sutton Sta SM2 218 A2
Suttons Way EC1 242 B5
Sutton Way
Hounslow TW5 129 B4
North Kensington W10 90 C2
Sutton Wlk
SE1 116 B5 250 D3
Swaby Rd SW17, SW18 158 A2
Swaffham Ct 1 RM6 58 C4
Swaffield Prim Sch SW18 158 A4
Swaffield Rd SW18 158 A4
Swain Cl SW16 181 B4
Swain Ho CR4 180 D3
Swain Rd CR7 205 A4
Swains Cl UB7 104 A4
Swain's La N6 71 B6
Swainson Ho N7 72 C4
Swainson Rd W3 111 D4
Swains Rd CR4, SW17 180 D3
Swain St NW8 92 C3 237 A6
Swakeleys Dr UB10 60 C3
Swakeleys Rd UB10 60 C5
Swakeleys Rdbt UB8, UB10 60 A4
Swakeleys Sch UB10 82 D5
Swaledale Cl N11 31 A4
Swallands Rd SE6 163 C1
Swallowbrook Bsns Ctr UB4 106 D5
Swallow Cl
Bushey WD23 8 A3
New Cross Gate SE14 140 D4
Swallow Ct
Chingford IG8 36 B3
Ilford IG2 56 D4
4 Paddington W9 91 C2
5 Ruislip HA4 40 C1
1 SE12 165 A4
Swallow Dr
Northolt UB5 85 C5
Willesden NW10 67 B2
Swallowfield NW1 231 D1
Swallowfield Rd SE7 121 B1
Swallowfield Way UB3 105 B4
Swallow Gdns SW16 181 D5
Swallow Ho
Hornsey N8 50 B6
NW8 230 A4
Swallow Pk KT6 214 B5
Swallow Pl
24 Poplar E14 97 B1
W1 238 D1
Swallows Ct 5 SE20 184 D3
Swallow St
Newham E6 100 A2
W1 115 C6 249 B5
Swaminarayan Sch The NW10 67 B2
Swanage Ct 5 N1 73 C1
Swanage Ho SW8 270 C3
Swanage Rd
Chingford E4 36 A3
Wandsworth SW18 158 A5
Swanage Waye UB4 84 C1
Swan And Pike Rd EN3 7 C5
Swan App E6 100 A2
Swanbourne SE17 262 A3
Swanbourne Ho NW8 237 A6
Swanbridge Rd DA7 147 C4
Swan Bsns Ctr 8 W4 111 B2
Swan Cl
Croydon CR0 205 C2
Feltham TW13 173 A6
Higham Hill E17 35 A3
Swan Ct
Chelsea SW3 257 B1
Parsons Green SW6 265 A3
Poplar E14 97 B1
Whetstone N20 14 A2
Swan Ctr SW17 158 A1
Swandon Way SW18 135 D1
Swan Dr NW9 27 C1
Swanfield St E2 95 D4
Swan Ho
De Beauvoir Town N1 73 B1
Enfield EN3 18 C6
Swan La
EC4 117 B6 252 D5
Loughton IG10 21 C4
Whetstone N20 14 A1
Swan Lane Pier EC4 117 B6 252 C5
Swanlea Sec Sch E1 96 B3
Swanley Ho SE17 263 B2
Swanley Rd DA16 146 C4
Swan Mead SE1 117 C3 263 A5
Swan Mews
Stockwell SW9 138 B3
SW6 265 A2
Swanmore Ct SW18 158 A5
Swann Ct 8 TW7 131 A2
Swanne Ho 12 SE10 142 A5
Swan Pas 5 E1 118 A6
Swan Pl SW13 133 D3
Swan Rd
Feltham TW13 173 A6
Greenwich SE18 121 D3
Rotherhithe SE16 118 C4
Southall UB1 85 D1
West Drayton UB7 104 A4
Swanscombe Ho
1 BR5 190 B1
11 Shepherd's Bush W11 112 D5
Swanscombe Point 7 E16 98 D2
Swanscombe Rd
5 Chiswick W4 111 C1
Shepherd's Bush W11 112 D5
Swansea Ct E16 122 D5
Swansea Rd
Enfield EN3 6 C1
Harlington TW14, TW6 149 B5
Swansland Gdns 2 E17 35 A2
Swan St
Isleworth TW7 131 B2
SE1 117 A4 252 B1
Swanston Ct TW1 152 D4
Swan The BR4 224 A6
Swanton Gdns SW19 156 D3
Swanton Rd DA8 147 D5
Swan Way EN3 6 D3
Swanwick Cl SW15 155 D4
Swan Wlk
Oatlands Pk TW17 193 C2
SW3 136 D6 267 C6
Swan Yd N1 72 D2
Swaton Rd E3 97 C3
Swaylands Rd DA17 147 C6
Swaythling Cl N18 34 B6
Swaythling Ho SW15 155 D5
Swedenborg Gdns E1 118 B6
Sweden Gate SE16 119 A2
Swedish Quays SE16 119 A3
Swedish Sch The SW13 134 A6
Sweeney Cres SE1 253 D1
Sweet Briar Gn N9 17 D1
Sweet Briar Gr N9 17 D1
Sweet Briar Wlk N18 33 D6
Sweetcroft La UB10 60 C1
Sweetmans Ave HA5 40 D6
Sweets Way N20 14 B2
Swell Ct E17 53 D3
Swetenham Wlk SE18 123 A1
Swete St E13 99 A5
Sweyn Pl SE3 143 A3
Swift Cl
Harrow HA2 63 D6
Hayes UB3 83 D1
Higham Hill E17 35 A3
Thamesmead SE28 124 B6
Swift Ct SM2 217 D1
Swift Ctr CR0 220 B1
Swift Ho
16 Stepney E1 96 C1
15 Stoke Newington N16 73 C5
1 SW9 138 C5
8 Wanstead E18 55 B6
Swift Rd
Feltham TW13 173 A6
Southall UB2 107 B3
Swiftsden Way BR1 186 C4
Swift St SW6 135 B4 264 C2
Swinbrook Rd W10 91 A2
Swinburne Cres CR0 206 C3
Swinburne Ct 4 SE5 139 B1
Swinburne Ho 15 E2 96 C4
Swinburne Rd SW15 134 A1
Swinderby Rd HA0 66 A2
Swindon Cl IG3 57 C1
Swindon Rd TW6 149 A6
Swindon St W12 112 C5
Swinfield Cl TW13 173 A6
Swinford Gdns SW9 138 D2
Swingate La SE18 145 C5
Swingfield Ct BR2 209 D4
Swingfield Ho 4 E9 96 C6
Swinley Ho NW1 231 D2
Swinnerton St E9 75 A3
Swinson Ho 12 N11 31 C5
Swinton Cl HA9 44 D1
Swinton Ho 21 E2 96 A4
Swinton Pl WC1 233 C2
Swinton St WC1 94 B4 233 C2
Swires Shaw BR2 225 D4
Swiss Cottage NW3 70 B1
Swiss Cottage Sch
South Hampstead NW3 70 B1
St John's Wood NW8 92 B6 229 D6
Swiss Cottage Sta NW3 70 B1
Swiss Re Building* EC2 95 C1 243 B2
Swiss Terr 7 NW3 70 B1
Switch Ho 4 E14 120 B6
Swithland Gdns SE9 188 C6
Swyncombe Ave W5 109 B2
Swynford Gdns 7 NW4 46 A5
Sybil Elgar Sch UB2 107 B3
Sybil Mews N4 50 D3
Sybil Phoenix Cl SE8 118 D1
Sybil Thorndike Casson Ho SW5 255 B1
Sybil Thorndike Ho 12 N1 73 A2
Sybourn Inf Sch Annexe E10 53 A1
Sybourn Jun & Inf Schs E17 53 B2
Sybourn St E17 53 B2
Sycamore Ave
DA15 167 D5
Ealing W5 109 D3
East Finchley N3 47 D6
Hayes UB3 105 C6
Old Ford E3 97 B6
Sycamore Cl
Carshalton SM5 218 D4
Chislehurst SE9 166 A2
East Acton W3 111 C5
Sycamore Cl *continued*
2 Edgware HA8 27 A6
Edmonton N9 34 A6
Feltham TW13 150 A1
New Barnet EN4 14 B5
Newham E16 98 C3
Northolt UB5 85 A6
South Croydon CR2 221 C3
Yiewsley UB7 104 B6
Sycamore Ct
4 Beckenham BR3 185 C2
Forest Gate E7 77 A2
3 Forest Hill SE26 184 C6
Golders Green NW11 47 A3
Hendon NW4 28 C1
Hillingdon UB8 82 C3
Hither Green SE12 164 D5
Hounslow TW4 129 A1
Kilburn NW6 91 C6
Surbiton KT6 198 A2
Tufnell Pk N19 71 D5
10 West Norwood SW16 182 C5
Sycamore Gdns
Hammersmith W6, W12 112 B3
Mitcham CR4 180 B1
Tottenham N15 51 D5
Sycamore Gr
Kingsbury NW9 45 A2
Kingston u T KT3 199 C6
Lewisham SE6 164 A5
Penge SE20 184 A2
Sycamore Hill N11 31 A4
Sycamore Ho
4 Buckhurst Hill IG9 21 D2
23 Finchley N2 30 B1
10 Maitland Pk NW3 70 D2
Penge SE20 184 D4
17 Rotherhithe SE16 118 D4
3 Shepherd's Bush W6 112 B4
2 Stoke Newington N16 73 B6
Teddington TW11 175 C3
Twickenham TW1 152 D2
Sycamore Lo
7 Ashford TW16 171 D3
Putney SW15 134 B2
Sycamore Lodge HA2 64 B6
Sycamore Mews 4 SW4 137 C2
Sycamore Rd SW19, SW20 178 C4
Sycamore St EC1 242 A5
Sycamore Way TW11 175 C4
Sycamore Wlk
Ilford IG6 57 A5
1 Kensal Town W10 91 A3
Sydcote SE21 161 A3
Sydenham Ave
Penge SE26 184 B5
Southgate N21 16 B6
Sydenham High Sch SE26 162 B1
Sydenham High Sch GDST SE26 184 B5
Sydenham Hill SE21, SE22, SE23, SE26, SE19 162 A1
Sydenham Hill Sta SE21 161 D1
Sydenham Ho 16 KT6 197 D2
Sydenham Ind Est SE26 185 B5
Sydenham Park Mans 2 SE26 162 C1
Sydenham Park Rd SE23, SE26 162 C1
Sydenham Pk SE26 162 C1
Sydenham Rd
Forest Hill SE26 185 A6
Thornton Heath CR0 205 B2
Sydenham Rise SE23 162 B2
Sydenham Sta SE26 184 C6
Sydenham Station App 4 SE26 184 C6
Sydmons Ct SE23 162 C4
Sydner Mews N16 73 D4
Sydner Rd N16 73 D4
Sydney Chapman Way EN5 1 B3
Sydney Cl SW3 256 D3
Sydney Cotts KT10 212 D2
Sydney Cres TW15 170 D4
Sydney Ct
Hayes UB4 84 C3
Surbiton KT6 214 A6
Sydney Gr NW4 46 C4
Sydney Ho
4 Chiswick W4 111 C2
Sydney Ho *continued*
Muswell Hill N10 31 B3
Sydney Mews SW3 256 D3
Sydney Pl SW7 257 A3
Sydney Rd
Abbey Wood SE2 124 D3
Bexley DA6 146 D1
Ealing W13 109 A4
East Bedfont TW14 150 A3
Enfield EN2 5 B1
Hornsey N8 50 C5
Muswell Hill N10 31 B3
Richmond TW10, TW9 132 A1
Sidcup DA14 189 C6
Sutton SM1 217 C4
Teddington TW11 174 D5
Wanstead E11 55 B3
West Barnes SW20 178 D1
Woodford IG8 37 A6
Sydney Russell Sch The RM9 80 D3
Sydney St SW3 114 C1 257 A2
Sydney Terr KT10 212 D2
Sylva Cotts 3 SE8 141 C4
Sylva Ct 3 SW15 156 D4
Sylvana Cl UB10 82 B6
Sylvan Ave
Church End N3 29 C1
Dagenham RM6 59 B3
Edgware NW7 27 D4
Wood Green N22 32 C3
Sylvan Ct
Finchley N12 29 D6
1 Kilburn NW6 91 D6
South Croydon CR2 221 A2
Sylvan Gdns KT6 197 D2
Sylvan Gr
Hampstead NW2 68 D4
SE15 140 B6
Sylvan Hill SE19 183 C2
Sylvan Ho N21 16 B6
Sylvan Rd
Ilford IG1 79 A6
South Norwood SE19 183 D2
Upton E7 77 B2
Walthamstow E17 53 C4
Wanstead E11 55 A4
Sylvan Way
Coney Hall BR4 224 C4
Dagenham RM8 80 B5
Sylvan Wlk BR1 210 B6
Sylverdale Rd CR0 220 D5
Sylvester Ave BR7 188 B4
Sylvester Ct HA0 65 D3
Sylvester Ho 7 E8 74 B2
Sylvester Path 8 E8 74 B2
Sylvester Rd
Finchley N2 30 B1
Hackney E8 74 B2
Walthamstow E17 53 B2
Wembley HA0 65 C3
Sylvestrus Cl KT1 176 C1
Sylvia Ave HA5 23 B4
Sylvia Ct
N1 235 C3
Wembley HA9 66 D1
Sylvia Gdns HA9 66 D1
Sylvia Lawla Ct N22 32 B1
Sylvia Pankhurst Ho
10 Dagenham RM10 81 C5
14 Globe Town E2 96 D4
Sylvia Young Theatre Sch NW1 237 B5
Symes Mews NW1 232 A4
Symington Ho SE1 262 C5
Symington Mews E9 74 D3
Symister Mews N1 95 C4
Symons St SW3 114 D2 257 D3
Symphony Cl HA8 26 D3
Symphony Mews 15 W10 91 A4
Syon Gate Way TW7, TW8 131 B5
Syon Ho & Pk* TW8 131 C4
Syon La
Brentford TW7, TW8 131 B5
Hounslow TW7 130 D6
Syon Lane Sta TW7 131 A5
Syon Lo 6 SE12 165 A4
Syon Park Cotts TW8 131 C4
Syon Park Gdns TW7 130 D5
Syon Park Sch TW7 131 B4
Syringa Ho SE4 141 B2

T

Tabard Ct 6 E14 98 A1
Tabard Ho
SE1 262 D6
Teddington KT1 175 C2
Tabard St SE1 117 B3 262 C6
Tabernacle Ave 7
E13 99 A3
Tabernacle St
EC2 95 B3 242 D6
Tableer Ave SW4 159 D6
Tabley Rd N7 72 A4
Tabor Ct 3 SM3 217 A2
Tabor Gdns SM2, SM3 217 B1
Tabor Gr SW19 179 B3
Tabor Rd W6 112 B3
Tachbrook Est
SW1 115 D1 259 D1
Tachbrook Mews
SW1 259 A4
Tachbrook Rd
East Bedfont TW14 149 D4
Southall UB2 106 D2
Tachbrook St
SW1 115 C2 259 B3
Tack Mews SE4 141 C2
Tadbourne Ct 1 HA8 27 A3
Tadema Ho NW8 236 D5
Tadema Rd
SW10 136 A5 266 B3
Tadlow KT1 198 C6
Tadmor Cl TW16 193 D5
Tadmor St W12 112 D5
Tadworth Ave KT3 199 D4
Tadworth Ct 5 N11 31 A4
Tadworth Ho SE1 251 C1
Tadworth Rd NW2 68 A6
Taeping St E14 119 D2
Taffrail Ho 2 E14 119 D1
Taffy's How CR4 202 C6
Taft Way 44 E3 97 D4
Taggs Ho KT1 175 D1
Tailors Ct 9 SW16 181 C6
Tailworth St 16 E1 96 A2
Tait 7 NW9 27 D3
Tait Ct
16 Old Ford E3 97 B6
SW8 269 D2
Tait Ho
SE1 251 B3
2 Tufnell Pk N19 71 C4
Tait Rd CR0 205 C2
Tait Rd Ind Est CR0 205 C2
Takhar Mews SW11 136 C3
Talacre Rd NW5 71 A2
Talbot Ave N2 48 B6
Talbot Cl N15 51 D5
Talbot Cres NW4 46 A4
Talbot Ct
EC3 252 D6
Neasden NW9 67 B5
Talbot Gdns IG3 80 A6
Talbot Grove Ho 10
W11 91 A1
Talbot Ho
Highbury N7 72 C5
Poplar E14 97 D1
Talbot Pl SE3 142 C3
Talbot Rd
Ashford TW15 170 A5
Camberwell SE22 139 C1
Dagenham RM9 81 B1
Ealing W13 109 A5
Forest Gate E7 77 A4
Harrow HA3 24 D1
Highgate N6 49 A3
Isleworth TW1, TW7 131 A1
Notting Hill W2 91 C1
Notting Hill W11 91 B1
Southall UB2 107 A2
South Norwood CR7 205 B5
Tottenham N15 51 D5
Twickenham TW2 152 D3
Wallend E6 100 C5
Wallington SM5 219 A3
Wembley HA0 65 D2
Wood Green N22 31 C2
Talbot Sq W2 92 B1 236 C1
Talbot Wlk
Notting Hill W11 91 A1
Willesden NW10 67 C2
Talbot Yd SE1 252 C3
Talcott Path 12 SW2 160 C3
Talfourd Pl SE15 139 D4
Talfourd Rd SE15 139 D4
Talgarth Rd
Hammersmith W6 112 C1
W14 113 A1 254 B2
Talgarth Wlk NW9 45 C4
Talia Ho E14 120 A3
Talina Ctr SW6 266 A1
Talisman Cl 2 IG3 58 B1
Talisman Sq SE26 184 A6
Talisman Way HA9 66 B5
Tallack Cl HA3 24 C3
Tallack Rd E10 53 B1
Tall Elms Cl BR2 208 D4
Talleyrand Ho SE5 139 A3
Tallis Cl E16 99 B1
Tallis Gr SE7 143 B6
Tallis St EC4 251 B6
Tallis View NW10 67 B2
Tallow Rd TW8 131 C5
Tall Trees SW16 204 B6
Talma Gdns TW2 152 C4
Talmage Cl SE23 162 C4
Talman Gr HA7 25 D4
Talma Rd SW2 138 C1
Talmud Torah Chaim
Meirim Sch N16 51 D1
Talmud Torah Machzikei
Hadass Sch E5 52 A2
Talmud-Torah Yetev-Lev
N16 52 A1
Talwin St E3 97 D4
Tamar Cl 24 E3 97 B6
Tamar Ho
10 Cubitt Town E14 120 A4
SE11 261 B2
Tamarind Ct 8 W3 89 A1
Tamarind Ho 4 SE15 140 A5
Tamarind Yd 5 E1 118 A5
Tamarisk Sq W12 111 D6
Tamar Sq IG8 37 B4
Tamar St SE7 122 A2
Tamar Way N17 52 A6
Tame Ho 3 UB5 85 B4
Tamesa Ho TW17 192 C2
Tamesis Gdns KT4 215 C6
Tamian Ind Est TW4 128 C1
Tamian Way TW4 128 C1
Tamil Ho SE6 163 C2
Tamworth N7 72 A2
Tamworth Ave IG8 36 C4
Tamworth La CR4 203 B6
Tamworth Pk CR4 203 B6
Tamworth Pl 3 CR0 221 A6
Tamworth Rd CR0 221 A6
Tamworth St
SW6 135 C6 265 A5
Tancred Rd N4 50 D3
Tandem Ctr SW19 180 B2
Tandridge Ct SM2 217 D2
Tandridge Dr BR6 211 B1
Tandridge Pl 2 BR6 211 B1
Tanfield Ave NW2 67 D5
Tanfield Rd CR0 221 A4
Tangier Rd TW10 132 D2
Tangleberry Cl BR1 210 B5
Tangle Tree Cl N3 29 D1
Tanglewood Cl
Hillingdon UB10 82 C3
South Croydon CR0 222 C5
Stanmore HA7 8 C2
Tanglewood Lo HA8 27 A4
Tanglewood Way
TW13 150 B1
Tangley Gr SW15 155 D4
Tangley Park Rd
TW12 173 B4
Tanglyn Ave TW17 192 D4
Tangmere
Tottenham N17 33 B1
WC1 233 C1
Tangmere Gdns UB5 84 C5
Tangmere Gr KT2 175 D5
Tangmere Way NW9 27 C1
Tanhurst Ho 27 SW2 160 A4
Tanhurst Wlk SE2 124 D3
Tankerton Rd KT6 214 B6
Tankerton St WC1 233 B1
Tankerton Terr CR0 204 B3
Tankerville Rd SW16 182 A3
Tankridge Rd NW2 68 B6
Tanner Ho
1 Merton SW19 180 A2
SE1 253 B1
Tanner Point E13 99 A6
Tanners Cl KT12 194 B3
Tanners End La N18 33 C5
Tanner's Hill SE8 141 C4
Tanners La IG6 57 A6
Tanners Mews SE8 141 B4
Tanner St
Barking IG11 79 A2
SE1 117 C4 253 B1
Tanners Yd 33 E2 96 B5
Tannery Cl
Beckenham BR3, CR0 206 D4
Dagenham RM10 81 D5
Tannery Ho 22 E1 96 A2
Tannington Terr N5 72 C5
Tannsfeld Rd SE26 184 D5
Tansley Cl N7 71 D3
Tanswell St SE1 251 A1
Tansy Cl E6 100 C1
Tantallon Rd SW12 159 A3
Tant Ave E16 98 D1
Tantony Gr RM6 58 D6
Tanworth Gdns HA5 22 C1
Tanyard Ho 8 TW8 131 C5
Tan Yard La DA5 169 C4
Tanza Rd NW3 70 D4
Tapestry Cl SM2 217 D1
Tapley Ho 11 SE1 118 A4
Taplow NW3 70 B1
Taplow Ct CR4 202 C5
Taplow Ho 36 E2 95 D4
Taplow Rd N13 33 A6
Taplow St N1 95 A5 235 B3
Tappesfield Rd SE15 140 C2
Tapping Cl 5 KT2 176 C3
Tapp St E1 96 B3
Tapster St EN5 1 B2
Tara Ct 4 BR3 185 D1
Taranto Ho 14 E1 96 D2
Tarati Ct HA0 65 D1
Tarbert Rd SE22 161 C6
Tarbert Wlk E1 118 C6
Target Cl TW14 149 C5
Target Ho W13 109 B5
Target Rdbt UB5 85 B6
Tariff Rd N17 34 A4
Tarleton Ct 2 N22 32 C1
Tarleton Gdns SE23 162 B3
Tarling Cl DA14 168 B1
Tarling Rd
Canning Town E16 98 D1
Finchley N2 30 A1
Tarling St E1 96 C1
Tarnbank EN2 16 A6
Tarnbrook Ct SW1 258 A3
Tarn St SE1 117 A3 262 A5
Tarns The NW1 232 A2
Tarnwood Pk SE9 166 B3
Tarplett Ho 22 SE14 140 D6
Tarquin Ho SE26 184 A6
Tarragon Cl SE14 141 A5
Tarragon Gr SE26 184 D4
Tarranbrae NW6 69 A1
Tarrant Ho E2 96 C4
Tarrant Pl W1 237 C3
Tarrantt Ho W14 254 A6
Tarriff Cres SE8 119 B2
Tarrington Cl SW16 159 D1
Tartan Ho 12 E14 98 A1
Tarver Rd
SE17 116 D1 261 D2
Tarves Way SE10 141 D5
Tash Pl N11 31 B5
Tasker Cl UB7 127 A5
Tasker Ho
3 Barking IG11 101 B5
17 Poplar E14 97 B2
Tasker Lo W8 245 A2
Tasker Rd NW3 70 D3
Tasman Ct
Ashford TW16 171 C3
9 Cubitt Town E14 119 D2
Tasman Ho 17 E1 118 B5
Tasmania Terr N18 33 A4
Tasman Rd SW9 138 A2
Tasman Wlk E16 99 D1
Tasso Rd W6 135 A6 264 A6
Tasso Yd W6 264 A5
Tatam Rd NW10 67 B1
Tatchbury Ho SW15 155 D5
Tate Britain*
SW1 116 A2 260 A3
Tate Gdns WD23 8 C4
Tate Ho 18 E2 96 D5
Tate Modern*
EC4 116 D5 251 D4
Tate Rd
Newham E16 122 B5
Sutton SM1 217 C3
Tatham Pl NW8 92 B5 229 D4
Tatnell Rd SE23 163 A5
Tattersall Cl SE9 166 A6
Tatton Cres E5, N16 51 D2
Tatum St SE17 117 B2 262 D3
Tauheed Cl N4 73 A6
Taunton Ave
Hounslow TW3 130 A3
Wimbledon SW20 178 B1
Taunton Cl SM3 201 C1
Taunton Dr
Enfield EN2 4 C2
Finchley N2 30 A1
Taunton Ho W2 236 A1
Taunton Mews NW1 237 C5
Taunton Pl
NW1 92 D3 237 C6
Taunton Rd
Greenford UB6 85 D6
Lewisham SE12 164 D6
Taunton Way HA7 26 A1
Tavern Cl SM5 202 C2
Tavern Ct SE1 262 B5
Taverner Ho N16 73 B5
Taverners Cl W11 244 A3
Taverners Ct HA9 66 B6
Taverners Lo EN4 15 A6
Taverner Sq 4 N5 73 A4
Taverners Way E4 20 C3
Tavern La SW9 138 C3
Tavistock Ave
Mill Hill NW7 28 D3
Walthamstow E17 53 A6
Wembley UB6 87 A5
Tavistock Cl N16 73 C3
Tavistock Cres
Mitcham CR4 204 A5
Notting Hill W11 91 B2
Tavistock Ct
1 Croydon CR0 205 B1
WC1 239 D6
Tavistock Gdns IG3 79 C4
Tavistock Gr CR0 205 B2
Tavistock Ho 3 W11 91 B2
Tavistock Mews 3
W11 91 B1
Tavistock Pl
Bloomsbury
WC1 94 A3 240 A6
East Barnet N14 15 B5
Tavistock Rd
4 Beckenham BR2 208 D5
Carshalton SM5 202 B1
Croydon CR0 205 B1
DA16 146 C4
Dagenham NW10 89 D5
Edgware HA8 26 C2
Leyton E7 76 D4
Notting Hill W11 91 B2
Stratford E15 76 D2
Tottenham N4, N15 51 B3
Uxbridge UB10 61 A3
Wanstead E18 55 A6
Tavistock Sq
WC1 93 D3 239 D6
Tavistock St
WC2 116 A6 250 B6
Tavistock Terr N19 71 D5
Tavistock Twr SE16 119 A3
Tavistock Wlk SM5 202 B1
Taviton St WC1 93 D3 239 C6
Tavy Bridge SE2 124 C4
Tavy Cl SE11 261 B2
Tawney Rd SE28 124 B6
Tawny Cl
Ealing W13 109 B5
Feltham TW13 150 A1
Tawny Way SE16 118 D2
Tayben Ave TW2 152 C5
Taybridge Rd SW11 137 A1
Tayburn Cl E14 98 A1
Tayfield Cl UB10 61 A5
Tay Ho 10 E3 97 B5
Tayler Ct NW8 229 C6
Taylor Ave TW9 132 D3
Taylor Cl
Deptford SE8 141 B6
Hampton TW12 174 A5
Hounslow TW3 130 A4
3 Orpington BR6 227 D4
Tottenham N17 34 A3
Taylor Ct
Ealing W13 109 C5
Penge SE20 184 C1
Stratford New Town E15 76 A3
Taylor Ho
Carshalton SM5 218 C6
10 Streatham SW2 160 C3
Taylor Rd
Mitcham CR4 180 C3
Wallington SM6 219 B3
Taylor's Bldgs SE18 122 D2
Taylors Cl DA14 167 D1
Taylors Ct TW13 150 A2
Taylor's Gn W3 89 C1
Taylor's La
Barnet EN5 1 B4
Forest Hill SE26 184 B6
Willesden NW10 67 C1
Taylorsmead NW7 28 A5
Taymount Grange 2
SE23 162 C2
Taymount Rise SE23 162 C2
Tayport Cl N1 72 A1
Tayside Ct 6 SE5 139 B1
Tayside Dr HA8 10 D2
Taywood Rd UB5 85 B3
Teak Cl SE16 119 A5
Tealby Ct N7 72 B2
Teal Cl
Enfield EN3 6 C6
Newham E16 99 D2
Teal Ct
30 SE8 141 B6
Wallington SM6 219 C3
Willesden NW10 67 B2
Teale St E2 96 A5
Tealing Dr KT19 215 B4
Teal Pl SM1 217 B3
Teal St 1 SE10 120 D3
Teasel Cl CR0 206 D1
Teasel Cres SE28 123 C5
Teasel Way E15 98 C4
Teather St 12 SE5 139 C5
Tebbs Ho 14 SW2 160 C4
Tebworth Rd N17 33 D3
Technology Pk NW9 45 C6
Teck Cl TW7 131 A3
Tedder 5 NW9 27 D3
Tedder Cl
Chessington KT9 213 C3
Hillingdon UB10 60 B1
Tedder Rd CR2 222 D1
TEDDINGTON 175 C5
Teddington Meml Hospl
TW11 174 C4
Teddington Park Rd
TW11 174 D6
Teddington Pk TW11 174 D5
Teddington Sch
TW11 175 C4
Teddington Sta
TW11 175 A4
Ted Hennem Ho RM10 81 D5
Tedman Ct SE13 142 A1
Ted Roberts Ho 25 E2 96 B5
Tedworth Gdns SW3 257 C1
Tedworth Sq
SW3 114 D1 257 C1
Tees Ave UB6 86 D5
Tees Ct W7 86 B1
Teesdale Ave TW7 131 A4
Teesdale Cl E2 96 B5
Teesdale Gdns
Isleworth TW7 131 A4
South Norwood SE25 183 C1
Teesdale Rd E11 54 D2
Teesdale St E2 96 B5
Teesdale Yd 34 E2 96 B5
Teeswater Ct DA18 124 D3
Tee The W3 89 C1
Teevan Cl CR0 206 A2
Teevan Rd CR0 206 A2
Teign Mews SE9 166 A2
Teignmouth Cl
6 Clapham SW4 137 D1
Edgware HA8 26 B1
Teignmouth Gdns UB6 87 A4
Teignmouth Par UB6 87 B5
Teignmouth Rd
Bexley DA16 146 C3
Brondesbury NW2 68 D2
Tejas Ct N3 47 A5
Tej Ct E7 77 D3
Telcote Way HA4 40 C2
Telegraph Hill NW3 69 D5
Telegraph La KT10 212 D3
Telegraph Mews
Ilford IG3 58 A1
Seven Kings IG3 57 D1
Telegraph Pl E14 119 D2
Telegraph Rd SW15 156 C4
Telegraph St EC2 242 C2
Telemann Sq SE3 143 B2
Telephone Pl SW6 264 D6
Telfer Cl 4 W3 111 A4
Telfer Ho
8 Dulwich SE21 183 C6
EC1 234 D1
Telferscot Prim Sch
SW12 159 D3
Telferscot Rd SW12 159 D3
Telford Ave SW12,
SW2 160 A3
Telford Avenue Mans 7
SW2 160 A3
Telford Cl
Penge SE19 183 D4
Walthamstow E17 53 A2
Telford Ct EN5 13 C6
Telford Dr KT12 194 C2
Telford Ho
2 Belvedere DA17 125 C3
8 Kensal Town W10 91 A2
SE1 262 A6
Telford Parade Mans 8
SW2 160 A3
Telford Rd
3 Hendon NW9 46 A3
Kensal Town W10 91 A2
Sidcup SE9 167 B2
Southall UB1 85 D1
Twickenham TW4 151 C4
Telford Rd (North Circular
Rd) N11 31 C5
Telford's Yd 21 SE1 118 A6
Telford Terr SW1 269 A6
Telford Way
Dagenham W3 89 C2
Hayes UB4 85 A2
Telham Rd E6 100 C5
Tell Gr SE22 139 D1
Tellson Ave SE18 144 A4
Telscombe Cl BR6 227 C6
Telscombe Ho SW11 268 A1
Temair Ho 1 SE10 142 A5
Temeraire Pl TW8 110 B1
Temeraire St SE16 118 C4
Tempelhof Ave NW2 46 C2
Temperley Rd SW12 159 A4
Templar Ct RM7 59 D5
Templar Dr SE28 102 D1
Templar Ho
Hampstead NW2 69 B2
7 Upper Clapton E5 74 C6
Templar Pl TW12 173 C3
Templars Ave NW11 47 B3
Templars Cres N3 29 C1
Templars Dr HA3 24 B4
Templars Ho E15 75 D3
Templar St SE5 138 D3
Temple Ave
Croydon CR0 223 B5
Dagenham RM8 59 C1
EC4 116 C6 251 B6
Oakleigh Pk N20 14 B4
Temple Cl
Finchley N3 29 B1
Leytonstone E11 54 C2
Woolwich SE18 123 A3
Templecombe Rd E9 96 C6
Templecombe Way
SM4 201 A4
Templecroft TW15 171 B4
Temple Ct
Stepney E1 96 D2
SW8 270 A3
Templedene BR2 186 B1
Temple Dwellings 7
E2 96 B5
TEMPLE FORTUNE 47 A4
Temple Fortune Ct 9
NW11 47 B4
Temple Fortune Hill
NW11 47 C4
Temple Fortune Ho 3
NW11 47 B4
Temple Fortune La
NW11 47 C3
Temple Fortune Par 5
NW11 47 B4
Temple Gdns
Dagenham RM8 80 D5
Edmonton N21 16 D2
Temple Fortune NW11 47 B3
Temple Gr
Enfield EN2 4 D2
Golders Green NW11 47 C3
Temple Hall Ct E4 20 B2
Temple Ho
13 Battersea SW11 136 C2
4 Tufnell Pk N7 71 C5
11 Walthamstow E17 53 D6
Temple La EC4 94 C1 241 B1
Temple Lo EN5 14 B4
Templeman Rd W7 86 D2
Templemead Cl W3 89 C1
Temple Mead Cl HA7 25 B4
Templemead Ho E9 75 A4
Temple Mill La E10,
E15 76 A4
TEMPLE MILLS 75 D3
Temple Mills Rd E9 75 C4
Templemore DA14 190 B5

Temple Par EN5 14 B4
Temple Pk UB8 82 C4
Temple Pl
WC2 116 B6 250 D6
Temple Rd
Acton Green W4 111 A3
Cricklewood NW2 68 C5
Croydon CR0 221 B4
Ealing W5 109 D3
Hornsey N8 50 B5
Isleworth TW3 130 A1
Newham E6 100 A6
Richmond TW9 132 B2
Temple Sheen SW14 155 A6
Temple Sheen Rd
SW14 133 A1
Temple St E2 96 B5
Temple Sta
WC2 116 C6 251 A6
Temple Terr N22 32 C1
Templeton Ave E4 35 D6
Templeton Cl
South Norwood SE19 183 B2
25 Stoke Newington
N16 73 C3
Templeton Ct
Enfield EN3 6 C5
Walthamstow E10 53 D1
Templeton Pl
SW5 113 C2 255 B3
Templeton Rd N4, N15 51 B3
Temple Way SM1 218 B5
Temple West Mews
SE11 261 C5
Templewood W13 87 B2
Templewood Ave NW3 69 D5
Templewood Gdns
NW3 69 D5
Templewood Point
NW2 69 B6
Tempsford Cl EN2 5 A2
Tempsford Ct HA1 42 D3
Temsford Cl HA2 24 A1
Tenbury Cl E7 77 D3
Tenbury Ct SW12 159 D3
Tenby Ave HA3 25 B1
Tenby Cl
Dagenham RM6 59 A3
Tottenham N15 51 D5
Tenby Ct E17 53 A4
Tenby Gdns UB5 63 C2
Tenby Ho
Hayes UB3 105 A3
Islington N7 72 C4
W2 236 A1
Tenby Rd
DA16 146 D4
Dagenham RM6 59 A3
Edgware HA8 26 B1
Enfield EN3 6 C1
Walthamstow E17 53 A4
Tench St E1 118 B5
Tenda Rd SE16 118 B2
Tendring Ho SW2 160 C5
Tendring Way RM6 58 C4
Tenham Ave SW2 159 D2
Tenison Ct W1 249 A6
Tenison Way SE1 251 A3
Tenniel Cl W2 245 D6
Tennison Ave WD6 10 D6
Tennison Rd SE25 205 D4
Tennis St SE1 117 B4 252 C2
Tenniswood Rd EN1 5 C4
Tennyson Ave
Kingsbury NW9 45 A6
Plashet E12 78 A1
Twickenham TW1 152 D3
Wanstead E11 55 A2
West Barnes KT3 200 B4
Tennyson Cl
DA16 145 D4
Enfield EN3 18 D6
Feltham TW14 150 A5
Tennyson Ct 3
TW10 175 D6
Tennyson Ho
2 Erith DA17 125 B1
SE17 262 B2
Southall UB1 85 C1
Tennyson Rd
Ashford TW15 170 A5
Ealing W7 108 D6
Hounslow TW3 130 A3
Kilburn NW6 91 B6
Leyton E10 75 D6
Mill Hill NW7 28 A5
Penge SE20 184 D3
Stratford E15 76 C1
Walthamstow E17 53 B3
Wimbledon SW19 180 A4
Tennyson St SW8 137 B3
Tensing Ct TW19 148 A3
Tensing Ho N1 72 D2
Tensing Rd UB2 107 C3
Tentelow La UB2 107 D3
Tenterden Cl
Hendon NW4 46 D6
SE9 188 B6
Tenterden Dr NW4 46 D6
Tenterden Gdns
Croydon CR0 206 A2
Hendon NW4 46 D6
Tenterden Gr NW4 46 D6
Tenterden Ho SE17 263 B2
Tenterden Rd
Croydon CR0 206 A2
Dagenham RM8 81 B6
Tottenham N17 33 D3
Tenterden St W1 238 D1
Tenter Ground E1 243 C3
Tent Peg La BR5 211 A4
Tent St E1 96 B3
Tenzing Ct 4 SE9 166 A2
Tequila Wharf E14 97 A1
Terborch Way 6
SE22 161 C6
Tercelet Terr NW3 70 A4
Teredo St SE16 118 D3
Terence Ct 6 DA17 147 B6
Teresa Mews E17 53 C5
Teresa Wlk N10 49 B4
Terling Cl E11 76 D5
Terling Ho 9 W10 90 C2
Terling Rd RM8 81 C6
Terling Wlk N1 235 A6
Terminal Four Rdbt
TW6 149 A5
Terminus Pl SW1 258 D5
Tern Ho 9 SE15 139 D4
Terrace Gdns SW13 133 D3
Terrace Ho 2 N20 14 A1
Terrace La TW10 154 A5
Terrace Rd
Hackney E9 74 C1
Newham E13 99 B6
Walton-on-T KT12 194 B3
Terraces The 6
SW20 178 D3
Terrace The
Barnes SW13, SW14 133 C3
Chingford E4 20 C1
Cranley Gdns N2 49 A5
EC4 241 B1
Kilburn NW6 91 C6
10 Rotherhithe SE8 119 B2
1 Woodford IG8 37 A4
Terrace Wlk RM9 81 A3
Terrall Apartments 7
N17 51 D6
Terrano Ho 1 TW9 132 D4
Terrapin Ct SW17 159 B1
Terrapin Rd SW17 159 B1
Terrapins KT6 197 D2
Terrick Rd N22 32 A2
Terrick St W12 90 B1
Terrilands HA5 41 B6
Territorial Ho SE11 261 B3
Terront Rd N15 51 A5
Terry Ct 8 SM6 219 C2
Terry Ho SW2 160 C3
Terry Lodge 2 CR7 204 C4
Tersha St TW9 132 B1
Tessa Sanderson Pl 6
SW8 137 B2
Tessa Sanderson Way
UB6 64 B3
Testerton Wlk 3
W11 112 D6
Testwood Ct W7 108 C6
Tetcott Rd
SW10 136 A5 266 A3
Tetherdown N10 49 A6
Tetherdown Prim Sch
N10 49 A5
Tetty Way BR1, BR2 187 A1
Teversham La
SW8 138 A4 270 B2
Teviot Cl DA16 146 B4
Teviot St E14 98 A2
Tewkesbury Ave
Forest Hill SE23 162 B4
Pinner HA5 41 A4
Tewkesbury Cl
Barnet EN4 2 B1
Tottenham N15 51 B3
Tewkesbury Ct N11 31 D4
Tewkesbury Gdns
NW9 44 D6
Tewkesbury Rd
Carshalton SM5 202 B1
Tewkesbury Rd *continued*
Ealing W13 109 A6
Tottenham N15 51 B3
Tewkesbury Terr N11 31 D4
Tewson Rd SE18 123 C1
Teyham Ct SW11 158 D5
Teynham Ave EN1 17 B5
Teynham Ct N12 30 A6
Teynham Gn BR2 209 A4
Teynham Ho SE9 167 B5
Teynton Terr N17 33 A2
Thackeray Ave N17 34 A1
Thackeray Cl
Hayes UB8 82 D1
Isleworth TW7 131 A3
Wimbledon SW19 178 D3
Thackeray Ct
Chelsea SW3 257 C2
Ealing W5 88 B1
West Kensington W14 254 A5
Thackeray Dr RM6 58 B2
Thackeray Ho
College Pk NW10 90 A4
WC1 240 A6
Thackeray Manor
SM1 218 A3
Thackeray Mews E8 74 A2
Thackeray Rd
Clapham SW8 137 B3
Newham E6 99 D5
Thackeray's Almshouses
SE6 163 D5
Thackeray St W8 255 D6
Thackery Lo TW14 149 B5
Thackrah Cl N2 30 A1
Thakeham Cl SE26 184 B5
Thalia Cl SE10 142 B6
Thame Rd SE16 118 D4
Thames Ave
Dagenham RM9 103 D3
Sands End
SW10 136 A4 266 B2
Wembley UB6 86 D5
Thames Bank SW14 133 A3
Thamesbank Pl SE28 102 C1
Thames Barrier Visitor
Ctr* SE18 121 D3
Thames Christian Coll
SW11 136 B2
Thames Circ E14 119 C2
Thames Cl TW12 173 D1
Thames Cnr TW16 194 C6
Thames Cres W4 133 C5
Thames Ct
Ealing W7 86 C1
Edmonton N9 18 C1
10 SE15 139 D5
West Molesey KT8 173 D1
THAMES DITTON 197 B2
Thames Ditton Fst Sch
KT7 196 D3
Thames Ditton Island
KT7 197 A3
Thames Ditton Jun Sch
KT7 196 D2
Thames Ditton Sta
KT7 196 D2
Thames Dr HA4 39 A3
Thames Eyot 8 TW1 153 A3
Thamesfield Ct TW17 193 A2
Thamesfield Ho
TW17 193 A2
Thamesfield Mews
TW17 193 A2
Thamesgate Cl TW10 175 B6
Thames Gateway Pk
RM9 103 B4
Thames Haven KT6 197 D4
Thames Hts SE1 253 C2
Thameside TW11 175 D3
Thameside Ctr TW8 132 B6
Thameside Ind Est
E16 121 D4
Thameside Pl KT1 175 D2
Thames Link Ho 7
TW9 132 A1
Thames Mdw KT12,
TW17 193 C1
THAMESMEAD 124 A5
Thames Mead KT12 194 A3
Thames Meadow KT8 195 C6
Thamesmead Sec Sch
TW17 193 B3
Thamesmead Sh Ctr
SE28 124 A6
Thamesmere Dr
SE28 124 A6
Thames Pl SW15 134 D2
Thamespoint TW11 175 D3
Thames Quay
Millwall E14 119 D4
SW10 266 B1
Thames Rd
Barking IG11 102 A4
Chiswick W4 132 D6
Newham E16 121 D5
Thames Reach
Fulham W6 134 C6
Woolwich SE28 123 C4
Thames Road Ind Est
E16 121 D4
Thames Row TW9 132 B6
Thames Side
Teddington KT1 175 D2
Thames Ditton KT7 197 B3
Thames St
Hampton TW12 173 D1
Kingston u T KT1, KT2 175 D1
SE10 141 D6
Sunbury TW16 194 B6
Walton-on-T KT12 193 D2
Thamesvale Cl TW3 129 C3
Thames Valley Univ
W5 109 D5
Thames View 2 IG1 79 A6
Thames View Ho
TW12 194 A3
Thames View Inf Sch
IG11 102 A5
Thames View Jun Sch
IG11 101 D5
Thames View Lo
IG11 101 C4
Thames Village W4 133 A4
Thames Wlk
SW11 136 C5 267 A4
Thane Mans N7 72 B5
Thanescroft Gdns
CR0 221 C5
Thanet Ct 14 W3 88 C1
Thanet Dr BR2 225 D5
Thanet Ho
WC1 233 A1
1 West Norwood
SE27 160 D1
Thanet Lo NW2 69 A2
Thanet Pl CR0 221 A4
Thanet Rd DA5 169 C4
Thanet St WC1 94 A4 233 A1
Thane Villas N7 72 B5
Thane Works N7 72 B5
Thanington Ct DA15 167 C5
Thant Cl E10 75 D5
Tharp Rd SM6 219 D3
Thatcham Ct N20 14 A4
Thatcham Gdns N20 14 A4
Thatcher Cl UB7 104 A4
Thatchers Way TW7 152 B6
Thatches Gr RM6 59 A5
Thavies Inn EC4 241 B2
Thaxted Ct N1 235 D3
Thaxted Ho
Bermondsey SE16 118 C2
Dagenham RM10 81 D1
Thaxted Lo 3 E18 55 B6
Thaxted Pl 9 SW20 178 D3
Thaxted Rd
Buckhurst Hill IG9 21 D4
SE9 167 A2
Thaxton Rd
W14 135 B6 264 D6
Thayers Farm Rd
BR3 185 A2
Thayer St W1 93 A1 238 B2
Theatre Sq E15 76 B2
Theatre St SW11 136 D2
Theberton St
N1 94 D6 234 C6
Theed St SE1 116 C5 251 B3
Thelbridge Ho 28 E3 97 D4
Thelma Gdns SE3 144 A4
Thelma Gr TW11 175 A4
Theobald Cres HA3 24 A2
Theobald Rd
Croydon CR0 220 D6
Walthamstow E17 53 C2
Theobalds Ave N12 30 A6
Theobalds Ct N4 73 A6
Theobalds Park Rd EN2 4 D6
Theobald's Rd
WC1 94 B2 240 C4
Theobald St SE1 262 C5
Theodora Way HA5 39 D6
Theodore Ct SE13 164 B5
Theodore Ho 1
SW15 156 A6
Theodore Rd SE13 164 B5
Therapia La
Thornton Heath CR0 204 A2
Therapia La *continued*
Thornton Heath CR0 204 A3
Wallington CR0 203 D2
Therapia Lane Sta
CR0 204 A2
Therapia Rd SE22 162 C5
Theresa Rd W6 112 A2
Therfield Ct N4 73 A6
Thermopylae Gate
E14 119 D2
Theseus Ho
2 South Bromley E14 98 B1
2 E14 98 B1
Theseus Wlk N1 234 D3
Thesiger Rd SE20 184 D3
Thessaly Ho SW8 269 A3
Thessaly Rd
SW8 137 C4 269 B2
Thetford Cl N13 32 D4
Thetford Ct
3 Dulwich SE21 162 B2
New Malden KT3 199 C4
Thetford Gdns RM9 103 A6
Thetford Ho SE1 263 C6
Thetford Rd
Ashford TW15 148 A1
Dagenham RM9 80 D1
New Malden KT3 199 C4
Thetis Terr TW9 132 C6
Theydon Gr IG8 37 C4
Theydon Rd E5 74 C6
Theydon St E17 53 B2
Thicket Cres SM1 218 A4
Thicket Ct 14 SM1 218 A4
Thicket Gr
Dagenham RM9 80 C2
Penge SE20 184 A3
Thicket Rd
Penge SE20 184 B3
Sutton SM1 218 A4
Thicket The UB7 82 A1
Third Ave
Chadwell Heath RM6 58 C3
Dagenham RM10 103 D5
East Acton W3 111 D5
Enfield EN1 17 D6
Hayes UB3 105 D5
Little Ilford E12 78 B3
3 Newham E13 99 A4
Walthamstow E17 53 C4
Wembley HA9 65 D6
West Kilburn W10 91 A4
Third Cl KT8 196 A5
Third Cross Rd TW2 152 B2
Third Way HA9 66 D4
Thirleby Rd
Hendon HA8 27 B2
SW1 115 C3 259 B5
Thirlestane Ct N10 31 A1
Thirlestane Ho TW12 173 D6
Thirlmere NW1 231 D2
Thirlmere Ave UB6 87 C4
Thirlmere Gdns HA9 43 D1
Thirlmere Ho
Isleworth TW1 152 D6
19 Stoke Newington
N16 73 B4
Thirlmere Rd
Muswell Hill N10 31 B2
Streatham SW16 181 D6
Thirlmere Rise BR1 186 D4
Thirsk Cl UB5 63 C2
Thirsk Rd
Clapham SW11 137 A1
Mitcham CR4 181 A3
South Norwood SE25 205 B5
Thistlebrook SE2 124 C3
Thistlebrook Ind Est
SE2 124 C4
Thistlecroft Gdns HA7 25 D1
Thistle Ct N17 52 B5
Thistledene KT7 196 C3
Thistledene Ave HA2 63 A5
Thistledown Ct SE25 205 C6
Thistlefield Cl DA5 168 D3
Thistle Gr SW7 256 B1
Thistle Ho 10 E14 98 A1
Thistlemead BR7 188 D1
Thistlewaite Rd E5 74 B5
Thistlewood Cl 3 N7 72 B6
Thistleworth Cl TW7 130 B5
Thistley Cl N12 30 C4
Thistly Ct SE8 141 D6
Thomas a' Beckett Cl
HA0 64 D4
Thomas Arnold Prim Sch
RM9 81 B1
Thomas Baines Rd
SW11 136 B2
Thomas Burt Ho 9 E2 96 B4
Thomas Buxton Jun & Inf
Sch E1 96 A3
Thomas Cribb Mews
E6 100 B1
Thomas Crowell Ct 29
N1 73 C3
Thomas Ct RM8 80 C6
Thomas Dean Rd
SE26 185 B6
Thomas Dinwiddy Rd
SE12 165 B2
Thomas Doyle St SE1 261 D6
Thomas Fairchild Com
Sch N1 95 A5 235 B4
Thomas Gamuel Prim Sch
E17 53 C3
Thomas Hardy Ho N22 32 B2
Thomas Hewlett Ho
HA1 64 C4
Thomas Ho
9 Belmont SM2 217 D1
3 Hackney E9 74 C2
4 Stockwell SW4 138 A1
Thomas Hollywood Ho 3
E2 96 C5
Thomas Jones Prim Sch
W11 91 A1
Thomas' La SE6 163 C4
Thomas Lo E17 53 D4
Thomas Milner Ho 8
SE15 140 A5
Thomas More Bldg The
HA4 39 C1
Thomas More Ho EC2 242 A3
Thomas More Sq E1 118 A6
Thomas More St E1 118 A5
Thomas More Way N2 48 A6
Thomas North Terr 4
E16 98 D2
Thomas Pl W8 255 C5
Thomas Pooley Ct
KT6 198 A2
Thomas Rd E14 97 C2
Thomas Road Ind Est 2
E14 97 C1
Thomas Shearley Ct
DA5 169 D4
Thomas's London Day
Schs SW11 136 B4 266 D1
Thomas's Prep Sch
Clapham SW11 158 D6
Thomas St SE18 122 D2
Thomas Tallis Sch
SE3 143 B2
Thomas Wall Cl SM1 217 D3
Thomas Watson Cottage
Homes The EN5 13 A6
Thompson Ave
Richmond TW9 132 C2
6 SE5 139 A5
Thompson Cl
Ilford IG1 79 A6
Morden SM3 201 C1
Thompson Ho
11 Kensal Town W10 91 A3
SE14 140 D6
Southall UB1 107 A6
Thompson Rd
Dagenham RM9 81 B5
Dulwich Village SE22 161 D5
Hounslow TW3 129 D1
Uxbridge UB10 60 A1
Thomson Cres CR0 204 C1
Thomson Ct 4 E8 74 A2
Thomson Ho
Pimlico SW1 259 D1
Walworth SE17 263 A3
Thomson Rd HA3 42 C6
Thorburn Ho SW1 248 A1
Thorburn Sq SE1 118 A2
Thorburn Way SW19 180 B2
Thoresby Ho N16 73 B5
Thoresby St N1 95 A4 235 B2
Thorkhill Gdns KT7 197 B1
Thorkhill Rd KT7 197 B2
Thornaby Gdns N18 34 B5
Thornaby Ho 15 E2 96 B4
Thorn Ave WD23 8 A3
Thornbill Ho 1 SE15 140 A5
Thornbridge Ct 10
EN5 13 D6
Thornbury 3 NW4 46 C5
Thornbury Ave TW7 130 B5
Thornbury Cl
Edgware NW7 28 D3
Stoke Newington N16 73 C3

Thornbury Ct
Croydon CR2 221 B3
Hounslow TW7 130 C5
W11 245 A6
Thornbury Ho N6 49 C1
Thornbury Lo EN2 4 D2
Thornbury Rd
Clapham Pk SW2 160 A5
Hounslow TW7 130 B4
Thornbury Sq N6 49 C1
Thornby Rd E5 74 C5
Thorn Cl
BR2 210 C3
Northolt UB5 85 B4
Thorncliffe Ct SW2 160 A5
Thorncliffe Rd
Clapham Pk SW2 160 A5
Southall UB2 107 B1
Thorncombe Rd
SE22 161 C6
Thorncroft HA2 64 A5
Thorncroft Rd SM1 217 D4
Thorncroft St
SW8 138 A5 270 A3
Thorndale BR7 188 B3
Thorndale Ho 10 N16 51 C1
Thorndean St SW18 158 A2
Thorndene Ave N11 15 A3
Thorndike Ave UB5 84 D6
Thorndike Cl
SW10 136 A5 266 A4
Thorndike Ho SW1 259 C2
Thorndike Rd 21 N1 73 B2
Thorndike St
SW1 115 D2 259 C3
Thorndon Cl BR5 189 D1
Thorndon Gdns KT19 215 C4
Thorndon Rd BR5 189 D1
Thorndyke Ct HA5 23 B3
Thorne Cl
Claygate KT10 213 A1
DA8 147 D6
Leyton E11 76 C4
Littleton TW15 171 A3
Newham E16 99 A1
Thorne Ho
34 Bethnal Green E2 96 C4
4 Cubitt Town E14 120 A3
Thorneloe Gdns CR0,
CR9 220 D3
Thorne Pas 7 SW13 133 D3
Thorne Rd
SW8 138 A5 270 B3
Thorne's Cl BR3 208 A6
Thorness Ct SW18 158 A5
Thorne St SW13,
SW14 133 C2
Thornet Wood Rd
BR1 210 C6
Thornewill Ho 8 E1 118 C6
Thorney Cres
SW11 136 B5 266 D3
Thorneycroft Cl KT12 194 C3
Thorneycroft Dr EN3 7 C6
Thorneycroft Ho 11
W4 111 C1
Thorney Ct W8 246 A1
Thorney Hedge Rd
W4 110 D2
Thorney St
SW1 116 A2 260 A4
Thornfield Ave NW7 29 A2
Thornfield Ct NW7 29 A2
Thornfield Ho 5 E14 119 C6
Thornfield Par NW7 29 A3
Thornfield Rd W12 112 B4
Thornford Rd SE13 164 A6
Thorngate Rd W9 91 C3
Thorngrove Rd E13 99 B6
Thornham Gr E15 76 B3
Thorn Ham Ho SE1 262 D6
Thornham St SE10 141 D6
Thornhaugh St WC1 239 D5
Thornhill Ave
SE18 145 C5
Surbiton KT6 214 A6
Thornhill Bridge Wharf
N1 233 C5
Thornhill Cres N1 72 B1
Thornhill Ct N8 49 D3
Thornhill Gdns
Barking IG11 79 C1
Leyton E10 75 D6
Thornhill Gr N1 72 C1
Thornhill Ho
12 Chiswick W4 111 C1
Islington N1 72 C1
Thornhill Mews
SW15 135 B1
Thornhill Prim Sch N1 72 C1
Thornhill Rd
Ickenham UB10 60 C4
Islington N1 94 C6 234 A6
Leyton E10 75 D6
Surbiton KT6 214 B6
Thornton Heath CR0 205 A2
Thornhill Sq N1 72 B1
Thornhill Way TW17 192 C4
Thornicroft Ho 12
SW9 138 B3
Thornlaw Rd SE27 182 D6
Thornley Cl N17 34 A3
Thornley Dr HA2 63 D6
Thornley Pl 2 SE10 120 C1
Thornsbeach Rd SE6 164 A2
Thornsett Pl SE20 184 B1
Thornsett Rd
Penge SE20 184 B1
Wandsworth SW18 157 D3
Thornsett Terr SE20 184 B1
Thornton Ave
Chiswick W4 111 C2
Streatham SW2 159 D3
Thornton Heath CR0 204 B3
West Drayton UB7 104 B3
Thornton Cl UB7 104 B3
Thornton Ct
Lower Holloway N7 72 A3
West Barnes SW20 200 D4
Thornton Dene BR3 185 C1
Thornton Gdns SW12 159 D3
Thornton Gr HA5 23 C4
THORNTON HEATH 204 D3
Thornton Heath Pond
CR7 204 C4
Thornton Heath Sta
CR7 205 A5
Thornton Hill SW19 179 A3
Thornton Ho
SE17 263 A3
7 Wanstead E11 55 A3
Thornton Lo
South Norwood CR7 205 A6
8 Wimbledon SW19 179 A3
Thornton Pl W1 237 D4
Thornton Rd
Barnet EN5 1 A2
Belvedere DA17 125 D2
BR1 187 A5
Carshalton SM5 202 B1
Ilford IG1 78 D4
Leyton E11 76 B6
Lower Edmonton N18 18 C1
Mortlake SW14 133 B2
Streatham SW12, SW2 159 D3
Thornton Heath CR0,
CR7 204 B3
Wimbledon SW19 178 D3
Thornton Rd E SW19 178 D4
Thornton Rd Ind Est
CR0 204 B3
Thornton Row CR7 204 C4
Thornton St SW9 138 C3
Thornton Way NW11 47 D4
Thorntree Ct W5 88 A2
Thorntree Prim Sch
SE7 121 D1
Thorntree Rd SE7 121 D1
Thornville Gr CR4 180 B1
Thornville St SE8 141 C4
Thornwell Ct W7 108 C4
Thornwood Cl E18 37 B1
Thornwood Gdns W8 245 A2
Thornwood Lo W8 245 A2
Thornwood Rd SE13 164 C6
Thornycroft Ct TW9 132 B3
Thorogood Gdns E15 76 C3
Thorold Ho
SE1 252 A2
6 Streatham SW2 160 A4
Thorold Rd
Ilford IG1 57 A1
Wood Green N22 32 A3
Thorparch Rd
SW8 137 D5 269 D3
Thorpebank Rd W12 112 A5
Thorpe Cl
BR6 227 C6
Forest Hill SE26 184 D6
Notting Hill W10 91 A1
Thorpe Coombe Hospl
E17 54 A6
Thorpe Cres E17 35 B1
Thorpe Ct
Enfield EN2 4 D2
Upper Tooting SW17 180 C6
Thorpedale Gdns IG6 56 D5
Thorpedale Rd N4 50 B1
Thorpe Hall W5 87 D2
Thorpe Hall Prim Sch
E17 36 B2
Thorpe Hall Rd E17 36 A2
Thorpe Ho N1 233 D5
Thorpe Rd
Barking IG11 79 B1
Chingford E17 36 A1
Kingston u T KT2 176 A3
Leyton E7 76 D4
Newham E6 100 B6
Tottenham N15 51 C3
Thorpewood Ave SE23,
SE26 162 B2
Thorpland Ave UB10 61 A5
Thorsden Way 2
SE19 183 C5
Thorverton Rd NW2 69 A5
Thoydon Rd E3 97 A5
Thrale Almshouses
SW16 182 A5
Thrale Rd SW16 181 C5
Thrale St SE1 252 B3
Thrasher Cl 20 E8 95 D6
Thrawl St E1 95 D2 243 D3
Thrayle Ho 2 SW9 138 B2
Threadgold Ho 8 N1 73 B2
Threadneedle St EC2,
EC3 95 B1 242 D1
Three Bridges Bsns Ctr
UB2 108 A4
Three Bridges Prim Sch
UB2 107 D3
Three Colts La E2 96 B3
Three Colt St E14 119 B6
Three Corners DA7 147 D3
Three Cups Yd WC1 240 D3
Three Kings Yd W1 248 C6
Three Meadows Mews
HA7 24 D2
Three Mill La E3 98 A4
Three Mills Studios
E14 98 A4
Three Nun Ct EC2 242 B2
Three Oak La SE1 253 C2
Three Oaks Cl UB10 60 B5
Threshers Pl W11 244 A6
Thriffwood SE23,
SE26 162 D1
Thrigby Rd KT9 214 B2
Thring Ho 2 SW9 138 B3
Throckmorten Rd E16 99 B1
Throgmorton Ave
EC2 95 B1 242 D2
Throgmorton St
EC2 95 B1 242 D2
Throwley Cl SE2 124 C3
Throwley Rd SM1 217 D3
Throwley Way SM1 217 D3
Thrupp Cl CR4 181 B1
Thrush Gn HA2 41 C5
Thrush St SE17 262 A2
Thunderer Rd RM9 103 B3
Thurbarn Rd SE6 185 D5
Thurbin Ho UB4 83 B2
Thurland Ho 3 SE16 118 B2
Thurland Rd SE16 118 A3
Thurlby Cl HA1 43 A3
Thurlby Croft NW4 46 C6
Thurlby Rd
Wembley HA0 65 D2
West Norwood SE27 182 C6
Thurleigh Ave SW12 159 A5
Thurleigh Ct SW12 159 A5
Thurleigh Rd SW12 159 A5
Thurleston Ave SM4 201 A4
Thurlestone Ave
Colney Hatch N12 30 D4
Ilford IG3 79 D4
Thurlestone Cl TW17 193 A3
Thurlestone Ct 1 UB1 85 D1
Thurlestone Par
TW17 193 A3
Thurlestone Rd SE27 182 C6
Thurloe Cl SW7 257 A4
Thurloe Ct SW3 257 A3
Thurloe Pl
SW7 114 B2 256 D4
Thurloe Place Mews
SW7 256 D4
Thurloe Sq
SW7 114 C2 257 A4
Thurloe St
SW7 114 B2 256 D4
Thurlow Cl E4 35 D4
Thurlow Ct 5 E11 55 A4
Thurlow Gdns HA0 65 D3
Thurlow Hill SE21 161 A2
Thurlow Ho 17 SW16 160 A1
Thurlow Park Rd SE21,
SE24 161 A2
Thurlow Rd
Hampstead NW3 70 B3
West Ealing W7 109 A4
Thurlow St
SE17 117 C1 263 A1
Thurlow Terr NW5 71 A3
Thurlow Twrs SE27 160 C1
Thurlow Wlk SE17 263 A1
Thurlston Rd HA4 62 A5
Thurnby Ct TW2 152 C1
Thurnscoe NW1 232 A5
Thursland Rd DA14 191 A5
Thursley Cres CR0 224 B1
Thursley Gdns SW19 156 D2
Thursley Ho
3 Kingston u T KT2 176 D3
10 Streatham SW2 160 B4
Thursley Rd SE9 166 B1
Thurso Ho NW6 91 D5
Thurso St SW17 180 B6
Thurstan Rd SW20 178 B3
Thurston Ho 4 BR3 185 D4
Thurston Ind Est
SE13 141 D2
Thurston Rd
Southall UB1 85 B1
St Johns SE8, SE13 141 D3
Thurtle Rd E2 95 D5
Thurza Ct TW7 130 D3
Thyer Cl BR6 227 A4
Thyme Cl SE3 143 C2
Thyme Ct NW7 29 A3
Thyra Gr N12 29 D4
Tibbatt's Rd E3 97 D3
Tibbenham Pl SE6 163 C2
Tibbenham Wlk E13 98 D5
Tibberton Sq N1 235 A6
Tibbets Cl SW19 156 D3
Tibbet's Corner
SW19 156 D4
Tibbet's Ride SW19 156 D4
Tiber Cl 10 E3 97 C6
Tiber Gdns N1 233 B5
Ticehurst Cl BR5 190 A3
Ticehurst Rd SE23 163 A2
Tickford Cl SE2 124 C4
Tickford Ho NW8 230 A1
Tidal Basin Rd E16 120 D6
Tidbury Ct SW8 269 A3
Tideham Ho SE28 123 B5
Tidelock Ho SE28 123 B4
Tidemill Prim Sch
SE8 141 C5
Tidenham Gdns CR0 221 C5
Tideside Ct SE18 122 A3
Tideslea Path SE28 123 B5
Tideslea Twr SE28 123 A4
Tideswell 10 NW5 71 B4
Tideswell Rd
Croydon CR0 223 C5
Putney SW15 134 C1
Tideway Cl TW10 175 C6
Tideway Ct 9 SE16 118 D5
Tideway Ho E14 119 C4
Tideway Ind Est
SW8 137 C6 269 B5
Tideway Wharf SW13 133 C3
Tideway Yd SW13 133 C3
Tidey St E3 97 C2
Tidford Rd DA16 145 D3
Tidworth Ho 13 SE22 139 C2
Tidworth Rd E3 97 C3
Tiepigs La BR2, BR4 208 D1
Tierney Ct 4 CR0 221 D6
Tierney Rd SW2 160 A3
Tierney Terr SW2 160 A3
Tiffin Girls' Sch The
KT2 176 A4
Tiffin Sch KT2 176 B1
Tiger Ho WC1 232 D1
Tiger La BR2 209 B5
Tiger Way E5 74 B4
Tignel Ct W3 110 C4
Tigris Cl N9 18 C2
Tilbrook Rd SE3 143 C2
Tilbury Cl
14 Camberwell SE15 139 D5
St Paul's Cray BR5 190 B1
Tilbury Ho 4 SE14 140 D6
Tilbury Rd
Leytonstone E10 54 A2
Newham E6 100 B5
Tildesley Rd SW15 156 C5
Tile Farm Rd BR6 227 B5
Tilehurst NW1 231 D1
Tilehurst Point 2
SE2 124 C4
Tilehurst Rd
Cheam SM3 217 A3
Wandsworth SW17,
SW18 158 B3
Tile Kiln La
Edmonton N13 33 A5
Harefield UB9 38 D2
Upper Holloway N6 49 C1
Tileyard Rd N7 72 A1
Tilford Ave CR0 224 A1
Tilford Gdns SW19 156 D3
Tilford Ho 8 SW2 160 B4
Tilia Cl SM1 217 B3
Tilia Rd E5 74 B4
Tilia Wlk 21 SW9 138 D1
Tiller Ho 28 N1 95 C6
Tiller Rd E14 119 C3
Tillet Sq SE16 119 A4
Tillett Cl NW10 67 A2
Tillet Way 6 E2 96 A4
Tilley Rd TW14 150 A3
Tillingbourne Gdns N3 47 B6
Tillingbourne Way N3 47 B5
Tillingham Way N12 29 D6
Tilling Ho 1 SE15 140 B2
Tilling Rd NW2 46 C2
Tilling Way HA9 65 D6
Tillman Ho 8 SW2 160 B3
Tillman St E1 96 B1
Tilloch St 9 N1 72 B1
Tillotson Ct SW8 269 D3
Tillotson Rd
Edmonton N9 17 D2
Harrow HA3 23 D3
Ilford IG1 56 C2
Tilney Ct
EC1 242 B6
Kingston u T KT6 197 D4
Woodford IG9 21 A2
Tilney Dr IG9 21 A2
Tilney Gdns 12 N1 73 B2
Tilney Rd
Dagenham RM9 81 B2
Southall UB2 106 C2
Woodford IG9 21 A2
Tilney St W1 248 B4
Tilson Cl 2 SE15 139 C5
Tilson Gdns SW2,
SW4 160 A4
Tilson Ho SW2 160 A4
Tilson Rd N17 34 A2
Tilston Cl E11 76 D5
Tilton St SW6 264 B5
Tiltwood The W3 111 A6
Tilt Yard App SE9 166 B5
Timber Cl BR7 188 C1
Timbercroft KT19 215 C4
Timbercroft La SE18 145 C5
Timbercroft Prim Sch
SE18 145 C5
Timberdene NW4 28 D1
Timberland Cl 16
SE15 140 A5
Timberland Rd E1 96 B1
Timber Mill Way
SW4 137 D2
Timber Pond Rd
SE16 118 D4
Timber St EC1 242 A6
Timberwharf Rd N16 52 A3
Time Sq E8 73 D3
Times Sq SM1 217 D3
Timor Ct UB1 107 D5
Timothy Cl
Bexley DA6 169 A6
1 Clapham Pk SW4 159 C6
Timothy Ho DA18 125 A4
Timsbury Wlk 5
SW15 156 A3
Tina Ct
Forest Hill SE6 163 B4
West Norwood SW16 160 C1
Tindal St SW9 138 D4
Tinniswood Cl N5 72 C3
Tinsley Cl SE25 206 B6
Tinsley Rd E1 96 C2
Tintagel Cres SE22 139 D1
Tintagel Ct EC1 241 C6
Tintagel Dr HA7 25 D6
Tintagel Ho SE20 184 A3
Tintern Ave NW9 44 D6
Tintern Cl
Putney SW15 157 A6
Wimbledon SW19 180 A4
Tintern Ct W13 109 A6
Tintern Gdns N14 16 A4
Tintern Ho
Belgravia SW1 258 C3
Regent's Pk NW1 231 D3
Tintern Path NW9 45 C3
Tintern Rd
Carshalton SM5 202 B1
Tottenham N22 33 A2
Tintern St SW4 138 A1
Tintern Way HA2 41 D1
Tinto Rd E16 99 A3
Tinwell Mews WD6 11 B6
Tinworth St
SE11 116 A1 260 B2
Tippett Ct E6 100 B5
Tippetts Cl EN2 5 A4
Tipthorpe Rd SW11 137 A2
Tipton Dr CR0 221 C4
Tiptree 7 NW1 71 B1
Tiptree Cl E4 20 A1
Tiptree Cres IG5 56 C6
Tiptree Ct EN2 5 B1
Tiptree Dr EN2 5 B1
Tiptree Rd HA4 62 B4
Tirlemont Rd CR2 221 A1
Tirrell Rd CR0 205 A3
Tisbury Ct W1 249 C6
Tisbury Rd SW16 182 A1
Tisdall Pl
SE17 117 B2 262 D3
Tissington Ct 4
SE16 118 D2
Titan Bsns Est 3 SE8 141 C5
Titan Ct TW8 110 B1
Titchborne Row W2 237 B1
Titchfield Rd
Carshalton SM5 202 B1
Enfield EN3 7 A6
Paddington
NW8 92 D6 230 C6
Titchfield Wlk SM5 202 B2
Titchwell Rd SW18 158 B3
Tite St SW3 136 D6 267 C6
Tithe Barn Cl KT2 176 B2
Tithe Barn Way UB5 84 B5
Tithe Cl
Hayes UB4 83 D2
Hendon NW7 28 A2
Walton-on-T KT12 194 B3
Tithe Ct NW4 28 A2
Tithe Farm Ave HA2 63 C5
Tithe Farm Cl HA2 63 C5
Tithe Wlk NW7 28 A2
Titian Ave WD23 8 C4
Titley Cl E4 35 C5
Titmus Cl UB8 83 A1
Titmuss Ave SE28 124 B6
Titmuss St W12 112 C4
Tivendale N8 50 A6
Tiverton Ave IG5 56 C6
Tiverton Cl CR0 205 D2
Tiverton Dr SE9 167 A3
Tiverton Prim Sch N15 51 B3
Tiverton Rd
Brondesbury Pk NW6,
NW10 90 D6
Edgware HA8 26 B1
Edmonton N18 33 C5
Hounslow TW3 130 A3
Ruislip HA4 62 A5
Tottenham N4, N15 51 B3
Wembley HA0 88 A5
Tiverton St
SE1 117 A3 262 A6
Tiverton Way
Chessington KT9 213 D3
Edgware NW7 28 D3
Tivoli Ct SE16 119 B5
Tivoli Gdns 11 SE7 122 A2
Tivoli Rd
Hornsey N8 49 D4
Hounslow TW4 129 A1
West Norwood SE27 183 A5
Toad La TW4 129 B1
Tobago St 12 E14 119 C4
Tobin Cl NW3 70 C1
Toby Ct N9 18 C4
Toby La E1 97 A3
Toby Way KT5, KT6 214 D6
Todber Ho W14 254 A6
Todd Ho 8 N2 30 B1
Todds Wlk N7 72 B6
Tokenhouse Yd EC2 242 C2
TOKYNGTON 66 D2
Tokyngton Ave HA9 66 C2
Toland Sq SW15 156 A6
Tolcairn Ct 2 DA17 125 C1
Tolcarne Dr HA5 40 B6
Tolchurch 2 W11 91 C1
Toldos Yakov Yosef sch
N16 51 C1
Toley Ave HA3, HA9 44 A2
Tolhurst Dr 4 W10 91 A4
Tollbridge Cl W10 91 A3
Tollesbury Gdns IG6 57 B6

Tollet St E1 96 D3
Tollgate Dr
Dulwich SE21 161 C2
Hayes UB4 106 D6
Tollgate Ho 1 NW6 91 D5
Tollgate Prim Sch
Croydon CR0 206 C3
Newham E13 99 C3
Tollgate Rd E6 100 A2
Tollhouse Way N19 71 C6
Tollington Ct N4 72 B6
Tollington Ho 4 N19 72 A5
Tollington Pk N4 72 B6
Tollington Pl N4 72 B6
Tollington Rd N7 72 B4
Tollington Way N7 72 A5
Tolmers Sq NW1 93 C3 239 B6
Tolpaide Ho SE11 261 A3
Tolpuddle Ave 1 E13 99 C6
Tolpuddle St N1 94 C5 234 A4
Tolsford Rd E5 74 B3
Tolson Ho 4 TW7 131 A2
Tolson Rd TW7 131 A2
Tolverne Rd SW20 178 C2
TOLWORTH 214 C6
Tolworth Broadway KT6 198 D1
Tolworth Cl KT6 198 D1
Tolworth Gdns RM6 58 D4
Tolworth Girls' Sch KT6 214 B5
Tolworth Hospl KT6 214 C6
Tolworth Inf Sch KT6 198 B1
Tolworth Junc KT6 214 D6
Tolworth Jun Sch KT6 198 B1
Tolworth Par RM6 59 A4
Tolworth Park Rd KT6 214 B6
Tolworth Rd KT6 214 A6
Tolworth Rise N KT5 198 D1
Tolworth Rise S KT5 198 D1
Tolworth Sta KT5 214 D6
Tolworth Underpass KT5, KT6 214 D6
Tomahawk Gdns 4 UB5 84 D4
Tom Coombs Cl SE9 144 A1
Tom Cribb Rd SE18, SE28 123 B3
Tom Groves Cl E15 76 B3
Tom Hood Cl E15 76 B3
Tom Hood Sch E11 76 D5
Tom Jenkinson Rd 5 E16 121 A5
Tomkyns Ho SE11 261 A3
Tomline Ho SE1 252 A3
Tomlin's Gr E3 97 C4
Tomlinson Cl
5 Gunnersbury W4 110 D1
Spitalfields E2 95 D4
Tomlins Orch IG11 101 A6
Tomlin's Terr E14 97 A1
Tomlins Wlk 4 N7 72 B6
Tom Mann Cl IG11 101 C6
Tom Nolan Cl E15 98 C5
Tompion Ho EC1 241 D6
Tompion St EC1 234 D1
Tom Smith Cl SE10 142 C6
Tom Smith Ho 3 E17 54 A4
Tomson Ho SE1 263 C6
Tom Williams Ho SW6 264 C5
Tonbridge Cres HA3 44 A5
Tonbridge Hos WC1 233 A1
Tonbridge Rd KT12, KT8 195 B5
Tonbridge St WC1 94 A4 233 A1
Toneborough 16 NW8 91 D6
Tonfield Rd SM3 201 B1
Tonge Cl BR3 207 C4
Tonsley Hill SW18 157 D6
Tonsley Pl SW18 157 D6
Tonsley Rd SW18 157 D6
Tonsley St SW18 157 D6
Tonstall Rd CR4 181 A1
Tony Law Ho SE12 165 A6
Tooke Cl HA5 23 A2
Tookey Cl HA3 44 B2
Took's Ct EC4 241 A2
Tooley St SE1 117 C5 253 A3
Toorack Rd HA3 24 B1
Tooting Bec Gdns SW16 181 D6
Tooting Bec Lido SW16 181 C6
Tooting Bec Rd
Furzedown SW17 181 B6
Streatham SW16 181 C5
Tooting Bec Sta SW17 159 A1
Tooting Broadway SW17 180 D5
Tooting Broadway Sta SW17 180 C5
Tooting Gr SW17 180 C5
TOOTING GRAVENEY 180 B5
Tooting High St SW17, SW19 180 C5
Tooting Mkts SW17 180 D6
Tooting Sta SW17 180 D4
Tootswood Rd BR2, BR3 208 C5
Topaz Ct TW13 149 D1
Topaz Ho KT4 199 B1
Topaz Wlk NW2 46 D2
Topcliffe Dr BR6 227 B4
Topham Ho 8 SE10 142 A5
Topham Sq N17 33 A2
Topham St EC1 241 A6
Top House Rise E4 20 A4
Topiary Sq TW9 132 B2
Topley St SE9 143 D1
Topmast Point 23 E14 119 C4
Top Pk BR3 208 C4
Topsfield Cl N8 49 D4
Topsfield Par N8 50 A3
Topsfield Rd N8 50 A4
Topsham Rd SW17 181 A6
Tora Ct 9 IG9 21 C2
Torbay Ct 13 NW1 71 B1
Torbay Mans NW6 91 B6
Torbay Rd
Brondesbury NW6 69 B1
Harrow HA2 63 A6
Torbay St 15 NW1 71 B1
Torbitt Way IG2 57 D4
Torbridge Cl HA8 26 A3
Torbrook Cl DA5 169 A5
Torcross Dr SE23 162 C2
Torcross Rd HA4 62 C5
Tor Ct W8 245 B2
Torfell 5 E18 36 D1
Tor Gdns W8 113 C4 245 A2
Tor Gr SE28 123 C5
Tor Ho N6 49 B3
Tormead Cl SM1 217 C2
Tormount Rd SE18 145 C6
Tornay Ho
Hackney E9 74 C1
N1 233 C4
Toronto Ave E12 78 B4
Toronto Rd IG1 57 A1
Torquay Gdns IG4 55 D5
Torquay Ho 1 SM6 219 D3
Torquay St W2 91 D2
Tor Rd DA16 146 C4
Torrence Ho 6 N19 71 C6
Torrens Ct SE5 139 B2
Torrens Rd
Clapham Pk SW2 160 B6
Stratford E15 76 D2
Torrens Sq E15 76 D2
Torrens St EC1 94 D5 234 C3
Torres Sq E14 119 C1
Torre Wlk SM5 202 C1
Torrey Dr SW9 138 C3
Torriano Ave NW5 71 D3
Torriano Cotts NW5 71 C3
Torriano Jun & Inf Schs NW5 71 D3
Torriano Mews NW5 71 C3
Torridge Gdns SE15 140 C1
Torridge Rd CR7 204 D4
Torridon Ct HA8 10 D2
Torridon Ho NW6 91 D5
Torridon Jun & Inf Schs SE6 164 B2
Torridon Rd SE13, SE6 164 B3
Torrington Ave N12 30 B5
Torrington Cl
Claygate KT10 212 C2
North Finchley N12 30 B6
Torrington Ct
Forest Hill SE26 184 A5
Harrow HA2 63 D5
North Finchley N12 30 B6
Torrington Dr HA2 63 D5
Torrington Gdns
Friern Barnet N11 31 C4
Wembley UB6 65 C1
Torrington Gr N12 30 C5
Torrington Pk N12 30 B6
Torrington Pl
Bloomsbury WC1 93 D2 239 C4
St George in t East E1 118 A5
Torrington Rd
Claygate KT10 212 C2
Dagenham RM8 59 B1
Ruislip HA4 62 A5
Wanstead E18 55 A6
Wembley UB6 87 C6
Torrington Sq
Bloomsbury WC1 93 D3 239 D5
Thornton Heath CR0 205 B2
Torrington Way SM4 201 C3
Torr Rd SE20 184 D3
Tortington Ho 1 SE15 140 B5
Torver Rd HA1 42 C5
Torver Way BR6 227 B5
Torwood Rd SW15 156 A6
Totham Lo SW20 178 B2
Tothill Ho SW1 259 D4
Tothill St SW1 115 D4 249 D1
Totland Ho SW18 157 D5
Totnes Rd DA16 146 C5
Totnes Villas N11 31 C5
Totnes Wlk N2 48 B5
Tottan Terr E1 96 D1
Tottenhall 5 NW1 71 A1
Tottenhall Inf Sch N13 32 C4
Tottenhall Rd N13 32 D4
TOTTENHAM 33 D1
Tottenham Court Rd W1 93 C2 239 B4
Tottenham Court Road Sta W1 93 D1 239 D2
Tottenham Gn E 3 N15 51 D5
Tottenham Gn E South Side 4 N15 51 D5
TOTTENHAM HALE 52 A6
Tottenham Hale N15 52 A5
Tottenham Hale Ret Pk N15 52 A5
Tottenham Hale Sta N17 52 B6
Tottenham La N8 50 B4
Tottenham Mews W1 239 B4
Tottenham Rd N1 73 C2
Tottenham St W1 93 C2 239 B4
Totterdown St SW17 180 D5
TOTTERIDGE 13 C3
Totteridge Comm N20 12 C3
Totteridge Gn N20 13 C2
Totteridge Ho
Barnet N20 13 B3
Battersea SW11 136 B3
Totteridge La N20 13 D3
Totteridge Pk N20 12 D3
Totteridge Rd EN3 6 D6
Totteridge Village N20 13 B3
Totteridge & Whetstone Sta N20 14 A2
Totternhoe Cl HA3 43 C4
Totton Rd CR7 204 C6
Toucan Cl NW10 88 C4
Touchard Ho N1 235 D1
Toulmin St SE1 117 A4 252 A1
Toulon St SE5 139 A5
Toulouse Ct 2 SE16 118 B1
Tounson Ct SW1 259 D3
Tournay Rd SW6 135 B5 264 D4
Toussaint Wlk 18 SE16 118 A3
Tovil Cl SE20 184 B1
Tovy Ho 6 SE1 118 A1
Towcester Rd E3 98 A3
Tower 42* EC2 95 C1 243 A2
Tower Bldgs 22 E1 118 B5
Tower Br App E1, EC3 253 C5
Tower Bridge* E1, EC3, SE1 117 D5 253 C4
Tower Bridge Bsns Complex SE16 118 B3
Tower Bridge Bsns Sq SE16 118 B2
Tower Bridge Mews HA0 64 D4
Tower Bridge Piazza SE1 253 C3
Tower Bridge Prim Sch SE1 117 D4 253 C2
Tower Bridge Rd SE1 117 C4 253 A1
Tower Bridge Sq SE1 253 C2
Tower Bridge Wharf SE1 118 A5
Tower Cl
Hampstead NW3 70 B3
Orpington BR6 227 D5
Penge SE20 184 B3
Tower Ct
Brockley SE4 141 A1
Stamford Hill E5 51 D2
St Giles WC2 240 A1
St John's Wood NW8 230 B4
Tower Gardens Rd N17 33 B2
Towergate SE1 263 A4
Towergate Cl UB8 60 A3
Towergate Ho 35 E3 97 B5
Tower Gateway Sta EC3 117 D6 253 C6
Tower Gdns KT10 213 A1
Tower Gr KT13 193 C1
TOWER HAMLETS 97 B2
Tower Hamlets Coll
Poplar E14 97 D1
Poplar E14 119 D6
Stepney E1 96 D1
Tower Hamlets Rd
Forest Gate E7 76 D3
Walthamstow E17 53 C6
Tower Hill EC3 117 D6 253 D5
Tower Hill Sta EC3 117 D6 253 C6
Tower La HA9 65 D5
Tower Mans SE1 263 C5
Tower Mews
Hackney E5 75 A3
Walthamstow E17 53 C5
Tower Millennium Pier EC3 117 C5 253 B4
Tower Mill Rd 1 SE15 139 C5
Tower Pl E EC3 253 B5
Tower Pl W EC3 253 B5
Tower Rd
DA7 147 D1
Orpington BR6 227 D5
Twickenham TW1, TW2 152 D1
Willesden NW10 68 A1
Tower Rise TW9 132 A2
Tower Royal EC4 252 C6
Towers Ave UB10 83 A4
Towers Bsns Pk HA9 66 D4
Towers Ct UB10 83 A4
Towers Pl TW10 154 A6
Towers Rd
Pinner HA5 23 A2
Southall UB1 85 C3
Tower St WC2 240 A1
Towers The
Dartmouth Pk NW5 71 B5
1 Richmond TW9 132 B1
Tower Terr
Brockley SE4 141 A1
Wood Green N22 32 B1
Tower The* EC3 117 D6 253 C5
Towerview SE13 163 C6
Tower View
Bushey WD23 8 C4
Croydon CR0 207 A2
Tower Wharf SE1 253 C2
Tower Wlk SE1 263 A4
Towfield Ct TW13 151 B2
Towfield Rd TW13 151 B2
Towncourt Cres BR5 211 B5
Towncourt La BR5 211 B2
Towncourt Path N4 51 A1
Townend Ct 6 BR1 186 D2
Towney Mead UB5 85 B5
Towney Mead Ct UB5 85 B5
Townfield Rd UB3 105 D5
Townfield Sq UB3 105 D6
Town Field Way TW7 131 A3
Town Hall Approach Rd N15 51 D5
Townhall Ave 3 W4 111 B1
Town Hall Rd SW11 136 D2
Townholm Cres W7 108 D3
Town Hos EC1 241 D5
Town La TW19 148 A2
Townley Ct E15 76 D2
Townley Gram Sch for Girls DA6 169 B6
Townley Rd
DA6 169 B6
Dulwich Village SE22 161 C6
Townley St SE17 117 B1 262 C2
Townmead Bsns Ctr SW6 136 A2
Town Meadow TW8 131 D5
Townmead Rd
Richmond TW9 132 D3
Sands End SW6 136 A3
Town Quay IG11 100 D6
Town Quay Wharf IG11 100 D6
Town Rd N9 18 B2
Townsend Ave N14 31 D6
Townsend Ct NW9 45 B2
Townsend Ho 14 SE1 118 A2
Townsend Ind Est NW10 89 A5
Townsend La NW9 45 B3
Townsend Mews 3 SW18 158 A2
Townsend Prim Sch SE17 117 C2 263 A4
Townsend Rd
Ashford TW15 170 A5
Southall UB1 107 A5
South Tottenham N15 51 D4
Townsend St SE1, SE17 117 C2 263 A4
Townsend Way HA6 22 A3
Townsend Yd N6 49 B1
Townshend Cl DA14 190 C4
Townshend Ct NW8 230 B4
Townshend Est NW8 92 C5 230 A4
Townshend Ho 16 SE18 122 B2
Townshend Rd
Chislehurst BR7 188 D5
Primrose Hill NW8 92 C6 230 A5
Richmond TW9 132 B1
Townshend Terr TW9 132 B1
Towns Ho 4 SW4 137 D2
Towson Ave UB5 84 B5
Townson Way UB5 84 A5
Town The EN2 5 B2
Town Tree Rd TW15 170 C5
Towpath TW17 192 B1
Towpath Way CR0 205 D4
Towpath Wlk E9 75 B3
Towton Rd SE27 161 A2
Toxteth Ho N4 51 A2
Toynbec Cl BR7 188 D6
Toynbee Rd SW19, SW20 179 A2
Toynbee St E1 95 D2 243 C3
Toyne Way N6 48 D3
Tracey Ave NW2 68 C3
Tracy Ct HA7 25 C3
Tracy Ho 15 E3 97 B4
Trade Cl N13 32 C6
Trader Rd E6 100 D1
Tradescant Ho 15 E9 74 C1
Tradescant Rd SW8 138 A5 270 B3
Trade Twr 8 SW11 136 A2
Trade Winds Ct 1 E1 118 A5
Trading Estate Rd NW10 89 A3
Traemore Ct SW16 160 C1
Trafalgar Ave
North Cheam KT4, SM3, SM4 200 D1
SE15 139 D6
Tottenham N17 33 C4
Trafalgar Bsns Ctr IG11 101 D3
Trafalgar Cl 1 SE16 119 A2
Trafalgar Ct
Barking E6 100 C6
Hounslow TW3 129 B2
West Barnes KT3 200 B6
Trafalgar Gdns
Stepney E1 96 D2
W8 255 D6
Trafalgar Gr SE10 142 B6
Trafalgar Ho
Barking IG11 102 B4
SE17 262 B2
Trafalgar Inf Sch TW2 152 B2
Trafalgar Jun Sch TW2 152 B2
Trafalgar Mews E9 75 B2
Trafalgar Pl
Edmonton N18 34 A5
Wanstead E11 55 A5
Trafalgar Point 2 N1 73 B1
Trafalgar Rd
Greenwich SE10 120 C1
Merton SW19 180 A3
Trafalgar Rd *continued*
Twickenham TW2 152 B2
Trafalgar Sq* SW1 115 D5 249 D4
Trafalgar St SE17 117 B1 262 D2
Trafalgar Terr HA1 42 C1
Trafalgar Trad Est EN3 7 A1
Trafalgar Way
Canary Wharf E14 120 A5
Croydon CR0 220 C6
Trafford Cl E15 75 D3
Trafford Ho N1 235 D4
Trafford Rd CR7 204 B4
Trafford Villas CR0 204 B4
Tragail SW15 157 A6
Traherne Lo 5 TW11 174 D5
Trahorn Cl E1 96 B3
Traitors Gate* EC3 117 D5 253 C4
Tralee Ct 31 SE16 118 B1
Tramsheds Ind Est The CR0, CR4 203 D2
Tramway Ave
Ponders End N9 18 C4
Stratford E15 76 B1
Tramway Cl SE20 184 C2
Tramway Path CR4 202 C5
Trance Way W3 110 C3
Tranmere Ct 5 SM2 218 A1
Tranmere Ho 7 N7 72 C3
Tranmere Rd
Edmonton N9 17 D4
Twickenham TW2 151 D4
Wandsworth SW17, SW18 158 A2
Tranquil Pas SE3 142 D3
Tranquil Vale SE3 142 C3
Transept St NW1 237 B3
Transmere Cl BR5 211 A3
Transmere Rd BR5 211 A3
Transom Cl SE16 119 A2
Transom Sq E14 119 D1
Transport Ave TW8 131 B6
Tranton Rd SE16 118 B3
Trappes Ho 2 SE16 118 B2
Traps La KT2, KT3 177 C2
Travellers Way TW5 128 C3
Travers Cl E17 34 D2
Travers Ho 6 SE10 142 B6
Travers Rd N7 72 C5
Travis Ho SE10 142 A4
Treacy Cl WD23 8 A2
Treadgold Ho 7 W11 112 D6
Treadgold St W11 112 D6
Treadway St E2 96 B5
Treasury Bldgs SW1 250 A2
Treasury Cl SM6 219 D3
Treaty Ctr TW3 129 D2
Treaty St N1 94 B6 233 C5
Trebeck St W1 248 C3
Treborough Ho W1 238 A4
Trebovir Rd SW5 113 C2 255 B3
Treby St E3 97 B3
Trecastle Way 2 N7 71 D4
Tredegar Mews 10 E3 97 B4
Tredegar Rd
Bow E3 97 B5
Wood Green N11 31 D3
Tredegar Sq E3 97 B4
Tredegar Terr E3 97 B4
Trederwen Rd E8 96 A6
Tredown Rd SE26 184 C5
Tredwell Cl BR2 210 A5
Tredwell Rd SE27 182 D6
Tree Cl TW10 153 D3
Treehouse Sch N10 49 A5
Treen Ave SW13 133 D2
Tree Rd E16 99 C1
Trees The N16 51 B2
Tree Tops 1 IG8 37 A6
Treetops Cl SE2 125 A1
Treetops Ct CR7 205 A4
Treetops View IG10 21 D4
Treeview Cl SE19 183 C2
Treewall Gdns BR1 187 B6
Trefgarne Rd RM10 81 C6
Trefil Wlk N7 72 A4
Trefoil Ho DA18 125 A4
Trefoil Rd SW18 158 A6
Trefusis Ct TW5 128 B4
Tregaron Ave N8 50 A3
Tregaron Gdns KT3 199 C5
Tregarvon Rd SW11 137 A1
Tregenna Ave HA2 63 C4

Tregenna Cl 1 N14 15 C6
Tregenna Cl HA2 63 C4
Tregony Rd BR6 227 D4
Trego Rd E9 75 C1
Tregothnan Rd SW9 138 A2
Treguntur Rd SW10 114 A1 256 A1
Treherne Ct
Brixton SW9 138 D4
Upper Tooting SW17 181 A6
Trehern Rd 12 SW14 133 B2
Trehurst St E5 75 A3
Trelawney Cl E17 53 D5
Trelawney Est E9 74 C2
Trelawney Ho SE1 252 A2
Trelawn Rd
Leyton E10 76 A5
Tulse Hill SW2 160 C6
Trellis Ho SW19 180 A3
Trellis Sq 1 E3 97 B4
Treloar Gdns SE19 183 B4
Tremadoc Rd SW4 137 D1
Tremaine Cl SE4 141 C3
Tremaine Rd SE20 184 B1
Trematon Ho SE11 261 B2
Trematon Pl TW11 175 C3
Tremlett Gr N19 71 C5
Tremlett Mews N19 71 C5
Trenance Gdns IG3 80 A5
Trenchard Ave HA4 62 B4
Trenchard Cl
Grahame Pk NW9 27 C2
Stanmore HA7 25 B4
Trenchard Ct SM4 201 C3
Trenchard St SE10 120 B1
Trenchold St SW8 138 A6 270 A5
Trend Ct W13 109 B5
Trendell Ho 8 E14 97 C1
Trenholme Cl 6 SE20 184 B3
Trenholme Rd SE20 184 B3
Trenholme Terr SE20 184 B3
Trenmar Gdns NW10 90 B4
Trent Ave W5 109 C3
Trent CE Prim Sch EN4 2 D1
Trent Ct
1 South Croydon CR2 221 A3
Wanstead E11 55 A4
Trent Ctry Pk* EN4 3 A3
Trent Gdns N14 15 B5
Trentham Ct W3 89 B2
Trentham Lo 8 EN1 17 C6
Trentham St SW18 157 C3
Trent Ho
4 Kingston u T KT2 175 D2
Nunhead SE15 140 C1
Trent Rd
Buckhurst Hill IG9 21 B3
Clapham Pk SW2 160 B6
Trent Way
Hayes UB4 83 C4
North Cheam KT4 216 C5
Trentwood Side EN2 4 B2
Treport St SW18 157 D4
Tresco Cl BR1 186 C4
Trescoe Gdns HA2 41 A2
Tresco Gdns IG3 80 A6
Tresco Ho SE11 261 A2
Tresco Rd SE15 140 B1
Tresham Cres NW8 92 C3 237 A6
Tresham Rd IG11 79 D1
Tresham Wlk E9 74 C3
Tresidder Ho 10 SW4 159 D4
Tresilian Ave N21 16 B6
Tressel Cl 20 N1 72 D1
Tressillian Cres SE4 141 C2
Tressillian Rd SE4 141 C2
Trestis Cl UB4 84 D2
Treswell Rd RM9 103 A6
Tretawn Gdns NW7 11 C1
Tretawn Pk NW7 27 C6
Trevallyn Lo 1 KT2 176 D2
Trevanion Rd W14 254 B2
Treve Ave HA1 42 B2
Trevelyan Ave E12 78 B4
Trevelyan Cres HA3 43 D2
Trevelyan Ct KT3 199 D2
Trevelyan Gdns NW10 90 C6
Trevelyan Ho
16 Globe Town E2 96 D4
SE5 138 D5
6 Twickenham TW1 153 C5
Trevelyan Rd
Leyton E15 76 D4
Trevelyan Rd continued
Upper Tooting SW17 180 D4
Trevenna Ho 13 SE23 162 D1
Trevera Ct EN3 19 A6
Treveris St SE1 251 D3
Treversh Ct 7 BR1 186 D2
Treverton St W10 90 D3
Treverton Twr W10 90 D2
Treves Cl N21 16 B6
Treves Ho E1 96 A3
Treville St SW15 156 B4
Treviso Rd SE23 163 A2
Trevithick Cl TW14 149 D3
Trevithick Ho
13 Bermondsey SE16 118 B2
3 Gospel Oak NW5 71 B4
SW8 269 C2
Trevithick St SE8 141 C6
Trevone Gdns HA5 41 A3
Trevor Cl
Harrow HA3 24 D3
Hayes BR2 209 A2
Isleworth TW7 152 D6
New Barnet EN4 14 B5
Northolt UB5 84 C5
Trevor Cres HA4 61 D4
Trevor Gdns
Hendon HA8 27 B2
Northolt UB5 84 C5
Ruislip HA4 62 A4
Trevor Pl SW7 114 C4 247 B1
Trevor Rd
Hayes UB3 105 C4
Hendon HA8 27 B2
Wimbledon SW19 179 A3
Woodford IG8 37 A3
Trevor Roberts Tutorial Coll NW8 70 B1
Trevor Sq SW7 114 C4 247 B1
Trevor St SW7 114 C4 247 B1
Trevose Ho SE11 260 D2
Trevose Rd E17 36 B2
Trewenna Dr KT9 213 D3
Trewince Rd SW20 178 C2
Trewint St SW18 158 A2
Trewsbury Ho 2 SE2 124 D4
Trewsbury Rd SE26 184 D5
Triandra Way UB4 84 D2
Triangle Ct
4 Newham E16 99 C2
SE1 252 B3
Triangle Ctr UB1 108 B5
Triangle Est The SE11 261 A1
Triangle Ho SE1 253 C2
Triangle Pl SW4 137 D1
Triangle Rd 7 E8 96 B6
Triangle The
Barking IG11 79 A2
Crouch End N19 49 D2
EC1 241 D6
Hackney E8 96 B6
Kingston u T KT3 177 A1
Tribune Ct 16 NW9 46 A5
Tricorn Ho SE28 123 B5
Trident Bsns Ctr SW17 180 D5
Trident Gdns 6 UB5 84 D4
Trident Ho
14 South Bromley E14 98 A1
Woolwich SE28 123 B5
Trident St SE16 118 D2
Trident Way UB2 106 B3
Trieste Ct SW12 158 D3
Trig La EC4 252 A6
Trigon Rd SW8 138 B5 270 D4
Trilby Rd SE23 162 D2
Trillington Ho W12 112 A5
Trillo Ct IG1 57 C2
Trimdon NW1 232 B5
Trimmer Ct TW7 130 D2
Trimmer Wlk 11 TW8 132 A6
Trim St SE8 141 B6
Trinder Gdns N19 50 A1
Trinder Mews 10 TW11 175 A5
Trinder Rd
Barnet EN5 12 C6
Finsbury Pk N4, N19 50 A1
Tring Ave
Ealing W5 110 B5
Southall UB1 85 B1
Wembley HA9 66 C2
Tring Cl IG2 57 B4
Tring Ct TW1 175 A6
Trinidad Ho 17 E14 119 B6
Trinidad St E14 119 B6
Trinity Ave
East Finchley N2 48 B6
Trinity Ave continued
Enfield EN1 17 D5
Trinity Church Rd SW13 134 B6
Trinity Church Sq SE1 117 A3 262 B6
Trinity Cl
3 Clapham SW4 137 C1
Hounslow TW4 129 A1
Keston Mark BR2 210 A1
Lewisham SE13 142 B1
Leyton E11 76 C6
Trinity Cotts TW9 132 B2
Trinity Cres SW17 159 A2
Trinity Ct
8 Chingford E4 20 A2
Edmonton N18 33 D4
Eltham SE9 166 D5
Finsbury WC1 240 C6
Forest Hill SE23 162 C1
Greenwich SE7 121 D2
2 Hoxton N1 95 C6
Rotherhithe SE16 119 A4
Southgate N21 16 D3
Thornton Heath SE25 205 C3
Twickenham TW2 152 C2
Wallington SM6 219 C1
Willesden NW2 68 C3
Wimbledon SW19 179 C4
Trinity Dr UB8 83 A1
Trinity Gdns
E16 98 D2
Stockwell SW2, SW9 138 B1
11 Wanstead E18 55 B6
Trinity Gn E1 96 C2
Trinity Gr 8 SE10 142 A4
Trinity Ho
SE1 262 B6
5 Walthamstow E17 53 D6
Trinity Homes 14 SW2 138 B1
Trinity Mews
Penge SE20 184 B2
SE9 167 B5
Wandsworth SW18 157 C3
Trinity Par TW3 129 D2
Trinity Pl
Bexleyheath DA6 147 B1
City of London EC3 253 C5
Trinity RC High Sch (Lower) IG8 37 A6
Trinity RC High Sch (Upper) IG8 37 A6
Trinity RC High Sch (Upper Sch) IG8 36 D6
Trinity Rd
East Finchley N2 48 B6
Ilford IG6 57 A6
Richmond TW9 132 B2
Southall UB1 107 A5
Wandsworth SW17, SW18 158 C4
Wimbledon SW19 179 C4
Wood Green N22 32 A3
Wood Green N22 32 B2
Trinity Rise SE24, SW2 160 D4
Trinity St Mary's CE Prim Sch SW12 159 A3
Trinity Sch
Croydon CR0 222 C6
Dagenham RM10 81 C4
Trinity Sq EC3 117 C6 253 B6
Trinity St
Enfield EN2 5 A3
9 Newham E16 99 A2
SE1 117 B3 262 C6
Trinity Terr IG9 21 B4
Trinity Way
East Acton W3 111 D6
Walthamstow E4 35 B4
Trio Pl SE1 117 A4 252 B1
Triscott Ho UB3 106 A5
Tristan Ct 34 SE8 141 B6
Tristan Sq SE3 142 C2
Tristram Cl E17 54 B6
Tristram Dr N9 18 A1
Tristram Rd BR1 186 D6
Triton Ct
EC2 242 D5
Woodford IG9 21 A2
Triton Ho 2 E14 119 D2
Triton Sq NW1 239 A6
Tritton Ave CR0 220 A4
Tritton Ho N21 17 B5
Tritton Rd SE21, SE27 161 B1
Triumph Cl UB7 127 A4
Triumph Ho IG11 102 A4
Triumph Rd E6 100 B1
Triumph Trad Est N17 34 A4
Trocette Mans SE1 263 B6
Trojan Ct
Brondesbury NW6 69 A1
9 Ealing W7 109 A5
Trojan Ind Est NW10 67 D2
Trojan Way CR0 220 B5
Troon Cl
34 Bermondsey SE16 118 B1
Erith SE28 102 D1
Troon Ct UB1 108 A6
Troon Ho 9 E14 97 A1
Troon St E1 97 A1
Tropical Ct 2 W10 90 D4
Trosley Rd DA17 147 C6
Trossachs Rd SE22 161 C6
Trothy Rd SE1 118 A2
Trotman Ho 1 SE14 140 C4
Trott Rd N10 31 A3
Trott St SW11 136 C4 267 A1
Trotwood Ho 3 SE16 118 B4
Troubridge Ct 12 W4 111 A1
Troughton Rd SE7 121 B1
Troutbeck NW1 231 D1
Troutbeck Rd SE14 141 A4
Trouville Rd SW4 159 C5
Trowbridge Rd E9 75 B2
Trower Ho 5 E9 75 A2
Trowlock Ave TW11 175 C4
Trowlock Island TW11 175 D4
Trowlock Way TW11 175 D4
Troy Ct
W8 255 A6
5 Woolwich SE18 122 D2
Troyes Ho NW3 70 D3
Troy Rd SE19 183 B4
Troy Town SE15 140 A2
Troy Town Flats SE15 140 A2
Trubshaw Rd UB2 107 D3
Trulock Ct N17 34 A3
Trulock Rd N17 34 A3
Truman Cl 2 HA8 27 A3
Truman's Rd 24 N16 73 C3
Trumpers Way W7 108 D3
Trumpeters Inn TW9 153 C6
Trumpington Rd E7 76 D4
Trump St EC2 242 B1
Trundlers Way WD23 8 C3
Trundle St SE1 252 A2
Trundleys Rd SE8 141 A6
Trundley's Rd SE8 118 D1
Trundley's Terr SE8 118 D2
Truro Ct 2 N8 49 D4
Truro Gdns IG1 56 A2
Truro Ho
25 Paddington W2 91 C2
Pinner HA5 23 B2
Truro Rd
Walthamstow E17 53 B5
Wood Green N22 32 B3
Truro St NW5 71 A2
Truro Way UB4 83 C4
Truscott Ho 3 CR7 204 C3
Trusedale Rd E6 100 B1
Truslove Rd SE27 182 D5
Trussley Rd W6 112 C3
Trust Wlk SE21 160 D3
Tryfan Cl IG4 55 D4
Tryon Cres E9 96 C6
Tryon St SW3 114 D1 257 C2
Trystings Cl KT10 213 A2
Tuam Rd SE18 145 B6
Tubbenden Cl BR6 227 C5
Tubbenden Dr BR6 227 B4
Tubbenden Jun & Inf Schs BR6 227 B4
Tubbenden La BR6 227 C5
Tubbenden La S BR6 227 B3
Tubbs Rd NW10 89 D5
Tudor Ave
Hampton TW12 173 C3
North Cheam KT4 216 B4
Tudor Cl
Ashford TW15 170 A6
BR7 188 B2
Cheam SM3 217 A2
Chessington KT9 214 A3
Crouch End N6 49 C2
Hampstead NW3 70 C2
Hampton TW12 174 A5
Hendon NW7 28 A4
Pinner HA5 40 A4
Tulse Hill SW2 160 B5
Wallington SM6 219 C1
Welsh Harp NW9 67 A6
Woodford IG8 37 B5
Tudor Coll WC1 233 A1
Tudor Court N HA9 66 C3
Tudor Court S HA9 66 C3
Tudor Cres EN2 5 A4
Tudor Ct
2 Barnet EN5 1 B1
3 Ealing W13 87 C1
Feltham TW13 172 C6
Kingsland N1 73 C2
5 Rotherhithe SE16 118 D5
Sidcup DA14 168 A1
South Acton W5 110 C4
4 Stanwell TW19 148 A5
Teddington TW11 174 D4
Walthamstow E17 53 B2
Tudor Dr
Kingston u T KT2 176 A5
Walton-on-T KT12 194 D1
West Barnes SM4 201 A3
Tudor Ent Pk HA3 42 B6
Tudor Est NW10 88 D5
Tudor Gables NW7 27 D6
Tudor Gdns
Acton W3 88 C1
Harrow HA3 24 B1
Mortlake SW14 133 C2
Twickenham TW1 152 D3
Welsh Harp NW9 67 A6
West Wickham BR4 224 A5
Tudor Gr E9 74 C1
Tudor Ho
Brook Green W14 112 D2
Feltham TW13 172 C6
34 Hackney E9 74 C1
Mitcham CR4 181 A2
6 Muswell Hill N10 31 A3
Queensbury NW9 44 C5
Tolworth KT6 198 C1
Tudor Lo 4 N12 29 D5
Tudor Mews
Walthamstow E17 53 B5
2 Willesden NW10 68 A2
Tudor Par
Dagenham RM6 58 D2
SE9 144 A1
Tudor Pl SW19 180 C3
Tudor Prim Sch
Finchley N3 30 A2
Southall UB1 107 A6
Tudor Rd
Ashford TW15 171 B4
Barking IG11 101 D6
Barnet EN5 1 D2
Beckenham BR3 208 A6
Chingford E4 35 D4
Croydon SE25 206 B4
Hackney E9 96 B6
Hampton TW12 173 C3
Harrow HA3 24 B1
Hayes UB3 83 B1
Isleworth TW3 130 B1
Kingston u T KT2 176 C3
Newham E6 99 C6
Penge SE20 183 D3
Pinner HA5 22 C1
Ponders End N9 18 C4
Southall UB1 107 A6
Tudor Sq UB3 83 B2
Tudor St EC4 116 C6 251 B6
Tudors The 2 BR3 185 D1
Tudor Way
BR5 211 B3
Hillingdon UB10 60 C2
Osidge N14 15 D3
South Acton W3 110 C4
Tudor Well Cl HA7 25 B5
Tudor Wlk DA5 169 A5
Tudway Rd SE3, SE9 143 C1
Tufnell Ct 19 E3 97 B6
Tufnell Mans 7 N7 71 D4
TUFNELL PARK 71 D4
Tufnell Park Mans 2 N7 72 A5
Tufnell Park Prim Sch N7 71 D4
Tufnell Park Rd N19, N7 71 D4
Tufnell Park Sta N19 71 C4
Tufton Ct SW1 260 A5
Tufton Gdns KT8 173 D1
Tufton Rd E4 35 C6
Tufton St SW1 116 A3 260 A5
Tugboat St SE28 123 C4
Tugela Rd CR0 205 B3
Tugela St SE6 163 B2
Tugmutton Cl BR6 226 D4
Tuke Sch SE15 140 B4
Tulip Cl
Croydon CR0 206 D1
Hampton TW12 173 B4
5 Newham E6 100 B2
Southall UB2 108 A4
Tulip Ct 1 HA5 40 C6
Tulip Gdns
Chingford E4 20 B1
Ilford IG1 78 D2
Tullis Ho 12 E9 74 C1
Tull St CR4 202 D2
Tulse Cl BR3 208 A6
TULSE HILL 160 D4
Tulse Hill
Tulse Hill SW2 160 C4
Tulse Hill SW27 160 D2
Tulse Hill Sta SE27 160 D2
Tulse Ho SW2 160 C5
Tulsemere Rd SE21, SE27 161 A2
Tumbling Bay KT12 194 A3
Tummons Gdns SE25 183 C1
Tump Ho SE28 123 C5
Tunbridge Ct 1 SE26 162 A1
Tunbridge Ho EC1 234 C2
Tuncombe Rd N18 33 C6
Tunis Rd W12 112 B5
Tunley Gn 12 E14 97 B2
Tunley Rd
Dagenham NW10 89 C6
Upper Tooting SW12, SW17 159 A2
Tunmarsh La E13 99 C4
Tunnan Leys E6 100 C1
Tunnel Avenue Trad Est SE10 120 B4
Tunnel Gdns N11 31 C3
Tunnel Link Rd TW6 148 C5
Tunnel Rd SE16 118 C4
Tunnel Rd E TW6 126 D3
Tunnel Rd W TW6 126 D4
Tunstall Cl BR6 227 C4
Tunstall Ct 14 TW9 132 B4
Tunstall Rd
Croydon CR0 205 C1
Stockwell SW9 138 B1
Tunstall Wlk 10 TW8 132 A6
Tunstock Way DA17 125 A3
Tunworth Cl NW9 45 A3
Tunworth Cres SW15 155 D5
Tun Yd SW8 137 B2
Tupelo Rd E10 75 D6
Tupman Ho 26 SE16 118 A4
Tuppy St SE28 123 A3
Turberville Ho 1 SW9 138 B2
Turene Cl SW18 136 A1
Turin Rd N9 18 C4
Turin St E2 96 A4
Turkey Oak Cl SE19 183 C2
Turkey St EN1, EN3 6 C6
Turkey Street Sta EN3 6 C6
Turks Cl UB8 82 C4
Turk's Head Yd EC1 241 C4
Turks Row SW3 114 D1 257 D2
Turle Rd
Finsbury Pk N4 72 B6
Thornton Heath SW16 182 A1
Turlewray Cl N4 50 B1
Turley Cl E15 98 C6
Turnagain La EC4 241 C2
Turnage Rd RM8 59 A1
Turnant Rd N17 33 A2
Turnberry Cl
24 Bermondsey SE16 118 B1
Hendon NW4 28 D1
Turnberry Quay 1 E14 119 D3
Turnberry Way BR6 211 B1
Turnbull Ho N1 234 D6
Turnbury Cl SE28 102 D1
Turnchapel Mews 1 SW4 137 B2
Turner Ave
Mitcham CR4 180 D2
Tottenham N15 51 C5
Twickenham TW2 152 A1
Turner Cl
7 Brixton SW9 138 D4
Hampstead Garden Suburb NW11 47 D3
Hillingdon UB4 83 A4
Wembley HA0 65 D2
Turner Ct
9 Herne Hill SE5 139 B1
24 Rotherhithe SE16 118 C4
Turner Dr NW11 47 D3
Turner Ho
Finsbury Pk N4 50 B1
24 Millwall E14 119 C4
St John's Wood NW8 230 A4
Strand WC2 250 B5
6 Twickenham TW1 153 D5
Westminster SW1 259 D3

Turner Lo 10 SW19 156 D3
Turner Mews SM2 217 D1
Turner Pl SW11 158 C6
Turner Rd
Edgware HA8 26 B1
New Malden KT3 199 B2
Walthamstow E17 54 A6
Turners Cl N20 14 D1
Turners Ct
Leyton E15 76 A4
New Barnet EN5 13 D5
Tottenham N15 51 B4
Turners Meadow Way
BR3 185 B2
Turner's Rd E3 97 B2
Turner St
Canning Town E16 98 D1
Stepney E1 96 B2
Turners Way CR0 220 C6
Turneville Rd
W14 135 B6 264 C6
Turney Prim & Sec Specl
Sch SE21 161 A4
Turney Rd SE21 161 B4
Turnham Green Sta
W4 111 C2
Turnham Green Terr
W4 111 C2
Turnham Ho SE4 141 A1
Turnham Prim Sch
SE4 141 A1
Turnham Rd SE4 141 A1
Turnmill Ho 8 SW2 160 C6
Turnmill St
EC1 94 D2 241 C4
Turnour Ho 31 E1 96 B1
Turnpike Cl SE8 141 B5
Turnpike Ct DA6 146 D1
Turnpike Ho EC1 234 D1
Turnpike La
Hornsey N8 50 C6
Sutton SM1 218 A3
Uxbridge UB10 82 A5
Turnpike Lane Sta
N15 50 D6
Turnpike Link CR0 221 C6
Turnpike Mews N8 50 C6
Turnpike Way TW7 131 A4
Turnpin La 3 SE10 142 A6
Turnstone Cl
Edgware NW9 27 C1
Newham E13 99 A4
Uxbridge UB10 60 D3
Turnstone Terr 11
W13 86 D3
Turpentine La
SW1 115 B1 258 D1
Turpin Cl 15 EN3 7 C6
Turpington Cl BR2 210 A2
Turpington La BR2 210 A3
Turpin Ho SW11 268 C2
Turpin Rd TW14 149 D5
Turpin Way
Upper Holloway N19 49 D1
Wallington SM6 219 B1
Turquand St SE17 262 B3
Turret Gr SW4 137 C2
Turret Ho KT2 176 A4
Turton Ho 5 SE18 144 D6
Turton Rd HA0 66 A3
Turville Ho NW8 237 A6
Turville St E2 243 C6
Tuscan Ho 36 E2 96 C4
Tuscan Rd SE18 123 B1
Tuscany Ho E17 35 B1
Tuskar St SE10 120 C1
Tutorial Coll of West
London UB1 107 B5
Tuttlebee La IG9 21 A2
Tuttle Ho SW1 259 D1
Tweedale Ct E15 76 A3
Tweed Ct W7 86 C1
Tweeddale Gr UB10 61 A5
Tweeddale Prim Sch
SM5 202 B2
Tweeddale Rd SM5 202 B1
Tweed Ho E14 98 A3
Tweedmouth Rd E13 99 B5
Tweedy Cl EN1 17 D6
Tweedy Rd BR1 187 A2
Tweezer's Alley WC2 251 A6
Twelve Acre Ho 5
E12 78 C5
Twelvetrees Bsns Pk
E16 98 B3
Twelvetrees Cres E3 98 A3
Twentyman Cl IG8 37 A5
Twice Times Montessori
Sch SW6 135 C3
TWICKENHAM 152 D4
Twickenham Bridge
TW9 153 C6
Twickenham Cl CR0 220 B5
Twickenham Gdns
Harrow HA3 24 C3
Wembley UB6 65 A3
Twickenham Pl KT7 212 D6
Twickenham Prep Sch
TW12 174 A2
Twickenham Rd
Isleworth TW1,TW7 131 A2
Leyton E11 76 B6
Richmond TW1,TW9 131 C1
Teddington TW11 175 A6
Twickenham TW13 151 B1
Twickenham Rugby
Football Union Ground
TW2 152 C5
Twickenham Sta
TW1 153 A4
Twickenham Trad Ctr
TW1 152 D5
Twig Folly Cl 21 E2 96 D5
Twilley St SW18 157 D4
Twine Cl IG11 102 B4
Twine Ct E1 118 C6
Twineham Gn N12 29 C6
Twining Ave TW2 152 B1
Twinn Rd NW7 29 A4
Twin Tumps Way
SE28 124 A6
Twisden Rd NW5 71 B4
Twiss Ho 6 SE18 122 D1
Twist Ho E10 75 D6
Two Bridges Ind Est
CR0 221 B2
Twybridge Way NW10 67 A1
Twyford Abbey Rd
NW10 88 B4
Twyford Ave
Acton W3 110 C6
Muswell Hill N2 48 D6
Twyford CE High Sch
W3 110 D5
Twyford Cres W3 110 C5
Twyford Ct
Acton W3 110 C6
Muswell Hill N10 49 A6
6 Wembley HA0 88 A5
Twyford Ho
Highbury N5 72 D5
6 Tottenham N15 51 C3
Twyford Par KT6 198 C1
Twyford Rd
Carshalton SM5 202 B1
Harrow HA2 41 D2
Ilford IG1 79 A3
Twyford St N1 94 B6 233 C6
Twynholm Mans SW6 264 A4
Tyas Rd E16 98 D3
Tybenham Rd SW19 201 C6
Tyberry Rd EN3 6 C2
Tyburn La HA1 42 D2
Tyburn Tree (site of)*
W2 247 C6
Tyburn Way W1 247 D6
Tye La BR6 227 A3
Tyer's Est SE1 253 A2
Tyers Gate
SE1 117 C4 253 A1
Tyers Ho 1 SW16 181 C5
Tyers St SE11 116 B1 260 C2
Tyers Terr
SE11 116 B1 260 D1
Tyeshurst Cl SE2 125 A1
Tylecroft Rd SW16 182 A1
Tylehurst Gdns IG1 79 A3
Tyler Cl
Erith DA8 147 D5
Haggerston E2 95 D5
Tyler Ho SE3 142 B3
Tyler Rd UB2 107 D3
Tylers Ct
4 Walthamstow E17 53 C5
5 Wembley HA0 88 A5
Tylers Gate HA3 44 A3
Tylers Path SM5 218 D4
Tyler St
Greenwich SE10 120 C1
SE10 142 C6
Tylney Ave SE19 183 D5
Tylney Ho 10 E1 96 B1
Tylney Rd
BR1 187 D1
Forest Gate E7 77 C4
Tymperley Ct SW19 157 A3
Tynamara KT1 197 D5
Tynan Cl TW14 150 A3
Tyndale La N1 72 D1
Tyndale Mans N1 72 D1
Tyndale Terr 13 N1 72 D1
Tyndall Gdns E10 76 A6
Tyndall Rd
DA16 145 D2
Leyton E10 76 A6
Tyne Ct W7 86 C1
Tyneham Cl 10 SW11 137 A2
Tyneham Rd SW11 137 A2
Tyne Ho 8 KT2 175 D2
Tynemouth Cl E6 100 D1
Tynemouth Dr EN1 6 A5
Tynemouth Rd
Mitcham CR4 181 A3
Plumstead Comm SE18 123 C1
Tottenham N15 51 D5
Tynemouth St SW6 136 A3
Tynemouth Terr 9
N15 51 D5
Tyne St E1 243 D2
Tynsdale Rd NW10 67 C2
Tynte Ct E9 75 A3
Tynwald Ho 14 SE26 162 A1
Type St E2 96 D5
Tyrawley Rd SW6 265 C2
Tyrell Cl HA1 64 C4
Tyrell Ct SM5 218 D4
Tyrells Ct 3 SE15 140 B2
Tyrols Rd SE23 162 D3
Tyrone Ct SW16 181 D5
Tyrone Rd E6 100 B4
Tyron Way DA14 189 D5
Tyrrell Ave DA16 168 B6
Tyrrell Ho
Catford BR3 185 D5
SW1 269 B6
Tyrrell Rd SE22 140 A1
Tyrrell Sq CR4 180 C2
Tyrrel Way NW9 46 A2
Tyrwhitt Rd SE4 141 C2
Tysoe Ave EN3 7 B6
Tysoe St EC1 234 B1
Tyson Rd SE23 162 C4
Tyssen Com Prim Sch
N16 52 A1
Tyssen Rd N16 73 D5
Tyssen St
Dalston E8 73 D2
Hoxton N1 95 C5
Tysson Ho E9 75 A1
Tytherton 29 E2 96 C5
Tytherton Rd N19 71 D5

U

Uamvar St E14 97 D2
Uckfield Gr CR4 181 A2
Uckfield Rd EN3 6 D6
Udall St SW1 259 B3
Udimore Ho 11 W10 90 C2
Udney Park Rd TW11 175 A4
Uffington Rd
West Norwood SE27 182 C6
Willesden Green NW10 90 B6
Ufford Cl HA3 23 D3
Ufford Rd HA3 23 D3
Ufford St SE1 116 C4 251 B2
Ufton Ct UB5 84 D4
Ufton Gr N1 73 B1
Ufton Rd N1 73 C1
Uhura Sq 19 N16 73 C5
Ujima Ct
Finsbury Pk N19 50 A1
Streatham SW16 182 A6
Ujima Ho SW16 182 A6
UK Coll of Bsns &
Computing IG2 56 C3
Uk Cotts UB3 105 B4
Ullathorne Rd SW16 181 C6
Ulleswater Rd N14 16 B1
Ullin St E14 98 A2
Ullswater SW15 156 D5
Ullswater Cl
Bromley BR1 186 C3
Hayes UB4 83 C5
Kingston u T KT2,
SW15 177 B6
Ullswater Cres SW15 177 B6
Ullswater Ct
Harrow HA2 41 C2
2 Woodford E18 37 A1
Ullswater Ho SE15 140 C6
Ullswater Rd
Barnes SW13 134 A5
West Norwood SE27,
SW16 160 D2
Ulster Ct KT2 175 D4
Ulster Gdns N13 33 A6
Ulster Pl NW1 238 C5
Ulster Terr NW1 238 C6
Ulundi Rd SE3 142 C6
Ulva Rd SW15 134 D1
Ulverscroft Rd SE22 162 A6
Ulverstone Rd SE27 160 D2
Ulverston Rd E17 36 B1
Ulysses Rd NW6 69 B3
Umberston St E1 96 B1
Umbria St SW15 156 A5
Umfreville Rd N4 50 D3
Umoja Ho N22 32 B1
Una Ho 7 NW5 71 B2
Undercliff SE10 142 A4
Undercliff Rd SE13 141 D2
UNDERHILL 13 C6
Underhill EN5 13 C6
Underhill Ct EN5 13 C6
Underhill Ho 7 E14 97 C2
Underhill Jun & Inf Schs
EN5 13 A6
Underhill Pas NW1 231 D6
Underhill Rd SE21,
SE22 162 B4
Underhill St NW1 231 D5
Underne Ave N14 15 B2
Undershaft EC3 95 C1 243 A1
Undershaw Rd BR1 164 D1
Underwood CR0 224 A3
Underwood Ct 3 E10 53 D1
Underwood Ho
East Molesey KT8 195 C4
Hammersmith W6 112 B3
Underwood Rd
Bethnal Green E1 96 A3
Chingford E4 35 D5
Woodford IG8 37 D3
Underwood Row N1 235 B2
Underwood St
N1 95 A4 235 B2
Underwood The SE9 166 B2
Undine Rd E14 119 D2
Undine St SW17 180 D5
Uneeda Dr UB6 86 B6
Unicorn Bldg 14 E1 118 D6
Unicorn Prim Sch
BR3 207 D4
Unicorn Sch TW9 132 B4
Unicorn Works N17 34 C3
Union Cl E11 76 B4
Union Ct
45 Paddington W2 91 C2
2 Richmond TW10 154 A6
South Lambeth SW4 138 A3
Union Dr E1 97 A3
Union Gr SW8 137 D3
Union Mews 32 SW9 138 A3
Union Pk 11 SE10 120 D1
Union Rd
BR2 209 D4
Clapham SW8 137 D3
Friern Barnet N11 31 D4
Northolt UB5 85 C5
Thornton Heath CR0 205 A2
Wembley HA0 66 A2
Union Sq N1 95 A6 235 B5
Union St
Barnet EN5 1 A2
Kingston u T KT1 175 D1
Mill Meads E15 98 B6
SE1 117 A5 252 A3
Union Terr HA2 41 C1
Union Wharf N1 235 B4
Union Wlk E2 95 C4
Union Yd W1 238 D1
Unity Cl
West Norwood SE19 183 A5
Willesden NW10 68 A2
Unity Mews NW1 232 C4
Unity Rd EN3 6 C6
Unity Terr HA2 63 D6
Unity Way SE18 121 D3
Univ Coll Jun Sch
NW3 70 A4
Univ Coll London
Bloomsbury
WC1 93 D3 239 C6
Bloomsbury
WC1 94 A3 240 B6
Univ Coll London
(Windeyer Inst)
W1 93 C2 239 B4
Univ Coll London
(Wolfson Ho)
NW1 93 C4 232 B1
University Cl NW7 27 D3
University Coll Hospl
WC1 93 C3 239 B6
University Coll Sch
NW3 70 A3
University Gdns DA5 169 B4
University Mans
SW15 134 D2
University Pl DA8 147 D5
University Rd SW19 180 B4
University St
WC1 93 C3 239 B5
University Way E16 122 D6
Univ of California
WC1 93 D2 239 D3
Univ of East London
Barking RM8 80 A4
Newham E16 122 C6
Stratford E15 76 C2
Univ of East London
(Duncan Ho) E15 98 B6
Univ of East London
(Holbrook Ctr) E15 98 D5
Univ of Greenwich
SE10 142 B6
Univ of Greenwich Avery
Hill Campus Mansion
Site SE9 167 A5
Univ of Greenwich Avery
Hill Campus Southwood
Site SE9 167 B4
Univ of Greenwich Rachel
Mcmillan Campus
SE8 141 C6
Univ of Greenwich
Riverside Ho Annexe
SE18 122 C3
Univ of London
WC1 93 D3 239 D5
Univ of London (King's
Coll Hall) SE5 139 B2
Univ of London Obsy
NW7 27 D4
Univ of London (Queen
Mary & Westfield Coll)
E1 97 A3
Univ of Westminster
NW1 93 C3 239 A6
Univ of Westminster
(Cavendish Campus)
W1 93 C2 239 A4
Univ of Westminster
(Harrow Campus)
HA1 43 A2
Univ of Westminster
(Marylebone Campus)
W1 93 A2 238 A4
Univ of Westminster
(Regent Campus)
W1 93 C2 239 A3
Univ of Westminster
(Regent Campus, Univ
HQ) W1 93 B1 238 D2
Uno Apartments 4
BR1 187 A2
Unwin Ave TW14 149 B6
Unwin Cl SE15 140 A6
Unwin Rd
Isleworth TW7 130 C2
SW7 114 B3 256 D6
Upbrook Mews
W2 92 A1 236 B1
Upcerne Rd
SW10 136 A5 266 B3
Upchurch Cl 8 SE20 184 B3
Upcott Ho
33 Bromley E3 97 D4
4 Hackney E9 74 C1
Upcroft Ave HA8 27 A6
Updale Rd DA14 189 D6
Upfield CR0 222 B5
Upfield Rd W7 86 D2
Upgrove Manor Way 12
SE24 160 C4
Uphall Prim Sch IG1 78 D3
Uphall Rd IG1 78 D3
Upham Park Rd W4 111 C2
Uphill Dr
Edgware NW7 27 C5
Kingsbury NW9 45 A4
Uphill Gr NW7 27 C6
Uphill Rd NW7 27 C6
Upland Ct SE23 162 C2
Upland Prim Sch
DA7 147 B2
Upland Rd
Croydon CR2 221 B3
DA7 147 B2
East Dulwich SE22 162 A5
8 Newham E13 99 A3
Sutton SM2 218 B1
Uplands
Beckenham BR3 185 C1
Woolwich SE18 122 D1
Uplands Ave E17 34 D1
Uplands Bsns Pk E17 52 D6
Uplands Cl SW14 154 D6
Uplands Ct N21 16 C4
Uplands Park Rd EN2 4 C3
Uplands Rd
East Barnet EN4 15 A3
Hornsey Vale N8 50 B4
Ilford RM6 58 D6
Woodford IG8 37 D3
Uplands The HA4 40 A1
Uplands Way N21 16 C6
Upnall Ho 16 SE15 140 C6
Upney Ct 2 IG11 79 D1
Upney La IG11 79 D1
Upney Sta IG11 79 D1
Upnor Way SE17 263 B2
Uppark Dr IG2 57 A3
Upper Abbey Rd
DA17 125 C2
Upper Addison Gdns
W14 113 A4 244 A2
Upper Bank St E14 119 D5
Upper Bardsey Wlk 7
N1 73 A2
Upper Belgrave St
SW1 115 A3 258 B6
Upper Berkeley St
W1 92 D1 237 D1
Upper Beulah Hill
SE19 183 C2
Upper Brighton Rd
KT6 198 A2
Upper Brockley Rd
SE4 141 B3
Upper Brook St
W1 115 A6 248 A6
Upper Butts TW8 131 C6
Upper Caldy Wlk 18
N1 73 A2
Upper Camelford Wlk 14
W10 91 A1
Upper Cavendish Ave
N3 47 C6
Upper Cheyne Row
SW3 136 C6 267 A6
UPPER CLAPTON 52 B1
Upper Clapton Rd E5 74 B6
Upper Clarendon Wlk 12
W11 91 A1
Upper Dengie Wlk N1 235 A6
UPPER EDMONTON 34 B5
UPPER ELMERS
END 207 B3
Upper Elmers End Rd
BR3 207 A4
Upper Farm Rd KT8 195 B5
Upper Fosters NW4 46 C5
Upper Gn W CR4 180 D1
Upper Gr SE25 205 D5
Upper Grosvenor St
W1 115 A6 248 A5
Upper Grotto Rd
TW1 152 D2
Upper Ground
SE1 116 C5 251 A4
Upper Grove Rd
DA17 147 B6
Upper Gulland Wlk 23
N1 73 A2
UPPER HALLIFORD 193 B5
Upper Halliford Rd
TW17 193 C6
Upper Halliford Sta
TW16 171 C1
Upper Hampstead Wlk 29
NW3 70 A4
Upper Ham Rd KT2,
TW10 175 D6
Upper Handa Wlk 2
N1 73 A2
Upper Harley St NW1 238 B5
Upper Hawkwell Wlk
N1 235 B6
UPPER HOLLOWAY 71 D6
Upper Holloway Sta
N19 71 D6
Upper Holly Hill Rd
DA17 125 D1
Upper James St W1 249 B6
Upper John St W1 249 B6
Upper Lismore Wlk 8
N1 73 A2
Upper Lodge Mews
TW12 174 A4
Upper Mall W6 112 B1
Upper Marsh
SE1 116 B3 260 D6

Upper Montague St
W1 92 D2 237 C3
Upper Mulgrave Rd
SM2 217 A1
Upper North St E3, E14 97 C2
UPPER NORWOOD 183 C3
Upper Park Rd
Belvedere DA17 125 D2
BR1 187 C2
Friern Barnet N11 31 C5
Kingston u T KT2 176 C4
Maitland Pk NW3 70 D3
Upper Phillimore Gdns
W8 113 C4 245 A1
Upper Pk IG10 21 D6
Upper Ramsey Wlk 19
N1 73 B2
Upper Rawreth Wlk
N1 235 B6
Upper Rd
Finchley N2 30 C2
Newham E13 99 A4
Wallington SM6 219 D3
Upper Richmond Rd
SW15 134 C1
Upper Richmond Rd W
TW10, SW14, SW15 133 A1
UPPER RUXLEY 191 C3
Upper St Martin's La
WC2 250 A6
Upper Selsdon Rd
CR2 221 D1
Upper Sheridan Rd 3
DA17 125 C2
UPPER SHIRLEY 222 D4
Upper Shirley Rd
CR0 222 D5
Upper Sq TW7 131 A2
Upper St N1 94 D6 234 C5
Upper Sunbury Rd
TW12 173 C2
Upper Sutton La
TW5 129 C4
UPPER SYDENHAM 184 A6
Upper Tachbrook St
SW1 259 B4
Upper Talbot Wlk 7
W10 91 A1
Upper Teddington Rd KT1,
KT8 175 C2
Upper Terr NW3 70 A5
Upper Thames St
EC4 117 A6 252 B6
Upper Tollington Pk
N4 50 C1
Upperton Rd DA14 189 D5
Upperton Rd E E13 99 C4
Upperton Rd W E13 99 C4
UPPER TOOTING 158 D1
Upper Tooting Park Mans
1 SW17 159 A2
Upper Tooting Pk
SW17 158 D2
Upper Tooting Rd
SW17 158 D1
Upper Town Rd UB6 85 D3
Upper Tulse Hill SW2 160 B3
Upper Vernon Rd
SM1 218 B3
UPPER WALTHAMSTOW 54 C6
Upper Walthamstow Rd
E17 54 B6
Upper Wickham La
DA16 146 B4
Upper Wimpole St
W1 93 A2 238 B4
Upper Woburn Pl NW1,
WC1 93 D4 232 D1
Uppingham Ave HA7 25 C1
Upsdell Ave N13 32 C4
Upshire Ho E17 35 B1
Upstall St SE5 138 D4
UPTON 77 B1
Upton Ave E7 77 A1
Upton Cl
Cricklewood NW2 69 A5
Sidcup DA5 169 B5
Upton Cross E13 99 A6
Upton Cross Prim Sch
E13 99 B6
Upton Ct
Penge SE20 184 C3
Southall UB1 107 D5
4 Wimbledon SW19 178 D3
Upton Day Hospl
DA6 147 A1
Upton Dene SM2 217 D1
Upton Gdns HA3 43 C3
Upton Hts E7 77 A1
Upton La E7 77 A1
Upton Lo E7 77 A2
Upton Lodge Cl WD23 8 A4
UPTON PARK 99 D6
Upton Park Rd E7 77 B1
Upton Park Sta E13 99 C6
Upton Prim Sch DA5 169 B6
Upton Rd
Bexley DA6 169 A6
Edmonton N18 34 A5
Hounslow TW3 129 C2
SE18 145 A6
South Norwood CR7 183 B1
Upton Rd S DA5 169 B5
Upton Villas 4 DA6 147 A1
Upway N12 30 C4
Upwood Rd
SE12 165 A5
Thornton Heath SW16 182 A2
Urban Mews N4 50 D2
Urlwin St SE5 139 A6
Urlwin Wlk SW9 138 D4
Urmston Dr SW19 157 A3
Urmston Ho 4 E14 120 A2
Urquhart Ct BR3 185 B3
Ursula Lo DA14 190 B5
Ursula Mews N4 51 A1
Ursula St
SW11 136 C4 267 A1
Ursuline High Sch
SW20 178 D2
Ursuline Prep Sch
SW19 178 D3
Urswick Gdns RM9 81 A1
Urswick Rd
Dagenham RM9 81 A1
Hackney E5, E9 74 C3
Usborne Mews SW8 270 D4
Usher Hall NW4 46 B5
Usher Rd E3 97 B5
Usk Rd SW11 136 A1
Usk St E2 96 D4
Utah Bldg 3 SE13 141 D4
Utopia Ho 3 NW2 68 A2
Utopia Village
NW1 93 A6 231 A6
Uvedale Rd
Dagenham RM10 81 C5
Enfield EN2 17 B6
Uverdale Rd
SW10 136 A5 266 B3
UXBRIDGE 82 A6
Uxbridge Coll
Hayes UB3 106 A6
Uxbridge UB8 60 A2
Uxbridge High Sch
UB8 82 A5
Uxbridge Rd
Acton W3, W5 110 C5
Ealing W13 109 C6
Feltham TW13 150 D2
Hampton TW12, TW13 173 D5
Hayes UB4 106 C6
Hillingdon UB10, UB4 83 C2
Kingston u T KT1, KT6 197 D4
Shepherd's Bush W12 112 B5
Southall UB1, UB2, W5,
W7 108 B5
Stanmore HA7 25 A5
Uxbridge Road (Harrow
Weald) HA3 24 B3
Uxbridge Road (Hatch
End) HA5 23 B3
Uxbridge Road (Pinner)
HA5 22 D1
Uxbridge St
W8 113 C5 245 A4
Uxendon Cres HA3,
HA9 44 A1
Uxendon Hill HA9 44 B2
Uxendon Manor Prim Sch
HA3 44 A4

V

Vadnie Bish Ho NW5 71 C2
Vaine Ho 4 E9 75 A2
Valance Ave E4 20 D3
Valan Leas BR2 208 C6
Vale Ave WD6 10 D6
Vale Cl
Muswell Hill N2 48 D6
Orpington BR6 226 C4
St John's Wood
W9 92 A4 229 A1
Twickenham TW1 153 A1
Vale Cres SW15 177 C6
Vale Croft
Claygate KT10 212 D1
Pinner HA5 41 A4
Vale Ct
Barnet EN5 1 D1
East Acton W3 111 D5
St John's Wood
W9 92 A4 229 A1
Wembley HA0 65 C5
Vale Dr EN5 13 C6
Vale End SE22 139 D1
Vale Est The W3 111 C5
Vale Farm Sports Ctr
HA0 65 B4
Vale Gr
Acton W3 111 B5
Stoke Newington N4 51 A2
Vale La W3 88 C2
Vale Lo SE23 162 C2
Valence Ave RM8 80 D6
Valence Cir RM8 81 A5
Valence House Mus*
RM8 81 A6
Valence Jun & Inf Schs
RM8 80 D6
Valence Wood Rd
RM8 81 A5
Valencia Rd HA7 25 C6
Valens Ho 1 SW2 160 C3
Valentia Pl SW9 138 C1
Valentine Ave DA5 169 A3
Valentine Ct
Elstree WD6 9 D5
3 Forest Hill SE23 162 D2
Valentine Ho
11 Clapham Pk SW4 159 C5
26 Old Ford E3 97 B6
Valentine Pl
SE1 116 D4 251 C2
Valentine Rd
Harrow HA2 64 A5
Homerton E9 74 D2
Valentine Row SE1 251 C1
Valentines High Sch
IG2 56 C3
Valentines Rd IG1 56 D1
VALE OF HEALTH 70 B5
Vale of Health NW3 70 B5
Vale Rd
BR1 188 C1
Claygate KT10 212 D1
Mitcham CR4 203 D5
Stoke Newington N4 51 A2
Sutton SM1 217 D4
Upton E7 77 B2
Worcester Pk KT19,
KT4 215 D5
Vale Rd N KT6 214 A6
Vale Rd S KT6 214 A6
Valerian Way E15 98 C4
Valerie Ct
Belmont SM2 217 D1
Bushey WD23 8 A4
Vale Rise NW11 47 B1
Vale Row N5 72 D5
Vale Royal N7 72 A1
Valery Pl TW12 173 C3
Vale Sch The SW7 256 A5
Valeside Ct 2 EN5 1 D1
Valeswood Rd BR1 186 D5
Vale Terr N4 51 A3
Vale The
Ashford TW16 172 A4
Cricklewood NW11 69 A6
Croydon CR0 222 D6
East Acton W3 111 C5
Feltham TW14 150 B5
Heston TW5 129 A6
Muswell Hill N10 31 A2
Ruislip HA4 62 C4
Southgate N14 16 A4
SW3 136 B6 266 D6
Woodford IG8 37 A3
Valetta Gr E13 99 A5
Valetta Rd W3 111 D4
Valette Ct N10 49 B5
Valette Ho E9 74 C2
Valette St E8 74 B2
Valiant Cl 13 UB5 84 D4
Valiant Ho
9 Cubitt Town E14 120 A4
5 Greenwich SE7 121 C1
SW11 266 D1
Valiant Way E6 100 B2
Vallance Rd
Bethnal Green E1 96 A3
Muswell Hill N22 31 C1
Vallentin Rd E17 54 A5
Valley Ave N12 30 B6
Valley (Charlton Athletic
FC) The SE7 121 C1
Valley Cl HA5 22 B1
Valley Ct IG8 37 B3
Valley Dr NW9 44 D3
Valleyfield Rd SW16 182 B5
Valley Fields Cres EN2 4 C3
Valley Gdns
Mitcham SW19 180 B3
Wembley HA0 66 B1
Valley Gr SE7 121 C1
Valley Ho
4 Edmonton N9 18 A1
Upper Clapton E5 52 C1
Valleylink Est EN3 19 A5
Valley Mews TW1 153 A2
Valley Pl KT6 198 A3
Valley Point Ind Est
CR0 204 A2
Valley Prim Sch BR2 186 D1
Valley Prospect 3
SE19 183 C4
Valley Rd
Beckenham BR2 186 C1
BR5 190 B2
Streatham SW16 182 B6
Uxbridge UB10 82 A5
Valleyside SE7 121 D1
Valley Side E4 19 C3
Valley Side Par E4 19 C2
Valley View EN5 13 A5
Valley Wlk CR0 222 C6
Valliere Rd NW10 90 A4
Valliers Wood Rd
DA15 167 C3
Vallis Way
Chessington KT9 213 D4
Ealing W13 87 A2
Val McKenzie Ave N7 72 C5
Valmar Rd SE5 139 A4
Valmar Trad Est SE5 139 A4
Valnay St SW17 180 D5
Valognes Ave E17 35 A2
Valois Ho SE1 263 C6
Valonia Gdns SW18 157 B5
Vambery Rd SE18 145 A6
Vanbern Ho NW5 71 A2
Vanborough Ct 4
SM2 218 A2
Vanbrough Cres UB5 84 C6
Vanbrugh Cl 2 E16 99 D2
Vanbrugh Ct SE11 261 B3
Vanbrugh Dr KT12 194 C3
Vanbrugh Fields SE3 142 D5
Vanbrugh Hill SE10,
SE3 142 D6
Vanbrugh Ho 8 E9 74 C1
Vanbrugh Mews
KT12 194 C2
Vanbrugh Park Rd
SE3 142 D5
Vanbrugh Park Rd W
SE3 142 D5
Vanbrugh Pk SE3 142 D5
Vanbrugh Rd W4 111 B3
Vanbrugh Terr SE3 142 D4
Vanburgh Cl BR6 211 C1
Vanburgh Ct 6 EN5 1 A1
Vanburgh Ho E1 243 C4
Vancouver Rd
Edgware HA8 26 D2
Forest Hill SE23 163 B2
Hayes UB4 84 B3
Richmond TW10 175 C6
Vancover Ho 33 E1 118 B5
Vanderbilt Rd SW18 158 A3
Vanderbilt Villas 1
W12 112 D4
Vanderville Gdns N2 30 B1
Vandome Cl E16 99 B1
Vandon Ct SW1 259 B6
Vandon Pas SW1 259 B6
Vandon St SW1 259 B6
Van Dyck Ave KT3 199 B2
Vandyke Cl SW15 156 D5
Vandyke Cross SE9 166 A6
Vandy St EC2 243 A5
Vane Cl
Hampstead NW3 70 B4
Harrow HA3 44 B3
Vane Ho 18 N2 30 B1
Vanessa Cl DA17 125 C1
Vane St SW1 259 B4
Vanfame Ct KT3 199 D6
Vange Ho 12 W10 90 C2
Van Gogh Cl 11 TW7 131 A2
Van Gogh Ct E14 120 B3
Vanguard Bldg 6
E14 119 C4
Vanguard Cl
Newham E16 99 B2
Thornton Heath CR0 204 D1
Vanguard Ho
11 Hackney E8 74 B1
7 Merton SW19 180 A3
6 Stanwell TW19 148 A5
Vanguard St SE8 141 C4
Vanguard Trad Ctr
E15 98 A6
Vanguard Way
Hatton TW6 127 C3
Wallington SM6 220 A1
Van Lang Ho EN3 18 D6
Vanneck Sq SW15 156 A6
Vanner Point 27 E9 74 D2
Vanoc Gdns BR1 187 A6
Vansittart Rd E7 77 A4
Vansittart St 7 SE14 141 A5
Vanston Pl
SW6 135 C5 265 B4
Vantage Ct
Harlington UB3 127 C5
4 South Norwood
SW16 182 B3
Vantage Mews 7
E14 120 A5
Vantage Pl W8 255 B5
Vant Rd SW17 180 D5
Vantrey Ho SE11 261 A3
Varcoe Rd SE16 118 C1
Vardens Rd SW11 136 B1
Varden St E1 96 B1
Vardon Cl W3 89 B1
Vardon Ho SE10 142 A4
Vardy Ho HA7 25 B5
Varey Ho E1 97 A4
Varley Ho 5 NW6 91 C6
Varley Par NW9 45 C5
Varley Rd E16 99 B1
Varley Way CR4 180 B1
Varma Ct SE3 143 A4
Varna Rd
Hampton TW12 173 D2
SW6 135 B5 264 C3
Varndell St
NW1 93 C4 232 A2
Varsity Dr TW1, TW7 152 D5
Varsity Row SW14 133 A3
Vartry Rd N15 51 C3
Vascroft Est NW10 88 D3
Vassall Ho 3 E3 97 A4
Vassall Rd SW9 138 C5
Vat Ho SW8 270 B4
Vauban Est SE16 263 D5
Vauban St
SE16 117 D3 263 D5
Vaudeville Ct N4 72 C6
Vaughan Almshouses
TW15 170 D5
Vaughan Ave
Chiswick W6 111 D2
Hendon NW4 46 A4
Vaughan Cl TW12 173 A4
Vaughan Est 3 E2 95 D4
Vaughan Fst & Mid Sch
HA1 42 A3
Vaughan Gdns IG1 56 B2
Vaughan Ho SE1 251 C2
Vaughan Rd
Camberwell SE5 139 A2
DA16 145 D3
Harrow HA1 42 B3
Stratford E15 76 D2
Thames Ditton KT7 197 B2
Vaughan St SE16 119 B4
Vaughan Way E1 118 A5
Vaughan Williams Cl
SE8 141 C5
VAUXHALL 116 A1
Vauxhall Bridge Rd
SW1 115 C2 259 B3
Vauxhall Cross SE1,
SW8 116 A1 260 B1
Vauxhall Gdns CR2 221 A2
Vauxhall Gr
SW8 138 B6 270 C6
Vauxhall Prim Sch
SE11 116 B1 260 D2
Vauxhall St
SE11 116 B1 260 D2
Vauxhall Sta
SE11 116 A1 260 B1
Vauxhall Wlk SE11 260 C2
Vawdrey Cl E1 96 C3
Vaynor Ho N7 72 A4
Veals Mead CR4 180 C2
Vectis Ct SW18 157 D5
Vectis Gdns SW17 181 B4
Vectis Rd SW17 181 B4
Veda Rd SE13 141 C1
Vega Cres HA6 22 A5
Vega Rd WD23 8 A4
Veitch Cl TW14 149 D4
Veldene Way HA2 63 B5
Velde Way 1 SE22 161 C6
Vellacott Ho 3 W12 90 B1
Velletri Ho 17 E2 96 D5
Vellum Dr SM5 219 A5
Venables Cl RM10 81 D4
Venables St
NW8 92 B2 236 D4
Vencourt Pl W6 112 A2
Venetian Rd SE5 139 A3
Venetia Rd
Ealing W5 109 D4
Harringay N4 50 D3
Venice Ct 14 SE5 139 A5
Venita Manor SE27 182 C5
Venmead Ct 7 DA17 125 C2
Venner Rd SE26 184 C5
Venn Ho N1 233 D5
Venn St SW4 137 C1
Ventnor Ave HA7 25 B1
Ventnor Dr N20 13 D2
Ventnor Gdns IG11 79 C2
Ventnor Mans IG11 79 C2
Ventnor Rd
Belmont SM2 217 D1
SE14 140 D5
Ventnor Terr N15 52 A5
Ventura Ho 12 SW2 138 A1
Venture Cl DA5 169 A4
Venture Ct 3 SE12 165 A4
Venue St E14 98 A2
Venus Ho
7 Millwall E14 119 C2
8 Old Ford E3 97 C6
Venus Mews CR4 202 C6
Venus Rd SE18 122 B3
Vera Ave N21 16 C6
Vera Ct
1 Kensington W2 91 D1
Tottenham N22 32 D2
Vera Lynn Cl 5 E7 77 A4
Vera Rd SW6 135 A4 264 B2
Verbena Cl E16 98 D3
Verbena Gdns 4 W6 112 A1
Verdant Ct 3 SE6 164 C4
Verdant La SE6 164 C3
Verdayne Ave CR0 222 D6
Verdi Cres W10 91 A5
Verdun Rd
Barnes SW13 134 A5
SE18 146 A6
Vere Bank SW19 157 B3
Vereker Dr TW16 194 A6
Vereker Rd W14 254 B1
Vere St W1 93 B1 238 C1
Verity Cl W11 91 A1
Verity Ct N9 18 D3
Verity Ho 20 E3 97 B4
Vermeer Ct E14 120 B3
Vermillion Ct TW13 149 D1
Vermont Cl EN2 4 D1
Vermont Ho E17 35 B1
Vermont Rd
Sutton SM1 217 D5
Wandsworth SW18 157 D5
West Norwood SE19 183 C4
Verne Ct 9 W3 111 A3
Verneer Gdns SE15 140 C1
Verney Gdns RM9 81 A4
Verney Ho
Isleworth TW3 130 A1
Lisson Gr NW8 237 A6
South Kensington SW10 266 A6
Verney Rd
Bermondsey SE16 118 B1
Dagenham RM9 81 A4
Verney St NW10 67 B5
Verney Way SE16 118 B1
Vernham Rd SE18 145 A6
Vernon Ave
Ilford E12 78 B4
West Barnes SW20 178 D1
Woodford IG8 37 B3
Vernon Cl
Stanwell TW19 148 A3
West Ewell KT19 215 A2
Vernon Cres EN4 15 A5
Vernon Ct
Child's Hill NW2 69 B5
Ealing W5 109 C6
Stanmore HA7 25 B2
Vernon Dr HA7 25 A2
Vernon Ho
Hyde The NW9 45 D4
SE11 260 D1

Vernon House Sch
NW10 67 B3
Vernon Mews W14 254 B3
Vernon Pl WC1 240 B3
Vernon Rd
Bow E3 97 B5
Feltham TW13 149 D2
Hornsey N8 50 C6
Ilford IG3 57 D1
Leytonstone E11 54 C1
Mortlake SW14 133 B2
Stratford E15 76 C1
Sutton SM1 218 B3
Walthamstow E17 53 B4
Vernon Rise
Greenford UB6 64 B3
WC1 233 D2
Vernon Sq WC1 233 D2
Vernon St
W14 113 A2 254 B3
Vernon Yd
W11 113 B6 244 C6
Veroan Rd DA7 147 A3
Verona Ct
Chiswick W4 111 C1
10 SE14 140 D6
Verona Dr KT6 214 A6
Verona Rd E7 77 A1
Veronica Gdns CR4,
SW16 181 C2
Veronica Ho
Brockley SE4 141 B2
46 Bromley E3 97 D4
Veronica Rd SW17 159 B2
Veronique Gdns IG6 57 A4
Verran Rd SW12 159 B4
Versailles Rd SE20 184 A3
Verulam Ave E17 53 B2
Verulam Bldgs WC1 240 D4
Verulam Ct
Hendon NW9 46 A2
4 Southall UB1 86 A1
Verulam Ho 1 W6 112 C4
Verulam Rd UB6 85 C3
Verulam St EC1 94 C2 241 A4
Vervain Ho 2 SE15 140 A5
Verwood Dr EN4 2 D2
Verwood Ho SW8 270 D3
Verwood Lo 1 E14 120 B2
Verwood Rd HA2 24 A1
Veryan Ct 3 N8 49 D4
Vesage Ct EC1 241 B3
Vesey Path 15 E14 97 D1
Vespan Rd W12 112 A4
Vesta Ct SE1 253 A1
Vesta Ho 9 E3 97 C6
Vesta Rd SE4, SE14 141 A3
Vestris Rd SE23 162 D2
Vestry House (Mus)*
E17 53 D5
Vestry Mews 12 SE5 139 C4
Vestry Rd
Camberwell SE5 139 C4
Walthamstow E17 53 D5
Vestry St N1 95 B4 235 C2
Vevey St SE23, SE6 163 B2
Veysey Gdns RM10 81 C5
Viaduct Pl 28 E2 96 B4
Viaduct Rd N2 30 C1
Viaduct St E2 96 B4
Viaduct The
Harrow HA2 64 A5
Woodford E18 37 B1
Vian St SE13 141 D2
Vibart Gdns SW2 160 B4
Vibart Wlk N1 233 B6
Vicarage Ave SE3 143 A5
Vicarage Cl
New Malden KT4 199 C1
Northolt UB5 63 B1
Ruislip HA4 39 B2
Vicarage Cres
SW11 136 B4 266 C1
Vicarage Ct
Beckenham BR3 207 A6
East Bedfont TW14 149 A4
Finchley N12 29 D5
7 Putney SW15 156 A4
W8 245 C2
Vicarage Dr
Barking IG11 79 A1
Beckenham BR3 185 C2
Mortlake SW14 155 B6
Vicarage Farm Ct
TW5 129 B5
Vicarage Farm Rd TW3,
TW4, TW5 129 A4
Vicarage Fields KT12 194 C3
Vicarage Field Sh Ctr The
IG11 79 A1
Vicarage Gate
W8 113 D5 245 C3
Vicarage Gdns
Mitcham CR4 202 C6
Mortlake SW14 155 B6
W8 245 B3
Vicarage Gr SE5 139 B4
Vicarage Ho 1 KT1 176 B1
Vicarage La
Ilford IG1 57 B1
Stratford E15 76 D1
Wallend E6 100 C4
Vicarage Mans N15 51 A5
Vicarage Pk SE18 123 A1
Vicarage Prim Sch
E6 100 B4
Vicarage Rd
Ashford TW16 171 D4
Croydon CR0 220 C5
DA5 169 D3
Dagenham RM10 81 D1
Hampton Wick KT1 175 C2
Hendon NW4 46 A3
Kingston u T KT1 175 D1
Mortlake SW14 155 B6
Stratford E15 76 D1
Sutton SM1 217 D5
Teddington TW11 175 A5
Tottenham N17 34 A2
Walthamstow E10 53 D1
Woolwich SE18 123 A1
Vicarage The N8 50 B3
Vicarage Way
Harrow HA2 41 C2
Neasden NW10 67 B5
Vicarage Wlk
SW11 136 B4 266 D2
Vicars Bridge Cl HA0 88 A5
Vicar's Cl
Enfield EN1 5 C3
Newham E15 99 A6
South Hackney E9 96 C6
Vicar's Green Prim Sch
HA0 87 C5
Vicars Hill SE13 141 D1
Vicar's Moor La N21 16 D4
Vicars Oak Rd SE19 183 C4
Vicar's Rd NW5 71 A3
Vicar's Wlk RM8 80 B5
Viceroy Cl N2 48 C6
Viceroy Ct
5 Croydon CR0 205 B1
NW8 230 B4
Viceroy Lo 6 KT6 198 A4
Viceroy Par N2 48 C6
Viceroy Rd
SW8 138 A4 270 A2
Vic Johnson Ho 21 E3 97 B6
Vickers Cl SM6 220 B1
Vickers Ct 10 TW19 148 A5
Vickery Ct EC1 242 B6
Vickery Ho 13 SW4 138 A1
Vickery's Wharf 3
E14 97 C1
Victor Cazalet Ho N1 234 C6
Victor Gr HA0 66 A1
Victor Ho 2 N20 14 D1
Victoria & Albert Mus*
SW7 114 B3 256 D5
Victoria Arc SW1 258 D5
Victoria Ave
Barnet EN4 2 B1
East Molesey KT8 195 D6
EC2 243 B3
Finchley N3 29 B2
Hackbridge SM5, SM6 219 A5
Hillingdon UB10 60 D1
Hounslow TW3, TW4 151 C6
Newham E6 99 D6
Surbiton KT6 197 D3
Wembley HA9 66 D2
Victoria Bglws DA14 191 B3
Victoria Bldgs 13 E8 96 B6
Victoria Bsns Ctr
DA16 146 B3
Victoria Chambers
EC2 243 A6
Victoria Cl
Barnet EN4 2 B1
East Molesey KT8 195 C6
Harrow HA1 42 D3
Hayes UB3 83 B1
Victoria Coach Sta
SW1 115 B2 258 C3
Victoria Coll WC2 241 A2
Victoria Cotts
Ilford IG6 57 A4
Muswell Hill N10 31 A1
7 Richmond TW9 132 C4
3 Spitalfields E1 96 A2
Victoria Cres
Tottenham N15 51 C4
West Norwood SE19 183 C4
Victoria Ct
5 Clapham Pk SW4 159 D5
3 Penge SE26 184 C4
South Acton W3 110 C4
4 St George in t East
E1 118 A6
1 Wanstead E18 55 B6
Wembley HA9 66 C2
Victoria Dock Rd E16 121 B6
Victoria Dr SW19 156 D3
Victoria Emb
WC2 116 C6 251 A5
Victoria Gdns
Heston TW5 129 A4
W11 113 C5 245 A4
Victoria Gr
North Finchley N12 30 B5
W8 114 A3 256 A6
Victoria Gr Mews W2 245 C5
Victoria Hall 15 E16 121 A5
Victoria Ho
6 Clapham Pk SW4 159 D5
Edgware HA8 26 D4
2 Shepherd's Bush
W12 112 A4
SW1 258 C2
Victoria Ind Est W3 89 C2
Victoria Jun Sch
TW13 150 B3
Victoria La
Barnet EN5 1 B1
Hayes UB3 105 B1
Victoria Lo 5 SW19 178 C3
Victoria Mans
8 Islington N7 72 C3
Willesden NW10 68 B1
Victoria Mews
Kilburn NW6 91 C6
Wandsworth SW18 158 A3
Victoria Mills 1 E15 98 B6
Victorian Gr N16 73 C5
Victorian Hts 7 SW8 137 B3
Victorian Rd N16 73 D5
Victoria Park Ct 11 E9 74 C1
Victoria Park Ind Ctr
E9 75 B1
Victoria Park Lofts E9 96 D6
Victoria Park Rd E9 74 D1
Victoria Park Sq E2 96 C4
Victoria Pas NW8 236 C6
Victoria Pl 17 TW10 153 D6
Victoria Place Sh Ctr
SW1 115 B2 258 D4
Victoria Point 10 E13 99 A5
Victoria Rd
Barking IG11 78 D2
Barnet EN4 2 B1
Bexley DA6 147 C1
Bromley Comm BR2 209 D4
Buckhurst Hill IG9 21 D2
Chingford E4 20 C3
Chislehurst West BR7 188 C5
Dagenham RM10 81 D3
Ealing W5 87 B2
Edgware NW7 27 D5
Edmonton N9 17 D1
Feltham TW13 150 B3
Finsbury Pk N4 50 B1
Hendon NW4 46 D5
Kensington
W8 114 A3 256 A6
Kilburn NW6 91 B6
Kingston u T KT1 176 B1
Leyton E11 76 C4
Mitcham CR4 180 D3
Mortlake SW14 133 B2
Muswell Hill N22 31 D2
Newham E13 99 A5
North Acton NW10 89 C3
Ruislip HA4 62 B4
Sidcup DA15 168 A1
Southall UB2 107 B3
Surbiton KT6 197 D3
Sutton SM1 218 B3
Teddington TW11 175 A4
Tottenham Hale N15 52 A5
Twickenham TW1 153 B4
Walthamstow E17 36 A1
Wanstead E18 55 B6
Victoria Ret Pk HA4 62 D3
Victoria Rise SW4 137 B2
Victoria Sq SW1 258 D6
Victoria St
Erith DA17 125 B1
Stratford E15 76 C1
SW1 115 C3 259 B5
Victoria Sta
SW1 115 B2 258 D4
Victoria Terr
Dagenham NW10 89 C3
Finsbury Pk N4 50 C1
Harrow HA1 42 C1
Victoria (Underground)
SW1 115 B3 258 D5
Victoria Villas TW9 132 B1
Victoria Way SE7 143 C6
Victoria Wharf E14 119 A6
Victoria Yd 28 E1 96 A1
Victor Mills Cotts
BR8 191 C3
Victor Rd
College Pk NW10 90 B4
Harrow HA2 42 A6
Penge SE20 184 D3
Teddington TW11 174 C6
Victors Dr TW12 173 A4
Victor Seymour Inf Sch
SM5 218 D4
Victors Way EN5 1 B2
Victor Villas N9 17 B1
Victory Ave SM4 202 A4
Victory Bsns Ctr The
TW7 130 D1
Victory Cl TW19 148 A3
Victory Ct IG11 102 B4
Victory Pl
6 Limehouse E14 119 A6
SE17 117 B2 262 C4
West Norwood SE19 183 C4
Victory Rd
Merton SW19 180 A3
Wanstead E11 55 B5
Victory Road Mews 5
SW19 180 A3
Victory Sch
SE17 117 A2 262 B4
Victory Way
Hounslow TW5 106 C1
Rotherhithe SE16 119 A4
Victory Wlk SE8 141 C4
Video Ct N4 50 A2
Vidler Cl KT9 213 C2
Vienna Cl IG5 37 D1
View Cl
Harrow HA1 42 B5
Highgate N6 48 D2
View Cres N8 49 D4
Viewfield Cl HA3 44 A2
Viewfield Rd
DA5 168 C3
Wandsworth SW18 157 B5
Viewland Rd SE18 123 D1
Viewpoint
Ealing W5 110 B6
3 Islington N5 72 D3
Lewisham SE3 142 D2
View Point N20 14 A4
Viewpoint Ct 8 HA5 22 C1
View Rd N6 48 D3
Viewside Lo N6 49 C3
View The SE2 125 A1
Viga Rd N21 16 C5
Vigilant Cl SE26 184 A6
Vignoles Rd RM7 59 C2
Vigo St W1 115 C6 249 A5
Vi & John Rubens Ho
IG2 56 C3
Viking Cl 13 E3 97 A5
Viking Ct
Hampton TW12 173 D2
New Barnet EN4 14 B6
Viking Gdns E6 100 A3
Viking Ho
3 Camberwell SE5 139 A3
3 Woolwich SE7 122 A2
Viking Pl E10 53 B1
Viking Prim Sch UB5 84 D4
Viking Rd UB1 107 A6
Villacourt Rd SE18 146 A6
Village Arc The 2 E4 20 B3
Village Cl
Chingford E4 36 A5
Hampstead NW3 70 B3
Village Ct
Blackheath SE3 142 C2
Walthamstow E17 53 D4
Village Gate TW17 192 D4
Village Home The IG6 57 A6
Village Hts IG8 36 D5
Village Inf Sch RM10 81 C1
Village Mount 19 NW3 70 A4
Village Park Cl EN1 17 C5
Village Rd
Enfield EN1 17 C6
Hendon N3 29 A1
Village Row SM2 217 C1
Village Sch The NW3 70 D2
Village The
Battersea SW11 136 D2
SE7 143 D6
Village Way
Ashford TW15 170 C6
Beckenham BR3 207 C6
Dulwich Village SE21 161 B5
Ilford IG6 57 A6
Pinner HA5 41 B2
Willesden NW10 67 B4
Village Way E HA2 41 C2
Villa Rd SW9 138 C2
Villas On The Heath
NW3 70 A5
Villas Rd SE18 123 A2
Villa St SE17 117 B1 262 D1
Villiers Ave
Kingston u T KT5 198 B5
Twickenham TW2 151 B3
Villiers Cl
Kingston u T KT5 198 B5
Leyton E10 75 C6
Villiers Ct
Oakleigh Pk N20 14 A4
SW11 267 B2
Villiers High Sch UB1 107 B5
Villiers Ho W5 109 D6
Villiers Rd
Isleworth TW7 130 C3
Kingston u T KT1 198 B6
Penge BR3 184 D1
Southall UB1 107 B5
Willesden NW2 68 A2
Villiers St WC2 250 B4
Vincam Cl TW2 151 C4
Vince Ct N1 235 D1
Vincent Ave KT5 215 A6
Vincent Cl
Avery Hill DA15 167 C3
Barnet EN5 1 D2
Bromley BR2 209 B5
Harmondsworth UB7 126 C6
Vincent Ct
Finsbury Pk N4 50 A1
Hendon NW4 46 D5
Marylebone W1 237 C2
Ruislip HA4 62 B3
South Lambeth SW9 270 D1
Vincent Dr
Hillingdon UB10 82 B6
Upper Halliford TW17 193 C6
Vincent Gdns NW2 67 D5
Vincent Ho KT3 199 D5
Vincent Mews 1 E3 97 C5
Vincent Rd
Acton Green W3 111 A3
Chingford E4 36 B4
Croydon CR0 205 C2
Dagenham RM9 81 A1
Hounslow West TW4 128 D2
Kingston u T KT1 198 C6
Osterley TW7 130 B4
Tottenham N15 51 A5
Wembley HA0 66 B1
Wood Green N22 32 C1
Woolwich SE18 122 D2
Vincent Row TW12 174 A5
Vincents Cl SE16 119 A4
Vincents Path UB5 63 A2
Vincent Sq
SW1 115 D2 259 C4
Wood Green N22 32 C1
Vincent St
Canning Town E16 98 D2
Westminster
SW1 115 D2 259 D4
Vincent Terr
N1 94 D5 234 D4
Vince St EC1 95 B4 235 D1
Vine Cl
Surbiton KT5 198 B3
Sutton SM1 218 A5
West Drayton UB7 104 C2
Vine Cotts
3 Ealing W7 108 C5
Southall UB2 107 D2
Vine Ct
Harrow HA3 44 A3
Spitalfields E1 96 A2
Vinegar St E1 118 B5
Vinegar Yd SE1 253 A2
Vine Gdns IG1 79 A3
Vine Gr UB10 60 C1
Vine Hill EC1 241 A5
Vine La
Hillingdon UB10 82 B6
SE1 117 C5 253 B3
Uxbridge UB10 60 B1
Vine Lo N12 30 A4
Vine Pl
Ealing W5 110 A5
Hounslow TW3 129 D1
Vine Rd
Barnes SW13 133 D2
BR6 227 D2
East Molesey KT8 196 A5
Stratford E15 76 D1
Vineries Bank NW7 28 B5
Vineries Cl
Dagenham RM9 81 B2
Harmondsworth UB7 126 C6
Vineries The
Enfield EN1 5 C2
Southgate N14 15 C5
Viners Cl KT12 194 C3
Vine St Bridge EC1 241 B5
Vines Ave N3 29 D2
Vine Sq W14 254 D1
Vines Sch The SW11 137 A1
Vine St
W1 249 B5
Whitechapel
EC3 95 D1 243 C1
Vinewood Ct E17 54 B4
Vineyard Ave NW7 29 A3
Vineyard Cl
Forest Hill SE6 163 C3
Kingston u T KT1 198 B6
Vineyard Gr N3 29 D2
Vineyard Hill Rd
SW19 179 C6
Vineyard Path SW14 133 B2
Vineyard Rd TW13 150 A1
Vineyard Row KT1,
KT8 175 C2
Vineyard Sch The
TW10 154 A5
Vineyards The TW13 150 A1
Vineyard Studios 3
E7 77 C1
Vineyard The TW10 154 A6
Vineyard Wlk EC1 241 A6
Viney Ct 9 SW4 159 D5
Vine Yd SE1 252 B2
Viney Rd SE13 141 D2
Vining St SW2, SW9 138 C1
Vinlake Ave UB10 60 C5
Vinson Ho N1 235 D3
Vinter Ct TW17 192 C4
Vintners Ct EC4 252 B6
Vintry Mews 3 E17 53 C5
Viola Ave
Feltham TW14 150 C5
SE2 124 B1
Stanwell TW19 148 A3
Viola Ct HA8 26 D3
Viola Sq W12 111 D6
Violet Ave
Enfield EN2 5 B5
Hillingdon UB8 82 B2
Violet Cl
Cheam SM3 201 A1
Hackbridge SM6 203 A1
Newham E16 98 C3
32 SE8 141 B6
Violet Ct 2 E15 76 C1
Violet Gdns CR0 220 D3
Violet Hill NW8 92 A5 229 A3
Violet Hill Ho NW8 229 A3
Violet La CR0 220 D3
Violet Rd
Bromley E3 97 D3
Walthamstow E17 53 C3
Woodford E18 37 B1
Violet St E2 96 B3
Violet Terr UB8 82 C2
Violette Szabo Ho 4
SE27 183 B6
VIP Trad Est SE7 121 C2
Virgil Pl W1 237 C3
Virgil St SE1 116 B3 260 D6
Virginia Cl KT3 199 A5
Virginia Ct
Ashford TW15 170 A6
7 Rotherhithe SE16 118 D4
Virginia Ho
3 Blackwall E14 120 A6
Teddington TW11 175 A5
Virginia Prim Sch E2 95 D4
Virginia Rd
South Norwood CR7 182 D2
19 Spitalfields E2 95 D4
Virginia St E1 118 A6
Virginia Wlk SW2 160 B5
Viridian Ct TW13 149 D1
Viscount Cl N11 31 B5

Viscount Ct
9 Kensington W11 91 C1
1 Littleton TW15 171 A3
Viscount Dr E6 100 B2
Viscount Gr 3 UB5 84 D4
Viscount Point 6
SW19 179 C3
Viscount Rd TW19 148 A3
Viscount St EC1 242 A4
Viscount Way TW6 127 C1
Vista Ave EN3 6 D3
Vista Bldgs 19 E3 97 B4
Vista Bldg The 14
SE18 122 C2
Vista Dr IG4 55 D4
Vista Ho 2 SW19 180 B2
Vista Hts SE23 163 A4
Vista The
Chingford E4 20 B4
SE9 165 D4
Sidcup DA14 189 D5
Vista Way HA3 44 A3
Vitae Apartments 7
W6 112 A3
Vita Et Pax Sch N14 15 B6
Vittoria Ho N1 233 D5
Vittoria Prim Sch
N1 94 C5 234 A4
Viveash Cl UB3 105 D3
Vivian Ave
Hendon NW4 46 B4
Wembley HA9 66 C2
Vivian Comma Cl 3
N4 72 D5
Vivian Ct
Finchley N12 29 D5
Paddington NW6 91 D5
Vivian Gdns HA9 66 C3
Vivian Ho N4 51 B2
Vivian Mans 1 NW4 46 B4
Vivian Rd E3 97 A5
Vivian Sq SE15 140 B2
Vivian Way N2 48 B4
Vivien Cl KT9 214 A1
Vivienne Cl TW1 153 D5
Voce Rd SE18 145 B5
Voewood Cl KT3 199 D3
Vogans Mill SE1 253 D2
Vogler Ho 3 E1 118 C6
Vogue Ct 8 BR1 187 B2
Vollasky Ho 5 E1 96 A2
Volta Cl N9 18 C1
Voltaire
2 Camberwell SE5 139 D4
15 Richmond TW9 132 B4
Voltaire Ct 13 SW11 137 A3
Voltaire Rd SW4 137 D2
Voltaire Way UB3 105 C6
Volt Ave NW10 89 C4
Volta Way CR0 204 B1
Voluntary Pl E11 55 A3
Vora Ho HA0 65 D2
Vorley Rd N19 71 C6
Voss Ct SW16 182 A4
Voss St E2 96 A4
Voyager Bsns Est 10
SE16 118 A3
Voyagers Cl IG11 102 C1
Voysey Cl N3 47 A6
Vulcan Cl E6 100 C1
Vulcan Gate EN2 4 C3
Vulcan Rd SE4 141 B3
Vulcan Sq E14 119 C2
Vulcan Terr SE4 141 B3
Vulcan Way N7 72 B2
Vyne Ho SM5 218 D2
Vyner Ct E5 74 A6
Vyner Rd W3 111 B6
Vyners Sch UB10 60 B4
Vyner St E2 96 B6
Vyners Way UB10 60 C3
Vyne The DA7 147 D2
Vyvyan Ho SE18 144 C4

W

Wadbrook St KT1 175 D1
Wadcroft Ct SE4 141 B2
Waddesdon Lo HA3 43 A3
Wadding St
SE17 117 B2 262 C3
Waddington Cl EN1 5 C1
Waddington Rd E15 76 B2
Waddington St E15 76 B2
Waddington Way
SE19 183 B2
WADDON 220 C4
Waddon Cl CR0 220 C5
Waddon Court Rd
CR0 220 C5
Waddon Inf Sch CR9 220 C3
Waddon Marsh Sta
CR0 220 C6
Waddon Marsh Way
CR0 204 B1
Waddon New Rd CR0 220 D6
Waddon Park Ave
CR0 220 C5
Waddon Rd CR0 220 D5
Waddon Sta CR0 220 C4
Waddon Way CR0, CR2,
CR9 220 D2
Wade Ct
Muswell Hill N10 31 B3
Wembley HA0 65 D5
Wade Ho
16 Bermondsey SE1 118 A4
1 Enfield EN1 17 C6
Wade's Gr N21 16 C4
Wade's Hill N21 16 C4
Wade's La TW11 175 A5
Wadeson St E2 96 B5
Wade's Pl E14 119 D6
Wadeville Ave RM6 59 B2
Wadeville Cl DA17 125 C1
Wadham Ave E17 35 D3
Wadham Cl TW17 193 A2
Wadham Gdns
Greenford UB6 64 B2
Primrose Hill
NW3 92 C6 230 A6
Wadham Ho N18 33 D5
Wadham Rd
Highams Pk E17 35 D2
Putney SW15 135 A1
Wadhurst Cl SE20 184 B1
Wadhurst Ct E6 100 C5
Wadhurst Rd W4 111 B3
Wadley Rd E11 54 C2
Wadsworth Bsns Ctr
UB6 87 C5
Wadsworth Cl
Enfield EN3 18 D6
Wembley UB6 87 C5
Wadsworth Ct E10 54 A3
Wadsworth Rd UB6 87 C5
Wager St E3 97 B3
Waggoners Rdbt
TW5 128 B4
Waggon Mews N14 15 C3
Waggon Rd EN4 2 B6
Waghorn Rd
Harrow HA3 43 D6
Newham E13 99 C6
Waghorn St SE15 140 A2
Wagner St SE15 140 C5
Wagon Rd EN4, EN5 1 D6
Wagstaff Gdns RM9 80 C1
Wagtail Cl NW9 27 C1
Wagtail Wlk BR3 208 A4
Waights Ct KT2 176 A2
Waikato Lo IG9 21 C3
Wainford Cl SW19 156 D3
Wainwright Gr TW7 130 B1
Wainwright Ho 3 E1 118 C5
Waite Davies Rd
SE12 164 D4
Waitelands Ho KT3 199 B5
Waite St SE15 139 D6
Waithman St EC4 241 C1
Wakefield Ct 4 SE26 184 C4
Wakefield Gdns
Redbridge IG1 56 A3
South Norwood SE19 183 C3
Wakefield Ho
Dulwich SE22 162 B3
6 Peckham SE15 140 A4
Wakefield Mews WC1 233 B1
Wakefield Rd
Friern Barnet N11 31 D5
20 Richmond TW10 153 D6
South Tottenham N15 51 D4
Wakefield St
Edmonton N18 34 A5
Newham E6 100 A6
St Pancras WC1 94 A4 233 B1
Wakeford Cl SW4 159 C6
Wakehams Hill HA5 41 B6
Wakeham St 9 N1 73 B2
Wakehurst Rd SW11 158 D6
Wakeling Ct E7 77 C2
Wakeling Ho 8 SE27 160 D1
Wakeling La HA0 65 B5
Wakeling Rd W7 86 D2
Wakeling St 11 E14 97 A1
Wakelin Ho
Forest Hill SE23 163 A4
19 Islington N1 72 D1
Wakelin Rd E15 98 C5
Wakeman Ho HA8 26 A6
Wakeman Rd NW10 90 D4
Wakemans Hill Ave
NW9 45 B4
Wakering Rd IG11 79 A1
Wakerley Cl 6 E6 100 B1
Wakley St EC1 94 D4 234 C2
Walberswick St SW8 270 B3
Walbrook
EC4 252 C6
10 Wanstead E18 55 A6
Walbrook Ct 32 N1 95 C5
Walbrook Ho N9 18 C2
Walbrook Wharf EC4 252 C6
Walburgh St E1 96 B1
Walcorde Ave SE17 262 B3
Walcot Ct CR0 222 A6
Walcot Gdns SE11 261 A4
Walcot Ho 9 SE22 139 C2
Walcot Rd EN3 7 B3
Walcot Sq
SE11 116 C2 261 B4
Walcott St SW1 259 B4
Waldair Ct E16 122 D4
Waldeck Gr SE27 160 D1
Waldeck Rd
Brentford W4 132 C6
Ealing W13 87 B1
Mortlake SW14 133 A2
Tottenham N15 50 D6
Waldeck Terr SW14 133 A2
Waldegrave Ct
11 Barking IG11 101 B6
1 Teddington TW11 174 D5
Waldegrave Gdns
TW1 152 D1
Waldegrave Ho 5
SW15 156 C6
Waldegrave Pk TW1 174 D6
Waldegrave Rd
BR1 210 B5
Dagenham RM8 80 C6
Ealing W5 110 B6
Hornsey N8 50 C6
Penge SE19 183 D3
Teddington TW11 174 D6
Waldegrave Sch TW2 152 B1
Waldegrove CR0 221 D5
Waldemar Ave
Ealing W13 109 C5
Fulham SW6 135 A3
Waldemar Avenue Mans
SW6 264 A1
Waldemar Rd SW19 179 C5
Walden Ave
BR7 188 B6
Edmonton N13 33 A6
Walden Cl DA17 125 B1
Walden Ct SW8 269 D2
Walden Gdns CR7,
SW16 204 B5
Walden Ho
Barnet EN4 2 C1
8 Clapham SW11 137 A3
SW1 258 B3
Walden Rd
BR7 188 B4
Tottenham N17 33 B2
Waldenshaw Rd SE23 162 C3
Walden St E1 96 B1
Walden Way NW7 28 D4
Waldo Cl SW4 159 C6
Waldo Ind Est BR1 209 D6
Waldo Pl SW19 180 C3
Waldo Rd
BR1 209 D6
College Pk NW10 90 B4
Waldorf Cl CR2 220 D1
Waldram Cres SE23 162 C3
Waldram Park Rd
SE23 162 D3
Waldram Pl 6 SE23 162 C3
Waldrist Way DA18 125 B4
Waldron Gdns BR2 208 B6
Waldron Ho 17 SW2 160 B6
Waldronhyrst CR0,
CR2 220 D4
Waldron Mews SW3 266 D6
Waldron Rd
Harrow HA1, HA2 42 C1
Wandsworth SW18 158 A1
Waldrons The CR0 221 A4
Waldron's Yd HA2 64 B6
Waldstock Rd SE28 124 A6
Waleran Cl HA7 24 D4
Walerand Rd SE13 142 A3
Waleran Flats SE1 263 A4
Wales Ave SM5 218 C3
Wales Cl SE15 140 B6
Wales Farm Rd W3 89 B2
Waleton Acres SM6 219 C2
Waley St 1 E1 97 A2
Walfield Ave N20 13 D4
Walfield Ho N20 14 A4
Walford Ho 28 E1 96 B1
Walford Rd N16 73 C4
Walfrey Gdns RM9 81 A1
Walham Ct 15 NW3 70 D2
Walham Gr
SW6 135 C5 265 A4
WALHAM GREEN 135 D5
Walham Green Arc
SW6 265 B4
Walham Rise 1
SW19 179 A4
Walham Yd SW6 265 A4
Walkden Rd BR7 188 C5
Walker Cl
Ealing W7 108 C5
East Bedfont TW14 149 D4
Friern Barnet N11 31 C6
Hampton TW12 173 B4
Plumstead SE18 123 A2
Walker Ho NW1 232 C3
Walker Mews 9
SW2 160 C6
Walker Prim Sch N14 15 D2
Walkerscroft Mead
SE21 161 A3
Walker's Ct W1 249 C6
Walkers Lo 18 E14 120 A4
Walker's Pl SW15 135 A1
Walkinshaw Ct 9 N1 73 A1
Walks The N2 48 B6
Walk The
Ashford TW16 171 D3
Palmers Green N13 16 C1
Walkynscroft 1 SE15 140 B3
Wallace Cl
SE28 124 D6
Upper Halliford TW17 193 B5
Uxbridge UB10 82 A5
Wallace Collection*
W1 238 A2
Wallace Cres SM5 218 D3
Wallace Ct
19 Enfield EN3 7 C6
NW1 237 B3
Wallace Ho N7 72 B2
Wallace Lo N4 50 C1
Wallace Rd N1, N5 73 A2
Wallasey Cres UB10 60 C5
Wallbrook Bsns Ctr
TW4 128 B2
Wallbutton Rd SE4 141 A3
Wallcote Ave NW2 46 D1
Wall Ct N4 50 B1
Walled Garden Cl
BR3 207 D5
Walled Gdn The*
TW16 194 B6
WALLEND 100 C6
Wall End Ct E6 100 C6
Wall End Rd E6 78 C1
Waller Dr HA6 22 A2
Waller Rd SE14 140 D3
Wallers Cl RM9 103 B6
Wallett Ct 11 NW1 71 C1
Wallflower St W12 111 D6
Wallgrave Rd SW5 255 C3
Wallingford Ave W10 90 D1
WALLINGTON 219 A2
Wallington Cl HA4 39 A3
Wallington Ct 10
SM6 219 B2
Wallington Cty Gram Sch
SM6 219 B5
Wallington Green
SM6 219 B4
Wallington Rd IG3 57 D2
Wallington Sq 4
SM6 219 C2
Wallington Sta SM6 219 B2
Wallis Alley SE1 252 B2
Wallis Cl SW11 136 B2
Wallis Ho
5 New Cross Gate
SE14 141 A4
Ruislip HA4 39 A1
Ruislip HA4 39 B1
Wallis Rd
Hackney Wick E9 75 C2
Southall UB1 85 D1
Wallorton Gdns
SW14 133 B1
Wallside EC2 242 B3
Wall St N1 73 B2
Wallwood Rd E11 54 B2
Wallwood St E14 97 B2
Walmar Cl EN4 2 B4
Walmer Cl
BR6 227 B4
Chingford E4 19 D2
Walmer Gdns W13 109 A4
Walmer Ho
8 North Kensington
W10 90 D1
8 Penge SE20 184 C3
Walmer Pl W1 237 C4
Walmer Rd
North Kensington W10 90 C1
W11 113 A6 244 A5
Walmer Terr SE18 123 B2
Walmgate Rd UB6 87 B6
Walmington Fold N12 29 C4
Walm La NW2 68 C2
Walmsley Ho 1
SW16 181 C6
Walney Wlk 6 N1 73 A2
Walnut Ave UB7 104 C3
Walnut Cl
Hayes UB3 105 C6
Ilford IG6 57 A5
SE8 141 B6
Wallington SM5 218 D3
Walnut Ct 2 E17 54 A5
Walnut Gdns E15 76 C3
Walnut Gr EN1 17 B6
Walnut Ho 11 E3 97 B6
Walnut Mews SM2 218 A1
Walnut Rd E10 75 D6
Walnut Tree Ave CR4 202 C6
Walnut Tree Cl
Barnes SW13 133 D4
Chislehurst BR7 189 A2
Walnut Tree Cotts
SW19 179 A5
Walnut Tree Ho SW10 265 D6
Walnut Tree Rd
Brentford TW8 132 A6
Charlton TW17 171 A1
Dagenham RM8 81 A6
Greenwich SE10 120 C1
Heston TW5 129 B6
Walnut Tree Walk Prim
Sch SE11 116 C2 261 A4
Walnut Tree Wlk
SE11 116 C2 261 A4
Walnut Way
Buckhurst Hill IG9 21 D1
Ruislip HA4 62 C2
Walpole Ave TW9 132 B3
Walpole Cl
Pinner HA5 23 C4
West Ealing W13 109 C4
Walpole Cres 10
TW11 174 D5
Walpole Ct
Ealing W5 109 D5
7 Hammersmith W14 112 D3
South Hampstead NW6 70 A1
Twickenham TW2 152 C2
2 Wallington SM6 219 B3
Walpole Gdns
Acton Green W4 111 A1
Twickenham TW2 152 C1
Walpole Ho
Chislehurst BR7 189 B2
East Molesey KT8 195 C4
Walpole Lo W13 109 C5
Walpole Mews NW8 229 C5
Walpole Pl
9 Teddington TW11 174 D5
3 Woolwich SE18 122 D2
Walpole Rd
BR2 209 D4
Mitcham SW19 180 B4
South Croydon CR0 221 B6
Surbiton KT6 198 A3
Teddington TW11 174 D5
Tottenham N17 33 A1
Tottenham N17 51 A6
Twickenham TW2 152 C2
Upton E6 77 C1
Walthamstow E17 53 A5
Woodford E18 36 D2
Walpole St
SW3 114 D1 257 D2
Walrond Ave HA9 66 A3
Walsham Cl
SE28 124 D6
Upper Clapton N16 52 A1
Walsham Ho
New Cross Gate
SE14 140 D3
SE17 262 C2
Walsham Rd
Feltham TW14 150 B4
New Cross Gate SE14 140 D3
Walsh Lodge HA4 40 B3
Walsingham NW8 229 D6
Walsingham Gdns
KT19 215 D3
Walsingham Ho
Chingford E4 20 B4
Twickenham TW2 152 B2
Walsingham Lo
SW13 134 A4
Walsingham Mans
SW6 265 D4
Walsingham Pk BR7 189 B1
Walsingham Pl SW4,
SW11 159 A5
Walsingham Rd
BR5 190 B2
Ealing W13 109 A5
Enfield EN2 17 B6
Mitcham CR4 202 D4
Shacklewell E5 74 A5
Walsingham Wlk
DA17 147 C6
Walter Besant Ho 20
E1 96 D4
Walter Ct 3 W3 89 A1
Walter Green Ho
SE15 140 C4
Walter Ho SW10 266 C4
Walter Hurford Par 5
E12 78 C4
Walter Northcott Ho 2
NW6 69 C3
Walter Rodney Cl E12 78 B2
Walter Savill Twr E17 53 C3
Walters Cl
Hayes UB3 105 D4
SE17 262 B3
Walters Ho
3 Camberwell SE5 139 C3
Islington N1 234 D6
10 Kennington SE17 138 D6
Walter Sickert Hall
N1 235 A3
Walters Rd EN3 6 C1
Walter's Rd SE25 205 C5
Walter St
Globe Town E2 96 D4
2 Kingston u T KT2 176 A2
Walters Way SE23 162 D5
Walters Yd BR1 187 A1
Walter Taylor Ct SE4 141 B1
Walter Terr E1 96 D1
Walterton Rd W9 91 C3
Walter Wlk HA8 27 A4
Waltham Ave
Hayes UB3 105 B3
Preston NW9 44 C3
Waltham Ct
Chingford E17 36 A2
Whetstone N20 14 B1
Waltham Dr HA8 44 C6
Waltham Forest Coll
E17 35 D1
Waltham Gdns EN3 6 C6
Waltham Green Ct
SW6 265 C3
Waltham Ho
NW8 229 A6
10 Stockwell SW9 138 B3
Waltham Park Way
E17 35 C3
Waltham Pk E17 35 C2
Waltham Rd
Carshalton SM5 202 C1
Southall UB2 107 A3
WALTHAMSTOW 53 D6
Walthamstow Acad
E17 35 B2
Walthamstow Ave E4 35 C3
Walthamstow Ave (North
Circular Rd) E4 35 B4
Walthamstow Bsns Ctr
E17 36 A1
Walthamstow Central Sta
E17 53 C4
Walthamstow Mkt E17 53 C5
Walthamstow Queens
Road Sta E17 53 C4
Walthamstow Sch for
Girls E17 53 D5
Waltham Way E4 19 C2
Waltheof Ave N17 33 B2
Waltheof Gdns N17 33 B2
Walton Ave
Cheam SM3 217 B5
Harrow HA2 63 B4
New Malden KT3 199 D5

Walton Ave *continued*
Wembley HA9 66 D5
Walton Bridge Rd KT12, TW17 193 C2
Walton Cl
Dollis Hill NW2 68 B6
Harrow HA1 42 B5
Lea Bridge E5 74 D5
SW8 138 A5 270 B4
Walton Croft HA1 64 C4
Walton Ct EN5 14 A6
Walton Dr
Harrow HA1 42 B5
Willesden NW10 67 B2
Walton Gdns
Acton W3 88 D2
Feltham TW13 171 D6
Wembley HA9 66 A6
Walton Gn CR0 224 A1
Walton Ho
E2 243 D6
Ealing W5 109 D2
1 Edmonton N9 34 A6
1 Kingston u T KT2 176 A3
Upper Holloway N7 72 B5
10 Walthamstow E17 53 D6
Wandsworth SW18 157 C5
Walton La
Oatlands Pk KT13, TW17 193 B1
Shepperton TW17 193 B2
Walton Oak Prim Sch KT12 194 C1
WALTON-ON-THAMES 194 C2
Walton Pl SW3 257 C6
Walton Rd
East Molesey KT8, KT12 195 C5
Harrow HA1 42 B5
Little Ilford E12 78 C4
Newham E13 99 C5
Sidcup DA14 168 C1
Tottenham N15 51 D5
Walton-on-T KT12&KT8 194 D4
Walton St
Enfield EN2 5 B4
SW3 114 C3 257 B5
Walton Way
Acton W3 88 D2
Mitcham CR4 203 C5
Walt Whitman Cl 6 SE24 138 D1
WALWORTH 117 B1
Walworth Pl SE17 117 A1 262 B1
Walworth Rd SE17 117 A1 262 B2
Walworth Sch SE17 117 C1 263 B1
Walwyn Ave BR1 209 D6
Wanborough Dr SW15 156 B3
Wanderer Dr IG11 102 C4
Wandle Bank
Mitcham SW19 180 B3
Wallington CR0 220 A5
Wandle Court Gdns CR0 220 A5
Wandle Ct
4 Bedford Pk W12 111 C4
Wallington CR0 220 A5
West Ewell KT19 215 A4
Wandle Ho
6 Catford BR1 186 B5
NW8 237 A4
Wandsworth SW18 157 D4
Wandle Lo CR0 220 A5
Wandle Lodge SM6 219 B6
Wandle Pk Sta CR0 220 C6
Wandle Rd
Croydon CR0 221 A5
Hackbridge SM6 219 B6
Morden SM4 202 B4
Upper Tooting SW17 158 C2
Wallington CR0 220 A5
Wandle Side
Hackbridge SM6 219 B5
Wallington CR0 220 B5
Wandle Tech Pk CR4 202 D2
Wandle Trad Est CR4 202 D2
Wandle Valley Sch SM5 202 C2
Wandle Way
Mitcham CR4 202 D4
Wandsworth SW18 157 D3
Wandon Rd SW6 135 D5 265 D3
WANDSWORTH 157 C5
Wandsworth Bridge Rd SW6 135 D4 265 C1
Wandsworth Common Sta SW12 158 D4
Wandsworth Common West Side SW18 158 A6
Wandsworth Gyratory SW18 157 D6
Wandsworth High St SW18 157 D6
Wandsworth Mus* SW18 157 D6
Wandsworth Plain SW18 157 D6
Wandsworth Rd SW8 138 A5 270 A3
Wandsworth Road Sta SW4 137 C3
Wandsworth Town Sta SW18 135 D1
Wangey Rd RM6 58 D2
Wangford Ho 13 SW9 138 D1
Wanless Rd SE24 139 A2
Wanley Rd SE5 139 B1
Wanlip Rd E13 99 B3
Wansbeck Ct EN2 4 D2
Wansbeck Rd E3, E9 75 B1
Wansdown Pl SW6 135 D5 265 C4
Wansey St SE17 117 A2 262 B3
Wansford Rd IG8 37 C2
WANSTEAD 55 C3
Wanstead Church Sch E11 55 A4
Wanstead Cl BR1 187 C1
Wanstead High Sch E11 55 C3
Wanstead Hospl E11 55 B5
Wanstead Hts 8 E11 55 A4
Wanstead La IG1 56 A3
Wanstead Park Ave E12 77 D6
Wanstead Park Rd IG1 56 A1
Wanstead Park Sta E7 77 B4
Wanstead Pl E11 55 A4
Wanstead Rd BR1 187 C1
Wanstead Sta E11 55 B3
Wantage Rd SE12 164 D6
Wantz Rd RM10 81 D3
WAPPING 118 B5
Wapping Dock St 19 E1 118 B5
Wapping High St E1 118 B5
Wapping La E1 118 B5
Wapping Sta E1 118 C5
Wapping Wall E1 118 C5
Warbank La KT2 177 D3
Warbeck Rd W12 112 B4
Warberry Rd N22 32 B1
Warboys App KT2 176 D4
Warboys Cres E4 36 A5
Warboys Rd KT2 176 D4
Warburg Ho E2 96 A4
Warburton Cl
6 Kingsland N1 73 C2
Stanmore HA3 24 B4
Warburton Ct
Peckham SE15 140 A2
Ruislip HA4 62 A6
Warburton Ho 5 E8 96 B6
Warburton Rd
8 Hackney E8 96 B6
Twickenham TW2 151 D3
Warburton St 6 E8 96 B6
Warburton Terr E17 35 D1
Wardalls Ho 12 SE8 141 B6
Ward Cl CR2 221 C3
Wardell Cl NW7 27 C3
Wardell Ct N2 48 B6
Wardell Ho 7 SE10 142 A6
Warden Ave HA2 41 B1
Warden Rd NW5 71 A2
Wardens Field Cl 2 BR6 227 D2
Wardens Gr SE1 252 A3
Wardle St E9 74 D3
Wardley Lo E11 54 D3
Wardley St SW18 157 D4
Wardlow 8 NW5 71 B4
Wardo Ave SW6 135 A4 264 A2
Wardour Mews W1 239 B1
Wardour St W1 93 D1 239 C1
Ward Point SE11 261 A3
Ward Rd
Camden Town N19 71 C5
Mill Meads E15 98 B6
Wardrew Ct 9 EN5 14 A6
Wardrobe Pl EC4 241 D1
Wardrobe Terr EC4 251 D6
Wardrobe The 3 TW9 153 D6
Wards Cotts TW19 148 B4
Wards Rd IG2 57 B2
Wards Wharf App E16 121 D4
Ware Ct
Cheam SM1 217 B4
Edgware HA8 26 A6
Wareham Cl TW3 129 D1
Wareham Ct 2 N1 73 C1
Wareham Ho SW8 270 C4
Warehouse W E16 121 B6
Waremead Rd IG2 56 D4
Ware Point Dr SE28 123 B4
Warfield Rd
East Bedfont TW14 149 C4
Hampton TW12 173 D2
Kensal Green NW10 90 D4
Warfield Yd 6 NW10 90 D4
Wargrave Ave N15 51 D3
Wargrave Ho 46 E2 95 D4
Wargrave Rd HA2 64 A5
Warham Rd
Croydon CR2 221 A3
Harringay N4 50 D4
Harrow HA3 24 D1
Warham St SE5 138 D5
Waring Cl BR6 227 D2
Waring Dr BR6 227 D2
Waring Ho 25 E2 96 A4
Waring Rd DA14 190 C4
Waring St SE27 183 A6
Warkworth Gdns TW7 131 A5
Warkworth Rd N17 33 B3
Warland Rd SE18 145 C5
Warley Ave
Dagenham RM8 59 B2
Hayes UB4 84 A1
Warley Cl E10 53 B1
Warley Ho N1 73 B2
Warley Rd
Hayes UB4 84 A2
Lower Edmonton N9 18 C2
Woodford IG8 37 B3
Warley St E2 96 D4
Warlingham Rd CR7 204 D5
Warlock Rd W9 91 C3
Warlow Cl 6 EN3 7 C6
Warlters Cl N7 72 A4
Warlters Rd N7 72 A4
Warltersville Mans N19 50 A2
Warltersville Rd N4, N8, N19 50 A2
War Meml Homes W4 133 B5
Warming Cl E5 74 D5
Warmington Rd SE24 161 A5
Warmington St 3 E13 99 A3
Warminster Gdns SE25 184 A1
Warminster Rd SE25 184 A1
Warminster Sq SE25 184 A1
Warminster Way CR4 181 B1
Warmsworth NW1 232 A6
Warmwell Ave NW9 27 C2
Warndon St SE16 118 C2
Warneford Rd HA3 44 A6
Warneford St E9 96 B6
Warne Pl 4 DA15 168 B5
Warner Ave SM3 217 A6
Warner Cl
Hampton TW12 173 B5
Harlington UB3 127 B5
Hendon NW9 46 A2
Stratford E15 76 C3
Warner Ct SM3 217 A6
Warner Ho
1 Beckenham BR3 185 D4
Harrow HA1 42 B2
4 Homerton E9 74 D2
Lewisham SE13 141 D3
NW8 229 A2
Warner Pl E2 96 A4
Warner Rd
Bromley BR1 186 D3
Camberwell SE5 139 A4
Hornsey N8 49 D5
Walthamstow E17 53 A5
Warners Cl IG8 37 A5
Warner St EC1 94 C3 241 A5
Warner Yd EC1 241 A5
Warnford Ho SW15 155 C5
Warnford Ind Est UB3 105 C4
Warnford Rd BR6 227 D3
Warnham WC1 233 C1
Warnham Court Rd SM5 218 D1
Warnham Ho 6 SW2 160 B4
Warnham Rd N12 30 C5
Warple Mews W3 111 C4
Warple Way W3, W12 111 C4
Warren Ave
Bromley BR1 186 C3
Leyton E11 76 B5
Mortlake SW14, TW10 132 D1
Orpington BR6 227 D3
South Croydon CR2 222 D1
Warren Cl
DA6 169 C6
Esher KT10 212 A4
Hayes UB4 84 C2
Ponders End N9 18 D4
Wembley HA9 65 D6
West Norwood SE21 161 A4
Warren Comp Sch The RM6 59 B4
Warren Cres N9 17 D4
Warren Ct
17 Beckenham BR3 185 C3
5 Croydon CR0 205 C1
6 Ealing W5 87 C2
Greenwich SE7 143 C6
N1 234 A4
Tottenham Hale N17 52 A6
Warren Cutting KT2 177 B3
Warrender Prim Sch HA4 39 D2
Warrender Rd N19 71 C4
Warrender Way HA4 40 A2
Warren Dr
Greenford UB6 86 A3
Ruislip HA4 40 D2
Warren Dr N KT5, KT6 198 D1
Warren Dr S KT5 199 A1
Warren Dr The E11 55 C2
Warren Farm Cotts RM6 59 B5
Warren Fields HA7 25 C6
Warren Gdns E15 76 B3
Warren Hill IG10 21 C6
Warren Ho 21 E3 97 D4
Warren Jun Sch RM6 59 B4
Warren La
Stanmore HA7 9 A2
Woolwich SE18 122 D3
Warren Mews W1 239 A5
Warren Park Rd SM1 218 C2
Warren Pk KT2 177 A4
Warren Pond Rd E4 20 D4
Warren Rd
Ashford TW15 171 C3
Bexleyheath DA6 169 C6
Bushey WD23 8 B3
Chingford E4 20 A2
Croydon CR0 205 D1
Hayes BR2 225 A6
Ickenham UB10 60 B4
Ilford IG6 57 B4
Isleworth TW2 152 B5
Kingston u T KT2 177 A4
Leyton E10 76 A5
Mitcham SW19 180 C4
Sidcup DA14 168 C1
Wanstead E11 55 C2
Willesden NW2 67 D6
Warren Rise KT3 177 B2
Warren Road Prim Sch BR6 227 D4
Warrens Shawe La HA8 10 D2
Warren St W1 93 C3 239 A5
Warren Street Sta NW1 93 C3 239 B6
Warren Terr RM6 58 D5
Warren The
Hayes UB4 84 A1
Heston TW5 129 B5
Manor Pk E12 78 A4
Worcester Pk KT19 215 B5
Warren Way
Edgware HA8 26 D1
Finchley NW7 29 A4
Warren Wlk 1 SE7 143 C6
Warren Wood Cl BR2 225 A6
Warriner Dr N9 18 A1
Warriner Gdns SW11 137 A4 268 A1
Warrington Cres W9 92 A3 236 A6
Warrington Ct
4 Croydon CR0 220 D5
13 Merton SW19 179 C3
Warrington Gdns W9 236 A5
Warrington Rd
Croydon CR0 220 D5
Dagenham RM8 81 A6
Harrow HA1 42 C4
22 Richmond TW10 153 D6
Warrington Sq RM8 80 D6
Warrior Cl SE28 123 C5
Warrior Sq E12 78 C4
Warsaw Cl HA4 62 B2
Warspite Ho 3 E14 119 D2
Warspite Rd SE18 122 A3
Warton Rd E15 98 A6
Warwall E6 100 D1
Warwick W14 113 B2 254 D3
Warwick Ave
Edgware HA8 11 A1
Harrow HA2 63 B4
Paddington W9 92 A3 236 A5
Warwick Avenue Sta W9 92 A3 236 A5
Warwick Bldg SW8 268 C5
Warwick Chambers W8 255 A6
Warwick Cl
Bushey WD23 8 C4
DA5 169 B4
Hampton TW12 174 A3
New Barnet EN4 14 B6
Warwick Cres
Hayes UB4 83 D3
Little Venice W2 92 A2 236 A4
Warwick Ct
1 Beckenham BR2 186 C1
Ealing W7 86 D1
5 East Finchley N2 48 A6
Friern Barnet N11 31 D4
Harrow HA1 42 C6
Merton SW19 179 B2
13 New Barnet EN5 13 D6
Northolt UB5 63 C3
Surbiton KT6 214 A6
3 Upper Clapton E5 74 B6
WC1 240 D3
2 Woodford E18 36 D1
Warwick Dene W5 110 A5
Warwick Dr SW15 134 B2
Warwick Gdns
Harringay N4 51 A4
Ilford IG1 56 D1
Thames Ditton KT7 196 D4
Thornton Heath CR7 204 C5
W14 113 B2 254 D4
Warwick Gr
Surbiton KT5 198 B2
Upper Clapton E5 52 B1
Warwick Ho
9 Acton W3 88 C1
10 Brixton SW9 138 C3
6 Kingston u T KT2 176 A2
6 Putney SW15 156 C4
Stoke Newington N4 51 A1
5 Wimbledon SW19 179 A3
Warwick House St SW1 249 D4
Warwick La EC4 94 D1 241 D1
Warwick Lo
Brondesbury NW2 69 A3
Cheam SM1 217 B4
Twickenham TW2 151 D1
Warwick Mans SW5 255 A4
Warwick Par HA7 25 B1
Warwick Pas EC4 241 D2
Warwick Pl
Ealing W5 109 D4
Little Venice W9 92 A2 236 A4
Warwick Pl N SW1 259 A3
Warwick Rd
Ashford TW15 170 A5
Barnet EN5 1 D1
Bexley DA16 146 C2
Chingford E4 35 C5
Ealing W5 110 A5
Edmonton N18 33 D6
Enfield EN3 7 B6
Friern Barnet N11 31 D4
Hounslow TW4 128 B2
Kingston u T KT3 199 A6
Penge SE20 206 B6
Plashet E12 78 A3
Sidcup DA14 190 B5
Southall UB2 107 B3
Stratford E15 76 D2
Sutton SM1 218 A3
Teddington KT1 175 C2
Thames Ditton KT7 196 D4
Thornton Heath CR7 204 C6
Twickenham TW2 152 C3
Walthamstow E17 35 B1
Wanstead E11 55 B4
Warwick Rd *continued*
West Kensington W14, SW5 113 B2 254 D4
Yiewsley UB7 104 A5
Warwick Row SW1 115 B3 258 D6
Warwick Sch for Boys E17 54 A5
Warwickshire Path SE8 141 B5
Warwick Sq
Holborn EC4 241 D2
Pimlico SW1 115 C1 259 A2
Warwick Sq Mews SW1 259 A3
Warwick St W1 115 C6 249 B6
Warwick Terr
Leytonstone E17 54 B4
SE18 145 B6
Warwick Way SW1 115 B2 258 D4
Warwick Yd EC1 242 B5
Wasdale NW1 231 D1
Washbourne Ct N9 18 A2
Washbrook Ho SW2 160 C5
Washington Ave E12 78 B4
Washington Bldg 1 SE13 141 D4
Washington Cl 45 E3 97 D4
Washington Ct SW17 180 D4
Washington Ho
SW1 247 C1
Walthamstow E17 35 B1
Washington Rd
Barnes SW13 134 A5
Kingston u T KT1 176 C1
North Cheam KT4 200 B1
Upton E6 77 C1
2 Woodford E18 36 D1
Wastdale Rd SE23 162 D3
Watchfield Ct 7 W4 111 A1
Watcombe Cotts TW9 132 C6
Watcombe Rd SE25 206 B4
Waterbank Rd SE6 186 A6
Waterbeach Rd RM9 80 C2
Water Brook La NW4 46 C4
Watercress Pl N1 73 C1
Waterdale Rd SE2 146 A6
Waterden Cres E9 75 C3
Waterden Rd E15 75 C2
Waterer Ho 7 SE6 186 A6
Waterer Rise SM6 219 D2
Waterfall Cl N14 15 C1
Waterfall Cotts SW19 180 B4
Waterfall Rd
Mitcham SW19 180 B4
New Southgate N11, N14 15 C1
Waterfall Terr SW17 180 C4
Waterfield Cl
Belvedere DA17 125 C3
Woolwich SE28 124 B5
Waterfield Gdns SE25 205 C4
Waterford Ct 16 W13 109 A5
Waterford Rd SW6 135 D5 265 C3
Waterford Way NW10 68 A3
Watergardens The
Kingston u T KT2 177 A4
Woodford IG8 37 A5
Water Gardens The W2 92 C1 237 B2
Watergate EC4 251 C6
Watergate Ho 5 SE18 122 C2
Watergate Sch SE6 185 D5
Watergate St SE8 141 C6
Watergate Wlk WC2 250 B4
Water Gdns HA7 25 B4
Waterglade Ctr The W5 109 D6
Waterhall Ave E4 36 C6
Waterhall Cl E17 34 D2
Waterhead NW1 232 A2
Waterhedge Mews EN1 17 D6
Waterhouse Cl
Hammersmith W6 112 D1
Hampstead NW3 70 B3
Newham E16 99 D2
Waterhouse Ct 7 TW11 174 D5
Wateridge Cl E14 119 C3
Wateringbury Cl BR5 190 B1

Water La
16 Camden Town NW1 71 B1
Edmonton N9 18 B4
Ilford IG3 79 D5
Richmond TW10, TW9 153 D6
SE14 140 C5
Sidcup DA14 169 B2
Stratford E15 76 C2
Teddington KT1 175 D2
Twickenham TW1 153 A3
Water Lane Ho 29 TW10 153 D6
Water Lily Cl UB2 108 A4
Waterloo Bridge SE1, WC2 116 B6 250 D5
Waterloo Cl
East Bedfont TW14 149 D3
Hackney E9 74 C3
Waterloo Ct 4 HA0 66 A2
Waterloo East Sta SE1 116 C5 251 B3
Waterloo Gdns
26 Islington N1 72 D1
South Hackney E2 96 C5
Waterloo Int Sta SE1 116 B4 250 D2
Waterloo Pier SE1 250 C2
Waterloo Pl
Kew TW9 132 C6
9 Richmond TW9 132 A1
SW1 115 D5 249 C4
Waterloo Rd
Dollis Hill NW2 68 A6
Forest Gate E7 76 D3
SE1 116 C4 251 B2
Sutton SM1 218 B3
Upton E6 77 C1
Walthamstow E10 53 C2
Waterloo Sta SE1 116 C4 251 A2
Waterloo Terr N1 72 D1
Waterlow Ct NW11 47 D2
Waterlow Rd N19 49 C1
Waterman Bldg 2 E14 119 C4
Watermans Ct
12 Brentford TW8 131 D6
2 Brentford TW8 132 A6
Watermans Mews 1 W5 110 A6
Waterman St SW15 134 D2
Waterman Way E1 118 B5
Watermark Ct RM6 58 B3
Watermead TW14 149 C3
Watermead Ho E9 75 B3
Watermead La CR4 202 D2
Watermeadow La SW6 136 A3
Watermead Rd SE6 186 A6
Watermead Way N17 34 B1
Watermen's Sq 1 SE20 184 C3
Water Mews SE15 140 C1
Watermill Bsns Ctr EN3 7 B3
Watermill Cl TW10 153 C1
Watermill Ct SE13 141 D2
Watermill La N18 33 C5
Watermill Way SW19 180 A2
Water Mill Way TW13 151 C2
Watermint Quay N16 52 A2
Water Rd HA0 88 B6
Watersedge KT19 215 A4
Water's Edge SW6 134 C4
Watersfield Way HA8 26 A3
Waters Gdns RM10 81 C3
Watershipdown Ho 4 E11 54 D2
Waterside
11 Beckenham BR3 185 C2
N1 235 A3
Walthamstow E17 52 C3
Waterside Ave BR3 207 D4
Waterside Cl
Barking IG11 80 A4
30 Bermondsey SE16 118 A4
Northolt UB5 85 B4
Old Ford E3 97 B6
Surbiton KT6 214 A6
Woolwich SE28 123 D5
Waterside Ct
3 Hackbridge SM6 219 A5
Lewisham SE13 142 B1
Waterside Dr KT12 194 B4
Waterside Pl NW1 231 B6
Waterside Point SW11 267 B4
Waterside Rd UB2 107 C3
Waterside Sch SE18 123 B1
Waterside Trad Ctr W7 108 C3
Waterside Way SW17 180 A5
Watersmeet Way SE28 102 D1
Waterson St E2 95 D4
Waters Pl SW15 134 C3
Watersplash Cl KT1 198 A6
Watersplash La
Hayes UB3 106 A2
Southall TW5 106 B1
Watersplash Rd TW17 192 C5
Waters Rd
Catford SE6 164 C1
Kingston u T KT1 176 D1
Waters Sq KT1 198 D6
Water St WC2 251 A6
Water Twr Cl UB8 60 A3
Water Twr Hill CR0 221 B4
Water Twr Pl N1 234 C5
Water View Cl DA6 168 D6
Waterview Ho 13 E14 97 A2
Waterville Lo 6 N12 30 A5
Waterways Bsns Ctr EN3 7 C5
Waterworks Cnr E17 36 C1
Waterworks La E5 74 D6
Waterworks Rd SW2 160 B5
Waterworks Yd 4 CR0 221 A5
Watery La
DA14 190 B4
Hayes UB3 105 B1
Merton SW19, SW20 179 B1
Northolt UB5 84 C5
Wates Way CR4 202 D3
Wateville Rd N17 33 A2
Watford Cl SW11 267 B2
Watford Rd
Elstree WD6 9 C5
Harrow HA1 43 A1
Newham E16 99 A2
Northwood HA6 22 A4
Sudbury HA0, HA1 65 B4
Watford Way NW4 46 A5
Watford Way (Barnet By-Pass) NW9 27 D3
Watkin Mews 18 EN3 7 C6
Watkin Rd HA9 66 D5
Watkins Ho
11 Cubitt Town E14 120 A4
Harrow HA1 42 D4
Watkinson Rd N7 72 B2
Watling Ave HA8 27 B2
Watling Ct
EC4 242 B1
1 Elstree WD6 9 D5
Watling Gate NW9 45 C5
Watling Gdns NW2 69 A2
Watling Ho 10 SE18 144 C6
Watlings Cl CR0 207 A3
Watling St
Bexleyheath DA7 147 D1
4 Camberwell SE15 139 C6
City of London EC4 95 A1 242 B1
Watlington Gr SE26 185 A5
Watney Cotts SW14 133 A2
Watney Mkt* E1 96 B1
Watney Rd SW14 133 A2
Watneys Rd CR4 203 D4
Watney St E1 96 B1
Watson Ave
Cheam SM3 217 A6
Wallend E6 78 C1
Watson Cl
Mitcham SW19 180 C3
Stoke Newington N16 73 B3
Watson Ho 3 SW2 160 A4
Watsons Lo 4 RM10 81 D2
Watsons Mews W1 237 B3
Watsons Rd N22 32 B2
Watson's St SE8 141 C5
Watson St E13 99 B5
Wattisfield Rd E5 74 C5
Watts Cl N15 51 C4
Wattsdown Cl E13 99 A6
Watts Gr E3 97 D2
Watts Ho 6 W10 91 A2
Watt's La
Chislehurst BR7 189 A2
Teddington TW11 175 A5
Watts Rd KT7 197 A2
Watts St
SE15 139 D4
Wapping E1 118 B5
Wat Tyler Ho N8 50 A6
Wat Tyler Rd SE10 142 B4
Wauthier Cl N13 32 D5
Wavel Ct
7 Streatham SW16 160 A1
7 Wapping E1 118 C5
Wavell Dr DA15 167 C5
Wavell Ho N6 49 A3
Wavel Mews
Hampstead NW6 69 D1
Hornsey N8 49 D5
Wavel Pl SE26 183 D6
Wavendon Ave W4 111 B1
Waveney Ave SE15 140 B1
Waveney Cl E1 118 A5
Waveney Ho SE15 140 B1
Waverley Ave
Chingford Hatch E4 35 B6
Sutton SM1 217 D6
Tolworth KT5 199 A3
Twickenham TW2, TW4 151 C3
Walthamstow E17 54 B6
Wembley HA9 66 B3
Waverley Cl
BR2 209 D4
East Molesey KT8 195 C4
Hayes UB3 105 B2
Woodford E18 37 C1
Waverley Cres SE18 123 B1
Waverley Ct
5 Brondesbury NW6 69 A1
Enfield EN2 5 A2
North Finchley N12 30 B6
W1 238 B4
Waverley Gdns
Barking IG11 101 C5
Ealing NW10 88 B5
Ilford IG6 57 B6
Newham E6 100 A2
Northwood HA6 22 A2
Waverley Gr N3 47 A6
Waverley Ind Pk HA1 42 B6
Waverley Pl
Finsbury Pk N4 50 D1
St John's Wood NW8 92 B5 229 C4
Waverley Rd
Croydon SE25 206 B6
Enfield EN2 4 D2
Finsbury Pk N8 50 A2
Harrow HA2 41 A1
Plumstead SE18 123 B1
Southall UB1 107 C6
Stoneleigh KT17, KT4 216 B3
Tottenham N17 34 B3
Walthamstow E17 54 A6
Woodford E18 37 C2
Waverley Sch EN3 6 C1
Waverley Way SM5 218 C2
Waverly Ct NW3 70 D2
Waverton Ho 2 E3 97 B6
Waverton Rd SW18 158 A4
Waverton St W1 115 B5 248 C4
Wavertree Ct 9 SW2 160 A3
Wavertree Rd
Streatham SW2 160 B3
Woodford E18 37 A1
Waxham NW5 70 D3
Waxlow Cres UB1 85 C1
Waxlow Ho UB4 84 C2
Waxlow Rd NW10 89 B5
Waxlow Way UB5 85 B3
Waxwell Cl HA5 22 D1
Waxwell La HA5 22 D1
Wayatt Point 1 SE28 123 A3
Wayborne Gr HA4 39 A3
Waye Ave TW5 128 A4
Wayfarer Rd UB5 85 A4
Wayfield Link SE9 167 B5
Wayford St SW11 136 C3
Wayland Ave E8 74 A3
Wayland Ho 12 SW9 138 C3
Waylands UB3 83 B2
Waylands Ct IG1 79 B4
Waylands Mead BR3 185 D2
Waylett Ho SE11 261 A1
Waylett Pl
Wembley HA0 65 D4
West Norwood SE27 160 D1
Wayman Ct E8 74 B2
Wayne Cl BR6 227 D5
Waynflete Ave CR0 220 D5
Waynflete Sq
18 North Kensington W10 90 D1
16 Shepherd's Bush W10 112 D6
Waynflete St SW18 158 A2
Wayside
Chislehurst BR7 189 B2
Golders Green NW11 47 A1
Mortlake SW14 155 A6
New Addington CR0 223 D2
Wayside Ave WD23 8 B5
Wayside Cl N14 15 C5
Wayside Commercial Est IG11 102 A5
Wayside Ct
Isleworth TW7 130 C3
Twickenham TW1 153 C5
Wembley HA9 66 C5
Wayside Gdns RM10 81 C3
Wayside Gr BR7, SE9 188 B6
Wayside Mews IG2 56 C4
Weald Cl
16 Bermondsey SE16 118 B1
BR2 226 A6
Weald Fst & Mid Schs HA3 24 D3
Weald La HA3 24 B2
Weald Rd UB10 82 C5
Weald Rise HA3 24 D2
Weald Sq E5 74 B6
WEALDSTONE 42 D6
Wealdstone Rd SM3 217 B6
Weald The BR7 188 B4
Weald Way
Hayes UB4 83 C4
Romford RM7 59 D3
Wealdwood Gdns HA5 23 D4
Weale Rd E4 20 B1
Weall Ct HA5 41 A5
Weardale Ct EN5 12 C6
Weardale Gdns EN2 5 B4
Weardale Ho N4 51 A2
Weardale Rd SE13 142 B1
Wearmouth Ho 1 E3 97 B2
Wear Pl 13 E2 96 B4
Wearside Rd SE13 141 D1
Weatherbury 6 W2 91 C1
Weatherbury Ho 3 N19 71 D5
Weatherill Ct SE25 206 B3
Weatherley Cl E3 97 B2
Weathersfield Ct SE9 166 B5
Weaver Cl
Newham E16 122 D6
South Croydon CR0 221 D4
Weaver Ct 2 E2 96 B3
Weaver Ho
12 Bethnal Green E1 96 A3
1 Northolt UB5 85 B3
Weavers Cl TW7 130 C1
Weavers Ho 4 E11 55 A3
Weaver's La SE1 117 C5 253 B3
Weaver St E1 96 A3
Weavers Way
6 Camden Town NW1 71 D1
NW1 232 C6
Weaver Wlk SE27 182 D6
Webb Cl NW10 90 C3
Webb Ct
6 SE28 124 B6
South Acton W3 110 D4
Webber Cl WD6 9 D5
Webber Ho 6 IG11 78 D1
Webber Row SE1 116 D4 251 C1
Webber St SE1 116 D4 251 C1
Webb Est E5 52 A2
Webb Gdns 1 E13 99 A3
Webb Ho
2 Dagenham RM10 81 C5
Feltham TW13 151 A1
SW8 269 D3
Webb Pl NW10 89 D4
Webb Rd SE3 142 D6
Webbscroft Rd RM10 81 D4
Webbs Rd UB4 84 B4
Webb's Rd SW11 158 D6
Webb St SE1 117 C3 263 A5
Webheath 6 NW6 69 B1
Webley Ct 22 EN3 7 C6
Webster Gdns W5 109 D5
Webster Ho 16 N16 73 C3
Webster Rd
Bermondsey SE16 118 A3
Leyton E11 76 A5
Weddell Ho 23 E1 96 D3
Wedderburn Rd
Barking IG11 101 C6
Hampstead NW3 70 B3
Wedgewood Ct
1 Beckenham BR2 208 D5
DA5 169 B4
Wedgewood Ho
SW1 259 A1
Thames Ditton KT7 196 D1
Wedgewood Mews W1 239 D1
Wedgewood Wlk NW3 69 D3
Wedgwood Ho
17 Globe Town E2 96 D4
SE11 261 A5
Wedgwood Way SE19 183 A3
Wedlake St W10 91 A3
Wedmore Gdns N19 71 D6
Wedmore Rd UB6 86 B4
Wedmore St N19 71 D5
Weech Rd NW6 69 C4
Weedington Rd NW5 71 A3
Weedon Ho W12 90 A1
Weekley Sq SW11 136 B2
Weeks Ho TW10 175 C6
Weigall Rd SE12, SE3 143 A1
Weighhouse St W1 238 B1
Weighton Rd
Harrow HA3 24 B2
Penge SE20 184 B1
Weihurst Ct SM1 218 C3
Weihurst Gdns SM1 218 B3
Weimar St SW15 135 A2
Weirdale Ave N20 14 D2
Weir Hall Ave N18 33 B4
Weir Hall Gdns N18 33 B5
Weir Hall Rd N18 33 B4
Weir Ho 8 SW12 159 C4
Weir Rd
Sidcup DA5 169 D4
Streatham SW12 159 C4
Walton-on-T KT12 194 A3
Wimbledon SW18, SW19 157 D1
Weir's Pas NW1 232 D2
Weiss Rd SW15 134 D2
Welbeck Ave
Grove Pk BR1 187 B6
Hayes UB4 84 B3
Sidcup DA15 168 A3
Welbeck Cl
New Malden KT3 199 D4
North Finchley N12 30 B5
Stoneleigh KT17 216 A1
Welbeck Ct
Hayes UB4 84 B3
W14 254 C4
Welbeck Mans 10 NW6 69 C3
Welbeck Rd
Carshalton SM1 218 B6
Carshalton SM5 202 C1
East Barnet EN4 14 C5
Harrow HA2 41 D1
Newham E6 99 D4
Welbeck St W1 93 B1 238 C2
Welbeck Villas N21 17 A3
Welbeck Way W1 238 C2
Welbeck Wlk SM5 202 B1
Welbourne Prim Sch N17 52 A6
Welbury Ct E8 73 C1
Welby Ho N19 49 D2
Welby St SE5 138 D4
Welch Pl HA5 22 C2
Welcome Ct E17 53 C2
Weldon Cl HA4 62 B2
Weldon Ct
Southgate N21 16 B6
St Johns SE8 141 C3
7 Sutton SM1 218 B3
Thornton Heath CR7 204 D4
Weldon Dr KT8 195 B5
Weld Pl N11 31 B5
Welfare Rd E15 76 C1
Welford Cl E5 74 D5
Welford Ct
12 Camden Town NW1 71 B1
7 Clapham SW8 137 C3
Welford Ho 4 UB5 85 B3
Welford Pl SW19 179 A6
Welham Rd SW16, SW17 181 B4
Welhouse Rd SM5 202 C1
Wellacre Rd HA3 43 B3
Wellan Cl DA15, DA16 168 B6
Welland Ct SE6 163 B2
Welland Gdns UB6 86 D5
Welland Ho SE15 140 C1
Welland Mews E1 118 A5
Wellands Cl BR1 188 B1
Welland St SE10 142 A6
Well App EN5 12 C6
Wellbrook Rd BR6 226 C4
Wellby Cl N9 18 A3
Wellby Ct 1 E13 99 C5
Well Cl
Ruislip HA4 63 A5
Streatham SW16 182 B6
Wellclose Sq E1 118 A6
Wellclose St 20 E1 118 A6
Well Cottage Cl E11 55 C2
Well Ct EC4 242 B1
Wellday Ho 2 E9 75 A2
Welldon Cres HA1 42 C3
Welldon Ct
Harrow HA1 42 C4
1 West Dulwich SE21 161 B2
Welldon Park Fst Sch HA2 64 A4
Welldon Park Mid Sch HA2 64 A4
Weller Ho 23 SE16 118 A4
Weller Mews 6 BR2 209 B5
Weller St SE1 252 A2
Welles Ct 15 E14 119 C6
Wellesley Ave W6 112 B3
Wellesley Cl 8 SE7 121 C1
Wellesley Court Rd 1 CR0 221 B6
Wellesley Cres TW2 152 C1
Wellesley Ct
Cheam SM3 201 A1
St John's Wood W9 92 A4 229 A2
Twickenham TW2 152 C1
Wellesley Gr CR0 221 B6
Wellesley Ho
NW1 232 C1
12 Wimbledon SW19 179 A3
Wellesley Park Mews EN2 4 D3
Wellesley Pl
Camden Town NW5 71 A3
NW1 232 C1
Wellesley Rd
Croydon CR0 205 A1
Gospel Oak NW5 71 A3
Gunnersbury W4 110 D1
Harrow HA1 42 C4
Ilford IG1 57 A1
Sutton SM2 218 A2
Twickenham TW2 152 C1
Walthamstow E17 53 C3
Wanstead E11 55 A4
Wood Green N22 32 C1
Wellesley Road Sta CR0 221 B6
Wellesley St E1 96 D2
Wellesley Terr N1 95 A4 235 B2
Wellfield Ave N10 49 B6
Wellfield Rd SW16 182 B6
Wellfit St 6 SE24 138 D2
Wellgarth UB6 65 B2
Wellgarth Rd NW11 47 D1
Well Gr N20 14 B3
Wellgrove Sch N20 14 B3
Well Hall Par SE9 144 B1
Well Hall Pleasaunce* SE9 144 A1
Well Hall Rd SE9 144 B1
Well Ho 11 N9 18 A1
Wellhouse Rd BR3 207 C5
Wellhurst Cl BR6 227 D1
WELLING 146 B2
Wellingfield Ct 1 DA16 146 A2
Welling High St DA16 146 B2
Welling Sch DA16 146 B4
Wellings Ho UB3 106 B5
Welling Sta DA16 146 A3
Wellington
1 Grahame Pk NW9 27 D3
Hornsey N8 50 A5
Wellington Arch* SW1 248 B2
Wellington Ave
Chingford E4 19 D2
DA15 168 A5
Edmonton N9 18 B1
Hounslow TW3, TW4 151 C6
North Cheam KT4 216 C5
Pinner HA5 23 B2
South Tottenham N15 52 A3
Wellington Bldgs
15 Bow E3 97 C4
SW1 258 B1
Wellington Cl
Kensington W11 91 C1
New Cross Gate SE14 140 D4
Walton-on-T KT12 193 D1
Wellington Cres KT3 199 A6
Wellington Ct
Ashford TW15 170 A6

Wellington Ct *continued*
Knightsbridge SW1 . . . . 247 C1
Stanwell TW19 . . . . 148 A4
St John's Wood NW8 . . . 229 D3
Strand WC2 . . . . 250 A6
5 Surbiton KT6 . . . . 198 A3
Teddington TW12 . . . . 174 B5
4 Upper Tooting
SW17 . . . . 180 C4
Wandsworth SW18 . . . . 158 C6
Wellington Gdns
Greenwich SE7 . . . . 121 C1
Teddington TW12,
TW2 . . . . 174 B6
Wellington Gr SE10 . . . 142 B5
Wellington Ho
4 Ealing W5 . . . . 88 A4
18 Maitland Pk NW3 . . . . 70 D2
Northolt UB5 . . . . 63 C1
6 Ruislip HA4 . . . . 40 C1
Stanmore HA7 . . . . 9 A1
Wellington Hospl The
NW8 . . . . 92 B5 229 D3
Wellington Mans
Shacklewell N16 . . . . 73 D4
1 Walthamstow E10 . . . . 53 C1
Wellington Mews
East Dulwich SE22 . . . . . 140 A1
3 Islington N7 . . . . 72 B2
SE7 . . . . 143 C6
Streatham SW16 . . . . . . 159 D1
Wellington Mus (Apsley
Ho)* SW1 115 A4 248 B2
Wellington Par DA15 . . 168 A6
Wellington Park Est
NW2 . . . . 68 A6
Wellington Pas 7 E11 . 55 A4
Wellington Pl
East Finchley N2 . . . . 48 C4
St John's Wood
NW8 . . . . 92 B4 229 D2
Wellington Prim Sch
Bow E3 . . . . 97 C4
Chingford E4 . . . . 19 D2
Hounslow TW3 . . . . 129 B3
Wellington Rd
Ashford TW15 . . . . 170 A5
Bexley DA5 . . . . 168 D6
Brentford W5 . . . . 109 C3
Bromley BR2 . . . . 209 C5
Enfield EN1 . . . . 17 C6
Erith DA17 . . . . 125 B1
Harrow HA3 . . . . 42 C6
Hatton TW14 . . . . 149 C6
Kensal Green NW10 . . . . . 90 D4
Leyton E7 . . . . 76 D4
Newham E6 . . . . 100 B5
Pinner HA5 . . . . 23 B2
St John's Wood
NW8 . . . . 92 B5 229 D3
Teddington TW12,
TW2 . . . . 174 B6
Thornton Heath CR0 . . . . 204 D2
Walthamstow E10 . . . . . . 53 A1
Walthamstow E17 . . . . . . 53 A5
Wanstead E11 . . . . 55 A4
Wimbledon SW19 . . . . . . 157 C2
Wellington Rd N TW4 . 129 B2
Wellington Rd S TW4 . . 151 B6
Wellington Row E2 . . . . 96 A4
Wellington Sq
SW3 . . . . 114 D1 257 C2
Wellington St
1 Barking IG11 . . . . 101 A6
WC2 . . . . 116 B6 250 C6
Woolwich SE18 . . . . 122 C2
Wellington Terr
Harrow HA1 . . . . 42 B1
2 Wapping E1 . . . . 118 B5
Wellington Way E3 . . . 97 C4
Welling Way DA16 . . . . 145 B2
Well La SW14 . . . . 155 A6
Wellmead IG3 . . . . 58 A2
Wellmeadow Rd
Brentford W7 . . . . 109 A2
Catford SE13, SE6 . . . . . 164 C3
Wellow Wlk SM5 . . . . . . 202 B1
Well Rd
Barnet EN5 . . . . 12 C6
Vale of Health NW3 . . . . . 70 B5
Wells Cl
2 Northolt UB5 . . . . 84 C4
South Croydon CR2 . . . . 221 C3
Wells Ct
21 Hampstead NW3 . . . . . 70 A4
4 Mitcham CR4 . . . . 180 C2
1 Paddington NW6 . . . . . 91 C5
Stoke Newington N1 . . . . 73 C3
Wells Dr NW9 . . . . 45 B1
Wells Gdns
Dagenham RM10 . . . . 81 D3
Redbridge IG1 . . . . 56 A2
Wells Ho
4 Barking IG11 . . . . 80 A1
Ealing W5 . . . . 109 D6
Finsbury EC1 . . . . 234 C2
12 Kensal Town W10 . . . . 91 A3
New Cross Gate SE4 . . . . 141 A3
Plaistow BR1 . . . . 187 B5
9 Rotherhithe SE16 . . . . 118 C3
Wells Ho The 2 NW3 . . 70 B4
Wells House Rd NW10 . . 89 C2
Wellside Gdns SW14 . . 155 A6
Wells Mews W1 . . . . . . 239 B2
Wellsmoor Gdns BR1 . . 210 C6
Wells Park Ct SE26 . . . . 184 B6
Wells Park Rd SE26 . . . 184 B6
Wells Pl SW18 . . . . 158 A4
Wells Prim Sch IG8 . . . . 37 A6
Wellspring Cres HA9 . . . 66 D5
Wells Rd
BR1 . . . . 188 B1
Hammersmith W12 . . . . . 112 C4
Wells Rise
NW8 . . . . 92 D6 230 C5
Wells Sq WC1 . . . . 233 D1
Wells St W1 . . . . 93 C1 239 B2
Well St
Hackney E9 . . . . 74 C1
Stratford E15 . . . . 76 C2
Wellstead Ave N9 . . . . . . 18 D4
Wellstead Rd E6 . . . . . . 100 C5
Wells Terr N4 . . . . 72 C6
Wells The N14 . . . . 15 D4
Wells Way
Brompton
SW7 . . . . 114 B3 256 C6
Camberwell SE5 . . . . 139 C6
Well Wlk NW3 . . . . 70 B5
Wellwood Ct SW15 . . . . 134 C1
Wellwood Rd IG3 . . . . . . 58 A2
Welmar Works SW4 . . . 137 D1
Welsby Ct W5 . . . . 87 C2
Welsford St SE1 . . . . . . 118 A2
Welsh Cl E13 . . . . 99 A4
WELSH HARP 45 C1
Welsh Harp Field Centre
NW9 . . . . 45 B1
Welsh Ho 14 E1 . . . . 118 B5
Welshpool Ho 22 E8 . . . . 96 A6
Welshpool St 1 E8 . . . . 96 B6
Welshside NW9 . . . . 45 C3
Welshside Wlk NW9 . . . . 45 C3
Welstead Ho 29 E1 . . . . . 96 B1
Welstead Way W4 . . . . . 111 D2
Weltje Rd W6 . . . . 112 A1
Welton Ct SE5 . . . . 139 C4
Welton Ho E1 . . . . 96 D2
Welton Rd SE18 . . . . 145 C5
Welwyn Ave TW14 . . . . . 149 D5
Welwyn St E2 . . . . 96 C4
Welwyn Way UB4 . . . . . . 83 C3
WEMBLEY 65 D2
Wembley HA0 . . . . 65 D2
Wembley Arena HA9 . . . 66 C4
Wembley Central Sta
HA9 . . . . 66 A3
Wembley Commercial Ctr
HA9 . . . . 65 D6
Wembley Conference Ctr
HA9 . . . . 66 C4
Wembley Exhibition Halls
HA9 . . . . 66 C4
Wembley High Tech Coll
HA0 . . . . 65 C5
Wembley Hill Rd HA9 . . 66 B4
Wembley Hospl HA0 . . . 65 D2
Wembley Mkt
1 Wembley HA0 . . . . 66 A3
1 Wembley Pk HA9 . . . . . 66 C4
WEMBLEY PARK 66 C5
Wembley Park Bsns Ctr
HA9 . . . . 66 D5
Wembley Park Dr HA9 . . 66 B5
Wembley Park Sta
HA9 . . . . 66 C5
Wembley Prim Sch
HA9 . . . . 66 A5
Wembley Rd TW12 . . . . 173 C2
Wembley Stadium
HA9 . . . . 66 C3
Wembley Stadium Ind Est
Wembley HA9 . . . . 66 C5
Wembley HA9 . . . . 66 D4
Wembley Stadium Sta
HA9 . . . . 66 B3
Wembley Way HA9 . . . . . 66 D2
Wemborough Rd HA7 . . 25 C3
Wembury Mews N6 . . . . 49 C2
Wembury Rd N6 . . . . 49 B2
Wemyss Rd SE3 . . . . 142 D3
Wendela Ct HA1 . . . . 64 C6
Wendell Park Prim Sch
W12 . . . . 111 D4
Wendell Rd W12 . . . . . . 111 D4
Wenderholme CR2 . . . . 221 B3
Wendle Ct SW8 . . . . 270 A5
Wendling NW5 . . . . 70 D3
Wendling Rd SM1 . . . . . 218 B6
Wendon Ct 13 SM6 . . . . 219 C2
Wendon St E3 . . . . 97 B6
Wendover
SE17 . . . . 117 C1 263 A1
Wendover Cl UB4 . . . . . . 85 A3
Wendover Ct
Acton W3 . . . . 88 D3
Becontree W3 . . . . 89 A3
Bromley BR2 . . . . 209 B6
4 Child's Hill NW2 . . . . . 69 C5
W1 . . . . 238 A3
Wendover Dr KT3 . . . . . 199 D3
Wendover Ho
Bowes Pk N22 . . . . 32 B5
W1 . . . . 238 A3
Wendover Lo NW9 . . . . . 45 D3
Wendover Rd
Blackheath SE9 . . . . 143 D2
Bromley BR1, BR2 . . . . . 209 B6
Dagenham NW10 . . . . 89 D5
Wendover Way
Bexley DA16 . . . . 146 A1
Bushey WD23 . . . . 8 A5
Wendy Cl EN1 . . . . 17 D5
Wendy Ho 3 N12 . . . . . . 30 B5
Wendy Way HA0 . . . . 88 A6
Wengham Ho W12 . . . . 112 A6
Wenham Ho SW8 . . . . . 269 A3
Wenlake Ho EC1 . . . . . . 242 A6
Wenlock Ct N1 . . . . 235 D3
Wenlock Gdns 13 NW4 . 46 A5
Wenlock Rd
Burnt Oak HA8 . . . . 27 A4
Shoreditch N1 . . 95 A5 235 B3
Wenlock St N1 . . 95 B5 235 C3
Wennington Rd E3 . . . . . 96 D5
Wensdale Ho E5 . . . . 74 A6
Wensley Ave IG8 . . . . 37 A3
Wensley Cl
6 Barnet N11 . . . . 31 A4
SE9 . . . . 166 B5
Wensleydale Gdns
TW12 . . . . 173 D3
Wensleydale Ho 8 N4 . 51 A2
Wensleydale Rd
TW12 . . . . 173 D3
Wensley Rd N18 . . . . 34 B4
Wentland Cl SE6 . . . . . . 164 B2
Wentland Rd SE6 . . . . . 164 B2
Wentway Ct W13 . . . . . . 87 A3
Wentwood Ho 1 E5 . . . 74 B6
Wentworth Ave
Borehamwood WD6 . . . . . 10 B6
Finchley N3 . . . . 29 C3
Wentworth Cl
Ashford TW15 . . . . 170 D6
Finchley N3 . . . . 29 D3
Hayes BR2 . . . . 225 A6
Long Ditton KT6 . . . . . . 213 D6
Morden SM4 . . . . 201 C2
Orpington BR6 . . . . 227 C3
Thamesmead SE28 . . . . . 102 D1
Wentworth Cres
Hayes UB3 . . . . 105 B3
SE15 . . . . 140 A5
Wentworth Ct
Barnet EN5 . . . . 1 A2
7 Chingford E4 . . . . 36 B5
20 Kingston u T KT6 . . . . 198 A4
Southall UB2 . . . . 106 C2
2 Surbiton KT6 . . . . 214 A6
Twickenham TW2 . . . . . . 152 C1
W6 . . . . 264 A5
Wandsworth SW18 . . . . 157 D5
Wentworth Dr HA5 . . . . . 40 A4
Wentworth Dwellings
E1 . . . . 243 C2
Wentworth Gdns N13 . . 16 D1
Wentworth Hall NW7 . . . 28 C5
Wentworth Hill HA9 . . . 44 B1
Wentworth Ho
Enfield EN1 . . . . 17 C5
4 Greenwich SE3 . . . . . 143 A5
Wentworth Lo N3 . . . . . . 29 D3
Wentworth Mews E3 . . . 97 B4
Wentworth Pk N3 . . . . . . 29 D3
Wentworth Pl HA7 . . . . . 25 B4
Wentworth Rd
Manor Pk E12 . . . . 77 D4
Southall UB2 . . . . 106 D2
Wentworth Rd *continued*
Temple Fortune NW11 . . . 47 B3
Thornton Heath CR0 . . . . 204 C2
Wentworth St
E1 . . . . 95 D2 243 D3
Wentworth Tutorial Coll
NW11 . . . . 46 D3
Wentworth Way HA5 . . . 41 A5
Wenvoe Ave DA7 . . . . . . 147 D3
Wepham Cl UB4 . . . . 84 D2
Wernbrook St SE18 . . . 145 A6
Werndee Rd SE25 . . . . . 206 A5
Werneth Hall Rd IG5 . . . 56 C6
Werrington St
NW1 . . . . 93 C5 232 B3
Werter Rd SW15 . . . . . . 135 A1
Wesleyan Pl NW5 . . . . . . 71 B4
Wesley Ave
Becontree NW10 . . . . 89 B4
Hounslow TW3 . . . . 129 B3
Newham E16 . . . . 121 B5
Wesley Cl
Finsbury Pk N7 . . . . 72 B6
Harrow HA2 . . . . 64 A6
SE17 . . . . 261 D3
Wesley Ct W1 . . . . 238 B3
Wesley Ho SE24 . . . . . . 161 B5
Wesley Rd
Becontree NW10 . . . . 89 A6
Finchley N10 . . . . 30 C2
Hayes UB3 . . . . 84 A1
Leytonstone E10 . . . . 54 A2
Wesley Sq W11 . . . . 91 A1
Wesley St W1 . . . . 238 B3
Wessex Ave SW19 . . . . . 201 C6
Wessex Cl
Hinchley Wood KT10,
KT7 . . . . 212 D6
Ilford IG3 . . . . 57 C3
Kingston u T KT1, KT2 . . . 176 D2
Wessex Ct
Putney SW15 . . . . 156 D6
5 Stanwell TW19 . . . . . 148 A5
Wembley HA9 . . . . 66 B6
Wessex Dr HA5 . . . . 23 A3
Wessex Gardens Prim Sch
NW11 . . . . 47 A1
Wessex Gdns NW11 . . . . 47 A1
Wessex Ho
SE1 . . . . 263 D1
4 Tufnell Pk N19 . . . . . . 71 D5
Wessex La UB6 . . . . 86 B5
Wessex St E2 . . . . 96 C4
Wessex Way NW11 . . . . . 47 A1
Wesson Ho 3 CR0 . . . . 206 A1
West 12 Sh Ctr W12 . . . 112 D4
Westacott UB4 . . . . 83 C2
Westacott Cl N19 . . . . . . 49 D1
WEST ACTON 88 C1
West Acton Prim Sch
W3 . . . . 88 D1
West Acton Sta W3 . . . . 88 C1
West App BR5 . . . . 211 A4
West Arbour St E1 . . . . . 96 D1
West Ave
East Finchley N2 . . . . 47 D6
Finchley N3 . . . . 29 C4
Hayes UB3 . . . . 105 D6
Hendon NW4 . . . . 46 D4
Pinner HA5 . . . . 41 B2
Southall UB1 . . . . 107 B6
Wallington SM6 . . . . 220 A3
Walthamstow E17 . . . . . . 53 D4
West Avenue Rd E17 . . . 53 D5
West Bank
Barking IG11 . . . . 100 D6
Enfield EN2 . . . . 5 A3
Stamford Hill N16 . . . . . . 51 C2
Westbank Rd TW12 . . . 174 A4
WEST BARNES 200 C4
West Barnes La KT3,
SW20 . . . . 200 B5
WEST BEDFONT 148 B4
Westbeech Rd N22 . . . . . 50 C6
Westbere Ct HA7 . . . . . . 25 D5
Westbere Dr HA7 . . . . . . 25 D5
Westbere Rd NW2 . . . . . 69 A3
West Block 18 E1 . . . . . 118 C6
Westbourne Ave
Cheam SM3 . . . . 217 A6
Dagenham W3 . . . . 89 B1
Westbourne Cl UB4 . . . . 84 C3
Westbourne Cres W2 . 246 C6
Westbourne Ct
Cheam SM3 . . . . 217 A6
W2 . . . . 236 A2
Westbourne Dr SE23 . . 162 D2
Westbourne Gdns W2 . . 91 D1
Westbourne Gr
Notting Hill W2, W11 . . . . 91 C1
Westbourne Gr *continued*
W11 . . . . 113 B6 244 D6
WESTBOURNE GREEN 91 D3
Westbourne Gr Mews 7
W11 . . . . 91 C1
Westbourne Gr Terr
W2 . . . . 91 D1
Westbourne Ho
Heston TW5 . . . . 129 C6
SW1 . . . . 258 C2
8 Twickenham TW1 . . . . 153 B4
Westbourne Par 4
UB10 . . . . 82 D3
Westbourne Park Rd
Notting Hill W2 . . . . 91 C1
Notting Hill W11 . . . . 91 B1
Westbourne Park Sta
W11 . . . . 91 B2
Westbourne Park Villas
W2 . . . . 91 D2
Westbourne Pl N9 . . . . . 18 B1
Westbourne Prim Sch
SM1 . . . . 217 C5
Westbourne Rd
Barnsbury N7 . . . . 72 B2
Croydon CR0 . . . . 205 D3
DA7 . . . . 147 A5
Feltham TW13 . . . . 149 D1
Hillingdon UB8 . . . . 82 D3
Penge SE26 . . . . 184 D4
Westbourne St
W2 . . . . 114 B6 246 C6
Westbourne Terr
W2 . . . . 92 A1 236 B2
Westbourne Terrace
Mews W2 . . . . 236 A2
Westbourne Terrace Rd
W2 . . . . 92 A2 236 A3
Westbridge Cl W12 . . . 112 A5
Westbridge Prim Sch
SW11 . . . . 267 A2
Westbridge Rd
SW11 . . . . 136 C4 267 A2
WEST BROMPTON . . . 135 D6
West Brompton Sta
SW5 . . . . 113 C1 255 B1
Westbrook Ave TW12 . . 173 B3
Westbrook Cl EN4 . . . . . . 2 B2
Westbrook Cres EN4 . . . . 2 B2
Westbrook Ct SE3 . . . . . 143 B4
Westbrooke Cres
DA16 . . . . 146 C2
Westbrooke Rd
Bexley DA16 . . . . 146 C2
DA15 . . . . 167 B2
Westbrooke Sch
DA16 . . . . 146 D2
Westbrook Ho
5 Bethnal Green E2 . . . . 96 C4
5 Clapham Pk SW4 . . . . 159 C6
Westbrook Rd
Heston TW5 . . . . 129 B5
SE3 . . . . 143 B4
South Norwood CR7 . . . . 183 B1
Westbrook Sq EN4 . . . . . . 2 B2
West Brow BR7 . . . . 188 D5
Westbury Ave
Claygate KT10 . . . . 212 D2
Southall UB1 . . . . 85 C3
Tottenham N22 . . . . 32 D1
Wembley HA0 . . . . 66 A1
Westbury Cl
Ruislip HA4 . . . . 40 A2
Shepperton TW17 . . . . . 192 D3
Westbury Ct
3 Barking IG11 . . . . 101 B6
Beckenham BR3 . . . . 185 D2
1 Buckhurst Hill IG9 . . . . 21 C2
Clapham SW4 . . . . 159 B5
11 New Barnet EN5 . . . . . 14 A6
Tottenham N22 . . . . 33 A1
Westbury Gr N12 . . . . . . 29 C4
Westbury Ho
1 Walthamstow E17 . . . . 53 C5
6 Willesden NW10 . . . . . 67 C1
Westbury House Sch
KT3 . . . . 199 B4
Westbury La IG9 . . . . 21 C2
Westbury Lodge Cl
HA5 . . . . 40 D6
Westbury Pl 2 TW8 . . . 131 D6
Westbury Rd
Barking IG11 . . . . 101 B6
Beckenham BR3 . . . . 207 A6
Bowes Pk N11 . . . . 32 A4
Bromley BR1 . . . . 187 D2
Buckhurst Hill IG9 . . . . . . 21 C3
Ealing W5 . . . . 88 A1
Feltham TW13 . . . . 150 D3
Westbury Rd *continued*
Finchley N12 . . . . 29 D5
Ilford IG1 . . . . 78 C6
New Malden KT3 . . . . . . 199 B4
Penge SE20 . . . . 184 D2
Thornton Heath CR0 . . . . 205 B3
Upton E7 . . . . 77 B2
Walthamstow E17 . . . . . . 53 C5
Wembley HA0 . . . . 66 A1
Westbury Terr E7 . . . . . . 77 B2
Westbush Ct 1 W12 . . 112 B4
West Carriage Dr
W2 . . . . 114 C5 247 A4
West Central St WC1 . . 240 A2
West Chantry HA3 . . . . . 23 D2
Westchester Ct NW4 . . . . 46 D6
Westchester Dr NW4 . . . 46 D6
Westchester Ho W2 . . . 237 C1
West Cl
Ashford TW15 . . . . 170 A6
Barnet EN5 . . . . 12 B6
Cockfosters EN4 . . . . 3 A1
Edmonton N9 . . . . 17 D1
Greenford UB6 . . . . 86 A5
Hampton TW12 . . . . 173 A4
Wembley HA9 . . . . 44 B1
Westcliff Ho 13 N1 . . . . . 73 B2
Westcombe Ave CR0 . . 204 B2
Westcombe Ct 1
SE3 . . . . 142 D5
Westcombe Dr EN5 . . . . 13 C6
Westcombe Hill SE3,
SE10 . . . . 143 A6
Westcombe Lodge Dr
UB4 . . . . 83 B2
Westcombe Park Rd
SE3 . . . . 142 D5
Westcombe Park Sta
SE3 . . . . 121 A1
West Common Rd
BR2 . . . . 225 B5
Westcoombe Ave
SW20 . . . . 177 D2
Westcote Rd SW16 . . . . 181 C5
Westcote Rise HA4 . . . . . 39 A2
Westcott Cl
BR1 . . . . 210 A4
2 South Tottenham
N15 . . . . 51 D3
Westcott Cres W7 . . . . . 86 C2
Westcott Ho 1 E14 . . . 119 D6
Westcott Rd SE17 . . . . . 138 D6
West Cotts NW6 . . . . 69 C3
Westcroft 1 SM5 . . . . . 219 A4
Westcroft Cl
Enfield EN3 . . . . 6 C5
West Hampstead NW2 . . . 69 A4
Westcroft Ct
3 Chiswick W6 . . . . 112 A2
Kingsbury NW9 . . . . 44 D4
Westcroft Gdns SM4 . . 201 B5
Westcroft Ho 2 SM5 . . 219 A4
Westcroft Rd SM5,
SM6 . . . . 219 A4
Westcroft Sq W6 . . . . . 112 A2
Westcroft Way NW2 . . . . 69 A4
West Cromwell Rd
W14 . . . . 113 B1 254 D2
West Cross Ctr TW8 . . . 131 B6
West Cross Route W10,
W11 . . . . 112 D6
West Cross Way TW8 . . 131 B6
West Croydon Sta
CR9 . . . . 205 A1
West Ct
Hounslow TW7 . . . . 130 A5
Sunbury TW16 . . . . 172 B1
Walthamstow E17 . . . . . . 53 D5
Wembley HA0 . . . . 65 C6
Westdale Rd SE18 . . . . . 144 D6
Westdean Ave SE12 . . . 165 C3
Westdean Cl SW18 . . . . 157 D5
Westdown Rd
Catford SE6 . . . . 163 C4
Leyton E15 . . . . 76 A4
West Dr
Stanmore HA3 . . . . 24 B4
Streatham SW16 . . . . . . 181 C6
WEST DRAYTON 104 B4
West Drayton Park Ave
UB7 . . . . 104 A3
West Drayton Prim Sch
UB7 . . . . 104 A4
West Drayton Rd UB8 . . 82 D1
West Drayton Sta
UB7 . . . . 104 A5
West Drive Gdns HA3 . . 24 B4

WEST DULWICH 161 A2
West Dulwich Sta
SE21 161 B3
WEST EALING 109 B5
West Ealing Bsns Ctr
W13 109 A6
West Ealing Sta W13 109 B6
West Eaton Pl SW1 258 A4
West Eaton Pl Mews
SW1 258 A4
West Ella Rd NW10 67 C1
West End Ave
Leytonstone E10 54 B4
Pinner HA5 40 D5
West End Cl
Stonebridge NW10 67 A1
Willesden NW10 67 A1
West End Ct
Hampstead NW6 69 D1
Pinner HA5 40 D5
West End Gdns UB5 84 C5
West End La
Hampstead NW6 69 D2
Harlington UB7 127 A5
Pinner HA5 40 D5
West End Rd
Ruislip HA4, UB5 62 A4
Ruislip UB5 62 C1
Southall UB1 107 A5
Westerdale Ct N5 72 D4
Westerdale Rd [2]
SE10 121 A1
Westerfield Rd [1] N15 51 D4
Westergate W5 88 A2
Westergate Rd SE2 147 A6
Westerham
[13] Kingston u T KT6 198 A4
NW1 232 A5
Westerham Ave N9 17 C1
Westerham Dr DA15 168 C5
Westerham Ho SE1 262 D6
Westerham Lo [10]
BR3 185 C3
Westerham Rd
Keston BR2 225 D2
Walthamstow E10 53 D2
Westerley Cres SE26 185 B5
Westerley Ct HA4 62 B3
Western Ave
Dagenham W3 89 B1
Hendon NW11 46 D3
Hillingdon HA4, UB4, UB5,
UB10 61 C1
Northolt UB5, UB6 85 B6
Ruislip UB8, UB9, UB10 60 B3
Wembley UB6 87 C4
Western Avenue Bsns Pk
W3 88 D3
Western Beach Apts
E16 121 A5
Western Ct
[4] Dagenham W3 89 B1
Finchley N3 29 C4
[3] Kilburn W9 91 B5
Southall UB2 107 A3
Western Dr TW17 193 B3
Western Eye Hospl The
NW1 92 D2 237 C4
Western Gateway
E16 121 A6
Western Gdns W5 110 C6
Western Ho [3] W9 91 B3
Western Hts SM1 217 C3
Western International
Market UB2 106 B2
Western La SW12 159 A4
Western Mews W9 91 B3
Western Par EN5 13 D6
Western Pl [19] SE16 118 C4
Western Rd
Becontree NW10 89 A3
Brixton SW9 138 C2
Ealing W5 109 D6
Fortis Green N2 48 D5
Mitcham CR4, SW19 180 C1
Newham E13 99 C5
Southall UB2 106 D2
Sutton SM1 217 C3
Walthamstow E17 54 A4
Wood Green N22 32 B1
Western Terr [3] W6 112 A1
Western View UB3 105 D4
Westernville Gdns IG2 57 A2
Western Way
New Barnet EN5 13 D5
Plumstead SE28 123 C4
Western Wharf [2]
SE15 140 A6
WEST EWELL 215 C1
West Ewell Inf Sch
KT19 215 B3
West Farm Ct EN4 2 D2
Westferry Cir E14 119 C5
Westferry Rd E14 119 C3
Westferry Sta E14 119 C6
Westfield
[1] BR6 227 A3
Loughton IG10 21 C6
West Hampstead NW3 69 C4
Westfield Cl
Cheam SM1 217 B4
Enfield EN3 7 A2
Kingsbury NW9 45 A6
SW10 266 A3
Westfield Ct
[1] Kensal Green W10 90 D4
Kingston u T KT6 197 D4
Westfield Dr HA3 43 D5
Westfield Gdns
Harrow HA3 43 D5
Ilford RM6 58 C3
Westfield Ho [6] SE16 118 D2
Westfield La HA3 43 D5
Westfield London Sh Ctr
W12 112 D5
Westfield Pk HA5 23 B3
Westfield Rd
Beckenham BR3 185 B1
Cheam SM1 217 B4
Croydon CR0 220 D6
Dagenham RM9 81 B4
Ealing W13 109 A5
Edgware NW7 11 C1
Kingston u T KT6 197 D4
Mitcham CR4 180 D1
Walton-on-T KT12 195 A2
Westfields SW13 133 D2
Westfields Ave SW13 133 C2
Westfields Rd W3 88 D2
Westfield St SE18 121 D3
Westfield Way
Mile End E1 97 A3
Ruislip HA4 61 D5
West Finchley Sta N3 29 D4
West Garden Pl W2 237 B1
West Gate W5 88 A4
Westgate Bsns Ctr
[2] Kensal Town W10 91 A3
North Kensington W10 90 D3
Westgate Ct
[6] Beckenham BR3 186 A2
[15] Brixton SW9 138 C2
Lewisham SE12 165 A3
Westgate Est TW14 148 D3
Westgate Rd
Beckenham BR3 186 A2
Croydon SE25 206 B5
Westgate St E8 96 B6
Westgate Terr
SW10 135 D6 265 D6
West Gdns
Mitcham SW19 180 C4
Stepney E1 118 B6
Westglade Ct HA3 43 D4
West Gr
Lewisham SE10 142 B4
Woodford IG8 37 C5
WEST GREEN 51 A5
West Green Pl UB6 86 B6
West Green Prim Sch
N15 51 A5
West Green Rd N15 51 B5
Westgrove La SE10 142 A4
West Grove Prim Sch
N14 15 D4
West Halkin St
SW1 115 A3 258 A6
West Hallowes SE9 166 A3
West Hall Rd TW9 132 D4
WEST HAM 99 B6
West Ham Church Prim
Sch E15 98 D6
West Ham La E15 76 C1
WEST HAMPSTEAD 69 C4
West Hampstead Mews
NW6 69 D2
West Hampstead Sta
NW6 69 C2
West Hampstead
Thameslink Sta NW6 69 C2
West Ham Sta E15 98 C4
West Harding St EC4 241 B2
WEST HARROW 42 A2
West Harrow Sta HA1 42 A3
West Hatch Manor
HA4 39 D2
Westhaven SM1 217 C3
Westhay Gdns SW14 154 D6
WEST HEATH 146 D6
West Heath Ave NW11 47 C1
West Heath Cl NW3 69 C5
West Heath Ct NW11 47 C1
West Heath Dr NW11 47 C1
West Heath Gdns NW3 69 C5
West Heath Rd
SE2, DA7 146 D6
West Hampstead NW3 69 D5
WEST HENDON 45 D3
WEST HILL 157 B5
West Hill
Harrow HA2 64 C6
Highgate N6 49 A1
Putney SW15 157 A5
South Croydon CR2 221 C1
Wembley HA9 44 B1
Westhill Ct W11 244 D6
West Hill Ct N6 71 A5
West Hill Hall HA2 64 C6
Westhill Pk
Dartmouth Pk N6 71 A6
Highgate N6 70 D6
West Hill Prim Sch
SW18 157 C6
West Hill Rd SW18 157 B5
West Hill Way N20 13 D3
West Ho
Barking IG11 78 D2
[4] Penge SE20 184 D3
[9] Streatham SW12 159 C4
Westholm NW11 47 D5
Westholme BR6 211 D2
Westholme Gdns HA4 40 A1
Westhope Ho [29] E2 96 A4
Westhorne Ave SE9,
SE12 165 C5
Westhorpe Gdns NW4 46 C6
Westhorpe Rd SW15 134 C2
West House Cl SW19 157 A3
Westhurst Dr BR7 188 D5
West India Ave E14 119 C5
West India Dock Rd
E14 119 C6
West India Ho [1] E14 119 C6
West India Quay Sta
E14 119 C6
WEST KENSINGTON 113 A2
West Kensington Ct
W14 254 C2
West Kensington Mans
W14 254 C1
West Kensington Sta
W14 113 B1 254 C2
WEST KILBURN 91 A4
West La SE16 118 B4
Westlake [12] SE16 118 C2
Westlake Cl
Hayes UB4 85 A3
Palmers Green N13 16 C1
Westlake Rd HA9 65 D6
Westland Cl TW19 148 A5
Westland Ct [9] UB5 84 D4
Westland Dr BR2, BR4 224 D6
Westland Ho [1] E16 122 C5
Westland Lo [1] BR1 187 C1
Westland Pl N1 235 C2
Westlands Cl UB3 106 A2
Westlands Ct KT8 196 C5
Westlands Terr [3]
SW12 159 C5
Westlea Rd W7 109 A3
West Lea Sch N9 17 C1
Westleigh Ave SW15 156 C6
Westleigh Ct
Finchley N12 29 D4
[16] Wanstead E11 55 A4
Westleigh Dr BR1 188 A2
Westleigh Gdns HA8 26 C1
West Links HA0 87 D4
Westlinton Cl NW7 29 A4
West Lodge Ave W3 110 C5
West Lodge Ct W3 110 C5
West Lodge Fst & Mid
Schs HA5 40 D5
West Lodge Sch
DA15 168 A1
West London Acad
Northolt UB5 63 A1
Northolt UB5 85 A6
West London Shooting
Grounds UB5 84 B5
Westly Ct NW2 68 D2
Westly Ho N9 18 B3
Westmacott Dr TW14 149 D3
Westmacott Ho NW8 236 D5
West Mall W11 245 B4
Westmark Point [13]
SW15 156 B3
Westmead SW15 156 B5
West Mead
Ruislip HA4 62 C4
West Ewell KT19 215 C2
Westmead Cnr SM5 218 C4
Westmead Rd SM1 218 B4
Westmeath Ho NW2 68 A5
Westmere Dr NW7 11 B1
West Mersea Cl [9]
E16 121 B5
West Mews SW1 259 A3
West Middlesex Univ
Hospl TW7 131 A3
Westmill Ct N4 73 A6
WESTMINSTER 115 C4
Westminster Abbey*
SW1 116 A3 260 A6
Westminster Abbey Choir
Sch SW1 115 D3 259 D6
Westminster Acad
NW1 92 C2 237 A4
Westminster Acad (Sch of
English) W1 93 C1 239 B2
Westminster Ave
CR7 182 D1
Westminster Boating Base
SW1 269 C6
Westminster Bridge SE1,
SW1 116 A4 250 B1
Westminster Bridge Rd
SE1 116 B4 250 C1
Westminster Cath*
SW1 115 C3 259 A5
Westminster Cath Choir
Sch SW1 115 C2 259 B4
Westminster Cath RC
Prim Sch
SW1 115 D1 259 D2
Westminster City Hall
SW1 259 B6
Westminster City Sch
SW1 259 B6
Westminster Cl
East Bedfont TW14 150 A3
Teddington TW11 175 A5
Westminster Coll of
Computing HA9 66 A3
Westminster Ct
[22] Rotherhithe SE16 118 D5
South Norwood CR7 183 A1
[5] Wandsworth SW18 157 C6
Wanstead E11 55 B3
Westminster Dr N13 32 A5
Westminster Gdns
Barking IG11 101 C5
Chingford E4 20 C3
SW1 260 A4
Westminster Ind Est
SE18 121 D3
Westminster Kingsway
Coll
Battersea
SW11 137 A4 268 B2
St Pancras WC1 94 B4 233 C1
Westminster Kingsway
Coll (Regent's Park Ctr)
NW1 93 C3 239 A6
Westminster Pier
SW1 250 B1
Westminster Rd
Carshalton SM1 218 B6
Ealing W7 108 C5
Edmonton N9 18 B3
Westminster Sch
SW1 116 A3 260 A6
Westminster Sta
SW1 116 A4 250 B1
Westminster Under Sch
SW1 115 D2 259 C3
Westmoat Cl BR3 186 A3
WEST MOLESEY 195 C5
Westmont Rd KT10 212 C6
Westmoor Gdns EN3 6 D3
Westmoor Rd EN3 6 D3
Westmoor St SE7 121 D3
Westmore Ct SW15 157 A6
Westmoreland Ave
DA16 145 C1
Westmoreland Dr
SM2 217 D1
Westmoreland Ho
NW10 90 A4
Westmoreland Pl
[5] Bromley BR1 209 A6
Ealing W5 87 D2
Pimlico SW1 258 D1
Westmoreland Rd
Barnes SW13 134 A4
Westmoreland Rd *continued*
Beckenham BR2, BR3 208 D5
Bromley BR2 209 A5
Camberwell SE17 139 B6
Queensbury NW9 44 B5
Westmoreland St W1 238 B3
Westmoreland Terr
[10] Penge SE20 184 B3
SW1 115 B1 258 D1
Westmorland Cl
[3] Twickenham TW1 153 B5
Wanstead E12 77 D6
Westmorland Ct
[12] Surbiton KT6 197 D2
Sutton SM1 218 A5
Westmorland Rd
BR2 209 A5
Harrow HA1 41 D4
Walthamstow E17 53 C3
Westmorland Way
CR4 203 D4
Westmount Ct W5 88 B2
Westmount Rd SE9 144 C1
WEST NORWOOD 161 A1
West Norwood Sta
SE27 160 D1
West Oak BR3 186 B2
Westoe Rd N9 18 B2
Weston Ave
East Molesey KT8 195 B5
Thames Ditton KT10,
KT7 196 C2
Westonbirt Ct [6]
SE15 139 D6
Weston Ct
Highbury N4 73 A5
[3] Kingston u T KT1 198 A6
Oakleigh Pk N20 14 A4
Weston Dr HA7 25 B2
Weston Ed Ctr The
SE5 139 A3
West One Ho W1 239 A3
Westone Mans [6]
IG11 79 D1
West One Sh Ctr
W1 93 B1 238 C1
Weston Gdns TW7 130 C4
Weston Gn
Dagenham RM9 81 B4
Thames Ditton KT7 196 C1
Weston Gr [1] BR1 186 D2
WESTON GREEN 196 D1
Weston Green Prep Sch
KT7 196 C1
Weston Green Rd
KT7 196 C2
Weston Ho
[6] Brondesbury NW6 69 A1
[8] South Hackney E9 96 C6
Weston Lo KT7 196 D1
Weston Park Cl KT7 196 C1
Weston Park Prim Sch
N8 50 B4
Weston Pk
Hornsey Vale N8 50 B3
Kingston u T KT1 176 A1
Thames Ditton KT10,
KT7 196 C1
Weston Rd
Acton Green W4 111 A3
Bromley BR1 186 D3
Dagenham RM9 81 A4
Enfield EN2 5 B3
Thames Ditton KT7 196 C1
Weston Rise N1,
WC1 94 B4 233 D2
Weston St
SE1 117 B4 252 D2
Weston Wlk [3] E8, E9 74 B1
Westover Hill NW3 69 C6
Westover Rd SW18 158 A5
Westow Hill SE19 183 D4
Westow St SE19 183 C4
Westpark W5 87 D1
West Park Ave TW9 132 D4
West Park Cl
Heston TW5 129 B6
Ilford RM6 58 D4
West Park Rd
Richmond TW9 132 C4
Southall UB2 108 B5
West Parkside
Greenwich SE10 120 D3
Greenwich SE10 121 A2
West Pk SE9 166 A3
West Pl SW19 178 C5
West Plaza E14 119 D5
Westpoint
Beckenham BR2 208 B6
Putney SW15 156 D5
West Point [2] SE1 118 A1
Westpoint Apartments
N8 50 B5
Westpoint Trad Est
W3 88 D2
Westpole Ave EN4 3 B1
Westport Ct UB4 84 C3
Westport Rd E13 99 B3
Westport St E1 96 D1
West Poultry Ave EC1 241 C3
West Quarters W12 90 A1
West Quay Dr UB4 85 A2
West Ramp TW6 126 C4
West Rd
Chelsea
SW3 136 D6 267 D6
Clapham Pk SW4 159 D6
Dagenham RM6 59 A3
Ealing W5 88 A2
East Barnet EN4 15 A3
East Bedfont TW14 149 B4
Finchley N2 30 B2
Kingston u T KT2, KT3 177 A2
Tottenham N17 34 B4
West Drayton UB7 104 B3
West Ham E15 98 D6
West Ridge Gdns UB6 86 A5
Westrow SW15 156 C5
West Row W10 91 A3
Westrow Dr IG11 80 A2
Westrow Gdns IG3 79 D5
WEST RUISLIP 61 B6
West Ruislip Ct HA4 61 B6
West Ruislip Elementary
Sch UB10 61 A5
West Ruislip Sta HA4 61 A6
West Sheen Vale
TW9 132 B1
Westside
[11] Hammersmith
W6 112 A2
Hendon NW4 28 B1
Muswell Hill N2 48 D6
West Side Comm
SW19 178 C5
Westside Ct [1] W9 91 C3
West Silvertown Sta
E16 121 A5
West Smithfield
EC1 94 D2 241 D3
West Sq SE11 116 D3 261 C5
West St
[30] Bethnal Green E2 96 B5
Bexleyheath DA7 147 B2
Bromley BR1 187 A1
Carshalton SM5 218 D4
Croydon CR0 221 A4
Harrow HA1 42 C1
Leyton E11 76 C5
Soho WC2 93 D1 239 D1
Sutton SM1 217 D3
Walthamstow E17 53 D4
West Street La SM5 218 D4
West Street Pl [1]
CR0 221 A4
West Surrey Est
TW15 171 A2
West Sutton Sta SM1 217 C4
West Temple Sheen
SW14 154 D6
West Tenter St
E1 95 D1 243 D1
West Terr DA15 167 C3
West Thames Coll
TW7 130 C4
West Thamesmead Bsns
Pk SE28 123 D3
West Thornton Prim Sch
CR0 204 B3
West Towers HA5 40 D3
West Twyford Prim Sch
NW10 88 C5
Westvale Mews W3 111 C4
Westview W7 86 C1
West View
Dagenham RM6 58 C4
East Bedfont TW14 149 A4
Westview Cl
North Kensington W10 90 C1
Willesden NW10 67 D3
Westview Cres N9 17 C4
Westview Ct
[3] Elstree WD6 9 D5
[1] Whetstone N20 14 A2
Westview Dr IG8 37 D1
West View Gdns WD6 9 D5
Westville Rd
Shepherd's Bush
W12 112 A4
Thames Ditton KT7 197 A2

Westward Rd E4 35 B5
Westward Way HA3 44 A3
West Warwick Pl SW1 259 A3
Westway
Shepherd's Bush W10, W12 112 A6
West Barnes SW20 200 C5
West Way
BR5 211 B4
Burnt Oak HA8 27 A4
Croydon CR0 223 A5
Edmonton N18 33 B6
Hounslow TW5 129 B4
Neasden NW10 67 B5
Pinner HA5 40 D5
Ruislip HA4 39 D1
Shepperton TW17 193 B3
West Wickham BR4 208 C3
Westway Cl SW20 200 B6
Westway Ct UB5 85 C6
Westway (Elevated Rd) W10 91 B2
West Way Gdns CR0 222 D6
Westway Lo 35 W2 91 C2
Westways KT19 215 D4
West Ways HA6 22 A1
Westwell 4 NW5 71 A2
Westwell Rd SW16 182 A4
Westwell Road App SW16 182 A4
Westwick 7 KT1 176 C1
Westwick Gdns
Cranford TW4, TW5 128 B3
Hammersmith W14 112 D4
WEST WICKHAM 224 C6
West Wickham Sta BR3 208 A2
West Wimbledon Prim Sch SW20 200 B6
West Wlk
East Barnet EN4 15 A3
Hayes UB3 106 A5
Westwood Ave
Harrow HA2 63 D4
South Norwood SE19 183 A2
Westwood Bsns Ctr NW10 89 C3
Westwood Cl
BR1 209 D6
Esher KT10 212 A5
Ruislip HA4 38 D3
Westwood Coll DA16 145 C1
Westwood Ct
Enfield EN1 17 C5
3 Forest Hill SE23 162 C3
7 Wimbledon SW19 179 B5
Westwood Gdns SW13 133 D2
Westwood Hill SE26 184 B6
Westwood Ho
6 Shepherd's Bush W12 112 C5
5 Stoke Newington N4 51 B2
Westwood La DA16 145 D1
Westwood Language College for Girls SE19 183 B3
Westwood Lo N12 30 C5
Westwood Park Trad Est W3 88 D3
Westwood Pk SE23 162 B4
Westwood Pl SE26 184 A6
Westwood Rd
Barnes SW13 133 D2
Ilford IG3 58 A2
Westwood Sch WD23 8 B2
West Woodside DA5 169 A3
Wetheral Ct SW17 180 B6
Wetheral Dr HA7 25 C1
Wetherby Cl UB5 63 D2
Wetherby Ct SE25 183 C1
Wetherby Gdns SW5 114 A2 256 A3
Wetherby Mans SW5 255 C2
Wetherby Mews SW5 255 D2
Wetherby Pl SW7 114 A2 256 B3
Wetherby Rd EN2 5 A4
Wetherby Way KT9 214 A1
Wetherden St E17 53 B2
Wetherell Rd E9 96 D6
Wetherill Rd N10 31 A2
Wevco Wharf SE15 140 B6
Wexford Ho 11 E1 96 C2
Wexford Rd SW12 158 D4
Weybourne St SW18 158 A2
Weybridge Ct 19 SE16 118 B1
Weybridge Ho N4 51 A2
Weybridge Point 11 SW11 136 D3
Weybridge Rd CR7 204 C5
Wey Ct KT19 215 A4
Weydown Cl SW19 157 A3
Weyhill Ho 26 SE5 139 A3
Weyhill Rd 11 E1 96 A1
Wey Ho
6 Northolt UB5 85 B3
NW8 236 D5
Weylands Cl KT12 195 B1
Weylond Rd RM8 81 B5
Weyman Rd SE3 143 C4
Weymarks The N17 33 B4
Weymouth Ave
Brentford W5 109 C3
Edgware NW7 27 C5
Weymouth Cl 1 E6 100 D1
Weymouth Ct
Belmont SM2 217 C1
5 Haggerston E2 95 D5
15 Streatham SW2 160 B4
Weymouth Ho
Bromley BR2 186 D1
Edgware HA8 26 B4
Fitzrovia W1 238 D4
South Lambeth SW8 270 C3
Weymouth Mews W1 93 B2 238 C4
Weymouth Rd UB4 83 C4
Weymouth St W1 93 B2 238 C4
Weymouth Terr E2 95 D5
Weymouth Wlk HA7 25 A4
Whadcoat St N4 72 C6
Whaddon Ho
10 Camberwell SE5 139 C2
SW1 247 D1
Whalebone Ave RM6 59 B3
Whalebone Gr RM6 59 B3
Whalebone La E15 76 C1
Whalebone Lane N RM6 59 A6
Whalebone Lane S RM6, RM8 59 B2
Whales Yd E15 76 C1
Wharfdale Cl N11 31 A4
Wharfdale Rd N1 94 A5 233 B4
Wharfedale Ct 5 E5 74 D4
Wharfedale Gdns CR7, SW16 204 B6
Wharfedale St SW10 255 C1
Wharf La
19 Poplar E14 97 B1
Twickenham TW1 153 A3
Wharf Pl E2 96 B6
Wharf Rd
Enfield EN3 19 A5
King's Cross NW1 93 D6 232 D5
Shoreditch N1 95 A5 235 A3
Wharf Road NW1 94 A5 233 A4
Wharfside HA0 88 A6
Wharfside Rd E16 98 C2
Wharf St E16 98 C2
Wharf View Ct 15 E14 98 A1
Wharncliffe Dr UB1 108 B5
Wharncliffe Gdns SE25 183 C1
Wharncliffe Ho 3 SW15 156 C6
Wharncliffe Rd SE25 183 C1
Wharton Cl NW10 67 C2
Wharton Ho SE1 263 C6
Wharton Rd BR1 187 B2
Wharton St WC1 94 B4 233 D1
Whateley Rd
East Dulwich SE22 161 D6
Penge SE20 184 D3
Whatley Ave SW20 201 A6
Whatman Ho 10 E14 97 B1
Whatman Rd SE23 162 D4
Wheatcroft Ct SM1 201 D1
Wheatfields
Enfield EN3 7 A3
Newham E6 100 D1
Wheatfield Way KT1 176 A1
Wheathill Ho SE20 184 B1
Wheathill Rd SE20 206 B6
Wheat Ho TW19 148 A3
Wheatland Ho 7 SE22 139 C2
Wheatlands TW5 129 C6
Wheatlands Rd SW17 159 A1
Wheatley Cl NW4 28 A1
Wheatley Cres UB3 106 A6
Wheatley Gdns N9 17 C2
Wheatley Ho
Gospel Oak NW5 71 B4
3 Putney SW15 156 A4
Wheatley Mans 8 IG11 80 A1
Wheatley Rd TW7 130 D2
Wheatley St W1 238 B3
Wheatsheaf Cl UB5 63 A3
Wheat Sheaf Cl E14 119 D2
Wheatsheaf La
Fulham SW6 134 C5
SW8 270 B4
Wheatsheaf Par 7 BR4 207 D1
Wheatsheaf Terr SW6 264 D3
Wheatstone Cl SW19 180 C2
Wheatstone Ho 7 W10 91 A2
Wheatstone Rd W10 91 A2
Wheeler 2 NW9 27 D3
Wheeler Ct 5 SW11 136 B2
Wheeler Gdns N1 233 B6
Wheeler La E1 243 C4
Wheeler Pl 2 BR2 209 B5
Wheelers Cross IG11 101 B5
Wheelers Dr HA4 39 A3
Wheeler's St SM1 217 C5
Wheelhouse The 4 E14 119 D1
Wheelock Cl DA8 147 D5
Wheelwright St N7 72 B1
Whelan Way SM6 219 D5
Wheldon Ct SE1 253 C2
Wheler Ho E1 243 C5
Wheler St E1 95 D3 243 C5
Whellock Rd W4 111 C3
Whernside Cl SE28 124 C6
WHETSTONE 14 A2
Whetstone Cl N20 14 B2
Whetstone Park WC2 94 B1 240 C2
Whetstone Rd SE3 143 D4
Whewell Rd N19 72 A6
Whichcote St SE1 251 A3
Whidborne Bldgs WC1 233 A1
Whidborne Cl SE8 141 C3
Whidborne St WC1 233 B1
Whimbrel Cl SE28 124 C6
Whimbrel Way UB4 84 D2
Whinchat Rd SE18, SE28 123 B3
Whinfell Cl SW16 181 D5
Whinyates Rd SE9 144 A2
Whippendell Cl BR5 190 B2
Whippendell Way BR5 190 B1
Whippingham Ho 22 E3 97 B4
Whipps Cross E17 54 B4
Whipps Cross Ho E17 54 B4
Whipps Cross Hospl E10, E11 54 B3
Whipps Cross Rd E11 54 C3
Whiskin St EC1 94 D4 234 C1
Whisperwood Cl HA3 24 C3
Whistler Gdns HA8 26 B1
Whistler Mews
Dagenham RM8 80 B3
23 SE15 139 D5
Whistlers Ave SW11 136 B5 266 D3
Whistler St N5 72 D3
Whistler Twr SW10 266 A3
Whistler Wlk SW10 266 B4
Whiston Ho 18 N1 72 D1
Whiston Rd E2 96 A6
Whitakers Lo EN2 5 B4
Whitbread Cl N17 34 A2
Whitbread Ctr EC1 242 C5
Whitbread Rd SE4 141 B1
Whitburn Rd SE13 142 A1
Whitby Ave NW10 88 D4
Whitby Ct
6 Lower Holloway N7 72 A4
3 New Southgate N11 31 A4
Whitby Gdns
Carshalton SM1 218 B6
Queensbury NW9 44 C6
Whitby Ho NW8 229 A5
Whitby Par HA4 62 C6
Whitby Rd
Carshalton SM1 218 B6
Harrow HA2 64 A5
Ruislip HA4 62 C6
Woolwich SE18 122 B2
Whitby St E1 243 C6
Whitcher Cl SE14 141 A6
Whitcher Pl NW1 71 C2
Whitchurch Ave HA8 26 B3
Whitchurch Cl HA8 26 B4
Whitchurch Ct SW17 180 B6
Whitchurch Fst & Mid Schs HA7 25 D3
Whitchurch Gdns HA8 26 B4
Whitchurch Ho
Catford SE6 164 A1
16 North Kensington W10 90 D1
Whitchurch La HA8 26 B3
Whitchurch Par HA8 26 C3
Whitchurch Rd W11 112 D6
Whitcomb Ct W1 249 D5
Whitcomb St WC2 115 D6 249 D5
Whitcome Mews TW9 132 D4
Whiteacre Mews SE11 261 B1
Whiteadder Way E14 119 D2
Whitear Wlk E15 76 B2
Whitebarn La RM10 103 C6
Whitebeam Ave BR2 210 C3
Whitebeam Cl SW9 270 D3
Whitebeam Ho 3 NW3 70 D2
White Bear Pl 1 NW3 70 B4
White Bear Yd EC1 241 A5
White Bridge Ave CR4 202 B6
White Bridge Cl TW14 149 D5
White Butts Rd HA4 62 D5
WHITECHAPEL 95 D1
Whitechapel High St E1 95 D1 243 D2
Whitechapel Mkt E1 96 A2
Whitechapel Rd E1 96 B2
Whitechapel Sta E1 96 B2
Whitechurch La 3 E1 96 A1
Whitechurch Pas 1 E1 96 A1
White City W10 90 C1
White City Cl W12 112 C6
White City Est W12 112 B6
White City Rd W12 112 C6
White City Sta W12 112 C6
Whitecliff Ho SW18 157 D5
White Conduit St N1 234 B4
Whitecote Rd UB1 86 A1
White Craig Cl HA5 23 C5
Whitecroft Cl BR3 208 B5
Whitecroft Way BR3 208 B5
Whitecross Pl EC2 242 D4
Whitecross St EC1 95 A3 242 B5
White Cube The, Art Gallery* N1 95 C4
Whitefield Ave NW2 46 C1
Whitefield Cl SW15 157 A5
Whitefield Sch
Chingford E17 36 A1
Hendon NW2 46 D2
Whitefoot La BR1 164 B1
Whitefoot Terr BR1 164 D1
Whitefriars Ave HA3 24 C1
Whitefriars Ct 9 N12 30 B5
Whitefriars Dr HA3 24 C1
Whitefriars Fst & Mid Sch HA3 24 C1
Whitefriars St EC4 94 C1 241 B1
Whitefriars Trad Est HA3 24 B1
White Gate Gdns HA3 24 D3
Whitegates 4 EN5 13 D6
White Gdns RM10 81 C2
Whitehall SW1 250 A2
Whitehall Cres KT9 213 D3
Whitehall Ct SW1 116 A5 250 B3
Whitehall Gdns
Acton W3 110 C5
Chingford E4 20 C3
Chiswick W4 132 D6
SW1 250 A3
Whitehall La IG9 21 A2
Whitehall Lo
Muswell Hill N10 49 A6
Woodford IG8 21 A1
Whitehall Mans 3 N19 49 C1
Whitehall Park Rd W4 132 D6
Whitehall Pk N19 49 C1
Whitehall Pl
Wallington SM5 219 B4
WC2, SW1 116 A5 250 A3
Whitehall Prim Sch E4 20 C2
Whitehall Rd
Bromley BR2 209 D5
Chingford E4 20 C2
Harrow HA1 42 C2
Thornton Heath CR7 204 C4
West Ealing W7 109 A4
Woodford IG8 21 A1
Whitehall St N17 33 D3
White Hart Ave SE28, SE18 123 D3
White Hart La
Mortlake SW13 133 C2
Willesden NW10 67 D2
White Hart Lane Sec Sch N22 32 D3
White Hart Lane Sta N17 33 D3
White Hart Lane (Tottenham Hotspur FC) N17 34 A3
Whitehart Lo SW19 180 A4
White Hart Rd SE18 123 C2
White Hart Rdbt UB5 84 D5
White Hart St
Holborn EC4 241 D2
Kennington SE11 116 C1 261 B2
White Hart Terr N17 33 D3
White Hart Yd SE1 252 C3
Whitehaven Cl BR2 209 A5
Whitehaven Ct 5 DA6 147 A1
Whitehaven St NW8 237 A5
Whitehead Cl
Edmonton N18 33 B5
Wandsworth SW18 158 A4
Whitehead Ct
Muswell Hill N10 31 A2
Twickenham TW1 152 D4
Whitehead Ho 8 SW15 156 D6
Whitehead's Gr SW3 114 C2 257 B3
White Heart Ave UB8 83 A2
Whiteheath Ave HA4 39 A2
Whiteheath Inf Sch HA4 39 A3
Whiteheath Jun Sch HA4 39 A2
White Heron Mews TW11 174 D4
White Ho
2 Battersea SW11 136 B3
Lower Edmonton N9 18 C2
3 Streatham SW4 159 D4
Whitehorn Ho 6 E1 118 C5
White Horse Hill BR7, SE9 188 C6
Whitehorse La SE25 205 C5
White Horse La E1 96 D2
Whitehorse Manor Inf Sch CR7 205 B5
Whitehorse Manor Jun Sch CR7 205 B5
Whitehorse Mews SE1 261 C6
Whitehorse Rd
South Norwood CR0, CR7 205 B3
Tower Hamlets E1 97 A2
White Horse Rd
Limehouse E1 97 A1
Newham E6 100 B4
White Horse St W1 115 B5 248 D3
White Horse Yd EC2 242 C2
White Ho The
NW1 238 D6
Tottenham N17 51 C6
Upper Tooting SW17 180 D5
White House Ct
1 Beckenham BR3 186 A2
Osidge N14 15 D2
White House Dr HA7 25 C6
Whitehouse Est E10 54 A3
White House La EN2 5 A4
Whitehouse Way N14 15 B1
White Kennett St E1 243 B2
Whitelands Cres SW18 157 A4
Whitelands Ho SW3 257 D2
Whiteledges W13 87 C1
Whitelegg Rd E13 98 D5
Whiteley Ho 9 SW4 159 D4
Whiteley Rd SE19 183 B5
Whiteleys Ctr 19 W2 91 D1
Whiteleys Ho TW13 151 C1
Whiteleys Par 5 UB10 82 D3
Whiteleys Way TW13 151 C1
White Lion Ct EC3 243 A1
White Lion Hill EC4 116 D6 251 D6
White Lion St N1 94 C5 234 B3
White Lo
7 Ealing W5 87 C2
Golders Green NW11 47 B1
South Norwood SE19 182 D3
Whitelock Ho 21 E9 74 D2
White Lodge Cl
Hampstead Garden Suburb N2 48 B3
Isleworth TW7 131 A3
Sutton SM2 218 A1
White Lodge Ct TW16 172 C2
Whitely Ct TW13 151 B1
White Lyon Ct EC2 242 A4
Whiteness Ho 18 SW9 138 C4
White Oak Dr BR3 186 A1
White Oak Gdns DA15 167 D4
Whiteoak Ho SE19 183 A3
Whiteoaks La UB6 86 B5
White Orchards
Barnet N20 13 B3
Stanmore HA7 25 A5
White Post La E9 75 C2
White Post St SE14, SE15 140 C5
White Rd E15 76 C1
Whites Ave IG2 57 C3
Whites Dr BR2 208 D2
White's Grounds SE1 117 C4 253 B2
White's Grounds Est SE1 253 B2
White's Mdw BR1 210 C5
Whitespar DA14 189 D6
White's Row E1 95 D2 243 C3
White's Sq SW4 137 D1
White St UB1 106 D4
Whitestile Rd TW8 109 D1
Whitestone La NW3 70 A5
Whitestone Wlk NW3 70 A5
Whitethorn Ave UB7 104 B6
Whitethorn Gdns
Croydon CR0 222 B6
Enfield EN2 17 B6
Whitethorn Pl UB7 104 B5
Whitethorn St E3 97 C2
Whiteways NW4 46 D5
Whitewebbs Way BR5 189 D2
Whitfield Ct
3 Dulwich SE21 183 C6
Redbridge IG1 56 B2
SW4 270 A1
West Barnes SW20 178 D1
Whitfield Gdns W1 239 B4
Whitfield Ho NW8 237 A5
Whitfield Pl W1 239 B5
Whitfield Rd
DA7 147 B5
Upton E6 77 C1
Whitfield St W1 93 C2 239 B4
Whitford Gdns CR4 202 D6
Whitgift Ave CR2 221 A3
Whitgift Ct CR2 221 A3
Whitgift Ctr CR0 221 A6
Whitgift Ho
Battersea SW11 267 A2
Croydon CR2 221 A3
Lambeth SE11 260 C4
Whitgift Sch CR2 221 A3
Whitgift St
Croydon CR0 221 A5
SE11 116 B2 260 C4
Whiting Ave IG11 78 D1
Whitings Hill Prim Sch EN5 12 C6
Whitings Rd EN5 12 C6
Whitings The IG2 57 C4
Whitings Way E6 100 C2
Whitington Ave EC3 243 A1
Whitland Rd SM5 202 B1
Whitley Cl TW19 148 A5
Whitley Ho SW1 269 B6
Whitley Rd N17 33 C1
Whitlock Dr SW19 157 A3
Whitman Ho 20 E2 96 C4
Whitman Rd E3 97 A3
Whitmead Cl CR2 221 C2
Whitmore Cl N11 31 B5
Whitmore Gdns NW10 90 C5

Whitmore High Sch HA1, HA2 ... 42 A1
Whitmore Ho
Friern Barnet N11 ... 30 D6
20 Hoxton E1 ... 95 C6
Whitmore Prim Sch N1 ... 95 B6 235 D5
Whitmore Rd
Beckenham BR3 ... 207 B6
Harrow HA1 ... 42 A2
Hoxton N1 ... 95 C6
Whitnell Ct 7 SW15 ... 156 D6
Whitnell Way SW15 ... 156 D6
Whitney Ave IG4 ... 55 D5
Whitney Ho 6 SE22 ... 139 C2
Whitney Rd E10 ... 53 D2
Whitney Wlk DA14 ... 191 A4
Whitstable Cl
Beckenham BR3 ... 185 B2
Ruislip HA4 ... 61 C6
Whitstable Ho 11 W10 ... 90 D1
Whitstable Pl 9 CR0 ... 221 A4
Whitsters Ho SE1 ... 253 C2
Whitstone La BR3 ... 207 D4
Whittaker 3 NW9 ... 27 D3
Whittaker Ave TW10, TW9 ... 153 D6
Whittaker Ct SW4 ... 270 B1
Whittaker Pl 28 TW10 ... 153 D6
Whittaker Rd
Cheam SM3 ... 217 B5
Forest Gate E6 ... 77 D1
Whittaker St SW1 ... 258 A3
Whittaker Way 19 SE1 ... 118 A2
Whittam Ho SE27 ... 183 A5
Whitta Rd E12 ... 77 D4
Whittell Gdns SE26 ... 162 C1
Whitten Lo N12 ... 30 C6
Whittingham 6 N17 ... 34 B3
Whittingham Com Prim Sch E17 ... 35 A2
Whittingham Ct W4 ... 133 C5
Whittingstall Mans SW6 ... 264 D1
Whittingstall Rd SW6 ... 135 B4 264 D1
Whittington Ave UB4 ... 83 D2
Whittington Ct
Fortis Green N2 ... 48 D4
Penge SE20 ... 184 B1
Whittington Hospl The N19 ... 71 C6
Whittington Mews N12 ... 30 A6
Whittington Rd N22 ... 32 A3
Whittington Way HA5 ... 41 A4
Whittle 4 NW9 ... 27 D3
Whittlebury Cl SM5 ... 218 D1
Whittlebury Ho N4 ... 51 A2
Whittle Cl
Southall UB1 ... 85 D1
Walthamstow E17 ... 53 A2
Whittle Rd
Heston TW5 ... 128 C5
Southall UB2 ... 107 D4
Whittlesea Cl HA3 ... 24 A3
Whittlesea Path HA3 ... 24 A2
Whittlesea Rd HA3 ... 24 A2
Whittlesey St SE1 ... 116 C5 251 B3
WHITTON ... 152 A4
Whitton NW3 ... 70 D1
Whitton Ave W UB5, UB6 ... 64 B3
Whitton Cl UB6 ... 65 B2
Whitton Dene TW3, TW7 ... 152 B6
Whitton Dr UB6 ... 65 A2
Whitton Manor Rd TW7 ... 152 A5
Whitton Rd
Hounslow TW3 ... 151 D6
Twickenham TW1 ... 153 A4
Whitton Road Rdbt TW1 ... 152 D5
Whitton Sch TW2 ... 151 D2
Whitton Sta TW2 ... 152 A4
Whitton Waye TW2, TW3 ... 151 C5
Whitton Wlk E3 ... 97 C4
Whitwell Ho 11 E5 ... 74 B6
Whitwell Rd E13 ... 99 A4
Whitworth Cres 1 EN3 ... 7 C6
Whitworth Ho SE1 ... 262 B5
Whitworth Rd
SE18 ... 144 C5
South Norwood SE25 ... 205 D5
Whitworth St SE10 ... 120 C1
Whorlton Rd SE15 ... 140 B2
Whychcote Point NW2 ... 46 C2
Whymark Ave N22 ... 50 D6
Whytecroft TW5 ... 128 D5
Whyteville Ho E7 ... 77 B2
Whyteville Rd E7 ... 77 B2
Whytlaw Ho 10 E3 ... 97 B2
Wickersley Rd SW11 ... 137 A3
Wickers Oake SE19 ... 183 D6
Wicker St 24 E1 ... 96 B1
Wicket Rd UB6 ... 87 A4
Wickets The TW15 ... 170 A6
Wicket The CR0 ... 223 C3
Wickfield Ho 32 SE16 ... 118 A4
Wickford Ho 5 E1 ... 96 C3
Wickford St E1 ... 96 C3
Wickford Way E17 ... 52 D5
Wickham Ave
Cheam KT4, SM3 ... 216 C3
Croydon CR0 ... 207 A1
Wickham Chase BR4 ... 208 C2
Wickham Cl
Enfield EN3 ... 6 C2
New Malden KT3 ... 199 D4
Stepney E1 ... 96 C2
Wickham Common Prim Sch BR4 ... 225 A4
Wickham Court Rd BR4 ... 224 A6
Wickham Court Sch BR4 ... 224 B4
Wickham Cres BR4 ... 224 A6
Wickham Ct DA16 ... 145 C3
Wickham Gdns SE4 ... 141 B2
Wickham Ho SW15 ... 156 D5
Wickham La SE2 ... 146 A6
Wickham Mews SE4 ... 141 B3
Wickham Rd
Beckenham BR3 ... 207 D6
Brockley SE4 ... 141 B2
Chingford E4 ... 36 A3
Croydon CR0 ... 207 B1
Harrow HA3 ... 24 B1
Wickham St
Bexley DA16 ... 145 C3
Vauxhall SE11 ... 116 B1 260 C2
Welling DA16 ... 146 A4
Wickham Way BR3 ... 208 A4
Wick Ho 1 KT1 ... 175 D2
Wick La
Hackney E3 ... 75 B1
Stratford Marsh E3 ... 97 C6
Wickliffe Ave N3 ... 29 A1
Wickliffe Gdns HA9 ... 66 D6
Wicklow Ct SE26 ... 184 C5
Wicklow Ho N16 ... 51 D1
Wicklow St WC1 ... 94 B4 233 C2
Wick Rd
Hackney E9 ... 74 D2
Hackney E9 ... 75 A2
Teddington TW11 ... 175 C3
Wicks Cl SE12 ... 187 D6
Wickstead Ho TW8 ... 110 B1
Wicksteed Ho SE1 ... 262 B5
Wickway Ct 7 SE15 ... 139 D6
Wickwood St SE5 ... 138 D3
Widdenham Rd N7 ... 72 B4
Widdicombe Ave HA2 ... 63 A6
Widdin St E15 ... 76 C1
Widecombe Ct N2 ... 48 B4
Widecombe Gdns IG4 ... 56 A5
Widecombe Ho 32 SE5 ... 139 A3
Widecombe Rd SE9 ... 166 A1
Widecombe Way N2 ... 48 B5
Widegate St E1 ... 243 B3
Widenham Cl HA5 ... 40 C4
Wide Way CR4 ... 203 D6
Widewing Cl TW11 ... 175 B3
Widford 8 NW1 ... 71 B2
Widford Ho N1 ... 234 C3
Widgeon Cl E16 ... 99 B1
Widgeon Path SE28 ... 123 B3
Widley Rd W9 ... 91 C3
Widmer Ct TW5 ... 129 A3
WIDMORE ... 188 A1
Widmore Lodge Rd BR1 ... 187 D1
Widmore Rd
BR1 ... 187 C1
Hillingdon UB8 ... 82 D3
Widnes Ho 6 N7 ... 72 C3
Wieland Rd HA6 ... 22 A3
Wigan Ho E5 ... 52 B1
Wigeon Way UB4 ... 84 D1
Wiggins La TW10 ... 153 C2
Wiggins Mead NW9 ... 27 D3
Wigginton Ave HA9 ... 66 D2
Wigham Ho IG11 ... 79 A1
Wightman Rd N4, N8 ... 50 C4
Wighton Mews TW7 ... 130 C3
Wigley Rd TW13 ... 150 D3
Wigmore Ct 4 W13 ... 109 A5
Wigmore Hall* W1 ... 238 C2
Wigmore Pl W1 ... 93 B1 238 C2
Wigmore Rd SM5 ... 202 C1
Wigmore St W1 ... 93 A1 238 B2
Wigmore Wlk SM5 ... 218 B6
Wigram Ct SW11 ... 267 A2
Wigram Ho 7 E14 ... 119 D6
Wigram Rd E11 ... 55 C3
Wigram Sq E17 ... 54 A6
Wigston Cl N18 ... 33 C5
Wigston Rd E13 ... 99 B3
Wigton Gdns HA7 ... 26 A2
Wigton Pl SE11 ... 261 B1
Wigton Rd E17 ... 35 B2
Wilberforce Ct
Edgware HA8 ... 26 B6
2 SE28 ... 124 C5
Wilberforce Ho 4 SW11 ... 136 B2
Wilberforce Mews 9 SW4 ... 137 D1
Wilberforce Prim Sch W10 ... 91 A4
Wilberforce Rd
Finsbury Pk N4 ... 72 D6
Hendon NW9 ... 46 A3
Highbury N4, N5 ... 73 A5
Wilberforce Way SW19 ... 178 D4
Wilbraham Ho SW8 ... 270 A3
Wilbraham Pl SW1 ... 258 A4
Wilbury Prim Sch N18 ... 33 B5
Wilbury Way N18 ... 33 B5
Wilby Mews W11 ... 113 B5 244 D4
Wilcox Cl SW8 ... 270 B4
Wilcox Gdns TW17 ... 192 B6
Wilcox Ho 5 E3 ... 97 B2
Wilcox Pl SW1 ... 259 B5
Wilcox Rd
Sutton SM1 ... 217 D4
SW8 ... 138 A5 270 A4
Teddington TW11 ... 174 B6
Wildcroft Gdns HA8 ... 25 D4
Wildcroft Manor SW15 ... 156 C4
Wildcroft Rd SW15 ... 156 C4
Wild Ct WC2 ... 94 B1 240 C2
Wilde Cl E8 ... 96 A6
Wilde Pl
Edmonton N13 ... 32 D4
Wandsworth SW18 ... 158 B4
Wilder Cl HA4 ... 40 B1
Wilde Rd DA8 ... 147 D5
Wilderness Mews SW4 ... 137 B1
Wilderness Rd BR7 ... 188 D3
Wilderness The
East Molesey KT8 ... 196 A4
Hampton TW12 ... 173 D6
Wilderton Rd N16 ... 51 C2
Wildes Cotts SM3 ... 217 A2
Wildfell Rd SE6 ... 163 D4
Wild Goose Dr SE14 ... 140 C4
Wild Hatch NW11 ... 47 C3
Wilding Ho 17 E9 ... 74 D2
Wild Marsh Ct EN3 ... 7 A6
Wild's Rents SE1 ... 117 C3 263 A6
Wild St WC2 ... 94 B1 240 C1
Wildwood Cl SE12 ... 164 D4
Wildwood Gr NW3 ... 48 A1
Wildwood Rd NW11 ... 48 A2
Wildwood Rise NW11 ... 48 A1
Wildwood Terr NW3 ... 48 A1
Wilford Cl EN2 ... 5 B2
Wilford Ho 3 SE18 ... 122 D1
Wilford Rd CR0 ... 205 A2
Wilfred Fienburgh Ho N7 ... 71 D4
Wilfred Owen Cl SW19 ... 180 A4
Wilfred St SW1 ... 115 C3 259 A6
Wilfrid Gdns W3 ... 89 A2
Wilkes Rd 3 TW8 ... 132 A6
Wilkes St E1 ... 95 D2 243 D4
Wilkie Ho SW1 ... 259 D2
Wilkins Cl
Hayes UB3 ... 105 D1
Wilkins Cl *continued*
Mitcham CR4 ... 180 C2
Wilkins Ho SW1 ... 269 A6
Wilkinson Cl UB10 ... 83 A6
Wilkinson Ct SW17 ... 180 B6
Wilkinson Gdns CR7 ... 183 C2
Wilkinson Ho
Isleworth TW7 ... 130 D2
N1 ... 235 D3
Twickenham TW2 ... 152 B2
Wilkinson Rd E16 ... 99 C1
Wilkinson St SW8 ... 138 B5 270 C3
Wilkinson Way W4 ... 111 B4
Wilkin St NW5 ... 71 B2
Wilks Gdns CR0 ... 207 A1
Wilks Pl N1 ... 95 C5
Willan Rd N17 ... 33 C1
Willan Wall E16 ... 120 D6
Willard St SW8 ... 137 B2
Willbury Ho 4 N7 ... 71 D3
Willcocks Cl KT9 ... 214 A5
Willcott Rd W3 ... 110 D5
Will Crooks Gdns SE9 ... 143 D1
Willenfield Rd NW10 ... 89 A5
Willenhall Ave EN5 ... 14 A5
Willenhall Ct EN5 ... 14 A5
Willenhall Dr UB3 ... 105 C6
Willenhall Rd SE18 ... 122 D1
Willersley Ave
Blackfen DA15 ... 167 D4
Orpington BR6 ... 227 B5
Willersley Cl DA15 ... 167 D3
WILLESDEN ... 67 D1
Willesden Community Hospl The NW10 ... 68 A1
WILLESDEN GREEN ... 90 B6
Willesden Green Sta NW2 ... 68 C2
Willesden Junction Sta NW10 ... 89 D4
Willesden La NW2, NW6 ... 68 D2
Willes Rd NW5 ... 71 B2
Willett Cl
BR5 ... 211 C3
3 Northolt UB5 ... 84 C4
Willett Ho
7 Newham E13 ... 99 A5
Stockwell SW9 ... 138 A2
Willett Pl CR7 ... 204 C4
Willett Rd CR7 ... 204 C4
Willett Way BR5 ... 211 C3
William Allen Ho HA8 ... 26 B3
William Ash Cl RM9 ... 80 B2
William Atkinson Ho N17 ... 33 C3
William Banfield Ho 10 SW6 ... 135 B3
William Barefoot Dr SE9 ... 166 C1
William Bellamy Jun & Inf Schs RM10 ... 81 C6
William Blake Ho 2 SE15 ... 140 A3
William Bonney Est 10 SW4 ... 137 D1
William Booth Meml Training Coll SE5 ... 139 B3
William Booth Rd SE20 ... 184 A2
William Brown Ct SE27 ... 160 D2
William Byrd Sch UB3 ... 127 A6
William Carey Way HA1 ... 42 C3
William Caslon Ho 28 E2 ... 96 B5
William Channing Ho 6 E2 ... 96 B4
William C Harvey Sch N17 ... 33 B1
William Cl
26 Finchley N2 ... 30 B1
Lewisham SE13 ... 142 A2
Southall UB2 ... 108 A4
William Covell Cl EN2 ... 4 B5
William Ct
4 Belvedere DA17 ... 125 C2
4 Ealing W5 ... 87 C2
Ilford IG6 ... 57 B5
William Davies Prim Sch E7 ... 77 D2
William Davis Prim Sch E2 ... 96 A3
William Dr HA7 ... 25 B5
William Dromey Ct NW6 ... 69 B1
William Dunbar Ho NW6 ... 91 B5
William Dyce Mews 1 SW16 ... 181 D6
William Ellis Sch NW5 ... 71 A5
William Ellis Way 16 SE16 ... 118 A3
William Evans Ho 9 SE8 ... 118 D2
William Ford CE Jun Sch RM10 ... 81 C1
William Gdns SW15 ... 156 B6
William Guy Gdns 47 E3 ... 97 D4
William Harvey Ho 1 SW19 ... 157 A3
William Ho N13 ... 32 D4
William Hogarth Prim Sch The W4 ... 111 C1
William Hunt Mans SW13 ... 134 C6
William IV St WC2 ... 116 A6 250 A5
William Margrie Cl 1 SE15 ... 140 A3
William Marsden Ho 2 SE27 ... 182 D6
William Mews SW1 ... 114 D4 247 D1
William Morley Cl E6 ... 99 D6
William Morris Acad W6 ... 112 D1
William Morris Cl E17 ... 53 B6
William Morris Gallery* E17 ... 53 C6
William Morris Ho W6 ... 134 D6
William Morris Prim Sch CR4 ... 203 D6
William Morris Sch E17 ... 35 A2
William Morris Way SW6 ... 136 A3
William Patten Prim Sch N16 ... 73 D6
William Perkin Ct UB6 ... 64 C2
William Pl 37 E3 ... 97 B5
William Rainbird Ho 9 N17 ... 33 D3
William Rathbone Ho 3 E2 ... 96 B4
William Rd
Regent's Pk NW1 ... 93 C4 232 A1
Sutton SM1 ... 218 A3
Wimbledon SW19 ... 179 A3
William Rushbrooke Ho 4 SE16 ... 118 A2
Williams Ave E17 ... 35 B2
William Saville Ho 2 NW6 ... 91 B5
William's Bldgs 1 E2 ... 96 C3
Williams Cl SW6 ... 135 A5 264 B4
Williams Coll EC1 ... 241 B3
Williams Dr TW3 ... 129 C1
Williams Gr
Kingston u T KT6 ... 197 C3
Wood Green N22 ... 32 C2
Williams Ho
10 Bow E3 ... 97 C4
9 Hackney E9 ... 96 B6
14 Streatham SW2 ... 160 C3
7 Tottenham N17 ... 33 D3
Willesden NW2 ... 68 C5
Williams La
Morden SM4 ... 202 A4
Mortlake SW14 ... 133 A3
William Smith Ho 10 DA17 ... 125 C3
Williamson Cl SE10 ... 120 D1
Williamson Ct SE17 ... 262 A1
Williamson Rd N4 ... 50 D3
Williamson St N7 ... 72 A4
Williamson Way NW7 ... 29 A4
William Sq 15 SE16 ... 119 A6
Williams Rd UB2 ... 107 A2
William's Rd W13 ... 109 A5
William St
Barking IG11 ... 79 A1
Carshalton SM5 ... 218 D5
SW1 ... 114 D4 247 D1
Tottenham N17 ... 33 D3
Walthamstow E10 ... 53 D3
Williams Terr CR0 ... 220 C2
William Torbitt Prim Sch IG2 ... 57 D4
William Tyndale Prim Sch N1 ... 72 D1
William Wilberforce Ho 1 SE27 ... 182 D6
William Winter Ct 29 SW2 ... 160 C4
William Wood Ho 3 SE26 ... 162 C1
Willifield Way NW11 ... 47 C4
Willingale Cl IG8 ... 37 C4
Willingdon Rd N22 ... 32 D1
Willingham Cl 4 NW5 ... 71 C3
Willingham Terr NW5 ... 71 C3
Willingham Way KT1 ... 176 C1
Willington Ct E5 ... 75 A5
Willington Prep Sch SW19 ... 179 B5
Willington Rd SW9 ... 138 A2
Willis Ave SM2, SM5 ... 218 C2
Willis Ct CR7 ... 204 C3
Willis Ho
2 Ilford E12 ... 78 C5
8 Poplar E14 ... 119 D6
Willis Rd
E15 ... 98 D5
Thornton Heath CR0 ... 205 A2
Willis St E14 ... 97 D1
Willis Yd N14 ... 15 D4
Willlows The CR0 ... 223 A6
Will Miles Ct 6 SW19 ... 180 A3
Willmore End SW19 ... 179 D1
Willoughby Ave CR0 ... 220 B4
Willoughby Gr N17 ... 34 B3
Willoughby Ho
EC2 ... 242 C3
34 Wapping E1 ... 118 B5
Willoughby La N17 ... 34 B3
Willoughby Mews N17 ... 34 B3
Willoughby Park Rd N17 ... 34 B3
Willoughby Rd
Hampstead NW3 ... 70 B4
Hornsey N8 ... 50 C5
Kingston u T KT2 ... 176 B2
Twickenham TW1 ... 153 D6
Willoughby St WC1 ... 240 A3
Willoughbys The SW14 ... 133 C1
Willoughby Way SE7 ... 121 B2
Willow Ave
Barnes SW13 ... 133 D3
DA15 ... 168 A5
Yiewsley UB7 ... 104 B6
Willowbank SW6 ... 135 A2
Willow Bank TW10 ... 153 B1
Willowbank Rd SE15 ... 139 D6
Willowbay Cl EN5 ... 12 D5
Willow Bridge Rd N1 ... 73 A2
Willow Brook Prim Sch E10 ... 53 C1
Willowbrook Rd
Southall UB2 ... 107 C3
Stanwell TW19 ... 148 A2
Willow Bsns Pk SE26 ... 162 C1
Willow Cl
BR2 ... 210 B4
Brentford TW8 ... 131 C6
Buckhurst Hill IG9 ... 21 D1
12 Catford SE6 ... 164 D3
Sidcup DA5 ... 169 B5
Willow Cotts
Carshalton CR4 ... 202 D2
Feltham TW13 ... 151 A1
Richmond TW9 ... 132 C6
Willowcourt Ave HA3 ... 43 B4
Willowcroft SE3 ... 142 D1
Willow Ct
Ashford TW16 ... 171 C3
5 Beckenham BR3 ... 185 C2
Brixton SW9 ... 138 C4
Chiswick W4 ... 133 C5
8 Dagenham RM8 ... 58 D2
EC2 ... 243 A6
Edgware HA8 ... 26 A6
6 Finchley N12 ... 29 D6
Harrow HA3 ... 24 D2
Headstone HA2 ... 24 A1
Ilford IG1 ... 79 A3
Islington N7 ... 72 B3
Kingston u T KT3 ... 198 D6
8 London E11 ... 76 C6
Mitcham CR4 ... 202 C5
40 Paddington W2 ... 91 C2
3 Streatham SW16 ... 160 B1
Thornton Heath CR7 ... 205 B4
Willow Ctr The CR4 ... 202 D3
Willow Dean HA5 ... 22 D1
Willowdene
Highgate N6 ... 48 D2
1 Peckham SE15 ... 140 B4
5 SE15 ... 140 B5

Willow Dene WD23 ... 8 C4
Willowdene Cl TW2 ... 152 A4
Willowdene Ct N20 ... 14 A4
Willow Dene Sch
SE18 ... 145 C4
Willow Dr EN5 ... 1 A1
Willow End
Northwood HA6 ... 22 A4
Surbiton KT6 ... 198 A1
Totteridge N20 ... 13 C2
Willow Farm La
SW15 ... 134 B2
Willowfields Cl SE18 ... 123 C1
Willowfield Sec Sch
E17 ... 52 D6
Willow Gdns
Heston TW5 ... 129 C4
Ruislip HA4 ... 61 D6
Willow Gn
Borehamwood WD6 ... 11 B6
Grahame Pk NW9 ... 27 C2
Willow Gr
BR7 ... 188 D4
Newham E13 ... 99 A5
Ruislip HA4 ... 39 D1
Willow Hall NW3 ... 70 B4
Willowhayne Dr KT12 ... 194 B2
Willowhayne Gdns
KT4 ... 216 C4
Willow Ho TW14 ... 150 B6
Willow Ho
17 Finchley N2 ... 30 B1
9 Maitland Pk NW3 ... 70 D2
North Kensington W10 ... 90 D3
Teddington TW11 ... 175 C3
Willow La
Mitcham CR4 ... 202 D3
Woolwich SE18 ... 122 C2
Willow Lo
6 Ashford TW16 ... 171 D3
Fulham SW6 ... 134 D4
New Barnet EN5 ... 14 A6
Putney SW15 ... 134 B2
Willow Lodge 10
SW8 ... 137 B2
Willow Manor SM1 ... 217 B4
Willowmead Cl W5 ... 87 D2
Willowmere
Esher KT10 ... 212 A4
Ladywell SE13 ... 163 D6
Willow Mount CR0 ... 221 C5
Willow Pl
SW1 ... 115 C2 259 B4
Willow Rd
Dagenham RM6 ... 59 A3
Ealing W5 ... 110 A4
Enfield EN1 ... 5 C3
Hampstead NW3 ... 70 B4
New Malden KT3 ... 199 A5
Wallington SM6 ... 219 B1
Willows Ave SM4 ... 201 D4
Willows Cl HA5 ... 22 C1
Willows Ct 3 SW19 ... 179 C3
Willows Sch The UB4 ... 84 D3
Willow St
Broadgate
EC2 ... 95 C3 243 A6
Chingford E4 ... 20 B4
Willows Terr NW10 ... 89 D5
Willows The
Beckenham BR3 ... 185 C2
Claygate KT10 ... 212 C2
Loughton IG10 ... 21 D6
Wallend E12 ... 78 C1
Whetstone N20 ... 14 A1
Willowtree Cl UB10 ... 61 A5
Willow Tree Cl
Hayes UB4 ... 84 C3
Northolt UB5 ... 63 A2
14 Old Ford E3 ... 97 B6
Wandsworth SW18 ... 157 D3
Willow Tree Ct
DA14 ... 189 D5
4 Wembley HA0 ... 65 D3
Willow Tree La UB4 ... 84 C3
Willow Tree Prim Sch
UB5 ... 63 A2
Willowtree Way
SW16 ... 182 C2
Willow Tree Wlk BR1 ... 187 B2
Willow Vale
BR7 ... 188 D4
Shepherd's Bush W12 ... 112 A5
Willow View SW19 ... 180 B2
Willow Way
Finchley N3 ... 29 D3
Forest Hill SE26 ... 162 C1
9 Shepherd's Bush
W11 ... 112 D6
Sunbury TW16 ... 194 A5
Willow Way *continued*
Twickenham TW2 ... 151 D2
Wembley HA0 ... 65 A5
West Ewell KT19 ... 215 B2
Willow Wlk
Bermondsey
SE1 ... 117 D2 263 C4
Cheam SM1, SM3 ... 217 B5
15 Finchley N2 ... 30 B1
Harringay N15 ... 50 D5
Locksbottom BR6 ... 226 D5
Southgate N21 ... 16 B5
Walthamstow E17 ... 53 B4
Willow Wood Cres
SE25 ... 205 C3
Willridge Ct E11 ... 54 B2
Willrose Cres SE2 ... 124 B1
Willsbridge Ct 1
SE15 ... 139 D6
Wills Cres TW3 ... 151 D5
Wills Gr NW7 ... 28 B5
Will Thorne Pav The
E16 ... 100 A1
Wilman Gr E8 ... 74 A1
Wilmar Cl UB4 ... 83 B3
Wilmar Gdns BR4 ... 207 D1
Wilmcote Ho W2 ... 91 D2
Wilment Ct NW2 ... 68 C5
Wilmer Cl KT2 ... 176 B5
Wilmer Cres KT2 ... 176 B5
Wilmer Gdns 22 N1 ... 95 C6
Wilmer Ho 6 E3 ... 97 A5
Wilmer Lea Cl E15 ... 76 B1
Wilmer Pl N16 ... 73 D6
Wilmers Ct 5 NW10 ... 89 B6
Wilmer Way N14 ... 31 D5
Wilmington Ave W4 ... 133 B5
Wilmington Ct SW16 ... 182 A3
Wilmington Gdns IG11 ... 79 C1
Wilmington Sq
WC1 ... 94 C4 234 A1
Wilmington St WC1 ... 234 A1
Wilmot Cl
Finchley N2 ... 30 A1
SE15 ... 140 A5
Wilmot Ho 14 SM2 ... 218 A2
Wilmot Pl
Camden Town NW1 ... 71 C1
Ealing W7 ... 108 C5
Wilmot Rd
Leyton E10 ... 75 D6
Tottenham N17 ... 51 B6
Wallington SM5 ... 218 D3
Wilmot St E2 ... 96 B3
Wilmount St SE18 ... 122 D2
Wilna Rd SW18 ... 158 A4
Wilnett Ct 4 RM6 ... 58 B2
Wilnett Villas 5 RM6 ... 58 B2
Wilsham St
W11 ... 113 A5 244 A4
Wilshaw Cl NW4 ... 46 A6
Wilshaw Ho 10 SE8 ... 141 C5
Wilshaw St SE14 ... 141 C4
Wilsmere Dr
Harrow HA3 ... 24 C3
Northolt UB5 ... 63 A3
Wilson Ave CR4 ... 180 C2
Wilson Cl
Croydon CR2 ... 221 B3
Wembley HA9 ... 44 B2
Wilson Ct 9 SE28 ... 123 A3
Wilson Dr HA9 ... 44 B2
Wilson Gdns HA1 ... 42 A2
Wilson Gr SE16 ... 118 B4
Wilson Ho
39 Clapham SW8 ... 137 D3
2 SE7 ... 143 C6
South Hampstead NW6 ... 70 A1
Wilson Rd
Camberwell SE5 ... 139 C4
Chessington KT9 ... 214 B2
Newham E6 ... 99 D4
Redbridge IG1 ... 56 B2
Wilson's Ave 4 N17 ... 33 D1
Wilson's Pl E14 ... 97 B1
Wilson's Rd W6 ... 112 D1
Wilson's Sch SM6 ... 220 A2
Wilson St
Broadgate
EC2 ... 95 B2 242 D4
Southgate N21 ... 16 C4
Walthamstow E17 ... 54 A4
Wilstone Cl UB4 ... 85 A3
Wiltern Ct NW2 ... 69 A2
Wilthorne Gdns RM10 ... 81 D1
Wilton Ave W4 ... 111 C1
Wilton Cres
Merton SW19 ... 179 B2
SW1 ... 115 A4 248 A1
Wilton Ct
3 Edgware HA8 ... 26 D5
Muswell Hill N10 ... 31 A1
4 Richmond TW10 ... 154 A6
7 Stepney E1 ... 96 B1
7 Woodford IG8 ... 37 A4
Wilton Est E8 ... 74 A2
Wilton Gdns
East Molesey KT8 ... 195 C6
Walton-on-T KT12 ... 194 D1
Wilton Gr
Merton SW19 ... 179 B2
New Malden KT3 ... 199 D3
Wilton Ho
8 Camberwell SE22 ... 139 C2
Chislehurst BR7 ... 189 B2
Ealing W13 ... 109 B6
Wilton Mews
SW1 ... 115 A3 258 B6
Wilton Par TW13 ... 150 B2
Wilton Pl
2 Beckenham BR3 ... 208 A6
4 Harrow HA1 ... 42 D3
SW1 ... 115 A4 248 A1
Wilton Rd
Abbey Wood SE2 ... 124 C2
Cockfosters EN4 ... 2 D1
Hounslow TW4 ... 128 D2
Mitcham SW19 ... 180 C3
Muswell Hill N10 ... 31 A1
Westminster
SW1 ... 115 C2 259 A4
Wilton Row SW1 ... 248 A1
Wilton Sq N1 ... 95 B6 235 C6
Wilton St SW1 ... 115 B3 258 C6
Wilton Terr SW1 ... 258 A6
Wilton Villas N1 ... 235 C5
Wilton Way E8 ... 74 A2
Wiltshire Cl
Edgware NW7 ... 27 D5
SW3 ... 257 C3
Wiltshire Ct
Barking IG11 ... 79 A2
2 Finsbury Pk N4 ... 50 B1
Wiltshire Gdns
Stoke Newington N4 ... 51 A3
Twickenham TW2 ... 152 A3
Wiltshire La
Pinner HA5 ... 40 A5
Ruislip HA4 ... 39 D6
Wiltshire Rd
Brixton SW9 ... 138 C2
Thornton Heath CR7 ... 204 C6
Wiltshire Row
N1 ... 95 B6 235 D5
Wilverley Cres KT3 ... 199 C3
Wimbart Rd SW2 ... 160 B4
WIMBLEDON ... 179 B4
Wimbledon Bridge
SW19 ... 179 B4
Wimbledon Central
SW19 ... 179 B4
Wimbledon Chase Prim
Sch SW20 ... 179 A2
Wimbledon Chase Sta
SW20 ... 179 A1
Wimbledon Cl 2
SW20 ... 178 D3
Wimbledon Coll
SW19 ... 178 D3
Wimbledon Common*
SW19 ... 178 B6
Wimbledon Common Prep
Sch SW19 ... 178 D3
Wimbledon High Sch
SW19 ... 179 A4
Wimbledon Hill Rd
SW19 ... 179 B4
Wimbledon Lawn Tennis
Mus* SW19 ... 157 A1
Wimbledon Park Ct
SW19 ... 157 B3
Wimbledon Park
Montessori Sch
SW18 ... 157 C2
Wimbledon Park Prim Sch
SW19 ... 157 D2
Wimbledon Park Rd SW18,
SW19 ... 157 B3
Wimbledon Park Side
SW19 ... 156 D3
Wimbledon Park Sta
SW19 ... 157 C1
Wimbledon Rd SW17 ... 180 A6
Wimbledon Sch of Art
SW19 ... 179 A2
Wimbledon Sch of Art
Annexe SW19 ... 179 C3
Wimbledon Sta SW19 ... 179 B4
Wimbledon Stad
SW17 ... 180 A6
Wimbledon Stadium Bsns
Ctr SW17 ... 157 D1
Wimbledon Windmill
Mus* SW19 ... 156 C1
Wimbolt St E2 ... 96 A4
Wimborne 2 DA14 ... 190 B6
Wimborne Ave
Hayes UB4 ... 84 B1
Southall UB2 ... 107 C2
St Paul's Cray BR5,
BR7 ... 211 D5
Wimborne Cl
Buckhurst Hill IG9 ... 21 C2
Lewisham SE12 ... 164 D6
North Cheam KT4 ... 200 C1
Wimborne Ct 1 UB5 ... 63 C2
Wimborne Dr
Pinner HA5 ... 41 A2
Queensbury NW9 ... 44 C6
Wimborne Gdns W13 ... 87 B2
Wimborne Ho
Canning Town E16 ... 120 D6
Croydon CR0 ... 206 C4
Marylebone NW1 ... 237 B5
South Lambeth SW8 ... 270 D3
Upper Tooting SW12 ... 159 C1
Wimborne Rd
Edmonton N9 ... 18 A2
Tottenham N17 ... 33 C1
Wimborne Way BR3 ... 207 A5
Wimbourne Ct
Mitcham SW19 ... 180 B3
N1 ... 235 C4
South Croydon CR2 ... 221 C2
Wimbourne St
N1 ... 95 B5 235 C4
Wimbush Ho 3 N12 ... 29 D5
Wimpole Cl
Bromley BR2 ... 209 C5
1 Kingston u T KT1 ... 176 C1
Wimpole Mews
W1 ... 93 B2 238 C3
Wimpole St W1 ... 93 B1 238 C2
Wimshurst Cl CR0 ... 204 A1
Winans Wlk SW9 ... 138 C3
Winant Ho 19 E14 ... 119 D6
Wincanton Cres UB5 ... 63 C3
Wincanton Ct 2 N11 ... 31 A4
Wincanton Gdns IG6 ... 56 D6
Wincanton Rd SW18 ... 157 B4
Winchcombe Rd SM5 ... 202 C1
Winchcomb Gdns
SE9 ... 143 D2
Winchelsea Ave DA7 ... 147 B5
Winchelsea Cl SW15 ... 156 D6
Winchelsea Ho 16
SE16 ... 118 C4
Winchelsea Rd
Becontree NW10 ... 89 B6
Forest Gate E7 ... 77 A4
Tottenham N17 ... 51 C6
Winchelsey Rise CR2 ... 221 D2
Winchendon Rd
Fulham SW6 ... 135 B4 264 D2
Teddington TW11,
TW12 ... 174 B6
Winchester Ave
Brondesbury NW6 ... 69 A1
Heston TW5 ... 129 B6
Queensbury NW9 ... 44 C6
Winchester Cl
Beckenham BR2 ... 208 D6
Enfield EN1 ... 17 C6
Kingston u T KT2 ... 176 D3
11 Newham E6 ... 100 B1
SE17 ... 261 D3
Winchester Ct
15 Belvedere DA17 ... 125 C1
5 Higham Hill E17 ... 35 A2
Richmond TW9 ... 132 B2
W8 ... 245 C2
Winchester Dr HA5 ... 40 D4
Winchester Ho
5 Barking IG11 ... 80 A1
Bayswater W2 ... 236 A1
Chelsea SW3 ... 266 D5
1 Greenwich SE18 ... 143 D5
24 Tower Hamlets E3 ... 97 B4
Twickenham TW1 ... 153 C4
Winchester Mews
KT4 ... 216 D6
Winchester Pal* SE1 ... 252 C4
Winchester Pk BR2 ... 208 D6
Winchester Pl
6 Dalston E8 ... 73 D3
Highgate N6 ... 49 B1
Winchester Rd
Beckenham BR2 ... 208 D6
Winchester Rd *continued*
Bexley DA7 ... 146 D3
Chingford E4 ... 36 A3
Edmonton N9 ... 18 A3
Harlington UB3 ... 127 C5
Harrow HA3 ... 44 A5
Highgate N6 ... 49 B1
Ilford IG1 ... 79 B5
Northwood HA6 ... 40 A6
South Hampstead NW3 ... 70 B1
St Margarets TW1 ... 153 B5
Twickenham TW13 ... 151 B1
Walton-on-T KT12 ... 194 A1
Winchester Sq SE1 ... 252 C4
Winchester St
Acton W3 ... 111 A4
SW1 ... 115 B1 258 D2
Winchester Wlk SE1 ... 252 C4
Winchet Wlk CR0 ... 206 C3
Winchfield Cl HA3 ... 43 C3
Winchfield Ho SW15 ... 155 D5
Winchfield Rd SE26 ... 185 A5
Winch Ho
Isle of Dogs E14 ... 119 D3
SW10 ... 266 B4
Winchilsea Cres KT8 ... 174 A1
Winchilsea Ho NW8 ... 229 D1
WINCHMORE HILL ... 16 D4
Winchmore Hill Rd N14,
N21 ... 16 A4
Winchmore Hill Sta
N21 ... 16 D4
Winchmore Sch N21 ... 17 A2
Winchmore Villas N21 ... 16 B4
Winchstone Cl TW17 ... 192 B5
Winckley Cl HA3 ... 44 B4
Wincott St
SE11 ... 116 C2 261 B3
Wincrofts Dr SE9 ... 145 B1
Windall Cl SE20 ... 184 A2
Windborough Rd
SM5 ... 219 A1
Windcott Ct HA3 ... 43 C2
Windermere
NW1 ... 231 D2
12 Putney SW15 ... 156 D5
Windermere Ave
Golders Green N3 ... 47 C6
Kensal Rise NW6 ... 91 A6
Merton SW19 ... 201 D6
Ruislip HA4 ... 40 D2
Wembley HA9 ... 43 C1
Windermere Cl
BR6 ... 226 D5
East Bedfont TW14 ... 149 D3
Stanwell TW19 ... 148 A2
Windermere Ct
Barnes SW13 ... 133 D6
Barnet EN5 ... 1 D1
Carshalton SM5 ... 219 A5
Wembley HA9 ... 43 C2
Windermere Gdns IG4 ... 56 A4
Windermere Gr HA9 ... 43 C1
Windermere Hall HA8 ... 26 B5
Windermere Ho
Isleworth TW1 ... 152 D6
Tower Hamlets E3 ... 97 B3
Windermere Point 3
SE15 ... 140 C5
Windermere Rd
Brentford W5 ... 109 C3
Croydon CR0 ... 205 D1
Kingston u T SW15 ... 177 C5
Mitcham SW16 ... 181 D1
Muswell Hill N10 ... 31 B2
Southall UB1 ... 85 B2
Upper Holloway N19 ... 71 C6
West Wickham BR4 ... 224 C6
Windermere Way
UB7 ... 104 B5
Winders Rd SW11 ... 136 C3
Windfield Cl SE26 ... 184 D6
Windham Rd TW9 ... 132 B2
Winding Way RM8 ... 80 C5
Windlass Pl SE8 ... 119 A2
Windlesham Gr
SW19 ... 156 D3
Windley Cl SE23 ... 162 C2
Windmill WC1 ... 240 C4
Windmill Alley 7
W4 ... 111 C2
Windmill Ave UB2 ... 108 A4
Windmill Bridge Ho 1
CR0 ... 205 C1
Windmill Bsns Ctr
UB2 ... 108 A5
Windmill Bsns Village
TW16 ... 171 C2
Windmill Cl
Ashford TW16 ... 171 C3
Windmill Cl *continued*
12 Bermondsey SE1 ... 118 A2
Kingston u T KT6 ... 197 C2
4 Lewisham SE13 ... 142 A3
Windmill Ct
Brentford W5 ... 109 C2
Brondesbury NW2 ... 69 A2
Bushey WD23 ... 8 B3
Windmill Dr
BR2 ... 225 C4
Clapham SW4 ... 159 B6
Cricklewood NW2 ... 69 A5
Windmill Gdns
Brixton SW2 ... 160 B5
Enfield EN2 ... 4 C2
Windmill Gr CR0 ... 205 A3
Windmill Hill
Enfield EN2 ... 5 A2
1 Hampstead NW3 ... 70 A4
Hampstead NW3 ... 70 A5
Ruislip HA4 ... 39 D1
Windmill Ho
4 Millwall E14 ... 119 C2
SE1 ... 251 B3
Windmill La
Barnet Gate EN5 ... 11 D5
Bushey WD23 ... 8 C3
Greenford UB6 ... 86 A2
Isleworth TW7, UB2,
W7 ... 108 C2
Southall UB2 ... 108 A4
Stratford E15 ... 76 B2
Thames Ditton KT7 ... 197 B2
Windmill Lo TW16 ... 171 C2
Windmill Pas 10 W4 ... 111 C2
Windmill Pl UB1 ... 108 A5
Windmill Rd
Brentford TW8, W5 ... 109 C1
Charlton TW16 ... 171 C2
Chiswick W4 ... 111 C2
Edmonton N18 ... 33 B6
Hampton TW12 ... 174 A5
Mitcham CR4 ... 203 C5
Roehampton SW19 ... 156 B1
Thornton Heath CR0 ... 205 A2
Wandsworth SW18 ... 158 B5
Windmill Rd W TW16 ... 171 C1
Windmill Rise KT2 ... 176 D3
Windmill Row SE11 ... 261 A1
Windmill St
Bloomsbury
W1 ... 93 D2 239 C3
Bushey WD23 ... 8 C3
Windmill Terr TW17 ... 193 C2
Windmill Trad Est
CR4 ... 203 C5
Windmill Way HA4 ... 39 D1
Windmill Wlk SE1 ... 251 B2
Windmore Cl HA0 ... 65 A3
Windrose Cl SE16 ... 118 D4
Windrush KT3 ... 199 A5
Windrush Cl
Battersea SW11 ... 136 B1
Chiswick W4 ... 133 A5
Ickenham UB10 ... 60 B4
Windrush Ho NW8 ... 236 D4
Windrush La SE23 ... 162 D1
Windrush Prim Sch
SE28 ... 124 B5
Windrush Rd NW10 ... 89 B6
Windsock Cl 1 SE16 ... 119 B2
Windsor Ave
Cheam SM3 ... 217 A5
East Molesey KT8 ... 195 C6
Edgware HA8 ... 10 D1
Higham Hill E17 ... 35 A1
Hillingdon UB10 ... 60 D1
Merton SW19 ... 180 A2
New Malden KT3 ... 199 A4
Windsor Cl
Brentford TW8 ... 131 B6
Chislehurst BR7 ... 188 D5
Harrow HA2 ... 63 C5
Hendon N3 ... 29 A1
Pinner HA6 ... 22 A1
West Norwood SE27 ... 183 A6
Windsor Cres
Harrow HA2 ... 63 C5
Wembley HA9 ... 66 D5
Windsor Ct
Battersea SW11 ... 136 B3
Bayswater W2 ... 245 C6
Bickley BR1 ... 210 A6
Bushey WD23 ... 8 A4
Chelsea SW3 ... 257 B2
2 Clapham SW4 ... 137 C1
Edgware HA8 ... 26 B3

Windsor Ct *continued*
Friern Barnet N11 30 D5
Fulham SW6 135 A2
Osidge N14 15 C4
20 Rotherhithe SE16 118 D5
17 Sidcup DA14 168 A1
South Norwood SE19 183 C2
Sunbury TW16 172 A3
Temple Fortune NW11 47 A3
Walthamstow E17 53 B6
4 Wandsworth SW18 157 C6
West Hampstead NW3 69 C4
5 West Wickham BR4 207 D1
Windsor Ctr The
SE27 183 A6
Windsor Dr EN4 14 D5
Windsor Gdns
Hayes UB3 105 B3
Paddington W9 91 C3
Wallington CR0 220 A5
Windsor Gr SE27 183 A6
Windsor Hall 11 E16 121 B5
Windsor Ho
4 Acton Green W4 111 A1
Brondesbury NW2 69 A2
4 Globe Town E2 96 D4
2 Hendon NW4 28 D1
7 Northolt UB5 63 C2
Queensbury NW9 44 C5
Regent's Pk NW1 231 D2
Shoreditch N1 235 B4
Stanmore HA7 25 B5
Stoke Newington N4 51 A1
Windsor Lo KT3 199 A4
Windsor Mews
Catford SE6 164 A3
Forest Hill SE23 163 A3
Windsor Park Rd
UB3 127 D5
Windsor Pk SW19 180 A2
Windsor Pl SW1 259 B4
Windsor Rd
Ashford TW16 172 A4
Barnet EN5 12 D5
Chingford E4 35 D6
Cranford TW4,TW5 128 C3
DA6 147 A1
Dagenham RM8 81 A5
Ealing W5 110 A6
Forest Gate E7 77 C3
Harrow HA3 24 B2
Hendon N3 29 A1
Ilford IG1 79 A4
Kingston u T KT2 176 A3
Leyton E10 75 D6
Palmers Green N13 16 C1
Richmond TW9 132 B3
Southall UB2 107 B3
South Norwood CR7 182 D1
Teddington TW11 174 B5
Tottenham N17 34 A1
Upper Holloway N7 72 A5
Wanstead E11 77 A6
Willesden NW2 68 B2
Worcester Pk KT4 216 A6
Windsor St N1 94 D6 234 D6
Windsor Terr
N1 95 A4 235 B2
Windsor Way
W14 113 A2 254 A4
Windsor Wharf E9 75 B3
Windsor Wlk
Camberwell SE5 139 B3
Walton-on-T KT12 194 D1
Windspoint Dr SE15 140 B6
Windus Rd N16 51 D1
Windus Wlk N16 51 D1
Windy Ridge BR1 188 A2
Windy Ridge Cl
SW19 178 D5
Wine Cl E1 118 C6
Wine Office Ct EC4 241 B2
Winery La KT1 198 B6
Winey Cl KT9 213 C1
Winfield Ho 3 SW11 136 B3
Winford Ct 16 SE15 140 A4
Winford Ho E3 75 B1
Winford Par 6 UB1 85 D1
Winforton St SE10 142 A4
Winfrith Rd SW18 158 A3
Wingate Cres CR0 204 A3
Wingate Ho
26 Bromley E3 97 D4
8 Stoke Newington
N16 73 B4
Wingate Rd
Hammersmith W6 112 B3

Wingate Rd *continued*
Ilford IG1 78 D3
Sidcup DA14 190 C4
Wingate Trad Est 11
N17 33 D3
Wingfield Ct
5 Blackwall E14 120 B6
Sidcup DA15 167 D3
Wingfield Ho
Paddington NW6 91 D5
16 Spitalfields E2 95 D4
Wingfield Mews
SE15 140 A2
Wingfield Prim Sch
SE3 143 B2
Wingfield Rd
Kingston u T KT2 176 C4
Leyton E15 76 C4
Walthamstow E17 53 D4
Wingfield St SE15 140 A2
Wingfield Way HA4 62 B2
Wingford Rd SW2 160 A5
Wingham 3 NW5 71 A2
Wingham Ho 6 SE26 184 B5
Wingmore Rd SE24 139 A2
Wingrad Ho 18 E1 96 C2
Wingrave SE17 262 C3
Wingrave Rd W6 134 C6
Wingreen 15 NW8 91 D6
Wingrove Ho E4 19 D4
Wingrove Rd SE6 164 C2
Wings Cl SM1 217 C4
Winicotte Ho W2 236 D4
Winifred Cl EN5 11 D5
Winifrede Paul Ho 7
NW5 71 B4
Winifred Pl N12 30 A5
Winifred Rd
Dagenham RM8 59 A1
Hampton TW12 173 C6
Merton SW19 179 C2
Winifred St E16 122 B5
Winifred Terr EN1 17 D4
Winkfield Rd
Newham E13 99 B5
Wood Green N22 32 C2
Winkley Ct
Cranley Gdns N10 49 B5
Harrow HA2 63 C5
Winkley St 6 E2 96 B5
Winkworth Cotts 14
E1 96 C3
Winlaton Rd BR1 186 B6
Winmill Rd RM8 81 B5
Winn Bridge Cl IG8 37 D2
Winn Common Rd
SE18 145 C6
Winnett St W1 249 C6
Winningales Ct IG5 56 A6
Winnings Wlk UB5 63 A2
Winnington Cl N2 48 B3
Winnington Ho
19 Kensal Town W10 91 A3
8 SE5 139 A5
Winnington Rd
Enfield EN3 6 C6
Hampstead Garden Suburb
N2 48 B3
Winnipeg Dr 3 BR6 227 D2
Winnipeg Ho UB4 84 B3
Winn Rd SE12 165 B3
Winns Ave E17 53 B6
Winns Mews N15 51 C5
Winns Prim Sch The
E17 35 B1
Winns Terr E17 53 C6
Winsbeach E17 36 B1
Winscombe Cres W5 87 D3
Winscombe Ct W5 87 D3
Winscombe St N19 71 B6
Winscombe Way HA7 25 A5
Winsford Rd SE6 163 B1
Winsford Terr N18 33 B5
Winsham Gr SW11 159 A6
Winsham Ho NW1 232 D2
Winslade Ho 4 E5 74 B6
Winslade Rd SW2 160 A6
Winslade Way SE6 163 D4
Winsland Mews W2 236 C2
Winsland St
W2 92 B1 236 C2
Winsley St W1 239 B2
Winslow SE17 263 A1
Winslow Cl
2 Neasden NW10 67 C5
Pinner HA5 40 B3
Winslow Gr E4 20 C2
Winslow Rd W6 134 C6
Winslow Way TW13 151 A1
Winsmoor Ct EN2 4 D2

Winsor Prim Sch E6 100 C1
Winsor Terr E6 100 C2
Winstanley Rd SW11 136 B2
Winston Ave NW9 45 C2
Winston Cl
Harrow HA3 24 D4
Romford RM7 59 D5
Winston Ct
7 BR1 187 B2
Harrow HA3 23 D3
Winston Ho WC1 239 D6
Winston Rd N16 73 B4
Winston Way IG1 79 A5
Winston Wlk 2 W4 111 B2
Winter Ave E6 100 A6
Winterberry Ct 22 N12 29 D6
Winterborne Ave
BR6 227 B5
Winterbourne Ho
W11 244 A5
Winterbourne Inf Sch
CR7 204 C5
Winterbourne Jun Boys'
Sch CR7 204 C5
Winterbourne Jun Girls'
Sch CR7 204 C5
Winterbourne Rd
Dagenham RM8 80 C6
Forest Hill SE6 163 B3
Thornton Heath CR7 204 C5
Winter Box Wlk
TW10 154 B6
Winterbrook Rd SE24 161 A5
Winterburn Cl N11 31 A4
Winterfold Cl SW19 157 A2
Wintergreen Cl 7
E6 100 A2
Winterleys 7 NW6 91 B5
Winter Lo 17 SE16 118 A1
Winter's Ct E4 19 D1
Winterslow Ho 20
SE5 139 A3
Winters Rd KT7 197 B2
Winterstoke Gdns
NW7 28 A5
Winterstoke Rd SE6 163 B3
Winterton Ct KT1 175 D2
Winterton Ho 15 E1 96 C1
Winterton Pl SW10 266 B6
Winterwell Rd SW2 160 A6
Winthorpe Rd SW15 135 A1
Winthrop Ho 10 W12 112 B6
Winthrop St E1 96 B2
Winthrop Wlk HA9 66 A5
Winton Ave N11 31 C3
Winton Cl N9 18 D4
Winton Ct 15 KT6 197 D2
Winton Gdns HA8 26 B3
Winton Prim Sch
N1 94 B5 233 C3
Winton Rd BR6 226 D4
Winton Way SW16 182 C5
Wintour Ho HA9 65 D6
Wirrall Ho 15 SE26 162 A1
Wirral Wood Cl BR7 188 C4
Wisbeach Rd CR0 205 B4
Wisbech 5 N4 50 B1
Wisden Ho SW8 270 D5
Wisdom Ct 7 TW7 131 A2
Wisdons Cl RM7, RM9 59 D1
Wise La NW7 28 A4
Wiseman Ct 12 SE19 183 C5
Wiseman Rd E10 75 C6
Wise Rd E15 98 B6
Wiseton Rd SW17 158 D3
Wishart Rd SE3 143 D3
Wishaw Wlk N13 32 A4
Wisley Ho SW1 259 C2
Wisley Rd
Balham SW11 159 A6
St Paul's Cray BR5 190 B3
Wistaria Cl BR6 226 D6
Wisteria Cl
Edgware NW7 27 D4
Ilford IG1 78 D3
Wisteria Ho SE4 141 A2
Wisteria Rd SE13 142 B1
Wistow Ho 14 E2 96 A6
Witanhurst La N6 49 A1
Witan St E2 96 B4
Witchwood Ho 10
SW9 138 C2
Witcombe Point 14
SE15 140 A4
Witham Ct
Leyton E10 75 D5
Upper Tooting SW17 158 D1
Witham Ho 33 SE5 139 A3
Witham Rd
Dagenham RM10 81 C3

Witham Rd *continued*
Ealing W13 109 B5
Hounslow TW7 130 B4
Penge SE20 206 C6
Witherby Cl CR0 221 C4
Witherington Rd N5 72 C3
Withers Cl KT9 213 C2
Withers Mead NW9 27 D2
Withers Pl EC1 242 B6
Witherston Way SE9 166 C1
Withington Rd N2 30 C2
Withycombe Rd
SW19 156 D4
Withy Ho 4 E1 96 D3
Withy La HA4 39 A4
Withy Mead E4 20 B1
Witley Cres CR0 224 A2
Witley Ct
Southall UB2 107 B2
WC1 240 A5
Witley Gdns UB2 107 B2
Witley Ho 2 SW2 160 B4
Witley Ind Est UB2 107 B2
Witley Point 8 SW15 156 B3
Witley Rd N19 71 C6
Witney Cl
Ickenham UB10 60 B4
Pinner HA5 23 B4
Witney Path SE23 162 D1
Wittenham Way E4 20 B1
Witten Ho KT3 199 B1
Wittering Cl KT2 175 D5
Wittering Ho 9
SW11 136 D3
Wittersham Rd BR1 186 D5
Witts Ho KT2 198 B6
Wivenhoe Cl SE15 140 B2
Wivenhoe Ct TW4 129 B1
Wivenhoe Rd IG11 102 B5
Wiverton Rd SE26 184 C5
Wixom Ho SE9 143 C1
Wix Prim Sch SW4 137 B1
Wix Rd RM9 102 D6
Wix's La SW4 137 B1
Woburn W13 87 B2
Woburn Cl
Bushey WD23 8 A5
SE28 102 D1
Wimbledon SW19 180 A4
Woburn Ct
32 Bermondsey SE16 118 B1
Croydon CR0 205 A1
1 DA6 147 A1
Richmond TW9 132 B2
4 Woodford E18 37 A1
Woburn Pl
WC1 94 A3 240 A5
Woburn Rd
Carshalton SM5 202 C1
Croydon CR0 205 A1
Woburn Sq
WC1 93 D3 239 D5
Woburn Twr 14 UB5 84 D4
Woburn Wlk WC1 232 D1
Wodeham Gdns 1 E1 96 B2
Wodehouse Ave
SE15 139 D4
Wodehouse Ct 10
W3 111 A3
Woffington Cl KT1,
KT8 175 C2
Woking Cl SW15 133 D1
Wolcot Ho NW1 232 B3
Woldham Pl BR2 209 C5
Woldham Rd BR2 209 C5
Wolds Dr BR6 226 C4
Wolfe Cl
Hayes BR2 209 A3
Yeading UB4 84 B4
Wolfe Cres
Greenwich SE7 121 D1
34 Rotherhithe SE16 118 D4
Wolfe Ho 19 W12 112 B6
Wolferton Rd E12 78 B4
Wolffe Gdns 2 E15 76 D2
Wolf Fields Prim Sch
UB2 107 B2
Wolfington Rd SE27 182 D6
Wolfram Cl SE13 164 C6
Wolfson Ct
4 Barnet EN4 14 D3
Golders Green NW11 47 A2
SE1 253 D2
Wolfson Hillel Prim Sch
N14 15 D5
Wolftencroft Cl
SW11 136 B2
Wollaston Cl SE1 262 A4
Wollotan Ho N1 234 B4
Wolmer Cl HA8 26 D6

Wolmer Gdns HA8 10 C1
Wolmer Rd HA8 26 D6
Wolseley Ave SW18,
SW19 157 C2
Wolseley Gdns W4 132 D6
Wolseley Rd
Acton W4 111 A2
Carshalton CR4 203 A2
Harrow HA3 42 C6
Hornsey N8 49 D4
Upton E7 77 B1
Wood Green N22 32 B2
Wolseley St
SE1 117 D4 253 D1
Wolsey Ave
Thames Ditton KT7 196 D4
Wallend E6 100 C4
Walthamstow E17 53 B6
Wolsey Cl
Isleworth TW3 130 A1
Kingston u T KT2 176 D2
Southall UB2 108 A3
Wimbledon SW20 178 B3
Worcester Pk KT19,
KT4 216 A4
Wolsey Cres SM4 201 B2
Wolsey Ct
Bromley BR1 186 D3
SE9 166 B5
South Hampstead NW6 70 A1
Wolsey Dr
Kingston u T KT2 176 A4
Walton-on-T KT12 194 D1
Wolsey Gr HA8 27 B3
Wolsey Ho
2 Hampton TW12 173 D4
3 Kentish Town NW5 71 D2
Wolsey Inf Sch CR0 224 A1
Wolsey Jun Sch CR0 224 A1
Wolsey Mews
Kentish Town NW5 71 C2
Orpington BR6 227 D3
Wolsey Rd
Ashford TW15 170 B6
East Molesey KT8 196 B5
Enfield EN1 6 B3
Hampton TW12 174 A4
Stoke Newington N1 73 B3
Sunbury Comm TW16 171 D4
Wolsey St E1 96 C2
Wolsey Way KT9 214 C3
Wolstenholme HA7 25 B5
Wolstonbury N12 29 C5
Wolvercote Rd SE2 124 D4
Wolverley St E2 96 B4
Wolverton SE17 263 A2
Wolverton Ave KT2 176 C2
Wolverton Gdns
Brook Green W6 112 D2
Ealing W5 110 B6
Wolverton Mans W5 110 B5
Wolverton Rd HA7 25 B3
Wolverton Way N14 15 C6
Wolves La N22 32 C4
Womersley Rd N4, N8 50 B3
Wonford Cl KT2, KT3 177 C2
Wontner Cl 5 N1 73 A1
Wontner Rd SW12,
SW17 158 D2
Wooburn Cl UB8 82 D3
Wooburn Ct N14 15 D3
Woodall Cl
Chessington KT9 213 D2
15 Poplar E14 119 D6
Woodall Ho TW7 130 D2
Woodall Rd EN3 18 D5
Woodbank Rd BR1 164 D1
Woodbastwick Rd
SE26 185 A5
Woodberry Ave
Edmonton N21 16 D2
Harrow HA2 42 A5
Woodberry Cl
Ashford TW16 172 A4
Mill Hill NW7 28 D3
Woodberry Cres N10 49 B6
Woodberry Down N4 51 A2
Woodberry Down Com
Prim Sch N4 51 A2
Woodberry Gdns N12 30 A4
Woodberry Gr
Finchley N12 30 A4
Stoke Newington N4 51 A2
Woodberry View N6 49 A3
Woodberry Way
Chingford E4 20 A4
Finchley N12 30 A4
Woodbine Cl TW2 152 B2
Woodbine Gr
Enfield EN2 5 B5

Woodbine Gr *continued*
Penge SE20 184 B3
Woodbine La KT4 216 C5
Woodbine Pl E11 55 A3
Woodbine Rd DA15 167 C3
Woodbines Ave KT1 197 D6
Woodbine Terr E9 74 C2
Woodborough Rd
SW15 134 B1
Woodbourne Ave
SW16 159 D1
Woodbourne Cl
SW16 160 A1
Woodbourne Dr
KT10 212 D2
Woodbourne Gdns
SM6 219 B1
Woodbridge Cl
4 Dollis Hill NW2 68 A5
10 Finsbury Pk N7 72 B6
Woodbridge Ct
Forest Gate E7 77 D3
Stoke Newington N16 73 B5
Woodbridge High Sch
IG8 37 B3
Woodbridge Ho E11 54 D1
Woodbridge Rd IG11 79 D3
Woodbridge St
EC1 94 D3 241 C6
Woodbrook Rd SE2 146 B6
Woodbrook Sch BR3 185 B2
Woodburn Cl NW4 46 D4
Woodbury Cl
Croydon CR0 221 D6
Wanstead E11 55 B5
Woodbury Ct 1 W13 87 B3
Woodbury Gdns
Bromley SE12 187 B6
Eltham SE12 165 B1
Woodbury Ho 4
SE26 162 B1
Woodbury Park Rd
W13 87 B3
Woodbury Rd E17 53 D5
Woodbury St SW17 180 C5
Woodchester Sq W2 91 D2
Woodchurch Cl DA14 167 B1
Woodchurch Dr BR1 187 D3
Woodchurch Ho 15
SW9 138 C4
Woodchurch Rd NW6 69 D1
Wood Cl
Bethnal Green E2 96 A3
Harrow HA1 42 B2
Kingsbury NW9 45 B2
Woodclyffe Dr BR7 188 C1
Woodcock Ct HA3 44 A2
Woodcock Dell Ave
HA3 43 D2
Woodcock Hill HA3 43 C3
Woodcock Ho 4 E14 97 C2
Woodcocks E16 99 D2
Woodcombe Cres
SE23 162 C3
Woodcote Ave
Mill Hill NW7 28 C4
Thornton Heath CR7 204 D5
Wallington SM6 219 B1
Woodcote Cl
Enfield N9 18 C5
Kingston u T KT2 176 B5
Woodcote Ct 14 SM6 219 B2
Woodcote Dr BR6 211 B2
Woodcote Ho 4 SE8 141 B6
Woodcote Mews
Loughton IG10 21 D4
Wallington SM6 219 B2
Woodcote Pl 1 SE27 182 D5
Woodcote Rd
Wallington SM6 219 C1
Wanstead E11 55 A2
Woodcott Ho 1
SW15 156 A4
Woodcroft
SE9 166 B1
South Croydon CR0 221 C5
Southgate N21 16 C3
17 Stanmore HA7 25 C5
Wembley UB6 65 A2
Woodcroft Ave
Edgware NW7 27 C4
Stanmore HA7 25 A2
Woodcroft Cres UB10 82 D6
Woodcroft Mews
SE8 119 A2
Woodcroft Prim Sch
HA8 27 C3
Woodcroft Rd CR7 204 D3
Wood Dene 6 SE15 140 B4
Wood Dr BR7 188 A4

Woodedge Cl E4 20 D3
Woodend
South Norwood SE19 183 A4
Sutton SM1 218 A6
Thames Ditton KT10 212 A6
WOOD END 83 D1
Wood End UB3 83 C1
Wood End Ave HA2 64 A4
Wood End Cl UB5 64 B3
Woodend Gdns EN2 4 A1
Wood End Gdns UB5 64 A3
WOOD END GREEN 83 C2
Wood End Green Rd
UB3 83 C1
Wood End Inf Sch UB5 64 B3
Wood End Jun Sch
UB6 64 B3
Wood End La UB5 63 D3
Wood End Park Com Sch
UB3 105 A6
Woodend Rd E17 36 A1
Wood End Rd HA1, UB5 64 B4
Wood End Way UB5 64 A3
Wooder Gdns E7 77 A4
Wooderson Cl SE25 205 C5
Wooderson Ct 9
BR3 185 C2
Woodfall Ave EN5 13 B6
Woodfall Rd N4 72 C6
Woodfall St SW3 257 C1
Woodfarrs SE5 139 B1
Woodfield SW16 182 B2
Wood Field NW3 70 D3
Woodfield Ave
Colindale NW9 45 C5
Ealing W5 87 C3
Streatham SW16 159 D1
Wallington SM5 219 A1
Wembley HA0 65 C5
Woodfield Cl
1 Enfield EN1 5 C1
South Norwood SE19 183 A3
Woodfield Cres W5 87 D3
Woodfield Ct SW16 159 D1
Woodfield Dr EN4 15 A3
Woodfield Gdns KT3 199 D4
Woodfield Gr SW16 159 D1
Woodfield Ho
11 Forest Hill SE23 162 D1
Hinchley Wood KT7 212 D6
New Malden KT3 199 D4
6 Upper Clapton E5 74 B6
Wood Green N11 31 D4
Woodfield Pl W9 91 B3
Woodfield Rd
Cranford TW4, TW5 128 B3
Ealing W5 87 C3
Hinchley Wood KT10,
KT7 212 D6
Kensal Town W9 91 B2
Woodfield Rise WD23 8 B4
Woodfield Sch NW9 45 C1
Woodfields Ct SM1 218 A5
Woodfield Way N11 31 D3
WOODFORD 37 D5
Woodford Ave IG2, IG4, IG5,
IG8 56 B5
Woodford Bridge Rd
IG4 56 A5
Woodford Cres HA5 22 B1
Woodford Ct 15 W12 112 D4
Woodford Cty High Sch
IG8 36 D4
Woodforde Ct UB3 105 B1
WOODFORD GREEN 37 B3
Woodford Green Prep Sch
IG8 37 A4
Woodford Green Sch
IG8 36 D5
Woodford Ho
13 SE18 144 D6
5 Wanstead E18 55 A5
Woodford New Rd
Upper Walthamstow
E17 54 C6
Woodford E18 36 D3
Woodford Pl HA9 44 A1
Woodford Rd
Forest Gate E7 77 B4
Wanstead E18 55 A6
Woodford Sta IG8 37 B4
Woodford Trad Est
IG8 37 D1
WOODFORD WELLS 21 B1
Woodgate Ave KT9 213 D3
Woodgate Cres HA6 22 A4
Woodgate Dr SW16 181 D3
Woodgate Ho 12 KT6 198 A3
Woodger Rd W12 112 C4
Woodget Cl E6 100 A1

Woodglen SM4 202 C4
Woodgrange Ave
Ealing W5 110 C5
Enfield EN1 18 A5
Finchley N12 30 B4
Harrow HA3 43 D4
Woodgrange Cl HA3 43 D4
Woodgrange Ct 1
BR2 208 D1
Woodgrange Gdns
EN1 18 A5
Woodgrange Ho W5 110 B5
Woodgrange Inf Sch
E7 77 B4
Woodgrange Mans
HA3 43 C4
Woodgrange Park Sta
E12 77 D3
Woodgrange Rd E7 77 A3
Woodgrange Terr EN1 18 A5
WOOD GREEN 32 B2
Wood Green Sh City
N22 32 C1
Wood Green Sta N22 32 C1
Woodhall NW1 232 A1
Woodhall Ave
Dulwich SE21 161 D1
Pinner HA5 23 A2
Woodhall Dr
Dulwich SE21 161 D1
Pinner HA5 23 A2
Woodhall Gate HA5 22 D3
Woodhall Ho SW18 158 B5
Woodhall La WD19 23 A6
Woodhall Prim Sch
WD19 23 A6
Woodhall Rd HA5 22 D4
Woodham Ct E11 54 D5
Woodham Rd SE6 164 A1
Woodhatch Cl 16 E6 100 A2
Woodhaven Gdns IG6 57 A5
Woodhayes BR7 188 D4
Woodhayes Rd SW19,
SW20 178 C4
Woodhead Dr BR6 227 C6
Woodheyes Rd NW10 67 C3
Woodhill SE7, SE18 122 A2
Woodhill Cres HA3 43 D3
Woodhill Prim Sch
SE18 122 A2
Wood Ho
4 Clapham SW4 137 D3
2 Paddington NW6 91 B5
Woodhouse Ave UB6 86 D5
Woodhouse Cl
Hayes UB3 105 C3
Wembley UB6 86 D5
Woodhouse Eaves
HA6 22 A5
Woodhouse Gr E12 78 A2
Woodhouse Rd
Colney Hatch N12 30 C4
Leyton E11 76 D5
Woodhouse Sixth Form
Coll N12 30 B4
Woodhurst Ave BR5 211 A3
Woodhurst Rd
Acton W3 111 A6
SE2 124 A2
Woodington Cl SE9 166 C5
Woodison St E3 97 A3
Woodknoll Dr BR7 188 B2
Wood La
Dagenham RM10 81 A5
Highgate N6 49 B3
Hounslow TW7 130 D5
Kingsbury NW9 45 B2
Ruislip HA4 61 C6
Shepherd's Bush W12 112 C6
Stanmore HA7 9 B2
Woodford IG8 36 D5
Woodland App UB6 65 A2
Woodland Cl
Kingsbury NW9 45 A3
Uxbridge UB10 60 D6
West Ewell KT19 215 C2
West Norwood SE19 183 C4
Woodford IG8 21 B1
Woodland Cres
18 Rotherhithe SE16 118 D4
SE10 142 C6
Woodland Ct
Cheam SM1 217 C2
Temple Fortune NW4 47 A4
13 Wanstead E11 55 A4
Woodland Gdns
Cranley Gdns N10 49 B4
Isleworth TW7 130 C2
Woodland Gr SE10 120 C1
Woodland Hill SE19 183 C4

Woodland Hts SE3 142 C6
Woodland Mews
SW16 160 A1
Woodland Rd
Chingford E4 20 A3
Friern Barnet N11 31 B5
Penge SE19 183 D4
Thornton Heath CR7 204 C5
Woodland Rise
Cranley Gdns N10 49 B5
Wembley UB6 65 A2
WOODLANDS 130 C2
Woodlands
Beckenham BR3 185 D3
Clapham SW4 137 B1
Finchley N12 30 A4
Harrow HA2 41 C5
Temple Fortune NW11 47 A4
Walthamstow E11 54 B2
West Barnes SW20 200 D5
Woodlands Ave
Acton W3 110 D5
DA15 167 C3
Dagenham RM6 59 A2
Finchley N3 30 A2
Kingston u T KT3 177 B2
Ruislip HA4 40 D2
Wanstead E11 55 B1
Worcester Pk KT4 216 A6
Woodlands Cl
BR1 188 B1
Claygate KT10 212 D1
Temple Fortune NW11 47 A4
Woodlands Ct
9 Bromley BR1 186 D2
Brondesbury Pk NW10 90 D6
Dulwich SE22 162 B4
Southall UB1 107 C6
Woodlands Dr
Harrow HA7 24 D4
Sunbury TW16 172 C1
Woodlands Fst & Mid Sch
HA8 26 B2
Woodlands Gdns E17 54 C5
Woodlands Gr TW7 130 C3
Woodlands Gt SW15 157 B6
Woodlands Jun & Inf Schs
IG1 79 B3
Woodlands Par TW15 171 A4
Woodlands Park Rd
SE10 142 C6
Tottenham N15 51 A4
Woodlands Rd
Barnes SW13 133 D2
Bexleyheath DA7 147 A2
Bickley BR1 188 B1
Enfield EN2 5 B4
Harrow HA1 42 D4
Ilford IG1 79 A5
Isleworth TW7 130 C3
Leyton E11 76 C6
Lower Edmonton N9 18 C3
Southall UB1 106 D5
Surbiton KT6 197 D2
Walthamstow E17 54 A6
Woodlands St SE13 164 B4
Woodland St 2 E8 73 D2
Woodlands The
East Barnet N14 15 B3
Harrow HA1 64 C6
Highbury N5 73 A4
12 Hornsey N8 50 A2
Isleworth TW7 130 D3
Lewisham SE13 164 B4
Mitcham CR4 203 A6
South Norwood SE19 183 A3
Stanmore HA7 25 B5
Thames Ditton KT10 212 A6
Woodlands Way
SW15 157 B6
Woodland Terr SE7 122 A2
Woodland Way
Abbey Wood SE2 124 D2
Croydon CR0 207 A1
Edgware NW7 27 D4
Merton SM4 201 B5
Mitcham CR4 181 A3
Petts Wood BR5 211 A4
Southgate N21 16 C2
Tolworth KT5 214 D6
West Wickham BR4 224 A5
Woodford IG8 21 B1
Woodland Wlk
Chessington KT19 214 C2
9 Greenwich SE10 120 C1
Hampstead NW3 70 C3
Wood Lane High Sch
W12 90 B1
Wood Lane Sta W12 112 C6
Woodlawn Cl SW15 157 B6

Woodlawn Cres TW2 151 D2
Woodlawn Dr TW13 150 D2
Woodlawn Rd SW6 134 D4
Woodlea Dr BR2 208 C4
Woodlea Lo EN1 17 C5
Woodlea Rd N16 73 C5
Woodleigh
1 Kingston u T KT5 198 B4
3 Woodford E18 37 A2
Woodleigh Ave N12 30 C4
Woodleigh Ct N22 32 B2
Woodleigh Gdns
SW16 160 A1
Woodley Cl SW17 180 D3
Woodley La SM1, SM5 218 C5
Woodlodge 4 SW19 179 B5
Wood Lodge Gdns
BR1 188 A3
Wood Lodge La BR4 224 A5
Woodman La E4 20 C6
Woodman Mews
TW9 132 D4
Woodman Par 4
E16 122 C5
Woodmans Ct HA7 44 A6
Woodmans Gr NW10 67 D3
Woodmans Mews W12 90 B2
Woodman St E16 122 C5
Woodmansterne Prim Sch
SW16 181 D2
Woodmansterne Rd
Mitcham SW16 181 D2
Sutton SM5 218 C1
Wood Mead N17 34 A4
Woodmere SE9 166 B3
Woodmere Ave CR0 206 D2
Woodmere Cl
11 Clapham SW11 137 A2
Croydon CR0 206 D2
Woodmere Ct N14 15 B4
Woodmere Gdns CR0 206 D2
Woodmere Way BR3 208 B4
Woodnook Rd SW16 181 B5
Woodpecker Cl
Bushey WD23 8 A3
Enfield N9 18 B5
Harrow HA3 24 D2
Woodpecker Ct TW2 151 D4
Woodpecker Ho E17 53 C6
Woodpecker Mews
SE13 142 B1
Woodpecker Rd
6 SE14 141 A6
Woolwich SE28 124 C6
Wood Point 8 E16 99 A2
Woodquest Ave SE24 161 A6
Wood Rd
Littleton TW17 192 C5
Willesden NW10 67 A1
Wood Retreat SE18 145 B5
Wood Ride
Barnet EN4 2 B4
Orpington BR5 211 C5
Woodridge Cl EN2 4 C4
Woodridge Prim Sch
N12 13 C1
Woodridings Ave HA5 23 B2
Woodridings Cl HA5 23 B3
Woodridings Ct N22 31 D2
Woodriffe Rd E11 54 B2
Wood Rise HA5 40 A4
Woodrow SE18 122 B2
Woodrow Ave UB4 83 D3
Woodrow Cl UB6 65 B1
Woodrow Ct 3 N17 34 B3
Woodruff Ho 12 SW2 160 C5
Woodrush Cl 4 SE14 141 A5
Woodrush Way RM6 58 D5
Woodseer St E1 96 A2
Woodsford SE17 262 C1
Woodsford Sq
W14 113 A4 244 B2
Woodshire Rd RM10 81 D5
Woods Ho SW8 269 A2
WOODSIDE 206 A4
Woodside
Buckhurst Hill IG9 21 C2
Hampstead Garden Suburb
NW11 47 C4
Muswell Hill N10 49 A6
Walton-on-T KT12 194 A1
Wimbledon SW19 179 B5
Woodside Ave
Chislehurst BR7 189 A5
Croydon SE25 206 B4
Fortis Green N6 48 D5
North Finchley N12 30 A6
Thames Ditton KT10 196 C2
Wembley HA0 88 A6

Woodside Cl
Ruislip HA4 39 B3
Stanmore HA7 25 B5
Tolworth KT5 199 A2
Wembley HA0 88 A6
Woodside Court Rd
CR0 206 A2
Woodside Cres DA15 167 C1
Woodside Ct
Ealing W5 110 A5
Enfield EN2 4 D4
10 Finchley N12 29 D6
Palmers Green N13 16 C1
Wanstead E12 55 C1
Woodside End HA0 88 A6
Woodside Gdns
Chingford E4 35 D4
Tottenham N17 33 D1
Woodside Gn SE25 206 A3
Woodside Gr N12 14 A1
Woodside Grange Rd
N12 29 D6
Woodside Ho SW19 179 B4
Woodside Jun & Inf Sch
CR0 206 A2
Woodside La
DA5 168 D5
Whetstone N12 14 A1
WOODSIDE PARK 29 C6
Woodside Park Ave
E17 54 B5
Woodside Park Int Sch
N11 30 D5
Woodside Park Rd
N12 30 A6
Woodside Pk SE25 206 B3
Woodside Pl HA0 88 A6
Woodside Rd
BR1 210 A4
Coombe KT3 177 C1
Croydon SE25 206 B3
Kingston u T KT2 176 A3
Newham E13 99 C3
Northwood HA6 22 A3
Sidcup DA15 167 C1
Sutton SM1 218 A5
Woodford IG8 37 A6
Wood Green N22 32 C3
Woodside Sch
Belvedere DA17 125 D2
Walthamstow E17 54 A6
Woodside Sta SE25 206 B3
Woodside Way
Croydon CR0 206 C3
Streatham CR4 181 C2
Wood's Mews
W1 115 A6 248 A6
Woodsome Rd NW5 71 B5
Wood's Pl SE1 263 B5
Woodspring Rd
SW19 157 A2
Wood's Rd SE15 140 B4
Wood St
Barnet EN5 1 A1
Carshalton CR4 203 A2
Chiswick W4 111 C1
City of London
EC2 95 A1 242 B2
Custom Ho E16 121 B6
Kingston u T KT1 175 D1
Kingston u T KT2 176 A2
Walthamstow E17 54 B5
Woodstar Ho 3 SE15 140 A5
Woodstead Gr HA8 26 A4
Woods The
Eastbury HA6 22 A5
Uxbridge UB10 60 D4
Woodstock Ave
Brentford W13 109 A3
Cheam SM3 201 B2
Golders Green NW11 47 A2
Isleworth TW7 153 A6
Southall UB1 85 B4
Woodstock Cl
DA5 169 B3
Stanmore HA7 26 A1
Woodstock Cres N9 18 B5
Woodstock Ct
Kingston u T KT2 176 D1
Lee SE12 165 A5
Vauxhall SE11 260 D2
Woodstock Dr UB10 60 B4
Woodstock Gdns
Beckenham BR3 185 D3
Hayes UB4 83 D2
Ilford IG3 80 A6
Woodstock Gr W12 112 D4
Woodstock Grange
W5 110 A5

Woodstock Ho
Hayes UB3 83 B2
2 Highbury N5 73 A4
Woodstock Lane N
KT6 213 C6
Woodstock Lane S KT6, KT9,
KT10 213 C4
Woodstock Mews W1 238 B3
Woodstock Rd
Bedford Pk W4 111 C3
Bushey WD23 8 D4
Chingford E17 36 B1
Finsbury Pk N4 50 C1
Golders Green NW11 47 B1
South Croydon CR0 221 B5
Upton E7 77 C1
Wallington SM5, SM6 219 A3
Wembley HA0 66 B1
Woodstock Rise SM3 201 B2
Woodstock St W1 238 C1
Woodstock Studios 17
W12 112 D4
Woodstock Terr E14 119 D6
Woodstock The SM3 201 B2
Woodstock Way CR4 181 C1
Woodstone Ave KT17,
KT4 216 A3
Wood Street Sta E17 54 B5
Woodsyre SE26 183 D6
Woodthorpe Rd
Ashford TW15 170 A6
Putney SW15 134 B1
Woodtree Cl NW4 28 C1
Wood Vale
Cranley Gdns N10 49 C4
Dulwich SE22 162 B4
Woodvale Ave SE25 183 D1
Woodvale Ct
BR1 187 B1
South Norwood SE25 205 D6
Woodvale Way NW11 68 D5
Woodvale Wlk SE27 183 A5
Woodview Ave E4 36 A6
Woodview Cl
Finsbury Pk N4 50 D2
Kingston u T SW15 177 B6
Orpington BR6 227 A6
Woodville SE3 143 B4
Woodville Cl
SE12 165 A6
Teddington TW11 175 A6
Woodville Ct
3 Lewisham SE10 142 A4
Southgate N14 15 C6
Woodville Gdns
Ealing W5 88 A1
Hendon NW11 46 D2
Ilford IG6 56 D5
Ruislip HA4 39 A2
Surbiton KT6 197 D2
Woodville Gr 2
DA16 146 A2
Woodville Ho
SE1 263 C6
Sutton SM1 217 D4
Woodville Rd
Barnet EN5 1 D2
Ealing W5 87 D1
Golders Green NW11 47 A2
Leytonstone E11 54 D1
Morden SM4 201 C5
Paddington NW6 91 B5
Richmond TW10 153 C1
South Norwood CR7 205 B6
Stoke Newington N16 73 C3
Walthamstow E17 53 B5
Woodford E18 37 B1
Woodville St 16 SE7 122 A2
Woodville The W5 87 D1
Woodward Ave NW4 46 A4
Woodward Cl KT10 212 D2
Woodwarde Rd SE22 161 C5
Woodward Gdns
Dagenham RM9 80 C1
Harrow HA7 24 D3
Woodward Rd RM9 80 C1
Wood Way BR6 226 C6
Woodway Cres HA1 43 A3
Woodwell St SW18 158 A6
Wood Wharf SE10 142 A6
Woodyard Cl NW5 71 A3
Woodyard La SE21 161 C4
Woodyates Rd SE12 165 B4
Woolacombe Rd SE3 143 C3
Woolacombe Way
UB3 105 C2

Woolcombes Ct 4
SE16 118 D5
Woolden Ho 2 E4 20 C4
Wooler St
SE17 117 B1 262 D2
Woolf Cl SE28 124 B5
Woolf Ct 7 W3 111 A3
Woolf Mews WC1 240 A6
Woollaston Rd N4 50 D3
Woolley Ho SW9 138 D2
Woollon Ho 1 E1 96 C1
Woolmead Ave NW9 46 A2
Woolmer Gdns N18 34 A5
Woolmer Ho 2 E5 74 B6
Woolmer Rd N18 34 A5
Woolmore Prim Sch
E14 120 A6
Woolmore St E14 120 A6
Woolneigh St SW6 135 D3
Woolpack Ho 1 E9 74 C2
Wool Rd SW20 178 B4
Woolridge Way E9 74 C1
Woolstaplers Way
SE16 118 A2
Woolston Cl E17 34 D1
Woolstone Ho 7 E2 96 A6
Woolstone Rd SE23 163 A2
Woolven Ho SE3 142 D6
WOOLWICH 122 D3
Woolwich Arsenal Sta
SE18 122 D2
Woolwich Church St SE7,
SE18 122 A3
Woolwich Comm
SE18 144 C6
Woolwich Ct EN3 7 C5
Woolwich Dockyard Ind
Est SE18 122 A3
Woolwich Dockyard Sta
SE18 122 B2
Woolwich High St
SE18 122 C3
Woolwich Manorway
E16 122 D4
Woolwich Manor Way
Beckton E6 100 C1
North Woolwich E16 122 D5
Woolwich New Rd
SE18 122 D2
Woolwich Poly Sch for
Boys SE28 124 A5
Woolwich Rd
Belvedere DA17 125 C1
DA7 147 C2
Erith SE2 125 B1
Greenwich SE7, SE10 121 C2
Wooster Gdns E14 98 B1
Wooster Mews HA2 42 A6
Wooster Pl SE1 262 D4
Wootton KT10 212 A4
Wootton Gr N3 29 C2
Wootton Ho SE9 167 B5
Wootton St
SE1 116 C5 251 B3
Worbeck Rd SE20 184 C1
Worcester Ave N17 34 A3
Worcester Cl
Croydon CR0 223 C6
Dollis Hill NW2 68 B5
Mitcham CR4 181 A1
Worcester Cres
Edgware NW7 11 C1
Woodford IG8 37 C6
Worcester Ct
Ashford TW15 170 D5
Ealing W7 86 D1
Finchley N12 29 D5
Harrow HA1 42 C6
44 Paddington W2 91 C2
12 Sutton SM2 217 D2
Walton-on-T KT12 194 C1
Worcester Pk KT4 215 C5
Worcester Dr
Ashford TW15 170 D5
Bedford Pk W4 111 C4
Worcester Gdns
Northolt UB6 64 B2
Redbridge IG1 56 A2
Wandsworth SW11 158 D6
Worcester Pk KT4 215 C5
Worcester Ho
Bayswater W2 236 A1
3 Islington N1 73 A1
Lambeth SE11 261 A5
9 Putney SW15 156 C4
Worcester Mews 2
NW6 69 D2
WORCESTER PARK 215 C4
Worcester Park Rd
KT4 215 B5
Worcester Park Sta
KT4 200 A1
Worcester Rd
Belmont SM2 217 D1
Higham Hill E17 34 D1
Ilford E12 78 B4
11 Wimbledon SW19 179 B5
Worcesters Ave EN1 6 A5
Worcesters Prim Sch
EN1 5 D5
Wordsworth N8 50 C5
Wordsworth Ave
Greenford UB6 86 B5
Plashet E12 78 A1
Snaresbrook E18 54 D6
Wordsworth Ct
Harrow HA1 42 B2
New Barnet EN5 14 A6
Wordsworth Dr KT4,
SM3 216 C4
Wordsworth Gdns
WD6 10 C6
Wordsworth Ho
Maida Vale NW6 91 C4
15 SE18 144 C6
Wordsworth Par 1
N15 50 D5
Wordsworth Pl 11
NW5 70 D3
Wordsworth Rd
Bermondsey SE1 263 D3
Bexley DA16 145 C4
Hampton TW12, TW13 173 B6
Penge SE20 184 D3
Stoke Newington N16 73 C4
Wallington SM6 219 D2
Wordsworth Way
UB7 104 B2
Wordsworth Wlk
NW11 47 C5
Worfield St
SW11 136 C5 267 B3
Worgan St
Rotherhithe SE16 118 D2
SE11 116 B1 260 C2
Working Men's Coll The
NW1 93 C5 232 B4
Worland Rd E15 76 C1
World Bsns Ctr TW6 127 A4
WORLD'S END 4 C1
Worlds End La BR6 227 D1
World's End La EN2 4 B1
World's End Pas
SW10 266 C4
World's End Pl SW10 266 B4
World Trade Ctr London
E14 119 D4
Worley Ct NW2 68 D5
Worleys Dr BR6 227 B4
Worlidge St W6 112 C1
Worlingham Rd SE22 139 D1
Wormholt Park Prim Sch
W12 112 A6
Wormholt Rd W12 112 A5
Wormwood St EC2 243 A2
Wornington Rd W10 91 A2
Woronzow Rd
NW8 92 C6 230 A5
Worple Ave
Isleworth TW7 153 A6
Wimbledon SW19 178 D3
Worple Cl HA2 41 B1
Worple Ct SW19 179 A4
Worple Prim Sch
TW7 131 A1
Worple Rd
Isleworth TW7 131 A1
Wimbledon SW19,
SW20 178 D2
Worple Road Mews
SW19 179 B4
Worple St SW14 133 B2
Worple Way
Harrow HA2 41 B1
Richmond TW10 132 A1
Worship St EC2 95 C3 243 A5
Worslade Rd SW17 180 B6
Worsley Bridge Jun Sch
BR3 185 C3
Worsley Bridge Rd BR3,
SE6 185 C5
Worsley Ct N3 29 D4
Worsley Gr E5 74 A4
Worsley Grange BR7 189 A4
Worsley Ho 9 SE23 162 B2
Worsley Rd E11 76 C4
Worsopp Dr SW4 159 C6
Worth Cl BR6 227 C4
Worthfield Cl KT19 215 B1
Worth Gr SE17 262 C1
Worthing Cl 5 E15 98 C6
Worthing Rd TW5 129 B6
Worthington Cl CR4 203 B6
Worthington Ho
EC1 234 B2
16 Streatham SW2 160 C4
Worthington Rd KT6 198 B1
Wortley Rd
Forest Gate E6 77 D1
Thornton Heath CR0 204 C2
Worton Ct TW7 130 C1
Worton Gdns TW7 130 B3
Worton Hall Ind Est
TW7 130 C1
Worton Rd TW7 130 C2
Worton Way TW3,
TW7 130 B3
Wotton Ct 14 E14 120 B6
Wotton Rd
Cricklewood NW2 68 C5
18 SE8 141 B6
Wouldham Rd E16 98 D1
Wragby Rd E11 76 C5
Wrampling Pl N9 18 A3
Wrangthorne Wlk
CR0 220 C4
Wray Ave IG5 56 C6
Wrayburn Ho 28
SE16 118 A4
Wray Cres N4 72 B6
Wray Ct N4 72 B6
Wrayfield Rd SM3 216 D5
Wray Ho 11 SW2 160 A3
Wraysbury Cl TW4 151 A6
Wrays Way UB4 83 C3
Wrekin Rd SE18 145 A5
Wren Ave
Cricklewood NW2 68 C4
Southall UB2 107 B2
Wren Cl
E16 98 D1
Lower Edmonton N9 18 D3
Wren Cres WD23 8 A3
Wren Ct
1 Barnet EN4 14 D3
Croydon CR0 221 B4
Wren Gdns RM9 80 D3
Wren Ho
29 Bow E3 97 A5
4 Hampton TW12 173 D4
SW1 259 C1
Wren Landing E14 119 C5
Wrenn Ho SW13 134 C6
Wren Path SE28 123 B4
Wren Rd
Camberwell SE5 139 B4
Dagenham RM9 80 D3
Sidcup DA14 168 C1
Wrens Ave TW15 171 A6
Wren's Park Ho E5 74 B6
Wren St WC1 94 B3 240 D6
Wrentham Ave NW10 90 D5
Wrenthorpe Rd BR1 186 C6
Wren View N6 49 C1
Wrenwood Way HA5 40 B5
Wrestlers Ct EC3 243 A2
Wrexham Rd E3 97 C5
Wricklemarsh Rd
SE3 143 D4
Wrigglesworth St
SE14 140 D5
Wright Cl SE13 142 B1
Wright Gdns TW17 192 C4
Wright Ho SW15 156 B6
Wrighton Ct SM1 217 B2
Wright Rd TW5 128 C5
Wrights Cl RM10 81 D4
Wright's Gn SW4 137 D1
Wright's La
W8 113 D3 255 C6
Wrights Pl NW10 67 A2
Wrights Rd SE25 205 C6
Wright's Rd E3 97 B5
Wright's Row SM5 219 B4
Wrights Wlk SW14 133 B2
Writtle Ho 36 NW9 27 D1
Wrotham Ho
Beckenham BR3 185 B3
SE1 262 D6
Wrotham Rd
Barnet EN5 1 A3
13 Camden Town NW1 71 C1
DA16 146 C4
Ealing W13 109 C5
Wrottesley Rd
SE18 145 A6
Willesden Green NW10 90 A5
Wroughton Rd SW11 158 D5
Wroughton Terr NW4 46 B5
Wroxall Rd RM9 80 C2
Wroxham Gdns N11 31 D3
Wroxham Rd SE28 124 D6
Wroxton Rd SE15 140 C3
Wrythe Gn 2 SM5 218 D5
Wrythe Green Rd
SM5 218 D5
Wrythe La SM1, SM5,
SM4 218 C5
WRYTHE THE 218 D6
Wulfstan St W12 89 D1
Wyatt Cl
Bushey WD23 8 C4
Feltham TW13 150 D3
Hayes UB4 84 A2
Rotherhithe SE16 119 B4
Wyatt Ct HA0 66 A1
Wyatt Dr SW13 134 B5
Wyatt Ho
Blackheath Vale SE3 142 D3
NW8 236 D5
Wyatt Park Mans 1
SW2 160 A2
Wyatt Park Rd SW2 160 B2
Wyatt Rd
Forest Gate E7 77 A2
Highbury N5 73 A5
Wyatt's La E17 54 A6
Wybert St NW1 239 A6
Wyborne Ho NW10 67 A1
Wyborne Prim Sch
SE9 166 D3
Wyborne Way NW10 67 A1
Wyburn Ave EN5 1 B2
Wyche Gr CR2 221 A1
Wycherley Cl SE3 142 D5
Wycherley Cres EN5 13 D5
Wychwood Ave
Edgware HA8 25 D4
South Norwood CR7 205 A6
Wychwood Cl
Ashford TW16 172 A4
Edgware HA8 25 D4
Wychwood End N6 49 C2
Wychwood Gdns IG5 56 C5
Wychwood Ho N4 51 A2
Wychwood Way SE19 183 B4
Wyclif Ct EC1 234 C1
Wycliffe Cl DA16 145 D4
Wycliffe Ho 13 N16 73 C4
Wycliffe Rd
Battersea SW11 137 A3
Wimbledon SW19 179 D4
Wyclif St EC1 234 C1
Wycombe Ct SE3 143 A5
Wycombe Gdns NW11 69 C6
Wycombe Ho NW8 237 A6
Wycombe Pl SW18 158 A5
Wycombe Rd
Redbridge IG2 56 B4
Tottenham N17 34 A2
Wembley HA0 88 C6
Wycombe Sq W8 245 A3
Wydehurst Rd CR0 206 B2
Wydell Cl SM4 200 D3
Wydeville Manor Rd
SE12 187 B6
Wye Cl
Ashford TW15 170 D6
BR6 211 D2
Ruislip HA4 39 A3
Wye Ct W13 87 B2
Wyemead Cres E4 20 C2
Wyersdale Ho N4 51 A2
Wye St SW11 136 B3
Wyevale Cl HA5 40 A6
Wyfold Ho 8 SE2 124 D4
Wyfold Rd
SW6 135 A5 264 A3
Wyke Cl TW7 130 D6
Wyke Gdns W7 109 A3
Wykeham Ave RM9 80 C2
Wykeham Cl UB7 126 C6
Wykeham Ct
Chislehurst BR7 189 C4
Hendon NW4 46 C4
Wykeham Gn RM9 80 C2
Wykeham Hill HA9 44 B1
Wykeham Ho SW19 179 C2
Wykeham Prim Sch
NW10 67 C5
Wykeham Rd
Harrow HA3 43 B5
Hendon NW4 46 C4
Wykeham Rise N20 13 A3
Wykehurst Ho SW17 180 B5
Wyke Rd
Hackney Wick E3 75 C1
Wyke Rd *continued*
Merton SW20 178 C1
Wylchin Cl HA5 39 D6
Wyldes Cl NW11 48 A1
Wyldfield Gdns N9 17 D2
Wyld Way HA9 66 D2
Wyleu St SE23 163 A4
Wylie Rd UB2 107 C3
Wyllen Cl E1 96 C3
Wylo Dr EN5 12 A5
Wymering Mans 9
W9 91 C4
Wymering Rd W9 91 C4
Wymondham Ct NW8 229 D6
Wymond St SW15 134 C2
Wynan Rd E14 119 D1
Wynash Gdns SM5 218 C3
Wynaud Ct N22 32 B4
Wynbourne Ct SE20 184 B1
Wyncham Ave DA15 167 C3
Wynchgate
Harrow HA3 24 C3
Southgate N14 16 A4
Wyncroft Cl BR1 210 B6
Wyndale Ave NW9 44 C3
Wyndcliff Rd SE7 143 B6
Wyndcroft Cl EN2 4 D2
Wyndham Cl
Belmont SM2 217 C1
Orpington BR6 211 A1
Wyndham Cres
Camden Town N19 71 C5
Hounslow TW4 151 C5
Wyndham Ct
Brentford W7 109 A2
1 Thornton Heath
CR0 204 D3
Wyndham Deedes Ho 30
E2 96 A5
Wyndham Ho SW1 258 A3
Wyndham Lo TW7 130 C4
Wyndham Mews W1 237 C3
Wyndham Pl W1 237 C3
Wyndham Rd
Barnet EN4 14 D3
Brentford W13 109 B3
Forest Gate E6 77 D1
Kingston u T KT2 176 B3
SE5 139 A5
Wyndhams Ct 4 E8 73 D1
Wyndham St
W1 92 D2 237 C4
Wyndham Yd W1 237 C3
Wyndhurst Cl CR2 220 D1
Wyneham Rd SE24 161 B6
Wynell Rd SE23 162 D1
Wynford Pl DA17 147 C6
Wynford Rd N1 94 B5 233 D4
Wynford Way SE9 166 B1
Wynlie Gdns HA5 22 B1
Wynndale Rd E18 37 B2
Wynne Ct 6 TW7 131 A2
Wynne Ho SE14 140 D4
Wynne Rd SW9 138 C3
Wynn's Ave DA15 168 A6
Wynnstay Gdns
W8 113 C3 255 B6
Wynter Ho 20 SW9 138 B3
Wynter St SW11 136 A1
Wynton Gdns SE25 205 D4
Wynton Pl W3 88 D1
Wynyard Ho SE11 260 D2
Wynyard Terr SE11 260 D2
Wynyatt Ho EC1 234 C2
Wynyatt St EC1 94 D4 234 C2
Wyre Gr
Edgware HA8 10 D1
Hayes UB3 106 A2
Wyresdale Cres UB6 86 D4
Wyteleaf Cl HA4 39 A3
Wytham Ho NW8 236 D5
Wythburn Ct W1 237 C2
Wythburn Pl W1 237 C2
Wythenshawe Rd
RM10 81 C5
Wythens Wlk SE9 166 D5
Wythes Cl BR1 188 B1
Wythes Rd E16 122 A5
Wythfield Rd SE9 166 B5
Wyvenhoe Rd HA2 64 A5
Wyvern Est The KT3 200 A5
Wyvil Prim Sch
SW8 138 A5 270 B4
Wyvil Rd SW8 138 A5 270 A4
Wyvis St E14 97 D2

X

Xavier Ho E17 35 B1

Y

Yabsley St E14 120 A5
Yaldam Ho SE1 263 A3
Yalding Ho 20 E5 74 B3
Yalding Rd SE16 118 A2
Yale Cl TW4 151 B6
Yale Ct NW6 69 D3
Yarborough Rd 1
SW19 180 B2
Yardley Cl E4 19 D6
Yardley Ct SM3 216 D4
Yardley La E4 19 D6
Yardley Prim Sch E4 20 A5
Yardley St WC1 234 A1
Yard The N1 233 B3
Yarlington Ct N11 31 A5
Yarmouth Cres N17 52 B4
Yarmouth Pl W1 248 C3
Yarnfield Sq 15 SE15 140 A4
Yarnton Way DA17,
DA18 125 B3
Yarrow Cres E6 100 A2
Yarrow Ho
12 Cubitt Town E14 120 A3
16 North Kensington
W10 90 C2
Yateley St SE18 121 D3
Yatesbury Ct E5 75 A3
Yates Ct NW2 68 D2
Yates Ho 22 E2 96 A4
Yatton Ho 15 W10 90 C2
YEADING 84 D3
Yeading Ave HA2 41 A1
Yeading Ct UB4 84 C3
Yeading Fork UB4 84 C3
Yeading Gdns UB4 84 B2
Yeading Ho UB4 84 D2
Yeading Jun & Inf Schs
UB4 84 C2
Yeading La
Hayes UB4 84 B2
Northolt UB4, UB5 84 C4
Yeadon Ho 14 W10 90 C2
Yeames Cl W13 87 A1
Yearby Ho W10 90 C3
Yeate St N1 73 B1
Yeatman Rd N6 48 D3
Yeats Cl NW10 67 C2
Yeend Cl KT8 195 C5
Yeldham Ho W6 112 D1
Yeldham Rd W6 112 D1
Yellowhammer Ct
NW9 27 C1
Yelverton Lo TW1 153 C4
Yelverton Rd SW11 136 B3
Ye Market CR0 221 B3
Yenston Cl SM4 201 C3
Yeoman Cl
Newham E16 122 D6
West Norwood SE27 160 D1
Yeoman Ct
Heston TW5 129 B5
8 Sutton SM1 218 B3
Yeoman Dr TW19 148 A3
Yeoman Rd UB5 63 A1
Yeomans Acre HA4 40 A3
Yeomans Mews TW7 152 B6
Yeoman's Row
SW3 114 C3 257 B5
Yeoman St SE8 119 A2
Yeomans Way EN3 6 C3
Yeoman's Yd E1 253 D6
Yeo St E3 97 D2
Yeovil Cl BR6 227 C6
Yeovil Ho
Finsbury Pk N7 72 B6
North Kensington W10 90 C3
Yeovilton Pl KT2 175 C5
Yerbury Prim Sch N19 71 D5
Yerbury Rd N19 71 D5
Yeshivo Horomo
Tadmudical Coll N16 51 B1
Yesodey Hatorah Sch
N16 51 D2
Yester Dr BR7 188 A3
Yester Pk BR7 188 B4
Yester Rd BR7 188 B3
Yet Lev Ct E5 52 A1
Yew Ave UB7 104 A6
Yew Cl IG9 21 D2
Yewdale Cl BR1 186 C4
Yewfield Rd NW10 67 D2
Yew Gr NW2 68 D4

Yew Ho SE14 141 B3
Yews The TW15 170 D6
Yew Tree Ave N2 47 D6
Yewtree Cl
Harrow HA2 41 D5
Wood Green N22 31 C2
Yew Tree Cl
DA16 146 A4
3 Lewisham SE13 142 A2
New Malden KT4 199 C1
Southgate N21 16 C4
Yew Tree Cotts KT10 212 B6
Yew Tree Ct
Elstree WD6 9 D5
8 Stoke Newington N16 73 B6
8 Sutton SM2 218 A1
4 Temple Fortune NW11 47 B4
Yew Tree Gdns RM6 59 A4
Yew Tree Grange 2 W5 109 C6
Yew Tree Ho
New Malden KT4 199 C1
5 Surbiton KT6 198 A1
Yew Tree Lo 10 SW16 181 C6
Yewtree Rd BR3 207 B6
Yew Tree Rd
East Acton W12 111 D6
Hillingdon UB10 82 B6
Yew Trees TW17 192 B5
Yew Tree Wlk TW4 151 B6
Yew Wlk HA1 42 C1
YIEWSLEY 104 A6
Yiewsley Ct UB7 104 A5
Yoakley Rd N16 73 C6
Yoke Cl N7 72 A2
Yolande Gdns SE9 166 A6
Yonge Pk N4, N7 72 C5
York Ave
Ealing W7 108 C5
Hayes UB3 83 A1
Mortlake SW14 155 A6
Sidcup DA15 167 D2
Stanmore HA7 25 B1
Walworth SE17 262 B2
York Bldgs
WC2 116 A6 250 B5
York Bridge
NW1 93 A3 238 A6
York Cl
17 Camberwell SE5 139 A3
Ealing W7 108 C5
Morden SM4 201 D5
Newham E6 100 B1
York Ct
Beckenham BR3 186 B2
Kingston u T KT2 175 D4
Palmers Green N13 16 A1
Wallington SM6 219 C3
York Gate
NW1 238 B5
Southgate N14 16 A4
York Gr SE15 140 C4
York Hill SE27, SW16 160 D1
York Ho
Acton W3 111 A6
Chelsea SW3 257 D2
Chingford E4 35 C6
Edgware HA8 26 B4
Enfield EN2 5 B4
Forest Hill SE26 184 C5
1 Hendon NW4 28 D1
York Ho *continued*
1 Ilford IG1 78 D6
Islington N5 72 C3
Kensington W8 245 C2
11 Kentish Town N7 71 D2
Kew TW9 132 C4
4 Kingston u T KT2 176 B3
Lambeth SE1 116 B3 260 D5
Marylebone W1 237 C4
Pentonville N1 233 C3
Richmond TW10 154 C6
South Norwood SE25 205 C5
10 West Acton W3 88 C1
York House Pl
W8 113 D4 245 C2
Yorkland Ave DA16 145 D1
Yorkley Ho 3 W10 90 C3
York Mans
Battersea SW11 268 B2
2 Hendon NW9 46 A3
Marylebone W1 238 A4
Walworth SE17 262 B2
York Mews
Camden Town NW5 71 B3
Ilford IG1 78 C5
York Par
Brentford TW8 109 D1
Hendon NW9 46 A3
York Pl
Battersea SW11 136 B2
Ilford IG1 78 C6
WC2 250 B5
York Place Mans NW1 237 D4
York Rd
Battersea SW11, SW18 136 B2
Belmont SM1, SM2 217 C1
York Rd *continued*
Brentford TW8 109 D1
Chingford E4 35 C5
Dagenham W3 89 B1
Ealing W5 109 C3
Edmonton N18 34 B5
Forest Gate E7 77 A2
Friern Barnet N11 31 D4
Hounslow TW3 129 D2
Ilford IG1 78 C6
Kingston u T KT2 176 B3
Leyton E10 76 A5
New Barnet EN5 14 B6
Pinner HA6 22 A1
4 Richmond TW10 154 B6
SE1 116 B4 250 D2
Southgate N21 17 B4
Teddington TW11 174 C6
Thornton Heath CR0 204 C2
Walthamstow E17 52 D4
Wimbledon SW19 180 A4
York Rise
BR6 227 C6
Dartmouth Pk NW5 71 B5
York Road Bsns Ctr
SW11 136 B3
York St Chambers
W1 237 C4
Yorkshire Cl N16 73 C5
Yorkshire Gdns N18 34 B5
Yorkshire Grey SE9 165 D6
Yorkshire Grey Pl 13
NW3 70 A4
Yorkshire Grey Yd
WC1 240 C3
Yorkshire Rd
Limehouse E14 97 A1
Yorkshire Rd *continued*
Mitcham CR4 204 A5
York Sq 12 E14 97 A1
York St
Carshalton CR4 203 A2
Paddington W1 92 D2 237 D4
Twickenham TW1 153 A3
York Terr EN2 5 A5
York Terr E
NW1 93 A3 238 B5
York Terr W
NW1 93 A3 238 A5
Yorkton St E2 96 A5
York Way
Barnsbury N1, N7,
NW1 72 A1
Chessington KT9 214 A1
Friern Barnet N20 14 D1
N1 233 B5
Twickenham TW13 151 B1
York Way Ct
Islington N1 233 C5
Islington N1 233 B5
Youngmans Cl EN2 5 A4
Young Rd E16 99 C1
Young's Bldgs EC1 242 B6
Youngs Brewery Visitor Ctr* SW18 157 D6
Youngs Ct SW11 268 B1
Youngs Rd IG2 57 B4
Young St W8 113 D4 245 C1
Yoxall Ho 2 W10 90 C3
Yoxford Ct 6 RM6 58 B4
Yoxley App IG2 57 A3
Yoxley Dr IG2 57 A3
Yukon Rd SW12 159 B4
Yunus Khan Cl E17 53 C4

Z

Zambezie Dr N9 18 C1
Zampa Rd SE16 118 C1
Zander Ct E2 96 A4
Zangwill Ho NW6 91 B5
Zangwill Rd SE18, SE3 143 D4
Zealand Ave UB7 126 A5
Zealand Ho
11 Camberwell SE5 139 A3
4 Woolwich SE7 122 A2
Zealand Rd E3 97 A5
Zenith Lo 7 N3 29 D3
Zennor Rd SW12 159 C3
Zenoria St SE22 139 D1
Zermatt Rd CR7 205 A5
Zetland Ho W8 255 C6
Zetland St E14 98 A2
Zeus Ho N1 235 C1
Zion Ho 6 E1 96 C1
Zion Pl CR7 205 B5
Zion Rd CR7 205 B5
Zircon Ct N11 31 D3
ZK Pk CR0 220 B5
Zoar St SE1 117 A5 252 A4
Zodiac Ct CR0 204 D1
Zodiac Ho 3 E3 97 C3
Zoffany St N19 71 D6

List of numbered locations

This atlas shows thousands more place names than any other London street atlas. In some busy areas it is impossible to fit the name of every place.

Where not all names will fit, some smaller places are shown by a number. If you wish to find out the name associated with a number, use this listing.

The places in this list are also listed normally in the Index.

34
A5 7 Cordwain Ho

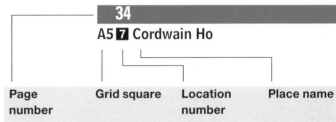

Page number | Grid square | Location number | Place name

1
A1 1 Hertswood Ct
2 Abingdon Lo
3 Sunbury Ct
4 Meriden Ho
5 Norfolk Ct
6 Vanburgh Ct
7 Morrison Ct
8 Kingshill Ct
9 Baronsmere Ct
10 Chartwell Ct
A2 1 Richard Ct
2 Alston Ct
3 Ridgeleigh Ct
4 Bartletts Cotts
5 Leathersellers Cl
6 Holkham Ho
7 Leinster Mews
B1 1 Olivia Ct
2 Tudor Ct
3 Gordon Mans
B2 1 Brake Shear Ho
2 Durham Ct
3 Huntingdon Ct
4 Cambridge Ct
5 Summit Ct
D1 1 Cranleigh Ct
2 Valeside Ct
3 Sherwood
4 Bradbury Ct
5 Chester Ho
6 Graham Ho
7 Highfield Ct
8 Amberley Ho
9 Hadley View
10 Stratton Lo
11 Gainsborough Ct
12 Christopher Ct
13 Bowmar Lo

2
A1 1 Hanover Ho
2 St Giles Ho
3 Henrietta Ho
4 Byron Ct
5 Preston Ct
6 Clivedon Ct
7 Battle House Mews
8 Phoenix Ct
9 Landsdown Cl
10 Comer Ho
11 Basil Ct
12 Russell Ct
13 Alice Cl
C1 1 Braeburn Ct
2 Bramley Ct
3 Cox Ct
4 Golden Ct
5 Pippin Ct
6 Russet Ct
7 High Birch Ct
8 Joystone Ct
9 Mark Lo
10 Edgeworth Ct

4
D3 1 Oakington Ct
2 Elderberry Ct
3 Blueberry Ct
4 Butterfield Ho

5
C1 1 Woodfield Cl
2 Fielders Cl

7
A2 1 Amethyest Ct
2 Bradmore Ct
3 Acer Ct
4 Cornell Ct
5 Durnsford Ct
6 Feldspar Ct
C6 1 Whitworth Cres
2 Polsten Mews
3 Aldis Mews
4 Dundas Mews
5 Colt Mews
6 Warlow Cl
7 Barrass Cl
8 Rigby Pl
9 Gunner Dr
10 Colgate Pl
11 Baddeley Cl
12 Sten Cl
13 Pritchett Cl
14 Rubin Pl
15 Turpin Cl
16 Island Centre Way
17 Hispano Mews
18 Watkin Mews
19 Wallace Ct
20 Needham Ct
21 Dryer Ct
22 Webley Ct
23 Frosbery Ct
24 Jacob Ct
25 Peabody Ct
26 Greener Ct
27 Bren Ct

9
D5 1 Watling Ct
2 Stuart Ct
3 Westview Ct
4 Potters Mews

13
D6 1 Rowan Wlk
2 Ford Ho
3 Glenwood Ho
4 Whitegates
5 Lisa Lo
6 South Lo
7 Hockington Ct
8 Lysander Ct
9 Ashwood Lo
10 Thornbridge Ct
11 Invergarry Ct
12 Eysham Ct
13 Warwick Ct
14 Chaucer Ct
15 Coleridge Ct
16 Springfields
17 Bure Ct
18 Florence Ct
19 Minetta Ct

14
A1 1 Belmont Ct
2 Terrace Ho
3 Croft Mews
4 Bluebell Ct
A2 1 Westview Ct
2 Oakleigh Mews
3 Mountview Ct
4 Mortimer Ct
5 Parklands
A6 1 Chiltern Ct
2 Gills Ct
3 Beaufort Ct
4 St Augustines Ct
5 Somerset Lo
6 Carlyle Lo
7 Stirling Lo
8 St Mirren Ct
9 Wardrew Ct
10 Apex Lo
11 Westbury Ct
B2 1 Davis Ct
2 Deerings Ct
3 Ashcroft Ct
B6 1 Redrose Trad Ctr
2 Lancaster Road Ind Est
C2 1 Mendip Ct
2 Purbeck Ct
3 Brendon Ct
4 Quantock Ct
5 Malvern Ct
6 Chiltern Ct
C5 1 Feline Ct
2 Brookhill Ct
3 Littlegrove Ct
4 Desmond Ho
D1 1 Springfield Ct
2 Victor Ho
3 Malborough Ho
4 Coopers Ct
5 Joiners Ct
D2 1 Bantock Ct
2 Burgess Ct
3 Heaton Ct
4 Bordley Ct
5 Garside Ct
6 Cranston Ct
7 Gleave Ct
D3 1 Wren Ct
2 Homerton Ct
3 Emmanuel Ct
4 Wolfson Ct
5 Robinson Ct
6 Gonville Ct

15
C6 1 Tregenna Cl
2 Catherine Ct
3 Conisbee Ct
4 Ashmead
D3 1 Dennis Par
2 Broadway The
3 Southgate Cir
4 Station Par
5 Bourneside
6 Bourneside Cres

17
C6 1 Wade Ho
2 Newport Lo
3 Halcyon Ho
4 Lerwick Ct
5 Anchor Ct
6 Grassmere Ct
7 Datchworth Ct
8 Trentham Lo
9 Austin Ct
10 Cedar Grange
11 Brookview Ct
12 Chestbrook Ct
13 Paddock Lo
14 Hamlet Ct
15 Haven Lo

18
A1 1 Plevna Ho
2 Lea Ho
3 Brook Ho
4 Valley Ho
5 Chiltern Ho
6 Blenheim Ho
7 Penn Ho
8 Romany Ho
9 Gilpin Ho
10 Anvil Ho
11 Well Ho
12 Passmore Ho
13 Durbin Ho
A2 1 Market Par
2 Beechwood Mews
3 Keats Par
4 Cedars Rd
5 Cross Keys Cl
6 Dorman Pl
7 Concourse The

20
1 Lea Ct
2 Park Ct
3 Conference Cl
4 Berrybank Cl
5 Russell Lo
6 Brunswick Lo
7 Kenilworth Ct
8 Trinity Ct
9 Kingsmead Lo
10 Fairlawns
A3 1 Knight Ct
2 Grant Ct
3 Chantry The
4 Bowyer Ct
5 Pineview Ct
6 Ellen Ct
7 Leeview Ct
8 Chelsea Ct
9 Bramley Ct
10 Garenne Ct
11 Kendal Ct
12 Fairways
13 Avon Ct
B3 1 Maddox Ct
2 Village Arc The
3 Cambridge Rd
4 Crown Bldgs
5 Pentney Rd
6 Scholars Ho
7 Cranworth Cres
C4 1 Connaught Ct
2 Woolden Ho
3 Fairmead Ct
4 Lockhart Lo
5 Cavendish Ct
6 Oakwood Ct
7 Plains The
8 Hadleigh Ct
9 Forest Ho
10 Mathieson Ho

21
B2 1 Stag Hts
2 Shore Point
3 Buckhurst Hill Ho
4 Beech Ave
5 High Road Buckhurst Hill
6 Highclears
C2 1 Westbury Ct
2 Palmerston Ct
3 Ibrox Ct
4 Richard Burton Ct
5 Queens Mews

6 Gunnels Ct & Hastingwood Ct
7 Marlborough Ct
8 Avenue The
9 Tora Ct
10 Somerset Ct
11 Mirravale Ct
C3 1 Rayburne Ct
2 Laurels The
3 Mablin Lo
4 Silvers
5 Makinen Ho
6 Roman Lo
D1 1 Highview Ho
1 Hornbeam Ho
2 Highview Ho
3 Bourne Ho
D2 1 Regency Lo
2 Kings Ct
3 Beech Ct
4 Sycamore Ho
5 Salisbury Gdns
6 Pegasus Ct
7 Buckhurst Ct
8 Mountbatten Ct
9 Atrium
D6 1 Richmond Ct
2 Highview Ct
3 Collins Ct
4 Lower Park Rd
5 Homecherry Ho

22

C1 1 Daniel Ho
2 Hawthorn Ct
3 Northcote
4 Edwin Ware Ct
5 Chalfont Wlk
6 Maple Ct
7 Montesole Ct
8 Viewpoint Ct

23

B3 1 Russettings
2 St Cuthberts Gdns
3 Cherry Croft Gdns
4 Claire Ct
5 Cornwall Ct
6 Falmouth Ho
7 Newlyn Ho
8 Chestnuts The
9 Dunford Ct
10 Stratton Ct
11 Hanover Ct

25

C5 1 Belgrave Gdns
2 Heywood Ct
3 Norfolk Ho
4 Garden Ct
5 Chatsworth Ct
6 Chartridge Ct
7 Hardwick Cl
8 Cheltenham Ct
9 Cargrey Ho
10 Holbein Ho
11 Goodwood Cl
12 Ascot Pl
13 Longchamp Ct
14 Halfacre
15 Burnham Ct
16 Dingle Ct
17 Woodcroft
18 Daneglen Ct
19 Buckingham Par
C6 1 Bickley Ct
2 Kelmscott Ct
3 Elstree Ho
4 Brompton Ct
5 Kenmare Ct
6 Burlington Park Ho
7 Gressenham Ct
8 Amora

26

D5 1 Penshurst Ct
2 Cranbourne Ct
3 Wilton Ct
4 Saxon Ct
5 Abbey Ct
6 Kenlor Ct
7 Daniel Ct
8 Hillcrest Ct
9 Hunters Lo
10 Orion Ct

27

A1 1 Colesworth Ho
2 Crokesley Ho
3 Curtlington Ho
4 Clare Ho
5 Kedyngton Ho
A3 1 Tadbourne Ct
2 Truman Cl
3 Lords Ct
4 Hutton Row
5 Compton Cl
6 Botham Cl
7 Bradman Row
A6 1 Iris Wlk
2 Sycamore Cl
3 Aster Ct
4 Firethorn Cl
5 Berberry Cl
6 Hibiscus Cl
B5 1 Monarchs Ct
2 Kensington Ct
3 Grosvenor Ct
4 Chasewood Ct
C2 1 Rufforth Ct
2 Riccall Ct
3 Lindholme Ct
4 Driffield Ct
5 Jack Ashley Ct
6 Folkingham La
7 Debden Cl
8 Holbeach Cl
9 Shawbury Cl
10 Daniel Ct
11 Leander Ct
12 Nimrod
13 Nisbet
14 Pixton
15 Rapide
16 Ratier
D1 1 Gauntlet
2 Guilfoyle
3 Grebe
4 Gates
5 Galy
6 Folland
7 Firefly
8 Halifax
9 Debussy
10 Crosbie
11 Grant Ct
12 Ham Ct
13 Deal Ct
14 Ember Ct
15 Canterbury Ct
16 Beaumont Ct
17 Cirrus
18 Defiant
19 Dessouter
20 Douglas
21 Cobham
22 Clayton
23 Camm
24 Bradon
25 Boarhound
26 Bodmin
27 Bleriot
28 Blackburn
29 Audax
30 Anson
31 Albatross
32 Arran Ct
33 Mavis Ct
34 Goosander Ct
35 Platt Halls (a)
36 Writtle Ho
37 Platt Halls (b)
38 Platt Halls (c)
D2 1 Slatter
2 Sopwith
3 Saimet
4 Sassoon
5 Roe
6 Orde
7 Osprey
8 Prodger
9 Randall
10 Porte
11 Norris
12 Nardini
13 Noel
14 Nicolson
15 Napier
16 Nighthawk
17 Moorhouse
18 Moineau
19 Mitchell
20 Lysander
21 Lillywhite
22 Martynside
23 March
24 Kemp
25 Mercury
26 Merlin
27 Hudson
28 Hawker
29 Hawfinch
30 Heracles
31 Hector
32 Concourse The
D3 1 Wellington
2 Wheeler
3 Whittaker
4 Whittle
5 Tedder
6 Cranwell Ct
7 Tait
8 Spooner

28

D1 1 York Ho
2 Windsor Ho
3 Regency Cres
4 Normandy Ho
5 Allerton Ct
6 Beaulieu Ho
7 Dewlands Ct
8 Knightshayes Ho

29

A3 2 Frances & Dick James Ct
3 Farthing Ct
4 Coniston Ct
B1 1 Carlisle Lo
2 Laburnum Lo
3 Eden Ct
4 Moorcroft Ct
5 Clifford Lo
6 Acacia Lo
7 Cumberland Ct
8 Little Dell Lo
9 Cyprus Ct
10 Cyprus Ho
C2 1 Sheringham Ct
2 St Ronan's
3 Crescent Rise
4 Elm Ct
5 Norman Ct
6 Marlow Ct
7 Dancastle Ct
8 Newman Ct
9 Station Mans
10 Alice Ct
D3 1 Hadley Ct
2 Sherbrook Ho
3 Shine Ho
4 Regent Ct
5 Lodge Mead Ct
6 Spencer Ct
7 Zenith Lo
8 Burberry Ct
D5 1 Silverbell Ct
2 Inverey Ho
3 Wimbush Ho
4 Tudor Lo
5 Duncan Ct
6 Phillipson Ho
D6 1 Brookfield Ct
2 Magnolia Ct
3 Dunbar Ct
4 Haughmond
5 Nansen Village
6 Willow Ct
7 Birch Ct
8 Beechcroft Ct
9 Speedwell Ct
10 Woodside Ct
11 Speedwell Ho
12 Rebecca Ho
13 Ashbourne Ct
14 Forest Ct
15 Beecholme
16 Greville Lo
17 St Johnstone Ho
18 Ashbourne Cl
19 Clements Cl
20 Station App
21 Montclair Ct
22 Winterberry Ct
23 Caroline Ct

30

A4 1 Sharon Ct
2 Lydia Ct
3 Beatrice Lo
4 Grange Ct
5 Blissland Ct
A5 1 Archgate Bsns Ctr
2 Robart Ho
3 Danescroft
4 Cornelius Ct
5 Gable Lo
6 Waterville Lo
7 Chand Ho
B1 1 New Trinity Rd
2 Garden Ho
3 Todd Ho
4 Sayers Ho
5 Mowbray Ho
6 Bouchier Ho
7 Cleveland Ho
8 Goodyear Ho
9 Lochleven Ho
10 Berwick Ho
11 Oak Ho
12 Hilton Ho
13 East View Ho
14 Myddleton Ho
15 Willow Wlk
16 Craven Ho
17 Willow Ho
18 Vane Ho
19 Adelphi Ct
20 Annette White Lo
21 Foskett Ho
22 Elmfield Ho
23 Sycamore Ho
24 Netherwood
25 Rew Lo
26 William Cl
B5 1 Murray Ho
2 Damon Ho
3 Wendy Ho
4 Lychgate Ct
5 Clarence Ct
6 Carley Ct
7 Hermiston Ct
8 Cardrew Ct
9 Whitefriars Ct
D5 1 Halliwick Ct
2 Halliwick Court Par
3 Queen's Par
4 St John's Villas
5 Hartland Ct
6 Kennard Mans
7 Bensley Cl
8 Leadbeaters Cl
9 Gibson Ct
10 Burton Ct
11 Knights Ct
12 Constable Cl
13 Alderman Ct

31

A3 1 Campe Ho
2 Betstyle Ho
3 Pymmes Brook Ho
4 Mosswell Ho
5 Cavendish Ho
6 Tudor Ho
7 Kingsfield Ho
8 Peacehaven Ct
9 Hatch Ho
10 Hampden Ct
11 Crown Ct
A4 1 Cheddar Cl
2 Wincanton Ct
3 Whitby Ct
4 Richmond Ct
5 Tadworth Ct
6 Wensley Cl
7 Howeth Ct
8 Kilnsey Ct
9 Harrogate Ct
10 Ripon Ct
B1 1 Cedar Ct
2 Carisbrook
3 St Ivian Ct
4 Barrington Ct
5 Essex Lo
B6 1 Grovefield
2 Lapworth
3 Stewards Holte Wlk
4 Sarnes Ct
5 Stanhope Ho
6 Holmsdale Ho
7 Crosby Ct
8 Leyland Ct
9 Boundary Ct
10 Stateland Ct
C5 1 Barbara Martin Ho
2 Jerome Ct
3 Limes Cl
4 Arnos Grove Ct
5 Cedar Ct
6 Betspath Ho
7 Curtis Ho
8 Mason Ho
9 Danford Ho
10 New Southgate Ind Est
11 Palmer's Ct
12 Swinson Ho
13 Jackson Ho

32

A4 1 Brownlow Lo
2 Brownlow Ct
3 Latham Ct
4 Fairlawns
5 Beaumaris
C1 1 Penwortham Ct
2 Tarleton Ct
3 Holmeswood Ct
4 Kwesi Johnson Ct
5 Sandlings The
6 Suraj Ho
C6 1 Hazelwood Ct
2 Ashbourne Lo
3 Mapledurham Ct

33

D1 1 Kenmare Dr
2 Ashling Ho
3 Honeysett Rd
4 Wilson's Ave
5 Palm Tree Ct
6 Stoneleigh Ct
7 Brook St
D3 1 Charles Ho
2 Moselle Ho
3 Ermine Ho
4 Kathleen Ferrier Ct
5 Concord Ho
6 Rees Ho
7 Williams Ho
8 Nursery Ct
9 William Rainbird Ho
10 Gibson Bsns Ctr
11 Wingate Trad Est
D4 1 Regan Ho
2 Isis Ho
3 Boundary Ct
4 Stellar Ho
5 Cooperage Cl

34

A5 1 Angel Pl
2 Cross St
3 Scott Ho
4 Beck Ho
5 Booker Rd
6 Bridport Ho
7 Cordwain Ho
8 St James's Ct
9 Highmead
A6 1 Walton Ho
2 Alma Ho
3 Brompton Ho
4 Field Ho
5 Bradwell Mews
6 Angel Corner Par
7 Paul Ct
8 Cuthbert Rd
9 Brockenhurst Mews
B3 1 Kenneth Robbins Ho
2 Charles Bradlaugh Ho
3 Woodrow Ct
4 Cheviot
5 Corbridge
6 Whittingham
7 Eastwood Cl
8 Alnwick
9 Bamburgh
10 Bellingham
11 Briaris Cl

35

A1 1 Clayton Ct
2 St Andrew's Ct
3 Aranya Ct
4 Fitzwilliam Ho
A2 1 Romany Gdns
2 Swansland Gdns
3 Garnett Way
4 Claymore Ct
5 Winchester Ct
C5 1 Ainslie Ho
2 Lewis Ho

36

B5 1 Hedgemoor Ct
2 Hewitt Ho
3 Castle Ho
4 Bailey Ct
5 Harcourt Ho
6 Gerboa Ct
7 Wentworth Ct
D1 1 Chatham Rd
2 Washington Rd
3 Cherry Tree Ct
4 Grosvenor Lo
5 Torfell
D2 1 Hillboro Ct
2 Dorchester Ct

37

A1 1 Chiltons The
2 Ullswater Ct
3 Leigh Ct
4 Woburn Ct
5 Alveston Sq
6 Eaton Ct
7 Regency Ct
8 Cowley Ct
9 High Oaks Lo
A2 1 Lindal Ct
2 Hockley Ct
3 Woodleigh
4 Milne Ct
5 Cedar Ct
6 Elizabeth Ct
7 Silvermead
8 Laurel Mead Ct
9 Mitre Ct
10 Pevensey Ct
11 Lyndhurst Ct
12 Manor Court Lo
A3 1 New Jubilee Ct
2 Chartwell Ct
3 Greenwood
4 Clementine Wlk
A4 1 Terrace The
2 Broomhill Ct
3 Clifton Ct
4 Fairstead Lo
5 Hadleigh Lo
6 Broadmead Ct
7 Wilton Ct
8 Fairfield Ct
9 Higham Ct
10 Aston Ct
A6 1 Tree Tops
2 Cranfield Ct
3 Percival Ho
4 Raine Gdns
B1 1 Station Est
2 Station App
3 James Ct
C3 1 Liston Way
2 Elizabeth Ct
3 Coopersale Cl
4 Sunset Ct
5 Lambourne Ct
C4 1 Hope Cl
2 Rex Par
3 Shalford
4 Rodings The
5 Lawrence Ct
6 Cowan Lo

40

C1 1 Salisbury Ho
2 Rodwell Cl
3 Pretoria Ho
4 Ottawa Ho
5 Swallow Ct
6 Wellington Ho
7 Canberra Ho
C6 1 Tulip Ct
2 Hyacinth Ct
3 Rose Ct
4 Iris Ct
D6 1 Ashburton Ct
2 Northend Lodge

42

D3 1 Nightingale Ct
2 St John's Ct
3 Gayton Ct
4 Wilton Pl
5 Murray Ct
6 Cymbeline Ct
7 Knowles Ct
8 Charville Ct
9 Lime Ct
10 Petherton Ct
11 Garth Ct
12 Chalfont Ct
13 Shepherds Ct
D4 1 Crystal Ctr The
2 Blue Point Ct
3 Ryan Ho
4 Rothwell Ct
5 Bruce Ho
6 Middlesex Ct
7 Ingram Ho
8 Arless Ho
9 Leaf Ho
10 Becket Fold
11 Brandan Ho
12 Robert Ho

46

A2 1 Milton Rd
2 Stanley Rd
A3 1 Mapesbury Mews
2 York Mans
3 Telford Rd
A5 1 Pilkington Ct
2 Cousins Ct
3 Seton Ct
4 Frensham Ct
5 Chatton Ct
6 Geraldine Ct
7 Swynford Gdns
8 Miller Ct
9 Roffey Ct
10 Peace Ct
11 Rambler Ct
12 Lion Ct
13 Wenlock Gdns
14 Dogrose Ct
15 Harry Ct
16 Tribune Ct
17 Bonville Gdns
18 Pearl Ct
B4 1 Vivian Mans
2 Parade Mans
3 Georgian Ct
4 Florence Mans
5 Park Mans
6 Cheyne Cl
7 Queens Par
8 Central Mans
C5 1 Courtney Ho
2 Golderton
3 Thornbury
4 Ferrydale Lo
5 Studio Mews
6 Brampton La
7 Short St
8 Belle Vue Rd
9 Longford Ct
10 Ashwood Ho
D5 1 Midford Ho
2 Rockfield Ho
3 Lisselton Ho
4 Acrefield Ho

47

B2 1 Berkeley Ct
2 Exchange Mans
3 Beechcroft Ct
4 Nedahall Ct
B3 1 Charlton Lo
2 Clifton Gdns
B4 1 Hallswelle Par
2 Belmont Par
3 Temple Fortune Ho
4 Yew Tree Ct
5 Temple Fortune Par
6 Courtleigh
7 Arcade Ho
8 Queens Ct
9 Temple Fortune Ct
B5 1 Monkville Par
2 Ashbourne Par

48

A6 1 St Mary's Gn
2 Dunstan Cl
3 Paul Byrne Ho
4 Longfield Ct
5 Warwick Ct
6 Branksome Ct
7 Sherwood Hall

49

B6 1 Dorchester Ct
2 Old Chapel Pl
3 Athenaeum Pl
4 Risborough Cl
5 Risborough Ct
C1 1 Calvert Ct
2 Academy The
3 Whitehall Mans
4 Pauntley St
5 Archway Hts
6 Pauntley Ho
D1 1 Louise White Ho

2 Levison Way
3 Sanders Way
4 Birbeck Ho
5 Scholars Ct
D2 1 Eleanor Rathbone Ho
2 Christopher Lo
3 Monkridge
4 Marbleford Ct
5 High London
6 Garton Ho
7 Hilltop Ho
8 Caroline Martyn Ho
9 Arthur Henderson Ho
10 Margaret Mcmillan Ho
11 Enid Stacy Ho
12 Mary McArthur Ho
13 Bruce Glasier Ho
14 John Wheatley Ho
15 Keir Hardie Ho
16 Monroe Ho
17 Iberia Ho
18 Lygoe Ho
19 Lambert Ho
20 Shelbourne Ho
21 Arkansas Ho
22 Lafitte Ho
23 Shreveport Ho
24 Packenham Ho
25 Orpheus Ho
26 Fayetville Ho
27 Bayon Ho
D4 1 Kelland Cl
2 Truro Ct
3 Veryan Ct
4 Coulsdon Ct

50

A1 1 Beeches The
2 Lambton Ct
3 Nugent Ct
4 Lambton Mews
5 Mews The
A2 1 Marie Lloyd Gdns
2 Edith Cavell Cl
3 Marie Stopes Ct
4 Jessie Blythe La
5 Barbara Rudolph Ct
6 Hetty Rees Ct
7 Leyden Mans
8 Brambledown
9 Lochbie
10 Lyngham Ct
11 High Mount
12 Woodlands The
A4 1 Margaret Hill Ho
2 Manray Ct
3 Hermiston Ct
4 Carleton Ho
A5 1 Mackenzie Ho
2 Stowell Ho
3 Campsbourne Ho
4 Palace Gate Mews
B1 1 Lawson Ct
2 Wiltshire Ct
3 Fenstanton
4 Hutton Ct
5 Wisbech
D5 1 Wordsworth Par
2 Spanswick Lo
3 Barker Ho
D6 1 Langham Cl
2 Sidi Ct
3 Ince Terr

51

A2 1 Finmere Ho
2 Keynsham Ho
3 Kilpeck Ho
4 Knaresborough Ho
5 Leighfield Ho
6 Lonsdale Ho
7 Groveley Ho
8 Wensleydale Ho
9 Badminton Ct
B2 1 Selwood Ho
2 Mendip Ho
3 Ennerdale Ho
4 Delamere Ho
5 Westwood Ho
6 Bernwood Ho
7 Allerdale Ho
8 Chattenden Ho
9 Farningham Ho
10 Oakend Ho
C1 1 Godstone Ct
2 Farnham Ct
3 Milford Ct
4 Cranleigh Ct
5 Haslemere Ct
6 Belmont Ct
7 Hockworth Ho
8 Garratt Ho
9 Fairburn Ho
10 Thorndale Ho
11 Oakdene Ho
12 Briardale Ho
C3 1 Oatfield Ho
2 Perry Ct
3 Henrietta Ho
4 Bournes Ho
5 Chisley Rd
6 Twyford Ho
7 Langford Cl
8 Hatchfield Ho
D1 1 Stamford Hill Mans
2 Montefiore Ct
3 Berwyn Ho
4 Clent Ho
5 Chiltern Ho
6 Laindon Ho
7 Pentland Ho
D2 1 Regent Ct
2 Stamford Lo
3 Holmwood Ct
D3 1 Sherboro Rd
2 Westcott Cl
3 Cadoxton Ave
D4 1 Westerfield Rd
2 Suffield Rd
D5 1 Laseron Ho
2 Greenway Cl
3 Tottenham Gn E
4 Tottenham Gn E South Side
5 Deaconess Ct
6 Elliot Ct
7 Bushmead Cl
8 Beaufort Ho
9 Tynemouth Terr
D6 1 Holcombe Rd
2 Rigby Ho
3 Chaplin Rd
4 Keswick Apartments
5 Ambleside Cl
6 Lauriston Apartments
7 Terrall Apartments
8 Old School Ct
9 Nicholson Ct
10 Reynardson's Ct
11 Protheroe Ho

52

A1 1 Stamford Gr E
2 Stamford Mans
3 Grove Mans
4 Stamford Gr W
B1 1 Hawkwood Mount
2 Holmbury View
3 High Hill Ferry
4 Leaside Ho
5 Courtlands
6 Ivy Ho
7 Shelford Ct

53

A4 1 Hammond Ct
2 St James Apartments
3 Grange The
A5 1 Bristol Park Rd
2 Stoneydown Ho
3 Callonfield
4 Hardyng Ho
C1 1 Wellington Mans
2 Clewer Ct
3 Cochrane Ct
C5 1 Westbury Ho
2 Hatherley Ho
3 Vintry Mews
4 Tylers Ct
5 Merchants Lo
6 Gillards Mews
7 Blacksmiths Ho
8 Central Par
D1 1 Fitzgerald Ct
2 Bechervaise Ct
3 Underwood Ct
D2 1 Staton Ct
2 Howell Ct
3 Atkinson Ct
4 Russell Ct
5 St Catherines Twr
6 St Lukes Ct
7 St Matthews Ct
8 St Mark's Ct
9 St Elizabeth Ct
10 Emanuel Ct
11 St Thomas Ct
12 Beaumont Ho
13 Shelley Ct
14 St Paul's Twr
15 Flack Ct
16 King Ct
17 Osborne Ct
18 Muriel Ct
19 All Saints Twr
20 St Josephs Ct
D5 1 Nash Ho
2 St Columbas Ho
3 Attlee Terr
4 Astins Ho
5 Lindens The
6 Kevan Ct
7 Squire's Almshouses
8 Berry Field Cl
9 Connaught Ct
10 Holmcroft Ho
11 St Mary's Church Ho
D6 1 Hallingbury Ct
2 Mace Ho
3 Gaitskell Ho
4 Hancocke Ho
5 Trinity Ho
6 Fanshaw Ho
7 Hilltop
8 Batten Ho
9 Bradwell Ho
10 Walton Ho
11 Temple Ho
12 Gower Ho
13 Maple Ho
14 Poplars Ho
15 Cedars Ho
16 Kimm Ho
17 O'Grady Ho
18 Latham Ho
19 Powell Ct
20 Crosbie Ho

54

A2 1 Ayerst Ct
2 Dare Ct
3 St Edwards Ct
A4 1 Collard's Almshouses
2 Ellen Miller Ho
3 Tom Smith Ho
A5 1 Northwood Twr
2 Walnut Ct
3 Albert Whicher Ho
4 Pelly Ct
5 Ravenswood Ind Est
6 Holland Ct
7 Emberson Ho
8 St Mark's Ho
9 Alfred Villas
10 Leonard Ho
11 Old Station Yard The
A6 1 St David's Ct
2 Golden Par
3 Chestnuts Ct
4 Matthew Ct
5 Gilbert Ho
6 Manning Ho
7 Southgate Ho
8 Boyden Ho
9 Prospect Ho
10 Newton Ho
D2 1 Buxton Ct
2 Hanbury Dr
3 Forest Lea
4 Watershipdown Ho

55

A3 1 Aldham Hall
2 Parkside Ct
3 Mapperley Cl
4 Weavers Ho
5 Cyna Ct
6 Reed Mans
7 Thornton Ho
8 Hardwick Ct
A4 1 Kingsley Grange
2 Station Par
3 Gwynne Ho
4 Staveley Ct
5 Thurlow Ct
6 Devon Ho
7 Wellington Pas
8 Wanstead Hts
9 Hollies The
10 Little Holt
11 Hunter Ct
12 Mountier Ct
13 Woodland Ct
14 Dudley Ct
15 Struan Ho
16 Westleigh Ct
A5 1 Shernwood Ho
2 Orwell Lo
3 Hermitage Ct
4 Gowan Lea
5 Woodford Ho
6 Eagle Ct
7 Newbury Ct
8 Shelley Ct
9 Hardy Ct
10 Dickens Ct
11 Byron Ct
A6 1 Millbrook
2 Half Acre
3 Elmbrook
4 Grange The
5 Glenavon Lo
6 Glenwood Ct
7 Ferndown
8 Embassy Ct
9 Orestes Ct
10 Walbrook
11 Helmsley
12 Snaresbrook Hall
B4 1 Nightingale Ct
2 Chelston Ct
3 Grosvenor Ct
4 Louise Ct
5 St Davids Ct
6 Cedar Ct
7 Shrubbery The
8 Nightingale Mews
B5 1 Great Hall The
2 Clock Ct
3 Langham Ho
B6 1 Victoria Ct
2 Kenwood Gdns
3 Thaxted Lo
4 Albert Rd
5 Albert Ho
6 Falcon Ct
7 Deborah Ct
8 Swift Ho
9 Pulteney Gdns
10 Spring Ct
11 Trinity Gdns

56

B4 1 High View Par
2 Spurway Par
3 Florence Root Ho
4 Rohan Pl
5 Homeheather Ho

57

A3 1 Catherine Ct
2 Lincoln Ct
3 Ivy Terr
4 Newbury Cotts

58

B1 1 Caledonian Cl
2 Talisman Cl
3 Norseman Cl
4 Frank Slater Ho
5 Brook's Mans
6 Brook's Par
B2 1 Mitre Ct
2 Coppins The
3 Stanetta Ct
4 Wilnett Ct
5 Wilnett Villas
B4 1 Sudbury Ct
2 Dunwich Ct
3 Cromer Terr
4 Norfolk Ct
5 Framlingham Ct
6 Yoxford Ct
C4 1 Swaffham Ct
2 Nacton Ct
3 Suffolk Ct
D2 1 Pavement Mews
2 Chadview Ct
3 Granary Ct
4 Bedwell Ct
5 Chapel La
6 Faulkner Cl
7 Maple Ct
8 Willow Ct
9 Cedar Terr

63

C2 1 Wimborne Ct
2 Haydock Green Flats
3 Brighton Dr
4 Blaydon Ct
5 Fakenham Cl
6 Rutland Ho
7 Windsor Ho

65

D3 1 Lowry Lo
2 Morritt Ho
3 Charles Goddard Ho
4 Snow Ct
5 Willow Tree Ct
6 Oak Lo

66

A2 1 Montrose Cres
2 Peggy Quirke Ct
3 Marylebone Ct
4 Waterloo Ct
5 Euston Ct
6 St Pancras Ct
7 Paddington Ct
8 Copland Mews
9 Coronet Par
10 Aylestone Ct
11 Charlotte Ct
A3 1 Wembley Mkt
2 Market Way
3 Lodge Ct
4 Central Sq
5 Manor Ct
6 Rupert Ave
7 Lily Ho
C4 1 Wembley Mkt

67

A5 1 Curie Ho
2 Darwin Ho
3 Priestley Ho
4 Rutherford Ho
5 Fleming Ho
6 Lister Ho
7 Edison Ho
B1 1 Biko Ho
2 Kingthorpe Terr
3 Scott Ho
4 Peary Ho
5 Shackleton Ho
6 Amundsen Ho
7 Brentfield Ho
8 Nansen Ho
9 Stonebridge Ct
10 Newcroft Ho
11 Magellan Ct
12 Leadbetter Ct
13 Jefferies Ho
14 Cowan Ct
15 Prothero Ho
16 Crawford St
17 Clark Ct
18 Diamond St
19 Mary Seacole Villas
C1 1 Beveridge Rd
2 Purcell Mews
3 George Lansbury Ho
4 Charles Hobson Ho
5 Reade Wlk
6 Westbury Ho
7 Bridge Ct
C4 1 Grange Ct
2 Green Ct
C5 1 Hazelwood Ct
2 Winslow Cl

68

A2 1 Regency Mews
2 Tudor Mews
3 Utopia Ho
4 Bell Flats
5 Angel Ct
A5 1 Bourne Ho
2 Carton Ho
3 Bidwell Ho
4 Woodbridge Cl
5 Mackenzie Ho
6 Banting Ho
C2 1 Rutland Park Gdns
2 Rutland Park Mans
3 Queens Par
4 Harcourt Ho
5 Solidarity Ho
6 Electra Ct
7 Cassandra Ct
8 Carlton Ct
D4 1 Oaklands Mews
2 Acer Ct
3 Maple Ct
4 Argyle Mans

69

A1 1 Christ Church Ct
2 Paul Daisley Ct
3 Fountain Ho
4 Kingston Ho
5 Waverley Ct
6 Weston Ho
7 Mapes Ho
8 Athelstan Gdns
9 Leff Ho
B1 1 Alma Birk Ho
2 Brooklands Ct
3 Brooklands Court Apartments
4 Cleveland Mans
5 Buckley Ct
6 Webheath
B5 1 Mortimer Cl
2 Primrose Ct
3 Sunnyside Ho
4 Sunnyside
5 Prospect Pl
C1 1 Linstead St
2 Embassy Ho
3 Acol Ct
4 Kings Wood Ct
5 Douglas Ct
6 King's Gdns
7 Carlton Mans
8 Smyrna Mans
9 New Priory Ct
10 Queensgate Pl
11 Brondesbury Mews
C2 1 Dene Mans
2 Sandwell Cres
3 Sandwell Mans
4 Hampstead West
5 Redcroft
C3 1 Orestes Mews
2 Walter Northcott Ho
3 Polperro Mans
4 Lyncroft Mans
5 Marlborough Mans
6 Alexandra Mans
7 Cumberland Mans
8 Cavendish Mans
9 Ambassador Ct
10 Welbeck Mans
11 Inglewood Mans
12 Dennington Park Mansions
C5 1 Portman Hts
2 Hermitage Ct
3 Moreland Ct
4 Wendover Ct
D2 1 Beswick Mews
2 Worcester Mews
3 Minton Mews
4 Doulton Mews
5 Laurel Ho
6 Sandalwood Ho
7 Iroko Ho
8 Banyan Ho
9 Rosewood Ho
10 Ebony Ho
11 Rosemont Mans
12 Exeter Mews

70

A1 1 Harrold Ho
2 Glover Ho
3 Byron Ct
4 Nalton Ho
A2 1 Petros Gdns
2 Heath Ct
3 Imperial Twrs
4 Fairhurst
5 St John's Ct
6 New College Ct
7 Chalford
8 Rosslyn Mans
9 Sutherland Ho
A4 1 Windmill Hill
2 Highgrove Point
3 Gainsborough Ho
4 Holly Bush Hill
5 Heath Mans
6 Holly Bush Steps
7 Pavilion Ct
8 Holly Berry La
9 New Campden Ct
10 Holly Bush Vale
11 Benham's Pl
12 Prospect Pl
13 Yorkshire Grey Pl
14 Gardnor Mans
15 Ellerdale Cl
16 Monro Ho
17 Prince Arthur Mews
18 Prince Arthur Ct
19 Village Mount
20 Perrin's Ct
21 Wells Ct
22 Bakers Pas
23 Spencer Wlk
24 Bird In Hand Yd
25 Kings Well
26 New Ct
27 Streatley Pl
28 Mansfield Pl
29 Upper Hampstead Wlk
A5 1 Hampstead Sq
2 Stamford Ct
3 Mount Sq The
B1 1 New College Par
2 Northways Par
3 Noel Ho
4 Campden Ho
5 Centre Hts
6 Hickes Ho
7 Swiss Terr
8 Leitch Ho
9 Jevons Ho
10 Langhorne Ct
11 Park Lo
12 Avenue Lo
B2 1 Belsize Park Mews
2 Baynes Mews
3 McCrone Mews
B3 1 Belsize Court Garages
2 Roscommon Ho
3 Akenside Ct
B4 1 White Bear Pl
2 Wells Ho The
3 Boades Mews
4 Flask Cotts
5 Coach House Yd
6 Pilgrim's Pl
7 Rosslyn Mews
C2 1 Banff Ho
2 Glenloch Ct
3 Havercourt
4 Holmefield Ct
5 Gilling Ct
6 Howitt Cl
7 Manor Mans
8 Straffan Lo
9 Romney Ct
10 Lancaster Stables
11 Eton Garages
D1 1 Hancock Nunn Ho
2 Higginson Ho
3 Duncan Ho
4 Mary Wharrie Ho
5 Rockstraw Ho
6 Cleaver Ho
7 Chamberlain St
8 Sharples Hall St
9 Primrose Mews
10 Rothwell St
11 St Georges Mews
D2 1 Alder Ho
2 Hornbeam Ho
3 Whitebeam Ho
4 Aspen Ho
5 Rowan Ho
6 Beech Ho
7 Chestnut Ho
8 Oak Ho
9 Willow Ho
10 Sycamore Ho
11 Maple Ho
12 Hazel Ho
13 Elaine Ct
14 Faircourt
15 Walham Ct
16 Stanbury Ct
17 Priory Mans
18 Wellington Ho
19 Grange The
D3 1 Cayford Ho
2 Du Maurier Ho

3 Isokon Flats
4 Palgrave Ho
5 Garnett Ho
6 Stephenson Ho
7 Park Dwellings
8 Siddons Ho
9 Mall Studios
10 Park Hill Wlk
11 Wordsworth Pl
12 Fraser Regnart Ct
13 St Pancras Almshouses

71

A1 1 Bridge Ho
2 Hardington
3 Mead Cl
4 Rugmere
5 Tottenhall
6 Beauvale
7 Broomfield
A2 1 Silverbirch Wlk
2 Penshurst
3 Wingham
4 Westwell
5 Chislet
6 Burmarsh
7 Shipton Ho
8 Stonegate
9 Leysdown
10 Headcorn
11 Lenham
12 Halstow
13 Fordcombe
14 Cannington
15 Langridge
16 Athlone Ho
17 Pentland Ho
18 Beckington
19 Hawkridge
20 Edington
B1 1 Ferdinand Ho
2 Harmood Ho
3 Hawley Rd
4 Hawley Mews
5 Leybourne St
6 Barling
7 Tiptree
8 Havering
9 Candida Ct
10 Lorraine Ct
11 Donnington Ct
12 Welford Ct
13 Torbay Ct
14 Bradfield Ct
15 Torbay St
16 Water La
17 Leybourne Rd
18 Haven St
19 Stucley Pl
20 Lawrence Ho
B2 1 Ashington
2 Priestley Ho
3 Leonard Day Ho
4 Old Dairy Mews
5 Monmouth Ho
6 Alpha Ct
7 Una Ho
8 Widford
9 Heybridge
10 Roxwell
11 Hamstead Gates
B4 1 Denyer Ho
2 Stephenson Ho
3 Trevithick Ho
4 Brunel Ho
5 Newcomen Ho
6 Faraday Ho
7 Winifrede Paul Ho
8 Wardlow
9 Fletcher Ct
10 Tideswell
11 Grangemill
12 Hambrook Ct
13 Calver
C1 1 Cherry Tree Ct
2 Chichester Ct
3 Durdans Ho
4 Philia Ho
5 Bernard Shaw Ct
6 Foster Ct
7 Bessemer Ct
8 Hogarth Ct
9 Rochester Ct
10 Soane Ct
11 Wallett Ct
12 Inwood Ct
13 Wrotham Rd
14 St Thomas Ct
15 Caulfield Ct
16 Bruges Pl
17 Reachview Cl
18 Lawfords Wharf
C3 1 Eleanor Ho
2 Falkland Pl
3 Kensington Ho
4 Willingham Cl
5 Kenbrook Ho
6 Aborfield
7 Great Field
8 Appleford
9 Forties The
10 Maud Wilkes Cl
11 Dunne Mews
12 Dowdeny Cl
C4 1 Benson Ct
2 Tait Ho
3 Manorfield Cl
4 Greatfield Cl
5 Longley Ho
6 Lampson Ho
7 Davidson Ho
8 Palmer Ho
9 Lambourn Cl
10 Morris Ho
11 Owen Ho
C5 1 Hunter Ho
2 Fisher Ho
3 Lang Ho
4 Temple Ho
5 Palmer Ho
6 Carlisle Ho
7 Durham Ho
8 Suffolk Ho
9 Lincoln Ho
10 Llewellyn Ho
11 Fell Ho
12 Aveling Ho
13 Merryweather Ct
14 Brennands Ct
15 St Christophers Ct
16 Francis Terrace Mews
C6 1 Flowers Mews
2 Archway Cl
3 Sandridge St
4 Bovingdon Cl
5 Cavell Ct
6 Torrence Ho
7 Rowan Wlk
8 Laurel Cl
9 Forest Way
10 Larch Cl
11 Pine Cl
12 Alder Mews
13 Aspen Cl
D1 1 Hillier Ho
2 Gairloch Ho
3 Cobham Mews
4 Bergholt Mews
5 Blakeney Cl
6 Weavers Way
7 Allensbury Pl
D2 1 Rowstock
2 Peckwater Ho
3 Wolsey Ho
4 Pandian Way
5 Busby Mews
6 Caledonian Sq
7 Canal Bvd
8 Northpoint Sq
9 Lock Mews
10 Carters Cl
11 York Ho
12 Hungerford Rd
13 Cliff Road Studios
14 Cliff Ct
15 Camelot Ho
16 Church Studios
17 Camden Terr
D3 1 Blake Ho
2 Quelch Ho
3 Lee Ho
4 Willbury Ho
5 Howell Ho
6 Holmsbury Ho
7 Leith Ho
8 Betchworth Ho
9 Rushmore Ho
10 Dugdale Ho
11 Horsendon Ho
12 Colley Ho
13 Coombe Ho
14 Ivinghoe Ho
15 Buckhurst Ho
16 Saxonbury Ct
17 Charlton Ct
18 Apollo Studios
19 Barn Cl
20 Long Meadow
21 Landleys Field
22 Margaret Bondfield Ho
23 Haywood Lo
D4 1 Fairlie Ct
2 Trecastle Way
3 Dalmeny Avenue Est
4 Hyndman Ho
5 Carpenter Ho
6 Graham Ho
7 Tufnell Mans
D5 1 Melchester Ho
2 Norcombe Ho
3 Weatherbury Ho
4 Wessex Ho
5 Archway Bsns Ctr
6 Harford Mews
7 Opera Ct
8 Rupert Ho
9 All Saints Church
D6 1 Bowerman Ct
2 Gresham Pl
3 Hargrave Mans
4 Church Garth
5 John King Ct
6 Ramsey Ct

72

A3 1 Kimble Ho
2 Saxonbury Ct
3 Poynder Ct
4 Pangbourne Ho
5 Moulsford Ho
A4 1 Arcade The
2 Macready Pl
3 Cardwell Rd
4 Mcmorran Ho
5 Crayford Ho
6 Whitby Ct
7 Prospect Pl
A5 1 Northview
2 Tufnell Park Mans
3 Fulford Mans
4 Tollington Ho
A6 1 Bracey Mews
2 Christie Ct
3 Ringmer Gdns
4 Kingsdown Rd
5 Cottenham Ho
6 St Paul's Ct
7 Rickthorne Rd
8 Stanley Terr
9 Arundel Lo
10 Landseer Ct
B1 1 Kerwick Cl
2 Rydston Cl
3 Skegness Ho
4 Frederica St
5 Ponder St
6 Kings Ct
7 Freeling St
8 Coatbridge Ho
9 Tilloch St
B2 1 Burns Ho
2 Scott Ho
3 Wellington Mews
4 Roman Ct
5 Piccadilly Ct
B3 1 Culverin Ct
2 Garand Ct
3 Mount Carmel
B4 1 Buckmaster Ho
2 Loreburn Ho
3 Cairns Ho
4 Halsbury Ho
5 Chelmsford Ho
6 Cranworth Ho
B6 1 Berkeley Wlk
2 Lazar Wlk
3 Thistlewood Cl
4 Tomlins Wlk
5 Andover Ho
6 Barmouth Ho
7 Chard Ho
8 Methley Ho
9 Rainford Ho
10 Woodbridge Cl
11 Allerton Wlk
12 Falconer Wlk
13 Sonderburg Rd
14 St Mark's Mans
15 Athol Ct
C1 1 Mountfort Terr
2 Avon Ho
3 Buckland Ho
4 Dovey Lo
5 Carfree Cl
6 Mitchell Ho
7 New College Mews
8 Lofting Ho
9 Brooksby Ho
10 Cara Ho
C3 1 Slaney Pl
2 Eastwood Cl
3 Milton Pl
4 Hartnoll Ho
5 St James School Flats
6 Widnes Ho
7 Tranmere Ho
8 Victoria Mans
9 Formby Ct
10 Mersey Ho
11 Birkenhead Ho
12 Drayton Park Mews
C6 1 Brookfield
2 Churnfield
D1 1 Islington Park Mews
2 Evelyn Denington Ct
3 Bassingbourn Ho
4 Cadmore Ho
5 Adstock Ho
6 Garston Ho
7 Flitton Ho
8 Datchworth Ho
9 Battishill St
10 Almeida St
11 Edward's Cotts
12 Hyde's Pl
13 Tyndale Terr
14 Spriggs Ho
15 Barratt Ho
16 Spencer Pl
17 Chadston Ho
18 Whiston Ho
19 Wakelin Ho
20 Tressel Cl
21 Canonbury Ct
22 Halton Ho
23 Shillingford St
24 Highburty Mans
25 Premier Ho
26 Waterloo Gdns
D2 1 Hampton Ct
2 Salisbury Ho
D3 1 De Barowe Mews
2 Fieldview Ct
3 Viewpoint
4 Ashurst Lo
D4 1 Chestnuts The
2 Bowen Ct
3 Peckett Sq
D5 1 Hurlock Ho
2 Blackstock Ho
3 Vivian Comma Cl
4 Monsell Ct

73

A1 1 Astey's Row
2 Lincoln Ho
3 Worcester Ho
4 Melville Pl
5 Wontner Cl
6 Hedingham Cl
7 Laundry La
8 Base Apartments
9 Walkinshaw Ct
10 New Bentham Ct
11 Bentham Ct
12 Haslam Ho
13 Horsfield Ho
14 Riverside Ho
15 Eric Fletcher Ct
16 Annette Cres
17 Ashby Ho
18 Lindsey Mews
19 Cardigan Wlk
20 Red House Sq
A2 1 Crowline Wlk
2 Upper Handa Wlk
3 Handa Wlk
4 Lismore Wlk
5 Bardsey Wlk
6 Walney Wlk
7 Upper Bardsey Wlk
8 Upper Lismore Wlk
9 Sark Ho
10 Guernsey Ho
11 Guernsey Rd
12 Sybil Thorndike Ho
13 Clephane Rd
14 Florence Nightingale Ho
15 Jersey Ho
16 Jethou Ho
17 Islay Wlk
18 Upper Caldy Wlk
19 Caldy Wlk
20 Alderney Ho
21 Gulland Wlk
22 Marquess Rd S
23 Upper Gulland Wlk
24 Church Rd
25 Oransay Rd
A3 1 Pearfield Ho
2 Larchfield Ho
3 Beresford Terr
4 Pondfield Ho
5 Ashfield Ho
6 Elmfield Ho
A4 1 Fountain Mews
2 Woodstock Ho
3 Henson Ct
4 Taverner Sq
B1 1 Downham Ct
2 Trafalgar Point
B2 1 John Kennedy Ct
2 John Kennedy Lo
3 Ball's Pond Pl
4 Haliday Wlk
5 Queen Elizabeth Ct
6 Canonbury Hts
7 Pinnacle The
8 Threadgold Ho
9 Wakeham St
10 Saffron Ct
11 Callaby Terr
12 Tilney Gdns
13 Westcliff Ho
14 Ilford Ho
15 Ongar Ho
16 Greenhills Terr
17 Romford Ho
18 Bute Wlk
19 Upper Ramsey Wlk
20 Rona Wlk
21 Thorndike Rd
B4 1 Ledo Ho
2 Salween Ho
3 Prome Ho
4 Arakan Ho
5 Rangoon Ho
6 Mandalay Ho
7 Karen Ho
8 Wingate Ho
9 Jubet Ho
10 Orde Ho
11 Chindit Ho
12 Mabel Thornton Ho
13 Crawshay Ho
14 Avon Ho
15 Connaught Mans
16 Jonson Ho
17 Herrick Ho
18 Donne Ho
19 Thirlmere Ho
20 Grasmere Ho
B6 1 Chestnut Ct
2 Sycamore Ho
3 Lordship Ho
4 Clissold Ho
5 Beech Ho
6 Laburnum Ho
7 Ormond Ho
8 Yew Tree Ct
9 Oak Ho
C1 1 Dorchester Ct
2 Wareham Ct
3 Dorset Ct
4 Stratton Ct
5 Swanage Ct
6 Blandford Ct
7 Portland Ct
8 Oscar Faber Pl
9 Metropolitan Bsns Ctr
10 Lancaster Cl
11 Palazzo Apartments
C2 1 Kingsland Gn
2 Kingsland Pas
3 Metropolitan Benefit Societies Almshouses
4 Nimrod Pas
5 De Beauvoir Pl
6 Warburton Cl
7 Buckingham Mews
8 Aztec Ct
C3 1 Hewling Ho
2 Matthias Ho
3 Port Royal Pl
4 Cressington Cl
5 King Henry's Yd
6 Bronte Ho
7 Sewell Ho
8 Lydgate Ho
9 Patmore Ho
10 Congreve Ho
11 Elton St
12 Conrad Ho
13 Southwell Ho
14 Neptune Ho
15 Campion Ho
16 Webster Ho
17 Meredith Ho
18 Beckford Ho
19 Ashley Ct
20 Hayling Cl
21 Millard Cl
22 Lydford Cl
23 Salcombe Rd
24 Truman's Rd
25 Templeton Cl
26 John Campbell Rd
27 Gillett Pl
28 Bradbury St
29 Thomas Crowell Ct
C4 1 Londesborough Ho
2 Knebworth Ho
3 Knebworth Rd
4 Bransby Ct
5 Imperial Ave
6 Leonard Pl
7 Shakspeare Mews
8 Binyon Ho
9 Shelley Ho
10 Browning Ho
11 Burns Ho
12 Andrew Marvell Ho
13 Wycliffe Ho
14 Blake Ho
15 Marlowe Ho
16 Fletcher Ho
17 Chaucer Ct
C5 1 Gujarat Ho
2 Marton Rd
3 Painsthorpe Rd
4 Selkirk Ho
5 Defoe Ho
6 Edward Friend Ho
7 Sheridan Ho
8 Barrie Ho
9 Arnold Ho
10 MacAulay Ho
11 Stowe Ho
12 Carlyle Ho
13 Shaftesbury Ho
14 Lillian Cl
15 Swift Ho
16 Dryden Ho
17 Scott Ct
18 Kingsfield Ho
19 Uhura Sq
20 Hartopp Ct
D1 1 Hilborough Rd
2 Shoreditch Ct
3 Evergreen Sq
4 Wyndhams Ct
5 Festival Ct
6 Fortune Ct
7 Rose Ct
8 Ability Plaza
D2 1 Prospect Ho
2 Woodland St
3 Crosby Wlk
4 Kirkland Wlk
5 Bowness Cl
6 Carlisle Wlk
7 Skelton Cl
8 Camerton Cl
9 Buttermere Wlk
10 Houghton Cl
11 Hayton Cl
12 Kingsland Sh Ctr
13 Springfield Ho
14 Parton Lo
15 Sanctuary Mews
D3 1 Miller's Terr
2 Chow Sq
3 Drysdale Flats
4 Gateway Mews
5 Birkbeck Mews
6 Winchester Pl
D4 1 Coronation Ave
2 Morris Blitz Ct
3 Shacklewell Ho
4 Alexandra Ct
D5 1 Lawrence Bldgs
2 Cottage Wlk
3 Batley Pl
D6 1 Garnham St
2 Garnham Cl
3 Sanford La
4 Sanford Wlk
5 Abney Gdns
6 Fleet Wood

74

A1 1 Aldington Ct
2 Bayton Ct
3 Rochford Wlk
A2 1 Burdon Ct
2 Thomson Ct
3 Bruno Ct
A3 1 Kingsdown Ho
2 Glendown Ho
3 Moredown Ho
4 Blakeney Cl
5 Beeston Cl
6 Benabo Ct
7 David Devine Ho
8 Kreedman Wlk
9 Hermitage Row
10 Grafton Ct
11 Lushington Terr
12 Aspen Ct
13 Pykewell Lo
14 Albion Works Studios
A5 1 Ravenscourt
2 Mellington Ct
3 Rendlesham Ho
4 Carroll Ct
A6 1 Cazenove Mans
2 Chedworth Ho
3 Aldergrove Ho
4 Abbotstone Ho
5 Briggeford Cl
6 Inglethorpe Ho
7 Ashdown Ho
8 Epping Ho
9 Cypress Cl
B1 1 Fortescue Ave
2 Pemberton Pl
3 Weston Wlk
4 Bayford St Ind Ctr
5 Bayford St
6 Sidworth St
7 Helmsley St
8 Cyntra Pl
9 Signal Ho
10 All Nations Ho
11 Vanguard Ho
12 Hacon Sq
B2 1 Bohemia Pl
2 Graham Mans
3 Marvin St
4 Boscobel Ho
5 Royal Oak Rd
6 Colonnades The
7 Sylvester Ho
8 Sylvester Path
9 Doctor Spurstowe Almshouses
10 Great Eastern Bldgs
11 Sojourner-Truth Cl
B3 1 Birchington Ho
2 Bicknor Ho
3 Boxley Ho
4 Adisham Ho
5 Cranbrook Ho
6 Marden Ho
7 Broome Ho
8 Crandale Ho
9 Cheriton Ho
10 Ditton Ho
11 Langley Ho
12 Dymchurch Ho
13 Elham Ho
14 Davina Ho
15 Pembury Pl
16 Downs Ct
17 Perrywood Ho
18 Staplehurst Ho
19 Pegwell Ho
20 Yalding Ho
21 Northbourne Ho
22 Monkton Ho
23 Milsted Ho
24 Athlone Cl
25 Clarence Pl

26 Gould Terr
27 Quested Ct
28 Brett Pas
29 Marcon Ct
30 Appleton Ct
B4 1 Ross Ct
2 Downs La
3 Gaviller Pl
4 Robert Owen Lo
5 Apprentice Way
6 Arrowe Ct
7 Gilwell Ct
8 Sutton Ct
9 St Andrews Mans
10 Kinnoull Mans
11 Rowhill Mans
12 Sladen Pl
13 Mothers Sq The
14 Richborough Ho
15 Sandgate Ho
16 Sheppey Ho
B5 1 De Vere Ct
2 Redcliffe Ct
3 Greville Ct
4 Anthony Kendal Ho
B6 1 Wentwood Ho
2 Woolmer Ho
3 Warwick Ct
4 Winslade Ho
5 Morriss Ho
6 Woodfield Ho
7 Rossendale Ho
8 Ettrick Ho
9 Charnwood Ho
10 Boyne Ho
11 Whitwell Ho
12 Scardale Ho
13 Hendale Ho
14 Brampton Cl
15 Aveley Ct
16 Aldeburgh Cl
17 Dennington Cl
C1 1 Pitcairn Ho
2 Lyme Grove Ho
3 Shakespeare Ho
4 Upcott Ho
5 Loddiges Ho
6 Parkinson Ho
7 Sloane Ho
8 Vanbrugh Ho
9 Cambridge Pas
10 Lyttleton Ho
11 Victoria Park Ct
12 Tullis Ho
13 Fairchild Ho
14 Forsyth Ho
15 Tradescant Ho
16 Mason Ho
17 Capel Ho
18 Cordwainers Ct
19 Bridgeman Ho
20 St Thomas's Pl
21 Barclay Ho
22 Clayton Ho
23 Danby Ho
24 Sherard Ho
25 Catesby Ho
26 Petiver Cl
27 Leander Ct
28 Philip Turner Est
29 Grendon Ho
30 Shore Mews
31 Shore Bsns Ctr
32 Kendal Ho
33 Classic Mans
34 Tudor Ho
35 Park Ho
36 Enterprise Ho
37 Alpine Gr
38 Clarendon Cl
39 Rotheley Ho
40 Bernie Grant Ho
C2 1 Woolpack Ho
2 Elvin Ho
3 Thomas Ho
4 Hockley Ho
5 Retreat Ho
6 Butfield Ho
7 Brooksbank Ho
8 Cresset Ho
9 Brooksbank St
10 Lennox Ho
11 Milborne Ho
12 Collent Ho
13 Middlesex Pl
14 Elsdale Ho
15 Devonshire Hall
16 Brent Ho
C6 1 Haybridge Ho
2 Framlingham Cl
3 Halesworth Cl
4 Harleston Cl
5 Lowestoft Cl
6 Howard Ho
7 Templar Ho
D1 1 Stuart Ho
2 Gascoyne Ho
3 Chelsfield Point
4 Sundridge Ho
5 Banbury Ho
6 Lauriston Ho
D2 1 Musgrove Ho
2 Cheyney Ho
3 Haynes Ho
4 Warner Ho
5 Gilby Ho
6 Gadsden Ho
7 Risley Ho
8 Baycliffe Ho
9 Sheldon Ho
10 Offley Ho
11 Latimer Ho
12 Ribstone Ho
13 Salem Ho
14 Fieldwick Ho
15 Lever Ct
16 Matson Ho
17 Wilding Ho
18 Rennell Ho
19 Dycer Ho
20 Granard Ho
21 Whitelock Ho
22 Harrowgate Ho
23 Cass Ho
24 Lofts on the Park
25 Heathcote Point
26 Ravenscroft Point
27 Vanner Point
28 Hensley Point
29 San Ho
D4 1 Cromford Path
2 Longford Ct
3 Overbury Ho
4 Heanor Ct
5 Wharfedale Ct
6 Ladybower Ct
7 Ilkeston Ct
8 Derby Ct
9 Rushmore Cres
10 Blackwell Cl
11 Belper Ct

75
A2 1 Chigwell Ct
2 Wellday Ho
3 Selman Ho
4 Vaine Ho
5 Trower Ho
B2 1 Mallard Cl
2 Merriam Ave
3 Gainsborough St
D6 1 Hammond Ct
2 Sorensen Ct
3 Hinton Ct

76
B1 1 Service Route No 2
2 Service Route No 3
B4 1 Mulberry Ct
2 Rosewood Ct
3 Gean Ct
4 Blackthorn Ct
5 Cypress Ct
C1 1 Stratford Office Village The
2 Violet Ct
3 Mandrake Way
4 Brimstone Ho
5 Hibiscus Lo
6 Glasier Ct
C3 1 Bordeaux Ho
2 Luxembourg Mews
3 Basle Ho
C5 1 Acacia Bsns Ctr
2 Brook Ct
3 Gainsfield Ct
4 Artesian Wlk
5 Doreen Capstan Ho
6 Apollo Pl
7 Peppermint Pl
8 Denmark St
9 Mills Ct
10 Paramount Ho
11 Robinson Cl
C6 1 Nansen Ct
2 Mallinson Ct
3 Barbara Ward Ct
4 Caradon Cl
5 Noel Baker Ct
6 Corigan Ct
7 Norman Ho
8 Willow Ct
9 Lime Ct
10 Owens Mews
11 Marnie Ct
12 Cotton Cl
D1 1 Flint Cl
2 St Matthews Ct
3 Ammonite Ho
4 Stone Ct
D2 1 Common The
2 Wolffe Gdns
3 College Pt
4 Onyx Mews
5 Candlelight Ct
6 Boltons The

77
A4 1 Bronte Cl
2 Anna Neagle Cl
3 Brownlow Rd
4 Carrington Gdns
5 Vera Lynn Cl
C1 1 Sarwan Ho
2 Bridgepoint Lofts
3 Vineyard Studios

78
C3 1 Stewart Rainbird Ho
2 Abraham Fisher Ho
3 Redo Ho
4 George Comber-ton Wlk
C4 1 Cardamom Ct
2 Annie Taylor Ho
3 Richard Fell Ho
4 Susan Lawrence Ho
5 Walter Hurford Par
6 John Cornwell VC Ho
7 Alfred Prior Ho
C5 1 Charlbury Ho
2 Willis Ho
3 Arthur Walls Ho
4 Blakesley Ho
5 Twelve Acre Ho
6 Beech Ct
7 Golding Ct
D1 1 Aveley Mans
2 Harlow Mans
3 Danbury Mans
4 Mayland Mans
5 Bowers Ho
6 Webber Ho
7 Paulson Ho
8 Collins Ho
9 Jack Cook Ho
D3 1 St Luke's Path
2 Springfield Ct
D5 1 Postway Mews
2 Oakfield Ho
3 Janice Mews
4 Kenneth More Rd
5 Clements Ct
6 Handforth Rd
7 Churchill Ct
8 Oakfield Lo
9 Langdale Ct
10 Ilford Chambers
D6 1 York Ho
2 Opal Mews
3 Florentine Ho
4 Kingsley Mews
5 Hainault Bridge Par

79
A6 1 Spectrum Twr
2 Thames View
3 City View
4 Centreway
5 Axon Pl
D1 1 Gibbards Cott
2 Upney Ct
3 Edgefield Ct
4 Manor Ct
5 Lambourne Gdns
6 Westone Mans
7 Loveland Mans
8 Edward Mans
9 Clarke Mans
10 Dawson Gdns
11 Sebastian Ct

80
A1 1 Bristol Ho
2 Canterbury Ho
3 Durham Ho
4 Wells Ho
5 Winchester Ho
6 Rosalind Ct
7 Exeter Ho
8 Wheatley Mans
9 Greenwood Mans
10 Plymouth Ho
11 Graham Mans
12 Portia Ct

81
C5 1 Markham Ho
2 Webb Ho
3 Preston Ho
4 Steadman Ho
5 Hyndman Ho
6 Clynes Ho
7 Henderson Ho
8 Blatchford Ho
9 Rogers Ho
10 Sylvia Pankhurst Ho
11 Mary Macarthur Ho
12 Ellen Wilkinson Ho
D2 1 Picador Ho
2 Centurion Lodge
3 Louis Ct
4 Watsons Lo
5 Carpenters Ct
6 Bell Ho
7 Rounders Ct
8 Oldmead Ho
9 Jervis Ct
10 Bartletts Ho
11 Royal Par
12 Richardson Gdns
13 Forsyth Ct
14 Eldridge Ct
15 Madison Ct
16 Bowery Ct
17 Rivington Ct

82
D3 1 Marlborough Par
2 Blenheim Par
3 Lea Ct
4 Westbourne Par
5 Whiteleys Par
6 Hillingdon Par
7 New Broadway

84
C4 1 Dilston Cl
2 Wells Cl
3 Willett Cl
4 Merlin Cl
5 Glyndebourne Ct
6 Albury Ct
7 Osterley Ct
8 Hatfield Ct
9 Gayhurst Ct
D4 1 Caravelle Gdns
2 Farman Gr
3 Viscount Gr
4 Tomahawk Gdns
5 Martlet Gr
6 Trident Gdns
7 Latham Ct
8 Jupiter Ct
9 Westland Ct
10 Seasprite Cl
11 Convair Wlk
12 Mayfly Gdns
13 Valiant Cl
14 Woburn Twr
15 Brett Cl
16 Friars Cl
D5 1 Medlar Cl
2 Cranberry Cl
3 Lely Ho
4 Girtin Ho
5 Cotman Ho
6 Raeburn Ho
7 Gainsborough Twr
8 Stanfield Ho
9 Millais Ct
10 Hunt Ct
11 Poynter Ct
12 Hogarth Ho
13 Constable Ho
14 Bonnington Ct
15 Romney Ct
16 Landseer Ho

85
B1 1 St Crispins Ct
B3 1 Weaver Ho
2 Caldon Ho
3 Ashby Ho
4 Welford Ho
5 Hertford Ho
6 Wey Ho
7 Middlewich Ho
8 Stourbridge Ho
B4 1 Netherton Ho
2 Keadby Ho
3 Tame Ho
4 Dorset Ct
D1 1 Thurlestone Ct
2 Disley Ct
3 Burgess Ct
4 Bayliss Cl
5 Lytham Ct
6 Winford Par
7 Brunel Pl
8 Rutherford Twr
9 Rountree Ct

86
A1 1 Farnham Ct
2 Gleneagles Twr
3 Birkdale Ct
4 Verulam Ct
5 Hartsbourne Ct
6 Ferndown Ct
7 Deal Ct
8 St David's Ct
9 Portrush Ct
10 Alnmouth Ct
11 Panmure Ct
12 Peterhead Ct
13 Sunningdale Ct
D2 1 Denbigh Ct
2 Devon Ct
3 Dorset Ct
4 Glamorgan Ct
5 Gloucester Ct
6 Hereford Ct
7 Merioneth Ct
8 Oxford Ct
9 Monmouth Ct
10 Paddington Ct
11 Pembroke Ct
12 Chadwick Cl
13 Cotts Cl
D3 1 Berkshire Ct
2 Buckingham Ct
3 Cardigan Ct
4 Carmarthen Ct
5 Cornwall Ct
6 Merlin Ct
7 Osprey Ct
8 Pelham Pl
9 Puffin Ct
10 Fulmar Ct
11 Turnstone Terr
D5 1 Medway Par
2 Brabstone Ho
3 Cotswold Ct

87
B3 1 Woodbury Ct
2 Edward Ct
3 Park Lo
C1 1 Hurley Ct
2 Amherst Gdns
3 Tudor Ct
4 Hilton Ho
C2 1 Hutton Ct
2 Cain Ct
3 Langdale Ct
4 William Ct
5 Castlebar Ct
6 Warren Ct
7 White Lo
8 Queen's Ct
9 King's Ct
10 Cheriton Cl
11 Stanley Ct
12 Juniper Ho
C3 1 Holtoake Ct
2 Pitshanger Ct
3 Holtoake Ho

88
A4 1 Nelson Ho
2 Gordon Ho
3 Frobisher Ho
4 Wellington Ho
5 Fairfax Ho
A5 1 Carlyon Mans
2 Ainslie Ct
3 Millers Ct
4 Priory Ct
5 Tylers Ct
6 Twyford Ct
7 Rose Ct
8 Laurel Ct
9 Sundew Ct
10 Campion Ct
11 Foxglove Ct
C1 1 Buckingham Ho
2 Chester Ct
3 Devon Ct
4 Essex Ho
5 Fife Ct
6 Gloucester Ct
7 Hereford Ho
8 Inverness Ct
9 Warwick Ho
10 York Ho
11 Suffolk Ho
12 Perth Ho
13 Norfolk Ho
14 Thanet Ct
15 Rutland Ct
16 Oxford Ct

89
A1 1 Avon Ct
2 Bromley Lo
3 Walter Ct
4 Lynton Terr
5 Acton Ho
6 Fells Haugh
7 Springfield Ct
8 Tamarind Ct
9 Lynton Ct
10 Aspen Ct
11 Pegasus Ct
12 Friary Park Ct
B1 1 Rosebank Gdns
2 Rosebank
3 Edinburgh Ho
4 Western Ct
5 Kilronan
B6 1 Carlyle Rd
2 Bernard Shaw Ho
3 Longlents Ho
4 Mordaunt Ho
5 Wilmers Ct
6 Stonebridge Ctr
7 Shakespeare Ave
C5 1 Futters Ct
2 Barrett Ct
3 Elms The
4 Fairlight Ct
D5 1 New Crescent Yd
2 Harlesden Plaza
3 St Josephs Ct
4 Jubilee Cl
5 Ellery Cl

90
B1 1 Holborn Ho
2 Clement Danes Ho
3 Vellacott Ho
4 O'Driscoll Ho
5 King Ho
6 Daley Ho
7 Selma Ho
8 Garrett Ho
C1 1 Latimer Ind Est
2 Pankhurst Ho
3 Quadrangle The
4 Nightingale Ho
5 Gordon Ct
6 Ducane Cl
7 Browning Ho
8 Pavilion Terr
9 Ivebury Ct
10 Olympic Ho
C2 1 Galleywood Ho
2 Edgcott Ho
3 Cuffley Ho
4 Addlestone Ho
5 Hockliffe Ho
6 Sarratt Ho
7 Firle Ho
8 Sutton Est The
9 Terling Ho
10 Danes Ho
11 Udimore Ho
12 Vange Ho
13 Binbrook Ho
14 Yeadon Ho
15 Yatton Ho
16 Yarrow Ho
17 Clement Ho
18 Danebury
19 Coronation Ct
20 Calderon Pl
21 St Quintin Gdns
C3 1 Princess Alice Ho
2 Yoxall Ho
3 Yorkley Ho
4 Northaw Ho
5 Oakham Ho
6 Markyate Ho
7 Letchmore Ho
8 Pagham Ho
9 Quendon Ho
10 Redbourn Ho
11 Ketton Ho
12 Hillman Dr
D1 1 Kelfield Ct
2 Downing Ho
3 Crosfield Ct
4 Robinson Ho
5 Scampston Mews
6 Girton Villas
7 Ray Ho
8 Walmer Ho
9 Goodrich Ct
10 Arthur Ct
11 Whitstable Ho
12 Kingsnorth Ho
13 Bridge Cl
14 Prospect Ho
15 St Marks Rd
16 Whitchurch Ho
17 Blechynden Ho
18 Waynflete Sq
19 Bramley Ho
20 Dixon Ho
D4 1 Westfield Ct
2 Tropical Ct
3 Chamberlayne Mans
4 Quadrant The
5 Queens Park Ct
6 Warfield Yd
7 Regent St
8 Cherrytree Ho
9 Artisan Mews
10 Artisan Quarter

91
A1 1 Malton Mews
2 Lancaster Lo
3 Manning Ho
4 Galsworthy Ho
5 Hudson Ho
6 Cambourne Mews
7 Upper Talbot Wlk
8 Kingsdown Cl
9 Lower Clarendon Wlk
10 Talbot Grove Ho
11 Clarendon Wlk
12 Upper Clarendon Wlk
13 Camelford Wlk
14 Upper Camelford Wlk
15 Camelford Ct
A2 1 Murchison Ho
2 MacAulay Ho
3 Chesterton Ho
4 Chiltern Ho
5 Lionel Ho
6 Watts Ho
7 Wheatstone Ho
8 Telford Ho
9 Golborne Mews
10 Millwood St
11 St Columb's Ho
12 Norfolk Mews
13 Lionel Mews
A3 1 Sycamore Wlk
2 Westgate Bsns Ctr
3 Buspace Studios
4 Bosworth Ho
5 Golborne Gdns
6 Appleford Ho
7 Adair Twr
8 Gadsden Ho
9 Southam Ho
10 Norman Butler Ho
11 Thompson Ho
12 Wells Ho
13 Paul Ho
14 Olive Blythe Ho
15 Katherine Ho
16 Breakwell Ct
17 Pepler Ho
18 Edward Kennedy Ho
19 Winnington Ho

A4 1 Selby Sq
2 Severn Ave
3 Stansbury Sq
4 Tolhurst Dr
5 John Fearon Wlk
6 Mundy Ho
7 Macfarren Ho
8 Bantock Ho
9 Banister Ho
10 Batten Ho
11 Croft Ho
12 Courtville Ho
13 Mounsey Ho
14 Bliss Mews
15 Symphony Mews
B1 1 Silvester Ho
2 Golden Cross Mews
3 Tavistock Mews
4 Clydesdale Ho
5 Melchester
6 Pinehurst Ct
7 Denbigh Ho
B2 1 Blagrove Rd
2 All Saints Ho
3 Tavistock Ho
4 Leamington Ho
B3 1 Octavia Mews
2 Russell's Wharf
3 Western Ho
4 Kelly Mews
B4 1 Boyce Ho
2 Farnaby Ho
3 Danby Ho
4 Purday Ho
5 Naylor Ho
6 St Judes Ho
7 Leeve Ho
8 Longhurst Ho
9 Harrington Ct
10 Mulberry Ct
11 Kilburn Ho
B5 1 Claremont Ct
2 William Saville Ho
3 Western Ct
4 Bond Ho
5 Crone Ct
6 Wood Ho
7 Winterleys
8 Carlton Ho
9 Fiona Ct
C1 1 Shottsford
2 Tolchurch
3 Casterbridge
4 Sandbourne
5 Anglebury
6 Weatherbury
7 Westbourne Gr Mews
8 Rosehart Mews
9 Viscount Ct
10 Hereford Mans
11 Hereford Mews
C2 1 Ascot Ho
2 Ashgrove Ct
3 Lockbridge Ct
4 Swallow Ct
5 Nightingale Lo
6 Hammond Lo
7 Penfield Lo
8 Harvey Lo
9 Hunter Lo
10 Barnard Lo
11 Falcon Lo
12 Johnson Lo
13 Livingstone Lo
14 Nuffield Lo
15 Finch Lo
16 Polesworth Ho
17 Oversley Ho
18 Derrycombe Ho
19 Buckshead Ho
20 Combe Ho
21 Culham Ho
22 Dainton Ho
23 Devonport Ho
24 Honwell Ho
25 Truro Ho
26 Sunderland Ho
27 Stonehouse Ho
28 Riverford Ho
29 Portishead Ho
30 Mickleton Ho
31 Keyham Ho
32 Moulsford Ho
33 Shrewsbury Mews
34 St Stephen's Mews
35 Westway Lo
36 Langley Ho
37 Brindley Ho
38 Radway Ho
39 Astley Ho
40 Willow Ct
41 Larch Ct
42 Elm Ct
43 Beech Ct
44 Worcester Ct
45 Union Ct
46 Leicester Ct
47 Kennet Ct
48 Oxford Ct
49 Fazerley Ct
C3 1 Westside Ct
2 Byron Mews
3 Sutherland Ct
4 Fleming Cl
5 Hermes Cl
C4 1 Pentland Rd
2 Nelson Cl
3 Pavilion Ct
4 Masefield Ho
5 Austen Ho
6 Fielding Ho
7 Argo Bsns Ctr
8 John Ratcliffe Ho
9 Wymering Mans
C5 1 Wells Ct
2 Cambridge Ct
3 Ely Ct
4 Durham Ct
C6 1 Ryde Ho
2 Glengall Pass
3 Leith Yd
4 Daynor Ho
5 Varley Ho
6 Sandby Ho
7 Colas Mews
8 Bishopsdale Ho
9 Lorton Ho
10 Marshwood Ho
11 Ribblesdale Ho
12 Holmesdale Ho
13 Kilburn Vale Est
14 Kilburn Bridge
D1 1 Vera Ct
2 Alexander Mews
3 Gurney Ho
4 Burdett Mews
5 Greville Lo
6 Hatherley Ct
7 Bridge Field Ho
8 Ralph Ct
9 Peters Ct
9 Pickering Mews
10 Riven Ct
11 Inver Ct
12 Cervantes Ct
13 Bishops Ct
14 Newbury Ho
15 Marlow Ho
16 Lynton Ho
17 Pembroke Ho
18 Pickering Ho
19 Whiteleys Ctr
D3 1 Ellwood Ct
D5 1 Tollgate Ho
2 Regents Plaza
3 Royal Langford Apartments
D6 1 Sylvan Ct
2 Birchington Ct
3 Farndale Ho
4 Abbey Rd Motorist Ctr
5 Greville Mews
6 Goldsmith's Pl
7 Remsted Ho
8 Bradwell Ho
9 Cheshunt Ho
10 Haliwell Ho
11 Broadoak Ho
12 Philip Ho
13 Hillsborough Ct
14 Sandbourne
15 Wingreen
16 Toneborough
17 Silverthorn
18 Kington Ho
19 Marrick Ho

95

C4 1 Pimlico Wlk
2 Aske Ho
3 Hathaway Ho
4 Haberdasher Pl
5 Fairchild Ho
6 Burtt Ho
7 Enfield Cloisters
8 McGregor Ct
9 Royal Oak Ct
10 Hoxton Mkt
11 Bath Pl
12 Chapel Pl
13 Standard Pl
14 Cleeve Workshops
15 Cleeve Ho
16 Printing House Yd
17 Perseverance Works
18 Crooked Billet Yd
19 Drysdale Ho
20 Castlefrank Ho
21 School App
22 Basing House Yd
23 Mail Coach Yd
C5 1 Bracer Ho
2 Scorton Ho
3 Fern Cl
4 Macbeth Ho
5 Oberon Ho
6 Buckland Ct
7 Crondall Ct
8 Osric Path
9 Caliban Twr
10 Celia Ho
11 Juliet Ho
12 Bacchus Wlk
13 Malcolm Ho
14 Homefield St
15 Crondall Pl
16 Blanca Ho
17 Miranda Ho
18 Falstaff Ho
19 Charmian Ho
20 Myrtle Wlk
21 Arden Ho
22 Sebastian Ho
23 Stanway Ct
24 Jerrold St
25 Rosalind Ho
26 Cordelia Ho
27 Monteagle Ct
28 John Parry Ct
29 James Anderson Ct
30 Ben Jonson Ct
31 Sara Lane Ct
32 Walbrook Ct
C6 1 Portelet Ct
2 Trinity Ct
3 Rozel Ct
4 St Helier Ct
5 Corbiere Ho
6 Kenning Ho
7 Higgins Ho
8 Cavell Ho
9 Girling Ho
10 Fulcher Ho
11 Francis Ho
12 Norris Ho
13 Kempton Ho
14 Nesham Ho
15 Crossbow Ho
16 Catherine Ho
17 Strale Ho
18 Horner Hos
19 Stringer Hos
20 Whitmore Ho
21 Nightingale Ho
22 Wilmer Gdns
23 Arrow Ho
24 Archer Ho
25 Meriden Ho
26 Rover Ho
27 Bowyer Ho
28 Tiller Ho
29 Canalside Studios
30 Kleine Wharf
31 Benyon Wharf
32 Quebec Wharf
33 Belvedere Ct
34 Portfleet Pl
D4 1 Gorsuch Pl
2 Strout's Pl
3 Vaughan Est
4 George Loveless Ho
5 Baroness Rd
6 James Brine Ho
7 Arthur Wade Ho
8 Robert Owen Ho
9 Sivill Ho
10 Georgina Gdns
11 Old Market Sq
12 Cuff Point
13 Bakers Rents
14 Leopold Bldgs
15 Dunmore Point
16 Wingfield Ho
17 Gascoigne Pl
18 Mandela Ho
19 Virginia Rd
20 Briggs Ho
21 Packenham Ho
22 Gowan Ho
23 Kirton Gdns
24 Chambord Ho
25 Ducal St
26 Strickland Ho
27 Alliston Ho
28 Gibraltar Wlk
29 Equity Sq
30 Shacklewell St
31 Rochelle St
32 Sonning Ho
33 Culham Ho
34 Hurley Ho
35 Palissy St
36 Taplow Ho
37 Chertsey Ho
38 Sunbury Ho
39 Sunbury Workshops
40 Datchett Ho
41 Hocker St
42 Coll Sharp Ct
43 Marlow Studio Workshops
44 Marlow Ho
45 Shiplake Ho
46 Wargrave Ho
47 Iffley Ho
D5 1 Queensbridge Ct
2 Godwin Ho
3 Kent Ct
4 Brunswick Ho
5 Weymouth Ct
6 Sovereign Mews
7 Dunloe Ct
8 Cremer Bsns Ctr
9 James Hammett Ho
10 Allgood St
11 Horatio St
12 Cadell Ho
13 Horatio Ho
14 Shipton Ho
D6 1 Hilborough Ct
2 Scriven Ct
3 Livermere Ct
4 Angrave Ct
5 Angrave Pas
6 Benfleet Ct
7 Belford Ho
8 Orme Ho
9 Clemson Ho
10 Longman Ho
11 Lowther Ho
12 Lovelace Ho
13 Harlowe Ho
14 Pamela Ho
15 Samuel Ho
16 Acton Ho
17 Loanda Cl
18 Phoenix Cl
19 Richardson Cl
20 Thrasher Cl
21 Mary Secole Cl
22 Canal Path
23 Pear Tree Cl
24 Hebden Ct
25 Charlton Ct
26 Laburnum Ct
27 Mansfield Ct
28 Garden Pl
29 Amber Wharf
30 Haggerston Studios

96

A1 1 Whitechurch Pas
2 Manningtree St
3 Whitechurch La
4 Naylor Bldg W
5 Morrison Bldgs
6 Nayor Bldg E
7 Mulberry St
8 Albany Ct
9 Cornell Bldg
10 Dryden Bldg
11 Weyhill Rd
12 Colefax Bldg
13 Fordham St
14 Myrdle Ct
15 Buckle St
16 Plough St
17 Goodman's Stile
18 Ropewalk Gdns
19 Skyline Plaza Bldg
20 Minet Ho
21 Mitali Pas
22 Basil Ho
23 Bernhard Baron Ho
24 Hogarth Ct
25 Delafield Ho
26 Chandlery Ho
27 Berner Terr
28 Victoria Yd
29 Batson Ho
30 Harkness Ho
31 Drewett Ho
32 Dowler Ho
33 Everard Ho
34 Bicknell Ho
35 Danvers Ho
36 Philchurch Pl
37 Hadfield Ho
38 Kindersley Ho
39 Langmore Ho
40 Halliday Ho
A2 1 Arthur Deakin Ho
2 Albert Cotts
3 Victoria Cotts
4 Boden Ho
5 Vollasky Ho
6 Daplyn St
7 Hobsons Pl
8 Hanbury Ho
9 Huguenot Ct
10 Links Yd
11 Casson Ho
12 Ramar Ho
13 Greatorex Ho
14 Chicksand Ho
15 Spelman Ho
16 Tailworth St
17 Monthope Rd
18 Evelyn Ho
19 Bloomfield Ho
20 Davenant Ho
21 Pauline Ho
22 Tannery Ho
23 Don Gratton Ho
24 Green Dragon Yd
25 Fieldgate Mans
26 Mosque Tower
A3 1 Bentworth Ct
2 Hawksmoor Pl
3 Kerbela St
4 Fuller Cl
5 Kinsham Ho
6 Menotti St
7 Barwell Ho
8 Grimsby St
9 Reflection Ho
10 Fleet Street Hill
11 Bratley St
12 Weaver Ho
13 Cornerstone Ct
14 Stuttle Ho
15 McGlashon Ho
16 John Pritchard Ho
A4 1 Providence Yd
2 Lygon Ho
3 Brabner Ho
4 Delta St
5 Delta Point
6 Tillet Way
7 Mullet Gdns
8 Lampern Sq
9 Kite Pl
10 Elver Gdns
11 Cobden Ho
12 Eversley Ho
13 Lorden Wlk
14 Rapley Ho
15 Dence Ho
16 McKinnon Wood Ho
17 Satchwell Rd
18 Dickinson Ho
19 Hutton Ho
20 Simmons Ho
21 Swinton Ho
22 Yates Ho
23 Johnson Ho
24 Jeremy Bentham Ho
25 Waring Ho
26 St James Ct
27 Ebony Ho
28 Azure Ho
29 Westhope Ho
30 Hague St
A5 1 London Terr
2 Sturdee Ho
3 Maude Ho
4 Haig Ho
5 Jellicoe Ho
6 Ropley St
7 Guinness Trust Bldgs
8 Ion Ct
9 Columbia Rd
10 Moye Cl
11 Morrel Ct
12 Courtauld Ho
13 Drummond Ho
14 Gurney Ho
15 Atkinson Ho
16 Halley Ho
17 Goldsmith's Sq
18 Shahjalal Ho
19 Ken Wilson Ho
20 April Ct
21 Crofts Ho
22 Sebright Ho
23 Beechwood Ho
24 Gillman Ho
25 Cheverell Ho
26 Besford Ho
27 Dinmont Ho
28 Elizabeth Mews
29 Sebright Pas
30 Wyndham Deedes Ho
31 Sheppard Ho
32 Mary James Ho
33 Hadrian Est
34 Blythendale Ho
35 George Vale Ho
36 Lion Mills
37 St Peter's Ave
38 Pritchard Ho
A6 1 Broke Wlk
2 Rochemont Wlk
3 Marlborough Ave
4 Rivington Wlk
5 Magnin Cl
6 Gloucester Sq
7 Woolstone Ho
8 Marsworth Ho
9 Cheddington Ho
10 Linslade Ho
11 Cosgrove Ho
12 Blisworth Ho
13 Eleanor Ct
14 Wistow Ho
15 Muscott Ho
16 Boxmoor Ho
17 Linford Ho
18 Pendley Ho
19 Northchurch Ho
20 Debdale Ho
21 Broadway Market Mews
22 Welshpool Ho
23 Ada Ho
B1 1 Peter Best Ho
2 Mellish Ho
3 Porchester Ho
4 Dickson Ho
5 Joscoyne Ho
6 Silvester Ho
7 Wilton Ct
8 Sarah Ho
9 Bridgen Ho
10 Tylney Ho
11 Greenwich Ct
12 Damien Ct
13 Philson Mans
14 Siege Ho
15 Jacob Mans
16 Proud Ho
17 Sly St
18 Barnett St
19 Kinder St
20 Richard St
21 Hungerford St
22 Colstead Ho
23 Melwood Ho
24 Wicker St
25 Langdale St
26 Chapman Ho
27 Burwell Cl
28 Walford Ho
29 Welstead Ho
30 Norton Ho
31 Turnour Ho
32 Luke Ho
33 Dunch St
34 Sheridan St
35 Brinsley St
B2 1 Wodeham Gdns
2 Castlemaine St
3 Court St
B3 1 Rochester Ct
2 Weaver Ct
3 Greenheath Bsns Ctr
4 Glass St
5 Herald St
6 Northesk Ho
7 Codrington Ho
8 Heathpool Ct
9 Mocatta Ho
10 Harvey Ho
11 Blackwood Ho
12 Rutherford Ho
13 Bullen Ho
14 Fremantle Ho
15 Pellew Ho
16 Ashington Ho
17 Dinnington Ho
18 Bartholomew Sq
19 Steeple Ct
20 Orion Ho
21 Fellbrigg St
22 Eagle Ho
23 Sovereign Ho
24 Redmill Ho
25 Berry Ho
26 Grindall Ho
27 Collingwood Ho
B4 1 Charles Dickens Ho
2 Adrian Bolt Ho
3 William Rathbone Ho
4 Southwood Smith Ho
5 Rushmead
6 William Channing Ho
7 John Cartwright Ho
8 Charles Darwin Ho
9 Thomas Burt Ho
10 John Fielden Ho
11 Gwilym Maries Ho
12 Joseph Priestley Ho
13 Wear Pl
14 John Nettleford Ho
15 Thornaby Ho
16 Stockton Ho
17 Barnard Ho
18 Gainford Ho
19 Stapleton Ho
20 James Middleton Ho
21 Kedleston Wlk
22 Queen Margaret Flats
23 Hollybush Ho
24 Horwood Ho
25 Norden Ho
26 Newcourt Ho
27 Seabright St
28 Viaduct Pl
29 Sunlight Sq
30 Providence Row Cl
B5 1 Dinmont St
2 Marian St
3 Claredale Ho
4 Keeling Ho
5 Maple St
6 Winkley St
7 Temple Dwellings
8 Argos Ho
9 Helen Ho
10 Lysander Ho
11 Antenor Ho
12 Paris Ho
13 Nestor Ho
14 Hector Ho
15 Ajax Ho
16 Achilles Ho
17 Priam Ho
18 Peabody Est
19 Felix St
20 Cambridge Cres
21 Peterley Bsns Ctr
22 Beckwith Ho
23 Brookfield Ho
24 Parminter Ind Est
25 Ted Roberts Ho
26 Cambridge Ct
27 Millennium Pl
28 William Caslon Ho
29 Hugh Platt Ho
30 West St
31 Mayfield Ho

32 Apollo Ho
33 Tanners Yd
34 Teesdale Yd
B6 1 Welshpool St
2 Broadway Ho
3 Regents Wharf
4 London Wharf
5 Warburton Ho
6 Warburton St
7 Triangle Rd
8 Warburton Rd
9 Williams Ho
10 Booth Cl
11 Albert Cl
12 King Edward Mans
13 Victoria Bldgs
14 Andrews Wharf
C1 1 Woollon Ho
2 Dundalk Ho
3 Anne Goodman Ho
4 Newbold Cotts
5 Kerry Ho
6 Zion Ho
7 Longford Ho
8 Bromehead St
9 Athlone Ho
10 Jubilee Mans
11 Harriott Ho
12 Brayford Sq
13 Clearbrook Way
14 Rochelle Ct
15 Winterton Ho
16 Swift Ho
17 Brinsley Ho
18 Dean Ho
19 Foley Ho
20 Robert Sutton Ho
21 Montpelier Pl
22 Glastonbury Pl
23 Steel's La
24 Masters Lo
25 Stylus Apartments
26 Arta Ho
C2 1 Fulneck
2 Gracehill
3 Ockbrook
4 Fairfield
5 Dunstan Hos
6 Cressy Ct
7 Cressy Hos
8 Callahan Cotts
9 Lindley Ho
10 Mayo Ho
11 Wexford Ho
12 Sandhurst Ho
13 Addis Ho
14 Colverson Ho
15 Beckett Ho
16 Jarman Ho
17 Armsby Ho
18 Wingrad Ho
19 Miranda Cl
20 Drake Ho
21 Ashfield Yd
22 Magri Wlk
23 Jean Pardies Ho
24 St Vincent De Paul Ho
25 Sambrook Ho
26 Louise De Marillac Ho
27 Dagobert Ho
28 Le Moal Ho
29 Odette Duval Ho
30 Charles Auffray Ho
31 Boisseau Ho
32 Clichy Ho
33 Paymal Ho
C3 1 William's Bldgs
2 Donegal Ho
3 Pelican Pas
4 Frederick Charrington Ho
5 Wickford Ho
6 Braintree Ho
7 Doveton Ho
8 Doveton St
9 Cephas Ho
10 Sceptre Ho
11 Bancroft Ho
12 Stothard St
13 Redclyf Ho
14 Winkworth Cotts
15 Amiel St
16 Hadleigh Ho
17 Hadleigh Cl
18 Ryder Ho
19 Mantus Cl
20 Kenton Ho
21 Colebert Ho
22 Ibbott St
23 Rickman Ho
24 Rickman St
25 Stothard Ho
26 Barbanel Ho
27 Stannard Cotts
28 St Peters Ct
29 Rennie Cotts
30 Pemell Cl
31 Pemell Ho
32 Leatherdale St
33 Gouldman Ho
34 Lamplighter Cl
35 Sherren Ho
36 Marlborough Lo
37 Hamilton Lo
38 Montgomery Lo
39 Cleveland Gr
40 Cromwell Lo
41 Bardsey Pl
42 Charrington Ho
43 Hayfield Yd
44 Allport Mews
45 Colin Winter Ho
C4 1 Mulberry Ho
2 Gretton Ho
3 Merceron Ho
4 Montfort Ho
5 Westbrook Ho
6 Sugar Loaf Wlk
7 Museum Ho
8 Burnham Est
9 Globe Terr
10 Moravian St
11 Shepton Hos
12 Mendip Hos
13 Academy Ct
14 Pepys Ho
15 Swinburne Ho
16 Moore Ho
17 Morris Ho
18 Burns Ho
19 Milton Ho
20 Whitman Ho
21 Shelley Ho
22 Keats Ho
23 Dawson Ho
24 Bradbeer Ho
25 Forber Ho
26 Hughes Ho
27 Silvester Ho
28 Rogers Est
29 Pavan Ct
30 Stafford Cripps Ho
31 Sidney Godley (VC) Ho
32 Butler Ho
33 Butler St
34 Thorne Ho
35 Bevin Ho
36 Tuscan Ho
C5 1 Evesham Ho
2 James Campbell Ho
3 Thomas Hollywood Ho
4 James Docherty Ho
5 Ebenezer Mussel Ho
6 Jameson Ct
7 Edinburgh Cl
8 Roger Dowley Ct
9 Sherbrooke Ho
10 Calcraft Ho
11 Burrard Ho
12 Dundas Ho
13 Ponsonby Ho
14 Barnes Ho
15 Paget Ho
16 Maitland Ho
17 Chesil Ct
18 Reynolds Ho
19 Cleland Ho
20 Goodrich Ho
21 Rosebery Ho
22 Sankey Ho
23 Cyprus Pl
24 Royston St
25 Stainsbury St
26 Hunslett St
27 Baildon
28 Brockweir
29 Tytherton
30 Malmesbury
31 Kingswood
32 Colville Ho
C6 1 Halkett Ho
2 Christchurch Sq
3 Helena Pl
4 Swingfield Ho
5 Greenham Ho
6 Dinmore Ho
7 Anstey Ho
8 Weston Ho
9 Carbroke Ho
10 Bluebell Cl
11 Cherry Tree Cl
12 Georgian Ct
13 Park Cl
14 Regency Ct
15 Norris Ho
D1 1 Pattison Ho
2 St Thomas Ho
3 Arbour Ho
4 Bladen Ho
5 Antill Terr
6 Majorie Mews
7 Billing Ho
8 Dowson Ho
9 Lipton Rd
10 Chalkwell Ho
11 Corringham Ho
12 Ogilvie Ho
13 Edward Mann Cl
14 Reservoir Studios
15 Lighterman Mews
D2 1 Roland Mews
2 Beatrice Ho
3 Morecambe Cl
4 Stepney Green Ct
5 Milrood Ho
6 Panama Ho
7 Galway Ho
8 Jacqueline Ho
9 Crown Mews
10 Caspian Ho
11 Darien Ho
12 Riga Ho
13 Flores Ho
14 Taranto Ho
15 Aden Ho
16 Master's St
17 Rosary Ct
D3 1 Raynham Ho
2 Pat Shaw Ho
3 Colmar Cl
4 Withy Ho
5 Stocks Ct
6 Downey Ho
7 Bay Ct
8 Sligo Ho
9 Pegasus Ho
10 Barents Ho
11 Biscay Ho
12 Solway Ho
13 Bantry Ho
14 Aral Ho
15 Pacific Ho
16 Magellan Ho
17 Levant Ho
18 Adriatic Ho
19 Genoa Ho
20 Hawke Ho
21 Palliser Ho
22 Ionian Ho
23 Weddell Ho
24 Carlyle Mews
25 Greencourt Ho
26 Sundra Wlk
D4 1 Stubbs Ho
2 Holman Ho
3 Clynes Ho
4 Windsor Ho
5 Gilbert Ho
6 Chater Ho
7 Ellen Wilkinson Ho
8 George Belt Ho
9 Ayrton Gould Ho
10 O'Brian Ho
11 Sulkin Ho
12 Jenkinson Ho
13 Bullards Pl
14 Sylvia Pankhurst Ho
15 Mary Macarthur Ho
16 Trevelyan Ho
17 Wedgwood Ho
18 Pemberton Ct
19 Leatherdale St
20 Walter Besant Ho
21 Barber Beaumont Ho
22 Brancaster Ho
23 Litcham Ho
D5 1 Kemp Ho
2 Piggott Ho
3 Mark Ho
4 Sidney Ho
5 Pomeroy Ho
6 Puteaux Ho
7 Doric Ho
8 Modling Ho
9 Longman Ho
10 Ames Ho
11 Alzette Ho
12 Offenbach Ho
13 Tate Ho
14 Norton Ho
15 St Gilles Ho
16 Harold Ho
17 Velletri Ho
18 Bridge Wharf
19 Gathorne St
20 Bow Brook The
21 Twig Folly Cl
22 Palmerston Ct
23 Lakeview
24 Peach Walk Mews
25 Caesar Ct

97

A1 1 Hearnshaw St
2 Berry Cotts
3 Causton Cotts
4 Elizabeth Blount Ct
5 Carr St
6 Shaw Cres
7 Darnley Ho
8 Mercer's Cotts
9 Troon Ho
10 Ratcliffe Ho
11 Wakeling St
12 York Sq
13 Anglia Ho
14 Cambria Ho
15 Caledonia Ho
16 Ratcliffe La
17 Bekesbourne St
18 John Scurr Ho
19 Regents Canal Ho
20 Basin App
21 Powlesland Ct
A2 1 Waley St
2 Edith Ramsay Ho
3 Andaman Ho
4 Atlantic Ho
5 Pevensey Ho
6 Solent Ho
7 Lorne Ho
8 Cromarty Ho
9 Dakin Pl
10 Greaves Cotts
11 Donaghue Cotts
12 Ames Cotts
13 Waterview Ho
14 Limehouse Fields Est
A3 1 Formosa Ho
2 Galveston Ho
3 Arabian Ho
4 Greenland Ho
5 Coral Ho
6 Anson Ho
7 Cambay Ho
8 Lindop Ho
9 Moray Ho
10 Azov Ho
11 Sandalwood Cl
12 Broadford Ho
A4 1 Imperial Ho
2 Newport Ho
3 Vassall Ho
4 Maurice Ct
5 Creed Ct
6 Christopher France Ho
7 Beaumont Ct
8 Pembroke Mews
A5 1 Nightingale Mews
2 Bunsen Ho
3 Bunsen St
4 Beatrice Webb Ho
5 Margaret Bondfield Ho
6 Wilmer Ho
7 Sandall Ho
8 Butley Ct
9 Josseline Ct
10 Dalton Ho
11 Brine Ho
12 Ford Cl
13 Viking Cl
14 Stanfield Rd
15 Stoneleigh Mews
16 Ruth Ct
17 School Bell Cloisters
18 Schoolbell Mews
19 Medhurst Cl
20 Olga St
21 Conyer St
22 Diamond Ho
23 Daring Ho
24 Crane Ho
25 Exmoor Ho
26 Grenville Ho
27 Hyperion Ho
28 Sturdy Ho
29 Wren Ho
30 Ardent Ho
31 Senators Lo
32 Hooke Ho
33 Mohawk Ho
34 Ivanhoe Ho
35 Medway Mews
B1 1 Dora Ho
2 Flansham Ho
3 Gatwick Ho
4 Ashpark Ho
5 Newdigate Ho
6 Midhurst Ho
7 Redbourne Ho
8 Southwater Cl
9 Andersens Wharf
10 Whatman Ho
11 Butler Ho
12 Fitzroy Ho
13 Salmon St
14 Mission The
15 Aithan Ho
16 Britley Ho
17 Cheadle Ho
18 Elland Ho
19 Wharf La
20 Docklands Ct
21 Park Heights Ct
22 Grosvenor Ct
23 Lime House Ct
24 Swallow Pl
25 St Anne's Trad Est
B2 1 Wearmouth Ho
2 Elmslie Point
3 Grindley Ho
4 Stileman Ho
5 Wilcox Ho
6 Huddart St
7 Robeson St
8 Couzens Ho
9 Perley Ho
10 Whytlaw Ho
11 Booker Cl
12 Tunley Gn
13 Callingham Cl
14 Bowry Ho
15 Perkins Ho
16 Printon Ho
17 Tasker Ho
B4 1 Trellis Sq
2 Sheffield Sq
3 Howcroft Ho
4 Astra Ho
5 Frye Ct
6 Byas Ho
7 George Lansbury Ho
8 Regal Pl
9 Coborn Mews
10 Tredegar Mews
11 Cavendish Terr
12 Lyn Mews
13 Buttermere Ho
14 Coniston Ho
15 Tracy Ho
16 Hanover Pl
17 St Clair Ho
18 Longthorne Ho
19 Vista Bldgs
20 Verity Ho
21 Icarus Ho
22 Whippingham Ho
23 Hamilton Ho
24 Winchester Ho
B5 1 Roman Square Mkt
2 John Bond Ho
3 McKenna Ho
4 Dennis Ho
5 McAusland Ho
6 McBride Ho
7 Libra Rd
8 Dave Adams Ho
9 Regency Ct
10 Tay Ho
11 Sleat Ho
12 Brodick Ho
13 Ewart Pl
14 Lunan Ho
15 Cruden Ho
16 Anglo Rd
17 Mull Ho
18 Sinclairs Ho
19 Driftway Ho
20 Clayhall Ct
21 Berebinder Ho
22 Partridge Ho
23 Barford Ho
24 Gullane Ho
25 Gosford Ho
26 Dornoch Ho
27 Dunnet Ho
28 Enard Ho
29 Fraserburgh Ho
30 Forth Ho
31 Stavers Ho
32 Rosegate Ho
33 Crowngate Ho
34 Queensgate Ho
35 Towergate Ho
36 Ordell Ct
37 William Pl
B6 1 Hampstead Wlk
2 Waverton Ho
3 Elton Ho
4 Locton Gn
5 Birtwhistle Ho
6 Clare Ho
7 Magpie Ho
8 Hornbeam Sq
9 Rowan Ho
10 Barge La
11 Walnut Ho
12 Birdsfield La
13 Atkins Ct
14 Willow Tree Cl
15 Jasmine Sq
16 Tait Ct
17 Ranwell Ho
18 Ranwell Cl
19 Tufnell Ct
20 Pulteney Cl
21 Vic Johnson Ho
22 Lea Sq
23 Iceni Ct
24 Tamar Cl
25 Roman Rd
26 Valentine Ho
C1 1 Landin Ho
2 Thomas Road Ind Est
3 Vickery's Wharf
4 Abbotts Wharf
5 Limehouse Ct
6 Charlesworth Ho
7 Gurdon Ho
8 Trendell Ho
9 Menteath Ho
10 Minchin Ho
11 Donne Ho
12 Old School Sq
13 Anglesey Ho
14 Gough Wlk
15 Baring Ho
16 Gladstone Ho
17 Hopkins Ho
18 Granville Ho
19 Overstone Ho
20 Pusey Ho
21 Russell Ho
22 Stanley Ho
C2 1 Bredel Ho
2 Linton Ho
3 Matthews Ho
4 Woodcock Ho
5 Limborough Ho
6 Maydwell Ho
7 Underhill Ho
8 Meyrick Ho
9 Ambrose Ho
10 Richardson Ho
11 Carpenter Ho
12 Robinson Ho
13 Bellmaker Ct
14 Lime Tree Ct
15 Bracken Ho
16 Bramble Ho
17 Berberis Ho
18 Bilberry Ho
19 Ladyfern Ho
20 Rosebay Ho
21 Invicta Cl
22 Phoenix Bsns Ctr
23 Metropolitan Cl
24 Busbridge Ho
C3 1 Fairmont Ho
2 Healy Ho
3 Zodiac Ho
4 Buick Ho
5 Consul Ho
6 Bentley Ho
7 Cresta Ho
8 Daimler Ho
9 Riley Ho
10 Jensen Ho
11 Lagonda Ho
12 Ireton St
13 Navenby Wlk
14 Burwell Wlk
15 Leadenham Ct
16 Sleaford Ho
17 Bow Triangle Bsns Ctr
C4 1 Bow Ho
2 Denmark Pl
3 Marsalis Ho
4 Lovette Ho
5 Drapers Almhouses
6 Mallard Point
7 Creswick Wlk
8 Bevin Ho
9 Huggins Ho
10 Williams Ho
11 Harris Ho
12 Marina Ct
13 Electric Ho
14 Matching Ct
15 Wellington Bldgs
16 Grafton Ho
17 Berkeley Ho
18 Columbia Ho
C5 1 Vincent Mews
2 Menai Pl
3 Heathfield Ct
4 Redwood Cl
5 Acorn Ct
6 Primrose Cl
7 Briar Ct
8 Springwood Cl
C6 1 Ironworks
2 Juno Ho
3 Chariot Cl
4 Saturn Ho
5 Hadrian Cl
6 Mercury Ho
7 Forum Cl
8 Venus Ho
9 Vesta Ho
10 Tiber Cl
11 Gemini Ho
12 Crown Close Bsns Ctr
13 Old Ford Trad Ctr
D1 1 Colebrook Ho
2 Essex Ho
3 Salisbury Ho
4 Maidstone Ho
5 Osterley Ho
6 Norwich Ho
7 Clarissa Ho
8 Elgin Ho
9 Shaftesbury Lo
10 Shepherd Ho
11 Jeremiah St
12 Elizabeth Cl
13 Chilcot Cl
14 Fitzgerald Ho
15 Vesey Path
16 Ennis Ho
17 Kilmore Ho
18 Cygnet House N
19 Cygnet House S
D2 1 Sumner Ho
2 David Hewitt Ho
3 St Gabriels Cl
4 Limehouse Cut
5 Colmans Wharf
6 Foundary Ho
7 Radford Ho
D3 1 Broxbourne Ho
2 Roxford Ho
3 Biscott Ho
4 Stanborough Ho
5 Hillstone Ct
D4 1 Bradley Ho
2 Prioress Ho
3 Alton Ho
4 Foxley Ho
5 Munden Ho
6 Canterbury Ho
7 Corbin Ho
8 Barton Ho
9 Jolles Ho

97 D4
10 Rudstone Ho
11 Baxter Ho
12 Baker Ho
13 Insley Ho
14 Hardwicke Ho
15 Glebe Ct
16 Priory St
17 Sadler Ho
18 Ballinger Point
19 Henshall Point
20 Dorrington Point
21 Warren Ho
22 Fairlie Ct
23 Regent Sq
24 Hackworth Point
25 Priestman Point
26 Wingate Ho
27 Nethercott Ho
28 Thelbridge Ho
29 Bowden Ho
30 Kerscott Ho
31 Southcott Ho
32 Birchdown Ho
33 Upcott Ho
34 Langmead Ho
35 Limscott Ho
36 Northleigh Ho
37 Huntshaw Ho
38 Chagford Ho
39 Ashcombe Ho
40 Shillingford Ho
41 Patrick Connolly Gdns
42 Lester Ct
43 Franklin St
44 Taft Way
45 Washington Cl
46 Veronica Ho
47 William Guy Gdns
48 Denbury Ho
49 Holsworthy Ho
50 Padstone Ho

98
A1 1 Glenkerry Ho
2 Carradale Ho
3 Langdon Ho
4 Balfron Twr
5 St Frideswides Mews
6 Tabard Ct
7 Delta Bldg
8 Findhorn St
9 Kilbrennan Ho
10 Thistle Ho
11 Heather Ho
12 Tartan Ho
13 Sharman Ho
14 Trident Ho
15 Wharf View Ct
A2 1 Mills Gr
2 St Michaels Ct
3 Duncan Ct
A4 1 Miller's House Visitor Ctr
B1 1 Lansbury Gdns
2 Theseus Ho
3 Adams Ho
4 Jones Ho
5 Sam March Ho
6 Arapiles Ho
7 Athenia Ho
8 Julius Ho
9 Jervis Bay Ho
10 Helen Mackay Ho
11 Gaze Ho
12 Ritchie Ho
13 Blairgowrie Ct
14 Circle Ho
15 Dunkeld Ho
16 Rosemary Dr
17 Sorrel La
18 East India Dock Road Tunnel
B3 1 Crescent Court Bsns Ctr
2 Ashmead Bsns Ctr
3 Forward Bsns Ctr The
B6 1 Victoria Mills
2 Hallings Wharf Studios
3 Poland Ho
4 Peter Heathfield Ho
5 Burford Rd
C5 1 Abbey Lane Commercial Est
2 Greenway Ct
C6 1 Barnby Sq
2 Barnby St
3 Brassett Point
4 David Lee Point
5 Worthing Cl
6 Bexhill Wlk
7 Old Barrowfield
8 Elmgreen Cl
9 Stafford Morris Ho
10 Nina Mackay Cl
11 Lime Wlk
D1 1 Newton Point
2 Sparke Terr
3 Montesquieu Terr
4 Crawford Point
5 Rathbone Ho
6 George St
7 Emily St
8 Fendt Cl
9 Sabbarton St
10 Briary Ct
11 Shaftesbury Ho
D2 1 Radley Terr
2 Bernard Cassidy St
3 Rathbone Mkt
4 Thomas North Terr
5 Mary St
6 Hughes Terr
7 Swanscombe Point
8 Rawlinson Point
9 Kennedy Cox Ho
10 Cooper St
D6 1 Harris Cotts
2 Moorey Cl
3 Euro Bsns Ctr
4 Ladywell St
5 Caistor Ho
6 Redfern Ho

99
A2 1 Odeon Ct
2 Edward Ct
3 Newhaven La
4 Ravenscroft Cl
5 Douglas Rd
6 Ferrier Point
7 Harvey Point
8 Wood Point
9 Trinity St
10 Pattinson Point
11 Clinch Ct
12 Mint Bsns Pk
A3 1 Webb Gdns
2 Eric Shipman Terr
3 Warmington St
4 Jellicoe Rd
5 Frank St
6 Seaton Cl
7 Tabernacle Ave
8 Upland Rd
9 Clove St
10 Edward St
A4 1 Bob Anker Cl
2 Lea Ct
3 Third Ave
4 Suffolk Rd
A5 1 Lettsom Wlk
2 Ashburton Terr
3 Grasmere Rd
4 Dimsdale Wlk
5 Rawstone Wlk
6 Scott Ho
7 Willett Ho
8 James Cl
9 Cordwainers Wlk
10 Victoria Point
11 Settle Point
12 Middle Rd
13 Steve Biko Lodge
14 Lady Helen Seymour Ho
A6 1 Royston Ct
B4 1 Barbers Alley
2 Grengate Lodge
3 Augurs La
4 Surrey St
5 Dongola Rd W
6 Bemersyde Point
7 Rowntree Clifford Cl
C2 1 Alliance Rd
2 Salomons Rd
3 Barnes Ct
4 Triangle Ct
5 Moorings The
C5 1 Wellby Ct
2 Northfield Ho
3 Bishop Wilfred Wood Ct
4 Castle Point
5 Moat Dr
C6 1 Tolpuddle Ave
2 Crown Mews
3 Lilac Ct
4 Hamara Ghar
5 Greenleaf Rd
6 Massey Ct
7 Florence Rd
8 Sissulu Ct
9 Austin Ct
D2 1 Partridge Cl
2 Vanbrugh Cl
3 Meadowsweet Cl
4 St Michaels Cl
5 Long Mark Rd
6 Congreve Wlk
D5 1 Foxcombe Cl
2 Rochford Cl
3 Kylemore Cl
4 Stondon Wlk
5 Imperial Mews
6 Dominica Cl
D6 1 Oldegate Ho
2 Gaitskell Ho
3 Cabot Way

100
A1 1 Hadleigh Wlk
2 Hawksmoor Cl
3 Fraser Cl
4 Moncrieff Cl
5 Burlington Cl
6 Dundonald Cl
7 Oakley Cl
8 Ashwell Cl
A2 1 Orchid Cl
2 Bellflower Cl
3 Partridge Sq
4 Larkspur Cl
5 Lobelia Cl
6 Stonechat Sq
7 Wintergreen Cl
8 Garnet Wlk
9 Mavis Wlk
10 Beacons Cl
11 Abbess Cl
12 Elmley Cl
13 Chetwood Wlk
14 Selby Cl
15 Denny Cl
16 Woodhatch Cl
A6 1 Oakwood Ct
2 Harrow Rd
3 Ray Massey Way
4 Madge Gill Way
5 Pilgrims Way
6 St Bartholomews Ct
B1 1 Bowers Wlk
2 Barton Cl
3 Clayton Cl
4 Dixon Cl
5 Gautrey Sq
6 Wakerley Cl
7 Canterbury Cl
8 Goose Sq
9 Coventry Cl
10 Butterfield Sq
11 Winchester Cl
B2 1 Fleetwood Ct
2 Lymington Cl
3 Holyhead Cl
4 Bondfield Rd
5 Tulip Cl
6 Ambrose Cl
7 Sage Cl
8 Lindwood Cl
D1 1 Weymouth Cl
2 Founder Cl
3 Admirals Ct

101
A6 1 Wellington St
2 St Ann's Rd
3 Cooke St
4 Gateway Ho
5 Ardleigh Ho
6 Skipper Ct
7 Hewetts Quay
B5 1 Anderson Ho
2 Rookwood Ho
3 Tasker Ho
4 Crispe Ho
5 Oban Ho
6 Earlsdown Ho
B6 1 Jarvis Cl
2 Mayflower Ho
3 Westbury Ct
4 Millicent Preston Ho
5 Louise Graham Ho
6 Grange Ho
7 Basing Ho
8 Barnes Ho
9 Lexham Ho
10 Ripple Ct
11 Waldegrave Ct
12 Howard Ct

104
A6 1 Milburn Dr
2 Cousins Cl
3 Leacroft Cl

108
C5 1 Marlow Ct
2 Andrewes Ct
3 Vine Cotts
4 Benjamin Ct
5 Broadway Bldgs
6 Clocktower Mews
7 Amberley Ho
8 Diamond Ct
D5 1 Silverdale Cl
2 Burdett Cl
3 Hopefield
4 Maunder Rd
5 Clare Ho

109
A5 1 Glastonbury Ct
2 Evesham Ct
3 Lacock Ct
4 Wigmore Ct
5 Melrose Ct
6 Brownlow Rd
7 Chignell Pl
8 Shirley Ct
9 Trojan Ct
10 Hatfield Rd
11 Pershore Ho
12 Hyde Ho
13 Hugh Clark Ho
14 Rosemoor Ho
15 Leeland Mans
16 Waterford Ct
17 O'Grady Ct
C6 1 Abbey Lo
2 Yew Tree Grange
3 Abinger Ct

110
A1 1 Burford Ho
2 Hope Cl
3 Centaur Ct
4 Phoenix Ct
A6 1 Watermans Mews
2 Hills Mews
3 Grosvenor Ct
4 Elton Lo
5 Hambledon Ct
C1 1 Surrey Cres
2 Forbes Ho
3 Haining Cl
4 Melville Ct
5 London Stile
6 Stile Hall Par
7 Priory Lo
8 Kew Bridge Ct
9 Meadowcroft
10 St James Ct
11 Rivers Ho
C5 1 Grosvenor Par
2 Oakfield Ct
3 Hart Grove Ct
4 Grosvenor Ct
D1 1 Churchdale Ct
2 Cromwell Cl
3 Cambridge Rd S
4 Oxbridge Ct
5 Tomlinson Cl
6 Gunnersbury Mews
7 Grange The
8 Gunnersbury Cl
9 Bellgrave Lo
D4 1 Cheltenham Pl
2 Beaumaris Twr
3 Arundel Ho
4 Pevensey Ct
5 Jerome Twr
6 Anstey Ct
7 Bennett Ct
8 Gunnersbury Ct
9 Barrington Ct
10 Hope Gdns
11 Park Road E
D5 1 Lantry Ct
2 Rosemount Ct
3 Moreton Twr
4 Acton Central Ind Est
5 Rufford Twr
6 Narrow St
7 Mount Pl
8 Sidney Miller Ct
9 Mill Hill Terr
10 Cheltenham Pl
11 Mill Hill Gr
12 Benjamin Ho
13 Arlington Ct
14 Lombard Ct
15 Steyne Ho

111
A1 1 Arlington Park Mans
2 Sandown Ho
3 Goodwood Ho
4 Windsor Ho
5 Lingfield Ho
6 Ascot Ho
7 Watchfield Ct
8 Belgrave Ct
9 Beverley Ct
10 Beaumont Ct
11 Harvard Rd
12 Troubridge Ct
13 Branden Lo
14 Fromow's Cnr
A2 1 Chiswick Green Studios
2 Bell Ind Est
3 Fairlawn Ct
4 Dukes Gate
5 Dewsbury Ct
6 Chiswick Terr
7 Mortlake Ho
A3 1 Blackmore Twr
2 Bollo Ct
3 Kipling Twr
4 Lawrence Ct
5 Maugham Ct
6 Reade Ct
7 Woolf Ct
8 Shaw Ct
9 Verne Ct
10 Wodehouse Ct
11 Greenock Rd
12 Garden Ct
13 Barons Gate
14 Cleveland Rd
15 Carver Cl
16 Chapter Cl
17 Beauchamp Cl
18 Holmes Ct
19 Copper Mews
A4 1 Belgrave Cl
2 Buckland Wlk
3 Frampton Ct
4 Telfer Cl
5 Harlech Twr
6 Corfe Twr
7 Barwick Ho
8 Charles Hocking Ho
9 Sunninghill Ct
10 Salisbury St
11 Jameson Pl
12 Castle Cl
A5 1 Rectory Rd
2 Derwentwater Mans
3 Market Pl
4 Hooper's Mews
5 Cromwell Pl
6 Locarno Rd
7 Edgecote Cl
8 Harleyford Manor
9 Coopers Ct
10 Avingdor Ct
11 Steyne Ho
B1 1 Chatsworth Lo
2 Prospect Pl
3 Townhall Ave
4 Devonhurst Pl
5 Heathfield Ct
6 Horticultural Pl
7 Merlin Ho
8 Garth Rd
9 Autumn Rise
B2 1 Disraeli Cl
2 Winston Wlk
3 Rusthall Mans
4 Bedford Park Mans
5 Essex Place Sq
6 Holly Rd
7 Homecross Ho
8 Swan Bsns Ctr
9 Jessop Ho
C1 1 Glebe Cl
2 Devonshire Mews
3 Binns Terr
4 Ingress St
5 Swanscombe Rd
6 Brackley Terr
7 Stephen Fox Ho
8 Manor Gdns
9 Coram Ho
10 Flaxman Ho
11 Thorneycroft Ho
12 Thornhill Ho
13 Kent Ho
14 Oldfield Ho
C2 1 Chestnut Ho
2 Bedford Ho
3 Bedford Cnr
4 Sydney Ho
5 Bedford Park Cnr
6 Priory Gdns
7 Windmill Alley
8 Castle Pl
9 Jonathan Ct
10 Windmill Pas
11 Chardin Rd
12 Gable Ho
C3 1 Fleet Ct
2 Ember Ct
3 Emlyn Gdns
4 Clone Ct
5 Brent Ct
6 Abbey Ct
7 Ormsby Lo
8 St Catherine's Ct
9 Lodge The
C4 1 Longford Ct
2 Mole Ct
3 Lea Ct
4 Wandle Ct
5 Beverley Ct
6 Roding Ct
7 Crane Ct
D1 1 Miller's Ct
2 British Grove Pas
3 British Grove S
4 Berestede Rd
5 North Eyot Gdns
D2 1 Flanders Mans
2 Stamford Brook Mans
3 Linkenholt Mans
4 Prebend Mans
5 Middlesex Ct
D3 1 Stamford Brook Gdns
2 Hauteville Court Gdns
3 Ranelagh Gdns

112
A1 1 Chisholm Ct
2 North Verbena Gdns
3 Western Terr
4 Verbena Gdns
5 Montrose Villas
6 Hammersmith Terr
7 South Black Lion La
8 St Peter's Wharf
A2 1 Hamlet Ct
2 Derwent Ct
3 Westcroft Ct
4 Black Lion Mews
5 St Peter's Villas
6 Standish Ho
7 Chambon Pl
8 Court Mans
9 Longthorpe Ct
10 Charlotte Ct
11 Westside
12 Park Ct
13 London Ho
A3 1 Elizabeth Finn Ho
2 Ashchurch Ct
3 King's Par
4 Inver Ct
5 Ariel Ct
6 Pocklington Lo
7 Vitae Apartments
A4 1 Becklow Gdns
2 Victoria Ho
3 Lycett Pl
4 Kylemore Ct
5 Alexandra Ct
6 Lytten Ct
7 Becklow Mews
8 Northcroft Ct
9 Bailey Ct
10 Spring Cott
11 Landor Wlk
12 Laurence Mews
13 Hadyn Park Ct
14 Askew Mans
15 Malvern Ct
B1 1 Prince's Mews
2 Aspen Gdns
3 Hampshire Hog La
4 Blades Ct
B2 1 Albion Gdns
2 Flora Gdns
3 Lamington St
4 Felgate Mews
5 Galena Ho
6 Albion Mews
7 Albion Ct
8 King Street Cloisters
9 Dimes Pl
10 Clarence Ct
11 Hampshire Hog La
12 Marryat Ct
13 Ravenscourt Ho
B3 1 Ravenscourt Park Mans
2 Paddenswick Ct
3 Ashbridge Ct
B4 1 Westbush Ct
2 Goldhawk Mews
3 Sycamore Ho
4 Shackleton Ct
5 Drake Ct
6 Scotts Ct
7 Raleigh Ct
8 Melville Court Flats
9 Southway Cl
B5 1 Arlington Ho
2 Lugard Ho
3 Shabana Ct
4 Sitarey Ct
5 Oaklands Ct
6 Davenport Mews
B6 1 Abercrombie Ho
2 Bathurst Ho
3 Brisbane Ho
4 Bentinck Ho
5 Ellenborough Ho
6 Lawrence Cl
7 Mackenzie Cl
8 Carteret Ho
9 Calvert Ho
10 Winthrop Ho
11 Auckland Ho
12 Blaxland Ho
13 Havelock Cl
14 Hargraves Ho
15 Hudson Cl
16 Phipps Ho
17 Lawson Ho
18 Hastings Ho
19 Wolfe Ho
20 Malabar Ct
21 Commonwealth Ave
22 Charnock Ho
23 Canning Ho
24 Cornwallis Ho
25 Commonwealth Ave
26 Champlain Ho
27 Grey Ho
28 Durban Ho
29 Baird Ho
30 Campbell Ho
31 Mitchell Ho
32 Denham Ho
33 Mackay Ho
34 Evans Ho
35 Davis Ho
36 Mandela Cl
C1 1 Bridge Avenue Mans
2 Bridgeview
3 College Ct
4 Beatrice Ho
5 Amelia Ho
6 Edith Ho
7 Joanna Ho
8 Mary Ho
9 Adela Ho
10 Sophia Ho
11 Henrietta Ho

12 Charlotte Ho
13 Alexandra Ho
14 Bath Pl
15 Elizabeth Ho
16 Margaret Ho
17 Peabody Est
18 Eleanor Ho
19 Isabella Ho
20 Caroline Ho
21 Chancellors Wharf
22 Sussex Pl
C2 1 Phoenix Lodge Mans
2 Samuel's Cl
3 Broadway Arc
4 Brook Ho
5 Hammersmith Broadway
6 Broadway Ctr The
7 Cambridge Ct
8 Ashcroft Sq
C4 1 Verulam Ho
2 Grove Mans
3 Frobisher Ct
4 Library Mans
5 Pennard Mans
6 New Shepherd's Bush Mkt
7 Kerrington Ct
8 Granville Mans
9 Romney Ct
10 Rayner Ct
11 Sulgrave Gdns
12 Bamborough Gdns
13 Hillary Ct
14 Market Studios
15 Lanark Mans
C5 1 Linden Ct
2 Frithville Ct
3 Blomfield Mans
4 Poplar Mews
5 Hopgood St
6 Westwood Ho
7 Stanlake Mews
8 Stanlake Villas
9 Alexandra Mans
D3 1 Grosvenor Residences
2 Blythe Mews
3 Burnand Ho
4 Bradford Ho
5 Springvale Terr
6 Ceylon Rd
7 Walpole Ct
8 Bronte Ct
9 Boswell Ct
10 Souldern Rd
11 Brook Green Flats
12 Haarlem Rd
13 Stafford Mans
14 Lionel Mans
15 Barradell Ho
D4 1 Vanderbilt Villas
2 Bodington Ct
3 Kingham Cl
4 Clearwater Terr
5 Lorne Gdns
6 Cameret Ct
7 Bush Ct
8 Shepherds Ct
9 Rockley Ct
10 Grampians The
11 Charcroft Ct
12 Addison Park Mans
13 Sinclair Mans
14 Fountain Ct
15 Woodford Ct
16 Roseford Ct
17 Woodstock Studios
D5 1 St Katherine's Wlk
2 Dorrit Ho
3 Pickwick Ho
4 Dombey Ho
5 Caranday Villas
6 Mortimer Ho
7 Nickleby Ho
8 Stebbing Ho
9 Boxmoor Ho
10 Poynter Ho
11 Swanscombe Ho
12 Darnley Terr
13 Norland Ho
14 Hume Ho
15 Boundary Ho
16 Norland Rd
17 Helix Ct
D6 1 Frinstead Ho
2 Hurstway Wlk
3 Testerton Wlk
4 Grenfell Wlk
5 Grenfell Twr
6 Barandon Wlk
7 Treadgold Ho
8 St Clements Ct
9 Willow Way
10 Florence Ho
11 Dora Ho
12 Carton Ho
13 Agnes Ho
14 Marley Ho
15 Estella Ho
16 Waynflete Sq
17 Pippin Ho
18 Baseline Business Studios

118

A1 1 Hope Ct
2 West Point
3 Centre Point
4 East Point
5 Proctor Ho
6 Tovy Ho
7 Avondale Pavement
8 Brettinghurst
9 Colechurch Ho
10 Harman Cl
11 Avondale Ho
12 Lanark Ho
13 George Elliston Ho
14 Eric Wilkins Ho
15 Six Bridges Ind Est
16 St James Ind Mews
17 Winter Lo
18 Fern Wlk
19 Ivy Ct
20 Fallow Ct
21 Culloden Cl
22 Archers Lo
A2 1 Cadbury Way
2 Robert Bell Ho
3 Robert Jones Ho
4 William Rushbrooke Ho
5 Helen Taylor Ho
6 Peter Hills Ho
7 Charles Mackenzie Ho
8 Drappers Way
9 Racs Flats
10 Abbey Gdns
11 Mayfair Ho
12 Windmill Cl
13 Maria Cl
14 Townsend Ho
15 Mason Ho
16 Kotree Way
17 Hannah Mary Way
18 Langdon Way
19 Whittaker Way
A3 1 Rudge Ho
2 Spenlow Ho
3 Darnay Ho
4 Carton Ho
5 Giles Ho
6 Bowley Ho
7 Casby Ho
8 Sun Pas
9 Ness St
10 Voyager Bsns Est
11 Dockley Road Ind Est
12 Spa Ct
13 Discovery Bsns Pk
14 Priter Road Hostel
15 Salisbury Ct
16 William Ellis Way
17 John McKenna Wlk
18 Toussaint Wlk
19 Gillison Wlk
20 Bromfield Ct
21 Ben Smith Way
22 Major Rd
23 Old Jamaica Bsns Est
A4 1 Providence
2 Springalls Wharf
3 Flockton St
4 Meridian Ct
5 East La
6 Luna Ho
7 Axis Ct
8 Farthing Alley
9 Peter Butler Ho
10 Brownlow Ho
11 Tapley Ho
12 Copperfield Ho
13 Dombey Ho
14 Fleming Ho
15 Parkers Row
16 Wade Ho
17 Bardell Ho
18 Nickleby Ho
19 John Felton Rd
20 Flockton St
21 Pickwick Ho
22 Oliver Ho
23 Weller Ho
24 Haredale Ho
25 Havisham Ho
26 Tupman Ho
27 Micawber Ho
28 Wrayburn Ho
29 Dartle Ct
30 Waterside Cl
31 Burnaby Ct
32 Wickfield Ho
33 Fountain Ho
34 Fountain Green Sq
35 St Saviours Ho
36 Providence Sq
A5 1 Trade Winds Ct
2 Spice Ct
3 Leeward Ct
4 Bridgeport Pl
5 Tamarind Yd
6 Cape Yd
7 Nightingale Ho
8 St Anthony's Cl
9 Stockholm Way
10 Miah Terr
11 Seville Ho
12 Douthwaite Sq
13 Codling Cl
14 Hermitage Ct
15 Capital Wharf
16 Cinnabar Wharf East
17 Cinnabar Wharf Central
18 Cinnabar Wharf West
19 Halcyon Wharf
A6 1 Conant Mews
2 Hanson Ho
3 Royal Tower Lo
4 Victoria Ct
5 Swan Pas
6 Royal Mint Pl
7 Peabody Est
8 Florin Ct
9 Flank St
10 Onedin Point
11 Liberty Ho
12 Ensign Ct
13 Sapphire Ct
14 Graces Alley
15 George Leybourne Ho
16 Fletcher St
17 Hatton Ho
18 Noble Ho
19 Shearsmith Ho
20 Wellclose St
21 Telford's Yd
22 Breezer's Ct
23 Pennington Ct
B1 1 Hockney Ct
2 Toulouse Ct
3 Lowry Ct
4 Barry Ho
5 Lewis Ct
6 Gainsborough Ct
7 Renoir Ct
8 Blake Ct
9 Raphael Ct
10 Rembrandt Ct
11 Constable Ct
12 Da Vinci Ct
13 Gaugin Ct
14 Michelangelo Ct
15 Monet Ct
16 Weald Cl
17 Jasmin Lo
18 Birchmere Lo
19 Weybridge Ct
20 Florence Ho
21 Gleneagles Cl
22 Sunningdale Cl
23 Muirfield Cl
24 Turnberry Cl
25 St Andrews Cl
26 Kingsdown Cl
27 St Davids Cl
28 Galway Cl
29 Edenbridge Cl
30 Birkdale Cl
31 Tralee Ct
32 Woburn Ct
33 Belfry Cl
34 Troon Cl
35 Holywell Cl
B2 1 Market Pl
2 Trappes Ho
3 Thurland Ho
4 Ramsfort Ho
5 Hambley Ho
6 Holford Ho
7 Pope Ho
8 Southwell Ho
9 Mortain Ho
10 Radcliffe Ho
11 Southwark Park Est
12 Galleywall Road Trad Est
13 Trevithick Ho
14 Barlow Ho
15 Donkin Ho
16 Landmann Ho
17 Fitzmaurice Ho
18 Dodd Ho
B3 1 Perryn Rd
2 Chalfont Ho
3 Prestwood Ho
4 Farmer Ho
5 Gataker Ho
6 Gataker St
7 Cornick Ho
8 Glebe Ho
9 Matson Ho
10 Hickling Ho
11 St Andrews Ho
B4 1 Butterfield Cl
2 Janeway Pl
3 Trotwood Ho
4 Maylie Ho
5 Cranbourn Pas
6 Cranbourn Ho
7 Cherry Garden Ho
8 Burton Ho
9 Morriss Ho
10 Dixon's Alley
11 King Edward The Third Mews
12 Cathay St
13 Mission The
14 Millstream Ho
B5 1 China Ct
2 Wellington Terr
3 Stevedore St
4 Portland Sq
5 Reardon Ho
6 Lowder Ho
7 Meeting House Alley
8 Farthing Fields
9 Oswell Ho
10 Park Lo
11 Doughty Ct
12 Inglefield Sq
13 Chopin's Ct
14 Welsh Ho
15 Hilliard Ho
16 Clegg St
17 Tasman Ho
18 Ross Ho
19 Wapping Dock St
20 Bridewell Pl
21 New Tower Bldgs
22 Tower Bldgs
23 Chimney Ct
24 Jackman Ho
25 Fenner Ho
26 Franklin Ho
27 Frobisher Ho
28 Flinders Ho
29 Chancellor Ho
30 Beechey Ho
31 Reardon Path
32 Parry Ho
33 Vancover Ho
34 Willoughby Ho
35 Sanctuary The
36 Dundee Ct
37 Pierhead Wharf
38 Scandrett St
39 St Johns Ct
B6 1 Newton Ho
2 Richard Neale Ho
3 Maddocks Ho
4 Cornwall St
5 Brockmer Ho
6 Dellow Ho
7 Bewley Ho
8 Artichoke Hill
9 Queen Anne Terr
10 King Henry Terr
11 King Charles Terr
12 Queen Victoria Terr
13 Sovereign Ct
14 Princes Court Bsns Ctr
15 Kingsley Mews
C2 1 Damory Ho
2 Antony Ho
3 Roderick Ho
4 Pedworth Gdns
5 Banner Ct
6 Rotherhithe Bsns Est
7 Beamish Ho
8 Corbetts Pas
9 Gillam Ho
10 Richard Ho
11 George Walter Ho
12 Westlake
13 Adron Ho
14 McIntosh Ho
C3 1 Blick Ho
2 Neptune Ho
3 Scotia Ct
4 Murdoch Ho
5 Edmonton Ct
6 Niagara Ct
7 Columbia Point
8 Ritchie Ho
9 Wells Ho
10 Helen Peele Cotts
11 Orchard Ho
12 Dock Offices
13 Landale Ho
14 Courthope Ho
15 Hithe Gr
16 China Hall Mews
C4 1 Mayflower St
2 St Mary's Est
3 Rupack St
4 Frank Whymark Ho
5 Adams Gardens Est
6 Hatteraick St
7 East India Ct
8 Bombay Ct
9 Stable Ho
10 Grannary The
11 Riverside
12 Cumberland Wharf
13 Seaford Ho
14 Hythe Ho
15 Sandwich Ho
16 Winchelsea Ho
17 Rye Ho
18 Kenning St
19 Western Pl
20 Ainsty St
21 Pine Ho
22 Beech Ho
23 Larch Ho
24 Turner Ct
25 Seth St
26 Risdon Ho
27 Risdon St
28 Aylton Est
29 Manitoba Ct
30 Calgary Ct
31 Irwell Est
32 St Olav's Sq
33 City Bsns Ctr
C5 1 John Rennie Wlk
2 Malay Ho
3 Wainwright Ho
4 Riverside Mans
5 Shackleton Ho
6 Whitehorn Ho
7 Wavel Ct
8 Prusom's Island
C6 1 Shadwell Pl
2 Gosling Ho
3 Vogler Ho
4 Donovan Ho
5 Knowlden Ho
6 Chamberlain Ho
7 Moore Ho
8 Thornewill Ho
9 Fisher Ho
10 All Saints Ct
11 Coburg Dwellings
12 Lowood Ho
13 Solander Gdns
14 Chancery Bldgs
15 Ring Ho
16 Juniper St
17 Gordon Ho
18 West Block
19 North Block
20 South Block
21 Ikon Ho
D2 1 John Kennedy Ho
2 Brydale Ho
3 Balman Ho
4 Tissington Ct
5 Harbord Ho
6 Westfield Ho
7 Albert Starr Ho
8 John Brent Ho
9 William Evans Ho
10 Raven Ho
11 Egret Ho
12 Fulmar Ho
13 Dunlin Ho
14 Siskin Ho
15 Sheldrake Ho
16 Buchanan Ct
17 Burrage Ct
18 Biddenham Ho
19 Ayston Ho
20 Empingham Ho
21 Deanshanger Ho
22 Codicote Ho
23 Buryfield Ct
D4 1 Schooner Cl
2 Dolphin Cl
3 Clipper Cl
4 Deauville Ct
5 Colette Ct
6 Coniston Ct
7 Virginia Ct
8 Derwent Ct
9 Grantham Ct
10 Serpentine Ct
11 Career Ct
12 Lacine Ct
13 Fairway Ct
14 Harold Ct
15 Spruce Ho
16 Cedar Ho
17 Sycamore Ho
18 Woodland Cres
19 Poplar Ho
20 Adelphi Ct
21 Basque Ct
22 Aberdale Ct
23 Quilting Ct
24 Chargrove Cl
25 Radley Ct
26 Greenacre Sq
27 Maple Leaf Sq
28 Stanhope Cl
29 Hawke Pl
30 Drake Cl
31 Brass Talley Alley
32 Monkton Ho
33 James Ho
34 Wolfe Cres
D5 1 Clarence Mews
2 Raleigh Ct
3 Katherine Cl
4 Woolcombes Ct
5 Tudor Ct
6 Quayside Ct
7 Princes Riverside Rd
8 Surrey Ho
9 Tideway Ct
10 Edinburgh Ct
11 Falkirk Ct
12 Byelands Cl
13 Gwent Ct
14 Lavender Ho
15 Abbotshade Rd
16 Bellamy's Ct
17 Blenheim Ct
18 Sandringham Ct
19 Hampton Ct
20 Windsor Ct
21 Balmoral Ct
22 Westminster Ct
23 Beatson Wlk
D6 1 Barnardo Gdns
2 Roslin Ho
3 Glamis Est
4 Peabody Est
5 East Block
6 Highway Trad Ctr The
7 Highway Bsns Pk The
8 Cranford Cotts
9 Ratcliffe Orch
10 Scotia Bldg
11 Mauretania Bldg
12 Compania Bldg
13 Sirius Bldg
14 Unicorn Bldg
15 Keepier Wharf

119

A2 1 Trafalgar Cl
2 Hornblower Cl
3 Cunard Wlk
4 Caronia Ct
5 Carinthia Ct
6 Freswick Ho
7 Graveley Ho
8 Husbourne Ho
9 Crofters Ct
10 Pomona Ho
11 Hazelwood Ho
12 Cannon Wharf Bsns Ctr
13 Bence Ho
14 Clement Ho
15 Pendennis Ho
16 Lighter Cl
17 Mast Ct
18 Rushcutters Ct
19 Boat Lifter Way
A5 1 Edward Sq
2 Prince Regent Ct
3 Codrington Ct
4 Pennington Ct
5 Cherry Ct
6 Ash Ct
7 Beech Ct
8 Hazel Ct
9 Laurel Ct
A6 1 St Georges Sq
2 Drake Ho
3 Osprey Ho
4 Fleet Ho
5 Gainsborough Ho
6 Victory Pl
7 Challenger Ho
8 Conrad Ho
9 Lock View Ct
10 Shoulder of Mutton Alley
11 Frederick Sq
12 Helena Sq
13 Elizabeth Sq
14 Sophia Sq
15 William Sq
16 Lamb Ct
17 Lockside
18 Adriatic Bldg
19 Ionian Bldg
20 Regents Gate Ho
B1 1 Gransden Ho
2 Daubeney Twr
3 North Ho
4 Rochfort Ho
5 Keppel Ho
6 Camden Ho
7 Sanderson Ho
8 Berkeley Ho
9 Strafford Ho
10 Richman Ho
11 Hurleston Ho
12 Grafton Ho
13 Fulcher Ho
14 Citrus Ho
B2 1 Windsock Cl
2 St George's Mews
3 Linberry Wlk
4 Lanyard Ho
5 Golden Hind Pl
6 James Lind Ho
7 Harmon Ho
8 Pelican Ho
9 Bembridge Ho
10 Terrace The
11 George Beard Rd
12 Colonnade The
13 Pepys Ent Ctr
B6 1 Hamilton Ho
2 Imperial Ho
3 Oriana Ho
4 Queens Ct
5 Brightlingsea Pl
6 Faraday Ho
7 Ropemaker's Fields
8 Oast Ct
9 Mitre The
10 Bate St
11 Joseph Irwin Ho
12 Padstow Ho
13 Bethlehem Ho

14 Saunders Cl
15 Roche Ho
16 Stocks Pl
17 Trinidad Ho
18 Grenada Ho
19 Kings Ho
20 Dunbar Wharf
21 Limekiln Wharf
22 Belgrave Ct
23 Eaton Ho
C1 1 Hudson Ct
2 Shackleton Ct
3 De Gama Pl
4 Mercator Pl
5 Maritime Quay
6 Perry Ct
7 Amundsen Ct
C2 1 Nova Bldg
2 Apollo Bldg
3 Gaverick Mews
4 Windmill Ho
5 Orion Point
6 Galaxy Bldg
7 Venus Ho
8 Olympian Ct
9 Poseidon Ct
10 Mercury Ct
11 Aphrodite Ct
12 Cyclops Mews
13 Neptune Ct
14 Artemis Ct
15 Hera Ct
16 Ares Ct
17 Ringwood Gdns
18 Dartmoor Wlk
19 Rothsay Wlk
20 Ashdown Wlk
21 Radnor Wlk
22 Ironmonger's Pl
23 Britannia Rd
24 Deptford Ferry Rd
25 Magellan Pl
26 Dockers Tanner Rd
C3 1 Bowsprit Point
2 St Hubert's Ho
3 John Tucker Ho
4 Broadway Wlk
5 Nash Ho
6 Fairlead Ho
7 Crosstrees Ho
8 Stanliff Ho
9 Keelson Ho
10 Clara Grant Ho
11 Gilbertson Ho
12 Scoulding Ho
13 Hibbert Ho
14 Cressall Ho
15 Alexander Ho
16 Kedge Ho
C4 1 Anchorage Point
2 Waterman Bldg
3 Jefferson Bldg
4 Pierpoint Bldg
5 Franklin Bldg
6 Vanguard Bldg
7 Edison Bldg
8 Seacon Twr
9 Naxos Bldg
10 Express Wharf
11 Hutching's Wharf
12 Tobago St
13 Bellamy Cl
14 Dowlen Ct
15 Cochrane Ho
16 Beatty Ho
17 Scott Ho
18 Laybourne Ho
19 Ensign Ho
20 Beaufort Ho
21 Spinnaker Ho
22 Bosun Cl
23 Topmast Point
24 Turner Ho
25 Constable Ho
26 Knighthead Point
C6 1 West India Ho
2 Berber Pl
3 Birchfield Ho
4 Elderfield Ho
5 Thornfield Ho
6 Gorsefield Ho
7 Arborfield Ho
8 Colborne Ho
9 East India Bldgs
10 Compass Point
11 Salter St
12 Garland Ct
13 Bogart Ct
14 Fonda Ct
15 Welles Ct
16 Rogers Ct
17 Premier Pl
18 Kelly Ct
19 Flynn Ct
20 Mary Jones Ho
21 Cannon Dr
22 Horizon Bldg
D1 1 Slipway Ho
2 Taffrail Ho
3 Platehouse The
4 Wheelhouse The
5 Chart House The
6 Port House The
7 Beacon Ho
8 Blasker Wlk
9 Maconochies Rd
D2 1 Brassey Ho
2 Triton Ho
3 Warspite Ho
4 Rodney Ho
5 Conway Ho
6 Exmouth Ho
7 Akbar Ho
8 Arethusa Ho
9 Tasman Ct
10 Cutty Sark Ho
D3 1 Turnberry Quay
2 Balmoral Ho
3 Aegon Ho
4 Marina Point
D6 1 Westcott Ho
2 Corry Ho
3 Malam Gdns
4 Blomfield Ho
5 Devitt Ho
6 Leyland Ho
7 Wigram Ho
8 Willis Ho
9 Balsam Ho
10 Finch's Ct
11 Poplar Bath St
12 Lawless St
13 Storey Ho
14 Abbot Ho
15 Woodall Cl
16 Landon Wlk
17 Goodhope Ho
18 Goodfaith Ho
19 Winant Ho
20 Goodspeed Ho
21 Lubbock Ho
22 Goodwill Ho
23 Martindale Ho
24 Holmsdale Ho
25 Norwood Ho
26 Constant Ho

120

A2 1 St John's Ct
2 Betty May Gray Ho
3 Castleton Ho
4 Urmston Ho
5 Salford Ho
6 Capstan Ho
7 Frigate Ho
8 Galleon Ho
9 Barons Lo
A3 1 Cardale St
2 Hickin St
3 John McDonald Ho
4 Thorne Ho
5 Skeggs Ho
6 St Bernard Ho
7 Kimberley Ho
8 Kingdon Ho
9 Killoran Ho
10 Alastor Ho
11 Lingard Ho
12 Yarrow Ho
13 Sandpiper Ct
14 Nightingale Ct
15 Robin Ct
16 Heron Ct
17 Ferndown Lo
18 Crosby Ho
A4 1 Llandovery Ho
2 Rugless Ho
3 Ash Ho
4 Elm Ho
5 Cedar Ho
6 Castalia Sq
7 Aspect Ho
8 Normandy Ho
9 Valiant Ho
10 Tamar Ho
11 Watkins Ho
12 Alice Shepherd Ho
13 Oak Ho
14 Ballin Ct
15 Martin Ct
16 Grebe Ct
17 Kingfisher Ct
18 Walkers Lo
19 Antilles Bay
A5 1 Lumina Bldg
2 Nova Ct W
3 Nova Ct E
4 Aurora Bldg
5 Arran Ho
6 Kintyre Ho
7 Vantage Mews
8 Managers St
9 Horatio Pl
10 Concordia Wharf
A6 1 Discovery Ho
2 Mountague Pl
3 Virginia Ho
4 Collins Ho
5 Lawless Ho
6 Carmichael Ho
7 Commodore Ho
8 Mermaid Ho
9 Bullivant St
10 Anderson Ho
11 Mackrow Wlk
12 Robin Hood Gdns
13 Prestage Way
B2 1 Verwood Lo
2 Fawley Lo
3 Lyndhurst Lo
4 Blyth Cl
5 Farnworth Ho
6 Francis Cl
B6 1 Quixley St
2 Romney Ho
3 Pumping Ho
4 Switch Ho
5 Wingfield Ct
6 Explorers Ct
7 Sexton Ct
8 Keel Ct
9 Bridge Ct
10 Sail Ct
11 Settlers Ct
12 Pilgrims Mews
13 Studley Ct
14 Wotton Ct
15 Cape Henry Ct
16 Bartholomew Ct
17 Adventurers Ct
18 Susan Constant Ct
19 Atlantic Ct
C1 1 Bellot Gdns
2 Thornley Pl
3 King William La
4 Bolton Ho
5 Miles Ho
6 Mell St
7 Sam Manners Ho
8 Hatcliffe Almshouses
9 Woodland Wlk
10 Earlswood Cl
D1 1 Baldrey Ho
2 Christie Ho
3 Dyson Ho
4 Cliffe Ho
5 Moore Ho
6 Collins Ho
7 Lockyer Ho
8 Halley Ho
9 Kepler Ho
10 Sailacre Ho
11 Union Pk
D3 1 Teal St
2 Maurer Ct
3 Mudlarks Blvd
4 Renaissance Wlk
5 Alamaro Lo

121

A1 1 Layfield Ho
2 Westerdale Rd
3 Mayston Mews
4 Station Mews Terr
A5 1 Capulet Mews
2 Pepys Cres
3 De Quincey Mews
4 Hardy Ave
5 Tom Jenkinson Rd
6 Kennacraig Cl
7 Charles Flemwell Mews
8 Gatcombe Rd
9 Badminton Mews
10 Holyrood Mews
11 Britannia Gate
12 Dalemain Mews
13 Bowes-Lyon Hall
14 Lancaster hall
15 Victoria Hall
A6 1 Clements Ave
2 Martindale Ave
3 Balearic Apts
4 Marmara Apts
5 Baltic Apts
6 Coral Apts
7 Aegean Apts
8 Capital East Apts
B1 1 Phipps Ho
2 Hartwell Ho
3 Nicholas Stacey Ho
4 Frank Burton Cl
B5 1 Beaulieu Ave
2 Charles Whincup Rd
3 Audley Dr
4 Julia Garfield Mews
5 Rayleigh Rd
6 Pirie St
7 Royal Victoria Pl
8 Pankhurst Ave
9 West Mersea Cl
10 Ramsgate Cl
11 Windsor Hall
12 Munning Ho
13 Drake Hall
14 Jane Austen Hall
15 Eastern Quay
C1 1 Ransom Rd
2 Linton Cl
3 Cedar Pl
4 Gooding Ho
5 Valiant Ho
6 Chaffey Ho
7 Benn Ho
8 Wellesley Cl
9 Gollogly Terr

122

A2 1 Harden Ct
2 Albion Ct
3 Viking Ho
4 Zealand Ho
5 Glenalvon Way
6 Parish Wharf
7 Elsinore Ho
8 Lolland Ho
9 Denmark Ho
10 Jutland Ho
11 Tivoli Gdns
12 Rance Ho
13 Peel Yates Ho
14 Rosebank Wlk
15 Paradise Pl
16 Woodville St
B2 1 Bowling Green Row
2 Sarah Turnbull Ho
3 Brewhouse Rd
4 Red Barracks Rd
5 Marine Dr
6 Hastings Ho
7 Centurion Ct
8 Cambridge Ho
9 Churchill Ct
10 Elizabeth Ct
11 Cambridge Barracks Rd
12 Len Clifton Ho
13 Granby Ho
14 Harding Ho
15 Rutland Ho
16 Townshend Ho
17 Rendlebury Ho
18 Milne Ho
19 Mulgrave Ho
20 Murray Ho
21 Chatham Ho
22 Biddulph Ho
23 Carew Ho
24 Eleanor Wlk
C2 1 Preston Ho
2 Lindsay Ho
3 Fraser Ho
4 Pickering Ho
5 Watergate Ho
6 Grinling Ho
7 Glebe Ho
8 Elliston Ho
9 Sir Martin Bowes Ho
10 Jim Bradley Cl
11 Bathway
12 Limavady Ho
13 Slater Cl
14 Vista Bldg The
C5 1 Westland Ho
2 Queensland Ho
3 Pier Par
4 Woodman Par
5 Shaw Ho
6 Glen Ho
7 Brocklebank Ho
D1 1 Branham Ho
2 Ford Ho
3 Wilford Ho
4 Parker Ho
5 Stirling Ho
6 Twiss Ho
7 Hewett Ho
8 De Haviland Dr
9 Schoolhouse Yd
D2 1 Beresford Sq
2 Central Ct
3 Walpole Pl
4 Anglesea Ave
5 Troy Ct
6 Ormsby Point
7 Haven Lo
8 Green Lawns
9 Eardley Point
10 Sandham Point
11 Bingham Point
12 Anglesea Mews
13 Masons Hill
14 Maritime Ho

123

A1 1 Glenmount Path
2 Claymill Ho
3 St James Hts
4 St Margaret's Path
5 George Akass Ho
A3 1 Wayatt Point
2 Albert Ho
3 Building 50
4 Building 49
5 Building 48
6 Building 47
7 Building 36
8 Blenheim Ho
9 Wilson Ct
B1 1 Bert Reilly Ho
B3 1 Apollo Way
2 Senator Wlk
3 Mallard Path
4 Fortune Wlk
C1 1 Fox Hollow Cl
2 Goldsmid St
C2 1 Gavin Ho
2 Richard Neve Ho
3 Bateson St
4 Lewin Ct

124

B5 1 Rowntree Path
2 MacAulay Way
3 Manning Ct
4 Chadwick Ct
5 Simon Ct
B6 1 Beveridge Ct
2 Hammond Way
3 Leonard Robbins Path
4 Lansbury Ct
5 Raymond Postgate Ct
6 Webb Ct
7 Curtis Way
8 Lytton Strachey Path
9 Keynes Ct
10 Marshall Path
11 Cross Ct
12 Octavia Way
13 Passfield Path
14 Mill Ct
15 Besant Ct
C3 1 Hermitage Cl
2 Chantry Cl
C4 1 Binsey Wlk
2 Tilehurst Point
3 Blewbury Ho
4 Coralline Wlk
5 Evenlode Ho
C5 1 Kingsley Ct
2 Wilberforce Ct
3 Shaftesbury Ct
4 Hazlitt Ct
5 Ricardo Path
6 Nassau Path
7 Malthus Path
8 Bright Ct
9 Cobden Ct
D4 1 Oakenholt Ho
2 Trewsbury Ho
3 Penton Ho
4 Osney Ho
5 St Helens Rd
6 Clewer Ho
7 Maplin Ho
8 Wyfold Ho
9 Hibernia Point
10 Duxford Ho
11 Radley Ho
12 Limestone Wlk
13 Masham Ho
14 Jacob Ho

125

A3 1 Harlequin Ho
2 Dexter Ho
3 Argali Ho
4 Mangold Way
5 Lucerne Ct
6 Holstein Way
7 Abbotswood Cl
8 Plympton Cl
9 Benedict Cl
B1 1 Shakespeare Ho
2 Tennyson Ho
3 Dickens Ho
4 Scott Ho
5 Lansbury Ho
6 Shaw Ho
7 Chestnuts The
C1 1 Stevanne Ct
2 Tolcairn Ct
3 Chalfont Ct
4 Alonso Ho
5 Ariel Ct
6 Miranda Ho
7 Prospero Ho
8 Laurels The
9 Camden Ct
10 Newnham Lo
11 Court Lo
12 Flaxman Ct
13 Hertford Wlk
14 Riverview Ct
15 Winchester Ct
C2 1 Brushwood Lo
2 Bletchington Ct
3 Upper Sheridan Rd
4 William Ct
5 Samson Ct
6 Cowper Rd
7 Venmead Ct
C3 1 Cressingham Ct
2 Telford Ho
3 Kelvin Ho
4 Faraday Ho
5 Jenner Ho
6 Keir Hardie Ho
7 Lennox Ho
8 Mary Macarthur Ho
9 Elizabeth Garrett Anderson Ho
10 William Smith Ho
11 Baden Powell Ho
12 Baird Ho
13 Boyle Ho

129

D1 1 Heathwood Ct
2 Aldermead
3 Northumberland Ct

130

C4 1 Osterley Lo
2 St Andrew's Cl
3 Parkfield
4 Fairways
5 Granwood Ct
6 Grovewood Ct

131

A2 1 Brewery Mews Bsns Ctr
2 Forge Lo
3 Pulteney Cl
4 Tolson Ho
5 Percy Gdns
6 Wynne Ct
7 Wisdom Ct
8 Swann Ct
9 Shrewsbury Wlk
10 King's Terr
11 Van Gogh Cl
12 Holme Ct
C5 1 Canute Ho
2 Spruce Ho
3 Moorings Ho
4 Jessops Wharf
5 Corsell Ho
6 Barnes Qtr
7 Dorey Ho
8 Tanyard Ho
9 Booth Ho
10 Oakbark Ho
11 Bordeston Ct
12 Shire Pl
D5 1 Galba Ct
2 Servius Ct
3 Maurice Ct
4 Leo Ct
5 Otho Ct
6 Nero Ct
7 Romulus Ct
8 Pump Alley
D6 1 Brockshot Cl
2 Westbury Pl
3 Brook La N
4 Braemar Ct
5 Brook Ct
6 Clifden Ho
7 Cedar Ct
8 Cranbrook Ct
9 Somerset Lo
10 Alexandra Rd
11 Berkeley Ho
12 Watermans Ct
13 Ferry Quays Ctyd

132

A1 1 St John's Gr
2 Michel's Row
3 Michelsdale Dr
4 Blue Anchor Alley
5 Clarence St
6 Sun Alley
7 Thames Link Ho
8 Benns Wlk
9 Waterloo Pl
10 Northumbria Ct
A6 1 Ferry Sq
2 Watermans Ct
3 Wilkes Rd
4 Albany Par
5 Charlton Ho
6 Albany Ho
7 Alma Ho
8 Griffin Ct
9 Cressage Ho
10 Tunstall Wlk
11 Trimmer Wlk
12 Running Horse Yd
13 Mission Sq
14 Distillery Wlk
B1 1 Towers The
2 Longs Ct
3 Sovereign Ct
4 Robinson Ct
5 Calvert Ct
6 Bedford Ct
7 Hickey's Almshouses
8 Church Estate Almshouses
9 Richmond International Bsns Ctr
10 Abercorn Mews
B4 1 Primrose Ho
2 Lawman Ct
3 Royston Ct
4 Garden Ct
5 Capel Lo
6 Devonshire Ct
7 Celia Ct
8 Rosslyn Ho
9 Branstone Ct
10 Lamerton Lo
11 Kew Lo
12 Dunraven Ho
13 Stoneleigh Lo
14 Tunstall Ct
15 Voltaire
C4 1 Clarendon Ct
2 Quintock Ho
3 Broome Ct
4 Lonsdale Mews
5 Elizabeth Cotts
6 Sandways
7 Victoria Cotts
8 North Ave
9 Grovewood
10 Hamilton Ho
11 Melvin Ct
12 Royal Par
13 Power Ho

14 Station Ave
15 Blake Mews
D1 1 Hershell Ct
2 Deanhill Ct
3 Park Sheen
4 Furness Lo
5 Merricks Ct
D4 1 Terrano Ho
2 Oak Ho
3 Aura Ho
4 Maple Ho
5 Cedar Ho
6 Saffron Ho
7 Lime Ho
8 Lavender Ho
9 Juniper Ho

133

B2 1 Rann Ho
2 Craven Ho
3 John Dee Ho
4 Kindell Ho
5 Montgomery Ho
6 Avondale Ho
7 Addington Ct
8 Dovecote Gdns
9 Firmston Ho
10 Glendower Gdns
11 Chestnut Ave
12 Trehern Rd
13 Rock Ave
D3 1 Melrose Rd
2 Seaforth Lo
3 St John's Gr
4 Sussex Ct
5 Carmichael Ct
6 Hampshire Ct
7 Thorne Pas
8 Brunel Ct
9 Beverley Path

134

D1 1 Olivette St
2 Mascotte Rd
3 Glegg Pl
4 Crown Ct
5 Charlwood Terr
6 Percy Laurie Ho
D6 1 Cobb's Hall
2 Dorset Mans
3 St Clements Mans
4 Bothwell St
5 Hawksmoor St

135

B3 1 Plato Pl
2 Mustow Pl
3 Laurel Bank Gdns
4 Ranelagh Mans
5 Churchfield Mans
6 Bear Croft Ho
7 Elysium Gate
8 Ethel Rankin Ct
9 Arthur Henderson Ho
10 William Banfield Ho
11 Melbray Mews
D3 1 Brightwells
2 Broughton Road App
3 Bulow Ct
4 Langford Rd
5 Elizabeth Barnes Ct
6 Snowbury Rd

136

A2 1 Molasses Ho
2 Molasses Row
3 Cinnamon Row
4 Calico Ho
5 Calico Row
6 Port Ho
7 Square Rigger Row
8 Trade Twr
9 Ivory Ho
10 Spice Ct
11 Sherwood Ct
12 Mendip Ct
13 Chalmers Ho
14 Coral Row
15 Ivory Sq
16 Kingfisher Ho
B1 1 Burke Ho
2 Fox Ho
3 Buxton Ho
4 Pitt Ho
5 Ramsey Ho
6 Beverley Cl
7 Florence Ho
8 Linden Ct
9 Dorcas Ct
10 Johnson Ct
11 Agnes Ct
12 Hilltop Ct
13 Courtyard The
14 Old Laundry The
15 Oberstein Rd
16 Fineran Ct
17 Sangora Rd
18 Harvard Mans
19 Plough Mews
B2 1 Benham Cl
2 Milner Ho
3 McManus Ho
4 Wilberforce Ho
5 Wheeler Ct
6 Sporle Ct
7 Holliday Sq
8 John Parker Sq
9 Carmichael Cl
10 Fenner Sq
11 Clark Lawrence Ct
12 Shaw Ct
13 Sendall Ct
14 Livingstone Rd
15 Farrant Ho
16 Jackson Ho
17 Darien Ho
18 Shepard Ho
19 Ganley Ct
20 Arthur Newton Ho
21 Chesterton Ho
22 John Kirk Ho
23 Mantua St
24 Heaver Rd
25 Candlemakers
B3 1 Archer Ho
2 White Ho
3 Winfield Ho
4 Powrie Ho
5 Morgan Ct
6 Fairchild Cl
7 Musjid Rd
C2 1 Kiloh Ct
2 Lanner Ho
3 Griffon Ho
4 Kestrel Ho
5 Kite Ho
6 Peregrine Ho
7 Hawk Ho
8 Inkster Ho
9 Harrier Ho
10 Eagle Hts
11 Kingfisher Ct
12 Lavender Terr
13 Temple Ho
14 Ridley Ho
15 Eden Ho
16 Hertford Ct
17 Nepaul Rd
C3 1 Meecham Ct
2 McKiernan Ct
3 Banbury St
4 Colestown St
5 Crombie Mews
6 Frere St
D3 1 Stevenson Ho
2 Ambrose Mews
3 Harling Ct
4 Southside Quarter
5 Latchmere St
6 Dovedale Cotts
7 Roydon Cl
8 Castlemaine
9 Wittering Ho
10 Berry Ho
11 Weybridge Point

137

A2 1 Shaftesbury Park Chambers
2 Selborne
3 Rush Hill Mews
4 Marmion Mews
5 Crosland Pl
6 Craven Mews
7 Garfield Mews
8 Audley Cl
9 Basnett Rd
10 Tyneham Cl
11 Woodmere Cl
A3 1 Hopkinson Ho
2 MacDonald Ho
3 Rushlake Ho
4 Bishopstone Ho
5 Dresden Ho
6 Millgrove St
7 Farnhurst Ho
8 Walden Ho
9 Kennard St
10 Langhurst Ho
11 Atkinson Ho
12 Kennard Ho
13 Voltaire Ct
14 Barloch Ho
15 London Stone Bsns Est
B2 1 Turnchapel Mews
2 Redwood Mews
3 Phil Brown Pl
4 Bev Callender Cl
5 Keith Connor Cl
6 Tessa Sanderson Pl
7 Daley Thompson Way
8 Rashleigh Ct
9 Abberley Mews
10 Willow Lodge
11 Beaufoy Rd
B3 1 St Philip Sq
2 Montefiore St
3 Gambetta St
4 Scott Ct
5 Radcliffe Path
6 Moresby Wlk
7 Victorian Hts
C1 1 Polygon The
2 Windsor Ct
3 Trinity Cl
4 Studios The
5 Bourne Ho
C2 1 Clapham Manor Ct
2 Clarke Ho
3 Gables The
4 Sycamore Mews
5 Maritime Ho
6 Rectory Gdns
7 Floris Pl
C3 1 Seymour Ho
2 Lucas Ho
3 Durrington Twr
4 Amesbury Twr
5 Fovant Ct
6 Allington Ct
7 Welford Ct
8 Ilsley Ct
9 Blake Ct
10 Brooklands Ct
D1 1 Kendoa Rd
2 Felmersham Cl
3 Abbeville Mews
4 Saxon Ho
5 Gifford Ho
6 Teignmouth Cl
7 Holwood Pl
8 Oaklands Pl
9 Wilberforce Mews
10 William Bonney Est
D2 1 Chelsham Ho
2 Lynde Ho
3 Greener Ho
4 Towns Ho
5 Hugh Morgan Ho
6 Roy Ridley Ho
7 Lendal Terr
8 Slievemore Cl
9 Cadmus Cl
10 Clapham North Bsns Ctr
D3 1 Haltone Ho
2 Surcot Ho
3 Kingsley Ho
4 Wood Ho
5 Dalemain Ho
6 Falloden Ho
7 Dartington Ho
8 Esher Ho
9 Kneller Ho
10 Lostock Ho
11 Croxteth Ho
12 Donnington Ho
13 Farnley Ho
14 Hardwick Ho
15 Bradfield Ho
16 Brocket Ho
17 Colchester Ho
18 Clive Ho
19 Chessington Ho
20 Rushbrook Ho
21 Stanmore Ho
22 Newton Ho
23 Netherby Ho
24 Oakwell Ho
25 Rydal Ho
26 Rushton Ho
27 Harcourt Ho
28 Metcalfe Ho
29 Lydwell Ho
30 Raleigh Ho
31 Spencer Ho
32 Shipley Ho
33 Naylor Ho
34 Mordaunt Ho
35 Stanley Ho
36 Alderley Ho
37 Effingham Ho
38 Grant Ho
39 Wilson Ho
40 Fraser Ho

138

A1 1 Morris Ho
2 Gye Ho
3 Clowes Ho
4 Thomas Ho
5 Stuart Ho
6 Storace Ho
7 Bedford Ho
8 Ascot Ct
9 Ascot Par
10 Ashmere Ho
11 Ashmere Gr
12 Ventura Ho
13 Vickery Ho
14 Stafford Mans
15 Beresford Ho
A2 1 Callingham Ho
2 Russell Pickering Ho
3 Ormerod Ho
4 Lopez Ho
5 Coachmaker Mews
A3 1 Barling Ct
2 Jeffrey's Ct
3 Brooks Ct
4 Dalmeny Ct
5 Fender Ct
6 Fishlock Ct
7 Bedser Ct
8 Gover Ct
9 Clarence Wlk
10 Barton Ct
11 Allom Ct
12 Garden Ho
13 Otha Ho
14 Hayward Ct
15 Surridge Ct
16 Knox Ct
17 Jephson Ct
18 Holmes Ct
19 McIntyre Ct
20 Richardson Ct
21 Cassell Ho
22 Pakington Ho
23 Bain Ho
24 Enfield Ho
25 Fawcett Ho
26 Sidgwick Ho
27 Jowett Ho
28 Beckett Ho
29 Arden Ho
30 Pinter Ho
31 Barrington Ct
32 Union Mews
B1 1 Freemens Hos
2 Roger's Alm-shouses
3 Gresham Alm-shouses
4 Exbury Ho
5 Glasbury Ho
6 Dalbury Ho
7 Fosbury Ho
8 Chalbury Ho
9 Neilson-Terry Ct
10 Pavilion Mans
11 Daisy Dormer Ct
12 George Lashwood Ct
13 Marie Lloyd Ct
14 Trinity Homes
15 Lethaby Ho
16 Edmundsbury Ct Est
17 Regis Pl
18 Marlborough Mews
19 Alpha Ho
20 Beta Pl
21 Cedars Ho
B2 1 Turberville Ho
2 Thrayle Ho
3 Percheron Ct
4 Draymans Ct
B3 1 Maurice Ho
2 Thring Ho
3 Paton Ho
4 Huxley Ho
5 Morell Ho
6 Mary Ho
7 Beale Ho
8 Rosa Parks Ho
9 Birrell Ho
10 Waltham Ho
11 Burford Ho
12 Thornicroft Ho
13 Addington Ho
14 Goffton Ho
15 Redmayne Ho
16 Norton Ho
17 Aytoun Ct
18 Colwall Ho
19 Burrow Ho
20 Wynter Ho
21 Crowhurst Ho
22 Lidcote Gdns
23 Cumnor Cl
24 Park View Mews
C1 1 Electric Mans
2 Electric La
3 Connaught Mans
4 Clifton Mans
5 Hereford Ho
6 Chaplin Ho
7 Brixton Oval
8 Lord David Pitt Ho
9 Marcus Garvey Way
10 Montego Cl
11 Bob Marley Way
12 Leeson Rd
C2 1 Buckmaster Cl
2 Albemarle Ho
3 Goodwood Mans
4 Angell Park Gdns
5 Fyfield Rd
6 Howard Ho
7 Harris Ho
8 Broadoak Ct
9 Burgate Ct
10 Witchwood Ho
11 Blacktree Mews
12 Chartham Ct
13 Chilham Ct
14 Northgate Ct
15 Westgate Ct
16 Dover Mans
C3 1 Norval Gn
2 Hilda Terr
3 Burton La
4 Church Gn
5 Lord Holland La
6 Sorrell Cl
7 Burton Rd
8 Holles Ho
9 Leys Ct
10 Warwick Ho
11 Fairfax Ho
12 Wayland Ho
13 Dudley Ho
14 Denchworth Ho
15 Fitzgerald Ho
16 Lambert Ho
17 Chute Ho
18 Bedwell Ho
19 Ferrey Mews
20 Serenaders Rd
21 Boatemah Wlk
22 Ireton Ho
23 Marston Ho
24 Morrison Rd
25 Fir Grove Rd
26 Shore Way
C4 1 Hector Ct
2 Jason Ct
3 Creon Ct
4 Hermes Ct
5 Argos Ct
6 Cadmus Ct
7 Appollo Ct
8 Mercury Ct
9 County Ho
10 Seasalter Ho
11 Downbarton Ho
12 Garlinge Ho
13 Moira Ho
14 Alvanley Ho
15 Woodchurch Ho
16 Durlock Ho
17 Hallam Ho
18 Whiteness Ho
19 Bromstone Ho
20 Penelope Ho
21 Melbourne Sq
22 Cloisters The
23 Cliffsend Ho
24 Sacketts Ho
25 Hanway Ho
26 Brickworth Ho
27 Redlynch Ho
28 Stodmarsh Ho
29 Kingsgate Ho
30 Chardin Ho
31 Annesley Ho
32 Knowlton Ho
33 Russell Gr
34 Eamann Casey Ho
C5 1 Swift Ho
2 Listowel Cl
3 Deal Wlk
4 Plover Ho
5 Aigburth Mans
6 Glencoe Mans
7 Glenshaw Mans
8 Cleveland Mans
9 Leda Ct
10 Jupiter Ct
11 Juno Ct
12 Healy Ho
13 Ashton Ho
14 Ramsey Ho
15 Annesley Ho
16 Cowley Rd
C6 1 Sherwin Ho
2 Pegasus Pl
3 Kilner Ho
4 Read Ho
5 Lohmann Ho
6 Hornby Ho
7 Abel Ho
8 Blythe Ho
9 Key Ho
10 Lockwood Ho
11 Alverstone Ho
12 Blades Ho
13 Rothesay Ct
D1 1 Mahatma Gandhi Ind Est
2 Dylan Rd
3 Bessemer Park Ind Est
4 Pablo Neruda Cl
5 Langston Hughes Cl
6 Walt Whitman Cl
7 James Joyce Wlk
8 Alice Walker Cl
9 Louise Bennett Cl
10 Chadacre Ho
11 Burwood Ho
12 Pyrford Ho
13 Wangford Ho
14 Ashford Ho
15 Kenwood Ho
16 Moyne Ho
17 Elveden Ho
18 Carrara Cl
19 Broughton Dr
20 Angela Davis Ind Est
21 Tilia Wlk
22 County Ho
D2 1 Mallams Mews
2 Amberley Ct
3 Harper Ho
4 Leicester Ho
5 Station Ave
6 Wellfit St
7 Loughborough Ct
8 Belinda Rd
9 Higgs Ind Est
D3 1 Langport Ho
2 Iveagh Ho
3 Newark Ho
4 Edgehill Ho
5 Hopton Ho
6 Ashby Ho
7 Nevil Ho
D4 1 Fairbairn Gn
2 Hammelton Gn
3 Foxley Sq
4 Silverburn Ho
5 Butler Ho
6 Dalkeith Ho
7 Turner Cl
8 Bathgate Ho
9 Black Roof Ho
D6 1 Faunce Ho
2 Garbett Ho
3 Harvard Ho
4 Doddington Pl
5 Kean Ho
6 Jephson Ho
7 Cornish Ho
8 Bateman Ho
9 Molesworth Ho
10 Walters Ho
11 Cruden Ho
12 Brawne Ho
13 Prescott Ho
14 Chalmer's Wlk
15 Copley Cl
16 King Charles Ct

139

A3 1 Bergen Ho
2 Oslo Ho
3 Viking Ho
4 Jutland Ho
5 Norvic Ho
6 Odin Ho
7 Baltic Ho
8 Nobel Ho
9 Mercia Ho
10 Kenbury Gdns
11 Zealand Ho
12 Elsinore Ho
13 Norse Ho
14 Denmark Mans
15 Dane Ho
16 Canterbury Cl
17 York Cl
18 Kenbury Mans
19 Parade Mans
20 Winterslow Ho
21 Lilford Ho
22 Bartholomew Ho
23 Guildford Ho
24 Boston Ho
25 Hereford Ho
26 Weyhill Ho
27 Lichfield Ho
28 Lansdown Ho
29 Honiton Ho
30 Pinner Ho
31 Baldock Ho
32 Widecombe Ho
33 Nottingham Ho
34 Witham Ho
35 Barnet Ho
36 Empress Mews
A4 1 Bertha Neubergh Ho
2 Mornington Mews
3 Badsworth Rd
4 Pearson Cl
5 Elm Tree Ct
6 Samuel Lewis Trust Dwellings
7 Milkwell Yd
8 Keswick Ho
9 Mitcham Ho
A5 1 Boundary Ho
2 Day Ho
3 Burgess Ho
4 Carlyle Ho
5 Myers Ho
6 Thompson Ave
7 Palgrave Ho
8 Winnington Ho
9 Brantwood Ho
10 Lowell Ho
11 Jessie Duffett Ho
12 Otterburn Ho
13 Crossmount Ho
14 Venice Ct
15 Bowyer St
16 Livingstone Ho
17 Gothic Ct
18 Coniston Ho
19 Harlynwood
20 Carey Ct
21 Finley Ct
22 Grainger Ct
23 Hayes Ct
24 Moffat Ho
25 Marinel Ho
26 Hodister Cl
27 Arnot Ho
28 Lamb Ho
29 Kipling Ho
30 Keats Ho
31 Kenyon Ho
32 New Church Rd
33 Sir John Kirk Cl
B1 1 Shaftesbury Ct
2 Mayhew Ct
3 Morris Ct
4 Swinburne Ct
5 Perth Ct
6 Tayside Ct
7 Matlock Ct

8 Hunter Ct
9 Turner Ct
B3 1 Selborne Rd
2 Hascombe Terr
B4 1 Joiners Arms Yd
2 Butterfly Wlk
3 Cuthill Wlk
4 Colonades The
5 Artichoke Mews
6 Peabody Bldgs
7 Brighton Ho
8 Park Ho
9 Peabody Ct
10 Lomond Ho
11 Lamb Ho
12 Kimpton Ct
13 Belham Wlk
14 Datchelor Pl
15 Harvey Rd
B5 1 Masterman Ho
2 Milton Ho
3 Pope Ho
4 Chester Ct
5 Marvel Ho
6 Flecker Ho
7 Landor Ho
8 Leslie Prince Ct
9 Evelina Mans
10 Langland Ho
11 Drinkwater Ho
12 Procter Ho
13 Shirley Ho
14 Drayton Ho
15 Bridges Ho
16 Cunningham Ho
17 Hood Ho
18 Herrick Ho
19 Dekker Ho
20 Houseman Way
21 Coleby Path
B6 1 Queens Ho
2 Arnside Ho
3 Horsley St
4 St Peter's Ho
5 St Johns Ho
6 St Marks Ho
7 St Stephens Ho
8 St Matthew's Ho
9 Red Lion Cl
10 Boyson Rd
11 Bradenham
C2 1 Harfield Gdns
2 Karen Ct
3 Seavington Ho
4 Appleshaw Ho
5 Birdsall Ho
6 Whitney Ho
7 Wheatland Ho
8 Wilton Ho
9 Walcot Ho
10 Whaddon Ho
11 Melbreak Ho
12 Ledbury Ho
13 Tidworth Ho
14 Riseholme Ho
15 Ringmer Ho
16 Petworth Ho
17 Stagshaw Ho
18 Ivybridge Ho
19 Inwood Ho
20 Gatcombe Ho
21 Felbridge Ho
22 Cowdray Ho
C3 1 Springfield Ho
2 Craston Ho
3 Walters Ho
4 Edgecombe Ho
5 Fowler Ho
6 Rignold Ho
7 Chatham Ho
C4 1 Barnwell Ho
2 Brunswick Villas
3 St Giles Twr
4 Bentley Ho
5 Dawson Ho
6 Dryden Ho
7 Mayward Ho
8 Longleigh Ho
9 Fairwall Ho
10 Bodeney Ho
11 Sandby Ho
12 Vestry Mews
13 Netley
14 Lakanal
15 Racine
C5 1 Tower Mill Rd
2 Tilson Cl
3 Granville Sq
4 Edgar Wallace Cl
5 Potters Cl
6 Dorton Cl
7 Samuel Jones Ind Est
8 Dibden Ho
9 Marchwood Cl
10 Pilgrims Cloisters
11 Beacon Ho
12 Teather St
13 Stacy Path
14 Rumball Ho
15 Ballow Cl
16 Rill Ho
C6 1 Downend Ct
2 Andoversford Ct
3 Pearse St
4 Watling St
5 Gandolfi St
D1 1 Dulwich Mews
2 St James's Cloisters
D4 1 Colbert
2 Voltaire
3 Finch Mews
4 Charles Coveney Rd
5 Bamber Rd
6 Crane St
7 Curlew Ho
8 Mallard Ho
9 Tern Ho
10 Crane Ho
11 Falcon Ho
12 Bryanston Ho
13 Basing Ct
14 Marcus Ho
15 Sheffield Ho
D5 1 Painswick Ct
2 Sharpness Ct
3 Mattingly Way
4 Hordle Prom N
5 Burcher Gale Gr
6 Calypso Cres
7 Hordle Prom S
8 Cinnamon Cl
9 Savannah Cl
10 Thames Ct
11 Shannon Ct
12 Amstel Ct
13 Danube Ct
14 Tilbury Cl
15 Hordle Prom E
16 Indus Ct
17 Oakcourt
18 Palm Ct
19 Rowan Ct
20 Blackthorn Ct
21 Pear Ct
22 Lidgate Rd
23 Whistler Mews
24 Boathouse Wlk
D6 1 Willsbridge Ct
2 Cam Ct
3 Quedgeley Ct
4 Saul Ct
5 Quenington Ct
6 Westonbirt Ct
7 Wickway Ct

140
A3 1 William Margrie Cl
2 William Blake Ho
3 Quantock Mews
4 Choumert Sq
5 Parkstone Rd
6 Atwell Rd
A4 1 Canal Head Public Sq
2 Angelina Ho
3 Jarvis Ho
4 Richland Ho
5 Honeywood Ho
6 Wakefield Ho
7 Primrose Ho
8 Hardcastle Ho
9 Dunstall Ho
10 Springtide Cl
11 Purdon Ho
12 Flamborough Ho
13 Lambrook Ho
14 Witcombe Point
15 Yarnfield Sq
16 Winford Ct
17 Portbury Cl
18 Robert Keen Cl
A5 1 Thornbill Ho
2 Vervain Ho
3 Woodstar Ho
4 Tamarind Ho
5 Hereford Retreat
6 Haymerle Ho
7 Furley Ho
8 Thomas Milner Ho
9 Applegarth Ho
10 Freda Corbett Cl
11 Rudbeck Ho
12 Henslow Ho
13 Lindley Ho
14 Collinson Ho
15 Sister Mabel's Way
16 Timberland Cl
17 Hastings Cl
18 Sidmouth Ho
19 Budleigh Ho
20 Stanesgate Ho
21 Breamore Ho
22 Ely Ho
23 Gisburn Ho
A6 1 Bowles Rd
2 Western Wharf
3 Northfield Ho
4 Millbrook Ho
5 Denstone Ho
6 Deerhurst Ho
7 Caversham Ho
8 Battle Ho
9 Cardiff Ho
10 Bridgnorth Ho
11 Exeter Ho
12 Grantham Ho
13 Aylesbury Ho
14 Royston Ho
B2 1 Tilling Ho
2 Goodwin Ho
3 Tyrells Ct
4 Citron Terr
5 Basswood Cl
6 Cheam St
B3 1 Walkynscroft
2 Ryegates
3 Hathorne Cl
4 Pilkington Rd
5 Russell Ct
6 Heaton Ho
7 Magdalene Cl
8 Iris Ct
B4 1 Willowdene
2 Pinedene
3 Oakdene
4 Beechdene
5 Hollydene
6 Wood Dene
8 Staveley Cl
9 Carnicot Ho
10 Martock Ct
11 Cherry Tree Ct
12 Kendrick Ct
B5 1 Tortington Ho
2 Credenhill Ho
3 Bromyard Ho
4 Hoyland Cl
5 Willowdene
6 Ashdene
7 Acorn Par
8 Havelock Ct
9 Springall St
10 Harry Lambourn Ho
11 Grenier Apartments
C3 1 Honiton Gdns
2 Selden Ho
3 Hathway Ho
4 Hathway St
5 Station Ct
C4 1 Trotman Ho
2 Boddington Ho
3 Heydon Ho
4 Boulter Ho
5 Astbury Bsns Pk
C5 1 Ambleside Point
2 Grasmere Point
3 Windermere Point
4 Roman Way
5 Laburnum Cl
6 Juniper Ho
7 Romney Cl
8 Hammersley Ho
9 Hutchinson Ho
10 Hammond Ho
11 Fir Tree Ho
12 Glastonbury Ct
13 Highbridge Ct
14 Filton Ct
15 Chiltern Ct
16 Cheviot Ct
C6 1 Penshurst Ho
2 Reculver Ho
3 Mereworth Ho
4 Camber Ho
5 Chiham Ho
6 Otford Ho
7 Olive Tree Ho
8 Aspen Ho
9 Lewis Silkin Ho
10 Richborough Ho
11 Dover Ho
12 Eynsford Ho
13 Horton Ho
14 Lamberhurst Ho
15 Canterbury Ind Pk
16 Upnall Ho
17 Sissinghurst Ho
18 Rochester Ho
19 Saltwood Ho
20 Leybourne Ho
21 Lullingstone Ho
D1 1 Laxton Path
2 Barlings Ho
3 Bayfield Ho
4 Coston Wlk
5 Coverham Ho
6 Gateley Ho
7 Dereham Ho
8 Greenwood Ho
9 Hilton Ho
10 Goodall Ho
11 Horsley Ho
12 Jordan Ho
D5 1 Richard Anderson Ct
2 Palm Tree Ho
3 Edward Robinson Ho
4 Antony Ho
5 Gerrard Ho
6 Palmer Ho
7 Pankhurst Cl
D6 1 Harrisons Ct
2 Grantley Ho
3 Sunbury Ct
4 Tilbury Ho
5 Graham Ct
6 Connell Ct
7 St Clements Ct
8 Henderson Ct
9 Jemotts Ct
10 Verona Ct
11 Heywood Ho
12 Francis Ct
13 Hind Ho
14 Donne Ho
15 Carew Ct
16 Burbage Ho
17 Newland Ho
18 Dobson Ho
19 Dalton Ho
20 Greene Ct
21 Redrup Ho
22 Tarplett Ho
23 Stunell Ho
24 Gasson Ho
25 Bryce Ho
26 Barnes Ho
27 Barkwith Ho
28 Bannister Ho
29 Apollo Ind Bsns Ctr

141
A4 1 Archer Ho
2 Browning Ho
3 Hardcastle Ho
4 Brooke Ho
5 Wallis Ho
A5 1 Batavia Ho
2 Marlowe Bsns Ctr
3 Batavia Mews
4 Woodrush Cl
5 Alexandra St
6 Primrose Wlk
7 Vansittart St
8 Granville Ct
9 Cottesbrook St
10 Ewen Henderson Ct
11 Fordham Ho
A6 1 Portland Ct
2 Phoenix Ct
3 Rainbow Ct
4 Hawke Twr
5 Chubworthy St
6 Woodpecker Rd
7 Hercules Ct
B5 1 Austin Ho
2 Exeter Way
3 Crossleigh Ct
4 Mornington Pl
5 Maple Ho
B6 1 Chester Ho
2 Lynch Wlk
3 Arlington Ho
4 Woodcote Ho
5 Cornbury Ho
6 Prospect Pl
7 Akintaro Ho
8 Mulberry Ho
9 Laurel Ho
10 Linden Ho
11 Ashford Ho
12 Wardalls Ho
13 Magnolia Ho
14 Howard Ho
15 Larch Cl
16 Ibis Ct
17 Merganser Ct
18 Wotton Rd
19 Kingfisher Sq
20 Sanderling Ct
21 Dolphin Twr
22 Mermaid Twr
23 Scoter Ct
24 Shearwater Ct
25 Brambling Ct
26 Kittiwake Ct
27 Diana Cl
28 Guillemot Ct
29 Marine Twr
30 Teal Ct
31 Lapwing Twr
32 Violet Cl
33 Skua Ct
34 Tristan Ct
35 Rosemary Ct
36 Cormorant Ct
37 Shelduck Ct
38 Eider Ct
39 Pintail Ct
C4 1 Admiralty Cl
2 Harton Lodge
3 Sylva Cotts
4 Pitman Ho
5 Heston Ho
6 Mereton Mans
7 Indiana Bldg
8 St John's Lodge
C5 1 Sandpiper Ct
2 Flamingo Ct
3 Titan Bsns Est
4 Rochdale Way
5 Speedwell St
6 Reginald Pl
7 Fletcher Path
8 Frankham Ho
9 Cremer Ho
10 Wilshaw Ho
11 Castell Ho
12 Holden Ho
13 Browne Ho
14 Resolution Way
15 Lady Florence Ctyd
16 Covell Ct
17 Albion Ho
C6 1 Dryfield Wlk
2 Blake Ho
3 Hawkins Ho
4 Grenville Ho
5 Langford Ho
6 Mandarin Ct
7 Bittern Ct
8 Lamerton St
9 Ravensbourne Mans
10 Armada St
11 Armada Ct
12 Benbow Ho
13 Oxenham Ho
14 Caravel Mews
15 Hughes Ho
16 Stretton Mans
D4 1 Washington Bldg
2 California Bldg
3 Utah Bldg
4 Montana Bldg
5 Oregon Bldg
6 Dakota bldg
7 Idaho Bldg
8 Atlanta Bldg
9 Colorado Bldg
10 Arizona Bldg
11 Nebraska Bldg
12 Alaska Bldg
13 Ohio Bldg
14 Charter Bldgs
15 Flamsteed Ct
16 Friendly Pl
17 Dover Ct
18 Robinscroft Mews
19 Doleman Ho
20 Plymouth Ho
D5 1 Finch Ho
2 Jubilee The
3 Maitland Cl
4 Ashburnham Retreat

142
A2 1 Bankside Ave
2 Elder Wlk
3 Yew Tree Cl
4 Mill Ho
A3 1 Ellison Ho
2 Pitmaston Ho
3 Aster Ho
4 Windmill Cl
5 Hertmitage The
6 Burnett Ho
7 Lacey Ho
8 Darwin Ho
9 Pearmain Ho
A4 1 Penn Almshouses
2 Jervis Ct
3 Woodville Ct
4 Darnall Ho
5 Renbold Ho
6 Lindsell St
7 Plumbridge St
8 Trinity Gr
9 Hollymount Cl
10 Cade Tyler Ho
11 Robertson Ho
A5 1 Temair Ho
2 Royal Hill Ct
3 Prince of Orange La
4 Lambard Ho
5 St Marks Cl
6 Ada Kennedy Ct
7 Arlington Pl
8 Topham Ho
9 Darnell Ho
10 Hawks Mews
11 Royal Pl
12 Swanne Ho
13 Maribor
14 Serica Ct
15 Queen Elizabeth's Coll
A6 1 Crescent Arc
2 Greenwich Mkt
3 Turnpin La
4 Durnford St
5 Sexton's Ho
6 Bardsley Ho
7 Wardell Ho
8 Clavell St
9 Stanton Ho
10 Macey Ho
11 Boreman Ho
12 Clipper Appts
B6 1 Frobisher Ct
2 Hardy Cotts
3 Palliser Ho
4 Bernard Angell Ho
5 Corvette Sq
6 Travers Ho
7 Maze Hill Lodge
8 Park Place Ho
D5 1 Westcombe Ct
2 Kleffens Ct
3 Ferndale Ct
4 Combe Mews
5 Mandeville Cl
7 Pinelands Cl

143
A5 1 Mary Lawrenson Pl
2 Bradbury Ct
3 Dunstable Ct
4 Wentworth Ho
A6 1 Nethercombe Ho
2 Holywell Cl
B6 1 Capella Ho
2 Collington Ho
C6 1 Warren Wlk
2 Wilson Ho
3 Priory Ho
4 Mar Ho
5 Langhorne Ho
6 Games Ho
7 Erskine Ho
8 Ducie Ho
9 Downe Ho
10 Bayeux Ho
11 Elliscombe Mount
12 Harold Gibbons Ct
13 Mascalls Ct
14 Leila Parnell Pl
15 East Mascalls
16 Birch Tree Ho
17 Cherry Tree Ct
18 Elm Tree Ct
19 Cedar Ct
D5 1 Winchester Ho
2 Brentwood Ho
3 Shenfield Ho
4 Chesterford Ho

144
A4 1 Master Gunner's Pl
2 Ross Ho
3 Dickson Ho
4 Horne Ho
5 Pendlebury Ho
6 Roberts Ho
7 Maple Tree Pl
C6 1 Lawson Ho
2 Mabbett Ho
3 Petrie Ho
4 Memess Path
5 Ruegg Ho
6 Nile Path
7 Leslie Smith Sq
8 Spearman St
9 Siedle Ho
10 Watling Ho
11 O'Neill Path
12 Old Clem Sq
13 Jefferson Wlk
14 Milward Wlk
15 Wordsworth Ho
16 Fenwick Cl
D6 1 Acworth Ho
2 Griffiths Ho
3 Squires Ho
4 Cowen Ho
5 Turton Ho
6 Alford Ho
7 Boxshall Ho
8 MacAllister Ho
9 Marvin Ho
10 Kelham Ho
11 Kimber Ho
12 Maxwell Ho
13 Woodford Ho
14 Penfold Ho

146
A2 1 Wellingfield Ct
2 Woodville Gr
3 Midwinter Cl
4 St Leonards Cl

147
A1 1 Woburn Ct
2 Arundel Ct
3 Longleat Ct
4 Upton Villas
5 Whitehaven Ct
6 Shirley Hts
7 Louise Ct
8 Bethany Ct
B6 1 Bevercote Wlk
3 Lullingstone Rd
4 Benjamin Ct
5 Charton Cl
6 Terence Ct
7 Renshaw Cl
8 Grove Rd
C1 1 Friswell Pl
2 Market Pl
3 Geddes Pl
4 Janet Ct
5 Broadway Sh Ctr
6 Mall The
7 Norwich Pl
8 Pincott Rd

148
A5 1 Stranraer Way
2 Deri Dene Cl
3 Lord Knyvetts Ct
4 Tudor Ct
5 Wessex Ct
6 Vanguard Ho
7 Shackleton Ct
8 Fleetwood Ct
9 Clifton Ct
10 Vickers Ct
11 Bristol Ct
12 Sunderland Ct

153
A3 1 Katharine Rd

2 Sandringham Ct
3 Garfield Rd
4 Arragon Rd
5 Flood La
6 John Wesley Ct
7 King Street Par
8 Thames Eyot
A4 1 Perryn Ct
2 Ivybridge Cl
3 Heritage Ho
4 Brook Ho
5 Neville Ho
6 Latham Cl
7 March Rd
8 Berkley Ct
9 Cole Court Lo
10 Cheltenham Ave
11 Railway App
A5 1 Greenways The
2 Cole Park View
B4 1 Melton Ct
2 Amyand Park Gdns
3 Crown Ct
4 Burrell Ho
5 Owen Ho
6 Brentford Ho
7 Leeson Ho
8 Westbourne Ho
9 Orleans Ct
10 Lebanon Ct
B5 1 Grove The
2 Cumberland Cl
3 Westmorland Cl
4 Sussex Cl
5 Norfolk Cl
6 Nicol Cl
7 Old Lodge Pl
8 Kelvin Ct
9 St Margaret's Ct
10 Park Cotts
11 St Margarets Bsns Ctr
12 Amyand Cotts
C1 1 Benson Ho
2 Bowes Lyon Ho
3 Cavendish Ho
4 Bentinck Ho
5 Clarke Ho
6 Secrett Ho
7 Edwards Ho
8 Field Ho
9 Greig Ho
10 Hawkins Ho
11 Newman Ho
12 Leyland Ho
13 Hornby Ho
14 Hatch Ho
C5 1 Howmic Ct
2 Sefton Lo
3 Ravensbourne Ho
4 Arlington Ct
5 Georgina Ct
6 Trevelyan Ho
7 Caradon Ct
8 Green Hedges
9 Old House Gdns
10 Queens Keep
11 Beresford Ct
12 Langham Ct
13 Poplar Ct
D5 1 Richmond Bridge Mans
2 Heatherdene Mans
3 Kenton Ct
4 Lennox Ho
5 Leicester Ct
6 Turner Ho
7 Blanchard Ho
8 Arosa Rd
9 Ashe Ho
10 Bevan Ct
11 Lawley Ho
12 Darling Ho
13 Richmond Mans
14 Beaulieu Cl
15 Roseleigh Cl
16 Mallard Ct
D6 1 Garrick Cl
2 Old Palace Yd
3 Wardrobe The
4 Maids of Honour Row
5 Hunters Ct
6 Queensberry Ho
7 Green The
8 Old Palace Terr
9 Paved Ct
10 Golden Ct
11 Brewers La
12 Square The
13 Lower George St
14 St James's Cotts
15 Church Wlk
16 Church Ct
17 Victoria Pl
18 Castle Yd
19 Lewis Rd
20 Wakefield Rd
21 Church Terr
22 Warrington Rd
23 Ormond Ave
24 Glovers Lo
25 Holbrooke Pl
26 Northumberland Pl
27 Heron Sq
28 Whittaker Pl
29 Water Lane Ho
30 Riverside Ho
31 St Helena Terr

154
A5 1 Lancaster Cotts
2 Lancaster Mews
3 Bromwich Ho
4 Priors Lo
5 Richmond Hill Ct
6 Glenmore Ho
7 Hillbrow
8 Heathshott
9 Friars Stile Pl
10 Spire Ct
11 Ridgeway
12 Matthias Ct
A6 1 Lichfield Terr
2 Union Ct
3 Carrington Lo
4 Wilton Ct
5 Egerton Ct
6 Beverley Lo
7 Bishop Duppa's Almshouses
8 Regency Wlk
9 Clear Water Ho
10 Onslow Avenue Mans
11 Michels Almshouses
12 Albany Pas
13 Salcombe Villas
B5 1 Chester Cl
2 Evesham Ct
3 Queen's Ct
4 Russell Wlk
5 Charlotte Sq
6 Jones Wlk
7 Hilditch Ho
8 Isabella Ct
9 Damer Ho
10 Eliot Ho
11 Fitzherbert Ho
12 Reynolds Pl
13 Chisholm Rd
B6 1 Alberta Ct
2 Beatrice Rd
3 Lorne Rd
4 York Rd
5 Connaught Rd
6 Albany Terr
7 Kingswood Ct
8 Selwyn Ct
9 Broadhurst Cl

156
A3 1 Farnborough Ho
2 Rushmere Ho
3 Horndean Cl
4 Highcross Way
5 Timsbury Wlk
6 Foxcombe Rd
7 Ryefield Path
8 Greatham Wlk
9 Gosport Ho
10 Stoatley Ho
11 Milland Ho
12 Clanfield Ho
13 Fareham Ho
14 Grayswood Point
A4 1 Woodcott Ho
2 Lyndhurst Ho
3 Wheatley Ho
4 Allbrook Ho
5 Bordon Wlk
6 Chilcombe Ho
7 Vicarage Ct
8 Shawford Ct
9 Eastleigh Wlk
10 Kings Ct
11 Somborne Ho
A6 1 Theodore Ho
2 Nicholas Ho
3 Bonner Ho
4 Downing Ho
5 Jansen Ho
6 Fairfax Ho
7 Devereux Ho
8 David Ho
9 Leigh Ho
10 Clipstone Ho
11 Mallet Ho
12 Arton Wilson Ho
B3 1 Ramsdean Ho
2 Purbrook Ho
3 Portsea Ho
4 Blendworth Point
5 Eashing Point
6 Hindhead Point
7 Hilsea Point
8 Witley Point
9 Buriton Ho
10 Grateley Ho
11 Hascombe Ho
12 Dunhill Point
13 Westmark Point
14 Longmoor Point
15 Cadnam Point
C4 1 Cumberland Ho
2 Devonshire Ho
3 Cornwall Ho
4 Norfolk Ho
5 Leicester Ho
6 Warwick Ho
7 Sutherland Ho
8 Carmarthen Ho
9 Worcester Ho
10 Rutland Ho
11 Paddock Way
C6 1 Inglis Ho
2 Ducie Ho
3 Wharncliffe Ho
4 Stanhope Ho
5 Waldegrave Ho
6 Mildmay Ho
7 Mullens Ho
D3 1 Sandringham Cl
2 Eastwick Ct
3 Oatlands Ct
4 Banning Ho
5 Grantley Ho
6 Caryl Ho
7 Duncombe Ho
8 Chilworth Ct
9 Kent Lo
10 Turner Lo
11 Marlborough
12 Parkland Gdns
13 Lewesdon Cl
14 Pines Ct
15 Ashtead Ct
16 Mynterne Ct
17 Arden
18 Stephen Ct
19 Marsham Ct
20 Doradus Ct
21 Acorns The
22 Heritage Ho
23 Conifer Ct
24 Spencer Ho
25 Chartwell
26 Blenheim
27 Chivelston
28 Greenfield Ho
29 Oakman Ho
30 Radley Lo
31 Simon Lo
32 Admirals Ct
D4 1 Brett Ho
2 Brett House Cl
3 Sylva Ct
4 Ross Ct
5 Potterne Cl
6 Stourhead Cl
7 Fleur Gates
8 Greenwood
D5 1 Balmoral Cl
2 Glenalmond Ho
3 Selwyn Ho
4 Keble Ho
5 Bede Ho
6 Gonville Ho
7 Magdalene Ho
8 Armstrong Ho
9 Newnham Ho
10 Somerville Ho
11 Balliol Ho
12 Windermere
13 Little Combe Cl
14 Classinghall Ho
15 Chalford Ct
16 Garden Royal
17 South Ct
18 Anne Kerr Ct
19 Ewhurst
D6 1 Geneva Ct
2 Laurel Ct
3 Cambalt Ho
4 Langham Ct
5 Lower Pk
6 King's Keep
7 Whitnell Ct
8 Whitehead Ho
9 Halford Ho
10 Humphry Ho
11 Jellicoe Ho

157
A3 1 William Harvey Ho
2 Highview Ct
3 Cameron Ct
4 Galgate Cl
5 Green Ho The
6 King Charles Wlk
7 Florys Ct
8 Augustus Ct
9 Albert Ct
10 Hertford Lo
11 Mortimer Lo
12 Allenswood
13 Ambleside
14 Hansler Ct
15 Roosevelt Ct
A6 1 Claremont
2 Downside
3 Cavendish Cl
4 Ashcombe Ct
5 Carltons The
6 Espirit Ho
7 Millbrooke Ct
8 Coysh Ct
9 Keswick Hts
10 Lincoln Ho
11 Avon Ct
B6 1 Keswick Broadway
2 Burlington Mews
3 Cambria Lo
4 St Stephen's Gdns
5 Atlantic Ho
6 Burton Lo
7 Manfred Ct
8 Meadow Bank
9 Hooper Ho
10 Aspire Bld
C6 1 Pembridge Pl
2 Adelaide Rd
3 London Ct
4 Windsor Ct
5 Westminster Ct
6 Fullers Ho
7 Bridge Pk
8 Lambeth Ct
9 Milton Ct
10 Norfolk Mans
11 Francis Snary Lo
12 Bush Cotts
13 Downbury Mews
14 Newton's Yd
D6 1 Fairfield Ct
2 Blackmore Ho
3 Lancaster Mews
4 Cricketers Mews
5 College Mews
6 Arndale Wlk

158
A2 1 Beemans Row
2 St Andrew's Ct
3 Townsend Mews
4 Sheringham Mews

159
A2 1 Upper Tooting Park Mans
2 Cecil Mans
3 Marius Mans
4 Boulevard The
5 Elmfield Mans
6 Holdernesse Rd
7 Lumiere Ct
A3 1 Heslop Ct
2 St James's Terr
3 Boundaries Mans
4 Station Par
5 Old Dairy Mews
A4 1 Hollies Way
2 Endlesham Ct
A5 1 Rayne Ho
2 St Anthony's Ct
3 Earlsthorpe Mews
4 Nightingale Mans
B3 1 Holbeach Mews
2 Hildreth Street Mews
3 Coalbrook Mans
4 Hub Buildings The
5 Metropolis Apartments
B4 1 Meyer Ho
2 Faraday Ho
3 Hales Ho
4 Frankland Ho
5 Graham Ho
6 Gibbs Ho
7 Dalton Ho
8 Ainslie Wlk
9 Rokeby Ho
10 Caistor Ho
11 Ivanhoe Ho
12 Catherine Baird Ct
13 Marmion Ho
14 Devonshire Ct
15 Blueprint Apartments
C4 1 Limerick Ct
2 Homewoods
3 Jewell Ho
4 Glanville Ho
5 Dan Bryant Ho
6 Olding Ho
7 Quennel Ho
8 Weir Ho
9 West Ho
10 Neville Ct
11 Friday Grove Mews
C5 1 Joseph Powell Cl
2 Cavendish Mans
3 Westlands Terr
4 Cubitt Ho
5 Hawkesworth Ho
6 Normanton Ho
7 Eastman Ho
8 Couchman Ho
9 Poynders Ct
10 Selby Ho
11 Valentine Ho
12 Gorham Ho
13 Deauville Mans
14 Deauville Ct
C6 1 Timothy Cl
2 Shaftesbury Mews
3 Brook Ho
4 Grover Ho
5 Westbrook Ho
6 Hewer Ho
7 Batten Ho
8 Mandeville Ho
9 George Beare Lo
D3 1 Sinclair Ho
2 MacGregor Ho
3 Ingle Ho
4 St Andrews Mews
D4 1 Riley Ho
2 Bennett Ho
3 White Ho
4 Rodgers Ho
5 Dumphreys Ho
6 Homan Ho
7 Prendergast Ho
8 Hutchins Ho
9 Whiteley Ho
10 Tresidder Ho
11 Primrose Ct
12 Angus Ho
13 Currie Ho
D5 1 Parrington Ho
2 Savill Ho
3 Blackwell Ho
4 Bruce Ho
5 Victoria Ct
6 Victoria Ho
7 Belvedere Ct
8 Ingram Lo
9 Viney Ct
10 Bloomsbury Ho
11 Belgravia Ho
12 Barnsbury Ho

160
A1 1 De Montfort Ct
2 Leigham Hall Par
3 Leigham Hall
4 Endsleigh Mans
5 John Kirk Ho
6 Raebarn Ct
7 Wavel Ct
8 Homeleigh Ct
9 Howland Ho
10 Beauclerk Ho
11 Bertrand Ho
12 Drew Ho
13 Dowes Ho
14 Dunton Ho
15 Raynald Ho
16 Sackville Ho
17 Thurlow Ho
18 Astoria Mans
A2 1 Wyatt Park Mans
2 Broadlands Mans
3 Stonehill's Mans
4 Streatleigh Par
5 Dorchester Ct
6 Picture Ho
A3 1 Beaumont Ho
2 Christchurch Ho
3 Staplefield Cl
4 Chipstead Ho
5 Coulsdon Ho
6 Conway Ho
7 Telford Avenue Mans
8 Telford Parade Mans
9 Wavertree Ct
10 Hartswood Ho
11 Wray Ho
A4 1 Picton Ho
2 Rigg Ho
3 Watson Ho
4 MacArthur Ho
5 Sandon Ho
6 Thorold Ho
7 Pearce Ho
8 Mudie Ho
9 Miller Ho
10 Lycett Ho
11 Lafone Ho
12 Lucraft Ho
13 Freeman Ho
14 New Park Par
15 Argyll Ct
16 Dumbarton Ct
17 Kintyre Ct
18 Cotton Ho
19 Crossman Hos
20 Cameford Ct
21 Parsons Ho
22 Brindley Ho
23 Arkwright Ho
24 Perry Ho
25 Brunel Ho
26 New Park Ct
27 Tanhurst Ho
28 Hawkshaw Cl
A6 1 King's Mews
2 Clapham Court Terr
3 Clapham Ct
4 Clapham Park Terr
5 Pembroke Ho
6 Stevenson Ho
7 Queenswood Ct
8 Oak Tree Ct
9 Park Lofts
10 Ashby Mews
B1 1 Carisbrooke Ct
2 Pembroke Lo
3 Willow Ct
4 Poplar Ct
5 Mountview
6 Spa View
B3 1 Charlwood Ho
2 Earlswood Ho
3 Balcombe Ho
4 Claremont Cl
5 Holbrook Ho
6 Gwynne Ho
7 Kynaston Ho
8 Tillman Ho
9 Regents Lo
10 Hazelmere Ct
11 Dykes Ct
B4 1 Archbishop's Pl
2 Witley Ho
3 Outwood Ho
4 Dunsfold Ho
5 Deepdene Lo
6 Warnham Ho
7 Albury Lo
8 Tilford Ho
9 Elstead Ho
10 Thursley Ho
11 Brockham Ho
12 Capel Lo
13 Leith Ho
14 Fairview Ho
15 Weymouth Ct
16 Ascalon Ct
17 China Mews
18 Rush Common Mews
B6 1 Beatrice Ho
2 Florence Ho
3 Evelyn Ho
4 Diana Ho
5 Brixton Hill Ct
6 Austin Ho
7 Manor Ct
8 Camsey Ho
9 Romer Ho
10 Gale Ho
11 Byrne Ho
12 Farnfield Ho
13 Marchant Ho
14 Rainsford Ho
15 Springett Ho
16 Mannering Ho
17 Waldron Ho
C3 1 Valens Ho
2 Loveday Ho
3 Strode Ho
4 Ethelworth Ct
5 Harbin Ho
6 Brooks Ho
7 Godolphin Ho
8 Sheppard Ho
9 McCormick Ho
10 Taylor Ho
11 Saunders Ho
12 Talcott Path
13 Derrick Ho
14 Williams Ho
15 Baldwin Ho
16 Churston Cl
17 Neil Wates Cres
18 Burnell Ho
19 Portland Ho
C4 1 Ellacombe Ho
2 Booth Ho
3 Hathersley Ho
4 Brereton Ho
5 Holdsworth Ho
6 Dearmer Ho
7 Cherry Cl
8 Greenleaf Cl
9 Longford Wlk
10 Scarlette Manor Wlk
11 Chandlers Way
12 Upgrove Manor Way
13 Ropers Wlk
14 Tebbs Ho
15 Bell Ho
16 Worthington Ho
17 Courier Ho
18 Mackie Ho
19 Hamers Ho
20 Kelyway Ho
21 Harriet Tubman Cl
22 Estoria Cl
23 Leckhampton Pl
24 Scotia Rd
25 Charles Haller St
26 Sidmouth Ho
27 Hunter Ct
28 Onslow Lo
29 William Winter Ct
30 Langthorne Lo
C5 1 Eccleston Ho
2 Scarsbrook Ho
3 Purser Ho
4 Rudhall Ho
5 Hardham Ho
6 Heywood Ho
7 Haworth Ho
8 Birch Ho
9 Lansdell Ho
10 Lomley Ho
11 Laughton Ho
12 Woodruff Ho
13 Bascome St
14 Dudley Mews
15 Herbert Mews
16 Blades Lo
17 Dick Shepherd Ct
18 Charman Ho
19 Morden Ho
20 Bishop Ct
21 Blackburn Ct
22 Leigh Ct
23 John Conwey Ho
24 Bristowe Cl
C6 1 Crownstone Ct
2 Brockwell Ct
3 Nevena Ct

4 St George's Residences
5 Hanover Mans
6 Fleet Ho
7 Langbourne Ho
8 Turnmill Ho
9 Walker Mews
10 Cossar Mews
11 Carter Ho
D1 1 Thanet Ho
2 Chapman Ho
3 Beaufoy Ho
4 Easton Ho
5 Roberts Ho
6 Lloyd Ct
7 Kershaw Ho
8 Wakeling Ho
9 Edridge Ho
10 Jeston Ho
11 Lansdowne Wood Cl
12 Rotary Lo

161
B2 1 Welldon Ct
2 Coppedhall
3 Shackleton Ct
4 Bullfinch Ct
5 Gannet Ct
6 Fulmar Ct
7 Heron Ct
8 Petrel Ct
9 Falcon Ct
10 Eagle Ct
11 Dunnock Ct
12 Dunlin Ct
13 Cormorant Ct
14 Oak Lodge
15 Corfe Lodge
C6 1 Velde Way
2 Delft Way
3 Arnhem Way
4 Isel Way
5 Kempis Way
6 Terborch Way
7 Steen Way
8 Deventer Cres
9 Nimegen Way
10 Hilversum Cres
11 St Barnabas Cl

162
A1 1 Tunbridge Ct
2 Harrogate Ct
3 Bath Ct
4 Leamington Ct
5 Porlock Ho
6 Cissbury Ho
7 Eddisbury Ho
8 Dundry Ho
9 Silbury Ho
10 Homildon Ho
11 Highgate Ho
12 Richmond Ho
13 Pendle Ho
14 Tynwald Ho
15 Wirrall Ho
16 Greyfriars
A6 1 Dorothy Charrington Ho
2 Keswick Ct
3 Kendall Ct
4 Halliwell Ct
B1 1 River Ho
2 Fordington Ho
3 Arbury Terr
4 Woodbury Ho
5 Gainsborough Mews
6 Forest Hill Ct
B2 1 Bromleigh Ct
2 Parfew Ct
3 Thetford Ct
4 Attleborough Ct
5 Dunton Ct
6 Frobisher Ct
7 Julian Taylor Path
8 Grizedale Terr
9 Worsley Ho
C1 1 Forest Lo
2 Sydenham Park Mans
3 William Wood Ho
C2 1 Fitzwilliam Hts
2 Taymount Grange
3 McLeod Ho
4 Featherstone Ave
5 Kingswear Ho
6 Salcombe Ho
7 Glynwood Ct
C3 1 Harlech Ct
2 Angela Ct
3 Westwood Ct
4 New Belmont Ho
5 Pearcefield Ave
6 Waldram Pl
7 Horniman Grange
8 South View Ct
9 Heron Ct
10 Katherine Ct
D1 1 Standlake Point
2 Radcot Point
3 Newbridge Point
4 Northmoor
5 Kelmscott
6 Radnor Ct
7 Heathwood Point
8 Ashleigh Point
9 Deepdene Point
10 Rosemount Point
11 Woodfield Ho
12 Clairville Point
13 Trevenna Ho
14 Hyndewood
D2 1 Pikethorne
2 Andrew Ct
3 Valentine Ct
4 Soper Cl

164
C4 1 Beaumont Terr
2 Littlebourne
3 Verdant Ct
D2 1 Kinross Ct
2 Montrose Ct
3 Rattray Ct
4 Rothesay Ct
D3 1 Edinburgh Ct
2 McMillan Ct
3 Rowallan Ct
4 Meridian Ct
5 Braemar Ct
6 Barrow Ct
7 Blair Ct
8 Darlington Ct
9 Hamilton Ct
10 Inverness Ct
11 Oak Cottage Cl
12 Willow Cl
13 Keswick Ct

165
A4 1 Swallow Ct
2 Honeysuckle Ct
3 Venture Ct
4 Cheriton Ct
5 Askham Lo
6 Syon Lo

166
A2 1 Portland Cres
2 Bourdillon Ct
3 Hillary Ct
4 Tenzing Ct
5 John Hunt Ct
6 Everest Ct
A6 1 Horsfeld Gdns
2 Foxhole Rd
C5 1 Roper St
2 Arcade The
3 Elm Terr
4 Imber Ct
5 Ashcroft Ct
6 Fairlands Ct
7 Brecon Ct
8 Newlands Ct
9 Harvard Ct
10 Garden Ct
11 Chiltern Ct
12 Fairway Ct

167
A2 1 Mervyn Stockwood Ho
2 Michael Marshall Ho
3 Keith Sutton Ho

168
A1 1 Ham Shades Cl
2 Aspen Ho
3 Medlar Ho
4 Cornel Ho
5 Stanton Ct
6 Hornbeam Ho
7 Beech Ho
8 Spindle Ho
10 Hunters Lo
11 Edam Ct
12 Monica James Ho
13 Oak Ho
14 Crescent Ct
15 Freeland Ct
16 Montague Ct
17 Windsor Ct
B5 1 Rochester Cl
2 Cobham Cl
3 Shorne Cl
4 Warne Pl

169
C4 1 Close The
2 Parkhurst Gdns
3 Chichester Ct
4 Pound Green Ct

170
B6 1 Station Par
2 Queens La
3 Copthorne Chase
4 Canterbury Ct
5 Church Par
C5 1 St Matthew's Ct
2 Dencliffe
3 Crest Ho
4 Bourne Ho
5 Elms The
6 Roxeth Ct
7 Rowland Hill Almshouses

171
A3 1 Viscount Ct
2 Blackthorne Ct
D3 1 Bishops Ct
2 Ash Lo
3 Lime Lo
4 Oak Lo
5 Elm Ct
6 Willow Lo
7 Sycamore Lo
8 Priscilla Ho
9 Sunbury Cross Ctr
10 Isobel Ho

173
A6 1 Gabriel Cl
2 Metcalfe Wlk
3 Dunmow Cl
4 Burgess Cl
5 Chamberlain Wlk
C2 1 Sherbourne Ct
2 Somerset Ct
3 Jubilee Ho
4 Rushbury Ct
5 Blenheim Ct
6 Hemming Cl
7 Ryedale Ct
8 Norman Ct
C4 1 Begonia Pl
2 Snowdrop Cl
3 Hyacinth Cl
4 Cyclamen Cl
5 Jonquil Gdns
6 Gladioli Cl
7 Daffodil Pl
8 Partridge Rd
D4 1 Acorn Cl
2 Wolsey Ho
3 Lytton Ho
4 Wren Ho
5 Faraday Ho

174
C5 1 Knaggs Ho
2 Keeling
3 Elizabeth Ct
4 Oakhurst Cl
5 Charles Ct
6 Harold Ct
D5 1 Waldegrave Ct
2 Luther Mews
3 Alice Mews
4 Gresham Ho
5 Traherne Lo
6 Fishers Ct
7 Waterhouse Ct
8 Oval Ct
9 Walpole Pl
10 Walpole Cres
11 Bychurch End

175
A5 1 Cherrywood Ct
2 Cambridge Ho
3 Cairngorm Cl
4 Gleneagles Ct
5 Christchurch Ave
6 Hales Ct
7 Plough La
8 Springfield Rd
9 Royal Oak Mews
10 Trinder Mews
C3 1 Belgravia Ho
2 Ash Ho
3 Crieff Ct
4 Maples The
D2 1 Wick Ho
2 Spinnaker Ct
3 Osiers Ct
4 Trent Ho
5 Arun Ho
6 Medway Ho
7 Avon Ho
8 Tyne Ho
9 Clyde Ho
10 Mersey Ct
11 Severn Ct
12 John William Cl
13 Henry Macaulay Ave
14 Seymour Lo
15 Falmouth Ho
16 Earlsfield Ho
D6 1 Byron Ct
2 Coleridge Ct
3 Tennyson Ct
4 Herrick Ct
5 Spenser Ct
6 Marlowe Ct
7 Brooke Ct
8 Gray Ct
9 Shelley Ct
10 Pope Ct
11 Dryden Ct

176
A1 1 Cleave's Almshos
2 Perry Ct
3 Drovers Ct
4 Gough Ho
5 Eden Wlk
6 Alderman Judge Mall
7 Lady Booth Rd
8 Caversham Ho
9 Littlefield Cl
10 Bentall Sh Ctr The
11 Adams Wlk
12 Ceres Ct
A2 1 Regents Ct
2 Walter St
3 Canbury Bsns Pk
4 Sigrist Sq
5 Ashway Ctr
6 Warwick Ho
7 Hedingham Ho
8 Alexander Ho
9 Bramber Ho
10 Carisbrooke Ho
11 Dartmouth Ho
12 Garland Ho
A3 1 Walton Ho
2 Berkeley Cl
3 Canbury Ct
4 King's Penny Ho
B1 1 Vicarage Ho
2 Rayleigh Ct
3 School Pas
4 Chippenham
5 Camm Gdns
B2 1 Onslow Ho
2 Dowler Ct
B3 1 McDonald Ho
2 Elm Ho
3 Dale Ct
4 York Ho
5 Florence Ho
6 Florence Rd
7 Roupell Ho
8 Delft Ho
C1 1 Wimpole Cl
2 Burwell
3 Caldecote
4 Fordham
5 Connington
6 Chesterton Terr
7 Westwick
8 Eureka Rd
9 Fulbourn
10 Comberton
11 Madingley
12 Grantchester
13 Cambridge Grove Rd
14 Oakington
15 Harston
16 Graveley
17 Croxton
18 Brinkley
19 Impington
20 Shelford
21 Duxford
22 Cascadia Ho
C2 1 Farthings The
2 Brae Ct
3 Princeton Mews
4 Station App
C3 1 Queen's Ct
2 St George's Rd
3 Park Road Ho
4 Dagmar Rd
5 Tapping Cl
6 Arthur Rd
7 Borough Rd
8 Belvedere Ct
9 Braywick Ct
10 Dean Ct
11 Rowan Ct
12 Richmond Ct
13 Sunningdale Ct
14 Hawker Ct
15 Cromwell Ct
16 Kings Ct
D2 1 Trevallyn Lo
2 Chichester Ho
3 Beechcroft
4 Cedars The
5 Liddlesdale Ho W
6 Liddlesdale Ho E
7 Deerhurst
8 Brockworth
9 Alderton
D3 1 Bramley Ho
2 Abinger Ho
3 Thursley Ho
4 Ridge Ho
5 Clone The
6 Mount Ct
7 Hillside Ct
8 Hill Ct
9 Royal Ct
10 Lakeside
11 High Ashton
D4 1 Godstone Ho
2 Hambledon Ho
3 Kingswood Ho
4 Leigh Ho
5 Milton Ho
6 Newdigate Ho
7 Farleigh Ho
8 Ockley Ho
9 Effingham Ho
10 Dunsfold Ho
11 Pirbright Ho
12 Clandon Ho
13 Ripley Ho

178
C3 1 Roskeen Ct
2 Chimneys Ct
3 Aston Ct
4 Rosemary Cotts
5 Victoria Lo
D2 1 Beaufort Ho
2 Kinnear Ct
3 Ranmore Ct
4 Lantern Ct
5 Crescent Ho
D3 1 Kings View Ct
2 Wimbledon Cl
3 Beryl Harding Ho
4 Upton Ct
5 Marian Lo
6 Terraces The
7 Lanherne Ho
8 Cumberland Cl
9 Thaxted Pl
10 Rathbone Ho
11 Princess Ct
12 Claremont Lo
13 Downs Ct
14 Ravenscar Lo
15 Haverley
16 Savona Cl
17 Beaumont Ct
18 Gordon Ct
D5 1 Lancaster Pl
2 Haygarth Pl
3 Allington Cl
4 Homefield Pl

179
A3 1 Stretford Ct
2 Brunswick Ct
3 Pavilion Ct
4 Louie Black Ho
5 Warwick Ho
6 Erica Ho
7 Adyar Ct
8 Thornton Lo
9 Ash Ct
10 Broughton Ho
11 Naomi Watts Ho
12 Wellesley Ho
13 Mayfair Ct
A4 1 Walham Rise
2 Grosvenor Ct
3 Sovereign Ho
4 Holly Lo
5 Florence Ct
6 Linden Cotts
7 Sheep Walk Mews
8 Emerson Ct
9 Hill Ct
10 Powell Ho
B4 1 Aspen Lo
2 Gladebury Ct
3 Centre Court Sh Ctr
B5 1 Lawns The
2 Prentice Ct
3 Catherine Ct
4 Woodlodge
5 Pixham Ct
6 Lake Cl
7 Westwood Ct
8 Brambles The
9 Lismore
10 Rose Ct
11 Worcester Rd
12 Leopold Ct
C3 1 Ashbourne Terr
2 Sir Cyril Black Way
3 Willows Ct
4 Harefield Ct
5 Broadway Ho
6 Viscount Point
7 Carrington Ho
8 Cloisters Ho
9 Downing Ho
10 Bickley Ct
11 Palmerston Gr
12 Gladstone Ct
13 Warrington Ct
D2 1 Gilbert Cl
2 Becket Cl
3 Priory Cl
4 Hudson Ct
5 Ryder Ho
6 Eleanor Ho
7 Ramsey Ho
8 Colborne Ct
9 Falcon Ho
10 Spur Ho
D3 1 Hamilton Road Mews
2 Dowman Cl
3 Burleigh Lo
4 Horatio Ho

180
A2 1 Tanner Ho
2 May Ct
3 Marsh Ct
4 Lovell Ho
A3 1 Fiske Ct
2 Mellor Ct
3 Olive Rd
4 Allerton Ho
5 Victory Road Mews
6 Will Miles Ct
7 Vanguard Ho
8 Mychell Ho
9 Merton Pl
10 De Burgh Ho
11 Norfolk Ho
12 Hotham Road Mews
B1 1 Ripley Ct
2 Brooklands Ct
3 Horner La
B2 1 Yarborough Rd
2 Vista Ho
3 Prospect Ho
4 Independence Ho
5 Nonsuch Ho
6 Baron Ho
C2 1 Linford Ct
2 Searle Ct
3 Gunnell Ct
4 Wells Ct
5 Hartley Ct
C3 1 Shere Ct
2 Goodwin Ct
3 Cairn Ho
C4 1 Douglas Ct
2 Lannock Ct
3 Gateway Ho
4 Wellington Ct
C5 1 Robertson Ho
2 Dewar Ho
3 Jean Ho
4 Marion Ct
5 Gravenel Gdns
6 Palladino Ho
D1 1 Elms Cotts
2 Sibthorp Rd
3 Armfield Cotts
4 Sir Arthur Bliss Ct
5 Fountain Ho
6 Gladstone Ho
7 Chart Ho

181
A1 1 Kennedy Cl
2 Pearce Cl
3 Mainwaring Ct
4 Coningsby Ct
5 Laburnum Ct
6 Beaumont Ct
7 Penfold Ct
8 Fitch Ct
10 Lea Cotts
A5 1 Osborne Terr
2 Limetree Wlk
C5 1 Tyers Ho
2 Boothby Ho
3 Adams Ho
4 Burney Ho
5 Boswell Ho
6 Chesterfield Ho
7 Garrick Ho
8 Levett Ho
9 Shelburne Ho
10 Marchmont Ho
11 Ryland Ho
12 Flather Cl
13 Bank Bldgs
14 Carriage Pl
15 Locarno Cl
C6 1 Walmsley Ho
2 Chambers Ho
3 Fordyce Ho
4 Percy Ho
5 Langton Ho
6 Moorfields Ct
7 Hidaburn Ct
8 Salter Ho
9 Tailors Ct
10 Yew Tree Lo
D6 1 William Dyce Mews
2 Doctor Johnson Ho

182
A3 1 Spa Central
A5 1 Oakdene Ct
2 Hopton Par
3 Merton Lo
4 Bouverie Ct
5 Deerhurst
6 Farnan Hall
A6 1 Central Mans
2 Central Par
B3 1 Marqueen Twrs
2 Shirley Ct
3 Sinclair Ho
4 Vantage Ct
5 Pavilion Ct
B6 1 Ashleigh Ho
2 Roseneath Pl
3 Shenley Ho
4 Blytheswood Pl
C5 1 Parkhill Ho
2 Ash Ct
3 Alder Ct
4 Beech Ct
5 Acacia Ct
6 Blackthorn Ct
7 Cypress Ct
8 Hawthorn Ct
9 Hazel Ct
10 Sycamore Ct
11 Maple Ct
12 Laburnam Ct
13 Fern Lo
14 Colyton La
C6 1 James Boswell Cl
2 St Albans Ho
3 Suffolk Ct
4 Rockhampton Cl
5 Delphian Ct
6 Heather Ct

D5 1 Woodcote Pl
2 Joe Hunte Ct
3 Cork Tree Ho
4 Lake Ho
5 Cedars Ho
6 Portobello Ho
7 Cooper Ho
8 Farnsworth Ho
9 Hook Ho
10 Crest The
11 Renshaw Ho
12 Ruscoe Ho
13 Sardeson Ho
D6 1 William Wilberforce Ho
2 William Marsden Ho
3 Samuel Ho
4 Morris Stephany Ho
5 Church Ct

183

A6 1 Moore Ho
2 Chaucer Ho
3 Bushell Ho
4 Bligh Ho
5 Hobbs Rd
6 Hogarth Ho
7 Goodbehere Ho
8 Astley Ho
9 Elder Gdns
10 Elderberry Gr
11 Pavement The
12 Dunkirk St
B6 1 Josef Perrin Ho
2 Jean Humbert Ho
3 Charles Staunton Ho
4 Violette Szabo Ho
5 Lilian Rolfe Ho
6 Odette Ho
7 Robert Gerard Ho
8 St Bernards Cl
9 Champness Cl
10 Pennington Cl
11 Queenswood Ct
C4 1 Northwood Way
2 High Limes
3 Valley Prospect
4 Plane Tree Wlk
5 City Prospect
6 Bankside Way
7 Ridge Way
8 Rochdale
9 Barrington Wlk
10 Gatestone Ct
11 Childs La
12 Carberry Rd
13 Norwood Heights Sh Ctr
C5 1 Oakdene
2 Thorsden Way
3 Oakfield Gdns
4 Georgetown Cl
5 Bridgetown Cl
6 Mountbatten Cl
7 Brabourne Cl
8 Alexandra Wlk
9 Compton Ct
10 Battenburg Wlk
11 Burma Terr
12 Wiseman Ct
C6 1 Linley Ct
2 Mellor Ho
3 Whitfield Ct
4 Michaelson Ho
5 Holberry Ho
6 Hovenden Ho
7 Huntley Ho
8 Telfer Ho
9 Markham Ho
10 Oldham Ho
11 Parnall Ho
12 Pierson Ho
13 Roper Ho
14 Roundell Ho
15 Sawyer Ho
16 Ransford Ho
17 Carmichael Ho
18 Bonne Marche Terr Mews
D3 1 Hetley Gdns
2 Claybourne Mews
3 Highland Lo
4 Mason Ct
5 Kendall Ct
6 High View
D5 1 Glenhurst Ct
2 Marlowe Ct
3 Grenville Ct
4 Raleigh Ct
5 Beechwoods Ct
6 Burntwood View

184

A3 1 Hanover Ct
2 Brunswick Ct
3 New Church Ct
4 Regency Ct
7 Owen Wlk
8 Bargrove Cl
9 Beaver Cl
B2 1 Dorset Ho
2 Collingwood Cl
3 Chartwell Way
4 Essex Twr
5 Appletree Cl
6 Ditton Pl
7 Kelvin Ct
8 Readman Ct
9 Glen Ct
10 Kingsbridge Ho
11 Carlton Ct
12 Benhurst Ct
13 Carole Ho
14 Dover Ho
15 Bettswood Ct
B3 1 Avery Ct
2 Rossal Ct
3 Oakdene Lo
4 Ridgemount Cl
5 Blakewood Ct
6 Trenholme Cl
7 Oakleigh Ct
8 Upchurch Cl
9 Devon Ho
10 Westmoreland Terr
11 Oakfield Road Ind Est
B5 1 Ragwort Ct
2 Firs The
3 Wingham Ho
4 Seath Ho
5 Ripley Ho
6 Lathwood Ho
7 Hurst Ho
8 George Ho
9 Browne Ho
10 Beacon Ho
11 Bailey Ho
12 Agate Ho
C2 1 Challin St
2 Rutland Ho
3 Pine Cl
C3 1 Watermen's Sq
2 St John's Cotts
3 Gladstone Mews
4 Middlesex Ho
5 Bethesda Ct
6 Ospringe Cl
7 Goudhurst Ho
8 Walmer Ho
9 Strood Ho
10 Greatstone Ho
11 John Baird Ho
C4 1 Midhurst
2 Oliver Ct
3 Victoria Ct
4 Wakefield Ct
5 Fountain Ct
6 Newlands Ct
C6 1 Homewalk Ho
2 Grace Path
3 Sycamore Ct
4 Sydenham Station App
5 Greenways
6 Faircroft
D3 1 Groombridge Ho
2 Provincial Terr
3 Smithers Ho
4 West Ho
5 Swallows Ct
6 Hornbeam Ho
7 Blenheim Centre

185

A1 1 Clock House Ct
2 Blandford Ave
3 Old School Cl
4 Lynsted Ct
5 Florence Rd
A6 1 Paxton Ct
2 Kenton Ct
3 Grove Ct
4 Shirley Lo
B2 1 Ashton Ct
2 Coombe Ct
3 Fontaine Ct
4 Richfield Ct
5 Sheridan Way
C1 1 Christ Church Rd
2 Lea Rd
3 Stanmore Terr
C2 1 Erindale Ct
2 Montgomerie Ct
3 Rebecca Ct
4 Sycamore Ct
5 Willow Ct
6 Marlborough Ct
7 Bearsted Terr
8 Berwick Ct
9 Wooderson Ct
10 Beck River Pk
11 Waterside
C3 1 Gardenia Ct
2 Brackendale Ct
3 Daniel Ct
4 Moliner Ct
5 Chartwell Lo
6 Randmore Ct
7 Dover Ho
8 Lucerne Ct
9 Malling Ho
10 Westerham Lo
11 Brasted Lo
12 Milton Ho
13 Bradsole Ho
14 Sandgate Ho
15 Adelaide Ct
16 Nettlestead Cl
17 Warren Ct
18 Alton Ct
19 Rockingham Ct
20 Camellia Ct
21 Sinclair Ct
22 Regents Ct
23 Minshull Pl
24 South Park Ct
D1 1 Parkside
2 Tudors The
3 Oakbrook
4 Tara Ct
5 Redlands The
6 Cambria
7 Hillworth
8 Kelsey Gate
9 Burrells
10 Lincoln Lo
11 Courtlands
12 Fairleas
13 Ashdown Cl
14 Barons
D2 1 Clifton Ct
2 Mayfair Ct
3 Lait Ho
4 Fire Station Mews
D4 1 Warner Ho
2 Clifford Ho
3 Lloyd Ho
4 Thurston Ho
5 Byron Ho
6 Blake Ho
7 Keats Ho

186

A2 1 White House Ct
2 Hunters The
3 Sandringham Ct
4 Glenhurst
5 Copperfields
6 Westgate Ct
A6 1 Dedham Ho
2 Flatford Ho
3 Langthorne Ct
4 Radley Ct
5 Hoover Ho
6 Brunner Ho
7 Waterer Ho
8 Marriott Ho
9 Bourbon Ho
B5 1 Longford Ho
2 Ingrebourne Ho
3 Brent Ho
4 Darent Ho
5 Beverley Ho
6 Wandle Ho
7 Rythe Ho
8 Ember Ho
9 Crane Ho
10 Ravensbourne Ho
C1 1 Warwick Ct
2 Maplehurst
3 Mount Arlington
4 Arundel Ct
D2 1 Weston Gr
2 Gibbs Ho
3 Longfield
4 Hammelton Ct
5 Bracken Hill Cl
6 Townend Ct
7 Treversh Ct
8 Cameron Ho
9 Woodlands Ct
10 Blythwood Pk
11 Bromley Pk
D3 1 Homecoppice Ho
2 Linden Ct
3 Kimberley Gate
4 Inglewood Ct
5 Mavery Ct
6 Glen Ct
7 Marlborough Ct
8 Cawston Ct
9 Blendon Path

187

A1 1 St James Ct
A2 1 Mitchell Way
2 Harrington Ho
3 Newman Ct
4 Uno Apartments
5 Bromley Ho
B2 1 Dainton Cl
2 Rothwell Ct
3 St Timothy's Mews
4 Andringham Lo
5 Kendall Lo
6 Summerfield
7 Winston Ct
8 Vogue Ct
9 Laurels The
C1 1 Westland Lo
2 Eastland Ct
3 Dairsie Ct
4 Northlands
5 Beechfield Cotts
6 Oasis The
7 Cromarty Ct
8 Silverstone Ct

188

A6 1 Beaconsfield Par
2 Cranley Par
3 Kimmeridge Gdns
4 King & Queen Cl
C2 1 Ivybridge Ct
2 Greenbank Lo

190

A6 2 Cyril Lo
3 Hazlemere
4 Milton Lo
5 Marlin Ct
6 Conroy Ct
7 Glenwood Ct
8 Culverton Ct
9 Holmbury Manor
B1 1 Swanscombe Ho
2 Haverstock Ct
3 Arrandene Ho
4 Broomfield Ho
5 Headley Ho
6 Kenley Ho
7 Ladywell Ho
B6 1 Chudleigh
2 Wimborne
3 St John's Par
4 Holly Ct
5 Rectory Bsns Ctr

193

D1 1 Orchard Ct
2 Bridge Ct

197

A2 1 Raleigh Ho
2 Leicester Ho
3 Gresham Ho
D2 1 Napier Ct
2 Darlington Ho
3 Charminster Ct
4 Mulberry Ct
5 Leander Ct
6 Clinton Ho
7 Hollingsworth Ct
8 Gloucester Ct
9 Palmerston Ct
10 Redwood Ct
11 Hursley Ct
12 Westmorland Ct
13 Lawson Ct
14 Alexander Ct
15 Winton Ct
16 Sydenham Ho
17 Caroline Ct
18 Ellswood Ct
19 Masefield Ct

198

A1 1 Ash Tree Cl
2 Shrubbery The
3 Malvern Ct
4 Gate Ho
5 Yew Tree Ho
A3 1 Station App
2 South Bank Lo
3 Bramshott Ct
4 Pandora Ct
5 Wellington Ct
6 Glenbuck Ct
7 Leighton Ho
8 Oakhill Ct
9 Downs View Lo
10 Osborne Ct
11 Surbiton Par
12 Woodgate Ho
13 Godwyn Ho
14 Ashby Ho
A4 1 Effingham Lo
2 Maple Ho
3 Channon Ct
4 Falconhurst
5 Ferndown
6 Viceroy Lo
7 Frensham Ho
8 Kingsley Ho
9 Rannoch Ct
10 Stratton Ct
11 Moray Ho
12 Dulverton Ct
13 Westerham
14 Hill Ct
15 Assheton-Bennett Ho
16 Hatfield Ho
17 Oxford Ct
18 Pennington Lo
19 Austin Ho
20 Wentworth Ct
21 Priory The
22 Sheraton The
23 Christopher Ct
24 Hobart Ho
25 St Mark's Hts
A5 1 Marquis Ct
2 Garrick Ho
A6 1 College Rdbt
2 Edinburgh Ct
3 Weston Ct
4 Grebe Terr
5 Heron Ct
6 Agar Ho
7 St James' Ct
8 Grove Ct
9 Springfield Ct
10 College Wlk
B3 1 Percy Ct
2 Holmwood
3 Middle Green Cl
4 Herbert Ct
B4 1 Woodleigh
2 Highcroft
3 Caernarvon Ct
4 Regency Ct
D1 1 Oakleigh Way
2 Chandler Ct

199

C2 1 Goodland Ho
2 Furzeland Ho
3 Oakcroft Ho
4 Meadcroft Ho
5 Newhouse
C4 1 Merryweather Ct
2 Roebuck Ct
3 Sable Ct
C5 1 Acacia Ho
2 Kingston Lo
3 Carrington Ct
4 Fairholme Ho
5 Marshall Ho
6 Norton Ho
7 Martin Ho

200

A1 1 Brookside Cres
2 Beverley Gdns
3 Purdey Ct
4 Avenue The
5 Briarwood Ct
6 Station App

202

D6 1 Fair Green Ct
2 Regal Ct
3 Lewes Ct
4 Esher Mews
5 Sibford Ct
6 Deseret Ho
7 Standor Ho
8 Langdale Par
9 Newman Terr

204

A2 1 Barcom Trad Est
2 Croydon Valley Trade Pk
C3 1 Rozelle Ct
2 Dunheved Ct
3 Truscott Ho
C4 1 Brigstock Par
2 Terry Lodge
3 Justin Ct
D3 1 Wyndham Ct
D5 1 Nutfield Pl
2 Braidwood Ho
3 Elliott Ho

205

B1 1 Tavistock Ct
2 Chartwell Cl
3 Speaker's Ct
4 Cumberland Ct
5 Viceroy Ct
6 Oriel Ct
7 Cherry Orchard Gdns
8 Sola Ct
9 Gamma Ct
C1 1 Windmill Bridge Ho
2 Squire Ct
3 Houston Ct
5 Warren Ct
D1 1 Hastings Pl
2 Grant Pl
3 Clive Ho
4 Havelock Ho
5 Bellmore Ct
6 Hereford Ct
7 Chequers Ct
8 Havelock Hall

206

A1 1 Farleycroft
2 Edgecumbe Ct
3 Wesson Ho
4 Sullivan Ct
5 Kenley Ho
6 Christopher Ct
7 Jayson Ct
A6 1 Leybourne Ct
2 Lestock Cl
3 Croftside The
D1 1 Cottongrass Cl
2 Oxlip Cl
3 Eyebright Cl

207

D1 1 North Rd
2 Sussex Rd
3 Riverside Wlk
4 Christie Ho
5 Windsor Ct
6 Sherwood Ct
7 Wheatsheaf Par
D6 1 Linden Ct
2 Park Ct
3 Chilchester Ct
4 Iveagh Ct

208

A6 1 Overbury
2 Wilton Pl
D1 1 Woodgrange Ct
2 Maycroft
3 Farnborough Cres
D4 1 Knowlton Gn
2 Speldhurst Cl
3 Bidborough Cl
4 Penshurst Wlk
D5 1 Wedgewood Ct
2 Birches The
3 Eccleshill
4 Tavistock Rd
5 Montpelier Ct

209

A5 1 Montague Terr
2 Chatsworth Ho
A6 1 Marina Cl
2 Cheveney Wlk
3 Bromley Manor Mans
4 Mall The
5 Westmoreland Pl
B5 1 Reflex Apartments
2 Wheeler Pl
3 Maxim Apartments
4 Exchange Apartments
5 Axiom Apartments
6 Weller Mews

211

B1 1 Gleneagles Gn
2 Tandridge Pl
3 Springfield Wlk
4 Pinehurst Wlk
5 Cromer Pl
6 Oakmont Pl

214

A6 1 St Bernards Ho
2 Wentworth Ct
3 Sunningdale Cl
4 Arklow Mews
5 Edward Pinner Ct

216

A6 1 Lansdowne Copse
2 Lansdowne Ct

217

A2 1 Cheam Court Flats
2 Farnham Ct
3 Tabor Ct
C1 1 Lancaster Ct
2 Redclyffe Terr
3 Kenilworth Terr
4 Lincoln Terr
5 Garden Ct
6 Ashwood Pk
7 Midsummer Apartments
8 Lyndhurst Ct
9 Lorraine Ct
10 Gloucester Ct
11 Banbury Ct
12 Camilla Ct
13 Lorac Ct
14 Kingswood Mans
15 Claremont Ho
16 Holly Ct
17 Castle Ho
18 Balmoral Ct
19 Davington Ct
20 Hereford Ct
C2 1 Norman Ho
2 Hawthorns The
3 Limes The
4 Alexa Ct
5 Kristina Ct
6 Beverley Ct
7 Chestnut Ct
D1 1 Holmeswood
2 Pebworth Lo
3 Addison Ct
4 Kingslee Ct
5 Raeburn Ho
6 Girtin Ho
7 Leith Towers
8 Courtlands
9 Thomas Ho
10 Grayshott Ct
11 Hadrian Ct
12 Sandown Ct
13 Magnolia Ct
14 Dunsfold Ct
15 Camberley Ct
16 Berrylands Ct
17 Brockham Ct
18 Alford Ct
19 Lansdowne Ho
20 Larchvale Ct
D2 1 Portland Ct
2 Durnston Ct
3 Barton Ct
4 Aplin Ct
5 Hannah Ct
6 Honeysuckle Ct
7 Rowans The
8 St Annes Ct
9 Bonnington Ho
10 Pamir Ct
11 Bradbourne Ct
12 Worcester Ct
D3 1 Marian Ct
2 Robin Hood Ct
3 Distin Ct
4 Queensmere
5 Grosvenor Ho
6 Cromer Mans
7 St Nicholas Ctr

D5 1 Dorothy Pettingel Ho
2 Margaret Ho

218

A1 1 Beauclere Ho
2 Melford Ct
3 Elmhurst Lo
4 Mansard Manor
5 Tranmere Ct
6 Beechcroft Lo
7 Savin Lo
8 Yew Tree Ct
9 Avondale Ct
10 Devonshire Ho
11 Hidcote Ho
12 Munstead Ct
13 Lodden Lo
14 Steetley Ct
15 Grampian Cl
16 Richard Sharples Ct
A2 1 Grosvenor Ct
2 Forest Dene Ct
3 Cedar Ct
4 Vanborough Ct
5 Shrub Ct
6 Evergreen Ct
7 Grasmere Ct
8 Heathfield Ct
9 Sherbourne Ct
10 Kinsale Grange
11 Linden Ct
12 Jubilee Ct
13 Langley Ct
14 Wilmot Ho
15 Farendon Ho
16 Alexander Ho
A3 1 Goossens Cl
2 Cliffe Wlk
3 Marlins Cl
4 Clowser Cl
5 Montana Gdns
6 Bournemouth Ct
7 Palmerston Ct
A4 1 Lodge The
2 Hazelwood Ho
3 Chesterton Ho
4 Clevedon Ho
5 Staincliffe Ho
6 Denewood Ho
7 Newlyn Ho
8 Manor Ct
9 Glenrose Ho
10 Oak Lo
11 Briar The
12 Fernhead
13 Branch Ho
14 Thicket Ct
15 Adam Ct
16 Arndell Ho
17 Oakwood Ct
B3 1 Hogarth Ho
2 Gillray Ho
3 Cramhurst Ho
4 Ronald Ho
5 Blythewood
6 Hillsde
7 Weldon Ct
8 Yeoman Ct
D5 1 Kynersley Cl
2 Wrythe Gn
3 Bedford Villas
4 Chateau The
5 Nelson Ct
6 Errington Manor
7 Leeds Ct
8 Blair Ct

219

A4 1 Westcroft
2 Westcroft Ho
A5 1 Burnside Ct
2 Millpond Pl
3 Waterside Ct
4 Stable Ct
5 Manor Ct
B2 1 Runnymede Ct
2 Dolphin Ct
3 Kings Ct
4 Cheyne Ct
5 Hendfield Ct
6 Ellerslie Ct
7 Embassy Ct
8 Chandler Ct
9 Hambledon Ct
10 Wallington Ct
11 Jasmine Ct
12 Napier Ct
13 Rosswood Ho
14 Woodcote Ct
15 Surrey Ct
16 Stag Ct
17 Moorlands
B3 1 Cornelion Cotts
2 Walpole Ct
3 Farmstead Ct
4 Derby Ho
5 Salisbury Ho
6 Chatham Ho
B4 1 Loraine Ho
2 Harcourt Lo
3 Coniston Ct
4 Alcester Ct
5 Friars Ct
6 Campbell Ho
7 Brodie Ho
8 Lesley Ct
9 Birch Ct
10 Airborne Ho
C2 1 Rossendon Ct
2 Mulberry Mews
3 Nairn Ct
4 Wallington Sq
5 Rosemount Twrs
6 Connell Ho
7 Ashby Grange
8 Terry Ct
9 Leigham Cl
10 Clyde Works
11 Chandos Bsns Ctr
12 Beech Ho
13 Wendon Ct
D3 1 Torquay Ho
2 Ashburton Ho
D5 1 Goodwood Lo
2 Haydock Lo
3 Kempton Lo

220

A1 1 Phoenix Ctr The
2 Ensign Way
3 Hunter Cl
4 Cirrus Cl
D5 1 Latimer Rd
2 Cromwell Ho
3 Arundel Ct
4 Warrington Ct
5 Grace Ct
6 Stuart Ct
7 Bridge Par

221

A3 1 Trent Ct
2 Sherwood Ct
3 Archers Ct
4 Keepers Ct
5 Lincoln Ct
6 Mount The
7 Fairhaven Ct
8 Brockham Ct
9 Chelwood Ct
10 Marey Ct
11 Landau Ct
A4 1 West Street Pl
2 Maple Ct
3 St Andrew's Rd
4 Albury Ct
5 Chestnut Ct
6 Elgin Ct
7 Beechfield Ct
8 Barham Ct
9 Whitstable Pl
10 Ledbury Pl
A5 1 Fellmongers Yd
2 Halstead Cl
3 Mann Cl
4 Waterworks Yd
5 Chanderia Ct
6 Katherine Ho
A6 1 Otterbourne Rd
2 Charrington Rd
3 Tamworth Pl
4 Priddy's Yd
5 Hospital of the Holy Trinity (Almshouses)
B6 1 Wellesley Court Rd
2 Norfolk Ho
3 Station App
4 Suffolk Ho
5 Cherry Orchard Gdns
6 Harrington Ct
D6 1 Cheyne Ct
2 Fourways
3 Princess Ct
4 Tierney Ct
5 Sinclair Ct
6 Guinness Ct
7 Mayfair Ct
8 Bishopscourt
9 Gloucester Lo
10 Beverley Hyrst
11 Melton Ct
12 Cecil Ct
13 Napier Ct

227

A3 1 Westfield
2 Farnborough Ct
3 Fern Hill Pl
4 Churchill Ct
5 Spencer Ct
6 Ladycroft Gdns
7 Crabbs Croft Cl
8 Clifton Cl
D2 1 Brittenden Cl
2 Wardens Field Cl
3 Winnipeg Dr
4 Superior Dr
5 Huron Cl
6 Manitoba Gdns
7 Lynne Cl
8 Flint Cl
9 Bakers Mews
D3 1 Osgood Gdns
2 Amberley Cl
3 Rawlings Cl
4 Beblets Cl
5 Fir Tree Cl
6 Raleigh Mews
7 King Henry Mews
D4 1 Healy Dr
2 Marsden Way
3 Taylor Cl
4 Strickland Way
5 Dryland Ave
6 Adcot Wlk
7 Lichlade Cl

Hospitals

Acton Hospital W3 110 C4
Ashford Hospital TW15 3AA 148 A2
Athlone House (The Middlesex Hospital) N6 48 D1
Atkinson Morley Hospital SW20 178 B3
Barking Hospital IG11 79 D1
Barnes Hospital SW14 133 C2
Beckenham Hospital BR3 185 B1
Bethlem Royal Hospital The BR3 207 C2
Blackheath Hospital SE3 142 C2
Bolingbroke Hospital The SW11 158 C6
Bowden House Hospital (Private) HA1 64 C6
British Home and Hospital for Incurables SW16 182 D5
Bromley Hospital BR2 9AJ 209 B5
Brompton Hospital SW3 114 B1 256 D2
BUPA Bushey Hospital WD2 8 D3
Carshalton, War Memorial Hospital SM5 218 D2
Cassel Hospital TW10 175 D6
Castlewood Day Hospital SE18 144 C4
Central Middlesex Hospital NW10 7NS 89 A4
Central Public Health Laboratory NW9 45 C6
Chadwell Heath Hospital RM6 58 B4
Charing Cross Hospital W6 8RF 112 D1
Charter Nightingale Hospital The NW1 92 C2 237 B4
Chase Farm Hospital EN2 8JL 4 C5
Chelsea Hospital for Women SW3 114 C1 257 A2
Chelsea and Westminster Hospital SW10 9NH 136 A6 266 B5
Chingford Hospital E4 20 A1
Chiswick Maternity Hospital W4 111 D1
Clayponds Hospital and Day Treatment Ctr TW8 110 A2
Clementine Churchill Hospital The HA1 64 D5
Colindale Hospital NW9 45 C6
Connaught Day Hospital E11 54 C3
Coppetts Wood Hospital N10 30 D2
Cromwell Hospital SW5 113 D2 255 C4
Devonshire Hospital W1 93 A2 238 B4
Dulwich Hospital SE22 139 C1
Ealing Hospital UB1 3HW 108 B4
East Ham Memorial Hospital E7 77 D1
Eastman Dental Hospital WC1 94 B4 240 C6
Edgware General Hospital HA8 26 D3
Elizabeth Garrett Anderson and Obstetric Hospital WC1 93 C3 235 B5
Farnborough Hospital BR6 226 C4
Finchley Memorial Hospital N12 30 A3
Fitzroy Nuffield Hospital W1 92 D1 237 C2
Garden Hospital The NW4 46 C6
Goldie Leigh Hospital SE2 146 C6
Goodmayes Hospital IG3 58 A4
Gordon Hospital The SW1 115 D2 259 C3
Great Ormond St Hospital for Children WC1 94 B3 240 C5
Grovelands Priory N14 16 A3
Guy's Hospital SE1 117 B5 252 D2
Hackney Hospital E9 75 A3
Hamlet (Day) Hospital The TW9 132 A2
Hammersmith Hospital W12 90 B1
Harrow Hospital HA2 64 C6
The Heart Hospital W1 93 B2 238 C3
Hillingdon Hospital UB8 82 B2
Homerton University Hospital E9 74 D3
Hornsey Central Hospital N8 49 D4
Hospital for Tropical Diseases WC1 232 C5
Hospital of St John and St Elizabeth NW8 92 B5 229 C3
Inverforth House Hospital NW3 70 A6
Jewish Home and Hospital at Tottenham The N15 51 D5
King George Hospital IG3 58 A4
King's College Hospital SE5 139 B3
Kings Oak Hospital (Private) The EN2 4 C5
Kingsbury Hospital NW9 44 C5
Kingston Hospital KT2 176 D2
Langthorne Hospital E11 76 B5
Lewisham Hospital SE13 163 D6
Lister Hospital SW1 115 B1 258 C1
London Bridge Hospital SE1 117 B5 252 D4
London Chest Hospital E2 96 C5
London Clinic NW1 93 A3 238 B5
London Foot Hospital W1 93 C3 239 A5
London Hospital (Mile End) The E2 96 D4
London Hospital (St Clements) The E3 97 B4
London Independent Hospital The E1 96 D2
Maida Vale Psychiatric Hospital W9 92 A3 236 B6
Manor House Hospital NW11 47 D1
Marlborough Day Hospital NW8 92 A5 229 A4
Maudsley Hospital The SE5 139 B3
Mayday University Hospital CR7 204 D3
Memorial Hospital SE18 144 C3
Mildmay Mission Hospital E2 95 D4
Molesey Hospital KT8 195 C4
Moorfields Eye Hospital EC1 95 B4 235 C1
Morland Road Day Hospital RM10 103 C6
National Hospital for Neurology and Neurosurgery N2 48 C5
National Hospital The WC1 94 A3 240 B5
National Physical Laboratory TW11 174 C4
Nelson Hospital SW20 179 B1
New Cross Hospital SE14 140 C5
New Victoria Hospital KT3 177 C2
Newham General Hospital E13 99 C3
Normansfield Hospital KT8 175 C3
North London Nuffield Hospital EN2 4 C3
North Middlesex University Hospital N18 33 C5
Northwick Park Hospital HA1 43 A2
Northwood Pinner and District Cottage Hospital HA6 22 A2
Norwood Hospital SE19 183 B4
Orpington Hospital BR6 227 D4
Paddington Com Hospital W9 91 C2
Penny Sangam Day Hospital UB2 107 B3
Plaistow Hospital E13 99 C5
Portland Hospital for Women and Children The W1 93 B3 238 D5
Princess Grace Hospital The W1 93 A3 238 A5
Princess Louise Hospital W10 90 C2
Princess Royal University Hospital BR6 226 C5
Priory Hospital The SW15 133 D1
Putney Hospital SW15 134 C2
Queen Charlotte's Hospital W12 90 B1
Queen Elizabeth Hospital for Children The E2 96 A5
Queen Elizabeth Hospital SE18 144 A5
Queen Mary's Hospital DA14 6LT 190 A4
Queen Mary's Hospital NW3 70 A5
Queen Mary's University Hospital SW15 156 A5
Queen's Hospital CR0 205 A3
Roding Hospital IG4 55 D6
Royal Brompton and Nat Heart Hospital The SW3 114 C1 257 A2
Royal Ear Hospital WC1 93 C3 239 B5
Royal Free Hospital NW3 70 C3
Royal Hospital SW15 157 A5
Royal London Homeopathic Hospital The WC1 94 A2 240 B4
Royal London Hospital(Whitechapel) E1 96 B2
Royal Marsden Hospital SW3 114 B1 256 D2
Royal Masonic Hospital W6 112 A2
Royal National Orthopaedic Hospital HA7 9 C2
Royal National Orthopaedic Hospital W1 93 B3 238 D5
Royal Nat TN&E Hospital The W5 87 C2
Royal Nat TN&E Hospital The WC1 94 B4 233 C2
St Andrew's Hospital E3 97 D3
St Ann's General Hospital N4, N15 51 A4
St Anthony's Hospital KT4 200 D1
St Bartholomew's Hospital EC1 94 D2 241 D3
St Charles' Hospital W10 90 D2
St Christopher's Hospice SE26 184 C5
St George's Hospital SW17 180 B5
St Giles Hospital SE5 139 C4
St Helier Hospital SM5 202 A1
St Joseph's Hospice E9, E8 96 B6
St Leonard's Hospital N1 95 C5
St Luke's Hospital W1 93 C3 239 A5
St Luke's Woodside Hospital N10 49 A5
St Mark's Hospital EC1 94 D4 234 D2
St Mark's Hospital HA1 43 A2
St Mary's Cottage Hospital TW12 173 B2
St Mary's Hospital W2 92 B1 236 D2
St Michael's Hospital EN2 5 B4
St Pancras Hospital NW1 93 D6 232 C5
St Thomas's Hospital SE1 116 B3 260 C6
St Vincent's Hospital HA5 39 D6
Samaritan Hospital for Women NW1 237 C4
Shirley Oaks Hospital CR0 206 C2
Sloane Hospital BR3 186 B2
South Western Hospital SW9 138 B2
Southwood Hospital (Geriatric) N6 49 A2
Springfield Hospital SW17 158 C1
Stepney Day Hospital E1 96 C1
Surbiton Hospital KT6 198 A3
Teddington Memorial Hospital TW11 174 C4
Thorpe Coombe Hospital E17 54 A6
Tolworth Hospital KT6 214 C6
Travel Clinic, Hospital for Tropical Diseases WC1 93 C3 239 B5
University College Hospital WC1 93 C3 239 B6
Upton Day Hospital DA6 147 A1
Wanstead Hospital E11 55 B5
Wellington Hospital (North) NW8 92 B5 229 D3
Wellington Hospital (South) NW8 92 B5 229 D3
Wembley Hospital HA0 65 D2
West Middlesex University Hospital TW7 6AF 131 A3
Western Hospital The NW1 92 D2 237 C4
Whipps Cross Hospital E11 1NR 54 B3
Whittington Hospital N19 5NF 71 C6
Willesden Community Hospital The NW10 68 A1
Winifred House Hospital EN5 11 D5

Hospitals with Accident and Emergency departments

Central Middlesex Hospital 89 A4
Acton Lane, Park Royal, London NW10 7NS
020 8965 5733

Charing Cross Hospital 112 D1
Fulham Palace Road, London W6 8RF
(A&E entrance off St Dunstan's Road)
020 8846 1234

Chase Farm Hospital 4 C5
The Ridgeway, Enfield, Middlesex EN2 8JL
020 8375 1010

Chelsea and Westminster Hospital 136 A6 266 B5
369 Fulham Road, London SW10 9NH
020 8746 8080

Ealing Hospital 108 B4
Uxbridge Road, Southall, Middlesex UB1 3HW
020 8967 5613

Hammersmith Hospital 90 B1
Du Cane Road, London W12 0HS
020 8383 1111

Hillingdon Hospital 82 B2
Pield Heath Road, Uxbridge, Middlesex UB8 3NN
01895 238282

Homerton University Hospital 74 D3
Homerton Row, E9 6SR
020 8510 5555

King George Hospital 58 A4
Barley Lane, Goodmayes, Ilford, Essex IG3 8YB
020 8983 8000

King's College Hospital 139 B3
Denmark Hill, (A&E in Ruskin Wing) SE5 9RS
020 3299 9000

Kingston Hospital 176 D2
Galsworthy Road, Kingston-upon-Thames, Surrey KT2 7QB
020 8546 7711

Lewisham Hospital 163 D6
High Street, Lewisham, London SE13 6JH
020 8333 3000

Mayday University Hospital 204 D3
Mayday Road, Thornton Heath CR7 7YE
020 8401 3000

Moorfields Eye Hospital (eyes only) 95 B4 235 C1
162 City Rd, London EC1V 2PO
020 7253 3411

Newham General Hospital 99 C3
Glen Road, Plaistow, London E13 8SL
020 7476 4000

North Middlesex University Hospital 33 C5
Sterling Way, Edmonton, London, N18 1QX
020 8887 2000

Northwick Park Hospital 43 A2
Watford Road, Harrow, Middlesex HA1 3UJ
020 8864 3232

Princess Royal University Hospital 226 C5
Farnborough Common, Orpington BR6 8ND
01689 863000

Queen Elizabeth Hospital 144 A5
Stadium Rd, Woolwich SE18 4QH
020 8836 6000

Queen Mary's Hospital 190 A4
Frognal Avenue, Sidcup,Kent DA14 6LT
020 8302 2678

Royal Free Hospital 70 C3
Pond Street, London NW3 2QG
020 7794 0500

Royal London Hospital (Whitechapel) 96 B2
Whitechapel Road, London E1 1BB
020 7377 7000

St George's Hospital 180 B5
Blackshaw Road, London SW17 0QT
020 8672 1255

St Helier Hospital 202 A1
Wrythe Lane, Carshalton, Surrey SM5 1AA
020 8296 2000

St Mary's Hospital 92 B1 236 D2
Praed Street, Paddington W2 1NY
(A&E entrance on South Wharf Rd)
020 7886 6666

St Thomas' Hospital 116 B3 260 C6
Lambeth Palace Road, London SE1 7EH
020 7188 7188

University College Hospital 93 C3 239 B6
235 Euston Rd, London NW1 2BU
0845 155 5000

West Middlesex University Hospital 131 A3
Twickenham Road, Isleworth, Middlesex TW7 6AF
020 8560 2121

Whipps Cross Hospital 54 B3
Whipps Cross Road, Leytonstone London E11 1NR
020 8539 5522

Whittington Hospital 71 C6
Highgate Hill, London, N19 5NF
020 7272 3070

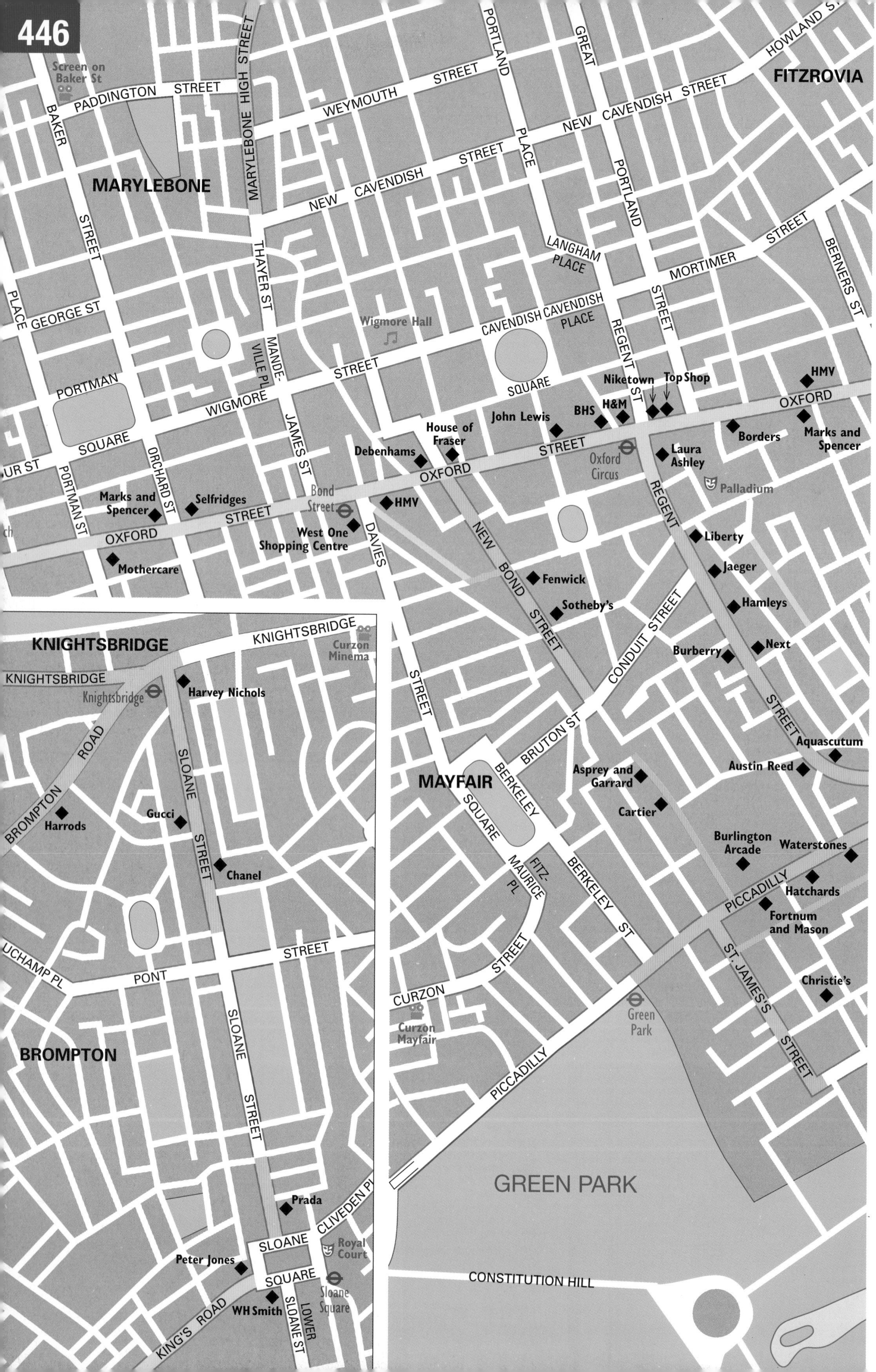

Screen on Baker St
PADDINGTON STREET
BAKER STREET
MARYLEBONE HIGH STREET
WEYMOUTH STREET
PORTLAND PLACE
GREAT PORTLAND STREET
HOWLAND ST
NEW CAVENDISH STREET
FITZROVIA
MARYLEBONE
NEW CAVENDISH STREET
THAYER ST
LANGHAM PLACE
MORTIMER STREET
BERNERS ST
PLACE
GEORGE ST
Wigmore Hall
CAVENDISH STREET
CAVENDISH PLACE
REGENT ST
MANDEVILLE PL
PORTMAN SQUARE
WIGMORE STREET
SQUARE
Niketown
Top Shop
HMV
UR ST
JAMES ST
John Lewis
BHS
H&M
OXFORD
House of Fraser
Borders
Marks and Spencer
ORCHARD ST
PORTMAN ST
Debenhams
STREET
Oxford Circus
Laura Ashley
Palladium
Marks and Spencer
Selfridges
Bond Street
OXFORD
HMV
STREET
OXFORD
West One Shopping Centre
DAVIES
NEW BOND STREET
REGENT STREET
Liberty
Mothercare
Fenwick
Jaeger
Sotheby's
Hamleys
CONDUIT STREET
Next
Burberry
KNIGHTSBRIDGE
KNIGHTSBRIDGE
Curzon Minema
KNIGHTSBRIDGE
Knightsbridge
Harvey Nichols
DAVIES STREET
BROMPTON ROAD
SLOANE STREET
BRUTON ST
Aquascutum
Austin Reed
MAYFAIR
BERKELEY SQUARE
Asprey and Garrard
Harrods
Gucci
Cartier
Burlington Arcade
Waterstones
Chanel
FITZMAURICE PL
BERKELEY ST
PICCADILLY
Hatchards
Fortnum and Mason
UCHAMP PL
PONT STREET
CURZON STREET
ST. JAMES'S STREET
Christie's
Curzon Mayfair
Green Park
BROMPTON
SLOANE STREET
PICCADILLY
GREEN PARK
Prada
CLIVEDEN PL
SLOANE SQUARE
Royal Court
Peter Jones
CONSTITUTION HILL
Sloane Square
WH Smith
KING'S ROAD
SLOANE ST
LOWER SLOANE ST

Cinemas, theatres shopping streets

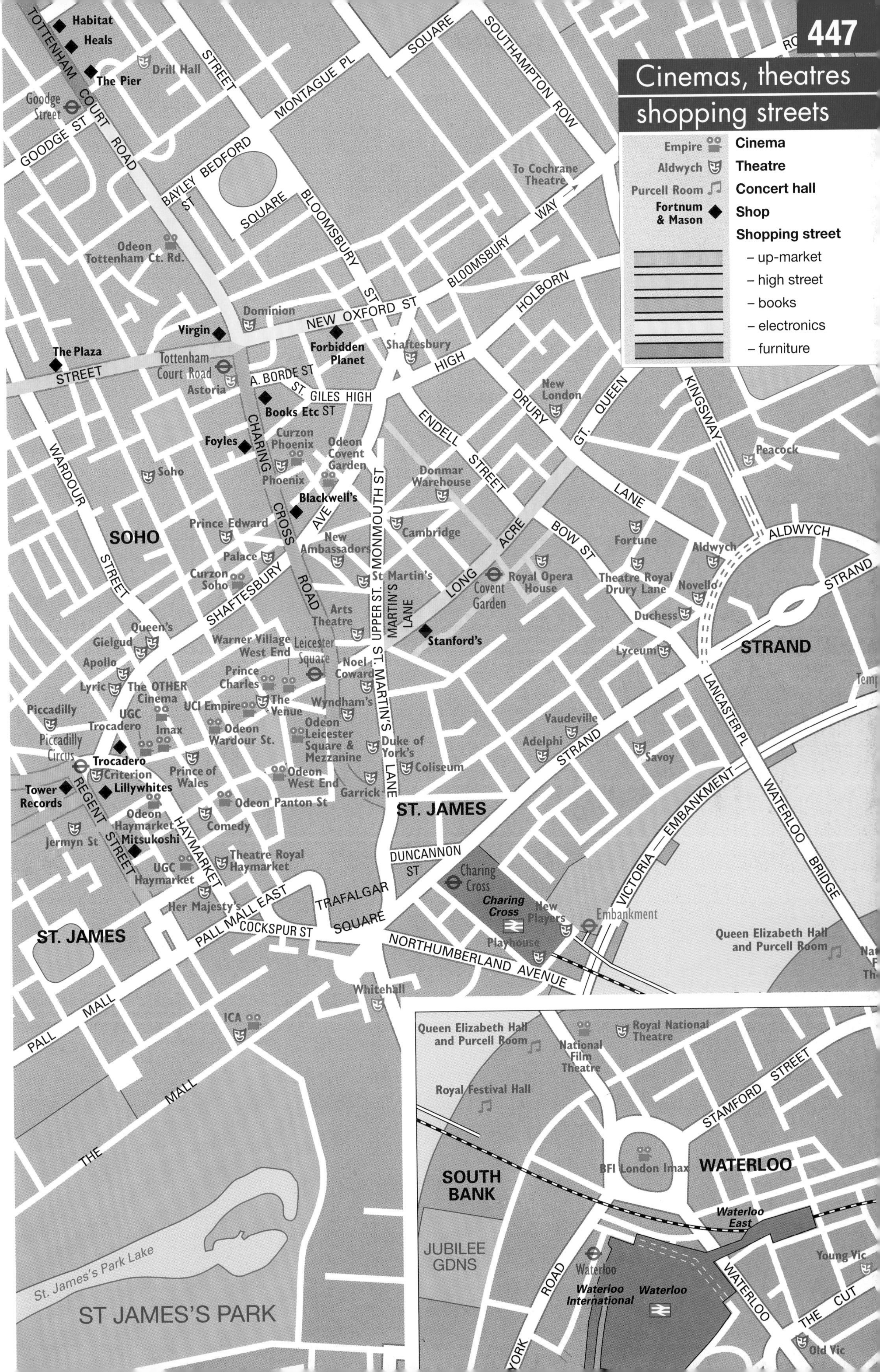

Empire Cinema
Aldwych Theatre
Purcell Room Concert hall
Fortnum & Mason Shop
Shopping street
– up-market
– high street
– books
– electronics
– furniture
Habitat
Heals
The Pier
Drill Hall
Goodge Street
TOTTENHAM COURT ROAD
GOODGE ST
STREET
MONTAGUE PL
SQUARE
SOUTHAMPTON ROW
BEDFORD SQUARE
BAYLEY ST
BLOOMSBURY ST
To Cochrane Theatre
BLOOMSBURY WAY
HOLBORN
Odeon Tottenham Ct. Rd.
Dominion
NEW OXFORD ST
Virgin
Forbidden Planet
Shaftesbury
HIGH
The Plaza
STREET
Tottenham Court Road
Astoria
A. BORDE ST
ST. GILES HIGH ST
Books Etc
New London
DRURY LANE
GT. QUEEN
KINGSWAY
ENDELL STREET
WARDOUR STREET
Foyles
CHARING CROSS ROAD
Curzon Phoenix
Odeon Covent Garden
Phoenix
Soho
Blackwell's
Donmar Warehouse
Peacock
SOHO
Prince Edward
AVE
New Ambassadors
Cambridge
ACRE
BOW ST
Fortune
Aldwych
ALDWYCH
Palace
SHAFTESBURY
UPPER ST. MARTIN'S LANE
MONMOUTH ST
St Martin's
LONG ACRE
Covent Garden
Royal Opera House
Theatre Royal Drury Lane
Novello
STRAND
Curzon Soho
Arts Theatre
Duchess
Queen's
Gielgud
Warner Village West End
Leicester Square
Stanford's
Lyceum
STRAND
Apollo
Prince Charles
Noel Coward
Lyric
The OTHER Cinema
The Venue
Wyndham's
Piccadilly
UGC Trocadero
UCI Empire
Odeon Leicester Square & Mezzanine
ST. MARTIN'S LANE
Vaudeville
LANCASTER PL
Imax
Odeon Wardour St.
Duke of York's
Adelphi
Piccadilly Circus
Trocadero
Criterion
Prince of Wales
Odeon West End
Coliseum
Savoy
Tower Records
Lillywhites
REGENT STREET
Garrick
VICTORIA EMBANKMENT
WATERLOO BRIDGE
Odeon Haymarket
Odeon Panton St
ST. JAMES
Jermyn St
Comedy
HAYMARKET
Mitsukoshi
DUNCANNON ST
UGC Haymarket
Theatre Royal Haymarket
Charing Cross
TRAFALGAR SQUARE
Her Majesty's
PALL MALL EAST
New Players
Embankment
Queen Elizabeth Hall and Purcell Room
COCKSPUR ST
Playhouse
ST. JAMES
NORTHUMBERLAND AVENUE
Whitehall
PALL MALL
ICA
THE MALL
St. James's Park Lake
ST JAMES'S PARK
Queen Elizabeth Hall and Purcell Room
National Film Theatre
Royal National Theatre
Royal Festival Hall
STAMFORD STREET
SOUTH BANK
BFI London Imax
WATERLOO
Waterloo East
JUBILEE GDNS
Young Vic
Waterloo
Waterloo International
Waterloo
YORK ROAD
WATERLOO
THE CUT
Old Vic

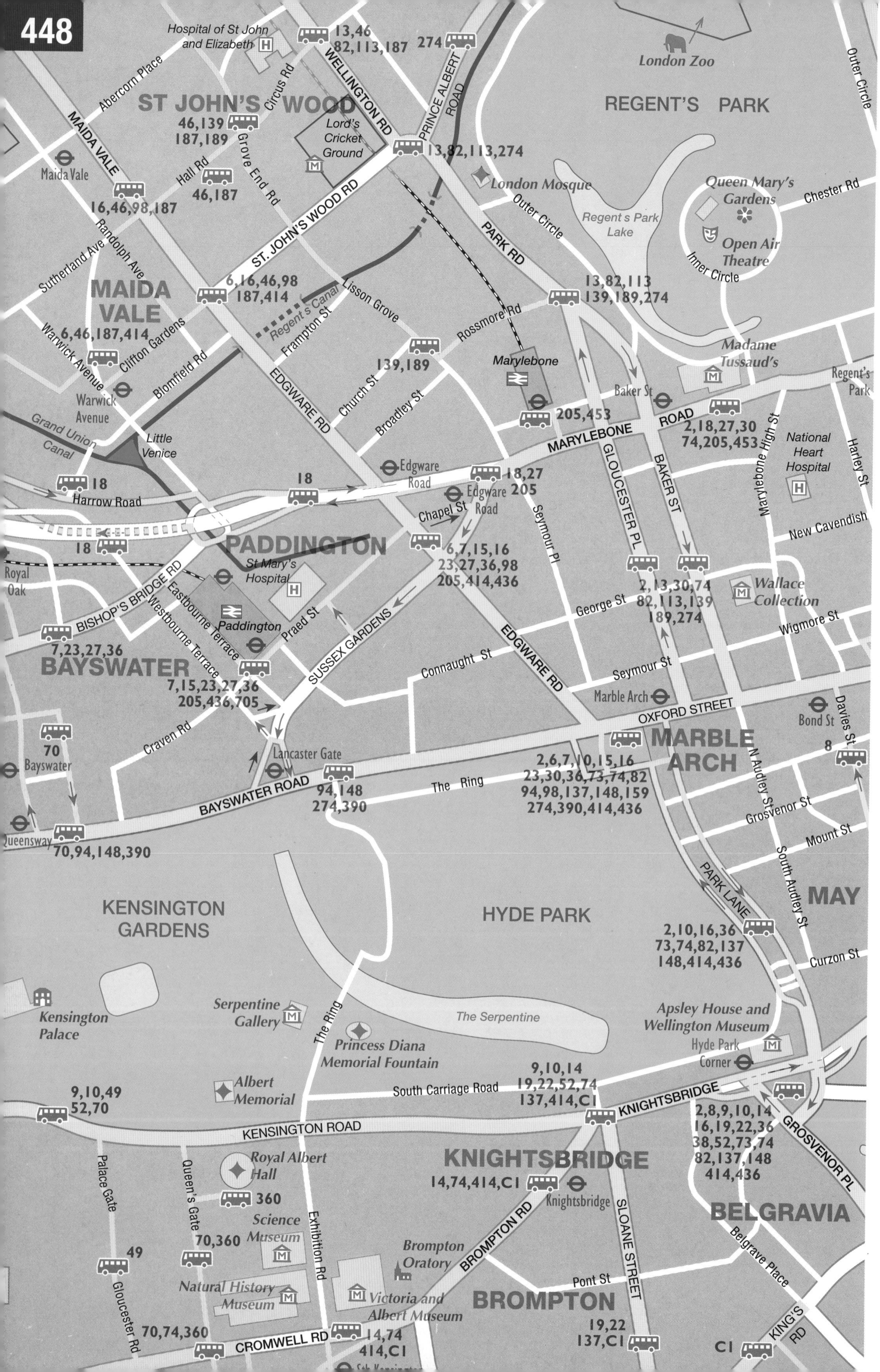
Hospital of St John and Elizabeth
13,46
82,113,187
274
London Zoo
Outer Circle
Abercorn Place
Circus Rd
WELLINGTON RD
PRINCE ALBERT ROAD
REGENT'S PARK
ST JOHN'S WOOD
46,139
187,189
Lord's Cricket Ground
13,82,113,274
MAIDA VALE
Maida Vale
Grove End Rd
Hall Rd
46,187
London Mosque
Outer Circle
Regent's Park Lake
Queen Mary's Gardens
Chester Rd
Open Air Theatre
Inner Circle
16,46,98,187
Randolph Ave
ST. JOHN'S WOOD RD
PARK RD
Sutherland Ave
MAIDA VALE
6,16,46,98
187,414
Regent's Canal
Lisson Grove
13,82,113
139,189,274
Frampton St
Rossmore Rd
Warwick Avenue
6,46,187,414
Clifton Gardens
Madame Tussaud's
Blomfield Rd
139,189
Marylebone
Warwick Avenue
EDGWARE RD
Church St
Baker St
Regent's Park
Grand Union Canal
Little Venice
Broadley St
205,453
MARYLEBONE
ROAD
2,18,27,30
74,205,453
National Heart Hospital
Harley St
Marylebone High St
18
Harrow Road
18
Edgware Road
18,27
205
Edgware Road
GLOUCESTER PL
BAKER ST
Chapel St
Seymour Pl
New Cavendish
18
PADDINGTON
St Mary's Hospital
6,7,15,16
23,27,36,98
205,414,436
Royal Oak
BISHOP'S BRIDGE RD
Eastbourne Terrace
Westbourne Terrace
Paddington
Praed St
SUSSEX GARDENS
2,13,30,74
82,113,139
189,274
Wallace Collection
George St
Wigmore St
7,23,27,36
BAYSWATER
EDGWARE RD
Connaught St
Seymour St
7,15,23,27,36
205,436,705
Marble Arch
OXFORD STREET
Bond St
Davies St
MARBLE ARCH
Craven Rd
70
Bayswater
Lancaster Gate
2,6,7,10,15,16
23,30,36,73,74,82
94,98,137,148,159
274,390,414,436
8
N Audley St
BAYSWATER ROAD
94,148
274,390
The Ring
Grosvenor St
Queensway
70,94,148,390
Mount St
PARK LANE
South Audley St
KENSINGTON GARDENS
HYDE PARK
MAY
2,10,16,36
73,74,82,137
148,414,436
Curzon St
Kensington Palace
Serpentine Gallery
The Ring
The Serpentine
Apsley House and Wellington Museum
Hyde Park Corner
Princess Diana Memorial Fountain
9,10,14
19,22,52,74
137,414,C1
9,10,49
52,70
Albert Memorial
South Carriage Road
KNIGHTSBRIDGE
KENSINGTON ROAD
2,8,9,10,14
16,19,22,36
38,52,73,74
82,137,148
414,436
GROSVENOR PL
Royal Albert Hall
KNIGHTSBRIDGE
14,74,414,C1
Knightsbridge
Palace Gate
Queen's Gate
360
Science Museum
BELGRAVIA
70,360
Exhibition Rd
Brompton Oratory
BROMPTON RD
SLOANE STREET
Belgrave Place
49
Natural History Museum
Victoria and Albert Museum
Pont St
BROMPTON
Gloucester Rd
70,74,360
CROMWELL RD
14,74
414,C1
19,22
137,C1
C1
KING'S RD

Central London buses

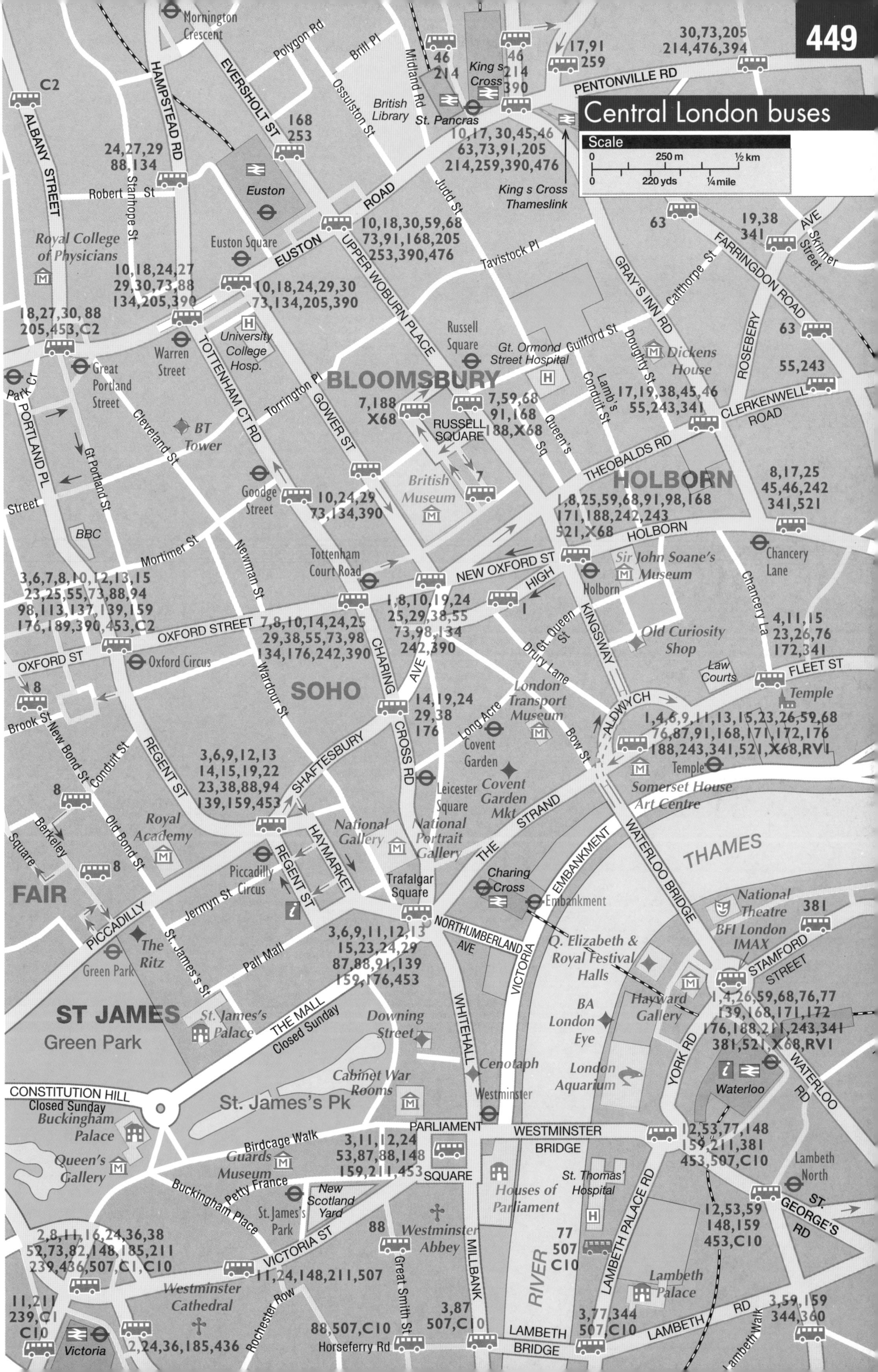

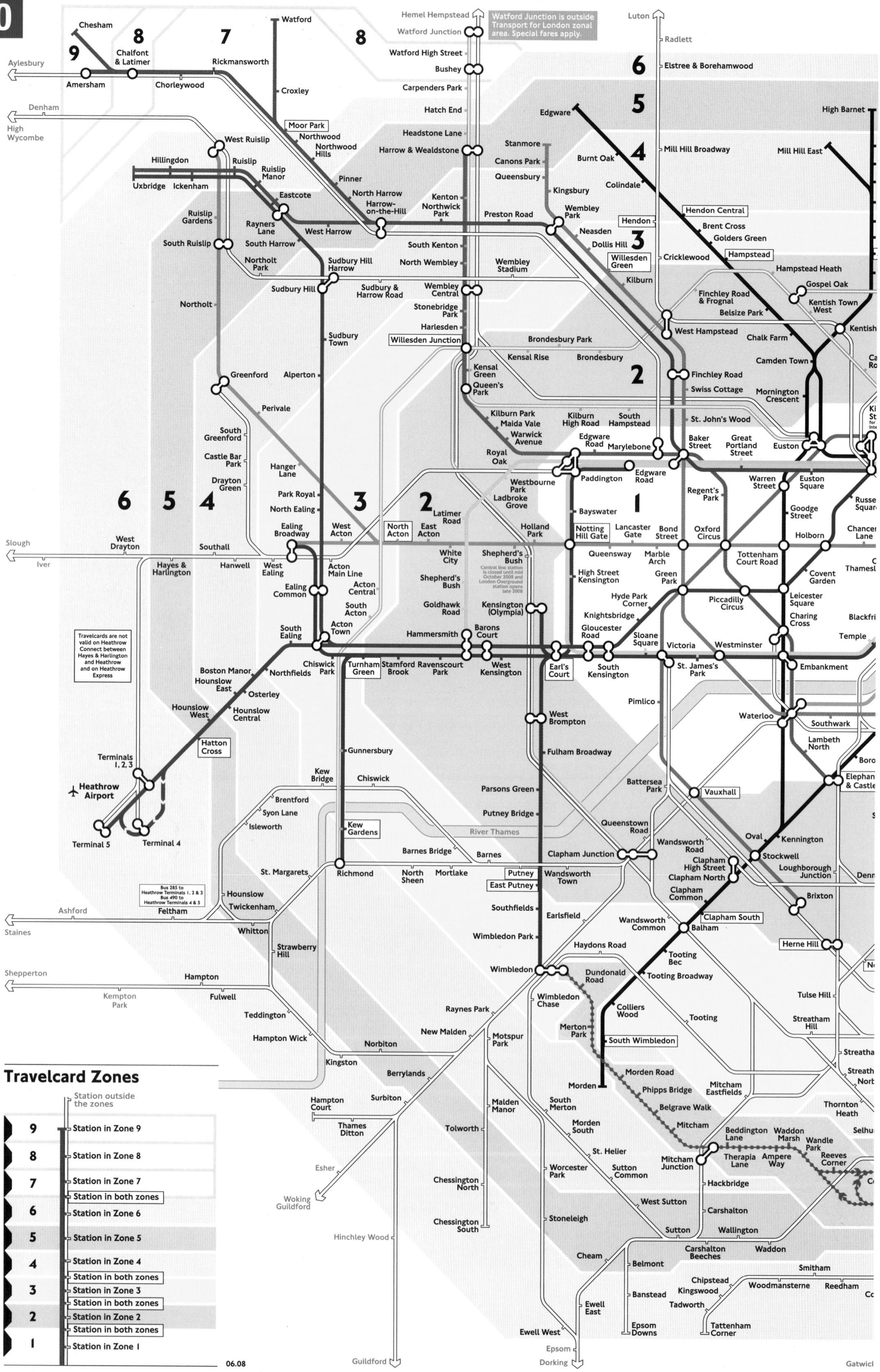
Watford Junction is outside Transport for London zonal area. Special fares apply.
Hemel Hempstead
Watford Junction
Watford High Street
Bushey
Carpenders Park
Hatch End
Headstone Lane
Harrow & Wealdstone
Luton
Radlett
Elstree & Borehamwood
Chesham
Chalfont & Latimer
Amersham
Aylesbury
Chorleywood
Rickmansworth
Watford
Croxley
Moor Park
Northwood
Northwood Hills
Pinner
North Harrow
Harrow-on-the-Hill
Denham
High Wycombe
West Ruislip
Ruislip
Ruislip Manor
Eastcote
Hillingdon
Uxbridge
Ickenham
Ruislip Gardens
Rayners Lane
South Harrow
West Harrow
South Ruislip
Northolt Park
Sudbury Hill Harrow
Sudbury Hill
Sudbury & Harrow Road
Northolt
Sudbury Town
Greenford
Alperton
Perivale
South Greenford
Castle Bar Park
Drayton Green
Hanger Lane
Park Royal
North Ealing
Ealing Broadway
West Acton
North Acton
East Acton
Slough
Iver
West Drayton
Hayes & Harlington
Southall
Hanwell
West Ealing
Acton Main Line
Ealing Common
Acton Central
South Acton
South Ealing
Acton Town
Travelcards are not valid on Heathrow Connect between Hayes & Harlington and Heathrow and on Heathrow Express
Boston Manor
Northfields
Chiswick Park
Osterley
Hounslow East
Hounslow West
Hounslow Central
Hatton Cross
Terminals 1, 2, 3
Heathrow Airport
Terminal 5
Terminal 4
Turnham Green
Stamford Brook
Ravenscourt Park
Gunnersbury
Kew Bridge
Chiswick
Brentford
Syon Lane
Isleworth
Kew Gardens
Richmond
St. Margarets
Bus 285 to Heathrow Terminals 1, 2 & 3
Bus 490 to Heathrow Terminals 4 & 5
Feltham
Hounslow
Twickenham
Ashford
Staines
Whitton
Strawberry Hill
Shepperton
Kempton Park
Hampton
Fulwell
Teddington
Hampton Wick
Kingston
Norbiton
Berrylands
Hampton Court
Surbiton
Thames Ditton
Esher
Woking
Guildford
Hinchley Wood
Guildford
Tolworth
Chessington North
Chessington South
Malden Manor
Motspur Park
New Malden
Raynes Park
Barnes Bridge
Barnes
Mortlake
North Sheen
River Thames
Edgware
Burnt Oak
Colindale
Stanmore
Canons Park
Queensbury
Kingsbury
Wembley Park
Neasden
Dollis Hill
Willesden Green
Kilburn
Hendon
Hendon Central
Brent Cross
Golders Green
Hampstead
Mill Hill Broadway
Mill Hill East
High Barnet
Cricklewood
Hampstead Heath
Gospel Oak
Kentish Town West
Kentish
Finchley Road & Frognal
Belsize Park
Chalk Farm
West Hampstead
Camden Town
Finchley Road
Swiss Cottage
Mornington Crescent
St. John's Wood
Kenton
Northwick Park
Preston Road
South Kenton
North Wembley
Wembley Stadium
Wembley Central
Stonebridge Park
Harlesden
Willesden Junction
Brondesbury Park
Kensal Rise
Brondesbury
Kensal Green
Queen's Park
Kilburn Park
Maida Vale
Warwick Avenue
Kilburn High Road
South Hampstead
Royal Oak
Edgware Road
Marylebone
Baker Street
Great Portland Street
Euston
Paddington
Edgware Road
Westbourne Park
Ladbroke Grove
Latimer Road
Regent's Park
Warren Street
Euston Square
Russell Square
Goodge Street
Bayswater
Notting Hill Gate
Lancaster Gate
Bond Street
Oxford Circus
Holborn
Chancery Lane
Holland Park
Queensway
Marble Arch
Tottenham Court Road
White City
Shepherd's Bush
Central line station is closed until mid October 2008 and London Overground station opens late 2008
Shepherd's Bush
High Street Kensington
Green Park
Covent Garden
Goldhawk Road
Kensington (Olympia)
Hyde Park Corner
Piccadilly Circus
Leicester Square
Knightsbridge
Charing Cross
Blackfriars
Hammersmith
Barons Court
Gloucester Road
Sloane Square
Victoria
Westminster
Temple
West Kensington
Earl's Court
South Kensington
St. James's Park
Embankment
Pimlico
Waterloo
Southwark
Lambeth North
West Brompton
Fulham Broadway
Parsons Green
Putney Bridge
Battersea Park
Vauxhall
Elephant & Castle
Queenstown Road
Oval
Kennington
Clapham Junction
Wandsworth Road
Stockwell
Clapham High Street
Clapham North
Loughborough Junction
Putney
Wandsworth Town
East Putney
Clapham Common
Brixton
Southfields
Earlsfield
Wandsworth Common
Clapham South
Balham
Herne Hill
Wimbledon Park
Haydons Road
Tooting Bec
Wimbledon
Dundonald Road
Tooting Broadway
Wimbledon Chase
Colliers Wood
Tooting
Tulse Hill
Merton Park
South Wimbledon
Streatham Hill
Morden
Morden Road
Phipps Bridge
Mitcham Eastfields
Streatham
Streatham Common
South Merton
Belgrave Walk
Thornton Heath
Morden South
Mitcham
Beddington Lane
Waddon Marsh
Wandle Park
Selhurst
St. Helier
Mitcham Junction
Therapia Lane
Ampere Way
Reeves Corner
Worcester Park
Sutton Common
Hackbridge
West Sutton
Stoneleigh
Carshalton
Sutton
Wallington
Cheam
Carshalton Beeches
Waddon
Belmont
Smitham
Chipstead
Kingswood
Woodmansterne
Reedham
Banstead
Tadworth
Ewell East
Epsom Downs
Tattenham Corner
Ewell West
Epsom
Dorking
Gatwick
Travelcard Zones
Station outside the zones
9 Station in Zone 9
8 Station in Zone 8
7 Station in Zone 7
Station in both zones
6 Station in Zone 6
5 Station in Zone 5
4 Station in Zone 4
Station in both zones
3 Station in Zone 3
Station in both zones
2 Station in Zone 2
Station in both zones
1 Station in Zone 1
06.08

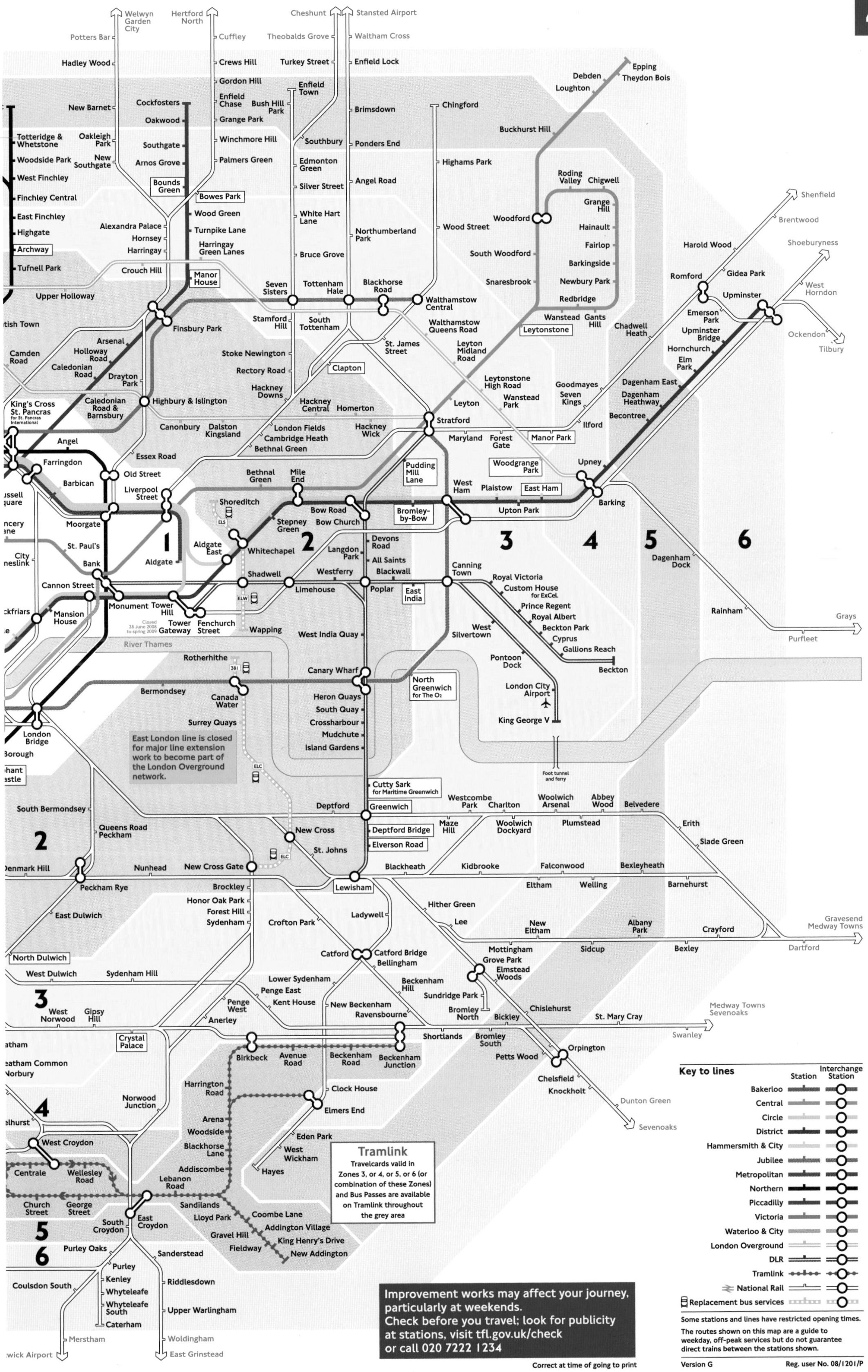
Welwyn Garden City
Hertford North
Cheshunt
Stansted Airport
Potters Bar
Cuffley
Theobalds Grove
Waltham Cross
Hadley Wood
Crews Hill
Turkey Street
Enfield Lock
Gordon Hill
Enfield Town
Epping
Theydon Bois
Debden
Loughton
New Barnet
Cockfosters
Enfield Chase
Bush Hill Park
Brimsdown
Chingford
Oakwood
Grange Park
Buckhurst Hill
Totteridge & Whetstone
Oakleigh Park
Southgate
Winchmore Hill
Southbury
Ponders End
Woodside Park
New Southgate
Arnos Grove
Palmers Green
Edmonton Green
Highams Park
West Finchley
Bounds Green
Silver Street
Angel Road
Roding Valley
Chigwell
Finchley Central
Bowes Park
Shenfield
East Finchley
Wood Green
White Hart Lane
Grange Hill
Brentwood
Highgate
Alexandra Palace
Turnpike Lane
Northumberland Park
Woodford
Wood Street
Hainault
Archway
Hornsey
Harringay Green Lanes
Shoeburyness
Harringay
Bruce Grove
South Woodford
Fairlop
Harold Wood
Tufnell Park
Crouch Hill
Barkingside
Manor House
Snaresbrook
Newbury Park
Gidea Park
Upper Holloway
Seven Sisters
Tottenham Hale
Blackhorse Road
Romford
West Horndon
Walthamstow Central
Redbridge
Upminster
Finsbury Park
Stamford Hill
South Tottenham
Walthamstow Queens Road
Wanstead
Gants Hill
Chadwell Heath
Emerson Park
Leytonstone
Ockendon
Kentish Town
Arsenal
Upminster Bridge
Tilbury
Camden Road
Holloway Road
Stoke Newington
St. James Street
Leyton Midland Road
Hornchurch
Caledonian Road
Drayton Park
Rectory Road
Clapton
Elm Park
Hackney Downs
Leytonstone High Road
Goodmayes
Dagenham East
King's Cross St. Pancras
for St. Pancras International
Caledonian Road & Barnsbury
Highbury & Islington
Hackney Central
Homerton
Wanstead Park
Seven Kings
Dagenham Heathway
Leyton
Canonbury
Dalston Kingsland
London Fields
Hackney Wick
Becontree
Stratford
Ilford
Angel
Cambridge Heath
Maryland
Forest Gate
Manor Park
Bethnal Green
Farringdon
Essex Road
Pudding Mill Lane
Woodgrange Park
Upney
Barbican
Old Street
Bethnal Green
Mile End
West Ham
Plaistow
East Ham
Russell Square
Liverpool Street
Shoreditch
Barking
Bow Road
Bromley-by-Bow
Upton Park
Chancery Lane
Moorgate
Stepney Green
Bow Church
Devons Road
1
2
3
4
5
6
St. Paul's
Aldgate East
Whitechapel
Langdon Park
All Saints
Dagenham Dock
City Thameslink
Bank
Aldgate
Canning Town
Shadwell
Westferry
Blackwall
Royal Victoria
Cannon Street
Limehouse
East India
Poplar
Custom House
for ExCeL
Blackfriars
Mansion House
Monument
Tower Hill
Prince Regent
Rainham
Grays
Royal Albert
Closed 28 June 2008 to spring 2009
Tower Gateway
Fenchurch Street
Beckton Park
Wapping
West Silvertown
Cyprus
West India Quay
Purfleet
River Thames
Gallions Reach
Rotherhithe
Pontoon Dock
Beckton
Canary Wharf
North Greenwich
for The O2
Bermondsey
London City Airport
Canada Water
Heron Quays
South Quay
Surrey Quays
King George V
Crossharbour
London Bridge
Mudchute
East London line is closed for major line extension work to become part of the London Overground network.
Island Gardens
Borough
Elephant & Castle
Foot tunnel and ferry
Cutty Sark
for Maritime Greenwich
Westcombe Park
Woolwich Arsenal
Abbey Wood
Belvedere
Deptford
Greenwich
Charlton
South Bermondsey
Maze Hill
Woolwich Dockyard
Plumstead
Erith
Queens Road Peckham
New Cross
Deptford Bridge
Elverson Road
Slade Green
St. Johns
Denmark Hill
Nunhead
New Cross Gate
Blackheath
Kidbrooke
Falconwood
Bexleyheath
Peckham Rye
Brockley
Lewisham
Eltham
Welling
Barnehurst
Honor Oak Park
Ladywell
Hither Green
Forest Hill
East Dulwich
Sydenham
Crofton Park
Lee
New Eltham
Albany Park
Crayford
Gravesend
Medway Towns
North Dulwich
Catford
Catford Bridge
Mottingham
Sidcup
Bexley
Dartford
Bellingham
Grove Park
West Dulwich
Sydenham Hill
Lower Sydenham
Elmstead Woods
Beckenham Hill
Penge East
Sundridge Park
West Norwood
Gipsy Hill
Penge West
Kent House
New Beckenham
Bromley North
Chislehurst
Medway Towns
Sevenoaks
Ravensbourne
Bickley
St. Mary Cray
Anerley
Swanley
Streatham
Crystal Palace
Shortlands
Bromley South
Orpington
Birkbeck
Avenue Road
Beckenham Road
Beckenham Junction
Petts Wood
Streatham Common
Norbury
Chelsfield
Knockholt
Harrington Road
Clock House
Norwood Junction
Dunton Green
Elmers End
Thornton Heath
Arena
Sevenoaks
Woodside
Eden Park
West Croydon
Blackhorse Lane
West Wickham
Centrale
Wellesley Road
Addiscombe
Hayes
Lebanon Road
Church Street
George Street
Sandilands
Coombe Lane
East Croydon
South Croydon
Lloyd Park
Addington Village
Gravel Hill
King Henry's Drive
Purley Oaks
Fieldway
Sanderstead
New Addington
Purley
Kenley
Coulsdon South
Whyteleafe
Riddlesdown
Whyteleafe South
Upper Warlingham
Caterham
Merstham
Woldingham
Gatwick Airport
East Grinstead
Tramlink
Travelcards valid in Zones 3, or 4, or 5, or 6 (or combination of these Zones) and Bus Passes are available on Tramlink throughout the grey area
Improvement works may affect your journey, particularly at weekends.
Check before you travel; look for publicity at stations, visit tfl.gov.uk/check or call 020 7222 1234
Key to lines
Station
Interchange Station
Bakerloo
Central
Circle
District
Hammersmith & City
Jubilee
Metropolitan
Northern
Piccadilly
Victoria
Waterloo & City
London Overground
DLR
Tramlink
National Rail
Replacement bus services
Some stations and lines have restricted opening times.
The routes shown on this map are a guide to weekday, off-peak services but do not guarantee direct trains between the stations shown.
Correct at time of going to print
Version G
Reg. user No. 08/1201/P

Places of interest

Central

West End

Admiralty Arch SW1 249 D4
Apple Market WC2 250 B6
Banqueting House SW1 250 A3
Big Ben SW1 250 B1
British Library NW1 93 D4 232 D2
British Mus WC1 94 A2 240 A3
BT Tower W1 93 C2 239 A4
Buckingham Palace SW1 115 C4 249 A1
Cabinet War Rooms SW1 115 D4 249 D2
Carnaby Street W1 93 C1 239 A1
Cenotaph SW1 250 A2
Changing of the Guard (site of) SW1 249 A1
Chinatown W1 115 D6 249 D6
Clarence House SW1 115 C5 249 B3
Cleopatra's Needle WC2 116 B5 250 C5
Courtauld Galleries WC2 250 C6
Covent Garden WC2 116 A6 250 B6
Dickens House Mus WC1 94 B3 240 D5
Downing Street SW1 116 A4 250 A2
Eros W1 115 D6 249 C5
Green Park SW1,W1 115 B4 248 D2
Guards Mus SW1 115 C4 249 B1
Holocaust Memorial Garden W2 114 D4 247 D2
Horse Guards Parade SW1 115 D5 249 D3
Houses of Parliament SW1 116 A3 260 B6
Hyde Park W2 114 D5 247 C3
Leicester Square WC2 115 D6 249 D5
London's Transport Mus WC2 250 B6
Marble Arch W1 114 D6 247 D6
Methodist Central Hall SW1 115 D4 249 D1
National Gallery W1 115 D6 249 D5
National Portrait Gallery W1 115 D6 249 D5
Nelson's Monument WC2 250 A4
New Scotland Yard SW1 115 D3 259 C6
Parliament Square SW1 116 A4 250 A1
Pepsi Trocadero W1 249 C5
Piccadilly Circus W1 115 D6 249 C5
Queen Victoria Memorial SW1 249 A2
Queen's Gallery SW1 115 B4 248 D1
Rotten Row SW1 114 D4 247 C2
Royal Academy of Arts W1 115 C6 249 A5
Royal Mews SW1 115 B3 258 D6
Royal United Services Mus SW1 250 A3
St James's Palace SW1 115 C5 249 B3
St James's Park SW1 249 C2
Serpentine Gallery W2 114 B4 246 D2
Soho W1 93 D1 239 C2
Somerset House WC2 116 B6 250 D6
Speakers' Corner W1 114 D6 247 D6
Tate Britain SW1 116 A2 260 A3
Trafalgar Square SW1 115 D5 249 D4
Tyburn Tree (site of) W2 247 C6
Wallace Collection W1 238 A2
Wellington Arch SW1 248 B2
Wellington Mus (Apsley House) SW1 115 A4 248 B2
Westminster Abbey SW1 116 A3 260 A6
Westminster Cathedral SW1 115 C3 259 A5

City

Bank of England EC2 242 C1
Barbican Arts and Conference Centre EC2 95 A2 242 B4
Central Criminal Court (Old Bailey) EC4 94 D1 241 D2
Custom House EC3 117 C6 253 A5
Dr Johnson's House EC4 241 B1
Gray's Inn WC1 94 B2 240 D4
Guildhall EC2 95 A1 242 B2
Inner Temple EC4 251 A6
John Wesley's House & Mus EC1 242 D6
Lincoln's Inn WC2 94 B1 240 D2
Lloyd's Building EC3 95 C1 243 A1
Mansion House EC4 242 C1
Merchant Taylors Hall EC2R 242 D1
Middle Temple EC4 116 C6 251 A6
Monument, The EC3 252 D6
Mus of London EC2 95 A2 242 A3
Nat West Tower EC2 243 A2
National Postal Mus EC1 95 A1 242 A2
Petticoat Lane Market EC2 95 D2 243 C3
Public Record Office Mus EC4,WC2 241 A2
Royal Exchange EC3 242 D1
St Katharine Dock E1 117 D5 253 D4
St Mary le Bow Church EC2 242 B1
St Paul's Cathedral EC4 95 A1 242 A1
Sir John Soane's Mus WC2 94 B1 240 C2
Spitalfields Market E1 95 D2 243 C4
Stock Exchange EC2 241 D1
Tower Bridge E1,EC3,SE1 117 D5 253 C4
Tower of London EC3 117 D6 253 C5
Traitors Gate EC3 117 D5 253 C4
Ye Olde Cheshire Cheese EC4 241 B2

Northern

Business Design Centre N1 94 C6 234 B5
Camden Market NW1 93 B6 231 D6
London Canal Mus N1 94 A5 233 B4
London Central Mosque NW8 92 C4 230 B1
London Zoo NW1 93 A5 231 A4
Lord's Cricket Ground NW8 92 B4 229 D2
Madame Tussaud's NW1 93 A3 238 A5
Open Air Theatre, Regent's Park NW1 231 A1
Planetarium NW1 93 A3 238 A5
Primrose Hill NW1 92 D6 230 C6
Queen Mary's Gardens NW1 231 A1
Regent's Park NW1 93 A4 231 A3
St George's Cathedral NW1 231 D2
Sherlock Holmes Mus NW1 92 D3 237 D5

Southern

Battersea Park SW11 137 A5 268 A3
Battersea Power Station SW8 137 B6 268 D6
Brompton Oratory SW7 114 C3 257 A5
Bear Gardens Mus SE1 117 A5 252 A4
Bermondsey Market SE1 117 C3 263 B8
Borough Market SE1 252 C3
Design Mus SE1 117 D4 253 D2
Florence Nightingale Mus SE1 250 D1
Gabriel's Wharf SE1 251 A4
George Inn SE1 252 C3
Globe Theatre SE1 252 A5
Hayward Gallery SE1 116 B5 250 D4
HMS Belfast SE1 253 B4
Imperial War Mus SE1 116 C3 261 B5
Lambeth Palace SE1 116 B3 260 C5
London Aquarium SE1 250 C1
London Dungeon SE1 117 B5 252 D4
London Eye SE1 116 B4 250 C2
London Peace Pagoda SW11 267 D4
Millennium Bridge SE1,EC4 252 A5
Mus of Garden History SE1 260 C5
National Film Theatre SE1 250 D4
National Theatre SE1 116 B5 250 D4
Old County Hall SE1 250 C2
Operating Theatre Mus and Herb Garret SE1 117 B5 252 D3
Oxo Tower SE1 251 B5
Royal Festival Hall SE1 116 B5 250 D3
Saatchi Gallery SE1 250 C2
St George's RC Cathedral SE1 116 C3 261 B6
Shakespeare's Globe Theatre (site of) SE1 252 B4
Southwark Cathedral SE1 117 B5 252 C4
Tate Modern SE1 116 D6 251 D4
Vinopolis SE1 117 B5 252 C4

Western

Albert Memorial SW7 114 B4 246 C1
Carlyle's House SW3 267 A5
Chelsea Barracks SW1 115 A1 258 B1
Chelsea Physic Garden SW3 115 A1 267 C6
Commonwealth Institute W8 113 C3 255 A6
Geological Mus SW7 114 B3 256 D5
Kensington Gardens W2 114 A5 246 B3
Kensington Palace W8 113 D5 245 D3
Leighton House W14 254 D6
Lindsey House SW10 266 D4
Little Venice W9 92 A2 236 A4
National Army Mus SW3 136 D6 267 D6
Natural History Mus SW7 114 B3 256 C5
Ranelagh Gardens SW1 115 A1 258 B1
Royal Albert Hall SW7 114 B4 246 C1
Royal Hospital (Army Pensioners) SW1 115 A1 258 A1
Science Mus SW7 114 B3 256 C5
Victoria and Albert Mus SW7 114 B3 256 D5

East

Canary Wharf E14 119 D5
Docklands Mus E14 119 D6
Epping Forest IG10 21 B6
Geffrye Mus E2 95 D5
London Docklands Visitor Centre E14 120 A4
London Gas Mus E16 98 B3
Mus of Childhood (V&A) E2 96 C4
Museum of the Great Eastern Railway E16 122 C4
Queen Elizabeth's Hunting Lodge Mus E4 20 D4
Ragged School Mus E3 97 A2
Vestry House (Mus) E17 53 D5
Whitechapel Art Gallery E1 95 D1

North

Alexandra Palace N22 31 D1
Barnet Mus EN5 1 A1
Battle of Britain Mus NW9 27 D1
Bruce Castle Mus N17 33 C2
Church Farm House Mus NW4 46 B6
Coppetts Centre N12 30 D3
Forty Hall EN2 5 D6
Freud Mus NW3 70 A2
Grange Mus of Community History NW10 67 D4
Hampstead Heath NW3 70 B6
Harrow Mus and Heritage Centre HA2 42 A6
Highgate Cemetery N19 71 B6
Kensal Green Cemetery (All Souls) NW10 90 C4
Kenwood House NW3 48 C1
Old Court (Mus and Library) HA0 65 C3
RAF Mus NW9 28 A1
Ruislip Lido HA4,HA5 39 B5
Ruislip Lido Railway HA4 39 B5
White Cube N1 95 C4

South east

Blackheath SE3 142 C4
Brockwell Park SE24 160 D5
Cutty Sark SE10 142 A6
Docklands Heritage Mus SE16 119 B5
Dulwich Picture Gallery SE21 161 C4
Eltham Palace SE9 166 A4
Flamsteed House SE10 142 B5
Gipsy Moth IV SE10 142 A6
Greenwich Park SE10 142 C5
Horniman Mus and Gardens SE23 162 B3
Livesey Mus SE15 140 B6
Meridian Building SE10 142 B5
Millennium Dome SE10 120 C5
National Maritime Mus SE10 142 B6
Old Royal Observatory Greenwich SE10 142 B5
Queen's House SE10 142 B6
Rotunda Mus SE18 122 B1
Scadbury Park Nature Reserve BR7 189 D4
South Norwood Country Park SE25 206 C5
Thames Barrier Visitor Centre SE18 121 D3
Well Hall Pleasaunce SE9 144 A1

South west

Barnes Common SW13 134 A2
Clapham Common SW4 137 C1
Fulham Palace SW6 135 A3
Hampton Court Palace KT8 196 D6
Kingston Mus KT1 176 A1
Wandsworth Mus SW15 135 A1
Wetland Centre SW13 134 B5
Wimbledon Common SW19 178 B6
Wimbledon Lawn Tennis Mus SW19 157 A1
Wimbledon Windmill Mus SW19 156 C1

West

Chiswick House W4 133 B6
Eel Pie Island TW1 153 A3
Gunnersbury Park Mus W3 110 C3
Ham House TW10 153 C2
Kew Bridge Steam Mus TW8 110 B1
Kew Gardens (Royal Botanic Gardens) TW9 132 A4
Kew Observatory TW9 131 C2
Kew Palace TW9 132 A5
London Butterfly House TW8 131 B4
Marble Hill TW1 153 C4
Mus of Richmond TW10 153 D6
Musical Mus TW8 132 A6
Osterley Park TW7 108 B1
Pitshanger Manor Mus and Art Gallery W5 109 D5
Portobello Road Market W10 91 A2
Richmond Park TW10 155 A3
Syon House TW8 131 C4
Walled Garden TW16 194 B6